The Reader's Adviser

The Reader's Adviser
14th EDITION

Marion Sader, Series Editor

Volume 1
The Best in Reference Works, British Literature, and American Literature
David Scott Kastan and Emory Elliott, Volume Editors

Books About Books • Bibliography • Reference Books: General • Reference Books: Literature • Medieval Literature • Renaissance Literature • Shakespeare • Restoration and Eighteenth-Century Literature • The Romantic Period • The Victorian Period • Modern British and Irish Literature • British Literature: Popular Modes • Early American Literature: Beginnings to the Nineteenth Century • Early Nineteenth-Century American Literature • Middle to Late Nineteenth-Century American Literature • Early Twentieth-Century American Literature • Middle to Late Twentieth-Century American Literature • Modern American Drama • American Literature: Some New Directions • American Literature: Popular Modes

Volume 2
The Best in World Literature
Robert DiYanni, Volume Editor

Introduction to World Literature • Hebrew Literature • Yiddish Literature • Middle Eastern Literatures • African Literatures • Literature of the Indian Subcontinent • Chinese Literature • Japanese Literature • Korean Literature • Southeast Asian Literatures • Greek Literature • Latin Literature • Italian Literature • French Literature • Spanish Literature • Portuguese Literature • German Literature • Netherlandic Literature • Scandinavian Literatures • Russian Literature • East European Literatures • Latin American Literatures • Canadian Literature • Literature of the Caribbean • Australian Literature • New Zealand Literature • Comparative Literature

Volume 3
The Best in Social Sciences, History, and the Arts
John G. Sproat, Volume Editor

Social Sciences and History: General Reference • Anthropology • Economics • Geography • Political Science • Psychology • Sociology • Education • World History • Ancient History • European History • African History • Middle Eastern History • History of Asia and the Pacific • United States History • Canadian History • Latin American History • Music and Dance • Art and Architecture • Mass Media • Folklore, Humor, and Popular Culture • Travel and Exploration

Volume 4
The Best in Philosophy and Religion
Robert S. Ellwood, Volume Editor

Philosophy and Religion: General Reference • General Philosophy • Greek and Roman Philosophy • Medieval Philosophy • Renaissance Philosophy • Modern Western Philosophy, 1600–1900 • Twentieth-Century Western Philosophy • Asian and African Philosophy, 1850 to the Present • Contemporary Issues in Philosophy • Ancient Religions and Philosophies • Eastern Religions • Islam • Judaism • Early and Medieval Christianity • Late Christianity, 1500 to the Present • The Bible and Related Literature • Minority Religions and Contemporary Religious Movements • Contemporary Issues in Religious Thought

Volume 5
The Best in Science, Technology, and Medicine
Carl Mitcham and William F. Williams, Volume Editors

Science, Technology, and Medicine: General Reference • A General View: Science, Technology, and Medicine • History of Science, Technology, and Medicine • Philosophy of Science, Technology, and Medicine • Ethics in Science, Technology, and Medicine • Science, Technology, and Society • Special Issues in Science, Technology, and Society • Engineering and Technology • Agriculture and Food Technology • Energy • Communications Technology • Medicine and Health • Illness and Disease • Clinical Psychology and Psychiatry • Mathematics • Statistics and Probability • Information Science and Computer Science • Astronomy and Space Science • Earth Sciences • Physics • Chemistry • Biological Sciences • Ecology and Environmental Science

Volume 6
Indexes

THE
Reader's Adviser®

14th EDITION

Volume 6
Indexes

Marion Sader, Series Editor

R. R. Bowker®
A Reed Reference Publishing Company
New Providence, New Jersey

Published by R. R. Bowker
A Reed Reference Publishing Company
Copyright © 1994 by Reed Publishing (USA) Inc.

International Standard Book Numbers
0-8352-3320-0 (SET)
0-8352-3321-9 (Volume 1)
0-8352-3322-7 (Volume 2)
0-8352-3323-5 (Volume 3)
0-8352-3324-3 (Volume 4)
0-8352-3325-1 (Volume 5)
0-8352-3326-X (Volume 6)
International Standard Serial Number 0094-5943
Library of Congress Catalog Card Number 57-13277

The paper used in this publication meets the minimum requirements
of American National Standard for Information Sciences—Permanence
of Papers for Printed Library Materials, ANSI Z39.48-1984.

∞™

ISBN 0-8352-3320-0

9 780835 233200

Contents

———————— ⚜ ————————

PREFACE   ix

Directory of Publishers   1

Name Index   27

Title Index   221

Subject Index   733

Preface

———————— ⟨⦿⟩ ————————

Volume 6 in *The Reader's Adviser* is a special index volume to accompany the 14th edition. While Volumes 1 through 5 give the user a comprehensive survey of the best of the literature in the humanities, sciences, and social sciences, Volume 6 provides, through its directory of publishers and its three cumulative indexes, a means of locating the publishers of titles cited throughout the first five volumes and easy access to author and editor names, book titles, and subjects as these appear in all the volumes.

The Directory of Publishers, arranged in alphabetical order by the abbreviated form used in the bibliographic entries, gives the publisher's full name. The listed publishers have been checked against the current *Books in Print* data file. For more detailed information on publishers, one can easily check the *Publishers* volume of the *Books in Print* set to secure current addresses and ISBNs for all publishers.

Some of the publishers listed in this directory may no longer be in business. The fact that a publisher is no longer publishing should not discourage the user of *The Reader's Adviser* from pursuing the acquisition of those books that have piqued his or her interest. Most of the titles chosen for inclusion in Volumes 1 through 5 were selected because of their ready availability through the facilities of public and university libraries, so these titles are accessible even if the publishing house is out of business or the title is presently out of print. For the reader who wants to purchase copies of titles that are out of print and finds that the publisher cannot be located, the local phone directory's "yellow pages" can be consulted for the names and addresses of bookstores that specialize in out-of-print or otherwise unavailable titles; such sources may even offer a search service for secondhand out-of-print books.

The three indexes are cumulations of those appearing in each of the five preceding volumes. In each index, the alphabetically arranged listings include volume and page numbers.

Name Index. This index lists names of authors appearing as main listings in the text (main-entry authors) and also names of authors and editors of the books listed in each of the bibliographies. Boldface type is used both for the name of each main-entry author and for the first page of the main listing.

Title Index. Titles of the books by main-entry authors are indexed here along with the titles of books listed in the bibliographies. Titles not indexed are those titles listed with a main-entry author that includes that author's name, e.g, *Collected Prose of T. S. Eliot,* or those broad generic titles such as "Complete Works," "Selections," "Poems." The only exception to this is Shakespeare (Volume 1), where all works by and about him are indexed. To locate all titles by and about a main-entry author, the user should look up that author in the Name Index to find the primary listing.

Subject Index. The Subject Index integrates the indexes in Volumes 1 through 5 using a detailed, multiple-approach access to the subject content of all five volumes. Because of the many new areas today that have evolved and borrowed from traditional disciplines, the user will find this index especially helpful in bridging the boundaries unavoidably imposed by the need for organized chapter divisions of traditional disciplines.

We hope this volume will prove useful in providing additional access to the material found in Volumes 1 through 5 of *The Reader's Adviser.*

Marion Sader
Publisher
Professional & Reference Books
R.R. Bowker
September 1993

The Reader's Adviser

Directory of Publishers

The following list includes the abbreviations and full names of publishers whose titles appear in *The Reader's Adviser*. The abbreviated form of a publisher's name as it appears throughout the five volumes is shown in boldface. The abbreviation is followed by the complete form of the name. The alphabetization method is letter-by-letter. For full information, addresses, and telephone and fax numbers, consult the Publishers Volume in the current edition of *Books in Print*. To locate information on many old publishers, small publishers, and organizations that publish materials, it may also be necessary to consult other sources.

A

A. A. Balkema *See* Ashgate Pub. Co.
Aames-Allen Aames-Allen Publishing Co.
AAP Association of American Publishers, Inc.
AASLH *See* Norton
A & C Black A & C Black Talman Co.
ABA American Booksellers Association
Abaris Bks. Abaris Books, Inc.
Abbeville Pr. Abbeville Press, Inc.
AB Bookman's Weekly AB Bookman's Weekly
ABC-CLIO ABC-CLIO, Inc.
Aberdeen U. Pr. Aberdeen University Press Books
Abingdon Abingdon Press, Div. of United Methodist Publishing House
Abjad Bk. Abjad Book Designers & Builders
Ablex Pub. Ablex Publishing Corp.
Abrams Harry N. Abrams, Inc.
Absolute Class. Absolute Classics
Academic Intl. Academic International Press
Academy Chi. Pubs. Academy Chicago Publishers, Ltd.
Acad. Pr. Academic Press, Inc.
A. capella Bks. A. capella Books, Div. of Chicago Review Press
Access Sec. Info. Access Security Information: A Security Information Service
Ace Bks. Ace Books, Div. of Berkley Publishing Group
Acrobat Acrobat Books
Acropolis Acropolis Books
Addison-Wesley Addison-Wesley Publishing Co., Inc.

Adler & Adler Adler & Adler Publishers, Inc.
Adlers Foreign Bks. Adler's Foreign Books, Inc.
Adonis Pr. Adonis Press
Adrienne Lee Adrienne Lee Press
Advent NY Advent Books, Inc.
Afr. Her. Pr. African Heritage Press
Africana Pub. *See* Holmes & Meier
Africa World Africa World Press
Ahmadiyya Anjuman Ahmadiyya Anjuman Ishaat Islam Lahore, Inc.
Aid-Research Associates Aid-Research Associates
Airmont Airmont Publishing Co., Inc.
ALA American Library Association
Alaska Northwest Alaska Northwest Books
Alba House Alba House, Div. of Society of St. Paul
Albatross Albatross
Aldine de Gruyter Aldine de Gruyter
Aldine Pub. *See* Aldine de Gruyter
Alfred Waller Ltd. Alfred Waller, Ltd.
Algonquin Bks. Algonquin Books of Chapel Hill
Alive Pubns. Alive Publications, Ltd.
Allanheld *See* Rowman
Allegro OR Allegro Publishing Co.
Allen & Unwin *See* Paul & Co. Pubs.
Allen Pr. Allen Press, Inc.
Allenson Allenson, Alec. R., Inc., Subs. of Aleph Press
Allerton Pr. Allerton Press, Inc.
Allison & Busby *See* Schocken
Allyn Allyn & Bacon, Inc.
Ally Pr. Ally Press

Almqvist & Wiskell SW   *See* Coronet Bks.
Alpha Pub. Co.   *See* Schocken
Alta Pr.   Alta Press
Alyson Pubns.   Alyson Publications, Inc.
AMA   American Medical Association
Am. Acad. Rome   American Academy in Rome
Amadeus CA   Amadeus Press
Amana Bks.   Amana Books
Am. Anthro. Assn.   American Anthropological Association
Am. Antiquarian   American Antiquarian Society
Am. Assn. Retire   American Association of Retired Persons
A. M. Best   A. M. Best Co.
Am. Bible   American Bible Society
Am. Bk. Pubs.   American Book Publishers, Inc.
Am. Chemical   American Chemical Society
Am. Classical Coll. Pr.   American Classical College Press
Am. Enterprise   *See* Univ. Pr. of Amer.
Amereon Ltd.   Amereon, Ltd.
Amer. Geophysical   American Geophysical Union
Amer. Historical Association   American Historical Association
Amer. Hospital   American Hospital Association
American Heritage Pr.   American Heritage Press, Div. of Forbes, Inc.
Americanist   Americanist Press
American Jewish Committee   American Jewish Committee
American Paper and Pulp Assoc.   American Paper and Pulp Association
American Theological Library Association   American Theological Library Association
Amer. Soc. for Info. Science   American Society for Information Science
Amer. Source Bks.   American Source Books
Amer. Type Founders Co.   American Type Founders Co.
Amer. U. of Beirut   American University of Beirut
Amer. W. Bks.   American West Books
Am. Family Foun.   American Family Foundation
Am. Fed. Arts   American Federation of Arts
Am. Fed. Astrologers   American Federation of Astrologers
Am. Geol.   American Geological Institute
Am. Herit. Pubns.   American Heritage Publications
Amherst Coll. Pr.   Amherst College Press
Am. Hist. Assn.   American Historical Association
Am. Inst. of Graphic Arts   American Institute of Graphic Arts
Am. Inst. Physics   American Institute of Physics

Am. Inst. Psych.   American Institute of Psychology
Am. Jewish Comm.   American Jewish Commonwealth
Am. Lib. Pub. Co.   American Library Publishing Co.
Am. Life Foun.   American Life Foundation & Study Institute
Am. Math.   American Mathematical Society
Am. Nuclear Soc.   American Nuclear Society
Am. Orient Soc.   American Oriental Society
Am. Petroleum   American Petroleum Institute Publications & Distribution Section
Am. Philos.   American Philosophy Society
Am. Phil. Soc.   *See* Am. Philos.
Am. Psychiatric   American Psychiatric Press, Inc., Subs. of American Psychiatric Association
Am. Psychol.   American Psychological Association
Am. Repr.-Rivercity Pr.   American Reprint Co./Rivercity Press
Am. Sch. Athens   American School of Classical Studies at Athens
Am. Schls. Oriental   American Schools of Oriental Research
Am. Soc. Civil Eng.   American Society for Civil Engineering
Am. Soc. Ed. & Rel.   American Society for Education & Religion, Inc.
AMS Pr.   AMS Press, Inc.
Am. Technical   American Technical Publishers, Inc.
Am. Trust Pubns.   American Trust Publications
Analytic Pr.   Analytic Press, Subs. of Lawrence Erlbaum Assocs., Inc.
Anchor   *See* Doubleday
Anchor Found.   Anchor Foundation, Inc.
And Bks.   And Books
Anderson MI   Anderson Publications
And/Or Pr.   And/Or Press, Inc.
Andrews & McMeel   Andrews & McMeel
Andrews Univ. Pr.   Andrews University Press
Andromeda   Andromeda Press
Angel Bks.   *See* Dufour
Angus & Robertson AT *See* HarpC
Anima Pubns.   Anima Publications, Div. of Conococheague Associates, Inc.
Anma Libri   Anma Libri
Ann Arbor   *See* U. of Mich. Pr.
Annual Reviews   Annual Reviews, Inc.
Anthology Film   Anthology Film Archives
Anthroposophic   Anthroposophic Press, Inc.
Anti-Defamation League   Anti-Defamation League of B'nai B'rith
Antiquarian Bookman Annual   Antiquarian Bookman Annual
Antique Collect.   Antique Collector's Club
Anvil Pr.   Anvil Press
Apalachee Pr.   Apalachee Press
Aperture   Aperture Foundation, Inc.
Apex Pr.   *See* New Horizons Press

Apollo Apollo Book
Appalach. Consortium Appalachian Consortium Press
Appel Paul P. Appel, Publisher
Applause Theatre Bk. Pubs. Applause Theatre Book Publishers
Appleton & Lange Appleton & Lange
Appleton-Century-Crofts *See* P-H
Applewood Applewood Books
Applied Arts Applied Arts Publishers
Apt Bks. Apt Books, Inc.
Aquarian Pr. UK *See* Thorsons SF
Aquila Poetry Aquila Poetry
A. R. Allenson Alec R. Allenson, Inc., Subs. of Aleph Press
Ararat Pr. Ararat Press
Arbit Arbit Books, Inc.
Arbor Hse. *See* Morrow
Arcade Pub. Inc. Arcade Publishing, Inc.
Arcadiensis Arcadiensis
Archimedia Archimedia
Architectural Hist. Found. Architectural Historical Foundation
Archon Bks. Archon Books
Arco Pub. *See* P-H
Arden Lib. Arden Library
Ardis Pubs. Ardis Publishers
Area Pubs. Area Publishers
A-R Eds. A-R Editions, Inc.
Ares Ares Publishers, Inc.
Arete Pr. Arete Press
Argosy Argosy
Argus Argus Motorbooks International, Publishers & Wholesalers, Inc.
Ariadne CA Ariadne Press
Aribus Asiae Aribus Asiae
Ariel Music Ariel Music
Ariel Pr. CA Ariel Press
Aries Rising Aries Rising Press
Arion Pr. Arion Press
Aris & Phillips UK *See* Oxbow Bks.
Arkham Arkham House Publishers
Arlington Pr. Arlington Press
Armenian Natl. Educ. Armenian National Education Committee
Arno Press Arno Press
Aronson Aronson, Jason, Inc.
Arrowood Pr. Arrowood Press, Div. of Budget Book Service, Inc.
Art Alliance Art Alliance Press
Art Direction Book Art Direction Book Co., Div. of Advertising Trade Publications, Inc.
Artech Hse. Artech House, Inc., Subs. of Horizon House, Microwave, Inc.
Artia *See* IBD Ltd.
Artisan Sales Artisan Sales
Artmans Pr. Artman's Press
Arts End Arts End Books
A. S. Barnes *See* Oak Tree Pubns.
Ashgate Pub. Co. Ashgate Publishing Co.
Ashod Pr. Ashod Press
Asia Bk. Corp. Asia Book Corp. of America

Asian Humanities Pr. Asian Humanities Press
Asia Pub. Hse. Asia Publishing House, Inc.
Aspen Aspen Publishers, Inc.
Assn. Am. Geographers Association of American Geographers
Assn. Am. Univ. Association of American University Presses
Assn. Chr. Lib. Association of Christian Libraries
Assn. for Childhood Ed. Assocation for Childhood Education
Assn. of Creative Writers Association of Creative Writers
Assn. of Syst. Coll. Association of Systematics Collections
Assoc. Faculty Pr. Associated Faculty Press
Association Pr. Association Press
Assoc. Pubs. D.C. Associated Publishers, Inc.
Assoc. Univ. Prs. Associated University Presses
Astor Bks. Astor Books, Div. of Astor Music, Inc.
Astor-Honor Astor-Honor, Inc.
Astragal Pr. Astragal Press
ASU Lat. Am. St. Arizona State University, Center for Latin American Studies
A. Sutton Pub. *See* Acadamy Chi. Pubs.
Ateneo de Manila U. Pr. Ateneo de Manila University Press, Cellar Book Shop
Atheneum Atheneum
Athlone Pr. Athlone Press
Atlantic Monthly Atlantic Monthly Press
Attic Pr. Attic Press
Auckland U. Pr. Auckland University Press
Augsburg Fortress Augsburg Fortress Publishers, Publishing House of the Evangelical Church in America
Augustana Coll. Augustana College Library
August Hse. August House
Augustinian Coll. Pr. Augustinian College Press
Aunt Lute Bks. Aunt Lute Books
Aura Pub. Co. Aura Publishing Co.
Auromere Auromere, Inc.
Austin Hill Pr. Austin Hill Press
Author Aid Author Aid
Autonomedia Autonomedia
Autumn Pr. Autumn Press
Avenel *See* Outlet Bk. Co.
Avery Pub. Avery Publishing Group, Inc.
Avon Avon Books
A. Wofsy Fine Arts A. Wofsy Fine Arts
Ayer Ayer Co. Publishers, Inc.

B

Baen Bks. Baen Books
Baha'i Baha'i Distribution Service
Bailiwick Bks. Bailiwick Books
Baker Bk. Baker Book House

Bald Eagle Mtn. Bald Eagle Mountain Press
Ballantine Ballantine Books, Inc.
Ball State Univ. Ball State University
Balsam Balsam Press, Inc.
Bancroft Parkman Bancroft Parkman, Inc.
Bandanna Bks. Bandanna Books
B & N Imports Barnes & Noble
  Books–Imports, Div. of Rowman & Little-
  field Publishers, Inc.
Banner of Truth The Banner of Truth
Banning Pr. Arthur J. Banning Press
Bantam Bantam Books, Inc., Div. of Bantam
  Doubleday Dell
Barber Pr. Lillian Barber Press
Barbour & Co. Barbour & Co., Inc.
Bard *See* Avon
Barnhart Bros. Barnhart Brothers
Barricade Bks. Barricade Books
Barrie and Rockliff Barrie & Rockliff
Barron Barron's Education Series, Inc.
Basic Basic Books
Batsford *See* Trafalgar
Battledore Ltd. Battledore, Ltd.
Baudry's European Lib. Baudry's European
  Library
Baylin Pubns. Baylin Publications
Bay Pr. Bay Press
B. Blom *See* Ayer
Beacham Pub. Beacham Publishing, Inc.
Beacon Pr. Beacon Press
Bear and Co. Bear & Co.
Bear Flag Bks. Bear Flag Books, Subs. of
  Padre Productions
Beaufort Bks. Beaufort Books
Be Bop Bks. Be Bop Books
Bedminster Pr. Bedminster Press
Beechhurst Beechhurst
Beekman Pubs. Beekman Publishers, Inc.
Behrman Behrman House, Inc.
Beil Frederick C. Beil Publisher, Inc.
Belknap Pr. *See* HUP
Bellerophon Bks. Bellerophon Books
Bellflower Bellflower Press
Belmont Music Pub. Belmont Music Pub-
  lishing
Bender Matthew Bender & Co., Inc.
Benjamin-Cummings Benjamin-Cummings
  Publishing Co., Subs. of Addison-Wesley
  Publishing Co.
Benjamins North Am. John Benjamins,
  North America, Inc.
Bennington Coll. Bennington College
Bentley Robert Bentley, Inc., Publishers
Benziger Benziger Publishing Co.
Beresford Bks. Beresford Books
Berg Pubs. Berg Publishers, Inc.
Berkeley Slavic Berkeley Slavic Specialties
Berkley Pub. Berkley Publishing Group
Berkshire Hse. Berkshire House Publishers
Berlitz Berlitz Publishing Company, Inc.
Bernan Pr. Bernan Press
Bethany Hse. Bethany House Publishers,
  Div. of Bethany Fellowship, Inc.

Beyond Words Pub. Beyond Words Publish-
  ing, Inc.
B. Franklin Burt Franklin, Publisher
Bhaktivedanta Bhaktivedanta Book Trust
Biblio NY Biblio Press, The Jewish Women's
  Publisher
Biblio. Soc. Amer. Bibliographical Society
  of America
Bibliotheca Bibliotheca Islamica, Inc.
Biblo Biblo & Tannen Booksellers & Pub-
  lishers, Inc.
Biling. Rev-Pr. Bilingual Press/Editorial Bi-
  lingue
Bingham Bros. Co. Bingham Brothers Co.
Birkhauser Birkhauser Boston, Div. of
  Springer-Verlag GmbH & Co. KG
Birth Day Birth Day Publishing Co.
Bk. Indus. Study Book Industry Study
  Group, Inc.
Bk. Sale Inc. Book Sales, Inc.
Bks. Demand Books on Demand
Bks. for Libraries Books for Libraries
Bks. Intl. VA Books International, Inc.
Black Letter Black Letter Press
Black Scholar Pr. Black Scholar Press
Black Sparrow Black Sparrow Press
Black Swan Black Swan Press
Black Swan CT Black Swan Books, Ltd.
Blackwell Pubs. Blackwell Publishers
Blackwell Sci. Blackwell Scientific Publica-
  tions, Inc.
Blackwood Blackwood Press
Blair John F. Blair Publisher
Blandford Pr. Blandford Press
Bloch Bloch Publishing Co.
Bloms Boktryckerll *See* Ayer
Bloodaxe Bks. *See* Dufour
Blue Moon Pr. Blue Moon Press, Inc.
Blue Water Pub. Blue Water Publishing
Blue Wind Blue Wind Press
Bnai Brith Bk. B'nai B'rith Book Service
Baobab Bks. Baobab Books
BOA Edns. BOA Editions, Ltd.
Bobbs Bobbs-Merrill Company
Boise St. U. W. Writ. Ser. Boise State Uni-
  versity Western Writers Series
Bolchazy-Carducci Bolchazy-Carducci Pub-
  lishers
Bonanza Pub. Bonanza Publishing
Book & Tackle Book & Tackle Shop
Bookbindery Bookbindery
Bookcraft Inc. Bookcraft, Inc.
Bookmark The Bookmark
Book Nest The Book Nest
Book-of-the-Month Club Book-of-the-Month
  Club
Bookpress Ltd. Bookpress, Ltd.
Booksellers Pub. Booksellers Publishing,
  Inc.
Bookworm Pub. Bookworm Publishing Co.,
  Inc.
Boosey & Hawkes Boosey & Hawkes, Inc.
Borden Borden Publishing Co.

Borderland Sciences Borderland Sciences Research Foundation, Inc.
Boreal Express Boreal Express
Borealis Pr. Borealis Press
Borgo Pr. Borgo Press
Borrego Pubns. Borrego Publications
Boston U. Pr. Boston University Press
Bottom Dog Pr. Bottom Dog Press
Boulevard Boulevard Books
Bowes & Bowes Bowes & Bowes
Bowker R. R. Bowker, A Reed Reference Publishing Co.
Bowker-Saur *See* K. G. Saur
Bowling Green Univ. Bowling Green University Popular Press
Boxwood Boxwood Press
Boyd & Fraser Boyd & Fraser Publishing Co., Div. of South-Western Publishing Co.
Boydell & Brewer Boydell & Brewer
Boynton Cook Pubs. Boynton Cook Publishers, Inc., Div. of Heinemann Educational Books
Bradbury & Evans Bradbury & Evans
Brady Books *See* P-H
Brady Compu. Bks. Brady Computer Books, Div. of Prentice-Hall Computer Publishing
Branden Pub. Co. Branden Publishing Co.
Brandywine Press Brandywine Press
Branford Charles T. Branford Co.
Brasseys *See* Macmillan
Braziller George Braziller, Inc.
Breitenbush Bks. Breitenbush Books, Inc.
Breslov Res. Inst. Breslov Research Institute
Brethren Brethren Press, Div. of Church of the Brethren
Brick Hse Pub. Brick House Publishing Co.
Brick Row Brick Row Book Shop
Bridge Pubns. Inc. Bridge Publications, Inc.
Bridgman Pubs. Bridgman Publishers
Brigham Brigham Young University Press
Bright Tyger Pr. Bright Tyger Press
Bristol Pr. Bristol Press
British Am. Books British American Books
British Amer. Pub. British American Publishing, Ltd.
British Bk. Ctr. British Book Center
British Film Inst. UK *See* Ind. U. Pr.
British Information Services British Information Services
British Lib. UK British Library
British Mus. Natural History British Museum of Natural History
British Standards Inst. British Standards Institute
Broadcasting Pubns. Broadcasting Publications, Inc., Book Division
Broadfoot Broadfoot Publishing Co.
Broadside Pr. Broadside Press
Broadview Pr. Broadview Press
Brockmeyer Brockmeyer
Brodart Brodart Co.
Bro-Dart Publishing Bro-Dart Publishing
Brookings Brookings Institute

Brooklyn Coll. Pr. Brooklyn College Press
Brooks-Cole Brooks/Cole Publishing Co., Div. of Wadsworth, Inc.
Brown & Benchmark Brown & Benchmark, Div. of William C. Brown Communications, Inc.
B. R. Pub. Co. TN B. R. Publishing Co.
Bruccoli Bruccoli, Clark, Layman, Inc.
Brunner-Mazel Brunner/Mazel Publishers
Bruter Inst. Bruter Institute
Bryn Mawr Coll. Lib. Bryn Mawr College Library
Bryn Mawr Commentaries Bryn Mawr Commentaries
B. T. Batsford *See* Trafalgar
Buccaneer Bks. Buccaneer Books
Bucknell U. Pr. Bucknell University Press
Bulfinch Pr. Bulfinch Press
Bull Pub. Bull Publishing Co.
Bunting Bunting & Lyon, Inc.
Buraff Pubns. Buraff Publications, Div. of Millin Publications, Inc.
Bureau of the Census Bureau of the Census
Burndy Lib. Burndy Library
Burn Hart Burn, Hart & Co., Publishers
Burning Deck Burning Deck
Busn. One Irwin Business One Irwin
Buttrwrth-Heinemann Butterworth-Heinemann, Subs. of Reed International Books
Buzzworm Buzzworm, Inc.

C

CAB Intl. CAB International
Cacho Hermanos Cacho Hermanos
Cadmus Eds. Cadmus Editions
Caesar Pr. Caesar Press
CA Health Pubns. California Health Publications
Calder Pr. Calder Press
Calico Bks. Calico Books
Calyx Bks. Calyx Books
Cambridge U. Pr. Cambridge University Press
Camden Hse. Camden House, Inc.
Cane Hill Pr. Cane Hill Press
Cape *See* Trafalgar
Capitalist Pr. OH Capitalist Press
Capra Pr. Capra Press
Capricorn Bks. Capricorn Books
Caratzas Aristide D. Caratzas, Publisher, Affil. of Melissa Media Associates, Inc.
Caravan Bks. Caravan Books, Subs. of Academic Resources Corp.
Carcanet Carcanet
Carey William Carey Library Publishers
Caribbean Authors Caribbean Authors
Carleton Pr. Carleton Press
Carleton U. Pr. Carleton University Press
Carnegie Inst. Carnegie Institution of Washington

Carnegie-Mellon   Carnegie-Mellon University Press
Carnegie Pr.   Carnegie Press
Carolina Biological   Carolina Biological Supply Co., Publications Department
Carol Pub. Group   Carol Publishing Group
Carolrhoda Bks.   Carolrhoda Books, Inc.
Carroll & Graf   Carroll & Graf Publishers
Carson Pub.   Carson Publishing
Case Western   Case Western Reserve University
Cassell   Cassell Publishing
Cassell UK   *See* Sterling
Castalia Pub.   Castalia Publishing Co.
Catbird Pr.   Catbird Press
Cath. Art Soc.   Catholic Art Society
Cath. Lib. Assn.   Catholic Library Association
Catholic Bibl. Assn.   Catholic Biblical Association of America
Catholic Bk. Agency   Catholic Book Agency
Cath. U. Pr.   Catholic University of America Press
Cato Inst.   Cato Institute
Caxton   Caxton Printers, Ltd.
Cayucos   Cayucos Books
C. C. Thomas   Charles C. Thomas, Publishers
Celestial Arts   Celestial Arts Publishing Corp., Subs. of Ten Speed Press
Cellar   Cellar Book Shop
Center Archaeo   Center Archaeo
Center for Afro-Amer. Studies   Center for Afro-American Studies
Center for Inter-Amer. Relations   Center for Inter-American Relations
Center Reform.   Center for Reformation Research
Central Conf. of Amer. Rabbis   Central Conference of American Rabbis
Centre d'Etudes Arcadiennes   Centre d'Etudes Arcadiennes
Centre for East Asian Cultural Studies   Centre for East Asian Cultural Studies
Centre of Southeast Asian Studies, Monash U.   Centre of Southeast Asian Studies, Monash University
Century Bookbindery   Century Bookbindery
C. E. Tuttle   Charles E. Tuttle, Co., Inc.
C. F. Peters   C. F. Peters
Chadwyck-Healey   Chadwyck-Healey
Chambers   Chambers, Div. of Chambers Kingpoker Graham Publishers, Inc.
Chameleon Bks.   Chameleon Books
Chapman & Hall   Chapman & Hall, Div. of Routledge, Chapman, & Hall, Inc.
Charioteer   Charioteer Press
Charles E. Merrill Bks.   Charles E. Merrill Books
Charles River Bks.   Charles River Books
Chartwell Bks.   Chartwell Books
Chatham Hse. Pubs.   Chatham House Publishers, Inc.
Chatra Bks.   Chatra Boooks
Chatto & Windus UK   *See* Trafalgar

Chelsea Green   Chelsea Green Publishing Co.
Chelsea Hse.   Chelsea House Publishers
Chelsea Pub.   Chelsea Publishing Co.
Chem. Heritage Fnd.   Chemical Heritage Foundation
Chem. Pub.   Chemical Publishing Co., Inc.
Cheng & Tsui   Cheng & Tsui Co.
Cherokee   Cherokee Publishing Co.
Cheshire Pub.   Cheshire Publishing Co.
Child. Bk. Coun.   The Children's Book Council, Inc.
Childrens   Children's Press, Div. of Grolier, Inc.
Chilmark Pr.   Chilmark Press
Chilton   Chilton Book Co., Subs. of Capital Cities/ABC, Inc.
China Bks.   China Books & Periodicals, Inc.
Chinese Lit. Pr.   Chinese Literature Press
Chinese Materials Ctr.   Chinese Materials Center
Chinese U. HK   Chinese University, Hong Kong
Chips   Chip's Bookshop, Inc.
Chiswick Book Shop   Chiswick Book Shop
C. H. Kerr   Charles H. Kerr, Publishing Co.
Choice Pubns.   Choice Publications
Chr. Classics   Christian Classics, Inc.
Christendom Pr.   Christendom Press
Christian Sci.   The Christian Science Publishing Society
Chronicle Bks.   Chronicle Books
Churchill   Churchill, Livingston, Inc., Subs. of Longman Group, Ltd.
Churton   Churton
Cinebooks   *See* NY Zoetrope
Cistercian Pubns.   Cistercian Publications
Citadel Pr.   Citadel Press
City Lights   City Lights Books
Claitors   Claitors Publishing Division
Clarendon Pr.   *See* OUP
Clark, Irwin   Irwin Clark, Inc.
Clark Boardman Callaghan   Clark Boardman Callaghan, Div. of Thomas Legal Publishing, Inc.
Clarke   Clarke Publishing
Clark U. Pr.   Clark University Press
Classical Coll. Pr.   Classical College Press
Clayhall   Clayhall
Clear Light   Clear Light Publications
Cleis Pr.   Cleis Press
Cleveland Mus. Art   Cleveland Museum of Art
Cloverdale Lib.   The Cloverdale Library
Clyde Pr.   Clyde Press
Coach Hse.   Coach House
Coast Pub.   Coast Publishing
Cockerel Pr.   Cockerel Press
Coffee Hse.   Coffee House Press
Colburn & Bentley   Colburn & Bentley
Cold Spring Harbor Pr.   Cold Spring Harbor Laboratory Press
Colleagues Pr. Inc.   Colleagues Press, Inc.
College-Hill   *See* Taylor & Francis

Colton Bk. Colton Book Imports
Col. U. Pr. Columbia University Press
Commerce Commerce Clearing House, Inc.
Compass Va. Compass Publications, Inc. (Virginia)
Computer Science Pr. Computer Science Press, W. H. Freeman & Co., Subs. of Scientific American, Inc.
Conch Mag. Conch Magazine, Ltd. Publishers
Concord Grove Concord Grove Press, Subs. of Institute of World Culture
Concordia Concordia Publishing House
Concourse Pr. Concourse Press, Subs. of East-West Fine Arts Corp.
Conference Bd. The Conference Board, Inc.
Confluence Pr. Confluence Press, Inc.
Congdon & Weed Congdon & Weed
Congr. Quarterly Congressional Quarterly, Inc.
Connecticut Hist. Soc. The Connecticut Historical Society
Conococheague Assoc. Conococheague Association
Consort Bk. Sales Consort Book Sales & Distribution
Constable *See* St. Mut.
Constructive Action Constructive Action, Inc.
Consumer Reports Consumer Reports Books, Div. of Consumer's Union of U.S., Inc.
Contemp. Bks. Contemporary Books, Inc.
Continuum Continuum Publishing Co.
Conway Data Conway Data, Inc.
Cooper Sq. Cooper Square Publishers, Inc.
Coord. Coun. Lit. Mag. Coordinating Council of Literary Magazines
Copper Beech Copper Beech Press
Copper Canyon Copper Canyon Press
Core Collection Core Collection
Corinth Bks. Corinth Books
Cormorant Bks. Cormorant Books
Cornell East Asia Pgm. Cornell East Asia Program
Cornell Maritime Cornell Maritime Press, Inc.
Cornell SE Asia Cornell University, Southeast Asia Program Publications
Cornell Univ. Pr. Cornell University Press
Corner Hse. Corner House Publishers
Cornwall Bks. Cornwall Books, Associated University Presses
Coronado Pr. Coronado Press, Inc.
Corona Pub. Corona Publishing Co.
Coronet Bks. Coronet Books
Council of State Govts. Council of State Governments
Coun. Oak Bks. Council Oak Books
Coun. Res. Values Council for Research in Values & Philosophy
Country Dance and Song Country Dance & Song Society of America

Courage Bks. Courage Books
Covent Garden Covent Garden
Coward-McCann Coward-McCann
Cowles Pub. Co. Cowles Publishing Co.
Cowley Pubns. Cowley Publications, Div. of Society of St. John the Evangelist
CQ Pr. Congressional Quarterly Press
Crane-Russak *See* Taylor & Francis
Creative Arts Bk. Creative Arts Book Company
Creative Ed. Creative Education, Inc.
Creighton U. Pr. Creighton University Press
Crescent Bks. Crescent Books
Cresset Pr. Cresset Press, Inc.
Croissant & Co. Croissant & Co.
Cromlech Bks. Cromlech Books, Inc.
Croom Helm UK *See* Routledge Chapman & Hall
Cross Cult. Cross-Cultural Communications
Crosscut Saw Crosscut Saw Press
Crossing Pr. The Crossing Press
Crossroad NY Crossroad Publishing Co.
Crown *See* Crown Pub. Group
Crown Bks. Yng. Read. Crown Books for Young Readers
Crown Pub. Group Crown Publishing Group
Crystal Clarity Crystal Clarity Publishers
CSUN California State University, Northridge Library
CSU Pr. Fresno CSU Press, Fresno
Ctr. Chinese Studies Center for Chinese Studies (University of Michigan)
Ctr. S&SE Asian University of Michigan, Center for South & Southeast Asian Studies
Ctr. Southeast Asian Studies Center for Southeast Asian Studies, Kyoto University, Japan
Ctr. Study Language Center for the Study of Languages & Information
Ctr. Western Studies Center for Western Studies
Curbstone Curbstone Press
Curley Pub. Curley Publishing, Inc.
Currency Pr. AT *See* St. Mut.

D

Dabor Science Pubns. Dabor Science Publications
Da Capo Da Capo Press, Inc.
Dalkey Arch. Dalkey Archive Press
Dallas Inst. Pubns. The Dallas Institute Publishers
Dance Horizons Dance Horizons
Dance Notation Bureau Dance Notation Bureau, Inc.
Dance Perspectives Dance Perspectives
Dancing Times Dancing Times
Dante U. Am. Dante University of America Press, Inc.
Darby Pub. Darby Publishing Co.

Dark Harvest Dark Harvest Books
Darling & Son Ltd. Darling & Son, Ltd.
Darwin Pr. Darwin Press, Inc.
David and Charles *See* Trafalgar
David & Warde David & Warde
David Brown David Brown
Davidson *See* Harlan Davidson
Davies Davies & Associates
Davis-Poynter Ltd. Davis-Poynter, Ltd.
Dawsons Dawson's Book Shop
Daystar Co. Carson Daystar Publishing Co.
Dearborn Trade Dearborn Trade
Decade Media Decade Media
December Pr. December Press, Inc.
De Gruyter Walter De Gruyter, Inc.
Dekker Marcel Dekker, Inc.
Delacorte Delacorte Press
De La Salle U. Pr. De La Salle University
  Press
Dell Dell Publishing Co., Inc.
Delmar Delmar Publishers, Inc., Div. of
  Thomson Education Publishing, Inc.
Delrey Arch. Delrey Architecture
Delta *See* Delacorte
Demos Pubns. Demos Publications, Inc.
Denali Press The Denali Press
Dent *See* St. Mut.
Deseret Bk. Deseret Book Co., Div. of Des-
  ert Management Corp.
Detroit Inst. Arts Detroit Institute of Arts
Devin Devin & Adair Publishers, Inc.
DeVorss DeVorss & Co.
Dewan Bahasa dan Pustaka Dewan Bahasa
  dan Pustaka
D.G.S. Skelton Dorothy Geneva Simmons
  Skelton
Dharma Pub. Dharma Publishing
Dial Dial, Div. of Penguin USA
Dial Bks. Young Dial Books for Young
  Readers, Div. of Penguin USA
Diamond Diamond Books
Diamond Farm Bk. Diamond Farm Book
  Publishers, Div. of Diamond Enterprises
Diana Pr. Diana Press
Diane Pub. Diane Publishing Co.
D. I. Fine Donald I. Fine, Inc.
Dillon *See* Macmillan
Diplomatic IN Diplomatic Press (Indiana)
Dixon & Sickels Dixon & Sickels
Documen Documen Press, Ltd.
Dolmen *See* Dufour
Dongsuhmunhaksa Dongsuhmunhaksa
Dorling Kindersley Dorling Kindersley, Inc.
Dorrance Dorrance Publishing Co., Inc.
Dorset Pr. Dorset Press
Dorsey The Dorsey Press, Div. of Wads-
  worth, Inc.
Doubleday Doubleday & Co., Inc., Div. of
  Bantam Doubleday Dell
Douglas & McIntyre CN *See* Sterling
Dover Dover Publications, Inc.
Dowden Pub. Dowden Publishing Co., Inc.
Down East Down East Books

Dragon's World Pub. Dragon's World Pub-
  lishing
Drama Bk. Drama Book Publishers
Dramatic Pr. Dramatic Press
Dramatic Pub. Dramatic Publishing Co.
Dramatists Play Dramatists Play Service,
  Inc.
Drapers Co. Research Drapers Co. Research
Dropsie Col. Dropsie College
Dryad Pr. Dryad Press
Dryden Pr. Dryden Press, Div. of Harcourt
  Brace College Publishers
D. Thomas Don Thomas
Duckworth *See* Focus Info. Gr.
Dufour Dufour Editions, Inc.
Duke Duke University Press
Dumbarton Oaks Dumbarton Oaks
Dunbury Pr. Dunbury Press
Duquesne Duquesne University Press
Dushkin Dushkin Publishing Group, Inc.
Dustbooks Dustbooks
Dutton Child. Bks. Dutton Children's Books
Duxbury Pr. Duxbury Press

E

EADS Pub. EADS Publishing Corp.
Eagle Pub. Corp. Eagle Publishing Corp.
Eakins Eakins Press Foundation
Earhart & Richardson Earhart & Richard-
  son
Earthworks Pr. Earthworks Press
Eason & Son Eason & Son
East African Pub. Hse. East African Publish-
  ing House
Eastern Acorn Eastern Acorn Press
Eastern Horizon Pr. Eastern Horizon Press
East Eur. Quarterly East European Quar-
  terly
East Ridge Pr. East Ridge Press
East-West Ctr. East-West Center
East-West Pub. East/West Publishing Co.
E.C.A. Associates E.C.A. Associates
Ecco Pr. Ecco Press
Eclipse Bks. Eclipse Books
ECW Pr. *See* InBook
Eden Pr. Eden Press/Art Reproductions
Ediciones Ediciones Universal
Ediciones Norte Ediciones del Norte
Edinburgh U. Pr. *See* Col. U. Pr.
Edit. Experts Editorial Experts, Inc.
Educ. Tech. Pubns. Educational Technology
  Publications, Inc.
Edward Arnold *See* Routledge Chapman &
  Hall
Eerdmans William B. Eerdmans, Publishing
  Co.
Eisenbrauns Eisenbrauns
E. J. Brill E. J. Brill, U.S.A., Inc.
Element MA Element Books, Inc.
Elias Pubs. Cairo *See* IBD Ltd.

Elizabeth Pr. Elizabeth Press
Elliots Bks. Elliot's Books
Elmete Press Elmete Press
Elsevier Elsevier Science Publishing Co., Inc.
ELT Pr. ELT Press
E.M. Coleman Ent. Earl M. Coleman Enterprises, Inc.
E. Mellen Edwin Mellen Press
Empire Bks. Empire Books
Emporia State Emporia State University Press
Ency. Brit. Inc. Encyclopaedia Britannica, Inc.
Enoch Pratt Enoch Pratt Free Library
Enquiry Pr. Enquiry Press
Enslow Pubs. Enslow Publishers, Inc.
Environ. Data Res. Environmental Data Research Institute
Environ. Ethics Bks. Environmental Ethics Books
E. O'Neill Eugene O'Neill Theater Center
Eridanos Library Eridanos Library
Eriksson Paul S. Eriksson, Publisher
Erlbaum Lawrence Erlbaum Associates, Inc.
Eskisehir Valiligi Eskisehir Valiligi
Essential Bks. Inc. Essential Books, Inc.
Estonian Hse. Estonian House
ETC Pubns. ETC Publications
Ethics & Public Policy Ethics & Public Policy Center
Eurasia Pr. Eurasia Press
Evergreen Evergreen Book Distributors
Everyman See C. E. Tuttle
Expansion Arts Expansion Arts
Exposition Pr. Exposition Press
Eyre & Spottiswood Eyre & Spottiswood

F

Faber & Faber Faber & Faber, Inc.
Facts on File Facts On File, Inc.
Fairleigh Dickinson Fairleigh Dickinson University Press
Fairmount Pr. Fairmount Press, Inc.
Fair Oaks CA Fair Oaks Publishing Co.
Far Eastern U. Far Eastern University
Farrar See FS&G
Fawcett Fawcett Book Group
Faxon The Faxon Company
Feedback Thea. Bks. Feedback Theatrebooks
Feldheim Philipp Feldheim, Inc.
Feminist Pr. Feminist Press at the City University of New York
Fermata The Fermata Press
Fertig Howard Fertig, Inc.
Finch Pr. Finch Press
Fine Arts Mus. See U. Ch. Pr.
Fine Comms. Fine Communications

Finnish Am. Lit. Finnish American Literary Heritage Foundation
Firebrand Bks. Firebrand Books
Firefly Bks. Ltd. Firefly Books, Ltd.
Fisher Inst. Fisher Institute
Fjord Pr. Fjord Press
Flammarion/APCI See Abbeville Pr.
Fleetway Pr. Fleetway Press
Flinders U. Flinders University
Flint Hills Flint Hills Book Co.
Floricanto Pr. Floricanto Press
Florida Atlantic Univ. Florida Atlantic University Press
FL St. U. Pr. See U. Press Fla.
Focal Pr. Focal Press
Focus Info. Gr. Focus Information Group, Inc.
Folcroft Folcroft
Folger Bks. Folger Books
Folklorica Pr. Folklorica Press
Fontana John M. Fontana Publishing
Fordham Fordham University Press
Fords Travel Fords Travel
Foreign Lang. Pr. China See Cheng & Tsui
Foreign Languages Pub. Hse. Foreign Languages Publishing House
Foreign Policy Foreign Policy Association
Forest Bks. See Dufour
Forsan Bks. Forsan Books
Fortress Pr. See Augsburg Fortress
Foundation Pr. Foundation Press, Inc.
Found. Class. Reprints The Foundation for Classical Reprints
Four Dimension Pub. Four Dimension Publishing
Four-G Pubs. Four-G Publishers, Inc.
Four Seasons Foun. Four Seasons Foundation
Four Square Four Square
Four Winds Pr. See Macmillan Child. Grp.
Franciscan Inst. Franciscan Institute Publications
Franciscan Pr. Franciscan Press
Fr. & Eur. French & European Publications, Inc.
Franklin Franklin Book Co., Inc.
Franklin Bks. Franklin Books
Fraunces Tavern Fraunces Tavern Museum
Frederick Muller Ltd. Frederick Muller, Ltd.
Freeman W. H. Freeman & Co.
Freeman Cooper Freeman Cooper
Free Pr. Free Press, Div. of Macmillan Publishing Co., Inc.
Fremantle ACP (AT) See Intl. Spec. Bk.
Fremont Pr. Fremont Press
French Samuel French, Inc.
French Forum French Forum Publishers, Inc.
Freshet Pr. Freshet Press, Inc.
Freundlich Freundlich Books
Friendship Pr. Friendship Press
Friends United Friends United Press

Friends Univ. Toledo   Friends of the University of Toledo Library
Frisch H.   Howard Frisch
Fromm Intl. Pub.   Fromm International Publishing Corp.
Fry and Kammerer   Fry & Kammerer
FS&G   Farrar, Straus & Giroux, Inc.
Fulcrum Pub.   Fulcrum Publishing
Funk & Wagnalls   Funk & Wagnalls
Future Tech. Surveys   Future Technology Surveys, Inc.
FWEW   Four Walls Eight Windows

G

Gabbard Writing & Photo   Gabbard Writing & Photography
Gadfly Pr.   Gadfly Press
GAF Intl.   G A F International
Gale   Gale Research, Inc.
Gallaudet U. Pr.   Gallaudet University Press
Gallopade Pub. Group   Gallopade: Publishing Group
Gambit   *See* Harvard Common Pr.
Gamut Pr.   Gamut Press
G&D   Grosset & Dunlap
Gannon   Gannon University Press
Garber Comm.   Garber Communications
Gardner Press, Inc.   Gardner Press, Inc.
Gareth Stevens Inc.   *See* Grey Castle
Garland   Garland Publishing, Inc.
Gaslight   Gaslight Publications
Gávea-Brown   Gávea-Brown Publications
Gay Sunshine   Gay Sunshine Press, Inc.
Gee Tee Bee   Gee Tee Bee
General Egyptian Book Organization   General Egyptian Book Organization
Genesis Pr.   Genesis Press
Geoffrey Bks.   Geoffrey Books
Geol. Soc. of Amer.   Geological Society of America, Inc.
George Allen   George Allen
Georgetown U. Pr.   Georgetown University Press
George Vickers   George Vickers
Gestalt Journal   Gestalt Journal Press
Gibbs Smith   Gibbs Smith, Publisher
Ginn & Co.   Ginn & Co.
Ginn Pr.   Ginn Press, Div. of Simon & Schuster Higher Educational Publishing Group
G. K. Hall   G. K. Hall, & Co., Div. of Macmillan Publishing Co., Inc.
Gleerup Lund   Gleerup Lund
Glencoe   Glencoe, Div. of Macmillan/McGraw-Hill School Publishing Co.
Gleneida Pub.   Gleneida Publishing Group
Global Hunger Project   Global Hunger Project
Globe Pequot   Globe Pequot Press
Globe Pr. Bks.   Globe Press Books
Gloucester Art   Gloucester Art Press

G. Mason Univ. Pr.   George Mason University Press
Gnomon Pr.   Gnomon Press
Godine   David R. Godine, Publisher, Inc.
Golden Leaves Pub.   Golden Leaves Publishing Co.
Golden Pond Pr.   Golden Pond Press
Golden Quill   The Golden Quill
Golden West Pub.   Golden West Publishers
Golemacher   Golemacher
Goodheart   Goodheart-Willcox Co.
Good Lion Pr.   Good Lion Press
Gordian   Gordian Press, Inc.
Gordon & Breach   Gordon & Breach Science Publishers, Inc.
Gordon Pr.   Gordon Press Publishers
Gorsuch Scarisbrick   Gorsuch Scarisbrick Publishers
Gotham   Gotham Book Mart
Gotham Hse.   Gotham House
Gower UK   Gower Publishing Co.
Grabhorn   Grabhorn
Graduate Theological Union   Graduate Theological Union
Grafton Bks.   Grafton Books
Granada   *See* Sheridan
Graphics Pr.   Graphics Press
Graylock   Graylock
Graywolf   Graywolf Press
Great Ocean   Great Ocean Publishers
Green   Warren H. Green, Inc.
Greenberg Pub. Co.   Greenberg Publishing Co., Inc.
Greenfld. Rev. Lit.   Greenfield Review Literary Center, Inc.
Greenhaven   Greenhaven Press, Inc.
Green Hill   Green Hill Publishers
Greenleaf   Greenleaf Books
Green Oak Pr.   Green Oak Press
Green River   Green River
Greenwich House   Greenwich House
Greenwood   Greenwood Publishing Group, Inc.
Gregg Intl.   Gregg International
Gresham Pub.   Gresham Publications
Grey Castle   Grey Castle Press
Grey Fox   Grey Fox Press
Grey Hse. Pub.   Grey House Publishing, Inc.
Griffon Hse.   Griffon House
Grolier Inc.   Grolier, Inc.
Grosset and Dunlap   Grosset & Dunlap
Grossman   Grossman Publishers, Inc.
Grove-Atltic.   Grove/Atlantic Monthly Press
Grove Pr.   Grove Press
Groves Dict. Music   Groves Dictionaries of Music, Inc.
Grove Weidenfeld   Grove Weidenfeld
Grune & Stratton   Grune & Stratton
Guilford Pr.   Guilford Press, Div. of Guilford Publications, Inc.
Gulf Pub.   Gulf Publishing Co.

H

Hacker   Hacker Art Books
Hackett Pub.   Hackett Publishing Co., Inc.
Hafner   Hafner Press
Hagley Museum   Hagley Museum & Library
Hale & Iremonger   Hale & Iremonger
Hale, Cushman & Flint   Hale, Cushman, & Flint
Halsted Pr.   Halsted Press, Div. of John Wiley & Sons, Inc.
Hambledon Press   Hambledon Press
Hamlyn Pub. Group UK   Hamlyn Publishing Group UK
Hammond Inc.   Hammond, Inc.
Hampton Roads Pub. Co.   Hampton Roads Publishing Co., Inc.
Hanging Loose   Hanging Loose Press
Hanover Hse.   Hanover House
Hanshin Pub.   Hanshin Publishing
Hanuman Bks.   Hanuman Books
Hapi Pr.   Hapi Press
Harbinger AZ   Harbinger House, Inc. (Arizona)
Harbor Hill Bks.   Harbor Hill Books, Div. of Purple Mountain Press
HarBraceJ   Harcourt Brace Jovanovich, Inc., Div. of Harcourt General Corp.
Harcourt   *See* HarBraceJ
Harlan Davidson   Harlan Davidson, Inc.
Harlequin Bks.   Harlequin Books
Harmonic Pk. Pr.   Harmonic Park Press
Harmony   *See* Crown Pub. Group
Harmony Raine   Harmony Raine & Company, Div. of Buccaneer Books, Inc.
HarpC   HarperCollins Publishers, Inc.
HarpC Child. Bks.   HarperCollins Children's Books, Div. of HarperCollins Publishers, Inc.
HarpCollege   HarperCollins College, Div. of HarperCollins Publishers, Inc.
Harper SF   Harper San Francisco, Div. of HarperCollins Publishers, Inc.
Harper's Mag. Found.   Harper's Magazine Foundation
Harper's Mag. Pr.   Harper's Magazine Press
Harrap   *See* P-H
Harrel Bks.   Harrel Books
Harrington Bk.   Harrington Books
Hartley & Marks   Hartley & Marks, Inc.
Hartmore   Hartmore House, Subs. of Media Judaica, Inc.
Hart Pubns.   Hart Publications
Harvard Business Sch.   Harvard Business School Press
Harvard Common Pr.   Harvard Common Press
Harvard U. Center Jewish   Harvard University Center for Jewish Studies
Harvester Pr. UK   Harvester Press
Harvest Pubns.   Harvest Publications, Div. of Baptist General Publications
Harvey Pub. Co.   Harvey Publishing Co.

Harwood Acad. Pubs.   Harwood Academic Publishers
Haskell   Haskell Booksellers, Inc.
Hastings   Hastings House Publishers, Div. of Eagle Publishing Corp.
Hastings Ctr.   Hastings Center
Hawkes Pub. Inc.   Hawkes Publishing, Inc.
Hawkshead Bk.   Hawkshead Book Distribution Co.
Haworth Pr.   The Haworth Press, Inc.
Hawthorne Bks.   Hawthorne Books
Hayden   Hayden, Div. of Prentice Hall Computer Publishing
HB Coll. Pubs.   Harcourt Brace College Publishers
Headwaters Pr.   Headwaters Press
Health Admin. Pr.   Health Administration Press, Div. of Foundation of the American College of Health Care Executives
Hearst Bks.   Hearst Books, Div. of William Morrow & Co.
Heath   D. C. Heath & Co.
Hebrew Pub.   Hebrew Publishing Co.
Hebrew Union Col. Pr.   Hebrew Union College Press
Heinemann Ed.   Heinemann Educational Books, Inc., Div. of Reed Publishing (USA) Inc.
Heinemann Nigeria   Heinemann Nigeria
Heinle & Heinle   Heinle & Heinle Publishers, Inc., Div. of Wadsworth, Inc.
Helene Obolensky Ent.   Helene Obolensky Enterprises
Hemisphere Pub.   Hemisphere Publishing Corp
Hemlock Soc.   Hemlock Society U.S.A.
Hendricks House   Hendricks House, Inc.
Hendrickson MA   Hendrickson Publishers, Inc. (Massachusetts)
Henry Carey Baird & Co.   Henry Carey Baird & Co.
Herald Pr.   Herald Press, Div. of Mennonite Publishing House, Inc.
Herbert Pr.   Herbert Press
Herder   *See* Fr. & Eur.
Herder and Herder   Herder & Herder
Heridonius   Heridonius Foundation, Div. of Amadeus Foundation
Heritage   Heritage Books, Inc.
Hermagoras Pr.   Hermagoras Press
Hermitage   Hermitage
Hermitage Pr.   Hermitage Press
Herndon Hse.   Herndon House
Heyday Bks.   Heyday Books
H. Holt & Co.   Henry Holt & Co., Inc.
Higginson Bk. Co.   Higginson Book Co.
High Text Pubs.   High Text Publications
Hilary Hse. Pubs.   Hilary House Publishers, Inc.
Hildebrandt   Hildebrandt, Inc.
Hill & Wang   Hill & Wang, Inc.
Hippocrene Bks.   Hippocrene Books, Inc.

Hispanic Seminary Hispanic Seminary of Medieval Studies
H. L. Levin Hugh Lauter Levin Associates
HM Houghton Mifflin Co.
Hodder & Stoughton *See* Trafalgar
Hogarth Pr. UK *See* Trafalgar
Holden-Day Holden-Day, Inc.
Holiday Holiday House, Inc.
Holland Pr. Holland Press
Holloway Holloway House Publishing Co.
Hollowbrook Hollowbrook Publishing
Hollow Pr. Hollow Press
Hollym Intl. Hollym International Corp.
Holmes & Meier Holmes & Meier Publishers, Inc.
Holmes Pub. Holmes Publishing Group
Holocaust Pubns. Holocaust Publications
Holt *See* H. Holt & Co.
Home Run Pr. Home Run Press
Hong Kong Univ. Pr. Hong Kong University Press
Hoover Inst. Pr. Hoover Institution Press
Horizon Pr. AZ Horizon Press
Horn Bk. Horn Book, Inc.
Howard U. Pr. Howard University Press
Howells Hse. Howells House
HR&W Holt, Rinehart & Winston, Inc.
HR&W Schl. Div. Holt, Rinehart & Winston, Inc., School Division
Hse. Fire Pr. House of Fire Press
Hudson & Goodwin Hudson & Goodwin
Hudson Hills Hudson Hills Press, Inc.
Huenefeld Huenefeld
Humana Humana Press
Humanities Humanities Press International
Human Kinetics Human Kinetics Publishers
Human Sci. Pr. Human Sciences Press, Inc.
Hungarian Cultural Hungarian Cultural Foundation
Hunt Botanical Lib. Huntington Botanical Library
Hunter Hse. Hunter House, Inc.
Huntington Lib. Huntington Library Publications
Hunt Inst. Botanical Huntington Institute for Botanical Documentation
HUP Harvard University Press
Hurst & Blackett Hurst & Blackett
Hutchinson Hse. Hutchinson House
Hutchinson UK *See* Trafalgar
Hy Cohen Hy Cohen
Hyland Hse. AT Hyland House
Hyperion Conn. Hyperion Press, Inc.

I

IBD Ltd. i.b.d., Ltd.
Ibis Pub. Ibis Publishing, Div. of ClassWorks, Inc.
ICS Pubns. ICS Publications, Institute of Carmelite Studies

Ideals Ideals Publications
I. E. Clark I. E. Clark, Inc.
IEEE Pr. Institute of Electrical and Electronics Engineers, Inc.
Ignatius Pr. Ignatius Press
IJP Index to Jewish Periodicals
IK Imprints IK Imprints
Illum. Way Pub. Illuminated Way Publishing, Inc.
Imperial Type Metal Co. Imperial Type Metal Co.
Imported Pubns. Imported Publications
Impossible Dream Impossible Dreams Publications
Imprint Pubns. Imprint Publications, Inc.
InBook InBook Distribution Co.
Ind. U. Pr. Indiana University Press
Ind. U. Pr. Asian Studies Research Institute Indiana University Press Asian Studies Research Institute
Ind. U. Res. Inst. Indiana University Research Institute
Index Pr. Index Press
Indiana Africa Indiana University, African Studies Program
Ind-US Inc. Ind-U.S., Inc.
Information Access Grp. Information Access Group
Info. USA Information U.S.A., Inc.
Inner Tradit. Intl. Inner Traditions International, Ltd.
In Pr. CO In Press
Ins. Econ. Finan. Institute for Economic and Financial Research, Div. of American Classical College
Inst. Amer. Music Institute of American Music
Inst. Byzantine Institute for Byzantine & Modern Greek Studies, Inc.
Inst. Econ. Pol. Institute for Economic & Political World Strategic Studies
Inst. for the Study of Human Issues Institute for the Study of Human Issues
Inst. Logo Institute of Logotherapy Press, Div. of Institute of Logotherapy
Inst. of Pacific Studies, U. of the South Pacific Institute of Pacific Studies, University of the South Pacific
Inst. Rational-Emotive Institute for Rational-Emotive Therapy
Inst. SE Asian Studies Institute of Southeast Asian Studies
Inst. Study Human Institute for the Study of Human Knowledge
Inst. Study Man Institute for the Study of Man, Inc.
Institute for Scientific Information Institute for Scientific Information
Institut Ricci Institut Ricci
Intemprte. Stage Intemperate Stage
Interlink Pub. Interlink Publishing Group, Inc.
International Ideas International Ideas

Interstate Interstate Publishers, Inc.
InterVarsity InterVarsity Press, Div. of Inter-Varsity Christian Fellowship of the USA
Intl. Bk. Ctr. International Book Centre
Intl. City-Cty Mgt. International City/County Management Association
Intl. General International General
Intl. Inst. Tech. International Institute of Technology, Inc.
Intl. Lrn. Syst. International Learning Systems, Inc.
Intl. Marine International Marine Publishing Co., Div. of McGraw-Hill, Inc.
Intl. Med. Pub. International Medical Publishing, Inc.
Intl. Pubns. Serv. International Publications Services, Div. of Taylor & Francis, Inc.
Intl. Pubs. Co. International Publishers Co.
Intl. Spec. Bk. International Specialized Books Services
Intl. Univs. Pr. International Universities Press, Inc.
Invisible-Red Hill Invisible City/Red Hill Press
IOP Pub. IOP Publishing
Iowa St. U. Pr. Iowa State University Press
IPPP Institute for Philosophy & Public Policy
Ipswich Pr. The Ipswich Press
Ir. Bks. Media Irish Books Media, Inc.
I. R. Dee Ivan R. Dee, Inc., Publisher
Irish Academic Pr. Irish Academic Press
Irish Bk. Ctr. Irish Book Center
Irvington Irvington Publishers
Irwin Richard D. Irwin, Inc.
ISI Pr. ISI Press
Isis Pr. CA Isis Press
Island Pr. Island Press, Div. of Center for Resource Economics
Italica Pr. Italica Press
Ithaca Pr. MA Ithaca Press
Ithaca UK *See* Paul & Co. Pubs.
Ivy Books Ivy Books, Div. of Ballantine Books, Inc.
I. Young Ione Young

J

Jahan Bk. Co. Jahan Book Co.
Jain Pub. Co. Jain Publishing Co.
Jai Pr. Jai Press, Inc.
James Louis & Samuel James Louis & Samuel
Janes Info. Pub. Janes Informational Publishing
Japan Pubns. Japan Publications (U.S.A.), Inc.
Jargon Soc. The Jargon Society, Inc.
JBK Pubs. JBK Publishers
J. Cape *See* Trafalgar

J. C. Brown John Carter Brown Library
J. Colet Pr. John Colet Press
Jenkins Jenkins Publishing Co.
Jennings Pr. Jennings Press, Inc.
Jesuit Hist. Jesuit Historical Institute Press
Jewish Hist. Jewish Historical Society of New York, Inc.
Jewish Lights Jewish Lights Publishing, Div. of LongHill Partners, Inc.
Jewish Pubns. Jewish Publications
Jewish Theol. Sem. of Amer. Jewish Theological Seminary of America
J. Heraty Assocs. Jack Heraty & Associates, Inc.
J. J. Augustin J. J. Augustin Publishers, Inc.
J. M. Dent and Sons J. M. Dent & Sons
J. Murray UK *See* Trafalgar
John Jay Pr. John Jay Press
John Knox *See* Westminster John Knox
John Muir John Muir Publications
Johns Hopkins Johns Hopkins University Press
Johnson Repr. Johnson Reprint Corp.
Joint Pub. Co. HK Joint Publishing Co. (Hong Kong)
Jonathan Cape *See* Trafalgar
Jonathan David Jonathan David Publishers, Inc.
Jones & Bartlett Jones & Bartlett Publishers, Inc.
Jordan & Sons Jordan & Sons
Joseph Pub. Co. Joseph Publishing Co.
Jossey-Bass Jossey-Bass Publishers, Inc.
Jove Pubns. Jove Publications, Inc.
JPS Phila. Jewish Publication Society
J. P. Tarcher Jeremy P. Tarcher, Inc., Div. of The Putnam Publishing Group
J. Simon Joseph Simon, Div. of Pangloss Press
J. S. Sanders J. S. Sanders & Co., Inc.
Judaica Pr. Judaica Press, Inc.
Julian Messner *See* S&S Trade
Juniper Pr. WI Juniper Press
J. Whitaker UK *See* Gale

K

Kala Prakashan *See* Nataraj Bks.
Kalimat Kalimat Press
Kampmann *See* M. Boyars Pubs.
Kardamitsas Pub. Kardamitsas Publishing
Karoma Karoma Publishers, Inc.
Karz-Cohl Pub. Karz-Cohl Publishing
Katydid Bks. Katydid Books
Kavanagh Peter Kavanagh, Hand Press
Kaye & Ward Kaye & Ward
Kayode Pubns. Kayode Publications, Ltd.
Kazi Pubns. Kazi Publications, Inc.
Keats Keats Publishing, Inc.
Kegan Paul *See* Routledge Chapman & Hall

Kelley   Augustus M. Kelley, Publishers
Kelly-Winterton Pr.   Kelly-Winterton Press
Kendall Coll. U. Pr.   Kendall College University Press
Kendall-Hunt   Kendall/Hunt Publishing Co.
Kennikat Pr.   Kennikat Press
Kent St. U. Pr.   Kent State University Press
Kerr   *See* C. H. Kerr
Kessinger Pub.   Kessinger Publishing Co.
Keter Pub.   *See* Coronet Bks.
Key Caribbean Pubs.   Key Caribbean Publishers
K. G. Saur   K. G. Saur, Subs. of R. R. Bowker
Khayats   Khayats
Kindersley   *See* Dorling Kindersley
King Fisher Bks.   King Fisher Books
Kingston Pr.   The Kingston Press, Inc.
Kiscadale Pubns. UK   *See* Seven Hills Bk. Dists.
Kitchen Table   Kitchen Table: Women of Color Press
Kluwer Ac.   Kluwer Academic Publishers, Subs. of Wolters Kluwer N.V.
Knightsbridge Pub.   Knightsbridge Publishing Co., Inc.
Knopf   Alfred A. Knopf, Inc., Subs. of Random House, Inc.
Knowledge Indus.   Knowledge Industry Publications, Inc.
Kodansha   Kodansha America, Inc.
Kodansha Ltd. Japan   Kodansha Ltd. Japan
Korean and Related Studies Pr.   Korean & Related Studies Press
Kosciuszko   Kosciuszko Foundation
Kosmos Edit. SA Mexico   *See* Ediciones
Kosovo   Kosovo
Kramer   H. J. Kramer, Inc.
Kraus   Kraus Reprint
Kraus Intl.   Kraus International Publications
Krieger   Krieger Publishing Co.
Krishnamurti   Krishnamurti Foundation of America
Krishna Pr.   Krishna Press, Div. of Garden Press
Ktav   Ktav Publishing House, Inc.
Kyle Cathie   Kyle Cathie
Kyoiku Shoseki   Kyoiku Shoseki
Ky. U. Pr.   Kentucky University Press

L

Labor Pubns. Inc.   Labor Publications, Inc.
Labyrinthos   Labyrinthos
Labyrinth Pr.   The Labyrinth Press, Inc.
Lacon Pubs.   Lacon Publishers
Lacy   Lacy Publishers
Lake Erie Col. Pr.   Lake Erie College Press
Landmark TX   Landmark Publications
Lane Bks.   Lane Books

Larchwood Pub.   Larchwood Publishing
Larson Pubns.   Laron Publications
La. State U. Pr.   Louisiana State University Press
Lat. Am. Lit. Rev. Pr.   Latin American Literary Review Press
Latitudes Pr.   Latitudes Press
Lawrence and Wishart   Lawrence & Wishart Humanities Press International, Inc.
Lea & Febiger   Lea & Febiger
Learned Pubns.   Learned Publications, Inc.
Learning Inc.   Learning, Inc.
Leaven Pr.   Leaven Press
Leetes Isl.   Leete's Island Books
Lehigh Univ. Pr.   Lehigh University Press
Leicester U. Pr.   Leicester University Press
L. Erlbaum Assocs.   Lawrence Erlbaum Associates, Inc.
Lerner Pubns.   Lerner Publications Co.
Lester & Orpen Dennys   Lester & Orpen Dennys
Lester Publshing Ltd.   Lester Publishing, Ltd.
Lewis   Lewis Publishers, Subs. of CRC Press, Inc.
Lexik Hse.   Lexik House Publishers
Lexington Bks.   Lexington Books
L. Hill Bks.   Lawrence Hill Books
Lib. Congress   Library of Congress, Div. of U. S. Government
Lib. Co. Philadelphia   Library Company of Philadelphia
Liberal Arts Pr.   The Liberal Arts Press
Liberty Fund   Liberty Fund, Inc.
Liberty Fund Glasgow   Liberty Fund Glasgow
Liberty Pr.   Liberty Press
Libra   Libra Publishers, Inc.
Librairie Droz   Librairie Droz
Libraries Board of South Australia   Libraries Board of South Australia
Library of America   The Library of America
Library of Armenian   Library of Armenian Studies
Lib. Soc. Sci.   Library of Social Science
Libs. Unl.   Libraries Unlimited, Inc.
Lieber-Atherton   Lieber-Atherton, Inc.
Lifetime   Lifetime Books, Inc.
Lightyear   Lightyear Press, Inc.
Liguori Pubns.   Liguori Publications
Limelight Edns.   Limelight Editions
Lime Rock Pr.   Lime Rock Press, Inc.
Limestone Pr.   Limestone Press
Lindisfarne Pr.   Lindisfarne Press
Linnet Bks.   Linnet Books
Lion USA   Lion Publishing
Lippincott   J. B. Lippincott Co.
Litarvan Lit.   Litarvan Literature
Lithuanian Days   Lithuanian Days
Little   Little, Brown, & Co.
Littlefield   Littlefield, Adams & Co.
Liturgical Pr.   The Liturgical Press
Liveright   Liveright Publishing Corp.

Liverpool U. Pr. Liverpool University Press
Llewellyn Pubns. Llewellyn Publications, Div. of Llewellyn Worldwide, Ltd.
Lockwood Trade Journal Co. Lockwood Trade Journal Co.
Locus Pr. Locus Press
Locust Hill Pr. Locust Hill Press
Lodestar Lodestar Books
Logbridge-Rhodes Logbridge-Rhodes, Inc.
London Hse. London House
London Pub. London Publishing Co.
Lone Eagle Lone Eagle Publishing
Longfellow Longfellow National Historic Site
Longman Longman Publishing Group
Longmeadow Pr. Longmeadow Press
Longshanks Bk. Longshanks Book
Longwood MA Longwood Press
Lontar Foundation Lontar Foundation
Lost Roads Lost Roads Publishers
Lothrop Lothrop, Lee & Shepard Books, Div. of William Morrow & Co., Inc.
Lotus Light Lotus Light Publications
Lowell Hse. Lowell House, Div. of RGA Publishing Group, Inc.
Loyola Loyola University Press
Lubrecht & Cramer Lubrecht & Cramer, Ltd.
Luce Robert B. Luce, Inc.
Lucis Lucis Publishing Co., Div. of Lucis Trust
Lumen Christi Lumen Christi Press
Lumen Inc. Lumen, Inc.
Lund U. Pr. Lund University Press
Lynne Rienner Lynne Rienner Publishers, Inc.
Lyons & Burford Lyons & Burford Publishers, Inc.

M

Macalaster College Macalaster College
McClelland & Stewart CN *See* Firefly Bks. Ltd.
Macedonian P.E.N. Centre Macedonian P.E.N. Centre
Macedonian Review Macedonian Review
McFarland & Co. McFarland & Co., Inc., Publishers
McGill CN University of Toronto Press
McGraw McGraw-Hill, Inc.
McKay David McKay Co., Inc.
MacKellar Smiths & Jordan MacKellar Smiths & Jordan
Macmillan Macmillan Publishing Co., Inc.
Macmillan Child. Grp. Macmillan Children's Book Group, Div. of Macmillan Publishing Co., Inc.
Madison Bks. UPA Madison Books Subs. of U. Pr. of Amer.
Madison Square Madison Square Press

Madrona Pubs. Madrona Publishers, inc.
Mage Pubs. Mage Publishers, Inc.
Magi Bks. Magi Books, Inc.
Magnolia Pr. Magnolia Press
Maison des Sciences de l'Homme Maison des Sciences de l'Homme
Maisonneuve Pr. Maisonneuve Press
Makati Trade Times Makati Trade Times
Management Advisory Pubns. Management Advisory Publications
Manchester Manchester Press
Manchester Univ. Pr. *See* St. Martin
Mansell *See* Cassell
Manual Arts Pr. Manual Arts Press
Manyland Manyland Books, Inc.
Map Collection Pubs. Map Collection Publications
Mapes Monde Mapes Monde Editore, Div. of Mapes Monde, Ltd.
Marboro Bks. Marboro Books
March of Dimes March of Dimes Birth Defects Foundation
Margun Music Margun Music
Marlboro Pr. The Marlboro Press
Marquette Marquette University Press
Marquis Who's Who Marquis Who's Who, A Reed Reference Publishing Co.
Marshall Cavendish Marshall Cavendish
Marsilio Pubs. Marsilio Publishers
Martinus Nijhoff *See* Kluwer Ac.
Math Assn. Mathematical Association of America
Mathesis Pubns. Mathesis Publications, Inc.
Math. Sci. Pr. Math-Sci Press
Mayfield Pub. Mayfield Publishing Co.
Maypop Pr. Maypop Press
Mazda Pubs. Mazda Publishers
Mazula Pubs. Mazula Publications
M. Boyars Pubs. Marion Boyars, Publishers, Inc.
Meadowbrook Pr. Meadowbrook Press
Meckler Meckler Corp.
Med. Econ. Data Medical Economic Data, Inc.
Medieval Acad. Medieval Academy of America
Medieval Inst. Medieval Institute Publications
Med. Physics Pub. Medical Physics Publishing Corp.
Melbourne University Pr. *See* Coronet Bks.
Memphis State U. Memphis State University
Mennonite Hist. Soc. Mennonite Historical Society
Mennonite Pub. Mennonite Publishing
Menorah Pub. Menorah Publishing Co., Inc.
Mercer Univ. Pr. Mercer University Press
Merck Merck & Co., Inc.
Merck-Sharp-Dohme Merck Sharp & Dohme International
Mercury Mercury Pfeiffer & Co.
Mercury Hse. Inc. Mercury House, Inc.

Meriden-Stinehour Pr. Meriden-Stinehour
Press
Meridian Bks. *See* NAL-Dutton
Mermaid Pr. Mermaid Press
Merriam-Webster Inc. Merriam-Webster,
Inc., Subs. of Encyclopaedia Britannica,
Inc.
Merrill Merrill Publishing Co.
Merrimack River Merrimack River Press
Merrion Pr. Merrion Press
M. E. Sharpe M. E. Sharpe, Inc.
Messner *See* S&S Trade
Methuen *See* Heinemann Ed.
Metro. Mus. Art Metropolitan Museum of
Art
M. Evans M. Evans & Co., Inc.
Mex. Am. Cult. Mexican American Cultural
Center
Meyer Stone Bks. Meyer Stone Books
Mho & Mho Mho & Mho Words
Micah Pubns. Micah Publications
Mich. Slavic Pubns. Michigan Slavic Publi-
cations
Mich. St. U. Pr. Michigan State University
Press
Microsoft Microsoft Press
Middle East Institute Middle East Institute
Midlands Bks. Midlands Books
Mid-Peninsula Lib. Mid-Peninsula Libary Co-
operation
Milkweed Ed. Milkweed Editions
Mills Sanderson Mills & Sanderson, Publish-
ers
Minerva *See* S. Asia
Minn. Hist. Minnesota Historical Society
Press
Minumsa Pub. Co. Sth Korea Minumsa
Publishing Co. of South Korea
MIT Pr. MIT Press
Mizan Pr. Mizan Press
Mnemosyne Mnemosyne Publishing Co., Inc.
MN Humanities Minnesota Humanities
Commission
Mockingbird Bks. Mockingbird Books
Modan-Adama Modan/Adama Books
Modern Humanities Res. Modern Humani-
ties Research Assocation
Modern Lang. Modern Language Association
of America
Modern Lib. Modern Library
Modoc Pr. Modoc Press
Mojave Bks. Mojave Books
M. O'Mara Bks. *See* Seven Hills Bk. Dists.
Monash University Monash University
Monitor Monitor Book Co., Inc.
Monthly Rev. Monthly Review Press
Moody Moody Press, Div. of Moody Bible In-
stitute
Morehouse Pub. Morehouse Publishing
Moretus Pr. Moretus Press
Morgan State Morgan State University Press,
English Department
Morrow William Morrow & Co., Inc.

Morrow Jr. Bks. Morrow Junior Books
Mosaic Pr. OH Mosaic Press
Mosby *See* Mosby Yr. Bk.
Mosby Yr. Bk. Mosby-Year Book, Inc.
Mountaineers The Mountaineers Books
Mountain Pr. Mountain Press Publishing Co.
Mouton Mouton de Gruyter
Movie Pubs. Servs. Movie Publisher Ser-
vices, Inc.
Moyer Bell Limited Moyer Bell Ltd.
MRTS MRTS
Muhlenberg Pr. Muhlenberg Press
Murray Murray Publications
Murton Pr. The Murton Press
Museum of Far Eastern Antiquities Muse-
um of Far Eastern Antiquities
Museum Pr. Museum Press
Museum Tusculanums Forlag Museum Tus-
culanums Forlag
Musical Scope Pub. Musical Scope Publish-
ing
Mus. Modern Art Museum of Modern Art
Mustang Mustang Publishing
Mutual Pub. HI Mutual Publisher
Myriade The Myriade Press, Inc.
Myrin Institute Myrin Institute, Inc.
Mysterious Pr. Mysterious Press
Mystic Seaport Mystic Seaport Museum,
Inc.

N

NAASR National Research for Armenian
Studies & Research
Naiad Pr. Naiad Press, Inc.
NAL-Dutton NAL/Dutton, Div. of Penguin
USA
N. American Heritage Pr. North American
Heritage Press
NASA National Aeronautics & Space Agency
Nash Steven J. Nash Publishing
Nataraj Bks. Nataraj Books
Natl. Acad. Pr. National Academy Press
Natl. Archives Records National Archives
Records Administration
Natl. Bk. Store Philippines National Book
Store Philippines
Natl. Bur. Econ. Res. National Bureau of
Economic Research, Inc.
Natl. Ctr. Constitutional National Center for
Constitutional Studies
Natl. Gallery Art National Gallery of Art
Natl. Geog. The National Geographic Society
Natl. Inst. of Educ. National Institute of
Education
Nat'l. Journal National Journal
Nat'l League Nurse National League for
Nursing
Natl. Museum Women National Museum of
Women in the Arts

Natl. Poet. Foun. National Poetry Foundation
Natl. Wildlife National Wildlife Federation
Natl. Woodlands Pub. National Woodlands Publishing Co.
Natural History Pr. Natural History Press
Naturegraph Naturegraph Publishers, Inc.
Nautical & Aviation Publ. Co. Nautical & Aviation Publishing Co. of America, Inc.
Nauwelaerts Nauwelaerts
Navajvan Publishing Hse. Navajvan Publishing House
Naval Inst. Pr. Naval Institute Press
NCSS National Council for the Social Studies
NCTE National Council of Teachers of English
NCTM National Council of Teachers of Mathematics
NCUP New College University Press
NEA National Education Assocation
Neal-Schuman Neal-Schuman Publishers, Inc.
Nelson Thomas Nelson, Publishers
Nelson Comm. Nelson Communications, Subs. of Thomas Nelson, Publishers
Nelson-Hall Nelson-Hall, Inc.
N. Eng. Pub. Assoc. New England Publishing Associates, Inc.
Neo Lao Haksat Pub. Neo Lao Haksat Publishing
NE U. Pr. Northeastern University Press
New Age New Age Books
New Amer. Lib. *See* NAL-Dutton
New Amer. Pr. New Americas Press
New Amsterdam Bks. New Amsterdam Books
Newbury Bks. Newbury Books
Newcastle Pub. Newcastle Publishing Co., Inc.
New Cent. Pubns. New Century Publications
New Clarion Pr. New Clarion Press
New Coll. U. Pr. New College University Press
Newcomen Society Newcomen Society
New Dir. Pr. New Directions Press
New English Library New English Library
New Era Pubns. MI New Era Publications, Inc.
New Horizons Pr. New Horizons Press
Newhouse Pr. Newhouse Press
New Ireland Pr. New Ireland Press
New London Pr. New London Press
New Market New Market Press
New Orleans Urban New Orleans Urban Folklore Society
New Press NY New Press
New Republic Bks. New Republic Books
New Rivers Pr. New Rivers Press
New Soc. Pubs. New Society Publishers
New World Lib. New World Library, Div. of Whatever Publishing, Inc.
New World Press NY New World Press

New York Graphic Society New York Graphic Society
Nijhoff Martinus Nijhoff Netherlands
N. Ill. U. Pr. Northern Illinois University Press
N. Mich. U. Pr. Northern Michigan University Press
No. Am. Trust Pub. North American Trust Publishing
Noble Pr. The Noble Press, Inc.
NOK Pubs. NOK Publishers, International
Nolo Pr. Nolo Press
Noontide The Noontide Press
Nordic Bks. Nordic Books
Nordland Pr. Nordland Press
Norris World Norris World Enterprises
North Atlantic North Atlantic Books
North Bks. North Books
North-Holland *See* Elsevier
North. Ill. U. Ctr. SE Asian Northern Illinois University, Center for Southeast Asian Studies
North River North River Press, Inc.
Northwestern U. Pr. Northwestern University Press
North Word NorthWord Press, Inc.
Norton W. W. Norton & Co., Inc.
Norwegian-Am. Hist. Assn. Norwegian American Historical Association
Nostos Bks. Nostos Books
Nova Sci. Pubs. Nova Science Publishers, Inc.
Noyes Noyes Publications
N. Point Pr. North Point Press
NSU Pr. LA Northwestern State University of Louisiana Press
NTC Pub. Grp. NTC Publishing Group
Nutt Nutt Studio
NW Pub. Northwest Publishing, Inc.
NY Acad. Sci. New York Academy of Science
NY Pub. Lib. New York Public Library
NY Times New York Times
NYU Pr. New York University Press
NY Zoetrope New York Zoetrope

O

Oak Knoll Oak Knoll Books
Oak Pub. Oak Publishing
Oak Tree Pubns. Oak Tree Publications, Inc., Div. of Vizcom, Inc.
Oberlin Coll. Pr. Oberlin College Press
Occidental Occidental Press
Oceana Oceana Publications, Inc.
Octagon *See* Hippocrene Bks.
October October House
Octopus Octopus Books
Oddo Oddo Publishing, Inc.
Odonian Pr. Odonian Press

Odyssey Pr.   Odyssey Press
OECD   Organization for Economic Cooperation & Development
O'Hara   J. Philip O'Hara Publishers, Inc., Subs. of Scross Press, Inc.
Ohio St. U. Pr.   Ohio State University Press
Ohio U. Ctr. Intl.   *See* Ohio U. Pr.
Ohio U. Pr.   Ohio University Press
Oil & Gas   Oil & Gas Consultants International, Inc.
Okla St. U. Pr.   Oklahoma State University Press
Okpaku Communications   Okpaku Communications Corp.
Old Mission Santa Barbara   Old Mission Santa Barbara
Oleander Pr.   The Oleander Press
Oliver & Boyd   Oliver & Boyd
Omega LA   Omega Publishing Service
Omenana   Omenana
Omnibus Pr.   Omnibus Press
Omnigraphics Inc.   Omnigraphics, Inc.
OMS   Office of Management Services, Div. of Association of Research Libraries
One World Pubns.   One World Publications, Ltd.
Ongpin Institute of Business   Ongpin Institute of Business
Ontario Rev. NJ   Ontario Review Press
Onyx   *See* NAL-Dutton
Open Court   Open Court Publishing Co., Div. of Carus Corp.
Open U. Pr.   *See* Taylor & Francis
Orbis Bks.   Orbis Books
Oreg. St. U. Pr.   Oregon State University Press
Oriental Bk. Store   The Oriental Book Store
Orientalia   Orientalia Art, Ltd.
Oriental Inst.   Oriental Institute Publications Sales, Div. of University of Chicago Press
Orient. Bk. Dist.   Oriental Book Distributors
Oryx   Oryx Press
Osborne-McGraw   Osborne/McGraw-Hill, Div. of McGraw-Hill, Inc.
OTA   Office of Technology Assessment
OUP   Oxford University Press, Inc.
Our Sunday Visitor   Our Sunday Visitor, Publishing Division
Outlet Bk. Co.   Outlet Book Co., Inc.
Overlook Pr.   Overlook Press
Owlswick Pr.   Owlswick Press
Ox Bow   Ox Bow Press
Oxbow Bks.   *See* David Brown
Oxbridge Comm.   Oxbridge Communications, Inc.
Oxford Bibliographical Soc., Bodleian Lib.   Oxford Bibliographical Society, Bodleian Library
Oxmoor Hse.   Oxmoor House, Inc.
Oyez   Oyez
Ozer   Jerome S. Ozer, Publisher, Inc.

P

Pace Intl. Res.   Pace International Research, Inc.
Pace Univ. Pr.   Pace University Press
Pachart   Pachart Publishing House, Div. of Pachart Foundation
Pacific Bks.   Pacific Books, Publishers
Pacific Pr. Pub. Assn.   Pacific Press Publishing Association
Paganiniana Pubns.   Paganiniana Publications, Inc.
Pa. Hist. & Mus. Commission   Pennsylvania Historical & Museum Commission
Paideia MA   Paideia Publishers
Pajarito Pubns.   Pajarito Publications
PAJ Pubns.   PAJ Publications
Panda Bks.   Panda Books
Pandit Pr.   Pandit Press, Ltd.
Panjandrum   Panjandrum Books
Pan Korea Bk. Corp.   Pan Korea Book Corp.
Pantheon   Pantheon Books
Paperbook Pr. Inc.   Paperbook Press, Inc.
Paper Pubns. Soc.   Paper Publications Society
Para   Para Publishing
Paragon Hse.   Paragon House Publishers
Parallax Pr.   Parallax Press
Parker Pub. IL   Parker Publishing
Parkwest Pubns.   Parkwest Publications, Inc.
Parramon Ediciones   Parramon Ediciones
Parsons Bks.   Parsons Books
Parthenon   The Parthenon Publishing Group, Inc.
Pastoral Pr.   Pastoral Press, Div. of National Association of Pastoral Musicians
Pa. St. U. Pr.   Pennsylvania State University Press
Pathfinder NY   Pathfinder Press
Patterson Smith   Patterson Smith Publishing Corp.
Paul & Co. Pubs.   Paul & Co. Publishers Consortium, Inc.
Paulist Pr.   Paulist Press
Paunch   Paunch
PB   Pocket Books
P. Bedrick Bks.   Peter Bedrick Books
PCA Enterp.   P.C.A. Enterprises
Peachpit Pr.   Peachpit Press
Peachtree Pubs.   Peachtree Publishers, Ltd.
Peacock Pubs.   F. E. Peacock Publishers, Inc.
Peeters Pr.   Peeters Press
Pegasus   Pegasus, Affil. of Bobbs-Merrill Co., Inc.
Pelican   Pelican Publishing Corp., Inc.
Pen Amer. Ctr.   PEN American Center
Pencil Point Pr. Inc.   Pencil Point Press
Pendle Hill   Pendle Hill Publications
Pendragon NY   Pendragon Press, Subs. of Camelot Publishing Co., Inc.
Penkevill   The Penkevill Publishing Co.

Penn. German Soc. Pennsylvania German Society
PennWell Bks. PennWell Books, Div. of PennWell Publishers Co.
Pentalic Corp. Pentalic Corp.
Penzler Bks. Penzler Books
People's Med. Soc. People's Medical Society
People's Pub. People's Publishing Co., Inc.
Performing Arts Performing Arts Network
Pergamon Pergamon Press, Inc.
Perigee Perigee Books
Peripatetic Peripatetic Press, Inc.
Perishable Pr. The Perishable Press, Ltd.
Perivale Pr. Perivale Press
Permaculture Permaculture Services International, Inc.
Permanent Pr. The Permanent Press, Affil. of Second Chance Press
Persea Bks. Persea Books, Inc.
Persephone Pr. Persephone Press
Personal Library Personal Library
Peters Corp. NM Peters Corp.
Peter Smith Peter Smith Publisher, Inc.
Petrocelli Petrocelli Books
Petronium Pr. Petronium Press
PG Partington Paul G. Partington
P-H Prentice Hall, Div. of Simon & Schuster, Inc.
P-H Gen. Ref. & Trav. Prentice-Hall General Reference & Travel, Div. of Simon & Schuster, Inc.
Phaeton Phaeton Press, Inc.
Phaidon UK Phaidon Press
Phanes Pr. Phanes Press
Pharos Bks. Pharos Books
Phi Beta Kappa Phi Beta Kappa
Philadelphia Patristic Foundation Philadelphia Patristic Foundation
Philos. Document Philosophy Documentation Center
Philos. Lib. Philosophical Library
Philosophia Pr. Philosophia
Philos. Sci. Assn. Philosophy of Science Association
P. Hunt Paul Hunt
Pickwick Pickwick Publication
Pierian Pr. Pierian Press
Pierpont Morgan Pierpont Morgan Library
Pierre Fauchard Academy Pierre Fauchard Academy
Pilgrim Bks. Pilgrim Books
Pilgrim Pr. Pilgrim Press
Pilot Bks. Pilot Books
Pimlico *See* Trafalgar
Pine River WI Pine River Press
Pinter *See* Wiley
Pitts. Theolog. Pittsburgh Theological Seminary
Plain Bks. Plain Books
P. Lang Pubs. Peter Lang Publishing, Inc.
Players Pr. Players Press, Inc.
Plenum Plenum Publishing Corp.
Plough The Plough Publishing House

Pluto Pr. Pluto Press
PNS Pubs. PNS Publishers
Pocket Bks. *See* PB
Poe Soc. Baltimore Poe Society of Baltimore
Poetry Miscellany Poetry Miscellany
Poets and Writers Poets & Writers
Poets Pr. The Poets Press
Point Loma Pub. Point Loma Publications, Inc.
Policy Studies Policy Studies Organization
Polish Inst. Arts & Sci. Polish Institute of Arts & Sciences of America, inc.
Polygon Pr. UK Polygon Press
Polytechnic Pr. Polytechnic Press
Pontifical Inst. of Medieval Studies Pontifical Institute of Medieval Studies
Pope John Ctr. Pope John Center
Popular Periodical Index Popular Periodical Index
Population Coun. The Population Council
Porcupine Pr. Porcupine Press, Inc.
Porcupine's Quill Porcupine's Quill
Porter Sargent Porter Sargent Publishers, Inc.
Poseidon Pr. Poseidon Press, Div. of Simon & Schuster, Inc.
Post Group The Post Group
Potala Potala Corp.
Potter Pubns. Potter Publications
Praeger *See* Greenwood
Prairie Poet Bks. Prairie Poet Books
Prelude Press Prelude Press
Prescott St. Pr. Prescott Street Press
Preservation Pr. The Preservation Press, Div. of National Trust for Historic Preservation
Presses de l'université du Quebec Presses de l'université du Quebec
Presses de l'université Laval Presses de l'université Laval
Press N. Amer. Press North America
Price Stern Price Stern Sloan, Inc.
Prima Pub. Prima Publishing
Princeton Arch. Princeton Architectural Press
Princeton Bk. Co. Princeton Book Co., Publishers
Princeton U. Pr. Princeton University Press
Priory Pr. Priory Press
Private Libs. Assoc. Private Libraries Association
Pro-Am Music Pro-Am Music
Pro Arte Libri Pro Arte Libri
Prod. Press The Productivity Press
Progressive Pubns. Progressive Publications
Prog. Studies Program Studies
Prometheus Bks. Prometheus Books
Proscenium Proscenium Press
PSG Pubns. PSG Publications
Psychohistory Pr. Psychohistory Press
Public Affairs Pr. Public Affairs Press

Public Management   Public Management In-
stitute
Puffin Bks.   Puffin Books
Purdue U. Pr.   Purdue University Press
Purple Mnt. Pr.   Purple Mountain Press, Ltd.
Pushcart Pr.   The Pushcart Press
Putnam Pub. Group   The Putnam Publishing
Group
P. V. Goldsmith   P. V. Goldsmith Publishing
Co.

Q

Quadrangle   *See* Brunner-Mazel
Quaker City Bks.   Quaker City Books
Quality Med. Pub.   Quality Medical Publish-
ing, Inc.
Quartet UK   *See* Interlink Pub.
Que Corp.   Que Corp., Div. of Prentice Hall
Computer Publishing
Queens Hse.-Focus Serv.   Queens
House/Focus Service
Quill and Brush   Quill & Brush
Quintessence   Quintessence Publications

R

Ragged Mountain Pr.   Ragged Mountain
Press
Rainy Day Oreg.   Rainy Day Press
Ramakrishna   Ramakrishna-Vivekananda
Center
Rand Corp.   The Rand Corp.
R & E Miles   R & E Miles
Rand McNally   Rand McNally & Co.
Random   Random House, Inc.
Random Bks. Yng. Read.   Random House
Books for Young Readers, Div. of Random
House, Inc.
Raven   Raven Press, Ltd., Subs. of Wolters
Kluwer U.S. Corp.
R. C. Packard   Rosa Covington Packard
Reader's Catalog   The Reader's Catalog
Readers Intl.   Readers International
Readex Bks.   Readex Books, Div. of Readex
Microprint Corp.
Real Comet   The Real Comet Press
Real People Pr.   Real People Press
Rebus   Rebus, Inc.
Reconstructionist Pr.   Reconstructionist
Press
Red Dust   Red Dust, Inc.
Redgrave Pub. Co.   Redgrave Publishing Co.
Red Gull Pr.   Red Gull Press
Red Hill Pr.   Red Hill Press
Red Rooster Pr.   Red Rooster Press
Red Sea Pr.   Red Sea Press
Reed Ref. Pub.   Reed Reference Publishing

Reference Pr. Intl.   Reference Press Interna-
tional
Ref. Press   Reference Press, Inc.
Regal Pubn.   Regal Publications
Regina Bks.   Regina Books
Regional Sci. Res. Inst.   Regional Science
Research Institute
Register Pr.   Register Press
Regnery Gateway   Regnery Gateway, Inc.
Reidel Pub.   *See* Kluwer Ac.
Reilly & Lee   Reilly & Lee
Reinhold   *See* Van Nos. Reinhold
**Religious and Theological Abstracts,
Inc.**   Religious & Theological Abstracts,
Inc.
Renfro Studios   Nancy Renfro Studios
Resc. Rehab.   Resources for Rehabilitation
**Research School of Pacific Studies, Austra-
lian National U.**   Research School of Pacif-
ic Studies, Australian National University
Res. Inst. Inner Asia Studies   Research In-
stitute for Inner Asia Studies
Resource Pub.   Resource Publications, Inc.
Res. Pubns. CT   Research Publications, Inc.
Reston   *See* P-H
Revisionist Pr.   Revisionist Press
Reynal & Hitchcock   Reynal & Hitchcock
R. H. Sommer   Robert H. Sommer, Publish-
er
Rice Univ.   Rice University Press
Richard Marek Pubs.   *See* Putnam Pub.
Group
Richard West   Richard West
Richwood Pub.   Richwood Publishing
Ridgeview   Ridgeview Publishing Co.
Ridgeway   Ridgeway Press
Rinehart   Roberts Rinehart, Publishers
Riverdale Co.   The Riverdale Co., Inc.
Riverrun NY   Riverrun Press, Inc.
Rizzoli Intl.   Rizzoli International Publica-
tions, Inc.
Rob Briggs   Rob Briggs, Associates
Robinson Bks.   Robinson Books
Rockefeller U. Pr.   Rockefeller University
Press
Rodale Pr. Inc.   Rodale Press, Inc.
Rodef Shalom Pr.   Rodef Shalom Press
Roehrs   Roehrs Co.
Ronald Pr.   Ronald Press
Ronin Pub.   Ronin Publishing
Rosenbach Mus. & Lib.   The Rosenbach Mu-
seum & Library
Rosen Group   The Rosen Publishing Group,
Inc.
Rosenkilde & Boyger   Rosenkilde & Boyger
Ross   Ross Books
Rossel Bks.   Rossel Books, Div. of Seymour
Rossel Co., Inc.
Rothman   Fred B. Rothman & Co., Inc.
Roth Pub. Inc.   Roth Publishing, Inc.
Roundwood Pr.   Roundwood Press
Routledge   Routledge, Div. of Routledge,
Chapman, & Hall, Inc.

Routledge Chapman & Hall Routledge, Chapman, & Hall, Inc., Subs. of International Thomson Organization

Rowman Rowman & Littlefield Publishers, Inc.

Royal Asiatic Society Royal Asiatic Society

RPI Rensselaer Polytechnic Institute

Rprt. Serv. Reprint Services Corp.

R. Rinehart Roberts Rinehart Publishers

R. S. Barnes Richard S. Barnes & Co., Books

Running Pr. Running Press Book Publishers

Russell Sage Russell Sage Foundation

Russell WV Russell Publishing Co.

Russica Pubs. Russica Publishers

Russ Walter Russ Walter, Publisher

Rutgers U. Pr. Rutgers University Press

S

Sachem Pr. Sachem Press

Sage Sage Publications, Inc.

Saifer Albert Saifer, Publisher

St. Alban Pr. Saint Alban Press

St. Ambrose U. Saint Ambrose University

St. Anthony Guild St. Anthony Guild

St. Bedes Pubns. Saint Bedes Publications

St. Dunstan's U. Pr. Saint Dunstan's University Press

St. James Pr. Saint James Press

St. Joseph College Saint Joseph College

St. Martin Saint Martin's Press, Inc., Subs. of Macmillan Publishing Co., Inc.

St. Paul Books Saint Paul Books

St. Sebastian Pr. Saint Sebastian Press

Salem Hse. Pubs. Salem House Publications

Salem Pr. Salem Press, Inc.

SamHar Pr. SamHar Press

Samisdat Samisdat

Sams Sams, Div. of Prentice Hall Computer Publishing

Sandhill Crane Sandhill Crane Press, Inc.

S&S Trade Simon & Schuster, Inc.

San Francisco Pr. San Francisco Press

Sanhedrin Sanhedrin Hebrew Publishing Co.

Sanskrit Classics Sanskrit Classics

Santa Barb. Mus. Art Santa Barbara Museum of Art

Saraswati Pustak Bhander Saraswati Pustak Bhander

S. Asia South Asia Books

Sathirakoses Nagapradipo Foundation Sathirakoses Nagapradipo Foundation

Saunders W. B. Saunders Co., Subs. of Harcourt Brace & Co.

Saunders and Otley Saunders & Otley

Saybrook Saybrook Publishing Co., Inc.

Sc. & Behavior Science & Behavior Books, Inc.

Scala Bks. Scala Books

S. Campbell Sandy M. Campbell

Scarecrow Scarecrow Press, Inc.

Schalkenbach Robert Schalkenbach Foundation

Schenkman Bks. Inc. Schenkman Books, Inc.

Schildge Pub. Schildge Publishing Co.

Schirmer Bks. Schirmer Books

Schocken Schocken Books, Inc.

Schoenhof Schoenhof's Foreign Books, Inc.

Scholar Bookshelf Scholar's Bookshelf

Scholarly Scholarly Press, Inc.

Scholarly Res. Inc. Scholarly Resources, Inc.

Scholars Pr. GA Scholars Press

Scholastic Inc. Scholastic, Inc.

Schol. Facsimiles Scholars' Facsimiles & Reprints

Scholium Intl. Scholium International, Inc.

Schreiber Schreiber & McLain Publisher

Science History Pubns. Science History Publications

Scientia Verlag Aalen Scientia Verlag Aalen

Sci. Tech. Pub. Science Tech Publishers

Scorpion *See* Interlink Pub.

Scot. Acad. Pr. UK *See* Mercer Univ. Pr.

Scott F. Scott, Foresman & Co.

Scream Pr. Scream Press

Scribner Charles Scribner's Sons

Scripta Scripta Humanistica

Script City Script City

Seabury Seabury Press, Inc.

Seal Pr. Feminist Seal Press-Feminist

Seaver Bks. Seaver Books

Secker & Warburg UK *See* Trafalgar

Second Chance Second Chance Press

Seely, Service & Co. Seely, Service & Co.

Select Bks. Select Books

Selene Bks. Selene Books

Self Realization Self Realization Fellowship

Seluzicki Fine Bks. Charles Seluzicki, Fine Books

Seminary Pr. Seminary Press

Senda Nueva Senda Nueva de Ediciones, Inc.

Seneca Bks. Seneca Books, Inc.

Sense Maker The Sense Maker

Sequoia Pub. Inc. Sequoia Publishing, Inc.

Serbia Pr. Serbia Press

Seven Hills Bk. Dists. Seven Hills Book Distributors

Seven Lakes Pr. Seven Lakes Press

Seven Locks Pr. Seven Locks Press

Seven Seas Pr. Seven Seas Press

Seventh Son Pr. Seventh Son Press

Severn Hse. Severn House Publishers, Ltd.

Seymour Pubns. Dale Seymour Publications

S. F. Vanni S. F. Vanni

S. G. Phillips S. G. Phillips, Inc.

Shaker Mus. Shaker Museum Foundation, Inc.

Shambhala Shambhala Publications, Inc.

Shapolsky Pubs. Shapolsky Publishers, Inc.

Sheba Pr. Sheba Press, Ltd.

Sheed & Ward MO   Sheed & Ward
Sheep Meadow   The Sheep Meadow Press
Sheffield Acad. Pr.   *See* Cornell Univ. Pr.
Shepherd Pub.   Shepherd Publishing House
Sheppard Pr.   Sheppard Press
Sheriar Pr.   Sheriar Press
Sheridan   Sheridan House, Inc.
Shiloh Bks.   Shiloh Books
Shilo Pub. Hse.   Shilo Publishing House, Inc.
Shire Pr.   Shire Press
Shoe String   Shoe String Press, Inc.
Shorey   Shorey Book Store
Siam Society   Siam Society
Sidgewick & Jackson   Sidgewick & Jackson
Sierra   Sierra Club Books
Sigma Fairport   Sigma Fairport Foundation, Inc.
Signature Bks.   Signature Books, Inc.
Signet   *See* NAL-Dutton
S. Ill. U. Pr.   Southern Illinois University Press
Silver Burdett Pr.   Silver Burdett Press
Sinauer Assocs.   Sinauer Associates, Inc.
Singapore U. Pr.   Singapore University Press
Singular Publishing   Singular Publishing Group, Inc.
Sixteenth Cent.   Sixteenth Century Journal Publishers, Inc.
S. J. Durst   Sanford J. Durst
S. Karger   S. Karger, AG
Sky Pub.   Sky Publishing Corp.
Slavica   Slavica Publishers, Inc.
Slosson Educational Pubs.   Slosson Educational Publishers
Slovene Studies   Slovene Studies
Small Pr. Dist.   Small Press Distribution, Inc.
Smiling Dolphins Pr.   Smiling Dolphins Press
Smithsonian Inst.   Smithsonian Institution Press
SMU Pr.   Southern Methodist University Press
Snow Lion   Snow Lion Publications, Inc.
Society of Typographic Arts   Society of Typographic Arts
Society Sp. & Sp-Am.   Society of Spanish & Spanish-American Studies
Soc. Indus.-Appl. Math.   Society for Industrial & Applied Mathematics
Sofia-Press   Sofia Press
Soho Press   Soho Press, Inc.
Soil & Water Conserv.   Soil & Water Conservation Society
Solaris Pr.   Solaris Press, Inc.
Solar Pub.   Solar Publishing
Solidaridad Pub.   Solidaridad Publishing
Solitaire Pub.   Solitaire Publishing
Somerset Pub.   Somerset Publishers, Inc.
Somerville Coll.   Somerville College
Soongsil U. Pr.   Soongsil University Press
Sophia Univ. Pr.   Sophia University Press
Sotheby Pubns.   Sotheby Publications
Soundings Pr.   Soundings Press

South Asia Bks.   *See* S. Asia
South End Pr.   South End Press
Spanish Lit. Pubns.   Spanish Literature Publications Co., Inc.
Spec. Child   Special Child Publications
Specific Pr.   Specific Press
Speedimpex   Speedimpex U.S.A., Inc.
Speller   Robert Speller & Sons, Publishers
Sphinx Pr.   Sphinx Press
Spinsters   Spinsters Book Co.
Spirit That Moves   The Spirit That Moves Us Press
Spoken Lang. Serv.   Spoken Language Services, Inc.
Spoon River   The Spoon River Press
Springer Pub.   Springer Publishing Co., Inc.
Springhouse   Springhouse Publishing Co.
Spring Pubns.   Spring Publications, Inc.
Spr.-Verlag   Springer-Verlag New York, Inc.
S. R. Guggenheim   Solomon R. Guggenheim Museum
Stackpole   Stackpole Books
Stanford U. Pr.   Stanford University Press
Starlight FL   Starlight Publishing Co.
Starmont Hse.   Starmont House
Starrhill Pr.   Starrhill Press
Starr King   Starr King
Star Rover   Star Rover House at Jack London Heritage House
Starwood Pub.   Starwood Publishing, Inc.
State House Pr.   State House Press
State U. NY Pr.   State University of New York Press
Station Hill Pr.   Station Hill Press
Stein & Day   Stein & Day
Steinbeck Society   Steinbeck Society
Stella Maris Bks.   Stella Maris Books
Stemmer Hse.   Stemmer House Publishers, Inc.
Stephen Greene Pr.   Stephen Greene Press
Sterling   Sterling Publishing Co., Inc.
Stewart Tabori & Chang   Stewart, Tabori & Chang, Inc.
St. Mut.   State Mutual Book & Periodical Service, Ltd.
Stokes   Stokes Publishing Co.
Stone Bridge Pr.   Stone Bridge Press
Stone Wall Pr.   Stone Wall Press
Storey Comm. Inc.   Storey Communications, Inc.
Stowe-Day   Stowe-Day Foundation
Strawberry   Strawberry Press
Studia Hispanica   Studia Hispanica Editors
Studio Pubns.   Studio Publications
Stuttman   H. S. Stuttman, Inc.
Styner & Cist   Styner & Cist
Sugden   Sherwood Sugden & Co.
Suhrkamp   *See* Fr. & Eur.
Summa Pubns.   Summa Publications
Summit Bks.   Summit Books, Div. of Simon & Schuster, Inc.
Summy-Birchard   Summy-Birchard, Inc.
Sun & Moon CA   Sun & Moon Press

Sunflower U. Pr. Sunflower University Press
Sun Pub. Sun Publishing Co.
SUNY Pr. *See* State U. NY Pr.
Surf Trav. Pubns. Surf Travel Publications
Surrey Bks. Surrey Books
Susquehanna U. Pr. Susquehanna University Press
Swallow Swallow Press
Swan Raven Swan Raven & Co.
Swaraj Pubn. (India) Swaraj Publications
Swedenborg Swedenborg Foundation, Inc.
Swets North Am. Swets North America
SW Pub. Southwest Publishing Co.
Sybex Sybex, Inc.
Synergistic Pr. Synergistic Press, Inc.
Syracuse U. Pr. Syracuse University Press
Szechenyi Society Szechenyi Society

T

TAB Bks. T A B Books, Div. of McGraw-Hill, Inc.
Tahrike Tarsile Quran Tahrike Tarsile Quran
Talon Pr. Talon Press
Tamarind Pr. Tamarind Press
Tamburitza Tamburitza Press
Tamesis Bks. Ltd. *See* Boydell & Brewer
TAN Bks. Pubs. TAN Books & Publishers, Inc.
Taplinger Taplinger Publishing Co., Inc.
Tashmoo The Tashmoo Press
Taunton Taunton Press, Inc.
Taylor & Francis Taylor & Francis, Inc.
Tchrs. Coll. Teachers College Press, Teachers College, Columbia University
T. C. Pub. T/C Publications
Technomic Technomic Publishing Co.
Telcraft Bks. Telcraft Books
Telegraph Bks. Telegraph Books
Templegate Templegate Publishers
Temple U. Pr. Temple University Press
TeNeues TeNeues Publishing Co.
Ten Speed Pr. Ten Speed Press
Tex. A & M Univ. Pr. Texas A & M University Press
Texas Ctr. Writers Texas Center for Writers Press
Tex. Christian Texas Christian University Press
Tex. St. Hist. Assn. Texas State Historical Association
Tex. Tech. Univ. Pr. Texas Tech University Press
TFH Pubns. TFH Publications, Inc.
Thames Hudson Thames & Hudson
Thammasat U. Pr. Thammasat University Press
Theatre Arts Bks. *See* Routledge, Chapman & Hall
Theatre Comm. Theatre Communications

Theobald Paul Theobald & Co.
Theosophy Theosophy Co.
Theos. Pub. Hse. Theosophical Publishing House
Theos. U. Pr. Theosophical University Press
The Smith The Smith
Thieme Med. Pubs. Thieme Medical Publishers, Inc.
Third Woman Third Woman Press
Third World Third World Press
Third World Center for Research and Publishing Third World Center for Research & Publishing
Thomas Charles C. Thomas, Publisher
Thorndike Pr. Thorndike Press
Thorsons SF Thorsons, Div. of Harper San Francisco
Thousand Autumns Pr. A Thousand Autumns Press
Three Continents Three Continents Press
Threshold VT Threshold Books
Thunders Mouth Thunder's Mouth Press
Ticknor & Fields Ticknor & Fields, Affil. of Houghton Mifflin Co.
Tidewater Tidewater Publishers
Timber Timber Press
Times Bks. *See* Random
Timken Pubs. Timken Publishers, Inc.
Tioga Pub. Tioga Publishing Co.
Tip Pubns. Tip Publications
Tiresias Pr. Tiresias Press, Inc.
Todd Pubns. Todd Publications
Tor Bks. Tor Books, Div. of Tom Doherty Associates, Inc.
Torstar Bks. Torstar Books
Touchstone Bks. Touchstone Books, Div. of Simon & Schuster, Inc.
Tourmaline Pub. Co. Tourmaline Publishing Co.
Trafalgar Trafalgar Square/David & Charles, Inc.
Transaction Pubs. Transaction Publishers
Trans-Atl. Phila. Trans-Atlantic Publications, Inc.
Transgravity Pr. Transgravity Press
Translation Pr. Translation Press
Trefoil Trefoil
Tribune Tribune Publishing
Trickster Pr. Trickster Press
Trillium Pr. Trillium Press
Trinity Press International Trinity Press International
Trinity U. Pr. Trinity University Press
Troll Assocs. Troll Associates, Subs. of Educational Reading Services
TSL Pr. Time & Space, Limited
Tundra Bks. Tundra Books of Northern New York
Turtle Isl. Foun. Turtle Island Foundation, Netzahaulcoyotl Historical Society
Twayne *See* Macmillan
Twelve Trees Pr. Twelve Trees Press
Twenty-Third Twenty-Third Publications

Twin Peaks Pr. Twin Peaks Press Berkeley, Chicano Studies Library
Tx. St. Direct Texas State Directory Press
Typophiles The Typophiles

U

Ubu Repertory Theater Pubns. Ubu Repertory Theater Publications
U. CA Pr. University of California Press
UC Berkeley Ctr. SE Asia University of California, Berkeley, Center for South & Southeast Asia Studies
UC Chicano Lib. University of California, Chicano Library
U. Ch. Pr. University of Chicago Press
U. CO Busn. Res. Div. University of Colorado Business Research Division
UH Pr. University of Hawaii Press
U. Kebangsaan Malaysia University of Kebangsaan Malaysia
Ukranian Acad. Ukranian Academic Press
Ukranian Arts Sci. Ukranian Academy of Arts & Sciences in the U.S.
Ultramarine Pub. Ultramarine Publishing Co., Inc.
Ulverscroft Ulverscroft Large Print Books, Ltd.
UMI Research UMI Research Collections
UN United Nations
Undena Pubns. Undena Publications
Underwood-Miller Underwood/Miller
Undiscovd. Worlds Pr. Undiscovered World Press
UNESCO *See* UNIPUB
U. New Haven Pr. University of New Haven Press
Unicorn Pr. Unicorn Press
Union Theological Seminary (Virginia) Union Theological Seminary
UNIPUB UNIPUB, Div. of Kraus Organization, Ltd.
United Bible *See* Am. Bible
United Syn. Bk. United Synagogue of America Book Service
United Western Pr. United Western Press
Univ. Central AR Pr. University of Central Arkansas Press
Univ. Chi. Lib. University of Chicago Library
Univelt Univelt, Inc.
Universe Universe Publishing, Inc.
Universe Pub. Co. Universe Publishing Co.
University MT University Press
Univ. Microfilms University Microfilms, Inc.
Univ. of Hull University of Hull Press
Univ. of Malaya Press University of Malaya Press
Univ. of New South Wales Pr. University of New South Wales Press
Univ. of South Pacific Pr. University of the South Pacific Press

Univ. Place University Place Book Shop
Univ. Pr. of Amer. University Press of America
Univ. Rochester Pr. University of Rochester Press
Univ. Sci. Bks. University Science Books
Unwin Hyman Unwin Hyman
U. of Adelaide Pr. University of Adelaide Press
U. of Ala. Pr. University of Alabama Press
U. of Ariz. Pr. University of Arizona Press
U. of Ark. Pr. University of Arkansas Press
U. of Brit. Col. Pr. University of British Columbia Press
U. of Conn. School of Education University of Connecticut School of Education
U. of Delaware Pr. University of Delaware Press
U. of Ga. Pr. University of Georgia Press
U. of Glasgow Pr. University of Glasgow Press
U. of Hawaii Pr. University of Hawaii Press
U. of Idaho Press University of Idaho Press
U. of Ife Pr. University of Ife Press
U. of Ill. Pr. University of Illinois Press
U. of Iowa Pr. University of Iowa Press
U. of Kyoto University of Kyoto
U. of London, School of Oriental and African Studies University of London, School of Oriental & African Studies
U. of Maine Pr. University of Maine Press
U. of Mass. Pr. University of Massachusetts Press
U. of Miami Pr. University of Miami Press
U. of Mich. Pr. University of Michigan Press
U. of Minn. Pr. University of Minnesota Press
U. of Miss. Pr. University of Mississippi Press
U. of Mo. Pr. University of Missouri Press
U. of NC Pr. University of North Carolina Press
U. of Nebr. Pr. University of Nebraska Press
U. of Nev. Pr. University of Nevada Press
U. of NM Pr. University of New Mexico Press
U. of Notre Dame Pr. University of Notre Dame Press
U. of Okla. Pr. University of Oklahoma Press
U. of Otago Pr. University of Otago Press
U. of Ottawa Pr. University of Ottawa Press
U. of Pa. Pr. University of Pennsylvania Press
U. of Pittsburgh Pr. University of Pittsburgh Press
U. of Queensland Pr. University of Queensland Press
U. of SC Pr. University of South Carolina Press
U. of Tenn. Pr. University of Tennessee Press
U. of Tex. Pr. University of Texas Press
U. of Tokyo Pr. University of Tokyo Press

U. of Toronto Pr.   University of Toronto Press
U. of Uppsala Pr.   University of Uppsala Press
U. of Utah Pr.   University of Utah Press
U. of Wales Pr.   University of Wales Press
U. of Wash. Pr.   University of Washington Press
U. of Wis. Pr.   University of Wisconsin Press
U. Pr. Colo.   University Press of Colorado
U. Pr. Fla.   University Press of Florida
U. Pr. of KS   University Press of Kansas
U. Pr. of Ky.   University Press of Kentucky
U. Pr. of Miss.   University Press of Mississippi
U. Pr. of New Eng.   University Press of New England
U. Pr. of Va.   University Press of Virginia
U. Pubns. Amer.   University Publications of America
Urban Inst.   Urban Institute
Urizen Books   Urizen Boks
US Games Syst.   United States Games Systems, Inc.
USGPO   United States Government Printing Office
U. TX Inst. Lat. Am. Stud.   University of Texas Institute for Latin American Studies
U. Wisc. Ctr. SE Asian   University of Wisconsin, Center for Southeast Asian Studies
U. Wisc.-River Falls Pr.   University of Wisconsin-River Falls Press

V

Vagabond Pr.   Vagabond Press
Vance Biblios.   Vance Bibliographies
Vanderbilt U. Pr.   Vanderbilt University Press
Van Gorcum   *See* Eisenbrauns
Vanguard   Vanguard
Van Nos. Reinhold   Van Nostrand Reinhold
Vanous   Arthur Vanous Co.
Vantage   Vantage Press, Inc.
VCH Pubs.   VCH Publishers, Inc.
Vedanta Pr.   Vedanta Press, Div. of Vedanta Society
Vendome   The Vendome Press
Ventnor   Ventnor Publishers
Venture Pr. FL   Venture Press
Verso   *See* Routledge Chapman & Hall
Victoria U. Pr.   Victoria University Press
Vienna Hse.   Vienna House, Inc.
Vignette   Vignette Multi Media
Vikas Pub. Hse. India   *See* Advent NY
Viking Penguin   Viking Penguin, Div. of Penguin USA
Vin.   Vintage Books, Div. of Random House, Inc.
Virago UK   *See* Trafalgar

Visible Ink Pr.   Visible Ink Press, Div. of Gale Research, Inc.
Vision Hse.   Vision House
Vision Pr.   Vision Press
Volcano Pr.   Volcano Press, Inc.
Vt. Folklife Ctr.   Vermont Folklife Center
VT Hist. Soc.   Vermont Historical Society

W

Wadsworth Pub.   Wadsworth Publishing Co.
Wake Forest   Wake Forest University Press
Walden Pr.   Walden Press
Wales U. Pr.   Wales University Press
Walker & Co.   Walker & Co., Div. of Walker Publishing Co., Inc.
Wall & Thompson   Wall & Thompson
Walter J. Johnson   Walter J. Johnson, Inc.
Wampeter Pr.   Wampeter Press
Wandmark Ent.   Wandmark Enterprises
Ward Hill Pr.   Ward Hill Press
Ward, Lock & Taylor   Ward, Lock & Taylor
Warne   Frederick Warne & Co., Inc.
Warner Bks.   Warner Books, Inc., A Time Warner Co.
Wash. St. U. Pr.   Washington State University Press
Water Info.   Water Information Center, Div. of Geraghty & Miller, Inc.
Watermill Pubs.   Watermill Publishers
Waterside Prodns.   Waterside Productions
Watson-Guptill   Watson-Guptill Publications, Inc.
Watson Publ. Intl.   Watson Publishing International
Watts   Franklin Watts, Inc., Subs. of Grolier, Inc.
Waveland Pr.   Waveland Press, Inc.
Wayland Pr.   Wayland Press
Wayne St. U. Pr.   Wayne State University Press
W. B. Saunders   W. B. Saunders & Co., Div. of Harcourt Brace & Co.
Weatherhill   Weatherhill, Inc.
Weber Systems   Weber Systems, Inc.
Wedgestone Pr.   Wedgestone Press
Weekly Graphic Pub.   Weekly Graphic Publisher
Weidenfeld & Nicolson UK   *See* Rothman
Weiner Pub. Inc.   Weiner Publishing, Inc.
Weiser Samuel   Samuel Weiser, Inc.
Wesleyan Univ. Pr.   *See* U. Pr. of New Eng.
Westburg   Westburg Associates, Publishers
West End   West End Press
Western Pub.   Western Publishing Co., Inc., Subs. of Western Publishing Group, Inc.
Western Reserve Univ.   Western Reserve University
Westminster John Knox   Westminster/John Knox Press
Westphal   Westphal Publishing

West Pub. West Publishing, College & School Division
Westview Westview Press
Weybright Weybright & Talley, Inc., Subs. of Random House, Inc.
W. H. Freeman W. H. Freeman & Co., Subs. of Scientific American, Inc.
Whirlwind Pr. Whirlwind Press
White Pine White Pine Press
White Rose Pr. White Rose Press
Whites Creek Pr. Whites Creek Press
Whitston Pub. Whitston Publishing Co., Inc.
Whittaker Whittaker
Wicklow Pr. Wicklow Press
Wiener Pub. Markus Wiener Publishing, Inc.
Wiley John Wiley & Sons, Inc.
Wilfion Bks. *See* Dufour
Wilfred Laurier U. Pr. Wilfred Laurier University Press
William Blackwood & Sons William Blackwood & Sons
William Lane William Lane
Williams & Wilkins Williams & Wilkins, Div. of Electronic Media
William Smith College Pr. William Smith College Press
Willis Locker & Owens Willis, Locker & Owens Publishing
Wilmans Wilmans
Wilshire Wilshire Book Co.
Wilson H. W. Wilson
Winchester Pr. Winchester Press
Windcrest *See* TAB Bks.
Windhover Pr. Windhover Press
Windsor NY Windsor Publishing Corp.
Wingbow Pr. Wingbow Press
Winston Pr. Winston Press
Wisdom MA Wisdom Publications
WIU Essays Lit. Western Illinois University Essays in Literature
Wm. C. Brown Co. Wm. C. Brown, Publishers
Wolfe Pub. Co. Wolfe Publishing Co.
Women's Pr. *See* InBook
Women Translation Women In Translation
Woodbine Hse. Woodbine House
Woodbridge Pr. Woodbridge Press
Woodhill Woodhill
Woodrose Pubns. Woodrose Publications
Word Bks. Word Books
Word Inc. Word, Inc.
Workmen's Circle Workmen's Circle, Education Department
Work Study Assn. Work Study Association, Inc.
World Bank The World Bank, Office of the Publisher
World Bk. World Book
World Health World Health Organization

World Pub. Co. World Publishing Co.
World Resources Inst. World Resources Institute
World Scientific Pub. World Scientific Publishing Co., Inc.
World Watch Institute World Watch Institute
Worth Worth Publishers, Inc.
Wrigley & Berriman Wrigley & Berriman
Writer Writer, Inc.
Writers & Readers Writers & Readers Publishing, Inc.
Writers Digest Writer's Digest Books
Wrld. Coun. Churches World Council of Churches
W. S. Hein William S. Hein & Co., Inc.
WSP Washington Square Press
W. T. Taylor W. Thomas Taylor Bookseller
W. W. Gaunt William W. Gaunt & Sons, Inc.

Y

Yale Russian Yale Russian & East European Publications
Yale U. Pr. Yale University Press
Yale U. SE Asia Yale University Southeast Asia Studies
Yankee Pub. Yankee Publishing, Div. of Ray Properties
Ye Galleon Ye Galleon Press
Ye Olde Printery Ye Olde Printery
YIVO Inst. YIVO Institute for Jewish Research
Yonsei U. Pr. Yonsei University Press
York Pr. York Press, Inc.
Yoseloff Yoseloff

Z

Zapizdat Pubns. Zapizdat Publications
Zebra Zebra Books, Div. of Kensington Publishing Corp.
Zed Bks. *See* Humanities
Zellerbach Family Fund Zellerbach Family Fund
Zephyr Pr. Zephyr Press
Zhaohua Pub Hse. Zhaohua Publishing House
Ziesing Bros. Ziesing Brothers Book Emporium
Ziff-Davis Ziff-Davis Press, Div. of Ziff-Davis Publishing Co.
Zondervan Zondervan Publishing Corp., Div. of HarperCollins Publishers, Inc.
Zone Bks. Zone Books

Name Index

This index cumulates in alphabetical sequence the Name Index of each of the five preceding volumes. The number of the volume in which a name appears is given with a colon followed by the page number on which the name can be located.

In addition to authors of books, this index includes the names of persons mentioned in introductory essays, section introductions, biographical profiles, general bibliographic entries, and "Books about" sections. Throughout, however, persons mentioned ·only in passing—to indicate friendships, relationships, and so on—are generally not indexed. Editors, translators, and compilers are not indexed unless there is no specific author given for the work in question. Writers of the introductions, forewords, afterwords, and similar parts of works are not indexed. The names of individuals who are represented by separate biographical profiles appear in boldface, as do the volume number(s) and page number(s) on which their profiles appear.

A

Aaboe, A., 5:38
Aalto, Alvar, 3:769
Aaron, Daniel, 1:712, 1:803, 1:928
Aaron, Frieda W., 2:30
Aaron, Henry J., 3:56, 5:327
Aaron, Jane, 1:295
Aaron, Richard I., 3:159, 4:179, 4:738
Aarons, Victoria, 2:46
Aaronson, Jerrold L., 4:384
Aasen, Ivar, 2:661
Aaserud, Finn, 5:674
Abadžiev, Georgi, 2:807
Abarbanel, Albert, 5:429
Abbate, Carolyn, 3:670
Abbey, Edward, 3:894, 5:131, 5:827
Abbey, Lloyd, 1:302
Abbot, Jacob, 1:1194
Abbott, Craig S., 1:63
Abbott, David, 5:4, 5:215, 5:652
Abbott, E. A., 1:216
Abbott, Nabia, 4:587
Abdalati, Hammudah, 3:442
'Abd al-Qaddus, Ihsan, 2:60
'Abd al-Ṣabūr, Ṣalāh, 2:60

Abdel-Aal, H. K., 5:635
Abdel-Fadil, M., 3:445
Abdel Wahab, Farouk W., 2:56
Abduh, Muhammad, 4:374, 4:375
Abdul, Raoul, 2:931
Abdul-Kadir, Abdullah bin, 2:323
Abdullah, Munshi, 2:323
Abdulrazak, Fawzi, 2:117
Abe Kōbō, 2:281, 2:284
Abel, Christopher, 2:871
Abel, Eli, 3:802
Abel, Elizabeth, 1:923
Abel, Emily K., 1:923
Abel, Ernest L., 5:375
Abel, Reuben, 4:19
Abelard, Peter, 4:93, 4:101, 4:105, 4:111
Abeles, R. H., 5:732
Abell, George, 5:587
Abella, Irving M., 3:616
Abelone, Henry, 4:789
Abelson, Joshua, 4:629
Abelson, Raziel, 4:19
Abe Masao, 4:363, 4:558
Aberbach, Alan David, 3:728
Aberbach, David, 2:12, 2:16
Abercrombie, John R., 5:564

Abercrombie, M. L. Johnson, 5:77
Aberle, David F., 4:467
Abernathy, Francis E., 3:862
Abernethy, Glenn, 3:536
Abeyasekere, Susan, 3:491
Able, Augustus H., 1:297
Ablin, David A., 3:490
Abokor, Axmed Cali, 2:117
Aboulafia, Mitchell, 4:308
Abraham, Antoine J., 4:577
Abraham, David, 3:376
Abraham, Gerald, 3:658, 3:718
Abraham, Henry J., 3:145
Abraham, Katharine G., 3:59
Abraham, Richard, 3:394
Abraham, Roberta, 3:463
Abraham of Troki, Isaac ben, 4:631
Abrahams, Cecil, 2:163, 2:165
Abrahams, Israel, 4:622, 4:628
Abrahams, Pete, 2:158
Abrahams, Roger D., 3:853, 3:862, 3:866, 3:867
Abrahams, William, 1:531, 1:921
Abrahamson, Irving, 1:1065
Abramowicz, Dina, 2:31

27

Abrams, David M., 5:417
Abrams, Meyer H., 1:129,
1:131, 1:265, 1:266, 1:306,
1:922, **1:930**
Abrams, Natalie, 5:118
Abramson, Doris E., 1:1071
Abramson, Edward A., 1:1032
Abramson, Jeffrey, 3:177,
3:183, 5:447
Abramson, Louis, 5:348
Abramson, Paul, 5:413
Abramson, Phyllis Leslie,
3:805
Abrash, Barbara, 2:106
Abse, Joan, 1:394
Abu al-'Ala' al-Ma'arri, 2:61
Abubakar, Ahmad, 3:416
Abulafia, David, 3:385
Abu-Lughod, Janet
L(ippman), 3:219, 3:274,
3:445
Abun-Nasr, J. M., 3:418
Abu Nuwas, 2:62
Abu Zayd, Layla, 2:58
Abzug, Robert H., 3:554,
3:598
Accad, Evelyne, 2:54
A-ch'eng, 2:236
Achebe, Chinua, 2:104,
2:125, **2:126**, 2:141, 2:142
Acheson, James M., 1:425
Achinstein, Peter, 5:61, 5:67,
5:662
Acholonu, Catherine Obianu-
ju, 2:138
Achtemeier, Paul J., 4:817
Achterberg, Jeanne, 5:318
Achtert, Walter S., 1:118
Acker, Alison, 3:638
Acker, Ally, 3:824
Ackerknecht, Erwin Heinz,
5:410
Ackerman, Bruce, 3:141
Ackerman, Diane, 1:931
Ackerman, James S., 3:785
Ackerman, Robert, 3:30,
3:878, 4:246, 4:477, 4:479
Ackerman, Susan E., 4:518
Ackerman, Terrence F.,
5:118
Ackermann-Engel, Ruby,
5:417
Ackland, Len, 5:109
Ackley, Katherine Anne,
1:539
Ackrill, J. L., 4:66
Ackroyd, Peter, 1:472, 1:872
Acland, Alice, 1:385
Acocella, Joan, 5:429
Adachi, Ken, 3:608
Adali-Mortty, G., 2:126
Adam, James Luther, 5:206
Adamczewski, Jan, 5:602

Adamovich, Anthony, 2:783
Adams, A. E., 3:292
Adams, Alice, 3:894
Adams, Anne V., 2:106
Adams, Anthony, 3:253
Adams, Charles C., 4:374
Adams, Charles D., 2:355
Adams, Charles F., 3:920
Adams, Charles F., Jr., 1:666
Adams, Charles J., 4:5, 4:533
Adams, Elise Bonita, 1:546
Adams, Evangeline, 4:860
Adams, Frank Dawson, 5:32,
5:622
Adams, Frederick, 4:22
Adams, George R., 3:515
Adams, Gerald, 3:208
Adams, Hazard, 1:490, 1:1133
Adams, Henry (Brooks),
1:710, 1:726, **1:728**, 1:937,
3:562
Adams, James L., 5:150,
5:191
Adams, James Truslow,
3:505, 3:512, 3:563
Adams, Jeffrey, 2:603
Adams, John, 1:645, 1:699
Adams, Jonathon S., 5:762
Adams, Laura, 1:1012
Adams, Marilyn Jager, 3:253
Adams, Marilyn McCord,
4:120
Adams, Michael, 1:56, 3:434
Adams, Michael J., 5:303
Adams, Nelson B., 2:523
Adams, Percy G., 3:891
Adams, Richard P., 1:836
Adams, Robert, 4:438
Adams, Robert M., 4:177
Adams, Robert McC., 3:449
Adams, Simon, 3:272
Adams, Stephen, 1:701
Adams, Thomas F., 1:6
Adams, Timothy D., 1:808
Adams, Walter, 3:61
Adams, William Taylor,
1:1194
Adams, Willi Paul, 3:541
Adams, W. Y., 3:418
Adamski, George, 4:870
Adamson, J. H., 3:907
Adamson, Jane, 1:214
Adamson, Walter L., 2:423
Adamthwaite, Anthony, 3:277
Adas, Michael, 5:24
Adato, Michelle, 5:239
Adcock, Frank E., 3:308,
3:313
Addams, (Laura) Jane,
1:726, **1:730**
Addeo, Edmond G., 5:372
Addiscott, T. M., 5:265

Addison, Joseph, 1:224,
1:228, 1:230, **1:232**, 1:257
Adelman, George, 5:758
Adelman, Irving, 1:427
Adelman, Janet, 1:208
Adelman, Morris A., 5:283,
5:290
Adelmann, F. J., 4:30
Adelson, Edward T., 5:429
Aderman, Ralph M., 1:681
Adkin, Mark, 3:633
Adkins, Arthur W., 4:47
Adkins, Jan, 1:13
Adler, Alfred, 5:430, 5:445
Adler, Bill, 3:719
Adler, Doris R., 1:176
Adler, Elkan N., 4:625
Adler, Hans G., 4:635
Adler, Jacques, 3:347
Adler, Leonore L., 3:178
Adler, Margot, 4:865
Adler, Morris, 4:620
Adler, Mortimer J., 1:116,
3:248, 3:263, 3:511, 4:66,
4:260, **4:269**
Adler, Renata, 3:805
Adler, Ruth, 2:43
Adler, Thomas P., 1:1083
Adoff, Arnold, 1:800, 1:914,
1:1196
Adonis, 2:62
Adorno, Theodor W.,
1:1132, 1:1151, 3:147,
3:177, 3:658, 4:271, 4:386,
4:390, **4:392**, 4:403, 5:88,
5:93
Adrian, Charles R., 3:148
Adrian, J., 5:260
Adriano, D. C., 5:616
Adshead, S.A.M., 3:466
Ady, Endre, 2:797, **2:799**
Aebi, Tania, 3:907
Aelred of Reivaulx, 4:101
Aepli, Martine, 3:481
Aeschylus, 1:517, **2:350**,
2:353, 2:366, 4:474
Aesop, 1:889, **2:351**, 2:485,
3:881
Afanasiev, Aleksandr, 2:691
Affifi, Abul E., 4:583
Afnan, Soheil M., 4:581
Afzal-Ur-Rehman, 3:442
Agassi, Joseph, 5:36, 5:62,
5:69, 5:79, 5:150, 5:684,
5:745
Agassiz, Louis, 3:130, 4:235,
5:785
Agazzi, Evandro, 5:67
Agee, James, 1:932, 3:533
Ager, Derek V., 5:622
Agera, Cassian R., 4:37
Aggeler, Geoffrey, 1:454

Agnew, John A., 3:122, 3:123, 3:124
Agnon, Shmuel Yosef, 2:8, 2:11
Agnon, S. Y., 4:599, 4:886
Agoratus, Steven, 4:532
Agosin, Marjorie, 2:848, 2:875
Agosta, Lucien L., 1:1205
Agrawal, Govind P., 5:303, 5:666
Agricola, Georgius, 5:627
Agrippa of Nettesheim, Henry Cornelius, 4:133
Aguilar Camín, Héctor, 3:638
Agus, Jacob, 4:657
Aḥmad, Jalāl Āl-i, 2:88
Ahad Ha-am, 2:12, 4:657
Aharoni, Yohanan, 4:809
Ahearn, Allen, 1:30, 1:76
Ahearn, Edward J., 2:499
Ahearn, Frederick L., Jr., 5:421
Ahern, Emily M., 4:530
Ahl, Frederick, 2:387, 2:390
Ahlgren, Andrew, 5:11
Ahlgren, Ernst, 2:671
Ahlsrom, Sydney E., 1:630
Ahlstrom, S. E., 4:750
Ahmad, Aziz, 4:372, 4:567, 4:577
Ahmad, Feroz, 3:452
Ahmad, Syed, 3:50
Ahmad, Viqar, 3:487
Ahmadjian, Vernon, 5:763
Ahmed, Abkar S., 3:487
Ahmed, A. Karim, 5:398
Ahmed, Rafiuddin, 3:486
al-Ahmed, Shahi, 4:579
Ahmed, Ziauddin, 3:442
Ahnebrink, Lars, 1:720, 1:751, 1:777
Aho, Alfred V., 5:549
Aho, Juhani, 2:657
Ahokas, Jaakko, 2:657
Ai Ch'ing, 2:237
Aichhorn, August, 5:416
Aichinger, Peter, 2:907
Aidoo, Ama Ata, 2:105, 2:129
Aiken, Conrad, 1:745, 1:809
Aiken, Henry D., 4:159
Aiken, Leona, 3:200
Aiken, Linda H., 5:337
Aiken, Riley, 3:853
Aiken, Robert, 2:276
Aiken, Susan Hardy, 2:649
Ailey, Alvin, Jr., 3:735
Ainsworth, Catherine H., 3:853, 3:858
Ainsworth, G. C., 5:758
Ainsworth-Davies, James R., 5:799

Airasian, Peter W., 3:256
Aisenberg, Ruth, 5:422
Aistis, Jonas, 2:804
Aitken, H., 3:606
Aitken, Hugh G. J., 5:228
Aitmatov, Chingiz, 2:695
Aizenberg, Edna, 2:857
Ajami, Fouad, 4:567, 4:577
Ajayi, Jacob Festus Ade, 3:415, 3:419, 3:425
Ajuwon, Bade, 2:126
Akatdamkoeng, 2:334
Akbar, M. J., 3:499
Akenson, Donald H., 3:608
Aker, Loren E., 3:206
Akeroyd, Richard H., 4:27
Akhavi, Shahrough, 4:567, 4:577
Akhmadulina, Bella, 2:695
Akhmatova, Anna, 2:683, 2:696, 2:703, 2:711, 2:733, 2:775
Akhtar, Shabbir, 3:442
Akiko, Yosano. *See* Yosano Akiko
Akin, John S., 5:330
Akinari, Veda. *See* Veda Akinari
Akira, Hirakawa, 4:512
Akira, Kurosawa, 2:285
Aksakov, Sergei, 2:697
Aksyonov (Aksenov), Vassily, 2:683, 2:697
Akutagawa Ryūnosuke, 2:281, 2:285
Aland, Barbara, 4:805
Aland, Kurt, 4:676, 4:794, 4:805, 4:817
Alan of Lille, 4:702
Alapuro, Risto, 3:381
Alas, Leopoldo (Clarín), 2:521 2:527
'Alavī, Bezorg, 2:86
al-Azmeh, Ariz, 4:584
Alazraki, Jaime, 2:857, 2:862
Alba, Richard D., 3:554
Alba, Victor, 3:386
Albanese, Catherine, 4:841
Albee, Edward, 1:1009, 1:1071, **1:1080,** 1:1102, 1:1122, 2:679
Albert, Daniel A., 5:79
Albert, Peter J., 3:520
Albert, Phyllis Cohen, 4:635
Albert, Richard N., 1:805
Alberti, Leon Battista, 2:404, 3:755
Alberti, Rafael, 2:521, 2:528, 2:531, 2:824
Alberts, A., 2:622
Albert the Great, 4:106
Alberty, Robert A., 5:735
Albrecht-Carrié, Rene, 3:277

Albright, Beth Parker, 5:318
Albright, Peter, 5:318
Albright, William F., 4:445, 4:806, 4:808, 4:822, **4:827**
Albright Donn, 1:1255
Albritton, Claude C., 5:622
Alchon, Suzanne Austin, 3:628
Alcock, Donald, 5:551
Alcott, Louisa May, 1:721, 1:731, 1:1193, 1:1195, **1:1197**
Aldcroft, Derek H., 3:325
Alden, John R., 3:519
Alder, D. D., 3:272
Alderson, Anthony D., 3:452
Alderson, Brian, 1:581
Aldhizer, T. Gerard, 5:399
Aldiss, Brian W., 1:611, 1:612
Aldiss, Margaret, 1:613
Aldred, Cyril, 3:300
Aldrich, Earl M., Jr., 2:845
Aldrich, Frank T., 5:620
Aldrich, Lawson, 3:857
Aldrich, Thomas Bailey, 1:731
Aldridge, Alfred Owen, 1:642, 4:767
Aldridge, John W., 1:420, 1:793, 1:916
Aldrin, Edwin Eugene, Jr., 3:911
Alegre, Edilberto N., 2:328
Alegria, Ricardo E., 4:466
Aleixandre, Vicente, 2:529
Aleksandrov, A. D., 5:480
Aleksandrov, Josip Murn, 2:834
Alemán, Mateo, 2:520, 2:529, 2:544
Alencar, José de, 2:891
Aleshkovsky, Yuz (Iosif), 2:698
Aletrino, L., 4:567
Alexander, Ann, 5:322
Alexander, Caroline, 3:901
Alexander, Charles C., 3:558
Alexander, E. Curtis, 1:45
Alexander, Edward, 1:1050
Alexander, Franz, 5:424
Alexander, Gordon J., 3:56
Alexander, Ian W., 4:27
Alexander, Jeffrey C., 3:209
Alexander, John T., 3:395
Alexander, John W., 3:122, 5:619
Alexander, Lamar, 3:901
Alexander, Michael, 1:143, 1:872
Alexander, Nigel, 1:213
Alexander, Pamela, 5:787
Alexander, Paul, 1:1031

Alexander, Peter, 4:179
Alexander, R. J., 3:295
Alexander, Robert L., 4:444
Alexander, Thomas G., 4:845
Alexandrov, Vladimir E.,
    2:701, 2:741
Alexandrova, Vera, 2:684
Alexandru, Ion, 2:823
Alfieri, Count Vittorio,
    2:399, **2:404,** 2:412, 2:424,
    2:425
Alford, C. Fred, 4:408, 5:94
Alford, John A., 1:154
Algar, Hamid, 2:57
Algarin, Joanne P., 3:853
Alger, Horatio, 1:1194
Algosaibi, Ghazi A., 2:56
Algren, West, 1:812
Ali, Abdullah, 3:442
Ali, Ahmed, 2:175, 2:176
Ali, Ameer, 3:442, 4:372
Ali, Syed A., 4:587
Āl-i Aḥmad, Jalāl, 2:85
Aliber, Robert Z, 3:44
Aliboni, R., 3:445
Aliotta, Antonio, 4:271
Alisjahbana, Sutan Takdir,
    2:316, **2:318**
Alkon, Paul, 1:240
Allaby, Michael, 5:758, 5:767,
    5:769, 5:815
Allain, Marie-Françoise, 1:489
Allan, D. F., 4:66
Allan, John J., 2:535
Allan, William, 5:264
Alland, Alexander, 3:822
Alland, Alexander, Jr., 5:794
Allard, Jean-Louis, 4:307
Allee, Warder C., 5:819
Allen, Beverly, 2:402, 2:432
Allen, Clarence W., 5:587
Allen, Daniel, 3:653
Allen, David, 1:438
Allen, David Grayson, 3:516,
    3:517
Allen, Don, 3:843
Allen, Donald M., 1:800,
    1:912, 1:915
Allen, Don C., 4:123
Allen, Don Cameron, 1:912
Allen, Elizabeth C., 2:770
Allen, Garland E., 5:47, 5:774
Allen, Gay Wilson, 1:654,
    1:670, 1:707, 1:718, 1:719,
    1:768, 1:878
Allen, George, 4:548
Allen, G. Freeman, 5:247
Allen, Henry E., 4:577
Allen, Hervey, 1:1244,
    1:1245
Allen, H. J., 4:71
Allen, Irving I., 3:872
Allen, Jeffner, 1:1183

Allen, Joan M., 1:840
Allen, J. W., 2:152
Allen, Lewis, 1:6
Allen, Margaret V., 1:673
Allen, Mark, 1:151
Allen, Mary, 1:916
Allen, Michael J. B., 1:205,
    4:141
Allen, Paul, 1:636
Allen, Paula Gunn, 1:1128,
    1:1130, **1:1135,** 1:1181,
    1:1185
Allen, Percy S., 4:139
Allen, Polly Wyn, 1:753
Allen, R. E., 4:50, 4:89
Allen, Ray, 3:866
Allen, Reginald, 1:357
Allen, Richard, 2:642
Allen, Richard H., 5:587
Allen, Robert, 1:1156, 3:212
Allen, Robert Loring, 3:76,
    3:105
Allen, Roger, 2:55
Allen, Walter, 1:269, 1:420
Allen, Woody, 1:933, 3:829,
    3:870
Allende, Isabel, 2:851
Allentuch, Harriet R., 2:508
Allentuck, Marcia, 2:48
Allibone, Samuel Austin,
    1:120, 1:126
Allinson, Francis G., 2:363
Allinson, Robert E., 4:522
Allione, Tsultrim, 4:543
Allison, Alexander W., 1:129
Allison, David, 4:246
Allison, Graham T., 3:277,
    5:109
Allison, Henry E., 4:187,
    4:206, 4:208
Allison, June W., 3:323
Allmon, Warren D., 3:18
Allott, Miriam, 1:302, 1:333
Allport, Gordon W(illard),
    3:168, 3:176, 3:177, **3:179,**
    3:202, 3:208, 3:237, **5:431**
Allport, Susan, 5:339, 5:774
Allsburg, Chris Van, 1:1194
al-Ma'arri, Abu al-'ala', 2:73
al-Marayati, Abid A., 3:449
Almenas, K., 5:239
Almond, Gabriel Abraham,
    3:141, **3:149**
Almond, Philip C., 4:488
Almqvist, Carl Jonas Love,
    2:671, **2:672**
Almy, Millie, 3:267
Alock, John, 5:825
Alon, Gedalyahu, 4:604
Alper, Ann Fitzpatrick, 3:942
Alpern, Henry, 4:16
Alpern, Kenneth D., 5:118
Alpers, Anthony, 4:461

Alpers, Antony, 2:970, 2:979
Alpers, Paul, 2:397
Alpers, Paul J., 1:198
Alpers, Svetlana, 3:788
Alperson, Philip, 3:756
Alpert, Hollis, 3:836
Alpert, Rebecca T., 4:659
Alphonso-Karkala, John,
    2:170
Alridge, A. Owen, 2:983
Alsen, Eberhard, 1:1043
Alsop, Joseph W., 2:344
Alster, Kristine B., 5:12
Alston, William P., 4:19
Altbach, Philip G., 1:48,
    3:253
Alter, Iska, 1:1013
Alter, Judy, 5:325
Alter, Reinhard, 2:568
Alter, Robert, 2:511, 2:989,
    4:816, 4:822
Althaus, Paul, 4:778
Altherr, Thomas L., 3:551
Altholz, Josef L., 3:353, 4:740
Althusser, Louis, 1:1126,
    3:290, 3:345, 4:242
Altick, Richard D., 1:30,
    1:86, 1:265, 1:271, 1:311,
    1:429, 1:928, 3:363
Altieri, Charles, 1:797, 1:912,
    1:923
Altieri, Miguel, 5:819
Altizer, Thomas J., 4:474
Altman, Bill, 1:815
Altman, Dennis, 1:1181
Altman, Mark, 3:829
Altman, Roberta, 5:367
Altman, Stuart A., 5:825
Altman, Stuart H., 5:332
Altmann, Alexander, 4:209,
    4:628
Altoma, Salih, 2:55
Altschul, Michael, 3:353
Altschul, Siri von Reis, 5:350
Altschull, J. Herbert, 3:805
Altshuler, Alan, 5:247
Altshuler, David, 4:638
Altwerger, Bess, 3:254
Aluri, Rao, 5:727
Alvarez, A., 1:417, 1:440
Alvarez, Alfred, 5:425
Alvarez, Luis W., 5:650
Alvarez, Walter C., 5:425
Alvarez-Pereyre, Jacques,
    2:106
Álvaro de Campos, 2:560
Alves, Rubem, 4:747
Alvey, Gerald, 3:860
Alwood, Martin S., 2:638
Alworth, E. Paul, 3:887
Amacher, Richard E., 1:1081
Amad, Shahnon, 2:323
Amadi, Elechi, 2:129

Amado, Jorge, 2:890, **2:891**
Amann, Dick, 5:577
Amantea, Carlos A., 3:901
Ambler, John S., 3:372
Ambrose, A., 4:22
Ambrose, Jamie, 1:821
Ambrose, St., 4:702
Ambrose, Stephen E., 3:533, 3:544
Ambrosius, Gerald, 3:345
Amend, Patricia, 5:347
Ames, Evelyn, 3:901
Ames, Roger T., 4:498, 4:502, 4:512, 4:522, 4:534
Ames, Van Meter, 4:33, 4:859
Amichai, Yehuda, 2:8, **2:13**, 2:17, 2:27
Amin, Karima, 1:954
Amir, Ali Syed, 4:567
Amirsadeghi, Hossein, 3:447
Amis, Kingsley, 1:414, 1:419, **1:431**, 1:466, 1:486, 1:507, 1:593
Amjad, Rashid, 3:487
Ammianus Marcellinus, 3:310
Ammons, A(rchie) R(andolph), 1:933
Ammons, Elizabeth, 1:788
Amore, Roy C., 4:503, 4:512
Ampalavanar, Rajeswary, 2:324
Amsel, A., 3:171
Amsterdam, Ezra A., 5:339
Amundsen, Darrel W., 4:893
Amundsen, Roald, 3:912, 3:936
Anagnostakos, Nicholas, 5:773
Anand, Mulk Raj, 2:177
Anantha Murthy, U. R., 2:177
Anastasi, Anne, 3:180
Anastasiow, Nicholas J., 5:321
Anaya, Rudolfo A., 1:805
Anbar, Michael, 5:370, 5:556
Al-Andalusi, Sa'id, 5:39
Anday, Melih Cevdat, 2:97, 2:98
Andaya, Barbara Watson, 3:492
Andaya, Leonard Y., 3:492
Andelson, Robert U., 3:80
Andersen, Benny Allen, 2:646
Andersen, Frank, 2:638
Andersen, Hans Christian, 1:577, 1:1206, 2:637, 2:644, **2:646**
Andersen, Richard, 1:963
Anderson, Benedict R., 2:336
Anderson, Bernhard W., 4:816

Anderson, Bonnie S., 3:325
Anderson, Bruce, 5:288
Anderson, Byron D., 5:651, 5:735
Anderson, C. Alan, 4:847
Anderson, C. Anthony, 4:324, 5:103
Anderson, Charles B., 1:39
Anderson, Charles R., 1:701, 1:746, 3:907
Anderson, D., 3:205
Anderson, David, 1:484
Anderson, David G., 2:875
Anderson, Donald K., 1:180
Anderson, Donald M., 1:13
Anderson, Dorothy D., 3:862
Anderson, Douglas R, 1:649
Anderson, E. W., 5:769
Anderson, Elliott, 3:801
Anderson, Emily, 3:707
Anderson, Eric, 3:580
Anderson, Fulton H., 4:165
Anderson, G. L., 2:311, 5:246
Anderson, G. W., 4:816
Anderson, Gerald H., 3:492
Anderson, Harriet, 2:849
Anderson, Herbert L., 5:652
Anderson, Hugh, 2:233
Anderson, Ingvar, 3:382
Anderson, J. K., 3:308, 3:324, 4:91
Anderson, J. R., 3:171
Anderson, Jack, 3:732, 3:740
Anderson, James E., 3:146
Anderson, James W., 5:381
Anderson, Jessica, 2:948
Anderson, John Q., 3:870
Anderson, Lindsay, 1:1166
Anderson, M., 2:128
Anderson, M. G., 5:626
Anderson, M. S., 3:340
Anderson, Madelyn K., 3:933
Anderson, Margaret, 4:875
Anderson, Margo J., 3:551
Anderson, Marian, 3:674
Anderson, Mary M., 5:354
Anderson, Maxwell, 1:1070, 1:1071, **1:1081**
Anderson, Norman, 3:442
Anderson, Odin W., 5:312
Anderson, Patricia, 5:378
Anderson, Paul R., 4:34
Anderson, Philip W., 5:670, 5:704
Anderson, Quentin, 1:649
Anderson, R. D., 3:372
Anderson, Richard, 3:253
Anderson, Robert, 1:1082, 3:694
Anderson, Robert M., Jr., 5:64
Anderson, Robert T., 3:381
Anderson, Scott, 4:845

Anderson, Sherwood, 1:802, **1:811**, 1:844, 1:858, 1:990
Anderson, Sydney, 5:758
Anderson, Virginia DeJohn, 1:627
Anderson, Walt, 4:859
Anderson, Wilda C., 5:43
Anderson, William T., 1:1209
Anderson-Imbert, Enrique, 2:845
Andersson, Christiane, 4:737
Andersson, T. M., 2:640
Andonian, Cathleen Culotta, 1:440
Andrade, E. N., 5:706, 5:712
Andrade, Eugénio de, 2:558
Andrade, Mário de, 2:889, **2:892**, 2:893
Andrade, Oswald de, 2:889, **2:893**
Andrae, Tor, 4:588
Andrew, Christopher, 3:395
Andrew, Dudley, 1:1156, 3:827
Andrew, Joe, 2:684
Andrew, Ray Vernon, 1:346
Andrewartha, H. G., 5:819
Andrewes, Antony, 3:301
Andrews, Barry, 2:947
Andrews, Edward D., 4:849
Andrews, Elmer, 1:495
Andrews, Henry N., 5:33
Andrews, John F., 1:221
Andrews, Joyce, 1:100
Andrews, Kenneth R., 3:358
Andrews, Lori B., 5:357
Andrews, Nancy, 5:554
Andrews, Paul, 5:543
Andrews, Robert, 1:116
Andrews, V(irginia) C(leo), 1:1239
Andrews, Walter G., 2:95
Andrews, William L., 1:86, 1:650, 1:659, 1:668, 1:727, 1:739, 1:808
Andreyev (Andreev), Leon-id, 2:698
Andrić, Ivo, 2:827, **2:828**
Andronicus, Livius, 2:378
Andrusyshen, C. H., 2:838
Anesaki, Masaharu, 4:534, 4:536
Angeles, Peter A., 4:2, 4:12
Angeli, Helen R., 1:392
Ângelo, Ivan, 2:889, **2:893**
Angelou, Maya, 1:934
Angoff, Charles, 2:106
Angus, Douglas, 1:921
Angus, Sylvia, 1:921
Angyal, Andras, 5:425
Anikouchine, William, 5:631
Ankori, Zvi, 4:631
Anna, Timothy E., 3:638

Annas, George J., 5:118, 5:343

Annas, Julia, 4:55, 4:58, 4:66, 4:78

Anouilh, Jean, 1:424, 1:1093, 2:445, **2:450**

Anozie, S. O., 2:142

Anscombe, G.E.M., 4:344

Anselm of Canterbury, St., 4:93, 4:100, **4:107, 4:703**

An-shih, Wang. *See* Wang An-shih

Ansky, S., 2:35, 4:657

Anstey, Roger, 3:361, 3:419

Anstruther, Ian, 3:938

Antébi, Elizabeth, 5:221

Antelyes, Peter, 1:681

Antenucci, John C., 3:120, 5:619

Anthony, Dick, 4:857

Anthony, Katharine S., 1:1199

Anthony, L. J., 5:215

Anthony, Michael, 2:932

Anthony, Piers, 1:1253

Anthony, Rayford G., 5:223

Antippas, A. P., 3:361

Antler, Joyce, 1:725

Antokoletz, Elliott, 3:665

Anton, John P., 4:47, 4:66, 4:78

Anton, Julie, 5:544

Antongini, Tom, 2:415

Antonioni, Michelangelo, 2:861 **3:830,** 3:843

Antonius, George, 3:434

Antonovsky, Aaron, 5:400

Antonozzi, Leopardo, 1:18

Antreassian, Antranig, 2:77

Antunes, António Lobo. *See* Lobo Antune, António

Anuman Rajadhon, 2:335

Anwar, Chairil, 2:316, **2:318**

Anyanwu, K. C., 4:369

Anyidoho, Kofi, 2:106

Anzaldua, Gloria, 1:1130, **1:1136,** 1:1147, 1:1184, 1:1185

Anzieu, D., 5:447

Anzovin, Steven, 5:109, 5:536

Apel, Karl-Otto, 4:249

Apfel, Roberta J., 5:350

Apicella, Vincent F., 1:62

Apollinaire, Guillaume, 2:427, 2:440, **2:450**

Apollodoros of Athens, 4:468

Apollonio, Umbro, 2:400

Apollonius of Perga, 5:497

Apollonius Rhodius, 2:352

Apostel, L., 4:26

Apostle, Richard A., 3:208

Apostol, Tom M., 5:490

Apostolic Fathers, 4:703

Apostolo, Giorgio, 5:218

Apparadurai, Arjun, 4:503

Appel, Alfred J., 1:1020, 2:692

Appel, Gersion, 4:599, 4:627

Appelbaum, Judith, 1:46

Appelbaum, R. P., 3:290

Appelfeld, Aron, 2:14

Apperson, George, 1:276

Appiah, Anthony, 4:19

Appian (Appianus), 2:380, **3:311**

Appignanesi, Lisa, 2:181, 4:27

Appignanesi, Richard, 5:447

Apple, Max, 1:909, **1:935**

Applebaum, Eleanor G., 5:780

Appleby, Joyce, 3:519

Appleby, R. Scott, 4:890

Appleman, Philip, 5:45, 5:831

ApRoberts, Ruth, 1:343

Apter, David E., 3:139

Apter, Emily S., 2:480

Aptheker, Herbert, 3:235, 3:511, 3:578

Apuleius, Lucius, 2:379, **2:382,** 4:60, **4:469**

Aquila, Richard E., 4:16

Aquinas, St. Thomas, 2:420, 4:19, 4:93, 4:101, 4:106, 4:108, 4:112, 4:113, **4:117,** 4:122, 4:136, 4:154, 4:260, 4:285, 4:305, 4:388, 4:695, 4:714, 4:882, 4:902

Aqvist, Lennart, 4:211

Arac, Jonathan, 1:325, 1:1133, 2:477, 4:400, 5:87

Aragon, Louis, 2:859

Aranda, Francisco, 3:832

Arata, Esther S., 1:123

Arbaugh, George E., 4:239

Arbena, Joseph L., 3:624

Arberry, Arthur J., 2:56, 2:83, 4:574, 4:587

Arblaster, Anthony, 3:340

Arbuthnot, May Hill, 1:50

Arce de Vázquez, Margot, 2:873

Archer, J. Clark, 3:123

Archer, John, 1:25

Archer, John Clark, 4:588

Archer, Sarah E., 5:337

Archimedes, 5:497, **5:498**

Archity, Kenneth J., 2:401

Arciniegas, Germán, 3:642

Ardagh, John, 3:345

Arden, John, 1:424, **1:433,** 1:531

Arden, Mary, 1:202

Arenas, Reinaldo, 2:843, **2:852,** 2:932

Arendt, Hannah, 3:139, **3:281,** 3:342, 3:347, 3:398, 4:271, 4:299, 4:386, **4:394, 5:81**

Arens, W., 4:466

Aretino, Pietro, 2:405

Arghezi, Tudor, 2:823, **2:824**

Arguedas, José Mariá, 2:844, **2:852**

Argyle, Michael, 3:172, 3:202

Aria, Barbara, 3:738

Arico, Santo L., 2:400

Aridjis, Homero, 2:852

Arie, Tom, 5:316

Arieli, Yehoshua, 1:627

Arieti, Silvano, 5:415, 5:420, 5:426

Arineri, S., 3:290

Ariosto, Ludovico, 2:398, 2:405, **2:406,** 2:426, 2:439, 2:558

Aris, Michael, 4:543

Aristophanes, 1:357, 2:342, 2:351, **2:352,** 4:91, 4:474

Aristotle, 1:168, 1:224, 1:1138, 2:343, 2:354, 2:364, 2:367, 2:369, 2:498, 3:150, **3:311,** 4:1, 4:44, 4:54, **4:64,** 4:76, 4:90, 4:93, 4:96, 4:98, 4:101, 4:103, 4:112, 4:115, 4:123, 4:136, 4:141, 4:150, 4:152, 4:153, 4:164, 4:221, 4:320, 4:363, 4:376, 4:401, 4:407,, 5:38, 5:105, 5:179, 5:203, 5:411, 5:687, 5:705, 5:758, 5:814

Ariyoshi Sawako, 2:281, **2:285**

Arjomand, Said A., 4:578

Arkin, Marian, 1:130

Arlen, Michael J., 3:810

Arlen, Shelley, 4:479

Arlington, Lewis Charles, 2:188

Arlt, Roberto, 2:844, **2:853**

Armah, Ayi Kwei, 2:105, 2:125, **2:130**

Armbrecht, H. James, 5:348

Armbruster, David L., 2:691

Armens, Sven, 1:246

Armes, Roy, 1:1156, 2:501

Armistead, J. M., 1:251

Armitage, Angus, 5:608

Armitage, Christopher M., 1:518

Armitage, Merle, 3:696, 3:743

Armor, David J., 5:427

Armour, Robert, 4:548

Armour, Robert A., 3:824

Armour, Rollin S., 4:723

Arms, George, 1:654, 1:759

Armstrong, Arthur H., 4:46, 4:55, 4:86

Armstrong, Brian G., 4:731, 4:761
Armstrong, Chris, 5:3
Armstrong, Christopher, 3:614
Armstrong, D. M., 4:93, 4:685, 5:62
Armstrong, David, 2:386, 5:312
Armstrong, Elizabeth Metzger, 5:312
Armstrong, Louis, 3:674
Armstrong, Michael, 2:766
Armstrong, Patrick, 5:794
Armstrong, Penny, 5:337
Armstrong, Scott, 3:544
Armstrong, T. J., 5:88
Arnason, H. H., 3:758
Arnauld, Antoine, 4:163, 4:176, 4:181
Arndt, Judy, 4:644
Arner, Robert D., 1:6
Arneson, Ben A., 3:380
Arnett, Willard Eugene, 4:327
Arnheim, Rudolf, 3:177, 3:756, 3:786, 5:191
Arni, Haim, 4:644
Arnold, David, 3:484
Arnold, Denis, 3:654, 3:678, 3:706
Arnold, E. Vernon, 4:59
Arnold, Edwin T., 1:819
Arnold, Eve, 3:738
Arnold, G. C., 5:521
Arnold, L. Eugene, 5:321
Arnold, Matthew, 1:309, 1:310, 1:314, 1:324, **1:327**, 1:336, 1:345, 1:661, 1:816, 1:975, 1:1129, 2:82, 2:89, 2:360, 2:512, 2:925, 5:798
Arnold, Stephen, 2:106, 2:111
Arnold, Thomas W., 4:567, 4:574
Arnold, Tom, 5:226
Arnold, William Harris, 1:30
Arnold, William J., 3:175
Arnoldi, M. J., 2:128
Arnot, Robert, 5:331
Arnott, Anne, 4:733
Arnott, Peter D., 2:349
Arnove, Robert F., 3:253
Arntzen, Etta, 3:756
Aron, Joseph, 4:644
Aron, Raymond, 3:199, 3:275, **3:282**, 3:398, 5:110
Aronovitz, David, 1:39
Aronowitz, Stanley, 3:213
Arons, Stephen, 5:422
Aronson, Eliot, 3:168, 3:169, 3:170
Aronson, Joseph, 3:766
Aronson, Ronald, 4:330

Arreola, Juan José, 2:853
Arrhenius, Svante, 5:733, 5:738
Arrian (Flavius Arrianus), 3:312
Arrich, Paul, 3:395
Arrington, Leonard J., 3:558, 4:845
Arrow, Kenneth Joseph, 3:68, 3:83
Arrowsmith, William, 2:349
Arsenault, Georges, 3:611
Art, Henry W., 5:815
Art, Robert J., 3:144
Artaud, Antonin, 1:864, 1:1008, 2:445, **2:451**
Arthur, Paul, 3:371
Arthurs, Peter, 1:442
Artin, Michael, 5:484
Artsimovich, L., 5:667
Artz, Frederick B., 3:326, 3:340, 4:96
Arundell, Dennis, 1:271, 1:426
Arvin, Newton, 1:683, 1:688
Arya, Atam P., 5:659
Arzt, Max, 4:599
Asada, Sadao, 3:473
Asals, Frederick, 1:1024
Asante, Molefi Kete, 4:368
Asbee, Sue, 1:526
Asbjørnsen, Peter C., 2:661, 2:662
Asbjornsen, Peter C., 3:854
Asch, Sholem, 2:29, 2:35, 2:42
Ascher, Marcia, 5:494
Aschheim, Steven E., 3:347
Aschkenasy, Nehama, 2:8, 4:649
Ascoli, Albert Russell, 2:406
Ash, Brian, 1:564
Ash, I., 5:724
Ash, M., 5:724
Ash, Niema, 3:901
Ashbery, John, 1:909, 1:911, 1:935, 1:1002
Ashbrook, William, 3:711
Ashby, Philip H., 4:507
Ashcraft, Morris, 4:831
Ashcroft, Bill, 1:1131
Ashe, Geoffrey, 3:356, 4:352
Asher, Herbert, 3:147
Asher, Shirley J., 5:421
Ashfield, Andrew, 1:268
Ashford, Janet Isaacs, 5:357
Ashkenazi, Michael, 4:539
Ashley, Franklin, 1:967
Ashley, Leonard R. N., 1:195, 1:323
Ashley, Maurice, 3:359, 3:372
Ashley, Robert, 1:167
Ashliman, D. L., 3:849

Ashman, Chuck, 4:768
Ashmore, Harry S., 3:264
Ashmore, Jerome, 4:327
Ashmore, Malcolm, 5:66
Ashraf, Syed A., 3:442
Ashtiany, Julia, 2:55
Ashton, Dore, 3:786
Ashton, Heather, 5:404
Ashton, Robert, 4:733
Ashton, Rosemary, 1:373
Ashton, Sir Frederick, 3:736, 3:738, 3:742, 3:745, 3:750, 3:754
Ashtor, Eliyahu, 3:434, 4:625
Ashworth, E. J., 4:123
Ashworth, William, 5:815
Asimov, Isaac, 1:282, 1:614, 1:1193, 1:1209, 1:1252, **1:1253**, 3:870, 5:6, **5:13**, 5:27, 5:60, 5:242, 5:484, 5:563, 5:587, 5:593, 5:599, 5:658, 5:724, 5:726, 5:727, 5:734, 5:758
Aske, Martin, 1:294
Askenasy, Alexander, 5:420
Aškerc, Anton, 2:834
Asmis, Elizabeth, 4:73
Aspin, Roy, 1:582
Aspiz, Harold, 1:707
Aspray, William, 3:112, 5:542, 5:582, 5:583
Asquith, Cynthia Mary Evelyn, 1:330
Asquith, Peter, 5:60
Asselineau, Roger, 1:707
Assis, Joaquim Maria Machado de. See Machado de Assis, Joaquim Maria
Asso, Doreen, 5:354
Ast, Freidrich, 4:79
Astaire, Fred, 3:736, 3:751
Astley, Thea, 2:949
Aston, Margaret, 3:332
Aston, W. G., 4:536
Astor, Gerald, 5:368
Astrov, Margot Luise Therese, 1:631
Asturias, Miguel Angel, 2:843, 2:844, 2:853
Atack, Jon, 4:869
Atanasijevic, Ksenija, 4:135
Atchity, John K., 1:1004
Ateek, Naim S., 4:896
Athanassakis, Apostolos N., 2:360
Atherton, Margaret, 4:191
Atherton, Stanley S., 1:547
Atiya, Aziz S., 4:676, 4:692
Atkins, Beryl T., 1:98
Atkins, C. Douglas, 1:1128
Atkins, John, 1:420, 1:467, 1:537, 1:592
Atkins, P. W., 5:659

Atkinson, A. B., 3:67
Atkinson, Brooks, 1:1071
Atkinson, Charles M., 3:151
Atkinson, Clarissa W., 1:153,
　4:698
Atkinson, Gary M., 5:780
Atkinson, James, 4:778
Atkinson, John W., 3:175
Atkinson, M. J., 4:86
Atlas, James, 3:253
Atmore, Anthony, 3:418
Atre, Shakuntala, 5:559
'Aṭṭār, Farīd al-Dīn, 2:84,
　4:574
Attenborough, David, 5:817
Atterbom, Per Daniel Ama-
　deus, 2:670
Attfield, Robin, 5:74, 5:113
Attig, Thomas, 5:116
Attridge, Derek, 1:505
Attridge, Harold W., 4:709
Attwater, Donald, 4:275,
　4:675, 4:755
Atulananda, Swami, 4:563
Atwater, W. Eastwood, 5:413
Atwell, Nancie, 3:253
Atwood, Margaret, 2:902,
　2:904, 2:905, 2:906
Atwood, Stephen J., 5:348
Atwood, William G., 2:505
Au, Susan, 3:732
Aubert, Claude, 5:344
Aubet, Maria E., 3:300
Aubrey, James R., 1:478
Auburn, Mark S., 1:254
Auchard, John, 1:121, 1:765
Auchincloss, Louis, 1:843,
　1:937
Auckett, Amelia D., 5:321
Auden, W(ystan) H(ugh),
　1:165, 1:416, 1:434, 1:444,
　1:467, 1:481, 1:486, 1:500,
　1:502, 1:507, 1:511, 1:517,
　1:552, 1:688, 1:935,
　1:1037, 2:348, 2:800, 4:47
Audi, Robert, 4:888
Audouze, Jean, 5:587
Audrey, Robert L., 5:262
Audubon, John James,
　3:894 5:786
Audubon, Maria, 3:907
Aue, Hartmann von, 2:562,
　2:582
Auerbach, Doris, 1:1111
Auerbach, Erich, 1:420,
　2:417, 2:985
Auerbach, Nina, 1:269, 1:318,
　1:322
Auerbach, Paul S., 5:381
Aufderheide, Patricia, 1:1128
Aufricht, Hans, 3:272
Augarde, A. J., 1:116
Augarten, Stan, 5:539

Augustine of Hippo, St.,
　2:430, 3:150, 4:63, 4:93,
　4:98, 4:107, 4:108, 4:114,
　4:116, 4:150, 4:155, 4:674,
　4:702, 4:704, 4:705, 4:757,
　4:786
Augustinos, Gerasimos, 3:391,
　3:393
Aukstakalnis, Steve, 5:564
Aulen, Gustaf, 4:678, 4:886
Auletta, Ken, 3:66, 3:810
Aune, Bruce A., 4:206, 4:262,
　4:380
Aune, David E., 4:795
Aung San Suu Kyi, 2:314
Aurelius, Marcus, 1:386,
　4:56, 4:59, 4:75
Austen, Jane, 1:235, 1:264,
　1:269, 1:274, 1:289, 1:451,
　1:468, 1:538, 1:1007,
　2:953, 3:827
Austen-Leigh, J. E., 1:276
Auster, Henry, 1:354
Auster, Paul, 2:448
Austin, Allan E., 1:448, 1:481
Austin, Bruce A., 3:824
Austin, John Langshaw,
　4:261, 4:271
Austin, Linda Marilyn, 1:394
Austin, Mary (Hunter),
　1:726, 1:732
Austin, Michel M., 3:299,
　3:307, 4:449
Austin, Norman, 2:361, 4:428
Austin, Ralph, 3:416
Austin, Scott, 4:52
Austin, William W., 3:658,
　3:695
Austrian, G. D., 5:576
Austrian, Robert, 5:368
Ausubel, Nathan, 2:33, 4:593
Auty, R., 2:684
Avedon, John, 4:906
Aveling, Harry, 2:317, 2:321
Aveni, Anthony F., 4:455,
　4:457
Averch, Harvey A., 5:180
Averill, James R., 5:413
Averroës, 4:96, 4:101, 4:580,
　4:581, 4:585
Avery, Donald, 3:614
Avery-Peck, Alan J., 4:609
Aviad, Janet, 3:439, 4:659
Avicenna, 4:96, 4:101, 4:149,
　4:580, 4:581, 4:582
Avineri, Shlomo, 4:232,
　4:242, 4:655, 4:657
Avins, Carol, 2:684
Avis, F. C., 1:13
Avi-Yonah, Michael, 4:606,
　4:808, 4:809
Avni, Haim, 4:635
Avrich, Paul, 3:248

Awkward, Michael, 1:803,
　1:850
Awoonor, Kofi, 2:106, 2:126,
　2:131
Awwad, Tewfiq Yussef, 2:58
Axelrad, Albert S., 4:648
Axelrad, Jacob, 1:639
Axelrod, Alan, 1:636, 3:516
Axelrod, Steven Gould,
　1:887, 1:1006, 1:1031
Axinn, Sidney, 4:388
Axline, Virginia M., 5:421
Ayala, Ramón Pérez de. See
　Pérez de Ayala, Ramón
Ayalon, Ami, 3:434
Ayckbourn, Alan, 1:424,
　1:436
Ayer, Michael, 4:179
Ayer, Sir Alfred Jules, 4:41,
　4:201, 4:237, 4:249, 4:262,
　4:272, 4:312, 4:324, 4:343,
　4:344, 4:370, 5:103
Ayers, David, 1:514
Ayers, Edward L., 3:531
Ayers, Michael, 4:162
Ayling, Alan, 2:192
Ayling, Stanley, 3:361
Aymé, Marcel, 2:452
Ayoub, Mahmoud M., 4:587
Ayre, Leslie, 3:654
Azad, Abu-l-Kalam, 4:372
Aziz, Robert, 5:455
Azrak, Michel G., 2:56
Azuela, Mariano, 2:843,
　2:854
Azzam, Abd-al-Rahman, 4:588

B

Ba'al Shem Tov (Israel Ben
　Eliezer), 4:631, 4:660,
　4:668
Ba, Mariama, 2:105, 2:132
Ba, Sylvia, 2:147
Baba, Ahmad, 2:124
Baba, Meher, 4:872
Babb, Lawrence A., 4:503,
　4:507
Babbage, Charles, 5:541,
　5:575, 5:578
Babbitt, Irving, 2:446
Babcock, Robert H., 3:614
Babel, Isaac (Isaak), 2:699
Baber, Robert L., 5:125
Babich, Wayne A., 5:549
Babin, Ronald, 5:109
Babits, Mihály, 2:798
Babkin, Boris P., 3:191,
　5:364
Bach, Johann Sebastian,
　2:431, 3:675, 3:706, 3:727

Bach, Julie S., 5:118
Bach, Robert L., 3:209
Bachelard, Gaston, 4:273
Bachelard, Suzanne, 4:234
Bachmann, Ingeborg, 2:568
Back, Kurt W., 5:421
Backscheider, Paula R.,
    1:240
Bacon, Addison, 1:373
Bacon, Francis, 1:166,
    1:203, 1:204, 1:922, 2:410,
    3:153, **4:164**, 4:173, 4:848,
    5:105, 5:259
Bacon, Roger, 4:110, 4:115
Bacovcin, Helen, 4:755
Bacovia, George, 2:823
Badash, Lawrence, 5:697
Badawi, M. M., 2:55
Badcock, C. R., 3:34
Bade, David H., 5:262
Baden, John, 5:114
Bader, Barbara, 1:27, 1:37
Badger, Anthony J., 3:533
Badham, Linda, 4:887
Badham, Paul, 4:887
Badi al-Zaman al-Hamdhani,
    2:58
Badian, E., 3:299
Badough, Rose Marie, 5:544
Badr, Liyanah, 2:58
Badt, Kurt, 3:772
Baeck, Leo, 4:615, **4:660**
Baehr, Stephen L., 2:684
Baer, George W., 3:277
Baer, Hans A., 3:212
Baer, Yitzhak, 4:623
Bagader, Abu Bakr, 2:56
Bagchee, Shyamal, 1:472
Bagdikian, Ben H., 3:802
Baggett, Nancy, 5:348
Baglow, John, 1:517
Bagnall, Roger, 3:299
Bagnani, Gilbert, 2:391
Bagnell, Roger, 4:449
Bagrow, Leo, 5:619
Baha'u'llah, 4:861
Bahadur, K. P., 4:501
Bahm, Archie J., 4:5
Bahn, Paul, 4:432, 4:436
Bahr, Ehrhard, 2:801
Bahusevič, Franišak, 2:783
Baier, Annette, 4:201
Baier, Sue, 5:391
Baigell, Matthew, 3:758
Bail, Murray, 2:947
Bailey, Alice A., 4:858
Bailey, Anthony, 3:898
Bailey, Betty J., 3:434
Bailey, Cyril, 2:388, 4:53,
    4:73
Bailey, D. R. Shackleton,
    3:313, 4:72
Bailey, D. Sherwin, 4:678

Bailey, E. B., 5:644
Bailey, Eric J., 3:201
Bailey, Frank E., 3:452
Bailey, Harry, 3:146
Bailey, Herbert S., Jr., 1:43,
    1:46
Bailey, James Osler, 1:323,
    1:362
Bailey, Kathryn, 3:729
Bailey, Kenneth D., 3:200
Bailey, Liberty Hyde, 5:787
Bailey, T. E., 5:549
Bailey, Thomas A., 3:512,
    3:514, 3:541, 3:544
Baillie, Joanna, 1:271, **1:276**
Baily, Martin Neil, 5:184
Bailyn, Bernard, 1:6, 1:627,
    3:511, 3:512, 3:519, 3:541,
    3:563
Bain, Alexander, 4:244
Bain, David L., 5:233
Bain, Joe, 3:57
Bain, Kenneth R., 3:439
Bain, Robert, 1:712
Bainbridge, William Sims,
    4:855
Bains, W., 5:74
Bainton, Roland H., 3:334,
    4:139, 4:676, 4:678, 4:681,
    4:691, 4:749, 4:778
Bair, Deirdre, 1:440, 2:458,
    2:460
Bair, Frank E., 5:7, 5:391,
    5:633
Baird, Forrest, 4:23
Baird, Henry M., 4:731
Baird, James R., 1:887
Baird, Robert D., 4:422,
    4:507, 4:516, 4:517, 4:562
Bairstow, Jeffrey, 3:733
Baitz, Jon R., 1:1076
Bajan, Helen, 1:549
Bak, Janos, 4:723
Bakalar, James B., 5:405
Bakan, David, 3:169, 4:628
Bakeless, John E., 1:187
Baker, Arthur E., 1:13, 1:401
Baker, Bevan Braithwaite,
    5:695
Baker, Blanche M., 1:123
Baker, Carlos, 1:797, 1:846,
    2:986
Baker, Christopher John,
    3:485
Baker, Daisy, 3:898
Baker, Derek, 4:725
Baker, Donald, 3:868
Baker, Ernest Albert, 1:269,
    1:318, 1:420
Baker, G. P., 4:229
Baker, George Pierce, 1:1070
Baker, Henry F., 5:486
Baker, Holly Cutting, 3:857

Baker, Houston A., Jr.,
    1:793, 1:824, 1:910, **1:937**,
    1:1128, 1:1131, **1:1136**
Baker, J. R., 5:799
Baker, James M., 3:717
Baker, James R., 1:484
Baker, Jeffrey, 1:294, 5:774
Baker, Josephine, 3:737
Baker, Joseph O., 2:599
Baker, Kendall L., 3:376
Baker, Larry, 5:616
Baker, Leonard, 4:661
Baker, M. Pauline, 5:564
Baker, Margret, 3:868
Baker, Michael, 1:492
Baker, Paul R., 3:277
Baker, Raymond W., 3:445
Baker, Robert S., 1:499
Baker, Ronald L., 3:861
Baker, Russell, 3:870
Baker, Stephen F., 5:492
Baker, William E., 2:494
Bakhash, Shaul, 4:578
Bakhtiar, Laleh, 4:375
Bakhtin, Mikhail, 1:923,
    2:497, 2:684, 2:714
Bakhurst, David, 4:30
Bakker, J., 1:803
Bakker, Robert, 5:638
Bakr, Salwa, 2:58
Balakian, Anna, 2:463, 2:986
Balakian, Nona, 1:916
Balanchine, George, 3:722,
    3:733, **3:737**, 3:738, 3:741,
    3:742, 3:745, 3:747, 3:750,
    3:752, 3:754
Balchin, W.G.V., 5:619
Bald, R. C., 1:178
Baldanza, Frank, 1:462, 1:524
Balderston, Daniel, 2:857
Baldick, Christopher, 1:301,
    1:311, 1:1126
Baldick, Julian, 4:574
Baldini, Gabriele, 3:726
Baldry, H. C., 4:47
Baldwin, Alice, 1:627
Baldwin, B., 3:320
Baldwin, Dean R., 1:538,
    1:569
Baldwin, Dorothy, 5:339
Baldwin, Hanson W., 3:277
Baldwin, James, 1:905,
    1:934, **1:938**, 1:974,
    1:1083, 1:1185, 4:862
Baldwin, James M., 4:13
Baldwin, John D., 4:309
Baldwin, John W., 4:695,
    4:698
Baldwin, Lewis, 4:772
Baldwin, Steve, 3:201
Baldwin, T. W., 1:215
Baldwin, Thomas, 4:312

Baldwin, William, 1:167, **1:171**
Bale, John, 1:157, 1:163, 1:168, **1:172**
Bales, Eugene F., 4:13
Bales, Robert F., 3:172
Balf, Miriam, 1:1076
Balfour, Henry H., Jr., 5:389
Balfour, Sebastian, 3:636
Balfour, Sir Graham, 1:397
Balibar, Etienne, 4:242
Balio, Tino, 3:824
Baliozian, Ara, 2:76
Balke, Willem, 4:761
Ball, Douglas, 1:21
Ball, Johnson, 1:13
Ball, Margaret, 1:299
Ball, Patricia M., 1:315
Ball, Stephen J., 5:88
Ball, Terence, 4:242
Ball, W. W., 5:495
Ballard, Bruce W., 4:292
Ballard, Edward G., 5:69, 5:127
Ballard, Robert Duane, 3:126, **5:640**
Ballestrem, K. G., 4:30
Ballet, Arthur H., 1:1076
Ballhatchet, Kenneth, 3:483, 3:484
Balliett, Whitney, 3:667, 3:672, 3:730
Ballou, Ellen B., 1:42
Ballou, Robert O., 4:5
Ball-Rokeach, Sandra J., 3:203, 3:803
Balmer, Randall, 4:752
Balogh, Brian, 5:109
Balogh, Sandor, 3:389
Balstan, Hayim, 1:99
Balston, Thomas, 1:4
Baltazar, Francisco, 2:327
Baltes, Paul B., 3:173
Balthasar, Hans Urs von, 4:63, 4:891, 4:904
Baltimore, David, 5:784
Baly, Monica E., 5:362
Balyuzi, M. M., 4:588
Balz, Albert G., 4:169, 4:187
Balzac, Honoré de, 1:835, 2:236, 2:445, **2:453**, 2:617
Balzer, Marjorie M., 4:430
Bambara, Toni Cade, 1:910, **1:939**
Bamberger, Bernard J., 4:596, 4:620, 4:648
Bamberger, Jeanne Shapiro, 3:664
Bance, Alan, 2:579
Band, Arnold J., 2:12
Bandarage, Asoka, 3:487
Bandeira, Manuel, 2:893
Bandler, Richard, 5:441

Bandura, Albert, 3:175, 5:413
Bandyopadhyaya, Manik, 2:177
Bane, Michael, 3:654
Banerian, James, 2:339
Banerji, Bibhutibhushan, 2:177
Banerji, P., 3:850
Bang, Herman, 2:645, **2:647**, 2:666
Bangs, Carl, 4:731
Banister, Keith, 5:758
Banister, Manley, 1:27
Banks, Ann, 3:534
Banks, David J., 2:324
Banks, James, 3:253
Banks, Michael A., 5:301
Banks, Olive, 3:217
Banks, Russell, 1:909, 1:916, **1:940**
Banner, Lois, 3:554
Bannerman, Patrick, 3:442
Bannerman, R. Leroy, 3:810
Banning, Lance, 3:519
Bannon, John F., 3:643
Banta, Martha, 1:712, 1:765
Banting, Sir Frederick Grant, 5:406
Banton, Michael, 3:22, 3:23, 4:422
Banulescu, Stefan, 2:823
Baqir As-Sadr, Muhammad, 4:373
Barabtarlo, Gennadi, 2:741
Barac, Antun, 2:785, 2:827, 2:835
Baraheni, Reza, 2:82, 2:84
Baraka, Imamu Amiri (Leroi Jones), 1:910, **1:940**, 1:954, **1:1084**, 1:1086
Barakat, Halim, 2:58, 3:434
Baran, Paul A., 3:50
Baranauskas, Antanas, 2:804, **2:805**
Barany, George, 3:389
Barasch, Marc, 1:921
Barash, Asher, 2:15
Barash, David P., 5:769
Barbeau, Charles Marius, 3:874
Barber, Bernard, 3:208, 3:213
Barber, C. L., 1:185, 1:210
Barber, E. A., 2:357
Barber, E. J., 3:767
Barber, Edwin, 3:765
Barber, G. G., 1:6
Barber, Gerald M., 3:119
Barber, J. P., 5:417
Barber, James D., 3:146
Barber, Peter, 5:191
Barber, Richard, 3:357

Barber, Samuel, 3:675, 3:709
Barber, W. H., 4:177
Barbera, Jack, 1:549
Barbour, Hugh, 4:733
Barbour, Ian, 4:388, 5:74, 5:127, **5:160**, 5:195, 5:196, 5:199
Barbour, James, 1:722
Barbu, Ian, 2:823
Barca, Calderón de la. *See* Calderón de la Barca, Pedro
Barcus, James E., 1:303
Bardeen, John, 5:670, 5:696
Bardes, Barbara, 1:722
Bardgett, Frank D., 4:735
Bardhan, Pranab, 3:485
Bareham, Terence, 1:289
Bareham, Tony, 2:919
Baretti, Giuseppe, 2:407
Barfield, Owen, 1:923, 4:776
Bargad, Warren, 2:9, 2:19
Bargainnier, Earl F., 1:606
Barineau, R. Maurice, 4:341
Baring, Maurice, 2:684
Baring-Gould, Sabine, 3:850
Barish, Jonas A., 1:169, 1:184
Baritz, Loren, 1:627
Bark, Melvin Van den, 1:92
Bark, W. C., 3:328
Barkan, Sandra, 2:106
Barkan, Stanley, 1:129, 2:672
Barker, Adele M., 2:684
Barker, Arthur E., 1:192
Barker, Christine, 2:607
Barker, Clive, 1:599, 1:602
Barker, Eileen, 4:855, 4:871
Barker, Ernest, 4:66, 4:79
Barker, Forrest L., 5:298
Barker, John W., 4:682
Barker, Nicolas, 1:6, 1:13, 1:35, 1:43
Barker, Wendy, 1:746
Barker-Barfield, G. J., 1:647
Barksdale, Richard K., 1:653, 1:717, 1:718, 1:725, 1:848
Barley, Tony, 1:596
Barlow, Connie, 5:285
Barlow, Frank, 3:356
Barlow, Harold, 3:654
Barlow, Horace, 5:191
Barlow, Joel, 1:626, **1:632**
Barlow, Judith E., 1:1071, 1:1076
Barman, Jean, 3:609
Barnard, Chester I., 3:210
Barnard, Christiaan, 5:339
Barnard, Ellsworth, 1:877
Barnard, Frederick, 4:199
Barnard, G. A., 5:530
Barnard, Henry, 3:258
Barnard, L. W., 4:703

Barnard, Max, 5:537
Barnard, Robert, 1:606
Barnavi, Eli, 4:593
Barneau, Michel, 2:471
Barner-Barry, Carol, 3:147
Barnes, Barry, 4:406, 5:53,
  5:150
Barnes, Benjamin, 5:79
Barnes, Christopher, 2:746
Barnes, Clive, 1:1077, 3:734,
  3:750
Barnes, Djuna, 1:812, 1:985,
  1:1002, 1:1185, 1:1190
Barnes, Harry E., 5:34
Barnes, Hazel E., 2:476,
  2:507, 4:262, 4:330
Barnes, J. A., 3:19
Barnes, James J., 1:54
Barnes, John, 2:953, 3:633
Barnes, Jonathan, 3:311,
  4:50, 4:56, 4:58, 4:66,
  4:108
Barnes, Marian E., 3:866
Barnes, Mary, 5:426
Barnes, Michael, 4:507, 4:509
Barnes, Mildred A., 5:627
Barnes, R.S.K., 5:758
Barnes, Robert J., 1:283
Barnes, Ruth, 3:207
Barnes, Timothy D., 3:302,
  4:709, 4:714
Barnes, Virgil E., 5:627
Barnes, William, 1:316
Barnet, Sylvan, 1:131, 1:205,
  1:206
Barnett, A(rthur) Doak,
  3:496
Barnett, Gene A., 1:1121
Barnett, George L., 1:296
Barnett, Lincoln, 5:682
Barnhart, B., 5:77
Barnouw, Adriaan, 3:382
Barnouw, Erik, 3:551, 3:802,
  3:810, 3:825
Barnstone, Aliki, 2:4
Barnstone, Willis, 2:4, 2:371,
  4:810
Barnu, Eugen, 2:823
Barnwell, H. T., 2:471
Baroja y Nessi, Pío, 2:530
Barolini, Teodolinda, 2:417
Baron, Frank, 2:608
Baron, Hans, 2:400, 4:29,
  4:123, 4:151
Baron, Jason D., 5:403
Baron, Naomi S., 5:549
Baron, Robert, 5:837
Baron, Salo W., 3:347, 4:593,
  4:596, 4:635
Baron, W. R., 1:146
Barondess, Jeremiah, 5:364
Barone, Michael, 3:541
Baronian, Hagop, 2:77

Barooshian, Vahan D., 2:739
Barr, Alfred H., 3:786
Barr, Avron, 5:569
Barr, James, 4:817
Barr, Stringfellow, 3:326
Barraclough, Geoffrey, 2:564,
  3:328, 4:691, 4:694
Barral, Mary R., 4:311
Barranger, Milly S., 1:271
Barratt, Andrew, 2:735
Barratt, Glynn R., 3:395
Barrell, John, 1:225, 1:290
Barrer, N. Gerald, 4:516
Barret, Robert B., 5:100
Barrett, Charles K., 4:617,
  4:810
Barrett, Cyril, 4:344
Barrett, David B., 4:3, 4:716,
  4:742
Barrett, Edward, 5:561
Barrett, Eileen, 1:808
Barrett, Elizabeth, 1:338
Barrett, James, 5:758
Barrett, Leonard E., 4:467
Barrett, Michele, 3:206
Barrett, Paul H., 5:758
Barrett, Stephen, 5:346
Barrett, Timothy, 1:4
Barrett, William, 2:988,
  4:262, 5:69
Barricelli, Gian Piero, 2:424,
  2:426
Barricelli, Jean-Pierre, 2:710,
  2:987
Barrie, Sir J(ames)
  M(atthew), 1:328, 1:580,
  1:586
Barro, Robert J., 3:49
Barron, Jerome A., 3:801
Barron, Neil, 1:599, 1:611
Barros, Joi, 2:328
Barrow, Geoffrey W., 3:368
Barrow, John D., 5:11, 5:196,
  5:594, 5:654
Barrow, Leo L., 2:530
Barrow, Reginald H., 4:490
Barrow, W. J., 1:21
Barry, Colman J., 4:680,
  4:719, 4:740
Barry, Dave, 3:891
Barry, Elaine, 2:948
Barry, John A., 5:536
Barry, John M., 5:373
Barry, Philip, 1:1070, 1:1085
Barry, Robert, 5:196
Barry, Roger G., 5:633
Bars, Henry, 4:307
Barson, Alfred T., 1:933
Barstow, David R., 5:549
Barth, Else M., 4:391
Barth, Fredrik, 3:22, 3:447
Barth, Friedrich G., 5:767,
  5:769

Barth, Gunther, 3:558
Barth, Jack, 3:894
Barth, John, 1:909, 1:916,
  1:941, 1:952, 1:985, 5:563
Barth, J. Robert, 1:287
Barth, Karl, 4:254, 4:742,
  4:757, 4:759, 4:783, 4:787
Barth, Michael C., 5:633
Barth, Richard B., 5:403
Barth, Roland S., 3:248,
  3:253
Bartha, Georges De, 1:23
Barthel, Diane L., 4:843
Barthelemy, Anthony G.,
  1:727
Barthelemy-Madaule, Made-
  leine, 5:802
Barthelme, Donald, 1:909,
  1:916, **1:943,** 3:891
Barthes, Roland, 1:1130,
  2:446, **2:454,** 2:485, 2:498,
  2:503, 2:515
Bartholomeusz, Dennis, 1:214
Bartholomew, Fletcher, 5:196
Bartholomew, James R.,
  3:476
Bartlett, C. J., 3:365
Bartlett, Irving H., 1:722,
  3:523
Bartlett, John, 1:116
Bartlett, John G., 5:386
Bartlett, Richard, 3:551
Bartlett, Thomas, 3:369
Bartók, Béla, 3:676, 3:850
Barton, Anne, 1:184
Bartov, Hanokh, 2:15
Bartram, Alan, 1:19
Bartusiak, Marcia, 5:593
Baruch, Dorothy W., 5:421
Bary, William Theodore de,
  4:358, 4:497, 4:521, 4:523,
  4:526, 4:540
Baryshnikov, Mikhail, 3:653,
  3:738, 3:753
Barzini, Luigi, 2:400, 3:342,
  3:385
Barzun, Jacques, 1:117,
  1:604, 1:768, **1:813,** 3:9,
  3:187, 3:275, 3:340, 3:658,
  3:664, 3:681, 4:237
Bascom, Willard, 5:631
Bascom, William, 3:866,
  4:462
Basford, Terry K., 4:866
Basham, A. L., 3:482, 4:351,
  4:498
Basheer, Vaikom Muham-
  mad, 2:177
Ba Shin, 2:313
Bashiri, Iraj, 2:90
Bashō, 2:271, 2:276, 2:278,
  2:280
Basie, William, 3:677, 3:700

Basil, Robert, 4:866
Basile, Robert M., 5:635
Basil of Caesarea, St.,
    4:704, 4:705
Basker, James G., 1:257
Baskin, Judith, 4:649
Bass, Dick, 3:906
Bass, Eben E., 1:392, 1:499
Bass, Rick, 5:817
Bassan, M., 1:742
Bassani, Giorgio, 2:407,
    2:423
Bassett, Jan, 3:493
Bassett, John E., 1:793
Bassin, A., 5:451
Bassnett-McGuire, Susan,
    2:990
Bassuk, Daniel E., 4:507
Bastian, Katherine, 1:1023
Bastos, Augusto Roa. See
    Roa Bastos, Augusto
Bataille, Georges, 2:455
Bataille, Gretchen M., 3:509
Batatu, John, 3:449, 4:578
Batchelor, John, 1:570
Bate, Jonathan, 1:265, 1:306
Bate, Walter J., 1:249, 1:267,
    1:287, 1:294
Bateman, Alan M., 5:636
Bates, E. S., 4:878
Bates, Marston, 5:817
Bates, Milton J, 1:887
Bates, Robert L., 5:616,
    5:635
Bates, Scott, 2:451
Bates, William, 5:539
Bates, William N., 2:368
Bateson, Frederick W., 1:306
Bateson, Gregory, 3:14, 3:15,
    4:461
Batey, Peter, 3:125
Batley, Edward, 4:208
Batschelet, Margaret W., 5:27
Batshaw, Mark L., 5:321,
    5:375
Battan, Louis J., 5:633
Batten, Charles, 1:231
Battestin, Martin C., 1:245
Battestin, Ruth K., 1:245
Battie, David, 3:765
Battiscombe, Georgina, 1:390
Baudelaire, Charles, 1:691,
    1:693, 2:206, **2:456**, 2:486,
    2:982, 4:329
Baudrillard, Jean, 3:211
Baudry, Leon, 4:104
Bauer, Arnold, 2:608
Bauer, Brian S., 3:627
Bauer, Dale M., 1:803
Bauer, Henry H., 5:9, 5:150,
    5:589
Bauer, Josephine, 1:273
Bauer, K. Jack, 3:523, 3:638

Bauer, Walter, 4:98, 4:685,
    4:794
Bauer, Yehuda, 4:635
Bauerlein, Mark, 1:707
Bauermeister, Benjamin, 1:62
Baugh, Albert C., 1:129
Baugh, Edward, 2:943
Baugh, Kenneth, 3:222
Baughman, Ernest W., 3:849
Baughman, James L., 3:551,
    3:816
Baughman, Judith S., 1:967
Baum, Alan, 4:210
Baum, Andrew, 5:321, 5:339
Baum, Charlotte, 4:649
Baum, F. J., 1:1200
Baum, Joan, 5:578
Baum, L(yman) Frank,
    1:1194, **1:1199**
Baum, Robert J., 5:73, 5:127
Bauman, Richard, 3:862
Bauman, Zygmunt, 3:211
Baumbach, Jonathan, 1:917
Baumgarten, Murray, 1:1041
Baumol, William J., 3:48,
    3:57, 3:64, 3:67
Bauschatz, Paul C., 4:437
Bautista, Lahul, 2:328
Bavsell, R. Barker, 3:6
Bawden, Lee D., 3:59
Baxandall, Michael, 5:191
Baxter, Craig, 3:487
Baxter, Edmund, 1:290
Baxter, James Keir, 2:972,
    2:973
Bay, A., 3:278
al-Bayati, 'Abd al-Wahab,
    2:63
Bayer, Edward J., 5:129
Bayerschmidt, Carl F., 2:669
Bayle, Malebranche, 4:176
Bayle, Pierre, 4:166, 4:173
Bayles, Michael D., 5:106
Bayley, John, 1:496, 2:765
Baylin, Frank, 5:228
Bayliss, R.I.S., 5:381
Bayliss-Smith, T. P., 5:262
Bayly, C. A., 3:485
Baym, M. I., 1:730, 3:563
Baym, Nina, 1:129, 1:627,
    1:653, 1:657, 1:676, 1:717,
    1:722, **1:944**, 1:1224
Baynes, C. F., 4:525
Baynes, Kenneth, 4:316,
    4:378, 5:191, 5:212
Baynes, Norman H., 4:682
Baynes-Cope, A. D., 1:22
Bazán, Emilia Pardo, 2:521
Bazin, André, 1:1156, 1:1161,
    1:1179, 3:827, 3:842
Beach, Joseph W., 1:435,
    1:765
Beach, Sylvia, 1:39

Beacham, Walton, 2:2
Beachler, Lea, 1:127
Beadle, George Wells, 5:788
Beaglehole, J. C., 3:493,
    3:918
Beagon, Mary, 5:810
Beahm, George, 1:1241
Beakley, George C., 5:227
Beale, Howard K., 3:594
Beales, D., 3:385
Beales, Peter, 5:767
Beals, Alan R., 4:503
Bean, Lee L., 3:205
Bean, William N., 5:312
Bear, John, 5:536
Beard, Charles A(ustin),
    3:141, 3:542, **3:564**
Beard, Mary R(itter), 3:564
Beard, Michael, 2:90
Beardsley, John, 3:786, 3:867
Beare, J. I., 4:47
Bearman, Frederick A., 1:22
Beasley, David R., 1:61
Beasley, Joseph D., 5:327
Beasley, W. G., 3:473, 3:476
Beason, Gordon, Jr., 1:1258
Beaton, Roderick, 2:371
Beattie, Ann, 1:916, **1:945**
Beattie, D.R.G., 4:609
Beattie, J. H., 3:29
Beatty, Arthur, 1:306
Beatty, J. Kelly, 5:592
Beatty, Richmond C., 1:685
Beatty, William K., 5:314
Beaty, Janice, 3:253
Beauchamp, Dan E., 5:401
Beauchamp, Edward R.,
    3:248
Beauchamp, Gorman, 1:774
Beauchamp, Thomas L.,
    4:19, 4:201, 5:106, 5:118,
    5:120, **5:131**
Beaucour, Ferrard, 3:445
Beaudiquez, Marcelle, 1:63
Beaujour, Elizabeth K., 2:744
Beauman, Sally, 1:426
Beaumarchais, Pierre-Au-
    gustin Caron de, 2:445,
    2:457, 2:471
Beaumont, Cyril, 1:271,
    3:733
Beaumont, Ernest V., 4:34
Beaumont, Francis, 1:172
Beaumont, Peter, 3:435
Beauroy, Jacques, 3:372
Beauvoir, Simone de,
    1:1186, **2:458**, 4:309, 4:329
Beaver, Harold, 1:783
Beaver, Paul, 5:238
Beaver, R. Pierce, 4:520
Bebchuk, Lucian Arye, 3:61
Becher, Jeanne, 4:894
Bechr, Edward, 3:390

Bechtel, Delphine, 2:38
Bechtel, William, 4:384
Beck, Aaron T., 5:432
Beck, Evelyn Torton, 1:1183
Beck, Horace, 3:868
Beck, James, 3:788
Beck, Jane C., 3:858
Beck, Leslie J., 4:169
Beck, Lewis White, 4:159,
4:206, 4:209, 4:219
Beck, Paul Allen, 3:143
Beck, Robert N., 4:19
Becker, A. L., 2:317
Becker, Carl, 4:159
Becker, Carl L(otus), 3:154,
3:275, 3:337, 3:519, **3:566**
Becker, Charlotte B., 4:2,
4:13
Becker, Gary Stanley, 3:56,
3:69, 3:206
Becker, George J., 1:1248,
2:986
Becker, Jared, 2:428
Becker, Jürgen, 4:824
Becker, Lawrence C., 4:2,
4:13
Becker, Lucille F., 2:508
Becker, M., 5:240
Becker, Michael G., 1:294
Becker, Reinhard P., 4:124
Becker, Robert O., 5:318
Becker, Wayne M., 5:775
Beckerman, Bernard, 1:217
Beckett, Derrick, 5:250
Beckett, Samuel, 1:412,
1:419, **1:438,** 1:526, 1:985,
1:1087, 2:435, **2:459,**
2:483, 2:855
Beckford, James A., 4:856
Beckford, William, 1:603
Beckler, Alfred W., 5:368
Beckley, Harlan R., 4:900
Beckman, Arnold Orville,
5:738
Beckman, William A., 5:284
Bécquer, Gustavo Adolfo,
2:521, **2:530,** 2:533, 2:542
Bedani, Gino, 4:216
Bedarida, François, 3:365
Bedau, Hugo A., 3:204, 4:386
Bédé, Jean-Albert, 1:131, 2:3,
2:446, 2:518
Bedell, Gary, 4:19
Bedell, Kenneth B., 4:5
Bedient, Calvin, 1:417, 1:893
Bedini, Silvio A., 5:43
Bednorowski, Mary F., 4:841
Bedrosian, Robert, 2:76
Beedham, R. John, 1:27
Beekman, E. M., 2:622
Beer, Gillian, 1:354
Beer, John, 1:287
Beer, Patricia, 1:269

Beer, Samuel H., 3:365
Beer, Thomas, 1:742
Beerbohm, Sir (Henry)
Max(imilian), 1:367, 1:392,
1:440
Beers, Henry A., 1:267
Beers, Henry P., 3:508, 3:509
Beers, William, 4:892
Beeston, A.F.L., 2:55
Beethoven, Ludwig van,
3:677, 3:699, 3:713, 3:741
Beetz, Kirk H., 1:398
Beevor, Antony, 3:386
Beezley, William H., 3:638
Begiebing, Robert J., 1:1012
Begin, Menachem, 4:642
Begnal, Michael H., 1:470,
1:601
Begović, Milan, 2:785
Behan, Brendan, 1:424,
1:441
Behler, Ernest, 4:292
Behn, Aphra, 1:228, **1:232,**
1:238
Behrangi, Samad, 2:86
Behrendt, Stephen C., 1:278,
1:301, 1:303
Behrens, C.B.A., 3:338
Beichman, Janet, 2:288
Beidelman, Thomas O., 4:492
Beiderwell, Bruce, 1:299
Beier, Ulli, 2:106, 2:113
Beigel, Hugo G., 5:413
Beilin, Yossi, 3:439
Bein, Alex, 3:347
Beinin, Joel, 3:439
Beiser, Arthur, 5:652
Beiser, Frederick C., 4:16,
4:159, 4:209, 4:233
Beit-Hallahmi, Benjamin,
4:643
Beizer, Janet, 2:454
Beja, Morris, 1:505
Beker, J. Christian, 4:824
Belfiore, Elizabeth, 4:67
Belford, Barbara, 3:805
Belich, James, 3:494
Belier, Wouter W., 4:472
Belitsos, Byron, 5:559
Belkin, Gary S., 1:46
Belkin, Lisa, 5:118, 5:343
Belkin, Samuel, 4:608
Belkind, Allen, 1:828
Bell, Arthur E., 5:695
Bell, Barbara L., 1:64
Bell, Bernard W., 1:722
Bell, Catherine, 4:426
Bell, Cheryl, 3:734
Bell, Daniel, 3:139, **3:219,**
5:150, 5:572
Bell, David, 4:229, 4:234
Bell, David F., 2:518
Bell, Diane, 4:461

Bell, E. Moberly, 1:341
Bell, Eric T., 5:30, 5:527
Bell, James K., 1:91
Bell, J. Bowyer, 3:370, 3:439
Bell, John Fred, 3:45
Bell, Judith, 3:730
Bell, Mackenzie, 1:390
Bell, Michael D., 1:510,
1:657
Bell, Michael J., 3:866
Bell, Millicent, 1:676, 1:765
Bell, Peter Robert, 5:767
Bell, Quentin, 1:570
Bell, Richard, 4:587
Bell, Robert, 5:9, 5:106
Bell, Roger, 5:327
Bell, Rudolph M., 4:698,
4:701
Bell, S. P., 5:216
Bell, Whitfield J., 5:312
Bellack, Alan S., 5:417
Bellah, Robert N(eelly),
3:220, 3:248, 3:474, 4:422,
4:424, 4:540, 4:752, 4:855,
4:890
Bellak, Leopold, 5:417, 5:421
Bellamy, Edward, 1:733,
5:563
Bellamy, Joe David, 1:912
Bellamy, John, 5:301
Bellas, Ralph A., 1:390
Bellay, Joachim du, 2:444
Bellegarde-Smith, Patrick,
3:637
Belli, Giuseppe Gioacchino,
2:408
Bellina, Joseph H., 5:357
Bellini, Vincenzo, 3:678
Bellman, Carl Michael,
2:637, 2:670
Belloc, Hilaire, 1:428, **1:442,**
1:457
Belloni, Lanfranco, 5:27
Bellow, Saul, 1:448, 1:725,
1:909, 1:916, 1:921, **1:945,**
1:996, 1:1040, 1:1044,
1:1049
Bellringer, Alan W., 1:326,
1:765
Bell-Villada, Gene H., 2:857,
2:867
Bellwood, Peter, 3:493, 3:495
Belok, Michael V., 1:38
Belsey, Catherine, 1:169,
1:1131
Belth, Nathan C., 4:638
Bely (Biely), Andrei, 2:683,
2:700, 2:747
Belz, Herman, 3:514
Bembo, Pietro, 2:408
Bemelmans, Ludwig, 3:894
Bemis, Samuel Flagg, 3:567
Bemister, Margaret, 3:864

Ben, Amos D., 3:868
Benacerraf, P., 5:492
Benardete, M. J., 2:536
Benardete, Seth, 4:89
Benavente, Jacinto, 2:531
Benayoun, Robert, 3:829
Benchley, Robert, 1:807,
1:814, 1:868
Ben-David, Joseph, 3:202,
3:213, 5:150
Bender, Arnold E., 5:261
Bender, Gray T., 5:735
Bender, John B., 1:229
Bender, Todd K., 1:364
Benderly, Beryl L., 5:379
Bendersky, Joseph W., 3:376
Benderson, Albert E., 3:836
Bendix, Reinhard, 3:214,
3:244
Benedict, Ruth, 3:15, 3:22,
3:26, 3:28, 3:34, 3:36, 3:39,
3:474, 4:477, 4:534
Benedict of Nursia, St.,
4:705
Benedictsson, Victoria, 2:671
Benediktson, D. Thomas,
2:392
Benes, Peter, 3:858
Benesch, Otto, 3:789
Benestad, Finn, 3:698
Benet, Diana, 1:181, 1:539
Benét, Stephen Vincent,
1:815
Benet, Sula, 3:850
Benét, William R., 1:129,
1:131, 1:815, 2:3
Benevolo, Leonardo, 3:762
Benfey, Christopher, 1:746
Benfey, O. Theodor, 5:731,
5:756
Bengtson, Hermann, 3:298
Ben Gurion, David, 3:439
Benhabib, Seyla, 4:404
Beniger, James R., 5:125
Benitez-Rojo, Antonio, 2:930
Benjamin, Anne Myra Good-
man, 2:8
Benjamin, Ben, 5:399
Benjamin, Curtis G., 1:48
Benjamin, Jessica, 3:217
Benjamin, Jules R., 3:8,
3:275, 3:636
Benjamin, Martin, 5:118
Benjamin, Walter, 2:457
Ben Jelloun, Tahar, 2:117
Benko, Stephen, 4:682
Benkovitz, Miriam J., 1:474
Benn, Charles D., 4:527
Benn, Gottfried, 2:564,
2:568
Bennani, Ben, 2:56
Bennassar, Bartolomé, 2:522

Bennett, Arnold, 1:413,
1:419, 1:423, 1:440, **1:443**
Bennett, Benjamin, 1:425
Bennett, David H., 3:542
Bennett, E. A., 5:455
Bennett, G., 3:422
Bennett, George N., 1:759
Bennett, Hal Z., 5:342, 5:724
Bennett, Henry S., 1:36,
1:146
Bennett, J.A.W., 1:146, 1:147
Bennett, J. H., 5:528
Bennett, James A., 3:796
Bennett, James R., 1:56
Bennett, Joan, 1:165, 1:176,
1:181, 1:188, 1:354
Bennett, John G., 4:875
Bennett, Jonathan, 3:337,
4:187, 4:206
Bennett, Judith A., 3:495
Bennett, Lerone, Jr., 3:519,
4:772
Bennett, Patrick, 1:1096
Bennett, Paul A., 1:6
Bennett, Paula, 1:912
Bennett, Robert, 1:885
Bennett, Robert J., 3:118
Bennett, Tony, 1:1131
Bennett, William, 5:344
Bennigsen, Alexandre, 4:567
Bennis, Warren, 3:812
Benoit, Pierre, 4:887
Ben-Sasson, Haim, 4:593
Bensel, Richard Franklin,
3:542
Bension, Ariel, 4:629
Benson, Brian Joseph, 1:891
Benson, Eugene, 1:555, 2:904
Benson, Ezra Taft, 5:267
Benson, Frederick R., 2:522
Benson, Gordon, Jr., 1:1259
Benson, Herbert, 5:400,
5:401
Benson, Hugh H., 4:89
Benson, Jackson J., 1:846,
1:885
Benson, Kathleen, 3:703
Benson, Larry, 1:156
Benson, Lee, 3:514, 3:566
Benson, Nettie Lee, 3:638
Benstock, Bernard, 1:505
Benstock, Shari, 1:86, 1:505
Benston, Kimberly W.,
1:1085
Bentham, Jeremy, 1:309,
1:323, 1:344, **3:150,** 4:158,
4:190, 4:243, 4:256
Bentley, Eric, 1:1071, 2:402,
2:526, 2:573
Bentley, Gerald E., 1:169,
1:184, 1:204, 1:217, 1:278
Bentley, Jerry H., 4:124
Bentley, Nicolas, 1:349

Bentman, Raymond, 1:280
Benton, Gregor, 2:233
Benton, Neville, 5:262
Benton, Tim, 3:778
Benudhar, Pradham, 3:499
Benveniste, Emile, 4:435
Benvenuto, Richard, 1:336,
1:856
Ben-Yehuda, Eliezer, 1:99
Ben Zion, Raphael, 4:629
Berberi, Dilaver, 1:100
Berberi, Edel A., 1:100
Berberoglu, Berch, 3:214
Berberova, Nina, 2:701
Bercaw, Mary K., 1:688
Berchman, Robert M., 4:670
Bercovitch, Sacvan, 1:627,
1:712, **1:948,** 1:1128
Berdichevsky, Micah
Joseph, 2:7, **2:15**
Berdoe, Edward, 1:339
Berdyaev, Nikolai A., 4:274,
4:334, **4:758**
Bereano, Philip L., 5:150
Berelson, Bernard, 3:6
Berenbaum, Michael, 1:1065
Berenbeim, Ronald E., 1:54
Berenson, Bernard, 3:332,
3:758
Beresford, Larry, 5:378
Beresford, M. W., 3:355
Berg, A. Scott, 1:43
Berg, Alban, 3:679, 3:705,
3:714, 3:729, 4:392
Berg, Howard C., 5:775
Berg, Paul, 5:777
Berg, Stephen, 1:915
Bergelson, David, 2:36
Bergendoff, Conrad J., 4:730
Berger, Adolf, 3:305
Berger, Bennett, 3:217
Berger, Carl, 3:606, 3:614,
3:618, 3:622
Berger, Charles, 1:887,
1:1015
Berger, Charles R., 3:172
Berger, David, 4:623
Berger, Gordon M., 3:476
Berger, Harry, Jr., 1:198
Berger, John, 3:786, 5:264,
5:821
Berger, Karen, 5:371
Berger, Melvin, 5:736
Berger, Morroe, 3:435, 3:687
Berger, Peter L(udwig),
3:212, **3:220,** 4:424, 4:890,
5:69, 5:128
Berger, Raoul, 3:542
Berger, Sidney E., 1:7, 1:61
Berger, Stuart M., 5:344
Berger, Thomas (Louis),
1:948
Bergere, Marie-Claire, 3:469

Bergeret, Annie, 3:854
Bergeron, David M., 1:182, 1:220
Bergerson, David M., 3:359
Berghorn, Forrest J., 5:316
Bergin, Thomas G., 2:410, 2:434, 2:441, 4:151
Bergman, Abraham B., 5:375
Bergman, David, 1:1181, 5:219
Bergman, Hjalmar, 2:671
Bergman, Ingmar, 2:614, 2:673, 3:824, **3:830**
Bergman, Jerry, 4:863
Bergman, Jules, 5:219
Bergmann, Emilie L., 2:525
Bergmann, Gustav, 4:222
Bergmann, Peter G., 5:664
Bergmen, Samuel Hugo, 4:646
Bergon, Frank, 1:742
Bergonzi, Bernard, 1:414, 1:420, 1:564
Bergquist, Charles W., 3:635
Bergreen, Laurence, 1:933
Bergson, Henri, 2:373, 2:440, **4:219,** 4:305, 4:314, 4:900, 5:96, 5:789
Bergsten, Gunilla, 2:602
Beringer, Richard, 3:526
Berio, Luciano, 3:680
Berke, J., 5:426
Berkeley, Edmund, Jr., 1:76
Berkeley, George, 3:159, 4:12, 4:158, 4:166, 4:182, **4:191,** 4:211, 4:255
Berkhof, Hendrikus, 4:718
Berkhofer, Robert F., Jr., 3:275, 3:554
Berkley, George, 5:339
Berkovits, Eliezer, 4:646, 4:648
Berkow, Ira, 2:30
Berkow, Robert, 5:405
Berkowitz, Edward D., 3:542
Berkowitz, Leonard, 3:170
Berkson, William, 4:409, 5:99
Berland, Theodore, 5:386
Berler, Alexander, 3:439
Berlin, Adele, 4:823
Berlin, Ira, 3:511, 3:523, 3:526
Berlin, Isaiah, 3:95, 3:290, 3:337, 4:199, 4:216, 4:242
Berlin, Laura, 5:566
Berlin, Normand, 1:1108
Berliner, Arthur K., 5:447
Berliner, Paul F., 3:669
Berlioz, Hector, 3:680
Berlo, Janet C., 4:457
Berman, A. K., 4:20
Berman, Jeffrey, 1:464
Berman, Larry, 3:536

Berman, Paul, 1:1128
Berman, Ronald, 1:220, 2:761
Berman, William C., 3:544
Bermant, Chaim, 4:635
Bermont, Hubert, 1:46
Bernadec, Marie-Louise, 3:786
Bernal, Ignacio, 3:627, 4:455
Bernal, J. D., 5:24
Bernal, Martin, 4:446
Bernanos, Georges, 2:460
Bernard, Auguste, 1:7
Bernard, Claude, 5:788
Bernard, G. W., 3:358
Bernard, H. Russell, 3:11
Bernard, Jessie, 3:206, 3:207, **3:221**
Bernard, Raymond, 3:915
Bernard, Richard M., 3:536
Bernardo, Aldo S., 2:400, 2:434
Bernard of Clairvaux, St., 4:106, **4:111,** 4:706
Bernasconi, Robert, 4:292, 4:901
Bernauer, James W., 4:400, 5:88
Berndt, Bruce C., 5:488
Berndt, Catherine H., 4:461
Berndt, Ronald M., 4:461
Berne, Eric Lennard, 5:424, **5:433**
Bernhard, Thomas, 2:568
Bernhard, Winfred, 3:868
Bernhardt-Kabisch, Ernest, 1:305
Bernice, Daniel D., 5:480
Bernikow, Louise, 1:923
Berninghausen, David K., 1:56
Berninghausen, John, 2:233
Bernini, Gianlorenzo, 3:770
Bernotas, Bob, 1:1085, 4:845
Bernoulli, Jakob, 5:525, **5:527**
Berns, Walter, 3:142
Bernstein, Carl, 3:540, 3:805
Bernstein, Eckhard, 4:124
Bernstein, Gail Lee, 3:474, 3:476
Bernstein, Iver, 3:526
Bernstein, Jeremy, 5:536, 5:650, 5:654, 5:668, 5:672, 5:682, 5:720
Bernstein, Leonard, 3:682, 3:720
Bernstein, Leonard S., 1:46
Bernstein, Michael A., 1:872
Bernstein, Peter L., 3:55, 3:62

Bernstein, Richard J., 3:261, 4:404, 4:225, 4:249, 4:262, 4:292, 4:378, 5:89
Bernstein, Robert, 1:48
Bernstein, Robert A., 3:138
Bernstein, Samuel, 3:372
Bernstein, Samuel J., 1:1071
Berque, Jacques, 3:445
Berquist, Thomas A., 5:396
Berra, Tim, 5:779
Berrey, Lester V., 1:92
Berrin, Kathleen, 4:457
Berry, Adrian, 5:567
Berry, Arthur, 5:31
Berry, Brian J. L., 3:126, 3:127, 5:619
Berry, Christopher J., 4:201
Berry, Donald L., 4:662
Berry, Edward I., 1:210, 1:211
Berry, Eliot, 1:986
Berry, Herbert, 1:217
Berry, Jack, 2:126
Berry, M., 1:418
Berry, Mary Elizabeth, 3:474, 3:554
Berry, Michael, 3:785
Berry, R. J., 5:794
Berry, Ralph, 1:217
Berry, Scott, 4:859
Berry, Thomas, 4:498, 4:512, 5:657
Berry, Thomas E., 2:684
Berry, W. Turner, 1:7, 1:16
Berry, Wendell, 5:113, 5:132, 5:265, **5:268,** 5:821, 5:823
Berryman, John, 1:742, 1:806, 1:909, 1:911, 1:946, **1:949**
Berryman, Philip, 4:747
Bersani, Leo, 2:457, 2:486, 5:447
Bertensson, Sergei, 3:712
Berthoff, Warner, 1:688, 1:823, 1:910
Berthold, Margot, 2:3
Bertholf, Robert, 1:971
Bertin, Celia, 3:842
Bertocci, Peter A., 4:34, 4:262
Bertolotti, M., 5:666, 5:718
Berton, Peter, 3:465
Berton, Pierre, 3:612, 3:616, 3:906
Bertsch, Sharon McGrayne, 5:4, 5:187, 5:727
Berwanger, Eugene H., 3:531
Berzelius, Jons Jakob, 5:727, 5:731, **5:738,** 5:755
Besancon, Robert M., 5:652
Besant, Annie, 4:548, 4:554, 4:858, 4:879
Besette, Alan E., 5:759

Bespaloff, R., 2:361
Bessa-Luís, Agustina, 2:557
Besser, Gretchen R., 2:506
Bessinger, Jess B., Jr., 1:144
Best, Geoffrey, 3:339
Best, Otto F., 2:615
Bester, William S., 5:35
Besterman, Theodore, 1:7,
    1:61, 1:63, 1:120
Beston, Henry, 3:894
Bestor, Arthur, 3:217
Beth, E. W., 5:493
Bethe, Hans Albrecht.,
    5:133, 5:605, **5:671**
Bethea, David M., 2:684,
    2:751
Bethell, Leslie, 3:625
Bethell, S. L., 1:217
Bethge, Eberhard, 4:760
Bethke, Robert D., 3:858
Beti, Mongo, 2:105, **2:132**
Betjeman, Sir John, 1:444
Betsky, Sarah Z., 2:33
Bett, Henry, 3:847, 4:149
Bettelheim, Bruno, 1:578,
    1:1195, 2:585, 3:183,
    3:347, 3:880, 4:430, **5:434**
Bettenson, Henry, 4:680
Betteridge, Harold, 1:99
Betti, Franco, 2:405
Betti, Ugo, 2:408, 2:418
Bettini, Maurizio, 4:448
Betts, Raymond F., 3:416
Betts, Richard K., 5:184
Betz, Hans Dieter, 4:451,
    4:490
Beum, Robert Lawrence,
    1:429
Bevan, David, 2:487
Bevan, E., 4:55
Bevan, Edwyn, 3:418
Beven, Keith, 5:626
Bever, Thomas, 3:171
Beveridge, W. I., 5:389
Beverly, John, 2:540
Beversluis, John, 1:513,
    4:776
Bevington, David M. 1:157,
    1:158, 1:161, 1:169, 1:205,
    1:206, 1:217, 1:220
Bevington, William, 1:10,
    1:53
Bevis, Richard W., 1:228
Bevis, William, 1:887
Bevlin, Marjorie Elliott,
    5:191
Bew, Paul, 3:371
Bewell, Alan, 1:307
Bewley, Marius, 1:722
Bey, Essad, 4:588
Beye, Charles R., 2:352,
    2:361
Beye, Klaus G., 3:766

Beyer, Harald, 2:662
Beyer, Karl H., 5:350
Beyerchen, Alan D., 5:47
Beyerlin, Walter, 4:810
Bezruč, Petr, 2:788
Bhabha, Homi, 1:1133
Bhagat, M. G., 4:501
Bhaktivedanta, Swami A. C.,
    4:862
Bhandari, Mannu, 2:177
Bhaskar, Roy, 4:413
Bhattacharya, Deben, 2:174
Bhattacharya, Sachchida-
    nanda, 3:483
Bhattacharyya, Narendra
    Nath, 4:497, 4:498
Bialoszewski, Tadeusz, 2:812
Biaderle, Susanna, 3:793
Biagio, John Melloni, 5:311
Bial, Morrison D., 4:601
Biale, David, 4:593, 4:672
Biale, Rachel, 4:650
Bialer, Seweryn, 3:396
Bialik, Hayyim Nahman,
    2:7, **2:16,** 2:17
Bianchina, Paul, 5:225
Bianci, Eugene, 4:742
Bianco, Frank, 4:752
Biancolli, Louis, 3:707
Biasini, Gian-Paolo, 2:400,
    2:433
Biberaj, Elez, 3:392
Bickel, Alexander M., 3:542
Bickel, Leonard, 5:270
Bickerman, Elias J., 3:298,
    4:604
Bickers, Bernard, 4:677
Bickers, Kenneth N., 3:44
Bickerton, Ian J., 3:435
Bickford, Sam, 1:101
Bickham, George, 1:13
Bickley, R. Bruce, 1:755
Bickman, Martin, 1:688,
    1:701
Bickner, Robert J., 2:335
Bida, Constantine, 2:841
Bidwell, John, 1:633
Bieber, Margaret, 2:344
Biebuyck, Daniel, 2:126,
    3:419
Biegeleisen, J. I., 1:27
Bielchowsky, Albert, 2:581
Bielefeldt, Carl, 4:537
Bieler, Ludwig, 3:328, 3:370
Bien, Peter, 2:371, 2:372,
    2:374
Biennes, Ranulph, 3:907
Bier, Robert A., Jr., 5:625
**Bierce, Ambrose (Gwin-
    nett),** 1:721, **1:734**
Bierhorst, John, 1:1196,
    2:848
Bierman, John, 3:938

Biermann, Wolf, 2:569,
    2:590
Biers, William R., 3:304
Biesanz, Richard, 3:635
Bigelow, Charles, 1:13
Bigelow, John, 1:661
Bigelow, W. G., 5:370
Bigg, Charles, 4:63, 4:116
Biggs, Donald A., 5:417
Biggs, Frederick M., 1:120
Biggs, John R., 1:7
Bigland, Eileen, 1:408
Bigmore, F. C., 1:7
Bigsby, C.W.E., 1:530,
    1:1072, 1:1081
Biguenet, John, 2:991
Bijker, Wiebe E., 5:24, 5:150,
    5:151
Bikle, Lucy L., 1:737
Biles, Jack I., 1:484
Bilinkoff, Jodi, 4:786
Bill, James, 3:447
Bill, Valentine T., 2:710
Billeskov-Jansen, F. J., 2:645,
    2:651
Billias, George A., 3:513
Billigheimer, Rachel V.,
    1:572
Billings, Charlene W., 5:577
Billings, Thomas H., 4:60
Billingsley, Phil, 3:469
Billington, David P., 5:191
Billington, J. H., 3:394
Billington, Michael, 1:437,
    1:554
Billington, Ray Allen, 3:599,
    3:870
Bills, Donald D., 5:222
Bilstein, Roger E., 3:547
Binder, Arnold, 5:417
Binder, Virginia, 5:417
Bindoff, S. T., 3:358
Binet, Alfred, 3:174, **3:180**
Binford, Lewis R., 3:13
Bingham, Don, 3:765
Bingham, Joan, 3:765
Bingham, John A. C., 5:302
Bingham, Marjorie Wall,
    4:578
Bingham, Millicent Todd,
    1:746
Bin Gorion, Micha J., 3:854
Binham, Philip, 2:658
Binnig, Gerd, 5:672
Binstock, Robert H., 3:200
Binswanger, Ludwig, 5:436,
    5:469
Binyon, T. J., 1:604
Bioy Casares, Adolfo, 2:855
Birch, Anthony H., 3:138
Birch, Beverly, 5:679
Birch, Charles, 5:196
Birch, Cyril, 2:188, 2:192

Birch, Gordon G., 5:262
Birch, John H., 3:381
Birch, L. C., 5:819
Bird, Charles S., 2:126, 4:462
Bird, Christopher, 5:318
Bird, Graham, 1:768, 4:206, 4:237
Bird, Isabella, 3:901
Bird, Robert Montgomery, 1:1244
Bird, Roy K., 1:1017
Bird, Thomas E., 2:783
Birdsall, Stephen S., 3:124
Birdsell, David S., 3:144
Bireley, Robert, 4:728
Birge, John K., 4:574
Birkhoff, Garrett, 5:484
Birkin, Andrew, 1:438
Birley, Anthony, 3:356
Birmingham, David, 3:419, 3:420, 3:423
Birmingham, Martin, 3:423
Birnbaum, Philip, 4:596, 4:599, 4:627, 4:631
Birnbaum, S. A., 2:31
Birnes, William, 5:539
Birnes, W. J., 5:549
Birney, (Alfred) Earle, 2:907
Birrell, Anne, 2:188, 2:192
Birren, James, 3:201
Birtel, Frank, 5:196
Birx, H. James, 4:336
Bisbee, Eleanor, 3:452
Bishai, Wilson B., 4:567
Bishop, Elizabeth, 1:950, 1:962, 2:890
Bishop, Ferman, 1:730
Bishop, Jerry E., 5:777
Bishop, John Lyman, 2:189, 2:198
Bishop, John Michael, 5:789
Bishop, Jonathan, 1:670
Bishop, Mary, 4:768
Bishop, Morris, 3:611
Bishop, Nicholas, 1:498
Bishop, Rand, 2:106
Bishop, Robert, 3:868
Bishop, Thomas, 2:436
Bishop, William W., Jr., 3:144
Bissoondath, Neil, 2:932
Bitov, Andrei, 2:702
Bittencourt, J. A., 5:667
Bitter, Gary, 5:539
Bittinger, Emmert F., 4:732
Bittinger, Marvin L., 5:485
Bitton, Davis, 4:845
Bitz, Ira, 3:490
Bixby, George, 1:491
Bixler, Frances, 1:1066
Bixler, Paul, 3:488
Bizarro, Salvatore, 2:875

Bjerknes, Vilhelm Friman Koren, 5:641
Bjork, Daniel W., 1:769, 3:188, 4:237
Bjorkman, James Warner, 4:507, 4:515
Bjorkman, Stig, 3:831
Björling, Elmer Diktonius Gunnar, 2:657
Bjorling, Joel, 4:861, 4:866
Bjørnson, Bjørnstjerne, 2:662, **2:663**
Bjornson, Richard, 2:106
Black, Earl, 3:542
Black, Edwin, 4:642
Black, George, 3:544
Black, George W., Jr., 5:27
Black, Jeremy, 3:338, 3:368
Black, Joseph L., 2:730
Black, Matthew, 4:819
Black, Max, 3:237, 4:344
Black, Merle, 3:542
Black, Michael H., 1:40
Black, Patti C., 1:895
Black, Peter E., 5:631
Black, T. D., 5:659
Blackburn, David, 5:2, 5:27
Blackburn, John O., 5:288
Black Elk, 4:464
Blacker, Carmen, 4:539
Blackham, Harold John, 4:262
Blackman, P., 4:609
Blackman, Sue A., 3:57
Blackmer, Donald L., 3:385
Blackmore, John T., 5:700
Blackmore, Stephen, 5:762
Blackmur, R(ichard) P(almer), 1:730, 1:765, 1:797, 1:808, **1:816**
Blackstone, Bernard, 1:278
Blackstone, Margaret, 5:357
Blackstone, William, 4:203, 5:74, 5:114
Blackwell, Alice Stone, 2:848
Blackwell, Jeannine, 2:566
Blackwell, Richard J., 4:142, 5:60
Blackwood, David, 3:906
Blackwood, R. T., 4:37
Blades, William, 1:7, 1:22
Blaedel, Niels, 5:674
Blaga, Lucian, 2:823
Blahut, Richard E., 5:302
Blaikie, Piers M., 5:821
Blain, Virginia, 1:127
Blainey, Ann, 1:292
Blair, Arthur H., 3:450
Blair, Dorothy S., 2:106
Blair, Gwenda, 1:1209
Blair, John, 5:280
Blair, Margaret M., 3:55
Blair, P. H., 3:356

Blair, Walter, 1:650, 3:854
Blake, Caesar R., 1:746
Blake, Casey Nelson, 5:171
Blake, Judith, 3:200
Blake, Nelson M., 1:803
Blake, N. F., 1:141, 1:216
Blake, Nigel, 5:109
Blake, Patricia, 2:692
Blake, R., 3:273
Blake, R. A., 3:831
Blake, Ralph M., 5:62
Blake, Robert, 1:351, 3:363
Blake, Stephen P., 3:484
Blake, William, 1:248, 1:255, 1:264, 1:266, **1:277,** 1:314, 1:397, 1:560, 1:568, 1:577, 1:580, 1:1008, 2:441, 2:870, 4:235
Blakeley, T. J., 4:30, 4:31, 4:34
Blakely, James, 5:262
Blakemore, Colin, 5:191
Blakeslee, Sandra, 5:406
Blakeslee, Thomas R., 5:339
Blakeway, Claire, 2:494
Blamires, David Malcolm, 1:502
Blamires, Harry, 1:414, 1:420
Blanch, Robert J., 1:154, 1:156
Blanchard, Dallas A., 4:894
Blanchard, Marc E., 2:500
Blanchard, Olivier, 3:52, 3:58
Blanchard, Paula, 1:673
Blanche, Jerry, 1:129, 1:717
Blanchot, Maurice, 2:446, **2:460,** 2:461, 2:477
Blanco, Richard L., 3:509
Bland, Alexander, 3:734
Bland, David, 1:28
Bland, Jeffrey, 5:325, 5:394
Bland, Kalman P., 4:130
Blank, G. Kim, 1:303
Blank, Marion, 5:566
Blank, Robert H., 5:118
Blanpied, John W., 1:211
Blansfield, Karen C., 1:757
Blanshard, Brand, 4:275, 4:297
Blasi, Anthony J., 4:425
Blass, F., 4:794
Blassingame, John W., 3:523, 3:554
Blassingame, Wyatt, 3:924
Blatt, Burton, 3:256
Blatt, Harvey, 5:622
Blatt, Sidney J., 5:426
Blau, Joseph L., 4:124, 4:601, 4:651, 4:652
Blau, Peter M., 3:208, 3:210, 3:215, 3:218

Blaug, Mark, 3:44, 3:45, 3:56, 3:73, 3:74, 3:87, 3:89, 3:96, 3:97, 3:101, 3:105
Blavatsky, Helena P., 4:548, 4:852, **4:873**, 4:879
Blaxter, Kenneth, 5:266
Blayac, A., 1:562
Blayney, Peter W. M., 1:207
Blazynski, George, 4:742
Bledsoe, Robert, 3:144
Blee, Kathleen M., 3:217
Blehl, Vincent, 4:782
Bleich, David, 1:923
Bleich, J. David, 4:598, 4:629
Bleicher, Josef, 1:924
Bleier, Ruth, 5:151, 5:187, 5:763
Bleikasten, Andre, 1:836
Bleser, Carol K. R., 3:523, 3:526, 3:531
Blesh, Rudi, 3:667
Blessing, Richard, 1:1038
Blessing, Tim H., 3:543
Blessington, John P., 3:266
Blewett, David, 1:240
Blewett, John, 4:225
Bley, Helmut, 3:423
Bleznick, Donald W., 2:523
Blicher, Steen Steensen, 2:644
Blinder, Alan S., 3:67
Blinkin, Meir, 2:36
Blinkoff, Jodi, 4:736
Blishen, Edward, 1:579, 1:1196
Bliss, Anne, 5:729
Bliss, Carolyn, 2:966
Bliss, Edward, Jr., 3:805
Bliss, Lee, 1:200
Bliss, Michael, 3:606, 5:47, 5:381, 5:407
Bliss, Shepherd, 5:318
Blissett, William, 1:46, 1:502
Bliven, Bruce, Jr., 1:46
Blixen, Karen, 2:648
Bloch, Abraham P., 4:598
Bloch, Ernest, 3:658
Bloch, Ernst, 4:276
Bloch, Felix, 5:672
Bloch, Marc, 3:9, 3:330
Bloch, Maurice, 3:23
Bloch, R. Howard, 2:446
Bloch, Sidney, 5:118
Blocher, Donald H., 5:417
Block, Adrienne F., 3:654
Block, Alan A., 1:803
Block, Andrew, 1:77, 1:269, 1:318
Block, Chana, 1:181
Block, Fred L., 3:61
Block, Haskell M., 2:4
Block, Marguerite, 4:851
Block, N. J., 3:174

Blocker, H. Gene, 4:24, 4:316
Blode, Eleanor S., 3:801
Bloesch, Donald, 4:742
Blofeld, John, 4:527
Blok, Aleksandr (Alexander), 2:683, 2:700, **2:702**
Blom, Eric, 3:707
Blom, Jan B., 3:850
Blom, John J., 4:169
Bloodworth, William, Jr., 1:880
Bloom, Alan, 1:1126
Bloom, Alfred, 4:537
Bloom, Allan, 3:248
Bloom, Benjamin S., 3:248
Bloom, Bernard L., 5:421
Bloom, Clive, 1:426, 1:593
Bloom, Floyd E., 5:339
Bloom, Harold, 1:129, 1:134, 1:267, 1:278, 1:303, 1:315, 1:318, 1:326, 1:328, 1:333, 1:343, 1:371, 1:394, 1:404, 1:407, 1:410, 1:464, 1:668, 1:719, 1:740, 1:742, 1:747, 1:765, 1:783, 1:788, 1:795, 1:798, 1:803, 1:821, 1:823, 1:836, 1:840, 1:842, 1:848, 1:895, 1:900, 1:904, 1:906, 1:1029, 1:1081, 1:1133, **1:1137**, 1:1150, 1:1260, 2:351, 2:361, 2:368, 2:417, 2:434, 2:460, 2:486, 2:487, 2:491, 2:500, 2:511, 2:513, 2:700, 2:715, 2:741, 2:751, 2:765, 2:867, 2:876, 2:984, 4:889
Bloom, Robert, 1:457
Bloomfield, B. C., 1:435, 1:508
Bloomfield, Leonard, 3:21, 3:27
Bloomfield, Morton W., 1:154, 3:854
Bloor, David, 5:66, 5:151
Blos, Peter, 3:173
Blotner, Joseph, 1:803, 1:836, 1:1043
Blouet, Brian W., 3:133, 5:32
Bloy, Colin H., 1:21
Bluefarb, Sam, 1:917
Bluestein, Gene, 2:31, 3:868
Bluestone, I., 3:59
Bluestone, Max, 1:219
Blum, D. Steven, 3:158
Blum, David, 3:659
Blum, Eleanor, 3:801, 3:802
Blum, Ethel, 3:891
Blum, John Morton, 3:512, 3:534, 3:594
Blum, Kenneth, 5:350, 5:401
Blum, Lawrence A., 2:516
Blum, Richard H., 5:421

Blum, Rudolf, 1:60
Blum, Stephen, 3:659, 3:666
Blumberg, Arnold B., 4:657
Blumell, Bruce, 4:846
Blumenberg, Hans, 2:581
Blumenson, John C., 3:762
Blumenson, Martin, 3:277
Blumenthal, David R., 4:622, 4:629
Blumenthal, Henry, 4:66
Blumenthal, H. J., 4:61
Blumenthal, Joseph, 1:7
Blumer, Herbert, 3:200, 3:208, **3:221**
Blunden, Edmund, 1:296
Blunt, Wilfred Scawen, 1:40, 4:567
Bly, Robert, 1:798, 1:801, **1:951**, 1:1053, 2:671
Blyth, F. G., 5:635
Blyth, John W., 4:341
Boak, Denis, 2:502
Board, Christopher, 5:191
Boardman, John, 2:344, 3:304, 3:758, 4:446
Boardman, Michael M., 1:240
Boas, Franz, 3:21, 3:26, **3:28**, 3:32, 3:34, 3:36, 3:188, 3:235, 3:758
Boas, Frederick S., 1:169, 1:182, 2:390
Boas, Guy, 3:870
Boas, Marie, 4:124
Boatner, Mark M., 3:508
Boatright, Mody C., 3:864, 3:868
Bober, Natalie S., 1:842
Bobrick, Benson, 5:247
Boccaccio, Giovanni, 1:970, 2:383, 2:398, **2:409**, 2:492, 3:332, 4:469
Bochenski, Innocentius Marie, 4:20, 4:27, 4:31, 4:262
Bock, Audrey, 3:828
Bock, Carl, 3:901
Bock, Hedwig, 1:1072
Bockris, Victor, 3:796
Bockus, Frank, 5:417
Boczek, Boleslaw, 3:144
Bodde, Derk, 4:467
Bode, Carl, 1:859
Bode, Mabel Haynes, 2:313
Boden, Margaret, 3:174, 5:74, 5:570
Bodenhamer, David J., 3:139
Bodenheimer, Rosemarie, 1:318
Bodian, Nat G., 1:46
Bodichon, Barbara (Leighton Smith), 1:310, 1:324, **1:330**, 1:341
Bodiford, William, 4:537

Bodin, Jean, **4:133**
Bodine, Jay F., 2:579
Bodkin, Maud, 2:984
Bodner, John Tyler, 5:758
Bodunrin, P. O., 4:368
Body, Jacques, 2:481
Boehm, Eric H., 3:272
Boehmer, Heinrich, 4:778
Boehner, Philotheus, 4:97, 4:120
Boeman, J. S., 3:277
Boer, Karl W., 5:290
Boesche, Roger, 3:165
Boeschenstein, Hermann, 2:565
Boethius, 4:93, 4:96, 4:98, 4:100, **4:112**, 4:155
Boff, Clodovis, 4:896
Boff, K., 3:177
Boff, Leonardo, 4:747, 4:896
Boffin, Tessa, 3:201
Bogan, Louise, 1:579, **1:952**, 1:1015, 1:1038, 1:1197
Bogard, Travis, 1:200, 1:1072, 1:1108
Bogart, Leo, 3:203
Bogary, Hamza, 2:58
Bogdan, Radu J., 4:395
Bogdanich, Walt, 5:332
Boger, H. Batterson, 3:765
Boger, Louise, 3:765
Boggs, Carl, 3:345, 4:287
Boggs, R. S., 1:102
Bogle, Darlene, 4:894
Bogle, Donald, 3:825
Bognanno, Mario F., 3:59
Bogue, Allan G., 3:526
Bogue, Donald J., 3:205
Bogus, Ronald, 1:94
Bohannon, Paul, 3:416, 5:33
Bohlman, Philip V., 3:659, 3:666, 3:667
Bohman, James, 4:378
Böhme, Gernot, 4:384
Bohner, Charles, 1:893
Bohr, Niels, 5:142, **5:673**, 5:675, 5:689, 5:693, 5:703, 5:708, 5:709, 5:714, 5:719, 5:734
Boia, Lucian, 3:272
Boire, Gary, 2:908
Bois, Mario, 3:731
Boisselier, Jean, 2:313
Boitani, Piero, 1:146, 1:150, 2:417
Bok, Bart Jan, 5:599
Boklund, Gunnar, 1:200
Bokser, Ben Zion, 4:630
Bok, Sissela, 5:84
Boland, Peter, 5:327
Bolander, D., 1:95
Bold, Alan Norman, 1:280, 1:491, 1:517, 1:552

Boldy, Stephen, 2:862
Bolen, Eric, 5:820
Bolger, F.W.P., 3:612
Bolick, Nancy O., 4:849
Boller, Paul F., 3:542
Bollinger, Lee C., 3:805
Böll (or Boell), Heinrich, 2:564, **2:569**
Bolshakoff, Sergius, 4:755
Bolt, Bruce A., 5:629, 5:635
Bolt, Robert, 1:194, **1:445**
Boltax, Robert S., 5:405
Bolter, Jay David, 5:561, 5:572
Bolton, Brenda, 4:691
Bolton, Geoffrey, 3:494
Bolton, Herbert E(ugene), 3:623, **3:642**
Bolton, H. Philip, 1:349
Bolton, J. L., 3:357
Bolton, R., 4:771
Bolton, W. F., 1:141, 1:531
Boltzmann, Ludwig, 5:674
Bombaci, Alessio, 2:95
Bombeck, Erma, 3:870, 3:907
Bonaccorso, Richard, 1:529
Bonadelia, Peter, 3:825
Bonansea, Bernardino M., 4:114, 4:137
Bonaparte, Felicia, 1:354
Bonaparte, Napoleon, 3:339
Bonaventure of Bagnorea, St., **4:112**, 4:706
Bonavia, David, 3:466
Bond, Edward, 1:204, 1:424, **1:445**, 1:446
Bond, George D., 4:505, 4:513, 4:515, 4:526
Bond, Otto F., 1:102
Bond, Peter, 5:4
Bond, Richard W., 2:402
Bond, Simon, 3:870
Bondurant, Joan V., 4:352, 4:553
Bone, Robert, 1:657, 1:722
Bonebakker, S. A., 2:70
Bonevac, Daniel, 4:349
Bonham-Carter, Victor, 1:36
Bonhoeffer, Dietrich, 2:570, 4:757, **4:759**, 4:784
Bonin, Jane F., 1:1072
Bonjour, Edgar, 3:378
Bonjour, Laurence, 4:380
Bonn, Charles, 2:124
Bonn, Thomas L., 1:38
Bonnefoy, Yves, 2:461, 3:866, 4:428
Bonnell, F. C., 1:810
Bonner, Arthur, 4:507
Bonner, Gerald, 4:109
Bonner, Raymond, 3:205
Bonner, Robert J., 2:344
Bonner, Thomas, Jr., 1:740

Bonnicksen, Andrea, 5:118
Bonnie, Michael E., 3:447
Bonomi, Patricia U., 3:516, 3:519
Bonser, Wilfrid, 4:431
Bonsirven, Joseph, 4:620
Bonsor, Jack A., 4:292
Bonta, Marcia Myers, 5:817
Bontemps, Arna, 1:719, 1:720, **1:816**
Bonwick, Colin, 3:519
Böök, Fredrik, 2:647
Booker, M. Keith, 1:793
Boole, George, 5:499, 5:541, 5:576
Boolos, George, 4:411
Boom, Michael, 5:564
Boon, Louis Paul, 2:621, **2:622**, 2:623
Boone, Joseph, 1:1183
Boorstin, Daniel J(oseph), 1:49, 1:627, 3:155, 3:512, 3:551, **3:568**, 5:24, 5:69
Boos, Florence Saunders, 1:121
Booth, Anne, 3:491
Booth, Charles, 3:222
Booth, James, 1:508
Booth, John, 3:727
Booth, Michael R., 1:271, 1:272, 1:322, 1:323
Booth, Newell S., 4:462
Booth, Richard, 1:31
Booth, Stephen, 1:206, 1:212, 1:215
Booth, Wayne, 1:420, 1:924, **1:1138**
Boots, B., 3:119
Bootzin, Richard R., 5:429
Bopp, Richard E., 1:73
Borchert, Wolfgang, 2:570
Borden, Carla M., 4:507
Borden, Gale, 5:399
Borders, Earl, Jr., 3:891
Bordley, James, III, 3:551
Bordman, Gerald Martin, 1:1072, 3:667, 3:703
Bordon, William S., 3:476
Bordwell, David, 1:1157, 3:825, 3:834
Boren, Lynda S., 1:740
Borgen, Peder, 4:604
Borges, Jorge Luis, 1:1055, 2:844, **2:855**, 2:951
Borgmann, Albert, 5:69, 5:212
Boring, Edwin G., 3:167, 5:34, 5:35, 5:413
Bork, Alfred, 5:566
Bork, Robert H., 3:61
Borkland, Elmer, 1:924
Borko, Hilda, 3:254
Borkowski, P., 1:101

Borlaug, Norman, 5:269
Borman, William, 4:553
Bormann, Herbert F., 3:47
Born, Max, 5:658, 5:682,
    5:693, 5:708
Borner, G., 5:656
**Bornkamm, Günther, 4:824,
    4:829**
Bornstein, George, 1:417,
    1:872
Bornstein, Marc H., 3:169
Borodin, Alexander, 3:683,
    3:707
Borowitz, Eugene, 4:598,
    4:652, **4:661,** 4:885
Borowski, Tadeusz, 2:812,
    3:344
Borroff, Marie, 1:798
Borrow, George, 3:912
Bort, Barry D., 2:272
Borthwick, Meredith, 3:485
Bortone, Sandro, 3:765
Bortz, Walter M., 5:316
Borum, Paul, 2:645
Borus, Daniel H., 1:712
Bosanac, S. D., 5:658
Bosanquet, Bernard, 3:284,
    4:303
Bosboom-Tousaint, 2:620
Bosch, Gulnar, 1:22
Boscherini, Emilia Giancotti,
    4:187
Boschetti, Anna, 2:507, 4:330
Bosco, Dominick, 5:310
Bosha, Francis J., 1:961
Bosley, Keith, 2:339
Boslough, John, 5:607, 5:654
Bosma, Bette, 3:847
Bosmajian, Haig A., 1:56
Boss, Medard, 5:436
Bosse, Raymond, 5:316
Bossy, John, 3:355, 4:736
Bostetter, Edward E., 1:267
Bostwick, John, III, 5:371
Boswell, James, 1:231,
    1:233, 1:249, 1:250, 3:919
Boswell, Jeanetta, 1:747,
    1:830, 1:851
Boswell, John, 1:1181, 4:678
Boswell-Stone, W. G., 1:219
Bosworth, A. B., 3:301
Bosworth, Barry P., 3:59
Bosworth, Clifford E., 2:82,
    3:442, 3:454, 4:572
Bosworth, Joseph, 1:96
Bosworth, Richard, 3:385
Botero, Giovanni, 4:124
Botev, Khristo, 2:780, 2:781
Bothwell, Robert, 3:608,
    3:616
Botkin, Benjamin A., 1:725,
    3:854, 3:858, 3:868
Botkin, Daniel B., 5:819

Botkin, James, 5:226
Botstein, David, 5:806
Botterweck, G. Johannes,
    4:817
Bottigheimer, Ruth B., 1:578
Botting, Gary, 4:863
Botting, Heather, 4:863
Botto, António, 2:557
Bottomore, Thomas B.,
    3:200, **3:222,** 3:290
Botwinick, Aryeh, 3:142
Boucher, Cyril T. G., 5:254
Boucher, Sandy, 4:512
**Boucicault, Dionysius
    (Dion) Lardner, 1:331,**
    1:1069
Boudjedra, Rachid, 2:117
Boudouris, C., 4:47
Boudreau, Richard, 1:752
Boug, J. W., 5:697
Bouhdiba, Abdelwahab, 4:894
Boulares, Habib, 3:442, 4:578
Boulding, Kenneth E., 3:46,
    3:53, **3:70,** 3:144, 3:604
Boulez, Pierre, 3:683
Boullata, Issa J., 2:55, 2:56
Boulter, Eric, 5:383
Boulting, William, 2:440
Boulton, James T., 1:250
Bouquet, A. C., 4:567
Bourbaki, Nicolas, 5:499
Bourden, David, 3:796
Bourdieu, Pierre, 3:22, 4:292
Bourgeois, Joanne, 5:617
Bourgeois, Patrick L., 4:309,
    4:311
Bourke, Vernon J., 3:330
Bourland, Caroline B., 2:522
Bourne, Edward Gaylord,
    1:631
Bourne, Larry S., 3:127
Bourne, R., 3:207
Bournonville, August, 3:739,
    3:747
Bourre, Jean-Marie, 5:345
Bourricaud, François, 3:237
**Boussingault, Jean-Baptiste,
    5:270**
Boutelle, Ann Edwards,
    1:517
Boutens, P. C., 2:620
Bouvier, Nicolas, 3:901
Bouwsma, O. K., 4:345
Bouwsma, William J., 3:333,
    3:334, 4:124, 4:761
Bouyer, Louis, 4:139, 4:676,
    4:783
Bovbjerg, Randall R., 5:333
Bove, Alfred A., 5:325
Bove, Cheryl Browning,
    1:524
Bove, Tony, 5:561

Bovill, Edward W., 3:418,
    3:419
Bowden, Henry W., 4:719
Bowden, John, 4:676, 4:719
Bowden, Mary E., 5:756
Bowden, Mary W., 1:681
Bowder, Diana, 3:298
Bowen, Alan C., 4:47, 5:38
Bowen, Catherine Drinker,
    1:86, 1:928, 3:141, 3:519,
    3:576
Bowen, Charles S., 5:558
Bowen, David, 3:916
Bowen, Elizabeth, 1:447,
    1:486, 1:523, 3:898, 5:9
Bowen, Harold, 4:569
Bowen, J. C., 2:84
Bowen, James, 3:253
Bowen, Margarita, 5:32
Bowen, Meirion, 3:725
Bowen, Merlin, 1:688
Bowen, Robert, 5:635
Bowen, Roger W., 3:476
Bowen, Zack R., 1:461,
    1:505, 2:987
Bowen-Moore, Patricia,
    4:394, 5:82
Bower, Gordon H., 3:171,
    3:175
Bower, T. G., 3:173
Bowermaster, Jon, 3:907
Bowers, Deloss H., 5:227
Bowers, Faubion, 2:272
Bowers, Fredson T., 1:61,
    1:62, 1:169, 1:207
Bowers, Jane P., 1:882, 3:659
Bowers, Neal, 1:967, 1:1038
Bowersock, G. W., 3:302
Bowes, Pratima, 4:37
Bowie, G. Lee, 4:20
Bowie, Malcolm, 2:486
Bowie, Norman, 4:388
Bowie, Robert R., 3:445
Bowker, John W., 4:568,
    4:608, 4:886, 4:887
Bowlby, John, 5:421
Bowle, John, 3:154
Bowler, Peter J., 5:45, 5:763
Bowles, Samuel, 3:79, 3:253
Bowman, Barbara, 3:828
Bowman, Isaiah, 3:128
Bowman, John, 4:618
Bowman, Steven B., 4:623
Bowman, Sylvia E., 1:734
Bowra, Cecil M., 1:362,
    2:344, 2:348, 2:361, 2:365,
    2:366, 2:368
Bowring, Richard John,
    2:279, 2:290
Box, Joan Fisher, 5:528
Boxer, Charles R., 3:335,
    3:382, 3:386, 3:474, 3:484,
    3:628, 4:540

Boxill, Anthony, 2:939
Boyajian, Zabelle C., 2:76
Boyarin, Daniel, 4:620
Boyce, Mary, 4:443, 4:444, 4:547
Boyce, Ronald Reed, 5:619
Boyd, Ann, 1:594
Boyd, Anne M., 1:108
Boyd, Brian, 2:741
Boyd, Elizabeth F., 1:282
Boyd, Gregory A., 4:289
Boyd, James W., 4:517, 4:547
Boyd, Kenneth M., 5:123
Boyd, Martin, 2:950
Boyd, Richard, 5:62
Boyd, Robert N., 5:732
Boyd, Robert W., 5:666
Boyd, S. J., 1:484
Boyde, Patrick, 2:417
Boyden, David D., 3:671
Boydston, Jo Ann, 4:225
Boyer, Carl B., 5:30, 5:491
Boyer, David L., 4:263
Boyer, Ernest L., 1:50, 3:248
Boyer, L. Bryce, 3:864
Boyer, Lester L., 5:225
Boyer, Paul, 3:558
Boyer, Paul S., 3:516
Boyer, Peter J., 3:805
Boyer, Rick, 3:118
Boyer, Robert D., 1:123
Boyers, Robert, 1:912, 5:460
Boyle, G., 5:212
Boyle, John H., 3:464
Boyle, Joseph, 4:743
Boyle, Marjorie O'Rourke, 2:434, 4:139, 4:151
Boyle, Robert, 5:635, 5:727, 5:739, 5:748
Boyle, T. Coraghessan, 1:909, 1:952
Boyne, Roy, 5:88
Boyne, Walter J., 5:219
Boynton, Henry W., 1:756
Boytinck, Paul W., 1:454, 1:550
Bozeman, Pat, 1:35
Božić, Mirko, 2:785
Brøndsted, Johannes, 2:640
Brønner, Hedin, 2:655
Braak, M. ter, 2:621
Braaten, Jane, 3:229, 4:404
Brace, Edward R., 5:310
Bracegirdle, Brian, 5:223, 5:256
Bracher, Frederick G., 1:965
Bracher, Karl D., 3:376
Brachfeld, F. Oliver, 5:431
Bracken, Harry M., 4:191
Bracken, James K., 3:801
Bracken, Jeanne M., 5:371
Bracken, Paul, 5:109
Bradbeer, Robin, 5:537

Bradbrook, Muriel C., 1:169, 1:200, 1:210, 1:331, 1:924
Bradbury, Malcolm (Stanley), 1:166, 1:414, 1:420, 1:422, 1:448, 1:803, 1:917, 1:947, 2:986
Bradbury, Ray, 1:1193, 1:1252, 1:1254
Braddon, Mary Elizabeth, 1:310, 1:317, 1:332
Braden, Charles S., 4:842, 4:847, 4:855
Bradford, Ernle, 2:361
Bradford, Sarah, 1:352
Bradford, William, 1:625, 1:633
Brading, D. A., 3:628
Bradley, A. C., 1:212
Bradley, Anthony, 1:418
Bradley, David, 3:898
Bradley, Francis Herbert, 4:220, 4:260, 4:303
Bradley, Harriet, 3:207
Bradley, Ian, 5:196
Bradley, J., 3:277
Bradley, James E., 4:738
Bradley, John, 3:396
Bradley, John L., 1:394
Bradley, Laurence A., 5:376
Bradley, Raymond, 4:345
Bradley, S.A.J., 1:143
Bradley, Van Allen, 1:78
Bradley, William, 1:296
Bradshaw, Leah, 3:282, 4:395, 5:82
Bradshaw, Michael, 3:126
Bradshaw, Paul F., 4:687
Bradsher, Earl L., 1:40
Bradsher, Henry S., 3:454
Bradstreet, Anne, 1:625, 1:634
Brady, Anna, 3:825
Brady, Ann P., 1:339
Brady, Frank, 1:227, 1:230, 1:1155
Brady, Kathleen, 3:823
Brady, N. C., 5:220, 5:266
Brady, Robert N., 5:247
Braham, Jeanne, 1:947
Brahe, Tycho, 5:599, 5:601, 5:608
Brahms, Johannes, 3:684, 3:713
Braidūnas, Kazys, 2:805
Braine, John, 1:419, 1:449
Braithwaite, Edward Kamau, 2:933
Braithwaite, Ronald L., 5:330
Brake, Laurel, 1:387
Brakhage, Stan, 1:1159, 1:1174, 3:832
Brakman, Willem, 2:621
Brams, Steven J., 3:48

Bramwell, Anna, 3:272, 5:819
Bramwell, Martyn, 5:616
Branch, Taylor, 3:536
Branco, Camilo Castelo, 2:557
Brand, Arie, 3:229
Brand, Juliane, 3:680
Brand, Max, 1:1212
Brand, Oscar, 3:850
Brand, Stewart, 5:539, 5:567
Brandão, Ignácio de Loyola, 2:889, 2:894
Brandell, Gunnar, 5:447
Brandes, Georg, 2:664, 4:246
Brandl, Alois, 1:287
Brandon, George, 4:868
Brandon, James R., 2:274, 2:311
Brandon, Robert N., 5:67
Brandon, Ruth, 4:850
Brandon, S. G., 4:3, 4:887
Brandt, Allan M., 5:389
Brandt, D. Scott, 5:543
Brandt, Ellen B., 1:643
Brandt, John C., 5:592
Brandt, Kate, 1:1183
Brandt, Reinhard, 4:179
Brandt, Richard, 4:19, 4:254
Brandt, Steven A., 3:416
Brandt, Wiegmund, 5:660
Brandwood, Leonard, 4:79
Branham, Robert Bracht, 4:485
Brann, Ross, 2:8
Branner, Hans Christian, 2:647
Brannigan, Michael C., 4:881
Branson, Noreen, 3:365
Brant, Irving, 3:161
Brante, Thomas, 5:151
Brantlinger, Patrick, 1:311, 1:1126, 1:1131, 3:872
Brant (or Brandt), Sebastian, 2:571
Braque, Georges, 2:560
Bras, Rafael L., 5:631
Brasch, Charles Orwell, 2:972
Brasil, Emanuel, 2:891
Brass, Paul R., 3:485
Brassell, Tim, 1:554
Bratcher, James T., 3:862
Bratman, Michael, 4:23
Bratt, James D., 4:752
Bratter, T. E., 5:451
Bratton, Jacqueline S., 1:322
Braude, Ann, 4:850
Braude, Benjamin, 4:568
Braude, William G., 4:610
Braudel, Fernand, 3:283, 3:336, 3:372, 3:399, 3:620
Braudy, Leo, 1:1012

Brauer, Jerald C., 4:675, 4:719
Braun, Alan G., 3:144
Braun, Ernest, 5:47, 5:669
Braun, Thomas, 1:352
Braund, S. H., 2:387
Braunmuller, A. R., 1:169, 1:175, 1:195
Bravmann, M. M., 4:574
Bravmann, Rene A., 4:568
Braxton, Joanne, 1:910
Bray, George A., 5:347
Bray, Gerald L., 4:714
Bray, John, 4:731
Braybrooke, David, 5:67
Braybrooke, Patrick, 1:438
Brayer, Menachem M., 4:650
Brazdžionis, Bernardos, 2:805
Brazelton, T. Berry, 5:321
Breasted, James H., 2:52
Breathnach, Breandan, 3:850
Breaux, Adele, 2:504
Brebner, John Bartlet, 3:607, 3:610, 3:611, 3:612
Brecher, Arline, 5:373
Brecher, Edward M., 5:429
Brecht, Arnold, 3:138
Brecht, Bertolt, 1:243, 1:246, 1:424, 1:450, 2:435, 2:483, 2:564, **2:571,** 2:603, 2:612, 2:665, 2:679, 2:791, 3:282, 5:604
Breck, J., 4:756
Bredahl, A. Carl, Jr., 1:712
Bredero, Gerbrand A., 2:620, **2:623**
Bredsdorff, Elias, 2:638, 2:645, 2:647
Bredvold, Louis I., 1:241
Brée, Germaine, 2:480
Breed, Paul F., 1:427
Breen, Christine, 3:901
Breen, T. H., 3:516
Bregman, Jay, 4:62, 4:63
Bréhier, Emile, 4:16, 4:86, 4:124, 4:159
Breit, William, 3:44, 3:45, 3:61, 3:69, 3:77, 3:88, 3:103, 3:108
Breitung, Joan, 5:316
Breitweiser, Mitchell Robert, 1:627
Bremner, Robert H., 3:526, 3:537
Brenan, Gerald, 2:522
Brennan, Bernard P., 1:769, 3:188
Brennan, James R., 5:777
Brennan, Richard P., 5:2, 5:12, 5:27
Brennan, Timothy, 2:181
Brenner, Charles, 5:426
Brenner, Geoffrey, 4:196

Brenner, Joseph Hayyim, 2:16
Brenner, Margaret J., 3:181
Brenni, Vito J., 1:759
Brentano, Franz, 4:67, **4:221,** 4:234, 4:395
Brenton, Howard, 1:424, **1:449,** 1:492
Brenton L. L., 4:796
Breslauer, S. Daniel, 4:648, 4:662
Breslaver, George W., 3:396
Breslaver, S. Daniel, 2:16
Bresler, Fenton, 2:508
Breslin, Herbert H., 3:672
Breslin, James E., 1:900, 1:912
Bresnahan, Roger J., 2:328
Bressler, Stacey E., 5:544
Bretherick, Leslie, 5:724
Breton, André, 2:462, 2:854
Brett, Bill, 3:863
Brett, David, 3:898
Brett, Michael, 3:442
Brett, Philip, 3:685
Brett, Vanessa, 3:767
Brettell, Richard, 3:775
Brettle, R. P., 5:389
Breuer, Mordechai, 4:653
Breuil, Henri, 4:432
Breunig, LeRoy C., 2:451
Brew, J. O., 3:11
Brewer, Annie, 3:7, 3:290
Brewer, Charles L., 3:168, 3:181
Brewer, David J., 1:727
Brewer, Derek, 1:150
Brewer, E. Cobham, 1:131
Brewer, Frances J., 1:28
Brewer, Gay, 1:1228
Brewer, J. Gordon, 5:619
Brewer, James G., 3:118
Brewer, James K., 5:521
Brewer, Jeutonne, 1:454
Brewer, Priscilla J., 4:849
Brewer, Roy, 1:13
Brewster, Barbara Marie, 3:901
Brewster, Paul G., 3:861
Brewton, John E., 1:1197
Brewton, Sara, 1:1197
Brick, Howard, 3:220
Bricker, Phillip, 4:184
Brickhouse, Thomas C., 4:89
Bricklin, Mark, 5:310, 5:325
Brickner, Philip, 5:328
Bridenbaugh, Carl, 1:627, 3:519, **3:569**
Bridenthal, Renate, 3:326
Bridge, F. R., 3:375
Bridger, David, 3:347, 4:593
Bridges, John H., 4:111

Bridgman, Percy Williams, 5:675
Bridgman, Richard, 1:701
Bridson, D. G., 1:514
Brieger, Gert H., 5:312
Brier, Peter A., 1:808
Brière, O., 4:358
Brierley, H. G., 5:298
Brierly, Harry, 5:429
Brigden, Susan, 4:725
Briggs, A.D.P., 2:735, 2:751
Briggs, Asa, 1:36, 1:311, 3:363
Briggs, Katherine M., 3:854
Briggs, Robin, 3:372
Bright, David F., 2:157
Bright, John, 4:806
Bright, Michael, 5:770
Bright, Susie, 1:1181
Bright, William, 3:864
Brightly, Charles, 1:14
Brightman, Harvey J., 5:521
Brigs, Dennie, 3:877
Brill, A(braham) A(rden), 5:437, 5:447
Brillantes, Gregorio, 2:329
Brilliant, Ashleigh, 3:870
Brilliant, Lawrence B., 5:382
Brim, John A., 3:12
Brim, Orville G., Jr., 3:173, 3:216
Brindle, Reginald Smith, 3:665
Brindley, James, 5:248
Bringuier, Jean-Claude, 3:267
Brink, André, 2:157, 2:158, **2:159**
Brink, Carol Ryrie, 1:1195
Brinkley, Alan, 3:512, 3:534
Brinkley, David, 3:534
Brinkley, Douglas, 3:537
Brinkmeyer, Robert H., Jr., 1:1024
Brinner, William M, 4:625
Brinnin, John Malcolm, 1:557, 1:882
Brisco, Paula, 5:382
Briscoe, Marianne G., 1:157
Briscoe, Mary L., 1:86
Brisson, Germain J., 5:345
Bristow, Joseph, 1:339, 1:1183
Brito, Bernardo Gomes de, 2:557
Brittain, John A., 3:66
Brittan, Gordon G., 5:64
Britten, Beth, 3:685
Britten, Lord Benjamin, 1:255, **3:684,** 3:736
Britten, Norman A, 1:861
Britton, Celia, 2:509
Britton, Davis, 3:558

Broad, Charles Dunbar,
4:192, **4:277**, 4:303, 4:304
Broad, William J., 5:143,
5:235
Broadbent, John, 1:192
Broadhead, Robert S., 5:336
Broadie, Alexander, 4:32
Broadie, Sarah, 4:67
Broberg, Gunnar, 5:805
Broch, Hermann, 2:573,
2:593
Brock, Arthur J., 5:38
Brock, Dan W., 4:25, 5:119
Brock, Erland J., 4:852
Brock, James W., 3:61
Brock, Michael, 3:361
Brock, Peter, 3:345
Brock, Thomas D., 5:783,
5:801
Brock, W. A., 3:63
Brockbank, Philip, 1:206
Brockelmann, C., 4:568
Brockett, Oscar G., 1:1072
Brockhaus, Richard R., 4:345
Brockman, James R., 4:747
Brockman, John, 4:18, 5:9
Brock-Utne, B., 3:277
Brod, Max, 2:596
Broda, Johanna, 4:457
Brode, Douglas, 3:829
Broder, Nathan, 3:676
Broderick, Francis L., 3:578
Broderick, Robert C., 4:716
Brodetsky, Selig, 5:706
Brodhead, Richard H., 1:688,
1:836
Brodie, Bernard, 5:236
Brodie, Fawn M., 1:640,
3:155, 3:520, 3:914, 4:845,
4:879, 5:236
Brodie, Howard, 4:388
Brodin, Dorothy, 2:452
Brodrick, James, 4:728,
4:736, 4:770
Brodsky, Archie, 5:382
Brodsky, Joseph (Iosif),
2:683, 2:685, **2:703**, 2:762,
3:898
Brodsky, Patricia P., 2:608
Brodwin, Stanley, 1:661,
1:681
Brody, David, 3:547
Brody, Elaine M., 3:654,
5:316
Brody, Jane E., 5:339, 5:345
Brody, Martin, 3:664
Brody, Robert, 2:862, 2:866
Broe, Mary L., 1:813
Brofsky, Howard, 3:664
Brogan, T.V.F., 1:125
Brogard, Jacqueline V., 1:887
Broglie, Louis de, 5:734
Brolsma, Reinder, 2:634

Bromberg, Joan L., 5:667
Brombert, Victor, 2:457,
2:476, 2:483
Brome, Vincent, 1:537,
5:447, 5:455
Bromiley, Geoffrey W., 4:725,
4:758, 4:791
Bromke, Adam, 3:390
Bromley, David G., 4:855,
4:856, 4:862, 4:871
Bronner, Edwin, 1:1072
Bronner, Simon J., 3:849
Bronowski, Jacob, 1:278,
4:159, 5:14, 5:24, 5:106,
5:132, **5:161**
Bronshtein, I. N., 5:478
Bronski, Michael, 1:1181
Bronson, Walter C., 1:660,
1:727
Bronstein, Herbert, 4:599
Brontë, Anne, 1:334
Brontë, Charlotte, 1:310,
1:317, **1:334**, 1:355, 1:451,
1:618, 2:940
Brontë, Emily Jane, 1:310,
1:317, **1:334**, 1:618
Bronz, Stephen H., 1:824,
1:857
Bronzino, Joseph D., 5:12,
5:119
Brook, Barry S., 3:654
Brook, G. L., 1:31
Brook, Richard J., 5:521
Brooke, Charles F., 1:171
Brooke, Christopher, 3:330,
3:356, 4:698
Brooke, Claire, 3:654
Brooke, Nicholas, 1:212
Brooke, Rosalind, 3:330,
4:698
Brooke, Rupert, 1:416,
1:450
Brooker, Peter, 1:872
Brookes, John, 5:767
Brookfield, Harold C., 5:821
Brookhauser, Patrick, 3:201
Brookner, Anita, 1:451
Brooks, Anna Marie, 5:323
Brooks, Charles R., 4:507,
4:862
Brooks, Cleanth, 1:128,
1:248, 1:417, 1:653, 1:798,
1:806, 1:836, 1:874, 1:912,
1:922, 1:924, **1:953**, 1:1154
Brooks, Frederick P., Jr.,
5:549
Brooks, Gwendolyn, 1:910,
1:911, 1:915, **1:953**
Brooks, H. Allen, 3:778,
3:798
Brooks, Harold F., 1:206
Brooks, Harvey, 5:180
Brooks, Jeffrey, 2:685

Brooks, John L., 5:45
Brooks, Michael, 5:629
Brooks, Michael W., 1:394
Brooks, Paul, 5:829
Brooks, Peter, 1:1143, 2:454
Brooks, Richard, 4:218
Brooks, Robert C., 3:151
Brooks, Roger, 4:620, 4:648
Brooks, Valerie, 3:738
Brooks, Van Wyck, 1:650,
1:759, 1:765, 1:783
Broome, Richard, 3:494
Broomfield, Olga R., 1:444
Broomhead, Frank, 1:22
Brooten, Bernadette J., 4:614
Brophy, Brigid, 1:474
Brophy, Elizabeth, 1:229,
1:253
Brophy, James, 1:548, 5:688
Bros, Peter, 5:661
Brose, Margaret, 1:956
Brosman, Catherine S.,
2:507, 4:330
Brosse, Jacques, 4:716
Brotherston, Gordon, 2:845,
2:848
Broude, Norma, 5:192
Broughton, Leslie N., 1:339
Broughton, Panthea Reid,
1:1029
Broughton, T.R.S., 3:298
Brouwer, Abe, 2:635
Brower, D. R., 3:274
Brower, Kenneth, 3:894
Brower, Michael, 5:278
Brower, Reuben A., 1:252,
2:990
Brower, Robert H., 2:273
Brown, Abram E., 3:858
Brown, Arthur W., 1:673
Brown, Barbara B., 5:401
Brown, C. Mackenzie, 4:503
Brown, C. V., 3:67
Brown, Calvin S., 3:659
Brown, Carleton, 1:149
Brown, Cary E., 3:103
Brown, Charles, 4:784
Brown, Charles Brockden,
1:598, 1:626, **1:635**, 1:1239
Brown, Charles H., 1:661
Brown, Charles N., 1:612
Brown, Christopher C., 1:429
Brown, Clarence, 2:692,
2:738
Brown, Colin, 4:818
Brown, Craig, 3:606
Brown, Curtis, 4:21
Brown, D. M., 3:485
Brown, David, 3:724, 5:262
Brown, Dee, 3:531
Brown, Deming, 2:685
Brown, Duncan, 2:158
Brown, E. K., 1:420, 1:821

Brown, Edward J., 2:685,
2:739
Brown, Frank C., 1:14, 3:860
Brown, Geoffrey, 5:125
Brown, George, 3:858
Brown, George W., 5:426
Brown, Gillian, 1:650, 1:713
Brown, H., 1:418
Brown, Hanbury, 4:384
Brown, Harcourt, 5:41
Brown, Harold I., 4:384
Brown, Herbert R., 1:657
Brown, Howard M., 3:333,
3:551
Brown, Ian, 2:324
Brown, J. D, 1:862
Brown, J. P., 4:574
Brown, Jack H. U., 5:332
Brown, James, 3:45
Brown, James F., 3:392
Brown, Janet, 1:1072
Brown, Jeffrey L., 5:322
Brown, Joan L., 2:522
Brown, John, 1:174
Brown, John F., 5:216
Brown, John Mason, 1:1075
Brown, John R., 1:214,
1:222, 1:1072
Brown, Jonathan, 3:795
Brown, Joseph E., 4:464
Brown, Judith E., 5:357
Brown, Judith M., 3:486,
4:553
Brown, Julia Polwitt, 1:276
Brown, K. C., 4:174
Brown, Karen M., 4:868
Brown, L. Carl, 3:435
Brown, Laura, 1:226
Brown, Laurie M., 5:662,
5:717
Brown, Lawrence A., 3:124,
3:129
Brown, Lawrence D., 5:328
Brown, Les, 3:811
Brown, Lester O., 5:636,
5:822
Brown, Lester Russell,
5:132, 5:151, 5:265, **5:828**
Brown, Lloyd W., 2:106,
2:930
Brown, Lucy M., 3:353
Brown, Malcolm H., 3:708
Brown, Marie A., 5:386
Brown, Marshall, 1:225
Brown, Maurice F., 1:775
Brown, Maurice John Edwin,
3:715
Brown, Michael, 1:600, 5:337
Brown, Michael F., 4:465
Brown, Michael S., 5:75
Brown, Millie, 5:325
Brown, Milton W., 3:758
Brown, Nathalie B., 2:483

Brown, Peter, 3:303, 3:306,
3:665, 4:109, 4:449, 4:687
Brown, Peter G., 5:115
Brown, Peter L., 5:590,
5:592, 5:606
Brown, Phil, 3:205
Brown, R. Allen, 3:356
Brown, R. Craig, 3:614
Brown, Raymond E., 4:685,
4:816, 4:819, 4:824, 4:887
Brown, Richard, 1:505
Brown, Richard D., 3:526,
3:801
Brown, Richard H., 5:570
Brown, Robert C., 5:369
Brown, Robert E., 3:566
Brown, Robert F., 4:252
Brown, Robert L., 4:503
Brown, Robert McAfee,
4:747, 4:769
Brown, Roger H., 3:520
Brown, Russell, 2:905
Brown, S., 3:277
Brown, S. C., 4:263
Brown, Samuel R., 3:5
Brown, Seyom, 3:144, 3:148
Brown, Sterling Allen, 1:954
Brown, Stuart C., 4:177
Brown, Terence, 3:370
Brown, Terrance, 5:415
Brown, Theodore L., 5:734
Brown, Trisha, 3:739
Brown, Wallace, 3:612
Brown, William E., 2:685
Brown, William R., 3:887
Browne, Douglas, 5:343
Browne, E. J., 5:60
Browne, E. Martin, 1:473
Browne, Edward G., 2:82
Browne, Janet, 5:819
Browne, Joseph, 1:531
Browne, Kevin, 3:872
Browne, Lewis, 4:5
Browne, Pat, 3:872
Browne, Ray, 3:846, 3:860,
3:872, 3:873, **3:875**
Browne, Terry, 1:426
Brownell, Morris, 1:250
Brownell, William Crary,
1:326, 1:669
**Browning, Elizabeth
Barrett**, 1:310, 1:314,
1:336, 1:390, 1:568
Browning, Gary, 2:748
Browning, Reed, 3:361
Browning, Robert, 1:310,
1:313, 1:314, 1:321, 1:336,
1:337, 1:568, 1:989, 4:682
Brownlow, Kevin, 3:827
Brownlow, Timothy, 1:286
Brownstone, David, 1:52, 5:6,
5:815
Brú, Hedin, 2:655, 2:656

Brubaker, Timothy H., 3:201
Bruccoli, Matthew J., 1:840,
1:965, 1:967, 1:1228
Bruce, Dickson D., 1:713
Bruce, F. F., 4:797
Bruce, Robert V., 3:558, 5:45
Bruch, Hilde, 5:394, 5:426
Bruchey, Stuart, 3:547
Brucker, Gene A., 3:333
Bruckner, Anton, 3:685
Bruder, Gerry, 3:906
Brue, Stanley, 3:45
Brueghel the Elder, Pieter,
3:768, **3:770**
Brues, Guy de, 4:124
Bruggencate, K. Ten, 1:98
Brugger, Robert J., 3:514
Bruhn, John, 3:201
Brumbaugh, James E., 5:225
Brumbaugh, Robert S., 4:46,
4:79, 4:341
Brumble, H. David, III, 1:87,
1:631
Brumfit, J. H., 2:516
Brumm, Ursula, 1:627
Brümmer, Vincent, 4:743
Brun, Viggo, 2:336
Brundage, Anthony, 1:345,
3:9, 3:275, 3:363
Brundage, Burr C., 4:457
Brundell, Barry, 4:173
Bruneau, Thomas C., 3:386
**Brunel, Sir Isambard King-
dom, 5:249**
Bruner, Jerome S., 3:175,
3:254
Bruni, Leonardo, 2:433,
4:124
Bruning, Nancy, 5:355,
5:371, 5:399
Brunn, Stanley D., 3:124
Brunner, Edward J., 1:823
Brunner, John, 5:563
Brunner, Karl, 3:65
Bruno, Giordano, 2:410,
4:123, 4:133, **4:134**, 4:137,
4:148
Bruns, Gerald L., 1:924,
4:292
Brunsdale, Mitzi, 1:611, 2:669
Brunt, P. A., 3:303
Brunvand, Jan H., 3:847,
3:868
Brush, Craig, 4:146
Brush, Stephen G., 5:27,
5:658, 5:701
Brushwood, John S., 2:845
Bruss, Elizabeth W., 1:927
Bruss, Paul, 1:1003
Brussel, James A., 5:415
Bruteau, Beatrice, 4:353
Brutus, Dennis, 2:157, **2:159**
Bruyne, Edgar de, 4:95

Bryan, George B., 2:666
Bryant, Arthur, 3:406
Bryant, Christopher, 3:227
Bryant, Donald C., 3:152
Bryant, Hallman Bell, 1:485
Bryant, John, 1:688
Bryant, Joseph A., 1:993
Bryant, Paul, 1:715
Bryant, William Cullen,
  1:653, 1:660, 1:1192,
  2:359, 2:360
Bryce, Ivar, 1:594
Bryce, James, 3:151
Bryer, Jackson, 1:751, 1:899
Bryer, Jackson R., 1:713,
  1:803
Bryks, Rachmil, 2:36
Bryson, Bill, 3:894, 3:898
Bryson, Gladys, 4:32
Bryusov (Briusov), Valery,
  2:704
Bub, Jeffrey, 5:67
Buber, Martin, 2:41, 4:304,
  4:334, 4:602, 4:632, 4:655,
  4:660, 4:661, 4:669, 4:671
Bubner, R., 4:28
Bucco, Martin, 1:854
Buchan, David, 3:854
Buchan, Elizabeth, 1:589
Buchanan, A. Russell, 3:534
Buchanan, James M., 3:67
Buchanan, Nina K., 3:169
Buchanan, R. A., 5:36
Buchanan, Robert W., 1:392
Buchanan-Brown, John,
  1:131
Buchen, Irving H., 2:48
Büchler, Adolph, 4:604,
  4:615
Buchler, Justus, 4:249
Buchner, Alexander, 3:666
Büchner, Georg, 2:564,
  2:573, 3:679
Buchsbaum, Herbert J.,
  5:355
Buchwald, Art, 3:870
Buchwald, Jed Z., 5:701
Buci-Glucksmann, Christine,
  1:1131
Buck, Claire, 1:827
Buck, Timothy, 1:99
Buckhout, Robert, 3:167
Buckingham, Robert W.,
  5:334, 5:376
Buckingham, Willis J., 1:747
Buckland, Michael Keeble,
  5:543
Buckland, W. R., 5:520
Buckland, W. W., 3:305
Buckle, Richard, 3:732,
  3:738, 3:741
Buckler, William E., 1:316,
  1:328, 1:339, 1:387, 1:401

Buckler, William Earl, 1:326
Buckley, George T., 4:124
Buckley, Jerome H., 1:315,
  1:318, 1:401
Buckley, Ken, 3:494
Buckley, Michael, S. J.,
  4:884
Buckley, William F., Jr.,
  3:907
Buckner, Michael D., 5:118
Bucky, Peter A., 5:683
Budd, Louis J., 1:783, 1:836
Budd, Malcolm, 3:659, 4:345
Budden, Julian, 3:726
Budge, Ernest A., 3:445
Budhamanda, Swami, 5:196
Budick, Sanford, 4:610
Budoff, Penny Wise, 5:355
Buehler, W. K., 5:508, 5:530
Buel, James W., 3:938
Buell, Lawrence, 1:650, 1:713
Buero Vallejo, Antonio,
  2:521, 2:531
Buffington, Albert F., 3:850
Buffington, Robert, 1:875
Bufithis, Philip H., 1:1012
Buford, Thomas O., 4:20
Bugental, James F. T.,
  5:437
Bugliarello, George, 5:70,
  5:250
Buhle, Paul, 3:648
Bührig, Marga, 4:749
Buijs, Gina, 3:217
Buitenhuis, Peter, 2:923
Bukhsh, S. K., 3:442
Bukofzer, Manfred F., 3:659
Bulas, Kazimierz, 1:101
Bulgakov, Mikhail, 2:490,
  2:705
Bulger, F.W.P., 3:609
Bulka, Reuven P., 4:654
Bulkin, Elly, 1:1183
Bull, John, 1:425, 5:758
Bull, Storm, 3:654
Bullard, E. John, 3:771
Bullard, Fred M., 5:629
Bullard, Robert D., 3:205
Bullen, Christine V., 5:557
Bullen, K. E., 5:629
Bullett, Gerald, 2:197
Bulliet, Richard, 3:435
Bullins, Ed, 1:1086
Bullock, Alan, 3:292, 3:344,
  3:376, 3:399
Bullock, Chris, 1:134
Bullock, Marcus, 4:253
Bullough, Bonnie, 5:337,
  5:429
Bullough, Geoffrey, 1:219
Bullough, Vern L., 5:119,
  5:337, 5:429
Bullwinkle, Davis A., 3:416

Bulman, J. C., 1:217
Bulmer, Martin, 3:200
Bulmer, Simon, 3:58
Bulosan, Carlos, 2:328
Bulsterbaum, Allison, 1:859
Bultmann, Rudolf, 4:366,
  4:617, 4:743, 4:807, 4:821,
  4:824, 4:827, 4:829, 4:832
Bulwer-Lytton, Edward,
  1:310, 1:312, 1:316, 1:332,
  1:340
Bumiller, Elisabeth, 4:508
Bump, Jerome, 1:364
Bumsted, J. M., 3:612
Bunch, Bryan, 5:6, 5:216
Bunge, Mario A(ugusto),
  5:62, 5:70, 5:82, 5:99,
  5:712
Bunin, Ivan, 2:683, 2:706
Buning, Sietze, 1:480
Bunker, J., 5:79
Bunnay, Jane, 4:519
Bunting, Basil, 1:452
Buñuel, Luis, 3:832
Bunyan, John, 1:173, 1:403,
  1:576, 1:1194, 2:125,
  2:166, 3:823
Bunzel, John H., 3:542
Buol, S. W., 5:262
Buolby, Mark, 2:595
Buranelli, Vincent, 1:693,
  4:250, 4:847
Burbage, Richard, 1:203
Burbank, Rex, 1:630, 1:812,
  1:899, 1:1116
Burbidge, John, 4:233
Burch, John G., 5:543
Burch, Noel, 1:1157, 3:825
Burchard, Ludwig, 3:791
Burchard, Rachael C., 1:1060
Burchfield, Joe D., 5:45,
  5:622
Burckhardt, Jacob, 2:400,
  3:325, 3:332, 3:333, 3:399,
  4:682
Burckhardt, Sigurd, 1:208,
  2:599
Burd, Van Akin, 1:394
Burdett, Eric, 1:22
Burdman, Geri Marr, 5:316
Burford, Alison, 3:304
Burger, Alfred, 5:350
Bürger, Peter, 4:379
Burger, Ronna, 4:79
Burgess, Anthony (John An-
  thony Burgess Wilson),
  1:204, 1:420, 1:453, 1:525,
  1:846, 2:310
Burgess, Eric, 5:592
Burgess, Jeremy, 5:767
Burgess, Ronald D., 2:845
Burgess, William A., 5:352
Burghart, Richard, 4:498

Burgin, Richard, 2:49
Burgis, Nina, 1:349
Burian, P., 2:356
Burian, Peter, 4:475
Burian, Richard, 4:381, 5:67
Buridan, John, 4:103
Burish, Thomas G., 5:376
Burke, Edmund, 3:152,
  4:192, 4:210, 4:578
Burke, Frank, 3:837
Burke, James, 5:24
Burke, James Henry, 1:51
Burke, John, 3:898
Burke, John G., 5:212
Burke, Kathleen, 1:1199
Burke, Kenneth, 1:817,
  1:955, 1:1153
Burke, Marie Louise, 4:563
Burke, Peter, 2:400, 3:275,
  3:333
Burke, Robert E., 3:509
Burke, T. E., 4:410
Burkert, Walter, 4:87, 4:429,
  4:450, **4:470**
Burkhardt, Hans, 4:159
Burkhardt, Richard W., Jr.,
  5:43, 5:803
Burkhart, Charles, 1:462
Burkholder, Mark A., 3:628
Burkholder, Robert E., 1:670,
  1:688
Burki, Shahid Javed, 3:487
Burkitt, Francis C., 4:685
Burks, Ardath W., 3:476
Burks, Herbert M., Jr., 5:417
Burley, Walter, 4:16
Burling, Robbins, 3:21
Burlingame, Roger, 1:43,
  1:44
Burn, Andrew R., 2:358
Burne, Neville B., 1:289
Burness, Donald, 2:106,
  2:113
Burnet, John, 4:50, 4:79
Burnett, Anne P., 2:366
Burnett, Constance Buel,
  1:1201
Burnett, David, 4:857
Burnett, Frances Hodgson,
  1:1200
Burnett, Vivian, 1:1201
Burney, Frances (or Fanny)
  (Mme D'arblay), 1:235
Burnham, David, 5:74, 5:572
Burnham, John C., 3:551
Burnham, Peter, 3:365
Burnham, Robert, Jr., 5:591
Burns, Allan F., 4:465
Burns, Arthur F., 3:49, 3:65
Burns, Bryan, 1:297
Burns, Deborah, 3:891
Burns, E. Bradford, 3:625,
  3:631, 3:634, 3:639

Burns, Edward M., 3:274
Burns, Grant, 5:109, 5:287
Burns, J. H., 4:98
Burns, J. Patout, 4:685
Burns, James Macgregor,
  3:512, **3:570**
Burns, John, 4:219
Burns, Ken, 3:530
Burns, Ric, 3:530
Burns, Richard Dean, 3:509
Burns, Robert, 1:279, 1:285,
  1:291
Burns, Stewart, 3:551
Burns, Tom, 3:228
Burns, Tom R., 5:180
Burnshaw, Stanley, 1:842, 2:9
Burnstein, Stanley M., 3:299
Burnyeat, Myles, 4:56, 4:58
Burr, Angela, 4:862
Burr, David, 4:101
Burr, John R., 4:6, 4:37,
  4:263
Burr, Nelson R., 4:750
Burrell, David, C.S.C., 4:884
Burridge, Kenelm, 4:467
Burrill, Richard, 5:114
Burris, Sidney, 1:495
Burrison, John A., 3:859,
  3:860
Burrough, Bryan, 3:48
Burrough, P. A., 3:120
Burroughs, Edgar Rice,
  1:594, 1:616, 1:1209,
  1:1251, **1:1255**
Burroughs, William S.,
  1:956, 1:958, 1:998, 1:1185
Burrow, John A., 1:146,
  1:156
Burrow, John W., 3:41, 3:403
Burrows, David L., 3:659
Burrows, William E., 5:596
Bursill-Hall, G. L., 4:101
Bursztajn, Harold, 5:339
Burt, Alfred, 3:612, 3:637
Burt, Eugene C., 3:758
Burt, Forrest D., 1:328, 1:520
Burt, John, 1:893
Burt, Nancy V., 1:1084
Burt, Ronald, 3:215
Burtchaell, James, 4:894
Burtle, James L., 3:59
Burtless, Gary, 3:60
Burton, Arthur, 5:421
Burton, C. Emory, 3:211
Burton, David, 1:877
Burton, David H., 3:594
Burton, Ernest J., 1:123
Burton, Hester, 1:331
Burton, Ian, 5:620
Burton, John H., 4:201
Burton, Paul F., 5:544
Burton, Philip, 5:539
Burton, R.W.B., 2:365

Burton, Richard, 2:172, 2:457
Burton, Robert, 5:825
Burton, Sir Richard, 3:913
Burtt, Edwin A., 4:29, 4:124,
  4:159, 5:41, 5:706
Burtt, J. O., 2:348
Buruma, Ian, 3:902, 4:539
Bury, John B., 2:380, 5:44
Busby, Linda J., 3:811
Busby, Mark, 1:715, 1:1121
Busch, Eberhard, 4:758
Busch, Frederick, 1:986
Busch, Hans, 3:726
Busch, Marie, 2:789
Busch, Thomas W., 4:330
Busch, Wilhelm, 2:574
Buscombe, Edward, 1:1166
Busenbark, E. J., 1:27
Bush, Douglas, 1:165, 1:166,
  1:215, 1:265, 1:294, 4:124
Bush, Richard C., 4:532
Bush, Ronald, 1:473, 1:872
Bush, Vannevar, 5:14, **5:199**,
  5:580
Bushell, Garvin, 3:668
Bushman, Richard L., 3:516,
  3:582, 4:845, 4:879
Bushnell, David, 3:631, 3:635
Buss, Robin, 3:825
Bussagli, Mario, 3:762
Bussanich, John, 4:86
Busse, Ewald W., 5:316
Bussell, Frederick W., 4:76
Buswell, Robert E., 4:537
Butcher, Philip, 1:653, 1:737,
  1:793
Butcher, S. H., 4:67
Butler, Alban, 4:675
Butler, Arthur J., 2:402
Butler, A.S.G., 1:341
Butler, C., 4:111
Butler, Charles H., 5:287
Butler, Christopher, 1:924,
  4:263, 4:391, 5:564
Butler, David E., 3:353
Butler, Deborah A., 3:490
Butler, Eamonn, 3:77
Butler, Edward Cuthbert,
  4:705
Butler, Francelia, 1:579,
  1:1197
Butler, Gareth, 3:353
Butler, Jon, 3:558
Butler, Joseph, 4:158, **4:193**
Butler, Josephine Grey,
  1:310, 1:324, **1:340**
Butler, Judith, 1:1133,
  1:1181, 3:207
Butler, Lord C. H., 3:499
Butler, Marilyn, 1:268, 1:276,
  1:297
Butler, Martin, 1:169
Butler, Matilda, 3:802

Butler, Samuel, **1:341**, 2:359, 2:360, 2:361, 5:563
Butler, Thomas, 2:785, 2:828
Butler-Evans, Elliott, 1:917
Butlin, Martin, 1:279
Butor, Michel, 2:463
Butrick, Richard, Jr., 4:279, 5:85
Butscher, Edward, 1:810, 1:1031
Butt, John, 2:522
Buttel, Robert, 1:495
Butterfield, Herbert, 3:337, 5:24, 5:602
Butterick, George F., 1:1027
Butters, Ronald R., 1:1183
Butterworth, Neil, 3:693
Buttimer, Annette, 5:619
Buttinger, Joseph, 3:490
Buttitta, Tony, 1:840, 1:1072
Buttrick, George A., 4:818
Butts, Leonard, 1:979
Butts, Robert E., 4:143
Butwin, Frances, 2:46
Butwin, Joseph, 2:46
Butzer, Karl W., 5:626
Buxton, H. W., 5:575
Buytaert, Eligius, 4:120
Buzan, Barry, 3:144
Buzzati, Dino, 2:411
Byars, Betsy, 1:1195
Byatt, A(ntonia) S(usan), 1:454, 1:468
Byerman, Keith Eldon, 1:917
Byers, James M., 5:410
Bykaŭ, Vasil, 2:783, 2:784
Bylebyl, Jerome, 5:361
Byles, Monica, 5:2
Bynagle, Hans E., 4:6, 4:13
Byng, Lucy M., 2:824
Bynum, Caroline Walker, 4:695, 4:698, 4:892
Bynum, William F., 5:24, 5:27, 5:60
Byock, Jesse L., 3:381
Byoung-Lo, Philo Kim, 3:481
Byrd, Don, 1:1027
Byrd, Richard E(velyn), 3:914
Byrd, Rudolph P., 1:891, 4:875
Byrne, C. Judith, 5:324
Byrne, Edmund, 5:73
Byrne, John, 5:281
Byrne, Josefa H., 1:92
Byrnes, Edward T., 1:147
Byrnes, R. F., 3:348
Byrnes, Timothy, 4:752
Lord Byron, George Gordon, 1:225, 1:264, 1:266, 1:271, 1:273, 1:277, **1:281**, 1:292, 1:297, 1:298, 1:300, 1:302, 1:304, 1:313, 1:373,

1:434, 1:587, 1:598, 1:601, 1:690, 1:1099, 2:370, 2:383, 2:406, 2:531, 2:734, 2:750, 2:802, 3:681, 5:541, 5:575, 5:577
Byron, Toby, 3:669
Bywater, Ingram, 4:67
Bywater, Tim, 3:827
Bywaters, David A., 1:241

C

Cabezas, Omar, 3:639
Cabezon, José Ignacio, 4:894
Cable, George Washington, 1:721, **1:735**, 1:1193
Cable, Thomas, 1:146
Cabrera Infante, Guillermo, 2:843, 2:844, **2:857**, 2:934
Cachia, Pierre, 2:74
Cachin, Francoise, 3:780
Cacoullos, Ann, 4:230
Cadet, J. M., 4:518
Cadogan, Peter H., 5:650
Cadorette, Curt, 4:747, 4:769
Cadoux, C. John, 4:688
Cadwallader, Martin, 3:124
Cady, Edwin H., 1:630, 1:722, 1:742, 1:759, 1:783
Cady, John Frank, 3:488, 3:489
Caesar, Julius, 1:898, 2:378, **2:383**, 2:387, 2:396, **3:312**, 3:313, 3:314, 3:319, 3:320, 4:75, 4:436, 4:452
Caesar, Michael, 2:400
Caetani, Marguerite, 2:402
Cafarelli, Annette Wheeler, 1:231, 1:273
Caffrey, Margaret M, 3:27
Cage, John, 3:685, 3:740
Cahan, Abraham, 1:721, **1:737, 2:37**
Cahan, William G., 5:369
Cahill, Holger, 3:868
Cahill, Kevin M., 1:430
Cahill, Lisa Sowle, 4:894
Cahill, Robert E., 3:858
Cahn, Robert, 3:894
Cahn, Sammy, 1:95
Cahn, Steven M., 3:249, 4:20
Cailliet, Rene, 5:376
Cain, A. J., 5:779
Cain, James M., 1:1227
Cain, Michael, 3:771
Cain, Michael Scott, 1:46
Cain, Seymour, 4:305
Cain, Thomas H., 1:198
Caird, Edward, 3:285, 4:223
Caird, John, 4:187
Cairncross, Sandy, 5:352

Cairns, Earle E., 4:675, 4:717, 4:720
Cairns, Francis, 2:397
Cairns, R. A., 5:667
Cairns-Smith, A. G., 5:732, 5:763
Caistor, Nick, 2:848
Cajal, Santiago Ramón y. See Ramón y Cajal, Santiago
Cajanello, Duchess di, 2:671
Cajetan, Cardinal, 4:136
Cajori, Florian, 5:30
Čaks, Aleksandrs, 2:803
Calabrese, Anthony, 3:729
Calabrese, Edward J., 5:345
Calbally, E. I., 5:262
Caldecott, Randolph, 1:578, **1:580**, 1:583
Calder, Bruce J., 3:636
Calder, Daniel G., 1:143
Calder, Nigel, 5:9, 5:222, 5:572, 5:592, 5:622, 5:633, 5:664, 5:683
Calder, William M., 4:479
Calderón de la Barca, Pedro, 2:520, 2:531, **2:532**
Calderwood, James L., 1:208, 1:211, 1:213, 1:214
Caldwell, Bruce J., 3:46
Caldwell, Daniel H., 4:874
Caldwell, Erskine, 1:818
Caldwell, Helen, 2:896
Caldwell, John, 3:659
Caldwell, Richard, 4:446
Caldwell, Ronald J., 3:339, 4:719
Caldwell, Sandra M., 4:719
Caldwell, Thomas, 1:316
Calhoun, Craig, 3:215, 4:404
Calhoun, Daniel H., 5:36
Calian, Carnegie Samuel, 4:759
Califano, Joseph A., Jr., 5:332
Calkins, Mary, 3:181
Calladine, Chris, 5:784
Callaghan, Morley, 2:907
Callahan, Daniel J., 4:894, 5:78, **5:83**, 5:119, 5:132
Callahan, John F., 1:803, 1:917, 4:47
Callahan, North, 1:878
Callahan, Sidney, 4:894
Callahan, Steven, 3:907
Callan, Edward, 1:435, 2:168
Callan, Ron, 1:900
Callanan, Maggie, 3:201
Callas, Maria, 3:686
Callen, Michael, 5:387
Callender, Sheila T., 5:385
Callery, Bernadette G., 1:22
Callicott, J. Baird, 5:834

Callimachus, 2:343, 2:352, **2:354**
Callinicos, Alex, 3:295, 4:263, 4:379, 4:391
Callus, D. A., 4:115
Calvert, Monte, 5:36
Calvez, Jean-Yves, 4:771
Calvin, Jack, 5:820
Calvin, John, 1:636, 3:334, 4:1, 4:729, **4:760**, 4:773, 4:780
Calvin, Melvin, 5:740
Calvino, Italo, 2:400, **2:411**
Calvocoressi, M. D., 3:708
Calvocoressi, Peter, 1:56, 3:278
Cambon, Glauco, 2:421, 2:428, 2:441
Cameron, A.G.W., 5:654
Cameron, Averil, 3:309, 3:442
Cameron, David, 3:152
Cameron, Elisabeth, 3:765
Cameron, Elspeth, 2:910
Cameron, Judy, 3:734
Cameron, Kenneth M., 1:272
Cameron, Kenneth N., 1:303
Cameron, Moven, 1:418
Cameron, Sharon, 1:747
Cammett, John M., 4:287
Camões, Luís Vaz de, 2:556, **2:558**
Camp, John, 3:868
Campa, Arthur L., 3:863
Campanella, Thomas, 5:688
Campanella, Tommaso, 4:123, **4:137**
Campbell, Ada M., 5:267
Campbell, Alastair V., 5:119
Campbell, Alistair, 1:96
Campbell, Andrew, 5:758
Campbell, Angus, 3:143, 3:208
Campbell, Anne, 3:170
Campbell, Bruce, 4:852, 5:758
Campbell, Colin, 3:209, 3:537
Campbell, D'Ann, 3:534
Campbell, David G., 5:817
Campbell, Donald T., 3:6, 3:7
Campbell, Helen, 1:634
Campbell, H. M., 1:876
Campbell, J. B., 3:308
Campbell, J. D., 5:626
Campbell, James L., 1:340
Campbell, Jeremy, 5:74, 5:567
Campbell, John Francis of Islay, 3:845, **3:875**
Campbell, Joseph, 3:847, **3:876**, 4:428
Campbell, Karlyn K., 3:803
Campbell, Lewis, 2:368, 4:79, 5:701

Campbell, Lily B., 1:211
Campbell, Neil A., 5:763
Campbell, Olwen W., 1:297
Campbell, Oscar J., 1:222
Campbell, Paul J., 5:494
Campbell, R. H., 3:107
Campbell, Robert, 4:388, 5:415
Campbell, Roy, 2:539
Campbell, Stephen K., 5:521
Campbell, T. D., 4:215
Campenhausen, Hans von, 4:98, 4:690, 4:814
Campion, Thomas, 1:174, 2:383
Campos-Boralevi, Lea, 3:151
Camps, W. A., 2:361, 2:397
Camurati, Mireya, 4:33
Camus, Albert, 1:1056, 2:459, **2:463**, 2:465, 2:509, 2:554, 4:329
Camusso, Lorenzo, 3:765
Canaday, John, 3:761
Canary, Robert H., 1:485
Canavaggio, Jean, 2:535
Canavan, Francis, 3:152
Canby, Henry S., 1:765, 1:783
Cancian, F. M., 3:278
Cancro, Robert, 3:174
Candelaria, Cordelia, 1:798
Candlin, Enid Saunders, 3:902
Canetti, Elias, 2:564, **2:574**, 2:596
Canfield, Cass, 1:40
Canfield, J. Douglas, 1:225
Canfield, John Y., 4:345
Cankar, Ivan, 2:834, **2:835**
Cannadine, David, 3:365
Cannistraro, Philip V., 3:385
Cannizzaro, Stanislao, 5:740
Cannon, Betty, 4:330
Cannon, Calvin, 2:526
Cannon, Carl L., 1:31
Cannon, Dorothy F., 5:811
Cannon, Geoffrey, 5:325
Cannon, Hal, 3:863
Cannon, H. Graham, 5:803
Cannon, JoAnn, 2:401
Cannon, John, 3:361
Cannon, Lou, 3:537
Canny, Nicholas, 3:370
Canovan, Margaret, 4:395, 5:82
Canter, David, 3:206
Canth, Minna, 2:657
Cantlie, Audrey, 4:498
Cantor, Geoffrey N., 5:10, 5:61, 5:745
Cantor, Georg, 5:31, **5:500**, 5:509
Cantor, Joel M., 3:811

Cantor, Milton, 3:511
Cantor, Mindy, 2:986
Cantor, Muriel, 3:811
Cantor, Norman F., 2:986, 3:275
Cantril, Hadley, 3:202
Cantu, Robert C., 5:396
Cantwell, Alan, Jr., 5:387
Cantzlaar, George L., 5:415
Capaldi, Nicholas, 4:20, 4:201
Čapek, Karel, 2:788, **2:789**
Capek, Milic, 4:220, 5:62
Capie, Forrest H., 3:54
Caplan, Arthur L., 5:77, 5:79, 5:312, 5:825
Caplan, David, 3:170
Caplan, Gerald, 5:421
Caplan, Ronald, 5:357
Caplow, Theodore, 3:231
Caponigri, A. Robert, 2:442, 4:124, 4:159, 4:216
Capote, Truman, 1:916, **1:958**, 1:1185
Capp, Bernard, 4:725
Capper, Charles, 3:559
Cappon, Lester J., 3:505
Capps, Donald, 4:890
Capps, Jack L., 1:747
Capra, Frank, 3:833
Capra, Fritjof, 4:866, 5:196
Capron, Alexander M., 5:79, 5:780
Capstick, Peter Hathaway, 3:902
Caputi, Anthony, 2:436
Caputo, John D., 4:292
Caramagno, Thomas C., 1:570
Caramello, Charles, 1:917
Caranfa, Angelo, 2:468
Caras, Roger, 5:826
Caras, Steven, 3:747
Caras, Tracy, 3:660
Carballido, Emilio, 2:858
Carberry, M. Sandra, 5:549
Carby, Hazel, 1:1139
Carcopino, Jerome, 2:380, 3:307
Cardenal, Ernesto, 2:858
Cardin, I., 1:102
Cardozo, Arlene Rossen, 4:599
Carducci, Giosuè (Joshua), 2:399, **2:412**, 2:414, 2:421, 2:431
Cardwell, Guy, 1:783
Cardwell, Richard, 2:867
Careless, J.M.S., 3:612, 3:614
Carens, James F., 1:505
Carew Hunt, R. N., 3:139
Carey, George, 3:860
Carey, John, 1:178, 1:404, 1:484

Carey, John O., 5:207
Carey, Peter, 2:951
Carey, S. Warren, 5:32
Carhart, Margaret, 1:277
Caris, Timothy N., 5:373
Carlen, Claudia, 4:891
Carley, James P., 1:877
Carling, Finn, 2:662
Carling, Paul, 5:626
Carlitz, Katherine, 2:226
Carlsmith, J., 3:168
Carlson, Elof Axel, 5:777, 5:808
Carlson, Eric W., 1:693
Carlson, Harry G., 2:680
Carlson, Raymond, 3:891
Carlsson, Percy, 4:194
Carlston, Douglas G., 5:542
Carlton, David, 5:109
Carlton, E., 3:278
Carlton, Eric, 5:429
Carlton, Peter L., 5:350
Carlyle, Thomas, 1:311, 1:323, 1:324, 1:343, 1:355, 1:368, 1:372, 1:392, 3:402, 4:588, 5:249
Carman, Bliss, 1:778, 2:908, 2:924
Carman, John, 4:26, 4:892
Carmi, T., 2:9, 2:17
Carmichael, Calum M., 4:627
Carmody, Denise, 1:637, 4:749, 4:892
Carmody, John, 4:743
Carnall, Geoffrey, 1:305
Carnap, Rudolf, 4:261, 4:278, 4:279, 4:313, 4:332, 4:411, 5:62, 5:84, 5:101
Carner, Mosco, 3:680, 3:711
Carne-Ross, D. S., 2:365
Carney, Raymond, 3:833, 3:834
Carniero, Robert L., 3:42
Carnley, Peter, 4:887
Caro, Robert A., 3:537
Carosso, Vincent P., 3:547
Carpelan, Bo, 2:658
Carpenter, Bogdana, 2:811
Carpenter, Cal, 3:860
Carpenter, Charles A., 1:427
Carpenter, Finley, 3:194
Carpenter, Frederic I., 1:851, 1:1108
Carpenter, Humphrey, 1:436, 1:559, 1:578, 1:872, 1:1195, 4:512, 4:776
Carpenter, K., 4:503
Carpenter, Kenneth E., 1:36
Carpenter, Kenneth J., 5:394
Carpenter, Rhys, 2:361, 3:759
Carpenter, Richard C., 1:362
Carpenter, Ronald H., 3:599

Carpentier, Alejo, 2:844, 2:859, 2:934
Carpineto, Jane F., 5:337
Carpio, Lope Felix de Vega. See Vega Carpio, Lope Felix de
Carr, Anne, 4:781
Carr, Archie, 5:770, 5:817
Carr, Arthur S., 1:316
Carr, David, 4:234, 4:391
Carr, Edward H., 3:139, 3:275, 3:278, 3:344, 3:376
Carr, H. W., 3:284
Carr, Ian, 3:691
Carr, John, 1:608
Carr, Joseph J., 5:9
Carr, Mary, 5:759
Carr, Melbert B., 1:14
Carr, Michael H., 5:592, 5:629
Carr, Raymond, 3:386, 3:640
Carr, Virginia S., 1:828, 1:1009, 1:1101
Carr, William H., 3:396
Carrasco, David, 4:454, 4:457, 4:474, 4:883
Carreras, José, 3:687, 3:692, 3:708
Carrighar, Sally, 5:817
Carringer, Robert, 1:1179
Carrington, Henry B., 3:505
Carrington, Ildiko de Papp, 2:907
Carrison, M. P., 2:315
Carrithers, Gale H., 1:889, 5:171
Carrithers, Michael, 4:509, 4:512, 4:526
Carrol, Deborah, 3:249
Carroll, David, 1:354, 2:128, 5:345
Carroll, David L., 5:391
Carroll, Joseph, 1:887
Carroll, Lewis, 1:344, 1:574, 1:581, 1:586, 1:1207, 2:858
Carroll, Noel, 1:1157
Carroll, Peter N., 3:512, 3:537
Carroll, Robert L., 5:639
Carroll, William, 1:210
Carruth, Gorton, 1:132, 1:1195, 3:508
Carruth, Hayden, 1:801, 1:915
Carruthers, Peter, 4:345, 4:382
Carson, Ada Lou, 1:645
Carson, Anne, 4:749
Carson, Barbara H., 1:895
Carson, Bonnie L., 5:350
Carson, Herbert L., 1:645
Carson, L. H., 5:399
Carson, Neil, 1:1104

Carson, Rachel Louise, 5:132, 5:271, 5:631, 5:828
Carson, Richard L., 3:52
Carson, Robert, 3:306
Carsten, Franz L., 3:376
Carswell, Donald, 1:299
Carswell, John, 1:22
Cartelli, Thomas, 1:187
Carter, Alan, 1:532
Carter, Albert Howard, III, 2:412
Carter, Angela, 1:420, 1:455, 3:207
Carter, Ashton, B., 5:184
Carter, Benny, 3:687
Carter, D.N.G., 1:486
Carter, Dan T., 3:527
Carter, Elliott, 3:687
Carter, Everett, 1:759
Carter, Harry, 1:14
Carter, Jimmy, 3:435, 3:537
Carter, John, 1:7, 1:22, 1:31, 1:35, 1:76, 1:496
Carter, Margaret, 1:603
Carter, R.W.G., 5:631
Carter, Robert A., 1:46
Carter, Robert E., 4:365
Carter, Steven D., 2:274
Carterette, Edward C., 3:177
Cartey, Wilfred, 2:930
Cartland, Barbara, 1:618
Cartledge, Paul, 3:301, 3:307
Cartwright, Dorwin, 3:172
Cartwright, Nancy, 5:67
Caruso, Dorothy, 3:688
Caruso, Enrico, 3:653, 3:688
Caruso, Enrico, Jr., 3:688
Carvalho, David Numes, 1:62
Carver, Norman F., Jr., 3:418
Carver, Raymond, 1:805, 1:916, 1:959
Carver, Terrell, 3:75, 4:227, 4:242
Cary, Joseph, 2:441
Cary, Joyce, 1:456
Cary, Max, 2:344, 2:380, 3:303
Cary, Richard, 1:770
Casanova, Richard, 5:638
Casares, Adolfo Bioy, 2:844
Cascardi, Anthony, 2:535
Casciato, Arthur D., 1:1057
Case, Gerard R., 5:638
Caseiro, Alberto, 2:560
Caserio, Robert L., 1:318
Casey, Daniel J., 1:804
Casey, Timothy, 5:70
Cash, Arthur H., 1:258
Cash, Wilson W., 4:568
Cashdollar, Charles, 4:740
Cashman, Sean Dennis, 3:512
Cashmore, E. Ellis, 3:204

Casillo, Robert, 1:872
Casimir, Saint, 2:806
Caspar, Max, 5:41
Casper, Bernard, 4:628
Casper, Leonard, 2:328
Cass, Joan, 3:732
Cassaday, Neal, 1:998
Cassara, Ernest, 3:510
Cassatt, Mary, 3:771
Cassedy, Edward S., 5:278
Cassedy, James H., 5:13,
    5:312
Cassell, Abayomi, 3:419
Cassell, Eric J., 5:119
Cassell, Richard A., 1:475
Cassels, J.W.S., 5:488
Cassian, St. John, 4:705,
    4:706
Cassidy, David C., 5:694
Cassiodorus, 4:98
Cassirer, Ernst, 2:402, 3:337,
    4:124, 4:153, 4:155, 4:156,
    4:160, 4:206, 4:261, 4:279,
    4:331, 4:695, 5:469
Cassis, A. F., 1:489
Casson, Lionel, 2:349, 3:304
Casson, Mark, 3:49
Cassuto, Umberto, 4:445
Castanien, Donald Garner,
    3:646
Castellan, Georges, 3:390,
    3:391
Castellanos, Rosario, 2:860
Castelli, Jim, 5:109
Castiglione, Baldassare,
    2:413
Castiglioni, Arturo, 5:35
Castile, Rand, 4:537
Castillo, Carlos, 1:102
Castle, Kate, 3:734
Castle, Terry, 1:253
Castle, Wilfrid T., 3:454
Castleman, Michael, 5:318,
    5:350
Castro, Americo, 3:386
Castro, Eduardo Viveiros de,
    4:466
Castro, Ferreira de, 2:557
Castro, Jan Garden, 2:907
Castro, Joveita Ventura,
    2:329
Castro, Michael, 1:631
Castro, Miranda, 5:318
Castro, Rosalía de, 2:521,
    2:533
Castronovo, David, 1:899,
    1:902
Čašule, Kole, 2:807
Catalano, Joseph S., 4:330
Cataldo, Corinne B., 5:345
Catchpole, Brian, 3:272
Cate, George Allan, 1:395
Cate, James L., 3:534

Cather, Willa (Sibert),
    1:769, 1:802, 1:819, 1:1185
Catherine of Siena, St.,
    4:706
Catich, Edward M., 1:14
Catledge, Turner, 3:806
Catlin, George, 3:554
Cato, 5:265
Caton, Charles E., 4:263
Cattanach, Ann, 5:416
Catteau, Jacques, 2:715
Cattell, Raymond B., 5:106
Cattermole, Peter, 5:622
Catton, Bruce, 3:527, 3:571,
    3:574
Catton, Chris, 5:763
Catton, William B., 3:574
Catullus (Gaius Valerius Ca-
    tullus), 1:164, 2:354,
    2:378, 2:383, 2:388, 2:437
Cauchy, Baron Augustin
    Louis, 5:490, 5:501
Caudill, Maureen, 5:242
Caufield, Catherine, 5:821
Caughie, John, 1:1158
Caughie, Pamela L., 1:570
Caulfield, Malachy, 3:370
Causley, Charles, 3:850
Cauthen, Irby B., 1:693
Cauwels, Janice M., 5:370
Cavadino, Michael, 3:204
Cavafy, Constantine P.,
    2:370, 2:372, 2:517
Cavalcanti, Guido, 2:413
Cavalcaselle, G. B., 3:759
Cavalier, Robert, 4:160
Cavalieri, Liebe F., 5:726,
    5:782
Cavarnos, Constantine, 4:29,
    4:312
Cave, John D., 4:474
Cave, Richard Allen, 1:381,
    1:425
Cavell, Stanley, 1:701, 4:345
Cavendish, Richard, 3:854,
    4:568
Caves, Richard E., 3:58
Cawelti, John, 1:1210
Cawley, A. C., 1:158
Cawlor, Eric, 3:452
Caws, Mary Ann, 2:462,
    2:463, 2:466
Caws, Peter, 2:507, 4:34,
    4:330
Cayley, David, 5:137
Cazamian, Louis F., 2:446
Cazden, Norman, 3:859
Ceadel, Eric B., 2:52
Cecil, David, 1:238
Cedra, C., 5:261
Cedrins, Inara, 2:804
Cegelka, Patricia T., 5:426

Cela, Camilo José, 2:521,
    2:533
Celan, Paul, 2:564, 2:575
Celik, Zeyneb, 3:452
Céline, Louis-Ferdinand,
    2:465, 2:872, 2:897
Cell, John W., 3:554
Celletti, Rodolfo, 3:672
Cellini, Benvenuto, 2:413,
    3:333, 3:768, 3:772
Ceplair, Larry, 3:558
Cercignani, Fausto, 1:216
Cerdonio, M., 5:775
Cerf, Bennett A., 1:40
Cernuschi, Claude, 3:787
Cerny, Jaroslav, 4:442
Cerny, Philip G., 3:372
Cernyak-Spatz, Susan E.,
    2:565
Cervantes Saavedra, Miguel
    de, 1:244, 1:256, 2:383,
    2:406, 2:520, 2:534, 2:554
Cervigni, D. S., 2:402
César, Julio Ortega, 2:845
Cevasco, G. A., 1:548
Cézanne, Paul, 3:769, 3:772,
    3:775, 3:781
Ch'en, C. J., 2:192
Ch'en, Jerome, 2:257
Ch'en, Kenneth, 4:529
Ch'en, Yung-Fa, 3:469
Ch'eng Nai-shan, 2:241
Ch'eng-ta, Fan. See Fan
    Ch'eng-ta
Ch'en Jo-hsi, 2:240
Ch'en Ying-chen, 2:241
Ch'i-ch'ao, Liang. See Liang
    Ch'i-ch'ao
Ch'i-chi, Hsin, 2:204, 2:213
Ch'ien, T'ao. See T'ao Ch'ien
Ch'ien Chung-shu, 2:243,
    2:268
Ch'un-ming, Huang. See
    Huang Ch'un-ming
Ch'ü Yüan, 2:195
Cha, Dia, 2:322
Chabot, C. Barry, 5:447
Chabrol, Claude, 1:1169
Chadha, Rajni, 1:885
Chadwick, Douglas H., 5:758
Chadwick, Henry, 4:63, 4:99,
    4:110, 4:112, 4:676, 4:685
Chadwick, J., 2:347, 4:446
Chadwick, Owen, 3:340,
    4:706, 4:722, 4:738, 4:740,
    4:755, 4:783
Chadwick, Sir Edwin, 1:310,
    1:325, 1:341, 1:344, 1:368,
    1:375, 1:377
Chadwick, Whitney, 3:759
Chafe, William H., 3:537,
    3:554
Chaffee, C. David, 5:303

Chaffee, John W., 3:467, 4:526
Chaffers, William, 3:765
Chagnon, Napoleon, 3:25
Chahin, M., 2:76
Chai, Ch'u, 2:192
Chai, Leon, 1:650
Chai, Winberg, 2:192
Chaigne, Louis, 2:468
Chaikin, Andrew, 5:592
Chaisson, Eric, 5:594
Chaitanya, 2:173, 2:174
Chaitanya, Krishna, 3:483
Chako, George K., 5:236
Chakrabarty, Dipesh, 3:486
Chakraborty, A. K., 3:500
Chakravarty, S. R., 3:487
Chalfant, Edward, 3:563
Chalfen, Israel, 2:575
Chalk, Rosemary, 5:151
Challis, Chris, 1:998
Chaloner, W. H., 3:353
Chamberlain, Basil Hall, 4:536
Chamberlain, Bobby J., 2:892
Chamberlain, Hal, 5:564
Chamberlain, Neville, 3:278
Chamberlain, Robert L., 1:289
Chamberlain, William Henry, 3:396
Chamberlin, Bill F., 3:803
Chambers, Colin, 1:426
Chambers, Edmund K., 1:147, 1:169, 1:204, 1:221, 1:287
Chambers, J., 1:1035
Chambers, John B., 1:840
Chambers, Jonathan D., 3:358, 3:361
Chambers, R., 1:893
Chambers, Raymond W., 1:144, 4:147
Chametzky, Jules, 1:713, 1:737
Chamish, Barry, 3:439
Chamisso, Adelbert von, 2:575, 2:591
Champagne, Anthony, 5:343
Champigneulle, Bernard, 3:791
Champion, Larry S., 1:220
Champlain, Samuel de, 3:908
Champney, Freeman, 1:42
Chan, Jeffrey P., 1:129
Chan, Mary, 1:184
Chan, Román Piña, 4:455
Chan, Ts'ao. See Ts'ao Chan
Chan, Wing-tsit, 4:358, 4:521, 4:522, 4:526, 4:532
Chance, Jane, 1:156
Chance, Thomas H., 4:79
Chancellor, John, 3:357

Chances, Ellen B., 2:685
Chandidās, 2:173, 2:174
Chandler, Alfred D., 3:49
Chandler, David L., 3:806
Chandler, David P., 2:315, 3:490
Chandler, Frank W., 2:524
Chandler, Glen, 3:488
Chandler, James K., 1:307
Chandler, Mary V., 3:806
Chandler, Raymond, 1:604, 1:1209, 1:1226, 1:1227, 1:1230, 1:1233, 1:1234
Chandler, Richard E., 2:522
Chandler, Russell, 4:866
Chandrasekhar, Subrahmanyan, 5:603, 5:676, 5:686
Chaney, Beverley D., 1:39
Chang, Chung-yuan, 4:527, 4:529
Chang, Chun-shu, 2:210
Chang, Hao, 2:252, 4:361
Chang, H. C., 2:192
Chang, K'ang-i Sun, 2:189
Chang, K. C., 3:466
Chang, Luh-Maan, 5:223
Chang, Shi-Kuo, 5:550
Chang Ai-ling, 2:238
Chang Chieh, 2:238
Changeux, Jean-Pierre, 5:339
Chang Heng, 2:195
Chang Hsien-liang, 2:239
Chang Hsin-hsin, 2:240
Chang T'ien-i, 2:240
Channell, David F., 5:27
Channing, Steven A., 3:527
Channing, William E., 1:702
Chantelou, Paul Freart de, 3:770
Chantikian, Kosrof, 2:879
Chao, Kang, 3:466
Chapell, Warren, 1:7
Chaplin, Charlie (Sir Charles Spencer), 1:792, 1:1160, 1:1167, 1:1170, 2:496, 3:833
Chaplin, Gordon, 3:894
Chaplin, J. P., 3:169
Chapman, Abraham, 1:129
Chapman, Alexander, 3:900
Chapman, Charles E., 3:386
Chapman, D., 3:292
Chapman, George, 1:175, 1:186, 2:359, 2:360
Chapman, John W., 3:164
Chapman, Kenneth C., 2:670
Chapman, R. W., 1:31, 1:276
Chapman, Robert D., 5:592
Chapman, Robert L., 1:92, 1:93
Chapman, Sara S., 1:765
Chapman, William, 5:635

Chappell, Vere, 4:27, 4:160, 4:170, 5:41, 5:502
Chapple, J.A.V., 1:356
Char, René, 2:446, 2:465
Charents, Eghishe, 2:78
Charig, Alan, 5:638
Charkrabarti, Alok K., 5:184
Charles, Amy, 1:181
Charles, David, 4:67
Charles, Ray, 3:689
Charlesworth, James H., 4:810
Charlesworth, Max, 4:461
Charlton, D. G., 4:28
Charnay, J. P., 3:442
Charney, Maurice, 1:212, 1:213, 1:530
Charron, Jean D., 4:125
Charron, Pierre, 4:125
Charters, Ann, 1:999
Charters, Samuel, 1:912
Chartier, Roger, 3:337
Chartrand, Robert L., 5:125
Charvat, William, 1:38, 1:650
Chase, Allan, 5:389
Chase, Alston, 5:821
Chase, Gilbert, 3:659, 3:671
Chase, Harold W., 3:141
Chase, Richard, 1:657, 1:722, 3:860
Chaska, Norma L., 5:337
Chastain, Kenneth, 3:254
Chateaubriand, François René, Vicomte de, 2:466
Chatellier, Louis, 4:728, 4:736
Chatfield, Charles, 3:505
Chatterjee, Margaret, 4:352, 4:553
Chatterjee, Upamanyu, 2:177
Chatterton, Thomas, 1:284, 1:285
Chattopadhyaya, D. P., 4:353
Chau, Phan Boi, 2:338
Chaucer, Geoffrey, 1:140, 1:149, 1:196, 2:341, 2:359, 2:387, 2:389, 2:394, 2:396, 2:409, 2:426, 3:877, 4:469
Chaudhuri, K. N., 3:483
Chaudhuri, Nirad C., 4:503
Chavel, Charles B., 4:669
Chaves, Jonathan, 2:214
Chavira, Juan A., 5:320
Chayanov, Alexander, 5:265
Chayanov, A. V., 3:16
Chazan, Robert, 4:622, 4:623, 4:669
Check, William A., 5:387
Checkland, Sydney, 3:355
Cheek, Dennis W., 5:151
Cheetham, Mark A., 1:1134
Cheever, John, 1:839, 1:909, 1:960

Cheever, Susan, 1:961
Chekhov, Anton, 1:424,
   1:1102, 1:1113, 1:1114,
   2:265, 2:705, **2:707**, 2:724,
   2:769, 4:335
Chelkowski, Peter J., 2:82
Chen, Ching-chih, 5:5, 5:544
Chen, Franklin S. C., 2:256
Chen, Pearl Hsia, 2:256
Chen, Yu-shih, 2:258
Cheney, Anne, 1:1092
Cheney, C. R., 3:8
Cheney, Frances N., 1:80
Cheney, O. H., 1:49
Cheng, Francois, 2:189
Cheng, Siok-hwa, 3:489
Cheng, Vincent, 1:505
Chenu, M. D., 4:101, 4:696
Cheny, David, 4:24
Cheraskin, Emanuel, 5:345
Cheremisinoff, Paul N., 5:222
Cherlin, Andrew, 3:206
Cherniss, Harold F., 4:67,
   4:79
Chernow, Ron, 3:55
Chernyshevsky, Nikolai,
   2:710, 2:727
Cherry, Colin, 5:305, 5:571
Cherry, Conrad, 1:627, 1:637,
   4:767
Cherry, John, 3:767
Cherry, Robert, 3:66
Chertkov, Vladimir G., 2:766
Chertok, Leon, 5:417
Cheselka, Paul, 2:857
Chesler, Evan R., 3:348
Chesnut, Glenn F., 4:709
Chesnut, Mary Boykin Mil-
   ler, 1:726, 1:738, 3:527
Chesnutt, Charles Wadell,
   1:738
Chesnutt, Helen M., 1:739
Chess, Stella, 5:416
Chessman, G. Wallace, 3:594
Chester, Robert, 3:671
Chesterfield (Philip Dormer
   Stanhope), 4th Earl of,
   1:235, 1:249
Chesterman, Charles W.,
   5:627
Chesterton, G(ilbert)
   K(eith), 1:349, 1:428,
   1:440, 1:442, **1:457**, 2:711
Chet, Llan, 5:222
Cheung, Dominic, 2:235
Cheung, King-Kok, 1:121
Chevigny, Bell Gale, 1:673
Chew, Samuel C., 1:398
Cheyne, William Watson,
   5:409
Chhibber, V. N., 3:500
Chi, Pang-yuan, 2:235
Chi, Wen Shun, 1:97

Chiang, Yang. See Yang
   Chiang
Chiang, Yee, 3:902
Chiang Tzu-lung, 2:242
Chia P'ing-wa, 2:242
Chiapelli, Fredi, 1:631
Chiarenza, Marguerite Mills,
   2:417
Chiari, Joseph, 2:448, 2:468,
   2:487, 4:28, 4:263
Chiat, Marilyn, 4:614
Chickering, Robert B., 1:54
Chicorel, Marietta, 1:124
Chidester, David, 4:867,
   4:893
Chidley, John, 1:31
Chiera, Edward, 2:52
Chih, Ts'ao. See Ts'ao Chih
Chi-ha, Kim, 2:298
Chih-chüan, Ju. See Ju Chih-
   chüan
Chih-mo, Hsü, 2:246
Chih-Yang, Chao, 5:559
Chikamatsu Monzaemon,
   2:271, **2:276**
Chilcote, Paul W, 4:738
Chilcote, Ronald H., 3:416
Child, Francis J(ames),
   3:850, **3:877**
Child, Heather, 1:14
Child, Irvin L., 3:15
Childe, V. Gordon, 4:438
Childe, Vera G., 3:13
Childers, Peter, 3:175, 5:569
Childress, Alice, 1:1071
Childress, James F., 4:2,
   4:718, 4:893, 5:118, 5:119
Childs, Brevard S., 4:795,
   4:827
Childs, David, 3:376
Childs, John, 3:360
Childs, John S., 1:873
Childs, Michael J., 3:363
Chiles, Frances, 2:879
Chilton, Bruce D., 4:602,
   4:608
Chilton, John, 3:668, 3:674,
   3:701
Chin, Richard M., 5:318
Chin-gôn, Hyôn, 2:298
Ching-tzu, Wu. See Wu
   Ching-tzu
Chinnici, Rosemary, 4:892
Chinweizu, 2:107, 2:113
Chirban, John T., 5:417
Chisholm, Roderick M.,
   4:222, 4:261, 4:263, 4:280
   4:395
Chissel, Joan, 3:716
Chittick, Kathryn, 1:349
Chittick, William C., 4:590,
   4:902
Chitty, Derwas J., 4:688

Chiu-ling, Chang, 2:225
Chi-wôn, Kim, 2:298
Chiyo, Uno. See Uno Chiyo
Chmielewski, Wendy, 4:843
Choate, F., 3:864
Choate, Julian E., 1:1219
Chodoff, Paul, 5:118
Chodorow, Nancy Julia,
   1:1140, 1:1152, 2:982
Choi In-hoon (Ch'oe In-
   hun), 2:300
Choksky, Jamsheed K., 4:517,
   4:547
Cholokian, Patricia F., 2:492
Chomsky, Noam, 3:21, 3:142,
   3:203, 3:807, 4:170
Chomsky, William, 2:8
Chông, Ch'ôl, 2:298
Chong, Ken Pin, 5:635
Chông-hui, O., 2:298
Chon-un, Kim, 2:299
Chopin, Frédéric, 2:504
   3:689, 3:701, 3:713, 3:717
Chopin, Kate, 1:711, 1:721,
   1:739, 1:802
Chopp, Rebecca S., 4:749,
   4:896
Chopra, Deepak, 5:319
Chopra, Pran Nath, 3:483,
   3:484
Choquette, Diane, 4:3, 4:854
Chorafas, Dimitris N., 5:296
Chorley, Richard J., 3:118,
   5:633
Chorpenning, Joseph, 4:786
Chothia, Jean, 1:1108
Chou, Chih-p'ing, 2:189
Chou, Min-chih, 2:247, 4:360
Choukri, Mohamed, 2:479
Chow, Tse-tsung, 2:233
Chow, Ven Te, 5:631
Chown, Jeffrey, 3:828
Choy, Dexter, 3:890
Chraibi, Driss, 2:116, 2:118
Chrétien de Troyes, 2:466
Chrisman, Robert, 3:212
Christ, Carol P., 4:650
Christ, Carol T., 1:315
Christ, Karl, 2:380
Christensen, A. M., 3:866
Christensen, Carl C., 4:737
Christensen, Darrel E., 4:28,
   4:263, 4:341, 4:379
Christensen, Larry B., 3:169
Christensen, Michael, 4:776
Christensen, Terry, 3:542
Christeson, R. P., 3:851
Christian, Barbara, 1:924
Christian, Gary D., 5:735
Christian, James L., 5:192
Christian, Rebecca, 5:405
Christian, Reginald F., 2:766

Christian, William A., 4:342, 4:728, 4:898
Christians, Clifford C., 3:803
Christians, Clifford G., 5:70, 5:125, 5:165
Christiansen, Inger, 2:645
Christiansen, Reidar T., 2:662
Christianson, Gale E., 4:184, 5:41, 5:706
Christianson, Jon B., 5:332
Christianson, Paul K., 4:725
Christie, Anthony, 4:522
Christie, C. J., 2:311
Christie, Clive, 2:311
Christie, Dame Agatha, 1:458, 1:604, **1:605,** 1:609
Christie, Ian R., 3:353, 3:361
Christie, John A., 1:702
Christie, J.R.R., 5:61
Christie, Richard, 3:160
Christie, Ronald J., 5:119
Christoffel, Tom, 5:343
Christopher, Joe R., 1:513
Christopher, John B., 3:442
Christophersen, Hans O., 4:179
Christopherson, Merrill G., 2:537
Chrysostom, St. John, 4:707
Chryssides, George D., 4:871
Chu, Ellen W., 5:106, 5:151
Chubak, Sadiq, 2:87
Chubb, John E., 3:254
Chubb, Thomas C., 2:410
Chubin, Daryl E., 5:106, 5:151
Chudakov, A. P., 2:710
Chudoba, F., 2:788
Chukovskaya, Lydia, 2:697, **2:711,** 2:712
Chukovsky, Kornei, 2:703, **2:711,** 2:742
Chün, Hsiao. *See* Hsiao Chün
Chung, Chong-wha, 2:298
Chung, Ling, 2:193
Chung-shu, Ch'ien. *See* Ch'ien Chung-shu
Church, Elihu Dwight, 3:510
Church, Ralph W., 4:201
Church, Thomas W., 5:184
Churchfield, Sara, 5:770
Churchill, Caryl, 1:458
Churchill, Winston Spencer, 1:879, 2:591, 3:365, **3:400,** 4:551, 4:750
Churchland, Patricia Smith, 4:382
Churgin, Jonah R., 3:254
Churgin, Pinchas, 4:609
Chusid, Martin, 3:727
Chuvin, Pierre, 4:449
Chyet, Stanley F., 2:9

Chyzhevskyi, Dmytro, 2:685
Cianci, R., 5:664
Ciardi, John, 1:1195
Cibbarelli, Pamela, 5:545
Cicero (Marcus Tullius Cicero), 2:354, 2:378, **2:384,** 3:310, **3:313,** 3:;317, 4:59, **4:72,** 4:75, 4:150
Ciciarelli, John A., 5:635
Cíger-Hronský, Jozef, 2:833
Ciklamini, Marlene, 2:643
Čingo, Živko, 2:807
Cipolla, Carlo, 3:335
Cipolla, Carlo M., 5:77, 5:382
Cirillo, Dennis P., 5:396
Cirillo, Renato, 3:100
Cirker, Blanche, 1:14, 1:28
Cirker, Hayward, 1:14
Citron, Stephen, 3:709
Cixous, Hélène, 1:1131, 1:1143, **2:467,** 2:895, 2:896
Cizevskij, Dmitrij, 2:685
Clagett, Marshall, 5:39, 5:499
Claghorn, Charles E., 3:654
Claiborne, Robert, 1:95
Clair, Colin, 1:7
Clampitt, Amy, 1:962
Clancy, Michael, 5:552
Clansky, Kenneth B., 5:724
Clapham, John, 3:693, 3:720
Clapp, Genevieve, 3:206
Clapp, Jane, 1:135
Clapperton, Robert H., 1:4
Clare, John, 1:264, 1:267, **1:285,** 1:446
Clarence-Smith, Gervase, 3:423
Claréus, Ingrid, 2:638
Clark, Alisa McGown, 5:769
Clark, Andrew Hill, 3:609, 3:611
Clark, Arthur, 1:927
Clark, Arthur M., 1:798
Clark, Audrey N., 5:621
Clark, Barrett H., 1:1089, 2:4, 2:526
Clark, C.M.H., 3:494
Clark, Carleen, 5:376
Clark, David L., 1:636
Clark, David R., 1:572
Clark, Desmond M., 5:502
Clark, Donald N., 3:481, 4:540
Clark, Edward B., 5:376
Clark, Edwin H., 5:635
Clark, Elizabeth A., 4:678, 4:712
Clark, Ella E., 3:864
Clark, Forrest D., 5:234
Clark, Grahame, 3:13
Clark, J. Desmond, 3:416
Clark, J. G., 4:433
Clark, J. P., 2:133

Clark, Jerome, 4:870
Clark, John Bates, 3:72
Clark, John J., 3:49
Clark, Katerina, 2:685
Clark, Kenneth, 3:208, 3:756, 3:779, 3:789
Clark, Margaret S., 3:177
Clark, Martin, 3:385
Clark, Martin L., 4:59
Clark, Merrian E., 3:891
Clark, Michael, 1:828
Clark, Miles, 3:908
Clark, Neil, 1:518
Clark, Norman, 5:180
Clark, Paul, 3:469
Clark, Priscilla P., 2:446
Clark, Robert, 4:199
Clark, Robert B., 5:631
Clark, Ronald, 4:324
Clark, Ronald W., 3:287, 5:45, 5:47, 5:103, 5:231, 5:252, 5:683, 5:794, 5:797
Clark, S. D., 3:609
Clark, Stephen R., 4:67
Clark, Terry Nicholas, 3:202
Clark, Thurston, 3:908
Clark, Tom, 1:999
Clark, VeVe A., 1:1163
Clark, W.A.V., 3:119
Clark, W. E., 3:18
Clark, William, 3:915, **3:927**
Clark, William B., 1:893
Clark, William George, 1:206
Clarke, Alan D., 5:426
Clarke, Ann M., 5:426
Clarke, Arthur C(harles), 1:611, **1:613,** 1:1252, 5:533, 5:563, **5:600**
Clarke, Austin, 1:416, **1:459,** **2:934**
Clarke, Dorothy, 2:549
Clarke, Gerald, 1:959
Clarke, Graham, 1:910
Clarke, Howard, 2:361
Clarke, J. I., 3:435
Clarke, James W., 3:542
Clarke, John H., 1:921
Clarke, Kenneth, 3:860
Clarke, Mary, 3:732, 3:733, 3:860
Clarke, Peter, 3:87
Clarke, Samuel, 4:158, **4:194,** 4:203, 4:210
Clarkson, Atelia, 3:847
Clarkson, Christopher, 1:22
Clarkson, Leslie A., 3:355
Clarkson, Sarah May, 3:891
Clarkson, Stephen, 3:607, 3:616
Clary, David A., 5:237
Clasen, Claus-Peter, 4:723
Claudel, Paul, 2:468, 2:541
Claus, Hugo, 2:621, **2:623**

Clausen, John A., 3:534
Clausen, Wendell, 2:397
Clausewitz, Karl von, 3:340
Clavelin, Maurice, 4:143
Clavell, James, 2:310
Clay, Diskin, 4:73, 4:75
Clay, Reginald S., 5:33
Clayre, Alasdair, 3:466
Clayton, Gary E., 3:44, 3:45
Clayton, Jan, 3:713
Clayton, John J., 1:947
Clayton, Thomas, 1:213
Cleal, Christopher J., 5:638
Cleary, Beverly, 1:1195
Cleary, J. C., 4:537
Cleary, John, 4:47, 4:67
Cleary, Thomas, 3:467, 4:527,
    4:529, 4:534
Cleary, Thomas R., 1:245
Cleaver, Bill, 1:1195
Cleaver, Dale G., 3:756
Clebsch, William A., 3:326,
    4:726
Clecak, Peter, 3:558
Clegg, Jerry S., 4:79
Clemen, Wolfgang H., 1:216
Clemence, Richard V., 3:105
Clemens, Samuel. See Twain,
    Mark
Clement, Catherine, 1:1131
Clemente, Carmine D., 5:772
Clements, Colleen D., 5:124
Clements, Frank A., 3:454
Clements, Frederic E., 5:819
Clements, Kendrick A.,
    3:531, 3:544
Clements, Patricia, 1:362,
    1:570, 2:990
Clements, Robert J., 2:417,
    2:983
Clements, Ronald E., 4:813
Clements, William M., 3:864
Clendening, Logan, 5:35
Clendenning, John, 4:250
Clendinnen, Inga, 3:627,
    4:457
Clerc, Charles, 1:1035
Clerke, Agnes M., 5:45
Cleugh, James, 2:406
Cleveland, William S., 5:521
Clifford, Anne, 5:547
Clifford, James, 1:1133, 3:12,
    3:22, 4:426
Clifford, James L., 1:928
Clifford, John, 1:808
Clifford, Martin, 5:229
Clifford, Terry, 4:890
Clifton, Chas S., 4:865
Clifton, Merritt, 1:46
Cline, Barbara L., 5:661
**Cline, Howard F(rancis),
    3:644,** 3:649
Clingham, Greg, 1:234

Clinton, Catherine, 1:647,
    3:523, 3:527, 3:554
Clissold, Stephen, 2:550,
    4:786
Clive, Geoffrey, 4:247
Clive, John, 1:273, 1:374
Clodd, Edward, 5:799
Clogg, Richard, 3:393
Cloonan, Michèle Valerie,
    1:22
Cloonan, William, 2:512
Clooney, Francis X., 4:872
Close, Frank, 5:662
Clothey, Fred W., 4:503
Cloud, Preston, 5:594, 5:622
Clough, Arthur Hugh, 1:310,
    1:327, **1:345**
Clover, Carol, 2:640
Cloward, Richard A., 3:144,
    3:212, 3:215
Clowes, Edith W., 2:685,
    2:726
Clubb, O. Edmund, 3:466
Clulee, Nicholas H., 4:125
Clurman, Harold, 1:1072,
    1:1076
Clyman, Toby W., 2:710
Co, Francesco Dal, 3:764
Coale, Samuel, 1:961
Coan, Otis W., 1:122
Coates, Donald R., 5:635
Coates, R.F.W., 5:298
Cobb, Carl W., 2:525
Cobb, John B., 4:263, 4:289,
    4:294, 4:379, 4:718, 4:743,
    5:822, 5:196
Cobb, Richard, 3:372
Cobb, William S., 4:79
Cobban, A. B., 4:101
Cobban, Alfred, 2:446
Cobbett, Walter Wilson,
    3:654
Cobbett-Steinberg, Steven,
    3:731
Cobbs, John L., 1:789
Cobden-Sanderson, Thomas
    James, 1:7
Cobe, Patricia, 4:602
Cobo, Bernabe, 4:458
Coburn, Jewell R., 3:854,
    3:857
Coburn, Kathleen, 1:287
Coburn, Robert C., 4:380
Coburn, Thomas B., 4:503
Cocchiara, Giuseppe, 3:854
Cochran, Thomas C., 3:523
Cochran, Wendell, 1:47
Cochrane, Arthur C., 4:761
Cochrane, Charles N., 4:99,
    4:683
Cochrane, Hamilton E.,
    1:235
Cockburn, Alexander, 5:822

Cockburn, Cynthia, 5:187
Cockburn, J. S., 3:355
Cockcroft, James D., 3:631
Cockerell, Douglas, 1:22
Cockerell, Sydney M., 1:22
Cocks, Raymond, 3:35
Cockshut, A. O., 1:87
Cocores, J. A., 5:404
Cocteau, Jean, 2:462, **2:468,**
    2:498, **3:833**
Codd, G. A., 5:783
Codding, George A., Jr.,
    3:803
Code, Lorraine, 4:391
Codrescu, Andrei, 3:895
Cody, John, 1:747
Coe, Michael D., 3:627, 4:455
Coe, Rodney M., 5:348
Coedes, George, 3:902
Coetzee, J(acobus) M.,
    2:157, 2:158, **2:160**
Coffin, Tristram P., 3:848,
    3:864, 3:868
Coffman, Edward M., 3:531
Cogdell, John R., 5:229
Coggins, R. J., 4:618
Cohen, A., 4:888
Cohen, Aaron I., 3:654
Cohen, Abraham, 4:620
Cohen, Amnon, 4:625
Cohen, Anne B., 3:851
Cohen, Arthur Allen, 1:8,
    3:264, 4:646, 4:648, 4:886
Cohen, A. Toni, 5:549
Cohen, Avner, 5:109
Cohen, B. Bernard, 1:676
Cohen, David S., 3:859
Cohen, Donna, 5:391
Cohen, Edmund D., 5:455
Cohen, Edward E., 3:305
Cohen, Elliot E., 4:651
Cohen, G. A., 3:290, 4:242
Cohen, Gerson D., 4:622
Cohen, Hennig, 3:848, 3:870
Cohen, Henry, 5:77
Cohen, Hermann, 4:662,
    4:673
Cohen, I. Bernard, 5:14,
    5:24, 5:41, 5:44, 5:361,
    5:706, 5:763
Cohen, J. M., 1:116
Cohen, James, 3:831
Cohen, Jane R., 1:349
Cohen, Jeremy, 4:623, 4:696
Cohen, Joel E., 5:522, 5:650
Cohen, Joseph, 1:541, 2:8
Cohen, Lenard J., 3:392
Cohen, Leonard, 2:909,
    2:915
Cohen, Linda R., 5:184
Cohen, Marjorie Griffin,
    3:613
Cohen, Mark R., 4:625

Cohen, Marshall, 1:1158, 3:731
Cohen, Martin, 5:589
Cohen, Michael P., 5:836
Cohen, Milton A., 1:825
Cohen, Mindy, 5:348
Cohen, Morris Raphael, 3:275, 3:49, **4:280**, 4:297, 4:313, 5:95
Cohen, Morton N., 1:582
Cohen, Nancy Wainer, 5:357
Cohen, Naomi W., 4:638, 4:657
Cohen, Norman, 3:851, 4:753
Cohen, Paul A., 3:466, 3:498, 4:532
Cohen, Paula Marantz, 1:318
Cohen, R. M., 5:523
Cohen, Ralph, 1:261
Cohen, Raquel E., 5:421
Cohen, Richard A., 4:901
Cohen, Robert S., 5:62, 5:700
Cohen, Ronald, 3:12
Cohen, Selma J., 3:732
Cohen, Shaye J. D., 4:604
Cohen, Stanley, 5:348, **5:790**, 5:804
Cohen, Stanley J., 3:870
Cohen, Steven M., 4:638, 4:651
Cohen, Walter, 2:523
Cohen, Warren, 3:464
Cohen-Mor, Dalya, 2:65
Cohen-Solal, Annie, 2:507, 4:330
Cohen-Stratyner, Barbara Naomi, 3:731
Cohn, Adrian, 1:91
Cohn, Alan M., 1:505
Cohn, Max Arthur, 1:27
Cohn, Norman, 4:698, 4:721
Cohn R., 2:448, 2:487
Cohn, Ruby, 1:1072
Cohn-Sherbok, Don, 4:568
Cohuh, Cahit, 5:630
Coindreau, Maurice Edgar, 1:917
Coiro, Ann B., 1:182
Coit, Margaret L., 3:523
Coke-Enguídanos, Mervin, 2:542
Coker, Jerry, 3:668
Colacurcio, Michael J., 1:676
Colaianne, A. J., 1:154
Colaneri, John, 1:100
Colbert, Edwin H., 5:638
Colbert, Roz, 1:850
Colburn, David R., 3:548
Colby, K. M., 5:570
Colby, Robert A., 1:404
Colby, Vineta, 2:3
Colchester, Chloe, 3:767
Coldewey, John C., 1:157

Coldoff, Harry, 2:29
Cole, B. C., 5:561
Cole, Bill, 3:690, 3:691
Cole, Douglas, 1:187
Cole, Francis J., 5:33
Cole, Franklyn W., 5:633
Cole, G.D.H., 1:342, 3:140
Cole, John Y., 1:38, 1:49
Cole, Jonathan R., 3:213
Cole, Juan R., 4:861
Cole, Leonard A., 5:180
Cole, Lesley, 1:465
Cole, Margaret I., 3:113
Cole, Michael, 3:171
Cole, Robert E., 3:476
Cole, Stephen, 3:213
Cole, Thomas R., 3:558
Cole, Toby, 1:1072
Cole, Wayne S., 3:534
Colecchia, Francesca, 2:848
Coleman, Alexander, 2:559
Coleman, Arthur, 1:427
Coleman, Arthur P., 2:822
Coleman, D. C., 3:45
Coleman, Francis, 4:185
Coleman, James S(amuel), 3:204, 3:209, **3:223**, 3:234, 3:249
Coleman, Kenneth M., 3:631
Coleman, Marion M., 2:811
Coleman, Richard M., 5:340
Coleman, William, 5:45
Colen, B. D., 5:338, 5:375
Coleridge, Samuel Taylor, 1:208, 1:236, 1:237, 1:264, 1:266, 1:271, 1:273, 1:277, 1:281, 1:284, **1:286**, 1:290, 1:292, 1:295, 1:297, 1:304, 1:305, 1:307, 1:309, 1:313, 1:386, 1:454, 1:598, 1:601, 1:653, 1:779, 1:940
Coles, Robert, 1:1029, 2:516, 3:182, 3:249, 4:765, 4:788, 5:416, 5:421, 5:442
Colette (Sidonie-Gabrielle), 2:469
Coletti, Theresa, 2:420
Colgan, Michael, 5:345
Colie, Rosalie L., 1:165, 1:214, 4:168
Collaer, Paul, 3:666
Collar, N. J., 5:769
Collcutt, Martin, 3:474
Collecott, Diana, 1:827
Colledge, Edmund, 2:621
Collett, Camilla, 2:662
Colley, Ann C., 1:401
Colley, Linda, 3:361
Collie, Michael, 1:359, 1:379, 3:913
Collier, Basil, 3:278, 3:476
Collier, Bruce, 5:575
Collier, C. G., 5:633

Collier, David, 3:631
Collier, Eugenia W., 1:130
Collier, Helen V., 5:417
Collier, J. G., 5:287
Collier, James Lincoln, 3:674
Collier, Jane F., 3:19, 3:24
Collier, Peter, 1:1133
Collier, Richard, 4:740
Collier, Ruth Berins, 3:631
Collier, Simon, 3:624, 3:633
Collingridge, David, 5:212
Collings, Michael R., 1:613
Collingwood, Robin George, 3:284, **4:281**
Collini, Stefan, 1:328
Collins, Ardis B., 4:141
Collins, Arthur S., 1:273
Collins, David R., 1:589
Collins, Harry M., 5:9, 5:66, 5:74, 5:151
Collins, James D., 4:160, 4:187, 4:239
Collins, John, 1:35, 1:35
Collins, Larry, 4:642
Collins, Michael, 5:596
Collins, N. Mark, 3:415
Collins, Patricia Hill, 1:1131
Collins, Philip Arthur William, 1:349, 1:404
Collins, R. O., 3:418, 3:419
Collins, Randall, 3:200, 3:204
Collins, Richard H., 3:595
Collins, Robert G., 1:961
Collins, Roger, 3:386
Collins, Steven, 4:887
Collins, Wilkie, 1:310, 1:317, 1:321, **1:345**
Collins, William, 1:227, **1:236**
Collins, William P., 4:861
Collinson, Diane, 4:13, 4:388
Collinson, Patrick, 4:733
Collison, Patrick, 3:334
Collison, Robert L., 1:31
Collison-Morley, Lacy, 2:407
Colloms, Brenda, 1:369
Collon, Dominique, 4:544
Colman, Bruce, 5:823
Colman, Steven M., 5:627
Colodny, Robert G., 5:62, 5:79
Colomb, Gregory G., 1:227
Colombotos, John, 5:336
Colomy, Paul, 3:215
Colon, Fernando, 3:916
Colquhoun, Daryl, 1:582
Colson, F. H., 4:810
Colton, Joel, 3:274, 3:327
Coltrane, John, 3:690, 3:691
Colum, Padraic, 1:460

Columbus, Christopher,
3:335, 3:384, 3:588, 3:696,
3:915, 3:934, 3:941, 5:596,
5:616
**Columella, Lucias Junius
Moderatus,** 5:265, **5:271**
Colville, Derek, 1:315
Comaroff, Jean, 4:467
Comaroff, John L., 4:467
Comber, Leon, 2:325
Combs, James E., 3:808
Combs, Josiah H., 3:860
Comer, James P., 3:249
Comerchero, Victor, 1:897
Commager, Henry Steele,
2:386, 3:249, 3:511, 3:514,
3:527, **3:572,** 3:576
Commins, Dorothy, 1:40
Commoner, Barry, 5:822
Commons, John Rogers,
3:54, 3:60, **3:73**
Compaine, Benjamin, 3:203
Comparato, Frank F., 1:8
Compton, Arthur H(olly),
5:678, 5:684
Compton, Carol J., 2:322
Compton, Linda F., 2:57,
2:525
Compton, Robert R., 5:636
**Compton-Burnett, Dame
Ivy, 1:461,** 1:474
Comstock, George, 3:811
Comte, Auguste, 1:372,
2:810, 3:198, **3:223,** 4:159,
4:222
Conacher, D. J., 2:356
Conacher, J. B., 3:363
Conant, James B., 5:809
Conant, Roger, 2:771
Conati, Marcello, 3:727
Condell, Henry, 1:203
Conder, John J., 1:804
**Condillac, Étienne Bonnot
de,** 4:157, **4:194**
Condivi, Ascanio, 3:782
Condon, Ann Gorman, 3:613
Condon, Eddie, 3:668
Condon, G. A., 1:95
Condor, John, 3:563
Cone, Carl B., 3:152
Cone, James H., 4:748,
4:749, **4:762,** 4:772, 4:896
Confucius, 4:360, 4:363
Congdon, Kirby, 1:123
Congdon, Peter, 3:125
Congdon, R. J., 5:213
Conger, Syndy M., 1:602
Congrat-Butlar, Stefan, 1:47
Congreve, William, 1:228,
1:236, 1:244, 1:254, 2:385
Conklin, Paul, 3:534, 3:537,
3:547
Conlon, D. J., 1:458

Conn, Peter, 1:650
Connell, Desmond, 4:182
Connelly, Owen, 3:339
Connely, Willard, 1:243,
1:263
Conners, C. Keith, 5:416
Connery, Donald S., 3:898
Conniff, Michael L., 3:639
Connolly, Joseph, 1:76
Connolly, Julian K., 2:707
Connolly, L. W., 2:904
Connolly, P., 3:308
Connolly, S. J., 3:370
Connolly, Thomas E., 1:836
Connor, Billie M., 1:124
Connor, Jack, 5:817
Connor, Steven, 1:440
Connor, W. Robert, 3:323,
4:448
Connors, Martin, 5:546
Conolly, Leonard W., 1:271
Conot, Robert E., 3:344,
5:252
Conovan, M., 3:282
Conquest, Robert, 2:746,
3:396
Conrad, Barnaby, 1:118
Conrad, Bryce, 1:900
Conrad, David R., 5:172
Conrad, Geoffrey W., 4:457
Conrad, Joseph, 1:412,
1:419, 1:423, 1:440, **1:462,**
1:474, 1:475, 1:741, 1:969,
1:1054, 2:310, 3:459, 4:321
Conrad, Lawrence, 3:442
Conrad, Peter, 3:670
Conradi, Peter J., 1:524
Conroy, Hilary, 3:464, 3:480
Conscience, Hendrik, 2:620
Considine, Douglas M., 5:2,
5:616, 5:724
Considine, Glenn D., 5:724
Consigliere Pedroso, Zophi-
mo, 2:557
Console, William A., 5:424
Consolmagno, Guy, 5:591
Constable, John, 3:769,
3:773, 3:793
Constable, Pamela, 3:634
Constanza, Angelo, 2:138
Constas, Dimitre, 3:452
Contento, William G., 1:612
Contopoulous, G., 5:654
Contosta, David R., 3:563
Conway, Anne, 4:166
Conway, D., 3:290
Conway, H. McKinley, 5:633
Conway, Joan, 4:593
Conway, Moncure D., 1:642
Conwell, Russell, 5:340
Conze, Edward, 4:512, 4:897
Conzelmann, Hans, 4:825,
4:827

Coogan, Michael D., 4:445,
4:818
Cook, Albert, 1:417, 2:360
Cook, Albert M., 5:370
Cook, Albert S., 1:248
Cook, Ann Jennalie, 1:217
Cook, Blanche Wiesen,
3:534, 3:537
Cook, Bruce, 1:912
Cook, Captain James, 3:917
Cook, Christopher, 3:7,
3:272, 3:326, 3:353, 3:354,
3:363, 3:365, 3:367
Cook, Cornelia, 1:457
Cook, Curtis R., 5:538
Cook, Edward Tyas, 5:362
Cook, Eleanor, 1:977
Cook, G. Ramsay, 3:617
Cook, George W., 1:655
Cook, Harold E., 3:851
Cook, Haruko Taya, 3:477
Cook, J. M., 3:300
Cook, James H., 3:895
Cook, John A., 2:523
Cook, Judith, 1:425
Cook, L. M., 5:770
Cook, M. A., 3:435
Cook, Mercer, 2:107
Cook, Michael, 4:512, 4:588
Cook, Miriam, 2:65
Cook, Nicholas, 3:659
Cook, Pam, 1:1158
Cook, Ramsay, 3:605, 3:622
Cook, Sylvia J., 1:819
Cook, Theodore F., 3:477
Cook, William R., 4:710
Cooke, Alistair, 3:513
Cooke, Deryck, 3:705
Cooke, Jacob E., 3:541
Cooke, John E., 2:460
Cooke, Michael G., 1:282
Cooke, Raymond, 2:732
Cooke, Virginia, 1:544
Cookson, J. E., 3:361
Cookson, William, 1:873
Cooley, Charles H(orton),
3:224, 3:232
Coomaraswamy, Ananda K.,
3:759, 4:503
Coombes, H., 1:558
Coombs, Jan, 5:376
Coombs, Jim, 5:732, 5:759
Coombs, Philip H., 3:249
Coon, Dennis, 5:413
Cooney, Barbara, 1:1194
Coontz, Stephanie, 3:206
Cooper, Barry, 3:678, 3:872,
4:311, 4:400
Cooper, Chester L., 5:180
Cooper, David S., 5:382
Cooper, Dennis, 1:1185
Cooper, Doug, 5:552
Cooper, Helen, 1:150

Cooper, Henry R., 2:836
Cooper, Henry S. F., Jr., 5:596, 5:628
Cooper, James Fenimore, 1:649, 1:656, **1:662,** 1:674, 1:695, 1:789, 1:1192, 1:1209, 1:1211, 1:1244
Cooper, Jane R., 1:1037
Cooper, John M., 3:531, 3:595, 4:67
Cooper, Joshua, 2:692
Cooper, Kenneth H., 5:325
Cooper, Lane, 2:349, 4:67
Cooper, Pamela, 1:478
Cooper, Peter L., 1:1035
Cooper, Robert M., 1:176
Cooper, S. E., 3:278
Cooper, T. G., 1:1072
Cooper, Wayne F., 1:857
Cooper, William J., Jr., 3:513, 3:527
Cooperman, Bernard, 4:629
Cooperman, Jehiel B., 2:33
Cooperman, Sara H., 2:33
Coote, Stephen, 1:1183
Cooter, Roger, 5:46
Coover, Robert, 1:535, **1:962,** 1:984
Cope, Zachary, 5:363
Copeland, Donna R., 5:416
Copeland, Ian, 3:500
Copeland, Jack, 4:382
Copeland, Rebecca L., 2:295
Copeland, Roger, 3:731
Copenhaver, Brian P., 4:125
Copernicus, Nicolaus, 4:135, 4:406, 5:40, 5:477, 5:586, 5:600, **5:601,** 5:687
Copland, Aaron, 3:690, 3:740
Copleston, Frederick Charles, 4:2, **4:38,** 4:94, 4:118, 4:125, 4:160, 4:247, 4:256, 4:263, 4:574, 4:676, 4:736
Copley, A., 4:553
Copp, Newton H., 5:226
Copp, Terry, 3:614
Copplestone, Trewin, 3:761
Coppola, Eleanor, 3:828
Copson, E. T., 5:695
Coquery-Vidrovitch, Catherine, 3:415
Corballis, Richard, 1:201, 2:978
Corbeil, Jean-Claude, 1:98, 1:102
Corbet, G. B., 5:759
Corbett, Mary Jean, 1:325
Corbin, Henry, 4:16, 4:582
Corbin, Richard, 1:1076
Corbitt, Robert A., 5:816
Corcoran, Neil, 1:495

Cordell, Helen, 2:311, 2:322
Cordell, Richard Albert, 1:367
Cordero, Albert, 5:67
Corea, Gena, 5:343, 5:357, 5:387
Corey, Elias James, 5:741
Corke, Bettina, 3:624
Corless, Inge, 5:387
Corlett, J. Angelo, 4:316
Cormack, Malcolm, 3:773, 3:775
Cormier, Ramona, 4:6
Cormier, Robert, 1:1193, 1:1195
Corn, Charles, 3:902
Corn, Joseph J., 3:547, 5:47, 5:231
Corneille, Pierre, 2:391, 2:414, **2:470,** 2:498, 2:537
Cornelison, Pam, 3:508
Cornell, James, 5:596
Cornell, Luis L., 1:372
Cornford, Francis M., 4:46, 4:50, 4:79
Cornman, James W., 4:20
Corns, Thomas N., 1:231
Cornwell, Patricia, 4:768
Cornwell, R. D., 3:274
Corpuz, Onofre D., 3:492
Corr, Charles A., 5:378
Corr, Donna M., 5:378
Corré, Alan D., 5:552
Corrigan, John, 4:738, 4:751
Corrigan, Robert W., 1:1079, 1:1104
Corrigan, Timothy, 3:828
Corrington, Gail Peterson, 4:451
Corris, Peter, 3:495
Corry, James M., 5:331
Corse, Taylor, 1:241
Corsini, Raymond J., 3:169, 5:413, 5:416, 5:420
Corso, Gregory, 1:963, 1:1051
Corson, J. C., 1:299
Corstius, Jan Brandt, 2:983
Cort, David, 3:816
Cortada, James W., 3:547, 5:27, 5:539
Cortázar, Julio, 2:843, 2:844, **2:861,** 2:885
Cortazzi, Hugh, 3:474
Cortés, Hernán, 3:628
Corti, Walter R., 4:309
Cortínez, Carlos, 2:857
Corwin, Charles, 1:100
Cory, Donald W., 3:551
Cose, Ellis, 3:806
Coser, Lewis A., 1:49, 3:200, 3:202, 3:203, 3:204, 3:215, 3:234

Ćosić, Dobrica, 2:827, **2:829**
Cosío Villegas, Daniel, 3:644
Cosman, Carol, 2:511
Costa, Betty, 5:544
Costa, Horacio de la, 2:333
Costa, Richard Hauer, 1:564
Costello, Donald P., 3:837
Costello, Frank B., 4:125
Costello, John, 3:534
Costello, V.F., 3:435
Costlow, Jane T., 2:770
Cotkin, George, 1:769, 4:237
Cotsell, Michael, 1:539
Cott, Jonathan, 1:578, 3:721, 3:908
Cott, Nancy F., 3:554, 3:566
Cotterell, Arthur, 1:133
Cotterill, Rodney, 5:213, 5:670
Cottingham, John, 4:170
Cottingham, W. M., 5:658
Cottom, Daniel, 1:270, 1:354, 1:622
Cotton, John, 1:1194
Cottrell, Jane E., 2:430
Cottrell, Leonard, 2:344
Cottrell, Philip L., 1:88
Cottrell, Robert D., 2:492
Couch, Leon W., 5:298
Coughlan, Michael J., 4:894
Coughlan, Neil, 4:225
Coughlin, Vince, 5:301
Couliano, Ioan P., 4:125
Coulson, Charles, 5:734
Coulson, Jessie, 1:102
Coulson, Noel J., 4:578
Coulton, Barbara, 1:518
Coulton, G. G., 4:96
Coultrap-McQuin, Susan, 1:650, 1:713, 1:722
Couniham, Martin, 5:636
Counter, S. Allen, 3:906, 3:933
Countryman, Edward, 3:520
Couper, Alastair D., 5:616
Coupland, Reginald, 3:422
Courant, Richard, 5:480
Courlander, Harold, 3:866
Cournand, Andre F., 5:312
Coursen, H. R., 1:217
Court, John, 4:807
Court, Kathleen, 4:807
Court, T. H., 5:33
Courtenay, William J., 4:103
Courthion, Pierre, 3:780
Courtice, Katie, 5:393
Courtivron, Isabelle de, 1:926, 2:486
Courtney, E., 2:387
Courtney, Winifred, 1:296
Courtright, Paul B., 4:503
Courtwright, David T., 5:403
Courvoisier, Jacques, 4:791

Couser, G. Thomas, 1:727, 1:927
Cousin, Geraldine, 1:459
Cousins, Ewert, 4:888
Cousins, Paul M., 1:755
Cousteau, Jacques-Yves, 3:889, 3:908, 3:918, 5:642
Cousteau, Jean Michel, 3:919
Coustillas, Pierre, 1:359, 1:483
Coutinho, Alfranio, 2:890
Couvalis, George, 4:399
Couzens, Tim, 2:158
Covatta, Anthony, 1:190
Covell, Alan C., 4:539
Covell, Mara B., 5:376
Covert, Nadine, 3:756
Covington, Michael, 5:539, 5:591
Cowan, Henry J., 4:774, 5:245
Cowan, I. B., 4:735
Cowan, Louise, 1:798, 1:912
Cowan, Lyn, 5:456
Cowan, Ruth Schwartz, 5:187
Coward, Berry, 3:360
Coward, Harold G., 4:398, 4:497, 4:503, 4:521, 4:533, 4:894, 4:898
Coward, Sir Noel (Pierce), 1:424, 1:464
Cowart, David, 1:979, 1:1035
Cowden, Robert H., 3:672
Cowdrey, H. E., 4:692
Cowell, Frank R., 3:240
Cowell, Henry, 3:702
Cowell, Pattie, 1:635
Cowell, Sidney, 3:702
Cowen, Anne, 4:635
Cowen, Roger, 4:635
Cowgill, George L., 4:546
Cowie, Alexander, 1:722
Cowie, Peter, 3:825, 3:828, 3:831
Cowley, Malcolm, 1:794, 1:808, 1:822, 1:835, 1:880, 1:896, 1:995
Cowling, Maurice, 3:365
Cowper, William, 1:237, 1:580, 2:360
Cox, C. Barry, 3:126, 5:759, 5:763, 5:819
Cox, David, 5:456
Cox, Donald D., 5:767
Cox, Gary, 2:715, 4:388
Cox, George W., 3:848
Cox, Harvey, 4:857
Cox, J. Randolph, 1:564
Cox, James M., 1:659, 1:727
Cox, Jeffrey N., 1:228, 1:271, 1:272
Cox, John, 1:208
Cox, Kevin R., 3:123

Cox, LaWanda, 3:527
Cox, Michael, 5:726
Coxeter, H. S., 5:486
Coxford, Arthur F., 5:486
Coyle, Wallace, 3:520
Coyle, William, 1:118
Coyne, George V., 5:198
Coyne, Joseph Stirling, 1:324, 1:347, 1:366
Coyne, S. J., 5:198
Cozzens, James Gould, 1:964
Cozzens, Susan E., 5:151
Crabb, Cecil V., Jr., 3:544
Crabbe, George, 1:288
Crabbe, George, Jr., 1:289
Crabtree, Adam, 4:847
Craft, Robert, 3:723, 3:723
Cragg, Gerald R., 4:738
Cragg, Kenneth, 4:373, 4:568, 4:574, 4:587
Craib, Ian, 3:227
Craig, Albert, 2:186, 3:474, 4:358
Craig, Austin, 2:333
Craig, E. Quita, 1:1072
Craig, George D., 2:848
Craig, Gerald, 3:613
Craig, Gordon A., 2:565, 3:340, 3:376
Craig, Gordon Y., 5:622
Craig, Jenny, 5:325
Craig, John Clark, 5:552
Craig, Maurice, 1:22
Craig, Patricia, 1:422, 1:448, 1:605
Craig, Paul P., 5:239
Craig, Robert D., 3:495
Craig, Warren, 3:654
Craig, William, 3:278
Craig, William L., 4:574
Craighead, Frank C., Jr., 5:820
Craighead, John J., 5:820
Craigie, E. Horne, 5:811
Craik, George L., 4:165
Craik, T. W., 1:169, 1:170
Crampton, R. J., 3:392
Cranbrook, Earl of, 5:769
Crandall, N., 1:336
Crandall, Rick, 5:107
Crandall, Robert W., 5:184
Crane, Diana, 3:213
Crane, (Harold) Hart, 1:806, 1:823, 1:1186, 2:499
Crane, Milton, 1:208, 1:805
Crane, Stephen, 1:711, 1:721, 1:739, 1:741, 1:757, 1:776, 1:960, 1:1193
Crane, W.J.E., 1:22
Crane, Walter, 1:578, 1:580, 1:583
Cranfill, Thomas M., 2:848

Crankshaw, Edward, 3:375
Cranmer, Thomas, 4:725, 4:726, 4:763
Cranor, Carl F., 5:74
Cranston, Maurice, 3:159, 3:337, 4:179, 4:213
Cranston, S. L., 4:887
Cranston, Sylvia, 4:853, 4:874
Cranton, Elmer M., 5:347, 5:373
Cranz, Galen, 3:549
Crapo, Lawrence, 5:772
Crashaw, Richard, 1:175, 1:643
Cravalho, Ernest G., 5:324
Craven, Avery O., 3:527
Craven, Roy C., 3:759
Craven, Wesley F., 3:534
Cravens, Hamilton, 5:48
Crawford, C., 3:170
Crawford, Donald, 4:206
Crawford, F. Marion, 1:1244
Crawford, Harriet, 3:300
Crawford, J., 2:524
Crawford, James, 3:249
Crawford, M., 3:178, 5:552
Crawford, Michael, 3:299
Crawford, Phyllis, 1:125
Crawford, S. Cromwell, 4:355
Crawford, Thomas, 1:280
Crawford, Walter B., 1:287
Crawley, J. Winston, 5:552
Creager, Joan G., 5:340
Creangă, Ion, 2:823
Crease, Robert P., 5:651, 5:691, 5:713
Creasey, William A., 5:371
Creasy, Robert K., 5:358
Creedman, Theodore S., 3:635
Creegan, Charles L., 4:345
Creel, Herrlee G., 4:358, 4:522
Creeley, Robert, 1:911, 1:965, 1:969, 1:1026
Creighton, Donald, 3:604, 3:617, 3:622
Creighton, Joanne V., 1:1023
Cremin, Lawrence A., 3:254, 3:558
Crenshaw, James L., 4:823, 4:838
Cressy, David, 3:358
Crew, Louie, 1:1128
Crew, P. Mack, 4:737
Crewe, Jonathan V., 1:195
Crews, Frederick C., 1:118, 1:130, 1:588, 1:677
Cribb, Robert, 3:491
Crichton, Michael, 5:537
Crick, Bernard, 3:138

Crick, Francis Harry Compton, 5:9, 5:777, 5:784, **5:790,** 5:812, 5:813
Crickmay, Anthony, 3:734
Crim, Keith R., 4:3, 4:818
Crimmins, James, 4:190
Crimp, Douglas, 1:1181
Cringely, Robert X., 5:542
Cripps, Thomas, 1:1157
Crisp, Clement, 3:733, 3:842
Crispell, Kenneth, 3:542
Crist, Judith, 3:828
Crist, Timothy J., 1:68
Critchfield, Howard J., 5:633
Critchfield, Margot A., 5:552
Critchley, Macdonald, 5:391
Critchley, Simon, 4:901
Crits-Cristoph, P., 5:417
Crnjanski, Miloš, 2:827
Croce, Arlene, 3:732
Croce, Benedetto, 2:398, **2:414,** 2:417, 2:423, 2:439, **3:283,** 3:401, 4:271, 4:281
Crocker, Chester A., 3:423
Crocker, Lester G., 4:160
Crocker, Richard L., 3:659
Crocombe, Ron, 3:495
Crofton, Ian, 3:654
Crombie, A. C., 4:97
Crombie, I. M., 4:79
Crompton, Don, 1:484
Crompton, Rosemary, 3:24, 3:207
Cromwell, Florence S., 5:338
Crone, Hugh, 5:736
Croner, Helga, 4:898
Cronin, Anthony, 1:526
Cronin, Audrey K., 3:375
Cronin, Gloria L., 1:1003
Cronin, James W(ilson), **5:678,** 5:686
Cronin, Richard, 1:303
Cronk, George, 4:309
Cronkite, Walter, 3:813
Cronon, E. David, 3:510
Cronon, William, 3:531, 3:549, 5:822
Cronyn, George W., 1:719
Crook, Eugene J., 2:984
Crook, J. A., 3:305
Crosby, Alfred W., 3:628, 5:820
Crosland, Andrew T., 1:742
Crosland, Maurice, 5:747
Crosman, Inge, 1:927
Cross, A. G., 2:730
Cross, Claire, 3:358, 4:726
Cross, Donna Woolfolk, 3:811
Cross, Frank L., 4:675, 4:716
Cross, Frank M., 4:810
Cross, Gilbert B., 1:322, 3:847

Cross, Hardy, 5:213
Cross, W. L., 1:420
Cross, Whitney R., 3:523, 4:841
Cross, Wilbur, 5:402
Crossley, Pamela Kyle, 3:467
Crossley-Holland, Kevin, 1:143
Crossman, R. S., 3:163
Crosson, Frederick J., 5:74
Crouch, Archie R., 4:532
Crouch, Martin, 2:685
Crouch, Tom D., 5:46
Crouse, Timothy, 3:806
Crow, Charles L., 4:841
Crow, Jeffrey J., 3:520
Crow, John A., 2:522, 2:526, 3:625
Crowcroft, Peter, 5:820
Crowder, Christopher, 4:694
Crowder, Michael, 3:415, 3:416, 3:419
Crowder, Richard, 1:878
Crowe, Joseph A., 3:759, 3:788
Crowe, Michael J., 5:598
Crowley, Frank, 3:494
Crowley, J. Donald, 1:677, 1:784
Crowley, James B., 3:477
Crowley, John W., 1:759, 1:812
Crownfield, David, 4:892
Crowther, J. G., 5:716
Croydon, Bent, 4:869
Crozier, Brian, 3:372
Crozier, Michael J., 5:636
Cru, R. Loyalty, 4:196
Cruickshank, John, 2:446, 2:464
Cruikshank, Margaret, 1:1128, 1:1183
Crump, G. B., 1:1018
Crump, J. I., 2:189
Crump, Rebecca W., 1:390
Crunden, Robert M., 3:531
Crunican, Paul, 3:614
Cruttwell, Patrick, 1:166
Cruttwell, Robert W., 2:397
Cruz, Sor Juana Inés de la, 2:844, **2:862**
Cuddihy, John Murray, 3:348
Cuddon, J. A., 1:132
Cudjoe, Selwyn R., 2:930, 2:939
Cudworth, Ralph, 4:167, 4:178
Cugno, Alain, 2:543
Cukier, Daniel, 5:371
Cullen, Countee, 1:797, **1:824,** 1:848
Cullen, J., 5:767
Cullen, Louis M., 3:369

Cullen, Patrick, 1:189
Culler, Arthur D., 1:401
Culler, Jonathan, 1:924, 1:1131, **1:1140,** 2:446, 2:455, 2:476
Culley, Margo, 1:727, 1:728, 1:1128
Cullingford, Elizabeth, 1:572
Cullmann, Oscar, 4:825, **4:831**
Culver, Charles M., 5:77
Culver, John H., 3:145
Culver, Roger, 5:587
Culyer, A. J., 3:57, 5:382
Culyer, A. K., 5:324
Cumano, Ellen, 3:828
Cumming, W. P., 1:631, 3:895
Cummings, Charles, 4:888
Cummings, E(dward) E(stlin), 1:824, 2:437, 2:646
Cummings, Mark D., 4:513, 4:519, 4:522, 4:530, 4:534, 4:537, 4:542, 4:543
Cummings, Michael R., 5:778
Cummings, Michael S., 3:217
Cummings, Paul, 3:761
Cummings, Stephen, 5:338
Cummins, Robert E., 5:74
Cumont, Franz, 4:450, 4:451
Cump, Andy, 5:815
Cuneo, Michael W., 4:425
Cunha, Burke A., 5:389
Cunha, Dorothy G., 1:22
Cunha, Euclydes da, 2:889, **2:894,** 2:898
Cunha, George M., 1:22
Cunliffe, Christopher, 4:194
Cunliffe, Marcus, 1:650, 1:713, 3:514
Cunliffe, Richard J., 2:361
Cunningham, Agnes, 4:683, 4:688
Cunningham, Gustavus W., 4:263
Cunningham, Hugh, 3:362
Cunningham, Isabel Shipley, 5:767
Cunningham, Lawrence, 4:710, 4:891
Cunningham, Merce, 3:739, 3:752
Cunningham, Noble E., Jr., 3:520
Cunningham, Patricia, 3:872
Cunningham, Valentine, 1:318
Cunningham, William P., 5:616
Cunningham-Burns, Kathleen M., 5:351
Curie, Eve, 5:679

Curie, Marie Sklodowska,
5:679
Curley, Dorothy N., 1:134
Curley, E. M., 4:56, 4:170
Curnow, Allen, 2:973
Curran, Charles, 4:743
Curran, Douglas, 4:870
Curran, Stuart, 1:268, 1:303
Current, Richard N(elson),
3:508, 3:513, 3:527, **3:573**
Current-Garcia, Eugene,
1:657, 1:725, 1:757, 1:921
Currie, Barton, 1:31
Curry, Jane L., 3:806
Curry, Kenneth, 1:305
Curry, Leonard P., 3:523
Curry, Melvin D., 4:863
Curry, Ralph, 2:918
Curry, Richard O., 3:552
Curry, Thomas J., 3:139
Curti, Merle, 3:558
Curtin, Jeremiah, 3:854
Curtin, Philip de Armond,
3:416, 3:417, 3:420, **3:425**
Curtis, Anthony, 1:520
Curtis, Anthony R., 5:6
Curtis, Charles P., 5:707
Curtis, Howard, 5:544
Curtis, J. A., 2:706
Curtis, Joy, 5:118
Curtis, L. Perry, Jr., 3:363
Curtis, Michael, 3:139, 3:435,
4:568
Curtis, Richard, 1:47
Curtis, Tony, 1:495
Curtis, William J. R., 3:762
Curwen, Harold, 1:28
Curwin, Henry, 1:36
Cushing, Frank H., 3:864
Cushing, Harvey W., 5:54,
5:364, 5:365
Cushing, James, 5:67
Cushing, William, 1:77
Cushman, Robert E., 4:80
Custen, George F., 3:825
Cutcliffe, Stephen H., 5:52,
5:60, 5:70, 5:149, 5:152
Cuthbert, John A., 3:860
Cuthbertson, Joanne, 5:322
Cutler, Allan H., 4:623
Cutler, Bradley D., 1:330
Cutler, Helen E., 4:623
Cutler, Norman, 4:506
Cutler, Winnifred Berg, 5:355
Cutright, Paul R., 3:595,
3:928
Cutter, Mary A., 5:79
Cuvier, Baron Georges,
5:791
Cuyas, Arturo, 1:102
Cyert, Richard M., 3:49,
3:210

Cyprian of Carthage, St.,
4:707
Cytowic, Richard E., 5:391
Čyževskyj, Dmytro, 2:838
Czigány, Lóránt, 2:798
Czitrom, Daniel J., 3:803

D

Dabashi, Hamid, 4:373
Dabney, Virginius, 1:640
Dabundo, Laura, 1:265
Dadd, Debra Lynn, 5:386
Daemmrich, Horst S., 2:565
Daen, Daniël, 2:634
Daffron, Carolyn, 1:861
Daghlian, Philip B., 1:87
Dağlarca, Fazil Hüsnü, 2:95,
2:97
Dahl, Robert A., 3:142
Dahlberg, Frances, 4:431
Dahlbom, Bo, 4:396
Dahlgren, Peter, 3:806, 3:872
Dahlhaus, Carl, 3:659, 3:660
Dahlie, Hallvard, 2:922
Dahlstrom, Fabian, 3:718
Dahm, Bernard, 3:491
Dahmen, Hans D., 5:660
Dahmus, Joseph H., 4:714
Dahrendorf, Ralf, 3:204
Daiches, David J., 1:280,
1:397, 1:417, 1:420, 1:430,
1:510
Daigh, Ralph, 1:41
Daigle, Jean, 3:606
Dailey, Janet, 1:1220
Daims, Diva, 1:122
Daintith, John, 5:4, 5:13,
5:28
Dair, Carl, 1:8
Daiute, Colette, 5:566
Dalafi, H., 5:713
Daleski, H. M., 1:464
Daley, Robert, 3:898
Dalgarno, Melvin, 4:211
Dalin, David G., 4:639
Dallas, Wendy, 3:709
Dallek, Robert, 3:537, 3:544
Dalley, Stephanie, 4:545
Dallmayr, Fred, 4:292
Dally, Ann, 5:312
Dally, Peter, 1:337
Dalrymple, William, 3:902
Dalton, Elizabeth, 2:715
Dalton, George, 3:16
Dalton, John, 5:56, 5:602,
5:734, 5:738, **5:741**
D'Alton, John F., 2:380
Dalton, Roque, 2:862
Dalton, Russell J., 3:141
Dalven, Rae, 2:371

Daly, Herman, 5:822
Daly, Herman E., 3:47
Daly, Lowrie J., 4:103
Daly, Mary, 1:1186, 4:423,
4:749, **4:764**
Daly, M. W., 3:419
Daly, Reginald A., 5:626
Daly, Robert, 1:627
Dam, Freark, 2:634
Dam, Hari, 3:815
Dameron, J. Lasley, 1:693
Damiani, Bruno, 2:984
D'Amico, Robert, 1:1131
Damien, Yvonne M., 3:11
Damodar, Singhat, 3:487
Damon, S. Foster, 1:279
Dampier, William C., 5:25
Damrell, Joseph D., 4:872
Damrosch, Leopold, Jr.,
1:225, 1:229, 1:231, 1:252
Dan, Joseph, 4:598, 4:630,
4:632
Dana, Richard Henry, Jr.,
1:665, 3:919
Danaher, Kevin, 3:854
Danby, Herbert, 4:610, 4:810
Dance, Daryl Cumber, 2:930,
3:866
Dance, Stanley, 3:668, 3:677,
3:695
Danchev, Alex, 3:633
Dancy, Jonathan, 4:192
Dancy, R. M., 4:67, 4:80
Dancz, Virginia H., 3:492
Dane, Barbara O., 5:387
Dan Fodio, Shehu Usman,
2:134
Danford, John W., 4:345
Dangerfield, George, 3:366
Daniel, Charles, 5:263
Daniel, Glyn, 4:432, 4:436
Daniel, Helen, 2:947
Daniel, Norman A., 4:568
Daniel, Pete, 3:534, 5:262
Daniel-Rops, Henri, 4:739
Daniels, Cora L., 3:849
Daniels, George H., 5:46
Daniels, M., 1:28
Daniels, Norman, 4:211,
4:388
Daniels, R. V., 3:292
Daniels, Robert, 3:275
Daniels, Roger, 3:534
Dānishvār, Sīmīn, 2:85, 2:87
Danker, Frederick W., 4:794,
4:795
Danly, Robert L., 2:287
Dann, Uriel, 3:362, 4:568
Danna, Sammy R., 3:872
Dannhauser, Werner J., 4:89
D'Annunzio, Gabriele, 2:414,
2:873
Danson, Lawrence, 1:212

Dante Alighieri, 1:277,
1:302, 1:391, 1:610, 2:359,
2:380, 2:387, 2:398, 2:405,
2:407, 2:408, 2:409, 2:413,
2:414, **2:415**, 2:424, 2:426,
2:430, 2:431, 2:433, 2:439,
2:453, 2:981
Danto, Arthur, 4:247
D'Antonio, Michael, 4:866
Dantzig, Tobias, 5:488
Danzger, Murray, 4:659
Danziger, Nick, 3:902
Darbari, J., 3:500
Darbari, R., 3:500
Darbishire, Helen, 1:307
Darby, H. C., 3:354
Darby, Phillip, 3:366
Darby, William J., 3:444
D'Arcy, Martin, 4:783
Darden, Lloyd, 5:629
Darder, Antonia, 3:254
Dare, Philip N., 4:843
Dargan, E. Preston, 2:454
Dargyay, Eva, 4:497, 4:521,
4:533
Darian, Steven G., 4:503
Darío, Rubén, 2:863
Darius, Jon, 5:9
Dark, Sidney, 1:357
Darling, Pamela W., 1:23
Darlington, William A., 1:254
Darlow, Michael, 1:540
Darnay, Arsen J., 5:815
Darnell, Donald G., 3:649
Darnell, James, 5:784
Darnell, Regna, 3:40
Darnton, Robert, 1:347, 1:36,
1:711, 1:1249, 2:517,
2:651, 2:810, 3:338, 4:281,
4:406, 4:740, 5:44
Darrah, William Culp, 5:646
Darrow, Whitney, 1:43
Darton, F. J. Harvey, 1:36,
1:578
Darwin, Charles Robert,
3:171, 3:240, 5:46, 5:178,
5:195, 5:525, 5:615, 5:638,
5:779, **5:792**, 5:799, 5:802,
5:811, **5:830**
Darwin, Francis, 5:794
Darwin, John, 3:345
Darwish, Mahmud, 2:58
Dary, David, 3:558
Das, A. C., 4:501
Das, G. K., 1:477
Das, J., 5:298
Das, Manas M., 1:362, 3:486
Dās, Sūr, 2:173, 2:174
Dasgupta, Gautam, 1:1074
Dasgupta, Surendranath,
2:824, 4:351, 4:498
Dash, Julie, 1:1162
Dashti, Ali, 2:92

Dass, Nirmal, 4:516
Dass, Peter, 2:661
Daston, Lorraine, 5:44
Date, C. J., 5:559
Dathorne, O. R., 2:107,
2:930, 2:931
Datlof, Natalie, 2:505
Datta, Dhirendra M., 4:553
Datta, V. N., 4:508
Daube, David, 3:305
Dauben, Joseph W., 5:28,
5:491, 5:501
Dauenhauer, Nora Marks,
1:631
Dauenhauer, Richard, 1:631,
2:658
Dauer, Dorothea W., 4:256
Daugherty, James, 1:1194
Daughterty, Sue, 1:95
Daumas, Maurice, 5:25
Davenport, Basil, 2:382
Davenport, Cyril, 1:23, 1:36
Davenport, T. R., 3:423
Davenport, Wilbur B., 5:298
Davenport-Hines, R. P., 3:463
Davern, Cedric I., 5:777
David, A. Rosalie, 4:442,
4:548
David, Charles-Philippe, 3:450
David, Deirdre, 1:376
David, Florence N., 5:30,
5:526
David, Hans T., 3:675
David, Stuart, 1:14
David, Zdenek V., 3:389
David of Sassoun, 2:78
Davidowicz, Lucy S., 3:348
Davidson, A., 5:284
Davidson, Arnold E., 2:904
Davidson, Basil Risbridger,
3:416, 3:417, 3:420, **3:426**,
3:523
Davidson, Cathy N., 1:643,
1:735
Davidson, Clifford, 1:157,
1:159, 1:160
Davidson, Donald Herbert,
4:282, 4:380, 4:396
Davidson, Donald L., 5:110
Davidson, Edward H., 1:637,
1:693, 4:767
Davidson, Frank Paul, 5:213
Davidson, G. C., 5:427
Davidson, Gustav, 4:3
Davidson, Herbert A., 4:96
Davidson, Hilda R. Ellis,
2:640, 4:437
Davidson, Hugh M., 4:185
Davidson, Israel, 2:9
Davidson, James West, 3:514
Davidson, Jeremy H.C.S.,
2:311
Davidson, Marshall B., 3:513

Davidson, Nicholas S., 3:207,
3:334
Davidson, Paul, 5:398
Davidson, R. H., 5:770
Davidson, Robert F., 4:20,
4:488
Davie, Donald, 1:225, 1:296,
1:362, 1:417, **1:466**, 1:873
Davies, Andrew, 3:366
Davies, C. Collin, 3:483
Davies, Carole Boyce, 2:107,
2:930
Davies, Charlotte A., 3:369
Davies, Geoffrey, 5:730
Davies, Horton, 4:698
Davies, Hugh S., 1:339
Davies, Hunter, 1:589
Davies, J. G., 4:675
Davies, J. K., 3:301
Davies, Jessie, 2:718
Davies, John, 3:870
Davies, John H., 3:655
Davies, Marie Helene, 4:698
Davies, Nigel, 3:335, 3:627,
4:457
Davies, Norman, 3:390
Davies, Paul B., 1:349
Davies, Paul C. W., 5:15,
5:197, 5:595, 5:650, 5:654,
5:660, 5:662, 5:665, 5:686
Davies, Philip, 4:807
Davies, Richard, 2:699
Davies, Robertson, 2:909
Davies, W. D., 4:596, 4:617
Davies, Walford, 1:557
Davin, Delia, 3:469
da Vinci, Leonardo, 1:386,
2:219, 2:424, 3:768, **3:779,**
3:787, 5:189, 5:218
Davis, A. R., 2:189, 2:223,
2:225
Davis, Allen F., 1:731, 3:558
Davis, Allison, 3:22
Davis, Angela, 3:218
Davis, Arthur P., 1:725
Davis, Audrey B., 5:370
Davis, Barbara K., 1:122
Davis, Bernard D., 5:782
Davis, Dan, 5:591
Davis, David B., 1:722, 3:335,
3:523, 3:559
Davis, Devra Lee, 5:353
Davis, Donald Edward, 5:815
Davis, E., 3:435
Davis, Edith M., 5:328
Davis, F. Hadland, 4:586
Davis, Francis, 3:668
Davis, Goode P., 5:340
Davis, Gordon, 5:4
Davis, Gregson, 2:386
Davis, Harold E., 4:33
Davis, Hubert J., 3:860
Davis, J. C., 4:125

Davis, J. Madison, 2:910
Davis, Jack, 2:947
Davis, Jefferson, 3:574
Davis, Jill, 1:1183
Davis, Jinnie Y., 1:14
Davis, Joel, 5:778
Davis, John W., 5:119
Davis, Kay, 1:873
Davis, Kenneth C., 1:38, 3:515
Davis, Kenneth R., 4:724
Davis, Lennard J., 1:230, 1:794
Davis, Lenwood G., 3:761
Davis, Lynn E., 3:278
Davis, Madeleine, 5:472
Davis, Martin, 5:480, 5:481
Davis, Miles, 3:691
Davis, Morton D., 5:571
Davis, Moshe, 4:655
Davis, Natalie Z., 4:731
Davis, Nuel P., 5:707
Davis, P. H., 3:452
Davis, Peter, 5:335
Davis, Ralph, 3:335
Davis, Rebecca Harding, 1:721, 1:743
Davis, Richard Beale, 1:627
Davis, Richard L., 3:467
Davis, Robert G., 1:423
Davis, Robert M., 1:562, 1:885
Davis, Sara, 1:740
Davis, Stanley N., 5:631
Davis, Stephen T., 4:887
Davis, Susan, 2:971
Davis, Thadious M., 1:784, 1:836, 1:917
Davis, Thomas D., 4:20
Davis, Varina, 3:574
Davis, W. Eugene, 1:362
Davis, Walter R., 1:167, 1:174
Davis, William C., 3:574
Davis, William Morris, 5:642
Davis, Winston, 4:534, 4:540
Davison, Peter, 1:49, 1:425
Davitz, Joel R., 5:337
Davitz, Lois L., 5:337
Davy, Sir Humphry, 5:683, 5:742, 5:744, 5:747
Dawasha, Adeed, 3:442
Dawes, Rosemary N., 5:343
Dawidoff, Robert, 1:727, 4:327
Dawidowicz, Lucy S., 2:30, 2:31, 4:635
Dawkins, M. S., 5:838
Dawkins, Richard, 5:763, 5:779, 5:838
Dawley, Alan, 3:552
Daws, Gavan, 3:495
Dawsey, James, 4:6

Dawson, Carl, 1:312, 1:429
Dawson, Christopher H., 3:328, 4:783
Dawson, Giles E., 1:14
Dawson, Jerry, 4:254
Dawson, M. M., 4:89
Dawson, R. M., 3:614
Dawson, Raymond, 4:512
Day, Alan Edwin, 1:537
Day, Arthur G., 1:719, 1:912
Day, David, 1:559
Day, Donald, 3:887
Day, Dorothy, 4:765
Day, Douglas, 2:919
Day, James M., 3:178
Day, John, 5:556
Day, John A., 5:556, 5:634
Day, Kenneth, 1:9
Day, Sebastian, 4:114
Dayan, Joan, 1:693
Dayan, Moshe, 3:439
Daydí-Tolson, Santiago, 2:525
Dayton, Doug, 5:556
Dayton, Robert L., 5:298
Dazai Osamu, 2:285, 2:294
D'Costa, David, 5:394
D'Costa, Gavin, 4:898
D'Costa, Jean, 2:931, 2:937
Deacon, Bob, 3:345
Deacon, Desley, 3:494
Deakin, Motley F., 1:566
Deal, Carl, 5:815
Dealy, Glen Caudill, 3:625
Dean, Edwin, 3:57
Dean, J. A., 5:724
Dean, Joan Fitzpatrick, 1:493
Dean, Roger A., 4:871
Dean, Susan, 1:362
Dean, William, 4:751
Deane, Herbert A., 3:156, 4:110
Deane, Phyllis, 3:338, 3:354
Deane, Seamus, 3:339, 3:362
Deanesly, Margaret, 4:691
Dearden, C. W., 2:353
DeArmey, Michael, 4:290
DeBakey, Michael E., 5:345
DeBary, William Theodore, 2:186, 3:464, 3:466
De Beauvoir, Simone, 5:421
Debeir, Jean-Claude, 5:278
De Bellis, Jack, 1:772
De Bertier Sauvigny, Guillaume, 3:372
Debicki, Andrew P., 2:525
de Blij, Harm J., 3:125
Debo, Angie, 3:554
De Boer, Tjize J., 4:567
Debreczeny, Paul, 2:685, 2:751
Debreu, Gerard, 3:63
Debrunner, A., 4:794
DeBuger, James, 3:205

de Bury, Richard, 1:31
Debus, Allen G., 4:125, 4:128, 4:150, 5:28, 5:40
Debussy, Claude, 3:691, 3:712
De Camp, L. Sprague, 5:38, 5:231
Decareau, Robert V., 5:229
Décarie, Thérèse G., 3:192
De Castro, Adolph, 1:735
Decharme, Paul, 2:356
Dechêne, Louise, 3:611
Decker, Barbara, 5:629
Decker, Robert, 5:629
Decker, William M., 1:730
DeConde, Alexander, 3:508, 3:544
DeCosta, Miriam, 2:845
De Costa, René, 2:876
DeCoster, Cyrus, 2:553
Dedmon, Emmett, 3:902
De Duve, Christian, 5:775
Deegan, Mary J., 1:731
DeeGee, Lester, 3:558
Deeney, John L., 2:235
Deetz, Stanley A., 3:142
De Felice, Renzo, 4:644
De Filippo, Eduardo, 2:418
DeFleur, Lois B., 3:809
DeFleur, Melvin L., 3:203, 3:801, 3:803
Defoe, Daniel, 1:203, 1:229, 1:238, 1:241, 1:395, 1:576, 2:432, 2:512
de Ford, Miriam Allen, 1:88
DeForest, John William, 1:721, 1:744
DeFries, M. H., 5:635
De Galindez, Suarez J., 3:636
DeGaulle, Charles, 3:372
Degen, Paula, 5:220
De Gennaro, Angelo A., 3:284
DeGeorge, Richard R., 4:388
De George, Richard T., 4:13
Degh, Linda, 3:854, 3:861
Degler, Carl N(eumann), 3:513, 3:554, 3:575
de Graef, Ortwin, 1:1143
de Grand, Alexander J., 3:385
De Grazia, Alfred, 5:243
de Grazia, Edward, 1:56
de Grazia, Sebastian, 3:160
DeGregori, Thomas R., 5:213
DeGregorio, William A., 3:506
DeHaas-Lorentz, Geertrudia, 5:699
De Hamel, Christopher, 3:766
De Hartmann, Thomas, 4:875
De Heusch, Luc, 4:429

Deidre, David, 1:318
Deindorfer, Robert G., 3:858
De Jackson, J. R., 1:713
Dejardin, Kathleen, 3:767
De Jean, Joan, 2:366, 2:447, 2:484, 2:503
Dejkunjorn, Vasit, 2:336
De Jonge, A., 3:292
De Jongh, James, 1:794
Deken, Joseph, 5:242, 5:537, 5:564
de Kiewiet, C. W., 3:423
Dekker, George, 1:650, 1:665
Dekker, Maurits, 4:534
Dekker, Thomas, 1:176, 1:177
Dekmejian, Hrair, 4:568
DeKoven, Marianne, 1:420, 1:794, 1:882
De Kruif, Paul, 5:783, 5:801
De la Croix, Horst, 3:756
De Lafayette, Jean M., 1:96
De la Grange, Henry-Louis, 3:705
Delahunty, R. J., 4:187
De La Mare, Walter, 1:451, **1:466**
DeLamarter, Richard T., 5:542
De la Mothe, John, 1:550
De Landa, M., 3:278
Delaney, C. F., 4:334
Delaney, Cornelius, 4:281
Delaney, John J., 4:719
Delaney, Paul, 1:554
Delaney, Samuel R., 1:1252, **1:1256**
Delaney, Shelagh, 1:531
de Lange, Jan, 5:521
DeLange, Nicholas, 4:634
Delany, Paul, 5:561, 5:562
Delarue, Paul, 3:854
De la Torre, Teodoro, 4:16
De Lattre, Roland, 4:767
DeLaura, David J., 1:325
De Lauretis, Teresa, 1:1133, 3:827, 5:187
Delavignette, R., 3:420
Delbanco, Andrew, 1:627, 3:527, 4:753
Delblanc, Sven, 2:671
DelBueno, Dorothy J., 5:337
Delderfield, R. F., 3:339
Deleage, Jean-Paul, 5:278
Deledda, Grazia, 2:400, **2:419**
Delehaye, Hippolyte, 4:678
De Lerma, Dominque René, 3:655
Deleuze, Gilles, 1:583, 1:1131, 2:477, 4:400
Delevoy, Robert L., 3:771
Del Hoyo, Joseph, 5:759

Delibes, Miguel, 2:521, 2:538
Deliman, Tracy, 5:319
Delisser, Herbert George, **2:934**
Delkeskamp-Hayes, Corinna, 5:79
Dell, Floyd, 1:880
Del Mar, Norman, 3:655
Deloney, Thomas, 1:167, **1:177**
DeLorenzo, Lorisa, 5:322
DeLorenzo, Robert, 5:322
Deloria, Vine, Jr., 3:554, 4:464
Delpar, Helen, 3:624
Delthier, David P., 5:627
DeLuca, Vincent, 1:279
De'Lucchi, Lorna, 2:403
Delumeau, Jean, 3:334, 4:728
Del Vecchio, Alfred, 5:235
Delzell, Charles F., 3:385
Demac, Donna A., 1:56
De Maegd-Soep, Carolina, 2:710
De Man, Paul, 1:922, 1:966, 1:1131, **1:1141,** 1:1150, 1:1152
De Marco, Joseph P., 1:832, 3:578
de Maré, Eric, 1:28
Demarest, Arthur A., 4:457
Demaria, Richard, 4:844
DeMarre, Dean A., 5:324
de Maupassant, Guy. See Maupassant, Guy de
Dembo, L. S., 1:798, 2:195
Dement, William C., 5:391
Demetz, Peter, 2:565
D'Emilio, John, 1:1181, 3:215, 3:552
DeMille, Agnes George, **3:740,** 3:744, 3:753
De Mille, Anna G., 3:80
Demir, Soliman, 3:451
Demko, George J., 3:891
DeMoivre, Abraham, 5:525, **5:527**
de Moor, Johanes C., 4:545
De Morgan, Augustus, 5:495
Demos, John, 1:630, 3:516
Demosthenes, 2:343, 2:354, 2:362, 2:378
De Mowbray, Stephen, 3:394
Dempsey, J. M., 5:262
Demsey, David, 3:730
Demuth, Norman, 3:712
Den Boeft, J., 3:310
d'Encoussee, Helene C., 3:398
Dendle, Brian J., 2:547
Dendurent, H. O., 1:286
Denevan, William H., 3:627
Deng, Francis Mading, 4:462

Dengler, Sandy, 5:363
Denham, H. M., 3:898
Denham, Robert D., 1:977
Denholz, Elaine, 5:340
Denholz, Melvin, 5:340
De Nicolas, Antonio, 4:770
Denis, Numa, 4:438
Denison, Edward F., 3:53
Denitch, Bogdar, 3:345
Denmark, Florence L., 3:178, 3:179
Dennett, Daniel C., 4:382, **4:396,** 5:74, 5:75, 5:570, 5:571
Dennett, Tyler, 3:595
Denning, Michael, 1:592, 1:722, 3:559
Dennis, Everett, 3:203
Dennison, Sally, 1:38
Denny, Frederick, 3:442, 4:883
Denny, Norman, 3:357
de Noblet, Jocelyn, 5:192
Denoon, Donald, 3:423
Denson, Lawrence, 1:441
Dent, N.J.H., 4:213
Dent, R. W., 1:215
Denton, Michael, 5:784
Denton, Virginia L., 3:270
Denvir, Bernard, 3:759
Denzin, Norman K., 3:216
DeOlivera, Marques Antonia H., 3:386
Deonna, Laurence, 3:454
DePaor, Liam, 3:369
Depastas, Apostolos N., 5:110
Depew, David J., 4:47, 5:763
DePorte, Michael V., 1:259
De Quincey, Thomas, 1:264, 1:273, **1:289**
Deren, Maya, 1:1162
Derfler, Leslie, 3:372
Der Hovanessian, Diana, 2:76
Dermout, Maria, 2:310
Der Nister, 2:37
De Romilly, Jacqueline, 2:345, 4:54
DeRosa, Gabriele, 4:771
DeRougemont, Denis, 3:326, 3:330
Derow, Peter, 3:299, 4:449
Derrick, Dan, 5:566
Derrida, Jacques, 1:966, 1:1130, 1:1131, 1:1141, 1:1143, 1:1150, 1:1152, 2:447, 2:461, 2:467, 2:471, 2:478, 2:479, 2:494, 3:211, 4:262, 4:283, 4:390, **4:396,** 4:414
Derrida, Paul, 1:1141
Derry, John W., 3:362
Derry, T. K., 5:36
Derry, Thomas, 3:380, 3:381

Dertouzos, Michael L., 3:49, 5:539
DeRuggiero, Guido, 3:340
Dervaes, Claudine, 3:890
Derzhavin, Gavril, 2:682
Desai, Anita, 2:178
Desai, Santosh N., 4:518
de Sade, Comte de (Marquis de Sade) . *See* Sade (Donatien Alphonse François), Comte de
De Sanctis, Francesco, 2:419
Desani, G. V., 2:177
De Santillana, Giorgio, 5:38
Desautels, Paul E., 5:628
Descartes, René, 2:471, 3:153, 3:337, 4:12, 4:122, 4:146, 4:157, 4:164, 4:167, **4:168,** 4:171, 4:172, 4:173, 4:181, 4:183, 4:186, 4:199, 4:314, 4:381, 5:41, 5:96, 5:483, 5:485, **5:502**
De Schill, Stefan, 5:417
Deser, S., 5:715
Deshen, Shlomo, 4:644
Deshpande, Shashi, 2:177
De Silva, Douglas S., 5:224
de Silva, K. M., 3:487
DesJardins, Joseph R., 5:114
Desjardins, R. L., 5:774
Desjardins, Rosemary, 4:80
Desmond, Adrian, 5:831
Desmond, David P., 5:403
Desmond, John F., 1:895
Desmond, S., 3:381
De Sousa, Geraldo U., 1:220
Desowitz, Robert S., 5:340, 5:389
Despopoulus, Agamemnon, 5:773
Des Pres, Terrence, 2:988
Dessauer, Friedrich, 5:85
Dessauer, John P., 1:47
Desser, David, 1:760
Dessouki, Ali, 3:442
Desti, Mary, 3:742
Detienne, Marcel, 4:429, 4:446
Detmer, David, 4:330
De Tolnay, Charles Q., 3:782
Detweiler, Robert, 1:1060
Detwiler, Donald S., 3:376
Deullmann, Stephan, 3:381
Deutcher, Isaac, 3:292
Deutelbaum, Marshall, 1:1169
Deutsch, Babette, 1:132
Deutsch, Charles, 5:401
Deutsch, Dennis S., 5:556
Deutsch, Eliot, 4:349
Deutsch, Helene, 5:421
Deutsch, J. A., 5:523

Deutsch, Morton, 3:168, 5:421
Deutsch, Otto E., 3:698, 3:707, 3:715
Deutscher, Isaac, 3:295, 3:344, 3:348, 3:396, 4:655
Devall, Bill, 5:114, 5:822
Devaney, Sheila Greeve, 4:289, 4:743
De Vecchi, Pierluigi, 3:782
Dever, G. E. Alan, 5:319
Dever, William G., 4:808
Deveraux, Jude, 1:1221
Devine, Betsy, 5:650, 5:651
Devine, Michael D., 5:287
De Vitis, A. A., 1:489, 1:537
De Vito, Joseph A., 3:801
Devkota, Laxmiprasad, 2:176
Devlin, Albert J., 1:895
Devlin, James E., 1:819
De Vogue, Adalbert, 4:688
Devore, Irven, 3:17
DeVorkin, David H., 5:28
DeVos, George A., 3:464, 4:531, 4:539
De Voto, Bernard, 1:684, 1:783, 3:523, **3:576**
Devoto, Giacomo, 2:401
DeVries, Herbert, 5:325
DeVries, J., 3:338
DeVries, Jan, 4:420
DeVries, Raymond G., 5:337
DeVries, Willem A., 4:16, 4:233
De Weever, Jacqueline, 1:804
Dewey, John, 1:668, 1:733, 3:232, 3:242, 3:246, **3:259,** 3:264, 4:28, **4:223,** 4:260, 4:297, 4:301, 4:308, 4:324, 4:360, 5:59, 5:95, 5:438
Dewey, Patrick R., 5:544
Dewhurst, C. Kurt, 3:861
Dewhurst, Kenneth, 2:609, 4:179
DeWiest, Roger J. M., 5:631
De Witt, Norman W., 2:388, 4:73
Dews, Peter, 1:1131, 3:194, 4:391
Dewsbury, Donald A., 5:826
Dharmasiri, Gunapala, 4:512, 4:884
Dharmatala, Damcho Gyatsho, 4:541
Diaghilev, Sergei, 1:547, 2:468, 3:722, 3:737, **3:741,** 3:747, 3:748, 3:749, 3:750
Diamant, Anita, 4:601
Diamant, Lincoln, 5:237
Diamond, Arthur, 4:877
Diamond, Cora, 4:345, 5:493
Diamond, Edwin, 3:803, 5:421

Diamond, Elin, 1:535
Diamond, Harold J., 3:655
Diamond, Irene, 4:391
Diamond, Larry, 3:142
Diamond, Malcolm L., 4:662
Diamond, Timothy, 5:334
Díaz, Bernal, 3:629
Díaz, Janet W., 2:545
Diaz-Mas, Paloma, 4:644
Dib, Mohammed, 2:119
Dibble, R. F., 4:588
Dibelius, Martin, 4:825
DiBernard, Barbara, 1:505
Di Cesare, Mario, 1:181, 1:184, 2:397
Dichter, Harry, 3:659
Dick, Auguste, 5:513
Dick, Bernard F., 1:484
Dick, Everett, 1:725, 3:531, 3:549
Dick, Philip K., 1:1256
Dick, Steven J., 5:31
Dickason, Olive P., 3:610
Dicken, Peter, 3:122
Dickens, Arthur G., 3:358, 4:722, 4:726, 4:728, 4:778
Dickens, Charles, 1:292, 1:310, 1:317, 1:321, 1:344, 1:346, **1:347,** 1:353, 1:355, 1:378, 1:389, 1:399, 1:577, 1:584, 1:679, 1:854, 1:994, 1:1019, 1:1039, 1:1150, 1:1193, 2:40, 2:432, 2:617, 2:646
Dickens, Homer C., 3:751
Dickens, Monica, 5:322
Dickens, William T., 3:60
Dickenson, Robert E., 3:118
Dickenson, Terence, 5:591
Dickey, Christopher, 3:902
Dickey, James, 1:912, 1:966
Dickey, Laurence, 4:233
Dickey, Marcus, 1:778
Dickie, Margaret, 1:798
Dickinson, A. T., Jr., 1:122
Dickinson, Asa Don, 1:75
Dickinson, Donna, 1:747
Dickinson, Emily (Elizabeth), 1:668, 1:718, 1:726, 1:745, 1:806, 1:954, 1:962, 1:965
Dickinson, G. Lowes, 2:345
Dickinson, H. T., 3:362
Dickinson, John A., 3:610
Dickinson, John P., 5:9, 5:107
Dickinson, R. E., 5:619
Dickinson, W. Croft, 3:355, 4:774
Dick-Larkham, Richard, 5:284
Dicks, D. R., 4:48, 5:38
Dickson, David, 5:73, 5:152, 5:181

Dickson, D. Bruce, 4:433
Dickson, Paul, 3:868, 3:870
Dickson, William J., 3:172
Dickstein, Morris, 1:294,
 1:924, 3:559
DiClerico, Robert E., 3:146
Diderot, Denis, 1:105, 1:253,
 2:444, 2:471, 2:472, 3:372,
 4:195, 4:212
Didion, Joan, 1:909, 1:916,
 1:968
Dieckman, Hans, 3:169
Diederich, Bernard, 3:637,
 3:639
Diehl, Edith, 1:23
Diehl, Richard A., 4:455,
 4:457
Diem, Doan Thi, 2:338
Diener, Edward, 5:107
Dienes, Leslie, 5:280
Dienstag, Jacob I., 4:668
Diethrich, Edward B., 5:374
Dietrich, Craig, 3:469
Dietrich, John, 5:326
Dietschy, Marcel, 3:692
Dietz, Tim, 5:770
Diffey, T. J., 2:766
Diffie, Bailey W., 3:386
DiGaetani, John Louis, 2:987,
 3:670, 3:728
Diggins, John P., 3:542
Diggory, Terrence, 1:798,
 1:901
Diggs, Ellen Irene, 1:88
Di Giovanni, Norman
 Thomas, 2:857
Dignan, James, 3:204
DiGregorio, Mario A., 5:799
Dijksterhuis, E. J., 4:125,
 5:25
Dijkstra, Bram, 1:240
Dijkstra, Edward W., 5:550
Dillard, Annie, 5:818
Dillard, Mabel Mayle, 1:891
Dillard, Philip H., 1:357
Diller, Hans-Jurgen, 1:159
Dilligan, Robert, 1:294
Dillingham, William B.,
 1:688, 1:777, 3:870
Dillistone, Frederick W.,
 4:833
Dillman, Don A., 3:6
Dillon, John M., 4:55, 4:60,
 4:62, 4:670
Dilman, Ilham, 3:184, 4:412,
 5:100, 5:447
Dilthey, Wilhelm, 4:158,
 4:226, 4:254, 4:661
Dilworth, David, 4:37, 4:263
Dilworth, Thomas, 1:503
Dimaras, C. T., 2:371
DiMaria, Salvatore, 2:407
Dimitrova, Blaga, 2:781

Dimnet, Ernest, 1:333
Dimock, Edward C., Jr.,
 2:170, 2:174
Dimock, Wai-chee, 1:688
Dinesen, Isak, 2:645, 2:648,
 2:656
Dinges, John, 3:639
Dinkmeyer, Don C., 5:418
D'Innocenzo, Michael, 1:661
Dinshaw, Carolyn, 1:150
Dinwiddy, John, 4:191
Dio Cassius, 3:314
Dio Chrysostom, 3:314
Diodorus Siculus, 3:314
Diogenes Laertius, 4:46
Diop, Chiekh Anta, 3:428,
 4:368
Diophantus, 5:503
Dioszegi, V., 4:541
DiPietro, J., 1:713
Dipple, Elizabeth, 1:524
Dirac, Paul Adrien Maurice,
 5:679, 5:714, 5:715, 5:716
Dircks, Richard J., 1:245
Dirda, Michael, 1:23
Diringer, David, 1:14, 1:36
Dirlik, Arif, 3:469
Disch, Thomas M., 1:1252
Di Scipio, Giuseppe, 2:417
Disher, Maurice W., 1:271
Disney, A. R., 3:484
Disney, Michael, 5:654
Disney, Walt(er) Elias,
 1:590, 1:1163, 3:834
Disraeli, Benjamin, 1:309,
 1:317, 1:351
Ditlea, Steve, 5:539
Ditlevsen, Tove, 2:649
Ditsky, John, 1:885, 2:985
Dittemore, J. V., 4:878
Dittmer, Lowell, 3:469
Ditton, Jason, 3:228
Divine, Robert A., 3:537,
 3:544
Divitto, Barbara, 5:322
Dix, Carol, 5:359
Dix, Dom G., 4:688
Dix, Griffin, 4:539
Dixon, Brenda, 3:731
Dixon, E. James, 4:454
Dixon, Geoffrey, 1:357
Dixon, J. I., 1:102
Dixon, Paul B., 2:896
Dixon, Peter, 1:247
Dixon, S., 5:523
DiYanni, Robert, 1:430,
 1:801, 1:808, 1:915, 2:4
Dizard, Wilson P., Jr., 3:803
Djebar, Assia, 2:105, 2:116,
 2:119
Djerassi, Carl, 5:743
Djilas, Aleska, 3:392
Djilas, Milovan, 2:829, 3:392

Djurhuus, J.H.O., 2:655
Doan, Laura L., 1:804
Doane, Mary Ann, 1:1157,
 1:1158
Dobb, Maurice H., 3:50
Dobbs, Betty J., 4:184, 5:41
Dobbs, Brian, 1:392
Dobbs, Charles M., 3:544
Dobbs, Judy, 1:392
Dobell, Clifford, 5:41, 5:804
Dobie, J. Frank, 3:854, 3:863
Dobkin, Bruce H., 5:313
Dobkin, David S., 5:769
Döblin, Alfred, 2:576, 4:635
Dobrée, Bonamy, 1:370,
 1:372, 1:429
Dobree, John H., 5:383
Dobrinsky, Herbert, 4:601
Dobrolyubov, N. A., 4:31
Dobroszycki, Lucjan, 2:30,
 4:635
Dobson, Andrew, 4:315
Dobson, E. J., 1:216
Dobson, Joanne, 1:747
Dobson, R. B., 3:357
Dobson, W. A., 1:97, 2:195
Dobyns, Henry F., 3:640
Dobzhansky, Theodosius,
 5:779
Docherty, James C., 3:494
Dock, George, Jr., 5:787
Dockrill, M. L., 3:345
Dockstader, Frederick, 1:86
Doctor, Gary L., 3:719
Doctorow, E(dgar)
 L(aurence), 1:909, 1:968
Dodd, Charles Harold,
 4:814, 4:825, 4:832
Dodd, James, 5:662
Dodd, Janet S., 5:727
Dodd, P., 3:55
Dodd, Robert T., 5:592
Dodd, Valerie, 1:354
Dodds, Eric R., 2:345, 2:356,
 4:48, 4:61, 4:63, 4:446,
 4:449, 4:683
Dodge, Robert K., 3:870
Dodgson, Campbell, 3:774
Dodgson, Charles Lutwidge.
 See Carroll, Lewis
Dodson, Daniel B., 2:919
Dodson, E. O., 4:337
Dodson, Fitzhugh, 5:322
Dodson, George R., 4:220
Doe, Paul, 3:723
Doelp, Alan, 5:381, 5:392
Doeppers, Daniel F., 3:492
Doerfliner, Thomas M., 3:520
Doering, Bernard, 4:307
Doernberg, Myrna, 5:392
Doerries, Hermann, 4:683
Doeser, Linda, 3:734
Doggett, Frank, 1:887

Doggett, Joella, 1:629
Doherty, J. E., 3:369
Dohmann, Barbara, 2:846
Dohrenwend, Barbara S., 3:214
Dohrenwend, Bruce P., 3:214
Doi, Takeo, 2:291
Doig, Desmond, 4:743
Dokmaisot, 2:336
Dolan, Edward F., Jr., 5:801
Dolan, Jay, 4:751
Dolan, John Patrick, 4:677, 4:720
Dolan, Kathleen H., 2:540
Dolan, Walter, 4:13
Dolbeare, Kenneth M., 3:140
Dolby, William, 2:192
Dole, George, 4:852
Dole, Gertrude E., 3:42
Dole, Nathan H., 4:76
Dolezelova-Velingerova, M., 2:189
Dolin, Arnold, 1:47
D'Olivo, J. C., 5:664
Doll, Mary Aswell, 1:440
Dollar, Charles M., 3:8
Dollard, John, 3:19, 3:170, 3:176
Dolle, Raymond F., 1:635
Dolley, Michael, 3:370
Dollimore, Jonathan, 1:208, 1:212, 1:1181
Dombrowski, Daniel, 4:736
Dombrowski, Robert S., 2:423
Domhoff, William G., 3:214
Domingo, Plácido, 3:687, **3:692,** 3:708
Dominguez Ortiz, Antonio, 3:795
Dominic, Zoe, 3:736
Dominick, Joseph, 3:801, 3:803, 3:811
Domotor, Tekla, 3:854
Donadoni, Eugenio, 2:401
Donagan, Alan, 4:187, 4:282
Donahue, John J., 4:373
Donahue, William H., 5:608
Donakowski, Conrad L., 3:873
Donald, David, 3:510, 3:527, 3:529
Donald, David H., 1:904
Donald, James, 1:1133
Donaldson, Dwight M., 3:442, 4:574
Donaldson, E. Talbot, 1:151, 1:154, 1:219
Donaldson, Gary A., 3:554
Donaldson, Gerald, 1:31
Donaldson, Gordon, 3:368, 4:735
Donaldson, James, 4:100

Donaldson, Laura E., 1:924
Donaldson, Mary C., 2:489
Donaldson, Peter S., 3:333
Donaldson, R. J., 5:389
Donaldson, Scott, 1:840, 1:962
Donaldson, Stephen, 4:894
Donato, Eugenio, 1:1134, 2:476
Donawerth, Jane, 1:216
Donelaitis, Kristijonas, 2:804, **2:805**
Doner, Dean, 5:70
Doney, Willis, 4:170
Doniach, N. S., 1:97
Donin, Hayim H., 4:599, 4:601
Donington, Robert, 2:605, 3:670
Donn, William L., 5:633
Donnachie, Ian, 3:368, 4:735
Donnahoe, Alan S., 5:521
Donne, John, 1:166, **1:177,** 1:643, 1:806, 1:1003, 5:616
Donner, Fred M., 4:568
Donner, Jorn, 3:831
Donno, Elizabeth S., 1:189
Donoghue, Denis, 1:425, 1:794, 1:924
Donohue, Joseph W., 1:271, 1:322
Donoso, José, 2:844, 2:845, **2:863**
Donovan, Bernard T., 5:340
Donovan, Josephine L., 1:713, 1:723, 1:770, 1:804, 1:924
Donovan, Robert J., 3:537
Donovan, Stephen K., 3:18
Doody, Francis S., 3:105
Doody, Margaret Anne, 1:227, 1:253
Dooley, Brendon M., 5:44
Dooley, D. J., 1:563
Dooley, Dennis, 1:1230
Dooley, Patrick, 1:742
Dooling, D. M., 4:464
Doolittle, Hilda. *See* H. D. (Hilda Doolittle)
Doran, George H., 1:41
Doran, Madeleine, 1:169, 1:216
Dordevic, Mihailo, 2:828
Dore, Mohammed, 3:112
Dore, Ronald P., 3:474, 3:477
Doren, Charles Van, 1:116
Dorey, T. A., 4:139
Dorf, Richard C., 5:213, 5:242
Dorfman, Ariel, 1:1164, 2:843, **2:864,** 3:631, 3:873
Dorfman, Joseph, 3:109, 3:243

Doria, Charles, 4:439
Dorian, James P., 5:280
Dorman, Jon, 5:391
Dorn, Edward, 1:969
Dornbusch, Charles E., 3:510
Dornbusch, Rudiger, 3:47
Dor-Ner, Zvi, 3:916
Doroshkin, Milton, 2:31
Dorris, Michael, 5:375
Dorros, Sidney, 5:392
Dorsey, David F., 2:107
Dorsey, Michael W., 5:345
Dorsey-Gaines, Catherine, 3:252
Dorson, Richard M., 2:352, 3:848, 3:853, 3:854, 3:858, 3:868, 3:871, **3:877,** 4:539
Dos Passos, John (Roderigo), 1:803, **1:827,** 2:432, 2:888
Dossa, Shiraz, 5:82
Dossey, Larry, 5:369
Dostoyevsky, Anna, 2:715
Dostoyevsky, Fyodor, 1:253, 1:486, 1:829, 1:1019, 1:1039, 2:419, 2:560, 2:604, 2:617, 2:683, 2:711, **2:712,** 2:734, 2:740, 2:750, 2:760, 4:335
Dott, Robert H., Jr., 5:743
Doty, Gresdna A., 1:426
Doty, Mark A., 1:933
Doty, William G., 4:428
Double, Richard, 4:380
Doubleday, Neal Frank, 1:657
Doubrovsky, Serge, 2:447
Dougherty, James E., 3:144
Dougherty, Margaret M., 1:95
Doughtie, Edward, 3:659
Doughty, Charles M., 3:902
Doughty, Howard, 1:691, 3:592
Doughty, Oswald, 1:288, 1:392
Doughty, Paul L., 3:640
Douglas, Allie, 5:681
Douglas, Andrew H., 4:154
Douglas, Ann, 1:650
Douglas, Auriel, 1:93
Douglas, George, 1:859, 1:902
Douglas, J. D., 4:3, 4:675, 4:717
Douglas, Martin J., 4:861
Douglas, Mary, 3:28, 3:29, 4:477, 5:128
Douglas, Matthew M., 5:763
Douglas, Richard M., 4:728
Douglas, Roy, 3:726
Douglas-Hamilton, Iain, 5:763
Douglas-Hamilton, Oria, 5:763

Douglass, Frederick, 1:659, **1:666**, 1:681, 1:726, 1:785, 1:831, 1:986, 3:527
Douglass, Jane D., 4:761
Douglass, Ralph, 1:14
Dove, George N., 1:593
Dove, Rita, 1:970
Dover, Kenneth, 2:345, 2:353
Dover, K. J., 3:309
Dover, Michael J., 5:265
Dovlatov, Sergei, 2:716
Dow, James, 4:465
Dowd, Douglas F., 3:110
Dowdy, Shirley, 5:521
Dower, John W., 3:473, 3:477, 3:534
Dowey, Edward A., 4:761
Dowley, Tim, 4:676, 4:720, 4:743
Dowling, David, 1:836
Dowling, Harry F., 5:328
Dowling, William C., 1:227, 1:1150
Downer, Alan S., 1:1072
Downes, David A., 1:364
Downes, Edward, 3:664
Downes, Kerry, 3:792, 3:796
Downing, Charles, 2:77, 2:96
Downing, Christine, 4:424
Downing, David, 1:95
Downing, Douglas, 5:539
Downs, Anthony, 3:67, 3:142, 3:147
Downs, John, 3:44
Downs, Philip G., 3:659
Downs, Robert B., 1:31, 1:57, 1:75, 3:259, 3:871
Downton, James V., Jr., 4:872
Dox, Ida, 5:311
Doyle, Arthur Conan, 1:352, 1:591, 1:592, 1:593, 1:594, 1:596, 1:604, 1:605, **1:606**, 1:1226, 4:850
Doyle, Charles, 1:887, 1:901
Doyle, Denis D., 3:250
Doyle, Helen MacKnight, 1:733
Doyle, Paul A., 1:529
Doyle, Robert E., 5:418
Doyle, Rodger Pirnie, 5:353
Doyle, William, 3:336, 3:338
Dozy, Reinhardt, 2:519
Drabble, Margaret, 1:132, 1:414, 1:444, 1:454, **1:467**
Drabeck, Bernard A., 1:858
Drabkin, I. E., 4:125, 5:40
Drach, Ivan, 2:838
Drachman, Virginia G., 5:313
Dragland, Stan, 2:926
Drago, Edmund L., 3:527
Drake, Alvin W., 5:353
Drake, Dana B., 2:535

Drake, Donald, 5:350
Drake, Frank, 5:598
Drake, Paul W., 3:634
Drake, Samuel A., 3:858
Drake, Sandra E., 2:936
Drake, Stillman, 4:125, 4:143, 4:172, 5:40, 5:41, 5:604, 5:688
Drakikis, John, 1:208
Drakopoulou, Theone, 2:372, 2:377
Drakul, Simon, 2:807
Drame, Kandioura, 2:133, 2:155
Drandl, Johannes, 4:345
Drapela, Victor J., 3:177
Draper, Hal, 4:242
Draper, James P., 1:713
Draper, Larry W., 4:845
Draper, Ronald P., 1:362, 1:510
Dray, W. H., 3:275
Drayton, Michael, 1:179
Dreifuss, Fritz E., 5:392
Dreiser, Theodore, 1:711, 1:739, 1:802, **1:829**
Dreizin, Felix, 2:685
Drekmeier, Charles, 4:501
Dresch, Paul, 3:454
Drescher, Seymour, 3:165, 3:528
Dresden, Max, 5:662
Dresner, Samuel H., 4:632
Dresser, A. G., 4:878
Dresser, Horatio W., 4:847
Dressler, Fritz, 5:562
Dressler, P. Claus, 2:109
Dretske, Fred, 5:74
Drew, Fraser Bragg, 1:519
Drew, Horace, 5:784
Drew, Philip, 1:339
Drews, R., 3:316
Dreyer, Carl, 3:824, **3:834**
Dreyer, John L., 5:31, 5:40, 5:600
Dreyfus, Hubert L., 4:234, 4:292, 4:400, 5:74, 5:571
Dreyfus, Jack, 5:350
Dreyfus, John, 1:43
Dreyfus, Stuart E., 5:571
Dreyfuss, Henry, 3:756
Dreyfuss, Hubert L., 5:90
Drigotas, Frank M., Jr., 3:908
Driscoll, J. Walter, 4:875
Driscoll, Walter G., 5:652
Driver, G. R., 4:445
Driver, Harold E., 3:25, 3:33, 4:464
Driver, Sam N., 2:752
Drogin, Marc, 1:14
Dron, Georg J. W., 5:83
Dronamraju, Krishna R., 5:778, 5:798, 5:799

Dronke, Peter, 1:149, 4:16, 4:94, 4:698
Drossin, Julius, 3:665
Droste-Hülshoff, Annette von, 2:564, **2:576**
Drower, Ethel A., 3:855
Druckman, Daniel, 5:283
Drugovac, Miodrag, 2:807
Drummond, Ian, 3:616
Drury, Francis K. W., 1:123
Druts, Yefim, 3:855
Dry, Murray, 3:543
Dryden, Edgar A., 1:657
Dryden, John, 1:223, 1:228, 1:232, **1:240**, 1:248, 1:251, 1:252, 1:373, 2:365, 2:385, 2:387, 2:391, 2:396, 3:711
Dryden, W., 5:460
Dryer, Bernard, 5:392
Držić, Marin, 2:784
D'Souza, Dinesh, 1:1126, 3:249
D'Souza, Frances, 1:57
Du, Nguyen, 2:338
Duara, Pransenjit, 3:470
Duban, James, 1:688
Duberman, Martin, 1:685, 1:1183, 3:554
Dubler, Nancy N., 5:119
Dubnow, Simon, 2:30, 4:657
DuBoff, Leonard D., 1:47
Dubois, Charles, 1:282
DuBois, Ellen C., 3:527
Dubois, M. M., 1:98
Dubois, Paul, 5:378
Du Bois, Shirley G., 3:578
Du Bois, W(illiam) E(dward) B(urghardt), 1:726, 1:771, 1:785, 1:807, **1:831**, 3:224, 3:269, 3:527, 3:576
Dubos, René Jules, 3:48, 5:107, 5:132, 5:152, 5:409, **5:795**, 5:809
Du Boulay, Shirley, 4:743
Dubrow, Heather, 1:215
Duby, Georges, 3:328
Ducasse, Curt J., 5:62
Ducat, Craig R., 3:141
Duche, Jacob, 1:626
Duchesne-Guillemin, Jacques, 4:443, 4:444
Dučić, Jovan, 2:827, **2:830**
Duckett, Eleanor S., 3:330, 3:356
Duckett, Margaret, 1:756
Duckitt, John, 3:176
Duckles, Vincent, 3:655
Duckworth, George E., 2:382
Duczynszka, Ilona, 2:798
Duden, Barbara, 5:187
Dudley, Donald R., 2:3, 2:380, 4:55

Dudley, Rosemary, 5:392
Dudley, Underwood, 5:488
Duellman, William E., 5:770
Duensing, Paul Hayden, 1:13
Duerden, Dennis, 2:112
Duerr, Hans P., 4:430
Duff, John W., 2:380
Duff, Robert A., 4:187
Duffey, Bernard, 1:655, 1:901
Duffie, John A., 5:284, **5:291**
Duffield, Gervase, 4:726,
    4:761
Duffus, Robert L., 3:110,
    3:243
Duffus, William M., 3:110
Duffy, Eamon, 3:358
Duffy, John, 5:78, 5:328
Dugan, Alan, 1:970
Dugdale, John, 1:1035
Duhem, Pierre, 4:97, 5:25
Duignana, Peter, 3:417
Dukas, Helen, 5:683
Duke, Alastair, 4:731
Duke, Daniel L., 3:249
Duke, Judith S., 1:47
Duke, Marshall, 5:426
Duke, Maurice, 1:713
Duke, Michael, 2:214, 2:233,
    2:235
Dukelow, Richard W., 5:770
Dukore, Bernard F., 1:437,
    1:1072
Dulbecco, Renato, 5:311,
    5:759
Duling, Dennis C., 4:816
Dulles, Avery, 4:153, 4:891
Dulles, Foster Rhea, 3:544
Dumas, Alexandre (fils),
    2:473
Dumas, Alexandre (père),
    1:388, 1:773, **2:472**
Du Maurier, Daphne, 1:352,
    1:619
Du Maurier, George, 1:352,
    1:619
Dumbauld, Edward, 3:541
Dumézil, Georges, 4:435,
    4:437, 4:443, **4:471**
Dumitriu, Petru, 2:823,
    2:824
Dummett, Michael, 4:229,
    4:382
Dumont, Louis, 3:19, 4:503
Dumont, Micheline, 3:608
Dumoulin, Heinrich, 4:537,
    4:558
Dunan, Marcel, 3:7
Dunaway, David King, 1:499
Dunaway, John M., 2:482
Dunbar, Gary S., 3:118, 5:28,
    5:620
Dunbar, Janet, 1:330, 1:438
Dunbar, Maurice, 1:31

Dunbar, Paul Laurence,
    1:718
Duncan, A. A., 3:355
Duncan, A. S., 5:119
Duncan, Alastair, 1:23
Duncan, Cynthia M., 3:211
Duncan, Dayton, 3:895
Duncan, G., 4:244
Duncan, Isadora, 1:827,
    2:718, **3:741**
Duncan, Jan, 1:299
Duncan, Otis Dudley, 3:214,
    3:218
Duncan, Ray, 5:554
Duncan, Robert (Edward),
    1:911, **1:971**, 1:1003,
    1:1026
Duncan, Theodore G., 5:316
Duncan-Jones, Katherine,
    1:196
Dundes, Alan, 3:848, 3:868,
    4:428
Dunham, Vera S., 2:685
Dunham, William, 5:481
Dunkel, Wilbur D., 1:388
Dunkley, Ernest H., 4:730
Dunlap, Thomas R., 3:549
Dunlap, William, 1:636,
    1:1072
Dunleavy, Janet Egleson,
    1:505
Dunlop, Bill, 3:908
Dunlop, J., 5:298
Dunlop, John B., 2:761
Dunn, Andrew, 5:679
Dunn, Charles W., 1:147
Dunn, George E., 1:357
Dunn, John, 3:159, 4:179
Dunn, L. C., 5:778
Dunn, Peter N., 2:522
Dunn, Richard, 1:134
Dunn, Richard S., 4:736
Dunn, Rita, 3:175
Dunn, Waldo H., 3:403
Dunne, Peter, 5:763
Dunne, Tom, 1:364
Dunnigan, J. F., 3:278
Dunnington, G. W., 5:508,
    5:530
Dunsany, Lord, 1:591, 1:611,
    1:615
Duns Scotus, John, 4:93,
    4:103, **4:113**, 4:708
Dunster, David, 3:770
Dunteman, Jeff, 5:552
Duong, Pham Cao, 3:490
Dupee, Frederick W., 1:766
Du Plessis, Robert S., 3:382
Du Plessix Gray, Francine.
    See Gray, Francine du
    Plessix
Dupont-Sommer, A., 4:810
Dupré, Catherine, 1:483

Dupree, A. Hunter, 5:48
Dupree, Louis, 3:454
Dupree, Robert S., 1:889
Dupuis, J., 4:680
Dupuy, T. N., 3:278
Durán, Gloria, 2:866
Duran, Jane, 4:391
Durán, Manuel, 2:535
Durand, Maurice M., 2:339
Durang, Christopher,
    1:1071, **1:1086**
Durant, Ariel, 3:326, 3:338,
    3:401
Durant, David S., 1:622
Durant, Jack D., 1:254
Durant, Mary, 5:787
Durant, Will(iam) (James),
    3:326, 3:338, **3:401**, 4:15,
    4:16, 4:722
Duras, Marguerite, 2:473
Durback, Renee, 1:372
Durbin, Paul T., 5:6, 5:28,
    5:60, 5:70, 5:73, 5:74,
    5:128, 5:149, 5:152
Durden, Robert F., 3:527
Dürer, Albrecht, 1:15, 3:768,
    3:773, 5:189
Durfee, Harold A., 4:264
Durgnat, Raymond, 3:832
Durham, Frank, 1:1109,
    5:656
Durham, Philip, 3:554
During, Ingemar, 4:67, 4:80
Durkheim, Émile, 3:23,
    3:164, 3:198, 3:200, 3:212,
    3:225, 3:237, 3:242, 3:243,
    4:210, 4:424, 4:425, 4:427,
    4:472, 4:491, 4:493
Durnbaugh, Donald F., 4:724,
    4:732
Durning, Alan T., 5:152
Durocher, René, 3:609
Durrell, Gerald, 5:818
Durrell, Lawrence, 1:420,
    1:468, 1:862, 2:80, 2:95,
    2:372, 3:899
Durrell, Lee, 5:818, 5:822
Durrenberger, E. Paul, 3:16,
    3:381
**Dürrenmatt (or Duerren-
    matt), Friedrich**, 2:564,
    2:577
Duschl, Richard A., 3:254
Dusek, Dorothy, 5:326
Dusenbery, Verne A., 4:516
Dusinberre, Janet, 1:209
Duska, Ronald, 4:388
Dussel, Enrique, 4:748
Dutt, Ashok K., 3:482
Dutton, Geoffrey, 2:963
Dutton, Gregory Battcock,
    3:665
Dutton, Richard, 1:184, 1:204

Dutton, Robert R., 1:947
Duus, Peter, 3:474, 3:477
Duval, Edwin M., 2:497
Duyckinck, Evert A., 1:132
Duyckinck, George L., 1:132
Dvořák, Antonín, 3:693
Dvorine, William, 5:340
Dvornik, Francis, 4:692
Dwight, Timothy, 1:632
Dworetz, Steven, 4:180
Dwork, Deborah, 4:635
Dworkin, Gerald, 3:174
Dworkin, Martin, 5:776
Dworkin, Rita, 1:427
Dworkin, Ronald, 4:386
Dwyer, Frank, 3:358
Dwyer, Judith A., 5:110
Dwyer, June, 1:519
Dwyer, Philip, 4:311
Dwyer, Thomas A., 5:552
Dych, William V., 4:904
Dyck, Martin, 2:605
Dyer, Alan, 1:665, 5:591
Dyer, Denys, 2:599
Dyer, James A., 3:138
Dyer, Richard, 1:1157,
  1:1181, 1:1183
Dygat, Stanisław, 2:812
Dykeman, Peter A., 5:767
Dykhuizen, George, 4:225
Dykstra, Darrell I., 3:445
Dykstra, Waling, 2:634
Dykstra, Yoshiko, 4:537
Dym, Barry, 3:206
Dynes, Wayne R., 1:1128,
  1:1181, 1:1183, 4:894
Dyos, H. J., 1:312
Dyson, A. E., 1:122
Dyson, Frank, 5:715
Dyson, Freeman J., 5:10,
  5:110, **5:132,** 5:589
Dyster, Barrie, 3:494
Dzuback, Mary A., 3:264

E

Eades, Mary Dan, 5:371,
  5:398
Eadie, John W., 3:868
Eadmer, 4:703
Eagle, Dorothy, 1:132
Eagle, Herbert, 2:685, 2:692
Eagleton, Terry, 1:209, 1:333,
  1:924, 1:1126, 1:1131,
  2:988, 3:202, 3:211
Eakin, Marshall C., 5:212
Eakin, Paul J., 1:727, 1:808,
  1:927
Eames, Wilberforce, 1:67
Eargle, John, 5:229

Earhart, H. Byron, 4:533,
  4:534, 4:540, 4:883
Earhart, John F., 1:21
Earl, D. C., 3:320
Earle, A. S., 5:35
Earle, Sylvia, 3:920
Earman, John S., 5:62, 5:67
Earp, Frank R., 2:368
Eason, Ron, 1:15
Easson, Angus, 1:356
East, W. Gordon, 3:272
Easterbrook, W. T., 3:606
Easterling, P. E., 4:46
Eastham, D. A., 5:697
Eastham, Scott Thomas,
  5:197
Easthope, Antony, 1:1127,
  3:207, 4:29
Eastin, Roy B., 1:108
Eastling, P. E., 2:345
Eastman, Charles A., 1:726,
  1:749
Eastman, Fred, 5:809
Eastman, Lloyd E., 3:467,
  3:470
Eastman, Mary, 3:864
Eastman, Max, 3:871
Easton, Brian, 3:494
Easton, David, 3:138, **3:153**
Easton, Phoebe Jane, 1:5
Easton, Stewart C., 4:111,
  4:858
Eastwood, Bruce S., 5:666
Eaton, Clement, 3:523, 3:574
Eaton, Walter P., 1:1073
Eatwell, John, 3:44
Eatwell, Roger, 3:366
Eban, Abba, 4:593
Ebeling, Gerhard, 4:821
Eberhard, Wolfram, 4:521
Eberhardt, Vernon C., 4:720
Eberhart, Richard, 1:719,
  1:912, **1:971**
Ebersole, Gary L., 4:536
Ebert, Katherine, 3:767
Eberwein, Jane D., 1:630,
  1:747
Ebisch, Walther, 1:220
Eble, Kenneth E., 1:759,
  1:783, 1:840
Ebrey, Patricia, 4:522
Ebrey, Patricia B., 3:465,
  3:466, 3:467
**Eça de Queiróz, José Ma-
  ria,** 2:557, **2:558**
Eccles, John C., 5:81
Eccles, Mark, 1:187, 1:204
Eccles, W. J., 3:611
Echeruo, Michael J. C.,
  1:457, 2:107, **2:134**
Echevarria, Roberto G.,
  2:931
Echols, Alice, 3:215

Eck, Diana L., 4:503
Eckert, Carter J., 2:298,
  3:481
Eckert, Kevin, 3:201
Eckert, Michael, 5:669
Eckert, Roger, 5:773
Eckes, Alfred E., 5:636
Eckhart, Meister, 4:708,
  4:788
Eco, Umberto, 2:400, **2:419,**
  4:95, 4:118
**Eddington, Sir Arthur
  Stanley,** 5:586, **5:602,**
  5:677, **5:680**
Eddleman, Floyd E., 1:134,
  1:1073
Eddy, Mary Baker, 4:842,
  4:843, 4:847, **4:874,** 4:878
Edel, Abraham, 4:67
Edel, (Joseph) Leon, 1:87,
  1:414, 1:420, 1:727, 1:766,
  1:804, 1:928, **1:972,** 2:989
Edelhart, Michael, 5:355,
  5:371
Edelman, Deborah S., 5:316
Edelman, Gerald M., 5:340
Edelman, Lee, 1:823
Edelman, Marc, 3:635
Edelsky, Carole, 3:254
Edelstein, Alex X., 3:803
Edelstein, Ludwig, 4:48, 4:56
Edelsward, L. M., 3:381
Edelwich, Jerry, 5:382
Eden, David, 1:357
Edes, Mary Elisabeth, 1:430
Edey, Maitland, 5:638
Edgar, Neal L., 3:902
Edge, David O., 5:150, 5:589
Edgecombe, Rodney Sten-
  ning, 1:289, 1:552, 2:966
Edgerton, Franklin, 2:172
Edgerton, William, 1:131,
  2:3, 2:446
Edgren-Leffler, Anne Char-
  lotte, 2:671
Edie, James M., 3:188, 4:31,
  4:235
Edip, Halide, 2:97
Edison, Thomas A(lva),
  5:226, 5:228, **5:251,** 5:742
Edmond, J. B., 5:262
Edmond, Rod, 1:315, 1:391
Edmonds, J. M., 2:348
Edmondson, Edna, 4:860
Edmunds, Desmond, 1:62
Edmunds, R. David, 3:555
Edström, Vivi, 2:677
Edward, Carolyn P., 3:15
Edward, James Patrick, 3:687
Edwardes, Michael, 3:500
Edwards, Anne, 1:1249
Edwards, Bruce L., 1:513
Edwards, C. H., Jr., 5:30

Edwards, Clive, 5:266
Edwards, Diana, 5:326
Edwards, Gwynne, 3:832
Edwards, Herbert W., 1:714
Edwards, I. E., 3:300, 4:806
Edwards, James C., 4:20
Edwards, John, 3:348
Edwards, John H., 1:873
Edwards, Jonathan, 1:626,
　1:630, **1:636, 4:766,** 4:783,
　4:899
Edwards, Julia, 3:806
Edwards, Margot, 5:357
Edwards, Mark U., 4:778
Edwards, Mark W., 2:361,
　4:483
Edwards, Michelle, 4:599
Edwards, Paul, 4:2, 4:13,
　4:20, 4:94, 4:160, 5:60
Edwards, Philip, 1:216
Edwards, Ralph, 3:766
Edwards, Rem B., 4:34
Edwards, Richard, 3:60
Edwards, Ruth Dudley, 3:358,
　3:369
Edwards, T. R., 2:685
Edwards, Walter, 4:540
Eeden, Frederik van, 2:624
Eekman, Thomas, 2:785,
　2:808, 2:827, 2:835
Eells, George, 3:709
Eells, John S., Jr., 1:328
Effersöe, Rasmus, 2:655
Efron, Arthur, 2:536
Egan, David R., 2:766
Egan, Howard T., 4:173
Egan, Kieran, 3:258
Egan, Louise, 5:252
Egan, Melinda A., 2:766
Egan, Ronald C., 2:215
Egejuru, Phanuel A., 2:107
Eger, Ernestina N., 1:121
Egerton, Frank N., III, 3:549
Eglinton, John, 1:430
Eglītis, Anšlāvs, 2:803
Egudu, Romanus, 2:107
Eheart, Brenda, 5:357
Ehnmark, Erland, 4:483
Ehre, Milton, 2:700, 2:723
Ehrenberg, A.S.C., 5:521
Ehrenberg, Victor L., 2:345,
　2:353, 2:368, 2:727, 3:301
Ehrenburg (Erenburg), Ilya,
　2:717
Ehrenfeld, David, 5:114,
　5:822
Ehrenpreis, Irvin, 1:260,
　1:719
Ehrenreich, Barbara, 3:218
Ehrenreich, Henry, 5:668
Ehrenzweig, Anton, 3:757
Ehrlich, Anne, 5:831
Ehrlich, David, 5:340, 5:384

Ehrlich, Eugene, 1:132
Ehrlich, Isaac, 5:330
Ehrlich, Paul Ralph, 3:121,
　5:110, 5:769, **5:831**
Ehrlich, Victor, 2:811
Ehrman, Eliezer L., 4:639
Eichendorff, Joseph, Frei-
　herr von, 2:563, **2:577**
Eichengreen, Barry, 3:60
Eicher, Don L., 5:629
Eicher, Joanne B., 3:207
Eichner, Hans, 4:253
Eichrodt, Walther, 4:827,
　4:833
Eickelman, Dale P., 3:435
Eidelberg, Ludwig, 5:424
Eidelberg, Shlomo, 4:623
Eigner, Edwin M., 1:322,
　1:397
Eijsvoogel, Juurd, 5:10
Eikhenbaum, Boris, 2:686,
　2:735
Eiland, Murray L., 3:767
Eilon, Daniel, 1:260
Ein, Marina Newmyer, 3:806
Einarsson, Stefán, 2:640
Einstein, Albert, 1:550,
　3:111, 5:17, 5:48, 5:59,
　5:133, 5:477, 5:602, 5:606,
　5:663, 5:665, 5:675, 5:678,
　5:680, **5:681,** 5:699, 5:701,
　5:702, 5:705, 5:708, 5:715,
　5:719
Einstein, Alfred, 3:659
Einstein, Samuel, 5:424
Einzig, Hetty, 5:325
Eire, Carlos M., 4:737
Eisberg, Robert, 5:660
Eisdorfer, Carl, 5:391
Eiseley, Loren, 5:46
Eiseman, Ben, 5:405
Eisen, Arnold M., 4:634,
　4:646
Eisenbach, Elizabeth, 1:81
Eisenberg, Arlene, 5:357
Eisenberg, Azriel, 3:348
Eisenberg, David, 5:319
Eisenberg, John F., 5:344
Eisenberg, Mickey, 5:374
Eisenbichler, Konrad, 4:141
Eisendrath, Craig R., 4:342,
　5:453
Eisenhart, Margaret A.,
　3:250, 3:254, 3:255
Eisenhower, John S., 3:278
Eisenstadt, Shmuel N., 3:209,
　3:348, 4:593
Eisenstein, Elizabeth L., 1:8,
　5:36
Eisenstein, Hester, 1:925
Eisenstein, Ira, 4:659

Eisenstein, Sergei, 1:1155,
　1:1157, 1:1161, 1:1165,
　3:824, **3:835**
Eisler, Paul E., 3:655
Eisner, Elliot W., 3:254
Eisner, Gilbert M., 5:311
Eisner, Lotte H., 3:840
Eiss, Harry, 1:578, 1:1195
Eissfeldt, Otto, 4:816
Ekelöf, Gunnar, 2:673
Ekins, Paul, 3:249
Ekman, Karl, 3:718
Ekman, Kerstin, 2:671
Ekmanis, Rolfs, 2:804
Ekstrom, Kjell, 1:737
Ekwensi, Cyprain, 2:135
El-Ashry, Mohamed T., 5:289
Elazar, Daniel J., 3:439,
　4:639, 4:644
Elbert, Sarah, 1:1199
Elbow, Peter, 1:1127
Elder, Glen H., Jr., 3:173
Elder, John, 5:629, 5:818
Elderfield, John, 3:781
Elders, L., 4:67
Eldredge, Niles, 5:638, 5:763,
　5:826
Eldridge, Richard, 1:891
Elert, Werner, 4:730
Elfenbein, Anna Shannon,
　1:740
Elgar, Sir Edward, 3:693
Elgin, Catherine Z., 4:382,
　4:403
Eliade, Mircea, 2:823, **2:824,**
　4:2, 4:4, 4:425, 4:427,
　4:430, 4:431, 4:461, **4:472,**
　4:486, 4:490, 4:497, 4:503,
　4:522, 4:524, 4:543, 4:545,
　4:547, 4:548, 4:717, 4:897
Elias, Julius A., 4:80
Elias, Sherman, 5:118
Elias, Thomas S., 5:767
Elimimian, Isaac I., 2:107
Elior, Rachel, 4:853
Eliot, George, 1:310, 1:317,
　1:330, **1:352,** 1:372, 1:385,
　1:974
Eliot, Thomas H., 3:534
Eliot, T(homas) S(tearns),
　1:169, 1:177, 1:241, 1:248,
　1:302, 1:346, 1:370, 1:412,
　1:416, 1:428, 1:434, 1:467,
　1:469, **1:470,** 1:480, 1:502,
　1:511, 1:513, 1:517, 1:521,
　1:547, 1:552, 1:570, 1:691,
　1:718, 1:795, 1:806, 1:832,
　1:870, 1:890, 1:936, 1:963,
　1:974, 1:1003, 1:1048,
　1:1129, 1:1151, 1:1154,
　2:72, 2:370, 2:416, 2:418,
　2:427, 2:543, 2:655, 3:878,
　4:88, 4:305, 4:476

Elison, George, 3:474
Elkin, Judith, 4:644
Elkin, Michael, 5:401
Elkin, Stanley, 1:921, 1:972
Elkind, David, 3:267
Elkins, Stanley M., 3:523
Elkins, Stanley R., 3:583
Elledge, Jim, 1:1025
Ellen, Roy, 3:36, 4:486
Ellenberger, Henri F., 5:34
Ellery, John B., 4:244
Elliger, K., 4:794
Ellington, Edward
    Kennedy ("Duke"), 3:687,
    3:694
Elliot, Bob, 3:871
Elliot, Jeffrey M., 3:148
Elliot, T. G., 3:310
Elliott, Brian, 1:28, 2:946,
    5:152
Elliott, Clark A., 5:28
Elliott, Claudia, 2:867
Elliott, Emory, 1:130, 1:134,
    1:628, 1:650, 1:713
Elliott, Glen R., 5:341
Elliott, J. H., 3:335, 3:387
Elliott, John R., Jr, 1:159
Elliott, Marianne, 3:370
Ellis, Albert, 5:429, 5:438
Ellis, Frank H., 1:228
Ellis, Frederick S., 1:303
Ellis, Harry V., 5:350
Ellis, Havelock, 5:440
Ellis, Jane, 4:755
Ellis, John, 1:1157
Ellis, John M., 2:599
Ellis, John Tracy, 4:751
Ellis, Keith, 2:863, 2:869
Ellis, Marc H., 4:765, 4:769,
    4:896
Ellis, Peter B., 3:370
Ellis, Robert Richmond,
    2:552
Ellis, Steve, 2:418
Ellis, William, 1:794
Ellison, Curtis W., 1:739
Ellison, David R., 2:464
Ellison, Fred P., 2:892, 2:897
Ellison, Harlan, 1:1252
Ellison, Julie, 1:670
Ellison, Ralph (Waldo),
    1:973
Ellman, Richard, 1:128,
    1:410, 1:418, 1:429, 1:655,
    1:719, 1:801, 1:974
Ellmann, Maud, 1:873
Ellner, Steve, 3:641
Ellsberg, Margaret R., 1:364
Ellsworth, P., 3:168
Ellul, Jacques, 3:213, 5:70,
    5:86, 5:133, 5:163, 5:200,
    5:572

Ellwood, Robert S., 4:4,
    4:535, 4:841, 4:855
Ellwood, Robert W., 4:883
El Madhy, Christine, 4:442
el-Mallakh, Ragaei, 3:451
Elmessiri, A. M., 2:57
Elon, Amos, 4:642, 4:658
Elon, Menachem, 4:627
Elrod, J. W., 4:239
El Saffar, Ruth, 2:536
Else, Gerald F., 2:345
Else, Gerald Frank, 4:68
Elsen, Albert E., 3:757
Elser, J., 3:290
El-Shamy, Hasan M., 3:855
Elsschot, Willem, 2:621,
    2:624
Elstein, Arthur, 5:79
Elster, Jon, 4:242
Elsworth, J. D., 2:701
Elton, Charles Isaac, 1:31
Elton, Geoffrey R(udolph),
    3:334, 3:358, 3:402, 3:515,
    4:722, 4:726
Elton, Mary Augusta, 1:31
Elton, William R., 1:214
Éluard, Paul, 2:462, 2:474,
    2:854, 2:859
Elvander, Nile, 5:330
Elvin, Mark, 3:467
Elvin-Lewis, P. F., 5:351
Elwell-Sutton, L. P., 3:447
Elwin, Malcolm, 1:296, 1:389
Ely, James W., Jr., 3:139
Elytis, Odysseus, 2:370,
    2:373
Elzinga, Aant, 5:107
Elzinga, Kenneth G., 3:61
Emants, Marcellus, 2:625
Ember, Ildiko, 3:660
Emboden, William A., 2:469,
    3:834
Embree, Ainslie T(homas),
    2:171, 3:462, 3:484, 3:485,
    3:497, 4:503
Embree, Lester, 5:70
Emecheta, Buchi, 2:105,
    2:136
Emeljanow, Victor, 1:322
Emerson, Arthur, 4:532
Emerson, E. H., 1:634
Emerson, Everett, 1:628,
    1:644, 1:783
Emerson, Michael, 3:345
Emerson, Ralph Waldo,
    1:649, 1:654, 1:659, 1:668,
    1:672, 1:675, 1:700, 1:704,
    1:705, 1:717, 1:772, 1:801,
    1:803, 1:933, 1:1192,
    1:1197, 2:908, 4:840, 5:836
Emerson, Robert M., 3:12
Emery, Alan E. H., 5:781
Emery, Edwin, 1:8, 3:806

Emery, Laura Comer, 1:354
Emery, Lynne Fauley, 3:733
Emery, Michael, 1:8, 3:806
Emery, Walter B., 3:300
Emiliani, Cesare, 5:11
Emilsson, Eyjolfur Kjalar,
    4:86
Emin, Gevorg, 2:76
Eminescu, Mihail, 2:823,
    2:824, 2:825
Emmanuel, Muriel, 3:761
Emme, Eugene M., 5:37
Emmerson, Richard K.,
    1:141, 1:147, 1:157
Emmet, Dorothy, 4:342
Emmett, Steven Wiley, 5:395
Empson, William, 1:192,
    1:925
Emrich, Duncan, 1:1197
Emsley, Clive, 3:362
Emy, H. V., 3:363
Enchi Fumiko, 2:286
Enck, John J., 1:887
Enckell, Rabbe, 2:657
Endō Shūsaku, 2:286, 4:540
Endress, Gerhard, 4:568
Eng, Robert Y., 3:470
Engel, Bernard F., 1:863
Engel, Eva L., 2:566
Engel, Lehman, 1:1073, 3:660
Engelhardt, H. Tristram,
    5:77, 5:78, 5:79, 5:80, 5:81,
    5:120, 5:133
Engelkes, James R., 5:418
Engell, James, 1:225, 1:265
Engels, Donald W., 3:308
Engels, Friedrich, 3:37,
    3:74, 3:94, 4:226, 4:228,
    4:241
Engen, Rodney K., 1:583
Engerman, Stanley L., 3:54,
    3:547
England, Eugene, 1:704,
    1:779
English, Ava C., 5:424
English, Horace B., 5:424
English, Jane, 4:527
English, John, 3:616
English, Mary P., 5:783
English, Raymond, 5:110
Englund, Steven, 3:558
Engman, Max, 3:381
Ennius, 2:378
Eno, Robert B., 4:688
Enquist, P(er) O(lov), 2:671,
    2:673
Enroth, Ronald M., 4:857,
    4:864
Enser, A. G., 3:825
Ensminger, M. Eugene, 5:263
Ensor, Robert C., 3:363
Entwistle, Harold, 4:287
Eoff, Sherman H., 2:522

Ephron, Delia, 3:871
Epicurus, 2:378, 2:388, 4:53, **4:73**, 4:75, 4:89, 4:172
Epp, Eldon J., 4:813
Epp, Ronald, 4:57
Epstein, Benjamin, 4:639
Epstein, Beryl, 5:246
Epstein, Daniel Mark, 4:753
Epstein, Dena J., 3:866
Epstein, Edmund L., 1:505
Epstein, Edward J., 3:806
Epstein, Julia, 1:1183
Epstein, Klaus, 3:341
Epstein, Melech, 4:656, 4:657
Epstein, Samuel S., 5:246, 5:636, 5:822
Equiano, Olaudah, 2:104, 2:125, **2:137**
Erasmus, Charles J., 3:217
Erasmus, Desiderius, 1:193, 1:196, 1:389, 2:617, 2:620, 2:625, 4:133, **4:138**, 4:147, 4:155, 4:709, 4:721, 4:790
Erdinast-Vulcan, Daphna, 1:464, 1:489
Erdman, Carl, 4:692
Erdman, David V., 1:279
Erdozain, Placido, 4:748
Erenberg, Lewis A., 3:559
Erens, Patricia, 1:1158
Eribon, Didier, 4:401
Erickson, Carolly, 3:368, 4:726
Erickson, Darlene W., 1:864
Erickson, Jim, 5:543
Erickson, Jon, 5:622
Erickson, Lee, 1:339
Erickson, Milton H., **5:441**
Ericsson, Ronald J., 5:358
Erigena, Johannes Scotus, 4:93, 4:100, **4:114**
Erikson, Erik H(omburger), 3:173, **3:181**, 3:334, 4:553, 4:778, **5:441**
Erkkila, Betsy, 1:707
Erlanger, Ellen, 5:14
Erlen, Jonathon, 5:28
Erlich, Victor, 2:686, 2:722, 2:746
Erman, Adolf, 2:52, 3:300
Ermann, M. David, 5:125
Ermolaev, Herman, 2:686, 2:756
Erndl, Kathleen M., 4:504
Ernst, Earle, 2:273
Ernst, Richard Robert, 5:216, **5:743**
Ernst, Wallace G., 5:616
Erodes, Richard, 3:864
Erofeev, Venedikt, 2:717
Eroschenko, Victor, 5:773
Errington, Jane, 3:613
Errington, Paul L., 5:826

Erro-Peralta, Nora, 2:848
Erskine, Andrew, 4:55, 4:57
Ervin, Sam J., Jr., 3:871
Erwin, J., 5:770, 5:772
Esar, Evan, 3:871
Escarpit, Robert, 3:202
Eschelbach, Claire, 1:499
Eschenbach, Wolfram von, 2:562, 2:582
Eschholz, Paul A., 1:759
Escott, Paul D., 3:575
Escott, T. H., 1:340
Esenin, Sergei, 2:718
Esherick, Joseph W., 3:470
Eskin, Stanley G., 2:508
Espanca, Florbela, 2:557
Esposito, John L., 3:442, 3:463, 4:373, 4:578
Esposito, Joseph L., 4:252
Esslemont, J. E., 4:568, 4:861
Esslin, Martin, 1:425, 1:1081, 2:448, 2:452, 2:460
Estees, Sylvia P., 1:951
Esteicher, Donna, 5:321
Estell, Doug, 3:249
Estep, William R., 4:733
Estes, William K., 3:169, 3:175
Esthus, Raymond A., 3:595
Etherege, Sir George, 1:228, **1:242**
Etheridge, J. W., 4:608
Etherington, Don, 1:26
Etherton, Michael, 2:107
Etkin, Bernard, 5:219
Etmekjian, James, 2:76, 2:77
Etter, D. M., 5:552
Ettinghausen, Maurice L., 1:31
Ettorre, Elizabeth, 5:403
Etulain, Richard, 1:1215, 1:1219
Euben, J. Peter, 4:48
Euclid, 5:38, 5:477, 5:485, **5:504**
Eugenio, Damiana L., 2:329
Euler, Leonhard, 5:489, **5:505**
Euripides, 1:483, 1:529, 1:1091, 2:342, 2:353, **2:355**, 2:367, **4:474**
Eusebius of Caesarea, 4:709
Evangeliou, Christos, 4:61
Evans, Arthur B., 3:834
Evans, Barbara, 1:425
Evans, Bergen, 1:91, 1:116
Evans, Bertrand, 1:210, 1:272
Evans, B. Ifor, 1:216
Evans, Charles, 1:67, 3:510
Evans, Christopher, 5:537
Evans, Cornelia, 1:91
Evans, Donald, 4:888
Evans, Elizabeth, 1:852

Evans, Frederick W., 4:849
Evans, G. Blakemore, 1:206
Evans, Gareth, 1:425
Evans, Gillian Rosemary, 4:16, 4:108, 4:110, 4:112, 4:676, 4:696, 4:702, 4:703, 4:710
Evans, Harry B., 2:390
Evans, J. A., 3:316, 3:319
Evans, J.A.S., 4:480
Evans, J. D., 4:68
Evans, J. P., 3:859
Evans, Joan, 3:765
Evans, John H., 1:289
Evans, Joseph Claude, Jr., 4:334
Evans, Linda, 5:318
Evans, Mark, 3:667
Evans, Michael, 2:509
Evans, Miriama, 2:971
Evans, Nancy, 1:46
Evans, Nathaniel, 1:626
Evans, Oliver, 1:1102
Evans, Patrick, 2:970
Evans, Paul M., 3:498
Evans, Peter, 3:685
Evans, Rand B., 3:167, 3:168
Evans, Richard I., 1:1104, 3:180, 3:182, 3:192, 3:193, 5:432, 5:442, 5:451, 5:468
Evans, Robert C., 1:184
Evans, Sara M., 3:513
Evans, Walker, 3:533
Evans-Pritchard, E(dward) E(van), 3:19, 3:20, 3:25, **3:29 4:475**
Evelyn-White, H. G., 2:360
Even, Ahmet O., 2:96
Evenari, Michael, 3:439
Evennet, H. O., 4:728
Everest, Kevin, 1:288
Everett, Barbara, 1:213
Everett, John Rutherford, 3:73
Evernden, Neil, 5:114, 5:822
Eversman, Sharon, 5:759
Everson, William, 1:851
Evert, Walter H., 1:294
Eves, Howard, 5:487, 5:492, 5:493
Evetts, L. C., 1:15
Ewald, Johannes, 2:644
Ewbank, Inga-Stina, 1:216
Ewen, Stuart, 3:873
Ewer, R. F., 5:770
Ewing, Alfred C., 4:20
Ewing, Katherine P., 4:578
Exman, Eugene, 1:41
Eyck, Erich, 3:341, 3:376
Eyck, F. Gunther, 3:380
Eynine, Simon, 4:283
Eysenck, H. J., 5:404, 5:426

Ezell, Margaret J. M., 1:225
Ezra, Moses Ibn, 2:23

F

Faas, Ekbert, 1:315, 1:498
Faber, Joseph, 3:785
Faber, M. D., 4:865
Faber, Rodney B., 5:229
Fabian, A.C., 3:18
Fabre, Jean Henri, 5:796
Fabre, Michel, 1:906
Fabricand, Burton F., 5:522
Fabricant, Carole, 1:260
Fabricius, Johan, 2:310
Fabry, Joseph B., 5:444
**Fackenheim, Emil, 4:647,
4:663**
Faden, Ruth R., 5:120
Faderman, Lillian, 1:1181,
3:552
Fadiman, Clifton, 1:75
Fadiman, James, 3:175,
5:319, 5:426
Faelton, Sharon, 5:386
Fagan, Brian M., 3:416,
3:516, 4:432, 4:454
Fage, J. D., 3:416, 3:417,
3:420
Fagin, Gerald, 4:685
Fain, Venjamin M., 5:697
Fainberg, Anthony, 5:278
Fainlight, Ruth, 1:547
Fairbank, Alfred, 1:15
Fairbank, J. D., 5:650
Fairbank, John King, 2:186,
3:461, 3:464, 3:466, 3:467,
3:468, 3:470, 3:471, **3:497,**
4:358, 4:532
Fairbridge, Rhodes W., 5:617
Fairburn, Miles, 3:495
Fairchild, Wilma B., 5:620
Fairclough, Adam, 3:537
Fairclough, Henry R., 1:798
Fairfield, Leslie, 1:172
Fairley, William B., 5:522
Fairweather, Eugene R., 4:94
Faiz, Ahmed Faiz, 2:175
Fajardo, Salvador J., 2:525
Fakhry, Majid, 4:97, 4:373,
4:574
Fakih, Kimberly O., 1:1195,
3:871
Falaturi, Abdolajawad, 4:572
Falcone, Vincent J., 4:20
Faldbakken, Knut, 2:662,
2:663
Falen, James E., 2:700
Falger, Vincent S., 3:204
Falk, David S., 5:666
Falk, Doris V., 1:1093, 1:1108

Falk, Nancy Auer, 4:504,
4:512, 4:529, 4:539
Falk, Signi L., 1:858, 1:1118
Falkus, Malcolm, 3:354
Fall, Aminata Sow, 2:105
Fallaci, Oriana, 2:400, **2:420**
Fallico, Arturo, 4:126
Fallis, Richard, 1:417
Fallon, Eileen, 1:618
Fallon, N., 3:435
Falls, Cyril, 3:278
Falstein, Linda D., 5:484
Falstein, Louis, 2:46
Faludi, Susan, 3:218
Fan Ch'eng-ta, 2:196, 2:213,
2:230
Fancher, Raymond E., 5:447
Fang, Chaoying, 3:465
Fang, J. A., 5:479, 5:500
Fanger, Donald, 2:715, 2:722
Fan Hichtum, Nynke, 2:636
Fann, K. T., 4:272
Fann, W. E., 5:426
Fanon, Franz, 2:121
Fant, Maureen B., 3:309
Faraday, Michael, 5:228,
5:578, 5:665, **5:683,** 5:700,
5:744
Faragher, John Mack, 3:508,
3:523, 3:908
Farah, Caesar E., 3:442,
4:574
Farah, Nuruddin, 2:121
Faraone, Christopher A.,
4:451
Farber, Daniel A., 3:141
Farber, Eduard, 5:728
Farber, Marvin, 4:34
Farber, Paul, 5:33
Farberon, Norman, 5:423,
5:427
Farcy, Robert S., 4:337
Fardon, David F., 5:396
Faris, Wendy B., 2:866
Farish, Donald, 5:763
Farley, Reynolds, 3:209
Farmaian, Sattareh F., 3:447
Farmer, D. H., 1:143
Farmer, Edward L., 3:463
Farmer, G., 5:634
Farmer, John S., 1:92
Farmer, Philip Jose, 1:1257
Farnell, Lewis R., 4:545
Farner, Oskar, 4:791
Farnes, Patricia, 5:187
Farnham, Charles H., 1:691,
3:592
Farnsworth, Susan H., 3:366
Farquhar, George, 1:243,
1:1069
Farquharson, Arthur, 4:76
Farquharson, John, 3:377
Farr, Dorothy M., 1:180

Farr, James, 4:242
Farrand, John, Jr., 5:759
Farrand, Max, 3:541
Farrar, Janet, 4:865
Farrar, Stewart, 4:865
Farrell, David, 1:44
**Farrell, James T(homas),
1:832**
Farrell, John C., 1:731
Farrell, Joseph, 2:397
Farrell Lee, Grace, 1:1050,
2:48
Farrer, Claire R., 3:848,
3:866
Farrias, Victor, 4:293
Farrier, Susan E., 3:372
Farrington, Benjamin, 4:165
Farris, William Wayne, 3:474
Farrokhzad, Forough, 2:88,
2:90, 2:94
Farrow, Frank, 5:335
Farry, Stephen, 1:301
Farson, Negley, 3:902
Farudi, Daryush, 1:77
al-Faruqi, Isma'il Ragi, 4:574
Farvar, M. Taghi, 5:213
Farwell, Byron, 3:363, 3:938
Fasching, Darrell J., 5:165
Fasciana, Guy S., 5:340
Fasel, George, 3:152
Fash, William L., 4:455
Fasick, Adele M., 1:32
Fasih, Isma'il, 2:84
Fass, Ekbert, 1:913
Fass, Paula S., 3:534
Fassbinder, Werner, 3:836
Fast, Howard, 1:1245,
1:1246
el-Fathaly, Omar I., 3:454
Fatout, Paul, 1:735
Fatula, Mary Ann, 4:707
Fauchard, Pierre, 5:407
Fauel, John, 5:30
Faulkner, Christopher, 3:842
Faulkner, Claude W., 1:283
Faulkner, Donald W., 1:823
Faulkner, Howard J., 5:464
Faulkner, Peter, 1:382, 1:415,
1:567
Faulkner, Peter T., 5:110
Faulkner, Raymond O., 2:52,
4:442
Faulkner, William, 1:635,
1:673, 1:683, 1:703, 1:736,
1:802, 1:811, 1:822, **1:834,**
1:844, 1:883, 1:892, 1:903,
1:946, 1:972, 1:1009,
1:1024, 1:1056, 1:1193,
2:87, 2:123, 2:258, 2:427,
2:432, 2:509, 2:794, 2:863,
2:882, 2:902, 2:913, 3:837,
4:321
Fauré, Gabriel, 3:695, 3:712

Faurot, Jeannette L., 2:233
Fausset, Hugh I., 1:238
Faust, Drew Gilpin, 3:523, 3:527
Faust, Langdon L., 1:121, 1:127
Fava, Claudio G., 3:837
Faverty, Frederic E., 1:315
Fawkes, Richard, 1:332
Faxon, Alicia Craig, 1:392
Fay, Francesca C., 5:357
Fayette, Mme de La, 2:445, 2:485
Feachem, Richard G., 5:352
Feagans, Lynne, 3:803
Fear, Ypk fan der, 2:634
Fears, J. Rufus, 4:452
Feather, Leonard, 3:668
Feather, Norman, 5:712
Featherman, David L., 3:214
Febvre, Lucien, 1:8, 2:497, 4:126
Feder, Bud, 5:418
Feder, Don, 4:655
Feder, J., 5:328
Feder, Lillian, 1:417, 1:913, 2:988
Federico, P. J., 5:503
Federoff, Nina, 5:806
Fedin, Konstantin, 2:718
Fedoryka, Damian, 4:895
Feduccia, Alan, 5:776
Fee, Elizabeth, 3:201, 5:387
Fee, Gordon D., 4:814
Feenberg, Andrew, 5:73, 5:152
Feenstra, Ronald J., 4:886
Feest, Christian F., 3:759
Fehrenbacher, Don E., 3:527
Feibleman, James Kern, 4:283, 4:523, 5:213
Feidelson, Charles N., 1:128, 1:650
Feierberg (Feuerberg), Mordecai Ze'ev, 2:17
Feifel, Eugene, 2:216
Feigenbaum, Edward A., 5:74, 5:567, 5:570
Feigl, Herbert, 4:264, 5:80
Fein, David A., 2:515
Fein, Leonard J., 4:642
Fein, Richard J., 2:30
Feinberg, Gerald, 5:650, 5:654
Feinberg, Joel, 4:19, 4:20, 4:386
Feinberg, Paul, 4:21
Feinbloom, Richard I., 5:358
Feingold, Carl, 5:552
Feingold, Henry L., 4:594, 4:639
Feinsilver, Lillian M., 2:31
Feinstein, Alvan, 5:79

Feis, Herbert, 3:278, 3:344, 3:534
Feiwel, George R, 3:103
Feld, Bernard T., 5:110
Feld, Eliot, 3:742
Feldberg, Michael, 3:523, 5:341
Feldhusen, John F., 3:169
Feldman, David M., 4:598, 4:895
Feldman, Elaine B., 5:349
Feldman, Julian, 5:570
Feldman, Lily G., 3:439
Feldman, Louis H., 4:604, 4:608
Feldman, Paula R., 5:561
Feldman, Rodney M., 5:626
Feldman, William H., 5:387
Feldstein, Martin, 3:50, 3:53, 3:58
Felgar, Robert, 1:906
Felici, James, 5:561
Fell, Joseph P., III, 4:330
Felleisen, Matthias, 5:552
Fellini, Federico, 3:836, 3:843
Fellman, M., 3:278
Fellman, Michael, 3:525, 4:844
Fellner, William, 3:57, 3:76
Fellow, Otis, 2:472
Fellows, Donald K., 3:126
Fellows, Jay, 1:395
Fellows, Otis, 4:196
Felman, Shoshana, 2:989
Felman, Yehudi M., 5:390
Felperin, Howard, 1:210, 1:213
Feltes, N. N., 1:318
Fenelon, K. G., 3:451
Feng, Gia-Fu, 4:527
Feng, Yuan-chun, 2:189
Feng Chi-ts'ai, 2:243
Feng Hsüeh-feng, 2:244
Feng Meng-lung, 2:188, 2:197
Fenichel, Carol H., 5:314
Fenlon, Iain, ed., 3:660
Fennell, Francis L., 1:392
Fennell, John, 2:686
Fenno, Richard F., Jr., 3:146
Fenollosa, Ernest F., 2:273
Fensch, Thomas, 1:891
Fenton, Carroll Lane, 5:622
Fenton, Charles A., 1:816, 1:846
Fenton, John Y., 4:508
Fenton, Martin S., 3:510
Fenton, Mildred Adams, 5:622
Fenton, Thomas P., 3:462, 5:261
Fenwick, M. J., 2:931

Ferber, Richard, 5:322
Ferejohn, Michael, 4:68
Ferguson, Charles A., 3:21
Ferguson, Chris D., 3:331
Ferguson, E. James, 3:510
Ferguson, Eugene S., 5:12, 5:192, 5:227, 5:231
Ferguson, Everett, 4:676, 4:807
Ferguson, J. De Lancey, 1:280
Ferguson, James, 4:194
Ferguson, John, 3:306, 4:48, 4:68, 4:110, 4:446, 4:449, 4:895
Ferguson, Kitty, 5:17
Ferguson, Margaret, 1:165
Ferguson, Robert, 1:650, 1:863
Ferguson, Russell, 1:1133
Ferguson, Sinclair B., 4:5
Ferguson, Suzanne, 1:993
Ferguson, Wallace K., 3:333
Fergusson, Francis, 2:418
Fergusson, Rosalind, 1:115
Fergusson, Thomas G., 3:363
Ferkiss, Victor, 5:74, 5:152
Ferlazzo, Paul J., 1:747
Ferm, Deane W., 4:718, 4:743
Ferm, Vergilius, 4:16
Fermat, Pierre de, 5:483, 5:485, 5:488, 5:506, 5:525
Fermi, Enrico, 3:111, 5:142, 5:677, 5:684, 5:708, 5:720
Fermi, Laura, 3:385, 5:685
Fermor, Patrick L., 3:899
Fern, Fanny, 1:671
Fernandez, Doreen G., 2:328
Fernandez, James W., 3:14, 4:426
Fernández Moreno, César, 2:845
Fernea, Elizabeth W., 3:439
Fernia, Joseph V., 4:287
Ferrante, Joan M., 2:512, 4:698
Ferranti, Philip, 3:841
Ferrari, G.R.F., 4:80
Ferrarini, Elizabeth, 5:547
Ferré, Frederick, 5:70, 5:114, 5:197
Ferrell, Keith, 1:885
Ferrell, Robert H., 3:537, 3:542
Ferrer, Daniel, 1:505, 1:570
Ferrier, J. P., 3:452
Ferris, Ina, 1:299
Ferris, Timothy, 5:587, 5:588, 5:593, 5:595, 5:603, 5:691, 5:713
Ferris, William, 3:509, 3:851
Ferro, Marc, 3:343, 3:396

Ferry, Anne, 1:165
Ferry, David, 1:307
Ferry, Luc, 4:293, 5:90
Ferry, Ted S., 5:244
Fesharaki, F., 5:280
Fesharaki, Fereidun, 3:447
Feshbach, H., 5:674
Feshbach, Murray, 5:353
Fessenden, Joan S., 5:732
Fessenden, Ralph J., 5:732
Fester, René, 5:820
Festinger, Leon, 3:171, 3:210, 4:870
Fetterley, Judith, 1:717
Fetterman, David M., 3:254
Fettner, Ann Giudici, 5:387
Fetzer, James H., 5:62
Fetzer, Mary, 1:108, 3:506
Feuchtwanger, E. J., 3:376
Feuchtwanger, Lion, 2:578
Feuer, Kathryn B., 2:761
Feuer, Lewis S., 4:187, 5:661
**Feuerbach, Ludwig
   Andreas, 4:227**, 4:740
Feuerberg, M. Z., 2:7
Feuerlicht, Ignace, 2:602
Feuerstein, Georg, 4:497
Feuerwerker, Albert, 3:470
Feuerwerker, Yi-tse Mei, 2:264
Feyerabend, Paul Karl,
   4:160, **4:398,** 4:409, 5:66, **5:86**
**Feynman, Richard
   P(hillips),** 3:908, 5:133, 5:650, **5:685,** 5:715, 5:717
Fichman, Martin, 5:812
Fichner-Rathus, Lois, 3:757
Fichte, Johann, 3:375
Fichte, Johann Gottlieb,
   4:158, **4:197,** 4:231, 4:251, 4:252, 4:254
Fichtelberg, Joseph, 1:727
Fichter, Joseph Henry, 4:154, 4:871
Ficino, Marsilio, 2:433, 4:80, 4:123, **4:140,** 4:152
Fido, Elaine Savory, 2:930
Fiechter, A., 5:222
Fiedler, Leslie A(aron),
   1:209, 1:628, **1:975**
Fieg, Eugene C., 4:6
Field, Andrew, 1:813, 1:1020
Field, Arthur, 4:126
Field, G. C., 4:80
Field, Harry, 3:203
Field, Leslie, 1:904
Field, Norma, 2:279
Field, Richard, 1:202
Field, Stephen, 4:524
Field, Sydney, 4:555

Fielding, Henry, 1:223, 1:229, **1:244,** 1:403, 2:383, 2:391
Fielding, K. J., 1:349
Fielding, Mantle, 3:761
Fields, Rick, 4:859
Fields, Willa L., 5:340
Fiell, Charlotte, 3:766
Fiell, Peter, 3:766
Fienberg, Stephen E., 5:523
Fierman, Morton, 4:665
Fierstein, Stephen K., 5:780
Fierz, Markus, 4:126, 5:708
Fifer, Elizabeth, 1:882
Fifoot, Richard, 1:548
Figgis, John N., 4:126
Figurovskii, Nikolai Aleksandrovich, 3:683
Filene, Peter, 3:552
Filipowicz, Halina, 2:821
Filmer-Sankey, Josephine, 3:357
Filoramo, Giovanni, 4:60, 4:685
Filoreto, Carl, 3:806
Filreis, Alan, 1:887
Finamore, John, 4:61
Finch, Michael, 1:458
Finch, Robert, 5:818
Findlater, Richard, 1:426
Findlay, Elsa, 3:745
Findlay, James, 3:759
Findlay, Robert R., 1:1072
Findley, Carter V., 3:452
Findley, Timothy, 2:903, **2:910**
Findling, John E., 3:138, 3:508
Findly, Ellison Banks, 4:426, 4:504, 4:513, 4:529, 4:532, 4:578
Fine, Gail, 4:68
Fine, John V. A., 3:301
Fine, Lawrence, 4:630
Fine, Michael R., 3:148
Fine, Reuben, 5:448
Fineberg, Harvey V., 5:390
Finegan, Jack, 4:439, 4:808, 4:811
Fineman, Joel, 1:215
Finer, S. E., 1:345
Fingard, Judith, 3:608
Fingarette, Herbert, 5:421, 5:424, 5:426
Fink, Augusta, 1:733
Fink, Eugen, 4:74
Fink, Paul Jay, 5:415
Fink, Roberts, 3:655
Finkbeiner, Ann K., 5:386
Finke, Wayne H., 2:849
Finkel, Avraham Y., 4:648
Finkel, Donald, 2:235
Finkelhor, David, 5:416

Finkelman, Paul A., 3:555
Finkelstein, Bonnie
   Blumenthal, 1:477
Finkelstein, Louis, 3:348, 4:594, 4:615, 4:620, 4:622
Finkelstein, R. J., 5:715
Finklepearl, Philip J., 1:173
Finlay, Michael, 1:15
Finley, John H., Jr., 2:351, 2:361, 2:365, 3:323
Finley, Moses I., 2:345, 2:361, 3:298, 3:301, 3:307
Finn, Chester E., Jr., 3:249
Finn, David, 4:446
Finn, Julio, 3:668
Finn, Susan, 5:345
Finnegan, Ruth, 4:460
Finneran, Richard J., 1:572
Finney, Brian, 1:429
Finney, Claude L., 1:294
Finnie, David H., 3:450
Finnis, John, 4:743
Finocchiaro, Maurice A., 4:143, 4:172
Finson, Jon W., 3:706, 3:716
Finson, Shelley Davis, 4:749
Finucane, Ronald C., 4:726
Fiore, Robert L., 2:524
Fiorenza, Elisabeth Schüssler, 4:750, 4:814
Fiorenza, Francis Schüssler, 4:891
Fiori, Gabriella, 2:516
Fiorina, Morris P., 3:146
**Firbank, (Arthur Annesley)
   Ronald, 1:473**
Firchow, Evelyn S., 2:640
Firchow, Peter Edgerly, 1:499
Firdawsī, 2:82, 2:89
Firestone, Bernard J., 3:537
Firkin, B. G., 5:5, 5:367
Firkins, Ina T., 1:124, 2:666
Firkins, Oscar W., 1:670, 1:759
First, Joan M., 3:250
Firth, C. H., 3:406
Firth, Katherine R., 4:726
Firth, Raymond, 3:16, 3:17, 3:19, 3:24, 3:25, **3:29,** 3:36, 4:461, 4:486
Fisch, Harold, 2:12
Fisch, Max H., 4:34, 4:34
Fisch, Menachem, 4:258, 5:57, 5:58
Fischel, Jack, 4:594
Fischel, W. J., 4:584
Fischer, Claude S., 3:208, **3:226**
Fischer, David Hackett, 3:9, 3:276, 3:516, 3:552
Fischer, David W., 5:759
Fischer, Dietrich, 3:149

Fischer, Fritz, 3:278, 3:376
Fischer, Heinz-Dietrich, 3:806
Fischer, K. D., 3:291
Fischer, Louis, 3:396
Fischer, Michael F. J., 4:426
Fischer, Michael M., 3:448
Fischer-Dieskau, Dietrich, 3:715, 3:716
Fischer-Pap, Lucia, 5:386
Fischhoff, Baruch, 3:213
Fischler, Alan, 1:358
Fischoff, Baruch, 5:128
Fish, Stanley E., 1:181, 1:192, 1:197, **1:975,** 1:1127, 1:1143
Fishbane, Michael, 4:610, 4:823, 4:883
Fishburn, Katherine, 3:873
Fisher, Albert L., 5:353
Fisher, Barbara, 1:457, 1:887
Fisher, Benjamin F., 1:693
Fisher, Charles H., 5:729
Fisher, Clay/Henry, Will, **1:1212**
Fisher, Clive, 1:465
Fisher, David, 5:110
Fisher, David E., 3:906
Fisher, Dexler, 1:1128
Fisher, Herbert A., 3:152
Fisher, Irving, 3:75, 3:76
Fisher, Jeffrey A., 5:334
Fisher, John H., 1:151, 1:152
Fisher, Judith Law, 1:322
Fisher, Leonard Everett, 1:15
Fisher, May, 3:510
Fisher, Michael H., 3:485
Fisher, Miriam, 5:319
Fisher, Peter, 1:279
Fisher, Rhoda L., 3:871, 5:422
Fisher, Richard B., 5:409
Fisher, Robin, 3:610
Fisher, Ronald Aylmer, 5:525, **5:528**
Fisher, Seymour, 3:871, 5:422
Fisher, Susan M., 5:350
Fisher, W.B., 3:435
Fisher-Wirth, Ann W., 1:901
Fishkin, James S., 3:143
Fishlock, David, 5:221
Fishlock, Trevor, 3:369
Fishman, Aryei, 4:654
Fishman, Joshua A., 2:30, 2:31
Fishman, K. D., 5:542
Fishman, Stephen, 1:118
Fishman, Sylvia B., 4:650
Fishman, William J., 4:656
Fishwick, Marshall W., 3:872, 3:873
Fisk, Erma J., 5:818
Fiske, Arland O., 3:381
Fiske, John, 3:873

Fitch, Brian T., 1:440, 2:464
Fitch, James Marsten, 3:762
Fitch, Noel R., 1:36
Fitch, Val Logsdon, 5:679, **5:686**
Fite, David, 1:1138
Fitts, Dudley, 2:349
Fitz, Earl E., 2:896
Fitzgerald, Charles P., 2:186
Fitzgerald, Frances, 1:49, 3:515, 3:537, 3:559
Fitzgerald, F(rancis) Scott **(Key), 1:838,** 2:907
Fitzgerald, Percy, 1:32
Fitzgerald, Robert, 2:359, 2:360
Fitzhardinge, L. F., 3:301
Fitzhugh, Louise, 1:1195
Fitzhugh, William, 3:517
Fitzmyer, Joseph A., 4:795, 4:811
Fitzpatrick, Sheila, 3:394
Fitzpatrick, Vincent, 1:860
Fitzsimmons, Linda, 1:459
Fjermedal, Grant, 5:372, 5:542
Flaceliere, Robert, 2:345
Flader, Susan L., 5:834
Flage, Daniel, 4:201
Flaherty, Joseph, 5:428
Flaherty, Leo, 3:912
Flahiff, F. T., 1:214
Flake, Chad J., 4:845
Flamm, Dudley, 1:404
Flamm, Kenneth, 5:184
Flanagan, Cathleen C., 3:849
Flanagan, Hallie, 1:1073
Flanagan, James K., 1:1104
Flanagan, John T., 1:859, 3:849
Flanagan, Owen, 3:168, 4:382, 4:388
Flanagan, Thomas, 3:615
Flanders, Helen H., 3:858
Flannery, Austin P., 4:743, 4:891
Flannery, Edward, 4:635
Flating, Sonja, 5:322
Flaubert, Gustave, 1:463, 1:1019, 2:445, **2:475,** 2:504, 2:506, 2:528, 2:651, 2:723, 2:886, 4:329
Flaxman, Edward, 5:231
Fleck, Jeffrey, 2:17
Fleck, Richard F., 1:804
Fleischer, Michael, 5:628
Fleishman, Avrom, 1:270
Fleishman, Lazar, 2:746
Fleming, E. McClung, 1:40
Fleming, Ian, 1:432, 1:592, **1:593,** 1:595
Fleming, John, 3:762, 3:765
Fleming, John F., 1:34, 1:43

Fleming, John V., 4:699
Fleming, Robert E., 1:771, 1:817
Fleming, Sir Alexander, **5:407**
Fleming, Stuart J., 5:192
Fleming-Williams, Ian, 3:773
Flemming, N. C., 5:631
Flesch, Rudolf, 1:118
Fletcher, A. J., 3:360
Fletcher, Anne B., 5:322
Fletcher, Anthony, 3:360
Fletcher, Arnold, 3:454
Fletcher, Banister, 3:761
Fletcher, Colin, 3:908
Fletcher, George P., 4:389
Fletcher, John, 1:172, 1:179, 1:524, 2:509, 2:535
Fletcher, Joseph, 5:120
Fletcher, Katy, 1:593
Fletcher, Miles, 3:477
Fletcher, Pauline, 1:315
Fletcher, Richard, 1:272, 2:537
Fletcher, Sally, 5:392
Fletcher, Steve, 1:123
Fletcher, W.J.B., 2:192
Fletcher, W. Y., 1:23
Flew, Antony G., 4:3, 4:13, 4:21, 4:202, 4:264
Flexner, Abraham S., 5:373
Flexner, Eleanor, 1:1073
Flinn, Caryl, 3:825
Flinn, Michael W., 3:341, 3:355
Flint, J. E., 3:417, 3:420
Flint, Richard F., 5:626
Flint, Valerie I., 3:916
Flock, Emil, 5:537
Floistad, Guttorm, 4:264, 5:60
Flora, Cornelia, 5:220, 5:266
Flora, Joseph M., 1:712, 1:794, 1:1217
Flores, Albert, 5:73, 5:128
Flores, Angel, 2:536, 2:566, 2:596, 2:849
Flores, Barbara, 3:254
Flores, Fernando, 5:571
Florin, John W., 3:124
Florit, Eugenio, 2:526
Florman, Samuel C(harles), 5:70, 5:165, **5:252**
Flory, Paul John, 5:745
Flory, Wendy S., 1:873
Flournoy, T., 4:237
Flower, Elizabeth, 4:160
Flower, John E., 2:489
Flower, Newman, 3:698
Floyd, Virginia, 1:1108
Fluegel, Jane, 3:682
Fluegelman, Andrew, 5:561
Fluegge, S., 5:652
Flygt, Sten G., 2:587

Flynn, Carol Houlihan, 1:254
Flynn, George Q., 3:538
Flynn, Richard, 1:993
Fo, Dario, 2:400, 2:420
Foakes, R. A., 1:288
Fodor, Alexander, 2:766
Foerster, Norman, 1:653, 1:713, 1:717
Foerster, Werner, 4:807, 4:811
Fogarty, Robert S., 4:844
Fogel, Daniel M., 1:766
Fogel, Ephim, 1:184
Fogel, Robert W., 3:54, 3:515, 3:547
Fogel, Stan, 1:943
Fogelin, Robert J., 4:202, 4:345
Fogg, Walter L., 4:23
Fogle, Richard H., 1:268, 1:303, 1:677
Fohrer, Georg, 4:816
Folb, Peter I., 5:350
Folejewski, Zbigniew, 2:811
Foley, H., 2:357
Foley, Helene P., 4:475
Foley, James D., 5:564
Foley, Martha, 1:806, 1:921
Foligno, Cesare, 2:401
Folkenflik, Robert, 1:225, 1:250
Folks, H., 3:278
Folks, J. Leroy, 5:522
Folland, H. F., 3:907
Follett, Wilson, 1:91
Foltz, Anne-Marie, 5:328
Foner, Eric, 1:642, 3:504, 3:508, 3:520, 3:527
Foner, Philip S., 1:783
Fontane, Theodor, 2:564, 2:578
Fontenrose, Joseph, 4:446
Fonteyn, Dame Margot, 3:742, 3:750
Foord, Peter, 2:508
Foot, Mirjam M., 1:23, 1:25
Foote, Peter G., 3:380
Foote, Shelby, 3:528
Forbes, Ernest, 3:615
Forbes, Esther, 1:1195, 1:1201
Forbes, Jack D., 3:555
Force, James, 4:184
Forcione, Alban K., 2:536
Ford, Arthur L., 1:633, 1:966
Ford, Boris, 1:318, 1:414
Ford, Brian J., 5:192, 5:804
Ford, Clellan S., 3:12
Ford, Dan, 1:1166
Ford, David F., 4:718, 4:888
Ford, Ford Madox, 1:413, 1:419, 1:474, 1:566, 1:741, 1:845, 2:940

Ford, George H., 1:294, 1:318, 1:350
Ford, Hugh D., 1:37
Ford, John (Film director), 1:1156, 1:1165, 3:837
Ford, John (Renaissance playwright), 1:179
Ford, Lacy K., 3:524
Ford, Lewis S., 4:342
Ford, Marcus P., 4:237
Ford, Margaret P., 1:836
Ford, Peter, 3:895
Ford, Worthington, 1:38
Forde, Daryll, 3:20, 3:420
Forde, Victoria, 1:452
Forehand, Walter, 2:395
Forell, George W., 4:688
Foreman, Alexa L., 3:825
Foreman, E. K., 3:6
Forester, Tom, 5:125, 5:296, 5:537, 5:539
Forkel, Johann N., 3:675
Forker, Charles R., 1:201
Forkner, Ben, 1:806
Forman, Betty Y., 5:358
Forman, George E., 3:267
Forman, Jack J., 1:1123
Forman, Robert K. C., 4:498, 4:523, 4:535, 4:543
Forman, Werner, 3:442
Formigari, Lia, 4:29
Formisano, Ronald P., 3:524
Fornara, Charles W., 3:299, 3:301
Fornatale, Peter, 3:811
Fornell, Earl W., 4:851
Forrest, D. W., 5:529
Forrest, Gary G., 5:426
Forrest, W. G., 3:302
Forsström, Tua, 2:658
Forster, Arnold, 4:639
Forster, E(dward) M(organ), 1:258, 1:419, 1:421, 1:447, 1:448, 1:476, 1:483, 1:542
Forster, John, 1:350
Forster, Leonard, 2:566
Forster, Margaret, 1:337
Forster, Michael, 4:233
Forster, Robert, 5:326
Forsyth, Adrian, 5:764
Forsyth, D., 3:172
Forsyth, Donelson R., 5:418
Forsythe, Ana M., 3:734
Fortenbaugh, William W., 4:90, 4:91
Fortes, Meyer, 3:24
Fortescue, Adrian, 4:755
Fortey, Richard, 5:638
Fortin, Nina, 1:320
Fortune, Nigel, 3:678, 3:706
Fortune, R. F., 3:26
Forty, Adrian, 5:192

Forucci, Samuel L., 3:851
Foscolo, Ugo, 2:398, 2:421
Fosdick, Howard, 5:544
Foshay, Toby, 4:398
Foss, Clive, 3:306
Foss, Kenelm, 1:255
Foss, Murray, 3:67
Fosse, Bob, 3:743
Fost, Norman, 5:12
Foster, Charles H., 1:699
Foster, David W., 2:526, 2:845, 2:846, 2:882, 2:890
Foster, Edward, 1:750, 1:695, 1:910
Foster, Frances Smith, 1:754
Foster, Gaines M., 3:531
Foster, Gerald L., 5:219
Foster, Gretchen M., 1:227
Foster, Hal, 1:1133, 3:202
Foster, J. J., 5:566
Foster, John, 4:273
Foster, John B., 2:741
Foster, Kenelm, 4:151
Foster, Lawrence, 4:841
Foster, M. B., 4:233
Foster, M. Marie, 1:713
Foster, M. S., 5:340
Foster, R., 1:876
Foster, Robert J., 5:626
Foster, Roy F., 3:369
Foster, Shirley, 1:326
Foster, Stephen, 1:628, 3:695
Foster, Thomas C., 1:495
Foster, Virginia R., 2:846
Fothergill-Payne, Louise, 2:524, 2:549
Fothergill-Payne, Peter, 2:524
Fotheringham, A. Stuart, 3:122
Foti, Veronique M., 4:293
Foucault, Michel, 1:1129, 1:1146, 1:1179, 1:1181, 2:461, 2:476, 3:167, 3:205, 3:208, 3:326, 4:262, 4:284, 4:390, 4:399, 5:78, 5:87, 5:442
Foulcher, Keith, 2:317
Foulkes, Richard, 1:322
Fournier, Robert, 3:766
Fouyas, Methodius, 4:755
Fowden, Leslie, 5:266
Fowke, Edith, 3:851, 3:855
Fowke, Vernon C., 3:616
Fowler, Alistair, 1:166
Fowler, Barbara H., 2:348
Fowler, D. H., 4:80
Fowler, David C., 1:142, 1:147, 1:149, 1:154
Fowler, Doreen, 1:836
Fowler, Edward, 2:282
Fowler, F. G., 1:91
Fowler, Henry W., 1:91, 1:92

Fowler, Kenneth, 3:357
Fowler, Roger, 1:132
Fowler, W. Warde, 2:380,
   4:4481
Fowler, William A., 5:686
Fowler, William M., Jr.,
   3:520
Fowles, John, 1:420, **1:477**,
   1:534
Fowlie, Wallace, 2:495, 2:986
Fowlie-Flores, Fay, 3:641
Fox, Alistair, 4:126, 4:147
Fox, Daniel, 3:201
Fox, Daniel M., 5:330, 5:387
Fox, Dian, 2:554
Fox, Douglas A., 4:512
Fox, Emmet, 4:847
Fox, John, 2:447
Fox, Karen L., 4:601
Fox, Levi, 1:222
Fox, Marvin, 4:598, 4:668
Fox, Michael, 4:389, 5:110
Fox, Paula, 1:1195
Fox, Richard G., 3:485,
   4:516, 4:553
Fox, Richard W., 3:559,
   4:784
Fox, R. L., 3:306
Fox, Robin L., 3:17, 4:683
Fox, Stephen R., 3:549, 5:822
Fox, Steven, 5:297
Foxbrunner, Roman A., 4:632
Foxe, John, 4:733
Fox-Genovese, Elizabeth,
   3:504, 3:524
Fox-Lockert, Lucia, 2:524
Fraade, Steven D., 4:610
Fraassen, Bas C. van, 5:62,
   5:67
Frady, Marshall, 4:768
Fraenkel, Eduard, 2:386
Frager, Robert, 3:175
Fraistat, Rose A., 1:983
Fraknoi, Andrew, 5:588
Frame, Donald M., 2:491,
   4:146
Frame, Janet, 2:969, **2:973**
France, Anatole, 2:477
France, Anna K., 2:746
France, Charles E., 3:738
France, Peter, 2:686, 4:196,
   4:213
Francès, Robert, 3:660
Franceys, R., 5:245
Francis, Charles, 5:220, 5:266
Francis, R. Douglas, 3:606
Francis, Richard, 3:740
Francisco, Gabriel Beato,
   2:327
Francis of Assisi, St., 4:709
Franck, Frederick, 4:363
Franck, Irene, 1:52, 5:6,
   5:815

Francke, Kuno, 2:565, 2:566
Francks, Penelope, 3:477
Franco, Jean, 2:846, 2:849
Frängsmyr, Tore, 5:44, 5:805
Frank, Armin Paul, 1:818,
   1:956
Frank, Bernhard, 2:9
Frank, Daniel H., 4:646
Frank, Elizabeth, 1:952, 3:787
Frank, Frederick S., 1:230
Frank, Helena, 2:33
Frank, Jerome D., 5:418
Frank, Joseph, 2:686, 2:715
Frank, Judith, 5:556
Frank, Robert, 1:296
Frank, Robert G., Jr., 5:41,
   5:361
Frank, Ruth S., 4:601
Frank, Tenney, 3:307
Frank, Waldo, 2:849
Frankel, Charles, 4:160
Frankel, Edith R., 2:686
Frankel, Ellen, 4:597
Frankel, Francine R., 3:486
Frankel, Hans, 2:189, 2:215
Frankel, Hermann, 2:345
Frankel, Jonathan, 4:656
Frankfort, Henri, 2:52, 3:300,
   4:439, 4:441, 4:442, 4:548
Frankfurt, Harry, 4:170
Frankiel, Sandra S., 4:677,
   4:883
Frankl, Viktor, 5:443
Franklin, Allan, 5:48
Franklin, Benjamin, 1:626,
   1:637, 1:641, 1:646, 1:726,
   1:785, 1:866, 3:106, 4:200,
   4:210, 4:848, 5:15, 5:720
Franklin, H. Bruce, 1:688,
   1:1258
Franklin, John Hope, 3:506,
   3:513, 3:555, **3:579**
Franklin, Jon, 5:313, 5:381,
   5:392
Franklin, Julian H., 4:134,
   4:180
**Franklin, Miles (Stella Ma-
   ria), 2:952**
Franklin, R. W., 1:747
Franklin, Wayne, 1:665
Franko, Ivan, 2:837, **2:838**
Franks, A. H., 3:750
Franks, Claudia Stillman,
   1:492
Frantz, Douglas, 5:225
Frantz, Joe B., 1:1219, 3:600
Frantz, Philip, 2:722
Franzius, Enno, 4:569
Frapa, Pierre, 5:344
Frappier, Jean, 2:467
Frascina, Francis, 3:787
Fraser, Alexander C., 4:180
Fraser, Angus, 3:913

Fraser, Antonia, 3:360, 3:368,
   4:733, 4:735
Fraser, George S., 1:421
Fraser, John, 3:734, 3:738
Fraser, Keath, 3:891
Fraser, Nancy, 3:218
Fraser, Nicholas, 3:633
Fraser, Rebecca, 1:335
Fraser, Robert, 2:126, 2:131,
   4:477
Fraser, Russell A., 1:171,
   1:204, 1:816
Fraser, Walter J., Jr., 3:860
Fraser, W. Hamish, 3:873
Frassanito, William A., 3:528
Frater, Alexander, 3:902
Frauerfelder, Hans, 5:704
Frazer, M. J., 5:107
Frazer, Sir James George,
   3:23, **3:30,** 3:847, **3:878,**
   3:882, 4:421, **4:476,** 4:479,
   4:485, 4:488, 4:490, 4:491
Frazer, William, 3:78
Frazier, Claude A., 5:386
**Frazier, E(dward) Franklin,
   3:226,** 3:547
Frazier, Kendrick, 5:636
Frears, J. R, 3:372
Frede, Michael, 4:48
Frederic, Louis, 3:475
Frederick, R., 3:49
Frederick, Richard G., 5:762
Frederick, William H., 2:317,
   3:491
Fredericks, Carlton, 5:395
Fredman, Stephen, 1:798,
   1:913
Fredrickson, George M.,
   3:528, 3:555
Fredro, Alexander, 2:813
Freeborn, Richard, 2:686
Freed, Donald, 2:430
Freeden, Michael, 3:363
Freedheim, Donald K., 5:413
Freedland, Michael, 3:703
Freedman, Alan, 5:540
Freedman, Anne, 3:210
Freedman, David Noel, 4:4,
   4:818, 4:828
Freedman, Estelle F., 3:552
Freedman, Jacob, 5:628
Freedman, Jonathan, 1:766
Freedman, Lawrence, 3:278,
   3:538
Freedman, Maurice, 3:30,
   3:467
Freedman, Ralph, 2:608
Freedman, Robert O., 3:435,
   3:439
Freedman, Russell, 1:1195
Freehling, Alison G., 3:524
Freehling, William W., 3:524,
   3:528

Freehof, Solomon Benner, 4:598, 4:627, 4:652
Freeman, David, 1:1169
Freeman, Derek, 3:37
Freeman, Dorothy R., 5:418
Freeman, Eugene, 4:187, 4:249
Freeman, Harrop A., 5:418
Freeman, James, 4:504
Freeman, Jo, 3:215
Freeman, Lucy, 3:184, 5:448
Freeman, Mary Eleanor (Wilkins), 1:721, **1:749**
Freeman, Michael, 3:44
Freeman, Richard Burke, 5:759
Freeman, Roger K., 5:358
Freeman, Roger L., 5:304, **5:306**
Freeman, T. W., 5:620
Freeman-Grenville, G. S., 3:274, 3:354
Freese, Arthur S., 5:380
Freethy, Ron, 5:767
Frégault, Guy, 3:611
Frege, Gottlob, 4:228, 4:234, 5:84, 5:493
Frei, Hans W., 4:739, 4:743, 4:885
Freiberger, Paul, 5:542
Freiberger, Steven Z., 3:445
Freidel, David, 3:628
Freidel, Frank, 3:506
Freidin, Gregory, 2:738
Freidus, Alberta Joy, 2:317
Freifelder, David, 5:784
Freire, Paulo, 3:261, 4:748
Freitag, Sandra B., 4:504
Freitas, William, 2:558
Fremantel, Anne, 2:849
Fremont, John Charles, 3:908
French, A. P., 5:674
French, Alfred, 2:788
French, Bevan M., 5:629
French, Christopher W., 1:118
French, Hannah Dustin, 1:23
French, Harold W., 4:872
French, John R. P., 3:218
French, Marilyn, 1:925
French, Peter A., 4:21, 4:389
French, Roger, 5:810
French, Warren G., 1:777, 1:804, 1:885, 1:1043
Frend, W. H., 4:681, 4:685
Freneau, Phillip, 1:626, **1:639,** 1:1192
Freney, J. R., 5:262
Frenkel, Karen A., 5:242
Frenkel-Brunswik, Else, 3:147
Frenz, Horst, 2:984
Freppert, Lucan, 4:120
Frere, Sheppard, 3:356

Fretz, Bruce R., 5:413
Freuchen, Peter, 3:921
Freud, Anna, 3:181, 3:183, **5:444**
Freud, Martin, 5:448
Freud, Sigmund, 1:203, 1:224, 1:434, 1:826, 1:968, 1:1140, 1:1150, 1:1181, 1:1249, 2:266, 2:445, 2:611, 2:617, 2:624, 2:627, 2:713, 2:775, 2:982, 3:156, 3:166, 3:179, **3:182,** 3:185, 3:779, 4:255, 4:423, 4:424, 4:427, 4:477, 5:94, 5:411, 5:430, 5:431, 5:434, 5:436, 5:437, 5:440, 5:444, **5:445,** 5:452, 5:454, 5:458, 5:465, 5:466
Freudberg, Frank, 5:389
Freudenthal, Juan R., 2:846
Freudenthal, Patricia M., 2:846
Freund, Cynthia M., 5:337
Freund, E. Hans, 4:22
Freund, Elizabeth, 1:1131
Freund, John E., 5:520
Freund, Peter E. S., 5:319
Frey, Charles H., 1:1197
Frey, Linda, 3:326
Frey, Marsha, 3:326
Frey, P. A., 5:732
Frey, Sylvia, 3:520
Freymann, Robert, 5:340
Freyre, Gilberto de Mello, 2:889, **2:894,** 3:209, **3:645**
Friar, Kimon, 2:371
Fricker, M., 3:56
Friday, Adrian, 5:759
Fridegård, Jan, 2:671
Friebert, Stuart, 1:913
Fried, Jerome, 3:855
Fried, John, 5:345
Fried, Lewis, 1:713, 1:834, 2:31
Fried, Peter, 5:358, 5:404
Friedberg, Anne, 3:827
Friedberg, Maurice, 2:686
Friedel, Robert, 5:229
Friedenberg, Daniel M., 3:517
Friedenberg, Edgar Z., 5:460
Friedenberg, Robert V., 3:595
Friedenreich, Kenneth, 1:187
Friedenthal, Richard, 2:580, 2:581
Friedl, Ernestine, 3:17
Friedlander, Albert H., 4:661
Friedlander, Henry, 3:348
Friedlander, Lee, 3:668
Friedlander, Paul, 4:80
Friedlander, Will, 3:668

Friedman, Alan Warren, 1:421, 1:470, 1:836, 2:887
Friedman, Arthur, 5:522
Friedman, Daniel P., 5:552
Friedman, Edward, 3:470
Friedman, Edward H., 2:525, 2:536
Friedman, Ellen G., 1:1023
Friedman, George, 4:264, 4:408, 4:394
Friedman, Herbert, 5:588, 5:593
Friedman, Jerome, 4:126
Friedman, Jo Ann, 5:377
Friedman, Jonathan, 3:209
Friedman, Lawrence J., 3:524, 5:464
Friedman, Lawrence M., 3:145
Friedman, Lawrence S., 2:48
Friedman, Lee M., 2:518
Friedman, Lenemaja, 1:993
Friedman, Lenore, 4:515
Friedman, Leon, 3:506
Friedman, Louis, 5:596
Friedman, Mary Lusky, 2:857
Friedman, Maurice S., 4:264, 4:662
Friedman, Melvin J., 1:1024, 1:1057
Friedman, Meyer, 5:401
Friedman, Michael, 4:206, 4:384, 5:67
Friedman, Milton, 3:46, 3:54, 3:65, **3:76,** 3:79, 4:387
Friedman, Morton P., 3:177
Friedman, Norman, 1:826
Friedman, Robert M., 5:350, 5:642
Friedman, Susan S., 1:827
Friedman, Thomas L., 3:439
Friedmann, Thomas, 4:654
Friedrich, Carl J., 3:143
Friedrich, Hugo, 2:491
Friedrich, Otto, 1:852, 5:426
Friedrich, Werner, 2:983
Friedrichs, Guenter, 5:572
Friel, Brian, 1:478
Friend, Theodore, 3:493
Friendly, Alfred, 5:353
Friendly, Fred W., 5:811
Frier, Bruce W., 3:305
Fries, Paul, 4:755
Fries, Walderman H., 5:787
Friesel, Evyatar, 3:348
Friesen, Gerald, 3:609
Friis, Erik J., 2:640, 2:645, 2:658, 2:672
Frisby, David, 3:239
Frisch, Karl von, 3:194, **5:796,** 5:825, **5:832,** 5:835
Frisch, Max, 2:564, **2:579**

Frisch, Ragnar, 3:64
Frischauer, Paul, 3:385
Fritshi, Gerhard, 2:107
Fritz, Angela DiPace, 1:827
Fritz, Jean, 1:1195
Fritz, Kurt von, 4:71
Fritze, Ronald H., 3:8, 3:358
Fritzsch, Harald, 5:654, 5:662
Frodsham, J. D., 2:192, 2:202
Frohock, Wilbur M., 1:917, 2:488
Frolov, Ivan, 3:274, 4:3, 4:13
Frolov, Yuril P., 5:365
Froman, Paul K., 5:387
Fromm, Erich, 3:184, 3:344, 5:422, 5:445, 5:448, **5:449**
Frontain, Raymond-Jean, 2:985
Frosch, John, 5:424
Frost, Bede, 2:543
Frost, Darrel R., 5:759
Frost, Robert (Lee), 1:459, 1:550, 1:557, 1:668, 1:700, 1:775, 1:796, **1:841,** 1:871, 1:934, 1:1067, 1:1195, 1:1202
Frost, S. E., Jr., 4:16
Frost, William, 1:242
Froude, James A(nthony), 3:402
Frow, John, 1:1127
Fruchtenbaum, Arnold G., 4:599
Frude, Neil, 5:416, 5:567
Frugé, August, 1:44
Fruman, Norman, 1:288
Frumkin, Norman, 3:44
Fruton, Joseph S., 5:10, 5:732
Fry, Christopher, 1:471, **1:479**
Fry, Donald K., 1:144
Fry, Fiona S., 3:368
Fry, Gerald, 3:495
Fry, Gladys-Marie, 3:524, 3:866
Fry, Michael, 3:368
Fry, Plantagenet, 3:368
Fry, Roger, 3:773
Fryba, Mirko, 4:512
Fryde, E. B., 3:354
Frye, (Herman) Northrop, 1:192, 1:209, 1:210, 1:213, 1:265, 1:279, **1:976,** 1:1130, 1:1153, 2:904, 2:988, 2:989
Frye, Keith, 5:617, 5:626, 5:628
Frye, Marilyn, 1:925
Frye, Roland Mushat, 1:213
Fryer, Jonathan, 1:501
Fryer, Judith, 1:657, 1:788

Fu, Charles Wei-hsun, 4:349, 4:358, 4:522
Fu, Shen. *See* Shen Fu
Fu, Tu. *See* Tu Fu
Fuchs, Daniel, 1:887, 1:947
Fuchs, Nan Kathryn, 5:355
Fuchs, Oswald, 4:120
Fuchs, Stephan, 4:384, 5:152
Fuchs, Victor, 5:332
Fudenberg, Drew, 3:63
Fuentes, Annette, 3:218
Fuentes, Carlos, 2:844, **2:865**
Fuerst, Norbert, 2:565, 2:608
Fuertes, Gloria, 2:521
Fuess, Claude M., 1:283
Fugard, Athol, 2:160
Fuger, J., 5:728
Fugita, Stephen S., 3:557
Fuglestad, F., 3:418
Fuhrman, Manfred, 4:72
Fukui, Haruhiro, 3:474
Fukuyama, F., 3:276
Fuld, James J., 3:655
Fulk, R. D., 1:142
Fullbrook, Kate, 1:804
Fuller, C. J., 4:504
Fuller, Graham, 3:143
Fuller, John, 1:436
Fuller, John F., 3:278
Fuller, Michael Anthony, 2:220
Fuller, R. Buckminster, 3:254
Fuller, Robert C., 4:841, 4:847
Fuller, Roy, 1:480
Fuller, (Sarah) Margaret, 1:672, 1:809
Fuller, Steve, 5:66, 5:151, 5:153
Fullmer, June Z, 5:742
Fung, Sydney S., 2:189
Fung Yu-Lan (Feng You-Lan), 4:358, **4:359**
Funicello, Theresa, 3:211
Funk, Charles E., 1:95, 1:96
Funk, Rainer, 5:451
Funk, Robert W., 1:501, 4:794
Funkenstein, Amos, 4:126, 4:160
Funston, Judith, 1:766
Furay, Conal, 3:9
Furbank, Philip, 4:196
Furbank, P. N., 1:240, 1:477, 2:439
Furber, Alan, 1:15
Furcher, Erik, 3:452
Furedi, F., 3:276
Furet, François, 3:339
Furley, David J., 4:48, 4:50, 4:74
Furlong, Monica, 4:781, 4:859, 4:881

Furman, N. Howell, 5:735
Furmanov, Dmitry, 2:718
Furnas, Joseph Chamberlain, 1:397
Furness, C. J., 4:879
Furness, Horace Howard, 1:206
Furphy, Joseph, 2:945, **2:952**
Furse, Margaret, 4:296
Furst, Viktor, 3:796
Furtak, Thomas, 5:666
Furth, Hans G., 3:192, 3:267
Fürüzan (Fürüzan Yerde-len), 2:97
Fusek, Lois, 2:192
Fusi, Juan P., 3:386
Fuss, Diana, 1:1133, 1:1184
Fuss, Peter L., 4:250
Fussell, Edwin, 1:655, 1:719, 1:798, 1:913
Fussell, Paul, 1:227, 1:250, 1:429, 3:278, 3:343, 3:892, 3:899, 3:908
Fusso, Susanne, 2:722
Fustel de Coulanges, Numa Denis, 4:438
Futabatei Shimei, 2:281, **2:286**
Futrell, May, 5:316
Fyfe, Christopher, 3:420
Fynsk, Christopher, 4:293
Fyzee, A. A., 4:373

G

Gabbard, Alex, 5:247
Gabbin, Joane V., 1:955
Gabe, Jonathan, 5:350
Gabin, Jane S., 1:772
Gabirol, Solomon Ibn, 2:6, 2:23
Gabor, D., 3:47
Gaboudigian, Sylva, 2:78
Gabre-Medhin, Tsegaye, 2:121
Gabriel, Ralph H., 4:34
Gabrieli, Francesco, 4:569, 4:588
Gaby, Alan, 5:345
Gacs, Ute, 3:10
Gadamer, Hans-Georg, 4:80, 4:226, 4:262, 4:284, 4:318, 4:390, **4:401**
Gadd, Bernard, 2:970, 2:971
Gadd, Irna, 5:398
Gadd, Laurence, 5:398
Gaddis, John Lewis, 3:534, 3:538, 3:545
Gaddis, Vincent H., 3:864
Gaddis, William, 1:977
Gado, Frank, 3:831

Gadol, Joan, 2:404
Gaehde, Christa M., 1:27
Gaer, Joseph, 1:735, 4:569
Gaffield, Chad, 3:615
Gaffney, M. P., 5:479
Gág, Wanda (Hazel), 1:1194, **1:1202**
Gagarin, Michael, 2:351
Gager, John, 4:683
Gagliardi, Robert M., 5:299
Gagne, Cole, 3:660
Gagné, Robert M., 3:175
Gagnier, Regenia, 1:325, 1:410
Gagnon, Serge, 3:606, 3:620, 3:621
Gaile, Gary L., 3:118, 3:125
Gailey, Harry A., Jr., 3:416, 3:417, 3:420
Gainer, Patrick W., 3:860
Gaines, James F., 2:490
Gaines, Steven, 3:665
Gainsborough, Thomas, 3:768, **3:774**
Gaite, Carmen Martin, 2:521
Gaj, Ljudevit, 2:785
Gakwandi, Shatto A., 2:107
Galambos, Louis, 3:547
Galand, René, 2:493
Galang, Zoilo M., 2:328
Galanter, Marc, 3:486, 4:856, 5:402
Galavaris, George, 3:767
Galbraith, John Kenneth, 3:52, 3:54, **3:78, 5:212**
Galbreath, Bob, 3:860
Galdon, Joseph A., 2:328
Galdós, Benito Pérez. *See* Pérez Galdós, Benito
Gale, Barry G., 5:794
Gale, George, 5:63
Gale, Robert L., 1:666, 1:677, 1:689, 1:766, 1:1213, 1:1216, 3:508
Gale, Steven H., 1:535, 1:869, 3:871
Galeano, Eduardo, 3:625
Galen, 4:58
Galich, Aleksandr, 2:719, 2:743
Galilei, Galileo, 2:399, 2:410, 2:421, 3:153, 4:123, 4:135, **4:141, 4:171,** 4:173, 4:406, 5:41, 5:178, 5:195, 5:601, **5:603,** 5:681, **5:687,** 5:695
Galison, Peter, 5:48, 5:153
Gall, Eric P., 5:398
Gall, Sandy, 3:455
Gallagher, Catherine, 1:312, 1:318
Gallagher, D. P., 2:846
Gallagher, J. A., 3:363
Gallagher, John, 3:418

Gallagher, Kenneth T., 4:305
Gallagher, Monique, 1:526
Gallant, Mavis (de Trafford Young), 2:903, **2:911**
Gallenkamp, Charles, 3:627
Gallie, Roger, 4:212
Gallie, W. B., 4:249
Gallix, Andrew, 1:530
Gallo, Robert M. D., 5:387, 5:783
Gallo, Rose A., 1:840
Gallop, David, 4:52
Gallop, Jane, 1:1143, 1:1147
Galloway, David D., 1:917
Gallup, Donald Clifford, 1:473, 1:873
Galluscio, Eugene H., 3:171
Galsworthy, John, 1:419, 1:423, 1:474, **1:481,** 1:537
Galton, Francis, 3:224, 5:525, **5:529**
Galton, Lawrence, 5:341, 5:368, 5:381
Galvin, Herman, 2:30
Galvin, John P., 4:891
Gamarra, Eduardo, 3:633
Gambetta, Diego, 3:208
Game, Ann, 3:211
Gamer, Helena M., 4:700
Gammond, Peter, 3:703
Gamow, George, 5:586, **5:605, 5:689**
Gandhi, Mohandas K(aramchand), 2:169, 2:171, 2:179, 3:182, 4:321, 4:351, 4:549, **4:551,** 4:559, 4:772
Gane, Mike, 5:88
Ganin, John, 1:147
Ganjoo, Satish, 3:7
Gann, L. H., 3:417
Gans, Herbert J., 3:226, 3:542, 3:806
Gant, Michael M., 3:143
Gantz, John, 5:541
Ganz, Arthur F., 1:535
Ganzfried, Solomon, 4:627
Gänzl, Kurt, 3:660
Gaon, Saadia. *See* Saadia Gaon
Garafola, Lynn, 3:734, 3:741
Garbarino, James, 3:201
Garber, Daniel, 4:170
Garber, Marjorie, 1:209, 1:1182
Garborg, Arne, 2:662
Garcia, Jorge J., 4:264, 4:379
Garcia, Mario T., 3:555
Garcia-Ayvens, Francisco, 1:806
García Canclini, Néstor, 3:638

García Lorca, Federico, 2:521, 2:531, **2:538,** 2:542
García Márquez, Gabriel, 2:24, 2:842, 2:850, **2:866,** 2:902, 2:913, 2:951
Garcilaso De La Vega, **3:645**
Gard, Richard A., 4:6
Gard, Robert E., 3:861
Gard, Roger, 1:766
Garden, Edward, 3:724
Gardiner, Alan H., 3:300
Gardiner, C. Harvey, 1:694
Gardiner, Patrick, 4:160, 4:240
Gardiner, Samuel R., 3:360
Gardiner, Stephen, 3:778
Gardlund, Torsten, 3:115
Gardner, Averil, 1:531, 1:567
Gardner, Burleigh B., 3:22
Gardner, E. E., 3:859
Gardner, Erle Stanley, **1:1228**
Gardner, Gerald, 3:542
Gardner, Helen, 1:166, 1:192
Gardner, Howard, 3:174, 3:192, 3:250, 5:567
Gardner, J. Anthony, 3:435
Gardner, James B., 3:515
Gardner, Jane F., 3:306
Gardner, John (C.), 1:593, 1:917, **1:978**
Gardner, John W., 3:250
Gardner, Lloyd C., 3:545, 3:601
Gardner, Martin, 1:1200, 4:866, 5:63, 5:495, **5:506**
Gardner, Mary R., 3:22
Gardner, Monica M., 2:817
Gardner, Philip, 1:433
Garebian, Keith, 2:914
Garfield, David, 1:1073
Garfield, Evelyn Picon, 2:849
Garfinkel, Harold, 3:227
Garfinkel, Paul E., 5:395
Gargan, E. T., 4:741
Gargano, James W., 1:744, 1:766
Garibaldi, Antoine, 3:254
Garin, Eugenio, 4:126
Garlan, Yvon, 3:308
Garland, Allan E., 5:807
Garland, (Hannibal) Hamlin, 1:721, **1:750,** 1:775
Garland, Peter, 3:699
Garland, Robert, 3:307, 4:447
Garmonsway, G. N., 1:143
Garms, Walter I., 3:250
Garneau, François-Xavier, 3:604, **3:619**
Garner, David M., 5:395
Garner, John S., 3:531
Garnett, Richard, 1:133

Garnett, Robert Reginald, 1:562

Garnett, William, 5:701

Garnsey, Peter, 3:307

Garon, Sheldon, 3:477

Garrard, John, 2:686, 2:735

Garraty, John A., 3:274, 3:508, 3:513, 3:542

Garrett, Albert, 1:28

Garrett, Almeida, 2:557

Garrett, Edmund H., 1:316

Garrett, George, 1:995, 2:403

Garrett, John, 1:622

Garrett, N., 3:511

Garrett, Peter K., 1:318

Garrett, R. C., 5:374

Garrett, Simon, 2:978

Garrick, David, 1:248, 1:254, 1:262

Garrison, Daniel, 2:384

Garrison, Fielding H., 5:50

Garrison, Robert H., 5:345

Garrity, Devin A., 1:423

Garro, Elena, 2:868

Garrod, H. W., 1:236, 1:307

Garrow, David J., 3:538, 4:772

Garry, Ann, 4:391

Garry, Jim, 3:863

Garshin, Vsevolod, 2:719

Garside, Charles, Jr., 4:737

Garson, Barbara, 5:572

Garson, Helen S., 1:959

Garstand, William, 5:764

Garstein, Oskar, 4:736

Gartley, Lynn, 1:1165

Gartman, David, 3:547

Gartner, Leslie P., 5:773

Garton, Janet, 2:662

Garver, John W., 3:470

Garvey, Catherine, 3:803

Garvey, John H., 3:139

Garvin, Tom, 3:370

Gary, James H., 5:285

Garza, Roberto J., 1:1076

Gasche, Rodolphe, 4:398

Gasiorowska, Xenia, 2:686

Gaskell, Elizabeth (Cleghorn Stevenson), 1:310, 1:317, 1:334, 1:335, 1:352, **1:355**

Gaskell, G. A., 4:4

Gaskell, Philip, 1:62

Gasper, Philip, 5:62

Gass, William, 1:916, **1:979,** 1:985

Gassée, Jean-Louis, 5:542

Gassendi, Pierre, 4:171, **4:172,** 5:42

Gasset, José Ortega y. *See* Ortega y Gasset, José

Gassner, John, 1:131, 1:158, 1:1077, 2:3

Gaster, Moses, 2:33, 4:618

Gaster, Theodor H., 2:52, 4:439, 4:477, 4:599, 4:811

Gaston, Edwin W., Jr., 1:723

Gaston, Georg, 1:557

Gaston, Jerry, 3:214

Gatchel, Robert, 5:339

Gates, Barbara T., 1:335

Gates, Henry Louis, Jr., 1:130, 1:922, 1:925, 1:1127, 1:1133, **1:1144**

Gates, Louis, 1:725

Gates, Robert A., 1:1077

Gatewood, Willard B., 3:555

Gatlin, Lila L., 5:571

Gatrell, Simon, 1:289, 1:362

Gatson, George M., 1:489

Gatti, Hilary, 4:135

Gatti, John, 1:644

Gatt-Rutter, J., 2:401, 2:439

Gaudefroy-Demombynes, Maurice, 4:569

Gauguin, Paul, 1:520, 3:769, **3:775**

Gaukroger, Stephen, 4:170, 5:503

Gaull, Marilyn, 1:265

Gaunt, William, 1:315, 3:789

Gaur, Albertine, 1:5

Gauss, Carl Friedrich, 5:486, **5:507,** 5:525, **5:529**

Gausted, Edwin S., 4:719, 4:751

Gauthier, David P., 3:154, 4:174

Gauthier, Howard L., 3:123

Gaver, Jack, 1:1077

Gavin, William J., 4:31, 4:34

Gaviria, Moises, 5:428

Gavronsky, Serge, 2:448

Gay, John, 1:228, **1:246,** 1:252

Gay, Peter, 1:634, 2:447, 2:516, 2:565, 3:184, 3:274, 3:276, 3:337, 3:376, 3:515, 4:160, 4:218, 4:635, 4:739

Gay, Robert M., 1:118

Gayle, Addison, Jr., 1:906, 1:913

Gayley, Charles M., 1:133

Gaylord, Susan A., 5:317

Gay-Lussac, Joseph-Louis, 5:747

Gaynor, Frank, 4:718

Gayron, Daniel, 3:440

Gazarian-Gautier, Marie-Lise, 2:873

Geach, P. T., 4:304

Geanakoplos, Deno J., 4:693

Gearhart, Bill R., 3:254

Gearhart, Carol J., 3:254

Geary, Patrick J., 4:699

Gebler, Karl von, 5:688

Gebo, Sue, 5:12, 5:345

Geckle, George L., 1:188

Geden, A. S., 4:819

Gedo, Mary M., 5:422

Geduld, Harry M., 1:44, 1:1161, 3:825

Gee, Chuck, 3:890

Gee, Maurice, 2:970, **2:975**

Geertz, Clifford, 1:980, 1:1131, 1:1145, 3:14, 3:19, 3:23, **3:30,** 3:443, **4:477,** 4:569

Geertz, Hildred, 3:19

Geesey, Patricia, 2:117

Gefvert, Constance J., 1:644

Gehrels, Tom, 5:589

Gehring, Wes D., 1:1158, 1:1161, 3:825

Geiger, Abraham, 4:647

Geiger, George R., 3:80, 3:261

Geiger, Theodore, 3:274

Geijer, Erik Gustaf, 2:670

Geikie, Sir Archibald, 5:622

Geipel, John, 2:31

Geiringer, Irene, 3:675, 3:699

Geiringer, Karl, 3:675, 3:699

Geis, Irving, 5:522

Geisel, Theodor Seuss, 1194, **1:1203,** 1:1206

Geisendorfer, James V., 4:717, 4:751

Geiser, Elizabeth, 1:47

Geisler, J., 5:303

Geisler, Norman L., 4:21

Geist, Christopher D., 3:873

Gelb, Norman, 3:520

Gelb, P. Arthur, 3:893

Gelber, Leonard, 3:509

Gelberg, Steven, 4:862

Gelder, George S., 1:510

Gelder, Michael G., 5:427

Gelderman, Carol, 1:1008

Gelfand, Toby, 5:44

Gell, William, 1:299

Geller, Janet A., 5:418

Gellert, Charles L., 4:636

Gellman, Barton, 3:584

Gell-Man, Murray, 5:690

Gellner, E., 3:276

Gelphi, Barbara, 1:1038

Gelpi, Albert J., 1:628, 1:655, 1:719, 1:720, 1:747, 1:798, 1:887

Gelso, Charles J., 5:413

Gelven, Michael, 4:293

Gelzer, M., 3:307

Gelzer, Matthias, 3:313

Gemery, Henry A., 3:420

Gendron, Bernard, 5:73, 5:153

Gendrop, Paul, 3:762

Genest, John, 1:272

Genet, Jean, 1:952, 2:435, 2:468, **2:478**, 2:506, 4:329
Genette, Gerard, 2:447
Geng, Veronica, 1:130
Gennep, Arnold van, 4:430
Genoble, Penelope B., 5:393
Genovese, Eugene D(ominick), 3:524, 3:547, **3:580**
Gensler, Harry J., 5:509
Gentile, Giovanni, 4:271, **4:284**
Gentry, Linnea, 1:13
Gentz, William H., 4:818
George, Alexander L., 3:470
George, Don, 3:695
George, Emery, 2:593
George, Henry, 3:79
George, Linda, 3:200
George, Stefan, 2:564, **2:579**, 2:982
George, Susan, 5:266
Georges, Robert A., 3:855
Georgescu, Vlad, 3:390
Georgescu-Roegen, Nicholas, 3:46
Gephart, Ronald E., 3:510
Geraghty, James J., 5:631
Gerard, Albert S., 2:107, 2:116
Gerard, David, 1:547
Gerber, David A., 4:639
Gerber, Helmut E., 1:362
Gerber, Philip L., 1:821, 1:830, 1:842
Gerbner, George, 3:801, 3:803
Gere, James M., 5:636
Gerhardstein, Virginia B., 1:124
Gerhartz, Wolfgang, 5:725
Gérin, Winifred, 1:334, 1:335, 1:336, 1:356
Germain, Gilbert G., 5:128
Gernet, Jacques, 3:468, 4:358, 4:532
Geroch, Robert, 5:664
Gerould, Daniel, 1:1077
Gerrish, Brian A., 4:254, 4:722, 4:741, 4:762, 4:778
Gersh, Stephen, 4:60
Gershoy, Leo, 3:338, 3:339
Gershwin, George, 3:696, 3:736, 3:751
Gerson, Lloyd, 4:55
Gersonides, 4:664
Gerstein, Dean R., 5:402
Gerstenberger, Donna, 1:555
Gerstenblith, Patty, 4:445
Gersuny, Carl, 5:353
Gert, Bernard, 5:77
Gertel, Elliot, 4:655
Gervais, Karen G., 4:389

Gesenius, William, 4:794
Gesler, Wilbert M., 3:121
Gesner, Carol, 1:219
Gessel, Van C., 2:282, 2:283
Gessler, Alexei, 3:855
Getis, A., 3:119
Getz, William L., 5:418
Geuss, Raymond, 4:264, 4:404, 5:89
Gever, John, 5:282
Gevitz, Norman, 5:13, 5:338
Gewirth, Alan, 4:386
Geyer-Ryan, Helga, 1:1133
Geyikdaqi, Mehmet Y., 3:452
Geyl, Pieter, 3:382, 4:731
Geymonat, Ludovico, 4:143, 4:172
Ghadegesin, Segun, 4:368
Ghadially, Rehana, 4:508
Ghālib, Mirza Asadullah Khan, 2:175
Ghanim, Fathi, 2:58
Ghanoonparvar, M. R., 2:83, 2:84
Ghareeb, Edmund, 3:450
al-Ghazālī, 4:582
Gherity, James A., 3:45, 3:85
Gherman, Beverly, 1:898
Ghiglione, Loren, 3:806
Ghirardo, Diane, 3:202
Ghiselin, Michael, 5:794
Ghitani, Jamal, 2:59
Ghodes, Clarence, 1:79
Gholson, Barry, 5:153
Ghose, Aurobindo, 4:352
Ghosh, Amitav, 2:177, 3:445
Ghougassian, Joseph P., 5:432
Giamatti, A. Bartlett, 3:255
Gianakaris, C. J., 1:544
Gianakos, Larry J., 3:811
Giancotti, Emilia, 4:188
Giannelli, Giulio, 2:380
Giannone, Richard, 1:1024
Gianos, Mary P., 2:371
Gibaldi, Joseph, 1:118, 1:1128, 2:987
Gibb, Alexander, 5:256
Gibb, E.J.W., 2:96
Gibb, Hamilton, A., 3:443, 3:456, 4:373, 4:566, 4:569
Gibb, Jocelyn, 4:776
Gibbon, Edward, 2:380, 3:303
Gibbon, Guy, 3:13
Gibbon, Peter, 3:371
Gibbons, Brian, 1:206
Gibbons, Reginald, 1:1128
Gibbs, A. M., 1:546
Gibbs, Donald A., 2:233
Gibbs, James, 2:149
Gibbs, Josiah Willard, 5:584, 5:735, **5:746**
Gibbs, Lewis, 1:255

Gibbs, Robert, 4:671
Gibilisco, Stan, 5:28
Gibney, Michael J., 5:345
Gibran, Jean, 2:67
Gibson, Arthur C., 5:768
Gibson, Bob, 5:591
Gibson, Charles, 3:335
Gibson, Donald B., 1:742, 1:913
Gibson, Gail McMurray, 1:159
Gibson, Graeme, 2:904
Gibson, H. B., 5:418, 5:422
Gibson, Ian, 2:539
Gibson, J. W., 3:278
Gibson, James, 4:180
Gibson, James J., 3:177
Gibson, Jerry D., 5:299
Gibson, John C., 4:545
Gibson, L., 5:619
Gibson, Margaret, 3:357
Gibson, Mary Ellis, 1:339
Gibson, N., 5:241
Gibson, Roger F., 4:412, 5:100
Gibson, Ronald, 3:575
Gibson, Walter S., 3:771
Gibson, William C., 5:563, 5:811
Gibson, William M., 1:759, 1:783, 3:595
Gidal, Peter, 3:796
Giddens, Anthony, 3:199, 3:209, 3:215, **3:227**
Giddings, Robert, 1:294, 1:301
Giddins, Gary, 3:668, 3:674
Gide, André, 1:291, 2:469, **2:479**, 2:486, 2:503, 2:508, 2:513, 2:675
Gideon, Siegfrid, 5:263
Gieck, Kurt, 5:216
Giedion, Sigfried, 3:762, 3:777, 5:25, 5:573
Gienapp, William E., 3:542
Giere, Ronald N., 5:63
Giergielewicz, Mieczyslaw, 2:822
Gieryn, Thomas F., 3:213, 5:151
Gies, Frances, 3:331, 4:699
Gies, Joseph, 3:331, 4:699
Giesbrecht, Martin Gerhard, 3:44, 3:45
Giese, Frank S., 2:448
Gifford, Barry, 1:999, 1:1110
Gifford, George E., 5:313
Gifford, Henry, 2:766
Gifford, Prosser, 3:417
Gifford, Terry, 1:498
Giguere, Ronald G., 2:108
Gikandi, Simon, 2:108, 2:129
Gilard, Hazel A., 3:855

Gilbaugh, James H., 5:341
Gilbert, A. H., 4:145
Gilbert, Alan, 4:242
Gilbert, Bentley B., 3:366
Gilbert, Cecile, 3:851
Gilbert, Felix, 3:342, 4:145
Gilbert, G. Nigel, 5:153
Gilbert, Grove Karl, 5:626,
5:643
Gilbert, James, 3:538, 3:559
Gilbert, Kevin, 2:947
Gilbert, Martin, 3:401, 4:636
Gilbert, Neal Ward, 4:126
Gilbert, Roger, 1:798
Gilbert, Sandra Mortola,
1:130, 1:270, 1:318, 1:414,
1:714, 1:925, 1:1131,
1:1143, **1:1145**
Gilbert, Scott F., 5:776
Gilbert, Sir William
Schwenck, 1:311, 1:321,
1:356, 1:409
Gilbert, Steven G., 5:776
Gilboa, Amir, 2:13, **2:17**
Gilboa, Yehoshua, 4:636
Gilby, Thomas, 4:118
Gilcher, Edwin, 1:381
Gilchrist, Alexander, 1:279
Gilchrist, John A., 5:636
Gilder, George F., 3:66,
5:573
Gildin, Hilail, 4:213
Giles, Bill, 5:633
Giles, Edward, 4:688
Giles, James Richard, 1:857,
1:995
Giles, Jane, 2:479
Giles, Paul, 1:823
Giles, Sarah, 3:737
Giles of Rome, 4:103
Gilkes, Michael, 2:930, 2:936
Gilkey, Langdon B., 4:744,
4:787, **5:200,** 5:422
Gill, Brendan, 3:798
Gill, David W., 5:165
Gill, Derek, 3:908
Gill, Dominic, 3:671
Gill, Eric, 1:8
Gill, Gillian, 1:606
Gill, Jerry H., 4:311
Gill, Joseph, 4:694
Gill, Mary Louise, 4:68
Gill, Sam D., 4:464
Gill, Stephen, 1:307
Gillan, Patricia, 5:429
Gillan, Richard, 5:429
Gillen, Charles H., 1:522
Giller, Ken E., 5:263
Gilles, Richard J., 5:424
Gillespie, Charles Guy, 3:641
Gillespie, John T., 1:74,
1:1195
Gillespie, Larrian, 5:406

Gillespie, Neal C., 5:46,
5:794
Gillespie, Patti P., 1:272
Gillet, Richard, 3:176
Gillett, Grant, 5:119
Gilliard, Charles, 3:378
Gillies, Alexander, 4:199
Gillies, Malcolm, 3:677
Gilligan, Carol, 3:250, 5:413
Gillingham, John, 3:345,
3:354
Gillings, Richard J., 5:38
Gillispie, Charles C., 5:4,
5:25, 5:28, 5:44, 5:46,
5:479
Gillman, Neil, 4:620, 4:655
Gillmor, Donald M., 3:801
Gillon, Adam, 1:464, 2:811
Gilluly, James, 5:622
Gilman, Charlotte Perkins,
1:721, 1:726, **1:752**
Gilman, Sander L., 4:247,
4:636
Gilman, Stephen, 2:536
Gilman, Susan, 1:783
Gilmartin, David, 3:487
Gilmer, Walker, 1:42
Gilmore, Grant, 3:145
Gilmore, Michael T., 1:628
Gilmore, Myron P., 4:696
Gilmore, Robert K., 3:860
Gilmore, T., 1:103
Gilot, Françoise, 3:786
Gilpin, George H., 1:421
Gilsenan, Michael, 3:445,
4:578
Gilson, Étienne, 4:94, 4:95,
4:104, 4:110, 4:112, 4:113,
4:118, 4:126, 4:170, 4:260,
4:285, 4:696, 4:721
Gimbel, John, 3:279, 3:376
Gimbutas, Marija, 4:434
Gimpel, Jean, 3:331, 5:39
Gindin, James, 1:421
Gingerich, Owen, 5:11, 5:48,
5:590, 5:602, 5:656
Gingrich, F. W., 4:794
Gino, Carol, 5:337, 5:392
Ginsberg, Allen, 1:900,
1:909, 1:911, 1:956, 1:963,
1:980, 1:998, 1:1105,
1:1187
Ginsberg, Benjamin, 3:143
Ginsberg, Elaine K., 1:570
Ginsberg, Jekuthiel, 5:31
Ginsburg, Henry, 4:518
Ginsburg, Herbert, 3:192
Gintis, Herbert, 3:253
Ginzberg, Eli, 5:328, 5:333,
5:334
Ginzberg, Lori D., 3:555
Ginzberg, Louis, 4:610, 4:620
Ginzburg, Carlo, 4:431

Ginzburg, G., 3:276
Ginzburg, Lydia, 2:686
Ginzburg, Natalia, 2:400,
2:421
Ginzburg, V. L., 5:588
Gioia, Ted, 3:668
Giono, Jean, 2:480
Gippius, V. V., 2:722
Girard, Rene, 4:429
Girardot, N. J., 4:528
Giraud, Marcel, 3:610
Giraudoux, Jean, 1:480,
2:445, **2:481**
Girgus, Sam B., 1:804, 1:917
Girouard, Mark, 3:355
Giroud, Francoise, 5:679
Giroux, Henry A., 3:255
Gish, Lillian, 1:1168
Gish, Nancy K., 1:517
Gissing, George (Robert),
1:309, 1:350, **1:358**
Gitler, Ira, 3:668
Gitlin, Todd, 3:203, 3:811
Gitter, George, 3:801
Gittings, John, 3:470
Gittleman, Edwin, 1:705
Gittleman, Sol, 2:46
Giuliano, Francis A., 5:241
Givner, Joan, 1:870
Gjellerup, Karl, 2:645
Gjerset, Knut, 3:381
Gjertsen, Derek, 5:805
Gjuzel, Bogumil, 2:807
Glacken, C. J., 5:114
Glad, John, 2:686, 2:692
Gladilin, Anatoly, 2:719
Gladkov, Alexander, 2:746
Gladkov, Fyodor, 2:720
Glahe, Fred R, 3:107
Glahn, Richard von, 3:469
Glaister, Geoffrey Ashall,
1:32, 1:52, 1:69
Glantz, Leonard H., 5:343
Glanville, Philippa, 3:767
Glare, P. G., 1:101
Glaser, Elizabeth, 5:387
Glaser, William A., 3:210
Glasgow, Douglas G., 3:212
Glasgow, Ellen, 1:802, **1:842,**
1:937
Glasgow, Joanne, 1:1184
Glashow, Sheldon Lee,
5:690, 5:713, 5:718
Glasner, David, 3:65
Glass, Gene V., 3:255
Glass, Hiram B., 5:107
Glass, Philip, 3:696
Glass, Robert H., 5:358
Glassberg, David, 3:559
Glasse, Cyril, 3:443, 4:4,
4:566
Glasser, Otto, 5:711
Glasser, Robert, 5:282

Glasser, William, **5:451**
Glassie, Henry, 3:851, 3:855, 3:859, 3:868
Glassman, Deborah, 2:474
Glassman, Jon D., 3:435
Glassman, Steve, 1:850
Glatstein, Jacob, 2:29, 2:33, **2:38**, 4:636
Glatzer, Nahum N., 4:596, 4:610, 4:620, 4:629, 4:671
Glazer, Mark, 1:115
Glazer, Myra, 2:9
Glazer, Myron P., 3:49
Glazer, Nathan, 4:639
Glazer, Penina M., 3:49
Gleason, Elizabeth G., 4:728
Gleason, John B., 4:126
Gleckner, Robert, 1:279, 1:283
Gledson, John, 2:897
Gleick, James, 5:686
Gleijeses, Piero, 3:637
Glen, Duncan, 1:517
Glen, William, 5:629
Glendinning, Victoria, 1:448, 1:542, 1:548, 1:566
Glendon, Mary Ann, 4:895
Glenisson, A., 3:272
Glenn, Edgar M., 2:390
Glenn, Jules, 5:448
Glenn, Menachem G., 4:654
Glenn, Michael L., 3:206
Glenn, Peggy, 1:47
Glennon, Michael J., 3:545
Gliauda, Jurgis, 2:805, **2:806**
Glick, William J., 1:8
Glicksman, Arvin Sigmund, 5:377
Glimm, James Y., 3:859
Glišić, Milovan, 2:827
Gloag, John, 3:766
Glock, Charles Y., 3:209, 4:855
Glossbrenner, Alfred, 5:547, 5:556
Glover, Donald E., 1:513
Glover, Jon, 1:430
Glover, Jonathan, 5:120
Glubb, John Bagot, 3:435, 4:569, 4:588
Gluck, Barbara Reich, 1:505
Gluck, Carol, 3:477
Glück, Louise, **1:981**
Gluckel of Hameln, **2:38**, 4:623
Gluckin, Doreen, 5:355
Glut, Donald F., 5:638
Glymour, Clark, 5:63, 5:75, 5:320
Gnanadesikan, Mrudulla, 5:522
Goa, David, 4:503
Gochet, Paul, 4:412, 5:100

Godard, Jean-Luc, **3:837**
Godbeer, Richard, 3:517
Godbold, E. Stanly, Jr., 1:843
Godbolt, Shane, 5:3
Goddard, Stephen, 5:620
Godden, Jon, 3:902
Godden, Malcolm, 1:143
Godden, Richard, 1:917
Godden, Rumer, 3:902
Gödel, Kurt, **5:508**, 5:516
Godelier, Maurice, 4:242
Godfrey, Thomas, 1:626
Godlee, Rickman J., 5:409
Godolphin, Francis R. B., 3:302
Godshalk, William, 1:220
Godwin, A. H., 1:358
Godwin, Joscelyn, 4:450
Godwin, Mary Wollstonecraft, 1:302
Goebner, Patricia A., 5:337
Goehlert, Robert U., 3:506, 3:510, 3:510
Goehring, Eleanor E., 3:861
Goeldner, Charles R., 3:890
Goell, Yohai, 2:8
Goethals, George R., 5:422
Goethe, Johann von, 1:327, 1:373, 1:602, 1:648
Goethe, Johann Wolfgang von, 2:25, 2:250, 2:421, 2:426, 2:439, 2:512, 2:531, 2:563, **2:580**, 2:588, 2:599, 2:601, 2:609, 2:612, 2:802, 2:826, 3:375, 3:681, 3:707, 4:198, 4:254, 4:879
Goetz, William R., 1:766
Goetzman, Robert, 3:403
Goetzmann, William H., 3:524, 3:912
Goff, Frederick Richmond, 1:66
Goff, Janet, 2:279
Goff, Richard, 3:274
Goffman, Erving, 3:21, 3:205, 3:210, 3:221, **3:227**
Gofman, John W., 5:324, 5:397
Goforth, Frances S., 3:849
Goggin, Malcolm L., 5:181
Gogh, Vincent Van. *See* Van Gogh, Vincent
Gogol, Nikolai, 2:682, 2:697, 2:700, 2:712, **2:720**, 2:740
Gohau, Gabrial, 5:617
Gohdes, Clarence, 1:121
Gohlke, Mary, 5:377
Gohlman, William, 4:582
Goins, David Lance, 1:15
Goitein, Shlomo Dov, 4:625
Gokalp, Ziya, 4:373
Golan, Galia, 3:436
Golant, Stephen M., 3:201

Gold, Herbert, 1:806, 1:921, 3:895
Gold, Mark S., 5:403
Gold, Thomas B., 3:52
Goldbarth, Albert, 1:912, **1:982**, 3:873
Goldberg, Adele, 5:552
Goldberg, Arnold, 5:458
Goldberg, David Theo, 1:1133
Goldberg, Hillel, 4:620, 4:654
Goldberg, Isaac, 2:33, 2:890
Goldberg, Jonathan, 1:198
Goldberg, Judith, 2:31
Goldberg, Kathy E., 5:341
Goldberg, Larry H., 5:358
Goldberg, Leah, 2:7, **2:18**
Goldberg, Richard T., 5:372
Goldberg, Sander M., 2:395
Goldberg, Stanley, 5:665
Goldberg, Susan, 5:322
Goldblatt, Howard, 2:247
Goldemberg, Isaac, 2:844, **2:868**
Golden, Frank, 3:395
Golden, Frederic, 5:655
Golden, Janet, 5:36
Golden, Kenneth L., 3:877
Golden, Leon, 4:68
Golden, Morris, 1:245, 1:248, 1:261
Golden, Richard L., 5:54
Golden, Samuel A., 1:704, 1:779
Golden, William T., 5:181
Goldenberg, Herbert, 5:413
Goldenberg, José, 5:282
Goldenson, Robert M., 5:422
Goldfarb, Clare R., 4:851
Goldfarb, Jeffrey C., 3:143
Goldfarb, Russell M., 4:851
Goldfarb, Sheldon, 1:404
Goldfarb, Theodore, 5:114
Goldfield, David, 3:555
Goldfield, Lea Naomi, 4:668
Goldfinger, Stephen E., 5:341
Goldhaber, Michael, 5:181
Goldhill, Simon, 2:351
Goldhizer, Ignaz, 4:575
Goldie, Terry, 2:904, 2:905
Goldin, Claudia, 3:547
Goldin, Frederick, 2:403
Goldin, Grace, 5:329
Goldin, Judah, 4:610
Golding, Jean, 5:375
Golding, Sue, 3:143
Golding, William (Gerald), 1:420, **1:483**
Goldman, A. Richard, 5:341
Goldman, Alvin, 4:380
Goldman, Bernard, 4:614
Goldman, Bob, 5:399
Goldman, Edward A., 4:652

Goldman, Eric A., 2:31
Goldman, L. H., 1:947
Goldman, Merle, 2:233,
  3:466, 3:470, 3:498
Goldman, Michael, 1:209,
  1:213
Goldman, Peter, 4:877
Goldman, Ralph M., 3:543
Goldman, Robert, 2:171
Goldman, Robert P., 4:504
Goldman, Shifra M., 3:759
Goldman, Steven L., 5:152,
  5:153
Goldman, William, 1:1073
Goldmann, Lucien, 2:447,
  2:498, 4:185, 5:90
Goldoni, Carlo, 2:399, **2:422**
Goldring, Roland, 5:638
Goldsborough, Jennifer F.,
  3:767
Goldscheider, Calvin, 4:634,
  4:639
Goldscheider, Frances K.,
  3:206
Goldscheider, Ludwig, 3:779
Goldschmidt, Arthur, Jr.,
  3:445
Goldschmidt, Bertrand, 5:658
Goldschmidt, E. P., 1:23
Goldsmith, Arnold, 1:804
Goldsmith, Donald, 5:589,
  5:590, 5:656
Goldsmith, Emanuel S., 2:31,
  4:657, 4:667
Goldsmith, M., 5:181
Goldsmith, Maurice, 3:154,
  4:174
Goldsmith, Oliver, 1:224,
  1:227, 1:228, 1:231, **1:246,**
  1:254, 1:580, 1:679
Goldsmith, T., 3:171
Goldstein, David I., 2:715
Goldstein, Doris Mueller,
  5:120
Goldstein, Doris S., 3:165
Goldstein, Fred R., 5:299
Goldstein, J. S., 3:279
Goldstein, Joseph, 4:519
Goldstein, Kenneth S., 3:848,
  3:868
Goldstein, Malcolm, 1:1073,
  1:1097, 1:1116
Goldstein, Marc, 5:341
Goldstein, Melvyn C., 4:543
Goldstein, Sidney, 4:639
Goldstein, Steven M., 3:470
Goldstein, Tom, 3:806
Goldstine, Herman H., 5:37,
  5:540, 5:583
Goldstone, Herbert, 1:532
Goldsworthy, Andy, 5:192
Goldthorpe, Rhiannon, 2:507
Goldwater, Robert, 3:775

Goldwyn, Robert M., 5:396
Goleman, Daniel, 5:341
Goley, George F., IV, 5:559
Golfman, Noreen, 2:915
Golino, Carlo L., 2:403,
  4:143, 4:172
Gollin, Alfred, 5:219
Gollin, Tira, 1:683
Golob, Richard, 5:6
Golubitsky, Martin, 5:199
Golzio, Vincent, 3:788
Gombrich, Ernst H., 3:757,
  5:192, 5:193
Gombrich, Richard, 4:513,
  4:515
Gombrowicz, Witold, 2:813
Gomery, Douglas, 1:1156,
  3:825
Gomes, Albert M., 2:935
Gomes, Michael, 4:853
Gomez, Carlos F., 3:542
Gomez, M. Guillermo L.,
  3:215
Gomme, A. H., 1:171
Gomme, A. W., 2:364, 3:323
Gomperz, Theodor, 4:46
Goncharov, Ivan, 2:723
Gonda, Jan, 4:501, 4:504
Gong, Victor, 5:387
Góngora y Argote, Luis de,
  2:521, **2:539,** 2:541
Gonzales, M., 3:168
Gonzales, Michael A., 3:665
Gonzales-Wippler, Migene,
  4:868
González, Edward, 2:871
González, Justo L., 4:677,
  4:718
González, Luis E., 3:641
González Echevarría,
  Roberto, 2:846, 2:860
Gooch, Steve, 1:425
Good, Edwin M., 3:672
Good, Graham, 1:429
Good, Howard, 1:804
Goodall, Jane van Lawick,
  5:770, **5:832**
Goodchild, Peter J., 5:707
Goode, John, 1:359, 1:362
Goode, William J., 3:206
Goodenough, Erwin R., 4:60,
  4:670
Goodenough, Ward H., 3:38
Goodfield, June, 5:32, 5:383
Goodfriend, Joyce D., 3:517
Goodheart, Eugene, 1:510
Goodheart, Lawrence B.,
  3:552
Gooding, David, 5:745
Goodkin, Richard E., 2:495
Goodlad, John I., 3:250,
  3:262
Goodman, Anthony, 3:357

Goodman, Danny, 5:554
Goodman, David, 3:47
Goodman, Dena, 2:472
Goodman, Grant K., 3:464
Goodman, John C., 5:330
Goodman, Jordan, 3:44,
  3:341
Goodman, Lenn E., 4:646,
  4:668
Goodman, Martin, 4:606
Goodman, Michael Barry,
  1:958
Goodman, Michael Harris,
  4:357, 4:561
Goodman, Nelson, 4:286,
  4:380, **4:402,** 5:63
Goodman, Philip, 4:599
Goodman, Richard M., 5:375
Goodman, Russell B., 4:34
Goodman, S. F., 3:345
Goodman, Saul L., 4:651,
  4:656
Goodman, Susan, 1:788
Goodman, Thomas, 5:399
Goodpaster, K. E., 5:128
Goodrich, L. Carrington,
  3:465
Goodrich, Samuel G., 1:1194
Goodrick, Edward W., 4:818
Goodridge, Celeste, 1:864
Goodsell, David S., 5:774,
  5:784
Goodspeed, Charles E., 1:41
Goodspeed, Edgar J., 4:690,
  4:703
Goodwin, Albert, 3:362, 3:372
Goodwin, Geoffrey, 5:110
Goodwin, George L., 4:289
Goodwin, H. Eugene, 3:806
Goodwin, Jason, 3:903
Goodwin, Ken, 2:946, 2:947
Goodwyn, Janet, 1:788
Goodwyn, Lawrence, 3:531
Goody, Jack, 4:460
Gookin, Dan, 5:555
Goor, Batya, 2:8, **2:18**
Gopal, Ram, 3:500
Gopal, Sarvepalli, 4:354
Goran, Morris, 5:728
Gordievsky, Oleg, 3:395
Gordimer, Nadine, 2:157,
  2:161, 2:989
Gordis, Robert, 4:598, 4:821
Gordon, Andrew, 3:477
Gordon, Caroline, 1:762,
  1:982
Gordon, Cyrus H., 2:361,
  4:439
Gordon, David J., 1:546
Gordon, Deborah, 5:289
Gordon, Douglas H., 4:196
Gordon, George, 1:434
Gordon, Hayim, 2:69

Gordon, James S., 5:319
Gordon, Joanne Lesley, 3:720
Gordon, Leonard A., 3:486
Gordon, Lois G., 1:535, 1:963
Gordon, Louis, 1:944
Gordon, Lyndall, 1:473, 1:570
Gordon, Patricia, 1:34
Gordon, R., 2:931
Gordon, Raoul, 3:382, 3:855
Gordon, Richard, 5:363
Gordon, Robert, 3:783
Gordon, Sarah, 4:636
Gordon, Stephen, 1:492
Gordon-Smith, Maria, 3:690
Gore, Al, 3:206, 5:822
Gore, Walter, 1:1129
Goreham, Gary A., 5:261
Gorenstein, P., 5:596
Gorenstein (Gorenshtein), Friedrich, 2:724
Gorer, Geoffrey, 3:22, 3:903
Gorion, Emanuel Bin, 3:854
Gorkin, J., 3:295
Gorky (Gorki), Maxim, 2:653, 2:665, 2:683, **2:724,** 2:729
Gorlin, Robert J., 5:375
Gorman, G. E., 4:716
Gorman, Lyn, 4:716
Gorman, Martyn L., 5:770
Gorman, Michael E., 5:153
Gorman, Peter, 5:514
Gorman, Robert A., 1:54
Gornick, Vivian, 5:10
Gorostiza, José, 2:868
Gorovitz, Samuel, 5:120
Gorra, Michael Edward, 1:487
Gorst, Tony, 3:366
Gortner, Susan R., 5:337
Goscilo, Helena, 2:692
Goslee, David, 1:401
Goslin, David A, 3:216
Gosling, David, 5:107
Gosling, J. C., 4:80
Gosnell, Harold Foote, 3:538
Goss, Charles Mayo, 5:360
Goss, Kathleen, 5:348
Goss, Linda, 3:866
Gosse, Edmund, 1:133
Gossen, Gary H., 3:865
Gosset, William Sealy, 5:525, **5:530**
Gossett, Suzanne, 1:722
Gossett, Thomas F., 1:699
Gossman, Lionel, 2:490
Gotesky, Rubin, 5:451
Gotoff, Harold C., 2:385
Gott, Richard, 3:625
Gottesfeld, Harry, 5:426
Gottfried, Barbara, 1:1041
Gottfried, Martin, 3:713, 3:720, 3:743

Gottfried, Ted, 5:685
Gottfried von Strassburg, 2:562, **2:581**
Gotthelf, Allan, 4:68
Gottlieb, Gilbert, 3:173
Gottlieb, Robin, 1:52
Gottlieb, Vera, 2:710
Gottmann, Jean, 3:129, 3:216
Gottschalk, Louis, 3:9
Gottschalk, Stephen, 4:843
Gottwald, Norman K., 4:816
Goubert, Pierre, 3:372
Goudie, Andrew, 5:620
Goudy, Frederic W., 1:15
Gougeon, Len, 1:670
Gough, Barry M., 3:610
Gough, Kathleen, 3:17, 3:20
Gough, Michael, 5:736
Gouinlock, James, 3:261, 4:160, 4:225
Goulart, Frances Sheridan, 5:348, 5:403
Gould, Alice B., 5:785
Gould, Carol C., 5:73, 5:125
Gould, James A., 4:20, 4:21
Gould, James L., 5:764
Gould, John, 3:316, 3:899, 4:480
Gould, Josiah B., 4:57
Gould, Julius, 3:4, 3:272
Gould, Karen L., 2:509
Gould, Lewis L., 3:531, 3:595
Gould, Peter, 5:620
Gould, Stephen Jay, 3:18, 3:174, 3:250, **5:15,** 5:638, 5:643, 5:645, 5:764, 5:765, 5:818
Gould, Thomas, 4:48
Goulden, Joseph C., 3:806, 3:868
Goulden, Steven L., 5:218, 5:232
Goulder, Michael, 4:885
Goulding, Ray, 3:871
Gouldner, Alvin, 3:200, 3:202, **3:228,** 5:70
Goulet, Denis, 5:128, 5:213
Gounard, Jean-François, 1:906
Gounod, Charles, 3:697
Gouri, Haim, 2:18
Gow, Andrew S., 2:348
Gow, James, 3:392
Gow, Kathleen M., 5:337
Gower, John, 1:140, **1:152**
Gowing, Lawrence, 3:757, 3:773, 3:781
Goya y Lucientes, Francisco José de, 3:776, 3:780
Goytisolo, Juan, 2:521, **2:540**
Grabar, Andre, 4:688
Grabbe, Lester, 4:604

Graber, Doris A., 3:147, 3:806
Graber, Eden, 5:354
Grabhorn, Jane, 1:8
Grabiner, Judith V., 5:502
Grabo, Carl A., 1:303
Grabo, Norman S., 1:636, 1:644
Grabowicz, George G., 2:838, 2:840
Grace, James H., 4:894
Grace, Patricia, 2:970, **2:975**
Gracia, Jorge J. E., 4:33, 4:101
Gracie, David M., 4:553
Grade, Chaim, 2:29, **2:38**
Gradenwitz, Peter, 3:682
Graebner, William, 3:559
Graedon, Joe, 5:350
Graef, Hilda, 4:678
Graetz, Heinrich, 3:348, 4:647
Graff, Gerald, 1:925, 1:1128
Graff, Henry F., 3:275
Grafton, Anthony, 1:35, 4:126
Grafton, Sue, 1:1229, 1:1230, 1:1235
Graham, A. C., 2:192, 4:522, 4:526, 4:528
Graham, Bruce, 4:508
Graham, Daniel W., 4:68
Graham, Don, 1:777
Graham, Douglas F., 3:451
Graham, George, 4:382
Graham, Janis, 5:358
Graham, Jory, 5:372
Graham, Lawrence S., 3:386
Graham, Loren R., 5:107
Graham, Martha, 3:735, 3:739, **3:743,** 3:752
Graham, Peter, 1:283
Graham, Philip, 1:772
Graham, Rigby, 1:25
Graham, Robin L., 3:908
Graham, Roger, 3:615
Graham, Shirley, 1:647
Graham, W. Fred, 4:762
Graham, William Franklin (Billy), 4:767
Grahame, Kenneth, 1:578, **1:584,** 1:588
Graham-White, Anthony, 2:108
Grahn, Judy Rae, 1:1182, **1:1187**
Gralla, Preston, 5:556
Gralnick, Alexander, 5:418
Gramsci, Antonio, 1:1127, **2:423, 4:286**
Gramwell, Franklin I., 4:289
Granatstein, J. L., 3:605, 3:606, 3:607, 3:608, 3:615, 3:616

Grandolfo, Anita, 1:582
Grandy, Richard E., 5:63
Grandy, Walter T., 5:698
Graneau, Neal, 5:706
Graneau, Peter, 5:706
Granger, Bruce Ingham, 1:628, 1:638
Granger, Byrd H., 3:868
Grannis, Chandler B., 1:8, 1:47
Gransden, K. W., 2:397
Grant, Alexander, 3:368
Grant, Brian W., 5:426
Grant, Bruce K., 1:101
Grant, Douglas, 1:806
Grant, Edward, 4:94, 4:97, 4:126, 5:39
Grant, Frederick C., 4:448
Grant, George M., 3:606, 3:908
Grant, George Parkin, 5:70, 5:128
Grant, Isabel, 3:368
Grant, John Webster, 3:609, 3:610
Grant, Judith Skelton, 2:912
Grant, Julius, 1:62
Grant, Marcia M., 5:324
Grant, Michael, 1:133, 2:348, 2:382, 3:298, 4:439
Grant, Patrick, 1:178, 1:200
Grant, Peter R., 5:764, 5:779
Grant, Robert M., 4:99, 4:116, 4:453, 4:681, 4:683, 4:685, 4:703, 4:811, 4:813, 4:825
Grant, Ruth W., 3:160, 4:180
Grant, Verne, 3:18
Grant, W. L., 1:631
Grant Duff, M. E., 3:35
Granville-Barker, Harley, 1:222
Grass, Günter, 2:564, **2:582,** 2:585, 2:616
Grassi, Ernesto, 4:127
Grassian, Victor, 4:21
Grattan-Guinness, Ivor, 4:324, 5:30, 5:516
Grau, Joseph A., 4:337
Graubard, Stephen, 1:49, 3:152, 5:75
Grauer, Robert T., 5:552
Grave, S. A., 4:32, 4:212
Gravell, Thomas L., 1:5
Graves, Anne A., 2:107
Graves, Donald H., 3:255
Graves, Edgar B., 3:354
Graves, Richard Perceval, 1:486, 1:496
Graves, Robert, 1:484, 1:502, 1:542, 1:546, 1:875, 2:345, 2:359, 3:320, **3:879,** 3:908, 3:926

Graves, William S., 3:396
Gray, Beryl, 1:354
Gray, Donald J., 1:326
Gray, Donald P., 4:337
Gray, Douglas, 1:146, 1:147
Gray, Francine du Plessix, 5:137
Gray, Henry, 5:360
Gray, J. M., 1:401
Gray, James, 2:313
Gray, Jeffrey A., 3:171, 3:191
Gray, Jeremy, 5:30
Gray, Martin, 1:132
Gray, Nicolete, 1:15
Gray, Peter, 5:759
Gray, R., 3:420
Gray, Richard, 1:798, 1:893
Gray, Rockwell, 4:315, 5:97
Gray, Roland P., 3:858
Gray, Ronald D., 2:565, 2:573, 3:796
Gray, Simon, 1:486
Gray, Stephen, 2:158
Gray, Thomas, 1:227, **1:248,** 1:262, 1:277
Gray, Virginia, 3:148
Graybeal, Jean, 4:293
Grayling, A. C., 4:192, 4:345
Grayson, A. Kirk, 4:545
Grayson, James Huntley, 3:481, 4:533
Grayson, Jane, 2:722, 2:741
Grayson, Martin, 5:223, 5:229
Grayzel, Solomon, 4:594, 4:624, 4:634
Grean, Stanley, 4:214
Greaves, Richard L., 3:274, 3:360, 4:734, 4:749
Grebanier, Bernard, 1:35
Grebstein, Sheldon N., 1:854, 1:867
Greeley, Andrew M., 4:751
Greeley, Ronald, 5:593
Green, Archie, 3:851
Green, Arthur, 4:630, 4:632, 4:648, 4:669
Green, Bernard, 5:403
Green, Carol H., 3:506
Green, Charles I., 1:1081
Green, D. Brooks, 3:272
Green, D. H., 2:617
Green, David E., 3:543
Green, Gayle, 1:925
Green, H. M., 2:946
Green, Harvey, 3:534
Green, Henry, 1:486
Green, Jack P., 3:517
Green, James H., 5:304
Green, John, 2:83, 2:84
Green, Jonathan, 1:57
Green, Jonathon, 5:240
Green, Julien, 2:481

Green, Katherine Sobba, 1:230
Green, Lila, 3:855
Green, M., 2:692
Green, Martin, 4:553
Green, Michael, 4:683
Green, Nancy L., 4:656
Green, Nancy S., 5:351
Green, Otis H., 2:522
Green, Paul, 1:1071, **1:1088**
Green, Paul Eliot, 5:303
Green, Peter, 1:584
Green, Robert, 1:475
Green, Robert L., 4:776
Green, Robert W., 4:722
Green, Roger L., 1:372
Green, Stanley, 1:1073, 3:655, 3:825
Green, Thomas Hill, 4:180, **4:230**
Green, Vivian H., 4:790
Green, William S., 4:610
Greenawalt, Kent, 4:386
Greenaway, Frank, 5:810
Greenaway, Kate, 1:578, 1:580, 1:583, **1:585**
Greenberg, Allan C., 3:344
Greenberg, Blu, 4:650
Greenberg, Cheryl, 3:535
Greenberg, Dan, 5:181
Greenberg, Eliezer, 2:33, 4:657
Greenberg, Harvey Roy, 3:827
Greenberg, Irving, 4:599
Greenberg, Janelle R., 3:361
Greenberg, Joseph H., 3:21, 3:417
Greenberg, Louis, 3:348, 4:636
Greenberg, Mark L., 1:279, 5:153
Greenberg, Martin H., 3:858
Greenberg, Marvin J., 5:504
Greenberg, Michael R., 5:383
Greenberg, Milton, 3:509
Greenberg, Sidney, 4:136
Greenberger, Evelyn B., 1:345
Greenblatt, Stephen J., 1:165, 1:209, 1:1128, 3:358
Greenblum, Joseph, 4:641
Greene, David H., 1:556
Greene, Diana, 2:759
Greene, Donald, 1:250
Greene, Gayle, 1:208, 1:1134
Greene, (Henry) Graham, 1:419, 1:420, **1:487,** 1:525, 1:536, 1:551, 1:1024, 2:179, 2:286, 2:310, 3:840, 3:892
Greene, Jack P., 3:508, 3:517, 3:520

Greene, John C., 5:33, 5:46
Greene, Laura, 5:577
Greene, Maxine, 3:255
Greene, Mott T., 5:46
Greene, Naomi, 2:432
Greene, Norman N., 4:330
Greene, Robert, 1:180, 1:185
Greenfeld, Howard, 1:47
Greenfield, Howard, 3:688
Greenfield, Kent R., 3:279
Greenfield, Richard, 3:422
Greenfield, Stanley B., 1:143
Greenhill, Maurice H., 5:418
Greenhill, Ralph, 5:213
Greenlee, J. Harold, 4:794
Greenslade, Stanley L., 4:683
Greenslet, Ferris, 1:732
Greenson, Ralph R., 5:425
Greenspan, Ezra, 1:707
Greenstein, Fred I., 3:138, 3:538
Greenwald, Elissa, 1:766
Greenwald, Howard P., 5:372
Greenwalt, Emmett A., 4:858
Greenway, John, 3:855
Greenwood, D. A., 5:658
Greenwood, Sadja, 5:355
Greer, Allan, 3:611
Greer, Germaine, 5:355
Greer, Margaret R., 2:533
Greer, Rowan A., 4:688, 4:814
Greer, Thomas H., 3:326
Greg, W. W., 1:37, 1:207, 1:221
Gregg, Charles T., 5:389
Gregg, Edward, 3:360
Gregg, Robert C., 4:685
Gregor-Dellin, Martin, 3:728
Gregorian, Vartan, 1:57
Gregory, Frederick, 5:46
Gregory, Horace, 1:510, 1:856
Gregory, John, 3:734
Gregory, Lady Isabella Augusta, 1:423, 1:460, **1:489**, 1:571
Gregory, Peter N., 4:529
Gregory, R., 3:169
Gregory, Richard L., 4:382, 5:193
Gregory, Richard P., 5:732
Gregory, Ross, 3:535
Gregory the Great (Pope Gregory I), 4:706, **4:710**
Greider, William, 3:55
Greiman, Algirdas J., 2:489
Greiner, Donald J., 1:986, 1:1060
Greitzer, S. L., 5:486
Grekova, Irina, 2:692, **2:726**
Grell, Ole P., 4:734
Grenander, M. E., 1:735

Grenard, Steve, 5:769
Grene, David, 2:349, 2:368, 4:80
Grene, Marjorie, 4:68, 4:163, 4:188, 4:264, 5:794, 5:826
Gresh, Alain, 3:436
Greshoff, Jan., 2:622
Gresset, Michael, 1:836
Greteman, James, 3:206
Greub, W. H., 5:484
Grewal, J. S., 3:484, 4:516
Grey, James, 5:763
Grey, Jeffrey, 3:494
Grey, Rowland, 1:357
Grey, Thomas C., 1:887
Grey, Zane, 1:1211, **1:1213**
Gribbin, John, 5:17, 5:607, 5:656, 5:692
Gribetz, Judah, 4:594
Griboyedov (Griboedov), Aleksandr, 2:726, 2:770
Grice, Paul, 4:287
Gridley, Mark C., 3:668
Gridley, Roy E., 1:339
Grieb, Kenneth J., 3:624
Grieder, Jerome B., 2:233, 2:247
Grieg, Edvard, 3:697
Grierson, Herbert, 1:299
Grierson, Sir George, 2:169
Griffen, Jasper, 4:483
Griffin, Alice, 1:219
Griffin, David Ray, 4:384, 4:743
Griffin, J., 2:344, 2:361
Griffin, James, 4:389
Griffin, Jasper, 2:380
Griffin, John Howard, 4:307, 4:781
Griffin, Miriam D., 4:88
Griffin, Miriam T., 2:394
Griffin, Nicholas, 4:324
Griffin, Penny, 1:367, 1:388
Griffin, Peter, 1:846
Griffin, Robert, 2:406
Griffin, Robert D., 5:764
Griffith, Charles C., 3:624
Griffith, Daniel, 3:120
Griffith, D(avid) (Lewelyn) W(ark), 1:792, 1:1161, 1:1165, **1:1166**, 1:1172, 1:1173, 1:1177, 3:837
Griffith, H. Winter, 5:399
Griffith, John W., 1:579, 1:1197
Griffith, Nancy S., 1:734
Griffiths, A. Phillips, 4:273, 4:345
Griffiths, Frederick T., 2:686
Griffiths, Gareth, 2:108
Griffiths, J. M., 5:299
Griffiths, Morwenna, 4:391
Griffiths, N.E.S., 3:606

Griffiths, Naomi, 3:611
Griffiths, Paul, 3:655, 3:665, 5:67
Griffiths, Ralph A., 3:357
Griffiths, Trevor R., 1:425
Grigg, David B., 3:274
Grigg, John, 3:366
Grigg, Richard, 4:787
Griggs, Barbara, 5:319, 5:351
Griggs, Gary B., 5:636
Grigorovich, Y., 3:734
Grilli, Peter, 3:473
Grillmeier, Aloys, 4:685
Grillo, Ernesto, 2:401
Grillparzer, Franz, 2:583, 2:587
Grim, John, 4:337
Grim, Mary E., 4:337
Grim, Patrick, 5:63
Grim, Richard E., 3:510
Grim, Ronald E., 5:620
Grimal, Nicolas, 3:445
Grimaldi, Alfonsina A., 4:216
Grimes, Janet, 1:122
Grimes, John A., 4:3, 4:13, 4:498
Grimes, Ronald L., 4:897
Grimm, Francis W., 1:23
Grimm, Harold J., 4:722
Grimm, Herman F., 3:782
Grimm, Jacob, 1:943, **2:584**, 3:845, 3:875, **3:879**, 3:887
Grimm, Reinhold, 2:574
Grimm, Wilhelm, 1:577, 1:943, 2:584, 3:845, **3:879**, 3:887
Grimmelshausen, Johann (Hans) Jakob Christoffel von, 2:563, **2:585**
Grimshaw, James A., Jr., 1:893, 1:1024
Grimshaw, Jean, 4:391
Grimsley, Ronald, 4:213
Grinder, John, 5:441
Grindle, Juliet, 1:362
Grinker, Roy R., Sr., 5:415
Grinnell, Frederick, 5:10, 5:107, 5:154
Grinnell, George B., 3:865
Grinspoon, Lester, 5:110, 5:405
Grinstein, Alexander, 5:425, 5:448
Grinstein, Louise S., 5:494
Grisez, Germain, 4:743
Griswold, Alexander B., 2:313
Griswold, Charles L., Jr., 4:81
Griswold, Ralph E., 5:552
Griswold, Rufus W., 1:728
Gritsch, Eric, 4:778
Groarke, Leo, 5:110

Grob, Alan, 1:307
Grob, Gerald N., 3:513,
  3:552, 5:415
Grobel, Lawrence, 3:838
Grodecki, Louis, 3:762
Grodzins, Morton, 5:111
Groebel, J., 3:170, 3:279
Groen, Janny, 5:10
Grogan, Denis, 5:216
Grogin, R. C., 4:220
Groh, Dennis E., 4:685
Gronbech, Bo, 2:647
Grondzik, Walter T., 5:225
Groom, Nigel, 5:730
Gropius, Walter, 2:615,
  3:776
Gropman, Donald, 4:649
Gros, François, 5:782
Grose, Francis, 1:92
Gross, Alan G., 5:154
Gross, David C., 1:99, 1:103,
  4:593
Gross, Francis L., Jr., 3:182
Gross, Gerald, 1:49
Gross, Harvey, 1:417
Gross, John J., 1:273, 1:429,
  1:430, 1:728, 1:809
Gross, Kenneth, 1:198
Gross, Larry, 5:125
Gross, Leonard, 4:724
Gross, Lynne S., 3:801
Gross, M. Grant, 5:631
Gross, Nathan, 2:490
Gross, Rita M., 4:504, 4:512,
  4:529, 4:539
Gross, Stanley, 5:335
Gross, Susan Hill, 4:578
Grossberg, Lawrence, 1:1128
Grosseteste, Robert, 4:115
Grossfeld, B., 4:608
Grossfeld, Stan, 3:906
Grosskurth, Phyllis, 5:448
Grossman, David, 2:8, **2:18**
Grossman, Gene M., 3:53
Grossman, James, 1:665
Grossman, James R., 3:555
Grossman, Pamela L., 3:255
Grossman, Peter Z., 5:278
Grossman, Reinhardt, 4:230
Grossman, Susan, 4:892
Grossman, Vasily, 2:727
Grossman, William L., 2:891
Grossvogel, David I., 2:448
Grosz, Elizabeth, 1:1132
Grosz, Katarzyna, 4:545
Grote, George, 4:68
Grote, Harriet, 4:29
Grote, Jim, 5:197
Groth, Janet, 1:903
Grotjahn, Martin, 5:424
Groulx, Lionel, 3:604, **3:619,**
  3:620

Grout, Donald J., 3:660,
  3:670
Grove, Andrew S., 5:234
Grove, David C., 4:455
Grover, Kathryn, 3:552
Groves, David, 1:292
Groves, Donald G., 5:617
Groves, Leslie M., 5:658
Grow, Michael, 3:624
Grubb, Andrew, 5:120
Grubb, Kevin B., 3:743
Grubb, Michael, 5:282
Grubbs, Henry A., 2:513
Grube, G. M., 2:345, 4:81
Gruber, Frank, 1:1214
Gruber, Helmut, 3:375
Gruen, Erich S., 3:303, 3:306
Gruenberg, Ernest M., 5:383
Gruenberg, Estrellita V.,
  2:329
Grun, Bernard, 3:7
Grünbaum, Adolf, 3:178,
  5:68, 5:80
Grundtvig, Nicolai Frederik
  Severin, 2:644
Grundy, Isobel, 1:225, 1:250,
  1:570
Grunebaum, Gustave E. von,
  4:573
Gruner, Charles R., 3:871
Grunfeld, Frederick V., 3:791
Grunin, Robert, 3:801
Grušas, Juozas, 2:805
Grusec, J., 3:173
Gruson, Lindsey, 4:862
Gruter, Margaret, 3:171, 5:33
Grzimek, Bernhard, 5:759
Guare, John, 1:1071, **1:1089**
Guaspari, David, 2:685
Gubar, Susan, 1:130, 1:270,
  1:318, 1:414, 1:714, 1:925,
  1:1131, 1:1143, 1:1145,
  1:1146
Gudiol, José, 3:776
Gudzii, Nikolai K., 2:686
Guedalla, Roger, 1:452
Guenther, Herbert V., 4:543
Guerard, Albert L(eon),
  3:403
Guerard, Albert T., 1:837
Guercio, Francis M., 2:403
Guergelewicz, Mieczyslaw,
  2:811
Guerin, Philip J., Jr., 5:418
Guerlac, Henry, 5:749
Guerlac, Suzanne, 2:483
Gueroult, Martial, 4:170
Guerrero, Leon M., 2:333
Guerry, Herbert, 4:13
Guest, Ann H., 3:739
Guest, Ivor, 3:733
Guffey, George R., 1:189
Gugelberger, Georg M., 2:108

Guggenheim, Hans G., 3:892
Guibert, Rita, 2:846
Guiccoli, Countess, 1:283
Guicharnaud, Jacques, 2:448,
  2:497
Guicharnaud, June, 2:448
Guida, Louis, 3:861
Guidics, Giovanni, 5:776
Guidoni, Enrico, 3:762
Guidos, Barbara, 5:6
Guignon, Charles B., 4:293
Guilds, John C., 1:697
Guilford, Joy P., 3:174
Guiliano, Edward, 1:583
Guilkey, David K., 5:330
Guillaume, Alfred, 4:567,
  4:575, 4:588
Guillemin, Jeanne, 5:120
Guillén, Jorge, 1:1055,
  2:521, 2:531, **2:541,** 2:542,
  2:543
Guillén, Nicolas, 2:844,
  2:869, 2:935
Guinagh, Kevin, 2:348
Guinevera, Nancy, 1:1041
Guisso, R., 4:539
Guiton, Jacques, 3:779
Guiton, Margaret, 2:485
Gulick, Edward V., 3:279
Gullace, Giovanni, 2:415
Gullery, Jonathan G., 4:877
Gulley, Norman, 4:81
Gullick, J. M., 3:492
Gulliver, Lucille, 1:1199
Gullotta, Thomas P., 3:208
Gumilev, Nikolai, 2:683,
  2:687
Gummere, Francis B., 1:149
Gummere, Richard M., 4:88
Gumperz, John J., 3:21
Günderrde, Karonline von,
  2:616
Gundersheimer, Werner L.,
  4:127
Gunderson, Keith, 5:75
Gundulić, Ivan, 2:784
Gunew, Sneja, 1:1134, 2:946
Gunkel, Hermann, 4:823,
  4:830, **4:834,** 4:837
Gunn, Alastair, 5:128
Gunn, Clare A., 3:890
Gunn, Drewey W., 1:1118
Gunn, Edward M., 2:233,
  2:235
Gunn, Giles, 1:630, 1:1127,
  1:1128, 2:989
Gunn, James, 1:1254
Gunn, Thom(son), 1:412,
  1:466, **1:491**
Gunnarsson, Gunnar, 2:641
Gunnell, John G., 4:81
Gunner, Elizabeth, 2:108
Gunter, Pete A., 4:309

Gunther, John, 3:921
Guntrip, Harry, 5:425
Guppy, Robert, 4:247
Gupta, Narayani, 3:485
Gupta, Sunil, 3:201
Gura, Philip F., 3:517
Gurdjieff, G(eorge)
  I(vanovich), 4:875
Gurevich, Inge, 5:389
Gurin, Joel, 5:341, 5:344
Gurney, A. R., 1:1090
Gurney, O. R., 3:300, 4:445
Gurr, Andrew, 1:169, 1:217
Gurr, Michael I., 5:345
Gurrie, Michael L., 5:296
Gurwitsch, Aron, 4:235
Guss, David M., 4:465
Gustafson, Alrik, 2:671
Gustafson, James M., 4:744,
  4:893, 4:899
Gustafson, James Paul, 5:418
Gustafson, Milton O., 3:506
Gustafson, Richard F., 2:766
Gustafsson, Lars, 2:671,
  2:674
Gustavson, Carl G., 3:382
Gutek, Gerald L., 3:255
Gutfreund, H., 5:673
Guth, De Lloyd J., 3:358
Guthmundsson, Barthi, 3:381
Guthrie, A. B., Jr., 1:1214
Guthrie, Douglas, 5:409
Guthrie, James W., 3:250
Guthrie, John, 2:576
Guthrie, K. S., 4:87
Guthrie, Stewart E., 3:212,
  4:540
Guthrie, William K., 2:345,
  4:46, 4:54, 4:89
Gutierrez, Claudia, 5:125
Gutierrez, Gustavo, 4:748,
  4:768, 4:896
Gutman, Herbert G., 3:531,
  3:547, 3:555
Gutmann, Amy, 3:255
Gutmann, Joseph, 4:614
Gutsche, George J., 2:687
Gutschick, Vincent P., 5:263
Gutting, Gary, 4:401, 4:406,
  5:53, 5:66, 5:88
Guttmann, Allen, 3:552
Guttmann, Julius, 4:601
Gutzwiller, Kathryn J., 2:369
Gutzwiller, M. C., 5:660
Guy, C. G., 5:302
Guy, J. A., 1:194
Guy, John, 3:484, 4:126
Guyer, Foster E., 2:467
Guyer, Paul, 4:206
Guyot, Arnold, 3:130
Gwin, Minrose C., 1:837
Gwynn, Frederick L., 1:1043
Gwynn, Stephen, 1:604

Gyatso, Geshe, 4:543
Gyekye, Kwame, 4:26, 4:369
Gygax, Franziska, 1:896
Gyi, Maung Maung, 3:489
Gyllensten, Lars, 2:671
Gysi, Lydia, 4:168

H

Haack, Dennis G., 5:522
Haak, Bob, 3:789
Ha-Am, Ahad, 2:7, 2:12, 2:16
Haaparanta, Leila, 4:230
Haar, Dik T., 5:698
Haas, Ernst B., 3:144
Haas, John D., 3:258, 3:279
Haas, Robert, 5:346
Haasse, Hella S., 2:625
Habegger, Alfred, 1:766
Haber, L. F., 5:728
Haberer, Joseph, 5:181
Haberler, Gottfried, 3:62
Habermas, Jürgen, 3:199,
  3:229, 4:288, 4:386, 4:390,
  4:403, 5:70, 5:88, 5:93
Habets, Alfred, 3:683
Habib, Irfan, 3:484
Habibi, Emile, 2:58
Habicht, Christian, 4:72
Haboush, Jahyuan K., 4:540
Hacker, Andrew, 3:506
Hacker, P.M.S., 4:229, 4:345
Hackett, Alice Payne, 1:51
Hackett, C. A., 2:500
Hackett, Edward J., 5:151
Hackett, Stuart C., 4:523
Hacking, Ian, 4:160
Hacking, Ian M., 4:160, 5:42,
  5:63, 5:526
Hacks, Peter, 2:603
Hadamard, Jacques, 5:494
Hadamitzky, Wolfgang, 1:100
Hadas, Moses, 2:345, 2:348,
  2:349, 2:381, 4:57, 4:451,
  4:647
Hadda, Janet, 2:31, 2:38
Haddad, Amy Marie, 5:328
Haddad, George M., 3:436,
  4:577
Haddad, Heskel M., 4:644
Haddad, Robert M., 4:569
Haddad, Yvonne Yazbeck,
  4:426, 4:504, 4:513, 4:529,
  4:532, 4:569, 4:578, 4:887
Haddakin, Lilian, 1:289
Hadden, Jeffrey K., 4:753
Haddox, John H., 4:33
Hadewijch, 2:626
Hadley, Charles D., 3:543
Hadlock, Richard, 3:668
Hadreas, Peter J., 4:311

Hadzsits, George D., 2:388,
  4:75
Haecker, Theodor, 2:397
Haenchen, Ernst, 4:821
Haenicke, Diether H., 2:565
Haerle, Tracy, 5:376
Haessler, Herbert A., 5:322
Haffenden, John, 1:436,
  1:950
al-Hafiz, 2:89, 2:93, 4:583
Hafner, Katie, 5:547
Hagan, William T., 3:555
Hagedorn, Hermann, 3:595
Hagedorn, Jessica, 2:329
Hagelman, Charles W., Jr.,
  1:283
Hagen, Victor Wolfgang von,
  3:131
Hagerman, Edward, 3:528
Hagg, Thomas, 2:363
Haggard, H. Rider, 1:592,
  1:594
Haggart, James A., 3:855
Haggin, B. H., 3:665
Hagopian, John V., 1:1033
Hagstrom, Jack W. C., 1:491
Hagstrom, Jerry, 3:507
Hagstrum, Jean H., 1:225,
  1:294
Hague, Eleanor, 3:851
Hague, René, 1:503
Hahm, David E., 4:55
Hahn, Beverly, 2:710
Hahn, Emily, 5:826
Hahn, Harley, 5:555
Hahn, Lewis, 5:100
Hahn, Lewis E., 4:273, 4:289,
  4:305, 4:338, 4:412
Hahn, Roger, 5:44, 5:698
Haig, Stirling, 2:484, 2:511
Haigh, Christopher, 3:355,
  4:726
Haight, Anne Lyon, 1:57
Haight, Elizabeth H., 2:383,
  4:469
Haight, Gordon Sherman,
  1:326, 1:354
Haight, M. R., 5:422
Haile, Berard, 3:865
Haile, H. G., 2:565
Hailey, Christopher, 3:680
Hailo, Jay L., 1:567
Hailstones, Thomas J., 3:62
Haim, Sylvia G., 3:440
Haimo, Ethan, 3:723
Haimson, Leopold, 3:396
Haines, Byron, 4:578
Haining, Peter, 1:1162
Haining, Robert, 3:120
Hainsworth, Peter, 2:401
Hair, Donald S., 1:401
Hajdu, David, 3:672

Hajime, Tanabe. *See* Tanabe
  Hajime
Hajnal, Peter I., 1:111
Hakim, Albert, 4:21
al-Hakim, Tawfiq, 2:63
Hakluyt, Richard, 3:922
Haksar, P. N., 3:500
Hakutani, Yoshinobu, 1:906
Halasa, Malu, 4:862
Halberstam, David, 2:340,
  3:538, 3:807
Halberstam-Rubin, Anna,
  2:46
Halbfass, Wilhelm, 4:508
Hald, Anders, 5:526
Haldane, Duncan, 1:23
Haldane, Elizabeth, 1:356
Haldane, John Burdon
  Sanderson, 5:788, 5:797
Haldeman, E. Julius, 1:41
Hale, Frederick, 4:15
Hale, George Ellery, 5:605
Hale, Jane A., 2:497
Hale, John R., 3:335
Hale, Lucretia, 1:1194
Hale, Nathan G., Jr., 3:184,
  5:448
Hale, Thomas, 2:108, 2:112
Hales, Dianne, 5:325, 5:326,
  5:358, 5:392
Hales, E. E., 4:741
Hales, Robert E., 5:326
Ha-levi, Judah. *See* Judah
  Ha-levi
Halévy, Elie, 1:265, 4:245
Haley, Allan, 1:62
Haley, Jay, 5:418, 5:441
Haley, Russell, 2:971
Haliburton, Thomas
  Chandler, 2:912
Halkett, Samuel, 1:77
Halkin, Hillel, 4:658
Halkin, Léon-E., 4:721
Halkin, Simon, 2:9
Halkovic, Stephen A., 4:542
Hall, Alfred Rupert, 5:25,
  5:42, 5:667, 5:706
Hall, B. C., 3:895
Hall, Blaine H., 1:1003
Hall, Bob, 5:815
Hall, Calvin S., 3:178, 3:184,
  5:414, 5:422, 5:448, 5:456
Hall, Daniel George Edward,
  3:489
Hall, David, 3:801
Hall, David A., 5:316
Hall, David D., 3:517
Hall, David L., 4:342
Hall, Donald, 1:655, 1:915,
  1:951, **1:983**
Hall, Edwin S., Jr., 3:855
Hall, G(ranville) Stanley,
  3:173, **3:185,** 5:453

Hall, Halbert, 1:1216
Hall, Harrison, 4:234
Hall, James, 1:421, 3:757
Hall, James M., 1:242
Hall, John R., 1:97, 4:867
Hall, John W., 3:474, 3:475
Hall, Kermit L., 3:145, 3:510
Hall, Louis B., 4:714
Hall, Maria Boas, 5:25, 5:40,
  5:41, 5:46, 5:740
Hall, Mary, 4:748
Hall, N. John, 1:407
Hall, Peter Dobkin, 3:559
Hall, Radclyffe, 1:492
Hall, Raymond L., 4:862
Hall, Robert A., Jr., 1:100,
  3:27
Hall, Robert W, 4:81
Hall, Roland, 4:180, 4:202
Hall, Spencer, 1:303, 1:307
Hall, Stewart G., 4:686
Hall, Thomas E., 3:50, 5:508
Hall, Thomas S., 5:33
Hallahan, Daniel P., 3:255
Hallam, Anthony, 5:617,
  5:622
Hallam, Arthur F., 5:514
Hallam, Elizabeth, 3:357
Hallberg, Peter, 2:640, 2:642
Halleck, Seymour, 5:422
Hallenbeck, William H.,
  5:351
Haller, Herman W., 2:403
Haller, Rudolf, 4:345
Haller, William, 4:734
Hallett, Judith P., 3:309
Hallett, Robin, 3:417, 3:418,
  3:419
Halley, Edmond, 5:586,
  5:606
Halley, J. Woods, 5:670
Halley, Pierre, 5:303
Hallgrímsson, Jónas, 2:639
Halliburton, David, 1:742,
  4:293
Halliburton, Richard, 3:892
Halliday, David, 5:650, 5:652,
  5:660
Halliday, Mark, 1:888
Halliday, T. R., 5:838
Hallie, Philip P., 4:58, 4:146
Halline, Allan G., 1:1077
Halliwell, Leslie, 3:825
Halliwell, S., 4:68
Hallo, William W., 3:300
Hallowell, A. Irving, 3:40
Hallowell, Christopher, 5:316
Hallwas, John E., 1:855
Halman, Talât, 2:96, 2:102
Halpenny, Frances, 3:605
Halper, Edward C., 4:68
Halper, Nathan, 1:505

Halperin, David M., 1:1182,
  3:309
Halperin, Herman, 4:671
Halperin, John, 1:276, 1:359,
  1:407
Halperin, Jonathan L., 5:374
Halpern, Alan A., 5:400
Halpern, Ben, 4:658
Halpern, Daniel, 1:655,
  1:720, 2:4
Halpern, Jack, 1:100
Halpern, Jeanne W., 3:801
Halpern, Martin, 1:775
Halpern, Moyshe-Leyb, 2:39
Halpern, Paul, 5:594
Halpern, Susan, 1:460
Halsband, Robert, 1:251
Halsey, David, 3:895
Halstead, Bruce W., 5:351,
  5:769, 5:770
Halstead, Robert H., 5:231
Halttunen, Karen, 3:559
Halverson, William H., 4:21
Hamacher, Werner, 1:1143
Hamady, Walter S., 1:41
Hamalian, Leo, 2:57, 2:76,
  2:84
Hamann, J. G., 4:216
Hambley, Allan R., 5:296
Hamburg, David A., 5:341
Hamburger, Jean, 5:313
Hamburger, Martin, 2:593
Hamburger, Michael, 2:565,
  2:566, 2:986
Hamby, Alonzo, 3:538
Hamelin, Jean, 3:605, **3:620**
Hamer, D. A., 3:363
Hamer, Mary, 1:407
Hamerton-Kelly, Robert G.,
  4:429
Hames, Peter, 3:827
Hamidullah, M., 4:373
Hamilton, Albert Charles,
  1:196, 1:198
Hamilton, Alexander, 3:141
Hamilton, Bernard, 4:691,
  4:699
Hamilton, Betty, 5:6
Hamilton, Charles, 1:35
Hamilton, Edith, 2:345,
  2:381, **3:880**
Hamilton, Eva M. N., 5:346
Hamilton, George Heard,
  3:759, 3:780
Hamilton, Helen, 5:382,
  5:397
Hamilton, Holman, 3:575
Hamilton, Ian, 1:1006, 1:1043
Hamilton, Michael P., 5:378
Hamilton, Nigel, 2:601, 3:538
Hamilton, Peter, 3:225,
  3:237, 4:309
Hamilton, R., 2:358

Hamilton, Richard, 4:481, 5:389
Hamilton, Richard S., 3:254
Hamilton, Scott, 1:873
Hamilton, Virginia, 1:1195, 3:866
Hamlett, Patrick W., 5:73
Hamlin, A. D., 3:765
Hamlin, Talbot, 3:762
Hamlyn, David W., 4:2, 4:16, 4:256
Hamm, Charles, 3:660
Hammacher, A. M., 3:794
Hammacher, Renilde, 3:794
Hammarberg, Gita, 2:730
Hammen, Scott, 3:838
Hammer, Louis, 2:527
Hammer, Reuven, 4:610
Hammer, T. R., 1:968
Hammersley, Martyn, 3:222
Hammett, Dashiell, 1:1092, 1:1226, **1:1230,** 1:1233, 1:1234, 2:794
Hammond, Allen L., 5:677
Hammond, Barbara, 3:403
Hammond, Bryan, 3:737
Hammond, Charles M., 3:811
Hammond, George S., 5:732
Hammond, Guyton B., 5:451
Hammond, John L., 3:370, **3:403,** 3:700
Hammond, John R., 1:564, 1:566, 1:693
Hammond, Kenneth A., 5:620
Hammond, Lansing, 1:259
Hammond, Mason, 4:439
Hammond, N. G., 2:345, 3:298, 3:302, 4:806, 4:818
Hammond, Norman, 3:627, 4:455
Hammond, Philip E., 3:212, 4:752, 4:855
Hammond, R. J., 3:423
Hamner, Robert D., 2:939, 2:943
Hamod, Syed A., 1:846
Hamori, Andras, 2:55, 2:70
Hamouda, O. F., 3:84
Hampden-Turner, Charles, 3:168
Hampshire, Stuart, 4:160, 4:188
Hampson, Norman, 4:210
Hampton, Cynthia, 4:81
Hampton, Jean, 4:174
Hamsun, Knut, 2:43, 2:662, **2:664**
Hanafusa, Hideo, 5:242
Hanak, Peter, 3:390
Hanan, Patrick, 2:189, 2:210
Han-ch'ing, Kuan. *See* Kuan Han-Ch'ing

Hanchett, William, 3:528
Hancock, Geoff, 2:904
Hancock, Graham, 3:422
Hancock, W. K., 3:423
Hand, D. J., 5:571
Hand, Wayland D., 3:869, 5:319
Handel, George Frideric, 3:698, 3:718
Handel, Gerald, 3:216
Handelman, Susan A., 4:610
Handke, Peter, 2:585
Handley, Graham, 1:354
Handley-Taylor, Geoffrey, 1:512, 1:519
Handlin, Oscar, 3:581, 4:225, 4:639
Hands, A. R., 3:307
Handwerk, Glenn E., 5:285
Hane, Mikiso, 3:474, 3:477
Haneman, Mary, 4:786
Haney, Wayne S., 3:872
Hanff, Helene, 1:32
Hanfling, Oswald, 4:264, 4:345
Hanford, James H., 1:192
Hangen, Eva C., 1:201
Hanghe, Ahmed Artan, 2:117
Hanh, Thich Nhat, 4:496
Hanham, H. J., 3:354
Hanigan, James P., 4:894
Hanisch, Gertrude S., 2:503
Hanke, Lewis, 3:515, 3:629, 3:643, **3:646**
Hankey, W. J., 4:118
Hankins, James, 4:127
Hankins, Thomas L., 5:44
Hanks, Joyce Main, 5:70, 5:165
Hanks, Maxine, 4:892
Hanley, David L, 3:373
Hanley, Eileen, 5:376
Hanley, Nick, 3:48
Hanley, Susan B., 3:464, 3:475
Hann, E. M., 3:140
Hannah, Richard W., 2:605
Hannay, Margaret P., 1:513
Hanover, Nathan, 4:624
Hans, James S., 4:293
Hansberry, Lorraine, 1:1071, **1:1091**
Hanscombe, Gillian E., 1:541
Hansen, Alvin, 3:80, 3:103
Hansen, Dirk, 5:537
Hansen, Elaine Tuttle, 1:151
Hansen, Eric, 3:903
Hansen, Martin A., 2:650, 2:656
Hansen, Olaf, 1:714
Hansen, Valerie, 3:468
Han Shan, 2:198
Hanslick, Eduard, 3:660

Hansma, Paul K., 5:672
Hanson, Diania, 3:455
Hanson, Elizabeth I., 1:1136, 1:1249, 2:284
Hanson, Glen, 5:352
Hanson, Katherine, 2:662
Hanson, Norwood R., 5:66
Hanson, Paul D., 4:823
Hanson, R., 4:713
Hanson, Victor D., 3:308
Han Yong-un, 2:298, **2:300**
Han Yü, 2:198, 2:205, 2:215
Hao Yen-p'ing, 3:468
Hapgood, Isabel F., 2:692
Hapgood, Robert, 1:209
Hapke, Laura, 1:714
Happel, Stephen, 4:891
Haqqi, Yahya, 2:64
Harari, Josue V., 1:925
Haraway, Donna Jeanne, 1:1132, **1:1146** 3:213, 5:33, **5:201**
Harbage, Alfred, 1:170, 1:206, 1:221, 1:222
Harbert, Earl N., 1:650, 1:730, 1:919
Harbert, Kenneth, 5:339
Harbin, Billy J., 1:426
Harbison, Peter, 3:370
Harbison, Winfred A., 3:541
Harcourt, Caroline, 3:415
Harcourt, Melville, 2:652
Harcourt, Peter, 2:970
Hardacre, Helen, 3:477, 4:540
Harden, Blaine, 3:903
Harden, Edgar F., 1:404
Harden, John, 3:861
Harden, Victoria A., 5:313
Harder, Uffe, 2:645
Hardesty, Larry L., 5:544
Hardie, W. F., 4:68
Hardimon, Michael, 4:233
Hardin, Garrett, 5:114, **5:134,** 5:822
Hardin, Richard F., 1:179
Hardin, Russell, 5:111
Harding, Gunnar, 2:672
Harding, Harry, 3:470
Harding, M. Esther, 5:422
Harding, Phillip, 3:299
Harding, Sandra G., 4:36, **4:39,** 4:391, 5:25, 5:66, 5:154, 5:187, 5:202
Harding, Vincent, 3:555
Harding, Walter, 1:702, 5:837
Hardinge, Emma, 4:851
Hardison, O. B., 1:157, 3:559, 4:68, 4:699, 5:154, 5:573
Hardon, John A., 4:717
Hardwick, Charles S., 4:345
Hardwick, Elizabeth, 1:925

Hardwick, Michael, 1:276,
1:350, 1:608
Hardwick, Mollie, 1:350
Hardwick, Steve, 5:299
Hardwick, Susan Wiley,
3:118
Hardy, Barbara, 1:354
Hardy, David A., 5:623
Hardy, Florence Emily
Dugdale, 1:362
Hardy, Godfrey H., 4:324,
5:494, 5:583
Hardy, K. A., 3:276
Hardy, Richard P., 2:543
Hardy, Thomas, 1:291,
1:310, 1:314, 1:317, **1:360,**
1:378, 1:444, 1:474, 1:475,
1:481, 1:507, 1:1067,
2:249, 2:427, 2:972, 3:841,
4:255
Hardy, W. Carey, 5:284
Hardyment, Christine, 3:899
Hare, A. Paul, 3:172
Hare, David, 1:424, 1:449,
1:492
Hare, Peter, 4:16
Hare, R. M., 4:81
Hare, Richard, 2:726, 3:395
Hare, Thomas Blenman,
2:280
Hareven, Shulamith, 2:8,
2:19
Hareven, Tamara K., 3:173
Hargreaves, J. D., 3:420
Hargrove, Eugene, 5:114,
5:135
Harich, Walther, 2:606
Harik, Iliya F., 3:445
Häring, Bernard, 4:718
Haring, C. H., 3:629
Haring, L. Lloyd, 5:620
Harjan, George, 2:819
Harkabi, Yehoshafat, 3:440
Harkányi, Katalin, 5:28
Harkavy, Alexander, 1:103
Harkins, William E., 2:687,
2:789, 2:790
Harkless, Lawrence B., 5:396
Harkness, Carla, 5:358
Harkness, David, 3:366
Harkness, Richard, 5:351
Harkness, Stanley, 1:342
Harlan, Louis R., 1:785,
3:270, 3:555
Harland, W. B., 5:623
Harlander, Susan K., 5:221,
5:267
Harlow, Victor E., 4:264
Harman, Eleanor, 1:47
Harman, Gilbert, 4:380
Harman, Peter M., 5:46
Harmon, Barbara L., 1:181
Harmon, Ginger, 3:899

Harmon, Maurice, 1:418,
1:460, 1:529
Harmon, Rebecca Lamar,
4:790
Harmon, Robert B., 1:61
Harmon, William, 1:656
Harms, Ernest, 5:416
Harnack, Adolf, 4:95, 4:677,
4:681, 4:686, 4:688, 4:741
Harner, James L., 1:61, 1:167
Harner, Michael J., 3:895
Harnoncourt, Nikolaus, 3:660
Harper, F., 5:263
**Harper, Frances E(llen)
W(atkins),** 1:721, **1:753**
Harper, George M., 1:307
Harper, Howard M., Jr.,
1:917
Harper, Jon, 1:1052
Harper, J. Russell, 3:609
Harper, Margaret M., 1:904
Harper, Michael, 1:984
Harper, Michael J. K., 5:358
Harper, R., 5:418
Harpsfield, Nicholas, 1:194
Harran, Marilyn J., 4:778
Harrari, Josue, 1:1134
Harré, Rom, 4:384, 5:31,
5:63
Harrell, Stevan, 4:892
Harrer, Heinrich, 3:923
Harrier, Richard C., 1:171
Harries, Richard, 4:784
Harrigan, John J., 3:148
Harriman, Philip L., 5:413
Harrington, Curtis, 1:1176
Harrington, Gary, 1:837
Harrington, Geri, 5:397
Harrington, John P., 1:440
Harrington, Karl P., 2:384
Harrington, Michael, 3:52,
3:66
Harriott, R., 2:353
Harris, A., 3:279
Harris, Ann, 5:626
Harris, Ann Sutherland,
3:761, 3:770
Harris, Bernard, 1:1072
Harris, C. Leon, 5:770
Harris, Charles B., 1:943
Harris, Chauncey D., 3:118,
3:125, 5:620
Harris, Christina, 3:446
Harris, Cyril M., 3:761
Harris, Daniel A., 1:364
Harris, David V., 5:626
Harris, Donald, 3:680
Harris, Eddy L., 3:417, 3:895,
3:903
Harris, Elizabeth, 1:8
Harris, Ellen T., 3:698
Harris, Errol E., 4:188, 5:63

**Harris, George Washington,
1:673,** 1:1193
Harris, H. A., 3:307
Harris, H. S., 4:233
Harris, Jane G., 2:687, 2:738
Harris, Jocelyn, 1:254
Harris, Joel Chandler,
1:721, **1:754,** 1:1193,
1:1194
Harris, John, 5:120
Harris, Julia C., 1:755
Harris, Kevin, 1:457
Harris, Leonard, 4:386
Harris, Lis, 4:632
Harris, Mark, 1:855, 1:947
Harris, Marvin, 3:12, 3:14,
3:31, 5:34
Harris, Mary Dee, 5:564
Harris, Michael, 1:35
Harris, R. Baine, 4:61
Harris, R. Cole, 3:605, 3:606,
3:611
Harris, Richard C., 1:757
Harris, Richard H., 1:123,
1:427
Harris, Sandra L., 5:427
Harris, Seymour E., 3:105
Harris, Sharon M., 1:744
Harris, Susan K., 1:723
Harris, Tirril, 5:426
Harris, Tomas, 3:776
Harris, Trudie, 1:917, 1:1019
Harris, William H., 3:547
Harris, William J., 1:941
Harris, William O., 1:448
Harris, William T., 4:21
Harris, William V., 3:308
Harris, Wilson, 2:930, **2:935**
Harris, Zellig, 3:21
Harrison, Ada, 1:334
Harrison, Antony H., 1:315,
1:391, 1:398
Harrison, B. W., 4:895
Harrison, Barbara Grizzuti,
3:899, 4:863
Harrison, Brian, 3:366
Harrison, Edward R., 5:595,
5:655
Harrison, Everett F., 4:718
Harrison, George B., 1:174,
1:222
Harrison, Gilbert A., 1:899,
1:1116
Harrison, Helen, 5:322
Harrison, James, 2:181
Harrison, Jane E., 2:345,
4:478, 4:491
Harrison, John, 3:483
Harrison, John R., 1:417
Harrison, Joseph, 3:387
Harrison, Lewis, 5:319
Harrison, Lou, 3:699
Harrison, Martin, 3:374

Harrison, Michael I., 3:210
Harrison, Michelle, 5:355
Harrison, Peter, 5:759
Harrison, R. K., 4:718
Harrison, Robert Pogue,
　2:418
Harrison, Ross, 4:191
Harrod, Roy, 3:87
Harrold, Charles F., 1:326,
　4:783
Harrow, Ken, 2:108
Harrow, Leonard, 3:436
Harsh, Philip W., 1:133,
　2:382
Harshav, Barbara, 1:720, 2:33
Harshav, Benjamin, 1:720,
　2:32, 2:33
Harss, Luis, 2:846
Hart, Alan, 3:455
Hart, Alfred, 1:219
Hart, Anna, 5:568
Hart, B. H., 3:926
Hart, Clive, 3:838, 5:219
Hart, Dabney Adams, 1:513
Hart, George L., 2:172
Hart, Henry H., 1:495, 2:558,
　3:934
Hart, Herbert L., 3:151
Hart, Ivor B., 3:780, 5:193
Hart, James D., 1:8, 1:51,
　1:132, 1:650, 1:714, 1:1210
Hart, Jane Sherron De, 3:513
Hart, John Mason, 3:638
Hart, Martin, 2:621, 2:626
Hart, Mary L., 3:851
Hart, Patricia, 2:851
Harte, (Francis) Bret(t),
　1:718, 1:721, **1:755**, 1:990,
　1:1193
Harte, John, 5:351, 5:736
Hartford, Kathleen, 3:470
Harth, Erich, 5:341
Harth, Philip, 1:242
Harthan, John, 1:23, 1:28,
　3:766
Hartl, Daniel L., 5:778
Hartland, Edwin S., 3:848
Hartley, Anthony, 2:448
Hartley, L(eslie) P(oles),
　1:493
Hartley, Sir Harold, 5:743
Hartlyn, Jonathan, 3:635
Hartman, Charles, 2:199,
　3:468
Hartman, David, 4:648, 4:668
Hartman, Donald K., 1:124
Hartman, Geoffrey H., 1:208,
　1:307, 4:610
Hartman, John G., 1:1073
Hartman, Rudolf, 3:721
Hartman, Susan, 1:54
Hartmann, Klaus, 4:330
Hartmann, Olga De, 4:875

Hartmann, William K., 5:588,
　5:592, 5:594
Hartmann von Aue, 586
Hartnack, Justus, 4:345
Hartnell, Tim, 5:568
Hartnoll, Phyllis, 1:272
Hartog, François, 3:316,
　4:480
Hartsfield, Mariella G., 3:861
Hartshorn, Truman A., 3:122,
　3:124
Hartshorne, Charles, 4:17,
　4:34, 4:41, 4:161, 4:260,
　4:288, 4:338, 4:342
Hartshorne, Richard, 3:118,
　5:620
Hartt, Frederick, 3:757,
　3:759, 3:782
Hartwell, David, 1:612
Hartz, Louis, 3:606
Haruki, Murakami. See Mu-
　rakami Haruki
Harvey, A. C., 3:63
Harvey, A. McGhee, 3:551,
　5:313
Harvey, Anthony P., 5:639
Harvey, Charles, 1:383
Harvey, David, 3:118, 3:123,
　3:211
Harvey, Elizabeth D., 4:391
Harvey, Irene E., 4:398
Harvey, Jonathan, 3:721
Harvey, L. P., 3:387
Harvey, P. L., 3:57
Harvey, Paul, 2:346, 2:447,
　3:298
Harvey, Robert, 4:330
Harvey, Van A., 4:675, 4:718
Harvey, William, 5:42, 5:360
Harvie, Christopher, 3:355,
　3:368
Harwin, Ronald, 5:353
Harwit, Martin, 5:590
Harwood, Michael, 5:787
Hasan, Mohammed Yusof,
　2:326
Hasan, Y. F., 3:418
Hasan-Ibn-Hasan, Fasa'l,
　3:448
Hašek, Jaroslav, 2:788,
　2:790
Hasel, Gerhard F., 4:827
Haskell, Arnold L., 3:732,
　3:741
Haskins, Charles H., 4:101,
　4:699, 5:39
Haskins, Charles Homer,
　3:331
Haskins, James S., 3:703,
　4:739
Haslam, Gerald, 1:1218
Hasluck, F. W., 3:452
Hass, Ernst B., 5:181

Hass, Robert, 1:984
Hassall, Anthony J., 2:964
Hassan, Ihab, 1:917
Hassan, Ihab Habib, 1:910
Hassan, M. H., 5:713
Hassan, Salem K., 1:508
Hassard, John, 3:210
Hassard, T. H., 5:521
Hassett, Constance W., 1:339
Hassett, Joseph M., 1:572
Hassig, Ross, 3:628
Hassinger, Edward W., 5:328
Hastings, Adrian, 4:744
Hastings, Arthur C., 5:319
Hastings, Baird, 3:734
Hastings, Diana, 5:377
Hastings, James, 4:4, 4:717
Haswell, Charles K., 5:224
Hata, Gohei, 4:709
Hatab, Lawrence J., 4:37
Hatch, Edwin, 4:63, 4:99,
　4:818
Hatch, James V., 1:1078
Hatch, Nathan O., 3:559,
　4:751, 4:767, 4:813
Hatcher, John, 3:357
Hatcher, William S., 4:861
Hathaway, Anne, 1:202
Hathaway, Baxter, 4:127
Hatje, Gerd, 3:761
Hattaway, Herman, 3:526,
　3:528
Hattaway, Michael, 1:170
Hattendorf, Lynn C., 1:82
Hattersley, John, 3:201
Hatton, John, 5:10
Hauer, Mary G., 1:61
Hauerwas, Stanley, 4:744,
　4:897
Haug, Marie R., 5:316, 5:331
Haugeland, John C., 4:382,
　5:75, 5:570
Haugen, Einar, 2:663
Haugen, Eva, 2:663
Haugh, Richard, 2:761
Haupt, Arthur, 3:121
Hauptmann, Gerhart (Jo-
　hann Robert), 2:564,
　2:586, 2:665
Hausdorff, Don, 5:451
Hauser, Arnold, 3:202, 3:757
Hauser, Robert M., 3:214
Hauser, William, 3:475
Hausman, Carl R., 5:194,
　5:374
Hausman, Patricia, 5:341,
　5:346
Haut, Rivka, 4:892
Havard, W. C., 4:257
Havas, M., 5:616
Have, Henk ten, 5:78
Havel, Václav, 2:596, 2:788,
　2:791, 3:389

Havelock, Eric A., 2:346, 2:349, 2:384, 4:48, 4:81, 4:460
Havens, Daniel F., 1:1073
Havens, Raymond D., 1:307
Havens, Thomas, 3:477
Haverkamp, Jenniver A., 5:635
Havighurst, Alfred F., 3:354, 3:366, 3:407
Havighurst, Clark C., 5:328
Havlice, Patricia P., 1:126
Hawes, Bess L., 3:861
Hawes, Donald, 1:404
Hawi, Khalil, 2:59
Hawke, David F., 3:520, 3:524
Hawkes, Jacquetta, 4:432
Hawkes, John, 1:984
Hawkes, Terence, 1:209, 1:1132
Hawkin, David J., 5:197
Hawking, Stephen William, 5:8, **5:16**, **5:606**, 5:665, **5:691**, 5:708, 5:713
Hawkins, Alma, 3:731
Hawkins, Donald, 3:891
Hawkins, Hugh, 1:785, 3:270, 3:578
Hawkins, Raymond, 3:224
Hawkridge, David G., 3:255
Hawks, Howard, 3:837
Hawley, Donald, 3:451
Hawley, John S., 2:174, 4:504, 4:516
Hawthorn, Jeremy, 1:464
Hawthorne, Edward Foster, 1:750
Hawthorne, Nathaniel, 1:598, 1:635, 1:649, 1:657, 1:671, **1:674**, 1:679, 1:686, 1:699, 1:704, 1:750, 1:762, 1:801, 1:1193, 1:1194, 1:1219
Hawting, G. R., 4:569
Hay, Malcolm, 1:446, 1:446
Hay, Peter, 4:555
Hay, Stephen, 3:484
Hayashi Tetsumaro, 1:180, 1:886
Haycox, Ernest, 1:1211, **1:1214**, 1:1218
Haycraft, Howard, 1:604, 1:714, 1:1196, 2:3
Hayden, George A., 2:189
Hayden, John O., 1:268, 1:274
Hayden, M. R., 5:392
Hayden, Robert E(arl), **1:986**
Haydn, Franz Joseph, 1:261, 3:678, **3:699**
Haydn, Hiram, 1:41, 2:401

Hayek, Friedrich August **von, 3:81**, 3:98, 4:245
Hayes, Carleton J., 3:341
Hayes, Colin, 5:353
Hayes, Elizabeth, 3:731
Hayes, Greg, 3:892
Hayes, Harold T. P., 3:909
Hayes, John H., 4:806
Hayes, John R., 4:569
Hayes, John T., 3:775
Hayford, Harrison, 1:689
Haykal, Muhammad Husayn, 4:588
Haykin, Simon S., 5:299, 5:302
Hayles, N. Katherine, 2:989
Hayman, David, 1:421, 1:423
Hayman, Ronald, 1:425, 2:495, 2:573, 2:596, 4:331
Haymes, Emily M., 5:341
Haynes, David, 5:540
Haynes, Gary, 5:779
Haynes, John, 2:108
Haynes, Roslynn D., 1:564
Haynes, Stephen, 4:648, 5:414
Hays, Samuel P., 3:550, 5:822
Hayter, Charles, 1:358, 3:670
Hayward, Arthur L., 1:350
Hayward, John, 1:31, 1:316
Hayward, Max, 2:687, 2:692
Hayward, Robert, 4:608
Hayward, Roger, 5:730
Hayward, Stephen, 2:158
Haywood, Helene, 3:766
Haywood, John, 2:57
Hazan, Haim, 4:642
Hazard, B. H., 3:481
Hazard, Paul, 4:161
Hazaz, Haim, 2:8, **2:19**
Hazen, Margaret Hindle, 3:660
Hazen, Robert M., 3:250, 3:660
Hazlitt, William, 1:32, 1:115, 1:264, 1:273, 1:284, **1:290**, 1:292, 1:305
Hazzard, Shirley, 2:953
H. D. (Hilda Doolittle), **1:826**, 1:873, 1:1187
Head, Bessie, 2:105, **2:163**
Head, Joseph, 4:887
Head, Sydney W., 3:811
Heal, Felicity, 4:726
Healan, Dan M., 4:457
Healy, J. J., 2:946
Healy, Thomas F., 1:176
Heaney, Seamus (Justin), 1:416, **1:494**, 2:411
Hearn, D. Donald, 5:564
Hearn, Lafcadio, 4:539
Heath, Angela, 5:377

Heath, Ernie, 3:890
Heath, Peter, 4:582
Heath, Shirley Brice, 3:250
Heath, Stephen, 1:1157
Heath, Thomas L., 4:68, 5:38
Heath, William, 1:268
Heather, Nick, 5:402
Heath-Stubbs, John F., 1:418
Heaton, John L., 3:821
Hebbel, Friedrich, 2:564, **2:587**, 2:605, 2:644
Hebblethwaite, Peter, 4:744, 4:771
Hebert, Alan P., 1:246
Hebert, Raymond G., 5:363
Hecht, Anthony, 1:986
Hecht, Hans, 1:280
Hecht, Jeff, 5:235, 5:666, 5:718
Hecht, Susanna, 5:822
Hecker, Helen, 3:890
Hedges, Inez, 2:986
Hedges, Lawrence E., 5:425
Hedges, William L., 1:681
Hedrick, Charles W., 4:453
Hedrick, Joan D., 1:775
Hedstrom, M. I., 5:523
Heehs, Peter, 4:353
Heer, Friedrich, 3:331
Heeren, Vern E., 5:481
Heermance, J. Noel, 1:739
Heesterman, J. C., 3:484, 4:501
Heezen, Bruce C., 5:631
Hefele, Bernhard, 3:668
Hefele, Karl J., 4:677
Heffron, Mary J., 3:462, 5:261
Hegel, Georg Wilhelm **Friedrich,** 2:406, 2:414, 2:442, 2:455, 2:461, 3:94, 3:198, **3:284**, 3:289, 3:375, 4:12, 4:17, 4:158, 4:197, 4:198, 4:216, 4:227, 4:230, **4:231**, 4:238, 4:249, 4:251, 4:254, 4:259, 4:279, 4:281, 4:303, 4:366, 4:385, 4:393, 4:401, 4:409, 4:600, 4:663, 5:88, 5:94
Hegel, Robert E., 2:189
Heidegger, Martin, 1:1150, 2:461, 4:50, 4:74, 4:206, 4:226, 4:234, 4:252, 4:261, **4:290**, 4:299, 4:304, 4:309, 4:318, 4:328, 4:331, 4:334, 4:363, 4:365, 4:367, 4:376, 4:390, 4:393, 4:394, 4:396, 4:401, 4:830, 4:900, 4:902, 5:71, 5:81, **5:90**, 5:93, 5:96, 5:436
Heidel, Alexander, 4:440
Heidenheimer, Arnold J., 3:141, 5:330

Heijden, Adri van der, 2:621
Heikal, Mohamed, 3:446
Heil, Kenneth D., 5:767
Heilbron, John L., 5:31, 5:48, 5:703, 5:710
Heilbroner, Robert, 3:45, 3:51, 3:52, 3:53, 3:62, 3:87, 3:92, 3:95, 3:101, 3:107
Heilbrun, Carolyn G., 1:925
Heilman, Joan R., 5:347
Heilman, Robert B., 1:214, 1:1073
Heilman, Samuel, 4:642, 4:654
Heilmann, Klaus, 5:354
Heim, Michael, 2:688, 5:561
Heimert, Alan, 4:753
Heimlich, Henry J., 5:381
Heimmlich, Richard A., 5:626
Heims, Steve V., 5:583, 5:584
Heine, Heinrich, 1:561, 1:772, 2:16, **2:587**
Heine-Geldern, Robert, 4:518
Heinemann, Helen, 1:408
Heinemann, Benno, 4:632
Heinemann, Margot, 1:190
Heinesen, William, 2:655, **2:656**
Heiney, Donald, 2:401
Heinlein, Robert A., 1:614, 1:1252, **1:1257,** 5:563
Heinrich, Bernd, 5:764
Heinrichs, Waldo H., 3:535
Heinz, Thomas A., 3:798
Heisenberg, Elisabeth, 5:694
Heisenberg, Werner, 5:659, 5:680, **5:693,** 5:715, 5:716, 5:719, 5:734
Heiserman, Arthur Ray, 1:197, 2:363
Heisig, James W., 4:366
Heissig, Walther, 4:541
Heitland, William E., 5:265
Heitler, Waleter, 5:717
Heitman, Annegret, 2:645
Heitzenrater, Richard P., 4:790
Hejib, Alaka, 4:509
Hejtmanek, Milan G., 4:533
Hekmat, Forough, 2:83
Hektorović, Petar, 2:784
Held, David, 4:264, 4:404, 4:405, 5:89, 5:90
Held, Gilbert, 5:304, 5:550
Held, Julius S., 3:789, 3:792
Held, Michael, 3:761
Heldt, Barbara, 2:687
Helgeland, John, 4:688
Helgerson, Richard, 1:165
Helgert, Hermann J., 5:299
Heliodorus of Emesa, 2:343, **2:357**

Hellemans, Alexander, 5:216
Hellenbrand, Harold, 1:640
Heller, Agnes, 4:127
Heller, Celia S., 3:348, 4:636
Heller, Erich, 2:565, 2:602
Heller, James, 1:118
Heller, Janet Ruth, 1:272
Heller, Joseph, 1:987
Heller, Michael, 1:913, 5:655
Heller, Monica, 3:21
Heller, Peter, 3:903
Heller, Tamar, 1:346, 1:599, 1:618
Heller, Terry, 1:599
Heller, W. P., 3:69
Hellman, John, 2:516
Hellman, Lillian, 1:1066, 1:1071, **1:1092,** 1:1105, 1:1120, 1:1230
Helly, Dorothy D., 3:930
Helm, Dieter, 3:84
Helm, Mike, 3:863
Helman, Ethel, 5:313
Helmholtz, Hermann Ludwig Ferdinand von, 5:452, 5:671, **5:692,** 5:734
Helmreich, William B., 4:654
Helms, H. L., 5:540
Helpman, Elhanan, 3:53
Helsinger, Elizabeth K., 1:395
Helterman, Jeffrey, 1:918, 1:1013
Helweg, Marianne, 3:834
Helyar, John, 3:48
Hemenway, Robert, 1:850
Hemery, Daniel, 5:278
Heminges, John, 1:203
Hemingway, Ernest, 1:474, 1:741, 1:779, 1:801, 1:811, **1:844,** 1:852, 1:881, 1:883, 1:946, 1:960, 1:1193, 2:530, 2:648, 2:794, 2:907
Hemingway, Maurice, 2:546
Heminway, John, 3:903
Hemlow, Joyce, 1:235
Hemming, Roy, 3:667, 3:672
Hemmings, F.W.J., 2:518
Hempel, Carl Gustav, 4:383, 4:384, 5:63, **5:91**
Hempenstall, Peter J., 3:495
Hemphill, Essex, 1:1188
Henbest, Nigel, 5:592, 5:655
Hench, John B., 1:6, 3:801
Hendel, Charles W., 4:202
Henderson, Bill, 1:47, 1:50
Henderson, Carter, 5:315
Henderson, G. D., 4:735
Henderson, George, 5:353
Henderson, Greig E., 1:818
Henderson, Harold G., 2:274
Henderson, Heather, 1:325
Henderson, John S., 4:455

Henderson, Katherine, 1:911
Henderson, Ronald W., 3:206
Henderson, Stephen E., 2:107
Henderson, Valerie L., 3:193
Henderson, W. O., 3:75, 3:377
Hendin, Josephine, 1:918
Hendler, Sheldon P., 5:349
Hendley, Brian, 4:324, 4:342
Hendley, Steve, 4:331
Hendrex, Clyde, 3:207
Hendrick, George, 1:870
Hendrickson, David C., 3:546
Hendrix, Scott H., 4:778
Hendry, John, 5:661, 5:674, 5:701
Henfrey, Colin, 3:895
Heng, Liang, 3:470
Hengel, Martin, 4:604, 4:807, 4:811
Henifin, Mary Sue, 5:354
Henig, Martin, 4:448
Henig, Robin A., 5:369
Henig, Robin M., 5:316, 5:322
Henige, David, 4:460
Henke, Suzette A., 1:505
Henkel, Gretchen, 5:355
Henkels, Robert M., Jr., 2:493
Henkin, Louis, 3:144
Henley, Beth, 1:1071, **1:1093**
Henley, Tracey B., 4:237, 5:453
Henley, W. E., 1:92
Hennecke, Edgar, 4:811
Henninger, Mark G., 4:104
Henricks, Robert G., 3:468, 4:528
Henry, Carl F. H., 4:718, 4:744
Henry, D. P., 4:88, 4:108
Henry, David D., 1:775
Henry, Denis, 2:394
Henry, Dewitt, 1:921
Henry, E., 4:88
Henry, Elisabeth, 2:394, 2:397
Henry, Eric, 2:210
Henry, George W., 5:415
Henry, O., 1:756
Henry, Patrick, 2:491
Henry, Peter, 2:719
Henry, S. C., 4:739
Henry, Sondra, 4:650
Henryson, R., 2:352
Henry, Will/Fisher, Clay, 1:1212
Hensel, Fanny, 3:700
Henslin, James M., 3:206
Henslowe, Philip, 1:170
Henthorn, William E., 3:481

Hentsch, Thierry, 3:436
Henyon, Debra K., 5:267
Hepworth, James R., 5:828
Heraclitus of Ephesus, 4:50,
4:52, 4:56, **4:74**
Herald, Diana T., 1:122
Herberg, Will, 3:213, 4:639,
4:649, 4:753
Herbert, Anthony B., 3:892
Herbert, Christopher, 1:407
Herbert, Frank, 1:1258,
1:1263, 5:537
Herbert, George, 1:180,
1:643
Herbert, John H., 5:285
Herbert, Nick, 5:662
Herbert, Patricia, 2:311
Herbert, R. A., 5:783
Herbert, Robert I., 5:193
Herbert, S., 3:869
Herbert, Victor, 5:327, 5:346
Herbert, Wally, 3:933
Herbert, Xavier, 2:954
Herbert, Zbigniew, 2:810,
2:814
Herbstrith, Waltraud, 4:744
Herculano, Alexandre, 2:557
Herdeck, Donald E., 2:108,
2:930
Herder, Johann Gottfried
von, 2:442, 2:563, 2:588,
3:285, 4:158, **4:198,** 4:204,
4:216, 4:459
Herder, Johann von, 1:648
Herdt, Gilbert H., 3:15, 4:430
Heredia, José Maria de,
2:537
Hergenhahn, B. R., 3:167,
3:175
Hergenhan, Laurie, 2:946,
2:947
Herington, C. J., 2:351
Herken, Gregg, 5:181
Herling, Gustaw (Herling-
Grudziński), 2:814
Herman, A. L., 3:484, 4:37,
4:504
Herman, C. Peter, 5:347
Herman, Edward S., 3:203,
3:204, 3:807
Herman, Lloyd, 3:765
Hermann, A., 5:708
Hermann, John Patrick,
1:143
Hermans, Willem F., 2:621,
2:626, 2:628
Hermodsson, Elisabet, 2:671
Hern, Nicholas, 2:586
Hernández, José, 2:844,
2:869
Hernández, Miguel, 2:541
Herndl, Diane Price, 1:927,
1:1134

Herndon, Marcia, 3:660
Hernon, Peter, 1:108
Hernton, Calvin, 3:555
Herodotus, 2:342, 2:357,
2:366, **3:315,** 3:322, 4:419,
4:479, 5:485
Herold, J. Christopher, 2:510
Heron, Craig, 3:607
Heron, Echo, 5:337
Heron, G. A., 2:156
Herr, Cheryl, 1:505
Herr, Richard, 3:165, 3:387
Herr, Stanley S., 5:422
Herren, Ray V., 5:261
Herrick, F. H., 5:787
Herrick, Robert, 1:181
Herrin, Judith, 3:328
Herring, George C., 3:538,
3:631
Herrmann, Dieter B., 5:31
Herrmann, Luke, 3:794
Herrmann, Paul, 3:892
Herrnstein, Richard J., 5:35
Herron, Nancy L., 3:5
Hersen, Michael, 5:107,
5:414, 5:417
Hersey, John, 1:974
Hersh, Reuben, 5:481
Hershatter, Gail, 3:470
Hershinow, Sheldon J.,
1:1013
Hershkowitz, Mickey, 3:808
Hershlag, Z. Y., 3:436
Herskovits, Melville Jean,
3:16, 3:28, **3:32,** 3:420
Herstein, I. N., 5:484
Herstein, Sheila R., 1:331
Hertsgaard, Mark, 3:543,
3:807
Hertz, Eli E., 5:554
Hertz, Heinrich, 5:228,
5:641, **5:694**
Hertz, Johanna, 5:694
Hertz, Martin F., 3:584
Hertzberg, Arthur, 3:348,
4:161, 4:639, 4:647, 4:658
Herz, Judith Scherer, 1:477
Herzberg, Judith, 2:627
Herzenberg, Caroline L., 5:28
Herzen (Gertsen), Alek-
sandr, 2:727
Herzfeld, Michael, 3:869
Herzl, Theodor, 4:658
Herzman, Ronald B., 1:147
Herzog, Chaim, 3:436, 3:440
Herzog, Elizabeth, 2:30,
4:625
Herzog, Kristin, 1:657
Herzstein, Robert E., 3:375
Heschel, Abraham Joshua,
4:664, 4:660, 4:668, 4:884
Heschel, Susannah, 4:650
Heseltine, Janet E., 2:447

Hesiod, 2:341, 2:357, 2:396,
4:446, **4:481**
Heslin, JoAnn, 5:347
Hess, Beth B., 3:201, 3:216
Hess, Earl J., 3:528
Hess, Fred C., 5:730
Hess, Gary R., 3:345
Hess, Linda, 2:174
Hess, Mary Abbott, 5:358
Hess, Robert D., 3:147
Hesse, Everett W., 2:524
Hesse, Hermann, 2:564,
2:589
Hesse, Mary B., 4:405, 5:63
Hessel, Eugene A., 2:333
Hessing, Siegfried, 4:188
Hession, Charles H., 3:79
Hessney, Richard C., 2:189
Hestenes, Marshal D., 5:484
Hetherington, Norriss S.,
4:13
Hettinga, Tsjebbe, 2:634
Heung-gil, Yun. *See* Yun
Heung-gil
Heurgon, J., 3:303
Heuscher, Julius E., 3:869
Heussner, Ralph C., 5:389
Hevly, Bruce, 5:48
Hewes, Henry, 1:1078
Hewes, Jeremy, 5:561
Hewett, Ed. A., 3:52
Hewison, Robert, 1:395
Hewitt, George, 3:368, 4:735
Hewitt, G. F., 5:287
Hewitt, Graily, 1:16
Hewitt, Margaret, 3:356
Hewitt-Bates, J. S., 1:23
Hexham, Irving, 4:857
Hexter, Jack H., 3:359, 4:147
Hey, A. J., 5:660
Heyden, Doris, 3:762
Heyen, William, 1:915
Heyer, Anna H., 3:655
Heyerdahl, Thor, 3:889,
3:923, 3:940
Heym, Stefan, 2:564, 2:590
Heyman, Barbara B., 3:676
Heyneman, Martha, 5:595
Heywood, Andrew, 3:140
Heywood, Christopher, 2:108,
2:158
Heywood, Thomas, 1:182
Hezel, Francis X., 3:495
Hiatt, James L., 5:773
Hibbard, Caroline M., 3:360
Hibbard, Howard, 3:770,
3:782
Hibberd, Dominic, 1:533
Hibbert, Christopher, 1:358,
3:360, 3:362, 3:520
Hibbett, Howard, 2:283

Hick, John Harwood, 4:36, **4:40**, 4:117, 4:380, 4:569, 4:885, 4:898
Hickey, D. J., 3:369
Hickey, Morgen, 1:910
Hickman, Hannah, 2:604
Hickman, Larry A., 3:261, 4:225, 5:71, 5:73, 5:128, 5:154
Hickock, Kathleen, 1:316
Hicks, D., 3:279
Hicks, Edward, 1:155
Hicks, Granville, 1:996
Hicks, Robert D., 4:55, 4:868
Hicks, S. D., 5:216
Hicks, Sir John Richard, 3:65, 3:68, 3:82, **3:83**
Hicks, Tyler, G., 5:216
Hidāyat, Sādiq, 2:87, **2:90**
Hiden, John, 3:377
Hidore, John J., 5:634
Hiebel, Friedrich, 2:605, 4:880
Hiebert, Elfrieda H., 3:253
Higgins, David, 1:747
Higgins, I. J., 5:222
Higgins, Kathleen, 4:247, 4:248
Higgins, Paul C., 5:380
Higgins, W. E., 4:91
Higham, John, 3:515, 4:639
Higham, Thomas F., 2:348
Highet, Gilbert, 2:346, 2:387
Highsmith, Patricia, 1:1231
Hightower, James Robert, 2:189
Hightower, Jim, 5:266
Higuchi Ichiyō, 2:287
Hijiya, James A., 1:744
Hijmans, B. L., Jr., 4:469
Hijuelos, Oscar, 1:910, **1:988**
Hikmet, Nazim, 2:95, **2:98**
Hilberg, Raoul, 3:348
Hilberg, Raul, 4:636
Hilbert, David, **5:509**, 5:511, 5:512, 5:513, 5:581
Hildebidle, John, 1:702
Hildebrand, Klaus, 3:377
Hildebrandt, Darlene M., 5:546
Hilden, John, 3:394
Hildesheimer, Wolfgang, 3:707
Hilen, Andrew, 1:683
Hilfer, Anthony C., 1:723
Hilgard, Ernest J., 3:175
Hilgard, Josephine R., 5:376
Hill, Alan, 4:783
Hill, Christopher, 1:174, 1:192, 3:336, 3:360, **3:404**, **4:734**
Hill, Claire O., 4:324, 5:103
Hill, Donna, 4:879

Hill, Errol, 1:1073, 2:943
Hill, George H., 3:811
Hill, Gerard, 3:767
Hill, Hamlin, 1:650, 1:783
Hill, Herbert, 3:555
Hill, Jonathan D., 4:454
Hill, Karen, 5:815
Hill, Leslie, 2:460
Hill, Lewis, 2:324
Hill, Mary, 5:626
Hill, Mary A., 1:47, 1:753
Hill, Michael, 3:366
Hill, R. D., 3:492
Hill, Richard, 3:419
Hill, Richard O., Jr., 5:484
Hill, Samuel S., 4:717, 4:751, 4:753
Hill, Sylvia, 3:811
Hill, Thomas E., Jr., 4:206
Hillaby, John, 3:899
Hillard, John, 3:87
Hillary, Sir Edmund, 3:889, **3:924**
Hillerbrand, Hans J., 4:722
Hillerman, Tony, **1:1231**
Hillgarth, J. N., 4:683
Hillgruber, Andreas, 3:279
Hillhouse, J. T., 1:300
Hillier, Bevis, 1:445
Hillier, Robert Irwin, 1:397
Hillman, James, 5:414
Hillman, Sheilah, 5:322
Hillmann, Michael C., 2:89, 2:90
Hillmer, Norman, 3:606
Hills, L. Rust, 1:921
Hills, Michael Turner, 5:301
Hills, P. C., 1:921
Hills, Philip, 5:544
Hills, Richard L., 1:5
Hillway, Tyrus, 1:689
Hilsendager, Sarah Chapman, 3:731
Hiltebeitel, Alf, 4:504
Hilton, Nelson, 1:279
Hilton, Timothy, 3:786
Hiltz, Starr Roxanne, 5:296, **5:306**
Himelstein, Shamvel, 4:596
Himmelfarb, Gertrude, 3:276, 3:362, 5:46
Himmelfarb, Milton, 4:639
Himsworth, Harold, 4:384
Hinchcliff, Peter, 4:708
Hinchliffe, Arnold P., 1:425, 1:532, 1:535
Hinckley, Ann, 1:81
Hinckley, Barbara, 1:51
Hinckley, Karen, 1:51
Hinde, R. A., 3:170, 3:279
Hindemith, Paul, **3:700**
Hindery, Roderick, 4:893
Hindle, Brooke, 5:44, 5:46

Hindleu, Geoffrey, 3:892
Hindman, Sandra L., 1:8, 1:28
Hinds, Martin, 1:97
Hinds, William A., 4:844
Hinds, William C., 5:353
Hindus, Milton, 1:707
Hine, Charles R., 5:236
Hine, Darlene Clark, 3:508
Hine, Ellen, 4:195
Hine, Robert V., 4:844, 5:384
Hines, Jerome, 3:672
Hingley, Ronald F., 2:687, 2:710
Hinman, Charlton, 1:206, 1:207
Hinnant, Charles H., 1:250, 3:154, 4:174
Hinnells, John R., 4:4, 4:444, 4:498, 4:517, 4:523, 4:535, 4:547
Hinsdale, Burke A., 3:265
Hinsie, Leland E., 5:415
Hinson, E. Glenn, 4:683
Hintikka, Jaakko, 4:68, 4:230
Hintikka, Merrill B., 4:283
Hinton, Thomas R., 2:566
Hipkiss, Robert A., 1:999
Hippius, **2:728**
Hiro, Dilys, 4:578
Hirsch, Edward D., 1:925, 1:1127, **1:1147**
Hirsch, Eva, 3:453
Hirsch, Foster, 1:1073, 1:1118, 3:830
Hirsch, Gordon, 1:397
Hirsch, Marianne, 2:463
Hirsch, Samson Raphael, **4:665**
Hirsch, Steven W., 3:324, 4:91
Hirsch, Werner Z., 3:61
Hirschberg, Edgar W., 1:1234
Hirschberg, Stuart, 1:498
Hirschfeld, Al, 1:1071
Hirschfelder, Arlene, 3:508
Hirschi, Travis, 3:205
Hirschman, Albert O., 3:53, 3:64
Hirschmann, Jane R., 5:348
Hirschmeier, Johannes, 3:477
Hirshaut, Yashar, 5:372
Hirshberg, Edgar U., 1:373
Hirshfeld, Alan, 5:591
Hirst, David L., 1:446
Hirst, Michael, 3:782
Hirst, Paul O., 5:789
Hischak, Thomas S., 1:798
Hiscocks, Richard, 3:377
Hiskes, Anne L., 5:181
Hiskes, Richard P., 5:181
Hiskett, Melville, 2:134
Hitchcock, Bert, 1:725

Hitchcock, Henry-Russell, 3:763, 3:790, 3:798
Hitchcock, H. Wiley, 3:655, 3:660, 3:702
Hitchcock, Peter, 1:547
Hitchcock, (Sir) Alfred (Joseph), 1:1156, 1:1166, **1:1168**, 3:838, 3:842
Hite, Molly, 1:1035
Hitler, Adolf, 3:377
Hitsman, J. M., 3:615
Hitti, Philip Khuri, 3:436, 3:443, **3:456**, 4:564, 4:569, 4:575
Hittleman, Richard, 5:319
Hixson, Walter F., 3:584
Hla Ludu U., 2:313
Hla Pe, 2:313
Hlasko, Marek, 2:814
Hlasta, Stanley C., 1:16
Ho, Li. See Li Ho
Hoadley, John F., 3:520
Hoag, John D., 3:763
Hoare, James, 3:481
Hobbes, Thomas, 2:359, **3:153**, 4:158, 4:167, **4:173**, 4:185, 4:193, 4:214, 5:144
Hobbs, Anne S., 1:589
Hobbs, Jack A., 3:757
Hobbs, Jerry R., 5:561
Hoberman, J., 4:657
Hobhouse, Henry, 5:768
Hobhouse, Janet, 1:882
Hobsbaum, Philip, 1:1006
Hobsbawm, Eric J., 1:312, 3:140, 3:341, **3:404**, 3:869, 4:242
Hobson, Anthony, 1:24
Hobson, E. W., 5:580
Hobson, Fred C., Jr., 1:860, 1:910
Hobson, John A., 3:343
Ho Ch'i-fang, 2:245
Hochberg, Herbert, 4:312
Hochfield, George, 4:753
Hochheiser, Sheldon, 5:728
Hochhuth, Rolf, 2:591
Ho Chi Minh, 2:338, 2:340
Hochman, Barbara, 1:777
Hochman, Baruch, 1:510, 2:12
Hochman, Stanley, 2:3
Hockey, Susan, 5:564
Hocking, Mary E., 3:439
Hocking, William Ernest, 4:295
Hocks, Richard A., 1:766
Hocutt, Max, 4:21
Hodder, Ian, 3:13, 3:304, 4:434
Hoddeson, Lillian, 5:662, 5:669, 5:717
Hodeir, André, 3:669

Hodgart, Matthew J., 1:149
Hodgdon, Barbara, 1:211
Hodge, Frederick W., 1:631
Hodge, M. S., 5:31, 5:61
Hodge, Norman, 2:158
Hodge, Sheila, 1:41
Hodgen, Margaret T., 3:12
Hodges, Andrew, 5:582
Hodges, Donald C., 3:633
Hodges, Herbert A., 4:226
Hodges, Michael P., 4:346
Hodges, William F., 5:416
Hodgins, Jack, 2:913
Hodgkin, Thomas, 3:420
Hodgkiss, Alan G., 5:617
Hodgson, Amanda, 1:383
Hodgson, Godfrey, 3:538
Hodgson, Marshall G., 4:570
Hodgson, Robert, 4:453
Hodgson, Thomas, 1:16
Hodowanec, George V., 1:42
Hodson, Gillian, 1:540
Hodson, Phillip, 3:728
Hoecher, James J., 5:753
Hoecker-Drysdale, Susan, 1:376
Hoel, Sigurd, 2:662
Hoem, Edvard, 2:662, 2:662
Hoensh, Jorg, 3:390
Hoequist, Charles, 1:93
Hoerr, John P., 3:547
Hoff, Benjamin, 4:528
Hoff, Frank, 3:851
Höffding, Harald, 4:161
Hoffer, Peter C., 3:517
Hoffer, Thomas, 3:249
Hoffman, Andrew J., 1:784
Hoffman, Anne Golomb, 2:12
Hoffman, Banesh, 5:683
Hoffman, Catherine, 5:6
Hoffman, Daniel G., 1:693, 1:742, 1:837
Hoffmann, E(rnst) T(heodor) A(madeus), 2:563, **2:591**, 2:731
Hoffman, Frank W., 3:873
Hoffman, Frederick J., 1:794, 1:804, 1:837
Hoffman, Heinrich, 2:592
Hoffman, Helmut, 4:543
Hoffman, Herbert H., 1:125
Hoffman, Marshall, 5:400
Hoffman, Michael J., 1:883
Hoffman, Nancy, 3:255
Hoffman, Nancy J., 1:198
Hoffman, Nancy Y., 5:374
Hoffman, R. Joseph, 4:683
Hoffman, Ronald, 3:520
Hoffman, Stephen A., 5:336
Hoffman, Ted, 1:1078
Hoffman, William M., 1:1184, 5:125
Hoffmann, Charles G., 1:475

Hoffmann, M., 3:49
Hoffmann, Roald, 5:748, 5:755
Hoffmaster, C. Barry, 5:119
Hoffner, Harry A., Jr., 4:545
Hofmann, Payl, 3:375
Hofmannsthal, Hugo von, 2:564, **2:592**
Hofstadter, Douglas R., 5:75, 5:570, 5:571
Hofstadter, Richard, 3:255, 3:511, 3:515, 3:517, 3:524, 3:531, 3:543, 3:566, 3:567, **3:582**, 3:599, 5:46
Hogan, Charles B., 1:218
Hogan, James C., 2:368
Hogan, Michael, 3:345
Hogan, Robert, 1:1109
Hogendorn, Jan S., 3:420
Hogg, James, 1:269, **1:291**
Hoggart, Richard, 1:312
Hogstel, Mildred O., 5:317
Hogwood, Christopher, 3:698
Hohenberg, John, 1:135
Hoijer, Harry, 3:42
Hoisington, Sona S., 2:752
Holahan, John, 5:333
Holberg, Ludvig, 2:637, 2:644, **2:650**, 2:661
Holborn, Hajo, 3:377
Holbrook, Clyde A., 4:767
Holbrook, David, 1:788, 1:1031, 4:776
Holbub, Robert C., 3:229
Holcombe, Lee, 3:364
Holden, Alan, 5:487, 5:734
Holden, David, 3:451
Holden, Jonathan, 1:799
Hölderlin, (Johann Christian) Friedrich, 2:563, **2:593**, 4:231, 4:251
Holderness, Graham, 1:211
Holdren, John P., 5:291
Holdsworth, D. W., 3:605
Hole, Francis D., 5:262, 5:626
Holiday, Billie, 3:700, 3:719
Holifield, E. Brooks, 3:559
Holister, Geoffrey, 5:2, 5:27
Holladay, William L., 4:795
Hollahan, Eugene, 1:947
Holland, Cecelia, 1:1246
Holland, Dorothy C., 3:250, 3:255
Holland, Norman N., 1:209, 1:842, 2:989, 3:871
Holland, R. F., 3:345
Hollander, Jack M., 5:289
Hollander, Jacob H., 3:73, 3:101
Hollander, John, 1:129, 1:417, 1:799, 2:987
Hollander, Lee, 2:640

Hollander, Myles, 5:522
Hollander, Rachelle D., 5:155
Hollander, Samuel, 3:97,
3:101, 3:107
Hollard, Charles D., 5:223
Holldobler, Bert, 5:770
Holleb, Arthur I., 5:372
Hollenbach, David, 5:111
Holler, Frederick L., 3:138
Hollerith, Herman, 5:541,
5:576
Holley, Margaret, 1:864
Holliday, Paul, 5:760
Hollier, Denis, 2:447, 2:456,
2:507
Hollingdale, R. J., 2:602
Hollinger, David A., 3:559
Hollinger, Robert, 4:413
Hollington, Michael, 2:583
Hollingworth, Leta, 3:185
Hollis, C. Carroll, 1:707
Hollis, Martin, 4:21, 4:405
Hollis, Susan T., 3:869
Holliss, Richard, 1:1165
Hollister, C. Warren, 3:331
Hollister, Charles D., 5:631
Holloway, James Y., 5:165
Holloway, Jean, 1:751
Holloway, John, 1:325
Holloway, Karla F., 1:850,
2:108
Holloway, Peter, 2:946
Holloway, Robin, 3:692
Holman, C. Hugh, 1:131,
1:723, 1:904
Holmberg, David H., 4:541
Holmer, Paul, 4:777
Holmes, Ann M., 5:339
Holmes, Ernest, 4:847
Holmes, Fenwick, 4:847
Holmes, Frederic L., 5:44,
5:46, 5:749, 5:789
Holmes, George A., 3:357
Holmes, Helen Bequaert,
5:120
Holmes, J. Derek, 4:677
Holmes, J. L., 3:671
Holmes, Lowell D., 3:37
Holmes, Oliver Wendell,
1:653, **1:677**, 1:717,
1:1192, 3:156
Holmes, Philip, 2:679
Holmes, Richard, 1:288,
1:303
Holmes, Robert L., 4:389
Holmes, Roger W., 4:285
Holmes, Ronald M., 3:205
Holmes, Urban T., 3:331
Holmesland, Oddvar, 1:487
Holmström, Lakshmi, 2:177
Holmstrom, Lynda Lytle,
5:120
Holoch, Naomi, 1:1184

Holoman, D. Kern, 3:682
Holquist, Michael, 2:685,
2:715
Holroyd, Michael, 1:546
Holroyd, Stuart, 4:555, 4:858
Holt, Edwin B., 4:264
Holt, Elizabeth, 3:757
Holt, Hazel, 1:539
Holt, James C., 3:357
Holt, John, 3:250
Holt, John G., 5:760
Holt, Lee E., 1:342
Holt, Michael F., 3:543
Holt, Pat M., 3:544
Holt, Peter M., 3:416, 3:419,
3:443, 3:446, 4:570
Holt, R. C., 5:582
Holt, Robert Lawrence, 1:47
Holtgrieve, Donald G., 3:118
Holton, Gerald, 5:17, 5:20,
5:25, 5:63, 5:107, 5:136,
5:166, 5:791, 5:813
Holton, Milne, 2:808, 2:811,
2:828
Holton, Robert J., 3:238,
3:244
Holtsmark, Erling B., 1:1256
Holtz, Barry, 4:601, 4:632
Holtz, William, 1:259
Holtzman, Neil, 5:75
Holub, Miroslav, 2:788,
2:792
Holub, Rand, 1:16
Holub, Robert C., 4:404
Holum, John R., 5:732
Holvik, Leonard C., 3:670
Holzer, Leslie, 5:340
Holzman, Arnold D., 5:377
Holzman, Donald, 2:202,
4:363
Holzman, Harvey N., 5:229
Homan, Paul T., 3:45, 3:73,
3:93, 3:98, 3:110
Homans, George C., 3:172
Homans, Margaret, 1:336
Homans, Peter, 4:424, 5:456
Homayun, Tahira, 5:357
Homberger, Eric, 1:794,
1:873, 3:396
Home, R. W., 5:28
Homer, 1:175, 1:223, 1:244,
1:252, 1:342, 1:661,
1:1026, 2:341, 2:357,
2:358, 2:378, 2:396, 2:416,
2:426, 2:439, 2:915, 2:981,
2:983, 3:315, 3:882, 4:446,
4:481, **4:482**, 4:492
Honan, Park, 1:328, 1:339
Honchar, Oleksander, 2:838,
2:839
Hone, Ralph E., 1:611
Honer, Stanley M., 4:21
Honey, Maureen, 3:535

Honeyman, Katrina, 3:341
Hongladarom, Gail G., 5:355
Honig, Edwin, 2:533
Honig, Emily, 3:470
Honig, Robert, 5:815
Honigmann, E.A.J., 1:204,
1:207
Honour, Hugh, 3:757, 3:762,
3:765
Hoobler, D., 3:292
Hoobler, T., 3:292
Hood, Hugh, 2:913
Hood, Marlowe, 3:490
Hoods, Leroy, 5:782
Hooft, P. C., 2:620
Hoog, Constance, 4:543
Hoogasian-Villa, Susie, 2:77
Hoogenboom, Gerda, 2:628
Hooglund, Eric J., 3:448
Hook, Andrew, 1:828
Hook, Brian, 3:465
Hook, J. N., 3:552
Hook, Jay M. van, 5:70,
5:165
Hook, Sidney, 3:261, 3:326,
4:34, 4:225, 4:260, 4:264,
4:265, **4:297**, 4:321, 5:80,
5:107
Hooke, Robert, 5:522
Hooke, S. H., 4:441, 4:545
Hooker, A. Thomas, 4:518
Hooker, Michael, 4:170,
4:177
Hooker, Richard, 4:734
Hooker, Thomas, 1:630
Hookham, S. K., 4:513, 4:543
Hooks, Bell, 3:212
Hookway, Christopher, 4:249,
4:382, 4:412
Hooper, C., 5:236
Hooper, Roy, 1:1227
Hooper, Walter, 4:776
Hoopes, James, 1:628
Hooton, Joy, 2:947
Hoover, Kevin D., 3:62
Hoover, L. Elaine, 2:548
Hoover, Marjorie L., 2:744
Hoover, Stewart M., 3:811
Hooykaas, R., 5:42
Hopcroft, John E., 5:549,
5:568
Hope, A. D., 2:955
Hope, Charles, 3:793
Hope, Vincent, 4:32, 4:212
Höpfl, Harro, 4:762
Hopkins, A. G., 3:420
Hopkins, Amy, 1:42
Hopkins, Andrea, 1:147
Hopkins, David, 1:242
Hopkins, Donald R., 5:36,
5:389
Hopkins, Dwight, 4:748
Hopkins, Edward W., 4:498

Hopkins, Gerard Manley,
1:314, **1:363**, 1:511, 2:427,
2:972
Hopkins, I. W., 3:440
Hopkins, Jack W., 3:625
Hopkins, Jasper, 4:108,
4:149, 4:703
Hopkins, Jeanne, 5:588
Hopkins, Jeffrey, 4:356,
4:543, 4:544, 4:887
Hopkins, John R., 1:995
Hopkins, Kenneth D., 3:255,
3:307
Hopkins, Sarah Winnemucca,
1:726
Hopkins, Thomas J., 4:504
Hopkins, Vivian C., 1:670
Hopkinson, Michael, 3:370
Hopko, Thomas, 4:693
Hoppenstand, Gary, 1:604
Hopper, David H., 5:154,
5:197
Hopper, Grace Murray,
5:576
Hoppin, Richard H., 3:660
Hopwood, Derek, 3:443,
3:451
Hora, Bayard, 5:760
Horace (Quintus Horatius
Flaccus), 1:224, 1:807,
2:359, 2:378, 2:383, **2:385**,
2:387, 2:389, 2:396
Hord, Fred, 2:108
Hordern, William E., 4:718,
4:744
Hordeski, Michael, 5:540
Horewitz, James S., 5:418
Horewitz, Tony, 3:903
Horgan, Paul, 3:723
Hori, Ichiro, 4:539
Horicke, Baldri van, 1:16
Horisberger, B., 5:324
Horkheimer, Max, 1:1132
Horn, Berthold K., 5:553
Horn, David, 1:47
Horn, Delton T., 5:230
Horn, Henry S., 5:779
Horn, Lyle H., 5:634
Horn, Michiel, 3:616
Hornblower, Simon, 3:302,
3:323
Hornby, Nick, 1:925
Horne, Alistair, 3:373
Horne, David H., 1:195
Horne, Gerald, 3:578
Horne, Jo, 5:317
Horne, Philip, 1:766
Hornell, W., 4:100
Horney, Karen, 3:185,
5:445, **5:452**
Hornsby, E. John, Jr., 5:481
Hornstein, Lillian H., 1:122
Hornum, M., 4:61

Hornung, Erik, 4:442
Horosko, Manan, 3:745
Horovitz, Israel, 1:1094
Horowitz, Asher, 3:337
Horowitz, Dan, 3:440
Horowitz, Francis D., 3:173
Horowitz, Helen Lefkowitz,
3:552
Horowitz, Irving, 3:235
Horowitz, Karen, 5:377
Horowitz, Vladimir, 3:701
Horricks, Raymond, 3:669,
3:677
Horsch, John, 4:733
Horsley, Richard, 4:864
Horton, Carolyn, 1:24
Horton, John, 3:698
Horton, Paul C., 5:415
Horton, Rod W., 1:714
Horwitz, Howard, 1:650
Horwitz, Robert Britt, 3:803
Hosain, Attia, 2:177
Hosking, Geoffrey, 2:687
Hosking, P. L., 3:119
Hoskins, Robert, 3:674
Hoskins, W. G., 3:359
Hosley, David H., 3:807
Hosley, Richard, 1:219
Hotchner, A. E., 1:846
Hothersall, David, 5:35
Hotson, J. Leslie, 1:187
Hotten, John Campden,
3:506
Hotz, Louis, 4:645
Houaiss, Antonio, 1:102
Hough, Graham, 1:510
Houghton, David D., 5:617
Houghton, Patricia, 1:115
Houghton, Walter Edwards,
1:312, 1:315, 1:316, 1:319,
1:345
Houle, Cyril O., 3:255
Houlgate, Stephen, 4:233
Houn, Franklin W., 3:470
Hounshell, David A., 5:48
Hountondji, Paulin J., 4:26,
4:369
Hourani, Albert, 3:436,
3:437, 3:443, **3:457**, 4:373
Hourani, George F., 4:575
House, Humphrey, 1:350
House, J. W., 3:123
Houseman, Susan N., 3:59
Housman, A(lfred)
E(dward), 1:495
Houston, John P., 1:216,
2:401, 2:483, 2:500
Houston, R. A., 3:337
Houston, S. D., 3:628
Hovannisian, Richard G.,
2:76
Hovde, B. J., 3:380
Hovland, Carl I., 3:176

Howard, Angela Falco, 4:530
Howard, D., 5:664
Howard, Donald R., 1:151,
1:156
Howard, Douglas, 1:189
Howard, Harry N., 3:453
Howard, Jane, 3:37
Howard, Jean, 3:709
Howard, Jean E., 1:208,
1:218
Howard, John R., 1:660,
1:728
Howard, John Tasker, 3:696
Howard, June, 1:723
Howard, Leon, 1:685, 1:689,
1:723
Howard, M., 3:276
Howard, Michael S., 1:40
Howard, Moss, 3:173
Howard, R. Palmer, 5:54
Howard, Richard, 1:913,
1:988
Howard, Robert E., 1:594
Howard, Roger, 2:233
Howard, Ronnalie R., 1:392
Howard, Roy J., 1:925
Howard, Sidney, 1:1070
Howard-Hill, Trevor H., 1:79,
1:120, 1:220
Howarth, David, 3:357
Howarth, O.J.R., 5:619
Howarth, Osbert, 3:118
Howarth, William, 1:693,
1:702, 1:1011
Howatson, M. C., 1:133,
2:346
Howe, Ellic, 1:24
Howe, Herbert M., 2:349
Howe, Irving, 1:362, 1:421,
1:651, 1:788, 1:837, 1:946,
1:960, **1:989**, 2:30, 2:33,
2:34, 2:989, 3:555, 4:639,
4:640, 4:657
Howe, M. DeWolfe, 1:678
Howe, Russel W., 3:481
Howell, David, 3:366
Howell, R. Patton, 1:32
Howell, Wilbur S., 4:127
Howells, William, 5:779
Howells, William Dean,
1:721, 1:726, 1:737, 1:749,
1:757, 1:769, 1:780, 1:833,
2:401, 2:403
Howes, Alan B., 1:259
Howes, Barbara, 2:849
Howes, Ruth, 5:278
Howes, Wright, 1:78
Howitt, Doran, 5:547
Howland, Marguerite S., 3:8,
3:507
Hoy, David, 5:443
Hoy, David C., 1:925, 4:401
Hoy, Pat C., III, 1:430

Hoy, Peter C., 1:522
Hoyningen-Huene, Paul, 5:53
Hoyt, Erich, 5:760, 5:770
Hoyt, William G., 5:609
Hrabal, Bohumil, 2:792
Hryciw, Carol A., 1:986
Hsi, Ch'eng, 2:192
Hsia, Chih-tsing, 2:189, 2:233
Hsia, R. Po-Chia, 4:722
Hsia, Y. Edward, 5:781
Hsiao, K. C., 3:471
Hsiao, Kung-Chuan, 4:361
Hsiao Chün, 2:245, 2:246
Hsiao Hung, 2:245, **2:246**
Hsiao Kang, 2:200
Hsieh, Chiao-min, 3:465
Hsieh, D. A., 3:63
Hsieh Ling-yün, 2:201, 2:214
Hsien-tzu, T'ang. *See* T'ang
 Hsien-tzu
Hsien-yung, Pai. *See* Pai
 Hsieng-yung
Hsi K'ang, 2:199
Hsin, Ho, 2:235
Hsin-wu, Liu. *See* Liu Hsin-
 wu
Hsiu, Ou-yang. *See* Ou-yang
 Hsiu
Hsiung, James Chieh, 3:471
Hsiung, Yang. *See* Yang Hsi-
 ung
Hsu, Francis L., 3:15
Hsu, Immanuel C. Y., 3:471
Hsu, Jeffrey, 5:550
Hsu, Kai-yu, 2:235
Hsu, Vivian Ling, 2:234
Hsün, Lu. *See* Lu Hsün
Hswei, Thaw-da, 2:313
Htin, Aung U., 4:519
Htin, Maung, 2:313
Htin Aung, 2:314
Hu, John Y., 2:266
Hu, P'in-ch'ing, 2:204
Huan, Nguyen Tran, 2:339
Huang, Chi-ch'ih, 2:190
Huang, Joe C., 2:234
Huang, Philip C., 2:253
Huang, Philip C. C., 3:471
Huang, Ray, 3:467
Huang Ch'un-ming, 2:247,
 2:233
Hubbard, L. Ron, Jr., 4:869
Hubbard, Ruth, 5:781
Hubbard, Thomas K., 2:353
Hubbard, William, 3:345
Hubbell, Jay B., 1:778
Hubbell, Sue, 5:818
Hubble, Edwin Powell,
 5:586, 5:602, **5:607**, 5:653
Huber, Jeffrey T., 5:387
Huber, Peter W., 5:184
Huber, Thomas M., 3:478
Huberman, Elizabeth, 1:522

Hubert, Henri, 4:429
Hubert, Judd D., 2:490
Hubner, John, 4:862
Hucker, Charles O., 2:190,
 3:465, 3:467
Hudak, Leona M., 1:38
Hudak, Thomas J., 2:335
Hudgens, Betty L., 1:1064
Hudman, Lloyd E., 3:125
Hudson, Alfred E., 3:12
Hudson, Anne, 4:714, 4:721
Hudson, C. Wayne, 4:277
Hudson, Deal W., 4:307
Hudson, Derek, 1:423, 1:583
Hudson, Gladys W., 1:337
Hudson, John, 5:728
Hudson, Kenneth, 3:757
Hudson, Mark, 3:903
Hudson, Robert P., 5:313
Hudson, Robert V., 3:801,
 3:803
Hudson, Theodore R., 1:941,
 1:1085
Hudson, William Henry,
 1:365, 4:211
Hudson, Wintrop, 4:751
Hudson-Weems, Clenora,
 1:1019
Huebert, Ronald, 1:180
Huebner, Steven, 3:697
Huelskoetter, M.M.W., 5:317
Huenefeld, John, 1:47
Huerta, Jorge A., 1:1073
Huey, Lynda, 5:326
Hufbauer, Karl, 5:44
Huff, Darrell, 5:522
Huff, Theodore, 1:1162
Huffman, Claire De C. L.,
 2:428
Hufford, Mary T., 3:859
Huggett, Richard J., 5:617
Huggins, Nathan Irvin, 1:668,
 1:794, 3:555, 3:559
Hughes, Agatha C., 5:172
Hughes, Andrew, 3:655
Hughes, Gertrude R., 1:670
Hughes, Glenn, 1:1073
Hughes, Gwyneth, 3:396
Hughes, H. Stuart, 3:276,
 3:291, 3:343
Hughes, Jonathan, 3:51
Hughes, Judith M., 3:373,
 5:457
Hughes, Kathleen, 3:370
Hughes, Langston, 1:720,
 1:797, **1:847**, 1:849,
 1:1092, 1:1119, 1:1188,
 1:1189, 1:1195, 3:866
Hughes, Linda K., 1:401
Hughes, Merritt Y., 1:192
Hughes, Peter, 2:939
Hughes, Philip E., 4:127,
 4:722, 4:726, 4:764

Hughes, R.I.G., 5:68
Hughes, Richard, 1:496
Hughes, Robert, 2:946, 3:771
Hughes, Serge, 3:385
Hughes, Sukey, 1:5
Hughes, Ted, 1:491, **1:497,**
 1:1030
Hughes, Thomas P(arke),
 3:443, 3:548, 4:566, 5:37,
 5:50, 5:151, 5:172, 5:229,
 5:252
Hugh of St. Victor, 4:101
Hugo, Richard, 1:990
Hugo, Victor, 1:399, 1:772
Hugo, Victor Marie, 2:236,
 2:370, 2:445, 2:465, **2:482,**
 2:537
Hui, Yiu H., 5:261, 5:395
Huidobro, Vicente, 2:869
Huizinga, Johan, 3:14, 3:331,
 3:382, 4:139, 4:691
Huldén, Lars, 2:657, 2:658
Hulet, Claude L., 2:890
Hull, Clark L(eonard),
 3:166, **3:186**
Hull, David L., 4:384, 5:46,
 5:68, 5:794
Hull, Richard, 3:417
Hull, Roger, 5:760
Hulme, Hilda M., 1:216
Hulme, Keri, 2:970, **2:976**
Hulse, Clarke, 1:215
Hultkrantz, Ake, 4:464
Humboldt, Alexander von,
 3:116, **3:130,** 3:134, 5:747
Hume, Anthea, 1:198
Hume, David, 3:91, 3:106,
 3:213, 4:12, 4:58, 4:157,
 4:158, 4:166, 4:182, 4:194,
 4:195, **4:199,** 4:203, 4:210,
 4:211, 4:212, 4:214, 4:230,
 4:255, 4:272, 4:410, 4:739,
 5:809
Hume, Robert D., 1:228,
 1:245
Hume, Robert E., 4:501
Humez, Alexander, 1:16
Humez, Jean M., 4:849
Humez, Nicholas, 1:16
Humm, Maggie, 1:134
Humma, John B., 1:510
Hummel, Arthur W., 3:465
Hummell, Sherilynn J., 5:372
Humphrey, Caroline, 4:509
Humphrey, Derek, 4:389
Humphrey, Doris, 3:735,
 3:744, 3:746, 3:752
Humphrey, Robert, 1:421
Humphreys, Anne, 1:378
Humphreys, Glyn W., 3:177
Humphreys, Laud, 3:208
Humphreys, S. C., 3:307
Humphries, Reynold, 3:840

Humphry, Derek, 5:378
Huneker, James G., 3:704
Hung, Eva, 2:235
Hung, Hsiao. *See* Hsiao
  Hung
Hungerford, Edward B.,
  1:265
Huning, Alois, 5:126
Hunley, J. D., 3:75
Hunnings, Gordon, 4:346
Hunnisett, Basil, 1:28
Hunsinger, George, 4:758
Hunt, Anne Elise, 5:358
Hunt, Candida, 5:2
Hunt, Charles B., 5:626
Hunt, Douglas G., 1:130
Hunt, E. Stephen, 5:111
Hunt, Ernest W., 4:726
Hunt, G. H., 4:809
Hunt, Gaillard, 3:161
Hunt, G. H., 4:809
Hunt, George W., 1:962
Hunt, H., 3:172
Hunt, Hugh, 1:527
Hunt, James D., 4:553
Hunt, (James Henry) Leigh,
  1:283, **1:292,** 1:300
Hunt, John Dixon, 1:315,
  1:395
Hunt, Lee M., 5:617
Hunt, Lynn, 3:373
Hunt, Michael H., 3:545
Hunt, Morton, 5:35
Hunt, Noreen, 4:699
Hunt, Thomas C., 4:21
Hunt, Tina, 1:999
Hunt, Todd, 3:803
Hunt, William, 3:360, 3:940
Hunt-Badiner, Allan, 5:197
Hunter, Beatrice T., 5:346
Hunter, Brian, 3:8
Hunter, Daniel, 5:121
Hunter, Dard, 1:5
Hunter, Edna, 5:121
Hunter, G. K., 1:216
Hunter, J. A., 5:496
Hunter, J. M., 4:346
Hunter, J. Paul, 1:225, 1:230,
  1:245
Hunter, James Davison,
  3:559
Hunter, Janet E., 3:473
Hunter, Lynette, 1:458
Hunter, Madeline, 3:256
Hunter, Robert Grams, 1:211
Hunter, Sam, 3:759
Hunter, Thomas A., 5:244
Hunter, Virginia J., 3:323
Hunter, William B., 1:192
Hunter, Yvonne L., 5:213
Huntington, C. W., 4:513
Huntington, Gale, 3:858
Huntington, Richard, 4:430

Huntley, H. Robert, 1:475
Huppert, George, 4:127
Hurd, John C., Jr., 4:796
Hurlbut, Cornelius S., Jr.,
  5:617, 5:628
Hurlbutt, Robert H., 4:184,
  4:202
Hurrelmann, Klaus, 3:173
Hurst, G. Cameron, 3:475
Hurst, Jane D., 4:859
Hurston, Zora Neale, 1:849,
  3:866
Hurt, C. D., 5:5
Hurt, James, 2:5
Hurt, R. Douglas, 3:548,
  5:263
Hurwitz, Howard L., 3:595
Hurwitz, Jane, 5:611
Hurwitz, Johanna, 2:677
Hurwitz, Simon, 4:627
Hurwitz, Sue, 5:611
Hus, John, 4:691, 4:711,
  4:714
Husayn, Taha, 2:61, 2:71,
  4:374
Husband, Janet, 1:122, 1:125
Husband, Jonathan K., 1:122
Huseboe, Arthur R., 1:243
Hu Shih, 2:247, 4:360
Husik, Isaac, 4:629
Huss, Richard E., 1:16
Hussain, Asaf, 4:578
Hussein, M. Kamal, 2:59
Hussein, Mahmoud, 3:446
Husserl, Edmund, 4:159,
  4:221, **4:233,** 4:261, 4:290,
  4:309, 4:318, 4:328, 4:331,
  4:334, 4:366, 4:376, 4:396,
  4:900, 5:90, 5:469
Hussey, Edward, 4:50
Hussey, J. M., 4:693
Hussey, Mark, 1:570
Hussey, S. S., 1:216
Hussman, Lawrence E.,
  1:830
Huston, Aletha C., 3:211,
  3:560
Huston, John, 3:838
Huston, Perdita, 5:313
Hutcheon, Linda, 2:909
Hutcheson, Francis, 4:158,
  4:203, 4:210, 4:214
Hutchings, Arthur, 3:715
Hutchings, Bill, 1:238
Hutchins, B. L., 1:345
Hutchins, Margaret, 1:80
**Hutchins, Robert
  M(aynard), 3:263,** 4:269
Hutchins, Williams M., 2:57
Hutchinson, Ann, 3:746
Hutchinson, Bruce, 3:607
Hutchinson, James, 1:16
Hutchinson, Walter, 3:382

Hutchison, Jane Campbell,
  3:774
Hutchison, John A., 4:37
Hutchison, William R.,
  4:753
Huters, Theodore, 2:233,
  2:243
Hutman, Norma L., 2:545
Hutson, Lorna, 1:195
Hutt, Allen, 1:16
Huttar, Charles A., 1:513
Huttman, Barbara, 5:331,
  5:337
Hutton, Edward, 2:406
Hutton, James, 5:644
Hutton, Sarah, 4:183
Huu, To, 2:338
Huxford, Marilyn, 3:204,
  3:802
Huxhold, William E., 3:120
Huxley, Aldous, 1:419,
  1:474, **1:498,** 1:500, 2:238,
  2:888, 2:990, 3:892, 4:776,
  4:853, 5:563, 798
Huxley, Anthony J., 5:820
Huxley, Elspeth, 3:422, 3:903,
  3:909
Huxley, G. L., 2:346
Huxley, Sir Julian Sorrell,
  1:563, 3:18, **5:798,** 5:830
Huxley, Thomas Henry,
  1:366, 1:498, 5:47, 5:798,
  5:799
Huygens, Christiaan, 5:525,
  5:527, **5:694,** 5:803
Huygens, Constantijn, 2:620
Huynh Sanh Thong, 2:339
Huysmans, Gide, 2:445
Hviezdoslav, 2:832
Hwang, David Henry,
  1:1071, **1:1094**
Hwang Sun-wôn, 2:302
Hyamson, Moses, 4:630
Hyde, Albert C., 3:147
Hyde, G. M., 1:510
Hyde, Sidney T., 1:48
Hyder, Clyde K., 1:398
Hyer, Paul, 4:542
Hyers, Conrad, 4:537
Hyim, Gila J., 4:331
Hyland, D., 4:50
Hyland, Paul, 3:903
Hyland, Peter, 1:184
Hyman, Anthony, 5:576
Hyman, Arthur, 4:94
Hyman, Herbert H., 3:216
Hyman, Louis, 3:348
Hyman, Paula, 3:348, 4:636
Hymes, Dell, 3:21
Hymes, Robert P., 3:468
Hynek, J. Allen, 5:598
Hyneman, Charles S., 3:520
Hynes, H. Patricia, 5:830

Hynes, Joseph, 1:552
Hynes, Samuel, 1:429, 1:436

I

I'tisami, Parvin, 2:90
Iacone, Salvatore J., 1:32
Iacopi, Robert, 5:629
Iamblicus, 5:514
Ianna, Philip, 5:587
Iannone, A. Pablo, 5:128
Ibach, H., 5:668
Ibn Al-Arabi, 4:582
Ibn Daud Abraham, 4:627, 4:628
Ibn Gabirol, Solomon Ben Judah, 2:19
Ibn Hazm, 4:583
Ibn-Hisham, 4:588
Ibn Khaldun, Abd al-Rahman, 3:434, 3:457, 4:584
Ibn Khallikan, 4:584
Ibn Tufayl, 4:585
Ibrahim, Sun' Allah, 2:65
Ibsen, Henrik, 1:331, 1:388, 1:423, 1:424, 1:565, 1:1070, 1:1098, 2:265, 2:531, 2:586, 2:637, 2:662, 2:665
Ibuse Masuji, 2:287
Icaza, Rosa M., 2:544
Ide, Nancy, 5:552
Ide, Richard S., 1:175
Idelsohn, A. Z., 4:599
Idol, John L., Jr., 1:904
Idrīs, Yūsuf, 2:65, 2:116, 2:122
Ienaga, Saburo, 3:478
Ife, B. W., 2:525
Ifkovic, Edward, 1:713
Iggers, Georg G., 3:276, 4:728
Ignatius of Loyola, St., 4:727, 4:769
Ignatow, David, 1:990
Ihara Saikaku, 2:271, 2:277
Ihde, Aaron J., 5:32, 5:728
Ihde, Don, 4:267, 4:392, 5:71, 5:92
Ihimaera, Witi, 2:970, 2:977
Ihle, Sandra N., 1:155
Ijsewijn, Jozef, 2:381
Ikegami, Kojiro, 1:24
Il-ch'ol Sin, 4:535
Ilf, Ilya, 2:728
Iliffe, John, 3:422
Illich, Ivan, 3:250, 5:79, 5:128, 5:136, 5:336
Illingworth, Valerie, 5:588
Illman, John, 5:339
Il-lo, Pak, 2:298
Illyés, Gyula, 2:798, 2:799

Imhof, Paul, 4:770
I-ming, Liu, 4:528
Immel, Myra, 1:1195
Immerwahr, Henry R., 3:316, 4:480
Inada, Kenneth K., 4:6
Inalcik, Halil, 3:458
Infante, Guillermo Cabrera. See Cabrera Infante, Guillermo
Infeld, Leopold, 5:48
Ing, Janet, 1:9
Ing, Nancy, 2:235
Ingalls, Daniel H., 2:172
Ingalls, Robert P., 5:426
Ingarden, Ramon, 4:235
Inge, M. Thomas, 1:689, 1:713, 1:784, 2:420, 3:871, 3:873
Inge, Thomas, 1:1210
Inge, William (Motter), 1:1095
Inge, W. R., 4:86
Ingersoll, Fern S., 2:336
Ingham, K., 3:422
Ingham, Patricia, 1:362
Ingleby, C. M., 1:221
Inglehart, Ronald, 3:141
Inglis, Andrew F., 3:811
Inglis, Brian, 5:319
Ingram, Arthur, 5:247
Ingram, David, 5:89
Ingram, David B., 4:405
Ingram, David S., 5:759
Ingram, James, 3:490
Ingram, John H., 1:187
Ingram, M. J., 5:634
Ingram, Paul O., 4:423
Ingram, William, 1:192
Ingstad, Helge, 3:380, 3:899
Ingwersen, Faith, 2:650, 2:653
Ingwersen, Niels, 2:650, 2:653
Inhelder, Barbel, 3:192
In-hoon, Choi, 2:298
Inkeles, Alex, 3:200
Inkster, Ian, 1:312, 5:25
Inlander, Charles B., 5:405
Inman, Billie Andrew, 1:387
Innes, Catherine L., 2:129
Innes, William C., 4:762
Innis, Harold Adams, 3:604, 3:618, 3:621
Inoue, Hirochika, 5:242
Inoue Yasushi, 2:287
Insdorf, Annette, 3:843
Instad, Helge, 3:610
Inwood, Brad, 4:53, 4:55
Inwood, Michael, 4:233
Inwood, M. J., 3:285
Ionesco, Eugene, 1:952, 1:1987, 2:483, 2:679

Ions, Veronica, 4:548
Ioppolo, Grace, 1:207
Iorio, Dominick A., 4:30
Iorizzo, Luciano J., 3:556
Iqbal, Afzal, 4:590
Iqbal, Sir Muhammad, 4:374, 4:375, 4:585
Irani, George, 3:436
Irani, Mauchehr, 2:84
Irbe, Andrejs, 2:803
Ireland, Alleyne, 3:821
Ireland, John deCourcy, 3:371
Ireland, Norma O., 5:4
Irele, Abiola, 2:108
Irigaray, Luce, 1:1182
Iriye, Akira, 3:464, 3:478
Irokawa, Daikichi, 3:478
Irvine, Demar, 3:730
Irvine, William, 5:794, 5:799, 5:831
Irving, Bryant, 1:649
Irving, Clive, 3:448, 5:219
Irving, Edward B., 1:144
Irving, John, 1:991
Irving, Robert Grant, 3:485
Irving, Washington, 1:656, 1:679, 1:1192, 4:588, 5:786
Irwin, Richard G., 2:219
Irwin, Terence, 4:46, 4:68
Irwin, William A., 4:439
Isaac, Frank, 1:16
Isaac, Glynn L., 3:13
Isaac, Jeffrey C., 3:282, 5:82
Isaac, Rhys, 3:520
Isaacman, Allen F., 3:423
Isaacman, Barbara, 3:423
Isaacs, Alan, 5:3, 5:540
Isaacs, Amanda, 5:13
Isaacs, Harold R., 2:235, 4:651
Isaacs, Neil David, 1:559
Isaacson, Walter, 3:538
Isabella, 2:820
Isager, Signe, 3:304
Isailovic, Jordan, 5:229
Isaku, Patia R., 3:851
Isao, Kumakura, 4:538
Isbister, J. N., 5:448
Iser, Wolfgang, 1:387, 1:421
Isherwood, Christopher, 1:434, 1:435, 1:500, 4:354, 4:563, 4:872
Ishii, Yoneo, 4:519
Ishikawa Takuboku, 2:288
Iskander, Fazil, 2:729
Islam, Jumal N., 5:595, 5:655
Islam, Khurshidul, 2:175
Ismael, Jacqueline S., 3:455
Ismael, Tareq Y., 3:448, 3:450
Ismail, Taufiq, 2:316
Israel, Fred L., 3:273, 3:506

Israel, Guy, 5:587
Israel, Jonathan, 3:348, 4:734
Israel, Lucien, 5:336
Israel, Milton, 4:516
Israeli, Raphael, 3:443, 4:570
Issa, Kobayashi. *See* Kobayashi Isssa
Issacs, Reginald, 3:777
Issahakian, Avedick, 2:77, **2:78**
Issawi, Charles, 3:436, 3:443, 3:448, 3:453
Isser, Natalie, 4:858
Itasaka, Gen, 4:534
I'tisami, Parvin, 2:90
Ito, Ken K., 2:294
Ito, Takatoshi, 3:52, 3:58
Itzin, Catherine, 1:425
Itzkoff, Donald M., 5:247
Itzkoff, Seymour W., 4:280
Itzkowitz, Norman, 4:570
Ivanits, Linda J., 2:687
Ivanov, Vsevolod, 2:729, 2:774
Ivanov, Vyacheslav I., 2:715
Ivask, Astrīda, 2:803
Ivask, Ivar, 2:862
Ives, Charles Edward, 1:668, 3:699, **3:701**
Ives, Christopher, 4:537
Ivins, William M., Jr., 1:28
Ivinskaya, Olga, 2:746
Iyayi, Festus, 2:105
Iyengar, K. Srinivasa, 2:177
Iyengar, Shanto, 3:811
Iyer, Pico, 3:903
Iyer, Raghavan Narasimhan, 4:352
Iz, Fahir, 2:96
Izard, Carroll E., 3:172
Izbicki, Thomas M., 4:694
Izod, John, 3:828
Izumi Shikibu, 2:277

J

Jabaley, Theresa, 5:428
Jablonski, David, 5:617
Jablonski, Edward, 3:656
Jablousky, David, 3:401
Jablow, Alta, 2:108
Jabra, Jabra Ibrahim, 2:59
Jack, Ian, 1:265
Jack, Ronald D. S., 1:330
Jackall, Robert, 3:218
Jacks, Lawrence, 5:681
Jackson, Blyden, 1:714
Jackson, Bruce, 3:866
Jackson, Carl T., 4:508, 4:841
Jackson, Carlton, 1:1214
Jackson, David K., 1:693

Jackson, Dennis, 1:510
Jackson, Donald Gale, 3:524
Jackson, Douglas W., 5:400
Jackson, Gabriel, 3:387
Jackson, George, 3:394
Jackson, George P., 3:851
Jackson, Helen Maria (Fiske) Hunt, 1:721, **1:760**
Jackson, Holbrook, 1:32, 1:76
Jackson, H. R., 3:493
Jackson, Joan S., 1:88
Jackson, John, 3:61
Jackson, J. R., 1:288
Jackson, J. R. de J., 1:268
Jackson, Julia A., 5:616, 5:635
Jackson, Kenneth T., 3:552
Jackson, Martin A., 3:560, 3:826
Jackson, Mary V., 1:578
Jackson, Nancy E., 3:252
Jackson, Peter, 3:67
Jackson, Philip W., 3:256
Jackson, Rebecca, 3:510
Jackson, Richard, 1:913
Jackson, Richard H., 3:125
Jackson, Richard L., 2:846
Jackson, Robert, 1:247, 5:219
Jackson, Robert L., 2:710
Jackson, Russell, 1:322
Jackson, Samuel M., 4:717
Jackson, Shirley, 1:992
Jackson, Wallace, 1:268
Jackson, Walter A., 3:99
Jackson, Wes, 5:272, 5:823
Jackson, William, 3:279
Jackson, William T., 2:4, 2:582
Jacob, François, 5:800
Jacob, Gordon, 3:660
Jacob, Judith M., 2:315
Jacob, Margaret C., 3:337, 3:338, 3:382, 5:42
Jacob, Satish, 4:517
Jacob, Walter, 4:627, 4:652
Jacob ben Isaac of Janow, 2:39
Jacobi, Jolande F., 5:456
Jacobs, Arthur, 3:656
Jacobs, David M., 4:870
Jacobs, George, 5:387
Jacobs, Harriet Ann, 1:681
Jacobs, Henry E., 1:220
Jacobs, Jack, 4:656
Jacobs, Jane, 3:216
Jacobs, Janet L., 4:856
Jacobs, Joseph, 1:577, 1:579, 2:352, 3:845, **3:881**
Jacobs, Louis, 4:596, 4:620, 4:627, 4:628, 4:629, 4:630, 4:632, 4:884
Jacobs, Melville, 3:865

Jacobs, Wilbur R., 1:691, 3:592, 3:600, 3:643
Jacobsen, C. G., 3:471
Jacobsen, Jørgen-Frantz, 2:655, **2:656**
Jacobsen, Jens Peter, 2:645, **2:651**
Jacobsen, Roy M., 5:261
Jacobsen, Thorkild, 2:52, 4:440, 4:441, 4:545
Jacobson, Beverly, 5:327
Jacobson, Daniel, 1:199
Jacobson, Jerome, 4:501
Jacobson, Michael, 5:346
Jacobus, John, 3:759, 3:781
Jacobus, Lee, 1:1078
Jacoby, Joseph E., 5:428
Jacoby, M., 5:458
Jacoby, Neil H., 3:436
Jacoby, Russell, 5:422
Jacoway, Elizabeth, 3:548
Jaeger, Werner, 2:346, 2:355, 3:311, 4:48, 4:50, 4:63, 4:69, 4:683
Jaenen, Cornelius J., 3:610
Jafari, Jafar, 3:890
Jaffe, Abram J., 5:522
Jaffe, Aniela, 5:456
Jaffe, Audrey, 1:350
Jaffe, Bernard, 5:25, 5:702
Jaffe, Jacqueline A., 1:608
Jaffe, Ludwig, 3:786
Jagchid, Sechin, 4:542
Jagendorf, Moritz A., 3:858, 3:865
Jagersma, Henk, 4:604
Jaggard, William, 1:203, 1:221
Jahadhmy, Ali A., 1:103
al-Jahiz, 2:65
Jahn, Janheinz, 2:109
Jahoda, Marie, 3:184
Jaimes, M. Annette, 3:212
Jain, Sushil Kumar, 2:170
Jaini, Padmanabh S., 4:509
Jakes, John, 1:1244, **1:1247**
Jaki, Stanley L., 5:202
Jakle, John A., 3:892
Jakobson, Roman, 2:687
Jakšić, Djura, 2:827
Jaksic, Iván, 3:634
Jalal, Ayesha, 3:487
Jalal Al-Din Al-Suyuti, 4:585
Jamalzadah, Muhammad 'Ali, 2:91
James, Adeola, 2:109
James, Alice, 1:726, **1:761,** 1:767, 1:1055, 3:187
James, Arthur M., 5:653
James, C(yril) L(ionel) R(obert), 3:637, **3:647**
James, D. G., 4:257
James, Daniel, 3:209

James, David, 1:24
James, David B., 3:701,
    3:718, 3:728
James, Donald, 3:398
James, Eugene M., 1:244
James, Frank M., III, 4:129
James, Glenn, 5:479
James, Henry, 1:203, 1:353,
    1:360, 1:419, 1:423, 1:463,
    1:475, 1:494, 1:635, 1:677,
    1:692, 1:711, 1:721, 1:726,
    1:741, 1:757, **1:761,** 1:767,
    1:769, 1:789, 1:843, 1:844,
    1:937, 1:972, 1:1027,
    2:447, 2:517, 2:768, 2:863,
    2:948, 2:953, 3:187, 3:899,
    4:235
James, Jeffery, 5:182
James, Josef, 3:486
James, Lewis, 1:319
James, Louis, 2:930, 2:941
James, M. R., 1:600, 1:601
James, Montague R., 4:811
James, Preston E., 5:32,
    5:620
James, Robert C., 5:479
James, T. G. H., 3:300
James, William, 1:474,
    1:668, 1:726, 1:761, **1:767,**
    1:881, 1:1055, **3:187,**
    3:224, 3:268, 3:814, 4:223,
    4:235, 4:237, 4:248, 4:249,
    4:260, 4:295, 4:301, 4:364,
    4:423, 4:424, 5:411, **5:452**
Jameson, Althusser, 1:1150
Jameson, Fredric, 1:993,
    1:1132, **1:1148,** 2:507,
    2:687, 2:988
Jameton, Andrew, 5:121
Jami, 4:585
Jamieson, Kathleen Hall,
    3:144, 3:146, 3:803
Jamieson, Perry D., 3:529
Jamieson, Robert H., 5:326
Jamison, A. Leland, 4:752
Jamison, D. M., 3:440
Jamison, Stephanie W., 4:501
Jammer, Max, 5:68, 5:661
Janáček, Leoš, 3:702
Janaway, Christopher, 4:256
Jandy, Edward D., 3:224
Janecek, Gerald, 2:687, 2:701
Janelle, Pierre, 4:728
Janelli, Dawnhee Y., 4:539
Janelli, Roger L., 4:539
Janevski, Slavko, 2:807,
    2:808
Janik, Del Ivan, 1:395
Janis, Harriet, 3:667
Jankowski, Martin Sanchez,
    3:216
Jannetta, Ann Bowman,
    3:475

Janney, Frank, 2:860
Janos, Leo, 5:220
Janosik, Ellen H., 5:337
Janovy, John, Jr., 5:764
Janowitz, Henry, 5:384
Janowitz, Morris, 3:229
Janowsky, Oscar I., 4:639
Jansen, Godfrey H., 4:570,
    4:579
Jansen, Marius B., 3:464,
    3:478
Janson, H. W., 3:757
Jansson, Tove, 2:658
Jantz, Ursula, 1:243
**Jaques-Dalcroze, Émile,
    3:744**
Jarausch, K. H., 3:276
Jardin, Andre, 3:165
Jardine, Alice, 1:1134
Jardine, Lisa, 1:209, 4:126,
    4:165
Jarman, Douglas, 3:680
Jarrell, Mary, 1:993
Jarrell, Randall, 1:909,
    1:993, 2:963
Jarvie, Ian C., 5:62
Jarvis, Debra, 5:388
Jarvis, Robert M., 5:388
Jary, David, 3:200, 3:227
Jary, Julia, 3:200
Jarzombek, Mark, 2:404
Jasanoff, Sheila, 5:182
Jasenas, Michael, 2:434
Jason, Philip K., 1:719
Jaspers, Karl, 2:580, 4:17,
    4:21, 4:188, 4:247, 4:261,
    4:298, 4:304, 4:318, 4:349,
    4:377, 4:394, 5:81, 5:111,
    5:137
Jaspert, W. Pincus, 1:16, 1:62
Jastrow, Robert, 5:240, 5:588,
    5:595
Javadi, Hasan, 2:83
Javitch, Daniel, 2:407
Jay, Elisabeth, 1:326
Jay, John, 3:141
Jay, Karla, 1:1184, 1:1184
Jay, Martin, 2:565, 4:394
Jay, Richard, 1:326
Jayakar, Pupul, 4:555
Jayatilleke, K. N., 4:898
Jayne, Sears R., 4:141
Jaynes, Julian, 5:80
al-Jayyusi, Salma al-Khadra,
    2:55, 2:57, 2:61
Jazzar, Bernard N., 1:45
Jebb, Richard C., 2:348,
    2:363
Jedin, Hubert, 4:677, 4:720,
    4:729
Jeffers, (John) Robinson,
    1:497, **1:851**
Jeffers, Thomas, 1:342

Jefferson, Ann, 2:511, 2:983
Jefferson, Thomas, 1:626,
    1:633, 1:638, **1:639, 3:154,**
    3:159, 3:161, 3:927, 5:265
Jeffery, Arthur, 4:566, 4:587
Jeffery, Lillian H., 3:302
Jefferys, Kevin, 3:401
Jeffrey, David, 2:913
Jeffrey, Ian, 3:759
Jeffrey, Julie Roy, 3:532
Jeffrey, Richard C., 5:63
Jeffrey, Robin, 3:488
Jeffreys, Alan E., 5:745
Jeffry, Keith, 3:371
Jehlen, Myra, 1:627, 1:1128
Jekyll, Walter, 2:931
Jelavich, Barbara, 3:391,
    3:394
Jelavich, C., 3:391
Jellema, Rod, 2:635
Jellicoe, Ann, 1:531
Jellicoe, Sidney, 4:796
Jelliffe, Derrick B., 5:346
Jelliffe, E. F. Patrice, 5:346
Jemie, Onwuchekwa, 1:848
Jencks, Charles, 3:779
Jencks, Christopher, 3:214
Jencks, W. P., 5:732
Jenkins, Anthony, 1:323,
    1:554
Jenkins, Barbara, 3:892
Jenkins, Harold, 1:206
Jenkins, J. J., 4:180
Jenkins, Peter, 3:892, 3:903
Jenkins, Richard L., 5:416
Jenkinson, Edward B., 1:57
Jenkinson, Hilary, 1:16, 1:17
Jenkyns, Richard, 2:387
Jenner, Philip N., 2:311
Jenner, W. J., 2:235
Jennett, Bryan, 5:121
Jennie, Keith, 3:24
Jennings, Elizabeth, 1:501
Jennings, Hargrove, 4:848
Jennings, Karla, 5:537
Jensen, Adolf E., 4:429,
    4:432
Jensen, Arthur R., 3:174
Jensen, Carl, 3:807
Jensen, Ejner, 1:188
Jensen, Henning, 4:203
Jensen, Joan M., 3:556
**Jensen, Johannes V(ilhelm),
    2:651**
Jensen, J. Vernon, 5:799
Jensen, Jytte, 3:835
Jensen, Karen, 5:341, 5:552
Jensen, Mead L., 5:636
Jensen, Merrill, 3:541
Jensen, Niels L., 2:651
Jensen, Paul U., 3:840
Jensen, Richard, 3:532
Jensen, Richard D., 5:261

Jensen, Richard J., 3:8
Jenson, Robert, 4:767
Jerde, Judith, 3:767
Jeremias, Joachim, 4:604, 4:807, 4:827
Jerome, St., 4:711, 4:800
Jerrold, Douglas William, 1:311, 1:320, 1:324, **1:366**
Jerrold, Walter, 1:367
Jerrold, W. Blanchard, 1:367
Jersild, P(er) C(hristian), 2:671, **2:674**
Jervis, Robin, 1:268
Jervolino, Domenico, 4:319
Jesse, Andreas, 5:653
Jessel, Camilla, 3:734
Jessop, Thomas E., 4:192, 4:202, 4:212
Jester, John L., 5:815
Jeter, Katherine, 5:384
Jetter, Judy, 5:398
Jevons, William Stanley, 3:84, 5:278
Jewell, Jeala Jane, 2:402
Jewell, Malcolm E., 3:148
Jewett, Sarah Orne, 1:698, 1:721, **1:769**, 1:1193
Jewkes, John, 5:226
Jeyaretnam, Philip, 2:324
Jezer, Marty, 3:538
Jhabvala, Ruth Prawer, 2:177
Jhally, Sut, 3:560
Jiménez, Juan Ramón, 2:542
Jing-Nuan, Wu, 4:524
Joachim, Harold L., 4:170
Joachim, H. H., 4:69
Joachim of Fiore, 4:712
Joad, Cyril E., 4:21
Joannides, Paul, 3:788
Joaquin, Nick, 2:329
Jobe, Brock, 3:766
Jobes, Gertrude, 3:757, 3:849
Jobling, James A., 5:769
Jochim, Christian, 4:523
Joe, Rita, 2:914
Joergensen, Joergen, 4:265
Joffrey, Robert, 3:745
Johannes von Saaz, 2:594
Johannsen, Robert W., 3:510, 3:524
Johansen, Hans C., 3:381
Johanson, Donald, 5:638
Johansson, Thomas B., 5:289
John, Murray, 5:623
Johnman, Lewis, 3:366
John of Paris, 4:101
John of Salisbury, 4:115
John of the Cross, St., 2:520, **2:543**, 4:736, 4:786, 4:788
Johnpoll, Bernard K., 3:538, 4:656

Johnpoll, Lillian, 3:538
Johns, Alger F., 4:795
Johns, Anthony H., 2:317
Johns, Richard, 3:451
Johnsgaard, Paul A., 5:770
Johnson, A. F., 1:16
Johnson, Allan G., 5:522
Johnson, Alvin, 3:5
Johnson, Arthur W., 1:24
Johnson, Beth, 3:895
Johnson, Carroll B., 2:536
Johnson, Chalmers A., 3:471, 3:478
Johnson, Charles, 1:17, 2:322
Johnson, Claudia D., 1:220
Johnson, Claudia L., 1:276
Johnson, Curtiss S., 1:661
Johnson, D., 2:741
Johnson, D. W., 5:223
Johnson, David G., 5:336
Johnson, David L., 5:227
Johnson, Deborah, 1:524, 5:125, 5:128
Johnson, Diane, 1:1230
Johnson, Donald B., 3:511
Johnson, Donald Clay, 3:488
Johnson, Edgar, 1:300, 1:350, **1:994**
Johnson, Elmer D., 1:904
Johnson, Eyvind (Olof Verner), 2:671, **2:675**
Johnson, Francis R., 5:40
Johnson, Fridolf, 1:28
Johnson, G. Timothy, 5:341
Johnson, Galen A., 4:311
Johnson, George, 5:568
Johnson, H. D., 5:774
Johnson, Harold J., 4:98
Johnson, Harry G., 3:53, 3:58, 3:62
Johnson, James Turner, 4:570
Johnson, James Weldon, 1:718, 1:720, 1:721, **1:771**
Johnson, Janet Buttolph, 3:138
Johnson, John J., 3:631, 3:811
Johnson, John W., 3:508
Johnson, Joyce, 1:913
Johnson, Judith Anne, 1:559
Johnson, Lawrence E., 5:115
Johnson, Lemuel, 2:109
Johnson, Leonard R., 5:773
Johnson, Linck C., 1:702
Johnson, Luke Timothy, 4:813
Johnson, Lyman L., 3:628
Johnson, Margaret, 1:32
Johnson, Mark, 3:21
Johnson, Mary Lynn, 1:279
Johnson, Michael, 1:1128

Johnson, Michael G., 4:237, 5:453
Johnson, Mohamed Ismail, 5:385
Johnson, Norman L., 5:520
Johnson, Oliver A., 4:21
Johnson, Paul, 3:345, 3:723
Johnson, Pauline, 1:24
Johnson, Penelope, 4:699
Johnson, Richard, 1:436
Johnson, Robert K., 1:1113
Johnson, Samuel, 1:164, 1:209, 1:224, 1:227, 1:231, 1:233, 1:235, 1:241, 1:246, **1:248**, 1:253, 1:254, 2:387, 2:407, 3:790, 5:833
Johnson, Stanley, 5:263
Johnson, Stephen L., 5:374
Johnson, Thomas H., 1:630, 1:747, 3:511, 3:513
Johnson, Timothy, 5:334
Johnson, Toni O'Brien, 1:556
Johnson, Trevor, 1:362
Johnson, Uwe, 2:564, **2:594**
Johnson, W. R., 2:387, 2:397
Johnson, W. Stacy, 1:328
Johnson, Warren T., 5:768
Johnson, Willard L., 4:514, 4:530, 4:538
Johnson, William H., 3:909
Johnson-Davies, Denys, 2:57
Johnson-Laird, Philip, 5:568
Johnston, Brian, 2:666
Johnston, Derek W., 5:427
Johnston, Donald F., 1:54, 1:118
Johnston, Edward, 1:17
Johnston, G. A., 4:32
Johnston, George, 2:640
Johnston, Harold W., 2:381
Johnston, Johanna, 1:409
Johnston, Kenneth, 1:307
Johnston, Les, 3:205
Johnston, Marjorie, 5:678
Johnston, Priscilla, 1:42
Johnston, Robert D., 1:392
Johnston, Ronald J., 3:118, **3:131**
Johnston, Rory, 5:568
Johnston, William, 4:858
Johnston, William M., 3:375
Johnstone, Richard, 1:421
John XXIII, Pope, 4:770
Jókai, Mór (also Móricz, Maurice), 2:799
Jolivet, Pierre, 5:760
Joll, James, 3:279, 4:287
Jolley, Elizabeth, 2:955
Jolley, Nicholas, 4:177, 4:180, 4:182
Jolowicz, H. F., 3:306

Jonas, Hans, 4:63, 4:453, 4:686, 4:811, 5:71, **5:93,** 5:129, 5:139
Jonas, Klaus W., 2:602
Jonas, Susanne, 3:637
Joncich, Geraldine, 3:269
Jones, Adam L., 4:34
Jones, A. H., 3:302, 4:684
Jones, Archer, 3:528
Jones, B. J., 1:101
Jones, Barry, 3:366
Jones, Bessie, 3:861
Jones, C. B., 1:326
Jones, C. Eugene, 5:761
Jones, C. P., 3:314, 4:485
Jones, Charles O., 3:146
Jones, Cheslyn, 4:678, 4:897
Jones, Christopher, 3:389
Jones, D. Gareth, 5:119
Jones, David, 1:502
Jones, Dick, 5:770
Jones, Doris Arthur, 1:367
Jones, Douglas C., 5:252
Jones, E. J., 5:622
Jones, Eldred, 1:214, 2:109, 2:149
Jones, Emrys, 1:165
Jones, Eric L., 3:274, 3:326
Jones, Ernest, 1:213, 3:184, 5:47, 5:448
Jones, Esnor, 3:253
Jones, Everett L., 3:554
Jones, G. William, 3:831
Jones, Gareth, 3:369, 4:831
Jones, Gareth Stedman, 1:312
Jones, Geoffrey, 3:463
Jones, Gwyn, 1:418, 2:640, 3:381
Jones, Hazel J., 3:478
Jones, Helen C., 5:403
Jones, Henry Arthur, 1:310, 1:320, 1:321, **1:367,** 1:423
Jones, Henry J., 1:307
Jones, Herbert, 1:17
Jones, Howard, 3:545, 3:608, 4:74
Jones, Howard Mumford, 1:651, 1:714, 1:723
Jones, J. A., 5:559
Jones, J.G.W., 5:263
Jones, J. Knox, Jr., 5:758
Jones, Jacqueline, 3:552, 3:556
Jones, James, 1:994
Jones, James E., Jr.,3:555
Jones, James H., 5:390
Jones, James Rees, 3:360
Jones, Jennifer, 5:222
Jones, John, 2:346, 4:69, 4:328
Jones, John Paul, 3:122
Jones, Joseph, 1:772

Jones, Judith, 1:1041
Jones, K.R.W., 2:503
Jones, Kenneth W., 3:486, 4:508, 4:516, 4:517
Jones, Kirkland C., 1:817
Jones, Larry E., 3:344
Jones, Lawrence, 2:971
Jones, Louis C., 3:859
Jones, Majorie, 2:109
Jones, Malcolm V., 2:715, 2:766
Jones, Maldwyn Allen, 3:556
Jones, Margaret E., 2:525
Jones, Mark, 5:193
Jones, Mary Lou, 5:770
Jones, Mary M., 4:274
Jones, Max, 3:674
Jones, Monica Loose, 5:322
Jones, Nancy C., 5:252
Jones, O. R., 4:383
Jones, Owen, 3:765
Jones, Peter, 4:32
Jones, Preston, 1:1071, **1:1095**
Jones, R. T, 1:354
Jones, Raymond A., 3:364
Jones, Richard, 3:606
Jones, Richard F., 5:42
Jones, Robert, 1:1074
Jones, Robert C., 1:212
Jones, Robert Edmond, 1:1073
Jones, Roger, 3:788
Jones, Rufus M., 4:734
Jones, Stanley, 1:28, 1:291
Jones, Stephen, 1:599, 1:600
Jones, Steven, 3:849, 3:873, 5:760
Jones, Thomas M., 3:357
Jones, W. T., 4:17, 4:46, 4:161
Jones, W. Glyn, 2:655, 2:656, 3:381
Jones, William B., 5:303
Jones, Willis Knapp, 2:849
Jonsen, Albert R., 5:13, 5:121
Jonson, Ben, 1:175, **1:183,** 1:228, 1:1097, 2:383, 2:385, 2:389, 2:391, 2:393
Joplin, Scott, 1:968, **3:703**
Jopling, Norman, 1:123
Joppien, Rudiger, 3:918
Jordak, Francis E., 4:13
Jordan, A. C., 2:158
Jordan, Constance, 2:401
Jordan, David K., 4:531
Jordan, Elaine, 1:401
Jordan, Frank, Jr., 1:265
Jordan, Gerald, 3:354
Jordan, Heather Bryant, 1:448
Jordan, John, 5:238
Jordan, John E., 1:290

Jordan, Louis Henry, 4:420
Jordan, Richard D., 2:947
Jordan, Robert F., 3:761
Jordan, Rosan A., 3:869
Jordan, Terry G., 3:121, **3:132**
Jordan, W. K., 3:359
Jordan, Wilbur K., 4:726
Jordan, William, 4:50
Jordan, Winthrop D., 3:513, 3:556
Jordan, Z. A., 4:30
Jordanova, L. J., 5:803
Jordan-Smith, Paul, 4:464
Jordy, William H., 3:563, 3:763
Jorgen, Moe, 3:854
Jorgens, Jack J., 1:218
Jorgensen, Danny L., 4:860, 4:865
Jorgensen, Eric P., 5:823
Jorgensen, Paul, 1:214
Jorgenson, Elizabeth Watkins, 5:434
Jorgenson, Henry Irvin, 5:434
Jorgenson, Joseph G., 4:467
Joris, Lieve, 3:903
Jorpes, J. Erik, 5:739
José, F. Sionil, 2:328, **2:331**
José, Sionil, 2:328
Joselit, Jenna W., 4:639
Joseph, Bertram., 1:218
Joseph, Gerhard, 1:402
Joseph, Horace W., 4:81
Joseph, J.K.S., 3:355
Joseph, Stephen, 5:388
Josephs, Arthur, 5:392
Josephs, Lawrence, 3:178
Josephson, Brian David, 5:670, **5:695**
Josephson, Martin M., 5:416
Josephson, Matthew, 3:54, 5:226, 5:252
Josephus, Flavius, 2:343, 2:362, **3:316,** 4:604, 4:607, 4:615, 4:616, 4:617, **4:666**
Josephy, Alvin M., 3:556
Joshi, Arun, 2:177
Joshi, Irene M., 2:171
Josipovici, Gabriel, 4:816
Joslyn, Richard A., 3:138
Jospe, Alfred, 4:647
Jost, François, 2:983
Joukowsky, Anatol M., 3:851
Jourdan, Eric, 4:307
Jouve, Nicole W., 2:470
Jovanovich, William, 1:50
Joyce, Bruce, 3:256
Joyce, David D., 3:515

Joyce, James, 1:412, 1:419, 1:438, 1:453, 1:459, 1:474, 1:502, **1:503**, 1:515, 1:525, 1:540, 1:762, 1:946, 1:963, 1:974, 1:977, 1:1019, 1:1020, 1:1034, 1:1116, 2:87, 2:95, 2:123, 2:359, 2:410, 2:432, 2:438, 2:439, 2:442, 2:467, 2:494, 2:496, 2:560, 2:675, 2:679, 2:858, 2:870, 2:888, 2:897, 2:907, 2:915, 3:680, 3:827, 3:838
Joyce, Joyce A., 1:725, 1:906
Joyce, Patrick, 3:364
Joyce, William L., 1:9, 3:801
Joyner, Charles, 3:524, 3:867
József, Attila, 2:798, 2:800
Juan Chi, 2:202
Jubran (Gibran), Khalil, 2:66
Ju Chih-chüan, 2:248, 2:266
Judaeus, Philo. *See* Philo Judaeus
Judah, J. Stillson, 4:841, 4:863
Judah Ha-levi, 2:6, 2:20, 2:23, 4:666
Judd, Gerrit, 1:263
Judge, H., 3:273
Judson, A. C., 1:198
Judson, Horace Freeland, 5:778, 5:791, 5:813
Judson, Katherine, 3:863
Judson, Lindsay, 4:69
Juergensmeyer, Mark, 4:504, 4:508, 4:516, 4:553, 4:892
Jugo, Miguel de Unamuno y. *See* Unamuno y Jugo, Miguel de
Juhász, Ferenc, 2:800
Juhasz, Suzanne, 1:747
Jules-Rosette, Bennetta, 3:23
Julian, John, 3:656
Julian of Norwich, 4:712
Juliar, Michael, 1:1020
Julien, Eileen, 2:109, 2:112
Julius, DeAnne, 3:58
July, Robert W., 3:417
Jump, James R., 1:103
Jun'ichirō, Tanizaki. *See* Tanizaki Jun'ichirō
Jung, C(arl) G(ustav), 1:968, 2:910, 2:982, 3:876, 4:423, 4:424, 4:427, 4:473, 4:483, 4:870, 5:430, 5:436, 5:437, 5:445, 5:454, 5:469
Jung, Hwa Jol, 4:307
Jüngel, Eberhard, 4:744
Jünger, Ernst, 2:595
Jungerman, John A., 5:239
Jungk, Robert, 5:658
Jungmann, Josef A., 4:689
Jurčič, Josip, 2:834

Jurgensen, Knud A., 3:739
Jurji, Nabil Na'um, 2:59
Jusdanis, Gregory, 2:372
Justice, Donald, 1:995
Justin Martyr, 4:99
Justus, James H., 1:893
Juvenal (Decimus Junius Juvenalis), 1:187, 1:227, 1:248, 1:807, 2:379, 2:386, 2:389, 2:392

K

K'ang, Hsi, 2:202
K'ang Yu-Wei, 4:360
Kaba, Lansine, 4:570
Kabdebo, Thomas, 2:799
Kaberry, Phyllis M., 3:420, 4:461
Kabir, Humayun, 2:173, 2:176
Kadare, Ismail, 2:779
Kadic, Ante, 2:785, 2:827
Kadir, Djelal, 2:846, 2:876
Kadish, Sanford H., 3:205
Kadlec, Nancy, 5:398
Kadomtsev, B. B., 5:667
Kadushin, Charles, 1:49
Kadushin, Max, 4:600, 4:620
Kaegi, Walter E., 3:303
Kael, Pauline, 1:1179
Kaelin, E. F., 4:293
Kafalos, M., 5:650
Kafka, Franz, 1:521, 1:896, 1:949, 1:985, 1:1056, 2:90, 2:494, 2:564, 2:595, 2:818, 2:982
Kafker, Frank A., 3:339
Kafu, Nagai. *See* Nagai Kafu
Kagan, B. A., 5:632
Kagan, Jerome, 3:168, 3:173, 3:173, 5:322, 5:416
Kagan, Norman, 3:839
Kagle, Stephen E., 1:660, 1:727
Kahin, Audrey R., 3:491
Kahl, Joseph A., 3:631
Kahn, Albert E., 3:754
Kahn, Alfred E., 3:57
Kahn, Charles H., 4:51, 4:74
Kahn, Coppélia, 1:208, 1:209, 1:925, 1:1134
Kahn, Herman, 5:111
Kahn, Lothar, 2:578, 4:636
Kahn, Louis I(sadore), 3:769, 3:777
Kahn, Madeleine, 1:230
Kahn, Margaret, 4:570
Kahn, Marvin W., 5:418
Kahn, Paul, 5:200, 5:543
Kahn, Sholom J., 1:784

Kahn, Tamar J., 5:61
Kahn, Victoria, 4:127
Kahn, Yitzhak, 2:32
Kail, Robert V., 3:174
Kainz, Howard P., 3:149
Kaiser, Georg, 2:596
Kaiser, Otto, 4:815
Kaiser, Robert G., 3:346
Kaivola, Karen, 1:813, 2:474
Kakar, Sudhir, 4:424, 4:890
Kaku, Michio, 5:111
Kalayaanaphong, Angkhan, 2:335
Kalb, Jonathan, 2:460
Kalcik, Susan J., 3:869
Kalck, Pierre, 3:421
Kalechofsky, Roberta, 2:849
Kalecki, Michael, 3:53
Kaledin, Eugenia, 3:560, 3:563
Kālidāsa, 2:172
Kalisch, Beatrice J., 5:337
Kalisch, Philip A., 5:337
Kalita, Dwight, 5:348
Kallen, Horace M., 4:34, 4:237, 4:265, 4:324
Kallmann, Helmutt, 3:609, 3:656
Kalma, Douwe, 2:634
Kalmin, Richard, 4:610
Kals, W. S., 5:341, 5:591
Kalson, Albert E., 1:537
Kalstone, David, 1:196, 1:913
Kalupahana, David J., 4:513
Kamban, 2:172
Kamen, Betty, 5:348
Kamen, Edward W., 5:296
Kamen, Gloria, 1:586
Kamen, Henry, 3:387
Kamen, Si, 5:348
Kamenetsky, Christa, 3:880
Kamenka, Eugene, 4:243
Kamien, Roger, 3:665
Kamin, Leon J., 5:826
Kaminski, Bartlomie, 3:390
Kaminsky, Alice R., 1:373
Kamm, Josephine, 1:380
Kammen, Michael, 3:142, 3:515, 3:520, 3:560
Kammerling, Robert C., 5:628
Kampler, Fritz, 3:766
Kamshad, Hassan, 2:83
Kamuf, Peggy, 1:922, 4:398
Kanafani, Ghassan, 2:67
Kanamori, H., 5:630
Kanarfogel, Ephraim, 4:622
Kane, George, 1:154
Kane, Gordon, 5:662
Kane, Grace F., 3:861
Kane, Israel, 4:629
Kane, Joe, 3:895

Kane, Joseph Nathan, 1:88, 3:148, 3:506
Kane, Robert S., 3:903
Kane, Thomas T., 3:121
Kanefsky, Morton, 5:299
Kanes, Martin, 2:454
Kang, Sôk-kyông, 2:298
Kang, W., 4:309
Kangro, Bernard, 2:796, **2:796**
Kang Shin-jae, 2:303
Kanigel, Robert, 5:313, 5:764
Kanik, Orhan Veli, 2:98
Kanint, Larry, 3:906
Kaniss, Phyllis, 3:807
Kaniuk, Yoram, 2:20
Kann, Robert A., 3:389
Kannappan, Sam, 5:224
Kannenburg, Ida, 4:870
Kannengiesser, Charles, 4:689
Kannenstine, Louis, 1:813
Kanner, Barbara, 3:354, 3:355
Kanner, Leo, 5:416
Kanof, Abram, 4:597
Kant, Immanuel, 2:442, 2:588, 2:599 3:156, 3:375, 4:158, 4:197, 4:198, 4:200, 4:203, **4:204,** 4:208, 4:216, 4:219, 4:229, 4:230, 4:231, 4:253, 4:255, 4:279, 4:301, 4:318, 4:333, 4:363, 4:387, 4:413, 4:600, 4:739, 4:771, 5:85, 5:88, 5:105
Kanter, Jerome, 5:556
Kanter, Rosabeth M., 3:217
Kanth, Rajani K., 3:51
Kantorowicz, Ernst H., 4:98, 4:696
Kanya-Forstner, A. S., 3:421
Kanzer, Mark, 5:448
Kao, George, 2:241, 2:251
Kao, Karl, S., 2:192
Kao Ch'i, 2:202
Kao Hsiao-sheng, 2:248
Kapferer, Bruce, 4:515
Kapitza, Peter Leonidovich, 5:696
Kaplan, Amy, 1:723, 1:804
Kaplan, Andrew, 5:341
Kaplan, Aryeh, 2:42, 4:669
Kaplan, Berton H., 5:427
Kaplan, Chaim A., 3:349
Kaplan, David, 3:14
Kaplan, E. Ann, 3:811, 3:840
Kaplan, Ellen S., 5:392
Kaplan, Fred, 1:343, 1:350
Kaplan, Frederic M., 3:465
Kaplan, Gisela, 4:395
Kaplan, Justin, 1:707, 1:784
Kaplan, Louis, 1:87
Kaplan, Louise, 2:476

Kaplan, Marion, 3:386, 4:650
Kaplan, Mordecai Mena-heim, 4:658, 4:663, **4:667**
Kaplan, Norman M., 5:374
Kaplan, Stuart B., 4:860
Kaplan, William, 3:609
Kapleau, Philip, 4:537, 4:860
Kaplon, Morton, 4:172
Kapp, Ernst, 5:69
Kapr, Albert, 1:17
Kapstein, Israel J., 4:610
Kaptchuk, Ted J., 5:319
Kapur, Rajiv A., 4:516
Kapuscinski, Gisele, 2:84
Karacan, Ismet, 5:428
Karadžić, Vuk, 2:826
Karamzin, Nikolai, 2:730
Karaosmanoğlu, Yakup Kadri, 2:99
Kardong, T., 4:706
Kargon, Robert H., 5:702
Karimi-Hakkak, Ahmad, 2:84
Kark, Sidney L., 5:328
Karkala, Leena, 2:170
Karl, Barry D., 3:162
Karl, Frederick R., 1:415, 1:421, 1:464, 1:837, 1:918
Karl, John H., 5:302
Karlfeldt, Erik Axel, 2:671
Karlin, Leonard, 5:311
Karlinsky, Simon, 2:687, 2:692, 2:722, 2:768
Karlsen, Carol F., 3:518
Karman, James, 1:851
Karnow, Stanley, 3:471, 3:532, 3:538
Karp, Abraham J., 4:639
Karp, Gerald, 5:775
Karp, Ivan, 4:462
Karpat, Kemal H., 3:436
Karpel, Bernard, 3:759
Karpeles, Maud, 3:852
Karpinski, Leszek M., 4:883
Karplus, Walter J., 5:10
Karsh, Efraim, 3:538
Karski, Jan, 3:390
Kart, Gary S., 5:349
Kasack, Wolfgang, 2:687
Käsemann, Ernst, 4:821, 4:825
Kasen, Vivian Loeb, 5:224
Kaser, M. C., 3:389
Kashap, S. Paul, 4:188
Kasravi, Ahmad, 4:575
Kass, Leon R., 5:121
Kass, Linda Stern, 5:345
Kassen, Ceza, 2:57
Kassis, Hanna E., 4:587
Kasson, John F., 1:628, 3:552, 3:560
Kass-Simon, G., 5:187
Kastan, Carren, 1:766

Kastan, David Scott, 1:170, 1:209
Kaštelan, Jure, 2:785
Kastenbaum, Robert, 5:317, 5:422
Kastner, Joseph, 5:818
Kasulis, T. P., 4:537
Kataev (Katayev), Valentin, 2:730
Katahn, Martin, 5:346
Kateb, George, 4:395, 5:82
Kates, Judith A., 2:440
Kates, Robert W., 5:620
Kati, Muhammad, 2:124
Katkov, George, 3:396
Kato, Shuichi, 2:271, 2:282
Katouzian, Homa, 2:90, 3:448
Katra, William H., 2:884
Katsell, J., 2:692
Katsh, Abraham I., 4:570, 4:643
Kattenburg, Paul M., 3:538
Katz, Barbara F., 5:343
Katz, Bernard S., 5:280
Katz, Bill, 5:547
Katz, C. T., 3:290
Katz, David, 2:30
Katz, Ephraim, 3:825
Katz, Jacob, 3:349, 4:624, 4:636
Katz, James E., 5:287
Katz, Jane, 5:326, 5:358
Katz, Jay, 5:79
Katz, Jeffrey, 2:846
Katz, Jonathan, 1:1182
Katz, Joseph, 1:743
Katz, Linda Sobel, 5:815
Katz, Linda Sternberg, 1:72
Katz, Michael, 3:211
Katz, Michael B., 3:616
Katz, Michael R., 2:687
Katz, Robert, 3:836
Katz, Ruth, 3:660
Katz, Ruth Cecily, 4:505
Katz, Samuel M., 3:440
Katz, Stephen, 4:648
Katz, Steven, 4:575
Katz, Steven T., 4:601, 4:646
Katz, Victor J., 5:31, 5:492
Katz, William A., 1:52, 1:72, 1:73, 1:81
Katzman, David J., 3:552
Kauffman, Henry J., 3:859
Kauffman, James M., 3:255
Kauffmann, Stanley, 1:1073
Kaufman, Burton I., 3:538
Kaufman, G. A., 5:283
Kaufman, George S., 1:1096
Kaufman, Gordon, 4:744
Kaufman, Joel, 5:351
Kaufman, L., 3:177
Kaufman, Martin, 5:313, 5:338

Kaufman, Sharon R., 5:313
Kaufman, Wallace, 5:631
Kaufman, Walter, 3:670
Kaufman, William E., 4:596,
    4:649
Kaufmann, Emil, 3:763
Kaufmann, Fritz, 2:602
Kaufmann, Ludwig, 4:744
Kaufmann, Robert, 5:282
Kaufmann, Walter, 4:161,
    4:247, 4:265
Kaufmann, William J., III,
    5:588, 5:655, 5:664
Kaul, A. N., 1:658
Kaun, Alexander S., 2:699
Kautsky, Karl, 4:147
Kautzsch, E., 4:794
Kavanagh, Patrick, 1:416,
    1:506, 1:507
Kavanagh, Peter, 1:507
Kaverin, Veniamin, 2:731
Kawabata Yasunari, 2:281,
    2:288, 2:295
Kawin, Bruce, 3:827
Kawman, D., 5:426
Kay, H., 3:386
Kay, Lily E., 5:784
Kay, Norman, 3:718
Kayal, Philip M., 5:388
Kaye, G. W., 5:653
Kaye, H. J., 3:276
Kaye, Jacqueline, 1:873,
    2:117
Kaye, Phyllis J., 1:1074
Kayman, Martin A., 1:604,
    1:873
Kayser, Rudolf, 2:20
**Kay-Shuttleworth, Sir
    James Phillips,** 1:310,
    1:324, **1:367,** 1:375, 1:377
Kazantzakis, Helen, 2:374
Kazantzakis, Nikos, 2:359,
    2:361, 2:370, **2:373,** 3:904
Kazdin, Alan E., 5:416
Kazhdan, Alexander P., 4:693
Kazin, Alfred, 1:50, 1:421,
    1:714, 1:723, 1:773, 1:804,
    1:918, **1:995,** 1:1019,
    1:1028
Kazlauskas, Edward J., 5:545
Keach, William, 1:303
Kealey, Gregory S., 3:615
Keane, Patrick J., 1:486,
    1:572
Keaney, John J., 4:69
Kearney, Colbert, 1:442
Kearney, Hugh F., 3:355
Kearney, Richard, 3:371, 4:27
Kearns, Cleo McNelly, 1:473
Kearns, David T., 3:250
Kearns, Doris, 3:538
Kearns, George, 1:873
Keary, Philip, 5:629

Keast, William R., 1:166
Keat, Russell, 3:229, 4:405,
    5:89
Keates, John S., 5:617
Keating, Michael, 3:366
Keating, P. J., 1:319
Keats, John, 1:264, 1:267,
    1:271, 1:273, 1:280, 1:284,
    1:285, 1:290, 1:292, **1:293,**
    1:302, 1:305, 1:313, 1:314,
    1:516, 1:598, 1:855, 1:868,
    1:910, 2:825, 2:983
Keay, J., 3:274
Keay, John, 3:892
Kebede, Ashenafi, 3:867
Keck, Leander E., 4:825
Keddie, Nikki R., 3:443,
    3:447, 3:448, 4:570, 4:575
Kedourie, Elie, 3:440, 4:594
Kedward, H. R., 3:373
Kee, Howard Clark, 4:617,
    4:689, 4:807, 4:811, 4:815,
    4:816
Kee, Robert, 3:369, 3:535
Keedy, Mervin L., 5:485
Keefe, Janice A., 1:387
Keefe, Robert, 1:387
Keefe, Terry, 2:518
Keegan, John, 3:279, 3:343
Keele, Kenneth D., 5:361
Keeler, Robert F., 3:807
Keeley, Edmund, 2:371
Keeley, Robin, 4:718, 4:744
Keen, Maurice, 3:357
Keen, Richard A., 5:10
Keenan, George, 3:396
Keene, Donald, 2:272, 2:273,
    2:274, 2:282, 2:283, 2:295,
    3:475
Keeney, Bradford P., 5:419
Keeny, Spurgeon M., Jr.,
    5:287
Keeton, William, 5:764
Kefauver, Weldon A., 1:50
Kegan, Robert, 3:174
Kegley, Charles W., Jr.,
    3:545
Kehler, George, 3:672
Kehoe, Brendan P., 5:547
Kehrer, Daniel M., 5:351
Kehrer, James P., 5:351
Keightley, David N., 3:468
Keightley, T., 3:848
Keiji, Nishitani. See Nishitani
    Keiji
Keillor, Garrison, 3:871
Keim, Albert, 5:809
Keir, David L., 3:355
Keiser, Bernhard E(dward),
    5:299, **5:307**
Keiser, Gerd, 5:303
Keisling, Bill, 5:289
Keith, Arthur B., 4:501

Keith, Jennie, 3:201
Keith, Nelson W., 3:638
Keith, Novella Z., 3:638
Keith, Sandra, 5:479
Keith, W. J., 1:429
Keithly, David, 3:377
Kekes, John, 4:389
Kellaghan, Thomas, 3:256
Kellas, James G., 3:355
Keller, Alex, 5:658
Keller, Dean H., 1:124
Keller, Evelyn Fox, 5:66,
    5:154, 5:187, 5:780, 5:806
Keller, Frances Richardson,
    1:739
Keller, Gary D., 1:130
Keller, Gottfried, 2:564,
    2:597
Keller, Howard H., 1:99
Keller, John E., 2:522, 2:526
Keller, Karl, 1:644, 1:748
Keller, Michael A., 3:655
Keller, Peter C., 5:628
Keller, Rosemary S., 4:749
Kellerman, Aharon, 4:594,
    4:642
Kellert, Stephen R., 3:47
Kelley, Donald R., 2:762,
    4:127
Kelley, Harold H., 3:176
Kelley, Karol L., 1:804
Kelley, Kitty, 3:719
Kelley, Laurence, 2:735
Kelley, Mary, 1:651
Kelley, Michael R., 1:161
Kelley, Patricia, 3:201
Kelley, Richard, 1:950
Kelley, Robert L., 3:543
Kellgren, Johan Henrik,
    2:670
Kellner, Douglas, 1:1150,
    1:1157, 3:812, 4:17, 4:408
Kellner, Menachem Marc,
    4:598
Kellogg, Susan, 3:553
Kelly, Aidan, 4:865
Kelly, Alfred H., 3:142, 3:541
Kelly, Derek, 5:242
Kelly, Edward J., 5:419
Kelly, Gail P., 3:253
Kelly, Gary, 1:270
Kelly, George Edward,
    1:1097
Kelly, J.N.D., 4:675, 4:678,
    4:686, 4:712
Kelly, James, 1:67
Kelly, Katherine E., 1:554
Kelly, Louis, 2:990
Kelly, Marjorie, 4:570
Kelly, Paula, 5:322
Kelly, Raymond C., 3:24
Kelly, Richard Michael,
    1:367, 1:583

Kelly, Robert, 3:925
Kelly, Rob Roy, 1:17
Kelly, Rosemary, 3:354
Kelly, Thaddeus E., 5:781
Kelly, William P., 1:665
Kelman, Charles D., 5:384
Kelman, Harold, 5:452
Kelman, Steven, 5:336
Kelsey, D. M., 3:938
Kelsey, John, 4:570
Kemal Yaşar, 2:99
Kemeny, John G., 5:552
Kemp, Ian, 3:725
Kemp, Martin, 3:780, 5:190,
5:193, **5:203**
Kemp, Sandra, 1:372
Kemp, Wolfgang, 1:395
Kempe, Frederick, 3:904
Kempe, Margery, 1:152
Kemper, John D., 5:227
Kemper, Robert V., 3:11
Kempf, James M., 1:823
Kendall, Alan, 3:662, 3:696,
3:724
Kendall, Edward C., 5:369
Kendall, Laurel, 4:539
Kendall, Maurice G., 5:520,
5:526
Kendall, Paul M., 1:87,
1:928, 3:357
Kendall, Richard, 3:783
Kendall, R. T., 4:726
Kendall, Willmoore, 4:180
Kendrick, Brent L., 1:750
Kendrick, John W., 5:234
Kendrick, Walter, 1:599
Keneally, Thomas, 2:957
Kenkō Yoshida, 2:269, 2:277
Kennan, George F(rost),
3:286, 3:545, **3:583**
Kennard, Joseph S., 2:423
Kennedy, A., 1:425
Kennedy, Alex, 4:513
Kennedy, David M., 3:512,
3:514, 3:532
Kennedy, George, 2:346,
2:381, 2:393, 5:299
Kennedy, Ian, 5:121
Kennedy, J. Gerald, 1:693
Kennedy, John, 1:330
Kennedy, John H., 4:752
Kennedy, Leonard A., 4:104,
4:127
Kennedy, Michael, 3:685,
3:694
Kennedy, Paul M., 3:149,
3:326, 3:341, 3:366
Kennedy, Peter, 3:63, 3:852
Kennedy, P. J., 5:674
Kennedy, Raymond, 3:12
Kennedy, Richard S., 1:826,
1:904
Kennedy, William, 1:996

Kennedy, X. J., 1:997
Kennedy-Skipton, Laetitia,
1:14
Kenner, Hugh, 1:415, 1:421,
1:505, 1:794, 1:799, 1:873
Kennett, James P., 5:631
Kenney, E. J., 1:37, 2:381,
3:298
Kennington, Richard, 4:188
Kenny, Anthony, 4:17, 4:69,
4:119, 4:147, 4:170, 4:346,
4:386
Kenny, Anthony J., 5:111,
5:564
Kenny, Shirley Strum, 1:228
Kenny, Vincent S., 1:1089
Kenschaft, Patricia C., 5:479
Kent, David A., 1:391
Kent, James A., 5:725
Kent, J. P., 3:306
Kent, Marian, 3:453
Kent, Rosamond, 4:54
Kent, William C., 1:350
Kenton, Leslie, 5:349
Kenyatta, Jomo, 3:422
Kenyon, Frederic G., 1:37
Kenyon, J. P., 3:354, 3:360
Kenyon, John S., 1:92
Kenyon, Timothy, 1:194
Keough, Carol, 5:398
Kepel, Gilles, 4:570
Kepler, Clive, 4:395
Kepler, Johannes, 5:42,
5:600, 5:601, **5:608**, 5:705
Kepnes, Steven, 4:662
Keppie, L., 3:308
Kepple, Robert J., 4:6
Keppler, C. F., 2:985
Ker, Ian, 4:783
Kerber, Linda K., 3:513
Kerby-Fulton, Kathryn, 1:154
Kerensky, Alexander, 3:396
Kerensky, Oleg, 1:425, 3:736
Kerényi, Károly, 2:346,
4:470, **4:483**
Keris, Mas, 2:325
Kerlin, Robert T., 2:369
Kerlinger, Frederick N., 3:6
Kerman, Cynthia Earl, 1:891,
3:72
Kerman, Joseph, 2:987,
3:660, 3:665, 3:670
Kerman, D. Ariel, 5:374
Kermode, Frank, 1:129,
1:189, 1:417, 1:421, 1:888,
4:816
Kern, Gary, 2:692, 2:775
Kern, Jerome, 3:703
Kern, John Dwight, 1:790
Kernan, Alvin B., 1:208,
1:209, 1:1074
Kerner, George C., 4:331
Kerner, Mary, 3:732

Kernfeld, Barry, 3:656
Kernighan, Brian W., 5:550,
5:553
Kernodle, George R., 1:1074
Kernodle, Portia, 1:1074
Kerns, Virginia, 4:466
Kerouac, Jack, 1:956, 1:981,
1:997, 1:1190, 2:465,
4:853, 4:860
Kerr, A. P., 3:373
Kerr, Chester, 1:50
Kerr, Clark, 3:60, 3:94, 3:250
Kerr, Donald, 3:605
Kerr, Fergus, 4:346
Kerr, H. T., 4:63
Kerr, Howard, 4:841, 4:851
Kerr, James, 1:300
Kerr, Lucille, 2:881
Kerr, M. E., 1:1195
Kerr, Malcolm H., 4:374
Kerr, Mary Lee, 5:815
Kerrigan, John, 1:207
Kerrins, Joseph, 5:387
Kersey, Ethel M., 4:6, 4:161
Kersnik, Janko, 2:834
Kersnowski, Frank L., 1:470
Kerson, Lawrence A., 5:377
Kerson, Toba S., 5:377
Kert, Bernice, 1:846
Kertesz, Louise, 1:1042
Kertzer, David L., 3:24, 3:201
Kertzer, J. W., 2:917
Kesey, Ken, 1:999
Keshavadas, Sadguru S.,
2:171
Kessler, David, 4:644
Kessler, Edward, 1:888
Kessler, Gary C., 5:299
Kessler, I., 5:372
Kessler, Jascha, 2:798
Kessler, Lauren, 3:807
Kessler, Seymour, 5:781
Kessler-Harris, Alice, 3:504,
3:515, 3:556
Kessner, Thomas, 4:640
Kesterson, David B., 1:677,
1:784
Ketcham, Charles B., 3:831
Ketcham, Michael G., 1:232,
1:257
Ketcham, Ralph, 3:161
Ketcham, Ralph L., 1:628
Ketchum, Robert Glenn,
3:894
Ketner, Kenneth L., 4:249,
4:282
Kettani, M. Ali, 4:570
Kette, Dragotin, 2:834
Ketten-Cremer, R. W., 1:248
Kettering, Emil, 4:294
Kettl, Donald F., 3:65
Kettle, Arnold, 1:208, 1:421
Ketz, Louise B., 3:509

Keul, M. K., 3:272
Kevles, Bettyann, 5:770
Kevles, Daniel J., 5:48,
    5:651, 5:677, 5:782
Kevorkian, Jack, 5:378
Key, V. O., Jr., 3:155
Keyes, Charles F., 3:490
Keyes, Claire, 1:1037
Keynes, Geoffrey, 1:451,
    1:543
Keynes, John Maynard,
    1:542, 1:569, 3:45, 3:83,
    3:85, 3:90, 3:92, 3:94,
    3:101, 3:104, 4:321
Keynes, John Neville, 3:46
Keynes, Sir Geoffrey, 5:362
Keyser, Herbert H., 5:355
Keyssar, Helene, 1:1074
Keyt, David, 4:69
Khadduri, M., 4:895
Khalidi, Tarif, 3:443
Khalifah, Sahar, 2:59
al-Khalil, Samir, 3:449
Khamsong Srinawk, 2:336
Khan, Mahmood, 3:890
Khan, Mohammad S., 3:443
Khanaad, Prayad S. Naa,
    2:337
Khanh, Huynh Kim, 3:490
Khanin, Yakov I., 5:697
Kharrat, Idwar, 2:59
Khatibi, Abdelkebir, 2:122
Khatri, Linda A., 5:217
Khaver-Paver, 2:39
Khayyam, Omar. *See*·Omar
    Khayyam
Kherdian, David, 1:913
**Khlebnikov, Velimir (Vik-
    tor), 2:731**
Khomeini, Imam, 4:579
Khosla, Jawaharlal, 3:904
Khouri, Fred J., 3:436
Khouri, Mounah A., 2:55,
    2:57
Khrakhuni, Zareh, 2:76
Khruschev, Nikita S., 3:396
**Khukrit Pramoj, 2:335,
    2:336**
Khumayni, Ruh A., 3:443
Khuri, Ilyas, 2:59
Khuri, Raif, 3:443
Khuyen, Nguyen, 2:338
Kibee, Josephine Z., 3:11
Kiberd, Declan, 1:556
Kibler, James E., Jr., 1:918
Kibre, Pearl, 4:153
Kidd, Alan J., 3:364
Kidd, Beresford J., 4:681
Kidd, I. G., 4:56
Kidd, Ronald, 3:859
Kidder, Rushworth M., 1:557
Kidder, Tracy, 3:250, 5:154,
    5:537

Kidson, Frank, 3:852
Kieckhefer, Richard, 4:505,
    4:513, 4:526, 4:696
Kieffer, William F., 5:734
Kieft, Lester, 5:753
Kiell, Norman, 5:422
Kielland, Alexander, 2:662
Kiely, Robert, 1:270
Kiener, Ronald C., 4:630
Kier, Kathleen E., 1:689
Kieran, J. A., 3:422
Kierkegaard, Søren, 2:637,
    2:644, 2:652, 2:870, 4:207,
    4:238, 4:261, 4:299, 4:328,
    4:334, 4:366, 4:757, 4:771
Kiernan, Brian, 2:968
Kiernan, Kevin S., 1:144
Kiernan, Robert F., 1:465,
    1:474, 1:910, 1:1062
Kiernan, Thomas P., 4:14
Kiersch, George A., 5:636
Kiestra, D. H., 2:634
Kightly, Charles, 3:855
Kihlman, Christer, 2:659
Kilbourn, William, 3:613
Kilbridge, Janet, 3:201
Kilcullen, John, 4:164, 4:166
Killam, G. D., 2:110, 2:129,
    2:152, 2:155
Killen, Harold B., 5:299,
    5:302, 5:303
Killens, John O., 1:921
Killham, John, 1:402
Killian, Lewis, 3:203
Killingsworth, M. Jimmie,
    1:707
Kilmister, Clive William,
    4:324, 5:681, 5:714
Kilpatrick, Anna, 3:863
Kilpatrick, Hilary, 2:55
Kilpatrick, Jack, 3:863
**Kilpatrick, William Heard,
    3:264**
Kilvington, Richard, 4:104
Kim, Chong-un, 2:298
Kim, Han-Kyo, 2:298
Kim, Jaihiun J., 2:299, 2:301
Kim, Jong-gil, 2:299
Kim, Key-Hiuk, 3:464
**Kim, Richard (Kim Ûn-
    guk),** 2:298, **2:304**
Kim, Uchang, 2:299
Kim, Won, 5:559
Kim, Young Ho, 2:301
Kimball, Arthur G., 2:282
Kimball, Robert, 3:709
Kimbell, David R. B., 3:670,
    3:727
Kimble, Daniel P., 3:168
Kimbrough, Emily, 3:899
**Kim Chi-ha (Kim Yong-il),
    2:303**
Kimel, Alvin F., 4:905

Kim Man-jung, 2:297, **2:304**
Kimpton, M. H., 3:55
Kimsma, Gerrit, 5:78
**Kim So-wôl (Kim Chông-
    shik),** 2:298, **2:305**
Kim Tong-ni, 2:298, **2:306**
Kincaid, Jamaica, 2:936
Kincaid, Suzanne, 1:836
Kincaid, Zoe, 2:273
Kindem, Gorham, 3:825
Kinder, Donald R., 3:811
Kindleberger, Charles P.,
    3:54, 3:58
King, Arthur, 1:45
King, B. Kay, 3:251
King, Bruce, 1:189, 2:930,
    2:939
King, Carolyn M., 5:771
King, Coretta S., 4:773
King, Cuchlaine A., 5:620
King, Francis, 1:477
King, Frank P., 3:495
King, H. H., 2:699, 4:100
King, Henry C., 5:32
King, J. E., 5:771
King, James, 1:238
King, Jeannette, 1:319
King, John N, 1:198, 4:726
King, Joseph H., 5:344
King, Karen L., 4:453
King, Kimball, 1:427, 1:684
King, Larry, 5:220, 5:266
King, Lester S., 5:42, 5:44,
    5:54, 5:78, 5:313
King, Martha, 2:403
King, Martin Luther, Jr.,
    1:700, 1:941, 2:763, 4:561,
    4:762, **4:771**
King, Mary C., 1:556
King, Peter, 2:629, 4:180
King, Philip B., 5:643
King, Preston T., 4:134
King, Robert C., 5:760
King, Sallie B., 4:513, 4:530
King, Stephen, 1:599,
    1:1239, **1:1240**
King, Thomas H., 4:337
King, T. J., 1:218
King, Wayne, 5:760
King, Woodie, 1:799
King, Y., 3:279
Kingdon, John W., 3:146
Kingdon, Robert M., 4:732,
    4:734
King-Hele, Desmont, 1:303
Kinglake, Alexander, 3:925
Kingman, Daniel, 3:661
Kingman, Lee, 1:29, 1:52,
    1:1196
Kingsland, William, 4:853
Kingsley, Charles, 1:310,
    1:355, **1:368,** 1:574, 1:577,
    5:211

Kingsley, Mary, 3:909
Kingston, Beverley, 3:494
Kingston, Frederick T., 4:265
Kingston, Maxine (Ting Ting) Hong, 1:1000, 1:1094, 3:909
Kinkade, Richard P., 2:522
Kinkle, Roger D., 3:656
Kinkley, Jeffrey C., 2:234, 2:262
Kinmonth, Earl, 3:478
Kinnamon, Kenneth, 1:653, 1:717, 1:718, 1:725, 1:906
Kinnard, John, 1:291
Kinne, Wisner P., 1:1074
Kinnell, Galway, 1:1000
Kinnell, S. K., 3:273
Kinnell, Susan B., 3:8
Kinney, Arthur F., 1:197, 1:868, 1:1024, 2:413
Kinney, James, 1:723
Ki No Tsurayuki, 2:277
Kinross, Lord, 3:453
Kinsley, David R., 4:505, 4:530, 4:536
Kinsley, Helen, 1:242
Kinsley, James, 1:242
Kintanar, Thelma B., 2:311
Kinzer, Stephen, 3:637
Kinzie, Mary, 3:801
Kinzley, W. Dean, 3:478
Kiple, Kenneth F., 5:368
Kipling, Rudyard, 1:317, **1:369**, 1:423, 1:574, 1:586,1:592, 1:594
Kipnis, David, 5:154
Kippenhahn, Rudolf, 5:594
Kiralifalvi, Bela, 2:802
Kirby, David, 3:381, 3:382
Kirby, Richard, 5:126
Kirchhoff, Frederick, 1:383, 1:395
Kirevald, Barbara C., 5:771
Kirilov, Nikolai, 2:781
Kirk, Clara M., 1:759
Kirk, Frank, 2:781
Kirk, Geoffrey S., 2:52, 2:361, 4:50, 4:75
Kirk, Irina, 2:710
Kirk, Neville, 3:364
Kirk, Robert, 4:412
Kirk, Roger E., 5:522
Kirk, Rudolf, 1:759
Kirk, Russell., 3:152
Kirk, Ruth, 3:896
Kirkby, Joan, 2:946
Kirkconnell, Watson, 2:798, 2:838
Kirkeby, W. T., 3:729
Kirk-Greene, A., 3:421
Kirkham, Michael, 1:558
Kirkham, Richard L., 4:381
Kirkpatrick, B. J., 1:477

Kirkpatrick, Daniel, 1:920, 1:1074, 2:4
Kirkpatrick, Jane, 3:909
Kirkpatrick, R., 2:418
Kirkwood, G. M., 2:368
Kirkwood, Mossie M., 4:327
Kirmmse, Bruce, 4:240
Kirp, David L., 3:251
Kirsch, Sarah, 2:598
Kirsch, Thomas, 4:519
Kirschenbaum, Howard, 3:193
Kirschten, Robert, 1:967
Kirsh, Yoram, 5:663
Kirshenblatt-Gimblett, Barbara, 2:30, 4:635
Kirst, Hans Hellmut, 2:598
Kirstein, Lincoln, 3:732, 3:738, **3:745**
Kirtzeck, James, 4:567
Kirven, Robert, 4:852
Kirwan, Christopher, 4:110
Kiš, Danilo, 2:827, **2:830**
Kiser, Lisa J., 1:151
Kish, George, 3:119, 5:32, 5:620
Kish, Leslie, 3:7
Kishlansky, Mark A., 3:360
Kishon, Ephraim, 2:21
Kishwar, Madhu, 4:508
Kisker, George W., 5:427
Kissam, Philip, 5:224
Kissane, James D., 1:402
Kissinger, Henry A., 3:341, 3:539, 3:545
Kister, Kenneth F., 1:73
Kistiakowsky, George B., 5:182
Kistner, A. L., 1:190
Kitagawa, Joseph M., 3:474, 4:498, 4:509, 4:513, 4:516, 4:518, 4:519, 4:522, 4:530, 4:534, 4:535, 4:537, 4:542, 4:543, 4:570
Kitarō, Nishida. *See* Nishida Kitarō
Kitchen, Martin, 3:344
Kitchen, Philip, 4:385
Kitchener, Richard F., 4:383
Kitcher, Patricia, 4:206
Kitcher, Philip, 5:25, 5:63, 5:68, 5:493, 5:826
Kitson Clark, G.S.R., 1:312
Kittel, Charles, 5:668
Kittel, Gerhard, 4:818
Kittel, Muriel, 2:402
Kitto, Humphrey D., 2:346
Kitton, Frederic G., 1:350
Kittredge, George L., 1:151, 3:858
Kittredge, Mary, 5:388
Kittredge, William, 3:896

Kitzinger, Celia, 1:1182, 3:218
Kitzinger, Rachel, 3:298, 4:439
Kitzinger, Sheila, 5:358
Kiver, Eugene P., 5:626
Kivi, Alexis, 2:657
Kivy, Peter, 3:661, 4:203
Kizer, Carolyn, 1:1001, 2:235
Kí-Zerbo, G., 3:416
Kjetsaa, Geir, 2:715
Klaassen, Walter, 4:724
Klagsbrun, Francine, 4:598
Klancher, Jon, 1:265
Klaniczay, Tibor, 2:798
Klass, Morton, 4:872
Klass, Perri, 5:336
Klass, Philip J., 5:598
Klatell, Jack, 5:341
Klauder, Francis J., 4:21
Klaus, Marshall H., 5:358
Klaus, Phyllis H., 5:358
Klauser, Theodor, 4:678
Klausner, Carla L., 3:435
Klausner, Joseph, 4:604
Klayman, Richard, 4:640
Klebaner, Benjamin J., 3:548
Kleberg, Lars, 2:687
Klehr, Harvey, 3:535
Klein, A(braham) M(oses), 2:915
Klein, Ann, 4:543
Klein, Barbro S., 3:855
Klein, Christian Felix, 5:486, **5:510**
Klein, D. B., 5:35
Klein, Dennis A., 1:544
Klein, Ernest, 1:96
Klein, Ethel, 3:207
Klein, George de Vries, 5:241
Klein, H. Arthur, 3:771
Klein, Herbert S., 3:633
Klein, Holger Michael, 1:537
Klein, Isaac, 4:602
Klein, Jacob, 4:81
Klein, Juliet, 1:246
Klein, Lawrence Robert, 3:63, **3:87**
Klein, Leonard S., 1:131, 2:3, 2:447
Klein, Marcus, 1:918
Klein, Melanie, 5:456
Klein, Miles V., 5:666
Klein, Norma, 1:1195
Klein, S. A., 5:284
Kleiner, Morris M., 3:59
Kleinig, John, 5:121
Kleinz, J., 4:102
Kleist, Heinrich von, 2:563, **2:598**, 2:616
Klejment, Alice, 4:765

Klejment, Anne, 4:765
Klemin, Diana, 1:29
Klemke, E. D., 4:22, 4:312
Klemm, David E., 4:319
Klemm, Friedrich, 5:37
Klenicki, Leon, 4:898
Kleper, Michael L., 5:561
Klepfiscz, Heszel, 4:636
Kletz, Trevor A., 5:244
Klevar, Harvey L., 1:819
Klickstein, Herbert S., 5:32
Kliebard, Herbert, 3:256
Klieman, Charles, 5:374
Kliever, Lonnie D., 4:719
Klima, Vladimir, 2:110
Klimenko, Michael, 2:717
Klimo, Jon, 4:866
Klimoff, Alexis, 2:761
Klinck, Carl F., 2:904, 3:605, 3:618
Kline, George L., 3:394, 4:188, 4:342
Kline, Morris, 5:31, 5:481, 5:490, 5:492
Kline, Paul, 5:448
Kline, Thomas J., 2:488
Klineberg, Otto, 3:174, 3:188
Kling, August, 3:917
Klinkowitz, Jerome, 1:911, 1:918, 1:944, 1:1064
Klipper, Miriam Z., 5:401
Kliuchevskii, Vasilii O., 3:394, 3:395
Kloe, Donald R., 1:93
Kloepfer, Deborah K., 1:827
Kloesel, Christian, 4:249
Klopp, Charles, 2:415
Klose, Kevin, 3:396
Klostermeier, Klaus K., 4:505
Klosty, James, 3:740
Klotman, Phyllis R., 3:867
Kluback, William, 2:513, 4:663
Klug, Eugene F., 4:730
Klug, William S., 5:778
Kluge, Pamela Hollie, 3:807
Kluger, Richard, 3:556, 3:807
Knapp, Bettina L., 1:693, 1:743, 1:866, 1:883, 2:452, 2:468, 2:469, 2:479, 2:518, 3:834
Knapp, Bliss, 4:843
Knapp, Gerhard Peter, 5:451
Knapp, Herbert, 3:869
Knapp, Mary, 3:869
Knapp, Peggy, 1:151
Kneale, Martha, 4:97
Kneale, William, 4:97
Knechtges, David R., 2:193, 2:230
Knei-Paz, B., 3:295
Knerr, Anthony D., 1:303
Knickerbocker, K. L., 1:339

Knief, Ronald A., 5:240
Knight, Alan, 3:638
Knight, Alanna, 1:397
Knight, David, 5:11
Knight, Douglas A., 4:814
Knight, Frank Hyneman, 3:47, 3:88
Knight, Franklin W., 3:626
Knight, G. Wilson, 1:213, 1:215
Knight, James W., 5:320
Knight, Roger, 1:522
Knights, Ben, 1:325
Knill, Harry, 3:863
Knipe, Daniel M., 4:884
Knipe, David M., 4:505
Knitter, Paul, 4:898
Knoepflmacher, U. K., 1:301
Knoerle, Jeanne, 2:223
Knoll, Robert E., 1:184, 1:1018
Knorr, Wilbur, 5:504
Knorr-Cetina, Karin, 5:154
Knowles, A. V., 2:766, 2:770
Knowles, David, 3:355, 3:357, 4:94, 4:696, 4:699, 4:721, 5:39
Knowles, Malcolm M., 3:256
Knowles, Owen, 1:464
Knowles, Sebastian D., 1:421
Knox, Bernard M., 2:345, 2:368, 4:46
Knox, John, 4:729, 4:735, 4:773, 5:579
Knox, Paul, 3:122
Knox, Ronald A., 4:737
Knuth, Donald E., 5:550, 5:562
Knutson, Harold C., 2:490
Knutson, Roslyn L., 1:218
Kobayashi, Takiji, 2:283
Kobayashi Issa, 2:278, 2:280
Kobler, Franz, 4:594, 4:636
Kobler, Jasper F., 2:979
Kōbō, Abe. See Abe Kōbō
Kobrak, Fred, 1:50
Kocbek, Edvard, 2:835
Koch, Adrienne, 3:161
Koch, (Jay) Kenneth, 1:911, 1:935, 1:1001, 1:1025
Koch, Klaus, 4:815, 4:823
Koch, Robert, 5:800
Koch, Sigmund, 3:167, 3:168
Koch, Tom, 3:807, 5:317
Koch, William E., 3:862
Kochan, Lionel, 3:349, 3:394, 4:636
Kochanovski, Jan, 2:809
Kocher, Paul H., 1:187
Kockelmans, Joseph J., 4:235, 4:293, 5:91
Kodjak, Andrej, 2:752
Kodras, Janet, 3:122

Koegler, Horst, 3:731
Koenig, Louis W., 3:147
Koenigsberger, Dorothy, 4:127
Koenigsberger, H. G., 3:336
Koeph, Herbert H., 5:266
Koepke, Wulf, 3:286, 4:199
Koerner, Konrad, 3:40
Koestenbaum, Wayne, 1:1182
Koester, Helmut, 4:449, 4:807, 4:816, 4:825
Koestler, Arthur, 4:161, 5:42, 5:193, 5:568, 5:608
Koff, Roberta G., 3:803
Koffka, Kurt, 3:177
Kogan, Barry S., 4:581, 4:895
Kogan, Norman, 3:385
Kogos, Fred, 1:103
Koh, Hesung Chun, 3:463
Kohak, Erazim, 5:115
Kohfeldt, Mary Lou, 1:490
Kohl, Benjamin G., 4:127
Kohl, Herbert, 3:251
Kohl, Wilfrid L., 3:279, 5:284
Kohler, Wolfgang, 3:177
Kohlman, Bernard, 5:485
Kohn, Gary J., 4:640
Kohn, Hans, 3:286, 3:288, 3:341, 3:377, 3:405
Kohn, Ingrid, 5:358
Kohn, Livia, 4:528
Kohn, Melvin L., 3:214, 3:215
Kohout, Pavel, 2:793
Kohr, Leopold, 3:342
Koht, Halvdan, 2:666, 3:381
Kohut, Heinz, 5:457
Koita, Mamadou, 2:126
Kojève, Alexandre, 4:233
Kökeritz, Helge, 1:216
Kolakowski, Leszek, 4:220
Kolar, Walter W., 3:392
Kolas, Jakub, 2:783
Kolb, David, 4:293, 5:91
Kolb, Harold H., Jr., 1:714, 1:723
Kolb, W. J., 3:4, 3:272
Kolchin, Peter, 3:524
Kolenda, Konstantin, 4:17, 4:34, 4:325, 4:413
Kolesnikoff, Nina, 2:767
Kolig, Erich, 4:467
Kolin, Phillip C., 1:1074
Koljević, Svetozar, 2:827
Kolker, Robert P., 3:828
Kollar, Jan, 2:788
Kollek, Teddy, 3:440
Koller, John M., 4:349, 4:351, 4:498, 4:522, 4:523, 4:570
Koller, Patricia, 4:498, 4:522
Kolmerten, Carol A., 4:844
Kolmogrorov, A. N., 5:480

Kolneder, Walter, 3:727, 3:730
Kolodny, Annette, 1:714, 3:518, 3:550
Koloski, Bernard, 1:740
Kolsky, Thomas A., 4:658
Koltun, Elizabeth, 4:650
Kolve, Carolee N., 5:556
Kolve, V. A., 1:151, 1:159
Komenský, Jan Amos, 2:788
Komo, John J., 5:302
Komonchak, Joseph, 4:4
Komroff, Manuel, 3:934
Kondo, Dorinne K., 3:22
Konecsni, Johnemery, 4:22
Koneski, Blaže, 2:807, **2:808**
Kongas-Maranda, Elli Kaija, 3:855
Konishi, Jin'ichi, 2:272
Konner, Melvin, 5:334, 5:336
Konstan, David, 2:381
Konuma, M., 5:717
Konwicki, Tadeusz, 2:815
Koon, George W., 3:871
Koontz, Dean, 1:1239, **1:1241**
Koonz, Claudia, 3:326
Koop, C. Everett, 5:314, 5:334
Koopmans, Tjalling C., 3:47
Kooyman, Mary, 3:491
Kopeck, Ronald F., 5:560
Kopf, David, 4:355
Kopit, Arthur, 1:1098
Kopitar, Jernej, 2:834
Kopper, Edward A., 1:490, 1:556
Koprowski, Hilary, 5:409, 5:809
Kopytoff, Igor, 3:418, 3:419
Korall, Burt, 3:669
Korbel, Josef, 3:389
Korchin, Sheldon, 5:419
Kordi, Gohar, 3:448
Korg, Jacob, 1:339, 1:415, 1:557
Korn, Francis, 3:34
Korn, I., 5:302
Korn, Rokhl (Rachel), 2:29, **2:39**
Kornai, Janos, 3:52
Kornberg, Jacques, 2:13
Kornbluth, Cyril, 1:1252
Korner, Stephan, 5:493
Kornhauser, A., 5:107
Kornhauser, William, 3:143, 3:202
Korolenko, Vladimir, 2:732
Korom, Frank J., 4:503
Korsch, Karl, 4:243
Korson, George G., 3:859
Korte, Diana, 5:359
Kortepeter, C. Max, 3:453

Korth, Henry F., 5:560
Koschmann, J. Victor, 3:475, 3:479
Kosinski, Jerzy, 1:1002
Kositsky, Ann, 5:322
Koskoff, Ellen, 3:666
Kosmač, Ciril, 2:834
Kosofsky, Rita N., 1:1014
Kosok, Heinz, 1:527
Kosovel, Srečko, 2:834
Koss, Stephen, 3:366
Kossmann, Ernst H., 3:380
Kosso, Peter, 5:63
Kostelanetz, Richard, 1:421, 1:883, 1:911, 1:921, 3:686, 3:740
Kosters, Marvin H., 3:60
Kostić, Laza, 2:827
Kostiner, Joseph, 3:451
Kostis, Nicholas, 2:482
Kostof, Spiro, 3:762
Koszarski, Richard, 1:1177
Koszegi, Michael A., 4:6, 4:7
Kotei, S. I., 2:110
Kotkin, Amy J., 3:857
Kotlyarevski, Ivan, 2:837
Kotsakis, D., 5:654
Kott, Jan, 1:209
Kotwal, Firoze M., 4:517, 4:547
Kotz, Samuel, 5:520, 5:522
Koubourlis, Demetrius J., 2:738
Kouchag, Nahabed, 2:79
Koury, Enver M., 3:448
Kousser, J. Morgan, 3:603
Kovach, Francis, 4:107
Kovach, Joseph K., 3:167
Kovacs, Diane, 5:548
Kovacs, Maureen Gallery, 4:545
Kovel, Joel, 5:419
Kovtun, George J., 2:789, 2:833
Kowalk, Wolfgang, 1:252
Kowalski, Robert E., 5:374
Kowateski-Wallace, Beth, 1:717
Kowles, Richard V., 5:778
Koyré, Alexandre, 3:163, 4:81, 4:128, 4:143, 4:161, 5:42, 5:656
Kozak, Ellen M., 1:54
Kozelka, Paul, 1:1078
Kozicki, Henry, 1:402
Kozloff, Sarah, 3:825
Kozol, Jonathan, 3:211, 3:251
Kozu, Toshiaka, 5:633
Kra, Siegfried J., 5:336, 5:374, 5:405
Kraay, Colin, 3:306
Kraeling, Carl H., 4:614
Kraeling, E. G., 4:813

Kraemer, David, 4:620, 4:627
Kraemer, Ross S., 4:449, 4:892
Kraft, Elizabeth, 1:230
Kraft, Kenneth, 4:537, 4:538
Kraft, Michael E., 5:154
Kraft, Richard J., 3:258
Kraft, Robert A., 4:615, 4:814
Kraft, R. Wayne, 4:337
Kragh, Helge S., 5:680
Krahn, Cornelius, 4:780
Krakauer, Jon, 3:909
Kramarae, Cheris, 5:188
Kramer, Aaron, 1:655, 2:34
Kramer, E. E., 5:481
Krämer, Hans Joachim, 4:81
Kramer, Jack, 5:767
Kramer, Jane, 1:981, 3:346
Kramer, Jonathan D., 3:661
Kramer, Lawrence, 2:988
Kramer, Leonie, 2:946
Kramer, Mark, 5:314
Kramer, Peter, 5:121
Kramer, Rita, 3:266
Kramer, Samuel Noah, 2:52, 4:428, 4:439, 4:440, 4:441, 4:545, 4:546
Kramer, Victor A., 1:794, 1:1029
Kramers, J. H., 3:443, 4:566
Krampen, M., 3:206
Kranjčević, Silvije Strahimir, 2:785
Krantz, David, 5:339
Kranzberg, Melvin, 3:326, 5:37, **5:51,** 5:129, **5:166**
Krasilovsky, M. William, 3:657
Krasiński, Zygmunt, 2:810, **2:815**
Krasko, Ivan, 2:832
Krasovskaya, Vera, 3:749
Kraszewski, Józef, 2:810
Kraus, Hans-Joachim, 4:821, 4:823
Kraus, Hans Peter, 1:42
Kraus, Michael, 3:338, 3:515, 4:282
Kraus, Richard G., 3:731
Kraus, T., 3:304
Krause, Sydney J., 1:784
Krauskopf, Konrad B., 5:628
Kraussz, Michael, 4:381
Krausz, Ernest, 3:440
Kraut, Richard, 4:69, 4:81, 4:89
Krautheimer, Richard, 4:684
Kravitz, Leonard, 4:668
Kravitz, Nathaniel, 2:9
Krebs, D., 3:170
Krebs, Hans Adolf, 5:801
Kreeft, Peter J., 4:23, 4:777
Kreider, Jan F., 5:289

Kreiger, Murray, 1:215
Kreiswirth, Martin, 1:837, 1:1134
Kreith, Frank, 5:289
Kreitman, Esther, 2:40, 2:47
Krejci, Jaroslav, 3:389
Krell, David F., 4:293
Kren, Claudia, 5:28
Kresh, Paul, 1:1050, 2:49
Kress, Stephen W., 5:760
Krettek, Thomas, 4:340
Kretzmann, Norman, 4:94, 4:95, 4:104, 4:119, 4:696
Kreuder, Manfred, 5:730
Krêvê, Vincas (Mickievičius), 2:804, **2:806**
Kreyche, Gerald F., 4:17
Kreyling, Michael, 1:896
Kreymborg, Alfred, 1:655
Kribbs, Jayne K., 1:709
Kridl, Manfred, 2:811, 2:817
Krieger, Leonard, 4:186
Krieger, Murray, 1:422, 1:977
Krier, Theresa M., 1:198
Krikorian, Yervant H., 4:265
Krimm, Bernard G., 1:572
Krimsky, Sheldon, 5:75, 5:782
Kring, Hilda A., 4:844
Krinsky, Carol Herselle, 4:597
Kripke, Saul, 4:300
Krippner, Stanley, 5:419
Kris, Ernst, 5:425
Krishan, V., 5:667
Krishnaiah, Paruchuri R., 5:526
Krishnamurti, Jiddu, 4:549, **4:554**, 4:858
Kristeller, Paul Oskar, 2:401, 4:30, 4:55, 4:128, 4:141, 4:697
Kristeva, Julia, 1:1141, 2:447, 3:21
Kristic, R. V., 5:773
Kritzeck, James, 2:57
Kritzer, Amelia Howe, 1:459
Krivatsy, Nati H., 1:22
Krleža, Miroslav, 2:785, **2:786**
Kroeber, Alfred L., 3:13, 3:17, 3:28, **3:32**
Kroeber, Karl, 1:270
Kroeber, Theodora, 3:33
Kroetsch, Robert, 2:915
Kroger, William S., 5:419
Krogh, David, 5:404
Krohn, Julius, 3:846, **3:882**, 3:887
Krohn, Kaarle, 3:846, **3:882**, 3:887
Krohn, Wolfgang, 5:214
Krois, John M., 4:280

Krol, Ed, 5:547
Kroll, Paul W., 2:215
Kronberg, Ruthhilde, 3:848
Kronenberger, Louis, 3:362
Kronenfeld, Jennie J., 5:333
Kronick, David A., 5:28
Kropf, Richard W., 4:337
Kropfinger, Klaus, 3:728
Kropotkin, Peter, 2:687
Krueger, Richard A., 3:7
Kruglinski, David, 5:560
Krugman, Paul, 3:62
Krugovoy, George, 2:706
Krull, Marianne, 5:448
Krummel, Donald W., 1:61, 3:656
Krupat, Arnold, 1:631, 1:632, 1:714, 1:727
Krupp, E. C., 4:434
Krupp, Edwin C., 5:590
Krushchev, N. S., 3:292
Kruskal, William H., 5:521
Krutch, Joseph Wood, 1:702, 5:139, 5:252, 5:626, **5:833**
Krych, Steven M., 5:396
Krystutek, Zdenek, 3:389
Kryzytski, Serge, 2:707
Krzyzanowski, Julian, 2:811
Krzyzanowski, Ludwik, 2:811
Kuan-chung, Lo, 2:218
Kuan Han-ch'ing, 2:203, 2:209, 2:263
Kubach, Han Erich, 3:763
Kubal, David L., 1:531
Kubayanda, Josaphat B., 2:110
Kubitschek, Missy D., 1:804
Kubler, George A., 1:17
Kübler-Ross, Elisabeth, 5:379, 5:422
Kubo, Sakae, 4:798
Kubrick, Stanley, 1:614, **3:839**
Kuc, Roman, 5:296
Kucich, John, 1:319
Kuebrich, David, 1:707
Kuechler, Manfred, 3:141
Kuehl, John, 1:840, 1:978, 1:986
Kuehn, Robert E., 1:500
Kuehn, Thomas J., 5:182
Kuenne, Robert E., 3:57, 3:64
Kuenzli, Rudolf E., 2:463
Kugel, James L., 4:814
Kuhn, Annette, 1:1157
Kuhn, Hilde, 1:24
Kuhn, Philip A., 3:468
Kuhn, Thomas S(amuel), 3:213, 4:383, 4:399, **4:406**, 4:409, 5:25, 5:42, 5:48, **5:52**, 5:61, 5:66, 5:93,

5:147, 5:155, 5:572, 5:573, 5:602
Kuhns, William, 5:71
Kuhrt, Amelie, 3:309
Ku Hua, 2:249
Kuietenbrouwer, Maarten, 3:382
Kuiper, Pieter C., 5:427
Kuisel, Richard F., 3:373
Kuitert, H. M., 4:744
Kuizenga, Donna, 2:484
Kujoth, Jean S., 1:50, 1:51, 3:871
Kukathas, Chandran, 4:316
Kuklick, Bruce, 4:34, 4:265
Kulik, Stephen, 5:760
Kulikoff, Allan, 3:518, 3:548
Kuliš, Mykola, 2:837, **2:839**
Ķuliš, Pantelejmon (also Kulish), 2:839
Kulkarni, Hemant Balvantrao, 1:553
Kulkarni, V. M., 4:509
Kulke, Eckehard, 4:518
Kumar, Krishnan, 3:217
Kumar, Nita, 4:508
Kumar, Shiv K., 1:422
Kumar, Shrawan, 5:244
Kümmel, Werner G., 4:814, 4:815, 4:816
Kummings, Donald D., 1:707
Kumove, Shirley, 2:32
Kundera, Milan, 1:1040, 2:788, **2:793**
Kunene, Mazisi, 2:164
Kunetka, James W., 5:707
Küng, Hans, 4:423, **4:774**, 4:887
Kung, Shain-dow, 5:222
Kunhardt, Philip B., 3:528
Kunitz, Stanley (Jasspon), 1:714, **1:1003**, 1:1196, 2:3, 2:4
Kunitz, Stephen J., 5:353
Kunsoo, Kim, 5:245
Kunst, Jaap, 3:666
Kunt, M., 5:302
Kuntz, Marian Leathers, 4:128
Kuntz, Marion, 4:303
Kuntz, Paul G., 4:303, 4:324, 4:342
Kunzer, Ruth G., 2:801
Kuo Mo-jo, 2:249
Kuong, Javier F., 5:556
Kuo-wei, Wang, 2:186
Kupala, Janka, 2:783
Kuper, Adam, 3:5
Kuper, Hilda, 3:26
Kuper, Jessica, 3:5
Kuper, Leo, 3:39, 3:205
Kupersmith, Judith, 3:745
Kuprin, Aleksandr, 2:732

Kuralt, Charles, 3:909
Kurian, George Thomas,
1:88, 3:483
Kurosawa, Akira, 2:285,
3:824, **3:839**
Kurpershoek, P. M., 2:65
Kursunoglu, Behram, 5:214
Kurtén, Bjorn, 5:639, 5:764
Kurth, Willi, 3:774
Kurtz, Barbara E., 2:533
Kurtz, Bruce D., 1:1165
Kurtz, Paul, 4:298
Kurtz, Thomas E., 5:552
Kurzweil, Baruch, 2:16
Kurzweil, Edith, 1:925
Kurzweil, Ray, 3:174
Kurzweil, Zvi, 4:654
Kuschner, David S., 3:267
Kush, Thomas, 1:514
Kushigian, Julia Alexis,
2:857, 2:884
Kushma, John J., 3:524
Kushner, Aleksandr, 2:733
Kushner, David Z., 4:277
Kushner, Lawrence, 4:630
Kussi, Peter, 2:789, 2:833
Kustanovich, Konstantin,
2:698
Kustas, George L., 4:47
Kutcher, Arthur, 3:440
Kutler, Stanley I., 3:539
Kutner, Marc L., 5:653
Kutsch, K. J., 3:656, 3:672
Kutscher, Austin, 5:379
Kuyk, Dirk, Jr., 1:837
Kuzdin, Alan E., 5:417
Kuzmin, Mikhail, 2:733
Kuznets, Lois R., 1:584
Kuznets, Simon Smith,
3:51, 3:53, 3:66, **3:89**
Kvaerne, Per, 4:543
Kwakernaak, Huibert, 5:299
Kwame, Safro, 4:369
Kwang-chung, Yü, 2:235
Kwitny, Jonathan, 3:545
5:344
Kybett, Harry, 5:230
Kyburg, Henry E., Jr., 5:60,
5:64
Kyd, Thomas, 1:184, 1:194
Kyi, Aung San Suu. See
Aung San Suo Kyi
Kyle, David T., 5:129
Kyle, Richard, 4:841

L

La Bahn, Kathleen J., 2:612
Laban, Rudolf, 3:746
Labanyi, Jo, 2:525
Labaree, Benjamin W., 3:361

Labarre, E. J., 1:5
LaBarre, Weston, 4:467
Labedz, Leopold, 2:687
Labella, Vincenzo, 3:788
Labelle, Charles, 5:556
LaBelle, Jenijoy, 1:1038
Labor, Earle, 1:775
Laboucheix, Henri, 4:211
Labov, William, 3:21
Labrie, Ross, 1:1021
Labrousse, Elizabeth, 4:166
Labuz, Ronald, 1:9
Labuza, Theodore P., 5:221,
5:267
Laby, T. H., 5:653
Lacan, Jacques, 1:1132,
2:982, **5:458**
LaCapra, Dominick, 1:1134
Lacey, A. R., 4:3, 4:14, 4:220
Lacey, Robert, 5:247
Lacey, W. K., 3:309
Lach, Donald F., 3:335
La Charité, Raymond, 4:146
Lachs, John, 4:22
Lack, Elizabeth, 5:758
Lackey, Douglas P., 5:111
Lackie, J. M., 5:760, 5:775
Laclau, Ernesto, 1:1132
**Laclos, Pierre Ambroise
François Choderlos de,
2:484**
Lacoff, Cheryl Klein, 4:854
Lacoue-Labarthe, Phillippe,
4:293
Lacouture, Jean, 2:340
LaCugna, Catherine M, 4:775
Lacy, Dan M., 1:50
Lacy, Edward A., 5:303
Lacy, Norris J., 2:467
Ladd, Everett, Jr., 3:543
Ladd, George T., 4:22
**Ladd-Franklin, Christine,
3:189**
**Lady Hong of Hyegyông
Palace,** 2:297, **2:301**
Laeuchli, Samuel, 4:689
La Farge, Ann, 1:883
LaFargue, Michael, 4:528
**Lafayette, Marie Madeleine
de la Vergne, Comtesse
de, 2:484**
LaFeber, Walter, 3:279,
3:513, 3:532, 3:545, 3:631,
3:640
Laffan, R. G., 3:392
LaFleur, William R., 2:272,
4:513, 4:520
LaFollette, Marcel C., 5:10,
5:64, 5:155
La Fontaine, Jean de,
1:889, **2:484**
Lafore, Laurence, 3:344
Lafore, Robert, 5:554

Lagercrantz, Olof, 2:680
**Lagerkvist, Pär (Fabian),
2:675**
**Lagerlöf, Selma (Ottiliana
Lovisa),** 2:608, 2:671,
2:676
Lago, Mary M., 2:183
La Guma, Alex, 2:164
Lahee, Frederic H., 5:636
Lahey, Benjamin B., 5:416
Lahr, John, 1:530
Lai, T. C., 3:670
Laidler, David E., 3:65
Laing, Jennifer, 3:356
Laing, Lloyd, 3:356
**Laing, R(onald) D(avid),
5:459,** 5:460
Laird, Charlton G., 1:94,
3:862
Laistner, Max, 4:100, 4:699
Laistner, M.M.W., 3:303
Laithwaite, Eric, 5:227
Laitin, David D., 4:467
Lajolo, Davide, 2:433
Lakatos, Imre, 5:53, 5:66,
5:493
Lake, David A., 3:59
Lake, E., 3:317
Lake, Kirsopp, 4:704
Lakoff, George, 3:21
Lakshin, Vladimir, 2:762
Lal, P., 2:172, 2:173
Lalić, Ivan V., 2:827
Lalla, Barbara, 2:931
Lama, Dalai. See Tenzin
Gyatso
La Mar, Virginia A., 1:206
**Lamarck, Jean Baptiste,
5:802**
Lamartine, Alphonse-Marie-
Louis de Prat, 2:531
Lamb, Charles, 1:197, 1:264,
1:273, 1:285, 1:290, 1:292,
1:295, 1:677
Lamb, David, 5:64
Lamb, Jonathan, 1:259
Lamb, Matthew L., 4:744
**Lamb, Willis Eugene, Jr.,
5:697**
Lamberg-Karlovsky, C. C.,
4:439, 4:454
Lambert, Audrey M., 3:383
Lambert, Douglas M., 1:49
Lambert, Karel, 5:64
Lambert, Malcolm, 4:699,
4:721
Lambert, Mark, 5:267
Lambert, Steve, 5:547, 5:554
Lambert, Wilfred G., 2:53
Lamberti, Jean-Claude, 3:165
Lambert-Legace, Louise,
5:348

Lamberton, Robert, 2:358, 4:482, 4:483
Lamborn, Kathleen R., 5:524
Lambright, W. Henry, 5:182
Lambropoulos, V., 2:371
Lambton, Ann K. S., 3:416, 3:419
Lamm, Martin, 2:680
Lamm, Maurice, 4:602
Lammens, Henri, 4:575
Lammers, Stephen E., 4:893, 5:121, 5:124
Lammers, Susan, 5:542
Lammers, William W., 5:317
Lamming, George, 2:936
Lamont, Corliss, 4:225
Lamont, Rosette C., 2:484
Lamoreaux, Naomi, 3:548
Lamotte, Etienne, 4:513
L'Amour, Angelique, 1:1216
L'amour, Louis Dearborn, 1:1209, 1:1210, **1:1215**
Lampe, Kenneth F., 5:311, 5:760
Lampedusa, Giuseppe Tomasi, 2:407, **2:423**, 2:438
Lampel, Zvi L., 4:627
Lampert, Catherine, 3:791
Lampert, Laurence, 4:247
Lamphere, Louise, 3:25
Lampo, Hubert, 2:621, **2:627**
Lamprecht, Sterling P., 4:17, 4:161
Lampton, Christopher, 5:588
Lamson, Peggy, 3:79
Lancashire, Ian, 5:562
Lancaster, Don, 5:550
Lancaster, F. Wilfrid, 5:544
Lancaster, H. Carrington, 2:447
Lancaster, Henry O., 5:521
Lancaster, John, 1:17
Lancaster, Lewis R., 4:534
Lance, James W., 5:392
Lanctôt, Gustave, 3:613
Land, Stephen K., 4:29
Landau, Ellen G., 3:787
Landau, Jacob M., 4:644
Landau, Misia, 5:800
Landau, Ralph, 5:234
Landau, Sidney, 1:94, 5:760
Landeira, Ricardo, 2:525
Landen, Robert G., 3:436
Lander, J. R., 3:358
Lander, Mary K., 4:91
Landes, David S., 3:446, 5:37, 5:231
Landess, Thomas H., 1:983
Landis, Joseph C., 2:34
Landman, Leo, 4:621
Landon, Grelun, 3:658, 3:853
Landon, H. C. Robbins, 3:678, 3:700, 3:707

Landor, Walter Savage, 1:277, **1:296**, 1:397
Landow, George P., 1:325, 5:561, 5:562
Landrum, Larry N., 3:873
Landry, Donna, 1:227
Landsberg, Hans, 5:282
Landsberg, P. T., 5:650
Landsberger, Franz, 4:597
Landsbergis, Algirdas, 2:805, **2:806**
Landwehr, James M., 5:522
Landynski, Jacob W., 3:543
Lane, Anne J., 1:753, 3:566
Lane, Arthur E., 1:533
Lane, Calvin Warren, 1:562
Lane, David Christopher, 4:856, 4:872
Lane, Eugene N., 4:449, 4:682
Lane, Gary, 1:826, 1:1031
Lane, Harlan, 5:380, 5:422
Lane, Lauriat, 1:350
Lane, Margaret, 1:335, 1:589
Lane, Michael, 4:245
Lane, Robert E., 3:140
Lane-Poole, S., 4:570
Lanes, Douglas M., 5:377
Lanes, Selma, 1:32, 1:1206
Lang, Andrew, 1:32, 1:579, 2:359, 3:845, 3:881, **3:882**
Lang, Cecil Y., 1:316
Lang, David Marshall, 4:542
Lang, Denise, 5:377
Lang, D. M., 2:3
Lang, Fritz, 3:839
Lang, Helen S., 5:39
Lang, Kenneth R., 5:48, 5:588, 5:590
Lang, Mabel, 3:316, 4:480
Lang, Olga, 2:260
Lang, Paul H., 3:661, 4:737
Lang, Serge, 5:481, 5:490
Langan, Thomas, 4:294
Langbaum, Robert, 1:268, 1:315, 1:417, 2:649
Langendijk, Pieter, 2:620
Langenfeld, Robert, 1:381
Langenkamp, Robert D., 5:636
Langer, Jiri, 4:632
Langer, William L., 3:7, 3:273, 3:326, 3:341, 3:421
Langford, Gerald, 1:744, 1:757
Langford, Jerome J., 5:604, 5:688
Langford, Walter M., 2:846
Langguth, A. J., 1:523
Langhorne, Richard, 3:279
Langlais, Jacques, 4:644
Langland, Elizabeth, 1:1129

Langland, William, 1:140, **1:153**
Langley, Kathleen M., 3:450
Langley, Lester D., 3:631
Langley, Patrick, 5:542
Langman, Larry, 3:825
Langmuir, Irving, 5:667, 5:748
Lango, John W., 4:342
Langone, John, 5:338
Langone, Michael D., 4:857
Langston, Deborah P., 5:390
Langston, Douglas, 3:759
Langwell, W. H., 1:24
Lanier, Sidney, 1:717, **1:771**
Lanier-Graham, Susan D., 5:816
Lankford, Nelson D., 3:528
Lankton, Stephen R., 5:441
Lannie, Vincent P., 3:259
Lansbury, Coral, 1:407
Lansdown, Richard, 1:283
Lanson, Gustav, 4:218
Lantier, Raymond, 4:432
Lantz, Kenneth, 2:710, 2:736
Lanyon, Barbara P., 5:419
Lanyon, Richard I., 5:419
Lanza, Robert, 5:330
Lanzinger, Klaus, 1:904
Lao, Joseph S. M., 2:266
Laor, Nathaniel, 5:79
Lao She, 2:250
LaPalombra, Joseph, 3:385
Lapedes, Daniel N., 5:617
Lapeyrouse, Norton J., 5:241
Lapidge, Michael, 1:143
Lapidus, Ira M., 3:436, 4:570, 4:578
Lapierre, Dominique, 4:642
LaPin, Dierdre, 3:861
Lapine, James, 1:1079
Laplace, Marquis Pierre Simon de, 5:525, **5:530, 5:698**
LaPlante, Eve, 5:392
Lapointe, François H., 4:331, 4:346
Laporte, Jean, 4:679
Laporte, Leo, 5:639
Lapp, John C., 2:485
Lappe, Marc, 5:121, 5:351, 5:782
Lappin, Lou, 1:446
Laqueur, Thomas W., 1:312, 3:364
Laqueur, Walter, 3:346, 3:349, 3:377, 3:398, 4:658
LaQuey, Tracy, 5:547
Lardner, Ring(gold Wilmer), 1:852, 1:1096
Large, Brian, 3:720
Large, David C., 3:728
Large, Stephen S., 3:478

Larina, Anna, 3:397
Larkin, Colin, 3:656
Larkin, Emmet, 3:371
Larkin, Joan, 1:1183
Larkin, Philip, 1:414, 1:416, 1:418, 1:444, 1:466, **1:507,** 1:538
Larner, Robert J., 3:61
La Rochefoucauld, François, Duc de, 2:485
Laroui, Abdallah, 4:571
Larrabee, Eric, 3:535
Larremore, Thomas A., 1:42
Larrissy, Edward, 1:799, 1:913
Larsen, Erling, 1:933
Larsen, Karen, 4:730
Larsen, Marianne, 2:645
Larsen, Nella, 1:852, 1:1139
Larsen, Otto N., 3:801
Larsen, Paul, 5:238
Larsen, Richard J., 5:522
Larsen, Robin, 4:852, 4:880
Larson, Charles R., 2:110
Larson, David E., 5:311
Larson, Donald R., 2:555
Larson, Gary O., 3:560
Larson, Gerald James, 4:349
Larson, Judy L., 1:29
Larson, Robin, 3:877
Larson, Stephen, 3:877
Lartegue, Jean, 2:310
Lasagna, Louis, 5:79
Las Casas, Bartolomé de, 3:629
Lascelles, Mary, 1:276
Lasch, Christopher, 1:731, 3:543, 3:552, 3:560
Lash, Scott, 3:209, 3:211
Lasker, Daniel J., 4:629, 4:697
Lasker-Schuler, Else, 2:10
Laski, Harold J., 3:155
Lass, A. H., 1:118
Lasser, William, 3:145
Lassner, Phyllis, 1:448
Lasson, Kenneth, 5:226
Lasswell, Harold D., 3:156, 3:178
Last, Murray, 3:421
Last, Rex W., 2:607
Laszlo, Ervin, 4:31, 4:265
Lateiner, Donald, 3:316
Latham, Aaron, 3:904
Latham, David, 1:383
Latham, Peter, 3:684
Latham, R. E., 1:101
Latham, Sheila, 1:383
Latham, William, 5:194
Lathem, Edward C., 1:842
Lathi, B. P., 5:299
Latimer, Louise, 1:579
Latner, Joel, 5:465

Latour, Alessandra, 3:777
Latour, Bruno, 5:53, 5:93, **5:166**
Latourette, Kenneth Scott, 4:677, 4:720, 4:741
Lattimore, Eleanor, 3:904
Lattimore, Owen, 3:904
Lattimore, Richmond, 2:346, 2:359, 2:360
Lau, D. C., 4:528
Lau, Joseph S., 2:193, 2:235
Lauber, John, 1:300, 1:784
Lauda, Donald P., 5:227
Laudan, Larry, 5:64, 5:78
Laudan, Rachel, 5:64
Lauder, Robert E., 3:831
Laudon, Kenneth C., 5:125
Lauer, Kristin O., 1:788
Lauer, Rosemary, 4:218
Lauersen, Niels H., 5:355, 5:359
Laufer, Berthold, 4:523
Laufer, William S., 3:178
Laurence, Clifford A., 5:235
Laurence, Dan H., 1:546
Laurence, (Jean) Margaret (Wemyss), 2:903, **2:916,** 2:925
Laurent, Monique, 3:791
Laurie, Peter, 5:560
Lauritzen, Paul, 5:121
Lause, Kevin, 3:874
Lauter, Paul, 1:130, 1:653, 1:717, 1:911
Lauterbach, Jacob Z., 4:610
Laux, James M., 3:339
La Valley, Albert J., 1:1169
Lavender, David Sievert, 3:521, 3:928
Lavers, Annette, 2:455
Lavers, Norman, 1:1003
LaVey, Anton S., 4:868
Lavin, Bebe, 5:331
Lavoisier, Antoine Laurent, 5:44, 5:739, **5:748**
Lavrent'ev, M. A., 5:480
Lavrin, Asunción, 3:629
Law, F. M., 5:245
Law, John, 5:150
Lawall, Sarah, 1:925
Lawes, John B., 5:272
Lawler, James R., 2:466, 2:513
Lawler, John Lawrence, 1:45
Lawler, Philip F., 5:111
Lawless, Edward W., 5:155, 5:214
Lawless, Ray M., 3:852
Lawlor, Eric, 3:896, 3:904
Lawrance, Alan, 4:362
Lawrence, Ada, 1:510
Lawrence, Amy, 3:827
Lawrence, Bruce, 4:579

Lawrence, Clifford H., 3:331, 3:355, 4:699
Lawrence, Clifford L., 5:666
Lawrence, D(avid) H(erbert), 1:253, 1:413, 1:419, 1:475, **1:508,** 1:651, 1:714, 1:861, 1:1013, 2:427, 2:441, 2:878, 2:955, 4:321, 4:334
Lawrence, D. Baloti, 5:319
Lawrence, Gale, 5:761
Lawrence, John Shelton, 1:54
Lawrence, Nathaniel, 4:342
Lawrence, Peter, 4:467
Lawrence, Peter A., 5:778
Lawrence, Robert Z., 3:59
Lawrence, T(homas) E(dward), 3:925
Laws, Priscilla W., 5:397
Lawson, Alan, 2:947
Lawson, Alexander, 1:17
Lawson, E. Thomas, 4:884
Lawson, Joan, 3:731, 3:733
Lawson, John, 4:704
Lawson, Lewis A., 1:1029
Lawson, Richard H., 2:583
Lawson, Robert, 1:1194
Lawton, Anna, 2:692
Lax, Eric, 3:830
Laxalt, Robert, 3:899
Laxness, Halldór Kiljan, 2:640, **2:641,** 2:643
Layard, G. S., 1:585
Laye, Camara, 2:138
Layman, Emma M., 4:860
Layman, Richard, 1:918, 1:1230
Laymon, Charles M., 4:819
Layton, Bentley, 4:453
Layton, Edwin T., 5:26, 5:48, 5:129, 5:214
Layton, Irving, 2:917
Layton, Robert B., 5:650
Layzer, David, 5:655
Lazar, Moshe, 4:622
Lazarević, Laza K., 2:827
Lazarsfeld, Paul F(elix), 3:200, 3:203, **3:230**
Lazarus, Arnold A., 5:460
Lazarus, Emma, 1:718, **1:772**
Lazarus, Neil, 2:110
Lazenby, Walter, 1:388
Lazer, Hank, 1:1048
Lazerowitz, M., 4:22
Lazzarini, John, 3:750
Lazzarini, Roberta, 3:750
Lea, Henry C., 4:699
Lea, Sydney, 1:987
Leach, Edmund R., 3:19, 3:26, 3:34, 4:486
Leach, Eleanor W., 2:397
Leach, Jerry W., 4:486
Leach, MacEdward, 3:859

Leach, Maria, 3:849, 3:855
Leach, Penelope, 5:323
Leach, R., 3:852
Leach, R. H., 1:21
Leacock, Stephen (Butler),
2:918
Leacroft, Helen, 1:272
Leacroft, Richard, 1:272
Leacy, F. H., 3:605
Leadbetter, Edward R., 5:783
Leaf, Murray J., 3:11
Leafgren, Fred, 5:423
Leahey, Thomas H., 5:35
Leahy, Joann M., 5:358
Leahy, Thomas, 3:167
Leake, David, Jr., 3:492
Leakey, Louis S. B., 5:35
Leal, Luis, 2:854
Leal, Richard L., 3:635
Leaman, Oliver, 4:97, 4:575
Leaming, Barbara, 1:1179
Leapman, Michael, 3:807
Lear, Edward, 1:577, **1:586**,
1:1207
Lear, Jonathan, 4:69
Learmonth, A.T.A., 3:483
Lears, T. Jackson, 3:559,
3:560
Learsi, Rufus., 4:640
Leary, David E., 3:167, 3:168
Leary, Lewis, 1:45, 1:121,
1:628, 1:639, 1:709
Leary, William M., 3:510
Lease, Benjamin, 1:651,
1:748
Leatherbarrow, William J.,
2:715, 4:31
Leatherwood, Stephen, 5:761
Leaton, Anne, 2:739
Leavis, Frank R., 1:319,
1:350, 1:417, 1:510, 1:767,
1:926
Leavis, Q. D., 1:350
Leavitt, Judith W., 5:36,
5:314
LeBaron, B., 3:63
LeBaron, Charles, 5:336
Lebeaux, Richard, 1:702
Leber, Max, 5:351
LeBlanc, Ronald D., 2:688
Le Bon, Gustave, 3:203
Le Bot, Marc, 3:789
Le Bourdais, Donat M., 3:940
Lebowitz, Naomi, 4:240
Lebra, Joyce, 3:464
Lebrecht, Norman, 3:671
Lebreton, Jules, 4:681
LeBrun, Annie, 2:503
Le Carré, John, 1:592, **1:595**
Lecker, Robert, 2:904
Leckie, Robert, 3:546
Leckie, William H., 3:532

Lecky, W(illiam) E(dward)
H(artpole), 3:405
LeClair, Tom, 1:918
Leclercq, Jacques, 5:240
Leclercq, Jean, 4:676, 4:699
Le Corbusier, 2:560, 3:769,
3:778
Lederberg, Joshua, 5:761
Lederer, Katherine, 1:1093
Lederman, Leon, 5:650,
5:663
Ledger, Gerald R., 4:81
Ledkovsky, Marina, 2:692
Lednicki, Waclaw, 2:811,
2:815, 2:822
Leduc, Violette, 2:485
Ledyard, John, 3:909
Lee, Anthony A., 4:861
Lee, A. Robert, 1:655, 1:658,
1:689, 1:693, 1:727, 1:805,
1:840, 1:846
Lee, Brian, 1:723
Lee, Carol, 3:733
Lee, Chong-sik, 3:464
Lee, Courtland D., 5:422
Lee, David R., 3:119
Lee, Edward A., 5:302
Lee, H.D.P., 4:52
Lee, Hector, 3:863
Lee, Hermione, 1:448, 1:821,
1:1041
Lee, James W., 1:449
Lee, J. M., 3:367
Lee, Joann F., 3:556
Lee, John J., 5:783
Lee, Joseph J., 2:226, 3:371
Lee, Ki-baik, 2:298
Lee, Lawrence, 1:999, 1:1110
Lee, Leo Ou-fan, 2:234, 2:256
Lee, Manwoo, 3:482
Lee, Maurice, Jr., 3:368
Lee, M. Owen, 2:397
Lee, Peter H., 2:299
Lee, Philip R., 5:352
Lee, Phyllis C., 5:769
Lee, R., 5:239
Lee, Raymond L. M., 4:518
Lee, Richard B., 3:17
Lee, Robert, 1:719, 1:723
Lee, Sherman, 3:759
Lee, Sidney, 1:205, 1:222
Lee, Spike, 1:1170, 3:840
Lee, Steven, 5:109
Lee, Sung-Il, 2:299
Lee, Thomas H., 5:282
Leebaert, Derek, 5:573
Leebron, Elizabeth, 1:1165
Leech, Clifford, 1:170, 1:187,
1:201
Leed, Eric J., 3:892
Leeds, Barry H., 1:1000
Leeming, David A., 3:855,
4:427

Leeming, Glenda, 1:480,
1:565
Leeper, Robert W., 3:190
Leeson, C. Roland, 5:773
Leeson, Kenneth W., 1:50
Leeuwenhoek, Anton van,
5:803
Le Fanu, J. Sheridan, 1:600,
1:601, 1:602
Lefanu, Sarah, 2:158
Lefebure, Molly, 1:288
Lefebvre, Georges, 3:339,
3:373
Lefer, Diane, 1:773
Lefever, Ernest W., 5:111
Lefevre, Andre, 2:990
Lefevre, M. J., 5:381
Leff, Gordon, 4:102, 4:104,
4:697
Leffler, William L., 5:286
Lefkowitz, Mary R., 3:309,
4:447
LeFontaine, Joseph Ray-
mond, 1:63, 1:79
Leftwich, Joseph, 2:34, 2:50
LeGassick, Trevor, 2:69
Leggatt, Alexander, 1:211
Leggett, Bobby Joe, 1:496,
1:888
Leggett, Glenn, 1:118
Legman, Gershon, 3:871
Le Goff, Jacques, 4:697
Legouis, Emile, 1:307
Legouis, Pierre, 1:189
Le Guin, Ursula, 1:615,
1:1256, **1:1259,** 1:1262
Lehan, Richard, 1:830
Lehman, B. H., 1:344
Lehman, David, 1:936, 1:1015
Lehmann, John, 1:451, 1:501
Lehmann-Haupt, Hellmut,
1:9, 1:24, 1:37, 1:38
Lehman-Wilzig, Sam, 4:642
Lehner, Sigmund, 1:21
Lehninger, Albert L., 5:774
Lehrer, Keith, 4:20, 4:22,
4:212, 4:381, 5:107
LeHurray, Peter, 4:737
Leibniz, Gottfried Wilhelm,
Baron von, 2:515, 4:12,
4:154, 4:155, 4:158, 4:164,
4:167, **4:175,** 4:183, 4:186,
4:194, 4:218, 4:229, 4:317,
5:489, 5:506, 5:541, 5:705,
5:803
Leibovitz, Annie, 3:734
Leibowitz, Rene, 3:714
Leicester, Henry M., 5:32,
5:33, 5:728
Leick, Gwendolyn, 4:545
Leidy, W. Philip, 3:506
Leif, Irving P., 1:5
Leighton, Angela, 1:337

Leighton, Douglas, 1:24
Leighton, Ralph, 3:904
Leighton, Walter L., 4:28
Leijonhufvud, Axel, 3:62
Leiman, Melvin, 3:51, 3:83,
    3:97
Leiman, Sid Z., 4:598
Leinbach, L. Carl, 5:490
Leippe, M., 3:176
Leiris, Michel, 3:787
Leishman, J. B., 1:215
Leitch, Vincent B., 1:794,
    1:1132
Leiter, Samuel L., 2:273
Leites, Nathan, 3:204
Leith, John H., 4:680, 4:719,
    4:762
Lejeune, Philippe, 1:927
Leki, Ilona, 2:501
Leland, Charles G., 3:858
Lelchuk, Alan, 2:10
Lellinger, David B., 5:761
Lem, Stanislaw, 2:815
Lemann, Nicholas, 3:212,
    3:556
LeMay, G. H., 3:364
Le May, Reginald, 2:336
Lemon, Lee T., 2:688
Lemonick, Michael D., 5:595,
    5:655
Lempriere, J. A., 2:346
Lenburg, Carrie B., 5:324
Lenchek, Tom, 5:225
Lenczowski, George, 3:436
Lender, Mark Edward, 3:552
L'Engle, Madeleine, 1:50
Lengyel, Jozsef, 2:800
Lenhoff, Gail, 2:688
Lenin, Vladimir Ilyich,
    1:445, 3:157, **3:286**, 3:291,
    3:294
Lenk, John D., 5:304
Lennep, Jacob van, 2:620
Lenngren, Anna Maria, 2:670
Lennon, Thomas, 4:183
Lennox, James, 4:68
Lenoir, Timothy, 5:47
Lenowitz, Harris, 4:439
Lensen, George Alexander,
    3:464
Lensing, George S., 1:888
Lenski, Branko, 2:786, 2:828,
    2:835
Lent, John A., 3:801
Lentricchia, Frank, 1:926,
    1:1134
Lenz, Carolyn, 1:208
Lenz, Wilhelm von, 3:672
Lenz, William E., 1:723
León, Adolfo, 2:537
Leon, D., 3:440
León, Fray Luis de, 2:520
Leonard, Elmore, 1:1232

Leonard, James S., 1:784
Leonard, John, 1:192
Leonard, J. S., 1:1060
Leonard, Peter, 3:262
Leonard, Thomas C., 3:807
Leonard, Thomas M., 1:88,
    3:631
Leonardo da Vinci. See da
    Vinci, Leonardo
Leone, Mark P., 4:846, 4:856
Leonhardt, Thomas W., 5:126
Leonov, Leonid, 2:734
León-Portilla, Miguel, 3:629,
    4:457
**Leontief, Wassily, 3:47, 3:63,
    3:90**
Leopardi, Giacomo, 2:424,
    2:426, 2:428, 2:431, 2:440
**Leopold, Aldo, 5:115, 5:139,
    5:834**
Leopold, Carl Gustaf af,
    2:670
Leopold, Luna B., 5:632
Leopold, Richard W., 4:844
Leov, Yordan, 2:807
LePage, Jane Weiner, 3:656,
    3:671
Lepelletier, Edmond A.,
    2:514
Lepeltier, Robert, 1:24
LePore, Ernest, 4:283, 4:381
Leppert, Richard, 3:661
Lercano, Giacomo, 4:771
LeRiche, W. Harding, 5:346
Lermontov, Mikhail, 2:734
Lerner, Alan Jay, 3:661
Lerner, Allan W., 3:251
Lerner, Daniel, 3:436
Lerner, Gerda, 3:524, 3:556
Lerner, Ralph, 4:95
Lerner, Richard M., 3:174
Lerner, Rita G., 5:650
Lerner, Robert E., 4:721
Lernoux, Penny, 3:632, 4:748
LeRoi-Gourhan, André, 4:433
Leroy, Andre L., 4:202
Leroy-Ladurie, Emmanuel,
    3:276, 4:699
LeShan, Lawrence, 5:319
Lesher, J. H., 4:52
Lesiak, Michaeline, Sister,
    1:17
Lesinš, Knuts, 2:803
Lesko, Matthew, 5:216, 5:331
Leskov, Nikolai, 2:735
Lesky, Albin A., 2:346
Leslau, Wolf, 4:644
Leslie, Edward E., 3:909
Leslie, Stuart W., 5:226
Lessa, William A., 4:426,
    4:897
Lesser, M. X., 1:637
Lessing, Doris, 1:419, 3:904

Lessing, Gotthold Ephraim,
    2:563, **2:599**, 4:197, **4:207**,
    4:208, 4:739, 4:775
Lester, DeeGee, 3:506
Lester, Julius, 3:867
Lester, R. K., 3:49
Lester, Robert C., 4:519,
    4:884
Lethbridge, Robert, 2:518
Letwin, Shirley R., 1:407
**Leuchtenburg, William
    E(dward),** 3:504, 3:514,
    3:535, 3:539, **3:585**
Leupin, Alexandre, 2:447
Leutz, Walter N., 5:317
Levack, Daniel J., 1:1259
Levaillant, Maurice, 2:510
Levant, Howard, 1:886
Levarie, Norma, 1:9, 1:37
Levenson, Dorothy, 5:314
Levenson, Frederick B.,
    5:372
Levenson, J. C., 1:730, 3:563
Levenson, Jon D., 4:815
Levenson, Joseph R., 2:253,
    3:471, 4:532
Levenson, Michael, 1:415
Levenson, Steven, 5:554
Leventhal, Herbert, 4:841
Lever, Janet, 3:634
Lever, J. W., 1:207
Levere, Trevor, 1:288
Leverenz, David, 1:651
Leverett, James, 1:1078
Levering, Miriam, 4:510,
    4:530
Levering, Ralph B., 3:539
Levertoff, Paul, 4:630
Levertov, Denise, 1:1003,
    2:174
Leveson, David, 5:623
Levey, Michael, 1:387
Levey, Samson H., 4:608
Levi, A., 4:128
Levi, Albert W., 4:22, 4:161
Levi, Carlo, 2:421, 2:424
Levi, Darrell E., 3:638
Levi, Isaac, 5:64
Levi, Ken, 4:867
Levi, Peter, 1:205, 2:828
Levi, Primo, 2:425
Levi, Werner, 3:144
Leviant, Curt, 2:10
**Levi-Montalcini, Rita, 5:790,
    5:804**
Levin, Alan Scott, 5:386
Levin, Beatrice S., 5:314
Levin, Daniel L., 2:726
Levin, David, 1:628, 1:660,
    4:767
Levin, Flora R., 5:514

Levin, Harry, 1:187, 1:213, 1:658, 1:677, 1:714, 1:926, 2:447

Levin, Henry M., 3:218

Levin, Michael Graubart, 4:659

Levin, Milton, 1:465

Levin, N. Gordon, 3:546

Levin, Nora, 3:349, 4:656

Levin, Richard, 1:170

Levin, Toby, 5:376

Levinas, Emmanuel, 4:235, **4:900**

Levine, Bruce, 3:552

Levine, Carol, 5:121

Levine, Daniel, 1:731

Levine, Daniel H., 3:641

Levine, Daniel U., 3:257

Levine, Ethan, 4:608

Levine, Gaynell S., 3:859

Levine, George, 2:990

Levine, George Lewis, 1:270, 1:301, 1:319, 1:325, 1:354

Levine, Howard, 5:568

Levine, Joseph M., 1:225

Levine, Lawrence W., 3:556, 3:560, 3:867

Levine, Lee I., 4:597, 4:614, 4:621

Levine, Madeline G., 2:811

Levine, Michael, 5:816

Levine, Mortimer, 3:354, 3:359

Levine, Paula L., 3:201

Levine, Philip, 1:1004

Levine, Richard, 5:374

Levine, Richard A., 1:315

LeVine, Robert A., 3:15

Levine, Robert J., 5:121

Levine, Robert M., 3:634

Levine, Robert S., 1:658

Levine, Saul, 4:856

Levinger, Elma, 4:172

Levins, Richard, 5:764

Levinson, Daniel, 5:422

Levinson, David, 3:11

Levinson, Henry S., 1:769, 4:237, 4:328

Levinson, Horace C., 5:523

Levinson, Marjorie, 1:307

Levinson, Nadine, 3:178

Levinson, Orde, 3:423

Lévi-Strauss, Claude, 1:1125, 1:1141, 2:486, 3:15, 3:17, 3:20, 3:24, **3:33,** 4:426, 4:427, 4:428, 4:465

Levit, Fred, 1:350

Levitt, Eugene E., 5:427

Levitt, Marcus C., 2:688

LeVitus, Bob, 5:537

Levonian, Lufty, 4:571

Levstik, Fran, 2:834

Levtzion, N., 3:421

Levtzion, Nehemia, 4:571

Levy, Anita, 1:325

Levy, Beryl Harold, 4:652

Levy, Charles K., 5:761

Levy, Dore, 2:190

Levy, Eugene, 1:771

Levy, Howard S., 2:274

Levy, Leonard W., 1:57, 3:142, 3:509, 3:807

Levy, Matthys, 5:12

Levy, Paul, 4:29

Levy, Peter B., 3:511

Levy, Reuben, 2:83, 3:437, 3:443

Levy, Robert I., 3:22

Levy, Steven, 5:543

Levy, William T., 3:833

Levy-Bruhl, Lucien, 3:224, 4:223

Lewald, H. Ernest, 2:849

Lewalski, Barbara K., 1:166, 1:178, 1:192

Lewell, John, 2:282, 5:564

Lewellen, T. C., 5:35

Lewenstein, Bruce V., 5:155

Lewes, George Henry, 1:353, **1:372,** 4:17, 4:161

Lewin, Ellen, 5:355

Lewin, Gertrud W., 3:204

Lewin, Kurt, 3:176, **3:189,** 3:204, 5:460

Lewin, Roger, 4:866

Lewin, Ronald, 3:279, 3:401

Lewine, Richard, 3:656

Lewins, Jeffery D., 5:240

Lewis, A. R., 3:328

Lewis, Arthur M., 5:805

Lewis, Arthur O., 1:130

Lewis, A. W, 1:25

Lewis, Benjamin R., 1:221

Lewis, Bernard, 3:276, 3:328, 3:331, 3:416, 3:419, 3:443, 3:453, **3:458,** 4:567, 4:568, 4:571, 4:575, 4:579, 4:594, 5:225

Lewis, C(ecil) Day, 1:362, 1:416, 1:434, 1:444, **1:511,** 1:517, 1:552

Lewis, Clarence Irving, 4:260, **4:301,** 4:317

Lewis, C(live) S(taples), 1:147, 1:162, 1:165, 1:167, 1:192, 1:201, **1:512,** 1:574, 1:586, 4:99, **4:775**

Lewis, David K., 4:381

Lewis, David L., 3:560, 4:773

Lewis, Edith, 1:821

Lewis, Ewart, 4:98

Lewis, Felice Flannery, 1:57

Lewis, Frank A., 4:69

Lewis, Gavin, 3:326

Lewis, Geoffrey, 2:96

Lewis, Geraint, 3:725

Lewis, Gilbert Newton, 5:733, **5:749**

Lewis, Gillian, 4:731

Lewis, H. Spencer., 4:848

Lewis, H. W., 5:12

Lewis, I. M., 3:421, 3:422, 3:443, 4:431, 4:571

Lewis, James R., 4:860, 4:866

Lewis, Jan, 3:521

Lewis, Jane, 3:343, 3:364

Lewis, John, 1:9, 1:29, 1:32

Lewis, John S., 5:596

Lewis, Judy, 2:322

Lewis, Justin, 3:560

Lewis, Marcia A., 5:122

Lewis, Martin W., 5:115, 5:823

Lewis, Matthew Gregory, 1:269, 1:598, 1:601, **1:601,** 1:603

Lewis, Meriwether, 3:927

Lewis, Michael, 3:478

Lewis, Milton, 5:36

Lewis, Moshe, 3:398

Lewis, Naphtali, 3:300, 3:303, 3:307

Lewis, Norman, 3:904

Lewis, Oscar, 3:34, 3:39

Lewis, (Percy) Wyndham, **1:513**

Lewis, Peter, 1:246, 1:596

Lewis, Philip E., 2:485

Lewis, Philippa, 3:765

Lewis, Richard J., 5:261

Lewis, Richard J., Sr., 5:725, 5:726

Lewis, R(ichard) W(arrington) B(aldwin), 1:651, 1:653, 1:761, 1:767, 1:787, 1:788, **1:1004**

Lewis, Robert, Jr., 1:846

Lewis, Roy Harley, 1:25, 1:32

Lewis, Ruth A., 5:596

Lewis, Sinclair, 1:802, 1:811, **1:853,** 1:858, 1:867

Lewis, Theresa, 2:931

Lewis, Walter H., 5:351

Lewis, W. Arthur, 3:53

Lewis, Wilmarth S., 1:263, 1:604

Lewis, Wyndham, 2:427

Lewisohn, Ludwig, 4:596

Lewontin, Richard, 5:764, 5:826

Ley, Charles D., 2:557, 3:335, 3:386

Ley, David, 3:119

Ley, J.W.T., 1:350

Leyda, Jay, 1:689, 1:748, 3:712, 3:835

Leyden, W. von, 3:154, 4:175, 4:181

Leyerle, Betty, 5:334

Leyland, Winston, 1:1184, 2:849
Leymarie, Jean, 3:775
Leypoldt, Frederick, 1:67
Leyser, Henrietta, 4:700
Lezhnev, A., 2:752
Li, Alice, 3:488
Li, Lillian M., 3:467, 3:471
Li, Tze-chung, 3:5
Li, Wen-Hsiung, 5:784
Li Ang, 2:251
Liang, John, 1:77
Liang Ch'i-ch'ao, 2:231, 2:234, 2:252
Liaqat, M. Muntaz, 4:375
Libby, Willard Frank, 5:749
Liber, Maurice, 4:671
Liberles, Robert, 4:654
Liberman, Alexander, 3:899
Libman, Lillian, 3:723
Libo, Kenneth, 4:640
Liboff, Richard L., 5:660
Libowitz, Richard, 4:667
Licastro, Emmanuele, 2:409
Li Ch'iao-p'ing, 5:728
Li Ch'ing-chao, 2:204
Lichello, Robert, 3:819, 5:685
Lichtenberg, Frank R., 3:49
Lichtendorf, Susan S., 5:356
Lichtenstadter, Ilse, 2:55, 4:571
Lichtheim, George, 3:373
Lichtheim, Miriam, 2:53, 3:300, 4:442
Lichtmann, Maria R., 1:364
Lickona, Thomas, 3:251
Liddell, Basil H., 3:279
Liddell, H. G., 1:99, 4:795
Liddell, Robert, 1:462
Liddiard, Jean, 1:541
Lide, David R., Jr., 5:725
Lidman, Sara, 2:671, 2:673
Lidoff, Joan, 2:964
Lidz, Theodore, 5:427
Lie, Jonas, 2:662, 2:666
Liebenow, J. G., 3:421
Lieber, Hugh G., 5:496
Lieber, Lillian R., 5:496
Lieberman, Adrienne, 5:323
Lieberman, Bernhard, 5:523
Lieberman, E. James, 5:466
Lieberman, Lawrence, 1:913
Lieberman, Nancy, 3:834
Lieberman, Saul, 4:606
Lieberman, Victor B., 3:489
Lieberman, William S., 3:784
Liebert, R., 3:178, 3:812
Liebert, Robert S., 3:782, 5:425
Liebeschuetz, J.H.W.G., 3:306, 4:448

Liebig, Justus von, 5:259, 5:270, **5:273,** 5:727, 5:747, 5:755
Liebling, A(bbott) J(oseph), 3:813, 3:896
Liebman, Arthur, 4:656
Liebman, Bonnie, 5:346
Liebman, Charles S., 4:640, 4:642, 4:654
Liebowitz, Nathan, 3:220
Liehm, Antonin J., 2:789, 2:833
Liem, Antonin, 2:789
Liemohn, E., 4:738
Lienhardt, Godfrey, 4:462
Lienhardt, Samuel, 3:215
Lietzmann, Hans, 4:682
Lieu, Samuel N., 4:686
Lifar, Serge, 3:741
Life, Page W., 1:155
Lifson, David S., 2:34
Lifton, Robert J., 3:276, 3:478, 4:532, 5:79, 5:414, 5:423
Lifton, Sarah, 3:852
Light, James F., 1:744
Light, Richard J., 5:523
Light, Stephen, 4:331
Light, William J., 5:402
Lightfoot, J. B., 4:704
Lightfoot, Sara L., 3:251
Lightman, Alan, 5:68
Lihn, Enrique, 2:870
Li Ho, 2:205, 2:208
Lilker, Shalom, 4:658
Lilla, Salvatore R., 4:63
Lillard, Paula P., 3:266
Lillard, Richard G., 1:122
Lilley, Dorothy B., 5:544
Lilley, George P., 5:261
Lillyman, William J., 2:612
Lillyquist, Michael J., 5:320, 5:341
Lim, Catherine, 2:324, 2:325
Lim, Patricia, 2:311
Lima, Carolyn W., 1:74, 1:1196
Lima, John A., 1:74, 1:1196
Lima, Robert, 2:553
Lima-De-Faria, José, 5:628
Limbacher, James L., 3:667
Limerick, Patricia, 3:532
Limón, José, 3:744, **3:746,** 3:752
Limonov, Edward, 2:736
Lin, Julia C., 2:234
Lin, Shuen-fu, 2:190
Lin, Yü-sheng, 2:247
Linacre, Edward, 3:126
Lincoff, Gary F., 5:761
Lincoln, Abraham, 1:698, 1:877, 1:1249

Lincoln, Bruce, 4:426, 4:430, 4:435, 4:472
Lincoln, C. Eric, 3:539, 4:571, 4:748, 4:862
Lincoln, Victoria, 4:786
Lincoln, W. Bruce, 3:397
Lind, Jakov, 2:600
Lind, L. R., 2:403
Lind, Peter, 4:408, 5:94
Lindahl, Ingemar B., 5:78
Lindbeck, George, 4:889
Lindberg, Bertil C., 5:305
Lindberg, David, 4:128
Lindberg, David C., 4:97, 5:26, 5:39
Lindberg, Gary, 1:651
Lindberg, Gladys, 5:346
Lindberg, Kathryne V., 1:873
Lindberg, Stanley W., 1:819
Lindbergh, Charles A(ugustus), Jr., 3:928
Lindberg-Seyerstad, Brita, 1:475
Lindegren, Erik, 1:17
Lindell, Kristina, 2:322
Lindemann, Albert S., 3:326, 3:341
Linden, G. M., 3:272
Linden, William, 5:381
Lindenberger, Herbert S., 1:307
Lindenmann, Jean, 5:371
Linden-Ward, Blanche, 3:506
Linder, Amnon, 4:604
Linder, Marc, 3:104
Linderman, Gerald F., 3:528
Lindfors, Bernth, 2:110, 2:126, 2:129, 2:150
Lindgren, Astrid, 2:677
Lindgren, J. Ralph, 4:215
Lindgren, Raymond E., 3:382
Lindgren, Torgny, 2:671
Lindhardt, Jan, 4:128
Lindley, David, 1:174, 5:650
Lindley, Kenneth, 1:29
Lindo-Fuentes, Héctor, 3:637
Lindop, Grevel, 1:290, 1:502
Lindorff, Dave, 5:333
Lindow, John, 3:856
Lindquist, Marie, 5:372
Lindsay, A. D., 3:143
Lindsay, Jack, 1:383, 3:775
Lindsay, Maurice, 1:280, 1:418
Lindsay, (Nicholas) Vachel, 1:854
Lindsey, Byron, 2:692
Lindsey, Gene, 3:451
Lindsey, Robert, 1:35
Lindstrom, Harold, 4:790
Lindstrom, Naomi, 2:846
Lindtner, Charles, 4:513

Lindzey, Gardner, 3:169, 3:178, 5:422
Lineback, Richard H., 4:5, 4:6, 4:14, 5:60
Linetski, Isaac Joel, 2:40
Linforth, Ivan M., 4:447
Ling, Amy, 1:714
Ling, Peter J., 3:553
Ling, Trevor, 4:571, 4:895
Lingeman, Richard, 1:830, 3:553, 5:423
Lingenfelter, Richard E., 3:863
Linggard, Robert, 5:230
Lings, Martin A., 4:575, 4:588
Ling-yün, Hsieh. See Hsieh Ling-yün
Link, Arthur S., 3:510, 3:513, 3:532
Link, Frederick M., 1:233
Link, Perry, 2:234, 2:235, 3:471
Link, Peter K., 5:286, 5:636
Link, William A., 3:513
Linn, J. W., 1:731
Linna, Väinö, 2:657
Linnaeus, Carolus, 5:804
Linney, Romulus, 1:1098
Linschoten, Hans, 5:453
Linteau, Paul-André, 3:609
Lintner, Bertil, 3:489
Linton, Alan H., 5:783
Linton, William J., 1:29
Lintott, Andrew, 3:306
Lin Yü-t'ang, 1:97, 2:211, 2:218, 2:220, 2:253
Lipner, Julius J., 4:894
Li Po, 2:187, 2:206, 2:214, 2:215, 2:225
Lipp, Solomon, 4:33
Lippert, Jack E., 1:43
Lippincott, Lillian, 1:877
Lippit, Noriko Mizuta, 2:282, 2:283
Lippman, Edward A., 3:661
Lippman, Thomas W., 3:437
Lippmann, Walter, 3:147, 3:157, 3:814, 4:783
Lippy, Charles H., 4:4
Lippy, John D., Jr., 5:730
Lipset, Seymour Martin, 3:140, 3:158, 3:214, 3:234
Lipshires, Sidney, 4:408, 5:94
Lipton, Gladys C., 1:100
Liptzin, Sol, 2:32, 2:50
Li Shang-yin, 2:208
Lisle, Laurie, 3:785
Lisle, Leconte de, 2:537
Lispector, Clarice, 2:889, 2:895
Lissak, Moshe, 3:440
Lister, Joseph, 5:408
Liston, Daniel P., 3:256

Liston, Linda L., 5:633
Liston, Maureen, 1:883
Liszka, James J., 4:428
Liszt, Franz, 2:504, 3:690, 3:701, 3:703, 3:717, 3:721, 3:728
Litan, Robert E., 5:184
Litchen, Frances, 3:859
Litoff, Judy B., 5:338
Litt, Jerome Z., 5:399
Littell, Franklin H., 4:720, 4:724, 4:780
Little, Daniel, 4:243, 4:385
Little, David, 4:893
Little, Judy, 1:294
Little, Kenneth, 2:110
Little, Lester K., 4:700
Little, R. John, 5:761
Little, Stephen, 4:528
Little, W. A., 5:673
Littlefield, Daniel F., 1:715
Littler, June D., 4:869
Littleton, C. Scott, 4:472
Littmann, Mark, 5:593
Litto, Fredric M., 1:123
Litwack, Leon F., 3:504, 3:513, 3:525, 3:528, 3:548
Litz, A. Walton, 1:127, 1:276, 1:888
Litzinger, Boyd, 1:339
Litzmann, Berthold, 3:716
Liu, Alan, 1:307
Liu, James J. Y., 2:190
Liu, James T., 2:215
Liu, Kwang-Ching, 3:468, 3:470
Liu, Ts'un-yan, 2:210
Liu, Tsun-yan, 2:190
Liu, Wu-chi, 2:190
Liu E., 2:210
Liu Hsin-wu, 2:232, 2:254
Liu Pin-yen, 2:254
Lively, Jack, 3:165
Livermore, Harold U., 3:386
Livezey, William E., 3:288
Livingston, Alan, 3:759
Livingston, Donald W., 4:202
Livingston, Dorothy Michelson, 5:702
Livingston, Jane, 3:867
Livingston, Myra C., 1:579, 1:1196, 1:1197
Livingstone, Alasdair, 4:545
Livingstone, Angela, 2:746
Livingstone, David, 3:929, 3:937
Livingstone, David N., 5:794
Livingstone, Elizabeth A., 4:675, 4:716, 4:717
Livingston-Wheeler, Virginia, 5:372
Livo, Norma J., 2:322

Livy (Titus Livius), 2:387, 3:310, 3:314, 3:317
Li Yü, 2:209
Lizhong, Liu, 4:543
Llewellyn, Richard, 3:369
Llewellyn-Jones, Margaret, 1:425
Llewelyn, John, 4:294, 4:391, 4:398
Llosa, Mario Vargas. See Vargas Llosa, Mario
Lloyd, A. C., 4:61
Lloyd, Elisabeth A., 5:780
Lloyd, Genevieve, 4:17
Lloyd, Geoffrey E., 3:311, 4:69, 5:38
Lloyd, G.E.R., 4:48
Lloyd, Margaret G., 1:901
Lloyd, Peter E., 3:122
Lloyd, Rosemary, 2:457
Lloyd, Seton, 3:763
Lloyd, T. O., 3:355, 3:367
Lloyd-Jones, Hugh, 2:346
Llull, Ramon, 4:102
Lo, Irving Yucheng, 2:190
Loader, Colin, 3:232
Loades, Ann, 4:896
Loades, David, 3:359
Lob, Susan, 3:872
Lobeck, Armin K., 5:626
Lobel, Anita, 1:1194
Lobel, Arnold, 1:1194
Lobel, Jerome, 5:556
Lobell, John, 3:777
Lobner, Corinna del Greco, 1:505
Lobo Antunes, Antonio, 2:557, 2:559
Locher, J. L., 5:193
Lochrie, Karma, 1:153
Locke, John, 1:224, 1:249, 1:573, 1:576, 1:636, 1:641, 1:656, 3:154, 3:158, 4:12, 4:122, 4:157, 4:168, 4:173, 4:176, 4:178, 4:193, 4:195, 4:211, 4:214, 4:217, 4:739, 4:766, 5:144
Locke, M. A., 2:215
Locker, David, 5:377
Lockhart, Greg, 3:491
Lockhart, James, 3:629
Lockhart, J.A.R., 5:263
Lockhart, Joan S., 5:771
Lockhart, John Gibson, 1:281, 1:300
Lockley, Ronald M., 5:826
Lockridge, Laurence, 1:265, 1:288
Locksley, Gareth, 3:70, 3:83, 3:91, 3:102
Lockwood, Dean P., 4:128
Lockwood, George B., 4:844

Lockwood, Michael, 4:19, 5:122
Lockwood, William W., 3:478
Lockwood, Yvonne R., 3:861
Lockyer, Judith, 1:837
Lockyer, Roger, 1:220
Lodge, David (John), 1:414, 1:415, 1:420, 1:422, **1:514,** 1:1007, 2:688
Lodge, Oliver Joseph, 5:694
Lodge, R. C., 4:81
Lodge, Thomas, 1:185
Lodisch, Harvey, 5:784
Loeb, Louis E., 4:161
Loeber, E. G., 1:5
Loeffler, Margaret H., 3:251
Loeffler, Reinhold, 4:579
Loehlin, John C., 3:175
Loemker, Leroy E., 4:177
Loesberg, Jonathan, 1:325, 1:387
Loesser, Arthur, 3:672
Loetscher, Lefferts A., 4:717
Loewe, H., 4:610
Loewe, Michael, 3:469, 4:524
Loewe, Raphael, 2:20
Loewenburg, Alfred, 3:670
Loewenich, Walter von, 4:779
Loewenstein, Joseph, 1:184
Loewenthal, Lillian, 3:742
Lofland, John, 4:871
Lofland, Lyn, 3:216, **3:231**
Löfstedt, Einar, 2:381
Loftin, John D., 4:465
Loftis, John, 1:255
Loftus, Richard J., 1:417
Logan, Carolynn M., 5:6
Logan, Eugenia, 1:288
Logan, F. Donald, 3:380
Logan, George M., 1:194, 4:147
Logan, John, 1:1005, 3:216
Logan, Terence P., 1:170
Logsdom, Tom, 5:242, 5:247
Logue, Christopher, 3:871
Lohff, Wenzel, 4:730
Lohfink, Gerhard, 4:815
Lohse, Bernhard, 4:677, 4:778
Lohse, Edward, 4:808, 4:816
Loizos, Peter, 3:455
Lo-Johansson, Ivar, 2:671, 2:672
Lo Jung-pang, 4:361
Lokos, Lionel, 4:773
Lo Kuan-chung, 2:211
Lo Liyong, Taban, 2:152
Lomas, Herbert, 2:658
Lomas, Peter, 5:423
Lomatuway'ma, Michael, 3:865

Lomax, Alan, 2:931, 3:852, **3:884**
Lomax, Judy, 5:219
Lomax, Louis E., 4:862
Lombardi, Cathryn, 3:625
Lombardi, John V., 3:641
Lombardo, Patrizia, 2:455
Lomie, I. M., 5:41
Lomonosov, Mikhail, 2:682
Londer, Randi, 5:775
London, Jack, 1:721, **1:773,** 1:1249
London, Joan, 1:775
Londre, Felicia H., 1:1118
Lonergan, Bernard, 4:119
Long, A. A., 4:55, 4:55
Long, Barbara, 3:506
Long, Charles H., 4:426, 4:427, 4:570
Long, E. B., 3:506
Long, Edward, Jr., 4:744
Long, E. Hudson, 1:1074
Long, James W., 5:351
Long, John, 1:221
Long, Priscilla, 3:548, 5:346
Long, Richard A., 1:130, 2:64
Long, Robert Emmet, 1:57, 1:867, 1:891, 1:897
Longenbach, James, 1:888
Longfellow, Henry Wadsworth, 1:675, **1:682,** 1:717, 1:1192, 2:659
Longfellow, Samuel, 1:683
Longford, Lord, 3:371
Longino, Helen E., 5:66, 5:155, 5:188
Longinus, 1:224, **2:362,** 3:315
Longland, Jean R., 2:557
Longley, Dennis, 3:802, 5:540, 5:546
Longley, Edna, 1:518
Longley, Kateryna O., 2:946
Longley, Lawrence D., 3:144
Longmire, R. A., 3:489
Longrigg, Stephen H., 3:450, 3:455
Longstreet, Augustus Baldwin, 1:683
Longstreet, Stephen, 3:773
Longus, 2:343, **2:363**
Longwell, Chester L., 5:623
Longyear, Marie, 1:118
Longyear, Rey M., 3:661
Lönnrot, Elias, 2:657, 2:659
Lönnroth, Lars, 2:642
Lonsdale, Roger, 1:227, 1:269
Looby, Christopher, 1:639
Loofbourow, John, 1:404
Loomis, Elisha S., 5:514
Loomis, Gertrude, 2:512
Looney, Robert E., 3:448
Loop, Liza, 5:544

Looper, Travis, 1:283
Lope de Vega Carpio, Felix. *See* Vega Carpio, Lope Felix de
Lopez, Barry Holstun, 3:906, 3:916, 5:765, 5:818
Lopez, Donald S., Jr., 4:513
Lopez, Robert S., 3:54
Lopinski, Maciej, 3:390
Lopreato, Joseph, 3:18
Lorca, Federico García. *See* García Lorca Federico
Lord, Albert B., 2:361, 2:827, 4:460
Lord, Carnes, 4:69
Lord, Louis E., 2:353
Lord, M. P., 5:653
Lord, Russell, 5:275
Lorde, Audre Geraldine, 1:910, 1:1005, 1:1150, 1:1182, **1:1189**
Lorentz, Hendrik Antoon, 5:698
Lorenz, Clarissa M., 1:810
Lorenz, Konrad, 3:170, 3:171, **3:190,** 3:194, 5:825, 5:832, **5:835,** 5:837
Lorenzatos, Zissimos, 2:371
Lorenzoni, A. B., 5:234
Lorie, J. H., 3:55
Loring, Rosamond B., 1:5
Lortz, Joseph, 4:722
Losee, John, 5:64
Loseff, Lev, 2:688, 2:704
Loss, Archie K., 1:505, 1:521
Lossing, Larry D., 5:129
Lossky, Nicholas O., 4:31, 4:161
Lossky, Vladimir, 4:693, 4:756
Loth, David, 1:337
Lott, B., 3:178
Lott, Robert E., 2:553
Lottman, Herbert, 2:464, 2:470, 2:476
Lotze, Rudolf Hermann, 4:229, **4:240**
Loubser, Jan J., 3:238
Louchheim, Katie, 3:535
Loud, Patricia C., 3:777
Lough, John, 4:180
Louis, Kam, 4:358
Louis, Margot Kathleen, 1:398
Louis, William R., 3:367, 3:417
Lounsbury, John F., 5:620
Lourdeaux, Lee, 3:828
Louria, Donald B., 5:342
Lourie, Richard, 2:758
Louth, Andrew, 4:63, 4:689
Loux, Michael J., 4:69
Lovallo, Len, 1:606

Love, Nancy S., 3:140
Lovejoy, Arthur Oncken, 4:95, 4:161, **4:302**
Lovejoy, Paul, 3:418
Lovejoy, Thomas, 5:775
Lovekin, David, 5:71, 5:165
Lovelace, Augusta Ada Byron, Countess of, 5:541, 5:548, **5:577**
Loveland, Marion F., 3:871
Lovell, Ernest J., Jr., 1:283
Lovell, John, 3:661
Lovell, Mary S., 3:909
Lovell, Sir A. C. Bernard, 5:590, 5:656
Lovell, Terry, 1:1127
Lovelock, J. E., 5:823
Lovelock, Yann, 2:83
Loveman, Brian, 3:635
Loveridge, Mark, 1:259
Lovett, Charles C., 1:583
Loving, Jerome, 1:655, 1:670, 1:707
Lovinger, Paul W., 5:403
Lovins, Amory B., 5:75, 5:289, 5:823
Low, D. Anthony, 3:422, 3:486
Low, Donald A., 1:265, 1:281
Low, Douglas B., 4:311
Lowance, Mason I., 1:628
Lowe, Carl, 5:320
Lowe, David A., 2:688, 2:770
Lowe, Fonda, 5:376
Lowe, Victor, 4:342
Lowell, Amy, 1:294, **1:855,** 1:876, 1:1005, 5:608
Lowell, James Russell, 1:649, 1:659, 1:661, **1:684,** 1:717, 1:855, 1:936, 1:1005, 1:1192
Lowell, Percival, 5:608
Lowell, Robert, 1:549, 1:806, 1:855, 1:900, 1:909, 1:911, 1:1003, **1:1005,** 1:1030, 1:1051
Lowenthal, David T., 5:325
Lower, A.R.M., 3:613
Lowery, Charles D., 3:509
Lowery, Shearon, 3:801
Lowes, John L., 1:288
Lowin, Joseph, 1:1028
Lowitt, Richard, 3:509, 3:535
Lowman, Paul D., Jr., 5:617
Lowndes, William Thomas, 1:68
Lowney, Kathleen S., 4:871
Lowrance, William W., 5:75, 5:107, 5:155
Lowrie, Donald A., 4:275
Lowrie, Walter, 4:240
Lowry, Malcolm, 2:918
Lowry, Richard J., 5:461

Lowry, Shirley, 3:856
Löwy, Ilana, 5:78
Loy, Rosetta, 2:400
Loyn, H. R., 3:356
Loyrette, Henri, 5:246
Lozano, Beverly, 3:60
Lu, Cary, 5:554
Lu, Lisa, 2:193
Lu, Tonglin, 2:190
Lubar, Steven, 5:46
Lubbock, Percy, 1:337, 1:788
Luber, Raymond F., 5:423
Lubis, Mochtar, 2:316, **2:319**
Luby, Barry J., 2:849
Lucan (Marcus Annaeus Lucanus), 2:379, **2:387,** 2:389, 2:393
Lucas, Alice, 2:322
Lucas, Elizabeth, 1:17
Lucas, Frank L., 2:357
Lucas, George R., 4:342
Lucas, George Walton, Jr., 1:1171, 3:840
Lucas, Jean M., 4:188
Lucas, John, 1:270, 1:315, 1:319, 1:350, 1:911
Lucas, W. Scott, 3:366
Lucchesi, Valerio, 2:401
Luce, A. A., 4:182, 4:192
Luce, Henry R(obinson), 3:804, **3:815**
Luce, R. Duncan, 3:63
Luce, Stanford L., 2:465
Luce, T. James, 2:346
Lucente, Gregory L., 2:401, 2:442
Lucey, Kenneth, 4:14, 4:265, 4:386
Lu Chi, 2:212
Luchsinger, Arlene E., 5:762
Luciano, Dorothy S., 5:773
Lucian of Samosata, 2:343, **2:363, 4:484**
Lucie-Smith, Edward, 3:757, 3:759
Luck, Georg, 4:451
Luck, J. Murray, 3:378
Luckenbill, D. D., 2:53
Luckett, Perry D., 3:929
Lucky, Robert W., 5:573
Luckyj, George S., 2:838, 2:839, 2:840
Lucretius (Titus Lucretius Carus), 2:378, **2:388,** 4:59, 4:73, **4:75**
Lud, Ned, 5:247
Ludden, David, 3:484
Ludeman, Lonnie C., 5:296
Ludlow, Daniel, 4:4, 4:717, 4:846
Ludlow, Noah M., 1:1074
Ludmerer, Kenneth M., 5:336
Ludovici, L. J., 5:408

Ludwig, Charles, 5:745
Ludwig, Richard M., 1:714
Ludwikowski, Rett, 3:390
Luey, Beth, 1:50, 1:118
Luft, David S., 2:604
Luhan, Mabel G., 1:510
Luhr, William, 3:826
Luhrman, T. M., 4:865
Lu Hsün, 2:232, 2:234, 2:244, 2:245, 2:246, 2:249, **2:255,** 2:256
Lukac, Emil Boleslav, 2:833
Lukács, György (also Georg, George), 2:602, 2:798, **2:801,** 4:162
Lukas, Ellen, 4:337
Lukas, Mary, 4:337
Lukasiewicz, Jan, 4:69
Luker, Nicholas J., 2:693, 2:733
Lukes, Steven, 4:243, 4:405
Lukes, Timothy J., 4:408, 5:94
Lukić, Sveta, 2:785, 2:827
Lumbera, Bienvenido, 2:328
Lumet, Louis, 5:809
Lumiansky, Robert M., 1:151, 1:155, 1:159
Lumsden, E. S., 1:29
Lundberg, Donald E., 3:890
Lundberg, Margaret J., 5:423
Lundgaard, Kris, 5:549
Lundkvist, Artur, 2:671, 2:672
Lundquist, James, 1:830, 1:854, 1:1043, 1:1064
Lundwall, Sam J., 1:612
Lupton, Kenneth, 3:932
Lupul, Manoly R., 3:615
Luria, A. R., 3:172
Luria, Salvador E., 5:765
Lurie, Alison, 1:1007
Lurie, Edward, 5:785
Lusardi, James P., 1:214
Luscombe, D. E., 4:106
Luske, Bruce, 3:201
Luskin, John, 3:815
Lustig, Nora, 3:59
Lusty, Robert, 1:42
Lutgendorf, Phillip, 4:505
Lutgens, Frederick K., 3:126
Luth, H., 5:668
Luther, Martin, 2:562, 2:601, 3:182, 3:333, 4:133, 4:136, 4:138, 4:725,4:727, 4:729, 4:730, 4:733, 4:755, 4:757, 4:760, **4:777,** 4:779, 4:790, 4:813
Lutherer, Otto L., 5:782
Luthi, Max, 1:579, 3:856, 3:869
Luti, J. Mary, 4:786
Lutoslawski, Wincenty, 4:82
Luttbeg, Norman L., 3:143

Luttwak, Edward N., 3:279, 3:308
Lutyens, Mary, 4:556, 4:858
Lutz, Catherine A., 3:15
Lutz, Donald S., 3:520
Lutz, Harald, 5:324
Lützow, Francis, 2:789
Lu Yu, 2:213, 2:230
Luzuriaga, Gerado, 2:849
Lvov-Rogachevsky, V., 2:688
Ly, Singko, 2:325
Lyday, Leon F., 2:847
Lydecker, Mia, 5:352
Lydenberg, Harry Miller, 1:25
Lyell, Charles, 5:644
Lyell, William A., 2:256
Lyles, William H., 1:41, 1:301
Lyly, John, 1:167, **1:185**
Lyman, Stanford M., 3:237
Lynam, Edward, 3:923
Lynch, Edward A., 3:632
Lynch, Gerald, 2:909, 2:918
Lynch, James J., 5:342
Lynch, John, 3:387, 3:632
Lynch, John E., 4:102
Lynch, John Patrick, 4:70
Lynch, Owen M., 4:505
Lynch, Wilfred, 5:370
Lynch, William F., 4:82, 5:151
Lynd, Helen Merrell, 3:231, 5:423
Lynd, Robert S., 3:231
Lyndberg, Steven D., 5:129
Lyne, R.O.A.M., 2:397
Lynen, John F., 1:628
Lyngstad, Sverre, 2:662, 2:667
Lynn, David H., 1:805
Lynn, Joanne, 5:122
Lynn, Kenneth Schuyler, 1:846, 1:918
Lynn, Ruth, 1:1196
Lynn, S. J., 5:427
Lynott, Bob, 5:633
Lyon, Bryce, 3:355
Lyon, Howard H., 5:768
Lyon, H. R., 3:331
Lyon, Hugh Lee, 3:709
Lyon, James K., 2:573
Lyon, John, 2:553 , 5:45
Lyon, Melvin, 1:730
Lyon, Thomas J., 1:715, 5:818
Lyon, W. F., 5:770
Lyons, Arthur, 4:868
Lyons, David, 4:191
Lyons, Francis S. L., 3:364, 3:371
Lyons, J. A., 4:337
Lyons, John O., 1:918

Lyons, Kimon, 4:82
Lyons, Martin, 3:495
Lyons, Mary E., 1:850
Lyons, Oren, 3:515
Lyons, Robert, 3:446
Lyons, Robert J., 3:830
Lyons, Thomas P., 3:471
Lyons, William, 4:325
Lyotard, Jean-François, 3:211, 4:265
Lystad, Mary, 1:1196
Lystra, Karen, 3:553
Lytle, Mark, 3:514
Lytton, H., 3:173

M

Ma, Wendy Y., 2:193, 3:902
Maar, Ingrid, 3:864
Maas, Selve, 2:796
Mabbet, Ian, 3:463
Mabie, Margot C., 5:122
Mabro, Robert, 3:446
MacAdam, Alfred J., 2:847
McAfee, Ward, 4:2
McAleer, John J., 1:1238
McAleer, Neil, 5:601
McAlester, A. Lee, 5:623, 5:629
McAlister, Linda, 4:222
McAlister, Lyle N., 3:335, 3:629
McAllester, David P., 3:666
McAllester, Mary, 4:274
McAllister, Robert M., 5:372
McAnany, Emile, 3:803
McArdle, William D., 5:326
MacArthur, Robert H., 5:820
Macaulay, Alastair, 3:736
Macaulay, David, 5:12, 5:193
Macaulay, Neill, 3:631, 3:634, 3:639
Macaulay, Thomas Babington, 1:309, 1:311, 1:323, 1:324, **1:373,** 2:405, **3:405,** 3:409, 3:410
McAuley, James, 2:945, 2:946, **2:958**
MacAvoy, Paul W., 5:280, 5:284
McBain, Ed, 1:1233
Macbeth, George (Mann), 1:515
McBirney, A. R., 5:630
McBride, David, 5:13
McBride, Joseph, 3:833, 3:838
McBride, William L., 4:331
McBrien, Richard P., 4:745
McBrien, William, 1:549
McCabe, C. Kevin, 5:553

MacCabe, Colin, 1:1158
McCabe, Herbert, 4:891
McCabe, James Patrick, 4:6
McCabe, Robert A., 5:835
McCaffery, Larry, 1:911, 1:944, 1:963, 1:980
McCaffery, Lawrence F., 1:122, 1:422
MacCaffrey, Isabel G., 1:198
McCaffrey, Lawrence J., 3:369
McCaffrey, Margo, 5:393
McCaffrey, Phillip, 5:448
MacCaffrey, Wallace, 3:359
McCagg, William O., 3:349
McCain, Marian van Eyk, 5:356
McCall, Christina, 3:616
McCall, Dan, 1:689
McCall, G.J.H., 5:623
McCall, M., 2:351
McCall, Raymond J., 5:427
MacCameron, Robert, 3:638
McCamic, Frances S., 1:243
McCammon, Robert R., 1:1242
MacCana, Proinsias, 4:436
McCann, David R., 2:298, 2:299
McCann, Gordon, 3:861
McCann, Graham, 3:830
McCann, John M., 5:557
McCann, Joy L., 5:350
McCann, Mary Ann, 5:311, 5:760
McCann, Michael, 5:736
MacCannell, Dean, 3:893
McCarthy, B. Eugene, 1:263
McCarthy, Desmond, 1:426
McCarthy, J., 5:553
McCarthy, John D., 3:215
McCarthy, John P., 1:443
McCarthy, Martha M., 3:251
McCarthy, Mary, 1:957, 1:995, **1:1007,** 1:1034, 3:333, 3:899
McCarthy, Paul, 1:886
McCarthy, Thomas A., 4:378, 4:405, 5:89
McCartney, George, 1:563
McCartney, J., 5:77
McCarty, Willard, 5:562
McCauley, Martin, 3:377
McCavitt, William E., 3:802
McChesney, Robert W., 3:812, 5:296
McClary, Susan, 3:661, 3:661
McClatchy, J. D., 1:1045
McClean, Ruari, 1:29
McClellan, Edwin, 2:282
McClellan, James E., III., 5:45
McClelland, David C., 3:175

McClelland, G. W., 1:129
McClelland, I., 2:522
McClintock, Barbara, 5:806
MacClintock, S., 4:97
McCloskey, H. J., 4:389
McCloskey, J. J., 5:115
McCloskey, Robert, 1:1194
McCloskey, Robert G., 3:145
McClosky, Herbert, 3:148
McClung, Jr., Kenneth A., 5:557
McClung, Christina J., 5:557
McClure, Charles R., 1:108
McClure, John, 1:372
McClure, Michael, 1:1008
McClymer, John F., 3:532
MacCoby, Eleanor E., 3:174
Maccoby, Hyam, 4:624
Maccoby, Michael, 5:422
McColley, Diane K., 1:192
McConkey, Edwin M., 5:778
McConnell, Frank, 1:564
McConnell, Scott, 3:491
McCord, David, 1:1195
McCorduck, Pamela, 5:74, 5:537, 5:567, 5:568
McCorkle, Beth, 4:876
McCorkle, Ruth, 5:355
MacCormack, Sabine, 4:449, 4:458
McCormick, Donald, 1:593
McCormick, John, 4:328
McCormick, Richard A., 4:745, 5:122
McCormick, Richard L., 3:532
McCormick, Thomas W., 4:319
McCosh, James, 4:32, 4:212
McCown, Joe, 4:305
McCoy, Alfred W., 3:464
McCoy, Drew, 3:525
McCoy, F. N., 3:9
McCoy, Ralph E., 1:57
McCoy, Richard C., 1:196
MacCracken, Calvin D., 5:226
McCracken, Charles, 4:182
McCracken, David, 3:899
McCracken, R. J., 5:262
McCrady, Edward, 5:776
McCredie, Kenneth B., 5:372
McCreless, Patrick P., 3:728
McCrie, Thomas, 4:774
McCrohan, Donna, 3:812
McCroskey, Mia, 5:557
McCrosson, Doris Ross, 1:467
McCullers, Carson, 1:1009, 1:1080, 1:1100
McCulloh, William E., 2:363
McCullough, David G., 3:532, 3:539, 3:595, 3:640, 3:935
McCullough, David W., 1:32

McCullough, Helen Craig, 2:273
McCullough, Joseph, 1:751
McCullough, Virginia, 5:341, 5:371
McCullough, W. Stewart, 4:684
McCully, Marilyn, 3:787
MacCunn, John, 3:152
MacCurdy, C., 2:541
McCurdy, Howard E., 5:597
McCusker, Brian, 5:663
McCusker, John J., 3:548
McCutcheon-Rosegg, Susan, 5:359
Maccuun, John, 4:193
McDaniel, Jay, 4:745
McDaniel, June, 4:505
McDaniel, Melissa, 5:692
McDermott, John, Jr., 5:415
McDermott, Charlene, 4:37
McDermott, Emily A., 4:475
McDermott, John, 1:433
McDermott, Robert A., 4:353, 4:859
MacDiarmid, Hugh, 1:516
McDiarmid, Lucy, 1:436
McDivitt, James F., 5:628
McDonagh, Don, 3:731, 3:732, 3:744
MacDonagh, Oliver, 3:364, 3:371
McDonagh, Sean, 5:197
MacDonald, Barry, 3:495
MacDonald, Charles G., 3:448
Macdonald, David, 5:761
MacDonald, Douglas, 4:20
MacDonald, Duncan B., 4:575
MacDonald, Dwight, 1:130
McDonald, Forrest, 3:142, 3:521, 3:543
MacDonald, Frank, 3:818
MacDonald, Fred J., 3:812
MacDonald, George, 1:574, 1:577, 1:586, 1:1206
MacDonald, Hugh, 3:682, 3:717
MacDonald, Ian, 3:718
MacDonald, Isobel, 1:328
MacDonald, James M., 2:544
MacDonald, John D., 1:1226, 1:1233
MacDonald, Margaret R., 3:869
MacDonald, Mary, 3:376
MacDonald, Nesta, 3:741
MacDonald, Norman, 3:615
McDonald, Peter, 1:518
MacDonald, Ross, 1:1226, 1:1230, 1:1234
MacDonald, Ruth K., 1:589, 1:1199

MacDonald, Scott, 3:828
MacDonald, Stephen, 1:543
MacDonald, Stuart, 5:47, 5:669
MacDonald, Susan, 1:407
McDonald, William J., 4:675, 4:717
MacDonald, William L., 3:304
McDonnell, Jacqueline, 1:563
McDonnell, Kilian, 4:762
McDonough, Richard, 4:346
McDonough, Thomas R., 5:598
McDougall, Bonnie S., 2:234
McDougall, Derek, 3:157
McDougall, Walter A., 5:597
MacDowell, Douglas M., 3:306
McDowell, Frederick P., 1:843, 1:876
McDowell, Margaret B., 1:788
McDowell, Robert Brendan, 3:370
McDuff, David, 2:658
Mace, Nancy L., 5:392
McEachran, F., 4:199
Macedonski, Alexandru, 2:823
McElderry, Bruce R., Jr., 1:905
McElroy, Bernard, 1:213
McElvaine, Robert S., 3:535
MacEoin, Denis, 4:579
McEvoy, James, 4:115
McEwan, Neil, 1:129
McEwen, Christian, 1:1184
McEwen, Fred B., 1:767
McEwen, James S., 4:774
McFague, Sallie, 4:745, 4:884
McFall, Russell P., 1:1200, 5:639
McFarland, David, 5:826
McFarland, Dorothy T., 1:1025, 2:516
McFarland, H. Neill, 4:541
McFarland, J. D., 4:206
McFarland, Judy L., 5:346
McFarland, Mary B., 5:324
McFarland, Thomas, 1:273, 1:307
McFarlane, Anthony, 3:629
Macfarlane, Gwyn, 5:408
McFarlane, James W., 2:662, 2:666, 2:986
McFarlane, John E., 2:931
McFarlane, Kenneth B., 4:721
MacFarquhar, Roderick, 3:471
McFeely, William S., 1:668, 3:528

MacGaffey, Wyatt, 3:421, 4:462, 4:467
McGaha, Michael D., 2:533
McGann, Jerome J., 1:265, 1:266, 1:283, 1:873
McGarry, Daniel D., 1:122, 1:125
McGee, David, 5:149
McGew, Mac, 1:17
McGill, Frances, 5:369
McGill, Raymond D., 1:1075
McGilton, Henry, 5:555
McGinley, Phyllis, 4:679
McGinn, Bernard, 4:679, 4:700, 4:708, 4:712
McGinn, Kerry A., 5:384
McGinn, Robert E., 5:149
McGinn-Campbell, Karen M., 5:340
McGinnis, Mary, 3:257
McGivering, John H., 1:372
McGlathery, James M., 2:592
McGlynn, Frank, 3:528
McGlynn, John H., 2:317, 2:318
McGovern, Art, 4:896
McGovern, Edythe M., 1:1113
MacGowan, Kenneth, 1:1074, 1:1078
McGowan, Margaret, 2:503
McGowen, Tom, 5:48
McGrade, A. S., 4:121
McGrady, Donald, 2:530
McGrath, Alister E., 4:679, 4:722, 4:762, 4:778
McGrath, Daniel, 1:78
McGrath, F. C., 1:387
McGrath, Patrick, 1:599, 1:618
MacGregor, Geddes, 4:4, 4:14, 4:717, 4:736, 4:774
McGregor, Graham, 2:971
McGuinness, Brian, 4:333, 4:346, 5:700
McGuire, Christopher H., 5:335
McGuire, J. E., 5:41
McGuire, Patrick L., 2:688
McGuire, Philip C., 1:218
McGuire, Steven, 5:109
McGuire, Stryker, 3:896
McGuirk, Bernard, 2:867
McGuirk, Carol, 1:352
Mach, Elyse, 3:672
Mach, Ernst, 5:699, 5:707
Macha, Karel Hynek, 2:788
Machado, Diamantino P., 3:386
Machado, Manuel, 2:537
Machado de Assis, Joaquim Maria, 2:889, **2:896**
Machado y Ruiz, Antonio, 1:560, **2:544**

McHaffie, Barbara J., 4:749
Machan, Tibor, 4:14, 4:265, 4:386
Machann, Clinton, 1:328, 1:870
Machar, Jozef Svatopluk, 2:788
McHarg, Ian L., 5:823
Machedlover, Helene, 1:124
McHenry, Leemon, 4:22
Macherey, Pierre, 1:1127
Machiavelli, Niccolò, 2:398, 2:413, 2:422, 2:425, 2:426, 2:435, **3:160**, 3:333, 3:383, 3:385, **4:144**
Machlin, Paul S., 3:729
Machlis, Joseph, 3:665
Machlup, Fritz, 1:50, 3:47, 3:83
McIlwain, Charles Howard, 3:142
McIlwee, Judith S., 5:188
McIlwraith, Archibald K., 1:171
McInerny, Ralph M., 4:119, 4:307
Macinko, George, 5:620
McInnis, Raymond G., 3:5
McIntosh, Carey, 1:225
McIntosh, Christopher, 4:848
McIntosh, Jane, 3:13
McIntosh, Mary, 3:206
McIntosh, Robert P., 5:820
McIntosh, Robert W., 3:890
McIntrye, J. L., 4:136
MacIntyre, Alasdair C., 4:387, **4:406**, 4:408, 4:897
McIntyre, H. G., 2:450
McIntyre, John R., 5:182
McIntyre, Michael P., 3:126
McIntyre, Robert J., 3:392
Maciuszko, Jerzy J., 2:811
McIver, Tom, 5:780
Mack, Gerstle, 3:773
Mack, John E., 3:437, 3:926
Mack, Mary Peter, 3:151
Mack, Maynard, 1:214, 1:252, 2:5, 2:349
Mack, M. P., 4:191
Mack, Robert D., 4:342
Mack, Sarah, 2:390
Mackail, Denis G., 1:330
Mackail, J. W., 1:383
MacKay, Agnes M., 2:513
MacKay, A. L., 5:6
McKay, Alexander G., 3:305
McKay, Claude, 1:856
McKay, Derek, 3:338
McKay, Frank, 2:972
McKay, John P., 3:61, 3:274
McKay, L. R., 5:305
McKay, Nellie Y., 1:891, 1:1019

McKay, Sandra Lee, 3:256
McKee, Bates, 5:626
McKee, Patrick, 3:869
MacKellar, Thomas, 1:9
McKeller, Peter, 5:427
MacKendrick, Louis K., 2:923
McKendrick, Melveena, 2:524
MacKendrick, Paul L., 2:346, 2:349, 2:381, 3:305, 4:59
McKenna, John W., 3:358
McKenzie, Alan T., 1:231, 1:248
McKenzie, Barbara, 1:1008, 1:1025
Mackenzie, Donald, 5:155
MacKenzie, James J., 5:289
Mackenzie, Jeanne, 1:350
MacKenzie, Norman H., 1:364
MacKenzie, Patrick T., 4:22
MacKenzie, William C., 3:368
McKeon, C. K., 4:102
McKeon, Michael, 1:230
McKeon, Richard, 4:95, 4:189
McKerns, Joseph P., 3:807
MacKerras, Colin, 2:234, 3:465
McKerrow, Ronald B., 1:62
McKerrow, W. S., 5:639
Mackey, Douglas A., 1:1257
Mackey, Robert, 5:60, 5:71, 5:129
McKibben, Bill, 5:115, 5:823
Mackie, J. L., 4:180, 4:202
McKillop, A. B., 3:609
McKim, Donald, 4:719, 4:758
Mackin, Dorothy, 1:323
Mackinder, Sir Halford John, 3:132, 3:326
McKinnell, Robert Gilmore, 5:776
McKinney, H., 5:803
McKinnon, Alastair, 4:240
MacKinnon, Barbara, 4:35
MacKinnon, Edward M., 5:68
McKinnon, James, 3:661
MacKinnon, Neil, 3:613
Mackintosh, Duncan, 2:192
McKirahan, Richard D., Jr., 4:46, 4:70, 4:82
McKissack, Frederick, 3:270
McKissack, Patricia C., 1:832, 3:270, 3:848
McKitrick, Eric L., 3:583
Macklin, John J., 2:546
McKnight, Brian E., 3:464
McKnight, Gerald, 3:705
McKnight, Tom L., 3:126
McKown, Delos B., 5:765
Macksey, Kenneth, 5:237
Macksey, Richard, 1:1134

Mack Smith, Denis, 3:385
McKusick, James, 1:288
MacLachlan, Colin M., 3:629
MacLachlan, Patricia, 1:1195
Maclane, Saunders, 5:484
McLaren, Angus, 3:608
McLaren, Arlene Tigar, 3:608
McLaren, Jay, 3:656
McLaren, John, 2:946
McLaren, Peter, 3:262
McLarsen, J. S., 5:263
McLauchlan, Gordon, 3:495
McLaughlin, Brian, 4:283,
    4:381
McLaughlin, Eleanor, 4:679
McLaughlin, Eugene, 3:204
McLaughlin, Loretta, 5:314
McLaughlin, Mary Martin,
    1:147
McLaughlin, Sigrid, 2:693
McLaurin, Melton A., 3:556
McLean, Albert F., Jr., 1:662
McLean, Andrew M., 1:221
Maclean, Angus, 3:863
MacLean, Douglas, 5:111,
    5:115, 5:129
Maclean, Fitzroy, 3:368,
    3:394
McLean, Hugh, 2:736, 2:766
Maclean, Ian, 3:333
Maclean, Norman, 5:761
McLean, Ruari, 1:9, 1:18,
    1:25
Maclear, Michael, 3:539
MacLeish, Archibald, 1:841,
    1:857, 1:877, 2:492, 3:818
McLeish, Kenneth, 2:353,
    3:665
McLeish, Valerie, 3:665
McLellan, David, 4:227, 4:243
McLellan, Hilary, 5:565
MacLennan, Robert S., 4:617
McLeod, Addison, 2:401
McLeod, A. L., 1:857
Macleod, Arlene, 3:446
McLeod, Karen, 2:961
MacLeod, Malcolm L., 1:182
MacLeod, Murdo J., 3:629
MacLeod, Robert B., 3:167
Macleod, Roy, 5:36
McLeod, W. H., 4:516, 4:517
McLerran, Jennifer, 3:869
McLoughlin, William G.,
    4:753, 4:768
McLuhan, Marshall, 3:203,
    3:621, **3:817**, 4:459, 5:572,
    5:573
MacLure, Millar, 1:187
McLynn, Frank, 3:914, 3:938
McMahon, Gregory, 4:445
McMahon, Judi, 5:397
McMahon, M., 5:230
McMahon, Marie P., 3:362

McMahon, Robert J., 3:515
McMahon, William, 3:859
McManaway, James G.,
    1:189, 1:221
McManners, John, 4:2, 4:675
Macmaster, Juliet, 1:407
McMath, Robert, 3:532
McMichael, George, 1:130,
    1:653, 1:795
Macmillan, W. M., 3:423
McMillen, Neil R., 3:532
McMillin, Arnold, 2:688
McMillin, Scott, 1:228
McMullen, David, 3:468
MacMullen, Edith N., 3:259
MacMullen, Ramsay, 3:306,
    3:308, 4:449, 4:682, 4:684
McMullin, Ernan, 4:48,
    4:143, 5:67
McMullin, Erwin, 5:688
McMullin, Neil, 3:475
McMullin, Stanley, 2:913
McMurray, George R., 2:847,
    2:864, 2:867
McMurray, William, 1:759
McMurtrie, Douglas C., 1:9,
    1:63
McMurtry, Larry, 1:1009,
    1:1053
McNair, Arnold D., 3:305
McNall, Scott G., 3:24
McNally, D., 1:999
McNally, Raymond T., 2:688
McNally, Robert E., 4:729
McNally, Terrence, 1:1071,
    1:1101
McNamara, Jo Ann, 4:689
McNamara, Martin, 4:608,
    4:609, 4:796
McNamee, Gregory, 5:828
McNaught, Kenneth, 3:607
McNaughton, L. William,
    2:193, 2:195
MacNaughton, William R.,
    1:784, 1:1061
McNay, Lois, 4:401
McNeal, R. H., 3:292
**MacNeice, (Frederick)
    Louis**, 1:416, 1:434, **1:517**,
    1:552
McNeil, Barbara J., 5:324
McNeil, Ian, 5:26
MacNeil, Robert, 1:896
McNeil, Robert A., 3:625
McNeil, W. K., 3:861
McNeill, John T., 4:94,
    4:700, 4:762
McNeill, William H(ardy),
    3:274, **3:288**, 3:326, 3:330,
    3:333, 5:820
McNeir, Waldo F., 1:198
McNichol, Stella, 1:570
MacNicholas, John, 1:1074

McNiece, Gerald, 1:288
McNitt, Lawrence, 5:557
MacNiven, Don, 4:221
McNiven, Peter, 4:721
MacNutt, W. S., 3:610, 3:613
Maconie, Robin, 3:721
McPhail, Clark, 3:203
McPhee, Colin, 3:904
McPhee, John, 1:1010,
    5:623, **5:645**, 5:823
McPheeters, D., 2:534
McPherow, William, 1:125
McPherson, Bruce, 1:325
MacPherson, Crawford B.,
    4:174, 4:180, 4:193
Macpherson, James, 4:459
McPherson, James M(unro),
    3:504, 3:526, 3:528, **3:585**,
    3:603
Macpherson, Jay, 2:919
MacPherson, Malcolm, 5:694
McQuade, Donald, 1:795
McQuaid, Gary, 5:515
McQuail, Denis, 3:803
Macquarrie, John, 4:2, 4:265,
    4:718, 4:719, 4:745, 4:893
McQueen, Harvey, 2:971
Macqueen, J. G., 4:445
MacQueen, John, 1:418
McQuillan, Melissa, 3:794
MacRae, George W., 4:813
McRae, John R., 4:530
Macrae, Robert, 5:261
MacRobert, Alan, 5:591
MacShane, Frank, 1:476,
    1:867
McSharry, Patra, 3:873
McSherry, Frank D., Jr.,
    3:858
McShine, Kynaston, 3:796
McSweeney, Kerry, 1:398,
    1:689, 2:924, 2:939
**McTaggart, John McTaggart
    Ellis**, 4:259, **4:303**
Macura, P., 1:102, 5:761
McVan, Barbara, 5:381
McVay, Gordon, 2:718
McVey, Ruth T., 3:489
McVey, Sheila, 1:48
McWhiney, Grady, 3:529
McWhinney, Will, 3:210
McWhirter, David, 1:767
McWhorter, La Delle, 4:294
McWilliams, Carey, 1:735
McWilliams, Dean, 2:463
McWilliams, John P., 1:651,
    1:665
McWilliams, Peter A., 5:537,
    5:557, 5:562
Macy, Sheryl, 3:717
Madách, Imre, 2:797, **2:802**
Madachy, Joseph S., 5:496
Madan, Falconer, 1:583

Madan, T. N., 4:505
Madaras, Lynda, 5:314
Madariaga, Salvador de, 2:522, 3:632
Madaus, George F., 3:256
Madden, David E., 1:918, 1:933, 1:1018, 1:1227
Madden, Edward H., 4:35, 5:62
Madden, W. A., 1:325
Maddock, Kenneth, 4:461
Maddock, Mary, 2:693
Maddox, Brenda, 1:505
Maddox, George L., 5:316
Maddux, James F., 5:403
Madge, John H., 3:200
Madigan, Michael T., 5:783
Madison, Charles A., 1:38, 1:42, 2:32
Madison, James, 3:141, **3:161**
Madsen, Axel, 3:919, 5:642
Madsen, Richard N., 3:248
Madsen, Richard P., 3:471
Madsen, Roy Paul, 3:828
Madsen, Stephen, 3:759
Maduakor, Obi, 2:149
Maes-Jelinek, Hena, 2:936
Magalaner, Marvin, 1:421
Mágalini, Sergio I., 5:367
Magat, Wesley A., 3:58
Magaziner, Ira C., 3:62
Magdol, Edward, 3:553
Magee, Bryan, 4:256, 4:410, 5:99
Magee, David, 1:32
Magee, Elizabeth, 3:728
Magee, Rosemary M., 1:794, 1:1025
Mageli, Paul, 3:556
Maghut, Muhammad, 2:59
Magi, Aldo P., 1:905
Magid, Alvin, 3:641
Magid, Henry M., 3:156
Magill, Frank N., 1:116, 1:122, 1:125, 1:126, 1:128, 1:132, 3:826, 4:2, 4:266, 5:11, 5:728
Magnarelli, Sharon, 2:847
Magnus, Bernd, 4:247
Magnus, Laurie, 2:990
Magnus, Philip, 3:364
Magnuson, Paul, 1:307
Magnusson, Arthur A., 3:381
Magnusson, Magnus, 2:640, 3:368
Magnússon, Sigurdur, 2:640
Magoulias, Harry J., 4:693
Maguire, Robert A., 2:688, 2:722
Mahajan, V. D., 3:486
Mahan, Alfred Thayer, 3:271, **3:287,** 3:338

Mahan, L. Kathleen, 5:348
Mahaney, William C., 5:623
Mahdi, Muhsin, 4:95, 4:584
Maher, John, 3:877
Mahesh Yogi, Maharishi, 4:873
Mahfuz, Najib, 2:67, 2:116, 2:122, 2:123
Mahler, Gustav, 3:705
Mahler, Raphael, 4:632, 4:634
Mahmud, S. F., 4:571
Mahon, Gigi, 3:807
Mahon, Michael, 5:88
Mahoney, Dennis J., 3:142
Mahoney, Dorothy, 1:17
Mahoney, Edward P., 4:128
Mahoney, Michael S., 5:506
Mahoney, Robert, 1:255
Mahony, Bertha E., 1:29, 1:579
Mahood, M. M., 1:216, 1:457
Mahowald, Mary B., 4:17
Maida, Patrick D., 1:606
Maidment, K. J., 2:348
Maienschein, Jane, 5:765, 5:807
Maier, Anneliese, 4:97
Maier, Carol, 2:523
Maier, David, 5:560
Maier, Henry W., 5:442
Maier, Mark H., 3:67
Maier, Pauline, 3:521
Maier, Walter A., III., 4:545
Mailer, Norman, 1:861, 1:908, 1:916, 1:935, 1:957, 1:1005, **1:1011**
Mailick, Mildred, 5:331
Maimonides, 4:208, 4:664, **4:667**
Main, Jackson Turner, 3:518, 3:541
Maina wa Kinyatti, 2:152
Maine, Barry, 1:828
Maine, Sir Henry (James) Sumner, 3:34, 3:39, 3:242
Mainiero, Lina, 1:121, 1:127
Mainstone, Madeleine, 3:336
Mainstone, Rowland, 3:336
Maiorano, Robert, 3:738
Mair, Victor H., 2:190
Mais, Roger, 2:937
Maisel, L. Sandy, 3:509
Maitland, Sara, 2:181
Maixner, Paul, 1:397
Maizell, Robert E., 5:727
Maizlish, Stephen E., 3:524, 3:554, 3:598
Maja-Pearce, Adewale, 2:110, 2:113
Majewski, Henry F., 2:476
Major, Charles, 1:1244
Major, John, 5:707

Majumdar, R. C., 3:484
Majzels, Robert, 2:329
Makens, James, 3:890
Makepeace, Chris E., 1:32
Maki, Z., 5:717
Makin, Peter, 1:873
Makinde, M. Akin, 4:26, 4:369
Makinen, Merja, 1:457
Makkreel, Rudolf A., 4:226
Makler, Harry M., 3:386
Makos, Christopher, 3:796
Makower, Joel, 5:816
Makowsky, Michael, 3:200
Makowsky, Veronica A., 1:983
Makriyannis, John, 2:374
Malachowski, Alan, 4:413
Malamud, Bernard, 1:1012
Malamud, Randy, 1:415, 1:473
Malandra, William W., 4:443, 4:547
Malcles, Louise N., 1:61
Malcolm, Andrew H., 3:896
Malcolm, Janet, 3:184, 5:425
Malcolm, John, 4:82
Malcolm, Norman, 4:346
Malcolm X, (Malcolm Little), 3:556, 4:566, 4:762, 4:861, 4:862, **4:876**
Malebranche, Nicolas, 4:157, 4:164, **4:181**
Malgonkar, Manohar, 2:178
Malik, Charles, 4:373, 4:575
Malin, David, 5:588
Malin, Irving, 1:918, 1:947, 1:1057, 2:49
Malin, Michael C., 5:593
Malino, Francis, 4:637
Malinowski, Bronislaw, 3:20, 3:23, 3:26, 3:29, **3:35,** **4:485**
Malinowsky, H. Robert, 5:5, 5:217
Malkin, Sol M., 1:76
Mallac, Guy de, 2:746
Mallarmé, Stéphane, 1:691, 2:441, 2:445, **2:486,** 2:514, 2:621
Malle, Louis, 3:840
Mallea, Eduardo, 2:844, **2:870**
Mallinson, Jean, 2:907
Mallinson, Vernon, 3:382
Mallowan, M. E. L., 3:301
Malloy, James M., 3:633
Malm, William P., 3:666
Malmgren, Carl Darryl, 1:805, 1:919
Malmstad, John E., 2:701
Malone, Bill C., 3:852
Malone, Dumas, 1:640, 3:155

Malone, Michael P., 3:515
Maloney, George A., 4:756
Maloney, H. Newton, 4:890
Malory, Sir Thomas, 1:146,
  1:152, **1:154**
Malotki, Ekkehart, 3:865,
  3:865
Malouf, David, 2:958
Malpas, J. E., 4:283
Malpezzi, Frances M., 3:864
Malraux, André, 2:310, **2:487**
Malter, Henry, 4:672
Malthus, Thomas Robert,
  1:375, 1:393, 3:54, **3:91,**
  3:95, 3:100, 3:106
Malti-Douglas, Fedwa, 2:56,
  2:74
Maltin, Leonard, 3:826
Maly, Kenneth, 4:75
Mamet, David, 1:1087,
  1:1101, 3:828
Mamiya, Lawrence, 4:748
Manchester, William R.,
  1:860, 3:539
Mancinelli, Fabrizio, 4:689
Mancing, Howard, 2:536
Mancini, Pat M., 2:849
Mandela, Nelson, 3:423
Mandelbaum, David G., 3:21
Mandelbaum, Maurice, 4:22,
  4:162, 4:187
Mandelbaum, Michael, 3:279
Mandelker, Ira L., 4:842,
  4:844
Mandelkern, Solomon, 4:818
Mandell, Gail, 1:87
Mandell, Lewis, 3:548
Mandell, Richard, 3:343
Mandelstam, Nadezhda, 2:738
**Mandelstam (Man-
  del'shtam), Osip,** 2:683,
  2:733, **2:737**
Mander, Jerry, 5:126, 5:129
Mandrou, Robert, 4:162, 5:40
Manes, Stephen, 5:543
Manet, Edouard, 2:456,
  3:769, 3:771, **3:780,** 3:783,
  3:789
Manfra, Jo Ann, 5:123
Manfred, Frederick, 1:1217
Mang, Karl, 3:766
Manganaro, Marc, 3:12,
  4:477
Mange, Maria A., 5:628
Mangel, Charles, 5:405
Manger, Itzik, 2:40
Mango, Cyril, 3:763
Manguel, Alberto, 2:849
Mangum, Garth, 4:846
Mangum, John M., 5:197
Mangunwijaya, Y. B., 2:316
Manheim, Michael, 1:1108
Manhire, Bill, 2:971

Manila, Quijano de, 2:329
Mani-Leib, 2:40
Man-jung, Kim. *See* Kim
  Man-jung
Mankin, Paul A., 2:481
Manlove, C. N., 1:513
Mann, Charles C., 5:651,
  5:691, 5:713
Mann, David D., 1:237, 1:243
Mann, Heinrich, 2:601,
  4:247
Mann, Horace, 3:259, **3:264**
Mann, Jacob, 4:626, 4:631
Mann, Jill, 1:150, 1:151
Mann, Jonathan, 5:388
Mann, Michael, 3:24, 3:207
Mann, Nicholas, 4:151
Mann, Peggy, 5:403
Mann, Thomas, 1:434, 1:945,
  2:494, 2:564, 2:586, **2:601,**
  2:606, 2:610, 2:644, 2:911,
  3:729, 4:255, 4:256
Manne, Alan, 3:48
Manners, Gerald, 5:628
Manners, Robert A., 3:14
Mannheim, Karl, 3:140,
  3:213, **3:231,** 3:244
Manning, Brian, 3:360
Manning, Carol S., 1:896
Manning, Clarence A., 2:780,
  2:838
Manning, Olivia, 2:824
Manning, Peter, 5:565
Manning, Peter J., 1:283
Manning, Rita, 4:391
Mannion, Antionette M.,
  5:823
Mannon, James M., 5:379
Manor, James, 3:487
Manosevitz, Martin, 3:178
Manschreck, Clyde L., 4:677,
  4:720, 4:730
Mansell, Darrel, 1:276
Manser, Anthony, 4:221,
  4:331
Mansergh, Nicholas, 3:371
Mansfield, Harvey C., Jr.,
  3:160, 4:145
Mansfield, Katherine, 1:422,
  1:447, 2:969, 2:977, **2:978**
Mansfield, Peter, 3:437, 3:453
Manso, Peter, 1:1012
Manson, Richard, 2:442,
  4:216
Mansuripur, Masud, 5:550
Mantle, Burns, 1:1074
Manto, Saadat Hasan, 2:178
Manton, Jo, 1:301
Manuel, Don Juan, 2:520
Manuel, Frank E., 4:128,
  4:184, 5:42
Manuel, Fritzie P., 4:128
Manuud, Antonio G., 2:328

Manvell, Roger, 3:832
Manwaring, M. G., 3:280
Manzalaoui, Mahmoud, 2:57
Manzoni, Alessandro, 2:425,
  2:442
Mao, Nathan K., 2:210, 2:260
Mao Tse-tung, 2:256, 3:102,
  4:359, 4:361
Mao Tun, 2:248, 2:249,
  2:258
Mapanje, Jack, 2:165
Mappes, Thomas A., 5:122
Maqay, Tamas, 1:100
Marable, Manning, 1:832,
  3:556, 4:877
Maraini, Dacia, 2:400, **2:426**
Maraniss, James E., 2:533
Marble, Duane F., 3:120
Marc'hadour, Germaine,
  1:194
Marc, David, 3:871, 3:873
Marcel, Gabriel, 4:250,
  4:304, 4:318, 4:331
Marcell, David W., 4:237
Marcellinus, Ammianus,
  2:379
March, James G., 3:49, 3:210
Marchalonis, Shirley, 1:651,
  1:715, 1:750
Marchand, Leslie A., 1:283,
  1:777
Marchand, Philip, 3:818
Marchand, Roland, 3:548
Marchione, Margherita, 2:403
Marchuk, Gurii I., 5:632
Marcil-Lacoste, Louise, 4:212
Marcinkevičius, Justinas,
  2:805
Marcou, Jules, 5:785
Marcum, J., 3:423
Marcus, Alan I., 5:263
Marcus, Geoffrey, 3:362
Marcus, George E., 1:1133,
  3:12, 4:426
Marcus, Greil, 3:513, 3:560
Marcus, Harold G., 3:422
Marcus, Jacob Rader, 4:623,
  4:637, 4:640, 4:650, 4:652
Marcus, Jane, 1:570
Marcus, Joyce, 3:628
Marcus, Leah, 1:209
Marcus, Mordecai, 1:842
Marcus, Philip L., 1:572
Marcus, Rebecca B., 5:362
Marcus, Steven, 1:312, 1:350,
  3:75, 3:184
Marcuse, Dietrich, 5:304
Marcuse, Herbert, 4:245,
  4:297, 4:305, 4:386, 4:390,
  4:403, **4:407,** 5:71, 5:88,
  5:93
Marcuse, Sibyl, 3:672
Mardersteig, Giovanni, 1:9

Mare, Margaret, 2:603
Marechera, Dambudzo,
2:165
Marek, George R., 3:690
Marenbon, John, 4:94, 4:100
Margenau, Henry, 5:68
Marget, Madeline, 5:370
Marglin, Frederique Apffel,
4:505
Margolies, Cynthia P., 5:372
Margolies, Edward, 1:794
Margolies, Susanna, 3:899
Margoliouth, David S., 4:571,
4:588
Margolis, Howard, 5:54
Margolis, Joseph, 4:294,
4:381, 5:64, 5:72, 5:75,
5:91
Margolis, Max, 4:594
Margolis, Simeon, 5:317
Margossian, Marzbed, 2:76
Margulis, Lynn, 5:768, 5:776,
5:820
Mariani, Paul J., 1:901
Marías, Julián, 2:552
Marias, Julian, 3:25, 4:17,
4:22, 4:162, 4:315, 5:97
Mariátegui, José C., 3:640
Marinello, Peter V., 2:407
Marinetti, Filippo Tomma-
so, 2:427, 2:440
Maringer, Johannes, 4:432
Marinković, Ranko, 2:785,
2:786
Marino, Giambattista, 1:175
Marion, Jean-Luc, 4:889
Maritain, Jacques, 2:988,
4:22, 4:220, 4:260, 4:285,
4:305
Marius, Richard, 1:194, 4:148
Marivaux, Pierre Carlet de
Chamblain de, 2:444,
2:488
Mark, Hans, 5:596
Mark, Thomas C., 4:189
Markel, Michael H., 1:443
Marker, Frederick J., 2:666,
3:832
Marker, Lise-Lone, 2:666,
3:832
Markert, Linda Rae, 5:149
Markey, Thomas L., 2:648
Markgraf, Carl, 1:330, 1:438
Markham, Clements R., 3:936
Markham, Felix, 3:339
Markle, Joyce B., 1:1061
Markley, Robert, 1:243
Markman, Peter T., 4:465
Markman, Roberta H., 4:465
Markoff, John, 5:547
Markov, Vladimir, 2:688,
2:732
Markovic, Mihailo, 4:33

Markovits, Claude, 3:486
Markovitz, I. L., 3:421
Markowitz, Hal, 5:826
Markowitz, Harry M., 3:56
Marks, Alfred H., 2:272
Marks, Barry A., 1:826
Marks, Carole, 3:556
Marks, Elaine, 1:926, 1:1184,
2:448, 2:458
Marks, Frederick W., III,
3:595
Marks, Geoffrey, 5:314
Marks, John L., 5:487
Marks, Lawrence, E., 3:177
Marks, Ronald, 5:399
Markson, Elizabeth W.,
3:201, 3:216
Markun, Patricia M., 5:278
Markus, Robert A., 4:110
Markusen, Ann, 3:548
Marlatt, G. Alan, 5:419
Marlin, Emily, 5:402
Marling, Karal A., 3:869
Marling, William H., 1:1228
Marlowe, Christopher,
1:157, 1:175, **1:186,** 1:203,
1:271, 2:393
Marmor, T. R., 3:57, 5:328
Marmorstein, Arthur, 4:621
Marney, John, 2:201
Marotti, Arthur F., 1:178
Marovitz, Sanford E., 1:79,
1:121
Marowitz, Charles, 1:425
Marquardt, Manfred, 4:790
Marqués, René, 2:843, **2:870,**
2:937
Marr, David G., 2:312, 2:339,
2:966, 3:491
Marr, Phebe, 3:450
Marranca, Bonnie, 1:1074,
1:1111
Marrer-Tising, Carlee, 2:590
Marrin, A., 3:292
Marriott, Alice, 1:631
Marriott, F.H.C., 5:521
Marrone, Steven P., 4:115
Marrou, H. I., 2:347, 3:306,
4:110
Marrow, Alfred J., 3:190
Marrs, Suzanne, 1:896
Marrus, Michael R., 3:349,
4:637
Marryat, Captain Frederick,
1:316, **1:374**
Marsack, Robyn, 1:518
Marschall, Larry, 5:594
Marsden, Brian, 5:593
Marsden, George M., 4:753
Marsden, Michael T., 3:873
Marsella, Joy A., 1:1199
Marsh, Carole, 1:48

Marsh, Clifton E., 4:579,
4:862
Marsh, Jan, 1:558
Marsh, Rosalind J., 2:688
Marshack, Alexander, 4:434
Marshall, A. J., 5:800
Marshall, Alfred, 3:86, **3:93,**
3:237
Marshall, Bruce, 4:753, 4:885
Marshall, Byron, 3:478
Marshall, Charles W., 5:346
Marshall, Cynthia, 1:587
Marshall, Daniel P., 5:342
Marshall, David, 2:472, 2:488
Marshall, Dorothy, 3:362
Marshall, Paule, 1:1014
Marshall, P. J., 3:362
Marshall, Richard H., Jr.,
4:572
Marshall, Roger, 5:238
Marshall, Sherrin D., 3:383
Marshall, Sybil, 3:856
Marshall, William H., 1:283
Marsot, A. L., 4:579
Marston, John, 1:187
Marszalek, John E., 3:509
Martel, Gordon, 3:344
Martel, Susan, 5:357
Martelli, George, 3:930
Martelli, Leonard, 5:388
Marten, Gerald G., 3:489
Marten, Harry, 1:810, 1:1004
Martí, José, 2:871, 2:937
Martial (Marcus Valerius
Martialis), 2:383, **2:388,**
2:392
Martin, Adrienne, 2:536
Martin, Bernard, 4:595,
4:600, 4:652
Martin, Bill, 4:398
Martin, Bruce, 1:508
Martin, Chester, 3:607
Martin, Christian, 5:725
Martin, Dolores Moyano,
3:625
Martin, E. A., 5:761
Martin, Edley Wainright,
5:544
Martin, F. X., 3:369
Martin, Fenton S., 3:506
Martin, Ged, 3:613
Martin, Geoffrey J., 3:128,
5:32, 5:620
Martin, George, 3:727
Martin, George W., 3:670
Martin, Gerald, 2:847
Martin, Gottfried, 4:177,
4:206
Martin, Helmut, 2:234
Martin, Henri-Jean, 1:8
Martin, J. L., 5:660
Martin, James, 5:302, 5:538,
5:557, 5:560

Martin, James Kirby, 3:521, 3:552
Martin, Jay, 1:715, 1:897, 1:1006
Martin, John, 3:732
Martin, Judy, 1:17
Martin, Kingsley, 3:156
Martin, Luther H., 4:450
Martin, Michael, 3:509, 5:129
Martin, Mike W., 4:389
Martin, Mildred, 1:473
Martin, M. Kay, 3:17
Martin, Pete, 1:1165
Martin, Philip W., 1:268, 1:283
Martin, Phyllis, 1:92
Martin, Phyllis M., 3:419
Martin, R., 3:321
Martin, Rafe, 4:514
Martin, Ralph G., 3:539, 3:816
Martin, Richard M., 4:403
Martin, Robert, 3:678
Martin, Robert B., 1:335, 1:402
Martin, Robert K., 1:707, 1:1182
Martin, Robert M., 4:14, 4:383
Martin, Roland, 3:763
Martin, Russell, 1:921, 5:393
Martin, Samuel, 1:100
Martin, Stephen-Paul, 1:794
Martin, T. W., 3:359
Martin, Terence, 1:677, 4:32, 4:35
Martin, Timothy Peter, 1:505
Martin, Waldo E., Jr., 1:668
Martin, Wallace, 1:1132
Martin, Walter, 4:858
Martin, Wendy, 1:628, 1:635, 1:740
Martin, William G., 3:424
Martin, William R., 3:665
Martin, W. R., 2:922
Martindale, Charles, 1:219
Martindale, Joanna, 4:128
Martindale, Michelle, 1:219
Martine, James J., 1:723, 1:919, 1:1104, 1:1108
Martineau, Harriet, 1:311, 1:317, 1:344, **1:375**
Martinez-Alier, Juan, 5:823
Marting, Diane E., 2:847
Martinich, A. P., 4:22
Martins, Peter, 3:747, 3:751
Martins, Wilson, 2:890
Martinson, Harry, 2:671, **2:677**
Martinson, Moa, 2:671, 2:672
Marty, Martin E., 4:753, 4:890, 4:893
Martyn, J. Louis, 4:825

Martz, John D., 3:636
Martz, Louis L., 1:166, 1:194, 1:200, 4:148
Martz, William J., 1:950
Marulić, Marko, 2:784
Maruyama, Masao, 3:478
Marvell, Andrew, 1:188
Marvick, Louis W., 2:487
Marvin, Carolyn, 5:297
Marvin, Francis S, 3:224
Marwah, Onkar S., 5:287
Marwick, Arthur, 3:367
Marx, Alexander, 4:594
Marx, Karl Heinrich, 1:434, 1:807, 2:453, 3:37, 3:50, 3:51, 3:74, **3:94,** 3:102, 3:112, 3:122, 3:198, 3:2223:232, 3:271, 3:284, **3:289,** 3:340, 3:601, 4:12, 4:158, 4:216, 4:227, 4:228, **4:241,** 4:261, 4:297, 4:309, 4:377, 4:385, 4:399, 4:407, 4:409, 4:424, 4:425, 4:740, 5:59, 5:69, 5:87, 5:94, 5:163
Marx, Leo, 1:651, 1:715
Marx, Leonie A., 2:646
Marx, Robert, 1:1078
Marx, Samuel, 3:713
Marx, Werner, 4:252
Marx, Wesley, 5:632
Marx Brothers, 1:1097
Marxsen, Willi, 4:825
Marzán, Julio, 2:849
Masani, Pesi, 5:584
Masaoka Shiki, 2:288, 2:291
Masaryk, Tomáš G., 2:788, 2:790
Mascaro, Juan, 4:501
Masefield, John, 1:474, **1:518**
Mashaw, J. L., 3:57
Masiak, Mary J., 5:342
Masing-Delic, Irene, 2:688
Maskaleris, Thanasis, 2:375
Maslin, Simeon J., 4:602
Maslow, Abraham H(arold), 3:175, **5:460**
Maslow, Bertha G., 5:461
Maslowski, Peter, 3:546
Mason, Brian, 5:628
Mason, Colin, 3:654
Mason, Francis, 3:738
Mason, H. T., 4:218
Mason, Jackie, 2:30
Mason, John, 1:5
Mason, Philip, 3:424
Mason, Robert J., 5:816
Mason, Shirley L., 5:33, 5:623
Mason, S. M., 4:210
Mason, Stephen F., 5:26
Mason, Steve, 4:616

Maspero, Henri, 4:528
Mass, Jeffrey P., 3:475
Masse, Henri, 4:572
Massey, Mary Elizabeth, 3:529
Massine, Léonide, 3:736, 3:741, 3:745, **3:747**
Massinger, Philip, 1:189
Masson, Jeffrey Moussaieff, 3:184
Masson, Michel C., 4:359
Mast, Gerald, 1:1158, 3:667, 3:838
Masters, Edgar Lee, 1:811, 1:855, **1:858,** 1:1067
Masters, Hardin W., 1:859
Masters, Jamie, 2:388
Masters, Roger, 4:213
Masters, Roger D., 3:164
Masters, William H., 5:429
Masud, Muhammad K., 4:375
Masuji, Ibuse. *See* Ibuse Masuji
Masunaga, Reiho, 4:538
Masur, Gerhard, 3:632
Masur, Louis P., 1:717
Matarazzo, Joseph D., 5:401
Matas, Julio, 2:848
Matczak, Sebastian A., 4:14
Matejić, Mateja, 2:781, 2:785, 2:827, 2:828, 2:835
Matejka, Ladislav, 2:688
Mates, Benson, 4:57
Mates, Julian, 3:661
Matheopoulous, Helena, 3:671
Mather, George A., 4:854
Mather, Kirtley F., 5:33, 5:623
Mathes, Valerie S., 1:761
Mathew, Andrew M., 5:427
Mathew, Gervase, 3:422
Mathews, Basil, 1:785
Mathews, Jane D., 1:1074
Mathews, Richard, 1:613
Mathews, Timothy, 2:451
Mathewson, Rufus W., 2:688
Mathias, Roland, 1:561
Mathies, Loraine, 5:544
Matich, Olga, 2:688
Matilsky, Barbara C., 5:193
Matisse, Henri, 3:769, **3:780,** 3:786
Matlaw, Myron, 1:1078
Matlin, Margaret, 3:178
Matlock, J. F., 3:292
Matoš, Antun Gustav, 2:785
Matossian, Mary K., 3:326
Matossian, Nouritza, 3:731
Matras, Christian, 2:655
Matschoss, Conrad, 5:217
Matsen, Herbert S., 4:128
Matson, Johnny L., 5:427

Matsumoto, Tomone, 2:283
Matsumoto Seicho, 2:289
Matt, Daniel Chanah, 4:630
Matt, L. von, 3:304
Mattei, Carlos R., 5:97
Mattelart, Armand, 1:1164
Matteo, Sherrie, 3:218
Matthews, Bruce, 4:518
Matthews, David, 3:725
Matthews, Eric, 4:211
Matthews, Fred, 3:237
Matthews, Glenna, 3:557
Matthews, Honor, 2:985
Matthews, James, 1:528
Matthews, Janet R., 3:168,
  3:181
Matthews, Jill Julius, 3:494
Matthews, John, 3:310
Matthews, John T., 1:837
Matthews, Nancy M., 3:772
Matthews, Richard, 1:454
Matthews, William F., 1:25,
  1:87
Matthews, William H., III,
  5:623, 5:639
Matthews, William Klees-
  mann, 2:796, 2:835
Matthias, John, 1:503
Matthiessen, F. O., 1:651,
  1:656, 1:715, 1:720, 1:761,
  1:767, 1:770, 2:990
Matthiessen, Peter, 3:904,
  3:930
Mattingly, Garrett, 3:359,
  4:732
Mattingly, Harold, 4:684
Mattison, Chris, 5:771
Mattock, Chris, 5:225
Matton, Mary Ann, 5:456
Mattson, Mark T., 5:816
Matual, David, 2:766
Matuska, Alexander, 2:790
Matusow, Allen J., 3:539
Matute, Ana María, 2:521,
  2:545
Mauchly, John, 5:578, 5:581
Maucini, Matthew J., 4:307
Maude, Aylmer, 2:766
Maududi, Abdul A., 4:575
Mauger, Thierry, 3:451
Maugham, Robin, 1:521
Maugham, W(illiam) Somer-
  set, 1:424, 1:432, **1:519,**
  1:537, 2:238, 2:310, 3:775
Maughan-Brown, David,
  2:152
Maulana, Muhammad Ali,
  4:575
Mauldin, John H., 5:597
Maung, Mya, 3:489
Maupassant, Guy de, 2:488,
  2:839
Maurer, Armand, 4:119

Maurer, David J., 3:510
Maurer, Heinz F. W., 5:628
Mauriac, François, 1:488,
  1:1064, **2:489**
Maurois, André, 1:283, 2:453,
  2:454, 2:466, 2:473, 2:483,
  2:495, 5:408
Maury, Matthew F., 5:632
Mauss, Armand L., 3:215
Mauss, Marcel, 3:16
Mauzy, Diane K., 3:492
Mavian, Vahram, 2:76
Mawell, Robyn, 3:767
Maxwell, Baldwin, 1:189
Maxwell, D.E.S., 1:479, 1:715
Maxwell, Grover, 5:64, 5:80
Maxwell, James Clerk,
  5:228, 5:659, 5:665, 5:674,
  5:683, 5:694, 5:699, **5:700**
Maxwell, J. C., 1:206
Maxwell, Mary, 5:826
Maxwell, Robert, 5:330
May, Antoinette, 3:807
May, Charles E., 1:693
May, Elizabeth, 3:666
May, Ernest R., 3:471, 3:515,
  3:546
May, Florence, 3:684
May, Gita, 2:511
May, Glenn Anthony, 3:493
May, Henry F., 3:518, 3:560
May, Herbert G., 4:809
May, John R., 1:919
May, Keith M., 1:546
May, Kenneth, 5:491
May, Lary, 3:560
May, Rollo, 5:462
May, William, 4:743
Mayakovsky, Vladimir, 2:95,
  2:683, 2:731, **2:738**
Mayberry, Katherine J., 1:391
Maycock, Paul D., 5:289
Mayer, Debby, 1:53
Mayer, Fanny H., 4:539
Mayer, Jacob B., 3:165
Mayer, J. P., 4:134
Mayer, Martin, 3:56
Mayer, Milton, 3:264
Mayer, Ralph, 3:757
Mayer, Thomas, 3:65
Mayers, David A., 3:546,
  3:584
Mayers, Janis, 2:106
Mayfield, Wendy M., 1:45
Mayhead, Robin, 1:300
Mayhew, David R., 3:146
Mayhew, Henry, 1:310,
  1:324, 1:347, 1:366, **1:376**
Mayle, Peter, 3:900
Maynard, Jeff, 5:305
Maynard, Joe, 1:958
Maynard, John R., 1:339
Mayne, Ethel C., 1:339

Mayne, Seymour, 2:918
Mayo, Deborah G., 5:155
Mayo, Gretchen W., 3:865
Mayo, Henry B., 3:143
Mayo, Robert S., 2:589
Mayr, Ernst, 5:34, 5:765
Mayr, Otto, 5:43
Mays, James L., 4:819
Mays, Wolf, 4:263
Mazar, Amihai, 4:808
Mazer, Norma Fox, 1:1195
Mazini, Ibrahim 'Abd al-
  Qadir, 2:59
Mazlish, Bruce, 4:159
Mazmanian, Daniel, 3:550
Mazo, Joseph H., 3:733
Mazrui, Ali Al Amin, 2:153
Mazur, Allan, 5:155, 5:214
Mažuranić, Ivan, 2:785
Mazzaro, Jerome, 1:913,
  2:418
Mazzeo, Joseph A., 2:418
Mazzotta, Giuseppe, 2:410,
  2:418
Mbalia, Doreatha D., 1:1019
Mbiti, John S(amuel), 4:370,
  4:463
Meacham, Standish, 3:367
Mead, Christopher, 5:826
Mead, Frank S., 4:6, 4:717,
  4:751
Mead, George Herbert,
  3:208, 3:221, **3:232,** 4:260,
  4:308
Mead, G. R., 4:87
Mead, Hunter, 4:22
Mead, Lawrence M., 3:212
Mead, Margaret, 3:15, 3:27,
  3:28, 3:34, **3:36,** 3:39,
  3:174, 3:235
Mead, Marion, 4:874
Mead, Philip, 2:947
Mead, Shepherd, 1:1118
Mead, Sidney E., 4:753
Mead, Walter H., 5:280
Meade, James E., 3:54, 3:59
Meade, Marion, 1:868
Meadowcroft, Sam, 5:262
Meadows, Dennis L., 5:823
Meadows, Donella H., 3:48,
  5:167, 5:573, 5:823
Meadows, Eddie S., 3:669
Meadows, Jack, 5:126
Meagher, John C., 1:184
Meagher, Robert, 4:475
Means, Barbara, 3:171
Mechanic, David, 5:335
Meckier, Jerome, 1:350
Meckler, Alan Marshall, 1:38
Medawar, Jean S., 5:18,
  5:761

Medawar, Sir Peter Brian, 4:385, **5:17**, 5:314, 5:761, 5:765
Medcalf, Stephen, 1:147
Medin, Doug, 3:175
Medina, Enrique, 2:844, **2:872**
Medina, Manuel, 5:152
Medley, D. J., 3:354
Medvedev, Grigori, 5:287
Medvedev, P. N., 2:684
Medvedev, Roy, 2:756, 3:346, 3:397
Medvedev, Zhores A., 3:346
Medvei, Victor C., 5:34
Meehan, Brenda, 4:756
Meehan, James W., 3:61
Meehan, Richard, 5:155
Meeks, Wayne A., 3:308
Meese, Elizabeth, 1:1182
Meeuse, Bastiaan, 5:768
Megeath, Joe D., 5:523
Megged, Aharon, 2:21
Megill, Allan, 4:398
Megill, Robert E., 5:286
Mehden, Fred von der, 4:518
Mehdi, Rubya, 4:579
Mehlman, Felice, 3:766
Mehra, Jagdish, 5:708, 5:714
Mehra, Parshotam, 3:483
Mehrotra, A. K., 2:176
Mehta, Ved, 4:266, 4:553
Mehtha, S. P., 1:25
Meier, August, 1:785, 3:270, 3:506, 3:557
Meier, Kenneth J., 3:256
Meier, Levi, 5:122
Meier-Graefe, Julius, 3:795
Meiggs, Russell, 3:302
Meigs, Anna S., 4:462
Meigs, Cornelia, 1:1196
Meikle, Jeffrey L., 5:193
Meilach, Dona Z., 5:538
Meillassoux, Claude, 3:16, 3:429
Meine, Curt, 5:835
Meine, Franklin J., 3:872
Meiners, Roger K., 1:889, 1:1006
Meinhart, Noreen T., 5:393
Meinig, Donald W., 3:121, 3:125, 3:133
Meinkoth, Norman A., 5:761
Meinwald, Constance C., 4:82
Meisami, Julie Scott, 2:83
Meisch, Lynn, 3:896
Meisel, Martin, 1:323
Meisel, Perry, 1:362, 3:211
Meiselman, Moshe, 4:650
Meisner, Maurice, 3:469, 3:471
Meister, Charles W., 2:710
Mei Yao-ch'en, 2:214

Melber, Jehuda, 4:663
Melby, Ernest O., 3:265
Melcher, Marguerite F., 4:849
Melchett, Sonia, 3:893
Meldola, R., 5:752
Melges, Frederick T., 5:415
Melhado, Evan M., 5:739
Melhem, D. H., 1:954
Mellaart, James, 3:301, 4:434
Mellard, James M., 1:919
Mellen, Joan, 3:832
Mellers, Wilfrid, 3:661, 3:665, 3:726
Mellin, Michael, 5:557
Mello, Nancy K., 5:402
Mellor, Anne K., 1:266, 1:301, 2:986
Mellor, Ronald, 3:321
Mellow, James R., 1:840, 1:883
Mellown, Elgin W., 1:522
Melman, Seymour, 3:67, 5:234
Melnick, Arthur, 4:206
Melnick, R. Shep, 5:184
Melosh, Barbara, 5:338
Melton, J. Gordon, 4:4, 4:6, 4:7, 4:717, 4:751, 4:848, 4:854, 4:856, 4:859, 4:865, 4:866, 4:895
Meltzer, A., 3:65
Meltzer, Alan S., 5:390
Meltzer, David, 4:630
Meltzer, Edmund, 4:569
Meltzer, Judith, 5:335
Melville, Arabella, 5:351
Melville, Herman, 1:598, 1:657, 1:674, 1:675, 1:685, 1:773, 1:803, 1:967, 1:977, 1:1054, 1:1192, 1:1193, 1:1219, 2:427, 2:432
Melvin, Patricia Mooney, 3:210
Melzack, Ronald, 5:393
Melzi, Robert C., 1:100
Memmi, Albert, 3:349
Menaker, Esther, 5:466
Menand, Louis, 1:415
Menander, 2:355, 2:364, 2:378, 2:395
Menard, Henry W., 5:630, 5:632, 5:636
Menard, Russell R., 3:548
Menard, Scott, 3:206
Mencken, H(enry) L(ouis), 1:117, 1:807, 1:859, 1:1230, 4:247
Mendel, Arthur, 3:675
Mendel, Gregor Johann, 5:525, 5:777, 5:806, 5:807, 5:808
Mendel, Roberta, 3:893

Mendeleev, Dmitrii Ivanovitch, 5:364, 5:657, 5:750
Mendele Mokher Seforim, 2:41
Mendelsohn, Ezra, 3:349, 4:637, 4:656, 4:658
Mendelsohn, Roy M., 5:419
Mendelson, Alan, 4:670
Mendelson, Edward, 1:435, 1:436, 1:1035
Mendelson, Jack H., 5:402
Mendelssohn, Felix, 3:675, 3:705, 4:209, 4:493
Mendelssohn, Moses, 4:204, 4:208, 4:219, 4:252, 4:493
Mendenhall, William, 5:523
Mendes-Flohr, Paul R., 3:349, 4:634, 4:662, 4:888
Méndez-M., Miguel, 2:843, 2:872
Mendiones, Ruchira, 2:336
Meneghini, Giovannibattista, 3:686
Meneghini, Robert, 5:633
Menemencioglu, 2:96
Menendez, Albert J., 1:125
Menges, M. C., 4:121
Mengham, Rod, 1:487
Meng Hao-jan, 2:214
Meng-lung, Feng. *See* Feng Meng-lung
Menninger, Karl Augustus, 5:463
Menno Simons, 4:779
Menton, Seymour, 2:847
Menzel, Donald H., 5:591
Menzel, Paul T., 5:79, 5:122
Mepham, John, 4:243
Meras, Icchokas, 2:805
Merchant, Carolyn, 3:550, 4:167, 5:188, 5:823
Merchant, Paul, 5:269
Mercier, Vivian, 2:493
Meredith, Dale D., 5:234
Meredith, David, 3:494
Meredith, George, 1:297, 1:352, 1:360, 1:378, 1:384, 1:390
Meredith, Margaret O., 5:182
Merezhkovsky, Dmitry, 2:728
Mergal, Angel M., 4:724
Merideth, Robert, 5:115, 5:816
Merk, Frederick, 3:525
Merk, Lois B., 3:525
Merkel, Ingrid, 4:128
Merkel, James A., 5:214
Merkle, John C., 4:665
Merklein, Helmut A., 5:284
Merlan, Philip, 4:61
Merleau-Ponty, Maurice, 4:234, 4:261, 4:309, 4:329

Mermin, Dorothy, 1:315, 1:337
Mernissi, Fatima, 2:56, 3:444, 4:579
Merod, Jim, 1:1127
Merrell, Floyd, 2:857, 4:266, 4:391
Merriam, Alan P., 3:666, 3:865
Merriam, Charles E., 3:162
Merril, Thomas F., 1:981
Merrill, George Perkins, 5:624
Merrill, James, 1:1014
Merrill, John C., 3:807
Merrill, Kenneth R., 4:35, 4:202
Merrill, Robert, 1:1012
Merrimum, Eve, 1:773
Merrin, Jeredith, 1:864
Merritt, A., 1:594
Merritt, James Douglas, 1:474
Merritt, Jeffrey, 1:88
Merryweather, F. Somner, 1:32
Mersereau, John, 2:735
Mertens, Wim, 3:665
Merton, Robert K(ing), 3:210, 3:213, 3:214, 3:215, 3:231, **3:233**, 5:43, 5:155
Merton, Thomas, 2:858, 4:561, **4:780**, 4:895
Merwe, Alwyn van der, 5:719
Merwin, Henry C., 1:756
Merwin, W(illiam) S(tanley), 1:912, **1:1015**, 2:175
Meryman, Richard, 5:402
Merz, John Theodore, 4:162, 4:177, 5:47
Merzbach, Uta, 5:508
Meserole, Harrison T., 1:630
Meserve, Mollie A., 1:1075
Meserve, Walter J., 1:1072, 1:1074, 1:1075
Meskell, David, 2:498
Meskill, John, 2:186, 2:225
Messadie, Gerald, 5:29
Messenger, Ann, 1:226
Messer, Robert L., 3:539
Messerli, Douglas, 1:921
Mesthene, Emmanuel G., 5:71, 5:156
Mestrovic, Stjepan, 3:225
Meszaros, I., 2:802
Metcalf, Barbara Daly, 3:485, 4:572, 4:575
Metcalf, E. W., 1:739
Metcalf, Linda J., 3:140
Metcalf, Peter, 4:430
Metcalf, Robert A., 5:771
Metcalf, Robert L., 5:771
Metcalf, Thomas R., 3:485

Metcalfe, Alan, 3:608
Methodius, 2:780, 2:784, 2:826, 2:834
Métraux, Alfred, 3:628, 4:467
Metraux, Daniel, 4:541
Metress, Seamus P., 5:349
Metropolis, N., 5:49, 5:543
Metz, Christian, 1:1157
Metz, Johannes, 4:904
Metzger, Bruce M., 4:798, 4:805, 4:818
Metzger, Michael M., 3:848
Metzger, Thomas A., 4:532
Metzker, Isaac, 2:34
Metzler, Lloyd, 3:81
Meudt, R., 5:324
Meulen, Tsjibbe Gearts van der, 2:634
Meuller-Vollmer, Kurt, 3:286
Meyendorff, John, 4:679, 693, 4:756
Meyenn, K. V., 5:708
Meyer, Arnold Oskar, 4:734
Meyer, B. E., 4:161
Meyer, Carol, 1:48
Meyer, Donald, 4:753
Meyer, Doris, 2:849
Meyer, Isidore S., 4:658
Meyer, J. J., 4:505
Meyer, Jeffrey F., 4:531
Meyer, Karl E., 3:808
Meyer, Leonard B., 3:661
Meyer, Lorenzo, 3:638, 3:639
Meyer, Marvin, 4:450
Meyer, Michael, 1:702, 2:666, 2:680, 3:349, 4:594, 4:634, 4:652
Meyer, Michael C., 3:639
Meyer, Priscilla, 2:716, 2:722, 2:741
Meyer, R. W., 4:177
Meyer, Reinhold, 3:300
Meyer, Robert G., 5:427
Meyer, Susan E., 1:29, 3:772
Meyerhoff, Hans, 3:276
Meyering, Sheryl L., 1:753
Meyers, Casey, 5:326
Meyers, H. P., 5:668
Meyers, Jeffrey, 1:464, 1:489, 1:510, 1:514, 1:531, 1:846, 1:1006, 2:979, 3:926
Meyers, Mary A., 4:852
Meyers, Robert A., 5:2, 5:29, 5:351
Meyers, Valerie, 1:531, 1:531
Meyerstein, Edward H., 1:285
Meynell, Sir Francis, 1:9, 1:43
Mezey, Robert, 1:915, 2:10
Mezu, Okechukwu S., 2:147
Miłosz, Czesław, 2:810, **2:817**
Miao, Ronald, 2:190
Micaud, Charles A., 3:373

Michael, George, 3:765, 4:505
Michael, Jane W., 5:346
Michael, Sami, 2:22
Michaelides, Solon, 3:656
Michaelis, Meir, 3:349
Michaels, David, 5:324
Michaels, Fern, 1:1221
Michaels, Meredith W., 4:20
Michaels, Walter B., 1:723, 3:553
Michalopoulos, A., 2:362
Michalos, Alex C., 4:381, 5:64
Michalowski, Piotr, 4:545
Michaud, Regis, 4:28
Micheaux, Oscar, 1:1171
Michel, Paul-Henri, 4:136
Michel, Sonya, 4:649
Michelangelo Buonarroti, 1:386, 1:501, 1:1249, 2:427, 3:768, **3:781**, 3:787, 3:791
Michell, John, 4:434
Michels, Robert, 3:234
Michelson, Albert A(braham), 5:701
Michener, James A(lbert), 1:1245, **1:1247**, 2:10, 3:390, 3:900, **3:931**, 5:597
Michie, David, 5:568
Michie, Helena, 1:312, 2:989
Michnik, Adam, 3:390
Mickelson, Alan R., 5:666
Mickelson, Sig, 3:808
Mickiewicz, Adam Bernard, 2:810, 2:815, **2:816**, 2:826
Mickler, Michael, 4:871
Middlebrook, Diane W., 1:799, 1:913, 1:1045
Middlekauff, Robert R., 1:628, 3:518, 3:521
Middlemiss, Ross R., 5:487
Middleton, Allen H., 5:393
Middleton, Bernard C., 1:25
Middleton, Gerard V., 5:622
Middleton, Jo A., 1:821
Middleton, Kent R., 3:803
Middleton, Massinger, 1:172
Middleton, Robert Hunter, 1:18
Middleton, Robin, 3:763
Middleton, Ruth, 4:544
Middleton, Thomas, 1:189, 1:199, 2:535
Middleton, W. E. Knowles, 5:33
Midelfort, H. C. Erik, 4:730
Midgley, Leslie, 3:808
Midgley, Mary, 4:389
Midlarsky, M. I., 3:280
Midwinter, John E., 5:304
Mieder, Wolfgang, 1:115
Mielziner, Moses, 4:610

Miers, Suzanne, 3:418, 3:419
Mies van der Rohe, Ludwig, 3:769, 3:782
Mieželaitis, Eduardas, 2:805
Migiel, Marilyn, 2:401
Mignani, Rigo, 1:181
Mignone, Mario B., 2:419
Miguéis, José Rodrigues, 2:557, 2:560
Mihailovich, Vasa D., 2:781, 2:785, 2:786, 2:808, 2:827, 2:828, 2:835
Mihajlov, Mihajlo, 2:688
Mihalić, Slavko, 2:785, 2:786
Mijnhardt, Wijnand W., 3:338, 3:382
Mikasinovich, Branko, 2:786, 2:808, 2:828, 2:835
Mikhail, E. H., 1:427, 1:442, 1:490, 1:527, 1:556
Mikhail, Mona, 2:65, 2:69
Mikkelsen, Edwin J., 3:205
Miko, Stephen J., 1:510
Mikolyzk, Thomas A., 1:848
Milani, Farzaneh, 2:83
Milavsky, J. Ronald, 3:170
Milazzo, Lee, 1:1023
Milbank, John, 3:213, 4:890
Milbauer, Asher Z., 1:1041
Milburn, Michael A., 3:148
Milder, Robert, 1:689
Mileck, Joseph, 2:590
Miles, Agnes, 5:13
Miles, Alfred H., 1:316
Miles, Andrew, 3:343
Miles, Barry, 1:958
Miles, Gary B., 2:397
Miles, Josephine, 1:307, 1:429
Miles, Patricia H., 5:223, 5:256
Miles, Wyndham D., 5:223
Milewski, Robert J., 1:999
Milford, Humphrey S., 1:430
Milgram, Stanley, 3:175
Milivojević, Dragan, 2:786, 2:808, 2:828, 2:835
Milkman, Harvey B., 5:401
Mill, Harriet Taylor, 1:323, 1:379
Mill, John Stuart, 1:297, 1:309, 1:344, 1:375, 1:379, 1:380, 1:393, 2:810, 3:93, 3:95, 3:100, 3:106, 3:162, 4:158, 4:223, 4:243, 4:257, 4:385
Mill, Joshua E., 3:811
Mill, Robert Christie, 3:890
Millar, Fergus, 3:303, 3:314, 4:452
Millar, T. B., 3:494
Millay, Edna St. Vincent, 1:860

Millburn, John R., 5:32
Miller, Alan R., 5:553
Miller, Alan W., 4:659
Miller, Alfred E., 5:335
Miller, Anita, 1:444
Miller, Arthur, 1:1071, 1:1103, 2:531
Miller, Arthur I., 5:49
Miller, Barbara Stoler, 2:172, 2:173, 4:505
Miller, Beth, 2:522
Miller, Charles D., 5:481
Miller, Charles E., 5:552
Miller, Christopher L., 2:110
Miller, Cristanne, 1:748
Miller, D. A., 1:319
Miller, Darrell, 5:263
Miller, David, 3:371
Miller, David J., 5:107
Miller, David L., 1:198, 4:309
Miller, David N., 1:1050, 2:49
Miller, Delbert C., 3:7
Miller, Diane, 1:1165
Miller, Donald E., 3:394, 3:455
Miller, Donald L., 5:172
Miller, Edwin Haviland, 1:167, 1:707
Miller, Elizabeth W., 3:510
Miller, Eugene E., 1:906
Miller, Eugene Willard, 3:419, 5:636
Miller, Francis T., 3:929
Miller, Fred, 4:24, 4:69
Miller, G. Tyler, 5:823
Miller, G. Wayne, 5:314
Miller, Gabriel, 1:1106
Miller, George, 1:5
Miller, George A., 3:167
Miller, Gilbert H., 1:1025
Miller, Henry, 1:468, 1:812, 1:861, 1:864, 2:465, 2:500
Miller, Hugh, 5:624
Miller, Irwin, 5:329
Miller, Jacqueline Y., 5:769
Miller, James, 3:164, 4:214, 4:401
Miller, James E., Jr., 1:707, 1:708, 1:717
Miller, Jean B., 5:414
Miller, J. Maxwell, 4:806
Miller, John, 3:360
Miller, John C., 3:521
Miller, Jonathan, 5:448
Miller, Jordan Y., 1:1108
Miller, Joseph, 3:424
Miller, Joseph C., 3:856
Miller, Joseph Hillis, 1:319, 1:350, 1:362, 1:417, 1:422, 1:794, 1:1141, 1:1150
Miller, J. R., 3:611, 3:615
Miller, Karl, 1:423, 2:985
Miller, Kenneth E., 3:381

Miller, Kenton, 5:823
Miller, Kerby A., 3:371, 3:557
Miller, Lawrence, 1:440
Miller, Lorna Touryar, 3:394
Miller, Lucien, 2:223
Miller, Marjorie M., 1:1254, 5:14
Miller, Mary E., 4:454
Miller, Merl, 5:538, 5:567
Miller, Milton H., 5:415
Miller, Miriam Youngerman, 1:156
Miller, Mitchell H., Jr., 4:82
Miller, Muriel, 2:909
Miller, Nancy K., 1:926, 1:928, 1:1127, 2:447
Miller, Nathan, 3:535, 3:595, 3:936
Miller, Neal E(dgar), 3:176, 3:190
Miller, Patrick D., Jr., 4:823
Miller, Perry, 1:629, 1:630, 1:651, 1:715, 3:511, 3:586
Miller, Perry G., 4:35, 4:753, 4:767
Miller, Peter, 5:88
Miller, Phyllis Z., 4:601
Miller, P. M., 3:7
Miller, Randall, 3:509
Miller, R. Baxter, 1:849
Miller, R. H., 1:489
Miller, Richard, 4:243
Miller, Richard K., 5:243, 5:620
Miller, Richard W., 4:389
Miller, Robert P., 1:151
Miller, Robin F., 2:716
Miller, Ronald Henry, 4:671
Miller, Ruby M., 3:419
Miller, Russell, 4:869
Miller, R. W., 3:290
Miller, Samuel O., 5:387
Miller, Stuart W., 1:93
Miller, Timothy, 4:842, 4:844
Miller, Tom, 3:896
Miller, Victor C., 1:633
Miller, Walter M., Jr., 1:1260
Miller, Warner Allen, 5:719
Miller, Warren E., 3:144
Miller, William D., 4:765
Miller, William H., 5:247
Miller, William L., 3:162
Miller, Yvette, 2:847
Millerd, Clara E., 4:53
Millet, Allan R., 3:546
Millett, Bella, 1:147
Millgate, Jane, 1:300
Millgate, Michael, 1:363, 1:837
Millgram, Abraham E., 2:10, 4:600, 4:897
Millichap, Joseph R, 1:886

Millikan, Robert Andrews, 5:678, **5:702**
Millington, Barry, 3:729
Millington, John P., 5:742
Millington, T. Alaric, 5:479
Millington, William, 5:479
Millman, Lawrence, 3:906
Millman, Lorrie, 3:506
Mills, C(harles) Wright, 3:234
Mills, David, 1:159
Mills, Hilary, 1:1012
Mills, Howard W., 1:297
Mills, Joy, 4:853
Mills, Kay, 3:808
Mills, Maldwyn, 1:147
Mills, Margaret A., 4:503
Mills, Patricia J., 4:391
Mills, Russell, 5:278
Mills, Sara, 1:325
Mills, Theodore M., 3:172
Mills, Watson E., 4:5, 4:818, 4:864
Millspaugh, Ben P., 5:219
Milne, A(lan) A(lexander), 1:587, 1:588
Milne, Anthony R., 2:315
Milne, Gordon, 1:919
Milne, Hammish, 3:677
Milne, Lesley, 2:706
Milne, R. S., 3:492
Milne, Tom, 3:837
Milner, Anthony, 2:311
Milner, Henry, 3:382
Milner, Murray, Jr., 5:329
Milsom, John, 5:630
Milsum, John H., 5:401
Milton, John, 1:57, 1:162, 1:164, 1:166, 1:188, **1:190,** 1:243, 1:251, 1:267, 1:277, 1:311, 1:324, 1:644, 1:775, 1:1137, 1:1214, 2:359, 2:380, 2:385, 2:396, 2:405, 2:620, 2:802
Milton, John P., 5:213
Milton, Joyce, 3:929
Milton, Mary Lee, 1:288
Milton, Nathan, 2:846
Milton, Sybil, 3:348
Milunsky, Aubrey, 5:377
Milward, Alan S., 3:280
Milward, Peter, 1:219
Mims, Edwin, 1:772
Minadeo, Richard, 4:75
Minar, Edwin L., Jr., 4:87
Minarik, Joseph J., 3:67
Minc, Alain, 5:573
Mindel, Eugene D., 5:428
Mindell, Earl, 5:320, 5:346
Minear, Richard, 3:478
Mineau, Geraldine, 3:205
Miner, Earl, 1:242, 2:272, 2:273, 2:273, 2:274

Mingay, Gordon E., 3:361, 3:362, 3:364
Minichiello, Sharon, 3:478
Mink, Louis O., 4:282
Minnaert, M., 5:634
Minnich, Nelson H., 4:729
Minnis, A. J., 1:152
Minogue, Valerie, 2:506
Minoli, Daniel, 5:305
Minor, Robert Neil, 4:354, 4:508
Minsky, Marvin, 5:568
Minta, Stephen, 2:867
Minter, David, 1:837
Minton, Arthur J., 4:22
Mintz, Alan, 1:354, 4:641
Mintz, Anne P., 5:126
Mintz, Jerome R., 4:633
Mintz, Lawrence E., 3:872
Mintz, Penny, 5:252
Mintz, Ruth F., 2:10
Mintz, Steven, 3:553
Miola, Robert S., 1:213, 1:219
Miošić, Andrija Kačić, 2:784
Miquelon, Dale, 3:612
Mirabito, Michael M., 5:297
Miranda, Francisco Sá de, 2:556
Mirandola, Giovanni Pico della. *See* Pico della Mirandola, Giovanni
Mirandola, Pico della, 2:398, 2:433, 2:434, 2:436
Mireaux, Emile, 2:362
Miriam Joseph, Sister, 1:217
Mirkin, Gabe, 5:347, 5:400
Miron, Dan A., 2:41, 2:46
Mirrielees, Edith, 3:576
Mirsky, Dimitry S., 2:689, 2:752
Mirsky, Mark Jay, 2:9
Mirzahi, Andree, 5:331
Miscamble, Wilson D., 3:546, 3:584
Mises, Ludwig W. von, 3:52
Mishan, E. J., 3:64, 3:67
Mishima Yukio, 2:289
Miskimin, Harry, 3:333
Misra, Jay, 5:559
Mistichelli, Judith A., 5:60, 5:149
Mistral, Gabriela, 2:873
Mistry, Rohinton, 2:903, **2:919**
Mitcham, Carl, 5:60, 5:71, 5:126, 5:129, 5:130, 5:197
Mitchell, Arthur, 3:370
Mitchell, Brian R., 3:327, 3:343, 3:354
Mitchell, David, 3:387
Mitchell, Donald, 3:705, 3:707

Mitchell, Edwin Valentine, 1:32
Mitchell, Geoffrey Duncan, 3:5
Mitchell, James E., 5:395
Mitchell, Joan P., 5:562
Mitchell, Lee C., 1:723, 1:743, 1:805, 3:550
Mitchell, L. S., 3:98
Mitchell, Margaret, 1:982, 1:1220, 1:1244, **1:1248**
Mitchell, Maria, 5:609
Mitchell, P. M., 2:645, 2:645
Mitchell, Richard P., 3:437, 4:572
Mitchell, Richard Scott, 5:618, 5:628
Mitchell, Sally, 1:312, 3:354, 3:364
Mitchell, Susan L., 1:381
Mitchell, Thomas N., 2:385, 4:72
Mitchell, W.J.T., 1:1129
Mitchell, Wesley Clair, 3:49, 3:50, **3:97,** 3:242
Mitchell, William B., 5:620
Mitchinson, David, 3:784
Mitchison, Rosalind, 3:368
Mitford, Jessica, 5:359
Mitler, Louis, 2:96
Mitman, Gregg, 3:550
Mitroff, Ian I., 3:812
Mitsios, Helen, 2:283
Mitsis, Phillip, 4:74
Mittelholzer, Edgar, 2:937
Mittelman, James H., 3:54
Mitter, Sara S., 4:508
Mitterling, Philip I., 3:511
Mittlefehldt, Pamela, 3:862
Mitton, Jacquelin, 5:618
Miura, Akira, 1:100
Miura, Kerstin Tini, 1:25
Miyata, Ken, 5:764
Miyoshi, Masao, 2:282, 3:478
Mizener, Arthur, 1:476, 1:841
Mlama, Penina Muhando, 2:110
Mňačko, Ladislav, 2:833, **2:833**
Moaddel, Mansoor, 3:448
Moayyad, Heshmat, 2:84
Moberg, (Carl Artur) Vilhelm, 2:678
Mobley, Marilyn S., 1:770
Moche, Dinah L., 5:588
Mochulsky, Konstantin, 2:703, 2:716
Moctezuma, Eduardo M., 4:457
Moddelmog, Debra, 1:464
Modell, Judith, 3:27
Modgil, Celia, 3:267
Modgil, Sohan, 3:267

Modigliani, Franco, 3:62
Modleski, Tania, 1:618,
 1:1169
Modrak, Deborah K. W., 4:70
Moduro, Otto, 4:769
Modzelewski, Michael, 3:896
Moe, Jørgen, 2:661, 2:662
Moe, Terry M., 3:254
Moeller, Bernd, 4:722, 4:730
Moeller, Dade, 5:353
Moen, Elizabeth, 3:206
Moench, Richard W., 4:579
Moers, Ellen, 1:699
Moffat, Mary J., 1:130
Moffatt, James, 4:802, **4:835**
Moffett, Judith, 1:1015
Moffett, Samuel Hugh, 4:677
Moffitt, Perry-Lynn, 5:358
Mofolo, Thomas, 2:157,
 2:166
Mogen, David, 1:715, 1:1255
Moglen, Helen, 1:259
Mohammad, Ovey N., 4:581
Mohammad, Yousuf H.,
 5:280
Mohammed, Imam W.,
 4:579, 4:862
Mohanty, J. N., 4:295
Moholy-Nagy, Laszlo, 3:760
Mohsen, Sofia, 4:579
Moi, Toril, 1:926, 1:1132
Moir, John S., 3:610
Mok, Robert, 3:670
Moked, Gabriel, 4:192
Mokhiber, Russell, 3:205
Moldenhauer, Hans, 3:730
Moldenhauer, Rosaleen,
 3:730
Mole, John, 1:418
Moler, Kenneth L., 1:276
Molesworth, Charles F.,
 1:864, 1:913, 1:944, 1:1052
Molière, 1:254, 1:263,
 1:1066, 2:95, 2:391, 2:422,
 2:444, 2:458, 2:470, **2:490,**
 2:644, 2:650
Molin, Paulette, 3:508
Molina, Tirso de, 2:520
Moline, Jon, 4:82
Mollen, Art, 5:349
Mollenkott, Virginia R.,
 4:749, 4:750
Mollison, Bill, 5:820
Molloy, James F., Jr., 5:557
Molloy, Peter M., 5:29
Molnár, Ferenc, 2:798
Molotch, Harvey, 3:216
Molyneux, J., 3:295
Momaday, N. Scott, 1:704,
 1:1016
Momen, Moojan, 4:861
Momigliano, Arnaldo, 3:307

Monaco, James, 1:1157,
 3:826, 3:828
Monaghan, David, 1:276
Monan, J. D., 4:70
Monego, Joan, 2:117
Monet, Claude, 3:769, **3:783,**
 3:789
Money, Keith, 3:750
Monk, Raymond, 3:694,
 4:346
Monkhouse, F. J., 5:618
Monmonier, Mark S., 5:620,
 5:621
Monneret, Sophie, 3:789
Monod, Sylvère, 1:350
Monroe, Marilyn, 1:1103
Monsma, Stephen V., 5:130,
 5:197
Monsman, Gerald, 1:296,
 1:387
Monson, Karen, 3:680
Montagnes, Ian, 1:47
Montagu, Ashley, 3:170,
 5:765, 5:831
Montagu, Ivor, 3:835
**Montagu, Lady Mary Wort-
 ley,** 1:250
Montague, John, 1:418
**Montaigne, Michel Eyquem
 de,** 1:677, 1:922, 2:444,
 2:491, 4:145
Montale, Eugenio, 1:1066,
 2:399, **2:427,** 2:437, 2:439
Montano, Rocco, 2:418
Montefiore, Alan, 4:28, 4:266,
 4:379
Montefiore, C. G., 4:610
Monteiro, Adolfo Casais,
 2:557
Monteiro, George, 1:842
Monteiro, Mariana, 3:856
Monteith, J. L., 5:774
Montell, William L., 3:861
Monter, E. William, 3:856,
 4:762
Montero, Oscar, 2:884
**Montesquieu, Charles de
 Secondat, Baron de la
 Brede et de,** 2:471, 2:492,
 3:162, 4:158, **4:209**
Montessori, Maria, 3:265
Monteverdi, Claudio, 3:706
Montgomery, Guy, 1:242
Montgomery, H., 2:355
Montgomery, M. R., 5:219
Montgomery, R., 3:59
Montgomery, Sy, 3:909, 5:833
Monzaemon, Chikamatsu. *See*
 Chikamatsu Monzaemon
Moodie, John Dunbar, 2:920
**Moodie, Susanna (Strick-
 land),** 2:903, **2:920**

Moody, Ernest Addison,
 4:121
Moody, J. Carroll, 3:515
Moody, Marily, 1:108
Moody, Raymond, 4:866
Moody, Raymond A., Jr.,
 3:872
Moody, Richard, 1:1072,
 1:1075
Moody, T. W., 3:369
Moody, William Vaughn,
 1:775
Moog, Clodomir V., 2:890
Mookerjee, R. N., 1:880
Moon, Eric, 1:57
Moon, Michael, 1:708
Moon, Ross A., 3:444
Moon, Sun Myung, 4:870,
 4:877
Moon, William L., 3:896
Mooney, Harry J., Jr., 1:870
Mooney, James E., 1:68
Mooney, Michael, 4:217
Moor, Cornelia Niekus, 2:317
Moor, Ruth, 5:674
Moorcock, Michael, 1:615
Moore, Carleton B., 5:628
Moore, Charles A., 4:37,
 4:351, 4:358, 4:363, 4:498
Moore, Christopher, 3:612
Moore, Clement, 1:1194
Moore, David C., 3:364
Moore, David S., 5:523
Moore, Deborah D., 4:640
Moore, Don, 1:201
Moore, Donald, 4:665
Moore, Donna M., 5:429
Moore, Doris L., 5:578
Moore, Dwight, 5:423
Moore, Edward C., 4:225,
 4:238, 4:249
Moore, Emerson, 1:934
Moore, Frank L., 3:670
Moore, Geoffrey H., 3:50
Moore, George, 1:380
Moore, George Edward,
 4:211, 4:221, 4:260, **4:311,**
 4:325, 4:343, 4:395
Moore, George Foot, 4:621
Moore, Gerald, 2:110, 2:113,
 2:149
Moore, Harry T., 1:510
Moore, Henry, 3:784
Moore, Honor, 1:1078
Moore, Jack B., 1:630
Moore, James, 4:876, 5:831
Moore, Jennifer Mills, 5:125
Moore, Jerrold Northrop,
 3:694, 3:726
Moore, John Hammond, 1:45
Moore, John J., 5:237
Moore, John R., 1:660, 1:728

Moore, Marianne, 1:560,
1:745, **1:863**
Moore, Michael, 1:196
Moore, Mick, 3:487
Moore, Patrick, 5:587,
5:591, 5:593, **5:609,** 5:622
Moore, Peter D., 3:126, 5:819
Moore, Rayburn S., 1:790
Moore, Raylyn, 1:1200
Moore, Rebecca, 4:867
Moore, R. I., 4:700
Moore, R. Laurence, 4:842,
4:851
Moore, Roger, 3:367
Moore, Ruth E., 5:624, 5:791,
5:813
Moore, Sally F., 3:217
Moore, Steven, 1:978, 1:978
Moore, Winfred B., Jr., 3:860
Moore-Gilbert, B. J., 1:372
Moorehead, Alan, 3:422
Moorey, Roger, 4:808
Moorhouse, Geoffrey, 3:904
Moorman, Frederick, 1:182
Moorman, Mary, 1:307
Moosa, Matti, 2:56
Mor, Menachem, 4:651
Morace, Robert A., 1:448,
1:515, 1:979
Moraczewski, Albert S., 5:780
Moraga, Cherie, 1:1184
Morajes, Resil B., 2:328
Morales, Alfredo T., 2:332
Morales Carrión, Arturo,
3:641
Moramarco, Fred, 1:799
Moran, James, 1:9
Moran, Mary Hurley, 1:468
Moran, Megan, 5:402
Morante, Elsa, 2:400, **2:428,**
2:429
Morante, Pedro Díaz, 1:18
Morantz-Sanchez, Regina M.,
5:314
Moravcsik, Edith, 3:21
Moravcsik, Julius, 4:82
Moravia, Alberto, 2:429
Moravscik, Michael, 4:385
Morawetz, Herbert, 5:732
Mordden, Ethan, 1:1075,
3:672, 3:713
Mordello, Salvatore, 3:556
More, Henry, 4:166, 4:168,
4:182, 4:184
More, Paul Elmer, 4:55, 4:82
More, Sir Thomas, 1:166,
1:193, 1:445, 4:138, **4:147**
Moreh, Shmuel, 2:56
Morehead, Joe, 1:108, 3:506
Morehead, Philip D., 1:94
Moreland, Richard C., 1:837
Morell, David, 3:550

Morenz, Siegfried, 4:442,
4:548
Morewedge, Parviz, 4:61,
4:576
Morey, Robert A., 3:444
Morgan, Ann L., 3:764
Morgan, Arthur E., 1:734
Morgan, Brian L. G., 5:347
Morgan, Catherine, 3:305
Morgan, Christopher, 5:565
Morgan, Edmund S(ears),
3:518, 3:521, **3:587**
Morgan, Elizabeth, 5:336
Morgan, George A., Jr.,
4:247
Morgan, H. Wayne, 3:553
Morgan, Janet P., 1:606
Morgan, John, 4:734
Morgan, Joy E., 3:265
Morgan, Kathleen O., 5:331
Morgan, Kenneth O., 3:367,
3:369
Morgan, Kenneth W., 4:499,
4:523, 4:535, 4:576
Morgan, Lewis Henry, 3:26,
3:37, 3:240
Morgan, Mary Elizabeth,
2:577
Morgan, Max, 3:549
Morgan, Meredith, 5:384
Morgan, Michael L., 4:82,
4:634, 4:649
Morgan, N. J., 3:767
Morgan, Rachel, 5:555
Morgan, Richard G., 1:1028
Morgan, Robert F., 5:317
Morgan, Robert P., 3:662,
3:665
Morgan, S. J., 3:280
Morgan, Susanne, 5:356
Morgan, Ted, 1:521
Morgan, Thomas Hunt,
5:788, **5:807,** 5:808
Morganbesser, Sidney, 4:225
Morgan-Witts, Max, 5:383
Morgenbesser, Sidney, 5:96
Morgenstern, Karl, 5:730
Morgenstern, Oskar, 3:47,
3:63
Morgenstern, Sam, 3:654
Moriarity, Brian, 5:244
Moricz, Szigmond, 2:802
Mörike, Eduard, 2:603
Morin, Alexander J., 5:182
Mori Ōgai, 2:281, **2:289**
Morison, Elting E., 5:71,
5:232
Morison, Robert S., 5:107
Morison, Samuel Eliot,
1:629, 1:631, 3:335, 3:513,
3:514, **3:588,** 3:916
Morison, Stanley, 1:9, 1:18,
1:63

Morkholm, Otto, 3:306
Morley, Christopher, 1:33
Morley, Henry, 4:133
Morley, Jane, 5:172
Morley, John, 2:516, 4:196
Morley, Patricia, 2:917
Morley, Sheridan, 1:465
Morone, Joseph G., 5:75,
5:156, 5:244, 5:287
Moroney, M. G., 5:523
Morowitz, Harold J., 5:765,
5:782
Morpurgo, J. E., 1:42
Morra, Marion, 5:372
Morrall, John B., 4:98
Morreale, Don, 4:7
Morrel, Robert E., 2:272
Morrell, David, 1:943
Morrell, Jack, 1:312
Morrell, W. P., 3:495
Morris, Adelaide K., 1:888
Morris, A. J., 3:280
Morris, Allison, 3:205
Morris, Benny, 3:440
Morris, Brenda, 5:415
Morris, Brian, 1:201, 4:422
Morris, C. Brian, 2:522,
2:526, 2:539
Morris, Charles G., 3:168
Morris, Charles R., 4:180,
4:266
Morris, Christopher, 5:29,
5:217
Morris, Colin, 4:695
Morris, David, 5:278
Morris, David B., 1:252
Morris, David Joseph, 5:302
Morris, D. R., 3:424
Morris, Edmund, 3:595,
3:936
Morris, George S., 4:29
Morris, Gregory L., 1:979
Morris, Ian, 3:305
Morris, Ivan, 2:283, 3:474,
3:475
Morris, James, 4:572
Morris, Jan, 1:312, 3:893,
3:904, 3:909
Morris, Jonas, 5:329
Morris, Kenneth, 4:760
Morris, Mark, 3:738, **3:748**
Morris, Mary, 1:92, 1:96
Morris, Phyllis S., 4:331
Morris, Randall C., 4:289
Morris, Richard B., 3:509,
3:511, 3:521
Morris, Richard J., 3:256
Morris, Robert C., 3:256
Morris, Robert K., 1:1057,
2:939
Morris, Rosamund, 3:872
Morris, Scott, 5:261
Morris, Sean, 5:768

Morris, Wesley, 1:837
Morris, William, 1:10, 1:92, 1:96, 1:309, 1:314, 1:367, **1:382,** 1:397, 1:570, 1:591, 1:611, **1:617,** 2:383, 2:644
Morris, Willie, 1:837
Morris, Wright, 1:1016
Morrison, Alastair, 3:890
Morrison, Blake, 1:415
Morrison, Clinton, 4:818
Morrison, David, 5:593
Morrison, Donald R., 4:91
Morrison, Hugh, 3:763, 3:792
Morrison, Perry, 5:125
Morrison, Philip, 5:588, 5:651
Morrison, Phyllis S., 5:651, 5:734
Morrison, Robert S., 5:121
Morrison, Robert T., 5:732
Morrison, Toni, 1:849, 1:916, **1:1018**
Morriss, Margaret, 1:563
Morrow, Bradford, 1:514, 1:599, 1:618
Morrow, Glenn R., 4:62, 4:82
Morrow, Patrick D., 1:756
Morsberger, Robert E., 1:891
Morse, Arthur D., 4:640
Morse, Stephen J., 5:419
Morse, Thomas S., 5:314
Morson, Gary S., 2:689, 2:716
Morss, L. R., 5:728
Mortimer, Charles G., 3:893
Mortimer, Edward, 4:579
Mortimer, John, 1:481
Mortimer, Mildred, 2:110, 2:111
Mortley, Raoul, 4:28, 4:266
Morton, Desmond, 3:607
Morton, Frederic, 3:376
Morton, H(enry Canova) V(ollam), 3:932
Morton, J. B., 1:443
Morton, Leah, 4:650
Morton, Leslie, 5:3
Morton, Miriam, 2:693
Morton, William Lewis, 3:604, **3:622**
Mosak, Harold H., 5:431
Mosca, Gaetano, 3:140
Moschus, 2:364, 2:369
Mosekilde, E., 3:171
Mosekilde, L., 3:171
Moseley, E. M., 1:167
Moseley, Frank, 5:636
Moseley, Henry Gwyn Jeffreys, 5:703
Moseley, James G., 3:518
Moseley, Michael E., 4:458
Moser, Barry, 1:801
Moser, Charles A., 2:689, 2:748, 2:781

Moser, Diane K., 5:45
Moser, Thomas, 1:476
Moses, Daniel David, 2:905
Moses, Joel, 5:539
Moses, Larry, 4:542
Moses, Lincoln E., 5:523
Moses, Montrose, 1:1075, 1:1078
Moses, Stephane, 4:671
Mosher, Frederic J., 1:77
Moshiri, Farrokh, 3:448
Mosimann, Elizabeth A., 1:22
Moskop, John C., 4:289
Mosley, Leonard, 3:539
Mosley, Philip, 3:832
Moss, Alfred A., Jr., 3:513, 3:580
Moss, Henry S., 3:328
Moss, John, 2:904, 2:926
Moss, Leonard, 1:863, 1:1104
Moss, M. O., 5:352
Moss, Norman, 1:91
Moss, Robert F., 1:372
Moss, Sanford A., 5:771
Mössbauer, Rudolf Ludwig, 5:703
Mossberg, Barbara, 1:748
Mosse, George L., 2:565, 3:327, 3:344, 3:346, 3:350, 3:377, 4:722
Mossell, N. F., 1:725
Mossiker, Frances, 2:508
Mossman, Jennifer, 3:120
Mossner, Ernest C., 4:202
Mosteller, Frederick, 5:79, 5:522, 5:523, 5:524
Mostowski, Andrej, 5:509
Mostwin, Danuta, 3:557
Mostyn, Trevor, 3:437
Mote, Frederick W., 2:203, 3:468
Mother of Fujiwara Michitsuna, 2:278
Motion, Andrew, 1:508
Motokiyo, Zeami, 2:271
Motoyama, Yukihiko, 4:363
Mott, Frank Luther, 1:51, 1:715
Mott, Sir Nevill Francis, 5:669, **5:704**
Mottahedeh, Roy, 4:572
Motto, A. L., 4:88
Mottram, Eric, 1:958
Mottram, Ron, 1:1111
Motz, Lloyd, 5:652
Mouffe, Chantal, 1:1132
Mould, Richaiel, 5:287
Moulder, Evelina, 3:148
Moulder, Frances V., 3:464
Moulton, Charles A., 1:134
Moulton, Charles W., 1:430
Moulton, F. P., 5:274
Moulton, W. F., 4:819

Mounce, H. O., 4:346
Mount, Ellis, 5:2, 5:217
Mourant, John A., 4:22
Mourelatos, Alexander P. D., 4:51, 4:52
Mourgues, Odette de, 2:485
Mousnier, Roland E., 3:373
Moustakas, Clark E., 5:416, 5:423
Moutinho, Luiz, 3:891
Mowat, Barbara A., 1:211
Mowat, Farley, 3:904, 3:906, 3:909
Mowery, David C., 5:234
Mowery, J. Franklin, 1:22
Mowinckel, Sigmund, 4:823
Mowlana, Hamid, 3:804
Mowry, George E., 3:595
Mowshowitz, Abbe, 5:565
Moxon, Joseph, 1:10
Moyal, Georges J., 5:503
Mo Yen, 2:258
Moyer, Albert E., 5:652
Moyer, Elgin, 4:720
Moyer, Greg, 5:346
Moyers, Bill, 5:342
Moyle, Peter B., 5:771
Moynahan, Brian, 3:397
Moynahan, Julian, 1:510
Możejko, Edward, 2:698, 2:783
Mozans, H. J., 5:10
Mozart, Wolfgang Amadeus, 1:543, 2:458, 3:699, **3:706,** 3:713, 4:757
Mphahlele, Es'kia (Ezekiel), 2:166
Mrożek, Slawomir, 2:810, **2:818**
Msika, Hangson, 2:126
Mtshali, Oswald Mbuyiseni, 2:157
Mudimbe, V. Y., 4:369
Mudrick, Marvin, 1:276
Mudroch, Vaclav, 4:714
Mueller, Friedrich Max, 4:354
Mueller, Ian, 5:505
Mueller, Janet M., 1:167
Mueller, John, 3:737
Mueller, J. P., 5:458
Mueller, Milton, 3:803
Mueller-Vollmer, Kurt, 4:28
Muendel, Renate, 1:379
Muensterberger, Werner, 5:425
Muether, John R., 4:6
Muggeridge, Malcolm, 1:342, 4:745
Muhammad, Haji Salleh, 2:317

Muhammad (or Mohammed), 1:679, 2:54, 2:81, 3:433, 4:374, 4:564, 4:577, **4:586**, 4:861
Muir, Edwin, **1:521**, 1:812, 4:774
Muir, Frank, 1:809
Muir, John, 3:896, 5:139, **5:835**, 5:837
Muir, Kenneth, 1:201, 1:205, 1:213, 1:215, 1:218, 1:219, 1:222
Muir, Percy, 1:7, 1:33, 1:579
Muir, William, 4:588
Muirden, James, 5:591
Muirhead, John Henry, 4:29, 4:351
Muise, D. A., 3:605
Mujica, Barbara, 2:984
Mukerji, Chandra, 3:874
Mukherjee, Arun, 1:805, 1:830
Mukherjee, Meenakshi, 2:178
Mulder, John M., 4:754
Mulder, Rodney, 1:1217
Mulder, Tiny, 2:634
Mulgan, R. G., 4:70
Mulhall, Stephen, 4:294, 4:346
Mulholland, Leslie, 4:206
Mulick, James A., 5:427
Mulisch, Harry, 2:621, 2:623, **2:628**
Mulkay, Michael J., 4:406, 5:153, 5:154, 5:156, 5:589
Mullahy, Patrick, 5:471
Mullaly, Edward J., 1:858
Mullaney, Stephen, 1:209
Mullaney, T., 4:154
Mullen, Barbara D., 5:384
Mullen, Edward J., 1:849
Muller, Ann, 3:207
Muller, Hans Wolfgang, 3:763
Müller, Heiner, 2:603
Muller, Herbert J., 3:327, 3:334, 5:573
Muller, Hermann Joseph, 5:808, 5:812
Muller, Jerry, 4:215
Muller, Peter O., 3:125
Muller, Richard A., 4:762
Muller, Robert H., 1:72
Mullin, Donald C., 1:323
Mullin, Glenn H., 4:544
Mulliner, K., 2:324, 3:492
Multatuli, 2:316, **2:628**
Multhauf, Robert P., 5:29, 5:728
Mumey, Jack, 5:402
Mumford, George S., 5:591

Mumford, Lewis, 3:216, 5:54, 5:71, 5:95, 5:147, **5:168**, 5:572, 5:573
Mumley, Annie, 5:379
Mun, Thomas, 3:45, 3:54
Munasinghe, Mohan, 5:284, 5:292
Munby, A.N.L., 1:33
Mundell, E. H., 1:1229
Mundwiler, Leslie, 2:922
Mundy, J. H., 3:331
Munevar, Gonzalo, 4:399
Mungeam, G. H., 3:422
Mungello, David E., 4:177
al-Munif, 'Abd al-Rahman, 2:69
Munitz, Milton K., 4:23
Munk, Kaj (Harald Leininger), 2:652
Munonye, John, 2:139
Muñoz, Braulio, 2:847
Munoz, Carlos, Jr., 3:557
Munro, Alice (Laidlaw), 2:921
Munro, Donald, 2:112
Munro, Donald J., 4:359, 4:524
Munro, H(ector) H(ugh) ("Saki"), 1:523, **1:522**
Munsell, Joel, 1:5
Munson, Richard, 3:919
Munson, Ronald, 5:79
Munson, T. N., 4:328
Munton, Ann, 2:916
Mun-yôl, Yi. See Yi Mun-yôl
Munz, Ludwig, 3:789
Munz, Peter, 4:410
Muolo, Paul, 3:56
Mura, David, 3:904
Murakami, Shigeyoshi, 4:541
Murakami Haruki, 290
Murasaki Shikibu, 2:270, **2:278**
Murav, Harriet, 2:716
Murdin, Lesley, 5:594
Murdin, Paul, 5:588, 5:594
Murdoch, D. R., 5:674
Murdoch, Iris, 1:419, 1:454, 1:474, **1:523**, 4:83, 4:331
Murdoch, John E., 5:39
Murdock, George P., 3:12, 3:17, 3:20, 3:25, **3:37**
Murdock, Kenneth B., 1:634
Mure, G.R.G., 4:70, 4:233
Muriel, C. B., 5:621
Murnane, William J., 4:548
Muro, James J., 5:418
Murphet, Howard, 4:874
Murphey, Murray G., 4:160, 4:249
Murphy, Bruce A., 3:543
Murphy, Charles T., 2:348
Murphy, Cliona, 3:371

Murphy, Dervla, 3:904
Murphy, Edmond, 5:80
Murphy, Gardner, 3:167
Murphy, George E., Jr., 1:921
Murphy, James F., 1:794
Murphy, John J., 1:821
Murphy, Joseph A., 4:868
Murphy, Margueritte S., 1:799, 1:913
Murphy, M. Gertrude., 4:705
Murphy, Paul L., 3:532, 3:543
Murphy, R. J., 5:297
Murphy, Roland E., 4:798, 4:887
Murphy-O'Connor, Jerome, 4:809
Murray, Augustus Taber, 2:359, 2:360
Murray, Bruce, 5:593
Murray, Dian H., 3:468
Murray, Edward, 1:1106
Murray, Gilbert, 2:347, 2:354, 2:357, 4:48
Murray, Henry A., 3:178, 3:237
Murray, John A., 5:771
Murray, Les, 2:959
Murray, Linda, 3:333, 3:757, 3:760, 3:782
Murray, Margaret P., 1:788
Murray, O., 2:344
Murray, Oswyn, 3:302
Murray, Peter, 3:333, 3:757, 3:763
Murray, Peter B., 1:185
Murray, Raymond, 5:622
Murray, Robert K., 3:543
Murray, Ruth B., 5:317
Murray, William, 3:900
Murrell, J. N., 5:658
Murrin, John M., 3:517
Murrow, Edward R(oscoe), 3:818, 3:819
Murry, John M., 1:279, 1:294
Murty, K. Satchidananda, 4:354
Musa, Mark, 2:418
Musa, Sabri, 2:59
Muscatine, Charles, 1:151
Musgrave, Alan, 5:53, 5:66
Musgrave, Peggy B., 3:67
Musgrave, Richard A., 3:67
al-Mushin Mad'a, al-Mud'aj, 3:454
Musil, Robert, 2:439, **2:604**, 2:606, 5:700
Musschenga, Bert, 5:107
Musselwhite, David E., 1:319
Mussen, P.H., 3:174
Musser, Charles, 1:1174, 3:827
Musset, Alfred de, 2:531

Musson, A. E., 5:232
Mussorgsky, Modest, 3:707,
  3:712
Musto, David F., 3:553
Musurillo, Herbert, 4:689
Mutahhari, Ayatollah M.,
  4:373
al-Mutanabbi, Abu al-Tayyib
  Ahmad Ibn al-Husayn,
  2:69
Mutloatse, Mothobi, 2:111
Mutswairo, Solomon, 2:158
Mycielska, Klara, 5:423
Myer, Valerie G., 1:254,
  1:259, 1:468
Myerhoff, Barbara G., 3:217,
  4:465
Myerowitz, Molly, 2:390
Myers, Alan, 2:693
Myers, A. R., 3:358
Myers, Gerald, 4:238
Myers, Gerald E., 1:769,
  3:188
Myers, Helen, 3:667
Myers, Jack, 1:799
Myers, Norman, 5:823
Myers, Ramon H., 3:465,
  3:478
Myers, Robert A., 5:217
Myers, Robert Manson, 3:529
Myers, Robin, 1:35
Myers, Rollo H., 3:712
Myers, Sylvia Harcstark,
  1:226
Myers, William, 1:563.
Myerson, Joel, 1:651, 1:670,
  1:670, 1:702, 1:708
Myint, Ni Ni, 3:489
Mylander, Maureen, 5:384
Myles, Colette G., 3:856
Myrdal, Gunnar, 3:66, 3:82,
  3:98, 3:114, 3:115, 3:209,
  3:235
Myrdal, Jan, 2:673
Myrick, Kenneth, 1:196

N

Naamani, Israel T., 4:643
Naar, Ray, 5:419
Naarden, Bruno, 3:394
Nabhan, Gary, 5:818
Nabholtz, John R., 1:274
Nabokov, Peter, 3:557, 3:763
Nabokov, Vladimir, 1:453,
  1:909, 1:985, 1:1019,
  1:1034, 2:536, 2:689,
  2:711, 2:722, 2:739, 2:750,
  2:858, 3:839
Nace, Ted, 5:561
Nachbar, Jack, 3:873, 3:874

Nachtigal, Paul M., 3:256
Nachtigall, Lila, 5:356
Nachtmann, O., 5:662
Naddaff, Sandra, 2:56
Nadeau, Maurice, 2:447
Nadeau, Robert L., 1:919,
  5:650
Nadel, Alan, 1:974
Nadel, Ira Bruce, 1:326
Nadel, Siegfried, 3:26
Nadelhaft, Ruth L., 1:464
Nadell, Pamela S., 4:655
Naden, Corinne J., 1:74,
  1:1195
Nadirpur, Nadir, 2:84
Nadler, Steven, 4:164, 4:182
Naess, Arne, 4:189, 5:115
Naess, Harald, 2:665
Naevius, Gnaeus, 2:378
Naff, Thomas, 4:572
Nagai Kafū, 2:281, 2:290
Nagata, Judith, 4:518
Nagel, Ernest, 4:313, 4:385,
  5:64, 5:95
Nagel, Gwen L., 1:122, 1:770
Nagel, James, 1:122, 1:743,
  1:751, 1:846, 1:847
Nagel, Paul C., 3:563
Nagel, Thomas, 4:379
Naginski, Isabelle Hoog,
  2:505
Nagler, Michael, 2:362
Nagy, Joseph Falaky, 4:436
Nagy, Sharon, 3:201
Nahal, Chaman, 1:847
Nahm, Andrew C., 3:481
Nahmanides, 4:628, 4:669
Nahman of Bratslav, 2:41,
  4:661, 4:668
Nai-an, Shih. See Shih Nai-
  an
Naifeh, Steven, 1:35, 3:787
Nails, Debra, 4:188
Naiman, Arnold, 5:523
Naiman, Arthur, 5:540, 5:555
Naimy, Mikhail, 2:59, 2:67
Naipaul, Shiva, 4:867
Naipaul, V(idiadhar)
  S(urajprasad), 2:938,
  3:641, 4:579
Naipaul, V. S., 3:641, 4:579
Naisbitt, John, 5:573
Najita, Tetsuo, 3:475, 3:479
Nakamura, Hajime, 4:37,
  4:349
Nakamura, Robert T., 5:184
Nakamura, Takafusa, 3:479
Nakhnikian, George, 4:23
Nalbantian, Suzanne, 2:986
Namier, Lewis B(ernstein),
  3:406
Namora, Fernando, 2:557
Nance, Guinevera A., 1:500

Nance, Sherri, 5:323
Nanda, B. R., 3:486, 4:553
Nantell, Judith, 2:529
Naoya, Shiga. See Shiga
  Naoya
Napier, John, 5:541, 5:579
Napier, J. R., 5:771
Napier, P. H., 5:771
Napoli, Maryann, 5:311,
  5:405
Naquin, Susan, 3:468
Narain, Virendra, 3:487
Narasimhan, Chakravarthi V.,
  2:172
Narayan, R. K., 2:171,
  2:172, 2:179
Narayanan, Vasudha, 4:26
Narboni, Jean, 3:837
Naremore, James, 1:1169,
  1:1179
Narit, Prince, 2:334
Narlikar, Jayant V., 5:655,
  5:665
Narmour, Eugene, 3:172
Narogin, Mudrooroo, 2:946,
  2:960
Naroll, Raoul, 3:12
Narveson, Jan, 4:386
Nash, Ernest, 2:381
Nash, Gary B., 1:629, 3:518,
  3:521
Nash, George H., 3:532
Nash, James, 4:745
Nash, Jane C., 3:793
Nash, Jay Robert, 3:826
Nash, June, 3:22, 3:633
Nash, Kathy, 5:326
Nash, Roderick F., 3:550,
  5:115, 5:824
Nashe, Thomas, 1:167,
  1:177, 1:180, 1:194, 2:405
Nasr, Hosein, 5:39
Nasr, Seyyed Hossein,
  3:444, 4:375, 4:576, 4:582,
  4:885, 4:888, 4:901
Nasr Allah, Ibrahim, 2:59
Nassar, Eugene Paul, 1:873
Nassif, Janet Z., 5:377
Nasta, Susheila, 2:111, 2:942
Nastasijević, Momčilo, 2:827
Natanson, Maurice, 4:235,
  4:331
Nathan, Joe, 3:251
Nathan, John, 2:289
Nathan, Leonard, 2:818
Nathan, Peter E., 5:419,
  5:427
Nathanson, Jerome, 3:261,
  4:225
Nathiri, N. Y., 1:850
Natoli, Joseph P., 1:926,
  1:1134
Natov, Nadine, 2:706

Natow, Annette B., 5:347
Natsume Sōseki, 2:281, 2:288, **2:291**
Nauert, Charles G., Jr., 4:133
Naughton, John T., 2:462
Naugle, Helen H., 1:250
Nault, Marianne, 1:947
Nauman, St. Elmo, Jr., 4:3, 4:14
Navarre, Marguerite de, 2:492
Navarro, Marysa, 3:633
Navia, Luis E., 4:51
Nayler, G. H., 5:236
Naylor, Colin, 3:761
Naylor, Gloria, 1:1020
Naylor, Mary D., 5:342
Naylor, Penelope, 3:893
Nayman, Anatoly, 2:697
Nazor, Vladimir, 2:785
Ne'eman, Yuval, 5:663
Neagu, Fanus, 2:823
Neal, Larry, 3:55
Neal, Mary, 3:852
Neale, Dorothea, 1:129
Neale, J. E., 3:373
Neale, John M., 5:427
Neale, Walter, 1:735
Neaman, Judith, 1:92
Neary, Peter, 3:616
Neatby, Hinda, 3:613, 3:614, 3:616
Neatby, L. H., 3:906
Nebeker, Helen E., 2:941
Nebelsick, Harold, 5:197
Nebylitsyn, V. D., 3:171
Nechas, Jim, 5:320
Nectoux, Jean Michel, 3:695
Nedreaas, Torborg, 2:662
Needham, Joseph, 3:466, 4:523, 5:26, 5:34
Needham, Paul, 1:10, 1:25, 1:383
Needleman, Jacob, 4:855
Neely, Carol Thomas, 1:208, 1:209
Neely, Charles, 3:862
Neely, Mark E., Jr., 3:509, 3:529
Nef, Jorge, 5:130
Neff, Donald, 3:440
Neff, Emery, 1:344, 4:245
Neff, Mary K., 4:874
Neft, David S., 5:523
Negri, Antonio, 4:189
Nehemas, Alexander, 4:247
Nehls, Edward H., 1:510
Nehru, Jawaharlal, 2:180, 3:290, **3:498**
Nei, Masatoshi, 5:784
Neill, A. S., 3:251
Neill, Catherine A., 5:376
Neill, Robin, 3:622

Neill, Samuel D., 5:544
Neill, Stephen C., 4:508, 4:720, 4:745, 4:746, 4:814
Neillands, Robin, 3:331
Neilsen, Kai, 4:386
Neilsen, Phillip, 2:959
Neilson, Francis, 3:294, 3:401, 4:337
Neisser, Edith G., 5:423
Nekrasov, Nikolai, 2:742
Nelkin, Dorothy, 3:214, 5:18, 5:73, 5:75, 5:108, 5:111, 5:122, 5:130, 5:139 **5:172**, 5:248
Nell, Victor, 1:33
Nelles, H. V., 3:614, 3:615
Nelsen, Hart M., 4:748
Nelson, Benjamin, 1:1118
Nelson, Beth, 1:289
Nelson, Cary, 1:914, 1:1129
Nelson, Dana D., 1:629, 1:651
Nelson, Douglas, 1:88
Nelson, Emmanuel S., 2:930
Nelson, G. K., 4:851
Nelson, Havelock, 3:665
Nelson, Howard, 1:952, 1:1001
Nelson, James B., 4:894
Nelson, John C, 4:136
Nelson, Joseph S., 5:761
Nelson, Nancy Melin, 1:55
Nelson, Raymond, 1:1028
Nelson, Robert M., 1:805, 1:1016
Nelson, Stanley, 1:1079
Nelson, Ted, 5:562
Nelson, Thomas A., 3:839
Nelson, Walter W., 1:323, 1:411
Nelson, William, 1:197
Nelson, Wilson E., 3:532
Nemenyi, Peter, 5:523
Nemerov, Howard, 1:1021
Németh László, 2:798, **2:802**
Nemeyer, Carol A., 1:50
Nemo, John, 1:507
Nemoy, Leon, 4:631
Nencel, Lorraine, 3:12
Nentwig, Joachim, 5:730
Nerlich, Michael, 2:536
Nersessian, Nancy, 5:64
Nersoyan, Tivan, 4:755
Neruda, Pablo, 1:705, 1:1057, 2:655, 2:824, 2:843, 2:844, 2:870, **2:873**, 2:877
Nesbitt, Alexander, 1:18
Nesin, Aziz, 2:100
Neske, Gunther, 4:294
Ness, Frederic W., 1:217
Ness, Sally Ann, 3:733

Nessi, Pio Baroja y. See Baroja y Nessi, Pio
Nestle, E., 4:794
Nestle, Joan, 1:1184
Netanyahu, B., 4:633
Neter, John, 5:523
Nethercot, Arthur H., 1:288, 4:550, 4:859
Nethersole, Reingard, 2:158
Netter, Thomas, 5:388
Nettl, Bruno, 3:667
Nettl, J. P., 3:377
Nettl, Paul, 4:738
Nettler, Ron, 4:626
Nettleship, Richard L., 4:83
Netton, Ian Richard, 3:444, 4:567
Neufeldt, Leonard N., 1:702
Neufeldt, Ronald W., 4:497, 4:521, 4:533, 4:887
Neufeldt, Victor A., 1:354
Neugebauer, Otto, 5:38, 5:40
Neugroschel, Joachim, 2:34
Neuhouser, Fred, 4:198
Neuls-Bates, Carol, 3:654
Neuman, A. R., 3:259
Neuman, Daniel M., 3:659, 3:666
Neuman, James R., 5:482
Neuman, Shirley, 1:883
Neuman, W. Russel, 3:804
Neumann, Erich, 2:383, 5:425, 5:456
Neumann, Franz L., 3:140
Neumann, John von, 3:63, **3:111**, 5:142, 5:541, 5:693
Neusner, Jacob, 4:594, 4:596, 4:597, 4:600,4:601, 4:602, 4:605, 4:606,4:611, 4:612, 4:614, 4:615, 4:616, 4:617, 4:621, 4:640, 4:646, 4:648, 4:649, 4:651, 4:652, 4:680
Neustadt, Richard E., 3:147, 3:515, 5:390
Neuville, H. Richmond, 2:716
Nevadomsky, Joseph-John, 3:488
Neve, J., 1:238
Nevell, Richard, 3:732
Nevers, Noel de, 5:214
Nevill, John C., 1:376
Neville, Robert Cummings, 4:391
Nevins, Allan, 3:511, 3:514, 3:529, **3:590**
Nevison, Jack M., 5:557
Nevius, Blake, 1:788
Nevo, Ruth, 1:211, 1:213
New, W. H., 2:904, 2:905, 2:923
Newall, Venetia J., 3:848, 3:869

Newberger, E., 3:207
Newbery, David N. G., 3:52
Newbury, Colin, 3:421, 3:495
Newby, Eric, 3:900, 3:905
Newby, I. A., 3:560
Newby, James Edward, 1:127
Newby, Peter, 1:422
Newcomb, Franc J., 3:865
Newcombe, Josephine M., 2:699
Newdigate, B. H., 1:179
Newell, John, 5:9
Newell, Nancy P., 3:455
Newell, Richard S., 3:455
Newell, William H., 3:465
Newey, Vincent, 1:238, 2:989
Newhall, Beaumont, 3:760
Newhall, Richard A., 3:331
Newhouse, Dora, 1:94
Newkirk, William, 5:381
Newlin, Dika, 3:662
Newman, Barbara, 3:734
Newman, Claire E., 5:523
Newman, Ernest, 3:729
Newman, Harold, 3:766
Newman, John Henry, Cardinal, 1:311, 1:324, 1:368, 1:383, **4:782**
Newman, Judie, 1:947
Newman, Karen, 1:211
Newman, Katherine S., 3:212
Newman, Kim, 1:599
Newman, Lea Bertani Vozar, 1:689
Newman, Louis I., 4:633
Newman, Peter C., 3:616
Newman, Stanley S., 3:40
Newman, William M., 5:565
Newman, William S., 3:678
Newmark, Peter, 2:990
Newsom, Carol A., 4:819
Newson, Adele S., 1:850
Newton, A. Edward, 1:33
Newton, David E., 5:108
Newton, Esther, 1:1182
Newton, Gerald, 3:383
Newton, Isaac, 1:636, 1:641
Newton, Jack, 5:591
Newton, James, 3:929
Newton, Judith Lowder, 1:319
Newton, Saul, 5:471
Newton, Sir Isaac, 3:796, 4:157, 4:176, **4:183**, 4:194, 4:195, 4:383, 4:406, 4:738, 4:766, 5:15, 5:43, 5:56, 5:203, 5:477, 5:489, 5:506, **5:511**, 5:527, 5:585, 5:601, 5:603, 5:606, 5:608, 5:649, 5:663, 5:665, 5:681, 5:687, 5:695, 5:698, **5:704**, 5:727
Newton-Smith, W. H., 5:68

Nexø, Martin Andersen, 2:645, **2:652**
Neyman, Jerzy, 5:602
Ng, Lorenz K. Y., 5:353
Ngara, Emmanuel, 2:111
Ngate, Jonathan, 2:111
Ngugi wa Thiong'o, 2:111, **2:153**, 2:322
Nguyen, Dihn-Hoa, 1:103
Nguyen, Dinh Tham, 2:339
Nguyen, Chi Thien, 2:339
Nguyen, Ngoc Bich, 2:339
Niall, Brenda, 2:951
Nicholas, Barry, 3:306
Nicholas of Autrecourt, 4:104
Nicholas of Cusa, 4:116, 4:138, **4:148**, 4:712
Nicholls, Ann, 3:757
Nicholls, Peter, 5:565
Nichols, Aidan, 4:756
Nichols, Bill, 1:1157, 1:1158
Nichols, Charles H., 1:849
Nichols, Charles Lemuel, 1:44
Nichols, Fred J., 2:382
Nichols, James H., Jr., 4:75, 4:739
Nichols, John A, 4:700
Nichols, Larry A., 4:854
Nichols, Lee, 2:111
Nichols, Margaret Irby, 1:75
Nichols, Mary P., 4:90
Nichols, Peter, 1:524
Nichols, Robert L., 3:394
Nichols, Roger, 3:712
Nichols, Sallie, 5:456
Nichols, Stephen G., Jr., 2:983
Nicholson, Graeme, 4:294
Nicholson, Harold G., 2:514
Nicholson, H. B., 4:455
Nicholson, Lewis E., 1:144
Nicholson, L. H., 4:584
Nicholson, Linda, 1:926
Nicholson, Margaret, 1:92
Nicholson, Norman, 1:238
Nicholson, Reynold A., 2:56, 2:57, 4:576, 4:583
Nicholson, Richard H., 5:122
Nicita, Michael, 5:540
Nickelsburg, George W. E., 4:613, 4:615, 4:811, 4:814
Nickerson, Eve, 5:380
Nickerson, Raymond, 5:12
Nickon, Alex, 5:725
Nicodemos, 4:756
Nicol, Charles, 2:741
Nicol, D. M., 4:693
Nicoll, Allardyce, 1:242, 1:272, 1:323
Nicolson, Harold, 3:280
Nicolson, Harold G., 1:283, 1:541

Nicolson, Marjorie H., 1:192
Nicosia, Gerald, 1:999
Nida, Eugene A., 2:990
Nie, Norman H., 3:148
Niebuhr, H. Richard, 3:213, 4:254, 4:679, 4:745, 4:753, 4:899
Niebuhr, Reinhold, 4:772, **4:783**, 4:787
Nieh, Hualing, 2:234
Nield, E. W., 5:639
Nield, J. A., 1:122
Nieli, Russell, 4:346
Nielsen, Aldon L., 1:799
Nielsen, Kai, 4:413
Nielsen, Niels, 4:756
Nieman, Donald G., 3:139
Niemi, Richard G., 3:144
Nienhauser, William H., 2:190
Nietzsche, Friedrich Wilhelm, 1:668, 1:807, 1:1150, 2:25, 2:415, 2:455, 2:461, 2:485, 2:510, 2:564, 2:605, 2:624, 2:664, 4:38, 4:159, **4:245**, 4:255, 4:256, 4:261, 4:314, 4:334, 4:367, 4:390, 4:399, 4:407, 4:741, 5:87, 5:96
Nieuwenhuys, Robert, 2:621
Niewenhuis, J. D., 5:624
Niewyk, Donald L., 3:350
Nightingale, Benedict, 1:427
Nightingale, Florence, 5:362
Nijinska, Bronislava, 3:734, 3:736, **3:748**
Nijinsky, Romola, 3:653, 3:749
Nijinsky, Vaslav, 3:653, 3:741, **3:748**
Nijō, Lady, 2:279
Nikolaos, Van Dam, 3:455
Niles, Bo, 3:900
Nilsson, Martin P., 2:362, 4:450, 4:470, 4:486, 4:487
Nilsson, Nils A., 2:687, 2:746
Nimmanhemint, Mom Luong Bubpha, 2:334
Nimmer, David, 1:55
Nimmer, Melville B., 1:55
Nimmo, Dan, 3:808
Nimmons, David, 5:119
Nims, John Frederic, 2:5
Nin, Anaïs, 1:812, **1:864**
Nini, Yehuda, 4:626
Nininger, H. H., 5:624
Nirala, 2:176
Nisan, Mordechai, 4:643
Nisbet, Hugh Barr, 4:199
Nisbet, Robert A., 3:209, 3:225, **3:235**
Nisbett, Alec, 5:835
Nisenson, Eric, 3:691

Nisetich, F., 2:365
Nishida Kitarō, 4:348, **4:364**, 4:365, 4:366, 4:888
Nishitani Keiji, 4:363, **4:365**, 4:541, 4:889
Nissen, Hans, 4:434, 4:441
Nissenbaum, Stephen, 3:516
Nissley, Meta, 1:55
Nister, Der. *See* Der Nister
Nitsch, Twylah, 3:865
Nitske, W. Robert, 5:240, 5:711
Niven, Ivan M., 5:488, 5:491
Niven, Larry, 1:1261
Niven, Penelope, 1:879
Niver, Kemp R., 3:826
Nivola, Pietro S., 5:284
Nixon, Bebe, 5:388
Nixon, Howard M., 1:25
Nixon, Nichola, 5:388
Nixon, Paul, 2:389
Nizhny, Vladimir, 3:836
Njegoš, Petar Petrović, 2:826, 2:829, **2:831**
Njoku, Benedict C., 2:129
Nketia, Joseph H., 3:670
Nkosi, Lewis, 2:111, 2:157
Nkrumah, Kwame, 4:26, **4:370**
Nober, Petrus, 4:796
Noble, David F., 5:73, 5:75, 5:562
Noble, David W., 3:512
Noble, Donald, 1:886
Noble, Elizabeth, 5:359
Noble, Gil, 3:808
Noble, Iris, 5:364
Noble, Janet, 1:1079
Noble, J. Kendrick, Jr., 1:49
Noble, M. E., 4:503
Noble, Park S., 5:768
Noble, Peter, 1:1177
Noble, Richmond S., 1:220
Noble, R. W., 5:775
Noble, Thomas F. X., 4:695
Noble, Virginia D., 5:562
Noble, Wilfred Vernon, 4:734
Noble, William, 1:57
Nobo, Jorge L., 4:342
Nock, Arthur Darby, 4:470, **4:487**
Noddings, Nel, 4:391
Nodelman, Perry, 1:1196, 3:256
Noel, Bernard, 3:781
Noer, Deliar, 4:373
Noether, Emiliana P., 3:385
Noether, Emmy, 5:511, **5:512**
Nof, Shimon Y., 5:242, 5:243
Nohrnberg, James, 1:198
Nokes, David, 1:228
Nolan, Frederick, 3:713

Nolan, Janne E., 5:184
Nolan, William F., 1:1212
Noll, Mark A., 4:751, 4:813
Noll, Michael A., 5:12
Nolletti, Arthur, Jr., 1:760
Nollman, Jim, 5:826
Nonnecke, Ib Libner, 5:263
Nooteboom, Cees, 2:621
Nora, Simon, 5:573
Norberg-Schulz, Christian, 3:763
Norcliffe, Glen B., 3:120
Nord, Deborah E., 3:113
Nordbrandt, Henrik, 2:653
Nordby, Vernon J., 5:414, 5:456
Nordenfelt, Lennart, 5:78
Nordenskiold, Erik, 5:34
Nordhoff, Charles, 4:844
Nordquist, J., 3:282
Nordquist, Joan, 4:277, 4:294, 4:395, 4:398, 4:401, 5:76, 5:82, 5:88, 5:91, 5:94
Nordstrom, Byron J., 3:380
Nordstrom, Karl F., 5:632
Norén, Lars, 2:671
Noreña, Carlos G., 4:128, 4:156
Norich, Anita, 2:49
Noriega, Chon A., 1:1157
Norman, Buford, 5:561
Norman, David, 5:639
Norman, Elizabeth, 3:539
Norman, E. R., 3:355
Norman, Floyd E., 3:867
Norman, Howard, 3:865
Norman, Marsha, 1:1071, 1:1087, **1:1105**
Norrie, Ian, 1:37
Norrie, Kenneth, 3:607
Norrington, A.L.P., 1:39
Norris, (Benjamin) Frank(lin), 1:726, 1:740, **1:776**, 1:802
Norris, Christopher, 1:926, 1:1143, 4:266, 4:391, 4:398
Norris, Geoffrey, 3:712
Norris, John, 4:180
Norris, Leslie, 1:561
Norris, Richard A., Jr., 4:99, 4:686
Norris, Ronald V., 5:356
Norris, Ruth, 5:353
North, Christopher R., 4:822
North, Helen, 4:48
North, Michael, 1:487
Northam, John, 2:666
Northcutt, Wayne, 3:373
Northedge, F. S., 3:344
Northouse, Cameron, 1:532
Northup, George T. 523
Norton, Bryan G., 5:115

Norton, Caroline Sheridan, 1:383
Norton, David F., 4:202
Norton, Donna, 1:579, 1:1196
Norton, Eloise S., 3:856
Norton, Mary Beth, 3:514, 3:521
Norton, Peter, 5:538, 5:555
Norton, William, 3:121, 3:273
Norwid, Cyprian, 2:810
Norwood, Christopher, 5:359
Norwood, Gilbert, 2:365, 2:391, 2:395
Norwood, Vera, 5:818
Nosco, Peter, 3:475, 4:541
Noss, David S., 4:2
Nossal, G.J.V., 5:782
Nota, John H., 4:332
Notelovitz, Morris, 5:356, 5:396
Noth, Martin, 4:807, 4:823, **4:835**
Nottingham, John, 3:423
Noue, Alec, 3:397
Nouvel, Walter W., 3:741
Novack, Cynthia Jean, 3:732, 3:733
Novadus of Ghent, 2:269
Novák, Arne, 2:789
Novak, David, 4:598
Novak, Maximillian E., 1:240
Novak, Michael, 3:143, 4:748, 5:111
Novalis, 2:605, 2:612
Noverre, Jean-Georges, 3:749
Novick, Nelson Lee, 5:323
Novick, Peter, 3:515
Novik, Mary, 1:966
Novikov, Igor D., 5:607
Novin, Donald, 5:347
Nowak, Ronald M., 5:761, 5:769
Nowell, Elizabeth, 1:905
Nowell-Smith, Simon, 1:767
Nowicki, Stephen, Jr., 5:426
Nowlan, Robert A., 3:826
Noxon, James, 4:202
Noy, Dov, 3:856
Noyes, Robert W., 5:593
Noyes, Russell, 1:266, 1:268
Nozick, Robert, 4:313
Nuchelmans, G., 4:97
Nuechterlein, Donald Edwin, 3:490
Nugent, Robert, 2:475
Nugent, Walter T. K., 3:9, 3:557
Null, Gary, 5:347
Nulman, Mary, 3:656
Numbers, Ronald L., 4:893, 5:36, 5:329, 5:698
Nunes, Maria Luisa, 2:897

Nungezer, J. M., 1:218
Nunn, Frederick M., 3:632
Nunn, G. Raymond, 3:462
Nuovo, Victor, 5:207
Nureyev, Rudolph, 3:653, 3:738, 3:742, **3:749**
Nurse, Derek, 3:422
Nussbaum, Bruce, 5:214
Nussbaum, Felicity, 1:226, 1:231
Nussbaum, Martha C., 2:988, 4:48, 4:70
Nuttgens, Patrick J., 3:762
Nutting, Wallace, 3:766
Nwapa, Flora, 2:105, **2:139**
Nwoga, Donatus, 2:142
Nyamndi, George, 2:126
Nyce, James M., 5:200, 5:543
Nye, Andrea, 4:392
Nye, Joseph S., Jr., 3:145, 5:111
Nye, Mary J., 5:32
Nye, Russell B., 1:629, 1:1200
Nyeko, Balaam, 3:423
Nýka-Niliūnas, 2:805

O

Oakes, George W., 3:900
Oakes, James, 3:525
Oakeshott, Michael, 4:174
Oaklander, L. Nathan, 5:103
Oakley, Francis, 4:105, 4:691, 4:721
Oates, Joyce Carol, 1:909, 1:921, **1:1021**
Oates, Stephen B., 1:87, 3:525, 3:529, 3:539, 4:773
Oates, Wallace E., 3:48
Oates, Whitney J., 2:348, 2:349, 4:56, 4:70
O'Barr, Jean, 3:218
Obbink, Dirk, 4:451
O'Beirne, T. H., 5:496
Ober, Josiah, 3:302
Ober, Kenneth, 2:645
Oberg, Alcestis, 5:597
Oberg, Arthur, 1:914
Oberg, Charlotte, 1:383
Oberg, James E., 5:597
Oberhelman, Harley D., 2:867
Oberleder, Muriel, 5:317
Oberman, Heiko A., 4:105, 4:128, 4:129, 4:697, 4:721, 4:779
Obeyesekere, Gananath, 3:24, 4:424, 4:462, 4:515
Obiechina, E. N., 2:107, 2:111, 2:126

Obolensky, Dimitri, 2:684, 2:693
Oboler, Eli M., 1:57
Obradović, Dositej, 2:826
Obregon, Mauricio, 3:909
Obremski, T. E., 5:523
O'Brien, Conor C., 3:362
O'Brien, Darcy, 1:507
O'Brien, David, 4:745
O'Brien, David J., 3:557
O'Brien, David M., 3:145
O'Brien, Denis, 4:53
O'Brien, Ed, 3:719
O'Brien, Flann, 1:525
O'Brien, George, 1:479
O'Brien, Michael, 3:560
O'Brien, Michael J., 4:90
O'Brien, Theresa K., 4:888
Obstfelder, Sigbjørn, 2:662, 2:663
Obudho, Constance E., 3:802
O'Callaghan, Joseph F., 3:387
Ocampo, Ambeth R., 2:333
O'Carroll, Michael, 4:675
O'Casey, Sean, 1:423, **1:526**
Ochberg, Richard L., 1:87
Ochshorn, Judith, 4:439
Ochshorn, Kathleen, 1:1014
Ochsner, Jeffrey Karl, 3:790
O'Clair, Robert, 1:418
O'Connell, Agnes N., 3:169, 3:181
O'Connell, Joseph T., 4:516
O'Connell, Marvin R., 4:737
O'Connell, Maurice, 3:370
O'Connell, Michael, 1:199
O'Connell, Robert J., 4:110
O'Connor, Barbara, 3:266
O'Connor, Bernard F., 4:300
O'Connor, Daniel J., 4:162
O'Connor, David, 4:69, 4:312
O'Connor, Egan, 5:397
O'Connor, Flannery, 1:635, **1:1023**
O'Connor, Frank, 1:527, 1:1032
O'Connor, Garry, 1:527
O'Connor, John E., 3:560, 3:826
O'Connor, June, 4:353, 4:766
O'Connor, M., 4:795
O'Connor, Marion, 1:208
O'Connor, Patrick, 3:737
O'Connor, Raymond J., 5:771
O'Connor, Richard, 1:757
O'Connor, Richard A., 3:489
O'Connor, William V., 1:422, 1:457
Odagiri, Hiroko, 2:272
O'Day, Rosemary, 4:726, 4:727, 4:734
Oddy, Andrew, 5:193

O'Dea, Thomas F., 4:754, 4:846, 4:890
Oded, Arye, 4:572
Odell, George C., 1:218, 1:1075
Odell, Peter R., 5:636
Odell, Rice, 5:816
Oden, Robert A., 4:485
Oden, Thomas, 4:885
Oderman, Kevin, 1:873
Odets, Clifford, 1:1071, **1:1105**
Odian, Yervant, 2:79
Odier, Daniel, 1:958
Odom, Keith C., 1:487
O'Donnell, Patrick, 1:986
O'Donoghue, Michael, 5:618
O'Donovan, Leo, 4:904
O'Driscoll, Dorothy L., 5:317
Odum, Eugene P., 5:820
Ody, Anthony J., 5:286
Oehlenschläger, Axel, 2:644
Ōe Kenzaburō, 2:292
Oemarjati, Boen S., 2:319
Oesterley, William O., 4:605
Oestreich, Gerhard, 4:129
O'Faolain, Sean, 1:422, **1:528**
O'Farrell, P. J., 3:355
Offen, K., 3:276
Offord, D. C., 4:31
O'Flaherty, Wendy Doniger, 2:171, 4:428, 4:501, 4:505, 4:890
Ofrat, Elisha, 3:440
Ōgai, Mori. *See* Mori Ōgai
Ogali, Ogali A., 2:125, **2:140**
O'Gara, Gordon C., 3:595
Ogbaa, Kalu, 2:129
Ogbu, John U., 3:256
Ogburn, William F., 5:156
Ogburn, William Fielding, 3:236
Ogden, J. M., 5:290
Ogden, Schubert M., 4:831
Ogg, Oscar, 1:18
Ogilvie, Marilyn B., 5:4, 5:29
Ogilvie, R. M., 2:381, 3:303, 4:448
Ogle, Jane, 5:317
Ogletree, Thomas W., 4:745
O'Gorman, Frank, 3:362, 4:193
O'Gorman, James F., 3:790
Ogot, B. A., 3:418, 3:422
Ogot, Grace Akinye, 2:151, **2:155**
Ogungbesan, Kolawole, 2:126
Oh, Bonnie B. C., 3:468, 4:532
O'Hear, Anthony, 4:385, 4:410
Ohkawa, Kazushi, 3:479

O'Hanlon, Redmond, 3:896
O'Hanlon, Rosalind, 3:485
O'Hara, Frank, 1:900,
 1:1002, **1:1025,** 1:1190
O'Hara, James J., 2:397
O'Hara, John, 1:866
O'Hara, Patricia, 1:354
Ohlin, Bertil, 3:59
Ohlin, Peter, 1:933
Ohmann, Richard, 1:1127
Oibner, Bern, 5:711
Oinas, Felix J., 3:856
Oizerman, Theodor, 4:18,
 4:23
Ojinmah, Umelo Reubens,
 2:978
Ojo-Ade, Femi, 2:111
Ojo-Arewa, E., 2:112
Oka, Yoshitake, 3:479
Okadigbo, Chuba, 4:371
Okara, Gabriel, 2:140
O'Keeffe, Georgia, 3:784
O'Kelly, Morton E., 3:122
Okere, Theophilus, 4:26,
 4:369
Okerstrom, D., 3:280
Okey, Joseph, 3:389
Okigbo, Christopher, 2:141,
 2:151
Okken, P. A., 5:634
Oko, Adolph S., 4:189
Okot P'bitek, 2:151, **2:155**
Okpaku, Joseph O., 2:111
Okpewho, Isidore, 2:111,
 2:113, **2:142**
Okrent, Mark, 4:294
Okri, Ben, 2:105, **2:143**
Okroi, Loren J., 3:79
Okruhlik, Kathleen, 4:391
Okudzhava, Bulat, 2:719,
 2:742
Okun, Barbara F., 5:419
Olafioye, Tayo, 2:111
Olby, Robert, 5:10, 5:26,
 5:49, 5:61, 5:791, 5:807,
 5:813
Olcott, Henry S., 4:853
Oldenburg, Veena Talwar,
 3:485
Older, Julia, 5:356
Olderman, Raymond, 1:919
Oldfather, W. A., 4:57
Oldham, Gabriella, 3:826
Oldsey, Bernard Stanley,
 1:531
O'Leary, Brian, 5:592
O'Leary, K. Daniel, 5:419
Oleksiw, Susan P., 1:604
Olen, Jeffrey, 4:23
Olenick, Richard, 5:653
Olesha (Olyesha), Yury,
 2:743, 2:774
Oleson, John P., 3:304, 5:29

Olgren, Christine H., 5:299
Olin, John C., 4:729, 4:779
Oliphant, Dave, 1:25, 2:527
Oliphant, Margaret, 1:332,
 1:385
Oliphant, Mark, 5:712
Olitzky, Kerry M., 4:652
Oliva, Judy Lee, 1:493
Olivares, Julián, 2:548
Olivas, Michael A., 1:1061
Oliver, Clinton S., 1:1079
Oliver, Douglas L., 4:462
Oliver, George, 5:515
Oliver, James H., 4:76
Oliver, John E., 5:634
Oliver, Lawrence J., 1:794
Oliver, Roland Anthony,
 3:416, 3:418, 3:419, 3:422,
 3:423, **3:429**
Oliver, W. H., 3:495
Oliver, William I., 2:849
Olivier, Daniel, 4:779
Olkin, Sylvia K., 3:207
Ollier, C. D., 5:628
Olmos, Margarite Fernández,
 2:849
Olmstead, John Charles,
 1:379
Olney, James, 1:473, 1:928,
 2:111
Olney, Marguerite, 3:858
Olrik, Axel, 3:848
Olscamp, Paul J., 4:23
Olschki, Leonardo, 3:934
Olsen, Donald J., 3:341
Olsen, Fred, 4:466
Olsen, John P., 3:382
Olsen, Lynn M., 5:494
Olsen, Michael, 3:890
Olsen, Solveig, 5:566
Olsen, Tillie, 1:743, 1:926,
 1:1025
Olshen, Barry N., 1:478
Olson, Carl, 4:355, 4:506,
 4:530, 4:536
Olson, Charles, 1:689, 1:911,
 1:969, **1:1026**
Olson, David M., 3:148
Olson, David R., 4:460
Olson, Eric, 3:276
Olson, James, 3:341
Olson, James S., 3:491
Olson, Julius E., 1:631
Olson, Paul R., 2:543
Olson, Raymond E., 4:31
Olson, Rodney D., 1:760
Olson, Sigurd F., 3:896,
 5:818
Olson, Steve, 5:222, 5:402
Olsson, Hagar, 2:657
Oltmanns, Thomas F., 5:427
Olupona, Jacob K., 4:463
Olyan, Saul M., 4:545

O'Mahony, Christopher, 4:741
O'Malley, Charles D., 5:40,
 5:365
O'Malley, Ernie, 3:371
O'Malley, Padraig, 3:371
Omar Khayyam, 1:522, **2:92**
Omarr, Sydney, 4:860
O'Meally, Robert G., 1:974,
 3:701
O'Meara, Dominic J., 4:62,
 4:87, 4:99, 5:515
O'Meara, John J., 4:115
Omer-Cooper, J. D., 3:424
Omotoso, Kole, 2:105,
 2:129, **2:143,** 2:149
Ondaatje, Michael, 2:903,
 2:922
O'Neel, Hank, 1:813
Onega Jaen, Susana, 1:478
O'Neil, Charles J., 4:286
O'Neil, Kevin, 4:538
O'Neil, Robert M., 3:251
O'Neill, Eugene, 1:1070,
 1:1106, 1:1116, 2:349,
 2:427, 2:679, 2:724
O'Neill, Gerard K., 5:214
O'Neill, Hugh B., 3:463,
 3:466
O'Neill, John, 4:311
O'Neill, Michael, 1:303
O'Neill, Onora, 4:206, 4:387
O'Neill, Peter, 5:736
O'Neill, T. P., 3:371
O'Neill, William L., 3:535,
 3:539
Onetti, Juan Carlos, 2:876
Ong, Aihwa, 3:22
Ong, Walter J., 4:129, 4:460
Ongkili, James P., 3:492
Onians, Richard B., 4:49
Onions, Charles T., 1:96,
 1:216, 1:222
Onn, Chin Kee, 2:324
Ono, Sokyo, 4:536
Ono, Kazuko, 3:471
Onwueme, Tess, 2:143
Ooka, Makoto, 2:273, 2:283
Ooms, Herman, 3:475
Oparin, Aleksandr Ivanovich,
 5:774
Opatoshu, Joseph, 2:42
Opdahl, Keith, 1:947
Ophir, Adi, 4:83
Opie, Iona, 1:579, **3:884**
Opie, Peter, 1:579, **3:884**
Oppel, Frances Nesbitt, 1:572
Oppenheim, A. Leo, 4:441
Oppenheim, Frank, 4:250
Oppenheim, Janet, 4:851
Oppenheim, Michael, 5:13,
 5:332

Oppenheimer, J. Robert,
5:133, 5:143, 5:211, 5:697,
5:706
Oppenheimer, Max Stul,
5:557
Opper, Sylvia, 3:192
Oppler, Ellen, 3:787
Optic, Oliver, 1:1194
Oraf, Alfred D., 5:761
Orayevskiy, A. N., 5:235
Orchin, Milton, 5:726
Orcutt, William Dana, 1:33
Ordon, Edmund, 2:812
Ordway, Frederick I., III,
5:37, 5:613
Ore, Oystein, 5:488
O'Regan, Daphne, 2:354
O'Reilly, John J., 5:297
O'Reilly, Kenneth, 3:557
Orel, Harold, 1:372, 1:566,
1:592, 1:608
Oren, Dan A, 4:640
Orenstein, Arbie, 3:712
Oresick, Peter, 1:801
Oreszkowa, Eliza, 2:810
Organ, Troy Wilson, 4:70,
4:354
Orgel, Stephen, 1:184
Orians, Gordon H., 5:765
Orieux, Jean, 4:218
Origen, 4:62, 4:93, 4:98,
4:116
Oring, Elliott, 5:448
Orlando, Francesco, 2:498
Orledge, Robert, 3:714
Orlova, Alexandra, 3:708
Ormerod, Beverley, 2:930
Ormiston, Gayle L., 5:66,
5:71, 5:156
Ormond, Leonée, 1:330,
1:352
Ormsby, Eric, 4:582
Orne, Jerrold, 1:69
Orni, Efraim, 3:440
Ornstein, Allan C., 3:257
Ornstein, Robert, 1:212
Orr, David W., 5:115
Orr, Eleanor Wilson, 3:257
Orr, James, 4:739
Orr, Leonard, 1:572
Orrego, Vicuna F., 5:238
Orrell, John, 1:217, 1:218
Orren, Gary, 3:214
Orrey, Leslie, 3:671, 3:679
Orrick, Sarah, 5:815
Orrill, Robert, 5:460
Orsini, Gian N., 2:414
Ortega, Julio, 2:845, 2:867
Ortega y Gasset, José,
2:545, 3:203, 3:294, 3:327,
4:177, 4:261, **4:314,** 4:331,
5:96
Ortiz, Alfonso, 3:864

Ortiz, Flora I., 3:257
Orton, Gavin, 2:675
Orton, Joe, 1:424, **1:529**
Ortzen, Len, 2:117
Oruka, J. Odera, 4:26, **4:371**
Orwell, George, 1:370,
1:414, 1:419, 1:428, **1:530,**
2:310, 2:774, 2:818, 5:563
Osamu, Dazai. See Dazai
Ozamu
Osberg, Lars, 3:66
Osbon, Diane, 3:877
Osborn, E. F., 4:63
Osborn, Elizabeth M., 1:1078
Osborn, James M., 1:196
Osborn, Kevin, 5:374
Osborne, Carol Margot, 1:29
Osborne, Catherine, 4:49
Osborne, Charles, 3:711,
3:727, 3:729
Osborne, Harold, 3:758,
3:760, 3:765, 4:465
Osborne, John, 1:414, 1:424,
1:433, 1:486, 1:524, **1:531**
Osborne, Milton, 2:339
Osborne, Yvonne Hardaway,
5:427
Osen, Lynn M., 5:29
Oser, Jacob, 3:45
Osers, Ewald, 2:808
Osgood, Charles G., 1:199
Osgood, Cornelius, 3:481
Osgood, William R., 5:557
Oshagan, Vahe, 2:76
O'Sharkey, Eithne M., 2:460
Osler, Margaret J., 4:56
Osler, Ruth, 1:32
Osler, Sir William, 5:54,
5:363
Oslin, George P., 5:297
Osman, Mohammed Taib bin,
2:324
Osmanćzyk, Edmund Jan,
1:111
Osmond-Smith, David, 3:680
Osofsky, Gilbert, 3:867
Ossman, Jennifer, 1:77
Ostaijen, Paul van, 2:629
Ostaszewski, Adam, 3:64
Oster, Judith, 1:842
Osterbrock, Don, 5:590
Ostow, Miriam, 5:334
Ostrauskas, Kostas, 2:805
Ostriker, Alicia S., 1:799,
1:926
Ostroff, Anthony, 1:914
Ostrovsky, Aleksandr, 2:744
Ostrow, David G., 5:390
Ostwald, Martin, 3:323
Ô, Suk-kwôn, 2:299
O'Sullivan, Gerry, 3:204
O'Sullivan, Noel, 3:138
O'Sullivan, Sue, 1:1184

O'Sullivan, Vincent, 2:971
Osumare, Halifu, 3:734
Oswald, John Clyde, 1:10
Oswald, Laura, 2:479
Otchere, Freda E., 3:416
Otfinoski, Steven, 3:928
O'Toole, Christopher, 5:769,
5:771
O'Toole, G.J.A., 3:532
O'Toole, L. M., 2:689
O'Toole, Patricia, 3:563
Otten, Willemien, 4:115
Otto, Herbert A., 5:320
Otto, Rudolf, 4:487
Otto, Simon, 3:862
Ottoboni, M. Alice, 5:736
Otto-Dorn, Katharina, 3:437
Ottoson, David, 5:342
Otway, Thomas, 1:251,
1:1069
Ouellet, Fernand, 3:613
Ouellette, R. P., 5:222
Oulanoff, Hongor, 2:731
Oulton, A. J., 5:566
Ouologuem, Yambo, 2:105,
2:125, **2:144**
Ourmette, Victor, 4:315
Ousby, Ian, 1:132, 1:270
Ousmane, Sembene, 2:125,
2:144
Ouspensky, Leonid, 4:693
Ouspensky, P. D., 4:876
Outka, Gene, 4:893
Outram, Dorinda, 5:792
Ou-yang Hsiu, 2:214, **2:215,**
2:225
Oved, Yaacov, 4:844
Overall, Christine, 5:122
Overbye, Dennis, 5:590
Overfield, James H., 4:129
Overman, J. Andrew, 4:617
Overmier, Judith, 5:29
Overmyer, Daniel L., 4:523,
4:531, 4:884
Overzee, Anne H., 4:337
Ovid (Publius Ovidius
Naso), 1:186, 1:224, 2:354,
2:359, 2:364, 2:366, 2:379,
2:388, **2:389,** 2:958
Owen, G. E., 4:49, 4:67, 4:80
Owen, J., 3:59
Owen, Mary A., 3:867
Owen, Roger, 3:437, 4:572
Owen, Stephen, 2:190, 2:190,
2:199
Owen, Tobias, 5:593
Owen, Wilfred, 1:413, 1:416,
1:511, **1:533,** 1:557, 3:685
Owens, Delia, 5:818
Owens, Joseph, 4:46, 4:70
Owens, Louis, 1:886
Owens, Mark, 5:818
Owens, W. R., 1:240

Owomeyela, Oyeka, 2:111
Owram, Doug, 3:607
Owusu, Martin, 2:111
Oxorn, Harry, 5:404
Oxtoby, Willard G., 4:516
O Yông-su, 2:307
Oyono, Ferdinand, 2:145
Oz, Amos, 2:22, 2:26, 4:643
Ozakin, Aysel, 2:96
Ozeri, Zion M., 4:644
Ozick, Cynthia, 1:1027
Ozima, Minoru, 5:618
Ozment, Steven E., 3:331,
    4:129, 4:697, 4:721, 4:722,
    4:724, 4:727
Ozmon, H., 4:18
Ozouf, Mona, 3:339

P

Paardt, R. T. Van der, 4:469
Pacanowsky, Michael E.,
    3:802
Pace, Nicholas, 5:402
Pace, Steve, 5:219
Pacey, Arnold, 5:37, 5:71,
    5:156, 5:232
Pach, Walter, 3:789
Pachai, Bridglal, 3:930
Pachauri, R. K., 5:280
Pacheco, Esther M., 2:329
Pacheco, José Emilio,
    2:844, 2:876
Pa Chin, 2:259
Pachmuss, Temira, 2:689,
    2:693
Pachter, Henry M., 4:150,
    5:751
Pachter, Marc, 1:87
Pacifici, Sergio, 2:401
Pack, Spencer J., 3:51
Packard, Alpheus S., 5:803
Packard, Rosa C., 3:266
Packe, Michael St. John,
    3:97
Packer, Jean Garrett, 1:468,
    1:566
Packer, J. I., 4:5
Packull, Werner O., 4:724
Padden, R. C., 3:629
Paden, William E., 4:422
Padgett, Ron, 1:915
Padgett, Stephen, 3:346
Padilla, Heberto, 2:877,
    2:939
Padley, G. A., 4:129
Padover, Saul K., 3:155,
    3:543
Paehlke, Robert, 5:76
Paepke, C. Owen, 5:156
Pagden, Anthony, 3:336

Page, Adrian, 1:426
Page, Christopher, 3:662
Page, Denys L., 2:348, 2:362,
    2:366
Page, Jake, 5:342
Page, James D., 5:427
Page, Joseph A., 3:633
Page, Malcolm, 1:434, 1:437,
    1:493, 1:544, 1:555
Page, Monte M., 3:175
Page, Norman, 1:283, 1:346,
    1:363, 1:552, 2:741
Pagel, Walter, 4:129, 4:150,
    5:362
Pagels, Elaine, 4:453, 4:686
Pagels, Heinz R., 5:573,
    5:595, 5:655, 5:660, 5:691,
    5:713
Pagis, Dan, 2:9, 2:23
Paglia, Camille, 3:539
Pagter, Carl R., 3:868
Pahl, R. E., 3:218
Pai, Anna C., 5:778
Pai, Inez Kong, 2:299
Paiewonsky, Michael, 3:916
Pai Hsien-yung, 2:260
Paine, Suzanne, 3:453
Paine, Thomas, 1:626, 1:632,
    1:641, 1:648, 1:705
Painter, Genevieve, 5:416
Painter, George, 2:495
Painter, Sidney, 3:331, 3:332
Painter, William M., 2:403
Pais, Abraham, 5:49, 5:658,
    5:683
Paisley, William, 3:802
Pakenham, Frank, 3:371
Pakenham, Thomas, 3:364,
    3:370, 3:418
Palais, Joseph C., 5:304
Palamas, Kostes, 2:370,
    2:375
Palandri, Angela C., 2:234
Palau i Fabre, Josep, 3:787
Palazzollo, Carlo, 3:779
Palencia-Roth, Michael, 2:868
Paley, William S(amuel),
    3:818, 3:819
Palic, Vladimir M., 1:111
Palisca, Claude V., 3:660,
    3:662
Palladio, Andrea, 3:755,
    3:763, 3:785
Pallis, Svend A., 4:441
Pallottino, Massimo, 3:305
Palm, Göran, 2:671
Palmer, Alan, 1:117, 3:273
Palmer, Bruce, Jr., 3:636
Palmer, Bryan, 3:607
Palmer, Carole, 3:873
Palmer, Christopher, 3:667,
    3:685
Palmer, David, 1:166, 1:420

Palmer, David Scott, 3:640
Palmer, Eustace, 2:109
Palmer, Francis H., 3:394
Palmer, Helen H., 1:123
Palmer, Howard, 3:610
Palmer, Katherine, 5:803
Palmer, Laura, 5:387
Palmer, Martin, 4:531
Palmer, Monte, 3:454
Palmer, R., 3:852
Palmer, Richard E., 4:402
Palmer, R. L., 5:395
Palmer, Robert R., 3:274,
    3:327
Palmer, Stanley H., 1:631
Palmer, Tamara, 3:610
Palmer, Trevor, 5:774
Palmieri, Anthony F., 1:1110
Palmore, Erdman, 5:317
Pálsson, Hermann, 2:640
Paludan, Philip S., 3:529
Paludi, Michele A., 3:178
Pamuk, Orhan, 2:96
Panchen, Alec L., 5:765
Panek, Leroy, 1:604
Pangborn, Cyrus R., 4:518,
    548
Pangle, Thomas, 4:210
Panichas, George A., 4:74
Panikkar, Raimundo, 4:501
Pannekoek, A., 5:32
Pannenberg, Wolfhart, 4:99,
    4:745
Pannick, Gerald J., 1:816
Pano, Nicholas, 3:392
Panofsky, Erwin, 3:760,
    3:774, 4:738
Panova, Vera, 2:744
Pantel, Pauline S., 3:307
Paolucci, Anne, 2:436
Paolucci, Henry, 5:688
Pap, Arthur, 4:20
Papacosta, Pangratios, 5:668
Papadaki, Stamo, 3:779
Papanek, Victor, 5:130
Papanghelis, Theodore D.,
    2:392
Papasogli, Giorgio, 4:787
Paperno, Irina, 2:711
Papert, Seymour, 3:251,
    5:566, 5:568
Papini, Giovanni, 2:427,
    2:430
Papke, Mary E, 1:740
Papp, Daniel S., 5:182
Pappas, Charles N., 5:314
Pappas, George S., 4:20
Pappe, H. D., 1:380
Paquet, Sandra Pouchet,
    2:937
Paracelsus, Philippus Au-
    reolus, 4:123, 4:149, 5:412,
    5:739, 5:750

Paracer, Surindar, 5:763
Paradis, James, 5:800
Paradise, Nathaniel B., 1:171
Paradiso, John L., 5:769
Paramahansa, Ramakrishna,
4:562
Paramahansa Yogananda,
4:556, 4:872, 4:873
Parandowski, Jan, 2:819
Parascandola, John, 5:351
Pardo Bazán, Emilia, 2:546
Pardoe, F. E, 1:18
Paredes, Americo, 3:856,
3:863
Paredes, Ruby R., 3:493
Paredi, Angela, 4:702
Parel, Anthony J., 4:145
Parent, David, 4:247
Parenti, Michael, 3:808
Pares, Bernard, 3:394
Pares, Susan, 3:481
Pareto, Vilfredo, 3:99, 3:237
Paretsky, Sara, 1:1229,
1:1230, **1:1235**
Parfit, Michael, 3:906
Parfitt, George, 1:184
Parfitt, Tudor, 3:440
Pargellis, Stanley, 3:354
Paringer, William, 4:225
Paringer, William A., 3:261
Parini, Giuseppe, 2:399,
2:430
Parini, Jay, 1:1038
Parins, James W., 1:715
Paris, Bernard J., 1:276
Paris, Gaston, 2:515
Paris, Peter, 4:748
Park, David, 5:10
Park, Edwards, 5:340
Park, Mungo, 3:932
Park, R. Graham, 5:624
Park, Robert Ezra, 3:199,
3:216, 3:221, 3:222, **3:236**
Parke, Catherine N., 1:250
Parke, H. W., 4:447
Parker, A. A., 2:523
Parker, Andrew, 1:1134
Parker, Arthur C., 3:865
Parker, Barry, 1:221, 5:665
Parker, Carolyn, 2:111
Parker, Charlie, 3:691, **3:708**
Parker, Donald L., 3:811
Parker, Donn B., 5:126
Parker, Dorothy, 1:814,
1:867, 1:868
Parker, Geoffrey, 4:732, 4:737
Parker, H. T., 3:276
Parker, Hershel, 1:689
Parker, Kenneth, 2:158
Parker, Muriel, 3:767
Parker, Patricia, 1:208, 1:636,
1:643
Parker, Robert D., 1:837

Parker, Ronald B., 5:624
Parker, Steve, 5:794
Parker, Sybil P., 5:2, 5:29,
5:217, 5:618, 5:653, 5:816
Parker, Thomas, 1:88
Parker, Thomas H. L., 4:727,
4:762
Parker, W. H., 3:133
Parker, William R., 1:192
Parkes, Graham, 4:294, 4:350
Parkes, James W., 3:350,
4:637
Parkin, David, 3:422
Parkin, John, 1:863
Parkinson, Claire L., 5:6
Parkinson, G.H.R., 4:162,
4:177
Parkinson, R. B., 2:53
Parkman, Francis, 1:659,
1:690, 3:576, **3:591**
Parkman, Patricia, 3:637
Parks, Edd Winfield, 1:693,
1:703, 1:772, 1:778
Parks, George B., 2:523,
3:923
Parks, Suzan-Lori, 1:1071
Parland, Oscar, 2:658
Parley, Peter, 1:1194
Parnes, Robert, 5:263
Parnwell, E. C., 1:103
Parpola, Simo, 4:545
Parr, Joy, 3:608
Parra, Nicanor, 2:870, **2:877**
Parrinder, Edward G., 4:572
Parrinder, Geoffrey, 4:5,
4:463, 4:885, 4:894, 4:898
Parrinder, Patrick, 1:564
Parrington, Vernon Louis,
1:651, 1:715, 1:854, 4:35
Parris, Leslie, 3:773
Parrish, Stephen M., 1:308,
2:738
Parron, Delores L., 5:341
Parry, Adam, 2:362, 3:323
Parry, J. H., 3:336, 3:893
Parry, Jonathan, 3:23
Parry, Milman, 4:460
Parry, R. B., 3:119
Parsegian, V. L., 5:243
Parsons, Denys, 3:657
Parsons, Elsie C., 3:507
Parsons, Kitty, 3:852
Parsons, Talcott, 3:15,
3:216, 3:233, **3:237,** 3:242,
3:257
Parsons, Thomas S., 5:773
Parsons, William Barclay,
5:232
Partee, Charles, 4:129
Partin, Harry, 4:855
Partington, James R., 5:32,
5:729
Partington, Paul G., 1:832

Partington, Paul W., 3:578
Partington, Wilfred, 1:35
Partnoy, Alicia, 2:850
Partridge, Colin, 1:359
Partridge, Edward B., 1:184
Partridge, Elinor Hughes,
1:660, 1:727
Partridge, Eric, 1:93, 1:96,
1:216
Partridge, Ernest, 5:115
Partridge, Monica, 2:728
Parun, Vesna, 2:785, **2:787**
Parvez, H., 5:789
Pasachoff, Jay M., 5:588,
5:591, 5:653
Pascal, Anne, 1:333
Pascal, Blaise, 2:492, 2:516,
3:337, 4:164, **4:185,** 5:506,
5:525, 5:541
Pascal, Roy, 1:928, 2:596
Paschke, Barbara, 2:850
Pasco, Allan H., 2:454
Pascoli, Giovanni, 2:431
Pasek, Jan Chryzostom,
2:809, **2:819**
Pasler, Jann, 3:723
Pasmantier, Jeanne, 2:526
Pasolini, Pier Paolo, 2:431
Pass, Christopher, 3:44
Passmore, John, 3:257, 4:168,
4:202, 4:266, 4:379, 5:115
Passwater, Richard A., 5:347
Pasternak, Alexander, 2:746
Pasternak, Boris, 2:745,
3:397
Pasteur, Louis, 5:221, 5:274,
5:408, **5:409, 5:808**
Patai, Daphne, 1:734, 2:890
Patai, Raphael, 3:444
Patchen, Kenneth, 1:1028
Patel, Essop, 2:158
Patel, Ishwarbhi, 5:198
Pater, Alan F., 1:117
Pater, Jason R., 1:117
Pater, Walter Horatio,
1:324, 1:363, **1:386,** 1:409,
4:83
Paterson, Antoinette M.,
4:136
Paterson, Katherine, 1:1195,
1:1204
Paterson, Thomas G., 3:540,
3:546
Paterson, William, 3:346
Patil, V. T., 3:500
Patinkin, Don, 3:65
Patke, Rajeev S., 1:888
Patner, Andrew, 3:808
Paton, Alan, 2:157, **2:167,**
3:424
Paton, H. J., 4:207
Paton, Lucy A., 5:786
Paton, William, 5:782

Patrick, Hugh, 3:479
Patrick, J. Max, 1:182
Patrick, Mary Mills, 4:58
Patrick, Rembert, 3:575
Patrick, St., 4:713
Patrick, Walton R., 1:852,
  1:921
Patrides, C. A., 1:181, 1:192
Patry, William F., 1:55
Pattee, Fred L., 1:658, 1:715,
  1:724
Patten, John, 3:130
Patten, Robert L., 1:350
Patterson, Alex, 1:1171
Patterson, Annabel M., 1:189,
  1:193, 1:209
Patterson, Bob E., 4:784
Patterson, C. H., 5:419
Patterson, Charles, 3:674
Patterson, Charlotte A., 1:124
Patterson, Elizabeth C., 5:742
Patterson, Graeme, 3:622
Patterson, Henry, 3:371
Patterson, James T., 3:514,
  3:548
Patterson, Jane, 5:314
Patterson, Lee, 1:151
Patterson, Lyman Ray, 1:55
Patterson, Richard, 4:83
Patterson, Thomas C., 3:628
Patterson, Walter C., 5:240
Patterson, Yolanda A., 2:459
Pattison, George, 4:240
Pattison, Robert, 1:402
Pattison, Walter T., 2:523
Patton, Cindy, 1:1182, 3:202
Patton, Phil, 5:220
Patursson, Jóhannes, 2:655
Patwardhan, Vinayak N.,
  3:444
Pauck, Marion, 4:788
Pauck, Wilhelm, 4:730, 4:788
Paul, Anthony M., 4:31
Paul, Betty, 5:419
Paul, Charles B., 5:45
Paul, Diana Y., 4:514
Paul, Ellen Frankel, 5:112
Paul, Henry P., 1:214
Paul, Jean, 2:605
Paul, John Rodman, 5:390
Paul, Norman L., 5:419
Paul, Olgesby, 5:369
Paul, Robert, 4:734
Paul, Sherman, 1:670
Paulaharju, Samuli, 2:658
Pauli, Wolfgang, 5:657,
  5:680, **5:707,** 5:715
Paulin, Thomas, 1:363
Pauling, Linus, 5:730, 5:734,
  5:751
Paulitschke, P. V., 2:112
Paul of Finland, Archbishop,
  4:755

Paul of Venice, 4:129
Paulou, Dmitrii V., 3:397
Paulson, Ronald, 1:261
Pauly, Reinhard G., 3:662
Pausanias, 2:347, 4:488
Paustovsky, Konstantin,
  2:746
Pavarotti, Adua, 3:709
Pavarotti, Luciano, 3:653,
  3:687, 3:692, **3:708**
Pavese, Cesare, 2:411, 2:421,
  2:432, 2:442
Pavić, Milorad, 2:827, 2:831
Pavier, Thomas, 1:203
Pavlos, Andrew J., 4:855
Pavlov, Ivan Petrovich,
  3:176, **3:191,** 5:364, 5:464
Pavlova, Anna, 3:736, 3:750
Pavlović, Miodrag, 2:827,
  2:831
Pavlovski, Radovan, 2:807
Pavlowitch, Steven K., 3:392
Pawlowska, Harriet, 3:852
Paxton, John, 3:138
Paxton, Nancy L., 1:354
Paxton, Robert O., 3:349,
  3:373
Payer, Pierre J., 4:700
Payn, Graham, 1:465
Payne, Alma, 1:1199
Payne, Christopher, 3:766
Payne, Darwin, 1:789, 1:1219
Payne, F. William, 5:288
Payne, John R., 1:366
Payne, Ladel, 1:724, 1:919
Payne, Robert, 2:193, 4:572
Payne, Stanley G., 3:387
Payne, Wardell, J., 4:7
Payne, William M., 1:660,
  1:727
Payne-Gaposhkin, Cecilia,
  5:587, **5:610**
Paz, D. G., 3:364
Paz, Octavio, 1:1055, 2:850,
  2:868, **2:878**
Pazstory, Esther, 4:457
P'bitek, Okot. *See* Okot
  P'bitek
Pe, Hla, 4:519
Pea, Roy D., 5:566
Peace, Richard, 2:722
Peacock, D. Keith, 1:426
Peacock, James, 3:29
Peacock, Sandra J., 4:479
Peacock, Thomas Love,
  1:264, 1:273, **1:296,** 1:303,
  1:635
Pearce, Charles, 1:18
Pearce, David W., 3:44
Pearce, Douglas, 3:890
Pearce, E. A., 5:634
Pearce, Frank, 3:225
Pearce, Jane, 5:471

Pearce, J. Gordon, 5:301
Pearce, Lynn, 1:315
Pearce, Richard, 1:837,
  1:1035, 1:1057
Pearce, R. M., 5:256
Pearce, Roy Harvey, 1:631,
  1:655, 1:719, 1:799
Pearce, T. M., 1:733
Pearcy, G. Etzel, 3:273
Pearl, Richard M., 5:624
Pearlman, Mickey, 1:911
Pearlman, Moshe, 3:440
Pears, David, 4:346
Pearsall, Derek, 1:147, 1:154
Pearsall, Robert B., 1:339
Pearse, Nancy C., 1:173
Pearson, Birger A., 4:453
Pearson, Carol S., 1:1196
Pearson, Edmund L., 1:33
Pearson, Egon Sharpe,
  5:525, 5:526, 5:530, **5:531**
Pearson, Hesketh, 1:358,
  1:411
Pearson, J. D., 3:482
Pearson, John, 1:548
Pearson, Karl, 5:525, 5:529,
  5:530, **5:531**
Pearson, Lionel, 2:347, 2:355
Pearson, Michael, 3:397
Pearson, M. N., 3:484
Pearson, Norman Holmes,
  1:129, 1:915
Pearson, Paul D., 3:770
Pearson, Richard, 3:476
Peary, Robert E(dwin),
  3:912, **3:932**
Pease, Donald E., 1:760
Pease, Jane H., 3:525
Pease, Otis A., 3:592
Pease, William H., 3:525
Peat, F. David, 5:11
Peattie, Donald C., 5:820
Peattie, Mark R., 3:465,
  3:478
Peattie, Noel, 1:50
Peck, Abraham J., 4:652
Peck, David, 1:134
Peck, Harry T., 1:695
Peck, H. Daniel, 1:665
Peck, Linda L., 3:360
Peck, Merton J., 3:52
Peckenham, Nancy, 3:638
Peckham, Howard Henry,
  1:34, 3:511
Peckham, Morse, 1:266
Peden, Margaret S., 2:847,
  2:858
Peden, William, 1:919
Pedersen, Roger A., 5:777
Pedersen, S. A., 5:78
Pederson, Johannes, 1:10
Peebles, Patrick, 3:488
Peebles, Peyton Z., 5:302

Peel, J. D., 3:241
Peel, Robert, 4:843, 4:875
Peele, George, 1:195
Peers, Edgar A., 2:524, 2:526
Peet, Richard, 3:119
Pegels, C. Carl, 5:317
Pehl, Erich, 5:230
Peirce, Charles Sanders,
  1:726, 4:211, 4:235, **4:248,**
  4:260, 4:317, 4:333, 5:95
Peirce, Neal, 3:507
Pei Tao, 2:260
Pekarik, Andrew, 2:279
Pekkanen, John, 5:370
Peled, Matityahu, 2:69
Pelensky, Olga Anastasia,
  2:649
Pelikan, Jaroslav, 2:418, 4:99,
  4:677, 4:720
Pelin, Elin, 2:780, **2:782**
Pellegrin, Pierre, 4:70
Pellegrini, Anthony L., 2:400
Pellegrino, Edmund D.,
  5:80, **5:97**, 5:139
Pellegrino, J. W., 3:174
Pelletier, Francis Jeffrey,
  4:83
Pelletier, Kenneth R., 5:353,
  5:401
Pelletier, Paul A., 5:4, 5:29
Pelling, Henry, 3:356, 3:364,
  3:367
Pells, Richard H., 3:561
Pels, Peter, 3:12
Pelto, Gretel H., 3:12
Pelto, Pertti J., 3:12
Pelzer, Karl, 3:492
Pemberton, Thomas Edgar,
  1:390, 1:756
Pemble, John, 3:485
Peña, Valeriano Hernández,
  2:327
Pencavel, John, 3:60
Pence, George, 5:122
Pence, Terry, 5:122
Pendle, Karin, 3:662
Pendlebury, John D., 2:347
Penelhum, Terence, 4:202
Penfield, Marjorie P., 5:267
Penfield, Wilder, 5:81
Penley, Constance, 1:1157,
  1:1158
Penner, Allen Richard, 1:547
Pennington, Anne, 2:828
Pennington, M. Basil, 4:112,
  4:700
Pennock, J. Roland, 3:140
Penny, Barbara, 3:766
Penny, Nicholas, 1:395,
  3:788, 3:790
Penrose, C., 5:255
Penrose, Edith, 3:450

Penrose, Ernest Francis,
  3:418
Penrose, Roger, 5:76, 5:574,
  5:691, **5:708**
Penrose, Roland, 3:787
Penton, M. James, 4:863
Peñuelas, Marcelino C., 2:531
Penueli, S. Y., 2:10
Penzer, Norman M., 3:914
Penzias, Arno, 5:574
Pepinsky, Harold B., 5:545
Peppard, Victor, 2:744
Pepys, Samuel, 3:919
Peratt, A. L., 5:667
Percas de Ponseti, Helena,
  2:536
Perces, Marjorie, 3:734
Percesepe, Gary J., 4:398
Percival, Anthony, 2:547
Percival, George, 1:25
Percival, John, 3:754
Percival, Milton O., 1:279
Percy, Eustace, 4:774
Percy, Walker, 1:909, **1:1028**
Pereira, Luiz C., 3:143
Perelman, S(idney)
  J(oseph), 1:807, **1:868,**
  1:897, 1:952
Perera, Frederica P., 5:398
Peretti, Burton W., 3:561
Peretz, Don, 3:440, 4:579
Peretz, Yitskhok Leybush,
  (I. L.), 2:7, 2:29, **2:42**
Perez, Joseph F., 5:419
Pérez, Louis A., Jr., 3:636
Pérez Brignoli, Héctor, 3:632
Pérez de Ayala, Ramón,
  2:546
Pérez Firmat, Gustavo, 2:523
Pérez Galdós, Benito, 2:521,
  2:527, 2:531, **2:546**
Pérez-López, Jorge F., 3:636
Perez Sanchez, Alfonso E.,
  3:776
Perfect, Christopher, 1:19
Perham, Margery, 3:421,
  3:905
Perin, Roberto, 3:608
Perjes, Z., 5:665
Perkell, Christine, 2:397
Perkin, Sir William Henry,
  5:752
Perkins, C. R., 3:119
Perkins, David, 1:266, 1:268,
  1:294, 1:308, 1:417, 1:719,
  1:799, 5:726
Perkins, D. N., 5:342
Perkins, Donald H., 5:662
Perkins, Edwin J., 3:548
Perkins, George, 1:133
Perkins, Merle, 4:214
Perkins, Robert, 3:906

Perkins, Robert L., 3:285,
  4:240
Perkinson, Henry J., 3:257
Perle, George, 3:665
Perlès, Alfred, 1:470
Perlin, Seymour, 5:427
Perlis, Vivian, 3:702
Perlman, Lawrence, 4:665
Perlmatter, Philip, 3:212
Perlmutter, Arnold, 5:214
Perlmutter, Nathan, 4:640
Perlmutter, Ruth Ann, 4:640
Perloff, Marjorie, 1:799,
  1:914, 1:1025, 2:500
Perlove, Shelley, 3:770
Perls, Frederick, 5:464
Permutter, Donna, 3:754
Pern, Stephen, 3:896
Perng, Ching-hsi, 2:190
Pernick, Martin S., 5:47,
  5:370
Peronal-Hugoz, Jean-Pierre,
  4:579
Perreiah, Alan R., 4:130
Perren, Richard, 3:473
Perret, Jacques, 2:386
Perret, Yvonne M., 5:321
Perrett, Geoffrey, 3:535,
  3:546
Perrin, James M., 5:333
Perrin, Noel, 1:57, 3:897
Perrin, Norman, 4:816
Perrin, Ron, 4:332
Perron, Edgar du, 2:621
Perrow, Charles, 3:214,
  5:156, 5:244
Perrucci, Robert, 3:208
Perry, Ben E., 2:352, 2:363
Perry, Charles, 3:561
Perry, Donald, 5:820
Perry, Glenn E., 3:437
Perry, John, 1:775, 4:23
Perry, Lewis, 3:514, 3:525
Perry, Margaret, 1:824
Perry, Ralph Barton, 1:769,
  4:27, 4:35, 4:238, 4:266
Perry, Ted, 3:830
Perry, William E., 5:557
Perrycuick, C. J., 5:775
Persall, Marilyn, 4:391
Persaud, T.V.N., 5:34
Perse, Saint-John. *See* Saint-
  John Perse
Persico, Joseph, 3:819
Persius (Aulus Persius Flac-
  cus), 2:379, **2:390**
Personick, Stewart D., 5:304
Perutz, Max, 5:10
Pervan, Anthony S., 5:399
Pescar, Susan C., 5:358,
  5:400
Pesce, Angelo, 3:451
Peseroff, Joyce, 1:952

Pessen, Edward, 3:543
Pessoa, Fernando, 2:557,
2:560
Peszke, Michael A., 5:419
Petchenik, Barbara Bartz,
3:121
Peterdi, Gabor, 1:29
Peterkiewicz, Jerzy, 2:812
Peterman, Michael, 2:910
Peter of Spain, 4:102
Peters, B. Guy, 3:147
Peters, Catherine, 1:404
Peters, Edward, 3:331, 4:693,
4:700, 4:721
Peters, Ellis, 1:608
**Peters, F(rancis) E(dward),
3:459**
Peters, Frederick G., 2:604
Peters, Fritz, 4:876
Peters, Hans F., 4:247
Peters, Jane S., 5:326
Peters, Jean, 1:33, 1:53, 1:69
Peters, Jonathan A., 2:129,
2:145, 2:147, 2:149
Peters, Lenrie, 2:145
Peters, Margot, 1:546
Peters, Marie, 3:362
Peters, Oneita B., 5:806
Peters, Phillis, 1:646
Peters, Richard S., 4:174
Peters, Robert, 1:921
Peters, Robert L., 5:775
Peters, Rudolph, 4:895
Peters, Uwe H., 5:445
Peters, William C., 5:238
Peters, William S., 5:523
Petersen, Clarence, 1:39
Petersen, Fridrikur, 2:655
Petersen, Kirsten H., 2:112
Petersen, Michael, 4:381
Petersen, Renée, 3:206
Petersen, William, 3:206
Peterson, Dale, 5:565
Peterson, Donald, 4:346
Peterson, Gwen Boardman,
2:282
Peterson, Haller Alvarey,
5:335
Peterson, Houston, 5:800
Peterson, K. H., 2:129
Peterson, Merrill D., 3:154,
3:155, 3:525
Peterson, Morris S., 5:624
Peterson, R. A., 5:229
Peterson, Richard F., 1:505
Peterson, Richard H., 3:548
Peterson, Richard S., 1:184
Peterson, Roger Tory, 5:761,
5:787, 5:818
Petersson, Torsten, 2:385,
4:72
Petherbridge, Guy, 1:22
Pethick, John, 5:627

Petie, J. Howard, 5:544
Petit, Philip, 4:316
Petöfi, Sándor, 2:797, **2:802**
**Petrarch (Francesco Petrar-
ca),** 1:163, 1:164, 1:201,
2:298, 2:405, 2:408, 2:409,
2:424, 2:426, **2:433,** 2:440,
4:145, **4:150**
Petras, Peter, 3:233
Petrek, Jeanne A., 5:373
Petrie, Barbara, 2:971
Petrie, Dennis W., 1:928
Petrie, Glenn, 1:341
Petrie, Jennifer, 2:434
Petrone, Penny, 2:905
**Petronius (Gaius Petronius
Arbiter),** 2:379, **2:390**
Petroski, Henry, 5:12, **5:174,**
5:214, 5:226, 5:253
Petrovic, Gajo, 4:33
Petrović, Rastko, 2:827
Petrowski, Dorothy D., 5:338
Petrusha, Ronald, 5:540
Petry, Ann, 1:1029
Petry, E., 3:49
Petry, M. D., 4:741
Petry, Ray C., 4:697
Petryanov, I. V., 5:750
Pettegree, Andrew, 4:731
Petterson, B.O.D., 5:266
Pettigrew, Jane, 3:343
Pettigrew, Thomas F., 3:209
Pettijohn, Francis J., 5:624
Pettijohn, Terry F., 3:169
Pettinato, Giovanni, 4:445
Pettit, Arthur G., 1:784
Petuchowski, Jakob J., 4:596,
4:600, 4:601, 4:613, 4:652
Petulla, Joseph M., 3:550
Petykiewicz, J., 5:666
Petzvold, Charles, 5:555
Peuquet, Donna J., 3:120
Pevsner, Nikolaus, 3:762,
3:763
Peyasantiwong, Patcharin,
2:335
Peyer, Bernd, 1:725
Peyre, Henri, 2:495
Peyser, Joan, 3:662, 3:683
Pfaelzer, Jean, 1:724
Pfaltzgraff, Robert L., Jr.,
3:144
Pfeiffer, Charles C., 3:437
Pfeiffer, Robert H., 4:605
Pfeil, Fred, 3:346
Pfeiler, William K., 2:565
Pfuetze, Paul, 4:309
Phaedrus, Gaius Julius, 2:379
Phan, Peter C., 4:689
Phangkham, Thao, 2:321
Phelan, John Leddy, 3:493
Phelps, Donald, 1:834
Phelps, Gilbert, 3:640

Phelps, William L., 1:268
Philip, Alex J., 1:25
Philip, Cynthia Owen, 5:248
Philip, James A., 4:87, 5:515
Philip, Neil, 1:418, 1:720
Philippi, Donald, 4:536
Philipson, David, 4:653
Philipson, Martin, 3:780
Phillips, Charles S., 4:741
Phillips, E. D., 3:304
Phillips, Elizabeth, 1:748,
1:864
Phillips, Esther R., 5:492
Phillips, George, 3:766
Phillips, Gregory D., 3:367
Phillips, Harry T., 5:317
Phillips, Herbert P., 2:335
Phillips, James M., 4:541
Phillips, John, 3:393
Phillips, John L., Jr., 5:524
Phillips, John R., 4:738
Phillips, J.R.S., 3:331
Phillips, Louis, 1:720
Phillips, Margaret M., 4:139
Phillips, Melba, 5:652
Phillips, Michael J., 1:522,
1:587
Phillips, Owen M., 5:624
Phillips, Robert, 1:583,
1:1216, 5:385
Phillips, Roger, 5:767
Phillips, Stephen H., 4:349,
4:353
Phillips, William, 1:925
Phillipson, John S., 1:905
Philo Judaeus, 2:343, 2:364,
4:45, 4:60, 4:489, 4:607,
4:614, **4:670**
Phimmasone, Phouvong,
2:322
Phinney, John F. S., 3:11
Phippard, Martin, 5:247
Phipps, Lenore B., 5:337
Phoumisak, Chitr, 2:335
Phu, Sunthorn, 2:334
Piaget, Jean, 3:174, 3:176,
3:191, 3:266, 5:465
Piattelli, Palmarini Massimo,
3:192
Piazza, Paul, 1:501
Picard, M. Dane, 5:624
Picasso, Pablo, 2:80, 2:440,
2:451, 2:462, 2:468, 2:560,
3:741, 3:769, 3:780, **3:785,**
3:795
Piccireli, Annette, 5:815
Pichanick, Valerie Kossew,
1:376
Pick, Daniel, 3:343
Pick, Herbert L., Jr., 3:172
Pick, Otto, 2:789
Pickard, Samuel T., 1:709

Pickard-Cambridge, A. W.,
   2:347, 2:355
Picken, Stuart D. B., 4:536
Pickering, Andrew, 5:67,
   5:156, 5:663
Pickering, F. P., 2:566
Pickering, K. T., 5:632
Pickering, Mary, 3:224, 4:223
Pickering, W. S., 3:225
Pickett, Calder, 3:808
Pickford, J., 5:245
Pickles, Dorothy, 3:373
Pickover, Clifford A., 5:565
Pickowicz, Paul, 2:234
Pickvance, Ronald, 3:795
Pico Della Mirandola, Gian-
   francesco, 4:151
Pico Della Mirandola, Giov-
   anni, 1:386, 2:398, 2:433,
   2:434, 2:436, 4:140, 4:147,
   4:151, 4:152, 4:156
Picon, Gaëtan, 2:447
Picon-Salas, Mariano, 4:752
Pidmohylny, Valerian, 2:840
Piepkorn, Arthur C., 4:717,
   4:751
Pierce, Christine, 5:76, 5:116
Pierce, Gilbert A., 1:350
Pierce, James L., 3:65
Pierce, John Robinson, 5:12,
   5:300, 5:581
Pierce, J. T., 5:263
Pierce, Judy, 5:374
Pierce, L. C., 3:250
Pierce, Peter, 2:947
Pierson, William H., 3:763
Pieterse, Cosmo, 2:112
Pietrzak, Jeanne, 5:403
Pifer, Ellen, 1:478, 2:741
Piggot, Juliet, 4:535
Piggott, Patrick, 3:712
Piggott, Stuart, 4:436
Pihl, Marshall R., 2:299
Pijoan, Teresa, 3:865
Pike, Frederick B., 3:632
Pike, Zebulon Montgomery,
   3:910
Pilcher, Rosamunde (Scott),
   1:620
Pilkey, Orrin H., 5:631
Pilkington, A. E., 4:220
Pilkington, James Penn, 1:39
Pilkington, John, 1:837
Pillai, Thakazhi Sivasankara,
   2:178
Pillar, Charles, 5:157, 5:182
Pillard, Richard, 5:422
Pillement, Georges, 3:900
Pillemer, David B., 5:523
Pilling, Ann, 3:856
Pilnyak, Boris, 2:747, 2:753
Piltz, Rick, 5:815
Pimentel, David, 5:278

Pimentel, Marcia, 5:278
Pinault, David, 2:56, 4:572
Pinch, Alan, 2:766
Pinch, Trevor J., 5:9, 5:66,
   5:151
Pinchbeck, Ivy, 3:356
Pinches, Charles, 4:745
Pinciss, Gerald M., 1:220
Pinckney, Cathy, 5:324
Pinckney, Edward R., 5:324
Pindar, 1:684, 2:342, 2:364,
   2:517
Pindell, Terry, 3:897
Pine, Richard, 1:470, 1:479,
   1:866
Pine, Stanley H., 5:732
Pinero, Sir Arthur Wing,
   1:311, 1:321, 1:367, 1:388,
   1:423, 1:465, 1:481
Pines, David, 5:671
Pines, Jim, 1:1158
Pinfold, Mike, 3:674
Pinget, Robert, 2:493
Ping Hsin, 2:261
Pinion, F. B., 1:335, 1:354,
   1:363, 1:402
Pinkerton, Edward C., 1:96
Pinkney, David H., 3:372
Pinkney, Tony, 1:473, 1:511
Pinsker, Sanford, 1:911,
   1:919, 1:988, 1:1028,
   1:1041, 2:32, 4:594
Pinsky, David, 2:43
Pinsky, Robert, 1:296, 1:417,
   1:914, 1:1030
Pinter, Harold, 1:412, 1:414,
   1:465, 1:480, 1:482, 1:486,
   1:532, 1:533, 1:543
Pinto, Fernão Mendes,
   2:556, 2:561
Piovesana, Gino K., 4:363,
   4:541
Pipa, Arshi, 2:779
Piper, David, 3:758
Piper, J.D.A., 5:630
Pipes, Richard, 2:730, 3:280,
   3:397
Pipkin, H. Wayne, 4:791
Pippin, Brigid, 1:29
Pippin, Robert, 4:207, 4:233,
   4:408, 5:95
Pirajno, Franco, 5:636
Pirandello, Luigi, 2:399,
   2:409, 2:418, 2:422, 2:434,
   2:438, 2:441
Pira Sudham, 2:336
Pirenne, Henri, 3:329, 3:331,
   3:333, 3:380, 3:382, 3:407
Pirog, Gerald, 2:703
Pirsig, Robert M., 5:72, 5:157
Piscatori, James P., 3:444
Pisemsky, Aleksei, 2:748
Pisetsky, David, 5:398

Pitcher, Harvey, 2:710
Pitkin, Hanna F., 3:160,
   4:145
Pitt, David C., 3:12
Pitt, Joseph C., 4:143, 4:334,
   5:64
Pitt, Valerie H., 1:402, 5:653
Pittman, Rita H., 2:706
Pittman-Lindeman, Mary,
   5:387
Pittock, Malcolm, 2:613
Pitts, John, 5:637
Pivar, David J., 3:553
Piven, Frances Fox, 3:144,
   3:212, 3:215
Pizarnik, Alejandra, 2:879
Pizer, Donald, 1:715, 1:724,
   1:752, 1:777, 1:829, 1:831,
   1:919
Pizer, Hank, 5:317, 5:320,
   5:359
Pizzigati, Sam, 3:808
Pizzo, S., 3:56
Place, Janey Ann, 1:1166
Placher, William C., 4:719
Placido, Bucolo, 3:100
Plackett, Robert L., 5:526,
   5:530
Placksin, Sally, 3:669
Placzek, Adolf K., 3:764
Plader, Edward L., 5:730
Plaks, Andrew, 2:191, 2:223
Planck, Max, 4:332, 5:673,
   5:702, 5:709, 5:714, 5:734
Planhol, Xavier De, 3:444
Plano, Jack C., 3:509
Plant, Moira L., 5:402
Plant, R., 3:285
Plantinga, Cornelius, 4:886
Plantinga, Leon, 3:662
Planty-Bonjour, G., 4:31
Plaskett, L. G., 5:290
Plaskin, Glenn, 3:701
Plaskow, Judith, 4:650, 4:784
Plath, Sylvia, 1:497, 1:909,
   1:911, 1:950, 1:982,
   1:1030, 1:1045, 2:880
Plato, 1:193, 1:807, 2:343,
   2:359, 2:362, 2:365, 2:366,
   2:378, 2:408, 3:163, 3:318,
   3:324, 4:11, 4:44, 4:52,
   4:54, 4:58, 4:64, 4:76, 4:88,
   4:91, 4:123, 4:140, 4:150,
   4:152, 4:208, 4:253, 4:257,
   4:281, 4:283, 4:401, 4:409,
   4:414, 4:482, 4:580, 4:581,
   4:848, 5:105
Platonov, Andrei, 2:748
Platt, Anthony, 3:226
Platt, Gerald, 3:257
Platt, Jerome J., 5:403
Plattner, Marc F., 3:142
Plauger, P. J., 5:550

Plaut, Martin E., 5:385
Plaut, W. Gunther, 4:653
Plautus, Titus Maccius,
1:168, 1:189, 2:364, 2:378,
2:391, 2:554
Playfair, John, 5:644
Pleasants, Henry, 3:671,
3:672
Pleck, Elizabeth H., 3:554
Plenderleith, H. J., 1:26
Pletcher, Barbara A., 3:893
Pletta, Dan H., 5:227
Pliny the Elder, 1:105,
3:317, **5:809**
**Pliny the Younger (Gaius
Plinius Caecilius Secun-
dus),** 2:364, 2:379, **2:391**,
3:317, 4:682
Plochmann, George Kimball,
4:83
Ploeg, Durk van der, 2:635
Plog, Stanley, 3:890
Plotch, Batia, 4:602
Plotinus, 4:61, **4:85**, 4:116,
4:123, 4:140, 4:489
Plotke, David, 3:345
Plotkin, Stanley A., 5:409,
5:809
Plotnik, Arthur, 1:53
Plouffe, Paul P., 5:10
Plough, Alonzo L., 5:370
Plous, S., 3:176
Plowden, David, 5:246
Plowman, George T., 1:29
Plumb, Cheryl J., 1:813
Plumb, J(ohn) H(arold),
3:276, **3:407**
Plumb, Lawrence D., 4:866
Plumbe, W. J., 1:26
Plummer, Brenda Gayle,
3:637
Plummer, Kenneth, 1:1184
Plunka, Gene A., 1:544
Plutarch, 2:343, 2:365, 2:381,
3:318, 4:60, **4:489**
Po, Li. *See* Li Po
Po Chü-i, 2:215
Pocock, J.G.A., 4:145
Podoksik, Anatoly, 3:787
Podro, Michael, 3:761
Poe, Edgar Allan, 1:591,
1:598, 1:604, 1:607, 1:635,
1:657, 1:679, 1:684, **1:691**,
1:717, 1:734, 1:1047,
1:1192, 1:1209, 1:1226,
1:1239, 1:1251, 2:90,
2:456, 2:591, 2:731, 2:982,
5:833
Poewe, Karla, 4:857
Pogash, Carol, 5:388
Pogel, Nancy, 3:830
Pogge, Thomas W., 4:316
Poggi, Isotta, 4:865

Poggie, John J., Jr., 3:12
Pogonowski, Iwo, 1:101,
3:390
Pogue, Forrest C., 3:280
Pogue, Leland, 1:1169
Pogue, William R., 5:597
Pohl, Frederik, 1:1252,
1:1261, 1:1261
Pohland, Frederick G., 5:245
Poinar, George O., 5:765
Poincaré, Jules Henri,
5:509, **5:513**
Poindexter, Jeanne S., 5:783
Poirier, Richard, 1:651,
1:769, 1:794, 1:842, 1:1012
Pojman, Louis P., 4:23
Pok, A., 3:276
Polanski, Roman, 3:841
Polansky, Barbara Friedman,
1:55
Polansky, Ronald M., 4:83
Polanyi, Karl, 3:16
Pole, J. R., 3:508, 3:517,
3:543
Pole, Kay, 5:109
Polhemus, Robert M., 1:319
Poliakov, Leon, 4:637
Polich, J. Michael, 5:427
Politis, Linos, 2:371
Polivy, Janet, 5:347
Poliziano, Angelo (Politian),
2:398, 2:433, **2:436**
Polk, Dora, 1:561
Polk, Ralph, 1:10
Polk, William R., 3:437
Polkinghorne, J. C., 5:660
Pollack, Frederick, 4:189
Pollack, Herman, 4:624
Pollack, Howard, 3:688
Pollack, John, 5:74
Pollack, Judith, 3:258
Pollak, Michael, 4:644, 5:111
Pollard, Albert F., 4:764
Pollard, Alfred W., 1:68,
1:207, 1:289
Pollard, Edward A., 3:575
Pollard, Graham, 1:26, 1:35
Pollard, Hazel M., 1:251
Pollard, John A., 1:709
Pollard, M., 1:37
Pollard, Michael, 3:266
Pollard, S., 3:341
Pollock, Bruce, 3:665
Pollock, Dale, 1:1171
Pollock, Jackson, 3:787
Pollock, John, 4:768
Pollock, R. H., 3:181
Polo, Marco, 2:436, 3:465,
3:933
Polome, Edgar C., 4:436,
4:472
Polonsky, Antony, 3:350
Polowy, Teresa, 2:752

Polsby, Nelson W., 3:138,
3:146
Polukhina, Valentina, 2:704
Polybius, 2:343, 2:347, 2:366,
3:318
Pomerleau, Cynthia, 5:314
Pomeroy, Sarah B., 3:309,
4:447
Pomorska, Krystyna, 2:688,
2:689, 2:693, 2:746
Pompa, Leon, 2:442, 4:217
Pomper, P., 3:287
Pomponazzi, Pietro, 4:123,
4:153
Ponge, Francis, 2:494
Ponomareff, Constantin V.,
2:689
Ponting, Clive, 3:367
Pontoppidan, Henrik, 2:645
Pontuso, James F., 2:762
Pooch, Udo W., 5:300
Poole, H. Edmund, 1:7
Poore, Benjamin Perley,
1:109
Poovey, Mary, 1:312
Popa, Vasko, 2:827, 2:831,
2:832
Pope, Alexander, 1:223,
1:235, 1:241, 1:246, 1:248,
1:250, **1:251,** 1:261, 1:281,
1:547, 1:949, 2:359, 2:360,
2:365, 2:385, 2:396
Pope, Carl, 5:636, 5:822
Pope, J. L., 5:424
Pope-Hennessy, Dame Una,
1:351
Pope-Hennessy, James, 1:407
Pope-Hennessy, John, 3:788
Popenoe, Chris, 5:540
Popkin, Richard H., 4:18,
4:23, 4:24, 4:130, 4:162,
4:202, 5:40
Poplasen, Ilija, 3:276
Poppel, Stephen M., 3:350,
4:658
Poppeliers, John, 3:763
Popper, Sir Karl Raimund,
3:163, 4:315, **4:408**, 5:64,
5:81, 5:86, **5:97**, 5:660
Porath, Jonathan D., 3:350
Porphyry, 4:62
Porte, Joel, 1:652, 1:670,
1:767
Porter, Alan L., 5:76, 5:182
Porter, Andrew, 3:662
Porter, A. P., 1:850
Porter, A. R., 5:130
Porter, Bernard, 3:367
Porter, Cathy, 3:397
Porter, Charles A., 2:466
Porter, Cole, 3:709, 3:740
Porter, David, 1:748
Porter, David H., 2:386

Porter, Duncan, 5:794
Porter, Edwin Stanton, **1:1173**
Porter, F., 3:317
Porter, Glenn, 3:509
Porter, Harry R., 3:208
Porter, Jadranka, 3:455
Porter, Katherine Anne, **1:869,** 2:571
Porter, M. Gilbert, 1:947, 1:1000
Porter, Robert, 2:685
Porter, Robert T., 5:45, 5:416
Porter, Roy S., 5:29, 5:33, 5:60
Porter, William E., 3:808
Porter, William Sidney. See Henry, O.
Porterfield, Amanda, 1:629
Porterfield, William W., 5:726
Portes, Alejandro, 3:209
Portnoy, Joan, 3:893
Portnoy, Samuel A., 4:656
Portnoy, Sanford, 3:893
Porton, Gary G., 4:613
Portuges, Catherine, 1:1128
Porush, David, 5:565
Posner, R., 2:9
Posner, Richard A., 3:61
Posnock, Ross, 1:767, 1:769
Post, Chandler R., 2:523
Post, Jerrold M., 5:314
Post, Jonathan F., 1:200
Post, Robert, 5:52
Poster, Mark, 4:266, 4:331, 5:126
Postgate, John, 5:783
Postma, Obe, 2:634
Postman, Leo, 3:176, 3:202
Postman, Neil, 3:252, 5:130, **5:139,** 5:157, 5:574
Poston, M., 3:331, 4:700
Poteat, Patricia Lewis, 1:1029
Poterba, James, 3:47
Potok, Chaim, 1:1032
Potter, Beatrix, 1:578, **1:588**
Potter, David M(orris), 3:529, **3:592**
Potter, Dennis, 1:535
Potter, Esther, 1:26
Potter, G. R., 4:791
Potter, Lois, 1:170
Potter, Robert, 1:161
Potter, Stephen, 1:288, 5:248
Potts, D. C., 4:28
Potts, Eve, 5:372
Potts, Stephen W., 1:988
Potts, T. C., 4:95
Po-tuan, Chang, 4:528
Pough, Frederick H., 5:628
Poulet, Georges, 2:448, 2:457, 2:496, 2:500

Poulin, A., Jr., 1:915
Poulton, Helen J., 3:8, 3:507
Poulton, Hugh, 3:392
Pouncey, Peter, 3:323
Pound, Ezra (Loomis), 1:413, 1:415, 1:452, 1:470, 1:502, 1:513, 1:560, 1:705, 1:718, 1:797, 1:806, 1:826, 1:855, **1:870,** 1:899, 1:909, 1:1067, 2:185, 2:194, 2:273, 2:427, 2:499, 2:911, 5:785
Pound, Louise, 3:862
Pound, Omar, 2:84
Pound, Roscoe, 3:145
Poundstone, William, 5:583
Poupard, Paul, 5:688
Poussaint, Alvin, 3:249, 5:416
Povey, John, 2:106
Powell, Anthony (Dymoke), 1:419, **1:536**
Powell, David, 1:94
Powell, John Wesley, 5:646
Powell, J. U., 2:357
Powell, Kerry, 1:411
Powell, Lawrence C., 1:33, 1:851
Powell, Lawrence N., 3:529
Powell, Lenore, 5:393
Powell, Lyman P., 4:875
Powell, Milton B., 4:754
Powell, Ronald R., 1:74
Powell, T.G.E., 4:436
Powell, Walter, 1:49
Powell, Walter W., 3:204
Powell-Cope, Gail M., 5:386
Powells, Randall L., 3:423
Power, Eileen E., 3:331, 3:358, 4:700
Power, Margaret, 3:172
Powers, Charles, 3:100
Powers, Eileen, 3:331
Powers, J(ames) F(arl), **1:1032**
Powers, Lyall H., 1:767
Powers, Richard Gid, 3:540
Powicke, F. M., 3:357
Powicke, Maurice R., 4:727
Powledge, Fred, 5:221, 5:267, 5:632
Powlson, D. S., 5:265
Pownall, David E., 1:120
Poynter, Dan, 1:48
Poznansky, Alexander, 3:724
Pradhan, Dhiraj K., 5:550
Prado Salmón, Gary, 3:634
Prager, Dennis, 4:596
Prager, Leonard, 2:30
Pramoj, Kukrit. See Khukrit Pramoj
Prance, Claude A., 1:297
Prance, Ghillean Tolmie, 5:768

Prange, Gordon W., 3:535
Prather, Ronald, 3:730
Pratolini, Vasco, 2:437
Pratson, Frederick, 3:893
Pratt, Annis, 2:985
Pratt, E(dwin) J(ohn), 2:922
Pratt, Frantz, 3:638
Pratt, John C., 1:354
Pratt, Joseph, 3:547
Pratt, Louis H., 1:1084
Pratt, Norman T., 2:394
Pratt, Ray, 3:662
Pratt, R. Cranford, 3:422
Pratt, Sarah, 2:771
Pratt, Terrence W., 5:550
Pratt, Willis, 1:284
Prawer, Siegbert Salomon, 1:404
Prawer, S. S., 2:984
Praz, Mario, 2:401, 2:986
Prebish, Charles, 4:860
Preda, Marin, 2:823
Prehm, Herbert J., 5:426
Prelinger, Catherine, 4:754
Premchand, 2:180
Preminger, Alex, 1:131, 2:3
Prendergast, Christopher, 2:476, 2:511
Prendergast, John M., 5:348
Prendergast, Karen A., 5:558
Prendergast, Roy M., 3:667
Prenshaw, Peggy W., 1:896
Prenter, Reginald, 4:779
Prentice, Alison, 3:607, 3:609
Prentky, R., 3:170
Preradović, Petar, 2:785
Prescott, David M., 5:373
Prescott, John R., 5:621
Prescott, Peter, 1:806
Prescott, William H(ickling), 1:694, 3:648
Prešeren, France, 2:834, 2:836, 2:837
Presniakov, K. U., 3:395
Press, Frank, 5:624
Press, John, 1:383, 1:417
Press, William, 5:550
Pressman, Jeffrey, 3:146
Pressman, Peter, 5:372
Prestige, George L., 4:686
Preston, Antony, 5:239
Preston, Dickson J., 1:668
Preston, Douglas J., 5:765
Preston, Richard., 5:590
Prestwich, Menno, 4:732
Prestwich, Michael, 3:358
Preto, René, 3:830
Preus, Anthony, 4:47, 4:66, 4:78
Preus, J. Samuel, 4:420
Preus, Robert D., 4:730
Prevelakis, Pandelis, 2:374

Prévert, Jacques, 1:1002,
2:494
Pribic, Rado, 1:135
Pribram, E. Deidre, 1:1159
Price, Alan, 1:556
Price, A. W., 4:83
Price, Derek J. de Solla,
3:214, 5:61, 5:149
Price, Henry H., 4:202
Price, Jonathan, 5:550
Price, Kenneth M., 1:708
Price, Larkin B., 2:496
Price, Leontyne, 3:709
Price, Martin, 1:227, 1:230
Price, Richard, 4:203, **4:210,**
5:427
Price, Robert, 4:852
Price, S.R.F., 4:452
Prickett, Stephen, 1:288
Prideaux, S. T., 1:26
Pridmore, Jay, 3:922
Priebe, Richard K., 2:108,
2:112
Priest, E. R., 5:667
Priestley, J(ohn) B(oynton),
1:536, 1:728
Priestley, Joseph, 4:210,
4:212, 5:739, 5:748,
5:752
Priestly, Brian, 3:708
Priestman, Martin, 1:238
Prigogine, Ilya, 5:68, 5:735
Primeau, Ronald, 1:859
Primeaux, Martha, 5:353
Primoratz, Igor, 4:387
Prince, F. T., 1:207
Prince, Stephen, 3:839
Pring, J. T., 1:99
Pringle, Elizabeth Allston,
3:532
Pringle, Henry, 3:595, 3:936
Pringle, R. M., 5:521
Prins, Gwyn, 3:280
Prior, William J., 4:83
Prishvin, Mikhail, 2:749,
2:774
Pritchard, Francis H., 1:728
Pritchard, James B., 2:53,
4:7, 4:439, 4:809, 4:812
Pritchard, William H., 1:799,
1:842, 1:993
Pritchett, Frances W., 2:175
Pritchett, Sir V(ictor)
S(awden), 1:443, **1:538,**
2:710, 2:770, 3:900
Pritchett, W. Douglas, 4:864
Pritikin, Nathan, 5:347
Pritt, Donald S., 5:396
Prittie, Terence, 3:377
Proakis, John G., 5:302
Probosz, Kathilyn Solomon,
3:736
Probst, Gerhard, 2:579

Proclus, 4:62
Procopius, 2:344, 2:366,
3:319
Procter-Smith, Marjorie,
4:849
Proctor, Robert N., 5:67,
5:80, 5:108, 5:123, 5:157
Proffer, Carl R., 2:685, 2:689,
2:693, 2:741
Proffer, Ellendea C., 2:706,
2:741, 2:768
Prokofiev, Sergei, 3:709
Pronko, Leonard C., 2:273,
2:449, 2:484
Propertius (Sextus), 2:379,
2:383, 2:389, **2:392**
Propp, Vladimir, 2:689,
3:848, 3:869
Proschan, Frank, 5:522
Prosser, Eleanor, 1:213
Prothro, Edwin T., 3:171
Proudhon, Pierre J., 3:140
Proust, Marcel, 1:395, 1:419,
1:540, 1:1019, 2:439,
2:445, 2:469, **2:494,** 2:507,
2:604, 2:675, 2:870, 4:255
Provine, William B., 5:34,
5:49, 5:780
Prucha, Francis P., 3:507
Prude, Jonathan, 3:548
Prueitt, Melvin L., 5:565
Pruitt, Virginia, 5:464
Prundy, Wyatt, 1:997
Prus, Bolesław, 2:810, **2:819**
Prusek, Jaroslav, 2:191,
2:234, 2:250
Prussia, Stanley E., 5:267
Pruter, Karl, 4:859
Pruyn, Carolyn S., 2:263
Pryke, Kenneth, 3:613
Prytherch, Ray, 1:69
Przyboś, Jan, 2:810
Przybylski, Ryszard, 2:738
Pucci, P., 2:358
Puccini, Giacomo, 3:710
Puckett, N. Niles, 3:867
Pudney, John, 4:790
Puente, Antonio E., 3:168,
3:181
Puette, William J., 2:279
Pufendorf, Samuel, 4:185
Pugh, Francis, 5:191, 5:212
Pugliese, Olga Z., 4:141
Pugsley, Alfred, 5:250
Puhvel, Jaan, 4:436
Puhvel, Martin, 3:849
Puig, Manuel, 2:843, 2:844,
2:880, 2:888
Pulaski, Mary Ann Spencer,
3:192
Pulitzer, Joseph, 3:799,
3:820
Pullapilly, Cyriac K., 4:572

Pullen, Ian, 5:781
Pulos, C. E., 1:303
Pumfrey, Stephen, 5:40
Puppi, Lionello, 3:785
Purcell, Gary R., 5:545
Purcell, Henry, 3:684,
3:711
Purdom, C. D., 4:873
Purdon, M. E., 3:731
Purdy, Al, 2:923
Purdy, James, 1:1033
Purdy, Laura M., 5:120
Puri, Rashimi-Sudha, 3:280
Purpel, David E., 3:257
Purrington, Robert D., 5:656
Pursell, Carroll W(irth), Jr.,
3:326, 5:37, **5:54**
Purser, B. H., 3:448, 3:450
Purser, Michael, 5:301
Purtill, Richard L., 1:559,
4:23
Purves, William K., 5:765
Purvis, James D., 4:618
Pusey, Nathan M., 3:257
Pushkin, Aleksandr, 2:682,
2:712, 2:720, 2:734, 2:740,
2:749, 2:770, 2:771, 2:816,
2:826, 3:724, 4:900
Pustilnik, Jack, 4:23
P'u Sung-ling, 2:217
Putnam, Hilary, 4:288,
4:315, 4:379, **4:410,** 5:64,
5:492
Putnam, Linda L., 3:802
Putnam, Michael C., 2:381,
2:386, 2:396, 2:397
Putnam, Rory, 5:771
Putnam, Samuel, 2:890
Putt, Samuel G., 1:767
Putzel, Max, 1:837
Putzer, Edward, 2:272
Pye, Lucian W., 3:463, 3:471
Pye-Smith, Charlie, 3:905
Pyle, Howard, 1:1194,
1:1205
Pyle, Kenneth B., 3:479
Pyle, Robert M., 5:761
Pym, Barbara, 1:414, 1:451,
1:538
Pym, Denis, 3:210
Pyman, Avril, 2:703
Pynchon, Thomas (Rug-
gles), 1:535, 1:909, 1:952,
1:1034
Pyne, Stephen J., 5:643
Pyron, Darden Asbury,
1:1249
Pythagoras (of Samos),
4:87, **5:514**
Pytlik, Edward C., 5:227

Q

Qabbani, Nizar, 2:60, **2:70,**
2:71
Quadir, C. A., 4:373
Quah, Jon S. T., 2:324
Quah, Stella R., 2:324, 3:492
Qualey, Carlton C., 3:110
Qualls, Barry, 1:319
Qualter, Terence H., 3:204
Quammen, David, 5:765
Quandt, William B., 3:455
Quantrill, Malcolm, 3:770
Quarles, Benjamin, 3:521,
3:529
Quartermain, Peter, 1:799
Quarterman, John, 5:547
Quasimodo, Salvatore,
1:1055, 2:403, 2:427,
2:437, 2:824
Quasten, Johannes, 4:689,
4:690
Qu'ayd, Muhammad Yusuf,
2:59
Quayle, Eric, 1:33
Queen, Ellery, 1:1236
Queen, Karen J., 1:143
Queirós, Raquel de, 2:889,
2:897
Queiróz, José Maria Eça de.
See Eça de Queiróz, José
Maria
Queller, Donald E., 4:694
Queneau, Raymond, 2:496
Quennel, Peter, 1:283
**Quental, Anthero Tarqüínio
de,** 2:557, **2:561**
Quester, George H., 3:280
**Quevedo y Villegas, Fran-
cisco Gómez de,** 2:520,
2:539, **2:547**
Quigley, Carroll, 3:327
Quill, Timothy E., 3:201,
5:379
Quiller-Couch, Arthur, 1:206,
1:396
Quimby, Ian M., 3:849
Quimby, Phineas P., 4:847,
4:874, **4:877**
Quinby, Lee, 4:391
Quincey, Thomas De, 3:681
Quine, Willard Van Orman,
4:14, 4:279, 4:282, 4:315,
4:317, 4:379, 4:410, **4:411,**
5:64, **5:99**
Quiney, Thomas, 1:203
Quinlan, Kieran, 1:875
Quinlan, Maurice J., 1:238
Quinlan, Michael, 5:113
Quinley, Harold E., 3:209
Quinn, Antoinette, 1:507
Quinn, Arthur Hobson,
1:629, 1:715, 1:1075, 2:818

Quinn, David B., 1:631
Quinn, Edward G., 1:131,
1:221, 1:222, 2:3
Quinn, George, 2:317
Quinn, Kenneth P., 1:143,
2:381, 2:384
Quinn, Sister Bernetta, 1:799
Quinn, Susan, 3:186
Quinnett, Paul G., 5:423
Quinones, Ricardo J., 2:985,
2:986
Quinsey, V., 3:170
Quint, Howard H., 3:514
Quintana, Ricardo, 1:247
**Quintilian (Marcus Fabius
Quintilianus),** 2:379,
2:389, **2:392**
Quirk, Tom, 1:722
Quirk, William J., 3:214
Quiroga, Horacio, 2:843,
2:881
Qutb, Sayyid, 4:576

R

Raabe, Tom, 1:33, 1:76
Raat, W. Dirk, 3:639
Raban, Jonathan, 3:897,
3:900
Rabaté, Jean-Michel, 1:506,
1:873
Rabb, T. K., 3:280
Rabe, David, 1:1071, **1:1108**
Rabelais, François, 2:444,
2:453, 2:465, **2:497**
Rabey, David I., 1:426
Rabil, Albert, Jr., 4:130,
4:139
Rabin, Jonathan, 1:130
Rabin, Roni, 5:393
Rabinovitz, Rubin, 2:460
Rabinowicz, Harry M., 4:658
Rabinowitch, Eugene, 5:111
Rabinowitsch, Wolf Zeev,
4:633
Rabinowitz, Nancy S., 3:309
Rabinowitz, O. K., 3:294
Rabinowitz, Paula, 1:805
Rabinowitz, Stanley J., 2:686,
2:689, 2:759
Rabins, Peter V., 5:392
Rabkin, Eric S., 1:423, 1:615
Rabkin, Gerald, 1:1075
Rabkin, Norman, 1:210
Rabon, Israel, 2:43
Raboteau, Albert J., 3:561
Raby, Peter, 1:342, 1:411
Rachbauer, M. A., 2:617
Rachel, V., 5:402
Rachels, James, 5:123
Rachin, R. L., 5:451

Rachlin, Carol K., 1:631
Rachman, Stanley J., 5:423
Rachmaninoff, Sergey,
3:701, **3:711**
Racin, Kosta, 2:807
Racine, Jean, 2:441, 2:444,
2:470, **2:497**
Rackin, Phyllis, 1:212
Racter, 5:565
Rad, Gerhard von, 4:823,
4:827, **4:836**
Radauskas, Henrikas, 2:805
Radcliffe, Ann, 1:269, 1:591,
1:602, 1:603, 1:617, 1:619,
1:621
Radcliffe, Elsa J., 1:122
Radcliffe, Philip, 3:706
Radcliffe-Brown, A. R.,
3:20, 3:25, **3:38**
Radcliff-Umstead, Douglas,
2:408, 2:421, 2:436
Rademacher, Hans, 5:489,
5:495
Rader, Dotson, 1:1118
Rader, Melvin, 4:23
Rader, Ralph W., 1:402
Rader, Rosemary, 4:689
Radetsky, Peter, 5:314
Radford, Jean, 1:541, 1:618
Radhakrishnan, Sarvepalli,
4:350, 4:351, **4:353,** 4:498
Radice, E. A., 3:389
Radice, Lisanne, 3:113
Radičević, Branko, 2:827
Radiguet, Raymond, 2:498
Radin, Max, 4:605
Radin, Paul, 1:632
Radl, Shirley, 5:417
Radley, Virginia L., 1:337
Radner, Daisie, 4:182, 5:65
Radner, Michael, 5:65
Radot, René V., 5:809
Radway, Janice A., 1:1151,
1:1210
Radzig, A. A., 5:653
Radzinowicz, Mary Ann,
1:193
Rae, John B., 3:107, 3:548
Rae, Welsey D., 1:185
Rae, W. Fraser, 1:255
Raeburn, Michael, 3:662
Raeff, Marc, 2:693
Rafael, Vicente L., 3:493
Raff, Elizabeth C., 5:776
Raff, Rudolph A., 5:776
Raffe, W. G., 3:731
Raffel, Burton, 1:806, 2:317,
2:318, 2:339
Raffel, Marshall, 5:331
Raggett, J., 5:74
Ragusa, Olga, 2:401, 2:436
Rahill, Frank, 1:1075
Rahlfs, A., 4:796

Rahman, Fazlur, 3:444, 4:373, 4:576
Rahman, Habib U., 4:567
Rahman, Razlur, 4:893
Rahman, Syedur, 3:487
Rahner, Karl, 4:423, 4:676, 4:719, 4:745, 4:770, 4:891, **4:902,** 5:198
Rahv, Philip, 1:996
Rai, Amrit, 2:180
Rai, Priya Muhar, 4:417
Raiffa, Howard, 3:63, 3:204
Railo, Eilo, 1:270
Raimo, John, 3:507
Raina, Badri, 1:351
Raina, Trilokinath, 2:176
Rainbow, Paul, 4:400
Raine, Kathleen, 1:303, 1:572
Rainer, Yvonne, 1:1174
Raines, Howell, 3:557
Rainey, Lawrence S., 1:874
Rains, Darell L., 5:230
Rainwater, Robert, 3:756
Raitt, Jill, 4:723, 4:732
Raiziss, Sona, 1:799
Rajadhon, Phya Anuman, 4:519
Rajagopalachari, C., 2:172
Rajak, Tessa, 3:317, 4:666
Rajanubhab, Prince Damrong, 2:334
Rajchman, John, 4:267, 4:379, 4:401, 5:443
Rajendra, Cecil, 2:325
Rajeshwar, M., 2:150
Rājjāka, Moḥ Ābadura, 3:487
Raju, P. T., 4:38
Rake, Alan, 3:418
Rakić, Milan, 2:827
Raleigh, Donald J., 3:397
Raleigh, John H., 1:1108
Raley, Harold, 4:315
Ralov, Kirsten, 3:739
Ralph, Philip L., 3:274
Ralston, Anthony, 5:540, 5:551
Ramakrishna, 4:354, 4:871
Ramanathan, Suguna, 1:524, 1:550
Ramanujan, A. K., 2:174, 2:176
Ramazani, Jahan, 1:572
Ramazani, Rouhollah K., 3:448
Rambler, Mitchell B., 5:820
Rambo, Lewis, 4:890
Ramchand, Kenneth, 2:930, 2:931
Ramirez, Bruno, 3:609
Ramler, Malia, 5:403
Rammohun Roy (Roy, Ram Mohan), 4:355

Ramón y Cajal, Santiago, 5:810
Ramos, Graciliano, 2:890, **2:897**
Ramos, Juanita, 1:1184
Rampersad, Arnold, 1:832, 1:849, 3:579
Rampton, David, 2:742
Ramraz-Ravich, Gilah, 2:9
Ramsay, Sir William, 5:710, 5:753
Ramsay, William M., 4:785, 4:905
Ramsden, Charles, 1:26
Ramsden, John, 3:367
Ramsey, Boniface, 4:690
Ramsey, Jonathan, 1:307
Ramsey, Paul, 4:745, 4:896, 5:112
Ranaivo, Flavien, 2:152, **2:156**
Ranchetti, Michele, 4:741
Rancour-Laferriere, Daniel, 2:689, 2:722
Rand, Benjamin, 4:192
Rand, C. C., 2:233
Rand, Edward K., 2:390, 4:99
Rand, Marguerite C., 2:546
Randall, Bridwell, R., 3:214
Randall, David, 5:773
Randall, David A., 1:34
Randall, James G., 3:529
Randall, John Herman, 4:55, 4:70, 4:83, 4:130, 4:162, 4:267
Randall, Phyllis R., 1:459
Randall, Stephen J., 3:635
Randel, Don M., 3:657
Randel, Fred, 1:296
Randers, Jorgen, 5:823
Randisi, Jennifer Lynn, 1:552, 1:896
Randolph, Blythe, 3:929
Randolph, Sallie G., 4:849
Randolph, Vance, 3:861, **3:885**
Randsberg, Klaus, 3:305
Ranelagh, John, 3:370, 3:546
Rangdrol, Tsele Natsok, 4:544
Range, Willard, 3:500
Ranger, Terence, 3:869
Rank, Otto, 5:465
Ránki, György, 3:677
Rankin, Arthur C., 1:549
Rankin, Mary Backus, 3:470, 3:471
Rannit, Aleksis, 2:796, **2:796**
Ransohoff, Paul, 4:890
Ransom, John Crowe, 1:476, 1:806, **1:874,** 1:968, 1:1005

Ransom, Roger L., 3:45, 3:529, 3:548, 3:549
Rao, B. V., 3:274
Rao, K. Bhaskara, 1:372
Rao, K. L., 4:553
Rao, Raja, 2:178
Rapaport, A., 3:280
Rapaport, David, 3:178, 3:184
Rapaport, Herman, 4:294
Raph, Jane, 3:193
Raphael, 3:787, 3:790
Raphael, Bertram, 5:568
Raphael, Chaim, 4:594, 4:600
Raphael, D. D., 4:174, 4:204, 4:215
Raphael, Frederic, 1:283
Raphael, Marc Lee, 4:634, 4:641, 4:651
Rapoport, L., 3:293
Rapp, Carl, 1:901
Rapp, Friedrich, 5:72
Rapp, George Robert, Jr., 5:618
Rappaport, Louis J., 5:419
Rappaport, Roy A., 3:24
Rarey, Kanute P., 5:398
Ras, J. J., 2:317
Rashid, Nasser I., 3:451
Rashi (Solomon Ben Isaac), 4:628, **4:670**
Rasmussen, David M., 4:400, 4:405, 5:88
Rasmussen, Richard M., 4:870
Rasmussen, Steen E., 3:762
Rasor, Eugene L., 3:354
Rasponi, Lanfranco, 3:671
Rasputin, Valentin, 2:752
Ratchford, Fannie E., 1:333
Ratcliff, Carter, 3:796
Ratcliffe, Ronald V., 3:672
Rathbun, Carole, 2:96
Rathenow, Lutz, 2:606, 2:616
Rather, Dan, 3:808
Rather, L. J., 3:729
Rathgeber, Eva Marie, 1:48
Ratkevich, Ronald, 5:638
Ratliff, Floyd, 5:700
Rattenbury, Ken, 3:695
Rattigan, Sir Terence (Mervyn), 1:424, 1:464, 1:529, **1:539**
Ratushinskaya, Irina, 2:752
Ratzinger, Joseph Cardinal, 4:746, 4:891
Ratzsch, Del, 5:198
Rauch, George Von, 3:395
Rauchhaupt, Ursula von, 3:662
Raup, David M., 5:624, 5:639
Rausch, David A., 4:864
Ravel, Maurice, 3:712

Raven, James, 1:230, 1:592
Raven, J. E., 4:50, 4:83, 4:87
Ravenel, Shannon, 1:921
Ravetz, J. R., 5:157
Ravindra, Ravi, 5:198
Ravitch, Diane, 3:252, 3:553
Raw, Anthony, 5:771
Rawidowicz, Simon, 4:646
Rawlence, Christopher, 3:826
Rawlings, Hunter R., III, 3:323
Rawlins, Jack, 1:404
Rawls, John, 4:313, **4:315,** 4:385, 4:412
Rawlyk, George A., 3:606, 3:613
Rawski, Evelyn S., 3:468, 4:531, 4:533
Rawski, Thomas G., 3:467
Rawson, Beryl, 4:72
Rawson, Claude Julien, 1:226, 1:261
Rawson, Elizabeth, 2:385, 4:72
Rawson, Philip, 3:760
Ray, Ajit, 4:509
Ray, Arthur, 3:611
Ray, Benjamin C., 4:463, 4:898
Ray, Christopher, 5:68
Ray, Gordon N., 1:29, 1:404
Ray, Martin, 1:362
Ray, M. S., 5:223
Ray, Nihar Ranjan, 4:519
Ray, Rajat Kanta, 3:486
Raychaudhuri, Tapan, 3:484
Raymo, Chet, 5:10
Raymond, Agnes, 2:481
Raymond, Eric S., 5:538
Raymond, Jack, 3:662
Raymond, Mike, 5:382
Raynack, Elton, 3:78
Re, Lucia, 2:412
Re, Richard Noel, 5:765
Read, Colin, 3:613
Read, Conyers, 3:354, 3:359
Read, Herbert, 3:760
Read, Oliver, 5:230
Reade, Charles, 1:321, **1:389,** 1:399
Reader, G. T., 5:236
Reader, Ian, 4:535, 4:541
Reader, John P., 4:893
Reader, W. J., 1:313
Reagan, Nancy, 5:403
Reale, Giovanni, 4:46, 4:55, 4:70
Reardon, Bernard M., 4:741
Reardon, B. P., 2:349
Reardon, James J., 5:397
Reardon, Joan, 1:123, 1:125
Reaske, Herbert, 2:766
Reason, James, 5:423

Reay, David A., 5:284
Rebay, Luciano, 2:403
Rebreanu, Liviu, 2:823, **2:825**
Rechenberg, Helmut, 5:708
Rechy, John, 1:1190
Reck, Andrew J., 4:238, 4:267
Reck, David B., 3:667
Reckford, Kenneth J., 2:354
Red, W. Edward, 5:228
Redclift, Michael, 3:47
Redeker, Martin, 4:741
Redfern, Ron, 5:618, 5:627, 5:630
Redfern, Walter D., 2:481
Redfield, James, 4:492
Redfield, James M., 2:362
Redfield, Robert, 3:14, 3:34, **3:39,** 3:242, 4:477
Redford, Donald B., 4:442
Redgrave, G. R., 1:68
Redlich, Hans F., 3:706
Redman, Ben, 1:877
Redman, Tim, 1:874
Redmont, Jane, 4:754
Redner, Harry, 5:10
Redol, Alves, 2:557
Redondi, Pietro, 4:143, 5:43, 5:688
Redpath, Henry A., 4:818
Redpath, Peter, 4:308
Redpath, Philip, 1:484
Redwood, Christopher, 3:694
Rée, Jonathan, 4:18, 4:162
Reed, David A., 4:863
Reed, Graham W., 2:808
Reed, Henry Hope, 3:785
Reed, Ishmael, 1:1036
Reed, John, 3:397
Reed, John R., 1:564
Reed, Maxine K., 3:812
Reed, Peter J., 1:1064
Reed, R., 5:245
Reed, Robert M., 3:812
Reed, Roger, 1:30
Reed, Ronald, 1:26
Reed, Talbot Baines, 1:19
Reed, T. J., 2:581
Reed, Walt, 1:30
Reed, William H., 3:694
Reeder, Roberta, 2:693
Rees, Alan M., 5:6, 5:311
Rees, Davis, 3:482
Rees, Ennis, 1:175
Rees, Jane M., 5:348
Rees, Joan, 1:392
Rees, John, 4:245
Rees, Robert A., 1:650, 1:715
Rees, Samuel, 1:503
Reese, Gustave, 3:662
Reese, Kenneth M., 5:729
Reese, William L., 4:14

Rees-Mogg, William, 1:33
Reesor, Margaret E., 4:57
Reeve, Franklin D., 2:694, 2:703
Reeves, Hubert, 5:595, 5:656
Reeves, Marjorie, 4:102
Reeves, Nigel, 2:609
Reeves, Randall R., 5:761
Reeves, Richard, 3:165
Regalado, Iñigo E., 2:327
Regan, Tom, 4:312, 4:389, 5:76, 5:116
Regenstein, Helen, 1:708
Regio, José, 2:557
Regis, Edward, 5:598
Regis, Pamela, 1:629
Regnery, Henry, 1:43
Regosin, Richard, 2:491, 4:146
Rehder, Harold A., 5:762
Rehr, Helen, 5:331
Reibetanz, Julia Maniates, 1:473
Reich, Nancy B., 3:716
Reich, Robert B., 3:62
Reich, Warren T., 4:893, 5:61, 5:123
Reichard, Gary W., 3:537
Reichard, Robert, 5:524
Reichardt, Mary, 1:750
Reichenbach, Hans, 4:278, 4:385
Reichert, Herbert W., 2:611
Reichmann, W. J., 5:524
Reicke, Bo, 4:605
Reid, Anthony, 3:489
Reid, Constance, 5:510
Reid, Daniel G., 4:5, 4:718
Reid, Ian W., 1:971
Reid, James H., 2:570
Reid, J. B., 1:281
Reid, John G., 3:612
Reid, Joyce M. H., 2:448
Reid, Mark A., 3:826
Reid, Robert, 2:690, 5:679
Reid, Stuart, 1:94
Reid, Thomas, 4:211, 4:259, 4:395
Reid, T. R., 5:230
Reid, V(ictor) S(tafford), **2:940**
Reid, William H., 5:427
Reid, W. Malcolm, 5:762
Reid, W. Stanford, 4:732, 4:736, 4:762, 4:774
Reigstad, Paul, 2:667
Reijnders, Jan Long, 3:50
Reik, Miriam, 4:175
Reik, Theodor, 5:466
Reilly, Edwin D., Jr., 5:551
Reilly, E. R., 5:540
Reilly, Elizabeth Carroll, 1:30
Reilly, John M., 1:906

Reilly, Patrick, 1:246, 5:403
Reiman, Donald H., 1:266, 1:274, 1:303
Reiman, Reuben, 5:326
Reimer-Torn, Susan, 3:732
Reinecke, Ian, 5:574
Reiner, Erica, 2:53
Reines, Frederick, 5:605
Reinfeld, Linda, 1:914
Reingold, Nathan, 5:47, 5:49
Reinhardt, Karl, 2:368
Reinhartz, Dennis, 1:631
Reinharz, Jehuda, 3:349, 3:350, 3:440, 4:130, 4:634, 4:637
Reinharz, Shulamit, 5:188
Reinhold, K. L., 4:204
Reinhold, Meyer, 4:605
Reino, Joseph, 1:1046
Reis, Marion J., 2:688
Reis, Ricardo, 2:560
Reis, Roberto, 2:890
Reischauer, Edwin O(ldfather), 2:186, 3:474, **3:500,** 4:358
Reiser, Stanley J., 5:123, 5:370
Reiser, Stanley M., 5:324
Reisin, Avraham, 2:44
Reisman, Barry, 5:386
Reisman, David, 3:94
Reisman, John M., 5:35, 5:423
Reisner, Marc P., 5:824
Reisner, Robert G., 1:57, 3:708
Reiss, Edmund, 4:112
Reith, Edward J., 5:773
Reitlinger, Gerald, 3:350
Rejai, Mostafa, 3:140
Rejwan, Nissim, 4:644
Reljković, Matija, 2:784
Remak, J., 3:280
Remarque, Erich Maria, 2:606
Rembar, Charles, 1:57
Rembrandt Harmensz van Rijn, 3:768, 3:776, **3:788,** 3:793
Reményi, Joseph, 2:798
Remer, Daniel, 5:557
Remini, Robert V., 3:525
Remizov, Aleksei, 2:735, 2:749, **2:753,** 2:774
Remnant, Mary, 3:672
Remnick, David, 3:398
Rempel, Warren F., 3:232
Renard, John, 4:576
Renault, Alain, 4:293, 5:90
Renault, Mary, 2:347
Rendel, Romilda, 2:403
Rendell, Ruth, 1:609
Render, Sylvia, 1:739

Rendra, W. S., 2:316, **2:320**
Rendtorff, Rolf, 4:817
Renehan, Edward J., Jr., 3:550
Renfrew, Colin, 3:13, 3:301, 4:432, 4:434, 4:436, 4:472
Renfro, Nancy, 3:869
Rennert, Hugo A., 2:524
Rennie, John, 5:253, 5:254
Rennie, Sir John, 5:254
Rennie, Ysabel, 5:423
Reno, Robert P., 1:602
Renoir, Jean, 3:780, 3:789, **3:841**
Renoir, Pierre Auguste, 3:780, **3:789,** 3:841
Renwick, W. L., 1:266
Replogle, Justin, 1:436
Reps, John W., 3:533
Rescher, Nicholas, 4:177, 4:185, **4:316,** 4:385, 4:389, 4:576, 5:92, **5:100,** 5:108, 5:130
Reschke, Klaus, 2:579
Resek, Carl, 3:37
Resing, Russell, 1:1127
Resnick, Abraham, 3:287
Resnick, Robert, 5:652, 5:660
Resnick, Seymour, 2:526
Resnik, Michael D., 4:230, 5:79
Ressler, Steve, 1:464
Restak, Richard M., 5:323, 5:342, 5:773
Restivo, Sal, 5:31
Reston, James, 3:808
Restuccia, Frances L., 1:506
Reuchlin, Johann, 4:130
Reutter, Edmund E., Jr., 3:257
Reveal, James L., 5:768
Revell, Peter, 1:778
Revill, David, 3:686
Revius, Jacobus, 2:629
Rewald, John, 3:760, 3:773
Rex, Walter E., 2:448
Rexroth, Kenneth, 1:875, 1:963, **1:1036,** 1:1067, 2:193, 2:274
Rey, H. A., 5:591
Reyes, Edgar, 2:328
Reyfman, Irina, 2:690
Reymont, Wladyslaw Stanislaw, 2:810, **2:820**
Reynolds, David K., 5:423, 5:427
Reynolds, David S., 1:652
Reynolds, Dennis, 5:545
Reynolds, Ernest E., 4:727
Reynolds, Frank E., 4:428, 4:887
Reynolds, Graham, 3:794
Reynolds, Janet, 5:317

Reynolds, J. F., 5:248
Reynolds, Jim, 3:905
Reynolds, John S., 5:236
Reynolds, L., 2:347
Reynolds, Larry J., 1:652
Reynolds, L. D., 3:300
Reynolds, Mary T., 2:418
Reynolds, Mike, 1:847
Reynolds, Nancy, 3:732
Reynolds, Paul R., 1:43, 1:48
Reynolds, Sir Joshua, 3:768, 3:774, **3:789**
Rezen, Susan V., 5:380
Rhees, Rush, 4:346
Rhein, Phillip H., 2:465
Rheingold, Howard, 5:565, 5:568
Rhie, Gene S., 1:101
Rhoads, David M., 4:666
Rhodes, Frank H. T., 5:624, 5:639
Rhodes, Jack W., 1:294
Rhodes, James Ford, 3:514
Rhodes, Martha E., 5:267
Rhodes, P. J., 3:312, 4:70
Rhodes, Richard, 5:658
Rhodes, Robert, 1:395
Rhyne, Nancy, 3:861
Rhys, Jean, 2:940
Riach, Alan, 1:517
Riasanovsky, Nicholas V., 1:268, 3:395
Ribeiro, Aquilino, 2:557
Ribeiro, Bernardim, 2:556
Ribeiro, Darcy, 2:889, **2:898**
Ribeiro, João Ubaldo, 2:889, **2:898**
Ribner, Irving, 1:212
Ricardo, David, 1:375, 1:393, 3:92, 3:93, 3:95, **3:100,** 3:106
Ricci, Robert, 3:655
Riccio, Peter, 2:401
Rice, Anne, 1:1239, **1:1242**
Rice, Bradley R., 3:536
Rice, David G., 4:446
Rice, David Talbot, 3:760
Rice, Edward, 3:914, 4:572, 4:781
Rice, Elmer, 1:1070, **1:1109**
Rice, Eugene F., Jr., 4:130
Rice, F. Philip, 3:257
Rice, Kym S., 3:518
Rice, Martin, 2:705
Rice, M. Katherine, 5:6
Rice, Philip, 1:135, 1:1134
Rice, Stanley, 1:10
Rice, Thomas Jackson, 1:506, 1:570
Rich, Adrienne, 1:910, 1:911, **1:1037,** 1:1038, 1:1187, 1:1191, 2:175
Rich, Daniel, 5:281

Rich, Donald, 1:1160
Rich, Doris L., 3:910
Rich, E. E., 3:613
Rich, J., 3:308
Rich, Vera, 2:784
Richard, Lucien J., 4:762
Richard, Yann, 3:448
Richards, Bernard, 1:316
Richards, David, 2:694
Richards, Graham, 5:35
Richards, Ivor Armstrong,
  1:926, 2:359
Richards, Jeffrey H., 1:629
Richards, John F., 5:824
Richards, K. S., 5:626
Richards, Marion K., 1:844
Richards, Robert J., 5:794
Richards, Ruth M., 2:540
Richards, Susan, 3:398
Richards, W. Graham, 5:730
Richardson, Alan, 1:272,
  4:676, 4:719
Richardson, Bernard L.,
  5:422
Richardson, Bonham C.,
  3:626
**Richardson, Dorothy (Mil-
  ler)**, 1:414, 1:503, **1:540**
Richardson, Emeline, 3:305
Richardson, Henry G., 4:624
Richardson, Henry Handel,
  2:945, **2:961**
Richardson, Henry Hobson,
  3:768, **3:790**
Richardson, Herbert W.,
  4:856
Richardson, Hugh E., 4:356
Richardson, James, 1:363
Richardson, James T., 4:856,
  4:857, 4:864, 4:868
Richardson, Jeanne M., 5:217
Richardson, Joan, 1:888
Richardson, John, 3:780,
  3:787
Richardson, John T., 4:346
Richardson, John V., 1:14
Richardson, Joseph, 4:294,
  5:91
Richardson, Lewis F., 3:149
Richardson, R. C., 3:353
Richardson, Robert D., Jr.,
  1:702
Richardson, Robert G., 5:374
Richardson, Ruth, 1:313
Richardson, Samuel, 1:223,
  1:229, 1:244, **1:252**, 1:618,
  1:622, 1:1209
Richardson, Thomas J.,
  1:737, 3:52
Richardson, Walter C., 4:727
Richardson, W. J., 5:458
Richels, Richard, 3:48
Richet, Xavier, 3:390

Richetti, John J., 1:240,
  1:592
Richie, Donald, 3:839
Richkards, Maurice, 1:33
Richler, Mordecai, 2:903,
  2:924
Richlin, Amy, 2:381, 3:309
Richman, Harold, 5:335
Richman, Paula, 4:506,
  4:514, 4:892
Richman, Sidney, 1:1014
Richmond, I. A., 3:356
Richmond, John, 3:446
Richmond, Mary L., 4:849
Richmond, Merle A., 1:647
Richmond, P. G., 3:193
Richmond, Winthrop E.,
  3:849
Richs, Stephen D., 4:625
**Richter, Charles Francis,
  5:646**
Richter, Gisela M., 2:347
Richter, Jean Paul, 2:591
Richter, M., 3:163
Richter, Melvin, 4:230
Richter, Peyton E., 4:23
Rickard, Teresa, 5:653
Rickels, Milton, 1:674, 1:703
Rickets, Edward, 5:820
Ricketson, William F., 1:642
Rickett, Adele A., 2:191
Rickett, Richard, 3:376
Ricketts, Edward F., 5:632
Ricketts, Mac L., 4:474
Ricketts, Martin J., 5:285
Rickman, H. P., 4:226
Rickman, John, 3:22
Ricks, Beatrice, 1:473, 1:838
Ricks, Christopher B., 1:193,
  1:294, 1:316, 1:402, 1:473
Ricks, David, 5:423
Ricks, Thomas M., 2:83
Rico, Francisco, 2:525, 2:530
Ricoeur, Paul, 4:18, 4:267,
  4:318, 4:426, 4:886, 5:92
Riddel, Joseph N., 1:512,
  1:888, 1:901
Ridderikhoff, J., 5:80
Ride, Sally, 3:934, 5:610
Ride, W.D.L., 5:762
Ridenour, George M., 1:284
Rideout, Walter B., 1:812
Rider, Frederick, 2:491
Rider, K. J., 3:273
Ridgely, Joseph V., 1:697
Ridgway, Chester E., 5:382
Ridgway, John, 3:719
Ridgway, Matthew B., 3:482
Riding, Alan, 3:639
Riding, Laura, 1:484, **1:875**,
  1:935
Ridley, Jasper G., 3:359,
  4:727, 4:736, 4:774

Ridley, Mark, 5:780
Ridley, M. R., 1:294
Ridolfi, Roberto, 3:160, 4:145
Ridpath, I., 5:591
Rieber, Robert W., 3:168,
  3:197
Riede, David G., 1:328,
  1:392, 1:398
Riedel, Marc, 3:205
Rieder, Jonathan, 4:641
Riedl, John O., 4:130
Riedman, Sarah R., 5:801
Riedt, Heinz, 2:423
Rieff, Philip, 3:178, 3:184
Rieger, James, 1:303
Riehl, Herbert, 5:634
Riemens, Leo, 3:656, 3:672
Riemersma, Trinus, 2:635
Riepe, Dale, 4:23
Ries, Ferdinand, 3:678
Riesman, David, 3:209,
  3:238, 3:243
Riess, Frank, 2:876
Rieu, Emil, 2:360
Riewald, Jacobus Gerhardus,
  1:441
Rifaat, Alita, 2:59
Rifbjerg, Klaus, 2:653
Rifkin, Jeremy, 5:824
Rigby, J. Keith, 5:624
Rigby, S. H., 4:227
Rigden, John S., 5:651
Rigdon, Walter, 1:1075
Riggins, Stephen Harold,
  3:204, 3:804
Riggio, Milla Cozart, 1:161
Riggs, David, 1:184
Riggs, Fred W., 3:490
Riggs, Gail Kershner, 5:398
Righter, Anne, 1:210
Rigney, Barbara Hill, 2:907
Riis, Jacob A(ugust), 3:821
Rike, R. L., 3:310
Riker, William H., 3:145
Riley, E. C., 2:536
Riley, Glenda, 3:553
Riley, Isaac W., 4:35
Riley, James Whitcomb,
  1:717, **1:777**
Riley, Matilda W., 3:201
Riley, P. W., 3:360
Riley-Smith, Jonathan S. C.,
  4:694
Rilke, Rainer Maria, 1:1005,
  2:468, 2:480, 2:564, 2:604,
  2:607, 2:613, 2:651, 2:662,
  3:791, 4:255
Rilliet, Jean, 4:791
Rima, Ingrid H., 3:102
Rimanelli, Giose, 2:401
**Rimbaud, (Jean Nicolas)
  Arthur**, 2:486, 2:445,
  2:499, 2:514

Rimbaut, Ruben G., 3:209
Rimer, J. Thomas, 2:272,
  2:273, 2:282
Rimland, Bernard, 5:417
Rimmer, Douglas, 3:421
Rimsky-Korsakov, Nikolay,
  3:707, 3:710, **3:712**, 3:722
Rinbochay, Lati, 4:887
Rindler, W., 5:664
Ring, Kenneth, 4:870
Ring, Melvin L., 5:194
Ringe, Donald A., 1:636,
  1:665, 1:715, 1:724
Ringe, Sharon H., 4:819
Ringer, Alexander L., 3:714
Ringgren, Helmer, 4:441,
  4:445, 4:616, 4:817
Ringwalt, J. Luther, 1:10
Rinzler, Carol A., 3:869
Ripp, Victor, 2:770
Rippe, James M., 5:347
Rippier, Joseph Storey, 1:529
Rippy, J. Fred, 3:632
Rips, Elizabeth, 1:108
Riquelme, John Paul, 1:473,
  1:506
Rischin, Moses, 4:641
Riskin, Carl, 3:472
Rist, John M., 4:57, 4:74,
  4:87
Ristelhueber, Rene, 3:392
Ritchey, S. J., 5:348
Ritchie, Anne Thackeray,
  1:404
Ritchie, Arthur, 5:681
Ritchie, David, 5:538, 5:568,
  5:579
Ritchie, Dennis M., 5:553
Ritchie, J. M., 2:566
Ritchie, J. R., 3:891
Ritchie, Ward, 1:45
Ritsos, Yannis, 2:370, **2:375**
Ritter, Gerhard, 3:377
Ritter, Karl, 3:116, **3:134**
Rittner, Carol, 1:1065
Rittner, Don, 5:547, 5:816
Rivera, José Eustasio, 2:881
Rivero, Albert J., 1:246
Rivers, Elias L., 2:523, 2:527
Rivers, Isabel, 1:226
Rivers, J. E., 2:742
Rivers, William H., 3:20
Rivlin, Robert, 5:565
Rix, Martyn, 5:767
Rizal, José, 2:327, **2:332**
Rizzo, Betty, 1:255
Roa Bastos, Augusto, 2:843,
  2:881
Roach, John, 3:327
Roads, Curtis, 5:565
Roaf, Christina, 2:401
Roaf, Michael, 4:809
Roan, Carol, 3:733

Roark, James L., 3:529
Roazen, Paul, 3:182, 5:448
Rob, Caroline, 5:317
Roback, A. A., 2:32
Roback, Abraham A., 5:423
Robb, John D., 3:863
Robb, Kevin, 4:49
Robb, Nesca A., 4:130
Robbe-Grillet, Alain, 1:988,
  2:448, **2:500**, 2:505, 2:540
Robbins, Bruce, 1:1129
Robbins, Harold, 1:1222
Robbins, Herbert, 5:480
Robbins, J. Albert, 1:652
Robbins, Jerome, 3:738,
  3:747, **3:750**
Robbins, Judd, 5:194
Robbins, Keith, 3:364
Robbins, Lionel, 3:47
Robbins, Richard, 3:204
Robbins, Rossell H., 1:149
Robbins, Thomas, 4:855,
  4:857
Robe, Stanley L., 2:854,
  3:863
Robert, Jean-Claude, 3:609
Robert, Marthe, 2:536
Roberts, Alexander, 4:100
Roberts, Allen D., 1:35
Roberts, Chalmers M., 3:808
Roberts, Charles G., 2:908,
  2:924
Roberts, D. A., 5:263
Roberts, D. D., 3:284
Roberts, David, 3:364, 3:910
Roberts, Denis, 4:576
Roberts, Elizabeth Madox,
  1:875
Roberts, Gerald, 1:364
Roberts, J. Deotis, 4:748
Roberts, J. M., 3:274, 3:339
Roberts, J. W., 1:734
Roberts, James D., 4:748
Roberts, Jane, 3:780
Roberts, Jeanne A., 1:221
Roberts, John R., 1:176,
  1:178, 1:181
Roberts, Julian, 4:28
Roberts, K. B., 5:194
Roberts, Ken, 3:364
Roberts, L.E.J., 5:112
Roberts, Marie E., 4:848
Roberts, Matt T., 1:26
Roberts, Michael, 3:382,
  4:731
Roberts, Morley, 1:366
Roberts, Moss, 2:193
Roberts, Nancy, 4:766
Roberts, Neil, 1:498
Roberts, Paul N., 3:446
Roberts, Philip, 1:446, 1:446
Roberts, R. S., 5:230
Roberts, Richard H., 4:277

Roberts, Robert, 3:444
Roberts, Samuel J., 3:440
Roberts, Sidney C., 1:374,
  3:406
Roberts, Steven, 5:230
Roberts, Thomas J., 1:592,
  1:1210
Roberts, Willard Lincoln,
  5:618
Robertson, Alec, 3:693
Robertson, Allen, 3:732
Robertson, Bruce, 3:766
Robertson, D. W., 1:141,
  1:151
Robertson, James Oliver,
  3:515, 3:553
Robertson, Janet C., 3:553
Robertson, John G., 2:600
Robertson, Nan, 3:808
Robertson, R. MacDonald,
  3:856
Robertson, T(homas)
  W(illiam), 1:311, 1:321,
  1:347, **1:389**
Robey, David, 2:401, 2:983
Robin, E. D., 5:789
Robin, Eugene, 5:405
Robin, Regine, 2:690
Robins, R. H., 5:35
Robins, Robert S., 5:314
Robins-Mowry, Dorothy,
  3:479
Robinson, Abraham, 5:490,
  5:515
Robinson, Andrew, 3:828
Robinson, Arthur, 3:120,
  3:121, **3:134**
Robinson, Charles A., 2:347,
  2:349
Robinson, Charles E., 1:284
Robinson, Christopher, 2:364,
  2:372, 4:485
Robinson, Cyril, 3:393
Robinson, Daniel N., 4:70
Robinson, Daniel S., 4:32,
  4:250
Robinson, David, 1:670,
  1:1162, 3:419
Robinson, David J., 3:629
Robinson, David M., 2:366
Robinson, Donald A., 3:521
Robinson, Edwin Arlington,
  1:668, 1:775, **1:876**, 1:1067
Robinson, Edwin S., 5:630
Robinson, Eric H., 5:232
Robinson, Forrest, 1:783
Robinson, Francis, 3:482,
  3:688, 4:567
Robinson, Franklin E., 4:83
Robinson, Fred C., 1:143
Robinson, Geroid T., 3:395
Robinson, Halbert B., 3:252

Robinson, Harlow Loomis,
  3:710
Robinson, Howard, 4:66
Robinson, H. S., 3:856
Robinson, J., 3:169
Robinson, James M., 4:294,
  4:453, 4:686, 4:812
Robinson, Janice S., 1:827
Robinson, Jeffrey Cane,
  2:987
Robinson, J. G., 2:566
Robinson, J. Gregg, 5:188
Robinson, Joan (Maurice),
  3:52, 3:58, 3:95, **3:101,**
  3:110, 5:110
Robinson, John, 1:364
Robinson, John A., 4:746
Robinson, John M., 4:47
Robinson, Joy M., 2:504
Robinson, Judith S., 1:108,
  5:727
Robinson, Kenneth, 1:346
Robinson, Mabel L., 5:786
Robinson, Michael E., 3:482
Robinson, Paul, 5:95, 5:440
Robinson, Paul A., 3:671
Robinson, Phyllis C., 1:821
Robinson, Richard H., 4:83,
  4:514, 4:530, 4:538
Robinson, R. K., 5:261
Robinson, Ronald, 3:418
Robinson, Roxana, 3:785
Robinson, Ruth E., 1:77
Robinson, Sally, 1:456
Robinson, Susan, 5:359
Robinson, T. M., 4:75, 4:83
Robinson, William H., 1:647
Robinson, William L., 5:820
Robson, Clifford B., 2:155
Robson, David, 5:552
Robson, John A., 4:104
Robson, John M., 3:97
Robson, S. O., 2:317
Robson, W. W., 1:284
Roby, Kinley E., 1:444,
  1:457, 1:473
Roche, Elizabeth, 3:657
Roche, J., 5:652
Roche, Jerome, 3:657, 3:662
Rochelle, Gerald, 4:304
Rochester, Jack B., 5:541
Rochford, E. Burke, 4:863
Rochlin, Harriett, 4:641
Rock, Irvin, 3:177, 5:194
Rock, Marcia, 3:808
Rock, Roger O., 1:716
Rocke, Alan J., 5:741
Rockefeller, Steven C., 4:225
Rockhart, John F., 5:557
Rockmore, Tom, 4:294, 5:72,
  5:91
Rockwood, Raymond O.,
  3:567

Rodale, J. I., 1:94
Rodale, Robert David, 5:274
Rodda, Annabel, 5:188
Roddy, D., 5:300
Roden, Donald J., 3:479
Rodes, Barbara K., 5:816
Rodger, Richard, 3:325
Rodgers, Andrew D., III,
  5:788
Rodgers, Bernard F., Jr.,
  1:1041
Rodgers, Buck, 5:543
Rodgers, Eugene, 3:915
Rodgers, Harrell, Jr., 3:66
Rodgers, Marion, 1:860
Rodgers, Richard, 3:713
Rodin, Auguste, 3:791
Rodino, Robert J., 2:407
Rodinson, Maxime, 3:444,
  4:579, 4:589
Rodney, Walter, 3:418,
  3:421, **3:430**
Rodowick, D. N., 1:1157
Rodrigues, Eusebio L., 1:948
Rodriguez-Consuegra, F. A.,
  5:103
Rodríguez-Luis, Julio, 2:857
Rodríguez Monegal, Emir,
  2:850, 2:857
Rodriquez, Jaime E., 3:629
Rodwell, Graham, 2:449
Rodwin, Marc A., 5:123
Roe, Anne, 3:18
Roe, Barbara, 1:944
Roe, Ivan, 1:303
Roe, John, 1:207
Roe, Keith E., 5:762
Roe, Shirley A., 5:45
Roebuck, Peter, 3:368
Roedell, Wendy C., 3:252
Roemer, John, 4:243
Roensch, Frederick J., 4:119
Roesdahl, Else, 3:329
Roethke, Theodore, 1:909,
  1:1038
Roethlisberger, F. J., 3:172
Roett, Riordan, 3:634, 3:640
Rofé, Hosein, 4:873
Roff, Merrill, 5:423
Roff, William R., 3:492,
  4:580
Roffman, Roger A., 5:351
Rogal, Samuel J., 1:133,
  1:134
Rogers, A. Robert, 3:273
Rogers, Alisdair, 3:6
Rogers, Bruce, 1:10
Rogers, Carl Ransom, 3:193,
  5:467
Rogers, Douglas, 1:812
Rogers, Everett M., 5:297
Rogers, G.A.J., 4:175
Rogers, Ginger, 3:736, 3:751

Rogers, Jack B., 4:23
Rogers, Joseph W., 1:26
Rogers, Katharine M., 1:272,
  1:629, 1:717
Rogers, May, 1:300
Rogers, Pat, 1:226, 1:246,
  1:252
Rogers, Robert, 2:989
Rogers, W. G., 1:44
Rogers, Will, 3:885
Rogerson, John, 4:807
Rogin, Michael P., 1:689,
  3:525
Roginski, Jim, 1:135
Rognoni, Luigi, 3:663
Rogosin, Elinor, 3:734
Rogow, Arnold A., 3:157,
  4:175
Rogow, Faith, 4:650
Rohatyn, Dennis, 4:312
Rohde, Erwin, 4:49
Rohdie, Sam, 3:830
Rohmer, Elizabeth, 1:597
Rohmer, Eric, 1:1169, 3:842
Rohmer, Sax, 1:591, 1:592,
  1:596, 1:597
Rohr, Janelle, 4:580, 5:198
Rohrich, Lutz, 3:849
Rojas, Fernando de, 2:520,
  2:548
Roland, Charles P., 3:529
Roland, Harold E., 5:244
Rolf, Asal, 5:165
Rolfe, Christopher, 1:564
Rolfe, John C., 2:385, 4:73
Rolfe, Sidney E., 3:59
Roll, Eric, 3:46
Rolland, Romain, 2:501
Roller, David C., 3:509
Rollin, Bernard E., 5:782
Rollin, Robert B., 1:182
Rollins, Carl Purington, 1:10
Rollins, H. E., 1:165, 1:207
Rollins, Ronald Gene, 1:527
Roloff, Michael E., 3:172
Rolston, Adam, 1:1181
Rolston, Holmes, III, 5:76,
  5:116, **5:140**
Rolt, L.T.C., 5:217, 5:249,
  5:250, 5:256
Rølvaag, Ole Edvart, 2:667
Romains, Jules, 2:502
Roman, Margaret, 1:770
Romanell, Patrick, 4:33,
  4:285
Romano, Frank J., 1:19
Romano, Richard, 3:51, 3:83,
  3:97
Romanyshyn, Robert D.,
  5:157
Romasco, Albert U., 3:535
Romberg, Bertil, 2:673
Rome, Beatrice, 4:182

Romeo, Felicia F., 5:395
Romer, Alfred S., 5:773
Romer, John, 4:442
Romero, Oscar, 4:748
Romero, Patricia W., 3:905
Romines, Ann, 1:724
Rommel, Erwin, 3:280
Rompf, Kraft, 2:4
Ronald, Ann, 1:1214, 5:828
Ronall, R., 5:418
Ronan, Charles E., 3:468, 4:532
Ronan, Colin A., 4:144, 5:26, 5:588, 5:656
Ronayne, John, 5:300
Ronda, James P., 3:928
Rondthaler, Edward, 1:19
Rone, David, 4:644
Ronsard, Nicole, 5:326
Ronsard, Pierre de, 2:502
Röntgen, Wilhelm, 5:710
Rontsh, Isaac Elchonon, 2:44
Roof, Judith, 1:1182
Rookledge, Gordon, 1:19
Rookledge, Sarah, 1:15
Room, Adrian, 1:77, 1:94
Rooney, Andy, 3:872
Roorbach, Orville Augustus, 1:67
Roosevelt, Theodore, 1:729, 1:789, 1:791, 1:876, 3:80, 3:287, 3:531, 3:593, 3:821, 3:823, 3:935
Root, Robert K., 1:220
Root-Berstein, Robert S., 5:10
Roper, Derek, 1:274
Roper, John H., 3:603
Roper, William, 1:194
Ropiequet, Suzanne, 5:554
Ropp, Paul S., 2:230
Roppolo, Joseph P., 1:1086
Rorem, Paul, 4:63
Rorig, Fritz, 3:331
Rorty, Amelie Oksenberg, 4:70, 4:170
Rorty, Richard McKay, 1:1132, 4:35, 4:267, 4:294, 4:320, 4:376, 4:390, 4:412
Rosa, João Guimarães, 2:890, 2:898
Rosaldo, Michael Z., 3:26
Rosaldo, Michelle Z., 3:25
Rosaldo, Renate, 4:426
Rosand, David, 3:793
Rosberg, Carl G., 3:423
Rosbottom, Ronald C., 2:488
Rosca, Ninotchka, 2:328, 2:329
Roscoe, Adrian, 2:126
Rose, Al, 3:669
Rose, Brian G., 3:812

Rose, Charles, 3:714
Rose, Charles L., 5:316
Rose, David J., 5:293
Rose, Edward J., 3:80
Rose, Ellen Cronan, 1:468
Rose, H. J., 2:347
Rose, J., 5:2
Rose, Jacqueline, 1:438, 1:1031
Rose, Jerry, 3:203
Rose, John, 5:395
Rose, Mary Beth, 1:170
Rose, Minnie B., 5:382, 5:397
Rose, Peter I., 3:216
Rose, Phyllis, 1:570, 1:1039, 3:737
Rose, Steven, 5:569
Rose, Willie Lee, 3:529
Rosebury, Brian, 1:559
Rosegg, Peter, 5:359
Rosemond, John, 5:323
Rosen, Allen, 4:207
Rosen, Charles, 3:663, 3:688
Rosen, Edward, 5:40
Rosen, Frederick, 3:151
Rosen, George, 5:36, 5:336
Rosen, Joe, 5:595
Rosen, Louis, 5:282
Rosen, Michael, 4:233
Rosen, Norma, 1:926
Rosen, Philip, 1:1159
Rosen, Robert C., 1:829
Rosen, Roger, 3:873
Rosen, Stanley, 4:83, 4:381
Rosen, Winifred, 5:404
Rosenau, James N., 3:145
Rosenbach, A.S.W., 1:33
Rosenbaum, Art, 3:861
Rosenbaum, Margo, 3:861
Rosenbaum, Stanford P., 1:748
Rosenberg, Alexander, 4:201, 4:385, 5:68
Rosenberg, Alfred, 4:247
Rosenberg, Betty, 1:122, 1:1210
Rosenberg, Charles E., 5:36
Rosenberg, Emily S., 3:549
Rosenberg, Isaac, 1:413, 1:541, 1:557
Rosenberg, Jakob, 3:789
Rosenberg, Jay, 4:23
Rosenberg, Jerry M., 3:802, 5:541
Rosenberg, Joel, 4:817
Rosenberg, John D., 1:395, 1:402
Rosenberg, Marvin, 1:213, 1:214
Rosenberg, Morris, 3:168
Rosenberg, Nathan, 5:157, 5:234
Rosenberg, R., 5:78

Rosenberg, Richard S., 5:126
Rosenberg, Rosalind, 3:557
Rosenberg, Roy A., 4:630
Rosenberg, Steven A., 5:373
Rosenberg, Stuart E., 4:641
Rosenblatt, Jon, 1:1031
Rosenbloom, Alfred A., 5:384
Rosenbloom, Noah H., 4:665
Rosenblum, Daniel, 5:373
Rosenblum, Dolores, 1:391
Rosenblum, Nancy L., 3:151
Rosenblum, Naomi, 5:37
Rosenbluth, Michael, 5:428
Rosenfeld, Isadore, 5:13, 5:332
Rosenfeld, Morris, 2:29, 2:44
Rosenfeld, Robert, 5:523
Rosenfield, Leonora, 4:162, 4:170
Rosengarten, Theodore, 3:529, 3:535
Rosenheim, James M., 3:362
Rosenkrantz, Barbara Gutman, 3:550
Rosenkrantz, Roger D., 5:65
Rosenmeier, Rosamond, 1:635
Rosenmeyer, Thomas G., 2:351, 2:369, 2:394, 4:59, 4:88
Rosenof, Theodore D., 3:510
Rosenstone, Robert A., 3:479
Rosenthal, Alan, 3:146, 3:148
Rosenthal, A. M., 3:893
Rosenthal, Bernard, 1:636
Rosenthal, David, 3:669
Rosenthal, Edwin J., 4:580
Rosenthal, Gilbert S., 4:649
Rosenthal, Macha L., 1:417, 1:799, 1:800, 1:914
Rosenthal, Michael, 3:773
Rosenthal, Sandra B., 4:302, 4:309, 4:311
Rosenthal-Schneider, Ilse, 5:683, 5:710
Rosenwald, George C., 1:87
Rosenwein, Robert, 3:147
Rosenzweig, Franz, 4:662, 4:671, 4:886
Rosett, Henry L., 5:402
Rosheim, David L., 3:862
Rosidi, Ajip, 2:316
Roskies, David G., 4:648
Rosmond, Babette, 1:815
Rosner, Fred, 4:668
Rosof, Patricia J., 3:437
Rosovsky, Henry, 3:479
Rosow, Irving, 3:216
Rosowski, Susan J., 1:822
Ross, Andrew, 1:800, 1:914, 1:1127, 4:866
Ross, Charles A., 5:637

Ross, D., 5:290
Ross, Dan, 4:645
Ross, Donald, 1:701
Ross, Dorothy, 3:185
Ross, E. Denison, 3:934
Ross, Floyd H., 4:536
Ross, G. MacDonald, 4:177
Ross, Ishbel, 3:575, 3:808
Ross, James Bruce, 1:147
Ross, Joan, 2:430
Ross, Joan Carol, 4:857
Ross, John A., 3:206
Ross, June R., 5:637
Ross, Kristin, 2:500
Ross, Malcolm, 2:905
Ross, Marlon B., 2:987
Ross, Michael H., 5:773
Ross, Morton, 2:926
Ross, Nathaniel, 5:424
Ross, Robert L., 2:946, 2:969
Ross, Robert M., 3:18
Ross, Shelley, 3:543
Ross, Sinclair, 2:925
Ross, Sir David, 4:207
Ross, Stanley, 3:826
Ross, Stephen, 1:838
Ross, Stephen D., 4:342
Ross, Timothy A., 2:235
Ross, W. D., 4:71, 4:84
Rossabi, Morris, 3:468
Rossant, Janet, 5:777
Rossbacher, Lisa A., 5:624,
  5:637
Rossel, Sven H., 2:638,
  2:645, 2:652
Rosselli, John, 3:663, 3:672
Rossen, Janice, 1:508
Rosser, Brenda Lewis, 4:557
Rosser, David, 3:369
Rosser, Sue V., 5:13, 5:188
Rossett, Lisa, 1:939
Rossetti, Christina, 1:310,
  1:390, 1:474
Rossetti, Dante Gabriel,
  1:310, 1:382, 1:386, 1:390,
  1:391, 1:397, 1:474, 1:561,
  2:402, 2:413, 2:514
Rossetti, William M., 1:392
Rossi, Alice S., 3:207
Rossi, Ernest Lawrence,
  5:419
Rossi, Lee D., 1:559
Rossi, Paolo, 4:130, 4:166
Rossi, Peter, 3:7
Rossi, Vinio, 2:480
Rossini, Gioacchino Antonio,
  2:458
Rossiter, A. P., 1:210
Rossiter, Frank, 3:702
Rossiter, Margaret, 5:49
Rossman, Charles, 2:866,
  2:887

Rossman, Parker, 3:252,
  5:126
Rost, T. L., 5:768
Rosten, Leo Calvin, 2:30,
  2:32
Rostenberg, Leona, 1:34,
  1:37, 1:78
Roston, Murray, 1:226
Rostovtzeff, Mikhail, 2:347,
  2:381, 3:302, 3:303
Rostow, Walt W., 3:54
Roszak, Theodore, 5:72,
  5:101, 5:126, **5:174,** 5:563,
  5:572, 5:574
Rotberg, Robert I., 3:280,
  3:424, 3:905
Rotblat, Joseph, 5:112
Rotenberg, Mordecai, 4:633
Rotenstreich, Nathan, 4:646,
  4:662
Roth, Cecil, 4:5, 4:594, 4:597,
  4:624
Roth, Gerhard, 5:683
Roth, Hal, 3:910
Roth, Henry, 1:1039
Roth, John, 4:2
Roth, Leland M., 3:764
Roth, Leon, 4:170, 4:189,
  4:596
Roth, Phillip, 1:909, 1:945,
  1:987, **1:1040**
Roth, Phyllis A., 2:742
Roth, Robert J., 3:261
Rothbart, Harold A., 5:236
Rothchild, Joseph, 3:389
Rothchild, Sylvia, 4:641
Rothenberg, Albert, 5:194
Rothenberg, David, 5:72
Rothenberg, Joshua, 3:350
Rothenberg, Marc, 5:29,
  5:232
Rothenberg, Michael B.,
  5:323
Rothenberg, Robert E., 5:311
Rothera, Ellen, 5:386
Rothfelder, Jerry, 5:569
Rothfield, Lawrence, 1:319
Rothgeb, John M., Jr., 3:145
Rothman, Barbara Katz,
  5:203, 5:359
Rothman, Ellen K., 3:553
Rothman, Milton A., 5:10
Rothman, Tony, 5:10
Rothman, William, 1:1169
Rothmyer, Karen, 3:821
Rothrock, George A., 4:732
Rothschild, Henry R., 5:383
Rothschild, Joan, 5:37,
  5:157, 5:186, 5:188, **5:204**
Rothschuh, Karl E., 5:34
Rothstein, Eric, 1:244
Rothstein, William G., 5:47
Rotoli, Nicholas J., 1:123

Rottman, Marcia L., 5:629
Roud, Richard, 3:837
Rouechè, Berton, 5:383
Roumain, Jacques, 2:146,
  2:941
Rouner, Leroy S., 4:297
Rourke, Constance, 1:652
Rourke, Robert E. K., 5:523
Rous, Stephen N., 5:344
Rouse, Blair, 1:844
Rouse, Irving, 3:629, 3:917
Rouse, John, 2:573
Rouse, Joseph, 5:67, 5:157
Rouse, Ruth, 4:746
Rouse, William Henry Den-
  ham, 2:360
Rousseau, G. S., 1:252, 5:45
Rousseau, Jean Jacques,
Rousseau, Jean-Jacques,
  1:253, 1:573, 1:576, 2:471,
  2:503, 3:91, **3:164,** 3:626,
  3:845, **4:195, 4:200, 4:212,**
  5:144,
Routh, C. R., 3:359
Routh, Harold V., 1:429
Roux, Georges, 3:301, 3:450
Rovit, E. H., 1:876
Rowan-Robinson, Michael,
  5:588, 5:656
Rowe, Dorothy, 5:427
Rowe, George E., Jr., 1:190
Rowe, H., 3:175
Rowe, Joyce A., 1:805
Rowe, Karen, 1:644
Rowe, William, 4:194, 4:212
Rowe, William T., 3:468
Rowe, W. W., 2:690
Rowell, George, 1:272, 1:323
Rowell, Henry Thompson,
  2:381
Rowland, Beryl, 1:151
Rowland, Peter, 3:367
Rowland, Wade, 5:392
Rowley, Charles K., 3:67
Rowley, H. H., 4:819
Rowntree, Derek, 5:524
Rowntree, Lester, 3:121
Rowse, A. L., 1:205, 3:276
Rowson, Susanna Haswell,
  1:642, 1:1209, 1:1219
Roxon, Lillian, 3:657
Roy, David Todd, 2:250
Roy, D. Elliot, 5:212
Roy, Emil, 1:426
Roy, F. Hampton, 5:317
Roy, Rustum, 5:176, 5:182,
  5:198, 5:205, 5:212
Royce, Anya P., 3:733
Royce, Josiah, 1:668, 1:726,
  4:248, **4:249,** 4:260, 4:295,
  4:301, 4:304, 5:469
Royle, Edward, 3:364

Roysdon, Christine M., 5:60, 5:149, 5:217
Royster, Charles, 3:529
Rozanov, Vasily, 2:716
Rozenblit, Marsha L., 4:637
Rozental, S., 5:674
Różewicz, Tadeusz, 2:810, **2:820**
Rozman, Gilbert, 3:465, 3:478
Ruben, Brent, 3:803
Ruben, David-Hillel, 4:227, 4:243
Ruben, Douglas H., 4:14
Rubens, Peter Paul, 3:768, 3:790, **3:791**
Rubenstein, Amnon, 4:658
Rubenstein, Carol, 2:325
Rubenstein, James M., 3:122
Rubenstein, Richard L., 3:344, 3:350
Rubenstein, Roberta, 1:919
Rubin, Louis D., Jr., 1:130, 1:652, 1:712, 1:716, 1:737, 1:779, 1:905, 1:919
Rubin, Miri, 4:697
Rubin, Ruth, 2:32, 3:852
Rubin, Vitaly A., 4:525
Rubin, William, 3:773, 3:787
Rubin-Dorsky, Jeffrey, 1:681
Rubinstein, Artur, **3:713**
Rubinstein, Charlotte S., 3:761
Rubinstein, Frankie, 1:216
Rubinstein, Herbert, 5:398
Rubinstein, Mark, 5:396, 5:424
Rubinstein, Robert L., 3:201
Rubulis, Aleksis, 2:796, 2:804
Ruch, E. A., 4:369
Ruck, Rob, 3:636
Rudall, Paul, 5:768
Rudavsky, David, 4:643, 4:651
Rudd, Margaret, 2:552
Rudden, M. N., 5:668
Rudder, Robert S., 2:849
Ruddick, Lisa, 1:883
Ruddick, Nicholas, 1:611
Rude, Charles, 3:339
Rudé, George, 3:363
Ruderman, David B., 4:624
Ruderman, Judith, 1:511, 1:1057
Rudin, Marcia R., 4:857
Rudisill, Marie, 1:959
Rudman, Mark, 1:1006
Rudney, R., 3:280
Rudnick, Norman, 5:387
Rudnytsky, Peter L., 5:472
Rudolf, Anthony, 2:10, 2:34
Rudolph, James D., 3:640
Rudolph, Kurt, 4:453, 4:686
Rudolph, Lloyd I., 3:486

Rudolph, Susanne H., 3:486
Rudwick, Elliott, 3:557
Rudwick, Martin J. S., 5:34, 5:194
Rudy, Stephen, 2:716
Rueckert, William H., 1:818
Rueschemeyer, D., 3:51
Ruether, Rosemary Rad-ford, 4:650, 4:679, 4:684, 4:742, 4:749, **4:784,** 4:896, **4:904**
Ruf, Henry L., 4:38
Ruffner, James A., 5:7
Ruffo-Fiore, Silvia, 4:145
Rugoff, Milton, 3:893, 3:934
Ruihley, Glenn R., 1:856, 2:989, 5:449
Ruitenbeck, Hendrik M., 2:989, 5:449
Ruiz, Antonio Machado y. See Machado y Ruiz, Antonio
Ruiz, Juan, **2:549**
Ruiz, Ramón Eduardo, 3:636, 3:639
Rukeyser, Muriel, **1:1041**
Rule, Jane, 1:1182
Rulfo, Juan, 2:844, **2:882**
Rumbold, Valerie, 1:252
Rūmī, Jalāl al-Dīn, 2:92, 2:101, 4:566, **4:589**
Rumney, Avis, 5:395
Rumney, Thomas A., 5:261
Rumrich, John O., 1:193
Runciman, Steven, 4:694
Rundle, Bede, 4:346
Runes, Dagobert D., 4:3, 4:15, 4:18, 5:227
Running, Leona Glidden, 4:828
Runte, Alfred, 3:550
Runyon, Randolph P., 1:894
Runyon, Richard P., 5:524
Ruoff, A. LaVonne Brown, 1:134, 1:716, 1:1129
Rupnow, Marcia E., 5:620
Rupp, Ernest Gordon, 4:724, 4:727, 4:779
Rupp, Richard H., 1:708, 1:920
Ruppersburg, Hugh, 1:894
Rusch, William G., 4:686
Ruse, Michael, 3:208, 4:385, 5:47, 5:68, 5:198
Rush, James R., 2:312
Rush, Theressa G., 1:128
Rushdie, Salman, **2:180**
Rushefsky, Mark, 5:736
Rushton, Julian, 3:663, 3:682
Rusinko, Susan, 1:540
Rusk, Ralph L., 1:671

Ruskin, John, 1:324, 1:355, 1:363, 1:386, **1:392,** 1:409, 1:560, 1:574, 3:764, 3:793, 4:551
Russ, Joanna, 1:1252, 1:1256, **1:1261**
Russel, Peter, 4:873
Russell, Bert, 3:863
Russell, Bertrand Arthur William, 3:86, 4:18, 4:23, 4:38, 4:162, 4:177, 4:220, 4:221, 4:229, 4:236, 4:260, 4:272, 4:278, 4:301, 4:302, **4:320,** 4:333, 4:340, 4:343, 4:377, 4:379, 5:84, **5:101,** 5:112, 5:140, 5:493, **5:516,** 5:583
Russell, Burton J., 3:332
Russell, Charles, 5:317
Russell, Colin A., 5:198
Russell, D. A., 3:318, 4:490
Russell, David S., 4:605, 4:824
Russell, Francis, 1:730
Russell, Jeffrey B., 4:687, 4:697, 4:700
Russell, John, 1:422
Russell, Letty M., 4:815
Russell, Louise B., 5:353
Russell, P. E., 2:536
Russell, Peter, 1:874
Russell, Peter J., 5:778
Russell, Ralph, 2:175
Russell, Robert, 2:731
Russell, Robert J., 5:198
Russell, Ross, 3:669, 3:708
Russell, Sandi, 1:130
Russo, Anthony, 1:778
Russo, Dorothy, 1:778
Russo, Nancy Felipe, 3:169, 3:181
Russo, Vito, 1:1182
Rutan, J. Scott, 5:414
Ruth, John L., 4:724
Rutherford, A., 2:129
Rutherford, Andrew, 1:284, 1:372
Rutherford, Ernest, 5:657, 5:673, 5:678, 5:679, 5:696, 5:710, **5:711,** 5:734
Rutherford, F. James, 5:11
Rutherford, R. B., 4:59, 4:76
Ruthven, K. K., 1:874, 1:926
Ruthven, Malise, 4:572
Rutland, Robert Allen, 3:521, 3:541
Rutledge, Paul J., 3:557
Rutman, Anita H., 3:518
Rutman, Darrett B., 3:518
Rutnin, Mattani, 2:335
Rutt, Richard, 2:299
Rutter, Carol, 1:218
Ruyslinck, Ward, **2:629**

Ryals, Clyde De L., 1:339
Ryan, Alan, 4:175
Ryan, Cornelius, 3:344
Ryan, Frank, 5:383
Ryan, John K., 4:114
Ryan, Judith, 2:989
Ryan, Mary P., 3:557
Ryan, Michael, 1:1157, 4:267,
    4:392
Ryan, Robert M., 1:294
Ryan, Selwyn D., 3:641
Ryan, Thomas E., 2:594
Ryan, William, 3:212
Ryan, William J., 5:336
Rybakov, Anatoly, 2:754
Rybczynski, Witold, 5:157,
    5:215
Rycroft, Michael, 5:3, 5:597
Rydel, Christine, 2:694, 2:742
Ryder, A. J., 3:377
Ryder, John, 1:10
Ryder, John Douglas, 5:230
Ryer, Jeanne C., 5:547
Ryle, Gilbert, 4:84, 4:261,
    4:325, 4:381
Ryman, Daniele, 5:320
Rypka, J., 2:83
Ryschkewitsch, George E.,
    5:730
Ryskamp, Charles, 1:238
Ryūnosuke, Akutagawa. See
    Akutagawa Ryūnosuke
Rzhevsky, Nicholas, 2:690

S

Sa'di, 2:89, 2:93
Sa'idi, Ghulam Husayn,
    2:93
Saadia Gaon, 4:600, 4:671
Saarikoski, Pentti, 2:659
Saatkamp, Herman J., Jr.,
    4:328
Saaz, Johannes von, 2:562,
    2:594
Sabahattin Ali, 2:100
Sábato, Ernesto, 2:882
Sabato, Larry J., 3:144, 3:148
Sabin, Joseph, 1:67, 3:507
Sabin, Margery, 1:415, 1:440
Sabine, Gordon, 1:34
Sabloff, Jeremy A., 3:628,
    4:439, 4:454, 4:456
Sabol, A. J., 1:166
Sabor, Peter, 1:253, 1:263,
    1:604
Sabra, A. I., 5:43
Sá-Carneiro, Mário de, 2:557
Saccio, Peter, 1:186, 1:212
Sachar, Abram, 4:643

Sachar, Howard M., 3:350,
    3:440, 4:634, 4:643, 4:645
Sachs, Curt, 3:663, 3:667,
    3:672, 3:732
Sachs, D., 5:559
Sachs, Hans, 2:608
Sachs, Harvey, 3:657
Sachs, Lothar, 5:521
Sachs, Nelly, 2:11, 2:564,
    2:608
Sachs, Wolfgang, 5:182
Sacilotto, Deli, 3:758
Sackett, S. J., 3:862
Sacks, Kenneth, 3:315
Sacks, Oliver, 5:315, 5:393,
    5:428, 5:569
Sacks, Richard S., 3:640
Sacksteder, William, 4:175
Sackville-West, Vita (Victo-
    ria Mary), 1:541, 1:568
al-Sa'dawi, Nawal, 2:71,
    2:116, 2:120
al-Sadat, A., 3:445
Saddhatissa, Hammalava,
    4:893
Saddlemyer, Ann, 1:490
Sade (Donatien Alphonse
    François), Comte de,
    2:503, 2:627
Sader, Marion, 1:81, 1:1195
Sadie, Stanley, 3:655, 3:657
Sadleir, Michael, 1:31, 1:340
Sadler, Lynn Vetch, 1:452,
    1:468
Sadler, M. J., 5:261
Sadler, Michael T., 1:255
Sadler, T. W., 5:773
Sadoff, Robert L., 5:423
Sadoul, Georges, 3:826
Sadoveanu, Mihail, 2:823,
    2:826
Safer, Elaine B., 1:920
Saff, Donald, 3:758
Safran, Alexandre, 4:630
Safran, Nadav, 3:440
Safranski, Rudiger, 4:256
Sagal, Paul T., 3:194
Sagan, Carl, 5:18, 5:588,
    5:611, 5:647
Sagan, Dorion, 5:776
Sagar, Keith M., 1:498, 1:511
Sage, Michael, 4:708
Sage, William W., 3:491
Saggs, H.W.F., 4:440
Sagoff, Mark, 5:76, 5:824
Sahai, Sachchidanand, 2:322
Sahgal, Nayantara, 2:181
Sahlins, Marshall D., 3:14,
    3:16, 3:17, 3:18, 3:25, 3:32,
    3:495, 4:462
Said, A. Samad, 2:323

Said, Edward E., 1:926,
    1:1042, 1:1132, 1:1147,
    1:1152, 3:437, 3:444,
    3:455, 3:459
Said, Edward W., 2:988,
    4:572, 4:643
Saikaku, Ihara. See Ihara
    Saikaka
Sainsbury, Mark, 4:324, 5:103
Saint Ambrose. See Ambrose,
    St.
Saint Anselm of Canterbury.
    See Anselm of Canterbury,
    St.
Saint Augustine of Hippo.
    See Augustine of Hippo,
    St.
Saint Basil of Caesarea. See
    Basil of Caesarea, St.
Saint Benedict of Nursia.
    See Benedict of Nursia,
    St.
Saint Bernard of Clairvaux.
    See Bernard of Clairvaux,
    St.
Saint Bonaventure of Bagno-
    rea. See Bonaventure of
    Bagnorea, St.
Saint Catherine of Siena. See
    Catherine of Siena, St.
St. Clair, William, 1:301
St. Denis, Ruth, 3:743,
    3:751, 3:752
Saint-Exupéry, Antoine de,
    2:503
Saint Francis of Assisi. See
    Francis of Assissi, St.
Saint Ignatius of Loyola. See
    Ignatius of Loyola, St.
Saint Jerome. See Jerome,
    St.
Saint John Cassian. See Cas-
    sian, St. John
Saint John of the Cross. See
    John of the Cross, St.
Saint-John Perse, 2:492,
    2:504
St. Pierre, Brian, 1:886
Saintsbury, George E., 1:242
Saint Teresa of Avila. See
    Teresa of Avila, St.
Saint Teresa of Jesus. See
    Teresa of Jesus, St.
Saint Thomas Aquinas. See
    Aquinas, St. Thomas
Saipradit, Kularb, 2:335
Sajdak, Bruce T., 1:221
Sakharov, Andrei, 3:397,
    3:398
Saki. See Munro, H(ector)
    H(ugh)
Salam, Abdus, 5:690, 5:713,
    5:718

Salam, M. H., 5:713
Salami, Mahmoud, 1:478
Šalamun, Tomaž, 2:835, **2:836**
Salanga, Alfredo, 2:329
Salas, Xavier de, 3:776
Saldarini, Anthony J., 4:613, 4:616
Saldivar, Ramon, 1:1132
Sale, Kirkpatrick, 3:550, 3:630, 5:824
Sale, William M., 1:254
Salem, Dorothy C., 3:511
Salem, James M., 1:427
Salerno, Roger, 3:245
Sales, Grover, 3:669
Salevouris, Michael J., 3:9
Salgado, Gamini, 1:171
Saliba, John A., 4:857
Salih, al-Tayib, **2:72**, 2:116, 2:123
Salinas, Pedro, 2:521, 2:526, 2:531, 2:542, **2:549**
Salinger, Herman, 2:611
Salinger, J(erome) D(avid), **1:1042**, 1:1193
Salinger, Leo, 1:211
Salinger, Wendy, 1:1066
Salinš, Gunars, 2:803
Salisbury, Harrison, 3:395, 3:397, 3:808, **3:822**
Salkever, Stephen G., 4:71
Salkey, Andrew, 2:931, **2:941**
Salkind, C. T., 5:496
Sallares, Robert, 3:308
Salleh, Muhammad Haji, 2:325
Saller, Richard, 3:307, 3:308
Sallis, John, 4:75, 4:294, 4:398
Sallust, 2:379, 3:310, **3:319**
Sally, Judith D., 5:513
Salmawi, Muhammad, 2:59
Salmon, Claudine, 2:317
Salmon, J. H., 4:732
Salmon, J. Warren, 5:320
Salmon, Marylynn, 3:557
Salmon, Merrilee, 5:65
Salmon, Nathan U., 4:411
Salmon, Patrick, 3:394
Salmon, Wesley Charles, 5:65, 5:68, **5:103**
Salmore, Barbara G., 3:144
Salomé, Lou A., 4:247, 5:449
Salomon, Jean-Jacques, 5:182
Salomon, J. H., 3:865
Salpeter, Judy, 5:566
Salska, Agnieszka, 1:748
Salter, Elizabeth, 1:147
Saltman, Judith, 1:579, 1:1197

Saltykov-Shchedrin, Mikhail, **2:754**
Salutati, Coluccio, 2:433
Salvadori, Mario, 5:12
Salvaggio, Ruth, 1:226
Salvato, Joseph A., 5:245
Salvato, Larry, 3:826
Salvatore, Nick, 3:549
Salwak, Dale, 1:433, 1:449, 1:539, 1:879
Salzberg, Hugh W., 5:729
Salzinger, Kurt, 3:168
Salzman, Eric, 3:663, 3:665
Salzman, Jack, 1:133
Salzman, Leon, 5:428
Samaraweera, Vijaya, 3:488
Sambrook, James, 1:226, 1:261, 1:315
Sambursky, Samuel, 4:49, 4:57
Samenow, Stanton, 5:428
Sammells, Neil, 1:555
Sammons, Jeffrey L., 2:588
Samons, L. J., 3:301
Sampon, Annette, 2:494
Sampselle, Carolyn M., 3:218
Sampson, Anthony, 3:367, 5:280
Sampson, George, 1:728
Sampson, Robert, 1:593
Sams, Jamie, 3:865
Samson, Jim, 3:663
Samson, John, 1:689
Samuel, Maurice, 2:43, 2:46
Samuel, Richard, 2:566
Samuelian, Thomas J., 2:77
Samuels, Andrew, 5:456
Samuels, Charles E., 1:732
Samuels, Ernest, 1:730, 3:563
Samuels, Marwyn S., 3:119
Samuels, Mike, 5:323, 5:342
Samuels, Nancy, 5:323
Samuels, Warren J., 3:46, 3:69, 3:74, 3:89
Samuels, Wilfred D., 1:1019
Samuelson, David A., 1:218
Samuelson, Paul Anthony, 3:46, 3:64, 3:89, **3:103**
Sanasarian, Eliz, 3:448
Sanborn, Margaret, 1:784
Sanchez, Alfonso E. Perez, 3:795
Sánchez, Luis Rafael, **2:883**, 2:941
Sanchez Salazar, L. A., 3:295
Sanchez, Sonia, **1:1044**
Sanctis, Francesco De, 2:398, 2:414, 2:423
Sand, George, **2:504**, 3:689
Sandars, Nancy K., 4:445
Sandbach, F. H., 2:364, 4:57
Sandberg, Karl, 4:166
Sandberg, Larry, 3:852

Sandberg-Diment, Erik, 5:538
Sandburg, Carl, **1:877**, 1:954, 1:1195, 1:1205, 3:530
Sandeen, Ernest R., 4:15, 4:754
Sandel, Cora, 2:662, **2:667**
Sandelowski, Margarete, 5:359
Sandemose, Axel, 2:662
Sander, Reinhard W., 2:931
Sanders, Andrew, 1:319
Sanders, Arthur, 3:143
Sanders, Charles, 1:521
Sanders, Dennis, 1:606
Sanders, E. P., 4:617, 4:621, 4:807, 4:826
Sanders, Gerald DeWitt, 1:356, 1:418, 1:915
Sanders, James A., 4:613
Sanders, Jo, 3:257
Sanders, Lawrence, **1:1236**
Sanders, Marlene, 3:808
Sanders, N. K., 4:546
Sanders, Norman, 1:10, 1:53
Sanders, Ronald, 2:30, 3:350, 3:557, 4:643
Sanders, Steven, 4:24
Sanders, Valerie, 1:325, 1:376
Sanders, Wilbur, 1:178, 1:187
Sanderson, Christiane, 5:429
Sanderson, George, 3:419, 3:818
Sanderson, Marie, 5:634
Sandewall, Erik, 5:549
Sandler, Norman, 3:803
Sandler, Stephanie, 2:752
Sandmel, Samuel, 4:60, 4:100, 4:605, 4:646, 4:670, 4:812
Sandor, Jakob, 3:389
Sandro, Paul, 3:832
Sandrow, Nahma, 2:32
Sands, Matthew L., 5:650
Sandstrom, Alan R., 1:5
Sandstrom, Pamela Effrein, 1:5
Sandweiss, Jack H., 5:400
Sandweiss, Samuel H., 4:873
Sandys, John Edwin, 2:402
Sanford, Nevitt, 5:414
Sangren, Steven, 4:531
Sang-sôp, Yôm, 2:298
Sangster, Joan, 3:609
Sangwan, R. S., 5:221, 5:267
Sangwan-Norreel, B. S., 5:221, 5:267
San Juan, Epifanio, Jr., 2:329, 2:331
Sankar, Andrea, 5:379
Sankhdher, B. M., 4:355
Sanmartín, José, 5:152
Sannella, Ted, 3:852

Sansom, Sir George B(ailey), 3:474, 3:476, **3:501**
Santas, Gerasimos X., 4:90
Santayana, George, 1:726, 3:157, 3:814, 4:29, 4:75, 4:241, 4:296, **4:325**, 5:95
Santer, M., 4:687
Santí, Enrico, 2:876
Santillana, Giorgio de, 4:130, 4:144, 5:43, 5:688
Santino, Jack, 3:55
Santirocco, Matthew S., 2:386
Santmire, H. Paul, 4:746, 5:116
Santore, Anthony C., 1:986
Santos, Aida, 2:328
Santos, Bienvenido N., 2:328
Santos, Lope K., 2:327
Santos, Rosario, 2:850
Santrock, John W., 3:174, 3:257
Saperstein, Marc, 4:628
Sapir, Edward, 3:14, 3:21, **3:39**, 3:42, 4:477
Sapolsky, Harvey M., 5:130
Saposnik, Irving S., 1:397
Sapp, Stephen, 4:894
Sappho, 1:1179, 1:1188, 2:342, **2:366**
Sarason, Seymour B., 5:336
Sarch, Ray, 5:560
Sarduy, Severo, 2:844, **2:883**, 2:941
Sarg, Michael, 5:367
Sargeant, Winthrop, 4:506
Sargeson, Frank, 2:979
Saridis, George N., 5:243
Sarjeant, William Antony S., 5:625
Sarkar, Sumit, 3:486
Sarkonak, Ralph, 2:509
Sarlos, Robert K., 1:1075
Sarmiento, Domingo Faustino, 2:884
Sarndal, C. E., 5:524
Sarno, Louis, 3:421
Saron, Gustav, 4:645
Saroyan, Aram, 1:1110
Saroyan, William, 1:525, **1:1110**, 2:80
Sarraute, Nathalie, 2:448, **2:505**
Sarris, Andrew, 1:1158, 1:1166, 1:1176
Sartain, E. M., 4:585
Sarti, Roland, 3:386
Sarton, George, 5:23, 5:39, 5:40, **5:55**
Sartore, Richard L., 3:877
Sartori, Giovanni, 3:143

Sartre, Jean-Paul, 1:523, 1:966, 1:1148, 2:146, 2:292, 2:435, 2:457, 2:458, 2:459, 2:464, 2:476, 2:478, 2:485, 2:487, 2:494, **2:506**, 3:350, 4:39, 4:234, 4:261, 4:299, 4:301, 4:309, 4:318, **4:328**, 4:377
Saso, Michael R., 4:528, 4:532, 4:538
Sasson, Jack, 2:52
Sasson, Sarah D., 4:850
Sassoon, Anne S., 4:287
Sassoon, Rosemary, 1:19
Sassoon, Siegfried, 1:533, **1:542**, 1:557
Sassoun, David of, 2:75
Sassower, Raphael, 5:66, 5:156, 5:157
Sater, William F., 3:635
Satie, Erik, 3:714, 3:741
Satin, Joseph Henry, 1:220
Sato, Giei, 4:538
Sato, Hiroaki, 2:274, 2:283
Sattelmeyer, Robert, 1:784
Sattler, Helen Roney, 5:639
Sauer, Carl Ortwin, 3:121, **3:135**, 3:630
Saul, John, 1:1243
Saul, Julie, 3:834
Saulson, Donald S., 5:261
Saulson, Elizabeth M., 5:261
Saum, Lewis O., 3:530
Saunders, Catherine E., 1:844
Saunders, David, 1:55
Saunders, Jason L., 4:130
Saunders, Paul L., 5:390
Saunders, S. A., 3:607
Saunders, Trevor J., 4:84
Sava, Saint, 2:826
Savage, C. Wade, 4:324, 5:103
Savage, George, 3:766
Savage, Leonard J., 5:79
Savage, Michael D., 3:893
Saville, John, 3:365
Savin, Maynard, 1:390
Savona, Jeannette L., 2:479
Savory, Roger M., 4:572
Savory, Theodore, 2:991
Sawa, Yuki, 2:283
Sawako, Ariyoshi. *See* Ariyoshi Sawako
Sawatski, Suchat, 2:335
Sawey, Orlan, 3:576
Sawicki, Jana, 4:401, 5:88
Sawkins, Frederick J., 5:238
Sawyer, Elizabeth, 3:732
Sawyer, Ken K., 3:265
Sawyer, W. W., 5:482, 5:491
Sax, Boria, 2:566, 2:585
Sax, Joseph L., 5:116
Sax, N. Irving, 5:726

Saxe, Stephen O., 1:11
Saxelby, F. Outwin, 1:363
Saxon, A. H., 1:272
Saxonhouse, Arlene W., 4:49
Saxton, Martha, 1:1199
Sayce, R. A., 2:491, 4:146
Sayer, Andrew, 3:123
Sayer, Derek, 3:210, 3:244
Sayer, Jeffrey A., 3:415
Sayers, Dorothy, 1:346, 1:605, **1:609**
Sayers, Janet, 3:178
Sayers, Scott, 3:719
Sayre, Eleanor A., 3:776
Sayre, John R., 3:510
Sayre, Kenneth M., 4:84, 5:128
Sayre, Robert F., 1:639
Sayre, Woodrow Wilson, 3:910
al-Sayyab, Badr Shakir, 2:72
al-Sayyid-Marsot, Afaf L., 3:445
Scaer, Roberta, 5:359
Scafella, Frank, 1:847
Scaglione, Aldo, 2:434
Scalapino, Robert A., 3:465, 3:472
Scalia, S. Eugene, 2:413
Scammell, Michael, 2:762
Scanlan, Tom, 1:1075
Scanlon, Phil, Jr., 4:519
Scanzoni, Letha, 4:750
Scarborough, John, 3:304, 5:39
Scarborough, Vernon L., 3:628, 4:456
Scarisbrick, J. J., 3:359, 4:727
Scarr, Deryck, 3:496
Scatton, Linda H., 2:776
Schaaf, William L., 5:496
Schabas, Margaret, 3:85
Schacht, Richard, 4:247
Schachterle, Lance, 5:153
Schact, Joseph, 4:572
Schacter-Shalom, Zalman, 4:649
Schaefer, David, 2:491
Schaefer, Dennis, 3:826
Schaefer, Jack, 1:1217
Schaefer, Vincent J., 5:634
Schaeffer, Dagmar, 3:336
Schaeffer, R. L., 5:522
Schaerf, Carlo, 5:109
Schafer, E. H., 2:191
Schafer, Roy, 5:469
Schaff, Adam, 5:572
Schaff, Philip, 4:100, 4:678
Schaffer, Arthur, 3:522
Schaffer, Ronald, 3:533
Schaffer, Simon, 4:175, 4:258, 5:58

Schaie, K. Warner, 3:173
Schakel, Peter J., 1:261,
  1:513
Schaller, George B., 5:771,
  5:824
Schaller, Michael, 3:479
Schama, Simon, 3:383
Schank, Roger C., 3:175,
  5:569, 5:570
Schaper, Eva, 4:207
Schapiro, J. Salwyn, 3:344
Schapiro, Leonard, 3:397
Schapiro, Meyer, 3:773, 3:795
Schapsmeier, Edward L.,
  5:261
Schapsmeier, Frederick H.,
  5:261
Scharer, Linda, 5:328
Scharf, Aaron, 5:194
Scharf, Martin, 5:406
Scharfetter, Christian, 5:428
Scharff, Edward E., 3:809
Scharff, Jill Savege, 5:425
Scharff, Stefan, 3:827
Scharfstein, Ben-Ami, 4:18,
  4:37, 4:350
Scharlemann, Robert, 4:731,
  4:889
Scharnhorst, Gary, 1:753
Schatt, Stanley, 1:1064, 5:297
Schattschneider, Doris, 5:495
Schatz, Thomas, 1:1158
Schatzman, Evry, 5:589,
  5:656, 5:657
Schaub, James H., 5:130
Schaub, Thomas H., 1:920,
  1:1035
Schauer, Frederick, 3:139
Schaumann, Wolfgang, 5:266
Schaupp, Zora, 4:195
Schauss, Hayyim, 4:600
Scheader, Catherine, 3:663
Scheaffer, R. L., 5:523
Schechter, Solomon, 4:621
Scheckner, Peter, 1:316
Scheer, A. W., 5:558
Scheer-Schaezler, Brigitte,
  1:948
Scheffler, Israel, 4:385, 5:65
Scheick, William J., 1:564,
  1:629, 1:644, 1:724
Schein, S., 2:362
Scheindlin, Raymond P., 2:10
Schele, Linda, 3:628
Scheler, Max Ferdinand,
  4:261, **4:331,** 5:469
Schell, Edgar, 1:161
Schell, Jonathan, 5:112
Schellenberg, James A.,
  3:184, 3:190, 3:194, 3:233,
  4:309
Schellenberg, Kathryn, 5:126

Scheller, William, 3:916,
  5:284
Schelling, Friedrich Wil-
  helm Joseph, 4:158,
  4:197, 4:231, **4:250**
Schelling, Thomas C., 3:62,
  3:64
Schenk, Margaret T., 5:217
Schenk, Wilhelm, 4:729
Schenker, Daniel, 1:514
Schenker, Hillel, 4:643
Scheper-Hughes, Nancy,
  5:428
Scher, Jonathan, 5:359
Scherer, Donald, 4:24, 5:116
Scherfig, Hans, 2:654
Scherle, Victor, 3:833
Scherr, Barry P., 2:690,
  2:726
Scherzer, Kenneth A., 3:172
Scheub, Harold, 3:869
Schevill, Susie, 5:322
Schick, Frank L., 1:38
Schickel, Richard, 1:1165,
  1:1168
Schiebinger, Londa, 5:26,
  5:188
Schierbeek, Bert, 2:630
Schiesari, Juliana, 2:401
Schiff, Ze'ev, 3:440
Schiffman, Lawrence H.,
  4:621, 4:812
Schiffman, Ruth, 3:393
Schild, Ulla, 2:110
Schildt, Goran, 3:770
Schildt, Runar, 2:657
Schillebeeck, Edward, 4:746
Schiller, Friedrich von, 1:772
Schiller, Herbert I., 3:804,
  5:558
Schiller, (Johann Christoph)
  Friedrich von, 2:531,
  2:563, 2:580, 2:591, 2:599,
  2:609, 2:734
Schilpp, Paul Arthur, 4:41,
  4:276, 4:277, 4:280,4:300,
  4:302, 4:305, 4:312, 4:324,
  4:331, 4:338, 4:343, 4:354,
  4:410, 4:412, 5:49, 5:85,
  5:99, 5:100, 5:103, 5:139,
  5:683
Schimmel, Annemarie, 2:83,
  2:93, 4:375, 4:572, 4:589
Schinzinger, Roland, 5:129
Schipani, Daniel S., 3:262
Schipper, Mineke, 2:112
Schirmer, Gregory A., 1:460
Schlachter, Gail Ann, 5:545
Schlagel, Richard, 5:65
Schlam, Carl C., 2:383, 4:469
Schlauch, Margaret, 1:167
Schlegel, August Wilhelm,
  2:610, 4:251

Schlegel, Friedrich, 2:563,
  2:610, 4:252, 4:253
Schleicher, Joan L., 5:681
Schleiermacher, Friedrich
  Daniel Ernst, 4:253,
  4:254, 4:421, 4:785, 4:882
Schlepp, Wayne, 2:191
Schlereth, Thomas J., 3:533
Schlesinger, Arthur M(eier),
  3:522, **3:596**
Schlesinger, Arthur
  M(eier), Jr., 3:147, 3:507,
  3:535, 3:543, 3:576, **3:596**
Schlesinger, George N., 5:68
Schlesinger, Stephen, 3:637
Schless, Howard, 2:418
Schlessinger, Bernard, 5:4
Schlessinger, June H., 5:4
Schleunes, Karl A., 3:350
Schlick, Moritz, 4:272,
  4:278, **4:332**
Schlipp, P. A., 4:279
Schlossberg, Edwin, 4:18
Schlossman, Beryl, 2:476
Schlotel, Brian, 3:698
Schlueter, June, 1:135, 1:214,
  1:1104
Schlueter, Paul, 1:135
Schlumberger, Jean, 2:480
Schlupmann, Klaus, 5:823
Schmeckebier, Laurence F.,
  1:108
Schmemann, Alexander,
  4:756
Schmid, Carol L., 3:378
Schmidheiny, Stephan, 5:282
Schmidt, Alexander, 1:216
Schmidt, Dennis J., 4:295
Schmidt, Elfriede, 3:376
Schmidt, J. D., 2:231
Schmidt, Josephine A., 2:471
Schmidt, M., 4:790
Schmidt, Michael, 1:502
Schmidt, Nancy J., 2:112
Schmidt, Peter, 1:901
Schmidt, Werner H., 4:817
Schmiel, Robert, 2:354
Schmitt, Arno, 4:894
Schmitt, Charles B., 4:71,
  4:125, 4:130, 4:152
Schmitt, Hans A., 3:346
Schmitt, Richard, 4:243
Schmoller, A., 4:819
Schnackenburg, Rudolf,
  4:822
Schnapp, Jeffrey T., 2:418
Schneer, Cecil J., 5:625
Schneewind, Jerome, 4:257
Schneidau, Herbert N., 1:795
Schneider, David M., 3:17,
  3:20
Schneider, Elisabeth, 1:288,
  1:364

Schneider, Georg, 1:61
Schneider, Herbert W., 4:35,
    4:267
Schneider, Ilya I., 3:742
Schneider, Joanne, 3:326
Schneider, J. Stewart, 5:558
Schneider, Laurence A.,
    2:196
Schneider, Marilyn, 2:408
Schneider, Myles J., 5:396
Schneider, Pierre, 3:781
Schneider, Richard I., 3:275
Schneider, Richard J., 1:702
Schneider, Robert G., 5:405
Schneider, Ronald M., 3:634
Schneider, Stephen H.,
    5:775, 5:824
Schneider, Susan, 4:650
Schneiderman, Leo, 3:869
Schneidermeyer, Wilma,
    1:524, 1:552
Schnell, George A., 5:621
Schneller, Beverly E., 5:9
Schnitman, Jorge, 3:803
Schnitzler, Arthur, 1:554,
    2:610
Schockley, Ann A., 1:716
Schodek, Daniel L., 5:224
Schodt, David W., 3:636
Schoeck, Richard J., 4:139
Schoedel, William, 4:704
Schoem, David, 4:641
Schoemaker, George H.,
    3:869
Schoemaker, Joyce M., 5:351
Schoenbaum, David, 3:377
Schoenbaum, Samuel, 1:190,
    1:205, 1:222
Schoenberg, Arnold, 3:679,
    3:683, 3:686, 3:699, 3:705,
    3:714, 3:729
Schoener, Allon, 4:641
Schoenfeld, Joachim, 4:624
Schoenfeld, Robert, 5:727
Schoenfeldt, Michael C.,
    1:181
Schoenfield, M., 4:50
Schoeps, Hans-Joachim,
    4:573, 4:603
Schoeser, Mary, 3:767
Schofield, Edmund, 5:837
Schofield, Malcolm, 4:53,
    4:56, 4:57
Schofield, Robert S., 5:45
Scholar, Nancy, 1:866
Scholem, Gershom, 2:6,
    3:350, 4:631, **4:672**
Scholes, Robert E., 1:430,
    1:926, 1:1127, 2:988
Scholezer, Boris de, 3:717
Schollar, Barbara, 1:130
Schomer, Karine, 4:517
Schonberg, Harold C., 3:663

Schonberger, Richard, 5:234
Schonhorn, Manuel, 1:240
Schonkron, Marcel, 1:102
Schooler, Carmi, 3:214
Schoolfield, George C., 2:658,
    2:661
Schoolman, Morton, 4:408,
    5:95
Schopen, Bernard A., 1:1235
Schopenhauer, Arthur,
    2:561, 2:624, 2:627, 4:38,
    4:245, **4:254**
Schopf, Thomas J. M., 5:639
Schopmeyer, Betty B., 5:376
Schopp, Claude, 2:473
Schor, Hilary M., 1:356
Schor, Naomi, 2:476, 2:518
Schorer, C. E., 3:865
Schorer, Mark, 1:279, 1:423,
    1:854
Schorr, Daniel, 3:252
Schorr, Lisbeth B., 3:252
Schorske, Carl E., 2:565,
    3:350, 3:376
Schott, James D., 3:258
Schouls, Peter A., 4:180
Schoultz, Solveig von, 2:660
Schowalter, Daniel N., 4:452
Schrade, Leo, 3:706
Schrader, Richard J., 2:566
Schram, Stuart R., 2:257,
    3:467, 4:362
Schramm, Gunter, 3:48
Schrecker, John E., 3:472
Schreiber, Fred, 1:11
Schreurs, Marc, 2:700
Schreyer, Alice D., 1:63
Schrieffer, John Robert,
    5:671
Schrift, Alan, 4:295
Schrödinger, Erwin, 5:659,
    5:675, 5:680, 5:693, **5:714**
Schroeder, Alan, 1:785, 3:737
Schroeder, David P., 3:700
Schroeder, Fred E., 3:874
Schroeder, Frederic M., 4:87
Schroeder, H. J., 4:729
Schroeder, W. Widick, 4:263,
    4:379
Schrotenboer, Kathryn,
    5:356, 5:359
Schubert, E. D., 5:380
Schubert, Franz, 3:715
Schubert, Helmut, 5:669
Schucking, Levin L., 1:220
Schudson, Michael, 3:809,
    3:874
Schuh, Fred, 5:497
Schuh, Willi, 3:722
Schuker, Eleanor, 3:178
Schull, Joseph, 3:614, 3:615
Schuller, Gunther, 3:669
Schulman, Brian, 5:393

Schulman, Elias, 2:32
Schulman, Grace, 1:864
Schulman, Howard, 5:537
Schulman, Ivan A., 2:845
Schulte, Hans, 2:991
Schulte, Joachin, 4:347
Schulte, Rainer, 2:991
Schultz, Bart, 4:257
Schultz, Fred, 3:252
Schultz, John, 3:607
Schultz, Marilyn Spigel,
    5:224
Schultz, Theodore W., 3:48,
    3:57, 3:66
Schulz, Hans Joachim, 4:694
Schulz, Max F., 1:920
Schulze, Franz, 3:783
Schumacher, Edgar, 1:251
Schumacher, Ernst F., 3:62,
    3:346, 5:76, 5:157, 5:824
Schumacher, Michael, 1:920
Schuman, Samuel, 1:1020
Schumann, Clara (Wieck),
    3:684, **3:715,** 3:716
Schumann, Ferdinand, 3:716
Schumann, Robert, 3:675,
    3:684, 3:713, 3:715, **3:716**
Schumm, Stanley A., 5:632,
    5:643
Schumpeter, Joseph Alois,
    3:46, 3:50, 3:75, 3:76, 3:87,
    3:94, 3:95, 3:98, **3:104,**
    3:140, 3:143
Schuon, Frithjof, 4:373,
    4:573, 4:576
Schur, Norman W., 1:91
Schürer, Emil, 4:605, 4:808
Schurer, Fedde, 2:634
Schurman, Reiner, 4:295
Schurr, Sam, 5:283
Schurts, Mary M., 4:5
Schutte, Ofelia, 3:632
Schutzer, Daniel, 5:569
Schuurman, Egbert, 5:72
Schuyler, George, 1:879
Schuyler, Hamilton, 5:224
Schwade, Arcadio, 4:534
Schwaderer, W. David, 5:302
Schwager, Jack, 3:56
Schwartz, Benjamin I., 3:468,
    3:472, 4:359, 4:525
Schwartz, Boris, 3:672
Schwartz, Charles, 3:696,
    3:709
Schwartz, Delmore, 1:946,
    1:1044
Schwartz, Edward, 1:870
Schwartz, Egon, 2:578
Schwartz, Elliot, 3:666
Schwartz, Helen J., 5:566
Schwartz, Henry, 3:864
Schwartz, Howard, 2:10,
    2:34, 2:42, 4:669

Schwartz, Jeffrey H., 5:780
Schwartz, Jerome, 2:497
Schwartz, Joseph, 5:11
Schwartz, Karlene V., 5:820
Schwartz, Kessel, 2:522,
2:526, 2:529, 2:847
Schwartz, Lawrence H.,
1:838
Schwartz, Leon, 4:196
Schwartz, Lita L., 4:858
Schwartz, Lloyd, 1:951
Schwartz, Mischa, 5:300
Schwartz, Murray M., 1:208
Schwartz, Narda L., 1:120
Schwartz, Regina M., 1:193
Schwartz, Ronald, 2:847
Schwartz, Sanford, 1:800
Schwartz, Seth, 4:666
Schwartz, Stephen L., 5:770
Schwartz, Stuart B., 3:634
Schwartz, Theodore, 3:15,
3:37
Schwartz, William B., 3:56,
5:327
Schwartzbach, Bertram,
4:218
Schwartzberg, Joseph E.,
3:482
Schwarz, Daniel R., 1:352
Schwarz, Leo W., 4:595
Schwarz, Michiel, 5:158
Schwarzchild, Bettina, 1:1034
Schwarzfuchs, Simon, 4:637
Schwarzlose, Richard A.,
3:809
Schwebel, Milton, 3:193
Schweber, William L., 5:300
Schwed, Peter, 1:44
Schweid, Eliezer, 4:673
Schweitzer, Albert, 4:740,
4:826
Schweitzer, Ivy, 1:629
Schweizer, Eduard, 4:822,
4:826
Schwendinger, Herman,
3:200
Schwendinger, Julia, 3:200
Schwenke, Karl, 5:266
Schwerdt, Lisa M., 1:501
Schwertner, Thomas M.,
4:107
Schwiebert, Ernest G., 4:779
Schwinger, Julian Seymour,
5:664, 5:685, 5:690, **5:715**,
5:717
Schyberg, Frederik, 1:708
Schyfter, Sara, 2:527
Sciacca, Michele F., 4:267
Sciascia, Leonardo, 2:400,
2:438, 2:441
Scigaj, Leonard M., 1:498
Scitovsky, Tibor, 3:64
Sclar, Deanna, 5:12

Scliar, Moacyr, 2:889, **2:899**
Scobbie, Irene, 2:671
Scobie, James R(alston),
3:633, **3:649**
Scodel, Ruth, 2:368
Scofield, Martin, 1:473
Scootin, Harry, 5:740
Scoppetone, Sandra, 1:1195
Scorer, Richard S., 5:634
Scott, A. C., 2:273
Scott, A. F., 1:132
Scott, Alan, 3:215, 4:63
Scott, Allen J., 3:135
Scott, Alma O., 1:1203
Scott, Andrew, 3:58, 5:783
Scott, Arthur L., 1:784
Scott, Bonnie Kime, 1:415
Scott, Charles, 5:437
Scott, Charles E., 4:22
Scott, Derek B., 3:663
Scott, Donald M., 3:512
Scott, Duncan Campbell,
2:926
Scott, Gini Graham, 4:865,
4:866
Scott, Harriet F., 3:280
Scott, H. G., 2:694
Scott, H. M., 3:338
Scott, James A., 5:762
Scott, J. F., 5:503
Scott, Joan E., 5:565
Scott, John A., 2:362
Scott, John P., 3:170
Scott, John S., 5:224
Scott, Judith A., 3:253
Scott, Mary Jane W., 1:261
Scott, Michael, 1:188, 3:687,
3:689
Scott, Patrick G., 1:345
Scott, R., 1:99, 4:795
Scott, Robert Falcon, 3:725,
3:889, 3:912, **3:936**
Scott, Ronald B., 5:368
Scott, Sir Walter, 1:204,
1:242, 1:264, 1:269, 1:275,
1:277, 1:281, 1:291, **1:298**,
1:316, 1:662, 1:690, 1:694,
1:695, 1:994, 1:1209,
1:1244, 2:406, 2:426,
2:578, 2:591, 2:826, 3:912
Scott, Tom, 1:418
Scott, William B., 1:392
Scott, William F., 3:280
Scott, William T., 5:714
Scott, W. R., 3:200
Scott-Kilvert, Ian, 1:127
Scotto, Robert M., 1:986
Scott-Stokes, Henry, 2:289
Scotus, John Duns. *See* Duns
Scotus, John
Scragg, Leah, 1:186
Scrascia, Euclide, 5:367

Screech, M. A., 2:497, 4:139,
4:146
Scriabin, Aleksandr, 3:717
Scribner, Charles, 3:792
Scribner, R. W., 3:334, 3:377
Scrimgeour, James, 1:527
Scriven, Michael, 4:24, 4:331,
5:80
Scrivener, Michael, 1:269
Scruggs, Charles, 1:860
Scruton, Roger, 4:189
Scudder, Horace E., 1:685
Scullard, H. H., 2:345, 2:380,
3:298, 3:303, 4:448, 4:818
Scully, James, 1:418
Scully, Marlan O., 5:698
Scully, Stephen, 4:483
Scully, Vincent, 3:798
Scult, Mel, 4:667
Seaborg, Glenn Theodore,
5:754
Seabrook, Jeremy, 5:423
Seabury, P., 3:280
Seager, Allen, 1:1038, 3:616
Seager, Joni, 5:116, 5:816
Seager, Robin, 3:311
Seal, John, 5:390
Seale, Patrick, 3:455
Sealts, Merton M., 1:671,
1:689
Sealy, I. Allan, 2:178
Seaman, L. C., 3:341
Sear, Frank, 3:305
Searle, Humphrey, 3:704
Searle, John, 4:383, 5:76
Searle, Townley, 1:358
Searles, George J., 1:1041
Sears, Donald A., 1:118
Sears, Jean L., 1:108
Sears, John F., 3:893
Sears, Minnie E., 1:125
Sears, Robert R., 3:170,
3:184
Seaton, Douglass, 3:663
Seaver, G., 4:275
Seaver, Paul S., 4:734
Seaver, Richard, 1:130
Sebag-Montefiore, Ruth,
4:637
Sebba, Gregor, 4:170
Sechler, Robert P., 1:381
Secor, Robert, 1:464
Secrest, Meryle, 3:798
Sedgewick, Robert, 5:551
Sedgwick, Alexander, 4:737
Sedgwick, Catharine Maria,
1:695, 1:1209, 1:1219
Sedgwick, Eve Kosofsky,
1:319, 1:1132, 1:1182
Sedgwick, Henry D., 4:74,
4:76
Sedley, D. N., 4:55
See, Fred G., 1:724

Seeberg, Peter, 2:646
Seed, David, 1:988
Seeger, Pete, 3:852
Seeger, Raymond J., 5:689,
    5:700, 5:747
Seeley, Frank F., 2:770
Seeley, John, 5:424
Seeley, Thomas, 5:771
Seelye, John, 1:629
Seeman, Jeffrey L., 5:729
Seeskin, Kenneth, 4:90, 4:596
Sefami, Jacobo, 1:123
Seferis, George, 2:370,
    2:375, **2:376**
Seforim, Mendele Mokher,
    2:7, 2:29, 2:40
Segal, Alan F., 4:605
Segal, Charles, 2:368, 2:388,
    2:394, 4:75, 4:475
Segal, Charles M., 1:632
Segal, Erich, 2:391
Segal, Gerald, 3:496
Segal, Hanna, 5:457
Segal, Julius, 3:168
Segall, Jacob, 3:856
Segall, J. B., 2:471
Segalman, Ralp, 3:378
Segel, Harold B., 2:690
Seghers, Anna, 2:564, **2:611**
Segraves, R. Taylor, 5:420
Segre, Emilio, 5:685, 5:716
Segre, Michael, 5:604, 5:689
Segur, Nicolas, 2:478
Sehmsdorf, Henning, 2:662
Seidel, Kathryn Lee, 1:850
Seidel, Ken, 5:553
Seidensticker, Edward G.,
    2:291, 3:479
Seidick, Kathryn, 5:406
Seidler, Victor J., 2:516
Seidman, Steven, 5:90
Seifert, Jaroslav, 2:788,
    2:794
Seifrid, Thomas, 2:749
Seigel, Catharine F., 1:810
Seigel, J. E., 4:131
Seigfried, Charlene H., 4:238
Seigneuret, Jean-Charles,
    1:132
Sein, Henneth, 2:313
Sei Shōnagon, 2:270, **2:279**
Seitz, Don C., 3:821
Seitz, William C., 3:783
Seixas, Judith S., 5:403
Selby, George, 5:393
Selden, Gary, 5:318
Selden, Kyoko Iriye, 2:283
Seldes, George, 1:117
Selig, Robert L., 1:359
Seligman, E.R.A., 3:5
Seligman, Milton, 5:420
Seligman, Paul, 4:51
Selimović, Meša, 2:827

Selinger, Suzanne, 4:762
Selkirk, Errol, 1:847
Selkitar, Ofira, 4:658
Sellar, William Young, 2:381
Sellari, Giuliano, 1:18
Sellars, Wilfrid, 4:162, 4:264,
    4:333
Sellars, W. V. Quine, 4:261
Sellassie, Sergew Hable,
    3:423
Seller, Maxine S., 1:1075
Sellers, Charles G., 3:514,
    3:525
Sellery, George C., 3:333
Sellery, J. M., 1:448
Sellin, Eric, 2:112, 2:452
Sellin, Thorsten, 3:205
Selons, Trista, 2:474
Selser, Gregorio, 3:639
Seltzer, Leon E., 5:618
Seltzer, Mark, 1:767
Seltzer, Robert M., 4:440,
    4:595, 4:667
Selver, Paul, 2:789, 2:833
Selvon, Samuel, 2:942
Selye, Hans, 3:171, 5:401
Selz, Jean, 3:794
Selz, Peter, 3:760
Selzer, Richard, 5:315
Selznick, Gertude J., 3:209
Selznick, Philip, 3:210
Semendyayev, K. A., 5:478
Semmel, Bernard, 3:363
Semmelweis, Ignaz, 5:390
Sen, Amartya K., 3:66
Sen, Samar, 2:176
Sen, Soshitsu, 4:538
Senanu, K. E., 2:113
Senasbaugh, George F., 1:180
Sendak, Maurice, 1:587,
    1:1194, **1:1206**
Seneca, Lucius Annaeus,
    1:168, 2:279, 2:387, 2:389,
    2:393, 2:393, 4:12, 4:59,
    4:87, 4:150, 4:760
Senelik, Lawrence, 2:710
Seng, Peter J., 1:221
Senghor, Leopold Sedar,
    2:104, 2:138, **2:146**
Senior, Donald, 4:798
Senior, Hereward, 3:612
Senior, John, 5:304
Senior, Michael, 3:358
Senior, Nassau William,
    1:344
Senkoro, F. E., 2:112
Senn, Fritz, 1:506
Sennett, Richard, 3:202,
    3:209, 3:217, **3:238**
Šenoa, August, 2:785, **2:787**
Septimus, Bernard, 4:629
Seredich, John, 5:816
Serels, M. Mitchell, 4:645

Serequeberhan, Tsenay, 4:26,
    4:369
Serge, Victor, 3:397
Sergeant, Elizabeth S., 1:822
Sergeant, John, 4:180
Sergios, Paul, 5:388
Serling, Robert J., 5:219
Serlio, Sebastiano, 3:755
Seroff, Victor, 3:710
Serrett, Karen D., 5:338
Serullaz, Maurice, 3:795
Serumaga, Robert, 2:156
Service, Elman R., 3:11,
    3:17, 3:18
Service, Robert, 3:287, 3:343
Sesiano, J., 5:504
Sesonske, Alexander, 3:842
Sessions, George, 5:822
Setchkarev, Vsevolod, 2:722,
    2:724
Seth, Andrew, 4:32, 4:203
Seth, Vikram, 2:178
Sethna, K. D., 4:337
Seton, Marie, 3:500
Seton-Watson, Christopher,
    3:386
Seton-Watson, Hugh, 3:395
Settar, S., 4:510
Settle, Mary Lee, 3:453,
    3:905
Setzer, Lynn, 3:806
Seuling, Barbara, 1:48
Seurat, Silvere, 5:215
Seuss, Dr., *See* Geisel, Theo-
    dor Seuss
Sevan-Schreiber, Jean
    Jacques, 3:346
**Ševčenko, Taras (also
    Shevchenko),** 2:837, **2:840**
Severin, Timothy, 3:905
Severo, Richard, 5:393
Sévigné, Mme de, 1:250,
    2:484, 2:485, **2:507**
Sewall, Gilbert T., 3:252
Sewall, Richard B., 1:748
Seward, Desmond, 3:376
Sewell, William H., 3:214
Sexton, Anne, 1:909, 1:911,
    1:950, 1:982, **1:1045**
Sexton, Linda, 1:1045
Sexton, Patricia Cayo, 5:338
Sextus Empiricus, 4:58
Seybold, John, 5:562
Seybold, Klaus, 4:824
Seyersted, Per, 1:740, 1:1047
Seyffert, Peter, 2:690
Seymour, Charles, 3:782
Seymour, Miranda, 1:767
Seymour, Raymond B., 5:729
Seymour, Richard J., 5:632
Seymour-Smith, Charlotte,
    3:11

Seymour-Smith, Martin,
1:132, 1:486, 2:3
Sforza, Carlo, 3:392
Shabad, Theodore, 5:280
Shabecoff, Philip, 3:206
Shackle, George L. S., 3:64
Shackleton, J. R., 3:70, 3:83,
3:91, 3:102
Shackleton, Robert, 3:163,
4:210
Shackleton Bailey, D. R.,
2:386
Shafarevich, I. R., 5:487
Shafer, Boyd C., 3:274
Shafer, Byron E., 3:144,
4:442
Shafer, Robert Jones, 3:9,
3:277
Shaffer, Ed, 5:241
Shaffer, E. S., 2:984
Shaffer, Howard J., 5:401
Shaffer, Jerome A., 4:383
Shaffer, John B., 5:414
Shaffer, Peter (Levin),
1:424, **1:543**
Shafii, Mohammed, 4:576
Shafritz, Jay M., 3:146, 3:147
**Shaftesbury, Anthony Ash-
ley Cooper,** 4:158, 4:203,
4:214
Shah, Haresh C., 5:636
Shah, Idries, 4:576
Shaham, Nathan, 2:23
Shahan, Robert, 4:107
Shahan, Robert G., 4:412
Shahan, Robert W., 4:35,
4:202, 4:295, 5:100
Shahane, Vasant Anant, 1:477
Shahar, David, 2:24
Shaheen, Esber I., 3:451
Shaheen, Naseeb, 1:220
Shahid, Irfan, 2:92
Shahnon Ahmad, 2:326
Shaikh, Shafi, 1:97
Shain, Michael, 3:802, 5:540,
5:546
Shakabpa, W. D., 4:356
Shaked, Gershon, 2:9, 2:10,
2:12
Shakespeare, William, 1:172,
1:183, 1:185, 1:186, 1:190,
1:202-222, 1:228, 1:236,
1:271, 1:286, 1:320, 1:397,
1:446, 1:448, 1:574, 1:686,
1:876, 1:970, 1:1069,
1:1129, 1:1193, 1:1226,
1:1253, 2:16, 2:95, 2:359,
2:367, 2:389, 2:391, 2:393,
2:406, 2:407, 2:414, 2:415,
2:416, 2:422, 2:426, 2:427,
2:440, 2:461, 2:531, 2:553,
2:610, 2:620, 2:981, 3:283,
3:318, 3:681, 3:746, 5:13

Shakow, David, 3:178, 3:184
Shalamov, Varlam, 2:755
Shaland, Irene, 1:1075
Shallcross, Martyn, 1:620
Shallis, Michael, 5:126
Shamberger, Raymond J.,
5:373
Shamir, Moshe, 2:24
Shammas, Anton, 2:24
Shan, Han, 2:184
Shanas, Ethel, 3:201
Shangold, Mona, 5:400
Shang-yin, Li, 2:205, 2:206
Shanin, Theador, 5:265
Shank, Michael H., 4:105
Shank, M. Thomas, 4:700
Shank, Theodore, 1:1076
Shanker, S. G., 4:347
Shanks, Susan J., 5:376
Shanley, J. Lyndon, 1:702
Shannon, Albert C., 4:700
Shannon, Barbara, 5:346
Shannon, Claude, 5:294,
5:542, 5:571, **5:580**
Shannon, Edgar F., 1:402
Shannon, Fred A., 3:600
Shannon, Thomas, 4:745,
5:123
Shapere, Dudley, 4:144, 5:65
Shapin, Steven, 4:175
Shapira, Anita, 4:658
Shapiro, Ann R., 1:724
Shapiro, Arnold, 5:485
Shapiro, Barbara, 1:268,
3:772
Shapiro, Charles, 1:422
Shapiro, David, 1:915, 1:936
Shapiro, Elliot, 3:659
Shapiro, Gilbert, 5:11, 5:711
Shapiro, Herbert, 3:557
Shapiro, Herman, 4:56,
4:121, 4:126
Shapiro, Howard I., 5:359
Shapiro, H. Svi, 3:257
Shapiro, Ian, 4:387
Shapiro, Judith, 3:470
Shapiro, Karl (Jay), 1:1045
Shapiro, Lamed, 2:44
Shapiro, Leonard, 2:770
Shapiro, Martin, 3:541
Shapiro, Mary B., 5:338
Shapiro, Michael, 1:170
Shapiro, Nat, 3:657, 3:669
Shapiro, Norman R., 2:931
Shapiro, Paul D., 5:338
Shapiro, Robert, 5:654, 5:765
Shapiro, Samuel, 1:666,
3:920
Shapiro, Stuart C., 5:76,
5:570
Shapland, David, 5:597
Shapley, Deborah, 5:182

Shapley, Harlow, 5:602,
5:612
Sharer, Robert J., 4:455
Sharma, Arvind, 4:355,
4:506, 4:509, 4:514, 4:526,
4:528, 4:553, 4:563, 4:892
Sharma, B. N., 4:506
Sharma, Jagdish, 4:498
Sharma, J. S., 3:500
Sharma, K. K., 2:183
Sharma, Nasira, 2:84
Sharot, Stephen, 4:630,
4:634, 4:651
Sharov, Alexander S., 5:607
Sharp, Cecil J., 3:852
Sharp, Dennis, 3:762, 3:764
Sharp, Gene, 3:145
Sharp, Harold, 3:731
Sharp, Marjorie Z., 3:731
Sharpe, Eric J., 4:420, 4:422
Sharpe, M. E., 3:79
Sharpe, Mitchell R., 5:613
Sharpe, Tony, 1:1020, 2:742
Sharpe, William F., 3:49,
3:56
Sharples, R., 4:90
Sharps, J. G., 1:356
Sharqawi, 'Abd al-Rahman,
2:59
Shattock, Joanne, 1:349
Shattuck, Charles H., 1:218
Shattuck, Roger, 2:451,
2:496, 3:663
Shatzkin, Leonard, 1:50
Shatzman, Avi-Yonah, 3:298
Shatzman, Israel, 3:298
Shaver, Philip, 3:169, 3:207
Shaviro, Steven, 2:461
Shavit, David, 3:437, 3:463,
3:509
Shaw, Anna M., 3:865
Shaw, Arnold, 3:657, 3:666
Shaw, Bradley A., 2:847
Shaw, Elizabeth M., 5:632
Shaw, George Bernard,
1:210, 1:321, 1:331, 1:356,
1:367, 1:388, 1:423, 1:438,
1:440, 1:442, 1:446, 1:492,
1:496, 1:532, **1:544,** 2:605,
2:665, 3:926
Shaw, Henry, 1:92
Shaw, J. Thomas, 2:752
Shaw, Marion, 1:402
Shaw, Patrick W., 1:822
Shaw, Paul, 1:19
Shaw, Ralph, 3:511
Shaw, Ralph R., 1:68
Shaw, Ronald E., 5:224
Shaw, S. J., 3:453
Shaw, T. E., 2:360
Shaw, W. David, 1:402
Shaw, W. H., 3:290
Shaw, William Napier, 5:647

Shawn, Ted, 3:743, 3:751, 3:752
Shawqi, Ahmad, 2:73
Shayevitz, Berton, 5:398
Shayevitz, Myra, 5:398
Shaykh, Hanan, 2:59
She, Lao, 2:266
Shea, Daniel B., 1:629
Shea, Thomas F., 1:526
Shea, William R., 4:144, 4:172, 5:43, 5:689, 5:712
Shead, James A., 1:838
Sheaffer, John R., 5:245, 5:632
Sheaffer, Louis, 1:1108
Sheaffer, Robert, 5:598
Sheagren, Thomas, 5:323
Shealy, Daniel, 1:1199
Shean, Glenn, 5:428
Shear, Howard J., 5:420
Shearer, Benjamin F., 3:204, 3:802
Shedd, Robert G., 2:4
Sheehan, Donald, 1:38
Sheehan, Edmund W., 4:859
Sheehan, John C., 5:315
Sheehy, Eugene P., 1:63, 1:74, 1:81, 4:716
Sheehy, Gail, 5:356
Sheets-Pyenson, Susan, 5:47
Sheffield, Margaret, 5:782
Shefter, Martin, 3:143
Shein, Louis J., 4:31, 4:335
Shelanski, Vivien B., 3:210
Shelden, Michael, 1:531
Sheldon, Garret Ward, 1:641
Sheldon, Jennifer W., 5:771
Sheldon, Sidney, 1:1222
Sheldrake, Rupert, 5:198
Shelford, Victor E., 5:821
Shellabarger, Samuel, 1:236
Shelley, Mary Wollstone-craft, 1:264, 1:269, 1:281, **1:300,** 1:591, 1:598, 1:603, 1:635, 1:1209, 1:1239, 1:1251, 5:563
Shelley, Percy Bysshe, 1:264, 1:267, 1:271, 1:273, 1:281, 1:297, 1:300, **1:301,** 1:313, 1:314, 1:598, 1:635, 2:250, 3:676
Shelov, Steven P., 5:323
Shelp, Earl E., 5:80, 5:123
Shelston, Alan, 1:429
Shelton, John S., 5:627
Shelton, Roy C., 2:594
Shelton, Suzanne, 3:752
Shemel, Sidney, 3:657
Shen Fu, 2:218, 2:253, 2:268
Shenker, Israel, 4:595
Shen Ts'ung-wen, 2:249, **2:262,** 2:263
Sheohmelian, O., 3:856

Shepard, Carroll A., 5:356
Shepard, Francis P., 5:632
Shepard, Mark, 4:553
Shepard, Martin, 5:465
Shepard, Sam, 1:1071, 1:1089, **1:1110**
Shepard, Sanford, 2:523
Shepard, Thomas H., 5:737
Shephard, Bruce D., 5:356
Shepherd, A. P., 4:880
Shepherd, Margaret, 1:19
Shepherd, Michael, 5:449
Shepherd, Simon, 1:170, 1:187
Shepherd, William C., 4:857
Shepherd, William R., 3:9, 3:273
Sheppard, Helen E., 5:3
Sheppard, John Tresidder, 2:990
Sheppard, J. T., 2:351, 2:368
Sheppard, Judith, 1:78
Sheppard, Roger, 1:78
Sheppherd, Joseph, 4:861
Sherbiny, Nalem A., 3:437
Sherbo, Arthur, 1:255
Sherburne, Donald W., 4:343
Shereshevsky, Esra, 4:671
Sheridan, Daniel P., 4:506
Sheridan, James, 3:472
Sheridan, Richard Brinsley, 1:228, **1:254,** 1:383
Sheridan, Thomas B., 5:243
Sheriff, Robert E., 5:618
Sherk, Robert K., 3:300
Sherlock, Helen, 2:931
Sherlock, Philip M., 2:931
Sherman, Eric, 3:828
Sherman, J., 3:178
Sherman, James H., 5:773
Sherman, Joan R., 1:655, 1:656, 1:719, 1:720, 1:775
Sherman, Sarah W., 1:771
Sherman, William L., 3:639
Shermis, Michael, 4:5
Sherrard, Philip, 2:371
Sherrill, Robert, 5:241
Sherry, Norman, 1:489
Sherry, Ruth, 1:1127
Sherry, Suzanna, 3:141
Sherwin, Byron L., 4:665
Sherwin, Martin J., 3:280, 3:535
Sherwin-White, A. N., 2:392, 3:306
Sherwood, Eva R., 5:807
Sherwood, John C., 1:743
Sherwood, M., 5:729
Sherwood, William R., 1:748
Shestov, Lev, 2:690, 2:716, 4:247, **4:334**
Shetter, William Z., 2:621, 3:383

Shevelow, Kathryn, 1:231
Shewfelt, Robert L., 5:267
Shi, David E., 3:514, 3:561
Shibutani, Tamotsu, 3:203
Shideler, Ross, 2:674
Shields, Carol, 2:921
Shields, Steven L., 4:846
Shiffert, Edith, 2:283
Shiflett, Lee, 1:78
Shifreen, Lawrence J, 1:863
Shiga Naoya, 2:281, **2:292**
Shih, Chung-wen, 2:191
Shih, Hu, 2:211, 2:232
Shih, Vincent, 2:191
Shih-chen, Wang. See Wang Shih-Chen
Shih Nai-an, 2:185, 2:212, **2:218**
Shiki, Masaoka. See Masaoka Shiki
Shikibu, Izumi. See Izumi Shikibu
Shikibu, Murasaki. See Murasaki Shikibu
Shillington, Kevin, 3:416, 3:424
Shillony, Ben-Ami, 3:479
Shiloah, Amnon, 4:597
Shils, Edward, 3:202, 3:214, **3:238**
Shilstone, Frederick, 1:284
Shilts, Randy, 5:388
Shimazaki Tōson (Shimazaki Haruki), 2:281, **2:292**
Shimei, Futatabei. See Futabatei Shimei
Shimer, John A., 5:627
Shimoda, Koichi, 5:666
Shimron, Binyamin, 4:480
Shindul, Judith, 5:318
Shine, Helen Chadwick, 1:274
Shine, Hill, 1:274
Shine, Ian B., 5:808
Shine, Ted, 1:1078
Shinkokai, Kokusai B., 2:283
Shinn, Larry D., 4:862, 4:863
Shinn, Roger L., 5:130, 5:198
Shipka, Thomas A., 4:22
Shipley, G., 3:308
Shipley, Joseph T., 2:3
Shipman, Harry L., 5:594, 5:597
Shipps, Jan, 4:846
Shipton, Clifford K., 1:68
Shirane, Haruo, 2:279
Shirer, William L., 3:344, 3:377, 4:553
Shires, Linda M., 1:313
Shirley, Peggy F., 1:177
Shirley, R. W., 5:33
Shirvanzadeh, 2:79
Shiva, Vandana, 5:188, 5:824

Shivers, Alfred S., 1:1082
Shluim, Leonard, 5:194
Shmeruk, Khone, 2:34
Shneiderman, Ben, 5:558
Shneidman, Edwin S., 5:428
Shneidman, N. N., 2:690
Shober, Joyce Lee, 1:499
Shockley, William, 5:671
Shoemaker, Adam, 2:946
Shoemaker, Richard H., 1:68, 3:511
Shoemaker, William H., 2:524
Shojai, Siamack, 5:280
Sholevar, Bahman, 2:84
Sholokhov, Mikhail, 2:755
Sholom Aleichem, 2:45
Shōnagon, Sei. *See* Sei Shōnagon
Shook, Lawrence K., 4:286
Shook, Robert, 5:543
Shore, John, 5:538
Shore, Kenneth, 3:257
Shore, Sammy, 3:872
Shores, Louis, 1:81
Shorey, Paul, 4:84
Shorley, Christopher, 2:497
Short, Douglas D., 1:144
Short, James F., Jr., 3:204
Short, Luke, 1:1218
Short, Sam, 3:867
Shorter, A. W., 4:548
Shorter, Clement K., 1:333
Shorter, Edward, 5:315
Shortliffe, Edward H., 5:80
Shortt, S.E.D., 3:615
Shostakovich, Dmitri, 3:710, 3:717
Shostrom, Everett, 5:424
Shoukri, Ghali, 3:446
Shoumatoff, Alex, 3:905
Showalter, Elaine, 1:319, 1:716, 1:926, 1:1046, 1:1132, 1:1134, 1:1143, 1:1152, 2:989
Showalter, English, 2:465
Showerman, Grant, 2:386
Showman, Richard, 3:506
Shrader-Frechette, Kristin S., 5:76, 5:116, 5:130, 5:140
Shreve, G. M., 2:112
Shri Priyadarsha, 4:510
Shrobe, Howard E., 5:549
Shrout, Richard N., 5:368
Shryock, Richard H., 5:36
Shu, Frank H., 5:589
Shucard, Alan R., 1:655, 1:800, 1:824
Shue, Vivienne, 3:472
Shuffelton, Frank, 1:641
Shukla, Srilal, 2:178
Shukshin, Vasily, 2:756

Shulman, Frank J., 3:473
Shulman, Julius, 5:384
Shulman, Lee S., 5:79
Shulman, Neil, 5:332
Shulman, Robert, 1:716
Shumway, David R., 4:401
Shuntaro, Tanikawa. *See* Tanikawa Shuntaro
Shupe, Anson D., Jr., 4:846, 4:855, 4:857, 4:871
Shurkin, Joel N., 5:538
Shūsaku, Endō. *See* Endō Shūsaku
Shusterman, David, 1:550
Shute, Nevil, 2:962
Shuttleworth, Ughtred James, 1:368
Shwadran, Benjamin, 3:437
Shweder, Richard, 3:15
Shy, John W., 3:511, 3:522
Sibelius, Jean, 2:659, 3:718
Sibley, Brian, 1:1165
Sibley, M.J.N., 5:304
Sibley, William F., 2:292
Siburapha, 2:335, 2:336
Sicari, Stephen, 1:874, 2:418
Sicher, Efraim, 2:700
Sichronovsky, Peter, 4:637
Sick, Gary, 3:546
Siculus, Diodorus, 5:485
Siddigri, A. H., 3:444
Siddiq, Muhammad, 2:67
Siddique, Kaukab, 3:448
Sidel, Ruth, 5:315, 5:329
Sidel, Victor W., 5:315, 5:329
Sidenbladh, Erik, 5:359
Sider, Ronald J., 5:112
Sidgwick, Henry, 4:158, 4:256
Sidhwa, Bapsi, 2:178
Sidney, Sir Philip, 1:163, 1:164, 1:167, 1:185, 1:195, 1:197
Sidorsky, David, 4:641
Sieber, Harry, 2:544
Siebold, Cathy, 5:379
Siebt, Johanna, 4:334
Siefert, Marsha, 3:801
Siegal, Frederick P., 5:388
Siegal, Marta, 5:388
Siegel, Ben, 2:36, 2:49
Siegel, Bernard J., 3:11
Siegel, Lee, 2:173
Siegel, Marcia B., 3:732, 3:733, 3:744
Siegel, Mary-Ellen, 5:373
Siegel, Paul N., 2:762
Siegel, Richard, 4:602
Siegel, Seymour, 4:655
Siegfried, Robert, 5:743
Siegman, Gita, 1:135
Siekevitz, Philip, 5:130

Sienkiewicz, Henryk, 2:810, 2:819, 2:821
Sieveking, Ann, 3:760
Siever, Raymond, 5:624
Sievers, David, 1:1076
Sievers, Joseph, 4:605
Sievers, Sharon L., 3:479
Siffin, William J., 3:490
Sigal, Phillip, 4:595, 4:655
Sigelman, Lee, 3:212
Sigerist, Henry E., 5:36
Sigg, Eric Whitman, 1:473
Sigmund, Paul E., 3:635, 4:149
Sigworth, Oliver F., 1:236, 1:289
Sikelianos, Angelos, 2:376
Sikes, Edward E., 2:388
Sikes, J. G., 4:106
Sikorsky, Robert, 5:248
Šilbajoris, Rimvydas, 2:766, 2:805
Silber, Nina, 3:527
Silberger, Julius, 4:875
Silberman, Bernard S., 3:463
Silberman, Charles E., 3:205, 3:252, 4:641
Silbermann, Marc D., 2:566
Silbernagl, Stefan, 5:773
Silberschatz, Abraham, 5:560
Silberschlag, Eisig, 2:9, 2:25
Silberstein, Laurence J., 4:643, 4:662
Silbey, Robert J., 5:735
Silet, Charles L., 1:752
Silitch, Clarissa M., 3:858
Silk, E., 4:756
Silk, Joseph, 5:594, 5:654, 5:656
Silk, Leonard, 3:72, 3:91, 3:104
Silkin, Jon, 1:430
Silko, Leslie Marmon, 1:1046, 1:1135
Sill, Geoffrey, 1:240
Sillanpää, Frans Eemil, 2:657, 2:660
Sillanpoa, Wallace P., 4:638
Sillery, Anthony, 3:424
Sillitoe, Alan, 1:419, 1:546
Sillitoe, Linda, 1:35
Sills, Beverly, 3:718
Sills, David L., 3:5, 3:210
Sills, Stephanie, 1:1079
Silone, Ignazio, 2:438
Silva, António José da, 2:557
Silva-Núñez, Caridad, 2:848
Silver, Alain, 3:826
Silver, Arnold Jacques, 1:546
Silver, Carole, 1:92, 1:383
Silver, Daniel, 5:428
Silver, Daniel J., 4:595, 4:598
Silver, Rollo G., 1:19, 1:38

Silverblatt, Irene, 4:458
Silveria, Terry, 5:305
Silverman, Hugh J., 4:267, 4:392, 4:398, 4:402
Silverman, Kaja, 1:1132, 1:1158
Silverman, Kenneth, 1:629, **1:1047**
Silverman, Milton M., 5:352
Silverman, Sydel, 3:11, 3:28
Silverman, William A., 5:123
Silversmith, Ernest F., 5:725
Silverstein, Arthur M., 5:315
Silverstein, Shel(by), 1:586, 1:1195, **1:1206**
Silverstein, Y., 4:602
Silz, Walter, 2:566, 2:599
Sim, Katharine, 2:324
Simak, Clifford, 1:1252, **1:1262**
Simenon, Georges, 2:508
Šimić, Antun Branko, 2:785
Simic, Charles, 1:910, **1:1047**
Simkin, Penny, 5:359
Simkin, Tom, 5:630
Simmel, Georg, 3:204, **3:239,** 3:242
Simmonds, James D., 1:200
Simmons, Charles, 1:916
Simmons, Ernest J., 2:710
Simmons, James C., 1:959
Simmons, Leo W., 3:12
Simmons, Richard C., 5:424
Simmons, William S., 3:858
Simms, Bryan R., 3:666
Simms, Norman, 2:971, 2:990
Simms, William Gilmore, 1:695, 1:1244
Simon, Alfred, 3:656
Simon, A. R., 5:558
Simon, Claude, 2:509
Simon, Eckehard, 1:157
Simon, George T., 3:669
Simon, Harvey B., 5:326
Simon, Herbert, 1:9, 1:11
Simon, Herbert A., 3:49, 3:147, 3:175, 3:210, 5:76
Simon, Kate, 3:553
Simon, Marc, 1:823
Simon, Marcal, 4:615, 4:616
Simon, Maurice, 4:630
Simon, Neil, 1:436, 1:1071, **1:1111**
Simon, Oliver, 1:11
Simon, Reeva, 3:419
Simon, Ruth B., 5:630
Simon, Yves R., 4:71, 4:307
Simone, Charles, 5:373
Simoneau, Karin, 4:466
Simonet, Henri, 3:382
Simonov, Konstantin, 2:756
Simons, Geoff, 5:574

Simons, Herbert W., 1:818
Simons, John, 1:177
Simons, Judy, 1:235
Simons, Thomas W., 3:346
Simonson, G. R., 5:219
Simonson, Harold P., 1:716
Simonson, Maria, 5:347
Simonsuuri, Kirsti, 2:658
Simony, Maggy, 3:893
Simopoulos, Artemis P., 5:327, 5:781
Simpkins, C. O., 3:690
Simpson, Claude M., 3:657
Simpson, David, 1:308, 1:652
Simpson, D. P., 1:101
Simpson, Eileen, 1:914
Simpson, George E., 3:32, 4:468
Simpson, George G., 3:18, 5:639
Simpson, Jeffrey, 3:616
Simpson, Lewis P., 1:652
Simpson, Louis, 1:951, **1:1048**
Simpson, Theodore R., 5:597
Simpson, William K., 2:53, 3:300, 4:442
Sims, James H., 1:187, 1:220
Sims, Janet L., 3:761
Sims, Norman, 1:808
Simson, Otto G. von, 4:701
Sinaiko, Herman L., 4:84
Sinasi, Ibrahim, 2:96
Sinatra, Frank, 3:719, 3:730
Sinatra, Nancy, 3:719
Sinclair, Andrew, 1:775, 1:1166
Sinclair, Brett J., 5:320
Sinclair, Clive, 2:49
Sinclair, Keith, 3:494, 3:495
Sinclair, L., 3:295
Sinclair, Patti, 5:816
Sinclair, Sandra, 5:771
Sinclair, Upton (Beall), 1:879, 2:624
Sinclair, W. A., 3:494
Sincovec, Richard, 5:553
Sinfield, Alan, 1:208
Singer, Beth, 4:328
Singer, Charles J., 5:26, 5:34, 5:36, 5:39
Singer, Dorothea W., 4:136
Singer, Howard, 4:649
Singer, Isaac Bashevis, 1:916, **1:1048,** 2:29, 2:40, **2:46,** 2:49
Singer, I(srael) J(oshua), 2:47, **2:49**
Singer, J. David, 3:149
Singer, Jerome E., 5:321
Singer, Kenneth S., 5:424
Singer, Kurt, 3:474
Singer, Merrill, 3:212

Singer, Michael, 3:829
Singer, Milton B., 4:506
Singer, Peter, 5:123
Singer, Peter Albert David, 4:37, **4:43,** 4:389
Singer, Sam, 5:765, 5:778
Singh, Amritjit, 2:171
Singh, Bhagwan B., 4:250
Singh, Chaitram, 3:637
Singh, G., 2:428
Singh, Karen Lee, 4:59
Singh, Khushwant, 2:178, 4:517
Singh, Shukdev, 2:174
Singleton, Carole, 1:1072
Singleton, Fred, 3:381, 3:393
Singleton, Loy A., 5:230, 5:297
Singleton, Marvin, 1:860
Sinn, Gerlinde, 3:52, 3:59
Sinn, Hans-Werner, 3:52, 3:59
Sinnott, Edmund Ware, 5:811
Sinnott, R. W., 5:591
Sinor, John, 3:893
Sinyard, Neil, 1:1165
Sinyavsky, Andrei, 2:690, 2:747, **2:757,** 2:772
Sipihri, Suhrab, 2:84
Sipra, Paul, 3:936
Sirat, Colette, 4:629
Sirk, Douglas, 1:1175, 3:842
Sirota, Adair, 5:359
Sisler, Harry H., 5:730
Sisson, Charles Jasper, 1:185
Sisson, Clint, 1:8
Sister Nivedita, 4:563
Sitarz, Daniel, 3:206
Sitkoff, Harvard, 3:540
Sitney, P. Adams, 1:1158
Sitter, John E., 1:226
Sittig, Marshall, 5:737
Situmorang, Sitor, 2:316
Sitwell, (Dame) Edith, **1:547,** 1:800, 1:971, 1:1033, 2:72
Sitwell, Sacheverell, 3:704
Siu, Helen F., 2:235
Sivan, Emanuel, 4:573
Sivan, Raphael, 5:299
Sivirine, Alexis, 3:908
Sizemore, Russell F., 4:896
Sizemore, Russell R., 4:514
Sizer, Theodore, 3:268
Sjoberg, Gideon, 3:217
Sjöberg, Leif, 2:673, 2:676
Sjöstrand, Östen, 2:671, 2:672
Skaggs, Calvin, 1:725, 1:806
Skaggs, Merrill M., 1:822
Skaggs, Peggy, 1:740
Skalbe, Kārlis, 2:803
Skard, Sigmund, 3:381

Skármeta, Antonio, 2:885
Skaryna, Francišak, 2:783
Skaug, R., 5:300
Skeat, Walter W., 1:96, 2:324
Sked, Alan, 3:367
Skelton, Geoffrey, 3:700,
  3:729
Skelton, John, 1:162, **1:196**
Skelton, R. A., 1:631, 3:900
Škema, Antanas, 2:805
Skemp, J. B., 4:84
Skempton, A. W., 5:255
Skendi, Stavro, 2:779
Skidmore, Felicity, 3:59
Skidmore, Max J., 3:140
Skidmore, Thomas E., 3:632,
  3:634
Skillend, William E., 2:298
Skillin, Marjorie E., 1:118
Skinner, A. S., 3:107
Skinner, Andrew, 4:215
Skinner, Brian J., 5:625,
  5:626, 5:637, 5:639
**Skinner, B(urrhus)
  F(rederic)**, 3:166, 3:176,
  3:193, 3:268, 5:81, 5:434,
  5:469
Skinner, G. William, 3:466,
  3:469
Skinner, John, 1:452
Skinner, Quentin, 4:105,
  4:131
Skinner, Robert E., 1:1228
Skirbekk, Gunnar, 4:32
Sklar, Bernard, 5:297
Sklar, Lawrence, 5:68
Sklar, Martin J., 3:549
Sklar, Mary, 1:921
Sklar, Robert, 3:553, 3:561,
  3:827
Sklare, Marshall, 4:641, 4:655
Skocpol, Theda, 3:215
Skole, David, 5:282
Skolimowski, Henryk, 4:38,
  5:72
Skolnick, Jerome H., 3:145
Skolnik, Herman, 5:729
Skolnikoff, Eugene B., 5:158
Skomal, Susan S., 4:436
Skorupski, John, 4:245
Skotheim, Robert Allen,
  3:566, 3:567, 3:590
Skousen, Eric N., 5:112
Skowronski, Joann, 3:867
Skram, Amalie, 2:662, **2:668**
Skrupskelis, Ignas K., 1:769
Skura, Meredith, 1:926
Skutch, Alexander F., 5:766
Škvorecký, Josef, 2:788,
  2:794
Skydsgaard, Erik, 3:304
Skyrms, Brian, 5:65

Slaby, Andrew Edmund,
  5:377
Slade, Ruth, 3:421
Sladovich, Hedy E., 5:158,
  5:215
Slater, Candace, 3:856
Slater, Michael, 1:349, 1:351
Slater, Niall W., 2:391
Slater, Robert, 3:812
Slater, Robert H., 4:573
Slatoff, Walter J., 1:795
Slaughter, Frank G., 1:1223
Slavens, Thomas P., 4:15
Slavin, Robert E., 3:257
Slavitt, David R., 2:397
Slavov, Atanas, 2:781
Sleeper, James A., 4:641
Sleeper, R. W., 4:225
Sleigh, Robert, 4:164, 4:178
Slessor, Kenneth, 2:945,
  2:962
Slinn, E. Warwick, 1:315,
  1:339
Sloan, David, 3:809
Sloan, Douglas, 5:566
Sloan, Frank A., 5:333
Sloan, Irving J., 3:507
Sloan, Philip, 5:45
Sloane, David A., 2:703
Sloane, David E., 1:784
Sloane, Eric, 5:634
Slobin, Greta N., 2:754
Slobin, Mark, 3:853, 3:869
Slobogin, Christopher, 3:139
Slocum, Joshua, 3:937
Slocum, Robert E., 5:198
Slocum, Victor, 3:937
Slodnjak, Anton, 2:835
Slomcynski, Kazimierz M.,
  3:215
Slonim, Marc, 2:690
Slonim, Morris J., 5:524
Slonimsky, Nicholas, 3:657
Sloss, Radha Rajogopal,
  4:556
Slosson, Edwin E., 5:513
Slote, Bernice, 3:857
Slote, Michael, 4:389
Slotkin, Richard, 1:652,
  1:724, 3:525
Slowacki, Juliusz, 2:810,
  2:819
Sluckis, Mykolas, 2:805
Sluga, Hans, 4:230
Slusser, George E., 1:615,
  2:762
Slusser, R. M., 3:293
Smakov, Gennady, 3:738
Small, Ian, 1:387
Small, John, 5:618
Small, Judy J., 1:748
Small, Melvin, 3:149
Small, Miriam R., 1:679

Small, R. J., 3:119
Small, Stuart G. P., 2:384
Smalley, Beryl, 4:102, 4:628,
  4:697
Smalley, Donald, 1:407
Smallman, R. E., 5:238
Smallwood, Philip, 1:430
Smal-Stocki, Roman, 2:780
Smarr, Janet L., 2:403
Smart, Christopher, 1:255
Smart, James R., 5:487
Smart, Ninian, 4:422, 4:426,
  4:499, 4:523, 4:535, 4:741,
  4:884
Smart, Thomas B., 1:328
Smeaton, John, 5:254
Smedinghoff, Thomas J.,
  5:558
Smeed, John William, 2:985
Smelik, K.A.D., 4:812
Smelser, Neil J., 3:200,
  3:203, 3:215
Smetana, Bedřich, 3:719
Smethurst, Richard J., 3:479
Smiles, Samuel, 5:218, 5:249,
  5:250, 5:256
Smiley, Jane, 1:909, **1:1050**,
  1:1053
Smirnitsky, A. I., 1:102
Smirnov, B. M., 5:653
Smit, Eefke, 5:10
Smit, J. W., 3:383
Smit, P., 3:383
Smith, A. J., 1:178
Smith, Adam, 3:93, **3:105**,
  4:158, 4:200, **4:214**
Smith, Alexander M., 3:857
Smith, Alistair, 3:774
Smith, Anne, 1:511
Smith, Annick, 3:896
Smith, Anthony, 3:905
Smith, B., 3:177
Smith, Barbara, 1:927, 1:1184
Smith, Bardwell L., 3:474,
  4:518
Smith, Bernard, 3:918
Smith, Bradley F., 3:377
Smith, Brian K., 4:501
Smith, Bruce L. R., 5:183
Smith, C. Alphonso, 1:757
Smith, C. G., 5:634
Smith, Carol H., 1:473
Smith, Charles H., 5:812
Smith, Charles P., 3:176
Smith, Charles W., 1:30
Smith, Christian, 4:747
Smith, Colin, 2:537, 4:28
Smith, Constance, 3:210
Smith, D. Moody, 4:826
Smith, Datus C., Jr., 1:48
Smith, Dave, 1:914
Smith, David, 3:369
Smith, David Eugene, 5:31

Smith, David G., 5:618
Smith, David N., 1:242
Smith, David W., 5:783
Smith, Dawn L., 2:524
Smith, Denis, 3:344, 3:608
Smith, Dennis, 3:200, 5:35
Smith, Denzell S., 1:170
Smith, Dick, 5:577
Smith, Donald B., 3:606
Smith, Doris C., 5:367
Smith, Dwight L., 3:511
Smith, Elizabeth H., 4:316
Smith, Elton E., 1:389
Smith, Emil L., 5:774
Smith, Evans Lansing, 2:985
Smith, F. B., 5:363
Smith, Frank, 1:368
Smith, G., 3:280
Smith, G. E. Kidder, 3:764
Smith, Gaddis, 3:546
Smith, George, 3:354
Smith, Gerard, 4:131
Smith, Gertrude S., 2:344
Smith, Goldwin, 3:615
Smith, Gordon Ross, 1:221
Smith, Gregory White, 1:35
Smith, Greg W., 1:35, 3:787
Smith, Grover, 1:858
Smith, Hallett D, 1:165
Smith, Hedrick, 3:398, 3:809
Smith, Henry Nash, 1:652,
   1:658, 1:784, 3:533
Smith, H. Shelton, 4:752
Smith, J., 3:274, 5:261
Smith, J. I., 4:887
Smith, James Allen, 5:184
Smith, James E., 5:806
Smith, James W., 4:752
Smith, Jane A., 5:123
Smith, Jeffrey A., 3:809
Smith, Jessie C., 3:507
Smith, John, Jr., 5:48
Smith, John D., 3:509, 3:557
Smith, John E., 4:35, 4:250,
   4:267, 5:352
Smith, John Maynard, 5:766,
   5:795
Smith, John W., 5:635
Smith, Jonathan E., 4:767
Smith, Jonathan Z., 4:438,
   4:451, 4:470, 4:473, 4:487,
   4:490
Smith, Joseph, Jr., 4:845,
   4:846, **4:878**
Smith, Joseph H., 1:440
Smith, Karlene V., 5:768
Smith, Keith A., 1:26
Smith, Kelly S., 5:357
Smith, Kenneth R., 5:332
Smith, Kerri S., 5:318
Smith, Lacey B., 3:359
Smith, Lawrence R., 2:403
Smith, Lendon, 5:347

Smith, Leslie, 1:388
Smith, Linda C., 1:73
Smith, Logan P., 1:96
Smith, M., 3:170
Smith, Margo L., 3:11
Smith, Marilyn, 4:25
Smith, Mark S., 4:824
Smith, Maxwell A., 2:489
Smith, Maynard, 5:798
Smith, Michael B., 4:311
Smith, Michael P., 3:669,
   3:867
Smith, Morton, 3:298, 4:451,
   4:604
Smith, Nathan M., 5:261
Smith, Nelson, 1:292
Smith, Nicholas, 3:217
Smith, Nicholas D., 4:89
Smith, Nigel, 1:630
Smith, Norman Kemp, 4:171,
   4:202, 4:206
Smith, Page, 3:522, 3:525,
   3:530, 5:263
Smith, Paul, 1:847, 1:1134
Smith, Peggy, 1:53
Smith, Peter, 4:383, 4:861
Smith, Peter H., 3:632
Smith, Philip, 1:26
Smith, Preserved, 4:139
Smith, Ralph Bernard, 3:359
Smith, Richard B., 5:352
Smith, Richard Bernard,
   3:491
Smith, Richard Furnald,
   5:729
Smith, Robert, 3:421
Smith, Robert J., 3:474,
   3:480, 5:428
Smith, Robert W., 5:49,
   5:590
Smith, Roch C., 4:274
Smith, Roger, 3:365, 3:491
Smith, Roger C., 5:762
Smith, Roger H., 1:48, 1:50
Smith, Roland, 2:112
Smith, Sally B., 3:820
Smith, Samuel, 3:168
Smith, Sarah W., 1:254
Smith, Sidonie, 1:376, 1:928
Smith, Stan, 1:558
Smith, Steven, 4:233
Smith, Stevie, 1:414, **1:548**
Smith, T. Burton, 5:315
Smith, Thomas, 5:505
Smith, Thomas C., 3:93,
   3:476, 3:480, **3:502**
Smith, Thomas V., 4:36,
   4:163
Smith, Timothy, 1:512, 4:754
Smith, Tony, 3:346
Smith, Valene, 3:891
Smith, Valerie, 1:920
Smith, Vassar W., 2:694

Smith, Vincent, 5:12
Smith, Warren Hunting,
   1:263
Smith, Warren Sylvester,
   1:546
Smith, Wilfred Cantwell,
   4:422, 4:423, 4:427, 4:573
Smith, William, 2:347
Smith, William A., 4:285
Smith, William J., 1:579,
   1:1197, 2:891
Smith, William Robertson,
   4:428, **4:491**
Smith, Wilson, 3:255
Smithberger, Andrew T.,
   1:728
Smithers, G. V., 1:147
Smithers, Peter, 1:232
Smock, Raymond W., 1:786
Smolan, Rick, 5:315
Smolar, Leivy, 4:609
Smolla, Rodney, 3:809
Smoller, Bruce, 5:393
Smollett, Tobias (George),
   1:229, **1:256,** 1:662, 2:383
Smolowe, John S., 5:319
Smoryński, Craig, 5:489
Smrek, Jan, 2:833
Smuts, R. Malcolm, 3:360
Smyth, Frank, 5:344
Smyth, Herbert W., 2:351
Smythe, Colin, 1:490
Snaith, Clifton U., 1:402
Snapper, Johan P., 2:621
Snapper, John, 5:159
Sneader, Walter, 5:352
Snell, Bruno, 2:347, 4:49
Snellgrove, David L., 4:356
Snelling, N. J., 5:625
Sniderman, Florence M.,
   1:427
Snikere, Velta, 2:803
Snipes, Katherine, 1:486,
   1:894
Snitow, Ann, 1:476, 1:1184
Snoddaigh, Padraig O., 3:370
Snodgrass, Adrian, 4:538
Snodgrass, Anthony M., 3:302
**Snodgrass, W(illiam)
   D(ewitt),** 1:1051
Snorgrass, J. William, 3:802
Snow, David A., 4:860
Snow, Edgar, 3:472
Snow, Edward (Rowe),
   3:937
**Snow, Lord C(harles)
   P(ercy),** 1:419, 1:536,
   1:549, 5:18, 5:49, 5:158,
   5:183, 5:534, 5:652, 5:686
Snow, Loudell F., 5:331
Snow, Philip, 1:550
Snow, Theodore P., 5:589
Snowden, Frank M., 3:299

Snowman, Daniel, 3:693
Snurr, Georgia H., 2:517
Snyder, Franklin B., 1:281
Snyder, Gary, 1:491, 1:911, 1:998, 1:1036, **1:1051,** 2:198, 4:853
Snyder, Graydon F., 4:689
Snyder, Louis L., 3:338, 3:351, 3:377
Snyder, Marilyn, 5:397
Snyder, Mary Hembrow, 4:785, 4:905
Snyder, Robert Lance, 1:290
Snyder, Solomon H., 5:428
Snyder, Susan, 1:213
Snyder, William S., 4:24
Sobchack, Thomas, 3:827
Sobel, B. Zvi, 4:643, 4:864
Sobel, Dava, 5:598
Sobel, Robert, 3:374
Sober, Elliott, 5:68
Soccio, Douglas J., 4:24
Socha, John, 5:555
Sô Chông-ju, 2:307
Socknat, Thomas, 3:608
Socrates, 2:343, 2:351, 2:353, 3:163, 3:323, 4:11, 4:44, 4:50, 4:52, 4:53, 4:76, **4:88,** 4:91, 4:238, 4:314
Södergran, Edith, 2:655, 2:657, **2:660**
Sodhi, Devinder S., 5:225
Sodi, Risa B., 2:425
Soelle, Dorothee, 4:750
Sofer, Tehoeda, 4:894
Soffer, Olga, 4:433
Sofola, Zulu, 2:147
Sofowora, Abayomi, 5:320
Sofue, Takao, 3:464, 4:531, 4:539
Sogliuzzo, A. Richard, 2:436
Sokoloff, B. A., 1:948, 1:1061
Sokoloff, Boris, 4:223
Sokolov, Raymond, 3:814
Sokolov, Sasha (Aleksandr), 2:758
Sokolov, Yury M., 2:690
Sokolow, Nahum, 3:351
Sokolowski, Robert, 4:235
Soled, Debra E., 4:532
Soll, Robert W., 5:393
Sollers, Werner, 1:941, 1:1085
Sollie, Eddie C., 5:356
Solmsen, Friedrich, 2:351, 2:358, 4:71, 4:84
Sologub, Fedor, 2:683, **2:758**
Solomon, Barbara H., 1:921
Solomon, Deborah, 3:787
Solomon, Maynard, 3:678
Solomon, Robert C., 4:20, 4:24, 4:248, 4:267
Solomos, Alexis, 2:354

Soloukhin, Vladimir, 2:759
Soloveitchik, Joseph, 4:673, 4:886
Soloveytchik, George, 3:378
Solow, Robert M., 3:49, 3:51, 3:60
Solowey, Fred J., 3:808
Soltes, Mordecai, 2:32
Soltis, Jonas F., 3:258
Solzhenitsyn, Aleksandr, 2:683, 2:718, 2:755, 2:756, **2:759,** 2:771, 2:772, 3:346, 3:395, 3:397
Somekh, Sasson, 2:69
Somer, Elizabeth, 5:345, 5:347
Somers, Gerald G., 3:74
Somerville, John, 4:31
Somit, Albert, 3:138
Sommer, Doris, 2:847
Sommers, Ronald K., 5:380
Sondheim, Stephen, 3:720
Sôn-do, Yun, 2:298
Sonne, Jørgen, 2:646
Sonnenberg, David, 5:374
Sonnevi, Göran, 2:672
Sontag, Frederick, 4:240
Sontag, Raymond J., 3:344
Sontag, Susan, 1:1052, 3:740
Soong, Stephen C., 2:191, 2:236
Šop, Nikola, 2:785
Sopa, Geshe Lhundup, 4:544
Sophocles, 1:1091, 2:342, **2:366,** 2:593, 4:474
Šopov, Aco, 2:807
Sorabji, Richard, 4:66, 4:71
Sorauf, Frank J., 3:143, 3:144
Sorden, L. G., 3:861
Sordi, Marta, 4:684
Sorel, Georges, 3:140
Sorensen, Roy A., 4:385
Sørensen, Villy, 2:394, **2:654**
Sorescu, Marin, 2:823
Sorin, Gerald, 4:656
Sorkin, Alan, 5:333
Sorochan, Walter D., 5:342
Sorokin, Pitirim A., 3:221, 3:233, **3:240**
Sorrell, Charles A., 5:628
Sorrell, Martin, 2:494
Sorrell, Tom, 4:175
Sorrentino, Fernando, 2:857
Sorrentino, Sandy, 5:374
Sosa, Ernest, 4:192, 5:101
Sōseki, Natsume. *See* Natsume Sōseki
Sot, Dokmai, 2:334
Souchon, Edmond, 3:669
Součkova, Milada, 2:789, 2:833
Soufas, Teresa S., 2:523
Souhami, Diana, 1:883

Soule, Michael E., 5:821
Soulen, Richard N., 4:815
Soulsby, Basil H., 5:806
Soumaoro, Bourama, 2:126
Souritz, Elizabeth, 3:734
Sours, John A., 5:395
Soustelle, Jacques, 4:455
South, Margaret Tudor, 2:206
Southern, David W., 3:99
Southern, Eileen, 3:658, 3:663
Southern, Richard, 1:161
Southern, Richard W., 4:96, 4:108, 4:691, 4:703
Southey, Herder, 2:537
Southey, Robert, 1:264, 1:273, 1:277, 1:281, **1:304,** 1:324, 2:406
Southgate, Minoo, 2:84
Southmayd, William, 5:400
Southwell, Samuel B., 1:339, 1:818
Southworth, E.D.E.N., 1:1219, **1:1224**
Souza, Márcio, 2:889, **2:899**
Souza, Raymond D., 2:847
So-wôl, Kim. *See* Kim So-wôl
Soyinka, Wole, 2:104, 2:112, 2:125, **2:147**
Spacks, Patricia Ann Meyer, 1:228, 1:230, 1:231
Spadaccini, Nicholas, 2:536
Spade, Paul Vincent, 4:104
Spaeth, Janet, 1:1209
Spahn, Janet M., 1:72
Spahn, Mark, 1:100
Spahn, Theodore J., 1:72
Spain, David H., 3:12
Spalding, Frances, 1:549
Spalding, Henry D., 3:867, 3:872
Spalding, J. Howard, 4:880
Spallone, Patricia, 5:188, 5:782
Spangenburg, Ray, 5:45
Spanos, William, 1:426, 3:258
Spargo, Emma J., 4:113
Spark, Muriel, 1:301, 1:414, 1:420, 1:519, **1:550**
Sparkes, Ivan G., 1:94
Sparks, Colin, 3:806, 3:872
Sparr, Arnold, 1:795
Spate, O.H.K., 3:483
Spatola, Adriano, 2:403
Spatz, Lois, 2:351
Speaight, Robert, 1:218
Spear, Percival, 3:486
Spear, Thomas, 3:422
Spearing, A. C., 1:147, 1:156
Spears, Monroe K., 1:418, 1:436
Spears, Richard A., 2:126

Specht, Walter, 4:798
Speck, W. A., 3:363
Spector, Robert, 1:257, 2:676
Spector, Ronald, 3:536
Spedding, C. R., 5:264
Speer, Albert, 3:378
Speigler, Gerhard, 4:254
Spek, Peter van der, 3:671
Speke, John H., 3:910
**Spence, Jonathan
D(ermott)**, 3:467, 3:469,
3:472, **3:502**
Spence, Kenneth W., 3:176
Spencer, Benjamin, 1:795
Spencer, Frank, 3:11
Spencer, Herbert, 1:11,
1:395, **3:240, 4:245**
Spencer, Isobel, 1:584
Spencer, Katherine, 3:865
Spencer, Michael, 2:463
Spencer, Robert F., 4:573
Spencer, Roger W., 3:44,
3:69, 3:77, 3:88, 3:103,
3:108
Spencer, Samuel R., 1:786
Spencer, Sharon, 1:866
Spencer, Terence J., 1:206,
1:220, 2:371
Spencer, Theodore, 1:178
Spencer, William, 3:437
Spencer-Carr, Virginia,
1:1009
Spender, Sir Stephen,
1:416, 1:418, 1:422, 1:434,
1:511, 1:517, **1:552**
Spengemann, William C.,
1:658, 1:716
Spengler, Oswald, 3:291,
3:345, 3:393
Spenser, Edmund, 1:163,
1:164, 1:179, 1:196, **1:197**,
2:368, 2:389, 2:396, 2:406,
3:877, 4:182
Sperber, A. M., 3:819, 4:796
Sperber, Manes, 5:431
Sperling, Daniel, 5:290
Spero, Joan E., 3:145
Spero, Moshe Halevi, 4:890
Sperry, Roger W., 5:108
Sperry, Stuart M., Jr., 1:294
Spevack, Martin, 1:216
Spicehandler, Ezra, 2:9
Spicker, Stuart F., 5:78, 5:79,
5:80, 5:81, 5:93, 5:123
Spidlik, Tomas, 4:679
Spiegel, Dixie L., 1:34
Spiegel, Henry William, 3:46,
3:69, 3:73, 3:74, 3:94,
3:110, 3:113
Spiegel, Shalom, 4:621
Spiegelberg, Herbert, 4:235,
4:267
Spiegelman, Art, 4:637

Spiegel-Rösing, Ina, 3:214,
5:61, 5:149
Spiegler, Gerhard E., 4:349
Spiegler, M., 3:178
Spielberg, Nathan, 5:651,
5:735
Spielmann, M. H., 1:585
Spier, Leslie, 3:40
Spies, Walter, 3:734
Spigel, Lynn, 3:812
Spignesi, Stephen J., 1:1241
Spilka, Mark, 1:511, 1:847
Spillane, Mickey, 1:1226,
1:1237
Spiller, Robert E., 1:134,
1:630, 1:716
Spillman, Carolyn V., 3:849
Spilner, Maggie, 5:325
Spindel, Carol, 3:905
Spink, John S., 4:28, 4:163
Spink, Kathryn, 4:746
Spink, Wesley W., 5:36
Spinka, Matthew, 3:334,
4:711, 4:721
Spinoza, Baruch, 2:630,
4:12, 4:158, 4:167, 4:171,
4:175, **4:186,** 4:197, 4:208,
4:209, 4:628, 4:673
Spirer, Herbert F., 5:522
Spires, Robert C., 2:525
Spiro, Audrey, 4:526
Spiro, Melford E., 3:24, 3:36,
4:519, 4:643, 4:890
Spitz, Lewis W., 4:691, 4:723,
4:730
Spitzberg, Irving J., 3:252
Spitzer, Lyman, 5:594
Spitzer, Robert L., 5:428
Spivak, Charlotte, 1:1260
**Spivak, Gayatri Chakravor-
ty,** 1:1132, **1:1152**
Spivey, Ted R., 1:810
Splash, Clive, 3:48
Splaver, Sarah, 5:524
Spleth, Janice, 2:147
Spletter, Mary, 5:373
Spock, Benjamin, 1:1003,
5:323
Spong, John, 4:746
Sposito, Garrison, 5:264
Spoto, Donald, 1:1170
Sprafka, Sarah A., 5:79
Sprague, Arthur Colby, 1:212,
1:218
Sprague, Paul E., 3:793
Sprague, Rosamond Kent,
4:54
Sprent, Peter, 5:524
Spriano, P., 3:293
Sprigge, Timothy, 4:328
Spriggs, D. G., 4:834, 4:838
Sprinchorn, Evert, 2:680
Spring, Joel, 3:258

Springarn, Natalie Davis,
5:369
Springer, Carolyn, 2:402
Springer, Marlene, 1:740
Sprinker, Michael, 1:365
Sprintzen, David A., 4:24
Sproat, John G., 3:533, 3:595
Sproul, Barbara C., 4:427
Sproull, Robert F., 5:565
Sproxton, Judy, 1:552
Spruill, Julia Cherry, 3:518
Spuhler, J. N., 3:175
Spurgeon, Caroline, 1:217
Spurling, Hilary, 1:462
Spurr, Daniel, 3:897
Squadrito, Kathleen M.,
4:181
Squire, Aelred, 4:690
Squires, E., 5:662
Squyres, Wendy, 5:332
Sremac, Stevan, 2:827
Srinawk, Khamsing, 2:335
Srinivas, M. N., 3:486
Srinivasan, Bhama, 5:513
Srzednicki, J., 4:222
Staar, Richard F., 3:389
Stabb, Martin S., 2:847,
2:857
Stableford, Brian, 1:612
Stacey, C. P., 3:608, 3:612
Stacey, John., 4:714
Stachel, J., 5:664
Stachniewski, John, 1:630
Stack, George J., 4:240
Stacy, Robert H., 2:690
Stade, George, 2:4
Stadter, Philip A., 3:312,
3:318
Staël, Mme de, 2:510
Stafford, Mark, 1:832
Stafford, Maureen, 3:765
Stafford, William, 3:707
Stafford, William (Edgar),
1:1053
Stagnelius, Erik Johan, 2:670
Staguhn, Gerhard, 5:595
Stahl, Hans-Peter, 2:392
Stahl, William H., 5:39
Staiger, Janet, 1:1157
Staines, David, 1:402
Stainton, Elsie Myers, 1:48
Stairs, Denis, 3:608
Staley, Thomas, 1:506, 1:541,
2:941
Stalin, Joseph, 1:530, 1:550,
3:291, 3:294, 3:394, 3:822,
4:321
Stalker, Douglas, 5:320
Stallabrass, Julian, 3:784
Stalley, R. F., 4:84
Stallings, William, 5:300
Stallknecht, Newton P., 2:984
Stallman, Robert W., 1:743

Stallsworth, Paul, 4:895
Stallworthy, Jon, 1:533
Stallybrass, Peter, 1:170
Stam, Robert, 1:1158
Stambaugh, Joan, 4:295, 4:538
Stambaugh, John E., 4:446
Stambler, Irwin, 3:658, 3:666, 3:853
Stambolian, George, 1:1184, 2:448
Stamm, James R., 2:523
Stamp, Dudley, 5:621
Stamp, Patricia, 5:188
Stampp, Kenneth M(ilton), 3:525, 3:530, **3:598**
Stanaszek, Mary, 5:6
Stanbury, Sarah, 1:156
Stancu, Zaharia, 2:823, **2:826**
Standard, Paul, 1:19
Standish, Paul, 4:295
Standley, Fred L., 1:1084
Stanesby, Derek, 5:198
Stanescu, Nichita, 2:823
Stanford, Ann, 1:635
Stanford, Barbara Dodds, 1:954
Stanford, Derek, 1:316, 1:334
Stanford, Donald, 1:800
Stanford, William Bedell, 2:362, 2:985
Stang, Sondra J., 1:476
Stange, G. Robert, 1:316, 1:328
Staniforth, Maxwell, 4:704
Stankiewicz, W. J., 3:140
Stanley, George F. G., 3:612, 3:615
Stanley, Julian C., 3:6
Stanley, Manfred, 5:73
Stanley, Sir Henry Morton, 3:929, 3:930, **3:937**
Stanley, Steven M., 5:624, 5:639
Stanley, William D., 5:300
Stanley-Baker, Joan, 3:760
Stannard, David E., 3:557, 3:917, 4:735
Stannard, Martin, 1:563
Stansell, Christine, 3:525
Stansfield, Jeoffrey, 3:758
Stansky, Peter, 1:383, 1:531, 3:341
Stanton, Domna, 2:448
Stanton, Edward F., 1:847, 2:539
Stanton, H. V., 4:587
Stanton, Robert J., 1:959, 1:1062
Stanton, Stephen S., 1:1118
Stanton, William B., 3:525, 3:897

Stanworth, Michelle, 5:188
Stapanian, Juliette R., 2:739
Stape, J. H., 1:567
Staples, Shirley, 3:874
Stapleton, Darwin H., 5:29
Stapleton, Laurence, 1:864
Stapleton, Margaret L., 1:445
Stares, Paul B., 5:597
Starhawk, 4:865
Stark, Freya, 3:938
Stark, Henry, 5:300
Stark, John O., 1:1035
Stark, Oded, 3:60
Stark, Rodney, 4:855, 4:857
Starke, Aubrey H., 1:772
Starkey, Edward D., 4:7
Starkie, Enid, 2:457, 2:500
Starkie, Walter, 2:436
Starobin, Robert, 3:525
Starobinski, Jean, 2:492, 3:338
Starosciak, Kenneth, 1:1043
Starr, Chester G., 3:299
Starr, John Bryan, 4:362
Starr, Paul, 3:553, 5:315
Starr, R. H., Jr., 5:416
Starr, R. M., 3:69
Starr, William T., 2:501
Starrett, D. A., 3:69
Starrett, Vincent, 1:34
Stassinopoulis, Arianna, 3:687
Staten, Henry, 4:398
Statius, Publius Papinius, 2:379, **2:394**
Statler, Oliver, 4:539
Statt, David, 3:169
Staub, Jacob J., 4:659
Staude, John-Raphael, 5:456
Staude, J. R., 4:332
Staudohar, Paul D., 3:60
Stauffer, Donald Barlow, 1:719
Staugaard, Andrew G., 5:569
Stavig, Mark, 1:180
Stavrianos, Leften, 3:274
Stavrou, Theofanis G., 2:375, 3:394
Stayer, James M., 4:724
Stea, David, 3:206
Stead, Christina, 1:418, 2:945, **2:963,** 2:971
Steadman, Susan M., 1:123
Steane, J. B., 1:187
Stearn, Colin, 5:639
Stearn, W. T., 5:806
Stearns, Jean, 3:733
Stearns, Marshall Winslow, 3:669, 3:733
Stearns, Peter N., 3:327, 4:741
Stearns, Stephen C., 3:18
Stebbins, G. Ledyard, 5:780
Stebbins, Lucy, 1:407

Stebbins, Richard, 1:407
Stechow, Wolfgang, 3:771
Ste.-Croix, G.E.M. de, 3:299
Stedman, Edmund C., 1:656
Stedman, Preston, 3:663
Steed, S. Paul, 5:327
Steegman, John, 3:790
Steegmuller, Francis, 2:451, 2:469, 2:476, 3:834
Steel, Danielle, 1:1223
Steel, Rodney, 5:639
Steel, Ronald, 3:158, 3:809, 3:815
Steele, Elizabeth, 1:570
Steele, Sir Richard, 1:230, 1:232, **1:257**
Steele, William Paul, 1:332
Steen, Lynn A., 5:479, 5:480, 5:482
Steenbergen, G. J., 4:15
Steenberghen, F. van, 4:97, 4:119
Steene, Birgitta, 2:680
Steene, Sara J., 1:190
Steenson, Gary, 3:481
Steere, Jane, 5:123
Steeves, Edna, 1:229
Steeves, Richard, 5:397
Stefaniszyn, B., 2:113
Stefanovski, Goran, 2:807, **2:809**
Stefansson, Vilhjalmur, **3:939**
Steffan, Truman Guy, 1:284
Steffen, Jerome O., 3:515
Stefflre, Buford, 5:417
Stefoff, Rebecca, 3:693
Steger, Will, 3:907
Stegman, S. J., 5:399
Stegmueller, Wolfgang, 4:29, 4:268
Stegner, Mary, 1:725, 1:806, 1:921
Stegner, Wallace, 1:725, 1:806, 1:921, **1:1053,** 3:525, 3:576, 5:646
Stein, Allen F., 1:724
Stein, Arnold S., 1:178, 1:181
Stein, Benjamin, 5:236
Stein, Burton, 3:484
Stein, Dorothy, 5:578
Stein, Edith, 5:816
Stein, Edward, 1:1184
Stein, Gertrude, 1:844, **1:880,** 1:1191, 2:432, 3:724
Stein, Herbert, 3:55, 3:62, 3:67
Stein, J. Stewart, 5:225
Stein, Laszlo, 5:428
Stein, Leonard, 3:351, 5:424
Stein, Maurice R., 3:217
Stein, Murray, 5:456
Stein, Richard L., 1:313

Stein, Robert M., 3:44
Stein, Rolf A., 4:356, 4:520,
    4:523, 4:534, 4:544
Stein, Stephen J., 3:561,
    4:754, 4:850, 4:389
Steinbeck, John (Ernst),
    1:803, **1:883**, 3:910, 5:632
Steinberg, Ada, 2:701
Steinberg, David Joel, 3:481,
    3:489, 3:493
Steinberg, Deborah Lynn,
    5:188
Steinberg, Franz U., 5:377
Steinberg, Jules, 4:181
Steinberg, Milton, 4:596,
    4:621, 4:634, 4:655
Steinberg, S. H., 1:11, 2:4
Steinberg, Stephen, 3:209
Steinberg, Theodore L., 2:41
Steinbock, Bonnie, 5:124
Steinbrink, Jeffrey, 1:784
Steinbrugge, Karl V., 5:625
Steiner, Gary A., 3:204
Steiner, George, 1:1054,
    2:766, 2:801, 2:985, 2:989,
    2:991, 4:295
Steiner, Jean Francis, 3:351
Steiner, Nancy H., 1:1031
Steiner, Peter, 2:690
Steiner, Richard P., 5:320,
    5:730
Steiner, Roger, 1:98
Steiner, Rudolf, 4:248,
    4:852, 4:858, **4:879**
Steiner, Wendy, 2:988
Steinfirst, Susan, 3:850
Steinhaus, Hugo, 5:495, 5:497
Steinkraus, Warren E., 4:192
Steinman, Lisa M., 1:800
Steinman, Michael, 1:528
Steinmann, Marion, 5:396
Steinmetz, David C., 4:779
Steinmetz, Sol, 2:30
Steinsaltz, Adin, 4:613, 4:669
Steintrager, James, 3:151
Stella, Joseph G., 3:789
Stellman, Jeanne, 5:354
Stelter, Benjamin F., 1:339
Stemberger, G., 4:613
Stempel, Tom, 3:812
Stenberg, Peter, 2:30, 4:637
Stendahl, Krister, 4:617
Stendhal (Henri Beyle),
    2:445, **2:510**
Stenerson, Douglas C., 1:860
Stengers, Isabelle, 5:68, 5:735
Stenius, Erik, 4:347
Stent, Gunther S., 5:108
Stenton, Doris M., 3:357
Stenton, Frank M., 3:356
Stepansky, Paul E., 5:431,
    5:458
Stephans, A., 5:262

Stephen, Leslie, 3:151, 4:175,
    4;245
Stephens, Edward M., 1:556
Stephens, E. H., 3:51
Stephens, J. D., 3:51
Stephens, John, 1:1196
Stephens, John Russell, 1:323
Stephens, Mitchell, 3:809
Stephens, W. P., 3:334, 4:791
Stephenson, Charles L., 4:217
Stephenson, F. Douglas,
    5:420
Stephenson, Jonathan, 5:194
Stepney, Rob, 5:404
Stepto, Robert B., 1:808,
    1:928, 1:1128
Sterba, James, 4:160, 5:112
Sterling, Bruce, 5:547, 5:563
Sterling, Keir B., 5:806
Stern, Bernhard J., 3:37
Stern, Chaim, 4:600
Stern, Curt, 5:807
Stern, David, 2:9, 4:613
Stern, Fritz, 3:378
Stern, Irwin, 2:890
Stern, Joseph P., 2:603,
    3:345, 3:378, 4:248
Stern, Madeleine B., 1:34,
    1:38, 1:78, 1:673, 1:1199
Stern, Paul C., 5:283
Stern, Zelda, 2:235
Sternberg, Josef von,
    1:1175, 3:843
Sternberg, R., 3:175
Sternberg, Richard, 5:631
Sterne, Harold E., 1:26
Sterne, Laurence, 1:225,
    1:247, 1:256, **1:258**, 2:471,
    2:730
Sternlicht, Sanford V., 1:461,
    1:483, 1:519, 1:549, 1:553
Stetkevych, Suzanne, 2:56
Stetler, Susan, 1:86
Stetson, Erlene, 1:720
Stevanovic, Bosiljka, 2:690
Stevans, C. M., 3:849
Stevens, Earl E., 1:483
Stevens, Halsey, 3:677
Stevens, H. Ray, 1:483
Stevens, John E., 3:663
Stevens, Laura J., 5:386
Stevens, Leonard A., 5:245,
    5:632
Stevens, Martin, 1:159
Stevens, Maryann, 5:376
Stevens, Michael, 1:542
Stevens, Paul, 3:605
Stevens, Peter S., 5:487
Stevens, Richard, 3:182
Stevens, Stuart, 3:905
Stevens, Victor, 5:826

Stevens, Wallace, 1:480,
    1:560, 1:668, 1:795, 1:806,
    1:886, 1:935, 1:954, 1:1138
Stevenson, Anne, 1:951
Stevenson, Bruce, 3:354
Stevenson, Burton Egbert,
    1:115, 1:117, 1:221
Stevenson, Catherine Barnes,
    1:325
Stevenson, David L., 1:806,
    1:921
Stevenson, Elizabeth, 1:730
Stevenson, J., 4:689
Stevenson, John, 3:326, 3:354
Stevenson, Lionel, 1:316,
    1:379, 1:404
Stevenson, Louise, 3:561
Stevenson, Robert Louis,
    1:332, **1:395**, 1:577, 1:589,
    1:598, 2:731
Stevick, Philip, 1:806, 1:922
Steward, Julian H., 3:14,
    3:18
Stewart, Allegra, 1:883
Stewart, Anthony, 3:371
Stewart, David, 4:24
Stewart, Desmond, 4:573
Stewart, Garrett, 1:351
Stewart, George R., 1:756
Stewart, Gordon T., 3:614
Stewart, Ian, 5:199, 5:497
Stewart, J. A., 4:71
Stewart, James B., 3:56,
    3:530, 3:549
Stewart, Joseph, Jr., 3:256
Stewart, M. A., 4:32
Stewart, R. D., 5:558
Stewart, Rachel, 3:742
Stewart, Seumas, 1:34
Stewart, Walter, 5:449
Stewart, Wilson N., 5:640
Sticht, Thomas G., 1:49
Stick, David, 3:518
Stiebing, William H., Jr.,
    5:598
Stigler, George Joseph,
    3:46, 3:58, 3:64, 3:101,
    3:107, 3:114
Stigler, James W., 3:15
Stigler, Stephen M., 5:524,
    5:526
Stilgoe, John R., 3:550, 3:553
Stiller, W., 5:738
Stillinger, Jack, 1:266
Stillman, John M., 4:150
Stillman, John Maxson, 5:729
Stillman, Norman A., 4:626,
    4:645
Stillman, Richard J., Jr.,
    3:147
Stillwell, Margaret Bingham,
    1:67
Stillwell, Richard, 3:298

Stilman, Leon, 2:722
Stimpson, Brian, 2:513
Stimson, Frederick S., 2:848
Stimson, James A., 3:148
Stinchcombe, Arthur L.,
3:205
Stineback, David C., 1:632
Stineman, Esther L., 1:733
Stinson, J., 1:538
Stinson, John J., 1:454
Stirewalt, Edward N., 5:289
Stitcher, Teresa L., 5:32
Stites, Frances N., 3:522
Stobaugh, Robert, 5:283
Stock, Catherine M., 3:536
Stock, Irvin, 1:1008
Stock, Janet C., 2:496
Stockenström, Göran, 2:680
Stockhausen, Karlheinz,
3:720
Stocking, George W., Jr.,
3:11, 3:12, 3:28
Stocks, John L., 4:71
Stockton, David, 3:314
Stoddard, Florence J., 3:857
Stoddard, Lothrop, 4:573
Stoddard, Philip, 4:573
Stoeger, William R., 5:198
Stoesz, William, 4:541
Stoianovich, Traian, 3:277,
3:392
Stoker, Bram, 1:591, 1:601,
1:602, 1:1239
Stoker, James J., 5:487
Stokes, Anthony, 2:686
Stokes, Donald W., 5:821,
5:827
Stokes, Lilian, 5:827
Stokes, Michael C., 4:51
Stokes, Roy, 1:61
Stokes, W. Lee, 5:625
Stoler, Ann Laura, 3:491
Stoll, Anita K., 2:524
Stoll, Clifford, 5:547
Stoll, John E., 1:511
Stoltzfus, Ben, 2:501
Stommel, Elizabeth, 5:634
Stommel, Henry, 5:634
Stone, Brian, 1:147
Stone, Christopher D., 5:76,
5:116, 5:141, 5:824
Stone, David, 5:770
Stone, Deborah A., 5:331
Stone, I. F., 3:481, 4:649
Stone, Irving, 1:775, 1:1249,
3:795
Stone, John L. S., 5:772
Stone, Julius, 3:145
Stone, Lawrence, 3:359,
3:408, 4:735
Stone, M. David, 5:548
Stone, Michael E., 2:77,
4:615, 4:616

Stone, Norman, 3:343
Stone, Richard O., 5:624
Stone, Robert, 1:1054
Stone, Roger D., 3:634, 3:897
Stone, Samuel Z., 3:626
Stonehill, Charles A., 1:77
Stonehill, H. Winthrop, 1:77
Stoneman, Elvyn A., 3:273
Stoneman, Patsy, 1:356
Stoner, K. Lynn, 3:625
Stoppard, Miriam, 5:360
Stoppard, Tom, 1:357,
1:424, 1:535, 1:553
Storey, Charles A., 2:83
Storey, David, 1:531
Storey, Edward, 1:286
Storey, Graham, 1:365
Storey, John, 3:874
Storing, Herbert J., 3:543
Storm, Colton, 1:34
Storr, Anthony, 5:456
Story, Norah, 3:606
Stouck, David, 2:905
Stough, Charlotte L., 4:58
Stout, Earl J., 3:862
Stout, Harry, 4:767
Stout, Jeffrey, 4:893
Stout, Rex, 1:1237
Stovall, Floyd, 1:708
Stove, D. C., 4:203, 5:54
Stover, Carl F., 5:72
Stow, Randolph, 2:964
Stowe, Charles Edward,
1:699
Stowe, Harriet Beecher,
1:697, 1:752, 1:1070
Stowe, William W., 2:454
Stower, Caleb, 1:11
Strabo, 4:492, 5:485
Strachan, Paul, 4:519
Strachan-Davidson, J. L.,
2:385
Strachey, Lytton, 1:542, 1:569
Strack, H. L., 4:613, 4:812
Strahan, Hew, 3:280
Strahler, Alan H., 3:126,
5:621
Strahler, Arthur N., 3:126,
5:621
Strand, David, 3:472
Strand, Mark, 1:912, 1:915,
1:995, 1:1048, 1:1055
Strand, Richard, 1:1079
Strandberg, Victor H., 1:894
Strandes, Justus, 3:423
Strange, Roderick, 4:891
Strangelove, Michael, 5:548
Strasberg, Lee, 1:1079
Strassberg, Richard E., 2:191
Strassburg, Gottfried von.
See Gottfried von Strass-
burg
Strasser, Susan, 3:549, 5:189

Strassfeld, Michael, 4:600,
4:602
Strassfeld, Sharon, 4:602
Strater, Felix R., 5:543
Strathern, Marilyn, 3:16
Stratman, Carl J., 1:157,
1:272
Stratton, G. M., 4:91
Straub, Kristina, 1:1183
Straub, LaVonne A., 5:333
Straub, Peter, 1:1239, 1:1243
Straumanis, Alfreds, 2:804
Straus, Erwin, 5:469
Straus, Joseph Nathan, 3:666
Straus, Murray A., 5:424
Straus, Ralph, 1:40
Strauss, Gerald, 4:731
Strauss, L., 2:354
Strauss, Leo, 3:154, 3:160,
3:163, 4:90, 4:91, 4:145,
4:175, 4:189
Strauss, Richard, 2:592,
3:721
Strauss, Walter L., 3:774
Strausz, Ivan K., 5:356
Stravinsky, Igor, 2:560,
3:722, 3:741, 3:749
Stravinsky, Theodore, 3:723
Stravinsky, Vera, 3:723
Straw, Carol, 4:711
Strawn, John, 5:565
Strawson, Galen, 4:203
Strawson, Peter F., 4:207,
4:261, 4:321, 4:335, 4:379,
4:413
Strayer, Joseph R., 3:332,
4:94
Strean, Herbert S., 3:184,
5:448
Strecker, Edward Adam,
5:415
Street, Annie, 3:638
Street, John, 5:158, 5:183
Street, P. R., 5:263
Strēlerte, Veronika, 2:803
Strelka, Joseph, 1:927
Streng, Frederick J., 4:423
Strenski, Ivan, 4:420, 4:427,
4:428
Stresemann, Erwin, 5:34
Streusand, Douglas E., 3:484
Stribley, Miriam, 1:19
Strickland, Edward, 3:666
Strickland, Geoffrey, 2:511
Strickland, Walter W., 3:857
Strieber, Whitley, 4:870
Strieder, Peter, 3:774
Strier, Richard, 1:181
Strike, Kenneth A., 3:258
Striker, Gisela, 4:56
Strindberg, (Johan) August,
1:1070, 2:637, 2:664,
2:665, 2:671, 2:675, 2:679

Stringer, Jenny, 1:132
Stritar, Josip, 2:834
Strizower, Schifra, 4:645
Strniša, Gregor, 2:835
Strobel, Darrell F., 5:624
Strober, Deborah H., 3:540
Strober, Gerald S., 3:540
Strode, Hudson, 3:575
Stroheim, Erich von,
1:1177, 3:844
Stroll, Avrum, 4:23, 4:24
Stromberg, Roland N., 3:327,
4:27
Strong, Carson, 5:118
Strong, Donald, 3:760
Strong, Polly, 3:418
Strong, Steven J., 5:284
Strong-Boag, Veronica, 3:616
Stross, Randall E., 3:472
Stroud, Barry, 4:203
Stroud, Richard H., 5:816
Stroup, Donna F., 5:522
Strouse, Jean, 1:761, **1:1055**
Strout, Cushing, 1:716, 1:928,
3:567
Strozier, Robert M., 4:74
Strugatsky, Arkady, 2:762
Struhl, Karsten J., 4:24
Struhl, Paula R., 4:24
Struik, Dirk J., 5:31, 5:492
Strumpf, Michael, 1:93
Strunk, Oliver, 3:663
Strunk, William, Jr., 1:118
Strutt, Robert John, fourth
Baron Rayleigh, 5:716
Struve, Gleb, 2:690
Stryer, Lubert, 5:732
Stuart, A. R., 1:45
Stuart, David, 1:757
Stuart, Eileen M., 5:400
Stuart, J. A., 4:84
Stuart, John, 1:323
Stuart, Reginald C., 3:522
Stuart, Sandra Lee, 1:135
Stuart-Fox, Martin, 3:491
Stubbings, Frank H., 2:362
Stubbs, Charles W., 1:369
Stubbs, Richard, 3:492
Stuckenschmidt, H. H., 3:715
Studlar, Gaylyn, 1:1177
Studley, Vance, 1:19
Stuernagel, Gertrude, 5:95
Stuewer, Robert H., 5:678
Stuhlmacher, Peter, 4:815,
4:826
Stuhr, John J., 4:36
Stukane, Eileen, 5:355
Stump, Eleonore, 4:95, 4:119
Stumpf, Harry P., 3:145
Stumpf, Samuel E., 4:18,
4:24
Stunkel, Kenneth R., 4:38

Sturluson, Snorri, 2:639,
2:642, **2:643,** 2:661, 4:437
Sturm, Terry, 2:971
Styan, J. L., 1:218
Styron, William, 1:1056
Suárez, Francisco, 4:105,
4:154
Subak-Sharpe, Genell J.,
5:356, 5:375, 5:382
Subotić, Dragutin P., 2:828
Subotnik, Rose Rosengard,
3:664
Subrahmanyam, Sanjay, 3:484
Subramanyam, Krishna,
5:218
Subramini, 2:971
Suckiel, Ellen Kappy, 3:188
Sudha, Rai, 2:939
Suehiro, Akira, 3:490
Suelzle, Marijean, 3:208
Suetonius (Caius Suetonius
Tranquillus), 2:379, 2:392,
2:394, 3:320
Sugar, Peter F., 3:392
Sugarman, Ellen, 5:354
Sugden, Auden, 5:762
Suggs, M. Jack, 4:798
Suh, Ji-moon, 2:300
Suhl, Benjamin, 4:331
Suhl, Yuri, 4:637
Suhr, Claus, 5:727
Suits, Gustav, 2:796
Sukenick, Ronald, 1:888
Sukhwal, B. L., 3:482
Suksamran, Somboon, 4:520
Suleiman, Susan R., 1:927
Sulimirski, T., 3:301
Sullivan, Alvin, 1:274
Sullivan, Arthur, 1:311
Sullivan, Colleen, 5:356
Sullivan, David R., 5:538
Sullivan, Debbie, 3:869
Sullivan, Edward D., 2:489
Sullivan, Harry Stack, 5:470
Sullivan, Henry W., 2:533
Sullivan, J. P., 2:381
Sullivan, Kaye, 3:826
Sullivan, Lawrence, 4:465,
4:466, 4:506, 4:514, 4:530,
4:536
Sullivan, Louis, 1:668
Sullivan, Louis Henry,
3:790, **3:792,** 3:797
Sullivan, Michael, 3:467
Sullivan, Nancy, 1:720, 1:806,
1:922
Sullivan, Richard E., 3:329
Sullivan, Richardson, 3:769
Sullivan, Robert R., 4:402
Sullivan, Roger, 4:207
Sullivan, Rosemary, 1:1038,
2:905

Sullivan, Soraya Paknazar,
2:84
Sullivan, Walter, 1:889,
1:920, 5:627, 5:630
Sullivan, William M., 3:248
Sulloway, Frank J., 3:184,
5:47
Sully, Melanie, 3:376
Summer, Benedict H., 3:395
Summers, Claude J., 1:184,
1:477, 1:1182
Summers, David, 3:782
Summerson, John, 3:363,
3:762
Sumrall, Amber Coverdale,
4:746
Sundaram, K., 4:280
Sundkler, Bengt, 4:468
Sundquist, Eric J., 1:652,
1:668, 1:699, 1:724, 1:805,
1:838
Sundquist, James, 3:544
Sungolowsky, Joseph, 2:458
Sunim, Kusan, 4:538
Sunstein, Emily, 1:301
Sunthorn Phu, 2:337
Super, Robert H., 1:296,
1:407
Supičič, Ivo, 3:664
Suppe, Frederick, 5:65
Suppes, Patrick, 5:65, 5:96
Surasingsaruam Chimphanao,
2:336
Surin, Kenneth, 4:886
Surmelian, Leon, 2:77
Surtees, Virginia, 1:392
Surtz, Edward L., 1:194,
4:148
Suryadinata, Leo, 2:311
Su Shih, 2:219
Susser, Mervyn, 5:80
Sussex, Elizabeth, 3:826
Susskind, Charles, 3:702,
5:72, 5:215, 5:232
Sussman, Allen, 5:380
Sussman, Henry, 2:987
Sussman, Mark D., 5:396
Sutch, Richard, 3:549
Sutcliffe, Barry, 1:229
Sutcliffe, Peter, 1:43
Suter, Ronald, 4:347
Sutermeister, Edwin, 1:6
Sutherland, David E., 3:530
Sutherland, Edwin H., 3:205
Sutherland, Gail Hinich,
4:506, 4:510, 4:514
Sutherland, Ian, 5:332
Sutherland, John, 1:404,
5:313
Sutherland, N. M., 4:732
Sutherland, N. S., 5:428
Sutherland, Zena, 1:50, 1:53,
1:579, 1:1196, 1:1197

Sutton, Christine, 5:657, 5:658, 5:662, 5:663
Sutton, Horace, 3:897
Sutton, James, 1:19
Sutton, Max K., 1:358
Sutton, Walter, 1:914
Sutulov, Alexander, 5:628
Sutzkever, Abraham, 2:29, **2:49**
Suwannathat-Pian, Kobkua, 3:489
Suzuki, D(aisetz) T(eitard), 3:476, 4:363, 4:364, **4:557**
Suzuki, David T., 5:778
Suzuki, Shunryu, 4:538
Svelto, Orazio, 5:698
Svevo, Italo, 2:438
Svirski, Grigory, 2:691
Swaan, Wim, 3:905
Swados, Harvey, 1:130
Swahn, Jan-Ojvind, 2:322
Swain, Joseph Peter, 3:664
Swain, Kathleen M., 1:192
Swain, Tony, 4:461
Swaine, Michael, 5:542
Swallow, Deborah, 3:484
Swami Atulananda, 4:563
Swami Satyeswarananda, Giri, 2:172
Swan, Maureen, 4:554
Swanberg, Jane M., 4:474
Swanberg, W. A., 1:831
Swank, Scott T., 3:849
Swann, Brian, 1:632
Swann, Thomas Burnett, 1:827
Swanson, Donald C., 1:99
Swanson, Paul L., 4:530
Swanson, R. N., 4:695
Swanton, Michael, 1:141, 3:177
Swarbrick, Andrew, 1:247
Swearer, Donald K., 4:514, 4:520, 4:896
Swearingen, Bethany C., 1:896
Swedberg, Richard, 3:105
Swedenborg, Emanuel, 2:680, 4:850, 4:851, 4:852, **4:880**
Swedenborg, H. T., 1:242
Sweeney, Amin, 2:324, 4:460
Sweeney, Leo, 4:51
Sweet, Henry, 1:143
Sweet, Leonard I., 4:754
Sweetman, Bill, 5:220
Sweetman, David, 3:795
Sweetman, James W., 4:573
Sweetser, Marie-Odile, 2:485
Sweezy, Paul M., 3:50, 3:95
Sweitzer, Letitia, 5:332
Swenson, May, 1:1057
Swerdlow, Noel M., 5:40

Swetnam, J., 4:796
Swezey, Charles M., 4:900
Swiderski, Edward M., 4:31
Swidler, Ann, 3:248
Swidler, Leonard, 4:423
Swietlicki, Catherine, 2:523
Swift, Bernard C., 2:489
Swift, David W., 5:598
Swift, Jim, 5:522
Swift, Jonathan, 1:228, 1:235, 1:236, 1:241, 1:250, 1:252, **1:259,** 1:576, 1:949, 2:363, 2:365, 2:387, 5:258
Swift, Louis J., 4:689
Swift, Ruth, 1:208
Swimme, Brian, 5:657
Swinburne, Algernon Charles, 1:279, 1:310, 1:314, 1:386, **1:397,** 2:350, 2:366, 2:457, 2:512, 2:514
Swinburne, Richard, 4:886
Swindells, Julia, 1:325
Swindler, Daris R., 5:772
Swingewood, Alan, 3:200, 5:35
Swingle, L. J., 1:407
Swinnerton, Frank, 1:444
Switzer, Richard, 2:466
Swope, Martha, 3:738
Swoyer, Chris, 4:412, 5:100
Swyhart, Barbara A., 4:895
Sybesma, R. P., 2:634
Sydney, Sheldon B., 5:342
Sykes, Christopher, 4:643
Sykes, Percy M., 3:449, 3:894
Sylvester, Edward J., 5:405
Sylvester, Richard S., 1:165, 1:166, 1:194
Sylvester, Robert D., 4:312
Syme, Ronald, 2:381, 2:390, 3:303, 3:311, 3:320, 3:321
Symonds, J. A., 2:402
Symonenko, Vasyl, 2:838
Symons, Arthur J., 1:316, 1:720, 2:987, 3:900
Symons, Julian, 1:608
Synge, John Millington, 1:423, 1:460, 1:526, **1:555,** 1:571, 2:514
Szabadvary, Ferenc, 5:735
Szarmach, Paul E., 4:697
Szarycz, Ireneusz, 2:731
Szasz, Ferenc Morton, 5:707
Szasz, Thomas S., 5:81, 5:429
Szekely, Istvan, 3:52
Szilassy, Zoltan, 1:1076
Szonyi, David M., 4:7
Sztompka, Piotr, 3:209, 3:233
Szumski, Bonnie, 5:13
Szwed, John F., 3:867

T

Taaffe, Edward J., 3:123
Taaffe, James G., 1:192
Al-Tabari, 3:434, **3:455**
Taber, Sara Mansfield, 3:897
Tabor, Stephen, 1:498
Tabori, Paul, 2:799
Tacey, David, 2:966
Tachau, Katherine, 4:121
Tachihara Masaaki, 2:293
Tacitus, Cornelius, 2:379, 2:390, 2:392, **2:395,** 2:562, 3:310, **3:320,** 4:437
Tadmor, Nephtali, 3:439
Taeuber, Conrad, 3:241
Taeuber, Irene B., 3:241
Tafdrup, Pia, 2:646
Taft, Robert, 1:30
Tafuri, Manfredo, 3:764
Taggart, James M., 4:465
Tagliacozzo, Giorgio, 2:442, 4:217
Tagore, Sir Rabindranath (also Ravindranatha Thakura), 2:182, 2:250, 2:262, 4:355
Taha, Mahmud Mohamed, 4:576
Taha Husayn, 2:73
Tahir, Maimunah Mohammed, 2:324
Tahiri, Amin, 4:580
Tahir-Kheli, 3:449, 3:450
Tai, Hue-Tam Ho, 3:491
Tai Hou-ying, 2:262
Taillandier, Yvon, 3:791
Taine, Hippolyte, 2:454, 2:810
Tait, Hugh, 3:766
Taitte, W. L., 5:130
Taitz, Emily, 4:650
Takaki, Ronald T., 3:557
Takaya, Ted T., 2:283
Takeuchi, H., 5:630
Takeuchi, Keij, 5:634
Takeuchi Yoshinori, 4:365
Tal, Uriel, 3:351, 4:637
Talashoma, Herschel, 3:865
Talbert, Richard J., 3:298
Talbot, Daniel, 3:826
Talbott, John, 3:374
Talese, Gay, 3:809
Taliman, Warren, 1:912
Tallant, Robert, 4:868
Talley, Thomas W., 3:867
Tallis, Thomas, 3:723
Tallmer, Margot, 5:378, 5:379
Talmage, Frank, 4:603, 4:630
Talmon, J. R., 3:341
Talmor, Ezra, 4:203
Tambiah, S. J., 3:488, 4:519
Tames, R., 5:250

Tamineaux, Jacques, 4:295
Tamir, Zakariya, 2:74
Tamminga, D. A., 2:634
Tammsaare, Anton Hansen, 2:796
Tammuz, Benjamin, 2:25
Tamney, Joseph B., 4:842, 4:860
Tamparo, Carol D., 5:122
Tamplin, Ronald, 1:495
Tamrat, Taddesse, 3:423
Tan, Kim, 5:264
Tanabe, George J., 4:538
Tanabe, Willa Jane, 4:538
Tanabe Hajime, 4:365, 4:366
Tanaka, Yukiko, 2:284
Tancock, John L., 3:791
Tancredi, Laurence, 5:75, 5:122
Tanenbaum, Andrew S., 5:551
Tanenhaus, Joseph, 3:138
Taner, Haldun, 2:101
T'ang Hsien-tzu, 2:209, 2:220
Tangley, Laura, 5:823
Tanikawa Shuntaro, 2:293
Tanimoto, Steven L., 5:569
Tanizaki Jun'ichirō, 2:281, 2:293
Tankard, J. W., Jr., 5:526
Tannenbaum, Frank, 3:626, 3:644, 3:649
Tannenbaum, Percy H., 3:204
Tannenbaum, Samuel A., 1:20
Tanner, Kathryn, 4:746
Tanner, Norman, 4:891
Tanner, Stephen L., 1:1000
Tanner, Thomas, 5:835
Tanner, Tony, 1:767, 1:795, 1:920
Tanselle, G. Thomas, 1:61, 1:62, 1:79, 1:645
Tantaquidgeon, Gladys, 3:859
Tanur, Judith M., 5:521, 5:524
T'ao Ch'ien, 2:214, 2:222
Taper, Bernard, 3:738
Taper, L. Janette, 5:348
Tappert, Theodore G., 4:779
Tapping, G. Craig, 1:460
Tarabishi, Georges, 2:72
Taran, Leonardo, 4:52
Tarantola, Daniel J., 5:388
Tarasov, L. V., 5:666
Tarbell, Ida, 3:823
Tarbox, Katherine, 1:478
Tarbuck, Edward J., 3:126
Tarczan, Constance, 5:414
Tarde, Gabriel, 3:176
Targ, William, 1:44
Tarlov, Edward, 5:394

Tarnas, Richard, 4:18
Tarrant, Harold, 4:58
Tarrow, Sidney, 3:385
Taruskin, Richard, 3:664
Ta-Shema, I., 2:9
Tashman, Leonard J., 5:524
Tashner, John, 5:567
Tasman, Allan, 5:415
Tassel, Cynthia L. van, 5:541
Tasso, Torquato, 2:398, 2:405, 2:439
Tatar, Maria M., 2:585, 4:847
Tatarkiewicz, Wladislaw, 4:131
Tate, Allen, 1:806, 1:810, 1:888, 1:1005
Tate, Claudia, 1:1019
Tate, James, 1:1057
Tate, Thad W., 3:517
Tateishi, J., 3:536
Tatham, Andrew F., 5:617
Taton, Rene, 5:26
Tatum, Charles, 2:847
Tatum, James, 2:383, 4:469
Taub, Herbert, 5:300
Taubert, Sigfred, 1:37, 1:69
Taubes, Gary, 5:663
Taubman, Jane A., 2:768
Tauns, Linards, 2:803
Tausky, Margaret, 3:702
Tausky, Vilem, 3:702
Taussig, Michael, 4:431
Tavard, George H., 4:679, 4:697, 4:788
Tavaststjerna, Karl August, 2:657
Tavčar, Ivan, 2:834
Tave, Stuart M., 1:276
Tavernier-Courbin, Jacqueline, 1:775, 1:847
Taviani, Paolo, 3:917
Tawa, Nicholas E., 3:664
Tawaststjerna, Erik, 3:718
Tawney, Richard H., 3:51, 3:55
Tayanin, Damrong, 2:322
Tayler, Edward, 1:178
Tayler, Irene, 1:334
Taylor, A. E., 4:84, 4:90, 4:203
Taylor, A(lan) J(ohn) P(ercivale), 3:345, 3:367, 3:378, 3:408
Taylor, Aline M., 1:251
Taylor, Archer, 1:77
Taylor, Arthur J. P., 3:341
Taylor, Basil, 3:773
Taylor, Benjamin, 3:869
Taylor, Bob P., 5:116
Taylor, Charles, 4:233, 4:414
Taylor, Charles L., 3:138
Taylor, David A., 5:239
Taylor, David D., 3:487

Taylor, Deems, 3:713
Taylor, Dennis, 1:363
Taylor, Denny, 3:252
Taylor, Edmund, 3:343
Taylor, Edward, 1:625, 1:643
Taylor, Eugene, 1:769, 3:188
Taylor, Gary, 1:206, 1:207, 1:214
Taylor, George, 1:229, 1:323
Taylor, George R., 3:600
Taylor, George Rogers, 3:55
Taylor, Harley U., 2:607
Taylor, Helen, 1:724
Taylor, Henry Osborn, 4:96, 4:131
Taylor, Ina, 1:586
Taylor, Isaac, 1:37
Taylor, J. Gorden, 1:716
Taylor, Jenny, 1:346
Taylor, John B., 1:11
Taylor, John F. A., 3:258
Taylor, John Russell, 1:426
Taylor, Lily R., 4:452
Taylor, Lonn, 3:864
Taylor, M. Brook, 3:607
Taylor, Margaret, 1:74
Taylor, Mark C., 4:268, 4:392, 4:889
Taylor, Martin C., 2:873
Taylor, Paul, 3:752
Taylor, Paul W., 5:76, 5:116
Taylor, Peter J., 3:123
Taylor, Richard, 4:381
Taylor, Richard K., 5:112
Taylor, Robert H., 3:489, 4:515
Taylor, Robert Saxton, 5:545
Taylor, Rodney L., 3:469, 4:526, 4:541
Taylor, Sandra E., 5:330
Taylor, Theodore, 1:404
Taylor, Thomas, 5:661
Taylor, Thomas J., 1:1076
Taylor, Tom, 1:320, 1:398
Taylor, Vincent, 4:826
Taylor, W. Thomas, 1:36
Taylor, Walter, 1:838
Taylor, Walter W., 3:13
Taylor, Wendell H., 1:604
Taylor, William N., 5:400
Tchaikovsky, Peter Ilich, 3:701, 3:711, 3:723
Tcherikover, Victor, 4:605
Tchernichovski (Tchernichowsky), Saul, 2:7, 2:25
Teaford, Jon C., 3:533
Teale, Edwin Way, 5:818
Tebbel, John, 1:38, 1:630, 1:652
Tec, Nechama, 4:638
Teck, Katherine, 3:732
Tedder, D. William, 5:245

Tedlock, Barbara, 4:456, 4:465
Tedlock, Dennis, 4:456, 4:465
Teece, Philip, 5:591
Teed, Peter, 3:7
Teets, Bruce E., 1:464
Teeuw, A., 2:317
Tegethoff, Wolf, 3:783
Tegnér, Esaias, 2:670
Teich, Albert H., 5:73, 5:131, 5:158
Teichler-Zallen, Doris, 5:124
Teilhard de Chardin, Pierre, 3:910, 4:335
Teiser, Stephen F., 4:531
Teitelboim, Volodia, 2:876
Tekeyan, Vahan, 2:80
Teleki, Geza, 5:827
Telford, Thomas, 5:254, 5:255
Teller, Edward, 5:112, 5:142
Teller, Walter M., 3:937
Telles, Lygia Fagundes, 2:889, 2:900
Telushkin, Joseph, 4:596
Temin, Peter, 3:50
Temkin, Owsei, 5:394
Temkin, Sefton D., 4:653
Tempels, Placide, 4:369
Temple, Ruth, 2:506
Temple, Ruth Z., 2:523
Templeman, W. D., 1:326
Tenenbaum, Elizabeth B., 2:511
Teng Ssu-yu, 3:472
Tennaille, Mabel, 3:854
Tennenhouse, Leonard, 1:210
Tennent, R., 5:551
Tennyson, Alfred, 1st Baron, 1:310, 1:313, 1:314, 1:321, 1:327, 1:356, 1:398, 1:399, 1:444, 1:450, 1:704, 1:779, 2:383, 2:396, 2:512
Tennyson, Charles, 1:402
Tennyson, G. B., 1:316, 1:326
Tennyson, Hallam T., 1:402
Tentler, T., 4:701
Tenzin Gyatso, 4:356, 4:496, 4:558, 4:905
Teodorsson, Sven Tage, 4:53
Tepl, Johannes von, 2:562, 2:594
Terborgh, John, 5:772
Terence (Publius Tertentius Afer), 1:168, 1:263, 2:364, 2:378, 2:391, 2:554, 2:395
Teresa of Avila, St., 4:728, 4:736, 4:785
Teresa of Jesus, St., 2:520, 2:543, 2:550
Teresi, Dick, 5:650, 5:663, 5:718
Ter Horst, Robert, 2:533

Terkel, Studs, 3:536
Terrace, Vincent, 3:812
Terras, Victor, 2:691, 2:716
Terrell, Carroll F., 1:452, 1:874, 1:901
Terrell, John Upton, 5:646
Terres, John K., 5:762
Terrill, Thomas E., 3:513
Terry, Edward D., 2:848
Terry, Megan, 1:1071, 1:1113
Terry, Patricia, 4:437
Terry, Wallace, 3:540
Terry, Walter, 3:733, 3:744, 3:752
Tertullian, 4:713
Terwiel, B. J., 3:490
Teska, P. T., 3:171
Teskey, Ayleen, 2:749
Test, Mary Ann, 5:424
Tetel, Marcel, 2:492
Tetsurō, Watsuji. See Watsuji Tetsurō
Teuscher, Gerhart, 2:991
Teutsch, Betsy P., 4:597
Tezla, Albert, 2:798, 2:799
Thackeray, Henry, 4:666, 4:812
Thackeray, William Makepeace, 1:310, 1:317, 1:323, 1:332, 1:352, 1:366, 1:378, 1:402
Thackray, Arnold W., 5:45, 5:56, 5:729, 5:742
Thagard, Paul, 5:65
Thalmann, William G., 2:351
Tham, Seong Chee, 2:312
Tharoor, Shashi, 2:178
Tharp, Twyla, 3:738, 3:753
Tharpe, Jac, 1:842, 1:943
Thayer, Carlyle A., 3:491
Thayer, Helen, 3:907
Thayer, Horace S., 4:225, 4:268
Thayer, William R., 2:402
Thein Pe Myint, 2:314
Theissen, Gerd, 4:618, 4:826
The Mother of Fujiwara Michitsuna, 2:278
The-Mulliner, Lian, 2:324, 3:492
Theocritus, 2:343, 2:368, 2:396
Theodoracopulos, Taki, 3:393
Theoharis, Athan, 3:544
Theophrastus of Eresus, 2:343, 2:364, 2:369, 4:65, 4:90
Thernstrom, Stephan, 3:514, 3:549
Theroux, Paul, 2:310, 2:939, 3:897, 3:900, 3:905, 3:940
Thesing, William B., 1:429

Thibault, Claude, 3:606
Thibault, Paul J., 2:742
Thich Nhat Hanh, 4:561
Thiebaux, Marcelle, 1:844
Thielicke, Helmut, 4:746
Thiemann, Ronald, 4:746
Thiep Nguyen H., 2:339
Thiher, Allen, 2:497
Thiong'o, Ngugi wa, 2:103, 2:118, 2:151
Thirring, Walter E., 5:698
Thirsk, Joan, 3:360
Thody, Philip, 2:455
Thom, James Alexander, 1:1244
Thomas, Alan G., 1:34
Thomas, Alexander, 5:423
Thomas, Benjamin P., 3:530
Thomas, Bob, 1:1165, 3:737
Thomas, Brian, 1:489
Thomas, Calvin, 2:609
Thomas, Charles, 3:356, 4:437
Thomas, David, 3:369, 4:211
Thomas, Diana, 1:81
Thomas, Donald Serrell, 1:274, 1:316, 1:339, 1:398
Thomas, Dwight, 1:693
Thomas, Dylan, 1:414, 1:466, 1:525, 1:547, 1:556, 1:560, 1:1038
Thomas, E. E., 4:241
Thomas, Eberle, 1:544
Thomas, Edward, 1:557
Thomas, Emory N., 3:530
Thomas, G. Scott, 3:119
Thomas, Gareth, 2:525
Thomas, Geoffrey, 4:230
Thomas, Gillian, 1:376
Thomas, Gordon K., 1:284
Thomas, Gordon, 3:549, 5:383
Thomas, H. Nigel, 3:867, 3:869
Thomas, Henry, 2:525
Thomas, Hugh, 3:367, 3:387
Thomas, Isaiah, 1:11
Thomas, J., 3:177
Thomas, J. C., 3:690
Thomas, J. M., 5:684, 5:745
Thomas, Jack Ray, 3:625
Thomas, John Bowman, 5:300
Thomas, Julian, 3:13, 4:434
Thomas, Keith, 4:727
Thomas, Lawrence L., 1:101
Thomas, Lewis, 5:18, 5:315, 5:766
Thomas, M. Wynn, 1:708
Thomas, Milton H., 4:225
Thomas, Northcote W., 3:850
Thomas, P. M., 4:509, 4:554, 4:563

Thomas, Pam, 3:732
Thomas, Peter, 2:916
Thomas, Peter D., 3:363
Thomas, R. George, 1:558
Thomas, Robert D., 4:844
Thomas, Rosalind, 4:460
Thomas, Rosemary H., 3:862
Thomas, Susie, 1:822
Thomas, Tenney A., 1:784
Thomas, Terry, 5:558
Thomas, W. Donald, 3:929
Thomas, W. S., 3:369
Thomas, W(illiam) I(saac),
    3:221, 3:235, **3:241**
Thomasma, David, 5:80
Thomas-Stanford, Charles,
    5:505
Thomis, Malcolm I., 3:365
Thompson, Ann, 1:217,
    1:220, 2:989
Thompson, Bard, 4:681
Thompson, Colin P., 2:544
Thompson, Doug, 2:433
Thompson, E. P., 1:313,
    1:383, 3:874
Thompson, Edward J., 2:183
Thompson, Edward Palmer,
    3:352, 3:365, **3:410**
Thompson, Ewa M., 2:691,
    2:814
Thompson, F. M., 1:313,
    3:365
Thompson, G. R., 1:693
Thompson, George A., Jr.,
    1:122
Thompson, Gladys S., 3:395
Thompson, Harold W., 3:859
Thompson, Henry O., 5:124
Thompson, Henry T., 1:704,
    1:779
Thompson, Ida, 5:640, 5:762
Thompson, J. Eric S., 4:456
Thompson, J. M., 3:340,
    3:374
Thompson, J. W., 3:277
Thompson, James R., 1:263,
    1:292
Thompson, James S., 5:781
Thompson, James Westfall,
    1:37
Thompson, John B., 4:405,
    5:90
Thompson, John C., 1:428
Thompson, John D., 5:329
Thompson, John Herd, 3:616
Thompson, John O., 1:217
Thompson, Joseph John,
    5:678
Thompson, Josiah, 4:240
Thompson, Joyce, 5:124
Thompson, K., 3:836
Thompson, Keith, 4:870

Thompson, Kenneth, 3:224,
    3:658
Thompson, Kenneth W.,
    5:112
Thompson, Kristin, 1:1157,
    3:825
Thompson, Laurence G.,
    4:522, 4:523
Thompson, Lawrence, 1:683,
    1:842
Thompson, Leonard M.,
    3:424
Thompson, Margaret W.,
    5:781
Thompson, Michael, 5:158
Thompson, Patricia J., 5:347
Thompson, Paul, 3:367
Thompson, Paul Van K.,
    1:383
Thompson, Richard F., 5:773
Thompson, Robert F., 4:26
Thompson, Rose, 3:867
Thompson, Stith, 3:846,
    3:850, 3:857, 3:865, 3:877,
    3:882, **3:887**
Thompson, Susan Otis, 1:11
Thompson, Tommy, 1:20
Thompson, Virgil, 3:724,
    1:881, 3:709, 3:736
Thompson, W. B., 5:667
Thompson, W. G., 5:385
Thoms, William John, 3:845,
    3:887
Thomsen, Harry, 4:541
Thomsen, Moritz, 3:910
Thomsett, Kay, 5:380
Thomson, Belinda, 3:776
Thomson, Dale C., 3:616
Thomson, George, 2:351
Thomson, George Paget,
    5:716
Thomson, Ian, 1:111
Thomson, J. A., 4:695
Thomson, J.A.K., 1:220,
    1:429
Thomson, James, 1:261
Thomson, Joseph, 3:932
Thomson, Joseph John, 5:673
Thomson, Judith J., 4:387
Thomson, M., 5:389
Thomson, Patricia, 1:201
Thomson, Peter, 1:218
Thomson, Sir Joseph John,
    5:657, **5:715**
Thorarensen, Bjarni, 2:639
Thórdarson, Thorbergur,
    2:643
Thoreau, Henry David,
    1:659, 1:668, 1:675, **1:699,**
    1:897, 1:965, 1:1192,
    1:1197, 3:897, 4:551,
    4:771, 4:840, 5:143, 5:762,
    5:833, **5:836**

Thoren, Victor E., 5:40,
    5:600
Thorlby, Anthony, 2:4, 2:766
Thorman, George, 5:428
Thorn, Colin E., 5:627
Thornberry, Terence P.,
    5:428
Thorndike, Ashley H., 1:173
Thorndike, Edward L(ee),
    3:268, 5:471
Thorndike, Lynn, 4:98, 4:102,
    4:131, 5:26
Thorne, Brian, 3:193
Thorne, Tony, 1:93
Thornton, A. P., 3:365
Thornton, Charles H., 5:246
Thornton, Weldon, 1:556
Thorp, N. Howard, 3:864
Thorpe, Michael, 1:345,
    1:543, 2:939
Thorpe, Thomas Bangs,
    1:702
Thorpe, Thomas E., 5:753
Thorpe, W. H., 5:34
Thorsen, Kristine A., 1:123
Thorslev, Peter, 1:284
Thorup, Kirsten, 2:645,
    2:654
Thro, Ellen, 5:570
Throckmorton, B. H., 4:798
Thrombley, Woodworth G.,
    3:490
Thrower, Norman J. W.,
    5:606
Thublon, Colin, 3:901
Thucydides, 2:342, 2:369,
    3 315, **3:321,** 3:323
Thuborn, Tony, 5:640
Thultrup, Niels, 4:240
Thunann, Albert, 5:284
Thumbo, Edwin, 2:324, 2:325
Thung, P. J., 5:78
Thurber, James, 1:807,
    1:889, 1:897
Thurman, Judith, 2:649
Thurman, Robert A. F., 4:888
Thurmin, Janet, 3:827
Thursfield, Richard E., 3:259
Thurston, Herbert, 4:701
Thwaite, Ann, 1:588, 1:1201
Thwaite, Anthony, 1:418,
    1:508
Thwaite, Lucy Mickle, 1:29
Thwaite, Mary F., 1:34, 1:37
Tibble, Anne, 2:112
Tibi, Bassam, 3:437
Tibullus (Albius), 2:379,
    2:395
Tice, Terrence N., 4:15
Tichi, Cecilia, 1:652, 1:795,
    5:205
Tick, Judith, 3:659
Tidcombe, Marianne, 1:26

Tieck, Ludwig, 2:610, **2:612**
Tiedt, Iris M., 3:258
Tiedt, Pamela, 3:258
Tierney, Brian, 3:332, 4:695
Tierra, Lesley, 5:320
Tierra, Michael, 5:320
Tietjen, Gary J., 5:521
Tietze, Heinrich, 5:497
Tiffney, Bruce H., 5:640
Tifonov, D. N., 5:750
Tighgman, B. R., 4:347
Tikku, Girdhari, 4:576
Tiles, J. E., 4:226, 4:414
Tiles, Mary, 4:274
Tillery, Tyrone, 1:857
Tillich, Hannah, 4:788
Tillich, Paul Johannes,
4:252, 4:366, 4:422, 4:678,
4:783, **4:787,** 5:131, **5:206**
Tillman, Hoyt Cleveland,
4:526
Tillotson, Geoffrey, 1:227,
1:404
Tillotson, Kathleen, 1:319
Tillyard, E.M.W., 1:212
Tilman, Rick, 3:110, 3:235
Tilman, Seth P., 3:437
Tilton, Eleanor M., 1:679
Timberg, Bernard, 1:54
Timberlake, Michael, 3:217
Timko, Michael, 1:344
Timm, Jeffrey R., 4:506,
4:510, 4:514, 4:517
Timmerman, John H., 1:886,
1:1217
Timmerman, Kenneth R.,
3:450
Timms, David, 1:508
Timrod, Henry, 1:703, 1:718,
1:778
Tinbergen, Jan, 3:59, 3:64
Tinbergen, Nikolaas, 3:171,
3:194, 5:825, 5:832, 5:835,
5:837
Tindall, George B., 3:514
Tindall, William York, 1:174,
1:415, 1:422
Tiner, John H., 5:786
Tingay, Lance, 1:407
Tingley, Donald F., 3:511
Ting Ling, 2:263
Tinkler, Keith J., 5:33
Tint, Herbert, 3:374
Tintner, Adeline R., 1:766,
1:767
Tipler, Frank J., 5:196, 5:654
Tippett, Maria, 3:610
Tippett, Sir Michael, 3:725
Tipton, David, 2:850
Tipton, Steven M., 3:248,
4:855
Tirion, Wil, 5:591
Tirman, John, 5:240

Tirole, Jean, 3:63
**Tirso de Molina (Fray Ga-
briel Téllez),** 2:520, **2:551**
Tiryakian, Edward A., 3:240
Tise, Larry E., 3:520
Titcombe, Marianne Fletcher,
1:27
Titian, 2:405, 3:768, 3:780,
3:790, **3:793,** 5:365
Titon, Jeff Todd, 3:670
Tittel, Ed, 5:537
Tittler, Jonathan, 2:848
Titus, Harold, 4:25
Titus, James G., 5:633
Tiwari, M. N., 4:510
Tjepkema, Sandra L., 3:666
Tjoa, Hock Guan, 1:373
Tjosvold, Dean, 5:420
Tlaba, Gabriel M., 5:82
Tlali, Miriam, 2:157, **2:168**
Tmeko, Phillip, 4:82
Tobias, Alice L., 5:347
Tobias, Henry J., 4:656
Tobias, Michael, 4:510
Tobias, Russell R., 5:597
Tobias, Sheila, 5:11
Tobin, Frank, 4:102, 4:709
Tobin, Gregory M., 3:600
Tobin, James, 3:62
Tobriner, Marian Leona,
4:156
Toby, Ronald P., 3:476
**Tocqueville, Alexis Charles
Henri Clérel de,** 2:511,
3:143, 3:151, **3:164,** 3:231,
3:242
Todd, David K., 5:618
Todd, D. J., 5:243
Todd, Emmanuel, 3:25
Todd, Janet M., 1:230
Todd, John M., 4:723
Todd, Loreto, 3:857
Todd, Richard, 1:524
Todd, R. Larry, 3:706
Todd, Stephen, 5:194
Todd, William B., 1:36, 4:203
Todd, William M., 2:691
Todhunter, Isaac, 5:31
Toelken, Barre, 3:849
Toenjes, Leonard P., 5:12
Toeplitz, Otto, 5:495
Toer, Pramoedya Ananta,
2:316, **2:321**
Toews, John, 4:233
Toffanin, G., 4:131
Toffler, Alvin, 5:158, 5:572,
5:574
Toké, Arun N., 5:278
Toksvig, Signe, 4:852, 4:880
Toland, John, 3:280, 3:480,
3:536
Tolchin, Neal L., 1:690
Tolegian, Aram, 2:77

Toliver, Harold E., 1:208
**Tolkien, J(ohn) R(onald)
R(euel), 1:558,** 1:574,
1:579, 1:589, 1:611, 1:617,
4:776
Toll, Robert C., 3:874
Toller, Ernst, 2:612
Tolles, Winton, 1:399
Tolley, A. T., 1:508
Tollison, Robert D., 5:404
Tolman, Edward, 3:166,
3:195
Tolstaia, Sophia Andreevna,
2:766
Tolstaya, Tatyana, 2:762
Tolstoy, Alexandra L., 2:766
Tolstoy, Leo (Tolstoi, Lev),
1:1019, 2:239, 2:683,
2:724, 2:735, 2:750, 2:755,
2:760, **2:763,** 4:255, 4:551,
4:756, 4:900
Tolzman, Don H., 3:557
Tomalin, Ruth, 1:366
Tomarken, Edward, 1:250
Tomasi, Wayne, 5:308
Tomasson, Richard F., 3:381
Tominaga, Thomas T., 1:524,
1:552
Tomizuka, Carl T., 5:11
Tomkeieff, S. I., 5:628
Tomlin, Dana, 5:621
Tomlinson, B. R., 3:485
Tomlinson, Charles, 1:560,
1:800, 2:5
Tomlinson, J.D.W., 5:194
Tomonaga, Sin-Itiro, 5:685,
5:715, **5:716**
Tomory, William M., 1:528
Tompkins, Jane, 1:630, 1:658,
1:927, 1:1134
Tong-ni, Kim. See Kim
Tong-ni
Tonnessen, Diana, 5:356
Tönnies, Ferdinand, 3:39,
3:242
Took, J. F., 2:418
Toolan, David, 4:858
Toole, Betty A., 5:578
Tooley, Michael, 5:124
Tooley, R. V., 1:30
Toomer, Jean, 1:891
Toomey, Alice F. A., 1:63
Toor, Frances, 3:857
Toothill, Elizabeth, 5:762
Topelius, Zacharias, 2:659
Topinka, Rudy, 3:862
Topsfield, L. T., 2:467
Torga, Miguel, 2:557
Tormes, Lazarillo de, 2:529
Tornberg, Astrid, 1:103
Torney, Judith V., 3:147
Torrance, Nancy, 4:460
Torrance, S., 5:570

Torre, Michael D., 4:271, 4:308
Torrens, Paul R., 5:329
Torrents, Nissa, 2:871
Torrey, E. Fuller, 5:428
Torrey, Norman L., 4:196, 4:218
Torsney, Cheryl B., 1:790
Tortora, Gerard J., 5:773
Torwesten, Hans, 4:872
Toson, Shimazaki. *See* Shimazaki Toson
Tossa, Wajuppa, 2:336
Toth, Emily, 1:740
Toth, Martin D., 3:857
Toth, Susan Allen, 3:901
Totman, Conrad, 3:476
Totten, George O., 3:480
Toulmin, Stephen, 4:25, 5:32, 5:65
Touponce, William F., 1:1254, 1:1259
Tourneur, Cyril, 1:199
Tournier, Michel, 2:445, **2:511**
Touryan, Lorna, 3:455
Toussaint-Samat, Maguelonne, 5:264
Tov, Ba'al Shem. *See* Ba'al Shem Tov
Tovey, Donald F., 3:664, 3:678
Towell, Julie E., 5:3
Towiański, 2:816
Townes, Charles H(ard), 5:717
Townsend, A.A.R., 5:305
Townsend, H. G., 4:36
Townsend, Jill, 3:853
Townsend, John Rowe, 1:579, 1:1196
Townsend, Kenneth N., 3:47
Townshend, Charles, 3:365
Toye, William, 2:905
Toynbee, Arnold J(oseph), 3:277, 3:288, **3:293,** 3:327, 3:393, 4:337
Toynbee, Paget, 2:418
Trachtenberg, Alan, 1:716, 3:516, 5:246
Trachtenberg, Joshua, 4:624, 4:630
Trachtenberg, Marvin, 3:762
Trachtenberg, Stanley, 1:944, 1:948
Tracy, Ann, 1:270
Tracy, David, 4:99, 4:428, 4:746, 4:813, 4:889, 4:891
Tracy, Jack, 1:608
Tracy, James D., 3:333
Tracy, Lisa, 5:347
Tracy, Patricia, 4:767
Tracy, Theodore J., 4:84

Tracy, Walter, 1:20
Trager, Frank N., 3:489
Trager, Helen Gibson, 3:489
Trahan, Elizabeth, 2:723
Trail, Florence, 2:402
Traill, Catharine Parr, 2:920
Train, Kenneth E., 3:58
Trainer, Jennifer, 5:111
Trakl, Georg, 2:564, **2:613**
TranstRömer, Tomas, 2:671, **2:680**
Tranter, John, 2:947
Trapp, J. B., 1:141
Trask, David F., 3:533
Traube, Elizabeth G., 3:827
Traubner, Richard, 3:671
Traugott, John, 1:259
Trautman, Thomas R., 3:20, 3:37
Travers, Morris William, 5:710, 5:754
Travers, P(amela) L(yndon), 1:578, **1:590**
Traversi, Derek, 1:210
Traves, Tom, 3:615
Travis, Anthony S., 5:752
Travis, Jack, 3:764
Travis, Peter W., 1:159
Trawick, Margaret, 3:20, 4:506
Traynham, James G., 5:732
Treasure, Geoffrey, 3:338, 3:355, 3:363
Trefil, James S., 3:250, 5:8, **5:19,** 5:595, 5:651, 5:656, 5:662, 5:782
Tregear, Mary, 3:760
Tregonning, Kennedy G., 3:488
Treitler, Leo, 3:664
Trelawny, Edward J., 1:284, 1:300, 1:304
Treml, Vladimir, 2:691
Tremlett, George, 1:557
Trenner, Richard, 1:969
Trensky, Paul I., 2:789
Trent, William, 1:697
Trepp, Leo, 4:602
Tresler, Kathleen M., 5:324
Trevelyan, George Macaulay, 1:378, 3:408, **3:410**
Trevelyan, Joanna E., 5:321
Treverton, Gregory, 3:346
Trevor, William, 1:423
Trevor-Roper, Hugh R(edwald), 3:361, **3:411,** 3:415
Trewartha, Glenn T., 5:634
Trewin, J. C., 1:218
Treyz, J., 3:273
Trezise, Thomas, 2:460
Tribe, Laurence H., 3:142
Tricker, R. A., 5:684, 5:701

Trieff, Norman M., 5:354
Trien, Susan F., 5:398
Trieschmann, Roberta B., 5:394
Triffin, Robert, 3:58, 3:59, 3:102
Trifonov, Yury, 2:767
Trigg, George L., 5:650, 5:697
Trigg, Joseph W., 4:117
Trigger, Bruce G., 3:13, 3:301, 3:611
Trikha, Manorama, 1:842
Trilling, Lionel, 1:129, 1:326, 1:328, 1:370, 1:922, **1:1058**
Trimble, Marshall, 3:864
Trimingham, J. Spencer, 3:444, 4:573, 4:577
Trimpi, Wesley, 1:184
Trinkaus, Charles, 4:131, 4:151, 4:697
Tripolitis, Antonia, 4:63
Tripp, Bernell, 3:809
Tripp, Rhoda Thomas, 1:117
Trisco, Robert, 4:751
Tritton, Arthur S., 4:577
Trobridge, George, 4:852, 4:880
Trocki, Carl, 3:492
Troeltsch, Ernst, 4:95, 4:742, 4:899
Trofimenkoff, Susan M., 3:610
Trollope, Anthony, 1:310, 1:317, 1:351, 1:385, **1:404,** 1:407, 1:447, 2:408, 4:73
Trollope, Frances Eleanor, 1:409
Trollope, Frances Milton, 1:405, **1:407**
Trompf, G. W., 4:468
Tropea, Gregory, 4:295
Trotman, James C., 1:906
Trotsky, Leon, 2:691, 3:292, **3:294,** 3:411
Trotter, Robert T., 5:320
Trouard, Dawn, 1:896
Troupe, Quincy, 1:939, 1:1084
Trousdale, Marion, 1:217
Trout, J. D., 5:62
Trow, Martin A., 3:234
Trowbridge, John P., 5:375
Trowell, H. C., 5:395
Troxell, Eugene A., 4:24
Troyat, Henri, 2:710
Troyes, Chrétien de, 2:445, 2:586, 2:616
Truax, Rhoda, 5:409
Trubar, Primož, 2:834
Trubo, Richard, 5:374
Truchtenberg, Stanley, 3:872
Trudeau, Pierre Elliott, 3:609

Trudel, Marcel, 3:612
Trueb, Linda, 5:770
Trueblood, Alan S., 2:555
Trueblood, Elton, 4:25
Trueblood, Paul Graham,
  1:284
Truesdell, C. A., 5:506
Truffaut, François, 1:1168,
  1:1170, 3:824, **3:842**
Trujillo, Carla, 1:1184
Trumbull, John, 1:632
Trump, D. H., 3:299
Trump, Martin, 2:158
Trungpa, Chögyam, 4:357,
  4:544
Truong-vinh-Ky, 2:338
Trussler, Simon, 1:425,
  1:426, 1:532, 1:535
Truxal, John G., 5:231, 5:297
Tryon, Warren S., 1:44
Trypanis, Constantine A.,
  2:349, 2:375
Ts'an Hsüeh, 2:264
Ts'ao Chan, 2:185, 2:218,
  2:223, 2:229
Ts'ao Chih, 2:187, **2:223**
Ts'ao Yü, 2:251, **2:265**
Ts'ung-wen, Shen. *See* Shen
  Ts'ung-wen
Tsai, Meishi, 2:234
Tsai, Shih-shan Henry, 3:558
Tsanin, Mordekhai, 2:50
Tschichold, Jan, 1:11, 1:20
Tseng, Wen-Shing, 5:415
Tse-tung, Mao. *See* Mao Tse-
  tung
Tsibul'Kiu, L. M., 5:235
Tsien, Tsuen-hsuin, 2:187
Tsinker, Gregory P., 5:239
Tsomo, Karma Lekshe, 4:515
Tsung-yüan, Liu, 2:261
Tsunoda, Ryusaku, 4:534
Tsurumi, E. Patricia, 3:480
Tsushima Yuko, 2:294
**Tsvetaeva (Tsvetayeva), Ma-
  rina, 2:767**
Tu, Kuo-ch'ing, 2:206
Tu, Wei-ming, 4:526
Tuana, Nancy, 5:158, 5:189
Tubbs, S., 3:173
Tucci, Giuseppe, 4:356, 4:544
**Tuchman, Barbara
  W(ertheim),** 3:295, 3:332,
  3:343, **3:411,** 3:522, 4:701
Tuchman, Gaye, 1:320
Tuck, Richard, 4:175
Tucker, Allen B., Jr., 5:551
Tucker, Edward L., 1:683
Tucker, Gene M., 4:814
Tucker, Herbert F., 1:402
Tucker, James, 1:536
Tucker, Lena L., 1:121
Tucker, Mark, 3:695

Tucker, Martin, 1:135
Tucker, Mary E., 4:337
Tucker, Paul Hayes, 3:784
Tucker, Richard P., 5:824
Tucker, Robert C., 3:397,
  4:243
Tucker, Robert W., 3:546
Tucker, William, 3:68
**Tuckerman, Frederick God-
  dard, 1:704,** 1:718, **1:779**
Tuckett, Christopher, 4:826
Tuckwell, W., 3:925
Tudor, Antony, 3:740, 3:752,
  3:753
Tufte, Edward R., 1:11, 3:7,
  5:194, 5:524, 5:558
Tu Fu, 1:1001, 2:187, 2:206,
  2:224, 2:225, 2:237
Tuggle, Robert, 3:671
Tukagi, Dana Y., 3:258
Tulchin, Joseph S., 3:633
Tuleja, Thaddeus F., 3:507
Tull, Robert M., 5:372
Tullett, Thomm, 5:343
Tulloch, Gordon, 3:67
Tully, Mark, 4:517
Tulsīdās, 2:173
Tuman, Myron C., 5:126,
  5:574
Tun, Mao. *See* Mao Tun
Tung-p'o, Su, 2:188, 2:214,
  2:225
Tunnell, Kenneth, 3:205
Tunney, Christopher, 3:281
Tuqan, Fadwa, 2:59
Turabian, Kate L., 1:118
Turbayne, Colin M., 4:192
Turco, Alfred, 1:546
Ture, Alfred C., 5:264
Turgenev, Ivan, 1:463,
  2:683, 2:723, **2:768**
Turiel, Isaac, 5:354
Turing, Alan Mathison,
  5:541, **5:581,** 5:583
Turing, Sarah, 5:582
Turk, R. W., 3:288
Turkington, Carol, 5:380
Turkle, Sherry, 5:158, 5:574
Turnbull, Andrew, 1:841
Turnbull, C. Mary, 3:492
Turnbull, Colin M., 3:26
Turnbull, David, 5:668
Turnbull, Eleanor L., 2:527
Turnbull, R. M., 5:658
Turnell, Martin, 2:457, 2:471,
  2:491, 2:498
Turner, A. C., 3:894
Turner, Alberta, 1:914
Turner, Arlin, 1:677, 1:737
Turner, B. L., II, 5:825
Turner, Bryan S., 3:208,
  3:238, 3:244
Turner, Darwin T., 1:891

Turner, David, 2:618
Turner, E. G., 3:300
Turner, Frederick, 2:990,
  3:897
Turner, Frederick Jackson,
  1:690, 3:516, **3:598,** 3:621,
  3:642, 3:769, 3:773, 3:783
Turner, Frederick W., III,
  1:653, 1:720
Turner, Gerard, 5:47
Turner, Graeme, 1:1132,
  1:1158
Turner, Harold W., 4:468
Turner, Henry A., Jr., 3:378
Turner, Henry E., 4:100,
  4:687
Turner, James Grantham,
  1:193
**Turner, Joseph Mallord
  William, 3:793,** 5:203
Turner, Louis, 5:281
Turner, Marjorie S., 3:103
Turner, Michael, 3:92
Turner, Michael R., 1:720
Turner, M. W. 1:393
Turner, N., 3:201
Turner, Ralph, 3:168, 3:200,
  3:203
Turner, Roland, 5:218, 5:232
Turner, Tom, 5:825
Turner, Victor Witter, 3:24,
  3:40, 4:429, 4:430, 4:463,
  4:477, 4:898
Turner, W. Craig, 1:896
Turoff, Murray, 5:296
Turow, Joseph G., 1:50
Turpin, John, 5:560
Tursman, Richard, 4:249
Turton, Peter, 2:871
Turville-Petre, E. Gabriel,
  3:381
Turville-Petre, E.O.G., 4:437
Tusquets, Esther, 2:521
Tussing, Arlon R., 5:285
Tuttle, Esther, 5:626
Tuttle, Merlin D., 5:818
Tuttle, William H., Jr., 3:552
Tuttle, William M., Jr., 3:579
Tuttleton, James W., 1:658,
  1:724
Tutuola, Amos, 2:150
Tuve, Rosemond, 1:165,
  1:181
Tu Wei-Ming, 4:362, 4:533
Tuwim, Julian, 2:810, **2:822**
Tver, David F., 5:618
Twain, Mark, 1:203, 1:673,
  1:683, 1:703, 1:721, 1:726,
  1:732, 1:736, 1:755, 1:757,
  1:769, **1:779,** 1:1193,
  1:1195, 1:1201, 2:45,
  2:427, 2:592, 2:711, 2:912,
  2:952, 3:576, 3:889, 3:894,
  3:910, 5:518

Tweed, Thomas A., 4:842
Tweedale, M., 4:106
Twersky, Isadore, 4:625,
    4:627, 4:629, 4:668, 4:669
Twiss, B. C., 5:231
Twiss, Sumner B., 4:893
Twitchell, James B., 1:270,
    1:599
Twitchell, Paul, 4:873
Twitchett, Denis, 3:466,
    3:468, 3:469
Twombly, Robert C., 3:793,
    3:798
Twort, A. C., 5:245
Twyman, Michael, 1:30
Twyman, Robert, 3:509
Tyack, David B., 3:258
Tyacke, Nicholas, 4:734
Tydeman, William, 1:157
Tyler, Anne, 1:909, **1:1058**
Tyler, Bruce M., 3:212
Tyler, Gary, 1:427
Tyler, Moses Coit, 1:630
Tyler, Parker, 1:1162
Tyler, Royall, 1:626, **1:645,**
    1:1069
Tyler, Stephen A., 4:506
Tylor, Sir Edward Burnett,
    3:14, 3:30, **3:41,** 3:240
Tymms, W. R., 1:30
Tynan, Kenneth, 1:426
Tyndale, John, 5:684
Tynyanov, Yury, 2:691,
    2:770
Tyrrell, Esther Quesada,
    5:772
Tyrrell, John, 3:671
Tyrrell, Joseph Burr, 5:647
Tyrrell, Robert A., 5:772
Tyson, Alan, 3:678
Tyson, Joseph B., 4:817
Tyson, Peter, 2:597
**Tyutchev (Tiutchev), Fyo-
    dor, 2:771**
Tzafestas, Spyros G., 5:243
Tzara, Tristan, 2:859
Tzou, H. S., 5:246

U

Ubayd Zakani, Nizam al-Din,
    2:84
Udall, Stewart I., 3:550
Udelson, Joseph H., 3:561
Uden, Grant, 1:34, 1:76
al-Udhari, Abdullah, 2:57,
    2:58
Udovitch, A. L., 3:444
Udvardy, M. D., 5:762
Ueberhorst, Reinhard, 5:180

Ueberweg, Friedrich, 4:18,
    4:163
Ueda, Makoto, 2:272, 2:276,
    2:283, 2:284, 2:289
Ueda Akinari, 2:280
Uffelman, Larry K., 1:369
Uffenheimer, Rivka, 4:633
Ugarte, Michael, 2:541
Ugolnik, Anthony, 4:756
Ugrinsky, Alexej, 1:531,
    3:537, 4:208
Uhde, Wilhelm, 3:795
Uhlman, Marian, 5:350
Uhr, Carl G., 3:115
Ujević, Augustin Tin, 2:785
Ukhmani, A., 2:10
Ukladnikov, Alexander, 3:734
Ukrajinka, Lesja, 2:837,
    2:840
Ulam, Adam Bruno, 3:397
Ulanov, Ann Belford, 5:456
Ulanova, Galina, 3:754
Ulansey, David, 4:450
Uldricks, Teddy J., 3:281
Ullman, Dana, 5:338
Ullman, Jeffrey D., 5:549,
    5:560, 5:568
Ullmann, Lisa, 3:746
Ullmann, Walter, 4:695
Ulman, Lloyd, 3:60
Ulmer, Diane, 5:401
Umansky, Ellen M., 4:653
Umegaki, Michio, 3:480
**Unamuno y Jugo, Miguel
    de,** 2:521, **2:551,** 3:642,
    4:261, 4:337
Under, Marie, 2:796, **2:797**
Underhill, Evelyn, 4:679
Underhill, Ruth M., 1:632,
    4:465
Underwood, Ashworth E.,
    5:36
Underwood, Edna, 2:931
Undset, Sigrid, 2:662, **2:668**
Ungaretti, Giuseppe, 2:427,
    2:437, **2:440**
Unger, Leonard, 1:128, 1:800,
    3:491
Unger, Rhoda K., 3:178,
    3:179
Unger, Richard, 2:594
Unger, Sanford J., 3:546
Unger, Stephen H., 5:131
Unger-Hamilton, Clive, 3:671
Ungerleider, J. Thomas,
    4:855
Ungerleider-Mayerson, Joy,
    4:597
Unno, Taitetsu, 4:365, 4:366
Uno Chiyo, 2:294
Unrue, Darlene H., 1:870
Unruh, John D., Jr., 3:526
Unterecker, John, 1:823

Untermeyer, Louis, 1:418,
    1:720, 1:801, 1:915
Unwin, Philip, 1:45, 1:50
Unwin, Sir Stanley, 1:45,
    1:50
Updike, Daniel Berkeley,
    1:20
Updike, John, 1:908, 1:909,
    1:916, 1:945, 1:961,
    1:1019, **1:1059**
Uphaus, Robert W., 1:227
Upshur, Jiu-Hwa L., 3:275
Upton, Arthur C., 5:354
Urbach, Peter, 4:166
Urbach, Reinhard, 2:611
Urbain, Walter M., 5:267
Urban, Joan, 1:907
Urban, Milo, 2:833
Urdang, Laurence, 1:92, 1:93,
    3:507
Urey, Diane F., 2:547
Urgo, Joseph R., 1:838
Urmson, J. O., 4:15, 4:192,
    4:268
Uroff, Margaret Dickie, 1:498,
    1:824
Urofsky, Melvin I., 3:142,
    3:533, 4:658
Urošević, Vlada, 2:807
Urquhart, John, 5:354
Urrutia, Virginia, 3:897
Urton, Gary, 4:458, 4:466
Urvoy, Dominque, 4:581
Usdin, Gene, 5:420
Usher, Abbott Payson, 5:56
Usman Awang, 2:326
Usque, Samuel, 2:556
U Tam'si, Tchikiya, 2:150
Utter, Jack, 3:507
Uvarov, E. B., 5:3
Uyeda, S., 5:630

V

Vaculík, Ludvík, 2:788,
    2:795
Vago, Bela, 3:350
Vaičiulaitis, Antanas, 2:805,
    2:807
Vail, Dennis, 1:842
Vail, Leroy, 3:424
Vail, R.W.G., 1:67
Vajda, Miklos, 2:799
Vajdi, Shadab, 2:84
Vakalo, Eleni, 2:377
Val, Edwardo R., 5:428
Valavanis, Kimon P., 5:243
Valencia, Mark J., 5:281
Valency, Maurice, 2:402
Valenta, Jiri, 3:389
Valentine, Lloyd M., 3:50

Valenzuela, Arturo, 3:634
Valenzuela, Luisa, 2:851, **2:885**
Valera y Alcalá Galiano, Juan, 2:552
Valeros, Florentino B., 2:329
Valéry, Paul, 1:691, 2:486, **2:513,** 2:541, 2:543
Valins, Linda, 5:356
Valis, Noel M., 2:523, 2:528
Valk, Barbara G., 3:625
Valla, Lorenzo, 2:433, **4:154**
Vallance, Aymer, 1:383
Valle-Inclán, Ramón del, 2:553
Vallejo, Antonio Buero. *See* Buero Vallejo, Antonio
Vallejo, César, 2:843, **2:885**
Vallery-Radot, René, 5:410
Vallet, Roxanne, 5:621
Vallins, G. H., 1:236
Vamos, Gejza, 2:833
Van Allsburg, Chris, 1:1207
Van Alstyne, William W., 3:139
van Andel, Tjeerd, 5:630, 5:632
Van Ash, Cay, 1:597
van Beeck, Frans Jozef, 4:901
Vanbrugh, Sir John, 1:261
van Buitenan, J.A.B., 2:172, 2:173, 4:506
Vance, Carole, 1:1185
Vance, Eugene, 2:467
Vance, Joel, 3:729
Van Cleave Alexander, Michael, 3:359
Van Croonenburg, Englebert J., 4:25
Van Dam, A., 5:564
Vande Kieft, Ruth M., 1:896
van den Berg, J. H., 5:471
Vanden Bossche, Chris, 1:344
Vanden Burgt, Robert J., 4:238
Van den Toorn, Pieter C., 3:723
Vander, Arthur J., 5:773
Vanderbilt, Byron M., 5:252
Vander Closter, Susan, 1:470
Van der Dennen, Johan M. G., 3:204
Van der Heyningen, W. E., 5:390
van der Leeuw, Gerardus, 4:427, 4:885
Van der Linde, Coby, 5:281
Van der Linden, Harry, 4:207
Van der Pligt, J., 5:113
Van der Post, Laurens, 3:941, 5:456

Van der Steen, Wim J., 5:78
Van der Waerden, Bartel L., 5:39, 5:485, 5:661
Vanderwalker, F. N., 1:21
Van der Zanden, James W., 5:414
Van Deursen, A. Th., 3:383
VanDeVeer, Donald, 5:76, 5:116
Van Doren, Carl, 1:297, 1:630, 1:639
Van Doren, Charles, 3:511, 4:2
Van Doren, Mark, 1:242, 1:877
Van Duong, Quyen, 3:857
Van Dusen, Albert E., 3:518
Van Duyn, Mona, 1:1061
Van Dyk, Bruno, 2:158
Vanek, Jaroslav, 3:68
Van Erven, Eugene, 2:312
Vang, Lue, 2:322
Vangelisti, Paul, 2:403, 2:811
Van Gennep, Arnold, 3:25
Van Gerpen, Maurice, 3:809
Van Ghent, Dorothy, 1:270, 1:295
Van Gogh, Vincent, 1:1249, 3:768, 3:769, 3:775, **3:794**
van Heijenoort, Jean, 5:31
van Helden, Albert, 5:32
Van Herik, Judith, 4:424
Van Hoesen, Henry B., 1:61
Vanhoozer, Kevin J., 4:320
Vanita, Ruth, 4:508
Van Itallie, Jean-Claude, 1:1114
Van Kirk, Sylvia, 3:611
Van Loggem, Manuel, 2:622
Vannatta, Dennis P., 1:897
Van Norman Baer, Nancy, 3:748
Van Nostrand, Albert, 1:50, 1:656
van Orden, Naola, 5:327
Van Over, Raymond, 4:525
Van Rensselaer, Mariana Griswold, 3:791
Van Schendel, Arthur, 2:630
Van Scotter, Richard D., 3:258
Vansina, Jan, 3:421, **3:431**
Vanslov, V., 3:734
Van Slyke, Lyman P., 3:467
Van Spanckeren, Kathryn, 2:907
Van Straaten, Zak, 4:414
van Tassel, Dennie, 5:541
Van Zandt, David E., 4:864
Van Zile, Judy A., 3:731
Var, Turgut, 3:890
Vardac, A. Nicholas, 1:1076
Varey, Simon, 1:230, 1:246

Vargas Llosa, Mario, 2:834, 2:844, **2:886,** 2:894
Varghese, Roy Abraham, 5:68
Varley, Paul, 3:474, 4:538
Varma, Devendra P., 1:270
Varmus, Harold, 5:778
Varner, John G., 3:646
Varo, 5:265
Varoufakis, Yanis, 3:204
Vartanian, Aram, 2:472, 4:197
Vartoogian, Jack, 3:733
Vartoogian, Linda, 3:733
Vasari, Giorgio, 3:761, 5:195
Vasey, Daniel E., 5:265
Vasilenko, G. I., 5:235
Vasta, Edward, 1:147
Vatikiotis, P. J., 3:419, 3:438, 3:446, 3:455
Vaughan, Adrian, 5:250
Vaughan, Alden T., 3:518
Vaughan, David, 3:731, 3:736
Vaughan, Henry, 1:199
Vaughan Williams, Ralph, 3:723, **3:725**
Vaughn, Karen I., 4:181
Vaux, Kenneth, 4:893, 5:124
Vaziri, Mostafa, 3:449
Vazov, Ivan, 2:780, 2:781, **2:782**
Vázquez, Josefina Zoraida, 3:639
Vazquez, Roland, 3:664
Veatch, Henry B., 4:71
Veatch, Robert M., 5:124, **5:143**
Veblen, Thorstein, 1:726, 1:733, 1:784, 3:72, 3:97, 3:108, **3:242, 5:169**
Vecchione, Patrice, 4:746
Vecsey, Christopher, 3:516, 4:7
Veeder, William R., 1:397
Vega Carpio, Lope Félix de, 2:520, 2:532, 2:533, 2:534, **2:553,** 2:859
Vego, Milan, 5:239
Veilleux, Armand, 4:690
Veit-Wild, Flora, 2:165
Velazquez, Diego Rodriguez de Silva, 3:768, 3:776, 3:780, **3:795**
Velde, Rink van der, 2:635
Velie, Alan R., 1:1047
Velkley, Richard, 4:207
Vellacott, Jo, 4:325
Vellacott, Philip, 2:357
Velz, John W., 1:221
Venables, Robert W., 3:516
Venclova, Thomas, 2:805
Vendler, Helen H., 1:295, 1:800, 1:888, 1:914
Vendler, Zeno, 4:171

Veninga, James F., 1:929
Vento, Arnold C., 4:33
Ventris, M., 2:347
Venturelli, Peter, 5:352
Venturi, Franco, 2:402
Verba, Sidney, 3:141, 3:148, 3:214
Verbeke, Gerald, 4:57
Verbrugghe, Gerald, 3:300
Verdi, Giuseppe, 2:473, 3:692, 3:710, 3:726
Verducci, Florence, 2:390
Verduin, Leonard, 4:724
Verduyn, Christl, 2:917
Verene, Donald P., 4:217, 5:71
Verga, Giovanni, 2:399, 2:415, 2:441
Verhage, Heleen, 5:521
Verhey, Allen, 4:746, 4:893, 5:121, 5:124
Veríssimo, Érico, 2:890, 2:900
Verkler, Linda A., 1:76
Verlaine, Paul, 2:499, 2:513, 2:621
Verlarde, Pablita, 3:866
Verleger, Phillip K., Jr., 5:285
Verma, Rajiva, 2:171
Vermazen, Bruce, 4:283
Vermes, Geza, 4:616, 4:618, 4:812
Vermeule, Emily T., 2:348, 3:302
Vernadsky, George, 3:395, 3:412
Vernant, Jean-Pierre, 4:49, 4:429, 4:492
Verney, Michael, 5:239
Vernon, John, 2:987
Verrall, Arthur W., 2:357
Versényi, Laszlo, 4:54, 4:84, 4:295
Vervliet, H.D.L., 1:14
Very, Jones, 1:704, 1:718
Vesaas, Tarjei, 2:662, 2:669
Vesalius, Andreas, 5:365
Veselinović, Janko, 2:827
Vesey, Godfrey, 4:25
Vesilind, P. Aarne, 5:128
Vespucci, Amerigo, 3:941
Vessey, David, 2:394
Vestdijk, Simon, 2:621, 2:628, 2:631
Vetter, Richard C., 5:632
Veverka, Joseph, 5:630
Vexler, Robert L., 3:381
Veyne, Paul, 2:381
Veysey, Laurence R., 4:844
Viano, Maurizio, 3:829
Vicente, Gil, 2:561

Vickers, Brian, 1:217, 1:221, 4:166
Vickery, Donald M., 5:342
Vickery, John, 2:988, 3:30, 3:879, 4:477
Vickery, Olga W., 1:838
Vickery, Walter N., 2:691, 2:703, 2:752
Vico, Giambattista, 2:398, 2:410, 2:442, 4:30, 4:158, 4:215
Vidal, Dominique, 3:436
Vidal, Gore, 1:916, 1:1061, 1:1191
Vidal-Naquet, Pierre, 3:307, 4:447
Vidler, Alexander R., 4:742
Vidyāpati, 2:173
Vieira, Sergio, 3:424
Vierra, Andrea, 3:258
Vig, Norman J., 5:154
Vigano, Aldo, 3:837
Vigar, Penelope, 1:363
Vignola, Giacomo Barozzi da, 3:755
Vik, Bjørg, 2:662, 2:670
Vilar, Pierre, 3:387
Villa, José Garciá, 1:548, 2:328
Villanueva, Marianne, 2:329
Villard, Henry Serrano, 1:847
Villegas, Franciso Gómez de Quevedo y. See Quevado y Villegas, Franciso Gómez de
Villoldo, Alberto, 5:419
Villon, François, 2:514
Vinaver, Eugène, 1:155
Vinay, Dharwadker, 2:176
Vincent, David, 3:343
Vincent, John, 1:352
Vincent, Theo, 2:113
Vincenti, Walter Guido, 5:49, 5:256
Vine, Frederick John, 5:648
Vine, Richard A., 1:943
Viner, Jacob, 3:43, 3:107, 3:110
Viney, Donald W., 4:289
Vinogradov, V. V., 2:723
Vinson, James, 1:422, 1:428, 1:920, 1:1076, 2:4
Vinterberg, H., 1:98
Vinton, John, 3:658
Vio, Riccardo, 3:779
Viola, Lynne, 3:394
Viorst, Milton, 3:540
Viravong, Maha Sila, 2:322
Virchow, Rudolf Karl, 5:410
Virgil or Vergil (Publius Vergilius Maro), 1:223, 1:252, 1:511, 2:352, 2:368, 2:383, 2:385, 2:388, 2:396, 2:437, 2:439, 2:558, 2:837

Viroli, Maurizio, 4:214
Virtanen, Reino, 2:478
Virza, Edvards, 2:803
Visconti, Luchino, 3:843
Viscusi, Robert, 1:441
Viscusi, W. Kip, 3:58, 5:404
Vishniac, Roman, 2:30
Visick, Mary, 1:336
Viswanathan, Gauri, 1:313
Vita, Finzi Claudio, 3:438
Vita-Finzi, Penelope, 1:788
Vital, David, 4:643, 4:658
Vitale, Charity Y., 5:351
Vitali, Gary J., 5:419
Vitruvius, 3:764
Vittorini, Domenico, 2:402, 2:436
Vittorini, Elio, 2:411, 2:421, 2:437, 2:442
Vitz, Evelyn B., 2:515
Vivaldi, Antonio, 3:727
Vivante, Paolo, 2:362
Vivas, Eliseo, 1:511
Vivekananda, Swami, 4:355, 4:557, 4:562
Vives, Juan Luis, 4:155, 5:412
Vladeck, Bruce C., 5:334
Vladimov, Georgy, 2:771
Vlastos, Gregory, 3:307, 4:85, 4:90
Vlastos, Stephen, 3:476
Vo-Dinh, 2:340
Voegelin, Eric, 4:85
Voeller, Bruce R., 5:779
Vogel, Cyrille, 4:701
Vogel, Dan, 1:773
Vogel, David, 2:26
Vogel, E. K., 4:809
Vogel, Lucy, 2:703
Vogel, Morris J., 5:329
Vogel, Steven, 5:342
Vogelweide, Walther von der. See Walther von der Vogelweide
Vogt, Evon Z., 4:426, 4:465, 4:897
Vogt, Thomas M., 5:383
Vogt, W. Paul, 5:521
Vogue, E. M. de, 2:691
Vohra, Ashok, 4:354
Vohra, Ranbir, 2:251
Voight, M., 3:273
Voinovich, Vladimir, 2:683, 2:772
Voisin, André, 5:264
Vojnović, Ivo, 2:785
Vold, George B., 3:205
Volkoff, Vladimir, 3:724
Volkov, Solomon, 3:738
Voll, John O., 4:573
Vollmar, Edward R., 4:752
Voloshin, Beverly R., 1:716

Volpe, Edmond, 1:838
Volpendesta, David, 2:850
Voltaire, 1:235, 2:363, 2:407,
2:444, 2:471, 2:477, **2:515**,
3:106, 3:159, 4:12, 4:15,
4:166, 4:173, 4:195, **4:217**
Volti, Rudi, 5:149
von Baeyer, Hans C., 5:651
von Braun, Wernher, 5:37,
5:612
Vondel, Joost van den,
2:620, **2:631**
Von Frank, Albert J., 1:677
Von Hagen, Victor Wolfgang,
1:6
Von Hallberg, Robert, 1:1027
Vonnegut, Kurt, Jr., 1:991,
1:1062, 2:290, 5:72
Vonnegut, Mark, 5:424
von Neumann, John, 5:582
Voorhees, David William,
3:509
Voorhies, Barbara, 3:17
Vo Phien, 2:339
Voragine, Jacobus de, 4:701
Voranc, Prežihov, 2:834
Vorgrimler, Herbert, 4:719
Vorpahl, Ben Merchant,
1:789
Vos, Howard F., 3:437
Voss, Arthur, 1:658, 1:724,
1:806
Voss, Greg, 5:551
Voss, Stephen, 4:171
Vowles, Richard B., 2:983
Voznesensky, Andrei,
1:1003, 1:1066, **2:773**
Vrana, Stan A., 1:127
Vraz, Stanko, 2:785
Vucinich, W. S., 3:453

W

Waage, Frederick O., 1:201
Waardenburg, Jacques, 4:422
Wace, Alan J. B., 2:362
Wach, Joachim, 4:493
Wachenroder, Wilhelm Hein-
rich, 2:612
Wachman, Alan, 4:533
Wachs, Harry, 3:267
Wachtel, Andrew B., 2:691
Wachterhauser, Brice R.,
4:268, 4:392
Wad, Atul, 5:183
Waddams, Herbert M., 4:731
Waddell, Helen, 2:382, 4:690
**Waddington, Miriam (Dwor-
kin)**, 2:915, **2:926**
Waddington, Raymond B.,
1:175

Wade, Bonnie C., 3:670
Wade, Ira O., 2:516, 4:28,
4:218
Wade, Mason, 1:673, 1:691,
3:592, 3:614
Wade, Michael, 2:162
Wade, Nicholas, 3:177, 5:195
Wade, Peter, 3:635
Wadler, Joyce, 5:373
Wadley, Susan Snow, 4:506
Wadlington, Warwick, 1:838
Wadman, Anne, 2:634, 2:635
Wadsworth, Philip A., 2:485
Wagar, Jeannine, 3:671
Wagar, W. Warren, 3:273
Wagenknecht, Edward C.,
1:151, 1:683, 1:685, 1:702,
1:724, 1:760, 1:773, 1:784,
3:533
Waggoner, Hyatt H., 1:655,
1:677, 1:719
Waggoner, Susan, 5:326
Waghorne, Joanne Punzo,
4:506
Wagner, Frederick B., 5:364
Wagner, Jean, 1:914, 1:955
Wagner, Lilya, 3:809
Wagner, Linda W., 1:829,
1:847, 1:1004, 1:1023
Wagner, Marsha L., 2:191,
2:228
Wagner, Melinda B., 4:855
Wagner, Richard, 2:512,
2:608, 2:617, 2:644, 3:685,
3:693, 3:704, 3:714, 3:717,
3:721, **3:727**, 3:741, 4:245,
4:255
Wagner, Rudolf G., 4:531
Wagner-Martin, Linda, 1:788,
1:805, 1:1004, 1:1032,
1:1045
Wagoner, Mary S., 1:606
Wagoner, Robert, 5:589,
5:656
Wahl, Jean A., 4:268
Wahlke, John C., 3:146
Wahrhaftig, Clyde, 5:630
Wai, Dunstan M., 3:455
Waidson, H. M., 2:567
Waife-Goldberg, Marie, 2:46
Waik, A. E., 4:848
Waingrow, Marshall, 1:227
Wainright, William J.,
4:888
Wainwright, Geoffrey, 4:5,
4:746, 4:897, 4:898
Waite, Gary K., 4:724
Waite, Linda, 3:206
Waite, Mitchell, 5:565
Waite, P. B., 3:614
Waites, Neville H., 3:373
Waith, Eugene, 1:173
Waithe, Mary Ellen, 4:163

Waitzkin, Howard B., 5:329
Wajcman, Judy, 5:155, 5:158,
5:189
Wakefield, Gordon S., 4:676,
4:718
Wakefield, Walter L., 4:701
Wakelyn, John L., 1:697,
3:553
Wakeman, Frederic, Jr.,
3:469, 3:472
Wakeman, Frederic E., 4:362
Wakeman, John, 2:4
Walbank, F. W., 3:302, 3:319
Walcott, Derek, 2:933, **2:942**
Walcott, P., 2:358, 4:482
Walcutt, Charles Child, 1:724
Walczak, Yvette, 3:207
Wald, Alan M., 1:834
Wald, Elijah, 5:781
Waldeland, Lynne, 1:962
Walden, Daniel, 1:920
Walden, Russell, 3:779
Walden, Sarah, 1:27
Waldenfels, Hans, 4:365
Waldhorn, Arthur, 1:34, 1:75
Waldman, Harry, 5:243
Waldman, Nell, 2:922
Waldmeyer, U. G., 5:374
Waldo, Dwight, 3:147
Waldock, Arthur J., 2:368
Waldorf, Mary, 5:357
Waldron, Arthur, 3:467,
4:523
Waldrop, M. Mitchell, 5:569
Walecka, John D., 5:673
Walesa, Lech, 3:390
Waley, Arthur, 2:208, 2:217,
2:274, 4:525, 4:526, 4:528
Walford, A. J., 1:74, 3:327
Walford, Roy L., 5:318
Walhout, Donald, 1:365
Wali, Kameshwar C., 5:677
Walicki, Andrzej, 4:30
Walker, Alan, 3:690, 3:704
Walker, Alice, 1:207, 1:849,
1:910, **1:1064**
Walker, Barbara K., 2:96,
2:126
Walker, Carol Kyros, 1:295
Walker, Charles A., 5:240
Walker, Cheryl, 1:655, 1:719,
1:720, 1:800
Walker, D. P., 4:131
Walker, David, 1:800, 3:369
Walker, David B., 3:148
Walker, Dorothea, 1:552
Walker, E. A., 3:424
Walker, Frank, 3:727
Walker, Franklin, 1:775,
1:777
Walker, Gay, 1:12
Walker, Graham, 5:236

Walker, Graham B., Jr.,
1:1066
Walker, Gregory, 1:51, 1:197
Walker, Helen M., 5:526
Walker, I. M., 1:693
Walker, Ian, 3:901
Walker, Imogene, 1:261
Walker, J., 1:95
Walker, James R., 3:866
Walker, Janet, 2:283
Walker, Jayne L., 1:883
Walker, Jeffrey, 1:800
Walker, John, 3:773, 3:794,
5:726
Walker, Katherine Sorley,
3:734
Walker, Lenore, 5:424
Walker, M. E., 5:801
Walker, Margaret, 1:907
Walker, Martin, 3:809
Walker, Morton, 5:375, 5:396
Walker, Peter M. B., 5:3
Walker, Ralph, 4:207
Walker, Richard, 3:123
Walker, Richard D., 5:5
Walker, Robert, 3:712
Walker, Robert H., 1:719
Walker, Samuel, 3:139
Walker, Shirley, 2:947, 2:968
Walker, Sydney, III., 5:417
Walker, Terri C., 5:243
Walker, Thomas W., 3:639
Walker, Tom, 3:910
Walker, Warren S., 1:665,
2:126
Walker, William O., 4:819
Walker, Williston, 4:678,
4:720
Walkiewicz, E. P., 1:943
Walkowitz, Judith R., 1:313
Wall, Bernard, 2:426
Wall, Cheryl A., 1:1134
Wall, Geoffrey, 3:890
Wall, John W., 1:200
Wall, Joseph Frazier, 3:549
Wall, Patrick D., 5:393
Wallace, Alfred Russel,
5:802, **5:811**
Wallace, Anthony F. C.,
3:526
Wallace, Bruce, 5:779
Wallace, C. M., 1:288
Wallace, David, 2:410
Wallace, Dewey D., 4:735
Wallace, Edgar, 1:591, **1:597**
Wallace, Henry, 5:274
Wallace, Irving, 1:1250
Wallace, James, 5:543
Wallace, James D., 1:665
Wallace, John M., 1:189
Wallace, Karl R., 4:166
Wallace, Lew, 1:1244, **1:1250**
Wallace, Michael, 3:511

Wallace, Michele, 3:874
Wallace, Richard E., 5:422
Wallace, Robert K., 2:988
Wallace, Ronald, 1:719, 1:920
Wallace, Ruth A, 4:892
Wallace, William A., 4:25,
4:74, 4:102, 4:132, 4:144,
4:256, 5:65
Wallace, W. Stewart, 3:606
Wallace-Hadrill, Andrew,
2:395, 3:320
Wallace-Hadrill, D. S., 4:687
Wallace-Hadrill, John Mi-
chael, 4:692
Wallach, Luitpold, 4:100
Wallack, F. Bradford, 4:343
Wallbridge, David, 5:472
Wallenchinsky, David, 1:88
Waller, "Fats," 3:729
Waller, David, 3:353
Waller, Gary F., 1:196
Waller, Julian A., 5:381
Waller, Maurice, 3:729
Waller, Ray, 5:524
Wallerstein, Immanuel,
3:234, **3:243**, 3:424
Waller-Zuckerman, Mary El-
len, 1:652
Walling, William, 1:301
Wallis, Brian, 3:202
Wallis, Lawrence B., 1:173
Wallis, L. W., 1:20
Wallis, Richard T., 4:62, 4:63
Wallis, Roy, 4:869
Wallraff, Charles F., 4:300,
5:139
Walls, Jerry G., 5:769
Walmsley, Dorothy, 2:228
Walmsley, Lewis C., 2:228
Walpole, Horace, 1:262,
1:373, 1:590, 1:598, 1:601,
1:603, 1:621
Walsh, Chad, 4:777
Walsh, Claudette M., 1:899
Walsh, Gregory, 5:393
Walsh, H. H., 3:612
Walsh, James J., 4:71, 4:94
Walsh, Jeffrey, 1:920
Walsh, Michael, 3:705, 4:676
Walsh, Thomas F., 1:870
Walsh, Thomas P., 1:532
Walsh, Townsend, 1:332
Walsh, William, 2:939
Walshe, Maurice, 4:514
Walski, Thomas M., 5:245
Waltari, Mika Toimi, 2:657,
2:661
Walter, Claire, 1:88
Walter, Frank K., 1:61
Walter, James J., 5:123
Walter, Maila L., 5:676
Walter, Russ, 5:538
Walters, D. Gareth, 2:548

Walters, F. P., 3:281
Walters, Gregory J., 4:300
Walters, J. Donald (Swami
Kriyananda), 4:557
Walters, LeRoy, 5:61, 5:118,
5:124
Walters, P., 5:660
Walters, R. H., 3:175
Walters, Ronald G., 3:526
Walther, Wiebke, 4:580
**Walther von der Vogel-
weide,** 2:562, **2:614**
Waltke, Bruce K., 4:795
Walton, Craig, 4:182
Walton, Douglas, 4:381
Walton, Geoffrey, 1:788
Walton, John, 5:368
Walz, Eugene P., 3:843
Walzer, Mary M., 3:901
Walzer, Michael, 3:361, 4:735
Walzer, Norman, 5:333
Wand, John W., 4:682, 4:687
Wandor, Michelene, 1:427
Wang, C. H., 2:195
Wang, Chamont, 5:524
Wang, Gungwu, 2:312, 3:492
Wang, James C., 3:472
Wang, Jing, 2:191
Wang, Te-wei, 2:234
Wang, Tso-Liang, 1:201
Wang An-i, 2:266
Wang An-shih, 2:214, 2:215,
2:220, **2:225**
Wang Ch'ang-ling, 2:225
Wangchen, Geshe Namgyal,
4:513
Wangerin, Ruth, 4:864
Wang Meng, 2:267
Wangsawarn, Rong, 2:335
Wang Shih-chen, 2:185,
2:226
Wang Shih-ching, 2:256
Wang Shih-fu, 2:226
Wang Wei, 2;187, 2:214,
2:225, **2:227**
Warburton, Nigel, 4:25
Ward, A. C., 2:4
Ward, Adolphus W., 3:363
Ward, Aileen, 1:295
Ward, Audrey, 1:48
Ward, Barbara, 3:48, 3:66,
3:112, **3:295**
Ward, Benedicta, 4:701
Ward, Charles E., 1:242
Ward, Christopher, 3:522
Ward, David, 3:124, **3:136**
Ward, Dederick C., 5:625
Ward, Elizabeth, 3:826
Ward, Gary L., 4:895
Ward, Geoffrey C., 3:530
Ward, Gerald W., 3:766,
3:767

Ward, Jerry W., 1:134, 1:716, 1:921, 1:1129
Ward, John T., 3:365
Ward, Margaret, 3:371
Ward, Paul T., 5:551
Ward, Peter, 3:609
Ward, Philip, 1:48, 2:523
Ward, Robert E., 3:480
Ward, Stephen A., 5:231
Ward, Theodore Van, 1:748
Ward, William S., 1:274
Warde, Beatrice, 1:12
Wardle, Ralph Martin, 1:291
Ward-Perkins, J. B., 3:764
Ware, Dora, 3:765
Ware, James R., 4:529
Ware, Louise, 3:822
Ware, Marsha, 5:396
Ware, Susan, 3:536
Ware, Timothy, 4:694, 4:756
Warf, James C., 5:241
Warfel, Harry R., 1:636
Warford, Jeremy J., 3:48
Warhol, Andy, 3:795
Warhol, Robyn R., 1:927, 1:1134
Warkentin, John, 3:606
Warmington, E. H., 2:382
Warner, Anne, 3:853
Warner, Craig, 1:1038
Warner, Kerstin P., 1:251
Warner, Marina, 4:679
Warner, Oliver, 1:375
Warner, Rex, 1:193, 2:348
Warner, Stephen, 4:197
Warner, William W., 5:818
Warnke, Georgia, 4:402
Warnke, Martin, 3:792
Warnock, Geoffrey J., 4:192, 4:268, 4:272
Warnock, Mary, 4:268
Warnock, Robert, 1:427
Warnow, Joan Nelson, 5:606
Warr, Wendy, 5:727
Warren, Austin, 2:984
Warren, Harris G., 3:640
Warren, James, 5:375
Warren, James Perrin, 1:708
Warren, John K., 5:625
Warren, Joyce W., 1:671, 1:724
Warren, Larry, 3:735
Warren, Leonard, 3:19
Warren, Michael, 1:214
Warren, Robert Penn, 1:128, 1:653, 1:708, 1:736, 1:806, 1:869, 1:870, 1:874, **1:892**, 1:953, 5:787
Warren, W. L., 3:357
Warrender, Howard, 4:175
Warrick, Patricia S., 5:566
Warshaw, M., 5:379
Warshow, Robert, 3:874

Wartofsky, Marx W., 4;228, 5:62, 5:65
Warwick, Ronald, 2:183
Washburn, Margaret, 3:195
Washburn, Mark, 5:593
Washburn, Wilcomb E., 3:512
Washington, Booker T(aliaferro), 1:726, **1:785**, 1:831, **3:269**, 3:577
Washington, George, 1:680
Washington, Joseph R., Jr., 4:749
Wasiolek, Edward, 2:766
Waskow, Arthur I., 4:600
Wasley, Terree P., 5:333
Wasserman, Anthony I., 5:551
Wasserman, Earl R., 1:304
Wasserman, Jack, 3:780
Wasserman, Loretta, 1:822
Wasserman, Neil H., 5:232
Wasserstein, Bernard, 4:637, 4:638
Wasserstein, Wendy, 1:1071, **1:1114**
Wasserstrom, Jeffrey N., 3:472
Wasserstrom, William, 1:730
Wassmo, Herbjørg, 2:662, 2:663
Wasson, Tyler, 5:729
Wästberg, Per, 2:672
Waswo, Ann, 3:480
Waswo, Richard, 4:132
Waszink, P. M., 2:723
Watanabe, Kazuko, 4:545
Watanabe, Susuma, 5:182
Waterbury, John, 3:446
Waterfield, Robin, 4:51
Waterhouse, Ellis, 3:790
Waterlow, Sarah, 4:71
Waterman, Amy, 4:218
Waters, Aaron C., 5:622
Waters, Donald J., 3:867
Waters, Peter, 1:27
Waters, Somerset R., 3:891
Wati, Arena, 2:323
Watkin, David, 3:763
Watkin, Donald M., 5:349
Watkins, Ann E., 5:522
Watkins, Floyd C., 1:894
Watkins, Glenn, 3:666
Watkins, John, 5:65
Watkins, J.W.N, 4:175
Watkins, Mary, 5:420
Watkins, M. H., 3:606
Watkins, Nicholas, 3:781
Watkins, Owen, 4:735
Watkins, Peter, 5:663
Watkins, Vernon (Phillips), 1:560
Watson, Alan, 3:626

Watson, Aldren A., 1:27
Watson, Burton, 2:191, 2:214, 4:358, 4:529
Watson, Charles N., 1:775
Watson, Derek, 3:685
Watson, Donald G., 1:1041
Watson, George, 1:121, 1:422
Watson, G. Llewellyn, 3:218
Watson, G. R., 3:309
Watson, Harry L., 3:526
Watson, Ian, 1:437, 2:710
Watson, James Dewey, 5:49, 5:732, 5:777, 5:790, 5:791, **5:812**, 5:813
Watson, James L., 3:466, 4:531, 4:533
Watson, John, 5:231
Watson, John B(roadus), 3:166, 3:176, **3:195**, 5:411
Watson, J. R., 1:268
Watson, Julia, 1:928
Watson, Philip S., 4:779
Watson, Richard A., 4:171
Watson, Robert G., 3:626
Watson, Robert I., 3:168, 5:35, 5:414
Watson, Robert N., 1:184
Watson, Roger, 1:345
Watson, Sara Ruth, 1:542
Watson-Williams, Helen, 2:506
Watsuji Tetsurō, 4:366, 4:367
Watt, David L., 5:261
Watt, Donald, 1:500
Watt, Donald C., 3:281
Watt, Norman F., 5:428
Watt, William Montgomery, 3:213, 4:97, 4:373, 4:573, 4:577, 4:582, 4:587, 4:589
Watteau, Jean-Antoine, 1:451
Watters, Carolyn, 5:480
Watts, Alan Wilson, 4:853, 4:860, **4:880**, 5:424
Watts, Charles H., 1:656
Watts, Emily, 2:988
Watts, Emily Stipes, 1:630, 1:655
Watts, Harold H., 1:500
Watts, Pauline Moffit, 4:149
Watzlawick, Paul, 5:420
Waugh, Alec, 3:897
Waugh, Charles G., 3:858
Waugh, Earle H., 4:887
Waugh, Evelyn, 1:412, 1:419, 1:429, 1:444, 1:448, 1:474, 1:536, **1:561**, 1:1040
Waugh, Patricia, 1:135, 1:1134
Waxman, Chaim I., 4:641
Waxman, Meyer, 2:32
Waxman, Mordecai, 4:655
Waxman, Robert, 5:558

Way, Brian, 1:841
Wayman, Alex, 4:514
Wayman, Hideko, 4:514
Wayne, Stephen J., 3:144,
  3:147
Weakland, Allen, 5:683
Wear, Andrew, 5:41
Wearden, Stanley, 5:521
Wearing, J. P., 1:427, 1:546
Weatherall, David, 3:101
Weatherall, M., 5:13
Weatherby, Harold L., 4:783
Weatherby, W. J., 1:939,
  1:1084
Weatherford, J. McIver, 3:23
Weatherford, Richard M.,
  1:743
Weatherhead, Andrew Kings-
  ley, 1:553
Weaver, Bennett, 1:304
Weaver, Donald B., 3:169
Weaver, Jack W., 3:558
Weaver, Jefferson Hane,
  5:678
Weaver, M., 1:901
Weaver, Muriel P., 3:13
Weaver, Robert, 2:905
Weaver, Suzanne, 3:61
Weaver, Warren, 5:571
Weaver, William, 3:727
Webb, Beatrice, 3:112
Webb, Clement C. J., 4:18,
  4:116
Webb, Eugene, 4:320
Webb, Eugene J., 3:7
Webb, James, 4:842, 4:856,
  4:876
Webb, Michael G., 5:285
Webb, Robert K., 1:313,
  1:376, 3:356
Webb, Sidney, 3:55, 3:112
Webb, Stephen, 3:518
Webb, Timothy, 1:304
**Webb, Walter Prescott,
  3:600**
Webb, William H., 3:5
**Webber, Andrew Lloyd,
  3:704**
Webber, Winslow L., 1:34
Weber, Alison, 2:550, 4:787
Weber, Brom, 1:812
Weber, Bruce H., 5:763
Weber, Carl J., 1:363
Weber, Charles L., 5:300
Weber, Julius, 5:618
**Weber, Max, 3:51, 3:55,
  3:198, 3:210, 3:213, 3:217,
  3:225, 3:229, 3:237, 3:242,
  3:243, 3:334, 4:424, 4:425,
  4:494, 4:759**
Weber, Olga S., 1:34, 1:135
Weber, R., 4:796
Weber, Robert J., 5:726

Weber, Robert L., 5:718
Weber, Ronald, 1:847
Weber, Samuel, 1:1127
Weber, William, 3:728
Webering, Damascene, 4:121
**Webern, Anton von, 3:705,
  3:714, 3:729**
Webster, Andrew, 5:149
Webster, Charles, 5:43
Webster, D. E., 3:453
Webster, Harvey C., 1:422
Webster, James K., 5:217
Webster, John, 1:200, 5:264
Webster, John G., 5:370
Webster, T. B., 2:348, 2:364,
  2:368, 3:302
Wechsler, David, 3:196
Weckmann, Luis, 3:630
Wecter, Dixon, 1:784
Wedberg, Anders, 4:18, 4:85,
  4:268
Wedde, Ian, 2:971
Wedding, Dan, 5:420
Wedeck, Harry E., 2:382
Wedeen, Richard P., 5:352
**Wedekind, Frank (Benja-
  min Franklin), 2:614,
  3:679**
Wedgwood, Cicely V., 3:361
Wedin, Michael V., 4:71
Weeks, Jeffrey, 1:1182
Weeks, John, 3:11, 3:640
Weeks, Lyman Horace, 1:6
Weeks, Mary Elvira, 5:729
Weeks, William Earl, 3:546
Wees, William C., 3:827
Wegeler, Franz Gerhard,
  3:678
Wegelin, O., 1:630
Wegener, Charles, 4:381
Weger, Karl-Heinz, 4:746
Wegs, J. Robert, 3:346
Wehr, Hans, 1:97
Wei, James, 5:223
Wei, Wang. See Wang Wei
Weibel, Adele C., 3:767
Wei Chuang, 2:228
Weidner, Marsha, 4:524,
  4:535
**Weierstrass, Karl Wilhelm
  Theodor, 5:490, 5:516**
Weigel, John A., 1:470
Weiger, John G., 2:536
Weightman, Judith M., 4:867
Weigl, Bruce, 1:968
Weigle, L. A., 4:798
Weigley, Russell F., 3:536
Weik, Martin H., 3:802
Weiker, Walter F., 3:453
Weil, André, 5:489
Weil, Andrew, 5:320, 5:404
Weil, Ben H., 1:55
Weil, Dorothy, 1:643

Weil, Judith, 1:187
Weil, Marsha, 3:256
**Weil, Simone, 2:362, 2:516,
  4:788**
Weil, Ulric, 5:558
Weil, Vivian, 5:159
Weiler, Paul C., 5:344
Weimann, Robert, 1:210
Weinberg, Alvin, 5:113
Weinberg, Bernard, 2:402,
  2:454, 2:498
Weinberg, David H., 4:638
Weinberg, Gerhard L., 3:378
Weinberg, Herman G., 3:840
Weinberg, Julius R., 4:94,
  4:163, 4:698
Weinberg, R. J., 4:104
Weinberg, Robert, 1:1216
**Weinberg, Steven, 5:596,
  5:665, 5:690, 5:713, 5:718**
Weinberger, Bernhard W.,
  5:407
Weinberger, Jerry, 4:166
Weinberger, Marvin I., 5:547
Weinberger, Norman S.,
  3:767
Weinbrot, Howard D., 1:226
Weinder, Lyu, 5:402
Weiner, Anita, 4:643
Weiner, Carolyn N., 3:825
Weiner, Charles, 5:606
Weiner, David A., 4:347
Weiner, Eugene, 4:643
Weiner, Herbert, 4:630, 4:643
Weiner, Irving B., 5:420
Weiner, Joan, 4:230
Weiner, Jonathan, 5:625
Weiner, Max, 4:653
Weiner, Michael E., 5:348
Weiner, Myron F., 5:420
Weiner, Philip P., 3:7
Weiner, Richard, 3:802
Weiner, Richard S., 5:553
Weinfield, Henry, 1:248
Weingarden, Lauren S., 3:793
Weingart, Richard E., 4:106
Weingartner, Charles, 3:252
Weingartner, Paul, 5:83,
  5:108
Weingast, David Elliott, 3:815
Weingreen, Jacob, 4:795
Weininger, Otto, 5:457
Weinlick, J. R., 4:740
Weinreich, Beatrice, 2:33
Weinreich, Max, 2:32
Weinreich, Regina, 1:999
Weinreich, Uriel, 2:33
Weinryb, Bernard, 4:625
Weinsheimer, Joel, 4:402
Weinstein, Bruce, 5:124
Weinstein, David A., 1:55
Weinstein, Donald, 4:701
Weinstein, Leo, 2:551

Weinstein, Marlene G., 5:558
Weinstein, Michael A., 4:33,
    4:36
Weinstock, John, 2:638,
    5:806
Weintraub, Pamela, 5:696
Weintraub, Sidney, 3:63
Weintraub, Stanley, 1:428,
    1:546, 1:929
Weintraub, Wiktor, 2:817
Weir, Robert F., 5:124
Weis, Elizabeth, 1:1170
Weisberg, Herbert F., 3:138,
    3:144
Weisbord, Robert G., 4:638
Weisbrot, Robert, 3:558,
    4:645
Weisbuch, Robert, 1:652,
    1:748
Weisenburger, Steven C.,
    1:1036
Weisenthal, Simon, 3:351
Weishahn, Mel W., 3:254
Weisheipl, James A., 4:107,
    4:119, 5:40
Weiss, Anita M., 3:487
Weiss, Beno, 2:439
Weiss, Daniel, 1:511
Weiss, Egon, 1:20
Weiss, Gaea, 5:321
Weiss, Johannes, 4:826
Weiss, Judy, 1:148
Weiss, Nancy J., 3:536
Weiss, Paul, 4:262, 4:288,
    4:338
Weiss, Peter, 2:603, **2:614**
Weiss, Piero, 3:664
Weiss, Raymond, 4:668
Weiss, Roberto, 2:402, 4:132
Weiss, Shandor, 5:321
Weiss, Sharlene M., 5:401
Weiss, Solomon, 5:359
Weissbort, Daniel, 2:692
Weisse, Allen B., 5:315,
    5:405
Weissglass, Julian, 5:525
Weisskopf, Victor F., 5:651,
    5:708
Weissman, Dick, 3:852
Weissmann, Gerald, 5:766
Weisstein, Ulrich, 2:984
Weitz, Morris, 4:268
Weitzman, David, 5:232
Weitzman, Kurt, 3:767
Weitzmann, Lenore J., 3:207
Weixlmann, Joseph, 1:943
Weizenbaum, Joseph, 5:77,
    5:126, **5:144,** 5:159, 5:570,
    5:571
Weizman, Ezer, 3:441
Weizmann, Chaim, 3:351
Welbon, Guy, 4:507
Welch, Claude, 4:742

Welch, Holmes, 4:530
Welch, John F., 5:220
Welch, Robert E., 1:418,
    1:752
Welch, Susan, 3:212
Welch, Walter L., 5:230
Welcher, Frank J., 5:735
Weld, Annette, 1:539
Welding, Peter, 3:669
Welfare, Simon, 3:396
Welfe, W., 3:63
Welhaven, Johan, 2:661
Welker, Anthony J., 5:286
Wellbery, David E., 2:600
Wellek, René, 1:135, 1:266,
    1:430, 1:927, 2:414, 2:984
Welles, E. R., 3:859
Welles, (George) Orson,
    1:1170, **1:1178,** 3:844
Wells, Carolyn, 1:131
Wells, Christine L., 5:341
Wells, Colin, 3:303
Wells, Deane, 5:123
Wells, Frank, 3:906
Wells, Harry K., 3:191
Wells, H(erbert) G(eorge),
    1:367, 1:412, 1:413, 1:423,
    1:428, 1:440, 1:475, 1:540,
    1:563, 1:565, 1:577, 1:611,
    1:761, 1:1178, 1:1209,
    1:1251, 2:475, 5:563
Wells, Kenneth E., 4:520
Wells, Malcolm, 5:278
Wells, Robin Headlam, 1:199
Wells, Stanley, 1:206, 1:207,
    1:221, 1:222
Wellwarth, George E., 2:524,
    2:526
Welsch, Roger, 3:862
Welsh, Alexander, 1:226,
    1:300, 1:351
Welshimer, Linda, 1:838
Welter, Barbara, 1:716
Welton, K. B., 4:895
Welty, Eudora, 1:447, **1:894**
Welty, Paul T., 3:463
Wemple, Suzanne F., 4:701
Wemyss, Courtney T., 1:531
Wendel, François, 4:762
Wender, Dorothea, 2:382
Wendorf, Richard, 1:236
Wendt, Albert, 2:970, **2:979**
Wenk, Arthur B., 3:692
Wenk, Edward, Jr., 5:159,
    5:183, 5:215
Wenke, Robert J., 4:432,
    4:439
Wenner, Manfred W., 3:451
Wensinck, Arent J., 4:577
Wentz, Walter Yeeling Evans,
    4:544
Wentzel, Kenneth B., 5:379
Wenyon, Michael, 5:235

Wenz, Peter S., 4:389, 4:895
Wenzel, Helene V., 2:459
Werblowsky, J. Z., 4:628
Werblowsky, Zwi, 4:595
Werfel, Franz, 2:564, **2:615**
Werhane, Patricia H., 4:347
Werkmeister, William H.,
    4:36
Wernblad, Annette, 3:830
Wernecke, Herbert H., 3:870
Werner, Craig H., 1:920
Werner, Eric, 4:597
Wernham, James, 1:769,
    4:335
Wernham, R. B., 3:359
Wershoven, Carol, 1:788
Wertenbaker, Lael T., 5:342
Werth, Alexander, 3:281
Wertheim, Albert, 1:1072
Wertheim, Gunther K., 5:704
Wertheimer, Alan, 4:387
Wertheimer, Jack, 3:351
Wertsman, Vladimir, 2:690
Wertz, Dorothy C., 3:202
Wescott, Lynanne, 5:220
Wesker, Arnold, 1:424,
    1:433, 1:526, 1:531, 1:543,
    1:564
Wesley, John, 4:738, 4:740,
    4:789
Wessinger, Catherine Low-
    man, 4:550
West, Cornel, 1:727, 1:772,
    4:267, 4:268, 4:379, 4:749
West, Dame Rebecca, 1:422,
    1:565
West, Darrell M., 3:812
West, David, 2:382
West, Delno C., 3:917
West, Edward N., 4:716
West, John F., 2:655
West, John O., 3:864
West, Luther S., 5:806
West, Nathanael, 1:802,
    1:896, 1:972
West, Rebecca J., 2:402,
    2:428
West, Richard C., 1:559
West, Ruth, 5:319, 5:321
West, Selno C., 4:712
West, Stephen G., 3:200
West, Stephen H., 2:190
West, Thomas H., 4:277
Westbrook, Francis Abeken,
    2:202
Westbrook, Perry D., 1:634,
    1:717, 1:750, 1:771
Westbrook, Robert B., 3:261,
    4:226
Westerby, Herbert, 3:704
Westergaard, Harald, 5:527
Westermann, Claus, 4:815,
    4:822, 4:824

Westermeyer, Joseph, 5:428
Westernhagen, Curt von, 3:729
Westerway, Peter, 5:297
Westerweel, Bart, 1:181
Westfall, Gloria, 1:111
Westfall, Richard S., 4:184, 5:43, 5:512, 5:706
Westfall, William, 3:610
Westkott, Marcia, 3:186, 5:452
Westlake, H. D., 3:323
Westling, Louise, 1:896
Westman, Robert S., 5:41
Westman, Walter E., 5:821
Westmore, Ann, 5:360
Westney, D. Eleanor, 3:480
Westoby, Adam, 4:18, 4:162
Weston, Alan J., 5:339
Weston, Corinne, 3:361
Weston, Rae, 5:637
Weston-Smith, Miranda, 5:191
Westphal, Fred A., 4:25
Westphal, Jonathan, 4:347
Westphal, Kenneth, 4:233
Westrum, Ron, 5:149
Westrup, Jack A., 3:711
Westrute, Bruce C., 3:438
Wetherbee, Winthrop, 1:151
Wetlesen, Jon, 4:189
Wetter, Gustav A., 4:31
Wettersten, John, 4:409, 5:99
Wetzel, Betty, 3:910
Wexelblatt, Richard L., 5:551
Wexford, Jane, 2:770
Wexman, Virginia W., 3:841
Weybright, Victor, 1:45
Whalen, James, 2:550
Whalen, Terry, 1:508
Whaley, Susan, 2:928
Whaling, Frank, 4:422
Wharton, C. E., 1:1060
Wharton, David A., 5:772
Wharton, Edith, 1:711, 1:726, 1:750, **1:786,** 1:937, 1:1004
Wharton, E. R., 1:99
Wheare, Jane, 1:570
Wheatley, Paul, 4:439
Wheatley (Peters), Phillis, 1:626, **1:646,** 2:125
Wheeler, Jesse, H., 5:621
Wheeler, John Archibald, 5:665, **5:719**
Wheeler, Lynde Phelps, 5:747
Wheeler, Marjorie, 5:625
Wheeler, Mary B., 3:9
Wheeler, Michael, 1:395, 5:525
Wheeler, Mortimer, 3:760
Wheeler, Post, 3:857
Wheeler, Richard P., 1:211

Wheelis, Allen, 5:414
Wheelock, Frederic M., 2:393
Wheelock, Keith, 3:446
Wheelwright, Phillip E., 4:75
Wheelwright, Ted, 3:494
Whewell, William, 4:257, **5:57,** 5:104
Wheye, Darryl, 5:769
Whibley, Leonard, 2:348
Whicher, George F., 1:748
Whicher, Stephen E., 1:671, 1:720
Whicker, Marcia L., 5:333
Whiffen, Marcus, 3:764
Whipple, Thomas K., 2:389
Whistler, L., 1:262
Whitaker, G. H., 4:810
Whitaker, Thomas, 1:901
Whitaker, Virgil K., 1:220
Whitby, M., 5:262
White, Alan, 4:252
White, Alan R., 4:312, 4:387
White, Augustus A., III, 5:394
White, Barbara A., 1:725, 1:789
White, Barbara Ehrlich, 3:789
White, Carl M., 3:273
White, Christopher, 3:789, 3:792
White, David A., 4:85, 4:295
White, Edmund, 1:1185
White, Edward G., 1:789
White, Elizabeth Wade, 1:635
White, E(lwyn) B(rooks), 1:118, 1:131, 1:807, 1:889, **1:897,** 1:1194, 1:1208
White, Eric W., 3:685, 3:723, 3:725
White, Florence M., 5:752
White, Geoffrey, 3:15
White, Gertrude, 1:533
White, Gilbert, 5:632, 5:637, 5:819
White, Graham, 3:368
White, Hayden V., 1:956, **1:1153**
White, James, 1:501
White, James W., 3:480
White, Joan, 3:734
White, John, 3:701, 5:195
White, Katherine S., 1:131
White, K. D., 3:304, 5:39
White, Ken, 1:48
White, Landeg, 2:939
White, Lawrence J., 3:56
White, Leonard, 3:162
White, Leslie Alvin, 3:14, 3:19, **3:41**
White, L. P., 5:290

White, Lynn, Jr., 3:332, 5:40, **5:58,** 5:117, 5:145, 5:199
White, Michael, 5:17, 5:607, 5:652, 5:656, 5:692
White, Morton, 4:36, 4:226, 4:268, 5:96
White, N. B., 5:523
White, Newman Ivey, 1:304
White, Nicholas P., 4:85
White, Norman, 1:365
White, Patrick, 2:945, 2:958, **2:964**
White, Randy Wayne, 3:898
White, Ray L., 1:811, 1:812, 1:1062, 2:676
White, R. E., 4:679
White, Richard, 3:551
White, R. J., 1:266
White, Robert W., 5:428
White, Sarah H., 1:122, 1:125
White, Sidney Howard, 1:437
White, Stephen, 3:398
White, Stephen K., 3:138, 3:229, 4:405
White, Steven F., 2:850
White, Theodore, 3:540, 3:809
White, Tony, 3:766
Whitebread, Charles H., 3:139
Whitehead, Alfred North, 3:13, 4:260, 4:288, 4:301, 4:302, 4:320, 4:338, **4:340,** 4:377, 4:379, 4:411, 5:27, 5:84, 5:101, 5:482, 5:516
Whitehead, David, 3:299
Whitehead, Henry, 4:507
Whitehead, John, 1:36, 1:520, 1:521
Whitehill, Clayton, 1:20
Whitelaw, William Menzies, 3:614
Whiteley, Nigel, 1:395
Whitelock, Dorothy, 1:143, 3:356
Whitemore, Hugh, 5:582
Whiten, Andrew, 4:383
Whiteside, Kerry H., 4:311
Whiteside, Thomas, 1:51
Whitfield, Francis J., 1:101
Whitfield, Jane S., 1:95
Whitfield, John H., 2:402
Whiting, Bartlett J., 1:115
Whiting, Beatrice B., 3:15, 5:417
Whiting, Helen A., 3:867
Whiting, John, 5:417
Whiting, John W., 3:15
Whiting, Robert, 4:727
Whiting, Roger, 5:195
Whiting, W. M., 3:12
Whitlow, Roger, 1:847

Whitman, Cedric H., 2:354, 2:357, 2:362, 2:368, 4:475
Whitman, Robert F., 1:546
Whitman, Ruth, 2:34
Whitman, Walt, 1:654, 1:668, **1:705**, 1:718, 1:796, 1:877, 1:908, 1:933, 1:981, 1:1042, 1:1048, 1:1057, 1:1192, 2:237, 2:250, 2:432, 2:711, 3:725
Whitmarsh, Anne, 2:459
Whitmarsh, Katherine, 4:355
Whitmore, A. P., 5:265
Whitnah, Donald R., 3:507
Whitney, Barry L., 4:289
Whitney, Charles A., 5:591
Whitney, Elinor, 1:29
Whitney, Phyllis A., 1:1238
Whitney, Steven, 5:355
Whitrow, G. J., 5:68, 5:683
Whitson, Robley E., 4:850
Whitt, Frank Rowland, 5:236
Whittaker, Alan, 5:242
Whittaker, Molly, 4:605
Whittaker, Thomas, 4:62
Whittall, Arnold, 3:664, 3:666, 3:685, 3:725
Whittemore, Katharine, 1:809
Whittemore, Reed, 1:914
Whittemore, Robert C., 4:284
Whitteridge, G., 5:362
Whittier, John Greenleaf, 1:708, 1:717, 1:1193
Whitton, Kenneth S., 2:577
Whittow, John B., 5:621, 5:637
Whitworth, Geoffrey, 3:749
Whitworth, J. A., 5:5, 5:367
Wholey, Denis, 5:403
Whorf, Benjamin L., 3:20, **3:42**
Whorton, James, 5:315
Whyte, Martin King, 3:207
Whyte, William F., 3:173
Wiant, Sarah, 1:118
Wiarda, Howard, 3:141
Wibha Senanan, 2:336
Wickens, G. M., 4:582
Wickersham, John, 3:300
Wickett, Ann, 4:389, 5:378
Wickham, Glynne, 1:158, 1:170
Wicks, George, 1:863
Wicksell, Knut, 3:114
Widdicombe, Toby, 1:734
Widdowson, Peter, 1:363
Widdowson, R. W., 5:266
Widmer, Kingsley, 1:863, 1:897
Widner, Doug, 5:305
Wiebe, Robert H., 3:526, 3:533
Wiebe, Rudy, 2:927

Wieczynski, Joseph L., 3:395
Wiedhaus, Peter, 1:69
Wiegand, Wayne A., 1:36
Wiener, Leo, 2:33, 2:694
Wiener, Martin, 3:368
Wiener, Norbert, 5:77, 5:159, 5:495, 5:541, 5:581, **5:583**
Wiener, Philip P., 3:9, 3:273, 4:3, 4:15, 4:163
Wienpahl, Paul, 4:189
Wiesel, Elie, 1:1064, 3:351, 4:633
Wiesenthal, J. L., 1:546
Wieser, Nora J., 2:850
Wiest, Jean-Paul, 4:533
Wiet, Gaston, 3:438
Wiget, Andrew O., 1:133, 1:717
Wiggins, Gary D., 5:727
Wiggins, Henry H., 1:40
Wightman, G.B.H., 2:58
Wightman, William P., 5:27, 5:41
Wigley, T.M.L., 5:634
Wigner, Eugene Paul, 5:142, **5:719**
Wigoder, Geoffrey, 4:5, 4:595, 4:597
Wigzell, Faith, 2:722
Wijaya, Putu, 2:316, 2:318
Wijetilleke, Lakdasa, 5:286
Wilber, C. Martin, 3:472
Wilber, Donald N., 3:449
Wilbert, Johannes, 4:466
Wilbur, Earl M., 4:724
Wilbur, J. B., 4:71
Wilbur, Richard, 1:1066
Wilcher, Robert, 1:565
Wilcox, David R., 3:628, 4:456
Wilcox, Earl J., 1:842
Wilcox, Ella W., 4:847
Wilcox, John C., 2:525, 2:543
Wilcox, Wayne A., 3:487
Wilczek, Frank, 5:651
Wild, Cynthia M., 5:426
Wild, John D., 4:85, 4:238
Wild, Peter, 5:816
Wildavsky, Aaron, 3:146, 3:147
Wilde, Alan, 1:477
Wilde, Oscar, 1:311, 1:324, 1:357, 1:363, 1:367, 1:386, 1:388, **1:409**, 1:423, 1:438, 1:974, 2:819
Wilde, William H., 2:947
Wildenstein, Daniel, 3:784
Wilder, Alec, 3:664, **3:730**
Wilder, Amos N., 1:899, 1:1116
Wilder, John, 1:212

Wilder, Laura Ingalls, 1:1195, **1:1208**
Wilder, Raymond, 5:492, 5:494
Wilder, Thornton, 1:897, **1:898**, 1:1070, **1:1115**, 2:508, 2:910
Wilder, Warren F., 2:448
Wildman, Eugene, 1:914
Wilen, Joan, 5:321
Wilen, Lydia, 5:321
Wilentz, Gay, 1:927
Wiles, Cheryl B., 5:336
Wiles, David, 1:219
Wiles, Maurice F., 4:687, 4:690
Wiley, Bell I., 1:738, 3:530
Wiley, Elizabeth, 1:694
Wiley, Roland J., 3:724
Wiley, Virginia, 1:47
Wilford, John Noble, Jr., 5:621, 5:640
Wilheim, J. J., 1:874
Wilhelm, Richard, 4:525, 4:529
Wilhoit, Frances, 3:801
Wilk, Harry, 5:628
Wilken, Robert L., 4:100, 4:684
Wilkerson, James A., 5:381
Wilkes, Paul, 4:781
Wilkie, Brian, 1:268, 1:279, 2:5
Wilkins, Burleigh, 3:285, 4:193
Wilkins, Ernest H., 2:402, 2:434, 4:151
Wilkins, Isabelle A., 5:358
Wilkins, Maurice Hugh Frederick, 5:777, 5:790, 5:812, **5:813**
Wilkinson, B., 3:355
Wilkinson, David O., 2:488
Wilkinson, Ian A. G., 3:253
Wilkinson, Jane, 2:112
Wilkinson, Loren, 4:746, 5:199
Wilkinson, L. P., 2:381, 2:386
Wilkinson, Myler, 1:847
Wilkinson, Rupert, 3:553
Wilks, Ivor, 3:421
Wilks, Michael J., 4:116
Will, Clifford M., 5:49
Willard, Dallas, 4:235
Willard, Nancy, 1:1195
Willard, Ruth, 2:484
Willcock, Malcolm L., 2:362
Willeford, Bennett R., Jr., 5:753
Willemen, Paul, 1:1158
Willemson, Eleanor W., 5:525
Willenson, Kim, 3:540

Willett, Frank, 3:760
Willey, Basil, 1:176, 1:226
Will-Harris, Daniel, 5:562
William, Joseph Mallard, 5:203
William, Douglas E., 4:410
William of Ockham, 4:93, 4:103, 4:113, **4:119**
William of Sherwood, 4:103
William of St. Thierry, 4:102
Williams, A. Roy, 5:324
Williams, Andrew T., 5:558
Williams, Anne, 1:227
Williams, Aubrey L., 1:237
Williams, Bernard, 4:171
Williams, Carolyn, 1:388
Williams, Cecil B., 1:683
Williams, Chris, 2:964, 5:398
Williams, Christine L., 3:207
Williams, D., 5:662
Williams, Dakin, 1:1118
Williams, Daniel D., 4:679
Williams, David, 1:373
Williams, Edwin B., 1:103
Williams, E. Neville, 3:327
Williams, Eric, 3:630
Williams, Frank J., 5:520
Williams, Frederick, 3:253, 5:297
Williams, Gareth, 5:593
Williams, Garth, 1:1194
Williams, Geoffrey Bernard, 1:473
Williams, George C., 5:800
Williams, George H., 4:724, 4:733, 4:747
Williams, George M., 4:563
Williams, George W., 1:176, 3:514
Williams, Glanmor, 3:369
Williams, Gordon, 2:381, 2:397
Williams, Gray, 5:341
Williams, Gwyn A., 3:369
Williams, Harley, 5:811
Williams, Harry, 1:1038
Williams, Henry B., 1:1076
Williams, Hermine Weigel, 3:670
Williams, Howel, 5:629, 5:630
Williams, Huntington, III, 3:812
Williams, Ioan, 1:379
Williams, Iolo A., 1:34
Williams, Jack, 3:124, 5:634
Williams, Jay, 3:793
Williams, Jed, 5:248
Williams, John Alden, 4:577, 4:580
Williams, Kenny J., 1:812
Williams, L. Pearce, 5:47, 5:684, 5:745

Williams, Linda, 3:832
Williams, Mark, 2:971
Williams, Martha E., 5:548
Williams, Martin, 3:669
Williams, Mary B., 5:125
Williams, Merryn, 1:363, 1:386
Williams, Michael J. S., 1:694
Williams, Michael R., 5:37
Williams, Niall, 3:901
Williams, Oscar, 1:419
Williams, Paul, 4:514, 5:350
Williams, Penly, 3:359
Williams, Peter W., 4:4
Williams, Philip M., 3:374
Williams, Pontheolla T., 1:986
Williams, R. H., 5:290
Williams, Raymond, 1:266, 1:274, 1:313, 1:422, 1:531, 1:1128, 3:341
Williams, Raymond Brady, 4:509, 4:510
Williams, Raymond Leslie, 2:848, 2:868, 2:887
Williams, Richard A., 5:300
Williams, Robert B., 3:261
Williams, Robert L., 5:428
Williams, Roger L., 1:21
Williams, Rowan, 4:678, 4:787
Williams, Sidney, 1:583
Williams, Stephen J., 5:329
Williams, Susan, 1:612, 5:381
Williams, T. Harry, 3:513, 3:530, 3:547
Williams, Tennessee, 1:532, 1:1071, 1:1087, 1:1098, 1:1112, **1:1116,** 1:1191, 2:679
Williams, Thomas A., 3:861
Williams, Trevor I., 5:27, 5:30, 5:36, 5:49
Williams, Ursula, 3:726
Williams, Victoria, 3:253
Williams, W. T., 1:236
Williams, Wiley J., 1:80
Williams, William Apple-man, 3:547, **3:601**
Williams, William Carlos, 1:560, 1:796, **1:899,** 1:934, 1:981, 1:990, 1:1026, 1:1057, 1:1067
Williams, William Proctor, 1:63
Williamson, Alan, 1:914, 1:1007
Williamson, David, 2:967
Williamson, Duncan, 3:857
Williamson, Edwin, 3:626
Williamson, G. A., 4:666
Williamson, Henry R., 2:225

Williamson, Hugh, 1:12
Williamson, Jeffrey G., 3:90
Williamson, Joel, 3:533, 3:558
Williamson, John B., 5:318
Williamson, Marilyn, 1:211
Williamson, Oliver E., 3:58
Williamson, Ray A., 3:866
Williamson, Roxanne K., 3:764
Willis, Diane J., 5:417
Willis, George, 3:512
Willis, Janice D., 4:544
Willis, Jerry, 5:538, 5:567
Willis, John, 1:1076, 3:826
Willis, Patricia C., 1:864
Willis, Paul, 3:23
Willis, R., 4:189
Willis, Sharon, 2:474
Willmott, Cort J., 3:118, 3:125
Willmott, Peter, 3:20
Wills, Christopher, 5:784
Wills, Garry, 3:522, 3:540, 3:544
Wills, Gary, 4:36
Wills, Geoffrey, 3:765
Wills, Kendall J., 1:135
Wills, Wolfram, 2:991
Willson, D. H., 3:361
Willumsen, Dorrit, 2:645, 2:646
Wilmore, Gayraud S., 4:749, 4:896
Wilmot, Chester, 3:345
Wilmut, Roger, 1:426
Wilshire, Bruce, 3:188, 5:454
Wilson, Adrian, 1:12
Wilson, A. N., 1:193, 1:300, 1:443, 1:513, 2:766, 4:777
Wilson, Angus, 1:351, 1:372, 1:419, 1:474, **1:566**
Wilson, Arthur M., 2:472, 3:338
Wilson, August, 1:1071, **1:1119**
Wilson, Bonnie, 3:891
Wilson, Bryan, 4:425
Wilson, Carroll L., 5:286
Wilson, Catherine, 4:178
Wilson, Charles, 3:336, 3:383, 3:509, 4:228
Wilson, Christopher P., 1:795, 1:805
Wilson, Colin, 1:567, 4:876
Wilson, Curtis, 4:104
Wilson, D. M., 3:380
Wilson, Daniel J., 4:303
Wilson, David, 5:236, 5:712
Wilson, Diana, 2:537
Wilson, Dick, 3:472
Wilson, E. A., 1:102

Wilson, Edmund, 1:370,
1:418, 1:474, 1:717, 1:744,
1:808, 1:839, 1:864, 1:897,
1:901, 1:938, 1:972,
1:1007, 2:448, 2:987, 3:95,
3:341, 3:591
Wilson, Edmund O., 5:770
Wilson, Edward, 3:907
Wilson, Edward A., 5:300
Wilson, Edward O., 3:171,
3:176, 5:117, 5:766, 5:819,
5:820, 5:821, 5:827
Wilson, Elizabeth, 3:217
Wilson, Frank P., 1:115,
1:207
Wilson, Garff B., 1:1076
Wilson, G.B.L., 3:731
Wilson, G. F., 1:366
Wilson, G. Terence, 5:419
Wilson, J., 5:668
Wilson, James D., 1:784
Wilson, Jane, 5:317
Wilson, Jason, 2:879
Wilson, Jeremy, 3:927
Wilson, Jerome D., 1:642
Wilson, John, 1:966, 4:379,
4:389
Wilson, John Dover, 1:186,
1:206
Wilson, John F., 3:163,
4:716, 4:754
Wilson, Josleen, 5:357, 5:397
Wilson, K., 3:856
Wilson, Katharina, 2:4
Wilson, Lanford, 1:1071,
1:1120
Wilson, Leonard G., 5:645
Wilson, Margaret, 4:25, 4:171
Wilson, Michiko N., 2:292
Wilson, Milton T., 1:304
Wilson, Mona, 1:279
Wilson, Monica, 3:25, 3:424
Wilson, N. G., 3:300
Wilson, Paul, 3:677
Wilson, Philip K., 5:375
Wilson, Richard W., 3:140
Wilson, Robert A., 1:34, 1:76
Wilson, Robert F., 1:699
Wilson, Robert R., 4:824
Wilson, Stephen, 3:351
Wilson, Thomas, 4:215
Wilson, Victor T., 1:20
Wilson, W., 2:347
Wilson, William Julius, 3:66,
3:212, **3:244**
Wilson, William Scott, 3:476
Wilson-Bareau, Juliet, 3:780
Wilt, Judith, 1:320
Wilton, Andrew, 3:794
Wilton, Tamsin, 5:388
Wiltshire, David, 3:241
Wiltshire, Martin G., 4:510,
4:514

Wimbush, Vincent L., 4:690
Wimsatt, Mary A., 1:697
Wimsatt, William Kurtz, Jr.,
1:927, **1:1154**
Win, Kanbawza, 2:314
Winch, Donald, 3:93
Winch, Peter, 2:516
Winchester, A. M., 5:779
Winchester, Simon, 3:906,
3:911
Winckler, Paul A., 1:12
Windeatt, Barry A., 1:151
Windelband, Wilhelm, 4:18,
4:163
Winder, Alan A., 5:300
Windham, Donald, 1:959
Windley, Brian F., 5:630
Windt, Peter Y., 4:25
Wine, Martin, 1:171
Wine, Sherwin T., 4:649
Winearls, Jane, 3:735
Winegarten, Renee, 2:510
Winfield, Betty H., 3:809
Wing, Donald Godard, 1:68
Wing, John K., 5:415
Wingler, Hans, 3:777
Winick, Charles, 3:11
Winick, Myron, 5:348, 5:356,
5:395
Winius, George D., 3:386
Winkler, Connie, 5:228
Winkler, John J., 3:309,
4:469
Winks, Robin W., 2:312,
3:607, 3:608
Winn, James A., 1:242
Winn, Ralph B., 4:36
Winner, Anthony, 1:464
Winner, Langdon, 3:214,
5:73, 5:104, 5:131, **5:145,**
5:148, 5:177
Winnicott, Donald Woods,
5:472
Winnifrith, Tony, 1:334
Winnington-Ingraham, R. P.,
2:368
Winny, James, 1:178
Winograd, Terry, 5:571
Winship, George Parker,
1:12, 1:37
Winslow, Ola E., 3:518,
4:767
Winsnes, Andreas H., 2:669
Winson, Anthony, 3:635
Winstedt, Richard, 2:324,
2:325, 3:492
Winston, David, 4:60, 4:670
Winston, Patrick Henry,
5:553, 5:558, 5:569, 5:570
Winston, Richard, 2:603
Wint, Guy, 3:278, 3:463
Winter, Robert, 3:678
Winter, Ruth, 5:404, 5:737

Winter, S. K., 1:1108
Winterich, John T., 1:12,
1:34, 1:37, 1:39
Winters, Yvor, 1:927
Winther, Per, 1:979
Winton, Calhoun, 1:257
Wippel, John F., 4:95, 4:103,
4:119
Wiredu, Kwasi, 4:27, **4:371**
Wirszubski, Chaim, 4:153
Wirth, Louis, 3:244
Wirth, Niklaus, 5:551, 5:552,
5:553
Wise, Boyd A., 2:394
Wise, David A., 3:60
Wiseman, Adele, 2:915
Wiseman, A.J.L., 5:263
Wiseman, Susan, 1:225
Wiseman, T. P., 2:384
Wiser, Charlotte, 4:509
Wiser, Charlotte Vially, 3:486
Wiser, William, 3:486, 4:509
Wishart, John, 5:530
Wishaw, B., 3:387
Wishaw, E. M., 3:387
Wishy, Bernard, 3:512
Wiskemann, Elizabeth, 3:386
Wisker, Alistair, 1:897
Wisse, Ruth R., 2:30, 2:33,
2:34
Wister, Owen, 1:789, **1:1218**
Wistrich, Robert S., 4:656
Wiswell, Ella Lury, 3:480
Witcover, Paul, 1:851
Witham, W. Tasker, 1:920
Witherick, Michael, 3:119,
5:618
Withey, Elsie Rathburn,
3:764
Withey, Henry F., 3:764
Withey, J. A., 2:313
Witke, Roxane, 3:472
Witkiewicz, Stanislaw Igna-
cy (Witkacy), 2:822
Witt, Charlotte, 4:72
Witt, Christine A., 3:891
Witt, R. E., 4:60
Witt, Reni L., 5:357
Witt, Ronald G., 4:127, 4:132
Witt, Stephen, 3:891
Wittels, Fritz, 5:449
Witters, Weldon L., 5:352
Wittfogel, Karl A., 3:140
Wittgenstein, Ludwig Josef
Johann, 4:12, 4:261,
4:271, 4:272, 4:278, 4:320,
4:325, 4:332, 4:333, 4:337,
4:343, 4:377, 4:381, 5:494
Wittig, Monique, 1:1133,
1:1182, 1:1183
Wittkopf, Eugene R., 3:545
Wittkower, Rudolf, 3:764,
3:770

Wittman, Sandra M., 2:339
Wittreich, J. A., 1:266
Wiznitzer, Arnold, 4:645
Wobbe, R. A., 1:489
Wogan-Browne, Jocelyn, 1:147
Wohl, Helmut, 2:558
Wohl, Stanley M., 5:329
Wöhler, Friedrich, 5:731, 5:747, **5:755**
Wojcic, Jan, 2:985
Wojciech, Hubert Zurek, 5:719
Wojtyla, Karol, 4:747
Wolberg, Lewis R., 5:420
Wolchik, Sharon L., 3:389
Wolf, Abraham, 4:189, 5:43
Wolf, Albert, 4:132
Wolf, Arnold Jacob, 4:649
Wolf, Arthur, 4:531
Wolf, Arthur P., 3:464
Wolf, Betje, 2:620
Wolf, C. P., 3:210
Wolf, Charles, 3:68
Wolf, Christa, 2:564, **2:615**
Wolf, Edward C., 5:265
Wolf, Edwin, II, 1:27, 1:34, 1:43
Wolf, E. L., 5:667, 5:672
Wolf, Eric, 3:17, 3:626
Wolf, George, 3:21, 5:340, 5:384
Wolf, Margery, 3:472
Wolf, Steven J., 5:400
Wolf, Theta H., 3:181
Wolfe, Alan, 2:286
Wolfe, Bertram, 2:726, 3:343
Wolfe, Charles K., 3:853
Wolfe, Gerard R., 1:39
Wolfe, John R., 3:57
Wolfe, Nancy T., 3:378
Wolfe, Peter, 1:596, 2:941, 2:967
Wolfe, Richard J., 1:6
Wolfe, Thomas (Clayton), 1:795, 1:892, **1:903**, 1:994, 1:998, 1:1056
Wolfe, Tom, 1:916, 5:597
Wolfenstein, E. Victor, 4:877
Wolfenstein, Martha, 3:204
Wolff, Christian, 4:207, **4:218**
Wolff, Cynthia G., 1:748, 1:789
Wolff, Egon, 2:887
Wolff, H. R., 5:78
Wolff, Joseph J., 1:360
Wolff, Kathryn, 5:5
Wolff, Konrad, 3:664
Wolff, Kurt H., 3:225
Wolff, Michael, 1:312
Wolff, Philippe, 4:100
Wolff, Robert Lee, 1:333

Wolff, Robert P., 4:25
Wolff, Tobias, 1:806, 1:915, 1:922
Wölfflin, Heinrich, 3:758, 3:774
Wolfgang, Marvin E., 3:204
Wolford, Chester L., 1:743
Wolfram von Eschenbach, 2:586, **2:616**
Wolfson, Harry Austryn, 4:60, 4:63, 4:100, 4:189, 4:670, 4:687
Wolheim, William, 4:601
Wolin, Richard, 4:295
Wolin, Sheldon S., 3:139
Wolk, Johannes van der, 3:795
Wolk, Samuel, 3:347, 4:593
Wolken, Jerome J., 5:766
Wolkers, Jan, 2:628, **2:632**
Wolkstein, Diane, 2:931, 3:857, 4:440, 4:546
Woll, Josephine, 2:691
Wollen, Peter, 1:1158
Wollin, Jay C., 5:639
Wolman, Benjamin B., 3:170, 5:414
Woloch, Nancy, 3:513
Wolosky, Shira, 1:748
Wolpe, David J., 4:600
Wolpe, Joseph, 5:472
Wolpert, Stanley A., 3:484, 3:487, 4:351
Wolter, Allan B., 4:95, 4:114
Wolters, Clifton, 1:148
Wolterstorff, Nicholas, 4:762
Wolverton, Van, 5:555
Womack, Brantly, 4:362
Womack, James, 5:247
Womer, Jan L., 4:690
Wong, Samuel S., 5:658
Wong, Sau-ling Cynthia, 3:256
Wong, Timothy, 2:230
Wong, Wang-chi, 2:234
Wongsawaan, Rong, 2:337
Wongthed, Suchit, 2:336
Wongthet, Sujit, 2:335
Woocher, Jonathan S., 4:641
Wood, Allen W., 4:207, 4:233, 4:243
Wood, C. T., 3:895
Wood, Carl, 5:360
Wood, Charles M., 4:494
Wood, Clement, 1:95
Wood, David, 4:398
Wood, Elizabeth A., 5:618
Wood, E. R., 1:229
Wood, Forrest, Jr., 4:290
Wood, Forrest G., 3:519
Wood, Gordon S., 3:522
Wood, John, 4:215

Wood, John Cunningham, 3:78, 3:83, 3:84, 3:85, 3:87, 3:94, 3:95, 3:101, 3:104, 3:105, 3:107
Wood, Laura N., 5:809
Wood, Lawrence C., 5:382
Wood, Marion, 3:866
Wood, Michael, 2:742, 2:868
Wood, Neal, 2:385, 4:59, 4:181
Wood, Nigel, 1:246
Wood, Norman, 5:342
Wood, Peter, 3:519
Wood, Robin, 1:1170
Wood, Thomas E., 4:501, 4:507, 4:514
Woodard, Charles L., 1:1016
Woodbridge, Frederick J., 4:72, 4:85
Woodbridge, H. C., 1:775
Woodcock, Bruce, 1:478
Woodcock, George, 3:607
Woodfield, Denis B., 1:37
Woodford, A. O., 5:622
Woodham-Smith, Cecil, 3:371, 5:363
Woodhead, A. D., 5:77
Woodhead, Peter, 3:305, 3:758
Woodhouse, A. S., 1:193
Woodhouse, C. M., 3:393
Woodhouse, Edward J., 5:75, 5:156, 5:240, 5:244, 5:287
Woodhouse, J. R., 2:401
Woodhouse, Mark B., 4:25
Woodhouse, Roger, 4:180
Woodiwiss, Kathleen, 1:1220, **1:1224**
Woodman, Tony, 2:382
Woodress, James, 1:652, 1:708, 1:725, 1:805, 1:822, 1:920
Woodring, Carl R., 1:268, 1:288
Woods, M. J., 2:540
Woods, Nancy F., 5:355
Woods, Ronald N., 3:78, 3:83, 3:84, 3:104
Woods, Samuel H., Jr., 1:247
Woodside, Alexander B., 3:465, 3:491
Woodward, Anthony, 4:328
Woodward, Bob, 3:540, 3:544, 3:805
Woodward, C(omer) Vann, 3:516, 3:533, 3:544, 3:585, **3:602**
Woodward, James B., 2:699, 2:707, 2:723
Woodward, Kim, 5:281
Woodward, Ralph L., Jr., 3:626, 3:637

Woodward, Robert Burns,
  5:748, **5:755**
Woodward, William H., 4:132
Woodwell, Donald R., 5:559
Woodworth, Steven E., 3:575
Woodyard, George W., 2:847
Wool, Robert, 3:870
Woolf, D. R., 3:361
Woolf, Harry, 5:45
Woolf, Leonard, 1:41
Woolf, Rosemary, 1:160
Woolf, Virginia, 1:337,
  1:413, 1:419, 1:428, 1:447,
  1:540, 1:541, **1:568,** 2:494,
  2:517
Woolgar, Steve, 5:159
Woolhouse, R. S., 4:181
Woolman, John, 1:626
Woolrych, Austin, 3:361
Woolsey, R. James, 5:113
Woolson, Constance Feni-
  more, 1:721, **1:789**
Wooten, Cecil W., 2:385
Wootton, Anthony, 5:772
Worchel, Stephen, 5:422
Worden, B., 3:361
Wordsworth, Dorothy, 1:308
Wordsworth, Jonathan, 1:266
Wordsworth, William, 1:199,
  1:237, 1:248, 1:264, 1:266,
  1:271, 1:273, 1:280, 1:281,
  1:284, 1:285, 1:286, 1:290,
  1:291, 1:295, 1:302, **1:305,**
  1:313, 1:327, 1:399, 1:416,
  1:434, 1:452, 1:454, 1:560,
  1:598, 2:908
Wormald, Jenny, 4:736
Worster, David, 5:117
Worster, Donald E., 3:551,
  5:821, 5:825
Worth, Cecilia, 3:207, 5:323
Worth, Katharine, 1:426
Worthen, John, 1:511
Worwood, Valerie Ann, 5:321
Wouk, Herman, 4:597
Wray, Harry, 3:480
Wray, William D., 3:473,
  3:480
Wrede, William, 4:826
Wren, Robert M., 2:129
Wren, Sir Christopher,
  3:768, **3:796**
Wrenn, John H., 1:859
Wright, Albert Hazen, 5:769
Wright, Andrew H., 1:246
Wright, Angus, 5:825
Wright, Arthur F., 4:530
Wright, Benjamin F., 3:815
Wright, Billie, 3:898
Wright, Charles, 1:995,
  1:1066
Wright, Charles S., 3:936
Wright, David, 1:269, 1:316

Wright, David F., 4:5
Wright, David G., 1:572
Wright, David H., 1:418
Wright, Deil S., 3:148
Wright, Dennis, 3:487
Wright, Derek, 2:131
Wright, Elizabeth, 1:927,
  1:1133
Wright, Frank Lloyd, 1:668,
  3:768, 3:769, 3:790, 3:792,
  3:793, **3:796**
Wright, G. E., 4:618
Wright, George T., 1:217,
  1:436
Wright, Georg H. von, 4:337
Wright, Gordon, 1:517, 3:281,
  3:374
Wright, Helen, 5:606, 5:609
Wright, James, 1:951,
  1:1053, **1:1067**
Wright, Joan, 3:892
Wright, John Lloyd, 3:798
Wright, Jonathan V., 5:347
Wright, Judith, 2:945, **2:968**
Wright, Kathleen, 4:402
Wright, Larry, 4:415
Wright, Louis, 1:630
Wright, Louis B., 1:206
Wright, Lyle H., 1:658, 1:725
Wright, M. R., 4:53
Wright, Mary C., 3:469
Wright, Quincy, 3:149
Wright, Richard, 1:802,
  1:905, 1:1009, 1:1029,
  1:1119
Wright, Richard A., 4:27,
  4:369
Wright, Robin, 4:573
Wright, Samuel, 1:388
Wright, Stuart, 1:466, 1:972,
  1:1029
Wright, T. R., 1:363
Wright, Walter Francis,
  1:379, 1:444
Wright, William Aldis, 1:206
Wright, Winthrop R., 3:641
Wrightsman, L., 3:169
Wrigley, E. A., 3:356
Wriothesley, Henry, 1:202
Wriston, Walter B., 5:127
Wrobel, Sylvia, 5:808
Wrong, Dennis H., **3:245**
Wroth, Lawrence C., 1:12,
  1:38
Wu, Eugene, 3:465
Wu, Kuang-Ming, 4:529
Wu Ch'eng-en, 2:229
Wu Ching-tzu, 2:188, **2:229**
Wulff, Donna Marie, 4:504
Wunderlich, Ray, 5:348
Wundt, Wilhelm, 3:166,
  3:185, 3:187, **3:196,** 5:411,
  5:452

Wurman, Richard Saul,
  5:554, 5:574
Wurthwein, Ernst, 4:806
Wuthnow, Robert, 4:747,
  4:754, 4:856
Wu Yuan-li, 3:466
Wyatt, Antony, 5:618, 5:625
Wyatt, David K., 3:490
Wyatt, M. Digby, 1:30
Wyatt (or Wiat), Sir
  Thomas the Elder, 1:163,
  1:164, **1:201**
Wyatt, Thomas, 2:406
Wyatt-Brown, Bertram, 3:526
Wybenga, Jan, 2:634
Wycherley, William, 1:228,
  1:263
Wyclif, John, 4:711, **4:714,**
  4:797, 4:799
Wye, Kenneth R., 5:762
Wyer, James, 1:81
Wyer, Mary, 3:218
Wykoff, Jerome, 5:625
Wylie, Hal, 2:112
Wylie, Ian, 1:288
Wyman, C.W.H., 1:7
Wyman, David, 3:536, 4:641
Wyman, Walker B., 3:862
Wymer, J. J., 4:433
Wynar, Bohdan S., 1:62, 1:74
Wyner, A. D., 5:581
Wynia, Gary W., 3:632, 3:633
Wynn, Graeme, 3:614
Wynn, Neil, 3:536
Wynne-Davies, Marion, 1:132
Wyrwicka, Wanda, 5:347
Wyschogrod, Edith, 4:295,
  4:392
Wyschogrod, Michael, 4:649,
  4:885
Wyss, Dieter, 5:425
Wyszkowski, Charles, 4:638

X

Xanthakos, Petros P., 5:246
Xenakis, Alan P., 5:343
Xenakis, Iannis, 3:730
Xenophon, 2:342, 2:370,
  3:312, 3:322, **3:323,** 4:88,
  4:91
Xuto, Somsakdi, 3:490

Y

Ya'ari, Ehud, 3:440
Yabes, Leopoldo Y., 2:333
Yablonsky, Lewis, 5:420
Yacine, Kateb, 2:123

Yacowar, Maurice, 1:1170, 3:830
Yadin, Yigael, 4:614
Yadin, Yvon, 3:309
Yahil, Leni, 3:351
Yalof, Ina L., 5:375
Yalom, Irvin D., 5:420
Yalom, Marilyn, 1:913
Yamada, Gayle K., 3:807
Yamamura, Kozo, 3:475, 3:476, 3:480
Yampolsky, Philip B., 4:538
Yanagisako, Sylvia J., 3:19
Yanak, Ted, 3:508
Yanchi, Liu, 4:522
Yancy, Preston M., 1:725
Yáñez, Agustin, 2:887
Yang, Benjamin, 3:472
Yang, Chen Ning, 5:720
Yang, C. K., 4:524
Yang, Vincent, 2:220
Yang Chiang, 2:243, 2:267
Yang Hsiung, 2:187, 2:230
Yang Wan-li, 2:230
Yankelovich, Daniel, 3:148
Yannella, Donald, 1:671
Yapp, Peter, 3:894
Yardley, Jonathan, 1:852, 3:898
Yardley, Michael, 3:927
Yariv, Amnon, 5:666
Yarnold, Edward, 4:678, 4:897
Yarwood, Edmund, 2:719
Yasushi, Inoue. *See* Inoue Yaushi
Yassif, Eli, 3:850
Yasuda, Kenneth, 2:274
Yasunari, Kawabata. *See* Kawabata Yasunari
Yates, Douglas, 2:584
Yates, Frances, 2:410, 5:41
Yates, Frances A., 4:132, 4:136, 4:848
Yates, Janelle, 1:851
Yates, Robin D. S., 2:228
Yavetz, Zvi, 3:313
Yazaki, Takeo, 3:476
Ye'or, Bat, 4:573
Yeager, Chuck, 5:220
Yeager, Jack A., 2:339
Yeager, Jeana, 5:220
Yeager, Patricia, 1:717
Yeager, Robert F., 1:144, 1:152, 1:152
Yearley, Lee, 4:897
Yearley, Steven, 5:159
Yeats, William Butler,
1:414, 1:416, 1:419, 1:423, 1:435, 1:450, 1:452, 1:459, 1:460, 1:471, 1:489, 1:502, 1:506, 1:507, 1:513, 1:517, 1:518, 1:521, 1:526, 1:555,

1:560, **1:570**, 1:968, 1:974, 1:1026, 1:1038, 1:1138, 2:972
Yeazell, Ruth Bernard, 1:230, 1:320, 1:761
Yedidia, Michael J., 5:338
Yee, Lee, 2:236
Yegulalp, Tuncel M., 5:245
Yeh, Michelle, 2:234
Yehiya, Eliezer Don, 4:642
Yehoshua, A(braham) B., 2:8, **2:26**
Yeo, Richard, 5:58
Yeo, Robert, 2:324
Yeoman, Guy, 3:418
Yerby, Frank, 1:1225
Yergin, Daniel, 5:279, 5:283, 5:293
Yerushalmi, Yosef Hayim, 4:595, 4:625
Yessayan, Zabel, 2:80
Yetiv, Jack Z., 5:348
Yevtushenko (Evtushenko), Yevgeny, 1:1003, **2:773**
Yi Mun-yŏl, 2:298, **2:308**
Ying-chen, Ch'en, 2:233
Yingling, Thomas E., 1:824, 1:1183
Yip, Wai-lim, 2:191
Yochelson, Samuel, 5:428
Yocum, Glen, 4:507
Yoder, Don, 3:849
Yoder, Joella G., 5:695
Yoder, John Howard, 4:896
Yoder, Jon A., 1:880
Yoder, Paton, 4:733
Yoffee, Norman, 4:546
Yogananda, Paramahansa. *See* Paramahansa Yogananda
Yogi, Stan, 1:121
Yohannan, John D., 2:57, 2:83, 2:84, 2:93
Yokomitsu Riichi, 2:295
Yolan, Jane, 1:1196
Yolton, John W., 4:163, 4:181, 4:740, 5:43
Yong-un, Han. *See* Han Yong-un
Yoo, Yushin, 3:482
York, Henry E., 3:138
York, Herbert F., 5:672
York, Neil Longley, 5:232
Yosa Buson (Taniguchi Buson), 2:280
Yosano, Akiko, 2:281, **2:295**
Yoshida, Kenko. *See* Kenko Yoshida
Yoshikawa, Kojiro, 2:191
Yoshikazu, Sakamoto, 3:480
Yoshino, M., 5:634
Yoshinori, Takeuchi. *See* Takeuchi Yoshinori

Yost, Robert, 4:178
Youcha, Geraldine, 5:403
Young, Alfred F., 3:522
Young, Allan M., 5:766
Young, Allen, 1:1184
Young, B. A., 1:540
Young, Brian, 3:610
Young, David, 1:913, 2:191
Young, Desmond, 3:345
Young, Frances, 4:687
Young, Frank W., 3:25
Young, G. M., 1:313
Young, George M., 3:365
Young, Gordon Davis, 4:445
Young, Heartsill, 5:545
Young, Howard T., 2:539, 2:543, 2:545, 2:552
Young, Hubert W., 3:438
Young, Hugo, 3:368
Young, Ian, 1:1185
Young, Ione D., 1:284
Young, James H., 5:315
Young, Jay A., 5:726
Young, John, 4:25
Young, Joseph A., 1:1173
Young, Julian, 4:248, 4:256
Young, Katherine K., 4:509, 4:892, 4:894
Young, Louise B., 5:11
Young, Margaret Labash, 5:4, 5:218
Young, Margaret W., 3:253
Young, Marilyn B., 3:540
Young, Michael, 3:20
Young, Oran R., 5:283
Young, Pamela Dickey, 4:749
Young, Peter, 3:281
Young, Philip, 1:847
Young, Robert, 1:1133
Young, Robert D., 3:277
Young, Robert M., 5:795
Young, Serinity, 4:892
Young, Stark, 1:1076
Young, Stuart H., 5:386
Young, Thomas Daniel, 1:805, 1:823, 1:875, 1:889, 1:920
Young, Trudee, 2:508
Young, Walter, 3:616
Youngberg, Ruth T., 1:611
Youngberg, Sylvia A., 5:351
Young-Bruehl, Elisabeth, 4:300, 4:395, 5:82
Younge, W. Arthur, 1:372
Youngs, Susan, 3:767
Yourcenar, Marguerite, 2:517
Yourdon, Edward, 5:551
Youtsey, John W., 5:398
Yovel, Yirmiahu, 4:207
Yovkov, Yordan, 2:780, 2:782
Yu, Anthony, 4:531

Yu, Beongcheon, 2:285, 2:301
Yu, Chai-Shin, 4:534, 4:539
Yu, David C., 4:522
Yu, George T., 3:472
Yü, Han. *See* Han Yü
Yu, Lu. *See* Lu Yu
Yu, Pauline, 2:192
Yü, Ts'ao. *See* Ts'ao Yü
Yüan, Ch'ü, 2:187, 2:201
Yuasa Yasuo, 4:367
Yudin, Florence, 2:541
Yudkin, Leon I., 2:9
Yü Hsin, 2:231
Yui, Tsunehiko, 3:477
Yukawa, Hideki, 5:716, 5:721
Yukio, Mishima. *See* Mishima Yukio
Yuko, Tsushima. *See* Tsushima Yuko
Yun, Sasson, 4:535
Yun Heung-gil (Yun Hûng-gil), 2:298, 2:308
Yunus Emre, 2:101
Yushij, Nima, 2:94
Yussen, Steven R., 3:257
Yü-t'ang, Lin. *See* Lin Yü-t'ang

Z

Zablocki, Benjamin, 3:217
Zach, Nathan, 2:26
Zacher, Christian K., 1:156
Zaehner, Robert C., 4:5, 4:501, 4:548, 4:574
Zaehnsdorf, Joseph W., 1:27
Zagorin, Perez, 3:334, 3:361
Zahan, Dominique, 4:463
Zahlan, Rosemarie S., 3:452
Zaidman, Louise B., 3:307
Zaimont, Judith Lang, 3:658
Zakai, Avihu, 1:630
Zakaria, Rafig, 3:487
Zaks, Rodnay, 5:553
Zald, Mayer N., 3:215
Zaller, John, 3:148
Zaller, Robert, 1:852, 3:361, 4:734
Zamyatin, Yevgeny, 2:735, 2:753, 2:774
Zander, Alvin, 3:172, 3:173
Zanella, Andrew W., 5:226
Zaner, Richard, 5:78
Zangwill, O. L., 3:169, 4:382
Zantop, Susanne, 2:566
Zapata, Luis, 2:888
Zapf, Hermann, 1:12, 1:20
Zaphiropoulos, Lela, 5:348
Zappala, Michael, 2:364

Zarate, Oscar, 5:447
Zarbock, Sarah F., 5:339
Zaret, Barry L., 5:375
Zaretsky, Irving I., 4:856
Zarian, Gostan, 2:80
Zarinš, Guntis, 2:803
Zarit, Steven H., 5:394, 5:429
Zarnecki, George, 3:760
Zarnowitz, Victor, 3:50
Zaroukian, Antranik, 2:81
Zaslavsky, Claudia, 5:495
Zaslaw, Neal, 3:664
Zasloff, Joseph J., 3:491
Zaslow, Morris, 3:610, 3:615, 3:616
Zavarzdeh, Mas'ud, 1:921
Zawadski, Rick T., 5:330
Zawojewski, Judith S., 5:525
Zboray, R., 5:559
Zborowski, Mark, 2:30, 4:625
Zea, Leopoldo, 2:848, 3:626, 4:33
Zeami, 2:280
Zecha, Gerhard, 5:108
Zeckhauser, Richard, 3:64, 3:65
Zedner, Lucia, 1:313, 3:365
Zee, Anthony, 5:651, 5:691
Zeeden, Ernest W., 4:731
Zeeman, Peter, 2:738
Zeichner, Kenneth M., 3:256
Zeig, Jeffrey K., 5:441
Zeig, Sande, 1:1183
Zeiger, Arthur, 1:34
Zeilik, Michael, 5:589, 5:590
Zeiller, Jacques, 4:681
Zeisel, Hans, 5:525
Zeitlin, Solomon, 4:605
Zeitlin, Steven J., 3:857
Zelazny, Roger, 1:1262
Zeldin, Jesse, 2:685, 2:723
Zeldin, Theodore, 3:374
Zelinsky, Wilbur, 3:122
Zell, Hans M., 2:112
Zellerbach, Merla, 5:386
Zeltner, Philip M., 3:261
Zeman, Z.A.B., 3:376
Zembaty, Jane S., 5:122
Zemer, Mosche, 4:627
Zempel, Edward N., 1:76
Zenkovsky, Serge A., 2:691, 2:694, 2:838
Zenner, Walter P., 4:644
Zernov, Nicholas, 2:691
Zerwick, Max, 4:795
Zesmer, David M., 1:141, 1:222
Zetlin, Mikhail, 3:664
Zetterbaum, Marvin, 3:165
Ziegler, Elsie B., 3:850
Ziegler, Philip, 3:332, 3:358, 3:365
Ziegler, Suzanne, 3:660

Ziemer, Rodger E., 5:302
Ziff, Larzer, 1:630, 1:725, 3:516
Zigrosser, Carl, 1:27
Zilahy, Lajos, 2:798
Zilboorg, Gregory, 5:415
Zim, Herbert S., 5:634
Ziman, John M., 5:20, 5:65, 5:104, 5:177
Zimbalist, Andrew, 3:640
Zimbardo, P., 3:176
Zimbardo, Philip G., 5:417, 5:424
Zimbardo, Rose A., 1:228
Zimdars-Swartz, Sandra, 4:712
Zimmer, Hans, 5:726
Zimmer, Heinrich, 4:351
Zimmerman, Bonnie, 1:1183
Zimmerman, Burke K., 5:783
Zimmerman, David R., 5:312
Zimmerman, Franklin B., 3:711
Zimmerman, Jan, 5:159, 5:189
Zimmerman, Judith E., 2:728
Zimmerman, Lee, 1:1001
Zimmerman, Martin B., 5:283
Zimmerman, Michael E., 4:295, 5:72, 5:91, 5:117
Zimmeth, Mary, 5:391
Zimunya, Musaemura, 2:113
Zinberg, Israel, 2:9, 2:33, 4:601
Zindel, Paul, 1:1122, 1:1195
Zink, Steven D., 1:110
Zinn, Howard, 3:514
Zinn, William V., 4:38
Zinner, Gauriel, 4:602
Zinner, Paul E., 3:389
Zinner, Stephen H., 5:390
Zinsser, Judith P., 3:325
Zinsser, William, 1:805, 5:538
Ziolkowski, Jan, 4:702
Ziolkowski, Margaret, 2:691
Ziomek, Henryk, 2:524
Zion, Claire, 5:358
Zion, William P., 5:122
Zipes, Jack, 2:566, 2:585, 3:870, 3:880
Zipperstein, Steven J., 4:638
Zirkel, Gene, 5:523
Ziv, Avner, 3:872
Zīverts, Mārtiņš, 2:803
Zlotnick, Dov, 4:613
Zmaj, Jovan Jovanović, 2:827
Znaniecki, Florian, 3:202
Zobarskas, Stepas, 2:805
Zobel, Hiller B., 5:344
Zochert, Donald, 1:1209
Zodhiates, Philip, 5:12
Zoete, Beryl de, 3:734

Zoff, O., 4:732
Zohrab, Krikor, 2:81
Zola, Émile, 1:380, 1:776, 2:445, **2:517**, 2:621, 2:854, 3:772
Zola, Irving Kenneth, 5:369
Zolotow, Maurice, 3:829
Zombeck, Martin, 5:589
Zorkoczy, Peter, 5:545
Zoshchenko, Mikhail, 2:696, 2:735, **2:775**
Zoubek, Charles E., 1:95
Zoubir, Abdelhamid, 2:117
Zuber, O., 2:991
Zuboff, Shoshana, 5:574
Zuck, Lowell H., 4:725

Zuck, Virpi, 2:638
Zuckerman, Alan, 4:634
Zuckerman, Harriet, 3:214, 5:11, 5:189
Zuckerman, Herbert S., 5:488
Zuckert, Catherine H., 1:725
Zuesse, Evan, 4:463
Zug, George R., 5:772
Zuidema, R. Tom, 4:458
Zukin, Sharon, 3:217
Zukofsky, Louis, 1:1067
Zukowsky, John, 3:783
Zunder, Theodore, 1:633
Zunser, Eliakum, 2:50

Zunz, Olivier, 3:549
Župančič, Oton, 2:834, **2:837**
Zusne, Leonard, 5:414
Zwalf, W., 4:515
Zwass, Adam, 3:52
Zweig, Paul, 2:985, 3:911
Zweig, Stefan, 2:501, 2:514, **2:617**
Zweingenshaft, Richard L., 3:214
Zwettler, Michael, 2:56
Zwicker, Steven N., 1:242
Zwinger, Ann, 3:898
Zwingli, Huldrych, 4:790
Zytkow, Jan M., 5:542

Title Index

This index cumulates in alphabetical sequence the Title Indexes of the preceding five volumes. The number of the volume in which a title appears is given with a colon followed by the page number on which the title can be located. The alphabetization method is letter-by-letter.

Titles of all books discussed in *The Reader's Adviser* are indexed here, except broad generic titles such as "Complete Works," "Selections," "Poems," "Correspondence." Also omitted is any title written by a profiled author that also includes that author's full name or last name as part of the title, such as *The Collected Papers of Charles Darwin.* The only exception to this is Shakespeare (Volume 1), where *all* works by and about him are indexed. To locate all titles by and about a profiled author, the user should refer to the Name Index for the author's primary listing (given in boldface). In general, subtitles are omitted unless two or more works have the same main title, or the main title consists of an author's full or last name (e.g., *Marie Curie: A Biography).* When two or more works by different authors have the same title, the authors' last names will appear in parentheses following the title.

A

A–Z Guide to Computer Graphics, 5:564
An A–Z Gynecology, 5:354
A–Z of Nuclear Jargon, 5:240
An A–Z of the Middle East, 3:436
AAAS Science and Technology Policy Yearbook 1991, 5:182
AAAS Science Book List, 1978–1986, 5:5
A. A. Milne: The Man behind Winnie-the-Pooh, 1:588
AAP Industry Statistics, 1:46
Aaron's Rod, 1:509
Abailard on Universals, 4:106
Abandoned: The Betrayal of the American Middle Class Since World War II, 3:214
The Abandonment of the Jews, 3:536, 4:641
Abba Hillel Silver: A Profile in American Judaism, 4:641
Abbasid Belles-lettres, 2:55
Abbé Groulx: Variations on a Nationalist Theme, 3:620

The Abbess, 1:408
The Abbess of Crewe, 1:551
AB Bookman's Yearbook, 1:51, 1:77
The Abbot, 1:298
ABC: The Alphabetization of the Popular Mind, 5:136
ABC Bunny, 1:1202
ABC et Cetera: The Life and Times of the Roman Alphabet, 1:16
ABC for Book Collectors, 1:31, 1:76
ABC of Color, 1:831
The ABC of Copyright, 1:54
ABC of Lettering and Printing Typefaces, 1:17
ABC of Reading, 1:871
The ABC of Relativity, 4:322, 5:102
ABC of the Book Trade, 1:76
ABCs of Type, 1:62
Abel and Bela, 2:493
Abe Lincoln: The Prairie Years and the War Years, 1:1205
Abe Lincoln Grows Up, 1:1195, 1:1205

Abel Sánchez, 2:552
Abingdon Dictionary of Living Religions, 4:3
Abinger Harvest, 1:476
The Abnormal Personality, 5:428
Abnormal Psychology (Gottesfeld), 5:426
Abnormal Psychology (Price), 5:427
Abnormal Psychology: A Community Health Perspective, 5:426
Abnormal Psychology: Current Perspectives, 5:429
Abolishing Death, 2:688
The Abolition, 5:112
The Abolitionist Legacy: From Reconstruction to the NAACP, 3:586
Aboriginal Australians: Black Responses to White Dominance, 1788–1980, 3:494
Aboriginal Population of Northwestern Mexico, 3:135
Aboriginal Religions in Australia: A Bibliographical Survey, 4:461

Aboriginal Women, Sacred and Profane, 4:461

Abortion: Law, Choice, and Morality, 5:83

Abortion: Understanding Differences, 4:894, 5:84

Abortion and Divorce in Western Law, 4:895

Abortion and Infanticide, 5:124

Abortion and the Ransom of the Sacred, 4:895

Abortion Is Not a Sin: A New-Age Look at an Age-Old Problem, 4:895

Abortion Rights as Religious Freedom, 4:895

The Abortive Revolution: China under Nationalist Rule, 1927–1937, 3:470

About Alphabets: Some Marginal Notes on Type Design, 1:20

About Islam, 3:444

About John Ford, 1:1166

About Philosophy, 4:25

About Science, 5:150

About Sleeping Beauty, 1:590

About That, 2:739

About the House, 1:435

Above the River: The Complete Poetry, 1:1067

Abraham Geiger and Liberal Judaism, 4:653

Abraham H. Maslow: A Memorial Volume, 5:461

Abraham Heschel's Idea of Revelation, 4:665

Abraham Joshua Heschel, 4:665

Abraham Lincoln: a Biography, 3:530

Abraham Lincoln: The Man behind the Myth, 3:529

Abraham Lincoln: The Prairie Years, 1:877, 1:878

Abraham Lincoln: The War Years, 1:877

Abraham Lincoln and the Second American Revolution, 3:586

Abraham Lincoln and the Union, 3:581

The Abraham Lincoln Encyclopedia, 3:509

Abraham Sutzkever: Partisan Poet, 2:50

An Abridgement of Universal Geography, Together with Sketches of History, 1:643

Abroad: British Literary Traveling between the Wars, 1:429, 3:892, 3:899, 3:908

Absalom, Absalom!, 1:834, 1:835

Absalom and Achitophel, 1:241

Absences, 1:1058

Absentee Ownership and Business Enterprise in Recent Times, 3:109

Absent Minded?, 5:423

Absent without Leave, 2:569

The Absolute at Large, 2:790

The Absolute beneath the Relative and Other Essays, 5:202

Absolute Nothingness: Foundations for a Buddhist-Christian Dialogue, 4:365

Absolute Zero Gravity, 5:650

The Absorbent Mind, 3:265

The Absorption of Immigrants, 3:209

Abstract Algebra, 5:484

Abstracting and Indexing Services Directory, 1:112

Abstract of a Treatise of Human Nature, 1740, 4:200

Abstract of British Historical Statistics, 3:354

Abstracts of English Studies, 1:119

Absurd ABC, 1:583

The Absurd Hero in American Fiction: Updike, Styron, Bellow, Salinger, 1:917

An Absurd Vice: A Biography of Cesare Pavese, 2:433

Abundance, 1:1093, 1:1094

Abundance for What?, 3:238

Abundance of Creation: An Artist's Vision of Creative Peace, 3:725

The Abuse of Casuistry: A History of Moral Reasoning, 5:121

Abusing Science: The Case against Creationism, 5:63

Abu Tammam and the Poetics of the Abbasid Age, 2:56

The Abyss, 2:517

The Abyss of Despair, 4:624

Abyss of Time, 5:622

The Acacia, 2:509

Academic American Encyclopedia, 1:106

The Academic Ethic, 3:239

Academic Freedom in the Age of the College, 3:582

The Academic Mind: Social Scientists in a Time of Crisis, 3:230

Academic Press Dictionary of Science and Technology, 5:2, 5:29

An Academic Question, 1:539

The Academic Scribblers: American Economists in Collision, 3:45

Acadia: The Geography of Early Nova Scotia to 1760, 3:611

Acadia, Maine, and New Scotland, 3:612

The Acadian Deportation: Deliberate Perfidy or Cruel Necessity?, 3:611

The Acadians of the Maritimes: Thematic Studies, 3:606

The Accents of Persuasion: Charlotte Brontë's Novels, 1:335

Acceptable Evidence: Science and Values in Risk Management, 5:155

Acceptable Risk, 3:213, 5:128

Acceptable Risks, 5:344

The Accident, 1:1065

Accident: A Day's News, 2:616

Accidental Death of an Anarchist, 2:420, 2:421

Accidental Empires, 5:542

The Accidental Tourist, 1:1058, 1:1059

The Accidental Universe, 5:654

Accident at Three Mile Island: The Human Dimensions, 3:210

Accidents of Influence: Writing as a Woman and a Jew in America, 1:926

Accommodating Protest, 3:446

The Accompanist, 2:702

Accomplices of Silence: The Modern Japanese Novel, 2:282

Accounting for United States Economic Growth, 1929–1969, 3:53

An Account of Corsica, 1:233

An Account of My Hut, 2:270

Account of the Three Kingdoms, 2:212

Acculturation: The Study of Culture Contact, 3:32

The Accumulation of Capital, 3:102

The Accursed Share, 2:455

The Acharnians, 2:353

Achebe or Soyinka? A Re-interpretation and a Study in Contrasts, 2:129, 2:149
Achebe's World, 2:129
Achievement in American Poetry, 1900–1950, 1:952
The Achievement Motive, 3:175
The Achievement of Christina Rossetti, 1:391
The Achievement of Galileo, 5:688
Achievement of Isaac Bashevis Singer, 2:48
The Achievement of John Henry Newman, 4:783
The Achievement of Literary Authority, 1:299
The Achievement of Margaret Fuller, 1:673
The Achievement of Robert Penn Warren, 1:893
The Achievement of Sherwood Anderson: Essays in Criticism, 1:812
The Achievement of William Faulkner, 1:837
The Achievement of William Styron, 1:1057
The Achievements of Michael Faraday, 5:744
The Achieving Society, 3:175
Achilleid, 2:394
Achilles' Heart, 2:773
Acidic Precipitation: Case Studies, 5:616
Acne: Advice on Clearing Your Skin, 5:399
The Acolyte, 2:949
The Acoustic Mirror: The Female Voice in Psychoanalysis and Cinema, 1:1158
Acquainted with the Night, 1:804
Acquanimitas, 5:363
Acquired Tastes, 3:900
Acres of Diamonds, 5:340
Acres of Flint: Sarah Orne Jewett and Her Contemporaries, 1:771
The Acrophile, 2:21
Across China, 3:903
Across New Worlds, 1:326
Across Spoon River: An Autobiography, 1:858
Across the Frontiers: Ireland in the 1990s, 3:371
Across the River and into the Trees, 1:845
Across the Top of the World, 3:906
Across the Tweed, 2:578

Across the Wide Missouri, 3:523, 3:576
Across Two Worlds, 2:78
The ACS Directory of Graduate Research 1991, 5:723
The ACS Style Guide: A Manual for Authors and Editors, 5:727
Act and Quality, 1:923
Acta Sanctorum, 2:800
Acting and Action in Shakespearean Tragedy, 1:213
Acting and Thinking: The Political Thought of Hannah Arendt, 3:282, 4:395, 5:82
Acting Is Believing, 2:554
Acting on Principle, 4:206
Acting Shakespeare, 1:218
Action Is Eloquence: Shakespeare's Language of Gesture, 1:217
The Action of Natural Selection on Man, 5:812
Actions and Events, 4:283, 4:381
Activation of Energy, 4:336
Activity of Philosophy: A Concise Introduction, 4:25
The Act of Creation, 5:193, 5:568
An Act of Terror, 2:159
The Actor's Nightmare, 1:1087
The Actors Studio: A Player's Place, 1:1073
Acts of Faith: A Journey to the Fringes of Jewish Identity, 4:645
Acts of King Arthur and His Noble Knights, 1:884
Acts of Literature, 4:397
Acts of Mind: Conversations with Contemporary Poets, 1:913
Acts of Regeneration, 1:1012
Acts of Supremacy: The British Empire and the Stage, 1790–1830, 1:322
The Acts of the Christian Martyrs: Text and Translations, 4:689
Acts of Will: The Life and Work of Otto Rank, 5:466
Ada: A Life and Legacy, 5:578
Ada, Countess of Lovelace: Byron's Legitimate Daughter, 5:578
Ada, or Ardor, 1:1019, 1:1020, 2:739, 2:740
Ada, the Enchantress of Numbers, 5:578
Adages, 4:138

Adam, Eve and the Serpent, 4:686
The Adam and Eve Diaries: Notes on Courtship and Marriage, 1:781
Adam and the Train, 2:570
Adam Bede, 1:353
Adam Mickiewicz: The National Poet of Poland, 2:817
Adam Mickiewicz, Poet of Poland: A Symposium, 2:817
Adam or Ape: A Sourcebook of Discoveries about Early Man, 5:35
Adam Resurrected, 2:21
Adams, An American Dynasty, 1:730
Adam's Breed, 1:492
Adam's Diary, 2:663
Adam Smith (Campbell), 3:107
Adam Smith (Raphael), 4:215
Adam Smith: Critical Assessments, 3:107, 4:215
Adam Smith and the Wealth of Nations, 3:107
Adam Smith in His Time and Ours, 4:215
Adam Smith's Science of Morals, 4:215
The Adaptable Man, 2:974
Adaptation and Intelligence: Organic Selection and Phenocopy, 3:266
Adapting to Life-Threatening Illness, 5:377
Adaptive Knowing, 4:284
The Added Dimension: The Art and Mind of Flannery O'Connor, 1:1024
The Addictions: Multidisciplinary Perspectives and Treatments, 5:401
The Adding Machine, 1:1109
Addresses and Presidential Messages, 1902–1904, 3:593
Addresses to the German Nation, 4:197
An Address to the German Nobility, the Babylonian Captivity, 4:777
Adelabu, 2:140
Adelchi, 2:426
The Adenauer Era, 3:377
An Adequate Response, 1:533
al-Adib, 2:74
Adieux: A Farewell to Sartre, 2:458, 4:330

Adirondack Voices: Woods-men and Woods Lore, 3:858

Adjustment and Human Relations, 5:422

Admetus, 1:773

Admetus and Other Poems, 1:772

The Administration of Justice from Homer to Aristotle, 2:344

Administrative Behavior, 3:49, 3:147, 3:210

The Administrative State, 3:147

The Admirable Crichton, 1:329, 1:438

Admiral of the Ocean Sea, 3:589, 3:916

Adolescence: An Introduction, 3:174

Adolescence, 3:173, 3:185

The Adolescent, 2:713

The Adolescent: Development, Relationships and Culture, 3:257

The Adolescent in the American Novel, 1920–1960, 1:920

The Adolescent Parent, 5:321

Adolescent Sexuality, 3:208

Adonais, 1:302

Adonis Garcia: A Picaresque Novel, 2:888

Adorno, 4:394

Adriatic, 1:518

The Adriatic: A Sea Guide to Venice, the Italian Shore and the Dalmatian Coast, 3:898

Adrienne Mesurat, 2:481

Adrienne Rich, 1:1038

Adrienne Rich's Poetry, 1:1038

Adrift: Seventy-Six Days Lost at Sea, 3:907

Adrift in the Old World, 1:681

The Adult Development of C. G. Jung, 5:456

The Advaitic Theism of the Bhagavata Purana, 4:506

Advanced Electronic Communications Systems, 5:308

Advanced Lectures in Econometrics, 3:63, 3:88

Advanced MS-DOS, 5:554

Advanced Research Methodology: An Annotated Guide to Sources, 3:6

Advanced Techniques of Hypnosis and Therapy, 5:441

The Advancement of Learning, 4:165

Advancement of Science, 5:25

The Advancement of Science and Its Burdens, 5:17

Advances in Agronomy, 5:220, 5:266

Advances in Biochemical Engineering—Biotechnology, Vol. 46, 5:222

Advances in Bioclimatology, Vol. 1., 5:774

Advances in Chemical Engineering, 5:223

Advances in Clinical Child Psychology, 5:416

Advances in Experimental Medicine, 5:789

Advances in Industrial Ergonomics and Safety, No. 4, 5:244

Advances in Nuclear Science and Technology, 5:240

Advances in Regional Demography: Forecasts, Information, Models, 3:125

Advances in the Drug Therapy of Mental Illness: Proceedings, 5:424

Advent at the Gates: Dante's Comedy, 2:418

The Advent of Sun Myung Moon, 4:871

Adventure in Freedom: Three Hundred Years of Jewish Life in America, 4:639

Adventure, Mystery, and Romance, 1:1210

The Adventure of Menahem-Mendl, 2:45

The Adventurer: The Fate of Adventure in the Western World, 3:911

The Adventurers, 1:1222

Adventures for Another World: Jonathan Trumble's Commonplace Book, 3:518

Adventures in Error, 3:939

Adventures in the Skin Trade and Other Stories, 1:557

Adventures in Value, 1:825

Adventures of a Ballet Historian, an Unfinished Memoir, 3:733

The Adventures of a Biographer, 1:86

The Adventures of a Fakir, 2:729

The Adventures of Alyx, 1:1262

Adventures of a Physicist, 5:650

Adventures of a Simpleton, 2:585

The Adventures of Augie March, 1:946

Adventures of a Young Man, 1:827

Adventures of Captain Bonneville, U.S.A., 1:679, 1:680

The Adventures of Ferdinand Count Fathom, 1:256

The Adventures of Harry Richmond, 1:378

The Adventures of Harry Richmond: The Unpublished Parts, 1:378

The Adventures of Huckleberry Finn, 1:780, 1:1193

Adventures of Huckleberry Finn: American Comic Vision, 1:784

Adventures of Ideas, 4:341

The Adventures of Mottel, the Cantor's Son, 2:45

The Adventures of Peregrine Pickle, 1:256

The Adventures of Roderick Random, 1:256

Adventures of the Dialectic, 4:310

The Adventures of Thomas Jefferson Snodgrass, 1:781

The Adventures of Tom Bombadil, 1:558

The Adventures of Tom Sawyer, 1:779, 1:780

Adventure with a Genius: Recollections of Joseph Pulitzer, 3:821

Adventure with a Microscope, 5:801

The Adventurous History of Hsi-men and His Six Wives, 2:226

The Adventurous Muse: The Poetics of American Fiction, 1789–1900, 1:658

Adversary in the House, 1:1250

Adverse Effects of Foods, 5:346

Adverse Reactions to Foods, 5:394

Adversity's Noblemen, 4:131

Adversus Marcionem, 4:713

Advertisements for Myself, 1:908, 1:1011, 1:1012

An Advertiser's Guide to Scholarly Publishing, 1:51

After Auschwitz: History, Theology and Contemporary Judaism, 3:350
After Babel, 1:1054
After Babel: Aspects of Language and Translation, 1:1054, 2:991
After Bakhtin: Essays on Fiction and Criticism, 1:515, 2:688
After Experience: Poems and Translations, 1:1051
After Foucault, 2:477, 4:400, 5:87
After Great Pain: The Inner Life of Emily Dickinson, 1:747
After Henry, 1:968
Afterimages of Modernity, 2:987
After Imperialism, 3:464
After Lebanon: The Israeli-Palestinian Connection, 4:643
After Magritte, 1:553
After Many a Summer Dies the Swan, 1:499
After Mao: Chinese Literature and Society, 1979–1981, 2:234
After Marx, 4:242
Afternoon of an Author: A Selection of Uncollected Stories and Essays, 1:840
After Philosophy, 4:378
After Restoration: The Beginning of Japan's Modern State, 3:480
After Russia—Posle Rossii, 2:767, 2:768
After Secession, 3:575
After the Demise of the Tradition, 4:413
After the Fact: The Art of Historical Detection, 3:514
After the Fall, 1:1103, 1:1104
After the Fall: The Demeter–Persephone Myth in Wharton, Cather, and Glasgow, 1:804
After the Fall: The Pursuit of Democracy in Central Europe, 3:143
After the Genteel Tradition: American Writers, 1910–1930, 1:794
After the Last Sky: Palestinian Lives, 3:460
After the Lost Generation, 1:793, 1:916
After the New Criticism, 1:926

After the Oil Price Collapse, 5:284
After the Trauma: Representative British Novelists since 1920, 1:422
After the Vows Were Spoken: Marriage in American Literary Realism, 1:724
After the Wake, 1:441
After the War: Essays on Recent Spanish Poetry, 2:525
After the World Broke in Two: The Later Novels of Willa Cather, 1:822
Afterthoughts from the U.S.S.R., 2:479
Afterthoughts on Materialism and Capitalism, 3:283
After Virtue: A Study in Moral Theory, 4:406, 4:407, 4:897
After You Mark Twain: A Modern Journey around the Equator, 3:910
After You Say Goodbye: When Someone You Love Dies of AIDS, 5:387
Against Apion, 3:316
Against Architecture: The Writings of Georges Bataille, 2:456
Against Epistemology—A Metacritique, 4:393
Against Interpretation, 1:1052
Against Mediocrity: The Humanities in America's High Schools, 3:249
Against Method, 4:399, 5:66, 5:86
Against Post-Modernism, 4:391
Against Racism: Unpublished Essays, Papers, Addresses, 1887–1961, 1:831, 3:577
Against Silence: The Voice and Vision of Elie Wiesel, 1:1065
Against the Academicians, 4:109
Against the Age: An Introduction to William Morris, 1:382
Against the American Grain, 4:800
Against the Apocalypse, 4:648
Against the Musicians, 4:58
Against the Nations: War and Survival in a Liberal Society, 4:744
Against Theory: Literary Studies and the New Pragmatism, 1:1129

Against the Self-Images of the Age, 4:407
Against the Stream: Critical Essays on Economics, 3:235
Again the Three Just Men, 1:598
Agamemnon, 1:517, 2:350
Agatha Christie, 1:606
Agatha Christie: A Biography, 1:606
Agatha Christie: An Autobiography, 1:606
The Agatha Christie Companion, 1:606
An Age Ago: A Selection of Nineteenth-Century Russian Poetry, 2:693
Age and Anthropological Theory, 3:24, 3:201
Agee on Film, 1:932
Ageless Aging: The Natural Way to Stay Young, 5:349
Ageless Body, Timeless Mind: The Quantum Alternative to Growing Old, 5:319
The Agency: The Rise and Decline of the CIA, 3:546
Agenda Twenty-one: The Earth Summit Strategy to Save Our Planet, 3:206
Agents of Power: The Role of the News Media in Human Affairs, 3:805
The Age of Access, 5:306
The Age of Adventure: The Renaissance Philosophers, 4:130
The Age of Alexander: Nine Greek Lives, 3:318
Age of Alignment: Electoral Politics in Britain, 1922–1929, 3:365
Age of Analysis: Twentieth-Century Philosophers, 4:268
The Age of Anxiety, 1:434
The Age of Balfour and Baldwin, 1902–1940, 3:367
The Age of Bede, 1:143
The Age of Capital, 1848–1875, 1:312, 3:404
The Age of Catherine de Medici, 3:373
The Age of Constantine the Great, 3:400, 4:682
An Age of Crisis, 4:160
The Age of Criticism: The Late Renaissance in Italy, 4:127
The Age of Dante, 2:402

The Age of Diminished Expectations: U.S. Economic Policy in the 1990s, 3:62
The Age of Doubt: American Thought and Culture in the 1940s, 3:559
The Age of Electronic Messages: Primer on the New Technologies, 5:231, 5:297
The Age of Empire, 1875–1914, 1:312, 3:341
The Age of Enlightenment, 3:337
Age of Erasmus, 4:139
The Age of Extravagance: An Edwardian Reader, 1:430
The Age of Grief, 1:1050, 1:1051
The Age of Gunpowder Empires: 1450–1800, 3:288
The Age of Ideology: The Nineteenth-Century Philosophers, 4:159
The Age of Improvement, 1783–1867, 1:311, 3:363
The Age of Innocence, 1:786, 1:787
Age of Intelligent Machines, 3:174
The Age of Jackson, 3:597
The Age of Nationalism: The First Era of Global History, 3:286
The Age of Plunder: The England of Henry VIII, 1500–1547, 3:359
The Age of Reason (Paine), 1:632
The Age of Reason (Sartre), 2:506
The Age of Reason (Snyder), 3:338
Age of Reason: The Seventeenth-Century Philosophers, 4:160
The Age of Reason Begins, 3:338
The Age of Reconnaissance: Discovery, Exploration and Settlement, 3:336
The Age of Reform: From Bryan to F.D.R., 3:531, 3:582
The Age of Reform 1250–1550, 3:331, 4:129, 4:697, 4:721
The Age of Religious Wars, 1559–1689, 4:736
Age of Revolution, 1789–1848, 3:404
The Age of Roosevelt, 3:535, 3:597
Age of Surrealism, 2:986

The Age of Suspicion, 2:448, 2:505, 2:506
The Age of Television, 3:203
The Age of the Academies, 3:268
The Age of the Reformation, 3:334
The Age of Wonders, 2:14
Ageproofing, 5:317
Agesilaos and the Crisis of Sparta, 3:301
The Ages of American Law, 3:145
The Ages of the World, 4:251
Aggression, 3:170
Aggression: A Social Psychological Analysis, 3:170
Aggression: Its Causes, Consequences, and Control, 3:170
Aggression and War: Their Biological and Social Bases, 3:170, 3:279
Aging and Mental Disorders, 5:429
Aging and Old Age: An Introduction to Social Gerontology, 3:201, 3:216
Aging and Public Health, 5:317
Aging and Public Policy: Social Control or Social Justice, 5:318
Aging and Society, 3:201
The Aging of the American Work Force: Problems, Programs, Policies, 3:59
The Aging Trap, 5:317
Agnes Grey, 1:334
Agon: Towards a Theory of Revisionism, 1:1138
The Agony and the Ecstasy, 1:1250
The Agony of Christianity, 2:551
Agoraphobia: Nature and Treatment, 5:427
The Agrarian Origins of American Capitalism, 3:548
The Agrarian Origins of Modern Japan, 3:476, 3:502
Agricola, 5:265
The Agricola and the Germania, 3:321
Agricultural and Animal Sciences Journals and Serials, 5:261
Agricultural Development and Tenancy Dispute in Japan, 1870–1940, 3:479

The Agricultural Handbook, 5:262
Agricultural Involution: The Processes of Ecological Change in Indonesia, 3:31
The Agricultural Revolution, 3:361
Agricultural Science and the Quest for Legitimacy, 5:263
Agricultural Statistics, 5:261
The Agricultural Systems of the World: An Evolutionary Approach, 3:274
Agriculture and Vegetation of the World, 5:261
The Agriculture Dictionary, 5:261
Agrippa and the Crisis of Renaissance Thought, 4:133
Agroecology: The Scientific Basis of Alternative Agriculture, 5:819
The Agunah, 2:39
Agunot, 2:11
Ah, but Your Land Is Beautiful, 2:167
Ahad Ha-Am, Asher Ginzberg: A Biography, 2:13
Aha! Gotcha: Paradoxes to Puzzle and Delight, 5:507
Aha! Insight, 5:507
A. H. Maslow: An Intellectual Portrait, 5:461
Ah Pook Is Here, 1:957
The AI Business: Commercial Uses of Artificial Intelligence, 5:558
AIDS: Facts and Issues, 5:387
AIDS: Intervening with Hidden Grievers, 5:387
AIDS: Principles, Practices, and Politics, 5:387
AIDS: The Burden of History, 5:387
AIDS: The Making of a Chronic Disease, 3:201, 5:387
AIDS: The Medical Mystery, 5:388
AIDS: The Mystery and the Solution, 5:387
AIDS Demo Graphics, 1:1181
The AIDS Directory, 5:387
The AIDS File, 5:387
AIDS in the World, 1992, 5:388
AIDS Law in a Nutshell, 5:388
AIDS-Proofing Your Kids, 3:206

The Aims of Education, 4:341

The Aims of Interpretation, 1:925, 1:1148

Ainsworth and Bisby's Dictionary of the Fungi, 5:758

Ain't Misbehavin': The Story of Fats Waller, 3:729

Air and Dreams: An Essay on the Imagination of Movement, 4:274

The Air-Conditioned Nightmare, 1:861, 1:862

Airman's Odyssey, 2:504

Air Pollution's Toll on Forests and Crops, 5:289

Airs, 2:160

Airs and Tributes, 2:160

Air Wars: Television Advertising in Political Campaigns, 1952–1992, 3:812

Aishah: The Beloved of Muhammad, 4:587

Aissa Saved, 1:456

Ake: The Years of Childhood, 2:148, 2:149

Akhenaton: The Heretic King, 4:442

Akiba: Scholar, Saint and Martyr, 4:620

Akritic Songs, 2:376

Aku-Aku, 3:923, 3:924

Akutagawa: An Introduction, 2:285

Aladdin, 1:321

ALA Glossary of Library and Information Science, 5:545

Alain Resnais, 3:828

Alain Robbe-Grillet, 2:501

Alan Ayckbourn, 1:437

Alan Ayckbourn: A Casebook, 1:437

Alan of Lille: The Frontiers of Theology in the Twelfth Century, 4:702

Alan of Lille's Grammar of Sex, 4:702

Alan Paton, 2:168

Alan Sillitoe, 1:547

Alan Sillitoe: A Critical Assessment, 1:547

Alan Sillitoe: An Annotated Bibliography, 1:547

Alan Turing: The Enigma, 5:582

Alaska, 1:1248, 3:931

Alban Berg, 3:680

Alban Berg: Master of the Smallest Link, 4:393

Albania, 3:392

Albania: A Socialist Maverick, 3:392

Albanian and South Slavic Oral Epic Poetry, 2:779

Albanian National Awakening, 2:779

Albee, 1:1081

Alberta: A New History, 3:610

Alberta Alone, 2:667, 2:668

Alberta and Freedom, 2:667, 2:668

Alberta and Jacob, 2:667, 2:668

Albert Camus, 2:465

Albert Camus: A Biography, 2:464

Albert Camus and the Literature of Revolt, 2:464

Albert Einstein: Philosopher-Scientist, 4:41, 5:49, 5:683

Albert Einstein, Historical and Cultural Perspectives, 5:17

Albert Einstein, the Human Side: New Glimpses from His Archives, 5:683

Alberto Moravia, 2:430

Albert the Great: Commemorative Essays, 4:107

Albertus Magnus and the Sciences, 4:107

Albinus and the History of Middle Platonism, 4:60

Albion's Fatal Tree: Crime and Society in Eighteenth-Century England, 3:410

Albion's Seed: Four British Folkways in America, 3:516

Albrecht Dürer: A Biography, 3:774

Albrecht Dürer: Engravings and Etchings, 3:774

Albrecht Dürer, Paintings, Prints, Drawings, 3:774

Album of American History, 3:512

Album of Science: From Leonardo to Lavoisier, 1450–1800, 5:24

Album of Science: The Nineteenth Century, 5:47

The Album of Science: The Physical Sciences in the Twentieth Century, 5:11

The Alcestiad or A Life in the Sun, 1:1116

Alcestis, 2:355, 2:356

The Alchemist, 1:183

Alchemy and Finnegans Wake, 1:505

Alcohol: Its Use and Abuse in America, 5:402

Alcohol and the Fetus: A Clinical Perspective, 5:402

Alcohol in America: Taking Action to Prevent Abuse, 5:402

Alcools, 2:451

Alcuin and Charlemagne: Studies in Carolingian History and Literature, 4:100

Alcyone, 2:415

Aldiss Unbound: The Science Fiction of Brian W. Aldiss, 1:613

Aldo Leopold: His Life and Work, 5:835

Aldo Leopold: The Man and His Legacy, 5:835

Aldo Leopold: The Professor, 5:835

Aldous Huxley, 1:500

Aldous Huxley: A Bibliography, 1916–1959, 1:499

Aldous Huxley: A Collection of Critical Essays, 1:500

Aldous Huxley: An Annotated Bibliography of Criticism, 1:499

Aldous Huxley: The Critical Heritage, 1:500

Aldus Manutius and the Development of Greek Script and Type in the Fifteenth Century, 1:13

Aleck Maury, Sportsman: A Novel, 1:983

Alec Wilder: A Bio-Bibliography, 3:730

Alec Wilder and His Friends, 3:730

Alejo Carpentier: The Pilgrim at Home, 2:860

Alejo Carpentier and His Early Works, 2:860

Aleksandr Blok, 2:703

Aleksandr Blok: A Biography. Vol. 1: The Distant Thunder. 1880–1908, 2:703

Aleksandr Blok and the Dynamics of the Lyric Cycle, 2:703

Aleksandr Blok Centennial Conference, 2:703

Aleksandr Blok's "Ital'janskie Stixi": Confrontation and Disillusionment, 2:703

Aleksandr Porfirevich Borodin: A Chemist's Biography, 3:683

Aleksandr Solzhenitsyn: Critical Essays and Documentary Materials, 2:761

Aleksej Remizov: Approaches to a Protean Writer, 2:754

The Aleph and Other Stories, 1933–1969, 2:856
The Aleph-Bet Book: Sefer Hamiddot, 2:42
The Aleph Weaver: Biblical, Kabbalistic and Judaic Elements in Borges, 2:857
Alessandro Achillini (1463–1512) and His Doctrine of Universals and Transcendentals, 4:128
Alessandro Manzoni, 2:426
Alexander Blok: An Anthology of Essays and Memoirs, 2:703
Alexander Blok: Between Image and Idea, 2:703
Alexander Blok as Man and Poet, 2:703
Alexander Fleming, the Man and the Myth, 5:408
Alexander Hamilton: A Biography, 3:521
Alexander Herzen 1812–1870, 2:728
Alexander Kuprin, 2:733
Alexander Ostrovsky, 2:744
Alexander Pope: A Life, 1:252
Alexander Pope: An Annotated Bibliography of Twentieth-Century Criticism, 1900–1979, 1:252
Alexander Pope: The Genius of Sense, 1:252
Alexander Pope: The Poetry of Allusion, 1:252
Alexander Pushkin (Bloom), 2:751
Alexander Pushkin (Vickery), 2:752
Alexander Pushkin: A Critical Study, 2:751
Alexander's Bridge, 1:820
Alexander's Path, 3:939
Alexander the Great and the Logistics of the Macedonian Army, 3:308
Alexandra David-Neel: Portrait of an Adventurer, 4:544
Alexandre Dumas: Genius of Life, 2:473
The Alexandria Quartet: Justine, Balthazar, Mountolive, Clea, 1:469, 2:372
Alexis, 2:517
Alexis de Tocqueville: A Biographical Study in Political Science, 3:165
Alfarabi, Avicenna and Averroës, 4:96

Alfred Adler: His Influence on Psychology Today, 5:431
Alfred Binet, 3:181
Alfred I. Du Pont: The Man and His Family, 3:549
Alfred Kroeber: A Personal Configuration, 3:33
Alfred Loisy: His Religious Significance, 4:741
Alfred Lord Tennyson, 1:402
Alfred Lord Tennyson: A Memoir by His Son, 1:402
Alfred Marshall: Critical Assessments, 3:94
Alfred North Whitehead: The Man and His Work, Vol. 1: 1861–1910, 4:342
Alfred North Whitehead: The Man and His Work, Vol. 2: 1910–1947, 4:342
Alfred Russel Wallace: An Anthology of His Shorter Writings, 5:812
Alfred Tennyson (Jordan), 1:401
Alfred Tennyson (Tennyson), 1:402
Alfred the Great: The King and His England, 3:356
Algebra, 5:484
Algebra and Trigonometry, 5:484
Algebra for College Students, 5:485
Algebra I, 5:500
Algebraic Calculations of the Rainbow and the Calculation of Chances, 4:187
Algebra II, 5:500
Algerie, 2:119
The Algerine Captive, 1:645
Algernon Charles Swinburne, 1:398
The Algonquin Legends of New England, 3:858
The Algorithmic Image: Graphic Visions of the Computer Age, 5:565
Algorithms, 5:551
Algorithms and Data Structures, 5:551
The Alhambra, 1:679, 1:680
Alias O. Henry: A Biography of William Sydney Porter, 1:757
Alibi, 2:916
The Alice Concordance, 1:582
Alice Doesn't: Feminism, Semiotics, Cinema, 3:827
Alice in Cartoonland, 1:1163
Alice in Westminster, 1:522

Alice in Wonderland, 1:581
Alice in Wonderland and Through the Looking Glass, 1:581
Alice James: A Biography, 1:761, 1:1056
Alice Munro: Paradox and Parallel, 2:922
Alice Munro and Her Works, 2:922
Alice's Adventures in Wonderland, 1:581, 1:582
Alice's Adventures Underground, 1:582
Alienation and Charisma, 3:217
The Alien Book of Truth: Who Am I? What Am I? Why Am I Here?, 4:870
The Alien Protagonist of Ford Madox Ford, 1:475
Alien Wisdom: The Limits of Hellenization, 3:307
Aline and Valcourt or The Philosophic Novel, 2:503
Alistair Cooke's America, 3:513
Alive and Writing: Interviews with American Authors of the 1980s, 1:911
All: The Collected Short Poems, 1956–1964, 1:1068
All: The Collected Short Poems, 1923–1958, 1:1068
All about H. Hatterr, 2:177
Allah's Commonwealth, 3:459
Allan Quatermain, 1:595
Allan's Wife, 1:595
All Backs Were Turned, 2:814
All Consuming Images: The Politics of Style in Contemporary Culture, 3:873
All Contraries Confounded, 1:813, 2:474
All Dressed Up and Nowhere to Go, 1:448
Allegories of Love: Cervantes', 2:537
Allegories of Reading, 1:966, 1:1142
Allegories of War: Language and Violence in Old English Poetry, 1:143
Allegory, Decalogue, and Deadly Sins in La Celestina, 2:549
Allegory, Myth and Symbol, 3:854
Allegory and Philosophy in Avicenna: Ibn Sina, 4:582

The Allegory of Love: A Study of Medieval Tradition, 1:147, 1:512

Allegria di naufragi, 2:440

Allen Ginsberg, 1:981

Allen Ginsberg in America, 1:981

Allen Lane, King Penguin: A Biography, 1:42

Allen Tate: A Recollection, 1:889

Allen Tate and the Augustinian Imagination: A Study of the Poetry, 1:889

The Allergy Self-Help Book, 5:386

Aller Retour New York, 1:862

All Faithful People: Change and Continuity in Middletown's Religion, 3:231

All Fall Down: America's Tragic Encounter with Iran, 3:546

All Fools, 1:175

All for Love, 1:251

All God's Children Need Traveling Shoes, 1:934

All God's Dangers: The Life of Nate Shaw, 3:535

All His Jazz: The Life and Death of Bob Fosse, 3:743

Allied Intervention in Russia, 1917–1920, 3:396

All I Survey, 1:457

All Men Are Brothers, 2:219

All My Friends Are Going to be Strangers, 1:1010

All My Pretty Ones, 1:1045

All My Road before Me: The Diary of C. S. Lewis, 1922–1927, 4:776

All My Sons, 1:1103, 1:1104, 2:659

All Our Children Learning, 3:248

All Our Yesterdays (Ginzburg), 2:421

All Our Yesterdays (Robertson), 3:553

All Over, 1:1080

All over Russia, 2:724

All Papa's Children, 2:935

All Passion Spent, 1:542

All Possible Worlds: A History of Geographical Ideas, 5:32, 5:620

All Quiet on the Western Front, 2:606

All-Romanized English-Japanese Dictionary, 1:100

All Said and Done, 2:458

All Scientists Now: The Royal Society in the Nineteenth Century, 5:46

All Silver and No Brass: An Irish Christmas Mumming, 3:868

All Strange Away, 2:459

All's Well That Ends Well, 1:205, 1:206

All That Glitters, 2:932

All That Heaven Allows, 1:1175

All That's Left to You: A Novella and Other Stories, 2:67

All That Swagger, 2:952

All the Colours of the Rainbow, 2:243

All the Conspirators, 1:500

All the King's Men, 1:892

All the Little Live Things, 1:1053

All the Paintings of Titian, 3:793

All the President's Men, 3:540, 3:805

All the Queen's Men: Power and Politics in Mary Stewart's Scotland, 4:735

All the Russians, 3:394

All the Way Home, 1:932

All the Year Round, 1:355

All Things Are Possible and Penultimate Words and Other Essays, 4:335

All Things Considered, 1:457

All Things New, 4:844

All Things Nuclear, 5:241

All Together Now, 1:425

The All-Too-Wise, 2:643

Allusions—Cultural, Literary, Biblical, and Historical: A Thematic Dictionary, 1:116

All Was Light: An Introduction to Newton's Opticks, 5:667, 5:706

All What Jazz: A Record Diary, 1:508

The Almanac of American History, 3:507, 3:597

The Almanac of American Politics, 1:81

Almanac of Famous People, 1:86

Almanac of Science and Technology: What's New and What's Known, 5:6

Almanacs of the United States, 1:81

Almayer's Folly, 1:463

Almost at the End, 2:774

The Aloe, 2:978

Alone, 3:915

Aloneness, 1:954

Alone of All Her Sex: The Myth and the Cult of the Virgin Mary, 4:679

Alone with America, 1:913, 1:989

Along the Road: Notes and Essays of a Tourist, 3:892

Along with Youth: Hemingway, the Early Years, 1:846

Alpha: The Myths of Creation, 4:427

Alpha and Omega, 4:479

The Alphabet, 1:15, 2:645

The Alphabet: A Key to the History of Mankind, 1:14

The Alphabet, and Elements of Lettering, 1:15

Alphabet Art: Thirteen ABCs from around the World, 1:15

Alphabet of Old Friends, 1:583

Alphabets and Birthdays, 1:881

Alphabet Thesaurus, 1:19

Alpha to Omega: The Life and Times of the Greek Alphabet, 1:16

The Alpine Christ and Other Poems, 1:851

Al Purdy and His Works, 2:923

Al Smith and His America, 3:581

The Altar and the City: A Reading of Virgil's Aeneid, 2:397

The Altarpiece in the Renaissance, 5:203

Altars of Unhewn Stone, 5:272

Altarwise by Owl-Light, 1:556

Altazor, 2:870

The Alteration, 1:432

Alterations of Personality, 3:180

Altered Egos: Authority in American Autobiography, 1:727, 1:927

Alternate Voices in the Contemporary Latin American Narrative, 2:845

Alternating Current, 2:878

Alternative Agriculture, 5:265

Alternative Alcott, 1:1198

Alternative Altars: Unconventional and Eastern Spirituality in America, 4:841

Alternative Health Care Resources: A Directory and Guide, 5:320

The Alternative Health
   Guide, 5:319
Alternative Medicine: A Bibli-
   ography of Books in En-
   glish, 5:321
Alternative Medicine and
   American Religious Life,
   4:841
Alternative Medicines: Popu-
   lar and Policy Perspec-
   tives, 5:320
Alternative Publishing: Five
   Modern Histories, 1:38
Alternative Shakespeare,
   1:208
Alternatives to Mental Hospi-
   tal Treatment, 5:424
Although, 2:792
Alton Locke, 1:369
Alvar Aalto: A Critical Study,
   3:770
Alvar Aalto: An Academy Ar-
   chitectural Monograph,
   3:770
Alvar Aalto: The Mature
   Years, 3:770
Alvar Aalto and the Interna-
   tional Style, 3:770
Alves and Co, 2:559
Alvin Ailey, Jr., 3:736
Always Astonished: Selected
   Prose, 2:560
Always Coming Home,
   1:1260
Always in Season: Folk Art
   and Traditional Culture in
   Vermont, 3:858
Alzheimer's, Stroke, and
   Twenty-Nine Other Neuro-
   logical Disorders, 5:391
Alzheimer's Disease: A Guide
   for Families, 5:393
Amadeus, 1:543
AMA Handbook of Poisonous
   and Injurious Plants, 5:760
Amalgamation, 1:723
Amana: From Pietist Sect to
   American Community,
   4:843
Amandla, 2:168
An Amateur Laborer, 1:829,
   1:830
The Amateur Naturalist,
   5:818
The Amazing Newborn, 5:358
The Amazing Universe, 5:588
The Amazon and Other Sto-
   ries, 2:736
Amazons and Warrior Wom-
   en, 1:170
The Ambassadors, 1:761,
   1:762

Ambassador World Atlas,
   1:84
The Ambidextrous Universe,
   5:507
The Ambiguous Compromise,
   2:117
The Ambiguous Relationship,
   3:288
Ambika in Jaina Art and Lit-
   erature, 4:510
The Ambivalence of Nation-
   alism, 3:480
The Ambivalent American
   Jew, 4:640
Ambrose Bierce, 1:735
Ambrose Bierce: A Biogra-
   phy, 1:735
Ambrose Bierce: The Devil's
   Lexicographer, 1:735
Ambrose Gwinnett Bierce: A
   Bibliography and Bio-
   graphical Data, 1:735
Ambrosio, or, the Monk,
   1:269
Ambulatory Care: Problems
   of Cost and Access, 5:332
Amelia, 1:245
Amelia Earhart: A Biography,
   3:910
Amen, 2:13
The Amen Corner, 1:938,
   1:939, 1:1083, 1:1084
The Amenities of Book-Col-
   lecting and Kindred Affec-
   tions, 1:33
America (Benét), 1:815
America (Baudrillard), 3:211
America: A Narrative History,
   3:514
America: History and Life,
   3:8
America, Russia, and the
   Cold War, 3:279, 3:545
America, Their America,
   2:133
America and Americans,
   1:884
America and I: Short Stories
   by American Jewish Wom-
   en Writers, 1:725
America and Russia: From
   Cold War Confrontation to
   Coexistence, 3:345
America and the Automobile,
   3:553
America and the Image of
   Europe: Reflections on
   American Thought, 3:568
America and the Uncon-
   scious, 4:841
America at 1750: A Social
   History, 3:582

America at 1750: A Social
   Portrait, 3:517
America by Design: Science,
   Technology, and Corporate
   Capital, 5:73
America Calling: A History
   of the Telephone to 1940,
   3:226
America Confronts a Revolu-
   tionary World: 1776–1976,
   3:601
America Faces the Future,
   3:565
America Goes to War: The
   Civil War and Its Meaning
   to Americans Today, 3:571
America Hurrah, 1:1114
America Hurrah and Other
   Plays, 1:1114
America in 1857: A Nation
   on the Brink, 3:530, 3:598
America in Europe: A Histo-
   ry of the New World in
   Reverse, 3:642
America in Fiction, 1:122
America in 1492, 3:556
America in Legend: Folklore
   from the Colonial Period
   to the Present, 3:848
America in Midpassage,
   3:565
America in Modern Italian
   Literature, 2:401
America in Our Time: From
   World War II to Nixon,
   3:538
America in Search of Itself:
   The Making of the Presi-
   dent, 1956–1980, 3:540
America in Space: An Anno-
   tated Bibliography, 5:597
America in the Great War:
   The Rise of the War Wel-
   fare State, 3:533
America in the Twentieth
   Century: A History, 3:514
America in Two Centuries:
   An Inventory, 3:568
America in Yiddish Poetry:
   An Anthology, 2:33
America Laughs: A Sampler,
   3:871
America Living with AIDS,
   5:388
The American, 1:762
American, African, and Old
   European Mythologies,
   3:866
American, Chinese, and Japa-
   nese Perspectives on War-
   time Asia, 1931–1949,
   3:464

Americana Anthology: Bicentennial Edition 1776–1976, Vol. 1, 1:129

The American Adam, 1:651

The American Age, 3:545

American Agricultural Implements, 5:262

American Alternative Theatre, 1:1076

American Anthology, 1787–1900, 1:656

American Architects and the Mechanics of Fame, 3:764

American Architectural Books, 3:763

American Architecture since 1780: A Guide to the Styles, 3:764

American Art, Painting, Sculpture, Architecture, Decorative Arts, 3:758

American Assassins: The Darker Side of Politics, 3:542

American Assimilation or Jewish Revival, 4:638

American Authors, 1600–1900, 1:127, 1:714

American Autobiography: Retrospect and Prospect, 1:927, 1:727, 1:808

The American Automobile Industry, 3:548

The American Backwoods Frontier, 3:132

American Ballads and Folk Songs, 3:884

American Ballet Theatre: The First Fifty Years, 3:734

American Best Sellers: A Reader's Guide to Popular Fiction, 1:51

The American Bibliography, 1:67, 3:510

American Bibliography: A Preliminary Checklist, 1:68

American Bibliography, 1801–1819, 3:511

The American Blood Supply: Issues and Policies of Blood Donation, 5:353

American Blues: Five One-Act Plays, 1:1117

American Book Collectors and Collecting from Colonial Times to the Present, 1:31

American Book Design and William Morris, 1:11

American Book of Days, 1:87

American Book Prices Current Annual, 1:78

American Book Prices Current Index, 1:78

The American Book Publishing Record Annual Cumulative, 1:70

American Book Trade Directory, 1:51, 1:69

The American-British, British-American Dictionary with Helpful Hints to Travelers, 1:91

American Buddhism, 4:860

American Buffalo, 1:1100

American Buildings and Their Architects, 3:763

The American Cancer Society's Complete Book of Cancer, 5:372

American Capitalism: The Concept of Countervailing Power, 3:78, 3:79

The American Catalogue of Books (Original and Reprints) (Kelly), 1:67

American Catalogue of Books (Original and Reprints) (Leypoldt), 1:67

The American Catholic Experience, 4:751

American Catholicism, 4:751

The American Census: A Social History, 3:551

The American Century, 3:513

American Ceramics: The Collection of Everson Museum of Art, 3:766

The American Challenge, 3:346

American Chameleon: Individualism in Trans-National Context, 3:552

American Chemists and Chemical Engineers, 5:223

American Christianity, 4:752

The American Cinema: Directors and Directions: 1929–1968, 1:1158

The American Civil Engineer: Origins and Conflict, 5:36

The American Civil War and the Origins of Modern Warfare, 3:528

The American Claimant, 1:780

The American Claimant Manuscripts, 1:676

The American Clock, 1:1103, 1:1104

American Cold War Strategy: Interpreting NSC 68, 3:546

American Commercial Banking: A History, 3:548

The American Commonwealth, 3:151

American Communes, 1860–1960: A Bibliography, 4:842, 4:844

American Communes to 1860: An Annotated Bibliography, 4:843

American Communities, 4:844

American Community Organizations: A Historical Dictionary, 3:210

American Composers: Dialogues on Contemporary Music, 3:666

The American Constitution: Its Origins and Development, 3:142, 3:541

American Constitutional Law, 3:142

American Counterpoint, 3:602

The American Cowboy, 3:864

The American Cowboy: The Myth and the Reality, 1:1219

The American Crisis, 1:641

American Critical Essays on "The Divine Comedy," 2:417

An American Crusade: The Life of Charles Wadell Chesnutt, 1:739

The American Curriculum, 3:512

The American Democrat, 1:664

The American Diaries, 1902–1926, 1:829

An American Diary, 1:331

American Dictionary of Printing and Bookmaking, 1:6

An American Dilemma, 3:98, 3:209, 3:235

American Diplomacy, 1900–1950, 3:545, 3:584

The American Disease: Origins of Narcotic Control, 3:553

American Dissertations on the Drama and the Theatre: A Bibliography, 1:123

American Drama and Its Critics: A Collection of Critical Essays, 1:1072

American Drama Criticism: Interpretations, 1890–1977, 1:134, 1073

American Drama from Its Beginning to the Present, 1:1074

The American Dramatist,
  1:1075
American Dramatists,
  1918–1945, 1:1072
The American Dream (Al-
  bee), 1:1080
An American Dream (Miller),
  1:1011
American Dreams: The Imag-
  ination of Sam Shepard,
  1:1111
American Dreams, American
  Nightmares, 1:918
American Dreams, Lost and
  Found, 2:240
American Earthquake, 1:902
The American Economy, 3:81
The American Economy in
  Transition, 3:53
American Education: The Co-
  lonial Experience,
  1607–1783, 3:254
American Education: The
  Metropolitan Experience,
  1876–1980, 3:558
American Education: The Na-
  tional Experience,
  1783–1876, 3:254
American Education in a
  Global Society, 3:255
The American 1890's: Life
  and Times of a Lost Gen-
  eration, 1:725
American Electoral Behavior,
  1952–1988, 3:143
The American Encounter
  with Buddhism,
  1844–1912, 4:842
American Encyclopaedia of
  Printing, 1:10
American Engineers of the
  Nineteenth Century: A
  Biographical Index, 5:217
American Environmental His-
  tory, 3:550
American Environmentalism:
  Readings in Conservation
  History, 3:550
The American Epic: Trans-
  forming a Genre,
  1770–1860, 1:651
American Epoch: A History
  of the United States since
  1900, 3:513
The American Ethos: Public
  Attitudes toward Capital-
  ism and Democracy, 3:148
The American Evasion of
  Philosophy, 1:727, 4:268
The American Experiment,
  Vol. 1: The Vineyard of
  Liberty, 3:512, 3:570

Vol. 2: The Workshop of
  Democracy, 3:512, 3:570
Vol. 3: The Crosswinds of
  Freedom, 3:512, 3:570
American Extremes, 3:644
The American Ezra Pound,
  1:873
American Farm Tools: From
  Hand Power to Steam
  Power, 5:263
American Fiction: A Contri-
  bution towards a Bibliog-
  raphy, 1:725
American Fiction: An Histori-
  cal and Critical Survey,
  1:715, 1:629
American Fiction: The Intel-
  lectual Background, 1:715
American Fiction, Eighteen
  Sixty-Five to Nineteen For-
  ty, 1:723
American Fiction, 1914–1945,
  1:803
American Fiction, 1900–1950:
  A Guide to Information
  Sources, 1:805, 1:920
American Fiction, 1774–1850:
  A Contribution toward a
  Bibliography, 1:630, 1:658
American Fiction in the Cold
  War, 1:920
American Fictions,
  1940–1980, 1:918
American Folk Art: A Guide
  to Sources, 3:849
American Folk Art: The Art
  of the Common Man in
  America, 1750–1900, 3:868
American Folklife, 3:849
American Folklore, 3:848,
  3:878
American Folklore: A Bibli-
  ography, 1950–1974, 3:849
American Folklore and the
  Historian, 3:868, 3:878
American Folk Medicine: A
  Symposium, 5:319
American Folk Poetry: An
  Anthology, 1:1197
American Folk Sculpture,
  3:868
American Folk Tales and
  Songs, 3:860
American Foreign Policy: A
  Global View, 3:545
American Foreign Policy:
  Patterns and Process,
  3:545
American Foreign Policy and
  the Blessings of Liberty,
  and Other Essays, 3:567

American Foreign Relations:
  A Historiographical Re-
  view, 3:514
American Free Verse: The
  Modern Revolution in Po-
  etry, 1:914
American Furniture with Re-
  lated Decorative Arts,
  1660–1830, 3:766
American Genesis: A Century
  of Invention and Techno-
  logical Enthusiasm, 3:548,
  5:50, 5:51
American Genesis: Captain
  John Smith and the
  Founding of Virginia,
  3:518
American Gothic, 1:715
American Graffiti, 1:1171
American Habitat: A Histori-
  cal Perspective, 3:550
American Handbook of Psy-
  chiatry, 5:415
American Health Quackery:
  Collected Essays, 5:315
American Herbalism, 5:320
The American Heritage Desk
  Dictionary, 1:89
American Heritage Dictio-
  nary, 1:91
The American Heritage Dic-
  tionary of the English Lan-
  guage, 1:89
American Heritage Larousse
  Spanish Dictionary, 1:102
American Heritage Picture
  History of the Civil War,
  3:571
American Heroine: The Life
  and Legend of Jane Ad-
  dams, 1:731, 3:558
American High: The Years of
  Confidence, 1945–1960,
  3:539
American Higher Education:
  A Documentary History,
  3:255
American Higher Education,
  1945–1970: A Personal Re-
  port, 3:257
American Historical Associa-
  tion Guide to Historical
  Literature, 3:325
American Historical Fiction,
  1:122
American Historical Pag-
  eantry, 3:559
The American Historical Ro-
  mance, 1:650
American History: A Survey,
  3:513
American History/American
  Film, 3:560, 3:826

American History—One Hundred Nutshells, 3:507
American Holocaust, 3:557, 3:917
American Hospital Association Guide to the Health Care Field, 5:367
American Humor: A Study of the National Character, 1:652
American Humorists, 1800–1950, 3:872
American Hunger, 1:905
American Ideals and Other Essays, Social and Political, 3:594
American Ideologies Today: Shaping the New Politics of the 1990s, 3:140
The American Idiom: A Correspondence, 1:900
The American Illustrated Book in the Nineteenth Century, 3:767
American Immigration, 3:556
American Immigration Collection, Series 1, 3:581
The American Indian and the United States: A Documentary History, 3:512
American Indian Autobiography, 1:87, 1:631
American Indian Environments, 3:516
American Indian Leaders: Studies in Diversity, 3:555
American Indian Literatures, 1:716, 1:1129
American Indian Myth and Legends, 3:864
American Indian Poetry: An Anthology of Songs and Chants, 1:719
American Indians, 3:555
American Indians: Answers to Today's Questions, 3:507
America 1941: A Nation at the Crossroads, 3:535
The American Inquisition: Justice and Injustice in the Cold War, 3:539
American Intellectual Histories and Historians, 3:566, 3:567, 3:590
The American Intellectual Tradition: A Source Book, 3:559
American Iron Hand Presses, 1:11
The Americanization of the Unconscious, 5:424

The American Jeremiad, 1:627, 1:948
American Jew, 4:639
The American Jew: A Zionist Analysis, 4:658
The American Jewish Album: 1654 to the Present, 4:641
The American Jewish Woman: A Documentary History, 4:650
The American Jewish Yearbook, 1:81
American Jews and the Separationist Faith, 4:639
American Jews and the Zionist Idea, 4:657
American Jews in Transition, 4:641
American Journalism History: An Annotated Bibliography, 3:809
The American Journalist: Paradox of the Press, 3:806
American Journey, 3:165
American Judaism, 4:639
American Judaism: Adventure in Modernity, 4:651
The American Judaism of Mordecai M. Kaplan, 4:667
American Judicial Politics, 3:145
The American Labor Movement, 3:548
The American Labor Movement: A Short History, 3:565
The American Language, 1:859
American Law: An Introduction, 3:145
American Library Directory, 1:51, 1:70, 1:104
American Literary Criticism from the Thirties to the Eighties, 1:794, 1:1132
American Literary Critics and Scholars, 1880–1900, 1:726
American Literary History: 1607–1830, 1:629
American Literary Naturalism, A Divided Stream, 1:724
The American Literary Revolution 1783–1837, 1:630
American Literary Scholarship: An Annual, 1:121, 1:652, 1:712
American Literature: A Prentice Hall Anthology, 1:130

American Literature: Essays and Opinions, 2:433
American Literature: The Makers and the Making, 1:653
American Literature, Culture, and Ideology, 1:716
American Literature, 1764–1789, 1:628
American Literature to Nineteen Hundred, 1:650, 1:713
American Lives, 3:534
American Log Buildings: An Old World Heritage, 3:132
American Medical Association Directory of Physicians in the United States, 5:367
American Medical Association Encyclopedia of Medicine, 5:5
The American Medical Association Family Medical Guide, 5:310
American Medical Association Handbook of Poisonous and Injurious Plants, 5:311
American Medical Association Pocket Guide to Emergency First Aid, 5:380
The American Medical Association's Book of Back Care, 5:396
American Medical Education: The Formative Years, 1765–1910, 5:313
American Medicine: The Power Shift, 5:334
American Medicine and Statistical Thinking, 1800–1860, 5:312
American Melodrama: Plays and Documents, 1:1077
American Men and Women of Science, 5:4, 5:723
American Mercury, 1:859
American Metal Typefaces of the Twentieth Century, 1:17
The American Midwife Debate: A Sourcebook on Its Modern Origins, 5:338
The American Mind, 3:572
The American Mind in the Mid-Nineteenth Century, 1:722
American Minimal Music, 3:665

The American Model: Influence and Independence in Australian Poetry, 2:946

American Modernity and Jewish Identity, 4:638, 4:651

The American Movie Industry: The Business of Motion Pictures, 3:825

American Music: A Panorama, 3:661

American Musical Theatre: A Chronicle, 3:667

The American Musical Theatre: A Consideration, 1:1073

American Musicians: Fifty-Six Portraits in Jazz, 3:667

American Music since 1910, 3:724

American Myth, American Reality, 3:515

The American Narcissus, 1:724

The American Nation, 3:513

American National Standard for Compiling Book Publishing Statistics, 1:52

The American Negro: A Study in Racial Crossing, 3:32

American Negro Poetry, 1:719

American Negro Short Stories, 1:921

The American Newness: Culture and Politics in the Age of Emerson, 1:651

The American 1960s: Imaginative Acts in a Decade of Change, 1:911

American Notebooks, 1:676

American Notes, 1:349, 1:371

The American Novel, 1789–1939, 1:630

The American Novel and Its Tradition, 1:657, 1:722

The American Novel and the Way We Live Now, 1:793, 1:916

American Novelists, 1:723

American Novelists, 1910–1945, 1:919

American Novelists since World War II, 1:918

American Novelists since World War II: Second Series, 1:918

The American Novel through Henry James, 1:723

The American Occupational Structure, 3:218

The American Occupation of Germany: Politics and the Military, 1945–1949, 3:376

The American Occupation of Japan: The Origins of the Cold War in Asia, 3:479

The American Pageant: A History of the Republic, 3:512

The American Peace Movement: Ideals and Activism, 3:505

The American People: A History, 3:513

American Philosophers at Work, 4:34

American Philosophy: A Historical Anthology, 4:35

American Philosophy: From Edwards to Quine, 4:35

American Philosophy and the Romantic Tradition, 4:34

American Philosophy Today and Tomorrow, 4:34, 4:265

American Photographers and the National Parks, 3:894

American Physicians in the Nineteenth Century: From Sects to Science, 5:47

American Physics in Transition, 5:652

American Picture Books: From Noah's Ark to the Beast Within, 1:27, 1:37

American Plays, 1:1077

American Playwrights: A Critical Survey, 1:1074

American Playwrights, 1918–1938, 1:1073

American Playwrights since 1945, 1:1074

American Poetry, 1:719

American Poetry: Texts and Meanings, 1:719

American Poetry: The Puritans through Walt Whitman, 1:655

American Poetry: Wildness and Domesticity, 1:798, 1:951

American Poetry, 1915–1945, 1:798

American Poetry and Prose, 1:653, 1:713, 1:717

The American Poetry Anthology, 1:655, 1:720

American Poetry in the Twentieth Century, 1:1036

American Poetry Observed: Poets on Their Work, 1:912

American Poetry of the Twentieth Century, 1:798

American Poetry through Nineteen Fourteen, 1:719

American Poets: From the Puritans to the Present, 1:655, 1:719

American Poets, 1880 to 1945, 1:799

American Policy toward Communist China, 1949–1969, 3:544

The American Political Dictionary, 3:509

The American Political Novel, 1:919

The American Political Tradition and the Men Who Made It, 3:543, 3:582

American Political Writing during the Founding Era, 1760–1805, 3:520

American Popular Culture: A Guide to Information Sources, 3:873

American Popular Song: The Great Innovators, 1900–1950, 3:664, 3:730

American Populism: A Social History, 1877–1900, 3:532

American Pragmatism: Peirce, James and Dewey, 4:225, 4:238, 4:249

The American Presidency: A Bibliography, 3:510

The American Presidency: Historical and Contemporary Perspectives, 3:146

American Press Opinion: Washington to Coolidge, 3:590

The American Primer (Boorstin), 3:568

An American Primer (Whitman), 1:706

The American Printer: A Manual of Typography, 1:9

An American Procession, 1:714, 1:996

American Profile, 1900–1909, 3:533

American Prose, 1:660, 1:727

American Prose and Criticism, 1820–1900, 1:660, 1:727

American Prose and Criticism, Nineteen Hundred to Nineteen Fifty, 1:808

American Prose Masters, 1:669

American Prosody, 1:654, 1:718

American Protestant Thought in the Liberal Era, 4:753

The American Psychological Association: A Historical Perspective, 3:167, 3:168

The American Puritan Imagination: Essays on Revaluation, 1:627

American Puritanism and the Defense of Mourning, 1:627

The American Puritans: Their Prose and Poetry, 1:630, 3:586

American Quest, 3:894

The American Rabbinate: A Century of Continuity and Change, 1883–1983, 4:652

The American Reading Public: What It Reads, Why It Reads, 1:50

American Realism: New Essays, 1:724, 1:805

American Realists and Naturalists, 1:919

American Red Cross First Aid and Safety Handbook, 5:12

American Reference Books Annual, 1:62, 1:74

American Reformers, 1815–1860, 3:526

The American Religion: The Emergence of the Post-Christian Nation, 1:1138, 4:889

American Religion and Philosophy: A Guide to Information Sources, 4:15

American Religious Empiricism, 4:751

American Renaissance, 1:651, 1:715

The American Revolution, 3:511, 3:519, 3:520

The American Revolution: An Encyclopedia, 3:508

The American Revolution: Changing Perspectives, 3:520

The American Revolution: Explorations in the History of American Radicalism, 3:522

The American Revolution: Its Character and Limits, 3:520

The American Revolution, 1775–1783, 3:519

American Rhyming Dictionary of Words and Phrases, 1:95

American-Russian Relations, 1781–1947, 3:601

The Americans (Boorstin), 3:512, 3:568

The Americans (Jakes), 1:1247

The Americans: A New History of the People of the United States, 3:581

The Americans: The Colonial Experience, 1:627

The American Scene, 1:764

An American Scene: A Reader, 1:859

American Scenes and Other Poems, 1:560

The American School: 1642–1985, 3:258

American Science and Technology: A Bicentennial Bibliography, 5:27

American Science in the Age of Jackson, 5:46

American Science in the Age of Jefferson, 5:46

The American Science of Politics: Its Origin and Conditions, 3:138

American Science Policy since World War II, 5:183

The American Secretaries of State and Their Diplomacy, 1776–1925, 3:567

The American Senator, 1:406

An American's Guide to English Parish Churches, 1:445

American Short Stories, 1:725, 1:921

American Short Stories of the Nineteenth Century, 1:725

The American Short Story, 1:725, 1:806

The American Short Story: A Critical Survey, 1:658, 1:724, 1:806

The American Short Story: Continuity and Change, 1940–1975, 1:919

The American Short Story before 1850: A Critical History, 1:657

The American Short Story, 1900–1945: A Critical History, 1:806

American Short Story Masterpieces, 1:805

American Singers, 3:667

American Singers: Twenty-seven Portraits in Song, 3:672

American Slavery, American Freedom: The Ordeal of Colonial Virginia, 3:518, 3:587

American Slavery, 1619–1877, 3:524

American Social History as Recorded by British Travellers, 3:590

American Society in the Buddhist Mirror, 4:842, 4:860

The American Society of Plastic and Reconstructive Surgeons' Guide to Cosmetic Surgery, 5:397

The American Songbag, 1:878

The American South: A History, 3:513

American Specimen Book of Type Styles, 1:13

The American Spirit: United States History as Seen by Contemporaries, 3:514

American State Politics: An Introduction, 3:155

The American States during and after the Revolution, 1775–1789, 3:590

American Statistics Index, 1:108

American Strategy in World War II: A Reconsideration, 3:279

The American Style of Foreign Policy, 3:544

The American Supreme Court, 3:145

The American T. S. Eliot: A Study of the Early Writings, 1:473

The American Theater: A Sum of Its Parts, 1:1076

American Theater and Drama Research, 1:1075

American Theater History, 1:1076

American Theater of the 1960s, 1:1076

American Theatre (Brown), 1:1072

The American Theatre (Mordden), 1:1075

American Theatre as Seen by Its Critics, 1752–1934, 1:1075

The American Thesaurus of Slang, 1:92

American Thought: The Civil War to World War I, 3:587

American Thought and Religious Typology, 1:627
American Thought from Puritanism to Pragmatism and Beyond, 4:35
American Tough: The Tough-Guy Tradition and American Character, 3:553
An American Tragedy, 1:829
American Transcendentalists: Their Prose and Poetry, 3:587
An American Triptych: Anne Bradstreet, Emily Dickinson, Adrienne Rich, 1:628
The American University, 3:257
The American Urban System: A Geographical Perspective, 3:131
An American Utopian, 3:234
American Values: Continuity and Change, 4:34
American Violence: A Documentary History, 3:511, 3:582
American Vision, 1:658
American Vision: The Films of Frank Capra, 3:833
The American Voter, 3:143
American War Literature: 1914 to Vietnam, 1:920
The American Way of Birth, 5:359
The American West: New Perspectives, New Dimensions, 3:515
American Wives: Thirty Short Stories by Women, 1:921
The American Woman, 3:554
American Women Artists: From Early Indian Times to the Present, 3:761
American Women in Jazz: Nineteen Hundred to the Present, 3:669
American Women in the 1960s, 3:506
American Women in the Nineties, 3:218
American Women Poets of the Nineteenth-Century: An Anthology, 1:720
American Women's Autobiography: Fea(s)ts of Memory, 1:727
American Women's Fiction, 1790–1870: A Reference Guide, 1:725
American Women Writers, 1:127

American Women Writers: A Critical Reference Guide, 1:121, 1:127
American Women Writers; Bibliographic Essays, 1:713
American Women Writers: Diverse Voices in Prose since 1845, 1:808
American Women Writers on Vietnam: Unheard Voices, 3:490
American Wood Engraving: A Victorian History, 1:29
American Wood Type: 1828–1900, 1:17
American Writers: A Collection of Literary Biographies, 1:127, 1:128
American Writers and Radical Politics, 1900–1939, 1:794
American Writers and the Great Depression, 1:130
American Writing since 1945: A Critical Survey, 1:910
American Writing Today, 1:911
American Yiddish Poetry, 1:720
American Yiddish Poetry: A Bilingual Anthology, 2:33
American Zionism from Herzl to the Holocaust, 4:658
America Revised: History Schoolbooks in the Twentieth Century, 1:49, 3:515
America's China Trade in Historical Perspective, 3:471
America's Families: A Documentary History, 3:512
America's Health Care Revolution: Who Lives? Who Dies? Who Pays?, 5:332
America's Humor: From Poor Richard to Doonesbury, 1:650
America's Jews, 4:641
America's Longest War: The United States and Vietnam, 1950–1975, 3:538
America's Misunderstood Welfare State, 3:57
America's Music: From the Pilgrims to the Present, 3:659
America's Musical Stage: Two Hundred Years of Musical Theatre, 3:661
America's Neighborhood Bats, 5:818

America's One Hundred One Most High Falutin', Big Talkin' Knee Slappin', Golly Whoppers and Tall Tales, 3:858
America's Paul Revere, 1:1202
America's Philosophical Vision, 4:35, 4:267
America's Quest for the Ideal Self, 3:558
America's Siberian Adventure 1918–20, 3:396
America's Struggle against Poverty, 1900–1980, 3:548
America's Theologian: A Recommendation of Jonathan Edwards, 4:767
America's Utopian Experiments, 3:127
America's Welfare State: From Roosevelt to Reagan, 3:542
America Takes the Stage, 1:1075
America through British Eyes, 3:590
America through Women's Eyes, 3:565
Amerika, 2:596
Amiable Autocrat: A Biography of Doctor Oliver Wendell Holmes, 1:679
Am I Blue, 1:1094
Am I My Parents' Keeper?, 4:388
Aminta, 2:440
Amiri Baraka, 1:1085
Amiri Baraka/LeRoi Jones: The Quest for "Popular Modernism," 1:941, 1:1085
A. M. Klein and His Works, 2:915
Ammianus and the Historia Augusta, 3:311
Ammianus Marcellinus: Seven Studies in His Language and Thought, 3:311
Ammianus Marcellinus and Fourth Century History, 3:310
Amok, 2:617
Among Friends: Hospice Care for the Person with AIDS, 5:376
Among My Books, 1:684
Among School Children, 3:250
Among the Believers: An Islamic Journey, 2:939, 4:579
Among the Gods, 4:446
Among the Hills, 1:708

Among Women, 1:923
Among Women Only, 2:432
Amor and the Psyche: The Psychic Development of the Feminine, 2:383
Amores, 2:389
Amoretti, 1:197
Amorous Fiametta, 2:409, 2:410
Amour Bilingue, 2:123
Amours, 2:502
Amours de Voyage, 1:345
Amphibian Species of the World, 5:759
Amphitryon and Two Other Plays, 2:391
Amritsar: Mrs. Gandhi's Last Battle, 4:517
A. M. Turing, 5:582
A. M. Turing's ACE Report of 1946 and Other Papers, 5:582
Amusing Ourselves to Death, 5:139
Amusing the Million: Coney Island at the Turn of the Century, 3:552
Amy Lowell, 1:856
Amyntas, 2:480
Anabaptism: A Social History, 1525–1618, 4:723
Anabaptism and Asceticism: A Study in Intellectual Origins, 4:724
Anabaptism in Outline: Selected Primary Sources, 4:724
Anabaptist Baptism, 4:723
The Anabaptist in South and Central Germany, Switzerland, and Austria, 4:723
Anabaptists and the Sword, 4:724
The Anabaptists and Thomas Müntzer, 4:724
The Anabaptist Story, 4:733
The Anabaptist View of the Church, 4:724
Anabaptist Writings of David Jovis, 1535–1543, 4:724
Anabasis, 2:492, 3:312, 3:323
The Anabasis of Alexander, Indica, 3:312
Anabolic Steroids and the Athlete, 5:400
An Anagram of Ideas on Art, Form and Film, 1:1163
Ana Hurrah, 2:60
Anais Nin, 1:866
Anais Nin: A Bibliography, 1:866
Anais Nin: An Introduction, 1:866

Anais Nin, Art and Artists: A Collection of Essays, 1:866
Analects, 4:526
The Analects of Confucius, 4:526
Analogical Imagination, 4:746
Analogy, 4:193
The Analogy of Names and the Concept of Being, 4:136
The Analogy of Religion, 4:193
The Analogy of The Faerie Queene, 1:198
The Analysis and Cognition of Melodic Complexity, 3:172
Analysis and Metaphysics, 4:414
The Analysis of Behavior: A Program for Self-Instruction, 3:194
The Analysis of Dreams, 5:436
Analysis of Knowledge and Valuation, 4:302
The Analysis of Mind, 4:322
The Analysis of Sensations and the Relation of the Physical to the Psychical, 5:700
The Analysis of the Self, 5:457
Analysis of Water Distribution Systems, 5:245
The Analyst and the Mystic, 4:424
Analytical Chemistry, 5:735
An Analytical Concordance to the Revised Standard Version of the New Testament, 4:818
Analytical Index of Presence Africaine: 1948–1972, 2:111
Analytical Index to Publications of the Texas Folklore Society, 3:862
Analytical Marxism, 4:243
Analytical Philosophy of Technology, 5:72
Analytical Psychology, Its Theory and Practice: The Tavistock Lectures, 5:454
The Analytic Attitude, 5:469
The Analytic Engine: Computers—Past, Present, and Future, 5:536
Analytic Geometry, 5:487
Analyzing Marx, 4:243
Analyzing Marx: Morality, Power and History, 3:290

Analyzing the Presidency, 3:146
Ana María Matute, 2:545
The Anarchiad: A New England Poem, 1:633
Anarchism: Nomos XIX, 3:140
The Anarchists in the Russian Revolution, 3:395
Anarchy, State and Utopia, 4:314
Anarke in Thucydides, 3:323
Anatahan, 1:1176
The Anathemata: Fragments of an Attempted Writing, 1:502
Anatole France, 2:478
Anatolian Tales, 2:100
Anatomy, Descriptive and Surgical, 5:360
The Anatomy Lesson, 1:1040, 1:1041
The Anatomy of an Egyptian Intellectual, Yahya Haqqi, 2:65
Anatomy of an Epidemic, 5:383
Anatomy of an Expedition, 5:632
The Anatomy of a Party: The National CCF, 1932–61, 3:616
The Anatomy of a Scientific Institution, 5:44
Anatomy of a Typeface, 1:17
The Anatomy of Bibliomania, 1:32, 1:76
Anatomy of Criticism, 1:976
Anatomy of Flowering Plants, 5:768
The Anatomy of God, 4:630
The Anatomy of Human Destructiveness, 5:449
The Anatomy of Inquiry, 5:65
The Anatomy of Judgment, 5:77
The Anatomy of Letters: A Guide to the Art of Calligraphy, 1:18
Anatomy of Love: A Study of the Tristan of Gottfried von Strassburg, 2:582
The Anatomy of Neoplatonism, 4:61
The Anatomy of Poverty, 3:614
Anatomy of Printing: The Influences of Art and History on Its Design, 1:9
The Anatomy of Racial Attitudes, 3:208
Anatomy of Racism, 1:1133

Anatomy of Terror, 3:292

Anatomy of the Human Body, 5:360

Anatomy of Wonder: A Critical Guide to Science Fiction, 1:611

Anaxagoras' Theory of Matter, 4:53

Anaximander and the Origins of Greek Cosmology, 4:51

Ancestors' Brocades, 1:746

Ancestor Worship and Korean Society, 4:539

Ancestral Voice: Conversations with N. Scott Momaday, 1:1016

Ancestral Voices: Fifty Books from the Romantic Period, 1:266

Anchor Anthology of Sixteenth-Century Verse, 1:165, 1:166

The Anchor Bible Dictionary, 4:4, 4:818, 4:820

The Anchor Companion to the Orchestra, 3:655

Anciene Wisse: English Text of the Anciene Riwle, 1:559

The Ancien Régime, 3:336, 3:338

The Ancien Régime: French Society, 1600–1750, 3:372

Ancient and Medieval Ethiopian History, 3:423

Ancient Architecture: Mesopotamia and Egypt, 3:763

Ancient Astronauts, Cosmic Collisions, and Other Popular Theories about Man's Past, 5:598

Ancient Athenian Maritime Courts, 3:305

The Ancient Child: A Novel, 1:1016

Ancient Christian Gospels: Their History and Development, 4:825

Ancient Christian Writers: The Works of the Fathers in Translation, 4:679

The Ancient City, 4:438

Ancient Civilizations: The Near East and Mesoamerica, 4:439, 4:454

The Ancient Concept of Progress and Other Essays on Greek Literature and Belief, 2:345

Ancient Concepts of Philosophy, 4:50

The Ancient Dialect: Thomas Carlyle and Comparative Religion, 1:343

The Ancient Economy, 3:307

Ancient Egypt: A Social History, 3:301

The Ancient Egyptian Book of the Dead, 4:442

Ancient Egyptian Literature: A Book of Readings, 2:53, 3:300, 4:442

The Ancient Egyptian Pyramid Texts, 2:52

Ancient Egyptian Religion: An Interpretation, 4:442, 4:548

The Ancient Egyptians: A Sourcebook of Their Writings, 2:52, 3:300

The Ancient Egyptians: Religious Beliefs and Practices, 4:442, 4:548

Ancient Engineers, 5:38

Ancient Evenings, 1:1011, 1:1012

Ancient Ghana and Mali, 3:421

Ancient Greece and Rome, 3:299

Ancient Greek Agriculture: An Introduction, 3:304

Ancient Greek Literature, 2:345

The Ancient Greeks: A Critical History, 3:301

The Ancient Greeks: An Introduction to Their Life and Thought, 2:345, 3:301

The Ancient History of Western Civilization, 3:298, 4:604

Ancient Indian Asceticism, 4:501

Ancient Iraq, 3:301, 3:450

Ancient Israel after Catastrophe, 4:606

Ancient Japan, 3:476

Ancient Judaism, 3:243

The Ancient Kingdoms of Mexico, 3:627

Ancient Law, 3:35

The Ancient Library of Qumran and Modern Biblical Studies, 4:810

Ancient Light: Our Changing View of the Universe, 5:68

Ancient Lives: Daily Life in Egypt of the Pharaohs, 4:442

Ancient Mariner, 1:305

Ancient Maya Civilization, 3:627, 4:455

Ancient Mesopotamia: Portrait of a Dead Civilization, 4:441

The Ancient Mysteries: A Sourcebook, 4:450

Ancient Mystery Cults, 4:450, 4:470

Ancient Myth in Modern Poetry, 1:417, 1:913, 2:988

Ancient Near East, 4:439

The Ancient Near East: A History, 3:300

Ancient Near Eastern Texts Relating to the Old Testament, 2:53, 4:812

Ancient Near Eastern Texts Relating to the Old Testament with Supplement, 4:439

The Ancient Near East in Pictures Relating to the Old Testament, 4:812

Ancient Near East in Pictures with Supplement, 4:439

Ancient Places: The Prehistoric and Celtic Sites of Britain, 4:436

Ancient Proverbs and Maxims from Burmese Sources, 2:313

The Ancient Quarrel between Poetry and Philosophy, 4:48

Ancient Records of Assyria and Babylonia, 2:53

Ancient Records of Egypt, 2:52

The Ancient Romances: A Literary-Historical Account of Their Origins, 2:352, 2:363

Ancient Roman Religion, 4:448

Ancients and Moderns, 5:42

Ancient Science and Modern Civilization, 5:56

Ancient Science through the Golden Age of Greece, 5:39

Ancient Skins, Parchments and Leathers, 1:26

Ancient Society, 3:37

Ancient Synagogues Revealed, 4:614

Ancient Synagogues: The State of Research, 4:614

Ancient Tales in Modern Japan, 4:539

The Ancient Theology, 4:131

The Ancient Wisdom, 4:549

Ancient Wisdom Revived: A History of the Theosophical Movement, 4:852

Ancient Writers: Greece and Rome, 2:346

Ancilla to Classical Reading, 2:345

The Ancrene Wisse, 1:146

And Again, 1:529

Andalusian Lyrical Poetry and Old Spanish Love Songs, 2:57, 2:525

The Andaman Islanders, 3:38

And a Threefold Cord, 2:164

And Call Me Coward, 1:1263

The Anderson Tapes, 1:1236

The Andes of Southern Peru, 3:128

And It Came to Pass, 2:16

And It Is Suddenly Evening, 2:437

And Justice for All, 3:536

And Keep Your Powder Dry: An Anthropologist Looks at America, 3:36

And Miss Reardon Drinks a Little, 1:1122, 1:1123

And Muhammad Is His Messenger, 4:589

And on the Eighth Day, 1:1236

Andorra, 2:579

And Other Neighborly Names, 3:862

And Quiet Flows the Don, 2:755, 2:756

The Andrassy Affair, 3:427

Andrea Palladio: The Complete Works, 3:785

Andreas Vesalius of Brussels, 1514–1564, 5:40, 5:365

André Breton: Magus of Surrealism, 2:463

André Breton Today, 2:463

André Gide, 2:480

André Gide and the Codes of Homotextuality, 2:480

Andrei Bely: The Major Symbolist Fiction, 2:701

Andrei Platonov: Uncertainties of Spirit, 2:749

André Malraux, 2:487

André Malraux: Towards the Expression of Transcendence, 2:487

André Malraux and the Metamorphosis of Death, 2:488

André Malraux and the Tragic Imagination, 2:488

Andrew Jackson, 3:525

Andrew Lloyd Webber, 3:705

Andrew Lloyd Webber: His Life and Works, 3:705

Andrew Marvell, 1:189

Andrew Marvell: Poète, Puritain, Patriote, 1621–1678, 1:189

Andrew Marvell: The Critical Heritage, 1:189

Andrey Bely: A Critical Review, 2:701

Andrey Bely: A Critical Study of the Novels, 2:701

Andrey Bely: Spirit of Symbolism, 2:701

Androcles and the Lion, 1:545

Andromache, 2:498

Andromache and Other Plays, 2:498

Andromaque, 2:498

And Still the Earth, 2:894

And the Band Played On: Politics, People and the AIDS Epidemic, 5:388

And the Bridge Was Love: Memories of a Lifetime, 2:615

And Then There Were None, 1:605

And the War Came, 3:530, 3:598

And the Wind Blows Free, 1:1218

And the Wolf Finally Came: The Decline of the American Steel Industry, 3:547

And Things Go Bump in the Night, 1:1103

And to Think That I Saw It on Mulberry Street, 1:1203

And We Sold the Rain: Contemporary Fiction from Central America, 2:850

Andy Goldsworthy: Collaboration with Nature, 5:192

Andy Warhol, 3:796

Andy Warhol: A Retrospective, 3:796

Andy Warhol: Films and Paintings—The Factory Years, 3:796

The Andy Warhol Diaries, 3:796

Anecdotes and Traditions, Illustrative of Early English History and Literature and Derived from Manuscript Sources, 3:888

Anecdotes of Destiny, 2:649

Anecdotes of Painting in England, 1:262

Anecdotes of Painting in England, 1700–1795, 1:262

An Angel at My Table, 2:973

The Angel at the Gate, 2:935

The Angelic Avengers, 2:649

Angel of Light, 1:1022

The Angel of the Tar Sands and Other Stories, 2:927

Angel Pavement, 1:537

Angels, 4:768

Angels and Aliens: UFOs and the Mythic Imagination, 4:870

Angels and Insects: Two Novellas, 1:454

The Angels and Us, 4:269

Angels, Apes and Man, 5:202

Angels Fall, 1:1120, 1:1121

Angels of Vision: Conversations on Philippine Literature, 2:328

Angel with Horns: Fifteen Lectures on Shakespeare, 1:210

Anger: How to Live with and without It, 5:438

Anger and After: A Guide to the New British Drama, 1:426

Anger and Aggression: An Essay on Emotion, 5:413

The Anger of Achilles: Homer's Iliad, 2:359

The Anger of Stephen Crane, 1:743

Angkor, 3:902

Angle of Repose, 1:1053

Anglish-Yinglish: Yiddish in American Life and Literature, 2:31

Anglo-American Encounters: England and the Rise of American Literature, 1:651

Anglo-Irish Essays, 1:430

Anglo-Norman England, 1066–1154, 3:353

Anglo-Norman Ireland, 1100–1318, 3:370

Anglo Saxon Attitudes, 1:567

The Anglo-Saxon Chronicle, 1:142, 1:143, 3:356

An Anglo-Saxon Dictionary, 1:96

Anglo-Saxon England, 3:356

Anglo-Saxon Poetry, 1:143

Anglo-Saxon Reader in Prose and Verse, 1:143

The Anglo-Saxon World: An Anthology, 1:143

The Angolan Revolution, 3:423

The Angry Gut: Coping with Colitis and Crohn's Disease, 5:385

The Anguish of the Jews: Twenty-three Centuries of Antisemitism, 4:635

Angus Wilson, 1:567

Angus Wilson: A Bibliography, 1:567

Angus Wilson: Mimic and Moralist, 1:567

Aniara, 2:678

Animadversiones, 4:172

Animal Behavior: An Evolutionary Approach, 5:825

Animal Behavior: Psychobiology, Ethology and Evolution, 5:826

Animal Crackers, 1:1097

The Animal Doctor, 2:674

Animal Farm, 1:530

The Animal in Its World: Explorations of an Ethologist, 1932–1972, 3:194

The Animal Kingdom, Arranged after Its Organization, 5:792

Animal Language, 5:770

Animal Liberation, 4:43

The Animal Mind: A Textbook of Comparative Psychology, 3:195

Animal Myths and Metaphors in South America, 4:466

Animal Physiology: Mechanisms and Adaptations, 5:773

Animal Rights and Human Obligations, 4:389

The Animal Rights-Environmental Ethics Debate, 5:114, 5:135

Animals and Why They Matter, 4:389

The Animals Arrival, 1:501

Animals as Navigators, 5:769

Animal Science, 5:263

Animal Species and Their Evolution, 5:779

Anita Brookner, 1:452

Anna (I) Anna, 2:653

Anna Christie, 1:1106, 1:1107

Anna Freud: A Life Dedicated to Children, 5:445

Anna Karenina, 2:763, 2:764

The Annals of America, 3:511

The Annals of a Publishing House, 1:385

Annals of English Drama, 975–1700, 1:170, 1:221

Annals of English Literature, 1475–1950, 1:120

The Annals of Imperial Rome, 3:321

Annals of Opera, 1597–1940, 3:670

Annals of Printing, 1:7

Annals of the American Academy of Political and Social Sciences, 1:48

Annals of the New York Stage, 1:1075

Anna of the Five Towns, 1:443

Anna Pavlova: Her Life and Art, 3:750

Anna's Book, 1:516

Anna Seghers' Exile Literature, 2:612

Anna Sokolow: The Rebellious Spirit, 3:735

Anne, 1:790

Anne Bradstreet, 1:635

Anne Bradstreet: A Reference Guide, 1:635

Anne Bradstreet: The Worldly Puritan, 1:635

Anne Bradstreet and her Time, 1:634

Anne Bradstreet Revisited, 1:635

Anne Bradstreet's Poetry: A Study in Subversive Piety, 1:635

Anne Brontë: A Biography, 1:334

Anne Brontë: Her Life and Work, 1:334

Anne Sexton: A Biography, 1:1045

Anne Sexton: A Self-Portrait in Letters, 1:1045

Anne Sexton: The Artist and Her Critics, 1:1045

Annette von Droste-Hülshoff: A Biography, 2:577

Annette von Droste-Hülshoff: A Reassessment of Her Life and Writings, 2:576

Annie Allen, 1:954

Annie Besant and Progressive Messianism, 4:550

Annie John, 2:936

Annie Kilburn: A Novel, 1:758

Anni Mirabiles, 1921–1925: Reason in the Madness of Letters, 1:816

Anniversaries: From the Life of Gesine Cresspahl, 2:594

Anniversaries II, 2:595

The Anniversary, 2:708

Ann Lee's and Other Stories, 1:447

The Annotated Alice, 1:582

An Annotated Bibliography of Edmund Spenser, 1:198

Annotated Bibliography of Expository Writing in the Mathematical Sciences, 5:479

An Annotated Bibliography of James Joyce, 1:506

Annotated Bibliography of John Updike Criticism, 1:1061

An Annotated Bibliography of Latin American Sports, 3:624

Annotated Bibliography of Musca Domestica Linnaeus, 5:806

Annotated Bibliography of Published Writings of W.E.B. Du Bois, 3:578

Annotated Bibliography of Puerto Rican Bibliographies, 3:641

An Annotated Bibliography of Shakespearean Burlesques, Parodies and Travesties, 1:220

An Annotated Bibliography of Sir Richard Francis Burton, 3:914

Annotated Bibliography of the Writings of William James, 4:238

An Annotated Bibliography on the Modern History of the Near East, 3:437

An Annotated Critical Bibliography of Alfred, Lord Tennyson, 1:402

An Annotated Critical Bibliography of Augustan Poetry, 1:228

Annotated Critical Bibliography of Feminist Criticism, 1:134

An Annotated Critical Bibliography of George Eliot, 1:354

An Annotated Critical Bibliography of Joseph Conrad, 1:464

An Annotated Critical Bibliography of Langland, 1:154

Annotated Critical Bibliography of Robert Browning, 1:339

An Annotated Critical Bibliography of Thomas Hardy, 1:362

An Annotated Critical Bibliography of William Morris, 1:383

The Annotated Gilbert and Sullivan, 1:357

An Annotated Guide to Current National Bibliographies, 1:64

Annotated Index to the Cantos of Ezra Pound: Cantos I–LXXXIV, 1:873

The Annotated Lolita, 1:1020, 2:740

The Annotated Sherlock Holmes, 1:607

The Annotated Snark, 1:582

Annotations for the Selected Works of William Makepeace Thackeray, 1:404

Ann Radcliffe's Novels: Experiments in Setting, 1:622

Annual Bibliography of English Language and Literature, 1:120

Annual Editions: Education 93–94, 3:252

The Annual Register 1989, 1:81

Annual Register of Grant Support: A Directory of Funding Sources, 1:104

Annual Review of Anthropology, 3:11

Annual Review of Astronomy and Astrophysics, 5:587

Annual Review of Fluid Mechanics, 5:257

Annual Review of Information Science and Technology, 5:545

Annual Review of Psychology, 3:168

Annual Review of Sociology, 3:200

Annual Review of Women in World Religions, Vol. 2: Heroic Women, 4:892

The Annual Survey of Psychoanalysis, 5:424

Ann Vickers, 1:854

Anonyma and Pseudonyma, 1:77

Anonymous Toil, 1:803

Anonyms: A Dictionary of Revealed Authorship, 1:77

Anorexia Nervosa: A Guide for Sufferers and Their Families, 5:395

Anorexia Nervosa: A Multidimensional Perspective, 5:395

Anorexia Nervosa and Bulimia: Diagnosis and Treatment, 5:395

Another Antigone, 1:1091

Another Birth, 2:88

Another Chance: Postwar America, 1945–1968, 3:538

Another Country, 1:938, 1:939, 1:1084

Another Ego, 1:510

Another Last Word, 2:152

Another Life, 2:767, 2:942, 2:943

Another Metamorphosis and Other Fictions, 2:654

Another Mother Tongue: Gay Words, Gay Essays, 1:1182

Another Mother Tongue: Gay Words, Gay Worlds, 1:1188

Another Nigger Dead, 2:152

Another Part of the Forest, 1:1092, 1:1093

Another Sheaf of White Spirituals, 3:851

Another Tale to Tell: Essays on Postmodern Culture, 3:346

Another View, 1:621

Anowa, 2:129

Anselm, 4:108

Anselm and a New Generation, 4:703

Anselm and Talking about God, 4:703

Anselm of Canterbury: Complete Treatises, 4:703

Anselm's Discovery, 4:288

Answered Prayers: The Unfinished Novel, 1:959

Antarctica: Accounts from Journals of Numerous Explorers, 3:915

Antarctica: The Extraordinary History of Man's Conquest of the Frozen Continent, 3:906

Antarctic Mineral Exploitation: The Emerging Legal Framework, 5:238

Antarctic Obsession, 3:936

Antecedents of the English Novel, 1400–1600: From Chaucer to Deloney, 1:167

Antechamber and Other Poems, 1:1008

Ante Kovačić, 2:785

The Ante-Nicene Fathers, 4:100, 4:680, 4:708, 4:713

Ante Pacem: Archaeological Evidence of Church Life before Constantine, 4:689

Antheil and the Treatise on Harmony, 1:871

Anthenaem, 2:610

Anthills of the Savannah, 2:127, 2:128

Anthologie de la Nouvelle Poésie Nègre et Malagache de la Langue Française, 2:146

An Anthology: Green River Review, 1968–1973, 1:567

Anthology of American Literature, 1:130

Anthology of American Literature. Vol. 1: Colonial through Romantic, 1:653

Anthology of American Literature. Vol. 2: Realism to the Present, 1:795

Anthology of Armenian Poetry, 2:76

An Anthology of Beowulf Criticism, 1:144

An Anthology of Canadian Literature in English, 2:905, 2:922, 2:927

An Anthology of Canadian Native Literature in English, 2:905

An Anthology of Chartist Poetry, 1:316

An Anthology of Chinese Literature, 2:192

An Anthology of Chinese Poetry from the Earliest Times to the Present Day, 2:193

An Anthology of Chinese Verse, 2:192

Anthology of Concretism, 1:914

An Anthology of Contemporary Chinese Literature, 2:235

Anthology of Contemporary Italian Prose, 2:403

Anthology of Contemporary Latin American Literature, 1960–1984, 2:849

An Anthology of Contemporary Malaysian Literature, 2:325

Anthology of Czechoslovak Literature, 2:789, 2:833

Anthology of Danish Literature, 2:645

Anthology of Fantastic Literature, 2:855

An Anthology of German Poetry from Holderlin to Rilke in English Translation, 2:566

Anthology of Greek Drama, 2:349

Anthology of Holocaust Literature, 2:33, 4:636

Anthology of Islamic Literature, 2:57, 4:567

An Anthology of Italian Lyrics from the 13th Century to the Present Day, 2:403

An Anthology of Italian Poems: 13th-19th Century, 2:403

An Anthology of Jacobean Drama, 1:171

Anthology of Japanese Literature: Earliest Era to Mid-Nineteenth Century, 2:273

Anthology of Korean Literature, 2:299

Anthology of Korean Writing, 2:297

An Anthology of Medieval Hebrew Literature, 2:10

Anthology of Medieval Music, 3:660

An Anthology of Medieval Serbian Literature in English, 2:828

An Anthology of Mexican Poetry, 2:850

An Anthology of Modern Arabic Poetry, 2:57, 2:73

Anthology of Modern Estonian Poetry, 2:796

Anthology of Modern Hebrew Poetry, 2:10

Anthology of Modern Indonesian Poetry, 2:318

Anthology of Modern Japanese Poetry, 2:283

An Anthology of Modern Kashmiri Verse 1930-1960, 2:176

The Anthology of Modern Korean Poetry, 2:298

An Anthology of Modern Persian Poetry, 2:84

An Anthology of Modern Swedish Literature, 2:672

An Anthology of Modern Turkish Short Stories, 2:96, 2:98, 2:100

An Anthology of Modern Yiddish Literature, 2:34

An Anthology of Modern Yiddish Poetry, 2:34

An Anthology of Neo-Latin Poetry, 2:382

Anthology of New Italian Writers: Selections from Botteghe Oscure, 2:402

Anthology of New York Poets, 1:915

An Anthology of Nineties' Verse, 1:316, 1:720

An Anthology of Religious Texts from Ugarit, 4:545

An Anthology of Roman Drama, 2:382

Anthology of Russian Literature from the Earliest Period to the Present, 2:694

An Anthology of Russian Neo-Realism, 2:693

An Anthology of Sacred Texts by and about Women, 4:892

Anthology of Serbian Poetry, 2:828

Anthology of Spanish Literature in English Translation, 2:526

An Anthology of Spanish Poetry, 2:526

An Anthology of the New England Poets from Colonial Times to the Present Day, 1:720

An Anthology of Twentieth Century Brazilian Poetry, 1:950, 2:890

An Anthology of Twentieth-Century New Zealand Poetry, 2:971

Anthology of Western Armenian Literature, 2:77

An Anthology of Wit, 3:870

Anthony Adverse, 1:1244, 1:1245

Anthony Burgess: A Bibliography, 1:454

Anthony Burgess: An Annotated Bibliography and Reference Guide, 1:454

Anthony Burgess: The Artist as Novelist, 1:454

Anthony Burgess Revisited, 1:454

Anthony Giddens, 3:227

Anthony Trollope, 1:407

Anthony Trollope's "Barchester Towers" and "The Warden," 1:407

The Anthropic Cosmological Principle, 5:196, 5:654

Anthropological Approaches to the Study of Religion, 3:23, 4:422

Anthropological Archaeology, 3:13

Anthropological Bibliographies: A Selected Guide, 3:11

The Anthropological Principle in Philosophy, 2:711

Anthropological Research: Process and Application, 3:12

Anthropological Research: The Structure of Inquiry, 3:12

Anthropological Studies of Religion: An Introductory Text, 4:422

An Anthropologist at Work: Writings of Ruth Benedict, 3:27

Anthropology: An Introduction to the Study of Man and Civilization, 3:41

Anthropology: Culture Patterns and Processes, 3:33

Anthropology, History, and Cultural Change, 3:12

Anthropology and Modern Life, 3:28

Anthropology and Roman Culture: Kinship, Time, Images of the Soul, 4:448

Anthropology as Cultural Critique, 4:426

Anthropology from a Pragmatic Point of View, 4:205

The Anthropology of Dance, 3:733

The Anthropology of Johannes Scottus Erigena, 4:115

The Anthropology of Music, 3:666

The Anthropology of Performance, 3:40

The Anthropology of Slavery: The Womb of Iron and Gold, 3:429

The Anthropology of War, 3:279

The Anti-Aesthetic: Essays on Postmodern Culture, 1:1133

Antibody Politic: AIDS and Society, 5:388

Antic Hay, 1:499

The Antichrist, 4:245, 4:246

Antichrist in the Middle Ages, 1:141

The Anti-Cult Movement in America: A Bibliographic History, 4:857

The Anti-Death League, 1:432

The Antidiabetic Functions of the Pancreas and the Successful Isolation of the Antidiabetic Hormone, Insulin, 5:407

Anti-Evolution: A Reader's Guide to Writings before and after Darwin, 5:780

The Antifederalists: Critics of the Constitution, 1781-1788, 3:541

Antigone, 2:367, 2:468

Antigone of Sophocles, 2:593

Antigones, 1:1054, 2:985

The Antiheroine's Voice, 2:525

Anti-Intellectualism in American Life, 3:524, 3:582

Anti-Memoirs, 2:487

The Antiphon, 1:812

Antipoems: New and Selected, 2:877

Anti-Politics in America, 3:542

Antiquarian Books: An Insider's Account, 1:32

The Antiquary, 1:298

Antiquities of the Jews, 3:316

Antiquity and the Middle Ages, 3:661, 5:39

The Antiquity of Man, 5:645

The Anti-Samuelson, 3:104

Anti-Semite and Jew, 3:350, 4:329

Anti-Semitism in America, 3:209

Anti-Semitism in American History, 4:639

Antisemitism in Modern France, 3:348

The Anti-Slavery Crusade in America, 3:586

Antislavery Reconsidered: New Perspectives on the Abolitionists, 3:525

The Anti-Social Family, 3:206

The Anti-Soviet Soviet Union, 2:772

Anti-Story: An Anthology of Experimental Writing, 1:922

The Anti-theatrical Prejudice, 1:169

Antitrust, the Market, and the State, 3:61

Antitrust Economics on Trial: A Dialogue on the New Laissez-Faire, 3:61

The Antitrust Paradox: A Policy at War with Itself, 3:61

Antitrust Penalty Reform: An Economic Analysis, 3:61

Antiworlds, 2:773

Antoine de Saint-Exupéry, 2:504

Antoine-Laurent Lavoisier: Chemist and Revolutionary, 5:749

Anton Chekhov, 2:710

Anton Chekhov: A Reference Guide, 2:710

Antonin Artaud, 2:452

Antonin Artaud: Man of Vision, 2:452

Antonio and Mellida, 1:188

Antonio Caso: Philosopher of Mexico, 4:33

Antonio Gramsci, 2:423, 4:287

Antonio Gramsci: Conservative Schooling for Radical Politics, 4:287

Antonio Gramsci and the Origins of Italian Communism, 4:287

Antonioni, 3:830

Antonio's Revenge, 1:188

Antonio Vivaldi: His Life and Work, 3:727

Antonio Vivaldi, Documents of His Life and Works, 3:727

Anton von Webern: A Chronicle of His Life and Work, 3:730

Anton von Webern: Perspectives, 3:730

Anton Webern: An Introduction to His Works, 3:730

Antony and Cleopatra, 1:205, 1:206, 3:318

Antony Tudor, 3:754

Antony van Leeuwenhoek and His "Little Animals," 5:41, 5:804

Ants, 5:770, 5:798

Anxiety, 2:820

Anxiety Disorders and Phobias, a Cognitive Perspective, 5:433

The Anxiety of Influence: A Theory of Poetry, 1:1138

Any Old Iron, 1:453

Anyone Can Fly, 5:219

Anything for Billy, 1:1010

Anza's California Expeditions, 3:643

Apartheid, 2:162

The "Apeiron" of Anaximander, 4:51

Apes, Angels, and Victorians, 5:794, 5:831

Apes and Angels: The Irishman in Victorian Caricature, 3:363

The Apes of God, 1:514

Apex Omnium: Religion in the Res Gestae of Ammianus, 3:310

Aphra Behn, 1:233

Aphrodite, 1:469

Apocalypse and Other Poems, 2:859

Apocalypse Delayed: The Story of Jehovah's Witnesses, 4:863

The Apocalyptic Imagination in Medieval Literature, 1:147

The Apocalyptic Premise: Nuclear Arms Debated, 5:111

The Apocalyptic Tradition in Reformation Britain 1530–1645, 4:726

Apocolocyntosis, 2:393

The Apocrypha, 2:493

Apocryphal New Testament, 4:811

Apollinaire: Poet among the Painters, 2:451

Apollo in Snow: Selected Poems, 2:733

Apollo in the Democracy, 3:777

Apollonius of Perga: Treatise on Conic Sections, 5:498

Apologetical Works, 4:713

Apologia and Florida, 2:383, 4:469

Apologia pro Vita Sua, 1:324, 4:782

Apologies to the Iroquois: The Iroquois and Their Neighbors, 1:902

Apology, 4:89, 4:152

Apology and Spectacles, 4:713

An Apology for Actors, 1:182

Apology for His Life, 1:230

Apology for Poesy, 1:163

The Apology for Raymond Sebond, 2:491, 4:146

Apostle of Culture: Emerson as Preacher and Lecturer, 1:670

The Apostolic Fathers, 4:704

The Apostolic Fathers: An American Translation, 4:703

The Apostolic Fathers: A New Translation and Commentary, 4:703, 4:811

The Apostolic Fathers, Clement, Ignatius, and Polycarp, 4:704

The Apostolic Preaching and Its Developments, 4:833

The Apotheosis of Captain Cook: European Myth-Making in the Pacific, 4:462

Appeal to Immediate Experience, 4:342

An Appeal to the People of England on the Recognition and Superintendence of Prostitution by Government, 1:341

Appearance and Reality: A Metaphysical Essay, 4:220, 4:221

The Apple Cart, 1:545

The Apple in the Dark, 2:895

The Apple Macintosh Book, 5:554

An Apple Pie, 1:585

Apples of Immortality: Folk Tales of Armenia, 2:77

The Application of Statistical Methods to Industrial Standardization and Quality Control, 5:531

Applications of Biotechnology, 5:222

Applications of Inductive Logic, 4:405

Applications of Weather Radar Systems, 5:633

An Applications-Oriented Approach to Artificial Intelligence, 5:569

Applied Cost Engineering, 5:234

Applied Hydrology, 5:631

Applied Lettering and Design, 1:16

Applied Science and Technology Index, 5:5

Applied Social Sciences Index and Abstracts, 3:5

Applied Statistics, 5:523

Appointment in Samarra, 1:866

An Appraisal of Walter Prescott Webb's "The Great Plains," 3:600

Appreciations: With an Essay on Style, 1:386, 1:387

Apprenticeship, 2:653

The Apprenticeship of Beatrice Webb, 3:113

The Apprenticeship of Duddy Kravitz, 2:924

The Apprenticeship of Ernest Hemingway, 1:846

An Apprenticeship or the Book of Delights, 2:895

Apprentice to Genius: The Making of a Scientific Dynasty, 5:313, 5:764

Approaches to Ancient Judaism: Theory and Practice, 4:610

Approaches to Canadian Economic History, 3:606

Approaches to E. M. Forster: A Centenary Volume, 1:477

Approaches to God, 4:306

Approaches to Gramsci, 4:287

Approaches to "Gravity's Rainbow," 1:1035

Approaches to Judaism in Medieval Times, 4:622

Approaches to Modern Judaism, 4:634

Approaches to Social Archaeology, 3:13

Approaches to Teaching Beowulf, 1:144

Approaches to Teaching Blake's Songs of Innocence and of Experience, 1:279

Approaches to Teaching Byron's Poetry, 1:284

Approaches to Teaching Chopin's The Awakening, 1:740

Approaches to Teaching Keats's Poetry, 1:294

Approaches to Teaching Medieval English Drama, 1:157

Approaches to Teaching Melville's Moby Dick, 1:688

Approaches to Teaching Shelley's Frankenstein, 1:301

Approaches to Teaching Shelley's Poetry, 1:303

Approaches to Teaching Sir Gawain and the Green Knight, 1:156

Approaches to Teaching Spanish Golden Age Drama, 2:524

Approaches to Teaching Whitman's Leaves of Grass, 1:707

Approaches to Teaching Wordsworth's Poetry, 1:307

Approaches to the Study of Social Structure, 3:215

Approaches to the Theater of Calderón, 2:533

Approaches to Translation: Aspects of Translation, 2:990

Approaches to Victorian Autobiography, 1:325

Approaching Simone, 1:1114

Approaching Vietnam, 3:545

An Approach to Congreve, 1:237

An Approach to Literature, 1:128

An Approach to Shakespeare, 1:210

Approach to the Metaphysics of Plato through the Parmenides, 4:82

The Approach to the New Testament. Hibbert Lectures, 4:1921, 4:835

Appropriate Visions, Technology, the Environment and the Individual, 5:213

Appropriating the Weather, 5:642

April, April, 1:1175

April Galleons, 1:936

April Twilights, 1:821

Aptitude Testing, 3:186

Apuleius and His Influence, 2:383, 4:469

Apuleius and the Golden Ass, 2:383, 4:469

An Aquarium of Women, 2:670

Aquinas (Copleston), 4:39

Aquinas (Kenny), 4:119

Aquinas: A Collection of Critical Essays, 4:119

Aquinas against the Averroists, 4:119

Aquinas on Human Action, 4:119

An Aquinas Reader, 4:117

Aquinas to Whitehead: Seven Centuries of Metaphysics of Religion, 4:288

The Aquinos of Tarlac: An Essay on History as Three Generations, 2:330

The Arab Awakening: The Story of the Arab National Movement, 3:434

The Arab Bureau: British Policy in the Middle East, 1916–1920, 3:438

The Arab Conquests in Central Asia, 3:456

Arabesque, 2:56

Arabesques (Gogol), 2:721

Arabesques (Shammas), 2:24

Arabian Love Poems, 2:71

The Arabian Nights, 2:58, 2:431, 2:648, 3:913

The Arabian Nights, Based on the Text of the Fourteenth-Century Syrian Manuscript, 3:913

The Arabian Peninsula: Society and Politics, 3:451

Arabic and Persian Poems, 2:84

The Arabic Book, 1:10

Arabic Literature: An Introduction, 2:55, 3:456

Arabic Literature in North Africa, 2:117

Arabic Literature to the End of the Umayyad Period, 2:55

The Arabic Novel: An Historical and Critical Introduction, 2:55

Arabic Poetry: A Primer for Students, 2:56

Arabic Short Stories, 2:57

Arabic Short Stories, 1945–1965, 2:57

Arabic Spain, 3:387

Arabic Thought in the Liberal Age, 1798–1939, 3:436, 3:443, 3:457, 4:373

Arabic Writing Today, 2:57

The Arab in Israeli Literature, 2:9

The Arab-Israeli Dilemma, 3:436

The Arab-Israeli Wars, 3:436

The Arab Mind, 3:444

Arab Oil: Impact on Arab Countries and Global Implications, 3:437

The Arab Revival, 4:569

The Arabs and the Sudan, 3:418

The Arabs in History, 3:328, 3:331, 3:458

The Arab World (The United States and the Arab World), 3:437

The Arab World: Society, Culture, and State, 3:434

The Arab World's Legacy, 3:443

The Arab World Today, 3:435, 3:437

Aracoeli, 2:429

Arafat: A Political Biography, 3:455

The Aramaic Bible: Targums in their Historical Context, 4:609

The Aramaic Version of Lamentations, 4:608

Aramis, or the Love of Technology, 5:167

The Arbat Trilogy, Vol. 2: Fear, 2:754

Arbiter of Elegance: A Study of the Life and Works of C. Petronius, 2:391

Arcadia, 1:167, 1:185, 1:196

Arcadian Adventures with the Idle Rich, 2:918

Arcana Mundi: Magic and the Occult in the Greek and Roman Worlds, 4:451

The Archaeological and Documentary Evidence, 4:446

Archaeological History of the Ancient Middle East, 4:439

Archaeology: Theories, Methods and Practice, 4:432

Archaeology and Language, 3:13, 3:301, 4:436, 4:472

The Archaeology of Easter Island, 3:923, 3:924

The Archaeology of Greece: An Introduction, 3:304

The Archaeology of Human Origins, 3:13

The Archaeology of Knowledge, 2:476, 2:477, 4:400, 5:87

The Archaeology of Palestine, 4:808, 4:828

The Archaeology of the Frivolous, 4:397

Archaeology of the Land of the Bible: 10,000–586 B.C.E., 4:808

Archaeology of the New Testament, 4:808

The Archaic and Ancient Ages, 2:272

Archaic and Classical Greece: A Selection of Ancient Sources in Translation, 3:299

Archaic and Classical Greek Coins, 3:306

Archaic Egypt, 3:300

Archaic Figure, 1:962

Archaic Greece: The Age of Experiment, 3:302

Archaic Greece: The City-States c.700–500 B.C., 3:302

Archaic Roman Religion, 4:471

Archbishop Romero: Martyr of Salvador, 4:748

The Archbishop's Ceiling, 1:1104

The Archeology of Crete, 2:347

Archer in Jeopardy, 1:1234

Archery at the Dark of the Moon: Poetic Problems in Homer's Odyssey, 2:361

Arches and Light: The Fiction of John Gardner, 1:979

Archetypal Images in Greek Religion, 4:483

Archetypal Patterns in Poetry: Psychological Studies of the Imagination, 2:984

Archetypal Patterns in Women's Fiction, 2:985

Archetype and Allegory in The Dream of the Red Chamber, 2:223

The Archetypes and the Collective Unconscious, 4:424

The Archetypes of Carlos Fuentes: From Witch to Androgyne, 2:866

Archetypes of Wisdom: An Introduction to Philosophy, 4:24

Archibald MacLeish (Falk), 1:858

Archibald MacLeish (Smith), 1:858

Archibald MacLeish: A Checklist, 1:858

Archibald MacLeish: Reflections, 1:858

The Archidoxes of Magic, 4:149

Archimedes in the Middle Ages, 5:499

Architects of Yiddishism at the Beginning of the Twentieth Century, 2:31, 4:657

Architectural Principles in the Age of Humanism, 3:764

Architectural Review, 1:444

Architecture: 19th and 20th Centuries, 3:756

Architecture, from Prehistory to Post-Modernism, 3:762

Architecture as a Home for Man: Essays for Architectural Record, 5:170

Architecture in the Age of Reason, 3:763

The Architecture of H. H. Richardson and His Time, 3:790

The Architecture of Hesiodic Poetry, 2:358, 4:481

The Architecture of Matter, 5:32

Architecture of Molecules, 5:730

The Architecture of Sir Christopher Wren, 3:796

The Architecture of the Intelligible Universe in the Philosophy of Plotinus, 4:86

The Architecture of the Italian Renaissance, 3:400

The Architecture of the Roman Empire, 3:304

The Architecture of the United States, 3:764

The Architecture of Wren, 3:796

The Archives of the Wullu Family, 4:545

Arctic Adventure: My Life in the Frozen North, 3:921

Arctic Dreams: Imagination and Desire in a Northern Landscape, 3:906, 5:765, 5:818
Arctic Twilight: Old Finnish Tales, 2:658
Arden on File, 1:434
The Arden Shakespeare, 1:206
The Arden Shakespeare: The Poems, 1:207
The Ardis Anthology of Russian Futurism, 2:693
The Ardis Anthology of Russian Romanticism, 2:694
An Area of Darkness, 2:938, 2:939
Arena: The History of the Federal Theatre, 1:1073
Arendt, Camus and Modern Rebellion, 3:282, 5:82
Areopagitica, 1:57, 1:191
Are There Really Tannaitic Parallels to the Gospels?, 4:617
Are You All Right?, 2:313
Are You Hungry?, 5:348
Are Your Dental Fillings Poisoning You?, 5:340
Are You Sure It's Arthritis: A Guide to Soft-Tissue Rheumatism, 5:398
Argentina: A City and a Nation, 3:633, 3:649
Argentina: Illusions and Realities, 3:633
Argentina and the Jews: A History of Jewish Immigration, 4:644
Argentina and the United States: A Conflicted Relationship, 3:633
Argentina's "Dirty War": An Intellectual Biography, 3:633
The Argonautica, 2:343, 2:352
Argonauts of the Western Pacific, 3:26, 3:35, 4:485
Argonauts to Astronauts, 3:909
Arguing with Historians: Essays on the Historical and the Unhistorical, 3:573
The Argument and the Action of Plato's Laws, 3:163
The Argument of the "Tractatus," 4:346
Arguments and Doctrines, 4:648, 4:886
Arguments of Augustan Wit, 1:226

Ariadne's Thread: Story Lines, 1:1151
Ariel, 1:1031
Ariel: Poems, 1:1031
Ariosto and Boiardo: The Origins of "Orlando Furioso," 2:407
Ariosto's Bitter Harmony: Crisis and Evasion in the Italian Renaissance, 2:406
Aristarchus of Samos: The Greek Copernicus, 5:38
Aristocracy of Art in Joyce and Wolfe, 1:904
Aristocrats, 1:479
Aristocrats of Color: The Black Elite, 1880–1920, 3:555
Aristophanes: A Study, 2:354
Aristophanes: His Plays and His Influence, 2:353
Aristophanes: Poet and Dramatist, 2:353
Aristophanes and the Comic Hero, 2:354
Aristophanes' Old and New Comedy. Vol. 1: Six Essays in Perspective, 2:354
Aristophanic Comedy, 2:353
The Aristos, 1:477, 1:478
The Aristotelian Ethics, 4:69
Aristotelianism, 4:71
The Aristotelians of Renaissance Italy: A Philosophical Exposition, 4:30
Aristotelian Theory of Comedy, 4:67
The Aristotelian Tradition and Renaissance Universities, 4:130
Aristotle (Barnes), 3:311, 4:66
Aristotle (Ferguson), 4:68
Aristotle (Grote), 4:68
Aristotle (Mure), 4:70
Aristotle (Randall), 4:70
Aristotle (Ross), 4:71
Aristotle: A Contemporary Appreciation, 4:71
Aristotle: Fundamentals of the History of His Development, 4:69
Aristotle: Growth and Structure of His Thought, 3:311, 4:69
Aristotle: History of Animals, Bks. VII–IX, 5:758
Aristotle: Selections, 4:71
Aristotle: The Collected Papers of Joseph Owens, 4:70
Aristotle: The Desire to Understand, 4:69

Aristotle: The Nicomachean Ethics: A Commentary, 4:69
Aristotle: The Power of Perception, 4:70
Aristotle and His Philosophy, 4:67
Aristotle and His World View, 4:67, 4:221
Aristotle and Logical Theory, 4:69
Aristotle and Plato in the Mid-Fourth Century, 4:67, 4:80
Aristotle and the Arabs, 3:459
Aristotle and the Human Good, 4:69
Aristotle and the Later Tradition, 4:66
Aristotle and the Problem of Value, 4:70
Aristotle and the Renaissance, 4:71, 4:131
Aristotle Dictionary, 4:13
Aristotle for Everybody, 4:66, 4:270
Aristotle on Eudaimonia, 4:66
Aristotle on Interpretation: Commentary by St. Thomas and Cajetan, 4:137
Aristotle on Memory, 4:71
Aristotle on Substance: The Paradox of Unity, 4:68
Aristotle on the Art of Poetry, 4:67
Aristotle on the Many Senses of Priority, 4:67
Aristotle on the Perfect Life, 4:69
Aristotle's Categories and Porphyry, 4:61
Aristotle's Classification of Animals, 4:70
Aristotle's Conception of Moral Weakness, 4:71
Aristotle's Concept of Dialectic, 4:68
Aristotle's Contribution to the Practice and Theology of Historiography, 4:71
Aristotle's Criticism of Plato and the Academy, 4:79
Aristotle's Criticism of Presocratic Philosophy, 4:67
Aristotle's "De Motu Animalium," 4:70
Aristotle's Ethical Theory, 4:68
Aristotle's First Principles, 4:68

Aristotle's Man: Speculations upon Aristotelian Anthropology, 4:67

Aristotle's Ontology: Essays in Ancient Greek Philosophy, V, 4:66

Aristotle's Philosophy of Action, 4:67

Aristotle's Physics, 4:69

Aristotle's Physics and Its Medieval Varieties, 5:39

Aristotle's Poetics, 4:68

Aristotle's Poetics: A Translation and Commentary for Students, 4:68

Aristotle's Poetics: The Argument, 4:68

Aristotle's Political Theory, 4:70

Aristotle's Prior and Posterior Analytics, 4:71

Aristotle's Psychology, 4:70

Aristotle's School: A Study of a Greek Educational Institution, 4:70

Aristotle's Syllogistic: From the Standpoint of Modern Formal Logic, 4:69

Aristotle's System of the Physical World, 4:71

Aristotle's Theology: A Commentary on the Book of Metaphysics, 4:67

Aristotle's Theory of Contrariety, 4:66

Aristotle's Theory of Poetry and Fine Art, 4:67

Aristotle's Two Systems, 4:68

Aristotle's Vision of Nature, 4:72

Aristotle the Philosopher, 4:66

Aristotle to Zoo: A Philosophical Dictionary of Biology, 5:18, 5:761

Arizona Adventure: Action Packed True Tales of Early Arizona, 3:864

Arizona Legends and Lore, 3:862

Arizona's Meteorite Crater: Past—Present—Future, 5:624

Arjuna in the Mahabharata: Where Krishna Is, There Is Victory, 4:505

The Ark of the Desert, 3:451

The Armada, 3:359, 4:732

Armadale, 1:346

Armchair Astronomy, 5:610

The Armed Forces of the USSR, 3:280

Armenia (Nordbrandt), 2:653

Armenia (Oshagan), 2:76

Armenia in Ancient and Medieval Times, 2:76

Armenian Folk-Tales and Fables, 2:77

The Armenian Image in History and Literature, 2:76

Armenian Legends and Poems, 2:76

Armenian Poetry Old and New, 2:77

The Armenians: A People in Exile, 4:542

The Armenians: Their History and Culture, 2:76

Armenia Observed, 2:76

Armies of the Night, 1:916, 1:1012

The Armies of the Night: History as a Novel, the Novel as History, 1:1011

Arminius: A Study in the Dutch Reformation, 4:731

Armoured Train 14-69, 2:729, 2:730

Arms and Independence, 3:520

Arms and Insecurity, 3:149

Arms and the Man, 1:544, 1:545

Arms Control: Alliances, Arms Sales, and the Future, 5:112

Arms for Arabs: The Soviet Union and War in the Middle East, 3:435

The Arms Race in the Era of Star Wars, 5:109

Armstrong's Last Goodnight, 1:433

The Army Air Forces in World War II, 3:534

Army-Chaplain Schmelzle's Journey to Flätz, 2:606

The Army, James II and the Glorious Revolution, 3:360

The Army of the Potomac: A Trilogy, 3:571

Arna Bontemps—Langston Hughes: Letters, 1925–1967, 1:849

Arnauld and the Cartesian Philosophy of Ideas, 4:164

Arnold, 1:328

Arnold Bennett, 1:444

Arnold Bennett: A Biography, 1:444

Arnold Bennett: A Last Word, 1:444

Arnold Bennett: An Annotated Bibliography, 1887–1932, 1:444

Arnold Bennett: Romantic Realist, 1:444

Arnold Bennett Himself, 1:566

Arnold J. Toynbee: A Life, 3:288

Arnold Schoenberg, 3:714

Arnold Schoenberg: His Life, World and Work, 3:715

Arnold Schoenberg: The Composer as Jew, 3:714

Arnold Toynbee on Judaism and Zionism: A Critique, 3:294

Aromatherapy, 5:320

Around 1981: Academic Feminist Literary Theory, 1:1144

Around Proust, 2:495

Around Theaters. 1898–1903, 1:440

Around the Cragged Hill: A Personal and Political Philosophy, 3:584

Around the Edge, 3:895

Around the World in Eighty Days, 3:820

Around the World in Eighty Ways, 3:892

Arrah-na-Pogue, or, The Wicklow Wedding, 1:331

The Arraignment of Paris, 1:195

Arrhenius Equation and Non-Equilibrium Kinetics, 5:738

Arrian of Nicomedia, 3:312

Arrighi's Running Hand, 1:19

The Arrivants: A New World Trilogy, 2:933

The Arrogance of Faith, 3:519

The Arrogance of Humanism, 5:822

The Arrogance of Race, 3:555

Arrogant Aussie: The Rupert Murdoch Story, 3:807

Arrogant Diplomacy: U.S. Policy toward Colombia, 1903–1922, 3:635

An Arrow in the Wall, 2:773

Arrow of God, 2:104, 2:127, 2:128

Arrowsmith, 1:853, 1:854

Ars Amatoris, 2:389

Ars Conjectandi, 5:527

Ars Poetica, 2:385

Art: A History of Painting, Sculpture, Architecture, 3:757

Art: An Introduction, 3:756

Art: Beauty in the Middle Ages, 4:95

Art and Architecture in Italy, 1600–1800, 3:756

The Art and Architecture of the Islamic World, 3:437

Art and Ceremony in Late Antiquity, 4:449

Art and Civilization, 3:757

Art and Glory: The Story of Elbert Hubbard, 1:42

The Art and History of Book Printing: A Topical Bibliography, 1:62

The Art and History of Books, 1:9, 1:37

Art and Ideology in the African Novel, 2:111

Art and Illusion: A Study in the Psychology of Pictorial Representation, 5:192

The Art and Imagination of Langston Hughes, 1:849

Art and Imagination of W.E.B. Du Bois, 1:832, 3:579

Art and Life in India: The Last Four Decades, 3:486

The Art and Mind of Shaw, 1:546

Art and Morality, 4:364

Art and Outrage: A Correspondence about Henry Miller, 1:470

Art and Philosophy: A Symposium, 4:264

Art and Photography, 5:194

Art and Physics: Experiments in Space, Time and Light, 5:194

The Art and Politics of Edward Bond, 1:446

Art and Prudence, 4:270

Art and Prudence: Studies in the Thought of Jacques Maritain, 4:307

Art and Reality: Ways of the Creative Process, 1:457

Art and Scholasticism: With Other Essays, 4:306

The Art and Science of Negotiation, 3:204

Art and Science of Book Preservation, 1:25

The Art and Science of Book Publishing, 1:46

The Art and Science of Love, 5:438

The Art and Science of Radio, 3:811

The Art and Science of Visual Illusions, 5:195

Art and Substance in George Meredith: A Study in Narrative, 1:379

Art and Technics, 5:169, 5:170

The Art and Technique of Simulation, 5:522

Art and the Artist: The Creative Urge and Personality Development, 5:465

Art and the Computer, 5:565

Art and the Reformation in Germany, 4:737

The Art and Thought of Heraclitus, 4:74

Art and Tradition in Sir Gawain and the Green Knight, 1:156

The Art and Vision of Flannery O'Connor, 1:1024

Art and Visual Perception: A Psychology of the Creative Eye, 3:177, 3:756

Art and Visual Perception, 5:191

Artapanos Comes Home, 2:50

Art Chronicles, 1954–1966, 1:1025

Arte Chicano, 3:759

Arte of English Poesie, 1:163

Art for Social Justice: The Major Novels of Upton Sinclair, 1:880

Art History in Africa, 3:431

Arthritis: Reducing Your Risk, 5:398

Arthritis Alternatives, 5:398

The Arthritis Book of Water Exercise, 5:398

Arthur and the Grail, 2:628

Arthur C. Clarke, 1:615

Arthur C. Clarke: The Authorized Biography, 5:601

Arthur C. Clarke's Mysterious World, 1:613

Arthur Conan Doyle, 1:608

Arthur Hugh Clough: Growth of a Poet's Mind, 1:345

Arthurian Poets: Edwin Arlington Robinson, 1:877

Arthur Meighen: A Biography, 3:615

Arthur Mervyn, 1:635, 1:636

Arthur Miller, 1:1104

Arthur Miller: A Collection of Critical Essays, 1:1104

Arthur O. Lovejoy: An Annotated Bibliography, 4:303

Arthur O. Lovejoy and the Quest for Intelligibility, 4:303

Arthur Rex, 1:949

Arthur Rimbaud, 2:500

Arthur Schnitzler, 2:611

Arthur Schopenhauer: Philosopher of Pessimism, 4:256

Arthur's Island, 2:428

Arthur Wing Pinero, 1:388

Arthur Wing Pinero and Henry Arthur Jones, 1:367, 1:388

Articles in American Literature, 1968–1975, 1:121

Articles on Aristotle, 4:66

Articles on Twentieth Century Literature, 1:120

Articles on Women Writers, 1976–1984: A Bibliography, 1:120

Articulation Disorders, 5:380

Art, Ideology, and the City of Teotihuacan, 4:457

Artifices of Eternity: Horace's Fourth Book of Odes, 2:386

Artificial Experts: Social Knowledge and Intelligent Machines, 5:74

Artificial Intelligence (Haugeland), 4:382

Artificial Intelligence (Winston), 5:569

Artificial Intelligence: An MIT Perspective, 5:570

Artificial Intelligence: The Very Idea, 5:75

Artificial Intelligence and Natural Man, 3:174, 5:570

Artificial Intelligence and Psychiatry, 5:571

The Artificial Intelligence Debate: False Starts, Real Foundations, 5:75

The Artificial Intelligence Dictionary, 5:570

Artificial Intelligence from A to Z: A Glossary of Artificial Intelligence, 5:74

Art in Achebe's Things Fall Apart, 2:128

Art in Context, 3:757

The Art Index, 3:756

Art in Our Times: A Pictorial History 1890–1980, 3:760

Art Inscribed: Essays on Ekphrasis in Spanish Golden Age Poetry, 2:525

The Artisans of Banaras: Popular Culture and Identity, 1880–1986, 4:508

Art Isn't Easy: The Achievement of Stephen Sondheim, 3:720

Art Isn't Easy: The Theater of Stephen Sondheim, 3:720

Artist and Audience: African Literature as a Shared Experience, 2:112

Artist and Society in Shakespeare's England, 1:169

The Artist as Critic: Critical Writings of Oscar Wilde, 1:974

Artist Beware, 5:736

The Artistic Evolution of Mikhail Zoshchenko: No Laughing Matter, 2:776

An Artist in the Rigging: The Early Work of Herman Melville, 1:688

The Artistry of Shakespeare's Prose, 1:217

Artists and Illustrators of the Old West: 1850–1900, 1:30

Artists and Revolution: Dada and the Bauhaus, 1917–1925, 3:344

Artists and Writers in the Evolution of Latin America, 2:848

Artist's Reminiscences, 1:583

The Art Museums of Louis I. Kahn, 3:777

Art Nouveau and Art Deco Bookbinding: French Masterpieces 1880–1940, 1:23

The Art Nouveau Book in Britain, 1:11

The Art of Aeschylus, 2:351

The Art of Animation, 1:1164

The Art of Art for Children's Books, 1:29

The Art of Autobiography in Nineteenth and Twentieth Century England, 1:87

The Art of Biblical Narrative, 2:989, 4:822

The Art of Biblical Poetry, 4:822

The Art of Biography, 1:87, 1:928

Art of Birds, 2:874

The Art of Bookbinding: A Practical Treatise, 1:27

The Art of Captain Cook's Voyages, 3:918

The Art of Cézanne, 3:772

The Art of Chinese Poetry, 2:190

The Art of Computer Management, 5:557

The Art of Computer Programming, 5:550

The Art of Contemporary English Culture, 1:421

The Art of Counseling, 5:462

The Art of D. H. Lawrence, 1:511

The Art of Demosthenes, 2:355

The Art of Desktop Publishing, 5:561

The Art of Discrimination, 1:261

The Art of Djuna Barnes: Duality and Damnation, 1:813

The Art of Easter Island, 3:924

The Art of Erotic Seduction, 5:439

The Art of Etching, 1:29

The Art of Excess: Mastery in Contemporary American Fiction, 1:918

The Art of Feeding Children Well, 5:348

The Art of Fiction, 1:515

The Art of Fine Lettering: Basic Skills and Techniques, 1:17

The Art of Frank Norris, Storyteller, 1:777

The Art of Greenaway: A Nostalgic Portrait of Childhood, 1:586

The Art of Grit: Ken Kesey's Fiction, 1:1000

The Art of Happiness: Teachings of Buddhist Psychology, 4:512

Art of Happiness or the Teachings of Epicurus, 4:74

The Art of I. Compton-Burnett: A Collection of Critical Essays, 1:462

The Art of Illuminating as Practised in Europe from the Earliest Times, 1:30

The Art of Jean Racine, 2:498

The Art of John Fowles, 1:478

The Art of John Gardner: Introduction and Exploration, 1:979

The Art of Knowing: The Poetry and Prose of Conrad Aiken, 1:810

The Art of Lettering, 1:17

The Art of Letters, 2:213

The Art of Life, 1:541

The Art of Listening: Developing Musical Perception, 3:664

The Art of Literary Publishing: Editors on Their Craft, 1:50

The Art of Literary Translation, 2:991

The Art of Living: Erich Fromm's Life and Works, 5:451

The Art of Living and Other Stories, 1:979

The Art of Love, 2:389

The Art of Loving, 5:450

The Art of Making Dances, 3:744

The Art of Mark Twain, 1:783

The Art of Maurice Sendak, 1:1206

The Art of Memory, 4:136

The Art of Mesoamerica, 4:454

Art of Nijinsky, 3:749

The Art of Oliver Goldsmith, 1:247

The Art of Paul Gauguin, 3:775

The Art of Persuasion in Greece, 2:346

The Art of Philosophizing and Other Essays, 4:322

The Art of Quartet Playing, 3:659

The Art of Recognition in Wolfram's "Parzifal," 2:617

The Art of Rhetoric in the Roman World, 300 B.C.-A.D. 300, 2:381

The Art of Science, 5:9

The Art of Seamus Heaney, 1:495

The Art of Southeast Asia, 3:760

The Art of Telling: Essays on Fiction, 1:421

Art of the Byzantine Era, 3:760

The Art of the Conservator, 5:193

Art of the Dance, 3:741

The Art of the Dramatist, 1:537

The Art of the Engineer, 5:191, 5:212

The Art of the French Illustrated Book, 1700–1914, 1:29

The Art of the Lyrical Ballads, 1:308

Art of the Medieval World, 3:760

The Art of the Novel, 1:762, 2:793

The Art of the Novel: Critical Prefaces, 1:764

The Art of the Odyssey, 2:361

The Art of the Printed Book, 1455–1955, 1:7

The Art of the Real: Muriel Spark's Novels, 1:552

The Art of the Renaissance, 3:333

The Art of the Tale: An International Anthology of Short Stories, 2:4

The Art of the Turkish Tale, 2:96

The Art of Thinking, 4:164

The Art of Thornton Wilder, 1:1116

The Art of Translation, 2:991

The Art of Travel, 1:764

The Art of Victorian Prose, 1:325

The Art of Walker Percy: Stratagems for Being, 1:1029

The Art of War, 3:160, 4:144, 4:145

The Art of Warfare in Biblical Lands, 3:309

The Art of William Morris, 1:383

The Art of Written Forms: The Theory and Practice of Calligraphy, 1:13

Art on Screen: A Directory of Films and Videos about the Visual Arts, 3:756

Art Poétique, 2:514

Arts, Sciences, Alloys, 3:730

Arts and Humanities Citation Index, 1:112

Arts in America: A Bibliography, 3:759

The Arts of Central Africa: An Annotated Bibliography, 3:419

The Arts of China, 3:467

Arts of India: 1550–1990, 3:484

Arts of India: Architecture, Sculpture, Painting, Music, Dance and Handicraft, 3:483

The Arts of Orpheus, 4:447

The Arts of the Beautiful, 4:285

Art That Works: The Decorative Arts of the Eighties Crafted in America, 3:765

As a Driven Leaf, 4:621

Asahel, 2:21

As a Man Grows Older, 2:439

Asante in the Nineteenth Century, 3:421

The Asbestos Strike, 3:609

ASCAP Biographical Dictionary, 3:654

The Ascendancy of Europe, 1815–1914, 3:340

The Ascent of F6, 1:435

The Ascent of Man, 5:24, 5:162

Ascent of Mount Carmel, 2:543

The Ascent of Mount Fuji, 2:695

The Ascent of Mount Ventoux, 4:150

Ascent to Omai, 2:935

Ascent to Orbit: A Scientific Autobiography, 5:601

Ascent to Truth: A Critical Examination of Quine's Philosophy, 4:412, 5:100

Ascetical Works, 4:704

Ascetic Behavior in Greco Roman Antiquity, 4:690

Ascetic Figures before and in Early Buddhism, 4:510, 4:514

ASEAN: A Bibliography, 2:311, 3:488

Aserah: Extrabiblical Evidence, 4:545

As Fine as Melanctha (Nineteen Fourteen to Nineteen Thirty), 1:882

As for Me and My House, 2:925

Ashenden, or The British Agent, 1:520

Asherah and the Cult of Yahweh in Israel, 4:545

Ashes in the Wind, 1:1225

Ash Wednesday, 1:471

The Ash Wednesday Supper, 4:135

Asia: A Handbook, 3:463

Asia and the Pacific: A Directory of Resources, 3:462

Asia in the Making of Europe, 3:335

Asia in Western Fiction, 2:312

Asian American Experiences in the United States, 3:556

Asian American Literature: An Annotated Bibliography, 1:121

Asian Drama, 3:98

Asian Drama: An Inquiry into the Poverty of Nations, 3:98, 3:235

The Asian Journal of Thomas Merton, 4:781

Asian Literature in English: A Guide to Information Sources, 2:311

Asian-Philippines Leader, 2:329

The Asian Plays: Fanshen, Saigon, and A Map of the World, 1:493

Asian Power and Politics: The Cultural Dimensions of Authority, 3:463

The Asians: Their Heritage and Their Destiny, 3:463

Asia—The Winning of Independence, 3:488

As If by Magic, 1:567

As I Lay Dying, 1:834, 1:835

Asimov's Annotated Don Juan, 1:282

Asimov's Biographical Encyclopedia of Science and Technology, 5:27, 5:724

Asimov's Chronology of Science and Discovery, 5:6

Asimov's New Guide to Science, 5:60, 5:726, 5:758

As It Happened: A Memoir, 3:820

As I Was Saying, 1:457

Asleep in the Sun, 2:855

As Long as Nothing Happens, Nothing Will: Stories, 2:239

As Old as the Moon: Cuban Legends and Folklore of the Antillas, 3:857

As Others See Us: The Armenian Image in Literature, 2:76

Aspects of Alice, 1:583

Aspects of Apuleius' Golden Ass, 4:469

Aspects of Athenian Democracy, 2:344

Aspects of Caste in South India, Ceylon and North West Pakistan, 3:19

Aspects of Death in Early Greek Art and Poetry, 3:302

Aspects of Góngora's Soledades, 2:540

Aspects of Modern Drama, 1:548

Aspects of Modern Poetry, 1:548, 1:800

Aspects of Modern Swedish Literature, 2:671

Aspects of Nature in Different Lands and Different Climates, 3:131

Aspects of Prehistory, 3:13

Aspects of Quantum Mechanics, 5:713

Aspects of Quantum Theory, 5:720

Aspects of Religion in the Soviet Union, 1917–1967, 4:572
Aspects of Scientific Explanation, 5:91
Aspects of South African Literature, 2:158
Aspects of the Novel, 1:419, 1:421, 1:476
Aspects of the Theory of Syntax, 3:21
Aspects of the Theory of Tariffs, 3:58
Aspects of Time, 5:68
The Aspern Papers and The Turn of the Screw, 1:762
An Aspirin a Day, 5:350
Aspirin Handbook: A User's Guide to the Breakthrough Drug of the 90s, 5:350
As Real as It Gets, 5:388
Assad: The Struggle for the Middle East, 3:455
Assassination of Light: Modern Saudi Short Stories, 2:56
The Assassins: A Book of Hours, 1:1022
The Assassins: A Radical Sect in Islam, 3:458, 4:571
The Assault, 2:621, 2:628
Assault on the Media: The Nixon Years, 3:808
The Assault on Truth: Freud's Suppression of the Seduction Theory, 3:184
Assembling California, 1:1010, 5:645
Assembly Language Primer for the IBM PC and XT, 5:554
The Assembly of Listeners: Jains in Society, 4:509
Assessing Health and Human Service Needs, 5:327
Assessing the Nuclear Age, 5:109
Asset Accumulation and Economic Activity, 3:62
The Assistant, 1:1012, 1:1013
The Associated Press Stylebook and Libel Manual, 1:118, 3:805
Assyrian Rulers of the Early First Millennium B.C. (1114–859), 4:545
Assyrian Rulers of the Third and Second Millennia B.C. (to 1115), 4:545
Astaire: The Man, the Dancer, 3:737
Astaire Dancing, 3:737
As the Story Was Told, 1:440

The Asthma Handbook, 5:386
The Asthma Self-Care Book: How to Take Control of Your Asthma, 5:397
Astoria, 1:679
Astoria, or Anecdotes of an Enterprize beyond the Rocky Mountains, 1:680
Astounding Days: A Science Fictional Autobiography, 1:615
The Astray, 2:81
Astrid Lindgren: Storyteller to the World, 2:677
Astroblemes-Cryptoexplosion Structures, 5:623
Astrology: True or False?, 5:587
Astrology and Religion among the Greeks and Romans, 4:451
Astrology in the Renaissance: The Zodiac of Life, 4:126
Astronomer by Chance, 5:590
The Astronomer's Sourcebook, 5:591
Astronomer's Universe: Stars, Galaxies and Cosmos, 5:593
Astronomiae Instauratae Mechanica, 5:600
The Astronomical Revolution: Copernicus-Kepler-Borelli, 5:42
Astronomical Thought in Renaissance England, 5:40
Astronomy: A Self-Teaching Guide, 5:588
Astronomy: From the Earth to the Universe, 5:588
Astronomy: The Cosmic Journey, 5:588
Astronomy: The Evolving Universe, 5:589
Astronomy and Optics from Pliny to Descartes, 5:666
Astronomy from Space: Sputnik to Space Telescope, 5:596
Astronomy Transformed: The Emergence of Radio Astronomy in Britain, 5:589
Astronomy with Binoculars, 5:591
Astrophil and Stella, 1:195
Astrophobia, 2:758
Astrophotography for the Amateur, 5:591
Astrophysical Data: Planets and Stars, 5:588
Astrophysical Formulae, 5:588

Astrophysical Quantities, 5:587
Astrophysics and Twentieth-Century Astronomy to 1950, 5:48, 5:590, 5:656
Astrophysics Today, 5:654
As We Know, 1:936
As We Saw Them: The First Japanese Embassy to America, 3:478
Asya, 2:769
Asylums, 3:205
Asylums: Essays on the Social Situation of Mental Patients and Other Inmates, 3:210, 3:228
The Asymmetric Society, 3:223
Asymmetric Typography, 1:11
As You Like It, 1:185, 1:205, 1:206, 1:210, 1:553
Atala and René, 2:466
Atalanta in Calydon, 1:397, 1:398
At Barstow, 1:560
At Dawn We Slept: The Untold Story of Pearl Harbor, 3:535
At Fault, 1:739, 1:740
At Heaven's Gate, 1:892
Atheism: Collected Essays, 1943–1949, 4:322
Atheism in the English Renaissance, 4:124
The Atheist's Tragedy, 1:199
The Athelings, 1:385
Athenaeum, 1:428, 4:252
Athenian Culture and Society, 3:302
The Athenian Empire, 3:302
Athens and Jerusalem, 4:335
Athens from Cleisthenes to Pericles, 3:301
Athens in the Age of Pericles, 2:347
At Her Best, 1:868
Athletes and Oracles, 3:305
At Home: Essays 1982–1988, 1:1062
At Home and Beyond: New Essays on Spanish Poets of the Twenties, 2:526
At Home in America: Second Generation New York Jews, 4:640
At Lady Molly's, 1:536
Atlanta Offering: Poems, 1:753
Atlantic City, 1:1090
The Atlantic Civilization: Eighteenth Century Origins, 3:338
Atlantic Double-Cross, 1:652

Atlantic High, 3:907

Atlantic Monthly, 1:732

The Atlantic Provinces: The Emergence of Colonial Society, 1712–1857, 3:613

The Atlantic Slave Trade: A Census, 3:420, 3:426

The Atlantic Slave Trade and British Abolition, 1760–1810, 3:361, 3:419

An Atlas of African History, 3:416

Atlas of American History, 3:505

Atlas of Ancient Archaeology, 4:432

Atlas of British History, 3:354

Atlas of China, 3:465

Atlas of Classical History, 3:298

Atlas of Early American History: The Revolutionary Era, 1760–1790, 3:505

Atlas of Histology, 5:773

An Atlas of Irish History, 3:369

Atlas of Maritime History, 5:239

Atlas of Modern Jewish History, 3:348

Atlas of Palaeobiogeography, 5:617

Atlas of Social Issues, 3:6

Atlas of South Asia, 3:482

Atlas of the Christian Church, 4:676

Atlas of the Islamic World since 1500, 4:567

Atlas of the Jewish World, 4:634

Atlas of the United States Environmental Issues, 5:816

Atlas of the World Economy, 3:44

Atlas of Twentieth-Century World History, 3:272

Atlas of World Cultures, 3:38

Atlas of World History, 3:272

At Last: A Christmas in the West Indies, 1:369

Atlas to the Life of Thomas Telford, 5:256

The Atmosphere: An Introduction to Meteorology, 3:126

Atmosphere, Weather, and Climate, 5:633

At Odds, 3:554, 3:575

Atom and Void: Essays on Science and Community, 5:707

The Atom Besieged, 5:111, 5:173

The Atom Bomb and the Future of Man, 4:299, 5:111

The Atomic Age: Forty-Five Scientists and Scholars Speak, 5:111

The Atomic Bomb: The Great Decision, 3:277

The Atomic Complex, 5:658

The Atomic Papers: A Citizen's Guide to Selected Books and Articles, 5:287

Atomic Physics, 5:658, 5:675

Atomic Physics of Lasers, 5:697

Atomic Quest: A Personal Narrative, 5:678

Atomic Structure and the Strength of Metals, 5:704

Atomic Theory and the Description of Nature, 5:673

Atoms and Power, 5:45, 5:56, 5:729

Atoms in the Family: My Life with Enrico Fermi, 5:685

Atoms of Silence: An Exploration of Cosmic Evolution, 5:595, 5:656

Atoms, Pneuma, and Tranquility, 4:56

Atoms, Stars, and Minds, 5:661

The Atom Station, 2:642

A to Z of Snake Keeping, 5:771

A to Zoo: Subject Access to Children's Picture Books, 1:74, 1:1196

At Paradise Gate, 1:1050

At Play in the Fields of the Lord, 3:930

Atra-Hasis: The Babylonian Story of the Flood, 2:53

At Random: The Reminiscences of Bennett Cerf, 1:40

At Swim-Two-Birds, 1:525

Attack and Die: Civil War Military Tactics and the Southern Heritage, 3:529

The Attack on Literature and Other Essays, 1:927

The Attack on the Mill and Other Stories, 2:518

Attack upon "Christendom," 4:239

Attempt at a Critique of All Revelation, 4:197

The Attempt of Infinite Man, 2:873

At the Back of the North Wind, 1:587

At the Bidding of the Heart: Essays, Sketches, Speeches, Papers, 2:756

At the Bottom of the River, 2:936

At the Crossroads: Essays on Ahad Ha'am, 2:13

At the Crossroads of Faith and Reason: An Essay on Pierre Bayle, 4:166

At the Crossroads of the Earth and the Sky: An Andean Cosmology, 4:458

At the End of the Open Road, 1:1048

At the Handles of the Lock, 2:12

At the Hand of Man: Peril and Hope for Africa's Wildlife, 3:205

At the Land, 1:1163

At the Origins of Modern Atheism, 4:884

At the Royal Court: Twenty-Five Years of the English Stage Company, 1:426

At the Sign of the Lion, and Other Essays, 1:442

At the Stone of Losses, 2:17

At the Threshold of Exact Science, 4:97

The Attic Orators, 2:348

Attitudes Toward History, 1:817

Attitudes toward Mental Patients, 5:420

The Attraction of the Contrary, 2:448

At War in the Gulf, 3:450

Aucassin and Nicolette, 2:452

Aucassin and Nicolette with other Romances, 2:452

Auctor and Actor: A Narratological Reading of Apuleius' Golden Ass, 4:469

Auden: A Carnival of Intellect, 1:435

Auden: A Collection of Critical Essays, 1:436

The Auden Generation: Literature and Politics in England in the 1930's, 1:436

Auden's Poetry, 1:436

The Audience for Children's Books, 1:49

The Audience in the Poem: Five Victorian Poets, 1:315

Audubon: A Vision, 1:892, 5:787

Audubon and His Journals, 3:907

Audubon Birds, 5:787

Audubon's Birds of America, 5:787

Audubon Society Encyclopedia of North American Birds, 5:762

Audubon Society Field Guide to North American Butterflies, 5:761

Audubon Society Field Guide to North American Fishes, Whales and Dolphins, 5:758

Audubon Society Field Guide to North American Fossils, 5:640, 5:762

Audubon Society Field Guide to North American Mushrooms, 5:761

Audubon Society Field Guide to North American Reptiles and Amphibians, 5:760

Audubon Society Field Guide to North American Rocks and Minerals, 5:627

Audubon Society Field Guide to North American Seashells, 5:762

Audubon Society Field Guide to North American Seashore Creatures, 5:761

Audubon Society Field Guide to the Natural Places of the Northeast, 5:760

Audubon Society Guide to Attracting Birds, 5:760

Audubon Society Guide to North American Birds: Eastern Region, 5:758

Audubon Society Guide to North American Birds: Western Region, 5:762

Audubon Society Handbook for Butterfly Watchers, 5:761

Audubon Society Master Guide to Birding, 5:759

Audubon the Naturalist, 5:787

Augie March, 1:946

Augsburg Commentary on the New Testament, 4:820

Augsburg Commentary on the Old Testament, 4:820

Auguste Comte: An Intellectual Biography, 3:224, 4:223

Auguste Comte: The Foundation of Sociology, 3:224

Auguste Comte and Positivism, 4:223

Auguste Comte and the United States 1816–1853, 3:224

Augustine (Chadwick), 4:110

Augustine (Kirwan), 4:110

Augustine: A Collection of Critical Essays, 4:110

Augustine and His Influence through the Ages, 4:110

Augustine of Hippo: A Biography, 3:306, 4;109

Augustine on Evil, 4:110

Augustine to Galileo, 4:97

August Nights, 2:913, 2:914

August 1914, 2:760, 3:395

Augusto Roa Bastos, 2:882

The August Sleepwalker, 2:261

August Strindberg, 2:680

Augustus Baldwin Longstreet, 1:684

Augustus to Constantine, 4:681

Auld Licht Idylls and Better Dead, 1:329

Aung San of Burma: A Biographical Portrait by His Daughter, 2:314

Aunt Carry's Ballads for Children, 1:384

Aunt Jo's Scrapbag, 1:1198

Aunt Julia and the Scriptwriter, 2:887

The Aunt's Story, 2:965, 2:966

Aura, 2:865

Au Revoir les Enfants, 3:841

Aurobindo's Philosophy of Brahman, 4:353

Aurora Floyd, 1:332

Aurora Leigh, 1:336, 1:337

The Aurora of the Philosophers, 4:149

The Auroras of Autumn, 1:886

Aus dem Tagebuch einer Schnecke, 2:582

Austerities, 1:1048

Austin Clarke: 1886–1974: A Critical Introduction, 1:460

Austin Clarke: A Study of his Writings, 1:460

Austin Clarke: His Life and Works, 1:460

Australia Feli, 2:961

Australia in Peace and War: External Relations, 1788–1977, 3:494

Australia in the International Economy in the Twentieth Century, 3:494

Australian Literary Criticism—1945–1988, 2:946

Australian Literature: An Historical Introduction, 2:946

Australian Religions: An Introduction, 4:461

The Australian Short Story: An Anthology from the 1890s to the 1980s, 2:947

The Austrian Mind: An Intellectual and Social History, 1848–1938, 3:375

Authenticity in Art: The Scientific Detection of Forgery, 5:192

The Authentic Mark Twain: A Literary Biography of Samuel L. Clemens, 1:783

Author and Agent: Eudora Welty and Diarmuid Russell, 1:896

Author and Critic, 1:482

Author and Editor at Work: Making a Better Book, 1:48

Author as Character in the Works of Sholom Aleichem, 2:46

Author Biographies Master Index, 1:126

The Authoress of the Odyssey, 1:342, 2:361

The Authoritarian Personality, 3:147, 3:177, 4:393

Authority, Liberty, and Automatic Machinery in Early Modern Europe, 5:43

Authority and the Individual, 4:322

Authority in the Modern State, 3:156

Author of the Prometheus Bound, 2:351

Author Price Guides, 1:78

Authors, Publishers, and Politicians, 1:54

Authors and Audiences in Traditional Malay Literature, 2:324

Authors by Profession, 1:36

Authorship and Copyright, 1:55

An Author's Primer to Word Processing, 1:46

Autobiographical Acts: The Changing Situation of a Literary Genre, 1:927

Autobiographical Memoir, 1:341

Autobiographical Notes: A Centennial Edition, 5:682

Autobiographical Notes and Notes on His Artistic and Poetic Circle of Friends, 1830–1882, 1:392

Autobiographical Reminiscences, with Family Letters and Notes on Music, 3:697
Autobiographical Sketches, 4:549
Autobiographical Statements in Twentieth-Century Russian Literature, 2:687
The Autobiographical Subject, 1:231
Autobiography (Cellini), 3:333
An Autobiography (Collingwood), 4:281
Autobiography (Eliade), 4:473
Autobiography (Franklin), 1:637
Autobiography (Martineau), 1:375
Autobiography (Mill), 1:380
An Autobiography (Muir), 1:521
Autobiography (Nkrumah), 4:370
Autobiography (Oliphant), 1:385
An Autobiography (Spencer), 3:240
Autobiography (Stanley), 3:938
An Autobiography (Trollope), 1:406
An Autobiography (Wright), 3:797
Autobiography (Zukofsky), 1:1068
Autobiography: A Soliloquy on Viewing My Life from the Last Decade of Its First Century, 3:577
An Autobiography: Centenary Edition, 3:499
Autobiography: Essays Theoretical and Critical, 1:928
Autobiography: Its Genesis and Phases, 1:927
Autobiography: The Story of My Experiments with Truth, 4:352
The Autobiography of Albert Einstein, 5:683
The Autobiography of Alice B. Toklas, 1:881, 1:882
The Autobiography of an American Novelist, 1:904
The Autobiography of an Ex-Colored Man, 1:771
The Autobiography of an Idea, 3:792
Autobiography of a Shaker and Revelation of the Apocalypse, 4:849

Autobiography of a Yogi, 4:556, 4:873
The Autobiography of John Stuart Mill, 4:243, 4:244
An Autobiography of Mahatma Gandhi, 4:552
Autobiography of Malcolm X, 4:876
The Autobiography of Malcolm X, as Told to Alex Haley, 3:556, 4:862
The Autobiography of St. Ignatius Loyola, with Related Documents, 4:770
The Autobiography of W.E.B. Du Bois, 1:831
The Autobiography of Will Rogers, 3:886
Autobiography Vol. 1: Journey East, Journey West, 1907 to 1937, 2:825
The Autocrat of the Breakfast-Table, 1:677, 1:678
Auto-da-Fé, 2:574, 2:575
Autographs and Manuscripts: A Collector's Manual, 1:76
Automagic: The Secret Life of Machines, 5:247
Automating Your Financial Portfolio, 5:559
Automotive and Small Truck Fuel Injection Systems: Gas and Diesel, 5:247
Autonomous Technology, 3:214, 5:73, 5:145, 5:146
Autonomy and Judaism, 4:646
Autopsy of Revolution, 5:163, 5:164
Autopsy on Surrealism, 2:886
Auto Repair for Dummies, 5:12
Auto Slavery, 3:547
Autumn, 2:259
Autumn across America, 5:818
The Autumn Garden, 1:1092
An Autumn Life: How a Surgeon Faced His Fatal Illness, 5:313
The Autumn of the Patriarch, 2:866, 2:867
Autumn Quail, 2:68
Availability: Gabriel Marcel and the Phenomenology of Human Openness, 4:305
Avant Garde: The Experimental Theater in France, 2:449
Avatamsaka Sutra, 4:529
Avatar and Incarnation, 4:885
Avataras, 4:549

The Avenue Bearing the Initial of Christ into the New World, 1:1001
Averroës and His Philosophy, 4:97
Averroës and the Metaphysics of Causation, 4:581
Averroës' Doctrine of Immortality: A Matter of Controversy, 4:581
Averting Catastrophe, 5:75, 5:156, 5:244
Averting the Apocalypse: Social Movements in India Today, 4:507
Avesta: The Hymns of Zarathustra, 4:443
Avicenna: His Life and Works, 4:581
Avicenna: Scientist and Philosopher, 4:582
Avicenna and the Visionary Recital, 4:582
The Avignon Quintet, 1:469
The Avila of Saint Teresa, 4:736, 4:786
Avril, 1:442
Awake and Sing, 1:1105
The Awakening, 1:739, 1:740, 1:802
The Awakening and Selected Stories, 1:740
The Awakening of Europe, 4:100
The Awakening of Intelligence, 4:554
The Awakening of Motek, 2:44
Awakenings, 2:321
Awakening to the Tao, 4:528
Awards, Honors and Prizes, 1:104, 1:135
Awash in a Sea of Faith, 3:558
Awash with Roses: The Collected Love Poems of Kenneth Patchen, 1:1028
Away, 2:941
The Awful Rowing toward God, 1:1045
Awit and Corrido: Philippine Metrical Romances, 2:329
A. W. Kinglake: A Biographical and Literary Study, 3:925
The Awkward Age, 1:762
The Axe, 2:795
Axe Handles, 1:1052
Axel's Castle, 1:901, 1:902
Axel's Castle: A Study in the Imaginative Literature of 1870–1930, 1:418, 2:448, 2:997

The Axion Esti, 2:373
Ayela's Angel, 1:406
Ayer, 4:273
Ayer Directory of Publica-
   tions, 1:72
Ayesha: The Return of She,
   1:595
Ayi Kwei Armah's Africa:
   The Sources of His Fic-
   tion, 2:131
al-Ayyam, 2:71, 2:74
Azi, 2:826
Azmari, 2:121
The Aztec and Maya Paper-
   makers, 1:6
The Aztec Empire: The Tol-
   tec Resurgence, 3:627
Aztec Image of Self and So-
   ciety: An Introduction to
   Nahua Culture, 4:457
The Aztecs: A History, 4:457
Aztecs: An Interpretation,
   3:627, 4:457
Aztecs, Maya, and Their Pre-
   decessors: Archaeology of
   Mesoamerica, 3:13
Azuela and the Mexican Un-
   derdogs, 2:854
Azul, 2:863

B

B-6: The Natural Healer,
   5:345
Baal, A Man's a Man, and
   The Elephant Calf, 2:572
Babbage's Calculating En-
   gines, 5:575
The Bab Ballads, 1:357
Babbitt, 1:854
Babel to Byzantium: Poets
   and Poetry Now, 1:912,
   1:967
Babes in the Wood, 1:580
Babies and Their Mothers,
   5:472
Baby: A Novel, 2:655
The Baby Checkup Book: A
   Parents' Guide to Well
   Baby Care, 5:322
Baby Doctor, 5:336
Baby, It's Cold Inside, 1:868
The Babylonian Akitu Festi-
   val, 4:441
Babylonian and Assyrian Re-
   ligion, 4:441, 4:545
The Babylonian Genesis: The
   Story of Creation, 2:53,
   4:440
Babylon Revisited and Other
   Stories, 1:839

Baby Massage: Parent-Child
   Bonding through Touch-
   ing, 5:321
Baby Skin, 5:323
Baby with the Bathwater,
   1:1087
The Bacchae, 2:356, 4:474
Bacchae, The Erpingham
   Camp, 1:529
The Bacchae of Euripides: A
   Communion Rite, 2:148
Bach, 3:675
Bachelard: Modern European
   Philosophy, 4:274
Bachelor Girls, 1:1115
The Bachelor of Arts, 2:179
The Bach Reader, 3:675
Back, 1:487
Back Attack, 5:394
Back Country, 1:1052
The Background of Ecology:
   Concept and Theory, 5:820
Backgrounds of American
   Literary Thought, 1:714
Backgrounds of Early Chris-
   tianity, 4:807
Backlash: The Undeclared
   War against American
   Women, 3:218
Back to Oegstgeest, 2:633
Back to the Congo, 3:903
Back to the Sources: Read-
   ing the Classic Jewish
   Texts, 4:601
A Backward Glance, 1:788
Backwater, 1:541
Back Where I Come From,
   3:814, 3:896
The Backwoods of Canada,
   2:920
Backwoods Utopia, 3:217
The Backyard Astronomer's
   Guide, 5:591
Backyard Astronomy, 5:591
Bacon: His Writings and His
   Philosophy, 4:165
Bacteria in Nature, Vol. 1:
   Bacterial Activities in Per-
   spective, 5:783
Bad Blood: The Tuskegee
   Syphilis Experiment, 5:390
A Bad Child's Book of
   Beasts, 1:442
Bad Dreams, 2:758, 2:759
Badenheim 1939, 2:14
The Badgers, 2:734
Bad Habits, 3:551
Badlands, 2:916
A Bad Man, 1:973
The Bad Place, 1:1241
The Bad Seed, 1:1081
Bad Trips, 3:891

The Bad War: An Oral Histo-
   ry of the Vietnam War,
   3:540
Baffling Phenomena, 4:317,
   5:101
Baga, 2:493
Baghdad: Metropolis of the
   Abbasid Caliphate, 3:438
A Baghdad Chronicle. Stud-
   ies in Islamic History,
   3:437
Baghdad without a Map,
   3:903
Bag Lady, 1:1114
The Baha'i Faith: An Histori-
   cal Bibliography, 4:861
The Bahai Faith: The Emerg-
   ing Global Religion, 4:861
The Bahai Religion: A Short
   Introduction to Its History
   and Teachings, 4:861
Baha'u'llah and the New
   Era, 4:861, 4:568
Bai Juyi, 2:200
Bailey's Cafe, 1:1020
The Bailiff Yerney and His
   Rights, 2:835
Baker's Biographical Dictio-
   nary of Musicians, 3:657
Baker's Dictionary of Chris-
   tian Ethics, 4:718
Baker's Dictionary of Theol-
   ogy, 4:718
The Bakufu in Japanese His-
   tory, 3:475
Balaam and His Master and
   Other Sketches and Sto-
   ries, 1:754
Balance and Swing, 3:852
Balance of Intrigue, 3:464
Balanchine, 3:738
Balanchine's Complete Sto-
   ries of the Great Ballets,
   3:733
Balanchine's Mozartiana: The
   Making of a Masterpiece,
   3:738
Balanchine's Tchaikovsky: In-
   terviews with George Bal-
   anchine, 3:738
Balancing Acts: Contempo-
   rary Stories by Russian
   Women, 2:692
The Balcony, 2:478
A Balcony over the Fakihani,
   2:58
The Bald Soprano, 2:483
The Balfour Declaration,
   3:351
Bali and Angkor: A 1930s
   Pleasure Trip Looking at
   Life and Death, 3:903

Balinese Character: A Photographic Analysis, 3:36
The Balkans: Minorities and States in Conflict, 3:392
A Ballade of the Scottysshe Kynge, 1:196
Ballades in Blue China, 3:882
The Ballad Mongers: Rise of the Modern Folk Song, 3:850
The Ballad of Carson McCullers, 1:1102
The Ballad of Peckham Rye, 1:551
The Ballad of Reading Gaol, 1:410
The Ballad of the Harp Weaver, 1:860
Ballad of the Hidden Dragon, 2:189
The Ballad of the Sad Cafe, 1:1009, 1:1080, 1:1102
The Ballad of the Sad Cafe and Other Stories, 1:1009
The Ballads, 1:149
Ballads and Blues: Poems, 2:320
Ballads and Lyrics of Old France, 3:882
Ballads and Songs of Indiana, 3:861
Ballads Migrant in New England, 3:858
Ballads of the English Border, 1:398
Ballantine Books: The First Decade, 1:39
Ball at the Opera, 2:822
Ball Courts and Ceremonial Plazas in the West Indies, 4:466
Ballet: An Illustrated History, 3:733
Ballet: Bias and Belief, 3:746
Ballet and Dance: The World's Major Companies, 3:734
Ballet and Modern Dance: A Concise History, 3:731
Ballet Art from the Renaissance to the Present, 3:733
Ballet Company, 3:734
The Ballet Goer's Guide, 3:733
A Ballet-Maker's Handbook: Sources, Vocabulary, Styles, 3:733
Ballet Mecanique (Mechanical Ballet), 1:1159
Balletomania: Story of an Obsession, 3:731

Ballets of Today, 3:733
Ballets Past and Present, 3:733
Balm in Gilead, 1:1121
Balm in Gilead and Other Plays, 1:1121
Baltic Drama: A Handbook and Bibliography, 2:804
Baltic Literature, 2:796, 2:804
The Baltic Nations and Europe, 3:394
Baltics, 2:681
The Baltic States, 3:395
Balzac: A Critical Study, 2:454
Balzac, James and the Realistic Novel, 2:454
Balzacian Montage: Configuring the Comédie Humaine, 2:454
Bambi, 1:1163
The Bamboo Grove: An Introduction to Sijo, 2:299
Banana Bottom, 1:856
Bananas, Labor and Politics in Honduras: 1954–1963, 3:638
Banaras: City of Lights, 4:503
Bancoop and the Bones of the Mammoth, 2:80
Bandits, 3:405
Bandits in Republican China, 3:469
The Bandit Wind, 2:808
Band of Angels, 1:892
The Bandura Player, 2:840
Bangladesh, 3:487
Bangladesh: A Select General Bibliography, 3:487
Bangladesh: Origins and Indian Ocean Relations, 1971–75, 3:487
Banished Immortal: Poems of Li T'ai-po, 2:207
Banjo, 1:856
Bankers and Pashas, 3:446
The Bannatyne Miscellany, 1:299
Banned Books: 387 B.C. to 1978 A.D., 1:57
Banner of Jerusalem, 4:657
The Banquet Years, 2:451, 3:663
The Bantam New College French and English Dictionary, 1:98
Bantam New College Italian and English Dictionary, 1:100
Bantam Shakespeare, 1:206

The Bantam Story: Twenty-Five Years of Paperback Publishing, 1:39
Banting: A Biography, 5:407
Bantu, Boer and Briton, 3:423
Bantu Philosophy, 4:367, 4:369
Bantu Prophets in South Africa, 4:468
Baotown, 2:266
The Baptism, 1:1085
The Baptism (and The Toilet), 1:941
Baptismal Instructions, 4:707
Baptism at the Savica, 2:836
Barabbas, 2:675
Baraka: The Renegade and the Mask, 1:1085
Barbara, 2:656, 2:657
Barbara Bodichon, 1827–1891, 1:331
Barbara Bodichon, George Eliot, and the Limits of Feminism, 1:331
Barbara Leighton Smith Bodichon and the Langham Place Group, 1:331
Barbara Pym, 1:539
Barbara Pym: A Reference Guide, 1:539
Barbara Pym and the Novel of Manners, 1:539
Barbarians at the Gate: The Fall of RJR Nabisco, 3:48
Barbarians of Mars, 1:616
Barbaric Comedies: Silver Face, Heraldic Eagle, and Romance of Wolves, 2:553
Barbarolexis: Medieval Writing and Sexuality, 2:447
The Barbary Shore, 1:1011, 1:1012
Barbed Wire and Mirrors: Essays on New Zealand Prose, 2:971
The Barber of Seville, 2:445, 2:457, 2:458
Barcelona and Beyond: The Disputation of 1263 and Its Aftermath, 4:669
Barchester Towers, 1:405
The Barclay Family Theatre, 2:913
The Bard, 1:248
Bardic Ethos and the American Epic Poem, 1:800
Bardo Thodol, 4:544
Bare-Faced Messiah: A Biography of L. Ron Hubbard, 4:869
Barefoot, 2:826
Barefoot in the Park, 1:1112

Barefoot to Balanchine: How to Watch Dance, 3:731

The Bark Tree, 2:496

Barnabo delle montagne, 2:411

Barnaby Rudge: A Tale of the Riots of Eighty, 1:348

The Barnabys in America, or Adventures of the Widow Wedded, 1:408

Barn Blind, 1:1050

Barnes and Noble Thesaurus of Physics, 5:653

Barney, Bradley, and Max: Sixteen Portraits in Jazz, 3:667

Barnhart Dictionary of Etymology, 1:95

The Baron in the Trees, 2:411

Barons Warres, 1:179

Baroque Architecture, 3:763

Baroque Music, 3:662

Baroque Music Today, 3:660

Barrack Room Ballads, 1:370

Barrel of a Pen: Resistance to Repression in Neo-Colonial Kenya, 2:154

Barren Ground, 1:843

Barren Lives, 2:897

Barrie: The Story of J.M.B., 1:330

Barriers to New Competition, 3:57

Bartholomew and the Oobleck, 1:1203

Bartholomew Fair, 1:183

Bartleby the Inscrutable 1:689

Bartlett's Familiar Quotations: Fifteenth and 125th Anniversary Edition, 1:116

Bartók, 3:677

Bartók and Kodály Revisited, 3:677

Bartók Remembered, 3:677

Bartolomé de las Casas: Bookman, Scholar, and Propagandist, 3:646

Bartolomé de las Casas in History, 3:646, 3:647

Baryshnikov, 3:738

Baryshnikov: From Russia to the West, 3:738

Baryshnikov at Work, 3:738

Bashō and His Interpreters: Selected Hokku, 2:276

Basic Algebraic Geometry, 5:487

BASIC and the Personal Computer, 5:552

Basic Bethe, 5:671

Basic Bookbinding, 1:25

Basic Book List, 1:52

The Basic Book of Antiques and Collectibles, 3:765

Basic Books in the Mass Media, 3:801

Basic Business Statistics for Managers, 5:521

Basic Christian Doctrine, 4:745

Basic Concepts in Relativity and Early Quantum Theory, 5:660

Basic Concepts in Sociology, 3:243

Basic Documents in American History, 3:511

Basic Engineering Principles, 5:214

The Basic English-Chinese, Chinese-English Dictionary, 1:97

Basic Exploration Geophysics, 5:630

Basic Forms of Prophetic Speech, 4:824

Basic Issues in Mass Communication, 3:203

Basic Japanese Conversation Dictionary, 1:100

Basic Judaism, 4:596

Basic Mathematics: You Can Count on Yourself, 5:484

Basic Methods for Mental Health Practitioners, 5:418

Basic Notions of Condensed Matter Physics, 5:670

Basic Number Theory, 5:489

Basic Petroleum Geology, 5:286, 5:636

Basic Plasma Processes on the Sun, 5:667

Basic Principles of Psychoanalysis, 5:437

The Basic Problems of Phenomenology, 4:290

BASIC Programming, 5:552

BASIC Programs for Scientists and Engineers, 5:553

Basic Psychiatry, 5:415

Basic Quantum Mechanics, 5:660

Basic Questions in Theology: Collected Essays, 4:99

Basic Reference Books, 1:81

Basic Reference Sources: A Self-Study Manual, 1:74

Basic Skills, 3:251

Basic Skills: A Plan for Your Child, A Program for All Children, 3:251

The Basic Teachings of the Great Philosophers, 4:16

The Basic Training of Pavlo Hummel, 1:1108, 1:1109

Basic Typography, 1:7

The Basic Works of Aristotle, 4:45

Basic Writings in the History of Psychology, 3:168

The Basic Writings of Bertrand Russell 1903–1959, 4:322

The Basic Writings of C. G. Jung, 5:454

Basic Writings of St. Augustine, 4:109

Basic Writings of St. Thomas Aquinas, 4:117

The Basic Writings of Sigmund Freud, 5:445

The Basil and Josephine Stories, 1:839

Basil Bunting, 1:452

Basil Bunting: A Bibliography of Works and Criticism, 1:452

Basil Bunting: Man and Poet, 1:452

Basin and Range, 5:623, 5:645

The Basis of Morality According to William of Ockham, 4:120

The Basques, 3:386

The Bass Saxophone, 2:794

The Batchelors, 1:551

Batfishing in the Rainforest, 3:898

Bath, 1:548

The Bathhouse, 2:739

The Battered Woman Syndrome, 5:424

Battered Women, 5:429

The Battle: Plays, Prose, Poems, 2:603

Battle: The Story of the Bulge, 3:280

Battle Chronicles of the Civil War, 3:586

Battle Circle, 1:1253

Battle Cry of Freedom: The Civil War Era, 3:528, 3:586

Battle for Batangas: A Philippine Province at War, 3:493

The Battle for Childhood: Creation of a Russian Myth, 2:691

The Battle for Guatemala: Rebels, Death Squads, and U.S. Power, 3:637

The Battle for Peace, 3:441

The Battle for the Control of U.S. Broadcasting, 1930–1935, 3:812

The Battle for the Elephants, 5:763

The Battle-Ground, 1:843

The Battle of Alcazar, 1:195

Battle of Angels, 1:1117

The Battle of Maldon, 1:142, 1:483

The Battle of Midway, 1:1166

The Battle of the Books: History and Literature in the Augustan Age, 1:225

Battle of the Books: What It Takes to Be Educated in America, 3:253

Battle-Pieces and Aspects of the War, 1:686, 1:687

The Battleship Potemkin, 3:835

Battles in the Desert and Other Stories, 2:877

Battles Lost and Won: Great Campaigns of World War II, 3:277

The Battle with the Slums, 3:821

Battling the White Lamb, 2:800

Baudelaire (Sartre), 2:457, 2:507

Baudelaire (Starkie), 2:457

Baudelaire: A Study of His Poetry, 2:457

Baudelaire: Lyric Poet in the Age of High Capitalism, 2:457

Baudelaire and Freud, 2:457, 5:447

Baudelaire and the English Tradition: Canonization of the Subversive, 2:990

Baudelaire in 1859: A Study in the Sources of Poetic Creativity, 2:457

Baudelaire on Poe: Critical Papers, 1:693

Baudelaire's Literary Criticism, 2:457

Bauhaus: Weimar, Dessau, Berlin, Chicago, 3:777

Baumgartner's Bombay, 2:179

The Bavli: The Talmud of Babylonia. An Introduction, 4:611

The Bay at Nice and Wrecked Eggs, 1:493

Bayes or Bust? Critical Examination of Bayesian Confirmation Theory, 5:62

The Bayeux Tapestry: The Norman Conquest, 3:1066, 3:357

Bayle, 4:166

Bayna al-Qasrayn, 2:67

The Bay of Noon, 2:953

Bayou Folk, 1:739, 1:740

The Beach, 2:432

The Beaches Are Moving: The Drowning of America's Shoreline, 5:631

Beachmasters, 2:949

Be a Good Neighbor and Leave Me Alone, 3:870

An Beal Bocht (The Poor Mouth: A Bad Story about the Hard Life), 1:525

Be All You Can Be! The U.S. Army Total Fitness Program, 5:326

The Bear, 2:709

The Beard, 1:1008

The Beards' New Basic History of the United States, 3:566

Beard's Roman Women, 1:453

Bearers of Bad Tidings, 2:626

The Bear Fell Free, 1:488

The Bear Flag, 1:1246

Bearing the Bad News: Contemporary American Literature and Culture, 1:911

Bearing the Cross, 3:538

Bearing the Unbearable, 2:30

Bearing Witness: Gay Men's Health Crisis and the Politics of AIDS, 5:388

The Bear's Dance, 2:800

Bear Went over the Mountain: Tall Tales of American Animals, 3:871

The Beast in Me and Other Animals, 1:890

The Beat Generation, 1:912

Beating the Bushes: Selected Essays, 1941–1970, 1:874

Beatrice, 2:611, 2:620

Beatrice and Sidney Webb: Fabian Socialists, 3:113

Beatrix Potter, 1:589

Beatrix Potter's Art, 1:589

Beatrix Potter's Lakeland, 1:589

Beauchampe; or, The Kentucky Tragedy, 1:696

Beauchamp's Career, 1:378

Beaumarchais, 2:458

The Beautiful and the Damned, 1:839

Beautiful Fables, 2:401

Beautiful Feathers, 2:135

Beautiful Losers, 2:909

Beautiful Machine: Rivers and the Republican Plan, 1755–1825, 1:629

The Beautiful Ones Are Not Yet Born, 2:130, 2:131

The Beautiful People, 1:1110

Beautiful Swimmers: Watermen, Crabs, and the Chesapeake Bay, 5:818

Beauty, Health, and Permanence: Environmental Politics in the United States, 1955–1985, 3:550, 5:822

A Beauty and Sensibility in the Thought of Jonathan Edwards, 4:767

Beauty and the Beast, 1:583, 1:1233

The Beauty and the Beast: Diary of a Film, 2:469

Beauty in Holiness: Studies in Jewish Ceremonial Art and Customs, 4:614

The Beauty of Doing Mathematics: Three Public Dialogues, 5:481

The Beaux' Stratagem, 1:243

Because It Is Bitter, and Because It Is My Heart, 1:1022

Because the Sea Is Black: Poems of Blaga Dimitrova, 2:781

Bech: A Book, 1:1060

Bechamp vs Pasteur, 5:809

Bech Is Back, 1:1060

Becket, 1:321, 2:450

The Becket Conflict and the Schools, 4:102

The Becket Controversy, 3:357

Beckett and Babel: An Investigation into the Bilingual Work, 1:440

Beckett and Joyce: Friendship and Fiction, 1:505

Beckett and Myth: An Archetypal Approach, 1:440

Beckett in Performance, 2:460

Beckett's Fiction: In Different Words, 2:460

Beckonings, 1:954

Becoming: Basic Considerations for a Psychology of Personality, 5:431

Becoming a Doctor: A Journey of Initiation in Medical School, 5:336

Becoming a Nation of Readers, 3:253

Becoming Browning, 1:339

Becoming Partners: Marriage and Its Alternatives, 3:193, 5:468

Becoming Visible: Women in European History, 3:326

The Bedbug, 2:739

Bed Number Ten, 5:391

The Bedroom and the State, 3:608

Beds in the East, 1:453

Beelzebub's Tales to His Grandson, 4:875

Been in the Storm So Long: The Aftermath of Slavery, 3:528

Bees: Their Vision, Chemical Senses and Language, 5:796

Bees of the World, 5:771

Beethoven, 3:678

Beethoven: His Life, Work and World, 3:678

Beethoven and the Creative Process, 3:678

The Beethoven Compendium, 3:678

Beethoven Essays, 3:678

Beethoven on Beethoven: Playing His Piano Music His Way, 3:678

The Beethoven Quartet Companion, 3:678

The Beethoven Reader, 3:678

Beethoven Remembered, 3:678

Beethoven Studies III, 3:678

Beethoven Studies II, 3:678

The Beetle Leg, 1:985

Be Faithful unto Death, 2:802

Before and After Socrates, 4:46

Before and After the Ch'ing Ming Festival, 2:258

Before Cannae, 2:652

Before Color Prejudice: The Ancient View of Blacks, 3:299

Before Eureka: The Presocratics and Their Science, 4:51

Before European Hegemony: The World System A.D. 1250–1350, 3:219, 3:274

Before Lift-Off: The Making of a Space Shuttle Crew, 5:596

Before Novels, 1:230

Before Philosophy, 3:300

Before Sexuality, 3:309

Before Sunrise, 2:775

Before the Armada: The Emergence of the English Nation, 1485–1588, 3:359

Before the Computer, 3:547

Before the Dawn, 2:292

Before the Mayflower: A History of Black America, 3:519

Before the Melting Pot, 3:517

Before the Nickelodeon, 1:1174

Before You Buy a Used Computer, 5:538

The Beggar, 2:68

A Beggar in Jerusalem, 1:1065

The Beggar Maid or Who Do You Think You Are?, 2:921

Beggar of Beauty, 2:800

Beggars and Prayers, 2:42, 4:669

The Beggar's Opera, 1:228, 1:246, 2:571

Beginner's Dictionary of Chinese-Japanese Characters, 1:97

The Beginner's Guide to Computers, 5:537

Beginning Again, 1:41, 1:569

Beginning Again: People and Nature in the New Millennium, 5:114

The Beginning and the End (Berdyaev), 4:275

The Beginning and the End (Manfuz), 2:68

A Beginning-Intermediate Grammar of Hellenistic Greek, 4:794

Beginning Italian Bilingual Dictionary, 1:100

The Beginning of the World of Books, 1450–1470, 1:67

Beginnings, 2:904

Beginnings: Intention and Method, 1:926, 1:1042

Beginnings in Ritual Studies, 4:897

The Beginnings of Astrology in America, 4:860

The Beginnings of English Society, 3:356

Beginnings of Naturalism in American Fiction, 1891–1903, 1:751

The Beginnings of New France, 1524–1663, 3:612

The Beginnings of Solid State Physics, 5:669

The Beginnings of Systematic Bibliography, 1:61

The Beginnings of the American People, 3:566

Beginnings of the English Romantic Movement, 1:268

The Beginnings of Western Science, 5:26

Beginning Statistics: A to Z, 5:523

Beginning Statistics with Data Analysis, 5:523

Beginning to Read: Thinking and Learning about Print, 3:253

Beginning to Read the Fathers, 4:690

Begriffschrift, 4:229

Behavior: An Introduction to Comparative Psychology, 3:196

Behavioral Approaches to Alcoholism, 5:419

A Behavioral Approach to Historical Analysis, 3:275

Behavioral Biology of Killer Whales, 5:771

Behavioral Health, 5:401

A Behavioral Theory of the Firm, 3:49, 3:210

Behavior and Evolution, 3:18

Behavior and Psychological Man, 3:195

Behavior in Public Places, 3:228

Behaviorism, 3:176, 3:196

Behaviorism, Neobehaviorism, and Cognitivism in Learning Theory, 3:171

Behavior of Captive Wild Animals, 5:826

Behavior of Organisms, 3:193

The Behavior of Organisms: Experimental Analysis, 3:176, 3:194

A Behavior System, 3:186

Behavior Therapy: A Clinical Introduction, 5:419

Behavior Therapy: Application and Outcome, 5:419

Behemoth: or the Long Parliament, 4:173

Behemoth: The Structure and Practice of National Socialism, 1933–1944, 3:140

Behind Closed Doors: Violence in the American Family, 5:424

Behind Mud Walls, 1930–1960, 3:486

Behind Mud Walls 1930–1960, with a Sequel, 4:506, 4:509

Behind Russian Lines: An Afghan Journal, 3:455
Behind the Door, 2:408
Behind the Lines—Hanoi, 3:822
Behind the Mask, 4:539
Behind the Mask of Innocence, 3:827
Behind the Mirror: A Search for a Natural History of Human Knowledge, 3:190
Behind the Painting and Other Stories, 2:336
Behind the Tube: History of Broadcasting, 3:811
Behold the Man, 1:616
Behold the Sign, 4:848
Behold the Spirit, 4:881
Being a Citizen in Ancient Rome, 3:306
Being Alive, 2:923
Being and Existence in Kierkegaard's Pseudonymous Works, 4:239
Being and Having: An Existentialist Diary, 4:304
Being and Knowing, 4:119
Being and Nothingness, 4:329
Being and Time, 4:291, 4:367, 5:90
Being a Philosopher: The History of a Practice, 4:2
Being Here: Poetry 1977–1980, 1:892
Being-in-the-World, 4:292
Being-in-the-World: A Commentary on Heidegger's Being and Time, 5:90
Being Jewish in America: The Modern Experience, 4:639
Being Peace, 4:561
Being There, 1:1002
The Bektashi Order of Dervishes, 4:574
Bel Ami, 2:488, 2:489
Belarmino and Apolonio, 2:546
A Beleaguered City, 1:385
Belgian Democracy: Its Early History, 3:382
Belgium, 3:382
Belgium, the Glorious, 3:382
Belgium and Western Germany in 1833, 1:408
Belgium in the Postwar Period: Partner and Ally, 3:382
Belief and History, 4:427
Belief and Worship in Native North America, 4:464

Believer's Church, 4:724, 4:732
Beli mugri, 2:807
Belinskij and Russian Literary Criticism, 2:691
The Bell, 2:727
Bell and Cohn's Handbook of Grammar, Style and Usage, 1:91
The Bell and the Drum: A Study of Shih Ching as Formulaic Poetry, 2:195
Belle de Jour, 3:832
Bellefleur, 1:1022
Bellini, 3:679
The Bell Jar, 1:1031
Bellman of London, 1:176
The Bells, 1:272, 1:732
Bells in Winter, 2:818
Bell System Technical Journal, 5:580
Bellum Civile, 2:387
The Belmont Report, 5:80
Belonging, 1:521
Belonging to the Universe, 5:196
Beloved, 1:916, 1:1018
Beloved Community, 5:171
Beloved Lady: A History of Jane Addams's Ideas on Reform and Peace, 1:731
The Belton Estate, 1:405
Bending the Bow, 1:971
A Bend in the River, 2:938
Bend Sinister, 2:740
Beneath the American Renaissance, 1:652
Beneath the Red Banner, 2:251
Benedetto Croce: Philosopher of Art and Literary Critic, 2:414
Benedetto Croce and the User of Historicism, 3:284
Benedict De Spinoza, 4:187
Benedictine Monasticism, 4:705
The Benediction of Brother Cadfael, 1:608
The Benefactor, 1:1053
The Bene Israel of Bombay: A Study of a Jewish Community, 4:645
The Benelux Countries: An Historical Survey, 3:380
Benét's Reader's Encyclopedia, 1:131, 2:3
Benét's Reader's Encyclopedia of American Literature, 1:133
Ben-Hur, 1:480, 1:1244, 1:1250, 1:1251

Benjamin Britten: His Life and Operas, 3:685
Benjamin Britten: Peter Grimes, 3:685
Benjamin Franklin, 1:639
Benjamin Franklin, An American Man of Letters, 1:638
Benjamin Franklin's Science, 5:15
Benjamin the Waggoner, 1:305
Ben Jonson, 1:184
Ben Jonson: A Life, 1:184
Ben Jonson: Public Poet and Private Man, 1:184
Ben Jonson: To the First Folio, 1:184
Ben Jonson and the Language of Prose Comedy, 1:184
Ben Jonson and the Poetics of Patronage, 1:184
Ben Jonson, Dramatist, 1:184
Ben Jonson's Parodic Strategy: Literary Imperialism in the Comedies, 1:184
Ben Jonson's Plays: An Introduction, 1:184
Ben Jonson's Poems: A Study of the Plain Style, 1:184
Benny Andersen: A Critical Study, 2:646
Benny Carter: A Life in American Music, 3:687
Ben's Dream, 1:1207
Bentham (Dinwiddy), 4:191
Bentham (Harrison), 4:191
Bentham (Steintrager), 3:151
Bentham and the Oppressed, 3:151
Bentham's Theory of the Modern State, 3:151
Benya Krik, The Gangster and Other Stories, 2:700
Beowulf, 1:141, 1:143, 1:144, 1:575, 1:978, 2:955
Beowulf: An Introduction, 1:144
Beowulf: The Monster and the Critics, 1:559
Beowulf and Other Old English Poems, 1:144
Beowulf and the Beowulf Manuscript, 1:144
Beowulf and the Fight at Finnsburg, 1:144
Beowulf Scholarship: An Annotated Bibliography, 1:144
Beppo, 1:281
Berdyaev's Philosophy of Hope, 4:759

Bérénice, 2:498
The Berg Companion, 3:680
Bergey's Manual of Systematic Bacteriology, 5:760
Bergman on Bergman: Interviews with Ingmar Bergman, 3:831
The Berg-Schoenberg Correspondence: Selected Letters, 3:680
Bergson, 4:220
Bergson and His Influence, 4:220
Bergson and Modern Physics: A Reinterpretation and Reevaluation, 4:220
Bergson and the Modern Spirit, 4:220
Bergson and the Stream of Consciousness Novel, 1:422
The Bergsonian Controversy in France, 1900–1914, 4:220
Bergsonian Philosophy and Thomism, 4:220, 4:306
Bergson to Sartre, 4:263
Berio, 3:680
Berkeley (Bracken), 4:191
Berkeley (Urmson), 4:192
Berkeley (Warnock), 4:192
Berkeley: An Introduction, 4:192
Berkeley: The Central Arguments, 4:192
Berkeley and Malebranche, 4:182
The Berkeley Conference on Dutch Literature, 1987, 2:621
Berkeley's American Sojourn, 4:192
Berkeley's Argument, 4:192, 4:277
Berkeley's Revolution in Vision, 4:191
Berlin, Alexanderplatz: The Story of Franz Biberkopf, 2:576
The Berlin Diary, 3:377
Berlin Ost, 2:606
The Berlin Stories, 1:500
Berlioz and His Century: An Introduction to the Age of Romanticism, 3:340, 3:681
Berlioz Orchestral Music, 3:682
Bernard Clare, 1:833
Bernard De Voto, 3:576
Bernard Foy's Third Castling, 2:674
Bernard Malamud (Hershinow), 1:1013

Bernard Malamud (Richman), 1:1014
Bernard Malamud: An Annotated Checklist, 1:1014
Bernardo Bertolucci, 3:828
Bernard Romans, 5:237
Bernard Shaw, 1:546
Bernard Shaw: A Bibliography, 1:546
Bernard Shaw: A Guide to Research, 1:546
Bernard Shaw: The Darker Side, 1:546
Bernard Shaw and the Actresses, 1:546
Bernard Shaw and the Comic Sublime, 1:546
Bernard Shaw on the London Art Scene, 1885–1950, 1:546
Bernard Spilsbury: Famous Murder Cases of the Great Pathologist, 5:343
Bernini, 3:770
Bernini and the Idealization of Death, 3:770
Bernstein: A Biography, 3:683
Bernstein Remembered, 3:682
Bertolt Brecht in America, 2:573
Bertram, or, The Castle of St. Aldobrand, 1:271
The Bertrams, 1:406
Bertrand Russell, 4:272, 4:324, 5:103
Bertrand Russell: A Psychobiography of a Moralist, 2:159
Bertrand Russell, A. S. Neill, Homer Lane, W. H. Kilpatrick, 3:264
Bertrand Russell and the Pacifists in the First World War, 4:325
Bertrand Russell and Trinity: A College Controversy of the Last War, 4:324
The Bertrand Russell Case, 4:324
Bertrand Russell's Best, 4:322
Best American Essays, 1:660, 1:728
Best American Plays
3rd Series, 1941–1951, 1:1077
4th Series, 1952–1957, 1:1077
5th Series, 1957–1963, 1:1077

6th Series, 1963–1967, 1:1077
7th Series, 1967–1973, 1:1077
Supplementary Volume, 1918–1958, 1:1077
Best American Short Stories, 1:921, 1:946, 1:950, 1:980
The Best and the Brightest, 3:538
Best Books for Children: Preschool through Grade 6, 1:74, 1:1195
Best Books for Junior High Readers, 1:74, 1:1195
Best Books for Public Libraries, 1:73
Best Books for Senior High Readers, 1:74, 1:1195
The Best Contemporary Fiction from Japan, 2:283
Best Encyclopedias: A Guide to General and Specialized Encyclopedias, 1:73
Best Ghost Stories, 1:601
The Best Hour of the Night, 1:1048
The Best in Children's Books, 1966–1972, 1:50
The Best Intentions, 3:831
The Best Man, 1:1062
The Best Man to Die, 1:609
The Best Medicine, 5:331
"The Best Men": Liberal Reformers in the Gilded Age, 3:533, 3:595
Best Nightmare on Earth: A Life in Haiti, 3:895
The Best of an Old Friend, 2:254
The Best of Disney, 1:1165
The Best of Fine Woodworking: Modern Furniture Projects, 3:766
The Best of Granta Travel, 3:907
The Best of Simple, 1:848
The Best of the Norwegian Heritage, 3:381
Best Plays of the Early American Theatre, 1:1077
Best Plays of the Modern American Theatre: 2nd Series, 1939–1946, 1:1077
The Best Plays Series, 1:1074
Best Science Fiction Stories, 1:564
Best-Selling Children's Books, 1:51
The Best Short Stories of Theodore Dreiser, 1:830
Best's Safety Directory, 5:724

Best Stories of Mary E. Wilkins, 1:750
Best Supernatural Tales of Arthur Conan Doyle, 1:607
The Best Tales of Hoffmann, 2:592
The Best Treatment, 5:332
The Betrayal (Micheaux), 1:1172
Betrayal (Pinter), 1:534
Betrayal of Health, 5:327
Betrayed by Rita Hayworth, 2:880
Betrothed (Agnon), 2:11
The Betrothed (Manzoni), 2:426
The Betsy, 1:1222
Better a Shield Than a Sword, 5:112, 5:143
Better Health Care for Less, 5:332
A Better Mousetrap: Improving Pest Management for Agriculture, 5:265
Better Think Twice about It: And Twelve Other Stories, 2:435
Between Berlin and Slobodka, 4:620
Between Boards: New Thoughts on Old Books, 1:34
Between Covers, 1:38
Between Cultures, 4:37
Between Dog and Wolf, 2:758
Between East and West, the Balkan and Mediterrean Worlds, 3:392
Between Exile and Return: S. Y. Agnon and the Drama of Writing, 2:12
Between Fantoine and Agapa, 2:493
Between Frieburg and Frankfurt: Toward a Critical Ontology, 4:292
Between God and Man: An Interpretation of Judaism, 4:664
Between Health and Illness, 5:401
Between Heaven and Earth, 2:615
Between Life and Death, 2:505
Between Man and Man, 4:662
Between Meals: An Appetite for Paris, 3:814
Between Men: English Literature and Male Homosocial Desire, 1:1182, 1:319

Between Oxus and Jumna, 3:293
Between Pacific Tides, 5:820
Between Past and Future, 3:282, 4:394, 5:82
Between Quantum and Cosmos, 5:719
Between Right and Right, 2:26
Between Science and Values, 5:107
Between Silence and Light: Spirit in the Architecture of Louis I. Kahn, 3:777
Between Tears and Laughter, 2:254
Between the Acts, 1:568, 1:569
Between the Library and the Laboratory, 5:43
Between the Sexes: Foundations for a Christian Ethics of Sexuality, 4:894
Between the Testaments, 4:605
Between Time and Eternity: The Essentials of Judaism, 4:596
Between Time and Timbuktu; or Prometheus Five: A Space Fantasy, 1:1063
Between Two Empires: The Ordeal of the Philippines, 1929–1946, 3:493
Between Two Gardens, 4:894
Between Two Worlds: The American Novel in the 1960s, 1:919
Between Two Worlds: Victorian Ambivalence about Progress, 1:325
Between Worlds: Woman Writers of Chinese Ancestry, 1:714
Beverly: An Autobiography, 3:719
Beware, Soul Brother, 2:128
Beware, Soul Brother and Other Poems, 2:127
Beware of Still Waters, 2:532
Beware the Cat: The First English Novel, 1:172
Beyond a Boundary, 3:647
Beyond Alcoholism: Alcohol and Public Health, 5:401
Beyond All Appearances, 4:338, 4:339
Beyond Amazement: New Essays on John Ashbery, 1:936
Beyond Anger: A Study of Juvenal's Third Book of Satires, 2:387

Beyond Appearance: Reflections of a Plastic Surgeon, 5:396
Beyond Baby Fat: Weight-Loss Plans for Children and Teenagers, 5:348
Beyond Belief: Essays on Religion in a Post-Traditional World, 4:424
Beyond Cellulite, 5:326
Beyond Conception: The New Politics of Reproduction, 5:782
Beyond Control: The Rise and Fall of ABC, 3:812
Beyond Culture, 1:1058
Beyond Diet: The 28-Day Metabolic Breakthrough Plan, 5:346
Beyond Economics, 3:71
Beyond Economics: Essays on Society, Religion, and Ethics, 3:71
Beyond Engineering, 5:174, 5:214
Beyond Fiction: The Recovery of the Feminine in the Novels of Cervantes, 2:536
Beyond Freedom and Dignity, 3:193, 5:81
Beyond Games and Scripts, 5:433
Beyond God the Father, 1:1186, 1:1187, 4:749, 4:764
Beyond Good and Evil, 4:245, 4:246
Beyond Humanism: Essays in the Philosophy of Nature, 4:288
Beyondism: Religion from Science, 5:106
Beyond Literacy: The Second Gutenberg Revolution, 1:32
Beyond Metaphor: The Theory of Tropes in Anthropology, 3:14, 4:426
Beyond Metaphysics?, 4:391
Beyond Objectivity and Relativism, 4:378
Beyond Occupation, 4:905
Beyond Oil: The Threat to Food and Fuel in the Coming Decades, 5:282
Beyond P. C.: Toward a Politics of Understanding, 1:1128
Beyond Power: On Women, Men, and Morals, 1:925
Beyond Psychology, 5:465

Beyond Realism: Turgenev's Poetics of Secular Salvation, 2:770

Beyond Reason, 4:399

Beyond Romanticism: Tuckerman's Life and Poetry, 1:779, 1:704

Beyond Socialist Realism: Soviet Fiction since Ivan Denisovich, 2:687

Beyond Spaceship Earth, 5:114, 5:135

Beyond Spoon River: The Legacy of Edgar Lee Masters, 1:859

Beyond Suffrage: Women in the New Deal, 3:536

Beyond Superfailure: America's Toxic Policy for the 1990s, 3:550

Beyond Symptom Suppression, 5:426

Beyond the Age of Waste: A Report to the Club of Rome, 3:47

Beyond the Barrier: The Story of Byrd's First Expedition to Antarctica, 3:915

Beyond the Black Hole: Stephen Hawking's Universe, 5:607

Beyond the Border: A New Age in Latin American Women's Fiction, 2:848

Beyond the Boundaries: Text and Context in African Literature, 2:112

Beyond the Chains of Illusion, 5:449, 5:450

Beyond the East Wind: Legends and Folktales of Vietnam, 3:857

Beyond the Fall of Night, 1:614

Beyond the Frontier: Writers, Western Regionalism and a Sense of Place, 1:716

Beyond the Horizon, 1:1106, 1:1107

Beyond the Hot Seat: Gestalt Approaches to Group, 5:418

Beyond the Hundredth Meridian, 5:646

Beyond the Limit (Ratushinskaya), 2:753

Beyond the Limits (Meadows), 3:48, 5:167, 5:168, 5:823

Beyond the Mechanical Universe: From Electricity to Modern Physics, 5:653

Beyond the Metafictional Mode, 2:525

Beyond the Mexique Bay, 1:499

Beyond the Milky Way, 5:606

Beyond the Nation-State: Functionalism and International Organization, 3:144

Beyond the Pleasure Principle, 5:445

Beyond Therapy, 1:1087

Beyond the Self: Wittgenstein, Heidegger, and the Limits of Language, 4:295

Beyond the Single Vision: Henry James, Michel Butor, Uwe Johnson, 2:463

Beyond the Tragic Vision, 1:266

Beyond the Veil: Male-Female Dynamics in a Modern Muslim Society, 2:56

Beyond the Wall: Essays from the Outside, 3:894

Beyond the Waste Land: The American Novel in the Nineteen-Sixties, 1:919

Beyond the Welfare State, 3:235

Beyond the Well of Loneliness: The Fiction of Radclyffe Hall, 1:492

Beyond This Horizon, 1:1258

Beyond Velikovsky: The History of a Public Controversy, 5:589

Beyond Vietnam: The United States and Asia, 3:501

Beyond Vision: One Hundred Historic Scientific Photographs, 5:9

Beyond Word Processing, 5:561

Beyond Words, 5:421

Be Your Own Power Company, 5:278

Bhagavad Gītā, 2:171, 2:172, 2:173, 4:502, 4:506

The Bhagavad Gita: An Interpretation, 4:552

The Bhagavad-Gita: Krishna's Counsel in Time of War, 4:505

The Bhagavadgita in the Mahabharata, 4:506

Bialik, 2:16

Bialik and Tshernichovsky, 2:16

Bias in Mental Testing, 3:174

The Bias of Communications, 3:621

The Bible, 1:480

Bible and Sword, 3:411, 3:412

The Bible in America: Essays in Cultural History, 4:813

The Bible in Aramaic Based on Old Manuscripts and Printed Texts, 4:796

The Bible in Early English Literature, 1:142

The Bible in Middle English Literature, 1:147

The Bible, Now I Get It: A Form Criticism Handbook, 4:815

The Bible Today, 4:814, 4:833

Biblia sacra iuxta vulgatam versionem, 4:796

Biblical Dialogues between a Father and his Family, 1:643

Biblical Interpretation in Ancient Israel, 4:823

Biblical Narrative in the Philosophy of Paul Ricoeur, 4:320

Biblical References in Shakespeare's History Plays, 1:220

Biblical References in Shakespeare's Tragedies, 1:220

Biblical Theology of the Old and New Testaments, 4:827

The Bibliographer's Manual of English Literature, 1:68

Bibliographia: An Inquiry into Its Definition and Designations, 1:60

Bibliographia Canadiana, 3:606

Bibliographia Cartesiana, 4:170

Bibliographical Dictionary of Latin American Historians and Historiography, 3:625

Bibliographical Guide to the Study of the Literature of the U.S.A., 1:79, 1:121

A Bibliographical Handbook of Bulgarian Authors, 2:781

Bibliographical Handbook on Tudor England: 1485–1603, 3:354

The Bibliographical History of Anonyma and Pseudonyma, 1:77

Bibliographical Introduction to the Study of John Locke, 4:179

Bibliographical Services throughout the World, 1:63

The Bibliographical Society of America, 1904-79, 1:60

A Bibliographical Survey for a Foundation in Philosophy, 4:13

Bibliographic Guide to Caribbean Mass Communication, 3:801

A Bibliographic Guide to Christian Feminist Liberation Theology, 4:749

A Bibliographic Guide to the Comparative Study of Ethics, 4:892

A Bibliographic Guide to the History of Computing, Computers, and the Information Processing Industry, 5:27

Bibliographic Index, 1:112

The Bibliographic Index: A Cumulative Bibliography of Bibliographies, 1:63, 1:120

Bibliographies: Their Aims and Methods, 1:61

Bibliographies in American History, 1942-1978, 3:509

Bibliographies on Tourism and Related Subjects, 3:890

Bibliography (La Bibliographie), 1:61

Bibliography and Genetic Study of American Realism, 4:264

Bibliography and Research Manual of the History of Mathematics, 5:491

A Bibliography of American Autobiographers, 1:87

A Bibliography of American Autobiography, 1945-1980, 1:86

The Bibliography of American Fiction, 1945-1988, 1:125

Bibliography of American Literature, 1:121

Bibliography of Asian Studies, 3:462

Bibliography of Bioethics, 5:61, 5:124

Bibliography of Black Music, 3:655

Bibliography of British History, 1851-1914, 3:354

Bibliography of British History, 1789-1851, 3:353

Bibliography of British History: The Eighteenth Century, 1714-1789, 3:354

Bibliography of British History: Tudor Period, 1485-1603, 3:354

Bibliography of British Literary Bibliographies, 1:120, 1:79

Bibliography of British Social and Economic History, 3:353

A Bibliography of Computer Music, 3:666

Bibliography of Creative African Writing, 2:109

Bibliography of Criticism of Contemporary Chicano Literature, 1:121

A Bibliography of David Hume and of Scottish Philosophy from Francis Hutcheson to Lord Balfour, 4:202, 4:212

Bibliography of Discographies, 3:653

Bibliography of Dr. William Harvey, 5:362

A Bibliography of E. M. Forster, 1:477

Bibliography of Early American Fiction, 1774-1830, 1:630

A Bibliography of Edith, Osbert, and Sacheverell Sitwell, 1:548

Bibliography of Editions, Translations, and Commentary on Xenophon's Socratic Writings, 1600 to Present, 4:91

A Bibliography of English History to 1485, 3:354

A Bibliography of English-language Source Materials on Thailand in the Humanities, Social Sciences, and Physical Sciences, 3:490

Bibliography of English Language Works on the Babi and Bahai Faiths 1844-1985, 4:861

A Bibliography of Epictetus, 4:57

Bibliography of European Economic and Social History, 3:325

A Bibliography of Evelyn Waugh, 1:562

Bibliography of Fifteenth Century Literature, with Special Reference to the History of English Culture, 1:121

Bibliography of Folklore, 1905-1907, 3:850

Bibliography of George Berkeley, 4:192

Bibliography of George Crabbe, 1:289

Bibliography of George Moore, 1:381

A Bibliography of Henry James, 1:766

Bibliography of History of Belgium, 3:407

Bibliography of Holy Land Sites, 4:809

Bibliography of Indo-English Literature, 2:170

A Bibliography of Isaac Bashevis Singer 1924-1949, 1:1050

A Bibliography of James Whitcomb Riley, 1:778

Bibliography of Matthew Arnold, 1:328

Bibliography of Medieval Drama, 1:157

Bibliography of Modern Hebrew Literature in English Translation, 2:8

A Bibliography of Modern History, 3:327

Bibliography of New Religious Movements in Primal Societies, 4:468

Bibliography of New Testament Bibliographies, 4:796

A Bibliography of Philosophical Bibliographies, 4:13

A Bibliography of Printing, 1:7

Bibliography of Publications on Old English Literature, 1:143

A Bibliography of Recreational Mathematics, 5:496

A Bibliography of Ronald Firbank, 1:474

A Bibliography of Rupert Brooke, 1:451

A Bibliography of Siegfried Sassoon, 1:543

Bibliography of Sir Walter Scott, 1:299

A Bibliography of Sir William Schwenck Gilbert, 1:358

Bibliography of Statistical Bibliographies, 5:521

A Bibliography of Studies and Translations of Modern Chinese Literature, 1918–1942, 2:233

A Bibliography of Targum Literature, 4:608

A Bibliography of the English Printed Drama to the Restoration, 1:221

A Bibliography of the Philosophy of Science, 1945–1981, 5:60

Bibliography of the Philosophy of Technology, 5:60

Bibliography of the Works of Dante Gabriel Rossetti, 1:392

Bibliography of the Works of John Stuart Mill, 4:245

A Bibliography of the Works of Louis MacNeice, 1:518

A Bibliography of the Writings and Criticisms of Edwin Arlington Robinson, 1:877

Bibliography of the Writings of Bret Harte, 1:756

A Bibliography of the Writings of W. H. Hudson, 1:366

A Bibliography of the Writings of Wyndham Lewis, 1:514

A Bibliography of Vico in English, 2:442

Bibliography of William Dean Howells, 1:759

Bibliography of Women and Literature, 1:121

Bibliography on Plato's Laws 1920–1970, with Additional Citations through May 1975, 4:84

Bibliography on Technology and Social Change in China and Japan, 3:463

Bibliography, Practical, Enumerative, Historical: An Introductory Manual, 1:61

Biblioholism: The Literary Addiction, 1:33, 1:76

Bibliomania in the Middle Ages, 1:32

Bibliotheca Americana, 1:67

Bibliotheca Botanica, 5:805

Bibliotheka, 4:468

Bibury's Weekly, 1:597

Bicycle and Other Poems, 2:958

Bicycling Science: Ergonomics and Mechanics, 5:236

Bid Me to Live, 1:826

Bid the Vassal Soar, 1:647

Bifurcated Politics: Evolution and Reform in the National Party Convention, 3:144

The Big Aiiieeeee!, 1:129

Big Backlands: Narrow Paths, 2:899

The Big Bands, 3:669

The Big Bang: The Creation and Evolution of the Universe, 5:656

Big Blue: IBM's Use and Abuse of Power, 5:542

Big Daddy from the Pedernales: Lyndon Baines Johnson, 3:537

The Big Fellow, 1:528

The Bigger Light, 2:934

The Big Grey Wolf, 2:240

The Big Horse and Other Stories of Modern Macedonia, 2:808

The Big Knife, 1:1105

The Big Knockover, 1:1230

Big Lin and Little Lin, 2:240

The Biglow Papers, 1:684

The Biglow Papers: First Series, 1:685

The Biglow Papers: Second Series, 1:685

The Big Money, 1:828

Big Muddy: Down the Mississippi through America's Heartland, 3:895

The Big Questions: A Short Introduction to Philosophy, 4:24

The Big Rock Candy Mountain, 1:1053

Big Science: The Growth of Large-Scale Research, 5:48

Big Science, Little Science, 3:214

The Big Season, 2:975

The Big Sky, 1:1214

The Big Sleep, 1:1226, 1:1228

Big Sur, 1:998

Big Sur and the Oranges of Hieronymus Bosch, 1:861, 1:862

Big Toys, 2:966

Big World, Small Screen, 3:560

The Bijak of Kabīr, 2:174

Bilbo's Last Song, 1:559

Billiards at Half-Past Nine, 2:569, 2:570

Billie Holiday, 3:701

Billie Holiday, Her Life and Times, 3:701

Billie's Blues: The Billie Holiday Story, 1933–1959, 3:701

Billion Year Spree: The True History of Science Fiction, 1:611, 1:612

A Bill of Rights for Future Generations, 3:918

A Bill of Rites, a Bill of Wrongs, a Bill of Goods, 1:1017

Billy Bathgate, 1:969

Billy Budd, 1:686, 2:989

The Billy-Club Puppets, 2:538

Billy Graham: America's Evangelist, 4:768

Billy Graham: A Parable of American Righteousness, 4:768

Billy Graham: Revivalist in a Secular Age, 4:768

Billy Phelan's Greatest Game, 1:996, 1:997

Billy Wilder in Hollywood, 3:829

Biloxi Blues, 1:1112

The Binary Brain: Artificial Intelligence in the Age of Electronics, 5:568

Binding Cultures: Black Women Writers in Africa and the Diaspora, 1:927

Binding Variants with More Binding Variants, 1:22

The Binghams of Louisville, 3:806

Bingo, 1:446

Bingo and The Sea: Two Plays, 1:446

A Bintel Brief, 2:34

A Bio-Bibliography of Andrea Vesalius, 5:365

Bio-Bibliography of Countee P. Cullen, 1903–1946, 1:824

A Biobibliography of Native American Writers 1772–1924, 1:715

Bioburst: The Impact of Modern Biology on the Affairs of Man, 5:765

Biochemistry, 5:732

The Biochemistry of Photosynthesis, 5:732

Biocultural Aspects of Disease, 5:383

Biodiversity, 5:821

Biodynamic Agriculture, 5:266

Bioelectric Measurements, 5:324

Bioengineering: An Engineering View, 5:251

Bioethical Decision-making: Releasing Religion from the Spiritual, 4:895

Bioethical Decision Making: Who Owns the Problem, 5:124

Bioethics: A Guide to Information Sources, 5:120

Bioethics: Basic Writings on the Key Ethical Questions That Surround Major, Modern Biological Possibilities and Problems, 5:123

Bioethics and Secular Humanism: The Search for a Common Morality, 5:134

Bioethics and the New Medical Technology, 5:122

Biofeedback and Sports Science, 5:400

Biofuture: Confronting the Genetic Era, 5:783

Biogeography: An Ecological and Evolutionary Approach, 3:126, 5:759, 5:763, 5:819

The Biographer's Gift: Life, Histories, and Humanism, 1:929

Biographia Literaria, 1:286, 1:287, 1:307

Biographical Dictionary of Afro-American and African Musicians, 3:658

Biographical Dictionary of American Architects (Deceased), 3:764

Biographical Dictionary of American Cult and Sect Leaders, 4:6, 4:854

Biographical Dictionary of American Journalism, 3:807

Biographical Dictionary of American Music, 3:654

Biographical Dictionary of American Science, 5:28

Biographical Dictionary of British Radicals in the Seventeenth Century, 4:734

Biographical Dictionary of Dance, 3:732

Biographical Dictionary of Jazz, 3:654

The Biographical Dictionary of Scientists (Abbott), 5:4

A Biographical Dictionary of Scientists (Williams), 5:30

The Biographical Dictionary of Scientists: Engineers and Inventors, 5:215

The Biographical Dictionary of Scientists: Physicists, 5:652

A Biographical Dictionary of the Characters in the Fiction of Henry James, 1:767

Biographical Dictionary of World War II, 3:281

Biographical Directory, 3:169

Biographical Directory of American Colonial and Revolutionary Governers, 1607–1789, 3:507

Biographical Directory of Fellows and Members, 3:169

Biographical Directory of the American Psychiatric Association, 5:414

Biographical Directory of the United States Congress, 1774–1989, 3:505

Biographical Directory of the United States Executive Branch, 1774–1989, 3:505

Biographical Encyclopedia of Scientists, 5:4, 5:28

Biographical History of Philosophy, 1:372, 1:373

The Biographical History of Philosophy from Its Origin in Greece down to the Present Day, 4:17, 4:161

A Biographical Index of British Engineers in the 19th Century, 5:216

Biographies of Meng Hao-jan, 2:215

Biography, 1:429

Biography: The Craft and the Calling, 1:86, 1:928

Biography Almanac, 3:7

Biography and Genealogy Master Index, 1:85

Biography and Truth, 1:929

Biography Index, 1:85, 1:126

Biography of an Atom, 5:162

A Biography of Philosophy, 4:17

Biological Aspects of Mental Disorder, 5:428

Biological Bases of Individual Behavior, 3:171

Biological Efficiency in Agriculture, 5:264

Biological Psychology, 3:168, 3:171

The Biological Roots of Human Nature, 3:171

Biological Science, 5:764

Biological Studies of Mental Processes, 3:170

A Biologist Remembers, 5:832

Biology, 5:763

Biology and Feminism: A Dynamic Interaction, 5:188

Biology and Knowledge, 3:266

The Biology Coloring Book, 5:764

Biology in the Nineteenth Century, 5:45

Biology of Amphibians, 5:770

Biology of Microorganisms, 5:783

The Biology of the Spirit, 5:811

Biomass as Fuel, 5:290

The Biomedical Basis of Gerontology, 5:316

Biomedical Ethics, 5:118, 5:122

Biometrika Tables for Statisticians, 5:531

Biophilia, 5:117, 5:819

Bio-Pics: How Hollywood Constructed Public History, 3:825

The Bio-Plan for Lifelong Weight Control, 5:327

Biosphere Politics: A New Consciousness for a New Century, 5:824

Biotechnics and Society: The Rise of Industrial Genetics, 5:75

Biotechnological Control of Plant Pathogens, 5:222

Biotechnology, 5:222

Biotechnology: Principles and Applications, 5:222

Biotechnology: Strategies for Life, 5:221

Biotechnology and Nutrition, 5:222

Biotechnology and Society: A Bibliography, 5:76

Biotechnology and the Human Genome: Innovations and Impact, 5:77

The Biotechnology Directory 1990, 5:732

Biotechnology in a Global Economy, 5:185

Biotechnology in Food Processing, 5:221, 5:267

Bird: The Legend of Charlie Parker, 3:708

Bird Behavior, 5:825

The Birder's Handbook, 5:831

A Bird in the House, 2:916, 2:917

Bird Lives: The High Life and Hard Times of Charlie (Yardbird) Parker, 3:708

Bird Migration, 5:826

Bird of the East, 2:64
The Birds (Aristophanes), 2:353
The Birds (Hitchcock), 1:1168
The Birds (McBain), 1:1233
Birds (Perse), 2:493
The Birds (Vesaas), 2:669
The Birds Fall Down, 1:566
The Birds Have Also Gone: A Novel, 2:99
Birds in Jeopardy, 5:769, 5:831
The Bird's Nest, 1:992
The Birds of America (Audubon), 5:786
Birds of America (McCarthy), 1:1007, 1:1008
Birds of Heaven, and Other Stories, 2:732
Birds through a Ceiling of Alabaster: Three Abbasid Poets, 2:58, 2:62
The Birnbaum Haggadah, 4:599
The Birodoa Plays, 2:133
The Birth and Death of the Miracle Man, 2:980
Birth and Development of the Geological Sciences, 5:32, 5:622
The Birth and Rebirth of Pictorial Space, 5:195
Birth at Dawn, 2:118
Birth Control in Jewish Law, 4:598, 4:895
Birth Control Technologies: Prospects by the Year 2000, 5:358
Birthday Book for Children, 1:585
The Birthday Party, 1:414, 1:534
The Birth of a Dilemma: Conflict and Settlement of Rhodesia, 3:424
The Birth of a Father, 3:207
The Birth of a Nation, 1:792, 1:1165, 1:1167, 1:1172
The Birth of a New Physics, 5:15, 5:41
The Birth of Modern Comedy of Manners, 2:364
The Birth of Pandora and the Division of Knowledge, 1:225
The Birth of Particle Physics, 5:662, 5:717
The Birth of Popular Heresy, 4:700
The Birth of Purgatory, 4:697
Birth of Reason and Other Essays, 4:326

The Birth of Romance: An Anthology, 1:148
The Birth of the Bill of Rights, 1776–1791, 3:541
Birth of the Clinic, 4:400
Birth of the Clinic: An Archaeology of Medical Perception, 5:78, 5:87, 5:443
The Birth of the Middle Ages, 3:395–814, 3:328
The Birth of the Nation, 3:522, 3:596
The Birth of the Palestinian Refugee Problem, 1947–1949, 3:440
The Birth of the Republic, 1763–1789, 3:521, 3:587
The Birth of the Talkies: From Edison to Jolson, 3:825
The Birth of Tragedy (and The Genealogy of Morals), 4:246
The Birth of Tragedy out of the Spirit of Music, 4:245
The Birth of Western Canada, 3:615
Birth Stories: The Experience Remembered, 5:357
The Bishop in the Church: Patristic Texts on the Role of the Episkopos, 4:688
Bishop of Everywhere: Bernard Shaw and the Life Force, 1:546
The Bishops and the Bomb: Waging Peace in a Nuclear Age, 5:109
Bismarck: The Man and the Statesman, 3:341, 3:409
Bismarck and the German Empire, 3:341, 3:376
Bit by Bit: An Illustrated History of Computers, 5:539
Bits and Pieces: The Ray Bradbury Bibliography, 1974–88, 1:1255
The Bitter Air of Exile: Russian Writers in the West, 1922–1972, 2:692
A Bitter Fate, 2:748
Bitter Fruit: The Untold Story of the American Coup in Guatemala, 3:637
Bitter Healing, 2:566
The Bitter Heritage: Vietnam and American Democracy, 1941–1966, 3:597
The Bitter Honeymoon, 2:429
Bitter Lemons, 1:469, 1:470
Bitter Medicine, 1:1235

The Bitter Woods: A Comprehensive Study of the War in Europe, 3:278
Black, White, and Southern, 3:555
The Black Aesthetic, 1:913
Black Africa, 2:110
Black Africa: The Economic and Cultural Basis for a Federated State, 3:428
Black African Literature in English: A Guide to Information Sources, 2:110
Black African Literature in English: 1982–1986, 2:110
Black African Literature in English: 1977–1981, 2:110
Black African Literature in English since 1952, 2:106
Black American Playwrights, 1:1800 to the Present: A Bibliography, 1:123
Black Americans' Views of Racial Inequality: The Dream Deferred, 3:212
Black American Writers Past and Present, 1:128
Black American Writing from the Nadir, 1:713
Black and Red, 3:578
Black and White Keys, 2:914
The Black Arrow, 1:396, 1:589
Black Artists in the United States, 3:761
Black Athena, 4:446
Black Australia: An Anthology of Aboriginal Poetry, 2:947
Black Authors: A Selected Annotated Bibliography, 1:127
The Black Band, or, The Mysteries of Midnight, 1:332
Black-Belt Diamonds, 1:785
Blackberry Winter: My Earlier Years, 3:36
Black Biography: 1790–1950, 1:85
Black Bo, 2:22
The Blackboard Jungle, 1:1233
Black-Body Theory and the Quantum Discontinuity, 1894–1912, 4:406, 5:48, 5:53
The Black Book, 1:469, 2:727
Black Bourgeoisie, 3:226, 3:547
Black Boy, 1:905

Black Byzantium: The Kingdom of Nupe in Nigeria, 3:26

Black Child Care, 5:416

Black Choreographers Moving: A National Dialogue, 3:734

Black Chronology: From 4,000 B.C. to the Abolition of the Slave Trade, 1:88

The Black Church in America, 4:748

The Black Church in the African American Experience, 4:748

The Black Cliffs, 2:641

Black Colleges and Universities: Challenges for the Future, 3:254

The Black Council, 2:839

Black Crane: An Anthology of Korean Literature, 2:299

Black Culture and Black Consciousness, 3:556, 3:867

Black Dance in the United States from 1619 to Today, 3:733

The Black Death, 3:332, 3:358

The Black Docker, 2:145

Black Drama of the Federal Theatre Era: Beyond the Formal Horizons, 1:1072

The Black Eel, 2:237

Black-Eyed Susan, 1:366

Blackeyes, 1:535

The Black Family in Slavery and Freedom, 1750–1925, 3:555

Black Feminist Criticism: Perspectives on Black Women Writers, 1:924

Black Feminist Thought, 1:1131

The Black Flame: A Trilogy, 1:832

Black Folk Art in America, 1930–1980, 3:867

Black Folktales, 3:867

Black Folk Then and Now, 1:831, 3:577

Blackfoot Lodge Tales: The Story of a Prairie People, 3:865

The Black Gulf, 2:747

The Black Heart: A Voyage into Central Africa, 3:903

The Black Heart's Truth: The Early Career of W. D. Howells, 1:759

The Black Heralds, 2:885, 2:886

The Black Hermit, 2:154

Black Holes, Gravitational Waves and Cosmology, 5:719

Black Holes, Quasars, and the Universe, 5:594

Black Holes and Baby Universes and Other Essays, 5:16, 5:607, 5:692

Black Holes and Warped Spacetime, 5:655

Black Humor Fiction of the Sixties, 1:920

The Black Hunter, 4:447

The Black Insider and Other Fragments, 2:165

Black Is My Truelove's Hair, 1:876

Black Is the Color of My True Love's Heart, 1:608

Black Is the Color of My TV Tube, 3:808

The Black Jacobins, 3:637, 3:648

Black Lamb and Grey Falcon: A Journey through Yugoslavia, 1:565

Black Leaders of the Twentieth Century, 3:506, 3:579

Black Letter Primer: An Introduction to Gothic Alphabets, 1:19

Black Light, 1:1000

Black Lightning, 2:937

Black Literature and Literary Theory, 1:1133, 1:1144, 1:1145

Black Literature Criticism, 1:713

Black Literature for High School Students, 1:954

Black Magic Poetry: Collected Poetry, 1961–67, 1:941

Blackmail, 1:1168

Black Majority, 3:519

Black Manhattan, 1:771

The Black Man's Burden: Africa and the Curse of the Nation State, 3:427

The Black Mind: A History of African Literature, 2:107

Black Mischief, 1:562

Black Mother: The African Slave Trade, 3:523

Black Music in America: A Bibliography, 3:867

The Black Muslims in America, 4:571, 4:862

Blackness and Race Mixture, 3:635

Black No More, 1:879

Black North in 1901: A Social Study, 3:577

Black Novelist as White Racist, 1:1173

Black Novelists and the Southern Literary Tradition, 1:919, 1:724

The Black Obelisk, 2:606

Black Odyssey: The Afro-American Ordeal in Slavery, 3:555

Black Poets of the United States, 1:914, 1:955

Black Politicians and Reconstruction in Georgia, 3:527

Black Popular Culture, 3:874

Black Power: A Record of Reactions in a Land of Pathos, 1:906, 1:905

The Black Prince, 1:523

Black Radio in Los Angeles, Chicago, and New York: A Bibliography, 3:811

Black Rain, 2:287

Black Rainbow: Legends of the Incas and Myths of Ancient Peru, 2:848

Black Reconstruction in America, 1860–1880, 1:832, 3:527, 3:577

Black Religions in the New World, 4:468

Black Religious Leaders: Conflict in Unity, 4:748

Black Rock Mining Folklore of the Pennsylvania Dutch, 3:859

Blacks, 1:954

The Blacks: A Clown Story, 2:478

Blacks and Media: A Selected, Annotated Bibliography, 1962–1982, 3:802

Blacks and Whites: Narrowing the Gap?, 3:209

Blacks and White TV: Afro-Americans in Television Since 1948, 3:812

Black Sects and Cults, 4:749

Black Separatism in the United States, 4:862

The Black Sheep, 1:347

Blacks in America: Bibliographic Essays, 3:586

The Blacks in America, 1492–1977: A Chronology and Fact Book, 3:507

Blacks in American Films and Television: An Encyclopedia, 3:825

Blacks in Antiquity: Ethiopians in the Greco-Roman Experience, 3:299

Blacks in Bondage: Letters of American Slaves, 3:525

The Blacks in Canada: A History, 3:607

Blacks in Hispanic Literature: Critical Essays, 2:845

Blacks in the White Establishment?, 3:214

Black Sister: Poetry by Black American Women, 1:720

Black Skin, White Masks, 2:121

The Black Snow, 2:705

Black Song, 3:661

Blacks on Television: A Selectively Annotated Bibliography, 3:811

Black Southern Voices, 1:921

Black Spring, 1:861

Black Star: A View of the Life and Times of Kwame Nkrumah, 3:427

Black Sunlight, 2:165

Black Theater, U.S.A.: Forty-Five Plays by Black Americans, 1847–1974, 1:1078

Black Theology: A Documentary History, 1966–1979, 4:749, 4:896

Black Theology: U.S.A. and South Africa, 4:748

Black Theology and Black Power, 4:763

Black Theology in Dialogue, 4:748

A Black Theology of Liberation, 4:748, 4:763

Black Theology Today: Liberation and Contextualization, 4:748

Black Thunder: Gabriel's Revolt: Virginia, 1:1800, 1:816, 1:817

The Black Underclass, 3:212

The Black Unicorn, 1:1190

Black Walls and Other Stories, 2:254

Black Water: A Novel, 1:1022

The Blackwell Companion to the American Revolution, 3:508

Blackwell's, 1879–1979: The History of a Family Firm, 1:39

Black Women in American History: From Colonial Times through the Nineteenth Century, 3:508

Black Women in American History: The Twentieth Century, 3:508

Black Women in White America: A Documentary History, 3:556

Black Women Writers at Work, 1:1019

Blackwoods, 1:324

Blackwood's Magazine, 1:366

Black Words, White Page: Aboriginal Literature 1929-1988, 2:946

Black Writers, White Audiences, 2:107

Black Writers in Latin America, 2:846

Black Writers of America: A Comprehensive Anthology, 1:653, 1:717, 1:725, 1:718

The Black Years of Soviet Jewry: 1939–1953, 4:636

Blade Runner, 1:1256, 1:1257

Blade Runner: A Movie, 1:957

Blades of Mars, 1:616

Blaise Pascal, 4:185

Blake: Prophet against Empire, 1:279

A Blake Dictionary: The Ideas and Symbols of William Blake, 1:279

Blake's Apocalypse, 1:278

Blake's Four Zoas: The Design of a Dream, 1:279

Blake's Job, 1:277

Blame, 2:885

Blaming Technology: The Irrational Search for Scapegoats, 5:70, 5:166, 5:253

Blaming the Victim, 3:212

Blaming the Victims: Spurious Scholarship and the Palestinian Question, 3:460

Blast and Counterblast, 4:735

Blasting and Bombardiering: An Autobiography, 1914–1926, 1:514

Blasts and Benedictions, 1:527

Blazing the Trail: Way Marks in the Exploration of Symbols, 3:41

Bleak House, 1:292, 1:348

Blessed Are You: Traditional Jewish Prayers for Children, 4:599

Blessed Rage for Order: The New Pluralism in Theology, 4:746

The Blessing Way, 1:1231

Blind Date, 1:1002

The Blind Devotion of the People: Religion and the English Reformation, 4:727

The Blindman's World and Other Stories, 1:734

The Blind Man Traces the Circle, 1:282

The Blind Musician, 2:732

Blindness, 1:487

Blindness and Autobiography: al-Ayyam of Taha Husayn, 2:74

Blindness and Insight, 1:966, 1:1142

Blindness and Visual Handicap: The Facts, 5:383

The Blind Owl, 2:90

The Blind Owl Forty Years After, 2:90

The Blind Watchmaker, 5:763

Blind White Fish in Persia, 3:905

Bliss, 2:951

Bliss and Other Stories, 2:978

Bliss Carman: A Reappraisal, 2:909

Bliss Carman: Quest and Revolt, 2:909

The Blithedale Romance, 1:674, 1:675

Blithe Spirit, 1:464, 1:465

Blix, 1:776

The Blob That Ate Oaxaca and Other Travel Tales, 3:901

The Blockbuster Complex, 1:51

Blonde Venus, 1:1176

Blood: The River of Life, 5:342

Blood and Tears, 2:325

Blood Disorders: The Facts, 5:385

Bloodhounds of Heaven, 1:270

Blood Knot, 2:161

The Blood of Abraham: Insights into the Middle East, 3:435

Blood of a Poet and the Testament of Orpheus, 3:834

The Blood of the Walsungs, 2:644

Blood of Unrequited Love, 2:880

Blood on the Dining-Room Floor: A Murder Mystery, 1:881

The Blood Oranges, 1:985

Blood Red, Sister Rose, 2:957

Bloods: An Oral History of the Vietnam War by Black Veterans, 3:540

Bloodshed, 1:1027

Bloodshed and Three Novellas, 1:1027

Blood Shot, 1:1235

A Bloodsmoor Romance, 1:1022

Blood Wedding, 2:538

The Bloody Chamber, 1:455

The Bloody Countess, 2:880

The Bloody Hoa, 2:46

Bloody Mary, 4:726

Blooming and Contending: Chinese Literature in the Post-Mao Era, 2:233

The Bloom in Spanish American Literature: A Personal History, 2:845

Bloomsbury: A House of Lions, 1:414

Bloomsbury's Prophet, 4:312

Blow Softly in Jericho, 2:21

Blow-Up and Other Stories, 2:861

The Blue and Brown Books, 4:343

The Blue and the Gray, 3:527, 3:572

The Blue Angel, 1:1176

Bluebeard, 1:583

The Blue Bedroom and Other Stories, 1:621

Blue Boy, 2:480

The Blue Dahlia, 1:1228

Blue Dragon White Tiger: Taoist Rites of Passage, 4:528

Blue Estuaries: Poems, 1:952

The Blue Fairy Book, 1:577, 1:579, 3:883

Blue Fire, 1:1238

The Blue Flowers, 2:496

The Blue Hammer, 1:1235

Blue Highways: A Journey into America, 3:896

The Blue Hotel and Other Stories (Maggie and Other Stories), 1:741

The Blue House, 2:242

The Blue Mother, 2:659

The Blue Mountains of China, 2:927

The Blue Nile, 3:422

Blueprint for a Cell: An Essay on the Nature and Origin of Life, 5:775

The Blue Room, 2:508

Blues, Ideology, and Afro-American Literature, 1:937, 1:1131, 1:1137

Blues for Bonnie, 2:320

Blues for Mister Charlie, 1:938, 1:939, 1:1084

Bluesland: Portraits of Twelve Major American Blues Masters, 3:669

The Bluesman, 3:668

The Bluest Eye, 1:1018

The Bluestocking Circle, 1:226

The Blue Swallows, 1:1021

Blundering to Glory: Napoleon's Military Campaigns, 3:339

Boarding House Blues, 1:833

Boards and Buckram, 1:47

The Boat in the Evening, 2:669

A Boat Load of Home Folk, 2:949

The Boatman, 2:919

The Boat of Longing: A Novel, 2:667

Bobby Deerfield, 2:607

Boccaccio, 2:410

The Bodhgaya Interviews, 4:560

Bodian's Publishing Desk Reference, 1:46

Bodies and Souls, 1:1191

Bodily Harm, 2:906

Bodin: On Sovereignty, 4:134

The Body: Toward an Eastern Mind-Body Theory, 4:367

Body, Boots, and Britches, 3:859

Body, Mind, and Spirit: The Journey toward Health and Wholeness, 5:318

Body, Movement, and Culture, 3:733

The Body and Society, 3:208

Body and Soul, 1:1172

The Body at Thirty: A Woman Doctor Talks to Women, 5:355

The Body Divine, 4:337

The Body Electric: Electromagnetism and the Foundation of Life, 5:318

Body Guards: The Cultural Politics of Gender Ambiguity, 1:1183

Body Healing, 5:320

The Body in Interpersonal Relations: Merleau-Ponty, 4:311

Body Language, 1:437

The Body Machine: Your Health in Perspective, 5:339

The Body of Beatrice, 2:418

The Body of Faith: God in the People Israel, 4:885

The Body of Faith: Judaism as Corporeal Election, 4:649

The Body Shop: Bionic Revolutions in Medicine, 5:370

Body Snatcher, 2:876

Body-Text in Julia Kristeva: Religion, Women, and Psychoanalysis, 4:892

The Boer War, 3:364

Boethius, 4:112

Boethius: The Consolations of Music, Logic, Theology and Philosophy, 4:112

The Bog People, 1:494

The Bohemian Register, 1:910

Bohin Manor, 2:815

Boi, 2:145

Bolívar, 3:632

Bolivia: The Evolution of a Multi-Ethnic Society, 3:633

Bolshevik Salute: A Modernist Chinese Novel, 2:267

Bolshevism: Practice and Theory, 4:322

The Bolshoi Ballet, 3:734

Bolts of Melody, 1:745

Bomb: Indonesian Short Stories, 2:318

The Bonanza Kings, 3:548

Bonaventure: A Prose Pastoral of Acadian Louisiana, 1:736

Bond: A Study of His Plays, 1:446

Bond on File, 1:446

The Bonds of Interest, 2:531

The Bonds of Love, 3:217

The Bone People, 2:976, 2:977

Bones of the Cuttlefish: Selected Poems in Translation, 2:428

Bonhoeffer's Ethic of Discipleship, 4:760

Bonifaz Caballero, Oscar, 2:861

Bonnie Prince Charlie, 3:368

Bontshe the Silent, 2:42

The Book, 2:486

The Book: Art and Object, 1:26

The Book: Its History and Development, 1:36

The Book: On the Taboo Against Knowing Who You Are, 4:881, 5:424

The Book: The Story of Printing and Bookmaking, 1:9, 1:63

A Book about Myself, 1:829

Book Auction Records 1988–1989, Vol. 86, 1:78

Bookbanning in America: Who Bans Books?—And Why?, 1:57

The Book before Printing: Ancient, Medieval, and Oriental, 1:36

Bookbinders and Their Craft, 1:26

Bookbinding, 1:23

Bookbinding: A Guide to the Literature, 1:62

Bookbinding: A Manual for Those Interested in the Craft of Bookbinding, 1:25

Bookbinding: Its Background and Technique, 1:23

Bookbinding, and the Care of Books, 1:22

Bookbinding and the Conservation of Books, 1:26

The Bookbinding Career of Rachel McMasters Miller Hunt, 1:27

Bookbinding for Amateurs, 1:22

Bookbinding in America, 1:24

Bookbinding in America: Three Essays, 1:23

Bookbinding in America 1680–1910, 1:22

Bookbinding in Early America: Seven Essays on Masters and Methods, 1:23

Bookbinding in England and France, 1:23

Bookbindings, 1:23

The Bookbindings of T. J. Cobden-Sanderson, 1:26

Book Buyer's Handbook, 1:52

Book Bytes: The User's Guide to 1200 Microcomputer Books, 5:540

Book Collecting, 1:31

Book Collecting: A Beginner's Guide, 1:34

Book Collecting: A Comprehensive Guide, 1:30, 1:76

Book Collecting: A Modern Guide, 1:33, 1:76

Book Collecting: An Introduction to Modern Methods of Literary and Bibliographical Detection, 1:31

Book Collecting: Four Broadcast Talks, 1:31

The Book-Collector, 1:32

The Book Collector's Handbook of Values 1982–83, 1:78

A Book Concluding with As a Wife Has a Cow: A Love Story, 1:881

Bookdealers in North America, 1:77

Book Design: Systematic Aspects, 1:10

Book Design: Text Format Models, 1:10

Book Distribution in the United States: Issues and Perspectives, 1:45

The Book-eddling Person, 1:45

Booker T. Washington, 1:785, 3:555

Booker T. Washington: Leader and Educator, 3:270

Booker T. Washington, Educator and Interracial Interpreter, 1:785

Booker T. Washington, Vol. 1: The Making of a Black Leader, 1856–1901, 1:785

Booker T. Washington and His Critics, 1:785, 3:270, 3:578

Booker T. Washington and the Adult Education Movement, 3:270

Booker T. Washington and the Negro's Place in American Life, 1:786

Booker T. Washington in Perspective: Essays of Louis R. Harlan, 1:786

The Book Fancier, or The Romance of Book Collecting, 1:32

Book Hunter's Holiday: Adventures with Books and Manuscripts, 1:33

Book Illustration, 1:28

Book Illustration of the 20th Century, 1:29

The Book in America, 1:38

Book Industry Trends, 1:47

Book Making in Diderot's Encyclopédie, 1:6

The Bookman's Glossary, 1:53, 1:69

A Bookman's Holiday, 1:32

Bookman's Holiday: The Private Satisfactions of an Incurable Collector, 1:34

The Bookman's Price Index, Vol. 48, 1:78

Bookman's Progress, 1:33

The Book Marketing Handbook, 1:46

The Book of America: Inside the 50 States Today, 3:507

The Book of American Negro Poetry, 1:720

Book of Americans, 1:815

The Book of a Thousand Plays, 1:123

The Book of Beliefs and Opinions, 4:672

The Book of Calendars, 1:87

The Book of Cats, 1:516

The Book of Changes, 2:62

The Book of Common Prayer (Cranmer), 1:162, 4:764, 4:773

A Book of Common Prayer (Didion), 1:968

The Book of Concord: The Confessions of the Evangelical Lutheran Church, 4:779

The Book of Concord: Thoreau's Life as a Writer, 1:702

Book of Curtesye, 1:575

The Book of Daniel, 1:968, 1:969

The Book of Dede Korkut, 2:96

The Book of Disquiet, 2:560

The Book of Dreams, 1:998

The Book of Examples, 4:584

The Book of Fantasy, 2:856

Book of Fire: Stories, 2:42

Book of Friends: A Tribute to Friends of Long Ago, 1:861

The Book of God: A Response to the Bible, 4:816

The Book of Good Love, 2:548, 2:549

The Book of Henry James; Appropriating the Classics, 1:767

Book of History, Book of Songs, Spring and Autumn Annals, Book of Rites, 4:524

The Book of IBM Software, 5:557

The Book of Indian Crafts and Indian Lore, 3:865

A Book of Ireland, 1:527

The Book of Irish Verse, 1:418

The Book of J, 1:1138

The Book of Jamaica, 1:940

The Book of Jewish Belief, 4:596

The Book of Jewish Books: A Reader's Guide to Judaism, 4:601

A Book of Jewish Ethical Concepts, 4:598

The Book of Job: Commentary, New Translation and Special Studies, 4:821

Book of Joyous Children, 1:777

The Book of Knowledge, 4:582, 4:667

The Book of Laughter and Forgetting, 2:793

The Book of Legends, 2:16

The Book of Life, 4:140

The Book of Light, 1:1032

The Book of Lists #3, 1:87

The Book of Lost Tales, 1:559

The Book of Margery Kempe, 1:146, 1:152

The Book of Masks, 2:303

Book of Mercy, 2:909

Book of Mormon, 1:659, 4:845, 4:846, 4:878, 4:879

Book of Negro Humor, 1:848, 3:866

Book of New England Legends and Folk Lore, 3:858

A Book of New Zealand Verse: 1923–45, 2:973

The Book of Nightmares, 1:1000, 1:1001

The Book of Odes, 2:194

Book of Paradise: The Wonderful Adventures of Shmuel Aba-Abervo, 2:40

The Book of Promethea, 2:467

The Book of Questions, 2:874

The Book of Religious and Philosophical Sects, 4:583

The Book of Repulsive Women, 1:812, 1:813

The Book of Saints, 4:719

The Book of Sand, 2:856

A Book of Scripts, 1:15

Book of Sin: From Golden Salakot to Red Hat, 2:330

The Book of Snobs, 1:403

The Book of Songs (McNoughton), 2:195

The Book of Songs (Waley), 2:185, 2:186, 2:187, 2:194

The Book of the Archpriest of Hita, 2:549

The Book of the Courtier, 2:413

The Book of the Dead (Egyptian), 2:115

Book of the Dead (Allen), 4:548

The Book of the Dead: The Papyrus of Ani in the British Museum, 2:53

The Book of the Duchess, 1:149

Book of the Eskimos, 3:921

The Book of the Glory of the Black Race, 2:66

The Book of the Goddess Past and Present, 4:506, 4:530, 4:536

The Book of Thel: A Facsimile and a Critical Text, 1:278

The Book of the Piano, 3:671

Book of the States, 1:110

The Book of the Subtyle Historyes and Fables of Esope, 1:575

Book of the Universal Concord, 4:361

The Book of the Violin, 3:671

The Book of Three, 1:1195

The Book of True Love, 2:549

The Book of Urizen, 1:278

A Book of Verse, 1:617

A Book of Women Poets from Antiquity to Now, 2:4, 2:377

Book of Wonder, 1:615

Book of Words, 1:371

The Book of World Famous Music: Classical, Popular and Folk, 3:655

Book of World Religions, 4:572

Book Publishers' Legal Guide, 1:47

Book Publishing: A Basic Introduction, 1:47

Book Publishing: What It Is, What It Does, 1:47

Book Publishing in America, 1:38

Book Publishing in the U.S.S.R., 1:48

Book Review Digest, 1:73, 1:112

Book Review Digest Author/Title Index, 1905–1984, 1:112

Book Review Index, 1:112

Books: From Writer to Reader, 1:47

Books: The Culture and Commerce of Publishing, 1:49, 3:202, 3:203

Books: Their History, Art, Power, Glory, Infamy, and Suffering, 1:31

Books, Libraries, and Research, 1:61

Books about Books, A Biobibliography for Collectors, 1:34

Books and Bidders: The Adventures of a Bibliophile, 1:33

Books and Book-Collecting, 1:31

Books and Bookmen, 1:32

Books and Book People in 19th-Century America, 1:38

Books and Collectors, 1:31

Books and Documents: Dating, Permanence and Preservation, 1:62

Books and History, 1:31

Books and Printing: A Treasury for Typophiles, 1:6

Books and Readers in Ancient Greece and Rome, 1:37

Books and Society in History, 1:36

Books and Their Readers in Eighteenth-Century England, 1:226

Book Selection and Censorship in the Sixties, 1:57

Bookselling, Reviewing and Reading, 1:49

Bookselling in America and the World, 1:39

Bookselling in Britain, 1:36

Books for College Libraries: A Core Collection of 50,000 Titles, 1:73, 3:273

Books for Public Libraries, 1:73

Books for the Millions, 1:8

Books in Action: The Armed Services Editions, 1:38

Books in Black or Red, 1:33

Books in My Baggage: Adventures in Reading and Collecting, 1:33

The Books in My Life, 1:861, 1:862

Books in Our Future: A Report from the Librarian of Congress to the Congress, 1:49

Books in Our Future: Perspectives and Proposals, 1:49

Books in Print, 1:71, 1:112

Books in Print, 1993–94, 1:52

Books in Print Supplement, 1:71

Books in Series 1985–1989, 1:112

Books in World History: A Guide for Teachers and Students, 3:273

Books of Blood, 1:599

Books of the Polish Nation, 2:817

Books That Changed America, 1:31

Books That Changed Our Minds, 1:822

Books That Changed the World, 1:31, 1:75

Books That Made a Difference: What People Told Us, 1:34

Bookstore Planning and Design, 1:48

The Book Today in Africa, 2:110

The Book Trade of the World, 1:37, 1:69

Book Traveler, 1:46

The Boom in Spanish-American Literature: A Personal History, 2:864

Border Beagles: A Tale of Mississippi, 1:696

Border Crossings, 1917–1934, 2:684

The Borderers, 1:271, 1:306

Borderland: Origins of the American Suburb, 1820–1939, 3:553

Borderlands—La Frontera: The New Mestiza, 1:1130, 1:1136

A Border of Blue, 3:897

The Border Town and Other Stories, 2:262

Borges and His Fiction: A Guide to His Mind and Art, 2:857

Borges and the Kabbalah and Other Essays on His Fiction and Poetry, 2:857

Borges on Writing, 2:857

Borges Revisited, 2:857

Borges the Poet, 2:857

Boris Godunov, 2:750, 2:751

Boris Pasternak: A Literary Biography: Volume One: 1890–1928, 2:746

Boris Pasternak: Essays, 2:746

Boris Pasternak: His Life and Art, 2:746

Boris Pasternak: The Poet and His Politics, 2:746

Boris Pasternak and His Times, 2:746

Boris Pasternak's Translations of Shakespeare, 2:746

Boris Pilnyak: Scythian at a Typewriter, 2:748

Born at Risk, 5:375

Born for Liberty: A History of Women in America, 3:513

Born in the Gardens, 1:525

Born in Tibet, 4:357

Born of the Same Roots: Stories of Modern Chinese Women, 2:234

Born Too Soon: Preterm Birth and Early Development, 5:322

Born to Sing: An Interpretation and World Survey of Bird Song, 4:288

Borodin and Liszt, 3:683

The Borough, 1:289

Borrowed Time: Artificial Organs and the Politics of Extending Lives, 5:370

Borstal Boy, 1:441

The Borzoi Anthology of Latin American Literature, 2:850

The Borzoi Book of French Folk Tales, 3:854

Bosnian Chronicle, 2:828

The Bosnian Story, 2:828

Bosoms and Neglect, 1:1090

The Boss: J. Edgar Hoover and the Great American Inquisition, 3:544

The Boss Girl: A Christmas Story, and Other Sketches, 1:778

Boss Kettering, 5:226

Boston: A Documentary Novel of the Sacco-Vanzetti Case, 1:880

The Boston Book Market, 1679–1700, 1:38

The Bostonians, 1:762

Boston's Immigrants: A Study of Acculturation, 3:581

Boston Studies in the Philosophy of Science, 5:700

Boswell: A Modern Comedy, 1:973

Boswell's Literary Art, 1:235

Botany: A Brief Introduction to Plant Biology, 5:768

Botchan, 2:291

The Bothie: The Text of 1848, 1:345

Both Your Houses, 1:1081

Botswana: A Short Political History, 3:424

The Botteghe Oscure Reader, 2:403

Bought and Sold, 2:429

Boundaries: Psychological Man in Revolution, 5:414

The Boundaries of Fiction: Carlyle, Macaulay, Newman, 1:325

The Boundaries of Genre, 2:716

Boundaries of Love: And Other Stories, 1:1040

Boundaries of the Self: Gender, Culture, Fiction, 1:919

Boundary and Space: An Introduction to the Work of D. W. Winnicott, 5:472

The Bounds of Race: Perspectives on Hegemony and Resistance, 1:1134

The Bounds of Reason: Cervantes, Dostoevsky, Flaubert, 2:535

The Bounds of Sense, 4:207, 4:414

Bound to Be Read, 1:42

Bound to Lead: The Changing Nature of American Power, 3:145

Bound to Violence, 2:144

Bourbaki, 5:500

Bourbon Spain: Seventeen Hundred to Eighteen Hundred Eight, 3:387

The Bourgeois Mind and Other Essays, 4:758

The Bourgeois Poet, 1:1045

The Bournonville Heritage, 3:739

The Bournonville School, 3:739

Bouvard and Pécuchet, 2:475

Bove-bukh, 2:28

The Bow and the Lyre: The Poem, 2:879

The Bowel Book: A Practical Guide to Good Health, 5:340, 5:384

The Bowels of the Earth, 5:629

Bowen's Court, 1:447

Bowker (R. R.) Memorial Lectures, 1:49

Bowker Annual Library and Book Trade Almanac, 1:51, 1:52, 1:70

Bowker's Complete Sourcebook of Personal Computing 1985, 5:539

The Bowl of Heaven, 4:860

Box of Delights: When the Wolves Were Running, 1:519

The Boy Castaways of Black Lake Island, 1:329

The Boy Changed into a Stag: Selected Poems, 1949–1967, 2:800

The Boy Changed into a Stag Cries Out at the Gate of Secrets, 2:800

The Boy David, 1:329

Boyhood on the Upper Mississippi: A Reminiscent Letter, 3:928

Boyhood with Gurdjieff, 4:876

The Boy in the Bush, 1:509

Boy's Life, 1:1242

The Boys on the Bus: Riding with the Campaign Press Corps, 3:806

A Boy's Town, 1:758

Bracebridge Hall: or, The Humourists, 1:679, 1:680

Bracebridge Hall, Tales of a Traveller, and The Alhambra, 1:680

Bradley's Moral Psychology, 4:221

Bradwardine and the Pelagians, 4:104

Brahma Sutra: The Philosophy of Spiritual Life, 4:353

The Brahmo Samaj and the Shaping of the Modern Indian Mind, 4:355

Brahms, 3:684

Brahms Letters, 1853–1896, 3:684

The Braided Dream: Robert Penn Warren's Late Poetry, 1:894

Braided Lives: An Anthology of Multicultural American Writing, 1:795

The Brain, 5:342, 5:773

The Brain: A User's Manual, 5:340

Brain, Mind, and Behavior, 5:339

Brain, Mind, and Computers, 5:202

Brainfood, 5:345

Brain Matters, 5:313

The Brain of Robert Frost: A Cognitive Approach to Literature, 1:842

Brainstorms, 4:396

Brainstorms: Philosophical Essays on Mind and Psychology, 5:74, 5:571

The Brainwashing/Deprogramming Controversy, 4:856

Brakes, 5:248

The Branch Will Not Break, 1:1067

Brand, 2:665, 2:666

The Brandeis/Frankfurter Connection, 3:543

Brander Matthews, Theodore Roosevelt, and the Politics of American Literature, 1880–1920, 1:794

A Brand New Life, 1:833

The Brass Butterfly, 1:484

The Brass Check: A Study of American Journalism, 1:880

Brassneck, 1:449

The Brass Serpent, 2:17

Brats, 1:997

Brave New World, 1:498, 1:499, 5:563

Brave New World Revisited, 1:499

Braving the Elements, 1:1015

The Bravo: A Tale, 1:662

Bravo of Venice, A Romance, 1:602

Brawny Wycherley, 1:263

Brazil, 1:950

Brazil: An Interpretation, 3:645

Brazil: Politics in a Patrimonial Society, 3:634

Brazilian Literature (Goldberg), 2:890

Brazilian Literature (Hulet), 2:890

Brazilian Literature: An Outline, 2:890

Brazilian Poetry (1950–1980), 2:891

Brazil on the Move, 1:828

Brazil's New Novel; Four Northeastern Masters, 2:892, 2:897

Breach of Faith: The Fall of Richard Nixon, 3:540

Bread, Hashish, and Moon: Four Modern Arab Poets, 2:56

Bread and Circuses: Theories of Mass Culture as Social Decay, 3:872

Bread and Rice, or Geometry in Yellow, 2:526

Bread and Wine, 2:438

Bread Not Stone: The Challenge of Feminist Biblical Interpretation, 4:814

Breakdown, 5:428

Breakdown and Bereavement, 2:16

The Breakdown of Cartesian Metaphysics, 4:171

The Breakdown of Nations, 3:342

Breakfast, Lunch, and Dinner of Champions, 5:346

Breakfast at Tiffany's, 1:958, 1:959

Breakfast of Champions, 1:1063

Breaking Boundaries, 4:689

Breaking Destructive Patterns, 5:418

Breaking Free, 2:672

Breaking Open: New Poems, 1:1042

Breaking the Code, 5:582

Breaking the Diet Habit: The Natural Weight Alternative, 5:347

Breaking the Land, 5:262

Breaking the Magic Spell, 2:566, 3:870

Breaking the Maya Code, 3:627

Breaking the Science Barrier: How to Explore and Explain the Sciences, 5:11

Breaking the Sound Barrier, 3:665

The Breaking Wave, 2:962

Break of Day, 2:470

The Break of Noon, 2:468

The Breakthrough, 1:620

Breakthrough: A Personal Account of the Egypt-Israel Peace Negotiation, 3:439

Breakthrough Fictioneers, 1:921

Breakthroughs, 5:6

Breakthroughs in Statistics, 5:520

The Break-up of the Hapsburg Empire, 1914–1918, 3:376

The Breast, 1:1040, 1:1041

Breast Cancer: Reducing Your Risk, 5:371

Breast Cancer, the Complete Guide, 5:372

Breastfeeding Secrets and Solutions, 5:358

Breast Implants: Everything You Need to Know, 5:355

The Breast of the Earth, 2:106, 2:132

The Breathing Cathedral: Feeling Our Way into a Living Cosmos, 5:595

Breathing Easy, 5:376

Breathing Lessons, 1:1059
Breathless, 3:837
A Breath of Life: Feminism in the American Jewish Community, 4:650
Brébeuf and His Brethren, 2:923
Brecht: A Biography, 2:573
Brecht and the West German Theater, 2:573
Brecht Memoir, 2:573
Brecht the Dramatist, 2:573
Brendan Behan: An Annotated Bibliography of Criticism, 1:442
Brentano and Intrinsic Value, 4:222, 4:395
Brentano and Meinong Studies, 4:222, 4:395
Bret Harte, 1:756
Bret Harte: Literary Critic, 1:756
The Brethren, 3:544
Breviario di estetica, 2:414
Breviloquium, 4:113
Brewer's Dictionary of Phrase and Fable, 1:131
Brewsie and Willie, 1:881
Brian Aldiss, 1:613
Brian Friel, 1:479
Brian Friel and Ireland's Drama, 1:479
The Bridal Canopy, 2:11
Bridal March and Other Stories, 2:663
The Bridal Wreath, 2:669
The Bride of Abydos, 1:281
The Bride of Innisfallen and Other Stories, 1:895
The Bride of Lammermoor, 1:298
The Bride of Messina, William Tell, and Demetrius, 2:609
The Bride Price, 2:136
Brideshead Revisited, 1:561, 1:562
Brides of Reason, 1:466
The Bridge, 1:823
Bridge Across the Sea: Seven Baltic Plays, 2:804
The Bridge and the Abyss, 2:726
Bridge at Andau, 3:390
The Bridge of Dreams: A Poetics of The Tale of Genji, 2:279
Bridge of Light: Yiddish Film between Two Worlds, 4:657
The Bridge of San Luis Rey, 1:898, 1:899

The Bridge on the Drina, 2:828, 2:829
Bridges, 2:669
Bridges: The Spans of North America, 5:246
Bridges and Boundaries: African Americans and American Jews, 1:989, 4:639
The Bridges at Toko-ri, 1:1248, 3:931
A Bridge to a Wedding, 2:139
Bridge to Terabithia, 1:1204
Bridge to the Future: A Centennial Celebration of the Brooklyn Bridge, 5:52
A Brief Account of Henry Gray, F.R.S., and His Anatomy, Descriptive, and Surgical, during a Century of Its Publication in America, 5:360
A Brief Chronicle Concerning the Examination and Death of Sir John Oldcastle, 1:172
Brief Counseling with Suicidal Persons, 5:418
Brief Demonstration of the Use of the Chronometer for Ascertaining Longitude, 2:620
Brief Encounter, 1:465
A Brief History of Central America, 3:632
A Brief History of Chinese Fiction, 2:234, 2:256
A Brief History of Science, 5:25
A Brief History of the Western World, 3:326
A Brief History of Time, 5:16, 5:607, 5:665, 5:691, 5:692, 5:713
A Brief Introduction to Hinduism, 3:484, 4:504
A Brief Life, 2:876
Brief Lives, 1:451
Brief Psychotherapy in Medical and Health Practice, 5:439
A Brief Summary in Plain Language of the Most Important Laws of England Concerning Women, 1:330, 1:331
A Brief Survey of Austrian History, 3:376
The Brigade (Wounds of Maturity), 2:15
Brigadier and Other Stories, 2:769
Brigadier Gerard, 1:607

Briggflatts, 1:452
Brigham Young, 4:845
Bright Air, Brilliant Fire: On the Matter of the Mind, 5:340
Bright Book of American Life, 1:995
The Bright Book of Life, 1:804, 1:918, 1:996
Bright Day, 1:537
A Brighter Coming Day: A Frances Ellen Watkins Harper Reader, 1:754
A Brighter Sun, 2:942
Brighter Than a Thousand Suns, 5:658
Bright Moon, Perching Bird: Poems, 2:208
Brighton Beach Memoirs, 1:1112
Brighton Rock, 1:488
Bright Orange for the Shroud, 1:1234
Bright Promises, Dismal Performances: An Economist's Protest, 3:76, 3:77
Bright Road to El Dorado, 2:932
Bright Shark, 5:641
Brigitte Bardot and the Lolita Syndrome, 2:458
Brik and Mayakovsky, 2:739
Brilliant Bylines, 3:805
Bring Forth the Mighty Men: On Violence and the Jewish Character, 4:649
Bringing Class Back In: Contemporary and Historical Perspectives, 3:24
Bringing Up Baby, 3:838
Bring Larks and Heroes, 2:957
Bring the Noise: A Guide to Rap Music and Hip-Hop Culture, 3:665
Britain: An Official Handbook, 1:82
Britain and the British Seas, 3:133
Britain and the Jews of Europe 1939–1945, 4:638
Britain in the Nineteen Twenties, 3:365
Britain in the Pacific Islands, 3:495
Britain in Transition: The Twentieth Century, 3:366
Britain since 1918, 3:366
Britain's Theatrical Periodicals, 1720–1967, 1:272
Britain through American Eyes, 3:572

Britannia: A History of Roman Britain, 3:356
The Britannia Bridge, 5:257
Britannica Book of the Year, 1:82, 1:107
Britannicus, 2:498
The British-Americans: The Loyalist Exiles in England, 1774–1789, 3:521
British and Irish Drama since 1960, 1:425
British and Irish Political Drama in the Twentieth Century, 1:426
British and Irish Women Dramatists since 1958: A Critical Handbook, 1:425
British Authors before Eighteen Hundred, 1:127
British Authors of the Nineteenth Century, 1:127
British Autobiographies, 1:87
British Books in Print (Whitaker's) 1993, 1:113
The British Broadside Ballad and Its Music, 3:657
British Business in Asia since 1860, 3:463
British Cultural Studies, 1:1132
The British Diplomatic Service, 1815–1914, 3:364
British Drama, 1:272
British Drama since Shaw, 1:426
British Dramatists: Since World War II, 1:428
The British Empire, 1558–1983, 3:355
The British Empire in the Middle East, 1945–1951, 3:367
British-English Language Dictionary, 1:91
British Factory, Japanese Factory, 3:477
British Fiction, 1750–1770, 1:230
British Folklorists: A History, 3:878
British Folktales, 3:854
British Historical Facts, 1688–1760, 3:354
British Investment in Latin America: 1822–1949, 3:632
The British Isles: A History of Four Nations, 3:355
British Literary Bibliography, 1970–79: A Bibliography, 1:120
British Literary Magazines: The Romantic Age, 1789–1836, 1:274

British Literature since 1945, 1:422
British Magazine, 1:256
British Military History: Military History Bibliographies, 3:354
British Military Intelligence, 1870–1914, 3:363
British Modern Fiction, 1920–1945, 1:1138
British Museum General Catalogue of Printed Books, Subject Catalogue Extracted from the: "Eighteenth-Century British Books," 1:66
British Museum General Catalogue of Printed Books and the Catalogues of The Bodleian Library and of the University Library Cambridge, an Author Union Catalogue Extracted from the: "Eighteenth-Century British Books," 1:66
The British Museum Is Falling Down, 1:515
The British Musical Theatre, 3:660
British National Bibliography, 1:68
British Natural History Books, 1495–1900: A Handlist, 5:759
British Paperback Books in Print, 1:71
British Plays of the Nineteenth Century, 1:323
British Poetry since 1960, 1:502
British Policy and the Turkish Reform Movement, 3:452
British Political Facts, 1900–1985, 3:353
British Population Growth, 1700–1850, 3:355
British Post-Structuralism: since 1968, 4:29
British Public Policy, 1776–1939, 3:355
British Rule in India: An Historical Sketch, 1:376
British Rule in Kenya, 3:422
British Science Fiction: A Chronology, 1478–1990, 1:611
British Social Democracy: A Study in Development and Decay, 3:366
British Society and the French Wars, 1793–1815, 3:362

British Society since 1945, 3:367
The British Spy Novel, 1:592
The British Theatre: Its Repertory and Practice, 1100–1900 A.D., 1:123
British Theatre, 1950–1970, 1:425
British Theatre in the 1890s: Essays on Drama and the Stage, 1:322
British Theatre since 1955: A Reassessment, 1:425
British Thought and Thinkers, 4:29
British Women Writers: A Critical Reference Guide, 1:127
British Wood Engraving of the 20th Century: A Personal View, 1:28
The British Working Class Reader, 1790–1848, 1:313
British Writers, 1:127
Britons: Forging the Nation, 1707–1837, 3:361
Britten, 3:685
The Britten Companion, 3:685
Broadband Coding, Modulation and Transmission Engineering, 5:299, 5:307
Broadcasting and Cable Yearbook 1993, 3:801
Broadcasting in America, 3:811
Broadcasting—Cable and Beyond, 3:811
A Broadside Treasury, 1965–1970, 1:915
Broadway Babies: The People Who Made the American Musical, 1:1075
Broadway Bound, 1:1112
The Broadway Musical: A Critical and Musical Survey, 3:664
Broadway Musicals of the Thirties, 1:1073
Brocade by Night, 2:273
Brocade Valley, 2:267
Broca's Brain: Reflections on the Romance of Science, 5:611
Brodsky's Poetics and Aesthetics, 2:704
Broken April, 2:779
The Broken Betrothal, 2:249
Broken Blossoms, 1:1167
Broken Bonds: The Rise and Fall of Yugoslavia, 3:392
Broken Bottles, Broken Dreams, 5:401

The Broken Calabash, 2:144
The Broken Code: The Exploitation of DNA, 5:782
The Broken Compass, 1:184
The Broken Cord, 5:375
The Broken Heart: A Tragedy, 1:179
The Broken Jug, 2:599
Broken Lights and Mended Lives, 4:688
The Broken Nest, 2:182
Broken Nuptials in Shakespeare's Plays, 1:209
Broken Promises: A History of Conscription in Canada, 3:615
Broken Promises, Mended Dreams, 5:402
Broken Scale Variance and the Light Cone, 5:690
The Broken Spears: The Aztec Account of the Conquest of Mexico, 3:629
A Broken World, 1919–1939, 3:344
Bronislava Nijinska: A Dancer's Legacy, 3:748
Bronislava Nijinska: Early Memoirs, 3:734
A Brontë Companion, 1:335
The Brontës, 1:333
The Brontës: Life and Letters, 1:333
The Brontës: The Critical Heritage, 1:333
The Brontës and Their Background: Romance and Reality, 1:334
The Brontës and Their Circle, 1:333
The Brontë Sisters, 1:333
The Brontë Story, 1:334, 1:335
The Brontë's Web of Childhood, 1:333
Brontosaurus, 1:1121
Bronze Age, Greek and Roman Technology, 5:29
The Bronze Horseman, 2:750
The Bronze Horseman and Other Poems, 2:750
Bronzeville Boys and Girls, 1:954
Brookings at Seventy-Five, 5:184
The Brook Kerith, 1:381
Brooklyn Bridge Fact and Symbol, 5:246
Brooklyn Is Not Expanding: Woody Allen's Comic Universe, 3:830
The Brothel in Rosenstrasse, 1:616

Brother, My Brother: A Collection of Stories, 2:334
Brother Francis, 4:710
The Brotherhood of the Rosy Cross, 4:848
Brother Jacob, 1:353
Brother Man, 2:937
The Brothers, 2:395
Brothers against the Raj, 3:486
Brothers and Sisters, 1:462
Brothers and Strangers, 3:347
The Brothers Ashkenazi, 2:49
The Brothers Grimm, 2:585, 3:880
The Brothers Grimm and Their Critics, 3:880
The Brothers Harper, 1817–1853, 1:41
The Brothers Karamazov, 2:535, 2:712, 2:713
The Brothers Mann, 2:601
The Brothers Singer, 2:49
Brother to Brother: New Writings by Black Gay Men, 1:1189
Brother to Dragons: A New Version, 1:893
The Brown Decades: A Study of the Arts in America, 1865–1895, 5:169, 5:170
The Brown Fairy Book, 3:883
Brown Girl, Brownstones, 1:1014
Brown Heritage: Essays on Philippine Cultural Tradition and Literature, 2:328
Browning and Italy, 1:339
Browning and the Fictions of Identity, 1:339
Browning and the Modern Novel, 1:339
The Browning Critics, 1:339
The Browning Cyclopedia, 1:339
The Brownings: A Victorian Idyll, 1:337
The Brownings and France: A Chronicle with Commentary, 1:339
Browning's Characters: A Study in Poetic Technique, 1:339
Browning's Heroines, 1:339
Browning's Later Poetry, 1881–1889, 1:339
Browning's Youth, 1:339
The Browning Version, 1:540
Bruce Rogers: A Life in Letters, 1870–1957, 1:7
Bruckner, 3:685

Bruegel (Delevoy), 3:771
Bruegel (Gibson), 3:771
Bruegel (Stechow), 3:771
Brunei: The Modern Southeast Asian Islamic Sultanate, 3:492
Brunel's Britain, 5:250
Bruno, or On the Natural and Divine Principle of Things, 4:251
Bruno's Dream, 1:523
The Brushwood Boy, 1:370
The Brute and Other Farces: Seven Short Plays, 2:709
Bruto Primo, 2:405
Bryce's American Commonwealth: Fiftieth Anniversary, 3:151
Bubbles: A Self-Portrait, 3:719
Bubbling April, 1:488
The Buccaneers, 1:787
Buckdancer's Choice, 1:967
The Buck Fever Papers, 1:811
Buckle at the Ballet: Selected Ballet Writings, 3:731
The Bucolics, 2:396
Buddenbrooks, 2:601, 2:602
The Buddha Eye: An Anthology of the Kyoto School, 4:363
A Buddha from Korea: The Zen Teachings of T'aego, 4:537
Buddha Nature, 4:513, 4:530
The Buddha Within, 4:513, 4:543
Buddhism (Berry), 4:498, 4:512
Buddhism (Lester), 4:884
Buddhism: A Cultural Perspective, 4:513, 4:520
Buddhism: Art and Faith, 4:515
Buddhism, Imperialism, and War. Burma and Thailand in Modern History, 4:895
Buddhism, Sexuality, and Gender, 4:894
Buddhism and Asian History, 4:513, 4:519, 4:522, 4:530, 4:534, 4:537, 4:542, 4:543
Buddhism and Politics in Thailand, 4:520
Buddhism and Society, 4:519, 4:890
Buddhism and Society in Southeast Asia, 4:520
Buddhism and the Spirit Cults in Northeast Thailand, 4:519

Buddhism and the State in Sixteenth-Century Japan, 3:475
Buddhism in America, 4:860
Buddhism in China, 4:529
Buddhism in the Tibetan Tradition, 4:543
The Buddhism of Tibet, 4:356, 4:560
Buddhism Transformed: Religious Change in Sri Lanka, 4:515
Buddhist America: Centers, Retreats, Practices, 4:7
Buddhist Art of the Tibetan Plateau, 4:543
The Buddhist Attitude to Other Religions, 4:898
Buddhist-Christian Dialogue: Mutual Renewal and Transformation, 4:423
A Buddhist Critique of the Christian Concept of God, 4:884
Buddhist Ethics: The Path to Nirvana, 4:893
Buddhist Hermeneutics, 4:513
Buddhist Meditation, 4:897
Buddhist Monk, Buddhist Layman, 4:519
Buddhist Philosophy, 4:513
The Buddhist Religion: A Historical Introduction, 4:514, 4:530, 4:538
The Buddhist Revival in Sri Lanka, 4:515
The Buddhist Saints of the Forest and the Cult of Amulets, 4:519
Buddhist Studies in the People's Republic of China, 4:532
Buddhist Thought in India, 4:512
A Buddhist Vision, 4:513
Budding Prospects: A Pastoral, 1:952
A Budget of Paradoxes, 5:495
Buenos Aires: From Plaza to Suburb, 1870–1910, 3:649
The Buenos Aires Affair: A Detective Novel, 2:880
Buff: Poems, 1:481
Buffalo Gals and Other Animal Presences, 1:1260
The Buffalo Soldiers: A Narrative of the Negro Cavalry in the West, 3:532
Buganda and British Overrule, 1900–1955, 3:422
The Bugbears, 2:402

Bugles in the Afternoon, 1:1215
Bugs, 5:563
Build a Literate Classroom, 3:255
Builders of the Bay Colony, 3:589
Building a Sustainable Society, 5:151
Building Domestic Liberty, 1:753
Building European Society, 3:343
Building Maintenance Engineering Price Book, 5:225
Building of Global Security through Cooperation, 5:292
The Building of the House: Houghton Mifflin's First Half Century, 1:42
Building the Universe, 5:658
Building Trades Dictionary, 5:12
Bulgakov: Life and Work, 2:706
Bulgakov's Last Decade: The Writer as Hero, 2:706
Bulgaria: Politics, Economics and Society, 3:392
Bulgaria, 1878–1918: A History, 3:392
Bulgaria under Communist Rule, 3:392
Bulletin of Science, Technology, and Society, 5:176
Bulletin of the Atomic Scientists, 5:108
Bullet Park, 1:960, 1:961
The Bull of Minos, 2:344
Bully for "Brontosaurus": Reflections in Natural History, 5:16
The Buln-Buln and the Brolga, 2:952
Bultmann: Towards a Critical Theology, 4:831
Bulwer: A Panorama, 1:340
A Bunch of Old Letters, 3:499
The Bundle, 1:445, 1:446
Buovo d'Antona, 2:28
A Burden for Critics, 1:816
The Burden of Southern History, 3:602
The Burden of the Past and the English Poet, 1:267
The Burdens of Formality: Essays on the Poetry of Anthony Hecht, 1:987
Bureaucratic Reform in the Ottoman Empire, 3:452
Burger's Daughter, 2:162

Burial and Ancient Society: The Rise of the Greek City-State, 3:305
Buried Alive, 1:443
Buried Child, 1:1110, 1:1111
The Buried Life, 1:404
The Buried Self: A Background to the Poems of Matthew Arnold, 1:328
Burke, 4:193
Burke, Disraeli, and Churchill: The Politics of Perseverance, 3:152
Burke and the Nature of Politics, 3:152
Burma, 4:519
Burma: Literature, Historiography, Scholarship, Language, Life, and Buddhism, 2:313
Burma: A Socialist Nation of Southeast Asia, 3:489
Burma, from Kingdom to Republic: A Historical and Political Analysis, 3:489
The Burma Road to Poverty, 3:489
Burma's Struggle against British Imperialism, 1885–1895, 3:489
Burma through Alien Eyes, 3:489
Burmese Administrative Cycles: Anarchy and Conquest, c.1580–1760, 3:489
Burmese Days, 1:530
Burmese Drama: A Study with Translations of Burmese Plays, 2:314
Burmese Folk-tales, 2:314
Burmese Monk's Tales, 2:314
Burmese Political Values: The Socio-Political Roots of Authoritarianism, 3:489
Burmese Supernaturalism, 3:24
The Burn, 2:697
Burn after Reading, 2:76
The Burned-Over District, 3:523, 4:841
Burnham's Celestial Handbook, 5:591
Burning Air and a Clear Mind: Contemporary Israeli Women Poets, 2:9
Burning Bright: A Play in Story Form, 1:885
Burning Grass, 2:135, 2:136
Burning Patience, 2:885
The Burning Plain and Other Stories, 2:882
The Burning Question, 2:546
Burn Marks, 1:1235

Burns: A Study of the Poems and Songs, 1:280
A Burns Companion, 1:280
The Burns Encyclopedia, 1:280
Burn This, 1:1120, 1:1121
The Burnt Ones, 2:966
A Burnt-Out Case, 1:488
Burnt Pearls: Ghetto Poems, 2:50
Burnt Water, 2:866
Burr, 1:1061, 1:1062
The Burroughs File, 1:958
A Burst of Light, 1:1190
Burton: Snow upon the Desert, 3:914
Bury My Heart at Wounded Knee, 3:531
The Bush Garden: Essays on the Canadian Imagination, 1:976, 2:904
The Bush Presidency: First Appraisals, 3:537
Business Cycles (Mitchell), 3:50
Business Cycles (Schumpeter), 3:104, 3:105
Business Cycles (Zarnowitz), 3:97
Business Cycles: the Nature and Causes of Economic Fluctuations, 3:50
Business Cycles and Business Forecasting, 3:50
Business Cycles and National Income, 3:81
Business Cycles and Their Causes, 3:50, 3:97
Business-Cycle Theory, 3:81
Business Decision Making for Higher Profits, 5:557
Business Ethics, 4:388
Business Fluctuations, Growth, and Economic Stabilization, 3:49
The Business of Bookbinding, 1:25
The Business of Book Publishing, 1:47
The Business of Good Government, 1:433
The Business of May Next: James Madison and the Founding, 3:162
The Business of the Enlightenment, 1:36
The Business One Irwin Handbook of Telecommunications, 5:304
Business Telematics: Corporate Networks for the Information Age, 5:559
Busman's Honeymoon, 1:610

Bus Stop, 1:1095
Bussy d'Ambois, 1:175
Bustan, 2:93
The Bus Trip Handbook, 3:891
The Busy House, 2:795
The Butcher's Wife, 2:251, 2:252
Butler's Ethics, 4:194
Butler's Lives of the Saints, 4:676
Butley, 1:486
The Butter and Egg Man, 1:1096
The Butter-Battle Book, 1:1203
Butterfield 8, 1:866
The Butterflies Carried Him Home and Other Indian Tales, 3:856
The Butterflies of North America: A Natural History and Field Guide, 5:762
Butterfly, 2:267
The Butterfly and Other Stories, 2:267
The Butterfly of Dinard, 2:428
The Butterfly Plague, 2:910, 2:911
The Butterfly's Evil Spell, 2:538
The Butts, 2:119
But What, 2:627
Buy Books Where—Sell Books Where, 1:77
Buyer's Guide to Modems and Communications Software, 5:305
Buying a Heart, 1:516
Buying Greenhouse Insurance, 3:48
Buying the Wind: Regional Folklore in the United States, 3:878
By Any Means Necessary, 4:876
By Avon River, 1:826
By Light, Light: The Mystic Gospel of Hellenistic Judaism, 4:670
By Line: Ernest Hemingway, 1:845
By Love Possessed, 1:964
Bylow Hill, 1:736
By Night Unstarred: An Autobiographical Novel, 1:506
By No Extraordinary Means, 5:122
Bypass: A Cardiologist Reveals What Every Patient Needs to Know, 5:374

Bypassing Bypass: The New Technique of Chelation Therapy, 5:373
Byron, 1:283
Byron: A Critical Study, 1:284
Byron: A Poet before His Public, 1:283
Byron: A Portrait, 1:283
Byron: The Years of Fame, 1:283
Byron and His Fictions, 1:283
Byron and the Bible: A Compendium of Biblical Usage, 1:283
Byron and the Myth of Tradition, 1:284
Byron and the Need of Fatality, 1:282
Byron and the Ruins of Paradise, 1:283
Byron as Poet, 1:284
A Byron Chronology, 1:283
The Byronic Hero: Types and Prototypes, 1:284
Byron in Italy, 1:283
Byron's Don Juan: A Critical Study, 1:282
Byron's "Don Juan": A Variorum Edition, 1:284
Byron's Historical Dramas, 1:283
Byron's Poetry: A Critical Introduction, 1:283
Byron's Political Verse Satire, 1:283
By the Bomb's Early Light, 3:558
By the Law of Nature: Form and Value in Nineteenth-Century America, 1:650
By the North Gate, 1:1023
By the Open Sea, 2:679, 2:680
By the Pen, 2:85
By the Shores of Silver Lake, 1:1208
By the Sweat of the Brow: Work in the Western World, 5:51
By the Waters of Babylon, 1:815
Byzantine and Early Islamic Near East, 3:442
Byzantine Architecture, 3:763
Byzantine Christianity: Emperor, Church and the West, 4:693
Byzantine Church, Society, and Civilization Seen through Contemporary Eyes, 4:693

The Byzantine Liturgy, 4:694
The Byzantine Theocracy,
    4:694
Byzantine Theology: Histori-
    cal Trends and Doctrinal
    Themes, 4:693, 4:756
Byzantium and the Decline
    of Rome, 3:303
Byzantium and the Rise of
    Russia, 4:693
Byzantium and the Roman
    Primacy, 4:692

C

The Cabala, 1:899
Cabbages and Kings, 1:756
Cabin Fever, 2:956
Cabot Wright Begins, 1:1033
The Cactus Primer, 5:768
Caddie Woodlawn, 1:1195
Cadillac Desert: The Ameri-
    can West and Its Disap-
    pearing Water, 5:824
Cadres, Bureaucracy, and Po-
    litical Power in Commu-
    nist China, 3:496
Caesar, Politician and States-
    man, 3:313
Caesar and Cleopatra, 1:544,
    1:545
Caesar as Man of Letters,
    3:313
Caesar or Nothing, 2:530
Café con Leche: Race, Class,
    and National Image in
    Venezuela, 3:641
The Caffeine Book, 5:403
Cage Cunningham Johns:
    Dancers on a Plane, 3:740
The Caged Ones, 2:313
Cain, 1:271, 1:281
Cain: The Biography of
    James M. Cain, 1:1227
Cain's Craft, 1:1227
Cairo: 1001 Years of the City
    Victorious, 3:445
Cakes and Ale, 1:520
The Calabrian Abbot: Joa-
    chim of Fiore in the His-
    tory of Thought, 4:712
The Calcium Bible: How to
    Have Better Bones All
    Your Life, 5:341
The Calculating Passion of
    Ada Byron, 5:578
Calculus, 5:490
Calculus: An Introductory
    Approach, 5:491
Calculus: An Intuitive and
    Physical Approach, 5:490

The Calculus of Consent,
    3:67
A Calculus of Suffering, 5:47,
    5:370
Calderón: The Secular Plays,
    2:533
Calderón and the Seizures of
    Honor, 2:533
Calderón in the German
    Lands and the Low Coun-
    tries, 2:533
Caleb Field, 1:385
The California and Oregon
    Trail, Being Sketches of
    Prairie and Rocky Moun-
    tain Life, 1:690
California Reefs, 3:919
California Suite, 1:1112
California's Utopian Colonies,
    4:844
Caligrammes: Poems of
    Peace and War, 2:451
The Caliph's Design, 1:514
Calked Boots and Other
    Northwest Writings, 3:863
Call for the Dead, 1:595
Calligraphic Alphabets, 1:13
Calligraphic Lettering with
    Wide Pen and Brush, 1:14
Calligraphy, 1:13
Calligraphy: A Sourcebook,
    1:14
Calligraphy: The Art of Beau-
    tiful Writing, 1:17
Calligraphy Now: New Light
    on Traditional Letters,
    1:19
Calligraphy's Flowering,
    Decay and Restora-
    tion, 1:19
The Calligraphy Source
    Book, 1:19
Calligraphy Techniques, 1:17
Calligraphy Today, 1:14
Callimachus: Hymns, Epi-
    grams, Select Fragments,
    2:354
Callimachus' Hymns One,
    Two, Five, Six, 2:354
The Calling of Sociology:
    And Other Essays on the
    Pursuit of Learning, 3:239
Call It Experience, 1:819
Call It Sleep, 1:1039
Call Me Ishmael, 1:689
The Call of Stories: Teaching
    and the Moral Imagina-
    tion, 3:249
The Call of the Curlew,
    2:74
The Call of the Minaret,
    4:568

Call of the Siren: Manatees
    and Dugongs, 5:770
The Call of the Wild, 1:773,
    1:774
The Call of the Wild, White
    Fang, and Other Stories,
    1:774
Call to Order, 2:469
Calvin: Institutes of the
    Christian Religion, 4:761
Calvin: Origins and Develop-
    ment of His Religious
    Thought, 4:762
Calvin: Theological Treatises,
    4:761
Calvin against Himself: An
    Inquiry in Intellectual His-
    tory, 4:762
Calvin and Classical Philoso-
    phy, 4:129
Calvin and English Calvinism
    to 1649, 4:726
Calvin and the Anabaptist
    Radicals, 4:761
Calvinism and the Amyraut
    Heresy, 4:731, 4:761
Calvinism in Europe,
    1555–1620: A Collection of
    Documents, 4:731
Calvinist Preaching and
    Iconoclasm in the Nether-
    lands, 1544–1569, 4:737
Calvino and The Age of Neo-
    realism: Fables of Es-
    trangement, 2:412
Calvin's Commentaries, 4:761
Calvin's Geneva, 4:762
Calvin's New Testament
    Commentaries, 4:761
Cal y canto, 2:528
The Cambodian Agony, 3:490
Cambodian Folk Stories from
    the Gatiloke, 2:315
Cambodia's Foreign Policy,
    3:491
The Cambridge Ancient His-
    tory, 3:298, 4:806
The Cambridge Atlas of As-
    tronomy, 5:587
Cambridge Bible Commen-
    tary, 4:820
The Cambridge Book of Po-
    etry for Children, 1:584
The Cambridge Chaucer
    Companion, 1:150
The Cambridge Companion
    to Aquinas, 4:119
The Cambridge Companion
    to Descartes, 4:170
The Cambridge Companion
    to English Renaissance
    Drama, 1:169

The Cambridge Companion to Hegel, 4:233

The Cambridge Companion to Kant, 4:206

The Cambridge Companion to Marx, 4:242

The Cambridge Companion to Old English Literature, 1:143

The Cambridge Companion to Plato, 4:81

The Cambridge Companion to Shakespeare Studies, 1:222

Cambridge Dictionary of Science and Technology, 5:3

Cambridge Economic History of Europe, 3:338

The Cambridge Economic History of India, Vol. 1: c.1200–c.1750, 3:484

The Cambridge Encyclopedia of China, 3:465

Cambridge Encyclopedia of Human Evolution, 5:760

The Cambridge Encyclopedia of India, Pakistan, Bangladesh, Sri Lanka, Nepal, Bhutan and the Maldives, 3:482

The Cambridge Encyclopedia of Latin America and the Caribbean, 3:624

Cambridge Encyclopedia of Space, 5:3

The Cambridge Encyclopedia of the Earth Sciences, 5:618

Cambridge Encyclopedia of the Life Sciences, 5:759

The Cambridge Encyclopedia of the Middle East, 3:437

Cambridge Essays 1888–1889, 4:322

Cambridge Guide to Literature in English, 1:132

The Cambridge Guide to the Material World, 5:213, 5:670

The Cambridge Handbook of American Literature, 1:133

The Cambridge Handbook of Contemporary China, 3:465

The Cambridge Historical Encyclopedia of Great Britain and Ireland, 3:355

The Cambridge History of Africa, 3:423

The Cambridge History of Africa, 1940–1975, 3:415

Cambridge History of American Literature, 1:133

The Cambridge History of China
Vol. 1, 3:466, 3:469
Vol. 3, 3:466, 3:469
Vol. 7, 3:466, 3:468
Vol. 10, 3:466, 3:468
Vol. 11, 3:466, 3:470
Vol. 12, 3:466, 3:470
Vol. 13, 3:466, 3:470
Vol. 14, 3:466, 3:471
Vol. 15, 3:466, 3:471

The Cambridge History of Classical Literature, 2:345, 4:46

Cambridge History of English Literature, 1:133

The Cambridge History of Iran, 3:301

The Cambridge History of Islam, 3:416, 3:443, 4:570

Cambridge History of Japan
Vol. 3: Medieval Japan, 3:476
Vol. 4: Early Modern Japan, 3:475
Vol. 5: The Nineteenth Century, 3:478
Vol. 6: The Twentieth Century, 3:477

The Cambridge History of Judaism, 4:596

The Cambridge History of Later Greek and Early Medieval Philosophy, 4:55, 4:93, 4:685

The Cambridge History of Later Medieval Philosophy, 4:94, 4:696

The Cambridge History of Latin America: Colonial Latin America, 3:625

The Cambridge History of Medieval Political Thought, c.350–c.1450, 4:98

The Cambridge History of Russian Literature, 2:689

The Cambridge History of the Bible, 4:676, 4:805, 4:813

Cambridge New Bibliography of English Literature, 1:79, 1:121

The Cambridge Platonists, 4:168

The Cambridge Press, 1638–1692, 1:12, 1:37

Cambridge Ritualists, 4:479

Cambridge Ritualists Reconsidered, 4:479

The Cambridge Shorter Bibliography of English Literature, 1:121

The Cambridge Translations of Medieval Philosophical Texts, 4:95

The Cambridge University History of Africa, 3:416

Cambridge University Press, 1584–1984, 1:40

Cambridge World History of Human Disease, 5:368

The Camel in Somali Oral Traditions, 2:117

Camel Xiangzi, 2:251

Camera Lucida, 2:455

The Camera Never Blinks: Adventures of a TV Journalist, 3:808

Camera Politica, 1:1157

Cameroon with Egbert, 3:904

Camilla, 1:235

Camille, 2:473

Camillus: A Study of Indo-European Religion as Roman History, 4:471

Camilo José Cela, 2:534

Camino Real, 1:1117

Camoens and His Epic, 2:558

The Campaign, 2:865

The Campaign of Maestrazgo, 2:547

The Campaigns of Alexander, 3:312

Campaspe and Sappho and Phao, 1:186

The Camphor Flame: Popular Hinduism and Society in India, 4:504

Campo di Marte, 2:437

Campos de Castilla, 2:544

Campus Life, 3:552

Camwood on the Leaves and Before the Blackout: Plays, 2:148

Canaanite Myths and Legends, 4:445, 4:545

Canada: Immigration and Colonization, 1841–1903, 3:615

Canada: The War of Conquest, 3:611

Canada, 1896–1920: A Nation Transformed, 3:617

Canada, 1922–1939: Decades of Discord, 3:616

Canada, 1939–1957: The Forked Road, 3:618

Canada, 1957–1967: The Years of Uncertainty and Innovation, 3:616

Canada and the Age of Conflict: A History of Canadian External Policies, 3:608

Canada and the American Revolution 1774–1783, 3:613

Canada and the Canadian Question, 3:615

Canada and the French-Canadian Question, 3:617

Canada and the Reagan Challenge, 3:607

Canada and the United States: The Civil War Years, 3:608

Canada before Confederation: A Study in Historical Geography, 3:606

Canada Learns to Play: The Emergence of Organized Sport, 1807–1914, 3:608

Canada's Balance of International Payments, 1900–1913, 3:110

Canada's First Nations, 3:610

Canada since 1945: Power, Politics, and Provincialism, 3:616

Canada's Smallest Province: A History of P.E.I., 3:609

Canada's War, 3:608

Canada under Louis XIV, 1663–1701, 3:611

Canadian Almanac and Directory 1985, 1:82

Canadian Books in Print, 1:113

Canadian Books in Print 1992, 1:72

Canadian Economic History, 3:606

The Canadian Encyclopedia, 3:605

The Canadian Frontier, 1534–1760, 3:611

The Canadian Identity, 3:622

The Canadian Jewish Chronicle, 2:915

The Canadian Labour Movement: A Short History, 3:607

Canadian Literature, 2:911

Canadian Native Literature in English, 2:903

The Canadian Novel: A Critical Anthology, 2:904

The Canadian Prairies: A History, 3:609

The Canadians, 3:607

Canadian Short Fiction, 2:905

The Canadian with Scott, 3:936

Canadian Women: A History, 3:607

Canadian Writers and Their Works: Fiction Series, 2:904

Canadian Writers and Their Works: Poetry Series, 2:904

Canadian Writers at Work, 2:904

The Canadian Zionist, 2:915

Can Africa Survive? Arguments against Growth without Development, 3:428

Canarsie: The Jews and Italians of Brooklyn against Liberalism, 4:641

Cancer, 5:372

Cancer: The Misguided Cell, 5:373

Cancer and Nutrition, 5:373

Cancer Control, 5:372

The Cancer Dictionary, 5:367

The Cancer Journals, 1:1189, 1:1190

A Cancer Patient's Guide to Radiation Therapy: A Cancer Patient's Primer, 5:397

The Cancer Patient's Handbook, 5:373

Cancer Ward, 2:718, 2:760

Canciones, 2:545

Candida, 1:438, 1:544, 1:545

Candidates, Parties, and Campaigns, 3:144

A Candid Critique of Book Publishing, 1:48

Candide, 2:515

Candide, or Optimism, 4:217

Candide, Zadig and Selected Stories, 2:515

Candide and Other Stories, 2:515, 4:217

Candle in the Wind, 2:760

Candles and Carnival Lights: The Catholic Sensibility of F. Scott Fitzgerald, 1:840

Candles in Babylon, 1:1004

The Candles of Your Eyes, 1:1034

Cane, 1:891

The Cannery Boat and Other Japanese Short Stories, 2:283

Cannery Row, 1:884

The Cannibal, 1:985

Cannibals and Kings, 3:14, 3:31

Cannibals and Missionaries, 1:1007, 1:1008

Can One Be Scientific and Yet Spiritual?, 5:196

The Canonization of Daniel Defoe, 1:240

The Canon of the New Testament, 4:805

Canons and Context, 1:911

Canons and Decrees of the Council of Trent, 4:729

Can Such Things Be?, 1:734, 1:735

Cantab, 1:389

The Canterbury Pilgrims, 1:277

The Canterbury Tales, 1:140, 1:145, 1:147, 1:149, 1:150, 2:409, 2:431

Can't Help Singin': The American Musical on Stage and Screen, 3:667

A Canticle for Leibowitz, 1:1260

Cántico, 2:541

Cantico Espiritual, 2:544

Canto General, 2:873, 2:874

Cantos, 1:413, 1:502, 1:797, 1:870, 1:899

The Cantos of Ezra Pound: The Lyric Mode, 1:873

Cantos of Mutabilitie, 1:197

Cantus Firmus, 2:797

Can't We Make Moral Judgments?, 4:389

Can Women Re-Image the Church?, 4:892

Can You Forgive Her?, 1:405

Cape Cod, 1:700

Cape Farewell, 2:678

Capital, 3:95, 3:290, 4:227, 4:241, 4:242

Capital, Vol. 1—A Critique of Political Economy, 3:51

Capital Accumulation in Thailand, 1855–1985, 3:490

Capital and Growth, 3:83

Capital and Its Earnings, 3:72

Capital and Time: A Neo-Austrian Theory, 3:83, 3:84

Capital Cities of Arab Islam, 3:457

Capital in Economic Theory, 3:50

Capital in the American Economy: Its Formation and Financing, 3:51, 3:90

Capitalism, Communism and Coexistence, 3:52, 3:79

Capitalism, Socialism, and Democracy, 3:104, 3:105, 3:140, 3:143

Capitalism and a New Social Order: The Republican Vision of the 1790s, 3:519

Capitalism and Confrontation in Sumatra's Plantation Belt, 1870–1979, 3:491

Capitalism and Freedom, 3:76, 3:77

Capitalism and Modernity: An Excursus on Marx and Weber, 3:210, 3:244

Capitalism and Modern Social Theory, 3:227

Capitalism and Nationalism in Prewar Japan, 3:478

Capitalism and Slavery, 3:630

Capitalism and Social Theory, 3:51

Capitalism and the State in Modern France, 3:373

Capitalism as a Moral System, 3:51

Capitalist Development and Democracy, 3:51

The Capitalist Manifesto, 4:270

The Capitalist Revolution, 3:221

The Capitalist World Economy, 3:243

Capital Theory and the Rate of Return, 3:51

Capote: A Biography, 1:959

The Capricious Cosmos: Universe beyond Law, 5:595

Capricornia, 2:954, 2:955

Caps and Bells, 2:435

The Capsule of the Mind: Chapters in the Life of Emily Dickinson, 1:748

Captain Brassbound's Conversion, 1:545

Captain Joshua Slocum, 3:937

Captain Mansana and Other Stories, 2:663

Captain Marryat: A Rediscovery, 1:374, 1:375

Captain Pantoja and the Special Service, 2:886, 2:887

Captains Courageous, 1:370

The Captain's Daughter, 2:750

The Captain's Daughter and Other Stories, 2:751

The Captain's Death Bed and Other Essays, 1:569

Captain Singleton, 1:239

Captain Sir Richard Francis Burton, 3:914

Captains of the Sands, 2:892

The Captain's Verses, 2:874

Captain Swing, 3:405

The Captive and the Free, 1:456

The Captive Mind, 2:817, 2:818

A Captive of the Caucasus, 2:702

A Captive of Time: My Years with Pasternak, 2:746

The Captive Soul of the Messiah: New Tales about Reb Nachman, 2:42, 4:669

A Captive Spirit: Selected Prose, 2:768

Captive Victors: Shakespeare's Narrative Poems and Sonnets, 1:215

Captures, 1:482

Caravan Journeys and Wandering in Persia, Afghanistan, Turkistan, and Beloochistan, 3:452

Caravans, 1:1248

The Cardboard Crown, 2:950

Cardenio, 1:204

Cardinal Cajetan Responds: A Reader in Reformation Controversy, 4:137

Cardinal Choices, 5:181

Cardinal Newman in His Age, 4:783

Carducci, 2:413

The Care and Repair of Books, 1:25

Career Change in Midlife: Stress, Social Support and Adjustment, 3:218

The Career of Dion Boucicault, 1:332

The Career of Philosophy, 4:162

The Career of Samuel Butler, 1835–1902, 1:342

Career Opportunities in Geology and the Earth Sciences, 5:637

Career Opportunities in Television, Cable, and Video, 3:812

Career Patterns in Education, 3:257

Careers in Engineering and Technology, 5:227

Careers in High Tech: Exciting Jobs in Today's Fastest-Growing Fields, 5:228

Careers of Opioid Users, 5:403

A Careful and Strict Enquiry into the Freedom of Will, 4:766

The Caregiver's Guide, 5:317

Caregiving: Helping an Aged Loved One, 5:317

The Careless Technology: Ecology and International Development, 5:213

Careless Widow and Other Stories, 1:538

Care of the Older Adult, 5:316

The Care of the Self, 5:87

The Care of the Sick: The Emergence of Modern Nursing, 5:337

The Caretaker, 1:534

Cargo Cults and Millennarian Movements, 4:468

The Caribbean, 3:931

Caribbean: A Novel, 1:1248

The Caribbean: The Genesis of a Fragmented Nationalism, 3:626

Caribbean, Sea of the New World, 3:642

Caribbean Folk Legends, 2:931

The Caribbean in the Wider World, 3:626

Caribbean Narrative, 2:931

Caribbean Verse: An Anthology, 2:931

Caribbean Women Writers, 2:930

Caribbean Writers: A Bio-Bibliographical Critical Encyclopedia, 2:930

Caring, 4:391

Caring and Compassion in Clinical Practice, 5:336

Caring and Curing, 4:893

Caring for a Loved One with AIDS, 5:386

Caring for Books and Documents, 1:22

Caring for the Burned: Life and Death in a Hospital Burn Center, 5:379

Caring for Your Aging Parents, 5:318

Caring for Your Baby and Young Child: Birth to Age 5, 5:323

Caring for Your Books, 1:23

Caritas, 1:565

Carl Becker's Heavenly City Revisited, 3:567

Carl Dreyer, 3:834

Carl Friedrich Gauss: A Bibliography, 5:508

Carl Friedrich Gauss: A Biography, 5:508

Carl Friedrich Gauss: Titan of Science, 5:508, 5:530

Carl Jona Love Almqvist, 2:673

Carlo Goldoni, 2:423

Carlos Fuentes, 2:866

Carlos Fuentes: A Critical View, 2:866

Carl Rogers, 3:193

Carl Rogers: Dialogues, 3:193

Carl Rogers: The Man and His Ideas, 3:193, 5:468

Carl Rogers on Encounter Groups, 5:468

A Carl Rogers Reader, 3:193

Carl Sandburg, 1:878

Carl Sandburg: A Biography, 1:879

Carl Sandburg: A Reference Guide, 1:879

Carl Sandburg: His Life and Works, 1:878

Carlton Fredericks' Nutrition Guide for the Prevention and Cure of Common Ailments and Diseases, 5:395

Carlyle and Mill, 1:344, 4:245

Carlyle and Tennyson, 1:344

Carlyle and the Search for Authority, 1:344

Carlyle's Theory of the Hero, 1:344

Carmichael's Manual of Child Psychology, 3:174

The Carnal Prayer Mat, 2:210

Carnap on Meaning and Analyticity, 4:279, 5:85

Carnival: Entertainment and Posthumous Tales, 2:649

A Carnival of Buncombe: Writings on Politics, 1:859

The Carnivores, 5:770

Caroli Linnaei, 5:805

Caroline Gordon: A Biography, 1:983

Caroline Gordon as Novelist and Woman of Letters, 1:983

Caroline Norton, 1:385

The Carousel, 1:621

The Carpathians, 2:974

The Carpentered Hen and Other Tame Creatures, 1:1059

Carpenter's Gothic, 1:977

Carrying the Fire: An Astronaut's Journey, 5:596

The Carter Years: The President and Policy Making, 3:536

Cartesian Linguistics: A Chapter in the History of Rationalist Thought, 4:170

Cartesian Meditations: An Introduction to a Phenomenology, 4:234

Cartographic Design and Production, 5:617

Cartographic Innovations, 3:134

Caruso, 3:688

Caruso: An Illustrated Life, 3:688

Caruso: His Life in Pictures, 3:688

Carving a Statue, 1:488

Caryl Churchill: A Casebook, 1:459

Casanova's Homecoming, 2:611

Cascadia: The Geologic Evolution of the Pacific Northwest, 5:626

A Casebook of Medical Ethics, 5:118

The Case for Animal Experimentation, 4:389

The Case for Animal Rights, 4:389

The Case for a Personal Psychotherapy, 5:423

The Case for Legibility, 1:10

The Case of Jonathan Drew, 1:1168

The Case of Peter Pan: or, The Impossibility of Children's Fiction, 1:438

The Case of the Daring Divorcee, 1:1229

The Case of the Fabulous Fake, 1:1229

The Case of the Mythical Monkeys, 1:1229

The Case of the Phantom Fortune, 1:1229

The Case of the Swinging Skirt, 1:1229

The Case of Walter Pater, 1:387

Cases in Bioethics: Selections from the Hastings Center Report, 5:144

Case Studies in Abnormal Behavior, 5:427

Case Studies in Abnormal Psychology, 5:427

Case Studies in Business, Society, and Ethics, 5:132

Case Studies in Medical Ethics, 5:144

Case Studies in Nursing Ethics, 5:144

Case Studies in Population Biology, 5:770

Cashel Byron's Profession, 1:545

Casino Royale, 1:593

Cassandra: A Novel and Four Essays, 2:615, 2:616

Cassandra's Daughters: The Women in Hemingway, 1:847

Cassell and the Publishers Association Directory of Publishing, 1:52, 1:69

The Cassell Book of Proverbs, 1:115

Cassell's Encyclopedia of World Literature, 1:131, 2:4

Cassell's French and English Dictionary, 1:98

Cassell's German-English, English-German Dictionary, 1:99

Cassell's Italian Dictionary: Italian-English, English-Italian, 1:100

Cassell's Latin and English Dictionary, 1:101

Cassell's New Dutch Dictionary: English-Dutch, Dutch-English, 1:98

Cassell's New German Dictionary (German-English and English-German), 1:99

Cassell's Spanish-English, English-Spanish Dictionary, 1:102

The Cassique of Kiawah, 1:696

Cassirer, Symbolic Forms and History, 4:280

Cassirer's Conception of Causality, 4:280

Cassius Dio, 3:314

Cass Timberlane, 1:853, 1:854

The Castaway, 1:237

Caste, 1:389

Caste, Conflict and Ideology, 3:485

Caste and Class in a Southern Town, 3:19

The Casting of the Bell, 2:794

Casting Shakespeare's Plays: London Actors and Their Roles, 1:1590–1642, 1:218

The Castle, 2:595, 2:596

Castle Corner, 1:456

Castle in Spain, 2:25

Castle Nowhere: Lake-Country Sketches, 1:790

The Castle of Crossed Destinies, 2:411

The Castle of Otranto, 1:262, 1:590, 1:603, 1:621

The Castle of Perseverance, 1:160

Castlereagh, 3:362

Castle Richmond, 1:406

Castles in the Air, 1:389

The Castles of Athlin and Dunbayne, 1:622

Castle to Castle, 2:465

Castro, 3:636

A Casual Brutality, 2:933
Casualties, Poems 1966–1968, 2:133
The Casualty, 2:570
The Cat, 2:508
A Cat, A Man, and Two Women, 2:294
The Catacombs: Rediscovered Monuments of Early Christianity, 4:689
Catacombs and Basilicas: The Early Christians in Rome, 4:689
Catal Huyuk: A Neolithic Town in Anatolia, 3:301
Catalog 25: Type Faces, Border Designs, Typecast Ornaments, Brass Rule, 1:13
Catalog of Books Relating to the Discovery and Early History of North and South America, 3:510
Catalog of Cometary Orbits 1993, 5:593
A Catalog of Crime, 1:604
A Catalog of Phonorecording of Music and Oral Data Held by the Archives of Traditional Music, 3:851
Catalog of Teratogenic Agents, 5:737
Catalog of the Hoose Library of Philosophy, 4:15
A Catalogue of American Watermarks 1690–1835, 1:5
Catalogue of Books in English on Japan, 1945–1981, 3:473
Catalogue of Books Printed in the XVth Century Now in the British Museum, 1:66
A Catalogue of Foreign Watermarks Found on Paper Used in America 1700–1835, 1:5
Catalogue of Nineteenth Century Bindery Equipment, 1:26
A Catalogue of Renaissance Philosophers: 1350–1650, 4:130
A Catalogue of the World of Linnaeus Preserved in the Libraries of the British Museum of Natural History, 5:806
The Catalpa Bow: A Study of Shamanistic Practices in Japan, 4:539

Catalyst of the Enlightenment: Gotthold Ephraim Lessing, 4:208
Cat and Mouse, 2:582
Cataracts: The Complete Guide from Diagnosis to Recovery for Patients and Families, 5:384
Cataracts: What You Must Know about Them, 5:384
Catastrophe, 2:411
Catastrophe and Other Stories, 2:411
Catastrophic Diseases: Who Decides What?, 5:79
Cat Country: A Satirical Novel of China in the 1930's, 2:251
Catch-22, 1:987, 1:988
Cat Chaser, 1:1232
The Catcher in the Rye, 1:1042, 1:1043
Catechism of the Catholic Church, 4:891
The Categorical Imperative, 4:207
The Categories of Dialectical Materialism: Contemporary Soviet Ontology, 4:31
Category Formation and the History of Religions, 4:422
The Category of the Aesthetic in the Philosophy of St. Bonaventure, 4:113
Catharine and Other Writings, 1:276
Catharine Maria Sedgwick, 1:695
The Cathedral, 2:839
The Cathedral Folk, 2:735, 2:736
Cathedrals of Science, 5:47
Catherine and Igor Stravinsky, 3:723
Catherine of Siena: The Dialogue, 4:706
Catherine of Siena's Way, 4:707
Catherine the Great and the Expansion of Russia, 3:395
Cather Studies, 1:822
Catholic Almanac: An Annual, 1:82
The Catholic Bishops and Nuclear War, 5:110
Catholic Bishops in American Politics, 4:752
The Catholic Church in America: An Historical Bibliography, 4:752
The Catholic Church in the Modern World, 4:741
The Catholic Crisis, 4:754

The Catholic Encyclopedia, 4:716
The Catholic Experience, 4:751
The Catholic Experience: An Interpretation of American Catholicism, 4:891
The Catholic Faith, 4:891
Catholic Girls, 4:746
Catholicism between Luther and Voltaire, 3:334, 4:728
Catholicism Study Edition, 4:745
The Catholicity of the Church, 4:891
The Catholic Modernists, 4:741
The Catholic Novel: An Annotated Bibliography, 1:125
The Catholic Periodical, 4:7
The Catholic Reformation, 4:728
The Catholic Reformation: Council, Churchmen, Controversies, 4:729
The Catholic Reformation: Savonarola to Ignatius Loyola, 4:729
Catholics, Anglicans and Puritans: Seventeenth Century Essays, 3:411
Catholic Social Thought: The Documentary Heritage, 4:745
The Catholic Study Bible, 4:798
A Catholic Vision, 4:891
Catholic Worker, 4:765
Catilina, 3:320
Catiline, 1:183
The Cat Inside, 1:957
The Cat in the Hat, 1:1203
Cato, 1:228
Cat on a Hot Tin Roof, 1:1117
Catriona, 1:396
Cats, 1:471
Cat's Cradle, 1:1063
Cat's Eye, 2:906
The Catullan Revolution, 2:384
Catullus: A Reader's Guide to the Poems, 2:384
Catullus: Poems—A Commentary, 2:384
Catullus and His Influence, 2:384
Catullus and His World: A Reappraisal, 2:384
Caucasian Chalk Circle, 1:446
Caucasian Journey, 3:902

Caudillos in Spanish America, 1800–1850, 3:632
Caurapañcāśikā, 2:173
Causality and Modern Science, 5:62, 5:83
Causality and Scientific Explanation, 4:102, 4:132
Cause, Experiment and Science, 4:143
Cause, Principle, and Unity: Five Dialogues, 4:135
Cause for Wonder, 1:1017
Cause of Death: The Story of Forensic Medicine, 5:344
Causes and Prevention of Cancer, 5:372
The Causes and Prevention of War, 3:148, 3:277
The Causes of Confederation, 3:613
Causes of Delinquency, 3:205
Causes of Evolution, 5:797
Causes of Evolution: A Paleontological Perspective, 3:18
The Causes of the Civil War, 3:598
The Causes of the Civil War: A Note on Historical Sentimentalism, 3:597
The Causes of the English Revolution, 3:408
Cautionary Tales, 1:442
Cavalcade of the American Novel, 1:724
Cavaliers and Roundheads: The English at War 1642–1649, 3:360
Cavalleria Rusticana, 2:441
Cavalleria Rusticana and Other Stories, 2:441
The Cave, 1:892
Cave and Shadows, 2:330
Cave Artists, 3:760
Cave Birds: An Alchemical Cave Drama, 1:498
The Cave Dwellers, 1:1110
The Cavendish Laboratory, 1874–1974, 5:716
The Cave of Making: The Poetry of Louis MacNeice, 1:518
The Cavern-Mystery Transmission, 4:527
Cawdor and Medea, 1:851
The Caxtons, 1:340
The Caxtons, A Family Picture, 1:340
CCH Congressional Index, 1:108
CD-ROM: The New Papyrus, 5:554

CD-ROM Licensing and Copyright Issues for Libraries, 1:55
C. Day Lewis, 1:512
C. Day Lewis, the Poet Laureate: A Bibliography, 1:512
Cebuano Literature: A Survey and Bio-Bibliography, 2:328
Cecilia, 1:235
Cecilia Payne-Gaposhkin: An Autobiography and Other Recollections, 5:610
The Celebrated Jumping Frog of Calaveras County, 1:781
The Celebration, 2:893
A Celebration for Edith Sitwell, 1:548
Celebration in Postwar American Fiction, 1945–1957, 1:920
A Celebration of American Family Folklore, 3:857
Celebration of Awareness: A Call for Institutional Revolution, 5:136
A Celebration of Demons, 4:515
Celebrations and Attacks, 1:989
Celebrations and Elegies, 1:501
Celebrations of Death: The Anthropology of Mortuary Ritual, 4:430
Celebrations of Life, 5:795
Celestial Mechanics, 5:530, 5:698
Celestial Navigation, 1:1059
The Celestial Worlds Discovered, 5:695
Celestina: A Novel in Dialogue, 2:548, 2:549
Céline and His Critics: Scandals and Parado, 2:465
Cell Biology, 5:775
Cell Movement and Cell Behavior, 5:775
The Cell of Self Knowledge: Seven Early English Mystical Treatises, 1:153
Cells, Development, and the Biology of Cancer, 5:778
Cellular Pathology, as Based upon Physiological and Pathological Histology, 5:410
The Celluloid Closet: Homosexuality in the Movies, 1:1182

Celluloid Sisters: Women and Popular Cinema, 3:827
Celsus: On the True Doctrine, 4:683
Celtic Britain, 3:356, 4:437
Celtic Fairy Tales, 3:882
Celtic Mythology, 4:436
Celtic Twilight and the Nineties, 1:460
The Celts, 4:436
Cement: A Novel, 2:720
The Cenci, 1:271, 1:302
Cenere, 2:419
Censored, 3:807
The Censoring of Diderot's Encyclopedia and the Reestablished Text, 4:196
Censorship, 1:57
Censorship: 500 Years of Conflict, 1:56, 1:57
Censorship: The Irish Experience, 1:56
Censorship and Education, 1:57
Censorship Landmarks, 1:56
Censorship, Libraries, and the Law, 1:56
Censorship Litigation and the Schools, 1:56
The Censorship of English Drama: 1737–1824, 1:271
Censors in the Classroom, 1:57
Census Bureau Catalog, 1:109
The Centaur, 1:1060
The Centaur in the Garden, 2:899
The Centaur Letters: Unpublished Letters by D. H. Lawrence, 1:509
Centenary Edition of the Works of Nathaniel Hawthorne Series, 1:674
Centennial, 1:1248, 3:931
Centennial Essays for Robinson Jeffers, 1:852
Centennial History of the Civil War, 3:527
Centennial Lectures, 5:751
Center and Periphery: Essays in Macro Sociology, 3:239
Center and Periphery: Spatial Variations in Politics, 3:129
Central America: A Nation Divided, 3:626
Central America and the United States: The Search for Stability, 3:631

Central America in the Nineteenth and Twentieth Centuries, 3:624

Centrality and Commonality (1989), Humanity and Self-Cultivation, 4:362

Centrality and Commonality: An Essay on Confucian Religiousness, 4:362

The Central Motion: Poems, 1968–1983, 1:967

The Central Philosophy of Tibet, 4:888

Centre and Labyrinth: Essays in Honour of Northrop Frye, 1:977

A Century of Biblical Archaeology, 4:808

Century of Chemistry, 5:729

A Century of Controversy, 3:11

A Century of Dishonor, 1:760

Century of Innovation, 1:1072

A Century of Political Cartoons, 3:590

Century of Progress, 3:565

A Century of Psychology as Science, 3:167, 3:168

The Century of Revolution, 1603–1714, 3:336, 3:404

A Century of the Essay, British and American, 1:430

The Century of Total War, 3:282

A Century of Yiddish Poetry, 2:34

Century's Ebb, 1:828

Ceramics of the World: From Four Thousand B.C. to the Present, 3:765

Ceremonies, 1:1189

Ceremony, 1:1047

Ceremony in Lone Tree, 1:1017

Certain, Lively Episodes, 1:231

A Certain Lucas, 2:861

A Certain Measure, 1:843

A Certain People: American Jews and Their Lives Today, 4:641

A Certain Realism: Making Use of Pasolini's Film Theory and Practice, 3:829

Cervantes (Canavaggio), 2:535

Cervantes (Durán), 2:535

Cervantes (Oliphant), 1:385, 1:386

Cervantes (Russell), 2:536

Cervantes, Aristotle, and the Persiles, 2:536

Cervantes across the Centuries: A Quadricentennial Volume, 2:536

Cervantes and the Burlesque Sonnet, 2:536

Cervantes and the Humanist Vision: A Study of Four Exemplary Novels, 2:536

Cervantes' Christian Romance: A Study of, 2:536

Cervantes's Exemplary Novellas and the Adventure of Writing, 2:536

Cervantes the Writer and the Painter of Don Quijote, 2:536

Cesare Pavese: A Study of the Major Novels and Poems, 2:433

Cézanne: A Biography, 3:773

Cézanne: A Study of His Development, 3:773

Cézanne: The Late Work, 3:773

Cézanne, the Early Years, 1859–1872, 3:773

C. G. Jung, 5:456

C. G. Jung: Letters, 1906–1950, 5:454

C. G. Jung and the Scientific Attitude, 5:455

C. G. Jung's Psychology of Religion and Synchronicity, 5:455

Chaadayev and His Friends, 2:688

Chaim Potok, 1:1032

Chaim Weizmann: The Making of a Zionist Leader, 3:440

The Chainbearer; or, The Littlepage Manuscripts, 1:663

The Chain of Chance, 2:816

Chain of Voices, 2:159

Chain Reaction, 5:109

The Chair Dance. Selected Poems, 2:658

Chairil Anwar: The Poet and His Language, 2:319

The Chairs, 2:483

Chaka, 2:166

The Challenge for Group Psychotherapy: Present and Future, 5:417

The Challenge of Comparative Literature, and Other Addresses, 2:983

The Challenge of Epilepsy, 5:392

The Challenge of German Literature, 2:565

The Challenge of Pain, 5:393

The Challenge of Peace: God's Promise and Our Response, 4:896

The Challenge of the American Revolution, 3:587

The Challenge of World Poverty, 3:66, 3:98

Challenges of Change, 3:813

Challenges of Humanistic Psychology, 5:438

Challenging, 1:753

Challenging Colonialism, 3:435

Challenging the Political Order, 3:141

Challinor's Dictionary of Geology, 5:618, 5:625

Chamber Music, 3:664

Chambers Atlas of World History, 3:272

Chambers Biology Dictionary, 5:759

Chambers' Journal, 1:607

The Champion, 1739–41, 1:244

Champlain: The Life of Fortitude, 3:611

Chamulas in the World of the Sun, 3:865

Chance, Love, and Logic, 4:248

A Chance Acquaintance, 1:758

Chance or Destiny: Turning Points in American History, 3:581

Chance or Reality and Other Essays, 5:202

Chandra: A Biography of S. Chandrasekhar, 5:677

The Change: Women, Aging and the Menopause, 5:355

Change and Continuity in Seventeenth-Century England, 3:404, 4:734

Change and Habit: The Challenge of Our Time, 3:293

Change and the Muslim World, 4:573

Change in View, 4:380

The Changeling (Middleton), 1:190

The Changeling (Lagerlöf), 2:676

A Change of Heart, 2:463

Change of Heart: The Bypass Experience, 5:374

A Change of Skin, 2:865

A Change of World, 1:1037

Changes, 1:1224

Changes: A Love Story, 2:129

Changes: Notes on Choreography, 3:740

Changes in the Land, 3:549, 5:822

The Changes of Cain, 2:985

Change Your Mind, Change Your World, 3:176

The Changing Anatomy of Britain, 3:367

Changing Cities: Urban Sociology, 3:219

Changing Course, 5:282

Changing Gods in Medieval China, 1127–1276, 3:468

Changing Health Care for an Aging Society, 5:317

The Changing Light at Sandover, 1:1015

The Changing Nature of Man, 5:471

Changing Order: Replication and Induction in Scientific Practice, 5:151

Changing Our Own Words, 1:1134

Changing Perspectives in Literature and the Visual Arts, 1650–1820, 1:226

Changing Places, 1:515

The Changing Population of the United States, 3:241

The Changing Rhythm: A Study of Najib Mahfuz's Novels, 2:69

The Changing Role of Women in Bengal, 1849–1905, 3:485

The Changing Roles of Occupational Therapists in the 1980s, 5:338

Changing States: Transformation in Modern Irish Writing, 1:418

Changing the Rules, 5:184

The Changing World of the Ice Age, 5:626

Chan Kom: A Mayan Village, 3:39

Channeling: A Bibliographic Exploration, 4:866

Channeling: Investigations on Receiving Information from Paranormal Sources, 4:866

The Chant of Jimmie Blacksmith, 2:957

Chants d'Ombre, 2:146

Chaos, 2:79

Chaos and Order: Complex Dynamics in Literature and Science, 2:989

Chaos in Classical and Quantum Mechanics, 5:660

Chapayev, 2:718, 2:719

Chapel Road, 2:623

Chaplin: Last of the Clowns, 1:1162

Chaplin, the Mirror of Opinion, 1:1162

Chaplinana: A Commentary on Charlie Chaplin's 81 Movies, 1:1161

The Chapman Report, 1:1250

Chapters from a Floating Life: The Autobiography of a Chinese Artist, 2:218

Chapter Two, 1:1112

Character and Conflict in Jane Austen's Novels, 1:276

Character and Consciousness in Eighteenth-Century Comic Fiction, 1:230

Character and Context, 2:17

The Character and Influence of the Indian Trade in Wisconsin, 3:599

Character and Opinion in the United States 1920, 4:326

Character and the Christian Life: A Study in Theological Ethics, 4:897

A Character Index and Guide to the Fiction of Iris Murdoch, 1:524

Characteristics of Men, Manners, Opinions, Times, 4:214

The Character of Melodrama, 1:332

Character of Physical Law, 5:685

The Character of Swift's Satire: A Revised Focus, 1:261

The Character of the Word: The Texts of Zora Neale Hurston, 1:850

Characters, 2:369, 4:90

The Characters in the Novels of Thomas Love Peacock, 1:297

Characters of the Reformation, 1:442

Character Structure and the Organization of Self, 3:178

Charcoal Sketches, and Other Tales, 2:821

Charismatic Religion in Modern Research: A Bibliography, 4:864

Charities and Social Aid in Greece and Rome, 3:307

Charlemont; or, The Pride of the Village: A Tale of Kentucky, 1:696

Charles A. Lindbergh: A Bio-Bibliography, 3:929

Charles Babbage: Pioneer of the Computer, 5:576

Charles Babbage and His Calculating Engines, 5:575

Charles Beard and the Constitution, 3:566

Charles Brockden Brown, 1:636

Charles Brockden Brown: American Gothic Novelist, 1:636

Charles Brockden Brown: An American Tale, 1:636

Charles Brockden Brown: A Reference Guide, 1:636

Charles Brockden Brown: Pioneer Voice of America, 1:636

Charles Chaplin, 1:1162

Charles Chaplin: A Bio-Bibliography, 1:1161

Charles Chesterfield, or, The Adventures of a Youth of Genius, 1:408

Charles Darwin: A Commemoration, 1882–1982, 5:794

Charles Darwin and Evolution, 5:794

Charles Darwin and the Problems of Creation, 5:46, 5:794

Charles Darwin as Geologist, 5:622

Charles Darwin in Western Australia, 5:794

Charles Dickens, 1:349

Charles Dickens: A Critical Introduction, 1:349

Charles Dickens: A Critical Study, 1:359

Charles Dickens: His Tragedy and Triumph, 1:350, 1:994

Charles Dickens: The World of His Novels, 1:350, 1:1150, 1:1151

Charles Dickens, 1812–1870, 1:351

Charles Dickens and His Original Illustrators, 1:349

Charles Dickens and His Publishers, 1:350

The Charles Dickens Encyclopedia, 1:350

Charles E. Merriam and the Study of Politics, 3:162

Charles Grant and British Rule in India, 3:485, 3:497

Charles Hartshorne and the Existence of God, 4:289

Charles Horton Cooley: His Life and His Social Theory, 3:224

Charles I and the Popish Plot, 3:360

Charles Ives and His America, 3:702

Charles Ives and His Music, 3:702

Charles Ives Remembered: An Oral History, 3:702

Charles Kingsley, 1:369

Charles Kingsley: His Letters and Memories of His Life, 1:369

Charles Kingsley: The Lion of Eversley, 1:369

Charles Kingsley and the Christian Social Movement, 1:369

Charles Lamb, 1:296

Charles Lamb and His Contemporaries, 1:296

Charles Lindbergh, 3:929

Charles Olson: The Scholar's Art, 1:1027

Charles Olson and Robert Creeley: The Complete Correspondence, 1:1027

Charles Olson's Maximus, 1:1027

Charles Peirce's Empiricism, 4:249

Charles Reade, 1:389

Charles Reade: A Biography, 1:389

Charles Reade: Dramatist, Novelist, Journalist, 1:389

Charles Ryder's School Days and Other Stories, 1:562

Charles Sanders Peirce: From Pragmatism to Pragmaticism, 4:249

Charles Stewart Parnell, 3:364

Charles Sumner and the Coming of the Civil War, 3:527

Charles W. Chesnutt: America's First Great Black Novelist, 1:739

Charles W. Chesnutt: A Reference Guide, 1:739

Charles Wadell Chesnutt, 1:739

Charles Wadell Chesnutt: Pioneer of the Color Line, 1:739

Charley's Aunt, 1:486

Charlie Chaplin: A Centenary Celebration, 1:1162

Charlie Parker, 3:708

Charlotte: A Tale of Truth, 1:642

Charlotte and Emily Brontë: An Annotated Bibliography, 1:333

Charlotte Brontë: The Evolution of Genius, 1:335

Charlotte Brontë and Her Family, 1:335

Charlotte Perkins Gilman, 1:753

Charlotte Perkins Gilman: A Bibliography, 1:753

Charlotte Perkins Gilman: The Making of a Radical Feminist 1860–1896, 1:753

Charlotte Perkins Gilman: The Woman and Her Work, 1:753

Charlotte's Daughter: or The Three Orphans, 1:643

Charlotte's Web, 1:898, 1:1194

Charlotte Temple, 1:642, 1:1209, 1:1219

Charlotte Temple: A Tale of Truth, 1:643

Charm: Early and Uncollected Poems, 1:965

Charmed Circle: Gertrude Stein and Company, 1:883

A Charmed Life, 1:1007, 1:1008

Charmes, 2:513

The Charm of Physics, 5:691

The Charnel Rose, Senlin: A Biography and Other Poems, 1:810

Charon's Cosmology, 1:1048

The Charterhouse of Parma, 2:511

Chartism, 3:365

The Charwoman's Shadow, 1:615

The Chase, 2:860

Chase's Annual Events, 1:88

Chaseworld: Foxhunting and Storytelling in New Jersey's Pine Barrens, 3:859

Chasing the Monsoon: A Modern Pilgrimage through India, 3:902

Chasin the Trane: The Music and Mystique of John Coltrane, 3:690

A Chaste Maid in Cheapside, 1:189, 1:190

Chateaubriand, 2:466

Chateaubriand: Composition, Imagination and Poetry, 2:466

Chateaubriand: Poet, Statesman, Lover, 2:466

Chattering Jack, 1:583

Chaucer: His Life, His Works, His World, 1:151

Chaucer: Modern Essays in Criticism, 1:151

Chaucer: Sources and Backgrounds, 1:151

Chaucer: The Canterbury Tales, 1:151

Chaucer: The Critical Heritage, 1:150

Chaucer and Dante, 2:418

Chaucer and His Poetry, 1:151

Chaucer and Medieval Estates Satire, 1:151

Chaucer and the Early Writings of Boccaccio, 2:410

Chaucer and the Fictions of Gender, 1:151

Chaucer and the Fifteenth Century, 1:146

Chaucer and the French Tradition, 1:151

Chaucer and the Imagery of Narrative, 1:151

Chaucer and the Italian Trecento, 2:417

Chaucer and the Poets: An Essay on Troilus and Criseyde, 1:151

Chaucer and the Social Context, 1:151

Chaucer and the Subject of History, 1:151

Chaucer's Dream Poetry: Sources and Analogues, 1:151

Chaucer's Sexual Poetics, 1:150

Chayanov Peasants, and Economic Anthropology, 3:16

C. H. Dodd: Interpreter of the New Testament, 4:833

The Cheapest Nights, 2:65

The Cheapest Nights: Short Stories, 2:122

Cheap Rooms and Restless Hearts, 1:757

Checklist of American Imprints, 1:68

A Checklist of Writings about Edwin Muir, 1:522

The Cheechako: Facts, Fables and Recipes, 3:857

Chekhov (Hahn), 2:710

Chekhov (Troyat), 2:710

Chekhov: A Biography, 2:710

Chekhov: A Collection of Critical Essays, 2:710

Chekhov: A Spirit Set Free, 2:710

Chekhov: The Silent Voice of Freedom, 2:710

Chekhov and Other Essays, 2:690, 4:335

Chekhov and Women: Women in the Life and Work of Chekhov, 2:710

A Chekhov Companion, 2:710

Chekhov Criticism, 1880 through 1986, 2:710

Chekhov in Performance in Russia and Soviet Russia, 2:710

The Chekhov Play: A New Interpretation, 2:710

Chekhov's Great Plays: A Critical Anthology, 2:710

Chekhov's Journey, 2:710

Chekhov's Poetics, 2:710

Chelation Therapy: The Key to Unclogging Your Arteries, 5:375

Chemcyclopedia, 5:724

Chemical and Physical Data, 5:653

The Chemical Arts of Old China, 5:728

Chemical Atomism in the Nineteenth Century, 5:741

Chemical Bonding and the Geometry of Molecules, 5:730

Chemical Engineering Design Project, 5:223

Chemical Evolution, 5:740

A Chemical Feast, 5:346

Chemical Formulary, 5:724

Chemical Formulary Series: Cumulative Index, Vols. 1–25, 5:724

The Chemical History of a Candle, 5:684, 5:744

Chemical Industry, 1900–1930, 5:728

Chemical Industry during the Nineteenth Century, 5:728

Chemical Information Management, 5:727

Chemical Information Sources, 5:727

Chemical Manipulation, 5:744

Chemical Manipulation of Crop Growth and Development, 5:263

Chemical Mediators of Inflammation and Immunity, 5:790

Chemical Metallurgy, 5:237

The Chemical Philosophy, 4:150

Chemicals and Society: A Guide to the New Chemical Age, 5:736

Chemistry, 5:752

Chemistry: The Central Science, 5:734

Chemistry, Alchemy and the New Philosophy, 1550–1700, 4:125

Chemistry Applied to Agriculture, 5:271

Chemistry for the Millions, 5:729

Chemistry Imagined: Reflections on Science, 5:748

Chemistry in America, Eighteen Seventy-Six to Nineteen Seventy-Six, 5:56

Chemistry in Modern Life, 5:738

Chemistry Made Easy, 5:730

Chemistry Made Simple, 5:730

Chemistry of Pulp and Paper Making, 1:6

The Chemistry of Soils, 5:264

The Chemistry of the Actinide Elements, 5:754

The Chemist's English: Say It in English, Please!, 5:727

Chemmeen, 2:178

Chem Sources International, 5:724

Chem Sources U.S.A., 5:724

The Chequer Board, 2:962

Chéri, 2:470

Chernobyl: The Real Story, 5:287

Chernyshevsky and the Age of Realism, 2:711

The Cherry Orchard, 2:707, 2:709

Chesapeake, 1:1248, 3:931

Chester Cycle, 1:158

The Chester Mystery Cycle, 1:159

The Chester Mystery Cycle: A New Edition with Modernized Spelling, 1:159

The Chester Mystery Cycle: Essays and Documents, 1:159

Chesterton: A Seer of Science, 5:202

The Chestnut Tree, 1:645

Chesty: A Tribute to a Legend, 1:1166

Chevengur, 2:748, 2:749

Chez Nous: A Domestic Comedy in Two Acts, 1:525

Chicago Guide to Preparing Electronic Manuscripts, 1:117, 5:545

The Chicago Manual of Style, 1:117

The Chicago School: A Liberal Critique of Capitalism, 3:200

The Chicago School of Sociology, 3:200

Chicana Lesbians: The Girls Our Mothers Warned Us About, 1:1184

The Chicano Anthology Index, 1:806

Chicano Narrative: The Dialectics of Difference, 1:1132

Chicano Poetry: A Critical Introduction, 1:798

Chicanos and Film: Essays on Chicano Representation and Resistance, 1:1157

Chicano Theater: Themes and Forms, 1:1073

The Chicken Book, 5:263

Chicken Soup and Other Folk Remedies, 5:321

Chicken Soup with Barley, 1:564

Chicorel Theater Index to Plays in Anthologies and Collections, 1:124

The Chief: Doctor William Osler, 5:54

The Chief Executive, 3:147

Chief Modern Poets of Britain and America, 1:418, 1:876, 1:915

The Chief Rabbi, the Pope, and the Holocaust, 4:638

The Chief Works and Others, 4:145

Chike and the River, 2:128

Chikuma River Sketches, 2:293

Child Abuse Prediction: Policy Implications, 5:416

The Child and Reality: Problems of Genetic Psychology, 3:267

The Child and the Curriculum, 3:260

Childbearing after 35: The Risks and the Rewards, 5:357

Childbirth with Insight, 5:359

Childbirth with Love, 5:359

Child Care: A Parent's Guide, 5:322

Child Christopher and Goldilind the Fair, 1:617

Child Development: An Introduction, 3:257

Child Development and Education: A Piagetian Perspective, 3:267

Childe Byron, 1:1099

Childe Harold, 1:266, 1:267, 1:281, 1:282
The Childermass, 1:514
Childhood (Nexø), 2:653
Childhood (Sarraute), 2:506
Childhood (Tolstoy), 2:763
Childhood, "Boyhood" and "Youth," 2:764
Childhood, Youth and Exile: My Past and Thoughts, 2:728
Childhood and Folklore: A Psychoanalytic Study of Apache Personality, 3:864
Childhood and Society, 3:173, 3:182, 5:442
Childhood Psychosis: Initial Studies and New Insights, 5:416
Childhood's End, 1:614, 1:1252
Childhood Socialization (Denzin), 3:216
Childhood Socialization, (Hendel), 3:216
Childhood Years: A Memoir (Yosho jidai), 2:294
The Child in the Family, 3:266
The Child in the House: An Imaginary Portrait, 1:387
Child-Lore: A Study in Folklore and Psychology, 3:869
Child of All Nations: A Novel, 2:321
Child of Fortune (Chuji), 2:294
Child of Light: A Reassessment of Mary Shelley, 1:301
Child of Man, 2:797
A Child of Sorrow, 2:328
The Child of the Islands: A Poem, 1:384
Child Psychiatry, 5:416
Children, 1:1091
The Children, 1:787
Children and Books, 1:50, 1:53
Children in English Society, 3:356
Children in Poverty: Child Development and Public Policy, 3:211
Children in the Hospital, 5:444
The Children of Aataentsic: A History of the Huron People to 1860, 3:611
The Children of Abraham: Judaism, Christianity, Islam, 3:459

Children of Abraham: The Short Stories of Sholem Asch, 2:36
Children of Alcoholism: A Survivor's Manual, 5:403
Children of Crisis: A Study of Courage and Fear, 3:249, 5:416
Children of Different Worlds: The Formation of Social Behavior, 3:15
Children of Dune, 1:1259
The Children of Frankenstein, 5:573
Children of Gebelawi, 2:68
The Children of God: A Make-Believe Revolution, 4:864
The Children of God/Family of Love: An Annotated Bibliography, 4:864
Children of Kaywana, 2:937, 2:938
Children of Light, 1:1055
The Children of Noisy Village, 2:677
The Children of Odin: The Book of Northern Myths, 1:461
Children of Paradise, 2:494
Children of Pride: A True Story of Georgia and the Civil War, 3:529
The Children of Sanchez, 3:34
Children of Six Cultures: A Psycho-Cultural Analysis, 5:417
Children of the Albatross, 1:865
Children of the Arbat, 2:754
The Children of the Dream, 5:434, 5:435
Children of the Jinn: In Search of the Kurds and Their Country, 4:570
The Children of the New Forest, 1:374
Children of the Poor, 3:822
Children of the Revels, 1:170
Children of the Sea, 1:1107
Children of the Tenements, 3:822
Children of the Uprooted, 3:581
Children of Wax: African Folk Tales, 3:857
The Children of Woot: A History of the Kuba Peoples, 3:431
Children's Book Awards International, 1:52

Children's Books: Awards and Prizes, 1:52
Children's Books and Class Society, 1:575
Children's Books in England: Five Centuries of Social Life, 1:36, 1:578
Children's Books in Print, 1:74
Children's Books of Yesterday, 1:579
Children's Books on Africa and Their Authors, 2:112
Children's Britannica, 1:106
Children's Catalog, 1:74
The Children's Crusade, 1:1063
Children's Games in Street and Playground, 3:884
The Children's Hour, 1:1092, 1:1093
Children's Island, 2:674
Children with a Star: Jewish Youth in Nazi Europe, 4:635
Children with Cancer: A Comprehensive Reference Guide for Parents, 5:371
Children with Handicaps: A Medical Primer, 5:321
Children with Tourette Syndrome: A Parents' Guide, 5:376
A Child's Christmas in Wales, 1:557
The Child's Conception of Number, 3:267
The Child's Conception of Physical Causality, 3:267
The Child's Conception of the World, 3:192, 3:267
The Child's Construction of Knowledge: Piaget for Teaching Children, 3:267
The Child's Discovery of Himself, 5:416
A Child's Garden of Verses, 1:396, 1:589
A Child's History of England, 1:349
Child's Play, 2:958, 2:959
Child Training and Personality: A Cross-Cultural Study, 3:15
Childworld, 1:1022
Chile: The Legacy of Hispanic Capitalism, 3:635
Chile and the United States: Empires in Conflict, 3:635
Chileno!, 2:885
The Chills, 2:695
Chilly Scenes of Winter, 1:945

Chimera, 1:942
The Chimes, 1:348
Chimes at Midnight, 1:1178
The Chimpanzees of Gombe:
  Patterns of Behavior,
  5:770, 5:833
China: A Critical Bibliogra-
  phy, 3:465
China: A Handbook, 3:466
China: A Macro History,
  3:467
China: A New History, 3:467,
  3:498
China: A Short Cultural His-
  tory, 2:186
China: Tradition and Trans-
  formation, 3:467, 3:498
China after Mao: With Se-
  lected Documents, 3:496
China and Christianity, 4:532
China and Japan at War,
  1937–1945: The Politics of
  Collaboration, 3:464
China and the Christian Im-
  pact, 3:468, 4:532
China and the Major Powers
  in East Asia, 3:496
Chinabound: A Fifty Year
  Memoir, 3:498
China Changes Faces: The
  Road from Revolution
  1949–1989, 3:470
China in Disintegration: The
  Republican Era in Chinese
  History, 3:472
China in World History,
  3:466
China Journal, 3:902
China Men, 1:1000
China Perceived: Images and
  Policies in Chinese Ameri-
  can Relations, 3:498
China's Continuous Revolu-
  tion: The Post-Liberation
  Epoch, 1949–1981, 3:469
China's Crisis, China's Hope,
  2:255
China's Economy in Global
  Perspective, 3:496
China's Imperial Past, 3:467
China's Intellectuals: Advise
  and Dissent, 2:233, 3:470
China's Own Critics, 2:247,
  4:360
China's Political Economy:
  The Quest for Develop-
  ment since 1949, 3:472
China's Response to the
  West, 3:472
China's Response to the
  West: A Documentary Sur-
  vey, 1839–1923, 3:498

China's Second Revolution:
  Reform after Mao, 3:470
China's Silk Trade: Tradition-
  al Industry in the Modern
  World, 1842–1937, 3:471
China to 1850: A Short His-
  tory, 2:190
The Chinese, 3:466
Chinese Alchemy, Medicine,
  and Religion in the China
  of A.D. 320, 4:529
Chinese Amusement: The
  Lively Plays of Li Yü,
  2:210
The Chinese and Japanese,
  3:464
Chinese Approaches to
  Literature from Confucius
  to Liang Ch'i-ch'ao, 2:191
Chinese Art, 3:760
Chinese Cinema: Culture and
  Politics since 1949, 3:469
Chinese Civilization: A
  Source Book, 4:522
Chinese Civilization and So-
  ciety: A Sourcebook, 3:465
The Chinese Communist
  Army in Action, 3:470
Chinese Communists and Ru-
  ral Society, 1927–1934,
  3:471
The Chinese Drama from the
  Earliest Times until Today,
  2:188
The Chinese Earth, 2:262
Chinese-English Dictionary of
  Contemporary Usage, 1:97
Chinese-English Dictionary of
  Idioms, 1:97
Chinese-English Dictionary of
  Modern Usage, 1:97
The Chinese Experience in
  America, 3:558
Chinese Fairy Tales and Fan-
  tasies, 2:193
Chinese Fiction from Taiwan:
  Critical Perspectives, 2:233
Chinese History and Litera-
  ture: Collections of Stud-
  ies, 2:191
Chinese History in Economic
  Perspective, 3:467
Chinese Ideas of Life and
  Death, 4:524
Chinese in Southeast Asia,
  3:488
Chinese Intellectuals in Cri-
  sis, 4:361
Chinese Literature, 2:193
Chinese Literature I: Popular
  Fiction and Drama, 2:192
Chinese Literature II: Nature
  Poetry, 2:192

Chinese Literature III: Tales
  of the Supernatural, 2:192
Chinese Local Elites and Pat-
  terns of Dominance, 3:470
Chinese Love Stories from
  "Ching-shih," 2:197
Chinese Lyricism, 2:191
Chinese Massage Therapy: A
  Handbook of Therapeutic
  Massage, 5:318
Chinese Middlebrow Fiction,
  2:190
The Chinese Mind: Essentials
  of Chinese Philosophy and
  Culture, 4:358
Chinese Mythology, 4:522
Chinese Narrative: Critical
  and Theoretical Essays,
  2:191
Chinese Narrative Poetry
  from the Late Han
  through T'ang Dynasties,
  2:190
Chinese Poetic Writing, 2:189
Chinese Poetry: Major Modes
  and Genres, 2:191
Chinese Profiles, 2:240
Chinese Religion: An Intro-
  duction, 4:523
Chinese Religion in Western
  Languages, 4:522
Chinese Religions, 4:523
The Chinese Renaissance,
  2:247, 4:360
The Chinese Revolution in
  Historical Perspective,
  3:472
Chinese Rhyme-prose, 2:191
Chinese Roundabout: Essays
  in History and Culture,
  3:467, 3:502
The Chinese Short Story,
  2:189
Chinese Society in the Eight-
  eenth Century, 3:468
Chinese-Soviet Relations
  1937–1945, 3:470
Chinese Stories from Taiwan
  1960–1970, 2:235
Chinese Story and Other
  Tales, 2:747
Chinese Theater in the Days
  of Kublai Khan, 2:189
The Chinese Theatre in Mod-
  ern Times: From 1840 to
  the Present Day, 2:234
Chinese Theories of Literature, 2:190
Chinese Thought: From Confucius to Mao Tse-tung,
  4:358, 4:522
Chinese Thought, Society,
  and Science, 3:467

The Chinese Vernacular Story, 2:189
Chinese Village, Socialist State, 3:470
The Chinese Wall, 2:579
The Chinese Way in Religion, 4:522
Chinese Women in a Century of Revolution, 1850–1950, 3:471
Ch'ing Administration: Three Studies, 3:498
Chinua Achebe: A Celebration, 2:129
The Chip, 5:230
Chips! Strategic Issues in Computer Industry Negotiations, 5:557
Chips with Everything, 1:565
Chiropractors: A Consumers' Guide, 5:338
Chirundu, 2:166, 2:167
Chitty-Chitty-Bang-Bang, 1:593
The Chivalric World of Don Quijote, 2:536
The Chocolate Deal, 2:18
Choice, 2:646
Choice and Chance: An Introduction to Inductive Logic, 5:65
Choice Humorous Satirical Works, 2:548
Choices: Realistic Alternatives in Cancer Treatment, 5:372
Choices and Decisions in Health Care, 5:120
Choices in Modern Jewish Thought: A Partisan Guide, 4:661
The Choking Doberman and Other "New" Urban Legends, 3:868
Cholera: The American Scientific Encounter, 1947–1980, 5:390
Choosing a Sex Ethic: A Jewish Inquiry, 4:598
Choosing a World Map: Attributes, Distortions, Classes, Aspects, 3:135
Choosing Crime, 3:205
Chopin, 3:690
The Chopin Companion: Profiles of the Man and the Musician, 3:690
The Chopin Playoffs, 1:1094
The Chorale, 4:738
Choreographer and Composer, 3:734

Choreography, the Art of the Body: An Anatomy of Expression, 3:735
A Chorus of Disapproval, 1:437
The Chosen, 1:1032
Chosen Country, 1:828
The Chosen People in America, 4:634, 4:646
The Chosen Place, the Timeless People, 1:1014
Chrestomathia, 4:190
Chrétien de Troyes: A Study of the Arthurian Romances, 2:467
Chrétien de Troyes: Inventor of the Modern Novel, 2:467
Chrétien de Troyes: The Man and His Work, 2:467
Chris Christofferson: A Play in Three Acts, 1:1107
Christ and Modernity: Christian Self-Understanding in a Technological Age, 5:197
Christ and the Decree, 4:762
Christ and the Moral Life, 4:900
Christ and Time, 4:832
The Christened Chinaman, 2:700, 2:701
Christening Pagan Mysteries: Erasmus in Pursuit of Wisdom, 4:139
Christiaan Huygens and the Development of Science in the Seventeenth Century, 5:695
Christian Antioch: A Study of Early Christian Thought in the East, 4:687
Christian Attitudes toward War and Peace, 4:678
Christian Blessedness, with Reflections upon a Late Essay Concerning Human Understanding, 4:180
The Christian Century in Japan, 1549–1650, 3:474, 4:540
The Christian Challenge, 4:775
The Christian Churches of the East, 4:755
The Christian Church in the Cold War, 4:755
The Christian Commitment: Essays in Pastoral Theology, 4:745
Christian Discourses, 4:239
Christian Ethics: The Historical Development, 4:679

The Christian Faith, 4:253, 4:680, 4:742
The Christian Fathers, 4:690
Christian Iconography: A Study of Its Origins, 4:688
The Christian Interpretation of the Cabala in the Renaissance, 4:124
Christianity: A Way of Salvation, 4:677, 4:883
Christianity, Communism, and the Ideal Society, 4:284
Christianity, Social Tolerance, and Homosexuality, 1:1179, 1:1181, 4:678
Christianity and Civilization, 3:293
Christianity and Classical Culture, 4:99, 4:683
Christianity and Culture, 1:472
Christianity and Democracy, 4:306
Christianity and Evolution, 4:336
Christianity and Islam under the Sultans, 3:452
Christianity and Judaism: The Formative Categories, 4:602
Christianity and Paganism, 350–750: The Conversion of Western Europe, 4:683
Christianity and Revolution: Radical Christian Testimonies, 1520–1650, 4:725
Christianity and the Encounter of the World Religions, 5:206
Christianity and the Scientist, 5:160
Christianity and World Religion, 4:423
Christianity in a Revolutionary Age, 4:741
Christianity in China, 4:532
Christianity in European History, 3:326
Christianity in Modern Japan, 4:540
Christianity in Modern Korea, 3:481
Christianity in the Roman Empire, 4:684
Christianity in the Twenty-First Century, 4:747
Christianity in Today's World: An Eerdmans Handbook, 4:744
Christianizing the Roman Empire, A.D. 100–400, 4:684

A Christian Looks at the
Jewish Question, 4:306
Christian Missions in Nigeria:
The Making of a New
Elite, 3:425
Christian Origins in Sociolog-
ic Perspective: Methods
and Resources, 4:617,
4:815
Christian Periodical Index,
4:7
The Christian Philosophy of
St. Augustine, 4:110
The Christian Platonists of
Alexandria: Eight Lectures,
4:63, 4:116
The Christian Polity of John
Calvin, 4:762
Christian Rite and Christian
Drama in the Middle Ages,
1:157, 4:699
Christians and Jews in Ger-
many, 3:351, 4:637
Christians and Jews in the
Ottoman Empire, 4:568
Christians and the Military:
The Early Experience,
4:688
The Christians and the Ro-
man Empire, 4:684
Christians and the World of
Computers, 5:126
The Christians as the Ro-
mans Saw Them, 4:100,
4:684
Christian Science: Its En-
counter with American
Culture, 4:843
Christian Science Today:
Power, Policy, Practice,
4:842
Christian Spirituality, 4:678
Christian Spirituality from
the Apostolic Fathers to
the Twelfth Century, 4:679
The Christian Tradition, 4:99,
4:720
Christian Tradition in Mo-
dern British Verse Drama,
1:426
Christian Uniqueness Recon-
sidered, 4:898
Christie in Love, 1:449
Christina Rossetti, 1:390
Christina Rossetti: A Bio-
graphical and Critical
Study, 1:390
Christina Rossetti: A Refer-
ence Guide, 1:390
Christina Rossetti: The Poet-
ry of Endurance, 1:391
Christina Rossetti and the
Poetry of Discovery, 1:391

Christina Rossetti in Context,
1:391
Christina Stead, 2:964
Christina Stead—A Life of
Letters, 2:964
Christine, 1:1240
Christ in East and West,
4:755
Christ in Eastern Christian
Thought, 4:679
Christ in the Christian Tradi-
tion, 4:685
Christ Legends, 2:677
Christmas Books, 1:348
A Christmas Carol, 1:348,
1:584
Christmas Customs around
the World, 3:870
A Christmas Garland, 1:440
A Christmas Memory, 1:959
Christmas Stories, 1:348
The Christological Contro-
versy, 4:686
Christology in Conflict: The
Identity of a Saviour in
Barth and Rahner, 4:885
The Christology of Rosemary
Radford Ruether, 4:785,
4:905
The Christology of the New
Testament, 4:825, 4:832
Christopher Columbus, 3:916
Christopher Columbus, A Ra-
dio Play, 1:518
Christopher Columbus, Mari-
ner, 3:589, 3:916
Christopher Fry, 1:480
Christopher Isherwood: A
Bibliography of His Per-
sonal Papers, 1:501
Christopher Isherwood: A
Personal Memoir, 1:501
Christopher Isherwood: A
Reference Guide, 1:501
Christopher Isherwood: Myth
and Anti-myth, 1:501
Christopher Marlowe, 1:187
Christopher Marlowe: An An-
notated Bibliography of
Criticism since 1950,
1:187
Christopher Marlowe: A
Study of His Thought,
Learning and Character,
1:187
Christopher Marlowe: Poet
for the Stage, 1:187
Christopher Marlowe and His
Associates, 1:187
Christopher Marlowe in Lon-
don, 1:187
Christopher Okigbo: Collect-
ed Poems, 2:142

Christopher Okigbo: Creative
Rhetoric, 2:142
Christopher Smart: An Anno-
tated Bibliography, 1:255
Christopher Smart: Scholar
of the University, 1:255
Christopher Unborn, 2:865
Christopher Wren and St.
Paul's Cathedral, 3:796
Christ Stopped at Eboli,
2:424
Christus Victor, 4:678, 4:886
Christ without Myth: A Study
Based on the Theology of
Rudolf Bultmann, 4:831
The Chromosome Theory of
Inheritance, 5:779
The Chronicle Historie of
Perkin Warbeck, 1:179
Chronicle of a Death Fore-
told, 2:866, 2:867
The Chronicle of King Ed-
ward the First, Surnamed
Longshanks, 1:195
Chronicle of Queens, 1:1187
A Chronicle of the Conquest
of Granada, 1:679, 1:680
A Chronicle of the English
Death, 1:469
Chronicle of the Indian
Wars, 3:516
A Chronicle of the Last Pa-
gans, 4:449
The Chronicle of Travnik,
2:828
The Chronicler of Baretshire:
A Life of Anthony Trol-
lope, 1:407
Chronicles in Stone, 2:779
The Chronicles of Aunt Min-
ervy Ann, 1:754
Chronicles of Barabbas,
1884–1934, 1:41
The Chronicles of Barset-
shire, or The Cathedral
Stories, 1:385, 1:405
Chronicles of Bustos Do-
mecq, 2:855, 2:856
The Chronicles of Corum,
1:616
The Chronicles of Narnia,
1:512, 1:578, 1:586, 4:776
Chronika, 4:468
A Chronological History of
World Theatre, 1:1075
A Chronological Outline of
American Literature, 1:134
A Chronological Outline of
British Literature, 1:133
A Chronology of English Lit-
erature, 1:132
A Chronology of Irish His-
tory since 1500, 3:369

Chronology of Islamic History, 4:567
The Chronology of Plato's Dialogues, 4:79
A Chronology of Printing, 1:7
The Chronology of the Geological Record, 5:625
Chronology of the Origin and Progress of Paper and Paper-Making, 1:5
A Chronology of World History, 3:274
The Chrysanthemum and the Sword, 3:22, 3:26, 3:27, 3:474, 4:534
Chrysanthemums and Other Stories, 2:244
Chthon, 1:1253
Chuang Tzu: A New Selected Translation with an Exposition of the Philosophy of Kuo Hsiang, 4:359
Chuang Tzu: Basic Writings, 4:529
Chuang Tzu: The Inner Chapters, 4:528
Chuang Tzu: World Philosopher at Play, 4:529
Chuang Tzu, The Seven Inner Chapters, 4:522, 4:526
Chu Hsi: New Studies, 4:526
Chu Hsi and Neo-Confucianism, 4:526
The Church, 4:774
Church, State and Jew in the Middle Ages, 4:623
The Church against Itself, 4:785
The Church and Abortion, 4:895
Church and People, 1450–1600, 3:358, 4:726
Church and Sect in Canada, 3:609
Church and Society in England: Henry VIII to James I, 4:726
Church and Society in England, 1770–1970: A Historical Survey, 3:355
Church and Society in Ireland, A.D. 400–1200, 3:370
Church and Society in the Last Centuries of Byzantium, 4:693
Church and State from Constantine to Theodosius, 4:683
Church and State in Tudor Ireland, 3:358
The Church and the Age of Reason, 4:738

The Church and the Jews in the Thirteenth Century, 4:624
The Church and the Left, 3:390
The Church and the Second Sex, 1:1186, 1:1187, 4:764, 4:765
Church Dogmatics: The Doctrine of God, 4:757
Churches and People in Australia and New Zealand, 1860–1930, 3:493
Churches in the Nineteenth Century, 4:740
The Churches Speak On: Abortion, 4:895
The Churches the Apostles Left Behind, 4:824
Churchill: A Life, 3:401
Churchill, Roosevelt, Stalin, 3:278, 3:344
Churchill, the Great Game and Total War, 3:401
Churchill, the Playwright, 1:459
Churchill as Warlord, 3:401
The Churchill Coalition, 1940–1945, 3:367
The Churchill Coalition and Wartime Politics, 1940–1945, 3:401
The Churchill Play, 1:450
Churchill's War Memoirs, 3:401
The Church in France, 1848–1907, 4:741
The Church in the British Era, 3:610
The Church in the Canadian Era: The First Century of Confederation, 3:609
The Church in the Eighteenth Century, 4:739
The Church in the French Era, 3:612
Church Manual of the Mother Church, 4:843, 4:874
The Church of Scientology and L. Ron Hubbard: A Bibliography, 4:869
The Church on the Mountain, 2:641
Church Order in the New Testament, 4:826
Chushingura: The Treasure of Loyal Retainers, A Puppet Play, 2:274
Ch'u Tz'u, 2:195
Ch'u Tz'u: The Songs of the South, 2:196
Chu Yuan; A Play in Five Acts, 2:250

Cicero, 3:313
Cicero (Bailey), 4:72
Cicero: A Biography, 2:385, 4:72
Cicero: A Portrait, 2:385, 4:72
Cicero: The Ascending Years, 2:385
Cicero: The Senior Statesman, 2:385, 4:72
Cicero, a Political Biography, 3:314
Cicero and His Influence, 2:385, 4:73
Cicero and the Fall of the Roman Republic, 2:385
Cicero and the Roman Republic, 4:72
The Cicerone, 3:400
Ciceronianus: Or, A Dialogue on the Best Style of Speaking, 4:138
Cicero Scepticus, 4:131
Cicero's Elegant Style: An Analysis of the Pro Archia, 2:385
Cicero's Philippics and Their Demosthenic Model: The Rhetoric of Crisis, 2:385
Cicero's Social and Political Thought, 2:385, 4:59
Cicero the Politician, 4:72
The Cid, Cinna, the Theatrical Illusion, 2:471
Cidean Ballads: Ballads about the Great Spanish Hero, El Cid, 2:537
The Cider House Rules, 1:991
Cimetière Marin, 2:513
Cincinnatus: George Washington and the Enlightenment, 3:522
Cinderellas of the Empire: Towards a History of Kiribati and Tuvalu, 3:495
Cinders, 4:397
The Cinema Book, 1:1158
The Cinema of Fritz Lang, 3:840
The Cinema of Jean Genet: Un Chant d'Amour, 2:479
The Cinema of Josef von Sternberg, 1:1176
A Cinema of Loneliness: Penn, Kubrick, Scorsese, Spielberg, Altman, 3:828
The Cinema of Stanley Kubrick, 3:839
Cinema Sequels and Remakes, 1903–1987, 3:826
Cinematics, 4:339
Cinna, 2:470

Cinnamon Skin, 1:1234
Cinque Maggio, 2:426
A Cinza das Horas, 2:893
The Circle Game, 2:906
The Circle of Baal Shem
  Tov: Studies in Hasidism,
  4:660
Circle of Paradox, 2:543
Circle of Unity: Baha'i Ap-
  proaches to Current Social
  Issues, 4:861
The Circling Song, 2:71,
  2:120
The Circulation of the Blood
  and Other Writings, 5:361
Circumference and Circum-
  stance, 1:748
The Circus, 1:1160
The Circus in the Attic and
  Other Stories, 1:892, 1:893
The Circus Valentine, 1:1105
CIS Congressional Committee
  Hearings Index, 1:109
CIS Index, 1:109
Cistercian Father Series,
  4:680
CIS U.S. Serial Set Index,
  1:109
The Citadel of the Senses
  and Other Essays, 5:391
Cities and Immigrants, 3:124,
  3:136
Cities and Sea-Coasts and
  Islands, 3:900
Cities and the Wealth of Na-
  tions: Principles of Eco-
  nomic Life, 3:216
Cities and Years, 2:718
Cities in Revolt: Urban Life
  in America, 1743–1776,
  3:519, 3:569
Cities in the Wilderness,
  3:569
The Cities of Ancient Mexi-
  co: Reconstructing a Lost
  World, 3:628
Cities of Salt, 2:69
Cities of the Interior, 1:865
Cities of the Red Night,
  1:957
Cities of the World: World
  Regional Urban Develop-
  ment, 3:124
Cities on a Hill: A Journey
  through Contemporary
  American Cultures, 3:559
The Citizen and the State:
  Essays on Regulation,
  3:108
Citizen Kane, 1:1178
The Citizen Kane Book:
  Raising Kane, 1:1179
Citizen Politics, 3:141

The City (Park), 3:216, 3:237
City (Simak), 1:1262
The City (Weber), 3:217,
  3:244
City, Class, and Culture,
  3:364
City and State Directories in
  Print, 1:104
The City and the Dogs (The
  Time of the Hero), 2:886
The City and the House,
  2:422
The City and the Mountains,
  2:559
The City and the Pillar,
  1:1061
The City and the Stars, 1:614
The City as a Work of Art:
  London, Paris and Vienna,
  3:341
City Classification Handbook:
  Methods and Applications,
  3:127
The City Hospitals: The Un-
  dercare of the Underprivi-
  leged, 5:328
The City in History, 3:216,
  5:169, 5:170
The City in Late Imperial
  China, 3:469
The City in Slang: New York
  Life and Popular Speech,
  3:872
The City in South Asia: Pre-
  Modern and Modern,
  3:483
The City in the Ancient
  World, 4:439
City Madam, 1:189
City of Discontent, 1:855
City of God, 1:1246, 1:1247
The City of God against the
  Pagans, 4:109
City of Many Days, 2:19
City of Night, 1:1190, 1:1191
City of Saffron, 2:59
City of Tears, 2:794
The City of the Heart: Yunus
  Emre's Verses of Wisdom
  and Love, 2:101
The City of the Saints, 3:913
City of the Sun, 2:410
The City of the Sun: A Poeti-
  cal Dialogue, 4:137
The City of Tomorrow and
  Its Planning, 3:778
City of Women: Sex and
  Class in New York City,
  1789–1860, 3:525
City of Words: American Fic-
  tion, 1950–1970, 1:920
City of Wrong, 2:59

City on a Hill, A History of
  Ideas and Myths in Ameri-
  ca, 1:627
A City on the Plain, 2:407
City People, 3:558
City Primeval: High Noon in
  Detroit, 1:1232
City without Walls, 1:435
The Civic Culture, 3:149,
  3:150
The Civic Culture Revisited,
  3:141, 3:150
The Civic Culture Study,
  1959–1960, 3:141
The Civic World of Early
  Renaissance Florence,
  3:333
Civil and Military Gazette,
  1:369
Civil Disobedience and Moral
  Law in Nineteenth-Century
  American Philosophy, 4:35
Civil Engineering Contracts:
  Practice and Procedure,
  5:224
Civilisation, Ma Mère!, 2:119
Civilité Types, 1:14
Civilization and Barbarism:
  Life of Juan Facundo Qui-
  roga, 2:884
Civilization and Capitalism,
  Fifteenth to Eighteenth
  Century, 3:283
Civilization before Greece
  and Rome, 4:440
Civilization of Europe, Sixth
  to Sixteenth Century,
  3:253
The Civilization of Experi-
  ence: A Whiteheadian
  Theory of Culture, 4:342
Civilization of the Ancient
  Mediterranean, 4:439
Civilization of the Ancient
  Mediterranean: Greece and
  Rome, 3:298
The Civilization of the
  Goddess: The World of
  Old Europe, 4:434
The Civilization of the Ren-
  aissance in Italy, 2:400,
  3:333, 3:400
Civilization or Barbarism: An
  Authentic Anthropology,
  3:429
Civilizations of the World:
  The Human Adventure,
  3:274
The Civilized Body: Social
  Domination, Control, and
  Health, 5:319
The Civilized Engineer,
  5:166, 5:253

The Civilized Imagination, 1:270, 1:622
Civilizing the Machine, 1:628
Civil Liberties, "Brainwashing" and "Cults", 4:857
The Civil War (Catton), 3:571
The Civil War (Cicero), 3:313, 3:571
Civil War (Lucan), 2:387
The Civil War: A Narrative, 3:528
The Civil War: An Illustrated History, 3:530
The Civil War and Reconstruction, 3:529
Civil War Books: A Critical Bibliography, 3:511
The Civil War Day by Day: An Almanac, 1861–1865, 3:506
The Civil War Dictionary, 3:508
The Civil War in France, 3:290
Civil Wars, 3:311
Civil War Treasury of Tales, 1:725
Claiming the Heritage, 1:804
The Claim of Reason: Wittgenstein, Skepticism, Morality, and Tragedy, 4:345
Claire Clairmont and the Shelleys, 1798-1879, 1:301
The Clairvoyant Eye: The Poetry and Poetics of Wallace Stevens, 1:888
Clamor, 2:541
Clamor of Innocence: Central American Short Stories, 2:850
Clamorous Voices: Shakespeare's Women Today, 1:218
Clandestine in Chile: The Adventures of Miguel Littin, 2:867
Clandestine Poems, 2:863
Clandestine Poems—Poemas Clandestinos: Bilingual Edition, 2:863
Clara Howard, 1:635
Clara Schumann: An Artist's Life, Based on Material Found in Diaries and Letters, 3:716
Clara Schumann: The Artist and the Woman, 3:716
Clara Schumann, A Dedicated Spirit: A Study of Her Life and Work, 3:716
Clara's Ole Man, 1:1086
Clare: The Critical Heritage, 1:286

Clarel: A Poem and Pilgrimage in the Holy Land, 1:687
Clarice Lispector, 2:896
Clarissa, 2:900
Clarissa Harlow, or The History of a Young Lady, 1:253, 1:1209
Clarissa's Ciphers: Meaning and Disruption in Richardson's Clarissa, 1:253
A Clash of Cultures, 3:485
Clash of Worlds, 4:857
Class, Politics, and Ideology in the Iranian Revolution, 3:448
Class, Status, and Power, 3:158
Class and Class Conflict in Industrial Society, 3:204
Class and Society in Early America, 1:629
Class Conflict in Egypt, 1945–1970, 3:446
Classes in Modern Society, 3:222
Classic, Romantic and Modern, 1:814
Classical American Philosophy, 4:36
Classical Approaches to the Study of Religion, 4:422
Classical Arabic Poetry, 2:62
Classical Arab Islam: The Heritage and Culture of the Golden Age, 3:443
Classical Armenian Culture: Influences and Creativity, 2:77
Classical Chinese Tales of the Supernatural and the Fantastic, 2:192
A Classical Dictionary, 2:346
Classical Dictionary of the Vulgar Tongue, 1:92
The Classical Era: From the 1740s to the End of the 18th Century, 3:664
Classical General Relativity, 5:677
The Classical Hollywood Cinema, 1:1157
Classical Influences on English Prose, 1:429
Classical Japanese Prose, 2:273
Classical Korean Poetry, 2:299
The Classical Language of Architecture, 3:762
The Classical Moment: Studies of Corneille, Molière, and Racine, 2:471, 2:491

Classical Music: A Concise History from Gluck to Beethoven, 3:663
Classical Music: The Era of Haydn, Mozart, and Beethoven, 3:659
Classical Mythology in Shakespeare, 1:220
Classical Probability in the Enlightenment, 5:44
Classical Scholarship, 3:298
The Classical Style: Haydn, Mozart, Beethoven, 3:663
The Classical Text: Aspects of Editing in the Age of the Printed Book, 1:37
Classical Thought, 4:46
The Classical Tradition, 2:346
Classical Traditions in Early America, 3:868
The Classical World Bibliography of Philosophy, Religion, and Rhetoric, 4:13
The Classical World of H. D., 1:827
Classic American Philosophers, 4:34
Classic American Short Stories, 1:806
Classic Ballroom Dances, 1:1048
Classic Black African Poems, 2:113
Classic Cases in Medical Ethics, 5:122
The Classic Chinese Novel: A Critical Introduction, 2:189
The Classic Fairy Tales, 1:579
The Classic Myths in English Literature and Art, 1:133
The Classic Noh Theatre of Japan, 1:871, 2:273
The Classic Odes, 2:194
Classic Philosophical Questions, 4:21
Classics, Staples, and Precursors in the History, Philosophy, and Sociology of Science, 5:56
Classics and Our Twentieth Century Poets, 1:798
Classics in Translation, 2:349
Classics of Children's Literature, 1:579, 1:1197
Classics of Public Administration, 3:147
Classics of Roman Literature, 2:382
The Classics of Science: A Study of Twelve Enduring Scientific Works, 5:805

Classics of Western Philosophy, 4:20

Classics of Western Spirituality, 4:680

The Classic Theatre: Six Italian Plays, 2:402

Classic Vision: The Retreat from Extremity in Modern Literature, 1:422

Classification, Evolution and the Nature of Biology, 5:765

Classified Shakespeare Bibliography 1936-1958, 1:221

The Class Mammalia, 5:792

Class Reunion, 2:615

Classrooms in the Crossfire, 3:251

The Class Struggle in the Ancient Greek World, 3:299, 3:308

Class Struggle in the Pale, 4:656

Claude Bernard and Animal Chemistry, 5:46, 5:789

Claude Bernard and the Internal Environment: A Memorial Symposium, 5:789

Claude Buffier and Thomas Reid: Two Common Sense Philosophers, 4:212

Claude Debussy and the Poets, 3:692

Claude Elwood Shannon: Collected Papers, 5:581

Claudel: Beauty and Grace, 2:468

Claude Lévi-Strauss, 3:34

Claude McKay, 1:857

Claude McKay: A Black Poet's Struggle for Identity, 1:857

Claude McKay: Centennial Studies, 1:857

Claude McKay: Rebel Sojourner in the Harlem Renaissance, 1:857

Claude Monet, 3:783

Claude Simon: And Fiction Now, 2:509

Claude Simon: Writing the Visible, 2:509

Claude Simon and the Transgressions of Modern Art, 2:509

Claude Simon's Mythic Muse, 2:509

Claudio Monteverdi: Life and Works, 3:706

Claudius, The God and His Wife Messalina, 3:879

Claudius the God, 1:485, 3:320

The Claverlings, 1:406

The Clayhanger Trilogy, 1:443

Clean Cheap Heat, 5:285

Cleaning and Preserving Bindings and Related Materials, 1:24

Cleaning Up the Mess, 5:184

Cleanness, 1:155

Clear Light of Day, 2:179

Clement of Alexandria: A Study in Christian Platonism and Gnosticism, 4:63

A Clergyman's Daughter, 1:530

Clever Gretchen and Other Forgotten Folktales, 1:1007

Client-Centered Therapy, 3:193, 5:468

Clifford Odets, 1:1106

Clifford Odets: The Thirties and After, 1:1106

Cliffs of Fall, 2:953, 2:954

Climate, Earth Processes, and Earth History, 5:617

Climate and Culture: A Philosophical Study, 4:367

Climate and Energy, 5:634

Climate and History: Studies in Past Climates and Their Impacts on Man, 5:634

Climate Change: Policy Initiatives, 5:186

Climate Change: The IPCC Response Strategies, 5:282

Climate Change: The IPCC Scientific Assessment, 5:289

Climate Change and Energy Policy, 5:282

Climate Data and Resources, 3:126

Clinical and Experimental Hypnosis, 5:419

The Clinical Application of Psychological Tests, 5:469

Clinical Applications of Rational-Emotive Therapy, 5:439

The Clinical Encounter, 5:80

Clinical Epidemiology: The Architecture of Clinical Research, 5:79

Clinical Ethics, 5:121

Clinical Genetics and Genetic Counseling, 5:781

Clinical Judgment, 5:79

Clinical Laboratory Tests: Significance and Implications for Nursing, 5:324

The Clinical Management of Nicotine Dependence, 5:404

Clinical Methods in Psychology, 5:420

The Clinical Performance Examination: Development and Implementation, 5:324

The Clinical Psychology Handbook, 5:414

The Clinical Psychology of Melanie Klein, 5:457

Clinical Studies in Psychiatry, 5:470

Clinician's Handbook of Childhood Psychopathology, 5:416

Clinton Street, and Other Stories, 2:39

Clio and the Doctors: History, Psycho-History, and Quanto-History, 1:814, 3:9, 3:275

Clive Barker's Shadows in Eden, 1:600

Cloak of Illusion, 2:812

The Clock, 2:753, 2:754

The Clockmaker (Haliburton), 2:912

Clockmaker (Simenon), 2:508

The Clockmaker from Cordoba, 2:858

Clock without Hands, 1:1009

A Clockwork Orange, 1:453

The Clockwork Testament, or Enderby's End, 1:453

The Clockwork Universe of Anthony Burgess, 1:454

The Cloister and the Hearth, 1:389

Cloning of Frogs, Mice and Other Animals, 5:776

Closed Circuit, 2:84

A Closed Eye, 1:451

Closely Watched Trains, 2:792

Close of Play and Pig in a Poke, 1:486

Close Quarters, 1:483

A Closer Look at Ariel: A Memory of Sylvia Plath, 1:1031

Close Sesame, 2:122

The Closing of the American Mind, 1:1124, 1:1126, 3:248

The Cloud Forest, 3:930

A Cloud in Trousers, 2:738

Cloud Nine, 1:458, 1:459, 1:1227

Cloud of Unknowing, 1:146

The Cloud of Unknowing and Other Works, 1:148

A Cloud over Bhopal, 5:243

The Clouds, 2:353

Clouds of Witness, 1:610

The Cloudy Night Book, 5:591

Clough: The Critical Heritage, 1:345

The Cloven Viscount, 2:411

The Clown, 2:569, 2:570

Clowns and Pantomimes, 1:271

C.L.R. James: The Artist as Revolutionary, 3:648

The Club, 2:967

Clues, Myths, and the Historical Method, 3:276

Clues to American Dance, 3:733

Cluniac Monasticism in the Central Middle Ages, 4:699

The Coach with the Six Insides, 1:504

Coal, Steel and the Rebirth of Europe, 1945–1955, 3:345

Coal-Bridge to the Future, 5:286

The Coal Question, 3:84, 3:85, 5:278

The Coal War, 1:880

Coastal Dunes, 5:632

Coast Environments, 5:631

Coasting: A Private Voyage, 3:900

A Coast of Trees, 1:934

A Coat of Many Colors, 2:738, 4:595

A Coat of Varnish, 1:550

Cobbett's Cyclopedic Survey of Chamber Music, 3:654

Cobblestone Leadership: Majority Rule, Minority Power, 3:570

The COBOL Environment, 5:552

Coca Cola Culture: Icons of Pop, 3:873

Cocaine Papers, 5:445

Cock-A-Doodle-Dandy, 1:526

The Cockatoos, Shorter Novels and Stories, 2:966

Cockerell, 1:40

Cockpit, 1:1002

Cock Pit, 1:964

Cock Robin, 1:583

The Cocktail Hour and Two Other Plays: The Perfect Party, 1:1091

The Cocktail Party, 1:471, 1:472, 1:480

Cocteau: A Biography, 2:469, 3:834

Code Blue: A Nurse's True-Life Story, 5:337

Code of Codes, 5:782

Code of Jewish Law, 4:627

Codeswitching: Anthropological and Sociolinguistic Perspectives, 3:21

Codex Atlanticus: A Facsimile of the Restored Manuscript, 3:779

The Cod Fisheries: The History of an International Economy, 3:621

Coelum Philosophorum: Or, the Book of Vexations, 4:149

Coercion, 4:387

The Coevolution of Climate and Life, 5:775

Coffee and Democracy in Modern Costa Rica, 3:635

Cogeneration, 5:287

Cogeneration and Decentralized Electricity Production, 5:287

Cogeneration Sourcebook, 5:288

The Cogito and Hermeneutics: The Question of the Subject in Ricoeur, 4:319

Cognition, 3:172

The Cognitive Computer: On Language, Learning and Artificial Intelligence, 3:175, 5:569

The Cognitive Connection: Thought and Language in Man and Machine, 5:568

Cognitive Development, 3:172

Cognitive Economy, 4:317

Cognitive Therapy in Clinical Practice: An Illustrative Casebook, 5:433

Cognitive Therapy of Depression, 5:433

Cognitive Therapy of Personality Disorders, 5:433

The Cognitive Turn, 5:153

A Coherent Splendor: The American Poetic Renaissance 1910–1980, 1:798

The Coil of Life, 5:791, 5:813

The Coincidental Art of Charles Brockden Brown, 1:636

A Coin in Nine Hands, 2:517

Coins of the Roman Empire, 3:306

The Cold and the Dark: The World after Nuclear War, 5:110

A Colder Eye: The Modern Irish Writers, 1:415, 1:421

Cold Fusion: The Making of a Scientific Controversy, 5:11

Cold Hearts, 5:370

Cold Nights, 2:259

Cold Regions Engineering: Proceedings of a Conference, 1991, 5:225

The Cold War: A Study in U.S. Foreign Policy, 3:157

The Cold War, 1945–1963, 3:345

The Cold War, 1945–1972, 3:539

The Cold War Begins, 3:278

The Cold War from Yalta to Peking, 5:293

Cole Porter: A Biography, 3:709

Coleridge, 1:287, 1:288

Coleridge: A Collection of Critical Essays, 1:287

Coleridge: The Critical Heritage, 1:288

Coleridge: The Damaged Archangel, 1:288

Coleridge, Lamb, Hazlitt, and the Reader of Drama, 1:272

Coleridge, Opium and Kubla Khan, 1:288

Coleridge and S. T. C.: A Study of Coleridge's Dual Nature, 1:288

Coleridge and the Power of Love, 1:287

Coleridge and Wordsworth, 1:288

Coleridge and Wordsworth: A Lyrical Dialogue, 1:307

Coleridge's Philosophy of Language, 1:288

Coleridge's Secret Ministry, 1:288

Coleridge's Variety: Bicentenary Studies, 1:287

Coleridge's Writings on Shakespeare, 1:208

Coleridge the Moralist, 1:288

Colette, 2:470

Colette: A Life, 2:470

Colin Clout, 1:196

Colin Clout's Come Home Again, 1:197

Collages, 1:865

The Collapse of Ancient States and Civilizations, 4:546

The Collapse of East German Communism, 3:377

The Collapse of State Socialism: The Case of Poland, 3:390

The Collapse of the Concert of Europe, 1890–1914, 3:279

The Collapse of the Weimar Republic: Political Economy and Crisis, 3:376
Collected Ancient Greek Novels, 2:349
Collected Articles on Ockham, 4:120
Collected Black Women's Narratives, 1:727
Collected Black Women's Poetry, 1:720
Collected Correspondence of J.M.W. Turner with an Early Diary and a Memoir by George Jones, 3:794
The Collected Dialogues of Plato, 4:45
The Collected Essays and Occasional Writings of Katherine Anne Porter, 1:869
The Collected Essays of Asa Briggs, 1:311
Collected Essays on Economic Theory. Vols. 1-3, 3:84
Collected Essays on Public Health and Epidemiology, 5:410
Collected Experimental Papers, 5:676
Collected Impressions, 1:447
Collected Papers on Mathematics, Logic, and Philosophy, 5:493
The Collected Works of Billy the Kid, 2:922
Collectible Books: Some New Paths, 1:76
Collecting American Pewter, 3:767
Collecting Himself, 1:890
Collecting Printed Ephemera, 1:33
The Collection, 1:534
A Collection of Chinese Lyrics, 2:192
A Collection of Classic Southern Humor Fiction and Occasional Fact by Some of the South's Best Story Tellers, 3:871
A Collection of Contemporary Gothic Fiction, 1:599
Collection of Modern Korean Literature, 2:307
Collective Behavior, 3:203
Collective Violence, 3:204
The Collector, 1:477
The Collector of Treasures, 2:163
The Collector's Book of Books, 1:33

The Collector's Bookshelf, 1:63
Collector's Choice, 1:34
The Collector's Guide to Antiquarian Bookstores, 1:77
The Colleen Bawn, or, The Brides of Garryowen, 1:272, 1:331
College Handbook, 1993, 3:249
The College Novel in America, 1:918
College of Dreams: The Writings of Anais Nin, 1:866
College Primer of Writing, 1:874
Collier's Encyclopedia, 1:106
Collin, 2:590
Colline, 2:480
Collins, 1:236
Collins COBUILD English Language Dictionary, 5:545
Collins-Robert French Dictionary, 1:98
The Colloquial Short Story in China: A Study of the San-yen Collection, 2:198
Colloquies, 4:138
Colloquium of the Seven about Secrets of the Sublime, 4:134
The Colloquy of Montbéliard, 4:723
The Colloquy of the Dogs, 2:535
Colombia and the United States: Hegemony and Interdependence, 3:635
Colombia before Independence, 3:629
The Colombian Novel, 1844-1987, 2:848
Colonel Jack, 1:239
The Colonel's Dream, 1:738, 1:739
Colonial American Poetry, 1:629
Colonial American Writing, 1:631
Colonial British America, 3:517
The Colonial Craftsman, 3:569
Colonialism in Africa, 1870-1960, 3:417
Colonialism in Africa, 1969-1975, 3:417
Colonialism in Sri Lanka, 3:487
Colonial Latin America, 3:628

Colonial Merchants and the American Revolution, 1763-1776, 3:596
The Colonial Physician and Other Essays, 5:312
The Colonial Printer, 1:12
Color, 1:824
Color and Democracy: Colonies and Peace, 3:577
Color Atlas of Physiology, 5:773
Color of Darkness, 1:1033
The Color of the Sky: A Study of Stephen Crane, 1:742
The Color Purple, 1:1064
Colors of a New Day: Writing for South Africa, 2:158
The Colors of Poetry: Essays in Classic Japanese Verse, 2:273
The Colossus and Other Poems, 1:1030, 1:1031
The Colossus of Maroussi, 1:861, 1:862
The Colossus of Roads: Myth and Symbol along the American Highway, 3:869
Colour: Some Philosophical Problems from Wittgenstein, 4:347
Colour and Colour Theories, 3:189
Colours of the Stars, 5:588
Coltrane: A Biography, 3:690
Columbella, 1:1238
The Columbiad: A Poem, 1:632, 1:633
Columbia Dictionary of Modern European Literature, 1:131, 2:3, 2:446
Columbia Encyclopedia, 1:107
The Columbia Granger's Index to Poetry, 1:125
The Columbia History of the American Novel, 1:628
The Columbia History of the World, 3:274
The Columbia Lippincott Gazetteer of the World, 5:618
Columbia-Lippincott Gazetteer of the World, With 1961 Supplement, 1:84
The Columbia Literary History of the United States, 1:134, 1:628, 1:650, 1:713
The Columbian Exchange, 3:628
The Columbian Muse of Comedy, 1:1073

Columbia University College of Physicians and Surgeons Complete Home Medical Guide, 5:5, 5:311

Columbia University Press, 1893–1983, 1:40

Columbus: The Great Adventurer: His Life, His Times, and His Voyages, 3:917

Columbus and the Age of Discovery, 3:916

Columbus and the Crowns, 3:916

Columbus Quincentenary Series, 3:917

The Combat, 2:143

Combating Your Child's Cholesterol: A Pediatrician Shows You How, 5:326

Combinatorial Programming, Spatial Analysis, and Planning, 3:136

Come Along with Me, 1:992

The Comeback, 1:1090, 1:1091

Come Back, Dr. Caligari, 1:944

Come Back, Little Sheba, 1:1095

Come Back to Erin, 1:529

Come Back Tomorrow and Other Plays, 2:59

Come Blow Your Horn, 1:1111, 1:1113

The Comedians, 1:488

The Comedy of Calisto and Melibea, 2:548

The Comdey of Errors, 1:205, 1:206

The Comedy That "Hoits": An Essay on the Fiction of Philip Roth, 1:1041

Come Marching Home, 1:1082

Come Sing, Jimmy Jo, 1:1204

Come Sit beside Me and Listen to Kouchag, 2:79

Comes the Voyager at Last, 2:131

Comet in Moominland, 2:658

The Comet Is Coming: The Feverish Legacy of Mr. Halley, 5:592

Come to Think of It, 1:457

Comets, Meteorites, and Men, 5:592

Come unto These Yellow Sands, 1:455

The Comforters, 1:551

The Comical Revenge, 1:242

The Comic Encyclopedia, 3:871

The Comic Matrix of Shakespeare's Tragedies, 1:213

Comics as Culture, 3:873

The Comic Spirit of Wallace Stevens, 1:887

The Comic Theatre: A Comedy in Three Acts, 2:422

Comic Transformations in Shakespeare, 1:211

Comic Visions: Television Comedy and American Culture, 3:871, 3:873

Coming Apart: An Informal History of America in the 1960s, 3:539

The Coming Crisis of Western Sociology, 3:200, 3:228

The Coming Fin de Siècle, 3:225

The Coming Fury. Centennial History of the Civil War, Vol. 1, 3:571

The Coming Health Care Crisis, 3:57

The Coming Information Age, 3:803

Coming into the Country, 1:1010

Coming of Age in Samoa, 3:36, 3:174

Coming of Age in the Milky Way, 5:593, 5:603, 5:691, 5:713

The Coming of Industrial Order, 1810–1860, 3:548

The Coming of Joachim Stiller, 2:627, 2:628

The Coming of Post-Industrial Society, 3:219, 3:220, 5:150, 5:572

The Coming of Stork, 2:967

The Coming of the Book: The Impact of Printing 1450–1800, 1:8

The Coming of the Civil War, 3:527

The Coming of the French Revolution, 3:339, 3:373

The Coming of the Mass Market, 1850–1914, 3:873

Comings Back: A Sequence of Poems, 1:982

Coming through Slaughter, 2:922

Coming to Light, 1:799, 1:913

The Coming to Power: Critical Presidential Elections in American History, 3:597

Coming to Public Judgment, 3:148

Coming to Writing and Other Essays, 2:467

Coming Up for Air, 1:530

Command, and I Will Obey You, 2:429

The Command and Control of Nuclear Forces, 5:109

The Commandant, 2:948

Commander-in-Chief: Franklin D. Roosevelt, His Lieutenants and Their War, 3:535

The Commedienne, 2:820

Commemorative Issue, 4:120

Commentaries on Benedict's Rule, 4:706

Commentaries on Living, 4:554

Commentaries on the Psalms, 4:709

A Commentary of the Plays of Sophocles, 2:368

Commentary on a Canzone of Benivieni, 4:152

Commentary on Being and Essence, 4:137

Commentary on "De Grammatico," 4:108

Commentary on Hegel's Logic, 4:303

A Commentary on Heidegger's Being and Time, 4:293

Commentary on Jean-Paul Sartre's Being and Nothingness, 4:330

A Commentary on Jean-Paul Sartre's Critique of Dialectical Reason, 4:330

A Commentary on Kant's Critique of Practical Reason, 4:206

A Commentary on Kant's Critique of Pure Reason, 4:206

Commentary on Macaulay's "History of England," 3:406

A Commentary on Plato's Meno, 4:81

Commentary on Plato's Symposium on Love, 4:80, 4:140

Commentary on Plato's Timaeus, 4:84

A Commentary on Plotinus: Ennead, 4:86

Commentary on Romans, 4:821

Commentary on the American Scene, 4:651

A Commentary on The Anathemata of David Jones, 1:503

A Commentary on the Aristotelian Athenaion Politeia, 3:312, 4:70

A Commentary on the Poems of Thomas Hardy, 1:363

A Commentary on the Satires of Juvenal, 2:387

A Commentary on Thucydides, 3:323

Commentary on True and False Religion, 4:791

Comments on Film, 3:836

Comments on Journalism, 2:252

Commerce and Government, 4:195

The Commercial Empire of the St. Lawrence, 3:618

The Commercial Revolution in Nineteenth Century China, 3:468

The Commercial Revolution of the Middle Ages, 950–1350, 3:54

Commercial Structure and Commercial Blight, 3:127

Commissioned Spirits, 1:325

Commitment and Community, 3:217

Commodore, 1:741

Common and Courtly Language, 1:225

Common Culture and the Great Tradition: The Case for Renewal, 3:873

A Common Faith, 3:260, 4:224

Common Flowering Plants of the Northeast, 5:767

The Common Glory, 1:1088

Common Landscape of America, 1580 to 1845, 3:550

Common Names of North American Butterflies, 5:769

The Common Press, 1:8

The Common Pursuit, 1:486

The Common Reader, 1:569

The Common School and the Negro American, 1:832

Common Sense, 1:641

Common Sense and Nuclear Warfare, 4:322, 5:112

Common Sense and the Fifth Amendment, 4:298

The Common Sense of Science, 5:162

A Common Story, 2:723

Commonwealth, 3:581

Commonwealth and Nehru, 3:500

The Commonwealth of Art: Style in the Fine Arts, Music and the Dance, 3:663

The Commonwealth of Learning, 3:249, 3:572

Commonwealth of Wings, 5:787

Commonwealth to Protectorate, 3:361

The Communal Experience, 4:844

Communalism: From Its Origins to the Twentieth Century, 1:1036

Communal Love at Oneida, 4:844

Communicating Vessels, 2:462

Communication and Culture, 3:803

Communication and Mass Media, 3:801

Communication and Organizations: An Interpretive Approach, 3:802

Communication and Persuasion: Psychological Studies of Opinion Change, 3:176

Communication and Social Structure, 3:803

Communication and the Evolution of Society, 3:229, 4:403, 5:89

The Communication Cord, 1:479

Communication for Command and Control Systems, 5:302

Communication for Dental Auxiliaries, 5:336

The Communication Handbook: A Dictionary, 3:801

Communications: A Guide to Information Sources, 3:801

Communications and Society, 3:204, 3:802

Communications Electronics: Systems, Circuits, and Devices, 5:298

Communications Standard Dictionary, 3:802

Communication Systems, 5:299

Communication Systems Analysis and Design: A Systems Approach, 5:300

Communication Techniques for Digital and Analog Signals, 5:299

Communication Technology, 5:297

A Communication to My Friends, 1:381

Communion: A True Story, 4:870

Communism and China: Ideology in Flux, 4:359

Communism in Italy and France, 3:385

Communist China: The Early Years, 1949–1955, 3:496

Communistic Societies of the United States, 4:844

The Communist Interpretation of the Philosophy of Karl Marx, 3:287

The Communist Manifesto, 3:74, 3:75, 3:95, 3:290

Communist Regimes in Eastern Europe, 3:389

Communist Strategy and Tactics in Czechoslovakia, 1918–1948, 3:389

Communities of Women: An Idea in Fiction, 1:269, 1:318

Community and Polity: The Organizational Dynamics of American Jewry, 4:639

Community and Revolution in Modern Vietnam, 3:491

Community and Society, 3:242

Community-Based Systems of Long-Term Care, 5:330

Community Conflict, 3:204, 3:223

Community Health Analysis: A Holistic Approach, 5:319

A Community in Conflict, 4:638

A Community on Trial: The Jews of Paris in the 1930's, 4:638

The Community Press in an Urban Setting, 3:230

Commutative Algebra, 5:500

Companeras: Latina Lesbians (An Anthology), 1:1184

A Companion to Aristotle's Politics, 4:69

Companion to a Sand County Almanac: Interpretive and Critical Essays, 5:834

A Companion to Beethoven's Pianoforte Sonatas, 3:678

A Companion to Chaucer Studies, 1:151

A Companion to Chinese History, 3:463, 3:466

A Companion to Greek Studies, 2:348

A Companion to Henry
James Studies, 1:766
A Companion to Homer,
2:362
A Companion to Joyce
Studies, 1:505
A Companion to Melville
Studies, 1:688
A Companion to Neo-Latin
Studies, 2:381
A Companion to Piers Plow-
man, 1:154
A Companion to Plato's
Republic, 4:85
A Companion to Russian
Studies, 2:684
A Companion to Scottish
History, 3:368, 4:735
A Companion to Shakespeare
Studies, 1:222
A Companion to the Cantos
of Ezra Pound, Vol. 2:
Cantos 74–120, 1:874
A Companion to the Grapes
of Wrath, 1:885
A Companion to the History
of Modern Science, 5:10,
5:26, 5:61
A Companion to the Iliad,
2:362
A Companion to the Physical
Sciences, 5:11
A Companion to the Study
of St. Anselm, 4:108, 4:703
The Companion to Twenti-
eth-Century Opera, 3:670
A Companion to Wittgen-
stein's "Tractatus," 4:344
A Company of Wolves, 1:455
The Company She Keeps,
1:1007, 1:1008
The Company Town: Archi-
tecture and Society in the
Early Industrial Age, 3:531
The Company We Keep: An
Ethics of Fiction, 1:1139
Comparatists at Work: Stud-
ies in Comparative Litera-
ture, 2:983
The Comparative Approach
to American History,
3:516, 3:602
Comparative Criticism: A
Yearbook, 2:984
Comparative Economic Sys-
tems, 3:52
Comparative Ethics in Hindu
and Buddhist Traditions,
4:893
Comparative Frontiers: A
Proposal for Studying the
American West, 3:516

The Comparative Geography
of Palestine and the Sinai-
tic Peninsula, 3:134
Comparative Health Systems,
5:331
Comparative Higher Educa-
tion Abroad: Bibliography
and Analysis, 3:253
Comparative History of Civi-
lizations in Asia, 3:463
A Comparative History of
Ideas, 4:37, 4:349
Comparative Literary Studies:
An Introduction, 2:984
Comparative Literature, 2:983
Comparative Literature: Mat-
ter and Method, 2:983
Comparative Literature:
Method and Perspective,
2:984
Comparative Literature and
Literary Theory: Survey
and Introduction, 2:984
Comparative Literature as
Academic Discipline, 2:983
Comparative Methods in Psy-
chology, 3:169
Comparative Musicology and
Anthropology of Music,
3:667
Comparative Philosophy: Se-
lected Essays, 4:37
Comparative Politics: A De-
velopmental Approach,
3:150
Comparative Politics: System,
Process, and Policy, 3:150
Comparative Public Policy,
3:141
Comparative Religion, 4:567
Comparative Religion: A His-
tory, 4:420
Comparative Religion: Its
Genesis and Growth, 4:420
Comparative Religious Eth-
ics, 4:893
Comparative Studies of How
People Think: An Intro-
duction, 3:171
The Comparative Study of
Religion, 4:494
Comparative Urbanization:
Divergent Paths in the
Twentieth Century, 3:127
A Compass for the Sunflow-
er, 2:58
Compassion, 2:547
Compassion in Tibetan Bud-
dhism, 4:543
Compendium of the Study of
Theology, 4:111

Competition among the Few:
Oligopoly and Similar
Market Structures, 3:57
Competitiveness in American
Society, 5:153
The Compleat Book of Yacht
Care, 5:239
The Compleat Computer,
5:541
The Compleat Jane Grab-
horn, 1:8
A Complete and Systematic
Concordance to the Works
of Shakespeare, 1:216
The Complete Anti-Federalist,
3:543
The Complete Bible: An
American Translation,
4:797
The Complete Book of Aller-
gy Control, 5:386
Complete Book of Ballets,
3:733
The Complete Book of Cos-
metic Facial Surgery,
5:396
The Complete Book of Den-
tal Care, 5:342
The Complete Book of Es-
sential Oils and Aromath-
erapy, 5:321
Complete Book of Home
Health Care, 5:334
The Complete Book of Jew-
ish Observance, 4:602
Complete Book of Marvels,
3:892
The Complete Book of Natu-
ral Foods, 5:345
The Complete Book of Silk
Screen Printing Produc-
tion, 1:27
The Complete Book of
Sleep: How Your Nights
Affect Your Days, 5:392
The Complete Book of the
Olympics, 1:88
The Complete Book of U.S.
Presidents, 3:506
The Complete Book of Wom-
en's Health, 5:355
The Complete Directory for
People with Disabilities,
5:368
Complete Drug Reference,
5:5
The Complete Encyclopedia
of Popular Music and
Jazz, 1900–1950, 3:656
The Complete Engravings,
Etchings, and Drypoints of
Albrecht Dürer, 3:774

The Complete Foot Book: First Aid for Your Feet, 5:396

Complete Freedom and Other Stories, 2:650

The Complete Greek Drama, 2:349

The Complete Greek Tragedies, 2:349

The Complete Grimms' Fairy Tales, 2:584, 3:880

The Complete Guide to Anti-Aging Nutrients, 5:349

The Complete Guide to Britain's National Theatre, 1:426

The Complete Guide to Calligraphy: Techniques and Materials, 1:17

A Complete Guide to Home Nursing, 5:377

The Complete Guide to Modern Dance, 3:732

The Complete Guide to Sherlock Holmes, 1:608

Complete Guide to Sports Injuries, 5:399

A Complete Guide to Therapy, 5:419

The Complete Guide to Women's Health, 5:356

The Complete Guide to Writing Fiction, 1:118

The Complete Handbook of Personal Computer Communications, 5:547

The Complete Handbook of Videocassette Recorders, 5:230

The Complete Health Club Handbook, 5:326

Complete Home Medical Guide, 5:311

The Complete Homeopathy Handbook, 5:318

The Complete Humorous Sketches and Tales, 1:781

The Complete Letters of Vincent Van Gogh, 3:794

The Complete Lyrics of Cole Porter, 3:709

The Complete Masques, 1:183

The Complete Maximus Poems, 1:1027

The Complete Modem Reference, 5:304

The Complete Operas of Puccini: A Critical Guide, 3:711

The Complete Paintings of Bruegel, 3:771

The Complete Paintings of Dürer, 3:774

The Complete Paintings of Raphael, 3:788

The Complete Parents' Guide to Telephone Medicine, 5:322

The Complete Pelican Shakespeare, 1:206

The Complete Plays of W. D. Howells, 1:758

The Complete Poems of Samar Sen, 2:176

The Complete Poetry and Prose of Geoffrey Chaucer, 1:150

The Complete Poor Richard's Almanac, 1:638

The Complete Psychological Works: Standard Edition, 5:445

The Complete Rhyming Dictionary, 1:95

The Complete Roman Drama, 2:382

The Complete Ronald Firbank, 1:474

Complete Roofing Handbook: Installation, Maintenance, Repair, 5:225

Complete Sherlock Holmes, 1:607

The Complete Signet Classic Shakespeare, 1:205

The Complete Sports Medicine Book for Women: Revised for the '90s, 5:400

The Complete Stephen King Encyclopedia, 1:1241

The Complete Sylvie and Bruno, 1:582

Complete Tales of Uncle Remus, 1:754

Complete Theories, 5:515

Complete Turbo Pascal, 5:552

The Complete University Medical Diet, 5:347

The Complete Walker III, 3:908

The Complete War Memoirs of Charles DeGaulle, 1940–1946, 3:372

The Complete Waterpower Workout Book, 5:326

The Complete White Oxen: Collected Short Fiction, 1:818

The Complete Woodcuts of Albrecht Dürer, 3:774

A Complete Word and Phrase Concordance to the Poems and Songs of Robert Burns, 1:281

The Complete Works: Globe Edition (Shakespeare), 1:206

The Complete Works of Aristotle: The Revised Oxford Translation, 5:38

Complete Works of Shakespeare, 1:205

The Complex Image: Faith and Method in American Autobiography, 1:727

Complexity: Life on the Edge of Chaos, 4:866

Complexity, Chaos and Biological Evolution, 3:171

The Complex Secret of Brief Psychotherapy, 5:418

Compliance Ideologies: Rethinking Political Culture, 3:140

The Composer and His Art, 3:660

The Composer in Hollywood, 3:667

A Composer's World: Horizons and Limitations, 3:700

The Composition of Aristotle's Athenaion Politeia, 4:69

The Composition of Mutanabbi's Panegyrics to Sayf al-Dawla, 2:70

A Comprehensible World, 5:720

Comprehensive Bibliography of American Constitutional and Legal History: Supplement, 1980–1987, 3:510

A Comprehensive Bibliography of American Constitutional and Legal History, 1896–1979, 3:510

A Comprehensive Bibliography of Yugoslav Literature in English, 1593–1980, 2:835, 2:785, 2:808, 2:827

Comprehensive Dictionary of Engineering and Technology, 5:216

A Comprehensive Dictionary of Psychological and Psychoanalytical Terms, 5:424

A Comprehensive Etymological Dictionary of the English Language, 1:96

A Comprehensive Index to Bibliographies in History Journals Published Worldwide, 3:8, 3:272

Comprehensive Index to English-Language Little Magazines,1890–1970, 1:124

The Compromise, 2:716

The Compton Effect: Turning Point in Physics, 5:678

Compulsions to Confess, 5:467

Compulsory Health Insurance: The Continuing American Debate, 5:329

The Compunctious Poet, 2:8

Computational Analysis of Kierkegaard's Samlede Vaerker, 4:240

The Computation of Style, 5:564

Computation Structures, 5:231

Computer: A Challenge for Business Administration, 5:558

The Computer Age: A Twenty-Year View, 5:539

Computer-Aided Instruction in the Humanities, 5:566

The Computer and Telecommunications Handbook, 5:305

Computer and the Brain, 5:583

The Computer and the Mind: An Introduction to Cognitive Science, 5:568

Computer-Assisted Legal and Tax Research, 5:558

Computer-Based Reference Service, 5:544

Computer Basics, 5:581

Computer Basics for Librarians and Information Scientists, 5:544

Computer Bits and Pieces: A Compendium of Curiosities, 5:574

Computer Books and Serials in Print, 1985–1986, 5:539

The Computer Cookbook, 5:539

Computer Dictionary for Beginners, 5:540

Computer Equity in Math and Science, 3:257

Computer Essays for Management, 5:556

The Computer Establishment, 5:542

Computer Ethics: Cautionary Tales and Ethical Dilemmas in Computing, 5:125

The Computer from Pascal to von Neumann, 5:37, 5:540, 5:583

The Computer Glossary: The Complete Illustrated Desk Reference, 5:540

Computer Graphics, 5:564

Computer Images: State of the Art, 5:564

The Computer in Education: A Critical Perspective, 5:566

The Computerization of Society: A Report to the President of France, 5:573

Computer Languages: A Guide for the Perplexed, 5:549

Computer Lib/Dream Machines, 5:562

Computer-Mediated Communication Systems: Status and Evaluation, 5:307

Computer Models of Thought and Language, 5:570

Computer Modern Typefaces, 5:562

Computer Networks and Distributed Processing, 5:557

Computer Pioneers, 5:577

The Computer Pioneers: The Making of the Modern Computer, 5:538, 5:579

Computer Power and Human Reason, 5:77, 5:126, 5:145, 5:159, 5:571

Computer Power for Your Law Office, 5:557

Computer Programs for Literary Analysis, 5:564

Computer Publishers and Publications, 5:545

Computer Readable Databases: A Directory and Data Sourcebook, 5:548

Computer Resource Guide for Nonprofits, 5:546

Computers, Ethics, and Society, 5:125

Computers and Composing, 3:801

Computers and Computing Information Resources Directory, 5:546

Computers and Telecommunications Networks, 5:301

Computers and the Imagination: Visual Adventures beyond the Edge, 5:565

Computers and Thought, 5:570

Computers and Typesetting, 5:562

Computers and Writing, 5:566

Computer Security, Auditing, and Internal Control Manual, 5:556

Computers for Everybody, 5:538, 5:567

Computers in Linguistics, 5:564

Computers in Medicine, 5:556

Computers in the Human Context, 5:539

Computer Solutions for Business, 5:556

Computer Studies: Computers in Society, 5:126

Computer Systems and Water Resources, 5:251

Computer Town: Bringing Computer Literacy to Your Community, 5:544

Computer Wimp, 5:536

Computing before Computers, 5:542

Computing Information Directory (CID), 5:546

Computing Reviews, 5:546

Computing Today: Microcomputer Concepts and Applications, 5:538

The Comrade, 2:432

Comrade Panchoonie, 2:79

Comrades: Russia in Revolution 1917–1992, 3:397

Comte: The Founder of Sociology, 3:224

Comte's Philosophy of Science, 1:372, 1:373

Comus, A Masque, 1:191

Conagher, 1:1216

Conan Doyle: Portrait of an Artist, 1:608

Concept and Empathy: Essays in the Study of Religion, 4:426

Conception, Pregnancy, and Birth, 5:360

The Conception of Immortality, 4:250

The Conception of Value, 4:288

Conceptions of Ether: Studies in the History of Ether Theories, 1740–1900, 5:31

Conceptions of God in Ancient Egypt, 4:442

Conceptions of Modern Psychiatry, 5:470

Conceptions of Reality in
    Modern American Poetry,
    1:798
Conceptions of State and
    Kingship in Southeast
    Asia, 4:518
The Concept of Anxiety,
    4:239
The Concept of Evidence,
    5:61
The Concept of First Philoso-
    phy and the Unity of the
    Metaphysics of Aristotle,
    4:70
The Concept of Irony: With
    Constant Reference to
    Socrates, 4:239
The Concept of Judgment in
    Montaigne, 4:146
The Concept of Man in Con-
    temporary China, 4:359
The Concept of Man in Early
    China, 4:524
The Concept of Matter in
    Greek and Medieval Phi-
    losophy, 4:48
The Concept of Mind, 4:325
The Concept of Nature,
    4:341
The Concept of Negritude in
    the Poetry of Leopold Se-
    dar Senghor, 2:147
The Concept of Univocity
    Regarding the Predication
    of God and Creature Ac-
    cording to William of
    Ockham, 4:121
Concepts, Theories, and the
    Mind-Body Problem, 5:80
The Concepts and Theories
    of Modern Democracy,
    3:138
Concepts in Film Theory,
    1:1156
Concepts in Solids: Lectures
    on the Theory of Solids,
    5:670
Concepts in Zoology, 5:770
Concepts of Chemistry, 5:726
Concepts of Criticism, 1:927,
    2:984
Concepts of Health and Dis-
    ease, 5:77
Concepts of Medicine, 5:77
Concepts of Modern Physics,
    5:652
Concepts of Space: The His-
    tory of Theories of Space
    in Physics, 5:68
Conceptual Astronomy: A
    Journey of Ideas, 5:590

Conceptual Blockbusting: A
    Guide to Better Ideas,
    5:191
The Conceptual Development
    of Quantum Mechanics,
    5:661
A Conceptual History of
    Modern Embryology, 5:776
Conceptual Notation and Re-
    lated Articles, 4:229
Conceptual Revolutions, 5:65
Concerning Consciousness,
    4:382
Concerning the Angels, 2:528
Concerning Vatican Council
    II, 4:423
Concert and Opera Singers:
    A Bibliography of Bio-
    graphical Materials, 3:672
Concertos and Choral Works,
    3:664
Concierto Barroco, 2:860
A Concise Anglo-Saxon Dic-
    tionary, 1:97
A Concise Biographical Dic-
    tionary of Singers, from
    the Beginning of Record-
    ed Sound to the Present,
    3:656, 3:672
Concise Book of World His-
    tory, 3:274
The Concise Cambridge Ital-
    ian Dictionary, 1:100
Concise Chemical and Tech-
    nical Directory, 5:724
A Concise Chronology of
    Typesetting Developments
    1886–1986, 1:20
The Concise Code of Jewish
    Law: A Guide to Prayer
    and Religious Observance
    on the Sabbath, 4:599
The Concise Code of Jewish
    Law: Daily Prayers and
    Religious Observances in
    the Life-Cycle of the Jew,
    4:627
The Concise Columbia Dic-
    tionary of Quotations,
    1:116
The Concise Columbia Ency-
    clopedia, 1:107
Concise Dictionary of Acro-
    nyms and Initialisms, 1:93
Concise Dictionary of Ameri-
    can History, 3:508, 3:509
A Concise Dictionary of As-
    tronomy, 5:618
A Concise Dictionary of Indi-
    an Philosophy: Sanskrit
    Terms Defined in English,
    4:3, 4:13, 4:498

Concise Dictionary of Mod-
    ern Japanese History,
    3:473
Concise Dictionary of Proper
    Names and Notable Mat-
    ters in the Works of
    Dante, 2:418
Concise Dictionary of Scien-
    tific Biography, 5:27
Concise Dictionary of the
    Christian World Mission,
    4:720, 4:745
A Concise Encyclopedia of
    Antiques, 3:765
The Concise Encyclopedia of
    Islam, 3:443, 4:4, 4:566
Concise Encyclopedia of
    Jewish Music, 3:656
Concise Encyclopedia of Liv-
    ing Faiths, 4:5
Concise Encyclopedia of Psy-
    chology, 3:169
Concise Encyclopedia of Sci-
    ence and Technology,
    5:217
The Concise Encyclopedia of
    Western Philosophy and
    Philosophers, 4:2, 4:15
A Concise English-Hungarian
    Dictionary, 1:100
Concise Etymological
    Dictionary of the English
    Language, 1:96
A Concise Exegetical Gram-
    mar of New Testament
    Greek, 4:794
Concise Guide to Jazz, 3:668
The Concise Guide to Type
    Identification, 1:62
A Concise Hebrew and Ara-
    maic Lexicon of the Old
    Testament, 4:795
A Concise History of Ameri-
    can Architecture, 3:764
A Concise History of Greece,
    3:393
A Concise History of Mathe-
    matics, 5:492
A Concise History of Modern
    Painting, 3:760
A Concise History of Scot-
    land, 3:368
Concise History of Spain,
    3:387
A Concise History of the
    American Republic, 3:585
A Concise History of the
    Arab-Israeli Conflict, 3:435
A Concise History of West-
    ern Architecture, 3:761
The Concise Illustrated Dic-
    tionary of Science and
    Technology, 5:28

Concise Introduction to Ceramics, 3:766

A Concise Introduction to Philosophy, 4:21

A Concise Introduction to the Philosophy of Nicholas of Cusa, 4:149

Concise Italian Dictionary, 1:100

The Concise Oxford Companion to English Literature, 1:132

Concise Oxford Companion to the Theatre, 1:272

The Concise Oxford Dictionary of Australian History, 3:493

The Concise Oxford Dictionary of Ballet, 3:732

Concise Oxford Dictionary of Botany, 5:767

The Concise Oxford Dictionary of Current English, 1:89

The Concise Oxford Dictionary of French Literature, 2:448

The Concise Oxford Dictionary of Proverbs, 1:115

The Concise Oxford Dictionary of Quotations, 1:116

The Concise Oxford Dictionary of the Christian Church, 4:675, 4:717

Concise Oxford Dictionary of Zoology, 5:769

The Concise Oxford English-Arabic Dictionary of Current Usage, 1:97

Concise Oxford Turkish Dictionary, 1:103

Concise Phonetic English-Hebrew/Hebrew-English Conversational Dictionary, 1:99

Concise Readings in Philosophy, 4:21

Concise Science Dictionary, 5:2

Concise Theological Dictionary, 4:719

Concluding, 1:487

The Concluding Unscientific Postscript, 4:239

Conclusive Evidence: A Memoir, 1:1020

A Concordance of the Qur'an, 4:587

Concordance to Byron's "Don Juan," 1:283

A Concordance to Darwin's "Expressions of Emotions in Man and Animals," 5:758

A Concordance to Milton's English Poetry, 1:192

A Concordance to the Complete Poems of Stephen Crane, 1:742

A Concordance to the Complete Poetical Works of Sir Thomas Wyatt, 1:201

A Concordance to the Complete Writings of George Herbert, 1:181

A Concordance to the English Poems of Andrew Marvell, 1:189

A Concordance to the English Poems of Thomas Gray, 1:248

A Concordance to the English Poetry of Richard Crashaw, 1:176

Concordance to the Gospel of Sri Ramakrishna, 4:355

A Concordance to the Greek Testament, 4:819

A Concordance to the Plays and Poems of Sir George Etherege, 1:243

A Concordance to the Plays of William Congreve, 1:237

A Concordance to the Poems of Ben Jonson, 1:184

A Concordance to the Poems of Edmund Spenser, 1:199

A Concordance to the Poems of Emily Dickinson, 1:748

A Concordance to the Poems of John Keats, 1:294

A Concordance to the Poems of Osip Mandelstam, 2:738

A Concordance to the Poems of Robert Browning, 1924–1925, 1:339

A Concordance to the Poems of Robert Herrick, 1:182

A Concordance to the Poems of Samuel Johnson, 1:250

A Concordance to the Poems of Sidney Lanier, 1:772

A Concordance to the Poetical and Dramatic Works of Alfred, Lord Tennyson, 1:401

A Concordance to the Poetical Works of John Dryden, 1:242

A Concordance to the Poetical Works of William Cowper, 1:238

A Concordance to the Poetry of Byron, 1:284

A Concordance to the Poetry of Edgar Allan Poe, 1:694

A Concordance to the Poetry of Samuel Taylor Coleridge, 1:288

A Concordance to the Septuagint and Other Greek Versions of the Old Testament (Including the Apocryphal Books), 4:818

A Concordance to the Sonnets of Góngora, 2:540

A Concordance to the Works of John Webster, 1:201

A Concordance to the Writings of William Blake, 1:279

Concordant Discord: The Interdependence of Faiths, 4:574

Concordia Mundi: The Career and Thought of Guillaume Postel, 1510–1581, 4:124

The Concubine, 2:130

The Condemned, Sentimental Memoirs of John Seaborne, 2:893

Conditioned Reflexes, 5:364

Conditioned Reflexes: An Investigation of the Physiological Activity of the Cerebral Cortex, 3:176, 3:191

The Condition of Jewish Belief, 4:648

The Condition of Postmodernity, 3:211

Condition of the Working Class in England, 4:227

The Condition of the Working Class in England: From Personal Observation and Authentic Sources, 3:74, 3:75

Conditions of Human Growth, 5:471

The Conditions of Learning and Theories of Instruction, 3:175

Conducting Research and Evaluation in Gifted Education, 3:169

Conduction of Electricity through Gases, 5:716

Conductivity and Magnetism: The Legacy of Felix Bloch, 5:673

The Conduct of War, 1789–1961, 3:278

Conductors in Conversation:
Fifteen Contemporary Con-
ductors Discuss Their
Lives and Profession,
3:671
Conductors in Conversation:
Herbert von Karajan, Sir
Georg Solti, Carlo Maria
Giulini, Claudio Abbado,
Eugene Ormandy, Riccar-
do Muti, James Levine,
3:671
Conductors on Record, 3:671
Conduct Problem/Emotional
Problem Interventions: A
Holistic Perspective, 5:419
Confabulario and Other In-
ventions, 1941–1961, 2:853
The Confederacy (Green),
1:1088
The Confederacy (Roland),
3:529
The Confederate Nation,
1861–1865, 3:530
The Confederates, 2:957
Confederate Women (Ches-
nut), 1:738
Confederate Women (Wiley),
3:530
Confederation, Constitution,
and Early National Period,
1781–1815, 3:510
The Conference of the Birds,
2:86
Confessio Amantis, 1:152
Confession, 2:763, 2:765
Confession; or, The Blind
Heart: A Domestic Story,
1:696
A Confession and Other Reli-
gious Writings, 2:765
The Confessions (St. Augus-
tine), 2:115, 4:109, 4:213,
4:786
Confessions of a Good Arab,
2:20
Confessions of a Hooligan,
2:718
Confessions of a Mask, 2:289
Confessions of an English
Opium Eater, 1:289, 1:290
Confessions of a Poet, 2:514
Confessions of a Prosaic
Dreamer, 1:296
Confessions of a Teenage Ba-
boon, 1:1122, 1:1123
Confessions of a Young Man,
1:380, 1:381
The Confessions of Brother
Haluin, 1:608
The Confessions of Jean
Jacques Rousseau, 3:164
Confessions of Love, 2:294

The Confessions of Nat Turn-
er, 1:1056
The Confessions of Zeno,
2:439
The Confidence-Man: His
Masquerade, 1:686
The Confidence Man in
American Literature, 1:651
Confidence Men and Painted
Women, 3:559
The Confidential Agent, 1:488
The Confidential Clerk, 1:472
A Confidential Matter, 3:721
Configurations, 2:878
Configurations of Culture
Growth, 3:17, 3:33
Confirmation, 5:91
Conflict, Power, and Politics
in the City: A Geographic
View, 3:123
Conflict and Compromise,
3:529, 3:548
Conflict and Consensus: A
Festschrift in Honor of
Lewis A. Coser, 3:204
Conflict and Consensus in
Switzerland, 3:378
Conflict and Crisis: The Pres-
idency of Harry S Tru-
man, 1945–1948, 3:537
Conflict and Defense, 3:71
Conflict and the Web of
Group Affiliations, 3:204
Conflict and War in the Mid-
dle East, 1967–1991, 3:437
The Conflicted Relationship,
3:274
Conflict in African Litera-
ture, 2:112
The Conflict in Education in
a Democratic Society,
3:263
Conflict in Modern Japanese
History: The Neglected
Tradition, 3:479
Conflict in the Middle East,
3:438
The Conflict of Interest be-
tween Physician as Thera-
pist and as Experimenter,
5:79
The Conflict of Interpreta-
tions: Essays on Her-
meneutics, 4:318
The Conflict of Love and
Honor, 2:512
Conflict of the Faculties,
4:205
Conflicts: Studies in Contem-
porary History, 3:406
Conflicts and Tensions in Islamic Jurisprudence, 4:578

Conflict Sociology: Toward
an Explanatory Science,
3:204
The Conformist, 2:429
Conformity's Children, 2:685
Confrontation, 2:801
Confrontations: Derrida-Heid-
egger-Nietzsche, 4:292
Confrontations with Myself,
5:421
Confronting Environmental
Racism, 3:205
Confronting Stravinsky: Man,
Musician, and Modernist,
3:723
Confucian Analects, 1:872
Confucian China and Its
Modern Fate, 3:471, 4:532
Confucian Discourse and
Chu Hsi's Ascendancy,
4:526
Confucianism and Family
Rituals in Imperial China,
3:467
Confucianism and Tokugawa
Culture, 3:475, 4:541
The Confucian Odes, 2:194
The Confucian Odes of Ezra
Pound, 2:195
Confucian Thought: Selfhood
as Creative Transforma-
tion, 4:362, 4:526
The Confucian Way of Con-
templation, 4:541
The Confucian World Ob-
served, 4:533
Confused Roaring: Evelyn
Waugh and the Modernist
Tradition, 1:563
Confusion, 1:964
The Congo, 1:855
The Congo and the Founding
of Its Free State, 3:938
Congress: Keystone of the
Washington Establishment,
3:146
Congress: The Electoral Con-
nection, 3:146
Congress and Law-Making:
Researching the Legislative
Process, 3:506
Congress and the Raj: Facets
of the Indian Struggle,
1917–47, 3:486
The Congressional Directory,
3:507
Congressmen's Voting Deci-
sions, 3:146
The Congresswomen, 2:353
Coningsby, 1:351
Conjectures and Refutations:
The Growth of Scientific
Knowledge, 5:98

Conjectures and Refutations, 4:409

Conjectures of a Guilty Bystander, 4:781

Conjugal Love, 2:429

Conjunctions and Disjunctions, 2:878

The Conjure Woman, 1:738, 1:739

A Connecticut Yankee at King Arthur's Court, 1:780

The Connection between Scientific Method and Metaphysics, or Logic and Mysticism, 4:322

The Conquerer in Constantinople, 2:832

Conquering Horse, 1:1217

The Conquerors, 2:487

Conquerors and Slaves, 3:307

The Conquest, 1:1221

The Conquest: The Story of a Negro Pioneer, 1:1172, 1:1173

Conquest and Empire: The Reign of Alexander the Great, 3:301

The Conquest of Cancer: Vaccines and Diet, 5:372

Conquest of Eden, 1493–1515, 3:916

The Conquest of Everest, 3:924

The Conquest of Gaul, 3:313

The Conquest of Granada, 1:228

The Conquest of Happiness, 4:322

The Conquest of New Spain, 3:629

The Conquest of Paradise, 3:630

The Conquest of the Perfect Love, 4:786

The Conquest of the Western Sudan, 3:421

Conquest of Violence: The Gandhian Philosophy of Conflict, 4:352, 4:553

Conrad Aiken: A Bibliography, 1:810

Conrad Aiken: Poet of White Horse Vale, 1:810

A Conrad Chronology, 1:464

Conrad Grebel: Son of Zurich, 4:724

Conscience in Medieval Philosophy, 4:95

The Conscience of the Eye, 3:202, 3:217, 3:238

The Conscience of Words, 2:575

Consciencism in African Political Philosophy, 4:371

Consciencism—Philosophy and Ideology for Decolonization and Development with Particular Reference to the African Revolution, 4:26, 4:371

Conscientious Objections, 5:140

Conscientization and Creativity: Paulo Freire and Christian Education, 3:262

The Conscious Brain, 5:569

The Conscious Lovers, 1:257

Consciousness, Introspection and the Operation of the Mind, 4:322

Consciousness and Change, 3:29

Consciousness and Revolution in Soviet Philosophy, 4:30

Consciousness and Society, 3:343

Consciousness and the Acquisition of Language, 4:310

Consciousness and the Physical World, 5:696

Consciousness Explained, 4:396

Consciousness in New England from Puritans and Ideas to Psychoanalysis and Semiotics, 1:628

The Conscious Universe: Part and Whole in Modern Physical Theory, 5:650

The Conscious Voice, 1:656

Consensus and Disunity, 3:367

The Consequences of Modernity, 3:215

Consequences of Phenomenology, 5:92

Consequences of Pragmatism: Essays 1972–1980, 4:35, 4:413

Consequently I Rejoice, 1:501

Conservation and Preservation of Humanities Research Collections, 1:25

Conservation and the Gospel of Efficiency, 3:550

The Conservation Atlas of Tropical Forests: Africa, 3:415

Conservation Biology: The Science of Scarcity and Diversity, 5:821

The Conservationist, 2:162

The Conservation of Books and Documents, 1:24

Conservation of Library Materials, 1:22

The Conservation of Orbital Symmetry, 5:755

Conservatism: Dream and Reality, 3:236

Conservative Judaism: An American Religious Movement, 4:655

Conservative Judaism: The New Century, 4:655

Conservative Judaism in America, 4:655

Considerations on Representative Government, 4:244

Considerations on the Doctrine of Phlogiston and the Decomposition of Water, 5:753

Consider the Lilies of the Field, 2:900

Consistency of the Continuum Hypothesis, 5:509

Consolação às Tribulações de Israel, 2:556

The Consolation of Philosophy, 4:112

Conspiracy and Romance, 1:658

The Conspiracy of Kings, 1:633

Constab Ballads, 1:857

Constable, 3:773

Constable: Pictures from an Exhibition, 3:773

Constable Paintings, Drawings and Watercolors, 3:773

Constance F. Woolson, 1:790

Constance Fenimore Woolson: Literary Pioneer, 1:790

Constance Fenimore Woolson: The Grief of Artistry, 1:790

Constance Ring, 2:668

Constancia and Other Stories for Virgins, 2:866

Constancy and Change in Human Development, 3:173

Constantine and Eusebius, 3:302, 4:709

Constantine and Religious Liberty, 4:683

Constantine and the Conversion of Europe, 4:684

Constantine Cavafy, 2:372

Constantine the Great and the Christian Church, 4:682

A Constitutional and Legal
History of Medieval England, 3:355
Constitutional Code, 4:190
Constitutional Diplomacy,
3:545
Constitutional Government
and Democracy, 3:143
Constitutional History of
Modern Britain since
1485, 3:355
The Constitutional Iniquity of
the Contageous Diseases
Acts, 1:341
Constitutional Interpretation,
3:141
Constitutionalism: Ancient
and Modern, 3:142
The Constitution in Crisis
Times, 1918–1969, 3:543
Constitution of Athens, 3:311
The Constitution of Society,
3:239
The Constitution of Society:
Outline of the Theory of
Structuration, 3:215
The Constitution of the United States and Related
Documents, 3:541
The Constitution Violated,
1:341
The Constraints of Desire,
3:309
A Constructed Roman Alphabet, 1:15
Constructing Knowledge: Authority and Critique in Social Science, 3:12
Constructing Quarks: A Sociological History of Particle Physics, 5:663
Constructing the Universe,
5:655
Construction Glossary: An
Encyclopedic Reference
and Manual, 5:225
The Construction of Modern
Science: Mechanisms and
Mechanics, 5:43
The Construction of Reality,
4:405
The Constructive Revolutionary, 4:762
Consuelo, 2:504, 2:505
Consumer Drug Digest, 5:310
Consumer Health: Facts,
Skills, and Decisions,
5:331
Consumer Health Information Source Book, 5:6
Consumer Index to Product
Evaluation and Information Sources, 1:113

Consumerism in Medicine:
Challenging Physician Authority, 5:331
The Consumers' Cooperative
Movement, 3:113
A Consumer's Dictionary of
Household, Yard and Office Chemicals, 5:737
Consumer's Guide to Package Travel around the
World, 3:893
Consuming Fears: The Politics of Product Risks,
5:130
Consuming Fiction, 1:1127
Contact and Conflict, 3:610
Contemplating Music: Challenges to Musicology,
3:660
Contemplating Music: Source
Readings in the Aesthetics
of Music, 3:660
Contemplating the Ancients,
4:526
The Contemplative Poetry of
Gerard Manley Hopkins,
1:364
Contemporaries, 1:995
Contemporaries, from the
Nineteenth Century to the
Present, 1:996, 1:421
Contemporaries of Marco
Polo, 3:934
Contemporary African Literature, 2:112
Contemporary Albanian Literature, 2:779
The Contemporary American
Comic Epic, 1:920
The Contemporary American
Fiction, 1:921
Contemporary American Literature, 1945–1972: An Introduction, 1:910
Contemporary American Philosophy: Second Series,
4:36, 4:267
Contemporary American Poetry (Hall), 1:915, 1:983
Contemporary American Poetry (Poulin), 1:915
Contemporary American
Poets: American Poetry
since 1940, 1:915
Contemporary American Reform Responsa, 4:652
Contemporary American
Short Stories, 1:921
Contemporary American
Theologies: A Critical Survey, 4:718, 4:743
Contemporary American
Writing, 1:925

Contemporary Approaches to
the Study of Religion,
4:422
Contemporary Architects,
3:764
Contemporary Artists, 3:761
Contemporary Australian
Drama: Perspectives since
1955, 2:946
Contemporary Authors, 1:126
Contemporary Authors: Permanent Series, 1:85
Contemporary Black Drama,
1:1079
Contemporary British Drama,
1950–1976, 1:427
Contemporary British Novelists, 1:422
Contemporary Calligraphy:
Modern Scribes and Lettering Artists, 1:14
Contemporary Chicano
Theatre, 1:1076
Contemporary China: A Research Guide, 3:465
Contemporary Chinese Literature, 2:233
Contemporary Chinese Novels and Short Stories,
1949–1974, 2:234
Contemporary Chinese Politics: An Introduction,
3:472
Contemporary Chinese
Theatre, 2:233
Contemporary Chinese Women Writers: Volume 2,
2:233
Contemporary Christologies:
A Jewish Response, 4:661,
4:885
Contemporary Classics in
Plant, Animal and Environmental Sciences, 5:758
Contemporary Clinical Psychology, 5:413
Contemporary Concert Music
by Women, 3:658
Contemporary Critique of
Historical Materialism,
3:227
Contemporary Croatian Literature, 2:785
Contemporary Danish Prose,
2:645
Contemporary Drama and
the Popular Dramatic Tradition in England, 1:425
Contemporary Dramatists,
1:126, 1:428, 1:1076
Contemporary Economic
Thought, 3:45, 3:73, 3:93,
3:98, 3:110

Contemporary Economists in Perspective, 3:46, 3:69

The Contemporary English Novel, 1:420

Contemporary European Philosophy, 4:27, 4:262

Contemporary Feminist Thought, 1:925

Contemporary Field Research: A Collection of Readings, 3:12

Contemporary Finnish Poetry, 2:658

Contemporary Foreign Language Writers, 2:4

Contemporary France: Politics and Society since 1945, 3:373

Contemporary French Literature: 1945 and After, 2:447

Contemporary French Philosophy: A Study in Norms and Values, 4:28

Contemporary French Poetry, 2:448

Contemporary German Philosophy, 4:28, 4:263, 4:379

Contemporary Halakhic Problems, 4:598

Contemporary Hermeneutics, 1:924

A Contemporary History of Austria, 3:376

Contemporary Illustrators of Children's Books, 1:29

Contemporary Indian Philosophy, 4:351

Contemporary Indian Tradition, 4:507

Contemporary International Law: A Concise Introduction, 3:144

Contemporary Irish Poetry, 1:418

Contemporary Islam and the Challenge of History, 4:569, 4:578

Contemporary Islamic Movements in Historical Perspective, 4:570

Contemporary Issues in Bioethics, 5:118

Contemporary Issues in Biomedical Ethics, 5:119

Contemporary Italian Poetry: An Anthology, 2:403

Contemporary Japanese Literature, 2:283

Contemporary Japanese Philosophical Thought, 4:363

Contemporary Jewish Ethics, 4:598

Contemporary Jewish Philosophies, 4:596, 4:649

Contemporary Jewish Religious Thought, 4:888

Contemporary Latin American Short Stories, 2:849

Contemporary Latvian Poetry, 2:804

Contemporary Literary Criticism Series, 1:134

Contemporary Literary Critics, 1:924

Contemporary Macedonian Poetry, 2:808

Contemporary Macedonian Writers, 2:807

Contemporary Moral Controversies in Technology, 5:128

Contemporary Nonlinear Optics, 5:666

Contemporary Novelists (Henderson), 1:126

Contemporary Novelists (Vinson, Kirkpatrick), 1:920

Contemporary Novelists of the English Language, 1:422

Contemporary Perspectives on Linnaeus, 5:806

Contemporary Philosophy: A New Survey, 4:264, 5:60

Contemporary Philosophy in Scandinavia, 4:31

Contemporary Photographers, 3:761

The Contemporary Poet as Artist and Critic: Eight Symposia, 1:914

Contemporary Poetry in America: Essays and Interviews, 1:912

Contemporary Poets, 1:126

Contemporary Poets in American Anthologies, 1960–1977, 1:123

Contemporary Polish Poetry, 2:811

Contemporary Portugal: The Revolution and Its Antecedents, 3:386

The Contemporary Praxis of the Fantastic: Borges and Cortázar, 2:857

Contemporary Problems in Statistics, 5:523

Contemporary Reform Jewish Thought, 4:652

Contemporary Roman Catholicism: Crises and Challenges, 4:785

Contemporary Russian Drama, 2:694

Contemporary Russian Literature, 1881–1925, 2:689

Contemporary Russian Prose: An Anthology, 2:693

Contemporary Serbian Literature, 2:827

Contemporary Spanish American Poets, 1:123

Contemporary Spanish Novel, 1939–1975, 2:525

Contemporary Spanish Poetry: Selections from Ten Poets, 2:527

Contemporary Spanish Poetry, 1898–1963, 2:525

Contemporary Technology: Innovations, Issues, and Perspectives, 5:149

Contemporary Turkish Literature: Fiction and Poetry, 2:96, 2:98, 2:99

Contemporary Turkish Writers, 2:96

Contemporary Urban Ecology, 3:127

Contemporary Women Writers: Hong Kong and Taiwan, 2:235

Contemporary Women Writers in Italy: A Modern Renaissance, 2:400

Contemporary Yugoslav Literature: A Sociopolitical Approach, 2:785, 2:827

Contemporary Yugoslav Poetry, 2:786, 2:808, 2:828, 2:835

Contending Theories of International Relations, 3:144

Contending with Kennan: Toward a Philosophy of American Power, 3:584

Content Analysis in Communications Research, 3:6

Content and Consciousness, 4:396

Content and Style of an Oral Literature, 3:865

The Content of Faith, 4:891, 4:903

The Content of the Form, 1:1154

Contes de ma mère l'oye, 1:576

Contestable Markets and the Theory of Industrial Structure, 3:57

The Contested Country, 3:392

The Contest of Faculties, 4:266, 4:391, 4:398

The Contest Problem Book:
Annual High School Math-
ematics Exams, 5:496
The Context of the Phenome-
nological Movement, 4:235
Contexts for Early English
Drama, 1:157
The Contexts of Acadian His-
tory, 1686–1784, 3:611
Contexts of Dryden's
Thought, 1:242
Contextual Realism: A Meta-
physical Framework for
Modern Science, 5:65
Continental Drift, 1:940
Continental Humanist Poet-
ics, 2:413
The Continental Op, 1:1230
Continental Stagecraft,
1:1074
Continents in Motion: The
New Earth Debate, 5:630
Contingency, Irony, and Soli-
darity, 1:1132, 4:413
Continuing Higher Educa-
tion: The Coming Wave,
3:251
The Continuing Presence of
Walt Whitman: The Life
after the Life, 1:707
The Continuing Silence of
the Poet, 2:26
Continuing the Revolution:
The Political Thought of
Mao, 4:362
Continuities in the Language
of Social Research, 3:230
Continuity and Change in
Modern Iran, 3:447
Continuity and Change in
Poland, 3:390
Continuity and Change in
Roman Religion, 3:306,
4:448
The Continuity of American
Poetry, 1:655, 1:719, 1:799
The Continuous and the Dis-
creet, 5:652
A Continuous Harmony,
5:269
Continuous Life, 1:1055
The Continuous Wave: Tech-
nology and American Ra-
dio, 5:228
Continuum: New and Later
Poems 1972–1988, 2:973
Contour in Time: The Plays
of Eugene O'Neill, 1:1108
The Contours of American
History, 3:601
Contours of Canadian
Thought, 3:609

The Contours of Masculine
Desire, 2:987
Contra Celsum, 4:116
A Contract, 2:439
Contracting Colonialism,
3:493
The Contrast, 1:645, 1:1069
The Contribution of A. L.
Kroeber to Culture Area
Theory and Practice, 3:33
Contributions of Faraday and
Maxwell to Electrical Sci-
ence, 5:684, 5:701
Contributions of Women in
Music, 3:663
Contributions to a History of
American State Geological
and Natural History Sur-
veys, 5:624
Contributions to a Philoso-
phy of Technology, 5:72
Contributions to the Ethnol-
ogy of the Kwakiutl, 3:28
Contributions to the Found-
ing of the Theory of
Transfinite Numbers, 5:500
Contributions to the Morning
Chronicle, 1:403
Contributions to the Natural
History of the United
States, 5:785
Contributions to the Theory
of Natural Selection, 5:812
Contributions towards a Bib-
liography of Epictetus: A
Supplement, 4:57
Contribution to the History
of Statistics, 5:527
Contribution to the Theory
of the Trade Cycle, 3:83
Controlling Technology: Eth-
ics and the Responsible
Engineer, 5:131
Control of Information in
the United States: An An-
notated Bibliography, 1:56
The Control of Nature,
1:1010
The Control of Oil, 5:280
The Control of Trusts, 3:72
The Control Revolution,
5:125
Controversaie, 2:393
Controversial Science: From
Content to Contention,
5:151
The Controversial Sholem
Asch: An Introduction to
His Fiction, 2:36
Controversies in Voting Be-
havior, 3:144

Controversy: Politics of Tech-
nical Decisions, 3:214,
5:73, 5:130, 5:172, 5:173
Controversy over Technology,
5:85
Convention Articles of Will
Rogers, 3:886
Convergences: Essays on Art
and Literature, 2:879
Conversation in Sicily, 2:443
Conversation in the Cathe-
dral, 2:886, 2:887
Conversations in Ebury
Street, 1:381
Conversations in Medicine,
5:315
Conversations with Adam
and Natasha, 5:459
Conversations with Akhmato-
va. Vol. 1: 1938–1941,
2:697
Conversations with Anatole
France, 2:478
Conversations with a Prince
and Other Poems, 2:820
Conversations with Ayck-
bourn, 1:437
Conversations with Erskine
Caldwell, 1:819
Conversations with Filipino
Writers, 2:328
Conversations with Flannery
O'Connor, 1:1025
Conversations with Isaac
Bashevis Singer, 2:49
Conversations with James
Baldwin, 1:1084
Conversations with James
Thurber, 1:891
Conversations with Jean
Piaget, 3:267
Conversations with Joyce
Carol Oates, 1:1023
Conversations with Malcolm
Cowley, 1:823
Conversations with Nietzsche:
A Life in the Words of
His Contemporaries, 4:247
Conversations with Robert-
son Davies, 2:910
Conversations with Thornton
Wilder, 1:899
Conversations with Walker
Percy, 1:1029
Conversations with Willie,
1:521
Conversations with Wright
Morris: Critical Views and
Responses, 1:1018
Conversation with a Cat and
Others, 1:442
Conversation with an Angel,
and Other Essays, 1:442

Conversation with My Uncle and Other Sketches, 2:979
Conversation with the Planet Earth: the World as a Comedy, 2:63
Conversion, 4:487
The Conversion of Saint Paul, 1:160
Conversion to Islam, 4:571
Convictions, 4:298
Conviction's Net of Branches, 1:913
Convivio, 2:416
Cool Energy—Renewable Solutions to Environmental Problems, 5:278
A Cool Million, 1:896
Coomassie and Magdala: The Story of Two British Campaigns in Africa, 3:938
Cooperation: The Basis of Sociability, 3:202
Cooperation and Competition among Primitive Peoples, 3:36
The Copernican Revolution, 4:406, 5:42, 5:53, 5:602
Copernicus and the Scientific Revolution, 5:40
Coping with a Hysterectomy: Your Own Choice, Your Own Solutions, 5:356
Coping with an Ostomy: A Guide to Living with an Ostomy, 5:385
Coping with Chemotherapy, 5:371
Coping with Chronic Disease: Research and Applications, 5:376
Coping with Crisis and Handicap, 5:377
Coping with Food Allergy: Symptoms and Treatment, 5:386
Coping with Hearing Loss: A Guide for Adults and Their Families, 5:380
Coping with High Blood Pressure, 5:374
Coping with Joyce: Essays from the Copenhagen Symposium, 1:505
Coping with Korea, 3:481
Coping with Lyme Disease, 5:377
Coping with Science, 4:384
Coping with Vulnerability: The Achievement of John Osborne, 1:532
Coppola, 3:828
The Copyright Clarification Act, 1:55

Copyright Handbook, 1:54, 1:118
Copyright Handbook: How to Protect and Use Written Works, 1:118
Copyright Law, 1:54
Copyright Registration for Derivative Works, 1:54
Copywriter's Handbook, 1:46
The Coquette, and Other Tales and Sketches, in Prose and Verse, 1:384
Coral Gardens and their Magic, 4:485
Cora Sandel: Selected Short Stories, 2:668
The Corbaccio, 2:409, 2:410
Corentyne Thunder, 2:937, 2:938
Corinne Kirchner, 5:336
Corinne of Italy, 2:510
Coriolanus, 1:205, 1:206, 3:318
Corneille and the Spanish Drama, 2:471
Cornélie, 1:185
Cornelius Agrippa: The Life of Henry Cornelius Agrippa von Nettesheim, 4:133
The Cornelius Chronicles, Vols. 1-3, 1:616
The Corner Drugstore, 5:351
Cornish Trilogy: The Rebel Angels, 2:910
Coronado: Knight of the Pueblos and Plains, 3:643
Coronado's Children, 3:863
Coronary Bypass Surgery: Who Needs It?, 5:374
Coronation of Love, 1:619
Corporate Crime and Violence, 3:205
Corporate Law and Economic Analysis, 3:61
The Corporate Reconstruction of American Capitalism, 1890-1916, 3:549
Corporate Takeovers and Productivity, 3:49
Corporations in the Moral Community, 4:389
Corpus Christi: A Theological Encyclopedia of the Eucharist, 4:675
Corpus Christi: The Eucharist in Late Medieval Culture, 4:697
Corpus Rubenianum Ludwig Burchard, 3:791
The Correlates of War, 3:149
Correlations in Rosenzweig and Levinas, 4:671
Correspondence and Papers of Edmond Halley, 5:606

Correspondence of Benedict De Spinoza, 4:189
The Correspondence of Boris Pasternak and Olga Freidenberg, 1910-1954, 2:746
The Correspondence of Charles Darwin: Vol. 1, 1821-1834, 5:793
The Correspondence of Samuel L. Clemens and William D. Howells, 1869-1910, 1:782
The Correspondence of Sargon II, Part I, 4:545
Correspondence of the French Ministers to the United States, 1791-1797, 3:599
The Correspondence of W.E.B. Du Bois, 1:832
Correspondence with Henry Huttleston Rogers, 1:780
Corridors of Deceit: The World of John le Carré, 1:596
Corridors of Time, 5:627
The Corsair, 1:281
The Corsican Brothers, 1:331
Corson's Inlet, 1:934
Cortisone: Memoirs of a Hormone Hunter, 5:369
Corydon, 2:480
Cosima, 2:419
Cosmetic Dermatologic Surgery, 5:399
The Cosmic Blueprint, 5:15
The Cosmic Christ in Origen and Teilhard de Chardin, 4:337
The Cosmic Code: Quantum Physics as the Law of Nature, 5:660, 5:691, 5:713
The Cosmic Cycle, 5:589
Cosmic Dawn: The Origins of Matter and Life, 5:594
Cosmic Discovery: The Search, Scope, and Heritage of Astronomy, 5:590
The Cosmic Frontiers of General Relativity, 5:655
Cosmic Horizons: Understanding the Universe, 5:589, 5:656
Cosmicomics, 2:411
Cosmic Wormholes: The Search for Interstellar Shortcuts, 5:594
The Cosmological Argument, 4:194
Cosmological Constants: Papers in Modern Cosmology, 5:654

The Cosmological Distance Ladder, 5:656

The Cosmological Eye, 1:861, 1:862

Cosmology (Contopoulous), 5:654

Cosmology (Rowan-Robinson), 5:656

Cosmology: The Science of the Universe, 5:595, 5:655

Cosmology, Fusion, and Other Matters, 5:605

The Cosmology of Giordano Bruno, 4:136

Cosmopolitan World Atlas, 1:84

The Cosmopolitan World of Henry James: An Intertextual Study, 1:767

Cosmos, 5:588, 5:611

Cosmos, Bios, Theos, 5:68

Cosmos, Earth, and Man: A Short History of the Universe, 5:594, 5:622

Cosmos and Creator, 5:202

Cosmos and Pornografia, 2:813

The Cosmos of Arthur Holly Compton, 5:678

Cosmotheoros, 5:695

Cossacks, Sevastopol, The Invaders and Other Stories, 2:764

The Costa Ricans, 3:635

Cost-Benefit Analysis, 3:67

Cost-Benefit Analysis and the Environment, 3:48

Cost Estimating with Microcomputers, 5:558

Costly Grace: An Illustrated Biography of Dietrich Bonhoeffer, 4:760

Costly Monuments, 1:181

The Cost of Discipleship, 4:760

Costs, Risks, and Benefits of Surgery, 5:79

Coulson's Valence, 5:734

The Council of Florence, 4:694

Counseling Adult Survivors of Child Sexual Abuse, 5:429

Counseling and Psychotherapy, 5:468

Counseling in Genetics, 5:781

Counseling in the United States, 5:418

Counseling Psychology, 5:413

Counseling Psychology in Community Settings, 5:417

Counseling Women: A Guide for Therapists, 5:417

Counselor Ayres Memorial, 2:896

Counsels and Maxims, 4:255

Counsels in Contemporary Islam, 4:373

Count Basie and His Orchestra, Its Music and Its Musicians, 3:677

Count Belisarius, 3:879

Count d'Orgel's Ball, 2:498, 2:499

Countee Cullen, 1:824

The Counterfeiters, 2:480

Counterfeit Lady, 1:1221

The Counterlife, 1:1041

A Counterpoint of Dissonance, 1:365

The Counter-Reformation (Davidson), 3:334

The Counter Reformation (Dickens), 4:728

The Counter Reformation: 1599–1610, 4:737

The Counter-Reformation Prince, 4:728

The Counter-Renaissance, 2:401

Counterrevolution and Revolt, 4:408, 5:94

The Counter-Revolution of Science: Studies on the Abuse of Reason, 3:82

The Countesse of Pembroke's Arcadia, 1:196

Counting for Something: Statistical Principles and Personalities, 5:523

Count Julian, 2:540

Count Lucanor, 2:520

The Count of Carmagnola, 2:426

The Count of Monte Cristo, 2:473

Country and Court: England, 1658–1714, 3:360

The Country and the City, 1:313

The Country Artist: A Story about Beatrix Potter, 1:589

Country By-Ways, 1:770

The Country Cousin, 1:937

A Country Doctor, 1:769, 1:770

Country Fair: Poems from Friesland since 1945, 2:635

The Country Girl, 1:1106

Country Life in Classical Times, 3:304

A Country Made by War, 3:546

Country Music, 1:1066, 1:1067

Country Music, U.S.A.: A Fifty Year History, 3:852

The Country of Streams and Grottoes, 3:469

The Country of the Blind, and Other Stories, 1:564

The Country of the Pointed Firs, 1:769, 1:770

Country Place, 1:1030

The Country Waif, 2:505

The Country Wife, 1:263

A Country Year: Living the Questions, 5:818

Count Zinzendorf, 4:740

The Coup, 1:1060

Coup de Grace, 2:517

Couples, 1:1059, 1:1060

Couples: Exploring and Understanding the Cycles of Intimate Relationships, 3:206

Couple Therapy, 5:417

The Courage to Be, 4:787, 5:206

The Courage to Change, 5:403

The Courage to Create, 5:462

The Course of Alcoholism: Four Years after Treatment, 5:427

The Course of Empire, 3:576

The Course of French History, 3:373

The Course of German History, 3:378, 3:409

The Course of Irish History, 3:369

A Course of Lectures on Dramatic Art, 2:610

The Course of Mexican History, 3:639

The Course of Modern Jewish History, 3:350, 4:634

The Court, 1:1059

Court, Kirk, and Community: Scotland, 1470–1625, 4:736

Court and Bakufu in Japan: Essays in Kamakura History, 3:475

Court and Country Politics in the Plays of Beaumont and Fletcher, 1:173

Court and Family in Sung China, 960–1279, 3:467

The Court and the Castle, 1:566

The Court and the Country: The Beginning of the English Revolution, 3:361

The Court Comedies of John Lyly: A Study in Allegorical Dramaturgy, 1:186

Court Cultures and the Origins of a Royalist Tradition in Early Stuart England, 3:360

The Courtesan's Jewel Box: Chinese Stories of the Xth-XVIIth Centuries, 2:198

The Courtier, 2:413

The Courting of Dinah Shadd and Other Stories, 1:371

Courting Poetry in Laos: A Textual and Linguistic Analysis, 2:322

Court of Appeal, 3:212

Court of Last Resort, 1:1109

Court Patronage and Corruption in Early Stuart England, 3:360

Courts and Modern Medicine, 5:343

Courtship, Love, and Marriage in Nineteenth-Century English Canada, 3:609

The Courtship Novel, 1740–1820: A Feminized Genre, 1:230

The Courtship of Miles Standish, 1:682

The Court Theatre, 1904–1907: A Commentary and Criticism, 1:426

Cousin Bazílio, 2:559

Cousin Bette, 2:453

Cousin Henry, 1:406

Cousin Phillis and Other Tales, 1:356

Cousin Pons, 2:453

Cousteau: An Unauthorized Biography, 3:919, 5:642

Cousteau: The Captain and His World, 3:919

Cousteau's Papua New Guinea Journey, 3:919

The Covenant, 3:931

A Covenant with Power, 3:545

The Covent-Garden Journal, 1:244, 1:245

Covering Islam, 3:444, 3:459, 3:460, 4:572

The Coverley Papers from The Spectator, 1:232, 1:257

Cover Stories: Narrative and Ideology in the British Spy Thriller, 1:592

The Cowards, 2:794

Cowboy Culture: A Saga of Five Centuries, 3:558

The Cowboy Philosopher on Prohibition, 3:886

The Cowboy Philosopher on the Peace Conference, 3:886

The Cow Jumped over the Moon, 2:907

Cowper's Poetry: A Critical Study and Reassessment, 1:238

Cowper's Task: Structure and Influence, 1:238

A Coyote Reader, 3:864

Coyote Waits, 1:1231

C. P. Cavafy, 2:372

The C Programming Language, 5:553

C. P. Snow, 1:550

C. P. Snow: A Reference Guide, 1:550

C. P. Snow and the Struggle of Modernity, 1:550

CQ Almanac, 1:82

Crabbe: The Critical Heritage, 1:289

Crabgrass Frontier: The Suburbanization of America, 3:552

Cracks in the Wall, 2:674

The Crack-up, 1:839, 1:840

The Cradle Will Rock, 1:1179

Craft, 2:767

Crafting Selves, 3:22

Crafting the Art of Magic, 4:865

The Craft of an Absolute Winner, 2:897

The Craft of Bookbinding: A Practical Handbook, 1:22

The Craft of Calligraphy, 1:17

The Craft of Ralph Ellison, 1:974

Craftsmen in Greek and Roman Society, 3:304

Craig's Wife, 1:1097, 1:1098

Crainquebille, 2:478

Crampton Hodnet, 1:539

Cranford and Other Tales, 1:355, 1:356

The Crater; or, Vulcan's Peak: A Tale of the Pacific, 1:663

Crazy Cock, 1:861

Crazy in Berlin, 1:948, 1:949

Crazy like a Fox, 1:868

The Created Legend, 2:758, 2:759

Created to Praise: The Language of Gerard Manley Hopkins, 1:364

Creating a Marriage, 3:206

Creating Community on College Campuses, 3:252

Creating Elizabethan Tragedy: The Theater of Marlowe and Kyd, 1:185

Creating Faulkner's Reputation, 1:838

Creating Minds, 3:174

Creating Rosie the Riveter, 3:535

Creating the Computer: Government, Industry, and High Technology, 5:184

Creation, 1:1062

Creation and Recreation, 1:976

Creation by Natural Law, 5:698

The Creation Controversy: Science or Scripture in the Schools, 5:173

Creationism on Trial: Evolution and God at Little Rock, 5:200

The Creation of Confederate Nationalism, 3:527

The Creation of Jazz: Music, Race, and Culture in Urban America, 3:561

The Creation of Matter: The Universe from Beginning to End, 5:654

The Creation of Mythology, 4:446

The Creation of Nikolai Gogol, 2:722

The Creation of Quantum Mechanics and the Bohr-Pauli Dialogue, 5:674

The Creation of the American Republic, 1776–1787, 3:522

The Creation of the Universe, 5:605

Creation of the World, 2:440

The Creation of the World According to Gersonides, 4:664

The Creation of the World and Other Business, 1:1103, 1:1104

The Creation of Tribalism in Southern Africa, 3:424

The Creation of Woman, 5:467

Creative Bookbinding, 1:24

Creative Democracy, 5:180

The Creative Element, 1:422, 1:553

Creative Evolution, 4:220

Creative History, 3:9

The Creative Imagination: Enlightenment to Romanticism, 1:265
Creative Intuition in Art and Poetry, 2:988, 4:306
The Creative Mind: An Introduction to Metaphysics, 4:220
The Creative Moment: How Science Made Itself Alien to Modern Culture, 5:11
The Creative Present: Notes on the Contemporary American Novel, 1:916
The Creative Process in the Autograph Musical Documents of Hector Berlioz, 3:682
Creative Tensions: The Life and Thought of Kenneth Boulding, 3:72
Creative Ventures, 4:338, 4:339
Creativity and Common Sense: Essays in Honor of Paul Weiss, 4:340
Creativity and Method: Studies in Honor of Rev. Bernard Lonergan, S.J., 4:744
Creativity and Taoism, 4:527
Creativity in American Philosophy, 4:34, 4:288
Creativity in George Herbert Mead, 4:309
The Creativity Question, 5:194
The Creators: A History of Heroes of the Imagination, 3:568, 5:69
Creature, 1:1243
Creatures of Habit and Creatures of Change, 1:514
The Credit Card Industry: A History, 3:548
Creeds of the Churches, 4:680
Crepuscular, 2:873
The Crescent in the East: Islam in Asia Major, 4:570
Crescent Moon and Other Stories, 2:251
The Cricket, 1:704
The Cricket beneath the Waterfall and Other Stories, 2:786
The Cricket on the Hearth, 1:348
Criers and Kibitzers, Kibitzers and Criers, 1:973
Cries, 2:372
Crime and Punishment, 2:712, 2:713

Crime and Punishment: Changing Attitudes in America, 3:205
Crime and Punishment in Medieval Chinese Drama, 2:189
Crimean Sonnets, 2:817
Crime in England, 3:355
Crime News and the Public, 3:806
Crimen Injuria, 2:168
The Crime of Galileo, 4:144, 5:43, 5:688
The Crime of Punishment, 5:463, 5:464
The Crime of Sylvester Bonnard, 2:477
The Crime of the Century, 1:432
Crimes of Conscience, 2:162
Crimes of the Heart, 1:1093, 1:1094
Criminal Gods and Demon Devotees, 4:504
The Criminally Insane, 5:428
The Criminal Personality: The Drug User, 5:428
The Criminal Prisons of London, and Scenes of Prison Life, 1:377
Criminal Procedure: An Analysis of Cases and Concepts, 3:139
Criminal Violence, Criminal Justice, 3:205
The Crimson Fairy Book, 3:883
Crises of the Republic, 3:282, 4:394, 5:82
Crisis and Transformation in Seventeenth-century China, 2:210
Crisis in Identity and Contemporary Japanese Novels, 2:282
Crisis in the Classroom: The Remaking of American Education, 3:252
The Crisis of Chinese Consciousness, 2:247
The Crisis of Church and State, 1050–1300, 4:695
The Crisis of Confidence: Ideas, Power and Violence in America, 3:597
The Crisis of European Sciences and Transcendental Phenomenology, 4:234
Crisis of Fear: Secession in South Carolina, 3:527
The Crisis of German Ideology, 2:565, 3:377

The Crisis of Political Modernism, 1:1157
The Crisis of Psychoanalysis, 5:450
Crisis of the Aristocracy, 1558–1641, 3:408
Crisis of the Early Italian Renaissance, 4:123
Crisis of the European Sciences, 4:234
Criss-Crossing Boundaries in African Literatures 1986, 2:108
Cristofano and the Plague, 5:382
Criterion, 1:428
The Critic, 1:254
A Critical and Exegetical Commentary on the Epistle to the Hebrews, 4:835
Critical and Historical Essays, 1:374
Critical and Interpretive Essays, 4:192
Critical Approaches to Federico Fellini's "8½", 3:836
Critical Approaches to Rubén Darío, 2:863
Critical Approaches to Teaching Swift, 1:261
The Critical Approach to Science and Philosophy, 5:99
Critical Bibliography of Religion in America, 4:750, 4:752
A Critical Cinema: Interviews with Independent Filmmakers, 3:828
A Critical Cinema 2: Interviews with Independent Filmmakers, 3:828
The Critical Circle, 1:925
Critical Concerns in Moral Theology, 4:743
Critical Connections: Communications for the Future, 5:185
Critical Dictionary of English Literature and British and American Authors, 1:120, 1:126
A Critical Dictionary of the French Revolution, 3:339
Critical Essays from The Spectator, 1:232, 1:257
Critical Essays in the Philosophy of Robin George Collingwood, 4:282
Critical Essays on Ambrose Bierce, 1:735
Critical Essays on Angus Wilson, 1:567

Critical Essays on Anne
Bradstreet, 1:635
Critical Essays on Anne Sex-
ton, 1:1045
Critical Essays on Anthony
Burgess, 1:454
Critical Essays on Arthur
Miller, 1:1104
Critical Essays on Cervantes,
2:536
Critical Essays on Charles
Brockden Brown, 1:636
Critical Essays on Charlotte
Brontë, 1:335
Critical Essays on D. H.
Lawrence, 1:510
Critical Essays on Dante,
2:418
Critical Essays on Denise
Levertov, 1:1004
Critical Essays on Dostoyev-
sky, 2:716
Critical Essays on E. M. For-
ster, 1:477
Critical Essays on Eduard
Mörike, 2:603
Critical Essays on Emily
Dickinson, 1:747
Critical Essays on Eudora
Welty, 1:896
Critical Essays on Eugene
O'Neill, 1:1108
Critical Essays on F. Scott
Fitzgerald's "The Great
Gatsby," 1:840
Critical Essays on Ford Ma-
dox Ford, 1:475
Critical Essays on Frank
Norris, 1:777
Critical Essays on Frederick
Douglass, 1:668
Critical Essays on Gabriel
García Márquez, 2:867
Critical Essays on George
Bernard Shaw, 1:546
Critical Essays on George
Orwell, 1:531
Critical Essays on George
Washington Cable, 1:737
Critical Essays on Gertrude
Stein, 1:883
Critical Essays on H. L.
Mencken, 1:860
Critical Essays on Hamlin
Garland, 1:751
Critical Essays on Harold
Pinter, 1:535
Critical Essays on Haw-
thorne's Short Stories,
1:677
Critical Essays on Haw-
thorne's "The Scarlet Let-
ter," 1:677

Critical Essays on Henry
Adams, 1:730
Critical Essays on Henry Da-
vid Thoreau's Walden,
1:702
Critical Essays on Henry
James: The Early Novels,
1:766
Critical Essays on Henry
James: The Late Novels,
1:766
Critical Essays on Herman
Melville's "Benito Cere-
no," 1:688
Critical Essays on Honoré de
Balzac, 2:454
Critical Essays on Ivan Tur-
genev, 2:770
Critical Essays on Jack Lon-
don, 1:775
Critical Essays on James
Baldwin, 1:1084
Critical Essays on James
Joyce, 1:505
Critical Essays on Joel
Chandler Harris, 1:755
Critical Essays on John
Cheever, 1:961
Critical Essays on John
Fowles, 1:478
Critical Essays on John
Greenleaf Whittier, 1:709
Critical Essays on John Up-
dike, 1:1061
Critical Essays on John Wil-
liam De Forest, 1:744
Critical Essays on Jorge Luis
Borges, 2:857
Critical Essays on Joyce
Carol Oates, 1:1023
Critical Essays on Langston
Hughes, 1:849
Critical Essays on Lawrence
Durrell, 1:470
Critical Essays on Lord
Byron, 1:283
Critical Essays on Louisa
May Alcott, 1:1199
Critical Essays on Margaret
Drabble, 1:468
Critical Essays on Mark
Twain, 1867–1910, 1:783
Critical Essays on Mary Wil-
kins Freeman, 1:750
Critical Essays on Melville's
"Billy Budd," 1:689
Critical Essays on Native
American Literature, 1:717
Critical Essays on Oscar
Wilde, 1:410
Critical Essays on Patrick
White, 2:967

Critical Essays on Philip
Roth, 1:1041
Critical Essays on Richard
Wright, 1:906
Critical Essays on Robert
Frost, 1:842
Critical Essays on Robert
Penn Warren, 1:893
Critical Essays on Robinson
Jeffers, 1:851
Critical Essays on Rudyard
Kipling, 1:372
Critical Essays on Sarah
Orne Jewett, 1:770
Critical Essays on Saul
Bellow, 1:948
Critical Essays on Simone de
Beauvoir, 2:458
Critical Essays on Sinclair
Lewis, 1:854
Critical Essays on Sir Arthur
Conan Doyle, 1:608
Critical Essays on Steinbeck's
"The Grapes of Wrath,
1:885
Critical Essays on T. S. Eliot:
The Sweeney Motif, 1:473
Critical Essays on the Poetry
of Tennyson, 1:402
Critical Essays on Thomas
Pynchon, 1:1035
Critical Essays on Tolstoy,
2:766
Critical Essays on Tom Stop-
pard, 1:554
Critical Essays on Toni Mor-
rison, 1:1019
Critical Essays on Vladimir
Nabokov, 2:742
Critical Essays on W. B.
Yeats, 1:572
Critical Essays on Wallace
Stevens, 1:887
Critical Essays on Walt Whit-
man, 1:708
Critical Essays on Washing-
ton Irving, 1:681
Critical Essays on William
Golding, 1:484
Critical Essays on William
Styron, 1:1057
A Critical Exposition of the
Philosophy of Leibniz,
4:177
A Critical Fable, 1:856
Critical Guide to Catholic
Reference Books, 4:6
The Critical Historians of
Art, 3:761
A Critical History of Chil-
dren's Literature, 1:1196
A Critical History of Western
Philosophy, 4:162

A Critical Introduction to Henry Green's Novels: The Living Vision, 1:487
A Critical Introduction to Modern Arabic Poetry, 2:55
A Critical Introduction to the Poems of Thomas Hardy, 1:362
A Critical Introduction to Twentieth-Century American Drama, 1:1072
Critical Issues in Medical Technology, 5:324
Critical Issues in Neo-Confucian Thought, 4:535
Critical Issues in the Information Age, 5:125
The Critical Muse: Selected Literary Criticism, 1:764
The Critical Path: An Essay on the Social Context of Literary Criticism, 1:976
The Critical Period in American Religion, 1875–1900, 3:596
Critical Perspectives in Modern Arabic Literature, 2:55
Critical Perspectives on Ngugi wa Thiong'o, 2:155
Critical Perspectives on Ayi Kwei Armah, 2:131
Critical Perspectives on Chinua Achebe, 2:129
Critical Perspectives on Christopher Okigbo, 2:142
Critical Perspectives on Leopold Sedar Senghor, 2:147
Critical Perspectives on Lusophone Literature from Africa, 2:106
Critical Perspectives on Modern Persian Literature, 2:83
Critical Perspectives on Naguib Mahfouz, 2:69
Critical Perspectives on Native American Fiction, 1:804
Critical Perspectives on Nigerian Literatures, 2:126
Critical Perspectives on Nonacademic Science and Engineering, 5:74, 5:152
Critical Perspectives on Sam Selvon, 2:942
Critical Perspectives on V. S. Naipaul, 2:939
Critical Perspectives on Wole Soyinka, 2:149
Critical Pilgrimages: Studies in the Arabic Literary Tradition, 2:56

Critical Practice, 1:1131
Critical Questions: On Music and Letters, Culture and Biography, 1:814, 3:658
The Critical Reception of Hamlin Garland, 1891–1978, 1:752
Critical Responses to Kenneth Burke, 1924–1966, 1:818
Critical Social Issues in American Education, 3:257
Critical Studies of Sir Gawain and the Green Knight, 1:156
Critical Studies of the Works of Charles Dickens, 1:350
A Critical Study of Condillac's Traite des Systemes, 4:195
Critical Survey of Drama: English Language, 1:123
Critical Survey of Long Fiction, 1:125
Critical Survey of Poetry, 1:125
The Critical Temper, 1:135
Critical Terms for Literary Study, 1:1134
Critical Theory and Post-Structuralism: In Search of a Context, 4:266
Critical Theory and Technology, 5:73, 5:152
The Critical Theory of Jürgen Habermas, 4:405, 5:89
Critical Theory since Plato, 1:1133
Critical Understanding: The Powers and Limits of Pluralism, 1:1139, 1:1138
Critical Views of Isaac Bashevis Singer, 2:49
The Critical Writing of James Joyce, 1:974
The Critical Years: The Union of British North America 1857–1873, 3:622
The Critic and Society: From Matthew Arnold to the New Historicism, 1:924
Criticism and Ideology: A Study in Marxist Literary Theory, 1:924
Criticism and Ideology: Second African Writers' Conference, Stockholm, 2:112
Criticism and Social Change, 1:926
Criticism and the Growth of Knowledge, 5:53, 5:66

Criticism in Action: Enlightenment Experiments in Political Writing, 2:472
Criticism in the University, 1:1128
Criticism of Milton's Paradise Lost, from The Spectator, 1711–1712, 1:232
Criticisms on Art, 1:290
Critics' Choice: New York Drama Critics' Circle Prize Plays, 1935–55, 1:1077
Critics of Capitalism: Victorian Criticism of Political Economy, 1:326
Critics of Consciousness: The Existential Structures of Literature, 1:925
Critics of Henry George, 3:80
Critics on Mark Twain, 1:784
Critics on Whitman, 1:708
Critics on William Dean Howells, 1:759
Critique, Norm, and Utopia, 4:404
Critique of Dialectical Reason, 2:507, 4:329
A Critique of Jean-Paul Sartre's Ontology, 4:331
Critique of Judgment, 4:204, 4:205
A Critique of Political Economy, 3:95
Critique of Practical Reason, 4:204, 4:205, 4:739
The Critique of Pure Modernity: Hegel, Heidegger, and After, 4:293, 5:91
Critique of Pure Reason, 4:204, 4:205, 4:206
A Critique of Pure Tolerance, 4:245, 4:408
Critique of the Human Potential Movement, 4:866
A Critique of the Study of Kinship, 3:20
Critiques and Essays on Modern Fiction, 1920–1951, 1:420
Critiques of Confucius in Contemporary China, 4:358
Critiques of Research in Social Sciences, 3:221
Crito, 4:89
Croce's Aesthetic, 3:284
Croce versus Gentile: A Dialogue on Contemporary Italian Philosophy, 4:285
Crofts Classics Series, 1:171
The Crohn's Disease and Ulcerative Colitis Fact Book, 5:385

Crome Yellow, 1:499
Cromwell (Hugo), 2:482
Cromwell (Fraser), 3:360
Cromwell: The Lord Protector, 4:733
Cromwell's Place in History, 3:360
Cronaca Familiare, 2:437
Cronache di Poveri Amanti, 2:437
Cronopios and Famas, 2:861
The Cross, 2:669
Cross-Cultural Perspectives in Medical Ethics: Readings, 5:144
Cross-Cultural Trade in World History, 3:426
Crosscurrents, 4:763
Crosscurrents: Interactions between Science and Faith, 5:198
Cross Fire: The Eight Years with Eisenhower, 5:268
Crossing Antarctica, 3:907
The Crossing of Antarctica, 3:925
Crossings: The Great Transatlantic Migrations, 1870–1914, 3:557
Crossing the Border, 1:1023
Crossing the Postmodern Divide, 5:69
Crossing the Water, 1:1031
Crossing to Safety, 1:1054
The Cross of Shaphan, 2:307
The Crossroad of Intentions, 2:515
The Crossroads in Folklore and Myth, 3:849
Crossroads of Civilization: Three Thousand Years of Persian History, 3:448
Crossroads to Israel 1917–1948, 4:643
Cross Ties: Selected Poems, 1:997
Crotchet Castle, 1:297
Crow: From the Life and Songs of the Crow, 1:497
The Crowd, 3:203
The Crowd in History, 3:339
Crowds and Power, 2:575
The Crow Eaters, 2:178
Crowell's Handbook of World Opera, 3:670
The Crowned Cannibals: Writings on Repression in Iran, 2:82
The Crown Guide to the World's Greatest Plays, 2:3
A Crown of Feathers, 2:47
The Crown of Life, 1:358

Crucial Instances, 1:786, 1:787
The Crucible, 1:1103, 1:1104
The Crucible of Europe, 3:328, 4:691
The Crucible of Race, 3:533
Crude Oil Prices—As Determined by OPEC and Market Fundamentals, 5:280
The Cruel Choice: A New Concept in the Theory of Development, 5:128
The Cruise of the Rolling Junk, 1:840
Cruise of the Snark, 1:774
Crumbling Idols, 1:751
The Crusade: Historiography and Bibliography, 4:692
Crusader in Crinoline: The Life of Harriet Beecher Stowe, 1:699
The Crusaders, 2:590
Crusaders for Fitness: A History of American Health Reformers, 5:315
The Crusades, 3:331
Crusoe's Footprints: Cultural Studies in Britain and America, 1:1126, 1:1131
Cry, the Beloved Country, 2:167
The Cry for the Dead, 2:968
The Crying of Lot 49, 1:1035
Cry of the Kalahari, 5:818
Cry of the People, 3:632, 4:748
Cry of the People and Other Poems, 2:304
A Crystal Age, 1:365
Crystal and Fox, 1:479
Crystal Boys, 2:260
The Crystal Desert: Summers in Antarctica, 5:817
The Crystal Goblet: Sixteen Essays on Typography, 1:12
Crystals, Electrons, and Transistors, 5:669
Crystals, Fabrics, and Fields, 1:1147, 1:1242, 5:201
Crystals and Crystal Growing, 5:734
Cry to Heaven, 1:1242
C. S. Lewis, 1:513
C. S. Lewis: A Biography, 1:513, 4:776, 4:777
C. S. Lewis: A Critical Essay, 4:777
C. S. Lewis: His Literary Achievement, 1:513
C. S. Lewis: The Art of Enchantment, 1:513

C. S. Lewis: The Shape of His Faith and Thought, 4:777
C. S. Lewis and the Search for Rational Religion, 1:513, 4:776
C. S. Lewis at the Breakfast Table, 4:781
C. S. Lewis on Scripture, 4:776
Cuando Yo Me Muera. Essays in Memory of Federico García Lorca, 2:539
Cuba: Between Reform and Revolution, 3:636
Cuba: The Making of a Revolution, 3:636
Cuba and the United States: Ties of Singular Intimacy, 3:636
Cuba's Nicolas Guillén: Poetry and Ideology, 2:869
The Cubist Painters, 2:451
The Cubs and Other Stories, 2:887
The Cuckoo's Egg: Inside the World of Corporate Espionage, 5:547
Cue, 1:1096
Cuentos: Based on the Folk Tales of the Spanish Californians, 3:863
Cuentos Chicanos: A Short Story Anthology, 1:805
The Cuisine of Sacrifice among the Greeks, 4:429, 4:493
Cujo, 1:1241
Culloden and the Forty Five, 3:368
Cult and Countercult, 4:866
Cult Controversies, 4:856
The Cult Controversy: A Guide to Sources, 4:856
The Cult Experience, 4:855
The Cultivation of Sagehood as a Religious Goal in Neo-Confucianism, 4:526
The Cult of Draupadi, 4:504
The Cult of Information, 5:126, 5:175, 5:574
The Cult of Optimism, 2:691
Cult of the Dead in a Chinese Village, 4:530
The Cult of the Saints: Its Rise and Function in Latin Christianity, 4:687
Cults: Faith, Healing and Coercion, 4:856
Cults: What Parents Should Know, 4:857
Cults, Converts and Charisma, 4:855

Cults, Culture and the Law: Perspectives on New Religious Movements, 4:857

Cults and New Religions, 4:854

Cults on Campus: Continuing Challenge, 4:857

Cultural Anthropology: A Guide to Reference and Information Sources, 3:11

Cultural Atlas of Mesopotamia and the Ancient Near East, 4:809

Cultural Contradictions of Capitalism, 3:220

Cultural Events from Africa, 2:156

The Cultural Geography of Health Care, 3:121

The Cultural Geography of the United States, 3:122

The Cultural Heritage of India, 4:498

Cultural History: Between Practices and Representations, 3:337

A Cultural History of India, 3:482, 4:498

A Cultural History of Spanish America from Conquest to Independence, 4:752

A Cultural History of Tibet, 4:356

Cultural Identity and Social Liberation in Latin American Thought, 3:632

The Cultural Landscape: An Introduction to Human Geography, 3:122

The Cultural Life of Modern America, 2:665

The Cultural Life of the American Colonies: 1607–1763, 1:630

Cultural Literacy: What Every American Needs to Know, 1:1124, 1:1127, 1:1148

Cultural Materialism: The Struggle for a Science of Culture, 3:12, 3:31

The Cultural Meaning of Popular Science, 5:46

Cultural Nationalism in Colonial Korea, 1920–1925, 3:482

Cultural Options and the Role of Tradition, 2:317

The Cultural Patterns in American Politics: The First Century, 3:543

Cultural Psychology: The Chicago Symposia on Human Development, 3:15

Cultural Studies, 1:1128

The Cultural Unity of Black Africa, 3:429

The Cultural Unity of Negro Africa, 3:428

Culture and Development: The Popular Theatre Approach in Africa, 2:110

Culture and History of the Bulgarian People, 3:392

Culture and Irony: Studies in Joseph Conrad's Major Novels, 1:464

Culture and Its Creators, 3:202

Culture and Modernity: East-West Perspectives, 4:349

Culture and National Identity in Republican Rome, 3:306

Culture and Personality: Contemporary Readings, 3:15

Culture and Power in Banaras, 4:504

Culture and Power in the Classroom, 3:254

Culture and Practical Reason, 3:14, 3:32

Culture and Society: Twenty-Four Essays, 3:38

Culture and Society, 1780–1950, 1:266, 1:313, 3:341

Culture and Society in Lucian, 4:485

Culture and the People, 2:725

Culture and Truth: The Remaking of Social Analysis, 4:426

Culture and Value, 4:343

Culture Clash: The Making of a Gay Sensibility, 1:1181

Culture, Class, and Development in Pakistan, 3:487

Culture, Conflict, and Crime, 3:205

Culture, Mind and Therapy: An Introduction to Cultural Psychiatry, 5:415

The Culture of Cities, 3:216, 5:169, 5:170

Culture of Compassion, 4:636

The Culture of Consumption, 3:559

The Culture of Criticism and the Criticism of Culture, 1:1127

The Culture of Narcissism, 3:560

The Culture of Renaissance Humanism, 4:124

The Culture of Science: Essays and Issues for Writers, 5:10

The Culture of Technology, 5:71, 5:156, 5:232

The Culture of the Meiji Period, 3:478

The Culture of the Renaissance in Italy, 3:399

The Culture of Western Europe: The Nineteenth and Twentieth Centuries, 3:327

Culture, People, and Nature: An Introduction to General Anthropology, 3:31

Culture, Power, and the State: Rural North China, 1900–1942, 3:470

Culture Shift in Advanced Industrial Society, 3:141

Culture, Technology and Society, 5:86

Culture Theory, 3:14

Culture, Tradition and Society in the West African Novel, 2:126

Culture Wars: The Struggle to Define America, 3:559

Cummings: The Growth of a Writer, 1:826

Cumulative Bibliography of Asian Studies, 1966–1970, 3:462

Cumulative Book Index, 1:113

The Cumulative Book Index, 1969–1985, 1:71

The Cumulative Paperback Index, 1939–59, 1:71

Cunning Intelligence in Greek Culture and Society, 4:493

The Cunning of History: The Holocaust and the American Future, 3:344, 3:350

Cupid and Psyche, 4:469

The Cup of Bitterness, 2:77

A Cup of Gold, 1:884

Curanderismo: Mexican American Folk Healing, 5:320

The Curate in Charge, 1:385

Curative Eurythmy, 4:879

The Cure at Troy: A Version of Sophocles' Philoctetes, 1:495

Cured to Death: The Effects of Prescription Drugs, 5:351

Curfew, 2:864

Curio, 2:302

The Curious Death of the Novel, 1:919

Curious Naturalists, 3:195, 5:837

Current Bibliography in the History of Technology, 5:24, 5:37

Current Biography, 5:467

Current Biography Yearbook, 1:85

Current Literary Terms, 1:132

The Current of Romantic Passion, 2:987

Current Perspectives in the Psychology of Religion, 4:890

Current Research in Philosophy of Science, 5:60

Currents in the Contemporary Argentine Novel, 2:845

Current Strategies for Containing Health Care Expenditure, 5:332

Curriculum Vitae, 1:552

The Curse of Kehama, 1:304

The Curse of the Wise Woman, 1:615

The Curtain and the Veil, 1:1074

A Curtain of Green and Other Stories, 1:895

Curtains, 1:426

Curtmantle, 1:480

Curve: Overlapping Narratives, 1:982

Custer Died for Your Sins: An Indian Manifesto, 3:554

Custom and Myth, 1:579, 3:882

The Custom of the Country, 1:786, 1:787

Customs in Common: Studies in Traditional Popular Culture, 3:410, 3:874

The Customs Union Issue, 3:110, 3:111

The Cut-outs of Henri Matisse, 3:781

Cuts, 1:448

The Cutting Edge: A Selection of Korean Poetry, Ancient and Modern, 2:299

Cutting Energy Costs, 5:284

Cutting through Spiritual Materialism, 4:357, 4:544

Cuttlefish Bones, 2:427

C. Vann Woodward, Southerner, 3:603

C. Wright Mills: An American Utopian, 3:235

C. Wright Mills: A Native Radical and His American Intellectual Roots, 3:235

Cybele, 1:1022

The Cyberiad: Fables for the Cybernetic Age, 2:816

The Cybernetic Imagination in Science Fiction, 5:566

Cybernetics, 5:584

Cyberpunk: Outlaws and Hackers on the Computer Frontier, 5:547

Cycle of American Literature, 1:716

The Cycles of American History, 3:597

Cycles of Fire: Stars, Galaxies, and the Wonder of Deep Space, 5:594

Cycling of Carbon, Nitrogen, Sulfur and Phosphorus in Terrestrial and Aquatic Ecosystems, 5:262

Cyclopean Song, 2:540

Cyclopedia of American Agriculture, 5:787

Cyclopedia of American Horticulture, 5:787

Cyclopedia of American Literature, 1:132

Cyclopedia of World Authors, 1:126, 1:128

Cymbeline, 1:205, 1:206

Cyprian, 4:708

Cyprian of Carthage and the Unity of the Christian Church, 4:708

Cyropaedia, 3:324

Czech and Slovak Literature in English: A Bibliography, 2:789, 2:833

Czech Literature, 2:789

Czech Literature since 1956: A Symposium, 2:789

Czech Opera, 3:671

Czechoslovakia at the Crossroads of European History, 3:389

Czechoslovakia in Transition: Politics, Economy and Society, 3:389

Czechoslovak Literature: An Outline, 2:789, 2:833

Czech Prose: An Anthology, 2:789

Czech Song and Dance: Parts, 3:853

Czech Song and Dance: Score, 3:853

Czech Writers and Politics, 1945–1969, 2:788

D

Daddy Jake, the Runaway, and Short Stories Told after Dark by Uncle Remus, 1:754

Daedalus, or Science and the Future, 5:797

The Daemonic Genius of Richard Wright, 1:907

Daggers and Javelins: Essays, 1974–1979, 1:941

Daguerreotypes and Other Essays, 2:649

Dahcotah: Or, Life and Legends of the Sioux around Fort Snelling, 3:864

The Dahomean, 1:1225

Dahomey, An Ancient West African Kingdom, 3:32, 3:420

Dai Greatcoat: A Self-Portrait of David Jones in His Letters, 1:502

The Daily Daily, 2:869

Daily Life in Ancient Rome, 2:380, 3:307

Daily Life in China on the Eve of the Mongol Invasion, 1250–1276, 3:468

Daily Life in Japan in the Age of the Samurai, 1185–1603, 3:475

Daily Life in the Time of Homer, 2:362

The Daily Life of Ku-poh the Novelist, 2:300

Daily Living in the Twelfth Century, 3:331

Daimon Life: Heidegger and Life-Philosophy, 4:293

The Dainty Monsters, 2:922

Daisy Mayme, 1:1098

Daisy Miller, 1:761, 1:762

Daisy Miller and Other Stories, 1:763

The Dalai Lama at Harvard, 4:560, 4:906

D'Alembert's Dream, 2:471

The Dalkey Archive, 1:525

Damaged Goods, 4:654

The Damages, 1:989

Dambudzo Marechera: A Source Book on His Life and Work, 2:165

Dame Trot and Her Comical Cat, 1:583

The Damned and the Beautiful: American Youth in the 1920's, 3:534

Damned for Despair, 2:551

Dan Barry's Daughter, 1:1212

Dance: A Short History of Classic Theatrical Dancing, 3:731

Dance and Drama in Bali, 3:734

The Dance and the Railroad, 1:1094

The Dance Anthology, 3:732

Dance Classics, 3:731

Dance Composition and Production, 3:732

Dance Hall of the Dead, 1:1232

The Dance Handbook, 3:732

Dance in India: An Annotated Guide to Source Materials, 3:733

Dance Language and Orientation of Bees, 5:796, 5:832

The Dance Makers: Conversations with American Choreographers, 3:734

The Dance of Death, 2:679, 2:680

The Dance of Leah: Discovering Yiddish in America, 2:30

The Dance of Life, 5:440

A Dance of Masks: Senghor, Achebe, Soyinka, 2:129, 2:147, 2:149

A Dance of the Forest, 2:148

Dance of the Happy Shades, 2:921

A Dance of the Painted Maidens, 2:141

Dance on the Earth, 2:917

The Dancer and the Dance, 3:740

A Dancer of Fortunes, 2:139

The Dancer's Heritage: A Short History of Ballet, 3:733

The Dancer's Survival Manual, 3:745

Dances of the Obscure, 2:659

The Dance Technique of Lester Hornton, 3:734

A Dance to the Music of Time, 1:536

Dance to the Piper and Promenade Home: A Two-part Autobiography, 3:740

Dance with the Music: The World of the Ballet Musician, 3:732

Dancing at Lughnasa, 1:479

The Dancing Bears, 1:1015

The Dancing Bees, 5:796, 5:832

The Dancing Girl, 1:320

Dancing in Chains: The Youth of William Dean Howells, 1:760

A Dancing Matrix: Voyages along the Viral Frontier, 5:369

The Dancing Socrates and Other Poems, 2:822

Dancing through History, 3:731

Dancing without Music: Deafness in America, 5:379

The Dandelion on the Imjin River, 2:303

Dandil: Stories from Iranian Life, 2:94

The Dandy and the Herald, 1:470, 1:866

Dandy Dick, 1:388

Dāneshvār's Playhouse: A Collection of Short Stories, 2:88

Danger: Memory!, 1:1103, 1:1104

Dangerous Aquatic Animals of the World, 5:770

Dangerous Corner, 1:537

Dangerous Diagnostics, 5:75, 5:122, 5:173

"Dangerous Foreigners," 3:614

Dangerous Properties of Industrial Materials, 5:726

Dangers of Deterrence: Philosophers on Nuclear Strategy, 5:109

Dangling Man, 1:946

Daniel Bell and the Agony of Modern Liberalism, 3:220

Daniel Bell and the Decline of Intellectual Radicalism, 3:220

Daniel Defoe, 1:240

Daniel Defoe: Ambition and Innovation, 1:240

Daniel Defoe: His Life, 1:240

Daniel Deronda, 1:353

Daniel Martin, 1:478

Daniel Webster, 3:523

Daniel Webster and the Rise of National Conservatism, 3:573

The Danish Economy in the Twentieth Century, 3:381

Danish-English, English-Danish Dictionary, 1:98

Danish-English Dictionary: Dansk-Engelsk Urdbog, 1:98

Danish Literature: A Short Critical Survey, 2:645

D'Annunzio, 2:415

Danny Goodman's Macintosh Handbook: Featuring System 7, 5:554

Dante (Bloom), 2:417

Dante (Eliot), 2:418

Dante: Poet of the Secular World, 2:417

Dante, Lyric Poet and Philosopher: An Introduction to the Minor Works, 2:418

Dante, Petrarch, Boccaccio, 2:400

Dante, Philomythus and Philosopher: Man in the Cosmos, 2:417

Dante and English Poetry: Shelley to T. S. Eliot, 2:418

Dante and Philosophy, 4:104

Dante Gabriel Rossetti, 1:392

Dante Gabriel Rossetti: An Alien Victorian, 1:392

Dante Gabriel Rossetti: An Annotated Bibliography, 1:392

Dante Gabriel Rossetti: Poet and Painter, 1:392

Dante Gabriel Rossetti and the Limits of Victorian Vision, 1:392

A Dante of Our Time, Primo Levi and Auschwitz, 2:425

Dante's Drama of the Mind: A Modern Reading of the Purgatorio, 2:418

Dante's Paradiso and the Limitations of Modern Criticism, 2:418

Dante's Poets: Textuality and Truth in the Comedy, 2:417

Dante's Thought and Poetry, 2:418

Dante the Philosopher, 4:286

Danton's Death, 2:573, 2:574

Danziger's Travels beyond Forbidden Frontiers, 3:902

Daphnis and Chloe, 2:348, 2:363

Daredevils of Sassoun, 2:78

Dare to Be Creative, 1:50

The Daring Muse: Augustan Poetry Reconsidered, 1:227

Daring to Be Bad: Radical Feminism in America, 1967–1975, 3:215

The Dark Ages: Life in the United States, 1945–1960, 3:538

Dark Ancestor: The Literature of the Black Man in the Caribbean, 2:930

Dark Angel, 1:1240

Dark as the Grave Wherein My Friend Is Laid, 2:919

The Dark at the Top of the Stairs, 1:1095

Dark Avenues, 2:707

The Dark Brain of Piranesi and Other Essays, 2:517

The Dark Child, 2:139

A Dark Comedy of Manners, 1:766

The Dark Design, 1:1257

The Dark Diamond, 2:799

The Darkening Glass, 1:395

The Darker Comedies, 2:391

The Darker Side of Virtue, 4:846

Darkfall, 1:1241

Dark Flower, 1:482

Dark Ghetto: Dilemmas of Social Power, 3:208

The Dark Glass, 1:392

The Dark Historic Page, 1921–1939, 1:499

Dark Horses, New Poems, 1:997

The Dark Is Light Enough, 1:480

Dark Journey: Black Mississippians in the Age of Jim Crow, 3:532

The Dark Labyrinth, 1:469

The Dark Lady, 1:937

Dark Laughter, 1:811

The Dark Light Years, 1:612

The Dark Lord, 4:863

Darkness, 1:1243

The Darkness and the Light, 4:288

Darkness Visible, 1:483

Darkness Visible: A Memoir of Madness, 1:1057

Darkness Visible: A Study of Virgil's Aeneid, 2:397

The Dark Night of the Soul, 2:543

A Dark Night's Passing, 2:292

Dark Paradise: Opiate Addiction in America before 1940, 5:403

Dark Pony, 1:1101

The Dark Romance of Dian Fossey, 3:909

The Dark Room (Narayan), 2:179

The Dark Room and Other Poems (Lihn), 2:870

The Dark Room of Damocles, 2:627

Dark Safari: The Life behind the Legend of H. M. Stanley, 3:938

The Dark Side: Tales of Terror and the Supernatural, 2:488

The Dark Side of Genius: The Life of Alfred Hitchcock, 1:1170

Dark Side of the Universe, 5:19, 5:595

The Dark Sun: A Study of D. H. Lawrence, 1:510

Dark Testament, 2:159

Dark Thoreau, 1:701

The Dark Tunnel, 1:1234

Dark Twins: Imposture and Identity in Mark Twain's America, 1:783

Darling of the Day, 1:443

Darsan: Seeing the Divine Image in India, 4:503

Darwin, 5:45, 5:831

Darwin: Competition and Cooperation, 5:831

Darwin, Marx, Wagner: Critique of a Heritage, 1:814

Darwin and His Critics, 5:46, 5:794

Darwin and Huxley in Australia, 5:800

Darwin and the Darwinian Revolution, 5:46

Darwin and the Novelists: Patterns of Science in Victorian Fiction, 1:319, 2:990

Darwiniana, 5:799

The Darwinian Paradigm, 5:198

The Darwinian Revolution: Science Red in Tooth and Claw, 5:47

Darwinism, 5:812

Darwin's Century: Evolution and the Men Who Discovered It, 5:46

Darwin's Forgotten Defenders, 5:794

Darwin's Metaphor: Nature's Place in Victorian Culture, 5:795

Darwin to DNA, Molecules to Humanity, 5:780

Dashiell Hammett, 1:1230

Dashiell Hammett: A Descriptive Bibliography, 1:1230

Dashiell Hammett: A Life, 1:1230

Da Silva's Cultivated Wilderness and Genesis of the Clowns, 2:935, 2:936

Das Kapital, 3:94

Das Narrenschiff, 2:571

Database: A Primer, 5:559

Data Base: Structured Techniques for Design, Performance and Management: with Case Studies, 5:559

Data Base Management Systems—MS-DOS, 5:560

Databases: How to Manage Information on Your Micro, 5:560

Databases in Theory and Practice, 5:559

Database System Concepts, 5:560

Data Communications: Beyond Basics, 5:560

Data Communications for Engineers, 5:302

Data Compression, 5:550

The Data Game: Controversies in Social Science Statistics, 3:67

Data Sourcebook for Food Scientists and Technologists, 5:261

Data Visualization, 5:521

Dating, Mating and Marriage, 3:207

Daughter Buffalo, 2:974

The Daughter of Jorio: A Pastoral Tragedy, 2:415

Daughter of Persia, 3:447

A Daughter of the Middle Border, 1:751

Daughters, 1:1014

Daughters and Sons, 1:462

The Daughter's Dilemma, 1:318

Daughters of the Covenant: Portraits of Six Jewish Women, 1:773

Daughters of the Dreaming, 4:461

Daughters of the Dust, 1:1162

Daughters of the King: Women and the Synagogue, 4:892

The Daughter's Seduction: Feminism and Psychoanalysis, 1:1144, 1:1143

Dave Barry's Only Travel Guide You'll Ever Need, 3:891

David and Other Poems, 2:907

David Balfour, 1:395

David Copperfield, 1:348

David Garrick, 1:389

David Hare, 1:493

David Hare: Theatricalizing Politics, 1:493

David Hume, 4:202

David Hume: An Introduction to His Philosophical System, 4:202
David Hume: Common Sense Moralist, Sceptical Metaphysician, 4:202
David Hume: Many-Sided Genius, 4:202
David Hume: Philosopher of Moral Science, 4:202
David Hume: The Newtonian Philosopher, 4:201
David Hume: The Philosophical Works, 4:230
David Hume and the Miraculous, 4:203
David Hume's Theory of Mind, 4:201
David Jones, 1:503
David Jones: An Annotated Bibliography and Guide to Research, 1:503
David Jones: Artist and Writer, 1:502
David Jones: Man and Poet, 1:503
David Lloyd George: A Biography, 3:367
David of Sassoun: The Armenian Folk Epic in Four Cycles, 2:78
David Ricardo, 3:101
David Ricardo (1772–1823), 3:101
David Ricardo: A Centenary Estimate, 3:101
David Ricardo: Critical Assessments, 3:101
The David Show, 1:1090, 1:1091
David Williamson—a Writer's Career, 2:968
Davita's Harp, 1:1032
Daw Aung San Suu Kyi The Nobel Laureate: A Burmese Perspective, 2:314
Dawn, 1:829, 1:1065, 1:1240
Dawn Blossoms Plucked at Dusk, 2:256
Dawning of the Cold War: The U.S. Quest for Order, 3:545
Dawning of the Theosophical Movement, 4:853
The Dawn of Apocalyptic, 4:823
The Dawn of Belief, 4:433
The Dawn of European Art, 4:433
Dawn of Humanism in Italy, 2:402, 4:132
Dawn over Suez, 3:445

Dawn to the West: Japanese Literature in the Modern Era, 2:282
The Day: Morning, Midday, Evening, Night, 2:431
Day after Day, 2:437
Daybreak, 2:611
The Daybreakers, 1:1216
Daybreak in China, 3:427
Day by Day, 1:1006
Day by Day
    The 40's, 1:88
    The 50's, 1:88
    The 60's, 1:88
    The 70's, 1:88
Day for Night, 3:843
A Day in Regensburg: Short Stories, 2:42
A Day in the Country and Other Stories, 2:488
A Day in the Death of Joe Egg, 1:524
The Day Lasts More Than a Hundred Years, 2:695
The Daylight Moon and Other Poems, 2:959
A Day of Pleasure: Stories of a Boy Growing Up in Warsaw, 2:47
Day of the Countess, 2:24
Day of the Leopards: Essays in Defense of Poems, 1:927, 1:1155
The Day of the Locust, 1:896, 1:897
The Day of the Owl, 2:438
The Day of the Storm, 1:621
Days and Nights (Koch), 1:1002
Days and Nights (Simonov), 2:756
Days of Awe, 2:12, 4:599, 4:886
Days of Dust, 2:58
The Days of Henry Thoreau: A Biography, 1:702
The Days of His Grace, 2:675
Days of Sadness, Years of Triumph, 1939–1945, 3:535
Days of Sorrow and Pain: Leo Baeck and the Berlin Jews, 4:661
Days of Wrath, 2:487
Days on Earth: The Dance of Doris Humphrey, 3:744
Days with Ulanova, 3:754
The Day's Work, 1:371
The Day the Bubble Burst, 3:549
The Day the Leader Was Killed, 2:68
The Day the Sun Rose Twice, 5:707

The Day the Universe Changed, 5:24
The Day the Whores Came Out to Play Tennis and Other Plays, 1:1098
The Day the World Ended, 1:597
De Aanslag, 2:628
The Dead City, 2:415
The Dead Father, 1:943, 1:944
The Dead Feel No Pain, 2:784
Dead Head, 1:450
Deadline: A Memoir, 3:808
Deadlock, 1:1235
The Dead Man, 2:654
Dead Man's Plack; An Old Thorn; and Miscellanea, 1:365
Dead Man's Ransom, 1:608
The Dead Sea Scriptures, 4:811
The Dead Sea Scrolls: Major Publications and Tools for Study, 4:811
The Dead Sea Scrolls in English: Qumran in Perspective, 4:616, 4:812
The Dead Secret, 1:346
Dead Secrets: Wilkie Collins and the Female Gothic, 1:599, 1:618, 1:346
Dead Souls, 2:721
Deafness and Mental Health, 5:428
The Deal Decade, 3:55
Dealers in Books, 1:77
Dealing with Data and Chance, 5:525
Dealing with Genes: The Language of Heredity, 5:777
Deal in Wheat and Other Stories of the New and Old West, 1:776
Dean Acheson: The Cold War Years, 1953–71, 3:537
Dean Colet and His Theology, 4:726
The Dean's December, 1:946
Dear Brutus, 1:329
Dear Carnap, Dear Van, 4:279, 5:85, 5:99
Dear John, Dear Coltrane, 1:984
Dear Milli, 2:584
Dear Miss Mansfield: Tribute to Kathleen Mansfield Beauchamp, 2:977
Dear Russell—Dear Jourdain, 4:324, 5:516

Dear Scott, Dear Max: The Fitzgerald-Perkins Correspondence, 1:840

Dear Theo: The Autobiography of Vincent Van Gogh, 3:794

Death: Beyond Whole-Brain Criteria, 5:78

Death: The Final Stage of Growth, 5:379

Death, Disease and Famine in Pre-Industrial England, 3:355

Death, Dissection, and the Destitute, 1:313

Death, Dying, and the Biological Revolution, 5:144

Death, Intermediate State and Rebirth in Tibetan Buddhism, 4:887

Death, Sex, and Fertility, 3:31

Death, Sleep and the Traveler, 1:985

Death, War, and Sacrifice: Studies in Ideology and Practice, 4:426, 4:472

Death and After, 4:549

Death and Afterlife, 4:887

The Death and Birth of Judaism, 4:606, 4:651

Death and Dignity: Making Choices and Taking Charge, 5:379

Death and Diplomacy in Persia, 2:771

Death and Dying: Making Choices and Taking Charge, 3:201

Death and Dying: The Tibetan Tradition, 4:544

Death and Immortality in the Religions of the World, 4:887

The Death and Letters of Alice James: Selected Correspondence, 1:761

The Death and Life of Malcolm X, 4:877

Death and Rebirth in Virgil's Arcadia, 2:397

Death and the Fool, 2:593

Death and the King's Horsemen: A Play, 2:148

Death and the Labyrinth, 4:400

Death and the Lover, 2:589

Death and the Maiden, 2:865

Death and the Optimistic Prophecy in Vergil's Aeneid, 2:397

Death and the Regeneration of Life, 3:23

Death Be Not Proud: A Memoir, 3:921

Death by Melancholy: Essays on Modern Southern Fiction, 1:920

Death by Migration, 3:426

Death Comes for the Archbishop, 1:820

Death in Beirut, 2:58

Death in Life: Survivors of Hiroshima, 5:423

Death in the Afternoon, 1:845

A Death in the Family, 1:932

Death in the Locker Room: Steroids and Sports, 5:399

Death in the Woods: And Other Stories, 1:811

Death in Venice, 2:601, 2:602, 2:911

Death Is Different, 4:386

Death Is Forever, 1:979

Death Jag, 5:439

Death Kit, 1:1053

The Death Lobby: How the West Armed Iraq, 3:450

Death Notes, 1:609

The Death of a Beekeeper, 2:674

The Death of Adam: Evolution and Its Impact on Western Thought, 5:33

Death of a Doxy, 1:1237

Death of a Dude, 1:1238

The Death of Ahasverus, 2:675, 2:676

Death of a Lady's Man, 2:909

Death of a Legend, 1:1212

Death of a Naturalist, 1:494, 1:495

Death of an Ex-minister, 2:71, 2:120

The Death of a Nobody, 2:502

The Death of a President, November 1963, 3:539

The Death of Artemio Cruz, 2:865

Death of a Salesman, 1:532, 1:1103, 1:1104, 2:531

Death of a Simple Giant and Other Modern Yugoslav Stories, 2:786, 2:828, 2:835

The Death of Bessie Smith, 1:1080, 1:1081

The Death of Christopher Marlowe, 1:187

The Death of Empedocles, 2:593

The Death of God Controversy, 4:745

The Death of Ivan Ilyich, 2:764

The Death of Methuselah and Other Stories, 1:1049, 2:47

The Death of Nature, 4:167

The Death of Nature: Women, Ecology, and the Scientific Revolution, 3:550 5:188, 5:823

The Death of Nora Ryan, 1:833

The Death of Ramon Gonzalez: The Modern Agricultural Dilemma, 5:825

The Death of Stéphane Mallarmé, 2:486

The Death of the Heart, 1:447

The Death of the Moth and Other Essays, 1:569

The Death of the Past, 3:276

The Death of the Playwright?: Modern British Drama and Literary Theory, 1:426

The Death of Tragedy, 1:1054

The Death of Virgil, 2:573

The Death of William Posters, 1:547

The Death of Woman Wang, 3:469, 3:502

Death on the Installment Plan, 2:465

Death on the Nile, 1:606

Death or Dialogue? From the Age of Monologue to the Age of Dialogue, 4:423

The Death Penalty in America, 3:204

Death Ritual in Late Imperial and Modern China, 4:531, 4:533

Death Sentence, 2:461

Death's Jest-Book, 1:271

Death under Sail, 1:550

Death Valley: Geology, Ecology, Archaeology, 5:626

Death without End, 2:868, 2:869

The Debacle, 2:518

DeBasil's Ballets Russes, 3:734

Debate about the Earth, 5:630

The Debate on the English Reformation, 4:727

The Debate over Stabilization Policy and Other Macroeconomic Issues, 3:62

Debates on American History, 3:580

Debates over Medical Authority and Challenges in Biomedical Experimentation, 5:118
Debating Archaeology, 3:13
Debating P. C., 1:1128
Deborah: A Novel, 2:40
Debridement, 1:984
The Debt and the Deficit: False Alarms and Real Possibilities, 3:62
Debussy and Wagner, 3:692
The Debut, 1:451
Decade, 1:915
Decadence, 2:725
Decadence in Thirteenth Century Provencal and Hebrew Poetry, 2:8
The Decadent Vision in Leopoldo Alas, 2:528
The Decade of Discovery in Astronomy and Astrophysics, 5:657
A Decade of Tongues, 2:133
The Decameron, 2:398, 2:409, 2:410, 2:431, 2:648, 3:332
The Decapitated Chicken and Other Stories, 2:881
Decayed Gods, 4:472
The Decay of the Angel, 2:289
December 7th, 1:1166
Deception, 1:1040, 1:1041
The Deceptive Realism of Machado de Assis, 2:897
Deciding What's News, 3:806
Decision-Making: The Modern Doctor's Dilemma, 5:336
Decisions and Revisions, 5:64
Decision to Prosecute, 3:61
De Cive or the Citizen, 3:153, 4:173
The Declaration of Independence, 3:519, 3:566
The Declaration of Independence and What It Means Today, 3:541
Declarations of Independence, 1:722
The Declassified Eisenhower, 3:537
De Clementia, 4:760
The Decline, Revival and Fall of the British Empire, 3:363
Decline and Fall, 1:561, 1:562
The Decline and Fall of the American Programmer, 5:551

The Decline and Fall of the British Aristocracy, 3:365
The Decline and Fall of the Roman Empire, 2:380, 3:303
The Decline of Bismarck's European Order, 3:584
The Decline of Modernism, 4:379
Decline of Radicalism: Reflections of America Today, 3:568
The Decline of the New, 1:990
The Decline of the West, 3:291, 3:345
Decline of the West? George Kennan and His Critics, 3:584
The Declining Significance of Race, 3:212, 3:244
Decoding the Rabbis: A Thirteenth-Century Commentary on the Aggadah, 4:628
Decolonization and African Independence, 3:417
Decolonizing Feminisms: Race, Gender, and Empire-Building, 1:924
Decolonizing the Mind, 2:111, 2:154
Decolonizing the Subject, 1:928
De conscribendis epistolis, 4:156
Deconstruction: Theory and Practice, 1:926, 4:266, 4:391
Deconstruction and Criticism, 1:1133, 1:1138, 1:1151
Deconstruction and Philosophy, 4:398
Deconstruction and the Interests of Theory, 4:266
Deconstruction in Context: Literature and Philosophy, 4:268, 4:392
Deconstruction Reframed, 4:266, 4:391
Deconstructive Criticism: An Advanced Introduction, 1:1132
The Deconstructive Turn: Essays in the Rhetoric of Philosophy, 4:266, 4:392
Decorated Book Papers: Being an Account of their Designs and Fashions, 1:5
Decorative Alphabets and Initials, 1:18
The Decorative Art of Today, 3:778

Decrees of the Ecumenical Councils, 4:891
De Dialectica, 4:109
Deed of Life: The Novels and Tales of D. H. Lawrence, 1:510
Deep Black: Space Espionage and National Security, 5:596
The Deep Blue Sea, 1:540
Deep Down in the Jungle, 3:866
Deep Ecology: Living as if Nature Mattered, 5:822
Deephaven, 1:769, 1:770
Deep Marine Environments, 5:632
Deep Range, 1:614
Deep Rivers, 2:852
The Deep Sleep, 1:1017
The Deeps of Deliverance, 2:624
Deep South: A Social Anthropological Study of Caste and Class, 3:22
Deep Space: A Guide to the Cosmos, 5:656
Deep Truth: A Study of Shelley's Scepticism, 1:303
The Deer and the Tiger: A Study of Wildlife in India, 5:771
Deerbrook, 1:375
The Deer Park, 1:1011, 1:1012
De erroribus philosophorum, 4:103
The Deerslayer, 1:662, 1:663, 1:1211
The Defeat of Che Guevara, 3:634
The Defeat of the Confederacy, 3:572
The Defence of Guenevere and Other Poems, 1:382
A Defence of Poesie, 1:195
A Defence of Poetry, 1:196, 2:414
Defenders of God, 4:579
Defenders of the Faith: Inside Ultra-Orthodox Jewry, 4:654
Defense, 2:740
Défense et Illustration de la Langue Française, 2:444
Defense of Galileo, 2:410
The Defense of Galileo, 4:137, 5:688
Defense of Poetry, 1:273
A Defense of Stage Plays, 1:185
The Defiant Muse, 2:448

Defining Biology: Lectures from the 1890's, 5:765

Defining Power, 3:145

Defining Science, 5:58

The Definition of Moral Virtue, 4:71

Definition of Suicide, 5:428

The Definitive Four Act Version of "The Importance of Being Earnest," 1:410

Defoe and Economics, 1:240

Defoe and Fictional Time, 1:240

Defoe and the Idea of Fiction, 1713–1719, 1:240

Defoe and the Uses of Narrative, 1:240

Defoe's Art of Fiction, 1:240

Defoe's Narratives: Situations and Structures, 1:240

Defoe's Politics: Parliament, Power, Kingship, and Robinson Crusoe, 1:240

De Gaulle, 3:372

De Gouden Swipe, 2:636

Degradation of the Democratic Dogma, 3:562

Degrees, 2:463

Degrees of Freedom: The Novels of Iris Murdoch, 1:455

De humani corporis fabrica, 5:365

Deirdre of the Sorrows, 1:555

De la grammatologie (Of Grammatology), 1:1152

De l'Allegmagne, 2:510

De la recherche du bien: A Study of Malebranche's Science of Ethics, 4:182

The Delectable History of Forbonius and Prisceria, 1:185

Delhi between Two Empires, 1803–1931, 3:485

A Delicate Balance, 1:1080

The Delights of Terror: An Aesthetics of the Tale of Terror, 1:599

Delineations of American Scenery and Character, 3:894, 5:786

Deliverance (Dickey), 1:967

The Deliverance (Glasgow), 1:843

Deliverance and Other Stories, 2:180

Delivering Primary Health Care: Nurse Practitioners at Work, 5:338

Dell Paperbacks, 1942 to Mid–1962: A Catalog-Index, 1:41

Del Romanzo Storico, 2:426

Delta of Venus, 1:865

Delta Wedding, 1:894, 1:895

De ludo globi: The Game of Spheres, 4:148

The Deluge: An Historical Novel of Poland, Sweden, and Russia, 2:821

Delusion and Dream and Other Essays, 5:445

Delusions, Confusions, and the Poggenpuhl Family, 2:578

The Demand for Money: Theories, Evidence, and Problems, 3:65

The Demand for Primary Health Services in the Third World, 5:330

Demented: The World of the Opera Diva, 3:672

The Demesne of the Swans–Lebedinyi Stan, 2:767, 2:768

Demeter and Other Poems, 1:400

Demian, 2:589

Demimondaine, 1:388

The Demise of American Nuclear Power, 5:75, 5:287

The Demise of Nuclear Energy?, 5:156

Democracy: An American Novel, 1:729, 3:562

Democracy, Italian Style, 3:385

Democracy and Classical Greece, 3:301

Democracy and Deliberation: New Directions for Democratic Reform, 3:143

Democracy and Education, 3:260, 4:224

Democracy and Its Discontents: Reflections on Everyday America, 3:568

Democracy and Liberty, 3:405

Democracy and Poetry, 1:893

Democracy and Social Ethics, 1:731

Democracy and the Novel, 1:658

Democracy and Totalitarianism, 3:282

A Democracy at War, 3:535

Democracy in America, 3:143, 3:151, 3:164, 3:165

Democracy in an Age of Corporate Colonization, 3:142

Democracy in a Technological Society, 5:73, 5:146

Democracy in Crisis, 3:156

Democracy on Trial, 3:510

The Democracy Trap, 3:143

A Democratic Catholic Church, 4:742

Democratic Education, 3:255

Democratic Ideas and Reality, 3:133

The Democratic Monarchies of Scandinavia, 3:380

Democratic Promise: The Populist Movement in America, 3:531

Democratic Theory, 3:143

The Democratization of American Christianity, 3:559, 4:751

Democratizing Japan: The Allied Occupation, 3:480

Demographic Yearbook, 1:111, 3:272

The Demon, 2:734

De Monarchia, 2:417

Demon Box, 1:999

The Demonology of Copyright, 1:49

Demons, Dreamers and Madmen, 4:170

Demos: A Story of English Socialism, 1:358

Demosthenes: The Origin and Growth of His Policy, 2:355

Demosthenes and His Influence, 2:355

Demosthenes and the Last Days of Greek Freedom: 384–322 B.C., 2:355

Demosthenes on the Crown, 2:355

De Motu Cordis, 5:42, 5:361

Denali Journal, 3:910

The Denatured Novel, 1:50

Denied a Country, 2:647

Denise Levertov, 1:1004

Denise Levertov: An Interview, 1:1004

Denmark: A Modern History, 3:381

Denmark: A Troubled Welfare State, 3:381

Denmark: Success of a Developing Nation, 3:381

Denmark and the Faroes, 2:656, 2:657

Denmark in History, 3:381

Dennett and His Critics, 4:396

Den of Thieves, 3:56, 3:549
Dental Ethics, 5:124
Dentistry: An Illustrated History, 5:194
De Officiis, 4:72
Deontology, 4:190
De Partibus Animalium, Book I, and De Generatione Animalium, Book I, with Passages from Book II, 1–3, 4:65
The Department, 2:967
Departures, 1:995
The Depraved Sleepers, 2:630
De Profundis, 1:409
De Profundis and Other Writings, 1:410
Deptford Trilogy—Fifth Business, 2:910
Depth Psychology and a New Ethic, 5:425
The Depths of the Universe, 5:606
The Deputy, 2:591
De Quincey's Art of Autobiography, 1:290
Der Arme Heinrich, 2:586
De reductione artium ad theologiam, 4:113
Deregulating the Health Care Industry: Planning for Competition, 5:328
Derek and Choruses from "After the Assassinations," 1:446
Derek Walcott, 2:943
De Re Metallica, 5:627
De Rerum Natura, 2:378, 2:388, 4:75
De Re Rustica, 5:265, 5:271
Der Gerechte Richter, 2:612
Derivation of the Laws, 5:499
Der Lohndrücker, 2:603
A Dermatologist's Guide to Home Skin Care, 5:340
Der Nister's Work, 1907–1929: A Study of a Yiddish Symbolist, 2:38
Derrida, 4:398
Derrida: A Critical Reader, 4:398
Derrida and Deconstruction, 4:398
Derrida and Negative Theology, 4:398
Derrida and the Economy of Difference, 4:398
Derrida on the Threshold of Sense, 4:398
A Derrida Reader: Between the Blinds, 1:1131, 4:398
Der Rosenkavalier, Ariadne auf Naxos, 2:592

The Dervishes, or Oriental Spiritualism, 4:574
D.E.S.: The Bitter Pill, 5:351
De Sanctis on Dante, 2:419
A Descant for Gossips, 2:949
Descartes, 4:171
Descartes: A Study of His Philosophy, 4:170
Descartes: Critical and Interpretive Essays, 4:170
Descartes: His Moral Philosophy and Psychology, 4:169
Descartes: Philosophy, Mathematics and Physics, 4:170
Descartes: The Project of Pure Enquiry, 4:171
Descartes against the Skeptics, 4:170
Descartes and Hume, 4:203
Descartes and the Modern Mind, 4:169
Descartes' Discourse on Method, 4:170
Descartes' Metaphysical Physics, 4:170
Descartes on Polyhedra: A Study of the "De Solidorum Elements," 5:503
Descartes' Philosophy, Mathematics and Physics, 5:503
Descartes' Philosophy Interpreted According to the Order of Reasons, 4:170
Descartes' Philosophy of Science, 5:502
Descartes' Rules for the Direction of the Mind, 4:170
The Descendant, 1:843
Descending Figure, 1:982
Descent from Glory: Four Generations of the John Adams Family, 3:563
The Descent of Man, 1:953, 5:792
The Descent of Man and Selection in Relation to Sex, 5:793
Deschooling Society, 3:250, 5:136, 5:137
Describing Early America, 1:629
Description of Greece, 2:347, 4:489
Description of New England, 1:1192
Descriptive Sketches, 1:306
The Desert a City, 4:688
The Deserted Village, 1:227
The Desert Encroaches, 2:144
The Desert Fathers, 4:690
The Desert of Love, 2:489

The Desert Smells like Rain: A Naturalist in Papago Indian Country, 5:818
Desert Solitaire: A Season in the Wilderness, 5:827
Desert Tracings: Six Classical Arabian Odes, 2:58
Desert Trails of Atacama, 3:128
The Desert Year, 5:833
Design and Analysis of Computer Algorithms, 5:549
Design and Intent in African Literature, 2:107
Design and Planning of Engineering Systems, 5:234
Design and Truth in Autobiography, 1:928
Design for the Real World: Human Ecology and Social Change, 5:130
Designing Classroom Research, 3:254
Designing "Dead Souls": An Anatomy of Disorder in Gogol, 2:722
Designing the User Interface, 5:558
Design in Puritan American Literature, 1:629
The Design of Bibliographies: Observations, References and Examples, 1:7, 1:61
The Design of Biographia Literaria, 1:288
The Design of Books, 1:12
The Design of Experiments, 5:528
The Design of Lettering, 1:20
The Design of Rabelais' "Pantagruel," 2:497
The Design of Rimbaud's Poetry, 2:500
The Design of the Present, 1:628
Design Paradigms, 5:174
Designs on Truth: The Poetics of the Augustan Mock-Epic, 1:227
Design through Discovery: The Elements and Principles, 5:191
Design with Nature, 5:823
Design With Type, 1:8
Desire and Love in Henry James: A Study of the Late Novels, 1:767
Desire and the Sign: Nineteenth-Century American Fiction, 1:724
Desire and Truth: Functions of Plot in Eighteenth-Century English Novels, 1:230

The Desire of My Eyes: The Life and Work of John Ruskin, 1:395

Desires, Right and Wrong: The Ethics of Enough, 4:270

The Desire to Desire: The Woman's Film of the 1940s, 1:1157

Desktop Publishing Skills, 5:561

Desktop Publishing with Style, 5:562

Desolación, 2:873

Desolate Angel: Jack Kerouac, the Beat Generation and America, 1:999

Despair, 2:740

Desperate Character and Other Stories, 2:769

Desperate Journeys, Abandoned Souls, 3:909

Desperate Remedies, 1:361

Destination Biafra, 2:136

A Destiny Apart: New Zealand's Search for National Identity, 3:495

Destiny His Choice: The Loyalism of Andrew Marvell, 1:189

Destiny of a King, 4:471

The Destiny of Man, 4:275, 4:758, 4:759

The Destiny of the Mother Church, 4:842, 4:843

Destroy, She Said, 2:474

Destroyer and Preserver: Shelley's Poetic Skepticism, 1:302

The Destroyers: The Underside of Human Nature, 4:284

The Destruction of Pompeii and Other Stories, 2:698

The Destruction of the European Jews, 3:348, 4:636

Destructive and Useful Insects: Their Habits and Control, 5:771

The Destructive Element: A Study of Modern Writers and Beliefs, 1:422, 1:553

The Destructive War, 3:529

Destry Rides Again, 1:1212

Detachment and the Writing of History: Essays and Letters of Carl L. Becker, 3:566

Details of a Sunset and Other Stories, 2:740

Detained: A Writer's Prison Diary, 2:155

Detecting Patterns, 5:523

The Detective in Distress: Philip Marlowe's Domestic Dream, 1:1228

Detente: Prospects for Democracy and Dictatorship, 2:761

Determined Fictions: American Literary Naturalism, 1:805, 1:723

Determining Risks to Health: Federal Policy and Practice, 5:329

Determinism and Freedom in the Age of Modern Science, 4:264

De Tsjerne, 2:634

Deus Destroyed: The Image of Christianity in Early Modern Japan, 3:474

Deuteronomy: A Commentary, 4:837

Deutsche Sagen: German Legends, 2:584

DeValera, 3:371

Developing Second-Language Skills: Theory and Practice, 3:254

Developing Variations: Style and Ideology in Western Music, 3:664

Development, Economic Distribution and Social Change in Rural Egypt, 1952–1970, 3:445

Developmental Biology, 5:776

Developmental Biology of the Bacteria, 5:776

Developmental Psychology: Historical and Philosophical Perspectives, 3:174

Development and Displacement: Women in Southeast Asia, 3:488

Development as an Evolutionary Process, 5:776

Development Assistance, Export Promotion, and Environmental Technology, 5:185

The Development Dictionary: A Guide to Knowledge as Power, 5:136, 5:182

Development in Infancy, 3:173

The Development of Academic Freedom in the United States, 3:582

The Development of a Conceptual System for Dealing with Problems of Curriculum and Instruction, 3:262

The Development of African Drama, 2:107

The Development of a Medicine, 5:352

The Development of American Pharmacology, 5:351

Development of American Political Science: From Burgess to Behavioralism, 3:138

The Development of American Romance: The Sacrifice of Relation, 1:657

The Development of American Social Comedy from 1787 to 1936, 1:1073

The Development of Arabic Logic, 4:317, 4:576

Development of Biochemical Concepts from Ancient to Modern Times, 5:33

The Development of Creole Society in Jamaica 1770–1820, 2:934

The Development of Economic Thought, 3:73, 3:74, 3:94, 3:110, 3:113

The Development of Economic Thought, Great Economists in Perspective, 3:46

The Development of Franz Brentano's Ethics, 4:222

Development of Freud's Thought, 5:448

The Development of Japanese Business, 1600–1980, 3:477

The Development of Logic, 4:97

Development of Logical Empiricism, 4:265

The Development of Logical Method in Ancient China, 2:247, 4:360

The Development of Mathematics, 5:30

Development of Mathematics in the Nineteenth Century, 5:511

The Development of Modern Chemistry, 5:32, 5:722, 5:728

The Development of Modern Indonesian Poetry, 2:317

Development of Peirce's Philosophy, 4:249

The Development of Physical Theory in the Middle Ages, 5:40

The Development of Political Attitudes in Children, 3:147

The Development of Printers'
  Mechanical Typesetting
  Methods 1822–1925, 1:16
The Development of Quan-
  tum Theory, 5:680
The Development of Samuel
  Beckett's Fiction, 2:460
The Development of Sex Dif-
  ferences, 3:174
The Development of Shake-
  speare's Imagery, 1:216
The Development of the
  American Short Story,
  1:658, 1:715, 1:724
The Development of the
  Foundation of Mathemati-
  cal Analysis from Euler to
  Riemann, 5:30
The Development of the Inca
  State, 3:627
The Development of the Ira-
  nian Oil Industry, 3:447
The Development of
  Thought: Equilibration of
  Cognitive Structures, 3:192
Developments in Statistics,
  5:526
Developments of Modern
  Medicine, 5:36
The Devil and Daniel Web-
  ster, 1:815
The Devil and the Jews,
  4:624
The Devil Drives: A Life of
  Sir Richard Burton, 3:914
Devil in the Flesh, 2:498,
  2:499
The Devil in the Hills, 2:432
The Devil in the Shape of a
  Woman: Witchcraft in Co-
  lonial New England, 3:518
The Devil Is an Ass, 1:183
The Devil Is a Woman,
  1:1176
Devil on the Cross, 2:154
The Devils, 2:713
The Devils and Canon Bar-
  ham, 1:902
The Devil's Church and Oth-
  er Stories, 2:896
The Devil's Dictionary, 1:734,
  1:735
The Devil's Disciple, 1:545
The Devil's Dominion: Magic
  and Religion in Early New
  England, 3:517
Devil's Elixir, 2:591
The Devil's Law-Case, 1:200
Devil's Mode, 1:453
The Devil's Yard, 2:829
Devil Theory of War, 3:565
The Devil to Pay in the
  Backlands, 2:898, 2:899

The Devil Tree, 1:1003
The Devil Within, 2:498
The Devil with James Bond,
  1:594
De Viris Illustribus (On Illus-
  trious Men), 3:320
De voluptate, 4:155
Devotion to the Cross, 2:532
The Devouring Fungus: Tales
  of the Computer Age,
  5:537
De Vulgari Eloquentia, 2:416,
  2:417
Dewey, 4:226
Dewey, Russell, Whitehead:
  Philosophers as Educators,
  4:324, 4:342
Dewey and His Critics, 4:225
D. Fiore's Atlas of Histology
  with Functional Correla-
  tions, 5:773
Dhalgren, 1:1256
Dharma, 4:549
The Dharma Bums, 1:998,
  4:860
Dharma Gaia, 5:197
Dharma's Daughters: Contem-
  porary Indian Women and
  Hindu Culture, 4:508
The Dhimmi: Jews and
  Christians under Islam,
  4:573
D. H. Lawrence, 1:510
D. H. Lawrence: A Biogra-
  phy, 1:510
D. H. Lawrence: A Calendar
  of His Works, 1:511
D. H. Lawrence: A Collec-
  tion of Critical Essays,
  1:511
D. H. Lawrence: A Compos-
  ite Biography, 1:510
D. H. Lawrence: A Literary
  Life, 1:511
D. H. Lawrence: An Unpro-
  fessional Study, 1:864,
  1:865
D. H. Lawrence: Language
  and Being, 1:510
D. H. Lawrence: Novelist,
  1:510
D. H. Lawrence: Novelist,
  Poet, Prophet, 1:511
D. H. Lawrence: Pilgrim of
  the Apocalypse, 1:510
D. H. Lawrence: The Critical
  Heritage, 1:510
D. H. Lawrence: The Failure
  and the Triumph of Art,
  1:511
D. H. Lawrence and Modern-
  ism, 1:511

D. H. Lawrence and the
  Devouring Mother, 1:511
D. H. Lawrence and the Idea
  of the Novel, 1:511
Diabetes, 5:381
Diabetes: Caring for Your
  Emotions as Well as Your
  Health, 5:382
Diabetes: Questions You
  Have—Answers You Need,
  5:382
Diabetes: The Comprehensive
  Self-Management Hand-
  book, 5:382
Diaboliad and Other Stories,
  2:706
Diaghileff: His Artistic and
  Private Life, 3:741
Diaghilev (Buckle), 3:741
Diaghilev Observed by Critics
  in England and the United
  States, 1911–1929, 3:741
Diaghilev's Ballets Russes,
  3:734, 3:741
Diagnosing Organizations,
  3:210
Diagnosis: Philosophical and
  Medical Perspectives, 5:79
Diagnostic Psychological
  Testing, 5:469
The Dialectical Biologist,
  5:764
Dialectical Disputations,
  4:155
Dialectical Materialism, 4:31
Dialectic of Enlightenment,
  1:1132, 4:393
The Dialectic of Ideology
  and Technology, 3:228,
  5:70
The Dialectic of Selfhood in
  Montaigne, 2:491
Dialectics: A Controversy-Ori-
  ented Approach to the
  Theory of Knowledge,
  4:317
Dialectics of Nature, 4:227
The Dialect of the Tribe,
  1:415, 1:440
Dial 800 for Health, 5:311
The Dialogic Imagination:
  Four Essays, 1:923
The Dialogic Novels of Mal-
  colm Bradbury and David
  Lodge, 1:448, 1:515
Dialogue and Dialectic: Eight
  Hermeneutical Studies on
  Plato, 4:80, 4:401
Dialogue and Disagreement,
  4:671
Dialogue and Discovery: A
  Study in Socratic Method,
  4:90

Dialogue between a Philosopher and a Student of the Common Laws of England, 4:174

A Dialogue between Philosophy and Religion, 4:300

Dialogue Concerning the Two Chief World Systems, Ptolemaic and Copernican, 4:142, 4:171, 4:172, 5:41, 5:604, 5:688

Dialogue in American Drama, 1:1072

A Dialogue of a Philosopher with a Jew and a Christian, 4:106

A Dialogue of Comfort against Tribulation, 4:147

Dialogue on Free Will, 2:402

A Dialogue on G. E. Moore's Ethical Philsophy, 4:312

Dialogue on John Dewey, 4:225

Dialogue on Poetry and Literary Aphorisms, 4:253

Dialogues, 3:722, 4:200, 4:706

Dialogues Concerning Natural Religion, 4:194, 4:200, 4:739

Dialogues Concerning Two New Sciences, 4:172, 5:604, 5:688

Dialogues in Paradise, 2:265

The Dialogues of Alfred North Whitehead, 4:341

The Dialogues of Guy de Brues, 4:124

Dialogues on Metaphysics, 4:182

Dialogues on Metaphysics and on Religion, 4:181

Dialogues with Leuco, 2:432

Dialogues with Mothers, 5:435

A Dialogue with Arnold Lazarus: "It Depends," 5:460

Dialogue with Deviance, 4:633

Dialogue with Erich Fromm, 5:451

Dialogue with Erik Erikson: And Reactions from Ernest Jones, 3:182, 5:442

Dialogue with Gordon Allport, 3:180

The Diamond Cutters, 1:1037

Diamonds Are Forever, 1:593

Diana of the Crossways, 1:378, 1:384

Diana's Hunt, Caccia di Diana: Boccaccio's First Fiction, 2:410

Dianetics: The Modern Science of Mental Health, 4:869

Diaries of Adam and Eve, 1:781

The Diaries of Sophia Tolstoy, 2:766

Diary, 2:813

Diary: Nineteen Twenty-Eight to Nineteen Fifty-Seven, 2:482

The Diary and Sundry Observations of Thomas Alva Edison, 5:227, 5:252

A Diary from Dixie, 1:738

A Diary in America, 1:374

Diary in Exile, 3:1935, 3:294

A Diary in the Strict Sense of the Term, 3:35

The Diary of a Country Priest, 2:460

Diary of a Madman, 2:721

Diary of a Madman and Other Stories, 2:256

Diary of a Mad Old Man, 2:293

Diary of an Unknown, 2:469, 3:834

The Diary of Beatrice Webb, 3:113

Diary of 1805–1828 (Thomas), 1:11

The Diary of George Templeton Strong, 1835–1875, 3:590

Diary of Philip Hone, 1828–1851, 3:590

The Diary of Polina Suslova, 2:713

Diary of the Cavaliere Bernini's Visit to France, 3:770

Diary of the Discovery Expedition to the Antarctic Regions, 1901–1904, 3:907

Diary of the Sinai Campaign, 3:439

Diary of the "Terra Nova" Expedition to the Antarctic: 1910–1912, 3:907

Diary of the Voyage of the H.M.S. Rattlesnake, 5:799

The Diary of the War of the Pig, 2:855

The Diary of Vaslav Nijinsky, 3:749

Diary of William Harvey, 5:313

Diaspora: An Inquiry into the Contemporary Jewish World, 4:645

Diaspora: The Jews among the Greeks and Romans, 4:605

Diaspora Jews and Judaism, 4:617

The Diaspora Story: The Epic of the Jewish People among the Nations, 4:593

The (Diblos) Notebook, 1:1015

Dibs: In Search of Self, 5:421

Diccionario Espanol-Ingles/English-Spanish Dictionary, 1:103

Dickens: A Biography, 1:350

Dickens: A Life, 1:350

Dickens: From Pickwick to Dombey, 1:350

Dickens: Interviews and Recollections, 1:349

Dickens: The Critical Heritage, 1:349

Dickens and His Illustrators, 1:350

Dickens and Other Victorians: Essays in Honor of Philip Collins, 1:349

Dickens and the Dialectic of Growth, 1:351

Dickens and the 1830's, 1:349

Dickens and the Trials of Imagination, 1:351

Dickens and Women, 1:351

The Dickens Circle, 1:350

The Dickens Critics, 1:350

The Dickens Dictionary, 1:350

Dickens Dramatized, 1:349

Dickens Encyclopedia, 1:350

A Dickens Glossary, 1:350

The Dickens Index, 1:349

The Dickens Pantomime, 1:322

Dickens Studies Annual 1970–1992: Essays on Victorian Fiction, 1:349

Dickens the Novelist, 1:350

The Dickens World, 1:350

The Dick Gibson Show, 1:973

Dickinson: Strategies of Limitation, 1:747

Dickinson: The Modern Idiom, 1:748

Dickinson and the Strategies of Reticence, 1:747

Dickinson's English Historical Fiction, 1:124

Dick Whittington, 1:321

Dictatorships and the Passage from Capitalism to Communism, 3:287

Dictionary (Johnson), 1:235, 1:249

Dictionary: Polish-English, English-Polish, 1:101

Dictionary and Encyclopaedia of Paper and Paper-making, 1:5

Dictionary and Thesaurus of the Hebrew Language, 1:99

Dictionary Buying Guide, 1:89

The Dictionary of Accepted Ideas, 2:475, 2:476

A Dictionary of Actors, 1:218

Dictionary of Afro-American Slavery, 3:509

Dictionary of Agriculture, 5:262

Dictionary of AIDS-Related Terminology, 5:387

Dictionary of All Scriptures and Myths, 4:4

Dictionary of American Art, 3:758

Dictionary of American Biography, 1:85

Dictionary of American Diplomatic History, 3:138, 3:508

Dictionary of American English on Historical Principles, 1:89, 1:90

A Dictionary of American-English Usage, 1:92

Dictionary of American History, 3:509

A Dictionary of Americanisms on Historical Principles, 1:90

Dictionary of American Painters, Sculptors and Engravers, 3:761

Dictionary of American Philosophy, 4:3, 4:14

Dictionary of American Pop/Rock, 3:657

Dictionary of American Proverbs, 1:115

Dictionary of American Religious Biography, 4:719

Dictionary of American Spelling, 1:95

A Dictionary of Ancient Near Eastern Mythology, 4:545

A Dictionary of Angels: Including the Fallen Angels, 4:3

Dictionary of Anonymous Literature, 1:77

Dictionary of Anthropology, 3:11

Dictionary of Antiques and the Decorative Arts, 3:765

Dictionary of Architecture and Construction, 3:761

Dictionary of Art and Artists, 3:757

Dictionary of Asian Philosophies, 4:3, 4:14

Dictionary of Audio, Radio and Video, 5:230

A Dictionary of Ballet, 3:733

Dictionary of Behavioral Science, 3:170, 5:414

The Dictionary of Bible and Religion, 4:818

Dictionary of Biotechnology, 5:759

A Dictionary of Birds, 5:758

A Dictionary of Book History, 1:63

Dictionary of Books Relating to America from Its Discovery to the Present Time, 1:67, 3:507

A Dictionary of Botany, 5:761

Dictionary of Brazilian Literature, 2:890

A Dictionary of British History, 3:354

Dictionary of Canadian Biography, 3:605, 3:619

A Dictionary of Catch Phrases, 1:93

Dictionary of Cell Biology, 5:760

A Dictionary of Chinese Symbols, 4:521

Dictionary of Christianity in America, 4:5, 4:718

Dictionary of Christian Theology, 4:719

Dictionary of Civil Engineering, 5:224

Dictionary of Collective Nouns and Group Terms, 1:94

A Dictionary of Collective Onomatopoeic Sounds, Tones and Noises in English and Spanish, 1:93

A Dictionary of Colonial American Printers' Ornaments and Illustrations, 1:30

A Dictionary of Comparative Religion, 4:3

Dictionary of Computers, Information, and Telecommunications, 3:802, 5:541

Dictionary of Computer Terms, 5:539

Dictionary of Concepts in the Philosophy of Science, 5:60

Dictionary of Contemporary American Artists, 3:761

Dictionary of Contemporary American English, 1:91

A Dictionary of Contemporary American Usage, 1:91

A Dictionary of Contemporary Brazilian Authors, 2:890

A Dictionary of Contemporary Latin American Authors, 2:845

The Dictionary of Contemporary Music, 3:658

Dictionary of Contemporary Slang, 1:93

Dictionary of Cults, Sects, Religions and the Occult, 4:854

Dictionary of Demography, 3:206

A Dictionary of Early Music, from the Troubadours to Monteverdi, 3:657

The Dictionary of Ecology and Environmental Science, 5:815

A Dictionary of Egyptian Arabic: Arabic-English, 1:97

A Dictionary of Energy, 5:636

Dictionary of Engineering and Technology: English-German, Vol. 2, 5:744

The Dictionary of English Furniture, 3:766

A Dictionary of Environmental Quotations, 5:816

Dictionary of Environment and Development, 5:815

Dictionary of Fictional Characters, 1:132

Dictionary of Films, 3:826

Dictionary of Genetics, 5:760

Dictionary of Genetics and Cell Biology, 5:761

A Dictionary of Geography, 5:618

Dictionary of Geological Terms, 5:616

Dictionary of Greek and Roman Antiquities, 2:347

Dictionary of Greek and Roman Biography and Mythology, 2:347

Dictionary of Greek and Roman Geography, 2:347

Dictionary of Historical Terms, 3:7, 3:272

Dictionary of History, 3:7

A Dictionary of Hymnology: Origin and History of Christian Hymns, 3:656

A Dictionary of Indian History, 3:483

Dictionary of Information Science and Technology, 5:480

Dictionary of Information Technology, 3:802, 5:540

A Dictionary of Islam, 3:443, 4:566

A Dictionary of Japanese and English Idiomatic Equivalents, 1:100

A Dictionary of Literary, Dramatic and Cinematic Terms, 1:131

Dictionary of Literary Biography, 1:126, 1:866, 1:917, 1:918, 1:919, 1:920, 1:938

Dictionary of Literary Biography Yearbook, 1:126

Dictionary of Literary Terms, 1:132

Dictionary of Literary Themes and Motifs, 1:132

A Dictionary of Marxist Thought, 3:222

Dictionary of Mathematics, 5:479

Dictionary of Mechanical Engineering, 5:235, 5:236

Dictionary of Medical Eponyms, 5:5, 5:367

Dictionary of Medical Ethics, 5:119

The Dictionary of Medical Folklore, 3:869

Dictionary of Medical Syndromes, 5:367

Dictionary of Medieval Latin from British Sources, 1:101

A Dictionary of Mexican American Proverbs, 1:115

Dictionary of Ming Biography 1368–1644, 3:465

A Dictionary of Minicomputing and Microcomputing, 5:539

A Dictionary of Modern Critical Terms, 1:132

A Dictionary of Modern English Usage, 1:92

A Dictionary of Modern Indian History, 1707–1947, 3:483

A Dictionary of Modern Written Arabic, 1:97

A Dictionary of Musical Quotations, 3:654

A Dictionary of Musical Themes, 3:654

Dictionary of Mysticism, 4:718

Dictionary of Mythology, Folklore and Symbols, 3:757, 3:849

Dictionary of National Biography, 1:85, 5:4

Dictionary of National Biography from the Earliest Times to 1900 (Smith), 3:354

A Dictionary of New Thought Terms, 4:847

A Dictionary of Non-Christian Religions, 4:3, 4:5

Dictionary of Nutrition and Food Technology, 5:261

A Dictionary of Opera and Song Themes, 3:654

Dictionary of Ornament, 3:765

The Dictionary of Paper, 1:4

Dictionary of Petrology, 5:628

Dictionary of Philosophy (Angeles), 4:2, 4:12

A Dictionary of Philosophy (Flew), 4:3, 4:13

Dictionary of Philosophy (Frolov), 4:3, 4:13

A Dictionary of Philosophy (Lacey), 4:3, 4:14

Dictionary of Philosophy (Runes), 4:3, 4:15

Dictionary of Philosophy and Psychology, 4:13

Dictionary of Philosophy and Religion: Eastern and Western Thought, 4:14

Dictionary of Physics, 5:652

Dictionary of Plant Pathology, 5:760

Dictionary of Problem Words and Expressions, 1:92

A Dictionary of Pseudonyms and Their Origins, with Stories of Name Changes, 1:77

Dictionary of Psychology (Chaplin), 3:169

Dictionary of Psychology (Harriman), 5:413

Dictionary of Psychology and Related Fields, 5:413

The Dictionary of Publishing, 1:52

Dictionary of Quotations, 1:116

Dictionary of Religion and Philosophy, 4:4, 4:14, 4:717

Dictionary of Robotics, 5:243

Dictionary of Rocks, 5:618

Dictionary of Russian Literature, 2:687

Dictionary of Russian Literature since 1917, 2:687

A Dictionary of Saints, 4:719

Dictionary of Scandinavian History, 3:380

Dictionary of Scandinavian Literature, 2:638

Dictionary of Science and Technology, 5:217

Dictionary of Scientific Biography, 5:4, 5:28, 5:408, 5:479, 5:728

A Dictionary of Scientific Bird Names, 5:769

Dictionary of Scientific Literacy, 5:2, 5:27

Dictionary of Scientific Quotations, 5:6

A Dictionary of Shakespeare's Sexual Puns and Their Significance, 1:216

A Dictionary of Slang and Unconventional English, 1:93

A Dictionary of Social Science Methods, 3:7

A Dictionary of Statistical Terms (Kendall), 5:520

A Dictionary of Statistical Terms (Marriott), 5:521

Dictionary of Statistics and Methodology, 5:521

Dictionary of Subjects and Symbols in Art, 3:757

A Dictionary of Superstitions, 3:885

A Dictionary of the Chinese Particles, with a Prolegomenon in Which the Problems of the Particles Are Considered and They Are Classified by Their Grammatical Functions, 1:97

Dictionary of the Dance, 3:732

Dictionary of the Ecumenical Movement, 4:5, 4:746

Dictionary of the English Language, 1:249

Dictionary of the Environment, 5:815

Dictionary of the History of Ideas, 3:7, 3:273, 4:3, 4:15, 4:163

Dictionary of the History of Science, 5:24, 5:27, 5:60

Dictionary of the Khazars, 2:831

A Dictionary of the Life Sciences, 5:761

Dictionary of the Middle Ages, 4:94

Dictionary of Theoretical Concepts in Biology, 5:762

Dictionary of the Physical Sciences: Terms, Formulas, Data, 5:11

Dictionary of the Russian Revolution, 3:394

Dictionary of the Vietnam War, 3:491

Dictionary of Twentieth Century History: 1914–1990, 3:7

A Dictionary of World Mythology, 1:133

Dictionary of Yiddish Slang, 1:103

Dictionary/Outline of Basic Statistics, 5:520

Diderot (Fellows), 2:472, 4:196

Diderot (France), 3:338

Diderot (Wilson), 4:196

Diderot: A Critical Biography, 4:196

Diderot, Interpreter of Nature: Selected Writings, 2:472

Diderot and Descartes, 2:472, 4:197

Diderot and the Encyclopedists, 4:196

Diderot and the Jews, 4:196

Diderot as a Disciple of English Thought, 4:196

Diderot's Early Philosophical Works, 2:472

Diderot's Pictorial Encyclopedia of Trades and Industry, 2:472

Diderot's Writings on the Theatre, 2:472

Didyma: Apollo's Oracle, Cult, and Companions, 4:446

Die Afrika-Literatur in der Zeit von 1500–1750, 2:112

Die Cellularpathologie in ihrer Begründung auf physiologische und pathologische Gewebelehre, 5:410

Die Erdkunde, 3:134

Die Frau ohne Schatten, 2:592

Die Gesammelten Werke, 5:527

Die Gestundete Zeit, 2:568

The Diehards: Aristocratic Society and Politics in Edwardian England, 3:367

Die Judenbuche: A Bilingual Edition, 2:576

Die Philosophie Franz Brentanos, 4:222

Diet, Nutrition, and Cancer, 5:394

Diet and Cancer, 5:371

Dietary Fibre, Fibre-Depleted Foods and Disease, 5:395

The Dieter's Dilemma: Eating Less and Weighing More, 5:344

The Diet for Runners, 5:347

Dieting Makes You Fat: A Guide to Energy, Food, Fitness and Health, 5:325

Dietrich Bonhoeffer, 4:760

The Difference between Fichte's and Schelling's System of Philosophy, 4:198, 4:232

A Different Existence: Principles of Phenomenological Psychopathology, 5:471

Different Fleshes, 1:982

The Different Forms of Flowers on Plants of the Same Species, 5:793

Differential Equations: Pure and Applied Math, 5:679

Differential Geometry, 5:487

Differential Psychology, 3:180

A Different Language: Gertrude Stein's Experimental Writing, 1:882

Difficult Freedom: Essays on Judaism, 4:901

Difficulties in the Path of Psychoanalysis, 5:444

Difficult Loves, 2:412

A Difficult Young Man, 2:950

Diffusion Processes and Location, 3:129

The Digby Plays, 1:160

Digging into Popular Culture, 3:872, 3:875

Digging Up the Mountains, 2:932, 2:933

Digha Nikaya, 4:514

Digital and Analog Communication Systems, 5:298

Digital and Data Communications, 5:308

Digital Communication (Lee), 5:302

Digital Communications (Haykin), 5:302

Digital Communications: Fundamentals and Applications, 5:297

Digital Communications with Fiber Optics and Satellite Applications, 5:302

Digital Communication Systems, 5:302

Digital Deli: The Lunch Group, 5:539

Digital Line-of-Sight Radio Links: A Handbook, 5:305

Digital Signal Processing, 5:302

Digital Telephony, 5:301

Digital Transmission of Information, 5:302

The Digital Word, 5:562

Dignity and Practical Reason, 4:206

The Dilemma of a Ghost, 2:129

The Dilemma of Qualitative Method: Herbert Blumer and the Chicago Tradition, 3:222

Dilemmas, 4:325

Dilemmas in Modern Jewish Thought, 4:634, 4:649

Dilemmas in the Study of Information, 5:544

The Dilemmas of an Upright Man, 5:48, 5:710

Dilemmas of Democracy: Tocqueville and Modernization, 3:165

Dilthey: Philosopher of the Human Studies, 4:226

Dilthey Today, 4:226

The Dimension of the Present Moment, and Other Essays, 2:792

Dimensions in Wholistic Healing, 5:320

Dimensions of a New Identity, 5:442

Dimensions of Darwinism, 5:794

Dimensions of Islam, 4:573, 4:576

The Dimensions of Liberty, 3:581

Dimensions of Orthodox Judaism, 4:654

Di Mishpokhe Mashber, 2:37

Dimity Convictions: The American Woman in the Nineteenth Century, 1:716

Ding Ling's Fiction, 2:264

Dining in America, 1850–1900, 3:552

The Dining Room, 1:1091

Dinka Folktales: African Stories from the Sudan, 4:462

Dinner Along the Amazon, 2:911

Dinner at Eight, 1:1097

Dinner at the Homesick Restaurant, 1:1058, 1:1059

Dinner Pieces: A Translation of the Intercenales, 2:404

The Dinosaur Heresies, 5:638

Dinosaurs in the Attic, 5:765

Dinosaurs in the Morning: Forty-One Pieces on Jazz, 3:667

Dinosaur Tracks, 5:640

Diodorus of Sicily, 3:314

Diodorus Siculus and the First Century, 3:315

Dion Boucicault, 1:332

The Dionysiac Mysteries of the Hellenistic and Roman Age, 4:450, 4:486

Dionysiac Poetics and Euripides' Bacchae, 4:475

Dionysus and the City: Modernism in Twentieth-Century Poetry, 1:418

Diophantus' Arithmetica, 5:504

Diophantus of Alexandria: A Study in the History of Greek Algebra, 5:503

Dioxin, Agent Orange: The Facts, 5:736

Diplomacy and Ideology, 3:281

Diplomacy in Ancient Greece, 3:308

The Diplomacy of Constraint, 3:608

Diplomacy of Fear: Canada and the Cold War, 1941–1948, 3:608

The Diplomacy of Imperialism, 3:421

The Diplomacy of the American Revolution, 3:567

A Diplomatic History of Europe: Since the Congress of Vienna, 3:277

Diplomatic History of Modern Iraq, 3:449

A Diplomatic History of the American People, 3:544

Dipsychus, 1:345

Dirac: A Scientific Biography, 5:680

Directing the Film: Film Directors on Their Art, 3:828

Directions in Catholic Social Ethics, 4:743

Directions in Euripidean Criticism: A Collection of Essays, 2:356, 4:475

Directories in Print, 1:104

Director's Theatre, 1:425

Directory of African American Religious Bodies, 4:7

Directory of American Philosophers, 4:5

Directory of American Research and Technology, 1994, 5:724

Directory of Electronic Journals, Newsletters and Academic Discussion Lists, 5:548

Directory of Historical Organizations in the United States and Canada, 3:9

Directory of Information Management Software for Libraries, Information Centers, Record Centers and Supplement 1984, 5:545

Directory of Literary Magazines, 1992–93, 1:52

The Directory of Museums and Living Displays, 3:757

Directory of Online Databases, 1:104, 1:113, 5:546

Directory of Physics and Astronomy Staff, 1990–1991, 5:652

Directory of Popular Culture, 3:873

A Directory of Religious Bodies in the United States, 4:717, 4:751

Directory of Specialized American Bookdealers, 1984–1985, 1:77

Directory of Special Libraries and Information Centers, 1:104, 1:70

Directory of Technical and Scientific Directories, 5:3

Directory of the History of Ideas, 3:9

The Directory of Tunes and Musical Themes, 3:657

Directory of United Nations Documentary and Archival Sources, 1:111

Dirty Silence: Aspects of Language and Literature in New Zealand, 2:971

Disability and Disadvantage: The Consequences of Chronic Illness, 5:377

Disappearance, 2:767

Disappearing through the Skylight, 3:559, 5:154, 5:573

Disasters: The Anatomy of Environmental Hazards, 5:637

The Discarded Image, 4:99

Discascalicon: A Medieval Guide to the Arts, 4:101

Discipleship of Equals: A Critical Feminist Ecclesiology of Liberation, 4:750

Disciplinary, Moral, and Ascetical Works, 4:713

Discipline and Punish, 4:400

Discipline and Punish: The Birth of the Prison, 2:476, 2:477, 3:205, 5:87

The Discipline of Curiosity: Science in the World, 5:10

Discipline of Power, 3:616

A Discipline of Programming, 5:550

The Discipline of Taste and Feeling, 4:381

Disciplining Foucault: Feminism, Power, and the Body, 4:401, 5:88

Discontinuities in Wave Guides, 5:715

Discord, Dialogue, and Concord, 4:730

Discordant Harmonies, 5:819

A Discourse Concerning the Being and Attributes of God, 4:194

A Discourse of Disenchantment: Reflections on Politics and Technology, 5:128

The Discourse of Self in Victorian Poetry, 1:315

The Discourse of Western Planting, 3:922

Discourse on Free Will, 4:138

Discourse on Metaphysics, Correspondence with Arnauld, Monadology, 4:164, 4:176

Discourse on Method, 4:168, 4:169, 5:503

Discourse on the Awakening of Faith in the Mahayana, 4:557

Discourse on the Natural Theology of the Chinese, 4:176

Discourse on the Origin of Inequality, 4:212

Discourse on the Sciences and Arts, 4:212

Discourse on Thinking, 4:291

Discourses (Dio Chrysostom), 3:314

The Discourses (Machiavelli), 3:160, 4:145

Discourses of Difference, 1:325

The Discourses of Rumi, 4:589

Discourses of the Devil's Advocate and Other Controversies, 2:330

Discourses on Livy, 4:144

Discourses on the Heroic Poem, 2:440

Discourses on Two New Sciences, 4:142

Discourses on Various Important Subjects, Nearly concerning the Affair of the Soul's Eternal Salvation, 1:637

Discourse upon Comedy in a Letter to a Friend, 1:243

The Discoverers, 5:24

The Discoverers: A History of Man's Search to Know His World and Himself, 3:568

The Discoverers: An Illustrated History of Man's Search to Know His World and Himself, 3:569

Discoveries and Opinions of Galileo, 5:42

Discovering, 5:10

Discovering Africa's Past, 3:417

Discovering Book Collecting, 1:31

Discovering Causal Structure, 5:75

Discovering Great Singers of Classic Pop, 3:672

Discovering Modernism: T. S. Eliot and His Context, 1:415

Discovering Plato, 3:163, 4:81

Discovering Reality, 4:40

Discovering Shakespeare: A New Guide to the Plays, 1:222

Discovering the News: A Social History of American Newspapers, 3:809

Discovering the Universe, 5:655

Discovery: The Story of the Second Byrd Antarctic Expedition, 3:915

The Discovery and Characterization of Transposable Elements, 5:806

Discovery, Development, and Delivery of New Drugs, 5:350

Discovery, Innovation and Risk, 5:226

Discovery in Russian and Siberian Waters, 3:906

The Discovery of Being, 5:462

The Discovery of Constable, 3:773

The Discovery of Egypt, 3:445

Discovery of India, 3:499

The Discovery of Insulin, 5:47, 5:381

The Discovery of North America, 1:631

The Discovery of Society, 3:200

The Discovery of Subatomic Particles, 5:718

The "Discovery" of Sudden Infant Death Syndrome, 5:375

Discovery of the Bismarck, 5:641

The Discovery of the Child, 3:266

Discovery of the Elements, 5:729

The Discovery of the Mind in Early Greek Philosophy and Literature, 2:347, 4:49

The Discovery of the Sea, 3:893

Discovery of the Titanic, 5:641

The Discovery of the Unconscious, 5:34

The Discreet Art of Luis Buñuel: A Reading of His Films, 3:832

Discrimination: Its Economic Impact on Blacks, Women, and Jews, 3:66

Discrimination and Reverse Discrimination, 4:386

Discriminations: Further Concepts of Criticism, 1:927, 2:984

Disease, Life, and Man, Selected Essays, 5:410

Disease, Medicine and Empire, 5:36

Disease and Its Control: The Shaping of Modern Thought, 5:313

Disease Change and the Role of Medicine: The Navajo Experience, 5:353

The Disease Detectives, 5:368

A Disease of Society: Cultural and Institutional Responses to AIDS, 5:173

Diseases, 5:367

Disembodying Women: Perspectives on Pregnancy and the Unborn, 5:187

Disguise and Role-Playing in Ben Jonson's Drama, 1:184

The Disguises of the Demon, 4:506, 4:510, 4:514

Dishonored, 1:1176

The Disinherited Lady, 2:547

Dismantling the Silence, 1:1048

Disneyland, 2:812

The Disney Studio Story, 1:1165

The Disney Version, 1:1165

Disobedience, 2:429

The Disorganized Personality, 5:427

Displacements: Women, Tradition, Literatures in French, 2:447

Displacing Homophobia, 1:1183

The Dispossessed, 1:1260

The Dispossessed: America's Underclasses from the Civil War to the Present, 3:552

Disputation against Astrology, 4:152

Disputation and Dialogue: Readings in the Jewish-Christian Encounter, 4:603

Disputed Questions: On Being a Christian, 4:785

Disputed Questions in Theology and the Philosophy of Religion, 4:380

Disputed Questions on the Mystery of the Trinity, 4:113

Disquisitiones Arithmeticae, 5:507, 5:530

Disraeli (Blake), 1:351, 3:363

Disraeli (McGuirk), 1:352

Disraeli's Fiction, 1:352

Disraeli's Grand Tour: Disraeli in the Holy Land, 1830–31, 1:352

Disraeli the Novelist, 1:352

Disseminating Whitman: Revision and Corporeality in Leaves of Grass, 1:708

Dissemination, 2:447, 4:397

Dissent and Reform in the Early Middle Ages, 4:700

Dissent in Early Modern China, 2:230

Dissent in Three American Wars, 3:589

Dissertations on Government: The Affairs of the Bank and Paper-Money, 1:641

The Dissident Press, 3:807

The Dissolution of the Medieval Outlook, 4:104

Dissonant Voices in Soviet Literature, 2:692

Distanced, 2:134

Distance from Loved Ones, 1:1058

Distances in Time: Selected Poems, 2:334

Distant Dominion, 3:610

Distant Drum, 2:178

Distant Encounters, 5:593

Distant Islands: Travels across Indonesia, 3:902

Distant Is the Sun, 2:829

A Distant Mirror: The Calamitous Fourteenth Century, 3:332, 3:411, 3:412, 4:701

Distant Neighbors: A Portrait of the Mexicans, 3:639

Distant Pleasures: Alexander Pushkin and the Writing of Exile, 2:752

Distant Relations, 2:865

Distant View of a Minaret and Other Stories, 2:59

Distinction: A Social Critique of the Judgement of Taste, 3:22

The Distinguishing Marks of a Work of the Spirit of God, 1:637

Distortions, 1:945

The Distribution of Wealth: A Theory of Wages, Income and Profits, 3:72

District of Columbia, 1:828

Disturber of the Peace: The Life of H. L. Mencken, 1:860

Disturbing Element, 2:954

Disturbing the Peace, 3:389

Disturbing the Universe, 5:133

The Disuniting of America, 3:597

Dithyramb, Tragedy and Comedy, 2:347

Ditte: Ditte, Daughter of Man, 2:653

The Divan, Written in the Fourteenth Century, 2:90

Diverse Paths to Modernity in Southeastern Europe, 3:391

Diversifications: Poems, 1:934

Diversions of Pleasure: Luis Buñuel and the Crises of Desire, 3:832

The Diversity of Life, 5:117, 5:766, 5:821

The Diversity of Normal Behavior, 5:415

Divers Voyages Touching the Discovery of America and the Islands Adjacent, 3:922

The Diverting History of John Gilpin, 1:580

Divided Existence and Complex Society: An Historical Approach, 5:471

The Divided Heaven, 2:615, 2:616

Divided Houses: Gender and the Civil War, 3:527

Divided Lives: American Women in the Twentieth Century, 3:557

The Divided Self, 5:459

Divided We Fall, 3:212

Divided We Stand: Redefining Politics, Technology, and Social Choice, 5:158

Divided We Stand: The Crisis of a Frontierless Democracy, 3:600

The Divine Aretino, 2:406

Divine Comedies, 1:1015

The Divine Comedy, 1:277, 1:682, 2:398, 2:409, 2:413, 2:416, 2:417

The Divine Comedy: Tracing God's Art, 2:417

The Divine Comedy and the Encyclopedia of Arts and Sciences, 2:417

The Divine Consort: Radha and the Goddesses of India, 4:504

Divine Dancer: A Biography of Ruth St. Denis, 3:752

Divine Dialogues, 4:183

Divine Disenchantment: Deconverting from New Religions, 4:856

Divine Disobedience: Profiles in Catholic Radicalism, 5:137

The Divine Hierarchy: Popular Hinduism in Central India, 4:503

The Divine Horseman: The Voodoo Gods of Haiti, 1:1163

The "Divine Man": His Origin and Function in Hellenistic Popular Religion, 4:451

Divine Milieu: An Essay on the Interior Life, 4:336

Divine Name and Presence: The Memra, 4:608

Divine Omniscience and Human Freedom, 4:289

Divine Passions: The Social Construction of Emotion in India, 4:505

The Divine Poems, 1:178

Divine Power: A Study of Karl Barth and Charles Hartshorne, 4:289

The Divine Principle and Its Application, 4:877

The Diviner, 1:479

The Divine Relativity: A Social Conception of God, 4:289

The Divine Romance, 4:556

The Divine Romance: Teresa of Avila's Narrative Theology, 4:786

The Diviners, 2:916, 2:917

The Divine Woman, 2:191

Diving Birds of North America, 5:770

Diving for Pearls, 1:450

Diving into the Wreck: Poems 1971–72, 1:1037

Divinity and Experience: The Religion of the Dinka, 4:462

The Divinity of the Roman Emperor, 4:452

Division and the Stresses of Reunion, 1845–1876, 3:593

The Division of Labor in Society, 3:225

Division of the Kingdoms: Shakespeare's Two Versions of King Lear, 1:214

The Divisions and Methods of the Sciences, 4:117

Divorce: An American Tradition, 3:553

Divorce and New Beginnings: An Authoritative Guide, 3:206

The Divorce of Catherine of Aragon, 3:403

The Divorce Revolution, 3:207

Diwan over the Prince of Emgión, 2:673

Djuna: The Life and Times of Djuna Barnes, 1:813

The DMSO Handbook, 5:351

The DNA Story: A Documentary History of Gene Cloning, 5:812

Do Androids Dream of Electric Sheep?, 1:1256

Dobson's Encyclopaedia, 1:6

The Doctor, 1:304, 1:305

The Doctor and the Court: The Physician's Guide to Surviving, 5:344

The Doctor and the Devils and Other Scripts, 1:557

The Doctor and the Soul: From Psychotherapy to Logotherapy, 5:443

Dr. Barnard as I Knew Him, 3:259

Dr. Berger's Immune Power Diet, 5:344

Dr. Bowdler's Legacy, 1:57

Doctor Criminale, 1:448

Doctor Faustus, 1:157, 1:186, 2:601, 2:602

Dr. Fisher of Geneva or the Bomb Party, 1:488

Dr. Graesler, 2:611

Dr. Heidenhoff's Process, 1:734

Dr. Heimlich's Guide to Emergency Medical Situations, 5:381

The Doctor in Spite of Himself and The Bourgeois Gentleman, 2:490

The Doctor Is Sick, 1:453

Dr. Jekyll and Mr. Hyde, 1:396, 1:589

Dr. Jekyll and Mr. Hyde: After One Hundred Years, 1:397

Dr. Kathryn Schrotenboer's Guide to Pregnancy over 35, 5:359

Dr. Mollen's Anti-Aging Diet, 5:349

Doctor No, 1:593

Dr. Samuel Clarke: An Eighteenth Century Heretic, 4:194

Doctor Sax, 1:998

The Doctor's Book on Hair Loss, 5:399

The Doctor's Dilemma, 1:544, 1:545

Doctors' Dilemmas: Moral Conflict and Medical Care, 5:120

A Doctor's Guide to Feeding Your Child, 5:348

The Doctor's Guide to Medication during Pregnancy and Lactation, 5:358

A Doctor's Guide to the Best Medical Care, 5:13, 5:332

The Doctor's Guide to You and Your Colon, 5:385

Doctor Slaughter, 3:940

Dr. Spock's Baby and Child Care, 5:323

The Doctor's Wife, 1:332

Dr. Thorne, 1:405

Dr. W. C. Röntgen, 5:711

Dr. William Hunter at the Royal Academy of Arts, 5:203

The Doctor Who Dared, William Osler, 5:364

Doctor Wooreddy's Prescription for Enduring the Ending of the World, 2:960, 2:961

Dr. Wright's Guide to Healing with Nutrition, 5:347

Doctor Zhivago, 1:445, 2:745, 3:397

Doctrine and Covenants of the Church of Jesus Christ of Latter-Day Saints, 4:846, 4:879

Doctrine and Practice in the Early Church, 4:686

The Doctrine of Chances, 5:528

Doctrine of Merits in Old Rabbinical Literature, 4:621

Doctrine of the Heart, 4:549

The Doctrine of the Soul in the Thought of Plotinus and Origen, 4:63

The Doctrine of the Sufis, 4:574

The Doctrines of American Foreign Policy, 3:544

Documentary: A History of the Non-Fiction Film, 3:551, 3:825

A Documentary History of American Industrial Society, 3:54, 3:73

A Documentary History of Art, 3:757

A Documentary History of Religion in America since 1865, 4:751

A Documentary History of Russian Thought, 4:31

Documentary History of the Constitution of the United States of America, 1786–1870, 3:541

Documentary History of the Modern Civil Rights Movement, 3:511

A Documentary History of the Negro People in the United States, 3:511

Documentary Life, 1:205

The Documentation of the European Communities: A Guide, 1:111

Document Catalog, 1:109

Documents Illustrating Papal Authority, A.D. 96–454, 4:688

Documents in Early Christian Thought, 4:687

Documents in Mycenaean Greek, 2:347

Documents in the History of American Philosophy, 4:36

Documents of American Catholic History, 4:751

Documents of American Constitutional and Legal History, 3:142

Documents of American History, 3:511, 3:572

Documents of the Christian Church, 4:680

The Documents of Vatican II, 4:891

Documents Relating to the Early History of Hudson Bay, 5:648

Dodsworth, 1:853, 1:854

Does God Exist? An Answer for Today, 4:775

Dogalypse, 2:773

The Dog Beneath the Skin, 1:435

Dogeaters, 2:329

Dogen's Manuals of Zen Meditation, 4:537

The Dog It Was That Died, and Other Plays, 1:554

Dogma and Compulsion, 5:467

The Dogma of Christ, and Other Essays on Religion, Psychology, and Culture, 5:450

Dogmas and Dreams: Political Ideologies in the Modern World, 3:140

Dogmatic and Polemical Works, 4:711

The Dogmatic Principles of Soviet Philosophy (as of 1958), 4:31

Dog Soldiers, 1:1055

Dog Star Man, 1:1160

Dog Years, 2:582, 2:583

Doing Evil to Achieve Good: Moral Choice in Conflict Situations, 4:745

Doing Literary Business, 1:713, 1:722, 1:650

Doing Philosophy Historically, 4:16

Doing Science, 5:9

Doing Things with Texts: Essays in Criticism and Critical Theory, 1:931

Doing What Comes Naturally, 1:976, 1:1127

Doin Wildcat, 2:960, 2:961

Do-It-Yourself Medical Testing, 5:324

Dojo: Magic and Exorcism in Modern Japan, 4:540

The Doll, 2:819, 2:820

Dollars and Deficits, 3:65

A Doll's House, 2:665

A Doll's House and Other Plays, 2:666

Dolores, 1:461, 1:462

The Dolphin, 1:1006

Dolphin Dreamtime: The Art and Science of Interspecies Communication, 5:826

Dolphins, 3:918

Dombey and Son, 1:310, 1:348

Dom Casmurro, 2:896, 2:897

The Dome and the Rock: Structure in the Poetry of Wallace Stevens, 1:887

A Dome of Many-Coloured Glass, 1:856

The Domestic and Heroic in Tennyson's Poetry, 1:401

The Domestication of Europe, 4:434

The Domestication of the Savage Mind, 4:460

Domestic Individualism, 1:650, 1:713

Domestic Manners of the Americans, 1:407, 1:408

Domestic Revolutions: A Social History of American Family Life, 3:553

Dominance, Self-Esteem, Self-Actualization, 5:461

Dominant Symbols in Popular Culture, 3:872

Domination and Power, 5:88

Dominations and Powers: Reflections on Liberty, Society and Government, 4:326

Domingo F. Sarmiento: Public Writer (Between 1839 and 1852), 2:884

Dom Pedro: The Struggle for Liberty in Brazil and Portugal, 1798–1834, 3:634

Doña Flor and Her Two Husbands, 2:892

Donald Barthelme, 1:944

Donald Barthelme: A Comprehensive Bibliography and an Annotated Secondary Checklist, 1:944

Donald Barthelme: A Study of the Short Fiction, 1:944

Donald Barthelme's Fiction, 1:944

Donald Davidson, 4:283

Donald Davie: A Checklist of His Writings, 1946–1988, 1:466

Doña Luz, 2:552

Doña Perfecta, 2:547

The Donatist Church: A Movement of Protest in Roman North Africa, 4:685

Don Gil of the Green Breeches, 2:551

Don Isaac Abravanel: Statesman and Philosopher, 4:633

Don Juan (Byron), 1:225, 1:281, 1:282

Don Juan (Molière), 2:490

Don Juan: Variation on a Theme, 2:985

Don Juan and Other Plays, 2:490

"Don Juan" and Regency England, 1:283

Don Juan in Context, 1:283

The Don Juan Legend, 5:466

The Donkey Inside, 3:894

Donne's Anniversaries and the Poetry of Praise, 1:178

Donne's Idea of a Woman, 1:178

Donor, 5:370

Don Perlimplín, 2:538

Don Quijote, 2:229, 2:520, 2:534, 2:536

Don Quijote, 1894–1970: A Selective and Annotated Bibliography, 2:535

Don Quixote: Hero or Fool? A Study in Narrative Technique, 2:535

Don Quixote, or the Critique of Reading, 2:866

Don Quixote and the Dulcineated World, 2:536

Don Quixote of the Microscope, 5:811

Don's Party, 2:967

Don't Ask, 1:1004

Don't Ask Me How the Time Goes By: Poems, 1964–1968, 2:876

"Don't Call Me Gentle Charles," 1:296

Don't Know Much About History, 3:515

Don't Let Him Die, 2:142

Don't Tell 'Em It's Good for 'Em, 5:348

Don't Tell the Grownups: Why Kids Love the Books They Do, 1:1007

Don't Tread on Me: The Selected Letters of S. J. Perelman, 1:868

Donum Estonicum, 2:797

Doom of Youth, 1:514

Doomsday Cult, 4:871

Door into the Dark, 1:495

The Doorman, 2:852

Dora, Doralina, 2:897

Dorland's Illustrated Medical Dictionary, 5:367

Dorothy and the Wizard, 1:1200

Dorothy Day: A Biography, 4:765

Dorothy Day: A Radical Devotion, 4:765

Dorothy Day: Selected Writings, 4:765

Dorothy Day and the Catholic Worker, 4:766

Dorothy Day and the Catholic Worker: Bibliography and Index, 4:765

Dorothy L. Sayers: A Literary Biography, 1:611

Dorothy L. Sayers: A Reference Guide, 1:611

Dorothy L. Sayers: Solving the Mystery of Wickedness, 1:611

Dorothy Parker, 1:868

Dorothy Parker: What Fresh Hell Is This?, 1:868

Dorothy Richardson, 1:541

Doruntine, 2:780

The D.O.'s: Osteopathic Medicine in America, 5:338

The Dose Makes the Poison: A Plain-Language Guide to Toxicology, 5:736

Dos Khsidishe yingl, 2:40

Dos Passos, 1:828

Dos Passos: A Collection of Critical Essays, 1:828

Dos Passos: A Life, 1:828

Dos Passos: Artist as American, 1:829

Dos Passos: The Critics and the Writer's Intention, 1:828

Dos Passos's Early Fiction, 1912–1938, 1:828

Dos Passos' U.S.A.: A Critical Study, 1:829

Dos Poylishe yingl, 2:40

Dossier Society, 5:125

Dostoevsky: His Life and Work, 2:716

Dostoevsky: The Seeds of Revolt, 1821–1849, 2:715

Dostoevsky: The Stir of Liberation. 1860–1865, 2:715

Dostoevsky: The Years of Ordeal. 1850–1859, 2:715

Dostoevsky, Tolstoy and Nietzsche, 2:716, 4:247, 4:335

Dostoevsky and Gogol: Texts and Criticism, 2:716

Dostoevsky and Romantic Realism, 2:715

Dostoevsky and The Idiot: Author, Narrator and Reader, 2:716

Dostoevsky and the Legend of the Grand Inquisitor, 2:716

Dostoevsky and the Novel, 2:715

Dostoyevsky: Reminiscences, 2:715

Dostoyevsky: "The Brothers Karamazov," 2:715

Dostoyevsky after Bakhtin: Readings in Dostoyevsky's Fantastic Realism, 2:715

Dostoyevsky and Andreyev: Gazers upon the Abyss, 2:699

Dostoyevsky and the Jews, 2:715

Dostoyevsky and the Process of Literary Creation, 2:715

Do the Americas Have a Common History?, 3:643

Do the Right Thing, 1:1170

Doting, 1:487

The Double, 2:713

Double: A Psychoanalytical Study, 5:466

The Double Agent: Essays in Craft and Elucidation, 1:816

The Doubleday Roget's Thesaurus in Dictionary Form, 1:94

The Double Dealer, 1:237

Double Dream of Spring, 1:936

Double-Edged Helix: Genetic Engineering in the Real World, 5:726

The Double-Edged Helix: Science in the Real World, 5:782

The Double Elephant Folio: The Story of Audubon's Birds of America, 5:787

Double Exile: African and West Indian Writing Between Two Cultures, 2:108

The Double Helix, 5:49, 5:732, 5:791, 5:812, 5:813

The Double History of Dr. Valmy, 2:532

The Double Image, 1:1003

Double Indemnity, 1:1228

Double Jeopardy: A Critique of Seven Yuan Courtroom Dramas, 2:190

The Double Man, 1:435

Doubles: Studies in Literary History, 2:985

A Double Singleness, 1:295

Double Talk: The Erotics of Male Literary Collaboration, 1:1182

The Double Vision: Language and Meaning in Religion, 1:976

Double Yoke, 2:137

Doubt and Dogmatism: Studies in Hellenistic Epistemology, 4:56

Doubt's Boundless Sea, 4:123

Douglas Jerrold, 1:367

Douglas Jerrold, Dramatist and Wit, 1:366, 1:367

Douglas Jerrold and "Punch," by Walter Jerrold, 1:367

Dove, 3:908

Dove on Fire: Poems on Peace, Justice and Ecology, 2:325

The Doves Bindery, 1:26

The Dove's Nest and Other Stories, 2:978

Do We Agree? A Debate, 1:457

The Dow Jones-Irwin Technical Reference Guide to Microcomputer Database Management Systems, 5:559

Down and Out in the Great Depression, 3:535

Down by the Riverside: A South Carolina Slave Community, 3:524, 3:867

Down Fall, 2:673

Downfall of Cartesianism, 4:171

The Downfall of Gerdt Bladh, 2:659

Downfall of Temlaham, 3:875

The Downfall of the Gods, 2:654

Downhill All the Way, 1:569

Downhill All the Way: An Autobiography, 1919–1939, 1:42

Down Home, 1:657, 1:722

Down Second Avenue: Growing Up in a South African Ghetto, 2:166, 2:167

Down the Rabbit Hole, 1:32

Down There on a Visit, 1:500

The Downtown Jews: Portraits of an Immigrant Generation, 2:30

Down under All Over: A Love Affair with Australia, 3:901

Doxology: The Praise of God in Worship, Doctrine, and Life, 4:898

Doy Laurel in Profile: A Philippine Political Odyssey, 2:330

Dracula, 1:591, 1:602, 1:603, 1:1239

Dracula: The Vampire and the Critics, 1:603

Dracula's Guest, 1:603

Dracula Unbound, 1:613

The Draft, 1940–1973, 3:538

A Draft of Shadows and Other Poems, 2:878

A Draft of XXX Cantos, 1:871

Drafts and Fragments, Cantos 110–117, 1:871

Drafts for the Essay Concerning Human Understanding and Other Philosophical Writings, 3:159, 4:179

The Dragon: Fifteen Stories, 2:775

Dragon Beard Ditch: A Play in Three Acts, 2:251

A Dragon Defiant: A Short History of Vietnam, 3:490

The Dragon in the Gate, 1:364

A Dragon in the House, 3:369

The Dragons of Eden, 5:611

The Dragons of Tiananmen: Beijing as a Sacred City, 4:531

Dragon's Teeth, 1:879, 1:880

Dragon within the Gates: The Once and Future AIDS Epidemic, 5:388

Drama and Commitment, 1:1075

Drama and Ethos: Natural Law Ethics in Spanish Golden Age Drama, 2:524

Drama Criticism, 1:427

Drama in the Middle Ages: Comparative and Critical Essays, 1:157

Drama of a Nation: Public Theater in Renaissance England and Spain, 2:523

The Drama of Black Africa, 2:108

The Drama of J. M. Synge, 1:556

The Drama of Language, 2:599

Drama of Lugi Pirandello, 2:436

Drama of the English Renaissance, 1:171

The Drama of the European Jews, 4:635

Drama of the Gods: A Study of Seven African Plays, 2:111

Drama of the Universe, 5:587

The Drama of Thought, 4:24

The Drama Review, 2:420

Dramas, Fields, and Metaphors: Symbolic Action in Human Society, 3:40

Drama Series, 2:349

A Dramatic Appearance: New Zealand Theatre, 2:970

Dramatic Art in Aeschylus's Seven Against Thebes, 2:351

Dramatic Bibliography, 1:123

Dramatic Character in the English Romantic Movement, 1:271

Dramatic Concepts of Antonin Artaud, 2:452

Dramatic Criticism Index, 1:427

Dramatic Design in the Chester Cycle, 1:159

Dramatic Documents from the Elizabethan Playhouses, 1:221

Dramatic Festivals of Athens, 2:347

Dramatic Idylls, 1:338

The Dramatic Imagination, 1:1073

The Dramatic Landscape of Steinbeck's Short Stories, 1:886

Dramatic Life As I Found It, 1:1074

Dramatic Re-Visions, 1:123

The Dramatic Symphony, 2:701

Dramatic Uses of Biblical Allusions in Marlowe and Shakespeare, 1:187, 1:220

The Dramatic Works of George Peele, 1:195

Dramatism and Development, 1:955

The Dramatist and the Received Idea, 1:187

Dramatist in America: Letters of Maxwell Anderson, 1912–1958, 1:1082

Dramatists in Revolt, 2:847

The Dramaturgy of Shakespeare's Romances, 1:211

Dramouss, 2:138

Drapier's Letters, 1:259

Drawing and Understanding Fossils, 5:639

Drawing Down the Moon, 4:865

The Drawing of America: Eyewitnesses to History, 3:513

Drawings and Plans of Frank Lloyd Wright: The Early Period (1893–1909), 3:797

Drawings of Albrecht Dürer, 3:774

The Drawings of Goya in the Prado Museum, 3:776

The Drawings of Louis Henry Sullivan, 3:793

The Drawings of Raphael: With a Complete Catalog, 3:788

Drawing the Line, 5:120

Dreadful Pleasures: An Anatomy of Modern Horror, 1:599

The Dream, and Other Poems, 1:384

Dream and Existence, 5:436

Dream and Reality: An Essay in Autobiography, 4:759

A Dreambook for Our Time, 2:815

Dream Days, 1:584

A Dreamer's Journey: The Autobiography of Morris Raphael Cohen, 4:280

Dreamer's Tales, 1:615

Dream Girl, 1:1109

Dreaming Identities: Class, Gender, and Generation in 1980's Hollywood Movies, 3:827

Dreaming the Dark: Magic, Sex, and Politics, 4:865

The Dream Life of Balso Snell, 1:896

The Dream Life of Balso Snell and A Cool Million: Two Novels by West, 1:897

The Dream Master, 1:1263

The Dream of a Common Language: Poems, 1974–1977, 1:1037

The Dream of a Rarebit Fiend, 1:1174

The Dream of d'Alembert, 4:195

Dream of Fair to Middling Women, 1:439

A Dream of Governors, 1:1048

The Dream of Nation: A Social and Intellectual History of Quebec, 3:610

The Dream of Santa María de las Piedras, 2:872, 2:873

The Dream of Success: A Study of the Modern American Imagination, 1:918

The Dream of the Golden Mountains: Remembering the 1930s, 1:822

The Dream of the Red Chamber, 2:185, 2:188, 2:218, 2:223, 2:229

The Dream of the Rood, 1:142

A Dream of Wings: Americans and the Airplane, 1875–1905, 5:46

Dream on Monkey Mountain and Other Plays, 2:943

Dream Palaces: Malcolm, The Nephew and 63 Dream Palace, 1:1034

A Dream Play, 2:679

A Dream Play and Four Chamber Plays, 2:680

Dreams and Delusions: National Socialism in the Drama of the German Past, 3:378

Dreams and Delusions: The Drama of German History, 3:378

Dreams and Discourses: Sueños y discursos, 2:548

Dreams and Symbols: Man's Unconscious Language, 5:462

Dreams and the Unconscious in Nineteenth-Century Russian Fiction, 2:687

The Dream Sellers: Perspectives on Drug Dealers, 5:421

Dreams in the Mirror: A Biography of E. E. Cummings, 1:826

The Dream Sleepers, 2:976

Dreams of a Final Theory, 5:665, 5:718

Dreams of Amazonia, 3:634, 3:897

Dreams of Equality: Women on the Canadian Left, 1920–1950, 3:609

Dreams of Leaving, 1:493

The Dreams of Our Generation and Selections from Beijing's People, 2:240

Dreams of Reason: Science and Utopias, 5:795

The Dreams of Reason: The Computer and the Rise of the Sciences of Complexity, 5:573

The Dreams of Scheherazade, 2:74

"Dreams of the Sea," 2:267

The Dream Songs, 1:949, 1:950

Dream Tales and Prose Poems, 2:769

Dreamtigers, 2:855, 2:856

Dreamtime, 4:430

Dream Visions and Other Selected Stories, 2:835

Dred: A Tale of the Great Dismal Swamp, 1:698

The Dred Scott Case: Its Significance in American Law and Politics, 3:527

Dreiser, 1:831

Dreiser and His Fiction: A Twentieth Century Quest, 1:830

Dress and Gender, 3:207

Dress and Popular Culture, 3:872

Dressed in Light, 2:794

The Dreyfus Case: A Documentary History, 3:351

Drift toward Dissolution: The Virginia Slavery Debate of 1831–1832, 3:524

Drinking in America, 3:552

Drive It Forever: Your Key to Long Automobile Life, 5:248

The Drivers, 2:754

The Driver's Seat, 1:551

Drives toward War, 3:195

Droppings from Heaven, 2:917

The Drowned and the Saved, 2:425

The Drowning of an Old Cat and Other Stories, 2:248

Drowning with Others, 1:967

Drudgery Divine, 4:490, 4:491

Drug Discovery: The Evolution of Modern Medicines, 5:352

Drug Interactions Guide Book, 5:351

Drug Policy in the Americas, 3:632

Drugs and Foods from Little-Known Plants, 5:350

Drugs and People, 5:350

Drugs and Society: A Biological Perspective, 5:352

Drugs from A to Z: A Dictionary, 5:423

Drugs in America: A Social History, 1800–1980, 3:553

The Drugstore Cat, 1:1030

The Druids, 4:436

The Drummer Boy, 2:135, 2:136

Drummin' Men, the Heartbeat of Jazz, the Swing Years, 3:669

Drums at Dusk, 1:816

The Drums of Affliction, 3:40

The Drums of Father Ned, 1:526

The Drunken Boat, 2:499

A Drunk Man Looks at the Thistle, 1:516

Drury's Guide to Best Plays, 1:123

Dryden, 1:242

Dryden: The Critical Heritage, 1:242

Dryden and His Poetry, 1:242

Dryden in Revolutionary England, 1:241

Dryden's Aeneid: The English Virgil, 1:241

Dryden's Poetry, 1:242

Dry Valley, 2:707

A Dry White Season, 2:159

Du'a al-Qayrawan, 2:74

Dubin's Lives, 1:1013

Dubious Maternal Affection, 5:471

Dubliners, 1:503, 1:504

Dublin's Trade in Books, 1550–1800, 1:37

Dublin University Magazine, 1:601

The Duchess of Malfi, 1:200

The Duck Hunt, 2:624

The Duck Variations, 1:1100, 1:1101

Duddy Kravitz, 2:924

The Duel, 2:732, 2:733

The Duel and Other Stories, 2:708

Due to Circumstances beyond Our Control, 3:811

Dugard of Rouen, 3:612

Duino Elegies, 2:607

The Duke, 2:872

Duke Ellington, Jazz Composer, 3:695

Duke Ellington in Person: An Intimate Memoir, 3:694

The Duke Longitudinal Studies of Normal Aging, 1955–1980, 5:316

The Duke of Newcastle, 3:361

The Duke's Children, 1:405

The Duke University Medical Center Book of Arthritis, 5:398

Dulay, 1:1097

Dulles, 3:539

Duluth, 1:1062

Dumping: A Problem in International Trade, 3:110, 3:111

Duncan Campbell Scott: A Book of Criticism, 2:926

Duncan Campbell Scott: Selected Poetry, 2:926

Dunciad, 1:252

Dune, 1:1259, 1:1263

Dune Master: A Frank Herbert Bibliography, 1:1259

Dune Messiah, 1:1259

The Dunne Family, 1:833

Duplicate Keys, 1:1050

The Durham Report and British Policy: A Critical Essay, 3:613

Durkheim, Bernard and Epistemology, 5:789

Durkheim's Sociology of Religion, 3:225

Dürrenmatt: Reinterpretation in Retrospect, 2:577

Dusklands, 2:160

The Dusk of Dawn: An Essay toward an Autobiography of a Race Concept, 1:832, 3:577

Dusk on the Campo: A Journey in Patagonia, 3:897

The Dust Bowl: An Agricultural and Social History, 3:548

Dust Bowl: The Southern Plains in the 1930s, 5:825

Dust Tracks on a Road: An Autobiography, 1:850

Dutch Anabaptism, 4:780

Dutch Calvinism in Modern America, 4:752

Dutch Civilization in the Seventeenth Century and Other Essays, 3:382

The Dutch Courtesan, 1:187, 1:188

Dutch-English, English-Dutch Dictionary, 1:98

Dutch-English Dictionary, 1:98

The Dutch Lover, 1:232

Dutchman, 1:1085

Dutchman and The Slave: Two Plays, 1:1085
The Dutch Republic and the Civilization of the Seventeenth Century, 3:336, 3:383
The Dutch Republic in the Eighteenth Century, 3:338, 3:382
The Dutch Revolt, 4:732
Dutch Schools of New Netherland and Colonial New York, 3:264
The Dutch Seaborne Empire, 1600–1800, 3:335, 3:382
Dutch Uncle, 1:486
Duties of the Heart by R. Bachya ibn Paquda, 4:630
The Duty of Genius, 4:346
Dvořák, 3:693
Dvořák: His Life and Times, 3:693
Dvořák in Love, 2:794
The Dwarf, 2:675, 2:676
Dwellers in the Land: The Bioregional Vision, 5:824
Dwell in the Wilderness: Selected Short Stories (1931–1941), 2:334
The Dybbuk: A Play, 2:35
The Dybbuk and Other Writings, 2:35, 4:657
The Dyer's Hand, 1:434, 1:435
Dying at Home: A Family Guide for Caregiving, 5:379
A Dying Colonialism, 2:121
The Dying Gaul and Other Writings, 1:502
Dying to Please: Anorexia Nervosa and Its Cure, 5:395
Dylan Thomas, 1:557
Dylan Thomas: A Reference Guide, 1:557
Dylan Thomas: In the Mercy of His Means, 1:557
Dylan Thomas: The Country of the Spirit, 1:557
Dylan Thomas in America, 1:557
Dynamical Theory of Crystal Lattices, 5:675
Dynamic Genome: Barbara McClintock's Ideas in the Century of Genetics, 5:806
Dynamic International Oil Markets, 5:281
Dynamic Judaism: The Essential Writings of Mordecai M. Kaplan, 4:667

Dynamic Meteorology and Hydrography, 5:641
The Dynamic of Social Movements, 3:215
The Dynamic Planet, 5:616
Dynamic Probabilistic Models and Social Structure, 3:215
The Dynamics of Aging, 5:316
Dynamics of Atmospheric Flight, 5:219
The Dynamics of Biblical Parallelism, 4:823
The Dynamics of Bureaucracy, 3:210
The Dynamics of Culture Change, 3:35
The Dynamics of Educational Change, 3:262
The Dynamics of Folklore, 3:849
Dynamics of Growth in a Finite World, 5:167, 5:168
The Dynamics of Mass Communication, 3:801, 3:803
The Dynamics of Medieval Iceland: Political Economy and Literature, 3:381
Dynamics of Ocean Tides, 5:632
The Dynamics of Science and Technology, 5:26, 5:214
The Dynamics of Social Systems, 3:215
The Dynamics of Technical Controversy, 5:155, 5:214
A Dynamic Theory of Personality, 3:189
The Dynamic Universe: An Introduction to Astronomy, 5:589
Dynamism in the Cosmology of Christian Wolff, 4:219
The Dynasts, 1:360
A Dynasty of Love, 1:619
The Dyskolos, 2:364

E

Each in His Darkness, 2:482
Each in His Own Way, 2:435
Eagle against the Sun: The American War with Japan, 3:536
The Eagle and the Lion, 3:447
Eagle or Sun? 2:878
The Eagle with Two Heads, 2:468

Earle Birney and His Works, 2:907
Earlier Philosophical Writings, 4:187
The Earlier Seventeenth Century, 1:166
The Earliest English Poems, 1:143
Earl Mindell's Herb Bible, 5:320
Earl Mindell's Vitamin Bible, 5:346
The Earl of Beaconsfield, 3:403
The Earl of Louisiana, 3:814
Early American Almanac Humor, 3:870
Early American Architecture, 3:763
Early American Bookbinding from the Collection of Michael Papantonio, 1:23
Early American Books and Printing, 1:12, 1:37, 1:39
Early American Jewry, 4:640
Early American Literature: A Collection of Critical Essays, 1:628
Early American Philosophers, 4:34
Early American Poetry, 1:630
Early American Proverbs and Proverbial Sayings, 1:115
Early Americans, 3:520, 3:569
Early American Scientific and Technical Literature, 5:27
Early American Sheet Music, 1768–1889, 3:659
Early American Taverns: Entertainment of Friends and Strangers, 3:518
Early American Women Printers and Publishers: 1639–1820, 1:38
Early Arabic Drama, 2:55
Early Arianism: A View of Salvation, 4:685
Early Auden, 1:436
Early Biblical Interpretation, 4:814
Early Bindings in Paper, 1:22
Early Bookbinding Manuals, 1:26
The Early Career of Malcolm Cowley: A Humanist Among the Moderns, 1:823
Early Christian and Byzantine Political Philosophy, 4:692
The Early Christian Attitude to War, 4:688

Early Christian Creeds, 4:686
The Early Christian Doctrine of God, 4:99
Early Christian Doctrines, 4:686
Early Christian Fathers, 4:680
Early Christianity, 4:681
Early Christianity and Greek Paideia, 4:63, 4:683
Early Christian Spirituality, 4:689
Early Christian Thought and the Classical Tradition: Studies in Justin, Clement, and Origen, 4:99, 4:685
Early Christian Thoughts and the Classical Tradition, 4:63
Early Christian Writings: The Apostolic Fathers, 4:704
The Early Church and the State, 4:683
The Early Church to the Dawn of the Reformation, 4:677
Early Cooper and His Audience, 1:665
The Early Days of Joel Barlow, A Connecticut Wit, 1:633
Early Democracies in the Low Countries, 3:333, 3:380, 3:407
The Early Development of Mohammedanism, 4:571
The Early Diary of Anais Nin: Vol. 1, 1914–1920, 1:865
The Early Editions of Arthur Hugh Clough, 1:345
Early Editions of Euclid's Elements, 5:505
Early English Drama: An Anthology, 1:161
Early English Lyrics, 1:148
Early English Prose Romances, 3:888
Early English Stages, 1:158, 1:170
Early Essays, 4:312
The Early Fathers on War and Military Service, 4:689
Early Gentile Christianity and Its Hellenistic Background, 4:487
Early German Philosophy: Kant and His Predecessors, 4:209, 4:219
Early Gothic Manuscripts, 3:767
Early Greece, 3:302
Early Greek Astronomy to Aristotle, 4:48, 5:38

Early Greek Elegists, 2:344
Early Greek Philosophy, 4:50
Early Greek Poetry and Philosophy, 2:345
Early Greek Science: Thales to Aristotle, 5:38
Early Greek Thinking: The Dawn of Western Philosophy, 4:50, 4:291
The Early Growth of the European Economy, 3:328
The Early H. G. Wells: A Study of the Scientific Romances, 1:564
Early Hellenistic Coinage from the Accession of Alexander to the Peace of Apamaea (336–188 B.C.), 3:306
Early History of Charles James Fox, 3:410
The Early History of God: Yahweh and the Other Deities in Ancient Israel, 4:824
Early History of Human Anatomy, 5:34
The Early History of Rome, 3:317
The Early History of the Ancient Near East, 9000–2000 B.C., 4:434, 4:441
Early History of Zionism in America, 4:658
The Early Illustrated Book: Essays in Honor of Lessing J. Rosenwald, 1:28
Early in the Summer of 1970, 2:26
Early Islam, 4:573
The Early Islamic Conquests, 4:568
The Early Italian Poets, 1:391, 2:402
Early Joys, 2:718
Early Judaism and Its Modern Interpreters, 4:615, 4:814
The Early Kabbalah, 4:630
The Early Life of Ou-yang Hsiu and His Relation to the Rise of the Ku-wen Movement of the Sung Dynasty, 2:215
Early Life of William Wordsworth, 1770–1798, 1:307
The Early Liturgy to the Time of Gregory the Great, 4:689
Early Man in China, 4:336

Early Medieval Philosophy, 480–1150: An Introduction, 4:94
Early Medieval Spain: Unity in Diversity, 3:400–1000, 3:386
Early Mesopotamia and Iran, 3:301
The Early Middle Ages, 2:272
Early Middle English Verse and Prose, 1:147
Early Modern Europe, 1500–1789, 3:336
Early Modern France, 1560–1715, 3:372
Early Morning, 1:445, 1:446
The Early Motion Pictures, 3:826
Early Netherlandish Painting, 3:760
Early Nineteenth-Century Diary Literature, 1:660
The Early Novel of the Southwest, 1819–1918, 1:723
Early Novels and Stories, 1:821
Early One Morning, 1:467
Early Philosophical Writings, 4:198
The Early Plays: Slag, the Great Exhibition, Teeth 'n' Smiles, 1:493
Early Plays from the Italian, 2:402
Early Poems of Walter Savage Landor, 1:296
The Early Poetry, 1:571
Early Pythagorean Politics in Practice and Theory, 4:87
The Early Reception of Berkeley, 1710–1733, 4:191
Early Rome and the Etruscans, 3:303
Early Russian Literature, 2:686
The Early Spanish Ballad, 2:526
The Early Spanish Main, 3:630
Early Sparta, 2:346
Early Spring, 2:649
Early Stationary Steam Engines in America, 5:55
Early Stevens: The Nietzschean Intertext, 1:888
Early Thematic Mapping in the History of Cartography, 3:135
Early Theological Writings, 4:232

Early Thomistic School, 4:119

The Early Universe: Facts and Fictions, 5:656

The Early Vasas: A History of Sweden, 1523–1611, 4:731

The Early Versions of the New Testament, 4:806

Early Victorian Government, 1830–1870, 3:364

Early Warnings: Three Related Short Plays, 1:1114

The Early Window: The Effects of Television on Children and Youth, 3:812

Earnest Atheist: A Study of Samuel Butler, 1:342

The Earnest Men: Republicans of the Civil War Senate, 3:526

The Ear of the Other, 4:397

Ears and Tales and Commonsense: More Stories from the Caribbean, 2:931

Earth (Press), 5:624

The Earth (Zola), 2:518

The Earth: An Introduction to the Geological and Geophysical Sciences, 5:623

Earth and Man, 3:130

Earth and Other Ethics, 5:76, 5:142

Earth and Sky: Visions of the Cosmos in Native American Folklore, 3:866

Earth and the Human Future: Essays in Honour of Harrison Brown, 5:292

The Earth as Transformed by Human Action, 5:825

Earth beneath the Sea, 5:632

Earthbound, 2:796

Earthbound: New Introductory Essays in Environmental Ethics, 5:76, 5:116

The Earthbreakers, 1:1214

Earth Erect, 2:832

Earth Follies, 5:116

Earth Horizon, 1:726, 1:732, 1:733

Earth House Hold, 1:1052

Earth in the Balance: Ecology and the Human Spirit, 3:206, 5:822

The Earth in the Looking Glass, 5:629

The Earth Is the Lord's: The Inner World of the Jew in Eastern Europe, 4:664

Earth Journal, 1993: Environmental Almanac and Resource Directory, 5:815

Earthkeeping in the Nineties: Stewardship and Creation, 4:746, 5:199

Earth Life. 1985, 1:1189

Earthlike Planets: Surfaces of Mercury, Venus, Earth, Moon, and Mars, 5:593

Earthly Delights, Unearthly Adornments, 1:1017

The Earthly Paradise, 2:383, 2:644

Earthly Powers, 1:453

The Earthly Republic: Italian Humanists on Government and Society, 4:127

Earth Might Be Fair: Reflections on Ethics, Religion and Ecology, 5:160

Earthquake Country: California, 5:629

Earthquake Interpretations: A Manual for Reading Seismograms, 5:630

Earthquakes, Volcanoes, and Tsunamis: Anatomy of Hazards, 5:625

The Earth Sciences: An Annotated Bibliography, 5:29

Earth's Energy and Mineral Resources, 5:637

Earth Shelter Technology, 5:225

Earth's History, Structure, and Materials, 5:625

The Earth's Problem Climates, 5:634

The Earth We Live On, 5:624

East Africa and Its Invaders, 3:422

East and West, 2:761

East Angels, 1:790

East Asia: The Modern Transformation, 4:358

East Asia: Tradition and Transformation, 2:186, 3:464, 3:498, 3:501

East Asian Civilizations: A Dialogue in Five Stages, 3:464, 4:523

The East Asian Region: Confucian Heritage and Its Modern Adaptation, 3:465

East Central Europe between the Two World Wars, 3:389

The Eastern Buddhist, 4:557

The Eastern Establishment and the Western Experience, 1:789

Eastern Europe, 1740–1985: Feudalism to Communism, 3:389

Eastern Life, Present and Past, 1:376

Eastern Religions and Western Thought, 4:353

The Eastern Schism, 4:694

The Easter Party, 1:542

The Easter Rebellion, 3:370

East German Poetry: An Anthology, 2:566

East India Fortunes: The British in Bengal in the Eighteenth Century, 3:362

East Is East, 1:952, 1:953

East Meets West: The Jesuits in China, 1582–1773, 3:468, 4:532

East of Eden (Singer), 2:49

East of Eden (Steinbeck), 1:884

East River, 2:35

East Side General, 1:1223

East to West: A Journey Round the World, 3:293

Eastward Ha! 1:868

Easy Chair, 3:576

Eating Chiefs, 2:152, 2:153

Eating for Two: The Complete Guide to Nutrition during Pregnancy, 5:358

Eating People Is Wrong, 1:448

Eat to Win: The Sports Nutrition Bible, 5:346

Ebla: A New Look at History, 4:445

Ebony Pictorial History of Black America, 3:506

The Ebony Tower, 1:478

E. B. White: Some Writer!, 1:898

E. B. White Boxed Set, 1:1208

Eça de Queiróz and European Realism, 2:559

Ecce Homo, 4:246

The Eccentric Design: Form in the Classic American Novel, 1:722

Eccentric Travelers, 3:892

Ecclesiastical Authority and Spiritual Power in the Church of the First Three Centuries, 4:690

Ecclesiastical History, 4:709

Ecclesiastical History of the English People, 1:141

Echad: An Anthology of Latin American Jewish Writings, 2:849

Echo and Narcissus: Women's Voices in Classical Hollywood Cinema, 3:827

Echo at Coole and Other Poems, 1:460

Echoes: After Heidegger, 4:294

Echoes from Vagabondia, 2:908

Echoes of Iranian Revolution: Poems of Revolt and Liberation, 1979, 2:84

Echoes of the Ancient Skies: The Astronomy of Lost Civilizations, 5:590

The Echoing Green, 1:797, 2:986

The Echoing Wood of Theodore Roethke, 1:1038

The Echo of Greece, 2:345

The Eclipse of a Great Power: Modern Britain, 1870–1975, 3:364

The Eclipse of Biblical Narrative, 4:739

The Eclipse of Community: An Interpretation of American Studies, 3:217

The Eclipse of Darwinism, 5:763

The Eclogues, 1:511, 2:396, 2:397

Ecocide in the USSR: Health and Nature under Siege, 5:353

Ecodynamics: A New Theory of Societal Evolution, 3:71

Ecolinking: Everyone's Guide to Online Environmental Information, 5:547, 5:816

Ecological Economics: Energy, Environment, and Society, 5:823

Ecological Ethics and Politics, 4:389, 5:115

An Ecological History of Agriculture, 10,000 B.C.–A.D. 10,000, 5:265

Ecological Imperialism: The Biological Expansion of Europe, 900–1900, 5:820

Ecological Literacy, 5:115

Ecological Revolutions: Nature, Gender, and Science in New England, 3:550

The Ecological Spirituality of Teilhard, 4:337

The Ecological Web, 5:819

Ecology, Community, and Lifestyle: Outline of an Ecosophy, 5:115

Ecology, Economics, Ethics: The Broken Circle, 3:47

Ecology, Impact Assessment, and Environmental Planning, 5:821

Ecology, Meaning and Religion, 3:24

Ecology and Evolution of Darwin's Finches, 5:764

Ecology and History: The Greening of the West since 1880, 5:819

The Ecology of Agricultural Systems, 5:262

The Ecology of Fossils: An Illustrated Guide, 5:639

The Ecology of North America, 5:821

The Ecology of School Renewal, 3:262, 3:263

The Ecology of the Ancient Greek World, 3:308

An Ecology of the Spirit, 4:507, 4:509

The Econometric Analysis of Time Series, 3:63

An Econometric Model of the United States, 1929–52, 3:87, 3:88

Economic Analysis, 3:71

Economic Analysis of Law, 3:61

Economic and Demographic Change in Preindustrial Japan, 1600–1868, 3:475

Economic and Medical Evaluation of Health Care Technologies, 5:324

Economic and Social History of Ancient Greece: An Introduction, 3:307

Economic and Social History of Medieval Europe, 3:331, 3:407

Economic and Social History of Quebec, 1760–1850, 3:613

Economic Anthropology and Development, 3:16

The Economic Approach to Human Behavior, 3:70

Economic Basis of Politics, 3:565

Economic Change, 3:90

Economic Change in Precolonial Africa: Senegambia in the Era of the Slave Trade, 3:426

Economic Change in Precolonial Africa: Supplementary Evidence, 3:426

Economic Change in Thailand 1850–1970, 3:490

The Economic Consequences of the Peace, 3:86, 3:87

Economic Development, the Family and Income Distribution, 3:53, 3:66, 3:90

Economic Development and Regional Cooperation: Kuwait, 3:451

The Economic Development of Japan, 3:478

Economic Doctrines of Islam, 3:442

The Economic Doctrines of Knut Wicksell, 3:115

Economic Essays Contributed in Honor of John Bates Clark, 3:73

Economic Geography (Alexander), 5:619

Economic Geography (Hartshorn), 3:122

Economic Growth and Structure, 3:90

Economic Growth in Prewar Japan, 3:479

Economic Growth of Nations, 3:53, 3:90

Economic History, 3:83

The Economic History of Eastern Europe, 1919–1975, 3:389

An Economic History of Europe since 1750, 5:57

Economic History of Iran, 1800–1914, 3:448

An Economic History of Ireland since 1660, 3:369

An Economic History of Modern Spain, 3:387

The Economic History of Scotland, 3:368

Economic History of the Jews, 4:593

The Economic History of the Maritime Provinces, 3:607

The Economic History of the Middle East: A Book of Readings, 3:436

An Economic History of the Middle East and North Africa, 3:436

An Economic History of the USSR, 3:397

The Economic History of Turkey, 1800–1914, 3:453

An Economic History of West Africa, 3:420

Economic Imperialism in China, 3:470

Economic Inequality and Poverty, 3:66

Economic Integration and Planning in Maoist China, 3:471

An Economic Interpretation of the Constitution of the United States, 3:141, 3:542, 3:565

Economic Mineral Deposits, 5:636

Economic Origins of the Iranian Revolution, 3:448

Economic Perspectives: Further Essays on Money and Growth, 3:84

Economic Philosophy, 3:102

Economic Policies toward Less Developed Countries, 3:53

Economic Policy in Postwar Japan: Growth versus Economic Democracy, 3:480

Economic Reforms in New Democracies, 3:143

Economics, 3:46, 3:103

Economics: An Awkward Corner, 3:102

Economics: Principles and Practices, 3:45

Economics and Antitrust Policy, 3:61

Economics and the Public Purpose, 3:78, 3:79

Economics as a Science, 3:46, 3:71

Economic Semantics, 3:47

Economics in Perspective: A Critical History, 3:79

The Economics of Adam Smith, 3:107

The Economics of Aging, 3:60

The Economics of Alfred Marshall, 3:94

The Economics of Being Poor, 3:66

Economics of Book Publishing in Developing Countries, 1:48

The Economics of Cuban Sugar, 3:636

The Economics of David Ricardo, 3:101

The Economics of Discrimination, 3:70

The Economics of Energy, 5:285

The Economics of Health, 3:57

The Economics of Human Betterment, 3:71

The Economics of Imperfect Competition, 3:58, 3:102

The Economics of John Hicks, 3:84

The Economics of John Stuart Mill, 3:97

Economics of Labor in Industrial Society, 3:60

The Economics of Oligopolistic Competition: Price and Nonprice Rivalry, 3:57

Economics of Power System Reliability and Planning, 5:292

The Economics of Regulation: Principles and Institutions, 3:57

The Economics of Supply and Demand, 3:88

The Economics of the Environment, 3:48

Economics of the Mishnah, 4:606

The Economics of Vilfredo Pareto, 3:100

An Economic Survey of Ancient Rome, 3:307

Economic Survey of the Book Industry 1930–1931, 1:49

Economic Theory and Econometrics, 3:88

Economic Theory and Operations Analysis, 3:48

Economic Theory and Underdeveloped Regions, 3:98

Economic Theory in Retrospect, 3:45, 3:96

An Economic Theory of Democracy, 3:67, 3:142

Economic Thought: A Historical Anthology, 3:45, 3:85

Economic Thought and the Problem of the Unity of the World, 3:287

The Economic Value of Education, 3:56, 3:57

Économie et société en Nouvelle-France, 3:620

The Economist: Henry Thoreau and Enterprise, 1:702

The Economist as Preacher and Other Essays, 3:108

Economist Atlas, 1:84

The Economists, 3:72, 3:91, 3:104

The Economist's Economist, 3:84

Economy and Society in Scotland and Ireland, 1500–1939, 3:368

The Economy of British America, 1607–1789, 3:548

The Economy of Colonial America, 3:548

The Economy of Early Renaissance Europe, 1300–1460, 3:333

The Economy of Earth: Philosophy, Law, and the Environment, 5:824

Economy of Europe in an Age of Crisis: 1600–1750, 3:338

The Economy of the Earth, 5:76

The Economy Spinning Faster and Faster, 2:672

Eco-Philosophy, 4:38

Ecophilosophy: A Field Guide to the Literature, 5:815

Ecoscience, Population, Resources, Environment, 5:292

Eco-Spirituality: Toward a Reverent Life, 4:888

Ecrits: A Selection, 1:1132, 5:458

Écrivains Noirs, 2:108

Ecstasies: Deciphering the Witches' Sabbath, 4:431

Ecstasy: Shamanism in Korea, 4:539

Ecstatic Antibodies: Resisting the AIDS Mythology, 3:201

Ecstatic Religion, 4:431

Ecuador: An Andean Enigma, 3:636

Edda, 2:643

Eddie the Coal City Boy, 2:140

Eddington: The Most Distinguished Astrophysicist of His Time, 5:603

Eddington's Statistical Theory, 5:681

Eden, 2:816

The Eden Express, 5:424

Edgar A. Poe: Mournful and Never-ending Remembrance, 1:1047

Edgar Allan Poe, 1:693

Edgar Allan Poe: A Bibliography of Criticism, 1827–1967, 1:693

Edgar Allan Poe: A Study of the Short Fiction, 1:693

Edgar Allan Poe: The Critical Heritage, 1:693

Edgar Allan Poe: The Design of Order, 1:693

Edgar Allan Poe as Literary Critic, 1:693

An Edgar Allan Poe Companion, 1:693

Edgar Huntly, 1:635, 1:636, 1:1239

Edgar Huntly: Memoirs of a Sleep Walker, 1:635

Edgar Lee Masters, 1:859

Edgar Lee Masters: A Biographical Sketchbook about a Great American Author, 1:859
Edgar Lee Masters: The Spoon River Poet and His Critics, 1:859
Edgar Rice Burroughs, 1:1256
The Edge Is What I Have: Theodore Roethke and After, 1:1038
The Edge of Infinity, 5:595
The Edge of Objectivity: An Essay in the History of Scientific Ideas, 5:25
The Edge of the Alphabet, 2:974
The Edge of the Sea, 5:631, 5:829
The Edge of the Storm, 2:888
The Edge of the Swamp, 1:779
Edging Women Out: Victorian Novelists, Publishers, and Social Change, 1:320
Edible Wild Mushrooms of North America: A Field to Kitchen Guide, 5:759
The Edible Woman, 2:906
The Edifice, 2:143
Edifying Discourses, 4:238
The Edinburgh Review, 1:323
Edison, 5:252
Edison: A Biography, 5:226
Edison: The Man Who Made the Future, 5:252
Edison and His Invention Factory, 5:252
Edison's Electric Light: Biography of an Invention, 5:229
Edith Sitwell: A Unicorn among Lions, 1:548
Edith Sitwell: The Symbolist Order, 1:548
Edith Södergran: Modernist Poet in Finland, 2:661
Edith Stein: A Biography, 4:744
Edith Wharton, 1:788
Edith Wharton: A Biography, 1:788, 1:1004
Edith Wharton: A Collection of Critical Essays, 1:788
Edith Wharton: A Critical Interpretation, 1:788
Edith Wharton: An Annotated Bibliography, 1:788
Edith Wharton: A Study of Her Fiction, 1:788

Edith Wharton: A Study of the Short Fiction, 1:789
Edith Wharton: Traveller in the Land of Letters, 1:788
Edith Wharton and Kate Chopin: A Reference Guide, 1:740
Edith Wharton and the Art of Fiction, 1:788
Edith Wharton's Argument with America, 1:788
Edith Wharton's Women: Friends and Rivals, 1:788
Editing Illustrated Books, 1:46
Editing of Emily Dickinson: A Reconsideration, 1:747
The Editorial Problem in Shakespeare, 1:207
The Editor's Choice: New American Stories, 1:921
Editor's Choice III, 1:921
Editors on Editing, 1:49
Edmond, 1:1100, 1:1101
Edmund Burke, 3:152
Edmund Burke: A Genius Reconsidered, 3:152
Edmund Burke: His Political Philosophy, 4:193
Edmund Burke: Prescription and Providence, 3:152
Edmund Burke and His Literary Friends, 3:152
Edmund Husserl: Philosopher of Infinite Tasks, 4:235
Edmund Husserl's "Origin of Geometry," 4:397
Edmund Husserl's Phenomenological Psychology, 4:235
Edmund Husserl's Phenomenology: A Critical Commentary, 4:235
Edmund L. Epstein, 1:505
Edmund Spenser, 1:198
Edmund Spenser: Protestant Poet, 1:198
Edmund Wilson, 1:902
Edmund Wilson: A Critic for Our Time, 1:903
Edmund Wilson's America, 1:902
Edna St. Vincent Millay, 1:861
Eduard Mörike: The Man and the Poet, 2:603
Educated Guessing: How to Cope in an Uncertain World, 5:522
Educated in Romance: Women, Achievement, and College Culture, 3:250, 3:255

Educating for Character, 3:251
Education, 3:269
The Educational Imagination, 3:254
Educational Psychology, 3:269
Educational Psychology: Theory into Practice, 3:257
Educational Rankings: Annual, 1:82
Education and Civilization, 4:284
Education and Culture in the Political Thought of Aristotle, 4:69
Education and Economic Productivity, 3:57
Education and the Democratic Ideal, 3:249
Education and the Significance of Life, 4:554
Education at the Crossroads, 4:306
Education for a Changing Civilization, 3:264
Education for Critical Consciousness, 3:262
Education for Freedom: The Philosophy of Education of Jacques Maritain, 4:307
Education for Peace: Issues, Principles, and Practice in the Classroom, 3:279
Education for Transformation, 5:172
Education Index, 3:254
Education in the Age of Science, 4:276
Education in the Forming of American Society, 1:627, 3:564
Education in Tokugawa Japan, 3:474
Education of a Christian Prince, 4:139
The Education of an Editor, 1:49
Education of a Wandering Man, 1:1216
The Education of Children, 5:430
The Education of Desire: Marxists and the Writing of History, 3:276
The Education of Free Man, 3:265
The Education of Henry Adams, 1:729
The Education of Man: Educational Philosophy, 4:306

The Education of Mrs. Henry Adams, 3:560, 3:563
The Education of T. C. Mits, 5:496
The Education of the Human Race, 4:208
Education of the Individual, 5:430
Education Today, 3:260
An Educator's Guide to Psychological Tests, 5:414
Edvard Grieg: The Man and the Artist, 3:698
Edward Albee, 1:1081
Edward Albee: An Annotated Bibliography, 1968–1977, 1:1081
Edward Bellamy, 1:734
Edward Bellamy: A Bibliography, 1:734
Edward Bellamy: An Annotated Bibliography of Secondary Criticism, 1:734
Edward Bellamy Abroad, 1:734
Edward Bond, 1:446
Edward Bond: A Companion to the Plays, 1:446
Edward Bulwer, First Baron Lytton of Knebworth, 1:340
Edward Bulwer-Lytton, 1:340
Edward Elgar: A Creative Life, 3:694
Edward Evans-Pritchard, 3:29
Edward FitzGerald's Salaman and Absal, 4:585
An Edwardian Childhood, 3:343
Edwardian Occasions: Essays on English Writing in the Twentieth Century, 1:429
The Edwardians, 1:542
The Edwardians: The Remaking of British Society, 3:367
Edwardians and Late Victorians: Essays of the English Institute, 1:974
Edward Jenner—The Cheltenham Years, 1795–1823, 5:390
Edward Johnston, 1:42
Edward Lear: King of Nonsense, 1:586
Edward Philip Prince: Type Punchcutter, 1:13
Edward R. Murrow: An American Original, 3:819
The Edward R. Murrow Heritage: Challenge for the Future, 3:809

Edward Sapir: Appraisals of His Life and Work, 3:40
Edward Sapir: Linguist, Anthropologist, Humanist, 3:40
Edward Taylor, 1:644
Edward Taylor: An Annotated Bibliography, 1668–1970, 1:644
Edward the Dyke and Other Poems, 1:1187, 1:1188
Edward the Second, 1:186
Edward VI: The Threshold of Power, 4:726
Edward VI: The Young King, 3:359, 4:726
Edward Thomas, 1:558
Edward Thomas: A Critical Study, 1:558
Edward Thomas: A Poet for His Country, 1:558
Edward Thomas: A Portrait, 1:558
Edwin Arlington Robinson, 1:877
Edwin Arlington Robinson: A Critical Study, 1:877
Edwin Arlington Robinson: Stages in a New England Poet's Search, 1:877
Edwin Chadwick, Poor Laws and Public Health, 1:345
Edwin Hubble: The Discoverer of the Big Bang Universe, 5:607
Edwin Muir, 1:522
Edwin Muir: A Master of Modern Poetry, 1:522
Edwin Muir: An Introduction to His Work, 1:522
E. E. Cummings, 1:826
Een Zwerver Verdwaald, 2:630
Een Zwerver Verliefd, 2:630
Eerdmans' Handbook to Christian Belief, 4:718
Eerdmans' Handbook to Christianity in America, 4:751
Eerdmans' Handbook to the History of Christianity, 4:676, 4:720, 4:743
Eerdman's Handbook to the World Religions, 4:520
The Effective Reference Librarian, 1:81
The Effect of Gamma Rays on Man-in-the-Moon Marigolds, 1:1122, 1:1123
The Effects of Cross and Self-Fertilisation in the Vegetable Kingdom, 5:793
Effi Briest, 2:578

E for Environment, 5:816
E. Franklin Frazier Reconsidered, 3:226
Efuru, 2:139, 2:140
The Egalitarians, Human and Chimpanzee, 3:172
An Egg at Easter: A Folklore Study, 3:869
Egil's Saga, 2:643
Ego, Hunger, and Aggression, 5:464
The Ego and the Id, 5:445
The Ego and the Mechanisms of Defense, 3:183
The Egoist, 1:297, 1:378
Egotism in German Philosophy, 4:29, 4:326
The Egotistical Sublime: A History of Wordsworth's Imagination, 1:307
Egypt, 3:445
Egypt: Portrait of a President—Sadat's Road to Jerusalem, 3:446
Egypt, 1798–1952: Her Advance toward Modern Identity, 3:446
Egypt and the Fertile Crescent, 1516–1922: A Political History, 3:419, 3:446
The Egyptian, 2:661
The Egyptian Army in Politics, 3:446
An Egyptian Childhood, 2:74
Egyptian Earth, 2:59
The Egyptian Economy, 1952–1972, 3:446
The Egyptian Gods: A Handbook, 4:548
An Egyptian Journal, 1:484
Egyptian Mythology, 4:548
Egyptian One-act Plays, 2:57
Egyptian Religion, 4:442, 4:548
The Egyptians, 3:300
Egyptian Short Stories, 2:57
The Egyptian Stamp, 2:737
Egyptian Tales and Short Stories of the 1970's and 1980's, 2:57
Egyptian Time, 3:446
Egypt in the Nineteenth Century, 3:445
Egypt in the Sudan, 1820–81, 3:419
The Egypt of Nasser and Sadat: The Political Economy of Two Regimes, 3:446
Egypt of the Pharoahs: An Introduction, 3:300
Egypt's Economic Potential, 3:445

Egypt's Liberal Experiment, 1922–1936, 3:445

Egypt's Uncertain Revolution under Nasser and Sadat, 3:445

Ehrenburg: An Attempt at a Literary Portrait, 2:717

Ehrengard, 2:649

Eichmann in Jerusalem: A Report of the Banality of Evil, 3:282, 3:347, 4:394

Eiger Dreams: Ventures among Men and Mountains, 3:909

Eight American Authors: A Review of Research and Criticism, 1:652, 1:725

Eight Black Horses, 1:1233

Eight Chinese Plays—from the 13th Century to the Present, 2:192

Eight Contemporary Poets, 1:417

Eight Cousins, 1:1198

Eight Days: An Elegy for Thomas Garrigue Masaryk, 2:794

1851, or, The Adventures of Mr. and Mrs. Sandbags, 1:377

Eighteen Forty-Eight: The British State and the Chartist Movement, 3:365

1800 Woodcuts by Thomas Bewick and His School, 1:28

1876, 1:1062

Eighteen Short Songs of the Bitter Motherland, 2:375

Eighteen Stories, 2:569

Eighteen Texts: Writings by Contemporary Greek Authors, 2:371

Eighteenth and Nineteenth Century American Drama, 1:1077

The Eighteenth Brumaire of Louis Bonaparte, 3:290

The Eighteenth Century: The Intellectual and Cultural Context of English Literature, 1:226

Eighteenth-Century Background, 1:226

Eighteenth-Century Encounters, 1:226

Eighteenth Century England, 1714 to 1784, 3:362

Eighteenth-Century English Literature, 1:227

Eighteenth Century Europe, 1700–1789, 3:338

Eighteenth-Century Philosophy, 4:159

Eighteenth-Century Satire, 1:226

The Eighteenth Century Short Title Catalogue, 1:66

Eighteenth-Century Women Poets: An Oxford Anthology, 1:227

The Eightfold Way, 5:690

Eight Great Hebrew Short Novels, 2:10

The Eighth Commandment, 1:1236

The Eighth Day, 1:898, 1:899

The Eighth Day of Creation, 5:778, 5:791, 5:813

The Eighth Day of the Week, 2:814

800-Cocaine, 5:403

Eight Issues in American History: Views and Counterviews, 3:593

Eight Little Piggies: Reflections in Natural History, 5:764

Eight Men, 1:906

Eight Philosophers of the Italian Renaissance, 4:30, 4:128

Eight Short, Short Stories and Sketches, 1:833

8 Steps to a Healthy Heart, 5:374

Eighty Appalachian Folk Songs, 3:852

Eighty Fairy Tales, 2:647

Eighty-four Charing Cross Road, 1:32

80 Years of Best Sellers, 1895–1975, 1:51

Eighty Years of Locke Scholarship, 1900–1980: A Bibliographic Guide, 4:180

Einstein, 5:682

Einstein: The Life and Times, 5:47, 5:683

Einstein: The Man and His Achievement, 5:683

Einstein and the Generations of Science, 5:661

Einstein and the History of General Relativity, 5:664

Einstein's Dream: The Search for a Unified Theory of the Universe, 5:665

Einstein's Legacy, 5:664, 5:715

Einstein's Theory of Relativity, 5:675, 5:682

Einstein's Universe, 5:664, 5:683

Eirik the Red and Other Icelandic Sagas, 2:640

Eisenhower: Soldier and President, 3:533

Eisenhower and the Cold War, 3:537

Eisenhower's Lieutenants, 3:536

Eisenstein on Disney, 1:1165

Eisenstein's Ivan the Terrible: A Neoformalist Analysis, 3:836

E Is for Evidence, 1:1229

Either and Me or "Just Relax," 3:886

E. J. Pratt and His Works, 2:923

El Aleph, 2:855

Elbow Room, 4:396

El Cid, 2:537

El Contemplado, 2:550

The Elder Edda, 2:642

Elderly Patients and Their Doctors, 5:316

The Elder Pitt: Earl of Chatham, 3:361

Elders and Betters, 1:462

Elders Living Alone: Frailty and the Perception of Choice, 3:201

The Elder Statesman, 1:472

El Diccionario del Espanol Chicano: The Dictionary of Chicano Spanish, 1:103

E. L. Doctorow: Essays and Conversations, 1:969

Eleanor Roosevelt: Volume One, 1884–1933, 3:534

Elective Affinities, 2:581

Electra, 2:355, 2:356, 2:367, 2:592

Electric City and Other Stories, 2:976

Electricity and Magnetism, 5:700

Electricity and Matter, 5:716

Electricity in the Seventeenth and Eighteenth Centuries, 5:731

Electricity Pricing, 5:292

Electric Language: A Philosophical Study of Word Processing, 5:561

Electric Waves, 5:694

Electron, 5:702

Electronic and Computer Music, 5:565

Electronic Communications, 5:300

Electronic Communications Systems: A Complete Course, 5:300

Electronic Communications Systems: Fundamentals through Advanced, 5:308

Electronic Communications Technology, 5:300

Electronic Communication Systems (Kennedy), 5:299

Electronic Communication Systems (Stanley), 5:300

The Electronic Cottage, 5:537

The Electronic Giant, 3:811

Electronic Hearth: Creating an American Television Culture, 5:205

Electronic Highways, 5:297

Electronic Illusions: A Skeptic's View of Our High-Tech Future, 5:574

Electronic Life: How to Think about Computers, 5:537

Electronic Music: A Listener's Guide, 3:666

The Electronic Nigger, 1:1086

The Electronic Oracle: Computer Models and Social Decisions, 5:168

Electronic Processes in Ionic Crystals, 5:704

Electronic Processes in Non-Crystalline Materials, 5:704

Electronic Structure, Properties, and the Periodic Law, 5:730

The Electronic Sweatshop, 5:572

Electronic Synthesis of Speech, 5:230

Electrons, Protons, Photons, Neutrons and Cosmic Rays, 5:702

Electrons and Holes in Semiconductors, 5:671

Elegiac Feelings American, 1:964

An Elegiac Poem on the Death of that Celebrated Divine and Eminent Servant of Jesus Christ the Reverend and Learned George Whitefield, 1:646

Elegies, 2:392

The Elegies, and the Songs and Sonnets, 1:178

Elegy for a Lady, 1:1104

Elegy on the Death of a Mad Dog, 1:580

Elegy Written in a Country Churchyard, 1:248

The Elementary Forms of the Religious Life, 3:23, 3:212, 3:225, 4:425

Elementary Logic, 4:411

Elementary Meteorology, 5:643

Elementary Number Theory, 5:488

Elementary Order: Mendeleev's Periodic System, 5:750

Elementary Particle Physics, 5:662

Elementary Particle Physics of TASI Lecture '84, 5:662

Elementary Physical Geography, 5:643

Elementary Principles in Statistical Mechanics, 5:746

Elementary Quantum Mechanics, 5:704

The Elementary School Library Collection, 1:74

Elementary Statistics for Geographers, 3:119

Elementary Structures of Kinship, 3:20, 3:33

Elementary Structures Reconsidered: Lévi-Strauss on Kinship, 3:34

The Elements, 5:38

Elements and Electrons, 5:710

The Elements beyond Uranium, 5:754

Eléments de Sémiologie, 2:454

Elements of Algebra, 5:505

Elements of Artificial Intelligence: An Introduction Using LISP, 5:569

Elements of Bibliography: A Simplified Approach, 1:61

The Elements of Book-Collecting, 1:34

Elements of Cartography, 3:121, 3:135

Elements of Chemistry, 5:44

Elements of Chemistry in a New Systematic Order, Containing All the Modern Discoveries, 5:749

Elements of Christian Philosophy, 4:286

The Elements of Cinema: Toward a Theory of Cinesthetic Impact, 3:827

Elements of Detection and Signal Design, 5:300

Elements of Early Modern Physics, 5:31

The Elements of Editing: A Modern Guide for Editors and Journalists, 1:53

The Elements of Ethics, 4:312

Elements of General and Biological Chemistry, 5:732

The Elements of Graphing Data, 5:521

The Elements of Law: Natural and Politic, 3:153, 4:174

Elements of Lettering, 1:15

Elements of Literature, 1:129

Elements of Mathematics, 5:500

Elements of Monetary Policy, 3:65

Elements of Morality Including Polity, 4:257

Elements of Newton's Philosophy, 4:217

The Elements of Philosophy: A Compendium for Philosophers and Theologians, 4:24, 4:25

The Elements of Programming Style, 5:550

The Elements of Sir Isaac Newton's Philosophy, 2:515

Elements of Social Organization, 3:17, 3:24, 3:30

Elements of Solid State Physics, 5:668

The Elements of Spreadsheet Style, 5:557

The Elements of Style, 1:897, 1:898

Elements of Style: With Index, 1:118

Elements of the Bahai Faith, 4:861

Elements of the Mathematical Theory of Electricity and Magnetism, 5:716

The Elements of Theology, 4:62

Elements of the Philosophy of Newton, 4:195

Elements of the Philosophy of Right, 4:231, 4:232

Elements of Wave Mechanics, 5:704

Elena, 1:142

Elenchus Bibliographies Biblicus, 4:796

The Elephant, 2:818, 2:819

Eleusis: Archetypal Image of Mother and Daughter, 4:484

Eleven Canadian Novelists, 2:904

Eleven One-Act Plays, 1:1095
El Filibusterismo, 2:327
El Gallo de Sócrates, 2:528
Elgar, 3:694
Elgar as I Knew Him, 3:694
An Elgar Companion, 3:694
Elgar Studies, 3:694
El Hijo Prodijo: A Critical
  Index of Twentieth-Centu-
  ry Mexican Thought, 4:33
Eliakum Zunser: Poet of His
  People, 2:50
Elias Portolu, 2:419
Elie Wiesel: A Challenge to
  Theology, 1:1066
Elie Wiesel: Between Memo-
  ry and Hope, 1:1065
Elijah Muhammad, 4:862
El Inca: The Life and Times
  of Garcilaso de la Vega,
  3:646
El Inca Garcilaso de la
  Vega, 3:646
Eliot's Early Years, 1:473
Eliot's New Life, 1:473
Elite Activism and Political
  Transformation in China,
  3:471
The Elixir of Life Manu-
  scripts, 1:676
Elizabethan and Metaphysical
  Imagery, 1:165
Elizabeth and Ivy, 1:462
Elizabethan Essays, 1:169,
  1:472
Elizabethan Fiction, 1:167
Elizabethan Handwriting,
  1500–1650: A Manual, 1:14
Elizabethan Poetry: A Study
  in Conventions, Meaning,
  and Expression, 1:165
Elizabethan Popular Theatre:
  Plays in Performance,
  1:170
The Elizabethan Prodigals,
  1:165
The Elizabethan Puritan
  Movement, 3:334, 4:733
Elizabethan Revenge Trage-
  dy, 1:169
An Elizabethan Song Book,
  1:165
The Elizabethan Stage, 1:169,
  1:221
Elizabeth Barrett Browning,
  1:337
Elizabeth Barrett Browning:
  A Biography, 1:337
Elizabeth Barrett Browning:
  A Psychological Portrait,
  1:337

Elizabeth Barrett Browning:
  The Origins of a New Po-
  etry, 1:337
Elizabeth Barrett Browning
  Concordance, 1:337
Elizabeth Barrett Browning
  in Her Letters, 1:337
Elizabeth Bishop, 1:951
Elizabeth Bishop and Her
  Art, 1:951
Elizabeth Bowen, 1:448
Elizabeth Bowen: A Descrip-
  tive Bibliography, 1:448
Elizabeth Bowen: An Estima-
  tion, 1:448
Elizabeth Bowen: A Study of
  the Short Fiction, 1:448
Elizabeth Bowen: Portrait of
  a Writer, 1:448
Elizabeth Cary Agassiz: A Bi-
  ography, 5:786
Elizabeth Gaskell, 1:356
Elizabeth Gaskell: A Biogra-
  phy, 1:356
Elizabeth Gaskell: A Portrait
  in Letters, 1:356
Elizabeth Madox Roberts,
  1:876
Elizabeth Madox Roberts:
  American Novelist, 1:876
Elizabeth the Queen, 1:1081
Elizabeth Tudor: Biography
  of a Queen, 3:359
Ellen Glasgow, 1:843, 1:844
Ellen Glasgow and the Iron-
  ic Art of Fiction, 1:843
Ellen Glasgow and the Wom-
  an Within, 1:843
Ellen Glasgow's Development
  as a Novelist, 1:844
Ellery Queen's Circumstantial
  Evidence, 1:1236
Ellington: The Early Years,
  3:695
Elliott Carter, 3:688
Ellipsoidal Figures of Equi-
  librium, 5:677
Elmer Gantry, 1:853, 1:854
Elmer Rice, 1:1109
Elmer Rice: A Playwright's
  Vision of America, 1:1110
Elmer Sperry, 5:50
Elmer Sperry: Inventor and
  Engineer, 5:51, 5:229
Eloisa to Abelard, 1:252
El Ombú and Other South
  American Stories, 1:365
The Eloquence of Frederick
  Jackson Turner, 3:599
Eloquent Zen: Daito and
  Early Japanese Zen, 4:537
El Poeta en la Calle, 2:528
Elric Saga

Book 1: Elric of Melni-
  boné, 1:616
Book 2: Sailor on the
  Seas of Fate, 1:616
Book 3: Weird of the
  White Wolf, 1:616
Book 4: The Vanishing
  Tower, 1:616
Book 5: Bane of the
  Black Sword, 1:616
Book 6: Stormbringer,
  1:616
Book 7: Fortress of the
  Pearl, 1:616
El Salvador's Decade of Ter-
  ror, 3:636
El Señor, 2:528
El Señor Presidente, 2:853,
  2:854
Elsevier's Dictionary of Bota-
  ny II: General Terms,
  5:761
Elsevier's Russian-English
  Dictionary, 1:102
Elsewhere Perhaps, 2:22
Elsie Venner: A Romance of
  Destiny, 1:678
Elton's Ecologists: A History
  of the Bureau of Animal
  Population, 5:820
Elucidations of the Search
  after Truth, 4:181
The Elusive Mr. Wesley:
  John Wesley His Own Bi-
  ographer, 4:790
The Elusive Self in the Poet-
  ry of Robert Browning,
  1:339
The Elusive Transformation,
  5:158
The Emancipation of the
  Jews of Alsace, 3:348
The Emancipation Proclama-
  tion, 3:579
The Emancipist: Daniel
  O'Connell, 1830–1847,
  3:371
Emanuel Swedenborg: A
  Continuing Vision, 4:852,
  4:880
Emanuel Swedenborg, Scien-
  tist and Mystic, 4:852,
  4:880
The Embargo, or Sketches of
  the Time, 1:660
The Embarrassment of
  Riches, 3:383
Embarrassments, 1:763
Embattled Courage: The Ex-
  perience of Combat in the
  American Civil War, 3:528
The Embers and the Stars,
  5:115

The Embezzler, 1:937
The Embezzlers, 2:730, 2:731
Embodiment of Knowledge, 1:900
Embryology and Genetics, 5:807
An Emendation of Collingwood's Doctrine of Absolute Presuppositions, 4:282
Emerald City, 2:967
The Emerald City of Oz, 1:1200
Emergence of a Free Press, 3:807
The Emergence of African Fiction, 2:110
The Emergence of Christian Science in American Religious Life, 4:843
The Emergence of Conservative Judaism, 4:655
The Emergence of Contemporary Judaism, 4:655
Emergence of Folklore in Everyday Life, 3:869
The Emergence of Latin America in the Nineteenth Century, 3:631
The Emergence of Liberation Theology, 4:747
Emergence of Modern America, 1865-1878, 3:590
The Emergence of Modern Turkey, 3:453, 3:458
The Emergence of Ornithology as a Scientific Discipline: 1760-1850, 5:33
The Emergence of Probability, 4:160, 5:63, 5:42, 5:526
The Emergence of Romanticism, 1:268
The Emergence of Social Space: Rimbaud and the Paris Commune, 2:500
The Emergence of Thackeray's Serial Fiction, 1:404
The Emergence of the Jewish Problem, 1878-1939, 4:637
The Emergence of the Labour Party, 1880-1924, 3:367
The Emergence of the Latin American Novel, 2:845
The Emergence of the Modern Middle East: Selected Readings, 3:436
The Emergence of Whitehead's Metaphysics, 1925-29, 4:342
Emergency Poems, 2:877

Emergent Issues in Education: Comparative Perspectives, 3:253
Emerging Cosmology, 5:656
Emerging Energy Technologies: Impacts and Policy Implications, 5:282
An Emerging Entertainment, 1:1074
Emerging from the Chrysalis: Studies in Rituals of Women's Initiation, 4:430
Emerging Literatures, 2:158
Emerging Medieval Europe, 3:328
Emerging Technologies in Hazardous Waste Management III, 5:245
The Emerging Worldwide Electronic University, 3:252
Emerson: An Annotated Secondary Bibliography, 1:670
Emerson, Whitman, and the American Muse, 1:655, 1:670, 1:707
Emerson Centenary Essays, 1:670
Emerson on the Soul, 1:670
Emerson's Angle of Vision: Man and Nature in American Experience, 1:670
Emerson's Demanding Optimism, 1:670
Emerson's "Nature": Origin, Growth, Meaning, 1:671
Emerson's Romantic Style, 1:670
E. M. Forster: A Guide to Research, 1:477
E. M. Forster: A Life, 1:477
E. M. Forster and His World, 1:477
The Emigrants, 2:678, 2:936, 2:937
Emigrants and Exiles, 3:371, 3:557
Émile, 1:576, 3:164, 4:212, 4:213
Emile Durkheim: Critical Assessments, 3:225
Emile Durkheim, 1858-1917, 3:225
Emile Verhaeren, 2:617
Émile Zola, 2:518
Emile Zola: An Introductory Study of His Novels, 1:567
Emilia Galotti: A Tragedy in 5 Acts, 2:600
Emilia Pardo Bazán: The Making of a Novelist, 2:546
Emilio Carballido, 2:858

Emily Brontë, 1:336
Emily Brontë: A Psychological Portrait, 1:336
Emily Brontë and Beethoven, 2:988
Emily Dickinson, 1:747, 1:748
Emily Dickinson: A Bibliography of Secondary Sources, with Selective Annotations, 1:1890 Through 1987, 1:747
Emily Dickinson: A Collection of Critical Essays, 1:748
Emily Dickinson: An Interpretive Biography, 1:747
Emily Dickinson: A Poet's Grammar, 1:748
Emily Dickinson: A Voice of War, 1:748
Emily Dickinson: Lives of a Poet, 1:746
Emily Dickinson: Personae and Performance, 1:748
Emily Dickinson: The Mind of the Poet, 1:747
Emily Dickinson: When a Writer Is a Daughter, 1:748
Emily Dickinson's Home, 1:746
Emily Dickinson's Poetry, 1:748
Emily Dickinson's Reading, 1836-1886, 1:747
Emily Dickinson's Readings of Men and Books, 1:748
Emily Dickinson's Reception in the 1890s: A Documentary History, 1:747
Eminent Chinese of the Ch'ing Period, 3:465
Eminent Domain, 1:974
Emma, 1:275, 1:335
Emma Lazarus, 1:773
Emma Lazarus: Woman with a Torch, 1:773
The Emmet Fox Treasury, 4:847
Emmy Noether, 5:513
Emmy Noether in Bryn Mawr, 5:513
Emotion, 3:177
Emotion in the Thought of Sartre, 4:330
The Emotions: Outline of a Theory, 4:329
Emotions, Cognition, and Behaviour, 3:172
Empedocles: The Extant Fragments, 4:53

Empedocles' Cosmic Cycle,
4:53
The Emperor and the Gods:
Images from the Time of
Trojan, 4:452
The Emperor and the Ro-
man Army, 3:308
The Emperor and the Witch,
2:593
The Emperor in the Roman
World, 3:303, 4:452
The Emperor Jones, 1:1106,
1:1107
The Emperor Julian, 4:682
Emperor Michael Palaeo-
logus and the West,
1258–1282, 4:693
The Emperor of America,
1:597
Emperor of China: Self-Por-
trait of K'ang-Hsi, 3:503
The Emperor of the Amazon,
2:899
Emperor of the Cossacks,
3:395
Emperor of the Earth: Modes
of Eccentric Vision, 2:818,
2:899
Emperor Shaka the Great,
2:164
The Emperor's Kites: A Morphology of Borges' Tales,
2:857, 2:864
The Emperor's New Mind,
5:76, 5:574, 5:709
The Emperor's Old Clothes,
2:864
Empire and Aftermath, 3:477
Empire and Commonwealth,
3:607
Empire and Islam, Punjab
and the Making of Pakis-
tan, 3:487
Empire as a Way of Life,
3:601
Empire for Liberty: Melville
and the Poetics of Individualism, 1:688
Empire of Liberty: The Statecraft of Thomas Jefferson,
3:546
The Empire of Reason, 3:572
Empire or Independence,
1760–1776: A British
American Dialogue, 3:361
The Empire's Old Clothes,
3:631, 3:873
The Empire Strikes Back,
1:1171
Empire to Welfare State:
English History,
1906–1976, 3:367

The Empire Writes Back,
1:1131
Empirical Inquiry, 5:101
Empiricism and Geographical
Thought, 5:32
The Emptiness of Emptiness:
An Introduction to Early
Indian Madhyamika, 4:513
The Empty Copper Sea,
1:1234
The Empty Fortress: Infantile
Autism and the Birth of
the Self, 5:434, 5:435
The Empty House, 1:621
The Empty Mirror: Early
Poems, 1:981
Empty Promise: The Growing
Case against Star Wars,
5:240
An Enabling Humility, 1:864
The Enchafed Flood, 1:434,
1:435, 1:688
Enchanted Images: American
Children's Illustration
1850–1925, 1:29
The Enchanted Pilgrim and
Other Stories, 2:736
The Enchanted Ring: The
Untold Story of Penicillin,
5:315
The Enchanted Wanderer,
2:736
The Enchanter, 2:740
Enchanting Beasts: An An-
thology of Modern Women
Poets in Finland, 2:658
The Enchantments of Juda-
ism, 4:600
Enchiridion Ethicum, 4:183
Enchiridion Metaphysicum,
4:183
Enchiridion of Erasmus,
4:139
Encircled Kingdom: Legends
and Folktales of Laos,
3:854
Encountering the Goddess,
4:503
Encountering the Universe,
5:655
Encounter on the Narrow
Ridge: A Life of Martin
Buber, 4:662
Encounters between Judaism
and Modern Philosophy,
4:663
Encounters with Conductors
of Today, 3:671
Encounters with Einstein,
5:693
Encounters with Kennan:
The Great Debate, 3:584

Encounters with Qi: Explor-
ing Chinese Medicine,
5:319
Encounters with Stravinsky:
A Personal Record, 3:723
Encounters with the Arch-
druid, 5:623, 5:823
Encounters with Verdi, 3:727
Encounter with Emancipa-
tion, 4:638
Encyclopaedia Britannica,
1:105
An Encyclopaedia of Africa,
3:416
The Encyclopaedia of Gay
and Lesbian Recordings,
3:656
Encyclopaedia of Indian Mu-
sic, with Special Refer-
ence to the Ragas, 3:670
The Encyclopaedia of Islam,
4:567
Encyclopaedia of the Social
Sciences, 3:5
The Encyclopaedia of Type
Faces, 1:16
The Encyclopaedia Sherlocki-
ana, 1:608
Encyclopedia: Selections,
2:472
The Encyclopedia Americana,
1:106
The Encyclopedia Dictionary
of Science, 5:2
Encyclopedia Judaica, 4:5,
4:594
Encyclopedia of African-
American Civil Rights,
3:509
The Encyclopedia of Aging
and the Elderly, 5:317
Encyclopedia of Allergy and
Environmental Illness: A
Self-Help Approach, 5:386
Encyclopedia of American
Agricultural History, 5:261
Encyclopedia of American
Economic History, 3:509
The Encyclopedia of Ameri-
can Facts and Dates, 3:508
Encyclopedia of American
Film Comedy, 3:825
Encyclopedia of American
Foreign Policy, 3:508
Encyclopedia of American
History, 3:509
Encyclopedia of American
Humorists, 3:871
The Encyclopedia of Ameri-
can Music, 3:656
Encyclopedia of American
Political History, 3:508

The Encyclopedia of American Religions, 4:4, 4:717, 4:751, 4:854
Encyclopedia of Aquatic Life, 5:758
Encyclopedia of Archaeological Excavations in the Holy Land, 4:808
The Encyclopedia of Artificial Intelligence, 5:76, 5:570
The Encyclopedia of Arts and Crafts, 3:765
Encyclopedia of Asian History, 3:462
Encyclopedia of Associations, 3:6
Encyclopedia of Associations: International Organizations, 1:104
Encyclopedia of Associations: National Organizations of the U.S., 1:104
Encyclopedia of Associations: Regional, State, Local, 1:104
The Encyclopedia of Atmospheric Sciences and Astrogeology, 5:617
Encyclopedia of Biblical and Christian Ethics, 4:718
Encyclopedia of Bioethics, 4:893 5:61, 5:123
Encyclopedia of Black Folklore and Humor, 3:867
The Encyclopedia of Censorship, 1:57
Encyclopedia of Chemical Trademarks and Synonyms, 5:724
Encyclopedia of Childbearing: Critical Perspectives, 5:204
Encyclopedia of China Today, 3:465
Encyclopedia of Colonial and Revolutionary America, 3:508
Encyclopedia of Community Planning and Environmental Management, 5:224
Encyclopedia of Comparative Letterforms for Artists and Designers, 3:767
Encyclopedia of Computer Science and Engineering, 5:540, 5:551
An Encyclopedia of Continental Women Writers, 2:4
Encyclopedia of Cosmology, 4:13

Encyclopedia of Crime and Justice, 3:205
The Encyclopedia of Dance and Ballet, 3:732
Encyclopedia of Deafness and Hearing Disorders, 5:380
Encyclopedia of Early Christianity, 4:676
Encyclopedia of Eastern Philosophy and Religion, 4:4
Encyclopedia of Environmental Information Sources, 5:616
The Encyclopedia of Environmental Studies, 5:815
The Encyclopedia of Ethics, 4:2, 4:13
Encyclopedia of Evolution, 5:759
The Encyclopedia of Folk, Country, and Western Music, 3:658, 3:853
Encyclopedia of Food Science, Food Technology, and Nutrition, 5:261
Encyclopedia of Food Science and Technology, 5:261
The Encyclopedia of Furniture, 3:766
The Encyclopedia of Geochemistry and Environmental Sciences, 5:617
Encyclopedia of Geographic Information Sources, 3:120
Encyclopedia of Geomorphology, 5:617
The Encyclopedia of Homosexuality, 1:1183
The Encyclopedia of Human Behavior, 5:422
Encyclopedia of Human Biology, 5:311, 5:759
Encyclopedia of India, 3:483, 4:498
Encyclopedia of Industrial Chemical Additives, 5:724
The Encyclopedia of Insects, 5:769
The Encyclopedia of Islam (Bosworth), 3:442
The Encyclopedia of Islam (Gibb), 3:456
Encyclopedia of Islam (Lewis), 3:443
Encyclopedia of Japan, 4:534
The Encyclopedia of Jazz, 3:668
The Encyclopedia of Jazz in the Seventies, 3:668
The Encyclopedia of Jazz in the Sixties, 3:668

Encyclopedia of Jewish Concepts (A Book of Jewish Concepts), 4:596
Encyclopedia of Jewish Symbols, 4:597
Encyclopedia of Judaism, 4:5
Encyclopedia of Latin America, 3:624
Encyclopedia of Library and Information Science, 5:544
The Encyclopedia of Logic, 4:232
The Encyclopedia of Mammals, 5:761
Encyclopedia of Marine Invertebrates, 5:769
Encyclopedia of Microbiology, 5:761
Encyclopedia of Mineralogy, 5:617
Encyclopedia of Minerals, 5:618
The Encyclopedia of Minerals and Gemstones, 5:618
Encyclopedia of Modern Architecture, 3:761
Encyclopedia of Mormonism, 4:4, 4:717, 4:846
Encyclopedia of Musical Film, 3:825
Encyclopedia of Music in Canada, 3:656
The Encyclopedia of Myths and Legends of All Nations, 3:856
The Encyclopedia of Native American Religions, 3:508
Encyclopedia of Neuroscience, 5:758
The Encyclopedia of Oceanography, 5:617
The Encyclopedia of Opera, 3:671
The Encyclopedia of Paleontology, 5:617
The Encyclopedia of Philosophy, 4:2, 4:13, 4:94, 4:160, 4:231, 5:60
Encyclopedia of Physical Science and Technology, 5:2, 5:29, 5:217, 5:724
Encyclopedia of Physics (Flueggs), 5:650
Encyclopedia of Physics (Lerner), 5:652
Encyclopedia of Plastics, Polymers and Resins, 5:724
Encyclopedia of Pop, Rock, and Soul, 3:666
Encyclopedia of Pottery and Porcelain, 3:1800-1960, 3:765

The Encyclopedia of Prehistoric Life, 5:639
Encyclopedia of Psychoanalysis, 5:424
Encyclopedia of Psychology, 5:413
An Encyclopedia of Quotations about Music, 3:657
The Encyclopedia of Religion, 4:4, 4:497, 4:522, 4:717
Encyclopedia of Religion and Ethics, 4:4, 4:717
Encyclopedia of Romanticism: Culture in Britain, 1780–1830, 1:265
Encyclopedia of Science and Technology, 5:618
The Encyclopedia of Sedimentology, 5:617
Encyclopedia of Semiconductor Technology, 5:229
The Encyclopedia of Sexual Behavior, 5:429, 5:439
Encyclopedia of Shells, 5:762
Encyclopedia of Sociology, 3:200
Encyclopedia of Southern Culture, 3:509
The Encyclopedia of Southern History, 3:509
Encyclopedia of Statistical Sciences, 5:520
Encyclopedia of Superstitions, Folklore and the Occult Sciences of the World, 3:849
The Encyclopedia of Tarot, 4:860
Encyclopedia of Television: Series, Pilots and Specials, 3:812
Encyclopedia of Textiles, 3:767
Encyclopedia of the American Constitution, 3:142
Encyclopedia of the American Presidency, 3:509
Encyclopedia of the American Religious Experience, 4:4
Encyclopedia of the American Revolution, 3:508
The Encyclopedia of the American Theatre, 1900–1975, 1:1072
The Encyclopedia of the Biological Sciences, 5:759
Encyclopedia of the Confederacy, 3:508
The Encyclopedia of the Dead, 2:830

An Encyclopedia of the History of Technology, 5:26
The Encyclopedia of the Jewish Religion, 4:595
Encyclopedia of the Modern Middle East, 3:435
Encyclopedia of the Musical Theatre, 3:655
Encyclopedia of Theology: The Concise Sacramentum Mundi, 4:676, 4:719
Encyclopedia of the Reformed Faith, 4:719
Encyclopedia of the Third Reich, 3:377
Encyclopedia of the United Nations and International Agreements, 1:111
The Encyclopedia of Type Faces, 1:62
The Encyclopedia of Visual Art, 3:757
Encyclopedia of World Art, 3:757
Encyclopedia of World Cultures, 3:11
An Encyclopedia of World History, 3:7, 3:273
Encyclopedia of World Literature in the 20th Century, 1:131, 2:3
The Encyclopedia of World Regional Geology, Part 1, 5:617
The Encyclopedia Yearbook of Jazz, 3:668
Encyclopedic Dictionary of Exploration Geophysics, 5:618
The Encyclopedic Dictionary of Physical Geography, 5:620
The Encyclopedic Dictionary of Psychology, 3:169
Encyclopedic Dictionary of Roman Law, 3:305
Encyclopedic Dictionary of Yoga, 4:497
The Encyclopedic Handbook of Cults in America, 4:4, 4:854
Encyclopédie, 1:105
Endangered Hope: Experiences in Psychiatric Aftercare Facilities, 5:423
The End Crowns All, 1:211
Endeavors of Art: A Study of Form in Elizabethan Drama, 1:169
Enderby, 1:453
Enderby Outside, 1:453
Enderby's Dark Lady: Or, No End to Enderby, 1:453

End Game, 1:439
Endgame, 2:459
Ending in Earnest, A Literary Log, 1:422
Ending Lives, 4:388
The Ending of Time, 4:554
Endings, 2:69
Endless Enemies: The Making of an Unfriendly World, 3:545
Endlesse Worke: Spenser and the Structure of Discourse, 1:198
Endless Frontiers: The Story of McGraw-Hill, 1:43
Endless Horizons, 5:199
The Endless Migrations, 5:826
Endocrine Disorders, 5:382
The End of American Innocence, 3:560
The End of an Alliance, 3:539
The End of Colonial Rule in West Africa, 3:420
The End of Days, 2:19
The End of Education: Toward Posthumanism, 3:258
The End of European Empire: Decolonization after World War II, 3:346
The End of History and the Last Man, 3:276
The End of Ideology, 3:139, 3:220
End of Lieutenant Boruvka, 2:795
The End of Life: Euthanasia and Morality, 5:123
The End of Me Old Cigar, 1:532
The End of Nature, 5:115, 5:823
The End of Obscenity, 1:57
The End of Physics: The Myth of a Unified Theory, 5:650
The End of the Affair, 1:488
The End of the Battle, 1:562
End of the British Empire: The Historical Debate, 3:345
End of the Cold War, 3:346
End of the Cold War: European Unity, Socialism and the Shift in Global Power, 3:345
The End of the Cold War: Its Meaning and Implications, 3:345
End of the European Era: 1890 to the Present, 3:342

The End of the Glory: An Interpretation of the Origins of World War II, 3:344

The End of the Soviet Empire—The Triumph of the Nations, 3:398

The End of the Summer, 1:621

The End of the World, 1:1098

The End of the World and Other Stories, 2:912

The End of the World News: An Entertainment, 1:453

The End of Utopia: A Study of Aldous Huxley's Brave New World, 1:499

Endometriosis, 5:356

Ends and Beginnings, 2:728

Ends and Odds, 1:439

The Ends of Science: An Essay in Scientific Authority, 5:10

The Ends of the Earth: Perspectives on Modern Environmental History, 3:551

An End to Innocence, 1:975

End to Torment: A Memoir of Ezra Pound, 1:827, 1:873

The Endurance of Frankenstein: Essays on Mary Shelley's Novel, 1:301

The Enduring Legacy: Alexander Pope Tercentenary Essays, 1:252

The Enduring Questions, 4:23

Endymion, 1:293

Endymion: The Man in the Moon, 1:186

Eneide, 2:619

Enemies: A Love Story, 1:1049, 2:48

Enemies: A Play, 2:725

The Enemies of Books, 1:22

Enemies of the Roman Order, 3:308

The Enemy: A Biography of Wyndham Lewis, 1:514

Enemy at the Gates, 3:278

The Enemy in the Blanket, 1:453

An Enemy of the People, 2:665

The Enemy That Never Was: A History of the Japanese Canadians, 3:608

The Energies of Art: Studies of Authors Classic and Modern, 1:814

Energy, 2:720

Energy: The Next Twenty Years, 5:282

Energy, Economics and the Environment, 5:278

Energy, Force and Matter, 5:46

Energy Aftermath, 5:282

Energy Analysis and Policy, 5:284, 5:292

Energy and American Values, 5:160

Energy and Equity, 5:136

Energy and the Environment: Policy Overview, 5:186

Energy and the Future, 5:115

Energy and the Way We Live, 5:52

Energy Economics, 5:284

Energy Economics, Demand Management, 5:292

Energy Efficiency: Optimization of Electric Power Distribution Losses, 5:292

The Energy-Environment Connection, 5:289

Energy for a Sustainable World, 5:282

Energy from Heaven and Earth, 5:143

Energy from the Waves, 5:290

Energy Future (Stobaugh), 5:283

Energy Future (Yergin), 5:293

Energy in America's Future: The Choices before Us, 5:283

The Energy of Slaves, 2:909

Energy Policy: An Economic Analysis, 5:284

Energy Resources in an Uncertain Future, 5:283

The Energy Source Book—A Guide to Technology, Resources and Policy, 5:278

Energy Transition in Developing Countries, 5:281

Energy Unbound: A Fable for America's Future, 5:75, 5:823

The Energy Within, 5:318

Eneyida, 2:837

Enfranchisement of Women, 1:380

Engaged, 1:356

Engaged in Writing: Two Novels, 1:553

Engaging Feminism, 3:218

Engels, 3:75

Engels, Manchester, and the Working Class, 3:75

Engels and the Formation of Marxism, 4:227

Engendering Men: The Question of Male Feminist Criticism, 1:1183

Engendering the Subject, 1:456

Engineering: The Career and the Profession, 5:228

Engineering and the Liberal Arts, 5:165, 5:166, 5:253

Engineering and the Mind's Eye, 5:12, 5:192, 5:227

Engineering as a Social Enterprise, 5:158, 5:215

Engineering Design for Safety, 5:244

Engineering Formulas, 5:216

Engineering Geology Case Histories, 5:636

Engineering Hydrology, 5:632

The Engineering Profession, 5:227

Engineering Professionalism and Ethics, 5:130

The Engineer of Human Souls, 2:795

Engineers and Electrons: A Century of Electrical Progress, 5:230

Engineers and Engineering in the Renaissance, 5:232

Engineers and Ivory Towers, 5:213

Engineers and Their Profession, 5:227

The Engineers and the Price System, 3:109, 3:242

Engineer's Witness, 5:213

Engines of Change: The American Industrial Revolution, 1790–1860, 5:46

Engines of Instruction, Mischief, and Magic, 1:578

Engines of the Mind: A History of the Computer, 5:538

England, 1870 to 1914, 3:363

England, Europe and the Upper Nile, 3:419

England and Englishness, 1:315

England and Ireland since 1800, 3:355

England and the Catholic Church under Queen Elizabeth, 4:734

England and the English, 1:312, 1:340

England in 1815, 1:265

England in the Age of the American Revolution, 3:406

England in the Age of Wycliffe, 3:410
England in the Eighteenth Century, 1714–1815, 3:408
England in the Late Middle Ages, 3:358
England's Earliest Protestants, 1520–1535, 4:726
England's Ireland, 1:492
England's "Prussian Minister," 1:345
England's Treasure by Forraign [sic] Trade, 3:45, 3:54
England under Queen Anne, 3:410
England under the Stuarts, 3:410
England under the Tudors, 3:358, 3:402, 4:726
The English, 3:402
English, August, 2:177
The English Alliterative Tradition, 1:146
English Almanacs, 1500–1800: Astrology and the Popular Press, 4:725
English and Scottish Ballads, 3:877
English and Scottish Popular Ballads, 1:148, 3:850, 3:877
English and Scottish Printing Types 1501–35, 1508–41, 1:16
English and Scottish Printing Types 1535–58, 1552–58, 1:16
English-Arabic Vocabulary: Students' Pronouncing Dictionary, 1:97
The English Auden: Poems, Essays, and Dramatic Writings, 1:435
English Bards and Scotch Reviewers, 1:281
English Blake, 1:278
English Books and Readers, 1:36
English Books with Coloured Plates, 1790 to 1860, 1:30
The English Catholic Community, 1570–1850, 3:355, 4:736
The English Church, 1000–1066: A Constitutional History, 3:356
The English Church and the Papacy in the Middle Ages, 3:355
The English Civil War, 3:359
The English Clergy, 4:734
The English Comic Characters, 1:537

The English Common Reader, 1:265
English Court Hand, A.D. 1066 to 1500, 1:17
English Culture and the Decline of the Industrial Spirit, 1850–1980, 3:368
English Deism: Its Roots and Its Fruits, 4:739
English Drama, 1:171
English Drama: Restoration and Eighteenth Century, 1660–1789, 1:228
The English Eccentrics, 1:548
English Fairy Tales, 3:882
English Fairy Tales and More English Fairy Tales, 1:579
English Fiction of the Romantic Period, 1789–1830, 1:270
English Folk-Song and Dance, 3:852
The English Heritage, 3:408
The English Hero 1660–1800, 1:225
The English Historical Novel: Walter Scott to Virginia Woolf, 1:270
English History, 1914–1945, 3:367, 3:409
The English History Play in the Age of Shakespeare, 1:212
English Humanism: Wyatt to Cowley, 4:128
The English Humorists, 1:403
English-Hungarian, Hungarian-English Dictionary, 1:100
English in America: A Radical View of the Profession, 1:1127
English in Ireland in the Eighteenth Century, 3:403
English in the West Indies; or The Bow of Ulysses, 3:403
The English Jewry under Angevin Kings, 4:624
English Journey, 1:537
English Justice between the Norman Conquest and the Great Charter, 1066–1215, 3:357
English-Korean/Korean-English Dictionary, 1:101
English Landed Society in the Eighteenth Century, 3:362
The English Language, 1:96

The English Language in Medieval Literature, 1:141
English Laws for Women in the Nineteenth Century, 1:384
English Literature: An Illustrated Record, 1:133
English Literature: A Period Anthology, 1:129
English Literature, 1789–1815, 1:266 1815–1832, 1:265
English Literature and Ideas in the Twentieth Century, 1:429
English Literature before Chaucer, 1:141
English Literature in Its Foreign Relations, 1300 to 1800, 2:990
English Literature in the Sixteenth Century, 1:165, 1:167
English Loanwords in Japanese: A Selection, 1:100
English Mail-Coach and Other Essays, 1:290
English Medieval Narrative in the Thirteenth and Fourteenth Centuries, 1:146
English Medieval Romance, 1:146
English Melodrama, 1:271, 1:322
The English Modernist Reader, 1910–1930, 1:415
The English Morality Play, 1:161
English Mystery Plays, 1:159
The English Mystery Plays (Woolf), 1:160
The English Mystical Tradition, 4:721
English-Norwegian Dictionary, 1:101
The English Novel, 1:537
The English Novel: A Short Critical History, 1:269
The English Novel: Form and Function, 1:270
The English Novel: Select Bibliographical Guides, 1:122
The English Novel: Twentieth-Century Criticism, Defoe through Hardy, 1:134
The English Novel, 1740–1850, 1:269, 1:318
The English Novel at Mid-Century: From the Leaning Tower, 1:487

English Novel from Dickens to Lawrence, 1:422

English Novel Twentieth-Century Criticism, 1:135

The English People and the English Revolution, 1640–1649, 3:360

The English Philosophers from Bacon to Mill, 4:29, 4:159

English Philosophy since 1900, 4:268

English Plays of the Nineteenth Century, 1:272, 1:323

English Poetry of the Romantic Period, 1789–1830, 1:268

An English-Polish Dictionary of Idioms and Phrases, 1:101

English Political Pluralism: The Problem of Freedom and Organization, 3:156

English Politics and the American Revolution, 3:362

English Poor Law History, 3:55, 3:113

English Portraits and Essays, 1:430

English Pronunciation, 1500–1700, 1:216

English Prose and Criticism, 1900–1950: A Guide to Information Sources, 1:429

English Prose and Poetry, 1660–1800: A Selection, 1:227, 1:230

English Prose of the Victorian Era, 1:326

English Proverbs and Proverbial Phrases, 1:115

English Publishers in the Graphic Arts, 1599–1700, 1:37

The English Reformation, 3:358, 4:726

English Reformations: Religion, Politics and Society under the Tudors, 4:726

English Reformers, 4:727

English Renaissance Prose Fiction: An Annotated Bibliography of Criticism, 1984–1990, 1:167

English Renaissance Prose Fiction, 1500–1660, 1:167

English Renaissance Song, 3:659

English Review, 1:474

English Revolution, 3:1640, 3:404

The English Revolution, 1688–1689, 3:410

English Romantic Drama, 1795–1843: A Critical History, 1:272

English Romantic Irony, 1:266

English Romanticism: The Human Context, 1:265

English Romantic Poetry, 1800–1835: A Guide to Information Sources, 1:266

English Romantic Poetry and Prose, 1:266, 1:268

The English Romantic Poets: A Review of Research and Criticism, 1:265

English Romantic Writers, 1:266

An English-Serbocroatian Dictionary, 1:102

English Social History, 3:410

English Society in the Early Middle Ages, 1066–1307, 3:357

English-Speaking Justice, 5:128

English-Tagalog, Tagalog-English Pocket Dictionary, 1:101

The English Utilitarians: Jeremy Bentham, James Mill, John Stuart Mill, 4:245, 3:151

English Works of John Gower, 1:152

English-Yiddish/Yiddish-English Concise Conversational Dictionary, 1:103

The Enigma of Arrival, 2:939

The Enigma of Faith, 4:102

The Enigma of Gogol, 2:722

The Enigma of Mary Stuart, 4:735

The Enigma of Time, 5:650

Enigmatic Eye, 2:899

Enjoyment of Laughter, 3:871

The Enjoyment of Mathematics, 5:495

The Enjoyment of Music: An Introduction to Perceptive Listening, 3:665

Enlarging the Temple, 1:912

Enlightened Absence: Neoclassical Configurations of the Feminine, 1:226

Enlightened Racism, 3:560

The Enlightenment: An Interpretation, 3:337, 4:160, 4:739

Enlightenment, Revolution and Romanticism, 4:159

The Enlightenment in America, 3:518

Ennin's Travels in T'ang China, 3:501

The Enormous Room, 1:824, 1:825

Enquiries Concerning Human Understanding and Concerning the Principles of Morals, 4:99, 4:200

An Enquiry Concerning Human Understanding: And Letter from a Gentleman to His Friend in Edinburgh, 4:199, 4:200

An Enquiry Concerning the Principles of Morals, 4:200

An Enquiry Concerning the Principles of Natural Knowledge, 4:341

Enquiry into Plants, 4:90

Enquiry into Plants, and Minor Works on Odours and Weather Signs, 2:369

An Enquiry into the Causes of the Late Increase of Robbers, and Related Writings, 1:245

An Enquiry into the Nature of Certain Nineteenth Century Pamphlets, 1:35

Enrico Caruso: His Life and Death, 3:688

Enrico Caruso: My Father and My Family, 3:688

Enrico Fermi, 5:685

Enrico Fermi: Father of the Atomic Bomb, 5:685

Enrico Fermi: Physicist, 5:685

Enter a Free Man, 1:553, 1:554

Enter and Exit, 2:569

Enter Foot and Horse, 1:272

Enterprise: The Dynamic Economy of a Free People, 3:547

The Entertainer, 1:524, 1:531, 1:532

Entertaining Mathematical Puzzles, 5:507

Entertaining Mr. Sloan, 1:529

Entertaining Satan: Witchcraft and the Culture of Early New England, 3:516

The Entertainment Functions of Television, 3:204

The Entertainment Machine: American Show Business in the Twentieth Century, 3:874

Enthusiasm, 4:737

The Enthusiast: A Life of Thornton Wilder, 1:899, 1:1116

The Enthusiasts, 2:604

Entrepreneurship, 3:49

Entrepreneurship and Industry in India, 1800–1947, 3:486

Entropy Law and the Economic Process, 3:46

Entry into the Realm of Reality: The Text, 4:529

Enuma-Elish, 2:53, 4:440

The Environmental Address Book, 5:816

Environmental Chemistry, 5:736

Environmental Economics and Sustainable Development, 5:292

Environmental Encyclopedia, 5:616

Environmental Engineering and Sanitation, 5:245

Environmental Ethics (Rolston), 5:76, 5:116, 5:140

Environmental Ethics (Shrader-Frechette), 5:141

Environmental Ethics: An Introduction to Environmental Philosophy, 5:114

Environmental Ethics: Duties to and Values in the Natural World, 5:116

Environmental Ethics for Engineers, 5:128

Environmental Geology, 5:635

Environmental Grantmaking Foundations: 1992 Directory, 5:815

Environmental Hazards, 5:636

Environmental Health, 5:353

Environmental Health Engineering in the Tropics: An Introductory Text, 5:352

Environmentalism and the Future of Progressive Politics, 5:76

Environmental Issues and Management of Waste in Energy and Materials Production, 5:245

The Environmentalist's Bookshelf: A Guide to the Best Books, 5:115, 5:816

Environmental Justice, 4:389

Environmental Management and Economic Development, 3:48

Environmental Philosophy: From Animal Rights to Radical Ecology, 5:117

Environmental Profiles: A Global Guide to Projects and People, 5:815

Environmental Restoration: Science and Strategies for Restoring the Earth, 5:821

Environmental Sourcebook, 5:816

Environmental Success Index 1992, 5:815

Environmental Systems: Philosophy, Analysis, and Control, 3:118

Environment and Health (Editorial Research Assoc.), 5:353

Environment and Health (Trieff), 5:354

Environment and Human Performance, 5:341

Envisioning Information, 3:7, 5:194, 5:524, 5:558

The Envoy from Mirror City, 2:973

Envy, 2:731, 2:743

The Envy of the American States: The Loyalist Dream for New Brunswick, 3:613

Eōthen, 3:925

Ephemera: A Book on Its Collection, Conservation and Use, 1:32

Epic and Folk Plays of the Yiddish Theater, 2:34

Epic and Romance in the Argonautica, 2:352

The Epic in Africa: Towards a Poetics of the Oral Performance, 2:111

The Epic in the Making, 2:827

Epicoene, 1:183

The Epic of Digenes Akritas, 2:344

The Epic of Gilgamesh, 2:53, 4:545, 4:546

The Epic of Kings: Shahnama, 2:89

The Epic of Latin America, 3:625

The Epic of Sheik Beddreddin and Other Poems, 2:98

Epic of the Finnish Nation, 3:381

Epic of the Wheat, 1:776

Epic Singers and Oral Tradition, 2:361

Epics of Everyday Life: Encounters in a Changing Russia, 3:398

Epics of the Philippines, 2:329

Epic Songs of Russia, 2:692

Epicurea, 4:73

Epicureanism: Chief Ancient Philosophies, 4:74

Epicurean Political Philosophy: The "De Rerum Natura" of Lucretius, 4:75

The Epicurean Tradition, 4:74

Epicurus, 4:74

Epicurus: An Introduction, 4:74

Epicurus and Hellenistic Philosophy, 4:74

Epicurus and His Philosophy, 2:388, 4:73

Epicurus' Ethical Theory: The Pleasures of Invulnerability, 4:74

Epicurus' Scientific Method, 4:73

Epidemics and Mortality in Early Modern Japan, 3:475

The Epidemic That Never Was, 5:390

Epidemiology, Health, and Society: Selected Papers, 5:80

Epigrams and Satirical Verse, 2:751

Epigrams from Martial: A Verse Translation, 2:389

Epilegomena to the Study of Greek Religion, 4:479

Epilegomena to the Study of Greek Religion, and Themis, 2:345

Epilepsy, 5:393

Episcopal Women, 4:754

Episodes from the Early History of Mathematics, 5:38

Episodios nacionales, 2:546

Epistemology and Cognition, 4:380

Epistemology and Inference, 5:64

Epistemology of G. E. Moore, 4:312

Epistemology of the Closet, 1:1132, 1:1182

The Epistle on Singing Girls, Vol. 2: Approaches to Arabic Literature, 2:66

Epistle to a Godson, 1:435

Epistle to a Godson and Other Poems, 1:435

An Epistle to the Hebrews, 1:773

The Epistle to the Romans, 4:758

The Epistolary Moment, 1:227

Epitaph for a Small Winner, 2:896

Epithalamion, 1:197

Épitomé, 2:151

The Epochal Nature of Process in Whitehead's Metaphysics, 4:343

Epoch and Artist, 1:502

An Epoch of Miracles: Oral Literature of the Yucatec Maya, 4:465

Epochs of Italian Literature, 2:401

Epsom Downs, 1:450

Equal in Monastic Profession: Religious Women in Medieval France, 4:699

Equality, 1:734

Equality and Achievement in Education, 3:223

Equality and Liberty, 4:386

Equality and Liberty: Analyzing Rawls and Nozick, 4:316

Equality in America: The View from the Top, 3:214

Equality of Educational Opportunity, 3:209

Equal Rights: The Jesuit Estates Act Controversy, 3:615

Equator: A Journey, 3:908

Equiano's Travels, 2:138

Equilibrist: A Study of John Crowe Ransom's Poems 1916–1963, 1:875

Equity of Educational Opportunity, 3:223

Equivocal Endings in Classic American Novels, 1:805

Equus, 1:543

The Era of Persuasion: American Thought and Culture, 1521–1680, 3:559

The Era of Reconstruction, 3:598

The Era of Reform Eighteen Thirty to Eighteen Sixty, 3:572

The Era of the French Revolution, 3:339

The Era of Trujillo: Dominican Dictator, 3:636

The Erasers, 2:500

Erasmus, 4:139

Erasmus: A Critical Biography, 4:721

Erasmus: A Study of His Life, Ideals and Place in History, 4:139

Erasmus: Ecstasy and the Praise of Folly, 4:139

Erasmus: Lectures and Wayfaring Sketches, 4:139

Erasmus: The Growth of a Mind, 3:333

Erasmus and His Times, 4:139

Erasmus and the Age of Reformation, 4:139

Erasmus and the New Testament: The Mind of a Christian Humanist, 4:139

Erasmus and the Northern Renaissance, 4:139

Erasmus grandescens, 4:139

Erasmus of Christendom, 4:139

Erasmus of Europe: The Making of a Humanist, 4:139

Erasmus on Language and Method in Theology, 4:139

Erato and Apollyon, 2:437

Erec, 2:586

Erec et Enide, 2:466

Erewhon, 1:342 5:563

Erewhon Revisited, 1:342

Erewhon Revisited (and Erewhon), 1:342

Eric, 2:562

Eric Berne: Master Gamesman—A Transactional Biography, 5:434

Eric Brighteyes, 1:595

Eric Gill: The Man Who Loved Letters, 1:13

Erich Fromm, 5:451

Erich Fromm: The Courage to Be Human, 5:451

Erich Maria Remarque, 2:607

Eric Rohmer: Realist and Moralist, 3:842

Erie Water West: A History of the Erie Canal 1792–1854, 5:224

Erik Erikson: An Introduction, 3:182

Erik Erikson: The Growth of His Work, 3:182, 5:442

Erik H. Erikson: The Power and Limits of a Vision, 3:182

Eriugena, 4:115

Erle Stanley Gardner: A Checklist, 1:1229

Ermita, 2:331

Ernest Haycox, 1:1215

Ernest Hemingway, 1:847

Ernest Hemingway: A Life Story, 1:846

Ernest Hemingway: A Reconsideration, 1:847

Ernest Hemingway: New Critical Essays, 1:846

Ernest Hemingway: Six Decades of Criticism, 1:847

Ernest Hemingway: The Writer in Context, 1:846

Ernest Hemingway, Cub Reporter, 1:845

Ernest Hemingway and His World, 1:846

Ernest Hemingway and the Arts, 2:988

Ernest Hemingway's A Moveable Feast: The Making of Myth, 1:847

Ernest Hemingway's Apprenticeship, 1:845

Ernest Holmes: His Life and Times, 4:847

Ernst Bloch, 4:277

Ernst Bloch: A Bibliography, 4:277

Ernst Cassirer: An Annotated Bibliography, 4:280

Ernst Cassirer: Scientific Knowledge and the Concept of Man, 4:280

Ernst Mach: His Work, Life, and Influence, 5:700

Ernst Mach: Knowledge and Error, 5:700

Ernst Mach—A Deeper Look: Documents and New Perspectives, 5:700

Ernst Toller, 2:613

Eroding Soils: The Off-Farm Impacts, 5:635

Eros and Civilization, 4:408

Eros and Civilization: A Philosophical Inquiry into Freud, 5:94

Eros and Magic in the Renaissance, 4:125

Eros and Psyche: Studies in Plato, Plotinus, and Origen, 4:87

Eros and Vision: The Restoration to Romanticism, 1:225

Erotica, 2:835

Erotic Art: An Annotated Bibliography with Essays, 3:758

Erotic Faith: Being in Love from Jane Austen to D. H. Lawrence, 1:319

The Erotic Poems, 2:389

Erotic Tales of Old Russia, 2:692

The Erotic Traveler, 3:913
Erotism: Death and Sensuality, 2:455
Errand into the Wilderness, 1:629, 3:587, 4:35
Erring: A Postmodern A/theology, 4:889
Erroneous Emotions, 2:812
Ersatz in the Confederacy, 3:529
Erskine Caldwell, 1:819
Erskine Caldwell and the Fiction of Poverty: The Flesh and the Spirit, 1:819
Erving Goffman, 3:228
Erwin Schrödinger: An Introduction to His Writings, 5:714
Erwin Schrödinger and the Rise of Wave Mechanics, 5:714
Esarhaddon and Other Tales, 2:764
Esau and Jacob, 2:896
Escape from Freedom, 3:344, 5:449, 5:450
Escape from Predicament, 4:532
Escape into Siege, 2:9
The Escape Motif in the American Novel, 1:917
Eschatology in Maimonidean Thought, 4:668
Escher: His Life and Complete Graphic Works, 5:193
Esenin: A Biography in Memoirs, Letters, and Documents, 2:718
Esenin: A Life, 2:718
The Eskimo Storyteller: Folktales from Noatak, Alaska, 3:855
The Esoteric Basis of Christianity or Theosophy and Christian Doctrine, 4:853
Esoteric Christianity, 4:549
The Esoteric Scene: Cultic Milieu and Occult Tarot, 4:860, 4:865
Essais critiques, 2:454
Essay and General Literature Index, 1:113
An Essay Concerning Human Understanding, 1:224, 3:159, 4:178, 4:179, 4:739
The Essayes or Counsels, Civill and Morall, 4:165
Essayists Past and Present, 1:728
An Essay of Dramatic Poesy and Other Critical Writings, 1:241

An Essay on African Philosophical Thought, 4:26, 4:369
An Essay on Anaxagoras, 4:53
The Essay on Comedy, and the Uses of the Comic Spirit, 1:378, 1:379
An Essay on Criticism, 1:251
An Essay on Hardy, 1:362
An Essay on Liberation, 4:408, 5:94
Essay on Man, 1:252
An Essay on Man: An Introduction to a Philosophy of Human Culture, 4:279
An Essay on Marxian Economics, 3:52, 3:95, 3:102
An Essay on Metaphysics, 4:281
Essay on Morals, 4:217
An Essay on Philosophical Method, 4:281
An Essay on Shakespeare's Sonnets, 1:215
Essay on the Active Powers of Man, 4:211
Essay on the Cause of Chemical Proportions, 5:738
Essay on the Intellectual Powers of Man, 4:211
An Essay on the Nature and Significance of Economic Science, 3:47
An Essay on the Origin and Progress of Stereotype Printing, 1:16
An Essay on the Origin of Human Knowledge, 4:195
An Essay on the Poetry of Osip Mandelstam: God's Grateful Guest, 2:738
An Essay on the Principle of Population, 3:54, 3:92
Essay on the Theory of the Earth, 5:792
An Essay on Typography, 1:8
Essays: British and American, 1:728
Essays: On Entrepreneurs, Innovations, Business Cycles and the Evolution of Capitalism, 3:50, 3:105
Essays: Physical and Chemical, 5:749
Essays, Principles, Dialogues: With Selections from Other Writings, 3:181
Essays 1958–1962, on Atomic Physics and Human Knowledge, 5:674
Essays and Addresses, 2:363

Essays before a Sonata, the Majority, and Other Writings, 3:701
Essays in Aesthetics, 4:329
Essays in American Life and Letters, 1:809
Essays in Analysis, 5:516
Essays in Ancient Greek Philosophy (Anton and Kustas), 4:47
Essays in Ancient Greek Philosophy (Anton and Preus), 4:47, 4:66, 4:78
Essays in Ancient Philosophy, 4:48
Essays in Bibliography, Text and Editing, 1:61
Essays in Biography, 3:45, 3:85, 3:86, 3:87, 3:92, 3:94
Essays in Canadian Economic History, 3:621
Essays in Comparative Literature, 1:926
Essays in Criticism, 1:327
Essays in Criticism and Literary Theory, 1:232
Essays in Economics: Theories, Theorizing, Facts and Policies, 3:91
Essays in Economics, Vol. 1: Macroeconomics, 3:62
Essays in Eighteenth-Century Biography, 1:87
Essays in Existentialism, 4:329
Essays in Honor of Carl G. Hempel, 5:92
Essays in Humanity and Technology, 5:71
Essays in London and Elsewhere, 1:764
Essays in Musical Analysis, 3:664
Essays in Persuasion, 3:86
Essays in Physics, 5:682
Essays in Political Philosophy, 4:282
Essays in Positive Economics, 3:46, 3:77
Essays in Pragmatism, 1:768, 4:236
Essays in Psychology, 4:236
Essays in Radical Empiricism and a Pluralistic Universe, 4:236
Essays in Religion and Morality, 4:236
Essays in Science and Philosophy, 4:341
Essays in Shakespearean Criticism, 1:208
Essays in Sociological Theory, 3:237

Essays in South Slavic Literature, 2:785
Essays in the History of Economics, 3:46, 3:101, 3:107, 3:108, 3:114
Essays in the History of Ideas, 4:302
Essays in the History of Mechanics, 5:506
Essays in the History of Publishing, 1:36
Essays in the Philosophy of History, 4:282
Essays in the Public Philosophy, 3:815
Essays in the Science of Culture in Honor of Leslie A. White, 3:42
Essays of a Biologist, 5:798
Essays of a Catholic, 1:442
Essays of Elia, 1:295
Essays Offered to G. H. Luce by His Colleagues and Friends in Honour of His Seventy-fifth Birthday, 2:313
Essays of Montaigne: A Critical Exploration, 2:491, 4:146
Essays on Actions and Events, 4:283, 4:396
Essays on Adam Smith, 4:215
Essays on American Antebellum Politics, 1840–1860, 3:524
Essays on Aristotle's De Anima, 4:70
Essays on Aristotle's Ethics, 4:70
Essays on Aristotle's Poetics, 4:71
Essays on a Science of Mythology, 4:484, 5:455
Essays on Bentham: Studies in Jurisprudence and Political Theory, 3:151
Essays on Biblical Interpretation, 4:318
Essays on C. S. Lewis and George MacDonald, 1:587
Essays on Chaplin, 1:1161
Essays on Contemporary American Drama, 1:1072
Essays on Davidson: Actions and Events, 4:283
Essays on Descartes' Meditations, 4:170
Essays on Developing Economies, 3:53
Essays on Early Modern Philosophers, 4:27, 4:160
Essays on Equality, Law, and Education, 1:380

Essays on Gogol: Logos and the Russian Word, 2:722
Essays on Hayek, 3:83
Essays on Heidegger and Others: Philosophical Papers, 4:294
Essays on Henry Sidgwick, 4:257
Essays on Islamic Philosophy and Science, 4:575
Essays on Karamzin, 2:730
Essays on Language, Mind and Matter, 1919–1926, 4:322
Essays on Latin Lyric, Elegy, and Epic, 2:381
Essays on Life, Art and Science, 1:342
Essays on Literature and Society in Southeast Asia, 2:312
Essays on Medieval German Literature and Iconography, 2:566
Essays on New Testament Themes, 4:825
Essays on Old Testament Hermeneutics, 4:815
Essays on Philosophical Subjects, 3:107, 4:215
Essays on Realism, 2:801
Essays on Religion and the Ancient World, 4:487
Essays on Sex Equality, 1:380
Essays on Shelley, 1:302
Essays on Thai Folklore, 2:335
Essays on the Active Powers of the Human Mind, 4:211
Essays on the Context, Nature, and Influence of Isaac Newton's Theology, 4:184
Essays on the Foundations of Aristotelian Political Science, 4:69
Essays on the History of North American Discovery and Exploration, 1:631
Essays on the Intellectual History of Economics, 3:111
Essays on the Mahabharata, 4:506
Essays on the Philippine Novel in English, 2:328
Essays on the Philosophy and Science of René Descartes, 4:171
Essays on the Philosophy of George Berkeley, 4:192

Essays on the Philosophy of Leibniz, 4:177
Essays on the Philosophy of Music, 3:658, 4:277
Essays on the Philosophy of Socrates, 4:89
Essays on the Philosophy of W. V. Quine, 4:412, 5:100
Essays on the Sociology of Knowledge, 3:213
Essays on Thomas Mann, 2:602
Essays on Tudor and Stuart Politics and Government, 3:402
Essays on Walter Prescott Webb, 3:600
Essay towards a New Theory of Vision, 4:191
The Essence of Christianity, 4:228, 4:660, 4:740
Essence of Decision: Explaining the Cuban Missile Crisis, 3:277
The Essence of Judaism, 4:660
The Essence of Philosophy, 4:226
The Essence of Religion, 4:228
The Essence of Stigler, 3:108
The Essene Writings from Qumran, 4:810
The Essential Alan Watts, 4:881
Essential Articles for the Study of Edmund Spenser, 1:198
Essential Articles for the Study of Francis Bacon, 4:166
Essential Articles for the Study of George Herbert, 1:181
Essential Articles for the Study of John Donne's Poetry, 1:178
Essential Articles for the Study of John Dryden, 1:242
Essential Articles for the Study of Thomas More, 1:194
Essential Articles for the Study of William Blake, 1970–1984, 1:279
The Essential Augustine, 4:109
The Essential Aurobindo, 4:352
The Essential Book of Traditional Chinese Medicine, 4:522

The Essential Chaucer, 1:151
The Essential Darwin, 5:793
The Essential Eddington, 5:681
The Essential Erasmus, 4:721
The Essential Gesture: Writing, Politics, Places, 2:162, 2:989
The Essential Guide to Prescription Drugs, 5:351
The Essential Guide to Vitamins and Minerals, 5:347
Essential Hypertension: A Strategy for Individualized Treatment, 5:373
Essential Liberty: First Amendment Battles for a Free Press, 3:806
Essential Marxism in Postwar France: From Sartre to Althusser, 4:267
Essential Medical Physiology, 5:773
The Essential Piaget, 3:192
Essential Readings in Logical Positivism, 4:264
The Essential Reinhold Niebuhr: Selected Essays and Addresses, 4:784
Essential Relativity, 5:664
The Essential Rudolf Steiner, 4:859
Essentials, 1:891
Essential Sacred Writings from around the World, 4:2, 4:473
The Essential Shakespeare, 1:220
Essential Skills and Strategies in the Helping Process, 5:418
Essentials of Earth History, 5:625
Essentials of Genetics, 5:778
Essentials of Molecular Biology, 5:784
Essentials of Nutrition and Diet Therapy, 5:395
Essentials of Solid-State Electronics, 5:229
Essentials of World History, 3:274
The Essential Tao, 3:467
The Essential Tension, 4:406, 5:25, 5:53, 5:66
The Essential Tillich: An Anthology of the Writings of Paul Tillich, 4:787
The Essential Wisdom of George Santayana, 4:328
The Essential Works of Stoicism, 4:57
The Essential Writings, 3:285

The Essential Writings of Fritjof Schuon, 4:375
The Establishment, 1:1246
The Establishment of the Balkan National States, 1804–1920, 3:391
The Estate, 2:48
The Estate of Poetry, 1:521
The Estates of the Higher Nobility in Fourteenth-Century England, 3:357
Esther, 1:729, 3:562
Esther Rabbath I: An Analytical Translation, 4:611
Esther Waters, 1:380, 1:381
Esthetics as Nightmare: Russian Literary Theory, 1855–1870, 2:689
Esthetics of Music, 3:659
Esthetics of Negligence: La Fontaine's Contes, 2:485
The Esthetics of the Middle Ages, 4:95
The Estiennes, 1:11
Estrangement, 2:130
Estrangement: America and the World, 3:546
Estranging Dawn: The Life and Works of William Vaughn Moody, 1:775
Estrogen: The Facts Can Change Your Life, 5:356
Etching and Other Graphic Arts: An Illustrated Treatise, 1:29
The Eternal Act of Creation: Essays 1979–1990, 1:976
The Eternal City, 1:1174
The Eternal Covenant, 4:254
Eternal Curse on the Reader of These Pages, 2:880
The Eternal Feminine, 2:860
Eternal Feminines: Three Theological Allegories in Dante's Paradiso, 2:418
Eternal Life? 4:775, 4:887
The Eternal Message of Muhammad, 4:588
The Eternal Moment and Other Stories, 1:477
The Eternal Smile, 2:676
Eternal Truths and the Cartesian Circle, 4:170
Ethan Frome, 1:786
Ethan Frome and Other Short Fiction, 1:787
Ethica, 4:489
Ethica Eudemia, 4:65
Ethical and Scientific Issues Posed by Human Uses of Molecular Genetics, 5:121

Ethical Conflicts in Information and Computer Science, Technology, and Business, 5:125, 5:126
The Ethical Foundations of Marxism, 4:243
Ethical Idealism: An Inquiry into the Nature and Function of Ideals, 4:317, 4:389
Ethical Issues Associated with Scientific and Technological Research for the Military, 5:130
Ethical Issues in Engineering, 5:128
Ethical Issues in Family Medicine, 5:119
Ethical Issues in Psychosurgery, 5:121
Ethical Issues in Social Science Research, 5:106
Ethical Problems in Engineering, 5:73
Ethical Self-Determination in Don José Ortega y Gasset, 5:97
Ethical Studies, 4:220
Ethical Writings of Maimonides, 4:668
Ethics (Abelard), 4:106
Ethics (Broad), 4:277
Ethics (Spinoza), 4:186
Ethics: A Bibliography, 4:14
Ethics: An Investigation of the Facts and Laws of the Moral Life, 3:197
Ethics, Wealth and Salvation: A Study in Buddhist Social Ethics, 4:514, 4:896
Ethics after Babel: The Languages of Morals and Their Discontents, 4:893
Ethics and Educational Policy, 3:258
Ethics and Engineering Curricula, 5:127
Ethics and Infinity, 4:901
Ethics and Nuclear Arms: European and American Perspectives, 5:110
Ethics and Nuclear Deterrence, 5:110
Ethics and Population Limitation, 5:84
Ethics and Problems of the 21st Century, 5:128
Ethics and Regulation of Clinical Research, 5:121
Ethics and Risk Management in Engineering, 5:128
The Ethics and Selected Letters, 4:187

Ethics and Social Responsibility in Science Education, 5:107

Ethics and Technology, 5:129

Ethics and Technology: Ethical Choices in the Age of Pervasive Technology, 5:130

Ethics and the Environment, 5:116

Ethics and the History of Philosophy: Selected Essays, 4:277

Ethics and the Management of Computer Technology, 5:125

Ethics from a Theocentric Perspective, 4:744, 4:900

Ethics in an Age of Pervasive Technology, 5:52, 5:129

Ethics in an Age of Technology, 4:388, 5:127, 5:160, 5:196

Ethics in Clinical Psychology, 5:123

Ethics in Engineering, 5:129

Ethics in Medicine: Historical Perspectives and Contemporary Concerns, 5:123

Ethics in Nursing, 5:118

Ethics in Nursing: An Annotated Bibliography, 5:122

Ethics in Social and Behavioral Research, 5:107

Ethics in the History of Western Philosophy, 4:160

The Ethics of Ambiguity, 2:458

The Ethics of Authenticity, 4:414

The Ethics of Competition and Other Essays, 3:89

The Ethics of Environmental Concern, 5:74, 5:113

The Ethics of Freedom, 5:163, 5:164

The Ethics of Intensity in American Fiction, 1:723

The Ethics of Jonathan Edwards: Morality and Aesthetics, 4:767

The Ethics of Life and Death with Heinrich von Kleist, 2:599

Ethics of New Reproductive Technologies, 5:120

The Ethics of Organizational Transformation, 3:49

The Ethics of Reading: Kant, de Man, Eliot, James, and Benjamin, 1:1151

The Ethics of Reproductive Technology, 5:118

The Ethics of Romanticism, 1:265

The Ethics of Socrates: A Compilation, 4:89

The Ethics of Teaching, 3:258

The Ethics of Teaching and Scientific Research, 5:107

The Ethics of the Aristocrats and Other Satirical Works, 2:84

The Ethics of Using Animals in Biomedical Research, 5:123

The Ethics of War and Nuclear Deterrence, 5:112

Ethics on Call, 5:119

Ethics since Nineteen Hundred, 4:268

Ethics Teaching in Higher Education, 5:84

Ethics with Aristotle, 4:67

Ethiopia, 3:422

Ethiopian Story, 2:357

Ethiopiques, 2:146

The Ethnic Chinese in the ASEAN States: Bibliographical Essays, 2:311

Ethnic Groups and Boundaries, 3:22

The Ethnic Image in Modern American Literature: 1900–1950, 1:793

Ethnicity, Race, and American Foreign Policy, 3:544

Ethnicity and Race in the U.S.A.: Toward the Twenty-First Century, 3:554

Ethnic Minority Media: An International Perspective, 3:204, 3:804

Ethnic Perspectives in American Literature, 1:713

Ethnic Survival in America, 4:641

Ethnic Theatre in the United States, 1:1075

Ethnographic Bibliography of North America, 3:38

Ethnomathematics: A Multicultural View of Mathematical Ideas, 5:494

Ethnomusicology, 3:667

Ethnomusicology: A Study of Its Nature, Its Problems, Methods and Representative Personalities to Which Is Added a Bibliography, 3:666

Ethnomusicology and Modern Music History, 3:659, 3:666

Ethnomusicology of the Flathead Indians, 3:865

Ethnoscapes: Transcultural Studies in Action and Place, 3:206

Étienne Gilson, 4:286

An Étienne Gilson Tribute, 4:286

Et in Arcadia Ego: Essays on Death in the Pastoral Novel, 2:984

The Etiology, Concept and Prophylaxis of Childbed Fever, 5:390

Etonian, 1:302

Etoro Social Structure: A Study in Structural Contradiction, 3:24

The Etruscan, 2:661

Etruscan Places, 1:510

The Etruscans, 3:305

The Etruscans: Their Art and Civilization, 3:305

Etymological Lexicon of Classical Greek, 1:99

Etymologies and Genealogies, 2:446

The Eucharistic Theology of Theodore Beza, 4:732

Euclid: His Life and His System, 5:505

Euclidean and Non-Euclidean Geometries: Development and History, 5:504

Eudora Welty, 1:895, 1:896

Eudora Welty: A Critical Bibliography, 1936–58, 1:896

Eudora Welty: Seeing Black and White, 1:896

Eudora Welty: The Eye of the Storyteller, 1:896

Eudora Welty: Thirteen Essays, 1:896

Eudora Welty: Two Pictures at Once in Her Frame, 1:895

Eudora Welty's Chronicle: A Story of Mississippi Life, 1:895

Eugen Duhring's Revolution in Science, 4:227

Eugene Ionesco, 2:484

Eugene Onegin, 2:740, 2:750, 2:751

Eugene Onegin: A Novel in Verse, 2:751

Eugene O'Neill, 1:1108

Eugene O'Neill: A Critical Study, 1:1108

Eugene O'Neill and the American Critic: A Bibliographical Checklist, 1:1108

Eugene O'Neill and the Tragic Tension: An Interpretive Study of the Plays, 1:1108

Eugene O'Neill's New Language of Kinship, 1:1108

Eugene V. Debs: Citizen and Socialist, 3:549

Eugénie Grandet, 2:453

Eugenio Montale (Becker), 2:428

Eugenio Montale (Singh), 2:428

Eugenio Montale: Poet on the Edge, 2:428

Eugenio Montale's Poetry: A Dream in Reason's Presence, 2:428

Eunuch, 2:395

Euphues: The Anatomy of Wit, 1:185, 1:186

Euphues and His England, 1:185, 1:186

Eupsychian Management: A Journal, 5:461

Eurhythmics, Art and Education, 3:744

Euripidean Drama: Myth, Theme and Structure, 2:356

Euripides and His Age, 2:357

Euripides and His Influence, 2:357

Euripides and the Full Circle of Myth, 2:357, 4:475

Euripides and the Spirit of His Dramas, 2:356

Euripides' Medea: The Incarnation of Disorder, 4:475

Euripides the Rationalist, 2:357

Europa Yearbook, 1:82, 1:104

Europe, 1815–1914, 3:340

European Alliances and Alignments, 1871–1890, 3:341

European Armies and the Conduct of War, 3:280

European Authors, 1000–1900, 1:126, 1:128, 2:3

European Bookdealers, 1:77

European Community, 3:345

The European Culture Area: A Systematic Geography, 3:132

Europe and America beyond Two Thousand, 3:346

European Decolonization, 1918–1981: An Introductory Survey, 3:345

The European Demographic System: 1500–1820, 3:341

European Discovery of America: The Northern Voyages, 1:631, 3:335, 3:589

The European Discovery of America: The Southern Voyages, 1:631, 3:335, 3:589

European Drama Criticism, 1900–1975, 1:123

Europe and the Middle East, 3:457

Europe and the People without History, 3:17

Europe and the World in the Age of Expansion, 3:274

European Encounters with the New World, 3:336

The European Folktale: Form and Nature, 3:856

European Historical Statistics, 1750–1970, 3:327, 3:343

European Imperialism and the Partition of Africa, 3:418

European Integration: The State of the Art, 3:58

European Intellectual History since 1789, 3:327, 4:27

European Jewry in the Age of Mercantilism, 1550–1750, 3:348

European Literature in the Nineteenth Century, 2:414

The European Miracle, 3:326

European Research Centres, 5:3

European Revolutions and the American Literary Renaissance, 1:652

The Europeans (Barzini), 3:342

The Europeans (James), 1:762

European Sources of Scientific and Technical Information, 5:3

European Thought in the Eighteenth Century, 4:161

European Union: From Hitler to DeGaulle, 3:346

The European Witch Craze in the Sixteenth and Seventeenth Centuries and Other Essays, 3:411

European Writers, 1:128, 2:4

Europe between the Wars: A Political History, 3:344

Europe in Crisis, 1589–1648, 4:737

Europe in Decay, 1936–40, 3:407

Europe in Review: Reading and Sources, 3:327

Europe in the High Middle Ages, 1150–1309, 3:331

Europe in Transition: The 12th Century Renaissance in Europe, 3:331

Europe of the Devout, 4:728, 4:736

Europe on a Saturday Night, 3:899

Europe's Classical Balance of Power, 3:279

Europe since Hitler: The Rebirth of Europe, 3:346

Europe since 1945: A Concise History, 3:346

Europe Transformed, 1878–1919, 3:343

Eusebius, Christianity and Judaism, 4:709

Eustace and Hilda, 1:493, 1:494

The Eustace Diamonds, 1:405

Eutaw: A Sequel to the Forayers, 1:696

Euthyphro, 4:89

Evaluation and Explanation in the Biomedical Sciences, 5:78

Eva Luna, 2:851

The Evangelical Tradition in America, 4:754

Evangeline: A Tale of Acadie, 1:682

Evangeline and Selected Tales and Poems, 1:682

Evangelism in the Early Church, 4:683

Evangelist of Desire: John Wesley and the Methodists, 4:789

The Evangelization of the Roman Empire: Identity and Adaptability, 4:683

Evan Harrington, 1:378

Eva Perón, 3:633

Evaporite Sedimentology, 5:625

Evaristo Carriego: A Book about Old-time Buenos Aires, 2:856

Evelina, or A Young Lady's Entrance in the World, 1:235

Evelyn Innes, 1:381

Evelyn Waugh, 1:562, 1:563

Evelyn Waugh: A Reference Guide, 1:563

Evelyn Waugh: New Directions, 1:562

Evelyn Waugh: The Critical Heritage, 1:563

Evelyn Waugh and the Problem of Evil, 1:563

Even a Fist Was Once an Open Palm with Fingers: Recent Poems, 2:13

Evening Land: Aftonland, 2:676

Evening Mail, 1:601

The Evening of the Holiday, 2:953

Evening Post: A Century of Journalism, 3:590

Evenings on a Farm near Dikanka, 2:720

The Evening Star, 1:1010

Evening Tales, 2:826

An Evening Walk, 1:306

The Event of the Koran: Islam and Its Scripture, 4:587

Events in the Twentieth Century, 1:88

The Eve of St. Agnes, 1:267, 1:293

The Eve of St. Venus, 1:454

The Eve of the Revolution: A Chronicle of the Breach with England, 3:566

The Everlasting Mercy, 1:518

Ever since Darwin: Reflections in Natural History, 5:16, 5:638, 5:764

Ever since Paradise, 1:537

Ever since Sinai: A Modern View of Torah, 4:601

The Ever White Mountain: Korean Lyrics in the Classical Sijo Form, 2:299

Everybody's Autobiography, 1:882

Everybody's Guide to Homeopathic Medicines, 5:338

Everybody Who Was Anybody: A Biography of Gertrude Stein, 1:882

Everybody Wins, 1:1104

Everyday Chinese-English Dictionary, 1:97

Everyday Life in Early America, 3:520

Everyday Spanish Idioms, 1:102

An Everyday Story: Norwegian Women's Fiction, 2:662

Every Good Boy Deserves Favor and Professional Foul, 1:554

Everyman, 1:161

Everyman and Medieval Miracle Plays, 1:158

The Everyman Book of Victorian Verse: The Post-Romantics, 1:316

Everyman His Own Historian: Essays on History and Politics, 3:275, 3:566

Every Man in His Humour, 1:183

Every Man out of His Humour, 1:183

Everyman's Book of English Folktales, 3:856

Everyman's Book of Nonsense, 3:870

Everyman's Talmud, 4:620

The Everything and the Nothing, 4:872

Everything to Be Endured, 1:889

Everything You Always Wanted to Know about Statistics, but Didn't Know How to Ask, 5:521

Everywhere and Nowhere: The Path of Alan Watts, 4:881

Everywhere Spoken Against: Dissent in the Victorian Novel, 1:318

Every Writer's Guide to Copyright and Publishing Law, 1:54

Eve's Journey: Feminine Images in Hebraic Literary Tradition, 2:8, 4:649

Eve's Journey: The Physical Experience of Being Female, 5:356

Eve's Ransom, 1:358

The Evidence of Things Not Seen, 1:939

Evil and the God of Love, 4:117

Evil and the Process God, 4:289

Evil Spirit, 2:79

Evita, First Lady: A Biography of Eva Perón, 3:633

Evolution, 5:780

Evolution: A Theory in Crisis, 5:784

Evolution: The History of an Idea, 5:45

Evolution: The Main Synthesis, 3:18

Evolution and Culture, 3:17, 3:18

Evolution and Ethics, 5:800

Evolution and Modification of Behavior, 3:171, 3:190

Evolution and Society: A Study in Victorian Social Theory, 3:41

Evolution and the Founders of Pragmatism, 4:163

Evolution and the Myth of Creationism, 5:779

Evolutionary Art and Computers, 5:194

Evolutionary Economics, 3:71

The Evolutionary Process, 3:18

The Evolutionary Synthesis: Perspectives on the Unification of Biology, 5:34

Evolution at a Crossroads: The New Philosophy of Science, 5:763

Evolution in Science and Religion, 5:702

Evolution Now: A Century after Darwin, 5:795

Evolution of a Chinese Novel: Shui Hu Chuan, 2:219

The Evolution of Balzac's "Comédie Humaine," 2:454

The Evolution of British Imperial Policy during the Mid-nineteenth Century, 3:366

Evolution of Chemistry: A History of Its Ideas, Methods, and Materials, 5:728

The Evolution of Chinese Tz'u Poetry, 2:189

The Evolution of Civilizations: An Introduction to Historical Analysis, 3:327

The Evolution of Culture: The Development of Civilization to the Fall of Rome, 3:14, 3:19, 3:41–42

The Evolution of Economic Society, 3:45

The Evolution of Economic Thought, 3:45

The Evolution of Irish Nationalist Politics, 3:370

Evolution of Keats's Poetry, 1:294

The Evolution of Labor Relations in Japan, 3:477

The Evolution of Life Histories, 3:18

Evolution of Mathematical Concepts, 5:492

The Evolution of Medieval Thought, 4:94, 4:696, 5:39

The Evolution of Nuclear Strategy, 3:278

The Evolution of Physics, 5:48, 5:682

The Evolution of Privlages, 3:421

The Evolution of Progress, 5:156

The Evolution of Rights in Liberal Theory, 4:387

The Evolution of Societies, 3:237

The Evolution of Society: Selections from Herbert Spencer's "Principles of Sociology," 3:240

The Evolution of the Euclidean Elements, 5:504

The Evolution of the Sikh Community: Five Essays, 4:516

Evolution of Urban Society: Early Mesopotamia and Prehispanic Mexico, 4:438

The Evolution of Useful Things, 5:174, 5:226

The Evolution of Walt Whitman, 1:707

The Evolution of Weapons and Warfare, 3:278

Evolution without Evidence: Charles Darwin and the Origin of Species, 5:794

Evolution—Social and Organic: Linnaeus, Darwin, Kropotkin, Marx, 5:805

The Evolving Continents, 5:630

The Evolving Self: Problem and Process in Human Development, 3:174

The Ewings, 1:866

The Exact Sciences in Antiquity, 5:38

Exaltation of Light, 2:853

The Exalted Faith, 4:628

An Examination of Dr. Reid's Inquiry into the Human Mind, 4:212

Examination of Ezra Pound, 1:874

An Examination of James Joyce, 2:459

Examination of McTaggart's Philosophy, 4:277, 4:304

An Examination of Plato's Doctrines, 4:79

An Examination of Sir William Hamilton's Philosophy, 4:244

The Examined Life: Philosophical Meditations, 4:314, 4:389

The Examined Self: Benjamin Franklin, Henry Adams, Henry James, 1:639

Examine Your Doctor: A Patient's Guide to Avoiding Medical Mishaps, 5:336

Examining Holistic Medicine, 5:320

The Example of Edward Taylor, 1:644

The Example of Melville, 1:688

Excavating in Egypt: The Egypt Exploration Society, 1882–1982, 3:300

Excellence: Can We Be Equal and Excellent Too?, 3:250

Excellence and Equality, 3:254

Excellent Women, 1:538, 1:539

Exceptional Children: Introduction to Special Education, 3:255

The Exceptional Students in the Regular Classroom, 3:254

Except the Lord, 1:456

The Excesses of God: Robinson Jeffers as a Religious Figure, 1:851

The Exchange, 2:767

The Exchange and Other Stories, 2:767

Exchange and Power in Social Life, 3:208

Exchanges: South African Literature in Translation, 2:158

Excitement and Fascination of Science, 5:10

The Excluded Americans: Homelessness and Housing Policies, 3:68

Exclusiveness and Tolerance, 4:624

The Ex-Convict, 1:1173

The Excursion, 1:266, 1:305, 1:306

Excursions in World Music, 3:667

The Executioner's Song, 1:1011, 1:1012

"The Execution of Justice in England," by William Cecil, and "A True, Sincere, and Modest Defense of English Catholics," by William Allen, 4:734

The Execution of Mayor Yin and Other Stories from the Great Proletarian Cultural Revolution, 2:241

Executive Computing: How to Get It Done on Your Own, 5:557

Executive Leadership: A Rational Approach, 5:439

Exegetical Method: A Student's Handbook, 4:815

Exegetic Homilies, 4:705

The Exemplary Novels, 2:535

The Exercise Exchange Program, 5:347

Exercise for the Elderly, 5:326

Exercise Injuries: Prevention and Treatment, 5:396

Exercise Medicine: Physiological Principles and Clinical Applications, 5:325

Exercise Physiology: Energy, Nutrition, and Human Performance, 5:326

Exercises in Style, 2:496

Exercitatio Anatomica de Motu Cordis et Sanguinis in Animalibus, 5:361

Exhumations, 1:500

Exile and Kingdom, 1:630

Exile and Marriages, 1:983

Exile and Other Poems, 2:493

Exile and Return: Selected Poems, 2:376

The Exile and the Kingdom, 2:464

Exile and Tradition: Studies in African and Caribbean Literature, 2:112

Exiled in the Land of the Free, 3:515

The Exile into Eternity, 2:408

The Exile of James Joyce, 2:467

The Exiles, 2:138

Exiles: A Play, 1:504

The Exiles and Other Stories, 2:881

Exile's Return: A Literary Odyssey of the 1920s, 1:822

Existence: A New Dimension in Psychiatry and Psychology, 5:462

Existence and Actuality: Conversations with Charles Hartshorne, 4:289

Existence and Being, 4:291

Existential Battles: The Growth of Norman Mailer, 1:1012

The Existential Dialectic of Marx and Merleau-Ponty, 4:311

Existential Foundation of Medicine and Psychology, 5:436

Existentialism (Macquarrie), 4:265

Existentialism (Solomon), 4:267

Existentialism (Warnock), 4:268

Existentialism and Human Emotions, 4:329

Existentialism and Humanism, 4:329

Existentialism of Alberto Moravia, 2:430

Existentialist Ethics, 4:262

The Existential Pleasures of Engineering, 5:70, 5:166, 5:253

Existential Psychoanalysis, 4:329

Existential Psychology, 5:462

Existential Psychotherapy, 5:420

The Existential Sociology of Jean-Paul Sartre, 4:331

Existential Technics, 5:71, 5:92

Exit, Voice and Loyalty, 3:64

Exit the King, 2:483

Exons, Introns and Talking Genes—The Science behind the Human Genome Project, 5:784

The Exorcism of Sex and Death in Julien Green's Novels, 2:482

The Expanding City, 3:130

Expanding the View, 4:769

The Expanding Universe, 5:681

The Expanding Universe: Astronomy's "Great Debate," 1900–1931, 5:49

The Expanse of Green, 2:84

The Expansion of Christianity in the First Three Centuries, 4:681

The Expansion of Everyday Life, 1860–1876, 3:530

The Expansion of Islam: An Arab Religion in the Non-Arab World, 4:568

Expats: Travels in Arabia, from Tripoli to Teheran, 3:902

Expectations in Economics, 3:64

The Expedient Utopian: Bandaranaike and Ceylon, 3:487

The Expedition of Humphrey Clinker, 1:256

Expedition to Earth, 1:614

The Expense of Greatness, 1:816

Expensive People, 1:1022

Experience, 1:277

Experience and Artistic Expression in Lope de Vega: The Making of, 2:555

Experience and Certainty, 4:296

Experience and Education, 3:260, 4:224

Experience and Nature, 3:260, 4:224

The Experience of Defeat: Milton and Some Contemporaries, 3:404

The Experience of Depression, 5:427

The Experience of Insight, 4:519

The Experience of Literature, 1:129

Experiencing Architecture, 3:762

Experiencing Erickson: An Introduction to the Man and His Work, 5:441

Experiencing Hypnosis: Therapeutic Approaches to Altered States, 5:441

Experiment, Theory, Practice, 5:697

Experimental and Quasi-Experimental Designs for Research, 3:6

Experimental Approaches to Mammalian Embryonic Development, 5:777

The Experimental Fictions of Ambrose Bierce, 1:735

Experimental Food Science, 5:267

Experimental Methodology, 3:169

Experimental Phenomenology: An Introduction, 5:92

The Experimental Psychology of Alfred Binet, 3:181

Experimental Researches in Chemistry and Physics, 5:684, 5:744

Experimental Researches in Electricity, 5:745

Experimentation in American Religion, 4:856

Experimentation with Human Beings, 5:79

Experiment in Autobiography, 1:563

Experimenting with Truth, 5:177, 5:198

Experiments and Considerations Touching Colours, 5:739

Experiments and Observations on Different Kinds of Air, 5:753

Experiments in Plant–Hybridization, 5:807

Expiation, 2:724

Explaining America: The Federalist, 3:544

Explaining Behavior: Reasons in a World of Causes, 5:74

Explaining Hitler's Germany: Historians and the Third Reich, 3:377

Explaining Religion: Criticism and Theory from Bodin to Freud, 4:420

Explaining Science: A Cognitive Approach, 5:63

Explanation and Understanding, 4:338

Explanation in Geography, 3:117, 3:118

An Explanation of America, 1:1030

The Explanation of Behavior, 4:414

The Explanation of Ideology: Family Structures and Social Systems, 3:25

The Exploded Form: The Modernist Novel in America, 1:919

Exploding Poetry: Baudelaire-Rimbaud, 2:457, 2:500

The Exploding Suns: Secrets of Supernovae, 5:593

Exploding the Gene Myth, 5:781

The Exploitation of East Africa, 3:422

Exploration and Empire, 3:524

Exploration and Mining Geology, 5:238

The Exploration of North America, 1630–1776, 3:895

The Exploration of Space, 5:601

The Exploration of the Colorado River and Its Canyons, 5:646

The Exploration of the Pacific, 3:493

Explorations, 1:572

Explorations in African Systems of Thought, 4:462

Explorations in Cultural Anthropology, 3:38

Explorations in General Theory in Social Science, 3:238

Explorations in Personality, 3:178

Explorations in Psychoanalysis, 5:425

Explorations in Psychohistory, 3:276

Explorations in Shakespeare's Language, 1:216

Explorations in the Understanding of Landscape, 3:121

Explorations in Whitehead's Philosophy, 4:342

Explorer of the Human Brain: the Life of Santiago Ramón y Cajal, 5:811

Explorer of the Universe, 5:606

Explorers and Settlers, 3:897

The Explorers of North America 1492–1806, 3:610

Explorers of the Black Box, 5:339, 5:774

Exploring Artificial Intelligence on Your IBM PC, 5:568

Exploring Data, 5:522, 5:523

Exploring Jewish Ethics: Papers on Covenant Responsibility, 4:661

Exploring Judaism: A Reconstructionist Approach, 4:659

Exploring Madness: Experience, Theory, and Research, 5:426

Exploring Our Living Planet, 3:126, 5:641

Exploring Probability, 5:523

The Exploring Spirit: America and the World, Then and Now, 3:569

Exploring Surveys and Information from Samples, 5:522

Exploring the Bismarck, 5:641

Exploring the Deep Frontier: The Adventure of Man in the Sea, 3:920

Exploring the Titanic, 5:641

Exploring Washington's Past: A Road Guide to History, 3:896

Explosion in a Cathedral, 2:860

Explosions and Other Stories, 2:259

Ex Ponto, 2:390

Exporting Workers: The Turkish Case, 3:453

Exposed Structure in Building Design, 5:246

Exposing Cults: Understanding the Rise of Gurus in North America, 4:856

Exposition of the System of the World, 5:698

Expositions and Developments, 3:722

Expressionism in German Life: Literature and the Theatre, 2:566, 3:171

The Expression of the Emotions in Man and Animals, 5:793

Expressions of Self in Chinese Literature, 2:189

Ex Prodigy: My Childhood and Youth, 5:495, 5:584

The Expulsion of the Triumphant Beast, 4:135

Extensional Tectonics Associated with Convergent Plate Boundaries, 5:648

Extension of Copyright Terms, 1:54

The Exterminating Angel, Nazarin, and Los Olvidados, 3:832

Exterminator, 1:957

Extinction, 5:831

Extraordinary Facts Relating to the Vision of Colors, 5:741

The Extraordinary Mr. Wilkes, 3:362

An Extraordinary Woman: Selected Writings of Germaine de Staël, 2:510

Extrapolations: Demonstrations of Ericksonian Therapy, 5:441

Extrapolations from Dystopia: A Critical Study of Soviet Science Fiction, 2:686

The Extraterrestrial Life Debate 1750–1900, 5:598

Extraterrestrials: Science and Alien Intelligence, 5:598

Extraterritorial: Papers on Literature and the Language Revolution, 1:1054

Extravagaria, 2:874

The Extreme Occident, 2:824

Eye, 2:740

The Eye: The Window of the World, 5:342

Eye and Brain: the Psychology of Seeing, 5:193

Eye in the Sky, 1:1257

Eyeless in Gaza, 1:499

Eyeless Sight: A Study of Extra-Retinal Vision and the Paroptic Sense, 2:502

Eye of the Heart: Short Stories from Latin America, 2:849

The Eye of the Scarecrow, 2:936

The Eye of the Storm, 2:965, 2:966

Eye of the Story: Selected Essays and Reviews, 1:895

Eye on the World, 3:813

The Eyesight of Wasps, 2:737

"Eyes of the Night," 2:267

Eyrbyggja Saga, 2:641

Eyvind Johnson, 2:675

Ezekiel: A Commentary, 4:834

Ezra Pound, 1:872, 1:873

Ezra Pound: A Bibliography, 1:873

Ezra Pound: The Critical Heritage, 1:873

Ezra Pound Among the Poets, 1:872

Ezra Pound and America, 1:873

Ezra Pound and Italian Fascism, 1:874

Ezra Pound and the Cantos: A Record of Struggle, 1:873

Ezra Pound and the Erotic Medium, 1:873

Ezra Pound and the Monument of Culture, 1:874

Ezra Pound and the Symbolist Inheritance, 1:873

Ezra Pound as Literary Critic, 1:874

Ezra Pound in London and Paris, 1908–1925, 1:874

F

Faber Book of Ballads, 1:148

The Faber Book of Contemporary Australian Short Stories, 2:947

The Faber Book of Contemporary Latin American Short Stories, 2:848

The Faber Book of Gay Short Fiction, 1:1183, 1:1185

The Faber Book of Twentieth Century Verse, 1:418
Fabergé and the Russian Master Goldsmiths, 3:767
A Fable (Faulkner), 1:834, 1:835
Fable (Pinget), 2:493
A Fable (Van Itallie), 1:1114
Fable about Man, 4:156
A Fable for Critics, 1:685
The Fable of Orpheus, 2:436
Fables, 2:245
Fables for Our Time, 1:890
The Fables of Aesop, 2:352, 3:882
Fables of Identity: Studies in Poetic Mythology, 2:988
Fables of La Fontaine, 2:485
Fables of Man, 1:780
Fables of Mind: An Inquiry into Poe's Fiction, 1:693
Fabrica, 5:365
Fabricating the Self: The Fictions of Jessica Anderson, 2:948
The Fabric of the Body: European Traditions of Anatomical Illustration, 5:194
Fabric of the Heavens: The Development of Astronomy and Dynamics, 5:32
The Fabrics of Geology, 5:622
The Fabulous Miss Marie, 1:1086
The Fabulous Riverboat, 1:1257
Façade, 1:547
Façades: Edith, Osbert, and Sacheverell Sitwell, 1:548
The Face behind the Face, 2:774
The Face of Another, 2:284
The Face of Battle, 3:279, 3:343
The Face of Creation: Contemporary Hungarian Poetry, 2:798
The Face of Europe, 3:327
The Face of the Deep, 5:631
The Face of Time, 1:833
Faces, 2:649
Faces in My Time, 1:536
Faces in the Clouds: A New Theory of Religion, 3:212
Faces in the Water, 2:974
Faces of Degeneration: Aspects of a European Disorder, 1848–1918, 3:343
The Faces of Eve: Women in the Nineteenth Century American Novel, 1:657

Faces of Feminism: A Study of Feminism as a Social Movement, 3:217
Faces of Hunger, 4:387
Faces of Islam in African Literature, 2:108
Faces of Medicine: A Philosophical Study, 5:78
Faces of Revolution, 3:519, 3:564
Face to Face, 2:161
Face to Face with Levinas, 4:901
Facing East, 3:407
Facing Mount Kenya, 3:422
Facing Starvation: Norman Borlaug and the Fight against Hunger, 5:270
Facing the Chair, 1:828
Facing West from California's Shores, 4:858
Fact, Fiction, and Forecast, 4:403, 5:63
Fact and Context: The News as Myth, 3:807
Fact and Fantasy in Freudian Theory, 5:448
Factions' Fictions: Ideological Closure in Swift's Satire, 1:260
A Factious People: Politics and Society in Colonial New York, 3:516
The Fact of a Door Frame: Poems Selected and New, 1950–1984, 1:1037
Factory Girls: Women in the Thread Mills of Meiji Japan, 3:480
The Facts: A Novelist's Autobiography, 1:1041
Facts about the Presidents, 1:88, 3:506
Facts about the States, 3:148, 3:506
Facts from Figures, 5:523
The Facts of Life: An Essay in Feelings, Facts and Fantasy, 5:459
The Facts of Life: Science and the Abortion Controversy, 5:782
The Facts of Reconstruction: Essays in Honor of John Hope Franklin, 3:580
Facts on File, 1:88
Facts on File Bibliography of American Fiction: 1866–1918, 1:122
The Facts on File Dictionary of Astronomy, 5:588
The Facts on File Dictionary of Biology, 5:762

The Facts on File Dictionary of Botany, 5:762
The Facts on File Dictionary of European History, 1485–1789, 3:327
The Facts on File Dictionary of Proverbs, 1:115
The Facts on File English-French Visual Dictionary, 1:98, 1:102
Facts on File Scientific Yearbook, 5:2
Facts on File Yearbooks, 1:82
Factual Fictions: The Origins of the English Novel, 1:230
Faculty and the Library: The Undergraduate Experience, 5:544
Fado Alexandrino, 2:559
Fads and Fallacies in the Name of Science, 5:63
Fads and Foibles of Modern Sociology and Related Sciences, 3:240
The Faerie Queene, 1:164, 1:197, 1:198
Fahrenheit 451, 1:1252, 1:1255
The Failing Distance: The Autobiographical Impulse in John Ruskin, 1:395
The Fail-Safe Society, 5:157, 5:182
The Failure, 2:430
The Failure of Modernism, 1:800, 1:914
The Fair, 2:853
Fairbank Remembered, 3:498
Fair Blows the Wind, 1:1216
Fair Greece, Sad Relic, 2:371
The Fair Haven, 1:342
Fair Land, Fair Land, 1:1214
A Fairly Good Time, 2:911, 2:912
A Fairly Honorable Defeat, 1:523
The Fair Maid of Perth, 1:298
The Fair Maid of the West, 1:182
Fair Trial: Rights of the Accused in American History, 3:139
Fair Use and Free Inquiry: Copyright Law and the New Media, 1:54
Fair Use of Unpublished Works, 1:55
The Fair Use Privilege in Copyright Law, 1:55
Fairy Mythology, 3:848

Fairy Ship, 1:583
The Fairy Tale as Art Form and Portrait of Man, 3:869
Fairy Tales, 1:825
Fairy Tales, Fables, Legends, and Myths, 3:847
Fairy Tales, Told for Children, 2:646
Fairy Tales and Society: Illusion, Allusion, and Paradigm, 1:578
Fairy Tales as Ways of Knowing, 3:848
Faith, Prayer and Grace: A Comparative Study in Ramanuja and Kierkegaard, 4:37
Faith, Reason and Theology, 4:117
Faith, Trinity, Incarnation, 4:63
Faith after the Holocaust, 4:648
Faith and Fratricide: The Theological Roots of Anti-Semitism, 4:684, 4:785
Faith and Knowledge: The Jew in the Medieval World, 4:629
Faith and Piety in Early Judaism: Texts and Documents, 4:615
Faith and Power: The Politics of Islam, 4:579
Faith and Reason: An Introduction to Modern Jewish Thought, 4:646
Faith and the Intifada: Palestinian Christian Voices, 4:896
Faith and Works: Cranmer and Hooker on Justification, 4:764
A Faith for All Seasons, 3:442
Faithful Ruslan, 2:772
The Faith Healer, 1:479
Faith in a Seed, 5:762
Faith in History and Society: Toward a Practical Fundamental Theology, 4:904
The Faith of a Liberal, 4:280
The Faith of John Knox, 4:774
The Faith of Qumran, 4:616
The Faith of Reason, 4:160
The Faith of Secular Jews, 4:651, 4:656
The Faith of the Scots, 3:368
Faith on Earth, 4:745
Faith Strengthened, 4:631

Fakes and Frauds: Varieties of Deception in Print and Manuscript, 1:35
Fake? The Art of Deception, 5:193
Falange: A History of Spanish Fascism, 3:387
Falasha Anthology, 4:644
The Falashas: The Forgotten Jews of Ethiopia, 4:644
Falconer, 1:961
Falkland, 1:340
Falkner: A Novel, 1:300
The Fall, 2:464
The Fallacy of Star Wars, 5:240
The Fall and Rise of Modern Italy, 3:385
Fallen from the Symboled World, 1:997
Fallen Hearts, 1:1240
Fallen Soldiers: Reshaping the Memory of the World Wars, 3:346
Fall from Grace, 3:543
Fallible Man: Philosophy of the Will, 4:318
Falling: May Day Sermon and Other Poems, 1:967
Falling from Grace, 3:212
The Falling Sickness, 5:394
The Fall of America: Poems of These States, 1965–1971, 1:981
The Fall of Camelot: A Study of Tennyson's Idylls of the King, 1:402
The Fall of Hyperion, 1:267
The Fall of Imperial China, 3:472
The Fall of Israel, 3:439
Fall of Moondust, 1:614
The Fall of Public Man, 3:209, 3:238
The Fall of Robespierre: An Historic Drama, 1:304
The Fall of the Dynasties: The Collapse of the Old Order, 1905–1922, 3:343
The Fall of the House of Usher, 1:1239
The Fall of the Imam, 2:71, 2:120
The Fall of the King, 2:652
The Fall of the Roman Republic: Six Roman Lives, 3:318
The Fall of the Russian Empire, 3:398
The False and True, 2:437
False Dawn: Persian Poems (1951–1984), 2:84
False Gods, 1:937

The False Messiah, 2:585
The False Prison, 4:346
Fam and Yam, 1:1080
Familiar Cacti of North America, 5:767
Familiar Faces, Hidden Lives, 3:551
The Familiar Letter as a Literary Genre in the Age of Pushkin, 2:691
Familiar Mysteries: The Truth in Myth, 3:856
Families Living with Drugs and HIV, 5:403
Families under the Influence: Changing Alcoholic Patterns, 5:401
The Family (Goode), 3:206
The Family (Is'ao Yü), 2:137
Family (Pa Chin), 2:259, 2:260, 2:265, 2:292, 2:422
Family, Drama, and American Dreams, 1:1075
Family, Fields, and Ancestors, 3:467
The Family, Sex and Marriage in England, 1500–1800, 3:359, 3:408, 4:735
Family, Socialization, and Interaction Process, 3:237
The Family, Women and Death, 3:307
A Family Affair, 2:744
A Family and a Fortune, 1:462
Family and Fortune, 3:408
Family and Friends, 1:451
Family and Kinship in Chinese Society, 3:467
Family and Kinship in East London, 3:20
Family and Population in East Asian History, 3:464
The Family Carnovsky, 2:49
A Family Chronicle (Aksakov), 2:697
Family Chronicle (Pratolini), 2:437
Family Counseling, 5:419
Family Devotions, 1:1094
The Family Foot Care Book, 5:396
The Family Gathering, 2:674
Family Guide to Natural Medicine, 5:319
The Family Idiot: Gustave Flaubert, 1821–1857, 2:476, 2:507
The Family in Classical Greece, 3:309
The Family in Renaissance Florence, 2:404

The Family Letters, 1:342
The Family Mashber, 2:38
The Family Moskat, 1:1049, 2:48
Family Names: How Our Surnames Came to America, 3:552
The Family of Leon Roch, 2:547
The Family of Pascual Duarte, 2:521, 2:533, 2:534
A Family Patchwork: Five Generations of an Anglo-Jewish Family, 4:637
Family Pictures, 1:954
Family Plot, 1:1169
Family Plots: Balzac's Narrative Generation, 2:454
Family Relationships in Later Life, 3:201
The Family Reunion, 1:471, 1:472
The Family Romance of the French Revolution, 3:373
Family Sayings, 2:422
Family Secrets: Life Stories of Adult Children of Alcoholics, 5:402
The Family Shadow: Sources of Suicide and Schizophrenia, 5:427
The Family Structure in Islam, 3:442
Family Therapy: Theory and Practice, 5:418
Family Ties, 2:895
Famine and Food Supply in the Graeco-Roman World, 3:307
The Famished Road, 2:105, 2:143
Famous Actor Families in America, 1:1075
Famous American Books, 1:75
Famous American Plays of the Nineteen Twenties, 1:1078
the Nineteen Thirties, 1:1076
the Nineteen Forties, 1:1078
the Nineteen Fifties, 1:1079, 1:1083
the Nineteen Sixties, 1:1076
the 1970s, 1:1078, 1:1086
the Nineteen Eighties, 1:1078
Famous First Facts, 1:88
Famous Last Words, 2:911

Famous Problems of Elementary Geometry and Other Monographs, 5:511
Famous Problems of Mathematics, 5:497
The Fan, 2:422
Fan: The Story of a Young Girl's Life, 1:365
The Fancy Dress Party, 2:429
Fancy's Craft: Art and Identity in the Early Works of Djuna Barnes, 1:813
Fanny Burney, 1:235
Fanny Fern: An Independent Woman, 1:671
Fanshen, 1:493
Fans of Swords, 2:59
Fantasia, 1:1163
Fantasies in Moonlight, 2:147
Fantastic Fables, 1:734, 1:735
Fantasy Literature: A Reader's Guide, 1:611
Fantasy Literature for Children and Young Adults, 1:1196
Fantoches, 2:900
Faraday as a Natural Philosopher, 5:684, 5:745
Faraday as Discoverer, 5:684
Faraday Rediscovered, 5:745
Faraday to Einstein: Constructing Meaning in Scientific Theories, 5:64
Far Away and Long Ago, 1:365, 1:366
A Faraway Time and Place: Lore of the Eastern Shore, 3:860
A Far Cry from Kensington, 1:551
Farewell, My Lovely, 1:1228
Farewell Sermon, 1:636
A Farewell to Arms, 1:844, 1:845
A Farewell to Marx: An Outline and Appraisal of His Theories, 3:290
Farewell to Matyora: A Novel, 2:752
Farewell to Reason, 4:399, 5:86
Farewell to the Party of Lincoln: Black Politics in the Age of FDR, 3:536
Farewell to the Sea, 2:852
Farewell—We're Good and Gone: The Great Black Migration, 3:556
Far from Denmark, 3:747
Far from the Madding Crowd, 1:360

Far from the Madding Crowd: An Authoritative Text, Backgrounds, Criticism, 1:361
Farm Chemicals Handbook, 5:725
Farmer Boy, 1:1208
Farmer Giles of Ham: A Short Story, 1:559
Farmers at the Crossroads, 5:268
The Farmer's Boy, 1:580
The Farmer Went a-Trotting, 1:578
Farming, Fertilizers and the Nitrate Problem, 5:265
The Farmstead at the Frontier, 2:782
Faroe and Cosmos, 2:655
The Faroes: Countryside and People, 2:656
Faroese Folktales and Legends, 2:655
Faroese Short Stories, 2:655
A Far Off Place, 3:941
The Far Side of Paradise: A Biography of F. Scott Fitzgerald, 1:841
The Far Side of the Dollar, 1:1235
The Farther Reaches of Human Nature, 5:461
The Farthest Shore, 1:1259, 1:1260
Far Tortuga, 3:930
Fascination: Faulkner's Fiction, 1919–1936, 1:837
The Fascination of Statistics, 5:521
Fascism and the Industrial Leadership in Italy, 1919–1940, 3:386
The Fasti, 2:389
Fast Talk and Flush Times: The Confidence Man as a Literary Convention, 1:723
The Fatal Environment, 1:652, 1:724
Fatal Half Measures: The Culture of Democracy in the Soviet Union, 2:774
The Fatal Shore: The Epic of Australia's Founding, 2:946
The Fatal Weakness, 1:1098
The Fateful Alliance, 3:584
Fate of a Cockroach and Other Plays, 2:63
The Fate of American Poetry, 1:799
The Fate of Liberty: Abraham Lincoln and Civil Liberties, 3:529
The Fate of Man, 1:564

The Fate of Man in the Modern World, 4:758

The Fate of Reason: German Philosophy from Kant to Fichte, 4:16, 4:159, 4:209

The Fate of the Earth, 5:112

Fate of the Elephant, 5:758

The Fate of the Forest, 5:822

The Fate of Vultures: New Poetry from Africa, 2:113

The Father, 2:679

Father and Son, 1:833

The Father Brown Omnibus, 1:457, 1:458

Father Eustace: A Tale of the Jesuits, 1:408

The Father Hunt, 1:1238

Fatherland or Promised Land, 3:350, 4:637

The Fathers According to Rabbi Nathan, 4:610, 4:611

Fathers and Children (Rogin), 3:525

Fathers and Children (Turgenev), 2:768, 2:769

Fathers and Daughters in Roman Society, 3:309

Fathers and Heretics, 4:686

Fathers and Sons, 2:769

Fathers and Sons in Virgil's Aeneid: Tum Genitor Natum, 2:397

Father Sergius, and Other Stories and Plays, 2:765

The Fathers of the Church, 4:680

The Fathers of the Greek Church, 4:98, 4:690

The Fathers of the Latin Church, 4:98, 4:690

Fathers Talking: An Anthology, 4:690

The Fat Man in History, 2:951

The Fat of the Land, 5:221, 5:267

Fats Waller, 3:729

Fats Waller: His Life and Times, 3:729

Fatu-Hiva: Back to Nature on a Pacific Island, 3:924

Faulkner: A Biography, 1:836

Faulkner: A Collection of Critical Essays, 1:836

Faulkner: Myth and Motion, 1:836

Faulkner: The House Divided, 1:838

Faulkner and Modernism: Revision and Rewriting, 1:837

Faulkner and Race, 1:836

Faulkner and the Novelistic Imagination, 1:837

Faulkner and Women, 1:836

A Faulkner Chronology, 1:836

The Faulkner-Cowley File: Letters and Memories, 1944–1962, 1:822

Faulkner's Apocrypha: A Fable, Snopes, and the Spirit of Human Rebellion, 1:838

Faulkner's Country Matters: Folklore and Fable in Yoknapatawpha, 1:837

Faulkner's Fables of Creativity: The Non-Yoknapatawpha Novels, 1:837

Faulkner's Mississippi, 1:837

Faulkner's "Negro": Art and the Southern Context, 1:836

Faulkner's Search for a South, 1:838

Faulkner's World, 1:836

Fault-Tolerant Computing: Theory and Techniques, 5:550

Faust, 2:563, 2:580, 2:602

Faust in Literature, 2:985

Favorite Stories from Cambodia, 2:315

Favorite Uncle Remus, 1:754

The Fawn, 1:188

The FBI and Martin Luther King, Jr., 4:772

F.D.R.: An Intimate History, 3:535

Fear, 2:754

Fear and Courage, 5:423

Fear and Fascination in the Tropics, 2:339

Fear and Temptation, 2:904

Fear and Trembling, 2:94

A Fearful Joy: A Novel, 1:456

Fearful Symmetry: A Study of William Blake, 1:279, 1:976

Fearful Symmetry: Doubles and Doubling in Literature and Film, 2:984

Fearful Symmetry: Is God a Geometer?, 5:199

Fearful Symmetry: The Search for Beauty in Modern Physics, 5:651, 5:691

Fear of Diversity: The Birth of Political Science in Ancient Greek Thought, 4:49

Fear of Fiction, 2:49

The Fear of the Dead in Primitive Religion, 4:476

Feasting and Social Oscillation, 4:519

Feast of Faith, 4:755

A Feast of History, 4:600

The Feast of the Poets, 1:292, 1:1814,

A Feast of Words: The Triumph of Edith Wharton, 1:789

Feasts of Fear and Agony, 2:629

Feather Woman of the Jungle, 2:150

Federal Domestic Outlays, 1983–1990: A Data Book, 3:44

The Federalist, 3:541

The Federalist Era, 1789–1800, 3:521

The Federalist Papers, 3:141, 3:161

The Federal Theatre, 1935–1939: Plays, Relief and Politics, 1:1074

Federico Fellini: "Variety Lights" to "La Dolce Vita," 3:837

Federico García Lorca: A Life, 2:539

Feeding the Mother and Infant, 5:348

Feeding Your Baby from Conception to Age Two, 5:348

Feed Yourself Right, 5:347

A Feeling for the Organism: The Life and Work of Barbara McClintock, 5:806

The Feign'd Curtezans, 1:232

Felicitous Space, 1:788

Felix Bloch and Twentieth-Century Physics, 5:673

Felix Holt, the Radical, 1:353

Fellini: A Life, 3:836

Fellini's Road, 3:837

Fellow Feelings, 1:989

The Fellowship of the Frog, 1:598

The Fellowship of the Ring, 1:559

The Female Advocate, 1:622

The Female Experience: An American Documentary, 3:556

The Female Experience and the Nature of the Divine, 4:439

The Female Intruder in the Novels of Edith Wharton, 1:788

The Female Malady: Women, Madness, and English Culture, 1930–1980, 1:1046

The Female Man, 1:1262
Female of the Species, 3:17
The Female of the Species:
  Sex and Survival in the
  Animal Kingdom, 5:770
Female Perversions: The
  Temptations of Madame
  Bovary, 2:476
Female Piety in Puritan New
  England, 1:629
Female Psychology, 3:178
Female Spectators: Looking
  at Film and Television,
  1:1159
The Female World, 3:207,
  3:221
The Feminine and Faulkner:
  Reading (Beyond) Sexual
  Difference, 1:837
Feminine Consciousness in
  the Fiction of Katherine
  Anne Porter, 1:870
Feminine Endings: Music,
  Gender, and Sexuality,
  3:661
Feminine Ground: Essays on
  Women and Tibet, 4:544
The Feminine in Jungian
  Psychology and in Chris-
  tian Theology, 5:456
Feminine Psychology, 5:452
Feminine Sexuality, 5:458
Feminism, Bakhtin, and the
  Dialogic, 1:803
Feminism and Film Theory,
  1:1158
Feminism and Foucault,
  4:391
Feminism and Psychoanalytic
  Theory, 1:1140
Feminism and Science,
  5:158, 5:189
Feminism and Suffrage,
  3:527
Feminism and Women's Is-
  sues, 1974 to 1986, 3:218
Feminism Confronts Technol-
  ogy, 5:158, 5:189
Feminism/Postmodernism,
  1:926
Feminisms: An Anthology of
  Literary Theory and Criti-
  cism, 1:927, 1:1134
Feminism within the Science
  and Health Care Profes-
  sions, 5:13
Feminist Approaches to Sci-
  ence, 5:151, 5:187
The Feminist Companion to
  Literature in English,
  1:127
Feminist Critics Read Emily
  Dickinson, 1:747

Feminist Drama: Definition
  and Critical Analysis,
  1:1072
Feminist Interpretation of
  the Bible, 4:815
Feminist Knowledge: Critique
  and Construct, 1:1134
The Feminist Legacy of Kar-
  en Horney, 3:186, 5:452
Feminist Literary Criticism:
  Explorations in Theory,
  1:924
Feminist Literary Studies: An
  Introduction, 1:926
Feminist Methods: Social Re-
  search, 5:188
A Feminist Perspective in
  the Academy: The Differ-
  ence It Makes, 1:1129
Feminist Perspectives in
  Medical Ethics, 5:120
Feminist Perspectives in Phi-
  losophy, 4:391
Feminist Perspectives on
  Peace and Peace Educa-
  tion, 3:277
Feminist Spirituality and the
  Feminine Divine, 4:749
Feminists Theorize the Politi-
  cal, 1:1133
Feminist Studies/Critical
  Studies, 1:1133
Feminist Theatre, 1:1074
Feminist Theology: A Reader,
  4:896
Feminist Theology/Christian
  Theology: In Search of
  Method, 4:749
Feminist Theory: The Intel-
  lectual Tradition of Ameri-
  can Feminism, 1:713
Feminist Theory and Simone
  de Beauvoir, 2:458
Feminist Theory and the
  Classics, 3:309
Feminist Theory and the Phi-
  losophies of Man, 4:392
Feminist Theory and the
  Study of Folklore, 3:869
The Feminization of Ameri-
  can Culture, 1:650
Fen, 1:458, 1:459
Fences, 1:1119, 1:1120
Fenimore Cooper: The Criti-
  cal Heritage, 1:665
Feodor Dostoevsky: A Refer-
  ence Guide, 2:715
Ferdinand Count Fathom,
  1:256
Ferdydurke, 2:813
The Ferment of Knowledge,
  5:45

The Fermi Solution: Essays
  on Science, 5:651
Fern Leaves from Fanny's
  Portfolio, 1:671
Ferocious Alphabets, 1:924
The Ferry Crossing, 2:662
Fertile Soil: A Grower's
  Guide to Organic and In-
  organic Fertilizer, 5:263
Fertility Change on the
  American Frontier, 3:205
Fertilization of Orchids by
  Insects, 5:830
The Fervent Years: The
  Group Theatre and the
  Thirties, 1:1072, 1:1076
Festivals and Calendars of
  the Roman Republic,
  4:448
Festivals in South India and
  Sri Lanka, 4:507
Festivals of India, 4:506
Festivals of Interpretation,
  4:402
Festivals of the Athenians,
  4:447
Festivals of the Jewish Year:
  A Modern Interpretation
  and Guide, 4:599
Festschrift for B. F. Skinner,
  3:194
Fetal Alcohol Syndrome,
  5:375
The Fetish and Other Sto-
  ries, 2:430
The Feud, 1:949
Feudalism in Japan, 3:474
The Feudal Kingdom of Eng-
  land: 1042–1216, 3:356
Feudal Society, 3:330
Feu de Brousse, 2:151
Feuerbach: Opposition of
  Materialistic and Idealistic
  Outlook, 4:228
Feuerbach and the Search
  for Otherness, 4:228
Fever Coast Log: At Sea in
  Central America, 3:894
A Few Figs from Thistles,
  1:860
A Few Green Leaves, 1:538,
  1:539
Feyerabend's Critique of
  Foundationalism, 4:399
The Feynman Lectures on
  Physics: Commemorative
  Issue, 5:650, 5:685
Fi al-Shi'r al-Jahili, 2:74
The Fiancee and Other Sto-
  ries, 2:708
Fiasco, 2:816
Fiber Crops, 5:262

Fiber Optic Communications, 5:303

Fiber-Optic Communication Systems, 5:303

Fiber Optic Networks, 5:303

Fiber Optics, 5:303

Fiber Optics Communications, 5:304

Fibre-Optic Systems, 5:303

Ficciones, 2:855, 2:856

The Fichtean Dynamic of Novalis' Poetics, 2:605

Fichte's Theory of Subjectivity, 4:198

Ficino and Renaissance Neoplatonism, 4:141

Fiction 1876–1983: A Bibliography of United States Editions, 1:122

Fiction against History: Scott as Storyteller, 1:300

Fictional Realism in Twentieth-century China, 2:234

Fictional Space in the Modernist and Post-modernist American Novel, 1:805, 1:919

The Fiction and Criticism of Katherine Anne Porter, 1:870

Fiction and Figures of Life, 1:980

Fiction and Folklore: The Novels of Toni Morrison, 1:1019

Fiction and Repetition, 1:422, 1:1151

Fiction and Society in the Age of Pushkin, 2:691

Fiction as Truth: Selected Literary Writings by Richard Hughes, 1:497

The Fiction Catalog, 1:73, 1:124

Fiction for the Working Man, 1830–1850, 1:319

The Fiction of Frank Norris: The Aesthetic Context, 1:777

The Fiction of J. D. Salinger, 1:1043

The Fiction of Joseph Heller: Against the Grain, 1:988

The Fiction of Philip Roth and John Updike, 1:1041

The Fiction of S. Y. Agnon, 2:12

The Fiction of Sādiq Hidāyat, 2:90

The Fiction of Singapore, 2:325

Fiction's Inexhaustible Voice: Speech and Writing in Faulkner, 1:838

The Fictions of Anita Brookner: Illusions of Romance, 1:452

Fictions of Capital: The American Novel From James to Mailer, 1:917

Fictions of Consciousness, 1:325

The Fictions of John Fowles: Power, Creativity, Femininity, 1:478

Fictions of Modesty: Women and Courtship in the English Novel, 1:230

Fictions of Reality in the Age of Hume and Johnson, 1:231

Fictions of Resolution in Three Victorian Novels, 1:318

Fictions of Sappho: 1546–1937, 2:366

The Fictive World of Conrad Aiken: A Celebration of Consciousness, 1:810

Fiddler on the Roof, 2:45

The Fiddle Rose: Poems, 1970–1972, 2:50

Fidelities, 1:561

Fiedler on the Roof: Apostle to the Gentiles, 1:975

A Fiedler Reader, 1:975

Field Geologist's Training Guide, 5:242

Field Geology, 5:636

Field Geophysics, 5:630

The Field God, 1:1088

Field Guide, 1:984

A Field Guide and Introduction to the Geology and Chemistry of Rocks and Minerals, 5:628

A Field Guide to Airplanes, 5:219

A Field Guide to Contemporary Poetry and Poetics, 1:913

Field Guide to North American Edible Wild Plants, 5:767

A Field Guide to Rocks and Minerals, 5:628

A Field Guide to the Atmosphere, 5:634

A Field Guide to the Birds, 5:818

A Field Guide to the Dangerous Animals of North America, 5:761

A Field Guide to the Familiar, 5:761

A Field Guide to the Stars and Planets, 5:591

A Field Guide to Western Birds, 5:818

Fielding's Moral Psychology, 1:245

A Field Manual of the Ferns and Fern Allies of the United States and Canada, 5:761

The Field of Life and Death and Tales of the Hulan River, 2:246

The Field of Vision, 1:1017

The Field of Yiddish, 2:31, 2:42

Fields of Applied Psychology, 3:180

Fields of Life and Death, 2:245, 2:246

The Fields Were Green, 1:654

Field Theory in Social Science, 3:189

Field Work, 1:495

Fierce, Fine World, 2:749

The Fierce Embrace: A Study of Contemporary American Poetry, 1:913

A Fierce Green Fire: The American Environmental Movement, 3:206

The Fiery Angel: A Sixteenth Century Romance, 2:704

Fiery Dust: Byron's Poetic Development, 1:283

Fifteen American Authors Before 1900, 1:650, 1:715

Fifteen American One-Act Plays, 1:1078

Fifteen Greek Plays, 2:349

Fifteen Sermons, 4:193

The Fifteenth Century, 3:332

Fifteen Years of a Drunken's Life, 1:366

Fifth Avenue: A Very Special History, 3:553

The Fifth Branch: Science Advisers as Policymakers, 5:182

Fifth Business, 2:910

The Fifth Column, 1:844

The Fifth Column and Four Stories of the Spanish Civil War, 1:846

The Fifth French Republic, 3:373

The Fifth Generation, 5:74, 5:567

Fifth of July, 1:1120, 1:1121

Fifth Pestilence with the History of the Tinkling Symbol and Sounding Brass, 2:754

The Fifth Queen, 1:475

The Fifth Son, 1:1065

The Fifth Sun: Aztec Gods, Aztec World, 4:457

Fifth Sunday, 1:970

The Fifth Wheel, 2:24

The Fifties: From Notebooks and Diaries of the Period, 1:902

Fifty Basic Civil War Documents, 3:572

Fifty Caribbean Writers: A Bio-Bibliographical Critical Sourcebook, 2:930

Fifty Challenging Problems in Probability with Solutions, 5:523

Fifty Contemporary Poets: The Creative Process, 1:914

Fifty Great American Short Stories, 1:805

Fifty Letters, 2:392

Fifty Major Philosophers: A Reference Guide, 4:13

50 Simple Things You Can Do to Save the Planet, 5:822

Fifty Southern Writers after 1900, 1:712, 1:794

Fifty Southern Writers before 1900, 1:712

A Fifty-Year History of the American Federation of Astrologers, 4:860

Fifty Years and Other Poems, 1:771

Fifty Years of American Poetry, 1:801

Fifty Years of Chinese Philosophy 1898–1950, 4:358

Fifty Years of Hume Scholarship, 4:202

Fifty Years of Russian Prose: From Pasternak to Solzhenitsyn, 2:693

Fifty Years of Thomas Mann Studies, 2:602

Fifty Years of War and Diplomacy in the Balkans, 3:392

Fifty Years on the Old Frontier as Cowboy, Hunter, Guide, Scout, and Ranchman, 3:895

Figaro in London, 1:376

Figaro's, 1:376

The Fight, 1:1011

Fighters and Lovers: Theme in the Novels of John Updike, 1:1061

Fighting with Gandhi, 4:553

The Figure Finaglers, 5:524

The Figure in the Carpet and Other Stories, 1:763

The Figure of Dante: An Essay on the Vita Nuova, 2:418

Figures de l'Étranger, 2:123

Figures in Black: Words, Signs, and the Racial Self, 1:1145

Figures of Desire: A Theory and Analysis of Surrealist Film, 3:832

Figures of Division: William Faulkner's Major Novels, 1:838

Figures of Literary Discourse, 2:447

Figures of Thought in Roman Poetry, 2:381

Fiji: A Short History, 3:496

File on Ayckbourn, 1:437

File on Churchill, 1:459

File on Hare, 1:493

File on Shaffer, 1:544

File on Stoppard, 1:555

The Filibuster: A Study of the Political Ideas of Wyndham Lewis, 1:514

Filipina I: Poetry, Drama, Fiction, 2:329

Filipino Writers in English, 2:329

The Fille de Chambre, A Novel, 1:643

Film: An Anthology, 3:826

Film: A Reference Guide, 3:824

Film about a Woman Who..., 1:1174

Film Art, 3:825

Film Art: An Introduction, 1:1157

Film as Social Practice, 1:1158

The Film Audience: An International Bibliography of Research, 3:824

Film Directors: A Complete Guide, 3:829

Filmed Books and Plays, 3:825

The Film Encyclopedia, 3:825

The Film Form, 1:1157, 3:835

Film Forum: 35 Top Filmmakers Discuss Their Craft, 3:828

Filmgoer's and Video Viewer's Companion, 3:825

Filmguide to Psycho, 1:1169

Film History: Theory and Practice, 1:1156

The Film Index: A Bibliography, 3:826

Film Language: A Semiotics of the Cinema, 1:1157

Film Music: A Neglected Art, 3:667

Film Music: From Violins to Video, 3:667

Film Noir: An Encyclopedic Reference to the American Style, 3:826

The Film Sense, 3:835

Films for, by, and about Women, 3:826

The Films in My Life, 3:843

The Films of Akira Kurosawa, 3:839

The Films of Alain Robbe-Grillet, 2:501

The Films of Carl Theodor Dreyer, 3:834, 3:835

The Films of Federico Fellini, 3:837

The Films of Frank Capra, 3:833

The Films of Ginger Rogers, 3:751

The Films of Ingmar Bergman, 3:831

The Films of Josef von Sternberg, 1:1176

The Films of Nicolas Roeg: Myth and Mind, 3:828

The Films of Werner Herzog, 3:828

The Films of Woody Allen, 3:829

The Films of Yvonne Rainer, 1:1175

Film Theory and Criticism: Introductory Readings, 1:1158

A Film Trilogy, 3:831

Filocolo, 2:409

The Filostrato, 2:410

Filters against Folly, 5:114, 5:135

Filumena, 2:419

Final Acts: The Creation of Three Late O'Neill Plays, 1:1071

The Final Days, 3:540

The Final Foucault, 4:400, 5:88

Final Gifts, 3:201

The Final Island: The Fiction of Julio Cortázar, 2:862

Finally Truffaut, 3:843

The Final Solution, 3:350

Finance and Investment Handbook, 3:44

The Financial Expert, 2:180

The Financier, 1:829, 1:830

Fin-de-Siècle Vienna: Politics and Culture, 2:565, 3:350, 3:376

Finding, Selecting, Developing, and Retraining Data Professionals through Effective Human Resource Management, 5:556

Finding Models, 5:523

Findings, 3:682

Findings: A Book of Poems, 1:989

Findings and Keepings: Analects for an Autobiography, 5:170

Finding the Islands, 1:1015

Finding the Mean: Theory and Practice in Aristotelian Political Philosophy, 4:71

Finding the Source in Sociology and Anthropology, 3:5

Find What the Sailor Has Hidden: Vladmir Nabokov's "Pale Fire," 2:741

Fine and Historic Bindings from the Folger Shakespeare Library, 1:22

The Fine Art of Copyediting, 1:48

Fine Bookbinding in the 20th Century, 1:25

Fine Books, 1:34

Fine Clothes to the Jew, 1:847

Fine Printing: The San Francisco Tradition, 1:8

Fine Print on Type: The Best of Fine Print Magazine on Type and Typography, 1:13

Fine Things, 1:1224

Fingering the Jagged Grain: Tradition and Form in Recent Black Fiction, 1:917

The Finitude of Being, 4:295

Finland: People, Nation State, 3:381

Finnegans Wake, 1:438, 1:504, 1:1034, 1:1116, 2:442

Finn Family Moomintroll, 2:658

Finnish American Folklore: Quantitative and Qualitative Analysis, 3:855

Firbankiana, 1:474

Fire: Six Writers from Angola, Mozambique, and Cape Verde, 2:113

Fire and Iron: Critical Approaches to Njál's Saga, 2:642

Fire and Night: Five Baltic Plays, 2:804

The Fire and the Sun: Why Plato Banished the Artists, 1:523, 4:83

Fire-Bell in the Night: The Crisis in Civil Rights, 3:581

The Firebrand: William Lyon Mackenzie and the Rebellion in Upper Canada, 3:613

The Firebugs, 2:579

Fire Down Below, 1:483

The Firedrake, 1:1246, 1:1247

The Fire-Dwellers, 2:916, 2:917

Firefall: Poems, 1:1061

Fire from the Mountain: The Making of a Sandinista, 3:639

Fire in the Lake: The Vietnamese and the Americans in Vietnam, 3:537

A Fire in the Mind: The Life of Joseph Campbell, 3:877

Fire in the Steppe, 2:821

Fire in the Streets: America in the 1960s, 3:540

Fire in the Valley: Ewe Folktales, 2:132

Fire in the Valley: The Making of the Personal Computer, 5:542

The Fire Next Time, 1:1084, 4:862

Fire on the Mountain, 2:178, 2:179

Fires, 2:517

Fires: Essays, Poems, Stories, 1:960

Fire Sermon, 1:1017

The Fires of Jubilee: Nat Turner's Fierce Rebellion, 3:525

Fires of Love, Waters of Peace, 2:173

The Fires of Spring, 1:1248

Firestarter, 1:1241

The Fires Within: Volcanism on the Earth and Other Planets, 5:623

Fireworks: Nine Stories in Various Disguises, 1:455

The Firm of Charles Ottley, Landon and Co.: Footnote to an Enquiry, 1:35

First, Do No Harm, 5:118, 5:343

First Aid Manual for Chemical Accidents, 5:381

The First Amendment: A Reader, 3:139

First Amendment: Cases and Materials, 3:139

The First America, 3:628

The First American Constitutions, 3:541

First and Last, 1:442

The First and Last Freedom, 4:554

The Firstborn (Fry), 1:480

Firstborn (Glück), 1:982

First Catch Your Eland, 3:941

First-Century Judaism in Crisis, 4:605

The First Christian Histories, 4:709

The First Circle: A Novel, 2:759, 2:760

The First Cities, 1:1190

First Considerations: An Examination of Philosophical Evidence, 4:338, 4:339

A First Course in Calculus, 5:490

The First Crusade, 4:693

The First Crusade and the Idea of Crusading, 4:694

First Cut: Conversations with Film Editors, 3:826

The First Deadly Sin, 1:1236

The First Dynasty of Islam: The Umayyad Caliphate A.D. 661–750, 4:569

First Editions: A Guide to Identification, 1:76

The First Encounter (Bely), 2:701

First Encounter (Dos Passos), 1:828

The First Encounter: The Beginnings in Psychotherapy, 5:424

The First Filipino: A Biography of José Rizal, 2:333

The First Five Lives of Annie Besant, 4:550, 4:859

The First Folio of Shakespeare, 1:207

First Footsteps in East Africa or, an Exploration of Harar, 3:913

The First Four Years, 1:1208

The First Freedoms, 3:139

The First Freedom Today, 1:57

First Fruits: A Harvest of 25 Years of Israeli Writing, 2:10

A First Glance at St. Thomas, 4:119

The First Gothics: A Critical Guide to the English Gothic Novel, 1:230

The First Hundred Million, 1:41

The First Hundred Years: Association of Book Travelers, 1884–1984, 1:39

First Images of America: The Impact of the New World upon the Old, 1:631

First Impressions: Cylinder Seals in the Ancient Near East, 4:544

The First Industrial Revolution, 1750–1850, 3:338

The First International and After, 4:242

The First Jew, 4:640

First Lady of the South: The Life of Mrs. Jefferson Davis, 3:575

First Lectures in Political Sociology, 3:234

First Letter Concerning Toleration, 4:178

First Light, 5:590

First Love, 2:769

First Loves, 2:324

The First Men in the Moon, 1:563

The First Millennium A.D. in Europe and the Mediterranean, 3:305

The First New Nation, 3:158

The First of the Tudors: A Study of Henry VII and His Reign, 3:359

The First One Hundred and Fifty Years, 1:45

The First One Hundred Years of American Geology, 5:624

First Part of the Life of the Pícaro Guzmán de Alfarache, 2:529

The First Person, 4:395

First-Person America, 3:534

First Person Singular: Studies in American Autobiography, 1:727

First Philosophy: An Introduction to Philosophical Issues, 4:21

First Poems, 1:1014

First Principles of Typography, 1:9

The First Salute: A View of the American Revolution, 3:412, 3:522

The First Sentimental Education, 2:475

The First Social Experiments in America, 3:646, 3:647

The First Step: A Guide for the New Jewish Spirit, 4:649

First Step in the Clouds, 2:814

First Steps in Modern Ballet, 3:731

The First Systematic Theologian, Origen of Alexandria, 4:63

The First Taint of Civilization, 3:495

The First Thirteen Centuries, 4:98

The First Three Minutes, 5:596, 5:718

The First Urban Christians: The Social World of the Apostle Paul, 3:308

The First World War: An Illustrated History, 3:409

First Year Baby Care, 5:322

Fiscal Policy and Business Cycles, 3:81

The Fiscal Revolution in America, 3:62

F Is for Fugitive, 1:1229

Fish: An Enthusiast's Guide, 5:771

The Fish Can Sing, 2:642

The Fisher King, 1:536

The Fisherman's Invocations and Other Poems, 2:141

Fishers of Books, 1:31

Fishes of the World, 5:761

Fishke the Lame, 2:41

Fitness after 50, 5:325

Fit to Print: A. M. Rosenthal and His Times, 3:806

The Five: The Evolution of The Russian School of Music, 3:664

Five Acre Virgin and Other Stories, 2:955, 2:956

Five Centuries of English Bookbinding, 1:25

Five Centuries of Polish Poetry, 1450–1970, 2:812

Five Decades: Poems 1925–1970, 2:874

Five Elizabethan Comedies, 1:171

Five Elizabethan Tragedies, 1:171

Five Essays on Philosophy, 4:361

Five Families: Mexican Case Studies in the Culture of Poverty, 3:34

Five Finger Exercise, 1:543

The Five Great Religions, 4:572

Five Hours with Mario, 2:538

Five Hundred Years of Chinese Poetry, 1150–1650, 2:191

Five Hundred Years of Printing, 1:11

Five Ideas That Changed the World, 3:295, 3:296

Five Images of the Soviet Future, 3:396

The Five Jars, 1:600

Five Kingdoms: An Illustrated Guide to the Phyla of Life on Earth, 5:768, 5:820

Five Metaphysical Poets, 1:165, 1:176, 1:181, 1:188

Five Modern Yugoslav Plays, 2:786

Five Mountains: The Rinzai Zen Monastic Institution in Medieval Japan, 3:474

Five New World Primates: A Study in Comparative Ecology, 5:772

Five of a Kind: The Third Nero Wolfe Omnibus, 1:1238

The Five of Hearts, 3:563

Five Plays: Comedies and Tragicomedies, 2:539

Five Plays by Langston Hughes, 1:848

Five Political Leaders of Modern Japan, 3:479

Five Posts in a Market Place, 2:806

Five Public Philosophies of Walter Lippmann, 3:815

Five Questions Concerning the Mind, 2:403

Five Seasons, 2:26

Five Seasons of a Golden Year, A Chinese Pastoral, 2:197

Five Sermons, 4:193

Five Stages of Greek Religion, 4:48

Five Stories of Ferrara, 2:408

Five Television Plays, 1:1100

Five Temperaments, 1:913

Five Thousand Years of Popular Culture: Popular Culture before Printing, 3:874

Five Types of Ethical Theory, 4:277
The Five Ways: St. Thomas Aquinas' Proofs of God's Existence, 4:119
Five Women Who Loved Love, 2:277
The Fixed Period, 1:406
The Fixer, 1:1013
Fixions, 2:152
A Flag for Sunrise, 1:1055
Flags, 2:786
Flags in the Dust, 1:835
Flamboyant Drama, 1:161
Flame and Shadow, 2:968
The Flame and the Flower, 1:1220, 1:1224, 1:1225
The Flame of the Candle, 4:274
Flames across the Border, 1813–1814, 3:612
The Flaming Heart, 2:401
The Flamingo's Smile: Reflections in Natural History, 5:16, 5:638, 5:764
Flaming Tree, 1:1238
The Flanders Road, 2:509
Flannery O'Connor, 1:1025
Flannery O'Connor: The Imagination of Extremity, 1:1024
Flannery O'Connor and the Mystery of Love, 1:1024
The Flannery O'Connor Companion, 1:1024
Flannery O'Connor's Georgia, 1:1025
Flannery O'Connor's Library: Resources of Being, 1:1024
Flann O'Brien, 1:526
Flann O'Brien's Exorbitant Novels, 1:526
Flash of the Spirit: African and Afro-American Art and Philosophy, 4:26
Flatlanders and Ridgerunners, 3:859
Flaubert: A Biography, 2:476
Flaubert: The Uses of Uncertainty, 2:476
Flaubert and Madame Bovary: A Double Portrait, 2:476
Flaubert and Postmodernism, 2:476
Flavius Josephus: Selections from His Works, 4:666
Flavius Josephus on the Pharisees: A Composition-Critical Study, 4:616
Flaws and Fallacies in Statistical Thinking, 5:521

Flaws in the Glass: A Self-Portrait, 2:966
The Flayed God: The Mythology of Mesoamerica, 4:465
A Fleet Street Comedy, 1:450
Flegeljahre, 2:606
Fleming: Discoverer of Penicillin, 5:408
Flesh and Blood, 2:489
The Fleshly School of Poetry, 1:391
The Fleshly School of Poetry and Other Phenomena of the Day, 1:392
The Flesh Made Word: Female Figures and Women's Bodies, 1:312
Fletcher, Beaumont and Company, 1:173
The Fleuron Anthology, 1:9
The Flies, 2:506
Flight and Bliss, 2:705
The Flight from Reason, 1:56
Flight in America: From the Wrights to the Astronauts, 3:547
The Flight into Inwardness, 4:408, 5:94
Flight of a Witch, 1:608
The Flight of Icarus, 2:496
The Flight of the Mind, 1:570
Flight of the Storm Petrel, 5:826
Flight of the Wind Horse: A Journey into Tibet, 3:901
Flights, 2:646
Flights of Fantasy: Arabic Short Stories, 2:57
Flights of Victory, 2:859
Flight to Arras, 2:504
Flight to Canada, 1:1036
Floating Dragon, 1:1243
Floating Island, 3:899
The Floating Opera, 1:942
The Floating Opera and The End of the Road, 1:942
Floating Ports—Design and Construction Practices, 5:239
Floating the River in Melancholy, 2:293
The Flood, 1:560
Flood: A Romance of Our Time, 1:892
Floods, 5:626
Floorshow, 1:458
Florante at Laura, 2:327
Flora of Turkey and the East Aegean Islands, 3:452
Florence Nightingale, 5:363
Florence Nightingale: Nurse to Soldiers, 5:363

Florence Nightingale: Reputation and Power, 5:363
Florence Nightingale: Saint, Reformer, or Rebel, 5:363
Florence Nightingale and the Doctors, 5:363
Florence Nightingale and the Nursing Legacy, 5:362
Florentine Histories, 3:385
The Florida of the Inca, 3:646
The Flounder, 2:583
Flow Chart, 1:936
The Flower in Drama and Glamour: Theatre Essays and Criticism, 1:1076
Flowering Cherry, 1:445
Flowering Earth, 5:820
Flowering in the Shadows, 4:524, 4:535
Flowering Nettle, 2:678
The Flowering of Byron's Genius: Studies in "Don Juan," 1:284
The Flowering of New England, 1815–1865, 1:650
The Flowering Peach, 1:1106
The Flowering Plum and the Palace Lady, 2:189
A Flower in Her Hair, 1:964
Flowers and Shadows, 2:143
Flowers and Trees, 1:1163
Flowers from Hell, 2:339
Flowers in Salt, 3:479
Flowers in the Attic, 1:1239, 1:1240
Flowers in the Rain, and Other Stories, 1:621
The Flowers of Evil, 2:456
The Flow of Information: An Experiment in Mass Communication, 3:801
Fluids and Electrolytes through the Life Cycle, 5:342
Flush: A Biography, 1:337, 1:568, 1:569
Flutes of Death, 2:119
The Fluvial System, 5:632
Fly, 2:792
Fly and the Fly-Bottle: Encounters with British Intellectuals, 4:266
Fly Away Peter, 2:959
Flying a Red Kite, 2:913, 2:914
Flying Buttresses, Entropy and O-Rings: The World of an Engineer, 5:150
Flying Colors, 1:320
Flying-Fox in a Freedom Tree, 2:980

Flying-Fox in a Freedom Tree and Other Stories, 2:980

Flying Hero Class, 2:957

Flying Modern Jet Fighters, 5:219

The Flying Phoenix: Aspects of Chinese Sectarianism in Taiwan, 4:531

Flying Saucers: A Modern Myth of Things Seen in the Sky, 4:870

The Flying Wasp, 1:527

FOB ("Fresh off the Boat"), 1:1095

Focus Groups: A Practical Guide for Applied Research, 3:7

Focus on Hitchcock, 1:1169

Focus on "Macbeth," 1:214

Foe, 2:160

Foiling the System Breakers: Computer Security and Access Control, 5:556

The Folger Library Shakespeare, 1:206

Folk and Traditional Music of the Western Continents, 3:667

Folk Art in Texas, 3:862

Folk Art Motifs of Pennsylvania, 3:859

Folk Beliefs of the Southern Negro, 3:867

Folk Culture of the Slaves in Jamaica, 2:934

The Folk Culture of Yucatán, 3:39

Folk Cultures and Little People, 3:345

Folk Elements in Burmese Buddhism, 4:519

The Folk Heroes of Britain, 3:855

Folklife Sourcebook, 3:849

Folk Literature of the British Isles, 3:856

Folk Literature of the Tehuelche Indians, 4:466

Folklore: A Handbook for Study and Research, 3:847

Folklore: An Annotated Bibliography and Index to Single Editions, 3:850

Folklore: Performance and Communication, 3:868

Folklore: What Is It and What Is the Good of It, 3:848

Folklore and Fakelore: Essays toward a Discipline of Folk Studies, 3:848

Folklore and Folklife: A Guide to English Language Sources, 3:850

Folklore and Folklife: An Introduction, 3:848

The Folklore and Folklife of New Jersey, 3:859

Folklore and Literature in the U.S., 3:849

Folklore and the Sea, 3:868

Folklore from Iowa, 3:862

Folklore from Kansas: Customs, Beliefs, and Superstitions, 3:862

Folklore from the Schoharie Hills, New York, 3:859

Folklore in America, 3:848

Folklore in Nigerian Literature, 2:110

Folklore Methodology, 3:882

Folklore of Canada, 3:855

The Folklore of Puerto Rico, 3:855

Folklore of the Oil Industry, 3:868

Folklore of the Sea, 3:868

The Folklore of World Holidays, 3:869

Folklore Studies in the Twentieth Century, 3:848

Folk Medicine: The Art and the Science, 5:320, 5:730

Folk Medicine of the Delaware and Related Algonquin Indians, 3:859

Folk Music and Dances of Ireland, 3:850

Folk Music and Modern Sound, 3:851

Folk Music in School, 3:852

Folk Music Instruments of the World, 3:666

The Folk Music Sourcebook, 3:852

Folk Poetry of Modern Greece, 2:371

Folk Religion in Japan, 4:539

Folk Roots and Mythic Wings in Sarah Orne Jewett and Toni Morrison, 1:770

Folksingers and Folksongs in America, 3:852

The Folk Society, 3:39

Folk Song: USA, 3:884

A Folk Song History of America: America through Its Songs, 3:851

Folksongs and Their Makers, 3:851

Folksongs of Britain and Ireland, 3:852

Folk Songs of French Canada, 3:875

The Folk Songs of North America, 3:852, 3:884

Folk Songs of the Catskills, 3:859

Folk Songs of the Southern United States, 3:860

The Folk Song Style and Culture, 3:852

The Folks That Live on the Hill, 1:432

Folk Stories of the Hmong, 2:322

The Folktale, 3:850, 3:857, 3:887

Folk Tale, Fiction and Saga in the Homeric Epics, 2:361

Folktales and Reality, 3:849

Folk Tales from Kammu: A Master Teller's Tales, 2:322

Folktales from Somalia, 2:117

Folktales of America, 3:853

Folk Tales of Ancient Persia, 2:83

Folktales of Egypt, 3:855

Folk Tales of Iraq, 3:855

Folktales of Mexico, 3:856

Folktales of Norway, 2:662

Folktales of the Irish Countryside, 3:854

Folktales Told around the World, 3:853, 3:854

Folk Visions and Voices: Traditional Music and Song in North Georgia, 3:861

Folkways, 3:38

Following the Equator, 1:780, 1:782, 3:910

Follow the Ecstasy: The Hermitage Years of Thomas Merton, 4:781

Foma Gordeyev, 2:724, 2:725

Fontamara, 2:438

Food, Energy, and Society, 5:278

Food, Hunger, Agribusiness: A Directory of Resources, 5:261

Food, Sex and Pollution: A New Guinea Religion, 4:462

Food Additives and Federal Policy: The Mirage of Safety, 5:346

Food Additives for Hyperactive Children, 5:416

Food Additives Handbook, 5:261

Food Additive User's Handbook, 5:261
Food in Chinese Culture: Anthropological and Historical Perspectives, 3:466
Food Irradiation, 5:267
The Food of Death: Fifty-one Tales, 1:615
The Food of the Gods, 1:563
Food Packaging Technology, 5:267
Food Protection Technology, 5:267
The Food Resource, 5:263
Food Science, 5:262
Food Strategies for Tomorrow, 5:266
Food Technology, 5:267
Foodways in the Northeast, 3:858
The Fool, 1:446
The Fool and We Come to the River, 1:446
Fool for Love, 1:1111
Foolish Wives, 1:1177
Fools, 1:1112, 1:1113
Fools Are Passing Through, 2:577
Fools of Time: Studies in Shakespearean Tragedy, 1:213
Fools Say, 2:506
Footnote to a Friendship: A Memoir of Truman Capote and Others, 1:959
Footsteps: A Novel, 2:321
Forage Crops, 5:263
For a New Novel, 2:448, 2:500
The Forayers; or, The Raid of the Dog-Days, 1:696
Forays and Rebuttals, 3:576
For Better or for Worse: Canada and the United States to the 1990s, 3:606
Forbidden Fruit and Other Plays, 1:331
Forbidden Knowledge, 4:317
Forced Options: Social Decisions for the Twenty-First Century, 5:130, 5:198
Force of Circumstance, 2:458
The Force of Knowledge: The Scientific Dimension of Society, 5:20
The Force of Reason, 3:229
Forces and Fields, 4:405
Forces in Modern British Literature, 1885–1946, 1:415, 1:422
The Forces of Matter, 5:684, 5:745
The Forces of Nature, 5:662

Forces of Production: A Social History of Industrial Automation, 5:75
The Force So Much Closer Home: Henry Adams and the Adams Family, 1:730
Ford, 3:590
Ford: The Men and the Machine, 5:247
Ford Madox Ford, 1:475
Ford Madox Ford: Prose and Politics, 1:475
Ford Madox Ford: The Critical Heritage, 1:476
Ford Madox Ford and the Voice of Uncertainty, 1:476
Ford's Freighter Travel Guide: 1980–81, 3:891
Forecasting for Technologists and Engineers, 5:231
Foreday Morning: Selected Prose 1946–1986, 2:942
Forefathers' Eve, 2:817
A Foregone Conclusion, 1:758
The Foreground of Leaves of Grass, 1:708
Foreign Affairs, 1:1007
Foreign Affairs 50-Year Index, 1922–1972, 3:272
The Foreigner, 2:177
The Foreign Legion, 2:896
Foreign Policy Failure in the White House, 3:450
The Foreign Policy of Hitler's Germany: Diplomatic Revolution in Europe, 1933–1936, 3:378
The Foreign Policy of Hitler's Germany: Starting World War II, 1937–1939, 3:378
The Foreign Policy of the Third Reich, 3:377
A Foreign Woman, 2:716
Forensic Science, 5:730
The Forerunners: Black Poets in America, 1:799
The Forerunners of Dante: A Selection from Italian Poetry before 1300, 2:402
Forerunners of the Reformation: The Shape of Late Medieval Thought, 4:128, 4:697, 4:721
Foresight and Understanding: An Enquiry into the Aims of Science, 5:65
The Forest and the Sea, 5:817
The Forest of Anykščiai, 2:805

Forest of a Thousand Demons: A Hunter's Saga, 2:149
A Forest of Kings: The Untold Story of the Ancient Maya, 3:628
The Forest of Symbols: Aspects of Ndembu Ritual, 3:40; 4:463
The Forest People, 3:26
Forest Physiography, 3:128
A Forest Song, 2:841
Forever Flowing, 2:727
Forever in Your Embrace, 1:1225
For Every Sin, 2:14
Forewords and Afterwords, 1:434, 1:435
The Forged Coupon, 2:764
Forged Documents: Proceedings of the 1989 Houston Conference, 1:35
The Forger, 1:598
Forgers and Critics: Creativity and Duplicity in Western Scholarship, 1:35
Forget-Me-Not-Lane, 1:524, 1:525
Forging Ahead, 1:35
Forging a Language: A Study of the Plays of Eugene O'Neill, 1:1108
The Forging of the Cosmic Race: A Reinterpretation of Colonial Mexico, 3:629
The Forging of the Union, 1781–1789, 3:521
Forging the American Curriculum, 3:256
The Forgotten Frontier, 3:533
The Forgotten Half, 3:252
The Forgotten Hume, Le Bon David, 4:202
The Forgotten Language, 5:450
The Forgotten Legend of Sleepy Hollow, Rip Van Winkle, President Van Buren and Brom, 3:859
Forgotten Life, 1:613
The Forgotten Peninsula: A Naturalist in Baja California, 5:833
The Forgotten Plague, 5:383
Forgotten Voyager: The Story of Amerigo Vespucci, 3:942
Forgotten Women of Computer History, 5:577
The Fork River Space Project, 1:1017

For Lizzie and Harriet, 1:1006

For Love: Poems, 1950–1960, 1:965

For Love Alone, 2:963, 2:964

Formal, Transcendental, and Dialectical Thinking: Logic and Reality, 5:63

Formal and Transcendental Logic, 4:234

Formalism and Marxism, 1:1131

Formalism in Ethics and Non-Formal Ethics of Values, 4:332

Formalized Music: Thought and Mathematics in Composition, 3:730

The Formal Method in Literary Scholarship, 2:684

Form and Freedom in Korean Poetry, 2:298

Form and History in American Literary Naturalism, 1:723

Form and Meaning in Drama, 2:346

Form and Meaning in the Novels of John Fowles, 1:478

Form and Thought in Herodotus, 3:316, 4:480

Form and Transformation: A Study in the Philosophy of Plotinus, 4:87

For Marx, 3:345, 4:242

The Formation of Ch'an Ideology in China and Korea, 4:537

The Formation of Christendom, 3:328

The Formation of Science in Japan: Building a Research Tradition, 3:476

The Formation of the Atomic Theory and Its Earliest Critics, 4:48

The Formation of the Christian Bible, 4:814

The Formation of the German Chemical Community, 1720–1795, 5:44

The Formation of the Gospel Tradition, 4:826

Formation of the Jewish Intellect, 4:606

The Formation of the Mughal Empire, 3:484

The Formation of the New Testament, 4:816

The Formation of Vegetable Mould, through the Action of Worms with Observation of Their Habits, 5:793

The Formative Period of Islamic Thought, 4:577

For Max Weinreich on His Seventieth Birthday, 2:31

Form in Fiction, 1:423

Forming the American Minds, 1:38

Forming the Critical Mind: Dryden to Coleridge, 1:225

The Form of American Romance, 1:657

The Form of the Book: Essays on the Morality of Good Design, 1:11

The Form of Victorian Fiction, 1:319, 1:1150, 1:1151

For Mothers and Daughters: A Guide to Good Nutrition for Women, 5:356

Forms of Desire, 1:1184

Forms of Farewell: The Late Poetry of Wallace Stevens, 1:887

Forms of Talk, 3:21

Formula of His Own: Henry Adams' Literary Experiment, 3:563

Formulas and Calculations for Drilling, Production and Workover, 5:241

For My Brother Jesus, 2:917

For My People, 4:763

Fors Clavigera, 1:393

Forster's India, 1:477

Forster's Women: Eternal Differences, 1:477

The Forsyte Saga, 1:481, 1:482

Fort Apache, 1:1165

Forthcoming Books, 1:113

For the Common Defense, 3:546

For the Common Good, 5:822

For the Good of the Cause, 2:727

For the Major, 1:790

For the Major and Selected Short Stories, 1:790

For the Patient's Good: The Restoration of Beneficence in Health Care, 5:97

For the Sake of Honor, 2:80

For the Union Dead, 1:1005

FORTH Fundamentals: Language Glossary, 5:553

For Those in Peril, 3:925

For Those Who Come After: A Study of Native American Autobiography, 1:727

The Forties: From Notebooks and Diaries of the Period, 1:902

The Fortnightly, 1:386

Fortress America, 5:237

Fortress Besieged, 2:243

Fortunata and Jacinta: Two Stories of Married Women, 2:547

The Fortunate Isles, 3:428

The Fortunate Traveller, 2:943

Fortune Is a Woman, 3:160, 4:145

Fortunes of a Fool, 2:21

The Fortunes of Nigel, 1:298

The Fortunes of Richard Mahony, 2:945, 2:961

Forty Centuries of Ink, 1:62

The Forty Days of Musa Dagh, 2:615

Forty-four Irish Short Stories, 1:423

The Forty Second Parallel, 1:828

Forty Thieves, 1:583

For Voice, 2:884

Forward from Liberalism, 1:553

For Whom the Bell Tolls, 1:844, 1:845

For Whom the Cloche Tolls: A Scrapbook of the Twenties, 1:567

For Wiktor Weintraub, 2:811

For Your Eyes Only, 1:594

The Fossil Evidence for Human Evolution, 3:18

The Fossil Hunters: In Search of Ancient Plants, 5:33

A Fossil-Hunter's Handbook: My Life with Dinosaurs and Other Friends, 5:638

The Fossil Record and Evolution, 5:639

Fossils (Eldredge), 5:638

Fossils (Rhodes), 5:639

Fossils: An Introduction to Prehistoric Life, 5:639

Fossils: The Key to the Past, 5:638

Fossils and the History of Life, 5:639

Fossils for Amateurs, 5:639

Fossils in the Field, 5:638

Foucault, 1:1131, 4:400

Foucault: A Critical Reader, 4:401, 5:443

Foucault–Blanchot: Maurice
    Blanchot—The Thought
    from Outside, 2:461, 2:477
Foucault and Derrida: The
    Other Side of Reason,
    5:88
Foucault and Education: Dis-
    ciplines and Knowledge,
    5:88
Foucault and Feminism,
    4:401
Foucault's Archaeology: Sci-
    ence and the History of
    Reason, 4:401, 5:88
Foucault's Nietzschean Ge-
    neology: Truth, Power,
    and the Subject, 5:88
Foucault's Pendulum, 2:420
Foundation (Asimov), 1:1254
The Foundation (Buero),
    2:532
Foundational Fictions: The
    National Romances of Lat-
    in America, 2:847
Foundational Reflections:
    Studies in Contemporary
    Philosophy, 4:264
Foundation and Earth,
    1:1254
Foundation and Empire,
    1:1254
Foundation and Limits of
    State Power in China,
    3:467
Foundation Directory, 1:104
Foundation Grants Index,
    1:104
The Foundation of Jacques
    Maritain's Political Phi-
    losophy, 4:307
Foundation of Space-Time
    Physics, 4:384
The Foundation Pit, 2:748
Foundations and Applications
    of Inductive Probability,
    5:65
Foundations and Basic Theo-
    ry, 5:520
Foundations and Fundamen-
    tal Concepts of Mathemat-
    ics, 5:493
Foundation's Edge, 1:1254
The Foundations of "African-
    ité" or "Negritude" and
    "Arabité," 2:147
The Foundations of Arithme-
    tic, 4:229
Foundations of Behavioral
    Research, 3:6
The Foundations of Bioeth-
    ics, 5:120, 5:134

Foundations of Christian
    Faith: An Introduction to
    the Idea of Christianity,
    4:745, 4:903
Foundations of Computer
    Music, 5:565
Foundations of Economic
    Analysis, 3:64, 3:103
Foundations of Education,
    3:257
Foundations of Electrical En-
    gineering, 5:229
Foundations of Environmen-
    tal Ethics, 5:114, 5:135
The Foundations of Ethology,
    5:835
Foundations of Genetics: A
    Science for Society, 5:778
Foundations of Geometry,
    5:510
Foundations of Gestalt Theo-
    ry, 3:177
Foundations of Judaism:
    Method, Teleology, Doc-
    trine, 4:606, 4:607
The Foundations of Justice,
    5:144
The Foundations of Know-
    ing, 4:395
The Foundations of Mao Ze-
    dong's Political Thought,
    1917–1935, 4:362
Foundations of Measurement,
    5:65
Foundations of Method: In-
    formed Talks on Teaching,
    3:264
The Foundations of Modern
    Political Thought: The
    Renaissance, 4:105, 4:131
The Foundations of Newton's
    Alchemy, 4:184, 5:41
Foundations of Philosophy of
    Science, 5:62
The Foundations of Psycho-
    analysis: A Philosophical
    Critique, 3:178, 5:80
Foundations of Quantum Me-
    chanics, 5:659
The Foundations of Scientific
    Inference, 5:103
Foundations of Social Theo-
    ry, 3:223
The Foundations of Sover-
    eignty, and Other Essays,
    3:156
Foundations of Space-Time
    Theories, 5:67
Foundations of the Metaphys-
    ics of Morals, 4:204, 4:205
Foundations of the Origin of
    Species, 5:793

Foundations of the Portu-
    guese Empire, 1415–1850,
    3:386
Foundations of T'ien-T'ai Phi-
    losophy, 4:530
The Founder: Cecil Rhodes
    and the Pursuit of Power,
    3:424
The Founders, 1:1088
Founders of Faith, 4:512,
    4:526
Founders of Geology, 5:622
Founders of Modern Medi-
    cine, 5:801, 5:809
The Founders of the Middle
    Ages, 4:99
Founding of Harvard Col-
    lege, 3:589
The Founding of New Socie-
    ties, 3:606
The Fountain, 1:1106
Fountain and Tomb, 2:68
Fountains of Paradise, 1:614
Four African Literatures:
    Xhosa, Sotho, Zulu, Am-
    haric, 2:107
Four against Everest, 3:910
Four American Indian Mas-
    ters, 1:1047
Four Arguments for the
    Elimination of Television,
    5:126
Four Black Revolutionary
    Plays, 1:1085
The Four Books of Architec-
    ture, 3:763, 3:785
Four Canzones, 2:141
Four Centuries of Fine Print-
    ing, 1:63
Four-Chambered Heart, 1:865
Four Champa Trees, 2:322
Four Contemporary Novel-
    ists, 1:420, 2:939
Four Contemporary Swedish
    Poets, 2:672
Four Critics: Croce, Valéry,
    Lukacs, and Ingarden,
    2:414
Four Decades of Scientific
    Explanation, 5:103
Four Dissertations, 4:210
Four Doctrines, 4:880
Four Flemish Poets, 2:624
The Fourfold Root of the
    Principle of Sufficient
    Reason, 4:254
Four for Tomorrow, 1:1263
The Four Fundamental Con-
    cepts of Psycho-Analysis,
    5:458
The Four Great Heresies,
    4:687

Four Greek Plays: Andromache, Iphigenia, Phaedra, Athaliah, 2:498
Four Hasidic Masters and Their Struggle against Melancholy, 4:633
The 400 Blows, 3:843
Fourier Transforms in a Complex Domain, 5:584
Four in America, 1:882
The Four Just Men, 1:598
Four Loves, 1:512
Four Middle English Mystery Cycles, 1:159
The Four Million, 1:756
Four Modern Prophets, 4:785, 4:905
Four Morality Plays, 1:161
Fournier: The Compleat Typographer, 1:16
The Four Novels of Chinua Achebe: A Critical Study, 2:129
The Four O'Clock Murders, 4:845
Four Old Plays, 3:877
Four Paths to One God, 4:649
Four Plays, 2:531, 2:561
Four Portraits and One Subject: Bernard De Voto, 3:576
Four Puppet Plays, 2:539
Four Quartets, 1:471, 1:472
Four Reasonable Men: Aurelius, Mill, Renan, Sidgwick, 4:276
Four Reigns, 2:336
Four Restoration Playwrights, 1:251
Four Saints in Three Acts, 2:550
Four Screenplays, 3:834
The Four Seasons, 1:565
Four Seasons North: A Journal of Life in the Alaskan Wilderness, 3:898
Four Sons, 1:1165
The Fourteen Sisters of Emilio Montez O'Brien, 1:988
Fourteen Sonnets and Polyphemus, 2:540
Fourteenth-Century English Poetry: Contexts and Readings, 1:147
The Fourth Crusade, 4:694
The Fourth Deadly Sin, 1:1236
Four Theories of Myth in Twentieth-Century History, 4:420, 4:428

The Fourth President: The Life of James Madison, 3:161
The Fourth Trimester: On Becoming a Mother, 5:357
Fourth Way, 4:876
Four Tragedies, nos. 1–4, Three Tragedies, no. 5, 4:474
Four Tragedies and Octavia, 2:393, 4:88
Four Views of Time in Ancient Philosophy, 4:47
Four Voyages to the New World, 3:916
Foxe's Book of Martyrs, 4:733
Foxes of Harrow, 1:1225
The Fox in the Attic, 1:496, 1:497
The Fox Jumps over the Farmer's Gate, 1:578
The Fox Jumps over the Parson's Gate, 1:580
Fox Mykyta, 2:839
Foxybaby, 2:956
Fragile Ecologies: Contemporary Artists' Interpretation and Solutions, 5:193
The Fragile Species: Notes of an Earth Watcher, 5:19
The Fragile X Child, 5:376
The Fragility of Goodness, 4:48
The Fragmented Life of Don Jacobo Lerner, 2:868
Fragment of a Great Confession, 5:467
A Fragment of Autobiography: The Fun of Writing Inside Books, 3:921
A Fragment on Government, 3:150
Fragments, 2:130, 2:131
Fragments from My Diary, 2:725
Fragments of a Journal, 2:483
Fragments of a Poetics of Fire, 4:274
Fragments of Perseus, 1:1008
Frame of the Universe, 5:656
Frames of Mind: The Theory of Multiple Intelligences, 3:174
A Framework for Political Analysis, 3:153
The Framing and Ratification of the Constitution, 3:142
Framing Disease: Studies in Cultural History, 5:36
Framley Parsonage, 1:405

France, 1848–1945: Anxiety and Hypocrisy, 3:374
France, 1870–1914: Politics and Society, 3:372
France and England in North America, 1:690, 3:592
France in America, 3:611
France in Modern Times, 3:374
France in the Giscard Presidency, 3:372
France Prešeren, 2:836
Francesca de Rimini, 2:415
France since 1918, 3:374
Frances Trollope, 1:408
Frances Trollope, Her Life and Literary Work from George III to Victoria, 1:409
The Franchiser, 1:973
Francis Bacon: Discovery and the Art of Discourse, 4:165
Francis Bacon: From Magic to Science, 4:166
Francis Bacon: His Career and His Thought, 4:165
Francis Bacon: Philosopher of Industrial Science, 4:165
Francis Bacon and Renaissance Prose, 4:166
Francis Bacon on the Nature of Man, 4:166
Francis Bacon's Philosophy of Science: An Account and Reappraisal, 4:166
Francisco de Quevedo, Love Poet, 2:548
Francis Galton: The Life and Work of a Victorian Genius, 5:529
Francis Hutcheson and Contemporary Ethical Theory, 4:203
Francis of Assisi, 4:710
Francis Parkman, 1:691, 3:592
Francis Parkman: Heroic Historian, 1:691, 3:592
Francis Parkman, Historian as Hero: The Formative Years, 1:691, 3:592
Francis Petrarch, Six Centuries Later, 2:434
Francis Ponge, 2:494
Francis Ponge: La Poetique du Figural, 2:494
François Mauriac, 2:489
François Mauriac: Visions and Reappraisals, 2:489
François Truffaut, 3:843

François Truffaut: A Guide to References and Resources, 3:843

François Villon, 2:515

François Villon and His Reader, 2:515

Francophone African Fiction: Reading a Literary Tradition, 2:111

The Frank C. Brown Collection of North Carolina Folklore, 3:860

Frank Capra: The Catastrophe of Success, 3:833

Frankenstein, 1:269, 1:281, 1:300, 1:302, 1:591, 1:603, 1:1209, 1:1239, 1:1251, 5:563

Frankenstein Unbound, 1:612, 1:613

The Frankfort Book Fair (1574), 1:37

The Frankfurt School and Critical Theory, 3:200

Frank Herbert, 1:1259

Frankie and Johnny in the Claire de Lune, 1:1103

The Frankish Church, 4:692

Frank Knight, 1885–1972, Henry Simmons, 1899–1946, and Joseph Schumpeter, 1883–1950, 3:89

Franklin and Newton, 5:44

Franklin D. Roosevelt and the New Deal, 1932–1940, 3:535, 3:585

Franklin Evans, 1:706

Frank Lloyd Wright, 3:798

Frank Lloyd Wright, His Life and His Architecture, 3:798

Frank Lloyd Wright, the Guggenheim Correspondence, 3:797

Frank Lloyd Wright and the Prairie School, 3:798

Frank N. Meyer: Plant Hunter in Asia, 5:767

Frank Norris, 1:777

Frank Norris: A Biography, 1:777

Frank Norris: A Study, 1:777

Frank Norris: Instinct and Art, 1:777

Frank O'Connor, 1:528

Frank O'Connor at Work, 1:528

Frank O'Hara: Poet among Painters, 1:1025

Frank O'Hara: To Be True to a City, 1:1025

Frank Sinatra, My Father, 3:719

Franny and Zooey, 1:1043

A Franz Boas Reader, 3:28

Franz Brentano's Analysis of Truth, 4:222

Franz Fanon's Uneven Ribs, 2:152

Franz Grillparzer, 2:584

Franz Kafka: A Biography, 2:596

Franz Liszt, 3:704

Franz Liszt: The Virtuoso Years, 1811–1847, 3:704

Franz Rosenzweig: His Life and Thought, 4:671

Fraternity, 1:482

The Fratricides, 2:373, 2:374

Fraud, 1:451

Fraulein, 2:893

Fraulein Else, 2:611

Fray Juan Crespi, Missionary Explorer on the Pacific Coast, 3:643

Freaks: Myths and Images of the Secret Self, 1:975

Freaks of Genius, 1:1199

Fred Astaire, 3:737

Freddy's Book, 1:979

Frédéric Chopin, 3:690

Frederick Ashton: A Choreographer and His Ballets, 3:736

Frederick Ashton and His Ballets, 3:736

Frederick Douglass, 1:668, 1:785

Frederick Douglass: New Literary and Historical Essays, 1:668

Frederick Douglass's Narrative of the Life of Frederick Douglass, 1:668

Frederick Goddard Tuckerman, 1:704, 1:779

Frederick Jackson Turner's Legacy, 3:599

Frederick Manfred, 1:1217

Frederick Manfred: A Bibliographic and Publication History, 1:1217

Free Agents, 1:935

Free Air, 1:854

The Free and the Unfree: A New History of the United States, 3:512

Free at Last, 3:511

Free Banking and Monetary Reform, 3:65

The Free Black in Urban America, 1800–1850: The Shadow of a Dream, 3:523

A Free Discussion of the Doctrines of Materialism and Philosophical Necessity, 4:210

Freedom, 4:270

Freedom: A Documentary History of Emancipation, 1861–1867, 3:526

Freedom, Emotion and Self-Substance, 4:189

Freedom, Loyalty, Dissent, 3:573

Freedom and Authority in French West Africa, 3:420

Freedom and Destiny, 5:463

Freedom and Fate: An Inner Life of Ralph Waldo Emerson, 1:671

Freedom and Its Limitations in American Life, 3:593

Freedom and Karl Jaspers' Philosophy, 4:300

Freedom and Morality and Other Essays, 4:272

Freedom and Nature: The Voluntary and Involuntary, 4:319

Freedom and Politics in Ethical Behaviour, 4:230

Freedom and Reform, 3:89

Freedom and Resentment, 4:414

Freedom and Responsibility in the American Way of Life, 3:567

Freedom and the End of Reason, 4:207

Freedom and the Modern World, 4:306

Freedom and the Spirit, 4:758

Freedom and the Tragic Life: A Study in Dostoevsky, 2:715

Freedom as a Value, 4:330

Freedom Bound: A History of America's Civil Rights Movement, 3:558

Freedom from Fear and Other Writings, 2:314

Freedom from Menstrual Cramps, 5:356

Freedom from the Known, 4:555

Freedom from the Self: Sufism, Meditation, and Psychotherapy, 4:576

Freedom in Exile: The Autobiography of the Dalai Lama, 4:356, 4:560, 4:906

Freedom in the Modern World, 4:271, 4:308

Freedom Is the Right to Choose, 1:858

The Freedom of the Christian Man, 4:777

The Freedom of the City, 1:479

The Freedom of the Poet, 1:950

Freedom of the Press, 4:296

Freedom or Death, 2:374

Freedom to Learn: A View of What Education Might Become, 3:193

Freedom to Learn for the Eighties, 5:468

Freedom to Publish, 1:56

Freedom with Justice: Catholic Social Thought and Liberal Institutions, 4:748

Free Fall, 1:483

Free Grass, 1:1215

Free-Hand Lettering, 1:20

The Freeholder, or Political Essays, 1:232

Free Joe and Other Georgian Sketches, 1:754

The Freeman and Other Poems, 1:843

The Free Negro in North Carolina, 1790–1860, 3:579

Free to Choose: A Personal Statement, 3:77

Free to Teach: Achieving Equity and Excellence in Schools, 3:251

Free Voices in Russian Literature, 1950s–1980s, 2:690

The Freeway, 1:525

Free Wheelin': A Solo Journey across America, 3:895

Free Will and the Theory of the Moral Desire, 4:230

Free Women, 1:804

Frege: Logical Excavations, 4:229

Frege: Philosophy of Language, 4:229

Frege: Philosophy of Mathematics, 4:229

Frege and the Philosophy of Mathematics, 4:230

Frege in Perspective, 4:230

Frege's Theory of Judgment, 4:229

Frege Synthesized, 4:230

Frémont: Pathmarker of the West, 3:591

French and Germans, Germans and French, 3:372

The French and Italian Notebooks, 1:676

The French Army and Politics, 1870–1970, 3:373

French-Canadian Nationalism: An Anthology, 3:617

The French Canadians: 1760–1945, 3:614

French Civilization from Its Origins to the Close of the Middle Ages, 3:403

French Civilization in the Nineteenth Century, 3:403

French Drama of the Revolutionary Years, 2:449

French Education of Henry Adams, 1:730, 3:563

French-English Dictionary, 1:98

French Enlightenment and the Jews, 3:348, 4:161, 4:647

French Existentialism: A Christian Critique, 4:265

French Free Thought from Gassendi to Voltaire, 4:28, 4:163

French Historical Method: The "Annales" Paradigm, 3:277

French Humanism: 1470–1600, 4:127

The French Lieutenant's Woman, 1:477, 1:478, 1:534

French Literature and Its Background, 2:446

French Literature and the Philosophy of Consciousness, 4:27

French Lyric Poetry: An Anthology, 2:448

Frenchman's Creek, 1:620

French Moralists: The Theory of the Passions 1585–1649, 4:128

French Nuclear Diplomacy, 3:279

The French Paracelsians, 4:150

French Philosophers in Conversation, 4:28, 4:266

French Philosophers—New England Transcendentalism, 4:28

French Poets and Novelists, 2:447

French Political and Intellectual History, 3:372

The French Revolution (Roberts), 3:339, 3:372

The French Revolution (Thackeray), 1:324, 1:343

French Revolution: A Concise History and Interpretation, 3:374

The French Revolution: Conflicting Interpretations, 3:339

The French Revolution: Its Causes, Its History and Its Legacy after Two Hundred Years, 3:339

The French Revolution and Enlightenment in England, 1789–1832, 3:362, 3:339

The French Revolution and the Napoleonic Era, 3:339

French Right and Nazi Germany, 1933–1939, 3:373

French Textiles: From 1760–present, 3:767

French Thought since Sixteen Hundred, 4:28

The French through Their Films, 3:825

The French Welfare State: Surviving Social and Ideological Change, 3:372

Frenzy, 1:1169

The Frenzy of Sweeney, 1:460

Freud, 5:449

Freud: A Dictionary of Psychoanalysis, 5:445

Freud: A Life for Our Time, 3:184

Freud: A Man of His Century, 5:447

Freud: An Introduction to His Life and Work, 5:448

Freud: Political and Social Thought, 5:449

Freud: The Man, His World, His Influence, 5:448

Freud: The Mind of the Moralist, 3:178, 3:184

Freud, Biologist of the Mind: Beyond the Psychoanalytic Legend, 3:184, 5:47

Freud, Jews, and Other Germans, 3:184, 3:376, 4:635

Freud and Dora: The Artful Dream, 5:448

Freud and His Disciples: The Struggle for Supremacy, 5:447

Freud and His Early Circle, 5:447

Freud and His Father, 5:448

Freud and His Followers, 5:448

Freud and His Patients, 5:448

Freud and His Time, 5:449

Freud and Man's Soul, 3:183, 5:435

Freud and Philosophy: An Essay on Interpretation, 4:319

Freud and the Americans, 3:184, 5:448

Freud and the Culture of Psychoanalysis, 3:184

Freud and the Dilemmas of Psychology, 3:184

Freud and the Mind, 3:184, 5:447

Freud and Women, 3:184, 5:448

Freud as We Knew Him, 5:449

Freud for Beginners, 5:447

The Freudian Left: Wilhelm Reich, Geza Roheim, Herbert Marcuse, 5:95

Freud on Broadway, 1:1076

Freud on Femininity and Faith, 4:424

Freud on Schreber: Psychoanalytic Theory and the Critical Act, 5:447

The Freud Scenario, 2:507

Freud's Contribution to Psychiatry, 5:437, 5:447

Freud's Self-Analysis, 5:447

Friar Bacon and Friar Bungay, 1:180

The Friars and the Jews: The Evolution of Medieval Anti-Judaism, 4:623, 4:696

Friar Thomas D'Aquino: His Life, Thought, and Work, 4:119

Friday, 2:512, 2:624

Friedrich A. Hayek: Critical Assessments, 3:83

Friedrich Engels, 4:227

Friedrich Engels: His Life and Thought, 4:227

Friedrich Hebbel, 2:587

Friedrich Nietzsche, 4:246

Friedrich Nietzsche: Fighter for Freedom, 4:248

Friedrich Nietzsche: Philosopher of Culture, 4:247

Friedrich Schiller, 2:609

Friedrich Schlegel, 4:253

Friedrich Schleiermacher: The Evolution of a Nationalist, 4:254

Friend and Foe, 3:610

A Friend from England, 1:451

The Friendly Arctic: The Story of Five Years in Polar Regions, 3:939

A Friendly Companion to Plato's "Gorgias," 4:83

A Friend of Kafka and Other Stories, 1:1049, 2:47

Friend of My Youth, 2:921

Friends, You Drank Some Darkness, 2:671

Friends and Relations, 1:447

Friendship and Sympathy: Communities of Southern Women Writers, 1:794

The Friendship of the Barbarians, 3:324, 4:91

The Friends of Liberty, 3:362

Friends of Thunder, Folktales of Oklahoma, 3:863

Friesche Rymlerye, 2:634

A Fringe of Leaves, 2:965, 2:966

Frisk: A Novel, 1:1186

Fritz, 5:465

Fritz Lang, 3:840

Fritz Lang: A Film Guide, 3:840

Fritz Lang: Genre and Representation in His American Films, 3:840

Frivolity Unbound: Six Masters of the Camp Novel, 1:474

A Frog He Would a-Wooing Go, 1:580

The Frog King, 2:585

Frog Prince, 1:583

The Frogs, 2:353

From a Crooked Rib, 2:122

From Advocacy to Allocation, 5:335

From Agar to Zenry: A Book of Plant Uses, Names, and Folklore, 5:767

From a Land Where Other People Live, 1:1190

From Alfred to Henry III, 871–1272, 3:356

From a Logical Point of View, 4:411, 5:64, 5:99

From a Mighty Fortress, 4:737

From an Ozark Mountain Holler: Stories of Ozark Mountain Folk, 3:885

From Approximately Coast to Coast: It's the Bob and Ray Show, 3:871

From a Realist Point of View: Essays on the Philosophy of Science, 5:65

From Artifact to Habitat, 5:71, 5:156

From a Swedish Homestead, 2:676

From Atoms to Quarks: The Strange World of Particle Physics, 5:662

From Beast Machine to Man Machine, 4:162, 4:170

From Behind the Veil: A Study of Afro-American Narrative, 1:928, 1:808

From Beirut to Jerusalem, 3:439

From Birth to Maturity, 3:173

From Black Muslims to Muslims, 4:579, 4:862

From Blues to Bop: A Collection of Jazz Fiction, 1:805

From Bow Street to Baker Street: Mystery, Detection, and Narrative, 1:604

From Caveman to Chemist: Circumstances and Achievements, 5:729

From Chocolate to Morphine, 5:404

From Class to Culture, 2:324

From Colony to Country, 1:628

From Colony to Empire, 3:601

From Conservation to Ecology, 5:55

From Copyright to Copperfield: The Identity of Dickens, 1:351

From Counter-Reformation to Glorious Revolution, 3:361, 3:411

From Creation to Doom: The York Cycle of Mystery Plays, 1:159

From Croatian Renaissance to Yugoslav Socialism, 2:785

From Crossbow to H-Bomb, 5:236

From Death to Morning, 1:903

From Descartes to Hume, 4:161

From Desire to Godot: Pocket Theater of Postwar Paris, 2:448

From Despotism to Revolution, 1763–1783, 3:338

From Dickens to Hardy, 1:318

From Dr. Mather to Dr. Seuss, 1:1196

From Doon with Death, 1:609

From Dreyfus to Vichy: The Remaking of French Jewry 1906–1939, 3:348 4:636

From Eros to Gaia, 5:10, 5:133, 5:589

From Exile to Redemption: The Fiction of Isaac Bashevis Singer, 1:1050, 2:48

From Ezra to the Last of the Maccabees, 4:604

From Father to Son, 2:661

From Feudalism to Capitalism, 3:290

From Folklore to Fiction, 3:867, 3:869

From Frege to Godel, 5:31

From Fringe to Flying Circus, 1:426

From Furmanov to Sholokhov, 2:693

From Galbraith to Economic Freedom, 3:79

From Gautama Buddha to the Triumph of Christianity, 4:524

From Gesture to Idea: Aesthetics and Ethics in Molière, 2:490

From Gorky to Moscow and Beyond, 3:398

From Gothic Windows to Peacocks, 1:27

From Grimes to Brideshead: The Early Novels of Evelyn Waugh, 1:562

From Harlem to Hollywood, 3:212

From Health Dollars to Health Services: New York City, 1965-1985, 5:333

From Hegel to Marx, 4:298

From Here to Absurdity: The Moral Battlefields of Joseph Heller, 1:988

From Here to Eternity, 1:994

From Heroics to Sentimentalism: A Study of Thomas Otway's Tragedies, 1:251

From Hippocrates to Virchow: Reflections on Human Disease, 5:410

From Homicide to Slavery: Studies in American Culture, 3:559

From Honey to Ashes: Introduction to a Science of Mythology, 4:428, 4:465

From Honey to Ashes, Vol. 2: Mythologiques, 3:33

From Humanism to Science, 1480 to 1700, 4:162, 5:40

From Humanism to the Humanities, 4:126

From Hunters to Farmers, 3:416

From Invention to Innovation, 5:232

From Iran East and West, 4:861

From Karamzin to Bunin: An Anthology of Russian Short Stories, 2:693

From LeRoi Jones to Amiri Baraka: The Literary Works, 1:1085, 1:941

From Lisbon to Goa, 1500-1750, 3:386

From Luther to Chemnitz on Scripture and the Word, 4:730

From Luther to Popper, 4:408

From Machismo to Mutuality, 4:785

From Mankind to Marlowe, 1:161, 1:169

From Mathematical Constructivity to Computer Science, 5:582, 5:583

From Maxwell to Microphysics, 5:701

From Medina to Metropolis, 3:435

From Memex to Hypertext, 5:200, 5:543

From Milton to McLuhan: The Ideas behind American Journalism, 3:805

From Mineralogy to Geology: The Foundations of a Science, 1650-1830, 5:64

From Modern to Contemporary: American Poetry, 1945-1965, 1:912

From Morality to Virtue, 4:389

From Muhammad to the Age of Reforms, 4:543

From Mysticism to Dialogue, 4:662

From Myth to Fiction, 4:471

From Napoleon to Stalin: Comments on European History, 3:409

From Natural History to the History of Nature, 5:45

From Nicaea to Chalcedon: A Guide to the Literature and Its Background, 4:687

From Nicaragua with Love: Poems 1979-1986, 2:859

From Ocean to Sky: Jet Boating, 3:925

From Paracelsus to Van Helmont, 4:150

From Paralysis to Fatigue, 5:315

From Persecution to Toleration, 4:734

From Philo to Origen: Middle Platonism in Transition, 4:670

From Plantation to Ghetto, 3:557

From Platonism to Neoplatonism, 4:61

From Politics to Piety: The Emergence of Pharisaic Judaism, 4:616

From Prague after Munich: Diplomatic Papers, 1938-1940, 3:584

From Prejudice to Destruction: Anti-Semitism, 1700-1933, 3:349

From Primer to Pleasure in Reading, 1:34, 1:37

From Primitives to Zen, 4:472

From Puritanism to the Age of Reason, 4:739

From Puzzles to Portraits: Problems of a Literary Biographer, 1:928

From Quark to Quasar, 5:650

From Radical Left to Extreme Right, 1:72

From Rebellion to Revolution, 3:580

From Religion to Philosophy: A Study of the Origins of Western Speculation, 4:50

From Renaissance to Renaissance: Hebrew Literature, 2:9

From Renaissance to Revolution, 2:679

From Revolution to Politics, Chinese Communists on the Long March, 3:472

From Ritual to Theatre: The Human Seriousness of Play, 3:40

From Roots . . . to Late Budding, 5:312

From Rousseau to Proust, 5:440

From Russia with Love, 1:594

From Sails to Satellite, 5:248

From Sarajevo to Potsdam, 3:409

From Sea to Shining Sea, 1:1244

From Shakespeare to Existentialism, 4:161, 4:265

From Slavery to Freedom: A History of Negro Americans, 3:513, 3:579

From Solon to Socrates, 3:301

From Spanish Court to Italian Ghetto, 4:625

From Story to Stage, 1:219

From Surabaya to Armageddon: Indonesian Short Stories, 2:317

From Targum to Testament, 4:608

From Testament to Torah: An Introduction to Judaism in Its Formative Age, 4:621

From Text to Action, 4:319

From Text to Tradition, 4:621, 4:812

From That Place and Time: A Memoir, 1938–1947, 2:30

From the Beginning: Resources and Guide for the Middle East Study, 3:434

From the Beginnings to the Threshold of the Reformation, 4:676

From the Circle of Alcuin to the School of Auxerre, 4:100

From the Closed World to the Infinite Universe, 4:128, 4:161, 5:42, 5:656

From the Country of Eight Islands, 2:274, 2:283

From the Deep Woods to Civilization, 1:749

From the End of the Peloponnesian War to the Battle of Ipsus, 3:299

From the Enemy's Point of View, 4:466

From the Exile to Christ: A Historical Introduction to Palestinian Judaism, 4:807

From the Fall of Jerusalem, 586 B.C. to the Bar-Kakhba Revolt, A.D. 135, 4:605

From the Fifteenth District, 2:912

From the First Nine: Poems, 1946–1976, 1:1015

From the Ghetto: The Fiction of Abraham Cahan, 1:737

From the Gracchi to Nero: A History of Rome from 133 B.C. to A.D. 368, 3:303

From the Ground Up: The Business of Building in an Age of Money, 5:225

From the Hand of the Hunter, 1:449

From the Heart of the People: The Theology of Gustavo Gutierrez, 4:769

From the Idyll to the Novel: Karamzin's Sentimentalist Prose, 2:730

From the Joke Shop, 1:481

From the Kingdom of Memory: Reminiscences, 1:1065

From the Lands of Sultan and Shah, 3:436

From the Maccabees to the Mishnah, 4:604

From the Many to the One, 4:47

From the Middle Ages to the Enlightenment, 4:130

From the Other Shore, 2:727, 2:728

From the Outer Court to the Inner Sanctum, 4:549

From the Poetry of Sumer: Creation, Glorification, Adoration, 2:52, 4:441

From the Reminiscences of Private Ivanov, and Other Stories, 2:719

From the Rising of the Sun: Christians and Society in Contemporary Japan, 4:541

From the Silent Earth: A Report of the Greek Bronze Age, 2:344

From the Stone Age to Christianity, 4:806, 4:828

From the Stone Age to the Eleusinian Mysteries, 4:545, 4:548

From the Terrace, 1:866

From the Vietnamese: Ten Centuries of Poetry, 2:339

From Time to Time, 4:788

From Tin Foil to Stereo, 5:230

From Topic to Tale: Logic and Narrativity in the Middle Ages, 2:467

From Tradition to Commentary, 4:610

From Tradition to Gospel, 4:825

From Trinidad: An Anthology of Early West Indian Writing, 2:931

From Twilight to Dawn: The Cultural Vision of Jacques Maritain, 4:308

From Two to Five, 2:712

From Union Square to Rome, 4:765

From Waterloo to Peterloo, 1:266

From Where the Sun Now Stands, 1:1212, 1:1213

From Whistle Stop to Sound Bite: Four Decades of Politics and Television, 3:808

From X-Rays to Quarks: Modern Physicists and Their Discoveries, 5:716

Frontier, 1:1216

Frontier and Metropolis, 3:614

The Frontier Experience and the American Dream, 1:715

The Frontier Humorists: Critical Views, 3:871

The Frontier in American History, 3:516, 3:599

Frontiers of American Culture, 3:875

Frontiers of Change: Early Industrialism in America, 3:523

Frontiers of Dance: The Life of Martha Graham, 3:744

Frontiers of Knowledge, 5:58

Frontiers of Science and Philosophy, 5:62

The Frontier Thesis: Valid Interpretation of American History?, 3:599

Frontier Women: The Trans-Mississippi West, 1840–1880, 3:532

Front Yard and Other Italian Stories, 1:790

Frost: A Literary Life Reconsidered, 1:842

Frost: Centennial Essays, 1:842

Froude and Carlyle: A Study of the Froude-Carlyle Controversy, 3:403

The Frozen Deep, 1:321

The Frozen Leopard: Hunting My Dark Heart in Africa, 3:904

The Fruits of Merchant Capital, 3:580

Frustration and Aggression (Dollard), 3:170

Frustration and Aggression (Miller), 3:191

Frustration and Aggression: An Experiment with Young Children, 3:189

F. Scott Fitzgerald, 1:840

F. Scott Fitzgerald: A Collection of Critical Essays, 1:841

F. Scott Fitzgerald: A Descriptive Bibliography, 1:840

F. Scott Fitzgerald and the Art of Social Fiction, 1:841

F. Scott Fitzgerald's The Great Gatsby, 1:840

F. Sionil José and His Fiction, 2:332

Fueling Development, 5:185

Fuente Ovejuna, 2:554

Fuera del Juego, 2:877

The Fugitive, 2:321

The Fugitive Group, 1:798, 1:912

Fugitive Dreams, 2:622

Fugitive Essays, 4:250

The Fugitive Group: A Literary History, 1:798, 1:912

Fugue and Fresco: Structures in Pound's Cantos, 1:873

The Führer Bunker: A Cycle of Poems in Progress, 1:1051

Fulfilment and Other Stories of Women and Men, 1:830

A Full Hearing: Orality and Literacy in the Malay World, 4:460

Full Metal Jacket, 3:839

Full Recovery or Stagnation?, 3:81

Fully Empowered, 2:874

A Functional Biology of Crop Plants, 5:263

A Functional Biology of the Nematodes, 5:772

Functionalism Historicized: Essays on British Social Anthropology, 3:11

The Function of Bibliography, 1:61

The Function of Criticism: From the Spectator to Post-Structuralism, 1:1126

The Function of Reason, 4:341

Functions of a Real Variable, 5:500

Functions of Folk and Fairy Tales, 3:868

The Functions of Social Conflict, 3:204, 3:239

The Functions of the Executive, 3:210

Fundamental Conceptions of Psychoanalysis, 5:437

Fundamental Freedoms and Jehovah's Witnesses, 4:863

Fundamentalism: A Bishop Rethinks the Meaning of Scripture, 4:746

Fundamentalism, Revivalists and Violence in South Asia, 4:507, 4:515

Fundamentalism and American Culture, 4:753

Fundamentalisms Observed: The Fundamentalism Project, 4:890

The Fundamentalist Phenomenon, 4:753

Fundamental Laws of Arithmetic, 4:229

Fundamental Problems of Philosophy, 4:364

The Fundamental Questions of Philosophy, 4:20

Fundamental Reference Sources, 1:80

Fundamentals of Buddhist Ethics, 4:512

Fundamentals of Chemical Reaction Engineering, 5:223

Fundamentals of Digital Signal Processing, 5:296

Fundamentals of Ecology, 5:820

Fundamentals of Electronic Communications Systems, 5:308

Fundamentals of Horticulture, 5:262

Fundamentals of Interactive Computer Graphics, 5:564

Fundamentals of Islamic Thought: God, Man and the Universe, 4:373

Fundamentals of Learning, 3:269

Fundamentals of Meteorology, 5:633

Fundamentals of Molecular Evolution, 5:784

Fundamentals of Philosophy, 4:24

Fundamentals of Physics, 5:650, 5:652

Fundamentals of Plant Pest Control, 5:263

Fundamentals of Plasma Physics, 5:667

Fundamentals of Psychoanalysis, 5:424

Fundamentals of Robot Technology, 5:243

Fundamentals of Statistical Mechanics, 5:673

Fundamentals of Structured COBOL Programming, 5:552

Fundamental Studies of Jean Bodin: An Original Anthology, 4:134

Funeral Dirges of Yoruba Hunters, 2:126

Funeral Music for Freemasons, 2:674

Funeral Rites, 2:478

Funeral Seasons, 1:770

Funeral Speech, Erotic Essay, Exordia, and Letters, 2:355

Fun in a Chinese Laundry, 1:1176

Funk and Wagnalls New Encyclopedia, 1:106

Funk and Wagnall's Standard Dictionary of Folklore, Mythology, and Legends, 3:849, 3:855

The Funniest Man in the World, 2:21

Fun with Fractals, 5:194

Fun with String Figures, 5:495

The Fur Hat, 2:772

The Furies, 1:1247

Furniture and Furnishings, 3:766

Furniture Treasury, 3:766

Furta Sacra: Thefts of Relics in the Central Middle Ages, 4:699

The Further Adventures of Nils, 2:677

Further Collection of Chinese Lyrics, 2:192

Further Confessions of Zeno, 2:439

Further Voices in Vergil's Aeneid, 2:397

The Fur Trade and the Northwest to 1857, 3:613

The Fur Trade in Canada, 3:621

The Fury of Rachel Monette, 2:159

Fusion: Science, Politics and the Invention of a New Energy Source, 5:667

The Fusion of Psychiatry and Social Science, 5:470

Future(s) of Philosophy: The Marginal Thinking of Jacques Derrida, 4:398

The Future Comes: A Study of the New Deal, 3:565

Future Impact of Automation on Workers, 3:91

Future Indefinite: An Autobiography, 1:465

Future Indicative: Literary Theory and Canadian Literature, 2:904

The Future Is Now: Last Talks in India, 4:555

The Future of an Illusion, 4:424, 5:446

The Future of an Illusion: Film, Feminism, and Psychoanalysis, 1:1157
The Future of Architecture, 3:797
The Future of Banking, 3:65
The Future of Culture in Egypt, 2:74
The Future of Evangelical Theology, 4:742
The Future of Government in the United States, 3:162
The Future of Humanity, 4:555
The Future of Intellectuals and the Rise of the New Class, 3:202, 3:228
The Future of Islam, 4:567
A Future of Lousy Jobs? 3:60
Future of Man, 4:336
The Future of Mankind, 5:138
The Future of Marriage, 3:206, 3:221
The Future of New Religious Movements, 4:855
The Future of Psychoanalysis: Essays in Honor of Heinz Kohut, 5:458
The Future of Religion, 2:631
The Future of Religion: Secularization, Revival and Cult Formation, 4:855
The Future of the American Jew, 4:667
The Future of the American Negro, 1:785
The Future of the Automobile, 5:247
The Future of the Jewish Community in America, 4:641
The Future of the Mass Audience, 3:804
The Future of the Past, 3:602
The Future of the Printed Word, 5:544
Future Shock, 5:158
Future Water, 5:632
Futurist Manifestos, 2:400
The Futurological Congress, 2:816
The FX Decision, 3:496
Fyodor Dostoevsky, 2:715
Fyodor Dostoevsky's Brothers Karamazov, 2:715
Fyodor Dostoevsky's Crime and Punishment, 2:715
Fyodor Dostoyevsky: A Writer's Life, 2:715

G

Gabriela, Clove and Cinnamon, 2:891, 2:892
Gabriela Mistral, 2:873
Gabriela Mistral: The Poet and Her Work, 2:873
Gabriela Mistral's Religious Sensibility, 2:873
Gabriel Conroy, 1:755
Gabriele D'Annunzio, 2:415
Gabriele D'Annunzio in France: A Study in Cultural Relations, 2:415
Gabriel Fauré: A Musical Life, 3:695
Gabriel García Márquez (Bloom), 2:867
Gabriel García Márquez (Williams), 2:868
Gabriel García Márquez: A Study of the Short Fiction, 2:867
Gabriel García Márquez: New Readings, 2:867
Gabriel García Márquez and the Powers of Fiction, 2:867
Gabriel Marcel, 4:305
Gabriel's Wing: A Study into the Religious Ideas of Sir Muhammad Iqbal, 4:375
Gabriel Tolliver: A Story of Reconstruction, 1:754
Gadamer: Hermeneutics, Tradition, and Reason, 4:402
Gadamer and Hermeneutics, 4:402
Gadamer's Hermeneutics, 4:402
Gaia: An Atlas of Planet Management, 5:824
Gaia: A New Look at Life on Earth, 5:823
Gaia and God, 4:749, 4:785, 4:905
Gaiety Transfigured, 1:1181
Gainful Pursuits: The Making of Industrial Europe, 1600–1914, 3:341
Gainsborough: His Life and Art, 3:775
The Galactic Novae, 5:610
Galaxies (Ferris), 5:593, 5:603
Galaxies (Shapley), 5:612
Galbraith, Harrington, Heilbroner, 3:79
Galdós: The Early Historical Novels, 2:547
Galdós and His Critics, 2:547

Gale Directory of Publications and Broadcast Media, 1:113
Gale Directory of Publications and Broadcast Media 94 and Update, 1:72
Gale Environmental Sourcebook, 5:815
A Galilean Rabbi and His Bible, 4:608
Galileo (Brecht), 1:450, 2:572, 5:604
Galileo (Drake), 4:143, 5:688
Galileo (Ronan), 4:144
Galileo: A Philosophical Study, 4:144
Galileo: Man of Science, 5:688
Galileo: Pioneer Scientist, 4:143, 4:172
Galileo, Bellarmine and the Bible, 4:142
Galileo, First Observer of Marvelous Things, 4:172
Galileo, Heretic, 4:143, 5:43, 5:688
Galileo, Human Knowledge, and the Book of Nature, 4:143
Galileo, Science, and the Church, 5:604, 5:688
Galileo, the Jesuits and the Medieval Aristotle, 4:144
The Galileo Affair: A Documentary History, 4:143, 4:172
Galileo and His Sources, 4:144
Galileo and the Art of Reasoning, 4:143
Galileo at Work, 4:172
Galileo at Work: His Scientific Biography, 4:143, 5:41, 5:604, 5:688
Galileo Galilei: A Biography and Inquiry into His Philosophy of Science, 4:143, 4:172
Galileo Galilei: His Life and His Works, 5:689
Galileo Galilei: Toward a Resolution of 350 Years of Debate 1633–1983, 5:688
Galileo Galilei and the Roman Curia from Authentic Sources, 5:688
Galileo Man of Science, 4:143
Galileo Reappraised, 4:143, 4:172
Galileo's Intellectual Revolution, 4:172, 5:43, 5:689

Galileo's Intellectual Revolution: Middle Period, 1610–1632, 4:144

Galileo's Logical Treatises, 4:144

Galileo's Logic of Discovery and Proof, 4:144

Galileo Studies: Personality, Tradition, and Revolution, 4:143, 4:172

Gallathea (and Midas), 1:186

Gallopin' Gaucho, 1:1163

The Galton Case, 1:1234

The Gambler, 2:409, 2:713

The Gambler and The Diary of Polina Suslova, 2:713

Gambrinus, and Other Stories, 2:733

The Game, 1:454

Game, Set and Math: Enigmas and Conundrums, 5:497

A Game at Chess, 1:190

Game Management, 5:834

Game of Love, 1:619

Games, Gods and Gambling, 5:30, 5:526

Games and Decisions: Introduction and Critical Survey, 3:63

Games at Twilight, 2:179

Games People Play: The Psychology of Human Relationships, 5:433

The Games Were Coming, 2:932

Game Theory, 3:63

Game Theory: A Nontechnical Introduction, 5:571

Gandavyuha, 4:529

Gandhi, 4:352

Gandhi: Against the Tide, 4:553

Gandhi: Prisoner of Hope, 3:486, 4:553

Gandhi: The South African Experience, 4:554

Gandhi, A Memoir, 4:553

Gandhi and Charlie, 4:553

Gandhi and Civil Disobedience, 4:553

Gandhi and His Critics, 4:553

Gandhi and Non-Violence, 4:553

Gandhi and the Nonconformists: Encounters in South Africa, 4:553

Gandhian Utopia: Experiments with Culture, 4:553

Gandhi on Non-Violence, 4:895

Gandhi on War and Peace, 3:280

Gandhi's Religious Thought, 4:352, 4:553

Gandhi's Rise to Power: Indian Politics 1915–1922, 4:553

Gandhi's Truth: On the Origins of Militant Nonviolence, 3:182, 4:553

Gandhi Today: The Story of Mahatma Gandhi's Successors, 4:553

Ganesa: Lord of Obstacles, Lord of Beginnings, 4:503

Ganesh: Studies of an Asian God, 4:503

The Ganges in Myth and History, 4:503

Gantenbein, 2:579

García Márquez: One Hundred Years of Solitude, 2:868

García Márquez: The Man and His Work, 2:867

García Márquez, Writer of Colombia, 2:867

The Garden: New and Selected Poetry, 2:696

Garden, Ashes, 2:830

The Garden and Farm Books of Thomas Jefferson, 5:265

The Gardener's Year, 2:790

Gardenia, 1:1090

The Garden of Abdul Gasazi, 1:1207

The Garden of Adonis, 1:982, 1:983

The Garden of Eden, 1:845

The Garden of Priapus: Sexuality and Aggression in Roman Humor, 2:381

Garden of Rama, 1:614

The Garden of the Finzi-Continis, 2:407, 2:408

The Garden Party and Other Stories, 2:978

Gardens and Grim Ravines, 1:315

The Gardens of Silihdar and Other Writings, 2:80

The Garden Where the Brass Band Played, 2:631

Gardner's Art through the Ages, 3:756

Gardner's Chemical Synonyms and Trade Names, 5:725

Gargantua, 2:497

Gargantua and Pantagruel, 2:497

Garibaldi, The Man and the Nation, 3:385

Garip, 2:98

A Garland for John Donne, 1631–1931, 1:178

A Garland of Country Song, 3:850

A Garland of Rational Songs, 5:439

Garland Shakespeare Bibliographies, 1:220

The Garments of Torah: Essays in Biblical Hermeneutics, 4:610

The Garrick Year, 1:467

Gary Null's Complete Guide to Health, 5:347

Gary Snyder: Dimensions of a Life, 1:1052

Gary Snyder's Vision: Poetry and the Real Work, 1:1052

The Gases of the Atmosphere, the History of Their Discovery, 5:710

Gas I, 2:596

Gasoline, The Vestal Ladies on Brattle, 1:964

Gassendi's View of Knowledge, 4:173

Gaston Bachelard, 4:274

Gaston Bachelard, Subversive Humanist, 4:274

Gaston de Blondeville, or the Court of Henry 3rd, 1:622

Gaston de Latour, 1:387

The Gate behind the Wall: A Pilgrimage to Jerusalem, 4:642, 4:654

The Gate of Heavenly Peace, 3:503

Gates, 5:543

Gates of Bronze, 2:19

Gates of Eden: American Culture in the 60s, 3:559

The Gates of Horn: A Study of Five French Realists, 2:447

Gates of Prayer for Weekdays and at a House of Mourning, 4:600

Gates of Repentance, 4:600

The Gates of the Forest, 1:1065

Gates of the Mountains, 1:1212, 1:1213

Gateway, 1:1261

Gateway to Reality: An Introduction to Philosophy, 4:25

Gateway to the Middle Ages: Monasticism, 3:330

A Gathering of Saints: A True Story of Money, Murder and Deceit, 1:35

The Gathering of Zion: The Story of the Mormon Trail, 3:525
Gathering Storm in the Churches, 4:753
Gather Together in My Name, 1:935
The Gaucho Martín Fierro, 2:869
Gaudete, 1:497
Gaudier-Brzeska: A Memoir, 1:871
Gaudy Night, 1:610
Gauguin (Goldwater), 3:775
Gauguin (Thomson), 3:776
Gauguin: Watercolors, Pastels, Drawings, 3:775
Gauguin's Letters from the South Seas, 3:775
Gauguin's South Seas, 3:775
The Gauntlet, Beyond our Power, 2:663
Gauss: A Biographical Study, 5:508, 5:530
The Gawain-Poet, 1:156
The Gay Academic, 1:1128
Gay American History: Lesbians and Gay Men in the U.S.A., 1:1182
Gay and Lesbian Themes in Latin American Writing, 2:845
Gay Fictions: Studies in a Male Homosexual Literary Tradition, 1:1182
The Gay Genius, 2:220
Gay-Lussac: Scientist and Bourgeois, 5:747
The Gay Nineties in America: A Cultural Dictionary of the 1890s, 3:508
Gay Plays, 1:1184
Gays and Films, 1:1183
The Gay Science, 4:245, 4:246
Gay Sunshine Interviews, 1:1184
The Gazelle: Medieval Hebrew Poems on God, Israel, and the Soul, 2:10
Gazing on Secret Sights, 1:198
G. B. Shaw: An Annotated Bibliography of Writings about Him, 1:546
Geared to the Stars, 5:32
Gedatsu-kai and Religion in Contemporary Japan, 4:540
Gedichte, 2:613
Geisha in Rivalry (Udekurabe), 2:291

Gemeinschaft und Gesellschaft, 3:242
Gemology, 5:628
G. E. Moore, 4:312
G. E. Moore: A Critical Exposition, 4:312
Gems of Chinese Verse and More Gems of Chinese Poetry, 2:192
Gemstones and Their Origin, 5:628
Gender, 5:136, 5:137
Gender, Genre, and Power in South Asian Expressive Traditions, 4:503
Gender, Race and Region, 1:724
Gender and Kinship: Essays toward a Unified Analysis, 3:19
Gender and Religion: On the Complexity of Symbols, 4:892
Gender and Stratification, 3:207
Gender and the Life Course, 3:207
Gender at Work: Four Women Writers of the Eighteenth Century, 1:226
Gender Differences at Work, 3:207
Gendered Subjects: The Dynamics of Feminist Teaching, 1:1128
The Gender of Breadwinners, 3:608
The Gender of Modernism: A Critical Anthology, 1:415
The Gender of the Gift, 3:16
Gender Politics, 3:207
Gender Sanity: The Case against Feminism, 3:207
Gender Stratification, 3:24
Gender Trouble: Feminism and the Subversion of Identity, 1:1181, 3:207
The Genealogy of Demons, 1:872
A Genealogy of Modernism, 1:415
Gene Civilization, 5:782
Gene Mapping: Using Law and Ethics as Guides, 5:118
Geneology, 2:377
The General and Other Stories, 2:339
General Anthropology, 3:28
General Catalogue of Printed Books: Compact Edition, 1:66
General Climatology, 5:633

General Competitive Analysis, 3:69
General Geology, 5:626
General History of Africa, 3:416, 3:425
A General History of the Robberies and Murders of the Most Notorious Pyrates, 1:239
A General History of the Sciences, 5:26
The General in His Labyrinth, 2:866, 2:867
Generally Speaking, 1:457
The General next to God, 4:740
The General of the Dead Army, 2:779, 2:780
General Philosophy, 4:25
General Psychopathology, 4:299
General Psychopathology: An Introduction, 5:428
General Reference Books for Adults, 1:73, 1:81, 1:89
General Relativity and Gravitational Physics, 5:664
General Relativity from A to B, 5:664
General Science Index, 5:5
General Selections from the Works of Sigmund Freud, 5:446
General Theory, 3:90, 3:105
The General Theory of Employment, Interest and Money, 3:86, 3:87
General Theory of Knowledge, 4:333
General Theory of Relativity, 5:680
General Topology, 5:500
General View of Positivism, 3:223, 4:222
General William Booth Enters Heaven, 1:855
Genera Plantarum, 5:805
The Generation of 2000: Contemporary American Poets, 1:915
A Generation of Materialism, 1871–1900, 3:341
Generation of Spanish Poets, 1920–1936, 2:522, 2:526
Generations: Selected Poems, 2:40
Generations of Men, 2:968
Generous Lives: American Catholic Women Today, 4:754

Genes, Organisms, Populations: Controversies over the Units of Selection, 5:67

Genes, Radiation and Society: The Life and Work of H. J. Muller, 5:808

Genesis: A Commentary, 4:822, 4:838

Genesis and Geology, 5:46

Genesis and Structure of Society, 4:285

The Genesis of a Painting: Picasso's Guernica, 3:786

The Genesis of Ezra Pound's Cantos, 1:872

The Genesis of Faith, 4:665

Genesis of German Conservatism, 3:341

The Genesis of Novel Behavior: Individual Development and Evolution, 3:173

Genesis of Structures in African Narrative, Dahomean Narratives, 2:112

Genesis of the Frontier Thesis: A Study in Historical Creativity, 3:599

The Genesis of the Novel in Thailand, 2:336

The Genesis of Wuthering Heights, 1:336

Genesis Rabbah: The Judaic Commentary on Genesis, 4:611

Genesis II: Creation and Recreation with Computers, 5:565

Genetic Alchemy, 5:75, 5:782

Genetic Counseling: Facts, Values and Norms, 5:780

Genetic Counseling: Psychological Dimensions, 5:781

Genetic Counseling, the Church, and the Law, 5:780

A Genetic Counseling Casebook, 5:780

Genetic Engineering Technology: Principles and Applications, 5:223

Genetic Epistemology, 3:267

Genetic Nutrition, 5:781

Genetic Nutrition: Designing a Diet Based on Your Family Medical History, 5:327

Genetic Revolution: Scientific Prospects and Public Perceptions, 5:782

Genetics: Readings from Scientific American, 5:777

Genetics: The Past and the Present, 5:778

Genetics, Medicine, and Man, 5:808

Genetics, Society and Decisions, 5:778

Genetics and Modern Biology, 5:788

Genetics and the Origin of Species, 5:779

Genetics in Medicine, 5:781

Genitri, 2:489

The Genius, 1:450, 1:830

Genius: The Life and Science of Richard Feynman, 5:686

Genius and Talent, 4:347

Genius and the Mobocracy, 3:793

The Genius of American Politics, 3:569

The Genius of Arab Civilization: Source of Renaissance, 4:569

The Genius of George Washington, 3:521, 3:588

Genius of Place: William Faulkner's Triumphant Beginnings, 1:837

The Genius of Spain, and Other Essays on Spanish Literature, 2:522

Genocide: Its Political Use in the Twentieth Century, 3:205

Genome, 5:777

Genreflecting, 1:122, 1:1210

Genre Terms, 1:69

Genteel Barbarism, 2:845

The Genteel Tradition and the Sacred Rage, 1:727, 4:327

The Genteel Tradition at Bay, 4:326

The Gentle Art of Murder, 1:606

The Gentle Barbarian: The Life and Work of Ivan Turgenev, 2:770

Gentle Bridges, 4:356

Gentle Conquest: The Botanical Discovery of North America, 5:768

The Gentle Craft, 1:177

The Gentle Grafter, 1:757

Gentle Jack, 1:445

The Gentleman Dancing Master, 1:263

"The Gentleman from San Francisco" and Other Stories, 2:707

Gentleman in a Dustcoat: A Biography of John Crowe Ransom, 1:875

Gentleman's Progress: The Itinerarium of Dr. Alexander Hamilton, 1744, 3:569

The Gentleman Usher, 1:175

The Gentlemen in Trollope: Individuality and Moral Conduct, 1:407

The Gentle Puritan: A Life of Ezra Stiles, 1727–1795, 3:588

Gentle Vengeance, 5:336

The Gentry: The Rise and Fall of a Ruling Class, 3:362

Geo-Data: The World Geographical Encyclopedia, 1:84

Geofroy Tory, 1:7

The Geographer at Work, 5:620

The Geographer's Craft, 5:620

A Geographical Bibliography for American Libraries, 3:118, 3:125, 5:620

Geographical Ecology: Patterns in the Distribution of Species, 5:820

Geographical Essays, 5:643

The Geographical Pivot of History, 3:326

Geographic Dimensions of United States Social Policy, 3:122

Geographic Information Systems, 5:620

Geographic Information Systems: A Guide to the Technology, 3:120, 5:619

Geographic Information Systems and Cartographic Modeling, 5:621

Geographic Perspectives on America's Past, 3:136

Geographic Perspectives on Global Problems, 5:619

Geographic Perspectives on Urban Systems, 3:127

Geography (Dorn), 1:970

Geography (Strabo), 4:492

Geography: An Outline for the Intending Student, 5:619

Geography: Regions and Concepts, 3:125

Geography, Resources, and Environment, 5:620

Geography and Cartography: A Reference Handbook, 5:621

Geography and Geographers, 3:131

Geography and Plays, 1:882

Geography and Resource Analysis, 5:620

Geography and the State: An Essay in Political Geography, 3:132

Geography behind History, 3:272

Geography in America, 3:118, 3:125

Geography Is Fun, 5:621

The Geography of Agriculture: A Selected Bibliography, 5:261

Geography of Europe, 3:130

Geography of Holiness: The Photography of Thomas Merton, 4:781

Geography of Housing, 3:127

Geography of Israel, 3:440

The Geography of Market Centers and Retail Distribution, 3:127

A Geography of Soils, 5:635

Geography of the Ozark Highland of Missouri, 3:135

The Geography of the World Economy, 3:122

A Geography of Transportation, 3:123

Geohistory-Global Evolution of the Earth, 5:618

Geological Hazards, 5:635

A Geological Miscellany, 5:622

Geological Observations on the Volcanis Islands and Parts of South America Visited during the Voyage of the H.M.S. Beagle, 5:793

Geological Oceanography, 5:632

Geological Sketches, 5:785

Geologic Factors and the Evolution of Plants, 5:640

Geologic Hazards, Resources, and Environmental Planning, 5:636

Geologic Reference Sources, 5:625

The Geologic Story of the National Parks and Monuments, 5:626

Geologic Structures and Moving Plates, 5:624

A Geologic Time Scale, 5:623

Geologists and the History of Geology, 5:625

Geology, 5:624

Geology, Resources, and Society: An Introduction to Earth Science, 5:636

Geology and Society, 5:635

Geology Field Guide: The Black Hills, 5:626

A Geology for Engineers, 5:635

Geology Illustrated, 5:627

Geology in the Field, 5:636

Geology in the Nineteenth Century: Changing Views of a Changing World, 5:46

Geology Made Simple, 5:623

Geology of Coal, 5:637

Geology of National Parks, 5:626

Geology of the Industrial Rocks and Minerals, 5:635

Geology of the Sierra Nevada, 5:626

The Geology of the Terrestrial Planets, 5:629

Geometrical Solutions Derived from Mechanics, 5:498

Geometrodynamics, 5:719

Geometry from Multiple Perspectives, 5:486

The Geometry of René Descartes, 5:502

Geometry Revisited, 5:486

Geomorphology: An Introduction to the Study of Landscapes, 5:626

Geomorphology from the Earth, 5:626

The Geopolitical Aesthetic: Cinema and Space in the World System, 1:1149

Georg Cantor: His Mathematics and Philosophy of the Infinite, 5:501

George Balanchine: Ballet Master, 3:738

George Bernard Shaw, 1:457

George Borrow: A Bibliographical Study, 3:913

George Borrow, Eccentric, 3:913

George C. Marshall, 3:280

George Crabbe, 1:289

George Crabbe and the Progress of Eighteenth-Century Narrative Verse, 1:289

George du Maurier, 1:352

George Eliot, 1:354

George Eliot: A Biography, 1:354

George Eliot: A Guide through the Critical Maze, 1:354

George Eliot: An Intellectual Life, 1:354

George Eliot: Her Mind and Her Art, 1:354

George Eliot: The Critical Heritage, 1:354

George Eliot and Herbert Spencer, 1:354

George Eliot and Music, 1:354

George Eliot and the Conflict of Interpretations, 1:354

George Eliot and the Novel of Vocation, 1:354

A George Eliot Companion: Literary Achievement and Modern Significance, 1:354

George Eliot's Creative Conflict: The Other Side of Silence, 1:354

George Eliot's Middlemarch Notebooks, 1:354

George F. Kennan and the Making of American Foreign Policy, 1947–1950, 3:546, 3:584

George Farquhar, 1:244

George Farquhar: A Reference Guide, 1:244

George IV: Prince of Wales, 1752–1811, 3:362

George IV: Regent and King, 1811–1830, 3:362

George Fox: Seeker and Friend, 4:734

George Gershwin: Man and Legend, 3:696

George Gershwin, A Biography, 3:696

George Gissing, 1:359

George Gissing: A Biography, 1:359

George Gissing: An Annotated Bibliography of Writings about Him, 1:360

George Gissing: Ideology and Fiction, 1:359

George Henry Lewes, 1:373

George Henry Lewes: A Victorian Mind, 1:373

George Henry Lewes as Literary Critic, 1:373

George Herbert: An Annotated Bibliography of Modern Criticism, 1905–1974, 1:181

George Herbert: The Critical Heritage, 1:181

George Herbert Mead: A Unifying Theory for Sociology, 4:309

George Herbert Mead: Critical Assessments, 4:309

George Herbert Mead: Essays on His Social Philosophy, 3:233

George Herbert Mead: Self Language and the World, 4:309

George Herbert Mead on Social Psychology, 4:308

George Herbert's Lyrics, 1:181

George Kennan and the Dilemmas of United States Foreign Policy, 3:546, 3:584

George MacDonald, 1:587

George Meredith, 1:379

George Meredith: A Bibliography, 1:379

George Meredith: An Annotated Bibliography, 1925-1975, 1:379

George Meredith and Thomas Love Peacock, 1:297

George Mills, 1:972, 1:973

George Moore, 1:381

George Moore: A Disciple of Walter Pater, 1:381

George Moore: An Annotated Secondary Bibliography of Writings about Him, 1:381

George Orwell, 1:531

George Orwell: A Collection of Critical Essays, 1:531

George Orwell: An Annotated Bibliography of Criticism, 1:531

George Orwell: The Critical Heritage, 1:531

George Peele, 1:195

George Pierce Baker and the American Theatre, 1:1074

George S. Kaufman: His Life, His Theater, 1:1097

George S. Kaufman and His Collaborators: Three Plays, 1:1097

George Sand: Writing for Her Life, 2:505

George Santayana: A Bibliographical Checklist, 1880-1980, 4:328

George Santayana: A Biography, 4:328

Georges Bernanos: A Study of Christian Commitment, 2:460

Georges Cuvier, 5:792

George Seurat (1859-1891): The Metro, 5:193

Georges Simenon, 2:508

Georges Simenon: A Bibliography, 2:508

George Steiner: A Reader, 1:1054

George Washington: A Biography, 3:519

George Washington Cable, 1:737

George Washington Cable: A Study of His Early Life and Works, 1:737

George Washington Cable: The Life and Times of a Southern Heretic, 1:737

George Washington Harris, 1:674

George Washington Slept Here, 1:1097

George Washington Williams, a Biography, 3:579

George W. Cable: A Biography, 1:737

George Whitefield: Wayfaring Witness, 4:739

Georgian Delights: The Pursuit of Happiness, 3:408

Georgian London, 3:363

Georgia O'Keeffe, 3:785

Georgia O'Keeffe: A Life, 3:785

Georgia Scenes, 1:683, 1:684

Georgics (Simon), 2:509

The Georgics (Virgil), 1:511, 2:396, 2:397

Georg Lukács, 2:801

Georg Simmel on Individuality and Social Form, 3:239

Geothermal Resources, 5:635

Gerald R. Ford and the Politics of Post-Watergate America, 3:537

Gerald's Game, 1:1241

Gerard Manley Hopkins, 1:364

Gerard Manley Hopkins: A Comprehensive Bibliography, 1:364

Gerard Manley Hopkins: The Classical Background and Critical Reception of His Work, 1:364

Gerhard von Rad, 4:838

The Germ, 1:391

German and Italian Lyrics of the Middle Ages, 2:403

German Classics, 2:566

The German Democratic Republic since 1945, 3:377

The German Dictatorship, 3:376

German-English Dictionary, 1:98, 1:99

German-French Annals, 4:228

German Holocaust Literature, 2:565

German Humanism, 4:124

German Humanism and Reformation: Selected Writings, 4:124

Germania, 1:139, 1:144

The German Immigrant in America, 3:557

German Liberalism and the Dissolution of the Weimar Party System, 1918-1933, 3:344

German Life and Manners as Seen in Saxony at the Present Day, 1:377

German Literature in the Nineteenth Century, 2:565

German Literature under National Socialism, 2:566

A German Love Story, 2:591

German Narrative Prose, 2:566

The German Peasant War of 1525, 4:723

The German People and the Reformation, 4:722

German Philosophy: An Introduction, 4:28

German Philosophy and Politics, 4:28

The German Reformation, 3:334

German Root Lexicon, 1:99

The Germans, 2:565

Germans and Jews, 3:350

German Short Stories, 2:567

German Sociology, 3:283

German-Soviet Relations between the Two World Wars, 1919-1939, 3:376

The German Tradition in Literature, 2:565

A German World Family Dictionary: Together with English Equivalents, 1:99

Germany: Revolution and Counter-Revolution, 3:74, 3:75

Germany, 1866-1945, 3:376

Germany and Europe, 1919-1939, 3:377

Germany and the Germans, 3:345

Germany and the Two World Wars, 3:279

Germany from Potsdam to Partition, 3:427

Germany's Aims in the First World War, 3:278, 3:376

Germany's First Bid for Colonies, 1884-1885, 3:409

Germany Transformed: Political Culture and the New Politics, 3:376
Germany—from Partition to Reunification, 3:378
Germinal, 2:517, 2:518
Germs That Won't Die, 5:351
Gerontian, 1:471
Gershom Scholem: Kabbalah and Counter-History, 4:672
Gershwin: His Life and Music, 3:696
Gertrude, or Family Pride, 1:408
Gertrude and Alice, 1:883
Gertrude Stein, 1:882, 1:883
Gertrude Stein: An Annotated Critical Bibliography, 1:883
Gertrude Stein Advanced: An Anthology of Criticism, 1:883
Gertrude Stein and the Making of Literature, 1:883
Gertrude Stein and the Present, 1:883
The Gertrude Stein First Reader and Three Plays, 1:882
Gerusalemme Liberata, 2:440
Gesammelte Abhandlungen, 5:510
Gesenius' Hebrew Grammar, 4:794
The Gestalt Approach and Eyewitness to Therapy, 5:465
Gestalt Psychology, 3:177
Gestalt Therapy: Excitement and Growth in the Human Personality, 5:465
The Gestalt Therapy Book, 5:465
Gestalt Therapy Primer: Introductory Readings in Gestalt Therapy, 5:420
Gestalt Therapy Verbatim, 5:465
Get Away Old Man, 1:1110
Get Shorty, 1:1232
Getting Books to Children: An Exploration of Publisher-Market Relations, 1:50
Getting Even, 1:933, 3:870
Getting Here: The Story of Human Evolution, 5:779
The Getting of Wisdom, 2:961
Getting On-Line: A Guide to Assessing Computer Information Services, 5:548
Getting Out, 1:1105

Getting Over Getting High, 5:403
Getting Personal, 1:928, 1:1127
Getting Pregnant in the 1980s, 5:358
Getting Published: A Guide for Business People and Other Professionals, 1:46
Getting Published: The Writer in the Combat Zone, 1:46
Getting Saved from the Sixties, 4:855
Getting Sued and Other Tales of the Engineering Life, 5:155
Getting Thin, 5:347
Getting to Be Mark Twain, 1:784
Getting to Know the General: The Story of an Involvement, 1:489
Getting Used to Dying: A Novel, 2:239
Gettysburg: A Journey in Time, 3:528
Gettysburg: The Final Fury, 3:571
Ghana: An African Portrait, 3:428
Gharbzadegi = Weststruckness, 2:85
Ghazals of Ghālib: Versions from the Urdu, 2:175
The Ghetto, 3:245
G. H. Lewes: A Life, 1:373
G. H. Mead's Concept of Rationality, 4:309
Ghost, Gales and Gold, 3:937
Ghost at Noon, 2:429
The Ghost Festival in Medieval China, 4:531
The Ghost from the Grand Banks, 1:614
The Ghost in the Atom, 5:660
Ghost in the Wheels: Selected Poems, 1920–1976, 2:907
The Ghost Lake: The True Story of Louis Agassiz, 5:786
The Ghost of Lumumba, 2:140
Ghosts, 1:1098
Ghosts along the Cumberland: Deathlore in the Kentucky Foothills, 3:861
Ghosts and Other Plays, 2:666
Ghosts of the Confederacy, 3:531

Ghosts of the Gothic: Austen, Eliot, and Lawrence, 1:320
Ghosts of the Stage, 2:204
Ghost Stories and Mysteries, 1:601
Ghost Stories of an Antiquary, 1:600
Ghost Stories of Edith Wharton, 1:787
The Ghost Writer, 1:1040, 1:1041
Giacomo Leopardi, 2:424
Giambattista Vico and the Foundations of a Science of the Philosophy of History, 4:217
Giambattista Vico's Science of Humanity, 4:217
Gianfrancesco Pico della Mirandola (1469–1533) and His Critique of Aristotle, 4:152
Gian Lorenzo Bernini: The Sculptor of the Roman Baroque, 3:770
The Giant Pandas of Wolong, 5:771
Giants in the Earth, 2:667
Giants of Geology, 5:622
A Giant Walked among Them, 3:855
The Giaour, 1:281
Giddens' Theory of Structuration: A Critical Appreciation, 3:227
Gide, 2:480
Gideon Planish, 1:853, 1:854
Gift: Form and Reason for Exchange in Archaic Societies, 3:16
The Gift (H.D.), 1:827
The Gift (Nabokov), 2:711, 2:739, 2:740
Gifted Children, 3:185
The Giftedness in Every Child, 3:175
Gifted Young Children, 3:252
The Gift of a Cow: A Translation of the Hindi Novel, Godaan, 2:180
The Gift of Asher Lev, 1:1032
The Gift of Black Folk, 3:577
The Gift of Black Folk: The Negroes in the Making of America, 1:832
A Gift of Courage, 5:314
A Gift of Life, 5:368
Gift of the Magi, 1:757
Gifts, 2:47
Gifts of Love, 2:372
The Gift to Be Simple, 4:849

Gigi, Julie de Carneilhan, Chance Acquaintances, 2:470

Gilbert and Sullivan (Hayter), 1:358, 3:670

Gilbert and Sullivan (Pearson), 1:358

Gilbert and Sullivan: A Critical Approach to the Savoy Operas, 1:358

Gilbert and Sullivan: The Creative Conflict, 1:357

Gilbert and Sullivan and Their Victorian World, 1:358

The Gilbert and Sullivan Companion, 3:654

The Gilbert and Sullivan Concordance, 1:357

A Gilbert and Sullivan Dictionary, 1:357

Gilbert and Sullivan in America, 1:357

Gilbert before Sullivan: Six Comic Plays, 1:357

Gilbert Ryle: An Introduction to His Philosophy, 4:325

The Gilded Age: A Tale of Today, 1:780

Giles Goat-Boy, 1:942, 5:563

Giles of Rome on Ecclesiastical Power, 4:103

Gilgamesh, 2:53, 4:440

The Gilgamesh Epic and Old Testament Parallels, 2:53

Gilkey on Tillich, 4:787

Gilles and Jeanne, 2:512

Gimpel the Fool and Other Stories, 1:1049, 2:47

Ginger, You're Barmy, 1:515

The Gingerbread Lady, 1:1113

Gingertown, 1:857

The Gingham Dog, 1:1121

Ginseng and Other Tales from Manila, 2:329

Giordano Bruno, 4:136

Giordano Bruno, His Life and Thought, 4:136

Giordano Bruno and the Hermetic Tradition, 2:410, 4:136, 5:41

Giovanni Gentile on the Existence of God, 4:285

Giovanni Pascoli: Convivial Poems, 2:431

Giovanni's Room, 1:938, 1:939, 1:1084

Giovanni Verga, 2:441

Giraffe and a Half, 1:1207

Giraffes, Black Dragons and Other Pianos, 3:672

Girl Alive! 2:653

The Girl from Samos, 2:364

Girl from the Coast, 2:321

The Girl Green as Elderflower, 2:964

The Girl in the Photograph, 2:900

A Girl in Winter, 1:507, 1:508

Girls at War and Other Stories, 2:127, 2:128

The Girls in the Balcony: Women, Men, and "The New York Times," 3:808

The Girls of Slender Means, 1:551

Girl with a Monkey, 2:949

Girolamo Cardano, 1501–1576, 4:126

G Is for Gumshoe, 1:1229

Gissing: A Life in Books, 1:359

Gissing: The Critical Heritage, 1:359

Gītagovinda, 2:170

Gitanjali, 2:182

Giuseppe Baretti, 2:407

Giuseppe Ungaretti, 2:441

Give Me Back My Rags, 2:832

Giving Emergency Care Competently, 5:381

Giving Good Weight, 1:1010

The Giving Tree, 1:1206, 1:1207

G. K. Chesterton, 1:458

G. K. Chesterton: A Half Century of Views, 1:458

G. K. Chesterton: Explorations in Allegory, 1:458

The G. K. Hall Encyclopedia of Modern Technology, 5:2, 5:27

Glacial and Quaternary Geology, 5:626

Gladstone, 3:364

Gladstone: A Progress in Politics, 3:341

Gladstone and the Irish Nation, 3:370, 3:403

Glaister's Glossary of the Book, 1:32, 1:52, 1:69

Glas, 2:479, 4:397

Glasnost: An Anthology of Russian Literature under Gorbachev, 2:692

Glass: A World History, 3:766

Glass: Five Thousand Years, 3:766

The Glass Cage, 1:568

The Glass House: The Life of Theodore Roethke, 1:1038

The Glass Menagerie, 1:1117

A Glass of Blessings, 1:538, 1:539

The Glass Palace Chronicle of the Kings of Burma, 2:312

Gleanings for the Writings of Baha'u'llah, 4:861

Gleanings in Europe
England, 1:664
France, 1:664
Italy, 1:664
Switzerland, 1:664
The Rhine, 1:664

Glengarry Glen Ross, 1:1100

Gli Asolani, 2:408

Glide Path, 1:614

Gliding into the Everglades: And Other Essays, 1:862

A Glimpse of Eden, 3:901

A Glimpse of Sion's Glory: Puritan Radicalism in New England, 1620–1660, 3:517

Glimpses of Old New England Life: Legends of Old Bedford, Massachusetts, 3:858

Glimpses of the Harvard Past, 3:564

Glimpses of World History: Centenary Edition, 3:499

Glinda of Oz, 1:1200

Global Companies and Public Policy, 3:58

Global Ecology: Readings towards a Rational Strategy for Man, 5:292

Global Ecology: Towards a Science of the Biosphere, 5:820

The Global Ecology Handbook, 5:114

The Global Environment, 5:634

Global Environmental Change: A Natural and Cultural Environmental History (Mannion), 5:823

Global Environmental Change: The Human Dimensions (Stern), 5:283

Global Environmental Change: Understanding the Human Dimensions (National Research Council), 5:824

Global Guide to Media and Communications, 3:802

A Global History: The Human Heritage, 3:274

A Global Impact: The New Telecommunication Technologies, 5:230

Global Insecurity: A Strategy for Energy and Economic Renewal, 5:293

The Global Media Debate: Its Rise, Fall and Renewal, 3:803

Global Perspectives on Causes and Remedies of Soil Erosion, 5:265

The Global Philosophy, 4:38

Global Problems of Civilization, 3:274

Global Responsibility: In Search of a New World Ethics, 4:775

The Global Resurgence of Democracy, 3:142

Global Shift: The Internationalization of Economic Activity, 3:122

Global Standards: Building Blocks for the Future, 5:185

Global Studies: Middle East, 3:437

Global Tectonics, 5:648

Global Tomorrow Coalition, 5:114

The Global Village, 3:818

Global Warming: Are We Entering the Greenhouse Century?, 5:824

Global Warming: Economic Policy Responses, 3:47

Global Warming and Biological Diversity, 5:775

Gloria, 2:547

Gloria Diaz and Other Delineations, 2:330

The Glorious Cause: The American Revolution, 1763–1789, 3:521

The Glorious Destiny of Marshal Nnikon Nnika, 2:151

The Glorious Ones: Classical Music's Legendary Performers, 3:663

Glory, 2:740

The Glory and the Dream: A Narrative History of America, 1932–1972, 3:539

The Glory of Israel, 4:608

Glossary of Astronomy and Astrophysics, 5:588

A Glossary of Geographical Terms, 5:621

Glossary of Geology, 5:616

A Glossary of Indian Religious Terms and Concepts, 4:497

A Glossary of Literary Terms, 1:131

Glossary of Mineral Species 1983, 5:628

A Glossary of Ocean Science and Undersea Technology Terms, 5:617

Glossbrenner's Guide to Shareware for Small Businesses, 5:556

Gloucester Moors, 1:775

Gloucester Sea Ballads, 3:852

Glue and Lacquer; Four Cautionary Tales, 2:198

The Gnat Is Older Than Man, 5:116, 5:142, 5:824

Gnomon: Essays in Contemporary Literature, 1:421

Gnosis: A Selection of Gnostic Texts, 4:811

Gnosis: The Nature and History of Gnosticism, 4:453, 4:686

The Gnostic Gospels, 4:453, 4:686

Gnosticism, 4:453, 4:685

Gnosticism, Judaism, and Egyptian Christianity, 4:453

The Gnostic Novel of Mikhail Bulgakov: Sources and Exegesis, 2:706

The Gnostic Religion, 4:63, 4:453, 4:686, 4:811, 5:93

The Gnostic Scriptures: A New Translation with Annotations, 4:453

Goa and the Blue Mountains: Or, Six Months of Sick Leave, 3:913

Goatfoot Milktongue Twinbird, 1:984

The Goatibex Constellation, 2:729

Goat Island, 2:409

The Go-Between, 1:494

Goblin Market, 1:390

God, Death, Art, and Love: The Philosophical Vision of Ingmar Bergman, 3:831

God, Revelation and Authority: God Who Speaks and Shows, 4:744

God, Sex, and the Social Project, 4:894

God, Some Conversations, 4:199

God and Creatures: The Quodlibetal Questions, 4:114

A God and His Gifts, 1:462

God and Man, 4:746

God and Man in Contemporary Islamic Thought, 4:373, 4:575

God and Philosophy, 4:286

God and the Astronomers, 5:595

God and the New Physics, 5:15, 5:197

God and World in Early Christian Theology, 4:99

Godard, 3:837

Godard on Godard, 3:837

God Be with the Clown: Humor in American Poetry, 1:719

God Bless You, Mr. Rosewater, 1:1063

God Desired and Desiring, 2:542

The Goddess: Mythological Images of the Feminine, 4:424

The Goddess Anath: Canaanite Epics of the Patriarchal Age, 4:445

The Goddess and Other Women, 1:1023

Goddesses, Whores, Wives and Slaves, 3:309, 4:447

The Goddesses' Mirror: Visions of the Divine from East and West, 4:505, 4:530, 4:536

Goddesses of Sun and Moon: Circe, Aphrodite, Medea, Niobe, 4:484

The Goddess in the Stones: Travels in India, 3:904

God Dies by the Nile, 2:71, 2:120

Gödel, Escher, Bach: An Eternal Golden Braid, 5:571

Gödel's Proof, 5:95

Gödel's Theorem Simplified, 5:509

God Emperor of Dune, 1:1259

Godet's Proof, 4:313

God Glorified in Man's Dependence, 1:636

God Glorified in the Work of Redemption, By the Greatness of Man's Dependence upon Him, 1:637

God Has Many Names, 4:40, 4:898

God in Himself, 4:118

God in Modern Philosophy, 4:160

A God in Patristic Thought, 4:686

God in Search of Man: A Philosophy of Judaism, 4:664, 4:884

God in the Teachings of Conservative Judaism, 4:655

God Is Green, 5:196

God Is Red: A Native View of Religion, 4:464

God Knows, 1:987, 1:988

Godly Learning, 4:734

The God-Man: The Life, Journeys, and Work of Meher Baba, 4:873

God of Daniel S. in Search of the American Jew, 4:659

God of Tarot, 1:1253

God of the Oppressed, 4:763

Go Down, Moses and Other Stories, 1:836

The God Particle: If the Universe Is the Answer, What Is the Question, 5:650, 5:663

Gods, Demons & Others, 2:171

Gods, Ghosts and Ancestors: The Folk Religion of a Taiwanese Village, 4:531

Gods, Oracles and Divination: Folkways in Chinua Achebe's Novels, 2:129

God's Altar: The World and the Flesh in Puritan Poetry, 1:627

Gods and Myths of Ancient Egypt, 4:548

Gods and Myths of Northern Europe, 2:640, 4:437

Gods and the One God, 4:683

The Gods Arrive, 1:787

God's Bits of Wood, 2:145

God's Country and Mine, 1:813, 1:814

God's Country and My People, 1:1017

God's Dust: A Modern Asian Journey, 3:902

The God-Seeker, 1:854

God Sends Sunday, 1:817

God's Englishman: Oliver Cromwell and the English Revolution, 3:404, 4:734

God's Favorite, 1:1112, 1:1113

God's Fool: The Life of Francis of Assisi, 2:482

God's Grace, 1:1013

God's Handiwork: Images of Women in Early Germanic Literature, 2:566

God's House, 2:653

God's Laughter: Man and His Cosmos, 5:595

God's Little Acre, 1:818, 1:819

Gods of Flesh and Gods of Stone: The Embodiment of Divinity in India, 4:506

The Gods of Mars, 1:1256

The Gods of Pegana, 1:615

The Gods of Prehistoric Man, 4:432

The Gods of Raquel, 2:899

Gods of the Ancient Northmen, 4:437, 4:471

The Gods of the Greeks, 4:484

God's Playground: A History of Poland, 3:390

God's Plot and Man's Stories, 1:229

God's Presence in History, 4:663

God's Shadow, 2:84

The Gods Themselves, 1:1254

God's Trombones: Seven Negro Sermons in Verse, 1:771

The Gods Will Have Blood, 2:477

God's World: An Anthology of Short Stories, 2:68

The God That Failed, 2:438

God Was in This Place and I, I Did Not Know, 4:630

God We Seek, 4:339

The Godwins and the Shelleys: A Biography of a Family, 1:301

God Within, 5:795

God without Being, 4:889

Goethe, 2:581

Goethe: His Life and Times, 2:581

Goethe and His Age, 2:801

Gogol (Erlich), 2:722

Gogol (Gippius), 2:722

Gogol (Stilman), 2:722

Gogol: His Life and Works, 2:722

Gogol and the Natural School, 2:723

Gogol Bibliography, 2:722

Gogol from the Twentieth Century: Eleven Essays, 2:722

Gogol's Dead Souls, 2:723

Gogol's "Overcoat": An Anthology of Critical Essays, 2:723

Goin'a Buffalo, 1:1086

Going Crazy, 5:426

Going Places: The Guide to Travel Guides, 3:889, 3:892

Going to Meet the Man, 1:939

Going to the Dance, 3:731

Going to the Sources, 3:9, 3:275

Going Under, 2:711

Going Wrong, 1:609

Gokhale, Gandhi and the Nehrus: Studies in Indian Nationalism, 3:486

Gold: History, and Genesis of Deposits, 5:635

Goldberg Street: Short Plays and Monologues, 1:1101

The Gold Crowned Jesus and Other Writings, 2:304

The Gold Diggers, 1:965

Gold Dust, 3:524

The Golden Age, 1:584

The Golden Age of Brazil, 1695–1750, 3:628

The Golden Age of Chinese Drama, 2:191

The Golden Age of Opera, 3:671

The Golden Age of Soviet Theatre: The Bedbug, Marya, The Dragon, 2:692

The Golden Age of the Chinese Bourgeoisie, 1911–1937, 3:469

The Golden Apples, 1:895

The Golden Apples of the Sun, 1:1255

The Golden Ass, or Metamorphoses, 2:379, 2:382, 2:383

The Golden Book of Modern English Poetry: 1870–1920, 1:316

The Golden Bough, 3:23, 3:30, 3:878, 4:476, 4:485, 4:490

The Golden Bowl, 1:761, 1:762

Golden Boy, 1:1106

The Golden Branch, 1:321

The Golden Cage: The Enigma of Anorexia Nervosa, 5:394, 5:426

Golden Cockerel and Other Fairy Tales, 2:751

Golden Codgers, 1:974

The Golden Door, 4:640

Golden Droplet, 2:512

The Golden Epistle: A Letter to the Brethren at Mont Dieu, 4:102

Golden Fleece (Colum), 1:461

The Golden Fleece (Graves), 3:879

The Golden Fleece (Gurney),
1:1090, 1:1091
Golden Fleece and the He-
roes Who Lived before
Achilles, 1:461
The Golden Fountain Café,
2:547
The Golden Fruits, 2:505,
2:506
The Golden Gate: A Novel,
2:178
Golden Horn, 3:427
The Golden Journey: 225
Poems for Young People,
1:579, 1:1197
The Golden Key, 1:587
The Golden Lands of
Thomas Hobbes, 4:175
Golden Latin Artistry, 2:381
The Golden Legend, 4:701
The Golden Lotus, 2:185,
2:188, 2:226
Golden Multitudes: The Story
of Best Sellers in the
United States, 1:51
The Golden Peacock: A
Worldwide Treasury of
Yiddish Poetry, 2:34
The Golden Scorpion, 1:597
The Golden Thread and Oth-
er Plays, 2:858
The Golden Trade of the
Moors, 3:418, 3:419
The Golden Tradition: An
Anthology of Urdu Poetry,
2:175
The Golden Tradition: Jewish
Life and Thought in East-
ern Europe, 3:348, 4:635
A Golden Treasury of Jewish
Tales, 2:15
The Golden Verses of Pytha-
goras, 5:514
The Golden Web: 1933 to
1953, 3:810
The Golden Whip, 2:635,
2:636
Golden Wings and Other
Stories, 1:617
The Golden Years of Fan
Ch'eng-ta, 2:197
The Golden Years of the
Hutterites, 4:724
Goldfinger, 1:594
Gold Medallion World Atlas,
1:84
The Gold of the Tigers,
2:856
Goldoni and the Venice of
His Time, 2:423
The Gold Rimmed Specta-
cles, 2:407
The Gold Rush, 1:1160

Goldsmiths, 3:767
The Gold Standard and the
Logic of Naturalism,
1:723, 3:553
The Golem, 1:1050, 2:48
The Golem: What Everyone
Should Know about Sci-
ence, 5:9, 5:66
Gollancz: The Story of a
Publishing House,
1928–1978, 1:41
The Golovlyov Family, 2:755
Gompers in Canada, 3:614
Gondal Poems, 1:336
Gondal's Queen: A Novel in
Verse, 1:336
Gone from the Promised
Land: Jonestown as Ameri-
can Cultural History, 4:867
Gone Indian, 2:915
Gone South, 1:1242
Gone to Another Meeting,
1893-1993, 4:650
Gone with the Wind, 1:982,
1:1220, 1:1244, 1:1248,
1:1249
Go Not Gently: Letters from
a Patient with Amyotroph-
ic Lateral Sclerosis, 5:369
The Good Americans: The
Loyalists in the American
Revolution, 3:612
Good and Mad Women,
3:494
Good as Gold, 1:987, 1:988
A Good Birth, a Safe Birth,
5:359
Goodbye, Goodbye, Europe,
2:541
Goodbye, Howard, 1:1099
Goodbye Columbus and Five
Short Stories, 1:1041
The Goodbye Look, 1:1235
Goodbyes and Other Mes-
sages: A Journal of Jazz,
1981–1990, 3:667
Goodbyes and Other Stories,
2:876
Goodbye to All That, 1:484,
1:485
Good-bye to All That: An Au-
tobiography, 3:879
Goodbye to Goodtime Char-
lie, 3:148
The Good Companions, 1:537
Good Company: A Study of
Nyakyusa Age-Villages,
3:25
The Good Conscience, 2:865
The Good Doctor, 1:1112,
1:1113

Goodenough's Jewish Sym-
bols: An Abridged Edition,
4:597, 4:614
The Good Health Fact Book,
5:311
The Good High School: Por-
traits of Character and
Culture, 3:251
The Good Man and the
Good: An Introduction to
Ethics, 3:181
The Good Man's Dilemma,
1:1013
Good Morning, Midnight,
2:940
Good Morning! and Other
Stories, 2:64
Good Morning Blues: The
Autobiography of Count
Basie, 3:677
The Good Neighbor, 3:544
Good News, 3:249
The Good News According
to Luke, 4:822
The Good News According
to Mark, 4:822
The Good News According
to Matthew, 4:822
Good News for Animals?
Christian Approaches to
Animal Well-Being, 4:745
Goodnight! 2:757
Good Old Cause: English
Revolution of 1640–1660,
3:404
A Good Old-Fashioned
Christmas, 1:814
Good Operations—Bad Oper-
ations, 5:405
Good Reading: A Guide for
Serious Readers, 1:34,
1:75
The Good Society (Bellah),
3:220, 4:890
The Good Society
(Lippmann), 3:815
The Good Soldier, 1:475
The Good Soldier Schweik,
2:788, 2:790, 2:791
Good Tiger, 1:447
"The Good War": An Oral
History of World War
Two, 3:536
Good Work, 3:346
Goody Two Shoes, 1:583
Goose and Tomtom, 1:1108,
1:1109
Goose Green: A Battle Is
Fought to Be Won, 3:633
Gopalpur: A South Indian
Village, 4:503

The Gorbachev Phenomena: A Historical Interpretation, 3:398

Gordon Allport: The Man and His Ideas, 3:180, 5:432

Gordon W. Allport's Ontopsychology of the Person, 5:432

Gore Vidal (Kiernan), 1:1062

Gore Vidal (White), 1:1062

Gore Vidal: A Primary and Secondary Bibliography, 1:1062

Gorf, 1:1009

Gorilla, My Love, 1:939, 1:940

Gorski Vijenac, 2:827

The Gospel According to Billy, 4:768

The Gospel According to Chegem, 2:729

The Gospel According to St. John, 4:822

The Gospel According to St. Matthew, 2:431

The Gospel According to Tolstoy, 4:756

The Gospel in Solentiname, 2:859

The Gospel of John: A Commentary, 4:821, 4:831

The Gospel of John and Judaism, 4:617

The Gospel of Wealth in the American Novel, 1:805, 1:830

Gospel Parallels: A Synopsis of the First Three Gospels, 4:798

The Gossamer Years, 2:278

Gossip from the Forest, 2:957

Gösta Berling's Saga, 2:677

Go Tell It on the Mountain, 1:938, 1:939

Go Tell It to Women: A Play, 2:144

Gothic and Renaissance Bookbindings, 1:23

Gothic Architecture, 3:762

The Gothic Cathedral, 4:701

Gothic Drama from Walpole to Shelley, 1:272

The Gothic Flame, 1:270

Gothic Immortals: The Fiction of the Brotherhood of the Rosy Cross, 4:848

The Gothic Novel (1790–1830), 1:270

Gothic Novels of the Twentieth Century: An Annotated Bibliography, 1:122

Gothic Strains and Bourgeois Sentiments in the Novels of Mrs. Ann Radcliffe and Her Imitations, 1:622

The Gothic Tales of the Marquis de Sade, 2:503

The Gothic Visions of Ann Radcliffe and Matthew G. Lewis, 1:602

Go to the Widow-Maker, 1:994

Gottfried Benn: The Artist and Politics (1910-1934), 2:568

Götz von Berlichingen, 2:580

The Göttingen Model Book, 1:9

Gottlob Frege, 4:230

Gottschalk and the Grande Tarantelle, 1:954

Götz von Berlichingen, 2:580

Goudy's Type Designs: His Story and Specimens, 1:15

Gouverneur Morris, 3:594

Governing Science and Technology, 5:182

Governing Science and Technology in a Democracy, 5:181

Government Agencies, 3:507

Government and Community: England, 1450–1509, 3:358

Government and Local Power in Japan, 500 to 1700, 3:475

Government and Politics of Thailand, 3:490

Government by the People, 3:570

The Government Inspector, 2:722

The Government Inspector and Other Russian Plays, 2:692

The Government of Associations, 3:210

The Government of Science, 5:180

The Government of the Tongue: Selected Prose 1978-1987, 1:495

Government Publications: A Guide to Bibliographic Tools, 1:111

Government Publications and Their Use, 1:108

Government Research Directory, 1:104

Governors and Legislatures: Contending Powers, 3:146, 3:148

Gower's Confessio Amantis: Responses and Reassessments, 1:152

Goya, 3:776

Goya: Lithographs and Engravings, 3:776

Goya and the Spirit of Enlightenment, 3:776

Grace Abounding, 1:173, 1:174

Grace and Gratitude: The Eucharistic Theology of John Calvin, 4:762

Grace and Reason: A Study in the Theology of Luther, 4:778

Grace before Plowing: Fragments of an Autobiography, 1:519

Grace Hopper: Navy Admiral and Computer Pioneer, 5:577

Grace Notes, 1:970

Gracious Laughter Ripe: The Meditative Wit of Edward Taylor, 1:644

The Gradual Vegetarian, 5:347

Graham Greene, 1:489

Graham Greene: A Bibliography and Guide to Research, 1:489

Graham Greene: An Annotated Bibliography of Criticism, 1:489

Graham Greene: A Revaluation, 1:489

Graham Greene's Childless Fathers, 1:489

The Grain of the Voice: Interviews, 1962–1980, 2:455

A Grain of Wheat, 2:153, 2:154

Grammar in Rhyme, 1:583

The Grammar of Justification, 4:346

A Grammar of Motives, 1:955

Grammar of Ornament, 3:765

A Grammar of Politics, 3:156

The Grammar of Science, 5:531

The Grammar of Silence, 2:492

Grammar of the Yiddish Language, 2:30

A Grammatical Analysis of Greek New Testament, 4:795

Grammatical Man: Information, Entropy, Language, and Life, 5:567

Grammatical Theory in Western Europe 1500–1700, 4:129

Gramsci and the State,
1:1131
Gramsci's Democratic Theo-
ry: Contributions to a
Post-Liberal Democracy,
3:143
Gramsci's Marxism, 4:287
Gramsci's Political Thought,
4:287
Gramsci's Politics, 4:287
Grand Babylon Hotel: A Fan-
tasia on Modern Themes,
1:443
Grand Canyon, 5:834
Grand Canyon: Today and
All Its Yesterdays, 5:626
The Grand Design, 1:827
The Grandissimes, 1:736
The Grandissimes: Centennial
Essays, 1:737
Grandissimo Pavarotti, 3:708
Grandmother's Path, Grandfa-
ther's Path, 2:322
The Grand Strategy of the
Roman Empire, 3:308
Granite and Rainbow, 1:569
Grant: A Biography, 3:528
Grant Moves South, 3:571
Grant Takes Command, 3:571
The Grapes of Wrath, 1:803,
1:883, 1:884, 1:1165
The Grapes of Wrath: Trou-
ble in the Promised Land,
1:886
Graphic Communication and
the Crisis in Education,
3:191
Graphic Designer's Produc-
tion Handbook, 1:10, 1:53
Graphics Primer for the IBM
PC, 5:565
The Graphic Work of Renoir:
A Catalogue Raisonné,
3:789
Graphic Worlds of Peter
Bruegel the Elder, 3:771
Graphite, 2:755
The Grasmere Journals,
1:308
The Grass, 2:509
The Grass Harp, 1:959
Grass of Parnassus, 3:882
Grass Productivity, 5:264
The Grass Roof, 2:305
Grass Systematics and Evolu-
tion, 5:740
Grave, 1:277
The Graveyard, 2:814
Graveyard of the Angels,
2:852
Gravitation, 5:719
Gravitation and Cosmology,
5:665, 5:719

Gravitation Theory and Gra-
vitational Collapse, 5:719
Gravity and Grace, 4:788
Gravity's Rainbow, 1:1035
A Gravity's Rainbow Com-
panion, 1:1036
Gray, Collins, and Their Cir-
cle, 1:236
Gray and Collins: Poetical
Works, 1:236
Gray Plays: One, 1:486
Gray's Anatomy of the Hu-
man Body, 5:772
Greasy Lake and Other Sto-
ries, 1:952, 1:953
The Great Age of Chinese
Poetry: The High T'ang,
2:190
The Great Age of Discovery,
3:892
Great Ages and Ideas of the
Jewish People, 4:595
Great Ages of Man, 4:573
The Great American History
Fact-Finder, 3:508
The Great American Medi-
cine Show, 5:312
The Great American Novel,
1:1041
The Great American Popular
Singers, 3:672
Great American Short Sto-
ries, 1:725, 1:806, 1:921
The Great American Stomach
Book, 5:384
The Great and Secret Show,
1:600
The Great Anglo-Boer War,
3:363
The Great Arab Conquests,
4:569
The Great Bear: Contempo-
rary Writings on the Griz-
zly, 5:771
The Great Book-Collectors,
1:31
Great Books and Book Col-
lectors, 1:34
Great Books of the Western
World, 4:270
Great Britain and Hanover:
Some Aspects of the Per-
sonal Union, 3:363
Great Britian's Woodyard,
3:613
The Great Caruso, 3:689
Great Cases in Psychothera-
py, 5:420
The Great Chain of Being: A
Study of the History of an
Idea, 4:95, 4:161, 4:303
Great Chemists, 5:728

The Great Chinese Revolu-
tion, 1800–1985, 3:468,
3:498
The Great Christian Doctrine
of Original Sin Defended,
4:766, 4:767
Great Chronicle, 2:312
The Great Code: The Bible
and Literature, 1:976,
2:989
The Great Columbia Plain: A
Historical Geography,
3:133
The Great Comic Book He-
roes and Other Essays,
2:924
Great Contemporaries, 3:400
The Great Contraction,
1929–1933, 3:54, 3:65,
3:77
The Great Copernicus Chase,
5:602
The Great Crash of 1929,
3:54, 3:79
The Great Cycle, 2:669
The Great Debate: Theories
of Nuclear Strategy, 3:283
The Great Depression,
1929–1939, 3:616
The Great Dictator, 1:1161
The Great Divide: A Walk
through America along the
Continental Divide, 3:896
The Great Divorce, 1:512
Great Dramatists, 1:428
Great Economists before
Keynes, 3:44
Great Economists since
Keynes, 3:44
Great Engineers, 5:217, 5:249
Great Engineers and Pio-
neers in Technology,
5:218, 5:232
The Great Enterprise, 3:469
The Greater City: New York,
1898 to 1948, 3:591
The Greater Inclination,
1:786
The Greater Roman Histori-
ans, 3:303
The Greatest Ever Bank Rob-
bery, 3:56
Greatest Fire: A Study of Au-
gust Strindberg, 2:680
The Greatest Plague of Life,
1:377
The Great Evasion, 3:601
The Great Exhibition, 1:492,
1:493
Great Expectations, 1:348
Great Exploration Hoaxes,
3:910

The Great Explorers: The European Discovery of America, 3:589

The Great Feast, 2:177

Great Feats of Modern Engineering, 5:231

Great Foreign Language Writers, 2:4

Great Forgers and Famous Fakes, 1:35

The Great Frontier, 3:600

The Great Gatsby, 1:801, 1:838, 1:839

Great Geological Controversies, 5:622

The Great Gilly Hopkins, 1:1204

The Great God Brown, 1:1106

Great Heresies, 1:442

Great Historians from Antiquity to 1800: An International Dictionary, 3:272

The Great Hunger, 1:506

The Great Hunger: Ireland, 1845–1849, 3:371

The Great Ideas: One Hundred Two Essays, 4:270

The Great Ideas Anthologies, 4:270

The Great Illusion, 2:661

The Great Indian Novel, 2:178

The Great Instauration, 4:165

The Great Instauration: Science, Medicine and Reform 1626–1660, 5:43

Great Instauration and New Atlantis, 4:165

Great Issues in American History: 1865–1981, 3:582

Great Issues in American History: From Settlement to Revolution, 1584–1776, 3:583

Great Jewish Short Stories, 1:725, 1:921, 1:947

The Great Journey, 3:516

Great Maria, 1:1246, 1:1247

Great Masters of the Violin, from Corelli to Stern, Zukerman, and Perlman, 3:672

The Great Meadow, 1:875, 1:876

The Great Melody: A Thematic Biography of Edmund Burke, 3:362

The Great Merger Movement in American Business, 1895–1904, 3:548

The Great Monkey Trial: Science versus Fundamentalism in America, 5:48

The Great Mother: An Analysis of the Archetype, 5:456

The Greatness and Limitations of Freud's Thought, 3:184, 5:450

Greatness in the White House, 3:543

Great North American Indians, 1:86

The Great Ore, 2:771

The Great Patriotic War of the Soviet Union, 3:292

The Great Philosophers, 4:299

The Great Physicists from Galileo to Einstein, 5:605

Great Pianists Speak for Themselves, 3:672

The Great Piano Virtuosos of Our Time, 3:672

The Great Plains, 3:600

The Great Ponds, 2:130

The Great Po Sein: A Chronicle of the Burmese Theater, 2:313

Great Power Politics and the Struggle over Austria, 1945–1955, 3:375

The Great Powers and Poland, 1919 to 1945, 3:390

The Great Powers and the End of the Ottoman Empire, 3:453

The Great Powers in the Middle East, 1919–1939, 4:568

The Great Psychologists: From Aristotle to Freud, 3:168, 5:35, 5:414

The Great Quotations, 1:117

The Great Railway Bazaar: By Train through Asia, 3:905, 3:940

The Great Rebellion: Mexico, 1905–1924, 3:639

The Great Reform Act, 3:361

The Great Religions, 4:568

Great Religions of Modern Man, 4:6

The Great Reporters: An Anthology of News Writing at Its Best, 3:809

The Great Republic: A History of the American People, 3:512

The Great Reversal: Ethics and the New Testament, 4:746

The Great Reversal: Politics and Art in Solzhenitsyn, 2:762

The Great Sacrifice: Studies in Hopkins, 1:364

Great Sanskrit Plays in Modern Translation, 2:173

Great Scientific Discoveries, 5:29

The Great Shakespeare Forgery, 1:35

The Great Singers: From the Dawn of Opera to Our Own Time, 3:671

The Great Singers, from Jenny Lind to Callas and Pavarotti, 3:672

Great Singers on Great Singing, 3:672

Great Slave Narratives, 1:817

The Great Sophists in Periclean Athens, 4:54

Great Soviet Short Stories, 2:694

The Great Symphonies, The Great Orchestras, The Great Conductors, 3:671

The Great Television Race, 3:561

The Great Temple of Tenochtitlan, 4:457

The Great Terror—Stalin's Purge of the Thirties, 3:396

Great Thinkers, Great Ideas: An Introduction to Western Thought, 4:20

The Great Tradition: George Eliot, Henry James, Joseph Conrad, 1:319, 1:767, 1:926

The Great Train Robbery, 1:1167, 1:1173

Great Tranquility: Questions and Answers, 2:13

Great Travelers, 3:893

The Great Treasury of Western Thought, 1:116, 4:270

The Great Trek, 3:424

The Great Triumvirate: Webster, Clay, and Calhoun, 3:525

The Great United States Exploring Expedition of 1838–1842, 3:897

The Great Wall of China: From History to Myth, 3:467, 4:523

The Great Wall of China: Stories and Reflections, 2:596

The Great War, 1914–1918, 3:278, 3:343

The Great War and Modern
  Memory, 3:278, 3:343
The Great Wheel: The World
  Monetary System, a Rein-
  terpretation, 3:59
The Great White Lie, 5:332
The Great World, 2:958,
  2:959
The Great World and Timo-
  thy Colt, 1:937
Great Writers of the English
  Language, 1:127
The Great Zoo and Other
  Poems, 2:869
Greece, Gods, and Art, 3:899
Greece and Babylon: A Com-
  parative Sketch, 4:545
Greece and Rome at War,
  3:308
Greece in the Bronze Age,
  2:348, 3:302
Greed, 1:1177
The Greek Accounts of East-
  ern History, 3:316
Greek-American Folk Beliefs
  and Narratives, 3:855
Greek and Latin Authors,
  1:800 B.C.–A.D. 1000,
  1:133
The Greek and Macedonian
  Art of War, 3:308
Greek and Roman Classics
  in Translation, 2:348
Greek and Roman Critics,
  2:345
Greek and Roman Technol-
  ogy, 3:304, 5:39
The Greek Anthology, 2:348
Greek Apologists of the Sec-
  ond Century, 4:683
Greek Architecture, 3:763
Greek Art, 3:758
Greek Atomists and Epicu-
  rus, 4:53, 4:73
Greek Biology and Greek
  Medicine, 5:39
Greek Bucolic Poets: Theo-
  critus, Bion, and Moschus,
  2:348, 2:369
The Greek City from Alexan-
  der to Justinian, 3:302
The Greek Concept of Jus-
  tice, 4:48
The Greek Cosmologists, 4:48
Greek Drama, 2:349
Greek Elegy, Iambus, and
  Anacreontea, 2:348
A Greek-English Lexicon,
  1:99, 4:795
A Greek-English Lexicon of
  the New Testament and
  Other Early Christian Lit-
  eratures, 4:794

The Greek Experience, 2:344
Greek Folk Religion, 4:486
The Greek Gift: Politics in a
  Cypriot Village, 3:455
Greek Gods and Heroes,
  3:879
A Greek Grammar of the
  New Testament and Other
  Early Christian Literature,
  4:794
The Greek Historians, 3:302
Greek Historical Documents:
  The Fourth Century B.C.,
  3:300
Greek Historical Documents:
  The Hellenistic Period,
  3:299, 4:449
Greek Homosexuality, 3:309
Greek in Jewish Palestine,
  4:606
The Greek Islands, 1:470,
  3:899
Greek Literature, 4:46
Greek Literature: An Anthol-
  ogy, 2:348
Greek Lyric, 2:348
Greek Lyric Poetry from Alc-
  man to Simonides, 2:366
The Greek Magical Papyri in
  Translation, Including the
  Demotic Spells, 4:451
Greek Medicine (Brock),
  5:38
Greek Medicine (Philips),
  3:304
The Greek Myths, 1:485,
  3:879
The Greek New Testament,
  4:794
The Greek Passion, 2:374
Greek Philosophers: From
  Thales to Aristotle, 2:345,
  4:46
Greek Philosophers of the
  Hellenistic Age, 4:55
Greek Plays in Modern
  Translation, 2:349
Greek Political Oratory,
  3:302
Greek Political Theory: The
  Image of Man in Thucy-
  dides and Plato, 4:80
Greek Religion, 4:470
Greek Revival Architecture
  in America, 3:762
The Greeks, 3:301
The Greeks and the Good
  Life, 4:47
The Greeks and Their Gods,
  2:345
The Greeks and the Irration-
  al, 2:356, 4:48, 4:446
The Greek Sceptics, 4:58

Greek Science after Aristotle,
  5:38
Greek Sculpture, 3:759
Greek Skepticism: A Study in
  Epistemology, 4:58
The Greeks of Asia Minor,
  3:393
The Greeks Overseas: Their
  Early Colonies and Trade,
  3:304
The Greek State, 3:301
The Greek Stones Speak,
  2:346, 3:305
Greek Theories of Elementa-
  ry Cognition from Alc-
  maeon to Aristotle, 4:47
Greek Thinkers: A History of
  Ancient Philosophy, 4:46
Greek Tragedies in New
  Translations, 2:349
Greek Tragedy, 2:346
Greek Tragedy and Political
  Theory, 4:48
The Greek-Turkish Conflict
  in the 1990s, 3:452
The Greek Upheaval: Kings,
  Demagogues and Bayonets,
  3:393
The Greek View of Life,
  2:345
The Greek Way, 3:881
The Greek Way of Death,
  3:307
The Greek Way of Life,
  3:307
The Greek World, 478-323
  B.C., 3:302
Green against Green: A His-
  tory of the Irish Civil
  War, 3:370
Green and Gold: Stories and
  Poems from Bengal, 2:176
The Green Cabinet: Theocri-
  tus and the European Pas-
  toral Lyric, 2:369
Green Centuries, 1:983
The Green Crow, 1:527
Green Days by the River,
  2:932
Green Delusions, 5:115,
  5:823
Green Eggs and Ham, 1:1203
The Green Encyclopedia,
  5:815
The Green Fairy Book,
  1:577, 3:883
The Green Fool, 1:506
Green Henry, 2:597
The Green Hills of Africa,
  1:845
The Green House, 2:886
Greenhouse Effect and Sea
  Level Rise, 5:633

The Greening of the Church, 5:197

Green Inheritance: The World Wildlife Fund Book of Plants, 5:820

Greenland, 1:450

The Greenlanders, 1:1050, 1:1051

The Green Machines, 5:222

The Green Man, 1:432

Green Mansions, 1:365

The Green Mare, 2:452

The Green Mountain Boys, 1:1244

The Green PC: Making Decisions That Make a Difference, 5:536

The Greenpeace Guide to Anti-Environmental Organizations, 5:815

Green Pharmacy: A History of Herbal Medicine, 5:319, 5:351

Green Plants: Their Origin and Diversity, 5:767

Green Products by Design: Choices for a Cleaner Environment, 5:185

The Green Revolution, 5:263

The Green Revolution: Peace and Humanity, 5:270

The Green Revolution: The Environmental Movement, 1962–1992, 3:550

Green Water, Green Sky, 2:911, 2:912

Green with Beasts, 1:1015

Gregarious Saints: Self and Community in American Abolitionism, 1830–1870, 3:524

Gregorius, 2:586

Gregory Nazianzus: Rhetor and Philosopher, 4:785, 4:905

Gregory the Great: Perfection in Imperfection, 4:711

Grendel, 1:978, 1:979

Grey Birds, 2:630

The Grey Fairy Book, 3:883

Grey Is the Color of Hope, 2:753

Grey Is the Color of Life, 2:753

A Grey Man, 2:300

Grey of Fallodon: Being the Life of Sir Edward Grey, 3:411

The Grey Whale, Eschrichtius Robustus, 5:770

The Grey Woman and Other Tales, 1:356

Grieg, 3:698

Griffith: An American Life, 1:1168

The Grimké Sisters from South Carolina: Rebels against Slavery, 3:524

Grit and Clay, 5:624

Groping for Ethics in Journalism, 3:806

Groping in the Dark: The First Decade of Global Modelling, 5:167, 5:168

Gropius: An Illustrated Biography of the Creator of Bauhaus, 3:777

Ground Anchors and Anchored Structures, 5:246

The Grounding with My Brothers, 3:430

Grounds for Comparison, 1:926

The Ground Work, 1:971

The Ground Work II: In the Dark, 1:971

The Group, 1:1007, 1:1008

Group Counseling: Theory and Practice, 5:418

Group Counseling and Group Psychotherapy with Rehabilitation Clients, 5:420

Group Dynamics, 3:172, 5:418

Group Dynamics: Research and Theory, 3:172

Group Portrait with Lady, 2:570

Group Psychology and the Analysis of the Ego, 5:446

Groups at Work: Unresolved Issues in the Study of Organizations, 3:173

Grove Karl Gilbert: A Great Engine of Research, 5:643

Grover Cleveland: A Study in Courage, 3:591

The Groves of Academe, 1:1007, 1:1008

Growing and Using the Healing Herbs, 5:321

Growing Old, Staying Young, 5:316

Growing Old in America, 3:552

Growing Up in New Guinea, 3:15, 3:36

Growing Up Literate: Learning from Inner-City Families, 3:252

Growing Up Stupid under the Union Jack, 2:934

Growing Younger, 5:317

Growth, Shortage and Efficiency, 3:52

Growth and Development of Birds, 5:771

The Growth and Structure of Elizabethan Comedy, 1:169, 1:210

The Growth of Biological Thought, 5:34, 5:765

The Growth of Economic Thought, 3:46

The Growth of Medical Knowledge, 5:78

The Growth of Philosophical Radicalism, 4:245

Growth of Political Stability in England, 1675–1725, 3:408

The Growth of Reform Judaism, 4:653

The Growth of Scientific Ideas, 5:27

The Growth of Southern Civilization, 1790–1860, 3:523

The Growth of the American Republic, 3:514, 3:589

Growth of the Biblical Tradition, 4:815

Growth of the Soil, 2:664

The Growth of Working-Class Reformism in Mid-Victorian England, 3:364

Growth Recurring: Economic Change in World History, 3:274

Growth through Reason, 5:439

Grundlagen der Geometrie, 5:509

Grundlinien einer Philosophie der Technik, 5:69

Grundrisse, 4:242

Gryll Grange, 1:297

Grzimek's Animal Life Encyclopedia, 5:759

Grzimek's Encyclopedia of Evolution, 5:759

Grzimek's Encyclopedia of Mammals, 5:759

G. Stanley Hall: The Psychologist as Prophet, 3:185

The Guarani, 2:891

The Guardian Angel (Holmes), 1:678

Guardian Angel (Paretsky), 1:1235

The Guardian of Every Other Right, 3:139

The Guardian of the Word, 2:139

Guardians of the Sacred Word: Ewe Poetry, 2:132

Guard of Honor, 1:964

Guatemalan Sociology, 2:854

The Gucci Bag, 2:917

Gudrun, 2:619

The Guerrilla Is Like a Poet: An Anthology of Filipino Poetry, 2:329

Guerrillas, 2:939

A Guest for the Night, 2:11

The Guest of Honor (Wallace), 1:1250

A Guest of Honour (Gordimer), 2:161, 2:162

Guest the One-Eyed, 2:641

The Guide: A Novel, 2:180

A Guidebook for Technology Assessment and Impact Analysis, 5:76, 5:130

Guidebook to Folk Literature, 3:849

A Guided Tour of the Living Cell, 5:775

A Guide for Collectors of Oral Traditions and Folk Cultural Material in Pennsylvania, 3:859

A Guide for Field Workers in Folklore, 3:848

The Guide for the Perplexed, 4:667, 4:668

Guidelines for Bias-Free Publishing, 1:47

Guidelines on Dialogue with People of Living Faiths and Ideologies, 4:899

Guidelines to Safe Drinking, 5:402

Guides to Biblical Scholarship, 4:814

Guide to Aesthetics, 2:414

The Guide to Amateur Astronomy, 5:591

A Guide to American Catholic History, 4:751

Guide to American Foreign Relations since 1700, 3:509

Guide to American Literature and Its Backgrounds since 1890, 1:714

Guide to American Scientific and Technical Directories, 5:3

A Guide to Animal Tracking and Behavior, 5:827

Guide to Buddhist Philosophy, 4:6

Guide to Chinese Philosophy, 4:358, 4:522

Guide to Chinese Religion, 4:522

A Guide to Computer Applications in the Humanities, 5:564

Guide to Congress, 3:505

A Guide to Critical Reviews Part III, 1:427

A Guide to Cults and New Religions, 4:857

A Guide to Econometrics, 3:63

Guide to Economic Indicators, 3:44

Guide to Economics and Business Journalism, 3:807

Guide to Electronics in the Home, 5:229

Guide to English Literature from Beowulf through Chaucer and Medieval Drama, 1:141

A Guide to Everyday Economic Statistics, 3:44

Guide to Ezra Pound's Selected Cantos, 1:873

A Guide to Folktales in the English Language, 3:849

Guide to Geologic Literature, 5:624

Guide to Greece, 4:489

A Guide to Historical Method, 3:9, 3:277

A Guide to Information Sources in the Geographical Sciences, 5:620

A Guide to Jane Austen, 1:276

Guide to Japanese Drama, 2:273

Guide to Japanese Poetry, 2:273

Guide to Japanese Prose, 2:272

A Guide to Jewish Religious Practice, 4:602

Guide to John Rae's Life of Adam Smith, 3:107, 3:111

A Guide to Keynes, 3:81

A Guide to Korean Characters: Reading and Writing Hangul and Hanja, 1:101

Guide to Kulchur, 1:871, 1:872

Guide to League of Nations Publications, 3:272

The Guide to Living with HIV Infection, 5:386

Guide to Marxist Literary Criticism, 1:134

Guide to Materials for the History of the United States in the Principal Archives of Mexico, 3:643

A Guide to Nature in Winter, 5:821

Guide to Official Publications of Foreign Countries, 1:111

A Guide to Personal Happiness, 5:439

Guide to Philosophy, 4:21

A Guide to Pound's Personae, 1:874

A Guide to Psychologists and Their Concepts, 5:414

Guide to Reference Books, 1:63, 1:74, 1:81, 4:716

Guide to Reference Books and Supplement, 1:121

Guide to Reference Books for School Library Media Centers, 1:75

Guide to Reprints: An International Bibliography of Scholarly Reprints, 1:71

Guide to Seventeenth-Century American Poetry: A Reference Guide, 1:629

Guide to Shakespeare, 1:222

A Guide to Statistics Methods and to the Pertinent Literature, 5:521

A Guide to Successful Marriage, 5:439

Guide to the Best Historical Novels and Tales, 1:122

Guide to the Bibliographies of Russian Literature, 2:691

A Guide to the Cantos of Ezra Pound, 1:873

A Guide to the Collecting and Care of Original Prints, 1:27

A Guide to the Culture of Science, Technology, and Medicine, 5:6, 5:28, 5:60, 5:149

A Guide to the Development of On-Site Sanitation, 5:245

Guide to the Diplomatic History of the United States, 1775–1921, 3:568

Guide to the History of Science, 5:55, 5:56

Guide to the Literature of Art History, 3:756

Guide to the Literature of Mathematics Today, 5:479

Guide to the Literature of the Biological Sciences, 5:762

A Guide to the Maximus Poems of Charles Olson, 1:1027

Guide to the New Medicine: What Works, What Doesn't, 5:320

A Guide to the Photovoltaic Revolution, 5:289

Guide to the Sources of the History of Nations, 3:272

Guide to the Study of United States History outside the U.S., 3:515

Guide to the Study of United States Imprints, 1:79

Guide to the Tale of Genji by Murasaki Shikibu, 2:279

Guide to the U.S. Supreme Court, 3:506

Guide to the Underworld, 2:673

A Guide to the Works of John Dewey, 4:225

A Guide to the Zoroastrian Religion, 4:517, 4:547

A Guide to Twentieth-Century Literature in English, 1:420

Guide to U.S. Elections, 3:506

Guide to U.S. Government Scientific and Technical Periodicals, 5:727

Guignol's Band, 2:465

Guillaume Apollinaire, 2:451

Guillaume Postel, Prophet of the Restitution of All Things, 4:128

Guilt, 2:802

Guinea Pig Doctors, 5:313

The Guinea Pigs, 2:795

The Guinness Book of World Records, 1:88

The Guinness Encyclopedia of Popular Music, 3:656

The Gulag Archipelago, 2:755, 2:760, 2:761, 3:346, 3:397

The Gulag Archipelago, Vol. 1, 2:761

The Gulag Archipelago, Vol. 2: 1918–1956, 2:761

The Gulag Archipelago, Vol. 3: 1918–1956: An Experiment in Literary Investigation, 2:761

The Gulag Archipelago Three: Katorga, Exile, Stalin Is No More, 2:761

The Gulf Conflict, 1990–1991, 3:538

The Gulistan, or Rose Garden, of Sa'di, 2:93

Gulliver's Travels, 1:259, 1:260, 1:574, 1:576

Gulliver's Travels and Other Writings, 1:260

The Gull's Hornbook, 1:176

A Gun for Sale, 1:488

The Gun in Politics: An Analysis of Irish Violence, 1916–1986, 3:370

Gunn and Hughes: Thom Gunn and Ted Hughes, 1:491

Gunnar Myrdal and America's Conscience, 3:99

Gunnar Myrdal and Black-White Relations, 3:99

Gunnlaug Wormtongue, 2:640

Guns, Sails and Empires, 3:335

Gunslinger, 1:969, 1:970

The Guns of August, 3:343, 3:411, 3:412

Günter Grass, 2:583

Günter Grass: The Writer in a Pluralist Society, 2:583

Gurdjieff: An Annotated Bibliography, 4:875

Gurdjieff: Making a New World, 4:875

Gurdjieff: The Anatomy of a Myth, 4:876

Gurdjieff: War against Sleep, 4:876

The Gurdjieff Years: 1929–1949, 4:876

Guru Nanak and the Sikh Religion, 4:516

Gustave Eiffel, 5:246

Gustav Mahler: An Introduction to His Music, 3:705

Gustav Mahler: The Early Years, 3:705

Gustavo Gutierrez, 4:769

Gustavus Vassa, the African, Written by Himself, 2:104, 2:137

Gutenberg and the Master of the Playing Cards, 1:9

Gutenberg Galaxy: The Making of Typographic Man, 3:818, 5:573

Gutenberg to Plantin: An Outline of the Early History of Printing, 1:12

Guyana: Politics in a Plantation Society, 3:637

Guy Mannering, 1:298

Guy of Warwick, 1:145

Guy Rivers: A Tale of Georgia, 1:696

Guzmán de Alfarache, 2:530, 2:544

Gwendolyn Brooks: Poetry and the Heroic Voice, 1:954

Gyn-Ecology, 4:423, 4:765, 1:1186, 1:1187

Gypsy Ballads, 2:538

The Gypsy Tribe, 2:826

H

Haa Shuka, Our Ancestors: Tlingit Oral Narratives, 1:631

Habad: The Hasidism of R. Shneur Zalman of Lyady, 4:632

Habermas: Critical Debates, 4:405, 5:90

Habermas and Modernity, 4:404, 5:89

Habermas and the Dialectic of Reason, 4:405, 5:89

Habermas and the Public Sphere, 3:215, 4:404

Habermas's Critical Theory of Society, 3:229, 4:404

Habitants and Merchants in Seventeenth-Century Montreal, 3:611

Habitat, Economy, and Society in the Central African Rainforests, 3:431

The Habitations of the Word, 1:980

The Habit of Being: Letters, 1:1024

Habits of the Heart, 3:220, 3:248, 4:752

The Hacker Crackdown: Law and Disorder on the Electronic Frontier, 5:547

Hackers, 5:543

Hadji Murat, 2:764

Hadrian's Memoirs, 2:517

Hagiography and Modern Russian Literature, 2:691

The Haidamaks, 2:840

The Haight-Ashbury: A History, 3:561

Hail and Farewell! 1:380, 1:381

Hail to the Emperor! 2:308

Haircut and Other Stories, 1:852

The Hairy Ape, 1:1106

Haiti: Guide to the Periodical Literature in English, 1800–1990, 3:638

Haiti: The Breached Citadel, 3:637

Haiti and the United States: The Psychological Moment, 3:637

Haji Agha: Portrait of an Iranian Confidence Man, 2:90

Halakhah in a Theological Dimension, 4:598

Halakhic Man, 4:673
The Halakhic Mind: An Essay on Jewish Tradition and Modern Thought, 4:673
H. A. Lorentz: Collected Papers, 1935–1939, 5:699
H. A. Lorentz: Impressions of His Life and Work, 5:699
Haldane and Modern Biology, 5:798
The Half-Blood, 1:724
A Half-Century of Eliot Criticism, 1:473
Half Moon Street, 3:940
Half of Man Is Woman, 2:239
Halford Mackinder: A Biography, 3:133
Halfway to the Moon, 1:620
Halldór Laxness, 2:642
Halley and His Comet, 5:606
Hall of Mirrors, 1:1055
Hallucinated City, 2:893
Hamburg Dramaturgy, 2:600
Hamilton Fish: The Inner History of the Grant Administration, 3:591
Hamilton Stark, 1:940
Hamlet, 1:205, 1:206, 1:212, 1:213, 1:554, 2:461
The Hamlet: A Novel of the Snopes Family, 1:835
Hamlet, King Lear, Othello, 1:221
Hamlet and Oedipus, 1:213
Hamlet and Revenge, 1:213
Hamlet Machine, 2:603
Hamlet Machine and Other Texts for the Stage, 2:603
Hamlin Garland, 1:751
Hamlin Garland: A Biography, 1:751
Hamlin Garland and the Critics: An Annotated Bibliography, 1:751
Hamlin Garland's Early Work and Career, 1:752
Hammer on the Rock: A Midrash Reader, 4:610
The Hammonds of Redcliffe, 3:523
Hampshire Days, 1:365
The Hand, 2:698
Hand Bookbinding: A Manual of Instruction, 1:27
Handbook for Academic Authors, 1:118
A Handbook for Booklovers, 1:79
A Handbook for Inventors, 5:226

Handbook for Mental Health Care of Disaster Victims, 5:421
Handbook for Research in American History, 3:507
A Handbook for Teaching African Literature, 2:108
A Handbook for the Study of Suicide, 5:427
Handbook in Applied Meteorology, 5:617
Handbook of Abusable Drugs, 5:350, 5:401
The Handbook of a Christian Soldier, 4:138
Handbook of Aging and the Social Sciences, 3:200
Handbook of Alligators and Crocodiles, 5:769
Handbook of American Film Genres, 1:1158, 3:825
Handbook of American Folklore, 3:848
Handbook of American-Jewish Literature, 1:713, 2:31
Handbook of American Popular Literature, 1:1210
The Handbook of Artificial Intelligence, 5:569
The Handbook of Association Publishing, 1:46
Handbook of Biblical Criticism, 4:815
Handbook of Borderline Disorders, 5:428
Handbook of British Chronology, 3:354
Handbook of Chemistry and Physics, 5:652, 5:725
A Handbook of Classical Drama, 1:133
Handbook of Common Foot Problems, 5:396
Handbook of Community Health Nursing: Essentials for Clinical Practice, 5:338
Handbook of Data Communications, 5:304
Handbook of Dates for Students of History, 3:8
Handbook of Denominations in the United States, 4:6, 4:717, 4:751
A Handbook of Dyes from Natural Materials, 5:729
Handbook of English-Arabic for Professionals, 1:97
Handbook of Food Engineering, 5:261
A Handbook of Greek Literature, 2:347

Handbook of Health, Health Care, and the Health Professions, 5:335
Handbook of Health Professions Education, 5:335
Handbook of Helpful Press Hints, 1:21
Handbook of Industrial Robotics, 5:243
Handbook of Intensive Brief and Emergency Psychotherapy, 5:417
The Handbook of International Financial Management, 3:44
Handbook of Latin American Literature, 2:845
Handbook of Latin American Studies, 2:846, 2:868
The Handbook of Latin American Studies (Hanke), 3:646, 3:647
Handbook of Latin American Studies (Martin), 3:625
A Handbook of Living Religions, 4:498, 4:523, 4:535
Handbook of Mathematics, 5:478
Handbook of Mental Retardation, 5:427
Handbook of Metaphysics and Ontology, 4:159
A Handbook of Method in Cultural Anthropology, 3:12
Handbook of Middle American Indians, 4:465
Handbook of New Nations, 3:273
Handbook of Nutrition, Health, and Aging, 5:349
Handbook of Optics, 5:652
Handbook of Organizations, 3:210
Handbook of Perception, 3:177
Handbook of Perception and Human Performance, 3:177
The Handbook of Political Science, 3:138
A Handbook of Printing Types with Notes on the Style of Composition and Graphic Processes Used by Cowells, 1:16
Handbook of Psychiatric Rehabilitation Practice, 5:415
Handbook of Psychological Terms, 5:413
Handbook of Rational-Emotive Therapy, 5:439

Handbook of Reactive Chemical Hazards, 5:724
Handbook of Recording Engineering, 5:229
Handbook of Regular Pattern, 5:487
Handbook of Research Design and Social Measurement, 3:7
Handbook of Russian Literature, 2:691
Handbook of Short-Term Dynamic Psychotherapy, 5:417
Handbook of Small Group Research, 3:172
Handbook of Snakes of the United States and Canada, 5:769
Handbook of Socialization Theory and Research, 3:216
The Handbook of Social Psychology, 3:169
Handbook of Sociology, 3:200
A Handbook of Space Astronomy and Astrophysics, 5:589
Handbook of Survey Research, 3:7
Handbook of Synagogue Architecture, 4:614
Handbook of Texas, 3:600
Handbook of the American Indian Languages, 3:21, 3:28
Handbook of the Birds of the World, 5:759
Handbook of the Indians of California, 3:33
A Handbook of Theological Terms, 4:675, 4:718
Handbook of the Psychology of Aging, 3:201
Handbook of Toxic and Hazardous Chemicals and Carcinogens, 5:737
Handbook of War Studies, 3:280
Handbook of Western Philosophy, 4:162
Handbook of World Philosophy: Contemporary Developments since 1945, 4:6, 4:37, 4:263
Handbook on American Popular Culture, 3:873
A Handbook to Literature, 1:131
Handel, 2:501, 3:698
Handel: A Documentary Biography, 3:698

Handel: His Personality and His Times, 3:698
Handel and the Pastoral Tradition, 3:698
A Handful of Dust, 1:561, 1:562
The Handmaid's Tale, 2:906
The Hand of Ethelberta: A Comedy in Chapters, 1:361
The Hand of Fu Manchu, 1:597
Hands and Hearts: A History of Courtship in America, 3:553
Hand's End: Technology and the Limits of Nature, 5:72
Hands-On Statistics: Exploring with a Microcomputer, 5:525
Hands Up, 1:970
The Handwriting of the Renaissance, 1:20
Hanging in There: Living Well on Borrowed Time, 5:369
Hangman's Holiday, 1:610
Hangover Mass, 1:997
Hangsaman, 1:992
Hania, 2:821
Han Joong Nok: Reminiscences in Retirement, 2:302
Hankow: Commerce and Society in a Chinese City, 1796–1889, 3:468
Hannah and Her Sisters, 3:829
Hannah Arendt, 4:395
Hannah Arendt: A Bibliography, 3:282, 4:395, 5:82
Hannah Arendt: A Reinterpretation of Her Political Thought, 3:282, 5:82
Hannah Arendt: For Love of the World, 5:82
Hannah Arendt: Politics, Conscience, Evil, 5:82
Hannah Arendt: Thinking, Judging, Freedom, 4:395
Hannah Arendt's Philosophy of Natality, 4:394, 5:82
Hannele, 2:586
Hanover and Britain, 1740–1760, 3:362
Hanoverian London, 1714–1808, 3:363
The Han Rhapsody: A Study of the Fu of Yang Hsiung, 2:230
Hans Bethe: Prophet of Energy, 5:672
Hans Christian Andersen, 2:647

Hans Reichenbach: Logical Empiricist, 5:103
Hanukah Money, 2:45
Hanukkah Anthology, 4:599
Han Yong-un and Yi Kwang-su, 2:301
Han Yü and the T'ang Search for Unity, 2:199, 3:468
Hanz Kuechelgarten, Leaving the Theater and Other Works, 2:722
Hapgood, 1:554
Happily Ever After: A Portrait of Frances Hodgson Burnett, 1:1201
The Happy Birthday of Death, 1:964
Happy Days (Beckett), 1:439, 2:459
Happy Days 1880–1892 (Mencken), 1:859
Happy Endings: Lesbian Writers Talk about Their Lives and Work, 1:1183
The Happy Isles of Oceania, 3:940
The Happy Prince and Other Stories, 1:410
Happy Times in Norway, 2:669
Happy Valley (Byrne), 5:434
Happy Valley (White), 2:945, 2:965, 2:966
The Hapsburg Monarchy among the Great Powers, 1815–1918, 3:375
The Hapsburgs: Portrait of a Dynasty, 3:375
Harbrace College Handbook, 1:118
Harbrace Guide to the Library and the Research Paper, 1:118
The Hard-Boiled Explicator, 1:1228
Hard-Boiled Wonderland and the End of the World: A Novel, 2:290
Hard Bop: Jazz and Black Music, 1955–1965, 3:669
Hard Cash, 1:389
Hard Drive: Bill Gates and the Making of the Microsoft Empire, 5:543
The Harder We Run: Black Workers since the Civil War, 3:547
The Hard Facts of Grimms' Fairy Tales, 2:585
Hard Heads, Soft Hearts; Tough-Minded Economics for a Just Society, 3:67

Hard Labor, 2:432

The Hard Life: A Novel, 1:525

Hard Money, 1:1218

Hard News: Women in Broadcast Journalism, 3:807

Hard Times (Hard Times for These Times), 1:348

Hard Times: An Oral History of the Great Depression, 3:536

Hard Tomatoes, Hard Times, 5:266

Hardy, the Creator: A Textual Biography, 1:362

Hardy and the Erotic, 1:363

Hardy in America: A Study of Thomas Hardy and His American Readers, 1:363

Hardy in History, 1:360, 1:363

Hardy of Wessex, 1:363

Hardy's Poetic Vision in the Dynasts: The Diorama of a Dream, 1:362

Hardy's Poetry, 1860–1928, 1:363

Hare Krishna and the Counterculture, 4:863

Hare Krishna in America, 4:863

The Hare Krishna Movement, 4:862

The Hare Krishnas in India, 4:507, 4:862

Haring, 1:1165

Harland's Half Acre, 2:958, 2:959

Harlan Hubbard: Life and Work, 5:269

Harlem Glory, 1:856

Harlem in Review, 1:793

The Harlem Renaissance, 1:794, 3:559

The Harlem Renaissance Re-Examined, 1:794

Harlem Shadows, 1:856

Harlequin's 30th Anniversary, 1949–1979, 1:41

Harlot's Ghost, 1:1011, 1:1012

Harmless Tales, 2:654

The Harmonics of Nicomachus and the Pythagorean Tradition, 5:514

The Harmonious Circle, 4:876

The Harmonists: A Folk-Cultural Approach, 4:844

Harmonium, 1:886

The Harmonizer, 1:21

Harmony and Unity: The Life of Niels Bohr, 5:674

Harmony of Dissonances: T. S. Eliot, Romanticism and Imagination, 1:473

Harold, the Last of the Saxons, 1:340

Harold Adams Innis: Portrait of a Scholar, 3:622

Harold Bloom: The Rhetoric of Romantic Vision, 1:1138

Harold D. Lasswell and the Study of International Relations, 3:157

Harold Hotelling, 1895–1973, Lionel Robbins, 1898–1984, Clark Warburton, 1896–1979, John Bates Clark, 1847–1938, and Ludwig von Mises, 1881–1973, 3:73

Harold Laski, 1893–1950: A Biographical Memoir, 3:156

Harold Pinter, 1:535

Harold Pinter: A Casebook, 1:535

Harold Pinter: An Annotated Bibliography, 1:535

Harold Pinter: Critical Approaches, 1:535

Harold's Years: Impressions of the Harold Wilson Era, 1:432

Haroun and the Sea of Stories, 2:181

The Harp and the Shadow, 2:860

Harper American Literature, 1:795

The Harper Atlas of the Bible, 4:7, 4:809

The HarperCollins Dictionary of Art Terms and Techniques, 3:757

The HarperCollins Dictionary of Sociology, 3:200

Harper Collins French Dictionary, 1:98

Harper Collins German Dictionary, 1:99

Harper Collins Italian Dictionary, 1:100

Harper Dictionary of Contemporary Usage, 1:92

The Harper Dictionary of Economics, 3:44

Harper's Bible Commentary, 4:819

Harper's Bible Dictionary, 4:817

Harper's Bible Pronunciation Guide, 4:819

Harper's New Testament Commentaries, 4:820

The Harps That Once: Sumerian Poetry in Translation, 2:52, 4:440

Harrap's Concise French Dictionary, 1:98

Harriet Beecher Stowe, 1:699

Harriet Beecher Stowe and American Literature, 1:699

Harriet Hume, 1:566

Harriet Martineau, 1:376

Harriet Martineau: A Radical Victorian, 1:376

Harriet Martineau: First Woman Sociologist, 1:376

Harriet Martineau: The Woman and Her Work 1802–76, 1:376

Harriet Martineau on Women, 1:376

Harrod's Librarian's Glossary and Reference Book, 1:69

Harrouda, 2:117

The Harrowing of Hubertus, 2:937, 2:938

Harry S Truman and the Modern American Presidency, 3:537

A Harsh and Dreadful Love, 4:766

Hart Crane, 1:823

Hart Crane: A Re-Introduction, 1:823

Hart Crane: The Contexts of the Bridge, 1:823

Hart Crane: The Patterns of His Poetry, 1:824

Hart Crane and the Homosexual Text, 1:824, 1:1183

The HART Program, 5:374

Hartshorne's Neo-Classical Theology, 4:290

Harvard Composers, 3:688

The Harvard Concordance to Shakespeare, 1:216

Harvard Guide to American History, 3:506

The Harvard List of Books in Psychology, 5:414

The Harvard Medical School Health Letter Book, 5:341

Harvard University Library: Theodore Roosevelt Collection, Dictionary Catalogue and Shelflist, 3:595

Harvest, 2:481

The Harvest and the Reapers: Oral Traditions of Kentucky, 3:860

The Harvest Gypsies: On the Road to the Grapes of Wrath, 1:885

Harvest of Hate, 4:637

The Harvest of Medieval Theology, 4:105, 4:129, 4:697, 4:721

A Harvest of Russian Children's Literature, 2:693

Harvest of the Lowlands, 2:622

Harvest on the Don, 2:756

Harvests of Change: American Literature, 1865–1914, 1:715

Harvey and the Oxford Physiologist, 5:41, 5:361

Has History a Future?, 3:399

Hasiddur Hashalem: Daily Prayer Book, 4:599

The Hasidic Anthology, 4:633

Hasidic Prayer, 4:632

Hasidic Thought, 4:632

Hasidism and Modern Man, 4:632

Hasidism and the Jewish Enlightenment, 4:632

Hasidism and the State of Israel, 4:658

Hasidism as Mysticism, 4:633

Has Man a Future?, 4:322

The Hasmoneans and Their Supporters, 4:605

The Hasty-Pudding: A Poem in Three Cantos, 1:633

Hateful Contraries: Studies in Literature and Criticism, 1:927, 1:1155

Hath Not a Jew, 2:915

Hatimi and His Encounter with Mutanabbi: A Biographical Sketch, 2:70

The Haunted Bookshop, 1:33

The Haunted Castle: A Study of the Elements of English Fiction, 1:270

The Haunted Hotel, 1:346

A Haunted House and Other Short Stories, 1:569

The Haunted Mirror, 1:876

Haunted New England, 3:858

The Haunted Pool, 2:504

The Haunted Study: A Social History of the English Novel, 1875–1914, 1:319

The Haunting of Hill House, 1:992

The Haunting of Sylvia Plath, 1:1031

Have His Carcase, 1:610

Havelok the Dane, 1:145

Haven and Home: A History of the Jews in America, 4:639

Haven in a Heartless World: The Family Besieged, 3:552

Have without Have-Nots: Six Essays on Democracy and Socialism, 4:270

Having a Baby without a Man, 5:359

Having Twins, 5:359

Having Your Baby with a Nurse Midwife, 5:337

Hawaii, 3:931

Hawkes: A Guide to His Fictions, 1:986

The Hawk in the Rain, 1:497

Hawks, Doves, and Owls: An Agenda for Avoiding Nuclear War, 5:109

Hawks, Owls, and Wildlife, 5:820

The Hawks and the Sparrows, 2:431

Hawks on Hawks, 3:838

The Haw Lantern, 1:495

Hawley's Condensed Chemical Dictionary, 5:726

Hawthorne, 1:677

Hawthorne: A Critical Study, 1:677

Hawthorne: The Critical Heritage, 1:677

Hawthorne's Fiction: The Light and the Dark, 1:677

Hawthorne's View of the Artist, 1:676

Hawthorne Tree: Some Papers and Letters on Life and the Theatre, 1:1089

Haydn: Chronicle and Works, 3:700

Haydn, a Creative Life in Music, 3:699

Haydn and the Enlightenment, 3:700

Hayduke Lives! 5:827

"The Hayek Story" in Critical Essays in Monetary Theory, 3:82

Hay Fever, 1:464, 1:465

Hayy ibn Yaqzan, 4:585

A Hazard of New Fortunes, 1:758

Hazardous Substances: A Reference, 5:736

Hazardous Waste in America, 5:636, 5:822

Hazlitt, 1:291

Hazlitt: A Life: From Winterslow to Frith Street, 1:291

H. C. Branner, 2:648

H. D., 1:827

H. D., The Life and Work of an American Poet, 1:827

H. D. and Freud: Bi-Sexuality and a Feminine Discourse, 1:827

Head above Water, 2:137

Head and Face Pain Syndromes, 5:376

Headbirths; Or, the Germans Are Dying Out, 2:583

Heading Home: With Weatherby and Dreams of Living, 1:493

Headlong Hall, 1:297

The Head of the District, 1:370

The Healer (Appelfeld), 2:14

The Healers (Armah), 2:131

The Healers: A History of American Medicine, 5:78

The Healers: Rise of American Medicine, 5:328

The Healer's Power, 4:388

The Healer's Tale, 5:313

Healing and Restoring, 4:506, 4:514, 4:530, 4:536

Healing and the Mind, 5:342

The Healing Blade: Neurosurgery on the Edge of Life and Death, 5:405

The Healing Herbs, 5:318

Healing Hypotheses, 4:847

Healing Song for the Inner Ear, 1:984

Healing the Planet: Strategies for Resolving the Environmental Crisis, 5:832

Health, Disease, and Causal Explanations in Medicine, 5:78

Health, Stress, and Coping, 5:400

Health, Stress and Illness: A Systems Approach, 5:401

Health, United States 1991, 5:311

Health and Behavior, 5:341

Health and Faith: Medical, Psychological and Religious Dimensions, 5:417

Health and Healing, 5:320

Health and Human Values, 5:132

Health and Medicine in the Christian Science Tradition, 4:843

Health and Medicine in the Islamic Tradition, 4:893

Health and Medicine in the Jewish Tradition: The Pursuit of Wholeness, 4:598

Health and Prevention of Disease in a Free Society, 5:353

Health and the Law: A Handbook for Health Professionals, 5:343

Health and Wealth: An International Study of Health-Care Spending, 5:330

Health Care and the Changing Economic Environment, 5:333

Health Care and the Elderly, 5:317

Health Care of Homeless People, 5:328

Health Care of the Elderly, 5:316

Health Care State Rankings, 1993: Health Care in the 50 United States, 5:331

The Health Care Survival Curve, 5:329

The Health Consequences of Smoking: A Report of the Surgeon General, 5:404

The Health Crisis: Opposing Viewpoints, 5:13

The Health Economy, 5:332

Health Education: Perspectives and Choices, 5:332

Health Facts, 5:311, 5:405

Health for the Whole Person: The Complete Guide to Holistic Medicine, 5:319

Healthful Aging, 5:316

Health Hazards Manual for Artists, 5:736

The Healthiest City: Milwaukee and the Politics of Health Reform, 5:314

Health in an Older Society, 5:316

Health Indicators, 5:382

Health Issues in the Black Community, 5:330

Health/Medicine and the Faith Traditions, 4:893

Health Planning in the United States: Selected Policy Issues, 5:328

Health Policies, Health Politics, 5:330

Health Policy: The Legislative Agenda, 5:333

Health Services in the United States: A Growth Enterprise since 1875, 5:312

Healthy Babies, Happy Kids, 5:348

Healthy Computing, 5:353

Healthy Homes, Healthy Kids, 5:351

Healthy Living in an Unhealthy World, 5:345

Healthy People in Unhealthy Places: Stress and Fitness at Work, 5:353

He and She: Men in the Eighties, 3:207

Heap of Ashes, 2:321

Hearing: Its Function and Dysfunction, 5:380

Hearing Out James T. Farrell, 1:834

Hearing Secret Harmonies, 1:536

Hear Me Talkin' to Ya: The Story of Jazz by the Men Who Made It, 3:669

The Heart: The Living Pump, 5:340

Heartbook, 5:373

Heartbreak House, 1:544, 1:545

Heartbreak Tango, 2:880

Heart Disease: Reducing Your Risk, 5:374

The Heart Is a Lonely Hunter, 1:1009, 1:1102

The Heart of a Child, 5:376

Heart of a Dog, 2:706

The Heart of a Woman, 1:935

The Heart of Buddhism, 4:366

The Heart of Buddhist Wisdom, 4:512

Heart of Darkness, 1:463

The Heart of Man: Its Genius for Good and Evil, 5:450

The Heart of Midlothian, 1:298

The Heart of O. Henry, 1:756

Heart of Oak: A Survey of British Sea Power in the Georgian Era, 3:362

The Heart of the Ancient Wood, 2:925

The Heart of the Dragon, 3:466

The Heart of the Hunter, 3:941

The Heart of the Matter (Greene), 1:488

The Heart of the Matter (Teilhard), 4:336

The Heart of the New Thought, 4:847

Heart of the World, 1:595

The Heart of Understanding, 4:561

The Heart of Yoknapatawpha, 1:837

Hearts and Minds in Guerilla Warfare, 1948–1960, 3:492

The Heart's Essential Landscape: Bernard Malamud's Hero, 1:1014

The Heart's Events: The Victorian Poetry of Relationships, 1:315

Heart-Shaped Leaves—American Writers during the Civil War, 1:717

Heart's Needle, 1:1051

The Heart-Stirrring Sermon and Other Stories, 2:44

Heartstones, 1:609

Heartwork: Selected Short Stories, 2:660

Hear us O Lord from heaven thy dwelling place, 2:919

Heat: And Other Stories, 1:1023

The Heath Anthology of American Literature, 1:130, 1:653, 1:717

Heathen Days, 1890–1936, 1:859

Heathen Valley, 1:1099, 1:1100

The Heat of the Day, 1:447

Heaven, 1:1240

Heaven and Hell, 4:880

Heaven in Transition, 4:518

The Heavenly City of the Eighteenth-Century Philosophers, 3:337, 3:567, 4:159

The Heavenly Hound, 2:242

The Heavenly Muse: A Preface to Milton, 1:193

Heaven My Blanket, Earth My Pillow, 2:230

Heaven on Earth: Dispatches from America's Spiritual Frontier, 4:866

The Heavens and the Earth: A Political History of the Space Age, 5:597

The Heavens Are Falling, 5:10

Heaven's My Destination, 1:898

Heavens to Betsy and Other Curious Sayings, 1:95

Heavy Minerals in Colour, 5:628

Heavy Sand, 2:754

Heavy Wings, 2:239

Hebrew: The Eternal Language, 2:8

Hebrew and Chaldee Lexicon to the Old Testament, 4:794

Hebrew Ballads and Other Poems, 2:10

The Hebrew Bible: A Socio-Literary Introduction, 4:816

The Hebrew Bible, the Old Testament, and Historical Criticism, 4:815

The Hebrew Bible and Its Modern Interpreters, 4:814

The Hebrew Book: An Historical Survey, 2:9

Hebrew Christianity: The Thirteenth Tribe, 4:864

Hebrew Ethical Wills, 4:628

Hebrew Melodies, 1:281

Hebrew Phrase Books, 1:99

Hebrew Poetry in the Middle Ages and the Renaissance, 2:9

The Hebrew Poetry of Hayyim Nahman Bialik and Modern Jewish Theology, 2:16

Hebrew Poetry of the Middle Ages and the Renaissance, 2:23

Hecuba, 2:355

Hedayat's Blind Owl as a Western Novel, 2:90

Hedda Gabler, 2:665

Hedda Gabler and Other Plays, 2:666

The Hedge, 2:538

Hedylus, 1:826

Hegel (Caird), 3:285

Hegel (Inwood), 4:233

Hegel (Plant), 3:285

Hegel (Taylor), 4:233, 4:414

Hegel: Religion, Economics and Politics of the Spirit, 1770–1807, 4:233

Hegel, Nietzsche and the Criticism of Metaphysics, 4:233

Hegel and Modern Society, 4:414

Hegel and Skepticism, 4:233

Hegel and the State, 4:671

Hegelianism, 4:233

Hegelian-Whiteheadian Perspectives, 4:341

Hegel's Critique of Liberalism, 4:233

Hegel's Development: Night Thoughts, 4:233

Hegel's Development: Toward the Sunlight, 4:233

Hegel's Dialectic, 4:402

Hegel's Dialectic and Its Criticism, 4:233

Hegel's Epistemological Realism, 4:233

Hegel's Ethical Thought, 4:233

Hegel's Idealism, 4:233

Hegel's Idea of a Phenomenology of Spirit, 4:233

Hegel's Ontology, 4:408

Hegel's Phenomenology of Spirit, 4:291

Hegel's Philosophy of History, 3:285

Hegel's Theory of Mental Activity, 4:233

Hegel's Theory of the Modern State, 4:232

Hegemony and Culture: Politics and Religious Change among the Yoruba, 4:467

Hegemony and Revolution, 2:423

Hegemony and Socialist Strategy, 1:1132

Heichal Hakodesh Concordance to the Old Testament, 4:818

Heidegger, 4:294, 5:91

Heidegger: Thought and Historicity, 4:293

Heidegger, Art and Politics: The Fiction of the Political, 4:293

Heidegger, Being, and Truth, 4:295

Heidegger and Asian Thought, 4:294, 4:350

Heidegger and Derrida: Reflections on Time and Language, 4:294

Heidegger and Modernity, 4:293, 5:90

Heidegger and Nazism, 4:293

Heidegger and the Earth: Issues in Environmental Philosophy, 4:294

Heidegger and the Language of Poetry, 4:295

Heidegger and the Poets: Poiesis/Sophia/Techné, 4:293

Heidegger and the Problem of Knowledge, 4:293

Heidegger and the Project of Fundamental Ontology, 4:295

Heidegger and the Question of Renaissance Humanism: Four Studies, 4:127

The Heidegger Case: On Philosophy and Ethics, 4:294, 5:91

The Heidegger Case: On Philosophy and Politics, 5:72

Heidegger on Being and Acting: From Principles to Anarchy, 4:295

Heidegger's Being and Time: A Reading for Readers, 4:293

Heidegger's Being and Time: The Analytic of Dasein as Fundamental Ontology, 4:293

Heidegger's Confrontation with Modernity, 4:295, 5:72, 5:91

Heidegger's Estrangements, 4:292

Heidegger's Pragmatism, 4:294

The Heidi Chronicles, 1:1115

The Heidi Chronicles and Other Plays, 1:1115

Heidi's Alps: One Family's Search for Storybook Europe, 3:899

The Heights of Machu Picchu, 2:874

Heimskringla, 2:639, 2:643, 2:661

The Heinemann Book of African Poetry in English, 2:113

Heinrich Böll: A German for His Time, 2:570

Heinrich Heine, 2:588

Heinrich Hertz: Memoirs, Letters, Diaries, 5:694

Heinrich von Kleist: Studies in His Works and Literary Character, 2:599

Heinrich von Ofterdingen, 2:605

The Heir, 1:542

Heirs of the Pharisees, 4:596

Heirs of the Roman Empire, 3:329

Heirs to the Past, 2:119

He Knew He Was Right, 1:406

Helen, 2:355

Helena, 2:896

Helen Hunt Jackson and Her Indian Reform Legacy, 1:761

Helen in Egypt, 1:826, 1:1187

Heliopolis, 2:595

The Heliotrope Wall and Other Stories, 2:545

Hellas, 1:271

The Hellbound Heart, 1:600

Hellenica, 3:323

Hellenika: I-II 3.10, 4:91

Hellenism: The History of a Civilization, 3:293

Hellenism in Jewish Palestine, 4:606
The Hellenistic Age from the Battle of Ipsos to the Death of Kleopatra VII, 3:299
Hellenistic Civilization and the Jews, 4:605
The Hellenistic Philosophers, 4:55
Hellenistic Philosophies, 4:55
Hellenistic Philosophy: Introductory Readings, 4:55
Hellenistic Philosophy: Selections from Epicureanism, Skepticism, and Neoplatonism, 4:56
Hellenistic Philosophy: Stoics, Epicureans, Skeptics, 4:55
Hellenistic Philosophy of Mind, 4:55
Hellenistic Poetry: An Anthology, 2:348
Hellenistic Religions: An Introduction, 4:450
The Hellenistic Stoa: Political Thought and Action, 4:55, 4:57
Hellenistic Ways of Deliverance and the Making of the Christian Synthesis, 4:55
The Hellenistic World and the Coming of Rome, 3:303
The Hellenistic World from Alexander to the Roman Conquest, 3:299, 4:449
The Hellenist World, 3:302
Hellfire and Lightning Rods: Liberating Science, Technology, and Religion, 5:197
Helliconia Summer, 1:613
Helliconia Winter, 1:613
Hello: A Journal, Feb. 29–May 3, 1976, 1:966
Hello, Dolly, 1:1116
Hello, Out There, 1:1110
Hell or Connaught: Cromwellian Colonization of Ireland, 1652–1660, 3:370
Helmets, 1:967
Heloïse and Abelard, 4:286
Help! For Small Press People, 1:46
Help for the Hyperactive Child, 5:417
Helping People: Karen Horney's Psychoanalytic Approach, 5:452

Helping Your Child Sleep through the Night, 5:322
Hemingway, 1:846
Hemingway: A Biography, 1:846
Hemingway: Essays of Reassessment, 1:847
Hemingway: The Critical Heritage, 1:846
Hemingway: The Paris Years, 1:847
Hemingway, the Writer as Artist, 1:846
Hemingway and His World, 1:846
Hemingway and Spain: A Pursuit, 1:847
Hemingway and Turgenev: The Nature of Literary Influence, 1:847
Hemingway for Beginners, 1:847
Hemingway in Love and War, 1:847
Hemingway on Love, 1:846
Hemingway's Art of Nonfiction, 1:847
Hemingway's First War, 1:847
Hemingway's Quarrel with Androgyny, 1:847
Hemingway's Reading, 1:847
The Hemingway Women, 1:846
Henceforward, 1:436
Henderson the Rain King, 1:946, 1:947
Henrik Ibsen, 2:666
Henri Matisse, 3:781
Henri Matisse, a Retrospective, 3:781
Henry Adams (Bishop), 1:730, 1:816
Henry Adams (Blackmur), 1:730, 1:816
Henry Adams (H. Adams), 3:562
Henry Adams (J. T. Adams), 3:563
Henry Adams (Samuels), 1:730
Henry Adams: A Biography, 1:730
Henry Adams: Scientific Historian, 3:563
Henry Adams and the American Experiment, 3:563
Henry and Cato, 1:523
Henry and Clare: An Intimate Portrait of the Luces, 3:816

Henry and June: From the Unexpurgated Diary of Anais, 1:865
Henry Arthur Jones and the Modern Drama, 1:367
Henry Barnard, 3:259
Henry Barnard: American Educator, 3:259
Henry Barnard's American Journal of Education, 3:259
Henry Brocken, 1:467
Henry David Thoreau, 1:702
Henry David Thoreau: What Manner of Man, 1:702
The Henry Davis Gift: A Collection of Bookbindings, 1:23
Henry Dunbar, 1:332
Henry Esmond, 1:403
Henry Fielding, 1:245, 1:246
Henry Fielding: A Life, 1:245
Henry Fielding: Political Writer, 1:245
Henry Fielding, Mask and Feast, 1:246
Henry Fielding and the London Theatre, 1728–1737, 1:245
Henry George, 3:80
Henry George, Citizen of the World, 3:80
Henry Green, 1:487
Henry Green and the Writing of His Generation, 1:487
Henry Handel Richardson, 2:961
Henry Hobson Richardson and His Works, 3:791
Henry Holt Handbook of Current Science and Technology, 5:6
Henry VIII (Dwyer), 3:358, 3:359
Henry VIII (Scarisbrick), 4:727
Henry VIII (Shakespeare), 1:204
Henry V, 1:205, 1:206, 1:207
Henry IV, 1:205, 1:206, 2:461
Henry James, 1:566, 1:765, 1:766, 1:972
Henry James: A Life, 1:766
Henry James: A Reader's Guide, 1:767
Henry James: A Reference Guide, 1:766
Henry James: A Study of the Short Fiction, 1:766
Henry James: The Conquest, 1:972

Henry James: The Critical Heritage, 1:766

Henry James: The Major Phase, 1:767

Henry James: The Master, 1:972

Henry James: The Middle Years, 1:972

Henry James: The Treacherous Years, 1:972

Henry James: The Untried Years, 1:766

Henry James: The Writer and His Work, 1:767

Henry James and Revision: The New York Edition, 1:766

Henry James and the Art of Power, 1:767

Henry James and The Darkest Abyss of Romance, 1:766

Henry James and the "Woman Business," 1:766

Henry James Encyclopedia, 1:766

Henry James in Westminster Abbey: The Address, 1:972

Henry James's Daisy Miller, The Turn of the Screw, and Other Tales, 1:765

Henry James's Portrait of the Writer as Hero, 1:765

Henry James's The Ambassadors, 1:765

Henry James's The Portrait of a Lady, 1:765

Henryk Sienkiewicz, 2:822

Henry Mayhew, 1:378

Henry Miller, 1:862, 1:863

Henry Miller: A Bibliography of Secondary Sources, 1:863

Henry Miller: A Life, 1:863

Henry Miller: The Modern Rabelais, 1:863

Henry Miller and the Critics, 1:863

Henry Miller on Writing, 1:861, 1:862

Henry Miller's Book of Friends: A Trilogy, 1:862

Henry Miller's Hamlet Letters, 1:862

Henry Miller—The Paintings: A Centennial Retrospective, 1:862

Henry Moore, 3:784

Henry Moore: My Ideas, Inspiration, and Life as an Artist, 3:784

Henry Moore: 60 Years of His Art, 3:784

Henry Moore: The Life and Work of a Great Sculptor, 1:983

Henry Moore on Sculpture, 3:784

Henry More (1614–1687) Tercentenary Studies, 4:183

Henry of Portugal, 3:386

Henry Purcell: His Life and Times, 3:711

Henry R. Luce and the Rise of the American News Media, 3:816

Henry Roth: The Man and His Work, 1:1039

Henry Sidgwick: Science and Faith in Victorian England, 4:257

Henry Sidgwick and Later Utilitarian Political Philosophy, 4:257

Henry VI, 1:205, 1:206, 1:211

Henry Steele Commager's The Story of the Second World War, 3:573

Henry Thoreau: A Life of the Mind, 1:702

Henry Timrod, 1:703, 1:778

Henry Timrod: Laureate of the Confederacy, 1:704, 1:779

Henry Vaughan: The Unfolding Vision, 1:200

Henry von Ofterdingen, 2:605

Henry Wadsworth Longfellow, 1:683

Henry Wadsworth Longfellow: His Poetry and Prose, 1:683

The Henry Wallaces of Iowa, 5:275

Henslowe's Diary, 1:170

Hen's Teeth and Horse's Toes, 5:16, 5:638, 5:764

A Hen Too Soon, 2:143, 2:144

The Heptameron, 2:492

Heptaplus, or Discourse on the Seven Days of Creation, 4:152, 4:153

Heraclitean Fragments: A Comparison Volume to the Heidegger-Fink Seminar on Heraclitus, 4:75

Heraclitus, 4:75

Heraclitus: Fragments: A Text and Translation with a Commentary, 4:75

Heraclitus: The Cosmic Fragments, 4:75

Heraclitus Seminar, 1966–1967, 4:74, 4:291

Heraldic Eagle, 2:553

Heralds of Promise, 1:1074

Herald to Chaos: The Novels of Elizabeth Madox Roberts, 1:876

Herbert Bayer: The Complete Work, 1:8

Herbert Eugene Bolton: The Historian and the Man, 1870–1953, 3:643

Herbert George Wells: An Annotated Bibliography of His Works, 1:564

Herbert Marcuse, 4:407, 4:408

Herbert Marcuse: A Bibliography, 5:94

Herbert Marcuse and the Crisis of Marxism, 4:408

Herbert Spencer, 3:241

The Herbs of Life, 5:320

Hercule Poirot's Casebook: Fifty Stories, 1:606

Hercules, 2:670

Hercules at the Crossroads: The Life, Works, Thought of Coluccio Salutati, 4:132

Herder, 4:199

Herder: His Life and Thought, 4:199

Herder and the Beginnings of Comparative Literature, 2:589

Herder and the Philosophy and History of Science, 4:199

Herder's Social and Political Thought, 4:199

Herder Today, 3:286

The Herdsman and the Linden Tree, 2:806

Here and Now, 1:1003, 2:904

Here Come the Clowns, 1:1085

Hereditary Genius: An Inquiry into Its Laws and Consequences, 5:529

Heredity, East and West: Lysenko and World Science, 5:798

Here Is New York, 1:898

Here I Stand: A Life of Martin Luther, 4:778

Here Lies Richard Brinsley Sheridan, 1:255

Heresy and Authority in Medieval Europe, 4:721

Heresy and Criticism, 4:825

Heresy and Politics in the Reign of Henry IV, 4:721

Heresy, Crusade, and Inquisition in Southern France, 1100–1250, 4:701

The Heresy of Self-Love: A Study of Subversive Individualism, 2:985

The Heresy of the Free Spirit in the Later Middle Ages, 4:721

Here the Country Lies, 3:558

Heretical Empiricism, 2:432

Heretic of Soana, 2:587

Heretics, 1:457

The Heretic's Apprentice, 1:608

Hereward the Wake, or The Watchful, 1:369

Her Eyes, 2:86

Heritage: Civilization and the Jews, 4:593

A Heritage and Its History, 1:462

Heritage and Promise: Perspectives on the Church of the Brethren, 4:732

The Heritage of African Poetry, 2:113, 2:142

Heritage of American Literature, 1:717

The Heritage of Copernicus: Theories "Pleasing to the Mind," 5:602

A Heritage of Her Own, 3:554

Heritage of Music, 3:662

Heritage of Our Times, 4:277

The Heritage of Russian Verse, 2:693

The Heritage of the Conquistadors, 3:626

Heritage of the Desert, 1:1213

Heritage of the Graphic Arts, 1:8

The Heritage of the Reformation, 4:730

The Heritage of Vietnamese Poetry, 2:339

The Heritage of Wisdom: Essays in the History of Philosophy, 4:17

Herland, 1:752

Herland: A Lost Feminist Utopian Novel, 1:752

Herman Hollerith: Forgotten Giant of Information Processing, 5:576

Herman Melville, 1:688, 1:689

Herman Melville: A Biography, 1:689

Herman Melville: Reassessments, 1:689

Hermann Cohen's Philosophy of Judaism, 4:663

Hermann Hesse: Biography and Bibliography, 2:590

Hermann Zapf and His Design Philosophy, 1:20

Hermeneia: A Critical and Historical Commentary on the Bible, 4:820

The Hermeneutical Theory of Paul Ricoeur: A Constructive Analysis, 4:319

Hermeneutics, 4:402

Hermeneutics: The Handwritten Manuscripts, 4:254

Hermeneutics and Deconstruction, 4:267, 4:392

Hermeneutics and Modern Philosophy, 4:268, 4:392

Hermeneutics and Praxis, 4:413

Hermeneutics and the Human Sciences, 4:319

The Hermeneutics Reader, 4:28

Hermetic Astronomy, 4:149

Hermetic Definition, 1:826

Hermeticism and the Renaissance, 4:128

Hermeticism and the Scientific Revolution, 5:41

Hermione, 1:826

The Hermit, 2:483

The Hermit and the Love-Thief, 2:173

The Hermit of Carmel, and Other Poems, 4:326

The Hermit of Eyton Forest, 1:608

The Hermits, 1:369

Hermits and the New Monasticism, 4:700

Hernani, 2:482

Hero and Chief: Epic Literature from the Banyangoa (Zaire Republic), 2:126

Hero and Leander, 1:186, 1:292

Hero and Leander: The Waves of the Sea and of Love, 2:583

The Hero and the Best of All Possible Worlds, 2:526

Herod: A Profile of a Tyrant, 4:605

Herod and Mariamne, 2:587

Herodias, 2:486

Herodotean Narrative and Discourse, 3:316, 4:480

Herodotus, 3:316, 4:480

Herodotus, Explorer of the Past: Three Essays, 3:316, 4:480

Heroes, Villains, and Ghosts: Folklore of Old California, 3:863

Heroes and Gods: Spiritual Biographies in Antiquity, 4:451

Heroes and Villains, 1:455

Heroes and Villains in Communist China, 2:234

Heroes Are Grazing in My Garden, 2:877

Heroes in Space: From Gagarin to Challenger, 5:4

The Heroes of Greek Fairy Tales for My Children, 1:369

Heroes of the Dark Continent, 3:938

Heroes of the Horizons, 3:906

Heroes' Twilight, 1:420

A Hero for Our Time: An Intimate Story of the Kennedy Years, 3:539

The Heroic Age of Scandinavia, 3:381

Heroicall Epistles, 1:179

The Heroic Enthusiasts, 2:410, 4:135

Heroic Epic and Saga, 3:856

The Heroic Temper: Studies in Sophoclean Tragedy, 2:368

Heroides, 2:389

Heroin Addiction: Theory, Research and Treatment, 5:403

The Hero in History: A Study in Limitation and Possibility, 3:326, 4:298

The Heron, 2:408

A Hero of Our Time, 2:734, 2:735

The Hero of the Waverley Novels, 1:300

The Hero Pony, 1:1101

The Hero Rises Up, 1:434

The Hero's Journey: Joseph Campbell on His Life and Work, 3:876

The Hero's Tale: Narration in the Early Modern Novel, 1:805

The Hero with a Thousand Faces, 3:876

The Hero Within: Six Archetypes We Live By, 1:1196

Herpes: A Complete Guide to Relief and Reassurance, 5:389

The Herpes Book, 5:389

Herpes Diseases and Your Health, 5:389

Herpetology: An Introductory Biology of Amphibians and Reptiles, 5:772

The Herring Gull's World, 3:195

Herself Surprised, 1:456

Her Share of Blessings, 4:449, 4:892

Her Story: Women in Christian Tradition, 4:749

Hertz and His Successors: Signalling across Space without Wires, 5:694

Her Victory, 1:547

Herzl, 4:658

Herzog, 1:946, 1:947

The Herzogenberg Correspondence, 3:684

Hesiod, 2:358, 4:482

Hesiod and Aeschylus, 2:351, 2:358

Hesiod and the Language of Poetry, 2:358

Hesiod and the Near East, 2:358, 4:482

He Sits at the Melting Pot, 2:652

Hesperides and Noble Numbers, 1:181

Het Been, 2:625

Het Behouden Huis, 2:626

The Heterdoxies of the Shi'ites According to Ibn Hazm, 4:584

Het Fregatschip Johanna Maria, 2:630

Het Reservaat, 2:629

Het Stenen Bruidsbed, 2:628

Het Vrome Volk, 2:626

Het woud der verwachting, 2:625

He Who Searches, 2:885

Hexadecimal Chronicles, 5:550

Hexaflexagons and Other Mathematical Diversions, 5:507

Hexameron, Paradise, Cain and Abel, 4:702

The Heyday of American Communism: The Depression Decade, 3:535

The Hey Diddle Diddle Picture Book, 1:581

Hey Diddle Diddle with Baby Bunting, 1:580

H.G.J. Moseley: The Life and Letters of an English Physicist, 1887-1915, 5:703

H. G. Wells, 1:564

H. G. Wells: A Reference Guide, 1:564

H. G. Wells: Discoverer of the Future, 1:564

H. G. Wells: Interviews and Recollections, 1:564

H. G. Wells and Rebecca West, 1:566

H. G. Wells under Revision, 1:564

H. H. Munro (Saki), 1:522

H. H. Richardson: Architectural Forms for an American Society, 3:790

H. H. Richardson, Complete Architectural Works, 3:790

The Hidden Doctrine of Maimonides' Guide for the Perplexed, 4:668

The Hidden Face of Eve: Women in the Arab World, 2:71, 2:72, 2:120

Hidden from History: Reclaiming the Gay and Lesbian Past, 1:1183

The Hidden God (Brooks), 1:953

Hidden God (Goldmann), 4:185

The Hidden-Hand Presidency: Eisenhower as Leader, 3:538

The Hidden Hinge, 3:266

Hidden History, 3:569

The Hidden History of the Korean War, 1950-1951, 3:481

Hidden Illness in the White House, 3:542

The Hidden Italy: A Bilingual Edition of Italian Dialect Poetry, 2:403

Hidden Laughter, 1:486

The Hidden Malpractice: How American Medicine Mistreats Women, 5:343

Hidden Music: Selected Poems, 2:672

The Hidden Order of Art: A Study in the Psychology of Artistic Imagination, 3:757

The Hidden Reader, 2:457, 2:476

Hidden Rivalries in Victorian Fiction: Dickens, Realism, and Revaluation, 1:350

Hidden Sun: Women of Modern Japan, 3:479

Hidden Treasures and Secret Lives, 4:543

The Hidden Universe, 5:654

The Hidden Victims of Alzheimer's Disease: Families under Stress, 5:394

Hide and Seek, 1:346

Hideous Progeny, 1:301

Hideyoshi, 3:474

Hiding, 1:619

Hiding the Universe, 2:227

Hi-Fi and The False Bottom, 2:809

Highbrow/Lowbrow, 3:560

The High Cost of Healing: Physicians and the Health Care System, 5:332

High Endeavours, 3:908

A Higher Kind of Loyalty: A Memoir by China's Foremost Journalist, 2:255

The Higher Learning in America, 3:242, 3:263

The Highest Apple, 1:1188

The Highest Stage of White Supremacy, 3:554

High in the Thin Cold Air, 3:924

The Highland Call, 1:1088

The Highlands and Isles of Scotland: A Historical Survey, 3:368

High Level: The Alps from End to End, 3:898

The High Middle Ages, 2:272

The High Middle Ages in England, 1154-1377, 3:355

High Noon in Southern Africa, 3:423

High Output Management, 5:234

The High Price of Bullion, a Proof of the Depreciation of Bank Notes, 3:100

High Renaissance and Mannerism, 3:760

The Highroad around Modernism, 4:391

The High Road to Pyrrhonism, 4:162, 4:202

High School: A Report on Secondary Education in America, 3:248

High Speed Flight, 5:220

High Tech Home Care: A Practical Guide, 5:328

High Technology Medicine: Benefit and Burdens, 5:121

The High-Tech Society, 5:537

High Theory/Low Culture, 1:1158

The High Walls of Jerusalem, 3:350, 4:643

The Highway and the City, 5:170

Highway Forty, 3:427

Highway Heavy Metal: The World's Trucks at Work, 5:247

A High Wind in Jamaica, 1:496, 1:497
The High Window, 1:1228
High Windows, 1:507
The Hikayat Abdullah, 2:323
Hilaire Belloc, 1:443
Hilaire Belloc: A Memoir, 1:443
Hilaire Belloc: Edwardian Radical, 1:443
Hilbert, 5:510
Hilda Lessways, 1:443
Hillel the Elder: The Emergence of Classical Judaism, 4:620
The Hill of Evil Counsel, 2:22
The Hills Beyond, 1:903
The Hills Were Joyful Together, 2:937
Himalayan Circuit: A Journey in the Inner Himalayas, 3:904
Him/Her/Self: Sex Roles in Modern America, 3:552
Himmerland Stories, 2:652
Himmo, King of Jerusalem, 2:20
Him with His Foot in His Mouth and Other Stories, 1:946
The Hind and the Panther, 1:241
A Hind in Richmond Park, 1:365
Hind in the Wood, 1:583
Hind Swaraj, or Indian Home Rule, 4:552
Hindu Ethics: Purity, Abortion, and Euthanasia, 4:894
Hindu Goddesses, 4:505
Hinduism, 4:884
Hinduism: A Cultural Perspective, 4:505
Hinduism: A Religion to Live By, 4:503
Hinduism: Experiments in the Sacred, 4:505
Hinduism in Thai Life, 4:518
Hindu Myths, 2:171
Hindu Myths: A Sourcebook Translated from the Sanskrit, 4:505
Hindu Nationalism and Indian Politics, 4:508
The Hindu Religious Tradition, 4:504
Hindu Scriptures, 4:501
The Hindu Temple: An Introduction to Its Meaning and Forms, 4:505
The Hindu Tradition, 3:497

The Hindu Tradition—Readings in Oriental Thought, 4:503
Hints and Disguises: Marianne Moore and Her Contemporaries, 1:864
Hints on the Study of the Bhagavad Gita, 4:549
Hippias Major, 4:78
Hippolytus, 1:1091, 2:355, 2:356
Hippolytus Temporizes, 1:827
Hireling, 1:494
Hiroshima, Mon Amour, 2:474
His Butler's Story, 2:736
His Daughter, 2:21
His Day Is Marching On: Memoirs of W.E.B. Du Bois, 3:578
His First Life, 1838–1862, 3:563
H Is for Homicide, 1:1229
His Majesty's Agent, 2:24
His Master's Voice, 2:816
Hispanic Caribbean Literature: Special Issue, 2:931
Hispanic Folk Music of New Mexico and the Southwest, 3:863
Hispanic Folktales from New Mexico, 3:863
Hispanics in the United States: An Anthology of Creative Literature, 1:130
The Hispanization of the Philippines, 3:493
Hispano-Jewish Culture in Transition, 4:629
His Religion and Hers, 1:752
Histoire du Canada depuis la découverte, 3:620
Histoire du Canada depuis sa découverte jusqu'à nos jours, 3:619
Histoire du catholicisme québécois, 3:621
Histoire économique du Québec, 1851–1896, 3:621
Histology: A Text and an Atlas, 5:773
Historia del corazón, 2:529
The Historian and the City, 3:581
Historia Naturalis, 1:105
Historians and the American West, 3:515
The Historian's Craft, 3:9
Historians' Fallacies: Toward a Logic of Historical Thought, 3:9, 3:276
Historian's Guide to Statistics, 3:8

The Historian's Handbook: A Descriptive Guide to Reference Works, 3:8, 3:507
Historical Abstracts, 3:8
Historical Americans: Books from Which Our Early History Is Written, 3:511
Historical Analysis in Geography, 3:273
Historical and Critical Dictionary: Selections, 4:166
Historical and Cultural Dictionaries of Asia, 3:462
Historical and Cultural Dictionary of India, 3:483
Historical and Political Essays, 3:405
The Historical Anthropology of Early Modern Italy, 2:400
Historical Atlas of Africa, 3:415
Historical Atlas of Britain, 3:354
Historical Atlas of Canada, 3:605
Historical Atlas of Crystallography, 5:628
Historical Atlas of Religion in America, 4:751
A Historical Atlas of South Asia, 3:482
A Historical Atlas of the Indian Peninsula, 3:483
A Historical Atlas of the Jewish People, 4:593
Historical Atlas of the Religions of the World, 4:4
Historical Background of Chemistry, 5:728
A Historical Commentary on Polybius, 3:319
A Historical Commentary on Thucydides, 3:323
Historical Criticism and Meaning of Texts, 1:713
Historical Criticism and Theological Interpretation of Scripture, 4:815
The Historical Development of Quantum Theory, 5:708
The Historical Development of the Calculus, 5:30
Historical Dictionary of Australia, 3:494
Historical Dictionary of Bangladesh, 3:487
Historical Dictionary of Costa Rica, 3:635
Historical Dictionary of Data Processing Organizations, 5:539

Historical Dictionary of European Imperialism, 3:341

Historical Dictionary of Fascist Italy, 3:385

Historical Dictionary of Indonesia, 3:491

Historical Dictionary of Laos, 3:491

Historical Dictionary of Oceania, 3:495

Historical Dictionary of Pakistan, 3:487

Historical Dictionary of Singapore, 2:324, 3:492

Historical Dictionary of the Central African Republic, 3:421

Historical Dictionary of the French Fourth and Fifth Republics, 1946-1990, 3:373

Historical Dictionary of Tudor England, 1485-1603, 3:358

An Historical Essay on Modern Spain, 3:387

Historical Essays, 3:411

Historical Geography: A Methodological Portrayal, 3:272

Historical Geography of the United States and Canada, 3:510, 5:620

A Historical Grammar of Poetic Myth, 1:485

Historical Introduction to Modern Psychology, 3:167

Historical Introduction to Philosophy, 4:21

An Historical Introduction to the Philosophy of Science, 5:64

Historical Introduction to the Study of Roman Law, 3:306

Historical Materialism and the Economics of Karl Marx, 3:284

Historical Metaphors and Mythical Realities, 3:495

The Historical Method of Herodotus, 3:316

The Historical Novel, 2:801

Historical Periodicals Directory, 3:272

Historical Register, 1:244

Historical Sets, Collected Editions, and Monuments of Music, 3:655

Historical Statistics of Canada, 3:605

Historical Statistics of U.S. Bureau of the Census, 1:109

Historical Tradition in the Fourth Gospel, 4:833

Historical Treatises, Abstracts and Papers on Stereotyping, 1:17

Historicism, the Holocaust, and Zionism, 4:646

Historicism and Knowledge, 1:1131

Historic Preservation: Curatorial Management of the Built World, 3:762

Historic U.S. Court Cases, 1690-1990: An Encyclopedia, 3:508

The Histories (Herodotus), 3:315, 3:316, 4:480

Histories (Polybius), 3:319

Histories (Sallust), 3:320

The Histories (Tacitus), 3:321

The Histories of Polybius, 2:347

Historiography, 3:8

The History (Herodotus), 3:316, 4:480

History (Lowell), 1:1006

History: A Novel, 2:429

History: Written and Lived, 4:339

History, Civilization and Culture, 3:240

History, Culture and Religion of the Hellenistic Age, 4:449, 4:807

History, Man, and Reason: A Study in Nineteenth-Century Thought, 4:162

The History and Adventures of an Atom, 1:256

History and American Society: The Essays of David Potter, 3:593

The History and Character of Calvinism, 4:762

History and Class Consciousness, 4:162

History and Communications, 3:622

History and Development of Human Genetics, 5:778

History and Literature of Early Christianity, 4:816

History and Magical Power in a Chinese Community, 4:531

The History and Management of Ocean Warfare, 3:288

The History and Philosophy of Technology, 5:70, 5:251

The History and Philosophy of the Metaphysical Movements in America, 4:841

The History and Present State of Discoveries Relating to Vision, Light and Colours, 5:753

The History and Present State of Electricity, with Original Experiments, 5:753

History and Prophecy: Oswald Spengler and the Decline of the West, 3:291

History and Root of the Principle of the Conservation of Energy, 5:700

History and System: Hegel's Philosophy of History, 3:285

The History and Technique of Lettering, 1:18

History and the Contemporary: Essays in Nineteenth-Century Literature, 1:723

History and the Homeric Iliad, 2:362

The History and Theology of Soka Gakkai: A Japanese New Religion, 4:541

A History and Theory of Informed Consent, 5:132

History and the Prism of Art: Browning's Poetic Experiments, 1:339

History and Truth, 4:319

History and Will: Philosophical Perspectives of Mao Tse-tung's Thought, 4:362

History as Art and as Science: Twin Vistas on the Past, 3:276

History as a System, 4:314, 5:96

History as High Adventure, 3:600

History as Romantic Art: Bancroft, Prescott, Motley, and Parkman, 1:660

History Begins at Sumer: Thirty-Nine Firsts in Man's Recorded History, 4:441

History in Ovid, 2:390

The History Man, 1:448

The History of Aesthetics as the Science of Expression, 3:284

The History of Africa (Fage), 3:417

A History of Africa (Gailey), 3:417

History of Africa (Shillington), 3:416

The History of Africa in
Maps, 3:416
The History of African-Americans in the Military, 3:554
A History of Afro-American
Literature, Vol. 1,
1746–1895, 1:714
History of Agricultural Education in the United States
1785–1925, 5:264
The History of a Hoax, 1:36
History of American Ecology:
An Original Anthology,
3:549
A History of American Literature, 1:630
A History of American Literature Since 1870, 1:715
A History of American Magazines, 1:715
A History of American Philosophy, 4:35
A History of American Physical Anthropology,
1930–1980, 3:11
The History of American Political Theories, 3:162
The History of American
Presidential Elections,
3:597
The History of American
Wars from 1745 to 1918,
3:547
History of Analytical Chemistry, 5:735
History of an Argentine Passion, 2:870
History of Ancient Egypt,
3:445
History of Ancient Greek Literature, 2:347
A History of Ancient Israel
and Judah, 4:806
A History of Ancient Mathematical Astronomy, 5:38
A History of Ancient Philosophy, 4:46
History of Ancient Western
Philosophy, 4:46
The History of Anthropology:
A Research Bibliography,
3:11
A History of Archaeological
Thought, 3:13
A History of Architecture:
Settings and Rituals, 3:762
History of Architecture,
3:761
History of Art, 3:757
History of a Staircase, 2:531
A History of Astronomy, 5:32

The History of Astronomy
from Herschel to Hertzsprung, 5:31
A History of Astronomy from
Thales to Kepler, 5:31
The History of a Town; Or,
The Chronicle of Foolov,
2:755
History of Auricular Confession and Indulgences in
the Latin Church, 4:699
History of Australia, 3:494
A History of Australian Literature, 2:946
The History of Bel Canto,
3:672
A History of Biology: A General Introduction to the
Study of Living Things,
5:34
The History of Biology: An
Annotated Bibliography,
5:29
The History of Biology: A
Survey, 5:34
History of Bohemian Literature, 2:789
The History of Bookbinding
525–1950 A.D., 1:23
The History of Bookbinding
and Design, 1:24
A History of Book Illustration, 1:28
A History of Book Publishing
in the United States, 1:38
A History of Book Publishing
in the United States: Volume 1, 1:630
The History of Books: A
Guide to Selected Resources in the Library of
Congress, 1:63
A History of Booksellers:
The Old and the New,
1:36
History of Brazil, 1:304,
3:634
A History of British Trade
Unionism, 3:356
A History of Broadcasting in
the United States, 3:810
The History of Bronze Age,
Greek and Roman Technology, 3:304
A History of Buddhist Philosophy: Continuities and
Discontinuities, 4:513
A History of Bulgarian Literature, 2:781
The History of Caliph Vathek, 1:269
A History of Canadian Literature, 2:904, 2:923

The History of Cardiac Surgery 1896–1955, 5:374
History of Cartography, 5:619
History of Central Africa,
3:419
The History of Chemical
Technology: An Annotated
Bibliography, 5:29
The History of Chemistry
(Hudson), 5:728
A History of Chemistry (Partington), 5:32, 5:729
A History of Chinese Civilization, 4:358
A History of Chinese Philosophy, 4:358, 4:359
The History of Christian
Doctrine, 4:677
History of Christian Ethics:
From the New Testament
to Augustine, 4:688
A History of Christianity,
4:677, 4:720
History of Christianity,
1650–1950: Secularization
of the West, 4:739
A History of Christianity in
Asia, 4:677
A History of Christianity in
India 1707–1858, 4:508
A History of Christianity in
the World, 4:677, 4:720
History of Christian Philosophy in the Middle Ages,
4:94, 4:126, 4:696, 4:721
History of Christian Spirituality, 4:676
A History of Christian Theology: An Introduction,
4:719
A History of Christian
Thought (González), 4:677,
4:718
A History of Christian
Thought (Tillich), 4:678
The History of Civil Engineering since 1600, 5:29
A History of Classical Malay
Literature, 2:324
The History of Classical
Physics: A Selected, Annotated Bibliography, 5:28
A History of Classical Scholarship, 2:402
A History of Clinical Psychology, 5:35, 5:423
History of Comparative Anatomy: From Aristotle to the
18th Century, 5:33
A History of Computing in
the Twentieth Century,
5:543

A History of Computing in the Twentieth Century: A Collection of Essays, 5:49

A History of Computing Technology, 5:37

The History of Conversion and Contemporary Cults, 4:858

A History of Cynicism from Diogenes to the Sixth Century A.D., 4:55

A History of Dance, 3:731

History of Danish Literature (Mitchell), 2:645

A History of Danish Literature (Rossel), 2:645

The History of Decorated Bookbinding in England, 1:25

The History of Deposit Banking in Mediterranean Europe, 5:57

The History of Doctor Johann Faustus, 2:565

History of Dogma, 4:95, 4:677

A History of Early Christian Literature, 4:690

A History of Early Nineteenth-Century Drama, 1800–1850, 1:323

History of Early Russian Literature, 2:686

History of East Africa, 3:422

History of Eastern Christianity, 4:676

History of Economic Analysis, 3:46, 3:104, 3:105

A History of Economic Thought (Bell), 3:45

A History of Economic Thought (Roll), 3:46

History of Education in Antiquity, 2:347, 3:306

The History of Egypt, 3:419

A History of Egypt under the Ptolemaic Dynasty, 3:418

A History of Eighteenth Century Russian Literature, 2:685

A History of Embryology, 5:34

A History of Endocrinology, 5:34

The History of Engineering Science: An Annotated Bibliography, 5:27

History of England, 1:324

History of England: From the Invasion of Julius Caesar to the Revolution of 1688, 4:201

History of England from the Accession of James II, 3:406

The History of England from the Fall of Wolsey to the Defeat of the Spanish Armada, 3:402, 3:403

History of England from the Roman Invasion to the Glorious Revolution, 4:199

History of England in the Eighteenth Century, 3:405

A History of English Craft Bookbinding Technique, 1:25

A History of English Drama, 1660–1900, 1:272

History of English Local Government, 3:113

A History of English Romanticism in the Eighteenth Century, 1:267

History of European Liberalism, 3:340

History of European Morals from Augustus to Charlemagne, 3:405

A History of European Printing, 1:7

A History of European Socialism, 3:326, 3:341

A History of European Thought in the Nineteenth Century, 4:162, 5:47

A History of Experimental Psychology, 3:167, 5:34, 5.413

A History of Exploration from the Earliest Times to the Present Day, 3:894

The History of Fanny Burney, 1:235

A History of Far Eastern Art, 3:759

A History of Finnish Literature, 2:657

History of Florence, 4:144

The History of Folklore in Europe, 3:854

A History of Food, 5:264

History of France, 3:372

A History of French Dramatic Literature in the Seventeenth Century, 2:447

A History of French Literature, 2:446

A History of Geology, 5:617

A History of German Literature, 2:566

History of German Literature as Determined by Social Forces, 2:565

A History of Gnosticism, 4:60, 4:685

A History of Greece, 3:393

A History of Greece to 322 B.C., 3:302

History of Greek Culture, 3:400

History of Greek Literature (Hadas), 2:345

A History of Greek Literature (Lesky), 2:346

A History of Greek Mathematics, 5:38

A History of Greek Philosophy, 2:345, 4:46

A History of Greek Religion, 4:486

History of Harlequin, 1:271

A History of Historical Writing, 3:277

History of Humanism, 4:131

A History of Hungarian Literature, 2:798

The History of Hungary after the Second World War, 1944–1948, 3:389

A History of Icelandic Literature, 2:640

History of Icelandic Prose Writers, 2:640

History of Illustrated Manuscripts, 3:766

The History of Impressionism, 3:760

History of Indian and Indonesian Art, 3:759

A History of Indian Buddhism: From Sakyamuni to Early Mahayana, 4:512

History of Indian Buddhism: From the Origins to the Saka Era, 4:513

A History of Indian Philosophy, 4:351, 4:498

History of Indonesia in the Twentieth Century, 3:491

The History of Invention: From Stone Axes to Silicon Chips, 5:27

History of Iranian Literature, 2:83

History of Ireland in the Eighteenth Century, 3:405

The History of Islam, 4:572

A History of Islamic Philosophy, 4:16, 4:97, 4:574

A History of Islamic Societies, 3:436

A History of Israel, 4:806

The History of Israel: Biblical History, 4:836

A History of Israel: From the Rise of Zionism to Our Time, 3:440, 4:643

A History of Israel from Alexander the Great to Bar Kochba, 4:604

A History of Italian Literature (Donadoni), 2:401, 2:402

History of Italian Literature (Wilkins), 2:419

History of Italian Renaissance Art: Painting, Sculpture, Architecture, 3:759

A History of Japan, 3:476

A History of Japan, 1334–1615, 3:501

A History of Japan, 1615–1867, 3:501

A History of Japanese Literature, 2:271, 2:272, 2:282

History of Japanese Religion, 4:534

History of Japan's Ethical Thought, 4:367

A History of Japan to 1334, 3:501

A History of Jewish Art, 4:597

A History of Jewish Literature, 2:9, 2:32, 2:33, 4:601

A History of Jewish Philosophy in the Middle Ages, 4:629

A History of Judaism, 4:595

The History of King Richard III and Selections from the English and Latin Poems, 1:194

A History of Knowledge: Past, Present, and Future, 4:2

History of Korea, 3:481

History of Labor in the United States, 3:60, 3:73

A History of Late Nineteenth-Century Drama, 1850–1900, 1:323

A History of Latin Literature, 2:381

A History of Lettering: Creative Experiment and Letter Identity, 1:15

A History of Literary Criticism in the Italian Renaissance, 2:402

A History of Magic and Experimental Science, 4:131, 5:26

A History of Malaysia, 3:492

A History of Malaysia, Singapore, and Brunei, 3:492

The History of Marxism, 4:242

History of Mathematical Notations, 5:30

A History of Mathematics (Boyer), 5:30, 5:491

A History of Mathematics (Katz), 5:31

A History of Mathematics. An Introduction, 5:492

The History of Mathematics: A Reader, 5:30

The History of Mathematics from Antiquity to the Present, 5:28, 5:491

A History of Mathematics in America before Nineteen Hundred, 5:31

A History of Mechanical Inventions, 5:57

A History of Mediaeval Jewish Philosophy, 4:629

A History of Medical Psychology, 5:415

A History of Medicine (Castiglioni), 5:35

A History of Medicine (Sigerist), 5:36

A History of Medieval Philosophy, 4:39, 4:94

A History of Medieval Spain, 3:387

A History of Melbourne's Hebrew Congregation, 4:644

The History of Metal Mining and Metallurgy: An Annotated Bibliography, 5:29

The History of Meteorology and Geophysics: An Annotated Bibliography, 5:27

The History of Mister Polly, 1:563

History of Modern Architecture, 3:762

History of Modern Art: Painting, Sculpture, Architecture, Photography, 3:758

The History of Modern Astronomy and Astrophysics, 5:28

History of Modern Bulgarian Literature, 2:780

A History of Modern Burma, 3:489

A History of Modern Chinese Fiction, 2:233

A History of Modern Criticism, 1750–1950, 1:430

History of Modern Criticism Series, 1700–1950, 1:135

A History of Modern France, 2:446

History of Modern Furniture, 3:766

The History of Modern Geography, 5:28, 5:620

A History of Modern Germany, 3:377

History of Modern Greek Literature (Dimaras), 2:371

A History of Modern Greek Literature (Politis), 2:371

A History of Modern Hungary, 1867–1986, 3:390

History of Modern India 1919–1982, 3:486

A History of Modern Jewry, 4:634

A History of Modern Philosophy, 4:161

The History of Modern Physics: An International Bibliography, 5:27

A History of Modern Poetry, 1:417, 1:719, 1:799

History of Modern Psychology, 3:167

The History of Modern Science, 5:27

A History of Modern Tibet, 1913–1951, 4:543

A History of Musical Style, 3:659

A History of Music in Canada, 1534–1914, 3:609

History of My Contemporary, 2:732

History of My Heart, 1:1030

A History of My Times, 3:324

A History of Nazi Germany, 3:376

History of Neurology, 5:50

A History of News, 3:809

History of New Testament Times, 4:605

History of New York, 1:679, 1:680

A History of Niger, 1850–1960, 3:418

History of Nineteenth-Century Russian Literature, 2:685

A History of Norway, 4:730

A History of Norwegian Literature, 2:662

A History of Old English Meter, 1:142

A History of Ornament: Ancient and Medieval, 3:765

A History of Orthodox Theology since 1453, 4:756

A History of Ottoman Poetry. Gibb Memorial, 1963–1984, 2:96

A History of Painting in Italy, Umbria, Florence, and Siena from the Second to the Sixteenth Century, 3:759

A History of Paper-Manufacturing in the United States, 1690–1916, 1:6

A History of Pentateuchal Traditions, 4:823, 4:836

A History of Persia, 3:449

A History of Persia under Quajar Rule, 3:448

A History of Philosophical Ideas in America, 4:36

History of Philosophical Systems, 4:16

History of Philosophy (Bréhier), 4:16, 4:159

History of Philosophy (Copleston), 4:2, 4:39, 4:94, 4:676

History of Philosophy (Marias), 4:162

A History of Philosophy (Ueberweg), 4:18, 4:163

History of Philosophy: Eastern and Western, 4:350

A History of Philosophy: From Bolzano to Wittgenstein, 4:268

History of Philosophy: Late Medieval and Renaissance Philosophy, 4:125

A History of Philosophy: With Especial Reference to the Formation and Development of Its Problems and Conceptions, 4:163

History of Philosophy and Philosophical Education, 4:286

A History of Philosophy in America, 4:160

History of Philosophy in Islam (De Boer), 4:373

The History of Philosophy in Islam (Fakry), 4:567

History of Photography: From 1839 to the Present, 3:760

History of Physiology, 5:34

History of Plymouth Plantation, 1:633

A History of Poliomyelitis, 5:390

A History of Polish Literature (Krzyzanowski), 2:811

The History of Polish Literature (Miłosz), 2:811

A History of Political Parties in the Province of New York, 1760–1776, 3:567

A History of Postwar Britain, 1945–74, 3:365

A History of Post-War Soviet Writing: The Literature of Moral Opposition, 2:691

The History of Printing in America, 1:11

A History of Printing Ink, Balls and Rollers 1440–1850, 1:21

A History of Probability and Statistics and Their Applications before 1750, 5:526

History of Programming Languages, 5:551

History of Psychology (Hothersall), 5:35

A History of Psychology (Leahey), 5:35

History of Psychology and Psychiatry, 5:423

A History of Psychology in Autobiography, 3:167

History of Psychotherapy: A Century of Change, 5:413

A History of Public Health, 5:36

The History of Pugachev, 2:751

The History of Quantum Mechanics and the Bohr-Pauli Dialogue, 5:661

History of Rasselas, Prince of Abissinia, 1:249

A History of Religion East and West: An Introduction and Interpretation, 4:571

History of Religions: Essays on the Problem of Understanding, 4:570

A History of Religious Ideas, 4:2, 4:473, 4:497, 4:524, 4:547

The History of Reynard the Fo, 2:629

History of Rocketry and Space Travel, 5:37

A History of Rome (Cary), 2:380, 3:303

History of Rome (Livy), 3:317

A History of Russia (Kliuchevskii), 3:394

A History of Russia (Riasanousky), 3:395

A History of Russia: Ancient Russia, 3:413

A History of Russian Jewish Literature, 2:688

A History of Russian Literature, 2:691

History of Russian Literature: From Its Beginnings to 1900, 2:689

History of Russian Literature from the Eleventh Century to the End of the Baroque, 2:685

A History of Russian Literature of the Romantic Period, 2:685

The History of Russian Philosophy, 4:31, 4:161

The History of St. Giles and St. James, 1:366

A History of Scandinavia, 3:380

A History of Scandinavian Literature: 1870 to 1980, 2:638

The History of Scepticism from Erasmus to Spinoza, 4:130, 4:162, 5:40

A History of Science, 5:25

A History of Science, Technology and Philosophy in the Sixteenth and Seventeenth Centuries, 4:132, 5:43

The History of Science and Technology: A Select Bibliography, 3:273

The History of Science and Technology in the United States, 5:29

The History of Science and the New Humanism, 5:56

The History of Science in the Eighteenth Century, 5:45

A History of Scientific Psychology, 5:35

History of Scotland, 3:882

The History of Scurvy and Vitamin C, 5:394

History of Seventeenth Century Russian Literature, 2:685

A History of Sexuality, 2:477, 4:400

The History of Sexuality An Introduction, Volume 1, 1:1181, 3:208, 3:326, 5:87

The Care of the Self, Volume 3, 3:208

The Uses of Pleasure, Volume 2, 3:208

A History of Sierra Leone, 3:420

The History of Sir Charles Grandison, 1:253

A History of Social Democracy in Postwar Europe, 3:346

A History of Socialist Thought, 3:140

The History of Solid State Physics, 5:669

A History of South Africa, 3:424

A History of South Africa: Social and Economic, 3:423

A History of South Africa to 1870, 3:424

A History of South-East Asia, 3:489

History of Southern Africa, 3:424

The History of Southern Literature, 1:652, 1:716

History of Soviet Literature, 2:684

A History of Spain and Portugal, 3:387

A History of Spain Founded on the Historia de España y de la Civilización Española of Rafael Altamira, 3:386

A History of Spanish Golden Age Drama: Studies in Romance Languages, 2:524

A History of Sparta 950–192 B.C., 3:302

The History of Spiritualism, 4:850

The History of Statistics: The Measurement of Uncertainty before 1900, 5:524, 5:526

The History of Statistics in the 17th and 18th Centuries against the Changing Background of Intellectual, Scientific and Religious Thought, 5:526

A History of Surrealism, 2:447

A History of Sweden, 3:382

A History of Swedish Literature, 2:671

A History of Switzerland, 3:378

History of Switzerland: From before the Beginnings to the Days of the Present, 3:378

A History of Technology, 5:26

A History of Technology and Invention: Progress through the Ages, 5:25

A History of the African People, 3:417

A History of the Alphabet, 1:14

The History of the American Aircraft Industry, 5:219

A History of the American Constitution, 3:141

A History of the American Drama: From the Beginning to the Civil War, 1:629, 1:1075

A History of the American Drama: From the Civil War to the Present Day, 1:1075

A History of the American Film, 1:1087

A History of the American People, 3:514

History of the American Theatre, 1700–1950, 1:1073

The History of the American Theatre and Anecdotes of the Principal Actors, 1:1072

History of the Americas, 3:643

A History of the Ancient World, 3:299

A History of the Arab Peoples, 3:436, 3:457

History of the Arabs, 3:436, 3:457, 4:569

History of the Balkan Peoples, 3:392

History of the Balkans from Mohammed the Conquerer to Stalin, 3:391

History of the Bank of New York and Trust Company, 1784–1934, 3:591

The History of the Barometer, 5:33

History of the Bible in English, 4:797

The History of the Calculus and Its Conceptual Development, 5:30

History of the Calculus of Variations in the Nineteenth Century, 5:31

A History of the Canadian Economy, 3:607

A History of the Christian Church, 4:678, 4:720

History of the Christian Church in Canada, 3:610

The History of the Church (Jedin), 4:677, 4:720

History of the Church (Smith), 4:879

A History of the Church in Latin America: Colonialism to Liberation, 4:748

A History of the Church to A.D. 461, 4:681

History of the Concept of Time: Prolegomena, 4:291

History of the Conquest of Mexico, 1:694

History of the Conquest of Mexico and History of the Conquest of Peru, 1:694, 3:649

History of the Conquest of Peru, 1:694

History of the Conspiracy of Pontiac, 1:690, 3:592

History of the Contemporary Jews from 1900 to the Present, 4:634

A History of the Council of Trent, 4:729

A History of the Councils of the Church from the Original Documents, 4:677

History of the Crusades, 4:694

History of the Dance in Art and Education, 3:732

A History of the Early Church, 4:682

History of the Early Church from A.D. 500, 4:682

The History of the Earth's Crust, 5:629

A History of the Ecumenical Movement, 1517–1948, 4:746

A History of the English Novel, 1:269, 1:318, 1:420

A History of the English-Speaking Peoples, 3:400

History of the Episcopal Church in America, 1607–1991, 4:719

The History of the Family at Borg, 2:641

History of the First World War, 3:279

A History of the Gambia, 3:420

The History of the Greek and Roman Theater, 2:344

A History of the Greek World: 323–146 B.C., 2:344

A History of the Guyanese Working People 1881–1905, 3:431

The History of the Health Care Sciences and Health Care, 1700–1980, 5:28

A History of the Human Community, 3:289

The History of the Illustrated Book: The Western Tradition, 1:28, 3:766

The History of the Incas, 3:628

History of the Indians of Connecticut, 1:744

A History of the Indians of the United States, 3:554

History of the Inductive Sciences, 4:257, 4:258, 5:57

A History of Their Own, 3:325

History of the Islamic Peoples, 4:568

History of the Italian People, 2:419

A History of the Jewish People (Ben-Sasson), 4:593

History of the Jewish People (Margolis and Marx), 4:594

A History of the Jewish People in the Age of Jesus Christ (175B.C.–135 A.D.), 4:808

The History of the Jewish People in the Age of Jesus Christ: A New English Edition, 4:605

A History of the Jews, 4:594

A History of the Jews: From Earliest Times through the Six-Day War, 4:594

A History of the Jews in Babylonia, 4:605

History of the Jews in Christian Spain, 4:623

A History of the Jews in England, 4:624

History of the Jews in Russia and Poland from the Earliest Times until the Present Day, 2:30

A History of the Jews in Venice, 4:624

A History of the Jews of Italy, 4:624

A History of the Jews of Tangier in the Nineteenth and Twentieth Centuries, 4:645

History of the Kings of Britain, 1:145

A History of the Later Roman Empire, 2:380

History of the Life and Voyages of Christopher Columbus, 1:679, 1:680

A History of the Maghrib, 3:418

The History of the Maghrib: An Interpretive Essay, 4:571

A History of the Marranos, 4:624

History of the Medieval Church, 590–1500, 4:691

The History of the Microscope, 5:33

A History of the Modern World, 3:274, 3:327

The History of the Navy of the United States of America, 1:664

The History of the Negro Race in America from 1619 to 1880, 3:514

A History of the Nonesuch Press, 1:43

History of the Norwegian People, 3:381

A History of the Old English Letter Foundries, 1:19

The History of the Order of Assassins, 4:569

A History of Theory of Informed Consent, 5:120

History of the Ottoman Empire and Modern Turkey, 3:453

History of the Persian Wars, 4:480

A History of the Physical Sciences since Antiquity, 5:31

The History of the Primitive Church, 4:681

The History of the Psychoanalytic Movement, 5:446

The History of the Reformation in Scotland, 4:735

History of the Reign of Ferdinand and Isabella the Catholic, 1:694

History of the Rise of the Huguenots of France, 4:731

A History of the Romanians, 3:390

History of the Roman World 753–146 B.C., 3:303

History of the Russian Revolution, 3:294, 3:397

History of the Russian State, 2:730

A History of the Sciences, 5:26

History of the Second World War, 3:279

A History of the Sikhs, 4:517

History of the Southern Luo, 3:422

The History of the Standard Oil Company, 3:823

A History of the Sudan, 3:419

A History of the Swedish People, 2:679

The History of the Synoptic Tradition, 4:824, 4:830, 4:831

The History of the Telescope, 5:32

The History of the Theory of the Beautiful, 3:284

A History of the Thermometer and Its Use in Meteorology, 5:33

History of the Transmission of Ancient Books to Modern Times, 1:37

A History of the Unification Church in the San Francisco Bay Area, 1960–1974, 4:871

History of the United States during the Administrations of Jefferson and Madison, 3:562

History of the United States from the Compromise of 1850 to the McKinley-Bryan Campaign of 1896, 3:514

History of the United States of America: A Guide to Information Sources, 3:510

A History of the Upper Guinea Coast, 1545–1800, 3:421, 3:431

A History of the Vikings, 2:640

History of the War in the Crimea, 3:925

A History of the Weimar Republic, 3:376

A History of the Work of Redemption, 1:637

A History of the World's Great Religions, 4:2

History of the Yiddish Language, 2:32

The History of Tom Jones, a Foundling, 1:245

The History of Trade Unionism, 3:55, 3:112, 3:113

The History of Turkish Literature, 2:95

A History of Twelfth-Century Western Philosophy, 4:16, 4:94

A History of Ukrainian Literature from the 11th to the End of the 19th Century, 2:838

A History of Unitarianism, 4:724

History of United States Naval Operations in World War II, 1939–1945, 3:589
History of U.S. Political Parties, 3:543
History of Violin Playing, from Its Origins to 1761 and Its Relationship to the Violin and Violin Music, 3:671
History of West Africa, 3:419, 3:425
A History of West Africa: An Introductory Survey, 3:420
A History of West Africa, 1000–1800, 3:428
A History of Western Education, 3:253
The History of Western Instruments, 3:672
A History of Western Music, 3:660
A History of Western Philosophy (Hamlyn), 4:16
A History of Western Philosophy (Jones), 4:17, 4:46
A History of Western Philosophy (Russell), 4:18, 4:162, 4:322
History of Western Technology, 5:37
A History of Witchcraft: Sorcerers, Heretics and Pagans, 4:700
A History of Women Philosophers, 4:163
History of World Exploration, 3:274
A History of World Societies, 3:274
A History of World Theater, 2:3
A History of Yiddish Literature, 2:32
The History of Yiddish Literature in the Nineteenth Century, 2:33
A History of Yugoslav Literature, 2:785, 2:827, 2:835
A History of Zen Buddhism, 4:537
A History of Zionism, 3:349, 4:658
History of Zionism, 1600–1918, 3:351
A History of Zoroastrianism, 4:444, 4:547
The History Plays: Plenty, Knuckle, and Licking Hitler, 1:493
History Remembered, Recovered, Invented, 3:276

Hist Whist and Other Poems for Children, 1:825
His Very Self and Voice: Collected Conversations of Lord Byron, 1:283
His Way: The Unauthorized Biography of Frank Sinatra, 3:719
Hitchcock, 1:1170, 3:843
Hitchcock: The First Forty-Four Films, 1:1169
Hitchcock: The Murderous Gaze, 1:1169
A Hitchcock Reader, 1:1169
Hitchcock's British Films, 1:1170
Hitchcock's Films, 1:1170
The Hitch-Hikers, 1:895
Hitler: A Study in Tyranny, 3:376, 3:399
Hitler: The Führer and the People, 3:345, 3:378
Hitler, Germans, and the "Jewish Question," 4:636
Hitler, the Germans and the Jews, 1:513
Hitler and Stalin: Parallel Lives, 3:292, 3:344, 3:399
Hitler Dances, 1:450
Hitler's Madman, 1:1175
Hitler's Social Revolution, 3:377
The Hittite Must Die, 2:24
Hittite Myths, 4:545
The Hittites, 3:300, 4:445
The Hittites and Their Contemporaries in Asia Minor, 4:445
The Hittite State Cult of the Tutelary Deities, 4:445
The Hive, 2:533, 2:534
The Hive of the Bee-Hunter: A Repository of Sketches (1854), 1:702
H.L.M.—The Mencken Bibliography, 1:860
H. L. Mencken, 1:859, 1:860
H. L. Mencken: Critic of American Life, 1:859
H. L. Mencken and the American Mercury Adventure, 1:860
Ho, 2:340
Hobbes (Peters), 4:174
Hobbes (Sorrell), 4:175
Hobbes (Stephen), 4:175
Hobbes (Tuck), 4:175
Hobbes: Morals and Politics, 4:174
Hobbes and His Critics, 3:154

Hobbes and Locke: The Politics of Freedom and Obligation, 3:154, 4:175, 4:181
Hobbes and the Social Contract Tradition, 4:174
Hobbes on Civil Association, 4:174
Hobbes's Science of Politics, 4:174
Hobbes's System of Ideas, 4:175
Hobbes Studies, 4:174
Hobbes Studies Bibliography: 1879–1979, 4:175
Hobbes to Hume, 4:161
The Hobbit, 1:559, 1:578, 1:589, 4:776
The Hobbit and The Lord of the Rings, 1:589
Ho Chi Minh: A Political Biography, 2:340
A Hodge-Podge of the Letters, Papers and Addresses Written during the Last Sixty Years, 1:10
Hoffman's Index to Poetry, 1:125
Hofmannsthal: Three Essays, 2:593
Hofmeyr, 3:424
The Hofstadter Aegis, a Memorial, 3:583
Hog on Ice and Other Curious Expressions, 1:96
Hogs in the Bottoms: Family Folklore in Arkansas, 3:861
Hölderlin Bicentennial Symposium, 2:593
Hölderlin's Major Poetry: The Dialectics of Unity, 2:594
Hölderlin's Silence, 2:594
The Holdup, 1:1105
Hold Your Tongue: Bilingualism and the Politics of "English Only," 3:249
A Hole Is to Dig, 1:1206
Holiday (Barry), 1:1085, 1:1086
The Holiday (Smith), 1:549
Holidays and Anniversaries of the World, 1:88
Holiness and Justice: An Interpretation of Plato's "Euthyphro," 4:84
Holiness and the Will of God, 4:714
Holiness of Life, 4:113
The Holistic Health Lifebook, 5:319
The Holistic Health Movement, 5:12

Holistic Medicine: Harmony of Body, Mind, Spirit, 5:319

Holland's Guide to Psychoanalytic Psychology and Literature-and-Psychology, 2:989

The Hollow Earth: The Greatest Geographical Discovery in History, 3:915

Hollywood, 1:1061, 1:1062

Hollywood Auteur: Francis Coppola, 3:828

Hollywood Genres: Formulas, Filmmaking, and the Studio System, 1:1158

Hollywood Scapegoat: The Biography of Erich von Stroheim, 1:1177

Holmes-Laski Letters, 3:156

Holmes of the Breakfast-Table, 1:678

The Holocaust: A History of the Jews of Europe during the Second World War, 4:636

The Holocaust: An Annotated Bibliography and Resource Guide, 4:7

The Holocaust: Ideology, Bureaucracy and Genocide, 3:348

The Holocaust: The Fate of European Jewry, 1932–1945, 3:351

The Holocaust, Israel, and the Jews, 4:636

The Holocaust in Historical Perspective, 4:635

The Holocaust in Yiddish Literature, 2:32

A Holocaust Reader, 3:348, 4:635

Holy Anorexia, 4:698

The Holy Bible: King James Version, 4:797

The Holy Bible: New International Version, Containing the Old Testament and New Testament, 4:797

The Holy Bible: The New Revised Standard Version, 4:797

Holy Days: The World of a Hasidic Family, 4:632

Holy Days and Holidays: The Medieval Pilgrimage to Compostela, 4:698

The Holy Earth, 5:787

The Holy Family of Father Moon, 4:871

Holy Feast and Holy Fast, 4:698

Holy Foolishness, 2:716

Holy Ghosts, 1:1099

Holy Ghosts: The Male Muses of Emily and Charlotte Brontë, 1:334

The Holy Land, 2:675, 2:676

The Holy Land: An Archaeological Guide from Earliest Times to 1700, 4:809

The Holy Land from the Persian to the Arab Conquests 536 B.C.–A.D. 640, 4:606

The Holy Roman Empire, 3:151

The Holy Scriptures According to the Masoretic Text, 4:801

The Holy Scriptures of the Old Testament: Hebrew and English, 4:794

The Holy Sinner, 2:586

The Holy Spirit, 4:685

Holy Terror: Inside the World of Islamic Terrorism, 4:580

The Holy Terrors, 2:469

The Holy War, 1:173, 1:174

Holy War in Ancient Israel, 4:838

The Holy War of Umar Tal, 3:419

Holy Warriors: The Abolitionists and American Slavery, 3:530

Holy Wars, 4:578

Holy Women of Russia, 4:756

Holy Writ or Holy Church: The Crisis of the Protestant Reformation, 4:697

The Holy Year of Jubilee, 4:701

Homage to Clio, 1:435

Homage to Daniel Shays: Collected Essays, 1952–1972, 1:1062

Homage to Galileo, 4:172

Homage to Georges Dumézil, 4:472

Homage to John Dryden, 1:241

Homage to Mistress Bradstreet and Other Poems, 1:950

Homage to the American Indians, 2:859

Homage to the Lame Wolf: Selected Poems 1956–1975, 2:832

Hombre, 1:1232

Hombre de Paso, Just Passing Through, 2:868

Home: Social Essays, 1:941

The Home Alternative to Hospitals and Nursing Homes, 5:376

The Home and the World, 2:182

Home as Found, 1:663

Home as Found: Authority and Genealogy in Nineteenth-Century American Literature, 1:652

Home at Grasmere: Part First, Book First, of "The Recluse," 1:306

Home before Dark: A Biographical Memoir of John Cheever, 1:961

Homebirth: The Essential Guide to Giving Birth Outside of the Hospital, 5:358

Home Book of Quotations: Classical and Modern, 1:117

Home Care for the Chronically Ill or Disabled Child, 5:322

The Homecoming (Pinter), 1:534

Homecoming (Sanchez), 1:1044

The Homecoming (Snow), 1:550

Homecoming at Twilight, 2:38

The Homecoming Game, 1:1021

Home Economics, 5:269

A Home for the Heart, 5:435

Home Free, 1:1121

Home Girls: A Black Feminist Anthology, 1:1184

Homegirls and Handgrenades, 1:1044

Home Ground, 2:973

Home Health Care: A Guide for Patients and Their Families, 5:377

The Home Health Care Solution: A Complete Consumer Guide, 5:377

Home Heath Care: Its Role in the Changing Health Services Market, 5:334

Home Is the Sailor, 2:891, 2:892

Home Is Where We Start From: Essays in Psychoanalysis, 5:472

The Homeless Imagination in the Fiction of Israel Joshua Singer, 2:49

The Homeless Mind: Modernization and Consciousness, 5:69
A Homemade World: The American Modernist Writers, 1:794
The Home of Man, 3:296
Home of the Gentry, 2:769
Homeopathy in America: The Rise and Fall of a Medical Heresy, 5:338
The Homeowner's Handbook of Solar Water Heating Systems, 5:289
The Home Place, 1:1017
The Home Plot: Women, Writing and Domestic Ritual, 1:724
Homer, 2:361, 2:362
Homer: Poet of the Iliad, 2:361, 4:483
Homer and Bible, 2:361
Homer and Mycenae, 2:362
Homer and the Epic, 2:361
Homer and the Heroic Tradition, 2:362
Homer and the Sacred City, 4:483
Homeric Hymns, 2:341, 2:359, 2:360, 4:482
Homer on Life and Death, 4:483
Homer's Odyssey, 2:361
Homer's Readers: A Historical Introduction to the Iliad and the Odyssey, 2:361
Homer's The Odyssey, 2:361
Homer the Theologian, 4:483
Homestead, 3:909
The Homesteader, 1:1172
Home Style: House Members in Their Districts, 3:146
Home to Harlem, 1:856
Home Truths, 2:911, 2:912
Homeward Bound; or, The Chase: A Tale of the Sea, 1:663
Homicide: A Screenplay, 1:1101
Homicide in American Fiction, 1798–1860: A Study in Social Values, 1:722
Homilies on Genesis, 4:707
Homilies on Psalms, 4:711
Homilies on Psalms and Other Texts, 4:711
Homo, Memento Finis, 1:157
Homo Faber, 2:579
Homo Hierarchicus: The Caste System, 4:503
Homo Hierarchicus: The Caste System and Its Implications, 3:19

Homo Ludens: A Study of the Play Element in Culture, 3:14
Homo Necans, 4:429, 4:470
Homonyms, "Sound Alikes," 1:94
Homosexual: Oppression and Liberation, 1:1181
The Homosexual in America: A Subjective Approach, 3:551
Homosexualities and French Literature, 2:448
Homosexualities and French Literature: Cultural Contexts/Critical Texts, 1:1184
Homosexuality, 3:208
Homosexuality: A Research Guide, 1:1128, 1:1181
Homosexuality: Power and Politics, 1:1184
Homosexuality: The Test Case for Christian Social Ethics, 4:894
Homosexuality and Religion and Philosophy, 4:894
Homosexuality and the Western Christian Tradition, 4:678
The Homosexual Tradition in American Poetry, 1:1182
Homo Viator: Introduction to a Metaphysic of Hope, 4:304
Hondo, 1:1216
Honduras: Portrait of a Captive Nation, 3:638
Honduras: The Making of a Banana Republic, 3:638
Honecker's Germany, 3:376
Honest Diplomat at the Hague: Private Letters, 1715–1716, 1:262
Honest John Vane, 1:744
The Honest Mind: The Thought and Work of Richard Price, 4:211
The Honest Rainmaker: The Life and Times of Colonel John Stingo, 3:814
Honest to God, 4:746
The Honest Whore, 1:176
Honeybee Ecology: A Study of Adaptation in Social Life, 5:771
The Honeycomb (Green), 1:1088
Honeycomb (Richardson), 1:541
Honey for the Bears, 1:453, 1:454
The Honeymoon, 2:663, 2:664

Honeymoon, Bittermoon, 2:546
The Honey Tree Song: Poems and Chants of Sarawak Dayaks, 2:325
Hong Kong, 3:904
Honkers and Shouters: The Golden Years of Rhythm and Blues, 3:666
The Honorable Beggars, 2:78
The Honorary Consul, 1:488
The Honorary Patron, 2:913
The Honor Plays of Lope de Vega, 2:555
The Honourable Schoolboy, 1:595
Hoogste Tijd, 2:628
Hooray for Yiddish, 2:32
Hoosier Folk Legends, 3:861
A Hoosier Holiday, 1:829
Hope: New Choices and Recovery Strategies for Adult Children of Alcoholics, 5:402
Hope Abandoned, 2:738
Hope against Hope, 2:738
Hope and Its Hieroglyph, 4:277
A Hope for Poetry, 1:511, 1:512
Hope Leslie, 1:695, 1:1209, 1:1219
Hope of Heaven, 1:866
The Hope of the Family, 1:347
Hopes and Impediments: Selected Essays, 2:128
Hopi Coyote Tales, 3:865
Hopitutuwutsi-Hopi Tales, 3:865
Hopkins: A Literary Biography, 1:365
Hopscotch, 2:861, 2:862
Horace, 2:386, 2:470
Horace and His Influence, 2:386
Horace and His Lyric Poetry, 2:386
Horace Chase, 1:790
Horace Liveright: Publisher of the Twenties, 1:42
Horace Mann, 3:265
Horace Mann: His Ideas and Ideals, 3:265
Horace Mann and the Common School Revival in the United States, 3:265
Horace's Compromise: The Dilemma of the American High School, 3:268
Horace's Poetic Journey: A Reading of Odes 1-3, 2:386

Horace's School: Redesigning the American High School, 3:268

Horace Walpole, 1:263

Horace Walpole: The Critical Heritage, 1:263, 1:604

Horace Walpole, Writer, Politician, and Connoisseur, 1:263

Horace Walpole's Memoirs, 1:263

Horeb: A Philosophy of Jewish Laws and Observances, 4:665

Horison, 2:316, 2:319

Hormones: The Messengers of Life, 5:772

Hormones and Human Behaviour, 5:340

Horn and Crescent, 3:423

Horologium Oscillatorium, 5:695

Horowitz: A Biography of Vladimir Horowitz, 3:701

Horrible Tango, 2:633

Horror: The One Hundred Best Books, 1:599

Horror Literature: A Reader's Guide, 1:599

Horsefeathers and Other Curious Words, 1:96

Horseman, Pass By, 1:1009, 1:1010

Horseman on the Roof, 2:481

The Horse of the Morning: A Life of Norman Washington Manley, 2:940

Horses, 5:639

The Horse's Mouth, 1:456

Horton Hatches the Egg, 1:1203

Horton Hears a Who, 1:1203

Hortus Cliffortianus, 5:805

Hortus Third, 5:787

The Hospice Alternative: A New Context for Death and Dying, 5:379

Hospice Care: Principles and Practice, 5:378

A Hospice Handbook, 5:378

The Hospice Handbook: A Complete Guide, 5:378

The Hospice Movement: Easing Death's Pains, 5:379

Hospice U.S.A., 5:379

The Hospice Way of Death, 5:378

The Hospital: A Social and Architectural History, 5:329

Hospitality and Travel Marketing, 3:890

Hospital Sketches, 1:1197, 1:1198

Hospital with a Heart, 5:313

The Hostage, 1:441

The Hostage Bride, 1:1220

Hosts and Guests, the Anthropology of Tourism, 3:891

The Hotel, 1:447

Hôtel du Lac, 1:451

The Hotel New Hampshire, 1:991

Hotel Universe, 1:1085, 1:1086

The Hot Gates, 1:483, 1:484

Hothouse, 1:1114

The Hot l Baltimore, 1:1120, 1:1121

The Hounds of Summer and Other Stories, 1:1008

The Hour and the Man, 1:375

Hourglass, 2:830

The Hour of Decision, 3:291

The Hour of the Lyn, 2:674

The Hour of the Star, 2:895

Hours of Idleness, 1:281

The House at Pooh Corner, 1:587, 1:588

The House behind the Cedars, 1:738, 1:739

Houseboat Days, 1:936

The Houseboy, 2:145

Housebreak House, 1:1178

The House by the Medlar Tree, 2:441

The House by the Sea, 2:131

House Divided: The Life and Legacy of Martin Luther King, 4:773

A House for Mr. Biswas, 2:938, 2:939

Household Words, 1:355

A House in Bali, 3:904

The House in Haarlem, 2:630

The House in Paris, 1:447

The House in the Sand, 2:874

House Made of Dawn, 1:1016, 1:1047

House of All Nations, 2:963

The House of Appleton, 1:39

The House of Atreus: Adapted from the Oresteia, 2:350

House of Babel, 2:675

The House of Bernarda Alba, 2:538

The House of Blue Leaves, 1:1089, 1:1090

A House of Children, 1:456

The House of Cobwebs, 1:359

The House of Connelly, 1:1088

The House of Fame, 1:149

House of Glass, 2:321

The House of Harper: One Hundred and Fifty Years of Publishing, 1:41

The House of Hunger, 2:165

House of Incest, 1:864, 1:865

The House of Intellect, 1:813, 1:814

The House of Islam, 4:568

The House of Life, 1:391

The House of Life: Rachel Carson at Work, 5:829

The House of Mirth, 1:786, 1:787

The House of Mirth: A Novel of Admonition, 1:788

The House of Morgan, 3:55

A House of Pomegranates, 1:409, 1:410

The House of Saud, 3:451

The House of Sleeping Beauties, 1:1095

The House of Stuart, 3:368

The House of the Dead, 2:713

House of the Liars, 2:428

The House of the Prophet, 1:937

The House of the Seven Gables, 1:674, 1:675

The House of the Solitary Maggot, 1:1034

The House of the Spirits, 2:851

The House of the Wolfings, 1:617

The House of Twilight, 2:309

The House of Warne: One Hundred Years of Publishing, 1:45

The House on Marshland, 1:982

The House on the Embankment, 2:767

The House on the Hill, 2:432

Houses, Villas and Palaces in the Roman World, 3:305

Houses without Doors, 1:1244

The House That Jack Built, 1:578, 1:580, 1:583

A House Undivided: Domesticity and Community in American Literature, 1:649

House upon the Sand, 2:806

The House with the Blind Glass Windows, 2:663

Housing America's Elderly, 3:201

Housman's Poems, 1:496

Hovering Fly and Other Essays, 1:889

The How and the Why, 5:10

How Animals See, 5:771

Howard Hawks, Storyteller, 3:838

Howard Nemerov, 1:1021

A Howard Nemerov Reader, 1:1021

Howard Pyle, 1:1205

Howard's End, 1:476

How Are Verses Made?, 2:739

How Brave a New World?: Dilemmas in Bioethics, 5:122

How Children Learn, 3:250

How Did We Find Out about Atoms?, 5:14

How Does Analysis Cure? Contributions to the Psychology of the Self, 5:457

How Do I Look: Queer Film and Video, 1:1158, 1:1184

How Do You Go to the Bathroom in Space?, 5:597

Howells: A Century of Criticism, 1:759

Howells: His Life and World, 1:759

Howells and the Age of Realism, 1:759

How Europe Underdeveloped Africa, 3:418, 3:430, 3:431

How Experiments End, 5:48, 5:153

How Far Can You Go?, 1:515

How Fast the Wind: Southern Africa, 1975–2000, 3:424

How Green Was My Valley (Ford), 1:1165

How Green Was My Valley (Llewelyn), 3:369

How I Found Livingstone, 3:930, 3:938

How Institutions Think, 3:28

How It Was in the War, 3:280

How Karl Barth Changed My Mind, 4:758

Howl, 1:980

Howl and Other Poems, 1:981

How Many Words Do You Want?, 3:808

How Movies Work, 3:827

How Much Is Enough? The Consumer Society and the Future of the Earth, 5:152

How New Will the Better World Be? A Discussion of Post-War Reconstruction, 3:567

How Nurses' Emotions Affect Patient Care: Self-Studies by Nurses, 5:337

How People Change, 5:414

How Plants Get Their Names, 5:787

How Prints Look: Photographs with a Commentary, 1:28

How Quaint the Ways of Paradox! 1:357

How the Church Can Minister to the World without Losing Itself, 5:200

How the Grinch Stole Christmas, 1:1203

How the Laws of Physics Lie, 5:67

How the North Won: A Military History of the Civil War, 3:528

How the Other Half Lives, 3:822

How the Swans Came to the Lake, 4:859

How the World Was One: Beyond the Global Village, 5:601

How Things Work in Your Home and What to Do When They Don't, 5:12

How to Avoid a Caesarean Section, 5:359

How to Be a Successful Computer Consultant, 5:558

How to Become a Professional Calligrapher, 1:14

How to Be Funny and Other Writings of Will Rogers, 3:886

How to Be Your Own Literary Agent, 1:47

How to Buy (and Survive!) Your First Computer, 5:556

How to Buy Rare Books, 1:33

How to Buy Software: The Master Guide to Picking the Right Program, 5:556

How to Choose a Winning Title, 1:46

How to Deep Freeze a Mammoth, 5:764

How to Do a Literature Search in Psychology, 3:169

How to Do Things with Words, 4:272

How to Eat Like a Child: And Other Lessons in Not Being a Grownup, 3:871

How to Find Chemical Information, 5:727

How to Find Information About AIDS, 5:387

How to Find Relief from Migraines, 5:392

How to Get Happily Published: A Complete and Candid Guide, 1:46

How to Get off Drugs, 5:404

How to Get the Most out of Philosophy, 4:24

How to Go around the World Overland, 3:893

How to Grow Science, 4:385

How to Lie with Maps, 5:620

How to Lie with Statistics, 5:522

How to Live with a Neurotic, 5:439

How to Live with a Problem Drinker and Survive, 5:426

How to Look at Dance, 3:732

How to Look It Up Online, 5:547

How to Make Nuclear Weapons Obsolete, 5:240

How to Make Sure Your Baby Is Well—And Stays That Way, 5:322

How to Master Your Fear of Flying, 5:439

How to Parent, 5:322

How to Protect Your Creative Work, 1:55

How to Publish, Promote, and Sell Your Own Book, 1:47

How to Publish and Market Your Own Book as an Independent Black Publisher, 1:45

How to Raise an Emotionally Healthy, Happy Child, 5:439

How to Read a Book, 4:270

How to Read a Film, 1:1157

How to Read Donald Duck, 1:1164, 2:864

How to Read Karl Barth: The Shape of His Theology, 4:758

How to Register a Copyright and Protect Your Creative Work, 1:54

How to Save Your Teeth and Your Money, 5:340

How to Sing, 3:688

How to Study History, 3:275

How to Survive on Fifty Thousand to One Hundred Fifty Thousand Dollars a Year, 3:870

How to Take a Chance, 5:522

How to Take Great Trips with Your Kids, 3:893

How to Talk Jewish, 2:30

How to Tell the Liars from the Statisticians, 5:522

How to Think about God: A Guide for the Twentieth-Century Pagan, 4:270

How to Think about Statistics, 5:524

How to Use a Research Library, 1:61

How to Use Statistics, 5:523

How to Watch TV News, 5:140

How to Write, 1:882

How to Write a Children's Book and Get It Published, 1:48

How to Write a Computer Manual, 5:550

How We Live, 1:921

How We Think, 3:260, 4:224

How Will the Heart Endure: Elizabeth Bowen and the Landscape of War, 1:448

How You Can Talk with God, 4:556

H.P.B.: The Extraordinary Life and Influence of Helena Blavatsky, 4:853, 4:874

Hrafnkel's Saga, 2:640

Hrafnkel's Saga and Other Stories, 2:640

Hrolf's Saga Kraka, 2:639

Hsiao Hung, 2:247

The Hsi-yu chi, 2:229

H₂O and the Waters of Forgetfulness, 5:136, 5:137

The Hubble Atlas of Galaxies, 5:607

Huck and Tom, 1:780

Huck Finn, 1:783

Huck Finn Among the Critics: A Centennial Selection, 1:784

Huckleberry Finn, 1:779, 2:916

Huckleberry Finn: Unwin Critical Library, 1:783

Hudson River Bracketed, 1:787

The Huenefeld Guide to Book Publishing, 1:47

The Huge Season, 1:1017

Hugh Hood and His Works, 2:914

Hughie, 1:1106, 1:1107

Hugh MacDiarmid: A Critical Survey, 1:517

Hugh MacDiarmid: The Man and His Work, 1:517

Hugh MacDiarmid: The Poetry of Self, 1:517

Hugh MacDiarmid's Epic Poetry, 1:517

Hugh Selwyn Mauberley, 2:911

Hugo and Dostoevsky, 2:483

Hugo von Hofmannsthal and His Time, 2:593

The Huguenots, 4:732

The Huguenots: A Biography of a Minority, 4:732

The Huguenot Struggle for Recognition, 4:732

The Human Age, 1:513

Human Aggression, 3:170

Human Anatomy and Physiology, 5:340

Human and Artificial Intelligence, 5:74

The Human and the Holy: The Spirituality of Abraham Joshua Heschel, 4:665

Human Associative Memory, 3:171

Human Biology, 5:763

The Human Body. The Kidneys: Balancing the Fluids, 5:406

Human Capital, 3:56, 3:70

The Human Comedy, 2:453, 2:547, 2:559

The Human Condition, 3:282, 4:394, 5:81, 5:82

The Human Costs of War, 3:278

Human Development, 5:414

The Human Dimension in International Relations, 3:188

Human Ecology: Problems and Solutions, 5:292

Human Energy, 4:336

Human Experimentation: A Guided Step into the Unknown, 5:123

The Human Factor, 1:488

The Human Factor in Changing Africa, 3:32

The Human Figure: The Complete "Dresden Sketchbook," 3:774

Human Genetics (Carlson), 5:777

Human Genetics (Winchester), 5:779

Human Genetics: An Introduction to the Principles of Heredity, 5:778

Human Genetics: Molecular Revolution, 5:778

The Human Group, 3:172

Humanhood: Essays in Biomedical Ethics, 5:120

Human Immortality and Pre-Existence, 4:303

Human Intelligence: Perspectives and Prospects, 3:174

Human Interests: Reflections on Philosophical Anthropology, 4:317, 5:101

Humanism and Scholasticism in Late Medieval Germany, 4:129

Humanism and Terror, 4:310

Humanism and the Physician, 5:97

Humanism in England during the Fifteenth Century, 4:132

Humanism in Italian Renaissance Musical Thought, 3:662

Humanism in Modern Chinese Literature: The Case of Dai Houying, 2:263

The Humanism of Leonardo Bruni: Selected Texts, 4:124

Humanistic and Political Literature in Florence and Venice at the Beginning of the Quattrocento, 2:400

Humanistic Education and Western Civilization 3:264

Humanistic Geography: Prospects and Problems, 3:119

Humanistic Psychology, 5:414

Humanistic Psychotherapy: The Rational-Emotive Approach, 5:439

Humanists and Bookbinders, 1:24

Humanists and Holy Writ, 4:124

The Humanities: A Selective Guide to Information Sources, 3:273

The Humanities Computing Yearbook
1988, 5:562
1989–1990, 5:562

Humanities Index, 1:113, 3:8

Humanities through the Black Experience, 3:867

Humanity and Self-Cultivation: Essays in Confucian Thought, 4:362, 4:526

The Humanity of God, 4:758

Human Knowledge: Its Scope and Limits, 5:102

Human Landscapes, 2:98

Human Learning, 3:269

The Human Mind, 5:464

The Human Mosaic, 3:121, 3:132

Human Nature, 5:472

Human Nature: Darwin's View, 5:794

Human Nature and Biocultural Evolution, 3:18

Human Nature and Collective Behavior, 3:203

Human Nature and Conduct, 3:260, 4:224

Human Nature and Human History, 4:282

Human Nature and Its Remaking, 4:296

Human Nature and the Social Order, 3:224

Human Nature in American Thought: A History, 3:558

Human Nonverbal Behavior: An Annotated Bibliography, 3:802

Human Physiology: The Mechanism of Body Function, 5:773

Human Poems, 2:886

The Human Predicament, 1:496

Human Rights, 4:386

Human Robots and Holy Mechanics, 5:129

The Human Search: An Introduction to Philosophy, 4:22

Human Sexual Aggression, 3:170

The Human Side of Diabetes: Beyond Doctors, Diets and Drugs, 5:382

Humans in Space: 21st Century Frontiers, 5:597

Human Universe and Other Essays, 1:1026

The Human Use of Human Beings: Cybernetics and Society, 5:77, 5:159

Human Values and Economic Policy: A Symposium, 4:265

Human Wishes, 1:984

A Humble Romance and Other Stories, 1:749, 1:750

Humboldt's Gift, 1:946, 1:947, 1:1044

Hume (Ayer), 4:201, 4:272

Hume (Stroud), 4:203

Hume, Hegel and Human Nature, 4:201

Hume, Newton, and the Design Argument, 4:184, 4:202

Hume and Locke, 4:180

Hume and the Enlightenment, 4:203

Hume and the Problem of Causation, 4:201

Hume's Intentions, 4:202

Hume's Moral Theory, 4:202

Hume's Philosophical Development: A Study of His Methods, 4:202

Hume's Philosophy of Common Life, 4:202

Hume's Skepticism in the Treatise of Human Nature, 4:202

Hume's Theory of the External World, 4:202

Hume's Theory of the Understanding, 4:201

The Humiliation of the Word, 5:163, 5:164

The Hummingbird and the Hawk, 3:629

Hummingbirds, 5:772

Humor in America: A Research Guide to Genres and Topics, 3:872

Humor of a Country Lawyer, 3:871

Humor of the Old Southwest, 3:870

The Humorous Verse of Lewis Carroll, 1:582

Humors of Blood and Skin: A John Hawkes Reader, 1:985

Humphrey Davy, 5:743

Humphrey Davy on Geology: The 1805 Lectures for the General Audience, 5:743

The Hunchback of Notre Dame, 2:482

A Hundred Years of Music, 3:658

A Hundred Years of Philosophy, 4:266

Hundred Years' War (Fowler), 3:357

The Hundred Years' War (Neillands), 3:331

Hungarian Authors: A Bibliographical Handbook, 2:798

Hungarian-English Dictionary, 1:100

Hungarian Folk Customs, 3:854

The Hungarian Folk Song, 3:850

Hungarian Helicon, 2:798

The Hungarian Model, 3:390

Hungarian Writers and Literature, 2:798

Hungary: An Economy in Transition, 3:52

Hunger: Basic Mechanisms and Clinical Implications, 5:347

Hunger, 2:664

Hunger and Health, 5:344

A Hunger for Home: Louisa May Alcott and Little Women, 1:1199

Hunger for Home: Louisa May Alcott's Place in American Culture, 1:1199

Hunger in a Land of Plenty, 1:879

Hungry Hill, 1:620

The Hungry Tigress: Buddhist Legends and Jataka Tales, 4:514

Hunters of the Great North, 3:939

Hunting Mister Heartbreak: A Discovery of America, 3:897

The Hunting of the Snark: A Musical Comedy, 1:582

Hunting the Wild Pineapple, 2:950

Huntington's Chorea, 5:392

Hunting Trips of a Ranchman, 3:594, 3:935

Hurlyburly, 1:1108, 1:1109

Hush Child, Can't You Hear the Music, 3:867

Hu Shih and Intellectual Choice in Modern China, 2:247, 4:360

Hu Shih and the Chinese Renaissance, 1917–1937, 2:247

Husserl, 4:234

Husserl: An Analysis of His Phenomenology, 4:319

Husserl: Intentionality and Cognitive Science, 4:234

Husserlian Meditations: How Words Present Things, 4:235

The Hustons, 3:838

Hutterian Brethren, 1528–1931, 4:733

Huxley: Prophet of Science, 5:800

Huxley and God: Essays on Mysticism, Religion, and Spirituality, 1:499

Huxley in Hollywood, 1:499

H. W. Wilson Company: Half a Century of Bibliographic Publishing, 1:45

The Hydra Head, 2:865

Hydrodynamic and Hydromagnetic Stability, 5:677

Hydrology, 5:631

Hydrology: An Introduction to Hydrolic Science, 5:631

Hydromagnetic Stability, 5:677

Hydrothermal Mineral Deposits, 5:636

Hymn of the Universe, 4:336

Hymns and Epigrams, 2:354

Hymns for the Drowning: Poems for Vishnu by Nammālvār, 2:174

Hymns of Zarathustra, 4:443

Hymns to the Night, 2:605

Hymn to Adversity, 1:248

Hypatia: New Foes with Old Faces, 1:368, 1:369

Hyperion, 1:293, 2:593

Hypermedia and Literary Studies, 5:561

Hypertext, 5:562

Hypnosis: Its Nature and Therapeutic Uses, 5:418

Hypnotherapy of Pain in Children with Cancer, 5:376

Hypothermia, Frostbite and Other Cold Injuries, 5:381

Hypothetical Reasoning, 5:101

I

i: six nonlectures, 1:825

I, Barbarian, 1:1247

I, Claudius, 1:484, 1:485, 1:1176, 3:320, 3:879

I, Robot, 5:563

I, the Jury, 1:1237

I, the Supreme, 2:882

I-Mary: A Biography of Mary Austin, 1:733

I Am: A Study of e. e. cummings' Poems, 1:826

I Am a Camera, 1:500

I Am a Mathematician: The Later Life of a Prodigy, 5:495, 5:584

I Am a Woman and a Jew, 4:650

Iamblichus and the Theory of the Vehicle of the Soul, 4:61

I Am Elijah Thrush, 1:1034

I Am Free and Other Stories, 2:60

I Am Not My Body: A Study of the International Hare Krishna Sect, 4:862

I Am the Darker Brother, 1:1196

I Am Wind, You Are Fire: The Life and Work of Rumi, 2:93

I and the "Not-I," 5:422

I and Thou, 4:662

Iannis Xenakis, the Man and His Music, 3:731

I Asked for Wonder: A Spiritual Anthology, 4:665

I Became Part of It: Sacred Dimensions in Native American Life, 4:464

Iberia: Spanish Travels and Reflections, 3:900, 3:931

The IBM Way, 5:543

Ibn Gabirol, 2:20

Ibn Khaldun: An Essay in Reinterpretation, 4:584

Ibn Khaldun and Tamerlane: Their Historic Meeting in Damascus, 4:584

Ibn Khaldun's Philosophy of History, 4:584

Ibn Rushd: Averroes, 4:581

Ibsen: A Critical Study, 2:666

Ibsen, A Biography, 2:666

Ibsen and Meaning: Studies, Essays and Prefaces, 2:666

Ibsen and Shaw, 1:546

Ibsen Companion, 2:666

Ibsen's Lively Art: A Performance Study of the Major Plays, 2:666

Icanchu's Drum, 4:466

Icastes: Marsilio Ficino's Interpretation of Plato's "Sophist," 4:141

The Ice Age, 1:468

Ice Around Our Lips: Finland-Swedish Poetry, 2:658

Iceland: The First American Republic, 3:939

Iceland: The First New Society, 3:381

Icelandic Aristocracy, 2:644

The Icelandic Family Saga: An Analytical Reading, 2:640

The Icelandic Saga, 2:640

Icelandic Short Stories, 2:640

The Iceman, the Arsonist, and the Troubled Agent, 1:1073

The Iceman Cometh, 1:1106, 1:1107, 2:724

The Ice Palace, 2:670

The Ice Storm, 1:936

I Ching, 4:525

The I Ching or Book of Changes, 4:525

Ichneutae, 2:367

I. Compton-Burnett, 1:462

The Icon and the Axe: An Interpretive History of Russian Culture, 3:394

Iconoclasm: The Way Out of the High Technology Dark Age, 5:196

Iconography in Medieval Spanish Literature, 2:522

Icon Programming for Humanists, 5:552

Icons of Popular Culture, 3:875

Ida: A Novel, 1:881

Ida Brandt, 2:647

Idanre and Other Poems, 2:149

Idea and Art in Elizabethan Fiction, 1:167

Idea and Essence in the Philosophies of Hobbes and Spinoza, 4:187

The Idea File of Harold Adams Innis, 3:622

The Ideal Book: Essays and Lectures on the Arts of the Book, 1:10

Ideal Forms in the Age of Ronsard, 2:503

An Ideal Husband, 1:409, 1:410

The Idealism of Giovanni Gentile, 4:285

Idealistic Argument in Recent British and American Philosophy, 4:263

The Idealistic Reaction against Science, 4:271

Idealists, 2:654

An Idealist View of Life, 4:354

Ideals and Realities: Selected Essays, 5:713

Ideals and Realities of Islam, 4:375, 4:576, 4:902

The Ideal Society and Its Enemies, 3:495

Ideals of the Samurai: Writings of Japanese Warriors, 3:476

The Idea of a Critical Theory: Habermas and the Frankfurt School, 4:264, 4:404, 5:89

The Idea of a Party System, 3:583

The Idea of a University, 4:782

The Idea of Christ in the Gospels; or God in Man, a Critical Essay, 4:326

The Idea of God in Homer, 4:483

The Idea of History, 3:284, 4:282

The Idea of History in Early Stuart England, 3:361

The Idea of Nationalism, 3:286

The Idea of Nature, 4:282

The Idea of Perfect History, 4:127

The Idea of Poverty: England in the Early Industrial Age, 3:362

The Idea of Prehistory, 4:432

The Idea of Principle in Leibnitz and the Evolution of Deductive Theory, 4:177

The Idea of Progress: An Inquiry into Its Origin and Growth, 5:44

The Idea of Progress in Classical Antiquity, 4:48

The Idea of Social Structure: Papers in Honor of Robert K. Merton, 3:215

The Idea of the Canterbury Tales, 1:151

The Idea of the Clerisy in the Nineteenth Century, 1:325

The Idea of the Good in Platonic-Aristotelian Philosophy, 4:80, 4:402

The Idea of the Holy, 4:487, 4:488

The Idea of the Jewish State, 4:658

The Idea of the Modern in Literature and the Arts, 1:989, 1:990

Ideas, Qualities and Corpuscles, 4:179

Ideas across Cultures, 3:466

Ideas and Ideals in the North European Renaissance, 4:132

Ideas and Information: Managing in a High-Tech World, 5:574

Ideas and Opinions, 5:682

Ideas and Styles in the Western Musical Tradition, 3:663

Ideas for a Philosophy of Nature, 4:251

Ideas from France: The Legacy of French Theory, 4:27

Ideas in Fiction: The Works of Hayim Hazaz, 2:19

Ideas of Jewish History, 3:349, 4:594

The Ideas of Le Corbusier: On Architecture and Urban Planning, 3:779

Ideas of Order in the Novels of Thomas Pynchon, 1:1035

The Ideas of Particle Physics: An Introduction for Scientists, 5:662

The Ideas of Richard Wagner, 3:728

Ideas of Statistics, 5:522

Ideas of the Great Psychologists, 3:168

Ideas Pertaining to a Pure Phenomenology and to a Phenomenological Philosophy, 4:234

Ideas toward a Pure Phenomenology, 4:234

Ideas toward the Philosophy of History of Humanity, 4:198

Identifying American Architecture, 3:762

Identity: Youth and Crisis, 5:442

Identity and the Life Cycle, 3:173, 3:182, 5:442

Identity Crisis, 1:1087

The Identity of France, 3:283

The Identity of Jesus Christ, 4:885

The Identity of Man, 5:162

Identity of Yeats, 1:974

The Identity Society, 5:451

The Ideological Origins of the American Revolution, 3:519, 3:564

Ideologies: Politics in Action, 3:140

Idéologies au Canada Français, 1850–1900, 3:620

Ideology: An Introduction, 3:211

Ideology, Society and Language: The Odyssey of Nathan Birnbaum, 2:31

Ideology and Classic American Literature, 1:627, 1:1128

Ideology and Discontent, 3:139

Ideology and Experience, 3:351

Ideology and Practice: The Evolution of Chinese Communism, 3:471

Ideology and the Image, 1:1157

Ideology and the New Social Movements, 3:215

Ideology and United States Foreign Policy, 3:545

Ideology and Utopia, 3:231, 3:232

Ideology and Utopia: An Introduction to the Sociology of Knowledge, 3:140

The Ideology of Order, 4:134

The Ideology of the Aesthetic, 3:211

The Ides of March, 1:898

I Didn't Notice the Mountain Growing Dark: Poems of Li Pai and Tu Fu, 2:208

The Idiom of the Time: The Writings of Henry Green, 1:487

Idioms and Phrases Index, 1:93

The Idiot, 2:712, 2:713, 2:714

Idiota de mente, 4:148

Idiots First, 1:1013

Idle Days in Patagonia, 1:365

Idle Fictions: The Hispanic Vanguard Novel, 1926–1934, 2:523

The Idler and His Works, 4:326

I Do Best Alone at Night, 2:673

Idols of the Tribe: Group Identity and Political Change, 4:651

I Dreamt Last Night, 5:436

Idu, 2:140

Idylls of the Bible, 1:753

Idylls of the King, 1:399, 1:400

Idylls of the King and a Selection of Poems, 1:400

Idylls of the Marketplace, 1:409, 1:411

IEEE Power Engineering Review, 5:286

Ifa Divination: Communication between Gods and Men in West Africa, 4:462

If Beale Street Could Talk, 1:938, 1:939

If I Am to be Remembered, 5:799

If I Could Preach Just Once, 4:322

If It Be Not I: Collected Poems, 1:1061

If It Really Were a Film, 2:646

If It Were Done: "Macbeth" and Tragic Action, 1:214

If Life Is a Bowl of Cherries, 3:870

If Not Now, When, 2:425

If on a Winter's Night a Traveler, 2:412

I. F. Stone: A Portrait, 3:808

If the Patient Is You (Or Someone You Love): Psychiatry Inside Out, 5:415

If There Are No More Heroes, There Are Heroines, 2:471

If the River Was Whiskey: Stories, 1:953

If You Lived Here . . . The City in Art, Theory, and Social Activism, 3:202

The Igbo Roots of Equiano (Gustavus Vassa), 2:138

Igbo Traditional Life, Culture and Literature, 2:107

Ignatius of Antioch: A Commentary on the Seven Letters of Ignatius, 4:704

Ignatius of Loyola, 4:770

Ignore Your Teeth and They'll Go Away, 5:342

I Have My Doubts, 4:744

I Know Why the Caged Bird Sings, 1:934, 1:935

The Ikons and Other Poems, 1:470

Il Convivio, 2:416, 2:417

Il Decamerone, 2:409

Ilesiod and the Homeric Hymns, 2:360

Il Fu Mattia Pascal, 2:435

Il Fuoco, 2:415

Il Gattopardo, 2:423

The Iliad, 1:175, 1:223, 2:252, 2:358, 2:359, 2:360, 2:378, 2:396, 2:416, 4:482

Iliad, or the Poem of Force, 2:362, 2:516

The Iliad, the Odyssey, and the Epic Tradition, 2:361

I Live under a Black Sun: A Novel, 1:548

Ill-Advised: Presidential Health and Public Trust, 3:542

Illegal Immigration: An Unfolding Crisis, 3:209

Ill Fares the Land: Essays on Food, Hunger and Power, 5:266

The Ill-Fated Peregrinations of Fray Servando, 2:852

Illiberal Education: The Politics of Race and Sex on Campus, 1:1126, 3:249

Illiterate America, 3:251

The Illiterate Digest, 3:886

Illness as Metaphor, 1:1052

I'll Take My Stand, 1:807

I'll Take Tomorrow, 5:377

I'll Tell You a Tale: An Anthology, 3:854

Illuminated Letter Designs in the Historical Style of the 13th and 15th Centuries, 3:767

Illuminated Manuscripts, 3:766

The Illuminating Icon, 4:756

Illuminations, 2:499

Illusion in Nature and Art, 5:193

Illusion Is More Precise Than Precision, 1:864

Illusion of Life: American Realism as a Literary Form, 1:714, 1:723

The Illusion of Technique, 5:69

The Illusion of Technique: A Search for Meaning in a Technological Civilization, 4:262

Illusions, 1:1162

Illustrated Atlas of World History, 3:272

The Illustrated Book: Its Art and Craft, 1:29

Illustrated Companion to a Brief History of Time, 5:17, 5:692

Illustrated Dictionary of Building Materials and Techniques, 5:225

An Illustrated Dictionary of Ceramics, 3:766

The Illustrated Dictionary of Microcomputers, 5:540

An Illustrated Dictionary of Ornament, 3:765

The Illustrated Dinosaur Dictionary, 5:639

Illustrated Encyclopedia of Architects and Architecture, 3:764, 3:762

The Illustrated Encyclopedia of Dinosaurs, 5:639

The Illustrated Encyclopedia of Helicopters, 5:218

Illustrated Encyclopedia of Human Histology, 5:773

The Illustrated Encyclopedia of New Zealand, 3:495

Illustrated Encyclopedia of the Classical World, 3:298

An Illustrated Guide to Fossil Collecting, 5:638

An Illustrated Guide to Modern Destroyers, 5:238

An Illustrated Guide to the American Economy, 3:67

An Illustrated Guide to the Protozoa, 5:783

The Illustrated Handbook of Desktop Publishing and Typesetting, 5:561

The Illustrated History of Canada, 3:606

The Illustrated Kama Sutra, Ananga-Ranga and Perfumed Garden, 3:914

Illustrated Lexicon of Agricultural Machines and Equipment, 5:261

The Illustrated Man, 1:1255

The Illustrated Petroleum Reference Dictionary, 5:636

Illustrating Children's Books, 1:46

Illustrating FORTRAN (The Portable Variety), 5:551

Illustration, 1:1151

Illustrations of Being: Drawing upon Heidegger and upon Metaphysics, 4:294

Illustrations of Political Economy, 1:317, 1:375

Illustrations of the Huttonian Theory of the Earth, 5:644

Illustrations on the Moral Sense, 4:203

The Illustrator and the Book in England from 1790–1914, 1:30

The Illustrator in America, 1880–1980, 1:30

The Illustrator's Notebook, 1:1196

Illustrators of Children's Books: 1744–1945, 1:579

Illustrators of Children's Books, 1967–1976, 1:29

The Illustrious House of Ramires, 2:559

Illustrious Men, 2:394

Illustrium Maioris Britanniae MB Scriptorum . . . MS Summarium, 1:163

Illywhacker, 2:951

I Love Myself When I am Laughing . . ., 1:850

Il Porto Sepolto, 2:440
Il Tempo, 2:437
The Image, 3:71
The Image: A Guide to Pseu-
do-Events in America,
3:551, 3:569
The Image: Knowledge in
Life and Society, 3:71
Image and Immortality: A
Study of Tristram Shandy,
1:259
The Image and Law, 1:1021
The Image and Other Sto-
ries, 2:47
Image and Pilgrimage in
Christian Culture, 3:40
Image and Reality in Plato's
Metaphysics, 4:83
Image and Symbol in the Sa-
cred Poetry of Richard
Crashaw, 1:176
Image before My Eyes, 2:30,
4:635
The Image Decade: Televi-
sion Documentary,
1965–1975, 3:811
The Image Empire: From
1950, 3:810
Image Ethics, 5:125
Imagemaker: Will Rogers
and the American Dream,
3:887
The Image of Africa, 3:417,
3:426
The Image of His Father, or,
One Boy Is More Trouble
than a Dozen Girls, Being
a Tale of a "Young Mon-
key," 1:378
The Image of Peter the
Great in Russian Fiction,
2:686
The Image of Women in
Contemporary Soviet Fic-
tion, 2:693
Image Recognition by Holog-
raphy, 5:235
Imagery in Healing: Shaman-
ism and Modern Medicine,
5:318
Imagery in Scientific
Thought: Creating Twenti-
eth-Century Physics, 5:49
The Imagery of Keats and
Shelley: A Comparative
Study, 1:303
The Imagery of the Cosmo-
logical Buddha, 4:530
Images and Understanding,
5:191
Images of a Free Press,
3:805

Images of Aleksei Remizov,
2:754
Images of Departure: Poetry,
1:461
Images of Kin: New and Se-
lected Poems, 1:984
Images of Science: A History
of Scientific Illustration,
5:192
Images of the Feminine in
Gnosticism, 4:453
Images of the New World,
2:848
Images of Wallace Stevens,
1:888
Images of Women in Antiq-
uity, 3:309
Imaginary Conversations,
1:296
Imaginary Friends, 1:1007
Imaginary Homelands: Essays
and Criticism 1981–1991,
2:181
The Imaginary Invalid, 2:490
An Imaginary Life, 2:958,
2:959
Imaginary Magnitude, 2:816
Imaginary Portraits, 1:386,
1:387
The Imaginary Signifier: Psy-
choanalysis and the Cine-
ma, 1:1157
The Imaginary Voyages,
1:692
The Imaginary Witness, 4:408
The Imaginary Witness: The
Critical Theory of Herbert
Marcuse, 5:95
Imagination: A Philosophical
Critique, 4:329
Imagination and Desire in
the Novels of Henry
James, 1:766
Imagination and Metaphysics
in St. Augustine, 4:110
Imagination and Reason in
Nineteenth Century Fic-
tion, 1:724
The Imagination as Glory:
Essays on the Poetry of
James Dickey, 1:968
The Imagination of Edward
Thomas, 1:558
The Imaginative Landscape
of Christopher Columbus,
3:916
The Imaginative World of
Alexander Pope, 1:252
Imagined Lives: A Study of
David Malouf, 2:959
Imaging American Women:
Idea and Ideals in Cultur-
al History, 1:712

Imagining India: Essays on
Indian History, 3:497
Imagining Religion: From
Babylon to Jonestown,
4:491
Imagining the Middle East,
3:436
Imagining the Penitentiary,
1:229
Imagining Tomorrow, 5:47,
5:231
Imajica: A Novel, 1:600
Imitation and Innovation,
3:480
Imitation and Praise in the
Poems of Ben Jonson,
1:184
Imitation of Life, 1:1175
Imitations, 1:1005, 1:1006
Imitations of Postmodernity,
3:211
Immediacy and Its Limits: A
Study in Martin Buber's
Thought, 4:662
Immediate Experience, 3:874
The Immigrant, 1:1160
Immigrant America: A Por-
trait, 3:209
The Immigrant Experience,
3:556
The Immigrants, 1:1246
The Immigrant's Daughter,
1:1246
Immigrants from Great Brit-
ain and Ireland, 3:558
The Immobilized Patient,
5:377
The Immoralist, 2:479, 2:480
Immoral Memories: An Auto-
biography, 3:835
Immortal, 1:1263
The Immortal Bartfuss, 2:14
Immortal Boy: A Portrait of
Leigh Hunt, 1:292
Immortality, 2:793
Immortality and Resurrec-
tion, 4:887
The Immortality of the Soul,
4:183
Immortal Rose: An Antholo-
gy of Persian Lyrics, 2:83
Immortal Shadows, 1:1076
Immortal Sisters: Secrets of
Taoist Women, 4:527
I'm Not Stiller, 2:579
Impact of Basic Research on
Technology, 5:214
The Impact of Biotechnology
on Agriculture, 5:221,
5:267
The Impact of Hitler: British
Politics and British Policy,
1933–1940, 3:365

Impact of Labour, Nineteen Twenty to Nineteen Twenty Four, 3:366

The Impact of Noise Pollution: A Socio-Technological Introduction, 5:251

Impact of Science on Society, 4:322

The Impact of the Intervention, 3:636

Impeachment: The Constitutional Problems, 3:542

The Impending Crisis, 1848–1861, 3:529, 3:593

The Imperative of Freedom: A Philosophy of Journalistic Autonomy, 3:807

The Imperative of Modernity, 5:97

The Imperative of Modernity: An Intellectual Biography of José Ortega y Gassett, 4:315

The Imperative of Responsibility, 5:71, 5:93, 5:129

Imperial Cities and the Reformation: Three Essays, 4:722, 4:730

The Imperial City of Potosi, 3:646, 3:647

Imperial Democracy: The Emergence of America as a Great Power, 3:546

Imperial Earth, 1:614

Imperial Germany and the Industrial Revolution, 3:109

The Imperial Idea and Its Enemies: A Study in British Power, 3:365

Imperialism, 3:343

Imperialism, the Highest Stage of Capitalism, 3:287

The Imperial Presidency, 3:147, 3:543, 3:597

The Imperial Self: An Essay in American Literary and Cultural History, 1:649

Imperial Spain, 1469–1716, 3:387

Imperial Texas: An Interpretive Essay in Cultural Geography, 3:133

An Imperial Vision: Indian Architecture and Britain's Raj, 3:485

The Imperiled Union: Essays on the Background of the Civil War, 3:598

Impermanence Is Buddha-Nature, 4:538

The Impersonal Sublime: Hugo, Baudelaire, Lautréamont, 2:483

The Impersonators, 2:948

Implants: Reconstructing the Human Body, 5:370

Implementation, 3:146

Implicit Meanings: Essays in Anthropology, 3:28

The Implied Reader, 1:421

The Importance of Being Earnest, 1:272, 1:409, 1:410, 1:554

The Importance of Living, 2:254

The Imported Bridegroom and Other Stories of the New York Ghetto, 1:737, 2:37

The Imposition of Method: A Study of Descartes and Locke, 4:180

The Impossible Dream: The Rise and Demise of the American Left, 3:538

The Impossible Dream: The Spirituality of Dom Helder Camara, 4:748

Impossible Sum of Our Tradition, 2:905

The Impostor, 2:646

Impressionism: A Feminist Reading, 5:192

Imprints on History: Book Publishing and American Frontiers, 1:38

The Improbable Machine, 5:74

The Improbable Origins of Modern Wall Street, 3:55

The Improbable Survivor: Yugoslavia and Its Problems, 1918–1988, 3:392

The Improvement of Mankind, 3:97

Improve Your Writing with Word Processing, 5:562

Improving Company Productivity, 5:234

Improving Doctor Performance, 5:336

Improving Health-Care Management in the Workplace, 5:329

Improving Instruction with Microcomputers, 5:567

Improving Safety in the Chemical Laboratory: A Practical Guide, 5:726

Improving Schools from Within, 3:253

Improving Your Reasoning, 4:381, 5:64

Improvisational Therapy, 5:419

Impure Science, 5:9, 5:106

IMS/Ayer Directory of Publications, 1:52

I'm Talking about Jerusalem, 1:565

In Abraham's Bosom, 1:1088

In a Dark Wood Wandering, 2:626

In a Different Voice, 3:250, 5:413

Inadmissible Evidence, 1:531, 1:532

In Advance of the Landing, 4:870

In a Far Country: Jack London's Western Tales, 1:774

In a Far Distant Land, 2:707

In a German Pension, 2:978

In a Hollow of the Hills, 1:756

In a Hundred Graves: A Basque Portrait, 3:899

In All His Glory: The Legendary Tycoon and His Brilliant Circle, 3:820

In a Minor Chord, 1:891

In an Antique Land, 3:445

In and out of the Garbage Pail, 5:465

Inanna, Queen of Heaven and Earth, 4:440, 4:546

In a Patch of Fireweed, 5:764

In a Shallow Grave, 1:1034

In a Strange Land, 2:732

In Bed One Night and Other Brief Encounters, 1:963

In Bluebeard's Castle: Some Notes toward the Redefinition of Culture, 1:1054

In Bolivia, 3:896

Inc. Magazine's Databasics, 5:547

Inca Civilization in Cuzco, 4:458

The Inca Empire, 3:628

Inca Religion and Customs, 4:458

Incarnation and Myth: The Debate Continued, 4:885

Incarnation in Hinduism and Christianity, 4:507

Incarnation of God: The Character of Divinity in Formative Judaism, 4:607

Incarnations: Poems, 1966–68, 1:893

The Incas and Their Ancestors: The Archaeology of Peru, 4:458

Incestuous Families, 5:428

Incident at Vichy, 1:1103, 1:1104

Incidents in the Life of a Slave Girl, 1:681, 1:682

In Circles, 1:881

Incitement to Nixonicide, 2:874

Incognita, 1:237, 1:244

Incognito, 2:824

The Incoherence of the Philosophers (Tahāfut al-Falāsifah), 4:582

In Cold Blood, 1:916, 1:958, 1:959

In Cold Type: Overcoming the Book Crisis, 1:50

Income, Employment and Public Policy, 3:81

In Command of France, 3:374

In Commemoration of William James, 1842–1942, 4:237

The Incomparable Atuk, 2:924

The Incomparable Land, 2:437

The Incompleat Folksinger, 3:852

The Incomplete Adult, 5:423

In Context, 5:52

In Corner B, 2:167

The Incorporation of America: Culture and Society in the Gilded Age, 1:716

The Incredible Bomb, 2:550

In Cuba, 2:859

Incunable Short-Title Catalogue, 1:66

Incunabula and Americana, 1450–1800: A Key to Bibliographical Study, 1:67

Incunabula in American Libraries, 1:66

In Custody, 2:179

Indecent Pleasures, 1:44

In Defense of American Liberties: A History of the ACLU, 3:139

In Defense of Animals, 4:43

In Defense of Decadent Europe, 3:283

In Defense of Historical Literature, 1:628

In Defense of Liberal Democracy, 3:142

In Defense of People's Temple, 4:867

In Defense of Reason: Three Classics of Contemporary Criticism, 1:927

In Defense of the Indians, 3:647

In Defense of Women: Susanna Rowson 1762–1824, 1:643

Indefinition, 1:212

Indemnity Only, 1:1236

Independence and After, 3:499

Independence and Nationhood: Scotland, 1306–1469, 3:368

Independence of Elmer Rice, 1:1109

The Independent Arab, 3:438

Independent People: An Epic, 2:641, 2:642

The Indeterminate World: A Study of the Novels of Joyce Cary, 1:457

Index Kewensis Plantarum Phanerogarum (Linnaeus to the Year 1885), 5:805

Index of American Periodical Verse, 1:1990, 1:125

Index of Middle English Verse, 1:149

Index of Plays Eighteen Hundred to Nineteen Twenty-Six, 1:124

The Index of Psychoanalytic Writings, 5:425

Index of Xenophontis Memorabilia, 4:91

Index Scholastico-Cartesian, 4:170

Index to Anthologies of Latin American Literature in English Translation, 2:846

Index to Aristotle, 4:70

Index to Biographies of Contemporary Composers, 3:654

Index to Book Reviews in Religion, 4:7

Index to Characters in the Performing Arts, 3:732

Index to Current Urban Documents, 1:110

Index to Full-Length Plays, 1895–1925, 1:124

Index to International Statistics, 1:111

Index to Jewish Periodicals, 4:8

Index to Literary Biography, 1:126

Index to Nietzsche, 4:247

Index to One-Act Plays, 1900–1924, 1:124

Index to Plays in Periodicals, 1977–1987, 1:124

Index to Poetry by Black American Women, 1:125

Index to Scientists of the World from Ancient to Modern Times, 5:4

Index to Social Sciences and Humanities Proceedings, 1979–, 3:8

An Index to the Collected Works of J. V. Stalin, 3:292

An Index to the Films of Josef von Sternberg, 1:1176

Index Translationum, 1:52

India, 3:484

India: An Anthropological Perspective, 4:506

India: A Wounded Civilization, 2:939

India and Europe, 4:508

India and Pakistan: A General and Regional Geography, 3:483

India and the West, 3:295

India in Eighteen Fifty-Seven: The Revolt against Foreign Rule, 3:497

Indiana, 2:504, 2:505

The Indiana Companion to Traditional Chinese Literature, 2:190

Indiana Folklore: A Reader, 3:861

Indiana Politics during the Civil War, 3:598

Indian Art: A Concise History, 3:759

Indian Boyhood, 1:726, 1:749

Indian Business and Nationalist Politics, 1931–1939, 3:486

Indian Currency and Finance, 3:86

Indian Days in the Canadian Rockies, 3:875

The Indian Fairy Book: From the Original Legends, 3:864

Indian Fairy Tales, 3:882

Indian Heroes and Great Chieftains, 1:749

Indian Journals: March 1962–May 1963, 1:981

The Indian Journals, Eighteen Fifty-Nine to Sixty-Two, 3:37

Indian Legends from the Northern Rockies, 3:864

Indian Legends of the Pacific Northwest, 3:864

Indian Literature in English: An Annotated Bibliography, 2:170

Indian Literature in English, 1827–1979: A Guide to Information Sources, 2:171

The Indian Mind: Essentials of Indian Philosophy and Culture, 4:351

Indian Philosophy, 4:351

Indian Religion, 4:498

An Indian Rural Economy, 1880–1955: The Tamiland Countryside, 3:485

Indians, 1:1098

Indians in the Fur Trade, 3:611

Indians of North America, 3:25, 4:464

Indian Summer, 1:758

Indian Summer: Lutyens, Baker, and Imperial Delhi, 3:485

Indian Tales of C. C. Trowbridge, 3:865

Indian Tales of North America: An Anthology for the Adult Reader, 3:864

The Indian To-Day, 1:749

The Indian Wants the Bronx, 1:1094

The Indian Way, 4:351, 4:498

Indian Writing in English, 2:177

India's Foreign Policy, 3:499

India Song, 2:474

India's Political Economy, 1947–1977, 3:486

India's Quest: Being Letters on Indian History, 3:499

India's Religion of Grace and Christianity Compared and Contrasted, 4:488

India's Search for National Identity, 3:497

Indica, 3:312

The Indifferent Children, 1:937

Indigestion, 5:384

The Individual and His Religion: A Psychological Interpretation, 5:432

The Individual and His Times, 1:481

Individual and Mass Behavior, 5:434

Individual and State in Ancient China, 4:525

The Individual and the Cosmos in Renaissance Philosophy, 4:124

The Individual and the Social Self, 4:308

The Individual and the Universe: An Introduction to Philosophy, 4:21

The Individual in Darwin's World, 5:16

Individualism and Economic Order, 3:82

Individualism and Nationalism in American Ideology, 1:627

The Individual Psychology of Alfred Adler, 5:430

Individuals, 4:414

The Individuated Self: Cervantes and the Emergence of the Individual, 2:537

Individuation and Narcissism: The Psychology of the Self in Jung and Kohut, 5:458

Indo-European Language and Society, 4:435

The Indomitable Mrs. Trollope, 1:408

Indonesia: Land under the Rainbow, 2:320

Indonesia: Social and Cultural Revolution, 2:318

Indonesian Dilemma, 2:320

Indonesian Economic History in the Dutch Colonial Era, 3:491

Indoor Air Quality and Human Health, 5:354

The Indoor Bicycling Fitness Program, 5:326

The Indoor Garden Book, 5:767

The Indra Hymns of the Rigveda, 4:501

In Dreams Begin Responsibilities, 1:1044

In Dubious Battle, 1:883, 1:884

Induction, 4:317

Induction, Physics, and Ethics, 5:108

Induction, Probability, and Confirmation, 5:64

Induction, Probability and Causation: Selected Papers, 4:277

Induction and Intuition in Scientific Thought, 5:18

Industrial Democracy, 3:112, 3:113

Industrial Design: Reflections of a Century, 5:192

Industrial Development and the Social Fabric, 3:61

Industrial Energy Conservation, 5:284

Industrial Harmony in Modern Japan: The Invention of a Tradition, 3:478

Industrialization as an Agent of Social Change: A Critical Analysis, 3:221

The Industrialization of Egypt, 1939–1973: Policy and Performance, 3:446

The Industrialization of Iraq, 3:450

Industrial Organization, 3:58

The Industrial Reformation of English Fiction, 1:318

Industrial Revolution, 3:565

Industrial Robot Handbook, 5:243

Industry and Empire, 3:405

Industry and Trade, 3:93

In English Ways, 3:516

Inequality: A Reassessment of the Effect of Family and Schooling in America, 3:214

Inequality, Poverty, and History, 3:90

Inequality and Heterogeneity: A Primitive Theory of Social Structure, 3:215

I Never Loved Your Mind, 1:1122, 1:1123

I Never Sang for My Father, 1:1082, 1:1083

I Never Wanted Fame, 2:545

In Evil Hour, 2:866, 2:867

Inevitable Revolutions: The United States in Central America, 3:545, 3:631

In Exile from the Land of Snows, 4:906

In Extremity, 1:364

In Face of Mystery: A Constructive Theology, 4:744

Infallible? An Inquiry, 4:774, 4:775

Infamy: Pearl Harbor and Its Aftermath, 3:536

The Infancy of Atomic Physics: Hercules in His Cradle, 5:658

Infante's Inferno, 2:858

Infantile Cerebral Paralysis, 5:446

The Infant Mind, 5:323

Infants of the Spring, 1:536

The Infant Sphinx: Collected Letters of Mary E. Wilkins Freeman, 1:750

In Favor of the Sensitive Man and Other Essays, 1:866

Infection and Communicable Diseases, 5:389

The Infection of Thomas De Quincey: A Psychopathology of Imperialism, 1:290

Infectious Diseases: A History of Their Control, 5:36
Inferences of Patients' Pain and Psychological Distress, 5:337
Inferential Statistics for Geographers, 3:120
Inferiority Feelings in the Individual and the Group, 5:431
Infernal Desire Machines of Doctor Hoffman, 1:455
The Infernal Machine and Other Plays, 2:469
Inferno, 2:413, 2:415, 2:416, 2:679
Inferno: From an Occult Diary, 2:680
Inferno I, 2:417
Inferno II, 2:417
The Infertility Book: A Comprehensive Medical and Emotional Guide, 5:358
The Infidel: A Story of the Great Revival, 1:332
Infinite in All Directions, 5:10, 5:133
The Infinite in Giordano Bruno, 4:136
Infinite Riches: The Adventures of a Rare Book Dealer, 1:32
The Infinite Worlds of Giordano Bruno, 4:136
Infinity and Continuity in Ancient and Medieval Thought, 4:104
Infinity in the Presocratics, 4:51
Inflation: Tax Rules and Capital Formation, 3:50
Influence of Beaumont and Fletcher on Shakespeare, 1:173
The Influence of Darwin on Philosophy and Other Essays, 4:224
The Influence of Emile Zola on Frank Norris, 1:777
The Influence of Existentialism on Ingmar Bergman, 3:831
The Influence of Freud on American Psychology, 3:178, 3:184
The Influence of Geography upon the History of Mankind, 3:130
The Influence of Greek Ideas on Christianity, 4:63, 4:99
The Influence of Islam upon Africa, 3:444, 4:573

The Influence of Islam upon Medieval Europe, 4:573
The Influence of Prophecy in the Later Middle Ages, 4:102
The Influence of Sea Power on History, 3:287, 3:288, 3:338
The Influence of Sea Power on the French Revolution and Empire, 3:287, 3:288
The Influence of Statius upon Chaucer, 2:394
Influenza, the Last Great Plague: An Unfinished Story of Discovery, 5:389
Infomania: The Guide to Essential Electronic Services, 5:547
Information, Freedom, and Censorship, World Report, 1:1991, Article 19, 1:57
Informational Approaches to Regulation, 3:58
Information and Information Systems, 5:543
Information Anxiety Is Produced by the Ever-Widening Gap between What We Understand and What We Think We Should Understand, 5:574
Information Ethics: Concerns for Librarianship and the Information Industry, 5:126
The Information Game: Ethical Issues in a Microchip World, 5:125
Information Industry Directory, 1:105
Information Management Technology: A Librarian's Guide, 5:544
Information Please Almanac, 1:82
Information Retrieval Systems: Characteristics, Testing and Evaluation, 5:544
Information Sources in Agriculture and Horticulture, 5:261
Information Sources in Cartography, 3:119
Information Sources in Engineering, 5:215
Information Sources in Information Technology, 5:540
Information Sources in the Life Sciences, 5:760
Information Sources in the Medical Sciences, 5:3

The Information Sources of Political Science, 3:138
Information Systems: Theory and Practice, 5:543
Information Systems in the 80s: Products, Markets, and Vendors, 5:558
An Information Systems Manifesto, 5:557
Information Technology: An Introduction, 5:545
Information Technology: It's for Everyone!, 5:126
Information Technology and the Individual, 5:126
The Information Technology Revolution, 5:296, 5:540
Information Theory: Fourth London Symposium, 5:306
Information Theory and the Living System, 5:571
Information through the Printed Word, 1:50
Information Transmission, Modulation, and Noise, 5:300
The Information Web, 5:125
An Informative Index to the Writings of Walter H. Pater, 1:388
An Informed Decision: Understanding Breast Reconstruction, 5:397
The Informed Heart: Autonomy in a Mass Age, 3:347, 5:435
The Informer, 1:1165
InfoTrac (Magazine Index), 1:113
In Frankenstein's Shadows, 1:301
In Freud's Shadow: Adler in Context, 5:431
Ingmar Bergman: A Critical Biography, 3:831
Ingmar Bergman: A Life in the Theater, 3:832
Ingmar Bergman: An Appreciation, 3:832
Ingmar Bergman: The Cinema as Mistress, 3:832
In God's Land, 2:653
In Gods We Trust: New Patterns of Religious Pluralism in America, 4:857
The Inhabitants, 1:1017
In Hazard, 1:496, 1:497
The Inheritance of Economic Status, 3:66
The Inheritors, 1:474, 1:483
In Her Own Words: Oral Histories of Women Physicians, 5:314

Inhibitions, Symptoms, and Anxiety (Problem of Anxiety), 5:446

In His Image, 4:608

The Inhuman Condition, 1:600

Initials and Pseudonyms: A Dictionary of Literary Disguises, 1:77

Initiation Ceremonies: A Cross-Cultural Study of Status Dramatization, 3:25

In Job's Balances: On the Sources of Eternal Truths, 4:335

In Joy and in Sorrow, 3:531

Injury Control: A Guide to the Causes and Prevention of Trauma, 5:381

In Just-Spring, 1:825

The Inklings, 4:776

The Ink of Melancholy, 1:836

The Ink Truck, 1:996, 1:997

In Labor: Women and Power in the Birthplace, 5:204, 5:359

An Inland Voyage, 1:395, 1:397

The Inland Waterways of England, 5:249

In Memoriam, 1:399, 1:400

In Memoriam Margaret Mead 1901–1978, 3:37

The Inmost Leaf: A Selection of Essays, 1:996

In My Father's Court, 1:1049, 1:1050, 2:48

In My Father's Den, 2:975

The Inn at Antimovo and Legends of Stara Planina, 2:782

The Inner Civil War: Northern Intellectuals and the Crisis of the Union, 3:528

The Inner Conflict of Tradition, 3:484, 4:501

The Inner Courtyard: Stories by Indian Women, 2:177

Inner Exile: Recollections of a Life with Werner Heisenberg, 5:694

The Inner Eye of Love: Mysticism and Religion, 4:858

The Inner Government of the World, 4:549

The Inner I: British Literary Autobiography of the Twentieth Century, 1:429

Inner Landscapes: The Theater of Sam Shepard, 1:1111

The Inner Room—Poems, 1:1015

The Inner Teachings of Taoism, 4:527

The Inner Theatre of Recent French Poetry, 2:462

The Inner World of American Psychiatry, 1890 to 1940, 5:415

The Inner World of Mental Illness, 5:427

In New York: A Selection, 2:39

Inni Sacri, 2:426

Innocence, 1:277

The Innocence of Age, 2:933

The Innocent, 2:305

Innocent Abroad: Charles Dickens' American Engagements, 1:350

Innocent Erendira and Other Stories, 2:867

Innocents Abroad, 1:780, 1:781, 3:894

The Innocents at Cedro, 3:110, 3:243

The Inn of the Cats, 2:531

The Inn of Tranquility: Studies and Essays, 1:482

Innovation and Growth in the Global Economy, 3:53

Innovation and the Productivity Crisis, 5:184

Innovation at the Crossroads between Science and Technology, 5:52

Innovation Diffusion: A New Perspective, 3:129

The Innovators: Rediscovering America's Creative Energy, 5:226

In One Newspaper, 2:717

In Orbit, 1:1017

In Other Words, 1:1057

In Other Worlds: Essays in Cultural Politics, 1:1132, 1:1153

In Our Image: America's Empire in the Philippines, 3:532

In Our Image and Likeness, 4:131

In Our Own Image: Building an Artificial Person, 5:242

In Our Time, 1:845

In Parenthesis, 1:502

In Place of the Flawed Diamond, 4:311

In Plain Russian, 2:773

In Polish Woods, 2:42

In Praise of Darkness, 2:856

In Praise of Idleness and Other Essays, 4:322

In Praise of Imperfection: My Life and Work, 5:804

In Praise of Krishna, 2:174

In Praise of Love, 2:402

In Praise of Our Lady, 1:501

In Praise of Philosophy, 4:310

In Praise of Shadows, 2:294

In Pursuit of Reason: The Life of Thomas Jefferson, 3:520

In Pursuit of Satan: The Police and the Occult, 4:868

Input-Output Economics, 3:47, 3:63, 3:91

In Quest of Identity, 2:847

In Quest of Telescopes, 5:589

In Quest of the Perfect Book, 1:33

In Quest of the Truth: A Survey of Medieval Jewish Thought, 4:629

Inquiries into Truth and Interpretation, 4:283, 4:380

The Inquiry, 2:409

An Inquiry Concerning Beauty, Order, Harmony, Design, 4:203

An Inquiry into Meaning and Truth, 4:322, 5:102

An Inquiry into the Authenticity of Moses Maimonides' Treatise on Resurrection, 4:668

An Inquiry into the Good, 4:364

An Inquiry into the Human Mind on the Principles of Common Sense, 4:211

An Inquiry into the Human Prospect, 3:53

Inquiry into the Nature of Peace, 3:109

Inquiry into the Original of Our Ideas of Beauty and Virtue, 4:203

Inquisition, 3:331

Inquisition and Society in Spain in the Sixteenth and Seventeenth Centuries, 3:387

The Inquisition in Hollywood, 3:558

The Inquisitor; or, Invisible Rambler, 1:643

The Inquisitory, 2:493

In Recognition of William Gaddis, 1:977, 1:978

In Red and Black, 3:580

In Respect to Egotism: Studies in American Romantic Writing, 1:652

In Retrospect: The History of a Historian, 3:596

Insanity: The Idea and Its Consequences, 5:81

Insatiability: A Novel in Two Parts, 2:822

In Science We Trust? Moral and Political Issues of Science in Society, 5:107

Inscrutable Earth: Explorations in the Science of the Earth, 5:624

In Search of a Better World: Lectures and Essays of Thirty Years, 4:409, 5:98

In Search of a Character, 1:489

In Search of a Cure: A History of the Pharmaceutical Discovery, 5:13

In Search of America: Transatlantic Essays, 1951–1990, 3:514

In Search of Ancient Astronomies, 4:434

In Search of Answers: Indian Women's Voices from Manushi, 4:508

In Search of Common Ground, 5:442

In Search of Florentine Civic Humanism, 4:29, 4:123

In Search of History: A Personal Adventure, 3:809

In Search of Human Nature, 3:575

In Search of Identity: An Autobiography, 3:445

In Search of J. D. Salinger, 1:1043

In Search of Light, 3:819

In Search of Melancholy Baby, 2:697, 2:698

In Search of My Beloved, 2:644

In Search of Omar Khayyam, 2:92

In Search of Peace, 3:278

In Search of Political Philosophy, 3:140

In Search of Southeast Asia: A Modern History, 3:489

In Search of Stevie Smith, 1:549

In Search of the City: Engels, Baudelaire, Rimbaud, 2:500

In Search of the Common Good: Utopian Experiments Past and Future, 3:217

In Search of the Miraculous: Fragments of an Unknown Teaching, 4:876

In Search of the Paper Tiger, 1:604

In Search of the Present, 2:879

In Search of Wagner, 4:393

In Search of Wealth and Power: Yen Fu and the West, 3:472

In Search of White Crows, 4:851

In Season, out of Season, 5:163

The Insect Comedy, 2:789

Insect Pests of Farm and Orchard, 5:770

Insects and Flowers: Biology of a Partnership, 5:767

Insects and Plants: Parallel Evolution and Adaptations, 5:760

Insects of the World, 5:772

Insects That Feed on Trees and Shrubs, 5:768

Insect Summer, 2:664

The Insecurity of Freedom: Essays on Human Existence, 4:665

Insei: Abdicated Sovereigns in the Politics of Late Heian Japan, 1086–1185, 3:475

Inshallah, 2:420

In Sicily, La Garibaldina, 2:443

Inside Africa, 3:922

Inside American Ballet Theatre, 3:734

Inside America's Most Powerful Newspaper Empires—From the Newsrooms to the Boardrooms, 3:806

Inside Asia, 3:922

Inside Bureaucracy, 3:147

Inside Europe Today, 3:922

Inside Information: Computers in Fiction, 5:565

Inside Insomnia: How to Get a Good Night's Sleep, 5:392

Inside Job: The Looting of America's Savings and Loans, 3:56

Inside Kasrilevke, 2:46

Inside Macintosh, 5:554

Inside Mr. Enderby, 1:454

Inside NASA, 5:597

Inside/Out: Lesbian Theories, Gay Theories, 1:1133, 1:1184

Inside Passage, 3:896

Inside Prime Time, 3:203, 3:811

The Insider: Stories of War and Peace from Nigeria, 2:127

Inside Russia Today, 3:921

Inside South America, 3:922

Inside the Black Box: Technology and Economics, 5:157, 5:234

Inside the Business Enterprise, 3:50

Inside the IBM PC, 5:555

Inside the Monster, 2:871

Inside the Onion, 1:1021

Inside the Royal Court Theatre, 1956–1981: Artists Talk, 1:426

Inside the Spaceships: UFO Experiences of George Adamski 1952–1955, 4:870

Inside the Third Reich, 3:378

Inside Us the Dead, 2:980

Inside War, 3:278

The Insidious Dr. Fu Manchu, 1:596, 1:597

Insidious Intent: An Interpretation of Fedor Sologub's "The Petty Demon," 2:759

Insight and Action: The Life and Work of Lion Feuchtwanger, 2:578

Insight and Responsibility, 3:182, 5:442

Insights and Oversights of Great Thinkers, 4:17, 4:161, 4:289

In Single Strictness, 1:381

Insolation, 2:118

In Southern Light: Trekking through Zaire and the Amazon, 3:905

Inspector Ali, 2:119

Inspector and Other Plays, 2:722

An Inspector Calls, 1:537

The Inspector General, 2:720, 2:722

Inspector Glebsky's Puzzle, 2:762

Inspector Imanishi Investigates, 2:289

In Speech and in Silence: The Jewish Quest for God, 4:600

Inspirations Unbidden: The "Terrible Sonnets" of Gerard Manley Hopkins, 1:364

Inspired Talks, My Master, and Other Writings, 4:562

Inspiriting Influences, 1:803

In Stalin's Time: Middle-Class Values in Soviet Fiction, 2:685

An Instant in the Wind, 2:159

Instant Spelling Dictionary, 1:95

Institutes of the Christian Religion, 4:760

Institutional Economics, 3:74

Institutional Economics: Its Place in Political Economy, 3:73

Institution and Interpretation, 1:1127

Institutionis Oratoriae, 2:393

The Institutions of France under the Absolute Monarchy, 1598–1789, 3:373

Instructed Vision, 4:32, 4:35

Instrumental Realism, 5:92

Instrument of Thy Peace, 2:167

Insulinde, 2:317

The Insulted and Injured, 2:714

The Insurrection, 2:885

In Suspect Terrain, 1:1010, 5:623, 5:645

Integrated Services Digital Networks, 5:299

Integrated Services Digital Networks: From Concept to Application, 5:300

Integrating Digital Services, 5:298

Integrating the City of Medicine, 5:13

Integration, 5:500

The Intellectual Adventure of Ancient Man, 2:52, 4:439

The Intellectual Cowardice of the American Philosophers, 4:34

The Intellectual Development of Karl Mannheim, 3:232

The Intellectual Development of Voltaire, 2:516, 4:218

The Intellectual Enterprise: Sartre and Les Temps Modernes, 2:507, 4:330

Intellectual Freedom Manual, 1:56, 1:57

Intellectual History of Europe from St. Augustine to Marx: A Guide, 3:326

An Intellectual History of Islamic India, 4:372

Intellectual Life in America: A History, 3:514

The Intellectual Life of Colonial New England, 1:629, 3:589

Intellectual Life of Jefferson's Virginia, 1:627

Intellectual Memoirs: New York 1936–1938, 1:1008

The Intellectual Migration: Europe and America, 1930–1960, 3:564

The Intellectual Milieu of John Dryden, 1:241

Intellectual Odyssey of Walter Lippmann, 3:815

Intellectual Origins of the English Revolution, 3:404

The Intellectual Origins of the European Reformation, 4:722

Intellectual Origins of the French Enlightenment, 4:28

Intellectuals, 3:345

Intellectuals: Aesthetics, Politics, Academics, 1:1129

The Intellectuals and the Powers: And Other Essays, 3:202, 3:214, 3:239

Intellectuals and the State in Modern China: A Narrative History, 2:233

Intellectual Trends in the Ch'ing Period, 2:234, 2:252

Intellectual Women and Victorian Patriarchy, 1:375, 1:376

Intelligence: Genetic and Environmental Influences, 3:174

Intelligence: Reconceptualization and Measurement, 3:175

Intelligence and Affectivity in Early Childhood, 3:192

An Intelligence Guide to Book Distribution, 1:46

The Intelligent Individual and Society, 5:676

The Intelligent Layman's Guide to Technology, 5:251

Intelligent Life in the Universe, 5:611

Intelligent Robotic Systems, 5:243

Intelligent Robotic Systems: Theory, Design, and Applications, 5:243

Intelligent Structural Systems, 5:246

Intelligibility and the Philosophy of Nothingness, 4:364

Intensive Care, 2:974

Intensive Care: The Story of a Nurse, 5:337

Intentionality, 4:383

Intentions and Uncertainty, 4:288

Inter-view: Talks with America's Writing Women, 1:911

The Interaction of the "Sibling" Byzantine and Western Cultures in the Middle Ages and Italian Renaissance (330–1600), 4:693

Interaction Process Analysis, 3:172

Interactions: A Journey through the Mind of a Particle Physicist and the Matter of This World, 5:691

Interactions: The Biological Context of Social Systems, 5:826

Interactive Programming Environments, 5:549

Interactive Writing, 5:566

Interbeing: Commentaries on the Tiep Hein Precepts, 4:561

Intercultural Attitudes in the Making, 3:264

Interdisciplinary Dimensions of African Literature, 2:106

Interest and Prices: A Study of the Causes Regulating the Value of Money, 3:114

The Interesting Narrative of the Life of Olaudah Equiano or Gustavus Vassa, the African, Written by Himself, 2:104, 2:137

The Interest of America in Sea Power, Present and Future, 3:288

Interferon: or, on Theater, 2:792

Interferon: The New Hope for Cancer, 5:371

Interferons: A Primer, 5:350

Interim, 1:1159

The Interior Castle, 2:550, 4:786

The Interior Landscape: Love Poems from a Classical Tamil Anthology, 2:174

Interludes, 2:535

Intermediate Algebra with Problem Solving, 5:485

Intermediate Greek-English Lexicon, 1:99

Intermediate Quantum Mechanics, 5:671

The Internal Constitution of Stars, 5:602, 5:681

Internal Constitution of the
  Earth, 5:647
The Internal Stance, 4:396
Internal Structure of the
  City, 3:128
International Acronyms, Ini-
  tialisms and Abbreviations
  Dictionary, 1:93, 5:3
International Atomic Energy
  Agency Publications Cata-
  log, 5:287
International Bibliography of
  the Historical Sciences,
  3:272
International Bibliography of
  the Social Sciences, 3:6
International Calvinism,
  4:732
International Code of Zoo-
  logical Nomenclature,
  5:762
International Dictionary of
  Anthropologists, 3:11
International Dictionary of
  Literary Awards, 1:135
International Dictionary of
  Medicine and Biology,
  5:760
International Directories in
  Print, 1:104
International Directory of
  Telecommunications, 5:230
The International Directory
  of Book Collectors,
  1985–1987, 1:78
International Directory of
  Little Magazines and Small
  Presses, 1:52
International Directory of
  Philosophy and Philoso-
  phers, 1990–92, 4:6
The International Economic
  Order, 3:58
International Encyclopaedia
  of Robotics, 5:242
International Encyclopedia of
  Population, 3:206
International Encyclopedia of
  Statistics, 5:521
International Encyclopedia of
  the Social Sciences, 3:5,
  3:272
International Encyclopedia of
  Women Composers, 3:654
The International Energy Re-
  lations of China, 5:281
An International Episode and
  Other Stories, 1:763
The International Farm Cri-
  sis, 3:47
International Film Guide,
  3:825

The International Flow of In-
  formation: A Trans-Pacific
  Perspective, 1:49
International Folk Dance at
  a Glance, 3:851
International Handbook of
  Behavior Modification and
  Therapy, 5:417
International Handbook of
  Historical Studies, 3:276
International Handbook on
  Aging, 5:317
International Issues in Ener-
  gy Policy, Development
  and Economics, 5:280
The International Kosher
  Cookbook, 4:602
International Law: Cases and
  Materials, 3:144
The International Law Dic-
  tionary, 3:144
International Literary Market
  Place, 1:52, 1:69
International Perspectives on
  the Falklands Conflict,
  3:633
International Rare Book
  Prices: Early Printed
  Books, 1:1988, 1:78
International Rare Book
  Prices: Modern First Edi-
  tions, 1:1988, 1:78
International Relations be-
  tween the Two World
  Wars, 1919–1939, 3:278,
  3:344
International Research Cen-
  ters Directory, 1:105
An International Sourcebook
  of Paper History, 1:5
The International Telecom-
  munication Union, 3:803
The International Thesaurus
  of Quotations, 1:117
International Trade and Eco-
  nomic Development, 3:111
The International Traveler's
  Security Handbook, 3:892
International Trotskyism,
  1929–1985, 3:295
The International Type Book,
  1:62
International Who's Who,
  1:86
International Who's Who in
  Energy and Nuclear Sci-
  ences, 5:652
International Who's Who in
  Music and Musician's Di-
  rectory 1990-91, 3:656
The Internet Companion: A
  Beginner's Guide to Glo-
  bal Networking, 5:547

Interpersonal Perception,
  5:459
The Interpersonal Theory of
  Psychiatry, 5:471
Interplay of East and West:
  Points of Conflict and Co-
  operation, 3:296
The Interplay of Influence:
  News, Advertising, Politics,
  and the Mass Media, 3:803
Interpretation, Deconstruc-
  tion, and Ideology, 1:924,
  4:391
An Interpretation of Brazil-
  ian Literature, 2:890
The Interpretation of Cul-
  tures, 1:980, 1:1131, 3:14,
  3:31, 4:263, 4:477, 4:478
The Interpretation of
  Dreams, 3:183, 5:446
Interpretation of Mass Spec-
  tra of Organic Com-
  pounds, 5:743
The Interpretation of Ordinary Landscapes: Geo-
  graphical Essays, 3:133
The Interpretation of Quan-
  tum Mechanics, 5:67
An Interpretation of Religion: Human Responses to
  the Transcendent, 4:40
Interpretation of Schizophre-
  nia, 5:426
The Interpretation of the
  Fourth Gospel, 4:825,
  4:833
Interpretation of the New
  Testament, 1861–1961,
  4:814
An Interpretation of Univer-
  sal History, 3:294, 3:327,
  4:314
An Interpretation of White-
  head's Metaphysics, 4:342
Interpretations and Forecasts,
  1922–1972, 5:170
Interpretations of American
  History, 3:513
Interpretations of Islam: Past
  and Present, 4:573
Interpretations of Life, 3:401
Interpretations of Marx,
  3:222, 3:290
Interpretations of Poetry and
  Religion: Critical Edition,
  4:326
Interpretation Theory: Disc-
  ourse and the Surplus of
  Meaning, 4:319, 4:426
The Interpreters, 2:148, 2:149
The Interpreter's Bible, 4:820
The Interpreter's Dictionary
  of the Bible, 4:818

The Interpreter's One-Volume Commentary on the Bible, 4:819

Interpreting across Boundaries: New Essays in Comparative Philosophy, 4:349

Interpreting Earth History, 5:624

Interpreting Folklore, 3:848

Interpreting Husserl: Critical and Comparative Studies, 4:234

Interpreting Maimonides, 4:668

Interpreting Modern Philosophy, 4:160

Interpreting the City: An Urban Geography, 3:124

Interpreting the Countertransference, 5:425

Interpreting the Indian, 1:631

Interpreting the Psalms, 4:823

Interpreting the Sacred: Ways of Viewing Religion, 4:422

Interpreting Wittgenstein: A Cloud of Philosophy, a Drop of Grammar, 4:347

Interregional and International Trade, 3:59

Interrelations of Literature, 2:987

Intersections, 1:1144

Intertextuality and the Reading of Midrash, 4:620

Intervention in the Caribbean: The Dominican Crisis of 1965, 3:636

Interventions for Children of Divorce: Custody, Access, and Psychotherapy, 5:416

Interview, 1:1114

Interviews (Barnes), 1:813

Interviews (Dorn), 1:970

Interviews and Conversations with 20th Century Authors Writing in English, 1:127

Interviews and Encounters, 1:1003

Interview with a Vampire, 1:1242

Interview with History, 2:420

In the Absence of Angels: A Hollywood Family's Courageous Story, 5:387

In the Absence of the Sacred, 5:129

In the African-American Grain: Call and Response in Twentieth-Century Black Fiction, 1:803

In the African-American Grain: The Pursuit of Voice in Twentieth-Century Black Fiction, 1:804, 1:917

In the Age of Prose: Literary and Philosophical Essays, 2:565

In the Age of the Smart Machine: The Future of Work and Power, 5:574

In the Beginning (Potok), 1:1032

In the Beginning (Ratushinskaya), 2:753

In the Beginning: Stories from the Bible, 2:36

In the Boom Boom Room, 1:1109

In the Burning Darkness, 2:532

In the Castle of My Skin, 2:936, 2:937

In the Cause of True Education, 3:259

In the Company of Others, 5:372

In the Course of Human Events, 3:521

In the Days of the Comet, 1:563

In the Ditch, 2:136, 2:137

In the Egg and Other Poems, 2:583

In the Eye of the Beholder, 2:65

In the Feminine Mode: Essays on Hispanic Women Writers, 2:523

In the Flesh, 1:600

In the Fog of the Season's End, 2:164

In the Footsteps of Le Corbusier, 3:779

In the Footsteps of Muhammed, 4:576

In the Freud Archives, 3:184

In the Glass Case: Essays on New Zealand Literature, 2:971

In the Heart of the Heart of the Country, 1:980, 2:160

In the Heart of the Seas: A Story of a Journey to the Land of Israel, 2:11

In the Heart's Last Kingdom, 1:893

In the Hills Where Her Dreams Live, 2:941

In the Interest of the Governed, 4:191

In Their Own Voices: African Women Writers Talk, 2:109

In Their Wisdom, 1:550

In the Land of Israel, 2:23, 4:643

In the Land of the Olmec, 4:455

In the Land of Unfrightened Birds, 2:749

In the Lap of Atlas: Stories of Morocco, 1:497

In the Margin of History, 3:407

In the Margins of Cervantes, 2:536

In the Matter of J. Robert Oppenheimer, 5:707

In the Mecca, 1:954

In the Middle: Writing, Reading and Learning with Adolescents, 3:253

In the Midst of Winter: Selections from the Literature of Mourning, 1:130

In the Mirror: Literature and Politics in the American Era, 2:336

In the Mirror of the Past, 5:136, 5:137

In the Moment: Jazz in the 1980s, 3:668

In the Name of Eugenics: Genetics and the Uses of Human Heredity, 5:48

In the Name of Science, 5:507

In the Nature of Materials, 1887–1941, 3:798

In the Night Kitchen, 1:1206

In the Palace of the King, 1:1244

In the Patient's Interest: Access to Hospital Care, 5:331

In the Presence of the Creator: Isaac Newton and His Times, 4:184, 5:41, 5:706

In the Rainforest: Report from a Strange, Beautiful, Imperiled World, 5:821

In the Realm of Pleasure, 1:1177

In the Secret Theatre of Home, 1:346

In the Servitude of Power—Energy and Civilization through the Ages, 5:278

In the Shade of Spring Leaves, 2:287

In the Shade of the Giant: Essays on Tolstoy, 2:766

In the Shadow of FDR: From Harry Truman to Ronald Reagan, 3:539, 3:585
In the Shadow of Man, 5:833
In the Shadow of Power: The Story of the Washington Post, 3:808
In the Shadow of the Enlightenment, 4:841
In the Shadow of the Mexican Revolution, 3:638
In the Shadow of the Sacred Grove, 3:905
In the Shadow's Light, 2:461
In the Shadows of Romance, 1:271
In the Skin of a Lion, 2:922
In the South Seas, 1:397
In the Spirit of William James, 1:769
In the Steps of the Master, 3:932
In the Storm, 2:45
In the Teeth of the Evidence, 1:610
In the Trail of the Wind, 1:1196
In the Village of Viger, 2:926
In the Village of Viger and Other Stories, 2:926
In the Vineyard of the Text, 5:136, 5:137
In the Wake of Galileo, 5:604, 5:689
In the Wet, 2:962
In the Wine Time, 1:1086
In the World of Sumer: An Autobiography, 4:441
In the Year of Jubilee, 1:358
In This Our Life, 1:843
In This World and the Next: Selected Writings, 2:43
The Intifada, 3:440
Intimate Exchanges, 1:436, 1:437
The Intimate Journal, 2:505
The Intimate Journals of Paul Gauguin, 3:775
Intimate Journeys: Stories from Life-Changing Therapy, 5:438
Intimate Letter to Millions, 2:874
The Intimate Machine: Close Encounters with Computers and Robots, 5:567
Intimate Matters: A History of Sexuality in America, 3:552
Intimate Memoirs, 2:508
Intimate Relations, 2:468

Intimate Things, 2:790
Intimations of Mortality, 4:293
Intolerance, 1:1167
Into Print: A Practical Guide to Writing, Illustrating, and Publishing, 1:47
Into the Breach: Samuel Beckett and the Ends of Literature, 2:460
Into the Great Solitude: An Arctic Journey, 3:906
Into the Heart of the Mind: An American Quest for Artificial Intelligence, 5:569
Into the Labyrinth: Essays on the Art of Lawrence Durrell, 1:470
Into the Mainstream: Conversations with Latin American Writers, 2:846
Into the World of Light, 2:977
In Transit, 2:912
Intricate and Simple Things: The Poetry of Galway Kinnell, 1:1001
Introducing Erik Erikson: An Invitation to His Thinking, 3:182
Introducing Jacques Ellul, 5:165
Introducing Liberation Theology, 4:896
Introducing New Gods: The Politics of Athenian Religion, 4:447
Introducing Persons, 4:382
Introducing Philosophy: A Text with Integrated Writings, 4:24
Introducing Religion: From Inside and Outside, 4:883
Introducing Shakespeare, 1:222
Introducing the Existentialists, 4:267
Introducing the Psalms, 4:824
Introducing the UNIX System, 5:555
Introducing Witi Ihimaera, 2:978
Introduction of Logic, 4:103
Introduction of Swedenborg's Religious Thought, 4:880
The Introduction of Western Literary Theories into Modern China 1919–1925, 2:234
An Introduction to African Literature, 2:106

Introduction to African Religion, 4:370, 4:463
An Introduction to American Literature, 2:856
An Introduction to Analog and Digital Communications, 5:299
Introduction to Ancient History, 3:298
An Introduction to Ancient Iranian Religions, 4:443, 4:547
An Introduction to Ancient Philosophy, 4:46
An Introduction to Anglo-Saxon England, 3:356
Introduction to Appropriate Technology: Toward a Simpler Life-Style, 5:213
Introduction to Automated Theory, Languages, and Computation, 5:568
An Introduction to Biblical Hebrew Syntax, 4:795
An Introduction to Bibliographical and Textual Studies, 1:63
An Introduction to Bibliography for Literary Students, 1:62
Introduction to Bibliography—Seminar Syllabus, 1:61
An Introduction to Child Psychiatry, 5:416
An Introduction to Chinese Civilization, 2:186
An Introduction to Chinese Literature, 2:190
Introduction to Classical Arabic Literature, 2:55
An Introduction to Classical Ballet, 3:733
Introduction to Classical Mechanics, 5:659
An Introduction to Climate, 5:634
Introduction to Climatology, 5:634
An Introduction to Coastal Geomorphology, 5:627
Introduction to Communications Engineering, 5:299
An Introduction to Communication Systems, 5:296
An Introduction to Communication Theory and Systems, 5:300
Introduction to Comparative Literature, 2:983
Introduction to Comparative Philosophy, 4:38

Introduction to Concepts and Theories in Physical Science, 5:17

Introduction to Contemporary Japanese Literature, 2:283

Introduction to Cosmology, 5:655

Introduction to Counseling, 5:418

Introduction to Critical Theory, 4:264, 4:404, 5:89

Introduction to Crop Husbandry, Including Grasslands, 5:263

An Introduction to Database Systems, 5:559

An Introduction to Democratic Theory, 3:143

Introduction to Digital Communication, 5:302

An Introduction to Digital Signal Processing (Karl), 5:302

Introduction to Digital Signal Processing (Kug), 5:296

An Introduction to Divine and Human Readings, 4:98

Introduction to Early Greek Philosophy, 4:47

An Introduction to Econometric Forecasting and Forecasting Models, 3:88

Introduction to Electrodynamics and Radiation, 5:698

Introduction to Energy—Resources, Technology, and Society, 5:278

Introduction to Existentialism, 4:264

An Introduction to Exploration Economics, 5:286

Introduction to Film Criticism, 3:827

An Introduction to Genetic Analysis, 5:778

An Introduction to Genetics, 5:788

Introduction to Geochemistry, 5:628

Introduction to Geographic Field Methods and Techniques, 5:620

Introduction to Geometry, 5:486

Introduction to Geophysical Exploration, 5:629

An Introduction to Haiku, 2:274

Introduction to Health Assessment, 5:340

An Introduction to Health Psychology, 5:339

Introduction to Health Services, 5:329

An Introduction to Hegel, 4:233

Introduction to High Energy Physics, 5:662

An Introduction to Homer, 2:361

Introduction to Information Theory, 5:550

Introduction to Information Theory: Symbols, Signals, and Noise, 5:581

Introduction to Interactive Computer Graphics, 5:565

An Introduction to Islam, 3:442, 4:568

Introduction to Islamic Civilization, 4:572

Introduction to Islamic Theology and Law, 4:575

An Introduction to Japanese Court Poetry, 2:273

Introduction to Jewish Bible Commentary, 4:628

An Introduction to Judaism. Textbook and Anthology, 4:596

Introduction to Korean History and Culture, 3:481

Introduction to Laser Physics, 5:666

Introduction to Library Research in Anthropology, 3:11

An Introduction to Literature in Brazil, 2:890

An Introduction to Logic, 5:101

Introduction to Logical Theory, 4:414

An Introduction to Logic and Scientific Method, 5:95

Introduction to Managerial Economics, 3:49

Introduction to Marine Engineering, 5:239

Introduction to Marx and Engels, 4:243

Introduction to Mathematical Philosophy, 4:323, 5:516

An Introduction to Mathematical Statistics and Its Applications, 5:529

Introduction to Mathematics, 4:341, 5:482

An Introduction to Medieval Islamic Philosophy, 4:97, 4:575

An Introduction to Metaphysics: The Creative Mind, 5:789

An Introduction to Metaphysics, 4:291

Introduction to Meteorology, 5:633

Introduction to Modern Bulgarian Literature, 2:781

An Introduction to Modern Economics, 3:102

Introduction to Modern Filipino Literature, 2:329

Introduction to Modern Greek Literature, 2:371

Introduction to Modern Polish Literature, 2:811

Introduction to Modern Spanish Literature, 2:526

Introduction to Mongolian History, 4:542

An Introduction to Motivation, 3:175

Introduction to Natural Language Processing, 5:564

An Introduction to Nichiren Shoshu Buddhism, 4:538

An Introduction to Nuclear Physics, 5:658

Introduction to Nuclear Power, 5:287

An Introduction to Numerical Reasoning, 5:524

Introduction to Object-Oriented Databases, 5:559

Introduction to Oil and Gas Technology, 5:241

Introduction to Optical Fiber Communication Systems, 5:303

Introduction to Paradise Lost, 1:192

Introduction to Pascal: Including Turbo Pascal, 5:553

An Introduction to Persian Literature, 2:83

An Introduction to Philo Judaeus, 4:60, 4:670

Introduction to Philosophy (Geisler), 4:21

An Introduction to Philosophy (Maritain), 4:22, 4:306

An Introduction to Philosophy (Nakhnikian), 4:23

An Introduction to Philosophy (Olscamp), 4:23

Introduction to Philosophy (Stroll and Popkin), 4:24

Introduction to Philosophy: A Case Study Approach, 4:23

Introduction to Philosophy: An Inquiry after a Rational System of Scientific Principles in the Relation to the Ultimate Reality, 4:22

Introduction to Philosophy: Classical and Contemporary Readings, 4:23

Introduction to Philosophy: From Wonder to World View, 4:24

An Introduction to Philosophy: Ideas in Conflict, 4:25

Introduction to Physical Gas Dynamics, 5:257

An Introduction to Physical Geography, 3:126

An Introduction to Piaget, 3:193

Introduction to Pipe Stress Analysis, 5:224

Introduction to Plane Geometry, 5:486

An Introduction to Plant Cell Development, 5:767

An Introduction to Plasma Physics, 5:667

An Introduction to Plato's Laws, 4:84

An Introduction to Plato's Republic, 4:78

An Introduction to Poetry, 1:1048

Introduction to Polish Versification, 2:811

An Introduction to Political Science Methods, 3:138

Introduction to Positive Philosophy, 3:224, 4:222

Introduction to Printing: The Craft of Letterpress, 1:11

Introduction to Psychoanalysis: Lectures for Child Analysts and Teachers, 5:444

Introduction to Psychology: Exploration and Application, 5:413

Introduction to Quantum Mechanics with Applications to Chemistry, 5:752

Introduction to Reference Work, 1:73, 1:80, 1:81

An Introduction to Rembrandt, 3:789

Introduction to Roman Law, 3:306

An Introduction to Ruskin, 1:394

Introduction to Scandinavian Literature, 2:638

Introduction to Scholarship in Modern Languages and Literatures, 1:1128

An Introduction to Science Studies, 5:20

Introduction to Scientific Geographic Research, 5:620

Introduction to Signals and Systems, 5:296

Introduction to Solid State Physics, 5:668

An Introduction to Sophocles, 2:368

Introduction to Spanish American Literature, 2:846

An Introduction to Spanish Literature, 2:523

An Introduction to Spatial Allocation Analysis, 3:136

Introduction to St. Thomas Aquinas, 4:117

An Introduction to Survey Research and Data Analysis, 3:138

Introduction to Symbolic Logic and Its Applications, 4:278

Introduction to Systems Philosophy—Toward a New Paradigm of Contemporary Thought, 4:265

Introduction to the Atmosphere, 5:634

Introduction to the Code of Maimonides (Mishneh Torah), 4:627

Introduction to the Dance, 3:731

An Introduction to the Development of Modern Malay Language and Literature, 2:324

Introduction to the English Novel, 1:421

An Introduction to the Foundations and Fundamental Concepts of Mathematics, 5:493

Introduction to the Foundations of Mathematics, 5:494

An Introduction to the Franciscan Literature of the Middle Ages, 4:699

An Introduction to the French Caribbean, 2:930

An Introduction to the Geometry of Numbers, 5:488

An Introduction to the History of Mathematics, 5:492

An Introduction to the History of Medicine, 5:50

An Introduction to the History of Psychology, 3:167

Introduction to the History of Religions, 4:494

Introduction to the History of Science, 5:39, 5:56

Introduction to the History of Sociology, 5:34

Introduction to the Human Sciences, 4:226

An Introduction to the Industrial History of England, 5:57

An Introduction to the Logic of the Sciences, 4:384

An Introduction to the Medieval Mystics of Europe, 4:697

Introduction to the Modern Economic History of the Middle East, 3:436

Introduction to the New Testament, 4:449, 4:816

Introduction to the Old Testament, 4:816

Introduction to Theoretical Geomorphology, 5:627

An Introduction to Theories of Learning, 3:175

Introduction to the Philosophy of History, 3:275

Introduction to the Philosophy of Science (Carnap), 5:62, 5:85

Introduction to the Philosophy of Science (Lambert), 5:64

Introduction to the Philosophy of Science (O'Hear), 4:385

Introduction to the Philosophy of Science (Salmon), 5:65

An Introduction to the Philosophy of Time and Space, 5:67

An Introduction to the Politics and Philosophy of José Ortega y Gasset, 4:315

An Introduction to the Principles of Morals and Legislation, 3:150, 4:190

Introduction to the Problem of Individuation in the Early Middle Ages, 4:101

Introduction to the Qur'an (Bell), 4:587

An Introduction to the Qur'an (Watt), 4:587

Introduction to the Reading of Hegel, 4:233

Introduction to the Reformed Tradition, 4:762
An Introduction to the Science of Comparative Mythology and Folklore, 3:848
Introduction to the Sociology of Music, 3:658, 4:393
Introduction to the Study of Comparative Literature, 2:983
An Introduction to the Study of Experimental Medicine, 5:789
An Introduction to the Study of Language, 3:27
Introduction to the Study of Philosophy, 4:21
An Introduction to the Study of Public Policy, 3:146
An Introduction to the Study of Stellar Structure, 5:677
An Introduction to the Study of Theravada Buddhism in Burma, 4:519
Introduction to the Talmud, 4:610
Introduction to the Talmud and Midrash, 4:613, 4:812
Introduction to the Technic of Child Analysis, 5:444
An Introduction to the Theology of Karl Barth, 4:758
An Introduction to the Theory of Atomic and Molecular Collisions, 5:658
Introduction to the Theory of Employment, 3:102
An Introduction to the Theory of Numbers, 5:488
An Introduction to the Theory of Random Signals and Noise, 5:298
An Introduction to the Theory of Seismology, 5:629
Introduction to the Work of Melanie Klein, 5:457
An Introduction to the Writings of Ngugi, 2:155
An Introduction to Tudor Drama, 1:169
Introduction to Typography, 1:11
Introduction to United States Government Information Sources, 1:108, 3:506
An Introduction to Urban Geographic Information Systems, 3:120
Introduction to Value Theory, 4:317, 5:101
An Introduction to Vietnamese Literature, 2:339

An Introduction to Virgil's Aeneid, 2:397
Introduction to William James: An Essay and Selected Texts, 4:238
Introduction to Wittgenstein's Tractatus, 4:344
Introduction to Yoga, 4:550
Introduction to Yugoslav Literature, 2:786, 2:808, 2:828, 2:835
An Introduction to Zen Buddhism, 4:558
An Introductory Bibliography for the Study of Scripture, 4:795
Introductory Bibliography to the Study of Hungarian Literature, 2:798
Introductory Biophysics, 5:775
Introductory Essays, 2:849
An Introductory Guide to Cultural Theory and Popular Culture, 3:874
Introductory Lectures on Psychoanalysis, 5:446
Introductory Nuclear Physics, 5:658
Introductory Philosophy, 4:25
Introductory Quantum Mechanics, 5:660
Introductory Readings in Geographic Information Systems, 3:120
Introductory Readings in Philosophy, 4:24
Introductory Solid State Physics, 5:668
Introspection and Contemporary Poetry, 1:914
Introspective Voyager: The Poetic Development of Wallace Stevens, 1:888
In Trouble Again: A Journey between the Orinoco and the Amazon, 3:896
Intruder in the Dust, 1:835
Intuition and Ego States: The Origins of Transactional Analysis, 5:434
Intuition and Reflection in Self-Consciousness, 4:364, 4:365
Intuitive Cognition: A Key to the Significance of the Later Scholastics, 4:114
Invalu, the Eskimo Wife, 3:921
The Invasion from Mars, 3:202
The Invasion of Canada, 1812–1813, 3:612

The Invasion of the Crimea, 3:925
Invasive Procedures: A Year in the World of Two Surgeons, 5:314
Invented Lives: The Marriage of F. Scott and Zelda Fitzgerald, 1:840
Inventing AIDS, 1:1182, 3:202
Inventing America: Jefferson's Declaration of Independence, 3:522, 3:544
Inventing a Word, 2:849
Inventing Reality: Politics and the Mass Media, 3:808
Inventing the NIH: Federal Biomedical Research Policy, 1887–1937, 5:313
Inventing the People, 3:521, 3:588
Invention: The Care and Feeding of Ideas, 5:584
Invention of Africa: Gnosis, Philosophy, and the Order of Knowledge, 4:369
The Invention of Li Yu, 2:210
The Invention of Morel, 2:855
The Invention of Morel and Other Stories, 2:855
The Invention of Physical Science, 5:32
The Invention of the Modern Hospital: Boston, 1870–1930, 5:329
The Invention of the World, 2:913
The Invention of Tradition, 3:405, 3:869
Inventions: Writing, Textuality, and Understanding in Literary History, 1:924
The Inventions of Mark Twain, 1:784
Inventive Minds: Profiles of Creativity in Science and Industry, 5:726
The Inverted Bell, 1:901
The Inverted Medical Dictionary, 5:6
Investigating Philosophy, 4:38
Investigating the Earth, 5:623
The Investigation, 2:614
Investing in People: The Economics of Population Quality, 3:57
Investments, 3:56
An Invincible Memory, 2:898
The Invisible Book: Epilogue, 2:716
Invisible Cities, 2:412

Invisible Colleges: Diffusion of Knowledge in Scientific Communities, 3:213

Invisible Criticism: Ralph Ellison and the American Canon, 1:974

The Invisible Epidemic: The Story of Women and AIDS, 5:387

Invisible Friends, 1:437

Invisible Guests: The Development of Imaginal Dialogues, 5:420

Invisible Invaders: The Story of the Emerging Age of Viruses, 5:314

The Invisible Land: A Study of the Artistic Imagination of Iurii Olesha, 2:744

Invisible Man (Ellison), 1:973, 1:974

The Invisible Man (Wells), 1:563

Invisible Poets: Afro-Americans of the Nineteenth Century, 1:655, 1:719

Invisible Reality, 2:542

Invisible Storytellers: Voiceover Narration in American Fiction Film, 3:825

Invisible Swords, 1:833

The Invisible Work Force, 3:60

Invitation to a Beheading, 2:739, 2:740

An Invitation to Book Collecting, 1:34

Invitation to Engineering, 5:227

An Invitation to Japanese Civilization, 4:535

Invitation to Midrash, 4:611

Invitation to Number Theory, 5:488

An Invitation to Philosophy (Capaldi), 4:20

Invitation to Philosophy (Hollis), 4:21

Invitation to Philosophy (Honer and Hunt), 4:21

Invitation to Physics, 5:653

An Invitation to Sociology: A Humanistic Perspective, 3:221

Invitation to Struggle: Congress, the President and Foreign Policy, 3:544

An Invitation to the Opera, 3:670

Invitation to the Talmud: A Teaching Book, 4:611

Invitation to the Theatre, 1:1074

Inviting Death: Indian Attitude towards the Ritual Death, 4:510

Involuntary Treatment of the Mentally Ill: The Problem of Autonomy, 5:419

The "Inward" Language, 1:165

In Which We Serve, 1:465

In Xanadu: A Quest, 3:902

Iola Leroy, 1:753, 1:1144

Ion, 2:355, 2:356, 2:825

Ionia: A Quest, 3:939

The Ionian Islands to Rhodes: A Sea Guide, 3:899

Ionian Philosophy, 4:47

I Ought to Be in Pictures, 1:1113

Iowa Legends of Buried Treasures, 3:862

Iphigenia in Aulis, 2:355, 2:356

Iphigenia in Tauris, 2:355, 2:356

Iphigénie, 2:498

I Presume: H. M. Stanley's Triumph and Disaster, 3:938

Iqbal: Manifestation of the Islamic Spirit, 4:375

Iqbal through Western Eyes, 4:375

The IQ Controversy, 3:174

Iracema. The Honey Lips, a Legend of Brazil, 2:891

Iran: From Religious Dispute to Revolution, 3:448

Iran as Imagined Nation, 3:449

Iranian Drama: An Anthology, 2:84

An Iranian Odyssey, 3:448

Iranian Short Story Authors: A Bio-bibliographic Survey, 2:83

Iranian Society: An Anthology of Writings, 2:86

The Iran-Iraq War: Old Conflicts, New Weapons, 3:449, 3:450

Iran Past and Present: From Monarchy to Islamic Republic, 3:449

Iran's Foreign Policy, 1941–1973, 3:448

Iraq: Economics, Oil and Politics, 3:450

Iraq, 1900–1950, 3:450

Iraq and Iran: Roots of Conflict, 3:448, 3:450

The Iraq-Iran War: A Bibliography, 3:435

Ireland, 1:375

Ireland: 1912–1985, Politics and Society, 3:371

Ireland: A History, 3:369

Ireland: An Illustrated History, 3:370

Ireland: A Social and Cultural History, 1922 to the Present, 3:370

Ireland: From Colony to Nation State, 3:369

Ireland: The Union and Its Aftermath, 3:364

Ireland and the Culture of Early Medieval Europe, 3:328, 3:370

Ireland and the Irish in Maritime History, 3:371

Ireland in the Age of Imperialism and Revolution, 1760–1801, 3:370

Ireland since the Famine, 3:371

I Remember: Sketch for an Autobiography, 2:746

I Remember Balanchine, 3:738

Iridion, 2:815

The Irish Beckett, 1:440

Irish Bookbindings, 1:22

Irish Elegies, 1:461

Irish Essays, 1:430

Irish Folk History Plays, 1:490

The Irish in Ontario: A Study in Rural History, 3:608

Irish Journal, 2:570

An Irishman in Dixie, 3:528

Irish Poetry after Yeats: Seven Poets, 1:418

Irish Political Documents, 1896–1916, 3:370

Irish Political Documents, 1916–1949, 3:370

Irish Politics and Social Conflict in the Age of the American Revolution, 3:370

Irish Renaissance, 1:417

Irish Studies: A General Introduction, 3:369

Iris Murdoch, 1:524

Iris Murdoch: Figures of Good, 1:524

Iris Murdoch: The Saint and the Artist, 1:524

Iris Murdoch: The Shakespearian Interest, 1:524

Iris Murdoch: Work for the Spirit, 1:524

Iris Murdoch and Muriel Spark: A Bibliography, 1:524, 1:552

Iron Cages: Race and Culture in 19th-Century America, 3:557

Iron Earth, Copper Sky, 2:100

The Iron Heel, 1:773, 1:774

The Iron Horse, 1:1165

Ironic Drama, 2:357

The Ironies of Progress: Henry Adams and the American Dream, 1:730

Iron John: A Book About Men, 1:951

Iron Lady, 3:368

The Iron Pillar—The Mishnah: Redaction, Form, and Intent, 4:613

The Iron Staircase, 2:508

Ironweed, 1:996, 1:997

Ironwood 22: Robert Duncan—A Special Issue, 1:971

Irony and Ideology in Rabelais: Structures of Subversion, 2:497

The Irony of Regulatory Form, 3:803

The Irrationality of History and the Tragedy of Mankind, 3:284

Irrational Man: A Study in Existential Philosophy, 2:988, 4:262

The Irreverent, but Indispensable, Guide to Hair Loss Solutions, 5:399

Irving Fisher: A Biography, 3:76

Irving Layton: The Poet and His Critics, 2:918

Irving to Irving: Author-Publisher Relations 1800–1974, 1:38

Isaac Asimov, 1:1254

Isaac Asimov: A Checklist of Works Published in the United States, 1:1254, 5:14

Isaac Asimov: Scientist and Storyteller, 5:14

Isaac Asimov: The Foundation of Science Fiction, 1:1254

Isaac Asimov's Treasury of Humor, 3:870

Isaac Babel (Bloom), 2:700

Isaac Babel (Ehre), 2:700

Isaac Babel: Russian Master of the Short Story, 2:700

Isaac Bashevis Singer (Malin), 2:49

Isaac Bashevis Singer (Siegel), 2:49

Isaac Bashevis Singer: A Study of the Short Fiction, 1:1050

Isaac Bashevis Singer: The Magician of West 86th Street, 2:49

Isaac Bashevis Singer: The Story of a Storyteller, 1:1050, 2:49

Isaac Bashevis Singer and the Eternal Past, 2:48

Isaac Bashevis Singer on Literature and Life: An Interview, 1:1050

Isaac Mayer Wise: Shaping American Judaism, 4:653

Isaac Rosenberg: The Half Used Life, 1:541

Isabella, 1:293

Isadora and Esenin, 2:718

Isadora Duncan: The Russian Years, 3:742

Isadora Speaks, 3:741

Isaiah, 4:709

Isaiah Thomas: Printer, Writer and Collector, 1:44

Isak Dinesen: The Life and Imagination of a Seducer, 2:649

Isak Dinesen: The Life of a Storyteller, 2:649

Isak Dinesen and the Engendering of Narrative, 2:649

Isak Dinesen's Art: The Gayety of Vision, 2:649

Isambard Brunel, 5:250

Isambard Kingdom Brunel: A Biography, 5:250

Isambard Kingdom Brunel: Engineering Knight-Errant, 5:250

Is Anyone Out There?, 5:598

Is Anyone Responsible? How Television Frames Political Issues, 3:811

Isara: A Voyage Around "Essay," 2:149

I Saw Two Englands, 3:932

ISDN, 5:299

ISDN and Broadband ISDN, 5:300

ISDN Design: A Practical Approach, 5:299

ISDN Explained: Worldwide Network and Applications Technology, 5:299

ISDN in Perspective, 5:299

I Served the King of England, 2:792

Isfahan Is Half the World: Memories of a Persian Boyhood, 2:92

Is Five . . . 1926, 1:825

Is He Popenjoy, 1:405

Isherwood: A Biography of Christopher Isherwood, 1:501

Isherwood's Fiction: The Self and Technique, 1:501

Ishmael, 1:333

Isis, 5:55

Isis Cumulative Bibliography, 1966–1975, 5:28

Isis Current Bibliography, 5:24, 5:37

Isis Unveiled, 4:852, 4:873, 4:874

Islam, 3:442

Islam (al Faruqi), 4:574

Islam (Denny), 4:883

Islam (Guillaume), 4:575

Islam (Masse), 4:572

Islam (Rahman), 4:576

Islam (Williams), 4:577

Islam: A Concise Introduction, 4:576

Islam: A Way of Life, 3:443, 3:457, 4:569

Islam: Belief and Practice, 4:577

Islam: Beliefs and Institutions, 4:575

Islam: Beliefs and Observances, 4:574

Islam: Continuity and Change in the Modern World, 4:573

Islam: From the Prophet Muhammad to the Capture of Constantinople, 4:571

Islam: Legacy of the Past, Challenge of the Future, 4:579

Islam: Politics and Religion in the Muslim World, 3:437

Islam: Social and Economic Structure, 3:443

Islam: The Fear and the Hope, 3:442, 4:578

Islam: The Religious and Political Life of a World Community, 4:570

Islam: The Straight Path, 3:442

Islam: The Straight Path—Islam Interpreted by Muslims, 4:576

Al-Islam: Unity and Leadership, 4:579, 4:862

Islam, Philosophy and Science, 4:373

Islam, Politics, and Social Movements, 4:578

Islam and Capitalism, 3:444, 4:579

Islam and Christianity, 4:571

Islam and Christian Theology, 4:573

Islam and Colonialism: The Doctrine of Jihad in Modern History, 4:895

Islam and Democracy: Fear of the Modern World, 3:444, 4:579

Islam and Development: Religion and Sociopolitical Change, 4:578

Islam and Its Cultural Divergence, 4:576

Islam and Modernism in Egypt, 4:374

Islam and Modernity: Transformation of an Intellectual Tradition, 3:444, 4:373

Islam and Nationalism, 4:372

Islam and Politics, 4:578

Islam and Revolution: Writings and Declarations of Imam Khomeini, 3:443

Islam and the Arab World: Faith, People, Culture, 3:459

Islam and the Modern Age, 4:571

Islam and the Plight of Modern Man, 4:375

Islam and the Political Economy of Meaning, 4:580

Islam and the West: A Historical Cultural Survey, 3:436, 3:457

Islam and the West, 3:443, 4:568

Islamic Architecture, 3:763

Islamic Art, 3:760

Islamic Bindings and Bookmaking, 1:22

Islamic Bookbindings in the Victoria and Albert Museum, 1:23

The Islamic Concept of Religion and Its Revival, 3:444

Islamic Culture and Socio-Economic Change, 3:442

Islamic Fundamentalism and Modernity, 4:373

Islamic History of the Middle East, 4:567

The Islamic Impact, 4:578

Islamic Iran: Revolution and Counterrevolution, 4:578

Islamic Middle East, 700–1900, 3:444

Islamic Modernism in India and Pakistan, 4:567, 4:577

Islamic Philosophical Theology, 4:576

Islamic Philosophy and Mysticism, 4:576

Islamic Philosophy and Theology, 4:97, 4:577

Islamic Reform, 4:374

Islamic Resurgence in the Arab World, 3:442

Islamic Revival in British India: Deoband, 1860–1900, 3:485, 4:572

Islamic Revolution: The Iranian Experiment, 3:448

Islamic Society and the West, 4:569

Islamic Society in the West, 3:456

Islamic Spain, 1250 to 1500, 3:387

Islamic Spirituality, 4:885, 4:888, 4:902

The Islamic Threat: Myth or Reality?, 4:578

The Islamic Tradition, 3:442

The Islamic Understanding of Death and Resurrection, 4:887

Islam in Asia: Religion, Politics, and Society, 3:463

Islam in Asia: Southeast and East Asia, 3:443

Islam in a World of Diverse Faiths, 4:568

Islam in East Africa, 3:444

Islam Inflamed, 4:572

Islam in Foreign Policy, 3:442

Islam in Modern History, 4:573

Islam in North America: A Sourcebook, 4:6

Islam in Perspective: A Guide to Islamic Society, 3:442

Islam in Practice, 4:579

Islam in Revolution: Fundamentalism in the Arab World, 4:568

Islam in South East Asia, 4:518

Islam in the Contemporary World, 4:572

Islam in the Modern National State, 4:580

Islam in the Modern World, 3:442, 4:579

Islam in the Political Process, 3:444

Islam in the World, 4:572

Islam in Transition: Muslim Perspectives, 4:373

Islam in Tropical Africa, 3:443, 4:571

Islam in Uganda, 4:572

The Islamization of Laws in Pakistan, 4:579

Islam Observed, 3:23, 3:31, 3:443, 4:478, 4:569

Islam Unveiled: The True Desert Storm, 3:444

The Island (Creeley), 1:965

The Island (Huxley), 1:499

The Island Acadians, 1720–1980, 3:611

Island Nights Entertainments, 1:396

The Island of Crimea, 2:697

Island of Cuba, 3:131

The Island of Dr. Moreau, 1:563

Island of History, 4:462

The Island of Tears, 2:155

The Island of the Mighty, 1:433, 1:434

The Island Press Bibliography of Environmental Literature, 5:817

The Islands (Alberts), 2:622

Islands (Fowles), 1:478

Islands: A Treasury of Contemporary Travel Writing, 3:892

The Islands in Between: Essays in West Indian Literature, 2:930

Islands in the Stream, 1:845

Islands in the Street, 3:216

The Islands of Boston Harbor: 1630–1971, 3:937

Islands of History, 3:496

Isla Negra: a Notebook, 2:875

The Isle Full of Noises: Modern Chinese Poetry from Taiwan, 2:235

Ismaelillo, 2:871

Isn't It Romantic, 1:1115

Is Objectivism a Religion?, 5:439

Is Prevention Better Than Cure?, 5:353

Israel: A Concise Political History, 3:439

Israel: An Echo of Eternity, 4:665

Israel: Its Politics and Philosophy, 4:643

Israel: Politics and People, 4:642

Israel—A Precarious Sanctuary: War, Death and the Jewish People, 4:643

Israel after Begin, 3:440
Israel at Vanity Fair, 1:404
Israel in America: A Too-Comfortable Exile, 4:640
Israel in Revolution 6–74 C.E., 4:666
Israel in the Begin Era, 3:439
The Israeli People, 3:440
Israeli Poetry: A Contemporary Anthology, 2:9
The Israelis: Founders and Sons, 4:642
Israelite and Judaean History, 4:806
Israel Jacobson: The Founder of the Reform Movement in Judaism, 4:652
Israel Potter, His Fifty Years of Exile, 1:686
Israel Salanter: Text, Structure, Idea, 4:654
Israel Salanter: The Story of a Religious-Ethical Current in Nineteenth-Century Judaism, 4:654
Israel's Fateful Hour, 3:440
Israel's Lebanon War, 3:440
Israel versus Jibril: The Twenty-Year War against a Master Terrorist, 3:440
Israfel: The Life and Times of Edgar Allan Poe, 1:1245
The Issa Valley, 2:818
Is Science Necessary? Essays on Science and Scientists, 5:10
Is Sex Necessary?, 1:890
Issues in Child Health and Adolescent Health, 5:321
Issues in Feminist Film Criticism, 1:1158
Issues in Health Services, 5:329
Issues in Marxist Philosophy, 4:243
Issues in Nursing: An Annotated Bibliography, 5:119
Issues in Nutrition for the 1980s: An Ecological Perspective, 5:347
Issues in Personality Theory, 5:414
Issues in Reproductive Technology I: An Anthology, 5:120
Issues in Science and Religion, 5:160
Issues in the Jewish-Christian Dialogue, 4:898
Issues in the Sociology of Religion: A Bibliography, 4:425

Is Surgery Necessary?, 5:405
Istanbul and the Civilization of the Ottoman Empire, 3:459
Is the Homosexual My Neighbor? Another Christian View, 4:750
Is There a Text in This Class?, 1:976
The Italian, 1:622
The Italian-Americans, 3:556
Italian and Irish Filmmakers in America, 3:828
Italian Authors of Today, 2:401
Italian Cinema: From Neorealism to the Present, 3:825
Italian Days, 3:899
Italian Dictionary, 1:100
Italian-English Dictionary, 1:100
Italian Fascism: Its Origins and Development, 3:385
Italian Folktales, 2:412
The Italian Girl, 1:523
Italian Hours, 3:899
Italian Hours: Travel Essays, 1:764
Italian Humanism: Philosophy and Civic Life in the Renaissance, 4:126
Italian Life, 3:386
Italian Literary Icons, 2:400
Italian Literature: From Ariosto to the Late Renaissance, 2:402
Italian Literature: Roots and Branches, 2:401
Italian Opera, 3:670
Italian Painters of the Renaissance, 3:332, 3:758
Italian Poetry, 2:403
Italian Poetry, 1960–1980: From Neo to Post Avant-Garde, 2:403
Italian Renaissance Tales, 2:403
The Italians, 2:400, 3:385
An Italian Story, 2:437
Italica: Studies in Italian Life and Letters, 2:402
The Italics Are Mine, 2:701, 2:702
Italo Calvino: Metamorphoses of Fantasy, 2:412
Italo Svevo, 2:439
Italo Svevo: A Double Life, 2:439
Italo Svevo: The Man and the Writer, 2:439
Italy: A Modern History, 3:385

Italy, Sicily and the Mediterranean, 1100–1400, 3:385
Italy and the Approach of the First World War, 3:385
Italy and the Enlightenment: Studies in a Cosmopolitan Century, 2:402
Italy from Liberalism to Fascism, 1870–1925, 3:386
Italy in the Twentieth Century, 3:385
Italy since 1945, 3:386
It Can't Happen Here, 1:853, 1:854
It Could Be Any One of Us, 1:437
An Item from the Late News, 2:949
It Is Never Too Late to Mend: A Matter-of-Fact Romance, 1:389
It Is So (If You Think So), 2:435
It Is Written, 2:577
It's a Battlefield, 1:488
It's a New Day, 1:1044
It Seemed Like Nothing Happened, 3:537
It's Good to Tell You: French Folk Tales from Missouri, 3:862
It's Hard to Be a God, 2:762
It's Me, Eddie: A Fictional Memoir, 2:736, 2:737
It's Only a Play, 1:1103
It's Raining in Mango, 2:949
It's Your Body: A Woman's Guide to Gynecology, 5:355
"It's Your Misfortune and None of My Own," 3:551
It Was the Nightingale, 1:475
Ivan Bunin, 2:707
Ivan Bunin: A Study of His Fiction, 2:707
Ivan Goncharov: His Life and His Works, 2:724
Ivanhoe, 1:298
Ivan Illich: In Conversation, 5:137
The Ivankiad, 2:772
Ivan Moscow, 2:747
Ivan P. Pavlov: Toward a Scientific Psychology and Psychiatry, 3:191
Ivan Pavlov, 3:191
Ivan the Terrible, 3:835
Ivan Turgenev, 2:770
Ives, 3:702
The Ivory Tower, 4:386
Ivy: The Life of I. Compton-Burnett, 1:462

Ivy Compton-Burnett, 1:462
I Wanted to Write a Poem,
    1:900
I Was a German: The Auto-
    biography of Ernst Toller,
    2:613
I Was There: Selected Dance
    Reviews and Articles,
    1936–1976, 3:732
Iwein, 2:586
I Will Fear No Evil, 1:1258
I Will Marry When I Want,
    2:154
I Will Not Rest, 2:501

J

Jacinto Benavente, 2:531
Jack: A Biography of Jack
    London, 1:775
Jack and Jill, 1:532, 1:1198
Jack and the Beanstalk,
    1:583
The Jackass, 2:526
Jack Hodgins and His
    Works, 2:913
Jack in Port: Sailortowns of
    Eastern Canada, 3:608
Jack Kerouac, 1:999
Jack Kerouac: An Annotated
    Bibliography of Secondary
    Sources, 1944–1979, 1:999
Jack Kerouac, Prophet of the
    New Romanticism, 1:999
Jack London, 1:775
Jack London: A Bibliography,
    1:775
Jack London: An American
    Myth, 1:775
Jack London: A Reference
    Guide, 1:775
Jack London: Sailor on
    Horseback, 1:775
Jack London and His Daugh-
    ters, 1:775
Jack London and His Times:
    An Unconventional Biogra-
    phy, 1:775
Jack London and the Klon-
    dike: The Genesis of an
    American Writer, 1:775
Jack of Newbery (1597–98),
    1:177
The Jackpot: A Folk-Play in
    Four Acts, 2:45
Jack's Book: An Oral Biogra-
    phy of Jack Kerouac,
    1:999
Jack Schaefer, 1:1218
Jackson Pollock (Frank),
    3:787

Jackson Pollock (Landau),
    3:787
Jackson Pollock: A Biogra-
    phy, 3:787
Jackson Pollock: An Ameri-
    can Saga, 3:787
Jackson Pollock: Meaning
    and Significance, 3:787
Jack Sprat's Legacy: The Sci-
    ence and Politics of Fat
    and Cholesterol, 5:346
Jack Straw's Castle, 1:491
Jack Tales, 3:860
Jack the Fatalist and His
    Master, 2:472
Jack the Giant Killer, 1:575
Jacob A. Riis: Photographer
    and Citizen, 3:822
Jacob A. Riis: Police Report-
    er, Reformer, Useful Cit-
    izen, 3:822
Jacob Berzelius: The Emer-
    gence of His Chemical
    System, 5:739
The Jacobean and Caroline
    Stage, 1:169
Jacobean Tragedies, 1:171
Jacob Faithful, 1:374
Jacob Have I Loved, 1:1204
The Jacobite's Journal,
    1747–48, 1:244
The Jacobite's Journal and
    Related Writings, 1:245
Jacobowsky and the Colonel,
    2:615
Jacob's Ladder and the Tree
    of Life, 4:303
Jacob's Room, 1:569
Jacopo Sadoleto, 1477–1547:
    Humanist and Reformer,
    4:728
Jacques and His Master,
    2:793
Jacques Cousteau's Calypso,
    3:908
Jacques Derrida: A Bibliogra-
    phy, 4:398
Jacques Ellul: A Comprehen-
    sive Bibliography, 5:70,
    5:165
Jacques Ellul: Interpretive
    Essays, 5:70, 5:165
Jacques Lacan: A Feminist
    Introduction, 1:1132
Jacques Maritain: Homage in
    Words and Pictures, 4:307
Jacques Maritain and the
    French Catholic Intellectu-
    als, 4:307
Jacques Prévert, 2:494
Jacques Prévert: Popular
    French Theater and Cine-
    ma, 2:494

Jacques the Fatalist, 4:195
Jade: Its History and Sym-
    bolism in China, 4:523
Jade Flute: The Story of Chi-
    nese Music, 3:670
The Jade Steps: A Ritual Life
    of the Aztecs, 4:457
Jadis et Naguère, 2:514
Jagua Nana, 2:135
Jaguar of Sweet Laughter:
    New and Selected Poems,
    1:931
Jaguar Skies, 1:1009
Jaime Ongpin, the Enigma: A
    Profile of the Filipino as
    Manager, 2:330
Jaina Debates on the Spiritu-
    al Liberation of Women,
    4:509
Jaina Yoga: A Survey of the
    Mediaeval Sravakacaras,
    4:510
Jain Ramayan, 4:510
Jakarta: A History, 3:491
Jake's Thing, 1:432
Jakob Berzelius: His Life and
    Work, 5:739
Jakobsonian Poetics and
    Slavic Narrative, 2:689
Jalal Al-Din Al-Suyuti, 4:585
Jamaica Inn, 1:620
Jamaica Song and Story,
    2:931
James Agee (Bergreen),
    1:933
James Agee (Larsen), 1:933
James Agee: Selected Jour-
    nalism, 1:932
James Anthony Froude: A
    Bibliography of Studies,
    3:403
James Baldwin, 1:939, 1:1084
James Baldwin: Artist on
    Fire, 1:939, 1:1084
James Baldwin: The Legacy,
    1:939, 1:1084
The James Bond Dossier,
    1:432
James Brindley and the Ear-
    ly Engineers, 5:249
James Bryce, 3:152
James Clerk Maxwell and
    the Theory of the Electro-
    magnetic Field, 5:701
James Comer, 5:416
James Dickey: A Checklist,
    1:967
James Dickey: A Descriptive
    Bibliography, 1:967
James Dickey: The Poet as
    Pitchman, 1:967

James Dickey and the Gentle Ecstasy of Earth: A Reading of the Poems, 1:967
James E. Keeler: Pioneer Astrophysicist, 5:590
The Jameses: A Family Narrative, 1:761, 1:767
The James Family Biography, 1:761
James Fenimore Cooper (Grossman), 1:665
James Fenimore Cooper (Ringe),
James Fenimore Cooper: An Annotated Bibliography of Criticism, 1:665
James Gould Cozzens: A Descriptive Bibliography, 1:965
James Gould Cozzens: A Life Apart, 1:965
James Gould Cozzens: New Acquist of True Experience, 1:965
James Hogg, 1:292
James Hogg: The Growth of a Writer, 1:292
James Hutton: Founder of Modern Geology, 5:644
James Jones, 1:995
James Jones: A Checklist, 1:995
James Joyce, 1:974
James Joyce: A Guide to Research, 1:506
James Joyce: Authorized Reader, 1:506
James Joyce: The Augmented Ninth, 1:505
James Joyce and Sexuality, 1:505
James Joyce and the Politics of Desire, 1:505
James Joyce's Italian Connection: The Poetics of the Word, 1:505
James M. Cain, 1:1227
James M. Gustafson's Theocentric Ethics: Interpretations and Assessments, 4:900
James Madison: A Biography, 3:161
James Madison and the Search for Nationhood, 3:521
James McAuley: Poetry, Essays and Personal Commentary, 2:958
James Merrill: An Introduction to the Poetry, 1:1015
James Merrill: Essays in Criticism, 1:1015

James Michener, 1:1248
James Russell Lowell, 1:685
James Russell Lowell: A Biography, 1:685
James Russell Lowell: Portrait of a Many-Sided Man, 1:685
James II: A Study in Kingship, 3:360
James Shore's Daughter, 1:815
James VI and the Gowrie Mystery, 3:882
James's Will-to-Believe Doctrine: A Heretical View, 1:769
James T. Farrell: The Revolutionary Socialist Years, 1:834
James the Fourth, 1:180
James Thomson (1700–1748), A Life, 1:261
James Thomson (B.V.), a Critical Study, 1:261
James Thomson, Anglo-Scot, 1:261
James Thurber, 1:891
Jamestown, 1544–1699, 3:569
James Truslow Adams: Historian of the American Dream, 3:591
James Watt and the Steam Revolution: A Documentary History, 5:232
James Weldon Johnson, 1:771
James Weldon Johnson: Black Leader, Black Voice, 1:771
James Weldon Johnson and Arna Wendell Bontemps: A Reference Guide, 1:817
James Whatman, Father and Son, 1:4
James Whitcomb Riley, 1:778
James Whitcomb Riley: An Essay, 1:778
Jami: The Persian Mystic and Poet, 4:586
Janáček: Leaves from His Life, 3:702
Janáček and Brod, 3:702
Jane Addams: A Biography, 1:731
Jane Addams and the Liberal Tradition, 1:731
Jane Addams and the Men of the Chicago School, 1:731
Jane and Prudence, 1:539
Jane Austen: A Study of Her Artistic Development, 1:276

Jane Austen: Facts and Problems, 1:276
Jane Austen: Irony as Defense and Discovery, 1:276
Jane Austen: Social Change and Literary Form, 1:276
Jane Austen: Women, Politics, and the Novel, 1:276
Jane Austen and Her Art, 1:276
Jane Austen and Mozart: Classical Equilibrium in Fiction and Music, 2:988
Jane Austen and the War of Ideas, 1:276
Jane Austen Dictionary, 1:276
Jane Austen in a Social Context, 1:276
Jane Austen's Art of Allusion, 1:276
Jane Brody's Good Food Book: Living the High Carbohydrate Way, 5:345
Jane Brody's the New York Times Guide to Personal Health, 5:339
Jane Ellen Harrison: The Mask and the Self, 4:479
Jane Eyre, 1:334, 1:335, 2:940
Jane Field, 1:750
Jane's Career, 2:934, 2:935
Jane Talbot, 1:635
Janos the Hero, 2:802
Jan Parandowski, 2:819
Jansenism in Seventeenth-Century France: Voices from the Wilderness, 4:737
Japan, 3:473
Japan: A Historical Survey, 3:474
Japan: A Short Cultural History, 3:474, 3:501
Japan: From Prehistory to Modern Times, 3:474
Japan: The Intellectual Foundations of Modern Japanese Politics, 3:479
Japan: The Story of a Nation, 3:501
Japan: Tradition and Transformation, 3:474, 3:501
Japan, China and the Modern World Economy, 3:464
Japan and China: From War to Peace, 1894–1972, 3:464
Japan and Korea: A Critical Bibliography, 3:463
Japan and Korea: The Political Dimension, 3:464

Japan and the World: Essays in Japanese History and Politics, 3:474

Japan and the World, 1853–1952, 3:473

Japan at War: An Illustrated History of the War in the Far East, 1931-45, 3:476

Japan at War: An Oral History, 3:477

Japan before Tokugawa, 3:475

Japan-China: A Journal of Two Voyages to the Far East, 3:904

The Japanese Achievement, 3:474

The Japanese American Experience, 3:557

The Japanese and Sun Yat-sen, 3:464

Japanese Art, 3:760

Japanese Blue Collar: The Changing Tradition, 3:476

Japanese Bookbinding: Instructions from a Master Craftsman, 1:24

The Japanese Chronicles, 3:901

The Japanese Colonial Empire, 1895–1945, 3:465, 3:478

Japanese Court Poetry, 2:273

Japanese Cultural Policies in Southeast Asia during World War II, 3:464

Japanese Culture: A Short History, 3:474

Japanese Culture: Tradition, Self, and the Social Order, 3:474

The Japanese Discovery of Europe, 3:475

Japanese Economic Growth: Trend Acceleration in the Twentieth Century, 3:479

The Japanese Economy, 3:52, 3:58

Japanese Film Directors, 3:828

Japanese Folk Literature: A Core Collection, 3:853

Japanese History and Culture from Ancient to Modern Times, 3:473

Japanese Industrialization and Its Social Consequences, 3:479

Japanese Landlords: The Decline of a Rural Elite, 3:480

Japanese Lantern, 3:905

Japanese Linked Poetry, 2:273

Japanese Literature: A Historical Outline, 2:272

Japanese Literature: An Introduction for Western Readers, 2:272

Japanese Manufacturing Techniques: Nine Hidden Lessons in Simplicity, 5:234

The Japanese Mind: Essentials of Japanese Philosophy and Culture, 4:363

Japanese Music: Another Tradition, Other Sounds, 3:670

Japanese Mythology, 4:535

A Japanese New Religion: Rissho Kosei-kai in a Mountain Village, 4:540

The Japanese Novel of the Meiji Period and the Ideal of Individualism, 2:283

Japanese Papermaking: Traditions, Tools, and Techniques, 1:4

Japanese Pilgrimage, 4:539

Japanese Poetic Diaries, 2:274

Japanese Religion: Unity and Diversity, 4:534

Japanese Religion and Philosophy, 4:363

Japanese Religion and Society: Paradigms of Structure and Change, 4:534

Japanese Religion in the Modern Century, 4:541

The Japanese Seizure of Korea, 1868–1910, 3:464

Japanese Spirituality, 4:558

Japanese Studies from Pre-History to 1990: A Bibliographical Guide, 3:473

Japanese Theatre, 2:272

The Japanese Today: Change and Continuity, 3:501

Japanese Women Writers: Twentieth Century Short Fiction, 2:283

Japanese Words and Their Uses, 1:100

Japan Examined: Perspectives on Modern Japanese History, 3:480

Japan in Asia, 3:465

Japan in Film, 3:473

Japan in the Muromachi Age, 3:475

Japan in Transition: From Tokugawa to Meiji, 3:478

Japan's Best-Loved Poetry Classic: Hyakunin Isshu, 2:274

Japan's Economy: A Bibliography of Its Past and Present, 3:473

Japan's Greater East Asia Co-Prosperity Sphere in World War II, 3:464

Japan's Modern Myths: Ideology in the Meiji Period, 3:477

Japan's Quest for Autonomy, 3:477

Jared's Story: A Boy in a Bubble and How His Family Saved His Life, 5:386

The Jargon of Authenticity, 4:393

Jason's Voyage: The Search for the Old World in American Literature, 1:904

Jataka, 2:315, 2:321

Jawaharlal Nehru, 3:499

Jawaharlal Nehru: A Descriptive Biography, 3:500

Jawaharlal Nehru: An Anthology, 3:499

Jawaharlal Nehru: Man of Letters, 3:500

Jawaharlal Nehru of India, 1889–1964, 3:500

Jawaharlal Nehru's World View: A Theory of International Relations, 3:500

Jawaharlal Nehru's Writings, 3:500

Jay's Treaty: A Study in Commerce and Diplomacy, 3:568

Jazz, 1:1018

Jazz: America's Classical Music, 3:669

Jazz: Its Evolution and Essence, 3:669

Jazz Bibliography, 3:668

Jazz Cleopatra: Josephine Baker in Her Time, 1:1039, 3:737

Jazz Dance: The Story of American Vernacular Dance, 3:733

Jazz from the Beginning, 3:668

The Jazz Heritage, 3:669

Jazz Masters in Transition, 1957–1969, 3:669

Jazz Masters of the Twenties, 3:668

The Jazz People of New Orleans, 3:668

Jazz Reference and Research Materials: A Bibliography, 3:669
Jazz Singing, 3:668
Jazz Styles: History and Analysis, 3:668
Jazz Styles in Kansas City and the Southwest, 3:669
The Jazz Tradition, 3:669
The Jazz Years: Earwitness to an Era, 3:668
J. B.: A Play in Verse, 1:858
J. B. Priestley, 1:537
J. B. Priestley: An Annotated Bibliography, 1:537
J. B. Priestley: The Last of the Sages, 1:537
J. B. Priestley's Plays, 1:537
JBS: The Life and Work of J.B.S. Haldane, 5:797
J. D. Salinger (French), 1:1043
J. D. Salinger (Lundquist), 1:1043
J. D. Salinger: A Thirty Year Bibliography, 1:1043
The Jealous God, 1:449
Jealousy, 2:500
Jean Baudrillard: From Marxism to Postmodernism and Beyond, 4:17
Jean Baudrillard: Selected Writings, 3:211
Jean Bodin and the Rise of Absolutist Theory, 4:134
Jean Bodin and the Sixteenth-Century Revolution in the Methodology of Law and History, 4:134
Jean-Christophe, 2:501
Jean Cocteau, 2:469, 3:834
Jean Cocteau, the Mimer and the Mask, 3:834
Jean Cocteau and His Films of Orphic Identity, 3:834
Jean d'Alembert: Science and the Enlightenment, 5:44
Jean Genet, 2:479
Jean Genet and the Semiotics of Performance, 2:479
Jean Genet in Tangier, 2:479
Jean Giraudoux: The Legend and the Secret, 2:481
Jean Giraudoux: The Theatre of Victory and Defeat, 2:481
Jean-Jacques: The Early Life and Work of Jean-Jacques Rousseau, 1712–1754, 4:213
Jean-Jacques Rousseau, 4:13

Jean-Jacques Rousseau: Transparency and Obstruction, 3:338
Jean-Jacques Rousseau and the Well-Ordered Society, 4:214
Jean Paul, 2:606
Jean-Paul Sartre, 2:507, 4:330
Jean-Paul Sartre: The Existentialist Ethic, 4:330
Jean-Paul Sartre: The Philosopher as a Literary Critic, 4:331
Jean-Paul Sartre and His Critics, 4:331
Jean Piaget: Consensus and Controversy, 3:267
Jean Piaget: The Man and His Ideas, 3:192
Jean Racine: Dramatist, 2:498
Jean Renoir, 3:842
Jean Renoir: A Life in Pictures, 3:842
Jean Renoir: The French Years 1924–1939, 3:842
Jean Rhys (James), 2:941
Jean Rhys (Wolfe), 2:941
Jean Rhys: A Critical Study, 2:941
Jean Rhys, Woman in Passage, 2:941
Jean Sibelius, His Life and Personality, 3:718
Jean Toomer, 1:891
Jean Toomer, Artist: A Study of His Literary Life and Work, 1894–1936, 1:891
Jean Toomer's Years with Gurdjieff: Portrait of an Artist, 1923–1936, 1:891, 4:875
Jedermann, 2:592
Jefferson, 3:155
Jefferson and His Time, 1:640, 3:155
Jefferson and His Time: The Sage of Monticello, 1:641
Jefferson and Madison: The Great Collaboration, 3:161
Jefferson and/or Mussolini, 1:871
Jefferson and the Ordeal of Liberty, 1:640
Jefferson and the Rights of Man, 1:640
Jefferson Davis, 3:574, 3:575
Jefferson Davis: His Rise and Fall, 1:889
Jefferson Davis: The Man and His Hour, 3:574
Jefferson Davis, a Memoir by His Wife, 3:574

Jefferson Davis and His Cabinet, 3:575
Jefferson Davis and His Generals, 3:575
Jefferson Davis and the Confederacy, 3:575
The Jeffersonian Persuasion: Evolution of a Party Ideology, 3:519
The Jefferson Image in the American Mind, 3:155
The Jefferson Scandals: A Rebuttal, 1:640
Jefferson the President: First Term, 1801–1805, 1:640
Jefferson the President: Second Term, 1805–1809, 1:640
Jefferson the Virginian, 1:640
Jehovah's Witnesses, 4:863
Jehovah's Witnesses and Kindred Groups, 4:863
Jehovah's Witness Literature, 4:863
Je Ne Parle Pas Français, 2:978
Jennie Gerhardt, 1:829, 1:830
Jenny, 2:668, 2:669
Jenny Craig's What Have You Got to Lose?, 5:325
Jenny Treibel, 2:579
Jens Peter Jacobsen, 2:651
Jeppe of the Hill and Other Comedies, 2:651
Jeptha, 2:632
Jeremy Bentham, 3:151
Jeremy Bentham: An Odyssey of Ideas, 4:191
Jeremy Bentham, His Life and Work, 3:151
Jeremy Bentham and Representative Democracy, 3:151
Jeremy's Version, 1:1034
Jerome: His Life, Writings and Controversies, 4:712
Jerome, Chrysostom and Friends: Essays and Translations, 4:712
Jerome Kern, 3:703
Jerome Kern: His Life and Music, 3:703
Jerusalem, 2:676, 2:677
Jerusalem: A History of Forty Centuries, 3:440
Jerusalem: A Study in Urban Geography, 3:440
Jerusalem: The Holy City, 3:459
Jerusalem; or, on Religious Power and Judaism, 4:208, 4:209

Jerusalem and Other Jewish Writings by Moses Mendelssohn, 4:647
Jerusalem Delivered, 2:398, 2:439, 2:440
Jerusalem in the Time of Jesus, 4:604, 4:807
Jerusalem the Golden, 1:468
Jerzy Kosinski, 1:1003
Jerzy Kosinski: An Annotated Bibliography, 1:1003
Jessie Phillips: A Tale of the Present Day, 1:408
A Jest of God, 2:916, 2:917
Jesuit and Savage in New France, 4:752
The Jesuits in North America, 3:592
Jesuit Thinkers of the Renaissance, 4:131
Jesus: A Jewish Dissent, 4:602
Jesus and Judaism, 4:617
Jesus and the Synoptic Gospels: A Bibliographic Study Guide, 4:795
Jesus and the Word, 4:825, 4:831
Jesus and the World of Judaism, 4:618
Jesus as Mother: Studies in the Spirituality of the High Middle Ages, 4:695
Jesus Christ and Mythology, 4:825, 4:831
Jesus in History, 4:807
Jesus of Nazareth, 4:824, 4:829
Jesus' Proclamation of the Kingdom of God, 4:826
Jesus Tales, 1:1100
Jesus the Jew: A Historian's Reading of the Gospels, 4:618
Jetport: The Boston Airport Controversy, 5:248
The Jew, 2:557
The Jew, and Other Stories, 2:769
Jew and Gentile in the Ancient World, 4:604
The Jew as Ally of the Muslim: Medieval Roots of Anti-Semitism, 4:623
The Jewel of the Seven Stars, 1:603
Jewels, 1:1223, 1:1224
The Jewels of Aptor, 1:1256
The Jew in America: A History, 4:640
The Jew in the Medieval Community, 3:350

The Jew in the Medieval World: A Source Book 315–1791, 4:623
The Jew in the Modern World: A Documentary History, 4:634
Jewish-American History and Culture: An Encyclopedia, 4:594
Jewish American Literature: An Anthology, 1:129
Jewish Americans: Three Generations in a Jewish Community, 4:639
Jewish and Female: Choices and Changes in Our Lives Today, 4:650
Jewish and Pauline Studies, 4:617
The Jewish Antiquities, 4:666
Jewish Art: An Illustrated History, 4:597
Jewish Art and Civilization, 4:597
Jewish Art and Religious Observance, 4:597
The Jewish Bible after the Holocaust: A Re-Reading, 4:663
Jewish Biblical Exegesis, 4:628
Jewish Bund in Russia from Its Origins to 1905, 4:656
The Jewish Catalog: A Do-It-Yourself Kit, 4:602
The Jewish-Christian Argument: A History of Theologies in Conflict, 4:603
The Jewish-Christian Debate in the High Middle Ages, 4:623
Jewish-Christian Relations: An Annotated Bibliography and Resource Guide, 4:5
Jewish Civilization, 3:348, 4:593
Jewish Communities in Frontier Societies, 4:644
The Jewish Community, 4:593
A Jewish Conservative Looks at Pagan America, 4:655
Jewish Continuity and Change: Emerging Patterns in America, 4:639
Jewish Education and Society in the High Middle Ages, 4:622
The Jewish Encyclopedia, 4:594
Jewish Ethics, Philosophy and Mysticism, 4:629
The Jewish Experience, 4:640

The Jewish Experience in America, 4:640
Jewish Family Celebrations: Shabbat Festivals and Traditional Ceremonies, 4:599
The Jewish Feminist Movement in Germany, 4:650
The Jewish Festivals: From Their Beginnings to Our Own Day, 4:600
Jewish Folk Art: From Biblical Days to Modern Times, 4:597
Jewish Folklore: An Annotated Bibliography, 3:850
Jewish Folkways in Germanic Lands (1648–1806), 4:624
The Jewish Government and Other Stories, 2:44
Jewish Historical Treasures, 3:348
The Jewish Holidays, 4:600
Jewish Identity on the Suburban Frontier, 4:641
Jewish Issues in Argentine Literature: from Gerchunoff to Szichman, 2:846
Jewish Law: History, Sources, Principles: Ha-Mishpat Ha-Ivri, 4:627
Jewish Laws of Childbirth, 4:602
Jewish Legends, 2:618
Jewish Life in the Middle Ages, 4:622
Jewish Life under Islam: Jerusalem in the Sixteenth Century, 4:625
Jewish Literature between the Bible and the Mishnah, 4:613, 4:811
Jewish Liturgy and Its Development, 4:599
Jewish Magic and Superstition, 4:630
Jewish Moral Philosophy, 4:598
Jewish Musical Traditions, 4:597
Jewish Mystical Testimonies, 4:630
The Jewish Mystical Tradition, 4:630
Jewish Mysticism: An Introduction to Kabbalah, 4:629
Jewish Mysticism and Jewish Ethics, 4:598
Jewish Nobles and Geniuses in Modern Hungary, 3:349

Jewish People, Jewish Thought: The Jewish Experience in History, 4:595

Jewish People in America, 4:594

Jewish Philosophers, 4:601

Jewish Philosophical Polemics against Christianity in the Middle Ages, 4:629, 4:697

Jewish Philosophy in a Secular Age, 4:596

Jewish Philosophy in Modern Times, 4:646

The Jewish Primer, 4:596

Jewish Publishing in America, 1:38

Jewish Radicals, 1875–1914: From Czarist Stetl to London Ghetto, 4:656

The Jewish Religion in the Soviet Union, 3:350

Jewish Sects, Religious Movements, and Political Parties, 4:651

Jewish Sects at the Time of Jesus, 4:615, 4:616

Jewish Self-Government in Medieval Egypt, 4:625

Jewish Self-Government in the Middle Ages, 4:622

Jewish Self-Hatred: Anti-Semitism and the Hidden Language of the Jews, 4:636

Jewish Socialist Movements, 1871–1917: While the Messiah Tarried, 4:656

Jewish Societies in the Middle East: Community, Culture, and Authority, 4:644

Jewish Spirituality from the Bible through the Middle Ages, 4:630

The Jewish State, 4:658

Jewish Thought in the Seventeenth Century, 4:629

Jewish Thought in the Sixteenth Century, 4:629

The Jewish Thought of Emil Fackenheim: A Reader, 4:664

Jewish Thought Today, 4:884

Jewish Travellers in the Middle Ages: Nineteen Firsthand Accounts, 4:625

Jewish Values in Bioethics, 5:122

The Jewish War, 3:316, 4:666

The Jewish War against the Jews, 4:648

The Jewish Way: Living the Holidays, 4:599

Jewish Way in Death and Mourning, 4:602

The Jewish Way in Love and Marriage, 4:602

The Jewish Wife and Other Short Plays, 2:572

Jewish Wit, 5:467

The Jewish Woman: New Perspectives, 4:650

The Jewish Woman in America, 4:649

Jewish Woman in Jewish Law, 4:650

Jewish Women in Historical Perspective, 4:649

Jewish Women in Rabbinic Literature, 4:650

The Jewish World: History and Culture of the Jewish People, 4:594

Jewish Worship, 4:600, 4:897

The Jew of Malta, 1:186

The Jew of Rome, 2:578

The Jews, 3:348

The Jews: Social Patterns of an American Group, 4:641

The Jews: Their History, Culture, and Religion, 4:594

The Jews, Are They Human? 1:513

Jews, Idols and Messiahs: The Challenge from History, 3:349

Jews, Judaism and the Classical World, 4:604

Jews against Zionism: The American Council for Judaism, 1942-1948, 4:658

The Jews among the Greeks and Romans, 4:605

Jews and Arabs: Their Contacts through the Ages, 4:625

Jews and Christians: Graeco-Roman Views, 4:605

Jews and Christians: The Myth of a Common Tradition, 4:603

Jews and French Quebecers: Two Hundred Years of Shared History, 4:644

Jews and Non-Jews in Eastern Europe, 1918-1945, 3:350

The Jews and the Crusaders, 4:623

The Jews and the Left, 4:656

The Jews from Alexander to Herod, 4:605

Jews in a Free Society: Challenges and Opportunities, 4:652

Jews in an Arab Land: Libya, 1835–1970, 4:644

The Jews in Christian Europe, 1400–1700, 3:348

Jews in Colonial Brazil, 4:645

The Jews in Egypt and in Palestine under the Fatimid Caliphs, with Preface and Reader's Guide to Shlomo Dov Goitein, 4:626

The Jews in Germany from the Enlightenment to National Socialism, 4:635

The Jews in Modern France, 4:637

Jews in Nineteenth-Century Egypt, 4:644

The Jews in Poland, 3:350

The Jews in Roman Imperial Legislation, 4:604

The Jews in Russia, 2:736

Jews in Russia: The Last Four Centuries, 3:350

The Jews in Russia: The Struggle for Emancipation, 3:348, 4:636

The Jews in South Africa: A History, 4:645

The Jews in Soviet Russia since 1917, 3:349, 4:636

Jews in the Hellenistic World, 4:608

The Jews in Their Land, 3:439

The Jews in the Modern World: A Documentary History, 3:349

The Jews in Weimar Germany, 3:350

The Jews of Arab and Islamic Countries, 4:644

The Jews of Arab Lands: A History and Source Book, 4:626

Jews of Arab Lands in Modern Times, 4:645

The Jews of Argentina. From the Inquisition to Peron, 4:645

The Jews of Byzantium, 1204–1453, 4:623

The Jews of East Central Europe between the World Wars, 3:349, 4:637

The Jews of Hope, 4:636

The Jews of Iraq: 3000 Years of History and Culture, 4:644

The Jews of Ireland from Earliest Times to the Year 1910, 3:348

The Jews of Islam, 3:459, 4:571, 4:594

Jews of Latin American Republics, 4:644

The Jews of Modernity, 4:639

The Jews of Moslem Spain, 4:625

The Jews of Odessa: A Cultural History, 1794–1881, 4:638

The Jews of Paris and the Final Solution, 1940–1944, 3:347

The Jews of Poland, 4:625

The Jews of Silence: A Personal Report on Soviet Jewry, 1:1065, 3:351

The Jews of the Renaissance, 4:624

The Jews of Vienna, 1867–1914: Assimilation and Identity, 4:637

The Jews of Washington, 4:638

The Jews of Yemen, 1800–1914, 4:626

The Jews under Roman and Byzantine Rule, 4:606

The Jew Süss, 2:578

JFK: Reckless Youth, 3:538

J. F. Powers, 1:1033

J. G. Frazer: His Life and Work, 3:30, 3:878, 4:477

J. G. Herder, 3:286

Jiddah: Portrait of an Arabian City, 3:451

Jig Cook and the Provincetown Players: Theatre in Ferment, 1:1075

Jig of Forslin, 1:810

Jig-Saw, 1:618

Jill, 1:508

The Jimmyjohn Boss and Other Stories, 1:789

Jimmy's Blues: Selected Poems, 1:939

The Jindyworobaks, 2:946

The Jingle Bell Principle, 2:792

Jinnah of Pakistan, 3:487

The Jivaro: People of the Sacred Waterfalls, 3:895

J. J. Thomson and the Cavendish Laboratory in His Day, 5:716

J. L. Austin, 4:272

J. M. Barrie, 1:330

J. M. Barrie: An Annotated Secondary Bibliography, 1:330, 1:438

J. M. Barrie: A Study in Fairies and Mortals, 1:438

J. M. Barrie: The Man behind the Image, 1:330, 1:438

J. M. Barrie and the Lost Boys, 1:438

J. M. Keynes in Retrospect: The Legacy of the Keynesian Revolution, 3:87

J. M. Synge, 1:555

J. M. Synge: Interviews and Recollections, 1:556

J. M. Synge: Literary Companion, 1:556

J. M. Synge, 1871–1909, 1:556

J. M. Synge and the Western Mind, 1:556

Joachim of Fiore: A Study in Spiritual Perception and History, 4:712

Joan of Arc, 2:984

Joan of Arc: An Epic Poem, 1:304

Joan of Arc: Personal Recollections, 1:780

Joan of Lorraine, 1:1081

Joan Robinson and the Americans, 3:103

The Joan Robinson Legacy, 3:102

The Job: Interviews with William Burroughs, 1:958

Job Security in America, 3:59

Jocelyn, 1:482

Joe Egg, 1:525

Joel Barlow, 1:633

Joel Barlow: Revolutionist, 1:633

Joel Chandler Harris, 1:755

Joel Chandler Harris: A Biography, 1:755

Joel Chandler Harris: A Reference Guide, 1:755

Joe Orton, 1:530

Joe Orton's Comedy of the Last Laugh, 1:530

Joe Turner's Come and Gone, 1:1119, 1:1120

Johan Ludvig Runeberg, 2:657

The Johanna Maria, 2:630

Johannes Kepler's New Astronomy, 5:608

Johannes V. Jensen, 2:652

Johann Gottfried Herder, 4:199

Johann Gutenberg and His Bible: A Historical Study, 1:9

Johannine Christianity: Essays on Its Setting, Sources, and Theology, 4:826

Johann Sebastian Bach: His Life, Art and Work, 3:675

John A. Macdonald, a Biography, 3:618

John Ashbery: An Introduction to the Poetry, 1:936

John Bale: Mythmaker for the English Reformation, 1:172

John Barleycorn: or Alcoholic Memoirs, 1:774

John Barth, 1:943

John Barth: An Annotated Bibliography, 1:943

John Barth: An Introduction, 1:943

John Barth: The Comic Sublimity of Paradox, 1:943

John Baskerville of Birmingham: Letter-Founder and Printer, 1:18

John Berryman, 1:950

John Berryman: A Checklist, 1:950

John Berryman: A Critical Commentary, 1:950

John Betjeman: A Life in Pictures, 1:445

John Braine, 1:449

John Braine and John Wain: A Reference Guide, 1:449

John Brown, 3:577

John Brown: The Making of a Martyr, 1:893

John Brown's Body, 1:815

John Bull's Other Island, 1:424

John Bunyan: A Study in Personality, 1:174

John Bunyan, 1628–1688: His Life, Times, and Work, 1:174

John Bunyan, Mechanick Preacher, 1:174

John Burroughs: An American Naturalist, 3:550

John C. Calhoun: American Portrait, 3:523

John Cage: An Anthology, 3:686

John Calvin, 4:761

John Calvin: A Biography, 4:762

John Calvin: A Sixteenth Century Portrait, 3:334, 4:761

John Calvin: His Influence in the Western World, 4:732, 4:762

John Calvin, the Church and the Eucharist, 4:762

John Case and Aristotelianism in Renaissance England, 4:71, 4:131

John Cassian: Conferences, 4:706

John Cheever, 1:961, 1:962

John Cheever: A Biography, 1:962

John Cheever: A Reference Guide, 1:961

John Cheever: The Hobgoblin Company of Love, 1:962

John Chrysostom and the Jews, 4:684

John Clare: A Reference Guide, 1:286

John Clare and the Picturesque Landscape, 1:286

John Colet, 4:126

John Colet and Marsilio Ficino, 4:141

John Coltrane, 3:690

John Company, 2:631

John Constable, 3:773

John Crowe Ransom: Critical Essays and a Bibliography, 1:875

John Crowe Ransom's Secular Faith, 1:875

John D. MacDonald, 1:1234

John D. Rockefeller: The Heroic Age of American Enterprise, 3:591

John Dalton, 5:742

John Dalton: Critical Assessments of His Life and Science, 5:56, 5:742

John Dalton and the Atomic Theory, 5:742

John Dee: The Mathematical Preface, 4:125

John Dee's Natural Philosophy: Between Science and Religion, 4:125

John Dewey, 3:261, 4:225

John Dewey: A Centennial Bibliography, 4:225

John Dewey: An Intellectual Portrait, 3:261, 4:225, 4:298

John Dewey: His Thought and Influence, 4:225

John Dewey: Recollections, 3:261

John Dewey: Religious Faith and Democratic Humanism, 4:225

John Dewey: The Reconstruction of the Democratic Life, 3:261, 4:225

John Dewey and American Democracy, 3:261, 4:226

John Dewey and Self-Realization, 3:261

John Dewey and the Paradox of Liberal Reform, 3:261, 4:225

John Dewey in Perspective, 3:261

John Dewey's Aesthetic Philosophy, 3:261

John Dewey's Challenge to Education, 3:581, 4:225

John Dewey's Philosophy of Value, 3:261, 4:225

John Dewey's Pragmatic Technology, 3:261, 4:225, 5:73

John Donne: A Life, 1:178

John Donne: An Annotated Biography of Modern Criticism, 1968–1978, 1:178

John Donne: Life, Mind and Art, 1:178

John Donne: The Critical Heritage, 1:178

John Donne, Coterie Poet, 1:178

John Donne and Francisco de Quevedo: Poets of Love and Death, 2:548

John Donne's Lyrics, 1:178

John Donne's Poetry, 1:178

John Dos Passos: Politics and the Writer, 1:829

John Dryden, 1:242

John Dryden: A Reference Guide, 1:242

John Dryden: Dramatist, Satirist, Translator, 1:242

John Dryden and His World, 1:242

John Duns Scotus, 1265–1965, 4:114

John Fairbank and the American Understanding of Modern China, 3:498

John Fell: The University Press and the "Fell" Types, 1:18

John Fell, 1745–1831, 1:18

John Fletcher's Chastity Plays: Mirrors of Modesty, 1:173

John Ford, 1:180, 1:1166

John Ford: Baroque English Dramatists, 1:180

John Ford and the Caroline Theatre, 1:180

John Ford and the Traditional Moral Order, 1:180

The John Ford Movie Mystery, 1:1166

John Fowles, 1:478

John Fowles: A Reference Companion, 1:478

John Fowles: A Reference Guide, 1:478

John Fowles's Fiction and the Poetics of Postmodernism, 1:478

John Gabriel Borkman, 2:665, 2:666

John Galsworthy, 1:483

John Galsworthy: A Biography, 1:483

John Galsworthy: An Annotated Bibliography of Writings about Him, 1:483

John Gardner: An Annotated Secondary Bibliography, 1:979

John Gardner: Critical Perspectives, 1:979

John Gay: An Annotated Checklist of Criticism, 1:246

John Gay: Dramatic Works, 1:246

John Gay, Social Critic, 1:246

John Gay and the Scriblerians, 1:246

John Gower: Moral Philosopher and Friend of Chaucer, 1:152

John Gower: Recent Readings, 1:152

John Gower's Poetic: The Search for a New Arion, 1:152

John Greenleaf Whittier, 1:709

John Greenleaf Whittier: Friend to Man, 1:709

John Gunther: Inside Journalism, 3:922

John Gunther's Inside Australia, 3:922

John Hawkes, 1:986

John Hawkes: An Annotated Bibliography, 1:986

John Hawkes and the Craft of Conflict, 1:986

A John Hawkes Symposium: Design and Debris, 1:986

John Henry Newman, 4:783

John Henry Newman: A Bibliographical Catalogue, 4:782

John Hus: A Biography, 3:334, 4:711, 4:721

John Hus at the Council of Constance, 4:711

John Huston, 3:838

John Keats, 1:294

John Keats: His Life and Writings, 1:294

John Keats: The Making of a Poet, 1:295

John Keats and Symbolism, 1:294

John Kennedy: A Political Profile, 3:571

John Kenneth Galbraith and His Critics, 3:79

John Kenneth Galbraith and the Lower Economics, 3:79

John Kepler, 5:608

John Knox (Percy), 4:774

John Knox (Ridley), 4:736

John Knox: Portrait of a Calvinist, 1:521, 4:774

John Knox: The Hero of the Scottish Reformation, 4:774

John Knox's History of the Reformation in Scotland, 4:774

John le Carré, 1:596

John Locke (Aaron), 3:159, 4:179, 4:738

John Locke (Squadrito), 4:181

John Locke: A Biography, 3:159, 4:179

John Locke: An Introduction, 4:181

John Locke: Economist and Social Scientist, 4:181

John Locke: Physician and Philosopher, 4:179

John Locke and the Doctrine of Majority Rule, 4:180

John Locke and the Theory of Sovereignty, 4:180

John Locke and the Way of Ideas, 4:181

John Locke's Liberalism, 3:160, 4:180

John Locke Symposium, 4:179

John Lyly, 1:186

John March: Southerner, 1:736

John Marshall: Defender of the Constitution, 3:522

John Marston, Dramatist, 1:188

John Marston Plays: Themes, Structure and Performance, 1:188

John Marston's Drama: Themes, Images, Sources, 1:188

John Masefield, 1:519

John Masefield, or, the Queen's Poet Laureate, 1:519

John Masefield's England, 1:519

John Maynard Keynes: Critical Assessments, 3:87

John Maynard Keynes: Life, Ideas, Legacy, 3:87

John Millington Synge, 1:555

John Milton, 1:193

John Milton: A Reader's Guide to His Poetry, 1:192

John Milton: Poet and Humanist, 1:192

John Muir and His Legacy, 3:549, 5:822

John Napier, 5:580

Johnno, 2:958, 2:959

Johnny Appleseed, Man and Myth, 4:852

Johnny Appleseed and Other Poems, 1:855

Johnny Johnson, 1:1088

Johnny Panic and the Bible of Dreams, 1:1031

Johnny Tremain, 1:1195, 1:1201, 1:1202

John of Paris on Royal and Papal Power, 4:101

John of Salisbury, 4:116

John O'Hara, 1:867

John Osborne, 1:532

John Osborne: A Reference Guide, 1:532

John Paul Jones: A Sailor's Biography, 3:589

John Paul II: A Man from Krakow, 4:742

John Paul II: A Pictorial Biography, 4:744

John Quincy Adams, 3:568

John Quincy Adams and American Global Empire, 3:546

John Randolph of Roanoke, 3:562

John Rawls' Theory of Social Justice: An Introduction, 4:316

John Reed and the Russian Revolution, 3:396

John Rennie, the Life and Work of a Great Engineer, 5:254

John Ruskin, 1:394, 1:395

John Ruskin: The Argument of the Eye, 1:395

John Ruskin: The Passionate Moralist, 1:393, 1:394

John Ruskin, a Reference Guide, 1:395

John Ruskin and Rose La Touche, 1:394

John Ruskin and Victorian Architecture, 1:394

John Sherman and Dhoya, 1:571

The Johns Hopkins Guide to the Medical Care of Patients with HIV Infection, 5:386

The Johns Hopkins Medical Handbook, 5:317

John Skelton, Laureate, 1:197

John Skelton, Priest as Poet: Seasons of Discovery, 1:197

John Skelton and the Politics of the 1520s, 1:197

John Skelton's Poetry, 1:197

John Smeaton FRS, 5:255

John Smeaton's Diary, 5:255

Johnson: The Critical Heritage, 1:250

Johnson and His Age, 1:225

Johnson over Jordan, 1:537

John Steinbeck, 1:886

John Steinbeck: The California Years, 1:886

John Steinbeck: The Voice of the Land, 1:885

John Steinbeck's Fiction: The Aesthetics of the Road Taken, 1:886

John Steinbeck's Re-Vision of America, 1:886

John Steinbeck's The Grapes of Wrath, 1:885

John Stuart Mill (Ellery), 4:244

John Stuart Mill (Skorupski), 4:245

John Stuart Mill: A Criticism with Personal Recollections, 4:244

John Stuart Mill: His Life and Works, 4:245

John Stuart Mill and Harriet Taylor, 1:380

John Stuart Mill and Harriet Taylor: Their Friendship and Subsequent Marriage, 4:245

John Stuart Mill and the Harriet Taylor Myth, 1:380

John Stuart Mill in Love, 1:380

John Stuart Mill's "On Liberty," 4:245

John XXIII: Simpleton or Saint? 4:771

John Updike, 1:1060

John Updike: A Comprehensive Bibliography, 1:1061
John Updike: The Cipher of the World, 1:1060
John Updike: Yea Sayings, 1:1060
John Updike's Novels, 1:1060
John von Neumann and Modern Economics, 3:112
John von Neumann and Norbert Wiener, 5:583, 5:584
John von Neumann and the Origins of Modern Computing, 3:112, 5:583
John Webster (Bradbook), 1:200
John Webster (Leech), 1:201
John Webster (Morris), 1:201
John Wesley: A Theological Biography, 4:790
John Wesley and His World, 4:790
John Wesley and the Women Preachers of Early Methodism, 4:738
John Wesley's Social Ethics: Praxis and Principles, 4:790
John William De Forest, 1:744
John William De Forest and the Rise of American Gentility, 1:744
John Winthrop's World: History as a Story/the Story as History, 3:518
John Wyclif and Reform, 4:714
John Wycliffe and the Beginnings of English Nonconformity, 4:721
Joining Charles and Other Stories, 1:447
Joining the Club: A History of Jews and Yale, 4:640
The Joke, 2:793
The Joker of Seville and O Babylon: Two Plays, 2:943
Jokes, 3:870
The Jokes of Sigmund Freud: A Study in Humor and Jewish Identity, 5:448
Joking Apart and Other Plays, 1:437
The Jolly Beggars, 1:280
The Jolly Corner: And Other Tales, 1:763
Jonah's Gourd Vine, 1:849
Jonas Lie, 2:667
Jonathan Cape: Publisher, 1:40
Jonathan Draws the Long Bow, 3:858

Jonathan Edwards, 3:587
Jonathan Edwards (Aldridge), 4:767
Jonathan Edwards (Lesser), 1:637
Jonathan Edwards (Miller), 4:767
Jonathan Edwards: A Profile, 4:767
Jonathan Edwards: Puritan, Preacher, Philosopher, 4:767
Jonathan Edwards: The Narrative of a Puritan Mind, 1:637, 4:767
Jonathan Edwards, 1703–1758: A Biography, 4:767
Jonathan Edwards, Pastor: Religion and Society in Eighteenth-Century Northampton, 4:767
Jonathan Edwards and the American Experience, 4:767
Jonathan Wild, 1:244, 1:245
The Jonsonian Masque, 1:184
Jorge Amado, 2:892
Jorge Guillén, 2:541
Jorge Luis Borges: A Literary Biography, 2:857
Jo's Boys, 1:1198
Jo's Boys and How They Turned Out, 1:1198
José Donoso, 2:864
José Martí: Architect of Cuba's Freedom, 2:871
José Martí: Revolutionary Democrat, 2:871
José Martí and the Cuban Revolution Retraced, 2:871
José Ortega y Gasset, 4:315
José Ortega y Gasset: Circumstances and Vocation, 5:97
José Ortega y Gasset: Philosophy of European Unity, 4:315
Joseph A. Schumpeter: Critical Assessments, 3:105
Joseph and His Brothers, 2:601, 2:602
Joseph and Koza, or The Sacrifice to the Vistula, 2:48
Joseph Andrews, 1:224, 1:229, 1:244, 1:245
Joseph Brodsky: A Poet for Our Time, 2:704
Joseph Butler's Moral and Religious Thought: Tercentenary Essays, 4:194

A Joseph Campbell Companion: Reflections on the Art of Living, 3:877
Joseph Campbell on Myth and Mythology, 3:877
Joseph Conrad, 1:464
Joseph Conrad: A Biography, 1:464
Joseph Conrad: An Annotated Secondary Bibliography, 1:464
Joseph Conrad: Consciousness and Integrity, 1:464
Joseph Conrad: Narrative Technique and Ideological Commitment, 1:464
Joseph Conrad: The Three Lives, 1:464
Joseph Conrad: The Way of Dispossession, 1:464
Joseph Conrad: Writing as Rescue, 1:464
Joseph Conrad and American Writers, 1:464
Joseph Conrad and the Modern Temper, 1:464
Josephine, 3:737
Josephine Baker, 3:737
Josephine Butler, Flame of Fire, 1:341
Joseph Karo: Lawyer and Mystic, 4:628
Joseph Lister, 1827–1912, 5:409
Joseph Lister, Father of Modern Surgery, 5:409
Joseph Mallord William Turner, 3:794
Joseph Priestley, 5:753
Joseph Priestley: Scientist, Theologian, and Metaphysician, 5:753
Joseph Priestley and the Idea of Progress, 5:753
Joseph Pulitzer, His Life and Letters, 3:821
Joseph Sheridan Le Fanu, 1:601
Joseph Smith, the First Mormon, 4:879
Joseph Smith and the Beginnings of Mormonism, 4:845, 4:879
Joseph Stalin, 3:292
Josephus: A Historical Romance, 2:578
Josephus: The Historian and His Society, 3:317, 4:666
Josephus: The Man and the Historian, 4:666, 4:812
Josephus and Judaean Politics, 4:666

Josephus and the Emperor, 2:578

Josephus with an English Translation, 4:812

Joseph von Eichendorff, 2:578

José Rizal on His Centenary, 2:333

Joshua Slocum, 3:937

Joshua Then and Now, 2:924

Josiah Royce, 4:250

Josiah Willard Gibbs: An American Physicist Par Excellence, 5:747

Josiah Willard Gibbs: The History of a Great Mind, 5:747

Josip Broz Tito, 3:393

Josip Kozarac, 2:785

Jou Pu Tuan, The Prayer Mat of Flesh, 2:210

Journalism and Popular Culture, 3:806, 3:872

Journal of a Cruise to the Pacific Ocean, 1842–1844, in the Frigate United States with Notes on Herman Melville, 3:907

The Journal of Albion Moonlight, 1:1028

Journal of American Culture, 3:875

Journal of a Mission to the Interior of Africa, 3:932

Journal of Asian Studies, 2:235

Journal of a Soul, 4:771

Journal of a Voyage to Lisbon, 1:244

Journal of H.M.S. Endeavour, 1768–1771, 3:917

The Journal of John Wesley, 4:740, 4:789

Journal of Popular Culture, 3:875

Journal of Regional Cultures, 3:875

Journal of Researches into the Natural History and Geology of the Countries Visited during the Voyage of the H.M.S. Beagle round the World under the Command of Captain Fitz Roy, 5:793, 5:830

The Journal of Richard Henry Dana, Jr., 3:919

Journal of the Discovery of the Source of the Nile, 3:910

Journal of the Federal Convention, 3:161

Journal of the Fictive Life, 1:1021

A Journal of the Plague Year, 1:239

Journals: Early Fifties–Early Sixties, 1:981

Journals 1939–1983, 1:553

The Journals of Lewis and Clark, 3:576

The Journals of Susanna Moodie: Poems, 2:906

The Journals of Thomas James Cobden-Sanderson 1879–1922, 1:7

The Journals of Zebulon Montgomery Pike, with Letters and Related Documents, 3:910

Journal to Stella, 1:259

Journey (Dygat), 2:812

The Journey (Landsbergis), 2:806

Journey (Michner), 3:931

The Journey Back, 1:938, 1:1137

Journey between Wars, 1:828

A Journey for Our Times, 3:808, 3:822

A Journey from London to Genoa, 2:407

The Journey Home: Some Words in Defense of the American West, 5:827

Journey into Barbary, 1:514

Journey into China, 3:903

A Journey into Gravity and Spacetime, 5:665, 5:719

Journey into Russia, 3:941

Journey into Summer, 5:818

The Journey of Ibn Fattouma, 2:68

The Journey of Life: A Cultural History of Aging in America, 3:558

The Journey of Niels Klim to the World Underground, 2:650

Journeys, 3:909

Journeys among the Dead, 2:483

The Journey's Echo, 3:939

Journeys in Dream and Imagination, 2:672

Journeys through Philosophy, 4:20

Journeys through the French African Novel, 2:110

Journeys through the Labyrinth, 2:847

The Journey through AIDS: A Guide for Loved Ones and Caregivers, 5:388

Journey through Genius: The Great Theorems of Mathematics, 5:481

Journey through Russia and Siberia, 1787–1788, 3:909

Journey through the Night, 2:600

Journey to Armenia, 2:737

A Journey to Arzrum, 2:751

Journey to a War, 1:500

Journey to Heartbreak, 1:544

Journey to Nowhere: A New World Tragedy, 4:867

Journey to Oblivion, 2:30, 4:637

Journey to Oneself, 2:781

Journey to Poland, 4:635

Journey to the Alcarria, 2:534

The Journey to the East, 2:589, 3:778

Journey to the End of the Night, 2:465

Journey to the Trenches: The Life of Isaac Rosenberg, 1890–1918, 1:541

Journey to the Vanished City: The Search for a Lost Tribe of Israel, 3:440

The Journey to the West, 2:188, 2:229, 4:531

A Journey to the Western Islands of Scotland (Boswell), 1:234

Journey to the Western Islands of Scotland and The Journal of a Tour to the Hebrides (Johnson), 1:249

Journey to Tradition: The Odyssey of a Born-Again Jew, 4:659

Journey Without Maps, 1:489

Joyce, Huston, and the Making of "The Dead," 3:838

Joyce and Dante: The Shaping Imagination, 2:418

Joyce and the Law of the Father, 1:506

Joyce Carol Oates (Creighton), 1:1023

Joyce Carol Oates (Friedman), 1:1023

Joyce Carol Oates: Novels of the Middle Years, 1:1023

Joyce Carol Oates's Short Stories between Tradition and Innovation, 1:1023

Joyce Cary, 1:457

Joyce Cary: A Descriptive Bibliography, 1:457

Joyce Cary: Liberal Principles, 1:457

Joyce Cary and Lawrence Durrell: A Reference Guide, 1:470
Joyce Cary and the Dimensions of Order, 1:457
Joyce Cary and the Novel of Africa, 1:457
Joyce Cary Remembered: In Letters and Interviews, 1:457
Joyce Cary's Africa, 1:457
Joyce in Context, 1:505
Joyce's Anatomy of Culture, 1:505
Joyce's Dislocutions: Essays on Readings as Translation, 1:506
Joyce's Visible Art, 1:505
Joyce upon the Void: The Genesis of Doubt, 1:506
The Joyful Wisdom, 4:246
The Joyless Economy: The Psychology of Human Satisfaction, 3:64
Joy of Man's Desiring, 2:481
The Joy of Music, 3:682
Joys of Italian Humor and Folklore, 3:872
The Joys of Motherhood, 2:137
The Joys of Yiddish, 2:32
The Joys of Yinglish, 2:30
Jozef Mak, 2:833
JR, 1:977
J.R.R. Tolkien: Myth, Morality, and Religion, 1:559
J.R.R. Tolkien: Six Decades of Criticism, 1:559
J. S. Bach, 4:740
Juan Carlos Onetti, 2:876
Juan de Mairena, 2:544, 2:545
Juan Luis Vives, 4:156
Juan Luis Vives and the Emotions, 4:156
Juan Ramón Jiménez, 2:543
Juan the Landless, 2:540
Juan Valera, 2:553
Juarez, 3:838
Jubiaba, 2:892
Jubilate Agno, 1:255
Jubilee of the Discovery of Mauve and of the Foundation of Coal-Tar Industry by Sir W. H. Perkin, 5:752
Judaeo-Christian Debates, 4:602
Judaic Ethics for a Lawless World, 4:598
Judaic Law from Jesus to the Mishnah, 4:617
The Judaic Tradition, 4:596
Judaism, 4:883

Judaism: A Portrait, 4:596
Judaism: A Sociology, 4:634
Judaism: Practice and Belief 63 B.C.E.–66 C.E, 4:621, 4:807
Judaism: The Classical Statement: The Evidence of the Bavli, 4:607, 4:611
Judaism: The Evidence of the Mishnah, 4:611
Judaism: The Evolution of a Faith, 4:595
Judaism and Christianity: A Guide to the Reference Literature, 4:7
Judaism and Christianity: Essays, 4:660
Judaism and Christianity in the Age of Constantine, 4:621
Judaism and Ethics, 4:598
Judaism and Hellenism, 4:604, 4:807
Judaism and Its History: In Two Parts, 4:647
Judaism and Its Social Metaphors, 4:607
Judaism and Modernization on the Religious Kibbutz, 4:654
Judaism and Modern Man, 4:649
Judaism and Mysticism According to Gershom Scholem, 4:673
Judaism and Psychology: Halakhic Perspectives, 4:890
Judaism and Scripture: The Evidence of Leviticus Rabbah, 4:607, 4:611
Judaism and Story, 4:607
Judaism and the Koran, 4:570
Judaism as a Civilization, 4:667
Judaism as Philosophy: The Method and Message of the Mishnah, 4:601
Judaism beyond God: A Radical Need to Be Jewish, 4:649
Judaism Despite Christianity, 4:671
Judaism from Cyrus to Hadrian, 4:604
Judaism in America: From Curiosity to Third Faith, 4:651
Judaism in Cold War America: 1945–1990, 4:640
Judaism in Society, 4:607, 4:611

Judaism in the Beginning of Christianity, 4:615
Judaism in the First Centuries of the Christian Era, 4:621
Judaism in the Matrix of Christianity, 4:621
Judaism on Trial: Jewish-Christian Disputations in the Middle Ages, 4:624
Judaisms and Their Messiahs in the Beginning of Christianity, 4:621
Judas at the Jockey Club and Other Episodes of Porfirian Mexico, 3:638
Jude, 1:360
Jude the Obscure, 1:310, 1:360, 1:361
The Judge, 1:566
The Judge and His Hangman, 2:577
The Judge's Chair, 2:801
Judging New Wealth, 1:592
Judgment and Reasoning in the Child, 3:267
A Judgment in Stone, 1:609
The Judgment of the Dead, 4:887
The Judicial Process, 3:145
Judicial Reform and Land Reform in the Roman Republic, 3:306
Judith, 1:833
Jugglers Three, 2:967
Jugurtha, 3:320
The Jugurthine War, 3:320
Jules and Jim, 3:843
Jules Romains, 2:502
Julia, 1:1243
Julian, 1:1061, 1:1062
Julian Huxley, 5:799
Julian the Apostate, 3:302
Juliette, 2:503
Julio Cortázar: Rayuela, 2:862
Julio Jurenito, 2:717
Julius Caesar, 1:205, 1:206, 1:1178, 2:461
Julius Caesar and His Public Image, 3:313
July's People, 2:162
Jumanji, 1:1207
The Jumblies, 1:586
Jump and Other Stories, 2:162
Jump at de Sun: The Story of Zora Neale Hurston, 1:850
Jumpers, 1:554

Jumpstart: The Economic
  Unification of Germany,
  3:52, 3:59
Jung: And the Story of Our
  Time, 5:456
Jung: Man and Myth, 5:455
Jung and Post-Jungians,
  5:456
Jung and Tarot: An Arche-
  typal Journey, 5:456
Jungian Analysis, 5:456
Jungian Psychology in Per-
  spective, 5:456
Jung in Context: Modernity
  and the Making of a Psy-
  chology, 5:456
The Jungle, 1:879, 1:880
The Jungle Book, 1:370,
  1:586
Jungle Fever, 1:1170
Jungle of Cities and Other
  Plays, 2:572
The Junior Book of Authors,
  1:1196
Junior High School Library
  Catalog, 1:74
Junkie, 1:956
Junky, 1:957
Juno and the Paycock, 1:526
Jupiter, 5:610
Jupiter Lights, 1:790
Jürgen Habermas, 4:404
Jürgen Habermas: Critic in
  the Public Sphere, 3:229
Jürgen Habermas on Society
  and Politics, 4:404, 5:90
Just Above My Head, 1:938,
  1:939
Just a Dream, 1:1207, 1:1208
"Just a Housewife": The Rise
  and Fall of Domesticity in
  America, 3:557
The Just and the Unjust,
  1:964
Just before Dawn, 2:143
Just before the Origin: Alfred
  Russel Wallace's Theory of
  Evolution, 5:45
Just Business, 4:389
Just Fate, 1:619
Just Health Care, 4:388
Justice, 1:481
Justice, Law, and Culture,
  4:284
Justice and Mercy, 4:599
Justice as Fairness, 4:316
Justice at Nuremberg, 3:344
Justice in Wartime, 4:323
The Justice of Zeus, 2:346
The Justices of the United
  States Supreme Court,
  1789–1991, 3:506

Justice without Trial: Law
  Enforcement in Democrat-
  ic Society, 3:145
Justice without Vengeance,
  2:554
Justification and Application:
  Remarks on Discourse
  Ethics, 5:89
Justifying Legal Punishment,
  4:387
Justine, 2:503
Justinian and the Later Ro-
  man Empire, 4:682
Just So Stories, 1:370, 1:371,
  1:586
Justus Lipsius: The Philoso-
  phy of Renaissance Stoi-
  cism, 4:130
The Just War: Force and Po-
  litical Responsibility,
  4:896, 5:112
Just War and Jihad, 4:570
Just Wild about Harry,
  1:861, 1:862
Juvenal the Satirist: A Study,
  2:387

K

The Kabbala: Law and Mysti-
  cism in the Jewish Tradi-
  tion, 4:630
Kabbalah and Criticism,
  1:1138
Kabuki: Five Classic Plays,
  2:274
Kabuki: The Popular Stage
  of Japan, 2:273
Kabuki Encyclopedia: An
  English Language Adapta-
  tion of Kabuki Jiten, 2:273
The Kabuki Theatre, 2:273
Kaddish and Other Poems,
  1958–1960, 1:981
Kafka: A Biography, 2:596
The Kafka Problem: An An-
  thology of Criticism about
  Franz Kafka, 2:596
Kafka's Narrators: A Study of
  His Stories and Sketches,
  2:596
Kafka's Other Trial: The Let-
  ters to Felice, 2:596
Kafu the Scribbler: The Life
  and Writings of Nagai
  Kafu, 1879–1959, 2:291
Kahlil Gibran: A Biography,
  2:67
Kahlil Gibran: His Life and
  World, 2:67
Kaifuso, 2:270

The Kalam Cosmological Ar-
  gument, 4:574
Kaleidoscope, 1:1223, 1:1224
The Kalevala, 2:657, 2:659
Kalevipoeg, 2:795
Kaligrunes, 2:773
Kalki, 1:1062
Kāma Sūtra, 2:172
The Kāma Sūtra of
  Vātsyāyana, 2:172
The Kama Sutra of Vatsyaya-
  ma Now Complete and
  Unexpurgated, 3:914
Kangaroo (Aleshkovsky),
  2:698
Kangaroo (Lawrence), 1:509
Kang Yu-wei: A Biography
  and a Symposium, 4:361
Kanji and Kana: A Handbook
  Dictionary of the Japanese
  Writing System, 1:100
Kansas Folklore, 3:862
Kant, 4:207, 4:299
Kant and the Claims of
  Knowledge, 4:206
Kant and the Claims of
  Taste, 4:206
Kant and the Exact Sciences,
  4:206
Kant and the Experience of
  Freedom, 4:206
Kant and the Nineteenth
  Century, 4:161
Kant and the Philosophy of
  History, 4:207
Kant and the Problem of
  Metaphysics, 4:206, 4:291
Kanthapura, 2:178
Kantian Ethics and Social-
  ism, 4:207
Kant's Aesthetic Theory,
  4:206
Kant's Analogies of Experi-
  ence, 4:206
Kant's Analytic, 4:206
Kant's Concept of Teleology,
  4:206
Kant's Dialectic, 4:206
Kant's Ethical Theory, 4:207
Kant's Life and Thought,
  4:206, 4:279
Kant's Metaphysics and
  Theory of Science, 4:206
Kant's Metaphysics of Experi-
  ence, 4:207
Kant's Moral Religion, 4:207
Kant's Moral Theory, 4:207
Kant's Rational Theology,
  4:207
Kant's Theory of Form,
  4:207
Kant's Theory of Freedom,
  4:206

Kant's Theory of Justice, 4:207

Kant's Theory of Knowledge, 4:206

Kant's Theory of Morals, 4:206

Kant's Theory of Rights, 4:206

Kant's Transcendental Psychology, 4:206

Kapitza, Rutherford and the Kremlin, 5:697

Kapitza in Cambridge and Moscow, 5:697

Kappa: A Satire, 2:285

Karaite Anthology: Excerpts from the Early Literature, 4:631

Karaites in Byzantium: The Formative Years, 970–1100, 4:631

Karaite Studies, 4:631

A Karamazov Companion, 2:716

Karamzin's Memoir on Ancient and Modern Russia, 2:730

Karel Čapek, 2:790

Karel ende Elegast, 2:619

Karl and Rosa, November 1918: A German Revolution, 2:576

Karl Barth: His Life from Letters and Autobiographical Texts, 4:758

A Karl Barth Reader, 4:758

Karl Jaspers: An Introduction to His Philosophy, 4:300, 5:139

Karl Jaspers: Basic Philosophical Writings, 4:299

Karl Jaspers and the Role of "Conversion" in the Nuclear Age, 4:300

Karl Marx (Appelbaum), 3:290

Karl Marx (Berlin), 4:242, 4:243

Karl Marx: A Reader, 3:290

Karl Marx: His Life and Environment, 3:95, 3:290

Karl Marx: His Life and Thought, 4:243

Karl Marx's Economics: Critical Assessments, 3:95

Karl Marx's Theory of History: A Defence, 3:290, 4:242

Karl Marx's Theory of Revolution, 4:242

Karl Pearson: An Appreciation of Some Aspects of His Life and Work, 5:531

Karl Popper, 4:410

Karl Rahner, 4:904

Karl Rahner: An Introduction to His Theology, 4:746

Karl Rahner: Theologian of the Graced Search for Meaning, 4:903

Karl Rahner in Dialogue, 4:745, 4:903

Karl Shapiro, 1:1046

Karma, 4:550

Karma and Rebirth: Post Classical Developments, 4:887

Karma and Rebirth in Classical Indian Traditions, 4:505

The Karma of Words, 2:272

Kaspar and Other Plays, 2:586

Kasper in de onderwereld, 2:627

Katallagete: Be Reconciled, 5:165

The Katana, 1:516

Kätchen von Heilbronn, 2:599

Katchikali, 2:145

Kate Beaumont, 1:744

Kate Bouverie, and Other Tales and Sketches, in Prose and Verse, 1:384

Kateb Yacine: "Nedjma," 2:124

Kate Chopin, 1:740

Kate Chopin: A Critical Biography, 1:740

Kate Chopin: A Life of the Author of The Awakening, 1:740

The Kate Chopin Companion, 1:740

A Kate Chopin Miscellany, 1:740

Kate Chopin Reconsidered: Beyond the Bayou, 1:740

Kate Greenaway, 1:585

Katerina: A Novel, 2:14

Katharine Walton; or, The Rebel of Dorchester, 1:696

Katherine Anne Porter, 1:870

Katherine Anne Porter: A Collection of Critical Essays, 1:870

Katherine Anne Porter: A Critical Biography, 1:870

Katherine Anne Porter: A Life, 1:870

Katherine Anne Porter: Conversations, 1:870

Katherine Anne Porter and Mexico: The Illusion of Eden, 1:870

Katherine Anne Porter and Texas: An Uneasy Relationship, 1:870

Katherine Mansfield, 2:979

Katherine Mansfield: A Biography, 2:979

Kathleen ni Houlihan, 1:490

Katinka, 2:647

Kavanaugh: A Tale, 1:683

Kaywana Blood, 2:937, 2:938

Kazantzakis: The Politics of the Spirit, 2:374

Kazantzakis and Linguistic Revolution in Greek Literature, 2:374

Keats, 1:294

Keats: The Myth of the Hero, 1:295

Keats: The Religious Sense, 1:294

Keats and Embarrassment, 1:294

Keats and Hellenism, 1:294

Keats and His Poetry: A Study in Development, 1:294

Keats and Shakespeare: A Study of Keats' Poetic Life from 1816–1820, 1:294

Keats and the Victorians, 1:294

Keats as a Narrative Poet: A Test of Invention, 1:294

Keats' Craftsmanship: A Study in Poetic Development, 1:294

Keats the Poet, 1:294

The Keeper of Sheep, 2:560

The Keeper of the Keys, 2:793

Keeping and Breeding Butterflies and Other Exotica, 5:772

Keeping Cool and Other Essays, 5:797

Keep the Aspidistra Flying, 1:530

Kekulé Centennial, 5:731

The Kempton-Wace Letters, 1:774

Kenilworth, 1:298

Ken Kesey, 1:1000

Kenneth Burke, 1:818, 1:956

Kenneth Burke: Literature and Language as Symbolic Action, 1:818

Kenneth Burke and Martin Heidegger, 1:818

Kenneth Burke and the Drama of Human Relations, 1:818
Kenneth Grahame, 1:584
Kenneth Grahame, 1859–1932, 1:584
Kenneth Patchen: A Collection of Essays, 1:1028
Kenneth Patchen and American Mysticism, 1:1028
Kenneth Slessor: A Biography, 2:963
Kentucky Country: Folk and Country Music of Kentucky, 3:853
Kentucky Folklore, 3:860
Kentucky Ham, 1:958
Kenya: A Political History, 3:422
The Kenyon Review, 1:874
Kepler, 5:41
Kept in the Dark, 1:406
Kerouac: A Biography, 1:999
Kerouac's Crooked Road: Development of a Fiction, 1:999
Kerygma and Myth, 4:743
Kesanli Ali Destani, 2:101
The Key, 2:293
Key Facts in Soviet History, 3:394
Keyguide to Information Sources in Archaeology, 3:305
Keyguide to Information Sources in Cartography, 5:617
Keyguide to Information Sources in Museum Studies, 3:758
The Keynesian Revolution in the Making, 1924–36, 3:87
Key Sources in Comparative and World Literature, 1:122
Keys to Nabokov, 2:741
The Key to Theosophy, 4:874
A Key to Uncle Tom's Cabin, 1:699
A Key to Whitehead's "Process and Reality," 4:343
Keywords in Evolutionary Biology, 5:780
KGB, 3:395
Khrushchev: The Years in Power, 3:346
Khrushchev Remembers: The Last Testament, 3:396
Khublai Khan: His Life and Times, 3:468
Kibbutz: New Way of Life, 3:440

Kibbutz: Venture in Utopia, 4:643
Kibbutz Judaism: A New Tradition in the Making, 4:658
Kicking the Leaves, 1:983
The Kid, 1:1160
Kid Auto Races at Venice, 1:1160
Kiddush ha-Shem: An Epic of 1648, 2:35
Kiddush Hashem: Cat in the Ghetto, 2:37
Kid Fitness, 5:325
Kidnapped, 1:395, 1:396, 1:589
Kids and Computers: A Parent's Handbook, 5:566
Kids and Drugs, 5:403
Kids Are What They Eat, 5:348
Kierkegaard (Gardiner), 4:240
Kierkegaard (Thompson), 4:240
Kierkegaard: A Collection of Critical Essays, 4:240
Kierkegaard: A Life of Allegory, 4:240
Kierkegaard: Construction of the Aesthetic, 4:393
Kierkegaard: The Aesthetic and the Religious, 4:240
Kierkegaard and Christendom, 4:240
A Kierkegaard Handbook, 4:240
Kierkegaard in Golden Age of Denmark, 4:240
Kierkegaard's Authorship: A Guide to the Writings of Kierkegaard, 4:239
Kierkegaard's Concluding Unscientific Postscript, 4:240
Kierkegaard's Existential Ethics, 4:240
Kierkegaard's Fear and Trembling: Critical Appraisals, 4:240
Kierkegaard's Relation to Hegel, 4:240
Kievan Russia, 3:395, 3:413
Killing Game, 2:483
The Killing Man, 1:1237
Killing the Messenger: One Hundred Years of Media Criticism, 3:806
Killing the Second Dog, 2:815
Killing Time, 1:948, 1:949
Killshot, 1:1232
Kim, 1:318, 1:370, 1:586

Kindergarten Chats, 3:792
The Kindly Ones, 1:536
Kindness, Clarity, and Insight, 4:560, 4:906
A Kindness Cup, 2:949
A Kind of Order, A Kind of Folly: Essays and Conversations, 1:1003
A Kind of Testament, 2:813
Kind Words: A Thesaurus of Euphemisms, 1:92
King: A Biography, 4:773
King, Queen, Knave, 2:740
King and Kin: Political Allegory in the Hebrew Bible, 4:817
A King and No King, 1:173
King and People in Provincial Massachusetts, 3:516
King Arthur and His Knights, 1:154
King Arthur's Death, 1:147
King Charles I, 4:733
King Coal: A Novel, 1:880
King David and His Wives, 2:43
The King David Report, 2:590
Kingdom and Colony: Ireland in the Atlantic World, 1560–1800, 3:370
Kingdom and Community: The Social World of Early Christianity, 4:683
The Kingdom and the Power, 3:809
The Kingdom by the Sea: A Journey around Great Britain, 3:900, 3:940
A Kingdom for a Stage, 1:212
The Kingdom of Armenia, 2:76
The Kingdom of Art, 1:821
The Kingdom of Books, 1:33
The Kingdom of God in America, 4:753
The Kingdom of God Is within You, 2:765
The Kingdom of the Earth, 2:656, 2:656
The Kingdom of This World, 2:859, 2:860
Kingdom's End and Other Stories, 2:178
Kingdoms of Gold, Kingdoms of Jade, 4:454
Kingdoms of the Savanna, 3:421, 3:431
Kingdoms of the Yoruba, 3:421
King Emene, 2:147
The Kingfisher, 1:962

King Forever! 2:136
King Gustav and the Devil, 1:979
King Harald's Saga, 2:643
King Hrolf and his Champions, 2:640
King Hunger, 2:699
King James VI and I, 3:361
King Johan, 1:172
King John (Shakespeare), 1:205, 1:206
King John (Warren), 3:357
King Lear, 1:205, 1:206, 1:212, 1:1050, 2:979
"King Lear" and the Gods, 1:214
"King Lear" in Our Time, 1:214
King Leopold, England and the Upper Nile, 1899–1909, 3:419
King Leopold's Congo, 3:421
King Leopold's Soliloquy, 1:780, 1:781
The King Must Die, 2:347
The King of Elfland's Daughter, 1:615
The King of Flesh and Blood, 2:24
King of Life, 2:819
King of Spades, 1:1217
King of the Beggars, 1:529
King of the Benighted, 2:84
The King of the Fields, 2:48
The King of Time, 2:732
King Ottocar: His Rise and Fall, 2:584
Kings and Kinsmen: Early Mbundu States in Angola, 3:424
Kings and Queens of Early Britain, 3:356
Kingsblood Royal, 1:853
The King's English, 1:91
The King's General, 1:620
Kingship and Community in Early India, 4:501
Kingship and the Gods, 4:441, 4:442
Kingship and Unity: Scotland, 1000 to 1306 A.D., 3:368
Kingsley Amis, 1:433
Kingsley Amis: An English Moralist, 1:433
Kingsley Amis: A Reference Guide, 1:433
Kingsley Amis: In Life and Letters, 1:433
Kingsley Amis: Modern Novelist, 1:433
King Solomon's Mines, 1:594, 1:595

King Solomon's Ring, 3:171, 3:190, 5:835
King's Peace, 3:361
The King's Quair, 1:150
The King Stag, 2:402
The King's Two Bodies: A Study of Medieval Political Theology, 4:98, 4:696
The King Who Was a King, 1:563
Kino: A History of the Russian and Soviet Film, 3:835
Kinship and Marriage among the Nuer, 3:19
Kinship and Marriage in Early Arabia, 4:492
Kinship and Social Organization, 3:20
Kinship in Bali, 3:19
Kinship Organization in Late Imperial China, 1000–1940, 3:466
Kipling: The Critical Heritage, 1:372
Kipling, Auden and Co.: Essays and Reviews, 1935–1964, 1:993
Kipling and Conrad: The Colonial Fiction, 1:372
Kipling and "Orientalism," 1:372
A Kipling Dictionary, 1:372
Kipling in India, 1:372
Kipling's Hidden Narratives, 1:372
Kipling's Mind and Art: Selected Critical Essays, 1:372
Kipling's South Africa, 1:372
Kipps, 1:563
Kirk-Othmer Concise Encyclopedia of Chemical Technology, 5:223, 5:725
Kirk-Othmer Encyclopedia of Chemical Technology, 5:725
The Kiss and Other Stories, 2:708
Kissinger: A Biography, 3:538
Kiss of the Spider Woman, 2:880
Kiss the Hand You Cannot Bite: The Rise and Fall of the Ceausecus, 3:390
Kister's Atlas Buying Guide, 1:74
Kitab al-Hayawan, 2:66
Kitab Fakhr al-Sudan 'ala al-Bidan, 2:66
Kit Brandon, 1:811

Kit Carson's Long Walk and Other True Tales of Old San Diego, 3:864
The Kitchen, 1:526, 1:565
Kiwi and Emu, 2:971
The Klansman, 1:792
The Kleptomaniac, 1:1174
Knife in the Water: With Repulsion and Cul-de-Sac, 3:841
The Knight of Olmedo, 2:554
Knight of Swords, 1:616
The Knight of the Burning Pestle, 1:173
The Knights, 2:353
Knight's Gambit, 1:835
The Knight's Tale, 1:150
The Knocker on Death's Door, 1:608
Knocking on the Door, 2:167
Knot and Other Plays, 2:161
Knots, 5:459
Knowing and Acting: An Invitation to Philosophy, 4:25
Knowing and the Known, 4:224
Knowing Everything about Nothing, 5:20
Knowing the Unknowable God: Ibn-Sina, Maimonides, Aquinas, 4:884
Knowledge, Goodness and Power, 4:130
Knowledge Acquisition for Expert Systems, 5:568
Knowledge and Human Interest, 3:229, 4:404, 5:89
Knowledge and Passion, 3:26
Knowledge and Power, 5:67, 5:157
Knowledge and Reflexivity, 5:159
Knowledge and Social Imagery, 5:66, 5:151
Knowledge and the Flow of Information, 5:74
Knowledge and the Good in Plato's Republic, 4:81
Knowledge and the Sacred: The Gifford Lectures, 1981, 4:375, 4:576, 4:902
Knowledge and Wonder: The Natural World as Man Knows It, 5:651
Knowledge as Desire: An Essay on Freud and Piaget, 3:267
Knowledge for What? The Place of Social Science in American Culture, 3:231

The Knowledge Machine: Artificial Intelligence and the Future of Man, 5:568
The Knowledge of God in Calvin's Theology, 4:761
The Knowledge That Endures, 1:288
Knowledge without Expertise: On the Status of Scientists, 5:157
Knut Hamsun, 2:665
Kodae Sosôl: A Survey of Korean Traditional Style Popular Novels, 2:298
Kodansha Encyclopedia of Japan, 3:473
Kohut's Legacy: Contributions to Self Psychology, 5:458
Kojiki, 2:269, 2:274
Ko-ji-ki (Chamberlain), 4:536
Kokinshu, 2:270, 2:274, 2:277
Kokin Wakashu, 2:275
Koko, 1:1243
Kokoro, 4:539
Kolyma Tales, 2:755
Kongi's Harvest, 2:148
Konoe Fumimaro: A Political Biography, 3:479
Konrad Lorenz, 5:835
Konrad Wallenrod, 2:817
Konrad Wallenrod, and Grazyna, 2:817
Konrad Wallenrod, and Other Writings, 2:817
Konspiva: Solidarity Underground, 3:390
Kon-Tiki, 3:923, 3:924
Koop: The Memoirs of America's Family Doctor, 5:314
The Koran, 4:586
The Koran Interpreted, 4:587
Korea, 3:481
Korea: An Introduction, 3:481
Korea: A Religious History, 3:481, 4:533
Korea: Tradition and Transformation: A History of the Korean People, 3:481
Korean and Asian Religious Tradition, 4:534
Korean and Japanese Women: An Analytic Bibliographical Guide, 3:463
The Korean Approach to Zen, 4:537
The Korean Buddhist Canon, 4:534
Korean Poetry Today, 2:299
The Koreans: Passion and Grace, 3:481

The Koreans and Their Culture, 3:481
A Korean Storyteller's Miscellany: The P'aegwan chapki, 2:299
Korean Studies Guide, 3:481
The Korean War, 3:482
Korea Old and New: A History, 2:298; 3:481
The Kosciuszko Foundation English-Polish, Polish-English Dictionary, 1:101
Kostis Palamas, 2:375
Kostis Palamas: A Portrait and an Appreciation, 2:375
Kotik Letev, 2:700, 2:701
Kovel's American Silver Marks, 3:767
Krakatit, 2:789, 2:790
Krane's Cafe: An Interior with Figures, 2:668
Krapp's Last Tape, 1:439, 2:459
Krapp's Last Tape and Other Dramatic Pieces, 1:439, 2:459
The Kreutzer Sonata and Other Stories, 2:764
Krishna: Myths, Rites, and Attitudes, 4:506
Krishna Consciousness in the West, 4:862
Krishnamurti: A Biography, 4:555
Krishnamurti: His Life and Death, 4:556
Krishnamurti: The Man, the Mystery and the Message, 4:555, 4:858
Krishnamurti: The Open Door, 4:556
Krishnamurti: The Reluctant Messiah, 4:555
Krishnamurti: The Years of Awakening, 4:556, 4:858
Krishnamurti: The Years of Fulfillment, 4:556, 4:858
The Kristeva Reader, 1:1132
Kristin Lavransdatter, 2:668, 2:669
Krsna: The Supreme Personality of Godhead, 4:862
Kubrick: Inside a Film Artist's Maze, 3:839
The Kula: New Perspectives on Massim Exchange, 4:486
Kulliyat, 2:93
Küng in Conflict, 4:775
Kuo Mo-jo: History of the Formative Years of His Life, 2:250

The Kurdish Question in Iraq, 3:450
Kurozumikyo and the New Religions of Japan, 4:540
Kurozumi Shinto: An American Dialogue, 4:541
Kurt Vonnegut (Klinkowitz), 1:1064
Kurt Vonnegut (Lundquist), 1:1064
Kurt Vonnegut, Jr. (Reed), 1:1064
Kurt Vonnegut, Jr. (Schatt), 1:1064
Kurt Vonnegut, Jr.: A Checklist, 1:1064
Kuwait: Dependency and Class in a Rentier State, 3:455
Kuwait, 3:454
The Kuwait Fund and the Political Economy of Arab Regional Development, 3:451
Kuyucakli Yusuf, 2:100
The Kuzari: An Argument for the Faith of Israel, 4:666, 4:667
Kyng Alisaunder, 1:145
Kyukhlya, 2:770

L

Labanotation: The System of Analyzing and Recording Movement, 3:746
La Bâtarde, 2:485, 2:486
L'Abbé C, 2:456
La Bella Estate, 2:432
La Bête Humaine, 2:518
Labor and an Integrated Europe, 3:60
Labor and Desire: Women's Revolutionary Fiction in Depression America, 1:805
Labor and Imperial Democracy in Prewar Japan, 3:477
The Laboratory Approach to Teaching Calculus, 5:490
Laboratory Life: The Construction of Scientific Facts, 5:166, 5:167
A Laboratory of Impure Forms: The Plays of Tadeusz Różewicz, 2:821
Laboratory Tests, 5:324
Labor Management and Social Policy, 3:74
The Labor Market as a Social Institution, 3:60

Labor Market Institutions and the Future Role of Unions, 3:59

Labor Markets under Trade Unionism: Employment, Wages, and Hours, 3:60

Labor of Love, Labor of Sorrow, 3:556

The Labor of Words: Literary Professionalism in the Progressive Era, 1:795

Labour and the British State, 3:366

The Labour Governments, 1945–1951, 3:366

Labour's Apprentices: Working-ClassLads in Late Victorian and Edwardian England, 3:363

La Brava, 1:1232

The Labyrinth of Solitude, 2:878, 2:879

Labyrinths, 2:141

Labyrinths: Selected Short Stories and Other Writings, 2:856

Labyrinths and Path of Thunder, 2:142

Labyrinths of Iron: A History of the Subways, 5:247

Lacan and Language: A Reader's Guide to Ecrits, 5:458

La Casa in Collina, 2:432

La Catedral, 2:886

Lacerba, 2:430

La Comédie Humaine, 2:445

La Convention Belzébir, 2:452

La Dame aux Camélias, 2:473, 2:473

Lad and Lass, 2:640

Ladders to Fire, 1:865

Ladies Almanack, 1:812, 1:813

Ladies at the Alamo, 1:1122, 1:1123

Ladies' Day (Thesmopheriazusae), 2:353

Ladies of the Press: The Story of Women in Journalism by an Insider, 3:808

La Dorotea, 2:554

A Lady, 1:855

The Lady and the Monk, 3:903

Lady Anna, 1:406

Lady Audley's Secret, 1:272, 1:332, 1:333

Lady Baltimore, 1:789

Lady Blessington's Conversations of Lord Byron, 1:283

Lady Chatterley's Lover, 1:508, 1:509

Lady Day: The Many Faces of Billie Holiday, 3:701

Lady Faustus, 1:931

The Lady from Dubuque, 1:1080

The Lady from Shanghai, 1:1178

The Lady from the Sea, 2:665, 2:666

Lady Gregory, 1:490

Lady Gregory: A Biography, 1:490

Lady Gregory: An Annotated Bibliography of Criticism, 1:490

Lady Gregory: Fifty Years After, 1:490

Lady Gregory's Journals, 1:490

The Lady in Kicking Horse Reservoir, 1:990

The Lady in the Lake, 1:1228

Lady Isabella Persse Gregory, 1:490

Lady Macbeth of the Mtsensk District and Other Stories, 2:736

The Lady of La Garaye, 1:384

The Lady of the Aroostook, 1:758

Lady of the Castle, 2:18

The Lady of the Lake and Other Poems, 1:299

Lady Oracle, 2:906

The Lady's Not for Burning, 1:480

The Lady Vanishes, 1:1168, 1:1169

Lady Windermere's Fan, 1:409, 1:410

Lady with the Dog, 2:708

La Favola di Orfeo, 2:436

Lafcadio, the Lion Who Shot Back, 1:1207

Lafcadio's Adventures, 2:480

La Fontaine, 2:485

La Fontaine: Poet and Counterpoet, 2:485

L'Age d'Or and an Andalusian Dog, 3:832

The Lagoon, 2:974

The Lagoon and Other Stories, 2:975

La Grande Illusion, 1:1177

La Grande Maison, 2:119

La Guerre, 2:440

La Habana para un Infante Difunto, 2:858

The Laird of Abbotsford: A View of Sir Walter Scott, 1:300

The Lair of the White Worm, 1:603

Lajar Terkembang, 2:318

La Jeune Parque, 2:513

The Lake, 1:381

The Lake and the Woods: or, Nature's Calendar, 2:749

Lakeboat, 1:1101

Lake Effect Country: Poems, 1:934

The Lake Region of Central Africa: A Picture of Exploration, 3:914

Lakota Myth, 3:866

Lak Tar Miyo Kinyero We Lobo, 2:155

La Légende des Siècles, 2:482

La Maison de Rendez-vous, 2:500

La Malatia Infantile (Childhood Disease), 2:437

La Mandragola, 4:144

Lamarck, 5:803

Lamarck: The Founder of Evolution, 5:803

Lamarck and Modern Genetics, 5:803

Lamarck the Mythical Precursor, 5:802

Lamarck to Darwin: Contributions to Evolutionary Biology, 1809–1859, 5:803

La Mémoire Tatouée, 2:122, 2:123

The Lamentation over the Destruction of Sumer and Ur, 4:545

Lamentations Rabbah: An Analytical Translation, 4:611

Lament Everlasting, 2:216

Lament for Adonis, 2:369

Lament for an African Pol, 2:132

Lament for a Nation: The Defeat of Canadian Nationalism, 3:606

Lament for the Death of a Bullfighter: And Other Poems, 2:539

The Lament for the South, 2:231

Lament of a Soldier's Wife, 2:338

Lament of the Lady of Ch'in, 2:228

Lament of the Masks, 2:141

L'Ameto, 2:409, 2:410

Lamia, 1:293

Lamia, Isabella, The Eve of
    St. Agnes . . . 1820, 1:293
The Lamp at Noon, 2:925
The Lamp at Noon and Oth-
    er Stories, 2:925
The Lamp Burns Low, 2:306
The Lamplighter, 1:1219
Lamp of Mahamudra, 4:544
The Lamp of Marvels, 2:553
The Lamp of Memory: Rus-
    kin, Tradition, and Archi-
    tecture, 1:395
La Nación, 2:870
Lancelot, 1:1029
Lancelot: The Knight of the
    Cart, 2:466, 2:467
Land, Freedom and Fiction:
    History and Ideology in
    Kenya, 2:152
Land, Love, Century: New
    and Selected Poems, 2:76
Land, Settlement, and Poli-
    tics on Eighteenth-Century
    Prince Edward Island,
    3:612
Land and Life: A Selection
    from the Writings of Carl
    Ortwin Sauer, 3:135
Land and Politics in the
    England of Henry VIII,
    3:359
Land and Power: The Zionist
    Resort to Force,
    1881–1948, 4:658
Land and Revolution in Iran,
    1960–1980, 3:448
The Land and the People of
    South Africa, 2:167
A Land Apart: A South Afri-
    can Reader, 2:158
Landaufenhalt, 2:598
The Land before Her, 3:518,
    3:550
Land behind Baghdad: A His-
    tory of Settlement on the
    Diyala Plains, 3:449
Land Degradation and Soci-
    ety, 5:821
Landfall, 2:972
The Landleaguers, 1:406
Landlords and Tenants in
    Imperial Rome, 3:305
Landmark Experiments in
    Twentieth-Century Physics,
    5:697
Landmarks in American Civil
    Engineering, 5:224
Landmarks of French Classi-
    cal Drama, 2:471
Landmarks of Modern British
    Drama, 1:427
Land of Fire, 2:78
Land of Hidden Fires, 2:670

Land of Hope: Chicago,
    Black Southerners, and
    the Great Migration, 3:555
The Land of Journey's End-
    ing, 1:733
The Land of Little Rain,
    1:732, 1:733
The Land of the Bible: A
    Historical Geography,
    4:809
Land of the Free, 2:663
Land of the Wooden Gods,
    2:671
The Land of Ulro, 2:818
The Land of Upside Down,
    2:612
Landor's Poetry, 1:296
A Landowner's Morning,
    Family Happiness, The
    Devil, 2:764
Landprints: On the Magnifi-
    cent American Landscape,
    5:627
Landscape, 1:534
Landscape Description in the
    Lyric Poetry and "Fuh on
    Dwelling in the Moun-
    tains," 2:202
The Landscape of Modernity:
    Essays on New York City
    1900–1940, 3:136
The Landscape of Nightmare,
    1:917
The Landscape of Soria,
    2:545
Landscape of the Body,
    1:1090
Landscape Painted with Tea,
    2:831
The Landscape Painter, 1:763
The Landscape Paintings of
    Thomas Gainsborough,
    3:775
Landscapes after the Battle,
    2:540
Landscapes of a New Land:
    Fiction by Latin American
    Women, 2:848
Landscapes of Learning,
    3:255
Landscapes of Power: From
    Detroit to Disney World,
    3:217
Landscape with Figures,
    1:1109
The Land's End: A Natural-
    ist's Impression in West
    Cornwall, 1:365
Landslides: Causes, Conse-
    quences, and Environ-
    ment, 5:636
Lands of Pleasure, 1:32

Landstörtzerin Courasche,
    2:585
Land Use, Environment, and
    Social Change, 3:551
Land Use, Food, Energy and
    Recreation, 5:270
Land without Evil, 3:625
Land without Justice, 2:830
Land without Thunder, 2:155
Lanford Wilson, 1:1121
Lanfranc of Bec, 3:357
L'Ange Déchu, 2:166
Langenscheidt New College
    German Dictionary, 1:99
Lange's Handbook of Chem-
    istry, 5:724
Langman's Medical Embryol-
    ogy, 5:773
Langston Hughes, 1:848
Langston Hughes: A Bio-Bib-
    liography, 1:848
Langston Hughes: An Intro-
    duction to the Poetry,
    1:848
Langston Hughes: The Poet
    and His Critics, 1:848
Langton Quartet, 2:950
Language, 3:21, 3:27
Language: An Introduction to
    the Study of Speech, 3:40
Language: The Unknown: An
    Initiation into Linguistics,
    3:21
Language, Counter-Memory,
    Practice, 2:477, 4:400
Language, Culture, and Per-
    sonality: Essays in Memory
    of Edward Sapir, 3:40
Language, Schooling, and
    Cultural Conflict, 3:615
Language, Sexuality, and Ide-
    ology in Ezra Pound's
    Cantos, 1:873
Language, Society, and
    Paleoculture:, 4:436
Language, Truth and Logic,
    4:273
Language and Desire in
    Seneca's Phaedra, 2:394
Language and Experience in
    Seventeenth Century Brit-
    ish Philosophy, 4:29
Language and Gesture: Es-
    says in Poetry, 1:797
Language and Ideology in
    Children's Fiction, 1:1196
Language and Information,
    3:21
Language and Insight, 5:469
Language and Learning,
    3:192

Language and Logic in the Post Medieval Period, 4:123

The Language and Logic of the Bible: The Earlier Middle Ages, 4:696

Language and Meaning in the Renaissance, 4:132

Language and Myth, 4:279

Language and Philosophy: A Symposium, 4:265

Language and Psychology in Pepita Jiménez, 2:553

Language and Silence, 2:801

Language and Silence: Essays on Language, Literature and the Inhuman, 1:1054

Language and Social Identity, 3:21

Language and Style in Leaves of Grass, 1:707

Language and the "Feminine" in Nietzsche and Heidegger, 4:293

Language and Theme: Essays on African Literature, 2:111

Language and the Poet: Verbal Artistry in Frost, Stevens, and Moore, 1:798

Language and Thought in Early Greek Philosophy, 4:49

The Language and Thought of the Child, 3:174, 3:192, 3:267

Language as Gesture: Essays in Poetry, 1:816

Language as Symbolic Action, 1:817, 1:956

Language Diversity, 3:256

Language in Culture, 3:42

Language in Dispute, 4:102

Language in Literature, 2:687

Language in Modern Literature: Innovation and Experiment, 1:415

Language in Wittgenstein's Later Philosophy, 4:345

Language in Wycherley's Plays, 1:263

The Language of 1984: Orwell's English and Ours, 1:531

The Language of Biotechnology: A Dictionary of Terms, 5:726

The Language of Canaan, 1:628

The Language of Change: Elements of Therapeutic Communication, 5:420

The Language of Fiction, 1:422, 1:515

Language of Life: An Introduction to the Science of Genetics, 5:788

The Language of Modernism, 1:415

The Language of Politics: Studies in Quantitative Semantics, 3:157

The Language of Shakespeare's Plays, 1:216

The Language of Social Research, 3:200, 3:230

The Language of the Book of Songs, 2:195

Language of the Earth, 5:624

The Language of the Foreign Book Trade: Abbreviations, Terms and Phrases, 1:69

Language of the Goddess, 4:434

The Language of the Heart: The Body's Response to Human Dialogue, 5:342

The Language of the Revenger's Tragedy, 1:199

The Language of the Self: The Function of Language in Psychoanalysis, 5:458

Language of the Street and Other Essays, 2:330

The Language of Twentieth-Century Music, 3:655

Language Planning for Modernization, 2:318

Language Poetry: Writing as Rescue, 1:914

Languages and Lore of the Long Island Indians, 3:859

The Languages of Africa, 1963, 3:417

Languages of Art, 4:403

The Languages of Italy, 2:401

The Languages of Literature in Renaissance Italy, 2:401

Languages of Revolt: Dada and Surrealist Literature and Film, 2:986

The Languages of Theatre, 2:991

Lanterna Magica, 2:656

The Lantern-Bearers and Other Essays, 1:397

Lanterns and Lances, 1:890

La Nuit, 1:1065

Laocoon: An Essay on the Limits of Painting and Poetry, 2:600

Laocoon, Nathan the Wise, Minna von Barnhelm, 4:208

Laocoon, or the Bounds of Painting and Poesy, 4:207

A Laodicean, 1:361

Laos, 2:322

Laos: A Bibliography, 3:491

Laos: Beyond the Revolution, 3:491

Lao She and the Chinese Revolution, 2:251

Lao Tzu: Tao Te Ching, 3:468, 4:527, 4:528, 4:529

Lao-Tzu: Te-Tao Ching, 4:528

La Peau de Chagrin, 2:453

La Pharisienne, 2:489

Laplace as a Newtonian Scientist, 5:698

Lapped Furrows: Correspondence, 1933–1967, 1:507

La Princesse de Clèves, 2:484

The Lapsed, 4:708

Lapse of Time, 2:267

Lara, 1:281

L'Arc Musical, 2:151

La Regenta, 2:528

La Répudiation, 2:118

La Revue Indigene, 2:941

The Large-Scale Structure of Space-Time, 5:692

Largo Desolato, 2:791

The Lark, 2:450

Larkin at Sixty, 1:508

La Rochefoucauld: The Art of Abstraction, 2:485

La Ronde, 2:610

Larousse Encyclopedia of Modern History, 3:7

Larousse Saturne French-English/English-French Dictionary, 1:98

Larval Forms and Other Zoological Verses, 5:764

La Salle and the Discovery of the Great West, 3:592

Laser: Supertool of the Eighties, 5:718

Laser Age in Optics, 5:666

The Laser Book: A New Technology of Light, 5:235, 5:666

The Laser Guidebook, 5:235, 5:666

Las Meninas, 2:532

L'Assommoir, 2:517, 2:518

The Last Adam, 1:964

Last Alternatives: Allen Tate, 1:889

Last and Lost Poems, 1:1044

The Last Atlantic Liners, 5:247

The Last Best Place: A Montana Anthology, 3:896

Last Book of Wonder, 1:615

Last Call, 2:628
The Last Chronicle of Barset, 1:405
Last Circle, 1:815
The Last Dalai Lama: A Biography, 4:357, 4:561
The Last Days, 2:496
Last Days: Stories, 1:1023
The Last Days of Alfred Hitchcock, 1:1169
The Last Days of Hitler, 3:411
The Last Days of Louisiana Red, 1:1036
The Last Days of Pompeii, 1:340
The Last Days of Socrates, 4:78
The Last Days of the New Yorker, 3:807
The Last Days of Tolstoy, 2:766
Last Decade: Essays and Reviews, 1965–1975, 1:1058
Last Diaries, 2:765
The Last Duty, 2:142, 2:143
Last Essays of Elia, 1:295
The Last Flower, 1:890
The Last Four Lives of Annie Besant, 4:550, 4:859
The Last Generation of the Roman Republic, 3:303
The Last Gentleman, 1:1029
The Lasting Elements of Individualism, 4:296
Lasting Impressions: Essays 1961–1987, 1:538
The Last Italian: Portrait of a People, 3:900
The Last Laugh, 1:868
The Last Laugh: Form and Affirmation in the Contemporary American Comic Novel, 1:920
The Last Letter Home, 2:678
Last Letters of Jacopo Ortis, 2:421
The Last Man, 1:300
The Last Man's Head, 2:948
The Last Meeting of the Knights of the White Magnolia, 1:1096
The Last Metro, 3:843
The Last of the Crazy People, 2:910, 2:911
The Last of the Empire, 2:145
The Last of the Fathers, 4:700
The Last of the Fathers: James Madison and the Republican Legacy, 3:525

The Last of the Mohicans, 1:662, 1:663, 1:1211
The Last of the Novelists: F. Scott Fitzgerald and "The Last Tycoon," 1:840
The Last of the Red-Hot Lovers, 1:1112, 1:1113
The Last One Hundred Days, 3:280
Last Orders, 1:613
The Last Panda, 5:771, 5:824
The Last Phase of the East Asian World Order, 3:464
The Last Picnic, 2:806
The Last Picture Show, 1:1010
Last Places: A Journey in the North, 3:906
Last Poems, 2:800
The Last Prima Donnas, 3:671
The Last Puritan: A Memoir in the Form of a Novel, 4:327
The Last Ride of Wild Bill, and Eleven Narrative Poems, 1:955
Last Rites: The Death of William Saroyan, 1:1110
The Last Romantic: Mihail Eminescu, 2:825
The Last Song of Manuel Sendero, 2:864
Last Songs from Vagabondia, 2:908
The Last Stand of Chinese Conservatism, 3:469
Last Talks at Saanen, 4:555
The Last Temptation of Christ, 2:373, 2:374
Last Theaters. 1904–10, 1:440
The Last Trial, 4:621
The Last Tycoon, 1:839
Last Voyage of Somebody the Sailor, 1:942
Last Waltz in Santiago and Other Poems of Exile and Disappearance, 2:864
The Last Word, 2:152
The Last Words of Dutch Schultz, 1:957
Last Writings: Nothingness and the Religious Worldview, 4:365, 4:888
Last Writings Vol. 1: Preliminary Studies for Part III of Philosophical Investigations, 4:343
Last Year at Marienbad, 2:500
Last Years of Henry Timrod, 1:778
Last Years of Nijinsky, 3:749

Late and Posthumous Poems, 1968–1974, 2:874
Late Augustan Poetry, 1:228
Late Augustan Prose, 1:231
Late Baroque and Rococo Architecture, 3:763
Late-Blooming Flowers and Other Stories, 2:708
Late Bourgeois World, 2:162
Late Call, 1:567
Latecomers, 1:452
A Late Divorce, 2:26
Late Marxism: Adorno, or the Persistence of the Dialectic, 1:1149
Late Medieval Mysticism, 4:697
The Late Medieval Plays of Bodleian MSS Digby 133 and e Museo 160, 1:160
Late Night Thoughts on Listening to Mahler's Ninth Symphony, 5:19, 5:766
Late Nineteenth-Century American Diary Literature, 1:727
Late Picasso: Paintings, Sculpture, Drawings, Prints, 1953–1972, 3:787
Later, 1:965
The Later Christian Fathers, 4:680
The Later Court Hands in England, 1:16
The Later Ghaznavids, 2:82, 3:454
The Later Heidegger and Theology, 4:294
The Later Jacobean and Caroline Dramatists, 1:170
Later Medieval Philosophy (1150–1350): An Introduction, 4:94
The Later Middle Ages, 1:147
The Late Romantic Era: From the Mid-19th Century to World War I, 3:663
The Later Philosophy of R. G. Collingwood, 4:282
The Later Philosophy of Schelling, 4:252
The Later Poetry of Osip Mandelstam: Text and Context, 2:738
Latin America: A Concise Interpretive History, 3:625
Latin America: A Cultural History, 3:642
Latin America: A Guide to the Historical Literature, 3:624
Latin America: Perspectives on a Region, 3:625

Latin America in Caricature, 3:631

Latin America in Its Literature, 2:845

Latin American History: A Teaching Atlas, 3:625

Latin American History: Essays on Its Study and Teaching, 1898–1965, 3:644

Latin American Literature in English, 1975–1978, 2:847

Latin American Literature in English Translation, 2:847

Latin-American Literature Today, 2:849

The Latin American Mind, 2:848, 4:33

Latin American Poetry, 2:845

The Latin Americans: Spirit and Ethos, 3:625

The Latin American Short Story: A Critical History, 2:847

Latin American Studies: A Basic Guide to Sources, 3:625

Latin American Thought: A Historical Introduction, 4:33

Latin American Women Writers: Yesterday and Today, 2:847

Latin America's Christian Democratic Parties: A Political Economy, 3:632

Latinas of the Americas: A Source Book, 3:625

Latin Journey: Cuban and Mexican Immigrants in the United States, 3:209

Latin Literature, 3:298

Latin Literature: An Anthology, 2:382

Latin Monasticism in Norman Sicily, 5:58

Latin Poets and Roman Life, 2:380

La Traviata, 2:473

The Latter Day Saints Churches: An Annotated Bibliography, 4:846

Latvian Literature under the Soviets, 2:804

Laughable Limericks, 1:1197

Laughable Loves, 2:793

Laugh after Laugh: The Healing Power of Humor, 3:872

Laughing: A Psychology of Humor, 3:871

Laughing Stock, 1:1099

Laughing Wild, 1:1087

Laughter: An Essay on the Meaning of the Comic, 4:220

Laughter in the Dark, 2:740

Laughter over the Left Shoulder, 2:759

Laughter through Tears: The Yiddish Cinema, 2:31

The Launching of Modern American Science, 3:558, 5:45

The Laundromat, 1:1105

Laura: The Life of Laura Ingalls Wilder, 1:1209

Laura Ingalls Wilder, 1:1209

Laura Ingalls Wilder Country, 1:1209

Laurence Sterne: Riddles and Mysteries, 1:259

Laurence Sterne: The Early and Middle Years, 1:258

Laurence Sterne: The Later Years, 1:259

Laurence Sterne and the Argument about Design, 1:259

Laurence Sterne's Sermons of Mister Yorick, 1:259

Laurier: The First Canadian, 3:615

Lautreamont, 4:274

La Vacanza, 2:426

Lavengro, 2:912

La Vida, 3:34

La Vie de Marianne, 2:488

La Voce, 2:430

Lavoisier and the Chemistry of Life, 5:749

Lavorare Stanca, 2:432

Law, Biology, and Culture: The Evolution of Law, 5:33

Law, Economics and Public Policy, 3:61

Law, Language, and Ethics, 5:142

Law and Bioethics: Selected Cases, 5:123

Law and Economics: An Introductory Analysis, 3:61

Law and Letters in American Culture, 1:650

Law and Life of Rome: 90 B.C. to A.D. 212, 3:305

Law and People in Colonial America, 3:517

Law and Philosophy: A Symposium, 4:265

Law and Society in Modern India, 3:486

Law and the Mind: Biological Origins of Human Behavior, 3:171

Law and the Social Order: Essays in Legal Philosophy, 4:280

Law and the State in Traditional East Asia, 3:464

The Law in Classical Athens, 3:306

The Law of Christ, 4:718

The Law of Medical Malpractice in a Nutshell, 5:344

The Law of Public Communication, 3:803

The Law of Success, 4:556

Lawrence and Oppenheimer, 5:707

Lawrence and the Arabs, 3:908

Lawrence and Women, 1:511

Lawrence Durrell, 1:470

Lawrence of Arabia (Hart), 3:926

Lawrence of Arabia (Lean), 1:445

Lawrence of Arabia: A Biographical Enquiry, 3:926

Lawrence of Arabia: The Authorized Biography of T. E. Lawrence, 3:927

The Laws, 3:163

The Laws: History, 4:78

The Laws and Custom of the Jewish Wedding, 4:602

Laws and Symmetry, 5:62

The Laws in the Pentateuch and Other Studies, 4:823, 4:836

The Laws of Imitation, 3:176

Laws of Man's Social Nature, 1:375

Laws of Thought, 5:499

Lawyers and Litigants in Ancient Athens, 2:344

Laxdaela Saga, 2:639, 2:641

Lay Buddhism in Contemporary Japan: Reiyukai Kyodan, 4:540

Lay-By, 1:449, 1:450, 1:492

The Layman's Dictionary of Psychiatry, 5:415

A Layman's Guide to Protestant Theology, 4:744

Layman's Guide to Protestant Thought, 4:718

The Layman's Guide to Psychiatry, 5:415

A Layman's Guide to Psychiatry and Psychoanalysis (The Mind in Action), 5:424, 5:434

A Layman's Introduction to Robotics, 5:242

The Lay of the Land, 1:714

Layout and Design for Callig-
raphers, 1:15
Lays of Ancient Rome and
Miscellaneous Essays and
Poems, 1:374
Lazarillo de Tormes, 2:530
Lazarus, As You Desire Me,
2:435
Lazri Meon: Daerah Zeni,
2:326
Lazy Dragon: Chinese Stories
from the Ming Dynasty,
2:198
Lazy River, 2:325
Leaden Wings, 2:238, 2:239
A Leader of Men, 2:65
Leadership and America's
Future in Space, 5:611
Leadership at the Fed, 3:65
Leaders of Public Opinion in
Ireland, 3:405
Leading American Essayists:
Biographies of Leading
Americans, 1:660, 1:727
Leading Indicators for the
1990s, 3:50
The Lead Soldier, 2:86
Leaflets: Poems 1965–68,
1:1037
Leaf Storm, 2:866
Leaf Storm, and Other Sto-
ries, 2:867
The League for Social Re-
construction, 3:616
The League of Nations, 3:281
League of Nations: Its Life
and Times, 1920–1946,
3:344
League of the Iroquois, 3:26,
3:37
League of Youth, 2:666
The Lean Lands, 2:888
Leaphorn and Chee, 1:1232
Leap of Action: Ideas in the
Theology of Abraham
Joshua Heschel, 4:665
Leaps, 5:419
Lear, 1:445
The Learned Ladies, 2:490
The Learned Presidency,
3:594
Learner's Swahili-Eng-
lish/English-Swahili Dictio-
nary, 1:103
Learning about Energy, 5:293
Learning by Heart: AIDS and
Schoolchildren in Ameri-
ca's Communities, 3:251
Learning from Accidents in
Industry, 5:244
Learning from Error, 4:409

Learning from Errors: Karl
Popper's Psychology of
Learning, 5:99
Learning How to Behave: A
Historical Study of Ameri-
can Etiquette Books, 3:596
Learning Laughter, 1:553
The Learning Society, 3:263
Learning to Heal: The Devel-
opment of American Medi-
cal Education, 5:336
Learning to Labor: How
Working Class Kids Get
Working Class Jobs, 3:23
Learning to Question: A
Pedagogy of Liberation,
3:262
Learning with Computers,
5:566
The Leatherstocking Tales,
1:663
Leaven of Malice, 2:910
Leaves, 5:768
Leaves from the Notebook of
a Tamed Cynic, 4:783,
4:784
Leaves of Grass, 1:654, 1:705,
1:706
Leaves of Grass: America's
Lyric-Epic of Self and De-
mocracy, 1:707
Leaves of Grass: The Original
1855 Edition, 1:706
Leaves of Grass and Selected
Prose, 1:706
Leaves of Grass One Hun-
dred Years After, 1:707
Leaves of the Banyan Tree,
2:979, 2:980
Leave Us Alone, 2:141
Leaving Cheyenne, 1:1010
Leaving Home: A Collection
of Lake Wobegon Stories,
3:871
Leaving the Highway: Six
Contemporary New Zea-
land Novelists, 2:971
Le Chant Écarlate, 2:132
Le Chiendent, 2:496
Le Cid: A Translation in
Rhymed Couplets, 2:471
Le Corbusier (Brooks), 3:778
Le Corbusier (Gardiner),
3:778
Le Corbusier: Architect,
Painter, Writer, 3:779
Le Corbusier and the Tragic
View of Architecture,
3:779
Le Corbusier Sketchbooks,
3:778
Lectionary of Music, 3:657
Lectures in Logic, 4:205

Lectures on, 2:536
Lectures on Art, 1:393
Lectures on Conditioned Re-
flexes, 3:191
Lectures on Don Quixote,
2:740
Lectures on Education, 3:265
Lectures on Elementary
Number Theory, 5:489
Lectures on Ethics, 4:205
Lectures on Human and Ani-
mal Psychology, 3:197
Lectures on Ideology and
Utopia, 4:319
Lectures on Kant's Political
Philosophy, 4:394
Lectures on Literature,
1:1020
Lectures on Literature: Brit-
ish, French and German
Writers, 2:741
Lectures on Modern Mathe-
matics, 5:480
Lectures on Philosophical
Theology, 4:205
Lectures on Political Econo-
my I, 3:114
Lectures on Political Econo-
my II, 3:114
Lectures on Russian Litera-
ture, 2:689
Lectures on the Early His-
tory of Institutions: A Se-
quel to Ancient Law, 3:35
Lectures on the English
Comic Writers, 1:291
Lectures on the English
Poets, 1:291
Lectures on the Ethics of
T. H. Green, Herbert
Spencer, and J. Martineau,
4:257
Lectures on the History of
Philosophy, 4:17, 4:232
Lectures on the History of
Religions, 4:573
Lectures on the Phenomena
of Life Common to Ani-
mals and Plants, 5:789
Lectures on the Philosophy
of Kant and Other Phi-
losophical Lectures and
Essays, 4:257
Lectures on the Philosophy
of Religion, 4:232
Lectures on the Philosophy
of World History: Intro-
duction, 4:232
Lectures on the Principles of
Political Obligation, 4:230
Lectures on the Religion of
the Semites, 4:491, 4:492

Lectures on the Republic of Plato, 4:83
Le Dance du Roi, 2:119
Led Astray, 1:331
Le Demantelement, 2:118
Le Devin du village, 4:212
The Leech, 2:668
The Leeuwenhoek Legacy, 5:804
Lefèvre: Pioneer of Ecclesiastical Renewal in France, 4:127
The Left Bank and Other Stories, 2:940
Left-Handed Calligraphy, 1:19
Left-Handed Liberty, 1:433
The Left Hand of Creation, 5:654
The Left Hand of Darkness, 1:1260
Left Politics and the Literary Profession, 1:794
Leftward Journey, 3:491
Legacies, 2:144
Legacies: Selected Poems, 2:877
The Legacy, 1:1246
The Legacy of an Empire, 3:214
The Legacy of Chrétien de Troyes, 2:467
The Legacy of Conquest: The Unbroken Past of the American West, 3:532
The Legacy of Erskine Caldwell, 1:819
The Legacy of George Ellery Hale, 5:606
The Legacy of H. Richard Niebuhr, 4:746
The Legacy of Hermann Cohen, 4:663
The Legacy of Islam, 4:567, 4:572
The Legacy of Kenneth Burke, 1:818
The Legacy of Luther, 4:731
The Legacy of St. Vladimir, 4:756
The Legacy of the Civil War, 1:893
The Legacy of Wittgenstein, 4:346
Legal Foundations of Capitalism, 3:74
The Legal Guide to Developing, Protecting and Marketing Software, 5:558
Legal Rights and Mental Health Care, 5:422
Legend and Legacy: The Story of Boeing and Its People, 5:219

Légendes Africaines, 2:151
The Legend of Ararat, 2:100
The Legend of Duluoz, 1:998
The Legend of Good Women, 1:150
The Legend of Maya Deren, 1:1163
The Legend of the Baal Shem, 4:660
The Legend of the Christmas Rose, 2:677
The Legend of the Master: Henry James as Others Saw Him, 1:767
The Legend of the Thousand Bulls, 2:100
Legends, 2:531
Legends and Folk Beliefs in a Swedish American Community, 3:855
Legends and Popular Tales of the Basque People, 3:856
Legends of Angria, 1:335
The Legends of Genesis: The Biblical Saga and History, 4:823, 4:835
Legends of Long Ago, 2:597
Legends of New England in Prose and Verse, 1:708
Legends of New York State, 3:858
Legends of Our Time, 3:351
Legends of Texas, 3:863
Legends of the California Bandidos, 3:863
Legends of the Hasidim, 4:633
Legends of the Jews, 4:610
Legends of the Old People of Dainava, 2:806
The Legends of the Saints, 4:678
Legends of the World, 3:854
The Legionnaires, 2:674
The Legislative System, 3:146
Legitimacy and the Military: The Yugoslav Crisis, 3:392
Legitimation Crisis, 3:229, 4:404, 5:89
Le Grand Recueil, 2:494
Legs, 1:996, 1:997
A Leg to Stand On, 5:315
Leibnitz and Locke, 4:177, 4:180
Leibniz, 4:177
Leibniz: An Introduction to His Philosophy, 4:177
Leibniz: Critical and Interpretive Essays, 4:177
Leibniz: Logic and Metaphysics, 4:177

Leibniz and Arnauld, 4:164, 4:178
Leibniz and Confucianism: The Search for Accord, 4:177
Leibniz and Philosophical Analysis, 4:178
Leibniz and the Seventeenth-Century Revolution, 4:177
Leibniz in France—From Arnauld to Voltaire, 4:177
Leibniz's Metaphysics: A Historical and Comparative Study, 4:178
Leibniz's Monadology: An Edition for Students, 4:317
Leigh Hunt, 1:292
Leisure, Gender, and Poverty, 3:366
Leisure in the Industrial Revolution, 1780–1880, 3:362
Leisure Travel: Making It a Growth Market . . . Again!, 3:890
Le Jeu de l'Amour et du Hasard, 2:488
Le Livre Blanc: The White Book, 2:469
Le Livre des Rois, 2:89
Le Livre du Sang, 2:123
Le Maître de la Parole: Kouma Lafolo Kuoma, 2:138
Le Mauvais Sang, 2:151
Le Métier à Tisser, 2:119
Lemon Sky, 1:1121
Le Morte d'Arthur, 1:154
Lendemain de conquête, 3:620
L'Enfant du Sable, 2:117
L'Enfant Noir, 2:138, 2:139
Lenin, 3:287
Lenin: A Political Life, 3:287
Lenin: Founder of the Soviet Union, 3:287
Lenin: Red Dictator, 3:413
Lenin, Trotsky and Stalin: The Intelligentsia and Power, 3:287
Lenin and Philosophy and Other Essays, 1:1126
Leningrad Nineteen Forty-One: The Blockade, 3:397
Leningrad's Ballet: Maryinsky to Kirov, 3:734
Lenin's Tomb: The Last Days of the Soviet Empire, 3:398
Leo Baeck: Teacher of Theresienstadt, 4:661
Leonard Bernstein, 3:682
A Leonard Bloomfield Anthology, 3:27

Leonard Cohen and His Works (Fiction), 2:909
Leonard Cohen and His Works (Poetry), 2:909
Leonard Maltin's Movie and Video Guide: 1993 Edition, 3:826
Leonardo, 2:430
Leonardo: A Portrait of the Renaissance Man, 5:195
Leonardo da Vinci (Clark), 3:779
Leonardo da Vinci (Wasserman), 3:780
Leonardo da Vinci: Artist, Scientist, Inventor, 5:203
Leonardo da Vinci: Aspects of the Renaissance Genius, 3:780
Leonardo da Vinci: A Study in Psychosexuality, 3:779, 5:446
Leonardo da Vinci: Life and Work, Paintings and Drawings, 3:779
Leonardo da Vinci: The Marvelous Works of Nature and Man, 5:203
Leonardo da Vinci, Engineer and Architect, 3:780
Leonardo da Vinci and a Memory of His Childhood, 1:1181, 3:779
Leonardo on Painting, 5:203
Leon Battista Alberti: Universal Man of the Early Renaissance, 2:404
Leonce and Lena, 2:573, 2:574
Leonid Andreyev (Kaun), 2:699
Leonid Andreyev (Newcombe), 2:699
Leonid Andreyev: A Study, 2:699
Leonid Andreyev: Photographs by a Russian Writer, 2:699
Leonid Andreyev, a Critical Study, 2:699
Leontiev, 4:275
Leon Trotsky's Theory of Revolution, 3:295
Leontyne Price: Highlights of a Prima Donna, 3:709
The Leopard, 2:407, 2:423, 2:940
A Leopardi Reader, 2:424
The Leopard's Spots, 3:525
Leopold Sedar Senghor, 2:147

Leopold Sedar Senghor and the Politics of Negritude, 3:421
Leo XIII and the Modern World, 4:741
Leo Tolstoy (Bloom), 2:765
Leo Tolstoy (Egan and Egan), 2:766
Leo Tolstoy (Gustafson), 2:766
Leo Tolstoy's Anna Karenina, 2:765
Leo Tolstoy's War and Peace, 2:765
Le Parti Pris des Choses, 2:494
Le Pauvre Christ de Bomba, 2:132
Le Paysan Parvenu, 2:488
The Leper and Other Stories, 2:829
Le Plaisir du Texte, 2:454
Le Portrait de Dora, 2:467
L'Era del Malessere, 2:426
Le Regard du Roi, 2:138
Le Retour au Bercail, 2:156
Lermontov: An Essay in Literary Historical Evaluation, 2:735
Lermontov: Tragedy in the Caucasus, 2:735
Le Roi des Aulnes, 2:512
The LeRoi Jones-Amiri Baraka Reader, 1:941
Le Roman Expérimental, 2:517
Le Sang des Autres, 2:458
Lesbia Brandon, 1:398
Lesbian Images, 1:1182
Lesbian Peoples: Material for a Dictionary, 1:1183
Lesbian Philosophy and Cultures, 1:1183
Lesbian Plays, 1:1183
Lesbian Poetry: An Anthology, 1:1183
A Lesbian's Heroine? 1:492
Lesbian Studies: Present and Future, 1:1128, 1:1183
Lesbian Texts and Contexts, 1:1184
Les Blancs, 1:1092
Les Boucs, 2:118
Les Brown's Encyclopedia of Television, 3:811
Les Caves du Vatican, 2:479
L'Esclavage en Afrique Précoloniale, 3:429
Les Fausses Confidences, 2:488
Les Fleurs du Mal, 2:456
Les Fleurs du Mal and Other Studies, 2:457

Lesko's New Tech Sourcebook, 5:216
Les Liaisons Dangereuses, 2:484
Leslie Marmon Silko, 1:1047
Les Mandarins, 2:458
Les Matinaux: The Dawn-Breakers, 2:465
Les Misérables, 2:482, 2:483
Les Orientales, 2:482
Les Précieuses Ridicules, 2:490
Lessing and the Enlightenment, 4:208
Lessing's Dramatic Theory, 2:600
Lessing's Laocoon: Semiotics and Aesthetics in the Age of Reason, 2:600
Lessing's Theological Writings: Selections in Translation, 2:600 4:739
A Lesson for Aloes, 2:161
The Lesson of Paul de Man, 1:1143
Lessons from Disaster, 5:244
Lessons in Formal Writing, 1:17
The Lessons of History, 3:276, 3:326, 3:402
The "Lessons" of the Past, 3:546
Lessons with Eisenstein, 3:836
Less Than Angels, 1:539
Less Than a Treason: Hemingway in Paris, 1:846
Less Than Glory, 3:520
Lester Ward and the Welfare State, 3:573
Les travailleurs québécois, 1851–1896, 3:621
Lesya Ukrainka: Life and Works, 2:841
Let Freedom Come: Africa in Modern History, 3:428
Let Me Hear You Whisper, 1:1122, 1:1123
Let My Children Work, 3:266
Let's Talk, 5:334
The Letter and the Spirit, 4:116
Letterbox: The Art and History of Letters, 1:13
A Letter Concerning Toleration, 4:179
Lettering, 1:16
The Letter on the Blind for the Benefit of Those Who See, 4:196
Letters, Speeches and Tracts on Irish Affairs, 3:152

The Letters and Diaries of John Henry Newman, 4:782

Letters and Lettering: A Treatise with 200 Examples, 1:14

Letters and Notes on the Manners, Customs and Conditions of the North American Indian, 3:554

Letters and Other Documents Illustrative of His Career (Vespucci), 3:942

Letters and Papers from Prison, 4:760

Letters Concerning the English Nation, 2:515

Letters from a Father and Other Poems, 1:1061

Letters from Africa: 1914–1931, 2:649

Letters from a Stoic, 2:393

Letters from a Traveller, 3:910

Letters from England by Don Manuel Alvarez Espriella, 1:305

Letters from Iceland, 1:517

Letters from Jenny, 5:432

Letters from Mexico, 3:628

Letters from Prison, 2:423

Letters from the Levant: During the Embassy to Constantinople, 1716–18, 1:251

Letters from the Russian Museum, 2:759

Letters from the Sandwich Islands, 1:782

Letters Home: Correspondence 1950–1963 (Plath), 1:1031

Letters I Never Mailed, 3:730

Letters in Two Volumes, 2:770

The Letters of Abu'l-'Ala, 2:62

Letters of a Russian Traveler, 1789–1790, 2:730

Letters of a Self-Made Diplomat to His President, 3:886

Letters of Credit: A View of Type Design, 1:20

Letters of Horace Walpole, Earl of Oxford, to Sir Horace Mann, 3:265

Letters of James Agee to Father Flye, 1:932

Letters of James Joyce, 1:974

Letters of Jews through the Ages, 4:594

Letters of John Henry Newman: A Selection, 4:782

Letters of Lenin, 3:287

The Letters of Lewis Carroll, 1:582

Letters of Medieval Jewish Traders, 4:626

The Letters of Mozart and His Family, 3:707

Letters of Pliny: A Historical and Social Commentary, 2:392

The Letters of St. Catherine of Siena, 4:707

The Letters of St. Cyprian of Carthage, 4:708

Letters of Sir Joshua Reynolds, 3:790

Letters of the Late Edward Bulwer, Lord Lytton, to His Wife, 1:340

The Letters of Thomas Chandler Haliburton, 2:912

Letters of Travel, 1892–1913 (Kipling), 1:371

The Letters of Vincent Van Gogh, 3:794

The Letters of Virginia Woolf and Lytton Strachey, 1:569

The Letters of William James, 4:236

The Letters of William S. Burroughs, 1945–1959, 1:958

Letters on Dancing and Ballet, 3:749

Letters on Demonology and Witchcraft, 1:299

Letters on England, 2:515

Letters on Familiar Matters: Rerum Familiarum Libri, 4:150

Letters on Literature and Politics, 1912–1972, 1:902

Letters on the Short Story, 2:710

Letters to A. C. Benson and Auguste Monod, 1:765

Letters to Anais Nin, 1:862

Letters to an American Jewish Friend: A Zionist's Polemic, 4:658

Letters to an American Lady, 1:513

Letters to a Niece and Prayer to the Virgin of Chartres, 3:562

Letters to Atticus, 3:313

Letters to a Young Doctor, 5:315

Letters to a Young Poet, 2:607

Letters to Felice, 2:596

Letters to Friends, Family, and Editors, 2:596

Letters to His Family: An Autobiography, 3:724

Letters to Lady Cunard, 1895–1933, 1:381

Letters to Malcolm: Chiefly on Prayer, 1:513

Letters to Marina, 2:427

Letters to Milena, 2:596

Letters to Mirabehn, 4:552

Letters to Olga, 2:791

Letters to Ottla and the Family, 2:596

Letters to the Future: An Approach to Sinyavsky-Tertz, 2:758

Letters to the New Island, 1:572

Letters to Tom Carter, 1:872

Letters to Vernon Watkins, 1:557

The Letters Trilogy, 3:797

A Letter to His Countrymen, 1:665

A Letter to Laura, 2:643

Letter to Rafael Sanchez, 3:916

Letter to the Grand Duchess Christina, 4:142

A Letter to the Queen on Lord Chancellor Cranworth's Marriage and Divorce Bill, 1:384

A Letter to the Right Reverend Lord Bishop of Exeter on the Custody of Infants, 1:384

Letter to the Soviet Leaders, 2:761

Let the Railsplitter Awake and Other Poems, 2:874

Let the Trumpet Sound: The Life of Martin Luther King, Jr., 3:539, 4:773

Lettice and Lovage: A Comedy, 1:543

Letting Go, 1:1040, 1:1041

Letty Fo, 2:963

Letty Fox: Her Luck, 2:963

"Let Us Begin Anew": An Oral History of Kennedy as President, 3:540

Let Us Now Praise Famous Men, 1:932, 3:533

Let Your Mind Alone, 1:890

The Levant at the Beginning of the Middle Bronze Age, 4:445

Levels of the Game, 1:1011

'Leven More Poems, 1:777

Le Ventre, 2:151

Léviathan, 2:482, 3:153, 4:174

Leviathan and the Air Pump: Hobbes, Bayle, and the Experimental Life, 4:175
The Levinas Reader, 4:901
Lévi-Strauss: Structuralism and Sociological Theory, 3:34
Levitating Trains and Kamikaze Genes: Technological Literacy for the 1990's, 5:12
Levitation: Five Fictions, 1:1027
The Levittowners, 3:226
L'Evolution du Royaume Rwanda des Origines a 1900, 3:431
Lew Archer, Private Investigator, 1:1235
Lewin's Topological and Vector Psychology: A Digest and a Critique, 3:190
Lewis: Sax's Dangerous Properties of Industrial Materials, 5:725
Lewis and Clark: Leading America West, 3:928
Lewis and Clark: Pioneering Naturalists, 3:928
Lewis and Clark among the Indians, 3:928
Lewis Carroll, 1:583
Lewis Carroll: An Annotated International Bibliography, 1960-1977, 1:583
Lewis Carroll: Interviews and Recollections, 1:582
Lewis Carroll and His Camera, 1:582
Lewis Carroll and the House of Macmillan, 1:582
The Lewis Carroll Handbook, 1:583
Lewis Henry Morgan: American Scholar, 3:37
Lewis Henry Morgan: Social Evolutionist, 3:37
Lewis Henry Morgan and the Invention of Kinship, 3:20, 3:37
Lewis Mumford: A Life, 5:172
Lewis Mumford: Public Intellectual, 5:51, 5:172
Lewis Percy, 1:452
A Lexical Concordance to the Poetical Works of Percy Bysshe Shelley, 1:303
A Lexicon of the Homeric Dialect, 2:361
Lexicon Plantonicum Sive Vacum Platonicarum Index, 1835-1838, 4:79

Lexicon Spinozanum, 4:187
The Liability Maze: The Impact of Liability Law on Safety and Innovation, 5:184
Liang Ch'i-ch'ao and Intellectual Transition in China 1890-1907, 2:252
Liang Ch'i-ch'ao and Modern Chinese Liberalism, 2:253
Liang Ch'i-ch'ao and the Mind of Modern China, 2:253, 3:471
Liang Chien Wen Ti, 2:201
The Liar, 2:422, 2:650
Liars: Australian New Novelists, 2:947
A Liberal Descent: Victorian Historians and the English Past, 3:403
The Liberal Imagination: Essays on Literature and Society, 1:1058
Liberalism and Its Challengers: From FDR to Bush, 3:538
Liberalism and the Challenge of Fascism, 3:344
Liberalism and the Social Problem, 3:400
Liberal Judaism, 4:661
Liberal Judaism at Home: The Practices of Modern Reform Judaism, 4:601
The Liberal Mind in a Conservative Age, 3:561
Liberal Politics in the Age of Gladstone and Roseberry, 3:363
Liberals, Radicals and Social Politics, 1892-1914, 3:363
The Liberal Tradition, 3:399
Liber Amicorum, 2:624
The Liberated Page: A Typographica [sic] Anthology, 1:11
Liberating Life: Contemporary Approaches to Ecological Theory, 5:196
Liberation and Change, 4:769
Liberation and Its Limits, 3:177, 3:183, 5:447
The Liberation of Life: From the Cell to the Community, 5:196
The Liberation of the Jew, 3:349
Liberation Theology: An Introductory Guide, 4:747
Liberation Theology: An Introductory Reader, 4:747

Liberation Theology: Human Hope Confronts Christian History and American Power, 4:785
Liberation Theology and Its Critics: Toward an Assessment, 4:896
Liberia: History of the First African Republic, 3:419
The Libertarian Idea, 4:386
Liberty, the Castle of Indolence and Other Poems, 1:261
Liberty, Virtue, and Progress: Northerners and Their War for Union, 3:528
Liberty and Peace, A Poem, 1:646
Liberty and Power: The Politics of Jacksonian America, 3:526
Liberty and Property: Political Ideology in Eighteenth Century Britain, 3:362
Liberty and Slavery: Southern Politics to 1860, 3:527
Liberty Denied: The Current Rise of Censorship in America, 1:56
Liberty Hyde Bailey, 5:788
Liberty in America, 1600 to the Present, 3:582
Liberty in the Modern State, 3:156
Liberty Lane: A Ballad Play of Dublin in Two Acts with a Prologue, 1:460
The Library, 4:469
Library and Information Science: A Guide to Information Sources, 5:544
Library Automation: Issues and Applications, 5:545
The Library of Christian Classics, 4:680
The Library of Henry James, 1:766
The Library of Literary Criticism of English and American Authors, 1:430
The Library of Pico della Mirandola, 4:153
Library Recommendations for Undergraduate Mathematics, 5:480
The Library World and the Publishing of Children's Books, 1:49
Libros de Poesía, 2:542
Li Ch'ing-chao, 2:204
Licking Hitler, 1:493
The Lie, 2:429
Liebig and after Liebig, 5:274

Lie Down in Darkness, 1:1056

Lie Groups and Lie Algebras, 5:500

A Lie of the Mind, 1:1111

Lies, Damn Lies and Statistics, 5:525

Lies, Language, and Logic in the Late Middle Ages, 4:104

Lieutenant Gustl, 2:610

Lieutenant Kije and Young Vitushishnikov, 2:771

A Life, 1:1017

Life: The Science of Biology, 5:765

The Life, as Written by Himself in His Letters and Memoirs, 3:681

The Life, Letters, and Literary Remains, 1:340

The Life, Letters and Labours of Francis Galton, 5:529

Life, Letters and Works of Louis Agassiz, 5:785

Life, Liberty, and the Pursuit of Land, 3:517

The Life, Manners, and Travels of Fanny Trollope: A Biography, 1:409

The Life, Music, and Times of Carlos Gardel, 3:633

Life above the Forest Floor: Tree Top World, 5:820

Life after Life, 4:866

Life among the Piutes, 1:726

Life among the Savages, 1:992

The Life and Adventures of a Clever Woman, 1:408

The Life and Adventures of Jonathan Jefferson Whitlaw, 1:408

The Life and Adventures of Michael Armstrong, the Factory Boy, 1:408

The Life and Adventures of Sir Launcelot Greaves, 1:256

The Life and Art of Albrecht Dürer, 3:774, 4:738

The Life and Campaigns of the Black Prince, 3:357

Life and Character of Rutherford B. Hayes, 1:758

Life and Confessions of a Psychologist, 3:185

The Life and Correspondence of David Hume, 4:201

Life and Death: Philosophical Essays in Biomedical Ethics, 5:119

The Life and Death of Andy Warhol, 3:796

The Life and Death of St. Thomas More, 1:194

The Life and Death of Yukio Mishima, 2:289

The Life and Extraordinary Adventures of Private Ivan Chonkin, 2:772

Life and Fate, 2:727

Life and Gabriella, 1:843

The Life and Hard Times of a Korean Shaman, 4:539

The Life and Labour of the People of London, 1890–1900, 3:222

The Life and Legend of an American Pioneer, 3:908

The Life and Letters of Charles Darwin, 5:794

Life and Letters of Emily Dickinson, 1:745

The Life and Letters of Erasmus and the Unknown Historical Significance of the Protestant Reformation, 3:403

Life and Letters of Joel Chandler Harris, 1:755

Life and Letters of John Greenleaf Whittier, 1:709

The Life and Letters of John Locke, with Extracts from His Journals and Common-place Books, 4:180

The Life and Letters of Sir Thomas Wyatt, 1:201

Life and Mind of John Dewey, 4:225

The Life and Minor Works of George Peele, 1:195

The Life and Morals of Jesus of Nazareth, 1:640

Life and Music of Béla Bartók, 3:677

The Life and Opinions of Tristram Shandy, Gentleman, 1:258

The Life and Opinions of Tristram Shandy, Gentleman: The Notes, 1:258

The Life and Opinions of Tristram Shandy, Gentleman: The Text, 1:258

The Life and Philosophy of J. McT. E. McTaggart, 1866–1925, 4:304

The Life and Philosophy of Johann Gottfried Herder, 4:199

The Life and Remains of Douglas Jerrold, 1:366, 1:367

Life and Science in the Twentieth Century, 5:47

The Life and Thought of Josiah Royce, 4:250

The Life and Thought of Friedrich Engels: A Reinterpretation, 3:75

The Life and Thought of Isaiah Bowman, 3:128

The Life and Time of Jehudah Halevi, 2:20

The Life and Times of Muhammad, 4:588

The Life and Times of Confederation, 1864–1867, 3:614

The Life and Times of Cotton Mather, 1:1047

The Life and Times of Edward I, 3:357

The Life and Times of Ernest Bevin, 3:399

Life and Times of Frederick Douglass, 1:667

The Life and Times of G. V. Black, 5:314

The Life and Times of Mary Tudor, 4:727

The Life and Times of Menelik II, 1844–1913, 3:422

The Life and Times of Michael K, 2:160

The Life and Times of Modern Physics, 5:652

The Life and Times of Po Chü-i, 2:217

The Life and Times of Richard II, 3:358

The Life and Times of Shehu Usman dan Fodio, 2:134

The Life and Times of Sir Edwin Chadwick, 1:345

The Life and Times of William Shakespeare, 1:205

The Life and Times of Zola, 2:518

The Life and Typography of William Caxton, England's First Printer, 1:7

The Life and Work of Muhammad Jalal-ud Din Rumi, 4:590

The Life and Work of Barbara Pym, 1:539

The Life and Work of Joanna Baillie, 1:277

The Life and Work of Roger Bacon: An Introduction to the Opus Majus, 4:111

The Life and Work of Sigmund Freud, 3:184, 5:47, 5:448

The Life of Graham Greene, Vol. 1: 1904–1939, 1:489

Life of Harriet Beecher Stowe Compiled from Her Letters and Journals, 1:699

The Life of Henri Brulard, 2:510

Life of Henry Wadsworth Longfellow, 1:683

The Life of Herbert Hoover: The Engineer, 1874–1914, 3:532

The Life of Horace Walpole, 1:604

Life of Ibsen, 2:666

The Life of Isaac Newton, 5:706

The Life of Isambard Kingdom Brunel: Civil Engineer, 5:250

Life of James Clerk Maxwell, 5:701

The Life of James K. Baxter, 2:972

Life of James Madison, 3:161

The Life of Jane Austen, 1:276

Life of Jefferson Davis, with a Secret History of the Southern Confederacy, Gathered behind the Scenes in Richmond, 3:575

The Life of Jesus, 4:254

The Life of Johannes Brahms, 3:684

The Life of John Berryman, 1:950

Life of John Bright, 3:411

A Life of John Calvin: A Study in the Shaping of Western Culture, 4:762

The Life of John Dryden, 1:242

The Life of John Knox, 4:774

The Life of John Maynard Keynes, 3:87

The Life of John Milton, 1:193

The Life of Johnny Reb, 3:530

The Life of John O'Hara, 1:867

Life of Johnson, 1:233, 1:234, 1:249, 1:250

The Life of John Stuart Mill, 3:97

The Life of Joseph Addison, 1:232

The Life of Katherine Mansfield, 2:979

The Life of Klim Samgin, 2:725

Life of Lady Mary Wortley Montgu, 1:251

The Life of Langston Hughes, 1:849

The Life of Lazarillo de Tormes, 2:544

The Life of Margaret Fuller, 1:673

The Life of Maxwell Anderson, 1:1082

The Life of Michelangelo (Condivi), 3:782

Life of Michelangelo (Grimm), 3:782

The Life of Monsieur de Molière, 2:795, 2:706

Life of Mr. Richard Savage, 1:249

The Life of Muhammad, 4:588

The Life of Muhammad from Original Sources, 4:588

The Life of Nelson, 1:304

Life of Nelson, the Embodiment of the Sea Power of Great Britain, 3:288

The Life of Niccolò Machiavelli, 3:160, 4:145

The Life of Olaudah Equiano, or Gustavus Vassa, the African, Written by Himself, 2:138

The Life of Oscar Wilde, 1:411

The Life of Pasteur, 5:410, 5:809

A Life of Picasso: Volume 1: 1881–1906, 3:787

The Life of Plotinus, 4:85

Life of Quintus Fixlein, 2:606

The Life of Ralph Waldo Emerson, 1:671

Life of Ramakrishna, 2:501

The Life of Reason, 4:327

Life of Robert Burns (Lockhart), 1:281

The Life of Robert Burns (Snyder), 1:281

The Life of Robert Louis Stevenson, 1:397

The Life of St. Anselm, Archbishop of Canterbury, 4:703

The Life of Saladin, 3:456

The Life of Samuel Butler: A Biography, 1:342

Life of Samuel Johnson, 1:233

Life of Science: Essays in the History of Civilization, 5:56

The Life of Sir Alexander Fleming: Discoverer of Penicillin, 5:408

The Life of Sir Arthur Conan Doyle, 1:608

The Life of Sir J. J. Thomson, O. M., Sometime Master of Trinity College, 5:716

The Life of Sir Walter Scott, 1:300

Life of Sir William Osler, 5:54, 5:364

A Life of Sir William Ramsay, 5:710, 5:754

The Life of Solitude, 4:150

The Life of Teresa of Jesus, 4:786

The Life of the Admiral Christopher Columbus, 3:915

The Life of the Automobile, 2:717

The Life of the Book, 1:37

The Life of the Mind, 4:394, 5:82

The Life of the Mind in America: From the Revolution to the Civil War, 1:629, 1:651, 3:587

The Life of the Sina, 4:582

The Life of the Spider, 5:796

A Life of Thomas Chatterton, 1:285

The Life of Thomas Hardy, 1:362

The Life of Thomas Love Peacock, 1:297

The Life of Thomas Paine, 1:642

The Life of Thomas Telford Written by Himself, 5:256

The Life of Tolstoy, 2:766

Life of Torah: Readings in the Jewish Religious Experience, 4:596

Life of Vivekanada, 2:501

The Life of Wesley; and the Rise and Progress of Methodism, 1:304

The Life of Wicksell, 3:115

The Life of Wilhelm Conrad Röntgen, Discoverer of the X-Ray, 5:240, 5:711

The Life of William Blake, 1:279

The Life of William Harvey, 5:362

The Life of William Morris, 1:383

A Life of William Shakespeare, 1:205

Life on Earth: A Natural History, 5:817

Life on the Mississippi, 1:779, 1:780, 1:782

A Life on the Road, 3:909

Life Pulse: Episodes from the Story of the Fossil Record, 5:763

Life's Blood: A Story of Medical Science and Human Courage, 5:370

Life Span: Values and Life-Extending Technologies, 5:144

Life-Span Developmental Psychology: Personality and Socialization, 3:173

Life Studies, 1:1005

Life Studies and For the Union Dead, 1:1006

The Life That He Led: A Biography of Cole Porter, 3:709

A Life through Poetry: Marina Tsvetaeva's Lyric Diary, 2:768

The Lifetime of a Jew: Throughout the Ages of Jewish History, 4:600

The Lifetime of a Landslide: Investigations in the French Alps, 5:624

The Lifetime Reading Plan, 1:75

Lifetimes under Apartheid, 2:162

The Life to Come: And Other Stories, 1:477

Life Together, 4:759, 4:760

Life to Those Shadows, 1:1157, 3:825

Life with Picasso, 3:786

Life with the Pneumococcus, 5:368

Lifeworld and Technology, 5:70

The Lifted Veil: The Book of Fantastic Literature by Women, 1:612

Lifting Belly, 1:882

Light and Enlightenment, 4:168

Light and Life Processes, 5:766

The Light and the Dark, 1:550

The Light around the Body, 1:951

The Light at the Edge of the Universe, 5:595, 5:655

The Lighter Side of Gravity, 5:665

The Lighthouses of New England, 1716–1973, 3:937

Light in August, 1:835

A Light in the Attic, 1:1207

Light Moving in Time: Studies in the Visual Aesthetic of Avant-Garde Film, 3:827

Lightning, 1:1233, 1:1241

Light of Common Day: Realism in American Fiction, 1:722

The Light of Lost Sons, 2:17

The Light of the Eyes: Homilies to Genesis, 4:633

The Light of the Soul, 4:182

Light on C. S. Lewis, 4:776

The Light Princess, 1:587

The Light Princess and Other Fantasy Stories, 1:587

Light Shining in Buckinghamshire, 1:458

The Light That Failed, 1:370

Light Up the Cave, 1:1003

Li Ho, 2:206

Li Ho: A Scholar-official of the Yüan-ho Period 806–821, 2:206

Lijmen, 2:625

Like Water, Like Fire, 2:784

The Lilac Fairy Book, 3:883

Lilies and Other Stories, 2:248

Lille and the Dutch Revolt: Urban Stability in the Era of Revolution, 1500–1582, 3:382

Lillian Hellman, 1:1093

Lily Montagu and the Advancement of Liberal Judaism, 4:653

The Lily of the Valley, 2:453

Limericks Historical and Hysterical, 3:870

The Lime Twig, 1:985

Limited, Inc., 4:397

The Limits of Analysis, 4:381

The Limits of Growth, 3:48

The Limits of Judicial Power: The Supreme Court in American Politics, 3:145

Limits of Land Settlement: A Report on Present-Day Possibilities, 3:128

The Limits of Mortality: An Essay on Wordsworth's Major Poems, 1:307

The Limits of Professional Power, 5:331

The Limits of Science, 4:317, 4:385, 5:18, 5:108

Limits of Scientific Inquiry, 5:107

The Limits to Capital, 3:123

The Limits to Growth, 5:167, 5:168, 5:573

L'Immortelle, 2:500

Limp Vellum Binding and Its Potential as a Conservation Type Structure for the Rebinding of Early Printed Books, 1:22

L'Incindie, 2:119

Lincoln, 1:1061

Lincoln: An Illustrated Biography, 3:528

Lincoln: A Novel, 1:1062

Lincoln: The Prairie Years and the War Years, 3:530

Lincoln and Black Freedom: A Study in Presidential Leadership, 3:527

Lincoln and His Generals, 3:530

Lincoln and His Party in the Secession Crisis, 3:593

Lincoln and the First Shot, 3:573

The Lincoln Murder Conspiracies, 3:528

The Lincoln Nobody Knows, 3:527, 3:573

Lincoln's Loyalists: Union Soldiers from the Confederacy, 3:573

Linda Tressel, 1:406

Lindbergh: His Story in Pictures, 3:929

Lindbergh and Commercial Aviation, 3:929

Linden Hills, 1:1021

Lindy, 3:427

Lineage, Life, and Labors of Jose Rizal, 2:333

Linear Algebra, 5:484

The Line in the Margin, 2:543

Linguistic Analysis and Phenomenology, 4:263

The Linguistic Turn: Recent Essays in Philosophical Method, 4:267, 4:413

Lining Up, 1:989

Lin McLean, 1:789, 1:1218

Linnaeus: Progress and Prospects in Linnean Research, 5:805

Linnaeus: The Man and His Work, 5:805

Linoleum Block Printing, 1:30

Linus Pauling: Scientist and Crusader, 5:752

L'Invitée, 2:458

The Linwoods; or "Sixty Years Since" in America, 1:695

Liolà, 2:435
The Lion, the Eagle and Upper Canada: A Developing Colonial Ideology, 3:613
Lion among Roses: A Memoir of Finland, 3:898
The Lion and the Honeycomb: Essays in Solicitude and Critique, 1:816
The Lion and the Jewel, 2:149
Lionel Lincoln; or, The Leaguer of Boston, 1:663
The Lioness and the Little One, 2:505
A Lion for Love: A Critical Biography of Stendhal, 2:511
Lions of the Punjab: Culture in the Making, 3:485, 4:516
The Lion's Roar of Queen Srimala, 4:514
The Lion's Share: A Short History of British Imperialism, 1850–1970, 3:367
Lipids in Human Nutrition: An Appraisal of Some Dietary Concepts, 5:345
Lippmann, Liberty and the Press, 3:815
Lipstick Traces: A Secret History of the Twentieth Century, 3:513
Lips Together, Teeth Apart, 1:1102, 1:1103
Lisa H: The True Story of an Extraordinary and Courageous Woman, 5:393
LISP, 5:553
LISP 1.5 Programmer's Manual, 5:553
Listen, 3:661, 3:665
The Listeners and Other Poems, 1:466
The Listener's Guide to Classical Music, 3:665
Listener's Guide to Folk Music, 3:852
The Listener's Musical Companion, 3:665
Listening to Jazz, 3:668
Listening to Korea: A Korean Anthology, 2:299
Listening to Prozac, 5:121
Listening to the Cicadas: A Study of Plato's Phaedrus, 4:80
Listening with the Third Ear: The Inner Experience of a Psychoanalyst, 5:466, 5:467
Listening Woman, 1:1232
Listen to Your Pain, 5:399

Lister and His Achievement, 5:409
A List of Benefits, 2:743
List of Depository Libraries, 1:109
Liszt, 3:704
Liszt, Composer, and His Piano Works, 3:704
Literacy: Reading the Word and the World, 3:262
Literacy and Orality, 4:460
Literacy and Orality in Ancient Greece, 4:460
Literacy and the Social Order, 3:358
Literacy in Early Modern Europe: Culture and Education, 1500–1800, 3:337
Literacy Online, 5:126, 5:574
The Literacy Underground of the Old Régime, 3:338
Literarni Listy, 2:795
Literary, Political, Scientific, Religious and Legal Publishing, Printing and Bookselling in England, 1551–1700, 1:37
The Literary Achievement of Rebecca West, 1:566
Literary Agents: A Writers' Guide, 1:53
Literary Agents of North America, 1:53
Literary Agents of North America Marketplace, 1984–1985, 1:53
Literary and Art Theories in Japan, 2:272
Literary and Library Prizes, 1:135
Literary Biography (Edel), 1:928
Literary Biography (Ellmann), 1:429
Literary Biography: Documentary Series, 1:126
The Literary Career of Charles W. Chesnutt, 1:739
Literary Criticism: A Short History, 1:953, 1:1155
Literary Criticism and Myth, 1:927
The Literary Criticism of Frank Norris, 1:776
Literary Democracy: The Declaration of Cultural Independence, 1:630
Literary Diseases: Theme and Metaphor in the Italian Novel, 2:400
Literary Disruptions, 1:918
Literary Dissent in Communist China, 2:233

Literary Essays of Ezra Pound, 1:871
The Literary Essays of Thomas Merton, 4:781
Literary Fortifications: Rousseau, Laclos, Sade, 2:484, 2:503
Literary France: The Making of a Culture, 2:446
Literary Friends and Acquaintances, 1:758
The Literary Guide to the Bible, 4:816
Literary History of Canada: Canadian Literature in English (Klinck), 2:904, 3:605, 3:618
Literary History of Canada: Canadian Literature in English (New), 2:905
The Literary History of England, 1:336, 1:385, 1:386
A Literary History of France, 2:447
A Literary History of New England, 1:717
A Literary History of Persia, 2:82
A Literary History of Rome, 2:380
A Literary History of Rome in the Silver Age, 2:380
A Literary History of the American West, 1:715, 1:716
A Literary History of the Arabs, 2:56
A Literary History of the Popular Ballad, 1:149
Literary History of the United States, 1:715
Literary History of the United States: Bibliography, 1:134
Literary History of the United States: History, 1:716
The Literary Impact of the Golden Bough, 3:30, 3:879, 4:477
Literary into Cultural Studies, 1:1127
Literary Journalism in the Twentieth Century, 1:808
The Literary Language of Shakespeare, 1:216
Literary Lapses, 2:918
The Literary Legacy of C. S. Lewis, 4:777
Literary Market Place (LMP): The Directory of American Book Publishing, 1:53, 1:69, 1:118

The Literary Mind: Its Place in an Age of Science, 1:808

The Literary Mind and the Carving of Dragons, 2:191

The Literary Miscellany, 1:273

Literary Politics in the Soviet Ukraine 1917–1934, 2:838

Literary Publishing in America, 1790–1850, 1:38

Literary Realism of William Dean Howells, 1:759

Literary Recordings, 1:123

Literary Reflections: A Shoring of Images, 1960–1993, 1:1004

The Literary Reputation of John Webster to 1830, 1:201

Literary Reviews and Essays on American, English and French Literature, 1:764

Literary Reviews in British Periodicals, 1798–1820: A Bibliography, 1:274

Literary Romanticism in America, 1:650

Literary Satellite: Czechoslovak-Russian Literary Relations, 2:833

The Literary South, 1:130

Literary Theory: An Introduction, 1:925, 1:1131

Literary Theory and Structure, 1:1155

Literary Theory Today, 1:1133

Literary Transcendentalism, 1:650

The Literary Underground of the Old Regime, 1:36

The Literary Universe of Jorge Luis Borges, 2:857

The Literary Use of the Psychoanalytic Process, 1:926

The Literary Vocation of Henry Adams, 1:730

The Literary Works of Ouyang Hsiu 1007–1072, 2:215

A Literate Passion: Letters of Anais Nin and Henry Miller, 1932–1953, 1:862

The Literate Revolution in Greece and Its Cultural Consequences, 2:346

Literature, 2:870

Literature, Obscenity and the Law, 1:57

Literature against Itself: Literary Ideas in Modern Society, 1:925

Literature and Cognition, 5:561

Literature and Evil, 2:455, 2:456

Literature and Existentialism, 4:329

Literature and History: Theoretical Problems & Russian Case Studies, 2:689

Literature and National Identity, 2:685

Literature and Nationalism, 2:989

Literature and Politics in the Age of Nero, 2:381

Literature and Psychoanalysis: The Question of Reading: Otherwise, 2:989

Literature and Psychoanalysis, 1:925

Literature and Religion, 2:989

Literature and Revolution, 2:691

Literature and Revolution in Soviet Russia, 1917–1962, 2:687

Literature and Science, 1:499, 2:990

Literature and Society in Imperial Russia, 2:691

Literature and Technology, 5:153

Literature and the Aborigine in Australia, 1770–1975, 2:946

Literature and the American Tradition, 1:723

Literature and Theology in Colonial New England, 1:634

Literature as National Institution, 2:371

Literature as Prophecy, 2:817

Literature for Young People on War and Peace, 1:578, 1:1195

Literature in America: An Illustrated History, 1:650

Literature in Malay by the Chinese of Indonesia, 2:317

Literature in South Vietnam: 1954–1975, 2:339

Literature in the Vernacular, 2:417

The Literature of Africa and the African Continuum, 2:111

The Literature of Ancient Egypt, 2:53, 4:442

The Literature of Change, 1:270, 1:319

The Literature of Controversy, 1:231

The Literature of Delight, 1:1195, 3:871

The Literature of Early America, 1:630

The Literature of Geography: A Guide to Its Organisation and Use, 3:118, 5:619

Literature of Medieval England, 1:141

The Literature of Modern Arabia: An Anthology, 2:57

Literature of the Early Republic, 1:630

Literature of the Hundred Flowers Period, 2:234

A Literature of Their Own, 1:319, 1:1046, 1:1132

Literature of the Low Countries, 2:627

The Literature of the Second Self, 2:985

The Literature of the Spanish People from Roman Times to the Present Day, 2:522

Literature of the Western World, 2:5

The Literature of the West Indies, 2:931

Literature of the Working World, 2:566

The Literatures of India: An Introduction, 2:170

Literatures of the East, 2:52

A Literature Without Qualities: American Writing Since 1945, 1:910

Lithographic Prints from Stone and Plate, 1:27

Lithography, 1800–1850, 1:30

Lithography for Artists, 1:28

Lithuanian Hasidism, 4:633

Lithuanian Short Story: Fifty Years, 2:805

Little America, 3:914

Little Angel and Other Stories, 2:699

Little Big Man, 1:948, 1:949

Little Birds, 1:865, 1:866

The Little Black Fish and Other Modern Persian Stories, 2:87

The Little Box, 2:832

A Little Boy Lost: Together with the Poems, 1:365

Little Caesar, 1:1185

The Little Community and Peasant Society and Culture, 3:14, 3:39

Little Dorrit, 1:348

The Little Drummer Girl, 1:595

The Little Engines That Could've, 5:575
Little Eyolf, 2:665
Little Flowers of St. Francis, 4:710
The Little Foxes, 1:1092, 1:1093
The Little Girls, 1:447
Little Golden America, 2:729
The Little Golden Calf, 2:729
Little Horses of Tarquinia, 2:474
Little House in the Big Woods, 1:1208
Little House on the Prairie, 1:1208
Little Jin, 2:757
A Little Learning, 1:561
The Little LISPer, 5:552
Little Lord Fauntleroy, 1:1200, 1:1201
A Little Love in Big Manhattan: Two Yiddish Poets, 2:30
The Little Magazine in America: A Modern Documentary History, 3:801
Little Magazines, 1:914
The Little Manual of Calligraphy, 1:19
Little Men, 1:1197, 1:1198
The Little Mermaid, 1:577
The Little Minister, 1:329
Little Mountain, 2:59
Little Novels, 1:346
Little Novels of Sicily, 2:441
A Little Pilgrim, 1:385
A Little Pretty Pocket Book, 1:576
The Little Prince, 2:504
The Little Princess, 1:1200, 1:1201
Little Red Riding Hood, 1:583
The Little Review, 1:428
The Little Savage, 1:374
Little Steel, 1:880
The Little Theater of the World, 2:593
A Little Touch of Drama, 2:839, 2:840
The Little Town, 2:601
Little Town on the Prairie, 1:1208
Little Tragedies, 2:750
Little Tree, 1:825
The Little Virtues, 2:422
Little Wars, 1:563
The Little White Bird, or, Adventures in Kensington Gardens, 1:329, 1:330
Little Women, 1:1193, 1:1195, 1:1197, 1:1198

Liturgies of the Western Church, 4:681
Live and Be Well: New Age and Old Folk Remedies, 5:321
Live and Let Die, 1:594
Live and Remember, 2:752
Live from Golgotha, 1:1062
Live Like Pigs, 1:433
The Lively Experiment: The Shaping of Christianity in America, 4:753
The Lively Years, 1920–1973, 1:1071
Live Machines: Hired Foreigners and Meiji Japan, 3:478
Live or Die, 1:1045
Lives, 1:177, 2:381
Lives and Letters, 1:86, 1:429, 1:928
The Lives and Times of Ebenezer Scrooge, 1:349
The Lives and Work of Anne Bradstreet, Emily Dickinson and Adrienne Rich, 1:635
Lives in the Shadow with J. Krishnamurti, 4:556
Lives in Transit: A Collection of Recent Russian Women's Writing, 2:692
The Lives of a Cell: Notes of a Biology Watcher, 5:19, 5:766
The Lives of Butterflies, 5:763
Lives of Eminent Philosophers, 4:46
Lives of Girls and Women, 2:921
The Lives of Jean Toomer: A Hunger for Wholeness, 1:891
Lives of Performers, 1:1174
Lives of the Caesars, 3:320
Lives of the Engineers, 5:2, 5:218, 5:250, 5:256
Lives of the Laureates, 3:44, 3:69, 3:77, 3:88, 3:103, 3:108
Lives of the Modern Poets, 1:799
Lives of the Most Eminent Painters, Sculptors, and Architects, 3:761
Lives of the Painters, 3:761
Lives of the Poets, 1:224, 1:234, 1:249
Lives of the Poets: Six Stories and a Novella, 1:969
Lives of the Saints, 4:675

The Lives of the Twelve Caesars, 2:394, 2:395
Living, 1:487
The Living and the Dead, 2:756, 2:757, 2:965, 2:966
The Living Aristophanes, 2:354
Living at the End of the Ages, 4:724
Living City, 3:797
A Living Covenant: The Innovative Spirit in Traditional Judaism, 4:648
The Living Dead: A Study of the Vampire in Romantic Literature, 1:270
The Living End, 1:973
The Living Flame of Love, 2:543
The Living God: Systematic Theology, 4:885
The Living Heart Diet, 5:345
Living in a World Revolution: My Encounters with History, 3:286
Living in the Environment: An Introduction to Environmental Science, 5:823
Living in the Eternal: A Study of George Santayana, 4:328
Living in the Maniototo, 2:974
Living Issues in Philosophy, 4:25
A Living Minstrelsy: The Poetry and Music of Sidney Lanier, 1:772
The Living of Charlotte Perkins Gilman, 1:752
The Living on the Dead, 2:21
Living Options in World Philosophy, 4:37
Living Peter: A Biographical Study of Pope John XXIII, 4:771
Living Philosophy: Eco-Philosophy as a Tree of Life, 5:72
The Living Planet, 5:817
Living Quarters, 1:479
Living Religions and a World Faith, 4:296
Living Richly in an Age of Limits, 5:114
The Living Room, 1:488
Living-Room War, 3:810
The Living Sea, 3:919, 5:642
A Living Soul, 2:675
Livingstone, Man of Africa: Memorial Essays, 1873–1973, 3:930
Livingstone's River, 3:930

Livingston's Legacy: Horace Waller and Victorian Mythmaking, 3:930

The Living Talmud: The Wisdom of the Fathers, 4:610

The Living Temple: George Herbert and Catechizing, 1:181, 1:976

The Living Theater, 1:1109

Living the Enlightenment, 3:337

The Living Thoughts of Nietzsche, 4:247

The Living Thoughts of St. Paul, 4:306

The Living Thoughts of Schopenhauer, 4:256

Living Together, 1:436

The Living U.S. Constitution, 3:543

Living Well with Emphysema and Bronchitis, 5:398

Living Well with Multiple Sclerosis, 5:391

Living with Death and Dying, 5:379

Living with Diabetes, 5:382

Living with Herpes, 5:390

Living within Limits: Ecology, Economic, and Population Taboos, 5:822

Living with Low Vision: A Resource Guide for People with Sight Loss, 5:384

Living with the Children of God, 4:864

Living with the Disabled: You Can Help—A Family Guide, 5:376

Living with Your Allergies and Asthma, 5:386

Livy: Hannibal the Scourge of Rome. Selections from Book XXI, 3:317

Li Yü, 2:210

Liza of Lambeth, 1:519

The Lizard's Tail, 2:885

Lizzie Leigh and Other Tales, 1:355

Local Assays: On Contemporary American Poetry, 1:914

Local Habitations: Regionalism in the Early Novels of George Eliot, 1:354

Local Health Policy in Action, 5:328

Local Knowledge: Further Essays in Interpretive Anthropology, 1:980, 3:31, 4:478

Local Religion in Sixteenth-Century Spain, 4:728

Location in Space: Theoretical Perspectives in Economic Geography, 3:122

Locations, 3:893

Locke (Ayer), 4:179

Locke (Fraser), 4:180

Locke (Woolhouse), 4:181

Locke, Berkeley, Hume, 4:180

Locke, Berkeley, Hume: Central Themes, 3:337

Locke, Rousseau, and the Idea of Consent, 4:181

Locke's Theory of Knowledge and Its Historical Relations, 4:180

Locke's Travels in France, 1675–1679, 4:180

The Lockwood Concern, 1:866

The Lodger, 1:1168

Loeb Class, 2:380

Logan's Medical and Scientific Abbreviations, 5:6

The Log Cabin Myth: The Social Backgrounds of the Presidents, 3:543

The Log from the Sea of Cortez, 1:884, 1:885

Logic (Lotze), 4:240

Logic (Salmon), 5:103

Logic: The Theory of Inquiry, 3:259, 3:260, 4:224

Logic, Laws, and Life, 5:79

Logic, Science, and Dialectic, 4:49

Logical and Philosophical Papers, 1909–1913, 4:323

The Logical Basis of Metaphysics, 4:382

Logical Foundations of Probability, 5:85

A Logical Introduction to Philosophy, 4:23

Logical Investigations, 4:229, 4:234

Logical Number Theory: An Introduction, 5:489

Logical Papers: A Selection, 4:176

Logical Positivism (Ayer), 4:262, 4:273

Logical Positivism (Hanfling), 4:264

Logical Positivism, Pragmatism and Scientific Empiricism, 4:266

The Logical Structure of the World and Pseudoproblems in Philosophy, 4:278, 5:85

Logical Works, 5:499

Logica Magna. Part I Fascicule 8, 4:129

Logica Magna. Part II Fascicule 3, 4:129

Logica Magna, Tractatus De Suppositione, 4:129

Logic and Knowledge: Essays 1901–50, 4:323, 5:102

Logic and Language Second Series, 4:264

The Logic and Limits of Trust, 3:208

Logic and Ontology in Heidegger, 4:295

Logic and Philosophy, 4:338

Logic and Reality in Leibniz's Metaphysics, 4:177

Logic and Rhetoric in England, 1500–1700, 4:127

Logic and the Objectivity of Knowledge: Studies in Husserl's Early Philosophy, 4:235

Logica Parva, 4:129

Logic in Three Books: Of Thought, of Investigation, and of Knowledge, 4:241

The Logic of Chemical Synthesis, 5:741

The Logic of Commands, 5:101

The Logic of Decision, 5:63

The Logic of Decision and Action, 4:317

The Logic of Deterrence, 5:111

The Logic of Divine Love, 4:106

Logic of Leviathan: The Moral and Political Theory of Thomas Hobbes, 3:154, 4:174

The Logic of Life, 5:800

The Logic of Modern Physics, 5:676

The Logic of Perception, 3:177

The Logic of Perfection and Other Essays in Neoclassical Metaphysics, 4:289

Logic of Pragmatism: An Examination of John Dewey's Logic, 4:225

The Logic of Reflection: German Philosophy in the Twentieth Century, 4:28

The Logic of Scientific Discovery, 4:409, 5:98

The Logic of Sense, 1:583

The Logic of St. Anselm, 4:108

The Logic of the Latifundio, 3:635

The Logic of William of Ockham, 4:121
Logico-Linguistic Papers, 4:414
Logics of Disintegration, 1:1131, 4:391
Logos and Ergon in Thucydides, 3:323
Loitering with Intent, 1:551
Lokotown and Other Stories, 2:136
Lolita, 1:1019, 1:1020, 2:740
L'Ombre et le Vent, 2:156
London, 1:227, 1:248
London and the Reformation, 4:725
London Assurance, 1:331
A London Bibliography of the Social Sciences, Twenty-fourth Supplement, 3:1989, 3:6
The London Bookbinders 1780–1806, 1:24
London Bookbinders 1780–1840, 1:26
London for Dickens Lovers, 1:350
London Labour and the London Poor, 1:377
The London Magazine, 1:324, 1:343
The London Magazine, 1820–29, 1:273
London Pride, or, When the World Was Younger, 1:333
The London Prodigal, 1:204
The London Stage 1940–1949: A Calendar of Plays and Players, 1:427
The Lone Heretic, 2:552
Loneliness, 5:423
Loneliness and Love, 5:423
The Loneliness at the Core: Studies in Thomas Wolfe, 1:904
The Loneliness of the Long-Distance Runner, 1:547
The Lonely Crowd, 3:209, 3:238
The Lonely Heart: A Biography of Carson McCullers, 1:1102
Lonely Hearts of the Cosmos, 5:590
The Lonely Hunter: A Biography of Carson McCullers, 1:1009
The Lonely Londoners, 2:942
The Lonely Voice: A Study of the Short Story, 1:527
A Lonely Woman: Forugh Farrokhzad and Her Poetry, 2:89

Lonesome Boy, 1:817
Lonesome Dove, 1:1010
Lonesome Traveler, 1:998
Lone Star Rising: Lyndon Johnson and His Times, 1908–1960, 3:537
The Long, Bitter Trail: Andrew Jackson and the Indians, 3:526
Long, Long Ago, 2:140
Long Ago: Selected Stories, 2:707
The Long Argument, 1:628
Long Black Song: Essays in Black American Literature and Culture, 1:938
The Long Conversation: A Memoir of David Jones, 1:502
Long Cycles: Prosperity and War in the Modern Age, 3:279
The Long Darkness (Grinspoon), 5:110
The Long Darkness (MacBeth), 1:516
Long Day's Journey into Night, 1:1106, 1:1107
The Long Day Wanes, 1:453, 1:454
Long-Distance Caregiving: A Survival Guide for Far Away Caregivers, 5:377
Long Distance Interrogation, 2:791
The Long Dream, 1:905
The Long Encounter, 1:688
The Longer Poems of Velimir Khlebnikov, 2:732
The Longest Day, 3:344
The Longest Journey, 1:476
Longest Years, 2:669
The Long Exile, 2:508
Longfellow: His Life and Work, 1:683
The Long Goodbye, 1:1228, 2:767
The Longhorns, 3:863
Longing for Harmonies, 5:651
The Long Journey, 2:652
A Long Journey: The Autobiography of Pitirim A. Sorokin, 3:240
Long Live Man, 1:964
Long Live Sandawara, 2:960, 2:961
The Long Loneliness: An Autobiography, 4:765
Longman Anthology of American Drama, 1:1078

The Longman Anthology of World Literature by Women, 1:130
Longman Atlas of Modern British History, 3:354
Longman Companion to Twentieth-Century Literature, 2:4
Longman Dictionary of Contemporary English, 1:90
The Longman Guide to Sources in Contemporary British History, 3:353
Longman Handbook of Modern European History, 1763–1985, 3:326
Longman Illustrated Dictionary of Botany, 5:762
The Long March, 1:1056
The Long March: The Epic of Chinese Communism's Survival, 3:472
Long Memory: The Black Experience in America, 3:554
The Long Peace: Inquiries into the History of the Cold War, 3:545
The Long Poems of Wallace Stevens: An Interpretive Study, 1:888
The Long Reach: New and Uncollected Poems 1948–1984, 1:972
The Long Revolution, 1:274
The Long Road to Freedom: Russia and Glasnost, 3:398
The Long Sigh the Wind Makes: Poems by William Stafford, 1:1053
Long Steel Rail: The Railroad in American Folksong, 3:851
A Long Time Burning: The History of Literary Censorship in England, 1:274
Longus, 2:363
The Long Valley, 1:884
The Long Voyage Home: Seven Plays of the Sea, 1:1107
Long-Wave Rhythms in Economic Development and Political Behavior, 3:127
Long Waves in Economic Development, 3:50
Long Way from Home, 1:857
The Long Winter, 1:1208
Long Years of Neglect, 1:697
The Look, 2:871
Look, Stranger!, 1:435
Look-Alike, Sound-Alike, Not-Alike Words: An Index of Confusables, 1:94

Look at the Harlequins!, 2:739, 2:740
Look at the Sky . . . and Tell the Weather, 5:634
Look Back, Mrs. Lot!, 2:21
Look Back Harder: Critical Writings of Allen Curnow 1935–84, 2:973
Look Back in Anger, 1:414, 1:531, 1:532
Look Homeward: A Life of Thomas Wolfe, 1:904
Look Homeward, Angel, 1:903
Looking at Art: An Introduction to Enjoying the Great Paintings of the World, 3:758
Looking Backward: 2000–1887, 5:563
Looking Backward, 1:733, 1:734
Looking Backward, Nineteen Eighty-Eight to Eighteen Eighty-Eight, 1:734
Looking for a Ship, 1:1011
Looking for Langston, 1:1188
Looking for Osman, 3:452, 3:904
Looking for Steinbeck's Ghost, 1:885
Looking-Glass Letters, 1:582
Looking Glass War, 1:596
Looking North for Health, 5:330
Looking on Darkness, 2:159
Looking Within, 1:734
The Look of Distance, 1:795
The Look of Maps: An Examination of Cartographic Design, 3:121
The Look of Russian Literature, 2:687
The Loom of Time: A Selection of His Plays and Poems, 2:172
Loon Lake, 1:969
Loose Canons: Notes on the Culture Wars, 1:925, 1:1127
Loot, 1:529
The Lorax, 1:1203
Lorca: An Appreciation of His Poetry, 2:539
Lord Burghley and Queen Elizabeth, 3:359
Lord Byron and Some of His Contemporaries, 1:283
Lord Byron as a Satirist in Verse, 1:283
Lord Byron's Iberian Pilgrimage, 1:284

Lord Chesterfield and His World, 1:236
Lord Chesterfield's Letters, 1:236
Lord Grey of the Reform Bill, 3:411
Lord Grizzly, 1:1217
L'Ordine Nuovo, 2:423
Lord Jim, 1:463, 1:741
Lord Kelvin and the Age of the Earth, 5:45, 5:622
Lord Lister, 5:409
Lord Lister, His Life And Doctrine, 5:409
Lord Liverpool's Administration: The Crucial Years, 1815–1822, 3:361
Lord Macaulay: The Pre-eminent Victorian, 1:374, 3:406
Lord North, 3:363
Lord of the Flies, 1:483
The Lord of the Isles, 1:299
The Lord of the Rings, 1:558, 1:559, 1:574, 1:578, 1:590, 4:776
The Lord of Uraniborg: A Biography of Tycho Brahe, 5:40, 5:600
Lord Peter: A Collection of All the Lord Peter Wimsey Stories, 1:610
Lord Peter Views the Body, 1:611
The Lord Protector, 4:734
Lord Rutherford, 5:712
Lord Shaftesbury, 3:404
Lord Weary's Castle, 1:1005, 1:1006
The Lore and Language of Schoolchildren, 3:884, 3:885
Lore and Science in Ancient Pythagoreanism, 4:470
Lorelei Two: My Life with Conrad Aiken, 1:810
Lorentz Transformations, 5:699
Lorenzo in Taos, 1:510
Lorraine Hansberry, 1:1092
Lorraine Hansberry: The Collected Last Plays, 1:1092
Losers, 1:479
Loser Take All: The Comic Art of Woody Allen, 3:830
Losing Battles, 1:894, 1:895
Loss of Eden: A Biography of Charles and Anne Morrow Lindbergh, 3:929
The Loss of El Dorado, 3:641

A Loss of Mastery: Puritan Historians in Colonial America, 1:634, 3:515
A Loss of Roses, 1:1095
The Loss of Self, 5:391
The Lost and Found Stories of Morley Callaghan, 2:908
Lost and Saved, 1:384
Lost at the Frontier, 5:176, 5:177, 5:182
Lost Borders, 1:732
The Lost British Policy, 3:411
The Lost Center and Other Essays in Greek Poetry, 2:371
The Lost Childhood and Other Essays, 1:488
Lost Cities of Africa, 3:428
The Lost Colony, 1:1088
The Lost Continent: Travels in Small Town America, 3:894
The Lost Eden, 2:332
The Lost Flying Boat, 1:547
The Lost Garden, 1:212
The Lost Girl, 1:509
The Lost Grove: Autobiography of a Spanish Poet in Exile, 2:529
The Lost Honor of Katharina Blum, 2:570
Lost Illusions, 2:453
Lost in a Book: The Psychology of Reading for Pleasure, 1:33
Lost in America, 2:48
Lost in the Crowd, 2:85
Lost in the Funhouse, 1:942, 1:943
Lost in Yonkers, 1:1113
Lost Island, 1:1238
A Lost Lady, 1:820
Lost Letters to Constantin Heger, 1:334
Lost Lhasa: Heinrich Harrer's Tibet, 3:923
Lost Love, 2:306
The Lost Musicians, 2:656
Lost Names, 2:305
The Lost Peace: International Relations in Europe, 1918–1939, 3:277
The Lost Pilot, 1:1057, 1:1058
Lost Possessions, 2:976, 2:977
Los Trabajos de Persiles y Sigismunda, 2:536
The Lost Rib: Female Characters in the Spanish-American Novel, 2:847
The Lost Road and Other Writings, 1:559

The Lost Soul of American Politics, 3:542

The Lost Steps, 2:859, 2:860

The Lost Summer: A Personal Memoir of F. Scott Fitzgerald, 1:840

Lost Tribes and Promised Lands: The Origins of American Racism, 3:557

The Lost Upland, 1:1015

The Lost World of the Kalahari, 3:941

The Lost World of Thomas Jefferson, 3:155, 3:569

Lost Years: Confessions of a Woman Alcoholic, 5:402

Lost Zoo, 1:824

Lothair, 1:351

Lotte in Weimar, 2:601

Lotte in Weimar: The Beloved Returns, 2:602

The Lottery: And Other Stories, 1:992

The Lottery; or The Adventures of James Harris, 1:992

A Lot to Ask: A Life of Barbara Pym, 1:539

The Lotus Boat, 2:191

Lotus in a Sea of Fire, 4:561

Lotus Petals: The Life and Work of Rudolph Steiner, 4:879

Lotus Sutra, 4:538

The Lotus Sutra in Japanese Culture, 4:538

Lotze's System of Philosophy, 4:241, 4:327

Lotze's Theory of Reality, 4:241

A Lou Harrison Reader, 3:699

Louis: The Louis Armstrong Story, 1900–1971, 3:674

Louis Agassiz, 5:785

Louis Agassiz: A Life in Science, 5:785

Louisa May Alcott, 1:1199

Louisa May: A Modern Biography of Louisa May Alcott, 1:1199

Louisa May Alcott: A Bibliography, 1:1199

Louisa May Alcott: A Reference Guide, 1:1199

Louis Armstrong: Biography of a Musician, 3:674

Louis Armstrong, an American Genius, 3:674

Louis Armstrong, His Life and Times, 3:674

Louisbourg Portraits: Life in an Eighteenth-Century Garrison Town, 3:612

Louis D. Brandeis and the Progressive Tradition in America, 3:533

Louis "David" Riel: Prophet of a New World, 3:615

Louise Bogan: A Portrait, 1:952

Louis H. Sullivan: The Banks, 3:793

Louis I. Kahn: Writings, Lectures, Interviews, 3:777

Louis Lambert, 2:453

Louis L'Amour, 1:1216

Louis L'Amour: His Life and Trails, 1:1216

The Louis L'Amour Companion, 1:1216

Louis MacNeice: A Study, 1:518

Louis MacNeice: The Poet in His Contexts, 1:518

Louis MacNeice in the BBC, 1:518

Louis Napoleon and the Second Empire, 3:374

Louis Pasteur, 5:809

Louis Pasteur: Free Lance of Science, 5:795, 5:809

Louis Riel, 3:615

Louis St. Laurent, Canadian, 3:616

Louis Sullivan: The Public Papers, 3:792

Louis Sullivan, His Life and Work, 3:793

Louis Sullivan, Prophet of Modern Architecture, 3:792

Louis the Fourteenth and the Greatness of France, 3:372

Louis Wirth: A Bio-bibliography, 3:245

Louis Wirth on Cities and Social Life, 3:245

Lou-lan and Other Stories, 2:287

Love (Carter), 1:455

Love (Stendhal), 2:511

Love, Death, and Exile, 2:63

Love, Knowledge, and Discourse in Plato, 4:84

Love, Lust, and Rebellion: New Approaches to Georg Büchner, 2:574

Love, Sex, Death and the Meaning of Life: The Films of Woody Allen, 3:830

Love & Solitude: Selected Poems, 1916–1923, 2:660

Love against Hate, 5:464

Love among the Cannibals, 1:1017

Love and Death in the American Novel, 1:628, 1:975

Love and Exile: The Early Years—A Memoir, 2:48

Love and Fame, 1:950

Love and Friendship in Plato and Aristotle, 4:83

Love and Mr. Lewisham, 1:563

Love and Responsibility, 4:747

Love and Science in Ancient Pythagoreanism, 4:87

Love and the Caribbean: Tales, Characters, and Scenes of the West Indies, 3:897

Love and War, 1:619

Love and Will, 5:463

Love Casts Out Fear, 1:619

The Loved and the Lost, 2:908

The Loved One, 1:561, 1:562

Love Elegies of the Renaissance, 2:503

Love Ethic of D. H. Lawrence, 1:511

Love for Love, 1:237

Love from Trieste, 2:655

Love in a Junk and Other Exotic Tales, 2:198

Love in Ancient Greece, 2:345

Love in a Tub, 1:242

Love in a Wood, 1:263

Love in the Ruins, 1:1029

Love in the Time of Cholera, 2:867

Love in the Western World, 3:326, 3:330

Love in Two Languages, 2:123

Love Is Colder Than Death, 3:836

Love Is Never Enough, 5:433

Love Is Not Enough, 5:435

Love Known: Theology and Experience in George Herbert's Poetry, 1:181

Love Letters and Two Other Plays: The Golden Age, 1:1091

Love Letters Between a Nobleman and His Sister, 1:233

Love Must Not Be Forgotten, 2:239

Love of Books: Philobiblon of Richard de Bury, 1:31

The Love of Learning and the Desire for God, 4:699

Love on a Barren Mountain, 2:267

Love Poems, 1:1044, 1:1045

The Love Poetry of Francisco de Quevedo, 2:548

The Lover, 2:26, 2:474

The Lovers (Farmer), 1:1257

Lovers (Friel), 1:479

Lovers in Paradise, 1:619

The Lovers Melancholy, 1:179

The Lover's Tale, 1:400

Love's Cross-currents, 1:398

Love's Knowledge: Essays on Philosophy and Literature, 2:988

Love's Labor's Lost, 1:205, 1:206

Love's Labor's Won, 1:204

Love's Last Shift, 1:261

Love's Martyr, 1:215

The Loves of Cass McGuire, 1:479

The Love Song of J. Alfred Prufrock, 1:416, 1:471

Love Song of the Dark Lord: Jayadeva's Gītagovinda, 2:173

The Love Songs of Chandidās, 2:174

The Love Songs of Vidyāpati, 2:174

Love Strikes a Devil, 1:619

The Love Suicide at Schofield Barracks, 1:1099

Love Visions, 1:150

Lovey Childs: A Philadelphian's Story, 1:866

The Love You Make: An Insider's Story of the Beatles, 3:665

Loving, 1:487

Loving a Woman in Two Worlds: Love Poems, 1:951

Loving-Living-Party Going, 1:487

Loving Nature: Ecological Integrity and Christian Responsibility, 4:745

Loving the Torah More Than God? Towards a Catholic Appreciation of Judaism, 4:901

Loving with a Vengeance, 1:618, 1:1151

Loving with a Vengeance: Mass-Produced Fantasies for Women, 1:618

Low City, High City: Tokyo from Edo to the Earthquake, 3:479

The Low Countries, 1780–1940, 3:380

Lowell and Mars, 5:609

The Lowensköld Ring, 2:677

Lower Canada, 1791–1840: Social Change and Nationalism, 3:613

The Lower Depths, 2:724

The Lower Depths and Other Plays, 2:725

Low-Stress Fitness, 5:325

Loyalties, 1:481

Loyalty, 4:389

L. Ron Hubbard: Madman or Messiah, 4:869

Lu Ann Hampton Laverty Oberlander, 1:1096

Lucan: An Introduction. Studies in Classical Philology, 2:387

Luchino Visconti—Three Screenplays, 3:843

Luchino Visconti—Two Screenplays: La Terra Treme, Senso, 3:843

Lucian, Satirist and Artist, 2:363

Lucian and His Influence in Europe, 2:364, 4:485

Lucian of Samosata in the Two Hesperias, 2:364

Lucien Leuwen, 2:511

Lucifer, 2:632

Lucifer: A Theological Tragedy, 4:327

Lucifer: The Devil in the Middle Ages, 4:697

Lucifer in Harness, 1:798

Lucifer in Harness: American Meter, Metaphor and Diction, 1:913, 1:655, 1:719

Lucinda Brayford, 2:950, 2:951

Lucinde, 2:610, 4:252

Lucinde and Fragments, 4:253

The Luck of Barry Lyndon, 1:403

The Luck of Roaring Camp, 1:756

Lucky Jim, 1:432, 1:507

Lucky Kristoffer, 2:650

Lucretius: De Rerum Natura, 2:388

Lucretius: Poet and Philosopher, 2:388

Lucretius and Epicurus, 4:73, 4:75

Lucretius and His Influence, 2:388, 4:75

Lucretius on Death and Anxiety, 2:388, 4:75

Lucy: The Beginnings of Humankind, 5:638

Lucy Church Amiably, 1:881

Lucy Gayheart, 1:820

Ludlow Fair, 1:1121

Ludovico Ariosto, 2:406, 2:407

Ludvig Holberg, 2:651

Ludwig Feuerbach and the Outcome of Classical German Philosophy, 4:228

Ludwig Wittgenstein: A Comprehensive Bibliography, 4:346

Ludwig Wittgenstein: Critical Assessments, 4:347

Ludwig Wittgenstein: Personal Recollections, 4:346

Lugard, 3:421

Lu Hsün, Writing for the Revolution: Essays, 2:256

Lu Hsün's Vision of Reality, 2:256

Luigi Pirandello, 2:436

Luigi Pirandello, 1867–1936, 2:436

Luigi Pirandello, Director: The Playwright in the Theater, 2:436

Luis Buñuel, 3:832

Luis Buñuel: A Critical Biography, 3:832

Luís de Camoens and the Epic of the Lusiads, 2:558

Lukács and Heidegger: Towards a New Philosophy, 5:90

Lukács' Concept of Dialectics, 2:802

Lullaby Land: Songs of Childhood by Eugene Field, 1:584

Lull and Bruno: Collected Essays, 2:411, 4:136

Lulu Plays and Other Sex Tragedies, 2:614

Lumbering Songs from the Northern Woods, 3:851

Lumea Romaneasca, 2:826

A Lume Spento, 1:870

Lunacy and Letters, 1:457

Lunacy of Light: Emily Dickinson and the Experience of Metaphor, 1:746

Lunar Caustic, 2:919

Lunar Landscapes, 1:985

The Lunar Light of Whitman's Poetry, 1:708

The Lunar Society of Birmingham, 5:45

Lung Cancer: The Facts, 5:398

L'Unité Culturelle de l'Afrique Noire, 3:428

Lupercal, 1:498

Lured, 1:1175

A Lure of Knowledge: Lesbian Sexuality and Theory, 1:1182

The Lure of the Land, 3:549

The Lusiads, 2:558, 2:559

Lust for Life, 1:1249, 1:1250, 3:795

Lustful Maidens and Ascetic Kings: Buddhist and Hindu Stories of Life, 4:503, 4:512

Lustra, 1:871

Luther, 1:531, 1:532

Luther: Man between God and the Devil, 4:779

Luther, Erasmus and the Reformation: A Catholic-Protestant Reappraisal, 4:779

Luther and Erasmus: Free Will and Salvation, 4:779

Luther and His Times: The Reformation from a New Perspective, 4:779

Luther and Music, 4:738

Luther and Staupitz, 4:779

Luther and the Papacy: Stages in a Reformation Conflict, 4:778

Lutheran Letters, 2:431

The Lutheran Milieu of the Films of Ingmar Bergman, 3:831

Luther in Context, 4:779

Luther on Conversion: The Early Years, 4:778

Luther's Faith: The Cause of the Gospel in the Church, 4:779

Luther's House of Learning, 4:731

Luther's Last Battles: Politics and Polemics, 1531–1546, 4:778

Luther's Progress to the Diet of Worms, 4:779

Luther's Theology of the Cross, 4:778

Lu Xun, A Biography, 2:256

Lu You, 2:214

Luzumiyat, 2:61

Lycidas, 1:191

Lyddie, 1:1204

Lydie Breeze, 1:1090

The Lyman Letters: New Light on Emily Dickinson and Her Family, 1:748

Lymphokines and the Immune Response, 5:790

Lyndon Johnson and the American Dream, 3:538

The Lyre of Orpheus, 2:910

The Lyre of Science: Form and Meaning in Lucretius's De Rerum Natura, 4:75

The Lyrical and the Epic: Studies of Modern Chinese Literature, 2:234

Lyrical Ballads, 1:305, 1:306

The Lyrical Poetry of Thomas Hardy, 1:362

The Lyric Encyclopedia of Raymond Queneau, 2:497

The Lyric Genius of Catullus, 2:384

Lyrics, 2:743

Lyrics from Arabia, 2:56

Lyrics of the Middle Ages: An Anthology, 1:148

Lyric Time: Dickinson and the Limits of Genre, 1:747

The Lyric Year, 1:860

Lysistrata, 2:353

The Lytle-Tate Letters, 1:889

M

Ma and Son: A Novel, 2:251

Maarten 't Hart, 2:626

Ma'aseh Book: Book of Jewish Tales and Legends, 2:33

Macaulay, 3:406

Macaulay: The Shaping of the Historian, 1:374

Macbeth, 1:205, 1:206, 1:212, 1:221

"Macbeth" and the Players, 1:214

Macbett, 2:483

The Macdermonts of Ballycloran, 1:406

MacDiarmid: A Critical Biography, 1:517

MacDiarmid: An Illustrated Biography, 1:517

MacDiarmid: The Terrible Crystal, 1:517

MacFlecknoe, 1:241

The MacGuffin: A Novel, 1:973

Machado, 2:545

Machado de Assis; The Brazilian Master and His Novels, 2:896

Mach Bands: Quantitative Studies on Neural Networks in the Retina, 5:700

The Machiavellian Cosmos, 4:145

Machiavelli and Guicciardini, 4:145

Machiavelli and Mystery of State, 3:333

The Machiavellian Moment, 4:145

Machiavelli in Hell, 3:160

Machiavelli's New Modes and Orders: A Study of the "Discourses on Livy," 3:160, 4:145

Machiavelli's "Prince" and Its Forerunners, 4:145

Machina ex Dea: Feminist Perspectives on Technology, 5:37, 5:157, 5:205

Machina ex Deo: Essays in the Dynamism of Western Culture, 5:58

Machina ex Deo: The Virgin and the Dynamo Reconsidered and Other Essays, 5:117

The Machine at the Bedside, 5:370

The Machine in the Garden: Technology and the Pastoral Idea in America, 1:651, 1:715

Machinery of Dominance: Women, Men, and Technical Know-How, 5:187

The Machinery of Life, 5:774, 5:784

The Machinery of Nature, 5:832

Machinery of the Mind: Inside the New Science of Artificial Intelligence, 5:568

Machines, Tools and Processes for Engineers, 5:236

Machines as the Measure of Man, 5:24

Machines Who Think, 5:568

A Machine That Would Go of Itself: The Constitution in American Culture, 3:520

Macho Camacho's Beat, 2:883

The Macintosh Bible, 5:555

Mackinder: Geography as an Aid to Statecraft, 3:133

Macmillan Anthology of Australian Literature, 2:947

The Macmillan Atlas History of Christianity, 4:720

The Macmillan Atlas of Rugs and Carpets, 3:767
The Macmillan Bible Atlas, 4:809
The Macmillan Book of Proverbs, Maxims and Famous Sayings, 1:115
The Macmillan Dictionary of Canadian Biography, 3:606
Macmillan Encyclopedia of Architects, 3:764
Macmillan Encyclopedia of Computers, 5:539
Macmillan Encyclopedia of Science, 5:29
The Macmillan Guide to Writing Research Papers, 1:118
Macro: Reindustrializing America and the World, 5:213
Macro Plays, 1:161
The Macro Plays: The Castle of Perseverance, Wisdom, Mankind, 1:161
Macroscope, 1:1253
Macunaíma, 2:892, 2:893
Madame Blavatsky: The Woman behind the Myth, 4:874
Madame Bovary, 2:475, 2:528, 2:559
Madame de La Fayette, 2:484
Madame Delphine, 1:736
Madame de Sévigné: A Life and Letters, 2:508
Madame de Sévigné: A Portrait in Letters, 2:508
Madame de Staël, 2:510
Madame de Treymes and Three Novellas, 1:787
Made from This Earth: American Woman and Nature, 5:818
Made in America, 3:49
Made in America: Science, Technology, and American Modernist Poets, 1:800
Madeleine and André Gide, 2:480
Mademoiselle de Seudéri, 2:591
Made to Order: The Myth of Reproductive and Genetic Progress, 5:188
Mad in Pursuit, 2:486
Mad Love, 2:462
Madly Singing, 2:302
The Madman and the Nun, and Other Plays, 2:822
Madman and the Nun and the Crazy Locomotive: Three Plays, 2:822

A Madman of Ch'u: The Chinese Myth of Loyalty and Dissent, 2:196
A Madman's Defense, 2:680
Mad Maria, 2:900
Madmen and Specialists, 2:149
Madness and Civilization: A History of Insanity in the Age of Reason, 2:477, 3:167, 3:205, 4:400, 5:87, 5:443
Madness and Lust: A Psychoanalytic Approach to Don Quixote, 2:536
The Madness of Lady Bright, 1:1121
The Madness of the Day, 2:461
The Madness of the Saints: Ecstatic Religion in Bengal, 4:505
The Mad Philosopher: Auguste Comte, 4:223
The Madrigal, 3:662
The Mad Trapper, 2:927
The Madwoman in the Attic, 1:318, 1:714, 1:925, 1:1131, 1:1145, 1:1146
A Mad World, My Masters, 1:190
Maenads, Martyrs, Matrons, Monastics, 4:449
The Maestro Myth: Great Conductors in Pursuit of Power, 3:671
Mafouz & Idris: Studies in Arabic Short Fiction, 2:65, 2:69
The Magazine in America, 1741–1900, 1:652
Magazines for Libraries, 1:52, 1:72, 1:113
Magazines for Young People, 1:72
The Maggid of Dubno and His Parables, 4:632
Maggie: A Girl of the Streets, 1:741
Maggie Cassidy, 1:998
Maghreb au Pluriel, 2:123
Maghrebian Literature in French, 2:117
Magic, Myth and Medicine, 3:868
Magic, Reason and Experience, 4:48, 5:38
Magic, Science and Religion and Other Essays, 3:23, 3:35, 4:485
Magic, Witchcraft and Paganism in America: A Bibliography, 4:865

Magical Medicine, 3:869
The Magic Barrel, 1:1013
Magic Bullets: A Revolution in Cancer Treatment, 5:372
The Magic Circle of Walden, 1:701
Magic from the Heart, 1:619
The Magic Gourd, 2:240
The Magician of Lublin, 2:47, 2:48
The Magicians, 1:537
The Magicians: A Study of the Use of Power in a Black Magic Group, 4:865
Magic in the Web: Action and Language in "Othello," 1:214
Magic into Science: The Story of Paracelsus, 4:150, 5:751
The Magic Kingdom, 1:973
The Magic Labyrinth, 1:1257
The Magic Lantern: An Autobiography, 3:831
The Magic Mirror: Law in American History, 3:145
The Magic Mountain, 2:601, 2:602
The Magic of Kindness, or, The Wondrous Story of the Good Huan, 1:378
The Magic of Minerals, 5:628
The Magic of Oz, 1:1200
The Magic Orange Tree: And Other Haitian Folktales, 2:931, 3:857
Magic Realism Rediscovered, 2:847
The Magic Toyshop, 1:455
The Magic World of Orson Welles, 1:1179
The Magic Years of Beatrix Potter, 1:589
Magika Hiera: Ancient Greek Magic and Religion, 4:451
Magill's Quotations in Context, 1:116
Magill's Survey's of Cinema, 3:826
Magill's Survey of Science, 5:11
Magister Ludi: The Glass Bead Game, 2:589
The Magistrate, The Second Mrs. Tanqueray, 1:388
Magistrates of the Roman Republic, 3:298
Magna Carta and the Idea of Liberty, 3:357
Magnalia Christi Americana, 1:1192
Magnetic North, 3:895

Magnetic Sleep: Mesmer and the Roots of Psychological Healing, 4:847
Magnificence (Brenton), 1:449
Magnificence (Skelton), 1:197
The Magnificent Ambersons, 1:1178
The Magnificent Obsession, 3:616
The Magus, 1:477, 1:478
The Mahabharata, 2:172, 4:502, 4:505
Mahan on Naval Strategy, 3:288
Mahan on Sea Power, 3:288
Mahatma Gandhi, 3:499
Mahatma Gandhi and Comparative Religion, 4:553
Mahatma Gandhi and His Apostles, 4:553
Mahayana Buddhism: The Doctrinal Foundations, 4:514
The Mahdist State in the Sudan, 1881–98, 3:419
Mahler, 3:705
Mahler: A Musical Physiognomy, 4:393
Mahogany and Other Stories, 2:747
Mahu, 2:493
Mahzor Hashalem: High Holyday Prayer Book, 4:599
The Maias, 2:559
Maiden of Orleans, 2:609
Maidens, Meal, and Money, 3:16, 3:429
Maidens' Vows, 2:813
Maiden Voyage, 3:907
The Maids, 2:478, 2:479
The Maid Silja, 2:660
The Maid's Tragedy, 1:173
Mail and Telephone Survey: The Total Design Method, 3:6
Mailer: A Biography, 1:1012
Mailer: His Life and Times, 1:1012
Maimonides, 4:668
Maimonides: Introduction to the Talmud, 4:627
Maimonides: Torah and Philosophic Quest, 4:668
Maimonides Ethics, 4:668
A Maimonides Reader, 4:668
Main Currents in American Thought, 1:715, 4:35
Main Currents in Contemporary German, British, and American Philosophy, 4:29, 4:268

Main Currents in Sociological Thought, 3:199
Main Currents of Indian History, 3:484
Main Currents of Korean Thought, 4:535
The Maine Woods, 1:700, 3:897
Mainly on the Air, 1:440
Main Problems in American History, 3:514
Main Street, 1:853, 1:854, 1:858
Main Street in Crisis, 3:536
Main Travelled Roads, 1:750, 1:751
Main Trends in Philosophy, 4:18, 4:23, 4:267, 4:319
Maíra, 2:898
Maitland, 3:402
Maitreya, 2:884
Máj, 2:788
Major Barbara, 1:544, 1:545
Major British Poets of the Romantic Period, 1:268
Major Canadian Authors, 2:905
The Major Comedies of Alexander Fredro, 2:813
Major Cuban Novelists: Innovation and Tradition, 2:847
The Major Fiction of William Gilmore Simms, 1:697
The Major Film Theories: An Introduction, 1:1156, 3:827
Major Hazards Onshore and Offshore, 5:241
Major Home Appliances: A Common Sense Repair Manual, 5:230
Major Inflations in History, 3:54
Majority Rule and Minority Rights, 3:573
Major Lyricists of the Northern Sung, 960–1126 A.D., 2:190
Major Operations of the Navies in the War of American Independence, 3:288
Major Peace Treaties of Modern History 1967–1979, 3:273
Major Poets of the Earlier Seventeenth Century, 1:166
Major Problems in the History of the Vietnam War, 3:515
Major Prophets of Today, 5:513

The Major Shakespearean Tragedies: A Critical Bibliography, 1:221
Major Soviet Writers: Essays in Criticism, 2:685
The Major Ternary Structural Families, 5:177
Major Themes in Modern Philosophies of Judaism, 4:646
Major Trends in Jewish Mysticism, 4:672
The Major Victorian Poets, 1:316
Major Writers in America, 3:587
Major Writers of Early American Literature, 1:628, 1:634, 1:644
Makar's Dream, and Other Stories, 2:732
Makbara, 2:540
Make Bright the Arrow, 1:860
Make It New: Essays, 1:871, 1:872
The Makepeace Experiment, 2:757
Maker of Heaven and Earth, 5:201
Make Room for TV: Television and the Family Ideal in Postwar America, 3:812
The Makers of Rome: Nine Lives by Plutarch, 3:318
Makers of the City, 1:834
Making a Difference: Feminist Literary Criticism, 1:925, 1:1134
Making a Living, 1:1160
Making America Corporate, 1870–1920, 3:549
Making American Tradition, 1:716
Making America's Budget Policy: From the 1980s to the 1990s, 3:67
The Making and Unmaking of a Soviet Writer, 2:720
Making Babies: The New Science and Ethics of Conception, 5:123
Making Cancer Policy, 5:736
Making Culture, 3:610
Making Face, Making Soul— Haciendo Caras, 1:1136
Making Gray Gold: Narratives of Nursing Home Care, 5:334
Making Health Decisions: An Epidemiologic Perspective on Staying Well, 5:383
Making Local News, 3:807

Making Medicine, Making Money, 5:350

The Making of a Ballerina, 3:754

The Making of a Black Leader, 1856–1901, 3:270

The Making of a Continent, 5:618, 5:630

The Making of a Counter Culture, 5:174, 5:175

Making of a Fly: The Genetics of Animal Design, 5:778

The Making of a History: Walter Prescott Webb and the Great Plains, 3:600

The Making of Americans, 1:881

The Making of a Modernist, 1:883

The Making of a Moonie: Choice or Brainwashing?, 4:871

The Making of a Musical, 3:660

The Making of an American, 3:821, 3:822

The Making of a Profession, 5:230

The Making of a Publisher: A Life in the 20th-Century Book Revolution, 1:45

The Making of a Saint: A Romance of Mediaeval Italy, 1:520

The Making of a Spiritual Movement, 4:872

The Making of a Statesman and Other Stories, 1:754

The Making of a Teacher: Teacher Knowledge and Teacher Education, 3:255

The Making of a Woman Surgeon, 5:336

Making of Christian Doctrine, 4:687

The Making of Citizen Kane, 1:1179

The Making of Colonial Lucknow, 1856–1877, 3:485

The Making of Economic Society, 3:51

The Making of English Reading Audiences, 1790–1832, 1:265

The Making of Europe, 3:328

The Making of Foreign Policy in China: Structures and Process, 3:496

The Making of Geography, 3:118, 5:619

The Making of Geology: Earth Science in Britain, 1660–1815, 5:33

The Making of Homeric Verse, 2:362, 4:460

The Making of Index Numbers, 3:75, 3:76

The Making of Mark Twain, 1:784

Making of Men, 4:339

The Making of Modern Colombia: A Nation in Spite of Itself, 3:635

The Making of Modern Europe, 1648 to 1780, 3:338

The Making of Modern Holland: A Short History, 3:382

The Making of Modern Japan: An Introduction, 3:479

The Making of Modern Korea, 3:482

The Making of Modern Russia, 3:394

The Making of Modern Society, 3:209, 3:236

The Making of Modern Turkey, 3:452

The Making of Modern Uganda, 3:422

The Making of Modern Zionism: Intellectual Origins of the Jewish State, 4:657

The Making of Religion, 3:882

The Making of Saudi Arabia, 3:451

The Making of T. S. Eliot's Plays, 1:473

The Making of the American Constitution, 3:541

The Making of the Atomic Bomb, 5:658

Making of the Auden Canon, 1:435

The Making of the "Canzoniere" and Other Petrarchan Studies, 4:151

The Making of the Creeds, 4:687

The Making of the Dutch Landscape, 3:383

The Making of the English Working Class, 1:313, 3:365, 3:410

The Making of "The Golden Bough": The Origins and Growth of an Argument, 4:477

Making of the Mexican Mind: A Study in Recent Mexican Thought, 4:33

The Making of the Modern Body, 1:312

Making of the Modern Gulf States, 3:452

The Making of the Modern Homosexual, 1:1184

The Making of the Modern Jew, 4:634

The Making of the Modern Mind, 4:162

The Making of the New Deal: The Insiders Speak, 3:535

The Making of the New Poor Laws, 3:363

The Making of the "Poema de Mío Cid," 2:537

The Making of the Pré by Francis Ponge, 2:494

The Making of the Roman Army, 3:308

The Making of Three Russian Revolutionaries, 3:396

The Making of Victorian Drama, 1:323

The Making of Victorian England, 1:312

The Making of Walden: With the Text of the First Version, 1:702

Making Peace with the Planet, 5:822

Making Revolution, 3:469

Making Science Our Own: Public Images of Science, 1910–1955, 5:10, 5:64

Making Sense of Marx, 4:242

Making Sense of the Jonestown Suicides, 4:867

Making Sense of Things: An Invitation to Philosophy, 4:24

Making the Classics in Judaism: The Three Stages of Literary Formation, 4:611

Making the Estrogen Decision, 5:355

Making Tracks: An American Rail Odyssey, 3:897

Making War—Making Peace: The Social Foundations of Violent Conflict, 3:278

The Makioka Sisters, 2:293

The Makropoulos Secret, 2:789, 2:790

Maksim Gorky: A Reference Guide, 2:726

The Malacia Tapestry, 1:613

The Malaise of Modernity, 4:415

The Malaria Capers, 5:389

Malaria Dreams, 3:905

Malavoglia, 2:441

The Malay Archipelago, 5:812
Malay Fishermen: Their Peasant Economy, 3:30
Malay Magic, 2:324
Malay Proverbs–Bidalan Melayu, 2:325
The Malays: A Cultural History, 3:492
Malaysia, 2:324
Malaysia: A Survey, 3:492
Malaysia: Economic Expansion and National Unity, 3:492
Malaysia: Tradition, Modernity, and Islam, 3:492
Malay Society in the Late Nineteenth Century: The Beginnings of Change, 3:492
The Malay World of Southeast Asia: A Select Cultural Bibliography, 2:311
Malcolm, 1:1033
Malcolm Lowry (Bareham), 2:919
Malcolm Lowry (Dodson), 2:919
Malcolm Lowry: A Biography, 2:919
Malcolm X, 1:1170
Malcolm X—A Voice for Black America, 4:877
The Malcolm X Reader: His Life, His Thought, His Legacy, 4:877
The Malcontent, 1:187, 1:188
The Maldive Mystery, 3:924
Malebranche: A Study of a Cartesian System, 4:182
Malebranche and British Philosophy, 4:182
Malebranche and Ideas, 4:182
The Malefactors, 1:983
Male Female Comedy Teams in American Vaudeville, 1865–1932, 3:874
The Male Muse, 1:1185
The Male Muse: A Gay Anthology, 1:1185
Male Mythologies: John Fowles and Masculinity, 1:478
Maler Nolten, 2:603
The Malformed Infant and Child: An Illustrated Guide, 5:375
Malign Fiesta, 1:514
Malina, 2:568
Malinowski and the Work of Myth, 4:486
Malinowski between Two Worlds, 3:36, 4:486

Mallarmé, or the Poet of Nothingness, 2:487
Mallarmé and the Art of Being Difficult, 2:486
Mallarmé and the Sublime, 2:487
Mallarmé's Prose Poems: A Critical Study, 2:487
Malone Dies, 2:459
Malory and Fifteenth-Century Drama, Lyrics, and Ballads, 1:147
Malory's Grail Quest, 1:155
Malory's Originality: A Critical Study of Le Morte d'Arthur, 1:155
Malraux: An Essay in Political Criticism, 2:488
The Maltese Falcon, 1:1226, 1:1230
Malthus, 3:93
Malthus and His Time, 3:92
Mama Day, 1:1021
Mama Lola: A Voodoo Priestess in Brooklyn, 4:868
The Mambo Kings Play Songs of Love, 1:988
Mame-Loshn: The Making of Yiddish, 2:31
Mammals of South-East Asia, 5:769
Mammolna: A Story about Maria Montessori, 3:266
Mammopart: An Essay in Economic Interpretation, 1:880
The Mammoth Book of Terror, 1:599
Mammoths, Mastodons, and Elephants, 5:779
Man (Hobbes), 4:174
The Man (Wallace), 1:1250
Man, Land and Myth in North Australia: The Gunwinggu People, 4:461
Man, Mind, and Science: A History of Anthropology, 3:11
Man, Science, Technology, 5:73
Man, the Manipulator, 5:424
Man, Time and World: The Anthropological Psychology of Erwin Straus, 5:470
Man Adapting, 5:795
Man against Himself, 5:464
The Man against the Sky, 1:876
Management and the Worker, 3:172

The Management of Pakistan's Economy, 1947–1982, 3:487
The Management of Smallpox Eradication in India, 5:382
A Manager's Guide to Computer Security, 5:126
Managing Business Microcomputer Systems, 5:556
Managing Change in Old Age, 4:642
Managing Gender, 3:494
Managing Hypertension, 5:375
Managing Incontinence, 5:406
Managing Industrial Enterprise: Cases from Japan's Prewar Experience, 3:480
Managing Information Technology: What Managers Need to Know, 5:544
Managing in the Emergency Medical Services: Principles and Practice, 5:381
Managing Nuclear Operations, 5:184
Managing the Commons, 5:114, 5:135
Man and Aggression, 3:170
Man and Beast in American Comic Legend, 3:871
Man and Boy, 1:540, 1:1017
Man and Crisis, 4:314, 5:96
Man and Culture, 4:486
Man and Culture: An Evaluation of the Work of Bronislaw Malinowski, 3:36
Man and His Approach to God in John Duns Scotus, 4:114
Man and His Bodies, 4:550
Man and His Myths: Tennyson's "Idylls of the King" in Critical Context, 1:401
Man and His Works, 3:269
Man and Land in Chinese History, 3:466
Man and Mouse: Animals in Medical Research, 5:782
Man and Nature: The Spiritual Crisis in Modern Man, 4:902
Man and Nature in the Renaissance, 4:125, 5:40
Man and People, 4:315
Man and Society: The Scottish Inquiry of the Eighteenth Century, 4:32
Man and Superman, 1:544, 1:545

Man and Technology:
Toward the Measurement
of a Culture, 5:69, 5:127
Man and the Environment,
5:272
The Man and the Fly, 2:526
Man and the Living World,
5:796
Man and the State, 4:296,
4:306
Man and World in the Light
of Anthroposophy, 4:858
Manassas: A Novel of the
War, 1:880
The Mandarin, 2:559
The Mandarin and the
Cadre: China's Political
Culture, 3:471
Mandarin Ducks and Butter-
flies, 2:234
Mandarins, Jews and Mis-
sionaries, 4:644
Mandatory Motherhood: The
True Meaning of "Right to
Life," 5:135
Mandela and Other Poems,
2:133
Mandela's Earth and Other
Poems, 2:148
The Mandelbaum Gate, 1:551
Mandelstam, 2:738
Mandeville's Used Book
Price Guide, 1:78
The Man Died: Prison Notes
of Wole Soyinka, 2:148,
2:149
Mandragola, 2:398, 2:435
The Mandrake, 2:402
The Mandukya Upanishad
and the Agama Sastra,
4:501, 4:507
The Man-Eating Myth: An-
thropology and Anthro-
pophagy, 4:466
Manet (Cachin), 3:780
Manet (Richardson), 3:780
Manet, 1832–1883, 3:780
Manet and His Critics, 3:780
Manet by Himself, 3:780
A Man for All Seasons,
1:194, 1:445
Man for Himself: An Inquiry
into the Psychology of
Ethics, 5:449, 5:450
Manfred, 1:271, 1:281
Manhattan Transfer, 1:828
Manhood and the American
Renaissance, 1:651
Manias, Panics, and Crashes,
3:54
Manichaeism in the Later
Roman Empire and Medi-
eval China, 4:686

Manifest Destiny and Mission
in American History: A
Reinterpretation, 3:525
Manifestoes of Surrealism,
2:462
Manifesto of the Communist
Party, 3:94
Manila: Sin City and Other
Chronicles, 2:330
Manila, 1900–1941: Social
Change in a Late Colonial
Metropolis, 3:492
Man in Estrangement: Paul
Tillich and Erich Fromm
Compared, 5:451
Man in His Time: The Best
Science Fiction Stories of
Brian W. Aldiss, 1:613
The Man in Leather
Breeches: The Life and
Times of George Fox,
4:734
Man in Nature: America be-
fore the Days of the White
Man, 3:135
The Man in the Black Coat
Turns: Poems, 1:951
The Man in the Brown Suit,
1:605, 1:606
The Man in the High Castle,
1:1257
Man in the Holocene, 2:579
Man in the Modern Age,
4:299, 5:138
The Man in the Sycamore
Tree, 4:781
"Man Is a Cause," 2:67
A Man Is Not a Flea: A Col-
lection of Stories, 2:775
Man Is the Measure, 4:19
Manitoba: A History, 3:622
Mankind, 1:157, 1:160
Mankind and Mother Earth:
A Narrative History of the
World, 3:293
Man-Machine Interface in
the Nuclear Industry,
5:111
Man-Made Minds, 5:569
Man-making Words, 2:869
Mannerhouse: A Play in a
Prologue and Four Acts,
1:904
Man of Feeling, 1:269
The Man of Letters in New
England and the South,
1:652
The Man of Mode, 1:242,
1:243
Man of Nazareth, 1:454
The Man of Reason: Male
and Female in Western
Philosophy, 4:17

Man of Reason: The Life of
Thomas Paine, 1:642
Man of Spain: A Biography
of Francis Suárez, 4:154
Man of the Moment, 1:437
A Man of the People, 2:127,
2:128
The Man-of-Words in the
West Indies, 3:853
The Manor, 1:1049, 2:48
The Manor House Novels,
1:405
The Man Outside, 2:571
Manscapes: An American
Journey, 3:895
Man's Conquest of the
Pacific, 3:493
Manservant and Maidservant,
1:462
Man's Estate: Masculine
Identity in Shakespeare,
1:209
Man's Fate, 2:487
Mansfield Park, 1:275
Man's Freedom, 4:338, 4:339
Man's Future Birthright: Es-
says on Science and Hu-
manity, 5:808
Man's Hope, 2:487
The Mansion, 1:835
The Mansions and the Shan-
ties: The Making of Mod-
ern Brazil, 2:895, 3:645
A Man Smiles at Death with
Half a Face, 2:560
Man's Place: An Essay on
Auden, 1:436
Man's Place in Nature, 4:332
Man's Place in Nature and
Other Essays, 5:799
Man's Responsibility for Na-
ture, 5:115
Man's Search for Himself,
5:463
Man's Search for Meaning:
An Introduction to Lo-
gotherapy, 5:443
Man Stands Alone, 5:798
Man's Woman, 1:776
Man the Hunter, 3:17
The Manticore, 2:910
A Mantis Carol, 3:941
Mantissa, 1:478
Mantissa Plantarum, 1767–71,
5:805
The Mantle of the Prophet:
Religion and Politics in
Modern Iran, 4:572
Mantra: Hearing the Divine
in India, 4:503
Manuale Typographicum,
1:12
A Manual for Manuel, 2:861

A Manual for Writers of Term Papers, Theses, and Dissertations, 1:118

A Manual of Comparative Typography: The Panrose System, 1:62

Manual of Cultivated Plants, 5:787

A Manual of Geology for Civil Engineers, 5:637

Manual of Hazardous Chemical Reactions, 5:725

Manual of Meteorology, 5:647

A Manual of Old English Prose, 1:143

A Manual of Parliamentary Practice for Use in the Senate of the United States, 1:640

Manual of Piety, 2:572

Manual of Political Economy, 3:99, 3:100

Manual of Ultrasound, 5:324

Manual of Zen Buddhism, 4:558

A Manual on Bookselling: How to Open and Run Your Own Bookstore, 1:45

The Manufacture and Testing of Durable Book Papers, 1:4

The Manufacture of Ink, 1:21

Manufacture of Madness, 5:429

Manufacturing Consent: The Political Economy of the Mass Media, 3:203, 3:807

Manuscripts and Documents: Their Deterioration and Restoration, 1:21

Manuscripts and Texts, 1:147

Manuscripts Don't Burn: Mikhail Bulgakov, 2:706

The Man Verdi, 3:727

The Man Who (Thought He) Looked like Robert Taylor, 2:334

The Man Who Invented Sin, 1:528

The Man Who Knew Too Much, 1:1168

The Man Who Lived His Life Over, 2:676

The Man Who Lost His Shadow, 2:58

The Man Who Loved Children, 2:963, 2:964

The Man Who Loved Laughter: The Story of Sholom Aleichem, 2:46

The Man Who Mistook His Wife for a Hat and Other Clinical Tales, 5:393, 5:428, 5:569

The Man Who Planted Hope and Grew Happiness, 2:481

The Man Who Planted Trees, 2:481

The Man Who Presumed: A Biography of Henry M. Stanley, 3:938

The Man Who Rediscovered America, a Biography of John Wesley Powell, 5:646

The Man Who Shot Liberty Valance, 1:1165

The Man Who Tasted Shapes, 5:391

The Man Who Trembled, 2:659

The Man Who Was Mark Twain: Images and Ideologies, 1:783

The Man Who Was There, 1:1017

The Man Who Would Be King and Other Stories, 1:371

The Man Who Would Be Perfect, 4:844

Man with Bags, 2:483

The Man Within, 1:488

The Man with Night Sweats: Poems, 1:491

The Man without Qualities, 2:604

The Man with the Golden Gun, 1:594

The Man with the Golden Touch, 2:799

A Many Colored Coat: Countee Cullen, 1:824

The Manyfacéd Glass: Tennyson's Dramatic Monologues, 1:401

Many Faces of Realism, 4:410

Many Inventions, 1:369

Many Loves and Other Plays, 1:900

Many Marriages, 1:811

Many Masks: A Life of Frank Lloyd Wright, 3:798

Many Moons, 1:890

Manyoshu, 2:270

The Man You Loved to Hate: Erich von Stroheim and Hollywood, 1:1177

Many Ramayanas: The Diversity of a Narrative Tradition in South Asia, 4:506

"Many Tender Ties," 3:611

Many-Windowed House, 1:822

Mao and China: A Legacy of Turmoil, 3:471

Mao and the Chinese Revolution, 2:257

Mao Papers: Anthology and Bibliography, 2:257

Mao's Harvest: Voices from China's New Generation, 2:235

Mao Tse-tung, 2:257

Mao Zedong: A Bibliography, 4:362

Map Appreciation, 5:621

A Map History of the Modern World, 3:272

Map Is Not Territory, 4:491

The Maple Leaf Forever: Essays on Nationalism and Politics in Canada, 3:617

The Mapmakers, 5:621

"The Map of All My Youth": Early Works, Friends, and Influences, 1:435

Map of Australian Verse, 2:946

A Map of Misreading, 1:1138

Map of Modern English Verse, 1:417

A Map of the World, 1:493

Mapping Literary Modernism: Time and Development, 2:986

Mapping of the World, 1472–1700: Early Printed World Maps, 5:33

Mapping Our Genes: Genome Projects—How Big, How Fast?, 5:778

Mapping the Code, 5:778

Maps, 2:122

Maps and Charts of the American Revolution, 3:505

Maps of the Mind, 3:168

Maps on File Annual Update, 1:84

The Maqamat of Badi' al-Zaman al-Hamadhani, 2:58

MA-RAI-EE, 2:324

Ma Rainey's Black Bottom, 1:1119, 1:1120

Marat/Sade, 2:614

Marbled Paper, 1:6

The Marble Faun, 1:674, 1:675

Marble Faun, and a Green Bough, 1:836

Marbles: A Play in Three Acts, 2:704

The Marble Threshing Floor, 2:371

Marbling: A History and a Bibliography, 1:5
Marcel Aymé, 2:452
Marcel Duchamp: Appearance Stripped Bare, 2:879
Marcel Proust (Peyre), 2:495
Marcel Proust (Shattuck), 2:496
Marcel Proust: A Biography (Hayman), 2:495
Marcel Proust: A Biography (Painter), 2:495
Marcel Proust: A Critical Panorama, 2:496
Marcel Proust: A Reference Guide, 2:496
March 1917, 2:760
Marching Men, 1:811
Marching to Armageddon: Canada and the Great War, 1914–1919, 3:607
Marching toward Freedom: Blacks in the Civil War, 1861–1865, 3:586
March Moonlight, 1:540
The March of Folly: From Troy to Vietnam, 3:412
The March of Literature, 1:475
March of Philosophy, 4:16
The March to Zion: United States Policy and the Founding of Israel, 3:439
Marcion: The Gospel of the Alien God, 4:686
Marco Polo: Venetian Adventurer, 3:934
Marco Polo and His Books, 3:934
Marco Polo's Asia, 3:934
Marco Polo Sings a Solo, 1:1090
Marco Zero, 2:893
Marcus Aurelius: A Biography, 4:76
Marcus Aurelius: Aspects of Civic and Cultural Policy in the East, 4:76
Marcus Aurelius: His Life and His World, 4:76
Marcus Aurelius and the Later Stoics, 4:76
Marcuse: Critical Theory and the Promise of Utopia, 4:408, 5:95
Marcuse and Freedom, 4:408, 5:94
Marcuse's Dilemma: From Marx to Freud and Beyond, 4:408, 5:94
Mardi, 1:686
Margaret Atwood, 2:907

Margaret Atwood: Vision and Forms, 2:907
Margaret Atwood and Her Works (Fiction), 2:907
Margaret Atwood and Her Works (Poetry), 2:907
Margaret Drabble, 1:468
Margaret Drabble: An Annotated Bibliography, 1:468
Margaret Drabble: A Reader's Guide, 1:468
Margaret Drabble: Existing within Structures, 1:468
Margaret Drabble: Puritanism and Permissiveness, 1:468
Margaret Fleming, 1:1070
Margaret Fuller, 1:673
Margaret Fuller: From Transcendentalism to Revolution, 1:673
Margaret Fuller: Whetstone of Genius, 1:673
Margaret Howth: A Story of Today, 1:743
Margaret Laurence: An Appreciation, 2:917
Margaret Laurence: The Long Journey Home, 2:917
Margaret Laurence and Her Works, 2:917
Margaret Mead: A Life, 3:37
Margaret Mead and Samoa, 3:37
Margaret Mitchell, 1:1249
Margaret Oliphant: A Critical Biography, 1:386
Margery Kempe and Translations of the Flesh, 1:153
The Marginal World of Ōe Kenzaburō: Themes and Techniques, 2:292
A Margin of Hope: An Intellectual Autobiography, 1:990
Margins of Philosophy, 4:397
Margot Fonteyn, 3:742
Marguerite de Navarre's Heptameron, 2:492
Marguerite Duras: Fascinating Vision and Narrative Cure, 2:474
Marguerite Duras: Writing on the Body, 2:474
Marguerite Yourcenar: A Reader's Guide, 2:517
Maria Callas: The Woman Behind the Legend, 3:687
Maria Meneghini Callas, 3:687
Maria Montessori, 3:266
Maria Montessori: A Biography, 3:266

Marian Anderson, 3:674
Marianela, 2:547
Marianne, 2:505
Marianne Moore, 1:863, 1:864
Marianne Moore: A Literary Life, 1:864
Marianne Moore: The Poetry of Engagement, 1:864
Marianne Moore: The Poet's Advance, 1:864
Marianne Moore: Vision into Verse, 1:864
Mariano Azuela, 2:854
Maria Stuart, 2:632
Marie, 2:655
Marie Curie, 5:679
Marie Curie: A Biography, 5:679
Marie Curie: A Life, 5:679
Marie Curie: The Polish Scientist Who Discovered Radium and Its Life-Saving Properties, 5:679
Marie Grubbe, 2:651
Marienbad, 2:46
Marienthal, 3:230
Marigolds in August and the Guest, 2:161
Marijuana, the Forbidden Medicine, 5:405
Marijuana Alert, 5:403
Marijuana as Medicine, 5:351
The Marijuana Question and Science's Search for an Answer, 5:403
Marilyn's Daughter, 1:1191
Marina Tsvetaeva: A Pictorial Biography, 2:768
Marina Tsvetaeva: The Woman, Her World, and Her Poetry, 2:768
Marine Geology, 5:631
Marine Mysteries and Dramatic Disasters of New England, 3:937
Marine Pollution, 5:631
Marinero en tierra, 2:528
Marino Faliero, The Two Foscari, Sardanapalus, 1:281
Mario and the Magician, 2:601, 2:602
The Marionette, 1:521
The Marion Press: A Survey and a Checklist, 1:42
Mario Vargas Llosa, 2:887
Mario Vargas Llosa: A Collection of Critical Essays, 2:887
Marital Crisis and Short-term Counseling: A Casebook, 5:418

Marital Love, 4:880

A Marital Puzzle: Trans-generational Analysis in Marriage Counseling, 5:419

Marital Therapy: A Combined Psychodynamic-Behavioral Approach, 5:420

The Maritime History of Massachusetts: 1783–1860, 3:589

The Maritime Political Boundaries of the World, 5:621

The Maritime Rights Movement, 1919–27: A Study in Canadian Regionalism, 3:615

The Maritimes and Canada before Confederation, 3:614

Marius the Epicurean, 1:386, 1:387

Marivaux's Novels, 2:488

Marjorie Daw and Other Stories, 1:732

Market, Plan, and State, 3:52

Market Centers and Retail Location: Theory and Applications, 3:127

Marketing Tourism Destinations, 3:890

The Marketing Workbench: Using Computers for Better Performance, 5:557

Marketplace Medicine: The Rise of the For-Profit Hospital Chains, 5:333

The Market Revolution: Jacksonian America, 1815–1846, 3:525

Markets or Governments: Choosing between Imperfect Alternatives, 3:68

Market Street: A Chinese Woman in Harbin, 2:246

A Market Theory of Money, 3:65, 3:84

The Mark of the Beast, 1:370

Marko Pasa, 2:100

Marko the Prince: Serbo-Croat Heroic Songs, 2:828

Marks and Monograms on European and Oriental Pottery and Porcelain, 3:765

Marks of Identity, 2:540

Mark the Evangelist, 4:825

Mark Twain, 1:783

Mark Twain: A Collection of Critical Essays, 1:784

Mark Twain: God's Fool, 1:783

Mark Twain: Selected Criticism, 1:784

Mark Twain: Social Critic, 1:783

Mark Twain: The Bachelor Years, 1:784

Mark Twain: The Development of a Writer, 1:784

Mark Twain: The Man and His Work, 1:784

Mark Twain and Bret Harte, 1:756

Mark Twain and the South, 1:784

Mark Twain as Critic, 1:784

Mark Twain at Work, 1:783

Mark Twain's Adventures of Huckleberry Finn, 1:783

Mark Twain's America, 3:576

Mark Twain's Hannibal, 1:780

Mark Twain's Last Years as a Writer, 1:784

Mark Twain's Mysterious Stranger: A Study of the Manuscript Texts, 1:784

Mark Twain's Pudd'n Head Wilson: Race, Conflict, and Culture, 1:783

Marlene Dietrich: Portraits, 1:1176

Marlowe: A Critical Study, 1:187

Marlowe: The Critical Heritage, 1:187

Marlowe and the Politics of Elizabethan Theatre, 1:187

Marmots: Social Behavior and Ecology, 5:769

The Marquise of O and Other Stories, 2:599

The Marriage, 2:813

Marriage, Divorce, Remarriage, 3:206

Marriage and Family in a Changing Society, 3:206

Marriage and Inequality in Classless Societies, 3:24

Marriage and Morals, 4:323

Marriage Blanc, 2:821

The Marriage of Bette and Boo, 1:1087

The Marriage of Figaro, 2:445, 2:457

The Marriage of Heaven and Hell, 1:278

The Marriage of Maria Braun, 3:836

The Marriage of Mr. Mississippi, 2:577

The Marriage of Zobeide, 2:593

The Marriage Proposal, 2:709

Marriages, 1:1243

Marriages and Infidelities, 1:1023

The Marriage Scenarios, 3:831

Married Life: A Novel, 2:26

The Marrow of Tradition, 1:738, 1:739

Marry Me, 1:1060

Mars, 5:609

Mars as the Abode of Life, 5:609

Marshall, Marx and Modern Times, 3:94

The Marshall Cavendish Encyclopedia of Family Health, 5:311

Marshall McLuhan: The Man and His Message, 3:818

Marshall McLuhan, the Medium and the Messenger, 3:818

The Mars Project, 5:612

Martha: The Life and Work of Martha Graham, 3:744

Martha Graham, 3:744

Martha Graham: The Early Years, 3:743

Martha Willis, 1:320

Martial and English Epigram from Sir Thomas Wyatt to Ben Jonson, 2:389

Martial and the Modern Epigram, 2:389

The Martian: A Novel, 1:352

The Martian Chronicles, 1:1252, 1:1255

Martin A. Hansen, 2:650

Martin and Malcolm and America: A Dream or a Nightmare, 4:763, 4:772

Martin Boyd: A Life, 2:951

Martin Buber: Jewish Existentialist, 4:662

Martin Buber: The Life of Dialogue, 4:662

Martin Buber on Myth: An Introduction, 4:662

Martin Buber's Social and Religious Thought, 4:662

Martin Chuzzlewit (The Life and Adventures of Martin Chuzzlewit), 1:348

Martin Eden, 1:773, 1:774

Martin Faber: The Story of a Criminal, 1:696

Martin Gardner's New Mathematical Diversions from Scientific American, 5:495

Martin Hart, 2:626

Martin Heidegger, 4:295

Martin Heidegger: A Bibliography, 4:294, 5:91

Martin Heidegger and National Socialism: Questions and Answers, 4:294
Martin Luther: An Introduction to His Life and Work, 4:778
Martin Luther: Road to Reform, 4:778
Martin Luther: The Man and His Work, 4:779
Martin Luther and the Birth of Protestantism, 4:778
Martin Luther and the Reformation, 4:778
Martin Luther King, Jr.: A Profile, 3:539
Martin Luther: Knowledge and Mediation in the Renaissance, 4:128
Martin Luther's Basic Theological Writings, 4:778
Martin Salander, 2:597
Martin—God's Court Jester: Luther in Retrospect, 4:778
Martí on the U.S.A., 2:871
Martyn Green's Treasury of Gilbert and Sullivan, 1:357
The Martyred, 2:305
The Martyred Princes Boris and Gleb, 2:688
Maru, 2:163
Marvell and the Civic Crown, 1:189
Marvell's Allegorical Poetry, 1:189
Marvelous Journey: A Survey of Four Centuries of Brazilian Writing, 2:890
The Marvelous Land of Oz, 1:1200
The Marvels of the Insect World, 5:796
Marx: An Introduction to "The Political Unconscious," 1:1150
Marx and Engels: The Intellectual Relationship, 4:227
Marx and Mill: Two Views of Social Conflict and Social Harmony, 4:244
Marx and the Marxists: The Ambiguous Legacy, 4:298
The Marxian Revolutionary Idea, 4:243
Marxism: For and Against, 3:52, 3:95
Marxism, Maoism, and Utopianism: Eight Essays, 3:471
Marxism & African Literature, 2:108

Marxism and Christianity, 4:407
Marxism and Deconstruction: A Critical Articulation, 4:267, 4:392
Marxism and Form, 1:1148, 1:1149
Marxism and Literary Criticism, 1:925, 3:202
Marxism and Literary History, 1:1127
Marxism and Literature, 1:1128
Marxism and Materialism, 4:227
Marxism and Morality, 4:243
Marxism and Philosophy (Callinicos), 4:263, 4:379
Marxism and Philosophy (Korsch), 4:243
Marxism and the Chinese Experience, 3:469
Marxism and the Philosophy of History, 3:284
Marxism in Modern France, 3:373
Marxist Literary Thought In China: The Influence of Ch'ü Ch'iu-pai, 2:234
Marxist Philosophy and the Sciences, 5:797
The Marxist Philosophy of Ernst Bloch, 4:277
Marxist Theories on Imperialism: A Critical Survey, 3:290
Marx's Concept of Man, 5:450
Marx's Politics, 4:242
Marx's Social Theory, 4:242
Marx's Theory of History, 3:290
Mary, 2:740
Mary: A History of Doctrine and Devotion, 4:678
Mary: The Feminine Face of the Church, 4:785
Mary, Queen of Scots, 3:368, 4:735
Mary, The Nazarene, The Apostle, 2:35
Mary Anne, 1:620
Mary Austin: Song of a Maverick, 1:733
Mary Austin: Woman of Genius, 1:733
Mary Baker Eddy (Bates), 4:878
Mary Baker Eddy (Eddy), 4:843
Mary Baker Eddy (Peel), 4:875

Mary Baker Eddy: A Life-Sized Portrait, 4:875
Mary Baker Eddy: An Interpretive Biography of the Founder of Christian Science, 4:875
Mary Barnes: Two Accounts of a Journey through Madness, 5:426
Mary Barton, 1:355
Mary Cassatt (Cain), 3:771
Mary Cassatt (Meyer), 3:772
Mary Cassatt: The Color Prints, 3:772
Mary Cassatt, Oils and Pastels, 3:771
Mary Chesnut's Civil War, 1:738, 3:527, 3:602
Mary E. Wilkins Freeman, 1:750
Mary Hunter Austin, 1:733
Maryknoll in China: A History 1918–1955, 4:533
Maryland Folklore, 3:860
Mary Lathrop/Who Died In/Boston/1831, 1:1194
Mary Magdalene, 1:160
Mary McCarthy (McKenzie), 1:1008
Mary McCarthy (Stock), 1:1008
Mary McCarthy: A Life, 1:1008
Mary of Scotland, 1:1081
Mary Poppins, 1:578, 1:590
Mary Poppins and the House Next Door, 1:590
Mary Poppins Comes Back, 1:590
Mary Poppins from A to Z, 1:590
Mary Poppins in Cherry Tree Lane, 1:590
Mary Poppins in the Park, 1:590
Mary Poppins Opens the Door, 1:590
Mary Ritter Beard: A Sourcebook, 3:566
Mary Shelley, 1:301
Mary Shelley: An Annotated Bibliography, 1:301
Mary Shelley: Her Life, Her Fiction, Her Monsters, 1:301
Mary Shelley: Romance and Reality, 1:301
Mary Stuart, 2:609
Mary Tjosvold, 5:420
Mary Tudor, the White Queen, 4:727
Mary Wilkins Freeman, 1:750

MASA: Medical Acronyms, Symbols and Abbreviations, 5:6

Masada: Herod's Last Fortress and the Zealots' Last Stand, 4:614

Masaoka Shiki, 2:288

Ma'sāt al-Hallāj, 2:61

Mascara, 2:864

Masers and Lasers: An Historical Approach, 5:666, 5:718

Mask and Tragedy: Yeats and Nietzsche, 1902–1910, 1:572

A Mask Dancing: Nigerian Novelists of the Eighties, 2:110

A Mask for Janus, 1:1015

The Mask of Comedy: Aristophanes and the Intertextual Parabasis, 2:353

The Mask of Fu Manchu, 1:597

The Mask of Keats, 1:294

The Mask of Power: Seneca's Tragedies and Imperial Power, 2:394, 4:88

Masks (Braithwaite), 2:933

Masks (Onnamen), 2:286

Masks and Faces, 1:272

The Masks Jews Wear: Self-Deceptions of American Jewry, 4:661

Masks of Conquest: Literary Study and British Rule in India, 1:313

Masks of Fiction in Dream of the Red Chamber, 2:223

The Masks of God, 3:876, 4:428

The Masks of "Hamlet," 1:213

The Masks of "King Lear," 1:214

Masks of Loneliness: Alfred Adler in Perspective, 5:431

The Masks of "Macbeth," 1:214

The Masks of "Othello," 1:214

Masks of the Universe, 5:595, 5:655

Masks Outrageous and Austere, 1:800

Maslow's Motivation and Personality, 3:175

Masnavi, 2:92

Masochism: A Jungian View, 5:456

Masonic Jurisprudence, 3:145

Mason Wade, Acadia and Quebec: The Perception of an Outsider, 3:606

The Masquerade (Clark), 2:133

Masquerade (Dailey), 1:1221

Masquerade Time, 2:136

Masques of God: Form and Theme in the Poetry of Henry Vaughan, 1:200

Mass, 2:331

Massageworks: A Practical Encyclopedia of Massage Techniques, 5:319

Mass and Elite in Democratic Athens, 3:302

Masscheroen, 2:623

Mass Communication: Producers and Consumers, 3:803

Mass Communication Law: Cases and Comments, 3:801

Mass Communications and American Empire, 3:804

Masses and Man: Nationalist and Fascist Perceptions of Reality, 3:344

Mass Extinctions: Processes and Evidence, 3:18

Mass Media, 3:801, 3:803

Mass Media and American Politics, 3:147

Mass Media Bibliography, 3:801, 3:802

The Mass of the Roman Rite: Its Origins and Development, 4:689

The Mastadon and the Condors, 2:320

Master Album of Pictorial Calligraphy and Scrollwork, 1:16

Master and Man and Other Stories, 2:764

The Master and Margarita, 2:705, 2:706

The Master Book of Mathematical Puzzles and Recreations, 5:497

The Master Builder, 2:665

The Master Builder and Other Plays, 2:666

The Master Builders, 5:245

Master European Realists of the Nineteenth Century, 2:986

Master Eustace, 1:763

Master Harold & the Boys, 2:161

Master Humphrey's Clock, 1:348

Mastering Italic Calligraphy, 1:13

The Master Key: An Electric Fairy Tale, 1:1199

Masterman Ready, 1:374

The Master of Ballantrae, 1:395, 1:396

The Master of Go, 2:288

The Master of Hestviken, 2:668, 2:669

The Master of Light: A Biography of Albert A. Michelson, 5:702

The Master of Modern French Criticism, 2:446

Master of the Moor, 1:609

Master of Villainy: A Biography of Sax Rohmer, 1:597

Master of Wisdom: Writings of the Buddhist Master Nagarjuna, 4:513

Masterpiece, 2:518

Masterpieces of African-American Literature, 1:132

Masterpieces of Hebrew Literature, 2:10

Masterpieces of Humor, 3:872

Masterpieces of Latin American Literature, 2:849

Masterpieces of Modern Chinese Fiction, 1919–1949, 2:256

Masterpieces of Modern Spanish Drama, 2:526

Masterpieces of World Literature, 1:122

Masterpieces of World Philosophy, 4:2

Master Poems from Modern Korea, 2:299

The Master Puppeteer, 1:1204

The Masters, 1:550

Masters, Princes, and Merchants, 4:698

The Masters and the Slaves: A Study in the Development of Brazilian Civilization, 2:894, 2:895, 3:209, 3:645

A Master's Bibliophile Bindings: Tini Miura 1980–1990, 1:25

The Master's House: A Tale of Southern Life, 1:703

Master Sijo Poems from Korea, 2:299

Masters of Ancient Comedy, 2:349

Masters of Light: Conversations with Contemporary Cinematographers, 3:826

Masters of Modern Drama, 2:4

Masters of Social Psychology: Freud, Mead, Lewin, and Skinner, 3:190, 3:184, 3:194, 3:233, 4:309

Masters of Sociological Thought: Ideas in Historical and Social Context, 3:200, 3:234

The Masters of the Dew, 2:941

Masters of the Keyboard, 3:664

Master Space: Film Images of Capra, Lubitsch, Sternberg and Wyler, 3:828

Masters without Slaves, 3:529

Masterworks of the No Theater, 2:274

Mastery Teaching, 3:256

Mastika, 2:326

Mastro-don Gesualdo, 2:441

The Matachines, 1:560

The Matador of the Five Towns and Other Stories, 1:444

The Matchmaker, 1:1116, 2:910

Mateo Alemán, 2:530

The Materials and Techniques of Painting, 5:194

Materials for the History of the Text of the Qur'an, 4:587

Maternal and Child Nutrition, 5:348

Maternal Care and Mental Health, 5:421

The Mathematical Analysis of Logic, 5:499

Mathematical Astronomy in Copernicus's De Revolutionibus, 5:40

The Mathematical Career of Pierre de Fermat, 5:506

Mathematical Carnival, 5:507

Mathematical Circus, 5:507

Mathematical Diversions, 5:496

Mathematical Economics: Twenty Papers of Gerard Debreu, 3:63

The Mathematical Experience, 5:481

Mathematical Ideas, 5:481

Mathematical Investigations in the Theory of Value and Price Appreciation and Interest, 3:76

Mathematical Logic, 4:411

Mathematical Magic Show, 5:496, 5:507

The Mathematical Papers of Isaac Newton, 5:512

The Mathematical Philosophy of Bertrand Russell, 5:103

Mathematical Principles of Natural Philosophy, 4:183

Mathematical Principles of Natural Philosophy and His System of the World, 5:706

The Mathematical Science of Christopher Wren, 3:796

Mathematical Snapshots, 5:495

The Mathematical Theory of Black Holes, 5:677

The Mathematical Theory of Communication, 5:571, 5:581

The Mathematical Theory of Huygen's Principle, 5:695

The Mathematical Theory of Relativity, 5:680, 5:681

Mathematical Thought: An Introduction to the Philosophy of Mathematics, 5:493

Mathematical Thought from Ancient to Modern Times, 5:31, 5:492

The Mathematical Works of Isaac Newton, 5:512

Mathematician's Apology, 5:494

Mathematico-Deductive Theory of Rote Learning, 3:186

Mathematics: An Introduction to Its Spirit and Use, 5:481

Mathematics—Its Contents, Methods and Meanings, 5:480

Mathematics, Magic, and Mystery, 5:507

Mathematics, Metaphysics and the Power of the Scientific Mind, 4:323

Mathematics and Science: An Adventure in Postage Stamps, 5:496

Mathematics and the Search for Knowledge, 5:31

Mathematics Dictionary, 5:479

Mathematics for the Non-Mathematician, 5:481

Mathematics in Aristotle, 4:68

Mathematics in Economics, 3:64

Mathematics in Society and History: Sociological Enquiries, 5:31

Mathematics in the Time of the Pharaohs, 5:38

Mathematics in Western Culture, 5:31, 5:481, 5:492

The Mathematics of Plato's Academy, 4:80

Mathematics Today: Twelve Informal Essays, 5:482

Mathematics Tomorrow, 5:482

Mathematische Annalen, 5:509

Mathematische Werke, 5:517

The Mathers: Three Generations of Puritan Intellectuals, 1596–1728, 1:628, 3:518

The Mathnawi of Jalalu'ddin Rumi, 4:589

Math Talk, 3:256

Matigari, 2:154

Matisse, 3:781

Matisse in the Collection of the Museum of Modern Art, 3:781

The Matriarch, 2:977

Matrilineal Kinship, 3:17, 3:20

The Matrix and Diamond World Mandalas in Shingon Buddhism, 4:538

Matrix and Line, 4:398

Matrix Computer Networks and Conferencing Systems, 5:547

The Matrix of Modernism, 1:800

Matsuo Bashō, 2:276

Matsuri: Festivals of a Japanese Town, 4:539

Matter, Energy and Life: An Introduction to Chemical Concepts, 5:774

Matter, Life and Generation, 5:45

Matter, Mind and Man: The Biology of Human Nature, 5:811

Matter and Memory, 4:220

Matter and Motion, 5:700

The Matter Myth, 5:15

Matter of Glory: A New Preface to Paradise Lost, 1:193

The Matter of My Book: Montaigne's "Essais" as the Book of the Self, 2:491, 4:146

Matter of Prejudice and Other Stories, 1:740

A Matter of Principle, 4:386

Matters Gray and White, 5:393

Matters of Life and Death: New American Stories, 1:806, 1:915, 1:922
Matters of Life and Death: Risks vs. Benefits of Medical Care, 5:405
Matthew Arnold, 1:328
Matthew Arnold: A Life, 1:328
Matthew Arnold: The Poet as Humanist, 1:328
Matthew Arnold and the Betrayal of Language, 1:328
Matthew Arnold in His Time and Ours, 1:328
Matthew Carey, Editor, Author and Publisher, 1:40
Matthew G. Lewis, Charles Robert Maturin and the Germans, 1:602
The Maturational Processes and the Facilitating Environment, 5:472
Maude: Prose and Verse, 1:390
Maugham: A Biography, 1:521
Maugham: A Reappraisal, 1:521
Maupassant: The Semiotics of Text, 2:489
Maupassant the Novelist, 2:489
Maurice, 1:476
Maurice Guest, 2:961
Maus: A Survivor's Tale, 4:637
Mauser, 2:603
Mavis Gallant and Her Works, 2:912
Max and Moritz, 2:574
Max and the Cats, 2:899
Max Beerbohm, Or The Dandy Dante: Rereading with Mirrors, 1:441
Max Beerbohm and the Act of Writing, 1:441
Max Brand, Western Giant: The Life and Times of Frederick Faust, 1:1212
Max Havelaar, 2:316, 2:621, 2:628
Maxim Gorky (Hare), 2:726
Maxim Gorky (Scherr), 2:726
The Maxims (La Rochefoucauld), 2:485
Maxims (Roosevelt), 3:594
Maximum Life Span, 5:318
Max Scheler: The Man and His Works, 4:332
Max Scheler, 1874–1928: An Intellectual Portrait, 4:332

Max Scheler's Concept of the Person: An Ethics of Humanism, 4:332
Max's Nineties: Drawings 1892–1899, 1:440
Max Weber: An Intellectual Portrait, 3:244
Max Weber on Economy and Society, 3:244
Maxwell Anderson, 1:1082
Maxwell Anderson: An Annotated Bibliography, 1:1082
Maxwell on Saturn's Rings, 5:701
Maxwell Perkins: Editor of Genius, 1:43
The Maya, 3:627
Maya: The Riddle and Rediscovery of a Lost Civilization, 3:627
Maya History and Religion, 4:456
Mayakovsky: A Poet in Revolution, 2:739
The Mayakovsky Case, 2:886
Mayakovsky My Love, 2:739
Mayakovsky's Cubo-Futurist Vision, 2:739
Maybe You Should Write a Book, 1:41
May Fourth Movement: Intellectual Revolution in Modern China, 2:233
May Man Prevail? 5:449, 5:450
The May Massee Collection: Creative Publishing for Children, 1923–1963, 1:42
Mayo Clinic Family Health Book: The Ultimate Home Medical Reference, 5:311
Mayonnaise and the Origin of Life, 5:765
The Mayor of Casterbridge, 1:360, 1:361
The Mayor of Zalamea, 2:532, 2:533
May You Be the Mother of a Hundred Sons, 4:508
The Maze of Ingenuity, 5:37, 5:232
The Maze of Justice, 2:63, 2:64
Mazeppa, 1:281
al-Mazini's Egypt, 2:59
M Butterfly, 1:1095
The McGraw-Hill Book of Poetry, 2:4
The McGraw-Hill Computer Handbook, 5:540

McGraw-Hill Concise Encyclopedia of Science and Technology, 5:2, 5:29, 5:725
McGraw-Hill Dictionary of Electrical and Electronic Engineering, 5:230
McGraw-Hill Dictionary of Electronics and Computers, 5:540
McGraw-Hill Dictionary of Engineering, 5:217
McGraw-Hill Dictionary of Information Technology and Computer Acronyms, Initials, and Abbreviations, 5:541
McGraw-Hill Dictionary of Science and Engineering, 5:216
McGraw-Hill Dictionary of Scientific and Technical Terms, 5:2, 5:216
McGraw-Hill Encyclopedia of Astronomy, 5:588
McGraw-Hill Encyclopedia of Chemistry, 5:725
McGraw-Hill Encyclopedia of Environmental Science and Engineering, 5:816
McGraw-Hill Encyclopedia of Geological Sciences, 5:617
McGraw-Hill Encyclopedia of Physics, 5:653
McGraw-Hill Encyclopedia of Science and Technology, 5:2, 5:29, 5:479, 5:653, 5:725
McGraw-Hill Encyclopedia of World Drama, 1:131, 2:3
McGraw-Hill Personal Computer Programming Encyclopedia, 5:539, 5:549
The McGraw-Hill Style Manual: Concise Guide for Writers and Editors, 1:118
McGraw-Hill Yearbook of Science and Technology, 1992, 5:2
McTeague, 1:776
Mead and Merleau-Ponty: Toward a Common Vision, 4:309, 4:311
Me Again: The Uncollected Writings of Stevie Smith, Illustrated by Herself, 1:549
Meaning and Action: A Critical History of Pragmatism, 4:268
Meaning and Being in Myth, 4:428

The Meaning and End of Religion, 4:422

Meaning and Medicine: A Doctor's Tales of Breakthrough and Healing, 5:369

Meaning and Method, 4:411

Meaning and Necessity: A Study in Semantics and Modal Logic, 4:278, 5:85

The Meaning and Uses of Polish History, 3:390

Meaning in Henry James, 1:765

The Meaning of Anxiety, 5:463

The Meaning of Contemporary Realism, 2:801

The Meaning of Criminal Insanity, 5:426

The Meaning of Evolution, 5:794

Meaning of Evolution: A Study of the History of Life and Its Significance for Man, 5:639

The Meaning of Fossils: Episodes in the History of Palaeontology, 5:34

The Meaning of Freedom, 3:528

The Meaning of God in Human Experience, 4:296

The Meaning of Heidegger, 4:294

The Meaning of Human History, 3:275, 4:281

The Meaning of Icons, 4:693

The Meaning of Immortality in Human Experience, Including Thoughts on Life and Death, 4:296

The Meaning of Independence, 3:588

The Meaning of Language, 4:383

The Meaning of Life: Essays by the Author of Language, Truth and Logic, 4:273

The Meaning of Life: Questions, Answers, and Analysis, 4:24

The Meaning of More's Utopia, 1:194, 4:147

Meaning of Relativity, 5:682

The Meaning of Stoicism, 4:56

The Meaning of the City, 5:163, 5:164

The Meaning of the Glorious Koran, 4:587

The Meaning of Treason, 1:566

The Meaning of Truth: A Sequel to Pragmatism, 4:236

The Meaning of Yiddish, 2:32

The Meanings of Death, 4:887

Measure for Measure, 1:205, 1:206, 1:210

Measurement of Adult Intelligence, 3:196

A Measure of Malpractice, 5:344

Measures of Personality and Social Psychological Attitudes, 3:169

Measuring Business Cycles, 3:49, 3:97

Measuring Personality Adjustment in Children Nine to Thirteen Years of Age, 5:468

Measuring the Universe: Cosmic Dimensions from Aristarchus to Halley, 5:32

Mechanic Accents: Dime Novels and Working-Class Culture in America, 1:722, 3:559

Mechanical and Electrical Equipment for Buildings, 5:236

The Mechanical Bride, 3:818

Mechanical Design and Systems Handbook, 5:236

The Mechanical Engineer in America, 1830–1910, 5:36

Mechanical Intelligence, 5:582

The Mechanical Investigations of Leonardo da Vinci, 3:780, 5:193

Mechanical Metamorphosis, 5:232

The Mechanical Universe: Introduction to Mechanics and Heat, 5:653

The Mechanic and the Gardener, 5:319

Mechanick Exercises on the Whole Art of Printing, 1:10

Mechanics: Classical and Quantum, 5:661

Mechanics in Sixteenth-Century Italy, 4:125, 5:40

Mechanics of Oil Shale, 5:635

The Mechanism of Mendelian Heredity, 5:807, 5:808

The Mechanization of the World Picture: Pythagoras to Newton, 4:125, 5:25

Mechanization Takes Command, 5:25, 5:263, 5:573

Medea, 2:355, 2:356, 2:431, 2:584

Media and the American Mind: From Morse to McLuhan, 3:803

The Media and the Gulf War: The Press and Democracy in Wartime, 3:809

Media Ethics: Cases and Moral Reasoning, 3:803, 5:125

The Media Lab: Inventing the Future at MIT, 5:567

The Media Monopoly, 3:802

Media Performance: Mass Communication and the Public Interest, 3:803

Media Speak: How Television Makes Up Your Mind, 3:811

The Mediating Self: Mead, Sartre, and Self-Determination, 4:308

Medicaid in the Reagan Era: Federal Policy and State Choices, 5:333

Medical and Health Information Directory, 5:6

Medical Applications of Clinical Nutrition, 5:394

A Medical Bibliography, 5:50

Medical Botany: Plants Affecting Man's Health, 5:351

Medical Care, Morbidity and Costs, 5:331

Medical Choices, Medical Chances, 5:339

Medical Costs, Medical Choices, 5:79

The Medical Detectives, 5:383

Medical Ethics, 5:144

Medical Ethics: A Clinical Textbook and Reference for the Health Care Professions, 5:118

Medical Ethics: The Moral Responsibilities of Physicians, 5:132

The Medical Industrial Complex, 5:329

Medical Informatics: Computer Applications in Health Care, 5:80

Medical Law, Ethics, and Bioethics in the Medical Office, 5:122

Medical Malpractice Litigation, 5:344

The Medical Messiahs, 5:315

Medical Nemesis: The Expropriation of Health, 5:79, 5:136, 5:137, 5:336

Medical Odysseys, 5:315

Medical Problem Solving: An Analysis of Clinical Reasoning, 5:79

Medical Quotes: A Thematic Dictionary, 5:13

The Medical Renaissance of the Sixteenth Century, 5:41

Medical Research with Children: Ethics, Law, and Practice, 5:122

Medical Science and the Advancement of World Health, 5:330

Medical Secretary's and Assistant's Encyclopedic Dictionary, 5:311

Medical Technician: The Layperson's Guide to Today's Medical Miracles, 5:368

Medical Technology and Society: An Interdisciplinary Perspective, 5:12, 5:119

Medical Thinking: A Historical Preface, 5:313

The Medical Triangle: Physicians, Politicians, and the Public, 5:334

The Medical Wars, 5:353

Medical Word Finder: A Reverse Medical Dictionary, 5:6

Medicinal Plants and Traditional Medicine in Africa, 5:320

Medicine, 5:13

Medicine: The State of the Art, 5:405

Medicine, Money, and Morals: Physicians' Conflicts of Interest, 5:123

Medicine and Its Technology, 5:370

Medicine and Society in America: 1660–1860, 5:36

Medicine and the Reign of Technology, 5:324

Medicine at the Crossroads, 5:334

Medicine for the Outdoors, 5:381

Medicine in America: A Short History, 5:13

Medicine's Great Journey: One Hundred Years of Healing, 5:315

Medieval and Tudor Drama, 1:158

Medieval Armenian Culture, 2:77

Medieval Aspects of Renaissance Learning: Three Essays, 4:128

Medieval Calligraphy: Its History and Technique, 1:14

The Medieval Charlemagne Legend: An Annotated Bibliography, 3:372

The Medieval Church, 4:691

Medieval Cities, 3:407

Medieval Cities: Their Origins and the Revival of Trade, 3:331, 3:407

Medieval Cosmology, Theories of Infinity, Place, Time, Void and the Plurality of Worlds, 4:97

Medieval Cultural Tradition in Dante's Comedy, 2:418

Medieval Drama, 1:158

Medieval Dream-Poetry, 1:147

Medieval England: An Aerial Survey, 3:355

The Medieval English Economy, 1150–1500, 3:357

Medieval English Literature, 1:141

Medieval English Lyrics: A Critical Anthology, 1:148

Medieval English Prose for Women, 1:147

Medieval English Verse, 1:148

Medieval Europe: A Short History, 3:331

The Medieval Expansion of Europe, 3:331

Medieval Handbooks of Penance, 4:700

Medieval Heresy: Popular Movements from Bogomil to Hus, 4:699, 4:721

The Medieval Heritage of Mexico, 3:630

Medieval Humanism and Other Studies, 4:96

Medieval Iceland: Society, Sagas and Power, 3:381

The Medieval Imagination, 4:697

The Medieval Inquisition, 4:700

The Medieval Inquisition: Foundations of Medieval History, 4:699

Medieval Islam: A Study in Cultural Orientation, 4:573

Medieval Japan: Essays in Institutional History, 3:475

Medieval Jewish Life, 4:622

Medieval Jewry in Northern France: A Political and Social History, 4:623

Medieval Liturgy: An Introduction to the Sources, 4:701

Medieval Logic: An Outline of Its Development from 1250–1400, 4:97

The Medieval Lyric, 1:149

The Medieval Machine: The Industrial Revolution of the Middle Ages, 3:331, 5:39

The Medieval Mind, 4:96

Medieval Monasticism, 3:331, 4:699

Medieval Music: The Sixth Liberal Art, 3:655

The Medieval Near East: Social and Economic History, 3:434

Medieval Netherlands Religious Literature, 2:621

The Medieval Papacy, 4:694

Medieval People, 3:331

Medieval Persian Court Poetry, 2:83

Medieval Philosophy, 4:39

Medieval Philosophy: From St. Augustine to Nicholas of Cusa, 4:95

Medieval Political Ideas, 4:98

Medieval Political Philosophy: A Sourcebook, 4:95

Medieval Reformation, 4:691

Medieval Religion and Technology: Collected Essays, 5:58, 5:199

Medieval Religious Women I: Distant Echoes, 4:700

Medieval Russian Laws, 3:413

Medieval Russia's Epics, Chronicles, and Tales, 2:694, 2:838

The Medieval Saga, 2:640

Medieval Science and Technology: A Selected, Annotated Bibliography, 5:28

Medieval Society, 3:331

Medieval Spanish Allegory, 2:523

Medieval Technology and Social Change, 3:332, 5:40, 5:58

The Medieval Theatre, 1:158

Medieval Theatre in the Round, 1:161

Medieval Thought from Saint Augustine to Ockham, 4:697

Medieval to Renaissance in English Poetry, 1:147

The Medieval Town, 3:331

The Medieval Tradition of Natural Law, 4:98

The Medieval Universities, 4:101

Medieval Wales, 3:369

Medieval Women, 3:331, 4:700

The Medieval World: Europe 1100 to 1350, 3:331

Medieval Writers and Their Work, 1:146

Meditating on the Word, 4:760

Meditation in Action, 4:357

Meditation on the Threshold: A Bilingual Anthology of Poetry, 2:861

Meditation on Violence, 1:1163

Meditations (Aurelius), 4:76

Meditations (Krishnamurti), 4:555

Meditations: Essays on Brecht, Beckett and the Media, 2:460

Meditations at 10,000 Feet: A Scientist in the Mountains, 5:19

Meditations at Sunset: A Scientist Looks at the Sky, 5:19

Meditations of a Maverick Rabbi, 4:648

The Meditations of Marcus Aurelius: A Study, 4:59, 4:76

Meditations of the Lover, 2:301

Meditations on First Philosophy, 4:168, 4:169

Meditations on Hunting, 4:315

The Mediterranean and the Mediterranean World in the Age of Philip II, 3:283, 3:336

A Mediterranean Society, 4:626

Mediterranean Valleys: Geological Change in Historical Times, 3:438

The Medium Is the Message, 3:818

Medium Rare: A Look at the Book and Its People, 1:49

Mediums, and Spirit-Rappers, and Roaring Radicals, 4:851

The Medusa and the Snail: More Notes of a Biology Watcher, 5:19, 5:766

Medusa's Hair: An Essay on Personal Symbols and Religious Experience, 3:24, 4:424

Meek Heritage, 2:660

The Meeting at Teltge, 2:583

Meeting at the Last Judgment, 2:824

A Meeting by the River, 1:500

Meeting Evil, 1:949

Meetinghouse Hill, 1630–1783, 3:518

The Meeting Point, 2:934

Meetings with Pasternak: A Memoir, 2:746

Meetings with Remarkable Men, 4:875

Meetings with Remarkable Women: Buddhist Teachers in America, 4:515

Meeting the Expectations of the Land, 5:269, 5:272, 5:823

Meet Me in the Green Glen, 1:892

Meg, 2:975

The Megalithic Monuments of Western Europe: The Latest Evidence, 4:434

Megalithomania, 4:434

Megalopolis: The Urbanized Northeastern Seaboard of the United States, 3:130, 3:216

Megascience and Its Background, 5:186

Megatrends: Ten New Directions Transforming Our Lives, 5:573

Me Grandad 'ad an Elephant: Three Stories of Muslim Life in South India, 2:177

The Meiji Restoration, 3:476

Mein Kampf, 3:377

Meister Eckhart: A Modern Translation, 4:708

Meister Eckhart: Teacher and Preacher, 4:708

Meister Eckhart: The Essential Sermons, Commentaries, Treatises, and Defense, 4:708

Meister Eckhart: Thought and Language, 4:102, 4:709

Mei Yao-ch'en and the Development of Early Sung Poetry, 2:214

Mekhilta According to R. Ishmael: An Analytical Translation, 4:611

Mekhilta According to R. Ishmael: An Introduction to Judaism's First Scriptural Encyclopaedia, 4:611

Mekilta Derabbi Ishmael, 4:610

Melancholy and the Secular Mind in Spanish Golden Age Literature, 2:523

Melancholy Man: A Study of Dickens' Novels, 1:350

Melanchthon: The Quiet Reformer, 4:730

Melanctha, 1:881

Melbourne, 3:365

Melincourt, 1:297

Mellichampe: A Legend of the Santee, 1:696

Melloni's Illustrated Medical Dictionary, 5:311

Melmouth the Wanderer, 1:269

Melodrama Classics: Six Plays and How to Stage Them, 1:323

The Melodramatic Imagination, 2:454

The Melodramatists, 1:1021

The Melody Lingers On, 3:667

Melon: A Play, 1:486

A Melville Encyclopedia: The Novels, 1:689

Melville J. Herskovits, 3:32

The Melville Log, 1:689

Melville's Later Novels, 1:688

Melville's Major Fiction: Politics, Theology, and Imagination, 1:688

Melville's Reading, 1:689

Melville's Sources, 1:688

A Member of the Third House, 1:751

The Member of the Wedding, 1:1009, 1:1101, 1:1102

Memed, My Hawk, 2:100

Memento Mori, 1:550, 1:551

Mémoires d'Outre-Tombe, 2:466

Memoir of a Revolution, 3:392

Memoir of a Russian Punk, 2:737

Memoir of a Thinking Radish: An Autobiography, 5:18, 5:314, 5:765

Memoir of Jane Austen, by Her Nephew, 1:276
Memoir of the Life and Labours of the Late Charles Babbage Esq., F.R.S., 5:575
A Memoir of the Warsaw Uprising, 2:812
Memoir on Heat, 5:749
Memoir on the Pancreas and on the Role of Pancreatic Juice in Digestive Processes, 5:789
Memoirs: Autobiography—First Draft and Journal (Yeats), 1:572
Memoirs, 1925–1963, 3:584
Memoirs Found in a Bathtub, 2:816
Memoirs from the Women's Prison, 2:72
Memoirs of a Dissident Publisher, 1:43
Memoirs of a Dutiful Daughter, 2:458
Memoirs of a Good-for-Nothing, 2:578
Memoirs of a Korean Queen, 2:302
The Memoirs of Alexander Herzen, 2:728
Memoirs of American Jews: 1775–1865, 4:640
Memoirs of a Midget, 1:466, 1:467
Memoirs of an Unregulated Economist, 3:108
Memoirs of an Unrepentant Field Geologist, 5:624
Memoirs of a Revolutionary, 3:397
Memoirs of a Tourist, 2:511
Memoirs of a Woman Doctor, 2:71
The Memoirs of Gluckel of Hamelin, 4:623
Memoirs of Hadrian, 2:517
Memoirs of Hecate County, 1:901, 1:902
Memoirs of Many in One, by Alex Xenophon Demirjian Gray, 2:966
Memoirs of My Dead Life, 1:380
The Memoirs of Sherlock Holmes, 1:607
Memoirs of Sir Walter Scott, 1:300
Memoirs of the Reign of King George II, 1:262
Memoirs of the Reign of King George III, 1:263

Memoirs of the Second World War, 3:365, 3:400
Memoirs on Fossil Elephants and on Reconstruction of the Genera Palaeotherium and Anoplotherium, 5:792
Memorabilia, 3:324, 4:91
The Memorandum, 2:791
Memorandum on Popular Education, 1:368
The Memorial, 1:500
Memorial Essays, 4:273
Memories, Dreams, Reflections, 5:455
Memories and Adventures, 1:608
Memories and Studies, 4:236
Memories for Paul de Man, 1:1143, 4:397
Memories of Evil Days, 2:482
Memories of Happy Days, 2:482
Memories of Home: The Writings of Alex La Guma, 2:165
Memories of Midnight, 1:1222
Memories of My Life, 5:529
Memory and Other Poems, 1:466
Memory Babe: A Critical Biography of Jack Kerouac, 1:999
Memory Gardens, 1:965
A Memory of Two Mondays, 1:1104
The Memory Palace of Matteo Ricci, 3:469
Men, Machines, and Modern Times, 5:71, 5:232
Men, Women, and Aggression, 3:170
Men, Women, and Boats, 1:741
Men, Women and Dogs, 1:890
Men, Women and Pianos, 3:672
The Menace, 1:491
The Menaechmus Twins and Two Other Plays, 2:391
Men and Angels: Three South American Comedies, 2:849
Men and Brethren, 1:964
Men and Centuries, 3:408
Menander: A Commentary, 2:364
Men and Masks: A Study of Molière, 2:490
Men and Not Men, 2:443
Men and Women, 1:338
Men at Arms, 1:562

Men at War, 1:845
Mencken and Sara: A Life in Letters, 1:860
Mendele Mocher Seforim, 2:41
Mendelssohn, 3:706
Mendelssohn and Schumann: Essays on Their Music and Its Context, 3:706
Men from Earth, 3:911
Meng Hao-jan, 2:215
Menina e Moça, 2:556
Men in Dark Times, 3:281, 3:282, 4:394
Men in Feminism, 1:1134
Men in the Sun and Other Palestinian Stories, 2:67
Menninger: The Family and the Clinic, 5:464
Men of Good Will, 2:502
Men of Iron, 1:1205
Men of Maize, 2:854
Men of Mathematics, 5:527
Men of Power, 5:809
Men of Science in America, 5:25
The Men of the Old Stone Age: Palaeolithic and Mesolithic, 4:432
The Menopause, 5:355
Menopause: A Guide for Women and the Men Who Love Them, 5:355
Menopause, Naturally: Preparing for the Second Half of Life, 5:355
Menopause and Midlife Health, 5:356
Mensius and Aquinas: Theories of Virtue and Conceptions of Courage, 4:897
Men's Lives: Surfmen and Baymen of the South Fork, 3:930
Men's Private Parts: An Owner's Manual, 5:341
Men's Work, Women's Work, 3:207
Mental and Physical Health Practices of Older People, 5:316
Mental Deficiency: The Changing Outlook, 5:426
Mental Handicap: Social Science Perspectives, 3:201
Mental Health: Philosophical Perspectives, 5:80
Mental Illness and American Society, 1875–1940, 3:552
Mental Illness and Psychology, 4:400, 5:443
Mentality and Machines, 5:75
Mental Machinery, 5:35

Mental Retardation: From Categories to People, 5:426

Mental Retardation: The Changing Outlook, 5:426

A Mental Theater: Poetic Drama and Consciousness in the Romantic Age, 1:272

The Mentor Book of Major British Poets, 1:419

Mentoria; or The Young Lady's Friend, 1:643

Men Who Made a New Physics: Physicists and the Quantum Theory, 5:661

Men without Art, 1:514

Men without Childhood, 2:81

Men without Mercy, 2:576

Men without Women, 1:844, 1:845

Merce Cunningham, 3:740

Merce Cunningham: Dancing in Space and Time, Essays 1944–1992, 3:740

Mercer Dictionary of the Bible, 4:5, 4:818

The Merchant, 1:565

The Merchant of Venice, 1:205, 1:206

Merci, or the Adventures of Shipov, 2:743

Merciful Disguises: Poems Published and Unpublished, 1:1061

Merck Index: An Encyclopedia of Chemicals, Drugs, and Biologicals, 5:725

The Merck Manual of Diagnosis and Therapy, 5:6, 5:405

Mercury Theatre of the Air, 1:1178

Mercy Philbrick's Choice, 1:760

Meredith: The Critical Heritage, 1:379

The Merger of Knowledge with Power: Essays in Critical Science, 5:157

Meridian, 1:1064

The Meridian Anthology of Early American Women Writers, 1:629, 1:717

Merit and Responsibility: A Study in Greek Values, 4:47

Merleau-Ponty and Marxism: From Terror to Reform, 4:311

Merleau-Ponty and Metaphor, 4:311

Merleau-Ponty and the Foundation of an Existential Politic, 4:311

Mermaids in the Basement: Poems for Women, 1:1001

The Merriam-Webster Dictionary, 1:90

Merriam-Webster's Collegiate Dictionary Tenth Edition, 1:90

The Merriam-Webster Thesaurus, 1:94

Merrily We Sing: One Hundred Five Polish Folksongs, 3:852

The Merry Adventures of Robin Hood, 1:1205

The Merry-Go-Round in the Sea, 2:964

The Merry Muses of Caledonia, 1:280

Merry Tales and Three Shrovetide Plays, 2:608

The Merry Wives of Windsor, 1:205, 1:206

Merton: A Biography, 4:781

Merton: By Those Who Knew Him Best, 4:781

Merton of the Movies, 1:1097

Mes Chansons de Toujours, 2:156

Meshes of the Afternoon, 1:1162

Mesmerism and the American Cure of Souls, 4:847

Mesmerism and the End of the Enlightenment in France, 5:44

The Mesoamerican Ballgame, 3:628, 4:456

Mesoamerican Writing Systems, 3:628

Mesolithic Prelude, 4:433

Message and Existence: An Introduction to Christian Theology, 5:201

The Message of Jesus Christ, 4:552

The Message of the Gita: With Text, Translation and Notes, 4:353

The Message of the Prophets, 4:823, 4:838

Messages: Poems from Ghana, 2:126

Messengers of God: Biblical Portraits and Legends, 1:1065

Messengers of the Day, 1:536

The Messiah: An Aramaic Interpretation, 4:608

The Messiah of Stockholm, 1:1027

The Messianic Idea in Israel, 4:604

The Messianic Idea in Judaism and Other Essays on Jewish Spirituality, 4:672

Messianic Judaism, 4:864

The Messianic Secret, 4:826

Messianism, Mysticism, and Magic, 4:630, 4:651

Messianism in the Talmudic Era, 4:621

Messias, 4:167

Metadrama in Shakespeare's Henriad: "Richard II" to "Henry V," 1:211

The Metafictional Muse, 1:944, 1:963, 1:980

Metafont: The Program, 5:562

Metaformations: Soundplay and Wordplay in Ovid and the Classical Poets, 2:390

Metahistory, 1:1153, 1:1154

Metal Deposits in Relation to Plate Tectonics, 5:238

Metal-Insulator Transitions, 5:704

The Metalogicon of John of Salisbury, 4:116

Metals Handbook, Desk Edition, 5:237

Metamagical Themas: Questing for the Essence of Mind and Pattern, 5:571

Metamora, 1:1069

Metamorphic Tradition in Modern Poetry, 1:799

Metamorphic Verse: The Elizabethan Minor Epic, 1:215

Metamorphoses (Apuleius), 4:469

Metamorphoses (Ovid), 2:379, 2:389

The Metamorphoses: Ovid's Roman Games, 2:390

The Metamorphoses of Apuleius: On Making an Ass of Oneself, 2:383, 4:469

The Metamorphoses of Shakespeare's Comedy, 1:210

The Metamorphoses of the Self, 2:482

The Metamorphosis of Galathea: A Study in Creative Adaptation, 1:186

The Metamorphosis of Pygmalion's Image, 1:187

Metaphor and Meaning in D. H. Lawrence's Later Novels, 1:510

Metaphor and Memory, 1:1028

Metaphors of Mind: Conceptions of the Nature of Intelligence, 3:175

Metaphors of Self: The Meaning of Autobiography, 1:928

Metaphors on Vision, 1:1160

Metaphors We Live By, 3:21

The Metaphysical and Geometrical Doctrine of Bruno as Given in His Work "De triplici minimo," 4:135

Metaphysical Disputations, 4:154

The Metaphysical Foundations of Logic, 4:291

The Metaphysical Foundations of Modern Physical Science, 4:124, 4:159, 5:41, 5:706

Metaphysical Foundations of Natural Science, 4:205

Metaphysical Meditations, 4:556

Metaphysical Passion, 1:799

Metaphysical Poetry, 1:166

The Metaphysical Poets, 1:166

Metaphysical Themes in Thomas Aquinas, 4:119

The Metaphysical Thought of Godfrey of Fontaines, 4:103

Metaphysics (Aune), 4:380

The Metaphysics (Avicenna), 4:581

Metaphysics (Lotze), 4:240

Metaphysics (Taylor), 4:381

Metaphysics, Materialism, and the Evolution of the Mind, 5:793

Metaphysics in Midwestern America, 4:855

Metaphysics in Three Books: Ontology, Cosmology, and Psychology, 4:241

The Metaphysics of Descartes: A Study of the Meditations, 4:169

The Metaphysics of Education, 4:323

The Metaphysics of Epistemology: Lectures by Wilfred Sellars, 4:333

The Metaphysics of G. E. Moore, 4:312

The Metaphysics of Good and Evil According to Suárez, 4:105

Metaphysics of Morals, 4:204, 4:205

The Metaphysics of Pragmatism, 4:298

The Metaphysics of Tractatus, 4:345

The Metaphysics of Transcendental Subjectivity, 4:334

Meteorite Craters, 5:623

Meteorology, 5:633

Meteorology of Air Pollution, 5:634

Methadone Maintenance: A Technological Fix, 5:173

Method, Model and Matter, 5:83

Method and Meaning in Jonson's Masques, 1:184

The Method and Message of Jewish Apocalyptic, 4:824

Method for the Easy Comprehension of History, 4:133, 4:134

Methodical Realism, 4:286

The Methodist Publishing House: A History, 1:39

The Methodist Revolution, 3:363

The Methodists, 4:739

The Method of Founding Stereotype, 1:14

Method of Henry James, 1:765

Methodology and Distribution, 5:520

Methodology of Economics and Other Social Sciences, 3:47

The Methodology of Herbert Blumer: Critical Interpretation and Repair, 3:222

Methods and Problems in Greek Science, 4:48

The Methods and Skills of History: A Practical Guide, 3:9

Methods in Analytical Psychology: An Introduction, 3:169

Methods in Field Geology, 5:636

Methods in Medicine: A Descriptive Study of Physicians' Behaviour, 5:80

Methods of Book Design: The Practice of an Industrial Craft, 1:12

The Methods of Ethics, 4:256, 4:257

Methods of Logic, 4:411

Methods of Research in Social Psychology, 3:168

Methods of Social Reform, 3:85

Methods of Social Research, 3:200

A Method to Their Madness: The History of the Actors Studio, 1:1073

The Metis in the Canadian West, 3:610

A Metrical History of Christianity, 1:644

Metropol, 2:695, 2:697, 2:773

Metropolis, 3:840

Metropolis: From Division of Labor to Urban Form, 3:136

Metropolis and Province: Science in British Culture, 1780–1850, 1:312

Metternich: The First European, 3:376

The Mexican Agrarian Revolution, 3:650

Mexican-American Folklore, 3:864

Mexican Americans: Leadership, Ideology, and Identity, 1930–1960, 3:555

The Mexican Empire of Iturbide, 3:638

Mexican Folktales from the Borderland, 3:853

Mexican Folkways, 3:857

The Mexican Novel Comes of Age, 2:846

The Mexican Revolution, 3:638

The Mexican War, 1846–1848, 3:523, 3:638

Mexico, 1:1248, 3:931

Mexico: From Revolution to Evolution, 1940–1960, 3:644

Mexico: Some Travels and Some Travelers There, 3:894

Mexico: The Struggle for Peace and Bread, 3:650

Mexico and the United States: Ambivalent Vistas, 3:639

Mexico City Blues, 1:998

Mexico in Its Novel: A Nation's Search for Identity, 2:845

Miau, 2:547

Michael and His Lost Angel, 1:367

Michael Drayton and His Circle, 1:179

Michael Drayton and the Passing of Elizabethan England, 1:179

Michael Faraday: A Biography, 5:684, 5:745
Michael Faraday: A List of His Lectures and Published Writings, 5:745
Michael Faraday: Father of Electronics, 5:745
Michael Faraday: Sandemanian and Scientist, 5:745
Michael Faraday and the Royal Institution, 5:684, 5:745
Michael Manley: The Making of a Leader, 3:638
Michaelmas Term, 1:190
Michael Ondaatje: Word, Image, Imagination, 2:922
Michael Ondaatje and His Works, 2:922
Michael Tippett, 3:725
Michael Tippett: An Introductory Story, 3:725
Michelangelo (De Tolnay), 3:782
Michelangelo (De Vecchi), 3:782
Michelangelo (Hartt), 3:782
Michelangelo (Hibbard), 3:782
Michelangelo (Murray), 3:782
Michelangelo: A Psychoanalytic Study of His Life and Images, 3:782, 5:425
Michelangelo: Sculptor-Painter-Architect, 3:782
Michelangelo, the Sistine Chapel Ceiling, 3:782
Michelangelo and His Drawings, 3:782
Michelangelo and the Language of Art, 3:782
Michelangelo Antonioni's Neo-Realism: A World View, 3:830
Michel Butor, 2:463
Michel de Montaigne's Essays, 2:491
Michelet, 2:455
Michel Foucault (Eribon), 4:401
Michel Foucault (Shumway), 4:401
Michel Foucault: A Bibliography, 4:401, 5:88
Michel Foucault: An Introductory Study of His Thought, 4:400
Michel Foucault: Beyond Structuralism and Hermeneutics, 4:400
Michel Foucault: The Freedom of Philosophy, 4:401, 5:443

Michel Foucault, Philosopher, 5:88
Michel Foucault's Force of Flight: Toward an Ethics for Thought, 4:400, 5:88
Michelson and the Speed of Light, 5:702
Michel Tournier, 2:512
Michigan Folklife Reader, 3:861
Mickelson's Ghosts, 1:979
Microbe Hunters, 5:783, 5:801
Microbes, Man and Animals: The Natural History of Microbial Interactions, 5:783
Microbes and Man, 5:783
Microbes in Extreme Environments, 5:783
Microcomputer Programming Languages, 5:550
Microcomputers for Lawyers, 5:558
Microcomputers for Legal Professionals, 5:557
Microcomputers in Business, 5:556
Microcomputers in Elementary Education: Perspectives on Implementation, 3:253
Microcomputers in Libraries, 5:544
Microcosm: The Quantum Revolution in Economics and Technology, 5:573
Microcosmos: Four Billion Years of Evolution from Our Microbial Ancestors, 5:776
Microeconomics, 3:64
Microelectronics and Society, 5:572
The Microelectronics Revolution, 5:540
A Micro Handbook for Small Libraries and Media Centers, 5:544
Micromegas and Other Stories, 2:515
The Micro Millennium, 5:537
Micromotives and Macrobehavior, 3:62
Micropublishing: A History of Scholarly Micropublishing in America, 1938–1980, 1:38
Microsoft COBOL, 5:553
The Microsoft Visual Basic Workshop, 5:552
Micro Software Evaluations, 1986–1988, 5:546
Micro-to-Mainframe Links, 5:560

Microwave Processing and Engineering, 5:229
Microwave Spectroscopy, 5:718
Microwave Technology, 5:230
Mid American Chants, 1:811
Midaq Alley, 2:68
The Middle-Aged Man on the Flying Trapeze, 1:890
The Middle Age of Mrs. Eliot, 1:567
The Middle Ages, 1:141, 1:1091
The Middle Ages: A Concise Encyclopedia, 3:331
The Middle Ages and the Renaissance, 4:124
Middle Ages to Romanticism, 2:645
Middle American Individualism, 3:227, 3:542
The Middle East, 3:434, 3:435, 4:580
The Middle East: A Geographical Study, 3:435
The Middle East: A Political and Economic Survey, 3:437
The Middle East: A Reader, 3:435
The Middle East: Fourteen Islamic Centuries, 3:437
Middle East: U.S. Policy, Israel, Oil and the Arabs, 3:435
The Middle East, Oil, and the Great Powers, 3:437
Middle East and Islam: A Bibliographical Introduction, 3:443
Middle East and North Africa (Gale), 1:82
Middle East and North Africa (Mansfield), 3:437
The Middle East and North Africa: Essays in Honor of J. C. Hurewitz, 3:419
The Middle East and North Africa: Medieval and Modern History, 3:437
Middle East Contemporary Survey, 3:434
Middle East in the World Economy, 1800–1914, 3:437
The Middle East in World Affairs, 3:436
Middle East Oil Money and Its Future Expenditure, 3:435
Middle East Organizations in Washington, D.C., 3:437

The Middle East since Camp David, 3:435

Middle English Literature, 1:146, 1:147

Middle English Lyrics, 1:148

The Middle English Mystery Play: A Study in Dramatic Speech and Form, 1:159

Middle English Survey: Critical Essays, 1:147

The Middle Ground, 1:468

Middle Man: The Adventures of a Literary Agent, 1:43

The Middleman, 1:322

Middlemarch, 1:353

The Middle Passage, 2:938, 2:939

Middle Platonism and Neoplatonism, 4:60

The Middle Platonists 80 B.C. to A.D. 220, 4:60

Middleton's Tragedies, 1:190

Middleton's Tragic Themes, 1:190

Middletown, 3:231

Middletown Families: Fifty Years of Change and Continuity, 3:231

Middletown in Transition: A Study in Cultural Conflicts, 3:231

The Middle Voice of Ecological Conscience, 4:294

The Middle Years, 1:762

Mid-Journey: An Unfinished Autobiography, 4:317

Midnight, 2:258

Midnight Folk, 1:519

Midnight Oil, 1:538

Midnight on the Desert, 1:537

Midnight's Children, 2:180, 2:181

Midnight Sun, 2:832

Midnight Was My Cry: New and Selected Poems, 1:1001

Midpassage: Alexander Herzen and European Revolution. 1847–1852, 2:728

Midrash: An Introduction, 4:611

Midrash and Literature, 4:610

Midrash Compilations of the Sixth and Seventh Centuries, 4:611

Midrash Reader, 4:611

Midsummer, 2:942, 2:943

Midsummer Night Madness and Other Stories, 1:528

A Midsummer Night's Dream, 1:205, 1:206

Midsummer Passion and Other Tales of Maine Cussedness, 1:819

The Mid-Tudor Crisis, 1545–1565, 3:359

Mid-Twentieth Century American Philosophy: Personal Statements, 4:34, 4:262

A Mid-Victorian Feminist: Barbara Leigh Smith Bodichon, 1:331

A Midwife's Story, 5:337

Mies Reconsidered: His Career, Legacy, and Disciples, 3:783

Mies van der Rohe: A Critical Biography, 3:783

Mies van der Rohe: European Works, 3:783

Mies van der Rohe: The Villas and Country Houses, 3:783

The Mighty and Their Fall, 1:461, 1:462

Migraine: The Evolution of a Common Disorder, 5:393

Migraine and Its Variants, 5:393

Migraine and Other Headaches, 5:392

Migrant: Farm Workers in America's Northwest, 5:172

Migrant Women: Crossing Boundaries and Changing Identities, 3:217

Migration and Residential Mobility: Macro and Micro Approaches, 3:124

Migration in Colonial Spanish America, 3:629

The Migration of Labor, 3:60

Miguel de Unamuno, 2:552

Miguel Street, 2:938, 2:939

Mihloti, 2:168

Mikhail Bakhtin, 2:685

Mikhail Bulgakov (Milne), 2:706

Mikhail Bulgakov (Natov), 2:706

Mikhail Lermontov, 2:735

Mikhail Sholokhov and His Art, 2:756

Mikrokosmos, 4:240

Milan Marjanović, 2:785

Mildred Pierce, 1:1227

Miles Davis: A Critical Biography, 3:691

Miles Davis: A Musical Biography, 3:691

Miles of Smiles, Years of Struggle: Stories of Black Pullman Porters, 3:55

Milestones in Mass Communications Research, 3:801

Milestones in Nigerian History, 3:425

Milestones in Science and Technology, 5:2

Militant Black Writer in Africa and the United States, 2:107

Militant Islam, 4:570, 4:579

The Militant South, 1800–1961, 3:579

Militarism, Imperialism, and Racial Accommodation, 3:237

The Militarization of Space: U.S. Policy, 1945–1984, 5:597

A Military and Historical Analysis of the Great Wars of the 17th and 18th Centuries, 3:288

Military Bibliography of the Civil War, 3:510

A Military History of Australia, 3:494

A Military History of Canada: From Champlain to the Gulf War, 3:607

The Military Industrial Complex, 5:55

Military Theory and Practice in the Age of Xenophon, 3:308

Militia Christi, 4:688

Milk and Honey, 2:956

Milk for Babes, Drawn out of the Breasts of Both Testaments, Chiefly for the Spiritual Nourishment of Boston Babes in either England, but may be of like Use for any Children, 1:1194

The Milkmaid, 1:580

The Milky Way, 5:599

The Miller of Old Church, 1:843

The Miller's Tale, 1:156

The Millionairess, 1:545

Millions of Cats, 1:1194, 1:1202, 1:1203

Millions of Strange Shadows, 1:987

The Mill on the Floss, 1:353

The Millstone, 1:468

Milton: A Biography, 1:192

Milton: Modern Essays in Criticism, 1:192

Milton and the English Revolution, 1:192

A Milton Encyclopedia, 1:192

Milton Friedman, 3:77

Milton Friedman: Critical Assessments, 3:78
A Milton Handbook, 1:192
Milton's Brief Epic: The Genre, Meaning, and Art of "Paradise Regained," 1:192
Milton's Eve, 1:192
Milton's God, 1:192
Milton's Grand Style, 1:193
Milton's "Lycidas": The Tradition and the Poem, 1:192
Mimekor Yisrael: Classical Jewish Folktales, 2:15, 3:854
Mimesis: The Representation of Reality in Western Literature, 1:420, 2:985
Mimosa and Other Stories, 2:239
Mind, Body Medicine: How to Use Your Mind for Better Health, 5:341
Mind, History, and Dialectic: The Philosophy of R. G. Collingwood, 4:282
Mind, Self, and Society: From the Standpoint of a Social Behaviorist, 3:208, 3:232, 4:308
The Mind and Art of Henry Adams, 1:730, 3:563
Mind and Body: A Categorical Relation, 5:134
Mind and Cosmos: Essays in Contemporary Science and Philosophy, 5:62
Mind and Imagination in Aristotle, 4:71
Mind and Medicine, 5:78
Mind and Nature, 4:281
The Mind and the Machine: Philosophical Aspects of Artificial Intelligence, 5:570
Mind and the World-Order: Outline of a Theory of Knowledge, 4:302
Mind as Healer, Mind as Slayer, 5:401
The Mind-Body Problem: A Psycho-Biological Approach, 5:83
Mind Breaths: Poems, 1972–1977, 1:981
Mind Design: Philosophy, Psychology and Artificial Intelligence, 5:75, 5:570
The Mind Has No Sex? Women in the Origins of Modern Science, 5:26, 5:188

The Mind in Conflict, 5:426
Minding America's Business, 3:62
Mind in Nature/Nobel Conference, 5:719
The Mind of a Poet: A Study of Wordsworth's Thought, 1:307
The Mind of Frederick Douglass, 1:668
The Mind of Germany, 3:377
The Mind of God: The Scientific Basis for a Rational World, 5:15
A Mind of Her Own: The Life of Karen Horney, 3:186
The Mind of Jawaharlal Nehru, 3:500
The Mind of John Paul II: Origins of His Thought and Action, 4:747
The Mind of Kierkegaard, 4:239
The Mind of Primitive Man, 3:28
The Mind of St. Bernard of Clairvaux, 4:112
The Mind of the Child Who Is Said to Be Sick, 5:416
The Mind of the Middle Ages: An Historical Survey, A.D. 200–1500, 4:96
The Mind of the Oxford Movement, 4:740
The Mind of the Talmud: An Intellectual History of the Bavli, 4:620, 4:627
The Mind of the Traveler from Gilgamesh to Global Tourism, 3:892
The Mind of Voltaire, 4:218
Mind of Winter: Wallace Stevens, Meditation, and Literature, 1:887
Mind Only: A Philosophical and Doctrinal Analysis of the Vijnanavada, 4:514
Mind over Machine, 5:571
The Mind Parasites, 1:568
The Mind-Reader, 1:1066
Minds, Machines, and Evolution, 4:382
The Mind's Best Work, 5:342
The Mind's Empire, 1:175
The Mind's Fate: Ways of Seeing Psychiatry and Psychoanalysis, 5:421
The Mind's I, 4:396
The Mind's I: Fantasies and Reflections on Self and Soul, 5:75, 5:570

The Mind's Journey to God, 4:113
The Mind's New Science: A History of the Cognitive Revolution, 5:567
Minds over Matter: A New Look at Artificial Intelligence, 5:569
Mindsplit: The Psychology of Multiple Personality and the Dissociated Self, 5:427
Minds That Came Back, 5:425
Mindstorms: Children, Computers, and Powerful Ideas, 3:251, 5:566
Mine: A Novel of Terror, 1:1242
The Mine at Fauln, 2:593
Mine Boy, 2:158, 2:159
Mine Eyes Have Seen the Glory, 4:752
The Miner, 2:291
The Mineral Kingdom, 5:628
Mineral Names: What Do They Mean?, 5:628
Minerals and Men, 5:628
Minerals in World Affairs, 5:628
A Mingled Yarn: The Life of R. P. Blackmur, 1:816
Mingo and Other Sketches in Black and White, 1:754
The Miniature Epic in Vandal Africa, 2:157
Minima Moralia, 4:393
Ministers of Reform, 3:531
The Minister's Wooing, 1:698
The Ministry in Historical Perspective, 4:679
Minna von Barnhelm, 2:600
Minnesota Folklife: An Annotated Bibliography, 3:862
The Minoan-Mycenaean Religion, 4:487
A Minor Apocalypse, 2:815
Minor Attic Orators, 2:348
Minor Characters, 1:913
Minorities in the Arab World, 3:443, 3:457
Minority Education and Caste, 3:256
The Minority Presence in American Literature 1600–1900, 1:653
Minor Latin Poets, 2:382
Minor Papers on the Currency Question, 3:101
Minor Prophecy: Walt Whitman's New American Religion, 1:707
Minotaur, 2:25

Minstrelsy of the Scottish Border, 1:299
The Mint, 3:925, 3:926
Mio My Son, 2:677
The Miracle, 1:1250
Miracle and Natural Law in Graeco-Roman and Early Christian Thought, 4:99
Miracle at Midway, 3:535
Miracle at Philadelphia, 3:141, 3:519
The Miracle Hater, 2:19
Miracle in the Early Christian World: A Study in Sociohistorical Method, 4:689
The Miracle of Love, 4:746
The Miracle of Mindfulness! A Manual on Meditation, 4:561
Miracle of the Rose, 2:478, 2:479
Miracles and Pilgrims: Popular Beliefs in Medieval England, 4:726
Miracles and the Medieval Mind: Theory, Record, and Event, 1000–1215, 4:701
Miracles of Courage, 5:322
The Miraculous Pigtail, 2:244
Miraculous Tales of the Lotus Sutra from Ancient Japan, 4:537
Miramar, 2:68
Mirandolina, 2:402
Mircea Eliade: The Romanian Roots, 1907–1945, 4:474
Mircea Eliade and the Dialectic of the Sacred, 4:474
Mircea Eliade's Vision for a New Humanism, 4:474
Mirgorod: Four Tales, 2:720, 2:721
Mirifici logarithmorum canonis descriptio, 5:579
Miroslav's Gospel, 2:826
Mirour de l'Homme, 1:152
Mirror, Sword and Jewel: The Geometry of Japanese Life, 3:474
The Mirror and the Lamp, 1:265, 1:931
Mirror and Veil: The Historical Dimension of Spenser's Faerie Queene, 1:199
A Mirror for Americanists: Reflections on the Idea of American Literature, 1:716
Mirror for Campus, 2:144
Mirror in the Roadway, 1:528

Mirror in the Shrine: American Encounters with Meiji Japan, 3:479
The Mirror Maker, 2:425
Mirror of a People: Canadian Jewish Experience in Poetry and Prose, 2:32
The Mirror of Art, Critical Studies, 2:457
The Mirror of Faith, 4:103
The Mirror of Herodotus, 3:316, 4:480
The Mirror of Magistrates, 1:172
The Mirror of Meaning, 4:283
The Mirror of Our Anguish, 2:436
The Mirror of Production, 3:211
Mirror of the Indies, 2:621
The Mirror of Vertue, or The Life of Thomas More, 1:194
Mirror on Mirror: Translation, Imitation, Parody, 2:990
Mirrors (Mahfuz), 2:68
Mirrors (Creeley), 1:965
Mirrorshades: The Cyberpunk Anthology, 5:563
Mirrors of Madness: Patrolling the Psychic Boarders, 3:201
Mirrors of Minds: Patterns of Experience in Educational Computing, 5:566
Mirrors of the Jewish Mind, 4:636
A Mirror to Nature: Transformations in Drama and Aesthetics, 1660–1732, 1:228
The Misalliance, 1:452
The Misanthrope, 1:263, 2:490
The Misanthrope and Other Plays, 2:490
Miscellaneous and Autobiographical Pieces, Fragments and Marginalia, 1:260
Miscellaneous Poems, 1:643
Miscellaneous Tracts Relating to Natural History, Husbandry, and Physick, 5:805
Miscellaneous Verdicts, 1:536
Miscellanies, 1:376
Miscellany of Men, 1:458
The Miser, 2:490
The Misfits, 1:1103
Misgivings, 1:989

Misha! The Mikhail Baryshnikov Story, 3:738
Mishima: A Biography, 2:289
Mishima: A Vision of the Void, 2:517
The Mishnah, 4:610, 4:810
Mishnah: A New Translation, 4:611
Mishnah: Introduction and Reader: An Anthology, 4:611
Mishnah's Division of Agriculture: A History and Theology of Seder Zeraim, 4:609
Mishnayoth, 4:609
Mishneh Torah: Maimonides' Code of Law and Ethics, 4:627
The Mismeasure of Man, 3:174, 3:250, 5:16, 5:638
The Miss Firecracker Contest, 1:1093, 1:1094
The Missing Bureaucrat, 2:654
The Missing Piece, 1:1207
The Missing Piece Meets the Big O, 1:1207
The Missing Reel: The Untold Story of the Lost Inventor of Moving Pictures, 3:826
Missing Words: The Family Handbook on Adult Hearing Loss, 5:380
The Mission, or Scenes in Africa, 1:374
Missionaries to Match Our Message, 5:268
The Missionary Enterprise in China and America, 3:498
The Missionary Enterprise in China and America, 4:532
Missionary Travels and Researches in South Africa, 3:929, 3:930
Mission to Earth: Landsat Views the World, 5:630
Mission to Gelele, King of Dahome, 3:914
Mission to Kala, 2:132
Mission to the Planets, 5:593
Mississippi Solo: A River Quest, 3:895
Mississippi Writings, 1:781
Miss Julie, 2:679
Miss Lonelyhearts, 1:896, 1:897
Miss Lonelyhearts and The Day of the Locust, 1:897
Miss Mackenzie, 1:406
Miss Marjoriebanks, 1:385

Miss Marple: The Complete Short Stories, 1:606
Miss Muriel and Other Stories, 1:1030
Miss Peabody's Inheritance, 2:956
Miss Ravenel's Conversion from Secession to Loyalty, 1:744
Miss Sara Sampson, 2:600
Miss Silver's Past, 2:794, 2:795
Miss Sophie's Diary, 2:263
Miss Sophie's Diary and Other Stories, 2:264
Mr. and Mrs. Baby and Other Stories, 1:1055
Mr. Arkadin, a Novel, 1:1179
Mr. Badman, 1:173
Mr. Basket-Knife and Other Khmer Folktales, 2:315
Mr. Britling Sees It Through, 1:563
Mr. Clemens and Mark Twain, 1:784
Mr. Gay's London, 1:246
Mr. George Eliot: A Biography of George Henry Lewes, 1:373
Mister Gustafsson Himself, 2:674
Mr. Happiness, 1:1101
Mister Jelly Roll, 3:884
Mister Johnson, 1:456
Mr. Jowialski, 2:813
Mr. Mani, 2:26
Mr. Midshipman Easy, 1:374
Mr. Palomar, 2:411
Mr. Rabbit Is Dead, 2:140
Mister Sammler's Planet, 1:946, 1:947
Mr. Scarborough's Family, 1:406
Mr. Scobie's Riddle, 2:956
Mr. Tompkins in Paperback, 5:605, 5:689
The Mistress, 2:290
Mistress Anne: The Exceptional Life of Anne Boleyn, 4:726
Mrs. Byrne's Dictionary of Unusual, Obscure, and Preposterous Words, Gathered from Numerous and Diverse Authoritative Sources, 1:92
Mrs. Caldwell Speaks to Her Son, 2:533, 2:534
Mrs. Dalloway, 1:568, 1:569
Mrs. Gaskell and Her Friends, 1:356
Mrs. Leicester's School, 1:295

The Mistress of Husaby, 2:669
Mrs. Peabody, 1:1168
Mrs. Reynolds, 1:881
Mistress to an Age: A Life of Mme de Staël, 2:510
Mrs. Trollope: The Triumphant Feminine in the Nineteenth Century, 1:408
Misused Statistics: Straight Talk for Twisted Numbers, 5:522
The Misuse of Alcohol, 5:402
Mit dem Schlimmsten wird schon gerechnet, 2:606
The MIT Dictionary of Modern Economics, 3:44
Miti and the Japanese Miracle: The Growth of Industrial Policy, 1925–1975, 3:478
The Mito Ideology, 3:475
Mitra-Varuna: An Essay on Two Indo-European Representations of Sovereignty, 4:471
Mitre, Sceptre: Transatlantic Faiths, Ideas, Personalities and Politics, 1:627
Mitre and Sceptre, 3:569
Mitterand: A Political Biography, 3:373
Mixed Blessings: Intensive Care for Newborns, 5:120
The Mixing of Colors and Paints, 1:21
A Mixture of Frailties, 2:910
MLA Handbook for Writers of Research Papers, 1:118
Mob, 1:482
Mo' Better Blues, 1:1171
Mobile: Study for a Representation of the United States, 2:463
Moby Dick, 1:686, 1:1254, 2:432
Moby Dick: Ishmael's Mighty Book, 1:689
Moby Dick as Doubloon: Essays and Extracts, 1:689
The Mocking of the President, 3:542
Model Assisted Survey Sampling, 5:524
Modeling and Forecasting Demand in Tourism, 3:891
Models, 5:65
Models and Analogies in Science, 4:405, 5:63
Models for the Multitudes, 1:804
Models in Paleobiology, 5:639

Models of God: Theology for an Ecological Nuclear Age, 4:745, 4:884
Models of Learning, Memory and Choice: Selected Papers, 3:175
Models of Power: Politics and Economics in Zola's "Rougon-Macquart," 2:518
Models of Teaching, 3:256
A Model to Be Put Together, 2:861
Modem Reference, 5:301
Modems and Communications on IBM PCs, 5:301, 5:302
The Mode of Information: Poststructuralism and Social Context, 4:267, 5:126
Moderna, 2:785
Modern Aesthetics, 4:131
Modern Africa, 3:417
Modern Africa: A Social and Political History, 3:428
Modern African Literature and the African Predicament, 2:107
Modern African Writers: Nadine Gordimer, 2:162
Modern Alphabets, 1:14
Modern American and British Prose, 1:430
Modern American Fiction: Form and Function, 1:805
Modern American Literature, 1:134
Modern American Lyric: Lowell, Berryman, Creeley and Plath, 1:914
The Modern American Novel, 1:803, 1:917
The Modern American Novel, 1914–1945, 1:805
The Modern American Novella, 1:805
Modern American Poetry, 1:801, 1:876, 1:915
Modern American Poetry, 1865–1950 (Moramarco), 1:799
Modern American Poetry, 1865–1950 (Shucard), 1:800
Modern American Poets, 1:801, 1:915
The Modern American Political Novel, 1:803
Modern American Prose: A Reader for Writers, 1:808
Modern American Religion, 4:753
Modern American Short Stories 1982, 1:806

Modern American Spiritualism, 4:851

The Modern American Theater: A Collection of Critical Essays, 1:1074

The Modern American Urban Novel: Nature as "Interior Structure", 1:804

Modern American Usage: A Guide, 1:91

Modern and Modernism: The Sovereignty of the Artist 1885–1925, 1:415

A Modern Approach to Islam, 4:373

Modern Arabic Drama in Egypt, 2:55

Modern Arabic Literature (Allen), 2:55

Modern Arabic Literature (Altoma), 2:55

Modern Arabic Literature, 1800–1970, 2:57

Modern Arabic Literature and the West, 2:55

Modern Arabic Poetry: An Anthology, 2:57

Modern Arabic Poetry 1800–1970, 2:56

Modern Arab Poets, 1950–1975, 2:56

Modern Arab Thought: Channels of the French Revolution to the Arab East, 3:443

Modern Architecture, 3:764

Modern Architecture since 1900, 3:762

Modern Arms and Free Men, 5:200

Modern Art, 3:759

Modern Black Poets: A Collection of Critical Essays, 1:913

Modern Bookbinding: A Survey and a Prospect, 1:24

Modern Book Collecting, 1:34, 1:76

Modern Book Design, 1:9

Modern Brazilian Short Stories, 2:891

Modern British Drama, 1:427

Modern British Dramatists, 1:1900 to 1945, 1:428

Modern British Essayists, 1:429

Modern British Farce, 1:388

Modern British Poetry, 1:418

Modern British Politics, 3:365

Modern Business Cycle Theory, 3:49

Modern Byelorussian Writing: Essays and Documents, 2:783

A Modern Catholic Dictionary, 4:717

Modern Catholicism, 4:744

Modern Chemical Magic, 5:730

Modern China, 3:498

Modern China and Its Revolutionary Process, 3:472

Modern China and the New World, 3:471, 4:361

Modern Chinese Literature in the May Fourth Era, 2:233

Modern Chinese Poetry: An Introduction, 2:234

Modern Chinese Poetry: Theory and Practice Since 1917, 2:234

Modern Chinese Society, an Analytical Bibliography, 3:466

Modern Chinese Stories, 2:235

Modern Chinese Stories and Novellas 1919–1949, 2:235

Modern Chinese Writers: Self-Portrayals, 2:234

Modern Christian Thinkers, 4:275

Modern Clinical Psychology, 5:419

Modern Communication Systems, 5:298

The Modern Concept of Nature, 5:808

Modern Congo Prophets: Religion in a Plural Society, 4:467

Modern Control Systems, 5:242

Modern Copyright Fundamentals, 1:55

Modern Critics in Practice: Critical Portraits of British Literary Critics, 1:430

Modern Democracies, 3:151

The Modern Democratic State, 3:143

A Modern Dictionary of Geography, 3:119, 5:618

Modern Digital and Analog Communication Systems, 5:299

Modern Dogma and the Rhetoric of Assent, 1:1139

Modern Drama: A Checklist of Critical Literature on 20th-Century Plays, 1:427

Modern Drama in America and England, 1:1950-1970, 1:123, 1:427

Modern Economic Growth, 3:53, 3:90

Modern Education: A Critique of Its Fundamental Ideas, 5:466

Modern Egypt: The Formation of a Nation State, 3:445

Modern Egyptian Drama: An Anthology, 2:56

The Modern Egyptian Novel, 2:55

Modern Electrical Communications: Analog, Digital, and Optical Systems, 5:300

Modern Electronic Communication Techniques, 5:299

Modern Elementary Particle Physics, 5:662

Modern England: 1901–1984, 3:354

Modern England: From the Eighteenth Century to the Present, 1:313, 3:356

Modern English Short Stories, 1:423

Modern Faith and Thought, 4:746

Modern First Editions: Their Value to Collectors, 1:76

Modern Folk Ballads, 3:850

Modern French Theatre: From Giraudoux to Genet, 2:448

Modern Furniture Classics since 1945, 3:766

Modern Geography: An Encyclopedic Survey, 3:118

Modern German Philosophy, 4:28

Modern Greece: A Short History, 3:393

Modern Greek Philosophers on the Human Soul, 4:29

Modern Greek Poetry (Dalven), 2:371, 2:373

Modern Greek Poetry (Friar), 2:371

Modern Greek Thought, 4:29

Modern Greek Writers, 2:371

Modern Hebrew Literature, 2:9

The Modern Hebrew Poem Itself: From the Beginnings to the Present, 2:9

Modern Hebrew Poetry, 2:9

Modern Hebrew Poetry: A Bilingual Anthology, 2:10

The Modern History of Japan, 3:473

The Modern History of Somaliland, 3:422

The Modern History of Iraq, 3:450

A Modern History of Tanganyika, 3:422

Modern Hungarian Poetry, 2:799

The Modern Impulse of Traditional Judaism, 4:654

Modern India: The Origins of an Asian Democracy, 3:486

Modern India, 1885–1947, 3:486

Modern Indian Interpreters of the Bhagavad Gita, 4:508

Modern Indian Poetry: An Anthology, 2:176

Modern Indian Responses to Religious Pluralism, 4:898

Modern Indonesian Literature, 2:317

A Modern Instance, 1:758

Modern Introduction to Philosophy, 4:20

Modern Ireland, 1600–1972, 3:369

Modern Irish American Fiction: A Reader, 1:804

Modern Islamic Literature, 2:57, 4:567

Modernism, 1:414

Modernism: 1890–1930, 2:986

Modernism and the Harlem Renaissance, 1:938, 1:1137

The Modernism of Ezra Pound: The Science of Poetry, 1:873

Modernist Anthropology: From Fieldwork to Text, 3:12

Modernist Form: Pound's Style in the Early Cantos, 1:873

The Modernist Idea, 2:890

The Modernist Movement in the Roman Church, 4:742

The Modernist Muslim Movement in Indonesia, 1900–1942, 4:373

The Modernist Trend in Spanish American Poetry, 2:848

The Modern Italian Novel: From Pea to Moravia, 2:401

The Modern Italian Novel, 2:402

Modern Italian Poets, 2:401, 2:403

Modern Italy, 1871–1982, 3:385

Modernity and Identity, 3:209

Modernity and Self-Identity, 3:209, 3:227

The Modernity of Tradition: Political Development in India, 3:486

Modernity within Tradition, 4:653

Modernization: The Transformation of American Life, 1600–1865, 3:526

The Modernization of French Jewry, 4:635

The Modernization of Sex, 5:440

The Modernization of Turkey from Ataturk to the Present Day, 3:453

The Modernizers: Overseas Students, Foreign Employees, and Meiji Japan, 3:476

Modernizing Shakespeare's Spelling, 1:207

Modern Japanese Drama: An Anthology, 2:283

Modern Japanese Fiction and Its Traditions: An Introduction, 2:282

Modern Japanese Literature: From 1868 to the Present Day, 2:283

Modern Japanese Novelists: A Biographical Dictionary, 2:282

Modern Japanese Poets and the Nature of Literature, 2:283, 2:289

Modern Japanese Stories: An Anthology, 2:283

Modern Japan through Its Weddings, 4:540

Modern Jewish Ethics: Theory and Practice, 4:598

Modern Jewish Religious Movements, 4:651

Modern Kongo Prophets: Religion in a Plural Society, 3:421

Modern Korean Literature, 2:299

Modern Language Association (MLA) International Bibliography of Books and Articles, 1:120

Modern Latin America, 3:632

Modern Latin American Art: A Bibliography, 3:759

Modern Latin American Literature, 2:846

Modern Latin American Narratives: The Dreams of Reason, 2:847

Modern Literary Theory: A Comparative Introduction, 2:983

Modern Literary Theory: A Reader, 1:135, 1:1134

Modern Love, 1:297, 1:390

Modern Malay Literary Culture: A Historical Perspective, 2:324

Modern Malaysian Chinese Stories, 2:325

Modern Man in Search of a Soul, 5:455

Modern Medicine, Its Theory and Practice, in Original Contributions by American and Foreign Authors, 5:363

A Modern Mephistopheles, 1:1198

Modern Mineralogy, 5:628

Modern Movements in European Philosophy, 4:27

Modern Music: A Concise History from Debussy to Boulez, 3:665

Modern Nordic Plays: Denmark, 2:645

Modern Nordic Plays: Finland, 2:658

Modern Nordic Plays: Iceland, 2:640

Modern Nordic Plays: Sweden, 2:672

Modern One-Act Plays from Latin America, 2:849

Modern Operating Systems, 5:551

Modern Painters, 1:324, 1:393, 1:394

Modern Persian Drama: An Anthology, 2:84

Modern Persian Prose Literature, 2:83

Modern Persian Short Stories, 2:84

Modern Philosophy: The French Enlightenment to Kant, 4:160

Modern Physical Geography, 3:126, 5:621

Modern Physical Metallurgy, 5:238

Modern Poems: An Introduction to Poetry, 1:801

Modern Poetics, 1:418

Modern Poetry: Essays in Criticism, 1:417, 1:799

Modern Poetry, 1:517, 1:518

Modern Poetry and the Tradition, 1:417, 1:798, 1:912, 1:924

Modern Poetry of the Arab World, 2:57
The Modern Poets: A Critical Introduction, 1:417, 1:799, 1:914
The Modern Prince, and Other Writings, 2:423, 4:287
Modern Prose Style, 1:429
Modern Proverbs and Proverbial Sayings, 1:115
The Modern Psychological Novel, 2:989
Modern Psychological Novel (The Psychological Novel, 1900–1950), 1:420
Modern Psychology: The Teachings of Carl Gustav Jung, 5:456
Modern Public Finance, 3:67
The Modern Researcher, 3:9, 3:275
Modern Residential Wiring, 5:229
Modern Revivalism: Charles Grandison Finney to Billy Graham, 4:753
Modern Romance and Transformations of the Novel, 1:299
The Modern Russian Dictionary for English Speakers: English-Russian, 1:102
Modern Russian Poets on Poetry, 2:685
Moderns and Contemporaries: Novelists, Poets, and Critics, 1:911
Modern Scandinavian Poetry: The Panorama of Poetry 1900–1975, 2:638
The Modern School Movement, 3:248
Modern Science and Christian Faith, 5:198
Modern Science and Human Values, 5:75, 5:107
Modern Scientists and Engineers, 5:217
Modern Scotland: The Nation since 1870, 3:355
Modern Scottish Poetry, 1:418
Modern Scribes and Lettering Artists, 1:18, 1:19
Modern Shakespearean Criticism, 1:208
The Modern Shepherd, 5:262
Modern Short Story in Peru, 2:845
Modern Signals and Systems, 5:299

Modern Slavic Literatures, 2:785, 2:808, 2:827, 2:835
The Modern Spanish Novel, 2:522
The Modern Spanish Novel, 1898–1936, 2:525
Modern Spanish Poems, 2:526
Modern Stylists: Writers on the Art of Writing, 1:983
Modern Switzerland, 3:378
Modern Syrian Short Stories, 2:56
Modern Thai Literature: The Process of Modernization and the Transformation of Values, 2:335
Modern Thai Literature: With an Ethnographic Interpretation, 2:335
The Modern Theme, 4:315
The Modern Theologians, 4:718, 4:888
Modern Therapies, 5:417
Modern Thought and Literature in France, 4:28
Modern Times (Chaplin), 1:1161
Modern Times (Moss), 2:904
The Modern Tradition: Backgrounds of Modern Literature, 1:128
Modern Trends in Hinduism, 4:507
Modern Trends in Islam, 3:456, 4:373, 4:569
Modern Turkish Drama, 2:101
Modern Turkish Drama: An Anthology of Plays in Translation, 2:96
Modern Ukrainian Short Stories, 2:838
A Modern Utopia, 1:564, 5:563
Modern Varieties of Judaism, 4:651
Modern Verse from Taiwan, 2:234
Modern Wales: A Concise History, 1485 to 1979, 3:369
The Modern West, Europe and the New World, 3:253
Modern Witchcraft and Psychoanalysis, 4:865
The Modern World: Ten Great Writers, 2:986
The Modern World System I–III, 3:243
The Modern Writer and His World, 1:421
The Modern Years, 2:282

Modern Yemen, 1918–1966, 3:451
Modes of Being, 4:338, 4:339
Modes of Production of Victorian Novels, 1:318
The Modes of Scepticism: Ancient Texts and Modern Interpretations, 4:58
Modes of Thought, 4:341
A Modest Proposal, 1:259
Modified Rapture: Comedy in W. S. Gilbert's Savoy Operas, 1:358
Moduor I and II, 3:778
Moeti Oa Bochabela, 2:166
The Moffats, 1:1195
Mogens, 2:651
Mogens: And Other Stories, 2:651
Mohamet and His Successors, 4:588
Mohammad (Bey), 4:588
Mohammad (Dibble), 4:588
Mohammad and the Course of Islam, 4:588
The Mohammadan Dynasties, 4:570
Mohammed and Charlemagne, 3:329, 3:407
Mohammedanism: An Historical Survey, 4:569
Mohn und Gedächtnis, 2:575
Moïra, 2:481
Molds, Molecules and Metazoa: Growing Points in Evolutionary Biology, 5:779
Mole Concept in Chemistry, 5:734
Molecular Biology of the Gene, 5:812
Molecular Cell Biology, 5:784
Molecular Evolutionary Genetics, 5:784
The Molecular Vision of Life, 5:784
The Molecules of Life, 5:784
Molière, 2:490, 2:705
Molière and the Comedy of Intellect, 2:490
Molletti: Poems of Love: The Motets of Eugenio Montale, 2:428
Moll Flanders, 1:238, 1:239
Moll Flanders: The Making of a Criminal Mind, 1:240
Molloy, 2:459
A Molna Elegy, 2:673
Moly and My Sad Captains, 1:491
Momentary Monsters: Lucan and His Heroes, 2:387

Moment in Peking, 2:253, 2:254

The Moment of Christian Witness, 4:904

The Moment of Creation, 5:19, 5:595, 5:656

The Moment of Poetry, 1:912

Moments of Grace, 1:501

Monadology, 4:167

The Monadology and Other Philosophical Writings, 4:176

Monarchia (On World Government), 2:416

Monarch Notes on Dostoyevsky's "The Brothers Karamazov," 2:716

Monarch Notes on Tolstoy's Anna Karenina, 2:766

Monarch Notes on Turgenev's Fathers and Sons, 2:770

The Monastery, 1:298

The Monastery of Saint Catherine at Mount Sinai, 3:767

Monet, 3:783

Monetary Economics, 3:65

Monetary Equilibrium, 3:98, 3:99, 3:115

Monetary History of the United States, 1867–1960, 3:76, 3:77

Monetary Mischief: Episodes in Monetary History, 3:77

Monetary Statistics of the United States: Estimates, Sources, Methods, 3:76, 3:77

Monetary Theory, 3:65

Monetary Theory and Fiscal Policy, 3:81

Monetary Theory and the Trade Cycle, 3:82

Monet at Argenteuil, 3:784

Monet by Himself: Paintings, Drawings, Pastels, Letters, 3:783

Monet's Years at Giverny: Beyond Impressionism, 3:784

Money, Credit and Commerce, 3:93

Money, Interest, and Prices: An Integration of Monetary and Value Theory, 3:65

Money and Banking in Islam, 3:442

Money and Fiction, 2:987

Money and Power in the New Religions, 4:857

Money for Maria, 2:752

Money in American Elections, 3:144

The Money-Order with White Genesis, 2:145

A Mongolian Living Buddha: Biography of the Kanjurwa Khutughtu, 4:542

The Mongols and Russia, 3:413

The Monikins, 1:663

The Monk, 1:601, 1:602

Monkey, 2:229

The Monkey Grammarian, 2:879

Monkey on a Stick, 4:862

The Monkey Wrench Gang, 5:828

Monks, Bishops, and Pagans: Christian Culture in Gaul and Italy, 4:700

Monk's Hood, 1:608

Monograms and Alphabetic Devices, 1:14

Monopolistic Competition and General Equilibrium Theory, 3:102, 3:58

Monopoly Capital: An Essay on the American Economic and Social Order, 3:50

Monopoly's Moment, 3:614

Monsieur Song, 2:493

Monsignor Quixote, 1:488

Montaigne, 2:491

Montaigne: A Biography, 2:491, 4:146

Montaigne: And Other Essays, Chiefly Biographical, 1:343

Montaigne and Bayle: Variations on the Theme of Skepticism, 4:146

Montaigne and Melancholy: The Wisdom of the Essays, 4:146

Montaigne in Dialogue, 2:491

Montaigne in Motion, 2:492

Montaigne's Discovery of Man: The Humanization of a Humanist, 2:491, 4:146

Montaillou: The Promised Land of Error, 4:699

Montale and the Occasions of Poetry, 2:428

Montcalm and Wolfe, 3:592

Mont-Cinère, 2:481

Montefiore: The Hospital as Social Instrument, 1884–1984, 5:314

Montenegro, 2:830

Montesquieu: A Critical Biography, 3:163, 4:210

Montesquieu, Rousseau and Marx: Politics and History, 3:290

Montesquieu and Rousseau: Forerunners of Sociology, 3:164, 4:210

Montesquieu and Social Theory, 4:210

Montesquieu's Idea of Justice, 4:210

Montesquieu's Philosophy of Liberalism: A Commentary on the Spirit of the Laws, 4:210

Montessori: A Modern Approach, 3:266

Montessori in Contemporary American Culture, 3:251

Montessori System Examined, 3:264

Monteverdi, 3:706

Monteverdi: Creator of Modern Music, 3:706

Monteverdi Companion, 3:706

Monte Walsh, 1:1217

A Month in the Country, 2:769, 2:770

Monthly Catalog of U.S. Government Publications, 1:109

Monthly Checklist of State Publications, 1:110

A Month of Sundays, 1:1060

Mont-St.-Michel and Chartres, 1:729, 1:730 3:562

The Monument, 1:1055

Monumenta Polonica, 2:811

Monumenta Serbocroatica, 2:785, 2:828

Moods, 1:1198

The Moods of Type, 1:20

Moominsummer Madness, 2:658

Moon, Sun and Witches, 4:458

The Moon and Sixpence, 1:520

The Moon and the Bonfire, 2:432

The Moon and the Zither: The Story of the Western Wing, 2:227

The Moon Bamboo, 4:561

The Moon Book: Exploring the Mysteries of the Lunar World, 5:629

The Moon by Whalelight and Other Adventures among Bats, Penguins, Crocodilians and Whales, 1:931

A Moon for the Misbegotten, 1:1106, 1:1107

The Moonies: A Psychological Analysis of the Unification Church, 4:871

Moonies in America: Cult, Church and Crusade, 4:871

The Moon in the Water: Understanding Tanizaki, Kawabata and Mishima, 2:282

The Moon Is a Harsh Mistress, 5:563

The Moon Is Down, 1:884

The Moonlight Bride, 2:137

Moonlighting with Your Personal Computer, 5:558

Moon of Wintertime, 3:610

The Moon Painters and Other Estonian Folk Tales, 2:796

Moonraker, 1:594

Moonrise, Moonset, 2:815

Moon Rocks, 5:628

Moons and Planets, 5:592

The Moonshine War, 1:1232

The Moons of Jupiter, 2:921

Moonsoon Country: Thailand in Transition, 2:336

The Moonstone, 1:346

Moore: G. E. Moore and the Cambridge Apostles, 4:29

Moorings and Metaphors, 2:108

The Moors: Islam in the West, 3:442

Moortown, 1:498

Moral Absolute: An Essay on the Nature and Rationale of Morality, 4:317

The Moral and Physical Condition of the Working Classes Employed in the Cotton Manufacture in Manchester, 1:368

The Moral and Political Thought of Mahatma Gandhi, 4:352

Moral Apostasy in Russian Literature, 2:687

The Moral Basis of Fielding's Art: A Study of Joseph Andrews, 1:245

Moral Clarity in the Nuclear Age, 5:111

Moral Conduct and Authority: The Place of Adab in South Asian Islam, 4:575

Moral Consciousness and Communicative Action, 4:404, 5:89

Moral Differences, 4:389

Moral Dilemmas in Modern Medicine, 5:122

Moral Education: Five Lectures, 3:268

Moral Emblems and Other Poems, 1:396

The Moral Essays: Operette Morali, 2:424

Moral Fables of Aesop, 2:352

Moralia, 4:489, 4:490

Morality, Reason, and Power: American Diplomacy in the Carter Years, 3:546

Morality and Ethics in Early Christianity, 4:690

Morality and Power in a Chinese Village, 3:471

Morality and the Bomb: An Ethical Assessment of Nuclear Deterrence, 5:110

Morality and the Human Future in the Thought of Teilhardde Chardin, 4:337

Morality as a Biological Phenomenon, 5:108

The Moral Judgment of the Child, 3:174, 3:192

Moral Knowledge and Its Methodology in Aristotle, 4:70

The Moral Limits of the Criminal Law, 4:386

A Morally Deep World, 5:115

Moral Man and Immoral Society: A Study in Ethics and Politics, 4:783, 4:784

A Moral Military, 4:388

The Moral Philosophy of T. H. Green, 4:230

The Moral Philosophy of Josiah Royce, 4:250

The Moral Philosophy of Richard Price, 4:211

The Moral Philsophy of G. E. Moore, 4:312

Moral Principles and Nuclear Weapons, 5:111

Moral Principles in Education, 3:261

Moral Reflections and Epistles, 2:650

Morals and Manners among Negro Americans, 3:578

The Moral Sense, 4:204

Morals on the Book of Job, 4:710

The Moral Tales, 2:528

Moral Value and the Human Zoo, 2:618

Moral Values in the Ancient World, 4:48

The Moral Vision of Dorothy Day: A Feminist Perspective, 4:766

Moran of the Lady Letty: A Story of Adventure off the California Coast, 1:776

A Morbid Taste for Bones, 1:608

Mordecai M. Kaplan and the Development of Reconstructionism, 4:667

Mordecai Richler and His Works, 2:924

More Alaska Bear Tales, 3:906

More Annotated Alice, 1:582

More Black American Playwrights: A Bibliography, 1:123

More Celtic Fairy Tales, 3:882

More English Fairy Tales, 3:882

More Ghost Stories of an Antiquary, 1:601

More Good Old Stuff, 1:1234

More Latin Lyrics: From Virgil to Milton, 2:382

More Letters of a Self-Made Diplomat, 3:886

More of My Life, 4:273

More Songs from Vagabondia, 2:908

More Stately Mansions, 1:1106, 1:1107

More's Utopia: The Biography of an Idea, 4:147

More Tales of Pirx the Pilot, 2:816

More than a Pantun: Understanding Malay Verse, 2:324

More than Fine Writing: Irene Wellington, Calligrapher (1904–84), 1:14

More Than One Universe: The Collected Stories of Arthur C. Clarke, 1:614

More Than the Ear Discovers: God in the Plays of Christopher Fry, 1:480

More Travels in a Donkey Trap, 3:898

More West Highland Tales, 3:876

More Women than Men, 1:462

More Work for Mother, 5:187

The Morgans: Private International Bankers, 1854–1913, 3:547

Morgan's Daughter, 2:935

Morgue, 2:568

Mori Ōgai and the Moderni-
zation of Japanese Cul-
ture, 2:290
Mori Sa'id, 2:19
Morley Callaghan and His
Works, 2:908
A Mormon Bibliography,
1830–1930, 4:845
The Mormon Experience: A
History of the Latter-day
Saints, 3:558, 4:845
Mormonism: The Story of a
New Religious Tradition,
4:846
Mormonism in Transition:
The Latter-Day Saints and
Their Church, 1890–1930,
4:845
The Mormon Murders: A
True Story of Greed, Forg-
ery, Deceit, and Death,
1:35
Mormons, 4:846
The Mormon's War on Pov-
erty: A History of L.D.S.
Welfare, 1830–1990, 4:846
Morning, Noon and Night,
1:964
A Morning at the Office,
2:937, 2:938
The Morning Glory: Prose
Poems, 1:951
Morning Hours, 4:209
Mornings on Horseback,
3:595, 3:935
Morning Star, 1:595
The Morning Watch, 1:932
The Moro Affair, 2:438
Morocco, 1:1176
Morocco Bound: Adrift
Among Books, 1:32
Morový Sloup: The Prague
Monument, 2:794
Morris Dictionary of Word
and Phrase Origins, 1:96
Morritz Schlick, 4:333
Mortal Acts, Mortal Words: A
Collection of Poems,
1:1001
A Mortal Antipathy, 1:678
The Mortal Danger: How
Misconceptions about Rus-
sia Imperil America, 2:761
The Mortal Hero: An Intro-
duction to Homer's Iliad,
2:362
Mortality, 2:134
Mortals and Immortals: Col-
lected Essays, 4:493
Mortal Vision: The Wisdom
of Euripides, 4:475
Morte Arthure (anonymous),
1:146

Morte d'Arthur (Malory),
1:146, 1:575
Morte d'Urban, 1:1033
Mortimeradios, 1:179
Mosaic, 2:773
A Mosaic of Life; or The
Magic Horn of Oberon,
2:731
The Mosby Medical Encyclo-
pedia, 5:311
Mosby's Memoirs and Other
Stories, 1:947
Moscow, 2:2042, 2:772
Moscow Notebooks, 2:737
Moscow of the Taverns,
2:718
Moscow Racetrack, 2:720
Moscow to the End of the
Line, 2:717
Moses, 2:838
Moses, Man of the Mountain,
1:849
Moses and Monotheism,
4:424, 5:446
Moses Ascending, 2:942
Moses Hess: Prophet of Com-
munism and Zionism,
4:655
Moses Mendelssohn: A Bio-
graphical Study, 4:209
Moses Migrating, 2:942
The Mosquito Coast, 3:940
Mosquitoes, 1:835
The Mössbauer Effect, 5:704
Mössbauer Effect: Principles
and Applications, 5:704
Mosses from an Old Manse,
1:675
The Most Ancient Testimony,
4:126
Most Secret, 2:962
A Most Wondrous Babble,
3:664
Motel, 1:1114
Mother (Asch), 2:35
The Mother (Brecht), 2:572
The Mother (Deledda), 2:419
Mother (Gorky), 2:724
Mother: The Great Revolu-
tionary Novel, 2:725
Mother and Son, 1:462
Mother Bombie, 1:186
Mother Camp: Female Im-
personators in America,
1:1182
Mother Comes of Age, 2:119
Mother Courage and Her
Children, 2:571, 2:572
Mother Earth: An American
Story, 4:464
Mother Goose, or, The Old
Nursery Rhymes, 1:585

Mother Goose in Prose,
1:1200
Motherhood: The Second
Oldest Profession, 3:870
Motherhood by Choice: Pio-
neers in Women's Health
and Family Planning,
5:313
Mother Hubbard, 1:583
Mother Is Gold: A Study in
West African Literature,
2:126
Motherlands, 2:111
The Mother Machine, 5:357
Mother Night, 1:1063
The Mother of Dreams and
Other Short Stories, 2:284
Mother Poem, 2:933
Mothers and Daughters: A
Lifelong Relationship,
5:423
Mother's First-Born Daugh-
ters: Early Shaker Writings
on Women and Religion,
4:849
Mothers of Psychoanalysis,
3:178
The Mother Spring, 2:119
The Mother's Recompense,
1:787
The Mother Syndrome in the
Russian Folk Imagination,
2:684
Mother Teresa: Her Work
and Her People, 4:743
Mothlight, 1:1159
Motif Index for Lost Mines
and Treasures, Applied
to Redaction of Arizona
Legends, and to Lost
Mines and Treasure Leg-
ends Exterior to Arizona,
3:868
Motif-Index of Folk-Litera-
ture, A Classification of
Narrative Elements in
Folk Tales, Ballads,
Myths, Fables, Medieval
Romances, Exempla,
Fabliaux, Jest-Books, and
Local Legends, 3:857,
3:882, 3:887
The Motion of History,
1:1085
The Motion Picture Guide,
3:826
Motivation and Personality,
5:461
Motivation and Personality: A
Handbook of Thematic
Content Analysis, 3:175,
3:176

Motivation and the Moral Sense in Francis Hutcheson's Ethical Theory, 4:203
Motives of Sound, 2:869
Motley, 1:482
The Motor Boys in Ottawa, 2:914
Motoring with Mohammed: Journey to Yemen and the Red Sea, 3:903
Mottke the Thief, 2:36
Mottoes, 1:117
Mouchette, 2:460
Moulton's Library of Literary Criticism of English and American Authors through the Beginning of the 20th Century, 1:134
The Mound Builders, 1:1121
The Mountain Giants, 2:435
Mountain Laurel, 1:1221
The Mountain of My Fear, 3:910
A Mountainous Journey: A Poet's Autobiography, 2:59
Mountain Storm, Pine Breeze: Folk Song in Japan, 3:851
Mountains without Handrails; Reflections on the Natural Parks, 5:116
The Mountain Wreath, 2:831
The Mount Sinai Medical Center Family Guide to Dental Health, 5:341
The Mourners Below, 1:1034
The Mournful Demeanor of Lieutenant Boruvka: Detective Tales, 2:795
Mourning, Gender, and Creativity in the Art of Herman Melville, 1:690
Mourning Becomes Electra, 1:1106
The Mourning Bride, 1:237
The Mousetrap and Other Plays, 1:606
Mouse Traps and Muffling Cups, 5:226
A Moveable Feast, 1:845
The Movement: English Poetry and Fiction of the 1950s, 1:415
Movement and Mental Imagery, 3:195
Movements and Issues in World Religions, 4:349
Movements in Art since 1945, 3:759
The Moviegoer, 1:1029
Movie-Made America: A Cultural History of American Movies, 3:561

Movies: A Psychological Study, 3:204
The Movies, Mr. Griffith, and Me, 1:1168
Movies and Methods, 1:1158
Moving and Shaking American Medicine, 5:334
The Moving Castle, 2:303
Moving from Within: A New Method for Dance Making, 3:732
The Moving Image, 2:968
A Moving Target, 1:484
Mozambique: From Colonialism to Revolution, 1900–82, 3:423
Mozambique: The Africanization of a European Institution, the Zambezi Prazeros, 1750–1902, 3:423
Mozart (Bloom), 3:707
Mozart (Hildesheimer), 3:707
Mozart: A Documentary Biography, 3:707
Mozart: Traces of Transcendence, 4:775
Mozart and Salieri, 2:738, 2:750
Mozart and Salieri: The Little Tragedies, 2:751
Mozart and Vienna, 3:707
The Mozart Companion, 3:707
The Mozart Handbook: A Guide to the Man and His Music, 3:707
Mozart in Prague: Thirteen Rondels, 2:794
Mozart's Death: A Corrective Survey of the Legends, 3:707
Mozart's Journey to Prague, 2:603
M. P., 1:389
MS—Something Can Be Done and You Can Do It, 5:393
Mtawa Mweusi, 2:154
Much Ado about Nothing (Grant), 4:126
Much Ado About Nothing (Shakespeare), 1:205, 1:206
Mudhakkirat Tabibah, 2:71
The Mud-Hut Dwellers, 2:826
Mūdīr-i Madrasah, 2:85
Mudun al-Milh, 2:69
Muhammad (Cook), 4:588
Muhammad (Lings), 4:588
Muhammad (Rodinson), 4:589
Muhammad: Prophet and Statesman, 4:589

Muhammad: The Man and His Faith, 4:588
Muhammad and the Conquests of Islam, 4:588
Muhammad and the Rise of Islam, 4:588
Muhammad at Mecca, 4:589
Muhammad at Medina, 4:589
Mulata, 2:853, 2:854
Mules and Men, 1:850, 3:866
Multatuli, 2:629
Multiculturalism and "The Politics of Recognition," 4:415
Multicultural Issues in Counseling: New Approaches to Diversity, 5:422
Multicultural Teaching, 3:258
The Multilingual Computer Dictionary, 5:540
Multinational Excursions, 3:58
Multinational Oil: A Study in Industrial Dynamics, 3:436
Multiple Authorship and the Myth of Solitary Genius, 1:266
Multiple Intelligences: The Theory in Practice, 3:250
Multiple Plot in English Renaissance Drama, 1:170
Multiple Regression, 3:200
The Multiple Stage in Spain during the Fifteenth and Sixteenth Centuries, 2:524
The Multiplicity of Dreams: Memory, Imagination, and Consciousness, 3:172
Multipurpose Tools for Bible Study, 4:795
Multivalence: The Moral Quality of Form in the Modern Novel, 1:421
Multi-Variable Calculus and Linear Algebra with Applications, 5:490
Multivariate Statistical Analysis in Geography, 3:132
Mulvaney Stories, 1:371
Mumbo-Jumbo, 1:1036
Mumby's Publishing and Bookselling in the 20th Century, 1:37
Mumford, Tate, Eiseley: Watchers in the Night, 1:889, 5:171
Mummies, Myth and Magic: In Ancient Egypt, 4:442
Mundane's World, 1:1188
The Munday Scheme, 1:479
Munera Pulveris, 1:324, 1:393, 1:394

Mungo Park: The African
Traveler, 3:932
Mungo Park and the Niger,
3:932
Municipal Government Reference Sources, 1:110
The Municipal Year Book,
3:1992, 3:148
The Muqaddimah, 3:458,
4:584
Murasaki Shikibu: The Tale
of Genji, 2:279
Murder and Assassination,
5:439
The Murder at the Vicarage,
1:605, 1:606
The Murder Book of J. G.
Reeder, 1:598
The Murderers among Us:
The Simon Wiesenthal
Memoirs, 3:351
Murder for Pleasure: The
Life and Times of the Detective Story, 1:604
Murder in Baghdad, 2:61
Murder in Mexico, 3:295
Murder in the Cathedral,
1:471, 1:472
Murder in the Ironsmiths'
Market, 2:100
Murder Must Advertise, 1:610
The Murder of Roger Ackroyd, 1:605, 1:606
Murder on the Orient Express, 1:606
Murder She Wrote: A Study
of Agatha Christies' Detective Fiction, 1:606
The Murders in the Rue
Morgue, 1:1226
Murder Trials, 2:384, 3:313
Murder Will Out: The Detective in Fiction, 1:604
Muriel at Metropolitan, 2:168
Muriel Spark, 1:552
Murky Business, 2:453
The Murmuring Stream: The
Life and Works of Hsieh
Ling-yün, 2:202
Murphy, 1:439, 2:459
Murrow: His Life and Times,
3:819
Murr the Tomcat, 2:591
Murther and Walking Spirits,
2:910
A Muse for the Masses,
3:873
The Muse in Mexico: A Mid-Century Miscellany, 2:848
The Muse Learns to Write,
4:460
The Muses of Resistance,
1:227

Museums and Women and
Other Stories, 1:1060
The Museum World of Henry James, 1:767
Music: An Appreciation,
3:665
The Music: Reflections on
Jazz and Blues, 1:941
Music, Gender, and Culture,
3:660
Music, Imagination, and Culture, 3:659
Music, Spirit and Language
in the Renaissance, 4:132
Musical Aesthetics: A Historical Reader, 3:661
Musicalalia: Sources of Information in Music, 3:655
Musical Allusion in the
Works of James Joyce,
2:987
Musical Applications of
Microprocessors, 5:564
Musical Elaborations, 1:1042
Musical Events: A Chronicle,
1983–1986, 3:662
Musical Instruments: A Comprehensive Dictionary,
3:672
Musical Instruments: An Illustrated History, from Antiquity to the Present,
3:672
Musical Instruments of the
World; An Illustrated Encyclopedia, 3:656
The Musical Language of
Berlioz, 3:682
The Musical Languages of
Elliott Carter, 3:688
Musical References in the
Chinese Classics, 3:670
A Musical Season: A Critic
from Abroad in America,
3:662
Musical Stages: An Autobiography, 3:713
The Musical Theatre: A Celebration, 3:661
Musical Tour through the
Land of the Past, 2:501
The Musical Woman: An International Perspective,
1986–1990, 3:658
Music and Ceremonies, 1:548
Music and Imagination,
3:691
Music and Literature: A
Comparison of the Arts,
3:659
Music and Musicians in
Nineteenth-Century Italy,
3:663

Music and Poetry, 1:772
Music and Poetry: The Nineteenth Century and After,
2:988
Music and Society: The Politics of Composition, Performance, and Reception,
3:661
Music and the Emotions:
The Philosophical Theories, 3:659
Music and the Historical
Imagination, 3:664
Music and the Reformation
in England: 1549-1660,
4:737
Music and Worship in Pagan
and Christian Antiquity,
4:689
Music at the Close: Stravinsky's Last Years, a Personal Memoir, 3:723
Music Criticism: An Annotated Guide to the Literature, 3:655
Music Cultures of the Pacific, the Near East and
Asia, 3:666
Music for Chameleons, 1:959
Music for the Dance: Reflections on a Collaborative
Art, 3:732
Music from a Blue Well,
2:662
The Music Guide to Austria
and Germany, 3:654
The Music Guide to Belgium, Luxembourg, Holland
and Switzerland, 3:654
The Music Guide to Great
Britain, 3:654
The Music Guide to Italy,
3:654
Music in a New Found
Land: Two Hundred Years
of American Music, 3:661
Music Industry Directory,
3:656
Music in Early Christian Literature, 3:661
Music in India: The Classical
Traditions, 3:670
Music in Painting, 3:660
Music in Society: A Guide to
the Sociology of Music,
3:664
Music in the 20th Century,
from Debussy through
Stravinsky, 3:658
Music in the Baroque Era:
From Monteverdi to Bach,
3:659

Music in the Classic Period, 3:662

Music in the Middle Ages, 3:662

Music in the New World, 3:660

Music in the Renaissance, 3:333, 3:662

Music in the Romantic Era, 3:659

Music in the Theatre of Ben Jonson, 1:184

Music in the United States: A Historical Introduction, 3:660

Music in the Western World: A History in Documents, 3:664

Music in Western Civilization, 3:661, 4:737

Music Is My Mistress, 3:695

The Music Lover's Literary Companion, 3:671

The Music Men, 3:660

The Music of Africa, 3:670

The Music of Alban Berg, 3:680

The Music of Alexander Scriabin, 3:717

The Music of Ancient Greece: An Encyclopedia, 3:656

The Music of Béla Bartók, 3:677

The Music of Benjamin Britten, 3:685

The Music of Black Americans: A History, 3:663

The Music of Britten and Tippett: Studies in Themes and Techniques, 3:666, 3:685, 3:725

The Music of Human Flesh, 2:58

The Music of Igor Stravinsky, 3:723

The Music of Jean Sibelius, 3:718

Music of Liszt, 3:704

Music of Many Cultures: An Introduction, 3:666

The Music of Sibelius, 3:718

The Music of Stockhausen: An Introduction, 3:721

Music of the Americas, 3:666

Music of the Twentieth Century: Style and Structure, 3:666

Music of the Twentieth Century, 3:665

Music of the Whole Earth, 3:667

Music of Three More Seasons, 3:662

Music of Three Seasons, 1974–1977, 3:662

Music Primer: Various Items about Music to 1970, 3:699

Music Reference and Research Materials: An Annotated Bibliography, 3:655

The Music School, 1:1060

Music since 1900, 3:657

Music through MIDI, 5:564

The Musk-Ox and Other Tales, 2:736

Muslim-Christian Encounters, 3:213

The Muslim Creed: Its Genesis and Historical Development, 4:577

The Muslim Discovery of Europe, 3:443, 3:459

Muslim Extremism in Egypt: The Prophet and the Pharaoh, 4:570

Muslim Institutions, 4:569

Muslim Intellectual: A Study of al-Ghazālī, 4:582

Muslim Minorities in the World Today, 4:570

Muslim Saints and Mystics, 2:86, 4:574

Muslim Theology, 4:577

Mussolini, 3:385

Mussolini: A Biography, 3:344

Mussolini and the Jews, 3:349

Mussorgsky, 3:708

Mussorgsky: In Memoriam, 1881–1981, 3:708

Mussorgsky's Days and Works: A Biography in Documents, 3:708

Mustaqbal al-Thaqafah al-Misriyah, 2:74

The Mute Stones Speak: The Story of Archaeology in Italy, 2:381, 3:305

Mutiny Within, 1:303

The Mutual Flame, 1:215

Mutuality: The Vision of Martin Buber, 4:662

Mutuwhenua: The Moon Sleeps, 2:976

Muzeeka, 1:1089, 1:1090

My Antonia, 1:820

My Antonia: The Road Home, 1:821

My Apprenticeship (Gorky), 2:724, 2:725

My Apprenticeship (Webb), 3:113

My Best Mary, 1:300

My Black Me, a Beginning Book of Black Poetry, 1:1196

My Bondage and My Freedom, 1:667, 3:527

My Bones and My Flute, 2:938

My Breast: One Woman's Cancer Story, 5:373

My Brilliant Career, 2:952

My Brother, My Executioner, 2:331

My Brother Benjamin, 3:685

My Brother's Keeper: James Joyce's Early Years, 1:974

My Career Goes Bung, 2:952

The Mycenaean Origins of Greek Mythology, 4:487

The Mycenaean World, 4:446

My Childhood, 2:724, 2:725

My Children! My Africa!, 2:161

Mycotoxins: Formation, Analysis, and Significance, 5:352

My Country and My People, 2:254

My Cousin Rachel, 1:620

My Darling, My Hamburger, 1:1122, 1:1123

My Darling Clementine, 1:1165

My Days of Anger, 1:833

My Dear Wister: The Frederick Remington-Owen Wister Letters, 1:789

My Deep Dark Pain Is Love, 2:849

My Early Life: A Roving Commission, 3:400

My Early Travels and Adventures in America, 3:938

My Father, Frank Lloyd Wright, 3:798

My Father, Irving Fisher, 3:76

My Father, Sholom Aleichem, 2:46

My Father's Moon, 2:956

My Father's Son, 1:528

My First Forty Years, 3:692

My First Summer in the Sierra, 5:836

My Friend Lawrence Durrell, 1:470

My Friend's Book, 2:477

My Guru and His Disciple, 4:872

My Half Century: Selected Prose, 2:697

My Heart Is Broken, 2:912

My Heart's in the Highlands, 1:1110
My House Is on Fire, 2:864
My Kalulu, Prince, King, and Slave: A Story of Central Africa, 3:938
My Lady Ludlow and Other Stories, 1:356
My Land and My People, 4:356
My Larger Education, 1:785
My Last Farewell, 2:332
My Last Sigh, 3:832
My Life, 3:294, 3:728, 3:742
My Life: Recollections of a Nobel Laureate, 5:675, 5:708
My Life, a Record of Events and Opinions, 5:812
My Life a Loaded Gun: Dickinson, Plath, Rich, and Female Creativity, 1:912
My Life and Hard Times, 1:890
My Life and My Films, 3:842
My Life and My Views, 5:675
My Life and Other Sketches, 2:836
My Life and the Times, 3:806
My Life as a Man, 1:1040
My Life as an Explorer, 3:912
My Life between Japan and America, 3:501
My Life in Pictures, 1:1161
My Life in the Bush of Ghosts, 2:150
My Life with Ishmael, 2:24
My Life with Martin Luther King, Jr., 4:773
My Life with Paper: An Autobiography, 1:5
My Literary Passions, 1:758
My Lives, 1:43
My Lost Mexico: The Making of a Novel, 3:931
My Love Affair with England, 3:901
My Many Years, 3:714
My Mark Twain, 1:758, 1:759, 1:780
My Memoirs, 2:473
My Michael, 2:22
My Mortal Enemy, 1:820
My Mother Gets Married, 2:672
My Mother's House, 2:470
My Mother's Sabbath Days: A Memoir, 2:39
My Musical Life, 3:713
My Name Is Asher Lev, 1:1032

My Name Is William Tell, 1:1053
My Oedipus Complex, 1:528
My Past and Thoughts, 2:727, 2:728
My People: Story of the Jews, 4:593
My Philosophical Development, 4:323, 5:102
My Proper Ground, 1:508
My Quest for Beauty, 5:463
Myra Breckenridge, 1:1061
"My Reader, My Fellow-Labourer", 1:274
My Recollections of Lord Byron, 1:283
My Religion, 4:552
Myricae, 2:431
Myron: A Novel, 1:1062
Myself I Must Remake: Life and Poetry of W. B. Yeats, 1:1152
Myself with Others; Selected Essays, 2:866
My Sister, Life, 2:745
My Sister Eileen, 1:897
My Son's Story, 2:162
My Soul Is Rested, 3:557
My Soul Looks Back, 4:763
My Soul's High Song: The Collected Writings of Countee Cullen, 1:824
Mysteries (Hamsun), 2:664
Mysteries (Wilson), 1:568
The Mysteries of Harris Burdick, 1:1207, 1:1208
The Mysteries of Mithra, 4:450
The Mysteries of Selflessness, 4:374
Mysteries of the Backwoods; or, Sketches of the Southwest, 1:702, 1:703
Mysteries of the Universe, 5:655
The Mysteries of Udolpho, 1:269, 1:602, 1:622
Mysteries of Winterthur, 1:1022
The Mysterious Affair at Styles, 1:605, 1:606
The Mysterious Mother, 1:262
The Mysterious Mr. Quin, 1:606
The Mysterious Mr. Ripley, 1:1231
The Mysterious North: Encounters with the Canadian Frontier 1947–1954, 3:906

The Mysterious Play of Kali: An Interpretive Study of Ramakrishna, 4:355
Mysterious Stranger and Other Stories, 1:781
Mysterium Cosmographicum, 5:608
Mystery, 1:1243
Mystery and Manners: Occasional Prose, 1:1024
The Mystery of Being, 4:304
The Mystery of Edwin Drood, 1:348
The Mystery of Fu Manchu, 1:596
The Mystery of Georges Simenon: A Biography, 2:508
The Mystery of Marie Rôget, 1:1226
The Mystery of the Mind, 5:81
Mystery Play, 1:1114
Mystery Religions in the Ancient World, 4:450
Mystery Train: Images of America in Rock 'n' Roll Music, 3:560
Mystical and Mythological Explanatory Works of Assyrian and Babylonian Scholars, 4:545
The Mystical Element in Heidegger's Thought, 4:292
Mystical Elements in Muhammad, 4:588
Mystical Islam: An Introduction to Sufism, 4:574
The Mystical Philosophy of Muhyid Din-Ibnul 'Arabi, 4:583
Mystical Poems of Rumi: Second Selection, 4:589
The Mystical Theology of St. Bernard, 4:112, 4:286
Mystic and Pilgrim, 1:153, 4:698
The Mystic Chords of Memory, 3:560
Mysticism: Christian and Buddhist, 4:558
Mysticism and Dissent, 4:724
Mysticism and Guilt-Consciousness in Schelling's Philosophical Development, 4:252
Mysticism and Logic and Other Essays, 4:323
Mysticism and Religious Tradition, 4:575
Mysticism and Sexuality: E.T.A. Hoffmann, 2:592

Mysticism and the Early South German-Austrian Anabaptist Movement, 1525–1531, 4:724

Mysticism East and West, 4:488

The Mystic Masseur, 2:938, 2:939

Mystics, Philosophers, and Politicians, 4:130

Mystics and Commissars, 4:567

Mystics and Zen Masters, 4:781

The Mystics of Islam: An Introduction to Sufism, 4:576

The Mystics of Spain, 2:526

The Mystics of the Church, 4:679

Mystifying Movies: Fads and Fallacies in Contemporary Film Theory, 1:1157

My Study Windows, 1:685

My Ten Years in a Quandary, 1:815

Myth: Its Meaning and Functions in Ancient and Other Cultures, 2:52

Myth, Cosmos, and Society: Indo-European Themes of Creation and Destruction, 4:435

Myth, Legend and Custom in the Old Testament, 4:477

Myth, Literature and the African World, 2:112, 2:149

Myth, Realism and the African Writer, 2:112

Myth, Rhetoric, and the Voice of Authority, 4:477

Myth, Ritual, and Kingship in Buganda, 4:463

Myth, Ritual and Religion, 3:882

Myth, Symbol, and Culture, 1:980

Myth and Cult among Primitive Peoples, 4:429, 4:432

Myth and Guilt, 5:467

Myth and History in the Contemporary Spanish Novel, 2:525

Myth and Ideology in Contemporary Brazilian Fiction, 2:890

Myth and Law among the Indo-Europeans, 4:436

Myth and Literature: Contemporary Theory and Practice, 2:988

Myth and Meaning in Early Taoism, 4:528

Myth and Metaphor: Selected Essays, 1974–1988, 2:988

Myth and Mystery, 4:811

Myth and Philosophy: A Contest of Truths, 4:37, 4:428

Myth and Religion of the North, 4:437

Myth and Ritual in Christianity, 4:881

The Myth and Ritual School: An Introduction, 3:879

The Myth and Ritual School: J. G. Frazer and the Cambridge Ritualists, 4:479

Myth and Society in Ancient Greece, 4:493

Myth and Symbol: Critical Approaches and Applications, 3:857

Myth and the Modern Novel: García Márquez, Mann, and Joyce, 2:868

Myth and Thought among the Greeks, 4:49, 4:493

Myth and Tragedy in Ancient Greece, 4:493

My Theatre Life, 3:739

The Mythical Man-Month: Essays on Software Engineering, 5:549

Mythical Past—Elusive Future: An Introduction to Historical Sociology, 3:276

Myth in Africa: A Study of Its Cultural and Aesthetic Relevance, 2:111, 2:142

Myth in Primitive Psychology, 4:486

Myth in the Poetry of Ted Hughes: A Guide to the Poems, 1:498

The Myth Makers, 1:538

Mythmaker's Magic: Behind the Illusion of "Creation Science," 5:765

Mythmaking and Metaphor in Black Women's Fiction, 1:804

The Mythmaking Frame of Mind: Social Imagination and American Culture, 3:559

The Myth of Christian Uniqueness, 4:898

The Myth of Deliverance: Reflections on Shakespeare's Problem Comedies, 1:210

The Myth of God Incarnate, 4:885

The Myth of Mau Mau, 3:423

The Myth of Meaning, 5:456

The Myth of Mental Illness: Foundations of a Theory of Personal Conduct, 5:81

The Myth of Senility: Misconceptions about the Brain and Aging, 5:316

The Myth of Sisyphus, 2:464

The Myth of Sisyphus and Other Essays, 2:464

The Myth of the Birth of the Hero, 5:466

Myth of the Eternal Return, 4:473

The Myth of the Judeo-Christian Tradition, 4:648

The Myth of the Machine, 5:71, 5:169, 5:171

The Myth of the Madding Crowd, 3:203

The Myth of the Modern, 3:211

The Myth of the Negro Past, 3:32

The Myth of the State, 4:279

Myth of Wild Africa: Conservation without Illusion, 5:762

Mythography: The Study of Myths and Rituals, 4:428

Mythologies: From Gingee to Kuruksetra, 4:504

Mythologies (Barthes), 2:454, 2:455

Mythologies (Bonnefoy), 4:428

Mythologies and Philosophies of Salvation in the Theistic Traditions of India, 4:505

Mythologies of the Ancient World, 2:52, 4:428, 4:439

Mythologiques, 4:428

Mythology, 2:345

Mythology: Timeless Tales of Gods and Heroes, 3:881

Mythology and Folktales: Their Relation and Interpretation, 3:848

Mythology and the Renaissance Tradition in English Literature, 1:215

Mythology and the Renaissance Tradition in English Poetry, 1:165

Mythology and the Romantic Tradition in English Poetry, 1:265

The Mythology of Mexico and Central America, 2:848

The Mythology of South America, 2:848

The Mythopoeic Reality: The
Postwar American Nonfic-
tion Novel, 1:921
Myths, Legends, and Folk
Tales from the Hmong of
Laos, 2:322
Myths, Models and Para-
digms, 5:160
Myths about St. Bartholo-
mew's Day Massacres,
1572–1576, 4:732
Myths and Folktales of the
Russians, Western Slavs,
and Magyars, 3:854
Myths and Legends of the
Great Dismal Swamp,
3:860
Myths and Legends of the
Mackinacs and the Lake
Region, 3:861
Myths and Legends of the
Pacific Northwest, 3:863
Myths and Realities: Societies
of the Colonial South,
3:570
Myths from Mesopotamia:
Creation, the Flood, Gil-
gamesh, and Others, 4:545
The Myths of Plato, 4:84
Myths of Power: A Marxist
Study of the Brontës,
1:333
Myths of the Hindus and
Buddhists, 4:503
Myths to Live By, 3:877
My Tibet, 4:560
My Uncle Dudley, 1:1016,
1:1017
My Universities, 2:724, 2:725
My View of the World, 5:714
My Voice Because of You,
2:550
My Wife, My Daughter, and
Poor Mary-Ann: Women
and Work in Australia,
3:494
My Wife Maria Callas, 3:686
My Works and Days: A Per-
sonal Chronicle,
1895–1975, 5:171
My World and Its Value,
4:345
My World and Welcome to
It, 1:890
My World Line: An Informal
Autobiography, 5:689
My World of Astrology, 4:860
My World of Bibliophile
Binding, 1:25
My Young Years, 3:714

N

Nabokov: His Life in Art,
1:1020
Nabokov: His Life in Part,
1:1020
Nabokov: The Critical Heri-
tage, 2:741
Nabokov and the Novel,
2:741
Nabokov's Ada: The Place of
Consciousness, 2:741
Nabokov's Art of Memory
and European Modernism,
2:741
Nabokov's Fifth Arc: Nabo-
kov and Others on His
Life's Work, 2:742
Nabokov's Otherworld, 2:741
Nabokov Translated, 2:741
A Nabokov Who's Who,
2:742
The Nabokov-Wilson Letters,
1:1020
Nada the Lily, 1:595
Nadja, 2:462
Nafrīn-i Zamīn, 2:85
The Nag, 2:41
Nag Hammadi, Gnosticism,
and Early Christianity,
4:453
The Nag Hammadi Library,
4:812
The Nag Hammadi Library
in English, 4:453, 4:686
Naguib Mahfouz's Egypt: Ex-
istential Themes in His
Writings, 2:69
Nahuat Myth and Social
Structure, 4:465
The Naive and Sentimental
Lover, 1:596
Nakahara: Family Farming
and Population in a Japa-
nese Village, 3:502
The Naked and the Dead,
1:1011, 1:1012
The Naked Computer, 5:541
Naked Earth, 2:238
Naked Emperors: Essays of a
Taboo Stalker, 5:135
The Naked Face, 1:1222
Naked in Exile: Khalil
Hawi's Threshing Floors of
Hunger, 2:59
Naked Lunch, 1:956, 1:957
Naked Masks: Five Plays,
2:435
Naked Music: Poems of Juan
Ramón Jiménez, 2:542
A Naked Needle, 2:122

Naked Poetry: Recent Ameri-
can Poetry in Open
Forms, 1:915
The Naked Year, 2:747
The Name above the Title:
An Autobiography, 3:833
The Name and Nature of Po-
etry: And Other Selected
Prose, 1:496
The Name Game: The Semi-
otic Intertext of De dondo
son los cantantes, 2:884
The Name of the Rose,
2:400, 2:419, 2:420
Names in the History of Psy-
chology: A Biographical
Sourcebook, 5:414
Naming and Necessity, 4:301
Naming in Paradise Lost:
Milton and the Language
of Adam and Eve, 1:192
Naming the Rose: Eco, Medi-
eval Signs, and Modern
Theory, 2:420
Naming the Rose: Essays on
Eco's "The Name of the
Rose," 2:420
Naming the Whirlwind: The
Renewal of God-Language,
4:744, 5:201
Nana, 2:517, 2:518
Napoleon, the Jews and the
Sanhedrin, 4:637
Napoleon and the Awakening
of Europe, 3:339
Napoleon and the Jews,
4:636
Napoleon and the Restora-
tion of the Bourbons,
3:406
Napoleon Bonaparte, 3:340
Napoleon from 18 Brumaire
to Tilsit, 1799–1807, 3:373
Napoleon from Tilsit to Wa-
terloo, 1807–1815, 3:373
Napoleon's Marshals, 3:339
Napoleon's Memoirs, 3:339
Napoleon Symphony, 1:454
The Narcissistic Text: A
Reading of Camus' Fic-
tion, 2:464
Narcissus and Goldmund,
2:589
Narrativas Trágico-marítimas,
2:557
Narrative, 1:681
Narrative, Apparatus, Ideolo-
gy: A Film Theory Reader,
1:1159
Narrative and Drama, 2:401
Narrative and Dramatic
Sources of Shakespeare,
1:219

The Narrative and Selected Writings, 1:667

Narrative Experiments, 5:66, 5:156

Narrative Irony in the Contemporary Spanish-American Novel, 2:848

Narrative Magic in the Fiction of Isabel Allende, 2:851

Narrative of an Expedition to the Zambesi and Its Tributaries, 3:930

The Narrative of Arthur Gordon Pym of Nantucket, 1:692

The Narrative of Realism and Myth, 2:442

Narrative of the Life of Frederick Douglass, 1:667

A Narrative of Travels on the Amazon and Rio Negro, 5:812

The Narrative Pattern in Ernest Hemingway's Fiction, 1:847

Narratives of Human Evolution, 5:800

The Narratives of Michel Butor: The Writer as Janus, 2:463

Narratives of the Travels and Adventures of Monsieur Violet, 1:374

Narrative Strategies in "La Princesse de Clèves," 2:484

Narrative Transvestism, 1:230

The Narrow Corner, 1:520

The Narrow Ground, 3:371

Narrow Road to the Deep North (Bond), 1:446

The Narrow Road to the Deep North and Other Travel Sketches (Bashō), 2:276

Narrow Rooms, 1:1034

The Narrows, 1:1030

Nasser and His Generation, 3:446

Nasser's New Egypt, 3:446

Natalia Ginzberg: Human Relationships in a Changing World, 3:399

The Natchez: An Indian Tale, 2:466

Nathalie Sarraute (Besser), 2:506

Nathalie Sarraute (Temple), 2:506

Nathalie Sarraute: The War of the Words, 2:506

Nathanael West, 1:897

Nathanael West: An Annotated Bibliography, 1:897

Nathanael West: The Art of His Life, 1:897

Nathanael West: The Ironic Prophet, 1:897

Nathaniel Hawthorne, 1:677

Nathaniel Hawthorne: A Biography, 1:677

A Nathaniel Hawthorne Encyclopedia, 1:677

Nathan the Wise, 2:600, 4:208

The National Archives and Foreign Relations Research, 3:506

National Atlas of the United States of America, 1:84

The National Book Awards: Forty One Years of Literary Excellence, 1:135

National Directory of Free Vacation and Travel Information, 3:891

The National Experience: A History of the United States, 3:512

National Fax Directory, 1:105

National Gazetteer of the United States of America, 1:84

National Geographic Atlas of the World, 1:84, 3:273

The National Health, 1:524, 1:525

National Health Care in Great Britain: Lessons for the U.S.A., 5:330

National Health Insurance: Conflicting Goals and Policy Choices, 5:328

National Health Policy: What Role for Government, 5:330

National Index of American Imprints through 1800: The Short-Title Evans, 1:68

Nationalism, Colonialism, and Literature, 2:988

Nationalism and History: Essays on Old and New Judaism, 4:657

Nationalism and Imperialism in the Hither East, 3:286

Nationalism and Realism, 1852–1879, 3:341

Nationalism and Revolution in Egypt, 3:446

Nationalism and the Jewish Ethic, 2:13

Nationalism and the Jewish Ethic: Basic Writings of Ahad Ha'am, 4:657

Nationalism in Modern Anglo-Irish Poetry, 1:417

Nationalism in the Horn of Africa, 3:421

Nationalisms and Sexualities, 1:1134

The Nationalist Movement, 3:485

The Nationalist Revolution in China, 1923–1928, 3:472

The Nationalization of the Masses, 2:565, 2:604, 3:377

National Leaders of American Conservation, 5:816

National List of Scientific Plant Names, 5:762

National Newspaper Index, 1:113

National Parks: The American Experience, 3:550

National Party Platforms, 1840–1976, 3:511

The National Playwrights Directory, 1:1074

The National Policy and the Wheat Economy, 3:616

National Styles of Humor, 3:872

National Union Catalog, 1:64

National Union Catalog, 1972, 1:65

National Union Catalog: A Cumulative Author List, 1953–57, 1:64

National Union Catalog: A Cumulative Author List, 1958–67, 1:64

National Union Catalog: A Cumulative Author List, 1968–72, 1:65

National Union Catalog: Audiovisual Materials, 1:65

National Union Catalog: Author List, 1973–77, 1:65

National Union Catalog: Books, 1:65

National Union Catalog: Cartographic Materials, 1:65

National Union Catalog: U.S. Books, 1:65

The National Union Catalog Pre-1956 Imprints, 1:65

Nation and Narration, 1:1133

A Nation at Risk: The Imperative for Educational Reform, 3:252

Nation Building in Malaysia, 1946–1974, 3:492

The Nation Comes of Age: A People's History of the Ante-Bellum Years, 3:525

Nation in Arms: The Origins of the People's Army of Vietnam, 3:491

The Nation in Crisis, 1861–1877, 3:510

A Nation of Behavers, 4:753

A Nation of Enemies: Chile under Pinochet, 3:634

Nations Negroes et Culture, 3:428

Native American Architecture, 3:763

Native American Folklore, 1879–1979: An Annotated Bibliography, 3:864

The Native American in American Literature, 1:716

Native American Literature, 1:133

Native American Myths and Mysteries, 3:864

Native American Reader, 1:129, 1:717

Native American Religions: An Introduction, 4:464

Native American Religions: North America, 4:465

Native American Testimony, 3:557

Native American Traditions: Sources and Interpretations, 4:464

Native American Women: A Bibliographic Dictionary, 3:509

Native Argosy, 2:907

Native Arts of North America, 3:759

Native Literature in Canada: From the Oral Tradition to the Present, 2:905

A Native of Winby, 1:769

Native of Winby and Other Tales, 1:770

The Native Population of the Americas in 1492, 3:627

Native Realm: A Search for Self-Definition, 2:818

Native Religions of North America, 4:464

Natives and Newcomers: Canada's "Heroic Age" Reconsidered, 3:611

Native Society and Disease in Colonial Ecuador, 3:628

The Natives of Hemsö, 2:679

Natives of My Person, 2:937

Native Son, 1:802, 1:905, 1:1029, 1:1088

Native Sons: A Critical Study of Twentieth-Century Negro American Authors, 1:794

Native Sources of Japanese Industrialization, 1750–1920, 3:480, 3:502

Native Stranger: A Black American's Journey into the Heart of Africa, 3:417, 3:903

The Native Tongue and the Word: Developments in English Prose Style, 1:167

The Natural, 1:1012, 1:1013

Natural Acts: A Sidelong View of Science and Nature, 5:765

Natural Agency: An Essay on the Causal Theory of Action, 5:790

The Natural Alien: Humankind and Environment, 5:114

The Natural and the Supernatural Jew, 4:646

Natural Childbirth: The Bradley Way, 5:359

Natural Classicism: Essays on Literature and Science, 2:990

A Natural Curiosity, 1:468

Natural Fictions: George Chapman's Major Tragedies, 1:175

Natural Gas: Governments and Oil Companies in the Third World, 5:284

The Natural Gas Industry: Evolution, Structure, and Economics, 5:285

Natural Hair Growth, 5:399

Natural Hazards: Local, National, Global, 5:637

Natural History, 5:810

Natural History of Deer, 5:771

The Natural History of H. G. Wells, 1:564

Natural History of Moles, 5:770

The Natural History of Religion, 4:201

The Natural History of Selborne, 5:819

Natural History of Shrews, 5:770

The Natural History of the Primates, 5:771

A Natural History of the Senses, 1:932

The Natural History of the Universe, 5:588

Natural History of Weasels and Stoats, 5:771

The Natural House, 3:797

Natural Inheritance, 5:529

Naturalism and Ontology, 4:333

Naturalism and the Human Spirit, 4:265

Naturalism in American Fiction: The Classic Phase, 1:804

The Naturalism of Condillac, 4:195

Natural Knowledge of God in the Philosophy of Jacques Maritain, 4:765

Natural Law, 4:232

Natural Law and Human Dignity, 4:277

The Natural Laws of Husbandry, 5:274

A Natural Perspective, 1:211, 1:976

The Natural Philosophy of Galileo, 4:143

The Natural Philosophy of Time, 5:68

Natural Regions of the United States and Canada, 5:626

Natural Relief for Arthritis, 5:398

Natural Right and the American Imagination, 1:725

The Natural Sciences and American Scientists in the Revolutionary Era, 5:28

Natural Selection, 5:793

Natural Supernaturalism, 1:265, 1:931

Natural Symbols: Explorations in Cosmology, 3:29

A Natural Theology for Our Time, 4:289

Natural Theories of Mind, 4:383

Nature, 1:669

Nature, Change and Agency in Aristotle's Physics: A Philosophical Study, 4:71

Nature, Man, and Society in the Twelfth Century, 4:101, 4:696

Nature, Technology, and Society, 5:74, 5:152

Nature and Culture in the Iliad: The Tragedy of Hector, 2:362

The Nature and Destiny of Man, 4:784

The Nature and Function of Scientific Theories, 5:62

The Nature and Growth of Modern Mathematics, 5:481

Nature and Life, 4:341

The Nature and Logic of Capitalism, 3:51

The Nature and Making of Parchment, 1:26

Nature and Man, 4:338, 4:339

Nature and Man's Fate, 5:135

The Nature and Purpose of the Universe, 1:1088

Nature and Religious Imagination: From Edwards to Bushnell, 1:627

Nature and Self, 2:220

Nature and the American Mind, 5:785

The Nature Catalog, 5:816

The Nature Directory: A Guide to Environmental Organizations, 5:816

Nature in Asian Traditions of Thought: Essays in Environmental Philosophy, 4:498, 4:502, 4:512, 4:522, 4:534

The Nature of a Crime, 1:474

The Nature of All Being: A Study of Wittgenstein's Modal Atomism, 4:345

The Nature of Belief, 4:783

The Nature of Change in Geographical Ideas, 5:619

The Nature of Copyright: A Law of Users' Rights, 1:55

The Nature of Doctrine: Religion and Theology in a Postliberal Age, 4:889

The Nature of Existence, 4:303

The Nature of Geography, 3:116, 3:118, 5:620

The Nature of Human Intelligence, 3:174

The Nature of Hypnosis and Suggestion, 5:441

The Nature of Light and Colour in the Open Air, 5:634

Nature of Man: A Reader, 5:450

The Nature of Man and His Relation with the Universe, 4:323

The Nature of Man in Early Stoic Philosophy, 4:57

The Nature of Maps: Essays toward Understanding Maps and Mapping, 3:121, 3:135

The Nature of Mathematical Knowledge, 5:493

The Nature of Physical Reality: A Philosophy of Modern Physics, 5:68

The Nature of Physical Theory (1936), 5:676

The Nature of Prejudice, 3:176, 3:179, 3:208, 5:432

The Nature of Scotland, 3:368

The Nature of Suffering: And the Goals of Medicine, 5:119

The Nature of the Chemical Bond and the Structure of Molecules and Crystals, 5:734, 5:752

The Nature of the Child, 5:322

The Nature of the Gods, 4:72

The Nature of the Physical World, 5:681

The Nature of Thermodynamics, 5:676

The Nature of the Stratigraphical Record, 5:622

The Nature of Thought, 4:276

Nature Religion in America: From the Algonkian Indians to the New Age, 4:841

Nature's Body: Gender in the Making of Modern Science, 5:188

Nature's Diary, 2:749

Nature's Economy: A History of Ecological Ideas, 3:551, 5:821

Nature's Metropolis: Chicago and the Great West, 3:531, 5:822

Nature's Nation, 3:587, 4:35

Nature's Sternest Painter: Five Essays on the Poetry of George Crabbe, 1:289

Nausea, 2:506

Navajo Coyote Tales: The Curly to Aheedliinii Version, 3:865

Navajo Folktales, 3:865

The Naval War of 1812, 3:594

Naven, 3:14, 4:461

The Navstar Global Positioning System, 5:247

The Nazarene, 2:35

The Nazi Doctors: Medical Killing and the Psychology of Genocide, 5:79

Near Changes, 1:1061

Near-Death Experiences: An Annotated Bibliography, 4:866

Near Eastern Religious Texts Relating to the Old Testament, 4:810

Nearest the Pole, 3:933

The Near-Johannesburg Boy, 1:954

The Nearness of You: Poems for Men, 1:1001

Near Shore Sediment Transport, 5:632

Near to the Wild Heart, 2:895

Near Zero: Frontiers of Physics, 5:650

Nebraska Folklore, 3:862

Nebraska Symposium on Motivation, 3:175

The Necessary Angel: Essays on Reality and the Imagination, 1:886, 1:887

The Necessary Blankness, 1:916

Necessary Doubt, 1:567

Necessary Lessons: Decline and Renewal in American Schools, 3:252

Necessary Questions: An Introduction to Philosophy, 4:19

Necessities of Life, 1:1037

The Necessities of War: A Study of Thucydides' Pessimism, 3:323

Necessity, Cause and Blame: Perspectives on Aristotle's Theory, 4:71

The Necessity of Pragmatism: John Dewey's Conception of Philosophy, 4:225

Nedjima, 2:123

Ned Myers; or, A Life Before the Mast, 1:663

The Need for Roots, 4:788

Needful Things, 1:1241

The Needle's Eye, 1:467, 1:468

The Need to Be Loved, 5:467

Negara: Theatre-State in 19th Century Bali, 3:31, 4:478

Negation in Baroja: A Key to His Novelistic Creativity, 2:530

Negations, 5:94

Negative Dialectics, 4:393

The Negev: The Challenge of a Desert, 3:439
The Neglect of Experiment, 5:48
Negotiating Democracy: Politicians and Generals in Uruguay, 3:641
Negotiation Games: Applying Game Theory to Bargaining and Arbitration, 3:48
Negritude: Black Poetry from Africa and the Caribbean, 2:931
Negritude and Humanism, 2:147
The Negro, 3:578
The Negro Almanac: A Reference Work on the Afro-American, 1:82
Negro-American Family, 1:832
The Negro and His Folklore in Nineteenth-Century Periodicals, 3:866
The Negro Artisan, 3:578
The Negro Caravan, 1:955
Negro Cowboys, 3:554
The Negro Family in the United States, 3:226
Negro Folk Music, U.S.A., 3:866
Negro Folk Rhymes, Wise and Otherwise: A Study, 3:867
Negro Folk Tales, 3:867
The Negro in America: A Bibliography, 3:510
The Negro in American Fiction, 1:955
Negro in Business, 3:578
Negro Intelligence and Selective Migration, 3:188
The Negro in the American Revolution, 3:521
The Negro in the Civil War, 3:529
The Negro in the South, 3:269
The Negro Mother: And Other Dramatic Recitations, 1:848
The Negro Newcomers in Detroit and The Negro in Washington, 1:955
Negro Playwrights in the American Theatre, 1925–1959, 1:1071
Negro Poetry and Drama, 1:955
The Negro's Civil War, 3:528, 3:586
Negro Thought in America, 1880–1915, 1:785, 3:270

Nehru: A Pictorial Biography, 3:500
Nehru: The Making of India, 3:499
Nehru's Vision of Peace and Security in a Nuclear Age, 3:500
Neighbor Rosicky, 1:820
Neighbors, 1:949
Neighbors in Turmoil: Latin America, 3:631
Neil Simon, 1:1113
Neil Simon: A Critical Study, 1:1113
Neither Angel nor Beast: The Life and Work of Blaise Pascal, 4:185
Neither Black nor White, 3:575
Neither Here nor There: Travels in Europe, 3:898
Nelson Mandela Speeches 1990, 3:423
Neo-African Literature: A History of Black Writing, 2:109
Neo-African Literature and Culture: Essays in Memory of Janheinz Jahn, 2:110
Neo-Assyrian Treaties and Loyalty Oaths, 4:546
Neoclassical and Nineteenth-Century Architecture, 3:763
A Neo-Classical Theory of Economic Growth, 3:54
Neo-Classic Drama in Spain, 2:523
Neo-Confucian Education: The Formative Stage, 4:526
Neo-Confucian Thought in Action: Wang Yang-ming's Youth, 4:362
Neo-Hindu Views of Christianity, 4:509, 4:553, 4:563
The Neolithic of the Near East, 4:434
Neoplatonism, 4:62
Neoplatonism and Christian Thought, 4:62, 4:99
Neoplatonism and Gnosticism, 4:62, 4:63
Neoplatonism and Islamic Thought, 4:61, 4:576
Neoplatonism and Jewish Thought, 4:646
Neoplatonism of the Italian Renaissance, 4:130
Neo-Platonists, 4:62
Neostoicism and the Early Modern State, 4:129

Nepali Visions, Nepali Dreams, 2:176
The Nephew, 1:1033, 1:1034
Neptune's Gift: A History of Common Salt, 5:728
Neruda: An Intimate Biography, 2:876
Nerve Cells: Transmitters and Behavior, 5:804
Nervous People and Other Satires, 2:775
A Nervous Splendour: Vienna 1888–89, 3:376
A Nest of Simple Folk, 1:528
A Nest of the Gentry, 2:768
The Netherlands: A Chronology and Fact Book, 3:383
The Netherlands: An Historical and Cultural Survey, 1795–1977, 3:383
The Netherlands and the Rise of Modern Imperialism, 3:382
The Netherlands in Perspective, 2:621
Netherwood, 2:966
The Nether World, 1:358
Netochka Nezvanova, 2:714
The Network Nation: Human Communication via Computer, 5:296, 5:307
Networks of Power: Electrification in Western Society, 1880–1930, 5:37, 5:51
Networks of Power, 3:208
Neurobiology of Alcohol Abuse, 5:402
Neurobiology of Arachnids, 5:769
Neurological Disorders, 5:393
Neuromancer, 5:563
Neuronal Man: The Biology of Mind, 5:339
Neurophilosophy, 4:382
The Neuroses, 5:427
Neurosis and Human Growth: A Study of Self-Realization, 5:452
Neurosis and Human Growth: The Struggle Toward Self-Realization, 3:186
Neurosis and Treatment: A Holistic Theory, 5:425
The Neurotic Constitution, 5:430
The Neurotic Personality of Our Time, 3:186, 5:452
The Neutral Yankees of Nova Scotia, 3:612
Never Again, 2:140

Never at Rest: A Biography
of Isaac Newton, 4:184,
5:43, 5:512
Never Call Retreat: Centenni-
al History of the Civil
War, Vol. 3, 3:571
Never Cry Wolf, 1:1165
Never Done: A History of
American Housework,
3:549, 5:189
Never Love a Stranger,
1:1222
Never Say Die: A Thousand
Years of Yiddish in Jewish
Life and Letters, 2:31
Never Say Goodby, 1:1039
Never Send Flowers, 1:979
Nevertheless: The Varieties
and Shortcomings of Reli-
gious Pacifism, 4:896
New Adventures, 2:646
New African Literature and
the Arts, 2:111
The New Age, 2:914
The New Age: Notes of a
Fringewatcher, 4:866
The New Age Encyclopedia,
4:4, 4:866
A New Age Now Begins,
3:522
The New Alchemists, 5:537
The New American Bible:
Revised New Testament,
4:798
The New American Bible:
Translated from the Origi-
nal Languages with Criti-
cal Use of All the Ancient
Sources, 4:798, 4:803
The New American Bible,
4:803
New American Dramatists,
1960–1990, 1:1072
New American Gothic, 1:918
The New American Medical
Dictionary and Health
Manual, 5:311
The New American Philoso-
phers, 4:267
New American Plays, 1:1079
New American Plays One,
1:1079
New American Plays Two,
1:1079
The New American Poetry,
1945–1960, 1:800, 1:915
The New American Poverty,
3:66
The New American Roget's
College Thesaurus in Dic-
tionary Form, 1:94
The New American Standard
Bible, 4:801

New American World, 1:631
New American Writing: Es-
says on American Litera-
ture Since 1970, 1:910
New and Collected Poems:
1917–1984, 1:857
New and Collected Poems,
1961–1983, 1:971
New and Collected Poems
1970–1985, 1:991
New and Original Extrava-
gances, 1:357
New and Selected Poems,
1923–1985, 1:893
New and Selected Poems,
1930–1990, 1:972
New and Selected Things
Taking Place, 1:1057
The New Anti-Semitism,
4:639
New Appleton's Cuyas Eng-
lish-Spanish and Spanish-
English Dictionary, 1:102
The New Archaeology and
the Ancient Maya, 4:456
New Architecture and the
Bauhaus, 3:777
New Arrivals, Old Encoun-
ters: Twelve Stories, 1:613
The New Aspects of Time:
Its Continuity and Novel-
ties, 5:62
The New Astronomy, 5:608
A New Athens, 2:914
New Ballads, 2:216
New Bearings in English Po-
etry: A Study of the Con-
temporary Situation, 1:417
The New Being, 4:787
Newbery and Caldecott Med-
al Books: 1956–1965,
1:1196
Newbery and Caldecott Med-
al Books, 1976–1985, 1:52,
1196
Newbery and Caldecott Med-
alists and Honor Book
Winners, 1:135
The New Book of Knowl-
edge, 1:106
The New Book of World
Rankings, 1:88
The New British Drama:
Fourteen Playwrights since
Osborne and Pinter, 1:425
New British Drama in Per-
formance on the London
Stage: 1970-1985, 1:425
New British Political Drama-
tists, 1:425
New Brunswick: A History,
1784–1867, 3:610

New Cambridge Bibliography
of English Literature,
1:120
The New Cambridge History
of American Literature,
1:712
The New Cambridge History
of India, 3:486
The New Cambridge History
of India: The Politics of
India since Independence,
3:485
The New Cambridge Shake-
speare: The Poems, 1:207
New Cambridge Shakespeare,
1:206
The New Capitalists, 4:270
The New Catholic Encyclope-
dia, 4:5, 4:93, 4:675
The New Cavalcade I: Afri-
can American Writing,
1:725
The New Century Bible
Commentary, 4:820
New Chapters in the History
of Greek Literature, 2:357
A New Checklist of English-
Language Fiction Relating
to Malaysia, Singapore and
Brunei, 2:324
The New Chemistry, 5:729
The New Church in the New
World, 4:851
New Classical Macroeconom-
ics, 3:62
The New Colony, 2:435
Newcomers: Negroes and
Puerto Ricans in a Chang-
ing Metropolis, 3:582
The Newcomes, 1:403
The New Communications
Technologies, 5:297
A New Companion to Shake-
speare Studies, 1:222
The New Comparative Myth-
ology, 4:472
The New Complete Guide to
Environmental Careers,
5:815
New Complete Walker, 3:908
New Conceptions, 5:357
A New Conscience and an
Ancient Evil, 1:731
The New Conservatism,
4:404
The New Conservatism: Cul-
tural Criticism and the
Historians' Debate, 3:229
The New Constellation,
4:262, 4:292
The New Country: A Social
History of the American
Frontier, 1776–1890, 3:551

The New Covenant: Jewish
Writers and the American
Idea, 1:804, 1:917
The New Cratylus, 2:955
A New Creation Story: The
Creative Spirituality of
Teilhard de Chardin, 4:337
New Critical Approaches to
the Short Stories of Ernest
Hemingway, 1:846
A New Critical History of
Old English Literature,
1:143
The New Criticism, 1:874
The New Criticism in
France, 2:447
The New Cults, 4:858
New Day, 2:940
The New Day Recalled,
3:616
The New Deal (Conklin),
3:534
The New Deal (Degler),
3:575
The New Deal: The Depres-
sion Years, 1933–1940,
3:533
The New Deal and the West,
3:535
New Departures in Linguis-
tics, 3:21
New Dictionary of American
Slang, 1:92
The New Dictionary of Exis-
tentialism, 4:3, 4:14
A New Dictionary of Quota-
tions on Historical Princi-
ples from Ancient and
Modern Sources, 1:117
New Dictionary of Theology,
4:4, 4:5
A New Dictionary of the So-
cial Sciences, 3:5
The New Dinosaur Diction-
ary, 5:638
New Directions in Bookbind-
ing, 1:26
New Directions in Compara-
tive Politics, 3:141
New Directions in European
Historiography, 4:728
New Directions in Psycholog-
ical Anthropology, 3:15
New Directions in Safety,
5:244
New Directions in Soviet
History, 3:398
The New Dramatists of Mexi-
co, 1967–85, 2:845
The New Eastern Europe:
Social Policy Past, Present
and Future, 3:345

The New Eighteenth Century:
Theory, Politics, English
Literature, 1:226
New Electric Power Technol-
ogies: Problems and Pros-
pects for the 1990's, 5:287
The New Empire: An Inter-
pretation of American Ex-
pansion, 1860–1898, 3:532
The New Encyclopaedia Bri-
tannica, 1:107
New Encyclopedia of Philos-
ophy, 4:15
New Encyclopedia of World
History in Convenient Tab-
ulated Form, 3:273
New England Bean Pot:
American Folk Stories to
Read and to Tell, 3:858
The New England Clergy
and the American Revolu-
tion, 1:627
New England Generation,
1:627
New England Literary Cul-
ture, 1:650, 1:713
New England Local Color
Literature: A Women's
Tradition, 1:723
The New England Merchants
in the Seventeenth Centu-
ry, 3:564
The New England Mind,
3:587, 4:753
A New England Nun and
Other Stories, 1:749, 1:750
New England's Outpost: Aca-
dia before the Conquest of
Canada, 3:611
New England's Strange Sea
Sagas, 3:858
A New-England Tale, 1:695
The New Era and the New
Deal, 1920–1940, 3:509
Newer Ideals of Peace, 1:731
New Essays by Henry Field-
ing, 1:245
New Essays Concerning Hu-
man Understanding, 4:176
New Essays on Adventures of
Huckleberry Finn, 1:783
New Essays on Moby Dick,
1:688
New Essays on Native Son,
1:906
New Essays on Sister Carrie,
1:831
New Essays on "The Ameri-
can," 1:765
New Essays on The Awaken-
ing, 1:740
New Essays on "The Great
Gatsby," 1:840

New Essays on Their Eyes
Were Watching God, 1:850
New Essays on The Portrait
of a Lady, 1:767
New Essays on the Red
Badge of Courage, 1:743
New Essays on The Rise of
Silas Lapham, 1:760
New Essays on "The Scarlet
Letter," 1:676
New Essays on Tolstoy,
2:766
New Essays on Uncle Tom's
Cabin, 1:699
New Essays on Winesburg,
Ohio, 1:812
The New Evolutionary Time-
table, 5:639
A New Face of Hinduism:
The Swaminarayan Reli-
gion, 4:509
The New Faith-Science De-
bate, 5:197
New Families, No Families?,
3:206
The New Farmer, 5:274
The New Feminist Criticism,
1:716, 1:926, 1:1046,
1:1134
Newfoundland in the North
Atlantic World, 1929–1949,
3:616
New France: The Last Phase,
1744–1760, 3:612
New France 1701–1744: "A
Supplement to Europe,"
3:612
New French Feminisms: An
Anthology, 1:926
The New Gardener's Hand-
book and Dictionary,
5:767
The New Generation in Meiji
Japan: Problems in Cultur-
al Identity, 3:479
New German Film: The Dis-
placed Image, 3:828
The New Golden Bough,
4:476
The New Gothic: A Collec-
tion of Contemporary
Gothic Fiction, 1:618
New Ground: Western Amer-
ican Narrative and the Lit-
erary Canon, 1:712
The New Grove Dictionary
of American Music, 3:655
The New Grove Dictionary
of Jazz, 3:656
The New Grove Dictionary
of Music and Musicians,
3:657

The New Grove Encyclopedia of Musical Instruments, 3:657

New Grub Street, 1:358

The New Guide to Modern World Literature, 2:3

A New Guide to Rational Living, 5:439

A New Guide to the Stars, 5:591

The New Hacker's Dictionary, 5:538

The New Harmony Communities, 4:844

The New Harvard Concise Dictionary of Music, 3:657

The New Harvard Dictionary of Music, 3:657

New Healthcare Market, 5:327

New Heaven, New Earth: A Study of Millenarian Activities, 4:467

The New Héloïse, 4:212

A New Historical Geography of England after 1600, 3:354

A New Historical Geography of England before 1600, 3:354

The New Historicism: Studies in Cultural Poetics, 1:713

The New History and the Old, 3:276

A New History of Australia, 3:494

A New History of French Literature, 2:447

A New History of India, 3:484, 4:351

A New History of Korea, 2:298

A New History of Portugal, 3:386

A New History of Spanish American Fiction, 2:847

A New History of Spanish Literature, 2:522

The New Holistic Health Handbook: Living Well in a New Age, 5:318

New Homage to John Dryden, 1:242

New Hope for Problem Pregnancies: Saving Babies before They're Born, 5:358

New Horizons in the Philosophy of Science, 5:64

New Ideas on the Structure of the Nervous System in Man and the Vertebrates, 5:810

The New Illustrated Encyclopedia of World History, 3:326

New Illustrated Science and Invention Encyclopedia, 5:2

The New Industrial State, 3:78, 3:79

New Information Technology in Education, 3:255

The New Intellectuals, 1:170

New International Atlas, 1:84

The New International Commentary on the New Testament, 4:820

The New International Commentary on the Old Testament, 4:820

New International Dictionary of New Testament Theology, 4:818

The New International Dictionary of the Christian Church, 4:675, 4:717

The New International Greek Testament Commentary, 4:821

A New Introduction to Bibliography, 1:62

A New Introduction to Philosophy, 4:20

The New Italian Poetry, 1945 to the Present: A Bilingual Anthology, 2:403

New Italian Women: A Collection of Short Fiction, 2:403

The New Jerome Biblical Commentary, 4:819

The New Jerusalem: Planning and Politics, 3:440

The New Jerusalem Bible, 4:798, 4:803

The New Jewish Encyclopedia, 3:347, 4:593

A New Jewish Ethics, 4:648

A New Jewish Theology in the Making, 4:661

The New Jewish Wedding, 4:601

The New Jews, 4:641

"A New Kind of War," 3:545

New Knowledge in Human Values, 5:461

The New Labor Press: Journalism for a Changing Union Movement, 3:808

The New Lafayette Theatre Presents the Complete Plays and Aesthetic Comments by Six Black Playwrights, 1:1086

A New Language for Psychoanalysis, 5:469

New Letters, 1:305

The New Leviathan: Man, Society, Civilization and Barbarism, 4:282

The New Liberalism: An Ideology of Social Reform, 3:363

A New Life, 1:1012, 1:1013

The New Life, 2:417

New Light on Boswell, 1:234

New Light on the Most Ancient East, 4:438

A New Look at the Dinosaurs, 5:638

The Newly Born Woman, 1:1131, 2:467

Newman, 4:783

Newman: His Life and Spirituality, 4:783

Newman after a Hundred Years, 4:783

Newman the Theologian: A Reader, 4:782

New Maps of Hell, 1:432

The New Market Wizards: Conversations with America's Top Traders, 3:56

New Masters, 3:529

The New Medicine and the Old Ethics, 5:13

New Mermaid Series, 1:170

New Methods of Measuring Marginal Utility, 3:64

The New Metropolis in the Arab World, 3:435

The New Music: The Avant-Garde since 1945, 3:665

The New Nationalism, 3:594

The New Net Goes Fishing, 2:977

The New Nietzsche, 4:246

The New Nightingales, 5:338

New Norwegian Plays, 2:662

The New Novel: From Queneau to Pinget, 2:493

New Orleans Jazz: A Family Album, 3:669

New Orleans Jazz Fest: A Pictorial History, 3:669

New Orleans Sketches, 1:835

The New Our Bodies, Ourselves, 5:355

The New Oxford Annotated Bible with the Apocryphal/Deuterocanonical Books, 4:798

The New Oxford Book of American Verse, 1:655, 1:719

The New Oxford Book of Australian Verse, 2:959, 2:960
The New Oxford Book of Eighteenth-Century Verse, 1:227, 1:269
The New Oxford Book of Romantic Verse, 1:266
The New Oxford Book of Seventeenth-Century Verse, 1:166
The New Oxford Book of Sixteenth-Century Verse, 1:165
The New Oxford Book of Victorian Verse, 1:316
The New Oxford Companion to Music, 3:654
New Oxford History of Music, 3:658
The New Palgrave: A Dictionary of Economics, 3:44
New Parenthood: The First Six Weeks, 5:323
New Paths in Book Collecting: Essays by Various Hands, 1:76
New Pathways in Science, 5:681
The New Penguin Shakespeare: The Rape of Lucrece, 1:207
The New Penguin Shakespeare: The Sonnets and A Lover's Complaint, 1:207
The New Penguin Shakespeare, 1:206
New People: Miscegenation and Mulattoes in the United States, 3:558
New Perspectives on Evolution, 3:19
New Perspectives on Galileo, 4:143
New Perspectives on Historical Writing, 3:275
New Perspectives on Israeli History: The Early Years of the State, 4:643
New Perspectives on Race and Slavery in America, 3:554, 3:598
New Perspectives on the Life and Art of Richard Crashaw, 1:176
The New Physics, 5:15
New Plays U.S.A.
No. 1, 1:1078
No. 2, 1:1078
No. 3, 1:1078
No. 4, 1:1076
The New Poetic: Yeats to Eliot, 1:418

New Poetic Mirror, 1:291
The New Poetics of the New American Poetry, 1945–1960, 1:1026
New Poetry, 1:481
New Poetry from a New Spain, 2:527
The New Poets: American and British Poetry since World War II, 1:418
New Poets of England and America, 1:983, 1:1048
The New Polish Poetry: A Bilingual Collection, 2:811
The New Politics of Poverty, 3:212
The New Politics of Science, 5:73, 5:152, 5:181
The New Politics of the Budgetary Process, 3:147
The New Psychotherapies, 5:418
The New Radicalism in America, 1889–1963, 1:731, 3:543
The New Rays of Professor Röntgen, 5:711
A New Reader's Guide to African Literature, 2:112
New Readings vs. Old Plays, 1:170
New Realism: Cooperative Studies in Philosophy, 4:264
The New Realism: Writings from China after the Cultural Revolution, 2:236
New Reform Responsa, 4:598
The New Religions: Insights into the Cult Phenomenon, 4:855
New Religions, 4:855
New Religions and Mental Health: Understanding the Issues, 4:856
New Religions and the Theological Imagination in America, 4:841
The New Religions of Africa, 3:23
The New Religions of Japan, 4:541
The New Religious Consciousness, 4:855
New Religious Movements: A Perspective for Understanding Society, 4:855
New Religious Movements: A Practical Introduction, 4:855
New Religious Movements in the United States and Canada, 4:3, 4:854

New Roots for Agriculture, 5:272
The New Russians, 3:398
The New Sabin, 1:67
The New Schaff-Herzog Encyclopedia of Religious Knowledge, 4:717
The New Schools of Spanish American Poetry, 2:848
The New Science, 2:442, 4:215
The New Scientific Spirit, 4:274
Newsday: A Candid History of the Respectable Tabloid, 3:807
New Selected Poems, 1:1004
New Serial Titles 1950–1970, 1:72, 113
News from Jerusalem, 2:24
News from Nowhere, 1:382, 3:806
The New Shakespeare, 1:206
The New Shelley: Later Twentieth-Century Views, 1:303
The New Shostakovich, 3:718
Newsmen Speak: Journalists on Their Craft, 3:821
The New Social Economy: Reworking the Division of Labor, 3:123
The New Solar System, 5:592
A New Song: Celibate Women in the First Three Christian Centuries, 4:689
New Songs from the Jade Terrace, 2:201
Newspaper Days, 1:829, 1:830
The Newspaper of Claremont Street, 2:956
Newspapers: A Reference Guide, 3:809
Newspapers in Microfilm: United States, 1948–1972, 1:115
New Spirituality and the Christ Experience of the Twenty-First Century, 4:879
News That Matters: Television and American Opinion, 3:811
New Studies in Berkeley's Philosophy, 4:192
The New System, 2:663
A New System of Chemical Philosophy, 1808–1827, 5:742
New Technological Era for American Agriculture, 5:185

The New Telecommunications: Infrastructure for the Information Age, 5:297

The New Television Technologies, 3:801

The New Testament: A Guide to Its Writings, 4:829

The New Testament: An Introduction, 4:816

The New Testament: The History of the Investigations of Its Problems, 4:814

New Testament Abstracts: A Record of Current Periodical Literature, 4:8, 4:796

The New Testament and Early Christianity, 4:817

The New Testament and Its Modern Interpreters, 4:813

The New Testament and Mythology, and Other Basic Writings, 4:743, 4:825, 4:831

New Testament Apocrypha, 4:811

New Testament Background: Selected Documents, 4:617, 4:810

The New Testament Environment, 4:808

The New Testament Era: The World of the Bible from 500 B.C. to A.D. 100, 4:605

New Testament Exegesis: A Handbook for Students and Pastors, 4:814

New Testament Message: A Biblical Theological Commentary, 4:821

The New Testament Octapla, 4:798

New Testament Theology: Basic Issues in the Current Debate, 4:827

The New Testament World, 4:807

The New Textiles, 3:767

New Theatre Voices of the Fifties and Sixties, 1:425

New Theatre Voices of the Seventies, 1:426

A New Theory of Value: The Canadian Economics of H. A. Innis, 3:622

The New Thoreau Handbook, 1:702

The Newtonian Revolution, 5:706

The Newtonians and the English Revolution, 5:42

Newton Rules Biology: A Physical Approach to Biological Problems, 5:775

Newton's Philosophy of Nature, 5:43

Newton versus Einstein, 5:706

New Towns in Israel, 3:439

A New Translation of Volney's Ruins, 1:633

New Translations, 2:849

New Transportation Fuels, 5:290

A New Treasury of Poetry, 1:418, 1:720

The New Turks: Pioneers of the Republic, 1920–1950, 3:452

New Twentieth-Century Encyclopedia of Religious Knowledge, 4:3, 4:717

The New University Wits and the End of Modernism, 1:422

A New Variorum Edition of Shakespeare, 1:206

The New Variorum "Poems," 1:207

The New Variorum "Sonnets," 1:207

New Vico Studies, 4:217

New Viewpoints in American History, 3:596

New Views of an Old Planet: Continental Drift and the History of the Earth, 5:630

New Vocabularies in Film Semiotics, 1:1158

New Voices: Immigrants in U.S. Public Schools, 3:250

The New Walt Whitman Handbook, 1:707

The New Wave: Truffaut, Godard, Chabrol, Rohmer, Rivette, 3:828

The New Wave Spanish Drama: An Anthology, 2:526

New Ways in Psychoanalysis, 3:186, 5:452

A New Way to Pay Old Debts, 1:189

New Webster's Spelling Dictionary, 1:95

New West African Literature, 2:126

The New Westminster Dictionary of Liturgy and Worship, 4:675

The New Westminster Dictionary of the Bible, 4:819

The New West of Edward Abbey, 5:828

The New Woman and the Old Academy, 3:254

The New Woman/New Earth: Sexist Ideologies and Human Liberation, 4:785

The New Women's Theatre, 1:1078

New World, New Earth, 1:652, 5:205

New World Avenue and Victory, 2:815

A New World Jerusalem, 4:852

New World Metaphysics, 1:630

The New World of Islam, 4:573

The New World of James Fenimore Cooper, 1:665

A New World Order: Grassroots Movements for Global Change, 3:249

New Worlds, New Technologies, New Issues, 5:70, 5:152

New Worlds from the Lowlands, 2:622

The New Writer, 5:562

New Writing from the Middle East, 2:57, 2:84

New Writing from the Philippines: A Critique and Anthology, 2:328

A New Year: Stories, Autobiography and Poems, 2:59

New Year's Eve 1929, 1:833

New York, 1:813

New York Ain't America, 2:21

New York Art of Writing Plays, 2:554

The New York City Draft Riots, 3:526

The New Yorker, 2:921

New York Jew, 1:996

The New York Philharmonic Guide to the Symphony, 3:664

The New York Public Library Book of 20th Century American Quotations, 1:117

The New York Public Library Book of How and Where to Look it Up, 1:61

The New York Public Library Desk Reference, 1:82

New York State Folktales, Legends and Ballads, 3:859

New York Times Atlas of the World, 1:84

New York Times Book Review 1896–1981, 1:114
The New York Times Index, 1:114
The New York University Medical Center Family Guide to Staying Healthy in a Risky Environment, 5:354
A New Zionism, 4:658
New Zionism and the Foreign Policy System of Israel, 4:658
Next to Shakespeare, 1:251
Next Week, Swan Lake: Reflections on Dance and Dances, 3:731
Next Week East Lynne: Domestic Drama in Performance, 1820–1874, 1:322
Nexus, 1:861
Ngaahika Ndeenda, 2:154
NgaBa, 2:313
Ngambika: Studies of Women in African Literature, 2:107
Ngugi Wa Thiong'o, 2:155
Nibelungenlied, 2:562, 2:604, 2:605, 2:619, 2:644
Nicaragua: The Land of Sandino, 3:639
Nicaraguan New Time, 2:859
Nicaraguan Sketches, 2:862
Niccolò Machiavelli, 4:145
The Nice and the Good, 1:523
Nice Jewish Girls: A Lesbian Anthology, 1:1183
Nice Work, 1:515
Nichiren: The Buddhist Prophet, 4:536
Nichiren Shoshu Buddhism and the Soka Gakkai in America, 4:859
Nicholas Karamzin and Russian Society in the Nineteenth Century, 2:730
Nicholas Nickleby, 1:348
Nicholas of Autrecourt, 4:104
Nicholas of Cusa, 4:149
Nicholas of Cusa and Medieval Political Thought, 4:149
Nicholaus Cusanus: A Fifteenth-Century Vision of Man, 4:149
Nick Adams Stories, 1:845
Nickel Mountain, 1:978, 1:979
Nick of the Woods, 1:1244
Nicodemos of the Holy Mountain: A Handbook of Spiritual Counsel, 4:756

Nicolas Berdyaev, 4:275
Nicolaus Copernicus and His Epoch, 5:602
Nicomachean Ethics, 4:66, 5:105
Niebuhr and His Age, 4:784
Niels Bohr: A Centenary Volume, 5:674
Niels Bohr: His Life and Work as Seen by His Friends and Colleagues, 5:674
Niels Bohr: Physics and the World, 5:674
Niels Bohr: The Man, His Science, and the World They Changed, 5:674
Niels Bohr's Philosophy of Physics, 5:674
Niels Bohr's Times: In Physics, Philosophy, and Polity, 5:658
Niels Klim, 2:650
Niels Lyhne, 2:651
Nietzsche (Heidegger), 4:291, 5:90
Nietzsche (Rosenberg), 4:247
Nietzsche (Salomé), 4:247
Nietzsche (Schacht), 4:247
Nietzsche: A Collection of Critical Essays, 4:248
Nietzsche: A Frenzied Look, 4:246
Nietzsche: An Introduction to His Philosophical Activity, 4:247
Nietzsche: A Self-Portrait from His Letters, 4:246
Nietzsche: Life as Literature, 4:247
Nietzsche: Philosopher, Psychologist, Antichrist, 4:247
Nietzsche and Asian Thought, 4:350
Nietzsche and the Question of Interpretation, 4:295
Nietzsche as Philosopher, 4:247
Nietzsche's Existential Imperative, 4:247
Nietzsche's Philosophy of Art, 4:248
Nietzsche's Teaching: An Interpretation of Thus Spoke Zarathustra, 4:247
Nietzsche's View of Socrates, 4:89
Nietzsche's Zarathustra, 4:247
Nigerian Folk Tales, 2:126
Nigerian Perspectives, 3:420
Nigeria since 1970: A Political and Economic Outline, 3:421

The Nigger of the Narcissus, 1:463
Night (Tournier), 2:512
Night (Wiesel), 1:1065
'night, Mother, 1:1105
Night and Day, 1:554
A Night at the Movies, 1:963
Night Creature: A Journal of Jazz, 1975–80, 3:667
Night Flight, 2:503, 2:504
A Night in Acadie, 1:740
The Nightingale, 1:577
The Nightingale, or The Saga of Yosele Solovey the Cantor, 2:45
The Nightingale's Burden, 1:655, 1:719
A Night in May, 2:26
Night Light, 1:995
Nightly Horrors: Crisis Coverage on Television Network News, 3:808
Nightmare Abbey, 1:297
The Nightmare Notebook, 1:862
Nightmares and Hobbyhorses, 1:259
Nightmares and Visions, 1:1025
The Night of the Iguana, 1:1117
The Night of the Long Knives, 2:598
The Night of the Prowler, 2:966
The Night of the Tribades: A Play from 1889, 2:674
Night Rider, 1:892
Night Riders in Black Folk History, 3:524, 3:866
Night Roamers and Other Stories, 2:665
A Night's Adventure, 1:389
Nights and Days, 1:1015
Nights at the Circus, 1:455
Night-Side, 1:1023
The Night's Journey; and, The Coming of the Messiah, 2:84
Nights of Serampore, 2:824
Nights with Uncle Remus: Myths and Legends of the Old Plantation, 1:754
Night Train to Turkistan: Modern Adventures along China's Ancient Silk Road, 3:905
Night Traveller, 2:61
The Night Trilogy: Night, Dawn, The Accident, 1:1065

A Night with the Hants and Other Alabama Experiences, 3:860
Nightwood, 1:812, 1:813, 1:985, 1:1002, 1:1190
al-Nihayat, 2:69
Nihon bungaku (Japanese Literature), 2:272
Nihongi, 4:536
Nihon Kodai Bunka, 4:366
Nihon Seishin-shi Kenkyū, 4:366
Niiwam and Taaw, 2:145
Nijinsky, 3:749
Nikolai Gogol (Nabokov), 2:722
Nikolai Gogol's Quest for Beauty: An Exploration into His Works, 2:723
Nikolai Leskov: The Man and His Art, 2:736
Nikolai Nikolaevich, 2:698
Nikolay Gogol (Grayson), 2:722
Nikolay Leskov, 2:736
Nikos Kazantzakis (Bien), 2:374
Nikos Kazantzakis (Kazantzakis), 2:374
Nikos Kazantzakis: A Biography Based on His Letters, 2:374
Nikos Kazantzakis and His Odyssey, 2:374
Nimmer on Copyright, 1:55
Nina, the Comic Actor and an Old Friend, 2:748
Nina Balatka, 1:406
Nine, 1:1098
Nine and a Half Mystics: The Kabbala Today, 4:630
A Nine Cloud Dream, 2:297, 2:304
Nine Faces of Kenya, 3:903
Nine Fairy Tales, 2:790
Nine Gates to the Chassidic Mysteries, 4:632
The Nine Guardians, 2:860
The 900 Days: The Siege of Leningrad, 3:397
The Nine Language Universal Dictionary, 1:96
Nine Men Who Laughed, 2:934
The Nine Questions People Ask about Judaism, 4:596
The Nine Songs; A Study of Shamanism in Ancient China, 2:196, 4:525
The Nine Tailors, 1:610
Nine Talmudic Readings, 4:901

Nineteen Ancient Poems, 2:187
Nineteen Eighty-Five, 1:454
1984, 1:530, 5:563
1984 and Beyond: Into the 21st Century, 5:572
The Nineteen Eighty-Four Election in Historical Perspective, 3:585
1940: Myth and Reality, 3:367
The Nineteen Letters of Ben Uziel on Judaism, 4:665
Nineteen Nineteen, 1:828
1991–1992 Green Index, 5:815
1993 Conservation Directory, 5:816
1993 Directory of Country Environmental Studies, 5:817
The 1993 Handbook of World Stock and Commodity Exchanges, 3:45
1993 Information Please Environmental Almanac, 5:817
The 1960s, 3:510
1939: In the Shadow of War, 3:535
Nineteenth and Twentieth Century Art: Painting, Sculpture, Architecture, 3:759
The Nineteenth Century, 2:566
Nineteenth-Century American Plays, 1:1078
Nineteenth-Century American Poetry, 1:655, 1:719
The Nineteenth-Century American Short Story, 1:658, 1:723
Nineteenth-Century American Women's Novels: Interpretive Strategies, 1:723
Nineteenth-Century Book Arts and Printing History, 1:10
Nineteenth-Century British Drama: An Anthology of Representative Plays, 1:323
Nineteenth-Century Essays, 1:728
Nineteenth-Century Literary Criticism Series, 1:134
Nineteenth-Century Music, 3:659
Nineteenth Century Ornamented Typefaces, 1:16
Nineteenth-Century Philosophy, 4:160

Nineteenth-Century Plays, 1:272
Nineteenth-Century Readers' Guide to Periodical Literature: 1890–1899, 1:114
Nineteenth-Century Religious Thought in the West, 4:741
Nineteenth-Century Romanticism in Music, 3:661
Nineteenth-Century Russian Literature: Studies of Ten Russian Writers, 2:429, 2:686
Nineteenth-Century Russian Literature in English, 2:689
Nineteenth-Century Scientific Instruments, 5:47
The Nineteenth Century Short Title Catalogue, 1:66
Nineteen Thirty-Eight . . . and the Consequences, 3:376
Ninth Wave, 2:717
A Nip in the Air, 1:444
Nirat Muang Klaeng, 2:337
Nirmala, 2:180
Nishida Kitarō, 4:365
Nitrogen Fixation in Tropical Cropping Systems, 5:263
NIV Exhaustive Concordance, 4:818
Nixon Agonistes: The Crisis of the Self-Made Man, 3:540
Njal's Saga: A Critical Approach, 2:642
Njál's Saga, 2:639, 2:642
Njegoš: Poet, Prince, Bishop, 2:830
N. M. Karamzin: A Study of His Literary Career (1783–1803), 2:730
No. 13, 1:1168
Noah's Ark Alphabet, 1:583
Noah Webster's American Spelling Book, 3:573
No and Bunraku: Two Forms of Japanese Theatre, 2:273
Noa Noa: The Tahitian Journal, 3:775
Noatun, 2:656
Nobel Dreams: Power, Deceit, and the Ultimate Experiment, 5:663
Nobel Laureates in Literature: A Biographical Dictionary, 1:135
The Nobel Lecture on Literature, 2:761, 2:818

The Nobel Peace Prize and
the Dalai Lama, 4:357
Nobel Prize Winners, 5:729
Nobel Prize Winners, Chem-
istry, 5:728
Nobel Prize Women in Sci-
ence, 5:4, 5:187, 5:727
The Nobility of Failure: Trag-
ic Heroes in the History
of Japan, 3:474
The Noble Gases, 5:734
The Noble Savage: Jean-
Jacques Rousseau, 1754–
1762, 4:213
Nobody Knows My Name,
1:1084
Nocturne: From the Notes of
Lt. Amiran Amilakhvari,
Retired, 2:743
Nocturnes, 2:146, 2:602
No Day without a Line,
2:743
Noel and Cole: The Sophisti-
cates, 3:709
Noel Coward, 1:465
Noel Coward and His
Friends, 1:465
No Enemy, 1:475
No Exit, 2:506
No Exit and Three Other
Plays, 2:507
No Fist Is Big Enough to
Hide the Sky, 3:428
No Fond Return of Love,
1:538, 1:539
No Friendly Voice, 3:263
No Gods and Precious Few
Heros: Scotland,
1914–1980, 3:368
No Harvest but a Thorn,
2:326
Noh Drama and the Tale of
Genji, 2:279
No Heaven for Priests, 2:140
No Heroics, Please: Uncol-
lected Writings, 1:960
No! In Thunder: Essays on
Myth and Literature, 1:975
The Noise of Change: Rus-
sian Literature and the
Critics (1891–1917), 2:689
No Laughing Matter, 1:567
No Laughing Matter: An
Analysis of Sexual Humor,
3:871
No Laughing Matter: Ration-
ale of the Dirty Joke,
3:871
No Laughing Matter: The
Life and Times of Flann
O'Brien, 1:526
Noli Me Tangere, 2:327

No Longer an Island: Britain
and the Wright Brothers,
1902–1909, 5:219
No Longer at Ease, 2:127,
2:128
No Longer Human (Ningen
shikkaku), 2:285
Nomads, Exiles, and Em-
igrés, 2:847
Nomads of South Persia: The
Basseri Tribe of the
Khamseh Confederacy,
3:447
"No Magic Bullet," 5:389
No Man Knows My History:
The Life of Joseph Smith,
4:845, 4:879
No Man's Land (Pinter),
1:534
No Man's Land (Heminway),
3:903
No Man's Land: An Antholo-
gy of Modern Danish
Women's Literature, 2:645
No Man's Land: The Place of
the Woman Writer in the
Twentieth Century, 1:414,
1:714, 1:1146
No More Dying Now, 1:609
No More Hot Flashes and
Other Good News, 5:355
No More War, 5:751, 5:752
Nomos: Essays in Athenian
Law, Politics, and Society,
3:307
Non-Adhesive Binding, 1:26
No Nature: New and Select-
ed Poems, 1:1052
Nonconformity in Modern
British Politics, 3:366
Non-Cycle Plays and Frag-
ments, 1:160
Non-Different Nature: Film
and the Structure of
Things, 3:835
None but the Brave, 2:611
None Genuine without This
Signature, 2:913, 2:914
None Is Too Many: Canada
and the Jews of Europe,
1933–1948, 3:616
Nones, 1:435
None Shall Look Back, 1:982
The Nonexistent Knight,
2:411
The Nonexistent Knight and
The Cloven Viscount,
2:412
The Nongraded Elementary
School, 3:263
Non-Ionising Radiation: Mi-
crowaves, Ultra Violet Ra-
diation, and Lasers, 5:703

The Non-Jewish Jew and
Other Essays, 3:348, 4:655
Nonlinear Dynamics, Chaos,
and Instability, 3:63
Nonreactive Measures in the
Social Sciences, 3:7
The Non-Reality of Free
Will, 4:380
Non-Renunciation: Themes
and Interpretations in Hin-
du Culture, 4:505
Nonsense Novels, 2:918
Non-Stop, 1:612, 1:613
Nontoxic, Natural and Earth-
wise, 5:386
Nontraditional Careers for
Women, 5:524
Nonviolent Insurrection in
El Salvador, 3:637
Non-Voting: Causes and
Methods of Control, 3:162
The Non-Western Films of
John Ford, 1:1166
Noon at a Country Inn,
2:807
No One Writes to the Colo-
nel, 2:866
No One Writes to the Colo-
nel and Other Stories,
2:867
No Ordinary Summer, 2:718
Noose of Laurels, 3:933
No Paradise for Workers,
3:494
No Peace beyond the Line:
The English in the Carib-
bean, 1624–1690, 3:570
No Place of Grace, 3:560
No Place on Earth, 2:616
The No Plays of Japan, 2:274
Nora: A Biography of Nora
Joyce, 1:505
Norbert Wiener: Eighteen
Ninety-Four to Nineteen
Sixty-Four, 5:584
The Nordic Mind: Current
Trends in Scandinavian
Literary Criticism, 2:638
No Respect: Intellectuals and
Popular Culture, 1:1127
Norito: A Translation of the
Ancient Japanese Ritual
Prayers, 4:536
Normal Accidents: Living
with High Risk Technolo-
gies, 3:214, 5:156, 5:244
The Norman Conquests,
1:436, 1:437
Norman Mailer (Bufithis),
1:1012
Norman Mailer (Merrill),
1:1012

Norman Mailer (Poirier), 1:1012

Norman Mailer: A Collection of Critical Essays, 1:1012

Normans and the Norman Conquest, 3:356

The Normative Grounds of Social Criticism: Kant, Rawls, and Habermas, 4:316

The Normative Theory of Individual Choice, 4:314

The Norms of Nature: Studies in Hellenistic Ethics, 4:56

The Norse Atlantic Saga, 3:381

North, 1:495

North African Literatures, 2:117

North African Villages: Morocco, Nigeria, and Tunisia, 3:418

North African Writing, 2:117

North America from Earliest Discovery to First Settlements, 1:631

North American Discovery, circa 1000–1612, 1:631

North American Free Trade, 3:59

North American Indian Life, 3:507

North American Indian Stories: More Earthmaker's Tales, 3:865

The North American Online Directory, 1987, 5:547

North American XB-70 Valkyrie, 5:219

North and South, 1:355

The North and the Secession Crisis, 1860–61, 3:530, 3:598

Northanger Abbey, 1:269, 1:275

The North Atlantic Triangle, 3:607

The North Atlantic Tribune, 1:970

The Norther, 2:858

Northern Enterprise: Five Centuries of Canadian Business, 3:606

Northern Europe in the Early Modern Period, 3:382

Northern Ireland since 1968, 3:371

Northern Ireland since Nineteen Twenty, 3:366

Northernizing the South, 3:573

The Northern School of and the Formation of Early Ch'an Buddhism, 4:530

Northfield Poems, 1:934

The Northland Expansion of Canada, 1914–1967, 3:616

The Northmen, Columbus, and Cabot, 1085–1503, 1:631

North of Slavery: The Negro in the Free States, 1790–1860, 3:525

The North Pole, 3:933

North Pole Legacy: Black, White, and Eskimo, 3:906, 3:933

Northrop Frye: An Enumerative Bibliography, 1:977

Northrop Frye: Myth and Metaphor, Selected Essays 1974–1988, 1:976

Northrop Frye and Critical Method, 1:977

Northrop Frye in Modern Criticism, 1:977

Northrop Frye on Shakespeare, 1:209

The North Ship, 1:507

The Northward Expansion of Canada, 1914–1967, 3:610

Northward over the Great Ice, 3:933

The Northwest Passage, 3:912

Northwest to Fortune, 3:939

North with the Spring, 5:818

Norton Anthology of Afro-American Literature, 1:130

The Norton Anthology of American Literature, 1:129, 1:653, 1:717

Norton Anthology of English Literature, 1:129, 1:266

Norton Anthology of Literature by Women: The Tradition in English, 1:130

The Norton Anthology of Modern Poetry, 1:418

The Norton Anthology of Poetry, 1:129

Norton Anthology of World Masterpieces, 1:130, 2:5

The Norton Book of American Short Stories, 1:806

The Norton Book of Nature Writing, 5:818

Norton Critical Editions, 2:713

Norton Facsimile: The First Folio of Shakespeare, 1:206

The Norton/Grove Concise Encyclopedia of Music, 3:657

Norton's 2000.0 Star Atlas and Reference Handbook, 5:591

Norway-Sweden: Union, Disunion and Scandinavian Integration, 3:382

Norwegian-English, English-Norwegian Pocket Dictionary, 1:101

Norwegian-English Dictionary, 1:101

Norwegian Folk Music, 3:850

Norwegian Folk Tales, 2:662, 3:854

No Safe Place: Toxic Waste, Leukemia, and Community Action, 3:205

No Siege Is Absolute, 2:465

Nos luttes constitutionnelles, 3:620

Nostalgia and Nightmare: A Study in the Fiction of S. Y. Agnon, 2:12

Nostalgia for the Present, 2:773

No Star Is Lost, 1:833

No State Shall Abridge, 3:139

No Stranger to Tears: A Surgeon's Story, 5:369

Nostromo, 1:463

No Survivors, 1:1212

No Sweetness Here, 2:129

Notable Americans: What They Did from 1620 to the Present, 3:506

Notable American Women: The Modern Period, 1:86

Notable American Women, 1607–1950: A Biographical Dictionary, 1:86

Notable Black American Women, 3:507

Notable Names in the American Theatre, 1:1075

Not about Heroes, 1:543

Not by Strange Gods, 1:876

Notebook, 1:1006

Notebooks (Ignatow), 1:990, 1:991

Notebooks (Maritain), 4:306

The Notebooks, 1930–1934 (Thomas), 1:557

Notebooks 1914–1916, 4:344

Notebooks for an Ethics, 4:329

The Notebooks for "A Raw Youth," 2:714

The Notebooks for "Crime and Punishment," 2:714

The Notebooks for "The Brothers Karamazov," 2:714
The Notebooks for "The Idiot," 2:714
The Notebooks for "The Possessed," 2:714
The Notebooks of Henry James, 1:762
The Notebooks of Malte Laurids Brigge, 2:607
The Notebooks of Serafino Gubbio, 2:435
Notes from China, 3:412
Notes from the Energy Underground, 5:278
Notes from the Underground, 2:711, 2:712, 2:714
Notes of an Apprenticeship, 3:684
Notes of a Native Son, 1:939, 1:974
Notes of a Son and Brother, 1:762
Notes of Debates in the Federal Convention of 1787, 3:161
Notes on a Dream, 1:1082
Notes on Child Study, 3:269
Notes on Life, 1:829
Notes on Love in a Tamil Family, 3:20, 4:506
Notes on Nursing: What It Is and What It Is Not, 5:362
Notes on Poems and Reviews, 1:397
Notes on Prints, 1:28
Notes on Science Technology and Science Education in the Development of the South, 5:713
Notes on the Cuff and Other Stories, 2:706
Notes on the History of Military Medicine, 5:50
Notes on the Life of Edmund Spenser, 1:198
Notes on the Nicomanchean Ethics of Aristotle, 4:71
Notes on the State of Virginia, 1:640
Notes on Thought and Vision, 1:827
Notes to Literature, 4:393
Not Free to Desist: The American Jewish Committee 1906–1966, 4:638
No Thanks, 1:825
Nothing, 1:487
Nothing at All, 1:1202, 1:1203
Nothing-Doting-Blindness, 1:487

Nothing Grows by Moonlight, 2:662
Nothing Is Hidden: Wittgenstein's Criticism of His Early Thought, 4:346
The Nothingness beyond God, 4:365
Nothing Sacred, 1:455
Nothing Stands Still: Essays by Arthur M. Schlesinger, 3:596
Nothing Venture, Nothing Win, 3:925
Not Honour More, 1:456
Not I, 1:439
Not in Heaven: The Nature and Function of Halachah, 4:648
Not in Our Genes, 5:826
Notions of the Americans: Picked Up by a Travelling Bachelor, 1:665
Not Necessarily the New Age: Critical Essays, 4:866
Not of This Time, Not of This Place, 2:13
Not Out of Hate, 2:313
Not Quite a Miracle, 5:392
No Traveller, 1:989
Notre-Dame de Paris, 2:482, 2:483
The Not-Right House, 1:1034
Not So Free to Choose, 3:78
Not So Simple Neil Simon, 1:1113
Not That You Asked . . . , 3:872
Not This Pig: Poems, 1:1004
Not to Disturb, 1:551
Not under Forty, 1:821
Not Wanted on the Voyage, 2:911
Nourishing Your Child, 5:348
Nova, 1:1256
Nova Express, 1:957
Novalis, 2:605
Novalis and Mathematics, 2:605
Nova Scotia and Confederation, 1864–1871, 3:613
Nova Scotian, 2:912
Nova Scotia's Massachusetts, 3:613
The Novel, 1945–1950, 1:422
The Novel, 3:931
The Novel and Contemporary Experience in Africa, 2:107
The Novel According to Cervantes, 2:536
The Novel and the Modern World, 1:420

The Novel and the Police, 1:319
The Novel as Transformation Myth, 2:133, 2:155
The Novel before the Novel, 2:363
Novel Epics: Gogol, Dostoevsky, and National Narrative, 2:686
The Novel Histories of Galdós, 2:547
The Novel in Antiquity, 2:363
The Novel in Javanese: Aspects of Its Social and Literary Character, 2:317
The Novel in Seventeenth-Century China, 2:189
A Novelist in the Making, 1:777
Novelists' America: Fiction as History, 1910–1940, 1:803
The Novelist's Responsibility, 1:494
The Novellas of Valentin Rasputin: Genre, Language and Style, 2:752
A Novel of Husbands and Wives, 1:853
The Novel of Manners in America, 1:658, 1:724
Novel of Thank You, 1:881
The Novel of the American West, 1:1214
The Novel of the Future, 1:865
A Novel of the Maid of Orleans, 2:957
The Novel of the Spanish Civil War, 1936–1975, 2:525
The Novel of Violence in America, 1:917
Novel on Yellow Paper, 1:548, 1:549
Novels, Mont-Saint-Michel, The Education, 1:729, 3:562
Novels, Readers, and Reviewers, 1:657, 1:944
Novels and Novelists, 1:422
Novels and Stories (London), 1:774
Novels in English by Women, 1891–1920: A Preliminary Checklist, 1:122
The Novels of Anthony Powell, 1:536
The Novels of Ayi Kwei Armah: A Study in Polemical Fiction, 2:131

The Novels of Barbara Pym, 1:539

The Novels of C. P. Snow: A Critical Introduction, 1:550

The Novels of Chinua Achebe, 2:129

Novels of D. H. Lawrence: A Search for Integration, 1:511

The Novels of Dashiell Hammett, 1:1230

The Novels of F. Scott Fitzgerald, 1:840

The Novels of Frank Norris, 1:777

The Novels of George Eliot, 1:354

The Novels of George Lamming, 2:937

The Novels of Jack London: A Reappraisal, 1:775

The Novels of James Gould Cozzens, 1:965

The Novels of Jane Austen: An Interpretation, 1:276

The Novels of John Gardner: Making Life as a Moral Process, 1:979

The Novels of John Steinbeck: A Critical Study, 1:886

The Novels of Julio Cortázar, 2:862

The Novels of Nathalie Sarraute, 2:506

Novels of Saul Bellow: An Introduction, 1:947

Novels of the Caribbean, 2:931

Novels of the 1840s, 1:310

The Novels of Theodore Dreiser: A Critical Study, 1:831

Novels of the Troubled Years, 2:326

The Novels of Thomas Hardy: Illusion and Reality, 1:363

The Novels of Thomas Love Peacock, 1:297

Novels of William Faulkner: A Critical Interpretation, 1:838

The Novels of William Golding, 1:484

The Novels of Wole Soyinka, 2:150

The Novels of Wright Morris: A Critical Interpretation, 1:1018

The Novel To-Day, 1:420

November Haggard: Uncollected Prose and Verse, 1:507

Novum Organum and Related Writings, 4:165

Novum Testamentum Graece, 4:794

Novus Ordo Seclorum: The Intellectual Origins of the Constitution, 3:142, 3:521

Novy Mir: A Case Study in the Politics of Literature 1952–1958, 2:686

Now and Then: Poems 1976–1978, 1:893

No Way, 2:422

Now Barabbas, 1:50

Now Don't Try to Reason with Me, 1:1139

Nowhere, 1:949

The Nowhere City, 1:1007

Nowhere to Play, 2:137

No Wit, No Help Like a Woman's, 1:190

Now It Can Be Told: The Story of the Manhattan Project, 5:658

Now That I Have OS/2 2.0 on My Computer, What Do I Do Next?, 5:554

Now the King is Dead, 2:61

Now the News: The Story of Broadcast Journalism, 3:805

Now the Volcano: An Anthology of Latin American Gay Literature, 2:849

Now We Are Six, 1:587, 1:588

Now You See It: Studies on Lesbian and Gay Film, 1:1157, 1:1181

The N-Town Play, 1:159

Nubia: Corridor to Africa, 3:418

The Nuclear Age, 5:240

Nuclear Age Thinking, 5:110

Nuclear and Practice Physics Source Book, 5:653

Nuclear Arms: Ethics, Strategy, Politics, 5:113

The Nuclear Arms Race: Technology and Society, 5:239

Nuclear Astrophysics, 5:687

Nuclear Blackmail and Nuclear Balance, 5:184

The Nuclear Connection, 5:113

The Nuclear Crisis Reader, 3:280

The Nuclear Delusion, 3:584

Nuclear Deterrence: Ethics and Strategy, 5:111

Nuclear Energy and Ethics, 5:112, 5:141

Nuclear Energy and the Public, 5:113

Nuclear Engineering: An Introduction, 5:239

Nuclear Engineering: Theory and Technology of Commercial Nuclear Power, 5:240

Nuclear Ethics: A Christian Moral Argument, 5:111

Nuclear Holocaust and Christian Hope, 5:112

Nuclear Physics, 5:685

Nuclear Power, 5:240

Nuclear Power: Technical and Institutional Options for Health, Safety, and the Environment, 5:287

Nuclear Power, Both Sides, 5:111

Nuclear Power and Public Policy, 5:76, 5:112, 5:141

Nuclear Power and Public Responsibility, 5:112

Nuclear-Powered Submarines, 5:238

The Nuclear Power Game, 5:109

Nuclear Power in an Age of Uncertainty, 5:288

Nuclear Power in Developing Countries: An Analysis of Decision Making, 5:287

Nuclear Power Issues and Choices, 5:287

The Nuclear Present, 5:109

Nuclear Proliferation: Breaking the Chain, 3:280

The Nuclear Question, 3:279

Nuclear Rights, Nuclear Wrongs, 5:112

Nuclear War: Philosophical Perspectives, 5:110

The Nuclear Waste Primer, 5:240

Nuclear Weapons and the American Churches, 5:110

Nuclear Weapons and the Future of Humanity, 5:109, 5:110

Nucleosynthesis in Massive Stars and Supernovae, 5:687

Nucleus: Reconnecting Science and Religion in the Nuclear Age, 5:197

Nude Descending a Staircase: Poems, Song, A Ballad, 1:997

Nuer, 3:25, 3:29
Nuer Religion, 3:29, 4:475
Number: The Language of
    Science, 5:488
Number One, 1:827
Numbers: Rational and Irra-
    tional, 5:488
Numbers and Ideals, 5:515
Number Theory for Begin-
    ners, 5:489
Numerical Recipes: The Art
    of Scientific Computing,
    5:550
The Nun, 2:471, 2:472
A Nun from T'aishan, 2:211
Nuns and Soldiers, 1:523
The Nun's Priest's Tale,
    1:150
Nureyev, 3:750
Nurse Norton's Affair, 1:524
A Nursery Companion, 1:579,
    3:885
Nursery Manual, 5:787
Nursery Rhymes and Tales:
    Their Origin and History,
    3:847
Nurses: A Political Force,
    5:337
Nurses: The Human Touch,
    5:337
The Nurse's Story, 5:337
Nursing and the Management
    of Pediatric Communica-
    tion Disorders, 5:376
Nursing Care of the Older
    Adult, 5:317
Nursing Implications of Lab-
    oratory Tests, 5:324
Nursing in the 1980s: Crises,
    Opportunities, Challenges,
    5:337
Nursing Practice: The Ethical
    Issues, 5:121
The Nursing Process in Later
    Maturity, 5:317
The Nursing Profession: A
    Time to Speak, 5:337
The Nutcracker, 2:592
Nutraerobics, 5:325
Nutrition: An Inquiry into
    the Issues, 5:346
Nutrition: Concepts and Con-
    troversies, 5:346
Nutrition, Diet, and Health,
    5:345
Nutrition, the Aged, and So-
    ciety, 5:349
Nutritional Intervention in
    the Aging Process, 5:348
Nutrition and Cancer, 5:373
Nutrition and Diet Therapy:
    Principles and Practice,
    5:345

Nutrition and Killer Diseases,
    5:395
The Nutrition Desk Refer-
    ence, 5:345
The Nutrition Detective,
    5:355
Nutrition for the Prime of
    Your Life, 5:347
Nutrition for Your Pregnan-
    cy: The University of
    Minnesota Guide, 5:357
Nutrition in Adolescence,
    5:348
Nutrition in Health and Dis-
    ease, 5:395
Nutrition in the Middle and
    Later Years, 5:349
Nuts and Bolts of the Past,
    3:524
Nutshell Library, 1:1206
Nyamba Nene and the Flying
    Bus, 2:154
Nyamba Nene's Pistol, 2:154
The Nymph of Fiesole, 2:409,
    2:410
Nymph Song, 2:409
Nyugat, 2:800, 2:802

O

The Oak and the Calf: A
    Memoir, 2:761
The Oak Openings; or, The
    Bee-Hunter, 1:663
O Albany! An Urban Tapes-
    try, 1:996
The Oasis, 1:1007, 1:1008
Obedience to Authority: An
    Experimental View, 3:175
Obi, 2:139
Objections to Astrology,
    5:599
Objections to Nuclear De-
    fence: Philosophers on De-
    terrence, 5:109
Objections to Sex and Vio-
    lence, 1:458
Objective Knowledge: An
    Evolutionary Approach,
    5:64, 5:98
Objective Knowledge, 4:409
Objectivity, Realism, and
    Truth: Philosophical Pa-
    pers, 4:413
Object-Oriented Program-
    ming: An Introduction,
    5:551
Objects of Desire: Design
    and Society since 1750,
    5:192
Oblomov, 2:723

Oblomov and His Creator:
    The Life and Art of Ivan
    Goncharov, 2:723
The Obscene Bird of Night,
    2:863, 2:864
Obscure Destinies, 1:821
Observation and Objectivity,
    4:384
Observations, 1:441
Observations in the Art of
    English Poesie, 1:174
Observers Observed: Essays
    on Ethnographic Field-
    work, 3:12
The Observing Self: Redis-
    covering the Essay, 1:429
O'Casey the Dramatist, 1:527
Occasional Form: Henry
    Fielding and the Chains of
    Circumstance, 1:245
Occasions, 2:427
Occasions for Philosophy,
    4:20
The Occasions of Poetry: Es-
    says in Criticism and Au-
    tobiography, 1:491
Occidentosis: A Plague from
    the West, 2:86
The Occult: A History, 1:568
The Occult Establishment,
    4:856
The Occult in America: New
    Historical Perspectives,
    4:841
The Occult Philosophy, 4:133
Occult Philosophy in the
    Elizabethan Age, 4:132
The Occult Underground,
    4:842
The Occult World of Ma-
    dame Blavatsky, 4:874
Oceana; or England and Her
    Colonies, 3:403
Ocean and Marine Diction-
    ary, 5:618
Ocean at the Window: Hun-
    garian Prose and Poetry
    since 1945, 2:799
Oceania: The Native Cultures
    of Australia and the Pacif-
    ic Islands, 4:462
Oceanic Islands, 5:630
Ocean of Wisdom: Guidelines
    for Living, 4:560
Oceanography: The Last
    Frontier, 5:632
Oceanography, 5:631
The Oceans, Our Last Re-
    source, 5:632
Ocean to Ocean, 3:908
The Ocean World, 3:919
The Ocean World of Jacques
    Cousteau, 3:918

Ockham, Descartes, and Hume, 4:163

Ockham's Theory of Propositions: Part II of the Summa Logicae, 4:120

Ockham's Theory of Terms: Part I of the Summa Logicae, 4:120

Ockham to Suarez, 4:736

O Come Ye Back to Ireland: Our First Year in County Clare, 3:901

The Octaroon, 1:272, 1:331

Octavio Paz: Homage to the Poet, 2:879

Octavio Paz: The Mythic Dimension, 2:879

Octavio Paz, 2:879

October 1916, 2:760

October 1917, 3:396

October Ferry to Gabriola, 2:919

October Light, 1:979

The October Revolution: A Collection of Articles and Speeches, 3:292

The October Revolution, 3:397

The Octopus: A Story of California, 1:776

The Octopus, 1:776

Octopussy, 1:594

The Octoroon, 1:1070

Octubre, 2:528

Oda Oak Oracle, 2:121

The Odd Couple, 1:1112, 1:1113

Odd Girls and Twilight Lovers, 1:1181, 3:552

The Odd Women, 1:358

Ode on the Intimations of Immortality, 1:305

Odes and Epodes: With the Centennial Hymn, 2:386

Odes et ballades, 2:482

The Odes of Horace: A Critical Study, 2:386

The Odes of John Keats, 1:295

Ode to Dejection, 1:286

Ode to Walt Whitman and Other Poems, 2:539

Odi Barbare (Barbarian Odes), 2:412

Odi Barbare: Italian Text with English Prose, 2:413

Odi et Amo: The Complete Poetry of Catullus, 2:383

Odysseus/Ulysses, 2:984

The Odyssey: A Modern Sequel (Kazantzakis), 2:361, 2:373, 2:374

The Odyssey, 1:175, 1:223, 1:252, 1:661, 2:358, 2:359, 2:360, 2:361, 2:378, 2:396, 2:416, 2:819, 2:916, 4:482, 4:483

The Odyssey of Korean Democracy: Korean Politics, 1987–1990, 3:482

The Odyssey of Shen Congwen, 2:262

Oedipus at Colonus, 2:367

Oedipus in Nottingham: D. H. Lawrence, 1:511

Oedipus in the Trobriands, 3:36

Oedipus Rex, 2:367, 2:431

Oedipus Trilogy, 1:553

Oedipus Tyrannus, 2:367

Oeroeg, 2:625

Of Acceptable Risk: Science and the Determination of Safety, 5:155

Of a Fire on the Moon, 1:1011

Of Age and Innocence, 2:936, 2:937

Of a World That Is No More, 2:49

Of Being and Unity, 4:153

Of Chameleons and Gods, 2:165

Off Broadway: Essays about the Theatre, 1:1071

Offending the Audience, 2:585

The Office of the Scarlet Letter, 1:948

Officers and Gentlemen, 1:561, 1:562

Office Work Can Be Dangerous to Your Health, 5:354

The Official American Board of Medical Specialties (ABMS) Directory of Board Certified Medical Specialists, 1994, 5:368

Official Congressional Directory, 1:109

Official Methods of Analysis of the AOAC, 5:735

The Official Museum Directory, 1:105, 3:1994, 3:757

The Official YMCA Fitness Program, 5:326

The Officina Bodoni, 1:9

Of Foxes and Hen Houses: Licensing and the Health Professions, 5:335

Offspring of Empire, 3:481

Off the Track, 5:247

Of Grammatology, 2:447, 4:397

Of Human Bondage: Coming of Age in the Novel, 1:521

Of Human Bondage, 1:520

Of Human Freedom, 1:814, 4:251

Of Love and Lust, 5:467

Of Love and Shadows, 2:851

Of Making Many Books: A Hundred Years of Writing and Publishing, 1:44

Of Media and People, 3:203

Of Men and Machines, 1:130

Of Mice and Men, 1:883, 1:884

Of Mind and Other Matters, 4:403

Of Nightingales That Weep, 1:1204

Of Poetry and Poets, 1:719, 1:912

Of Predation and Life, 5:826

Of Revelation and Revolution, Vol. 1, 4:467

Of Sondry Folke: The Dramatic Principle in the "Canterbury Tales," 1:151

Of Spirit: Heidegger and the Question, 4:397

Of Stars and Men: Human Response to an Expanding Universe, 5:612

Of the Decorative Illustration of Books Old and New, 1:583

Of Thee I Sing, 1:1097

Of the Farm, 1:1060

Of the Just Shaping of Letters, 1:15

Of the Laws of Ecclesiastical Polity, 4:734

Of the Standard of Taste and Other Essays, 4:201

Of the Vanitie and Uncertaintie of Artes and Sciences, 4:133

Of Time and the River, 1:903

Of Tyranny, 2:405

Of Wisdom, 4:125

Of Woman Born: Motherhood as Experience and Institution, 1:1037

The Ogre, 2:512

Oh Dad, Poor Dad, Mamma's Hung You in the Closet and I'm Feeling So Sad, 1:1098

O. Henry, 1:757

O. Henry: A Biography of William Sydney Porter, 1:757

O. Henry: The Legendary
Life of William Sydney
Porter, 1:757
O. Henry Biography, 1:757
O, How the Wheel Becomes
It! 1:536
Oh! Pascal! 5:552
Oh, What a Lovely War,
1:524
Oh What a Paradise It
Seems, 1:961
Oil! 1:880
The Oil and Gas Book, 5:286
Oil and World Power, 5:636
Oil Companies in the Inter-
national System, 5:281
The Oil Follies of 1970–1980,
5:241
The Oil Man of Obange,
2:139
The Oil Markets in the
1980s: A Decade of De-
cline, 5:280
Oil Markets in Turmoil: An
Economic Analysis, 5:285
The Oil Sketches of Peter
Paul Rubens: A Critical
Catalogue, 3:792
O Jerusalem, 4:642
Okeke, the Magician, 2:140
Oku no Hosomichi, 2:276
Olavus Petri and the Ecclesi-
astical Transformation in
Sweden (1521–1552),
4:730
Old, Sick, and Helpless:
Where Therapy Begins,
5:317
Old Age in Myth and Sym-
bol: A Cultural Dictionary,
3:869
Old and New Poems, 1:983
The Old and New World Ro-
manticism of Washington
Irving, 1:681
Old and Rare: Forty Years in
the Book Business, 1:78
The Old and the New: From
Don Quixote to Kafka,
2:536
Old Arts and New Theology,
4:696
The Old Bachelor, 1:237
The Old Beauty and Others,
1:820
The Old Catholic Source-
book, 4:859
Old Clemens and W.D.H.,
1:759, 1:783
Old Courtier, 1:583
Old Creole Days, 1:736
The Old Curiosity Shop,
1:348

The Old Devils, 1:432
Old Diary Leaves, 4:853
The Older Sophists, 4:54
The Oldest Biography of Spi-
noza, 4:188
The Oldest Living Graduate,
1:1096
The Oldest Stories in the
World, 2:52
Old European Order, 1660 to
1800, 3:338
The Old Farmer and His Al-
manack, 3:858
The Old Farmer's Almanac,
1:83
The Old Farmer's Almanac
Book of Old Fashioned
Puzzles, 3:858
An Old-Fashioned Girl,
1:1198
An Old Fashioned Thanksgiv-
ing, 1:1198
Old Father Storyteller, 3:866
Old Flames and a Month in
the Country, 1:486
Old Floating Cloud: Two No-
vellas, 2:265
The Old Glory, 1:1006
Old Glory's Course, 1:1034
Old Goriot, 2:453
The Old Gringo, 2:865
Old Icelandic Poetry. Eddic
Lay and Skaldic Verse,
2:640
Old Indian Days, 1:749
Old Iowegian Legends, 3:862
Old Jewish Folk Music, 3:853
The Old Judge, or, Life in a
Colony, 2:912
Old Love and Other Stories,
2:47
Old Maids to Radical Spin-
sters: Unmarried Women
in the Twentieth-Century
Novel, 1:804
The Old Man, 2:439, 2:767
The Old Man and His Sons,
2:655, 2:656
The Old Man and the Bu-
reaucrats, 2:825
The Old Man and the Medal,
2:145
The Old Man and the Sea,
1:845
Old Man Joseph and His
Family, 1:1099
Old Man Rubbing His Eyes,
1:951
An Old Man's Confession,
2:439
An Old Man's Love, 1:406
The Old Man Who Does as
He Pleases, 2:214

The Old Man Who Does as
He Pleases: Poems and
Prose, 2:213
The Old Men at the Zoo,
1:567
Old Mortality, 1:298
Old New York, 1:787
The Old Ones, 1:565
The Old Patagonian Express:
By Train through the
Americas, 3:897, 3:940
Old Possum's Book of Practi-
cal Cats, 1:471, 1:472
The Old Protestantism and
the New, 4:741
The Old Rabbinic Doctrine
of God, 4:621
The Old Red Sandstone, or
New Walks in an Old
Field, 5:624
Old Regime and the French
Revolution, 3:164, 3:165
The Old Revolutionaries: Po-
litical Lives in the Age of
Samuel Adams, 3:521
Old Rosa: A Novel in Two
Stories, 2:852
Old Sir Douglas, 1:384
Old Snow, 2:261
The Old Social Classes and
the Revolutionary Move-
ments of Iraq, 3:449,
4:578
An Old Sweetheart of Mine,
1:777
The Old Swimmin'-Hole,
1:777
The Old Testament: An In-
troduction, 4:816, 4:817
Old Testament Abstracts, 4:8,
4:796
Old Testament Books for
Pastor and Teacher, 4:795
Old Testament Introduction,
4:817
Old Testament Library, 4:821
Old Testament Message,
4:821
The Old Testament Pseudepi-
grapha, 4:810
The Old Testament since the
Reformation, 4:813
Old Testament Theology:
Basic Issues in the Cur-
rent Debate, 4:827, 4:838
Old Testament Women in
Western Literature, 2:985
The Old Testament World,
4:807
The Old Time Fiddler's Rep-
ertory: 245 Traditional
Tunes, 3:851
Old Times, 1:534

Oldtown Folks, 1:698
Old Wines are Tasty, 2:147
The Old Wives' Tale, 1:195, 1:443
The Old World and the New, 1:408
The Old World and New, 1492–1650, 3:335
The Old World's New World, 3:602
The Olive Fairy Book, 3:883
Oliver Evans: Inventive Genius of the Industrial Revolution, 5:231
Oliver Goldsmith: A Biography, 1:680
Oliver Goldsmith: A Georgian Study, 1:247
Oliver Goldsmith: Essays Towards an Interpretation, 1:247
Oliver Goldsmith, A Reference Guide, 1:247
Oliver Goldsmith Revisited, 1:247
Oliver Twist, 1:348
Oliver Wendell Holmes, 1:679
The Olmec: Mother Culture of Mesoamerica, 4:455
The Olmecs: The Oldest Civilization in Mexico, 4:455
The Olmec World, 3:627, 4:455
Olney Hymns, 1:237
-Ologies and -Isms: A Thematic Dictionary, 1:93
The Olympic Discus, 2:819
Oman and Its Renaissance, 3:451
Omar Khayyam: The Philosopher-Poet of Medieval Islam, 2:92
Omega Project, 4:870
Omensetter's Luck, 1:980
Ominous Years, 1774–1776, 1:234
O Mistress Mine, 1:540
Omneros, 2:119
Omniana, 1:304
The Omni Interviews, 5:696
Omnipotence and Other Theological Mistakes, 4:289
Omnivore, 1:1253
Omoo, 1:685, 1:687
On, 1:442
On Adolescence: A Psychoanalytic Interpretation, 3:173
On a Field Azure, 2:754
On Aggression, 3:170, 3:190, 5:835
On Agriculture, 5:265

On a Note of Triumph: Norman Corwin and the Golden Years of Radio, 3:810
On Another Man's Wound, 3:371
On Anything, 1:442
On Aphasia, 5:446
On Aristotle and Greek Tragedy, 2:346, 4:69
On Aristotle's Categories, 4:62
On Art and Literature: Critical Writings, 2:871
On Autobiography, 1:927
On Becoming a Biologist, 5:764
On Becoming a Novelist, 1:979
On Becoming a Person, 5:468
On Being a Jewish Feminist, 4:650
On Being and the One, 4:152
On Being Black and Healthy, 5:339
On Being Blue: A Philosophical Inquiry, 1:980
On Being Christian, 4:774
On Being in the World, 4:294, 4:346
On Being the Right Size and Other Essays, 5:797, 5:798
On Bended Knee: The Press and the Reagan Presidency, 3:543, 3:807
On Buildings, 3:319
On Calderón, 2:533
Once-Born, Twice-Born Zen: The Soto and Rinzai Schools of Japan, 4:537
Once Five Years Pass and Other Dramatic Works, 2:539
Once in a Lifetime, You Can't Take It with You, The Man Who Came to Dinner, 1:1097
On Certainty, 4:344
Once There Was a War, 1:884, 1:885
Once upon a Time: A Fairy Tale for Grown-ups, 1:588
Once upon a Time: On the Nature of Fairy Tales, 1:579
Once Upon a Time: Yeki Bud, Yeki Nabud, 2:92
On Christian Doctrine, 4:109
On Compiling an Annotated Bibliography, 1:61
On Conjectures, 4:148

On Contemporary Literature, 1:421
On Copia of Words and Ideas, 4:139
On Culture and Social Change: Selected Papers, 5:156
On Death and Dying, 5:422
On Deconstruction, 1:924, 1:1141
On Difficulty and Other Essays, 1:1054
Ondine, 2:481
On Directing Film, 3:828
On Directing Shakespeare: Interviews with Contemporary Directors, 1:217
On Disobedience and Other Essays, 5:450
On Double Consciousness, 3:181
On Dreaming: An Encounter with Medard Boss, 5:437
On Duties, 2:384
One Across, Two Down, 1:609
The One and Its Relation to Intellect in Plotinus, 4:86
One and Many in Aristotle's Metaphysics: The Central Books, 4:68
One and Many in Presocratic Philosophy, 4:51
The One Best System: A History of American Urban Education, 3:258
One Book, Five Ways: Procedures of Five University Presses, 1:46
One Boy at War: A Life in the AIDS Underground, 5:388
One Boy's Boston: 1887–1901, 3:589
On Economics and Society: Selected Essays, 3:62
One Day, 1:1017
One Day at a Time, 1:728
One Day in the Life of Ivan Denisovich, 2:760
One Day on Beetle Rock, 5:817
One-Dimensional Man, 4:408, 5:71, 5:94
On Editing Shakespeare, 1:207
One Dry Season: In the Footsteps of Mary Kingsley, 3:901
On Education, 4:224
One Earth, Four or Five Worlds, 2:879
One Fat Englishman, 1:432

One Fault, 1:408

One Flesh, 1:193

One Flew over the Cuckoo's Nest, 1:999

One Foot in Eden, 1:521

One for the Road: A Play, 1:534

One Generation After, 1:1065

One-Handed Basket Weaving: Poems on the Theme of Work, 4:589

One Hundred and One More Uses for a Dead Cat, 3:870

One Hundred Armenian Tales and Their Folkloristic Significance, 2:77

One Hundred Billion Suns, 5:594

One Hundred Books about Bookmaking, 1:9

150 Careers in the Health Care Field, 5:335

The 158-Pound Marriage, 1:991, 1:992

One Hundred Love Sonnets: Cien sonetos de amor, 2:874

One Hundred Poems from the Chinese, 2:193

One Hundred Problems in Elementary Mathematics, 5:497

The One Hundredth Anniversary 1–23 Presentation Box, 1:589

One Hundred Twenty Days of Sodom and Other Writings, 2:503

One Hundred Years of Anthropology, 3:11

One Hundred Years of Homosexuality and Other Essays on Greek Love, 1:1182, 3:309

One Hundred Years of Huckleberry Finn, 1:784

One Hundred Years of Negro Freedom, 1:817

One Hundred Years of Old Testament Interpretation, 4:813

One Hundred Years of Solitude, 2:842, 2:851, 2:866, 2:867, 2:913

One Hundred Years of Theosophy, 4:853

The One I Know Best of All, 1:1201

O'Neill: Son and Artist, 1:1108

O'Neill: Son and Playwright, 1:1108

One in Three: Women with Cancer Confront an Epidemic, 5:372

One Is Enough, 2:140

One Kind of Freedom: The Economic Consequences of Emancipation, 3:549

One Little Boy, 5:421

One Man Alone across the Atlantic in a Nine-foot Boat, 3:908

One Man's Initiation—1917, 1:828

One Man's Meat, 1:898

One More Sunday, 1:1234

One Nation under Television: The Rise and Decline of Network TV, 3:812

On Enchantments, 4:153

On English Poetry, 1:485

One of Ours, 1:820

One Potato, Two Potato: The Secret Education of American Children, 3:869

Oneself as Another, 4:319

One Thing More, or Caedmon Construed, 1:480

1,001 Health Tips, 5:341

One Thousand and One Things Everyone Should Know about Science, 5:19

One Thousand Journeys to the Rivers, Lands and Seas of Seven Continents, 3:894

One Thousand Souls, 2:748

One Thousand Years: A Concise History of Hungary, 3:390

One Time, One Place, 1:895

One Two, Buckle My Shoe, 1:583

One Two Three . . . Infinity: Facts and Speculations, 5:605, 5:689

One Universe: An Armchair Guide, 5:588

One-Variable Calculus with an Introduction to Linear Algebra, 5:490

On Every Front: The Making and Unmaking of the Cold War, 3:540, 3:546

On Everything, 1:442

On Evolution and Fossil Mammals, 5:639

One Way to Heaven, 1:824

One Word to the Other, 2:879

One Writer's Beginnings, 1:894, 1:895

On Extended Wings: Wallace Stevens' Longer Poems, 1:888

On Extended Wings, 1:932

On Fate, Free Will and Predestination, 4:153

On Faulkner: The Best from American Literature, 1:836

On Feeling, Knowing, and Valuing: Selected Writings, 4:332

On First Principles: Being Koetschau's Text of the De Principiis, 4:116

On Foreign Shores: American Images in Indonesian Poetry, 2:318

On Formal and Universal Unity, 4:105, 4:154

On Formally Undecidable Propositions of Principia Mathematica. . . ., 5:509

On Free Choice of the Will, 4:109

On Free Will, 4:138, 4:155

Ongoing Journey, 4:317

On Hegel's Logic, 4:233

On Her Majesty's Secret Service, 1:594

On Heroes, Hero-Worship and the Heroic in History, 1:343, 4:588

On Heroes and Hero-Worship, 1:343

On Heroes and Tombs, 2:882, 2:883

On Her Way Rejoicing: The Fiction of Muriel Spark, 1:552

On Hindu Ritual and the Goddess, 4:504

On His Blindness, 1:191

On His Own Ignorance, 2:402

On His Own Ignorance and That of Many Others, 4:150

On History, 3:283

On History and Philosophies of History, 3:275

On Human Communication: A Review, a Survey, and a Criticism, 5:306, 5:571

On Ideas: Aristotle's Criticism of Plato's Theory of Forms, 4:68

Onions and Cucumbers and Plums: Forty-six Yiddish Poems in English, 2:33

On Jews and Judaism in Crisis: Selected Essays, 3:350, 4:672

On Job: God-Talk and the Suffering of the Innocent, 4:769

On Judaism, 4:662

On Keynesian Economics and the Economics of Keynes, 3:62

On Kingship to the King of Cyprus, 4:117

On Knowing: Essays for the Left Hand, 3:175

On Law, Morality, and Politics, 4:118

On Learned Ignorance, 4:148, 4:149

On Leon Battista Alberti: His Literary and Aesthetic Theories, 2:404

On Lewis Mumford: An Annotated Bibliography, 5:172

On Liberty, 1:380, 3:96, 4:244

On Lies, Secrets, and Silence: Selected Prose, 1966–1978, 1:1037

On Life and Letters, 2:477

Online: A Guide to America's Leading Information Services, 5:547

Online Communities: A Case Study of the Office of the Future, 5:307

On Literature, 2:725

On Louis Simpson: Depths Beyond Happiness, 1:1048

On Love and Happiness, 4:336

Only a Miner: Studies in Recorded Coal Mining Songs, 3:851

Only a Mother, 2:672

The Only Chaos and Other Essays, 5:202

An Only Child, 1:527, 1:528

The Only Daughter, 2:948

The Only Kangaroo Among the Beauty: Emily Dickinson and America, 1:748

Only One Earth: The Care and Maintenance of a Small Planet, 3:48, 5:795

The Only Problem, 1:551

The Only Son, 2:139

Only the Dreamer Can Change the Dream, 1:1005

On Mach's Theories, 5:700

On Mark Twain: The Best from American Literature, 1:783

On Metaphysics, 4:395

On Method: Toward a Reconstruction of Psychological Investigation, 3:169

On Miracle Ground: Essays on the Fiction of Lawrence Durrell, 1:470

On Modern Marriage, 2:649

On Moral Fiction, 1:917, 1:978, 1:979

On Moral Medicine: Theological Perspectives in Medical Ethics, 4:893, 5:121

On Motion and on Mechanics, 4:142

On Native Grounds, 1:723, 1:773, 1:804, 1:918, 1:995, 1:996

On Nothing and Kindred Subjects, 1:443

On Old Age and on Friendship, 4:72

Onomasticon, 4:709

On Oratory and Orators, 2:384

On Philosophical Style, 4:276

On Poetic Imagination and Reverie, 4:274

On Poetry and Poets, 1:472

On Poets and Others, 2:879

On Psychological Prose, 2:686

On Racine, 2:498

On Reading Ruskin, 1:395, 2:495

On Religion: Speeches to Its Cultured Despisers, 4:253, 4:254

On Religion, 4:425, 4:575

On Responsibility, 5:421

On Revolution, 3:282, 3:342, 4:394

On Revolution: Selected Writings, 1920–1966, 2:340

On Rhetoric, 4:66

On Russian Poetry, 2:687

On Sepulchres, 2:421

On Shakespeare, Modern Poetry, Plato and Other Subjects, 1:417

On Shame and the Search for Identity, 5:423

On Socialists and "The Jewish Question" after Marx, 4:656

On Something, 1:443

The Onstage Christ: Studies in the Persistence of a Theme, 2:985

On Stage in America, 1:1072

On Symbols and Society, 1:817, 1:956

On the Accuracy of Economic Observations, 3:47

On the Art of Medieval Arabic Literature, 2:55

On the Art of the Kabbalah, 4:130

On the Banks of Plum Creek, 1:1208, 1:1209

On the Basis of Morality, 4:255

On the Beach, 2:962

On the Beneficence of Censorship, 2:688

On the Cause, Principle and One, 4:135

On the Causes of Plants, 4:90

On the Church of Christ: The Person of the Church and Her Personnel, 4:306

On the Commonwealth, 2:384

On the Composition of Images, Signs and Ideas, 4:135

On the Contrary, and Other Poems, 2:792

On the Crown, 2:343

On the Dark Side of Russian Literature. 1709–1910, 2:689

On the Destruction and Conquest of Britain, 1:145

On the Dignity of Man, on Being and the One, Heptaplus, 4:153

On the Duty of Man and Citizen According to Natural Law, 4:186

On the Edge, 1:467

On the Edge of Destruction, 3:348, 4:636

On the Edge of Reason, 2:786

On the Edge of the Cliff and Other Stories, 1:538

On the Epistemology of the Inexact Sciences, 5:101

On the Equilibrium of Heterogeneous Substances, 5:746

On the Essence of Finite Being as Such, on the Existence of the Essence, and Their Distinction, 4:105, 4:154

On the Eternal in Man, 4:332

On the Eternity of the World, 4:118

On the Eve, 2:768, 2:769

On the Eve of Uncertain Tomorrows, 2:933

On the Existence of God,
4:221

On the Fourfold Root of the
Principle of Sufficient
Reason, 4:255

On the Frontier, 1:435

On the Frontiers of Science:
How Scientists See Our
Future, 5:9

On the Genealogy of Morals,
4:245, 4:246

On the Glassy Sea, 5:589

On the Glaubenslehre: Two
Letters to Dr. Leucke,
4:254

On the Golden Porch, 2:762,
2:763

On the Good Life, 2:384

On the Historical Novel,
2:426

On the History and Method
of Economics, 3:47, 3:89

On the Iliad, 2:361

On the Imagination, 4:152

On the Immortality of the
Soul, 2:403

On the Infinite, the Universe
and Worlds, 4:135

On the Interpretation of Empedocles, 4:53

On the Kabbalah and Its
Symbolism, 4:672

On the Law of Nature and
Nations, 4:186

On the Limits of Poetry:
1928 to 1948, 1:889

On the Literary Genetics of
Shakespeare's Poems and
Sonnets, 1:215

On the Lives and Characters
of the Philosophers, 4:16

On the Logic of the Social
Sciences, 4:404, 5:89

On the Making of Apocalypse
Now, 3:828

On the Marble Cliffs, 2:595

On the Modernist Long
Poem, 1:798

On the Moral Reclaimability
of Prostitutes, 1:341

On the Most Ancient Wis-
dom of the Italians, 4:30,
4:216

On the Motion and Immobil-
ity of Douve, 2:461

On the Motion of the Heart
and Blood in Animals,
5:361

On the Motives Which Led
Husserl to Transcendental
Idealism, 4:235

On the Move, 3:609

On the Movements and Hab-
its of Climbing Plants,
5:793

On the Musically Beautiful,
3:660

On the Natural State of Men,
4:186

On the Nature of Health: An
Action-Theoretic Approach,
5:78

On the Nature of the Uni-
verse, 2:388

On the Nature of Things,
2:388, 4:75

On the Origin of Species: A
Facsimile of the First Edition, 5:793

On the Origin of Species,
5:792

On the Other Side: A Journey through Soviet Central
Asia, 3:904

On the Penitentiary System
in the United States,
3:164, 3:165

On the Philosophy of His-
tory, 4:306

On the Plantation, 1:754

On the Plurality of Worlds,
4:381

On the Poet and His Craft,
1:1038

On the Poetry of Galway
Kinnell: The Wages of Dy-
ing, 1:1001

On the Poetry of Matthew
Arnold: Essays in Critical
Reconstruction, 1:328

On the Power of God, 4:118

On the Progress of Sanitation, Civil and Military, to
the year 1888, 1:344

On the Proof by Spirit and
Power, 4:207

On the Psychology of Wom-
en: A Survey of Empirical
Studies, 3:178

On the Remedies of Good
and Bad Fortune, 4:150

On the Revolution of the
Heavenly Spheres, 5:601

On the Right Lines: The
Limits of Technological
Innovation, 5:248

On Thermonuclear War,
5:111

On the Road, 1:981, 1:997,
1:998, 1:1190

On the Road with John
James Audubon, 5:787

On the Secret Conflict of My
Worries, 4:150

On the Several Senses of Being in Aristotle, 4:67,
4:221

On the Shoulders of Giants,
3:233

On the Side of the Apes,
5:826

On the Solitary Life, 4:150

On the Soul and Life, 4:156

On the Structure and Distribution of Coral Reefs,
5:794

On the Study Methods of
Our Time, 4:215, 4:216

On the Study of Celtic Literature and Other Essays,
1:327

On the Sublime, 2:362

On the Sublime and Beautiful, 4:192

On the Supreme Good, 4:96

On the Theory of Contingency and Its Relation to Association and Normal
Correlation, 5:531

On the Trial of the Arawaks,
4:466

On the True Good, 4:155

On the Truth of Being,
4:293, 5:91

On the Truth of the Catholic
Faith, 4:118

On the Unity of the Intellect,
4:118

On the Use of Philosophy:
Three Essays, 4:306

On the Vanity of Pagan
Learning, 4:151

On the Various Forces of
Nature, 5:745

On the Various Kinds of Dis-
tinctions, 4:105, 4:154

On the Way Home, 1:1208

On the Way to Language,
4:291

On the Way Toward a Phe-
nomenological Psychology,
5:453

On the Wings of Occasions,
1:754

On Thinking, 4:325

On Thought and Life: Con-
versations with Karel
Čapek, 2:790

On Time and Being, 4:291

Ontogeny and Phylogeny,
3:18, 5:16, 5:638

The Ontological Argument,
4:108

The Ontological Argument of
Charles Hartshorne, 4:289

Ontological Relativity, 4:411

Ontological Relativity and Other Essays, 5:99
Ontology, 4:284
Ontology and Alterity in Merleau-Ponty, 4:311
On Top of Old Smoky, 3:859
On Translating Homer, 1:327, 2:360
On Trial, 1:1109
On True and False Ideas, 4:164
On Truth, 4:118
On Understanding Japanese Religion, 3:474
On Universals: The Tractatus de Universalibus, 4:714
On University Studies, 4:252
On Violence, 3:282
On Virginity: Against Remarriage, 4:707
On Vision and Colors, 4:254
On War, 3:340
On War and Morality, 4:389
On Women and Judaism: A View from Tradition, 4:650
On Wordsworth's Prelude, 1:307
On Work: Historical, Comparative and Theoretical Approaches, 3:218
On World Government, 2:417
On Writing, Editing and Publishing: Essays Explicative and Hortatory, 1:814
The Open Boat: And Other Tales of Adventure, 1:741
An Open Book, 3:838
Open Doors and Three Novellas, 2:438
An Open Elite? England, 1540–1880, 3:408
Open Form and the Feminine Imagination, 1:794
The Open Hand: Essays on Le Corbusier, 3:779
Open Heart Surgery: A Guidebook for Patients and Families, 5:375
Open Horizons, 3:896
Opening Doors: The Life and Work of Joseph Schumpeter, 3:105
The Opening of American Society, 3:526
The Opening of the Canadian North, 1870–1914, 3:615
The Opening of the Field, 1:971
Opening Pandora's Box: A Sociological Analysis of Scientists' Discourse, 5:153

Openings in the Old Trail, 1:756
Open Letters: Selected Writings, 2:791
An Open Life: Joseph Campbell in Conversation with Michael Toms, 3:877
Open Season, 5:357
Open Secret: Versions of Rumi, 4:589
Open Secrets, 4:859
The Open Society and Its Enemies, 3:163, 4:409, 5:98
Open to the Sun: A Bilingual Anthology of Latin American Women Poets, 2:850
The Open Universe, 4:409
The Open Universe: An Argument for Indeterminism, 5:98
Open Veins of Latin America, 3:625
Opera, 4:77
Opera: A Concise History, 3:671
Opera: Enneades, 4:86
Opera and Ideas: From Mozart to Strauss, 3:671
Opera and Its Symbols: The Unity of Words, Music, and Staging, 3:670
Opera as Drama, 2:987, 3:670
Opera Omnia, 5:505
Opera on the Beach, 3:697
Opera Posthuma, 4:186
The Operas of Charles Gounod, 3:697
The Operas of Puccini, 3:711
The Operas of Verdi, 3:726
Operations of the Geometric and Military Compass, 4:142
The Operators, 2:147
Opera Woyonsi, 2:149
Operetta: A Theatrical History, 3:671
The Opinions of Mr. Jerome Coignard, 2:477
O Pioneers!, 1:820
Opium, 2:469
Opium and Empire: Chinese Society in Colonial Singapore, 1800–1910, 3:492
The Opium-Eater: A Life of Thomas De Quincey, 1:290
Oppenheimer: The Years of Risk, 5:707
The Oppenheimer Case: The Trial of a Security System, 5:707

The Oppenheimer Hearing, 5:707
The Oppermanns, 2:578
Opportunities in Chemistry, 5:726
Opportunity and Change, 3:214
The Opposing Self: Nine Essays in Criticism, 1:1058
Opposites: Poems and Drawings, 1:1066
Oppositions of Religious Doctrines, 4:898
Opposition to Sovietization in Byelorussian Literature, 1917–1957, 2:783
Oppression and Liberty, 2:516, 4:788
Optical Communications, 5:304
Optical Electronics, 5:666
Optical Fiber Communications: Principles and Practice, 5:303, 5:304
Optical Fibers, 5:303
Optical Fibers for Transmission, 5:304
Optical Fiber Transmission Systems, 5:304
Optical Fibres and Sources for Communications, 5:303
Opticks, 5:43, 5:705, 5:706
Optics, 5:666
Optics Today, 5:666
Optimal Regulation: The Economic Theory of Natural Monopoly, 3:58
The Optimist's Daughter, 1:894, 1:895
The Optimum Quantity of Money and Other Essays, 3:77
Options in Health and Health Care, 5:335
Optoelectronics and Lightwave Technology, 5:304
Opus Maius, 4:111
Opus Posthumous, 1:887
Opus Postumum, 4:204, 4:205
O.R.: The True Story of Twenty Four Hours in a Hospital Operating Room, 5:338
Oral and Written Poetry in African Literature Today, 2:109
Oral Historiography, 4:460
Orality and Literacy: The Technologizing of the World, 4:460

Oral Poetry: Its Nature, Significance and Social Context, 4:460

Oral Torah: The Sacred Books of Judaism: An Introduction, 4:612

Oral Tradition as History, 3:432

The Oral Tradition of Classical Arabic Poetry, 2:56

The Orange Fairy Book, 3:883

Oranges, 1:1011

The Oranging of America, and Other Stories, 1:935

Oration on the Dignity of Man, 2:403, 4:153

The Orators: An English Study, 1:435

The Orchid Boat: Women Poets of China, 2:193

Orchid Book, 5:767

The Ordeal, 2:784

Ordeal by Fire: The Civil War and Reconstruction, 3:528, 3:586

Ordeal by Labyrinth: Conversations with Claude-Henri Rocquet, 4:473

The Ordeal of Civility, 3:348

The Ordeal of George Meredith, 1:379

The Ordeal of Gilbert Pinfold, 1:562

The Ordeal of Mark Twain, 1:783

The Ordeal of Richard Feverel, 1:297, 1:378, 1:379

The Ordeal of the Constitution, 3:541

The Ordeal of the Union, 3:529, 3:591

The Ordeal of Thomas Hutchinson, 3:519, 3:564

The Ordeal of Total War, 1939–1945, 3:281

Ordeal Therapy: Unusual Ways to Change Behavior, 5:418

Order and Chance: The Pattern of Diderot's Thought, 4:196

"Order and Progress": A Political History of Brazil, 3:634

Order and Progress: Brazil from Monarchy to Republic, 2:895, 3:645

Ordered by Words: Language and Narration in the Novels of William Faulkner, 1:837

Order from Confusion Sprung, 1:226

Order in Paradox: Myth, Ritual, and Exchange among Nepal's Tamang, 4:541

Orderly Chaos: The Mandala Principle, 4:357

The Order of Assassins, 4:570

The Order of Mimesis: Balzac, Stendhal, Nerval and Flaubert, 2:476

The Order of the Day: An Unidentified Flying Opus, 2:900

The Order of Things (Foucault), 4:400

The Order of Things: A Life of Joseph Furphy, 2:953

The Order of Things: An Archaeology of the Human Sciences, 2:476, 2:477, 5:87, 5:443

Order Out of Chaos: Man's New Dialogue with Nature, 5:68, 5:735

Ordinary Christians in a High-Tech World, 5:198

Ordinary Differential Equations, 5:501

Ordinary Lives: Voices of Disability and Disease, 5:369

Ordinary Love and Good Will, 1:1051

An Ordinary Lunacy, 2:948

Ordinary People and Everyday Life, 3:515

An Ordinary Story, 2:723

Ordine Nuovo, 2:423

Or Does I Explode: Black Harlem in the Great Depression, 3:535

Oregon's Ghosts and Monsters, 3:863

The Oregon Trail: Sketches of Prairie and Rocky Mountain Life, 3:592

The Oregon Trail, 1:690

The Oregon Trail and The Conspiracy of Pontiac, 1:690

Or Else: Poems 1968–1973, 1:893

Or Else, the Lightning God and Other Stories, 2:325

The Oresteia, 2:350

Orestes, 2:355

Organic Chemistry: The Name Game; Modern Coined Terms and Their Origins, 5:725

Organic Chemistry, 5:732

Organic Chemistry in Its Application to Agriculture and Physiology, 5:273

Organic Gardening, 5:274

Organic Nomenclature: A Programmed Introduction, 5:732

Organism, Medicine, and Metaphysics, 5:78, 5:93

The Organizational Revolution: A Study in the Ethics of Economic Organization, 3:71

The Organization of American Culture, 1700–1900, 3:559

The Organization of Industry, 3:58, 3:108

The Organization of Thought, Educational and Scientific, 4:341

Organizations, 3:210

Organizations Master Index, 1:104

Organized Democracy, 3:382

Organized Labor in Venezuela, 1958–1991, 3:641

Organized Miracles, 4:864

Organized Workers and Socialist Politics in Interwar Japan, 3:478

Organ Transplants: A Patient's Guide, 5:370

Oriental Architecture I: India, Indonesia, Indochina, 3:762

Oriental Architecture II: China, Korea, Japan, 3:762

Oriental Despotism: A Comparative Study of Total Power, 3:140

Orientalism, 1:1042, 1:1132, 3:437, 3:459, 3:460

Orientalism in the Hispanic Literary Tradition, 2:857, 2:884

The Orientalizing Revolution, 4:471

Oriental Philosophies, 4:349, 4:523, 4:570

Oriental Philosophy: A Westerner's Guide to Eastern Thought, 4:523

The Oriental Religions and American Thought, 4:508, 4:841

Oriental Rugs: A New Comprehensive Guide, 3:767

Orientations: Collected Writings, 3:684

Orient Express, 1:488, 1:828

The Orient of Style: Modernist Allegories of Conversion, 2:476

Origen: Spirit and Fire: A Thematic Anthology of His Writings, 4:63

Origen: The Bible and Philosophy in the Third Century Church, 4:117

Origen and the Life of the Stars: A History of an Idea, 4:63

The Origin, 1:1250

Original Intent and the Framers' Constitution, 3:142

Original Light: New and Selected Poems 1973–1983, 1:982

The Original Lists of Persons of Quality, 3:506

The Original Teachings of Ch'an Buddhism, 4:529

Origin and Development of Psychoanalysis, 5:446

The Origin and Early Form of Greek Tragedy, 2:345

The Origin and Goal of History, 4:299, 5:138

The Origin and Growth of Plato's Logic, 4:82

The Origin and Meaning of Hasidism, 4:632

The Origin and Prevention of Major Wars, 3:280

Origin and Treatment of Schizophrenic Disorders, 5:427

Origin and Virtues of Gems, 5:739

Origin of Dewey's Instrumentalism, 4:226

The Origin of Genetics: A Mendel Source Book, 5:807

The Origin of Life, 5:774

The Origin of Our Knowledge of Right and Wrong, 4:222

The Origin of Philosophy, 4:315, 5:96

Origin of Sedimentary Rock, 5:622

The Origin of Species, 5:830

The Origin of Table Manners, Vol. 3: Mythologiques, 3:33

The Origin of the Brunists, 1:962, 1:963

The Origin of the Gods: A Psychoanalytic Study of Greek Theogonic Myth, 4:446

The Origin of the Icelanders, 3:381

The Origin of the Idea of Crusade, 4:692

The Origin of the Jesuits, 4:770

The Origin of the Serif: Brush Writing and Roman Letters, 1:14

The Origin of the Soul in St. Augustine's Later Works, 4:110

Origins, 3:18

Origins: A Short Etymological Dictionary of Modern English, 1:96

Origins: A Skeptic's Guide to the Creation of Life on Earth, 5:765

Origins: Canadian History to Confederation, 3:606

Origins: Creation Texts from the Ancient Mediterranean, 4:439

The Origins and Development of Classical Hinduism, 4:498

Origins and Development of the Turkish Novel, 2:96

The Origins and Growth of Communication, 3:803

The Origins and Rise of Ethnology, 5:34

The Origins and Rise of the Filipino Novel, 2:328

The Origins of Academic Geography in the United States, 5:32

Origins of American Political Parties, 1789–1803, 3:520

The Origins of American Politics, 3:541, 3:564

The Origins of Aristotelian Science, 4:68

The Origins of Biblical Law, 4:627

The Origins of Calvin's Theology of Music, 1536–1553, 4:737

The Origins of Canadian Politics: A Comparative Approach, 3:614

The Origins of Cauchy's Rigorous Calculus, 5:502

The Origins of Certainty: Means and Meanings in Pascal's Pensées, 4:185

The Origins of Chemistry, 5:729, 5:751

The Origins of Chinese Civilization, 3:468

The Origins of Chinese Communism, 3:469

The Origins of Christianity: Sources and Documents, 4:617, 4:811

The Origins of Consciousness in the Breakdown of the Bicameral Mind, 5:80

The Origins of Culture, 3:41

The Origins of Entrepreneurship in Meiji Japan, 3:477

The Origins of European Thought about the Body, the Mind, the Soul, the World, Time and Fate, 4:49

The Origins of Greek Thought, 4:49, 4:493

The Origins of Intelligence in Children, 3:267

The Origins of Isma'ilism, 4:575

The Origins of Judaism: Religion, History, and Literature in Late Antiquity, 4:605

Origins of Life, 5:133

The Origins of Malay Nationalism, 3:492

The Origins of Mendelism, 5:807

The Origins of Modern Arabic Fiction, 2:56

The Origins of Modern Germany, 2:564

The Origins of Modern Science, 5:24, 5:602

The Origins of Nonviolence, 4:553

The Origins of Philosophy, 4:50

Origins of Pragmatism, 4:237, 4:249, 4:273

The Origins of Psychoanalysis, 5:446

Origins of Religious Art and Iconography in Preclassic Mesoamerica, 4:455

Origins of Scientific Sociology, 3:200

Origins of Scientific Thought from Anaximander to Proclus, 600 B.C.–500 A.D., 5:38

Origins of Southern Radicalism, 3:524

The Origins of Stoic Cosmology, 4:55

The Origins of the American Constitution: A Documentary History, 3:142

Origins of the Black Press: New York, 1827–1847, 3:809

The Origins of the Christian Mystical Tradition: From Plato to Denys, 4:63, 4:689
Origins of the Cold War, 3:597
The Origins of the Druze People and Religion, with Extracts from Their Sacred Writings, 4:575
The Origins of the English Novel, 1600–1740, 1:230
The Origins of the Family, Private Property and the State, 3:37, 3:74, 3:75, 4:227
The Origins of the First World War, 3:279
Origins of the Israeli Polity: Palestine under the Mandate, 3:440
Origins of the Kabbalah, 4:672
The Origins of the Marshall Plan, 3:279
Origins of the Medieval World, 3:328
The Origins of the Mithraic Mysteries, 4:450
Origins of the Modern Japanese State: Selected Writings of E. H. Norman, 3:477
The Origins of the Modern Jew, 3:349, 4:634
Origins of the New South, 1877–1913, 3:533, 3:602
The Origins of Theoretical Population Genetics, 5:49
The Origins of the Platonic Academy of Florence, 4:126
The Origins of the Republican Party, 1852–1856, 3:542
The Origins of the Romantic Movement in Spain, 2:522
The Origins of the Second World War (Remak), 3:280
The Origins of the Second World War (Taylor), 3:345, 3:409
The Origins of the Second World War in Asia and the Pacific, 3:478
Origins of the Second World War Reconsidered, 3:344
The Origins of the Sexual Impulse, 1:567
The Origins of Totalitarianism, 3:139, 3:281, 3:282, 4:394, 5:82

The Origins of Violence: Approaches to the Study of Violence, 3:280
Orion, 2:925
The Orkneyinga Saga, 2:640
Orlando: A Biography, 1:569
Orlando, 1:568
Orlando Furioso, 2:398, 2:406
Orley Farm, 1:405
Orloff and His Wife: Tales of the Barefoot Brigade, 2:725
Ormand, 1:635, 1:1239
Ormand, or The Secret Witness, 1:635
Ormond, 1:636
Orn, 1:1253
Ornithological Biography, 5:786
Ornithology: From Aristotle to the Present, 5:34
Oroonoko, 1:232, 1:233
The Orphan: A Play in Two Acts, 1:1109
The Orphan, 1:251
Orphan Warriors: Three Generations and the End of the Qing World, 3:467
Orphée, 2:468
Orpheu, 2:557
Orpheus Descending, 1:1117
Orrie's Story, 1:949
Orsinian Tales, 1:1260
Orson Welles: A Biography, 1:1179
Orson Welles: A Critical View, 1:1179
Orson Welles on Shakespeare: The W.P.A. and Mercury Theater Playscripts, 1:1179
Orta Oyunu, 2:95
Orthodox Church, 4:694, 4:756
The Orthodox Church: Its Past and Its Role in the World Today, 4:679, 4:756
The Orthodox Church in the Byzantine Empire, 4:693
The Orthodox Eastern Church, 4:755
Orthodox Theology: An Introduction, 4:693, 4:756
Orthodoxy, Roman Catholicism and Anglicanism, 4:755
Orthodoxy and Heresy in Earliest Christianity, 4:98, 4:685
Orthodoxy in American Jewish Life, 4:654

Orthodoxy in Late Imperial China, 3:468
The Orton Diaries, 1:530
Orwell: The Authorized Biography, 1:531
The Orwellian World of Jehovah's Witnesses, 4:863
Or You Can Let Him Go, 5:406
Oscar and Lucinda, 2:951
Oscar Wilde, 1:409, 1:410, 1:411
Oscar Wilde: A Collection of Critical Essays, 1:974
Oscar Wilde and the Dramatic Critics: A Study in Victorian Theatre, 1:411, 1:323
Oscar Wilde and the Theatre of the 1890's, 1:411
Oscar Wilde's Oxford Notebooks: A Portrait of a Mind in the Making, 1:410
Oscar Wilde's "The Importance of Being Earnest," 1:410
O Singapore: Stories in Celebration, 2:325
Osip Mandelstam, 2:738
Os Lusíadas, 2:558
Osteoporosis: Your Head Start to the Prevention of Fractures, 5:396
The Ostomy Book, 5:384
Oswald Spengler, 3:291
O The Chimney, 2:608
Othello, 1:157, 1:205, 1:206, 2:989
"Othello" as Tragedy: Some Problems of Judgment and Feeling, 1:214
Othello's Countrymen: The African in English Renaissance Drama, 1:214
The Other America, 3:66
The Other American Traditions: Nineteenth-Century Women Writers, 1:725
The Other Bible, 4:810
The Other Bostonians, 3:549
The Other Civil War: American Women in the Nineteenth Century, 3:554
Other Council Fires Were Here before Ours, 3:865
The "Other" Eighteenth Century: English Women of Letters, 1660–1800, 1:227
Other Exiles, 2:933
Other Fires: Short Fiction by Latin American Women, 2:849

The Other Heading: Reflections on Today's Europe, 3:211, 4:397
Other Healers, 5:13
Other Inquisitions, 1937–1952, 2:856
The Other John Updike, 1:1060
The Other Man: Conversations with Graham Greene, 1:489
The Other Mexico, 2:878
The Other Pareto, 3:100
The Other Paris, 2:912
Other People's Myths: The Cave of Echoes, 4:428
Other People's Trades, 2:425
The Other Pushkin: A Study of Alexander Pushkin's Prose Fiction, 2:751
The Other Revolution, 3:555
The Other Side of Midnight, 1:1223
The Other Side of the Wall: Three Novellas, 2:23
The Other South: Southern Dissenters in the Nineteenth Century, 3:575
Other Spaces: New Theatre and the Royal Shakespeare Company, 1:426
The Other Victorians, 1:312
Other Voices: New Writers and Writing in New Zealand, 2:970, 2:971
Other Voices, Other Rooms, 1:958, 1:959
Other Weapons, 2:885
Otherwise: Last and First Poems of Eugenio Montale, 2:428
Otherwise Engaged, 1:486
Otherwise Engaged and Other Plays, 1:486
Otherwise Than Being or Beyond Essence, 4:901
The Other Woman (Ogot), 2:155
The Other Woman (Selons), 2:474
Other Women: The Writing of Class, Race, and Gender, 1832–1898, 1:325
The Other World, 4:851
Other Worlds: Space, Superspace and the Quantum Universe, 5:660
Otho the Great, 1:271
Ottemiller's Index to Plays in Collections, 1:124
The Ottoman Centuries: The Rise and Fall of the Turkish Empire, 3:453

The Ottoman Empire: Conquest, Organization, and Economy, 3:458
The Ottoman Empire: Its Record and Legacy, 3:453
The Ottoman Empire: The Classical Age 1300–1600, 3:458
Ottoman Empire and Islamic Tradition, 4:570
The Ottoman Empire and Its Successors, 3:437, 3:453
Ottoman Imperialism during the Reformation, 3:453
Ottoman Turkish Writers, 2:96
The Ottoman Turks: Nomad Kingdom to World Empire, 3:453
Otto of the Silver Hand, 1:1205
Otto Rank: A Rediscovered Legacy, 5:466
Otto Warburg: Cell Physiologist, Biochemist, and Eccentric, 5:802
"O un Amy!" Essays on Montaigne in Honor of Donald M. Frame, 4:146
An Ounce of Prevention: Child Health Politics under Medicaid, 5:328
Our America, 2:871
Our American Cousin, 1:399
Our Common Future, 5:825
Our Country: The Shaping of America from Roosevelt to Reagan, 3:541
Our Dead Behind Us: Poems, 1:1190
Our Debt and Duty to the Farmer, 5:275
Our Decentralized Literature, 1:713
Our Environment: An Introduction to Physical Geography, 3:126
Our Expanding Universe, 5:589, 5:656, 5:657
Our Friend James Joyce, 1:461
Our Friend Manso, 2:547
Our Gang, 1:1040
Our Gang: Jewish Crime and the New York Jewish Community, 1900–1940, 4:639
Our Genetic Future: The Science and Ethics of Genetic Technology, 5:782
Our Golden Ironburg, 2:698

Our Grandmother's Drums: A Portrait of Rural African Life and Culture, 3:903
Our House in the Last World, 1:988
Our House in the New World, 1:988
Our Inner Conflicts: A Constructive Theory of Neurosis, 3:186, 5:452
Our International Monetary System: Yesterday, Today and Tomorrow, 3:59
Our Irish Theatre, 1:490
Our Kind, 3:31
Our Knowledge of the External World, 4:323
Our Knowledge of the External World, as a Field for Scientific Method in Philosophy, 5:84
Our Knowledge of the Growth of Knowledge, 4:410
Our Lady of the Flowers, 2:478, 2:479
Our Last First Poets: Vision and History in Contemporary American Poetry, 1:914
Our Life with Mr. Gurdjieff, 4:875
Our Limits Transgressed: Environmental Political Thought in America, 5:116
Our Man in Havana, 1:488
Our Man in Panama, 3:639
Our Mark Twain: The Making of His Public Personality, 1:783
Our Masters Taught Rabbinic Stories and Sayings, 4:613
Our Medical Future, 5:334
Our Modern Stone Age, 5:635
Our Mutual Friend, 1:348
Our Naked Frailties: Sensational Art and Meaning in "Macbeth," 1:214
Our National Parks, 5:836
Our Next Frontier: A Personal Guide for Tomorrow's Lifestyle, 5:274
Our Nig, 1:1144
Our Old Home, 1:675, 1:676
Our Philosophical Traditions, 4:17, 4:161
Our Philosophy, 4:373
Our Public Life, 4:339
Our Right to Choose: Toward a New Ethic of Abortion, 4:895
Ours, 1:389

Ours: A Russian Family Album, 2:716

Our Sages, God, and Israel: An Anthology of the Jerusalem Talmud, 4:612

Our Selves/Our Past: Psychological Approaches to American History, 3:514

Our Singing Country, 3:884

Our Singing Strength: An Outline of American Poetry (1620–1930), 1:655

Our Sister Kill Joy, 2:129

Ours Once More: Folklore Ideology, and the Making of Modern Greece, 3:869

Our Stagflation Malaise: Halting Inflation and Unemployment, 3:63

Our Three Selves: The Life of Radclyffe Hall, 1:492

Our Town, 1:1115, 1:1116

Our Twisted Hero, 2:308

Our Uncertain Heritage: Genetics and Human Diversity, 5:778

Ousmane Sembene: Contemporary Griot, 2:145

Outbreak of Love, 2:950, 2:951

The Outbreak of the English Civil War, 3:360

Outbreaks, 3:203

Outcast London, 1:312

An Outcast of the Islands, 1:463

Outcasts and Other Stories, 2:725

The Outcasts of Poker Flat, The Luck of Roaring Camp, and Other Sketches, 1:756

Outdoor Pastimes of an American Hunter, 3:594, 3:935

Outerbridge Reach, 1:1055

The Outer Circle: Women in the Scientific Community, 5:11, 5:189

The Outermost House: A Year of Life on the Great Beach of Cape Cod, 3:894

The Outer Path: Finding My Way in Tibet, 3:905

Out from Underdevelopment: Prospects for the Third World, 3:54

Out from under Gogol's "Overcoat," 2:722

Out in the Midday Sun, 3:909

Outland, 1:732

The Outlaw and Other Stories, 2:319

The Outlaws of Medieval Legend, 3:357

Outlaws of the Marsh, 2:185, 2:188, 2:211, 2:218, 2:219

An Outline History of American Drama, 1:1074

An Outline History of Classical Chinese Literature, 2:189

Outline of Comparative Literature from Dante Alighieri to Eugene O'Neill, 2:983

Outline of Cultural Materials, 3:12, 3:38

Outline of European Architecture, 3:763

Outline of History, 1:563

An Outline of Philosophy, 4:23

An Outline of Russian Literature, 2:684

An Outline of the Theology of the New Testament, 4:827

Outline of World Cultures, 3:38

Outlines of a Critique of Political Economy, 3:74

Outlines of a Philosophy of Art, 4:282

Outlines of Mahayana Buddhism, 4:557, 4:558

Outlines of Organic Chemistry, 5:755

Outlines of Psychology, 3:197

Outlines of the History of Ethics, 4:257

Out of Africa, 2:648

Out of Africa and Shadows on the Grass, 2:649

Out of a Whirlpool, 1:547

Out of India: Selected Stories, 2:177

Out of Italy: 1450–1650, 3:283

Out of My Later Years, 5:682

Out of Order? The Policing of Black People, 3:204

Out of Our Past: The Forces That Shaped America, 3:513, 3:576

Out of Site: A Social Criticism of Architecture, 3:202

Out of Step: An Unquiet Life in the Twentieth Century, 4:298

Out of the Closet: Voices of Gay Liberation, Twentieth-Anniversary Edition, 1:1184

Out of the Depths, 2:17

Out of the Ghetto: The Social Background of Jewish Emancipation, 1770–1870, 3:349, 4:636

Out of the Kumbla: Caribbean Women and Literature, 2:930

Out of the Night: A Biologist's View of the Future, 5:808

Out of the Shadows, 1:1188

Out of the Shelter, 1:515

Out of the Silent Planet, 1:512

The Outpost, 2:819

Outside Over There, 1:1206

The Outsider (Borchert), 2:570

The Outsider (Wilson), 1:567, 1:568, 1:905

Outsiders in a Hearing World: A Sociology of Deafness, 5:380

Outside the IBM PC and PS/2: Access to New Technology, 5:555

Outside the Whale: George Orwell's Art and Politics, 1:531

Outstanding International Press Reporting, 3:806

Out the Other Side, 1:1184

Out There: Marginalization and Contemporary Cultures, 1:1133

Out to Work: A History of Wage-Earning Women in the United States, 3:556

Outward Signs: The Language of Christian Symbolism, 4:716

Out West: American Journey along the Lewis and Clark Trail, 3:895

Ou-yang Hsiu: An Eleventh-century Neo-Confucianist, 2:215

Ovarian and Uterine Cancer: Reducing Your Risk, 5:372

Over 55: A Handbook on Aging, 5:316

The Overcoat and Other Short Stories, 2:721

The Overcoat and Other Tales of Good and Evil, 2:721

Overcoming Our Obsessions, 3:841

Overcoming Procrastination, 5:440

Overcoming Resistance: Rational-Emotive Therapy with Difficult Clients, 5:440

Over Fifty-Five, Healthy, and Alive, 5:317

Overhead in a Balloon, 2:911, 2:912

Over Here: The First World War and American Society, 3:532

Overload: The New Human Condition, 5:421

Overlord: Normandy, 1944, 3:279

Overnight to Many Distant Cities, 3:891

The Overreacher: A Study of Christopher Marlowe, 1:187

Over Sea, under Stone, 1:578

Over the Brazier, 1:485

Over-the-Counter Pills That Don't Work, 5:351

Over the Frontier, 1:549

Over the Teacups, 1:677, 1:678

Overview of the Psychotherapies, 5:420

Ovid, 2:390

Ovid and the Elizabethans, 2:390

Ovid's Games of Love, 2:390

Ovid's Toyshop of the Heart: Epistulae Heroidum, 2:390

Owen Barfield on C. S. Lewis, 4:776

Owen the Poet, 1:533

Owen Wister, 1:789, 1:1219

Owen Wister: Chronicler of the West, Gentleman of the East, 1:789, 1:1219

The Owl, 1:985

The Owl among Colophons: Henry Holt as Publisher and Editor, 1:42

The Owl and the Nightingale, 1:145, 1:148

The Owl and the Pussy Cat, 1:586

Owls and Artificers: Oxford Lectures on Poetry, 1:481

Owls Do Cry, 2:974

The Owl's Insomnia: Poems, 2:528

Owners, 1:458

Owning Scientific and Technological Information: Value and Ethical Issues, 5:159

Oxford American Dictionary, 1:90

The Oxford Anthology of American Literature, 1:129

Oxford Anthology of Canadian Literature, 2:905

The Oxford Anthology of English Literature, 1:129

Oxford Bible Atlas, 4:809

Oxford Book of American Light Verse, 1:656

Oxford Book of American Verse, 1:656, 1:720

The Oxford Book of Aphorisms, 1:115

The Oxford Book of Ballads, 1:148

Oxford Book of Canadian Short Stories in English, 2:905

The Oxford Book of Children's Verse in America, 1:655

The Oxford Book of English Detective Stories, 1:605

The Oxford Book of Essays, 1:430, 1:728, 1:809

Oxford Book of Greek Verse in Translation, 2:348

The Oxford Book of Humorous Prose, 1:809

The Oxford Book of Irish Short Stories, 1:423

The Oxford Book of Late Medieval Verse and Prose, 1:147

Oxford Book of Modern Verse, 1892–1935, 1:419

The Oxford Book of Narrative Verse, 3:885

Oxford Book of Poetry for Children, 1:579, 1:1196

Oxford Book of Scottish Verse, 1:418

Oxford Book of the Sea, 1:130

The Oxford Book of Twentieth Century English Verse, 1:418

The Oxford Book of Verse in English Translation, 2:5

The Oxford Book of Welsh Verse in English, 1:418

The Oxford Chekhov, 2:708, 2:709

Oxford Classical Dictionary, 1:133, 2:345, 3:298, 4:818

The Oxford Companion to American History, 3:513

The Oxford Companion to American Literature, 1:132, 1:650, 1:714

The Oxford Companion to American Theatre, 1:1072

The Oxford Companion to Animal Behavior, 5:826

The Oxford Companion to Art, 3:758

The Oxford Companion to Australian Literature, 2:947

The Oxford Companion to Canadian History and Literature, 3:606

The Oxford Companion to Canadian Literature, 2:905

The Oxford Companion to Canadian Theatre, 2:904

The Oxford Companion to Children's Literature, 1:1195

The Oxford Companion to Classical Literature (Harvey), 2:346, 3:298

The Oxford Companion to Classical Literature (Howatson), 1:133, 2:346

The Oxford Companion to English Literature, 1:132

The Oxford Companion to French Literature, 2:447

The Oxford Companion to Medicine, 5:368

The Oxford Companion to Spanish Literature, 2:523

The Oxford Companion to the Bible, 4:818

The Oxford Companion to the Decorative Arts, 3:765

The Oxford Companion to the Mind, 3:169, 4:382

The Oxford Companion to the Supreme Court of the United States, 3:145

Oxford Companion to the Theatre, 1:272

The Oxford Companion to Twentieth-Century Art, 3:760

The Oxford Dictionary of Art, 3:758

The Oxford Dictionary of Byzantium, 4:693

The Oxford Dictionary of English Etymology, 1:96

The Oxford Dictionary of English Proverbs, 1:115

The Oxford Dictionary of Modern Greek: Greek-English, English-Greek, 1:99

The Oxford Dictionary of Modern Quotations, 1:116

Oxford Dictionary of Natural History, 5:758

The Oxford Dictionary of Nursery Rhymes, 1:579, 3:884, 3:885

The Oxford Dictionary of
  Popes, 4:675
The Oxford Dictionary of
  Quotations, 1:117
The Oxford Dictionary of the
  Christian Church, 4:675,
  4:716
The Oxford-Duden Pictorial
  English and Chinese Dic-
  tionary: Simplified Charac-
  ter Edition, 1:98
The Oxford-Duden Pictorial
  English Dictionary, 1:90
Oxford-Duden Pictorial
  French and English
  Dictionary, 1:98
The Oxford-Duden Pictorial
  German-English Diction-
  ary, 1:99
The Oxford-Duden Pictorial
  Japanese and English
  Dictionary, 1:100
Oxford-Duden Pictorial Por-
  tuguese and English Dic-
  tionary, 1:102
Oxford-Duden Pictorial Ser-
  bo-Croat and English Dic-
  tionary, 1:102
Oxford-Duden Pictorial Span-
  ish and English Diction-
  ary, 1:103
Oxford Encyclopedia of
  Trees of the World, 5:760
The Oxford English-Arabic
  Dictionary of Current Us-
  age, 1:97
Oxford English Dictionary:
  Being a Corrected Re-
  Issue, 1:90
Oxford English Dictionary,
  1:89, 1:216, 2:584
Oxford Guides to Chaucer:
  The Canterbury Tales,
  1:150
The Oxford History of Aus-
  tralia, 3:494
The Oxford History of Aus-
  tralian Literature, 2:946
Oxford History of East Afri-
  ca, 3:422
The Oxford History of Eng-
  lish Literature Series,
  1:133
The Oxford History of Eng-
  lish Music, 3:659
The Oxford History of Hun-
  garian Literature from the
  Earliest Times to the
  Present, 2:798
The Oxford History of Mod-
  ern India, 1740–1975,
  3:486

The Oxford History of New
  Zealand, 3:495
The Oxford History of New
  Zealand Literature in Eng-
  lish, 2:971
The Oxford History of South
  Africa, 3:424
The Oxford History of the
  American People, 3:513,
  3:589
The Oxford History of the
  Classical World, 2:344,
  3:298
The Oxford History of the
  Popes, 4:678
The Oxford Ibsen, 2:665
Oxford Illustrated Encyclope-
  dia: World History from
  the Earliest Times, 3:273
Oxford Illustrated Encyclope-
  dia, 5:726
Oxford Illustrated Encyclope-
  dia of Invention and Tech-
  nology, 5:2
The Oxford Illustrated His-
  tory of Christianity, 4:2,
  4:675
The Oxford Illustrated His-
  tory of New Zealand,
  3:495
The Oxford Illustrated Liter-
  ary Guide to Great Britain
  and Ireland, 1:132
The Oxford Illustrated Liter-
  ary Guide to the United
  States, 1:132
Oxford Latin Dictionary,
  1:101
Oxford Mail, 1:612
The Oxford Nursery Rhyme
  Book, 1:579, 3:884, 3:885
The Oxford Paperback Italian
  Dictionary: Italian-En-
  glish/English-Italian, 1:100
Oxford Picture Dictionary of
  American English, 1:103
The Oxford Shakespeare,
  1:206
The Oxford Study Bible: Re-
  vised English Bible with
  the Apocrypha, 4:798
The Oxford University Press:
  An Informal History, 1:43
The Oxford University Press
  and the Spread of Learn-
  ing, 1:43
The Oyster and the Eagle:
  Selected Aphorisms and
  Parables, 2:629
Ozark Baptizings, Hangings,
  and Other Diversions,
  3:860

Ozark Folklore: An Annotat-
  ed Bibliography, 3:861
Ozark Folksongs, 3:861
Ozark Mountain Folks, 3:885
The Ozarks: An American
  Survival of Primitive Soci-
  ety, 3:885
Ozark Superstitions, 3:885
Ozidi, 2:133
Ozma of Oz, 1:1200

P

Pablo Neruda (Agosin), 2:875
Pablo Neruda (Bloom), 2:876
Pablo Neruda: All Poets the
  Poet, 2:875
Pablo Neruda: The Politics
  of Prophecy, 2:876
Pablo Picasso: A Retrospec-
  tive, 3:787
Pablo Picasso, 3:786
Pa Chin, 2:260
Pa Chin and His Writings:
  Chinese Youth Between
  Two Revolutions, 2:260
Pachomian Koinonia, 4:690
The Pacific Alliance, 3:476
Pacific Basin and Oceania,
  3:495
Pacific Islanders under Ger-
  man Rule, 3:495
Pacific Rising, 3:906
Pacific Street, 1:1246, 1:1247
The Pacific War, 3:534
The Pacific War, 1931–1945,
  3:478
Pacing the Void: T'ang Ap-
  proaches to the Stars,
  2:191
Packaging the Presidency,
  3:146
A Packet of Letters, 4:782
Pack My Bag, 1:487
Pack of Wolves, 2:784
PAC Power: Inside the
  World of Political Action
  Committees, 3:144
Padraic Colum, 1:461
Padraic Colum: A Biographi-
  cal-Critical Introduction,
  1:461
Pagan: Art and Architecture
  of Old Burma, 4:519
Pagan and Christian in an
  Age of Anxiety, 4:63,
  4:449, 4:683
Paganism and Christianity,
  100–425 C.E.: A Source-
  book, 4:449, 4:682

Paganism in the Roman Empire, 3:306, 4:449
A Pagan Prophet: William Morris, 1:383
The Pagan Rabbi and Other Stories, 1:1028
Pagan Rome and the Early Christians, 4:682
Pagans and Christians, 3:306, 4:683
Paideia: The Ideals of Greek Culture, 2:346, 4:48
Paideia Problems and Possibilities, 4:270
The Paideia Program: An Educational Syllabus, 4:270
The Paideia Proposal: An Educational Manifesto, 3:248, 4:270
Pain: A Nursing Approach to Assessment and Analysis, 5:393
Pain, Pleasure, and American Childbirth, 5:359
Pain and Its Conquest, 5:422
Pain Control: The Bethesda Program, 5:393
The Painful Prescription: Rationing Health Care, 3:56
The Painful Prescription: Rationing Hospital Care, 5:327
Pain Management, 5:377
The Painted Bird, 1:1002, 1:1003
Painted Desert: Poems, 2:836
Painted Lace and Other Pieces, 1914–1937, 1:882
Painterly Abstraction in Modernist American Poetry, 1:797
The Painter of Modern Life and Other Essays, 2:457
The Painting, 2:528
Painting in Canada: A History, 3:609
Paintings: A Man and His Art, 3:719
The Paintings of Henry Miller, 1:861
The Paintings of Thomas Gainsborough, 3:775
Paint It Today, 1:827
A Pair of Blue Eyes, 1:360, 1:361
A Pair of Patient Lovers, 1:758
A Pair of Spectacles, 1:272
Pakistan, 3:487
Pakistan: The Consolidation of a Nation, 3:487

Pakistan: The Modern Nations in Historical Perspective, 3:487
The Palace, 2:509
Palace of Desire, 2:68
The Palace of Pleasure, 1:166, 2:403
The Palace of Shattered Vessels, 2:24
Palace of the Peacock, 2:935, 2:936
The Palace of the White Skunks, 2:852
Palace Walk, 2:68
Palaver: Three Dramatic Discussion Starters, 2:149
Pale Fire, 1:1020, 2:740
Paleobotany and the Evolution of Plants, 5:640
Paleoceanography, 5:639
The Paleolithic Age, 4:433
Paleomagnetism and the Continental Crust, 5:630
Paleontology, the Record of Life, 5:639
Paleontology and Paleoenvironments, 5:639
Palestine and Israel in the Nineteenth and Twentieth Centuries, 3:440
Palestine's Children, 2:67
Palestinian Judaism in the Time of Jesus Christ, 4:620
The Palestinian Uprising—Israel's Third Front, 3:441
The Palestinian Wedding, 2:57
The Pali Literature of Burma, 2:313
Palimpsest, 1:826
Paliques, 2:527
Palisandriia, 2:758
Pal Joey, 1:867
Palladio, 3:785
Palladio's Architecture and Its Influence: A Photographic Guide, 3:785
Palladius: Dialogue on the Life of St. John Chrysostom, 4:707
The Palm at the End of the Mind: Selected Poems and a Play, 1:887
Palm Sunday: An Autobiographical Collage, 1:1063
The Palm-Wine Drinkard and His Dead Palm-Wine Tapster in Dead's Town, 2:150
Palomino, 2:955, 2:956
Pamela, 1:223, 1:229, 1:253, 1:1209
Pamela Part II, 1:253

Pamphilus and Galatea, 2:549
Pamphlets of the American Revolution, 1750–1776, 3:511
Pan, 2:664
Panama and the United States: The Forced Alliance, 3:639
Panama at the Crossroads, 3:640
The Panama Canal: The Crisis in Historical Perspective, 3:545, 3:640
The Panama Canal and the Sea Power in the Pacific, 3:288
The Panchatantra Reconstructed, 2:172
The Panda's Thumb: More Reflections in Natural History, 5:16, 5:638
Pandemonium: The World of Clive Barker, 1:600
Panditji: A Portrait of Jawaharlal Nehru, 3:500
Panic Spring, 1:469
The Panjandrum Picture Book, 1:581
Pan Michael: An Historical Novel of Poland, the Ukraine, and Turkey, 2:821
Panslavonic Folklore, 3:857
Pan Tadeusz, 2:817
Pantaloon, 1:329
Pantelejmon Kuliš: A Sketch of His Life and Times, 2:839
Panther in the Sky, 1:1244
The Panther Woman: Five Tales from One Cassette Recorder, 2:598
The Papacy and the Middle East, 3:436
Papa Doc: Haiti and Its Dictator, 3:637
The Papal Encyclicals, 4:891
The Papal Monarchy: The Western Church from 1050 to 1250, 4:695
The Paper: The Life and Death of the Herald Tribune, 3:807
Paper, 1:4
Paper and Ink Relationships, 1:21
Paperback Parnassus, 1:48
Paperbark: A Collection of Black Australian Writings, 2:947
The Paperbound Book in America, 1:38
Paperbound Books in Print, 1:71

Paper Flowers: A Play in Six
Scenes, 2:887
Paper Heroes: A Review of
Appropriate Technology,
5:215
Paper Houses, 2:645
Papermaking: Art and Craft,
1:5
Papermaking: The History
and Technique of an An-
cient Craft, 1:5
Paper Making as an Artistic
Craft: With a Note on Ny-
lon Paper, 1:5
Papermaking in Britain
1488–1988: A Short His-
tory, 1:5
Papermaking in Pioneer
America, 1:5
The Paper Men, 1:484
Paper Mould and Mould-
maker, 1:5
The Papers and Correspon-
dence of William Stanley
Jevons, 3:85
Papers from a Conference
on Thai Studies in Honor
of William J. Gedney,
2:335
Papers of John von Neu-
mann on Computing and
Computer Theory, 5:583
Papers on African Literature,
2:108
Papers on Fuchsian Func-
tions, 5:513
Papers on Literature and Art,
1:672, 1:673
Papers Presented at the
Longfellow Commemora-
tive Conference, 1:683
Pappy: The Life of John
Ford, 1:1166
Parable for a Season, 2:144
Parables and Paradoxes,
2:596
Parables in Midrash: Narra-
tive and Exegesis in Rab-
binic Literature, 4:613
The Parables of the King-
dom, 4:833
Parabola, 2:773
Paracelsus, 4:150
Parade's End, 1:475
Paradigm Change in Theol-
ogy: A Symposium for the
Future, 4:775
Paradigms and Barriers: How
Habits of Mind Govern
Scientific Belief, 5:54
Paradigms and Revolutions,
4:406, 5:53, 5:66

Paradise Lost, 1:164, 1:191,
1:277, 1:293, 1:1105
The Paradise Myth in Eight-
eenth-Century Russia,
2:684
Paradise News, 1:515
Paradise Reclaimed, 2:641
Paradise Regained, 1:191
The Paradise Within: Studies
in Vaughan, Traherne, and
Milton, 1:200
Paradiso, 2:416
The Paradoxes of Freedom,
4:298
The Paradoxical Ascent to
God, 4:853
Paradoxical Resolutions:
American Fiction since
James Joyce, 1:920
Paradox of Order: Some Per-
spectives, 2:939
Paragraphs on Printing, 1:10
Paraguay: An Informal Histo-
ry, 3:640
Paraguay: The Personalist
Legacy, 3:640
Parallel Lives: Five Victorian
Marriages, 1:1039
Parallel Lives: Spanish and
English Drama, 2:524
Parallel Lives of Greeks and
Romans, 3:318
Paramahansa Yogananda: In
Memoriam, 4:557
Paramedic, 5:338
The Paranoid Style in Ameri-
can Politics and Other Es-
says, 3:543, 3:583
A Paraphrase and Notes on
the Epistles of St. Paul,
3:159
Parapsychology, New Age
and the Occult: A Source
Encyclopedia, 4:854
The Parasite, 2:41
Parasites and Western Man,
5:389
Parat Dictionary of Food and
Nutrition, 5:260
Par-dessus l'Épaule, 2:123
Pardon Me, You're Stepping
on My Eyeball, 1:1122,
1:1123
Parent-Child Group Therapy,
5:321
Parent-Child Interaction:
Theory, Research and
Prospects, 3:206
Parent Power, 5:323
The Parent's Desk Reference,
5:6
The Parent's Guide to Educa-
tional Software, 5:566

Parents Matter, 3:207
Parerga and Paralipomena:
Short Philosophical Essays,
4:255
Paris, France, 1:882
Paris and Oxford Universities
in the 13th and 14th Cen-
turies, 4:102
Paris and the Parisians,
1:408
Paris Bound, 1:1085
The Parisian Prowler: Le
Spleen de Paris. Petits
Poèmes en Prose, 2:456
Parisian Sketches: Letters to
the New York Tribune,
1875–1876, 1:764
Parisina, 1:281
Paris Spleen, 2:456
Parkinson's: A Patient's View,
5:392
Parkman's History: The His-
torian as Literary Critic,
3:592
Park's Quest, 1:1204
Pär Lagerkvist in America,
2:676
The Parliamentary Novels,
1:405
The Parliament of 1621: A
Study in Constitutional
Conflict, 3:361
The Parliament of England,
1559–1581, 3:402
The Parliament of Fowls,
1:149
Parlour Poetry: A Casquet of
Gems, 1:720
Parmenides: A Text with
Translation, Commentary
and Critical Essays, 4:52
Parmenides: Being, Bounds
and Logic, 4:52
Parmenides, 4:291
Parmenides, Plato and the
Semantics of Not-Being,
4:83
Parmenides of Elea: Frag-
ments, 4:52
Parnassus Corner: A Life of
James T. Fields, Publisher
to the Victorians, 1:44
The Parnassus of a Small
Nation: An Anthology of
Slovene Lyrics, 2:835
Parnassus on Wheels, 1:33
Parodies: An Anthology from
Chaucer to Beerbohm and
After, 1:130
A Parody Anthology, 1:131
Paroles, 2:494

The Parsees in India: A Minority as Agent of Social Change, 4:518
The Parthenon and Its Sculptures, 4:446
Partial Hospitalization: A Current Perspective, 5:423
Participation in America: Political Democracy and Social Equality, 3:148
The Participatory Economy, 3:68
The Particle Connection, 5:663
The Particle Explosion, 5:662
The Particle Hunters, 5:663
Particle Physics in Japan 1930–1950, 5:717
Particles, Sources, and Fields, 5:715
Particles and Ideas: Bishop Berkeley's Corpuscularian Philosophy, 4:192
Particles and Sources, 5:715
Particles and Waves: Historical Essays in the Philosophy of Science, 5:67, 5:662
Particularities: Readings in George Eliot, 1:354
Particulars of My Life, 3:194
Parties Out of Power in Japan, 1931–1941, 3:476
Partings Welded Together, 1:319
Parting the Waters: America in the King Years, 1954–63, 3:536
The Partisan, 1:695, 1:696
A Partisan Guide to the Jewish Problem, 4:655
Partisan Picture, 3:427
Partition and Independence of India, 3:486
The Partners, 1:937
Partners in Crime, 1:606
Part of My Life, 4:273
Part of Nature, Part of Us: Modern American Poets, 1:800, 1:914
A Part of Speech, 2:704
Party and Political Opposition in Revolutionary America, 3:519
Party Games, 2:598
Party Going, 1:487
The Party of Fear, 3:542
The Party of Humanity: Essays in French Enlightenment, 2:447
Party Politics in America, 3:143

Parzival, 2:562, 2:586, 2:616, 2:617
Parzival of Wolfram von Eschenbach, 2:617
Pascal for the Humanities, 5:552
Pascal's Wager: A Study of Practical Reasoning in Philosophical Theology, 4:185, 4:317
Pascal User Manual and Report, 5:552
Páscoa Feliz, 2:560
The Pasha's Concubine and Other Tales, 2:829
Pasión de la Tierra, 2:529
Passacaglia, 2:493
Passage, Port and Plantation, 3:495
A Passage for Dissent: The Best of SIPAPU, 1970–1988, 1:50
Passage from India: Asian Indian Immigrants in North America, 3:556
The Passage of Nature, 4:342
Passages from the Life of a Philosopher, 5:575, 5:578
The Passages of Joy, 1:491
A Passage to France, 2:74
A Passage to India, 1:419, 1:476
The Passenger, 3:830
Passing, 1:853
The Passing of Traditional Society, 3:436
Passing the Time in Ballymenone: Culture and History of an Ulster Community, 3:855
Passing Time, 2:463
The Passion According to G.H., 2:895
Passion and Excess: Blanchot, Bataille and Literary Theory, 2:461
Passion and Pain, 2:617
The Passion Artist, 1:985
Passionate Exiles: Madame de Staël and Madame Recamier, 2:510
Passionate Quests: Five Modern Women Travelers, 3:893
Passionate Virtuosity: The Fiction of John Barth, 1:943
Passionate Women, Passive Men: Suicide in Yiddish Literature, 2:31
A Passion for Books, 1:33
The Passion for Jazz, 3:668
A Passion for Truth, 4:665

The Passion of Ingmar Bergman, 3:831
The Passion of Michael Foucault, 4:401
The Passion of New Eve, 1:455
The Passion of the Western Mind, 4:18
Passion Play, 1:524, 1:525, 1:1002
Passions and Impressions, 2:875
Passions and Other Stories, 2:47
Passions of the Mind (Byatt), 1:454, 1:455
The Passions of the Mind (Stone), 1:1250
The Passions of the Soul: The Third Book of "De anima et vita," 4:156
A Passion to Know: Twenty Profiles in Science, 5:677
Passover Anthology, 4:599
A Passover Haggadah, 4:599
A Passover Haggadah for Jewish Believers, 4:599
The Passport of Malam Ilia, 2:135
Passport to Heaven: Gender Roles in the Unification Church, 4:871
Password: Poems, 1:1053
The Past, 1:1001
Past and Present, 1:343, 1:368
Past and Process in Herodotus and Thucydides, 3:323
The Past and the Future, 3:399
The Past and the Present, 3:408
The Past before Us: Contemporary Historical Writing in the United States, 3:515
Pasternak: A Collection of Critical Essays, 2:746
Pasternak: Doctor Zhivago, 2:746
The Pasternak Affair: Courage of Genius, 2:746
Pasteur and Modern Science, 5:409
The Pasteurization of France, 5:167
Pasteur's and Tyndall's Study of Spontaneous Generation, 5:809
The Past in the Present, 1:920
Past Masters, and Other Papers, 2:602
Pastoral Care, 4:710

A Pastoral Novel, 1:978
Pastors and Masters, 1:462
Past Tense: The Cocteau Diaries, 2:469
The Pastures of Heaven, 1:884
Patent Alternative Dispute Resolution Handbook, 5:226
Pater in the 1990s, 1:387
Paternalism in Early Victorian England, 3:364
Paterson, 1:796, 1:899
Pater's Portraits: Mythic Pattern in the Fiction of Walter Pater, 1:387
The Path: A Spiritual Autobiography, 4:557
The Path between the Seas, 3:532, 3:640
Pather Panchali, 2:177
The Pathfinder, 1:662, 1:663, 1:1211
The Pathless Way: John Muir and American Wilderness, 5:836
The Pat Hobby Stories, 1:839
The Path of a Pioneer, 4:877
The Path of Carbon in Photosynthesis, 5:740
Path of Discipleship, 4:550
The Path of Subud, 4:873
Path of Thunder, 2:141, 2:159
The Path on the Rainbow, 1:719
Paths in the Rainforest, 3:421, 3:431, 3:432
Paths in Utopia, 4:655
Paths of Change: Strategic Choices for Organizations and Society, 3:210
Paths of Resistance: The Art and Craft of the Political Novel, 1:805
Paths to the Present, 3:596
The Path to Hope: Fragments from a Theologian's Journey, 4:747
The Path to the Double Helix, 5:49, 5:791, 5:813
The Path to the Nest of Spiders, 2:411, 2:412
Patience, 1:155, 1:409
The Patient as Partner: A Theory of Human-Experimentation Ethics, 5:144
Patient Education and Health Promotion in Medical Care, 5:332
The Patient-Physician Relation: The Patient as Partner, Part 2, 5:144

The Patient's Advocate, 5:331
The Patient Stone: A Persian Folktale, 2:90
The Patient Stone, 2:87
Patriarch and Folk: The Emergence of Nicaragua, 1798–1858, 3:639
The Patriarch's Wife: Literary Evidence and the History of the Family, 1:225
The Patriarchy of Shakespeare's Comedies, 1:211
Patrice Lumumba, 2:140
Patrick Kavanagh, 1:507
Patrick Kavanagh: A Critical Study, 1:507
Patrick Kavanagh: Born-Again Romantic, 1:507
Patrick Kavanagh: Man and Poet, 1:507
Patrick White: A Life, 2:966
Patrick White: Fiction and the Unconscious, 2:966
Patrick White's Fiction: The Paradox of Fortunate Failure, 2:966
Patrimony: A True Story, 1:1040, 1:1041
A Patriot for Me, 1:532
Patriotic Gore: Studies in the Literature of the American Civil War, 1:717, 1:744, 1:902
Patriotic Pacifism: Waging War on War in Europe, 1815–1914, 3:278
Patriotism, Inc. and Other Tales, 2:629
Patrology, 4:690
Patronage and Principle: A Political History of Modern Scotland, 3:368
Patrons and Protégées: Gender, Friendship, and Writing in Nineteenth-Century America, 1:651, 1:715
Pattern: A Study of Ornament in Western Europe from 1180 to 1900, 3:765
Pattern and Growth in Personality, 5:432
Pattern in the Material Folk Culture of the Eastern United States, 3:868
The Pattern of Christian Truth, 4:100, 4:687
Pattern of Politics, 4:415
Pattern of the Chinese Past, 3:467
The Pattern of Tragicomedy in Beaumont and Fletcher, 1:173
Patterns, 1:855

Patterns and Patterning: A Study of Four Poems by George Herbert, 1:181
Patterns in Comparative Religion, 4:472
Patterns in Nature, 5:487
Patterns in Prehistory: Humankind's First Three Million Years, 4:432, 4:439
Patterns in Russian Literature II: Notes on Classics, 2:690
Patterns of Action: Religion and Ethics in Comparative Perspective, 4:893
Patterns of Childhood, 2:615, 2:616
Patterns of Culture, 3:15, 3:26, 3:27
Patterns of Decay: Shakespeare's Early Histories, 1:211
Patterns of Discovery, 5:66
Patterns of Human Heredity: An Introduction to Human Genetics, 5:777
Patterns of Hypnotic Techniques of Milton H. Erickson, M.D., 5:441
Patterns of Intention: On the Historical Explanation of Pictures, 5:191
Patterns of Kingship and Authority in Traditional Asia, 3:463
Patterns of Language: Structure, Variation, Change, 3:21
Patterns of Learning: New Perspectives on Life Span Education, 3:255
Patterns of Nationality: Twentieth-Century Versions of America, 1:795
Patterns of Race in the Americas, 3:31
Patterns of Reformation, 4:724
Patterns of Renewal, 3:941
Patterns on Our Planet: Concepts and Themes in Geography, 3:118
The Patton Papers, 3:277
Paul, 4:824, 4:829
Paul: Apostle to the Gentiles, 4:824
Paul A. Samuelson: Critical Assessments, 3:104
Paula Gunn Allen, 1:1136
Paul among the Jews and Gentiles, 4:617
Paul and His Interpreters: A Critical History, 4:826

Paul and Mary: Two Case Histories of Truants from Life, 5:435

Paul and Palestinian Judaism: A Comparison of Patterns of Religion, 4:617, 4:826

Paul and Rabbinic Judaism: Some Rabbinic Elements in Pauline Theology, 4:617

Paul Celan: A Biography of His Youth, 2:575

Paul Cézanne, 3:773

Paul Cézanne: The Watercolors—A Catalogue Raisonné, 3:773

Paul Claudel, 2:468

Paul Claudel: The Man and the Mystic, 2:468

Paul de Man: Deconstruction and the Critique of Aesthetic Ideology, 1:1143

Paul Éluard, 2:475

Paul Gauguin: Letters to His Wife and Friends, 3:775

Paul Green, 1:1089

Paul Hindemith: The Man behind the Music, 3:700

Pauline, 1:338

Paulo Freire: A Critical Encounter, 3:262

Paul of Venice: A Bibliographical Guide, 4:130

Paul Revere and the World He Lived In, 1:1201

Paul Robeson: A Biography, 3:554

Paul Samuelson and Modern Economic Theory, 3:103

Paul's Awakening, 2:624

Paul the Apostle: The Triumph of God in Life and Thought, 4:824

Paul Tillich: His Life and Thought, 4:788

Paul Tillich and the Christian Message, 4:788

Paul Tillich's Philosophy of Culture, Science, and Religion, 5:206

Paulus, 5:463

Paul Valéry (Bloom), 2:513

Paul Valéry (Grubbs), 2:513

Paul Valéry: Philosophical Reflections, 2:513

Paul Valéry and Music, 2:513

Paul Verlaine, 2:514

Pauper, Brawler and Slanderer, 2:150

Pavannes and Divagations, 1:872

Pavarotti: Life with Luciano, 3:709

Pavarotti: My Own Story, 3:708

Pavlov: A Biography, 3:191, 5:364

Pavlova: A Collection of Memoirs, 3:750

Pavlova: Repertoire of a Legend, 3:750

Pavlov and His School, 5:365

Paying Guest, 1:358

PC/Computing Guide to Shareware, 5:556

The PDR Family Guide to Prescription Drugs, 5:311

Peace, 2:353

Peace: An Idea Whose Time Has Come, 3:280

Peace, from War to War, 3:277

Peace and Bread in Times of War, 1:731

Peace and Disarmament, 4:896

The Peace and War Reader, 3:280

Peace by Ordeal: The Negotiation of the Anglo-Irish Treaty, 3:1921, 3:371

Peace by Revolution: An Interpretation of Mexico, 3:650

Peaceful Conquest: The Industrialization of Europe, 1760–1970, 3:341

The Peacemakers: The Great Powers and American Independence, 3:521

Peacemaking 1919, 3:280

Peace Research in Western Europe: A History Guide, 3:280

Peace Shall Destroy Many, 2:927

Peace with God, 4:768

Peacock: His Circle and His Age, 1:297

Peacock Displayed: A Satirist in His Context, 1:297

Peacock Pie: A Book of Rhymes, 1:467

Peacock's Memoir of Shelley, with Shelley's Letters to Peacock, 1:303

The Peacocks of Baboquivari, 5:818

Peake's Commentary on the Bible, 4:819

Pearl (Anonymous), 1:145, 1:155

The Pearl (Steinbeck), 1:884

Pearl: A New Verse Translation, 1:155

The Pearl Canon, 2:90

Pearl Harbor Reexamined: Prologue to the Pacific War, 3:480

The Pearl Maiden, 1:595

The Pearl of Orr's Island, 1:698

Pearl Poems: An Omnibus Edition, 1:155

Peasant, Lord, and Merchant, 3:611

Peasant and Peasant Societies, 5:265

Peasant China in Transition, 3:472

Peasant History in South India, 3:484

Peasant Nationalism and Communist Power, 3:471

Peasant Protests and Uprising in Tokugawa Japan, 3:476

The Peasant Rebellion, 2:787

The Peasants, 2:820

Peasants, Rebels, and Outcasts: The Underside of Modern Japan, 3:477

Peasants in History: Essays in Honour of Daniel Thorner, 3:405

The Peasants' Revolt of Thirteen Eighty One, 3:357

Peasant State and Society in Medieval South India, 3:484

The Peasant War in Germany, 3:74, 3:75

The Peculiar Institution, 3:525, 3:598

Pedagogical Anthropology, 3:266

A Pedagogy for Liberation: Dialogues on Transforming Education, 3:262

Pedagogy of the Oppressed, 3:262, 4:748

The Peddlars, 2:742

Peddlers and Princes, 3:31

Peder Paars, 2:650, 2:651

Peder Victorious, 2:667

Peder Victorious: A Tale of the Pioneers Twenty Years Later, 2:667

Pediatric Epileptology, 5:392

Pedro Páramo, 2:882

The Peelites and the Party System, 1846–52, 3:363

Peer Gynt, 2:586, 2:665, 2:666

Peerless Science: Peer Review and U.S. Science Policy, 5:151

The Pegnitz Junction, 2:911, 2:912

Peirce, 4:249

Peirce, Semiotics, and Pragmatism: Essays by Max H. Fisch, 4:249

Peirce and Pragmatism, 4:249

Peirce's Philosophy of Science, 4:317

Peirce's Theory of Scientific Discovery, 4:249

Peking Man, 2:266

Pelagius: A Historical and Theological Study, 4:110

Pelham, 1:340

Pelham, or, The Adventures of a Gentleman, 1:340

The Pelican History of Art, 3:756, 3:758

Pelican History of Canada, 3:607

The Pelican History of the World, 3:274

Pelican New Testament Commentaries, 4:821

The Pelican Shakespeare, 1:206

Pelle the Conqueror, 2:652, 2:653

The Peloponnesian War, 3:322

Pembroke, 1:750

Pen, Sword and Camisole, 2:892

The Penal System: An Introduction, 3:204

The Pen and the Faith: Eight Modern Muslim Writers and the Qur'an, 4:574

The Pencil, 5:174, 5:226

Pencil Letter, 2:753

Pendennis, 1:403

The Pendulum Clock, 5:695

Penetrating Wagner's Ring: An Anthology, 3:728

The Penguin Book of British Comic Stories, 1:422

The Penguin Book of Chinese Verse: Poets Series, 2:189

Penguin Book of Contemporary New Zealand Poetry, 2:971

Penguin Book of Contemporary New Zealand Short Stories, 2:971

The Penguin Book of English Romantic Verse, 1:269

The Penguin Book of First World War Prose, 1:430

Penguin Book of French Verse, 2:448

The Penguin Book of German Verse, 2:566

The Penguin Book of Greek Verse, 2:349, 2:373

The Penguin Book of Hebrew Verse, 2:9, 2:17

The Penguin Book of Homosexual Verse, 1:1183

The Penguin Book of Modern African Poetry, 2:113

The Penguin Book of Modern Australian Poetry, 2:947

The Penguin Book of Modern British Short Stories, 1:422

The Penguin Book of Modern Yiddish Verse, 2:34

The Penguin Book of New Zealand Verse, 2:973

The Penguin Book of Russian Short Stories, 2:694

The Penguin Book of Southern African Verse, 2:158

The Penguin Book of Turkish Verse, 2:96

The Penguin Companion to Classical, Oriental and African Literature, 2:3, 2:4

The Penguin Companion to European Literature, 2:3, 2:4

The Penguin Dictionary of Architecture, 3:762

The Penguin Dictionary of Decorative Arts: New Edition, 3:765

The Penguin Dictionary of Modern History, 1789–1945, 3:273

The Penguin Dictionary of Modern Quotations, 1:116

The Penguin Dictionary of Musical Performers, 3:656

The Penguin Dictionary of Physical Geography, 5:621

The Penguin Dictionary of Physics, 5:653

The Penguin Dictionary of Religions, 4:4

The Penguin Dictionary of Saints, 4:675

The Penguin Dictionary of Science, 5:3

The Penguin Guide to Ancient Egypt, 4:548

The Penguin History of Latin America, 3:626

The Penguin History of New Zealand Literature, 2:970

The Penguin History of the Church, 4:677

Penguin Island, 2:477

The Penguin New Literary History of Australia, 2:946

Penguin Psychology: or, The Mystery of Bridge Building, 1:815

Penguin Spanish Dictionary, 1:103

The Penguin World Omnibus of Science Fiction, 1:612

Penhally, 1:982

Penicillin, Its Practical Application, 5:408

The Penitent, 2:48

Pennies from Heaven, 1:535

Pennsylvania Dutch American Folk Art, 3:859

Pennsylvania Dutch Folklore, 3:859

The Pennsylvania Edition of Sister Carrie, 1:829

Pennsylvania German Secular Folk Songs, 3:850

Pensées, 3:337, 4:185

Pensieri, 2:424

The Pensive King, 2:409

The Pentagon of Power, 5:169

The Peony Pavilion, 2:221, 2:222

People, Books and Book People, 1:32

People, Penguins, and Plastic Trees, 5:76, 5:116

People, State and Fear, 3:144

People, Years, Life, 2:717

The People, Yes, 1:878

A People and a Nation: Brief Edition, 3:514

A People and a Proletariat: Essays in the History of Wales, 1780–1980, 3:369

People and Information, 5:545

People and Places, 3:36

People Called Shakers: A Search for the Perfect Society, 4:849

The People Could Fly: American Black Folktales, 3:866

People in Glass Houses, 2:953, 2:954

People in the Summer Night: An Epic Suite, 2:660

People in World History, 3:273

People Live Here: Selected Poems, 1949–1983, 1:1048

The People Look at Radio, 3:203

The People Look at Television, 3:204

A People Numerous and Armed, 3:522

The People of Aristophanes: A Sociology of Old Attic Comedy, 2:353

People of Great Russia: A Psychological Study, 3:22

The People of Hamilton, Canada West, 3:616

People of Plenty: Economic Abundance and the American Character, 3:593

The People of Roman Britain, 3:356

People of Seldwyla, 2:597

People of the City, 2:135, 2:136

People of the Dawn, 2:671

People of the Puszta, 2:799

The People of the United States in the Twentieth Century, 3:241

People One Ought to Know, 1:501

People or Monsters?, 2:255

The People's Cause: A History of Guerrillas in Africa, 3:428

The People's Champion, 1902–1911, 3:366

A People's Charter: The Pursuit of Rights in America, 3:571

People's China: A Brief History, 3:469

The People's Choice, 3:230

"A People's Contest": The Union at War, 1861–1865, 3:529

The People's Guide to Vitamins and Minerals from A to Zinc, 5:310

A People's History of the United States, 3:514

The Peoples of Ireland: From Prehistory to Modern Times, 3:369

The Peoples of the Eastern Hapsburg Lands, 1526–1918, 3:389

People with AIDS, 5:388

The Peopling of British North America: An Introduction, 3:564

Pepita Jiménez, 2:552

Perceiving, 4:395

Perception, Expression and History, 4:311

The Perception of Music, 3:660

The Perception of Women in Spanish Theater of the Golden Age, 2:524

Perceptrons: An Introduction to Computer Geometry, 5:568

Perceptual Acquaintance from Descartes to Reid, 4:163

The Perceptual World: Readings from Scientific American Magazine, 5:194

Perceval: The Story of the Grail, 2:466, 2:467

Perchance to Dream: The Patient's Guide to Anesthesia, 5:369

Perched on Nothing's Branch, 2:800

Percival Keene, 1:374

Percy Bysshe Shelley, 1:303

Percy Bysshe Shelley: A Literary Life, 1:303

Père Goriot, 2:453

Peregrinação, 2:556, 2:561

Peregrine Pickle, 1:256, 1:662

Perelandra, 1:512

Perennial Philosophical Issues, 4:21

The Perfectionist, 2:967

Perfection of Exile: Fourteen Contemporary Lithuanian Writers, 2:805

Perfection Proclaimed, 1:630

The Perfect Lady by Mistake and Other Stories, 2:198

Perfect Markets and Easy Virtue: Business Ethics and the Invisible Hand, 3:57

The Perfect Party, 1:1091

A Perfect Peace, 2:22

A Perfect Spy, 1:596

Perfect Symmetry: The Search for the Beginning of Time, 5:595, 5:655, 5:714

A Perfect Vacuum, 2:816

The Perfect Wagnerite, 2:605

The Performers and Their Plays, 1:228

The Performing Self, 1:794

Perfumed Garden of Shagkh Nefzawi, 3:914

The Perfume Handbook, 5:730

Peribáñez, 2:554

Pericles, 1:204, 1:205, 1:206

The Perilous Vision of John Wyclif, 4:714

The Perils of Politeness, 2:77

The Perils of Prosperity, 1914–32, 3:585

Periodical Title Abbreviations, 1:114

The Periodic Table, 2:425

Periphyseon: The Division of Nature, 4:115

Peri theōn, 4:468

Perkin Warbeck, 1:179

Permaculture: A Practical Guide for a Sustainable Future, 5:820

Permanence and Change: An Anatomy of Purpose, 1:817

Permanence/Durability of the Book: A Two-Year Research Program, 1:4

Permanence/Durability of the Book—II–VII, 1:4, 1:5

The Permanent Revolution: Results and Prospects, 3:295

The Permanent Revolution: The French Revolution and Its Legacy, 3:339

The Permanent War Economy: American Capitalism in Decline, 3:67

Per Olov Enquist. A Critical Study, 2:674

Perón: A Biography, 3:633

Perpetua and the Habit of Unhappiness, 2:132

The Perpetual Curate, 1:385

Perplexing Puzzles and Tantalizing Teasers, 5:507

Perplexities and Paradoxes, 2:552

The Persecuting Imagination, 1:630

The Persecution and Assassination of Jean-Paul Marat as Performed by the Inmates of the Asylum of Charenton under the Direction of the Marquis de Sade, 2:615

Persecution and Trial of Gaston Naessens, 5:318

The Persecution of Peter Olivi, 4:101

The Persian Empire, 3:300

The Persian Expedition, 3:324

The Persian Gulf, 3:448, 3:450

The Persian Gulf TV War, 3:812

The Persian Letters, 3:162, 3:163, 4:209

Persian Literature: A Bio-Bibliography Survey, 2:83

Persian Mythology, 4:444, 4:547

Persian Oil: A Study in Power Politics, 3:447

Persian Poetry in England and America: A Two Hundred Year History, 2:83

A Persian Requiem, 2:88

The Persians, 2:350

A Persian Stronghold of Zoroastrianism, 4:547

The Persian Wars, 3:316

Persiles and Sigismunda, 2:537

The Persistent Desire: A Femme-Butch Reader, 1:1184

The Persistent Problems in Psychology, 3:167

The Persisting Osler, 5:364

Persona and Shame, 3:831

Personae: Collected Poems, 1:871

The Personal Computer Book, 5:537

Personal Computers and the Disabled, 5:557

Personal Health Reporter, 5:6, 5:311

Personal Influence, 3:230

Personalities and Powers, 3:407

Personality, 5:413

Personality: A Psychological Interpretation, 3:177, 3:179

Personality: Strategies and Issues, 3:178

Personality: The Need for Liberty and Rights, 5:451

Personality and the Social Encounter: Selected Essays, 3:177, 3:179, 5:432

Personality Theory, Moral Development, and Criminal Behavior, 3:178

A Personal Matter, 2:292

Personal Memoirs of H. P. Blavatsky, 4:874

Personal Narrative of a Pilgrimage to Al-Madinah and Meccah, 3:914

Personal Narrative of Travels to Equinoctial Regions of America during the Years 1799–1804, 3:131

Personal Patronage under the Early Empire, 3:308

Personal Philosophy: The Art of Living, 4:20

Personal Psychopathology: Early Formulations, 5:471

Personal Reminiscences of a Great Crusade, 1:341

Person and Community: Ghanaian Philosophical Studies I, 4:371

Person and Community in American Philosophy, 4:34

Person and Object, 4:395

The Person and the Common Good, 4:306

The Person in Psychology, 5:432

Person/Planet: The Creative Disintegration of Industrial Society, 5:175

Persons and Minds: The Prospects of Nonreductive Materialism, 5:75

Persons and Places: The Autobiography of George Santayana, 4:327

Persons and Their World: An Introduction to Philosophy, 4:23

Persons of the Drama: Theatre Criticism and Comment, 1:1073

Person to Person: The Problem of Being Human, 5:468

Perspective in Whitehead's Metaphysics, 4:342

The Perspective of the World: Civilization and Capitalism, Vol. III, 3:283

Perspective on the Nature of Geography, 3:116, 3:118

Perspectives by Incongruity, 1:956

Perspectives in Philosophy: A Book of Readings, 4:19

Perspectives in the History of Religions, 4:420

Perspectives on African Literature, 2:108

Perspectives on AIDS: Ethical and Social Issues, 5:122

Perspectives on American Folk Art, 3:849

Perspectives on American Furniture, 3:766

Perspectives on American Labor History: The Problem of Synthesis, 3:515

Perspectives on Max Frisch, 2:579

Perspectives on Paul, 4:825

Perspectives on Peirce: Critical Essays on Charles Sanders Peirce, 4:249

Perspectives on Population, 3:206

Perspectives on Publishing, 1:48

Perspectives on Quine, 5:100

Perspectives on Technology, 5:234

Perspectives on the New Age, 4:866

Perspectives on Thomas Hobbes, 4:175

Persuasion, 1:275

Persuasion and Healing: A Comparative Study of Psychotherapy, 5:418

Persuasion and Politics: The Social Psychology of Public Opinion, 3:148

Persuasions of the Witch's Craft, 4:865

Perturbed Spirit: The Life and Personality of Samuel Taylor Coleridge, 1:288

Peru: A Cultural History, 3:640

Peru: The Evolution of a Crisis, 3:640

Peru: The New Poetry, 2:850

Peru under Fire: Human Rights Since the Return to Democracy, 3:640

Perversity and Error, 4:97

Pesikta De-Rab Kahana, 4:610

Pesiqta deRab Kahana: An Analytical Translation and Explanation, 4:612

Pesni-Poems, 2:808

Pesticides and Human Health, 5:351

Pesticides in the Diets of Infants and Children, 5:736

Petals of Blood, 2:154

Petals on the Wind, 1:1240

Peter Abelard, 4:106

Peterbell, 1:306

Peterborough Chronicle, 1:140

Peter Camenzind, 2:589

Peter Freuchen's Book of the Seven Seas, 3:921

Peter Handke, 2:586

Peter Ibbetson, 1:352

Peter Martins, Prince of the Dance, 3:747

Peter Maurin: Prophet in the Twentieth Century, 4:765

The Peter Norton Programmer's Guide to the IBM PC, 5:555

Peter Norton's Assembly Language Book for the IBM PC, 5:555

Peter Norton's DOS Guide, 5:538

Peter Norton's Guide to Unix, 5:555

Peter of Ailly and the Harvest of Fourteenth-Century Philosophy, 4:104, 4:127

Peter Pan, 1:329, 1:437, 1:438

Peter Pan and Cricket, 1:438

Peter Pan and Wendy, 1:329

Peter Paul Rubens: Life and Work, 3:792

Peter Paul Rubens: Man and Artist, 3:792

Peter Paul Rubens, 3:792

Petersburg, 2:700, 2:701

Peter Schlemihl: The Shadowless Man, 2:576

Peter Shaffer, 1:544

Peter Shaffer: A Casebook, 1:544

Peter Shaffer: An Annotated Bibliography, 1:544

Peter Shaffer: Roles, Rites, and Rituals in the Theater, 1:544

Peter Simple, 1:374

Peterson's First Guide to Birds, 5:761

Peterson's First Guide to Wildflowers, 5:761

Peter the Great and the Emergence of Russia, 3:395

Peter Weiss, 2:615

Petite Palace of Pettie His Pleasures, 1:166

Petrarch (Bergin), 2:434, 4:151

Petrarch (Bloom), 2:434

Petrarch (Mann), 4:151

Petrarch (Petrie), 2:434

Petrarch: An Introduction to the Canzoniere, 4:151

Petrarch: Poet and Humanist, 4:151

Petrarch: The Augustan Poets, the Italian Tradition and the "Canzoniere," 2:434

Petrarch, Laura, and the "Triumphs," 2:434

Petrarch in America, 2:434

Petrarch's Eight Years in Milan, 4:151

Petrarch's Genius: Pentimento and Prophecy, 2:434, 4:151

Petrarch's Later Years, 4:151

Petrarch's "Secretum": Its Making and Its Meaning, 4:151

Petrography: An Introduction to the Study of Rocks in Thin Sections, 5:629

Petroleum Economics and Engineering, 5:635

Petroleum Price Regulation: Should We Decontrol?, 3:69

Petroleum Refining: Technology and Economics, 5:285

Petroleum Refining for the Nontechnical Person, 5:286

The Petty Demon, 2:758, 2:759

The Peyote Cult, 4:467

Peyote Hunt: The Sacred Journey of the Huichol Indians, 4:465

The Peyote Religion among the Navaho, 4:467

Phadaeng Nang Ai: A Translation of a Thai-Isan Folk Epic in Verse, 2:336

Phaedo, 4:89

The Phaedo: A Platonic Labyrinth, 4:79

Phaedo, or on the Immortality of the Soul, 4:208

Phaedon; or, the Death of Socrates, 4:209

Phaedra and Other Plays, 2:498

Phaidon Guide to Glass, 3:766

Phantom of Fact: A Guide to Nabokov's PNIN, 2:741

The Phantom Rickshaw, 1:370

Phantoms, 1:1241

Phantoms, and Other Stories, 2:769

The Phantom Lady, 2:532

The Phantom Ship, 1:374

The Pharaoh, 2:820

Pharisaism in the Making: Selected Essays, 4:615

The Pharisees: The Social Background of Their Faith, 4:615

The Pharisees, 4:615

Pharisees, Scribes and Sadducees in Palestinian Society: A Sociological Approach, 4:616

Pharsalia, 2:387

Phases of Rilke, 2:608

Phèdre, 2:498

The Phenomenological Movement: An Historical Introduction, 4:235, 4:267

Phenomenological Psychology, 5:470

Phenomenology and the Foundation of the Sciences, 4:234

Phenomenology and Treatment of Depression, 5:426

Phenomenology and Treatment of Schizophrenia, 5:426

The Phenomenology of Perception, 4:310

The Phenomenology of Spirit, 4:231, 4:232

The Phenomenon of Life: Toward a Philosophical Biology, 5:93

Phenomenon of Man, 4:336

The Phenomenon of Man Revisited, 4:337

Phi Beta Kappa in American Life: The First Two Hundred Years, 3:574

Phi Delta Kappan, 3:257

Philadelphia, Here I Come!, 1:478, 1:479

The Philadelphia Negro: A Social Study, 3:578

The Philadelphia Story, 1:1085, 1:1086

Philanthropy and Social Progress: Seven Essays, 1:731

Philaster, or, Love Lies a-Bleeding, 1:173

Philip Barry, 1:1086

Philip Freneau: Champion of Democracy, 1:639

Philipino Concise Dictionary, 1:101

Philip K. Dick, 1:1257

Philip Larkin, 1:508

Philip Larkin: A Bibliography, 1933–1976, 1:508

Philip Larkin: A Writer's Life, 1:508

Philip Larkin: His Life's Work, 1:508

Philip Larkin: Writer, 1:508

Philip Larkin and English Poetry, 1:508

Philip Larkin and His Contemporaries: An Air of Authenticity, 1:508

Philip Massinger: A Critical Reassessment, 1:189

Philip Massinger and the Restoration Drama, 1:189

Philippics, 2:343, 2:384

Philippine Collaboration in World War II, 3:493

Philippine Colonial Democracy, 3:493

The Philippines: A Singular and a Plural Place, 3:493

The Philippines, 3:492

Philip Roth (Jones), 1:1041

Philip Roth (Lee), 1:1041

Philip Roth: A Bibliography, 1:1041

A Philip Roth Reader, 1:1041
Philip II, 4:737
Phillipps Studies, 1:33
Phillis Wheatley: A Bio-Bibliography, 1:647
Phillis Wheatley in the Black American Beginnings, 1:647
Philo: Foundations of Religious Philosophy in Judaism, Christianity and Islam, 4:60, 4:100, 4:670
Philo, John and Paul: New Perspectives on Judaism and Early Christianity, 4:604
Philoctetes, 2:355, 2:367
Philological and Historical Commentary on Ammianus Marcellinus, 3:310
Philo of Alexandria: An Introduction, 4:60, 4:100, 4:670, 4:812
Philosopher at Large: An Intellectual Autobiography, 4:270
The Philosophers: Life and Thought, 4:18
Philosophers Ancient and Modern, 4:25
Philosophers and Pamphleteers: Political Theorists of the Enlightenment, 3:337
The Philosopher's Annual, 4:263
Philosophers at War: The Quarrel between Newton and Leibniz, 5:42
The Philosopher's Dictionary, 4:14
The Philosopher's Game, 4:18
The Philosopher's Guide to Sources, Research Tools, Professional Life, and Related Fields, 4:13
Philosopher's Index: An International Index to Philosophical Periodicals, 4:8
The Philosopher's Index, 1990 Cumulative Edition, 5:60
The Philosopher's Index, 4:14
The Philosopher's Index Thesaurus, 4:14
Philosophers Lead Sheltered Lives: A First Volume of Memoirs, 4:284
Philosophers of Consciousness, 4:320
Philosophers of the Scottish Enlightenment, 4:32, 4:212

The Philosopher's Pupil, 1:523
Philosophers Speak for Themselves: Berkeley, Hume, and Kant, 4:163
Philosophers Speak for Themselves: From Descartes to Locke, 4:163
Philosophers Speak of God, 4:289
Philosophia Botanica, 5:805
Philosophiae Moralis Institutio, 4:203
Philosophiae Naturalis Principia Mathematica, 5:705
Philosophical Analysis: Its Development between the Two World Wars, 4:268
Philosophical Analysis in Latin America, 4:264, 4:379
Philosophical and Historical Roots of Occupational Therapy, 5:338
The Philosophical Anthropology of George Herbert Mead, 4:309
Philosophical Apprenticeships, 4:402
The Philosophical Basis of Biology, 5:797
A Philosophical Basis of Medical Practice, 5:80, 5:97
The Philosophical Books of Cicero, 4:59
Philosophical Consequences of Quantum Theory, 5:67
Philosophical Correspondence, 4:205
Philosophical Dictionary, 2:515, 4:15, 4:217, 4:218
Philosophical Dimensions of the Neuro-Medical Sciences, 5:81
The Philosophical Discourse of Modernity, 4:404, 5:89
A Philosophical Enquiry into the Origin of Our Ideas of the Sublime and Beautiful, 3:152
A Philosophical Essay on Probabilities, 5:530, 5:698
Philosophical Essays, 4:176, 4:273
Philosophical Essays: From Ancient Creed to Technological Man, 5:93, 5:129
Philosophical Ethics: An Introduction to Moral Philosophy, 5:132
Philosophical Explanations, 4:314

Philosophical Foundations of Soviet Aesthetics, 4:31
Philosophical Fragments (Kierkegaard), 4:239
Philosophical Fragments (Schlegel), 2:610, 4:253
Philosophical Fragments: 1901–1914 and the Philosopher and Peace, 4:304
Philosophical Grammar, 4:344
Philosophical Hermeneutics, 4:402
Philosophical Ideas in the United States, 4:36
The Philosophical Imagination: An Introduction to Philosophy, 4:19
Philosophical Investigations in the U.S.S.R., 4:30
The Philosophical Irony of Laurence Sterne, 1:259
Philosophical Issues in Aristotle's Biology, 4:68
Philosophical Letters, 4:169, 4:217, 4:218
The Philosophical Movement in the Thirteenth Century, 4:97
Philosophical Perspectives: History of Philosophy, 4:162, 4:333
Philosophical Perspectives: Metaphysics and Epistemology, 4:333
Philosophical Perspectives on Newtonian Science, 4:184
Philosophical Perspectives on Peace, 3:149
Philosophical-Political Profiles, 5:89
Philosophical Problems, 4:24
Philosophical Problems and Arguments: An Introduction, 4:20
Philosophical Problems of Space and Time, 5:68
Philosophical Profiles: Essays in a Pragmatic Mode, 4:262, 4:379
The Philosophical Propaedeutic, 4:232
Philosophical Questions: An Introductory Anthology, 4:23
Philosophical Radicals of 1832, 4:29
Philosophical Remarks, 4:344
Philosophical Studies, 4:304
Philosophical Subjects, 4:414
The Philosophical Theology of Duns Scotus, 4:114

Philosophical Theories, 4:22
Philosophical Thought in
America, 4:33
Philosophical Thoughts, 4:195
Philosophical Trends in the
Contemporary World,
4:267
Philosophical Works, 4:201
Philosophical Works Includ-
ing the Works of Vision,
4:191
Philosophical Writing: An In-
troduction, 4:22
The Philosophic Mind, 1:307
Philosophic Problems, 4:22
Philosophic Thought in
France and the United
States, 4:34
Philosophic Way of Life in
America, 4:36
Philosophies and Cultures,
4:39
Philosophies Men Live By,
4:20
Philosophies of India, 4:351
The Philosophies of Science,
4:384
Philosophizing with Socrates:
An Introduction to the
Study of Philosophy, 4:19
Philosophy, 4:300, 5:138
Philosophy: A Guide to the
Reference Literature, 4:6,
4:13 .
Philosophy: A Modern En-
counter, 4:25
Philosophy: An Introduction,
4:20, 4:21, 4:25
Philosophy: An Introduction
through Original Fiction,
Discussion and Readings,
4:20
Philosophy: An Introduction
to the Art of Wondering,
5:192
Philosophy: A Select, Classi-
fied Bibliography of Eth-
ics, Economics, Law, Poli-
tics, Sociology, 4:14
Philosophy: East and West,
4:37
Philosophy: Paradox and Discovery, 4:22
Philosophy: The Basic Issues,
4:22
Philosophy: The Basics, 4:25
Philosophy, Poetry, History:
An Anthology of Essays,
2:414
Philosophy, Religion and Science in the Seventeenth
and Eighteenth Centuries,
4:740, 5:43

Philosophy, Rhetoric, and the
End of Knowledge, 5:66,
5:148, 5:153
Philosophy, Science and
Method: Essays in Honor
of Ernest Nagel, 5:96
Philosophy, Social Theory,
and the Thought of
George Herbert Mead,
4:308
Philosophy, Technology and
the Arts in the Early Mod-
ern Era, 4:130
Philosophy after Darwin,
4:162, 4:267
Philosophy and AI: Essays at
the Interface, 5:74
Philosophy and an African
Culture, 4:27, 4:372
Philosophy and Contempo-
rary Problems: A Reader,
4:23
Philosophy and Culture, East
and West, 4:37
Philosophy and Environmen-
tal Crisis, 5:74, 5:114
Philosophy and Feminist
Thinking, 4:391
Philosophy and History: A
Symposium, 4:265
Philosophy and Human
Geography, 3:119
Philosophy and Humanism,
4:128
Philosophy and Ideology,
4:30
Philosophy and Its Past, 4:18,
4:162
Philosophy and Knowledge:
A Commentary on Plato's
Theaetetus, 4:83
Philosophy and Literature in
Latin America, 4:33
Philosophy and Logical Syn-
tax, 4:278
The Philosophy and Method-
ology of Economics, 3:46
Philosophy and Ordinary
Language, 4:263
The Philosophy and Poetics
of Gaston Bachelard, 4:274
The Philosophy and Psychol-
ogy of Pietro Pomponazzi,
4:154
The Philosophy and Psychol-
ogy of Sensation, 4:289
Philosophy and Public Poli-
cy, 4:298
Philosophy and Romantic
Nationalism: The Case of
Poland, 4:30
Philosophy and Science in
the Islamic World, 4:373

Philosophy and Science in
the Scottish Enlighten-
ment, 4:32
Philosophy and Spacetime
Physics, 5:68
Philosophy and Technology:
Readings in the Philosoph-
ical Problems of Technol-
ogy, 5:71, 5:129
Philosophy and Technology
II: Information Technology
and Computers in Theory
and Practice, 5:126
Philosophy and the Human
Condition, 4:19, 5:132
Philosophy and the Idea of
Freedom, 4:413
Philosophy and the Mirror of
Nature, 4:378, 4:413
Philosophy and the Modern
World, 4:161
Philosophy and Theology in
the Middle Ages, 4:16
Philosophy and the Origin
and Evolution of the Uni-
verse, 5:67
Philosophy and the Real
World, 4:410
Philosophy and the Real
World: An Introduction to
Karl Popper, 5:99
Philosophy and the Social
Problem, 3:401
Philosophy and the World,
4:300, 5:138
Philosophy and Tradition,
4:359
Philosophy as Metanoetics,
4:366
Philosophy before Socrates,
4:46
Philosophy Born of Struggle,
4:386
Philosophy East/Philosophy
West, 4:37, 4:350
Philosophy for a New Gener-
ation, 4:20
Philosophy for Everyman:
From Socrates to Sartre,
4:18
A Philosophy for Living: A
Sketch of Aquinate Philos-
ophy, 4:22
Philosophy from the Renais-
sance to the Romantic
Age, 4:124
Philosophy from the Roman-
tic Age to the Age of Rea-
son, 4:159
Philosophy Gone Wild: Es-
says in Environmental
Ethics, 5:116, 5:140

Philosophy in Africa: Trends and Perspectives, 4:368
Philosophy in America, 4:35
Philosophy in America from Puritans to James, 4:34
Philosophy in and out of Europe, 4:264
Philosophy in France Today, 4:28, 4:266, 4:379
Philosophy in Medicine, 5:77
Philosophy in Process, 4:339
Philosophy in Russia: From Herzen to Lenin and Berdyaev, 4:39
Philosophy in the Bedroom, 2:503
Philosophy in the Middle Ages: The Christian, Islamic and Jewish Traditions, 4:94
Philosophy in the Soviet Union: A Survey of the Mid-Sixties, 4:31, 4:265
Philosophy in the Twentieth Century, 4:262, 4:273
Philosophy in World Perspective, 4:37, 4:263
Philosophy Journals and Serials: An Analytical Guide, 4:14
Philosophy Looks to the Future: Confrontation, Commitment and Utopia, 4:23
Philosophy Now, 4:24
The Philosophy of A. J. Ayer, 4:273
The Philosophy of a Biologist, 5:797
The Philosophy of Alfred North Whitehead, 4:41, 4:343
The Philosophy of Andy Warhol: From A to B and Back Again, 3:796
Philosophy of Aristotle, 4:66
Philosophy of Arithmetic, 4:234
The Philosophy of Art, 4:252
Philosophy of Artificial Intelligence, 5:74
The Philosophy of Atomism and Other Essays, 1914–1919, 4:323
The Philosophy of Auguste Comte, 3:224, 4:223
The Philosophy of Baruch Spinoza, 4:188
Philosophy of Benedetto Croce: An Introduction, 3:284
The Philosophy of Bergson, 4:220

The Philosophy of Bertrand Russell, 4:42, 4:324, 5:103
Philosophy of Biological Science, 4:384
Philosophy of Biology, 5:68
Philosophy of Biology Today, 4:385, 5:68
The Philosophy of Brand Blanshard, 4:42, 4:276
The Philosophy of C. D. Broad, 4:42, 4:277
The Philosophy of C. I. Lewis, 4:42, 4:302
The Philosophy of Charles Hartshorne, 4:289
The Philosophy of Chrysippus, 4:57
The Philosophy of Clement of Alexandria, 4:63
The Philosophy of David Hume, 4:202
The Philosophy of Dr. Samuel Clarke and Its Critics, 4:194
Philosophy of Education, 4:224
The Philosophy of Edward Bellamy, 1:734
The Philosophy of Ernst Cassirer, 4:42, 4:280
Philosophy of Existence, 4:300, 4:304, 5:138
The Philosophy of Existentialism, 4:305
The Philosophy of F. H. Bradley, 4:221
The Philosophy of F.W.J. Schelling: History, System, and Freedom, 4:252
The Philosophy of Franz Brentano, 4:222
The Philosophy of Friedrich Nietzsche, 4:247
The Philosophy of G. E. Moore, 4:42, 4:312
The Philosophy of Gabriel Marcel, 4:42, 4:305
The Philosophy of George Herbert Mead, 4:309
The Philosophy of George Santayana, 4:42
The Philosophy of Georg Henrik von Wright, 4:42, 4:338
The Philosophy of Giambattista Vico, 2:414
The Philosophy of Henry George, 3:80
Philosophy of History (Aron), 3:283
The Philosophy of History (Croce), 3:284

The Philosophy of History (Hegel), 3:285
The Philosophy of History (Voltaire), 2:515, 4:218, 4:253
The Philosophy of History in Our Times, 3:276
The Philosophy of Jean-Paul Sartre, 4:42, 4:331
The Philosophy of John Dewey, 4:42
Philosophy of Judaism, 4:601
The Philosophy of Karl Jaspers, 4:42, 4:300, 5:139
The Philosophy of Karl Popper, 4:42, 4:410, 5:99
The Philosophy of Language in Britain, 4:29
The Philosophy of Leibniz, 4:323, 5:101
The Philosophy of Lev Shestov, 1866–1938: A Russian Religious Existentialist, 4:335
The Philosophy of Life, and Philosophy of Language, in a Course of Lectures, 4:253
The Philosophy of Literary Form, 1:818, 1:956
Philosophy of Logic, 4:410, 4:411, 5:99
The Philosophy of Love in Spanish Literature, 2:523
The Philosophy of Loyalty, 4:250
Philosophy of Mahatma Gandhi, 4:553
The Philosophy of Malebranche, 4:182
The Philosophy of Marsilio Ficino, 4:141
The Philosophy of Martin Buber, 4:42
The Philosophy of Mathematics: An Introductory Essay, 5:493
Philosophy of Mathematics: Selected Readings, 5:492
Philosophy of Mathematics (Baker), 5:492
Philosophy of Mathematics (Putnam), 4:410
Philosophy of Mathematics and Deductive Structure in Euclid's "Elements," 5:505
The Philosophy of Medicine: The Early Eighteenth Century, 5:44, 5:313
Philosophy of Medicine, 5:78
The Philosophy of Mind, 4:232, 4:382, 4:383

Philosophy of Modern Music, 4:393

The Philosophy of Money, 3:239

The Philosophy of Natural Magic, 4:133

Philosophy of Natural Science, 4:384, 5:63, 5:92

Philosophy of Nature, 4:232

The Philosophy of Nicholas Rescher: Discussion and Replies, 5:101

The Philosophy of Nietzsche, 4:247

The Philosophy of Paul Ricoeur: An Anthology of His Work, 4:319

The Philosophy of Phineas P. Quimby, 4:878

Philosophy of Physics, 5:83

Philosophy of Plato and Aristotle, 4:583

Philosophy of Plotinus: The Gifford Lectures at St. Andrews, 1917–1918, 4:86

The Philosophy of Popper, 4:410

Philosophy of Psychology, 5:83

The Philosophy of Robert Grosseteste, 4:115

The Philosophy of Rousseau, 4:213

The Philosophy of Rudolph Carnap, 4:42, 4:279, 5:85

The Philosophy of Sarvepalli Radhakrishnan, 4:43, 4:354

The Philosophy of Schleiermacher, 4:254

The Philosophy of Schopenhauer, 4:256

Philosophy of Science (Bechtel), 4:384

Philosophy of Science (Boyd), 5:62

Philosophy of Science (Fetzer), 5:62

Philosophy of Science: The Natural Sciences in Christian Perspective, 5:198

Philosophy of Science, Cognitive Psychology, and Educational Theory and Practice, 3:254

Philosophy of Science and Its Discontents, 5:153

Philosophy of Science and Technology, 5:83

Philosophy of Science and the Occult, 5:63

Philosophy of Social Science (Braybrooke), 5:67, 5:68

Philosophy of Social Science (Rosenberg), 4:385

The Philosophy of Socrates: A Collection of Critical Essays, 4:90

The Philosophy of Spinoza: The Unity of His Thought, 4:189

The Philosophy of Spinoza: Unfolding the Latent Processes of His Reasoning, 4:189

The Philosophy of St. Bonaventure, 4:113, 4:286

The Philosophy of St. Thomas Aquinas, 4:118, 4:286

Philosophy of Subjective Spirit, 4:232

The Philosophy of Symbolic Forms, 4:279

The Philosophy of Teaching, 3:257

Philosophy of Technology, 5:70

Philosophy of Technology: An Introduction, 5:71, 5:92

Philosophy of Technology: The Problem of Its Realization, 5:86

The Philosophy of the Act, 4:308

The Philosophy of the American Revolution, 4:36

The Philosophy of the Church Fathers: Faith, Trinity, Incarnation, 4:63, 4:100, 4:687

The Philosophy of the Enlightenment, 3:337, 4:160, 4:279

The Philosophy of the Inductive Sciences, 4:257, 4:258, 5:57

The Philosophy of the Present, 4:308

Philosophy of the Recent Past, 4:27, 4:35, 4:266

Philosophy of the Sixteenth and Seventeenth Centuries, 4:130, 4:162

The Philosophy of the Visual Arts, 3:756

The Philosophy of Thomas Reid, 4:211

The Philosophy of W. V. Quine, 4:43, 4:412, 5:100

The Philosophy of Wealth, 3:72

The Philosophy of Wilhelm Dilthey, 4:226

Philosophy of William James, 4:237

Philosophy of Woman: An Anthology of Classic and Current Concepts, 4:17

Philosophy's Journey: From the Presocratics to the Present, 4:17

Philo with an English Translation, 4:810

Phineas Finn, 1:405

Phineas Redux, 1:405

Phoebe Junior, 1:385

The Phoenicians and the West: Politics, Colonies and Trade, 3:300

Phoenissae, 2:355

The Phoenix and the Turtle, 1:215

A Phoenix Too Frequent, 1:480

Phormio, 2:395

The Photograph, 2:262

Photographs and Words, 1:1017

Photography: A Concise History, 3:759

Photosynthesis of Carbon Compounds, 5:740

Phra Chai Suriya, 2:337

Physical Chemistry, 5:735

Physical Distribution, 1:49

Physical Geography: A Landscape Appreciation, 3:126

Physical Geography (King), 5:620

Physical Geography (McIntyre), 3:126

The Physical Geography of the Sea, and Its Meteorology, 5:632

The Physical Geography of William Morris Davis, 5:643

Physical Geology, 5:626

Physical Opinions, 4:90

Physical Optics, 5:666

Physical Order and Moral Liberty, 4:327

Physical Science in the Middle Ages, 4:97, 5:39

The Physical Universe, 5:589

Physical World of the Greeks, 4:49

Physician Assistants: Present and Future Models of Utilization, 5:339

Physicians and Social Change, 5:336

Physicians' Guide to Rare Diseases, 5:367

The Physician's Hand: Work Culture and Conflict in American Nursing, 5:338

Physicians in the Making, 5:336

Physicians Signers of the Declaration of Independence, 5:313

The Physicists, 1:550

The Physicists: A Generation That Changed the World, 5:686

The Physicists: The History of a Scientific Community in Modern America, 5:48, 5:652, 5:677

A Physicist's ABC on Plasma, 5:667

Physicist's Conception of Nature, 5:693

Physicists Look Back: Studies in the History of Physics, 5:652

Physics, Philosophy, and Theology: A Common Quest for Understanding, 5:198

Physics and Astrophysics: A Selection of Key Problems, 5:588

Physics and Beyond, 5:693

Physics and Philosophy: The Revolution in Modern Science, 5:693

Physics and the Ultimate Significance of Time, 4:384

Physics in My Generation, 5:675

The Physics of High Pressure, 5:676

Physics of the Plasma Universe, 5:667

Physics of the Stoics, 4:57

The Physics of Time Asymmetry, 5:650

Physics Terminology, 5:653

Physics through the 1990s, 5:651

Physics Vade Mecum, 5:652

Physics without Math: A Descriptive Introduction, 5:11

Physiological Theory and the Doctrine of the Mean in Plato and Aristotle, 4:84

Physiology of the Nervous System, 5:342

Piaget and His School: A Reader in Developmental Psychology, 3:192

Piaget and Knowledge: Theoretical Foundations, 3:192

Piaget in the Classroom, 3:193

Piaget's Theory of Intellectual Development, 3:192

Piaget's Theory of Knowledge, 4:383

The Piano in Concert, 3:672

The Piano Lesson, 1:1119, 1:1120

The Pianoplayers, 1:454

The Piano Tuner, 2:242

The Piazza Tales, 1:687

The Piazza Tales and Other Prose Pieces, 1839–1860, 1:687

Pic, 1:998

Picasso (Jaffe), 3:786

Picasso (Palau), 3:787

Picasso (Podokski), 3:787

Picasso (Stein), 1:882

Picasso: Art as Autobiography, 5:422

Picasso: Fifty Years of his Art, 3:786

Picasso: His Life and Works, 3:787

A Picasso Anthology: Documents, Criticism, Reminiscences, 3:787

Picasso Line Drawings and Prints, 3:786

Picasso Lithographs: Sixty-One Works, 3:786

The Picasso Museum, Paris, 3:786

Picasso on Art: A Selection of Views, 3:786

Picasso's Guernica, 3:787

Picasso's Vollard Suite, 3:786

The Pickwick Papers, 1:349

Picnic, 1:1095

Pico della Mirandola's Encounter with Jewish Mysticism, 4:153

Pictorial Bookbindings, 1:23

Pictorial Calligraphy and Ornamentation, 1:18

Pictorial Dictionary of Ancient Rome, 2:381

A Pictorial Encyclopedia of Trades and Industry, 4:196

A Pictorial Guide to Fossils, 5:638

Pictorial History of the Jewish People from Biblical Times to Our Own Day throughout the World, 4:593

Pictorial History of W.E.B. Du Bois, 3:578

Pictorial Human Embryology, 5:776

Pictor's Metamorphoses and Other Fantasies, 2:590

A Picture, 2:246

Picture America, 1:1017

A Picture Book, 1:528

The Picture Book of Quantum Mechanics, 5:660

The Picturegoers, 1:515

The Picture of Dorian Gray, 1:409, 1:410

Picture Palace, 3:940

Pictures, Images and Conceptual Change, 4:334

Pictures from a Brewery, 2:15

Pictures from an Institution, 1:993

Pictures of Fidelman, 1:1013

Pictures of Romance: Form against Context in Painting and Literature, 2:988

Picturesque Expressions: A Thematic Dictionary, 1:117

Picture This, 1:988

Pidginization and Creolization of Languages: Proceedings, 3:21

A Piece of Blue Sky: Scientology, Dianetics and L. Ron Hubbard Exposed, 4:869

A Piece of My Mind, 1:525

Piece of the Wind: And Other Stories to Tell, 3:848

Pieces and Pontifications, 1:1011, 1:1012

Pieces of the Action, 5:200

The Pied Piper of Hamelin, 1:338

Pied Piper of Lovers, 1:469

Pier Paolo Pasolini: Cinema as Heresy, 2:432

Pier Paolo Pasolini: The Poetics of Heresy, 2:432

Pierre, 2:989

Pierre; or, the Ambiguities, 1:686, 1:687

Pierre, Israel Potter, The Confidence-Man, Tales, and Billy Budd, 1:687

Pierre and Jean, 2:488, 2:489

Pierre Auguste Renoir, 3:789

Pierre Bayle and Voltaire, 4:218

Pierre Corneille, 2:471

Pierre de Ronsard, 2:503

Pierre Didot the Elder and French Book Illustration 1789–1822, 1:29

Pierre Fauchard, Surgeon-Dentist, 5:407

Pierre Gassendi: From Aristotelianism to a New Natural Philosophy, 4:173

Pierre Teilhard de Chardin's Philosophy of Evolution, 4:336
Pierrot Mon Ami, 2:496
Piers Plowman, 1:140, 1:145, 1:147, 1:153
Piers Plowman: An Annotated Bibliography of Editions and Criticism, 1:154
Piers Plowman: The A Version, 1:153
Piers Plowman: The B Version, 1:153
Piers Plowman: The C-Text and Its Poet, 1:154
Piers Plowman: The Evidence for Authorship, 1:154
Piers Plowman as a Fourteenth Century Apocalypse, 1:154
Piers Plowman by William Langland: An Edition of the C-Text, 1:153
Piers the Plowman: Literary Relations of the A and B Texts, 1:154
Pietro Aretino: The Scourge of Princes, 2:406
Pig Earth, 5:264
The Pigeon, 1:482
Pigeon Feathers and Other Stories, 1:1060
The Pigman, 1:1122, 1:1123
Pigs, a Guide to Management, 5:262
Pigsty, 2:431
Pilgrimage, 1:540
The Pilgrimage of Eternity, 4:374
The Pilgrimage of Henry James, 1:765
The Pilgrimage of Western Man, 3:326
Pilgrim at Sea, 2:675, 2:676
Pilgrim at Tinker Creek, 5:818
Pilgrims in Aztlán, 2:872, 2:873
Pilgrim's Progress, 1:173, 1:174, 1:574, 1:576, 1:1194, 2:125, 2:166
Pilgrim's Regress, 4:776
Piling Blood, 2:923
The Pill, John Rock, and the Church: The Biography of a Revolution, 5:314
The Pill, Pygmy Chimps and Degas' Horse, 5:743
Pillar of the Sky, 1:1247
The Pillars of Society, 2:665

The Pillars of Society: Six Centuries of Civilization in the Netherlands, 3:383
Pillars of the Community, 2:666
The Pill Book of High Blood Pressure, 5:374
The Pillow Book, 2:270, 2:279
The Pillows, 2:646
Pills, Pesticides, and Profits: The International Trade in Toxic Substances, 5:353
Pills and Potions, 5:351
Pills to Purge Melancholy, 1:246
The Pilot, 1:662, 1:663, 1:1244
Pima Indian Legends, 3:865
Pinball, 1:1002, 1:1003
Pincher Martin (The Two Deaths of Christopher Martin), 1:484
Pinckney's Treaty: America's Advantage from Europe's Distress, 1783–1800, 3:568
Pindar, 2:365
Pindar and Aeschylus, 2:351, 2:365
Pindar and Homer, 2:365
Pindarique Odes, 2:365
Pindar's Pythian Odes, 2:365
The Pine Barrens, 5:623, 5:645
Pine River and Lone Peak, 2:298
Pink and White Tyranny, a Society Novel, 1:698
The Pink Fairy Book, 3:883
Pinocchio, 1:1163
Pinocchio in Venice: A Novel, 1:963
Pinter: A Collection of Critical Essays, 1:535
Pinter's Comic Play, 1:535
The Pinyin Chinese-English Dictionary, 1:98
Pioneer Conservationists of Eastern America, 5:816
Pioneer Conservationists of Western America, 5:816
The Pioneer Fringe, 3:128
Pioneering Space: Living on the Next Threshold, 5:597
Pioneer Jews: A New Life in the Far West, 4:641
The Pioneers, 1:662, 1:663, 1:1211
Pioneers of France in the New World, 3:592
Pioneers of Public Health, 5:801

Pioneers of Science: Nobel Prize Winners in Physics, 5:718
Pions to Quarks: Particle Physics in the 1950s, 5:662
Pious Brief Narrative in Medieval Castilian and Galician Verse, 2:526
Pipá, 2:528
The Piper and the Bard: A Study of William Blake, 1:279
The Piper Dies and Other Short Stories, 2:65
Pipers at the Gates of Dawn: The Wisdom of Children's Literature, 1:578
The Pipes Are Calling: Our Jaunts through Ireland, 3:901
Pippi Goes on Board, 2:677
Pippi in the South Seas, 2:677
Pippi Longstocking, 2:677
Pirandello and the Crisis of Modern Consciousness, 2:436
Pirandello and the French Theater, 2:436
Pirandello's Theater, 2:436
The Pirate, 1:662
Pirates, Shipwrecks, and Historic Chronicles, 3:937
Pirates of the Cell: The Story of Viruses from Molecule to Microbe, 5:783
Pirates of the South China Coast, 1790–1810, 3:468
The Pirenne Thesis, 3:407
Pirouette: Pierre Trudeau and Canadian Foreign Policy, 3:608
The Pisan Cantos, 1:870
Pisemsky: A Provincial Realist, 2:748
Pissing in the Snow and Other Ozark Folk Tales, 3:861, 3:885
The Pistol, 1:994
The Pit, 1:776
Piter Jelles Troelsra, 2:634
Pitseng, 2:166
Pitt and Popularity, 3:362
Pity the Monsters: The Political Vision of Robert Lowell, 1:1007
Pivot of the Four Quarters, 4:439
Place and Politics: The Geographical Mediation of State and Society, 3:123

Place and Vision, 1:805, 1:1016

A Place Called School: Prospects for the Future, 3:262, 3:263

A Place for Ann, 1:1238

A Place in the News: From the Women's Pages to the Front Page, 3:808

A Place in Time: Caregivers for Their Elderly, 5:317

A Place in Time: Middlesex County, Virginia, 1650–1750, 3:518

Place Migration and Development in the Third World, 3:124, 3:129

The Place of Dead Roads, 1:957

The Place of Emotion in Argument, 4:381

The Place of St. Thomas More in English Literature and History, 4:147

The Place of the Skull, 2:695

The Place of the Stage, 1:209

A Place on the Magdalena Flats, 1:1096

Place Over Time: The Continuity of Southern Distinctiveness, 3:576

Places for Learning, Places for Joy: Speculations on American Schooling, 3:268

Places Rated Almanac, 3:118

A Place to Come To, 1:892

Plácido Domingo, 3:693

The Plague, 2:464

Plague, Population and the English Economy, 1348–1530, 3:357

Plagued by the West, 2:86

Plagues and People, 3:289

A Plain Account of Christian Perfection, 4:789

The Plain Dealer, 1:263

Plain Folk: The Life Stories of Undistinguished Americans, 3:552

Plain Folk in the New South, 3:560

Plain Language from Truthful James, 1:756

A Plain Letter to the Lord Chancellor on the Infant Custody Bill, 1:383, 1:384

Plain Lives in a Golden Age, 3:383

The Plains Across, 3:526

Plains Indian Mythology, 1:631

Plains Song, 1:1017

Plain Tales from the Hills, 1:371

Plane Crazy, 1:1163

The Planetarium, 2:506

Planetary Geology in the 1980s, 5:630

The Planetary System, 5:593

Planet Earth, 5:625

Planet Earth: An Encyclopedia of Geology, 5:617

Planet News: Poems, 1961–1964, 1:981

The Planets, 5:592

The Planets: A Comic Pastoral, 1:931

Planets Beyond: Discoveries in Our Outer Solar System, 5:593

The Planet We Live On: An Illustrated Encyclopedia of the Earth Sciences, 5:617

A Plan for Escape, 2:855

Planning and Control Guides and Forms: For Small Book Publishers, 1:47

Planning a Tragedy: The Americanization of the War in Vietnam, 3:536

Plans for Departure, 2:182

The Plantagenet Encyclopedia, 3:357

Plantation, Town, and County, 3:580

The Plantation Mistress: Woman's World in the Old South, 3:523

Plantation Pageants, 1:755

Plant Competition: An Analysis of Community Functions, 5:819

Plant Engineers' and Managers' Guide to Energy Conservation, 5:284

Plant Fossils in Geologic Investigation: The Paleozoic, 5:638

Plant Morphogenesis, 5:811

Plaques and Peoples, 5:820

Plasma Physics, 5:667

Plasmas and Controlled Fusion, 5:293

Plastic Surgery for Men: The Complete Illustrated Guide, 5:397

Platero and I, 2:542

Plate Tectonics: Unraveling the Mysteries of the Earth, 5:622

Platinum: Ten Filipino Stories, 2:332

Plato (Hall), 4:81

Plato (Hare), 4:81

Plato: An Introduction, 4:80

Plato: Dramatist of the Life of Reason, 4:83

Plato: The Man and His Work, 4:84

Plato: The Midwife's Apprentice, 4:80

Plato, One: Metaphysics and Epistemology; a Collection of Critical Essays, 4:85

Plato, Two: Ethics, Politics, and Philosophy of Art and Religion; a Collection of Critical Essays, 4:85

Plato and Aristotle, 4:85

Plato and Aristotle on Poetry, 4:68

Plato and Augustine, 4:300

Plato and His Contemporaries, 4:80

Plato and Parmenides, 4:79

Plato and Platonism, 1:387, 4:82, 4:83

Plato and Socrates: A Comprehensive Bibliography, 1958–1973, 4:82

Plato and the Foundations of Metaphysics, 4:81

Plato in the Italian Renaissance, 4:127

The Platonic Epistles, 4:78

Platonic Piety: Philosophy and Ritual in Fourth-Century Athens, 4:82

The Platonic Renaissance in England, 4:279

Platonic Studies, 4:85

Platonic Studies of Greek Philosophy: Form, Arts, Gadgets, and Hemlock, 4:46

Platonic Theology, 4:140

The Platonic Theology (Six Books of Proclus on the Theology of Plato), 4:62

Platonic Tradition in Anglo-Saxon Philosophy, 4:29

Platonism, 4:79, 4:82

Platonism and Cartesianism in the Philosophy of Ralph Cudworth, 4:168

The Platonism of Marsilio Ficino, 4:141

The Platonism of Philo Judaeus, 4:60

Platonov and Fyodorov, 2:749

Plato on Beauty, Wisdom and the Arts, 4:82

Plato on Justice and Power: Reading Book I of Plato's Republic, 4:82

Plato on Knowledge and Reality, 4:85

Plato on the Self-Prediction of Forms, 4:82
Plato's Analytic Method, 4:84
Plato's Cosmology, 4:79
Plato's Defence of Poetry, 4:80
Plato's Dialectical Ethics, 4:402
Plato's Earlier Dialectic, 4:83
Plato's Euthydemus: Analysis of What Is and Is Not Philosophy, 4:79
Plato's Invisible Cities: Discourse and Power in the Republic, 4:83
Plato's Mathematical Imagination, 4:79
Plato's Parmenides: The Conversion of the Soul, 4:82
Plato's Penal Code, 4:84
Plato's Philebus, 4:283
Plato's Philosophy of Mathematics, 4:85
Plato's Progress, 4:84, 4:325
Plato's Psychology, 4:83
Plato's Slavery in Its Relation to Greek Law, 4:82
Plato's Sophist: The Drama of Original and Image, 4:79, 4:83
Plato's Symposium, 4:84
Plato's Theology, 4:84
Plato's Theory of Art, 4:81
Plato's Theory of Education, 4:82
Plato's Theory of Ethics: The Moral Criterion and the Highest Good, 4:82
Plato's Theory of Ideas, 4:84
Plato's Theory of Knowledge: The Theaetetus and the Sophist of Plato, 4:79, 4:81
Plato's Theory of Man, 4:85
Plato's Theory of Understanding, 4:82
Plato's Thought, 4:81
Plato's Thought in the Making, 4:83
Plato's Trilogy: Theaetetus, the Sophist, and the Statesman, 4:81
Plato's Universe, 4:85
Plato Today, 3:163
Plautus and Terence, 2:391, 2:395
Plautus in Performance: The Theatre of the Mind, 2:391
Plave Legende–Blue Legends, 2:830
Play, 1:389
Play, Dreams and Imitation in Childhood, 3:176, 3:192, 3:267

Playback, 1:425
The Playboy of the Western World, 1:555
Play by Play, 2:868
The Play Called Corpus Christi, 1:159
The Player on the Other Side, 1:1236
Player Piano, 1:1063, 5:72
Players and Performances in the Victorian Theatre, 1:323
A Play for Giants, 2:148, 2:149
Playful Revolution: Theatre and Liberation in Asia, 2:312
Playgoing in Shakespeare's London, 1:169, 1:217
Play Index, 1:124
Playing and Reality, 5:472
Playing God: Medieval Mysteries on the Modern Stage, 1:159
Playing God in Yellowstone, 5:821
Playing With Mischief, 1:744
Play It As It Lays, 1:968
The Playmaker, 2:957
The Play of Allegory in the Autos Sacramentales of Pedro Calderón de la Barca, 2:533
The Play of Faulkner's Language, 1:837
A Play of Mirrors: Eight Major Poets of Modern Japan, 2:283
The Play of Power, 2:533
The Play of the Sacrament, 1:160
The Play of Wisdom: Its Texts and Contexts, 1:161
Plays: Major Barbara, Heartbreak House, Saint Joan, Too True to Be Good, 1:545
Plays and Players in Modern Italy, 2:401
Plays by American Women: 1900–1930, 1:1076
Plays by David Garrick and George Colman the Elder, 1:229
Plays by George Colman the Younger and Thomas Morton, 1:229
Plays by Samuel Foote and Arthur Murphy, 1:229
Plays by W. S. Gilbert, 1:357
Plays by Women, 1:427
Plays for the Poor Theatre: Five Short Plays, 1:450

Plays in Periodicals, 1:124
Plays in Review, 1956–1980, 1:425
The Plays of Caryl Churchill: Theatre of Empowerment, 1:459
Plays of Confession and Therapy, 2:680
The Plays of Eugene O'Neill, 1:1108
The Plays of Eugene O'Neill: A New Assessment, 1:1108
Plays of Gods and Men, 1:615
The Plays of Harold Pinter: An Assessment, 1:535
The Plays of Henry Fielding: A Critical Study of His Dramatic Career, 1:246
The Plays of John Galsworthy, 1:482
The Plays of John Osborne: An Assessment, 1:532
The Plays of Mary Pix and Catherine Trotter, 1:229
Plays of Protest, 1:880
Plays of the Natural and Supernatural, 1:830
Plays on the Passions, 1:271
Plays Unpleasant, 1:545
Play Therapy with Abused Children, 5:416
The Playwright as Magician, 1:209
Playwrights for Tomorrow: A Collection of Plays, 1:1076
Playwrights on Playwriting: The Meaning and Making of Modern Drama, 1:1072
Playwright's Theatre: The English Stage Company at the Royal Court, 1:426
Plaza Suite, 1:1112, 1:1113
Pleasurable Instruction, 1:231
Pleasure, Knowledge, and Being: An Analysis of Plato's Philebus, 4:81
Pleasure and Danger: Exploring Female Sexuality, 1:1185
The Pleasure Bond: A New Look at Sexuality and Commitment, 5:429
The Pleasure Garden, 1:1168
Pleasures and Days: And Other Writings, 2:495
Pleasures and Speculations, 1:467
The Pleasures of Book Collecting, 1:32
The Pleasures of Children's Literature, 1:1196, 3:256

The Pleasures of Japanese
  Literature, 2:272
Pleasures of Music, 3:664
The Pleasures of Philosophy,
  3:402
Plenty, 1:493
Pletzl of Paris: Jewish Immi-
  grant Workers in the
  Belle Époque, 4:656
Plexus, 1:861
Plotinus, 4:87
Plotinus: The Road to Reali-
  ty, 4:87
Plotinus on Sense-Perception:
  A Philosophical Study,
  4:86
Plots and Characters in Ma-
  jor Russian Fiction, 2:684
Plots and Characters in the
  Fiction and Narrative Po-
  etry of Herman Melville,
  1:689
Plots and Characters in the
  Fiction of James Fenimore
  Cooper, 1:665
Plotting America's Past,
  1:665
Plotting Women: Gender and
  Representation in Mexico,
  2:846
Plough, Sword, and Book:
  The Structure of Human
  History, 3:276
The Plough and the Pen:
  Writing from Hungary,
  1930–1956, 2:798
The Plough and the Stars,
  1:526
Ploughman and Other
  Poems, 1:506
The Ploughshares Reader:
  New Fiction for the 80's,
  1:921
The Plowman from Bohemia,
  2:562, 2:594
Pluck and Luck, 1:815
Plumb, 2:975
Plumed Serpent, 1:509
Plunder of the Arts in the
  Seventeenth Century,
  3:411
A Pluralistic Universe, 4:236
Plurality and Ambiguity: Her-
  meneutics, Religion, Hope,
  4:889
Plurality of Worlds, 5:31
Plutarch, 3:318, 4:490
Plutarch and His Times,
  4:490
Plutarch's Ethical Writings
  and Early Christian Litera-
  ture, 4:490

Plutarch's Historical Meth-
  ods: An Analysis of the
  Mulierum Virtues, 3:318
Pluto's Republic: Incorporat-
  ing "The Art of the Solu-
  ble" and "Induction and
  Intuition in Scientific
  Thought," 5:18
PMS: Premenstrual Syn-
  drome, 5:356
PMS: Premenstrual Syn-
  drome and You, 5:355
PMS: What Every Woman
  Should Know about Pre-
  menstrual Syndrome,
  5:357
Pnin, 1:1020, 2:740
Po Chü-i as a Censor, 2:216
The Pocket Aquinas, 3:330
Pocket Dictionary of Saints,
  4:719
A Pocket Guide to Astrono-
  my, 5:591
A Pocket Guide to Food Ad-
  ditives, 5:261
A Pocket History of the Unit-
  ed States, 3:573, 3:591
The Pocket Mirror, 2:974
The Pocket Oxford Russian
  Dictionary: Russian-En-
  glish/English-Russian,
  1:102
Poe: A Critical Study, 1:693
Poe, Death, and the Life of
  Writing, 1:693
Poe and His Times: The Art-
  ist and His Milieu, 1:693
The Poe Log: A Documenta-
  ry Life of Edgar Allan
  Poe, 1809–1849, 1:693
The Poem of Angkor 'Vat,
  2:315
The Poem of Empedocles: A
  Text and Translation with
  an Introduction, 4:53
Poem of the Deep Song,
  2:539
Poem of the Elder Edda,
  4:437
Poem of the End, 2:767
Poem of the Mountain, 2:767
Poems: Descriptive, Dramat-
  ic, Legendary and Con-
  templative, 1:697
Poems, Chiefly in the Scott-
  ish Dialect, 1:279, 1:280
Poems, Plays, and the Bri-
  ton, 1:257
Poems All Sizes, 1:998
The Poems and Lyrics of
  Last Lord Lee: A Transla-
  tion, 2:209

Poems and Texts: An Anthol-
  ogy of French Poems,
  2:448
Poems Before and After: Col-
  lected English Transla-
  tions, 2:792
Poems by Faiz, 2:175
Poems Chiefly Lyrical, 1:399
Poems Descriptive of Rural
  Life, 1:285
Poems from Oby, 1:516
Poems from Prison, 2:148
Poems from the Book of
  Hours, 2:607
Poems from the Hebrew,
  2:10
Poems in Prose, 2:769
The Poems of Ancient Tamil,
  2:172
Poems of Black Africa, 2:149
The Poems of Doctor Zhiva-
  go, 2:745
Poems of East and West,
  1:541
Poems of Endre Ady, 2:799
The Poems of George
  Crabbe: A Literary and
  Historical Study, 1:289
Poems of Love and Death,
  1:516
Poems of Love and War,
  2:174
Poems of Rita Joe, 2:914
Poems of Robert Frost: An
  Explication, 1:842
Poems of Solitude, 2:192
Poems of the Elder Edda,
  2:642
Poems of the Late T'ang,
  2:192
The Poems of the Pearl
  Manuscript, 1:155
Poems on Miscellaneous
  Subjects, 1:753
Poems on Various Subjects,
  Religious and Moral,
  1:646, 1:647
Poems to Eat, 2:288
Poems Twice Told: Contain-
  ing The Boatman and
  Welcoming Disaster, 2:919
The Poem's Two Bodies: The
  Poetics of the 1590 Faerie
  Queene, 1:198
Poems Written between the
  Years 1768 and 1794,
  1:639
Poems Written in Early
  Youth, 1:472
Poem without a Hero, 2:696
Poe Poe Poe Poe Poe Poe
  Poe, 1:693

Poe's Fiction: Romantic Irony in the Gothic Tales, 1:693

Poesía de Paso, 2:870

Poet and Painter: The Aesthetics of E. E. Cummings's Early Work, 1:825

The Poet and the Dream Girl, 1:878

The Poet and the Gilded Age, 1:719

The Poet and the Hangman: Nekrasov and Muravyov, 2:742

The Poet and the Mystic, 2:544

The Poet and the Natural World in the Age of Góngora, 2:540

The Poet as Analyst: Essays on Paul Valéry, 2:513

The Poet as Mythmaker, 2:840

The Poet as Philosopher, 4:151

The Poet at the Breakfast-Table, 1:677

The Poetic Achievement of Ezra Pound, 1:872

Poetical, Dramatic, and Miscellaneous Works, 1:246

The Poetic Art of A. E. Housman: Theory and Practice, 1:496

The Poetic Avant-Garde in Poland, 1918–1939, 2:811

Poetic Diction: A Study in Meaning, 1:923

Poetic Drama of Paul Claudel, 2:468

The Poetic Edda, 2:642

Poetic Form and British Romanticism, 1:268

The Poetic Mirror, 1:291

Poetics, 1:1138

Poetics of Aristotle, 4:67

The Poetics of Cavafy, 2:372

The Poetics of Gender, 1:926

The Poetics of Impersonality: T. S. Eliot and Ezra Pound, 1:873

The Poetics of Indeterminacy, 1:799, 2:500

Poetics of Music in the Form of Six Lessons, 3:722

Poetics of Reverie: Childhood, Language and Cosmos, 4:274

Poetics of Space, 4:274

The Poetics of the New American Poetry, 1:912

Poetics of Valentin Kataev's Prose of the 1960's and 1970's, 2:731

A Poetics of Women's Autobiography, 1:376

The Poetics of Yury Olesha, 2:744

The Poetics of Yves Bonnefoy, 2:462

Poetic Thinking: An Approach to Heidegger, 4:293

The Poetic Vision of Muriel Rukeyser, 1:1042

The Poetic Vision of Robert Penn Warren, 1:894

The Poetic Works of Flavien Ranaivo, 2:156

The Poet in America, 1:1650 to Present, 1:720

Poet in New York, 2:538, 2:539

The Poet in the World, 1:1003

The Poet Kao Ch'i, 1336–1374, 2:203

Poetry, Language, Thought, 4:291

The Poetry and Career of Li Po, 2:208

Poetry and Civil War in Lucan's Bellum Civile, 2:388

Poetry and Experience, 4:226

Poetry and Literature: An Introduction to the Criticism and History, 2:414

Poetry and Metamorphosis, 1:560, 1:800

Poetry and Militancy in Latin America, 2:863

Poetry and Opinion, 1:858

The Poetry and Poetics of Amiri Baraka: The Jazz Aesthetic, 1:941

The Poetry and Poetics of Jorge Luis Borges, 2:857

Poetry and Politics; The Life and Works of Juan Chi (A.D. 210–263), 2:202

Poetry and Politics in the Age of Augustus, 2:382

Poetry and Pragmatism, 1:769

Poetry and Reform, 1:269

Poetry and Repression: Revisionism from Blake to Stevens, 1:267

Poetry and Society: The Role of Poetry in Ancient Greece, 2:347

Poetry and the Making of Modern Egypt (1882–1922), 2:55

Poetry and Truth in Robert Browning's "The Ring and the Book," 1:339

Poetry by American Women, 1:125

Poetry by American Women, 1900–1975: A Bibliography, 1:123

Poetry by American Women, 1975–1989: A Bibliography, 1:123

Poetry by Canadian Women, 2:905

Poetry Criticism Series, 1:134

Poetry Handbook: A Dictionary of Terms, 1:132

Poetry in America, 1:655

Poetry Index Annual, 1:125

Poetry in Modern Ireland, 1:460

The Poetry of Adam Mickiewicz, 2:817

The Poetry of Africa: An Introduction for Students, 2:108

The Poetry of American Women from 1632 to 1945, 1:630, 1:655

The Poetry of Auden: The Disenchanted Island, 1:436

The Poetry of Austin Clarke, 1:460

The Poetry of Black America: Anthology of the Twentieth Century, 1:800, 1:914, 1:1196

The Poetry of Byron, 1:283

The Poetry of Clough, 1:345

The Poetry of Commitment in South Africa, 2:106

The Poetry of Crabbe, 1:289

The Poetry of Dante, 2:414, 2:417

The Poetry of Dante Gabriel Rossetti: Modes of Self-Expression, 1:392

Poetry of Discovery: The Spanish Generation of 1956–1971, 2:525

The Poetry of Edwin Muir: The Field of Good and Ill, 1:522

Poetry of Exile, 2:389

The Poetry of Experience, 1:268, 1:315, 1:417

The Poetry of Ezra Pound, 1:873

A Poetry of Force and Darkness: The Fiction of John Hawkes, 1:986

The Poetry of Greek Tragedy, 2:346

The Poetry of John Dryden, 1:242

The Poetry of Leopold Sedar Senghor, 2:147

The Poetry of Li Shang-yin, Ninth Century Baroque Chinese Poet, 2:208

The Poetry of Marianne Moore: A Study in Voice and Value, 1:864

The Poetry of Meditation, 1:166

The Poetry of Meng Chiao and Han Yü, 2:199

The Poetry of Okot p'Bitek, 2:156

The Poetry of Pablo Neruda, 2:876

A Poetry of Presence: The Writing of William Carlos Williams, 1:901

Poetry of Randall Jarrell, 1:993

The Poetry of Resistance: Seamus Heaney and the Pastoral Tradition, 1:495

The Poetry of Samuel Taylor Coleridge, 1:288

The Poetry of Seamus Heaney, 1:495

The Poetry of Singapore: Anthology of ASEAN Literature, 2:325

The Poetry of Sir Philip Sidney, 1:196

Poetry of Stephen Crane, 1:742

The Poetry of Stevie Smith: "Little Girl Lost," 1:549

The Poetry of Tennyson, 1:401

The Poetry of the Aeneid, 2:397

Poetry of the Early T'ang, 2:190

Poetry of the First World War, 1:533

Poetry of the Negro, 1746–1970, 1:720

Poetry of the Romantic Period, 1:268

The Poetry of Thomas Hardy, 1:362

The Poetry of W. B. Yeats, 1:517

The Poetry of William Cowper, 1:238

The Poetry of Yevgeny Yevtushenko, 2:774

Poetry Realized in Nature, 1:288

Poetry's Voice, Society's Song: Ottoman Lyric Poetry, 2:95

The Poet Sa'di: A Persian Humanist, 2:93

The Poet's Africa, 2:110

Poet's Alphabet, 1:952

The Poets and the Poetry of the Nineteenth Century, 1:316

The Poet's Circuits, 1:461

The Poet's Discovery: Nineteenth-Century Australia in Verse, 2:947

Poets in Their Youth: A Memoir, 1:914

A Poet's Journal: Days of 1945–1951, 2:376

A Poet's Notebook, 1:548

The Poets of Haiti, 2:931

Poets of Modern Russia, 2:686

Poets of Nicaragua: A Bilingual Anthology, 1918–1979, 2:850

Poets of Prague: Czech Poetry between the Wars, 2:789

Poets of Reality: Six Twentieth-Century Writers, 1:417

Poets of Transcendentalism: An Anthology, 1:655

Poet's Prose: The Crisis in American Verse, 1:798, 1:913

The Poet's Testament: Poems and Two Plays, 4:327

The Poet's Truth: A Study of the Poet in Virgil's Georgics, 2:397

The Poet's Work: An Introduction to Czesław Miłosz, 2:818

The Poet Without a Name: Gray's "Elegy" and the Problem of History, 1:248

The Poet Wordsworth, 1:307

Poganuc People, 1:698

Poinciana, 1:1238

The Point Loma Community in California, 1897–1942, 4:858

Point of View for My Work as an Author, 4:238

Points and Lines, 2:289

Points of Contact, 2:990

Points of Departure, 2:23

Points of View: Five Essays, 1:520

Poison, Play, and Duel: A Study in "Hamlet," 1:213

The Poisoned Well: New Strategies for Groundwater Protection, 5:823

Poisoning Our Children: Surviving in a Toxic World, 5:351

Poison in the Pot: The Legacy of Lead, 5:352

Poisonous and Venomous Marine Animals of the World, 5:769

Poisons of the Past: Molds, Epidemics, and History, 3:326

Poland, 3:931

Poland: An Historical Atlas, 3:390

The Połaniecki Family, 2:821

Polar Dreams, 3:907

The Polar Express, 1:1207, 1:1208

The Polarity of Mexican Thought, 4:33

The Policeman's Beard Is Half Constructed, 5:565

Police Power and Colonial Rule: Madras, 1859–1947, 3:484

Policies and Procedures of a Cardiac Rehabilitation Program, 5:375

Policies for Prosperity: Essays in a Keynesian Mode, 3:62

Policing a Socialist Society: The German Democratic Republic, 3:378

Policraticus: The Statesman's Book, 4:116

Policy and Police, 3:402

Policy for Land: Law and Ethics, 5:141

Policy Implications of Greenhouse Warming, 5:282, 5:736

A Policy of Kindness, 4:560

Policy Options in Long-Term Care, 5:335

Policy Papers in International Affairs, 4:570

The Policy Sciences: Recent Developments in Scope and Method, 3:157

Polifemo y Galatea, 2:540

Polish-American Folktales, 3:853

The Polish Complex, 2:815

Polish Flowers, 2:822

Polish Jews: A Pictorial Record, 2:30

The Polish Lad, 2:40

The Polish Land, 2:811

The Polish Peasant in Europe and America, 3:241

Polish Romantic Literature, 2:811

The Polish School of Philosophy of Medicine, 5:78

Polish Short Story in English: A Guide and Critical Bibliography, 2:811

Political, Electoral and Spatial Systems: An Essay in Political Geography, 3:132

Political and Economic Encyclopedia of the Pacific, 3:496

Political and Historical Writings, 2:333

Political and Social Change in Modern Egypt, 3:446

The Political and Social Ideas of Saint Augustine, 4:110

Political and Social Thought in the Contemporary Middle East, 3:436

Political Anthropology: An Introduction, 5:35

Political Buddhism in Southeast Asia, 4:520

The Political Career of Richard Brinsley Sheridan, 1:255

Political Change and Industrial Development in Japan, 3:502

Political Change in the Metropolis, 3:148

Political Development and Social Change in Libya, 3:454

The Political Economy of Commerce: Southern India, 1500–1650, 3:484

The Political Economy of Development in India, 3:485

The Political Economy of Global Energy, 5:280

The Political Economy of International Technology Transfer, 5:182

The Political Economy of Modern Iran: Despotism and Pseudo-Modernism, 3:448

The Political Economy of Postwar Reconstruction, 3:365

The Political Economy of Science and Technology, 5:180

The Political Economy of Slavery, 3:547, 3:580

The Political Economy of the Raj, 1914–1947, 3:485

The Political Element in the Development of Economic Theory, 3:98, 3:99

Political Essay on the Kingdom of New Spain, 3:131

A Political Fable, 1:963

Political Geography: Recent Advances and Future Directions, 3:123

Political Handbook of the World, 1:83

Political Hermeneutics: The Early Thinking of Hans-Georg Gadamer, 4:402

A Political History of Post-War Italy, 3:385

Political Ideals, 4:323

The Political Ideas of Harold J. Laski, 3:156

Political Ideologies: An Introduction, 3:140

Political Ideologies: Comparative Approach, 3:140

Political Ideology, 3:140

The Political Illusion, 5:163, 5:164

Political Innovation in America: The Politics of Policy Initiation, 3:146

Political Justice in a Republic: James Fenimore Cooper's America, 1:665

The Political Language of Islam, 3:459, 4:579

Political Man: The Social Bases of Politics, 3:140, 3:158

Political Mobilization of Peasants: A Study of an Egyptian Community, 3:445

The Political Ontology of Martin Heidegger, 4:292

Political Parties, 3:585

Political Parties: A Sociological Study of the Oligarchical Tendencies of Modern Democracy, 3:234

Political Parties and American Political Development from the Age of Jackson to the Age of Lincoln, 3:543

Political Parties and Elections in American States, 3:148

Political Parties and Elections in the United States, 2:871

Political Parties and Elections in the U.S.: An Encyclopedia, 3:509

Political Parties in Turkey: The Role of Islam, 3:452

The Political Philosophies of Plato and Hegel, 4:233

Political Philosophy and Time: Plato and the Origins of Political Vision, 4:81

Political Philosophy as Therapy: Marcuse Reconsidered, 5:95

The Political Philosophy of Burke, 3:152, 4:193

The Political Philosophy of Hobbes: His Theory of Obligation, 4:175

Political Philosophy of Hobbes: Its Basis and Its Genesis, 3:154, 4:175

The Political Philosophy of Hobbes: The Rationale of the Sovereign State, 3:154

The Political Philosophy of Luis De Molina, S. J., 4:125

The Political Philosophy of Montaigne, 2:491

The Political Philosophy of Rousseau, 3:164, 4:213

The Political Philosophy of the Frankfurt School, 4:264, 4:394, 4:408

The Political Philosophy of Thomas Jefferson, 1:641

The Political Poetry and Ideology of F. I. Tiutchev, 2:771

Political Power: Its Composition and Incidence, 3:162

The Political Reason of Edmund Burke, 3:152

The Political Responsibility of the Critic, 1:1127

Political Satire in the American Revolution, 1763–1783, 1:628

Political Science: A Guide to Reference and Information Sources, 3:138

Political Science Research Methods, 3:138

Political Shakespeare: New Essays in Cultural Materialism, 1:208

Political Socialization: A Study in the Psychology of Political Behavior, 3:216

Political Sociology, 3:222

The Political Stage: American Drama and Theater of the Great Depression, 1:1073
Political Structures and Democracy in Uruguay, 3:641
The Political System: An Inquiry into the State of Political Science, 3:138, 3:153
The Political System of the Anuak of the Anglo-Egyptian Sudan, 3:29
Political Systems of Highlands Burma: A Study of Kachin Social Structure, 3:26
Political Theory: The Foundations of Twentieth Century Political Thought, 3:138
Political Theory and Postmodernism, 3:138
The Political Theory of John Wyclif, 4:103
The Political Theory of Montesquieu, 3:163
The Political Theory of Possessive Individualism: Hobbes to Locke, 4:174, 4:180
Political Thought from Gerson to Grotius: 1414–1625, 4:126
Political Thought in Medieval Islam: An Introductory Outline, 4:580
Political Thought in Medieval Times, 4:98
The Political Thought of Abraham Lincoln, 3:574
The Political Thought of John Locke, 3:159, 4:179
The Political Thought of Pierre D'Ailly, 4:105
Political Thought of Plato and Aristotle, 4:66, 4:79
The Political Thought of Sallust, 3:320
The Political Thought of Thomas Aquinas, 4:118
The Political Thought of William of Ockham, 4:121
The Political Unconscious, 1:1132, 1:1149
Political Violence in Ireland: Government and Resistance since 1848, 3:365
Political Writings, 4:196, 4:205, 4:232
Political Writings of Thomas Jefferson, 3:154
The Politician and Other Stories, 2:335, 2:336

The Politics, 3:311
Politics: Who Gets What, When, and How, 3:157
Politics, Culture and Class in the French Revolution, 3:373
Politics, Markets and America's Schools, 3:254
Politics, Parties, and Pressure Groups, 3:155
Politics, Personality and Social Science in the Twentieth Century, 3:157
Politics, Philosophy, Culture, 4:400
Politics and a Belly-Full: The Journalistic Career of William Cullen Bryant, 1:661
Politics and Belief in Herodotus, 4:480
Politics and Culture in Wartime Japan, 3:479
Politics and Freedom, 5:82
Politics and Health Care Organization: HMO's as Federal Policy, 5:328
Politics and History, 3:283
Politics and Ideology in the Age of the Civil War, 3:527
Politics and Language in Dryden's Poetry, 1:242
Politics and Literature in Shanghai, 2:234
Politics and Nationhood: Post-Revolutionary Portugal, 3:386
Politics and Petroleum in Ecuador, 3:636
Politics and Policy: The Eisenhower, Kennedy, and Johnson Years, 3:544
Politics and Script, 1:18
Politics and Society in De Gaulle's Republic, 3:374
Politics and Society in Israel, 3:440
Politics and Technology, 5:158, 5:183
Politics and the Military in Jordan, 3:455
Politics and the Novel, 1:421, 1:990, 2:989
Politics and the Restraint of Science, 5:180
Politics and Vision: Continuity and Innovation in Western Political Thought, 3:139
Politics by Other Means: The Declining Importance of Elections in America, 3:143

Politics in African Poetry, 2:111
Politics in Brazil, 1930–1964: An Experiment in Democracy, 3:634
Politics in English Romantic Poetry, 1:268
Politics in the American States: A Comparative Analysis, 3:148
Politics in the Ancient World, 3:298
Politics in the Poetry of Coleridge, 1:288
Politics in the Tokugawa Bakufu, 1600–1853, 3:476
The Politics of a Literary Man: William Gilmore Simms, 1:697
The Politics of Alternative Technology, 5:152
The Politics of American English, 1776–1850, 1:652
The Politics of Assimilation, 3:349, 4:637
The Politics of Being: The Political Thought of Martin Heidegger, 4:295
The Politics of Bureaucracy, 3:147
The Politics of Chaos: Canada in the Thirties, 3:616
The Politics of Coalition Rule in Colombia, 3:635
The Politics of Conscience: T. H. Green and His Age, 4:230
The Politics of Culture, 2:789
The Politics of Deference, 3:364
The Politics of Developing Areas, 3:149
The Politics of Development: Forests, Mines and Hydro-Electric Power in Ontario, 1849–1941, 3:615
The Politics of Development: Perspectives on Twentieth-Century Asia, 3:465
The Politics of Discretion, 4:186
The Politics of Education: Culture, Power, and Liberation, 3:262
The Politics of Electoral College Reform, 3:144
The Politics of Energy Conservation, 5:284
The Politics of Energy Research and Development, 5:281

Politics of Eurocommunism: Socialism in Transition, 3:345

The Politics of Experience, 5:459

The Politics of Fantasy: C. S. Lewis and J. R. R. Tolkien, 1:559

The Politics of Friendship: Pompey and Cicero, 4:72

The Politics of Futility, 4:656

The Politics of God: Christian Theologies and Social Justice, 4:746

The Politics of God and the Politics of Man, 5:163, 5:164

The Politics of Hispanic Education, 3:256

The Politics of Hope, 3:597

The Politics of International Economic Relations, 3:145

The Politics of Latin American Development, 3:632

The Politics of Locke's Philosophy, 4:181

The Politics of Mass Society, 3:143, 3:202

The Politics of Military Rule in Brazil, 1964–1985, 3:634

The Politics of Moderation: An Interpretation of Plato's "Republic," 3:163

The Politics of Narration, 1:837

The Politics of Nonviolent Action, 3:145

Politics of Nursing, 5:337

The Politics of Palestinian Nationalism, 3:455

The Politics of Park Design: A History of Urban Parks in America, 3:549

The Politics of Philo Judaeus: Practice and Theory, 4:670

The Politics of Prose: Essay on Sartre, 2:507

The Politics of Pure Science, 5:181

The Politics of Reality: Essays in Feminist Theory, 1:925

The Politics of Recovery: Roosevelt's New Deal, 3:535

The Politics of Samuel Johnson, 1:250

The Politics of Social Theory, 4:405, 5:89

The Politics of Social Theory: Habermas, Freud and the Critique of Positivism, 3:229

The Politics of State Courts, 3:145

The Politics of Story in Victorian Social Fiction, 1:318

The Politics of Technology, 5:212

The Politics of the Developing Areas, 3:150

The Politics of the Family and Other Essays, 5:459

The Politics of Therapy, 5:422

Politics of the World Economy, 3:243

Pollen and Fragments, 2:605

Polling and the Public, 3:147

Pollock and After: The Critical Debate, 3:787

Polyethnicity and National Unity in World History, 3:289

Polyeuctus, 2:470

Polyhymnia: The Rhetoric of Horatian Lyric Discourse, 2:386

Polymers: The Origins and Growth of a Science, 5:732

The Polynesians, 3:495

Poly-Olbion, 1:179

The Pompadours, 2:755

Pompeii and Herculaneum: The Living Cities of the Dead, 3:304

Pompilia, 1:339

The Pond, 2:753

The Ponder Heart, 1:894, 1:895

The Pooh Perplex: A Freshman Casebook, 1:588

Poole's Index to Periodical Literature, 1:114

The Pool Hall, 1:1105

Po-on, 2:331

The Poor Christ of Bomba, 2:132

Poore's Descriptive Catalogue of the Government Publications of the United States, Sept. 4, 1774–March 4, 1881, 1:109

Poor Fellow My Country, 2:954, 2:955

Poor Folk, 2:712, 2:714

The Poorhouse Fair, 1:1059, 1:1060

Poor Laws and Paupers, 1:375

The Poor Man and His Lady, 1:360

Poor Miss Finch: A Novel, 1:346

The Poor Mouth: A Bad Story about the Hard Life, 1:525

The Poor of New York, 1:331

Poor Pearl, Poor Girl, 3:851

Poor People's Movements: Why They Succeed, How They Fail, 3:215

Poor Richard's Almanac, 1:637, 1:638

Poor White, 1:811

Poor Women, Poor Families, 3:66

Pope John XXIII: Shepherd of the Modern World, 4:771

Popes, Monks and Crusaders, 4:692

The Popes and European Revolution, 4:738, 4:740

Popes and Princes 1417–1517, 4:695

The Popish Plot, 3:360

Popol Vuh, 4:456

Popper and After: Four Modern Irrationalists, 5:54

Popper Selections, 4:409

Poppy, 1:525

Pops, 1:1099

Popular Anti-Catholicism in Mid-Victorian England, 3:364

The Popular Ballad, 1:149

Popular Beliefs and Folklore Tradition in Siberia, 4:541

The Popular Book: A History of America's Literary Taste, 1:1210, 1:51

Popular Buddhism in Siam and Other Essays on Thai Studies, 4:519

Popular Culture, 1:982, 3:873

Popular Culture: An Introductory Text, 3:874

Popular Culture and Curricula, 3:875

Popular Culture and Libraries, 3:873

Popular Culture and Popular Movements in Reformation Germany, 3:377

Popular Culture and the Expanding Consciousness, 3:875

The Popular Culture Explosion, 3:875

Popular Culture in Early Modern Europe, 3:333

Popular Culture Reader, 3:873

A Popular Dictionary of Islam, 3:444, 4:567

Popular Ethics in Ancient Greece, 2:347

Popular Fiction before Richardson: Narrative Patterns, 1:592

Popular Fiction in England, 1914–1918, 1:592

A Popular Guide to Government Publications, 3:506

A Popular Guide to Medical Language, 5:310

A Popular History of Astronomy in the Nineteenth Century, 5:45

Popular History of Philosophy, 4:16

A Popular History of the Reformation, 4:722

The Popular Mood of Pre-Civil War America, 3:530

Popular Nutritional Practices: A Scientific Appraisal, 5:348

Popular Periodical Index, 1:114

Popular Politics and Society in Late Victorian Britain, 3:364

Popular Religion in the Middle Ages, 3:330, 4:698

The Popular School, 1:170

Popular Scientific Lectures (Mach), 5:700

Popular Scientific Lectures, (Helmholtz), 5:692

Popular Songs and Ballads of Han China, 2:188

Popular Tales of the West Highlands, Orally Collected, 3:876

Popular Works, 4:198

Population, Disease and Land in Early Japan, 645–900, 3:474

Population, Economy, and Society in Pre-Industrial England, 3:358

Population, Evolution, and Birth Control, 5:135

Population and Politics since 1750, 3:289

Population and Society, 3:245

The Population Bomb, 3:121, 5:831, 5:832

The Population Explosion, 5:832

The Population Handbook, 3:121

The Population History of England, 1541–1871: A Reconstruction, 3:356

The Population of Japan, 3:241

The Population of the United States: Historical Trends and Future Projections, 3:205

Populations of the Middle East and North Africa, 3:435

The Pop World of Henry James: From Fairy Tales to Science Fiction, 1:767

Porphyry's Isagoge, 4:62

Porphyry's Launching-Points to the Realm of the Mind, 4:61

The Portable Abraham Lincoln, 3:527

The Portable Arthur Miller, 1:1104

The Portable Darwin, 5:794

The Portable Dorothy Parker, 1:868

The Portable Faulkner, 1:822, 1:835

The Portable Graham Greene, 1:489

The Portable Greek Reader, 2:348, 4:47

The Portable Karl Marx, 3:290

The Portable Malcolm Cowley, 1:823

The Portable Mark Twain, 3:576

The Portable Medieval Reader, 1:147

The Portable Nietzsche, 4:246, 4:741

The Portable North American Indian Reader, 1:653, 1:720

Portable Plato, 3:163

The Portable Roman Reader, 2:382

The Portable Sherwood Anderson, 1:811

The Portable Twentieth Century Russian Reader, 2:692

The Portable Veblen, 3:242

The Portable Victorian Reader, 1:326

Portable Voltaire, 4:218

The Portable World Bible, 4:5

Portfolio Selection: Efficient Diversification of Investments, 3:56

Portnoy's Complaint, 1:987, 1:1040, 1:1041

Port of Saints, 1:957

Portrait, 1:505

The Portrait of a Lady: Maiden, Woman and Heroine, 1:767

The Portrait of a Lady, 1:763

Portrait of a Man Unknown, 2:506

Portrait of Ambrose Bierce, 1:735

Portrait of a Muckraker, 3:823

Portrait of an Age: Victorian England, 1:313, 3:365

Portrait of an Artist: A Biography of Georgia O'Keeffe, 3:785

Portrait of an Obsession, 1:33

Portrait of a Publisher, 1915–1965, 1:42

A Portrait of Aristotle, 4:68

Portrait of Barrie, 1:330

A Portrait of Claude Debussy, 3:692

Portrait of Edith Wharton, 1:788

Portrait of Elgar, 3:694

Portrait of Emily Dickinson: The Poet and Her Prose, 1:747

Portrait of George Moore in a Study of His Work, 1:381

A Portrait of Isaac Newton, 5:42

Portrait of Josephine Butler, 1:341

Portrait of Mr. B: Photographs of George Balanchine with an Essay, 3:738

A Portrait of the Artist: The Plays of Tennessee Williams, 1:1118

Portrait of the Artist as a Young Dog, 1:557

A Portrait of the Artist as a Young Man, 1:503, 1:504

Portrait of the Artist as Filipino, 2:331

A Portrait of the Royal Ballet, 3:734

A Portrait of Twenty-Five Years, 5:62

A Portrait of Wittgenstein as a Young Man, 4:338

Portraits, Political and Personal, 3:295

Portraits from Life, 1:475

Portraits of American Women, 1:647

Portraits of Destiny, 2:652

Portraits of France, 3:898

Portraits of Russian Personal-
ities between Reform and
Revolution, 3:395
Portraits of Yiddish Writers,
2:32
Portugal, 2:558
Portugal and Africa,
1815–1910, 3:423
The Portuguese: The Land
and Its People, 3:386
Portuguese Africa, 3:416
Portuguese-English, English-
Portuguese Dictionary,
1:102
Portuguese-English Diction-
ary, 1:101
Portuguese Exploration to
the West and the Forma-
tion of Brazil: 1450–1800,
3:336
Portuguese Folk Tales, 2:557
Portuguese India in the Mid-
Seventeenth Century,
3:484
The Portuguese in India,
3:484
The Portuguese Period in
East Africa, 3:423
Portuguese Voyagers to
America in the Fifteenth
Century, 3:589
Portuguese Voyages,
1498–1663, 2:557, 3:335,
3:386
Posidonius: The Fragments,
4:56
Positions, 4:397
The Positive Analysis of So-
cial Phenomena, 4:222
Positive As Sound: Emily
Dickinson's Rhyme, 1:748
The Positive Hero in Russian
Literature, 2:688
Positive History of the New
Social Order and Histori-
cal Analysis of Social Phe-
nomena, 4:222
Positive Parenting Fitness,
3:207
Positive Philosophy, 4:222
The Positive Philosophy of
Auguste Comte, 1:376
Positives: Verses by Thom
Gunn, 1:491
The Positive Thinkers, 4:753
The Positivist Dispute in Ger-
man Sociology, 4:393
Possessed: Or the Secret of
Myslotch, 2:813
The Possessed, 2:712, 2:714
Possessed with Greatness,
1:175

Possessing the Secret of Joy,
1:1064
Possession: A Romance,
1:454, 1:455
The Possible and the Actual,
5:800
Possible Worlds: And Other
Papers, 5:797
Post-Analytic Philosophy,
4:267, 4:379
The Post-Card: From Soc-
rates to Freud and Be-
yond, 3:211
The Post Card, 4:397
The Post-Civil War Spanish
Social Poets, 2:525
The Post-Colonial Critic,
1:1153
Postharvest Handling: A Sys-
tems Approach, 5:267
Post-Holocaust Dialogues:
Critical Studies in Modern
Jewish Thought, 4:648
A Posthumous Confession,
2:625
Postindustrial Possibilities: A
Critique of Economic
Discourse, 3:61
The Post-Industrial Prophets:
Interpretations of Technol-
ogy, 5:71
The Postman Always Rings
Twice, 1:1227
Post Metaphysical Thinking,
4:404
Postmodern American Poet-
ry, 1:913
The Postmodern Condition:
A Report on Knowledge,
3:211
The Postmodern Explained:
Correspondence 1982–85,
4:265
Postmodern Fiction: A Bio-
bibliographical Guide,
1:122, 1:422
Postmodernism, or, the Cul-
tural Logic of Late Capi-
talism, 1:1149
Postmodernism and Demo-
cratic Theory, 3:142
Postmodernism/Jameson/
Critique, 1:1150
Postmodern Italian Fiction,
2:401
The Post Modern Poets,
1:915
Postscript Language Refer-
ence Manual, 5:562
Postscript Language Tutorial
and Cookbook, 5:562

Post-structuralist Joyce: Es-
says from the French,
1:505
Postwar American Economy:
Performance and Prob-
lems, 3:81
Post War Britain: A Political
History, 3:367
Postwar Britain, 1945–1964,
3:366
Postwar British Fiction,
1:421
Postwar German Literature:
A Critical Introduction,
2:565
The Postwar Japanese Econ-
omy: Its Development and
Structure, 3:479
Postwar Korean Short Sto-
ries, 2:298
Postwar Kuwait—The Middle
East, 3:455
Postwar Poetry of Iceland,
2:640
Postwar Polish Poetry: An
Anthology, 2:811
Potestas Calvium, 4:335
Potiki, 2:976
The Pot of Gold and Other
Plays, 2:391
The Potter's Field, 1:608
The Pottery and Porcelain of
the United States and
Marks of American Pot-
ters, 3:765
The Potting Shed, 1:488
Pouliuli, 2:979, 2:980
Pounamu, Pounamu, 2:977
Pound: The Cantos, 1:873
The Pound Era, 1:415, 1:799,
1:873
Pound-Ford: The Story of a
Literary Friendship, 1:475
Pound's Cantos, 1:873
Pound's Epic Ambition:
Dante and the Modern
World, 1:874, 2:418
Poverty, Ethnicity, and the
American City, 1840–1925,
3:136
Poverty and Famines: An Es-
say on Entitlements and
Deprivation, 3:66
Poverty and Plenty on the
Turkish Farm, 3:453
The Poverty Debate: Politics
and the Poor in America,
3:211
The Poverty of Historicism,
4:409
The Poverty of Nations, 3:53
Poverty of Philosophy, 3:95,
3:290

Praise in The Faerie Queene, 1:198
The Praise of Folly, 4:138, 4:139, 4:147
The Praise of Pleasure, 1:194, 4:148
Praises and Dispraises: Poetry and Politics, the Twentieth Century, 2:988
Praisesong for the Widow, 1:1014
The Prancing Nigger, 1:474
Prancing Novelist, 1:474
Prater Violet, 1:500
Pravda, 1:450, 1:493
Praxeology: An Anthology, 4:32
Praxis, 4:33
Praxis of Liberation and Christian Faith, 4:769
The Praxis of Suffering, 4:896
Prayer and Power: George Herbert and Renaissance Courtship, 1:181
Prayerbook Reform in Europe, 4:652
A Prayer for Owen Meany, 1:992
Prayer in Judaism, 4:600
Prayers for Dark People, 1:832, 3:578
The Praying Man, 2:333, 2:334
The Preaching of Islam, 4:567, 4:574
Precalculus Mathematics, 5:480
Precaution: A Novel, 1:663
Precepts and Counsels on Scientific Investigation, 5:810
Pre-Christian Ireland: From the First Settlers to the Early Celts, 3:370
Precious Irony: The Theatre of Jean Giraudoux, 2:481
The Precipice, 2:723
Precolonial Africa: An Economic and Social History, 3:417
Pre-Colonial African Trade, 3:420
Precolonial Black Africa, 3:429
Pre-Columbian Architecture of Mesoamerica, 3:762
The Predatory Behavior among Wild Chimpanzees, 5:827
The Predecessors of Shakespeare, 1:170

Predestination, God's Foreknowledge, and Future Contingents, 4:120
The Predicament of Culture, 3:22
Predictions for the Ensuing Year, 1:259
Prefaces to English Nineteenth-Century Theatre, 1:322, 1:323
Prefaces to the Experience of Literature, 1:129, 1:1058
The Prefaces to the Waverley Novels, 1:299
Preface to a Twenty Volume Suicide Note, 1:941
Preface to Chaucer: Studies in Medieval Perspectives, 1:151
Preface to Democratic Theory, 3:142
A Preface to Donne, 1:178
A Preface to Grants Economics: The Economy of Love and Fear, 3:71
A Preface to Hardy, 1:363
A Preface to Hopkins, 1:365
A Preface to Metaphysics: Seven Lectures on Being, 4:307
A Preface to Morality, 4:389
A Preface to Morals, 3:158, 3:815
A Preface to Philosophy, 4:25
Preface to Plato, 4:81
A Preface to Politics, 3:158, 3:814, 3:815
Preface to Shakespeare, 1:249
Pregnancy, Birth, and the Early Months: A Complete Guide, 5:358
Pregnancy, Childbirth, and the Newborn, 5:359
Pregnancy and Life-Style Habits, 5:358
The Pregnancy Book for Today's Woman, 5:359
Pregnant Is Beautiful, 5:357
A Prehistoric Bibliography, 4:431
Prehistoric Textiles, 3:767
The Prehistory of Flight, 5:219
The Prehistory of the Mediterranean, 3:299
Preindustrial City: Past and Present, 3:217
Pre-Inferno Plays, 2:680
Prejudice, 3:209
Prejudices, 1:807

Preliminary Discourse on Philosophy in General, 4:219
Preliminary Stocktaking, 2:767
Preliminary Survey of British Literature on South-East Asia in the Era of Colonial Decline and Decolonisation, 2:311
Prelude (Mansfield), 2:978
The Prelude (Wordsworth), 1:305, 1:306
Prelude to Bolshevism, 3:396
Prelude to Civil War, 3:524
Prelude to Galileo, 4:144
Prelude to Independence: The Newspaper War on Britain, 1764–1776, 3:596
Prelude to Mathematics, 5:482
Prelude to Space, 1:614
Prelude to the Partition of West Africa, 3:420
Premature Babies: A Handbook for Parents, 5:323
The Premature Baby Book, 5:322
Premchand, a Life, 2:180
The Premie Parents' Handbook, 5:323
Prenn Drifting, 2:801
The Prentice Hall Encyclopedia of World Proverbs, 1:115
Prentice-Hall Guide to English Literature, 1:132
Prentice-Hall Handbook for Writers, 1:118
Preparation for the Gospel, 4:709
Preparing for Childbirth: A Couple's Manual, 5:359
Preparing for Construction in the 21st Century, 5:223
Preparing to Enter Dental School, 5:335
Prepositions: The Collected Critical Essays of Louis Zukofsky, 1:1068
The Pre-Raphaelite Dream (The Pre-Raphaelite Tragedy), 1:315
The Pre-Raphaelite Imagination, 1848–1900, 1:315
The Pre-Raphaelite Poets, 1:315, 1:316
The Pre-Raphaelites and Their Circle, 1:316
Pre-Raphaelite Writing, 1:316
Pre-Raphaelitism: A Collection of Critical Essays, 1:315

Preromanticism, 1:225
Preschool: Appropriate Practices, 3:253
Prescott and His Publishers, 1:694
Prescription Medicide: The Goodness of Planned Death, 5:378
Prescriptions for Death: The Drugging of the Third World, 5:352
The Presence of Ford Madox Ford: A Memorial Volume of Essays, 1:476
Presence of Grace, 1:1033
The Presence of Hawthorne, 1:677
The Presence of René Char, 2:466
The Presence of Stoicism in Medieval Thought, 4:57
The Present, 1:414
The Present Age in British Literature, 1:417
The Present and Past, 1:462
The Presentation of Self in Everyday Life, 3:228
A Present for Young Ladies: Containing Poems, 1:643
Present Indicative: An Autobiography, 1:465
Presenting Paul Zindel, 1:1123
Present Philosophical Tendencies, 4:266
Present Status of the Philosophy of Law and of Rights, 4:296
Present Tense, 2:904
The Preservation of Books in Tropical and Subtropical Countries, 1:26
The Preservation of Leather Bookbindings, 1:26
The Preservation of the Species: The Value of Biological Diversity, 5:115
Preservation Planning Program, 1:23
The Presidency: A Research Guide, 3:506
The Presidency of James Earl Carter, Jr., 3:538
The Presidency of Theodore Roosevelt, 3:531, 3:595
The Presidency of Woodrow Wilson, 3:531
Presidential Addresses and State Papers, 3:594
Presidential Anecdotes, 3:542
Presidential Campaigns, 3:542

The Presidential Character: Predicting Performance in the White House, 3:146
Presidential Debates: The Challenge of Creating an Informed Electorate, 3:144
Presidential Economics, 3:55
Presidential Mission, 1:879
Presidential Power and the Modern Presidents, 3:147
President Masaryk Tells His Story, 2:790
President Reagan: The Role of a Lifetime, 3:537
President Roosevelt and the Coming of the War, 1941, 3:565
The Presocratic Philosophers, 4:50
The Presocratic Philosophers: A Critical History with a Selection of Texts, 4:50
The Presocratic Philosophers: An Annotated Bibliography, 4:51
The Presocratics, 4:50
The Pre-Socratics: A Collection of Critical Essays, 4:51
The Press and America: An Interpretative History of the Mass Media, 1:8, 3:806
The Press and Public, 3:203
The Press and the American Revolution, 1:6, 3:564
Press Control around the World, 3:806
Pressure Drop, 2:159
The Pretenders, 2:331
Pretender to the Throne: The Further Adventures of Private Ivan Chonkin, 2:772
Pretend the World Is Funny and Forever, 3:871, 5:422
Pretty Lady, 1:443
Preventing War in the Nuclear Age, 3:149
The Prevention Guide to Surgery and Its Alternatives, 5:405
Prevention of Child Maltreatment, 5:417
Prevent Your Heart Attack, 5:374
The Price, 1:1103, 1:1104
The Price of the Ticket: Collected Nonfiction 1948–1985, 1:939
Prices and Production, 3:82
Pricksongs and Descants, 1:963

Prick Up Your Ears: The Biography of Joe Orton, 1:530
Pride and Passion: Robert Burns, 1759–1796, 1:280
Pride and Prejudice, 1:275
Priest and A Dead Priestess Speaks, 1:826
Priest and Revolutionary, 4:741
Priestley in America, 1794–1804, 5:753
A Priest of Consciousness: Essays on Conrad Aiken, 1:810
The Priest of Love: A Life of D. H. Lawrence, 1:510
Priests, Warriors and Cattle: A Study in the Ecology of Religions, 4:435
Priests and Politicians: Manitoba Schools and the Election of 1896, 3:614
A Priest's Diary, 2:663
Prima che il gallo canti, 2:432
The Primacy of Perception, 4:310
The Primal Curse: The Myth of Cain and Abel in the Theatre, 2:985
Primal Myths: Creating the World, 4:427
Primal Vision, Selected Writings, 2:568
Primary Elections, 3:162
The Primary English Class, 1:1094
Primary Health Care of the Older Adult, 5:316
Primary Ousia: An Essay on Aristotle's Metaphysics Z and H, 4:69
Primary Philosophy, 4:24
The Primary Source: Tropical Forests and Our Future, 5:823
The Primary World of the Senses, 5:470
Primate Visions, 1:1147, 5:33, 5:201
The Prime Minister, 1:405
Prime Movers: The Makers of Modern Dance in America, 3:733
Prime Moves: Low-Impact Exercises for the Mature Adult, 5:326
The Prime of Life, 2:458
The Prime of Miss Jean Brodie, 1:551

A Primer in Data Reduction:
An Introductory Statistics
Textbook, 5:521
A Primer of Behavioral Phar-
macology, 5:350
A Primer of Book Collecting,
1:34
A Primer of Freudian Psy-
chology, 3:178, 3:184
A Primer of Freudian Psy-
chology: Twenty-Fifth An-
niversary Edition, 5:448
A Primer of Group Psycho-
therapy, 5:419
A Primer of Jungian Psychol-
ogy, 5:456
A Primer of Soto Zen, 4:538
A Primer of Statistics for Po-
litical Scientists, 3:155
A Primer on Chemical De-
pendency, 5:428
A Primer to Bookbinding,
1:23
Prime Time, Our Time,
3:812
Prime-Time Television: Con-
tent and Control, 3:811
Primitive Architecture, 3:762
Primitive Art, 3:28, 3:758
Primitive Christianity: In Its
Contemporary Setting,
4:617, 4:807, 4:831
Primitive Classification, 3:225
Primitive Culture, 3:14, 3:30
Primitive Polynesian Econo-
my, 3:16
Primitive Rebels, 3:405
The Primitive World and Its
Transformations, 3:14, 3:39
Primo Vere, 2:415
The Prince, 2:398, 2:413,
3:160, 3:333, 4:144, 4:145
The Prince and the Letters,
2:405
The Prince and the Pauper,
1:780
Prince Edward Island and
Confederation, 1863–1873,
3:612
Prince Friedrich von Hom-
burg, 2:599
Prince Hagen: A Phantasy,
1:880
Prince Jin-Gim's Textbook of
Tibetan Buddhism, the
"Sesbya Rab-Gsal," 4:543
Prince of Darkness, 1:1033
Prince of Darkness and Oth-
er Stories, 1:1033
A Prince of Our Disorder:
The Life of T. E. Law-
rence, 3:437, 3:926
The Prince of Parthia, 1:626

Prince of Publishers: A Study
of the Work and Career of
Jacob Tonson, 1:44
A Prince of the Church,
4:254
Prince of the Ghetto, 2:43
The Prince of the House of
David, 1:1244
Princeps a Diis Electus,
4:452
Princeps Concordiae: Pico
della Mirandola and the
Scholastic Tradition, 4:153
Princes and Peasants: Small-
pox in History, 5:36, 5:389
Princess, 1:356
The Princess and Curdie,
1:587
The Princess and Other Sto-
ries, 2:708
The Princess and the Goblin,
1:587
Princess Bell Etoile, 1:583
The Princess Casamassima,
1:763
The Princess of Clèves, 2:484
A Princess of Mars, 1:1256
The Princess Waits, 2:61
The Princeton Companion to
Classical Japanese Litera-
ture, 2:272
The Princeton Encyclopedia
of Classical Sites, 3:298
The Princeton Encyclopedia
of Poetry and Poetics,
1:131, 2:3
Princeton Studies on the
Near East, 4:569
Princeton University Press,
1905–1980, 1:43
Principal Navigations, Voy-
ages, Traffiques, and Dis-
coveries of the English
Nation, 3:922
The Principal Upanishads,
4:354
Principia Ethica, 4:312
Principia Mathematica, 4:323,
4:341, 4:738, 5:84, 5:102,
5:516, 5:606, 5:705
Principi di una scienza nuo-
va, 2:442
Principium Sapientiae: The
Origins of Greek Philo-
sophical Thought, 4:50
Principle and Practice, or
The Orphan Family: A
Tale, 1:375
The Principle of Hope, 4:277
Principle of Lasers, 5:698
The Principle of Reason,
4:291

Principles, Dialogues and
Philosophical Correspon-
dence, 4:191
The Principles and Practice
of Medicine, 5:54, 5:363,
5:364
Principles and Proofs: Aris-
totle's Theory of Demon-
strative Science, 4:70
Principles for Oral Narrative
Research, 3:848
Principles of Anatomy: Physi-
ology, 5:773
Principles of a New Science
on the Nature of Nations,
2:442
Principles of Animal Ecol-
ogy, 5:819
Principles of Arable Crop
Production, 5:263
The Principles of Art, 4:282
Principles of Art History,
3:758
Principles of Behavior: An
Introduction to Behavior
Theory, 3:187
Principles of Bibliographical
Description, 1:62
Principles of Biochemistry,
5:774
Principles of Biochemistry:
General Aspects, 5:774
Principles of Biochemistry:
Mammalian Biochemistry,
5:774
Principles of Biomedical Eth-
ics, 5:118, 5:132
Principles of Catholic Theol-
ogy: Building Stones for a
Fundamental Theology,
4:746, 4:891
Principles of Chemical In-
strumentation, 5:735
Principles of Chemistry,
5:750
Principles of Christian Theol-
ogy, 4:719
The Principles of Classical
Dance, 3:732
Principles of Classical Japa-
nese Literature, 2:272
Principles of Communication
Systems, 5:300
Principles of Compiler De-
sign, 5:549
Principles of Computer Sci-
ence, 5:549
Principles of Data-Base Man-
agement, 5:560
Principles of Database Sys-
tems, 5:560
The Principles of Descartes'
Philosophy, 4:171, 4:186

Principles of Digital and Analog Communications, 5:299

Principles of Economics, 3:93

Principles of Electrical Engineering, 5:200

Principles of Electromagnetic Compatibility, 5:307

Principles of Electron Tunneling Spectroscopy, 5:672

Principles of Geochemistry, 5:628

Principles of Geographical Information Systems for Land Resources Assessment, 3:120

Principles of Geology, 5:645

Principles of Gestalt Psychology, 3:177

Principles of Group Treatment, 5:434

Principles of Interactive Computer Graphics, 5:565

Principles of Literary Criticism, 1:926

Principles of Logic, 4:220

The Principles of Mathematics, 4:323, 5:102, 5:493, 5:516

The Principles of Mechanics, 5:694

The Principles of Nature: Her Divine Revelation and a Voice to Mankind, 4:850

Principles of Nuclear Magnetic Resonance in One and Two Dimensions, 5:744

Principles of Optical Fiber Measurements, 5:304

Principles of Paleontology, 5:624, 5:639

Principles of Philosophy, 4:168, 4:169, 5:41

The Principles of Physical Optics, 5:700

Principles of Physiological Psychology, 3:197

Principles of Political Economy, 4:244

The Principles of Political Economy, Considered with a View to Their Practical Application, 3:92, 3:96

The Principles of Political Economy and Taxation, 3:101

Principles of Polymer Chemistry, 5:746

Principles of Programming Languages, 5:551

The Principles of Psychology, 1:768, 3:187, 3:240, 4:255, 4:236, 5:453

Principles of Quantum Electrodynamics, 5:698

The Principles of Quantum Mechanics, 5:680

Principles of Scientific Thinking, 5:63

Principles of Soil Chemistry, 5:264

Principles of Stellar Systems, 5:677

The Principles of the Most Ancient and Modern Philosophy, 4:167

Principles of the Philosophy of the Future, 4:228

Principles of the Theory of Heat, 5:700

Principles of Topological Psychology, 3:189

The Printed Book in America, 1:7

Printed Ephemera, 1:32

The Printer and the Pardoner, 1:10

Printers and Press Freedom, 3:809

The Printer's Composition Matrix, 1:16

The Printer's Manual, an Abridgment of Stower's Grammar, Comprising all the Plans in that Work for Imposing Forms, Several Tables and other Useful Articles, 1:11

Printing, Book Collecting and Illustrated Books, 1:7

The Printing and Proof-reading of the First Folio Shakespeare, 1:207

Printing and Society in Early America, 1:9, 3:801

Printing and the Mind of Man, 1:7

Printing for Pleasure, 1:10

The Printing Ink Manual, 1:21

Printing in the Americas, 1:10

Printing in the Fifteenth Century, 1:12

The Printing Press as an Agent of Change, 1:8, 5:36

Printing Presses, 1:9

The Printing Revolution in Early Modern Europe, 1:8

Printing the Written Word, 1:8

Printing Types: An Introduction, 1:17

Printing Types: Their History, Forms, and Use, 1:20

Printing Types and How to Use Them, 1:16

Printing With the Handpress, 1:6

Printmaking: History and Process, 3:758

Printmaking Methods Old and New, 1:29

Prior Analytics, 4:66, 4:164

The Prism of Piety, 4:738

Prisms, 4:393

Prison Diary, 2:340

Prisoner of Grace, 1:456

The Prisoner of Second Avenue, 1:1113

The Prisoner of Sex, 1:1011

The Prisoner of War, 1:366

The Prisoner of Zenda, 1:1244

Prisoner's Dilemma, 5:583

Prisoners without Trial: Japanese Americans in World War II, 3:534

The Prison-House of Language, 1:1149, 2:687

Prison Notebooks: Selections, 4:287

The Prison Papers of Bozorg Alavī: A Literary Odyssey, 2:86

The Pritikin Promise: 28 Days to a Longer, Healthier Life, 5:347

Privacy, 4:339

The Private Albert Einstein, 5:683

Private Domain, 3:753

The Private Ear and the Public Eye, 1:543

The Private Life of Florence Nightingale, 5:363

Private Life of the Romans, 2:381

Private Lives, 1:465

The Private Lives and Professional Identity of Medical Students, 5:336

The Private Lives of Victorian Women, 1:325

The Private Mary Chesnut: The Unpublished Civil War Diaries, 3:602

The Private Memoirs and Confessions of a Justified Sinner, 1:269, 1:291, 1:292

Private Orations, 2:355

The Private Papers of Henry Ryecroft, 1:358

A Private Practice, 5:403

Private Redevelopment of the Central City, 3:128

The Private Self: Theory and Practice of Women's Autobiographical Writings, 1:86

Privates on Parade, 1:524, 1:525

Private Theatricals: The Lives of the Victorians, 1:322

Private View: Behind the Scenes with American Ballet, 3:734, 3:738

Private View: Essays on Literature, 1:467

Private Woman, Public Stage, 1:651

The Private World of Daphne du Maurier, 1:620

The Private World of Jean Giono, 2:481

Privileged Communication and the Press, 3:809

The Privileged Playgoers of Shakespeare's London, 1576–1642, 1:217

The Prize (Wallace), 1:1250

The Prize (Yergin), 5:279, 5:293

The Prizegiving, 2:96

Prize Stories 1988: The O. Henry Awards, 1:921

Prize-Winning American Drama: A Bibliographical and Descriptive Guide, 1:1072

Pro and Contra Wagner, 3:729

Probability: The Foundation of Eugenics, 5:529

Probability and Hume's Inductive Skepticism, 4:203

Probability without Tears, 5:524

The Probable and the Marvelous, 1:268

The Problematic Self, 2:511

The Problem Child, 5:430

The Problem of Burke's Political Philosophy, 4:193

The Problem of Knowledge: Philosophy, Science, and History since Hegel, 4:273, 4:279

The Problem of Pain, 4:776

The Problem of Slavery in the Age of Revolution, 1770–1823, 3:523

The Problem of Slavery in Western Culture, 3:335

Problem of Stagflation, 3:62

The Problem of the Criterion, 4:395

The Problem of the Hexateuch and Other Essays, 4:824, 4:838

The Problem of Unbelief in the Sixteenth Century: The Religion of Rabelais, 2:497, 4:126

The Problem of Verse Language, 2:691

The Problem of World History and the Destiny of Mankind, 3:291

Problems and Other Stories, 1:1060

Problems and Projects, 4:403

Problems from Locke, 4:180

Problems in Materialism and Culture, 1:1128

Problems in Philosophy: West and East, 4:37

Problems in the History of Philosophy, 4:18

Problems in the Literary Biography of Mikhail Sholokhov, 2:756

Problems of a Sociology of Knowledge, 4:332

The Problems of Biology, 5:766

Problems of Cartesianism, 4:183

The Problems of Chemistry, 5:730

The Problems of China, 4:323

The Problems of Christianity, 4:250

The Problems of Consciousness, 4:364

Problems of Dostoevsky's Poetics, 2:714

Problems of Life and Mind, 1:373

Problems of Men, 4:224

Problems of Modern Physics, 5:699

The Problems of Neurosis: A Book of Case Histories, 5:430

The Problems of Philosophers: An Introduction, 4:22

The Problems of Philosophy: Introductory Readings, 4:19, 4:22, 4:23, 4:323

The Problems of Philosophy in Their Interconnection, 4:333

Problems of Religious Pluralism, 4:41

Problems of Russian Romanticism, 2:690

Problems of Soviet Literature, 2:694

Problems of Suffering in the Religions of the World, 4:568, 4:886

Problem-Solving Strategies for Men in Conflict, 5:423

Problem-Solving Therapy: New Strategies for Effective Family Therapy, 5:418

Problem Solving with Structured FORTRAN 77, 5:552

Procedures for Salvage of Water-Damaged Library Materials, 1:27

Procedures from Underground, 2:906

Procedures of Montage in Isaak Babel's "Red Cavalry," 2:700

Proceedings of the 1960 Heat Transfer and Fluid Mechanics Institute, 5:257

Proceedings of the Boston Area Colloquium in Ancient Philosophy, 4:47

Proceedings of the First Italian International Congress on Spinoza, 4:188

Proceedings of the International Congress of Applied Mechanics, 5:257

Proceed with Caution, 5:75

Process and Reality: An Essay in Cosmology, 4:341

The Process Engraver's Compendium for Users of Photo-Process Engraving, 1:29

Processes of Graphic Reproduction in Printing, 1:28

Procession, 3:921

The Process of Capitalist Production as a Whole, 3:51, 3:95

The Process of Circulation of Capital, 3:51, 3:95

The Process of Economic Development in Australia, 3:494

Process Philosophy and Political Ideology, 4:289

Process Philosophy and Social Thought, 4:263, 4:379

Process Theology: An Introductory Exposition, 4:743

Proclaiming a Classic: The Canonization of the Orlando Furioso, 2:407

Proclamation Commentaries: The New Testament Witnesses for Preaching, 4:821

Proclamation Commentaries: The Old Testament Witnesses for Preaching, 4:821

Proclus: A Commentary on the First Book of Euclid's Elements, 4:62

Proclus' Commentary on Plato's Parmenides, 4:62

Procopius, 3:319

Procopius' History of His Own Time, 3:319

Procreation or Pleasure? Sexual Attitudes in American History, 3:551

The Prodigal Land, 2:888

Production, Work, Territory, 3:136

The Productivity Prescription, 5:233

Profane Prose, 2:863

Professional and Reference Books: A Guide for Booksellers, 1:46

Professional Ethics, 5:106

Professional Ethics and Civic Morals, 3:225

Professional Ethics and Law in the Health Sciences, 5:121

Professionalizing Modern Medicine, 5:44

The Professional Quest for Truth, 4:384, 5:152

The Professional Soldier, 3:230

The Professional Writer in Elizabethan England, 1:167

The Profession of Authorship in America, 1800–1870, 1:650

The Profession of Eighteenth-Century Literature, 1:225

The Profession of Letters, 1780–1832, 1:273

The Profession of the Playwright: British Theatre, 1800–1900, 1:323

"The Profession of the Religious" and the Principal Arguments from "The Falsely-Believed and Forged Donation of Constantine," 4:155

Professions of Taste, 1:766

The Professor, 1:334, 1:335

The Professor, the Institute, and DNA, 5:795

The Professor at the Breakfast-Table, 1:677

The Professor at the Breakfast-Table, with the Story of Iris, 1:678

Professor Bernhardi, 2:610, 2:611

The Professor Challenger Adventures: The Lost World and the Poison Belt, 1:607

The Professor of Desire, 1:1041

Professors and Gods, 1:481

The Professor's House, 1:819, 1:820

Professor Unrat, 2:601

Pro File: The Official Directory of the American Institute of Architects, 3:764

Profile of Horace, 2:386

A Profile of Twentieth-Century American Poetry, 1:799

Profiles, Pathways, and Dreams, 5:729

Profiles in American Judaism, 4:651

Profiles in Belief, 4:717, 4:751

Profiles in Jazz: From Sidney Bechet to John Coltrane, 3:669

Profiles of Eleven, 4:656, 4:657

Profiles of Eminent American Chemists, 5:729

Profile Trinidad: A Historical Survey from the Discovery to 1900, 2:932

The Profit Outcast: Trotsky, 1929–1940, 3:295

Profits, Interest, and Investment, 3:82

Profits without Production, 5:234

A Profusion of Spires: Religion in Nineteenth-Century Ontario, 3:609

Program Design with Pseudocode, 5:549

Programmers at Work, 5:542

Programming in Ada, 5:553

Programming Language Design, 5:551

Programming Languages: Design and Implementation, 5:550

Programming Languages, 5:551

Programming on Modula-2, 5:553

Programming Windows 3.1, 5:555

Programs for Profit: How to Really Make Money with a Personal Computer, 5:559

Progress, Coexistence and Intellectual Freedom, 3:397

Progress and Archaeology, 3:13

Progress and Its Problems: Towards a Theory of Scientific Growth, 5:64

Progress and Poverty, 3:80

Progress and Power, 3:567

Progress and Pragmatism, 4:237

Progresse of the Soule, 1:177

Progress for a Small Planet, 3:296

Progress in Animal Biometeorology, 5:774

Progress in Neuroscience: Readings from Scientific American, 5:773

Progress in Optics, 5:667

The Progressive Era and the Great War, 1896–1920, 3:510

The Progressive Historians, Turner, Beard, Parrington, 3:515, 3:566, 3:567, 3:583, 3:599

The Progressive Movement, 1900–1915, 3:583

The Progressive Party in Canada, 3:622

Progressivism, 3:532

The Progress of Love, 2:921

The Progress of Poesy, 1:248

The Progress of Romance: The Politics of Popular Fiction, 1:618

A Progress of Sentiments: Reflections on Hume's Treatise, 4:201

Project for a Revolution in New York, 2:500

Projective and Introjective Identification and the Use of the Therapist's Self, 5:425

Projective Testing and Psychoanalysis, 5:469

Projective Verse, 1:1026

The Project of Reconciliation, 4:233

Project Solar Sail, 1:614

Prolegomena to Any Future Metaphysics, 4:204, 4:205

Prolegomena to Ethics, 4:230

Prolegomena to the Study of Greek Religion, 2:346, 4:479

The Proletarian Moment: The Controversy over Leftism in Literature, 1:794

Proletarian Writers of the Thirties, 1:918

A Proliferation of Prophets, 2:565

Prologue to Revolution, 3:588

Promethean Ethics: Living with Death, Competition, and Triage, 5:135

Prometheus: The Life of Balzac, 2:454

Prometheus Bound, 2:350

Prometheus Unbound: An Interpretation, 1:303

Prometheus Unbound, 1:267, 1:271, 1:302

Prominent Scientists: An Index to Collective Biographies, 5:4, 5:29

The Promise, 1:1032

The Promised City: New York's Jews, 1870–1914, 4:641

The Promised Land, 2:155, 2:820, 2:881

The Promised Land: The Great Black Migration and How It Changed America, 3:212, 3:556

The Promise of Destiny, 1:1199

The Promise of the New South: Life after Reconstruction, 3:531

Promises to Keep, 3:139

A Promise to Keep: The American Encounter with Anti-Semitism, 4:638

Promoters, Patriots, and Partisans, 3:607

Promoting Experimental Learning, 5:41

Promoting Your Health, 5:342

Pronouncing Dictionary of American English, 1:92

Proofreading Manual and Reference Guide, 1:53

Proofs and Refutations: The Logic of Mathematical Discovery, 5:493

Propaganda: The Formation of Men's Attitudes, 5:163, 5:164

Propaganda Technique in the World War, 3:156

The Proper Role of Government, 5:268

Properties as Processes: A Synoptic Study of Wilfred Sellars' Nominalism, 4:334

The Properties of "Othello," 1:214

Propertius: A Hellenistic Poet on Love and Death, 2:392

Propertius: Love and War, 2:392

Propertius: Modernist Poet of Antiquity, 2:392

Prophecy and Politics, 4:656

Prophecy and Society in Ancient Israel, 4:824

Prophecy Deliverance! An Afro-American Revolutionary Christianity, 4:749

Prophet (Hareven), 2:19

The Prophet (Jubran), 2:66

The Prophet Armed, 3:396

The Prophetic Faith, 4:662

The Prophetic Minority: American Jewish Immigrant Radicals, 1880–1920, 4:656

Prophetic Strain: The Greater Lyric in the Eighteenth Century, 1:227

The Prophetic Tradition in American Poetry, 1835–1900, 1:655

Prophetic Waters: The River in Early American Life and Literature, 1:629

The Prophets, 4:823

Prophets of Doom, 2:83

Prophets of Extremity, 4:398

The Prophets of Israel, 3:881

The Prophets of Israel and Their Place in History, 4:492

Prophets of Past Time: Seven British Autobiographers, 1880–1914, 1:429

Prophets of Prosperity: America's First Political Economists, 3:547

A Proposal for Correcting the English, Polite Conversations, etc., 1:260

The Prosecution of John Wyclif, 4:714

The Prose Edda, 2:642, 2:643

The Prose Edda of Snorri Sturluson: Tales from Norse Mythology, 4:437

Prose Fiction of the Cuban Revolution, 2:847

The Prose Fiction of Veniamin A. Kaverin, 2:731

Prose in the Age of Poets, 1:231, 1:273

Proselytism in the Talmudic Period, 4:620

Prose Observations, 1:342

Prose of the British Romantic Movement, 1:274

Prose of the Victorian Period, 1:326

The Prose of the World, 4:310

The Prose Poems and La Fanfarlo, 2:456

Prose Works, 4:843, 4:875

Prose Writers of America, 1:728

The Pro-Slavery Argument, 1:696

The Prospect before Us, 1:828

A Prospect of Ferrara, 2:407

Prospects for a Common Morality, 4:893

Prospects for Interstellar Travel, 5:597

Prospects for Post-Holocaust Theology, 4:648

Prospero's Cell, 1:470, 2:95

The Prostitute in African Literature, 2:112

Prostitution and Victorian Society: Women, Class, and the State, 1:313

Protagoras, 4:78

Protecting Our Children's Teeth, 5:340

Protection or Free Trade, 3:80

Protector of the Faith, 4:694

Protectors of the Land, 5:114

Protect Yourself, 5:556

Protestant, Catholic, Jew: An Essay in American Religious Sociology, 3:213, 4:639, 4:753

Protestant and Roman Catholic Ethics, 4:893, 4:900

The Protestant Ethic and the Spirit of Capitalism, 3:51, 3:55, 3:213, 3:244, 3:334, 4:425

Protestantism and Capitalism and Social Science, 4:722

Protestant Poetics and the Seventeenth-Century Religious Lyric, 1:166

The Protestant Reformation 1517–1559, 4:722, 4:723

Protestants: Birth of a Revolution, 4:722

Protestant Thought in the Nineteenth Century, 4:742

Protocols of Reading, 2:988

Proto-Indo-European: The Archaeology of a Linguistic Problem, 4:436

Proud Empires, 2:934

Proud Flesh, 1:1034

The Proud Tower, 3:343, 3:412

Proust, 2:460

Proust: A Biography, 2:495

Proust: Portrait of a Genius, 2:495

Proust and the Psychology of Decadence in History, 3:284

Proustian Space, 2:496

Providence in the Philosophy of Gersonides, 4:664

Province of Piety: Moral History in Hawthorne's Early Tales, 1:677

Provincial Autonomy: Minority Rights and the Compact Theory, 1867–1921, 3:617

The Provincial Deputation in Mexico, 3:638

The Provincial Letters, 4:185

A Provincial Tale, 2:774

Provisions—A Reader from Nineteenth Century American Women, 1:717

The Provoked Wife, 1:261, 1:262

Prufrock and Other Observations, 1:547

Pruning Manual, 5:787

Prussian Nights: Bilingual Edition, 2:761

The Prussian Officer, and Other Stories, 1:509

The Psalms: A Form-Critical Introduction, 4:823, 4:835

Psalms, 2:859

Psalms 1–59: A Commentary; Psalms 60–150: A Commentary, 4:821

The Psalms in Israel's Worship, 4:823

The Pseudepigrapha and Modern Research with a Supplement, 4:810

Pseudo-Dionysius, 4:63

Pseudonyms and Nicknames Dictionary, 1:77

Psyche: The Cult of Souls and Belief in Immortality among the Greeks, 4:49

Psyche and Symbol, 4:424

Psyche Reborn: The Emergence of H. D., 1:827

Psychiatric Dictionary, 5:415

Psychiatric Ethics, 5:118

Psychiatric Interview, 5:471

Psychiatric Patient Rights and Patient Advocacy: Issues and Evidence, 5:421

A Psychiatric Study of Myths and Fairy Tales, 3:869

A Psychiatrist Discovers India, 5:436

Psychiatry and the Cults: An Annotated Bibliography, 4:857

Psychiatry in Broad Perspective, 5:415

Psycho, 1:1168

Psychoanalysis: The First Ten Years, 1888–1898, 5:449

Psychoanalysis: The Impossible Profession, 5:425

Psychoanalysis, Its Theories and Practical Application, 5:437

Psychoanalysis, Psychology and Literature: A Bibliography, 5:422

Psychoanalysis, Scientific Method, and Philosophy, 5:80

Psychoanalysis, Scientific Method and Philosophy: A Symposium, 4:265

Psychoanalysis and Cultural Theory: Thresholds, 1:1133

Psychoanalysis and Dasein-analysis, 5:437

Psychoanalysis and Faith, 5:446

Psychoanalysis and Interpersonal Psychiatry, 5:471

Psychoanalysis and Literature, 2:989

Psychoanalysis and Society: The Social Thought of Sigmund Freud, 5:447

Psychoanalysis for Teachers and Parents, 5:444

Psychoanalysis of Fire, 4:274

The Psycho-Analytical Treatment of Children: Lectures and Essays, 5:444

Psychoanalytic Criticism: Theory in Practice, 1:927, 1:1133

A Psycho-Analytic Dialogue, 5:446

Psychoanalytic Explorations in Art, 5:425

Psychoanalytic Interpretation in Rorschach Testing, 5:469

Psychoanalytic Pioneers, 5:424

Psychoanalytic Psychology: The Development of Freud's Thought, 5:447

Psychoanalytic Psychology of Normal Development (1970–1980), 5:444

Psychoanalytic Schools from the Beginning to the Present, 5:425

The Psychoanalytic Study of Society, 5:425

A Psychoanalytic Study of the Double in Literature, 2:989

Psychoanalytic Theory, Therapy, and the Self, 5:425

The Psychoanalytic Vocation: Rank, Winnicott, and the Legacy of Freud, 5:472

The Psychobiology of Mind-Body Healing, 5:419

Psychodrama: Resolving Emotional Problems through Role-playing, 5:420

Psychological Approaches to Child Abuse, 5:416

Psychological Aspects of Genetic Counseling, 5:781

Psychological Investigations, 4:315

Psychological Modeling: Conflicting Theories, 5:413

The Psychological Novel, 1:804

Psychological Perspectives on Literature, 1:926

Psychological Perspectives on Politics, 3:147

Psychological Reflections: A New Anthology of His Writings, 1905–1961, 5:455

Psychological Testing, 3:180

The Psychological World of Natsume Sōseki, 2:291

Psychology: A Biosocial Study of Behavior, 3:171

Psychology: An Introduction, 3:168

Psychology: The Briefer Course, 1:768, 5:453

Psychology: The Science of Mental Life, 3:167

Psychology and Arthur Miller, 1:1104

Psychology and the Human Dilemma, 5:462, 5:463

Psychology and the Soul, 5:466

Psychology from an Empirical Standpoint, 4:222

Psychology from the Standpoint of a Behaviorist, 3:196

Psychology of Adjustment: Personal Growth in a Changing World, 5:413

The Psychology of Adolescence, 3:185

The Psychology of Anxiety, 5:427

The Psychology of Aristotle, 4:67

The Psychology of Attitude Change and Social Influence, 3:176

The Psychology of C. G. Jung, 5:456

The Psychology of Composition, 3:835

The Psychology of Computer Vision, 5:570

The Psychology of Death, 5:422

The Psychology of Dementia Praecox, 5:455

The Psychology of Habit According to William Ockham, 4:120

Psychology of Imagination, 4:329

The Psychology of Intelligence, 3:267

The Psychology of Interpersonal Behavior, 3:172

Psychology of Invention in the Mathematical Field, 5:494

The Psychology of Judgment and Decision Making, 3:176

The Psychology of Learning and Motivation, 3:175, 3:176

The Psychology of Myth, Folklore and Religion, 3:869

Psychology of Radio, 5:432

The Psychology of Reasoning, 3:174, 3:181

Psychology of Religion: A Guide to Information Sources, 4:890

The Psychology of Rumor, 3:176, 3:180, 3:202, 5:432

The Psychology of Science: A Reconnaissance, 5:461

Psychology of Science: Contributions to Metascience, 5:153

The Psychology of Sex: A Manual for Students, 5:440

The Psychology of Subnormal Children, 3:185

Psychology of the Child, 3:192

The Psychology of the Sickbed, 5:472

The Psychology of Wants, Interests and Attitudes, 3:269

The Psychology of Women: Future Directions in Research, 3:178

The Psychopath, 5:427

The Psychopath in Society, 5:428

Psychopathology: A Case Book, 5:428

Psychopathology: The Science of Understanding Deviance, 5:427

Psychopathology and Politics, 3:157

Psychopathology and Society, 5:427

The Psychopathology of Everyday Life, 5:447

Psychopharmacology and Psychotherapy, 5:418

The Psychosocial Aspects of AIDS: An Annotated Bibliography, 3:201

The Psychosocial Dimensions of Cancer, 5:372

Psychosomatic Disorders, 5:414

Psychotherapies: A Comparative Casebook, 5:419

Psychotherapy and Existentialism: Selected Papers on Logotherapy, 5:443

Psychotherapy and Personality Change, 5:468

Psychotherapy and Process, 5:438

Psychotherapy by Reciprocal Inhibition, 5:473

Psychotherapy East and West, 4:881, 5:424

Psychotherapy for the 1990s, 5:414

Publica Carmina: Ovid's Books from Exile, 2:390

Public Access Microcomputers: A Handbook for Librarians, 5:544

Public Access Microcomputers in Academic Libraries, 5:544

Public Access to Governmental Information, 1:108

Public Administration: Concepts and Cases, 3:147

Public Affairs Information Service Bulletin, 3:5

The Public and Its Problems: An Essay in Political Inquiry, 4:224

Public and Private High Schools: The Impact of Communities, 3:249

The Publication of Joel Barlow's Columbiad, 1:633

The Public Burning, 1:963

The Public Career of Sir Thomas More, 1:194

Public Choice Theory, 3:67

The Public Commission of the University, 3:258

Public Enemy, 2:666

Public Finance in Theory and Practice, 3:67

The Public Good: Philanthropy and Welfare in the Civil War Era, 3:526

The Public Health Agitation, 1833–48, 1:345

Public Health and the Medical Profession in the Renaissance, 5:77

The Public Image, 1:551

Public Investment, the Rate of Return and Optimal Fiscal Policy, 3:69

Publicity for Books and Authors, 1:47

Public Knowledge: An Essay Concerning the Social Dimension of Science, 5:20

Public Library Catalog, 1:73

Public Opinion, 3:147, 3:158, 3:815

Public Opinion and American Democracy, 3:155

Public Opinion in America: Moods, Cycles, and Swings, 3:148

Public Policy and Politics in America, 3:146

Public Policy and the Aging, 5:317

The Public Realm and the Public Self, 5:82

Public Religion in American Culture, 4:754

Public School Law: Teachers' and Students' Rights, 3:251

Public Sector Economics, 3:67

Published in Paris, 1:37

Publishers, Distributors, and Wholesalers of the United States, 1993–1994, 1:69

Publishers Directory, 1:53, 1:69, 1:114

Publishers for Mass Entertainment in Nineteenth-Century America, 1:38

Publishers' International ISBN Directory, 1:69

Publishers on Publishing, 1:49

Publishers' Trade List Annual, 1:71, 1:114

Publishing: A Complete Guide for Schools, Small Presses and Entrepreneurs, 1:47

Publishing: Inside Views, 1:50

Publishing Children's Books in America, 1919–1976, 1:52

Publishing from the Desktop, 5:562

Publishing in the Third World: Knowledge and Development, 1:48

Publishing in the Third World: Trend Report and Bibliography, 1:48

The Publishing Unwins, 1:45

The Publish-It-Yourself Handbook: Literary Tradition and How To, 1:47

Puccini: A Critical Biography, 3:711

Pudd'nhead Wilson and Other Tales, 1:780

Pueblo Sites in Southeastern Arizona, 3:135

Puella, 1:967

The Puerto Rican Journey, 3:234

Puerto Rico: A Colonial Experiment, 3:640

Puerto Rico: A Political and Cultural History, 3:641

The Pugnacious Presidents: White House Warriors on Parade, 3:541

Pujangga Baru: Literature and Nationalism in Indonesia, 1933–1942, 2:317

Pulitzer Prizes, 1:1990, 1:135

The Pulitzer Prize Story, 1:135

The Pulitzer Prize Story II: 1959–1980, 1:135

Pulling Up the Ladder, 4:345

Punch, 1:324, 1:352, 1:377

Pundits, Poets, and Wits: An Omnibus of American Newspaper Columns, 3:808

The Puppet's Tale, 2:177

Puppets U.S.A.-Texas: Exploring Folklore, Music and Crafts with Puppets, 3:869

Puppet Theatre of Japan, 2:273

Purcell, 3:711

The Purcell Papers, 1:601

The Purchasing Power of Money, 3:76

Pure and Applied Science Books, 1876–1982, 5:5

Pure Gold, 2:667

Pure Logic, 3:84

Pure Lust: Elemental Feminist Philosophy, 1:1187, 4:764, 4:765

Pure Mathematics, 5:582

Pure Politics and Impure Science: The Swine Flu Affair, 5:315

Pure Pragmatics and Possible Worlds: The Early Essays of Wilfrid Sellars, 4:333

The Pure Theory of Capital, 3:82

Pure Theory of Foreign Trade and the Pure Theory of Domestic Values, 3:93

A Purgatorial Flame: Seven British Writers in the Second World War, 1:421

Purgatorio, 2:416

Purim Anthology, 4:599

The Puritan Dilemma: The Story of John Winthrop, 3:518, 3:588

The Puritan Experience, 4:735

The Puritan Family, 3:588

Puritan Influences in American Literature, 1:628

Puritanism and Theatre, 1:190

Puritanism and the Rise of Modern Science: The Merton Thesis, 5:15

Puritanism in America: New Culture in a New World, 1:630

Puritanism in America, 1620–1750, 1:628

The Puritan Lectureships: The Politics of Religious Dissent, 1560–1662, 4:734

The Puritan Moment: The Coming of Revolution in an English County, 3:360

The Puritan Ordeal, 1:627

The Puritan Origins of the American Self, 1:627, 1:948

The Puritans: A Sourcebook of Their Writings, 1:630, 3:511

Puritans, Indians and Manifest Destiny, 1:632

Puritans and Adventurers: Changes and Persistence in Early America, 3:516

Puritans and Predestination, 4:735

The Puritans in America: A Narrative Anthology, 4:753

The Puritan Way of Death: A Study in Religion, Culture, and Social Change, 4:735

Purity and Danger, 3:28, 3:29

Purity and Pollution in Zoroastrianism: Triumph over Evil, 4:547

Purity Crusade: Sexual Morality and Social Control, 1868–1900, 3:553

Purity of Diction in English Verse, 1:225, 1:296, 1:466

Purity of Heart, 4:239

The Purloined Letter, 1:1226

The Purple Land, 1:365

The Purpose and Meaning of Jewish Existence, 4:663

Purposes of Art: An Introduction to the History and Appreciation of Art, 3:757

Purposive Behavior in Animals and Men, 3:195

Pursuing Melville: Nineteen Forty to Nineteen Eighty, 1:689

Pursuing Parenthood: Ethical Issues in Assisted Reproduction, 5:121

The Pursuit, 2:859

The Pursuit of Equality in American History, 3:543

The Pursuit of Happiness: Family and Values in Jefferson's Virginia, 3:521

The Pursuit of Meaning: Viktor Frankl, Logotherapy, and Life, 5:444

The Pursuit of Power, 3:289

The Pursuit of Salvation, 1:489

The Pursuit of Science in Revolutionary America, 1735–1789, 5:44

The Pursuit of Signs, 1:924, 1:1141

Pursuit of the Millennium, 4:698, 4:721

Pursuit of the Prodigal, 1:937

Pursuit of Truth, 4:411, 5:100

Pursuits of Happiness, 3:517

Push Comes to Shove: An Autobiography, 3:753

Pushkin, 2:752

Pushkin: A Concordance to the Poetry, 2:752

Pushkin: Literature and Social Ideas, 2:752

The Pushkin House, 2:702

Pushkin Plus: Lyric Poems of Eight Russian Poets, 2:694

Pushkin's I. P. Belkin, 2:752

Pushkin's Prose, 2:752

Pushkin Today, 2:751

Puss-in-Boots, 1:583

Put Out More Flags, 1:562

Putting Dell on the Map: A History of Dell Paperbacks, 1:41
Puttin' on Ole Massa, 3:867
Puzzles, Paradoxes and Problems: A Reader for Introductory Philosophy, 4:21
Puzzles, Problems and Enigmas, 5:20
Puzzles and Paradoxes, 5:496
Puzzling Shakespeare: Local Reading and Its Discontents, 1:209
Pygmalion, 1:425, 1:544, 1:545
Pylon, 1:835
Pynchon: A Collection of Critical Essays, 1:1035
Pynchon: The Voice of Ambiguity, 1:1035
Pynchon's Fictions, 1:1035
The Pyramid, 1:483, 1:484
The Pyramids of Egypt, 3:300
Pyramids of Sacrifice: Political Ethics and Social Change, 5:128
Pythagoras: A Life, 5:514
Pythagoras: The Reality of the New Computer Age, 5:515
Pythagoras and Early Pythagoreanism, 4:87, 5:515
Pythagoras Revived: Mathematics and Philosophy in Late Antiquity, 5:515
Pythagorean Proposition, 5:514
Pythagoreans and Elatics, 4:87
The Pythagorean Sourcebook and Library, 4:87, 5:514
The Pythagorean Triangle: The Science of Numbers, 5:515
The Pythagorean Writings, 5:514

Q

Qasr al-Shawq, 2:67
QED: The Strange Theory of Light and Matter, 5:685
Qian Zhongshu, 2:243
"Qindil Umm Hashim," 2:64
Quad, 1:439
The Quakers in Puritan England, 4:733
Qualitative Analysis: Historical and Critical Essays, 3:230

Qualitative and Quantitative Social Research, 3:231
Quality of Life: The New Medical Dilemma, 5:123
A Quality of Violence, 2:941
The Quality School: Managing Students without Coercion, 5:451
Quanta: A Handbook of Concepts, 5:659
The Quantifying Spirit in the Eighteenth Century, 5:44
The Quantitative Analysis of Social Problems, 5:524
Quantitative Laws in Biological Chemistry, 5:738
Quantitative Methods for Historians: A Guide to Research Statistics, 3:276
Quantities, 1:989
Quantum Concepts in Space and Time, 5:709
Quantum Electronics, 5:697
Quantum Gravity 2: A Second Oxford Symposium, 5:709
Quantum Kinematics and Dynamics, 5:715
Quantum Mechanics, 5:660
Quantum Mechanics of One and Two Electron Atoms, 5:672
Quantum Physics of Atoms, Molecules, Solids, Nuclei and Particles, 5:660
Quantum Reality, 5:662
Quantum Theory and Measurement, 5:719
Quantum Theory and Nonlocal Fields, 5:721
Quantum Theory and the Schism in Physics, 4:409, 5:98, 5:660
The Quantum Theory of Radiation, 5:717
The Quantum Universe, 5:660
The Quantum World, 5:660
The Quare Fellow, 1:424, 1:441
Quarks: The Stuff of Matter, 5:662
The Quarrel over Future Contingents (Louvain, 1465–1475), 4:104
Quarrels That Have Shaped the Constitution, 3:542
The Quarterly Review, 1:323
"The Quarterly Review" under Gifford, 1:274
Quartermaine's Terms, 1:486
Quartet, 2:627

Quartet in Autumn, 1:538, 1:539
Quartet of the Quarter Moon, 2:330
Quasars, Pulsars, and Black Holes: A Scientific Detective Story, 5:655
Quasi Una Fantasia: Essays on Music and Culture, 4:393
Quaternary Dating Methods, 5:623
Quebec: A History 1867–1929, 3:609
Quebec: The Revolutionary Age, 1760–1791, 3:613
Quebec, 1759: The Siege and the Battle, 3:612
Quebec, Where Ancient France Lingers, 3:875
Quebec and Its Historians: The Twentieth Century, 3:606, 3:621
Quebec and Its Historians 1840–1920, 3:606, 3:619, 3:620
Quebec Women: A History, 3:608
Queen Anne, 3:360
Queen Mary, 1:321
The Queen of Hearts, 1:346, 1:580
The Queen of Spades, 2:750
Queen of Spades and Other Stories, 2:751
The Queen of Swords, 1:1187, 1:1188
The Queen of the Damned, 1:1242
The Queen of Wands, 1:1187, 1:1188
The Queen's Diadem, 2:672
Queen's Rebels: Ulster Unionism in Historical Perspective, 3:371
Queneau's Fiction: An Introductory Study, 2:497
Quentin Durward, 1:298
The Quest: History and Meaning in Religion, 4:474
Quest for an American Sociology, 3:237
Quest for An Island, 2:698
A Quest for a Non-Violent Russia, 2:766
The Quest for Being and Other Studies in Naturalism and Humanism, 4:298
The Quest for Certainty, 4:223
The Quest for Christa T., 2:615, 2:616

The Quest for Community, 3:236
The Quest for El Cid, 2:537
Quest for Eros: Browning and "Fifine," 1:339
Quest for Identity, 5:414
Quest for Kerouac, 1:998
The Quest for Love of Lao Lee, 2:251
The Quest for Meaning of Swami Vivekananda, 4:563
The Quest for Mind, 3:192
The Quest for Permanence, 1:268, 1:294, 1:308
The Quest for Political and Spiritual Liberation, 4:353
The Quest for Quarks, 5:663
The Quest for Shakespeare's Globe, 1:218
Quest for the Human: An Exploration of Saul Bellow's Fiction, 1:948
Quest for the Killers, 5:383
Quest for the Origins of the First Americans, 4:454
Quest for the Real Samoa: The Mead-Freeman Controversy and Beyond, 3:37
Questing Fictions: Latin America's Family Romance, 2:846
Questionable Shapes, 1:758
The Question Concerning Technology and Other Essays, 4:292, 5:90
The Question of Being, 4:291
The Question of "Eclecticism": Studies in Later Greek Philosophy, 4:55
The Question of Hamlet, 1:213
The Question of Henry James, 1:766
A Question of Heroes, 2:330
The Question of Hu, 3:503
The Question of Jean-Jacques Rousseau, 4:279
The Question of Language, 2:109
The Question of Language in Heidegger's History of Being, 4:292
The Question of Palestine, 3:455, 3:460, 4:643
A Question of Power, 2:163
The Question of Value, 4:293
Questions, 2:332
Questions of Cinema, 1:1157
Questions of Third Cinema, 1:1158
Questions of Travel, 1:950
Questions on Wittgenstein, 4:345

Questions Patients Most Often Ask Their Doctors, 5:342
The Quest of the Historical Jesus, 4:826
The Quest of the Quiet Mind: The Philosophy of Krishnamurti, 4:555
The Quest of the Silver Fleece, 1:832, 3:578
Quests for a Promised Land: The Works of Martin Andersen Nexø, 2:653
A Quick and Dirty Guide to War, 3:278
A Quick Graph: Collected Notes and Essays, 1:966
Quicksand, 1:853
Quick Scientific Terminology, 5:2
Quiddities: An Intermittently Philosophical Dictionary, 4:14, 4:411, 5:100
The Quiet American, 1:489, 2:339
The Quiet American and the Ugly American, 1950–1960, 2:311
Quiet Chameleon: Modern Poetry from Central Africa, 2:126
The Quiet Crisis and the Next Generation, 3:550
Quiet Days in Clichy, 1:861, 1:862
The Quiet Don, 2:756
The Quiet Man, 1:1165
The Quimby Manuscripts, 4:847
Quine: Language, Experience, and Reality, 4:412
Quine on Ontology, Necessity, and Experience, 4:412
Quine on Ontology, Necessity and Experience: A Philosophical Critique, 5:100
Quinn's Book, 1:996, 1:997
Quintilian, 2:393
Quintilian as Educator, 2:393
Quintus Fixlein, 2:605
Qui Se Souvient de la Mer, 2:119
Quixotic Scriptures: Essays on the Textuality of Hispanic Literature, 2:523
Quodlibetal Questions, 4:120
Quotations in History, 1:117
Quo Vadis? A Narrative of the Time of Nero, 2:821
The Quran (Khan), 4:587
The Quran (Palmer), 4:587

The Qur'an: A New Translation with a Critical Rearrangement of the Surahs, 4:587
The Qur'an and Its Interpreters, 4:587
The Qur'an as Scripture, 4:587
Qur'ans and Bindings from the Chester Beatty Library, 1:24

R

Raag Darbari, A Novel, 2:178
Rabad of Posquieres: A Twelfth-Century Talmudist, 4:627
Rabat: Urban Apartheid in Morocco, 3:219
Rabbi Moses Nahmanides, 4:669
A Rabbinic Anthology, 4:610
The Rabbinic Class of Roman Palestine in Late Antiquity, 4:621
Rabbinic Fantasies: Imaginative Narratives from Classic Hebrew Literature, 2:9
Rabbinic Lay Confrontations in Jewish Law, 4:627
Rabbinic Political Theory: Religion and Politics in the Mishnah, 4:607
The Rabbinic Traditions about the Pharisees before 70, 4:616
Rabbis and Wives, 2:39
Rabbit, Run, 1:1059, 1:1060
Rabbit at Rest, 1:1059, 1:1060
Rabbit Is Rich, 1:1059, 1:1060
Rabbit Redux, 1:1059, 1:1060
Rabbits and Boa Constrictors, 2:729
Rabdologiae; seu Numerationes per Virgulas libri duo, 5:579
Rabdology, 5:580
Rabelais, 2:497
Rabelais and His World, 2:497
Rabi: Scientist and Citizen, 5:651
Rabindranath Tagore: Perspectives in Times, 2:183
Rabindranath Tagore: Poet and Dramatist, 2:183
Rabindranath Tagore's Aesthetics, 2:183

Race: Science and Politics, 3:27

Race, Culture, and Evolution, 3:11, 3:28

Race, Gender, and Desire, 1:917

Race, Law, and American History, 1700–1990, 3:555

Race, Reform, and Rebellion, 3:556

Race, Sex, and Class under the Raj, 3:484

Race and Colour in Islam, 3:443, 4:571

Race and History: Selected Essays, 1938–1988, 3:555, 3:579

Race and Nationalism in Trinidad and Tobago, 3:641

The Race and Other Stories, 2:925

Race and Representation, 3:212

Race and Slavery in the Middle East, 3:459

Race Differences, 3:174, 3:188

Race Differences in Intelligence, 3:175

Race in America: The Struggle for Equality, 3:555

Rachel Ray, 1:406

Rachel Vernhagen: The Life of a Jewish Woman, 4:394

Rachel Weeping: The Case against Abortion, 4:894

Rachmaninoff: His Life and Times, 3:712

Rachmaninoff, 3:712

Racial Determinism and the Fear of Miscegenation Pre-1900, 3:557

The Racial Economy of Science: Toward a Democratic Future, 5:25

Racial Equality in America, 3:579

Racial Hygiene: Medicine under the Nazis, 5:80, 5:123

"Racial Matters": The FBI's Secret File on Black America, 1960–1972, 3:557

The Racial Problem in the Works of Richard Wright and James Baldwin, 1:906

Racine: A Theatrical Reading, 2:498

Radhakrishnan: A Biography, 4:354

Radhakrishnan: A Religious Biography, 4:354, 4:508

Radhakrishnan: His Life and Ideas, 4:354

Radhakrishnan and the Ways to Oneness of East and West, 4:354

Radhasoami Reality: The Logic of a Modern Faith, 4:508

The Radiant City (La Ville Radieuse), 3:778

The Radiant Way, 1:468

Radiation and Human Health, 5:324

Radiative Transfer, 5:677

Radical Artifice: Writing Poetry in the Age of Media, 1:914

Radical Departures: Desperate Detours to Growing Up, 4:856

The Radical Durkheim, 3:225

The Radical Empiricism of William James, 4:238

Radical Geography, 3:119

Radical Innocence: Studies in the Contemporary Novel, 1:917

Radicalism and the Origins of the Vietnamese Revolution, 3:491

The Radicalism of the American Revolution, 3:522

The Radical Kingdom: The Western Experience of Messianic Hope, 4:785

The Radical Left and American Foreign Policy, 3:546

The Radical Reformation, 4:724, 4:733

Radicals, Secularists and Republicans, 3:364

The Radical Spinoza, 4:189

Radical Spirits, 4:850

Radical Stages: Alternative History in Modern British Drama, 1:426

Radical Tragedy, 1:212

Radical Visions and American Dreams, 3:561

The Radical Whigs, John Trenchard and Thomas Gordon, 3:362

Radioactive Waste Disposal, 5:177

Radio and Television: A Selected, Annotated Bibliography, 3:802

Radio and the Printed Page, 3:203, 3:230

Radio Broadcasts of Will Rogers, 3:886

Radiocarbon Dating, 5:750

Radio in the Television Age, 3:811

Radio Listening in America: The People Look at Radio Again, 3:203

Radiology of the Foot and Ankle, 5:396

Radio Research, 1941, 3:230

Radio's Golden Years, 3:812

Radio System Design for Telecommunications (1–100 GHz), 5:306

The Ra Expeditions, 3:924

Rafael Alberti's Poetry of the Thirties: The Poet's Public Voice, 2:529

Rafael Carrera and the Emergence of the Republic of Guatemala, 1821–1871, 3:637

R. A. Fisher: The Life of a Scientist, 5:528

The Raft, 2:133

The Raft Is Not the Shore, 4:562

The Raft of Muhammad, 4:579

Ragazzi di Vita, 2:431

Rage of Angels, 1:1223

A Rage to Live, 1:867

Ragged Dick, 1:1194

Ragtime, 1:968, 1:969

Rahner, Heidegger and Truth, 4:292

A Rahner Reader, 4:745

The Raid and Other Stories, 2:764

Railways: Past, Present and Future, 5:247

Rain, 1:520

The Rainbow, 1:508, 1:509

The Rainbow and the Rose, 2:962

Rainbow in the Mist, 1:1238

The Rainbow Makers, 5:752

Rainbow of Hope: A Guide for the Special Needs Child, 5:376

Rainbow's End, 1:608

Rainer Maria Rilke, 2:608

Rain One Step Away, 2:97

Rain on Fire: The Murder of Chico Mendes and the End of the Amazon, 2:900

Rains in the Jungle, 2:322

The Rainy Spell and Other Korean Stories, 2:300

Raise High the Roof Beam, Carpenters, 1:1043

Raise High the Roof Beam, Carpenters and Seymour: An Introduction, 1:1043

Raise Race Rays Raze: Essays since 1965, 1:941
Raising Black Children, 3:249
Raising Demons, 1:992
Raising Standards for American Education, 3:251
A Raisin in the Sun, 1:1092
The Raj: India and the British 1600–1947, 3:485
The Raj, the Indian Mutiny, and the Kingdom of Oudh, 1801–1859, 3:485
Rakhmaninoff, 3:712
The Rakish Stage: Studies in English Drama, 1660–1800, 1:228
Ralph Cudworth: An Interpretation, 4:168
Ralph Ellison: A Collection of Critical Essays, 1:974
Ralph the Heir, 1:406
Ralph Waldo Emerson, 1:670, 1:671
Ralph Waldo Emerson: A Biography, 1:670
Ramakerti, 2:315
Ramakien: The Thai Epic, 4:518
Ramakrishna: His Life and Sayings, 4:354
Ramakrishna and His Disciples, 4:354, 4:563
Ramakrishna and His Message, 4:355
Ramakrishna and Vivekananda: New Essays, 4:355
Ramanujan's Notebooks, 5:488
Rāmāyana, 2:171, 2:172, 2:315, 2:321, 2:337, 4:502, 4:509
Rāmāyana at a Glance, 2:171
The Ramayana in Laos: A Study of the Gvay Dvorahbi, 2:322
The Rāmāyana of R. K. Narayan, 2:172
The Ramayana of Valmika, 4:504
The Rāmāyana of Vālmīki: Balakanda, 2:171
The Rāmāyana of Vālmīki, 2:172
Ramban (Nahmanides) Commentary on the Torah, 4:669
Ramban: His Life and His Teachings, 4:669
Rameau's Nephew, 2:471, 2:472, 4:195
Rameau's Nephew and D'Alembert's Dream, 4:196

Ram Mohan Roy: Social, Political, and Religious Reform in 19th Century India, 4:355
Ram Mohan Roy, the Apostle of Indian Awakening, 4:355
Ramona, 1:760
Ramón del Valle-Inclán, 2:553
Ramón Pérez de Ayala, 2:546
Ramus, Method, and the Decay of Dialogue, 4:129
Ran, 3:839
Ranch Life and the Hunting Trail, 3:594
Randall Jarrell: A Literary Life, 1:993
Randall Jarrell and The Lost World of Childhood, 1:993
Randall Jarrell's Letters: An Autobiographical and Literary Selection, 1:993
Rand McNally Atlas of the Oceans, 5:616
Rand McNally Goode's World Atlas, 1:84
Rand McNally Road Atlas, 1:1993, 1:84
The Random House Basic Dictionary: Italian, 1:100
The Random House Book of Early Perennials, 5:767
The Random House Book of Late Perennials, 5:767
The Random House Book of Twentieth-Century Poetry, 2:448
Random House Dictionary of the English Language, 1:90
The Random House Encyclopedia, 1:107
The Random House Handbook, 1:118
The Random House Speller/Divider, 1:95
Random House Thesaurus, 1:94
Random House Treasury of Best Loved Poems, 1:720
Random Signal Analysis in Engineering Systems, 5:302
Random Thoughts, 2:260
Random Walks in Biology, 5:775
The Range of Human Capacities, 3:196
Ransoming the Time, 4:307
The Ransom of Red Chief, 1:757
Ranthorpe, 1:373
Rape and Revelation, 2:985

Rape and Writing in the "Heptameron" of Marguerite de Navarre, 2:492
The Rape of Bunny Stuntz, 1:1090, 1:1091
The Rape of Lucrece, 1:202, 1:203, 1:215
Rape of Shavi, 2:137
The Rape of the Lock, 1:251, 1:252
Raphael, 3:788
Raphael: His Life, His Art, His Fortunes, 3:788
Raphael, His Life and Works, 3:788
The Rapids, 3:427
A Rare Benedictine, 1:609
Rare Books 1983–84: Trends, Collections, Sources, 1:77
A Rare Book Saga: The Autobiography of H. P. Kraus, 1:42
Rare Books and Royal Collectors: Memoirs of an Antiquarian Bookseller, 1:31
The Rash Act, 1:475
Rashi: His Life and Works, 4:671
Rashi: The Man and His World, 4:671
Rashi and the Christian Scholars, 4:671
Rashomon and Other Stories, 2:285
Rasselas, 1:247
The Rastafarians: Sounds of Cultural Dissonance, 4:467
The Rat, 2:583
Ratcatcher, 2:767
Rate of Interest, 3:75
The Rate of Interest and Other Essays, 3:102
Rates of Chemical Weathering of Rocks and Minerals, 5:627
Rates of Exchange, 1:448
Rating America's Corporate Conscience, 5:129
The Rating Guide to Life in America's Small Cities, 3:119
Rational Conflict, 3:204
Rational-Emotive Approaches to Problems of Childhood, 5:440
The Rational Enterprise: Logos in Plato's Theaetetus, 4:80
The Rationale of Judicial Evidence, Specially Applied to English Practice, 3:150
Rationalism, Empiricism, and Pragmatism, 4:262, 4:380

Rationality: A Philosophical Inquiry into the Nature and Rationale of Reason, 4:317, 5:101

Rationality: The Critical View, 5:62

Rationality, Relativism and the Human Sciences, 4:381

Rationality, Religious Belief and Moral Commitment, 4:888

Rationality and Irrationality in Economics, 4:242

Rationality and Relativism, 4:405

The Rational Society: A Critical Reading of Santayana's Social Thought, 4:328

Rat Jelly, 2:922

The Rattigan Version: Sir Terence Rattigan and the Theatre of Character, 1:540

Ravel, 3:712

Ravel: His Life and Works, 3:712

Ravel: Man and Musician, 3:712

A Ravel Reader: Correspondence, Articles, Interviews, 3:712

The Raven and the Whale, 1:651, 1:715, 3:587

The Raven in the Foregate, 1:609

The Ravenous Hyenas and the Wounded Sun, 4:501

The Ravished Image: Or How to Ruin Masterpieces by Restoration, 1:27

The Ravishing of Lol V. Stein, 2:474

The Raw and the Cooked, Vol. 1: Mythologiques, 3:33

Rawls: A Theory of Justice and Its Critics, 4:316

Raw Material, 1:547

Ray Bradbury, 1:1255

Raymond Chandler, 1:1228

Raymond Chandler: A Checklist, 1:1228

Raymond Chandler: A Descriptive Bibliography, 1:1228

The Raymond Chandler Omnibus, 1:1228

Raymond Queneau, 2:497

A Ray of Hope: Coping with Radiation Therapy, 5:371

The Ray of the Microcosm, 2:831

Rays of Positive Electricity and Their Application to Chemical Analyses, 5:716

The Razor's Edge, 1:520

Razzle Dazzle: The Life and Work of Bob Fosse, 3:743

R. Buckminster Fuller on Education, 3:254

R. D. Laing, 5:460

R. D. Laing and Anti-Psychiatry, 5:460

The Reaches of Heaven: A Story of the Baal Shem Tov, 2:47

Reach for Tomorrow, 1:614

Reaching for the Moon: On Asian Religious Paths, 4:499, 4:523, 4:535

Reaching Judgment at Nuremberg, 3:377

Reaching Tin River, 2:950

The Reach of Philosophy, Essays in Honor of James Kern Feibleman, 4:284

Reach to Eternity, 2:829

Reaction and Revolution, 1814–1832, 3:340

The Reactionaries—Yeats, Wyndham, Lewis, Pound, Eliot, Lawrence, 1:417

Reactionary Essays on Poetry and Ideas, 1:889

Read All Your Life: A Subject Guide to Fiction, 1:122

Reader, I Married Him, 1:269

A Reader in Bureaucracy, 3:210, 3:233

Reader in Comparative Religion: An Anthropological Approach, 4:426, 4:897

Reader in the History of Books and Printing, 1:12

The Reader in the Text, 1:927

A Reader on Islam, 4:566

Reader-Response Criticism: From Formalism to Post-Structuralism, 1:927, 1:1134

The Reader's Adviser, 1:75, 4:419

The Reader's Catalog, 1:75

The Reader's Companion to American History, 3:508

The Reader's Companion to World Literature, 1:122

Reader's Digest Almanac and Yearbook, 1:1985, 1:83

The Reader's Encyclopedia of Shakespeare, 1:222

The Reader's Encyclopedia of World Drama, 1:131, 2:3

A Reader's Guide to Auden, 1:436

A Reader's Guide to Canadian History 1: Beginnings to Confederation, 3:605

A Reader's Guide to Canadian History 2: Confederation to the Present, 3:605

A Reader's Guide to Fifty British Plays: 1660–1900, 1:428

A Reader's Guide to Fifty Modern British Plays, 1:427

A Reader's Guide to Gerard Manley Hopkins, 1:364

Reader's Guide to Great Britain: A Bibliography, 3:354

A Reader's Guide to Great Twentieth-Century English Novels, 1:421

A Reader's Guide to Gunnar Ekelöf's "A Molna Elegy," 2:673

Reader's Guide to Jack London, 1:774

A Reader's Guide to Japanese Literature, 2:272, 2:282

The Reader's Guide to Microcomputer Books, 5:540

Readers' Guide to Periodical Literature, 1:114

A Reader's Guide to Robert Lowell, 1:1006

A Reader's Guide to Shakespeare's Plays: A Discursive Bibliography, 1:220

A Reader's Guide to the Classic British Mystery, 1:604

A Reader's Guide to the Contemporary English Novel, 1:421

A Reader's Guide to the Great Religions, 4:5, 4:533

Reader's Guide to the Short Stories of Ernest Hemingway, 1:847

A Reader's Guide to the Short Stories of Herman Melville, 1:689

A Reader's Guide to the Short Stories of Mark Twain, 1:784

A Reader's Guide to William Faulkner, 1:838

A Reader's Guide to William Gaddis's "The Recognitions," 1:978

Reading, Writing and Recon-
struction, 3:256
Reading Adrienne Rich: Re-
views and Revisions,
1951–81, 1:1037
Reading America: Essays on
American Literature, 1:794
Reading American Photo-
graphs, 3:516
Reading and Fiction in Gold-
en Age Spain, 2:525
Reading Apollinaire: Theories
of Poetic Language, 2:451
Reading Billy Budd, 1:689
Reading Black, Reading Fem-
inist: A Critical Anthology,
1:1133
Reading Capital, 4:242
Reading Chekhov's Text,
2:710
Reading Chinua Achebe: Lan-
guage and Ideology in Fic-
tion, 2:129
Reading Educational Re-
search, 3:258
Reading Faulkner, 1:837
Reading Faulknerian Trage-
dy, 1:838
Reading for Pleasure: Guide-
lines, 1:34
Reading Gertrude Stein:
Body, Text, Gnosis, 1:883
Reading Habermas, 4:405
Reading Heidegger: Com-
memorations, 4:294
Reading in the 1980s, 1:49
Reading Lists for College-
bound Students, 3:249
Reading Nietzsche, 4:248
A Reading of Eliot's Four
Quartets, 1:473
A Reading of George Her-
bert, 1:181
The Reading of Imagery in
the Chinese Poetic Tradi-
tion, 2:192
A Reading of Paradise Lost,
1:192
A Reading of Proust, 2:495
A Reading of Sir Gawain
and the Green Knight,
1:156
Reading Petronius, 2:391
Reading Philip Roth, 1:1041
Reading Pound Reading:
Modernism after
Nietzsche, 1:873
Reading Race, 1:799
Reading Realism in Stendhal,
2:511
Reading Rorty, 4:413
Readings, 2:467

Readings from the New
Book of Nature, 1:919
Reading Shakespeare in Per-
formance: "King Lear,"
1:214
Readings in African Philoso-
phy: An Akan Collection,
4:369
Readings in Church History,
4:680, 4:719, 4:740
Readings in Eastern Reli-
gions, 4:497, 4:521, 4:533
Readings in Ethical Theory,
4:334
Readings in Ethnomusicol-
ogy, 3:666
Readings in Medieval Poetry,
1:147
Readings in Modern Jewish
History, 4:639
Readings in Philosophical
Analysis, 4:264, 4:334
Readings in Russian Philo-
sophical Thought, 4:31
Readings in Russian Poetics:
Formalist and Structuralist
Views, 2:688
Readings in the History of
Christian Theology, Vol. 2,
4:719
Readings in the Philosophy
of Moses Maimonides,
4:668
Readings in the Qur'an,
4:588
Reading the African Novel,
2:108
Reading the Ashes: An An-
thology of the Poetry of
Modern Macedonia, 2:808
Reading the Book of Nature:
An Introduction to the
Philosophy of Science,
5:63
Reading the Mind of God,
5:19
Reading the Past: Current
Approaches to Interpreta-
tion in Archaeology, 3:13,
3:304
Reading the Past: Maya
Glyphs, 3:628
Reading the Romance: Wom-
en, Patriarchy, and Popu-
lar Literature, 1:1151,
1:1152, 1:1210
Reading the World: Selected
Writings, 1935–1976, 1:977
Reading Twentieth-Century
Poetry, 1:799, 1:913
Reading Wagner: A Study in
the History of Ideas, 3:729

Reading William Blake,
1:278
Reading with Clarice Lispec-
tor, 2:467, 2:896
A Ready Reference to Philos-
ophy East and West, 4:13
Reagan's America, 3:540
Reagent Chemicals, 5:726
The Real Anti-Semitism in
America, 4:640
The Real Inspector Hound,
1:553
The Real Inspector Hound
and After Magritte, 1:554
Realism: A Critique of Bren-
tano and Meinong, 4:222
Realism, History, and Myth
in Defoe's Fiction, 1:240
Realism and Allegory in the
Early Fiction of Mao Tun,
2:258
Realism and Naturalism in
Nineteenth-Century Litera-
ture, 1:715, 1:724
Realism and Reality, 2:566
Realism and the Aim of Sci-
ence, 4:409, 5:98
Realism and the Background
of Phenomenology, 4:263,
4:395
Realism and the Romance,
1:766
Realism in European Theater
and Drama, 1870–1920: A
Bibliography, 1:123
Realism in Modern Litera-
ture, 2:986
The Realism of William
Dean Howells, 1:759
Realism to the Present, 2:645
Realism with a Human Face,
4:410
The Realist at War, 1:759
The Realistic Imagination,
1:270
Realistic Revolt in Modern
Poetry, 1:798
Realistic Romance: The
Prose Fiction of Thomas
Deloney, 1:177
The Realistic Spirit: Wittgen-
stein, Philosophy and the
Mind, 4:345
A Realist Philosophy of Sci-
ence, 4:384
The Realists, 1:550
The Realities behind Diplo-
macy, 3:366
Reality, 4:338, 4:339
Reality, Knowledge and the
Good Life: A Historical In-
troduction to Philosophy,
4:16

Reality and Fiction in Modern Japanese Literature, 2:282

Reality and Scientific Truth, 5:683, 5:710

Reality and the Heroic Pattern, 2:368

Reality and the Poet in Spanish Poetry, 2:526, 2:550

The Reality of the Historical Past, 4:319

Reality Sandwiches: Poems, 1953–1960, 1:981

Reality Therapy: A New Approach to Psychiatry, 5:451

The Reality Therapy Reader, 5:451

Realizing Rawls, 4:316

The Real Life Nutrition Book, 5:345

The Real Life of Sebastian Knight, 2:740

Really Reading Gertrude Stein, 1:1188

The Real Menstrual Cycle, 5:354

The Realm of Algebra, 5:484

The Realm of Rights, 4:387

The Realm of Spirit and the Realm of Caesar, 4:275, 4:758

Realm of the Immortals: Daoism in the Arts of China, 4:528

The Realm of the Nebulae, 5:607

Realms of Gold, 1:468

Realms of Gold: Myths and Legends from around the World, 3:856

The Realms of Healing, 5:419

Real Presences: Is There Anything in What We Say?, 1:1054, 2:989

The Real Thing, 1:554

Real Thing and Other Tales, 1:763

The Real Work: Interviews and Talks, 1964–1978, 1:1052

Reamker (Ramakerti): The Cambodia Version of the Ramayana, 2:315

Reappraisals in History, 3:359

Reappraisals in Renaissance Thought, 4:131

The Rear Column and Other Plays, 1:486

Rear Window, 1:1168

Reason, Grace, and Sentiment, 1:226

The Reason, the Understanding, and the Time, 4:303

The Reasonable Man: Trollope's Legal Fictions, 1:407

The Reasonableness of Christianity and a Discourse on Miracles, 4:178, 4:179, 4:739

Reason and Analysis, 4:276

Reason and Authority in the Eighteenth Century, 4:739

Reason and Belief, 4:276

Reason and Emotion in Psychotherapy, 5:440

Reason and Goodness, 4:276

Reason and Hope: Selections from the Jewish Writings of Hermann Cohen, 4:663

Reason and Human Good in Aristotle, 4:67

Reason and Life: The Introduction to Philosophy, 4:22

Reason and Nature: An Essay on the Meaning of Scientific Method, 4:281

Reason and Rationality in Natural Science: A Group of Essays, 4:317

Reason and Relativism: A Sartrean Investigation, 4:331

Reason and Religious Belief, 4:381

Reason and Responsibility, 4:20

Reason and Revelation: From Paul to Pascal, 4:27

Reason and Revolution: Hegel and the Rise of Social Theory, 4:408, 5:94

Reason and Right: A Critical Examination of Richard Price's Moral Philosophy, 4:211

Reason and the Search for Knowledge, 5:65

Reason and Tradition in Islamic Ethics, 4:575

Reason and Violence: A Decade of Sartre's Philosophy, 1950–1960, 5:459

Reason Awake: Science for Man, 5:107, 5:795

Reason in Art, 4:327

The Reason in a Storm, 1:473

Reasoning and the Logic of Things, 4:248

Reasoning in Medicine: An Introduction to Clinical Inference, 5:79

Reasoning Things Out, 4:25

Reason in Madness: Critical Essays, 1:889

Reason in Science, 4:327

Reason in Society, 4:327

Reason in the Age of Science, 4:402

The Reason of Following: Christology and the Ecstatic I, 4:889

The Reason of State and the Greatness of Cities, 4:124

Reason over Passion, 1:375, 1:376

Reasons for Moving, 1:1055

Reasons of State, 2:860

Reasons to Believe: New Voices in American Fiction, 1:920

Reason to Hope, 4:337

Reassessing the Henrician Age: Humanism, Politics and Reform, 1500–1550, 4:126

The Reawakening, 2:425

Rebecca, 1:619, 1:620

Rebecca Harding Davis and American Realism, 1:744

Rebecca's Children: Judaism and Christianity in the Roman World, 4:605

Rebecca West, 1:566

Rebecca West: A Life, 1:566

Rebecca West: An Annotated Bibliography, 1:566

The Rebel: An Essay on Man in Revolt, 2:464

The Rebel Angels, 2:910

Rebellion: The Rising in French Canada, 3:614, 3:1837

Rebellion and Democracy in Meiji Japan, 3:476

Rebellion in the Backlands, 2:894

A Rebellious Prophet: A Life of Nicolai Berdyaev, 4:275

The Rebels, 1:1247

Rebels and Gentlemen: Philadelphia in the Age of Franklin, 3:570

Rebels and Rulers, 3:334

Rebels of the Heavenly Kingdom, 1:1204

The Rebel's Silhouette, 2:175

Rebirth of a Nation: Wales, 1880–1980, 3:369

The Rebirth of Nature, 5:198

The Rebirth of Private Policing, 3:205

Rebuilding Russia: Toward
    Some Formulations, 2:761
Rebuilding Shakespeare's
    Globe, 1:217
Recent American Philosophy:
    Studies of Ten Representa-
    tive Thinkers, 4:267
Recent Archaeological Dis-
    coveries and Biblical Re-
    search, 4:808
Recent Developments in
    Alcoholism, 5:402
Recent Japanese Philosophi-
    cal Thought, 4:541
Recent Mammals of the
    World, 5:758
Recent Philosophers, 4:266,
    4:379
Recent Poetry of Spain: A
    Bilingual Anthology, 2:527
Recent Revolutions in Geol-
    ogy, 5:624
Recent Social Trends in the
    United States, 3:162, 3:236
Recent Theories of Narrative,
    1:1132
Recent Work in Philosophy,
    4:14, 4:265, 4:386
The Recent Work of Jürgen
    Habermas, 3:229, 4:405
The Reception of Hermann
    Hesse by Youth in the
    United States, 2:590
Recessional, 1:370
Reckless Character, and Oth-
    er Stories, 2:769
Reckless Disregard: West-
    moreland v. CBS et al.;
    Sharon v. Time, 3:805
Reclaiming Birth: History
    and Heroines of American
    Childbirth Reform, 5:357
Recognition and Regulation
    in Cell-Mediated Immuni-
    ty, 5:813
The Recognition of Edgar Al-
    lan Poe: Selected Criticism
    since 1829, 1:693
Recognition of Emily Dickin-
    son: Selected Criticism
    since 1890, 1:746
Recognition of Health Haz-
    ards in Industry, 5:352
The Recognition of Herman
    Melville, 1:689
The Recognition of Nathaniel
    Hawthorne: Selected Criti-
    cism since 1828, 1:676
The Recognitions, 1:977
Recognizing Islam, 4:578
Recollections and Reflec-
    tions, 3:721, 5:435, 5:716

Recollections of My Life,
    5:811
Recollections of the Last
    Days of Shelley and By-
    ron, 1:284
Recollections of the New
    Deal: When the People
    Mattered, 3:534
Recollections of Things to
    Come, 2:868
Recombinant DNA: A Short
    Course, 5:813
Reconciliation, Law and
    Righteousness: Essays in
    Biblical Theology, 4:826
Reconsiderations, 3:293
Reconstructing American Lit-
    erary History, 1:712
Reconstructing Judaism: An
    Autobiography, 4:659
Reconstructing Memory:
    Black Literary Criticism,
    2:108
Reconstructing Scientific
    Revolutions, 5:53
Reconstructing Womanhood,
    1:1139, 1:1140
Reconstruction: America's
    Unfinished Revolution,
    1863–1877, 3:528
Reconstruction: An Antholo-
    gy of Revisionist Writings,
    3:598
Reconstruction after the Civil
    War, 3:579
Reconstruction in Philoso-
    phy, 4:223, 4:224
A Reconstruction of Eco-
    nomics, 3:71
The Reconstruction of Reli-
    gious Thought in Islam,
    4:375
Recordings: Art, Spectacle,
    Cultural Politics, 3:202
Record of a Life: An Autobi-
    ographical Sketch, 2:801
A Record of Crying Blood, A
    Record of Sorrow, 2:301
A Record of World Events,
    3:7
Records of Shelley, Byron,
    and the Author, 1:304
The Records of the Federal
    Convention of 1787, 3:541
Re-Counting Plato, 4:81
Recovering from a C Sec-
    tion, 5:357
Recovering Literature's Lost
    Ground, 1:659, 1:727
Recovering the Canon: Es-
    says on Isaac Bashevis
    Singer, 2:49

Recovering the Stoics: The
    Spindel Conference 1984,
    4:57
Recovering the Word: Essays
    on Native American Liter-
    ature, 1:632
Recovery, 1:950
Recovery, Reorientation and
    Reformation: Wales,
    1415–1642, 3:369
Recreating Japanese Women,
    1600–1945, 3:476
Recreating Motherhood: Ide-
    ology of Technology in a
    Patriarchal Society, 5:204
The Recruiting Officer, 1:243
The Rector and the Doctor's
    Family, 1:385
The Rector of Justin, 1:937
The Recurring Silent Spring,
    5:830
Red, White, and Black: The
    Peoples of Early America,
    3:518
The Redaction of the Babylo-
    nian Talmud: Amoraic or
    Saboraic, 4:610
The Red and the Black,
    2:511
The Red and the Green,
    1:523
The Red Ape: Orang-utans
    and Human Origins, 5:780
The Red Badge of Courage,
    1:741, 1:1193
The Red Badge of Courage:
    Redefining the Hero,
    1:742
Red Bamboo, 2:337
Red Blizzard and The Oldest
    Maiden Lady in New Mex-
    ico, 1:1212
The Red Book and the Great
    Wall: An Impression of
    Mao's China, 2:430
Redburn, His First Voyage,
    1:686, 1:687
Redburn, White-Jacket, Moby
    Dick, 1:687
The Red Carnation, 2:443
Redcoats and Rebels, 3:520
Red Cross, 1:1089
Redefining American Literary
    History, 1:134, 1:716,
    1:1129
Redefining Black Film, 3:826
Redefining Death, 4:389
Redefining the Past, 3:545,
    3:601
Red Empire—The Forbidden
    History of the USSR,
    3:396

The Redemption of the Un-
wanted, 4:643
Redemptive Encounters:
Three Modern Styles in
the Hindu Tradition, 4:507
Redesigning the World, 1:383
The Red Fairy Book, 3:883
Redgauntlet, 1:298
Red Giants and White
Dwarfs, 5:588
The Red Glove, 2:820
Red Gloves, 2:506
Red Harvest, 1:1226, 1:1230
Red Hunters and the Animal
People, 1:749
Redirecting Science, 5:674
Rediscovering Judaism: Re-
flections on New Theol-
ogy, 4:649
The Rediscovery of the
Mind, 5:76
The Red Lamp of Incest: An
Inquiry into the Origins of
Mind and Society, 3:17
The Red Laugh, 2:699
The Red Limit: The Search
for the Edge of the Uni-
verse, 5:595, 5:603
Red Man's Religion: Beliefs
and Practices of the Indi-
ans North of Mexico,
4:465
The Red Pony, 1:884
Redrawing the Boundaries,
1:1128
The Red Room, 2:671, 2:679
Red Roses for Bronze, 1:826
The Red Rover: A Tale,
1:663
The Redskins; or, Indian and
Injin, 1:663
Red Sorghum: A Family
Saga, 2:259
Red Star in Orbit, 5:597
Red Star over China, 3:472
Red Stars: Political Aspects
of Soviet Science Fiction,
2:688
Red Victory: A History of
the Russian Civil War,
3:397
Red Vienna: Experiment in
Working-Class Culture,
1919–1934, 3:375
Red Virgin Soil: Soviet Liter-
ature in the 1920's, 2:688
The Red Wheel, 2:760
Redwood: A Tale, 1:695
Redwood Curtain, 1:1121
Reed, Pen, and Brush Alpha-
bets for Writing and Let-
tering, 1:14
A Reed in the Tide, 2:133

Re-editing Shakespeare for
the Modern Reader, 1:207
The Reef, 1:786, 1:787
Reel Politics: American Polit-
ical Movies from "Birth of
a Nation" to "Platoon,"
3:542
Reel Women: Pioneers of
the Cinema, 1896 to the
Present, 3:824
Reena and Other Stories,
1:1014
Reenacting the Heavenly Vi-
sion, 4:531
The Reeve's Tale, 1:140
Reference and Essence,
4:411
Reference and Information
Services: An Introduction,
1:73
Reference and Online Ser-
vices Handbook, 5:547
Reference Books for Young
Readers, 1:74, 1:81, 1:89
Reference Data on Atoms,
Molecules and Ions, 5:653
Reference Manual for Tele-
communications, 5:306
Reference Sources for Small
and Medium-Sized Librar-
ies, 1:74
Reference Sources in His-
tory: An Introductory
Guide, 3:8
Reference Sources in Library
and Information Services,
5:545
Reference Works for Theo-
logical Research, 4:6
Refiguring America, 1:900
Refiguring the Father: New
Feminist Readings of Pa-
triarchy, 1:717
Refiguring the Hero, 2:554
Refiguring Women: Perspec-
tives on Gender and the
Italian Renaissance, 2:401
Reflecting on The Well of
Loneliness, 1:492
Reflection on the Philosophy
of Sir Arthur Eddington,
5:681
Reflections, 3:892
Reflections at Fifty and Oth-
er Essays, 1:834
Reflections from Captivity,
2:340
Reflections in a Golden Eye,
1:1009
Reflections of an Economic
Policy Maker, 3:65
Reflections of a Non-Political
Man, 2:601, 2:602

Reflections of a Physicist,
5:676
Reflections of Social Life in
the Navaho Origin Myth,
3:865
Reflections on a Marine
Venus, 1:470
Reflections on America,
4:307
Reflections on Black, 1:1159
Reflections on Frege's Phi-
losophy, 4:230
Reflections on Gender and
Science, 5:154, 5:187
Reflections on History (Force
and Freedom), 3:400
Reflections on Human Na-
ture, 4:303
Reflections on Philosophy:
Introductory Essays, 4:22
Reflections on Rebellion,
2:317
Reflections on Resemblance,
Ritual, and Religion, 4:501
Reflections on Suicide, 2:510
Reflections on the Civil War,
3:571
Reflections on the Constitu-
tion, 3:156
Reflections on the Death of
a Porcupine, 1:510
Reflections on the May
Fourth Movement: A Sym-
posium, 3:472
Reflections on the Philoso-
phy of the History of Man-
kind, 2:588, 2:589, 3:286,
4:199
Reflections on the Principles
of Psychology: William
James after a Century,
5:453
Reflections on the Revolu-
tion in France, 3:152,
4:192, 4:210
Reflections on the Revolu-
tion of Our Time, 3:156
Reflections on the Way to
the Gallows: Rebel Wom-
en in Prewar Japan, 3:477
Reflections on Violence,
3:140
The Reflexive Thesis: Wright-
ing Sociology of Scientific
Knowledge, 5:66
Reform and Reformation:
England 1509–1558, 3:334,
4:726
Reform and Reformation:
England and the Continent
1500–1750, 4:725

Reform and Regulation: American Politics from Roosevelt to Wilson, 3:531

Reform and Renewal: Thomas Cromwell and the Common Weal, 3:402

Reform and Revolution in China: The 1911 Revolution in Hunan and Hubei, 3:470

The Reformation (Chadwick), 4:722

The Reformation (Durant), 4:722

The Reformation (Elton), 3:334, 3:402

The Reformation (Mosse), 4:722

Reformation (Todd), 4:723

The Reformation: A Narrative History Related by Contemporary Observers and Participants, 4:722

Reformation and Revolution 1558–1660, 4:733

Reformation and Society in Sixteenth-Century Europe, 4:722

The Reformation Era: 1500–1650, 4:722

Reformation Europe: A Guide to Research, 4:722

Reformation Europe, 1517–1559, 4:722

The Reformation in Denmark, 4:730

The Reformation in England, 4:727

The Reformation in Germany, 4:722

The Reformation in Medieval Perspective, 4:721

The Reformation in the Cities, 4:722

The Reformation of Reform Judaism, 4:652

Reformation Thought: An Introduction, 4:722

Reformatory Education, 3:259

Reformed Confessions of the Sixteenth Century, 4:761

Reformed Reader: A Sourcebook in Christian Theology, 4:719

Reformers and Babylon, 4:725

Reformers in Profile, 4:722

Reform in Eastern Europe, 3:52, 3:58

Reforming American Education, 4:270

Reforming Medicine: Lessons from the Last Quarter Century, 5:315, 5:329

Re-forming the Narrative: Toward a Mechanics of Modernist Fiction, 1:421

Reforming the Soviet Economy, 3:52

Reform in the Provinces: The Government of Stuart England, 3:360

Reformist Apocalypticism and Piers Plowman, 1:154

Reform Judaism: A Historical Perspective, 4:652

Reform Judaism, a Historical Perspective: Essays from the Yearbook of the Central Conference of American Rabbis, 4:652

Reform Judaism in America, 4:652

Reform Judaism in America: A Study in Religious Adaptation, 4:652

Reform Judaism Today, 1973–77, 4:652

Reform Movement in Judaism, 4:653

Reform of Education, 4:285

Reform Responsa for Our Time, 4:652

Reform Thought in Sixteenth-Century Italy, 4:728

Refuge, 2:22

The Refugee in America, 1:407, 1:408

Refugee Scholars in America: Their Impact and Their Experiences, 3:200

Refutation of Helvetius, 4:195

Regarding Television: Critical Approaches, 3:811

Regeneration, 2:439

Regeneration through Violence, 1:652, 3:525

The Regenerators: Social Criticism in Late Victorian English Canada, 3:617

The Regents Renaissance Drama Series, 1:170

Regiment of Women, 1:948, 1:949

Reginald Pole: Cardinal of England, 4:729

Region, Race, and Reconstruction: Essays in Honor of C. Vann Woodward, 3:586, 3:603

Regional Dynamics of the Indonesian Revolution: Unity from Diversity, 3:491

Regional Geography of the World, 5:621

Regional Landscapes of the United States and Canada, 3:124

Regional Perspectives on the Olmec, 4:455

Regional Sketches, 1:699

Regno, 2:430

Regulae, 4:164

Regulating Birth: Midwives, Medicine and the Law, 5:337

Regulating Pesticides in Food: The Delaney Paradox, 5:736

Regulating the Poor: The Functions of Public Welfare, 3:212

Regulating Toxic Substances: A Philosophy of Science and the Law, 5:74

Regulation and the Courts: The Case of the Clean Air Act, 5:184

Regulatory Environment for Science: A Technical Memorandum, 5:726

Rehearsal for Reconstruction, 3:529

Reichswehr and Politics: 1918–1933, 3:376

Reigen, 2:610

The Reign of Henry VI, 3:357

The Reign of Mary Tudor, 3:359

The Reign of Wazobia, 2:144

Reilly's Woman, 1:1221

Reincarnation, 4:550

Reincarnation: The Phoenix Fire Mystery, 4:887

Reinhart in Love, 1:948, 1:949

Reinhart's Women, 1:948, 1:949

Reinhold Niebuhr, 4:784

Reinhold Niebuhr: A Biography, 4:784

Reinhold Niebuhr and Issues of Our Time, 4:784

A Reinhold Niebuhr Reader: Selected Essays, Articles, and Book Reviews, 4:784

Reinventing Technology: Policies for Democratic Values, 5:181

Reinventing Womanhood, 1:925

The Reivers, 1:835

Rejoice in the Lamb, 1:255

The Relapse, 1:261, 1:262

Relational Database: Selected Writings, 5:559

Relational Databases, 5:559

Relations: Medieval Theories, 1250–1325, 4:104

Relations of Indian, Greek and Christian Thought in Antiquity, 4:38

Relativity: The Special and the General Theory, 5:48, 5:682

Relativity and Cosmology, 5:664

Relativity and Gravitation— Classical and Quantum, 5:664

Relativity Theory of Protons and Electrons, 5:681

Relativity Today, 5:665

The Relaxation Response, 5:401

The Relevance of Charles Peirce, 4:249

The Relevance of Education, 3:254

The Relevance of the Beautiful, 4:402

Reliable Knowledge, 5:20, 5:65

The Relic, 2:559

Religio Laici, 1:241

Religion: A Dialogue, and Other Essays, 4:255

Religion, Ideology and Heidegger's Concept of Falling, 4:295

Religion, Law and Power: The Making of Protestant Ireland, 1660–1760, 3:370

Religion, My Own: The Literary Works of Najib Mahfuz, 2:69

Religion, Nationalism and Politics in Bangladesh, 3:486

Religion, Science, and Public Policy, 5:196

Religion, Society, and Utopia in Nineteenth-Century America, 4:842, 4:844

The Religion, Spirituality, and Thought of Traditional Africa, 4:463

Religion, Values, and Development in Southeast Asia, 4:518

Religion and Art, 4:340

Religion and Change in Contemporary Asia, 4:573

Religion and Empire: The Dynamics of Aztec and Inca Expansion, 4:457

Religion and Family in East Asia, 3:464

Religion and Freedom in the Modern World, 3:334

Religion and Freedom of Thought, 3:587

Religion and Hopi Life in the Twentieth Century, 4:465

Religion and Legitimation of Power in Thailand, Laos, and Burma, 4:518

Religion and Modernization in Southeast Asia, 4:518

Religion and Neoplatonism in Renaissance Medicine, 4:129

Religion and Nothingness, 4:365, 4:541, 4:889

The Religion and Philosophy of the Veda and Upanishads, 4:501

Religion and Politics in Contemporary Iran, 4:567, 4:577

Religion and Politics in Iran: Shi'ism from Quietism to Revolution, 3:448, 4:570

Religion and Politics in Israel, 4:642

Religion and Politics in Israel: The Interplay of Judaism and Zionism, 3:439

Religion and Politics in Latin America, 3:641

Religion and Politics in Muslim Society: Order and Conflict in Pakistan, 3:487

Religion and Politics in the Middle East, 4:568

Religion and Public Education, 3:268

Religion and Respectability, 3:364

Religion and Ritual in Chinese Society, 4:531

Religion and Ritual in Korean Society, 4:539

Religion and Science, 4:323

Religion and Sexism, 4:650, 4:679

Religion and Sexuality: The Shakers, the Mormons, and the Oneida Community, 4:841

Religion and Society in Central Africa: The Bakongo of Lower Zaire, 3:421, 4:462

Religion and the Decline of Magic, 4:727

Religion and the Environmental Crisis, 5:115, 5:136

Religion and the Family in East Asia, 4:531, 4:539

Religion and the One: Philosophies East and West, 4:574

Religion and the Rise of Modern Science, 5:42

Religion and the Rise of Capitalism, 3:51, 3:55

Religion and the Scientific Future, 5:201

Religion as a Social Vision, 4:508

Religion in Aboriginal Australia: An Anthology, 4:461

Religion in America, 4:751

Religion in American History: Interpretive Essays, 4:754

Religion in American Life, 4:751, 4:752

Religion in an Age of Science, 5:160, 5:161, 5:196

Religion in Ancient Egypt: Gods, Myths, and Personal Practice, 4:442

Religion in China, 3:244

Religion in Chinese Society, 4:524

Religion in Communist China, 4:532

Religion in Contemporary Japan, 4:535, 4:541

Religion Index One: Periodicals, 4:8

Religion Index Two: Multi-Author Works, 4:8

Religion in Economics: A Study of John Bates Clark, 3:73

Religion in Essence and Manifestation, 4:427, 4:885

Religion in Greece and Rome, 2:347

Religion in Japanese History, 4:535

Religion in Modern India, 4:507, 4:516, 4:517, 4:562

Religion in Native North America, 4:7

Religion in Primitive Culture, 3:41

Religion in Relation: Method, Application, and Moral Location, 4:427

Religion in Roman Britain, 4:448

Religion in Sociological Perspective, 4:425

Religion in the Age of Romanticism, 4:741

Religion in the Ancient Greek City, 3:307

Religion in the Andes: Vision and Imagination in Early Colonial Peru, 4:458
Religion in the Japanese Experience, 4:533
Religion in the Making, 4:341
Religion in the Medieval West, 4:691
Religion Journals and Serials: An Analytical Guide, 4:6
The Religion of Isaac Newton: The Fremantle Lectures 1973, 4:184
The Religion of Islam, 4:575
The Religion of Japan's Korean Minority, 4:540
The Religion of Java, 3:23, 3:31, 4:478
Religion of Reason out of the Sources of Judaism, 4:663
The Religion of Solidarity, 1:733, 1:734
The Religion of the Greeks and Romans, 2:346, 4:484
The Religion of the Manichees: Donnellan Lectures for 1924, 4:685
Religions, Values and Peak Experiences, 5:461
Religions of Africa, 4:884
Religions of Antiquity, 4:440
Religions of Asia, 4:498, 4:499, 4:523, 4:535, 4:543
The Religions of China, 4:523, 4:884
The Religions of India, 4:498
Religions of Japan, 4:534, 4:883
The Religions of Mankind, 4:573
Religions of Mesoamerica, 4:454, 4:883
The Religions of Mongolia, 4:541
Religions of the Ancient Near East, 4:441, 4:445
Religions of the East, 4:570
The Religions of the Roman Empire, 3:306, 4:449
The Religions of Tibet, 4:356, 4:543
Religion, Revolution and English Radicalism, 4:738
Religion within the Bounds of Plain Reason, 4:204
Religion within the Limits of Reason Alone, 4:205, 4:739
Religion without Revelation, 5:798

Religious and Anti-Religious Thought in Russia, 3:394
Religious and Inspirational Books and Serials in Print, 1985, 4:716
Religious and Spiritual Groups in Modern America, 4:855
Religious and Theological Abstracts, 4:8
Religious Attitude and Life in Islam, 4:575
Religious Bodies in the United States: A Directory, 4:6, 4:854
Religious Conflict in Social Context, 4:654
The Religious Dimensions of Confucianism, 3:469
Religious Encounters with Death, 4:887
Religious Essays: A Supplement to "The Idea of the Holy," 4:488
Religious Evolution, 4:422
The Religious Experience, 4:884
Religious Experience and Truth: A Symposium, 4:265
The Religious Experience of Mankind, 4:422
The Religious Experience of the Roman People, 2:380
The Religious Fringe: A History of Alternative Religions in America, 4:841
A Religious History of America, 4:751
A Religious History of the American People, 4:750
Religious Information Sources: A Worldwide Guide, 4:7
The Religious Investigations of William James, 4:237
Religious Leaders, 4:716
Religious Leaders of America, 4:7
Religious Life in Seventeenth-Century Scotland, 4:735
The Religious Life of Man: Guide to the Basic Literature, 4:883
Religious Lyrics of the Thirteenth, Fourteenth, and Fifteenth Centuries, 1:148
Religious Movements: Genesis, Exodus, and Numbers, 4:857
Religious Movements in Contemporary America, 4:856

The Religious Orders in England, 3:355
Religious Outsiders and the Making of America, 4:842
The Religious Philosophy of Nishitani Keiji, 4:365
The Religious Philosophy of Plotinus and Some Modern Philosophies of Religion, 4:86
The Religious Philosophy of Tanabe Hajime, 4:366
The Religious Philosophy of William James, 4:238
Religious Platonism, 4:284
Religious Poverty and the Profit Economy in Medieval Europe, 4:700
Religious Publishing and Communication, 1:47
Religious Radicals in Tudor England, 3:359
Religious Reading: The Annual Guide, 4:716
The Religious Roots of Rebellion: Christians in Central American Revolutions, 4:747
Religious Thought and Economic Society, 3:111
Religious Thought in the Nineteenth Century, 4:741
The Religious Thought of José Rizal, 2:333
The Religious Traditions of Asia, 4:498, 4:509, 4:513, 4:516, 4:518, 4:522, 4:534, 4:542, 4:543
Religious Traditions of the World, 4:883
Religious Trends in Modern China, 4:532
Religious Violence and Abortion: The Gideon Project, 4:894
Reliques of Ancient English Poetry, 1:148
The Reluctant Naturalist: A Study of G. E. Moore's Principia Ethica, 4:312
The Reluctant Patron, 3:560
Remains of Elmer, 1:498
The Remaking of Istanbul, 3:452
Re-making Poetry: Ted Hughes and a New Critical Psychology, 1:498
Remaking the Past, 3:666
A Remarkable Medicine Has Been Overlooked, 5:350
Remarkable Providences: Readings on Early American History, 1:630

Remarks on Colour, 4:344
Remarks on Frazer's Golden Bough, 4:344
Remarks on Marx, 4:400
Remarks on the Foundations of Mathematics, 4:344, 5:494
Remarks on the Philosophy of Psychology, 4:344
Rembrandt, 3:789
Rembrandt: Rembrandt Harmensz van Rijn, 3:789
Rembrandt, Life and Work, 3:789
Rembrandt Fecit: A Selection of Rembrandt's Etchings, 3:789
Rembrandt's Drawings, 3:789
Rembrandt's Enterprise: The Studio and the Market, 3:788
Rembrandt's Hat, 1:1013
Remembering and Repeating: Biblical Creation in Paradise Lost, 1:193
Remembering Anna Akhmatova, 2:697
Remembering James Agee, 1:933
Remembering Laughter, 1:1054
Remembering Poets: Reminiscences and Opinions, 1:984
Remembering Rosario, 2:861
Remembering the University of Chicago: Teachers, Scientists and Scholars, 3:239
Remember Ruben, 2:133
Remember to Remember, 1:861
Remembrance and Pantomime, 2:943
Remembrance of Things Past, 2:445, 2:495
Remembrances, 2:190
Reminiscences, 1:343
Reminiscences about a Great Physicist: Paul Adrien Dirac, 5:720
Reminiscences and Reflections, 5:802
Reminiscences in Retirement, 2:301
Reminiscences of Clara Schumann from the Diary of Her Grandson Ferdinand Schumann, 3:716
Reminiscences of Rudolf Steiner, 2:701
Reminiscences of Sir Walter Scott's Residence in Italy, 1832, 1:299

Reminiscences of Swami Vivekananda, 4:563
Reminiscences of the English Lake Poets, 1:290
Reminiscences of Tolstoy, Chekhov and Andreev, 2:725
Remizov's Fictions, 1900–1921, 2:754
Remorse, 1:271
The Removalists, 2:967
The Renaissance, 1:386, 1:387
Renaissance, 3:402
The Renaissance: From the 1470s to the End of the 16th Century, 3:660
Renaissance: Its Nature and Origin, 3:333
The Renaissance, the Reformation and the Erratic Behavior of Desiderius Erasmus, 4:140
Renaissance and Baroque Poetry of Spain, 2:527
The Renaissance and English Humanism, 4:124
Renaissance and Reformation, 4:691
Renaissance Architecture, 3:763
Renaissance Concepts of Method, 4:126
Renaissance Drama, 1:171
Renaissance Drama as Cultural History, 1:170
The Renaissance Drama of Knowledge: Giordano Bruno in England, 4:135
Renaissance Essays, 3:411
Renaissance Exploration, 3:335
Renaissance Feminism: Literary Texts and Political Models, 2:401
The Renaissance "Hamlet": Issues and Responses in 1600, 1:213
Renaissance Humanism, 4:127
Renaissance Humanism: Studies in Philosophy and Poetics, 4:127
Renaissance Humanism, Vols. 1–3: Foundations, Forms and Legacy, 4:130
Renaissance Humanism 1300–1550: A Bibliography of Materials in English, 4:127
The Renaissance Idea of Wisdom, 4:130

The Renaissance in Historical Thought, 3:333
The Renaissance in Italy, 2:402
Renaissance Man, 4:127
Renaissance Man and Creative Thinking, 4:127
Renaissance Man from Louisiana, 1:817
The Renaissance Notion of Women, 3:333
The Renaissance of Islam, 3:442
Renaissance of Sciences in Islamic Countries, 5:713
The Renaissance of the Twelfth Century, 4:101, 4:699, 5:39
Renaissance Philosophy (Copenhaver), 4:125
Renaissance Philosophy (Fallico), 4:126
Renaissance Philosophy: New Translations of Lorenzo Valla, Paul Cortese, Cajetan, T. Bacciliere, Juan Luis Vives, Peter Ramus, 4:127
The Renaissance Philosophy of Man, 2:402, 4:125, 4:153, 4:155, 4:156, 4:279, 4:695
Renaissance Self-Fashioning: From More to Shakespeare, 1:165
Renaissance Theory of Love, 4:136
Renaissance Thought: The Classic, Scholastic and Humanistic Strains, 4:697
Renaissance Thought and Its Sources, 2:401, 4:128
Renaissance Thought and the Arts: Collected Essays, 4:128
Renascence and Other Poems, 1:860
Rendering Things Visible, 2:158
Render Me My Song, 1:130
Rendezvous in Space: The Science of Comets, 5:592
Rendezvous with Rama, 1:614
René Char, 2:466
René Char: The Myth and the Poem, 2:466
René Descartes, 5:502
René Descartes: Critical Assessments, 5:503
Renegade in Power: The Diefenbaker Years, 3:616

Renewable Energy: Sources
    for Fuels and Electricity,
    5:289
The Renewable Energy Alter-
    native, 5:288
Renewing Philosophy, 4:410
Renga, 2:878
Renoir, 3:789
Renoir, His Life, Art and
    Letters, 3:789
Renoir, My Father, 3:789
The Repairing of Books, 1:22
The Repeating Island: The
    Caribbean, 2:930
The Repertory of Shake-
    speare's Company,
    1594–1613, 1:218
Reportage on Crime, 2:330
Reportage on Lovers, 2:330
Reportage on the Marcoses,
    1964–1970, 2:330
Reported Sightings, 1:936
Report from Part I, 1:954
Report from the Besieged
    City, 2:814
Report of the Exploring Ex-
    pedition to the Rocky
    Mountains in the Year
    1842, 3:908
Report of the Geology of the
    Henry Mountains, 5:626,
    5:643
A Report on American Uni-
    versity Presses, 1:50
Report on the Conditions
    and Needs of the Mission
    Indians, 1:760
Report on the Poor Laws,
    1:344
Report on the Sanitary Con-
    dition of the Labouring
    Population of Great Brit-
    ain, 1:344
Reports of My Death: An Au-
    tobiography, 1:1046
Report to Greco, 2:374
Representation and Reality,
    4:411
Representations of Women:
    Nineteenth-Century British
    Women's Poetry, 1:316
Representative Essays: En-
    glish and American, 1:660,
    1:728
Representative Government
    and the Degeneration of
    Democracy, 4:244
Representative Man: Ralph
    Waldo Emerson in His
    Time, 1:670
Representative Men, 1:670
Representative Modern Plays:
    British, 1:427

Representative Plays, 1:367,
    1:482
Representative Plays by
    American Dramatists,
    1:1078
Representative Spanish Au-
    thors, 2:523
Representing and Interven-
    ing, 5:63
Representing Femininity,
    1:325
Representing Kenneth Burke:
    Selected Papers from the
    English Institute, 1:956
Representing Shakespeare:
    New Psychoanalytic Es-
    says, 1:208
Repression in Victorian Fic-
    tion, 1:319
The Reprieve, 2:506
Reproduction: The Cycle of
    Life, 5:341
Reproduction and Develop-
    ment, 5:770
The Reproduction of
    Mothering: Psychoanalysis
    and the Sociology of Gen-
    der, 1:1140
Reproduction of Copyrighted
    Works by Educators and
    Librarians, 1:54
Reproductive Health Hazards
    in the Workplace, 5:737
Reproductive Technologies:
    Gender, Motherhood and
    Medicine, 5:188
The Republic, 1:193, 3:163,
    4:78
The Republican Roosevelt,
    3:594
The Republic in Peril, 3:520
The Republic of Austria,
    1918–1934, 3:376
Republic of Fear: The Inside
    Story of Saddam's Iraq,
    3:449
The Republic of Korea: Eco-
    nomic Transformation and
    Social Change, 3:481
The Republic of Many Man-
    sions, 1:637
The Republic of Mass Cul-
    ture, 3:551
The Republic of Plato, 4:79
The Republic of St. Peter,
    680–825, 4:695
The Republic of the South-
    ern Cross and Other Sto-
    ries, 2:705
Requiem, 2:696
Requiem for a Nun, 1:835
Requiem for Na'aman, 2:25

Required Writing: Miscella-
    neous Pieces, 1955–1982,
    1:508
Rereading Beowulf, 1:144
Re-reading Levinas, 4:901
Rereading Russell: Essays on
    Bertrand Russell's Meta-
    physics and Epistemology,
    4:324, 5:103
Res Cogitans: An Essay in
    Rational Psychology, 4:171
Rescued Readings, 1:882
Rescue the Dead, 1:991
Rescuing Horace Walpole,
    1:604
The Research Center Direc-
    tory, 1:105, 5:3
Research Design in Anthro-
    pology, 3:12
A Researcher's Guide to
    Sources on Soviet Social
    History in the 1930's,
    3:394
Research Fraud in the Be-
    havioral and Biomedical
    Sciences, 5:107
Research Guide to Biography
    and Criticism: Literature,
    2:2
Research Guide to Biography
    and Criticism: World Dra-
    ma, 2:3
Research Guide to Central
    America and the Carib-
    bean, 3:624
A Research Guide to English
    Translation of Chinese
    Verse, 2:190
Research Guide to Philoso-
    phy, 4:15
Research Guide to Religious
    Studies, 4:716
Research in African Litera-
    ture, 2:130
Researching and Writing in
    History: A Practical Hand-
    book for Students, 3:9
Research in Philosophy and
    Technology, 5:70, 5:165
Research in the History of
    Economic Thought and
    Methodology, Vols. 1 and
    8, 3:89
Research in the Sociology of
    Health Care, 3:202
Research Methods in Cultur-
    al Anthropology, 3:11
Research on Chemical La-
    sers, 5:235
Research on Human Sub-
    jects, 3:213
Research Services Directory,
    5:3

The Reservoir, 2:974
Reservoir Ravine, 2:914
Reshaping America: Society and Institutions, 1945–1960, 3:537
Reshaping Life: Key Issues in Genetic Engineering, 5:782
Reshaping the Psychoanalytic Domain, 5:457
Residence on Earth, 2:873, 2:875
Residential Energy Conservation, 5:284
Resistance, Rebellion and Death, 2:464
Resistance and Caribbean Literature, 2:930
Resistance in Postcolonial African Fiction, 2:110
Resistance in Vichy France, 3:373
The Resistance to Theory, 1:1131, 1:1142, 1:1143
Resisting Images: Essays on Cinema and History, 3:553, 3:827
Resist Much, Obey Little: Some Notes on Edward Abbey, 5:828
The Resolution of Conflict: Constructive and Destructive Processes, 5:421
Resolving Social Conflicts, 3:176, 3:189, 3:204
Resort to Arms: International and Civil Wars, 1816–1980, 3:149
Resource Book for the Teaching of Astronomy, 5:588
Resource Directory for the Disabled, 5:368
Resources of American Musical History, 3:656
The Resources of Kind: Genre-Theory in the Renaissance, 1:165
Respected Sir, 2:68
Respect for Nature: A Theory of Environmental Ethics, 5:76, 5:116
Respirable Particles, 5:398
Respiratory Disorders, 5:397
Respiratory Patient Care, 5:398
Responsa Anthology, 4:648
The Responsa Literature and a Treasury of Responsa, 4:627
The Responsa of Solomon Luria, 4:627

Responses: On Paul de Man's Wartime Journalism, 1:1143
Responses: Prose Pieces, 1948–1976, 1:1066
Responses of the Presidents to Charges of Misconduct, 3:544, 3:602
Responses to 101 Questions on the Bible, 4:816
Responses to 101 Questions on the Dead Sea Scrolls, 4:811
Responses to Industrialization: The British Experience, 1780–1850, 3:365
Response to Modernity: A History of the Reform Movement in Judaism, 4:652
Responsibilities, 1:571
Responsibilities of the American Book Community, 1:49
Responsibilities of the Novelist and Other Literary Essays, 1:776
Responsibilities to Future Generations: Environmental Ethics, 5:115
Responsibility and Atonement, 4:886
The Responsibility of the Artist, 4:307
The Responsible Electorate: Rationality in Presidential Voting, 1936–1960, 3:155
Responsible Technology: A Christian Perspective, 5:130, 5:197
Responsive Readings, 1:184
Rest is Silence, 2:900
The Restless Earth: A Report on the New Geology, 5:622
The Restlessness of Shanti Andía, 2:530
The Restless Ocean, 1:289
A Restless Spirit: The Story of Robert Frost, 1:842
Restless Universe, 5:675
Restless Youth, 2:720
The Restoration: Problems and Perspectives in History, 3:360
Restoration and Eighteenth-Century Comedy, 1:228
Restoration and the Cat, 1:446
Restoration of Leather Bindings, 1:25
The Restoration of Self, 5:457

The Restorer's Handbook of Drawings and Prints, 1:24
The Restructuring of American Religion, 4:754
The Resurrection (Gardner), 1:978
Resurrection (Tolstoy), 2:763, 2:764
The Resurrection of Joseph Bourne, 2:913
Rethinking Democracy, 5:73
Rethinking Early Greek Philosophy, 4:49
Rethinking Employment Policy, 3:59
Rethinking History and Myth, 4:454
Rethinking Popular Culture: Contemporary Perspectives in Cultural Studies, 3:874
Rethinking Progress, 3:209
Rethinking Scripture: Essays from a Comparative Perspective, 4:510, 4:530
Rethinking the Neolithic, 3:13, 4:434
Rethinking the South: Essays in Intellectual History, 3:560
Rethinking Working-Class History: Bengal 1890–1940, 3:486
Retired Dreams, 2:896
Retornos de lo vivo lejano, 2:528
The Retreat, 2:14
Retreat from Love, 2:470
The Retreat from Race: Asian Admissions and Racial Politics, 3:258
Retreat from Reform: Patterns of Political Behavior in Interwar Japan, 3:478
Retreat into the Mind: Victorian Poetry and the Rise of Psychiatry, 1:315
Retribution (Blok), 2:702
Retribution (Southworth), 1:1219, 1:1224
Return from the Stars, 2:816
Return from the U.S.S.R., 2:479
Returning to Tradition: The Contemporary Revival of Orthodox Judaism, 4:659
The Return of Consciousness, 2:64
The Return of Eden: Five Essays on Milton's Epics, 1:192
The Return of Eva Peron, 2:939
The Return of Imray, 1:370

The Return of Lanny Budd,
  1:879
Return of Lieutenant Boruv-
  ka, 2:795
The Return of Philip Lati-
  nowicz, 2:786
The Return of the Amasi
  Bird: Black South African
  Poetry, 1891–1981, 2:158
Return of the Jedi, 1:1171
The Return of the King,
  1:559
The Return of the Native,
  1:360, 1:361
The Return of the Reader:
  Reader-Response Criticism,
  1:1131
The Return of the Soldier,
  1:566
The Return of the Spring,
  2:63
The Return to Camelot: Chi-
  valry and the English Gen-
  tleman, 3:355
Return to Diversity, 3:389
Return to Earth, 3:912
Return to Essentials: Reflec-
  tions on the Present State
  of Historical Study, 3:402
Return to Judaism: Religious
  Renewal in Israel, 4:659
A Return to Moral and Reli-
  gious Philosophy in Early
  America, 4:34
Return to the Red Planet,
  5:592
Return to the Shadows,
  2:156
Return to Tsugaru: Travels
  of a Purple Tramp, 2:286
Return to Yesterday, 1:474,
  1:475
Reuben and Rachel; or,
  Tales of Old Times, 1:643
Reuben Gold Thwaites: A
  Memorial Address, 3:599
Reunion, 1:1101
Reunion and Reaction, 3:602
Revaluation: Essays on Phil-
  ippine Literature, Cinema,
  and Popular Culture, 2:328
Revelation and Divination in
  Ndembu Ritual, 3:40
Revelation and Reason in
  Islam, 4:574
The Revelations of a Prosti-
  tute, 2:155
The Revels History of Drama
  in English, 1:271, 1:322
The Revels History of Drama
  in English, 1500–1576,
  1:169

The Revels History of Drama
  in English, 1613–1660,
  1:170
The Revels Plays, 1:170
Revenge, 1:450
Revenge of the Rose, 1:616
The Revenger's Comedies,
  1:437
The Revenger's Tragedy,
  1:199
The Reveries of the Solitary
  Walker, 4:213
Reverse Acronym, Initialisms
  and Abbreviations Dictio-
  nary, 1:93
Reverse International Acro-
  nyms, Initialisms and Ab-
  breviations Dictionary, 5:3
Reverse Thunder, 1:932
Review and Evaluation of
  Smoking Cessation Meth-
  ods, 5:404
Reviewing before "The Edin-
  burgh," 1788–1802, 1:274
Reviewing Classics of Joyce
  Criticism, 1:505
Reviewing Romanticism,
  1:268
Review of Child Develop-
  ment Research, 3:173
Review of Digital Communi-
  cation, 5:298
Review of National Litera-
  ture: Norway, 2:662
A Review of Personality
  Theories, 3:177
Reviews of Plasma Physics,
  5:667
The Revised English Bible
  with the Apocrypha, 4:798
Revising Mythologies: The
  Composition of Thoreau's
  Major Works, 1:701
Revising Shakespeare, 1:207
Re-Vision: Essays in Feminist
  Film Criticism, 1:1158
Revisionary Play: Studies in
  the Spenserian Dynamics,
  1:198
Revisioning Psychology,
  5:414
Revisions in Mercantilism,
  3:45
Revivalism and Social Re-
  form, 4:754
The Revolt, 4:642
The Revolt against Dualism:
  An Inquiry Concerning the
  Existence of Ideas, 4:303
Revolt in the Desert, 3:925,
  3:926
The Revolt of Aphrodite,
  1:469

The Revolt of the Engineers,
  5:48, 5:129, 5:214
The Revolt of the Masses,
  3:203, 4:315, 5:96
The Revolt of the Nether-
  lands, 1555–1609, 3:382,
  4:731
Revolution, No. 9, 2:159
Revolution and Convention
  in Modern Poetry, 1:800
Revolution and Counterrevo-
  lution, 3:158
Revolution and Reaction: Bo-
  livia 1964–1985, 3:633
Revolution and Romanticism,
  1:651
The Revolution and the
  Word: The Rise of the
  Novel in America, 1:643
Revolutionaries, 3:140, 3:405
Revolutionary America,
  1763–1789: A Bibliogra-
  phy, 3:510
Revolutionary Immortality:
  Mao Tse-tung and the Chi-
  nese Revolution, 4:532
Revolutionary Jews from
  Marx to Trotsky, 4:656
Revolutionary Literature in
  China: An Anthology,
  2:233
Revolutionary Mexico, 3:638
The Revolutionary Origins of
  Modern Japan, 3:478
Revolutionary Writers: Litera-
  ture and Authority in the
  New Republic, 1:628
A Revolution in Earth Sci-
  ence, from Continental
  Drift to Plate Tectonics,
  5:623
Revolution in Iran: A Reap-
  praisal, 3:448
Revolution in Miniature,
  5:47, 5:669
Revolution in Science, 5:15,
  5:25, 5:763
The Revolution in Science
  1500–1750, 5:42
Revolution in Time: Clocks
  and the Making of the
  Modern World, 5:37
The Revolution of 1688 in
  England, 3:360
The Revolution of Hope:
  Toward a Humanized
  Technology, 5:450
The Revolution of Moral
  Consciousness, 2:685
The Revolution of the Saints:
  A Study in the Origins of
  Radical Politics, 3:361,
  4:735

The Revolution of Things, 2:812

Revolution on the Pampas, 3:649

Revolution or Reform, 4:408, 5:94

Revolutions and Dictatorships, 3:286

Revolutions and Military Rule in the Middle East, 3:436

Revolutions and Reconstructions in the Philosophy of Science, 4:405

Revolutions in Eastern Europe: The Religious Roots, 4:756

Revolutions in Modern English Drama, 1:426

The Revolutions of 1848, 4:242

Revulsion, 2:802

R. E. Walton's Weekly, 1:597

The Rewiring of America: The Fiber Optics Revolution, 5:303

Reworlding: The Literature of the Indian Diaspora, 2:930

Rewriting the Renaissance, 1:165

Rewriting the Victorians: Theory, History and the Politics of Gender, 1:313

Rex Stout: A Biography, 1:1238

Reynard the Fox, 2:620, 2:629

Reynard the Fox and Other Medieval Netherlands Secular Literature, 2:621

Reynart the Foxe, 1:575

Reynolds, 3:790

Reynolds Stone, 1:18

Rhapsody: A Dream Novel, 2:611

Rhesos, 2:356

Rhetoric, Comedy and Violence of Language in Aristophanes' Clouds, 2:354

Rhetoric, Prudence and Skepticism in the Renaissance, 4:127

Rhetoric and Philosophy in Renaissance Humanism, 4:131

Rhetoric and Reality in Plato's Phaedrus, 4:85

Rhetoric and Reform: Erasmus' Civil Dispute with Luther, 4:139

Rhetoric as Philosophy: The Humanist Tradition, 4:127

The Rhetoric of Alcuin and Charlemagne, 4:100

The Rhetoric of Chin P'ing-mei, 2:226

The Rhetoric of Confession, 2:282

The Rhetoric of Fiction, 1:420, 1:924, 1:1139

A Rhetoric of Irony, 1:1139

The Rhetoric of Morality and Philosophy, 4:89

A Rhetoric of Motives, 1:956

The Rhetoric of Poetry in the Renaissance and Seventeenth Century, 2:401

The Rhetoric of Religion: Studies in Logology, 1:818, 1:956

The Rhetoric of Romanticism, 1:966, 1:1143

The Rhetoric of Science, 5:154

Rhetorics of Order: Ordering Rhetorics in English Neoclassical Literature, 1:225

Rheumatic Diseases: Rehabilitation and Management, 5:398

Rhinoceros, 2:483

Rhinoceros and Other Plays: The Leader, The Future Is in Eggs, 2:483

Rhyme or Reason: A Limerick History of Philosophy, 4:16

The Rhymes (Bécquer), 2:530, 2:531

Rhymes (Dante), 2:417

Rhythm and Intent, 4:503

Rhythm and Movement: Applications of Dalcroze Eurhythmics, 3:745

Rhythm and Resistance: Explorations in the Political Uses of Popular Music, 3:662

Rhythm and Tempo: A Study in Music History, 3:663

Rhythm-a-ning: Jazz Tradition and Innovation in the '80s, 3:668

Rhythm in the Novel, 1:420

Ricardian Poetry: Chaucer, Gower, Langland, and the Gawain Poet, 1:146

The Rice Industry of Burma, 1852–1940, 3:489

Rice in Malaya: A Study in Historical Geography, 3:492

The Rice-Sprout Song, 2:238

Riceyman Steps, 1:443

Rich and Famous, 1:1090

Rich and Strange: Gender, History, Modernism, 1:420, 1:794

Richard and Cosima Wagner: Biography of a Marriage, 3:729

Richard Brinsley Sheridan, 1:254

Richard Brinsley Sheridan: A Reference Guide, 1:255

Richard Crashaw, 1:176

Richard Eberhart: A Descriptive Bibliography, 1921–1987, 1:972

Richard Hakluyt and His Successors, 3:923

Richard Hakluyt and the English Voyages, 3:923

The Richard Harding Davis Years: A Biography of a Mother and Son, 1:744

Richard Henry Dana (Adams), 1:666, 3:920

Richard Henry Dana, Jr. (Gale), 1:666

Richard Henry Dana, Jr.: 1815–1882 (Shapiro), 1:666, 3:920

Richard Hurdis; or, The Avenger of Blood, 1:696

Richard Palmer Blackmur, 1:816

Richard Price as Moral Philosopher and Political Theorist, 4:211

Richard's Cork Leg, 1:441

Richard II, 1:205, 1:206

Richard Strauss: A Chronicle of the Early Years, 1864–1898, 3:722

Richard Strauss: The Staging of His Operas and Ballets, 3:721

Richard the Lion-Hearted, 1:145

Richard III, 1:205, 1:206, 1:211, 1:1069

Richard III: The Great Debate, 3:357

Richard Wagner: His Life, His Work, His Century, 3:728

Richard Wagner and His World, 3:729

Richard Wagner and the Modern British Novel, 2:987

Richard Wagner and the Nibelungs, 3:728

Richard Wilbur: A Reference Guide, 1:1066

Richard Wilbur's Creation, 1:1066

Richard Wright, 1:906, 1:907
Richard Wright: Books and Writers, 1:906
Richard Wright: Myths and Realities, 1:906
Richard Wright: Ordeal of a Native Son, 1:906
Richard Wright: The Critical Reception, 1:906
A Richard Wright Bibliography, 1:906
Richard Wright's Art of Tragedy, 1:906
Richard Wright's Native Son, 1:906
Riches of the Wild: Land Mammals of South-East Asia, 5:769
Rich Like Us, 2:182
Richmond Lattimore, 2:349
The Rich Nations and the Poor Nations, 3:66, 3:296
Rickshaw: The Novel Lo-t'o Hsiang-tzu, 2:251
Rickshaw Beijing: City People and Politics in the 1920s, 3:472
The Ricoeur Reader: Reflection and Imagination, 4:319
The Riddle of Gravitation, 5:664
The Riddle of the Dinosaur, 5:640
The Riddle of the Early Academy, 4:79
Riders in the Chariot, 2:965, 2:966
Riders of Judgment, 1:1217
Riders of the Purple Sage, 1:1210, 1:1213
Riders on the Earth: Essays and Recollections, 1:858
Riders to the Sea, 1:555
The Riding Master, 2:648
Riding the Iron Rooster: By Train through China, 3:940
Riding with the Dolphins, 5:770
Riegel's Handbook of Industrial Chemistry, 5:725
Rienzi, 1:340
Rigby's Romance, 2:952
Right and Wrong: A Philosophical Dialogue between Father and Son, 4:340
The Right Brain, 5:339
The Righteous Remnant: The House of David, 4:844
The Right Madness on Skye: Poems, 1:990
Rights, 4:387

Rights, Restitution, and Risk, 4:387
Rights at Work: Employment Relations in the Post-Union Era, 3:60
The Rights of Doctors, Nurses and Allied Health Professionals, 5:343
Rights of Man, 1:641
Rights of Man: Part the Second, 1:641
Rights of Man and Natural Law, 4:307
The Rights of Nature: A History of Environmental Ethics, 3:550, 5:824
Rights of Passage, 2:933
The Rights of Patients: The Basic ACLU Guide to Patient Rights, 5:343
The Right Stuff, 5:597
The Right to an Answer, 1:453, 1:454
The Right to Die, 4:389, 5:378
The Right to Dream, 4:274
A Right to Song: The Life of John Clare, 1:286
The Rig Veda: An Anthology, 4:501
Rigvedic India, 4:501
Rilke, 2:608
Rimbaud: A Critical Introduction, 2:500
Rimbaud: Visions and Habitations, 2:499
Rime disperse, 2:434
Rime e ritmi, 2:412
Rime Nuove, 2:412
Rime of the Ancient Mariner, 1:267
Rime or Canzoniere, 2:433
The Rimers of Eldritch, 1:1121
The Rimers of Eldritch and Other Plays, 1:1121
Rinconete and Cortadillo, Man of Glass, 2:535
The Ring, 1:1224
Ring: A Biography of Ring Lardner, 1:852
The Ring and the Book, 1:338
Ring Lardner, 1:852
A Ring of Conspirators: Henry James and his Literary Circle, 1895–1915, 1:767
The Ring of the Dove: A Treatise on the Art and Practice of Arab Love, 4:583
The Ring of the Nibelungs, 2:644, 3:728

Rings of Burnished Brass, 2:65
Rings of Burnished Brass and Other Stories, 2:122
Ringworld, 1:1261
The Ringworld Engineers, 1:1261
Rio Grande, 1:1165
Rioters and Citizens: Mass Protest in Imperial Japan, 3:478
Riot in Heaven, 2:144
The Ripening Seed, 2:470
Ripley Underground, 1:1231
Ripley Under Water, 1:1231
Riprap and Cold Mountain Poems, 1:1052
Rip Van Winkle, 1:332, 1:1069
Risalat al-Ghufran, 2:61
Risalat al-Qiyan, 2:66
Risalāt al-Tauhīd, 4:374
Rise and Decline of Western Liberalism, 3:340
The Rise and Destiny of the German Jew, 4:637
The Rise and Fall and Rise of Modern Dance, 3:731
The Rise and Fall of Athens: Nine Greek Lives, 3:318
The Rise and Fall of British Naval Mastery, 3:341
The Rise and Fall of the Judean State, 4:605
The Rise and Fall of the British Documentary, 3:826
The Rise and Fall of the Communist Party in Burma, 3:489
The Rise and Fall of the Confederate Government, 3:574
The Rise and Fall of the Great Powers, 3:149, 3:326
The Rise and Fall of the Man of Letters, 1:273, 1:429
The Rise and Fall of the Plantation Complex: Early Atlantic History, 3:426
The Rise and Fall of the Third Reich, 3:344
The Rise and Fall of the Well-Made Play, 1:426
The Rise of American Civilization, 3:566
"The Rise of American Edition Binding," 1:26
The Rise of American Philosophy, 4:34, 4:265

The Rise of Anthropological Theory: A History of Theories of Culture, 3:32, 5:34

The Rise of Christian Europe, 3:411

The Rise of Christianity, 4:681

The Rise of David Levinsky, 1:737, 2:37

The Rise of Financial Capitalism, 3:55

The Rise of German Industrial Power, 1834–1914, 3:377

The Rise of Historical Sociology, 5:35

The Rise of Managerial Computing, 5:557

The Rise of Modern China, 3:471

The Rise of Modern Industry, 3:404

The Rise of Modern Japan, 3:476

The Rise of Music in the Ancient World: East and West, 3:663

The Rise of Neo-Confucianism in Korea, 4:540

The Rise of Puritanism, 4:734

The Rise of Reform Judaism: A Sourcebook of Its European Origins, 4:653

The Rise of Respectable Society, 1:313, 3:365

The Rise of Robert Millikan: Portrait of a Life in American Science, 5:702

The Rise of Romance, 1:155

The Rise of Rome to 264 B.C., 3:303

The Rise of Science and the Enlightenment, 3:337

The Rise of Scientific Philosophy, 4:385

The Rise of Silas Lapham, 1:758

The Rise of the American Novel, 1:722

The Rise of the Anglo-German Antagonism: 1860–1914, 3:366

The Rise of the Atlantic Economies, 3:335

The Rise of the City, 1878–1898, 3:596

The Rise of the Common Player, 1:169

The Rise of the Computer State, 5:74, 5:572

The Rise of the Corporate Commonwealth, 3:547

The Rise of the Great Powers, 3:338

The Rise of the Greek Epic, 2:347

The Rise of the Gunbelt: The Military Remapping of Industrial America, 3:548

The Rise of the Monophysite Movement, 4:685

The Rise of the New Model Army, 3:360

The Rise of the New West, 1819–1829, 3:599

The Rise of Theodore Roosevelt, 3:595, 3:936

The Rise of the Papacy, 4:688

The Rise of the Roman Empire, 3:319

The Rise of the Romanovs, 3:395

The Rise of the Russian Novel, 2:686

The Rise of the West, 3:326

The Rise of the West: A History of the Human Community, 3:274, 3:289

The Rise of Universities, 3:331, 4:101

The Rise of Western Rationalism, 4:160

Rise to Globalism: American Foreign Policy since 1938, 3:544

Rising from the Plains, 5:623, 5:645

The Rising Gorge, 1:868

The Rising in Western Upper Canada, 1837–38, 3:613

The Rising Sun, 3:280, 3:480

Risk, 4:317

Risk: A Philosophical Introduction to the Theory of Risk Evaluation and Management, 5:130

Risk, Uncertainty and Profit, 3:88, 3:89

Risk Acceptability According to the Social Sciences, 5:128

Risk Analysis and the Scientific Method, 5:76, 5:141

Risk and Blame: Essays in Cultural Theory, 3:29

Risk and Rationality: Philosophical Foundations for Populist Reforms, 5:76

The Risks of Nature: A History of Environmental Ethics, 5:115

Risk Watch: The Odds of Life, 5:354

The Risorgimento and the Unification of Italy, 3:385

Rites and Symbols of Initiation, 4:430, 4:897

The Rites of Assent, 1:948

Rites of Passage (Golding), 1:484

Rites of Passage (Van Gennep), 3:25, 4:430

Ritual, Myth and Magic in Early Modern Europe, 3:856

Ritual Cosmos: The Santification of Life in African Religions, 4:463

Ritual in the Dark, 1:567, 1:568

Ritual in Transfigured Time, 1:1163

Ritual Irony: Poetry and Sacrifice in Euripides, 2:357, 4;475

The Ritual of Battle: Krishna in the Mahabharata, 4:504

Ritual Poetry and the Politics of Death in Early Japan, 4:536

The Ritual Process: Structure and Anti-Structure, 3:24, 3:41, 4:430, 4:898

Rituals and Power: The Roman Imperial Cult in Asia Minor, 4:452

Rituals and Ritualism in Popular Culture, 3:875

Rituals of Manhood: Male Initiation in Papua New Guinea, 4:430

Ritual Theory, Ritual Practice, 4:426

The Rivals, 1:254

River (Hughes), 1:498

River (Leonov), 2:734

The River Between, 2:151, 2:153, 2:154

The River Breaks Up, 2:49

River in the Desert, 3:446

The River Ki, 2:285

River Morphology, 5:632

River of Life, and Other Stories, 2:733

Rivers and Mountains, 1:936

The Riverside Anthology of Children's Literature, 1:579, 1:1197

The Riverside Anthology of Literature, 1:130

The Riverside Chaucer, 1:150

The Riverside Shakespeare, 1:206

Rivers of Empire: Water, Aridity, and the Growth of the American West, 3:551

River Sumida, 2:291
Rivers West, 1:1216
Rizal without an Overcoat, 2:333
R.L.S. in the South Seas: An Intimate Photographic Record, 1:397
R.N., 5:337
The Road (London), 1:774
The Road (Martinson), 2:678
The Road (Soyinka), 2:149
The Road Back, 2:606
The Road Back to Paris, 3:814
Road Belong Cargo, 4:467
The Road Between, 1:833
The Road from Babylon: The Story of Sephardic and Oriental Jews, 4:594
The Road from Los Alamos: Collected Essays of Hans A. Bethe, 5:672
The Road of Science and the Ways to God, 5:202
Road Scholar: Coast to Coast Late in the Century, 3:895
Roadside Geology of Virginia, 5:626
Roadside Picnic, 2:762
Roads to Freedom: Socialism, Anarchism and Syndication, 4:323
The Road through the Wall, 1:992
The Road to Bithynina, 1:1223
The Road to Cibola, 3:135
The Road to Confederation. The Emergence of Canada: 1863–1867, 3:618
The Road to Disunion Vol. I: Secessionists at Bay, 1776–1854, 3:528
The Road to East Slope: The Development of Su Shi's Poetic Voice, 2:220
The Road to Jaramillo: Critical Years of the Revolution in Earth Science, 5:629
The Road to Medical Enlightenment, 1650–1695, 5:42
Road to Nirvana, 1:1098
The Road to Oz, 1:1200
Road to Pearl Harbor, 3:534
The Road to Realism, 1:759
The Road to Revolution: Scotland under Charles I, 1625–37, 3:368
The Road to Serfdom, 3:82

The Road to Tara: The Life of Margaret Mitchell, 1:1249
The Road to the City, 2:421, 2:422
The Road to the Never Land, 1:330
The Road to the White House 1992: The Politics of Presidential Elections, 3:144, 3:147
The Road to Total Freedom, 4:869
The Road to Tryermaine, 1:288
The Road to Wellsville, 1:953
The Road to Xanadu: A Study in the Ways of the Imagination, 1:288
The Road to Yalta: 1944–45, 3:396
Road with No End, 2:320
Roald Amundsen and Robert Scott: Race for the South Pole, 3:936
Roald Amundsen and the Quest for the South Pole, 3:912
Roanoke Island: The Beginning of English America, 3:518
The Roaring Girl, 1:190
The Roaring Silence: A Biography of John Cage, 3:686
The Robber Barons, 3:54
The Robber Bridegroom, 1:895
The Robbers, 2:563, 2:609
The Robbers, Wallenstein, 2:609
Robert, Duke of Normandy, 1:185
Robert A. Heinlein: America as Science Fiction, 1:1258
Robert Anderson, 1:1083
Robert Anson Heinlein, 1:1258
Robert Bellarmine, Saint and Scholar, 4:736
Robert Benchley: A Biography, 1:815
Robert Benchley: His Life and Good Times, 1:815
Robert Bly: An Introduction to the Poetry, 1:952
Robert Bly: When Sleepers Awake, 1:952
Robert Boyle: Founder of Modern Chemistry, 5:740
Robert Boyle and Seventeenth-Century Chemistry, 5:740

Robert Boyle on Natural Philosophy, 5:739
Robert Boyle's Experiments in Pneumatics, 5:739
Robert Browning, 1:339, 1:457
Robert Browning: A Bibliography, 1830–1950, 1:339
Robert Browning: A Life within Life, 1:339
Robert Browning: His Poetry and His Audiences, 1:339
Robert Bruce and the Community of the Realm of Scotland, 3:368
Robert Burns, 1:280
Robert Burns: The Critical Heritage, 1:281
Robert Burns: The Man, His Works, the Legend, 1:280
Robert Burns: The Man and His Work, 1:280
Robert Burns and His World, 1:280
Robert Burns Woodward and the Art of Organic Synthesis, 5:756
Robert Coover, 1:963
Robert Coover: The Universal Fictionmaking Process, 1:963
Robert Creeley, 1:966
Robert Creeley: An Inventory, 1:966
Robert Creeley's Life and Work: A Sense of Increment, 1:966
Robert Dale Owen, 4:844
Robert Duncan: A Descriptive Biography, 1:971
Robert Duncan: Scales of the Marvelous, 1:971
Robert E. Peary and the Fight for the North Pole, 3:933
Robert Frost, 1:842
Robert Frost: A Biography, 1:842
Robert Frost: An Anthology of Recent Criticism, 1:842
Robert Frost: The Man and the Poet, 1:842
Robert Frost: The Work of Knowing, 1:842
Robert Frost and the New England Renaissance, 1:842
Robert Frost Himself, 1:842
Robert Frost Poetry and Prose, 1:842
Robert Frost's Imagery and the Poetic Consciousness, 1:842

Robert Fulton: A Biography, 5:248

Robert Graves, 1:485, 1:486

Robert Graves: An Annotated Bibliography, 1:485

Robert Graves: His Life and Works, 1:486

Robert Graves: The Lasting Poetic Achievement, 1:486

Robert Graves: The Years with Laura, 1926–1940, 1:486

Robert Greene Criticism: A Comprehensive Bibliography, 1:180

Robert Grosseteste: Scholar and Bishop, 4:115

Robert Hayden: A Critical Analysis of His Poetry, 1:986

Robert Herrick: A Biographical and Critical Study, 1:182

Robert Herrick's Hesperides and the Epigram Book Tradition, 1:182

Robert Hunter Middleton, 1:18

Robert K. Merton's Social Theory, 3:233

Robert Kennedy and His Times, 3:597

Robert Kennedy in His Own Words, 3:597

Robert Koch: A Life in Medicine and Bacteriology, 5:801

Robert Kroetsch, 2:916

Robert Kroetsch and His Works, 2:916

Robert Laird Borden: A Biography, 3:614

Robert Louis Stevenson, 1:397

Robert Louis Stevenson: The Critical Heritage, 1:397

Robert Louis Stevenson and Romantic Tradition, 1:397

Robert Lowell, 1:1006

Robert Lowell: A Biography, 1:1006

Robert Lowell: An Introduction to the Poetry, 1:1006

Robert Lowell: Interviews and Memoirs, 1:1006

Robert Lowell: Life and Art, 1:1006

Robert M. Hutchins: Portrait of an Educator, 3:264

Robert Maynard Hutchins: A Memoir, 3:264

Robert Musil, Master of the Hovering Life, 2:604

Robert Musil and the Crisis of European Culture, 2:604

Robert Musil and the Culture of Vienna, 2:604

Robert Oppenheimer: Letters and Recollections, 5:707

Robert Oppenheimer: Shatterer of Worlds, 5:707

Robert Penn Warren, 1:893, 1:894

Robert Penn Warren: A Collection of Critical Essays, 1:893

Robert Penn Warren: A Descriptive Bibliography, 1922–1979, 1:893

Robert Penn Warren and American Idealism, 1:893

Robert Penn Warren and the American Imagination, 1:894

Robert Penn Warren's All the King's Men, 1:893

Robert Pinget: The Novel as Quest, 2:493

Robert Schumann and the Study of Orchestral Composition, 3:716

Robert Schumann Words and Music: The Vocal Compositions, 3:716

Robertson Davies, 2:910

Robertson Davies: An Appreciation, 2:910

Robert Southey, 1:305

Robert Southey: A Reference Guide, 1:305

Robert Southey and His Age: The Development of a Conservative, 1:305

Robespierre, 3:374

Robin Goodfellow, 1:332

Robinson Crusoe, 1:238, 1:239, 1:374, 1:574, 1:576, 2:512

Robinson Jeffers, 1:851

Robinson Jeffers: The Man and His Work, 1:851

Robinson Jeffers and the Critics, 1912–1983, 1:851

Robotics and AI: An Introduction to Applied Machine Intelligence, 5:569

Robotics in Non-industrial Environments, 5:243

Robotics Research, 5:242

The Robot Revolution, 5:242

Robots: Machines in Man's Image, 5:242

Rob Roy, 1:298

The Rock, 1:471

Rock Encyclopedia, 3:657

Rocket Ship Galileo, 1:1258

The Rocket Team, 5:613

Rock Formation: Music, Technology, and the Production of Culture, 3:873

Rock Garden, 2:374

The Rocking Chair, 2:915

Rockinghorse, 2:21

Rocking the Ship of State: Towards a Feminist Peace Politics, 3:279

Rock Music in American Popular Culture, 3:872

Rodale's Encyclopedia of Natural Home Remedies, 5:310

Roderick Hudson, 1:763

Roderick M. Chisholm, 4:395

Roderick Random, 1:256, 1:662

Rodgers and Hammerstein, 3:713

Rodgers and Hammerstein: The Men and Their Music, 3:713

Rodgers and Hart: Bewitched, Bothered, and Bedeviled, 3:713

Rodin, 3:791

Rodin: A Biography, 3:791

Rodin: Sculpture and Drawings, 3:791

Rodman the Keeper: Southern Sketches, 1:790

Rodogune: The French Text with a Facing English Translation, 2:471

The Roeblings: A Century of Engineers, Bridge-Builders and Industrialists, 5:224

Roger Bacon and His Search for a Universal Science, 4:111

Roger Bacon's Letter Concerning the Marvelous Power of Art and of Nature and Concerning the Nullity of Magic, 4:111

Roger Mais, 2:937

Roger's Version, 1:1060

Roger Williams: The Church and the State, 3:588

Roget's II: The New Thesaurus, 1:94

Roget's International Thesaurus, 1:93

Roget's University Thesaurus, 1:94

The Rogue, 1:1221

The Rogue; or The Life of Guzmán de Alfarache, 2:529

Rohm and Haas: History of a Chemical Company, 5:728

Roland Barthes, 1:1131, 2:455

Roland Barthes: A Conservative Estimate, 2:455

Roland Barthes: Structuralism and After, 2:455

Roland-Michel Barrin de La Galissonière 1693–1756, 3:620

Role of Fats in Food and Nutrition, 5:345

The Role of Mood in Heidegger's Ontology, 4:292

The Role of Providence in the Social Order, 3:110, 3:111

The Role of the Americas in History, 3:626

The Role of the Emotions and the Will in the Process of Mental Phenomena, 4:323

The Role of the Mythic West in Some Representative Examples of Classic and Modern American Literature, 1:803

The Role of the Priest in the Novels of Georges Bernanos, 2:460

The Role of Value in Karl Mannheim's Sociology of Knowledge, 3:232

The Role of Women in Early Christianity, 4:679

Roll, Jordan, Roll: The World the Slaves Made, 3:524, 3:580

Rølvaag: His Life and Art, 2:667

The Roly-Poly Pudding, 1:588

Romain Rolland: The Man and His Works, 2:501, 2:617

Romain Rolland and a World at War, 2:501

Romaji Diary and Sad Toys, 2:288

The Roman, 2:661

Roman Architecture, 3:305, 3:764

Roman Art, 3:760

Roman Art and Architecture, 3:760

Roman Augury and Etruscan Divination, 4:448

Roman Britain, 3:356

Roman Britain and Early England, 55 B.C. to A.D. 871, 3:356

The Roman Catholic Church and the Creation of the Modern Irish State, 1878–1886, 3:371

The Roman Catholic Church and the North-West School Question, 3:615

Roman Catholic Modernism, 4:741

Romance Literatures, 2:523

The Romance of a Plain Man, 1:843

The Romance of Sorcery, 1:597

A Romance of the Equator, 1:613

The Romance of the Forest, 1:622

Romance of the Jade Bracelet and Other Chinese Operas, 2:193

The Romance of the Rose, 1:150, 2:502

Romance of the Three Kingdoms, 2:188, 2:211, 2:212, 2:219

The Romance of the Western Chamber, 2:188, 2:226, 2:227

The Romance of Tristan and Iseult as Retold by Joseph Bédier, 2:512

The Romance of Tristan and Isolt, 2:512

The Romance of William Morris, 1:383

Romance of Wolves, 2:553

Romances and Narratives, 1:240

Romances of Roguery: The Picaresque Novel in Spain, 2:524

The Romances of William Morris, 1:383

The Romance Tradition in Urdu, 2:175

The Roman Citizenship, 3:306

Roman Civilization, 3:300

Roman Coins, 3:306

Roman Comedy, 2:381

Roman Elegies and Other Poems, 2:581

The Roman Empire, 3:303

The Roman Empire: Economy, Society and Culture, 3:307

The Roman Empire and Its Neighbors, 3:303

The Roman Empire of Ammianus, 3:310

Roman Erotic Elegy: Love, Poetry, and the West, 2:381

Romanesque Architecture, 3:763

Roman Farming, 3:304

The Roman Festivals of the Period of the Republic, 4:448

Roman Fever: And Other Stories, 1:787

Roman Historical Coins, 3:306

Roman History (Ammianus), 3:310,

Roman History (Appian), 2:380, 3:311

Roman History (Dio Lassus), 3:314

Romanian-English/English-Romanian Dictionary, 1:102

The Romanians: A History, 3:390

Romanian Short Stories, 2:824

Roman Laughter: The Comedy of Plautus, 2:391

Roman Law, 3:305

Roman Law and Common Law: A Comparison in Outline, 3:305

Roman Lettering, 1:15

Roman Literary Portraits: Aspects of the Literature of the Roman Empire, 2:381

Roman Literary Theory and Criticism, 2:380

Roman Literature and Society, 2:381

Roman Medicine, 3:304, 5:39

The Roman Mind, 4:59

Roman Nature: The Thought of Pliny the Elder, 5:810

Roman Nights and Other Stories, 2:432

The Roman Nobility, 3:307

Roman Poems: Bilingual Edition, 2:431

Roman Poetry: From the Republic to the Silver Age, 2:382

The Roman Poets of the Republic, 2:381

Roman Polanski, 3:841

Roman Quarry and Other Sequences, 1:502

The Roman Revolution, 2:381, 3:303

The Romans, 2:380

The Romans: An Introduction to Their History and Civilization, 2:380

The Romans and Their Gods in the Age of Augustus, 4:448

Roman Science, 5:39

The Romans in Britain, 1:450

Roman Social Relations, 50 B.C. to A.D. 284, 3:308

The Roman Soldier, 3:309

Romans on the Rhine: Archaeology in Germany, 3:305

Roman Stoicism: Being Lectures, 4:59

Roman Tales, 2:429

The Romantic Age, 1:266

The Romantic Agony, 2:401, 2:986

Romantic Bards and British Reviewers, 1:268, 1:274

The Romantic Body, 1:294

The Romantic Comedians, 1:843

Romantic Cruxes: The English Essayists and the Spirit of the Age, 1:273

Romantic Ecology: Wordsworth and the Environmental Tradition, 1:306

The Romantic Ethic and the Spirit of Modern Consumerism, 3:209

The Romantic Exiles: A Nineteenth-Century Portrait Gallery, 3:139

The Romantic Foundations of the American Renaissance, 1:650

The Romantic Generation of Modern Chinese Writers, 2:234

The Romantic Heritage of Marxism, 2:566

The Romantic Ideology: A Critical Investigation, 1:265

The Romantic Image, 1:417

Romanticism and Anthony Trollope, 1:407

Romanticism and Feminism, 1:266, 2:986

Romanticism and Marxism, 4:253

Romanticism and Revolt, 3:341

The Romantic Lady, 1:1201

Romantic Legends of Spain, 2:531

The Romantic Mother: Narcissistic Patterns in Romantic Poetry, 1:268

Romantic Music: A Concise History from Schubert to Sibelius, 3:664

Romantic Music: A History of Musical Style in Nineteenth-Century Europe, 3:662

Romantic Narrative Art, 1:270

The Romantic Novel in England, 1:270

Romantic Poets and Prose Writers, 1:268

Romantic Poets and the Epic Tradition, 1:268

The Romantic Revolution in America, 1800–1860, 1:651

Romantics, Rebels, and Reactionaries, 1:268

The Romantic School and Other Essays, 2:588

The Romantics on Milton: Formal Essays and Critical Asides, 1:266

The Romantics Reviewed, 1:266, 1:274

The Romantic Ventriloquists, 1:267

The Roman Way, 2:381, 3:881

The Roman World of Dio Chrysostom, 3:314

The Romany Rye, 3:912, 3:913

Rome and Italy, 3:317

Rome and the Counter-Reformation in Scandinavia, 4:736

Rome and the Greek East to the Death of Augustine, 3:300

Rome and the Mediterranean, 3:317

Rome in Canada, 3:608

Rome in the Augustan Age, 2:381

Romeo and Juliet, 1:179, 1:205, 1:206

Rome on the Euphrates, 3:938

Romiosyne, 2:375

Rommel: The Desert Fox, 3:345

Rommel Papers, 3:280

Romola, 1:353

Ronald Firbank, 1:474

Ronald Firbank: A Biography, 1:474

Ronia, the Robber's Daughter, 2:677

The Roofing Ceremony, 2:679

The Roofing Ceremony and The Silver Lake, 2:680

Rookledge's International Typefinder, 1:19

Rookledge's International Handbook of Type Designers, 1:15

Room at the Top, 1:449

A Room of One's Own, 1:569

Room's Dictionary of Confusibles, 1:94

Room's Dictionary of Distinguishables and Confusibles, 1:94

A Room with a View, 1:476

Room without Walls, 2:658

Roosevelt: The Lion and the Fox, 3:571

Roosevelt: The Soldier of Fortune, 3:571

Roosevelt after Inauguration, 1:957

Roosevelt and the Isolationists, 1932–1945, 3:534

The Roosevelt Family of Sagamore Hill, 3:595

Roosevelt Research, 3:506

Rootabaga Stories, 1:878

Rootabaga Stories, Pt. 1, 1:1205

Rootabaga Stories, Pt. 2, 1:1205

Roots, 1:425

Roots and Branches, 1:971

The Roots of American Bureaucracy, 1830–1900, 3:532

The Roots of American Psychology, 3:168

Roots of Black Music, 3:867

The Roots of Civilization, 4:434

The Roots of English: A Reader's Handbook of Word Origins, 1:95

The Roots of Ethics: Science, Religion, and Values, 5:84

The Roots of Fundamentalism, 4:754

Roots of Modern Mormonism, 4:846

Roots of Negro Racial Consciousness, 1:824, 1:857

The Roots of Reference, 4:411, 5:100

Roots of Revolution: An Interpretive History of Modern Iran, 3:448

The Roots of the Modern American Empire, 3:601

Rope, 1:1168

The Rope and Other Plays,
2:391
A Rope for Dr. Webster,
1:965
The Ropemakers of Plym-
outh, 3:589
Rope of Ash, 2:326
Rorty's Humanistic Pragma-
tism, 4:413
Rosalind, 1:329
Rosa Luxemburg, 3:377
Rosalynde, 1:185
Rosary of the White Lotuses,
4:541
Rose, Blanche, and Violet,
1:373
Rose, Where Did You Get
That Red?, 1:1001, 1:1002
Rose and Lotus: Narrative of
Desire in France and Chi-
na, 2:190
Rose in Bloom, 1:1198
A Rose in Winter, 1:1225
Rosenbach: A Biography,
1:34, 1:43
A Rosen by Any Other
Name, 1:1094
Rosencrantz and Guilden-
stern, 1:357
Rosencrantz and Guilden-
stern Are Dead, 1:553,
1:554
The Rosendorf Quartet: A
Novel, 2:23
Rose of Dutcher's Coolly,
1:751
A Rose of Flesh, 2:633
The Rose of Life, 1:333
The Rose Rent, 1:609
Roses: An Illustrated Ency-
clopedia and Grower's
Handbook, 5:767
Roses and Thorns, 2:235
The Rose Tattoo, 1:1117
Rosh Hashanah Anthology,
4:599
The Rosicrucian Enlighten-
ment, 4:848
Rosicrucianism in America,
4:848
Rosicrucian Questions and
Answers, 4:848
The Rosicrucians: Their Rites
and Mysteries, 4:848
Rosmersholm, 2:665, 2:666
Rossetti and His Circle,
1:392
Rossetti's Portrait Drawings
of Elizabeth Siddall, 1:392
Ross Macdonald (Kenneth
Millar), 1:1235
The Rosy Cross Unveiled,
4:848

The Rosy Crucifixion, 1:861
Rothamsted Memoirs on Ag-
ricultural Chemistry and
Physiology, 5:273
Rotting Hill, 1:514
Roubles in Words, Kopeks in
Figures and Other Stories,
2:756
The Rouge of the North,
2:238
Rough Crossing and On the
Razzle, 1:554
Roughing It, 1:781
Roughing It in the Bush,
2:903, 2:920
Rough Magic: A Biography
of Sylvia Plath, 1:1031
The Rough Riders, 3:594,
3:935
The Rougon-Macquart, 2:517
Roumanian Folktales Retold
from the Original, 3:856
Roumanian Stories, 2:824
Roumeli: Travels in Northern
Greece, 3:899
Round about Midnight: A
Portrait of Miles Davis,
3:691
Round and Round the Gar-
den, 1:436
Round Ireland in Low Gear,
3:900
The Round Table, 1:291
Rousseau: An Introduction to
His Psychological, Social
and Political Theory, 4:213
Rousseau: Confessions, 4:213
Rousseau: Dreamer of De-
mocracy, 3:164, 4:214
Rousseau: Totalitarian or
Liberal, 3:164
Rousseau, Judge of Jean-Jac-
ques, 4:213
Rousseau, Nature and His-
tory, 3:337
Rousseau and Revolution,
3:402
Rousseau and the Religious
Quest, 4:214
Rousseau's Social Contract:
The Design of the Argu-
ment, 4:213
The Route of Parmenides,
4:52
The Rover, 1:233
The Rover, Part II, 1:233
The Rowley Poems, 1:285
Roxana, 1:239
The Royal Ballet: A Picture
History, 3:734
The Royal Ballet: The First
Fifty Years, 3:734

Royal Charles: Charles II
and the Restoration, 4:734
Royal Commentaries of the
Incas, and General History
of Peru, 3:646
Royal English Bookbindings,
1:23
The Royal Family, 1:1097
Royal Family, Royal Lovers,
3:359
The Royal Game, 2:617
The Royal Guest: And Other
Classical Danish Narrative,
2:645
Royal Highness, 2:602
The Royal Hunt of the Sun,
1:543
Royall Tyler, 1:645
The Royal Pardon, 1:434
The Royal Play of "Mac-
beth," 1:214
The Royal Road to Ro-
mance, 3:892
The Royal Shakespeare Com-
pany: A History of Ten
Decades, 1:426
Royce and Hocking: Ameri-
can Idealists, 4:250
Royce's Logical Essays, 4:250
Royce's Mature Philosophy
of Religion, 4:250
Royce's Metaphysics, 4:250,
4:305
Royce's Social Infinite: The
Community of Interpreta-
tion, 4:250
Roy Fuller, 1:481
R. R. Bowker: Militant Lib-
eral, 1:40
Rubaiyat (Hikmet), 2:98
The Ruba'iyat of Omar
Khayyam, 1:522, 2:92
Rubens, 3:792
Ruddigore, 1:272
Rudeness and Civility: Man-
ners in Nineteenth-Century
Urban America, 3:560
Rudin, 2:768, 2:769
Rudolf Bultmann, 4:831
Rudolf Otto: An Introduction
to His Philosophical The-
ology, 4:488
Rudolf Otto's Interpretation
of Religion, 4:488
Rudolf Steiner: Herald of a
New Epoch, 4:858
Rudolf Virchow: Doctor,
Statesman, Anthropologist,
5:410
Rudolph Steiner: Scientist of
the Invisible, 4:880
Rudyard Kipling, 1:371,
1:432

Rudyard Kipling: Realist and Fabulist, 1:372

Rudyard Kipling and the Fiction of Adolescence, 1:372

Rudyard Kipling's India, 1:372

Rudyard Kipling's "Kim," 1:372

Rudy Wiebe and His Works, 2:928

The Ruffian on the Stair, 1:529

Rufino Tamayo: Myth and Magic, 2:879

Rugged Individualism Reconsidered: Essays in Psychological Anthropology, 3:15

The Ruined Map, 2:284

Ruin the Sacred Truths, 1:1138

Rule, Britannia, 1:261

Rule of Darkness: British Literature and Imperialism, 1830–1914, 1:311

The Rule of Metaphor, 4:319

The Rule of Saint Benedict: A Doctrinal and Spiritual Commentary, 4:688

The Rule of St. Benedict in Latin and English with Notes, 4:705

The Rule of the Master, 4:705

Rulers, Townsmen, and Bazaars, 3:485

The Rules of Sociological Method, 3:200, 3:225

The Ruling Class, 3:140

The Ruling Race: A History of American Slaveholders, 3:525

Rumi: Poet and Mystic, 4:589

Rum Island, 2:631

Rumors of Rain, 2:159

Rumor Verified: Poems, 1979–1980, 1:893

The Rump Parliament, 1648–1653, 3:361

Run, River, Run, 3:898

Runaway Horses, 2:289

Runestaff, Number 1: Jewel in the Skull, 1:616

Runestaff, Number 2: Mad God's Amulet, 1:617

Runestaff, Number 3: Sword of the Dawn, 1:617

Runestaff, Number 4: Runestaff, 1:617

Rungless Ladder: Harriet Beecher Stowe and New England Puritanism, 1:699

Runner of the Mountain Tops: The Life of Louis Agassiz, 5:786

The Runner's World Knee Book, 5:400

Running for President: The Candidates and Their Images, 3:597

Running in the Family, 2:922

Running MS-DOS, 5:555

Running the Amazon, 3:895

Run School Run, 3:248

Rupert Brooke and the Intellectual Imagination, 1:451

Rural Education: In Search of a Better Way, 3:256

Rural Electrification for Development: Analysis and Policy Applications, 5:292

Rural Health Care: Innovation in a Changing Environment, 5:333

Rural Heath Organization: Social Networks and Regionalization, 5:328

Rural Life in Victorian England, 3:364

Rural Poverty in America, 3:211

Rural Russia under the Old Regime, 3:395

The Rural Tradition, 1:429

R.U.R. and The Insect Play, 2:790

The Rushdie File, 2:181

Rushes, 1:1191

Rush Hour of the Gods, 4:541

Ruskin and the Art of the Beholder, 1:395

Ruskin's Drawings in the Ashmolean Museum, 1:395

Ruskin's Maze: Mastery and Madness in His Art, 1:395

Russell, 4:324, 5:103

Russell and Moore: The Analytical Heritage, 4:273, 4:312, 4:324

Russell's Idealist Apprenticeship, 4:324

Russia, 3:395

Russia, Poland and the West: Essay in Literary and Cultural History, 2:811

Russia, the Atom and the West, 3:584

Russia, the Soviet Union, and the United States: An Interpretive History, 3:545

Russia 1917: The Karnilov Affair, 3:396

Russia 1917—The February Revolution, 3:396

Russia According to Women, 2:692

Russia and America: A Philosophical Comparison, 4:31, 4:34

Russia and the Russians: Inside the Closed Society, 3:396

Russia and the West under Lenin and Stalin, 3:584

Russia at the Dawn of the Modern Age, 3:413

Russia at War, 3:281

The Russia House, 1:596

Russian and Polish Women's Fiction, 2:692

A Russian Beauty and Other Stories, 2:740

A Russian Civil War Diary: Alexis V. Babine in Saratov, 1917–1922, 3:397

A Russian Cultural Revival, 2:693

Russian Culture in the 1980's, 2:686

Russian Drama from Its Beginnings to the Age of Pushkin, 2:687

Russian Empire 1801–1917, 3:395

Russian-English Dictionary, 1:102

Russian Expansion to the Pacific 1641–1850, 3:395

Russian Fairy Tales, 2:691

Russian Folk Belief, 2:687

Russian Folk Epos in Czech Literature: 1800–1900, 2:789

Russian Folklore, 2:690

Russian Folk Lyrics, 2:693

The Russian Forest, 2:734

Russian Formalism: A Metapoetics, 2:690

Russian Formalism: History-Doctrine, 2:686

Russian Formalism and Anglo-American New Criticism, 2:691

Russian Formalist Criticism: Four Essays, 2:688

Russian Formalist Film Theory, 2:685

Russian Formalist Theory and Its Poetic Ambience, 2:689

The Russian Frontier, 3:395

Russian Futurism: A History, 2:688

Russian Futurism through Its Manifestos, 1912–1928, 2:692

A Russian Gentleman, 2:697

Russian Gypsy Tales, 3:855
The Russian Idea, 4:275
Russian Intellectual History:
    An Anthology, 2:693
The Russianization of Gil
    Blas: A Study in Literary
    Appropriation, 2:688
The Russian Jewry Reader,
    3:348
The Russian Jew under Tsars
    and Soviets, 4:635
A Russian Journal, 1:884,
    1:885
Russian Life in Town and
    Country, 3:394
Russian Literary Criticism: A
    Short History, 2:690
Russian Literary Politics and
    the Pushkin Celebration of
    1880, 2:688
Russian Literature: Ideals
    and Realities, 2:687
Russian Literature and Ideol-
    ogy, 2:690
Russian Literature and Psy-
    choanalysis, 2:689
Russian Literature in the
    Nineteenth Century, 2:18
Russian Literature of the
    Twenties: An Anthology,
    2:693
Russian Literature since the
    Revolution, 2:685
Russian Literature under Le-
    nin and Stalin 1917–1953,
    2:690
The Russian Master and Oth-
    er Stories, 2:708
Russian Metaphysical Roman-
    ticism: The Poetry of Tiut-
    chev and Boratynskii,
    2:771
Russian Mystics, 4:755
The Russian Novel from
    Pushkin to Pasternak,
    2:686
The Russian Novelists, 2:691
The Russian Orthodox
    Church: A Contemporary
    History, 4:755
Russian Orthodoxy under the
    Old Regime, 3:394
The Russian People and So-
    cialism, 2:728
Russian Philosophical Termi-
    nology, 4:30
Russian Philosophy, 4:31
Russian Poetry: Meter,
    Rhythm and Rhyme, 2:690
The Russian Proprietor and
    Other Stories, 2:764
Russian Prose, 2:686

The Russian Revolution (Ber-
    dyaev), 4:275
The Russian Revolution
    (Chamberlin), 3:396
Russian Revolution: The
    Overthrow of Czarism and
    the Triumph of the So-
    viets, 3:295
The Russian Revolution,
    1900–1927, 3:343
The Russian Revolutionary
    Novel: Turgenev to Paster-
    nak, 2:686
The Russian Revolution from
    Lenin to Stalin,
    1917–1929, 3:396
The Russian Revolutions of
    1917: The Origins of Mod-
    ern Communism, 3:397
Russian Romantic Prose: An
    Anthology, 2:693
Russian's Balkan Entangle-
    ments, 1806–1914, 3:394
A Russian Schoolboy, 2:697
The Russian Soul and the
    Jew: Essays in Literary
    Ethno-Criticism, 2:685
Russian Themes, 2:688
Russian Theology, 1920–1965:
    A Bibliographic Survey,
    4:756
Russian Views of Pushkin's
    Eugene Onegin, 2:752
Russian Women: Two Sto-
    ries, 2:726
Russian Writers and Society:
    1825–1904, 2:687
Russian Writers and Soviet
    Society, 1917–1978, 2:687
Russian Writing since Nine-
    teen Fifty-Three: A Critical
    Survey, 2:688
Russia on the Way, 3:822
Russia under Peter the
    Great, 2:515
The Rustle of Language,
    2:455
Rusty's Story, 5:392
Ruth, 1:355
Ruth Benedict, 3:27
Ruth Benedict: Patterns of a
    Life, 3:27
Ruth Benedict: Stranger in
    This Land, 3:27
Rutherford: Recollections of
    the Cambridge Days, 5:712
Rutherford: Simple Genius,
    5:712
Rutherford and Boltwood:
    Letters on Radioactivity,
    5:712

Rutherford and Physics at
    the Turn of the Century,
    5:712
Rutherford and the Nature
    of the Atom, 5:712
Ruth Hall and Other Writ-
    ings, 1:671
Ruth Rabbah: An Analytical
    Translation, 4:612
Ruzzante Returns from the
    Wards, 2:402
R.V.W.: A Biography of
    Ralph Vaughan Williams,
    3:726
Ryan's Daughter, 1:445
Ryder, 1:812, 1:813

S

S, 1:1060
Saadia Gaon: His Life and
    Works, 4:672
Sabbatai Sevi: The Mystical
    Messiah, 2:36, 4:631
The Sabbath: Its Meaning for
    Modern Man, 4:665
Sabbatical: A Romance,
    1:942
The Sachertorte Algorithm
    and Other Antidotes to
    Computer Anxiety, 5:538
The Sackett Companion: A
    Personal Guide to the
    Sackett Novels, 1:1216
Sackett's Land, 1:1216
Sacramentum Mundi: An En-
    cyclopedia of Theology,
    4:719
The Sacred and Profane
    Love Machine, 1:523
The Sacred and the Profane:
    The Nature of Religion,
    4:472, 4:474
The Sacred Bridge: Liturgical
    Parallels in Synagogue and
    Early Church, 4:597
Sacred Canopy: Elements of
    a Sociological Theory of
    Religion, 3:212, 3:221,
    4:424, 4:890
A Sacred Circle, 3:523
The Sacred Fount, 1:763
Sacred Fragments: Recovering
    Theology for the Modern
    Jew, 4:620
The Sacred Hoop, 1:1130,
    1:1135, 1:1181
The Sacred in a Secular Age,
    3:212

Sacred Journeys: Conversion and Commitment to Divine Light Mission, 4:872
Sacred Keeper: A Biography of Patrick Kavanagh, 1:507
Sacred Narrative: Reading in the Theory of Myth, 4:428
The Sacred Night, 2:117
The Sacred Pipe, 4:464
Sacred Places: American Tourist Attractions in the Nineteenth Century, 3:893
The Sacred Portal: A Primary Symbol in Ancient Judaic Art, 4:614
Sacred Rage: The Crusade of Modern Islam, 4:573
Sacred Survival: The Civil Religion of American Jews, 4:641
A Sacred Thread, 4:509
The Sacred Void, 3:422
Sacred Wood, 1:472
Sacrifice: Its Nature and Function, 4:429
Sacrifice in Africa: A Structuralist Approach, 4:429
Sacrificial Smoke, 2:672
Sad Are the Eyes of William Tell, 2:526
The Saddest Pleasure: A Journey on Two Rivers, 3:910
The Saddest Story: A Biography of Ford Madox Ford, 1:476
Saddle and Ride, 1:1215
Sade: A Sudden Abyss, 2:503
Sade-Fourier-Loyola, 2:455, 2:503
The Sadeian Woman and the Ideology of Pornography, 1:455, 1:456, 3:207
Sadeq Hedayat: The Life and Literature of an Iranian Writer, 2:90
A Sad Heart at the Supermarket: Essays and Fables, 1:993
The Sad Lament of Pecos Bill on the Eve of Killing His Wife, 1:1111
Sadness and Happiness: Poems, 1:1030
Saeculum: History and Society in the Theology of St. Augustine, 4:110
Safe Conduct, 2:745, 2:746
Safe Delivery: Protecting Your Baby during High-Risk Pregnancy, 5:358

The Safe Deposit and Other Stories about Grandparents, Old Lovers, and Crazy Old Men, 2:47
Safed Spirituality, Rules of Mystical Piety and Elijah de Vidas' Beginning of Wisdom, 4:630
Safe Food, 5:346
Safeguarding Civil Liberty Today, 3:567
Safeguarding Intellectual Property, 1:54
A Safe Sea of Women: Lesbian Fiction 1969–1989, 1:1183
The Safety of Medicines: Evaluation and Prediction, 5:350
Safety Second: The NRC and America's Nuclear Power Plants, 5:239
Saga of Gisli the Outlaw, 2:640
The Saga of the Völsungs, 2:644
The Saga of Tristram and Isönd, 2:639
The Sage and the Way: Studies in Spinoza's Ethics of Freedom, 4:189
The Sage in Harlem: H. L. Mencken and the Black Writers of the 1920s, 1:860
Sage Philosophy, 4:26, 4:371
Sages and Dreamers, 1:1065
Sagesse, 2:514
Sagital Section: Poems by Miroslav Holub, 2:792
Sahil al-Jawad al-Abyad, 2:74
Sai Baba: The Holy Man and the Psychiatrist, 4:873
Saigon: Year of the Cat, 1:493
Sailing Alone around the World, 3:937
Sailing into the Unknown: Yeats, Pound, and Eliot, 1:800
Sailor Historian, 3:589
A Sailor's Guide to Production Sailboats, 5:238
St. Albert the Great, 4:107
St. Ambrose: His Life and Times, 4:702
Saint and Singer, 1:644
Saint and Sufi in Modern Egypt: An Essay in the Sociology of Religion, 3:445
St. Anselm: A Portrait in a Landscape, 4:703

Saint Anselm and His Biographer, 4:108
St. Anselm's Proslogion, 4:703
Saint Anthony and Other Stories, 2:488
St. Augustine of Hippo: Life and Controversies, 4:109
St. Augustine's Early Theory of Man, A.D. 386–391, 4:110
St. Augustine's Platonism, 4:110
Saint Basil and Monasticism, 4:705
St. Bernard of Clairvaux, 4:112
Saint-Exupéry in America, 1942–1943: A Memoir, 2:504
Saint Francis, 2:373, 2:374
St. Francis Xavier, 1506–1552, 4:728
Saint-Genet: Actor and Martyr, 2:507
Saint Genet, Comedian and Martyr, 2:478
Sainthood: Its Manifestations in World Religions, 4:505, 4:513, 4:526
St. Ignatius Loyola: The Pilgrim Years, 1491–1538, 4:770
St. Ives, 1:396
Saint Jack, 3:940
Saint Joan, 1:544, 1:545
Saint Joan of the Stockyards, 2:571, 2:572
St. John of the Cross, 2:543
St. John of the Cross: An Appreciation, 4:736
St. John of the Cross: Reflections on Mystical Experience, 2:543
Saint-John Perse, 2:493
Saint Judas, 1:1067
St. Martin's Dictionary of Twentieth-Century Composers, 1910–1971, 3:658
St. Mawr, 1:509
Saint Maybe: A Novel, 1:1059
St. Peter Canisius, 4:728
St. Petersburg, 2:700, 2:701
St. Peter's Fair, 1:609
The Saint Play in Medieval Europe, 1:160
St. Roman's Well, 1:298
Saints, Scholars, and Schizophrenics: Mental Illness in Rural Ireland, 5:428
Saints and Postmodernism, 4:392

Saints and Rebels: Seven Nonconformists in Stuart England, 3:360

Saints and Revolutionaries: Essays on Early American History, 3:517

Saints and Society, 4:701

Saints and Strangers, 1:455

Saint Servatius Legend, 2:619

The Saint's Lamp, 2:64

The Saint's Lamp and Other Stories, 2:64

St. Teresa of Avila (Clissold), 2:550, 4:786

St. Teresa of Avila (Papasogli), 4:787

St. Thérèse of Lisieux: By Those Who Knew Her, 4:741

St. Thomas and the Gentiles, 4:270

Saint Thomas and the Problem of Evil, 4:307

Saint Thomas and the World State, 3:263

St. Thomas Aquinas: On Charity, 4:118

St. Thomas Aquinas: On Spiritual Creatures, 4:118

St. Thomas Aquinas: Philosophical Texts, 4:118

St. Thomas Aquinas: Theological Texts, 4:118

Saint Urbain's Horseman, 2:924

Saint Watchings, 4:679

Saki, a Life of Hector Hugh Monroe, 1:523

Sakyadhita: Daughters of the Buddha, 4:515

Salamander: The Story of the Mormon Forgery Murders, 1:35

Salam Benua: Greetings to the Continent, 2:327

Salammbô, 2:475

Salazar and Modern Portugal, 3:386

Salem Chapel, 1:385

Salem Possessed, 3:516

Sales Publication Reference File, 1:109

Salina, 2:325

Salinger's Glass Stories as a Composite Novel, 1:1043

Salka Valka, 2:642

Sallust, 3:320

Sally Ride: Shooting for the Stars, 5:611

Salma-gundi, 2:161

Salman Rushdie, 2:181

Salman Rushdie and the Third World, 2:181

Salmonia, 5:742

Salomé, 1:409, 1:410

Salons, 2:472

Salt: The Brand Name Guide to Sodium Content, 5:346

The Salt Eaters, 1:940

Salterton Trilogy–Tempest Tost, 2:910

The Salt Garden, 1:1021

Salt Water Poems and Ballads, 1:518, 1:519

Salvat Encyclopedia of Science and Technology, 5:29

Salvation, 2:36

Salvation and Suicide, 4:867

The Salvation Hunters, 1:1176

Salvation in History, 4:832

Samaritan Documents: Relating to Their History, Religion and Life, 4:618

The Samaritan Pentateuch and the Origin of the Samaritan Sect, 4:618

The Samaritan Problem, 4:618

The Samaritans: History, Doctrines and Literature, 4:618

Samaritans and Jews: The Origins of Samaritanism Reconsidered, 4:618

Sam Clemens of Hannibal, 1:784

Same Door, 1:1060

Sam Holman, 1:833

Sam Lawson's Oldtown Fireside Stories, 1:699

Sammy Cahn's Rhyming Dictionary, 1:95

Sampler of Book Illustration Processes Issued in Connection with an Exhibition of Techniques in Book Illustration, 1:30

Sampling: A Quick, Reliable Guide to Practical Statistics, 5:524

Sam Shepard, Arthur Kopit, and the Off-Broadway Theater, 1:1111

Samskara: A Rite for a Dead Man, 2:177

Samson Agonistes, 1:191

Samuel Barber, 3:676

Samuel Barber: The Composer and His Music, 3:676

Samuel Beckett, 1:440, 2:460

Samuel Beckett: A Biography, 1:440

Samuel Beckett: A Reference Guide, 1:440

Samuel Beckett: Repetition, Theory, and Text, 1:440

Samuel Beckett: The Expressive Dilemma, 1:440

Samuel Beckett's Molloy, Malone Dies, The Unnamable, 2:460

Samuel Butler, 1:342

Samuel Butler Revalued, 1:342

Samuel Johnson, 1:249

Samuel Johnson: An Analysis, 1:250

Samuel Johnson, Biographer, 1:250

Samuel Johnson and Biographical Thinking, 1:250

Samuel Johnson and the Life of Writing, 1:250

Samuel Johnson and the Scale of Greatness, 1:250

Samuel Johnson on Shakespeare, 1:209, 1:250

Samuel Johnson's Attitudes to the Arts, 1:250

Samuel Richardson, 1:253, 1:254

Samuel Richardson: A Man of Letters, 1:254

Samuel Richardson: A Reference Guide, 1:254

Samuel Richardson: Master Printer, 1:254

Samuel Richardson: Passion and Prudence, 1:254

Samuel Richardson: Tercentenary Essays, 1:253

Samuelson and Neo-Classical Economics, 3:103

Samuel Taylor Coleridge: A Biographical Study, 1:287

Samuel Taylor Coleridge: A Bondage of Opium, 1:288

Samuel Taylor Coleridge: An Annotated Bibliography of Criticism and Scholarship, 1900–1939, 1:287

Samuel Taylor Coleridge, Lectures 1808–1819: On Literature, 1:288

Samuel Taylor Coleridge and the English Romantic School, 1:287

San Camilo, 1936, 2:534

San-ch'ü: Its Technique and Imagery, 2:191

The Sanctified Church, 1:850

Sanctorum Communio, 4:759

Sanctuary, 1:835

The Sanctuary Sparrow, 1:609

Sand and Other Poems, 2:58

The Sandbox, 1:1080, 1:1081

Sandburg Treasury: Prose and Poetry for Young People, 1:878
The Sand Castle, 1:523
The Sand Child, 2:117
A Sand County Almanac, 5:115, 5:834
Sandino, 3:639
The Sandino Affair, 3:639
The S and L Debacle: Public Policy Lessons for Bank and Thrift Regulation, 3:56
Sandra Street and Other Stories, 2:932
Sandro from Chegem, 2:729
The Sands of Mars, 1:614
The Sands of Time, 1:1223
Sandstone Depositional Models for Exploration for Fossil Fuels, 5:241
Sandstorms: Days and Nights in Arabia, 3:940
The Sane Positivist: A Biography of Edward L. Thorndike, 3:269
The Sane Society, 5:450
Sangha, State and Society: Thai Buddhism in History, 4:519
Sang-i Sabur, 2:87
Sang Thong, 2:336
Sanitary Report, 1:368
Sanshirō: A Novel by Natsume Sōseki, 2:291
Sanskrit Love Lyrics, 2:173
Sanskrit Poetry from Vidyākara's "Treasury," 2:172
Santa Fe Sunshine, 1:1096
Santander Regime in Gran Colombia, 3:635
Santayana: An Examination of His Philosophy, 4:328
Santayana: Saint of the Imagination, 4:327
Santayana, Art, and Aesthetics, 4:327
Santayana, Pragmatism and the Spiritual Life, 4:328
Santayana and the Sense of Beauty, 4:327
Santería: African Spirits in America, 4:868
Santería: The Religion, 4:868
The Santería Experience: A Journey into the Miraculous, 4:868
Santería from Africa to the New World, 4:868
The Sants: Studies in a Devotional Tradition of India, 4:517
Sapphira and the Slave Girl, 1:820

Sappho, 2:584
Sappho and Alcaeus, 2:366
Sappho and Her Influence, 2:366
Sappho to Valery, 2:5
Saqt al-Zand, 2:61
Sarah, or the Exemplary Wife, 1:643
Sarah Orne Jewett (Donovan), 1:770
Sarah Orne Jewett (Matthiessen), 1:770
Sarah Orne Jewett: Reconstructing Gender, 1:770
Sarah Orne Jewett, an American Persephone, 1:771
Sarapiqui Chronicle: A Naturalist in Costa Rica, 5:766
Sara Videbeck–The Chapel, 2:672
Sardines, 2:122
Saroyan: A Biography, 1:1110
Sartoris, 1:835
Sartor Resartus, 1:324, 1:343
Sartor Resartus and On Heroes and Hero-Worship, 1:343
Sartre (Caws), 4:330
Sartre (Hayman), 4:331
Sartre: A Life, 2:507, 4:330
Sartre: A Philosophic Study, 4:331
Sartre: Literature and Theory, 2:507
Sartre: Romantic Moralist, 4:331
Sartre: The Origins of a Style, 1:1148, 1:1149, 2:507
Sartre and Flaubert, 2:476, 2:507, 4:330
Sartre and Psychoanalysis, 4:330
Sartre's Concept of a Person, 4:331
Sartre's Existential Biographies, 4:331
Sartre's Marxism, 4:331
Sartre's Ontology, 4:330
Sartre's Political Theory, 4:331
Sartre's Second Critique, 4:330
Šarūnas, 2:806
Sarvodaya: The Welfare of All, 4:552
Satan: The Early Christian Tradition, 4:687
Satanic Bible, 4:868
The Satanic Rituals, 4:868
The Satanic Verses, 2:181
Satan in Goray, 1:1049, 2:48
The Satanism Scare, 4:868

Satanstoe; or, The Littlepage Manuscripts: A Tale of the Colony, 1:663
Satan Wants You! The Cult of Devil Worship in America, 4:868
Satchmo, 3:674
Satchmo: My Life in New Orleans, 3:674
Satellites, 2:145, 2:146
Satellites Today: The Complete Guide to Satellite Television, 5:228
Sati: Historical and Phenomenological Essays, 4:509
Sati: Widow Burning, 4:508
Satie the Composer, 3:714
The Satin Slipper, 2:468
Satire in Persian Literature, 2:83
Satire or Evasion?: Black Perspectives on Huckleberry Finn, 1:784
Satires of Decimus Junius Juvenalis, 2:387
Satirical Sketches, 4:484
Satisfaction Guaranteed: The Making of the American Mass Market, 3:549
Satori in Paris, 1:998
Saturday, Sunday, Monday, 2:419
Saturday Evening Post, 1:834
A Saturday Life, 1:492
Saturday Morning Murder: A Psychoanalytic Case, 2:18
Saturday Night and Sunday Morning, 1:547
Saturday Review, 1:869
Saturn, 5:610
Satyagraha in South Africa, 4:552
Satyajit Ray: The Inner Eye, 3:828
The Satyricon, 2:379, 2:390
Saudi Arabia, 3:451
Saudi Arabia and the Gulf War, 3:451
Saudi Arabia Unveiled, 3:451
Saul Bellow (Bradbury), 1:947
Saul Bellow (Dutton), 1:947
Saul Bellow (Scheer-Schaezler), 1:948
Saul Bellow: A Comprehensive Bibliography, 1:948
Saul Bellow: Drumlin Woodchuck, 1:947
Saul Bellow: His Works and His Critics—An Annotated International Bibliography, 1:947

Saul Bellow: In Defense of
    Man, 1:947
Saul Bellow: Vision and Re-
    vision, 1:947
Saul Bellow and History,
    1:947
Saul Bellow and the Struggle
    at the Center, 1:947
Saul Bellow's Fiction, 1:947
Saul Bellow's Moral Experi-
    ences, 1:947
Saul Tschernichovsky: Poet
    of Revolt, 2:25
Sauna as Symbol: Society
    and Culture in Finland,
    3:381
Sauve Qui Peut, 1:470
The Savage Anomaly: The
    Power of Spinoza's Meta-
    physics and Politics, 4:189
The Savage God: A Study of
    Suicide, 5:425
Savage Holiday, 1:905
Savage Inequalities, 3:211,
    3:251
Savage Landor, 1:296
Savage Mind, 3:15, 3:33
A Savage Place, 1:1223
A Savage War of Peace: Al-
    geria, 1954–1962, 3:373
Saved, 1:445, 1:446
Save Three Lives, a Plan for
    Famine Prevention, 5:274
Saving America's Wildlife,
    3:549
Saving Civilization: Yeats,
    Eliot, and Auden Between
    the Wars, 1:436
Saving the Appearances: A
    Study in Idolatry, 1:923
The Saviors of God, 2:374
Savushun: A Novel about
    Modern Iran, 2:88
Sawbones Memorial, 2:925
Saxe Holm's Stories, First
    Series, 1:760
Saxe Holm's Stories, Second
    Series, 1:760
Say Cheese!, 2:698
The Sayings and Doings of
    Samuel Slick of Slickville,
    2:912
Sayings and Riddles in New
    Mexico, 3:863
Say It with Figures, 5:525
Sayonara, 3:931
The Scalpel and the Heart,
    5:374
Scandinavia: Denmark, Nor-
    way, Sweden, 1319–1974,
    3:381
Scandinavian Ballads, 2:638

Scandinavian Countries,
    1720–1865, 3:380
The Scandinavians, 3:898
Scandinavian Women Writ-
    ers, 2:638
The Scapegoat, 1:620
The Scaremongers: The Ad-
    vocacy of War and Rear-
    mament, 1896–1914, 3:280
The Scarlet City, 2:626
The Scarlet Empress, 1:1176
The Scarlet Letter, 1:657,
    1:674, 1:675
The Scarlet Letter: A Read-
    ing, 1:676, 1:945
The Scarlet Song, 2:132
The Scar of Montaigne: An
    Essay in Personal Philoso-
    phy, 4:146
The Scene-Four, 1:1079
The Scene-One: Plays from
    Off-Off Broadway, 1:1079
Scenes from American Life,
    1:1090, 1:1091
Scenes from American Life:
    Contemporary Short Fic-
    tion, 1:921
Scenes from Deep Time,
    5:194
Scenes from Russian Life,
    2:759
Scenes from the Anti-Nazi
    War, 3:428
Scenes from the Bathhouse:
    And Other Stories of Com-
    munist Russia, 2:775
Scenes of Clerical Life,
    1:353, 1:385
Scenes of Nature, Signs of
    Man, 1:795
The Scene-Three: Annual An-
    thology of Off-Off Broad-
    way Plays, 1:1079
The Scene-Two, 1:1079
The Scenic Art, 2:914
Scent, Smile and Sorrow: Se-
    lected Verse, 2:77
The Scented Garden Men's
    Hearts to Gladden, 3:913
Scented Gardens for the
    Blind, 2:974
Scent of Apples: A Collection
    of Stories, 2:334
A Scent of Onions, 2:144
Scent Smile and Sorrow: Se-
    lected Verse, 1891–1957,
    2:79
The Sceptical Chemist, 5:739,
    5:740
Sceptical Essays, 4:323
Scepticism, Man and God,
    4:58

Scepticism, Rules, and Pri-
    vate Languages, 4:347
Scepticism and Animal Faith:
    Introduction to a System
    of Philosophy, 4:327
Scepticism or Platonism: The
    Philosophy of the Fourth
    Academy, 4:58
Scheherezade in the Market-
    place, 1:356
Schelling: An Introduction to
    His System of Freedom,
    4:252
Schelling's Idealism and Phi-
    losophy of Nature, 4:252
Schelling's Treatise on the
    Essence of Human Free-
    dom, 4:252, 4:292
Schindler's Ark, 2:957
Schindler's List, 2:957
Schism and Continuity in an
    African Society, 3:41
Schizophrenia, 5:427
Schizophrenia: A Develop-
    mental Analysis, 5:426
Schizophrenia: An Introduc-
    tion to Research and
    Theory, 5:428
Schizophrenia: A Source of
    Social Insight, 5:426
Schizophrenia as a Human
    Process, 5:471
Schleiermacher: Life and
    Thought, 4:741
Schleiermacher on Christ
    and Religion, 4:254
The Schlemiel as Metaphor,
    1:919, 2:32
The Schlemiel as Modern
    Hero, 2:33
Schoenberg and His School,
    3:714
The Scholar Adventurers,
    1:30
Scholarly Communication:
    The Report of the Nation-
    al Enquiry, 1:50
Scholarly Reprint Publishing
    in the United States, 1:50
The Scholars, 2:188, 2:229,
    2:231
Scholars, Saints and Sufis:
    Muslim Religious Institu-
    tions since 1500, 3:443,
    4:575
Scholars and Their Publish-
    ers, 1:50
A Scholar's Guide to Aca-
    demic Journals in Reli-
    gion, 4:6

Scholars' Guide to Washington, D.C., for Latin American and Caribbean Studies, 3:624

Scholarship on Philo and Josephus, 1937–1962, 4:608

Scholastic: A Publishing Adventure, 1:43

The Scholastic Culture of the Middle Ages: 1000–1300, 4:695

Scholasticism and Politics, 4:307

Scholastic Miscellany: Anselm to Ockham, 4:94

Scholastic Rabbinism, 4:613

School, 1:389

The School and Society, 3:259, 3:261, 4:224

Schooldays in Imperial Japan: A Study in the Culture of a Student Elite, 3:479

School Daze, 1:1170

School Effectiveness: A Reassessment of the Evidence, 3:256

School Finance: The Economics and Politics of Public Education, 3:250

A School for Fools, 2:758

The School for Scandal, 1:254

The School for Wives, 2:490

Schoolgirl Murder Case, 1:568

Schooling and Achievement in American Society, 3:214

Schooling and the Struggle for Public Life, 3:255

Schooling in Capitalist America, 3:253

The School of Peter Abelard, 4:106

School of the Sun, 2:545

The School Principal: A Novel, 2:85

The School Promoters, 3:609

Schools and Scholars in Fourteenth-Century England, 4:103

The Schools We Deserve, 3:252

Schopenhauer, 4:256

Schopenhauer and Nietzsche, 3:239

Schopenhauer and the Wild Years of Philosophy, 4:256

Schopenhauer as Educator, 4:256

Schopenhauer as Transmitter of Buddhist Ideas, 4:256

Schrodinger: Centenary Celebration of a Polymath, 5:714

Schubert, 3:715

Schubert: A Critical Biography, 3:715

Schubert: A Documentary Biography, 3:715

Schubert's Songs: A Biographical Study, 3:715

Schumpeter: A Biography, 3:105

Schumpeter, Social Scientist, 3:105

The Schumpeterian System, 3:105

Science: A History of Discovery in the Twentieth Century, 5:49

Science: The Very Idea, 5:159

Science, American Style, 5:49

Science, Conflict, and Society, 5:135

Science, Culture and Popular Belief in Renaissance Europe, 5:40

Science, Ethics, and Medicine, 5:78, 5:134

Science, Faith, and Politics, 4:166

Science, Folklore, and Ideology, 5:38

Science, Metaphysics, and the Chance of Salvation, 1:769

Science, Perception and Reality, 4:334

Science, Politics and Society in Eighteenth-Century Italy, 5:44

Science, Reason, and Religion, 5:198

Science, Technology, and Development, 5:183

Science, Technology, and National Policy, 5:182

Science, Technology, and Policy Decisions, 5:181

Science, Technology, and Social Change, 5:159

Science, Technology, and Social Progress, 5:153

Science, Technology, and Society, 5:149

Science, Technology, and Society: A Cross-Disciplinary Perspective, 3:214, 5:61, 5:149

Science, Technology, and Society: Emerging Relationships, 5:151

Science, Technology, and Society: New Directions, 5:149

Science, Technology, and the Art of Medicine, 5:79

Science, Technology and Society in Seventeenth Century England, 3:233

Science, Technology and Society in Seventeenth Century England, 5:43

Science, the Endless Frontier: A Report to the President, 5:200

Science Advice to the President, 5:181

Science after Forty, 5:56

Science à la Mode: Physical Fashions and Fictions, 5:10

Science and Building, 5:245

Science and Civic Life in the Italian Renaissance, 4:126

Science and Civilisation in China, 3:466, 4:523, 5:26

Science and Civilization in Islam, 5:39

Science and Common Understanding, 5:707

Science and Corporate Strategy: Du Pont R&D, 1902–1980, 5:48

Science and Creation: From Eternal Cycles to an Oscillating Universe, 5:202

Science and Creationism, 5:765

Science and Cultural Crisis, 5:676

Science and Engineering Literature: A Guide to Reference Sources, 5:217

Science and Ethical Values, 5:107

Science and Ethics, 5:107

Science and Everyday Life, 5:797

Science and Gender: A Critique of Biology and Its Theories on Women, 5:763

Science and Government, 1:550, 5:183

Science and Health with Key to the Scriptures, 4:842, 4:843, 4:874, 4:875

Science and Human Affairs, 5:108

Science and Human Life, 5:797

Science and Human Values, 5:106, 5:161, 5:162

Science and Immortality, 5:54, 5:364

Science and Immortality:
The Eloges of the Paris
Academy of Sciences
(1699–1791), 5:45
Science and Its Public: The
Changing Relationship,
5:17
Science and Life, 5:702
Science and Metaphysics:
Variations on Kantian
Themes, 4:334
Science and Morality: New
Directions in Bioethics,
5:124
Science and Moral Priority:
The Merging of Mind,
Brain, and Values, 5:108
Science and Philosophy in
Classical Greece, 4:47,
5:38
Science and Politics, 5:182
Science and Polity in France
at the End of the Old Re-
gime, 5:44
Science and Relativism, 5:64
Science and Religion, 5:798
Science and Religion: A Crit-
ical Survey, 5:140
Science and Religion: Oppos-
ing Viewpoints, 5:198
Science and Religion in Sev-
enteenth-Century England,
5:43
Science and Scepticism, 5:65
Science and Scientific Re-
searchers in Modern Soci-
ety, 5:9, 5:107
Science and Secularity: The
Ethics of Technology,
5:161
Science and Sentiment in
America, 4:36
Science and Social Struc-
ture: A Festschrift for
Robert K. Merton, 3:213
Science and Society: Select-
ed Essays in the Sociology
of Science, 5:150
Science and Spirit, 5:198
Science and Subjectivity,
4:385
Science and Synthesis, 4:337
Science and Technology,
5:12
Science and Technology: An
Introduction to the Litera-
ture, 5:216
Science and Technology Ad-
vice to the President,
Congress, and Judiciary,
5:181

Science and Technology An-
nual Reference Review,
5:5
Science and Technology
Desk Reference, 5:7, 5:726
Science and Technology in
History, 5:25
Science and Technology in
New York City for the
21st Century, 5:250, 5:251
Science and Technology Is-
sues in Coastal Ecotour-
ism, 5:185
Science and Technology Poli-
cy, 5:181
Science and the Common
Understanding, 5:211
Science and the Enlighten-
ment, 5:44
Science and the Human
Imagination, 4:405
Science and the Modern
World, 4:341, 5:27
Science and the New Civili-
zation, 5:702
Science and the Renaissance,
5:41
Science and the Revenge of
Nature, 4:408, 5:94
Science and the Social Or-
der, 3:213
Science and the Sociology of
Knowledge, 4:406
Science and the Unseen
World, 5:681
Science and Thought in the
Fifteenth Century, 4:131
Science and Unreason, 5:65
Science and Wisdom, 4:307
Science as a Process, 4:384,
5:68
Science as Intellectual Prop-
erty: Who Controls Scien-
tific Research?, 3:214,
5:108, 5:172
Science as Power, 3:213
Science as Practice and Cul-
ture, 5:67, 5:156
Science as Social Knowl-
edge, 5:66, 5:155, 5:188
Science at the Bedside,
5:313
Science Awakening 1: Egyp-
tian, Babylonian, and
Greek Mathematics, 5:39
Science Awakening 2: The
Birth of Astronomy, 5:39
Science Education and Ethi-
cal Values, 5:7, 5:107
Science Education in the
United States: Issues, Cri-
ses, Priorities, 5:11
Science Ethics, 5:108

Science Fiction, Fantasy, and
Horror: 1990, 1:612
The Science Fiction Encyclo-
pedia, 5:565
The Science Fiction of H. G.
Wells, 1:564
Science for All Americans,
5:11
Science for Public Policy,
5:180
Science from Your Airplane
Window, 5:618
The Science Gap, 5:10
Science in Action, 5:167
Science in a Free Society,
4:399
Science in America: A Docu-
mentary History,
1900–1939, 5:49
Science in Context: Readings
in the Sociology of Sci-
ence, 5:150
Science in History, 5:24
Science in Nineteenth-Cen-
tury America: A Documen-
tary History, 5:47
Science in Society: An Anno-
tated Guide to Resources,
5:149
Science in the Early Roman
Empire, 5:810
Science in the Federal Gov-
ernment, 5:48
Science in the Medieval
World: "Book of the Cate-
gories of Nations," 5:39
Science in the Middle Ages,
4:97, 5:39
Science Is Not Enough,
5:200
Science Matters: Achieving
Scientific Literacy, 3:250
Science Observed: New Per-
spectives on the Social
Study of Science, 5:154
The Science of Animal Hus-
bandry, 5:262
The Science of Art, 5:193,
5:203
The Science of Chance:
From Probability to Statis-
tics, 5:523
The Science of Culture, 3:41,
3:42
The Science of Culture: A
Study of Man and Civiliza-
tion, 3:14
The Science of Dreams,
5:421
The Science of English
Verse, 1:772
The Science of Ethics, 4:198

Science off the Pedestal: Social Perspectives on Science and Technology, 5:106, 5:151
The Science of Knowledge, 4:198
Science of Life, 1:563
The Science of Living, 5:431
Science of Logic, 4:231, 4:232
The Science of Mechanics, 5:700
The Science of Mechanics in the Middle Ages, 5:39
Science of Political Economy, 3:80
The Science of Religion, 4:557
The Science of Rights, 4:198
The Science of the Mind, 3:168, 4:382
The Science of Translation: Theoretical and Applicative Aspects, 2:991
The Science of Winning: A Random Walk on the Road to Riches, 5:522
Science Policy, Ethics, and Economic Methodology, 5:76, 5:130, 5:141
Science Policy and Politics, 5:182
The Science Question in Feminism, 4:40, 4:391, 5:66, 5:154, 5:187
Science Reorganized: Scientific Societies in the 18th Century, 5:45
Science Responds to Environmental Threats: Country Studies, 5:186
Science Responds to Environmental Threats: Synthesis Report, 5:186
Sciences and the Vedas, 5:198
Sciences of the Artificial, 3:175, 5:76
Science Year, 1993: The World Book Annual Science Supplement, 5:3
Scientific and Technical Books and Serials in Print, 1994, 5:5
Scientific and Technical Information Resources (Subramanyam), 5:218
Scientific and Technical Information Sources (Chen), 5:5
Scientific and Technical Literature: An Introduction for Communication, 5:5

Scientific and Technical Organizations and Agencies Directory, 5:4, 5:218
Scientific and Technological Periodicals of the Seventeenth and Eighteenth Centuries: A Guide, 5:28
The Scientific Attitude, 5:10, 5:107, 5:154
Scientific Autobiography and Other Papers, 5:709
The Scientific Case against Smoking, 5:404
Scientific Controversies, 5:134
Scientific Discovery: Computational Explorations of the Creative Process, 5:542
Scientific Elite: Nobel Laureates in the United States, 3:214
Scientific Explanation and Atomic Physics, 5:68
Scientific Explanation and the Causal Structure of the World, 5:65, 5:103
Scientific Growth, 5:150
Scientific Healing Affirmations: Theory and Practice of Concentration, 4:557
The Scientific Image, 5:63
The Scientific Imagination, 5:17
Scientific Knowledge and Philosophic Thought, 4:384
The Scientific Letters and Papers, Vol. 1: 1846–1862, 5:700
Scientific Literacy and the Myth of the Scientific Method, 5:9, 5:150
The Scientific Marx, 4:243
Scientific Materialism, 5:83
Scientific Materialism in Nineteenth-Century Germany, 5:46
Scientific Organizations in Seventeenth-Century France, 1620–1680, 5:41
Scientific Papers of Arthur Holly Compton, 5:678
Scientific Progress, 4:318, 5:100, 5:101
The Scientific Renaissance 1450–1630, 4:124, 5:40
Scientific Research, 5:83
Scientific Revolutions, 5:63
Scientific Romance in Britain: Eighteen-ninety to Nineteen-fifty, 1:612
A Scientific Theory of Culture, 3:35

The Scientific Work of René Descartes, 5:503
Scientist and Catholic: Pierre Duhem, 5:202
A Scientist at the Seashore, 5:19
A Scientist at the White House, 5:182
A Scientist Explores Spirit, 4:852
Scientists and World Order, 5:181
Scientists Confront Velikovsky, 5:590
Scientists in Quest for Peace: A History of the Pugwash Conferences, 5:112
The Scientist's Role in Society: A Comparative Study, 5:150
The Scientist's Role in Society: A Comparative Study with a New Introduction, 3:213
Scientists under Hitler, 5:47
Scientology: The Fundamentals of Thought, 4:869
Scilla's Metamorphosis, 1:185
Scoop, 1:561, 1:562
The Scope and Method of Political Economy, 3:46
The Scope of Renaissance Humanism, 4:131, 4:697
The Scope of Total Architecture, 3:777
The Scorched-Wood People, 2:927
The Scorpion God: Three Short Novels, 1:484
Scotch Reviewers: "The Edinburgh Review," 1802–1815, 1:273
Scotland: The Making of the Kingdom, 3:355
Scotland: The Shaping of a Nation, 4:735
Scotland and Nationalism: Scottish Society and Politics, 1707–1977, 3:355
Scotland from the Earliest Times to 1603, 3:355
Scotland Reformed: The Reformation in Angus and the Mearns, 4:735
The Scott, Foresman Anthology of Children's Literature, 1:579, 1:1196, 1:1197
Scott and Ernest: The Authority of Failure and the Authority of Success, 1:840
Scott and His Circle, 1:299
Scott and Scotland, 1:521

Scott Fitzgerald, 1:841
Scott Fitzgerald: The Prom-
ises of Life, 1:840
The Scottish Covenanters,
1660–1688, 4:735
Scottish Historical Docu-
ments, 3:368
Scottish Journey, 1:522
Scottish Philosophy, 4:32,
4:203
The Scottish Philosophy, Bio-
graphical, Expository, Crit-
ical, from Hutcheson to
Hamilton, 4:32, 4:212
The Scottish Philosophy of
Common Sense, 4:32,
4:212
The Scottish Reformation,
4:735
The Scottish Stories and Es-
says, 1:397
Scottish Tradition: A Collec-
tion of Scottish Folklore,
3:854
Scott Joplin, 3:703
Scott Joplin and the Ragtime
Era, 3:703
Scott's Last Expedition, 3:936
The Scourge of Villainie,
1:187, 1:188
The Scout, or the Black Rid-
ers of Congaree, 1:696
The Scramble for Africa,
3:416, 3:418
Screening History, 1:1062
Screening Out the Past,
3:560
Screen Memories: Hollywood
Cinema on the Psychoana-
lytic Couch, 3:827
The Screens, 2:479
Screen World, 3:826
The Screwtape Letters, 1:512,
4:776
Scriabin: Artist and Mystic,
3:717
Scribblers and Scoundrels,
1:35
Scribes, Warriors and Kings:
The City of Copan and the
Ancient Maya, 4:455
Scribes and Scholars, 2:347,
3:300
The Scribner-Bantam English
Dictionary, 1:90
The Script Letter: Its Form,
Construction and Applica-
tion, 1:20
The Script of Decadence,
2:476
Scripture, Sects and Visions,
4:615, 4:616

A Scroll of Agony: The War-
saw Diary of Chaim A.
Kaplan, 3:349
Sculpture and Sculptors of
the Greeks, 2:347
The Sculpture and Sculptors
of Yazilikava, 4:444
The Sculpture of Auguste
Rodin, 3:791
Scum, 2:48
The Sea, 1:445
The Sea, the Sea, 1:523
The Sea and the Bells, 2:875
The Sea and the Honey-
comb, 1:951
The Sea around Us, 5:631,
5:828, 5:829
Seabirds: An Identification
Guide, 5:759
The Sea Birds Are Still
Alive, 1:939, 1:940
The Sea-Crossed Fisherman:
A Novel, 2:100
Sea Grapes, 2:942, 2:943
The Sea Gull (Chekhov),
2:707, 2:709
Seagull (Kemal), 2:100
The Sea Lions; or, The Lost
Sealers, 1:664
Seals of the World, 5:771
Seamus Heaney, 1:495
Seamus Heaney, Poet of
Contrary Progressions,
1:495
The Séance and Other Sto-
ries, 2:47
Sean O'Casey, 1:527
Sean O'Casey: A Life, 1:527
Sean O'Casey and His Crit-
ics: An Annotated Bibliog-
raphy, 1916–1982, 1:527
Sean O'Casey's Drama: Veri-
similitude and Vision,
1:527
Sean O'Faolain, 1:529
Sean O'Faolain: A Critical
Introduction, 1:529
Sean O'Faolain's Irish Vision,
1:529
Sea of Cortez: A Leisurely
Journal of Travel and Re-
search, 1:884, 1:885, 5:632
Sea of Death, 2:892
The Sea of Fertility, 2:289
The Sea Peoples: Warriors of
the Ancient Mediterrane-
an, 1250 to 1150, 4:445
The Search, 2:68
The Search after Truth and
Elucidations of the Search
after Truth, 4:181, 4:182
The Searchers, 1:1165

Searchers and Seizures,
1:973
Search for a Father: Sartre,
Paternity, and the Ques-
tion of Ethics, 4:330
Search for a Method, 4:329
The Search for a New Or-
der, 3:477
The Search for an Ideal,
3:615
The Search for Authenticity,
5:438
The Search for Concrete-
ness—Reflections on He-
gel and Whitehead, 4:341
Search for Consensus: The
Story of the Democratic
Party, 3:543
The Search for Criminal
Man, 5:423
The Search for Existential
Identity, 5:438
The Search for Extraterrestri-
al Life in the Cosmos,
5:598
The Search for Gravity
Waves, 5:665
The Search for Isadora: The
Legend and the Legacy of
Isadora Duncan, 3:742
The Search for Jewish Iden-
tity in America, 4:641
The Search for Jewish Theol-
ogy, 4:648
The Search for Modern Chi-
na, 3:472, 3:503
The Search for Nothing: The
Life of John of the Cross,
2:543
The Search for Order,
1877–1920, 3:533
The Search for Self-Defini-
tion in Russian Literature,
2:691
The Search for the Elements,
5:727
Search for the Gene, 5:779
The Search for the Origins
of Christian Worship,
4:687
A Search for Wisdom and
Spirit: Thomas Merton's
Theology of the Self, 4:781
Searching, 2:71, 2:120
Searching between the Stars,
5:594
Searching for a Cure, 5:329
Searching the Heart, 3:553
The Searching Wind, 1:1092
The Search Within: Inner
Experiences of a Psycho-
analyst, 5:467
Seascape, 1:1080, 1:1081

The Season: A Candid Look at Broadway, 1:1073

Season at the Point: The Birds and Birders of Cape May, 5:817

A Season in Hell, 2:499

Season of Adventure, 2:936, 2:937

Season of Anomy, 2:148

Season of Giants 1492–1508: Michelangelo, Leonardo, Raphael, 3:788

Season of Migration to the North, 2:72

Season of Youth: The Bildungsroman from Dickens to Golding, 1:318

A Season on the Earth: Selected Poems of Nirala, 2:176

The Seasons (Donelaitis), 2:806

The Seasons (Thomson), 1:261

Seasons for Celebration, 4:601

The Seasons of a Man's Life, 5:422

Seasons of Our Joy: A Handbook of Jewish Festivals, 4:600

Season Songs, 1:498

Sea Tales, 1:664

The Seated Train: Lenin's Eight-Month Journey from Exile to Power, 3:397

Seat of Empire: The Political Role of Eighteenth-Century Williamsburg, 3:570

The Sea Turtle: So Excellent a Fishe, 5:770

The Sea Urchin Embryo: A Developmental Biological System, 5:776

The Sea Wall, 2:473, 2:474

The Sea Wolf, 1:773

The Sea-Wolf and Other Stories, 1:774

Sebastian im Traum, 2:613

The Sebastopol Sketches, 2:764

Secondary Cities of Argentina, 3:649

Secondary Schools at the Turn of the Century, 3:268

Second Chance, 3:544

Second-Class Citizen, 2:136, 2:137

The Second Coming, 1:1029

The Second Coming: Satanism in America, 4:868

The Second Common Reader, 1:569

The Second Creation, 5:651, 5:691, 5:713

The Second Curtain, 1:481

The Second Ewings, 1:867

A Second Flowering: Works and Days of the Lost Generation, 1:822

Second Generation, 1:1246

Second Hymn to Lenin, 1:516

The Second Isaiah Introduction, Translation and Commentary to Chapters 40–55, 4:822

The Second Jewish Catalogue: Sources and Resources, 4:602

The Second Jungle Book, 1:370

The Second Lady, 1:1250

Second Lieutenant Kije, 2:770

The Second Life of Art: Selected Essays, 2:428

Second Look at Science and Government, 5:214

A Second Look in the Rear-View Mirror, 4:270

The Second Message of Islam, 4:576

The Second Mrs. Tanqueray, 1:322, 1:388

Second Nature: Forty-Six Poems, 2:745

Second Opinion, 5:13

The Second Round, 2:145, 2:146

The Second Scientific American Book of Mathematical Puzzles and Diversions, 5:496, 5:507

The Second Scroll, 2:915

The Second Self: Computers and the Human Spirit, 5:158, 5:574

The Second Sex, 2:458

The Second Shepherd's Play, 1:140, 1:159

The Second Sickness: Contradictions of Capitalist Health Care, 5:329

Second Sight, 5:384

Second Skin, 1:985

The Second Son, 1:1186

The Second Tongue, 2:325

The Second Treatise of Civil Government, 4:179

The Second Tree from the Corner, 1:898

The Second Twenty Years at Hull House, 1:730

The Second Vienna School: Expressionism and Dodecaphony, 3:663

The Second Wave: British Drama for the Seventies, 1:426

The Second World War: A Military History, 3:278

The Second World War and the Atomic Age, 1940–1973, 3:510

Secrecy and Power: The Life of J. Edgar Hoover, 3:540

Secret, 2:434

The Secret Adversary, 1:605, 1:606

The Secret Affairs of Mildred Wild, 1:1122, 1:1123

The Secret Agent, 1:347, 1:463

The Secret and Lily Hart: Two Tales, 1:335

Secret and Sacred, 3:526

Secretary of Praise: The Poetic Vocation of George Herbert, 1:181

Secretary Stimson: A Study in Statecraft, 3:574

The Secret Brother and Other Poems, 1:501

The Secret Connexion: Causation, Realism, and David Hume, 4:203

The Secret Doctrine: The Synthesis of Science, Religion, and Philosophy, 4:852, 4:873, 4:874

The Secret Garden, 1:1200, 1:1201

The Secret Garden: An Anthology on the Kabbalah, 4:630

Secret Gardens, 1:578

The Secret Guide to Computers, 5:538

Secret History of Procopius, 3:319

The Secret House of Death, 1:609

The Secret Life of Saeed, the Ill-Fated Pessimist, 2:58

The Secret Life of Walter Mitty, 1:890

A Secret Meeting in Rome, 3:915

The Secret of Childhood: A Book for All Parents and Teachers, 3:266

The Secret of Chimneys, 1:605, 1:606

The Secret of Dr. Honigberger, 2:824

The Secret of Happiness and Other Fantastic Fables, 1:735
The Secret of the Kingdom, 2:661
The Secret of the Universe: Mysterium Cosmographicum, 5:42
A Secret Past, 2:336
The Secret Pilgrim, 1:596
The Secret Rapture, 1:493
The Secret Ring: Freud's Inner Circle and the Politics of Psychoanalysis, 5:448
Secrets, 1:1224
Secrets and Surprises, 1:945
The Secret Self: Psychoanalytic Experiences in Life and Literature, 5:467
The Secret Sharer, 1:463
Secrets of Life, Secrets of Death, 5:66, 5:154, 5:187
Secrets of the Heart, 2:67
Secrets of the Lotus, 4:520
Secrets of the Self, 4:375
Secrets of the Temple: How the Federal Reserve Runs the Country, 3:55
Secret Wars, 3:319
Secret Weavers, 2:848
Section and Party, 3:123
The Secular Ark: Studies in the History of Biogeography, 5:819
Secular Education in Philo of Alexandria, 4:670
The Secular Is Sacred, 4:141
Secularization and Moral Change, 4:407
The Secularization of the European Mind in the Nineteenth Century, 3:340
The Secular Journal of Thomas Merton, 4:781
The Secular Pilgrims of Victorian Fiction: The Novel as Book of Life, 1:319
The Secular Scripture: A Study of the Structure of Romance, 1:977
Secular Utilitarianism, 4:190
The Security Gamble: Deterrence Dilemmas in the Nuclear Age, 5:111
Sedimentary Facies in Geologic History, 5:623
Seduction and Betrayal: Women and Literature, 1:925
The Seduction and Other Stories, 1:1023
Seduction of the Minotaur, 1:865

The Seed and the Spring Night, 2:670
Seeds of Change: Five Plants That Transformed Mankind, 5:768
Seeds of Corruption, 2:59
The Seeds of Decadence in the Late Nineteenth-Century Novel, 2:986
Seeds of Destruction: Nationalist China in War and Revolution, 3:470
Seeds of Italian Nationalism, 1700–1815, 3:385
Seeing Is Believing, 1:560
Seeing the Gawain-Poet: Description and the Act of Perception, 1:156
Seeing the Light, 5:666
Seeing Things: Poems, 1:495
See It Now, 3:819
The Seeker, 2:608
Seeking Spiritual Meaning: The World of Vedanta, 4:872
Seeking the Path to Life, 4:649
Seek My Face, Speak My Name: A Contemporary Jewish Theology, 4:648
Seek the Stars, 1:619
The Seer & Other Norwegian Tales, 2:666
See under Love, 2:19
Sefer ha-Qabbalah: The Book of Tradition, 4:627
The Seigneurial Regime in French Canada: A Geographical Study, 3:611
Seismicity of the Earth, 5:647
Seized: Temporal Lobe Epilepsy as a Medical, Historical, and Artistic Phenomenon, 5:392
Seize the Day, 1:946
Seize the Day, with Three Short Stories and a One-Act Play, 1:947
The Seizure of Power, 2:818
Sejanus, 1:183
A Select Bibliography of the Negro American, 3:578
Select Dissertations from Amoenitates Academicae, 5:805
A Selected Bibliography of Modern History, 3:276
Selected Critical Writings of George Santayana, 4:327
Selected Czech Tales, 2:789
Selected Drawings of Gian Lorenzo Bernini, 3:770

Selected Essays from the Tatler, the Spectator, and the Guardian, 1:257
Selected Essays in the History of Letter Forms in Manuscript and Print, 1:18
Selected from Twentieth-Century American Poetry: An Anthology, 1:801
Selected Highland Folktales, 3:856
Selected Imaginary Conversations of Literary Men and Statesmen, 1:296
Selected Latin American One-Act Plays, 2:848
Selected Modern English Essays, 1:430
Selected One-Act Plays, 1:545
Selected Papers on Economic Theory, 3:114
Selected Papers on Hysteria and Other Psychoneuroses, 5:447
Selected Papers on Quantum Electrodynamics, 5:715, 5:717
Selected Passages from Correspondence with Friends, 2:721, 2:722
Selected Philosophical Essays, 4:332
Selected Philosophical Russian Contemporary Essays, 4:31
The Selected Plays: The Broken Heart, 'Tis Pity She's a Whore, Perkin Warbeck, 1:1166
Selected Poems from the Goddesses, 2:250
Selected Poems of Duncan Campbell Scott, 2:926
Selected Poems of Pak Mogwol, 2:299
Selected Poems of Tudor Arghezi, 2:824
Selected Poems of Zareh Khrakhouni, 2:76
Selected Stories of Thein Pe Myint, 2:314
Selected Studies in Bibliography, 1:61
Selected Subaltern Studies, 1:1153
Selected Tales of Liao Zhai, 2:217
Selected Works of Ramon Llull (1232–1316), 4:102
Selected Writings from a Connectionist's Psychology, 3:269

Selected Writings of Edward Sapir in Language, Culture, and Personality, 3:14, 3:21

Selected Writings of the New England Transcendentalists, 4:753

Selected Writings of Vahram Mavian (1926–1983), 2:76

Selected Writings on the History of Science, 4:258, 5:57

Select English Writings, 4:714

Selecting and Organizing State Government Publications, 1:110

A Selection from Poems of Rural Life in the Dorset Dialect, 1:316

Selection of African Poetry, 2:113

Selection of Refined Literature, 2:193, 2:201

A Selection of Religious Lyrics, 1:149

A Selection of the Correspondence of Linnaeus and Other Naturalists, 5:806

Selections from Contemporary Portuguese Poetry, 2:557

Selections from Cultural Writings, 1:1127, 4:287

Selections from Distribution and Abundance of Animals, 5:819

Selections from English Wycliffite Writings, 4:714, 4:721

Selections from Medieval Philosophers, 4:95

Selections from the Scottish Philosophy of Common Sense, 4:32

Selections from Three Works of Francisco Suárez, 4:154

Selections of Refined Literature, 2:195

Selective Bibliography of Shakespeare, 1:221

Selective Nontreatment of Handicapped Newborns, 5:124

A Select Library of the Nicene and Post-Nicene Fathers of the Christian Church, 4:100, 4:680, 4:702, 4:705, 4:706, 4:707, 4:709, 4:710, 4:712

Select Passages Illustrating Neoplatonism, 4:61

The Self, Its Body, and Freedom, 4:296

Self, Society, Existence, Human Nature and Dialogue in the Thought of George Herbert Mead and Martin Buber, 4:309

Self-Analysis, 3:186, 5:452

Self and Image in Juan Ramón Jiménez, 2:543

The Self and Its Brain, 4:409, 5:81, 5:98

Self and Nature in Kant's Philosophy, 4:207

The Self and Others, 5:459

Self and Sensibility in Contemporary American Poetry, 1:912

Self and Society in Southeast Asian Fiction, 2:311

The Self and the World in the Philosophy of Josiah Royce, 4:250

Self and World in Schopenhauer's Philosophy, 4:256

The Self as Agent, 1:967

Self Condemned: A Novel of Exile, 1:514

Self-Consciousness, 1:1060

Self-Consuming Artifacts, 1:976

Self-Crowned Laureates: Spenser, Jonson, and the Literary System, 1:165

Self-Deception, 5:422

Self-Deception and Morality, 4:389

Self-Directed Learning: A Guide for Learners and Teachers, 3:256

Self-Direction and Political Legitimacy: Rousseau and Herder, 4:199

Self-Discovery and Authority in Afro-American Narrative, 1:920

Self-Fulfilling Prophecy: Exile and Return as the History of Judaism, 4:594

Self-Help for Premenstrual Syndrome, 5:355

The Self-Inflicted Wound: Southern Politics in the Nineteenth Century, 3:527

Self-Interviews, 1:967

The Selfish Gene, 5:779

Self-Knowledge in Plato's Phaedrus, 4:81

Selfless Persons: Imagery and Thought in Theravada Buddhism, 4:887

The Self-Made Man in Meiji Japanese Thought, 3:478

The Self-Observed: Swift, Johnson, Wordsworth, 1:261

The Self on Transformation, 5:424

The Self-Overcoming of Nihilism, 4:365

Self-Portrait in a Convex Mirror, 1:936

Self-Portrait of the Other: A Memoir, 2:877

Self-Portraits: Tales from the Life of Japan's Great Decadent Romantic, 2:286

Self Publishing By the Seat of Your Pants!, 1:48

The Self-Publishing Manual: How to Write, Print and Sell Your Own Book, 1:48

Selling Science, 5:172

Selling the Book: A Bookshop Promotion Manual, 1:48

Selma Lagerlöf, 2:677

Selo zad sedumte jaseni, 2:807, 2:808

Semantics of Biblical Language, 4:817

(Sem)Erotics: Theorizing Lesbian: Writing, 1:1182

The Semiotic of Myth: A Critical Study of the Symbol, 4:428

Semites and Anti-Semites, 3:459

Semites and Anti-Semites: An Inquiry into Conflict and Prejudice, 4:571

Semper Fidelis: The History of the United States Marine Corps, 3:546

The Senate Speeches, 1:572

Send My Roots Rain, 1:365

Send These to Me: Jews and Other Immigrants in Urban America, 4:639

Seneca, 4:88

Seneca: A Philosopher in Politics, 2:394, 4:88

Seneca: The Humanist at the Court of Nero, 2:394, 2:654

Seneca and Celestina, 2:549

Seneca Myths and Folklore, 3:865

Senecan Drama and Stoic Cosmology, 2:394, 4:59, 4:88

Seneca's Drama, 2:394

Seneca the Philosopher and His Modern Message, 4:88

Senescence: The Last Half of Life, 3:185

Senilità, 2:438

Senior High School Library Catalog, 1:75

Sensational Designs, 1:630, 1:658

Sensational Victorian: The Life and Fiction of Mary Elizabeth Braddon, 1:333

Sensations and Images and the Strange Deviations of the Mind, 4:323

Sense and Contradiction: A Study in Aristotle, 4:67

Sense and Non-Sense, 4:310

Sense and Nonsense in Psychology: The Challenge of Hypnosis, 5:417

Sense and Nonsense of Statistical Inference, 5:524

Sense and Sensibilia, 4:272

Sense and Sensibility, 1:275

Sense and Subjectivity: A Study of Wittgenstein and Merleau-Ponty, 4:311

Sense of an Ending: Studies in the Theory of Fiction, 1:421

The Sense of Beauty: Critical Edition, 4:327

A Sense of Detachment, 1:532

The Sense of Movement, 1:491

The Sense of Order: A Study in the Psychology of Decorative Art, 5:192

The Sense of Power, 3:606, 3:614

A Sense of Story: Essays on Contemporary Writers for Children, 1:579, 1:1196

A Sense of the Earth, 5:623

A Sense of the Future: Essays in Natural Philosophy, 5:162

Sense of the Past, 1:763

The Sense of Wonder, 5:829

The Senses Considered as Perceptual Systems, 3:177

The Senses of Walden, 1:701

The Sensible Spirit: Walter Pater and the Modernist Paradigm, 1:387

Sensory Processes: The New Psychophysics, 3:177

The Sensuous Person: Critique and Corrections, 5:440

Sentences Undecidable in Formalized Arithmetic, 5:509

Sentimental Comedy: Theory and Practice, 1:228

The Sentimental Education, 2:475

Sentimental Journey, 1:256, 1:258, 2:421

Sentimental Memoirs of John Seaborne, 2:893

The Sentimental Novel in America, 1789–1860, 1:657

Sentimental Tommy, 1:438

The Separate Notebooks, 2:818

Separate Pasts: Growing Up White in the Segregated South, 3:556

A Separate Rose, 2:875

Separate Spheres: The Opposition to Woman Suffrage in Britain, 3:366

Separate Tables, 1:540

Separation: Anxiety and Anger, 5:421

The Sephardic Tradition: Ladino and Spanish-Jewish Literature, 4:622

Sephardim: The Jews from Spain, 4:644

September, 1:621

September Blackberries, 1:1009

Septuaginta, 4:796

The Septuagint and Modern Study, 4:796

The Septuagint Version of the Old Testament and Apocrypha, 4:796

Sequels: An Annotated Guide to Novels in Series, 1:122, 1:125

A Sequel to an Enquiry into the Nature of Certain Nineteenth Century Pamphlets by John Carter and Graham Pollard, 1:35

The Seraglio, 1:1015

Seraphim Grosse Pointe, 2:893

Séraphita, 2:453

Seraph on the Suwanee: A Novel, 1:849

The Serapion Brethren, 2:591

The Serapion Brothers: A Critical Anthology, 2:692

Serbian Poetry from the Beginnings to the Present, 2:828

The Serbs: Guardians of the Gate, 3:392

Serenading Louie, 1:1121

Serenading the Reluctant Eagle: American Musical Life, 1925–1945, 3:664

Serenity in Crisis: A Preface to Paul de Man, 1939–1960, 1:1143

Sergeant Getúlio, 2:898

Serge Diaghilev: His Life, His Work, His Legends, 3:741

Sergei Prokofiev: A Biography, 3:710

Sergei Prokofiev: A Soviet Tragedy, 3:710

Sergei Prokofiev: Materials, Articles, Interviews, 3:710, 3:717

Sergei Rachmaninoff: A Lifetime in Music, 3:712

Serial Composition and Atonality, 3:665

Serial Murder, 3:205

Serious and Tragic Elements in the Comedy of Thomas Dekker, 1:177

A Serious Character: The Life of Ezra Pound, 1:872

Serious Daring from Within, 1:896

A Serious Fall in the Value of Gold, 3:84

Serious Money, 1:459

Serjeant Musgrave's Dance, 1:433

Sermo Lupi ad Anglos, 1:142

Sermones y moradas, 2:528

Sermons (Butler), 4:193

Sermons (Donne), 1:177

Sermons (Edwards), 1:637

Sermons and Homilies of the Christ of Elqui, 2:877

Sermons and Soda Water, 1:867

Sermons of Mr. Yorick, 1:258

Serowe: Village of the Rain-Wind, 2:163

The Serpent, 1:1114

The Serpent and the Staff, 1:1225

Serpentina's Petticoat, 2:633

Serpent in Eden: H. L. Mencken and the South, 1:860

The Servant, 1:534

Servant of Two Masters, 2:402, 2:422

Serving End-Users in Science-Technology Libraries, 5:217

Seryozha: Several Stories from the Life of a Very Small Boy, 2:744

Sesame and Lilies: The Two Paths and the King of the Golden River, 1:394

Sessanta Racconti, 2:411

Set Free in China: Sojourns on the Edge, 3:903
SETI Pioneers, 5:598
Set Theory and Its Logic, 4:411
Set This House on Fire, 1:1056, 1:1057
Setting Free the Bears, 1:991, 1:992
Setting Limits: Medical Goals in an Aging Society, 5:84
The Setting Sun, 2:285, 2:286
Setting the World on Fire, 1:567
The Settlers, 2:678
The Set-Up: An Anatomy of the English Theatre Today, 1:425
Sevastopol Stories, 2:763
Ševčenko and the Critics, 1861–1980, 2:840
Seven against Thebes, 2:350, 2:351
The Seven Ages of Romulo, 2:330
Seven Brothers, 2:657
Seven Clues to the Origin of Life: A Scientific Detective Story, 5:732, 5:763
Seven Comedies, 2:488
Seven Contemporary Chinese Women Writers, 2:234
Seven Conversations with Jorge Luis Borges, 2:857
Seven Exegetical Works, 4:702
Seven Famous Greek Plays, 2:349
The Seven Good Years and Other Stories, 2:43
Seven Gothic Dramas: 1789–1825, 1:228, 1:272
Seven Great Religions, 4:550
Seven Ideas That Shook the Universe, 5:651, 5:735
Seven Interpretive Essays on Peruvian Reality, 3:640
Seven Japanese Tales, 2:294
The Seven Lamps of Architecture, 1:324, 1:393, 1:394, 3:764
The Seven Madmen, 2:853
Seven Modern American Poets: An Introduction, 1:800
Seven Nights, 2:856
Seven One-Act Plays, 2:651
The Seven Pillars of Wisdom, 3:925, 3:926
Seven Plays, 2:613
Seven Poets, 1:517
Seven Poor Men of Sydney, 2:963, 2:964

Seven Principles of Man, 4:550
Seven Science Fiction Novels, 1:564
The Seven Seas, 1:370
Seven Short Novels, 2:709
The Seven Sisters, 5:280
The Seven Storey Mountain, 4:780, 4:781
Seven Summits, 3:906
Seventeenth and Eighteenth Century British Philosophers, 4:160
The Seventeenth Century, 3:336
Seventeenth-Century American Poetry, 1:630
Seventeenth-Century English Poetry, 1:166
Seventeenth-Century Natural Scientists, 5:41
Seventeenth-Century New England, 3:517
The Seventh Commandment, 1:1237
The Seventh Cross, 2:611, 2:612
The Seventh Night, 2:834
The Seventh Sense, 4:203
77 Dream Songs, 1:949
Seventy Three Poems, 1:825
Seven Victorian Poets, 1:316
Seven Viking Romances, 2:640
Seven Voices, 2:846
Seven Winters, 1:447
Seven Women, 1:1166
Seven Years in Tibet, 3:923
Seven Years War, 3:592
The Several Israels, and an Essay: Religion and Modern Man, 4:646
Several Perceptions, 1:455
A Severed Head, 1:523
Sewall Wright and Evolutionary Biology, 5:780
Sex, Economy, Freedom, and Community: Eight Essays, 5:269
Sex, Sin and Grace, 4:784
Sex and Gender, 3:207
Sex and Racism in America, 3:555
Sex and Repression in Savage Society, 3:20, 3:35, 4:486
Sex and Temperament in Three Primitive Societies, 3:36
Sex and the Liberated Man, 5:440

Sex and the Penitentials: The Development of a Sexual Code 550–1150, 4:700
The Sex Diary of Gerald Sorme, 1:567
Sex Ethics in the Writings of Moses Maimonides, 4:668
Sex in Human Loving, 5:434
Sex in Nature, 5:763
Sex in the Golden Years: What's Ahead May Be Worth Aging For, 5:316
Sex in the World's Religions, 4:894
Sexism and God-Talk: Toward a Feminist Theology, 4:785, 4:905
The Sex Life of Flowers, 5:768
The Sex Researchers, 5:429
Sextet: His Later Writings under One Cover, 1:862
Sex Therapy Today, 5:429
Sexual Anarchy: Gender and Culture at the Fin de Siècle, 1:1046, 2:989
Sexual Anxiety: A Study of Male Impotence, 5:429
Sexual Dissidence: Augustine to Wilde, Freud to Foucault, 1:1181
Sexuality, the Bible, and Science, 4:894
Sexuality and Eroticism among Males in Moslem Societies, 4:894
Sexuality and Its Discontents: Meanings, Myths, and Modern Sexualities, 1:1182
Sexuality and Life-Threatening Illness, 5:378
Sexuality and Marriage in Colonial Latin America, 3:629
Sexuality and Psychoanalysis, 5:429
Sexuality and War: Literary Masks of the Middle East, 2:54
Sexuality in Islam, 4:894
The Sexual Labyrinth of Nikolai Gogol, 2:722
Sexual Life in Ancient India, 4:505
The Sexual Life of Savages in North-Western Melanesia, 3:35
Sexually Transmitted Disease: Guidelines for Physicians and Health Workers, 5:390
Sexually Transmitted Diseases in Homosexual Men, 5:390

Sexually Victimized Children, 5:416

The Sexual Outlaw, 1:1191

Sexual Personae, 3:539

Sexual Perversity in Chicago, 1:1100, 1:1101

Sexual Politics, Sexual Communities, 1:1181, 3:215

Sexual Sameness: Textual Differences in Lesbian and Gay Writing, 1:1183

Sexual/Textual Politics, 1:926

Sexus, 1:861

Sex without Guilt, 5:440

Seyidu Kamara: Ka Donkiliw, 2:126

Shaarei Mitzvah: Gates of Mitzvah, 4:602

Shadow and Act, 1:974

Shadow Country, 1:1135

The Shadow Lines, 2:177

Shadow of a Doubt, 1:1168

The Shadow of a Gunman, 1:526

The Shadow of Cain, 1:548

The Shadow of God and the Hidden Imam, 4:578

Shadow of Paradise: Sombra del Paraiso, 2:529

The Shadow of the Glen, 1:555

Shadowplay: The Life of Antony Tudor, 3:754

Shadows, 1:1243

Shadows of a Sound, 2:303

Shadows of Forgotten Ancestors, 5:611

Shadows of Heaven: The Life of Lester Pearson, 3:616

Shadows on the Grass, 2:648

Shadows on the Rock, 1:820

Shadows Uplifted, 1:1144

The Shadows Within: Essays on Modern Jewish Writers, 2:9

Shadow Train: Fifty Lyrics, 1:936

Shadow Work, 5:136, 5:137

The Shaft, 1:560

Shaftesbury's Philosophy of Religion and Ethics, 4:214

Shahjahanabad: The Sovereign City in Mughal India, 1639–1739, 3:484

Shahnamah, 2:89

The Shaker Adventure, 4:849

Shaker Communities, Shaker Lives, 4:849

The Shaker Experience in America, 3:561, 4:754, 4:850

Shaker Literature: A Bibliography, 4:849

Shaker Music: A Manifestation of American Folk Culture, 3:851

The Shakers: Two Centuries of Spiritual Reflection, 4:850

The Shaker Spiritual Narrative, 4:850

Shaker Villages, 4:849

Shakespeare, 1:220

Shakespeare: A Biographical Handbook, 1:204

Shakespeare: Annotated Bibliographies and Media Guide for Teachers, 1:221

Shakespeare: A Study and Research Guide, 1:220

Shakespeare: Man of the Theater, 1:218

Shakespeare: Meaning and Metaphor, 1:217

Shakespeare: Select Bibliographical Guides, 1:221

Shakespeare: The Critical Heritage, 1:221

Shakespeare: The Globe and the World, 1:222

Shakespeare: The Theatre-Poet, 1:209

Shakespeare: The Theatrical Dimension, 1:218

Shakespeare, the Later Years, 1:204

Shakespeare, the Lost Years, 1:204

The Shakespeare Allusion-Book, 1:221

Shakespearean Bibliography, 1:220

Shakespearean Criticism, 1:287

Shakespeare and Classical Tragedy: The Influence of Seneca, 1:219

Shakespeare and Company, 1:39

Shakespeare and His Forerunners, 1:772

Shakespeare and His Sources, 1:220

Shakespeare and His Theater, 1:217

Shakespeare and Jonson, Their Reputations in the Seventeeth Century Compared, 1:184

Shakespeare and the Actors: The Stage Business in His Plays, 1660–1905, 1:218

Shakespeare and the Classical Tradition, 1:221

Shakespeare and the Classics, 1:220

Shakespeare and the Comedy of Forgiveness, 1:211

Shakespeare and the Dramaturgy of Power, 1:208

Shakespeare and the Energies of Drama, 1:209

Shakespeare and the English Romantic Tradition, 1:265

Shakespeare and the Goddess of Complete Being, 1:498

Shakespeare and the Greek Romance: A Study of Origins, 1:219

Shakespeare and the Homilies, 1:219

Shakespeare and the Idea of the Play, 1:210

Shakespeare and the Nature of Women, 1:209

Shakespeare and the New Bibliography, 1:207

Shakespeare and the Popular Dramatic Tradition, 1:217

Shakespeare and the Popular Tradition in the Theater, 1:210

Shakespeare and the Popular Voice, 1:209

Shakespeare and the Problem of Meaning, 1:210

Shakespeare and the Question of Theory, 1:208

Shakespeare and the Rhetoricians, 1:217

Shakespeare and the Shapes of Time, 1:209

Shakespeare and the Sixteenth-Century Study of Language, 1:216

Shakespeare and the Stoicism of Seneca, 4:88

Shakespeare and the Traditions of Comedy, 1:211

Shakespeare and the Uses of Antiquity, 1:219

A Shakespearean Grammar, 1:216

The Shakespearean Imagination, 1:209

Shakespearean Meanings, 1:208

Shakespearean Negotiations, 1:209

The Shakespearean Promptbooks: A Descriptive Catalogue, 1:218

Shakespearean Representation, 1:213

Shakespearean Romance, 1:210

The Shakespearean Stage, 1574–1642, 1:170, 1:217

Shakespearean Staging, 1599–1642, 1:218
Shakespearean Tragedy, 1:212
Shakespeare at the Globe, 1599–1609, 1:217
Shakespeare Bibliography, 1:220, 1:221
Shakespeare Documents, 1:221
The Shakespeare First Folio: Its Bibliographical and Textual History, 1:207
The Shakespeare Folger Filmography, 1:221
Shakespeare Folios and Quartos, 1:207
Shakespeare Glossary, 1:216
The Shakespeare Handbook, 1:222
Shakespeare in a Changing World, 1:208
Shakespeare Index, 1:221
Shakespeare in the Theater, 1701–1800, 1:218
Shakespeare in Warwick-shire, 1:204
Shakespeare Lexicon, 1:216
Shakespeare on Film, 1:218
Shakespeare on Television, 1:217
Shakespeare on the American Stage, 1:218
Shakespeare on the English Stage, 1900–1964, 1:218
Shakespeare on the Stage, 1:218
Shakespeare Our Contemporary, 1:209
Shakespeare Quarterly, 1:221
Shakespeare Reproduced: The Text in History and Ideology, 1:208
Shakespeare's Art: Seven Essays, 1:208
Shakespeare's Art of Orchestration, 1:218
Shakespeare's Bawdy, 1:216
Shakespeare's Biblical Knowledge and Use of the Book of Common Prayer, 1:220
Shakespeare's Chaucer: A Study in Literary Origins, 1:220
Shakespeare's Clown: Actor and Text in the Elizabethan Playhouse, 1:219
Shakespeare's Comedies, 1:210
Shakespeare's Comedy of Love, 1:211

Shakespeare's Comic Rites, 1:210
Shakespeare's Development and the Problem Comedies, 1:211
Shakespeare's Dramatic Language, 1:216
Shakespeare's Early Tragedies, 1:212
Shakespeare's England: An Account of the Life and Manners of His Age, 1:222
Shakespeare's English Kings, 1:212
Shakespeare's Festive Comedy, 1:210
Shakespeare's Ghost-Writers: Literature as Uncanny Causality, 1:209
Shakespeare's Histories: Mirrors of Elizabethan Policy, 1:211
Shakespeare's Histories: Plays for the Stage, 1:212
Shakespeare's History, 1:211
Shakespeare's History Plays, 1:212
Shakespeare's Holinshed, 1:219
Shakespeare's Imagery and What It Tells Us, 1:217
Shakespeare's Language: An Introduction, 1:216
Shakespeare's Lives, 1:205
Shakespeare's Mature Tragedies, 1:213
Shakespeare's Metrical Art, 1:217
Shakespeare's Names: A Pronouncing Dictionary, 1:216
Shakespeare's Perjured Eye, 1:215
Shakespeare's Playhouses, 1:217
Shakespeare's Plays in Quarto, 1:205
Shakespeare's Plutarch, 1:220
Shakespeare's Progress, 1:527
Shakespeare's Pronunciation, 1:216
Shakespeare's Proverbial Language: An Index, 1:215
Shakespeare's Religious Background, 1:219
Shakespeare's Rhetoric of Comic Character, 1:211
Shakespeare's Roman Plays: The Function of Imagery in the Drama, 1:212
Shakespeare's Rome, 1:213
Shakespeare's Sentences: A Study in Style and Syntax, 1:216

Shakespeare's Sisters: Feminist Essays on Women Poets, 1:635, 1:1145, 1:1146
Shakespeare's Sonnets, 1:215
Shakespeare's Sonnets, Edited with Analytic Commentary, 1:206
Shakespeare's Stagecraft, 1:218
Shakespeare's Styles: Essays in Honour of Kenneth Muir, 1:216
Shakespeare's Theatre, 1:218
Shakespeare's Tragic Sequence, 1:213
Shakespeare's Use of Learning, 1:220
Shakespeare's Use of Music: Comedies, 1:221
Shakespeare's Use of Music: Final Comedies, 1:221
Shakespeare's Use of Music: Histories and Tragedies, 1:221
Shakespeare's Use of the Arts of Language, 1:217
Shakespeare's Wordplay, 1:216
Shakespeare's Works and Elizabethan Pronunciation, 1:216
Shakespeare's World: Background Readings in the English Renaissance, 1:220
Shakespeare—From Betterton to Irving, 1:218
The Shakespearian Moment and Its Place in the Poetry of the Seventeenth Century, 1:166
The Shaking of the Foundations, 4:787
Shakti: Power in the Conceptual Structure of Karimpur Religion, 4:506
Shakubuku, 4:860
Shall We Gather at the River?, 1:1067
Shamanism: Archaic Techniques of Ecstasy, 4:431, 4:474
Shamanism: Soviet Studies of Traditional Religion in Siberia and Central Asia, 4:430
Shamanism: The Spirit World of Korea, 4:539
Shamanism, Colonialism, and the Wild Man: A Study in Terror and Healing, 4:431
Shaman of Visions, 2:980

Shamans, Housewives and Other Restless Spirits, 4:539

Shamans, Mystics, and Doctors, 4:890

The Shaman Sorceress, 2:306, 2:307

The Shaman's Touch: Otomi Indian Symbolic Healing, 4:465

Shame, 2:181

Shamela, 1:229

Shane, 1:1210, 1:1211, 1:1217

Shane: The Critical Edition, 1:1217

Shanghai Express, 1:1176

Shanna, 1:1224, 1:1225

Shantung Compound, 5:201, 5:422

The Shape of Apocalypse in Modern Russian Fiction, 2:684

The Shape of Death: Life, Death, and Immortality in the Early Fathers, 4:99

The Shape of Hawthorne's Career, 1:945

The Shape of Meaning in the Poetry of David Jones, 1:503

The Shape of the Liturgy, 4:688

Shapes, Space and Symmetry, 5:487

The Shapes of Change: Images of American Dance, 3:733

Shapes of the Voice, 2:630

A Shaping Joy: Studies in the Writer's Craft, 1:953

The Shaping of America, 3:125, 3:133

The Shaping of American Diplomacy, 3:601

The Shaping of Longfellow's John Endicott, 1:683

The Shaping of the Elizabethan Regime, 3:359

The Shaping of the Swedish Health System, 5:330

Shaping Political Consciousness, 3:543

Shaping Technology/Building Society: Studies in Sociotechnical Change, 5:150

Shaping the Political Arena, 3:631

Shaping the World Economy: Suggestions for an International Economic Policy, 3:59

Shared Pleasures: A History of Movie Presentation in the United States, 3:825

The ShareWare Book: Using PC-Write, PC-File, and PC-Talk, 5:537

Shari'at and Ambiguity in South Asian Islam, 4:578

Sharing Literature with Children: A Thematic Anthology, 1:579, 1:1197

Sharing the Dance: Contact Improvisation and American Culture, 3:731, 3:733

Sharks: An Introduction for the Amateur Naturalist, 5:771

Sharp Gravel, 2:319

Shattered Hope, 3:637

Shattered Peace: Origins of the Cold War and the National Security State, 5:293

The Shattered Spectrum: A Survey of Contemporary Theology, 4:719

The Shaughraun, 1:331, 1:332

The Shavuot Anthology, 4:599

Shaw and the Nineteenth Century Theater, 1:323

Shaw and the Play of Ideas, 1:546

The Shawl, 1:1028, 1:1101

Shaw on Shakespeare, 1:210

al-Shawqiyat, 2:73

Shaw's Moral Vision: The Self and Salvation, 1:546

Shaw's Sense of History, 1:546

She, 1:594, 1:595

She, Who, 1:1187, 1:1188

She and Allan, 1:594

Shechem: Biography of a Biblical City, 4:618

The Sheep Well, 2:554

She Has No Place in Paradise, 2:71, 2:120

Shelley (Raine), 1:303

Shelley (White), 1:304

Shelley: A Critical Reading, 1:304

Shelley: A Voice Not Understood, 1:304

Shelley: His Thought and Work, 1:303

Shelley: The Critical Heritage, 1:303

Shelley: The Golden Years, 1:303

Shelley: The Last Phase, 1:303

Shelley: The Pursuit, 1:303

Shelley and Byron: The Snake and the Eagle Wreathed in Flight, 1:284

Shelley and His Audiences, 1:303

Shelley's Adonais: A Critical Edition, 1:303

Shelley's Annus Mirabilis: The Maturing of an Epic Vision, 1:303

Shelley's Cenci: Scorpions Ringed with Fire, 1:303

Shelley's Later Poetry, 1:304

Shelley's Mythmaking, 1:303, 1:1137

Shelley's Poetic Thoughts, 1:303

Shelley's Style, 1:303

The Shell Seekers, 1:620, 1:621

The Sheltered Life, 1:843

The Sheltered Quarter: a Tale of a Boyhood in Mecca, 2:58

The Shepheardes Calendar (Spenser), 1:163, 1:197

The Shepherd of the Ocean: Sir Walter Raleigh and His Times, 3:907

The Shepherd's Calendar (Clare), 1:285

The Shepherd's Calendar: With Village Stories and Other Poems, 1:1827, 1:285

Shepherd's Historical Atlas, 3:9, 3:273

A Shepherd's Life: Impressions of the South Wiltshire Downs, 1:365

Shepherds of the Night, 2:892

Shepherd's Pipe, and Other Stories, 2:611

Sheridan, 1:254, 1:255

Sheridan and the Drama of Georgian England, 1:255

Sheridan's Comedies: Their Contexts and Achievements, 1:254

Sherlock Holmes: The Complete Novels and Stories, 1:608

Sherlock Holmes and the Case of Doctor Freud, 5:449

Sherwood Anderson, 1:812, 1:989

Sherwood Anderson: A Biographical and Critical Study, 1:812

Sherwood Anderson: A Collection of Critical Essays, 1:812

Sherwood Anderson: A Selective, Annotated Bibliography, 1:812

The Sherwood Anderson Diaries, 1936–1941, 1:811

Sherwood Anderson's Memoirs: A Critical Edition, 1:811

She's Gotta Have It, 1:1170

She Stoops to Conquer, 1:246, 1:247

The She-Wolf and Other Stories, 2:441

She Wore a Yellow Ribbon, 1:1165

She Would If She Could, 1:242, 1:243

Shifting Gears: Technology, Literature, Culture in Modernist America, 1:795, 5:205

Shifting Landscape, 1:1040

Shifting Lines in the Sand, 3:450

The Shiga Hero, 2:292

Shih Ching: The Classic Anthology Defined by Confucius, 2:195

The Shi'ite Religion: A History of Islam in Persia and Irak, 3:442, 4:574

The Shi'ites, 4:572

Shin Buddhism, 4:558

Shingling the Fog and Other Plains Lies, 3:862

The Shining, 1:1240, 1:1241

The Shining Path of Peru, 3:640

Shinran's Gospel of Pure Grace, 4:537

Shinto: Japan's Spiritual Roots, 4:536

Shinto: The Kami Way, 4:536

Shinto: The Way of Japan, 4:536

Shinto and the State, 1868–1988, 3:477, 4:540

Shinto-Bibliography in Western Languages, 4:534

The Ship, 2:59

Ship of Fools, 1:869

Ships and Seamanship in the Ancient World, 3:304

Shipwreck, 1:478

Shipwreck Narratives, 2:557

The Shipyard, 2:876

Shira, 2:12

Shirley, 1:335

Shirley Jackson, 1:993

Shirley Radl, 5:424

Shirot Bialik, 2:16

Shiva's Pigeons: An Experience of India, 3:902

Shmuel Yosef Agnon: a Revolutionary Traditionalist, 2:12

Shoal of Time: A History of the Hawaiian Islands, 3:495

Shobogenzo: Zen Essays by Dogen, 4:534

The Shock of Recognition, 1:902

Shock-Trauma, 5:381

The Shockwave Rider, 5:563

The Shoemaker's Holiday, 1:176, 1:177

The Shoemaker's Prodigious Wife, 2:538

Sholom Aleichem, 2:46

Sholom Aleichem: A Non-Critical Introduction, 2:46

Sholom Aleichem: The Writer as Social Historian, 2:46

Sholom Aleichem in America: the Story of a Culture Hero, 2:46

Sholom Aleichem's Wandering Star, and Other Plays of Jewish Life, 2:45

Sholom Aleykhem: Person, Persona, Presence, 2:46

Shooting an Elephant, 1:530

The Shooting Party: A Novel, 2:709

Shore of Love, 2:839

Shores of Darkness, 1:265

A Short Account of the Destruction of the Indies, 3:629

A Short Dictionary of Furniture, 3:766

Shorter Encyclopedia of Islam, 3:443, 3:456, 4:566

A Shorter Finnegans Wake, 1:504

The Shorter Oxford English Dictionary on Historical Principles, 1:90, 1:96

The Shorter Science and Civilisation in China, 5:26

The Shortest Way with Dissenters, 1:239

The Short Fiction of Caroline Gordon: A Symposium, 1:983

The Short Fiction of Ernest Hemingway: A Study in Major Themes, 1:846

Short Friday and Other Stories, 1:1049, 2:47

A Short Grammar of Biblical Aramaic, 4:795

A Short History of American Poetry, 1:719

A Short History of Astronomy, 5:31

A Short History of Biology, 5:14

A Short History of Chemistry, 5:14

Short History of Chinese Communism: Completely Updated, 3:470

A Short History of Christian Doctrine, 4:677

Short History of Czech Literature, 2:788

A Short History of Ethics, 4:407

A Short History of Existentialism, 4:268

A Short History of Finland, 3:381

Short History of Genetics, 5:778

A Short History of Geomorphology, 5:33

A Short History of Greek Literature, 2:345

A Short History of Irish Literature: A Backward Look, 1:527

A Short History of Islam, 4:571

A Short History of Italian Literature, 2:402

A Short History of Linguistics, 5:35

Short History of Medicine, 5:36

A Short History of Medieval Philosophy, 4:94, 4:698

Short History of Modern Korea, 3:482

A Short History of Modern Bulgaria, 3:392

A Short History of Norway, 3:381

A Short History of Opera, 3:670

A Short History of Quebec: A Socio-Economic Perspective, 3:610

A Short History of Scientific Ideas to 1900, 5:26

A Short History of Sociological Thought, 3:200, 5:35

A Short History of Spanish Literature, 2:523

A Short History of Switzerland, 3:378

A Short History of Syriac
  Christianity to the Rise of
  Islam, 4:684
A Short History of Technol-
  ogy: From the Earliest
  Times to 1900 A.D., 5:36
A Short History of the Amer-
  ican Nation, 3:513
A Short History of the Arab
  People, 3:435
A Short History of the Arabs,
  3:457
A Short History of the Cath-
  olic Church, 4:677
A Short History of the Egyp-
  tian People, 3:445
A Short History of the Inter-
  pretation of the Bible,
  4:99, 4:813
A Short History of the Lab-
  our Party, 3:367
A Short History of the Liber-
  al Party, 1900–1975, 3:363
A Short History of the Near
  East, 3:436
A Short History of the Papa-
  cy in the Middle Ages,
  4:695
A Short History of the Print-
  ed Word, 1:7
A Short History of the Unit-
  ed States, 3:514
A Short History of the West-
  ern Liturgy, 4:678
A Short History of the Yugo-
  slav Peoples, 3:393
A Short History of Twenti-
  eth-Century Technology,
  1900–1950, 5:49
Short History of World War
  Two, 1939–1945, 3:281
A Short Introduction to Mor-
  al Philosophy, 4:203
The Short Life: A Novel,
  2:21
Short Life of Kierkegaard,
  4:240
The Short Narratives of
  E. M. Forster, 1:477
The Short Novels of John
  Steinbeck: Critical Essays,
  1:885
Short Reign of Pippin IV: A
  Fabrication, 1:884
Short Sentimental Journey
  and Other Stories, 2:439
The Short Stories of Sean
  O'Faolain, 1:529
The Short Stories of Yūsuf
  Idrīs: A Modern Egyptian
  Author, 2:65
Short Story Index, 1:114

Basic Volume, 1900–1949,
  1:125
Collections Indexed
  1900–1978, 1:125
The Short Story in South
  East Asia: Aspects of a
  Genre, 2:311
The Short Story in Spain in
  the Seventeenth Century,
  2:522
Short Story Masterpieces,
  1:806
Short Talks with the Dead,
  and Others, 1:443
A Short-Title Catalogue of
  Books Printed in England,
  Scotland and Ireland, and
  of English Books Printed
  Abroad, 1475–1640, 1:68
A Short-Title Catalogue of
  Books Printed in England,
  Scotland, Ireland, Wales
  and British America and
  of English Books Printed
  in Other Countries,
  1641–1700, 1:68
A Short View of the Immo-
  rality and Profaneness of
  the English Stage, 1:237
A Short Walk in the Hindu
  Kush, 3:905
Shosha, 2:48
Shostakovich, 3:718
The Shot, 2:532
Shots without Guns: The Sto-
  ry of Vaccination, 5:801
The Shoulders of Atlas, 1:750
Should Trees Have Standing?
  Toward Legal Rights for
  Natural Objects, 5:116,
  5:142
The Showa Anthology, 2:283
Showdown, 2:892
Showers, 3:27
The Showman of Vanity Fair:
  The Life of William Mak-
  epeace Thackeray, 1:404
Show Me the Good Parts:
  The Reader's Guide to Sex
  in Literature, 1:57
Show Music on Record: The
  First 100 Years, 3:662
The Show-Off, 1:1097, 1:1098
Show People, 1:426
The Shows of London, 1:271
Shrapnel and the Poet's
  Year, 1:516
Shrivings, 1:543
A Shropshire Lad, 1:496
The Shtetl, 2:34
A Shtetl and Other Yiddish
  Novellas, 2:34
Shtetl Memories, 4:624

Shuckin' and Jivin': Folklore
  from Contemporary Black
  Americans, 3:866
A Shuttle in the Crypt,
  2:148, 2:149
Shuzo Kuki and Jean-Paul
  Sartre, 4:331
The Shy Child, 5:417
Shyness: What It Is, What to
  Do about It, 5:424
Siamese Tales Old and New:
  With Some Reflections on
  the Tales, 2:336
The Siamese Theatre, 2:335
Siam Rath, 2:336
Sibelius, 3:718
Siberia: A Poem, 2:50
Siberian Odyssey: Voyage
  into the Russian Soul,
  3:904
The Siberians, 3:904
The Sibyl, 2:675, 2:676
Sic et non: A Critical Edi-
  tion, 4:106
Sicilian Carousel, 1:470
The Sicilian Relatives, 2:438
Sicilian Romance, 1:622
Sickness and Health in
  America, 5:36
The Sickness unto Death,
  4:239
Siddhartha, 2:589
Sidelights on Relativity,
  5:682
Sidereus Nuncius, or the Si-
  dereal Messenger, 5:42,
  5:604
Sidewalks of America, 3:868
Sidgwick's Ethics and Victo-
  rian Moral Philosophy,
  4:257
Sidney Hook: Philosopher of
  Democracy and Human-
  ism, 4:298
Sidney Hook and the Con-
  temporary World, 4:298
Sidney Lanier, 1:772
Sidney Lanier: A Biographi-
  cal and Critical Study,
  1:772
Sidney Lanier: The Man, the
  Poet, the Critic, 1:772
Sidney's Poetry, 1:196
Siebenkäs, 2:605
The Siege of Corinth, 1:281
The Siege of Leningrad,
  3:822
The Siege of Thebes, 1:146
Siegfried, 2:481
Siegfried Sassoon: A Critical
  Study, 1:543
Sierra Club: 100 Years of
  Protecting Nature, 5:825

The Sierra Club Handbook of Whales and Dolphins, 5:761

Sifra: An Analytical Translation, 4:612

Sifra in Perspective, 4:612

Sifre: A Tannaitic Commentary on the Book of Deuteronomy, 4:610

Sifré to Deuteronomy: An Analytical Translation, 4:612

Sifré to Deuteronomy: An Introduction to the Rhetorical, Logical, and Topical Program, 4:612

Sifré to Numbers: An American Translation, 4:612

Sigismund, 2:674

Sigmund Freud, 5:449

Sigmund Freud: His Personality, His Teaching and His School, 5:449

Sigmund Freud: Man and Father, 5:448

Sigmund Freud: Reminiscences of a Friendship, 5:436

Sigmund Freud and the Jewish Mystical Tradition, 4:628

Sigmund Freud's Dreams, 5:448

Sigmund Freud's Mission: An Analysis of His Personality and Influence, 5:448

Signal Driver, 2:966

Signals: The Science of Communications, 5:12

Signals: The Science of Telecommunications, 5:300

Signals: The Telephone and Beyond, 5:300

Signatures of the Visible, 1:1150

Signeponge-Signeponge, 2:494, 4:397

The Signet Classic Book of American Short Stories, 1:806

The Signet Classic Book of Eighteenth and Nineteenth Century British Drama, 1:272

The Signet Classic Shakespeare, 1:206

The Significance of Neoplatonism, 4:61

The Significance of Psychoanalysis for the Mental Sciences, 5:466

The Significance of Sections in American History, 3:599

The Significance of the Frontier in American History, 3:599

The Significance of Theory, 1:1127

Significations, 4:426

The Signifying Monkey, 1:1145

The Sign in Sidney Brustein's Window, 1:1092

The Sign of Angellica: Women, Writing, and Fiction, 1660–1800, 1:230

Sign of Misfortune, 2:784

The Sign of the Chrysanthemum, 1:1204, 1:1205

The Sign of the Hamster, 2:624

Signposts in a Strange Land, 1:1029

Signs, 4:310

Signs and Meaning in the Cinema, 1:1158

Signs and Symptoms, 1:1035

Signs in Action, 1:872

The Signs Reader: Women, Gender, and Scholarship, 1:923

Sigrid Undset, 2:669

Sigrid Undset: A Study in Christian Realism, 2:669

Sigrid Undset: Chronicler of Norway, 2:669

Sigurd the Völsung, 2:644

The Sikh Diaspora: Migration and the Experience beyond the Punjab, 4:516

Sikh History and Religion in the Twentieth Century, 4:516

Sikhism and the Sikhs: An Annotated Bibliography, 4:517

The Sikhs: History of Religion and Society, 4:516

Sikh Separatism: The Politics of a Faith, 4:516

The Sikhs of the Punjab, 3:484

Sikh Studies: Comparative Perspectives on a Changing Tradition, 4:516

Silas Downe, Forgotten Patriot: His Life and Writings, 3:570

Silas Marner, 1:353

Silence (Endō), 2:286, 4:540

Silence (Pinter), 1:534

Silence: Lectures and Writings of John Cage, 3:686

Silence and Invisibility, 2:971

Silence and Power: A Reevaluation of Djuna Barnes, 1:813

Silence in Henry James: The Heritage of Symbolism and Decadence, 1:765

Silence in the Snowy Fields, 1:951

The Silence of Bartleby, 1:689

The Silence of History, 1:833

The Silence of Love, 2:299, 2:300

Silences, 1:926, 1:1026

The Silences Between (Moeraki Conversations), 2:976

Silent Bomb: A Guide to the Nuclear Energy Controversy, 5:110

The Silent Cry, 2:292

Silent Night, Lonely Night, 1:1083

Silent Operas: Wusheng Xi, 2:210

The Silent Passage: Menopause, 5:356

Silent Revolution, 4:467

The Silent Scream: Alfred Hitchcock's Sound Track, 1:1170

Silent Snow, Secret Snow, 1:810

A Silent Sorrow, 5:358

Silent South, 1:736

Silent Spring, 5:829

The Silent Traveller in Japan, 3:902

The Silent World, 3:918, 3:919, 5:642

The Silent World of Doctor and Patient, 5:79

Silex Scintillans, 1:199

Silicon Dreams: Information, Man, and Machine, 5:573

The Silicon Idol: The Micro Revolution and Its Social Implications, 5:126

Silicon Mirage: The Art and Science of Virtual Reality, 5:564

Silico Sapiens: The Fundamentals and Future of Robots, 5:242

The Silken Thread, 2:668

Silks, Spices and Empire, 3:904

Silk-Screen Printing, 1:28

The Silk Screen Printing Process, 1:27

Silk Screen Techniques, 1:27

Silly Symphonies, 1:1163

Silmarillion, 1:559

Silvae, Thebaid or Thebais, Achilleid, 2:394
The Silver Age of Russian Culture: An Anthology, 2:693
The Silver Box, 1:481, 1:482
Silver Branch, 1:529
The Silver Chalice, 1:1244
The Silver Desert, 1:1215
The Silver Dove, 2:700, 2:701
Silver Face, 2:553
The Silver King, 1:367
Silverless Mirrors: Book, Self and Postmodern American Fiction, 1:917
Silver Plume, 1:1217
The Silver Tassie, 1:424, 1:526
Simas, 2:806
Simbi and the Satyr of the Dark Jungle, 2:150
Simenon: A Critical Biography, 2:508
Simians, Cyborgs, and Women, 1:1132, 1:1147, 3:213, 5:33, 5:201
Simmel and Since, 3:239
The Simon and Schuster Book of the Ballet, 3:732
Simon Bolívar, 3:632
Simone de Beauvoir: A Biography, 2:458
Simone de Beauvoir: Witness to a Century, 2:459
Simone de Beauvoir and the Demystification of Motherhood, 2:459
Simone de Beauvoir and the Limits of Commitment, 2:459
Simone Weil, 2:516
Simone Weil: A Modern Pilgrim, 2:516, 4:788
Simone Weil: An Intellectual Biography, 2:516
Simone Weil: An Introduction to Her Thought, 2:516
Simone Weil: The Just Balance, 2:516
Simone Weil Reader, 4:788
Simon Wheeler, Detective, 1:781
Simple and Direct: A Rhetoric for Writers, 1:117, 1:813
Simple Justice, 3:556
The Simple Life: Plain Living and High Thinking in American Culture, 3:561
A Simple Lust, 2:160
The Simple Past, 2:119

Simple Speaks His Mind, 1:848
A Simple Story, 2:12
Simple's Uncle Sam, 1:848
Simple Takes a Wife, 1:848
The Simpleton, 2:748
The Simpleton of the Unexpected Isles, 1:544
Simplicissimus, 2:585
Simplified Proofreading, 1:53
Simulating Science, 5:153
Sin, Sickness, and Sanity: A History of Sexual Attitudes, 5:429
Sin and Confession on the Eve of the Reformation, 4:701
Sinatra, the Man and His Music, 3:719
Sinatra, the Man and the Myth: An Unauthorized Biography, 3:719
The Sinatrafile, 3:719
The Sinatra Scrapbook, 3:719
Sincerity and Authenticity: Six Lectures, 1:1058
Sincerity and Truth: Essays on Arnauld, Bayle, and Toleration, 4:164, 4:166
Since Socrates: Studies in the History of Western Educational Thought, 3:257
Sinclair Lewis, 1:854
Sinclair Lewis: Our Own Diogenes, 1:854
Sinclair Lewis, an American Life, 1:854
Sinclair Ross: A Reappraisal, 2:926
Sinclair Ross and His Works, 2:926
The Sinful Knights: A Study of Middle English Penitential Romance, 1:147
Sinful Tunes and Spirituals: Black Folk Music to the Civil War, 3:866
Singapore, 2:324, 3:492
Singapore: The Legacy of Lee Kuan Yew, 3:492
Sing a Song of Sixpence, 1:580, 1:583
Sing a Song of Sixpence: The English Picture Book Tradition and Randolph Caldecott, 1:581
The Singer of Tales, 2:362, 2:827, 4:460
The Singer of the Eclogues: A Study of Virgilian Pastoral, 2:397
Singers of Italian Opera: History of a Profession, 3:672

Singin' and Swingin' and Gettin' Merry like Christmas, 1:935
The Singing Bourgeois, 3:663
The Singing Detective, 1:535
Singing for Power, 1:632
Singing from the Soul: An Autobiography, 3:687
Singing from the Well, 2:852
Singing Guns, 1:1212
Singing in the Spirit, 3:866
The Singing Men at Cashel, 1:460
The Singing of the Real World, 1:570
The Singing Spirit: Early Short Stories by North American Indians, 1:725
The Singing Wilderness, 5:818
Singing with Sai Baba: The Politics of Revitalization in Trinidad, 4:872
A Single Man, 1:500
Single Sparks: China's Rural Revolution, 3:470
Sing Song: A Nursery Rhyme Book, 1:390
A Singular Iniquity, 1:341
A Sinking Island: The Modern English Writers, 1:415, 1:466
The Sinner (Cosic), 2:829
The Sinners (Idrīs), 2:65
Sinners in the Hands of an Angry God, 1:636, 1:637, 4:766, 4:767
The Sin of Father Amaro, 2:559
The Sin of Father Mouret, 2:518
The Sin of Henry R. Luce: An Anatomy of Journalism, 3:816
Sino-Soviet Relations since Mao: The Chairman's Legacy, 3:471
Sins for Father Knox, 2:795
Sins of Omission, 1:1221
The Sins of the Fathers: Hawthorne's Psychological Themes, 1:677
Sin Xay, 2:321
Sir Arthur Eddington, 5:681
Sir Arthur Eddington, Man of Science and Mystic, 5:681
Sir Arthur Pinero: A Critical Biography with Letters, 1:388
Sir Bevis of Hampton, 2:28
Sir Charles Grandison, 1:253
The Sirens of Titan, 1:1063

Sir Gawain and Pearl: Critical Essays, 1:156
Sir Gawain and the Green Knight, 1:140, 1:145, 1:146, 1:155
Sir Gawain and the Green Knight, Pearl, Cleanness, Patience, 1:155
Sir George Etherege, 1:243
Sir George Etherege: A Reference Guide, 1:243
Sir George Goldie and the Making of Nigeria, 3:420
Sir George Mackenzie, 3:882
Sir Harry Johnston and the Scramble for Africa, 3:422
Sir Henry Maine: A Brief Memoir of His Life, 3:35
Sir Henry Maine: A Study in Victorian Jurisprudence, 3:35
Sir Humphrey Davy's Published Works, 5:742
Sir Isaac Newton, 5:706
Sir James Frazer and the Literary Imagination, 4:477
Sir James M. Barrie, 1:330
Sir John Betjeman: A Bibliography of Writings by and about Him, 1:445
Sir John Hicks: Critical Assessments, 3:84
Sir John Vanbrugh, Architect and Dramatist, 1664–1726, 1:262
Sir Joshua Reynolds, 3:790
Sir Joshua Reynolds: Discourses, 3:790
Sir Launcelot Greaves, 1:256
Sir Nigel, 1:607
Sir Philip Sidney, 1:196
Sir Philip Sidney: Courtier Poet, 1:196
Sir Philip Sidney: Rebellion in Arcadia, 1:196
Sir Philip Sidney and the Interpretation of Renaissance Culture, 1:196
Sir Philip Sidney as a Literary Craftsman, 1:196
Sir Richard Burton's Travels in Arabia and Africa, 3:914
Sir Richard Steele, M. P.: The Later Career, 1:257
Sir Robert Walpole, 3:408
Sir Thomas Malory: His Turbulent Career—A Biography, 1:155
Sir Thomas Malory and the Morte d'Arthur, 1:155
Sir Thomas More, 1:204

Sir Thomas More, or, Colloquies on the Progress and Prospects of Society, 1:304
Sir Thomas Wyatt and His Background, 1:201
Sir Walter Raleigh: The Renaissance Man and His Roles, 3:358
Sir Walter Scott (Bart), 1:299
Sir Walter Scott (Lauber), 1:300
Sir Walter Scott: The Great Unknown, 1:300, 1:994
Sir Walter Scott: The Making of a Novelist, 1:300
Sir Walter Scott as a Critic of Literature, 1:299
Sir William Osler: An Annotated Bibliography, 5:54
Sister Aimee: The Life of Aimee Semple McPherson, 4:753
Sister Carrie, 1:829, 1:830
Sisterly Feelings, 1:437
Sister Mary Ignatius Explains It All for You, 1:1087, 1:1088
Sister/Outsider, 1:1182, 1:1190
Sisters and Strangers: Women in the Shanghai Cotton Mills, 1919–1949, 3:470
Sister's Choice, 1:716, 1:1046
Sisters of the Spirit, 1:727
The Sisters' Tragedy, 1:496, 1:497
Sister Teresa, 1:381
A Sister to Scheharazade, 2:120
Siswe Bansi Is Dead, 2:161
Sitt Huda, 2:73
Sitting in the Bay Window: A Book for Parents of Young Alcoholics, 5:402
A Situation in New Delhi, 2:182
The Situation Is Hopeless, but Not Serious: The Pursuit of Unhappiness, 5:420
The Situation of Poetry, 1:417, 1:914, 1:1030
Situations, 2:506
The Sitwells: Edith, Osbert, and Sacheverell, 1:548
Siva: The Erotic Ascetic, 4:505
Six Armies in Normandy: From D-Day to the Liberation of Paris, 3:279
The Six Bookes of a Commonweale, 4:133, 4:134
Six by Six, 2:971
Six Chapters, 2:218

Six Chapters from My Life "Downunder," 2:268
Six Chapters of a Floating Life, 2:218, 2:253
Six Chapters of Life in a Cadre School, 2:268
Six Characters in Search of an Author, 2:435
Six Days, 2:58
Six Degrees of Separation, 1:1090
Six Dramatists in Search of a Language, 1:425
Six Dynasties Poetry, 2:189
Six Existentialist Thinkers, 4:262
Six Feet of Country, 2:162
Six Great American Plays, 1:1078
Six Great Ideas: Truth, Goodness, Beauty, Liberty, Equality, Justice, 4:270
Six Lectures on Modern Natural Philosophy, 5:506
Six Lives, Six Deaths: Portraits from Modern Japan, 3:478
Six Makers of English Religion, 1500–1700, 4:727
Six Memos for the Next Millenium, 2:412
Six Modern American Plays, 1:1078
Six Months in Hawaii, 3:901
Six Months Off: An American Family's Australian Adventure, 3:901
Six Moral Tales, 3:842
Six Novelists Look at Society, 1:420
Six Parts Love: A Family's Battle with Lou Gehrig's Disease (ALS), 5:393
The Sixpenny Magazine, 1:332
Six Perspectives on New Religions: A Case Study Approach, 4:855
Six Pillars: Introduction to the Major Works of Sri Aurobindo, 4:353
Six Plays, 1:389
Six Plays of the Yiddish Theatre, 2:33
Six Poems from the Greek of Sikelianos and Seferis, 2:377
Six Poets of Modern Greece, 2:371, 2:376
Six Poets of the San Francisco Renaissance: Portraits and Checklists, 1:913

Six Problems for Don Isidro Parodi, 2:855

Six Records of a Floating Life, 2:218

Six Sections from Mountains and Rivers without End Plus One, 1:1052

Six Tales of the Jazz Age and Other Stories, 1:839

Sixteen Modern American Writers: A Survey of Research and Criticism, 1:803

1676: The End of American Independence, 3:518

Sixteenth-Century North America, 3:135

The Sixties: From Notebooks and Diaries of the Period, 1:902

Sixty-Five Songs; Sixty-Five Pesen, 2:743

Sixty Poems, 2:803

Sixty-three: Dream Palace, Selected Stories, 1956–1987, 1:1034

Sixty-two: A Model Kit, 2:861

Six Wings: Men of Science in the Renaissance, 5:40, 5:56

Six World Religions, 4:567

S. J. Perelman: Critical Essays, 1:869

The Skalds: A Selection of Their Poems with Introduction and Notes, 2:640

The Skeleton: Fantastic Framework, 5:341

A Skeleton in the Darkroom: Stories of Serendipity in Science, 5:711

The Skeleton in the Wardrobe, 4:776

Skelton and Satire, 1:197

Skepsis, Dogma, and Belief: Uses and Abuses in Medicine, 5:80

A Skeptical Biochemist, 5:10, 5:732

Skeptical Sociology, 3:245

The Skeptical Tradition, 4:58

Skepticism: A Critical Appraisal, 4:318

Skepticism and Dissent: Selected Journalism, 1898–1901, 1:735

Skepticism and Naturalism, 4:414

The Sketch Book of Geoffrey Crayon, Gent., 1:679, 1:680

Sketches and Stories, 2:724

Sketches by Boz, 1:347, 1:349

Sketches from a Hunter's Album, 2:768, 2:769, 2:770

Sketches from a Life, 3:584

Sketches of Peasant Life, 2:748

Sketches of the Sixties, 1:755, 1:756

Sketch of the Evolution of Our Native Fruits, 5:787

A Sketch of the Life and Writings of Sidney Lanier, 1:772

The Skilled Labourer, 1760–1832, 3:403

The Skin Doctor's Skin Doctoring Book, 5:399

The Skinner Primer: Behind Freedom and Dignity, 3:194

Skinner's Philosophy, 3:194

The Skin of Our Teeth, 1:1116

Skins and Bones: Poems 1979–87, 1:1135

Skinwalkers, 1:1231

Skirgaila, 2:806

Skryabin, 3:717

Skull Beneath the Skin: The Achievement of John Webster, 1:201

Skutarevsky, 2:734

Sky Atlas 2000.0: Twenty-six Star Charts Covering Both Hemispheres, 5:591

Sky Catalogue 2000.0, 5:591

The Sky Clears: Poetry of the American Indians, 1:719, 1:912

The Sky Is My Tipi, 3:864

Skyscrapers, and Other Essays, 3:407

Skyscrapers Hide the Heavens, 3:611

Skywalking: The Life and Films of George Lucas, 1:1171

Skyward, 3:914

Skywatch East: A Weather Guide, 5:10

Skywatchers of Ancient Mexico, 4:455, 4:457

Slag, 1:493

Slang and Its Analogues, Past and Present, 1:92

Slapstick, 1:1063

Slaughterhouse-Five, 1:1063

The Slave (Baraka), 1:1085

The Slave (Singer), 2:48

Slave and Citizen: The Life of Frederick Douglass, 1:668

Slave and Citizen: The Negro in the Americas, 3:650, 3:626

The Slave Community: Plantation Life in the Antebellum South, 3:523

The Slave Girl, 2:137

The Slaveholders' Dilemma, 3:580

Slave Law in the Americas, 3:626

Slave Religion: The "Invisible Institution" in the Antebellum South, 3:561

Slavery: A Problem in American Institutional and Intellectual Life, 3:523

Slavery: Letters and Speeches, 3:265

Slavery in Africa: Historical and Anthropological Perspectives, 3:418

Slavery in the Structure of American Politics, 1765–1820, 3:521

Slaves, Peasants, and Rebels: Reconsidering Brazilian Slavery, 3:634

The Slave's Dream and Other Stories, 2:59

Slave Ship, 1:1085

Slaves in Algiers, or A Struggle for Freedom, 1:642, 1:643

Slaves No More: Three Essays on Emancipation and the Civil War, 3:526

Slaves of Love and Other Norwegian Short Stories, 2:662

Slaves Today: A Story of Liberia, 1:879

Slaves without Masters: The Free Negro in the Antebellum South, 3:523

Slavic Excursions: Essays on Russian and Polish Literature, 1:466

The Slavs beneath Parnassus, 2:832

Slav Soul, and Other Stories, 2:733

The Slayers of Moses, 4:610

Sleep Disorders: Diagnosis and Treatment, 5:428

Sleepers Joining Hands (Shadow Mothers), 1:951

Sleeping Beauty, 1:583

The Sleeping Beauty in the Wood, 1:321

Sleeping Fires, 1:359

The Sleeping Lord, 1:502

The Sleeping Lord and Other Fragments, 1:502
The Sleeping Prince (Faldbakken), 2:664
The Sleeping Prince (Rathgan), 1:540
Sleeping Tiger, 1:621
Sleep My Love, 1:1175
A Sleep of Prisoners, 1:480
The Sleep of Reason, 2:532
Sleepwalker in a Fog: Stories, 2:762, 2:763
The Sleepwalkers (Broch), 2:573
Sleepwalkers (Koestler), 4:161
The Sleepwalkers: A History of Man's Changing Vision of the Universe, 5:42
The Sleepwatchers, 5:391
Sleuth, 1:543
A Slight Ache, 1:534
Slogans, 1:117
The Slopes of Lebanon, 2:23
Slope Stability, Geotechnical Engineering, and Geomorphology, 5:626
A Slot Machine, a Broken Test Tube, 5:765
Slouching towards Bethlehem, 1:968
Slow Chrysanthemums, 2:299
Slow Fade to Black: The Negro in American Film, 1900–1942, 1:1157
Slow Homecoming, 2:586
Slow Learner: Early Stories, 1:1035
Slowly, by Thy Hand Unfurled, 1:1100
Slowly, Slowly in the Wind, 1:1231
The Slow Natives, 2:950
A Small Alpine Form: Studies in Nabokov's Short Fiction, 2:741
A Small Boy and Others, 1:762
Small Change, 3:843
Small Craft Warnings, 1:1117
Small Escapes under the Sun, 3:893
A Small Family Business, 1:437
The Small Farm in the Steppe, 2:731
The Small Giant: Sweden Enters the Industrial Era, 3:382
The Small House at Allington, 1:405

Small Is Beautiful: Economics as if People Mattered, 3:62, 5:76, 5:157, 5:824
The Small Publisher: A Manual and Case Histories, 1:48
Smalltalk-80: The Interactive Programming Environment, 5:552
Smalltalk-80: The Language, 5:552
Small Town America: A Narrative History, 1620 to the Present, 3:553
A Small Town in Germany, 1:596
Small World, 1:515
The Smart Set, 1:859
The Smell of Hay, 2:408
The Smell of It, 2:65
Smetana, 3:720
Smile, Please: An Unfinished Autobiography, 2:940
Smile Awhile, 2:140
Smile of the Gods: A Thematic Study of Cesare Pavese's Work, 2:433
Smile of the Lamb, 2:19
Smiley's People, 1:596
Smith of Wooton Major and Farmer Giles of Ham, 1:559
The Smithsonian Book of Flight, 5:219
Smoke, 2:768, 2:769
Smoke and Other Early Stories, 1:813
Smoking: Making the Choice under Uncertainty, 5:404
Smoking: Psychology and Pharmacology, 5:404
Smoking: The Artificial Passion, 5:404
Smoking, Personality, and Stress, 5:404
Smoking and Aging, 5:316
Smoking and Society: Toward a More Balanced Assessment, 5:404
Smoking for Two: Cigarettes and Pregnancy, 5:404
Smoking Tobacco and Health: A Fact Book, 5:404
Smuts, 3:423
The Snail on the Slope, 2:762
The Snake, 1:1237
A Snapshot Album, 1:895
Snapshots of a Daugher-in-Law, 1:1037
Sneaky People, 1:949

The Sneeze and Other Plays, 2:709
The Snobol4 Programming Language, 5:552
SNOBOL Programming for the Humanities, 5:564
The Snooty Baronet, 1:514
Snorri Sturluson, 2:643
Snow, 2:836
Snow and Summers, 2:660
Snowball Berry and Other Stories, 2:756
Snow-Bound: A Winter Idyl, 1:708
Snow Country, 2:288
Snow in May: An Anthology of Finnish Writing, 1945–1972, 2:658
Snow Leopard (Forsström), 2:658
The Snow Leopard (Matthiessen), 3:930
The Snow Maiden, 2:744
Snowman, Snowman, 2:974
The Snow Poems, 1:934
The Snows of Kilimanjaro and Other Stories, 1:845
Snow White, 1:943, 1:944
Snow White and Rose Red, 1:1233
Snow White and the Seven Dwarfs, 1:1163, 1:1202, 1:1203
Sobre los Ángeles, 2:528
Sob Sister Journalism, 3:805
Soccer Madness, 3:634
Social Amnesia, 5:422
Social and Cultural Dynamics, 3:240
Social and Economic History of the Hellenistic World, 2:347, 3:302
Social and Economic History of the Roman Empire, 2:381, 3:303
Social and Economic History of Twentieth-Century Europe, 3:345
The Social and Political Thought of Alexis de Tocqueville, 3:165
The Social and Political Thought of Herbert Spencer, 3:241
Social and Political Thought of Karl Marx, 3:290, 4:242
The Social and Political Thought of Leon Trotsky, 3:295
A Social and Religious History of the Jews, 3:347, 4:593, 4:596
The Social Animal, 3:170

Social Anthropology, 3:29

Social Anthropology of Complex Societies, 3:22

The Social Anthropology of Radcliffe-Brown, 3:39

A Social Basis for Prewar Japanese Militarism, 3:479

Social Behavior: Its Elementary Forms, 3:172

Social Behavior and Personality, 3:242

Social Behavior in Animals: With Special Reference to Vertebrates, 3:195, 5:838

Social Change: With Respect to Culture and Original Nature, 3:236

Social Change and Prejudice, 3:230, 5:435

Social Change and the City in Japan, 3:476

Social Change in Modern India, 3:486

Social Change in Tikopia, 3:30

Social Character in a Mexican Village, 5:422, 5:450

Social Choice and Individual Values, 3:69

Social Choice and Multicriterion Decision-Making, 3:68, 3:69

Social Choice and Public Decision Making, 3:69

The Social Cinema of Jean Renoir, 3:842

Social Cognition and Communication, 3:172

Social Commitment in Literature and the Arts, 2:317

Social Communication among Primates, 5:825

Social Concern in Calvin's Geneva, 4:762

Social Conflicts in the Roman Republic, 3:303

The Social Construction of American Realism, 1:723, 1:804

The Social Construction of Lesbianism, 1:1182, 3:218

The Social Construction of Reality, 3:220, 3:221

The Social Construction of Technological Systems, 5:24, 5:151

The Social Context of Dentistry, 5:335

The Social Context of Modern English Literature, 1:414

The Social Contract, 3:164, 4:212

Social Contract and Discourses, 4:213

The Social Control of Technology, 5:212

The Social Creation of Nature, 5:822

Social Criticism and Nineteenth-Century American Fictions, 1:716

Social Darwinism in American Thought, 3:583, 5:46

The Social Democratic Movement in Prewar Japan, 3:480

Social Development, 3:173

Social Dimensions of Law and Justice, 3:145

Social Epistemology, 5:66, 5:153

Social Figures: George Eliot, Social History and Literary Representation, 1:354

Social Foundations of Education, 3:258

Social Framework: An Introduction to Economics, 3:83

The Social History of Art, 3:202, 3:757

A Social History of England, 1851–1975, 3:365

Social History of the United States: A Guide to Information Sources, 3:511

The Social Impact of Computers, 5:126

Socialism: An Economic and Sociological Analysis, 3:52

Socialism: Ideals, Ideologies, and Local Practice, 3:140

Socialism: Past and Future, 3:52

Socialism and the Jews, 4:656

Socialism in England, 3:113

Social Issues: Meditative Thinking and the Threefold Social Order, 4:879

Socialist Europe and Revolutionary Russia, 3:394

Socialist Realism: An Impossible Aesthetic, 2:690

The Socialist Thought of Jawaharlal Nehru, 3:499

Socialization after Childhood: Two Essays, 3:216

Socialization and the Life Cycle, 3:216

Socialization as Cultural Communication, 3:37

Socialization to Old Age, 3:216

The Social Laws of the Qoran, 3:444

Social Learning and Imitation, 3:176, 3:191

Social Learning and Personality Development, 3:175

Social Life in the Insect World, 5:796

The Social Mission of English Criticism, 1:311, 1:1126

Social Mobility in Industrial Society, 3:158, 3:214

Social Movements and Protest in France, 3:372

Social Movements of the 1960s: Searching for Democracy, 3:551

Social Movements of the Sixties and Seventies, 3:215

Social Networks: A Developing Paradigm, 3:215

The Social Novel at the End of an Era, 1:804

Social Organization: A Study of the Larger Mind, 3:224

Social Organization: Essays Presented to Raymond Firth, 3:30

The Social Organization of Australian Tribes, 3:38

The Social Origins of Democratic Socialism in Jamaica, 3:638

Social Origins of Depression: A Study of Psychiatric Disorder in Women, 5:426

Social Philosophy and Religion of Comte, 4:223

The Social Philosophy of Adam Smith, 4:215

Social Plays, 1:388

Social Policy and the Welfare State in New Zealand, 3:494

Social Problems as Social Movements, 3:215

Social Process, 3:224

Social Psychology: Sociological Perspectives, 3:168

The Social Psychology of Prejudice, 3:176

Social Realism in the Novels of John Steinbeck, 1:885

Social Responsibility in Science, Technology, and Medicine, 5:73, 5:152

The Social Role of the Man of Knowledge, 3:202

The Social Science Encyclopedia, 3:5

Social Science Reference Sources, 3:5

Social Science Research Handbook, 3:5

The Social Sciences: A Cross-Disciplinary Guide to Selected Sources, 3:5

Social Sciences Citation Index, 1:114, 3:6

Social Sciences Index, 1:114, 3:6

Social Semiotics: Text, Meaning, and Nabokov's "Ada," 2:742

The Social Setting of Pauline Christianity: Essays on Corinth, 4:618, 4:826

The Social Shaping of Technology: How the Refrigerator Got Its Hum, 5:155

The Social Sources of Denominationalism, 3:213

Social Statics, 3:240

Social Statistics without Tears, 5:522

Social Status and Psychological Disorder: A Causal Inquiry, 3:214

Social Stratification in Polynesia, 3:25

Social Stratification in Science, 3:213

Social Structure, 3:17, 3:20, 3:25, 3:38

Social Structure, Work, and Personality, 3:215

Social Structure and Personality, 3:15

Social Structure and Personality Development, 3:173

The Social Structure of Islam, 3:443

Social Structures in Molière's Theatre, 2:490

The Social System, 3:216, 3:237

The Social Teaching of the Christian Churches, 4:95

Social Text, 1:1148

The Social Theories of Talcott Parsons: A Critical Examination, 3:237

Social Theory and Modern Sociology, 3:227

Social Theory and Social Structure, 3:215, 3:233

Social Thought, 4:689

The Social Thought of Jane Addams, 1:731

The Social Thought of John XXIII: Mater et Magistra, 4:771

The Social Thought of Lu Hsün, 1881–1936, 2:256

The Social Thought of Rousseau and Burke: A Comparative Study, 3:152

The Social Thought of W.E.B. Du Bois, 1:832, 3:578

The Social Transformation of American Medicine, 3:553, 5:315

Society and Civilization in Greece and Rome, 2:345

Society and Culture in Early Modern France, 4:731

Society and Economy in Colonial Connecticut, 3:518

Society and Religion in Elizabethan England, 4:734

Society and Settlement: Jewish Land of Israel in the Twentieth Century, 4:594, 4:642

Society and Technological Change, 5:149

Society and the Environment: A Soviet View, 5:697

Society and the Holy in Late Antiquity, 4:449

Society and the Sexes in Medieval Islam, 4:579

Society and the Writer: Essays on Literature in Modern Asia, 2:310, 2:312

Society in America, 1:376

Society in Crisis: France in the Sixteenth Century, 4:732

The Society of Mind, 5:568

The Society of Text, 5:561

Society of the Muslim Brothers, 4:572

The Sociobiological Imagination, 5:826

Sociobiology: The New Synthesis, 3:171, 3:176, 5:827

Sociobiology and Conflict, 3:204

Sociobiology and Psychology: Ideas, Issues, and Findings, 3:170

The Sociobiology Debate, 5:825

Sociocultural Theory, Values, and Sociocultural Change, 3:240

Socioeconomic Background and Achievement, 3:214

The Socioeconomics of Sustainable Agriculture, 5:261

Sociolinguistic Patterns, 3:21

Sociological Ambivalence and Other Essays, 3:215, 3:233

Sociological Ideas and Social Facts, 3:233

The Sociological Imagination, 3:234

Sociological Impressionism, 3:239

Sociological Theory and Modern Society, 3:237

Sociological Theory and Social Research, 3:224

Sociologie d'une Révolution, 2:121

The Sociologists of the Chair, 3:200

Sociology and the Jesus Movement, 4:864

Sociology as an Art Form, 3:236

Sociology as Social Criticism, 3:222

A Sociology of Age Stratification, 3:201

The Sociology of Early Palestinian Christianity, 4:618

The Sociology of Emile Durkheim, 3:225

The Sociology of Literature, 3:202

The Sociology of Postmodernism, 3:211

The Sociology of Race Relations: Reflection and Reform, 3:209

The Sociology of Religion (Wach), 4:494, 4:890

Sociology of Religion (Weber), 3:213, 3:244

The Sociology of Science, 3:233

Sociology of Science: A Sociological Pilgrimage, 5:156

The Sociology of Science: Theoretical and Empirical Investigations, 5:155

The Sociology of Science in Europe, 3:214

The Sociology of Small Groups, 3:172

The Sociology of Talcott Parsons, 3:237

The Sociology of the American Jew, 4:641

Sociology of Urban Women's Image in African Literature, 2:110

Sociomedia, 5:561

Socio-Religious Reform Movements in British India, 4:508, 4:516, 4:517

Socrates (Guthrie), 2:345, 4:89

Socrates (Santas), 4:90

Socrates, Buddha, Confucius and Jesus, 4:17, 4:300, 4:349

Socrates, Ironist and Moral Philosopher, 3:307, 4:90

Socrates and Aristophanes, 2:354, 4:90

Socrates and Legal Obligation, 4:89

Socrates and the Political Community: An Ancient Debate, 4:90

Socrates and the State, 4:89

Socrates on Trial, 4:89

Socrates to Sartre: A History of Philosophy, 4:18

Socratic Humanism, 4:54

The Socratic Paradoxes and the Greek Mind, 4:90

Socratic Satire: An Essay on Diderot and Le Neveu de Rameau, 4:197

The Sod-House Frontier, 1854–1890, 3:531

Sofia Petrovna, 2:711

Softcops, 1:459

Soft Energy Paths: Toward a Durable Peace, 5:289

The Soft Machine, 1:957

The Soft Machine: Cybernetic Fiction, 5:565

The Soft Side, 1:763

Software Configuration Management, 5:549

The Software Encyclopedia, 1993, 5:541

Software People: Inside the Computer Business, 5:542

Software Reflected, 5:125

Software Tools in Pascal, 5:550

So Human an Animal, 5:152, 5:795

Soil Genesis and Classification, 5:262

Soil Landscape Analysis, 5:626

Soil Taxonomy, 5:263

Sokoto Caliphate, 3:421

Solace: The Missing Dimension in Psychiatry, 5:415

Solar Building Architecture, 5:288

The Solar Electric House, 5:284

Solar Energy Handbook, 5:289

Solar Energy Research, 5:291

Solar Energy Thermal Processes, 5:291

Solar Engineering of Thermal Processes, 5:291

Solar Heat in Design by the f-Chart Method, 5:284, 5:291

Solar Hydrogen: Moving beyond Fossil Fuels, 5:290

Solaria, 2:421, 2:437

Solaris, 2:816

The Solar Period and the Price of Corn, 3:84

Soldier and Civilian in the Later Roman Empire, 3:308

The Soldiers, 2:591

Soldiers Are Not Born, 2:756

A Soldier's Embrace, 2:162

Soldiers' Pay, 1:835

Soldiers Three, 1:370

Soldier Stories, 1:371

Soldiers Women, 2:954

The Sole Spokesman, 3:487

Sole Survivor, 2:975

Solidarity, 2:331

Solid Clues, 5:650

The Solid Gold Cadillac, 1:1097

The Solid Mandala, 2:965, 2:966

Solid Philosophy, 4:180

Solid State Physics, 5:671

Solids and Surfaces, 5:748

Solid-State Physics: An Introduction to Theory and Experiment, 5:668

Solid State Physics, Vol. 46: Advances in Research and Applications, 5:668

Solid-State Physics Source Book, 5:669

Soliloquies in England and Later Soliloquies, 4:327

Solitaire/Double Solitaire, 1:1082, 1:1083

Solitary Comrade: Jack London and His Work, 1:775

The Solitary Singer: A Critical Biography of Walt Whitman, 1:707

Solitude and Society, 4:275

Solitudes of Luis de Góngora, 2:539, 2:540

Solo: An American Dreamer in Europe, 1933–1934, 1:1017

Solo: Life with an Electric Car, 3:897

Sologub's Literary Children: Keys to a Symbolist's Prose, 2:759

Solomon Gursky Was Here, 2:924

Solomon Maimon: An Autobiography, 4:647

So Long, Schoolboy! 2:742

So Long a Letter, 2:132

Solos, 2:527

Soloveitchik on Repentance, 4:886

Solstice, 1:1022

Solve Your Child's Sleep Problems, 5:322

Solzhenitsyn, 2:801

Solzhenitsyn: A Biography, 2:762

Solzhenitsyn: A Collection of Critical Essays, 2:761

Solzhenitsyn, Tvardovsky and Novy Mir, 2:762

Solzhenitsyn at Harvard, 2:761

Solzhenitsyn in Exile: Critical Essays and Documentary Materials, 2:761

The Solzhenitsyn-Sakharov Dialogue: Politics, Society, and the Future, 2:762

Solzhenitsyn's Political Thought, 2:762

So Many Versions? 4:798

Some Account of the English Stage from the Restoration in 1660 to 1830, 1:272

Some Americans: A Personal Record, 1:560

Some Aspects and Problems of London Publishing between 1550 and 1650, 1:37

Some Aspects of Hittite Religion, 4:445

Some Aspects of Rabbinic Theology, 4:621

Some Came Running, 1:994

Some Champions, 1:852

Some Day Been Dey: West African Pidgin Folktale, 3:857

Some Dogmas of Religion, 4:304

Some Enchanted Evenings: The Story of Rodgers and Hammerstein, 3:713

Some Facets of "King Lear": Essays in Prismatic Criticism, 1:214

Some Final Words of Advice, 2:277

Some Freaks, 1:1101

Some Honorable Men, 1:1011

Some Intellectual Consequences of the English Revolution, 3:404

Some Kind of Love Story, 1:1104

Some Laughter, Some Tears: Tales from the Old World and New, 2:45

Some Memories of W. B. Yeats, 1:519

Some Modern Writers, 1:430

Some Must Watch While Some Must Sleep, 5:391

Some Notes on Bookbinding, 1:22

Some of the Reasons against Woman's Suffrage, 1:690

Someone, 2:493

Some Passages in the Life of Mrs. Margaret Maitland of Sunnyside, 1:385

Some People, Places, and Things That Will Not Appear in My Next Novel, 1:961

Some Poems and Some Poets, 1:912

Some Prefer Nettles, 2:294

Some Presidents: Wilson to Nixon, 3:601

Some Problems of Philosophy, 4:236

Some Questions about Language, 4:271

Some Sort of Epic Grandeur: The Life of F. Scott Fitzgerald, 1:840

Some Spanish-American Poets, 2:848

Some Tame Gazelle, 1:538, 1:539

Something Beautiful for God: Mother Teresa of Calcutta, 4:745

Something Childish and Other Stories, 2:978

Something Happened, 1:987, 1:988

Something in Common and Other Stories, 1:848

Something I've Been Meaning to Tell You, 2:921

Something Like an Autobiography, 3:839

Something of Myself and Other Autobiographical Writings, 1:371

Something Out There, 2:162

Something to Love: Barbara Pym's Novels, 1:539

Something to Remember Me By—Three Tales, 1:947

Something Wicked This Way Comes, 1:1255

Some Thoughts Concerning Education, 1:576, 3:159, 4:178

Some Thoughts on the Present Aspect of the Crusade, 1:341

Sometimes a Great Notion, 1:999

Some Traditions of the Thai, 4:519

Some Trees, 1:936

Some Turns of Thought in Modern Philosophy, 4:327

Some Versions of Pastoral, 1:925

Some Views and Reviews of Ashton's Choreography, 3:736

Somewhere a Master: Further Tales of the Hasidic Masters, 4:633

Some Words of Jane Austen, 1:276

Some Write to the Future, 2:864

Somnium: The Dream, or Posthumous Work on Lunar Astronomy, 5:608

Somnium et vigilia in Somnium Scipionis, 4:156

Somoza and the Legacy of U.S. Involvement in Central America, 3:639

A Son, Come Home, 1:1086

Sonata Forms, 3:663

Sonata of Icarus, 2:806

Sonata Pathetique, 2:839

Sonatas, 2:553

Song, Dance, and Customs of Peasant Poland, 3:850

Song, Dance and Storytelling, 3:851

The Song at the Sea, 4:610

Song at Twilight, 1:465

The Songbook of Absences, 2:541

Song from the Forest: My Life among the Ba-Benjelle Pygmies, 3:421

Song Index: An Index to More than 12,000 Songs, 1:125

The Song of a Goat, 2:133

Song of a Maiden, 2:147

Song of a Prisoner, 2:155, 2:156

The Song of Bernadette, 2:615

Song of Eskasoni: More Poems of Rita Joe, 2:914

The Song of Hiawatha, 1:682, 2:659

Song of Lawino, 2:155

Song of Lawino & Song of Ocol, 2:156

Song of Liang Chou, 2:215

A Song of Love and Death: The Meaning of Opera, 3:670

Song of Ocol, 2:155

The Song of Roland, 2:509, 2:510, 2:537

Song of Solomon, 1:1018

Song of Songs Rabbah: An Analytical Translation, 4:612

The Song of the Lark, 1:820

Sóngoro Cosongo, 2:869

Songs and Ballads of the Maine Lumberjacks, 3:858

Songs and Hurts, 2:78

Songs before Sunrise, 1:398

Songs by the Ettrick Shepherd, 1:292

Songs from the Ghetto, 2:29, 2:44

Songs from Vagabondia, 2:908

Songs from Xanadu: Studies in Mongol Dynasty Song Poetry (San Ch'u), 2:189

Songs of a Semite: The Dance to Death, and Other Poems, 1:773

Songs of Castelvecchio, 2:431

Songs of Childhood, 1:467

Songs of Home, 2:886

Songs of Innocence, 2:977

Songs of Innocence and Experience, 1:278, 1:577, 1:580

Songs of Jerusalem and Myself, 2:13

Songs of Kabir from the Adi Granth, 4:516

Songs of Life and Hope, 2:863

The Songs of Seydou Camara, Vol. I: Kambili, 2:126

Songs of Summer, 1:777

Songs of the American West, 3:863

Songs of the Bards of Bengal, 2:174

Songs of the Cowboys, 3:864

Songs of the Flying Dragons, 2:299

Songs of the Saints of India, 4:504, 4:516

Songs of the South, 2:195, 196, 2:201

Songs of the Theater, 3:656

A Song to David, 1:255

Song without Music: Chinese Tz'u Poetry, 2:191

Sonnets, 2:416

Sonnets from the Portuguese, 1:337, 1:390

Sonnets pour Hélène, 2:502
Sonnets to Orpheus, 2:607
The Son of Apollo: Themes of Plato, 4:85
Son of a Smaller Hero, 2:924
Son of Man, 2:882
The Son of Perdition, 1:964
The Son of the Bondwoman (Los Pasos de Ulloa), 2:546
Son of the Male Muse: New Gay Poetry, 1:1185
A Son of the Middle Border, 1:751
Son of the Morning, 1:1022
Son of the Revolution, 3:470
The Son of the Wolf, 1:774
Sonovagun Stew: A Folklore Miscellany, 3:862
Sons and Lovers, 1:508, 1:509
Sons for the Return Home, 2:979, 2:980
Sons of Cain, 2:967, 2:968
Sons of the Shaking Earth, 3:626
Sons of the Wind, 2:847
Sophie's Choice, 1:1056, 1:1057
The Sophismata of Richard Kilvington, 4:104
Sophisms on Meaning and Truth, 4:103
The Sophisticated Traveler: Winter, Love It or Leave It, 3:893
Sophisticate's Primer of Relativity, 5:676
The Sophists, 4:54
Sophoclean Tragedy, 2:368
Sophocles (Bloom), 2:368
Sophocles (Reinhardt), 2:368
Sophocles (Scodel), 2:368
Sophocles: An Interpretation, 2:368
Sophocles: A Study of Heroic Humanism, 2:368
Sophocles, Poet and Dramatist, 2:368
Sophocles and Pericles, 2:368
Sophocles the Dramatist, 2:368
Sophrosyne: Self-Knowledge and Self-Restraint in Greek Literature, 4:48
Sorcerers of Dobu, 3:26
Sordello: A Marginally Annotated Edition, 1:338
Sore Throats and Sonnets of Love and Opposition, 1:450

Sor Juana: Or, the Traps of Faith, 2:879
Sororophobia: Differences among Women in Literature and Culture, 2:989
Sorraya in a Coma, 2:84
A Sorrow beyond Dreams, 2:586
The Sorrow of Belgium, 2:623, 2:624
Sorrow's Kitchen: The Life and Folklore of Zora Neale Hurston, 1:850
The Sorrows of Frederick, 1:1099
The Sorrows of Rosalie: A Tale, with Other Poems, 1:384
The Sorrows of Young Werther, 2:563, 2:580, 2:602
Sorry . . . But you didn't send us everything we need to register your claim to copyright, and we're going to have to start all over, 1:55
Sorties, 1:967
A Sort of Columbus: The American Voyages of Saul Bellow's Fiction, 1:947
A Sort of Life, 1:489
Sotheby's Concise Encyclopedia of Furniture, 3:766
Sotheby's Concise Encyclopedia of Glass, 3:765
The Sotheby's Directory of Silver: 1600–1940, 3:767
Soto Zen in a Japanese Town, 4:537
The Sot-Weed Factor, 1:942
Soul Clap Hands and Sing, 1:1014
The Soul of a New Machine, 5:154, 5:537
The Soul of Denmark, 3:381
The Soul of Man under Socialism, 1:409, 1:410
The Soul of Mbira, 3:669
The Soul of the Indian, 1:749
Soul of Wood, 2:600
Souls and the Structure of Being in Late Neoplatonism—Syrianus, Proclus and Simplicius, 4:61
The Souls of Black Folk, 1:726, 1:807, 1:831, 1:832, 3:578
Souls on Fire: Portraits and Legends of Hasidic Masters, 1:1065, 4:633

Soulstealers: The Chinese Sorcery Scare of 1768, 3:468
Soulstorm: Stories, 2:896
The Soul under the Influence of Technology, 5:86
Soumchi, 2:22
Sound, Speech, and Music, 3:659
Sound and Form in Modern Poetry, 1:417
The Sound and the Fury, 1:834, 1:835
Soundings: Music in the Twentieth Century, 3:666
Soundings: Some Early American Writers, 1:628
The Sound of a Voice, 1:1095
The Sound of Their Music: The Story of Rodgers and Hammerstein, 3:713
The Sound of the Mountain, 2:288
The Sound of the Wind: The Life and Works of Uno Chiyo, 2:295
The Sound of Two Hands Clapping, 1:426
The Sound of Wings: The Life of Amelia Earhart, 3:909
Soundpieces: Interviews with American Composers, 3:660
Sound Sentiment, 3:661
The Sound That Remains: A Historical Collection of Frisian Poetry, 2:635
Soundtrack: The Music of the Movies, 3:667
The Source, 1:1248, 3:931
Source Book in Animal Biology, 5:33
A Sourcebook in Asian Philosophy, 4:498, 4:522
A Source Book in Astronomy 1900–1975, 5:590
A Source Book in Astronomy and Astrophysics, 1900–1975, 5:48
A Source Book in Chemistry, 1400–1900, 5:32
A Source Book in Chemistry, 1900–1950, 5:728
Source Book in Chinese Philosophy, 4:358, 4:521
A Source Book in Geography, 3:119, 5:32, 5:620
A Source Book in Geology, 1400–1900, 5:33, 5:623
Sourcebook in Indian Philosophy, 4:351, 4:498

Source Book in Mathematics: Twelve Hundred to Eighteen Hundred, 5:31

A Source Book in Medieval Science, 4:94, 5:39

Source Book in the History of Psychology, 5:35

Source Book of Medical History, 5:35

Sourcebook on the Environment: A Guide to the Literature, 5:620

Source Readings in Music History from Classical Antiquity throughout the Romantic Era, 3:663

Sources: An Anthology of Contemporary Materials Useful for Preserving Personal Sanity While Braving the Great Technological Wilderness, 5:175

Sources and Documents Illustrating the American Revolution, 1764–1788, and the Formation of the Federal Constitution, 3:589

Sources for the Study of Greek Religion, 4:446

Sources of Anglo-Saxon Literary Culture: A Trial Version, 1:120

Sources of Art Nouveau, 3:759

Sources of Chinese Tradition, 2:186, 3:466, 4:358, 4:521

Sources of Contemporary Philosophical Realism in America, 4:35, 4:267

Sources of Indian Tradition, 2:171, 3:484, 4:497

Sources of Information in the Social Sciences, 3:5, 3:273

Sources of Invention, 5:226

Sources of Japanese Tradition, 4:534

Sources of Quantum Mechanics, 5:661

The Sources of Shakespeare's Plays, 1:219

The Sources of Ten Shakespearean Plays, 1:219

Sources of the Self, 4:415

The Sources of the White Devil, 1:200

South Africa, 1:406

South Africa: A Modern History, 3:423

The South African Novel in English: Essays in Criticism and Society, 2:158

South America Called Them, 3:131

South American Mythology, 4:465

The South and the Concurrent Majority, 3:593

The South and the Sectional Conflict, 3:529, 3:593

South Asia: A Systematic Geographic Bibliography, 3:482

South Asian Bibliography: A Handbook and Guide, 3:482

South by Southeast, 3:813

The South Country, 1:558

Southeast Asia: A Bibliography for Undergraduate Libraries, 3:488

Southeast Asia: A Critical Bibliography, 3:488

Southeast Asia: A Cultural Study through Celebration, 4:519

Southeast Asia: Bibliographic Directions in a Complex Area, 3:488

Southeast Asia: Its Historical Development, 3:488

Southeast Asia in the Age of Commerce, 1450–1680, Vol. 1, 3:489

South-East Asia Languages and Literatures: A Select Guide, 2:311

Southeast Asia Literature in Translation: A Preliminary Bibliography, 2:311

South East Asian Seas: Oil under Troubled Waters, 5:281

Southeast Asian Transitions: Approaches through Social History, 3:489

Southeast Asia under Japanese Occupation, 3:464

Southeastern Europe under Ottoman Rule, 1354–1804, 3:392

Southern African Literature: An Introduction, 2:158

Southern Africa since 1800, 3:423

A Southern Appalachian Reader, 1:795, 1:904

Southern Black Creative Writers, 1829–1953, 1:713

Southern Businessmen and Desegregation, 3:548

Southern Churches in Crisis, 4:753

The Southern Common People, 3:553

Southern Daughter: The Life of Margaret Mitchell, 1:1249

The Southern Enigma: Essays on Race, Class, and Folk Culture, 3:860

The Southern Experience in the American Revolution, 3:520

Southern Folk Ballads, 3:861

Southern Honor: Ethics and Behavior in the Old South, 3:526

Southern Literary Studies, 1:724

Southern Mail, 2:504

Southern Mountain Folksongs, 3:861

A Southern Odyssey—Travelers in the Antebellum North, 3:579

Southern Politics, 3:155

Southern Politics in State and Nation, 3:155

Southern Road, 1:954

The Southern Sudan: The Problem of National Integration, 3:455

The Southern Sudan, 1883–1898, 3:418

The Southern Writer in the Postmodern World, 1:910

Southern Writers: A Biographical Dictionary, 1:712

Southey, 1:305

South Jersey Towns: History and Legend, 3:859

South Light: A Journey to the Last Continent, 3:906

South of Nowhere, 2:559, 2:560

The South Pacific: An Introduction, 3:495

South Pacific Literature: From Myth to Fabulation, 2:971

The South Seas Fiction of Robert Louis Stevenson, 1:397

South Sea Tales, 1:774

South to Destiny, 2:829

Southwest: Three Peoples in Geographical Change 1600–1970, 3:134

South-West Africa under German Rule, 3:423

South Wind, 2:338

Souvenir Portraits: Paris in the Bell Epoque, 2:469

Souvenirs, 1:481

Souvenirs entomologiques, 5:796

Sovereign Reason: And Other Studies in the Philosophy of Science, 5:95

The Sovereign Sun: Selected Poems, 2:373

Sovereignty and Liberty, 3:521

The Sovereignty of Good, 1:523

Soviet-American Relations, 1917–1920, 3:396, 3:584

Soviet Attitudes toward Authority, 3:36

Soviet Book Publishing Policy, 1:51

Soviet Choreographers in the 1920s, 3:734

Soviet Civilization: A Cultural History, 2:690

Soviet Dissident Literature: A Critical Guide, 2:691

The Soviet Energy System: Resource Use and Policies, 5:280

Soviet Fiction since Stalin: Science, Politics and Literature, 2:688

A Soviet Heretic: Essays, 2:775

Soviet Ideology, 4:31

Soviet Influence in Eastern Europe, 3:389

Soviet Intervention in Czechoslovakia, 1968, 3:389

Soviet Literary Structuralism: Background, Debate, Issues, 2:690

Soviet Literary Theories, Nineteen Seventeen to Nineteen Thirty-Four, 2:686

Soviet Literature in the 1980s: Decade of Transition, 2:690

Soviet Literature in the Nineteen Seventies, 2:690

Soviet Marxism, 4:408

Soviet Marxism: A Critical Analysis, 5:94

Soviet Navy Tactics, 5:239

The Soviet Novel: History as Ritual, 2:685

Soviet Philosophy: A General Introduction to Contemporary Soviet Thought, 4:30

Soviet Philosophy: A Study of Theory and Practice, 4:31

Soviet Policy toward the Middle East since 1970, 3:435

The Soviet Regime in Czechoslovakia, 3:389

Soviet Relations with South-East Asia: An Historical Survey, 3:489

Soviet River, 2:734

Soviet Russian Dialectical Materialism, 4:31

Soviet Russian Literature: Writers & Problems, 1917–1977, 2:690

Soviet Russian Literature since Stalin, 2:685

Soviet Scholasticism, 4:30

Soviet Women Writing: Fifteen Short Stories, 2:692

Soweto Stories, 2:168

So Worthy, My Love, 1:1225

Space, 3:931, 5:597

Space, Time, and Gravitation: An Outline of the General Theory, 5:603, 5:681

Space, Time, and Motion: A Philosophical Introduction, 5:68, 5:104

Space, Time, Infinity, 5:596

Space, Time and Architecture: The Growth of a New Tradition, 3:762

Space Almanac, 5:6

Space and Geometry, 5:700

Space and the Eighteenth-Century English Novel, 1:230

Space and Time in the Modern Universe, 5:686

Spaceborne Weather Rader, 5:633

Space Cadet, 1:1258

Spacelab: Research in Earth Orbit, 5:597

The Space Merchants, 1:1252, 1:1261

The Space Odysseys of Arthur C. Clarke, 1:615

The Space of Literature, 2:446, 2:461

Space Resources: Breaking the Bonds of Earth, 5:596

Space Sciences, 5:588

Spaceship Neutrino, 5:657

Spaceshots: The Beauty of Nature beyond Earth, 5:588, 5:603

The Space Station: An Idea Whose Time Has Come, 5:597

The Space Station: A Personal Journey, 5:596

The Space Telescope, 5:590

Space-Time Information Processing, 5:300

Space-Time Physics, 5:719

Space-Time Structure, 5:714

Space Travel: A History, 5:613

Space 2000: Meeting the Challenge of a New Era, 5:597

Spain (Guillén), 2:869

Spain (Herr), 3:387

Spain: A Brief History, 3:387

Spain: Dictatorship to Democracy, 3:386

Spain: The Root and the Flower, 2:522

Spain, 1808–1975, 3:386

Spain, Let This Cup Pass from Me, 2:886

Spain, the Jews and Franco, 4:635

Spain and Portugal in the New World, 1492–1700, 3:335, 3:629

Spain and the Western Tradition, 2:522

Spain in America, 3:335

Spain in the Heart, 2:874, 2:875

Spain under the Hapsburgs, 3:387

Spangled Unicorn, 1:465

The Spaniards: An Introduction to Their History, 3:386

Spanish-American Folk-Songs, 3:851

Spanish American Literature: A History, 2:845

Spanish-American Literature in Translation, 2:849

Spanish American Literature since Independence, 2:846

The Spanish American Revolutions, 1808–1826, 3:632

Spanish American Women Writers: A Bio-Bibliographical Source Book, 2:847

Spanish American Writing Since 1941: A Critical Survey, 2:847

Spanish and Portuguese Romances of Chivalry, 2:525

Spanish and Portuguese South America during the Colonial Period, 3:626

Spanish Bayonet, 1:815

The Spanish Brabanter, 2:623

Spanish Central America: A Socioeconomic History, 1520–1720, 3:629

The Spanish Character, 2:522

Spanish Christian Cabala, 2:523

The Spanish Civil War (Beevor), 3:386

The Spanish Civil War (Mitchell), 3:387

Spanish Civil War (Thomas), 3:387

Spanish Drama before Lope de Vega, 2:524

The Spanish Empire in America, 3:629

Spanish-English Dictionary, 1:102

Spanish Exploration in the Southwest, 3:643

Spanish Explorers in the Southern United States, 1528–1543, 1:631

Spanish Golden Age in Poetry and Drama, 2:524

Spanish-Language Philosophy of Technology, 5:71

The Spanish Pastoral Drama, 2:524

Spanish Peru, 1532–1560: A Colonial Society, 3:629

The Spanish Picaresque Novel, 2:522

The Spanish Picaresque Novel and the Point of View, 2:525, 2:530

Spanish Poetry, 2:526

Spanish Republic and the Civil War, 1931–1939, 3:387

Spanish Revolution, 3:387

Spanish Short Stories, 2:849

The Spanish Stage in the Time of Lope de Vega, 2:524

The Spanish Struggle for Justice in the Conquest of America, 3:646, 3:647, 3:629

The Spanish Temper: Travels in Spain, 3:900

The Spanish Tragedy, 1:184, 1:185

Spanish Underground Drama, 2:524

The Spanish War: An American Epic, 1898, 3:532

Spanner and Pen: An Autobiography, 1:481

Span of the Year, 2:744

Spartacus, 1:1245

The Spartans, 3:301

Spatial Data Analysis in the Social and Environmental Sciences, 3:120

Spatial Interaction Models: Formulations and Applications, 3:122

Spatial Point Pattern Analysis, 3:119

Speak, Memory: An Autobiography Revisited, 2:741

Speaking from the Heart, 4:391

Speaking of a Personal God: An Essay in Philosophical Theology, 4:743

Speaking of Chaucer, 1:151

Speaking of Galbraith: A Personal Portrait, 3:79

Speaking of Gender, 1:1046

Speaking of Literature and Society, 1:1058

Speaking of Shiva, 2:174

Speaking the Christian God, 4:905

Speaking the Language of Desire: The Films of Carl Dreyer, 3:834

Speaking Truth to Power: The Art and Craft of Policy Analysis, 3:146

Speak to the Hills, 1:418

Special Children—Special Risks, 3:201

Special Education: Research and Trends, 3:256

The Special Education Handbook, 3:257

A Special Flower, 2:975

A Special Legacy, 4:641

The Special Relationship between West Germany and Israel, 3:439

Species Plantarum, 5:805

Specimen Book and Catalogue, 1:13

The Spectacle of Empire: Style, Effect and the Pax Britannica, 1:312

The Spectator, 1:232, 1:257, 1:550

The Spectator Bird, 1:1054

Spectral Theories, 5:500

Spectrum, 1:432

Speculation and Revelation, 4:335

Speculations about Jacob, 2:594, 2:595

Speculative Grammars of the Middle Ages, 4:101

Speculum Mentis, or the Map of Knowledge, 4:282

Speculum Spinozanum: 1677–1977, 4:188

Speech and Language in Psychoanalysis, 5:458

Speech and Phenomena, 4:397

Speeches, 1946–1964, 3:499

Speech for the Liberty of Unlicensed Printing, 1:191

Speed-the-Plow, 1:1101

The Spell (and From Beginning to End), 2:801

The Spell: An Extravaganza, 1:335

Spellbound, 1:1168

Spellbound: Studies on Mesmerism and Literature, 4:847

Spelling the Word: George Herbert and the Bible, 1:181

Spenser, Marvell, and Renaissance Pastoral, 1:189

The Spenser Encyclopedia, 1:198

Spenserian Poetics: Idolatry, Iconclasm and Magic, 1:198

Spenser's Allegory: The Anatomy of Imagination, 1:198

Spenser's Faerie Queene and the Cult of Elizabeth, 1:199

Spenser's Pastorals: The Shepheardes Calendar and "Colin Clout," 1:198

Spenser's Poetry and the Reformation Tradition, 1:198, 4:726

Sphere: The Form of a Motion, 1:934

Sphinx: Iceland and the Icelanders from the Settlement to the Present, 3:381

The Sphinx and the Commissar, 3:446

The Sphinx in the City, 3:217

Spider: The Story of a Predator and Its Prey, 5:770

Spider Woman's Granddaughters, 1:1135

Spike Lee, 1:1171

Spinal Cord Injuries: Psychological, Social, and Vocational Adjustment, 5:394

Spinors and Space-Time, 5:709

Spinoza (Caird), 4:187

Spinoza (Jaspers), 4:188

Spinoza (Scruton), 4:189

Spinoza: A Collection of Critical Essays, 4:188

Spinoza: Dictionary, 4:15

Spinoza: Essays in Interpretation, 4:187

Spinoza: His Life and Philosophy, 4:189

Spinoza: His Life, Correspondence and Ethics, 4:189

Spinoza, Descartes and Maimonides, 4:189

Spinoza and the Rise of Liberalism, 4:187
Spinoza and the Sciences, 4:188
A Spinoza Bibliography, 4:189
Spinoza in Soviet Philosophy: A Series of Essays, 4:188
The Spinoza of Market Street, 2:47
The Spinoza of Market Street and Other Stories, 1:1049
Spinoza on Nature, 4:187
Spinoza's Critique of Religion, 4:189
Spinoza's Philosophy: An Outline, 4:188
Spinoza's Political and Ethical Philosophy, 4:187
Spinoza's Theory of Truth, 4:189
Spin the Spin, 5:717
The Spiral Dance: Rebirth of the Ancient Religion of the Goddess, 4:865
The Spiral Path: Essays and Interviews on Women's Spirituality, 4:888
The Spire, 1:483, 1:484
Spires of Form: A Study of Emerson's Aesthetic Theory, 1:670
The Spirit and the Future of Islam, 3:442
Spirit in Ashes: Hegel, Heidegger, and Man-Made Mass Death, 4:295
The Spirit of American Philosophy, 4:36
The Spirit of Chinese Philosophy, 4:358, 4:359
The Spirit of Democratic Capitalism, 3:143
Spirit of Flame: A Collection of the Works of Lesya Ukrainka, 2:841
The Spirit of Islam, 3:442, 4:372, 4:567, 4:587
A Spirit of Joy, 1:40
The Spirit of M. Spinoza, or the Three Imposters, Moses, Jesus, and Mohammed, 4:188
The Spirit of Medieval Philosophy, 4:95, 4:286, 4:696
The Spirit of Mediterranean Places, 2:463
The Spirit of Modern Philosophy, 4:250
The Spirit of Music, 2:703
The Spirit of Place: Letters and Essays on Travel, 1:470

The Spirit of Romance, 1:871, 1:872
The Spirit of St. Louis, 3:928, 3:929
The Spirit of '76: The Growth of American Patriotism before Independence, 3:520, 3:570
The Spirit of '76: The Story of the American Revolution as Told by Participants, 3:573
The Spirit of '76 and Other Essays, 3:567
The Spirit of System: Lamarck and Evolutionary Biology, 5:43, 5:803
The Spirit of the Age or Contemporary Portraits, 1:291
The Spirit of the Counter Reformation, 4:728
The Spirit of the Enterprise, 1:49
The Spirit of the Laws, 3:162, 3:163, 4:209, 4:210
Spirit of the New England Tribes: Indian History and Folklore, 3:858
The Spirit of the Oxford Movement, 4:783
The Spirit of the Ten Commandments, 4:620
The Spirit of Youth and the City Streets, 1:731
Spirit Rebellious, 2:67
Spirits, Heroes and Hunters from North American Indian Mythology, 3:866
Spirits in Rebellion: The Rise and Development of New Thought, 4:847
Spirits of Resistance and Capitalist Discipline, 3:22
Spiritual and Anabaptist Writers, 4:724
Spiritual and Demonic Magic from Ficino to Campanella, 4:132
Spiritual Autobiography in Early America, 1:629
The Spiritual Background of Islam, 4:574
Spiritual Canticle, 2:543
Spiritual Exercises, Spiritual Diary, Autobiography, 4:769, 4:770
Spiritual Friendship, 4:101
Spiritualism and Nineteenth-Century Letters, 4:851
Spiritualism and Society, 4:851
The Spiritualists, 4:850

Spirituality and Human Nature, 4:888
The Spirituality of John Calvin, 4:762
The Spirituality of St. Teresa of Avila, 4:786
The Spirituality of Teilhard de Chardin, 4:337
The Spirituality of the Christian East: A Systematic Handbook, 4:679
The Spirituality of the Future, 4:337
The Spiritual Life, 4:550
The Spirituals and the Blues: An Interpretation, 4:763
The Spiritual Situation in Our Technical Society, 5:131, 5:206
The Spiritual Teachings of Teresa of Avila and Adrian Van Kaam, 2:550
Spiritus Creator, 4:779
Spiritus Mundi: Essays on Literature, Myth, and Society, 1:977, 2:988
Spirit World, 3:867
Spit Delaney's Island, 2:913
Splendid Failure: Hart Crane and the Making of The Bridge, 1:823
The Splendid Voyage, 5:668
The Splendor of Longing in the Tale of Genji, 2:279
A Splintered Mirror: Chinese Poetry from the Democracy Movement, 2:235
Spoiled, 1:486
The Spoils of Poynton, 1:763
The Sponsor: Notes on a Modern Potentate, 3:810
Spontaneity and Tradition: A Study in the Oral Art of Homer, 2:362
The Spontaneous Poetics of Jack Kerouac: A Study of The Fiction, 1:999
Spooky Poems, 1:825
Spoon River Anthology, 1:858
Sport: A Cultural History, 3:343
Sport: A Philosophic Inquiry, 4:340
Sport in Greece and Rome, 3:307
A Sport of Nature, 2:162
Sports Health: The Complete Book of Athletic Injuries, 5:400
Spreading the American Dream, 3:549

Spread Spectrum in Communication, 5:300
Spring, 2:259
Spring and Weight of the Air, 5:739
Spring Awakening: A Play, 2:614
Spring Silkworms and Other Stories, 2:258
Spring Snow, 2:289
Spring Tide, 2:646
Springtime and Harvest, 1:880
Spring Torrents, 2:769
Spurs: Nietzsche's Styles, 4:397
The Spy, 1:662, 1:664, 1:1244
Spy Fiction: A Connoisseur's Guide, 1:593
A Spy in the House of Love, 1:865
Spy Thrillers: From Buchan to LeCarré, 1:593
The Spy Who Came in from the Cold, 1:596
The Spy Who Loved Me, 1:594
The Square, 2:300
The Square Root of Wonderful, 1:1009, 1:1101, 1:1102
Squaring the Circle (Kataev), 2:730
Squaring the Circle (Stoppard), 1:554
Squirrels, 1:1101
Srengenge: A Novel from Malaysia, 2:326
Sri Aurobindo: A Brief Biography, 4:353
Sri Aurobindo and Karl Marx, 4:353
Sri Lanka, 3:488
Sri Lanka: A Handbook of Historical Statistics, 3:488
Sri Lanka: A Survey, 3:487
Sri Lanka: Ethnic Fratricide and the Dismantling of Democracy, 3:488
S. S. San Pedro, 1:964
Stability and Strife: England, 1714–1760, 3:363
The Stability of Shakespeare's Text, 1:207
The Stage and the Mirrors, 2:62
Stagecoach, 1:1165, 1:1166
Stagecoach: BFI Film Classics, 1:1166
Stage Door, 1:1097
The Stage of Aristophanes, 2:353

Stages in the Revolution: Political Theatre in Britain since 1968, 1:425
The Stages of Economic Growth: A Non-Communist Manifesto, 3:54
Stages of History: Shakespeare's English Chronicles, 1:212
Stages on the Road, 2:669
Stage to Screen: Theatrical Method from Garrick to Griffith, 1:1076
Staging the Renaissance, 1:170
The Stakes of Diplomacy, 3:815
The Stakes of the Warrior, 4:472
Stalin, 3:292
Stalin: A Political Biography, 3:292, 3:344
Stalin: Man and Ruler, 3:292
Stalin: Man of Steel, 3:292
Stalin: Russia's Man of Steel, 3:292
Stalin: The Man and His Era, 3:397
Stalin and His Generals: Soviet Military Memoirs of World War II, 3:396
Stalin and His Times, 3:292
Stalin and the European Communists, 3:293
Stalin as Revolutionary 1879–1929, 3:397
Stalin in October: The Man Who Missed the Revolution, 3:293
Stalin's War against Jews: The Doctor's Plot and the Soviet Solution, 3:293
Stalkers of the Infinite, 2:762
Stalky and Company, 1:371
The Stamp Act Crisis: Prologue to Revolution, 3:588
Stan Brakhage—A Retrospective, 1:1160
The Standard Book of Shakespeare Quotations, 1:221
Standard English-Korean and Korean-English Dictionary for Foreigners, 1:101
Standard First Aid, 5:380
Standard Handbook of Engineering Calculations, 5:216
Standard Methods of Chemical Analysis, 5:735
The Standard Periodical Directory, 1:72, 1:114
Standing at the Crossroads: Southern Life since 1900, 3:534

Standing on the Shoulders of Giants: A Longer View of Newton and Halley, 5:606
Standing Still and Walking in New York, 1:1025
Stand Still Like the Hummingbird, 1:861, 1:862
Stand Tall! Every Woman's Guide to Preventing Osteoporosis, 5:396
Stanley: The Making of an African Explorer, 3:938
Stanley and the Women, 1:432
Stanley Morison, 1:6
Stanley Morison: A Portrait, 1:19
Stanley Morison Displayed, 1:17
Stanley's Story, or Through the Wilds of Africa, 3:938
Stanzas in Meditation and Other Poems (Nineteen Twenty-Nine to Nineteen Thirty-Three), 1:882
Stanze, 2:436
Star and Planet Spotting, 5:590
The Star-Apple Kingdom, 2:943
A Starchamber Quiry: A James Joyce Centennial Volume, 1882–1982, 1:505
The Star Diaries, 2:816
Stares, 1:481
Starfishes of the Atlantic, 5:769
Stargazing: Astronomy without a Telescope, 5:610
Star Names: Their Lore and Meaning, 5:587
The Star of Redemption, 4:671, 4:886
Starry Messenger, 4:142
The Stars: A New Way to See Them, 5:591
Starsailing: Solar Sails and Interstellar Travel, 5:596
Stars and Atoms, 5:681
Stars and Clusters, 5:610
The Stars and Other Korean Short Stories, 2:303
Stars and Planets, 5:591
Starship, 1:612
The Starship and the Canoe, 3:894
Stars of the New Curfew, 2:143
The Stars Shine Down, 1:1223
Starswarm, 1:613
Starting Out in the Thirties, 1:995, 1:996

The Star Turns Red, 1:526
Starving to Death in a Sea of Objects, 5:395
Star Wars, 1:1171
The Star Wars: From the Adventures of Luke Skywalker, 1:1171
The Star Wars Debate, 5:109
State and Diplomacy in Early Modern Japan, 3:476
The State and Enterprise, 3:615
The State and Labor in Modern Japan, 3:477
The State and Local Government Political Dictionary, 3:148
State and Local Politics, 3:148
State and Local Statistics Sources, 1:110
The State and Peasant Politics in Sri Lanka, 3:487
State and Revolution, 3:287
State and Revolution in Finland, 3:381
State and Salvation, 3:609
State and Scholars in T'ang China, 3:468
The State and Social Revolution in Iran: A Theoretical Perspective, 3:448
State and Society in Roman Galilee, A.D. 132–212, 4:606
State and Society in the Taiwan Miracle, 3:52
State Government Research Directory, 1:105
The State in Burma, 3:489, 4:515
The State in Northern Ireland, 1921–72, 3:371
The State in Relation to Labor, 3:85
Statements, 2:161
State of Emergency, 2:320
The State of Food and Agriculture, 1987–1988, 5:262
The State of Latin America, 3:642
The State of Music 1939, 3:724
The State of Native America: Genocide, Colonization and Resistance, 3:212
The State of Nature: Ecology, Community, and American Social Thought, 3:550
The State of Nutrition in the Arab Middle East, 3:444
State of Revolution, 1:445
A State of Siege, 2:974

State of the Ark: An Atlas of Conservation in Action, 5:822
The State of the Book World, 1:50
The State of the Earth Atlas, 5:816
State of the Nation, 1:828
The State of the Union, 2:133
State of the World, 5:828
State of War, 2:329
States and Social Revolutions, 3:215
A Statesman of the Republic of Books, 1:44
Statesman's Yearbook, 1:83
The Statesman's Year-Book 1991–1992, 3:8
The Statesman's Yearbook World Gazetteer, 3:138
Statesmen and Gentlemen, 3:468
States of Emergency, 2:159
States of Mind: A Personal Journey through the Mid-Atlantic States, 3:898
The State Universities and Democracy, 3:591
The Static Element, Selected Poems, 2:27
Station Island, 1:495
Statistical Abstract, 1:109
Statistical Abstract of the United States, 1:83
Statistical Abstract of the United States, 1878–present, 3:6, 3:505, 3:507
Statistical Analysis for Geographers, 3:120
The Statistical Exorcist: Dispelling Statistics Anxiety, 5:522
Statistical Explanation and Statistical Relevance, 5:104
Statistical Inference and Analysis, 5:528
Statistical Issues: A Reader for the Behavioral Sciences, 5:522
Statistical Literacy: A Guide to Interpretation, 5:522
Statistical Mechanics of Chain Molecules, 5:746
Statistical Methods and Scientific Inference, 5:528
Statistical Methods for Geographers, 5:119
Statistical Methods for Research Workers, 5:528
Statistical Methods in Education and Psychology, 3:255

Statistical Methods in Psychological Research, 3:169
Statistical Physics and the Atomic Theory of Matter, from Boyle and Newton to Landau and Onsager, 5:658
The Statistical Pioneers, 5:526
Statistical Record of the Environment, 5:815
Statistical Reference Index, 1:110
Statistical Tables for Biological, Agricultural and Medical Research Workers, 5:528
Statistical Yearbook, 1:83
Statistics: A Guide to the Unknown, 5:524
Statistics: Concepts and Controversies, 5:523
Statistics and Public Policy, 5:522
Statistics by Example, 5:523
Statistics for Research, 5:521
Statistics from Scratch, 5:523
Statistics in Action, 5:524
Statistics in Plain English, 5:521
Statistics in the Real World: A Book of Examples, 5:522
Statistics of Deadly Quarrels, 3:149
Statius and the Thebaid, 2:394
The Statue Within, 5:800
Staying Alive: Women, Ecology, and Development, 5:188, 5:824
Staying Healthy without Medicine, 5:342
Staying Well: Your Complete Guide to Preventive Medicine, 5:326
Stay Well, 5:342
STD: Sexually Transmitted Diseases, 5:390
Stealing into Print, 5:155
Stealing the Language: The Emergence of Women's Poetry in America, 1:799
Stealing the Market, 3:56
Steamboat Willie, 1:1163
Steel and Iron, 2:49
Steel-Engraved Book Illustration in England, 1:28
Steerage and Ten Other Stories, 2:560
Steered by the Falling Stars, 3:897

Steering a New Course, 5:289

Stefansson: A Biography of Vilhjalaur, Canadian Arctic Explorer, 3:940

Stefansson: Ambassador of the North, 3:940

Steinbeck: A Collection of Critical Essays, 1:885

Steinbeck and Film, 1:886

The Steinbeck Question: New Essays in Criticism, 1:886

Steinbeck's The Grapes of Wrath: "Essays in Criticism," 1:886

Steinway, 3:672

Stendhal, 2:511

Stendhal: The Education of a Novelist, 2:511

Stendhal: The Red and the Black, 2:511

Stendhal and the Age of Napoleon: An Interpretive Biography, 2:511

The Stepchildren of the Reformation, 4:724

Stéphane Mallarmé, 2:486

Stephanos, 2:704

Stephen Crane, 1:742, 1:743, 1:950

Stephen Crane: A Biography, 1:743

Stephen Crane: A Collection of Critical Essays, 1:742

Stephen Crane: A Critical Bibliography, 1:743

Stephen Crane: A Critical Biography, 1:742

Stephen Crane: An Annotated Bibliography, 1:743

Stephen Crane: An Annotated Bibliography of Secondary Scholarship, 1:742

Stephen Crane: A Study of the Short Fiction, 1:743

Stephen Crane: The Critical Heritage, 1:743

Stephen Crane and Literary Impressionism, 1:743

Stephen Crane in Transition: Centenary Essays, 1:743

Stephen Crane's Artistry, 1:742

Stephen Crane's The Red Badge of Courage, 1:742

Stephen Foster, America's Troubadour, 3:696

The Stephen Foster Story, 1:1088

Stephen Hawking: A Life in Science, 5:17, 5:607, 5:656, 5:692

Stephen Hawking: Physicist, 5:692

Stephen Hawking: Quest for a Theory of the Universe, 5:17

Stephen Hawking's Universe, 5:654

Stephen Hero, 1:504

The Stephen King Story: A Literary Profile, 1:1241

Stephen Leacock: Humor and Humanity, 2:918

Stephen Leacock and His Works, 2:918

Stephen Sondheim, 3:720

Stephen Spender, 1:553

Stephen Spender, Works and Criticism: An Annotated Bibliography, 1:553

Stephen Spender and the Thirties, 1:553

Stephen Szechenyi and the Awakening of Hungarian Nationalism, 1791–1841, 3:389

Stephen Vincent Benét, 1:815

Stephen Vincent Benét: The Life and Times of an American Man of Letters, 1898–1943, 1:816

Step It Down, 3:861

The Step Not Beyond, 2:461

The Steppe and Other Stories, 2:708

Steppenwolf, 2:589, 2:590

Stepping Westward, 1:448

Steppin' Out, 3:559

Steps, 1:1002, 1:1003

Steps to an Ecology of the Mind, 3:15

Sterling A. Brown: Building the Black Aesthetic Tradition, 1:955

Sterne's Fiction and the Double Principle, 1:259

Steroid Reactions: An Outline for Organic Chemists, 5:743

Steroids Made It Possible, 5:743

Stevens and Simile: A Theory of Language, 1:887

Stevens and the Interpersonal, 1:888

Stevenson and the Art of Fiction, 1:397

Stevie: A Biography of Stevie Smith, 1:549

Stevie Smith, 1:549

Stevie Smith: A Bibliography, 1:549

Stevie Smith: A Biography, 1:549

Stewards of Excellence: Studies in Modern English and American Poets, 1:417

Stick, 1:1232

Sticks and Bones, 1:1108, 1:1109

Sticks and Stones: A Study of American Architecture and Civilization, 5:169, 5:171

Sticks in the Knapsack and Other Ozark Folk Tales, 3:885

Stiff Upper Lip, 1:470

Stigma, 3:228

Stigma and Mental Illness, 5:415

Stikhi, Poems, Poèmes, 2:753

Still Another Day, 2:875

Still Harping on Daughters: Women and Drama in the Age of Shakespeare, 1:209

Still Life: A Novel, 1:455

Still Life with a Bridle, 2:814

A Still Moment: Essays on the Art of Eudora Welty, 1:895

The Stillness of the World Before Bach, 2:674

Stillwell and the American Experience in China, 1911–1945, 3:411, 3:412

The Stinehour Press: A Bibliographical Checklist of the First Thirty Years, 1:44

Stirling Engines, 5:236

Stockhausen: Conversations with the Composer, 3:721

The Stock Market: Theories and Evidence, 3:55

Stocktakings from an Apprenticeship, 3:684

The Stoic, 1:829, 1:830

Stoic and Epicurean, 4:55

The Stoic and Epicurean Philosophers, 4:56

Stoichiometry, 5:710

The Stoic Idea of the City, 4:57

Stoic Logic, 4:57

Stoic Philosophy, 4:57

The Stoics, 4:57

Stoics and Skeptics, 4:55

Stolen Mind: The Slow Disappearance of Ray Doernberg, 5:392

Stolen Spring, 2:654

A Stone, a Leaf, a Door: Poems, 1:904

Stone, Clay, and Glass, Basics for Building, 5:635

Stone Age Economics, 3:16
The Stone and the Violets, 2:829
The Stone Angel, 2:917
The Stone Bridal Bed, 2:628
The Stone Country, 2:164
Stones, 2:911
The Stones of Chile, 2:875
The Stones of Florence, 1:1008, 3:333, 3:899
Stones of the Sky, 2:875
Stones of the Wall, 2:263
The Stones of Venice, 1:324, 1:393, 1:394
Stonewall Jackson: The Good Soldier, 1:889
Stoppard The Playwright, 1:554
Stopping by Woods on a Snowy Evening, 1:1202
Storied Lives: The Cultural Politics of Self Understanding, 1:87
Stories by American Authors, 1:658, 1:725
Stories by Iranian Women since the Revolution, 2:84
Stories for Children, 1:1050, 2:47
Stories from a Ming Collection, 2:198
Stories from Ancient Canaan, 4:445
Stories from Iran 1921–1991: A Chicago Anthology, 2:84
Stories from the Country of Lost Borders, 1:733
Stories from the Warm Zone and Sydney Stories, 2:948
Stories in Prose, Stories in Verse, Shorter Poems, Lectures and Essays, 1:382
Stories of Chinese Young Pioneers, 2:240
The Stories of Eva Luna, 2:851
Stories of Five Decades, 2:590
Stories of Georgia, 1:755
Stories of Happy People, 2:674
The Stories of Heinrich Böll, 2:570
The Stories of John Cheever, 1:960, 1:961
The Stories of Kleist: A Critical Study, 2:599
Stories of Life and Death, 2:542
Stories of Lost Israel in Folklore, 3:855
Stories of Modern America, 1:806, 1:921

The Stories of the Greeks, 2:348
Stories of the Modern South, 1:806
Stories of the Nineteen Twenties, 2:775
Stories of the Seen and the Unseen, 1:385
Stories of the Steppe, 2:725
Stories of the West, 3:935
Stories of Three Decades, 2:602
Stories on a String: The Brazilian Literature de Cordel, 3:856
The Storm, 2:744
The Storm and Other Poems, 2:428
The Storm and Other Things, 2:427, 2:428
Storm Center: The Supreme Court in American Politics, 3:145
Storm in Chandigarh, 2:182
Storm in the West, 1:854
Storm of Fortune, 2:934
The Storm of Steel, 2:595
Stormy Petrel: The Life and Work of Maxim Gorky, 2:726
Story: A Critical Anthology, 1:423
Story: News Stories, Editorials, Cartoons, and Pictures from the Pulitzer Prize Collection at Col. University, 1:135
The Story of a Bad Boy, 1:732
The Story of Adèle H., 3:843
The Story of Alchemy and Early Chemistry, 5:729
A Story of a Life, 2:747
Story of a Page, 3:821
The Story of Architecture, 3:762
The Story of Art, 3:757
The Story of a Shipwrecked Sailor, 2:867
The Story of Børge, 2:648
The Story of Civilization, 3:401, 3:402
The Story of Dr. Dolittle, 1:578
Story of Dr. Faustus, 2:565
The Story of Earth, 5:622
The Story of Emin's Rescue as Told in Stanley's Letters, 3:938
Story of Fritz Haber, 5:728
The Story of Geology: Our Changing Earth through the Ages, 5:625

The Story of Giuseppe Verdi, 3:726
The Story of Gösta Berling, 2:676
The Story of Great Aunt Shlomzion, 2:21
The Story of Handwriting, 1:15
The Story of Jazz, 3:669
The Story of Jewish Philosophy, 4:601
The Story of Judaism, 4:596
The Story of King Arthur and His Knights, 1:1205
The Story of Medicine in America, 5:314
The Story of Mt. Desert Island, Maine, 3:589
The Story of My Boyhood and Youth, 5:836
The Story of My Life (Andersen), 2:647
Story of My Life (Sand), 2:504
Story of My Life and Work (Washington), 1:785
The Story of Nigeria, 3:419
The Story of Papermaking, 1:6
The Story of Phillis Wheatley, 1:647
Story of Philosophy, 3:401, 4:15, 4:16
The Story of Phra Abhai Mani, 2:337
The Story of Physics, 5:652
The Story of Psychology, 5:35, 5:188
The Story of Rama in Jain Literature, 4:509
The Story of Rimini, 1:292
The Story of Sadler's Wells, 1683–1977, 1:271, 1:426
The Story of Scottish Philosophy, 4:32
The Story of Stone, 2:191
The Story of Telecommunications, 5:297
The Story of Telford, 5:256
Story of the Eye, 2:455, 2:456
The Story of the Glittering Plain, 1:382, 1:383
Story of the Great Geologists, 5:622
The Story of the Ingalls, 1:1209
The Story of the Jesus People: A Factual Survey, 4:864
Story of Theseus, 2:409
The Story of the Stone, 2:218, 2:223

The Story of the Synagogue: A Diaspora Museum Book, 4:597

Story of the W and Z, 5:663

The Story of Two Souls, 4:307

The Story of Utopias, 5:169, 5:171

The Story of Walt Disney, 1:1165

The Story of Weather, 5:633

The Story of Yiddish Literature, 2:32

The Story of Zahra, 2:59

Storyology Essays in Folklore, Sea-Lore, and Plant-Lore, 3:869

Story Patterns in Greek Tragedy, 2:346

The Storyteller (Robbins), 1:1222

Storyteller (Silko), 1:1047

A Storyteller and a City: Sherwood Anderson's Chicago, 1:812

Storytellers: Folktales and Legends from the South, 3:859, 3:860

A Story-Teller's Holiday, 1:381

A Story Teller's Story, 1:811

Storytellers to the Nation: A History of American Television Writing, 3:812

Story-telling Techniques in the Arabian Nights, 2:56

The Stove, 2:600

The Straight Mind and Other Essays, 1:1133, 1:1182

Straight-Talk No-Nonsense Guide to Heart Care, 5:373

Straight Talk with Your Gynecologist, 5:356

Strains of Utopia: Gender, Nostalgia, and Hollywood Film Music, 3:825

Strait Is the Gate, 2:479, 2:480

Strands, 2:977

The Strands Entwined: A New Direction in American Drama, 1:1071

Strange Bride, 2:155

The Strange Career of Jim Crow, 3:533, 3:603

The Strange Case of Dr. Jekyll and Mr. Hyde, 1:395, 1:396

The Strange Children, 1:983

Strange Country: A Study of Randolph Stow, 2:964

The Strange Death of Liberal England, 1910–1914, 3:366

The Strange Destiny of Rupert Brooke, 1:451

Strange Gods: The Great American Cult Scare, 4:855

Strange Interlude, 1:1106, 1:1107

The Strange Liberalism of Alexis de Tocqueville, 3:165

Strange Nation of Rafael Mandies, 2:899

Strange Necessity: Essays and Reviews, 1:566

The Strangeness of the Ordinary, 4:380

The Stranger (Camus), 2:464

The Stranger (Van Allsburg), 1:1208

The Stranger: Humanity and the Absurd, 2:465

Stranger and Brother: A Portrait of C. P. Snow, 1:550

Stranger at Home, 4:646, 4:649

The Strange Ride of Rudyard Kipling, 1:372, 1:567

Stranger in a Strange Land, 1:1258

The Stranger in Shakespeare, 1:209

Stranger in the Forest: On Foot across Borneo, 3:903

A Stranger in Tibet: The Adventures of a Wandering Zen Monk, 4:859

The Strangers All Are Gone, 1:536

Strangers and Brothers, 1:536, 1:550

Strangers and Brothers: Omnibus Edition, 1:550

Strangers and Pilgrims: From the Castle of Perseverance to King Lear, 1:161

Strangers at the Gate: Social Disorder in South China, 1839–1861, 3:469

Strangers from a Different Shore: A History of Asian Americans, 3:557

Strangers in a Christian Land, 4:894

Strangers in Their Own Lands, 4:637

Strangers on a Train, 1:1231

Strangers within the Realm: Cultural Margins of the First British Empire, 3:564

Stranger Violence: A Theoretical Inquiry, 3:205

Strange Stories: An Examination of Victorian Literature, 1:340

Strange Stories from a Chinese Studio, 2:218

A Strange Story and the Haunted and the Haunters, 1:340

Strange Tales from Make-do Studio, 2:217, 2:218

Strange Things Happen Here, 2:885

Strange Ways and Sweet Dreams, 3:867

Strange Weather, 4:866

A Strategic Analysis of Science and Public Policy, 5:180

Strategic Defense and the Future of the Arms Race, 5:17, 5:292

Strategic Minerals: A World Survey, 5:637

Strategies for Europe: Proposals for Science and Technology Policies, 5:181

Strategies for Public Health: Promoting Health and Preventing Disease, 5:353

Strategies of American Water Management, 5:632

Strategy: The Logic of War and Peace, 3:279

Strategy and Choice, 3:64, 3:65

The Strategy of Conflict, 3:64

The Strategy of Economic Development, 3:53

The Strategy of Life, 5:47, 5:169

Stravinsky: Glimpses of a Life, 3:723

Stravinsky: In Pictures and Documents, 3:723

Stravinsky: The Composer and His Works, 3:723

Stravinsky Retrospectives, 3:723

Straw Sandals: Chinese Stories of Social Realism, 2:235

Stray Papers: Reviews, Verses, Sketches, 1:404

Streamers, 1:1109

Stream of Consciousness in the Modern Novel, 1:421

The Stream of Days, 2:74

The Stream of Life, 2:895

The Street (Petry), 1:1029, 1:1030

The Street (Rabon), 2:44

The Street (Richler), 2:924

A Streetcar Named Desire,
1:532, 1:1117, 1:1119
A Streetcar to Subduction
and Other Plate Tectonic
Trips by Public Transport
in San Francisco, 5:630
Street Corner Society: The
Social Structure of an
Italian Slum, 3:173
A Street in Bronzeville,
1:954
The Street of Red Dawns,
2:724
Street Scene, 1:1109
Streets of Conflict, 2:932
Streets with No Names: A
Journey into Central and
South America, 3:896
Streit um die Technik, 5:85
The Strength of Fields, 1:967
Strenuous Life: Essays and
Addresses, 3:594
The Stress of My Life: A Sci-
entist's Memoirs, 3:171
Stress without Distress, 5:401
The Stricken Deer or the
Life of Cowper, 1:238
Strictly Business, 1:756
Stride, The Music of Fats
Waller, 3:729
Strife, 1:481
The Strife of Systems, 4:318
Strike the Black Flag, 1:1247
Striking a Balance: Dancers
Talk about Dancing, 3:734
Striking Chords: Multicultur-
al Literary Interpretations,
2:946
Strindberg: A Biography,
2:680
Strindberg and the Poetry of
Myth, 2:680
Strindberg as Dramatist,
2:680
Strindberg's Dramaturgy,
2:680
The String, 2:695
The Strings Are False, 1:518
String Too Short to Be
Saved, 1:984
The Stripping of the Altars:
Traditional Religion in
England, 1400–1580, 3:358
Striptease, Tango, Vatzlav:
Three Plays, 2:819
Stroke: An Owner's Manual:
The Invaluable Guide to
Life after Stroke, 5:392
A Stroll with Pushkin, 2:757
A Stroll with William James,
1:768, 1:813, 3:187, 4:237
Strong Hearts, 1:736

Strong Medicine: The Ethical
Rationing of Health Care,
5:122
Strong Opinions, 2:740
Strong Poison, 1:610
Strong Representations, 1:226
Structural Anthropology,
3:17, 3:33, 4:426
Structural Geology of Fold
and Trust Belts, 5:624
Structuralism and Semiotics,
1:1132
Structuralism in Literature:
An Introduction, 1:926
The Structuralist Controver-
sy, 1:1134
Structuralist Poetics, 1:924,
1:1131, 1:1141, 2:446
The Structural Transforma-
tion of the Public Sphere,
4:404
Structure, Style and Interpre-
tation in the Russian
Short Story, 2:689
Structure and Dynamics of
Organizations and Groups,
5:434
Structure and Form in the
Babylonian Talmud, 4:620
Structure and Function in
Primitive Society, 3:25,
3:38
Structure and History in
Greek Mythology and Ritu-
al, 4:470, 4:471
The Structure and Interpreta-
tion of Quantum Mechan-
ics, 5:68
A Structured Approach to
FORTRAN, 5:552
Structured COBOL: A Prag-
matic Approach, 5:552
Structured FORTRAN 77 for
Engineers and Scientists,
5:552
Structured Walkthroughs,
5:551
Structure in Science and Art:
Proceedings of Taunus,
May 1979, 5:18
The Structure of American
Medical Practice,
1875–1941, 5:336
The Structure of Appearance,
4:403
The Structure of Behavior,
4:310
The Structure of Being: A
Neoplatonic Interpretation,
4:61
The Structure of Byron's Ma-
jor Poems, 1:283

The Structure of Complex
Words, 1:925
The Structure of Empirical
Knowledge, 4:380
The Structure of Internation-
al Publishing in the 1990s,
1:50
The Structure of Jewish His-
tory and Other Essays,
3:348, 4:647
The Structure of Lutheran-
ism, 4:730
The Structure of Matter,
5:658
The Structure of Modern
Ideology, 3:138
The Structure of Philosophy,
4:23
The Structure of Plato's Phi-
losophy, 4:79
Structure of Politics at the
Accession of George III,
3:407
The Structure of Portuguese
Society: The Failure of
Fascism, 3:386
The Structure of Resurrec-
tion Belief, 4:887
The Structure of Science,
4:313, 4:385, 5:64, 5:95,
5:96
The Structure of Scientific
Inference, 4:405
The Structure of Scientific
Revolutions, 3:213, 4:406,
5:25, 5:53, 5:66, 5:147,
5:155, 5:573
The Structure of Scientific
Theories, 5:65
The Structure of Social Ac-
tion, 3:216, 3:237
The Structure of Society,
3:25, 4:315
The Structure of the Ameri-
can Economy, Nineteen
Nineteen to Nineteen Thir-
ty-Nine, 3:91
The Structure of the Canter-
bury Tales, 1:150
Structure of the Novel, 1:521
The Structure of the Otto-
man Dynasty, 3:452
The Structure of the Uni-
verse, 5:655
The Structure of Thucydides'
History, 3:323
The Structure of Time, 5:68
Structuring the Void, 1:918
The Struggle and the Tri-
umph: An Autobiography,
3:390
The Struggle for Black
Equality, 1954–1992, 3:540

The Struggle for Democracy in Chile, 1982–1990, 3:634

The Struggle for Europe, 3:345

Struggle for Greece, 1941–1949, 3:393

The Struggle for Mastery in Europe: 1848–1918, 3:409

The Struggle for Power in Syria, 3:455

Struggle for Synthesis, 4:177

The Struggle for the American Curriculum: 1893–1958, 3:256

The Struggle for the Border, 3:607

The Struggle in Afghanistan, 3:455

The Struggle of the Modern, 1:418, 1:552

The Struggle of the Naga Tribe, 2:320

Struggles for Justice: Social Responsibility and the Liberal State, 3:552

The Struggles for Peace: Israelis and Palestinians, 3:439

Struwwelpeter, 2:592

The Stuart Age, 3:360

Stuart England, 3:360

Stuart Little, 1:898

Stuart of Dunleath, 1:384

Stuart Wales, 3:369

The Stubborn Earth, 3:472

Stubborn Hope: Selected Poems of South Africa and a Wider World, 2:160

Stubborn Weeds, 2:235

Student: A Statistical Biography of William Sealy Gosset, 5:530

A Student at the Azhar, 4:374

A Student Guide to Engineering Report Writing, 5:216

Student Life, and Other Essays, 5:364

The Student Physician, 3:233

Student Protests in Twentieth-Century China: The View from Shanghai, 3:472

Students, Scholars, and Saints, 4:620

"Students'" Collected Papers, 5:530

The Student's Catullus, 2:384

A Student's Guide to History, 3:8, 3:275

A Student's Guide to the Selected Poems of Ezra Pound, 1:872

The Studhorse Man, 2:915, 2:916

Studies in Aeschylus, 2:351

Studies in African Literature, 2:155

Studies in African Religion, 4:570

Studies in American Indian Literature, 1:1128, 1:1135

Studies in Ancient Israelite Wisdom, 4:823

Studies in Arthur Schnitzler, 2:611

Studies in Beaumont, Fletcher and Massinger, 1:189

Studies in Biography, 1:928

Studies in Chinese Buddhism, 4:530

Studies in Chinese Literary Genres, 2:188

Studies in Chinese Literature, 2:189

Studies in Chinese Poetry and Poetics, 2:190

Studies in Classical and Ottoman Islam (7th–16th Centuries), 3:453

Studies in Classic American Literature, 1:651, 1:714

Studies in Contemporary Arabic Literature, 3:456

Studies in Contemporary Arabic Poetry and Criticism, 2:55

Studies in East European Folk Narrative, 3:854

Studies in Eighteenth-Century Islamic History, 4:572

Studies in Ethnomethodology, 3:227

Studies in Expressive Movement, 5:432

Studies in Folklore, 3:849

Studies in Hegelian Cosmology, 4:304

Studies in Hegelian Dialectic, 4:304

Studies in Henry James, 1:765

Studies in History and Jurisprudence, 3:151

Studies in Human Time, 2:448

Studies in Islamic and Judaic Traditions, 4:625

Studies in Islamic Mysticism, 4:583

Studies in Islamic Philosophy and Science, 4:576

Studies in Japanese Folklore, 4:539

Studies in Jewish Folklore, 3:856

Studies in Jewish History, 4:604

Studies in Jewish Law and Philosophy, 4:628

Studies in Jewish Mysticism, 4:630

Studies in Jewish Thought: An Anthology of German Jewish Scholarship, 4:646, 4:647

Studies in Joyce, 1:505

Studies in Kant's Aesthetics, 4:207

Studies in Later Greek Comedy, 2:348

Studies in Literature from the Ancient Near East, 2:52

Studies in Logical Theory, 4:225

Studies in Lucian's De Syria Dea, 4:485

Studies in Luke—Acts, 4:825

Studies in Machiavellianism, 3:160

Studies in Medieval and Renaissance Literature, 1:147

Studies in Medieval Jewish History and Literature, 4:625

Studies in Medieval Philosophy, Science, and Logic, 4:121

Studies in Medieval Thought, 4:96

Studies in Modern Italian Literature, 2:401

Studies in Muslim-Jewish Relations, 4:626

Studies in Optics, 5:702

Studies in Ottoman Social and Economic History, 3:458

Studies in Pessimism, 4:256

Studies in Phenomenological Psychology, 4:235

Studies in Philippine Church History, 3:492

Studies in Philosophy: A Symposium on Gilbert Ryle, 4:325

Studies in Post-Medieval Semantics, 4:123

Studies in Pre-Socratic Philosophy, 4:50

Studies in Renaissance Philosophy and Science, 4:131

Studies in Ruskin: Essays in Honor of Van Akin Burd, 1:395

Studies in Russian and Polish Literature in Honor of Waclaw Lednicki, 2:811

Studies in Sin and Atonement, 4:615

Studies in Social Anthropology, 3:29

Studies in Social History, 3:408

Studies in Soviet Thought, 4:31

Studies in Spanish Renaissance Thought, 4:128

Studies in Spinoza: Critical and Interpretive Essays, 4:188

Studies in Structure of American Economy, 3:91

Studies in Targum Jonathan to the Prophets, 4:609

Studies in Tennyson, 1:402

Studies in the Apostolic Fathers and Their Background, 4:703

Studies in the Archaeology of India and Pakistan, 4:501

Studies in the Cartesian Philosophy, 4:171

Studies in the Civilization of Islam, 4:569

Studies in the Contemporary Spanish-American Short Story, 2:846

Studies in the Development of Capitalism, 3:50

Studies in the Early History of Judaism, 4:606

Studies in the Economic History of the Middle East, 3:435

Studies in the History of Arabic Logic, 4:318

Studies in the History of Mathematics, 5:492

Studies in the History of Probability and Statistics, 5:526

Studies in the History of Statistical Method, 5:526

Studies in the History of Statistics and Probability, 5:526

Studies in the History of the Renaissance, 1:386

Studies in the Institutional History of Early Modern Japan, 3:475

Studies in the Life and Works of Petrarch, 2:434, 4:151

Studies in the Making of the English Protestant Tradition, 4:727

Studies in the Philosophy of David Hume, 4:202

Studies in the Philosophy of Kant, 4:206

Studies in the Philosophy of the Scottish Enlightenment, 4:32

Studies in the Psychology of Sex, 5:440

Studies in the Text History of the Life and Fables of Aesop, 2:352

Studies in the Theory of Ideology, 4:405

Studies in the Theory of International Trade, 3:111

Studies in the Theory of Public Finance, 3:114

Studies in the Variety of Rabbinic Cultures, 4:622

Studies in the Ways of Words, 4:288

Studies in Thucydides and Greek History, 3:323

Studies in Words, 1:512

Studies in Zen, 4:558

Studies on Canadian Literature: Introductory and Critical Essays, 2:904

Studies on Fermentation, 5:809

Studies on Hysteria, 3:183

Studies on Korea: A Scholar's Guide, 2:298

Studies on Mario Bunge's Treatise, 5:83

Studies on the Civilization of Islam, 2:55

Studies on the Near East, 4:571

Studies on Vietnamese Language and Literature, 2:339

Studies on Voltaire, 4:218

Studies on William Harvey, 5:361

Studs Lonigan, 1:833

A Study and Translation of Harry Mulisch's "Inspection," 2:628

A Study in Choreography for Camera, 1:1163

Study in Consciousness, 4:550

Studying Animal Behavior: Autobiographies of the Founders, 5:826

Studying History: How and Why, 3:275

Studying Women's Writing: An Introduction, 1:1127

A Study in Scarlet, 1:607

The Study of American Indian Religions, 4:465

Study of Ancient Judaism, 4:612

A Study of Archaeology, 3:13

A Study of Bellow, Salinger, Mailer, Baldwin, and Updike, 1:917

A Study of Dōgen: His Philosophy and Religion, 4:364

A Study of English Romanticism, 1:265, 1:977

The Study of Folklore, 3:848

A Study of History, 3:277, 3:293, 3:327

Study of Husserl's Formal and Transcendental Logic, 4:234

The Study of Instinct, 3:171, 3:195, 5:838

The Study of Liturgy, 4:678, 4:897

A Study of Nietzsche, 4:248

A Study of Self-Deception, 5:422

The Study of Sociology, 3:240

A Study of Sophoclean Drama, 2:368

A Study of Spinoza's Ethics, 4:187

The Study of the Bible in the Middle Ages, 4:628, 4:697

Study of the History of Science, 5:55

A Study of the Novels of George Moore, 1:381

A Study of the "Summa philosophiae" of the Pseudo-Grosseteste, 4:102

A Study of War, 3:149

Stupid PC Tricks, 5:537

Sturlunga Saga, 2:643

Style and Consciousness in Middle English Narrative, 1:147

Style and Music: Theory, History, and Ideology, 3:661

Style and Proportion: The Language of Prose and Poetry, 1:429

Style and Structure in the Prose of Isaak Babel, 2:700

Style and Symbolism in Piers Plowman: A Modern Critical Anthology, 1:154

Style in "Hamlet," 1:213
Style in History, 3:276
Style in Modern British Fiction, 1:422
The Style of "Don Juan," 1:284
The Style of Lu Hsün: Vocabulary and Usage, 2:256
Style of Sophocles, 2:368
Styles of Radical Will, 1:1052
Stylistic Relationship between Poetry and Prose in the Cántico Espiritual of San Juan de la Cruz, 2:544
Suárez on Human Freedom, 4:154
Suárez on Individuation, 4:105
Suasoriae, 2:393
Subcommittee on Patents, Copyrights, and Trademarks, 1:55
Subject and Predicate in Logic and Grammar, 4:414
Subject Catalogue of the History of Medicine and Related Sciences, 5:29
Subject Collections, 1:70, 1:105
Subject Collections in European Libraries, 1:70
Subject Guide to Books in Print, 1:71
Subject Guide to Children's Books in Print, 1:75
Subject Guide to Humor, 3:871
The Subjection of Women, 1:380, 3:96, 4:244
Subjective Criticism, 1:923
Subjectivities: A History of Self-Representation in Britain, 1832–1920, 1:325
The Subject of Semiotics, 1:1132
The Subject of Tragedy: Identity and Difference in Renaissance Drama, 1:169
Subjects and Sovereigns, 3:361
Subject to Change: Women's Writing–Feminist Reading, 2:447
Substance and Essence in Aristotle: An Interpretation of Metaphysics VII–IX, 4:72
Substance and Function and Einstein's Theory of Relativity, 4:279
Substance and Predication in Aristotle, 4:69

The Substance of Cervantes, 2:537
The Substance of the Descent of Man, 5:794
The Subterraneans, 1:998
The Subtle Connection between the Theory of Experience and the Logic of Science, 4:409
Subtle Is the Lord: The Science and Life of Albert Einstein, 5:49, 5:683
A Subtreasury of American Humor, 1:131
Suburbs of Hell, 2:964
Subversions of Desire: Prolegomena to Nick Joaquin, 2:331
The Subversive, 2:332
Subversive Genealogy: The Politics and Art of Herman Melville, 1:689
Success, 2:578
The Success and Failure of Picasso, 3:786
Successful Small-Scale Farming: An Organic Approach, 5:266
Such a Long Journey, 2:920
Such Is Life, 2:945, 2:952, 2:953
Such Is My Beloved, 2:908
Such Things Happen in the World, 2:723
Sudden Cardiac Death in the Community, 5:374
Sudden Infant Death: Patterns, Puzzles, and Problems, 5:375
Suddenly Last Summer, 1:1098, 1:1117, 1:1118
Suetonius: The Biographer of the Caesars, 3:320
Suetonius: The Scholar and His Caesars, 2:395, 3:320
Suez, 3:367
Suez, 1956, 3:445
Suffering and Evil in the Plays of Christopher Marlowe, 1:187
The Sufferings of Young Werther, 2:581
Suffer the Children, 1:1243
Suffixes: and Other Word-Final Elements of English, 1:92
Suffocating Mothers, 1:208
Sufi Essays, 4:902
The Sufi Orders in Islam, 4:577
The Sufi Path of Love: The Spiritual Teachings of Rumi, 4:590

The Sufis, 4:576
A Sufi Saint of the Twentieth Century, 4:575
Sug, the Trickster Who Fooled the Monk, 2:336
Sugar and Other Stories, 1:455
Sugar Creek: Life on the Illinois Prairie, 3:523
The Sugar Mother, 2:956
Sugar Street, 2:68
The Sugar Trap and How to Avoid It, 5:346
Suggestions towards the Further Government of India, 1:376
Suicidal Narrative in Modern Japan: The Case of Dazai Osamu, 2:286
Suicide, 3:225
Suing the Press: Libel, the Media, and Power, 3:809
The Suitcase, 2:717
Sukkariyah, 2:67
The Sukkot and Simhat Torah Anthology, 4:599
Sula, 1:1018, 1:1019
Sumatran Contributions to the Development of Indonesian Literature, 1920–1942, 2:317
Sumer and the Sumerians, 3:300
Sumerian Flood, 2:53
Sumerian Mythology, 4:441, 4:545
A Summary of Catholic History, 4:720
A Summary View of the Rights of British America, 1:639, 1:640
Summer, 1:446, 1:786, 1:787
Summer and Smoke, 1:1117, 1:1118
The Summer Anniversaries, 1:995
Summer at Lonely Beach: Selected Short Stories, 2:927
A Summer Bird-Cage, 1:467, 1:468
Summer Brave, 1:1095
Summer Glory: A Collection of Contemporary Chinese Poetry, 2:235
Summerhill: A Radical Approach to Child Rearing, 3:251
A Summer in London, 2:578
Summer in the Street of the Prophets and A Voyage to Ur of Chaldees, 2:24

Summer Knowledge: New and Selected Poems, 1938–1958, 1:1044

The Summer of the Danes, 1:609

Summer of the Seventeenth Doll, 2:945

Summer on the Lakes, in 1843, 1:673

Summing Up: The Science of Reviewing Research, 5:523

The Summing Up, 1:520

The Sun, Our Star, 5:593

The Sun Also Rises, 1:844, 1:845

Sun and Steel, 2:289

Sunbelt Cities: Politics and Growth since World War II, 3:536

The Sun Dance Religion: Power for the Powerless, 4:467

Sunday after the War, 1:861

The Sunday of Life, 2:496

The Sundial, 1:992

Sunflower Splendor: Three Thousand Years of Chinese Poetry, 2:190, 2:224

The Sunken Bell, 2:586

Sunken Oboe, 2:437

Sunlight, Moonlight, 2:303

Sunlight and Health, 5:320, 5:341

The Sunlight Dialogues, 1:978, 1:979

Sunlight on a Broken Column, 2:177

The Sun My Heart: From Mindfulness to Insight Contemplation, 4:562

The Sun Never Sets, 3:911

Sun Placed in the Abyss and Other Texts, 2:494

Sun Poem, 2:934

Sunrise: A Play in Four Acts, 2:265, 2:266

Sunset in Biafra, 2:130

The Sunset Maker: Poems/Stories/A Memoir, 1:995

The Sunshine Boys, 1:1112, 1:1113

Sunshine Sketches of a Little Town, 2:918

The Sun Shines over the Sangkan River, 2:264

Sunstone–Piedra de Sol, 2:878

Supercharging MS-DOS, 5:555

Superfairness: Applications and Theory, 3:67

Superforce: The Search for a Grand Unified Theory of Nature, 5:15

Superinsulated Design and Construction, 5:225

The Super-Intelligent Machine: An Electronic Odyssey, 5:567

Superiority and Social Interest: A Collection of Later Writings, 5:431

Supernatural Mysteries and Other Tales, 3:937

Supernovae, 5:594

The Supernova Story, 5:594

Superstrings: A Theory of Everything, 5:15

Supplementary Copyright Registration, 1:55

A Supplement for the Years 1930–1935, 1:220

Supplement to E. J. Labarre, Dictionary and Encyclopaedia of Paper and Paper-making, 1:5

The Suppliants, 2:350, 2:351

The Supply and Price of Natural Gas, 5:290

Support Systems and Community Mental Health, 5:421

Supposes, 2:402

Suppressed Commentaries on The Wisean Forgeries, 1:36

The Suppression of the African Slave Trade, 3:578

The Supreme Court: Justice and the Law, 3:542

The Supreme Court and the Idea of Progress, 3:542

The Supreme Court's Impact on Public Education, 3:257

The Supreme Identity, 4:881

Sūr Dās: Poet, Singer, Saint, 2:174

"Surely You're Joking, Mr. Feynman!": Adventures of a Curious Character, 3:908, 5:685

The Surface of Mars, 5:592

Surfacing, 2:906

Surgery in America: From the Colonial Era to the Twentieth Century, 5:35

Surpassing the Love of Men, 1:1181

Surprised by Joy: The Shape of My Early Life, 1:512

Surprised by Sin: The Reader in Paradise Lost, 1:192, 1:976

The Surprise of Being, 2:560

The Surprise of Excellence: Modern Essays on Max Beerbohm, 1:441

The Surprising Effects of Sympathy, 2:472, 2:488

Surprising Narrative, 2:138

Sur Racine, 2:454

Surrealism: The Road to the Absolute, 2:986

Surrealism Pro and Con, 1:818

Surreptitious Printing in England, 1550–1640, 1:37

Surveying for Civil Engineers, 5:224

Survey of Allied Health Professions, 5:339

Survey of American Philosophy, 4:36

Survey of American Poetry: Twilight Interval, 1890–1912, 1:798

Survey of British Poetry, 1:418

Survey of Compensation and Personnel Practices in the Publishing Industry, 1:46

Survey of Geometry, 5:487

A Survey of Hinduism, 4:505

Survey of Modern Algebra, 5:484

A Survey of Modernist Poetry, 1:485, 1:875

Survey of Objective Studies of Psychoanalytic Concepts, 3:184

A Survey of Polish Literature and Culture, 2:811

A Survey of Recent Christian Ethics, 4:744

Survey of Semiconductor Physics, 5:291

Survey Sampling, 3:7

Survey Sampling Principles, 3:6

Surveys from Exile, 4:242

Survival: A Thematic Guide to Canadian Literature, 2:904

Survival and the Bomb: Methods of Civil Defense, 5:720

Survival Guide to Computer Systems: A Primer for Executives, 5:557

Survival in Auschwitz: The Nazi Assault on Humanity, 2:425

A Survival Manual for the Independent Woman Traveler, 3:893

Survival of a Counterculture, 3:217

The Survival of Charles Darwin, 5:45, 5:794

The Survival of the Bark Canoe, 1:1011

Survival or Hegemony? The Foundations of Israeli Foreign Policy, 3:440

Surviving AIDS, 5:387

Surviving and Other Essays, 5:435

Surviving Exercise, 5:325

Surviving Schizophrenia: A Family Manual, 5:428

The Survivor, 1:516

The Survivor and Other Poems, 2:820

Survivors: An Oral History of the Armenian Genocide, 3:394, 3:455

The Survivors of the Crossing, 2:934

"Susanna," "Jeanie," and the "Old Folks at Home," 3:695

Susanna, Mother of the Wesleys, 4:790

Susanna Haswell Rowson, America's First Best-Selling Novelist, 1:643

Susanna Moodie: Voice and Vision, 2:921

Susanna Rowson, 1:643

A Susan Sontag Reader, 1:1052

Susie Sexpert's Lesbian Sex World, 1:1181

Suspect Chemicals Sourcebook, 5:724

The Suspect in Poetry, 1:967

Suspended Fictions: Reading Novels by Manuel Puig, 2:881

Suspense in the Formula Story, 1:593

Suspicions about Some Hidden Qualities of the Air, 5:739

Sustainability: Economics, Ecology, and Justice, 4:743

Sustainable Agricultural Systems, 5:266

Sustainable Agriculture and the Environment in the Humid Tropics, 5:824

Sustainable Agriculture in Temperate Zones, 5:220, 5:266

Sut Lovingood: Yarns Spun by a "Nat'ral Born Durn'd Fool," 1:673, 1:674

Sutpen's Design: Interpreting Faulkner's "Absalom, Absalom!" 1:837

Suttapitaka, 2:315

Su Único Hijo, 2:528

Suzanne and the Pacific, 2:481

The Swahili, 3:422

Swahili Phrasebook: For Travelers in Eastern and Southern Africa, 1:103

The Swallow and the Tom Cat: A Love Story, 2:892

The Swallow Book, 2:613

Swamiji and His Message, 4:563

Swami Vivekananda in the West: New Discoveries, 4:563

The Swan at the Well: Shakespeare Reading Chaucer, 1:219

The Swan's Wide Waters: Ramakrishna and Western Culture, 4:872

The Swazi: A South African Kingdom, 3:26

Sweden: Its People and Industry, 3:382

Sweden: Social Democracy in Practice, 3:382

Swedenborg: Life and Teachings, 4:852, 4:880

Swedenborg and His Influence, 4:852

The Swedish Church, 4:731

Swedish-English Dictionary, 1:103

Swedish-English, English-Swedish Dictionary: Svensk-Engelsk-Svensk Ordbok, 1:103

The Swedish Imperial Experience, 1560–1718, 3:382

Swedish Legends and Folktales, 3:856

Swedo-Finnish Short Stories, 2:658

Sweeney Astray, 1:495

Sweeney's Flight, 1:495

Sweeper in the Sky, 5:609

Sweet and Lowdown: America's Popular Song Writers, 3:654

Sweet and Sour: An Anthology of Comic Verse, 3:871

Sweet and Sour Milk, 2:122

Sweet Bird of Youth, 1:1118

The Sweet Dove Died, 1:538, 1:539

Sweet Eros, 1:1103

The Sweet Flypaper of Life, 1:848

Sweethearts, 1:356

The Sweet Hereafter: A Novel, 1:940

Sweet Man: The Real Duke Ellington, 3:695

Sweet Promised Land, 3:899

Sweet-Scented Name and Other Fairy Tales and Stories, 2:759

The Sweet Science, 3:814

Sweet Sue, 1:1091

Sweet Thursday, 1:884

The Sweet Trap, 2:147

The Swell Season, 2:795

Swift: The Man, His Works, and the Age, 1:260

Swift's Landscape, 1:260

Swimming through Your Pregnancy, 5:358

Swinburne, 1:398

Swinburne: A Study in Romantic Mythmaking, 1:398

Swinburne: The Critical Heritage, 1:398

Swinburne: The Poet of His World, 1:398

Swinburne and His Gods: The Roots and Growth of an Agnostic Poetry, 1:398

Swinburne's Medievalism: A Study in Victorian Love Poetry, 1:398

The Swindler, 2:548

The Swing Era: The Development of Jazz, 1930–1945, 3:669

A Swinger of Birches: Poems of Robert Frost for Young People, 1:1202

The Swing in the Garden, 2:914

Swing That Music, 3:674

The Swiss Way of Welfare: Lessons for the Modern World, 3:378

Switzerland in Perspective, 3:378

Sword and Scalpel, 1:1223

The Sword and the Flute, 4:505

The Sword and the Scepter: The Problem of Militarism in Germany, 3:377

Sword Blades and Poppy Seed, 1:855

Sword of Honor (Men at Arms), 1:561

The Sword of Welleran and Other Stories, 1:615

S. Y. Agnon, 2:12

Sybil, 1:351, 1:937

Sydney, 3:904

Sylvia: A Novel, 1:880

Sylvia Beach and the Lost
Generation, 1:36
Sylvia Plath: A Biography,
1:1032
Sylvia Plath: Method and
Madness, 1:1031
Sylvia Plath: New Views on
the Poetry, 1:1031
Sylvia Plath: Poetry and Exis-
tence, 1:1031
Sylvia Plath: The Poetry of
Initiation, 1:1031
Sylvia Plath: The Wound and
the Cure of Words, 1:1031
Sylvia Plath and Ted Hughes,
1:498
Sylvia's Lovers, 1:355
Sylvie and Bruno, 1:582
Symbiosis: An Introduction
to Biological Associations,
5:763
Symbiosis: Popular Culture
and Other Fields, 3:875
Symbiosis in Cell Evolution,
5:776
Symbol, Myth, and Culture,
4:280
Symbol and Empowerment:
Paul Tillich's Post-Theistic
System, 4:787
Symbol and Idea in Henry
Adams, 1:730
Symbol and Politics in Com-
munal Ideology: Cases and
Questions, 3:217
Symbol and Theology in Ear-
ly Judaism, 4:614
The Symbolic Art of Gogol:
Essays on His Short Fic-
tion, 2:723
Symbolic Interactionism: Per-
spective and Method,
3:200, 3:208, 3:222
Symbolic Wounds: Puberty
Rites and the Envious
Male, 4:430, 5:435
Symbolism: Its Meaning and
Effect, 4:341
Symbolism from Poe to Mal-
larmé, 2:487
Symbolism in American Lit-
erature, 1:650
Symbolism in Religion and
Literature, 5:463
The Symbolism of Evil,
4:319, 4:886
The Symbolist Movement: A
Critical Appraisal, 2:986
The Symbolist Movement in
Literature, 2:987
The Symbol of the Soul
from Holderlin to Yeats: A
Study in Metonymy, 2:986

Symbol Sourcebook, 3:756
Symlog: A System for the
Multiple Level Observation
of Groups, 3:172
Sympathy and Science:
Women Physicians in
American Medicine, 5:314
Symphonies and Other Or-
chestral Works, 3:664
The Symphony, 3:662, 3:663
Symphorien Champier and
the Reception of the Oc-
cultist Tradition in Renais-
sance France, 4:125
Symposium (Plato), 4:78
Symposium (Spark), 1:551
The Symposium (Xenophon),
4:91
Symposium on J. L. Austin,
4:272
The Synagogue: Studies in
Origins, Archaeology, and
Architecture, 4:614
The Synagogue in Late An-
tiquity, 4:597
Synagogue Life: A Study in
Symbolic Interaction,
4:654
Synagogues of Europe: Archi-
tecture, History, Meaning,
4:597
Synge, the Medieval and the
Grotesque, 1:556
Synge and Anglo-Irish Dra-
ma, 1:556
Synge and the Irish Lan-
guage, 1:556
Synnove Solbakken, 2:663
The Synonym Finder, 1:94
A Synopsis of American His-
tory, 3:514
Synopsis of the Four Gos-
pels, 4:794
A Synoptic Classification of
Living Organisms, 5:758
The Synoptic Vision: Essays
on the Philosophy of Wil-
frid Sellars, 4:334
Syntactic Structures, 3:21
Syntagma philosophicum,
4:173
Syntax, 2:703
Syria and Lebanon under
French Mandate, 3:455
Syrian Christians in Muslim
Society: An Interpretation,
4:569
The Syrian Goddess, 4:484
Syrian Pageant: The History
of Syria and Palestine,
3:454
A System Analysis of Politi-
cal Life, 3:153

Systema Naturae: Tomus II
Vegetabilia, 5:805
System and Revelation: The
Philosophy of Franz Ro-
senzweig, 4:671
Systematic Programming: An
Introduction, 5:553
Systematics, Evolution and
Anatomy, 5:772
Systematic Theology: Life
and the Spirit, History and
the Kingdom of God,
4:787, 5:206
Systematic Theology: Roman
Catholic Perspectives,
4:422, 4:745, 4:891
Système de la Mode, 2:454
The System of Dante's Hell,
The Dead Lecturer, and
Tales, 1:941
System of Inorganic Chemis-
try, 5:754
A System of Logic, 3:96
System of Logic: Ratiocina-
tive and Inductive, 4:243,
4:244
System of Moral Philosophy,
4:203
System of Natural Philoso-
phy, 4:194
System of Positive Polity,
3:224, 4:223
A System of Pragmatic Ideal-
ism, 4:318
System of Transcendental
Idealism, 4:251, 4:252
System Safety Engineering
Management, 5:244
Systems Analysis for Data
Transmission, 5:302
A Systems Approach to Poli-
tics, 3:153
A Systems Approach to
Small Group Interaction,
3:173
Systems Development with-
out Pain, 5:551
The Systems of the Hellenis-
tic Age: A History of An-
cient Philosophy, 4:55
Systems Theory Applied to
Agriculture and the Food
Chain, 5:263
S-Z, 2:454

T

Tabibito, 5:721
Table Manners, 1:436

Tables for Statisticians and Biometricians, Parts I and II, 5:531

Tables of Physical and Chemical Constants, 5:653

Table Talk: 1821–22, 1:291

Tachtiger-beweging, 2:624

The Taciturn Text: The Fiction of Robert Penn Warren, 1:894

Tacitus, 3:321

Tactical Exercise, 1:562

A Tagore Reader, 2:183

Taha Husayn: His Place in the Egyptian Literary Renaissance, 2:74

Tahiti: Memoirs of Arii Taimai, 3:562

Tahitians: Mind and Experience in the Society Islands, 3:22

Tahiti Nui: Change and Survival in French Polynesia 1767–1945, 3:495

The Tail of the Dragon: New Dance, 1976–82, 3:732

The Tailor of Gloucester, 1:588

The Tain of the Mirror, 4:398

The Tainos: Rise and Decline of the People Who Greeted Columbus, 3:629, 3:917

Take 22: Moviemakers on Moviemaking, 3:828

Take a Girl Like You, 1:432

Take Care of Your Heart, 5:339

Take Care of Yourself: The Consumer's Guide to Medical Care, 5:342

Take Charge of Your Health: The Complete Nutrition Book, 5:346

Take Heart, 5:369

Taking Center Stage: Feminism in Contemporary U.S. Drama, 1:1072

The Taking of Miss Janie, 1:1086

Taking Shelter, 2:948

Taking Sides: Clashing Views on Controversial Bioethical Issues, 5:121

Taking Sides: Clashing Views on Controversial Environmental Issues, 5:114

Taking Sides: The Fiction of John le Carré, 1:596

Taking Steps, 1:437

Taking the Curtain Call: The Life and Letters of Henry Arthur Jones, 1:367

Tala, 2:873

Talbot Road, 1:491

Talcott Parsons, 3:237

Talcott Parsons on Economy and Society, 3:238

The Talented Mr. Ripley, 1:1231

A Talent to Deceive: An Appreciation of Agatha Christie, 1:606

A Tale of a Tub, 1:259, 1:260

A Tale of a Tub with Other Earlier Works, 1696–1707, 1:260

The Tale of Benjamin Bunny, 1:588

The Tale of Fatuhmeh, 2:673

A Tale of Flowering Fortunes, 2:275

Tale of Genji, 2:269, 2:270, 2:278, 2:279, 2:286

Tale of Heike, 2:270, 2:275

Tale of Igor's Campaign, 2:682, 2:837

The Tale of Jemima Puddle-Duck, 1:588

The Tale of Kieu, 2:338

A Tale of Manchester Life, 1:355

The Tale of Mr. Jeremy Fisher, 1:588

The Tale of Mr. Tod, 1:588

The Tale of Mrs. Tiggy-Winkle, 1:588

The Tale of Mrs. Tittlemouse, 1:588

A Tale of Mystery, 1:320

The Tale of Peter Rabbit, 1:578, 1:588, 1:589

A Tale of Poor Lovers, 2:437

The Tale of the Body Thief, 1:1243

The Tale of the Heike, 2:275

The Tale of the Heike: Heike Monogatari, 2:275

The Tale of the Mandarin Ducks, 1:1205

The Tale of the Seven Who Were Hanged, 2:699

The Tale of the Tribe: Ezra Pound and the Modern Verse Epic, 1:872

A Tale of Three Heads, 2:753

The Tale of Tom Kitten, 1:588

The Tale of Two Bad Mice, 1:588

A Tale of Two Cities, 1:349

The Tales, 2:41

Tales, 1812, and Other Selected Poems, 1:289

Tales and Songs of Southern Illinois, 3:862

Tales for Fifteen; or Imagination and Heart, 1:664

Tales from Africa, 3:855

Tales from a Troubled Land, 2:167

Tales from China, 3:854

Tales from Firozsha Baaq, 2:920

Tales from Hispanic Lands, 3:855

Tales from Jókai, 2:800

Tales from Shakespeare, 1:295

Tales from Thailand: Folklore, Culture, and History, 3:857

Tales from the Argentine, 2:849

Tales from the First Americans, 3:865

Tales from the Japanese Storytellers as Collected in the Ho Dan Zo, 3:857

Tales from the Map Room, 5:191

Tales from the United States, 3:855

Tales of Abdullah's Voyage, 2:323

Tales of Adventurous Enterprise, 1:681

Tales of a Long Night, 2:576

Tales of a Low-Rent Birder, 5:763

Tales of Ancient India, 2:173

Tales of an Old Ocean, 5:632

Tales of a Traveller, 1:679, 1:680

Tales of a Wayside Inn, 1:682

Tales of Belkin, 2:750, 2:751

The Tales of Ensign Stål, 2:657

Tales of Hoffmann, 2:591, 2:592

Tales of Ise: Lyrical Episodes from Tenth-Century Japan, 2:275

Tales of Love, 2:447

Tales of Madness, 2:435

Tales of Mexican California, 3:863

Tales of Moonlight and Rain: Japanese Gothic Tales, 2:280

Tales of My Native Town, 2:415

Tales of My People, 2:36

Tales of New England, 1:770

Tales of Old-Time Texas, 3:863

Tales of Rabbi Nachman, 4:669

The Tales of Rabbi Nahman of Bratslav, 4:669

Tales of Secret Egypt, 1:597

Tales of Suicide, 2:435

Tales of Tenderness and Power, 2:163

Tales of Terror and Mystery, 1:607

Tales of the Argonauts and Other Sketches, 1:756

Tales of the Cochiti Indians, 3:27

Tales of the Dervishes, 4:576

Tales of the Frontier: From Lewis and Clark to the Last Roundup, 1:725

Tales of the Grotesque and Arabesque, 1:692

Tales of the Hasidim, 4:632

Tales of the Hodja, 2:96

Tales of the Home Folks in Peace and War, 1:755

Tales of the Middle Border, 1:751

Tales of the North American Indians, 3:865

Tales of the Pacific, 1:774

Tales of the Sacred and the Supernatural, 2:825, 4:474

Tales of the Seal People: Scottish Folk Tales, 3:857

Tales of the South Carolina Low Country, 3:861

Tales of the South Pacific, 1:1247, 3:931

Tales of the Tobacco Country, 3:861

Tales of the Wilderness, 2:748

Tales of the Wolf, 1:1237

Tales of the Working Girl, 1:714

Tales of Times Now Past, 2:275

Tales of Two Countries, 2:725

Tales of War, 2:826

The Talisman, 1:299

Talking All Morning, 1:952

Talking God, 1:1232

Talking Minds: The Study of Language in Cognitive Sciences, 3:171

Talking Mysteries: A Conversation with Tony Hillerman, 1:1232

Talking of Wales: A Companion to Wales and the Welsh, 3:369

Talking to Strange Men, 1:609

The Talking Tree. Poems in Prose, 2:672

Talking with African Writers, 2:112

Talking with Ingmar Bergman, 3:831

Talking with Robert Penn Warren, 1:894

Talking with Texas Writers: Twelve Interviews, 1:1096

Talkin' Moscow Blues, 2:795

Talks on Book-Collecting, 1:33

Talks to Teachers on Psychology, 3:187, 5:453

Talk That Talk: An Anthology of African-American Storytelling, 3:866

Tall Betsy and Dunce Baby: South Georgia Folktales, 3:861

Talley and Son, 1:1120, 1:1121

Talley's Folly, 1:1120, 1:1121

Tallis, 3:723

The Tall Men, 1:1213

Tall Tale America: A Legendary History of Our Humorous Heroes, 3:854

Tall Tales of the Catskills, 3:859

Tall Tales of the Southwest, 3:872

A Tally of Types: With Additions by Several Hands, 1:18

Talmud: A Close Encounter, 4:612

The Talmud: The Steinsaltz Edition, Vol. I, 4:613

Talmudic Thinking: Language, Logic, and Law, 4:621

Talmud of Babylonia: An American Translation, 4:612

Talmud of the Land of Israel: A Preliminary Translation and Explanation, 4:612

Tamburlaine the Great, 1:186

The Tamil Veda: Pillan's Interpretation of the Tiruvaymoli, 4:26

The Taming of the Shrew, 1:205, 1:206, 2:406

Taming the Tiger: The Struggle to Control Technology, 5:157, 5:215

Tanakh, of the Holy Scriptures, 4:798

Tancred, 1:351

Tangi, 2:977

Tangled Hair: Selected Tanka from Midaregami, 2:295

Tangled Vines, 1:1221

A Tangled Web, 1:619

Tanglewood Tales, 1:675, 1:1194

Tango, 2:818, 2:819

Tangsir, 2:87

The Tank Corps, 2:794

Tantra in Tibet, 4:560

Tantric Art and Meditation: The Tendai Tradition, 4:538

The Tantric Distinction: An Introduction to Tibetan Buddhism, 4:356

Taoism: The Road to Immortality, 4:527

Taoism and Chinese Religion, 4:528

Taoism and the Rite of Cosmic Renewal, 4:528

Taoist Meditation and Longevity Techniques, 4:528

The Tao of Pooh, 4:528

The Tao of the Tao Te Ching: A Translation and Commentary, 4:528

T'ao Yüan-ming: His Works and Their Meaning, 2:223

Tapping the Government Grapevine, 1:108

Taps at Reveille, 1:839

Taras Bulba, 2:721

Tar Baby, 1:1018, 1:1019

Targeted: The Anatomy of an Animal Rights Attack, 5:782

Targeting the Computer, 5:184

Targets of Satire in the Comedies of Etherege, Wycherley and Congreve, 1:243

Targumic Approaches to the Gospels, 4:608

The Targum Neofiti to Genesis, 4:796

The Targum of Jeremiah, 4:608

The Targums and Rabbinic Literature, 4:608

Targums of Onkelos and Jonathan Ben Uzziel on the Pentateuch with the Fragments of the Jerusalem Targum from the Chaldee, 4:608

Tar Heel Ghosts, 3:861

Ta'rikh ar-Rusul wa-al-Muluk, 3:434, 3:456

Tarjei Vesaas, 2:670

Tarjuma'n Al-Ashwa'q, 4:583

Tarpaulin Muster, 1:519
Tarr, 1:513, 1:514
Tarry Flynn, 1:506
Tars va Larz, 2:94
Tartuffe, 2:490
Tarzan Adventures, 1:616
Tarzan and Tradition: Classi-
  cal Myth in Popular Liter-
  ature, 1:1256
Tarzan of the Apes, 1:1255,
  1:1256
Tasks and Masks: Themes
  and Styles of African Lit-
  erature, 2:111
Tasman Relations: New Zea-
  land and Australia,
  1788–1988, 3:494
Tasso and His Times, 2:440
Tasso and Milton, 2:440
Tasso's Dialogues, 2:440
Tasso's Jerusalem Delivered,
  2:440
Taste and Technique in
  Book Collecting, 1:31, 1:76
A Taste of Liberty, 2:743
The Taste of Power, 2:833,
  2:834
The Taste of the Pineapple,
  1:513
The Taste of Yiddish, 2:31
The Tatler, 1:232, 1:257
Tattered Cloak and Other
  Novels, 2:702
Ta T'ung Shu, The One-
  World Philosophy of K'ang
  Yu-Wei, 4:361
Tauq al-Hamama, 4:583
Tawfiq al-Hakim, Playwright
  of Egypt, 2:64
The Taxi, 2:486
The Tax Inspector, 2:951
Ta'ziyeh, Ritual and Drama
  in Iran, 2:82
Tchaikovsky, 3:724
Tchaikovsky: A Biography,
  3:724
Tchaikovsky: A Self-Portrait,
  3:724
Tchaikovsky: Quest for the
  Inner Man, 3:724
Tchaikovsky: The Crisis
  Years, 3:724
Tchaikovsky's Ballets: Swan
  Lake, Sleeping Beauty,
  Nutcracker, 3:724
Tea and Sympathy, 1:1082,
  1:1083
The Teacher. The Free
  Choice of the Will. Grace
  and Free Will, 4:109
Teacher Education and the
  Social Conditions of
  Schooling, 3:256

Teacher in America, 1:813,
  1:814
Teachers for Our Nation's
  Schools, 3:263
Teaching: The Imperiled Pro-
  fession, 3:249
Teaching and Learning about
  Science and Society, 5:20
Teaching and Research in
  Philosophy: Africa, 4:26
Teaching and Worship of the
  Liberal Catholic Church,
  4:859
Teaching as a Conserving
  Activity, 3:252, 5:140
Teaching as a Subversive Ac-
  tivity, 3:252, 5:140
Teaching Authority in the
  Early Church, 4:688
Teaching Ethics, the Human-
  ities, and Human Values
  in Medicine, 5:97
Teaching Humanities in the
  Microelectronic Age, 3:253
The Teaching of African Lit-
  erature, 2:108
The Teaching of Computer
  Appreciation and Library
  Automation, 5:566
The Teaching of Ethnic
  Dance, 3:851
The Teaching of Humanae
  Vitae: A Defense, 4:743
The Teaching of the Catholic
  Church, 4:891
The Teaching of the Qur'an,
  4:587
Teaching Psychology in
  America: A History, 3:168,
  3:181
Teachings from the Ameri-
  can Earth: Indian Religion
  and Philosophy, 4:465
The Teachings of Hasidism,
  4:632
The Teachings of Pope John
  XXIII, 4:771
The Teachings of the Magi:
  A Compendium of Zo-
  roastrian Beliefs, 4:548
Teaching Strategies for the
  Social Studies, 3:253
Teaching Technology from a
  Feminist Perspective: A
  Practical Guide, 5:205
Teaching World History,
  3:272
Tea in Japan: Essays on the
  History of Chanoyu, 4:538
Tea Life, Tea Mind, 4:538
A Tear and a Smile, 2:67

The Tearoom Trade: Imper-
  sonal Sex in Public
  Places, 3:208
The Technical, Scientific and
  Medical Publishing Market,
  1:47
Technical Manifesto, 2:427
Technics and Civilization,
  5:169, 5:171, 5:573
Technics and Human Devel-
  opment, 5:169
Technics and Praxis, 5:71,
  5:92
Technique, Discourse, and
  Consciousness, 5:71, 5:164,
  5:165
Technique and Ideas in the
  Aeneid, 2:397
The Technique of Psycho-
  therapy, 5:420
Techniques of Differential
  Topology in Relativity,
  5:709
Techniques of Subversion in
  Modern Literature, 1:793
Technobabble, 5:536
The Technological Bluff,
  5:163, 5:164
Technological Change: Its
  Impact on Man and Soci-
  ety, 5:156
The Technological Con-
  science, 5:73
Technological Education—
  Technological Style, 5:52
Technological Innovation: A
  Critical Review of Current
  Knowledge, 5:52
The Technological Order,
  5:72
Technological Powers and
  the Person, 5:129
Technological Risk, 5:12
The Technological Society,
  3:213, 5:70, 5:163, 5:165,
  5:572
The Technological System,
  5:163, 5:165
The Technological Woman:
  Interfacing with Tomor-
  row, 5:159, 5:189
Technologies and Societies:
  The Shaping of People
  and Things, 5:149
Technology: Man Remakes
  His World, 5:162
Technology: Philosophical
  and Social Aspects, 5:36,
  5:69, 5:150
Technology, Change and So-
  ciety, 5:227
Technology, Gender, and
  Power in Africa, 5:188

Technology, Institutions, and Government Policies, 5:182

Technology, Society, and Man, 5:213

Technology, the Environment, and Human Values, 5:74, 5:160, 5:161

Technology, Theology, and the Idea of Progress, 5:197

Technology, the University, and the Community, 5:251

Technology 2001: The Future of Computing and Communications, 5:573

Technology and Agricultural Development in Pre-War Japan, 3:477

Technology and American Economic Growth, 5:234

Technology and Change, 5:212

Technology and Culture: An Anthology, 5:52

Technology and Justice, 5:70

Technology and Politics, 5:154

Technology and Power, 5:154

Technology and Reality, 5:213

Technology and Religion, 5:197

Technology and Responsibility, 5:70, 5:128

Technology and Social Change, 5:71

Technology and Social Process, 5:152

Technology and Social Shock, 5:155, 5:214

Technology and Society, 5:214

Technology and the Character of Contemporary Life, 5:69, 5:212

Technology and the City, 5:205

Technology and the Environment, 5:114

Technology and the Future, 5:73, 5:131, 5:158

Technology and the Future: A Philosophical Challenge, 5:72

Technology and the Human Condition, 5:73, 5:153

Technology and the Idea of Progress, 5:154

Technology and the Lifeworld: From Garden to Earth, 5:71, 5:92

Technology and the Wealth of Nations, 5:234

Technology and Values in American Civilization, 5:60, 5:149

Technology and Women's Voices Keeping in Touch, 5:188

Technology as a Human Affair, 5:71, 5:128, 5:154

Technology as a Social and Political Phenomenon, 5:150

Technology as Meaning and Destiny, 5:86

Technology as Symptom and Dream, 5:157

The Technology Edge: Opportunities for America in World Competition, 5:214

Technology in America: A History of Individuals and Ideas, 5:37, 5:55

Technology in Education: Looking toward 2020, 5:12

Technology in the Nineteen Nineties—Agriculture and Food, 5:266

Technology in War, 5:237

Technology in Western Civilization, 3:326, 5:37, 5:52, 5:55

Technology in World Civilization, 5:232

Technology Management, 5:236

The Technology Pork Barrel, 5:184

Technology Review, 5:165

Technology Transfer: A Realistic Approach, 5:215

The Techno/Peasant Survival Manual, 5:215

Technopoly: The Surrender of Culture to Technology, 5:130, 5:140, 5:157, 5:574

Ted Hughes, 1:498

Ted Hughes: A Bibliography, 1946–1980, 1:498

Ted Hughes: A Critical Study, 1:498

Ted Hughes: The Unaccommodated Universe, 1:498

Ted Shawn: Father of American Dance, 3:752

Teens with AIDS Speak Out, 5:388

Teeth n' Smiles, 1:492, 1:493

Teilhard (Lucas), 4:337

Teilhard de Chardin (King), 4:337

Teilhard de Chardin: A Short Biography, 4:337

Teilhard de Chardin's Vision of the Future, 4:337

Teilhard, Scripture and Revelation, 4:337

Te Kaihau: The Windeater, 2:976, 2:977

Tektites, 5:627

T. E. Lawrence: A Biography, 3:927

Telecommunications, 5:298

Telecommunication Principles, 5:297

Telecommunications: Equipment Fundamentals and Network Structures, 5:301

Telecommunications: Voice/Data with Fiber Optic Applications, 5:308

Telecommunications, Mass Media, and Democracy, 5:296

Telecommunications and Networking, 5:300

Telecommunications Engineering, 5:298

Telecommunications in Crisis, 3:803

Telecommunications in the Information Age, 5:297

Telecommunications Networks: A Technical Introduction, 5:297

Telecommunications Switching, 5:301

Telecommunications Switching Principles, 5:301

Telecommunications Technology Handbook, 5:305

Telecommunication System Engineering, 5:304

Telecommunication Transmission Handbook, 5:304, 5:306

Teleconferencing Technology and Applications, 5:299

Teleguide: A Handbook on Video-Teleconferencing, 5:305

The Telematic Society: A Challenge for Tomorrow, 5:538

Teleological Explanations, 4:415

Teleology Revisited and Other Essays in the Philosophy and History of Science, 4:313, 5:96

The Telephone, 2:712

Telephony: Today and Tomorrow, 5:296

Telerobotics, Automation, and Human Supervisory Control, 5:243

Telescopes, Tides and Tactics, 4:143, 5:688

Television, the Book, and the Classroom, 1:49

Television and Aggression: Results of a Panel Study, 3:170

Television Drama Series Programming, 3:811

Television in America, 3:811

Teller's War, 5:235

Tell Freedom, 2:158, 2:159

Telling Classical Tales: Chaucer and the "Legend of Good Women," 1:151

Telling Lies in Modern American Autobiography, 1:808

Telling Lives, 1:972

Telling Lives: The Biographer's Art, 1:87

The Telling of Lies, 2:911

Telling Tales, 4:603

Tell Me, Africa: An Approach to African Literature, 2:111

Tell Me a Riddle: A Collection, 1:1026

Tell Me Who I Am: James Agee's Search for Selfhood, 1:933

Tell My Horse, 1:850

The Tell-Tale Heart, 1:1239

"Tell the World": What Happened in China and Why, 2:255

The Tempest, 1:205, 1:206, 1:210

Tempest-Tost, 2:910

The Temple, 1:180

The Temple of Dawn, 2:289

The Temple of My Familiar, 1:1064

The Temple of the Golden Pavilion, 2:289

Temples and Elephants: Travels in Siam in 1881–1882, 3:901

Tempo: The Impact of Television on the Arts, 1:567

Temporal Modalities in Arabic Logic, 4:318

Temporal Relations and Temporal Becoming, 5:103

Temptation, 2:791

The Temptation of St. Anthony, 2:475

Temptations: A Book of Short Stories, 2:43

The Temptations of Big Bear, 2:927

The Tenacity of Prejudice: Anti-Semitism in Contemporary America, 3:209

The Tenant of Wildfell Hall, 1:334

The Tenants, 1:1013

The Ten Books on Architecture, 3:764

Ten Colloquies, 4:139

Ten Contemporary Polish Stories, 2:812

Ten Days That Shook the World, 3:397

Tendencies in Modern American Poetry, 1:856

Tender Buttons, 1:882

Tender Is the Night, 1:838, 1:839

The Tenderness of the Wolves, 1:1185, 1:1186

Tendi: A Swahili Classical Verse Form, 2:152

Ten Economic Studies in the Tradition of Irving Fisher, 3:76

Tenement Songs: The Popular Music of Jewish Immigrants, 3:869

Ten Essays on Zionism and Judaism, 2:13

Tengo, 2:869

Ten Great Economists from Marx to Keynes, 3:46, 3:76, 3:87, 3:94, 3:95, 3:98, 3:105

Ten Keys to Latin America, 3:650

Ten Modern Masters, 1:423

Tennessee: Cry of the Heart, 1:1118

Tennessee Folk Culture: An Annotated Bibliography, 3:861

Tennessee Red Berry Tales, 3:860

Tennessee Williams, 1:1118

Tennessee Williams: A Bibliography, 1:1118

Tennessee Williams: A Collection of Critical Essays, 1:1118

Tennessee Williams: An Intimate Biography, 1:1118

The Tennis Court Oath: A Book of Poems, 1:936

The Tennis Players, 2:674

Ten North Frederick, 1:866, 1:867

Tennyson, 1:402

Tennyson: The Growth of a Poet, 1:401

Tennyson: The Unquiet Heart, 1:402

Tennyson and Clio: History in the Major Poems, 1:402

Tennyson and Madness, 1:401

Tennyson and Swinburne as Romantic Naturalists, 1:398

Tennyson and the Doom of Romanticism, 1:402

Tennyson and the Reviewers, 1:402

Tennyson and the Text: The Weaver's Shuttle, 1:402

Tennyson and Tradition, 1:402

A Tennyson Companion: Life and Works, 1:402

Tennyson Laureate, 1:402

Tennyson's Camelot, 1:402

Tennyson's Characters: "Strange Faces, Other Minds," 1:401

Tennyson's Language, 1:401

Tennyson's Maud: The Biographical Genesis, 1:402

Tennyson's Style, 1:402

The Tenors, 3:672

Ten Philosophical Mistakes, 4:271

Ten Plus One, 1:1233

Ten Rungs: Hasidic Sayings, 4:632

Tensions Affecting International Understanding: A Survey of Research, 3:188

Ten Sixty Six: The Year of the Conquest, 3:357

The Tentative Pregnancy, 5:204

The Tenth Muse: The Psyche of the American Poet, 1:628, 1:655, 1:719, 1:798

The Tenth Muse Lately Sprung Up in America, 1:634

The Ten Thousand Day War: Vietnam, 1945–1975, 3:539

The Ten Thousand Leaves, 2:275

Tent of Miracles, 2:892

The Te of Piglet, 4:528

Teotihuacan (Berrin), 4:457

Teotihuacan: The City of Gods (Moctezuma), 4:457

Tepoztlán, a Mexican Village: A Study of Folk Life, 3:39

Terence, 2:395

Terence Rattigan, 1:540

Terence Rattigan: The Man and His Work, 1:540

Teresa, A Woman: A Biography of Teresa of Avila, 4:786

Teresa of Avila, 4:787

Teresa of Avila and the Rhetoric of Femininity, 2:550, 4:787

Teresa of Avila's Way, 4:786

Tereza Batista: Home from the Wars, 2:892

Terminations, 1:764

Terms for Order, 1:956

Terms of Endearment, 1:1010

Terra Non Firma: Understanding and Preparing for Earthquakes, 5:636

Terra Nostra, 2:865

Terrible Perfection: Women and Russian Literature, 2:687

Terrible Swift Sword: Centennial History of the Civil War, Vol. 2, 3:572

The Terrible Threes, 1:1036

The Terrible Twos, 1:1036

The Terrible World, 2:702

Territorial Rights, 1:551

The Territory Ahead: Critical Iinterpretations in American Literature, 1:1017

The Territory of the Historian, 3:276

The "Terrorism" Industry, 3:204

Terror out of Zion: The Fight for Israeli Independence, 1929–1949, 3:439

Tertia Vigilia, 2:704

Tertullian: A Historical and Literary Study, 4:714

Tess of the d'Urbervilles, 1:360, 1:361

A Testament, 3:798

Testament of Cresseid, 1:146

A Testament of Hope: The Essential Writings of Martin Luther King, Jr., 4:772

Test Case: Italy, Ethiopia and the League of Nations, 3:277

Testing Scientific Theories, 5:62

Testing-Tree: Poem, 1:1003

The Test of Honor, a Novel by a Young Lady, 1:643

Test-Tube Conception, 5:360

The Teutonic Knights, 2:821

Teutonic Mythology, 2:585

Tevye the Dairyman and the Railroad Stories, 2:45

Tewodros, 2:121

TEX: The Program, 5:562

Texas, 1:1088, 3:931

Texas and Southwestern Lore, 3:863

Texas Fury, 1:1222

Texas Graveyards: A Cultural Legacy, 3:132

Texas Heat, 1:1222

Texas in the Middle Eighteenth Century, 3:643

A Texas-Mexican Cancionero: Folksongs of the Lower Border, 3:863

The Texas Rangers: A Century of Frontier Defense, 3:600

Texas Rich, 1:1222

A Texas Trilogy, 1:1096

Texfake, 1:36

Text and Supertext in Ibsen's Drama, 2:666

The Text as Thou, 4:662

Text-Atlas of Histology, 5:773

The TEXtbook, 5:562

The Textbook in American Society, 1:49

A Textbook of Econometrics, 3:88

A Text-Book of Roman Law from Augustus to Justinian, 3:305

Text, ConText, and Hyper-Text: Writing with and for the Computer, 5:561

The Text of the New Testament: Its Transmission, Corruption, and Restoration, 4:805, 4:806

The Text of the Old Testament, 4:806

Texts, Hebrew Translation, Commentary, and Introduction, 4:445

Texts and Contexts: The Roman Writers and Their Audience, 2:381

Texts and Dialogues, 4:310

Texts and Studies in Jewish History and Literature, 4:631

Texts in Context: Traditional Hermeneutics in South Asia, 4:506, 4:510, 4:514, 4:517

A Textual Commentary on the Greek New Testament, 4:806

The Textual Condition, 1:873

Textual Criticism Since Gregg: A Chronicle, 1950–1985, 1:62

Textual Power: Literary Theory and the Teaching of English, 1:1127

Textual Problems of the First Folio, 1:207

Textual Sources for the Study of Sikhism, 4:516

Textual Sources for the Study of Zoroastrianism, 4:443, 4:547

Textual Strategies: Perspectives in Post-Structuralist Criticism, 1:925, 1:1134

T for Texas: A State Full of Folklore, 3:862

Thackeray: Interviews and Recollections, 1:404

Thackeray: Prodigal Genius, 1:404

Thackeray: The Critical Heritage, 1:404

Thackeray and Form of Fiction, 1:404

Thackeray at Work, 1:404

Thackeray's Canvass of Humanity: An Author and His Public, 1:404

Thackeray's Critics, 1:404

Thackeray's Novels: A Fiction That Is True, 1:404

Thackeray's Universe: Shifting Worlds of Imagination and Reality, 1:404

Thackeray the Humorist and the Man of Letters, 1:404

Thai Buddhism, 4:520

The Thai Bureaucracy: Institutional Change and Development, 3:490

Thailand: A Short History, 3:490

Thailand: Buddhist Kingdom as Modern Nation-State, 3:490

Thailand: Politics, Economy and Socio-cultural Setting, 3:490

Thailand: The Modernization of a Bureaucratic Policy, 3:490

Thailand and the Struggle for Southeast Asia, 3:490

Thai-Malay Relations, 3:489

Thai Manuscript Painting, 4:518

Thalaba the Destroyer, 1:304

Thames and Hudson Dictionary of Art and Artists, 3:758

The Thames and Hudson Dictionary of Art Terms, 3:757

The Thames and Hudson Encyclopaedia of 20th-Century Music, 3:655

Thames and Hudson Encyclopedia of Graphic Design and Designers, 3:759

The Thames and Hudson Encyclopedia of Impressionism, 3:759

The Thames and Hudson Manual of Bookbinding, 1:24

Thames and Hudson Manual of Typography, 1:11

That Bowling Alley on the Tiber: Tales of a Director, 3:830

That Hideous Strength, 1:512

That Long Silence, 2:177

That Mighty Sculptor, Time, 2:517

That Noble Dream, 3:515

That Rascal Freneau, 1:639

That Shakespeherian Rag: Essays on a Critical Process, 1:209

That Summer in Paris, 2:907, 2:908

That Sunny Dome: A Portrait of Regency England, 1:265

That Uncertain Feeling, 1:432

That Voice, 2:493

The Thaw, 2:717

The "Thaw" in Bulgarian Literature, 2:781

The Theaetetus of Plato, 4:79

The Theater and Its Double, 2:445, 2:451, 2:452

Theater and Literature in Russia Nineteen Hundred to Nineteen Thirty, 2:687

Theater Enough, 1:629

Theater in Southeast Asia, 2:311

The Theater of Devotion, 1:159

The Theater of Edward Albee, 1:1080

The Theater of the Absurd, 1:1081

Theatre and Crisis, 1:169

Theatre and Playhouse, 1:272

Theatre as Problem: Modern Drama and Its Place in Literature, 1:425

Theatre at Work, 1:425

The Theatre Guild: The First 10 Years, with Articles by the Directors, 1:1073

Theatre in Spain: 1490–1700, 2:524

Theatre in the Age of Kean, 1:272, 1:322

The Theatre in the Middle Ages, 1:157

Theatre in the Victorian Age, 1:322

The Theatre of Aristophanes, 2:353

The Theatre of Black Americans, 1:1073

The Theatre of Dionysus in Athens, 2:347

The Theatre of Jean Anouilh, 2:450

A Theatre of Love, 1:619

The Theatre of Medieval Europe: New Research in Early Drama, 1:157

Theatre of Nature, 4:134

The Theatre of the Absurd, 1:425, 2:448

The Theatre of Tom Stoppard, 1:554

The Theatre of Valle-Inclán, 2:553

Theatre Past and Present: An Introduction, 1:271

Theatre World, 1:1076

Theatrewritings, 1:1074

Theatre Year, 1:427

Thebaid, 2:394

Their Eyes Were Watching God, 1:849

Their Fathers' God, 2:667

Their Very Own and Golden City, 1:565

Their Wedding Journey, 1:758

Theism in Medieval India, 4:503

Them, 1:1022

Thematic Catalogs in Music: An Annotated Bibliography, 3:654

A Thematic History of Indonesian Poetry: 1920–1974, 2:317, 2:321

Thematic Origins of Scientific Thought: Kepler to Einstein, 5:17, 5:25, 5:63

Theme, Embodiment and Structure in the Poetry of George Crabbe, 1:289

Theme and Structure in Swift's Tale of a Tub, 1:261

Theme and Style in African Poetry, 2:107

Theme Is Freedom, 1:828

Themes and Conventions of Elizabethan Tragedy, 1:169

Themes and Images in the Fictional Works of Mme de Lafayette, 2:484

Themes and Settings in Fiction: A Bibliography of Bibliographies, 1:124

Themes and Variations in Pasternak's Poetics, 2:746

Themes and Variations in Shakespeare's Sonnets, 1:215

Themes in Contemporary Physics II, 5:715

Themes in Soviet Marxist Philosophy, 4:30

Themes of Islamic Civilization, 4:580

Themes of Work and Love in Adulthood, 3:182

Themis: A Study of the Social Origins of Greek Religion, 4:479

Then and Now: The Personal Past in the Poetry of Robert Penn Warren, 1:894

Theocritus in English Literature, 2:369

Theocritus' Pastoral Analogies: The Formation of a Genre, 2:369

Theodicy in Islamic Thought, 4:582

Theodore Beza's Doctrine of Predestination, 4:731

Theodore Dreiser, 1:830

Theodore Dreiser: His World and His Novels, 1:830

Theodore Dreiser, Vol. 1: At the Gates of the City, 1871–1907, 1:830

Theodore Dreiser, Vol. 2: An American Journey, 1908–1945, 1:830

Theodore Dreiser and the Critics, 1911–1982, 1:830

Theodore Low De Vinne, 1:10

Theodore Parker: Yankee Crusader, 3:573

Theodore Roethke: An American Romantic, 1:1038

Theodore Roethke: The Garden Master, 1:1038

Theodore Roethke: The Journey from I to Otherwise, 1:1038

Theodore Roethke's Dynamic Vision, 1:1038

Theodore Roosevelt, 3:595, 3:936

Theodore Roosevelt: A Life, 3:595, 3:936

Theodore Roosevelt, Culture, Diplomacy, and Expansion, 3:595

Theodore Roosevelt, the Making of a Conservationist, 3:595

Theodore Roosevelt among the Humorists, 3:595

Theodore Roosevelt and Japan, 3:595

Theodore Roosevelt and Labor in New York State, 1880–1900, 3:595

Theodore Roosevelt and the Politics of Power, 3:594

Theodore Roosevelt and the Progressive Movement, 3:595

Theodore Roosevelt and the Rhetoric of Militant Decency, 3:595

Theodore Roosevelt and the Rise of America to World Power, 3:594

Theodore Roosevelt and the Rise of the Modern Navy, 3:595

Theodore Roosevelt and the Russo-Japanese War, 3:595

Theodore Roosevelt's Caribbean, 3:595

Theodor Fontane: The Major Novels, 2:579

Theodor Herzl: A Biography of the Founder of Modern Zionism, 3:347

Theogony, 2:342, 2:357, 2:358

Theogony: Translated with Introduction, Commentary and Interpretative Essay, 4:228, 4:481

Theogony and Works and Days, 4:481

Theological and Dogmatic Works, 4:702

A Theological and Historical Introduction to the Apostolic Fathers, 4:704

Theological and Religious Reference Materials, 4:716

Theological Anthropology, 4:685

Theological Dictionary of the New Testament, 4:818

Theological Dictionary of the Old Testament, 4:817

Theological Essays, 4:744

Theological Investigations, 4:423, 4:903

The Theological Methodology of Hans Küng, 4:775

Theological Political Tractatus, 4:186

Theological Voices in Medical Ethics, 5:124

Theology after Freud: An Interpretive Inquiry, 4:424

Theology after Vedanta: An Experiment in Comparative Theology, 4:872

Theology after Wittgenstein, 4:346

Theology and Autonomy, 5:207

Theology and Bioethics: Exploring the Foundations and Frontiers, 5:123

Theology and Dialogue: Essays in Conversation with George Lindbeck, 4:753

Theology and Science in Mutual Modification, 5:197

Theology and Social Theory, 3:213, 4:890

Theology and Technology: Essays in Christian Analysis and Exegesis, 5:197

Theology and the Cain Complex, 1:497

Theology and the Problem of Evil, 4:886

Theology and the Scientific Imagination from the Middle Ages to the Seventeenth Century, 4:126, 4:160

Theology at the End of Modernity, 4:743

Theology for the Third Millennium, 4:775

Theology in America, 1:630

Theology in the Responsa, 4:629

Theology in the Russian Diaspora, 4:756

Theology of Culture, 5:206

Theology of Discontent, 4:373

The Theology of Jonathan Edwards: A Reappraisal, 1:637, 4:767

A Theology of Liberation: History, Politics, and Salvation, 4:748, 4:769, 4:896

The Theology of Martin Luther, 4:778

The Theology of Paul Tillich, 4:787

The Theology of Post-Reformation Lutheranism, 4:730

The Theology of St. Luke, 4:825

The Theology of Schleiermacher, 4:254

The Theology of the Early Greek Philosophers: The Gifford Lectures, 4:1936, 4:50

Theology of the English Reformers, 4:726

The Theology of the New Testament, 4:827, 4:831

Theology of the Old Testament, 4:827, 4:834

Theology of the Psalms, 4:823

The Theology of Unity, 4:374

Theophilus North, 1:898, 1:899

Theophrastean Studies, on Natural Science, Physics and Metaphysics, Ethics, Religion and Rhetoric, 4:90

Theophrastus and the Greek Physiological Psychology before Aristotle, 4:91

Theophrastus Bombastus von Hohenheim Called Paracelsus, 4:150

Theophrastus of Eresus: On His Life and Work, 4:91

Theorems on Essence and Existence, 4:103

Theoretical Criminology, 3:205

Theoretical Philosophy 1755–1770, 4:205

Theoretical Physics and Philosophical Problems: Selected Writings, 5:675

Theoretical Physics in the Twentieth Century, 5:708

Theories and Observation in Science, 5:63

Theories and Things, 4:411, 5:100

Theories in Social Psychology, 3:168

Theories of Africans: Francophone Literature and Anthropology in Africa, 2:110

Theories of Authorship, 1:1158

Theories of Counseling, 5:417

Theories of Counseling and Psychotherapy, 5:419

Theories of Explanation, 5:64

Theories of High Temperature Superconductivity, 5:670

Theories of Learning, 3:175

Theories of Light from Descartes to Newton, 5:43

Theories of Mass Communication, 3:203, 3:803

Theories of Personality, 5:422

Theories of Personality: Primary Sources and Research, 3:178

Theories of Primitive Religion, 4:475

Theories of Reading in Dialogue: An Interdisciplinary Study, 4:319

Theories of Science in Society, 5:151

Theories of Scientific Method, 5:62

Theories of the Earth and Universe, 5:32

Theories of the Proposition, 4:97

Theories of Translation: An Anthology of Essays from Dryden to Derrida, 2:991

Theories of Truth, 4:381

Theories of Vision from al-Kindi to Kepler, 4:128

Theory and Evidence, 5:63

Theory and History of Bibliography, 1:61

Theory and History of Folklore, 2:689, 3:848, 3:869

The Theory and Philosophy of Organizations, 3:210

Theory and Practice, 3:229, 4:404, 5:89

Theory and Practice in American Medicine, 5:312

The Theory and Practice of Communism, 3:139

The Theory and Practice of Infection Control, 5:389

The Theory and Practice of Modem Design, 5:302

The Theory and Practice of Translation, 2:990

Theory and Religious Understanding, 4:494

Theory and Treatment of Anorexia Nervosa and Bulimia, 5:395

Theory between the Disciplines: Authority/Vision/Politics, 1:1134

Theory in the Classroom, 1:1129

Theory Now and Then, 1:1151

The Theory of Alfred North Whitehead: A Logical and Ethical Vindication, 4:341

A Theory of Almost Everything, 5:196

The Theory of Atomic Collisions, 5:704

The Theory of Business Enterprise, 3:109

Theory of Capitalist Development, 3:95

The Theory of Categories, 4:222

A Theory of Cognitive Dissonance, 3:171

Theory of Collective Behavior, 3:203, 3:215

Theory of Colors, 2:581

The Theory of Communicative Action, 4:404, 5:70, 5:89

Theory of Culture Change, 3:14, 3:18

The Theory of Customs Unions, 3:59

Theory of Demonstration According to William Ockham, 4:121

Theory of Economic Development, 3:104, 3:105

The Theory of Economic Growth, 3:53

Theory of Economic History, 3:83, 3:84

The Theory of Fiction: Henry James, 1:764

Theory of Games and Economic Behavior, 3:63, 3:112

Theory of Heat, 5:701

The Theory of Heat Radiation, 5:709

A Theory of Indigenous Southeast Asian Urbanism, 3:489

The Theory of Interest, 3:75, 3:76

The Theory of International Economic Policy: Vol. II, Trade and Welfare, 3:59

The Theory of Intuition in Husserl's Phenomenology, 4:235

Theory of Island Biogeography, 5:820

A Theory of Justice, 4:316

Theory of Knowledge (Chisholm), 4:395

Theory of Knowledge (Lehrer), 4:22, 4:381

Theory of Knowledge: The 1913 Manuscript, 4:22, 4:323, 4:381, 4:395

The Theory of Knowledge of Giambattista Vico, 2:442, 4:216

The Theory of Knowledge of Hugh of St. Victor, 4:102

The Theory of Knowledge of Vital du Four, 4:102

The Theory of Legislation, 3:150

A Theory of Literary Production, 1:1127

Theory of Literature, 2:984

A Theory of Medical Ethics, 5:124, 5:144

The Theory of Moral Life, 4:225

The Theory of Moral Sentiments, 3:106, 3:107, 4:214, 4:215

The Theory of Motion in Plato's Later Dialogues, 4:84

The Theory of Peasant Cooperatives, 5:265

The Theory of Peasant Economy, 3:16

The Theory of Political Coalitions, 3:145

The Theory of Political Economy, 3:85

The Theory of Price, 3:64, 3:107, 3:108

A Theory of Price Control: The Classic Account, 3:79

Theory of Production, 3:64

The Theory of Properties of Metals and Alloys, 5:704

The Theory of Psychoanalysis, 5:455

The Theory of Relational Databases, 5:560

Theory of Relativity, 5:708

Theory of Science, 4:197, 5:63

Theory of Sets, 5:500

The Theory of Social and Economic Organization, 3:210, 3:244

The Theory of Superconductivity, 5:671

A Theory of Technology: Continuity and Change in Human Development, 5:213

Theory of the American Romance, 1:794

Theory of the Consumption Function, 3:77

Theory of the Earth, with Proofs and Illustrations, 5:644

The Theory of the Gene, 5:807

The Theory of the Leisure Class, 3:109, 3:242

Theory of the Novel, 2:801

The Theory of the Properties of Metals and Alloys, 5:704

Theory of the Spirit and the Egocentric Propensities of Man, 4:285

Theory of Valuation, 4:225

The Theory of Value: An Axiomatic Analysis of Economic Equilibrium, 3:63

The Theory of Wages, 3:83

Third Barnhart Dictionary of New English, 1:91
The Third Book about Achim, 2:594
The Third Force in Seventeenth-Century Thought, 4:18, 4:162
The Third French Republic, 1870–1940, 3:372
Third International after Lenin, 3:295
The Third Jewish Catalogue: Building Community, 4:602
The Third Kiss, 1:460
The Third Life of Per Smevik, 2:667
The Third Mind, 1:957
Third Notch and Other Stories, 2:326
The Third Planet, 5:617
The Third Policeman, 1:525
The Third Portuguese Empire, 1825–1975, 3:423
The Third Rose: Gertrude Stein and Her World, 1:882
The Third Voice: Modern British and American Verse Drama, 1:425
The Third Wave, 5:158, 5:574
The Third Wave: Russian Literature in Emigration, 2:688
Third World Film Making and the West, 1:1156
Third World Poems, 2:934
Third World Urbanization, 3:219
The Third World—North Africa: A Bibliography, 3:419
A Thirsty Evil: Seven Short Stories, 1:1062
The Thirteen Books of Euclid's Elements, 5:504
Thirteen Clocks, 1:890
Thirteen O'Clock, Stories of Several Worlds, 1:815
The Thirteen Pragmatisms and Other Essays, 4:303
The Thirteen Principal Upanishads, 4:501
Thirteen Stories, 1:895
Thirteenth Century, 1216–1307, 3:357
Thirteen Thinkers: A Sampler of Great Philosophers, 4:17
Thirteenth Night and A Short Sharp Rock, 1:450
The Thirties: From Notebooks and Diaries of the Period, 1:902

The Thirties and After: Poetry, Politics, People, 1930s–1970s, 1:553
The Thirtieth Year, 2:568
Thirty Indian Legends of Canada, 3:864
The 39 Steps, 1:1168
31 Letters and 13 Dreams: Poems, 1:990
Thirty Seconds, 3:810
The Thirty-Six Hour Day, 5:392
Thirty-Six Lectures in Biology, 5:765
Thirty Strange Stories, 1:564
Thirty Years of Yugoslav Literature, 1945–1975, 2:785, 2:808, 2:827, 2:835
Thirty Years That Shook Physics: The Story of Quantum Theory, 5:689
The Thirty Years War, 4:737
This . . . Is CBS: A Chronicle of 60 Years, 3:812
This and That and the Other, 1:443
This Body Is Made of Camphor and Gopherwood, 1:952
This Book-Collecting Game, 1:33
This Bridge Called My Back, 1:1136, 1:1184
This Business of Music, 3:657
This Calder Sky, 1:1221
This Cybernetic World: Of Men, Machines, and Earth Systems, 5:243
This Earth, My Brother, 2:131
This Earth, That Sky: Poems by Manuel Bandeira, 2:894
This Earth of Mankind, 2:321
This Great Stage: Image and Structure in "King Lear," 1:214
This Hallowed Ground, 3:572
This I Can Not Forget: The Memoirs of Nikolai Bukharin's Widow, 3:397
This Incomparable Lande: A Book of American Nature Writing, 5:818
This Indolence of Mine, 2:439
This Is It, 4:881
This Is Lagos and Other Stories, 2:140, 2:140
This Island, Now, 2:158
This Is London, 3:819
This Is My God, 4:597
This Is Not a Pipe, 4:400

This Is Not a Story and Other Stories, 2:472
This Is the Rill Speaking, 1:1121
This Journey, 1:1067
This Kind of Woman, 1960–1976, 2:284
This Land, This Time, 2:829
This Left Hand of Creation, 5:594
This Ol' Drought Ain't Broke Us Yet (But We're All Bent Pretty Bad), 3:863
This People Israel, 4:660
This Quiet Dust: And Other Writings, 1:1057
This Real Night, 1:566
This Religion of Islam, 4:576
This Sculptured Earth: The Landscape of America, 5:627
This Sex Which Is Not One, 1:1182
This Side Jordan, 2:916, 2:917
This Side of Paradise, 1:838, 1:839
This Solemn Mockery: The Art of Literary Forgery, 1:36
This Sunday, 2:863, 2:864
Thistle and Rose: A Study of Hugh MacDiarmid's Poetry, 1:517
This Tree Will Be Here for a Thousand Years, 1:952
This Unfriendly Soil: The Loyalist Experience in Nova Scotia, 1783–1791, 3:613
This Very Earth, 1:819
This Was America, 3:582
This Was a Poet: A Critical Biography of Emily Dickinson, 1:748
This Was Publishing, 1:38
This Way for the Gas, Ladies and Gentlemen, 2:812, 3:344
Thomas Alva Edison, 5:252
Thomas Alva Edison: A Streak of Luck, 5:252
Thomas and Beulah, 1:970
Thomas Aquinas, 4:118
Thomas Aquinas and John Gerhard, 4:731
Thomas Aquinas and Radical Aristotelianism, 4:119
Thomas Bailey Aldrich, 1:732
Thomas Becket, 3:357
Thomas Campion, 1:174
Thomas Carlyle, 1:343

Thomas Carlyle: A Biography, 1:343

Thomas Carlyle: A History of His Life in London, 1834–1881, 3:403

Thomas Carlyle: A History of the First Forty Years of His Life, 3:403

Thomas Chandler Haliburton and His Works, 2:913

Thomas Cranmer, 4:725, 4:727

Thomas Cranmer and the English Reformation 1489–1556, 4:764

Thomas D. Clark Lectures 1990: The Rediscovery of North America, 3:916

Thomas Dekker: A Reference Guide, 1:176

Thomas De Quincey: Bicentenary Studies, 1:290

Thomas De Quincey, Literary Critic, 1:290

Thomas Edison: Inventing the Future, 5:252

Thomas Edison: Professional Inventor, 5:252

Thomas Edison, Chemist, 5:252

Thomas Gray, 1:248

Thomas Gray: A Biography, 1:248

Thomas Gray: A Reference Guide, 1:248

Thomas H. Huxley, 5:799

Thomas Hardy, 1:362, 1:1150

Thomas Hardy: A Biography, 1:360, 1:363

Thomas Hardy: An Annotated Bibliography of Writings about Him, 1:362

Thomas Hardy: Distance and Desire, 1:362, 1:1151

Thomas Hardy: The Offensive Truth, 1:362

Thomas Hardy: The Poetry of Necessity, 1:363

Thomas Hardy: The Poetry of Perception, 1:363

Thomas Hardy: The Return of the Repressed—A Study of the Major Fiction, 1:362

Thomas Hardy: The Writer and His Background, 1:363

Thomas Hardy and British Poetry, 1:362, 1:417

Thomas Hardy and the Cosmic Mind, 1:362

A Thomas Hardy Dictionary, 1:363

Thomas Hardy—Poet of Tragic Vision, 1:362

Thomas Hart Benton, 3:594

Thomas Henry Huxley, 5:799

Thomas Henry Huxley: Communicating for Science, 5:799

Thomas Heywood, 1:182

Thomas Heywood's Pageants: A Critical Edition, 1:182

Thomas Hill Green: Philosopher of Rights, 4:230

Thomas Hobbes, 4:174

Thomas Hobbes: A Reference Guide, 3:154

Thomas Hobbes: Radical in the Service of Reaction, 4:175

Thomas Hunt Morgan: A Scientific Biography, 5:807

Thomas Hunt Morgan: Pioneer of Genetics, 5:808

Thomas J. Wise: Centenary Studies, 1:36

Thomas Jefferson: An Intimate History, 1:640, 3:155, 3:520

Thomas Jefferson, 1981–1990. An Annotated Bibliography, 1:641

Thomas Jefferson and the New Nation: A Biography, 3:155

Thomas Kyd, 1:185

Thomas Lodge, 1:185

Thomas Lodge and Other Elizabethans, 1:185

Thomas Love Peacock, 1:297

Thomas Mann (Feuerlicht), 2:602

Thomas Mann (Stern), 2:603

Thomas Mann: A Critical Study, 2:602

Thomas Mann: The Ironic German, 2:602

Thomas Mann: The Making of an Artist, 2:603

Thomas Mann: The World as Will and Representation, 2:602

Thomas Mann's Doctor Faustus, 2:602

Thomas Merton, Spiritual Master: The Essential Writings, 4:781

A Thomas Merton Reader, 4:781

Thomas Middleton: A Reference Guide, 1:190

Thomas Middleton and the New Comedy Tradition, 1:190

Thomas Middleton's City Comedies, 1:190

Thomas More, 4:147

Thomas More: A Biography, 1:194, 4:148

Thomas More: History and Providence, 4:147

Thomas More: The Search for the Inner Man, 1:194, 4:148

Thomas More and Erasmus, 4:727

Thomas More and His Utopia, 4:147

Thomas Nashe in Context, 1:195

Thomas of Reading, 1:177

Thomas Otway, 1:251

Thomas Paine, 4:273

Thomas Paine (Wilson), 1:642

Thomas Pynchon, 1:1035

Thomas Pynchon: Allusive Parables of Power, 1:1035

Thomas Pynchon: The Art of Allusion, 1:1035

Thomas Reid, 4:212

Thomas Reid and the "Way of Ideas," 4:212

Thomas Reid on Freedom and Morality, 4:212

Thomas Reid's Inquiry, 4:211

Thomas Telford, 5:223, 5:256

Thomas Telford: Civil Engineer, 5:256

Thomas White's De Mundo Examined in First English Translation, 4:174

Thomas William Robertson: His Plays and Stagecraft, 1:390

Thomas Wolfe, 1:904, 1:905

Thomas Wolfe: A Biography, 1:905

Thomas Wolfe: A Checklist, 1:904

Thomas Wolfe: A Collection of Critical Essays, 1:905

Thomas Wolfe: A Reference Guide, 1:905

Thomas Wolfe and His Editors, 1:904

A Thomas Wolfe Companion, 1:904

Thomas Wolfe Interviewed, 1929–1938, 1:905

Thom Gunn: A Bibliography, 1:491

Thomist Realism, 4:286

Thoreau, as Seen by His Contemporaries, 1:702, 5:837

Thoreau as World Traveler, 1:702

Thoreau's Complex Weave, 1:702

Thoreau's Seasons, 1:702

Thoreau's World and Ours: A Natural Legacy, 5:837

Thoreau the Poet–Naturalist: With Memorial Verses, 1:702

Thor Heyerdahl: Viking Scientist, 3:924

The Thorn in the Starfish: The Immune System and How It Works, 5:340

The Thorn of a Rose: Amy Lowell Reconsidered, 1:856

Thornton Wilder, 1:899, 1:1116

Thornton Wilder: A Reference Guide, 1:899

Thornton Wilder and His Public, 1:899, 1:1116

The Thorny Gates of Learning in Sung China, 3:467

Thorpe: Humorist of the Old Southwest, 1:703

Thorstein Veblen: A Critical Interpretation, 3:243

Thorstein Veblen: A Critical Reappraisal, 3:110

Thorstein Veblen: The Carleton College Veblen Seminar Essays, 3:110

Thorstein Veblen and His America, 3:109, 3:243

Thorstein Veblen and His Critics, 1891–63, 3:110

Those Terrible Carpetbaggers, 3:574

Those Twentieth Century Blues: An Autobiography, 3:725

Though He Slay Me, 2:15

Thought, Fact, and Reference, 4:312

Thought and Behavior in Modern Japanese Politics, 3:478

The Thought and Character of William James, 4:238

Thought and Expression in the Sixteenth Century, 4:131

Thought and Letters in Western Europe, A.D. 500–900, 4:100, 4:699

Thought and Vision: A Critical Reading of H. D.'s Poetry, 1:827

Thought Experiments, 4:385

Thought Forms, 4:550

The Thought of Gregory the Great, 4:710

The Thought of Jacques Ellul: A Systematic Exposition, 5:163, 5:164, 5:165

The Thought of Mao Tsetung, 4:362

The Thought of Paul Tillich, 5:206

Thought Power: Its Control and Culture, 4:550

Thoughts and Suggestions on Certain Social Problems, Contained Chiefly in Addresses to Meetings of Workmen in Lancashire, 1:368

Thoughts on Death and Immortality, 4:227, 4:228

Thoughts on Machiavelli, 3:160, 4:145

A Thousand Acres, 1:1050, 1:1051

A Thousand Cranes, 2:281, 2:288

A Thousand Days: John F. Kennedy in the White House, 3:597

A Thousand-Mile Walk to the Gulf, 5:836

A Thousand Years of Vietnamese Poetry, 2:339

A Thousand Years of West African History, 3:425

The Threat and the Glory: Reflections on Science and Scientists, 5:18

Threatened Birds of the Americas: The ICBP/IUCN Red Data Book, 5:769

Threatened Primates of Africa: The IUCN Red Data Book, 5:769

Three American Literatures, 1:1128

Three Apples from Heaven: Armenian Folk Tales, 3:856

Three Archaic Poets: Archilochus, Alcaeus, Sappho, 2:366

Three Argentine Thinkers, 4:33

Three Bears, 1:583

Three Blind Mice, 1:1233

Three Blind Mice: How the Television Networks Lost Their Way, 3:810

Three Books of Occult Philosophy or Magic, 4:133

Three Books on Life, 4:141

Three by Flannery O'Connor, 1:1024

The Three Caballeros, 1:1164

Three Centuries and the Island, 3:609

Three Centuries of Harvard, 1636–1936, 3:589

Three Cheers for the Paraclete, 2:958

Three Children's Plays, 1:1101

Three Chilean Thinkers, 4:33

Three Christian Capitals: Topography and Politics, 4:684

Three Cities: Petersburg, Warsaw, Moscow, 2:35

Three Classic African-American Novels, 1:725

Three Classical Poets: Sappho, Catullus and Juvenal, 2:387

The Three Clerks, 1:406

Three Comedies: Mine Hostess, The Boors, The Fan, 2:422

Three Contemporary Novelists, 1:986

Three Copernican Treatises, 5:40

The Three-Cornered World, 2:291

The Three Cousins, 1:408

The Three Cuckolds, 2:402

Three Days and a Child, 2:26

Three Degrees above Zero: Bell Labs in the Information Age, 5:537, 5:668

Three Dialogues between Hylas and Philonous, 4:191

Three Dialogues on Knowledge, 4:399, 5:86

Three Discourses on Imagined Occasions, 4:239

The Three Edwards: War and State in England, 1272–1377, 3:358

Three Egyptian Short Stories, 2:65

Three Essays on Religion, 4:244

Three Essays on the State of Economic Science, 3:47

Three Essays on the Theory of Sexuality, 1:1181, 3:183, 5:447

Three Essays on Thucydides, 3:323

Three Exemplary Novels, 2:535, 2:552

Three Eyes on the Past: Exploring New York State Folk Life, 3:859

Three Faces of Hermeneutics, 1:925
Three Faces of Imperialism, 3:366
Three Faces of Power, 3:144
Three Faiths—One God: A Jewish, Christian, Muslim Encounter, 4:41, 4:569
Three Famous Plays, 2:770
Three Famous Short Novels: Spotted Horses, Old Man, and The Bear, 1:835
Three Faroese Novelists, 2:655
The Three Fat Men, 2:743
Three Filipino Women, 2:331
Three Greek Plays for the Theatre, 2:349
Three Greek Romances, 2:348
Three Guineas, 1:569
Three Hours after Marriage, 1:252
Three Hundred Poems, 1903–1953, 2:542
Three Hundred Years of American Drama and Theatre, 1:1076
Three in Bed: Fiction, Morals and Politics, 2:162
Three Italian Chronicles, 2:511
Three Jacobean Tragedies, 1:171
Three Jewish Philosophers, 4:628
The Three Jovial Huntsmen, 1:580
The Three Kentucky Presidents: Lincoln, Taylor, Davis, 3:575
Three Kings: Three Stories from Today's China, 2:237
Three Last Plays, 1:490
Three Latin American Sociologists, 3:631
Three Laws, 1:172
The Three Little Pigs, 1:1163
Three Lives, 1:881
Three Major Texts, 1:387
The Three Marias, 2:897
Three Middle English Arthurian Romances, 1:147
Three Minutes of Silence, 2:771, 2:772
Three Modern Italian Poets: Saba, Ungaretti, and Montale, 2:441
Three Modern Novelists: Soseki, Tanizaki, Kawabata, 2:282
Three Modes of Modern Southern Fiction, 1:904

Three More Plays: Silver Tassie, Purple Dust, and Red Roses for Me, 1:527
Three Mughal Poets. Mīr, Mīr Hasan and Saudā, 2:175
The Three Musketeers, 2:473
Three Muslim Sages: Avicenna, Suhwardi, Ibn-'Arabi, 4:582
Three Novels: Ferdydurke, Pornografia, and Cosmos, 2:813
The Three Paradoxes of Roland Barthes, 2:455
Threepenny Opera, 1:246, 2:571, 2:572
Three Philosophical Moralists: Mill, Kant, and Sartre, 4:331
Three Philosophical Poets, 4:75, 4:327
The Three Pillars of Zen: Teaching, Practice, Enlightenment, 4:537, 4:860
Three Plays: Absurd Person Singular; Absent Friends; Bedroom Farce, 1:437
Three Plays: Broken Calabash, The Reign of Wazobia, and Parables for a Season, 2:144
Three Plays: Exit the King, The Killer, Macbett, 2:483
Three Plays: Juno and the Paycock, The Shadow of a Gunman, and The Plough and the Stars, 1:527
Three Plays: Our Town, The Skin of Our Teeth, The Matchmaker, 1:1116
Three Plays: Phaedra, Andromaque, Britannicus, 2:498
Three Plays: The Black Maskers, The Life of Man, The Sabine Woman, 2:699
Three Plays: The Last Carnival; Beef, No Chicken; A Branch of the Blue Nile, 2:943
Three Plays: The Weavers, Hannele, The Beaver Coat, 2:587
Three Poems, 1:936
Three Prefaces to Linnaeus and Robert Brown, 5:806
Three Prophetic Novels, 1:563
Three Reformers: Luther, Descartes, Rousseau, 4:307
Three Rival Versions of Moral Enquiry, 4:407

Three Russian Prophets: Khomiakov, Dostoevsky, Soloviev, 2:691
Three Russian Women Poets, 2:693
Three Russian Writers and the Irrational, 2:685
Three Sisters, 2:707, 2:709
Three Sketches of Chinese Literature, 2:250
Three Soldiers, 1:828
Three Spanish American Poets: Pellicer, Neruda, Andrade, 2:875
Three Studies in Current Philosophical Questions, 4:303
Three Styles in the Study of Kinship, 3:19
Three Theban Plays, 2:367
Three Theories of Child Development, 5:442
Three Thousand Leagues, 2:305
3000 Years of Black Poetry: An Anthology, 2:931
Three Thousand Years of Hebrew Literature, 2:9
Three Tragedies: Antigone, Oedipus the King, and Electra, 2:367
Three Tragedies: Blood Wedding, Yerma, Bernarda Alba, 2:539
Three Tragedies: Trojan Women, Medea, and Phaedra, 2:393
Three Trapped Tigers, 2:857
Three Travelers Watch a Sunrise, 1:886
Three Treatises, 4:778
Three Treatises on the Nature of Science, 4:58
Three Treatments of Universals by Roger Bacon, 4:111
Three Uneasy Pieces, 2:966
Three Ways of Thought in Ancient China, 4:525
Three Who Made a Revolution, 3:343
Three Winters, 2:817
Threshold of War, 3:535
The Thrill of Fear: Two Hundred Fifty Years of Scary Entertainment, 1:599
Thro' the Vision of the Night, 1:401
Through a Lens Darkly, 3:831
Through a Maze of Colour, 2:935
Through Russia, 2:725

Through the Dark Continent, or The Sources of the Nile, around the Great Lakes of Equatorial Africa, and down the Livingstone River to the Atlantic Ocean, 3:938

Through the Eyes of a Child, 1:579, 1:1196

Through the Looking Glass, 1:581, 1:582

Through the Open Door: A New Look at C. S. Lewis, 1:513

Through the Russian Prism: Essays on Literature and Culture, 2:686

Through Travellers' Eyes, 3:490

Thucydides, 3:323

Thunderball, 1:594

Thunder from the Mountains: Poems and Songs from the Mau Mau, 2:152

The Thundering Scot: A Portrait of John Knox, 4:736, 4:774

Thunderstorm, 2:266

Thunderstorms and Shooting Stars: The Meaning of Meteorites, 5:592

Thurber Carnival, 1:890

Thurber Country, 1:890

Thurber on Crime, 1:890

Thurms and the Barrie Country, 1:330

Thursday's Universe, 5:593

Thus Have I Heard: The Long Discourses of the Buddha, 4:514

Thus Spake Zarathustra, 4:245, 4:246

Thus to Revisit: Some Reminiscences, 1:475

The Thwarting of Baron Bolligrew, 1:445

Thymus Vulgaris, 1:1121

Thyroid Disease: The Facts, 5:381

Thyrsis, 1:327

Thyrza: A Tale, 1:359

Tiananmen Diary, 3:822

Tian Wen: A Chinese Book of Origins, 4:524

Tibet: A Political History, 4:356

The Tibetan Book of the Dead, 1:1114

Tibetan Buddhism in Western Perspective, 4:543

Tibetan Buddhist Medicine and Psychiatry: The Diamond Healing, 4:890

Tibetan Civilization, 4:356

Tibet Bon Religion: A Death Ritual of the Tibetan Bonpos, 4:543

Tibet Is My Country, 3:923

Tibullus: A Commentary, 2:396

The Ticket-of-Leave Man, 1:272, 1:320, 1:399

The Ticket That Exploded, 1:957

Ticket to Ride, 1:535

Tides, 2:143

The Tidewater Tales: A Novel, 1:942

The Tidings Brought to Mary, 2:468

Tieta, 2:892

Tiger!, 2:319, 2:320

The Tiger and the Horse, 1:445

Tiger at the Gates, 1:480, 2:481

Tiger Beat, 1:1186

Tiger Lilies, 1:771

Tiger of the Pampas, 2:884

The Tiger's Bones and Other Plays for Children, 1:498

The Tiger's Fang, 4:873

Tigers on the Tenth Day and Other Stories, 2:75

Tigrela: And Other Stories, 2:900

Till We Have Faces: A Myth Retold, 1:512

Tilting the Jar, Spilling the Moon, 2:299

Timber Colony, 3:614

Time, 2:13

Time, Forward!, 2:730, 2:731

Time, Narrative, and History, 4:391

Time, Space and Philosophy, 5:68

Time and Free Will, 4:220

Time and History in Contemporary Philosophy with Special Reference to Bergson and Croce, 3:284

Time and Idea: The Theory of History in Giambattista Vico, 2:442, 4:216

Time and Narrative, 4:319

Time and Necessity: Studies in Aristotle's Theory of Modality, 4:68

Time and Social Structure and Other Essays, 3:24

Time and Space: A Poetic Autobiography, 2:542

Time and the Artist in Shakespeare's English Histories, 1:211

Time and the Gods, 1:615

Time and the Highland Maya, 4:456, 4:465

Time and the Inner Future, 5:415

The Time and the Place and Other Stories, 2:68

Time and the Wind, 2:901

Time and Tide, 1:526

Time and Western Man, 1:514

Time Bomb: Fermi, Heisenberg, and the Race for the Atomic Bomb, 5:694

Time Enough for Love, 1:1258

Time for a Tiger, 1:453

A Time for Remembering: The Story of Ruth Bell Graham, 4:768

Time for Tea: Travels through China and India in Search of Tea, 3:903

A Time in Rome, 1:447, 3:898

The Time Machine, 1:563, 1:611, 5:563

Time of Decision with Rudolf Steiner: Experience and Encounter, 4:880

Time of Desecration, 2:429

The Time of Hope, 1:550

The Time of Indifference, 2:429

The Time of Man, 1:875, 1:876

The Time of Music, 3:661

The Time of My Life, 4:412, 5:100

The Time of the Angels, 1:523

The Time of the Assassins: A Study of Rimbaud, 1:861, 1:862, 2:500

Time of the Butcherbird, 2:164

The Time of the Generals, 3:632

The Time of the Land Surveyors, 2:803

The Time of William Faulkner, 1:917

The Time of Your Life, 1:1110

A Time on Earth, 2:678

Time on the Cross: The Economics of American Negro Slavery, 3:54, 3:547

Time Remembered, 2:450

Times, 2:420

Time's Arrow, Time's Cycle, 5:645

The Times Atlas of the
  Oceans, 5:616
Times Atlas of the World,
  1:85, 5:618
The Times Books World
  Weather Guide, 5:634
Time's Glory: Original Essays
  on Robert Penn Warren,
  1:893
The Timetables of American
  History, 3:507
The Timetables of History: A
  Horizontal Linkage of Peo-
  ple and Events, 3:7
The Timetables of Jewish
  History, 4:594
The Timetables of Science,
  5:216
Time to Act, 1:858
A Time to Be Born and a
  Time to Die: The Ethics
  of Choice, 4:895
A Time to Choose: America's
  Energy Future, 5:282
A Time to Dance, 3:731
A Time to Hear, a Time to
  Help: Listening to People
  with Cancer, 5:373
Time to Murder and Create:
  The Contemporary Novel
  in Crisis, 1:420
Time Travel and Other Math-
  ematical Bewilderments,
  5:507
The Time Wanderers, 2:762
Timoleon Etc., 1:688
Timon of Athens, 1:205,
  1:206
The Timothy Files, 1:1237
Tina, 2:647
The Tinbergen Legacy, 5:838
The Tin Drum, 2:582, 2:583
Tinker, Tailor, Soldier, Spy,
  1:596
A Tinker and a Poor Man:
  John Bunyan and His
  Church, 1628–1688, 1:174
The Tin Pot Foreign General
  and the Old Iron Woman,
  1:574
Tintern Abbey, 1:305
The Tin Woodman of Oz,
  1:1200
Tiny Alice, 1:1080, 1:1081
The Tio Kingdom of the
  Middle Congo, 1880–1892,
  3:432
Tippett: The Composer and
  His Music, 3:725
Tippett and His Operas,
  3:725
Tips for the Savvy Traveler,
  3:891

Tirade, 2:627
Tirra Lirra by the River,
  2:948
'Tis Pity She's a Whore,
  1:179
Tis So: Negro Folk Tales,
  3:867
A Tissue of Lies: Eudora
  Welty and the Southern
  Romance, 1:896
The Titan (Dreiser), 1:829,
  1:830
Titan (Paul), 2:606
The Titans, 1:1247
The Titans: A Three-Genera-
  tion Biography of the
  Dumas, 2:473
Titian, 3:793
Titurel, 2:616, 2:617
Titus Andronicus, 1:205,
  1:206, 1:212
TMJ Syndrome: The Over-
  looked Diagnosis, 5:341
The TM Technique, 4:873
To Acknowledge the Won-
  der, 5:662
The Toad Is the Emperor's
  Uncle: Animal Folk-Tales
  from Viet-Nam, 2:340
Toad of Toad Hall, 1:588
To a God Unknown, 1:884
To All Nations: The Billy
  Graham Story, 4:768
To Asmara, 2:958
Tobacco and Slaves, 3:518
Tobacco Road, 1:818, 1:819
To Be a Jew: A Guide to
  Jewish Observance in Con-
  temporary Life, 4:601
To Be an American, 3:522
To Be and Not to Be: Nega-
  tion and Metadrama in
  "Hamlet," 1:213
To Be a Publisher, 1:48
To Bedlam and Part Way
  Back, 1:1045
To Be Young, Gifted and
  Black, 1:1092
Tobias George Smollett,
  1:257
Tobias Smollett, Critic and
  Journalist, 1:257
To Change China: Western
  Advisers to China,
  1620–1960, 3:503
To Change Place: Aztec Cer-
  emonial Landscapes, 4:457
To Change the World: Chris-
  tology and Cultural Criti-
  cism, 4:785
Tocqueville: A Biography,
  3:165

Tocqueville and the Old Re-
  gime, 3:165
Tocqueville and the Problem
  of Democracy, 3:165
Tocqueville and the Two De-
  mocracies, 3:165
To Criticize the Critic and
  Other Writings, 1:472
To Crush the Serpent, 2:99
To Cuba and Back, 3:920
To Damascus I, 2:679
Today, I Am a Fountain Pen,
  1:1094
To Do No Harm: DES and
  the Dilemmas of Modern
  Medicine, 5:350
To Dwell among Friends,
  3:208, 3:226
To Engineer Is Human, 5:12,
  5:174, 5:226
To Fear a Painted Devil,
  1:609
To Form a More Perfect
  Union, 3:514
To Free the Mind: Libraries,
  Technology and Intellectu-
  al Freedom, 1:57
To Give and to Have, 2:437
To Have and Have Not,
  1:844, 1:845
To Have or to Be? 5:450
To Herland and Beyond,
  1:753
To His Coy Mistress, 1:188
The Toilet, 1:1085
The Toils of Scepticism, 4:58
To Jerusalem and Back: A
  Personal Account, 1:947
Tokagawa Religion, 4:540
To Keep the Ball Rolling,
  1:536
To Kill a Man's Pride and
  Other Stories from South-
  ern Africa, 2:158
To Know a Woman, 2:22
Tokugawa Ideology: Early
  Constructs, 1570-1680,
  3:475
Tokugawa Religion: The Val-
  ues of Pre-Industrial Ja-
  pan, 3:474
Tokyo Rising: The City since
  the Great Earthquake,
  3:479
Told by Uncle Remus, 1:755
To Lhasa and Beyond: Diary
  of the Expedition to Tibet
  in the Year 1948, 4:544
To Live and to Write: Selec-
  tions by Japanese Women
  Writers, 1913–1938, 2:284
To Live in Pronouns, 2:549

To Live in Pronouns: Selected Love Poems, 2:550
To Live until We Say Goodbye, 5:379
A Tolken for Children, 1:576
Tolkien: A Biography, 1:559
Tolkien: A Critical Assessment, 1:559
Tolkien: New Critical Perspectives, 1:559
Tolkien: The Illustrated Encyclopaedia, 1:559
Tolkien Criticism: An Annotated Checklist, 1:559
Tolstoy (Gifford), 2:766
Tolstoy (Wilson), 2:766
Tolstoy: A Critical Introduction, 2:766
Tolstoy: A Life of My Father, 2:766
Tolstoy: Anna Karenina, 2:766
Tolstoy: The Critical Heritage, 2:766
Tolstoy and the Novel, 2:765
Tolstoy on Education: Tolstoy's Educational Writings, 1861-62, 2:766
Tolstoy or Dostoevsky: An Essay in the Old Criticism, 2:766
Tolstoy's Aesthetics and His Art, 2:766
Tolstoy's Major Fiction, 2:766
Tolstoy's Translation of the Gospels: A Critical Study, 2:766
Tolstoy's "What Is Art?": An Essay in the Philosophy of Art, 2:766
The Toltec Heritage: From the Fall of Tula to the Rise of Tenochtitlan, 4:457
The Toltecs, until the Fall of Tula, 4:457
To Make the Wounded Whole, 4:772
Tombee: Portrait of a Cotton Planter, 3:529
A Tomb for Boris Davidovich, 2:830
The Tombs, 2:872
The Tombs of Atuan, 1:1260
To Mend the World: Foundations of Future Jewish Thought, 4:664
Tom Jones, 1:223, 1:244
Tom Jones: Adventure and Providence, 1:246
Tom Jones: A Film Script, 1:532

Tommaso Campanella: Renaissance Pioneer of Modern Thought, 4:137
The Tomorrow Makers: A Brave New World of Living-Brain Machines, 5:542
Tomorrow's Miracle, 1:1223
To Moscow—And Beyond, 3:822
Tom Paine and the American Revolution, 1:642, 3:520
Tom Sawyer, Detective, 1:781
Tom Sawyer Abroad, 1:781
Tom Stoppard: An Assessment, 1:554
Tom Stoppard: The Artist as Critic, 1:555
Tom Stoppard: The Moral Vision of the Major Plays, 1:554
Tom Stoppard and the Craft of Comedy: Medium and Genre at Play, 1:554
Tom Taylor and the Victorian Drama, 1:399
Tom Watson: Agrarian Rebel, 3:603
The Tongue Set Free: Remembrance of a European Childhood, 2:575
Tongues of Fire, 2:159
Tongues Untied, 1:1188
The Tongues We Speak: New and Selected Poems, 1:982
Tonight at 8:30, 1:465
Tonight We Improvise and "Leonora, Addio," 2:436
Toni Morrison, 1:1019
Toni Morrison's Developing Class Consciousness, 1:1019
Tono-Bungay, 1:564
Tony's Book, 2:914
Too Clever by Half or The Diary of a Scoundrel, 2:744
Too Far to Go, 1:1060
Too Hot to Handle? Social and Policy Issues in the Management of Radioactive Wastes, 5:240
Too Late the Phalarope, 2:167
Too Loud a Solitude, 2:793
Tools for Conviviality, 5:128, 5:136, 5:137
Tools for Thought, 5:568
Too Serious a Business, 3:281
The Tooth of Crime, 1:1008, 1:1110, 1:1111
Too True to Be Good, 1:544

Topaz, 1:1169
Top Girls, 1:458, 1:459
A Topical Dictionary of Statistics, 5:521
Topical Reference Books, 1:74
Topical Reference Works, 1:81
Topics in Chinese Literature: Outlines and Bibliographies, 2:189
Topics in West African History, 3:425
To Please a Child, 1:1200
Topological Vector Spaces, 5:500
To Pray as a Jew, 4:599
To Present the Pretence: Essays on the Theatre and Its Public, 1:433
To Promote, Defend and Redeem, 1:795
Top Silk, 2:967, 2:968
To Purge This Land with Blood: A Biography of John Brown, 3:529
Torah and Canon, 4:613
Torah from Our Sages: Pirke Avot, 4:612
Torah through the Ages: A Short History of Judaism, 4:607
The Torch, 2:802
The Torch-Bearers, 1:1097, 1:1098
The Torch in My Ear, 2:575
Torch of Life, 5:795
To Redeem the Soul of America, 3:537
Tormented Master: A Life of Rabbi Nahman of Bratslav, 4:669
Tornado, 1:1165
Toronto Workers Respond to Industrial Capitalism 1867-1892, 3:615
To Roosevelt, 2:863
Torquato Tasso, 2:439, 2:580
Torquemada, 2:547
The Torrents of Spring, 1:844, 1:845
Torrents of Spring, etc., 2:769
Torrey's Morphogenesis of the Vertebrates, 5:776
Tortilla Flat, 1:883, 1:884
Tortillas for the Gods: A Symbolic Analysis of Zinacanteco Rituals, 4:465
The Tosa Diary, 2:277, 2:278
To Save the Phenomena, 5:25

To Scorch or Freeze: Poems About the Sacred, 1:466
To Secure the Blessings of Liberty, 4:857
Tosefta: An Introduction, 4:612
Tosefta: Translated from the Hebrew, 4:612
To Space and Back, 3:935, 5:611
To Take Place: Toward Theory in Ritual, 4:491
Total Child Care: From Birth to Age Five, 5:322
Total Institutions, 3:228
Totality and Infinity: An Essay on Exteriority, 4:901
The Totality of Man's Philosophical System, 4:323
The Total Traveler by Ship: The Cruise Traveler's Handbook, 3:891
Total War: Causes and Courses of the Second World War, 3:278
To Tell a Free Story, 1:86, 1:659
Totem and Taboo, 4:424, 5:447
The Totem and the Tricolor, 3:495
Totemism, 3:34
Totemism and Exogamy, 4:476
Totems and Teachers: Perspectives on the History of Anthropology, 3:11, 3:28
To the Air, 1:491
To the Ends of the Earth, 3:907, 3:941
To the Finland Station, 3:95, 3:341
To the Halls of Montezuma, 3:524
To the Happy Few: Selected Letters of Stendhal, 2:511
To the Islands, 2:964
To the Land of the Cattails, 2:14
To the Lighthouse, 1:413, 1:568, 1:569
To the Maginot Line, 3:373
To the Memory of Childhood, 2:712
To the Reformation, 4:676
To the Slaughterhouse, 2:481
To the Webster-Ashburton Treaty, 3:608
To Those Who Need It Most, Hospice Means Hope, 5:379
Tottel's Miscellany, 1:163, 1:165, 1:201

Touching Peace: Practicing the Art of Mindful Living, 4:562
Touch Magic, 1:1196
Touch of Evil, 1:1178
A Touch of the Poet, 1:1106
Touchpoints, 5:321
Touchstone, 1:787
The Touchstones of Matthew Arnold, 1:328
Tough Guys Don't Dance, 1:1011, 1:1012
Tough Guy Writers of the Thirties, 1:918
Toujours Provence, 3:900
To Urania, 2:704
Tourism: Principles, Practices and Philosophies, 3:890
Tourism: The International Business, 3:890
Tourism Marketing and Management Handbook, 3:891
Tourism Planning, 3:890
The Tourist: A New Theory of the Leisure Class, 3:893
The Tourist: Travel in Twentieth Century North America, 3:892
The Tourist Business, 3:890
Tourist Development, 3:890
Tourist in Africa, 1:562
Tourists, Travellers, and Pilgrims, 3:892
The Tourist System, 3:890
Tourmaline: A Novel, 2:964
Tour of Duty, 1:828
A Tour on the Prairies, 1:679, 1:680
A Tour through the Whole Island of Great Britain, 1:239
Toward a Black Feminist Criticism, 1:927
Toward a Feminist Epistemology, 4:391
Toward a Freudian Theory of Literature, 2:498
Toward a Functioning Federalism, 3:148
Toward a General Theory of Action, 3:237
Toward a History of Needs, 5:136, 5:137
Toward a History of Ukrainian Literature, 2:838
Toward a Male Spirituality, 4:743
Toward a More Natural Science: Biology and Human Affairs, 5:121
Toward a New Earth: Apocalypse in the American Novel, 1:919

Toward a New Economics, 3:71
Toward a New Psychology of Women, 5:414
Toward a Perfected State, 4:340
Toward a Psychology of Being, 5:461
Toward a Rational Society, 4:404
Toward a Rational Society: Student Protest, Science, and Politics, 5:89
Toward a Recognition of Androgyny, 1:925
Toward a Sociology of the Novel, 2:447
Toward a Structural Theory of Action, 3:215
Toward a Theory of Growth, 3:90
Toward Defining the African Aesthetic, 2:109
Toward Global Equilibrium: Collected Papers, 5:167, 5:168
Toward Reunion in Philosophy, 4:268
Toward Robert Frost: The Reader and the Poet, 1:842
Towards a Better Life: Being a Series of Epistles, or Declamations, 1:956
Towards a Cosmic Music, 3:720
Towards a Critique of Foucault, 5:88
Towards a Literature of Knowledge, 1:873
Toward Samson Agonistes: The Growth of Milton's Mind, 1:193
Towards an African Literature, 2:158
Towards a New American Poetics, Essays and Interviews, 1:913
Towards a New Architecture, 3:778
Towards a New Israel: The Jewish State and the Arab Question, 4:643
Towards a New Theatre: The Lectures of Robert Edmond Jones, 1:1073
Towards a People's Literature, 2:329
Towards a World Theology: Faith and the Comparative History of Religion, 4:423

Towards Holistic Agriculture: A Scientific Approach, 5:266

Towards the African Revolution, 2:121

Towards the Decolonization of African Literature, 2:107

Towards the Discovery of Canada: Selected Essays, 3:618

Towards the Last Spike, 2:923

Towards the Mountain, 2:167

Towards the Stars, 2:653

Towards Understanding Islam, 4:575

Toward the Final Solution: A History of European Racism, 3:350

Toward the Future, 4:336

Toward the Poems of Mallarmé, 2:487

Toward the Radical Center: A Karel Čapek Reader, 2:790

Toward the Splendid City: Nobel Lecture, 2:875

Toward the Understanding of Shelley, 1:304

Toward Women in Love: The Emergence of a Lawrentian Aesthetic, 1:510

To Weave and Sing, 4:465

The Tower, 2:592

The Tower and the Bridge: The New Art of Structural Engineering, 5:191

Tower at the Edge of the World, 2:656

The Tower of Glass, 2:893

The Town, 1:835

Town and Country in Brazil, 3:32

The Town and the City, 1:998

The Town beyond the Wall, 1:1065

A Town Called Hibiscus, 2:249

Towneley Plays, 1:158

The Town Labourer, 1760–1832: The New Civilization, 3:404

A Town Like Alice, 2:962, 2:962

The Townshends of Raynham, 3:362

Toxicology and Biological Monitoring of Metals in Humans, 5:350

Toxics A to Z: A Guide to Everyday Pollution Hazards, 5:351, 5:736

Toynbee's Study of History, 3:294

Toys and Reasons: Stages in the Ritualization of Experience, 3:182

Toys in the Attic, 1:1092, 1:1093

Trace Element Geochemistry in Health and Disease, 5:628

Trace Elements, Hair Analysis, and Nutrition, 5:347

The Tracery Gleam: Selected Prose, 1:1009

Traces on the Rhodian Shore, 5:114

Trachiniae, 2:367

Tracing Back the Radiance: Chinul's Korean Way of Zen, 4:537

Tracing Literary Theory, 1:1134

Track of the Grizzly, 5:820

Tractates, De consolatione philosophiae, 4:112

Tractatus Logico-Philosophicus: German Text with English Translation, 4:344

Tractatus Theologico-Politicus, 4:189

Tract for the Times, 4:782

A Tract on Monetary Reform, 3:86

Tracts and Pamphlets, 1:257

Tracts and Treatises of the Reformed Faith, 4:761

Tracts on Hydraulics, 5:255

Trade, Plunder and Settlement, 3:358

Trade and Civilization in the Indian Ocean, 3:483

Trade and Conflict in Angola, 3:423

Trade and Diplomacy on the China Coast, 3:498

Trade and Economic Structure, Models and Methods, 3:58

Trade and Market in the Early Empires, 3:16

Trade Book Marketing, 1:46

Tradeoffs: Imperatives of Choice in a High-Tech World, 5:159, 5:183, 5:215

Trading with the Enemy: A Yankee Travels through Castro's Cuba, 3:896

Tradition, 3:239

Tradition, Innovation, Conflict, 4:643

Tradition, Trade and Transformation: Southeast Asian Textiles, 3:767

Traditional Agriculture in Southeast Asia: A Human Ecology Perspective, 3:489

Traditional American Folk Songs from the Anne and Frank Warner Collection, 3:853

Traditional Chinese Poetry and Poetics: Omen of the World, 2:190

Traditional Chinese Stories: Themes and Variations, 2:193

Traditional Islam in the Modern World, 3:444, 4:375

Traditional Japanese Poetry, 2:274

Traditional Korean Verse since the 1990s, 2:299

Traditional Moral Values in the Age of Technology, 5:130

Traditional Papermaking and Paper Cult Figures of Mexico, 1:5

The Traditional Tunes of the Child Ballads, 1:149

Tradition and Change (Kuhn), 5:53

Tradition and Change (Waxman), 4:655

Tradition and Change in Contemporary Malay-Indonesian Poetry, 2:317

Tradition and Crisis: Jewish Society at the End of the Middle Ages, 4:624

Tradition and Design in the Iliad, 2:361

Tradition and Interpretation, 4:816

Tradition and Interpretation in Matthew, 4:829

Tradition and Originality in Roman Poetry, 2:382

Tradition and Transition, 4:733

Tradition in an Age of Reform, 4:665

Tradition in Science, 5:693

The Tradition of Freedom in Croatian Literature, 2:785

The Tradition of Scottish Philosophy, 4:32

A Tradition of Subversion, 1:799, 1:913

Traditions of American Education, 3:254

The Traditions of Fine Book-
binding in the Twentieth
Century, 1:22
Traditions of Meditation in
Chinese Buddhism, 4:529
The Tragedies of George
Chapman, 1:175
Tragedy, 1:212
Tragedy and Civilization: An
Interpretation of Sopho-
cles, 2:368
Tragedy in the Victorian
Novel, 1:319
The Tragedy of American Di-
plomacy, 1900–1950,
3:547, 3:601
The Tragedy of Cambodian
History: Politics, War, and
Revolution since 1945,
3:490
The Tragedy of Man, 2:802
Tragedy of Paraguay, 3:640
The Tragedy of Pudd'nhead
Wilson, 1:780
The Tragedy of Sohrab and
Rostam, 2:89
The Tragicall History of
Christopher Marlowe,
1:187
Tragic Alphabet: Shake-
speare's Drama of Lan-
guage, 1:212
The Tragical Reign of Seli-
mus, 1:180
The Tragic Comedians,
1:421, 1:494
The Tragic Comedians: A
Study in a Well-Known
Story, 1:379
Tragic Drama in Aeschylus,
Sophocles and Shake-
speare: An Essay, 2:368
The Tragic Drama of Corn-
eille and Racine: An Old
Parallel Revisited, 2:471
Tragic Form in Shakespeare,
1:213
The Tragic Life: Bessie Head
& Literature in Southern
Africa, 2:163
Tragic Muse, 1:765
The Tragic Muse of John
Ford, 1:180
The Tragic Myth: Lorca and
Cante Jondo, 2:539
Tragi-Comedy, 2:548
Tragic Pleasures: Aristotle on
Plot and Emotion, 4:67
The Tragic Pursuit of Being:
Unamuno and Sartre,
2:552
Tragic Satire of John Web-
ster, 1:200

The Tragic Sense of Life,
2:551
Tragic Wisdom and Beyond,
4:305
Tragic Writers, 2:81
Trailerpark, 1:940
A Trail of Memories: The
Quotations of Louis
L'Amour, 1:1216
Trails: Toward a New West-
ern History, 3:532
Trail Town, 1:1215
Training in Christianity,
4:239
The Training of Pauper Chil-
dren, 1:368
The Training of the Zen
Buddhist Monk, 4:558
Train to H, 2:526
The Train to Pakistan, 2:178
The Traité de mécanique
céleste (Celestial Mechan-
ics), 5:698
The Tramp, 1:1160
Tranquillisers: Social, Psy-
chological and Clinical
Perspectives, 5:350
Transactional Analysis and
Family Therapy, 5:418
Transactional Analysis in Psy-
chotherapy, 5:434
The Transatlantic Review,
1:474
Transatlantic Sketches, 1:764
Transcendence and Wittgen-
stein's Tractatus, 4:346
The Transcendence of the
Ego: An Existentialist
Theory of Consciousness,
4:329
Transcendentalists: An An-
thology, 3:587
The Transcendentalists: A
Review of Research and
Criticism, 1:651
Transcendental Meditation,
4:873
Transcendental Wild Oats,
1:1199
Transcending Madness: The
Experience of the Six Bar-
dos, 4:357
Transcultural Health Care,
5:353
Trans Europe Express, 2:500
The Transfer Agreement,
4:642
The Transfer of Power in Af-
rica: Decolonization,
1940–60, 3:417
The Transfiguration of His-
tory at the Center of
Dante's Paradise, 2:418

Transfigured World: Walter
Pater's Aesthetic Histori-
cism, 1:388
Transformation of Judaism
from Philosophy to Reli-
gion, 4:607
The Transformation of Politi-
cal Culture: Massachusetts
Parties, 1790s–1840s, 3:524
The Transformation of Sin,
1:178, 1:200
Transformation of the Ameri-
can Party System, 3:543
The Transformation of the
Jews, 4:634
Transformation of the Lover,
2:63
The Transformation of Theol-
ogy, 1830–1890, 4:740
The Transformation of Vir-
ginia, 1740–1790, 3:520
Transformations, 1:1045
Transformations in American
Medicine, 5:54, 5:78
Transformations in Slavery:
A History of Slavery in Af-
rica, 3:418
Transformations of Romanti-
cism in Yeats, Eliot and
Stevens, 1:417
Transformations of the Word:
Spenser, Herbert, Vau-
ghan, 1:200
Transformation through
Menopause, 5:356
The Transformed Cell: Un-
locking the Mysteries of
Cancer, 5:373
The Transformed Metamor-
phosis, 1:199
Transforming Modernity:
Popular Culture in Mexi-
co, 3:638
Transforming the Revolution:
Social Movement and the
World System, 3:243
Transforming Traditional
Agriculture, 3:48
Transforming Traditions in
American Biology, 5:807
Transition: Essays on Con-
temporary Literature,
1:522
Transition in Spain from
Franco to Democracy,
3:386
Transitions: The Family and
the Life Course in Histori-
cal Perspectives, 3:173
The Transit of Venus, 2:953
The Transits of Venus: A
Study of Eighteenth-Cen-
tury Science, 5:45

A Transit to Narcissus: A Facsimile of the Original Typescript, 1:1012

Translated Documents of Greece and Rome, 3:299

Translating Literature, 2:990

Translating the Classics of Judaism: In Theory and in Practice, 4:612

Translation, An Elizabethan Art, 2:990

Translation and Translators, 1:47

Translation Determined, 4:412

A Translation of the Orpheus of Angelo Politian and the Aminta of Torquato Tasso, 2:436

A Translation of the Tenth-Century Anthology of Ts'u Lyrics, the Hua Chien Chi, 2:192

Translations, 1:479, 1:560

Translations of Eastern Poetry and Prose, 2:57

The Translations of Ezra Pound, 1:871

Translation Studies, 2:990

Transmemberment of Song: Hart Crane's Anatomies of Rhetoric and Desire, 1:823

Transparent Designs, 1:232, 1:257

The Transparent Lyric, 1:800

The Transparent Man, 1:987

Transparent Things, 2:741

The Transplanted Family, 3:557

Transplanting Religious Traditions: Asian Indians in America, 4:508

The Transportation Revolution, 1815–1860, 3:55

The Transport of Love, 2:173

Transuranium Elements: A Half Century, 5:728

Transuranium Elements: Products of Modern Alchemy, 5:755

Transvestism, 5:429

Transylvania, 2:802

Trappings of Power: Ballistic Missiles in the Third World, 5:184

Traps, 1:458

The Trauma of Birth, 5:465, 5:466

The Travail of Nature, 4:746, 5:116

The Travel Dictionary, 3:890

A Traveler at Forty, 1:829

A Traveler Disguised, 2:41

A Traveler from Altruria, 1:758

Travelers: The American Tourist from Stage Coach to Space Shuttle, 3:897

Travelers and Travel Liars, 1600–1800, 3:891

A Traveler's Guide to El Dorado and the Inca Empire, 3:896

Travelers of a Hundred Ages, 2:272

The Traveler's Reading Guide: Ready-made Reading Lists for the Armchair Traveler, 3:889, 3:893

A Traveler's Tale: Memories of India, 3:902

Travel for the Disabled, 3:890

A Travel Guide for the Disabled: Western Europe, 3:901

Travel in Asia: A Guide to Information Sources, 3:902

The Travel Industry, 3:890

Travel Industry World Yearbook: The Big Picture, 3:891

Traveling Companions, 2:724

The Traveling Entertainer and Other Stories, 2:956

The Travel Journal of Si Tenggang II, 2:325

The Traveller & His Road, 2:80

A Traveller in Little Things, 1:365

A Traveller in Rome, 3:932

A Traveller in Southern Italy, 3:932

The Traveller of the East, 2:166

Traveller's Dictionary of Quotations, 3:894

Traveller's Health Guide, 3:894

A Traveller's History of Scotland, 3:898

Travelling Companions, 1:764

Travelling North, 2:967, 2:968

Travel Literature and the Evolution of the Novel, 3:891

Travels, 2:13, 2:884

The Travels and Adventures of Benjamin the Third, 2:41

Travel Sense: A Guide for Business and Professional Women, 3:893

Travels in Alaska, 3:896, 5:836

Travels in Arabia Deserta, 3:902

Travels in Nepal: The Sequestered Kingdom, 3:905

Travels in Nihilon, 1:547

Travels in North America, in the Years 1841–42, with Geological Observations on the United States, Canada, and Nova Scotia, 5:645

Travels in the Interior Districts of Africa, 3:932

Travels into the Poor Man's Country: The Work of Henry Mayhew, 1:378

Travels in West Africa: Congo Français, Corsico and Cameroons, 3:909

Travel Sketches, 2:588

Travels of Charlie, 3:893

Travels of Lao Can, 2:211

The Travels of Lao Ts'an, 2:210, 2:211, 2:211, 2:231

The Travels of Marco Polo, 3:934

Travels through France and Italy, 1:256

Travels to Hallowed Ground, 3:530

Travels with a Donkey, 1:395

Travels with Charley, 1:884, 1:885

Travels with Charley in Search of America, 3:910

Travels with Cole Porter, 3:709

Travels with My Aunt, 1:489

Travesties, 1:554

Travesty, 1:985

Treason against God: A History of the Offense of Blasphemy, 1:57

Treasure Island, 1:395, 1:396, 1:589

The Treasurer's Report: And Other Aspects of Community Singing, 1:815

Treasures against Time: Paramahansa Yogananda with Doctor and Mrs. Lewis, 4:557

The Treasures of Darkness: A History of Mesopotamian Religion, 4:441, 4:545

A Treasury of African Folklore, 3:866

Treasury of Alphabets and Lettering, 1:20

Treasury of American Folklore, 3:854

Treasury of American Pen-and-Ink Illustrators, 1:1881 to 1938, 1:28

The Treasury of American Poetry, 1:720

Treasury of American Short Stories, 1:806, 1:922

A Treasury of Chinese Literature, 2:192

A Treasury of Irish Folklore, 1:461

A Treasury of Jamaican Poetry, 2:931

A Treasury of Jewish Folklore, 2:33

A Treasury of Jewish Folksong, 3:852

A Treasury of Jewish Humor, 2:33

A Treasury of Nebraska Pioneer Folklore, 3:862

Treasury of New England Folklore, 3:858

A Treasury of Sephardic Laws and Customs, 4:601

A Treasury of the Great Children's Book Illustrators, 1:29

Treasury of Well-Turned Verse, 2:172

A Treasury of Yiddish Poetry, 2:33

A Treasury of Yiddish Stories, 2:33

Treating Type A Behavior—and Your Heart, 5:401

A Treatise, Concerning the Causes of the Magnificence and Greatness of Cities, 4:124

Treatise against Hermogenes, 4:713

A Treatise Concerning Eternal and Immutable Morality, 4:168

A Treatise Concerning Religious Affections, 1:637

A Treatise Concerning the Principles of Human Knowledge, 4:191

A Treatise of Annuities on Lives, 5:528

Treatise of Human Nature, 3:106, 4:199, 4:201, 4:739

Treatise of Man, 4:169

A Treatise on Basic Philosophy, 5:70, 5:83

A Treatise on Free Will, 4:168

Treatise on God as First Principle, 4:114

A Treatise on Money, 3:86, 3:87

Treatise on Nature and Grace, 4:181, 4:182

A Treatise on Probability, 3:86

Treatise on Resurrection, 4:668

Treatise on Sensations, 4:195

Treatise on Separate Substances, 4:118

A Treatise on Systems, 4:195

Treatise on the Calculus of Finite Differences, 5:499

A Treatise on the Family, 3:56, 3:70, 3:206

Treatise on the Immortality of the Soul, 4:153

A Treatise on the Motion of Vortex Rings, 5:716

Treatises, 4:708

Treatises II: The Steps of Humility and Pride, on Loving God, 4:111

Treatises on Marriage and Remarriage, 4:713

Treatises on Penance, 4:714

Treatment of the Obsessive Personality, 5:428

Treat Me Right: Essays in Medical Law and Ethics, 5:121

Treblinka, 3:351

The Tree (Fowles), 1:478

Tree (José), 2:331

Tree and Leaf, 1:559, 1:579

The Tree Climber, 2:63, 2:64

The Tree of Knowledge, 2:530

A Tree of Life: Diversity, Flexibility, and Creativity in Jewish Law, 4:627

The Tree of Man, 2:965, 2:966

A Tree of Night and Other Short Stories, 1:959

Tree of Song, 2:539

Tree on Fire, 1:547

Trees of Life: Essays in Philosophy of Biology, 5:67

Trees of Life: Saving Tropical Forests and Their Biological Wealth, 5:823

Trees on the Cliff, 2:303

Trees on the Mountain: An Anthology of New Chinese Writing, 2:236

A Tree Within, 2:878

Trelawney of the "Wells," 1:388

The Tremendum: A Theological Interpretation of the Holocaust, 4:648

Tremordyn Cliff, 1:408

Tremor of Intent, 1:453, 1:454

The Trench, 2:69

Trends and Movements in Modern Arabic Poetry, 2:55, 2:61

Trends in Textbook Markets 1984, 1:49

The Trial, 1:949, 2:595, 2:596

The Trial and Death of Socrates, 4:78

Trial and Error: The Autobiography of Chaim Weizmann, 3:351

The Trial Begins, 2:757

Trial by Fire: A People's History of the Civil War and Reconstruction, 3:530

Trial by Jury, 1:357

Trial by Medicine: The Insanity Defense in Victorian England, 3:365

The Trial of Christopher Okigbo, 2:153

The Trial of Curiosity, 1:767, 1:769

The Trial of Dedan Kimathi, 2:154

Trial of Faith: Religion and Politics in Tocqueville's Thought, 3:165

The Trial of Rizal, 2:333

The Trials and Tribulations of Little Red Riding Hood, 3:870

Trials of Jawaharlal Nehru, 3:500

The Trials of Life; Vol. 1, 5:817

Trials of the Human Heart, 1:643

Tribal Scars and Other Stories, 2:145

Tribes, Government, and History of Yemen, 3:454

Tribes on the Hill: The United States Congress—Rituals and Realities, 3:23

The Tribune's Visitation, 1:502

Tribute to Freud: With Unpublished Letters by Freud to the Author, 1:826

Tribute to Freud: Writing on the Wall, 1:827

Tribute to Gyula Illyés: Poems, 2:799

A Tribute to Menno Simons, 4:780

Tribute to Sándor Petöfi on the 150th Anniversary of His Birth, 2:803

A Triche-Coeur, 2:151

The Trickster: A Study in American Indian Mythology, 1:632
The Trickster of Seville, 2:551
Trickster of Seville and the Stone Guest, 2:551
A Trick to Catch the Old One, 1:189, 1:190
The Triggering Town: Lectures and Essays on Poetry and Writing, 1:990
Trilby, 1:352
Trilce, 2:886
Trillion Year Spree, 1:611, 1:612
Trilogy, 1:826
Trilogy of Treason: An Intertextual Study of Juan Goytisolo, 2:541
The Trimmed Lamp, 1:756
The Trinitarian Controversy, 4:686
Trinitas: A Theological Encyclopedia of the Holy Trinity, 4:675
Trinity, Incarnation, and Atonement, 4:886
Trinity, Incarnation and Redemption, 4:108
Trinity and Process, 4:289
Tripitaka, 2:315
The Triple Thinkers and the Wound and the Bow, 1:902
Tripmaster Monkey: His Fake Book, 1:1000
A Trip to Parnassus; or the Judgement of Apollo, 1:643
Triptych, 2:509
The Triptych and the Cross, 1:354
Tristan, 2:512, 2:562, 2:581, 2:582
Tristana (Buñuel), 3:832
Tristana (Peréz Galdós), 2:547
Tristan and Isolde, 2:512, 2:581
Tristan and Isolt: A Study of the Sources of the Romance, 2:512
Tristessa, 1:998
Tristes Tropiques, 3:34
Tristia, 2:390
Tristram, 1:876
Tristram of Lyonesse, 1:398
Tristram Shandy, 1:225, 1:247, 1:258, 2:471
Tristram Shandy's World: Sterne's Philosophical Rhetoric, 1:259

The Triumph of Death, 2:415
Triumph of Evolution, 5:48
The Triumph of Life, 1:302
The Triumph of the Darwinian Method, 5:794
The Triumph of the Egg, 1:811
The Triumph of the Goddess, 4:503
Triumph of the Image, 3:804
The Triumph of the Novel: Dickens, Dostoevsky, Faulkner, 1:837
The Triumph of Wit: Molière and Restoration Comedy, 2:490
Triumph over Evil: Purity and Pollution in Zoroastrianism, 4:517
Triumph over Silence: Women in Protestant History, 4:749
Triumphs and Tragedy: A History of the Mexican People, 3:639
Triumph without Victory, 3:540
Troades, 2:394
Troilus and Cressida (Shakespeare), 1:205, 1:206
Troilus and Criseyde (Chaucer), 1:149, 1:150, 1:152, 2:394
The Trojan War Will Not Take Place, 1:480
The Trojan Women, 2:355, 2:356
The Troll Garden, 1:821
Trollope: A Biography, 1:407
Trollope: The Critical Heritage, 1:407
Trollope and Comic Pleasure, 1:407
Trollope Centenary Essays, 1:407
The Trollope Critics, 1:407
The Trollopes: The Chronicle of a Writing Family, 1:407
Trollope's Palliser Novels: Theme and Pattern, 1:407
The Trollope Student, 1:407
Trolls and People, 2:676
Tropes, Parables, Performatives: Essays on Twentieth-Century Literature, 1:794
Tropica: Color Cyclopedia of Exotic Plants and Trees, 5:761
Tropical Baroque: Four Manileño Theatricals, 2:331
Tropical Gothic, 2:331
Tropical Madness: Four Plays, 2:822

Tropical Nature, 5:764
Tropical Night Falling, 2:881
Tropic of Baseball: Baseball in the Dominican Republic, 3:636
Tropic of Cancer, 1:861, 1:862
Tropic of Capricorn, 1:862
Tropics of Discourse, 1:1154
Tropisms, 2:505, 2:506
Trotsky: A Bibliography, 3:295
Trotsky, Stalin and Socialism, 3:292
Trotskyism, 3:295
The Trotter-nama, 2:178
The Troubled Crusade: American Education, 1945–1980, 3:252, 3:553
The Troubled Dream of Life: Living with Mortality, 5:84
Troubled Eden: An Anatomy of British Jewry, 4:635
A Troubled Feast: American Society since 1945, 3:585
The Troubled People Book: A Comprehensive Guide to Getting Help, 5:423
Troubled Sleep, 2:506
The Troublemaker, 2:731
Troubleshooting Communications Facilities, 5:305
The Trouble with Nigeria, 2:128
Truants from Life: The Rehabilitation of Emotionally Disturbed Children, 5:435
The Trucial States, 3:451
Trudeau and Our Times, 3:616
The True Adventures of John Steinbeck, Writer: A Biography, 1:885
The True and Only Heaven: Progress and Its Critics, 3:560
True Christian Religion, 4:852, 4:880
True Humanism, 4:307
The True Intellectual System of the Universe, 4:168
The True Interpreter, 2:990
The True Patriot, 1:244, 1:245
A Truer Liberty: Simone Weil and Marxism, 2:516
True Stories from History and Biography, 1:676
True to Life Adventure Stories, 1:1188
True West, 1:1111
Truffaut by Truffaut, 3:843

The Truly Disadvantaged,
3:66, 3:244
Truman, 3:539
Truman Capote, 1:959
Truman Capote: A Reference
Guide, 1:959
Truman's Crises: A Political
Biography of Harry S Tru-
man, 3:538
Trumpeter of God: A Biogra-
phy of John Knox, 4:736,
4:774
Trumpet in the Land, 1:1089
The Trumpet-Major, 1:361
The Trumpet of the Swan,
1:897, 1:898
Trust, 1:1027
Trust: Making and Breaking
Cooperative Relations,
3:208
Trust to Good Verses: Her-
rick Tercentenary Essays,
1:182
Truth, Freedom, and Evil:
Three Philosophical Dia-
logues, 4:108
Truth, Hope, and Power,
4:410
Truth, Knowledge, and Mo-
dality: Philosophical Pa-
pers, 4:338
Truth, Love, and Immortali-
ty: An Introduction to
McTaggart's Philosophy,
4:304
The Truth about AIDS: Evo-
lution of an Epidemic,
5:387
The Truth about a Publisher,
1:45
The Truth about Chernobyl,
5:287
The Truth about Publishing,
1:50
The Truth about STD, 5:389
Truth and Actuality, 4:555
Truth and Existence, 4:329
Truth and Interpretation,
4:283
Truth and Justice, 2:796
Truth and Method, 4:402
Truth and Symbol, 4:300
Truth and Vision in Kathe-
rine Anne Porter's Fiction,
1:870
The Truth in Painting, 4:398
Truth in Religion: The Plu-
rality of Religions and the
Unity of Truth, 4:271
The Truth of Poetry, 2:986
Truth of the Gospel: An Ex-
position of Galatians,
4:821

Truth Tales: Contemporary
Stories by Women Writers
of India, 2:177
Truth to Life: The Art of Bi-
ography in the Nineteenth
Century, 1:87
Trying Conclusions: New and
Selected Poems, 1:1021
Ts'ao Yin and the K'ang-Hsi
Emperor, Bondservant and
Master, 3:503
Ts'ao Yü, 2:266
The Tsardom of Moscow,
1547–1682, 3:413
Tsardom of Muscovy, 3:395
T. S. Eliot: A Bibliography,
1:473
T. S. Eliot: A Bibliography of
Secondary Works, 1:473
T. S. Eliot: A Life, 1:472
T. S. Eliot: A Study in Char-
acter and Style, 1:473
T. S. Eliot: A Voice Descant-
ing: Centenary Essays,
1:472
T. S. Eliot: Essays from the
Southern Review, 1:473
T. S. Eliot: The Poems, 1:473
T. S. Eliot and Indic Tradi-
tions: A Study in Poetry
and Belief, 1:473
T. S. Eliot and Prejudice,
1:473
T. S. Eliot's Drama: A Re-
search and Production
Sourcebook, 1:473
T. S. Eliot's Dramatic Theory
and Practice, 1:473
Tsewa's Gift: Magic and
Meaning in an Amazonian
Society, 4:465
T. S. Kuhn and Social Sci-
ence, 4:406, 5:53
Tsotsi, 2:161
Tube of Plenty: The Evolu-
tion of American Televi-
sion, 3:551, 3:811
The Tudor Age, 3:359
The Tudor Constitution: Doc-
uments and Commentary,
3:402
Tudor Drama and Politics: A
Critical Approach to Topi-
cal Meaning, 1:169
Tudor Dynastic Problems,
1462–1571, 3:359
Tudor England, 3:358
The Tudor Facsimile Texts
Series, 1:171
The Tudor Regime, 3:359
The Tudor Revolution in
Government, 3:402

Tudor Rule and Revolution,
3:358
Tudor School Boy Life,
4:156
Tu Fu, 2:225
Tula: The Toltec Capital of
Ancient Mexico, 4:457
Tula of the Toltecs: Excava-
tions and Survey, 4:457
Tumultuous Years: The Presi-
dency of Harry S Truman,
1949–1953, 3:537
T'ung Shu, 4:531
Tungsten: A Novel, 2:886
Tunhuang Popular Narra-
tives, 2:190
The Tunnel, 2:883
Tunneling Spectroscopy,
5:672
Tunnels, 5:246
Tup-i Elastik, 2:87
Turbines, 2:837
Turbulence: A Novel, 2:242
Turbulence in World Poli-
tics: A Theory of Change
and Continuity, 3:145
Turbulent Currents, 2:259
The Turbulent Era: Riot and
Disorder in Jacksonian
America, 3:523
Turgenev: A Reading of His
Fiction, 2:770
Turgenev: His Life and
Times, 2:770
Turgenev's Russia: From
Notes of a Hunter to Fa-
thers and Sons, 2:770
The Turing Language: For-
mal and Informal Defini-
tions, 5:582
Turing's Man: Western Cul-
ture in the Computer Age,
5:572
Turing's Man, Turing's Wom-
an, or Turing's Person?
5:205
Turkey: A Modern History,
3:452
Turkey, the Straits, and U.S.
Foreign Policy, 3:453
Turkey Faces West, 2:97
The Turkey of Ataturk: So-
cial Process in the Turkish
Reformation, 3:453
Turkish Delight, 2:633
Turkish-English Dictionary,
1:103
Turkish National and West-
ern Civilization, 4:373
Turkish Reflections: A Biog-
raphy of a Place, 3:453,
3:905

Turkish Stories for Four Decades, 2:100

Turkish Transformation: A Study in Social and Religious Development, 4:577

Turn Again Tiger, 2:942

Turner, 3:794

Turner: Paintings, Watercolours, Prints and Drawings, 3:794

Turner, Bolton, and Webb, 3:600, 3:643

Turner and Beard: American Historical Writing Reconsidered, 3:514, 3:566

Turner in His Time, 3:794

The Turner Thesis Concerning the Role of the Frontier in American History, 3:600

Turning East: The Promise and Peril of the New Orientalism, 4:857

Turning Japanese: Memoirs of a Sansei, 3:904

Turning Point: A Candidate, a State, and a Nation Come of Age, 3:537

Turning the Pages: An Insider's Story of Simon and Schuster, 1924–1984, 1:44

Turning the Wheel: American Women Creating the New Buddhism, 4:512

A Turn in the South, 2:938, 2:939

Turn Left at Orion, 5:591

Turn Left at the Pub, 3:900

The Turn of the Screw, 1:763

The Turn of the Years, 1:538

Turn Right at the Fountain, 3:900

Turn West, Turn East: Mark Twain and Henry James, 1:765, 1:783

The Turquoise Mask, 1:1238

Tuttle Dictionary of Antiques and Collectible Terms, 3:765

Tuttle Dictionary of Quotations for Speeches, 1:117

Tutu: Voice of the Voiceless, 4:743

Tuva or Bust: Richard Feynman's Last Journey, 3:904

TV, 1:1114

TVA and the Grass Roots: A Study of Politics and Organization, 3:210

TV Genres: A Handbook and Reference Guide, 3:812

Twain's Heroes, Twain's Worlds, 1:784

Twelfth Night, 1:205, 1:206

Twelve African Writers, 2:110

Twelve American Plays, 1920–1960, 1:1076

Twelve American Poets, 1:720

The Twelve Caesars, 3:320

Twelve Centuries of Bookbindings 400–1600, 1:25

The Twelve Chairs, 2:729

Twelve Contemporary Economists, 3:70, 3:83, 3:91, 3:102

Twelve Great Western Philosophers, 4:18

Twelve Little Housemates, 5:796

Twelve Men, 1:830

Twelve Million Black Voices, 1:905, 1:906

Twelve Modern Indian Poets, 2:176

The Twelve-Note Music of Anton Webern: Old Forms in a New Language, 3:729

The Twelve Pound Look, 1:329

The Twelve Seasons, 5:834

Twelve Therapists: How They Live and Actualize Themselves, 5:421

Twelve Thousand Words, 1:91

Twelve to Sixteen: Early Adolescence, 5:416

The Twelve Words of the Gypsy, 2:375

Twelve Years Away from Constantinople, 2:79

The Twenties: American Writing in the Postwar Decade, 1:804, 1:794

The Twenties: From Notebooks and Diaries of the Period, 1:902

The Twentieth Century, 1:129, 1:414

The Twentieth Century: A Brief Global History, 3:274

Twentieth-Century American Dramatists, 1:1074

Twentieth-Century American-Jewish Fiction Writers, 1:920

Twentieth-Century American Literary Naturalism: An Interpretation, 1:919

Twentieth-Century American Literature, 1:134, 1:795

Twentieth Century American Nicknames, 1:88

Twentieth Century Architecture: A Visual History, 3:764

Twentieth-Century Authors, 1:126, 2:3, 2:4

The Twentieth-Century Book, 1:29

The Twentieth-Century Book: Its Illustration and Design, 1:9

Twentieth-Century British Criticism, 1:134

Twentieth-Century British Literature, 1:129

Twentieth-Century China, 3:466

Twentieth-century Chinese Drama: An Anthology, 2:235

Twentieth-century Chinese Poetry: An Anthology, 2:235

Twentieth-Century Culture: Modernism to Deconstruction, 2:986

Twentieth Century Czechoslovakia: The Meaning of Its History, 3:389

Twentieth-Century Dance in Britain, 3:732, 3:734

Twentieth-Century Encyclopedia of Religious Knowledge, 4:717

Twentieth-Century English Literature, 1:414

Twentieth-Century French Drama, 2:448

Twentieth-Century French Thought: From Bergson to Levi-Strauss, 4:28, 4:263

Twentieth-Century Germany: From Bismarck to Brandt, 3:377

Twentieth-Century Indian Interpretations of Bhagavad Gita, 4:509, 4:554, 4:563

Twentieth Century Interpretations of All the Kings Men, 1:893

Twentieth-Century Interpretations of Poe's Tales, 1:693

Twentieth-Century Iran, 3:447

Twentieth-Century Italian Poetry: A Bilingual Anthology, 2:403

Twentieth-Century Limited: Industrial Design in America, 1925–1939, 5:193

Twentieth-Century Literary Criticism: A Reader, 1:415

Twentieth-Century Literary
Criticism Series, 1:135
Twentieth-Century Music,
3:665
Twentieth-Century Music: A
History of Musical Style in
Modern Europe and Amer-
ica, 3:662, 3:665
Twentieth-Century Music: An
Introduction, 3:663, 3:665
Twentieth-Century Music:
The Sense behind the
Sound, 3:662
Twentieth-Century Philoso-
phy: The Analytic Tradi-
tion, 4:268
Twentieth Century Pleasures,
1:984
Twentieth-Century Popular
Culture in Museums and
Libraries, 3:874
Twentieth-Century Religious
Thought, 4:266, 4:745
Twentieth-Century Russian
Drama from Gorky to the
Present, 2:690
Twentieth-Century Russian
Literary Criticism, 2:686
Twentieth Century Russian
Poetry, 2:692
The Twentieth-Century Scien-
tists, 5:791, 5:813
Twenty Best Plays of the
Modern American Theatre,
1:1077
Twenty-eight Science Fiction
Stories, 1:564
Twenty-five Best Plays of the
Modern American Theatre:
Early Series, 1:1077
Twenty-five Engineers and
Inventors, 5:232
Twenty-five T'ang Poets: In-
dex to English Transla-
tions, 2:189
Twenty-five Years of Des-
cartes Scholarship,
1960–1984, 4:170
Twenty Letters to a Friend:
A Memoir, 3:292
Twenty Love Poems and a
Song of Despair, 2:875
Twenty Modern British Play-
wrights: A Bibliography,
1:1956 to 1976, 1:427
Twenty-one Stories, 1:489
Twenty Plays of the No
Theatre, 2:274
Twenty Poems of Love and a
Song of Despair, 2:873
Twenty Questions: An Intro-
duction to Philosophy,
4:20

Twenty-six and One: And
Other Stories, 2:725
The 26 Letters, 1:18
Twenty Thousand Leagues
under the Sea or David
Copperfield, 1:815
Twenty Thousand Quips and
Quotes, 3:871
Twenty Thousand Words,
1:95
Twenty Years at Hull-House,
1:730, 1:731
Twice around the Black
Church, 1:460
Twice as Less, 3:257
Twice Blessed, 2:328, 2:329
The Twice-born Fiction,
2:178
Twilight, 1:1065
Twilight and Other Stories,
2:19
Twilight in Delhi, 2:176
Twilight in Djakarta, 2:320
Twilight of Authority, 3:236
The Twilight of Sovereignty,
5:127
The Twilight of the Gods:
The Music of the Beatles,
3:665
Twilight of the Idols, 4:245
Twilight of the Pepper Em-
pire, 3:484
Twilight of the Tenderfoot: A
Western Memoir, 1:932
The Twilight Years, 2:285
The Twilight Years of Lady
Osler: Letters of a Doc-
tor's Wife, 5:364
Twin of Ice, 1:1221
The Twisted Road to
Auschwitz:, 3:350
Two: A Phallic Novel, 2:429
The Two Admirals: A Tale,
1:664
Two against Cape Horn,
3:910
Two Ages: The Age of Revo-
lution and the Present
Age, 4:239
Two Autobiographical Plays:
The True History of
Squire Jonathan, 1:433
Two Bad Ants, 1:1208
Two-Bit Culture: The Paper-
backing of America, 1:38
Two Bites at a Cherry, with
Other Tales, 1:732
Two Brothers, 2:437
Two Centuries of American
Medicine, 1776–1976,
3:551
Two Centuries of Philosophy,
4:34

Two Cheers for Democracy,
1:476
Two Chinese Poets: Vignettes
of Han Life and Thought,
2:195
Two-colored Brocade: The
Imagery of Persian Poetry,
2:83
Two Concepts of Rules,
4:316
The Two Cultures: And a
Second Look, 5:49, 5:158
The Two Cultures and the
Scientific Revolution,
1:550
The Two Deaths of Quincas
Wateryell: A Tall Tale,
2:892
Two Decades of Hamady and
the Perishable Press Limit-
ed, 1:41
Two-Edg'd Weapons, 1:243
Two Essays on Entropy,
4:278
The Two Faces of Ionesco,
2:484
Two Filipino Women, 2:332
The Two Forgers, 1:35
Two French Moralists, 2:485
The Two Gentlemen of Vero-
na, 1:205, 1:206
Two Hundred Decorative
Title Pages, 1:18
Two Hundred Years of
American Communes,
4:844
Two Hundred Years of Flight
in America, 5:37
Two Hundred Years of Geol-
ogy in America, 5:625
Two Hundred Years of Great
American Short Stories,
1:806, 1:921
Two Hundred Years of The-
ology: Report of a Person-
al Journey, 4:718
Two Interviews with Rossana
Dalmonte and Balint An-
dras Varga, 3:680
Two Jamaicas: The Role of
Ideas in a Tropical Colo-
ny, 1830–1865, 3:426
Two Japanese Novelists: So-
seki and Toson, 2:282
Two Koreas in Development,
3:481
Two Lives: The Story of
Wesley Clair Mitchell and
Myself, 3:98
Two Loves and a Life, 1:399
The Two Mas, 2:251

Two Men and Their Contributions in Two Countries, 5:255
The Two Metropolises Rhapsody, 2:195
Two Minutes of Silence: Selected Short Stories, 2:648
Two Moral Essays: Human Personality and On Human Obligations, 2:516
Two New Sciences, 4:142, 4:171
The Two Noble Kinsmen, 1:204
Two Novels of Mexico: The Flies and The Bosses, 2:854
The Two-Ocean War, 3:589
Two Old Testament Theologies, 4:834, 4:838
Two on a Big Ocean, 3:910
Two on a Tower: A Romance, 1:361
Two Pair of Shoes, 1:590
Two-Part Inventions, 1:989
Two Picaresque Novels, 2:548
Two Plays, 1:1088
Two Plays of Ancient India, 2:173
The Two Revolutions: Antonio Gramsci and the Dilemmas of Marxism, 4:287
Two Roads to Sumter, 3:572, 3:574
Two Romantic Trios: A Sextet of Extraordinary Musicians, 3:717
Two Roses, 1:272
Two Russian Thinkers: An Essay on Berdyaev and Shestov, 4:335
The Two Sources of Morality and Religion, 4:220
Two Studies in the Early Academy, 4:80
Two Studies in the Greek Atomists, 4:74
Two Tales of the Occult, 2:824
Two Thackerays, 1:404
2001: A Space Odyssey, 1:614, 5:563
2061: Odyssey Three, 1:614
2010: Odyssey Two, 1:614
Two Thousand Seasons, 2:130, 2:131
Two Thousand Word Manifesto, 2:795
Two Thousand Years of Textiles, 3:767
The Two Towers, 1:559

Two Tracts on Government, 4:179
Two Trains Running, 1:1120
Two Treatises of Government, 3:158, 3:159, 4:178, 4:179
Two Treatises of Philo of Alexandria, 4:60, 4:670
Two Trips to Gorilla Land and the Cataracts of the Congo, 3:914
Two Types of Faith: The Interpretation of Judaism and Christianity, 4:602, 4:662
Two Views of Freedom in Process and Thought, 4:342
Two Views of Two Ghost Towns, 1:560
Two Wheels and a Taxi: A Slightly Daft Adventure in the Andes, 3:897
Two Women, 2:429, 2:628
Two Women in One, 2:71, 2:120
Two Worlds: The Protestant Culture of Nineteenth Century Ontario, 3:610
Two Worlds and Their Ways, 1:462
Two Writers and the Cultural Revolution: Lao She and Chen Jo-hsi, 2:241, 2:251
Two Years Ago, 1:369
Two Years before the Mast, 1:666, 3:919, 3:920
The Twyborn Affair, 2:965, 2:966
Tycho Brahe, 5:40, 5:600
Tynan Right and Left: Plays, Films, Places, People and Events, 1:426
The Type 1/Type 2 Allergy Relief Program, 5:386
Type and Motif Index of the Folktales of England and North America, 3:849
Typee, 1:685, 1:687
Typee, Omoo, Mardi, 1:687
Typefaces for Books, 1:19
Type for Books: A Designer's Manual, 1:20
Typefounding in America, 1787–1825, 1:19
Type Metals: Their Characteristics and Their Performance, 1:20
The TypEncyclopedia: A User's Guide to Better Typography, 1:19

Types and Problems of Philosophy, 4:22
Types of Christian Theology, 4:743
Types of Economic Theory: From Mercantilism to Institutionalism, 3:97
Types of Religious Experience: Christian and Non-Christian, 4:494
Types of Scenery and Their Influence on Literature, 5:622
The Typewriter and the Men Who Made It, 3:574
Typographia; or, The Printer's Instructor. A Brief Sketch of the Origin, Rise, and Progress of the Typographic Art. . . ., 1:6
The Typographic Book, 1450–1935, 1:9
Typographic Years, 1:7
Typography: Design and Practice, 1:9
Typography and Typesetting, 1:9
Typologia, 1:15
The Tyranny of Kindness, 3:211
The Tyranny of Survival: And Other Pathologies of Civilized Life, 5:84, 5:119
Tyrant and Victim in Dostoevsky, 2:715
The Tyrants, 2:422
Tyrants Destroyed and Other Stories, 2:740
Tz'enah ur'enah, 2:39
T Zero, 2:412
Tzili: The Story of a Life, 2:14

U

Über die Sprache und Weisheit der Indier, 2:610
The Ubiquity of the Finite, 4:295
Ufifune: Love in the Tale of Genji, 2:279
UFO-Abductions—A Dangerous Game, 5:598
The UFO Controversy in America, 4:870
The UFO Experience: A Scientific Inquiry, 5:598
The UFO Literature, 4:870
UFOs: The Public Deceived, 5:598

UFOs—A Scientific Debate, 5:611

The UFO Verdict—Examining the Evidence, 5:598

The Ugaritic Poem of AGHT, 2:54

Ugarit in Retrospect: Fifty Years of Ugarit and Ugaritic, 4:445

Ugetsu Monogatari, 2:280

The Ugly Duckling, 1:577

Ugo Bénzi, Medieval Philosopher and Physician 1376–1439, 4:128

Ugo Betti: An Introduction, 2:409

Ugo Foscolo, 2:421

Ugo Foscolo: Poet of Exile, 2:421

Ukrainian Literature: Studies of the Leading Authors, 2:838

The Ukrainian Poets, 2:838

Ûlhwa, 2:306

Ûlhwa the Shaman, 2:306

Ullmann's Encyclopedia of Industrial Chemistry, 5:725

Ulrich's International Periodicals Directory, 1:53, 1:72, 1:115

The Ultimate Fate of the Universe, 5:595, 5:655

Ultimate Hope without God: The Atheistic Eschatology of Ernst Bloch, 4:277

Ultimately Fiction: Design in Modern American Literary Biography, 1:928

The Ultimate Weapon, 5:111

Ultima Thule, 2:961

Ultralight Airman's Manual, 5:219

Ultramarine, 2:919

Ultrasound: Biological Effects and Potential Hazards, 5:324

Ulysses, 1:413, 1:419, 1:503, 1:504, 1:946, 1:963, 1:977, 1:1020, 1:1022, 1:1034

Ulysses Found, 2:361

Ulysses on the Liffey, 1:974

Ulysses Theme, 2:362

The Ulysses Theme: A Study in the Adaptability of a Traditional Hero, 2:985

Umbertino, 2:439

An Umbrella from Picadilly, 2:794

Um Homem sorri à morte com meia cara, 2:560

The Unadjusted Girl, with Cases and Standpoints for Behavior Analysis, 3:242

The Unanswered Question: Six Talks at Harvard, 3:682

Unanswered Questions: Theological Views of Jewish-Catholic Relations, 4:648

Unassigned Frequencies: American Poetry in Review, 1964–1977, 1:913

Unattainable Earth, 2:818

The Unbearable Lightness of Being, 2:793

The Unbounded Community, 3:172

The Unbounded Frame, 4:844

The Unbound Prometheus, 5:231

The Unbroken Chain: An Anthology of Taiwan Fiction Since 1926, 2:235

Uncertain Glory: Folklore and the American Revolution, 3:868

The Uncertain Promise, 5:213

Uncertainty: The Life and Science of Werner Heisenberg, 5:694

The Uncertainty of Everyday Life, 1915–1945, 3:534

Uncivil Wars: Ireland Today, 3:371

The Unclassed, 1:359

Uncle Remus: His Songs and His Sayings, 1:755

Uncle Remus Stories, 1:755

Uncle Sam Presents: A Memoir of the Federal Theatre, 1935–1939, 1:1072

Uncle's Dream and Other Stories, 2:714

Uncle Shelby's Story of Lafcadio, the Lion Who Shot Back, 1:1206

Uncle Silas, 1:601

Uncle Tom's Cabin, 1:698, 1:1070, 1:1083

Uncle Tom's Cabin and American Culture, 1:699

Uncle Tom's Children: Four Novellas, 1:905

Uncle Valentine and Other Stories, 1:821

Uncle Vanya, 2:707, 2:709

The Uncollected Poems 1936–1959 (Layton), 2:917

Uncollected Prose (Yeats), 1:572

Uncollected Writings from Household Words, 1850–1859, 1:349

Uncollected Writings on Russian Literature, 2:689

Uncomfortable Wars: Toward a New Paradigm of Low-Intensity Conflict, 3:280

The Uncommercial Traveler, 1:349

Uncommon Friends, 3:929

The Uncommon Market, 3:420

Uncommon Sense, 5:707

Uncommon Therapy, 5:441

Uncommon Wisdom, 4:866

Uncommon Women and Others, 1:1114, 1:1115

Uncompensated Health Care: Rights and Responsibilities, 5:333

The Uncompromising Fictions of Cynthia Ozick, 1:1028

The Unconditioned in Human Knowledge: Four Early Essays, 1794–1796, 4:252

The Unconscious, 4:407

The Unconscious in Culture and Elementary Structures Reconsidered, 3:33

Unconscious Structure in Dostoevsky's "The Idiot," 2:715

Unconventional Wisdom, Essays in Honor of John Kenneth Galbraith, 3:79

Under a Colored Cap, 1:527

Under a Glass Bell, 1:864, 1:866

Under an Open Sky: Rethinking America's Western Past, 3:531

Under Briggflatts: A History of Poetry in Great Britain, 1:466

The Underclass, 3:66

Under Cover: An Illustrated History of American Mass Market Paperbacks, 1:38

The Underdogs, 2:843, 2:854

Under Eastern Eyes, 2:688

Under Gemini, 1:621

An Underground Fate, 1:489

Under Milk Wood: A Play for Voices, 1:557

Under Observation, 2:668

The Undersea, 5:631

Undersea Discoveries of Jacques-Yves Cousteau, 5:642

The Undersea World of Jacques Cousteau, 3:918

Under Siege in Kuwait, 3:455

Understanding Albert Camus, 2:464

Understanding American Jewry, 4:641

Understanding American Judaism, 4:651

Understanding and Helping the Schizophrenic, 5:426

Understanding Anorexia Nervosa, 5:395

Understanding Arnold Wesker, 1:565

Understanding Art, 3:757

Understanding Arthritis, 5:398

Understanding Bernard Malamud, 1:1013

Understanding Book-Collecting, 1:34, 1:76

Understanding Carson McCullers, 1:1009, 1:1102

Understanding Chronic Illness, 5:377

Understanding Claude Simon, 2:509

Understanding Computers, 5:577

Understanding Computers: Input-Output, 5:538

Understanding Computers and Cognition, 5:571

Understanding Cults and New Religions, 4:857

Understanding Denise Levertov, 1:1004

Understanding Disturbed Children, 5:416

Understanding DNA: The Molecule and How It Works, 5:784

Understanding Donald Barthelme, 1:944

Understanding Drama, 1:953

Understanding Enzymes, 5:774

Understanding Fiction, 1:953

Understanding Graham Greene, 1:489

Understanding History: A Primer of Historical Method, 3:9

Understanding Holography, 5:235

Understanding Human Nature, 5:431

Understanding Intergovernmental Relations, 3:148

Understanding Isaac Bashevis Singer, 2:48

Understanding Islam, 4:373, 4:573, 4:576

Understanding Jewish Mysticism: A Source Reader, 4:629

Understanding Jewish Prayer, 4:600

Understanding Jewish Theology: Classical Issues and Modern Perspective, 4:646

Understanding John Barth, 1:943

Understanding John Hawkes, 1:986

Understanding Joseph Heller, 1:988

Understanding Katherine Anne Porter, 1:870

Understanding Laughter: The Workings of Wit and Humor, 3:871

Understanding Leukemia, 5:372

Understanding Locke, 4:180

Understanding Male Sexual Health, 5:339

Understanding Maritain: Philosopher and Friend, 4:307

Understanding Media: The Extensions of Man, 3:203, 3:818

Understanding Natural Language, 5:571

Understanding New Media, 3:203

Understanding Non-Western Philosophy: Introductory Readings, 4:349

Understanding Oriental Philosophy, 4:284, 4:523

Understanding Pacemakers, 5:374

Understanding Philip Roth, 1:1041

Understanding Physics: The Electron, Proton, and Neutron, 5:658

Understanding Piaget: An Introduction to Children's Cognitive Development, 3:192

Understanding Poetry, 1:798, 1:953

Understanding Popular Culture, 3:873

Understanding Psychotherapy: A Paradox of Being, 5:420

Understanding Rabbinic Midrash: Texts and Commentary, 4:613

Understanding Randall Jarrell, 1:993

Understanding Reality: A Taoist Alchemical Classic, 4:528

Understanding Relativity: Origin and Impact of a Scientific Revolution, 5:665

Understanding Religion, 4:422

Understanding Scientific Reasoning, 5:63

Understanding Soviet Politics through Literature, 2:685

Understanding Statistical Reasoning, 5:525

Understanding Statistics, 5:523

Understanding Technological Politics, 5:73

Understanding Technology, 5:72, 5:215

Understanding Terence, 2:395

Understanding the Beats, 1:910

Understanding the Central American Crisis, 3:631

Understanding the Chinese Mind: The Philosophical Roots, 4:522

Understanding the Dairy Cow, 5:264

Understanding the Gender Gap, 3:547

Understanding the New Age, 4:866

Understanding the New Testament, 4:816

Understanding the Old Testament, 4:816

Understanding Vision, 3:177

Understanding Whitehead, 4:342

Understanding Wittgenstein: Studies of Philosophical Investigations, 4:346

The Undertaker's Gone Bananas, 1:1122, 1:1123

Under the Colors, 2:830

Under the Cope of Heaven, 3:516

Under the Ether Dome, 5:336

Under the Evening Sky, 2:662

Under the Greenwood Tree, 1:360, 1:361

Under the Jaguar Sun, 2:412

Under the Lilacs, 1:1198

Under the Mountain Wall, 3:930, 3:931

Under the Net, 1:523

Under the North Star, 1:498

Under the Roofs of Paris, 1:861, 1:862

Under the Sea Wind, 5:828, 5:829

Under the Tree, 1:876

Under the Volcano, 2:918, 2:919

Under the Window, 1:578, 1:585

Under the Yoke, 2:782

Under Western Eyes, 1:464

Under Western Skies: Nature and History of the American West, 3:551

Underworld, 1:1176

The Undeserving Poor, 3:211

The Undiscovered Continent: Emily Dickinson and the Space of the Mind, 1:747

The Undiscovered Self, 5:455

The Undivine Comedy, 2:815

UNDOC: Current Index: United Nations Documents Index, 1:111

Undoing the Social: Towards a Deconstructive Sociology, 3:211

The Undying Grass, 2:100

The Undying One, 1:384

The Undying One, and Other Poems, 1:384

Unease, 2:821

The Uneasy Chair: Biography of Bernard De Voto, 3:576

Unended Quest: An Intellectual Autobiography, 4:409, 5:99

The Unending Lightning, 2:541, 2:542

Unequal Care: A Case Study of Interorganizational Relations, 5:329

UNESCO Dictionary of the Social Sciences, 3:4, 3:272

UNESCO Sourcebook in Climatology, 5:634

UNESCO Statistical Yearbook, 1:53

Un Été à Stockholm, 2:123

Uneven Developments, 1:312

Unexpected Hanging and Other Mathematical Diversions, 5:496

The Unexpected Vista: A Physicist's View of Nature, 5:651

Unfinished Autobiography, 4:858

The Unfinished Journey: America since World War II, 3:537

The Unfinished Nation: A Concise History of the American People, 3:512

The Unfinished Quest of Richard Wright, 1:906

The Unfinished Revolution, 1:640

Unfinished Synthesis, 5:638

Unfinished Tales, 1:559

The Unfinished Universe, 5:11

The Unforeseen Wilderness, 5:269

The Unfortunate Traveller, 1:167, 1:194

The Unfortunate Traveller and Other Stories, 1:195

The Unfortunate Treasure, 1:433

Unframed Originals: Recollections, 1:1016

Unhappy Families, 3:207

The Unhappy Medium: Spiritualism and the Life of Margaret Fox, 4:851

The Unheard Cry for Meaning: Psychotherapy and Humanism, 5:444

The Unheeded Cry: Animal Consciousness, Animal Pain, and Science, 5:782

The Unheralded Triumph: City Government in America, 1870–1900, 3:533

Unholy Loves, 1:1022, 1:1023

The Unicorn, 1:523

Unification and the Fundamentals of Quantum Mechanics, 5:713

The Unification Church in America: Sects and Cults in America, 4:871

The Unification of South Africa, 1902–10, 3:424

The Unifying Concept, 2:536

The Unifying Moment, 4:342, 5:453

Union Democracy, 3:234

Union in Peril: The Crisis over British Intervention in the Civil War, 3:545

Union Jack—the New York City Ballet, 3:738

Union List of Film Periodicals, 3:825

Union List of Item Numbers Selected, 1:110

Union List of Serials in Libraries of the United States and Canada, 1:115

The Union of Bliss and Emptiness, 4:560

The Union of England and Scotland, 3:360

A Union Officer in the Reconstruction, 1:744

The Union of the Canadas, 3:612

The Uniqueness of the Individual, 5:18

The United Arab Emirates: An Economic and Social Survey, 3:451

United Artists: The Company Built by the Stars, 3:824

The United States, 3:513

The United States, Great Britain and British North America from the Revolution to the Establishment of Peace after the War of 1812, 3:612

The United States and Democracy in Chile, 3:635

United States and Israel, 3:440

The United States and Latin America, 3:632

The United States and Mexico, 3:639, 3:644

The United States and Porfirio Díaz, 3:645

The United States and the Caribbean in the Twentieth Century, 3:631

The United States and the Control of World Oil, 5:241

The United States and the End of the Cold War, 3:538, 3:545

The United States and the Global Struggle for Minerals, 5:636

The United States and the Middle East, 3:437

The United States and the Origins of the Cold War, 1941–1947, 3:534

The United States and the Origins of the Cuban Revolution, 3:636

The United States and World War Two: Military and Diplomatic Documents, 3:534

The United States Catalog: Books in Print, 1:71

The United States Congress: A Bibliography, 3:510

United States Government Publications Catalogs, 1:110

The United States in 1800, 3:563

The United States in Asia: A Historical Dictionary, 3:463

The United States in Latin America: A Historical Dictionary, 3:509

The United States in the Middle East: A Historical Dictionary, 3:437

The United States in the World Economy, 3:58

The United States in the World Economy: A Regional Geography, 3:124

Uniting the Dual Torah: Sifra and the Problem of the Mishnah, 4:612

Unity, Heresy, and Reform, 1378–1460, 4:694

Unity and Design in Horace's Odes, 2:386

Unity and Development in Plato's Metaphysics, 4:83

Unity in Diversity: Italian Communism and the Communist World, 3:385

Unity in the Ghazals of Hafez, 2:90

The Unity of Homer, 2:362

The Unity of Mankind in Greek Thought, 4:47

The Unity of Plato's Thought, 4:84

Unity of the Stream, 1:561

The Universal Baseball Association, 1:962, 1:963

Universal Dance: Selection from the Critical Prose Writings, 2:973

Universal Elements of Jurisprudence, 4:186

The Universal Humanity of Giambattista Vico, 4:216

The Universal Machine: Confessions of a Technological Optimist, 5:537

The Universal Penman: Engraved by George Bickham, London 1743, 1:13

The Universal Self: A Study of Paul Valéry, 2:513

Universals of Human Language, 3:21

The Universals Treatise of Nicholas of Autrecourt, 4:104

The Universe (Asimov), 5:587

Universe (Kaufmann), 5:588

The Universe of Dr. Einstein, 5:682

The Universe of Time, 1:833

The Universe Story, 5:657

University, Academics, and the Great Schism, 4:695

The University and Military Research; Moral Politics at M.I.T., 5:173

The University and the Public Interest, 3:255

The University of Chicago Spanish Dictionary, 1:102

The University of Utopia, 3:263

University Records and Life in the Middle Ages, 4:102

Unix and Libraries, 5:543

UNIX Primer Plus, 5:555

UNIX Programmer's Manual, 5:554

An Unkindness of Ravens, 1:609

The Unknowable Gurdjieff, 4:875

The Unknown Artist, 2:731

Unknown Greece, 3:900

The Unknown Mayhew, 1:377

The Unknown Murderer, 5:467

The Unknown Orwell, 1:531

The Unknown Russian Theater, 2:692

The Unknown Swedes, 2:679

"Unless You Believe, You Shall Not Understand," 4:105

Unlikely Heroines, 1:724

The Unlit Lamp, 1:492

Unloving Care: The Nursing Home Tragedy, 5:334

Unmanageable Revolutionaries: Women and Irish Nationalism, 3:371

Unmapped Territories: New Women's Fiction from Japan, 2:284

The Unnamable, 2:459

Unnatural Death, 1:610

Unofficial China, 3:471

An Unofficial Rose, 1:523

The Unpleasantness at the Bellona Club, 1:610

Unpopular Essays on Technological Progress, 4:318, 5:101, 5:130

The Unpredictable Past: Explorations in American Cultural History, 3:560

The Unpublished Cole Porter, 3:709

The Unpublished Velins of Lamarck, 5:1802 to 1809, 5:803

Unquiet Souls: Fourteenth-Century Saints and Their Religious Milieu, 4:696

The Unraveling of America: A History of Liberalism in the 1960s, 3:539

The Unreality Industry, 3:812

Unredeemed Rhetoric: Thomas Nashe and the Scandal of Authorship, 1:195

The Unreformed Church, 4:729

The Unresolved Question, 3:371

Unrolling Time: Huygens and the Mathematization of Nature, 5:695

Unruly Eloquence: Lucian and the Comedy of Traditions, 4:485

Unruly Practices, 3:218

Unruly Times: Wordsworth and Coleridge in Their Time, 1:455

Unseasonable Truths: The Life of Robert Maynard Hutchins, 3:264

The Unseen Elderly: A Study of Marginally Subsistent Hotel Dwellers, 3:201

The Unseen Hand and Other Plays, 1:1111

The Unseen World, 5:795

Unselfishness, 4:318

Unsettling Europe, 3:346

The Unsettling of America: Culture and Agriculture, 5:113, 5:265, 5:269, 5:821

Unsewn Binding, 1:25

An Unsocial Socialist, 1:546

Unsolved Mysteries of the Arctic, 3:940

The Unspeakable Curll, 1:40

The Unspeakable Mother, 1:827

Unspeakable Practices, Unnatural Acts, 1:944

Unspoken Worlds: Women's Religious Lives, 4:504, 4:512, 4:529, 4:539

UN Statistical Yearbook, 1:111

Unsui: A Diary of Zen Monastic Life, 4:538

An Unsuitable Attachment, 1:539

Unsung Voices: Opera and Musical Narrative in the Nineteenth Century, 3:670

The Untamed, 1:1212

Unthinking Social Science: The Limits of Nineteenth Century Paradigms, 3:243

Unthinking Thinking, 2:857

Until Justice and Peace Embrace, 4:762

The Untilled Field, 1:381

Until the Mashiach: Rabbi Nachman's Biography, 2:42

Until the Mashiach: Rabbi Nachman's Biography, an Annotated Chronology, 4:669

Until the Morning After: Selected Poems 1963–1985, 2:131

Until the Sun Falls, 1:1246, 1:1247

Untimely Thoughts, 2:724, 2:725

Untitled Subjects, 1:989

Unto a Good Land, 2:678

Unto Death: "Crusade" and "Late Love," 2:22

The Untold Story: The Life of Isadora Duncan, 1921–1927, 3:742

Unto This Last, 1:324, 1:393

Unto This Last, and Other Writings, 1:394

Untouchable, 2:177

Untouchable: An Indian Life History, 4:504

The Untuning of the Sky: Ideas of Music in English Poetry, 1500–1700, 2:987

The Unusable Past: Theory and the Study of American Literature, 1:1127

The Unvanquished, 1:835

The Unvarnished Doctrine, 4:180

The Unwanted, 1:1243

The Unwanted Symbol, 3:544

The Unwavering Eye: Selected Poems 1969–1975, 2:917

Unwelcome Muse: Chinese Literature in Shanghai and Peking 1937–1945, 2:233

Unwelcome Strangers: East European Jews in Imperial Germany, 3:351

The Unwritten War: American Writers and the Civil War, 1:712

Up and Down and Around: A Publisher Recollects the Time of His Life, 1:40

Upanishads, 4:501

Upbuilding Discourses in Various Spirits, 4:239

Up from Paradise, 1:1104

Up from Slavery, 1:726, 1:785, 3:269

Upheaval and Continuity: A Century of German History, 3:376

Uplift the Race: The Construction of School Daze, 1:1171

Upon the Sweeping Flood and Other Stories, 1:1023

Upper Canada: The Formative Years, 1784–1841, 3:613

The Upper Paleolithic of the Central Russian Plain, 4:433

Upright Practices: The Light of the Eyes, 4:632

Uprising, 2:825

The Uprooted, 3:582

Uprooted Americans: Essays to Honor Oscar Handlin, 3:582

Upstate: Records and Recollections of Northern New York, 1:902

Upton Sinclair, 1:880

Upton Sinclair: A Study in Social Protest, 1:880

The U.P. Trail, 1:1213

Urban African American Health Care, 3:201

The Urban Crucible, 3:521

Urban Fortunes, 3:216

Urbanization and Cancer Mortality, 5:383

Urbanization and Settlement Systems: International Perspectives, 3:128

Urbanization and Urban Planning in a Capitalist Society, 3:136

Urbanization in the Middle East, 3:435

Urbanization in the World Economy, 3:217

Urbanization of an African Community, 3:429

The Urban Land Nexus and the State, 3:136

Urban Nationalism: A Study of Political Development in Trinidad, 3:641

The Urban Prospect, 5:171

Urban Systems: Strategies for Regulation, 3:128

The Urban Villagers, 3:226, 3:227

An Urchin in the Storm: Essays about Books and Ideas, 5:16

Ursula K. Le Guin, 1:1260

Ursule Mirouet, 2:454

U.S.: A Statistical Portrait of the American People, 3:506

U.S. Book Publishing Yearbook and Directory, 1:53

U.S. Books Abroad: Neglected Ambassadors, 1:48

U.S. Code, 1:110

U.S. Cultural History: A Guide to Information Sources, 3:511

The Use and Abuse of Art, 1:813, 1:814

Use and Abuse of Statistics, 5:524

A Useful Inheritance, 4:318, 5:101

Useful Knowledge, 1:882

Use of Efficiency Standards in Energy Policy, 5:186

The Use of History, 3:276

The Use of Human Beings in Research, 5:123

The Use of Personal Documents in Psychological Science, 3:180, 3:168, 5:432

The Use of Pleasure, 5:87

The Use of Poetry and the Use of Criticism, 1:472

The Use of Rhyme in Shakespeare's Plays, 1:217

Uses of Comparative Mythology: Essays on the Work of Joseph Campbell, 3:877

The Uses of Disorder: Personal Identity and City Life, 3:217, 3:238

The Uses of Enchantment, 1:578, 1:1195, 2:585, 3:880, 5:436

The Uses of Literacy, 1:312

The Uses of the Past, 3:327

The Uses of the University, 3:250

U.S. Foreign Policy, 3:815

U.S. Foreign Policy: The Search for a New Role, 3:144

U.S. Government Manual, 1:110, 3:507

U.S. Government Publications, 1:108

U. S. Grant and the American Military Tradition, 3:572

Ushant: An Essay, 1:810

The U.S. Health Care System: A Look at the 1990s, 5:334

U.S. Iana, 1:78

Using Folk Tales in Multicultural Education, 3:869

Using Government Publications, 1:108

Using Historical Sources in Anthropology and Sociology, 3:12

Using New Communications Technologies; A Guide for Organizations, 5:305

U.S. National Health Policy: An Analysis of the Federal Role, 5:333

U.S. 1: America's Original Main Street, 3:896

U.S. Politics and Elections: A Guide to Information Sources, 3:510

U.S.-Soviet Relations in the Era of Détente: A Tragedy of Errors, 3:280

Utah Folk Art: A Catalog of Material Culture, 3:863

Utilitarianism, 3:96, 4:244

Utopia, 1:167, 1:193, 4:147

Utopia: An Elusive Vision, 4:147

Utopia and the Ideal Society, 4:125

Utopian Communism and Political Thought in Early Modern England, 1:194

The Utopian Function of Art and Literature: Selected Essays, 4:277

Utopianism, 3:217

The Utopian Novel in America, 1886–1896, 1:724

Utopian Studies II, 3:217

Utopian Thought in the Western World, 4:128

The Utopian Vision of D. H. Lawrence, 1:510

Utopia of Usurers, and Other Essays, 1:458

Utopias in Conflict: Religion and Nationalism in Modern India, 3:497

Uwe Johnson, 2:595

V

V, 1:1034, 1:1035

Vaccinating against Brain Dysfunction Syndromes, 5:383

Vachel Lindsay: A Poet in America, 1:855

Václav Havel or Living in Truth, 2:791

Vadim, 2:735

The Vagabond, 2:470

Vagabond Stars: A World History of Yiddish Theater, 2:32

Vailima Letters, 1:397

Vainglory, 1:474

Vale Ave, 1:826

Valence and the Structure of Atoms and Molecules, 5:749

Valentina, 2:807

Valentine, 2:505

Valentine and Orson, 1:583

Valentin Kataev, 2:731

Vale of Tears, 3:634

Valery Briusov and the Rise of Russian Symbolism, 2:705

Valiant for Truth: The Story of John Bunyan, 4:733

Validity in Interpretation, 1:1148

The Validity of Values—A Normative Theory of Evaluative Rationality, 4:318

Valle-Inclán: The Theater of His Life, 2:553

Valley of Darkness: The Japanese People and World War Two, 3:477

The Valley of Decision, 1:786, 1:787

The Valley of Fear, 1:607

The Valley of the Assassins: And Other Persian Travels, 3:939

The Valley of the Kings: Horizon of Eternity, 4:442

The Valley of Vision: Blake as Prophet and Revolutionary, 1:279

Valmouth, 1:474

Value, Capital and Rent, 3:114, 3:115

Value-added Processes in Information Systems, 5:545

Value and Capital, 3:83, 3:84

Value-Free Science? Purity and Power in Modern Knowledge, 5:67, 5:108, 5:157

Values Americans Live By, 4:36

Values and Imperatives: Studies in Ethics, 4:302

Values as Integrating Forces in Personality, Society, and Culture, 2:318

Values at Risk, 5:129

Values at War: Selected Tanner Lectures on the Nuclear Crisis, 5:110, 5:133

Values in Geography, 5:619

Valuing the Earth: Economics, Ecology, Ethics, 3:47

The Vampire Lestat, 1:1242

The Vampyre, 1:269, 1:300

Vandaleur's Folly: An Anglo-Irish Melodrama, 1:434

Vandover and the Brute, 1:776

Van Gogh (Hammacher), 3:794

Van Gogh (Uhdes), 3:795

Van Gogh: His Life and His Art, 3:795

Van Gogh: Twenty-Five Masterworks, 3:794

Van Gogh in Saint-Remy and Auvers, 3:795

The Vanished Imam: Musa al Sadr and the Shia of Lebanon, 4:567, 4:577

A Vanished Present: The Memoirs of Alexander Pasternak, 2:746

Vanished Supremacies, 3:407

The Vanishing American, 1:1213

The Vanishing Hero, 1:422, 1:529

The Vanishing Hitchhiker: American Urban Legends and Their Meanings, 3:868

The Vanishing Lung Syndrome, 2:792

Vanishing Points, 2:950

Vanishing Points: Dickens, Narrative, and the Subject of Omniscience, 1:350

The Vanishing Subject: Early Psychology and Literary Modernism, 2:989

Vanity Dies Hard, 1:609

Vanity Fair, 1:403

The Vanity of Human Wishes, 1:248, 2:387

Van Nostrand Reinhold Dictionary of Information Technology, 5:546

Van Nostrand's Scientific Encyclopedia, 5:2, 5:480, 5:616, 5:724

Vanquished Nation, Broken Spirit, 4:607

Van Sickle's Modern Airmanship, 5:220

A Vaquero of the Brush Country, 3:863

Variable Directions, 2:23

Variation, Transformation and Meaning, 2:317

Variation of Animals and Plants under Domestication, 5:794

The Varied Sociology of Paul F. Lazarsfeld, 3:231

The Varieties of Abnormality: A Phenomenological Analysis, 5:427

Varieties of Civil Religion, 4:752

Varieties of Experience: An Introduction to Philosophy, 4:22
Varieties of Moral Personality, 4:388
Varieties of Protestantism, 4:718
The Varieties of Religious Experience, 1:768, 3:187, 4:236, 4:237, 4:424, 5:453
Varieties of Social Explanation, 4:385
Variety of Attempt, 1:657
A Variety of Catholic Modernists, 4:742
Variorum, 1:571
A Variorum Commentary on the Poems of John Milton, 1:192
The Various Contrivances by Which Orchids Are Fertilised by Insects, 5:794
Vasari on Technique, 5:195
Vasconselos: A Romance of the New World, 1:696
The Vasectomy Book: A Complete Guide to Decision Making, 5:341
Vasilii Trediakovsky: The Fool of the "New" Russian Literature, 2:690
Vasily Pavlovich Aksënov: A Writer in Quest of Himself, 2:698
The Vatican, the Law, and the Human Embryo, 4:894
Vatican Council II: The Conciliar and Post-Conciliar Documents, 4:743
Vatzlav, 2:819
Vaughan Williams, a Life in Photographs, 3:726
Vaughan Williams and the Vision of Albion, 3:726
Vaulting Ambition: Sociobiology and the Quest for Human Nature, 4:385, 5:68, 5:826
Vedanta: Heart of Hinduism, 4:872
Vedanta for the Western World: A Symposium on Vedanta, 4:872
The Vedic Experience: Mantramanjari, 4:501
Vega and Other Poems, 1:470
The Vegetable, 1:840
Vegetable Production, 5:263
Vegetation, 2:494
Vegetation and the Atmosphere, 5:774
The Veil, 1:466

Veiled Images: Titian's Mythological Paintings for Philip II, 3:793
The Veiled One, 1:609
Veils and Words, 2:83, 2:91
Vein of Iron, 1:843
Velazquez, 3:795
Velazquez, Painter and Courtier, 3:795
Velga, 2:707
Velimir Khlebnikov: A Critical Study, 2:732
Velvet on Iron: The Diplomacy of Theodore Roosevelt, 3:595
The Vendor of Sweets, 2:180
The Venetian Vespers, 1:987
Venezuela: The Search for Order, the Dream of Progress, 3:641
Vengeance, 2:813
Vengeance and the Victim, 2:408
Venice: The Hinge of Europe, 1081–1797, 3:289, 3:333
Venice and the Defense of Republican Liberty, 3:333
Venice Observed, 1:1008, 3:333, 3:899
Venice Preserved, 1:251
The Venice Train, 2:508
Venture of Islam: Conscience and History in World Civilization, 4:570
Ventures in Book Collecting, 1:30
Venture to the Interior, 3:941
Venus: An Errant Twin, 5:592
Venus and Adonis, 1:202, 1:203, 1:215
Venus Observed, 1:480
Vera; or, the Nihilist, 1:410
The Veracious Imagination, 1:928
Veranilda: A Romance, 1:359
Verbal Behavior, 3:194
The Verbal Icon, 1:927, 1:1154, 1:1155
Verb Synonyms and Related Words, 1:94
Verbum: Word and Idea in Aquinas, 4:119
Verdi, 3:726
Verdi: A Documentary Study, 3:727
Verdi: A Life in the Theatre, 3:727
Verdi: His Music, Life and Times, 3:727
The Verdi Companion, 3:727

Verdi in the Age of Italian Romanticism, 3:727
Verdi's Aïda: The History of an Opera in Letters and Documents, 3:726
Verdi's Otello and Simon Boccanegra in Letters and Documents, 3:727
Vergil's Georgics and the Traditions of Ancient Epic, 2:397
Verging on the Abyss, 1:740
The Vermilion Bird: T'ang Images of the South, 2:191
Vermilion Gate, 2:254
Vermont Folksongs and Ballads, 3:858
The Vernacular Republic, 2:959
Vernon Watkins, 1:561
Vernon Watkins and the Spring of Vision, 1:561
Veronica, My Daughter and Other Onitsha Plays and Stories, 2:140
Verseform: A Comparative Bibligraphy, 1:125
Verses on the Beautiful Lady, 2:702
Versos Sencillos, 2:871
Versus: Philippine Protest Poetry, 1983–1986, 2:329
The Vertebrate Body, 5:773
Vertigo, 1:1168, 1:1169
Very: The Effective Years 1833–1840, 1:705
A Very Decided Preference: Life with Peter Medawar, 5:18
A Very Easy Death, 2:458, 5:421
The Very Eye of Night, 1:1163
Very Far Away from Anywhere Else, 1:1260
Very Old Bones, 1:997
Very Private Eye: An Autobiography in Diaries and Letters, 1:539
Vested Interests: Cross-Dressing and Cultural Anxiety, 1:1182
Veteris Testamenti concordantiae Hebraicae atque Chaldaicae, 4:818
Vexed and Troubled Englishmen, 1590–1642, 3:570
Via Augustini, 4:129
Via de' Magazzini, 2:437
The "Vibrant Silence" in Jorge Guillén's Aire Nuestro, 2:541

The Vicar of Bullhampton, 1:406
The Vicar of Wakefield, 1:247
The Vicar of Wrexhill, 1:408
Vicente Aleixandre, 2:529
Vichy France: Old Guard and New Order, 1940–1944, 3:373
Vichy France and the Jews, 3:349
Vicious Modernism: Black Harlem and the Literary Imagination, 1:794
Vico: A Study of the New Science, 2:442, 4:217
Vico: Past and Present, 4:217
Vico and Contemporary Thought, 4:217
Vico and Herder: Two Studies in the History of Ideas, 4:216
Vico and Herder: Two Studies in the Philosophy of History, 4:199
Vico and Marx, 2:442, 4:217
Vico in the Tradition of Rhetoric, 4:217
Vico Revisited: Orthodoxy, Naturalism and Science in the Scienzia Nuova, 4:216
Vico's Science of Imagination, 4:217
The Victim, 1:946, 1:947
A Victim of Circumstances and Other Stories, 1:359
The Victim of Love, 2:79
The Victims, 2:142, 2:143
Victims: A True Story of the Civil War, 3:529
Victims: Textual Strategies in Recent American Fiction, 1:1003
Victims of a Map, 2:58
The Victims of Democracy, 4:877
Victor Hammer: Artist and Printer, 1:12
Victor Hugo (Houston), 2:483
Victor Hugo (Maurois), 2:483
Victor Hugo and the Visionary Novel, 2:483
Victoria (Rowson), 1:643
Victoria (Hamsun), 2:664
The Victorian Age: Essays in History and in Social and Literary History, 1:315
Victorian Age in Literature, 1:457
The Victorian Age of English Literature, 1:386

The Victorian Age of German Literature, 2:565
Victorian America: Transformations in Everyday Life, 1876–1915, 3:533
Victorian and Edwardian London, 1:445
Victorian and Modern Poetics, 1:315
Victorian Biography: A Collection of Essays from the Period, 1:326
Victorian Book Design and Colour Printing, 1:9, 1:29
Victorian Book Illustration, 1:28
Victorian Britain: An Encyclopedia, 1:312, 3:354, 3:364
Victorian Cities, 1:312
The Victorian City, 1:312
The Victorian Constitution, 3:364
Victorian Devotional Poetry: The Tractarian Mode, 1:316
Victorian England, 1:313
Victorian England: Aspects of English and Imperial History, 1837–1901, 3:341
Victorian England, 1837–1901, 3:353
The Victorian Experience: The Poets, 1:315
Victorian Fiction, 1:318
Victorian Fiction: A Second Guide to Research, 1:318
The Victorian Frame of Mind, 1830–1870, 1:312, 1:315
The Victorian Historical Novel, 1840–1880, 1:319
The Victorian Homefront: American Thought and Culture, 1860–1880, 3:561
The Victorian Interpretation of Racial Conflict, 3:494
Victorian Jews through British Eyes, 4:635
Victorian Knight-Errant, 1:685
Victorian Ladies at Work, 3:364
Victorian Literature: Prose, 1:326
The Victorian Multiplot Novel: Studies in Dialogical Form, 1:318
Victorian Noon: English Literature in 1850, 1:312
Victorian Parlour Poetry: An Annotated Anthology, 1:720

Victorian People, 3:363
Victorian People: A Reassessment of Persons' Themes, 1851–67, 1:312
Victorian People and Ideas, 1:311, 3:363
Victorian Plays, 1837–1901, 1:323
Victorian Poetry: Clough to Kipling, 1:316
Victorian Poetry and Poetics, 1:316
Victorian Poetry and the Romantic Religion, 1:315
Victorian Poets: A Guide to Research, 1:315
Victorian Poets and Romantic Poems: Intertextuality and Ideology, 1:315
Victorian Popular Dramatists, 1:322
Victorian Prose: A Guide to Research, 1:325
Victorian Prose and Poetry, 1:326
Victorian Prose Masters, 1:326
Victorian Publishers' Bindings, 1:21
Victorian Publishers' Bookbindings in Paper, 1:25
A Victorian Romantic: Dante Gabriel Rossetti, 1:392
The Victorian Sage: Studies in Argument, 1:325
The Victorian Sages: An Anthology of Prose, 1:326
The Victorian Self: Autobiography and Biblical Narrative, 1:325
Victorian Songs, 1:316
The Victorian Temper: A Study in Literary Culture, 1:315
Victorian Theatre, 1:322
The Victorian Theatre, 1792–1914, 1:323
Victorian Things, 1:312
Victorian Women Travel Writers in Africa, 1:325
The Victorian Woodblock Illustrators, 1:28
Victorian Writing and Working Women, 1:325
Victoria's Year: English Literature and Culture, 1837–1838, 1:313
The Victorious Expression, 2:539, 2:545, 2:552
Victorious in Defeat: The Loyalists in Canada, 3:612
Victor's Justice: The Tokyo War Crimes Trial, 3:478

Victory: How a Progressive
Democratic Party Can Win
and Govern, 3:143
Victory Celebrations, Prison-
ers, and the Love-Girl and
the Innocent, 2:761
Victory to the Mother, 4:504
Videodisc Systems: Theory
and Applications, 5:229
Video Night in Kathmandu
and Other Reports from
the Not-So-Far-East, 3:903
Vienna and the Austrians,
1:408
The Viennese: Splendour,
Twilight and Exile, 3:375
Viennese Idylls, 2:611
Viennese Novelties, 2:611
Vietnam: History, 3:538
Vietnam and the Chinese
Model, 3:465
Vietnam and the West, 3:491
Vietnamese Anti-Colonialism,
1885–1925, 3:491
Vietnamese Communism,
1925–1945, 3:490
Vietnamese-English Diction-
ary, 1:103
The Vietnamese Experience
in America, 3:557
The Vietnamese Novel in
French, 2:339
Vietnamese Peasants under
French Domination,
1861–1945, 3:490
Vietnamese Short Stories: An
Introduction, 2:339
Vietnamese Tradition on
Trial, 1920–1945, 2:339
The Vietnamization of New
Jersey, 1:1088
The Vietnam Trauma in
American Foreign Policy,
1945–1975, 3:538
The Vietnam Wars,
1945–1990, 3:540
Viet Rock, 1:1113, 1:1114
The View from Afar, 3:34
The View from Ararat: Twen-
ty-five Years of Armenian-
American Writing, 2:76
The View from Coyaba,
2:159
The View from Eighty, 1:823
The View from Goffman,
3:228
The View from Nowhere,
4:379
A View from the Bridge,
1:1104
A View from the Spire: Wil-
liam Golding's Later Nov-
els, 1:484

A View of All the Russias,
3:941
View of Dawn in the Trop-
ics, 2:858
A View of Life, 5:765
A View of the Present State
of Ireland, 1:198
Viewpoints on Supply-Side
Economics, 3:62
Views and Reviews on Amer-
ican Literature, History,
and Fiction, 1:695
Views from a Window: Con-
versations with Gore
Vidal, 1:1062
Views on Capitalism, 3:51,
3:83, 3:97
A Vigorous Spirit of Enter-
prise, 3:520
The Vigour of Prophecy: A
Study of Virgil's Aeneid,
2:397
The Viking Achievement,
3:380
The Vikings (Bröndsted),
2:640
The Vikings (Roesdahl),
3:329
The Vikings in Britain, 3:356
The Vikings in History, 3:380
Vile Bodies, 1:561, 1:562
Vilfredo Pareto, 3:100
Vilhelm Moberg, 2:679
The Village, 2:707
The Village Beyond the Sev-
en Aspen Trees, 2:807,
2:808
The Village Gods of South
India, 4:507
The Village in 1970, 3:486
Village in August, 2:245,
2:246
The Village in the Turkish
Novel and Short Story,
1920 to 1955, 2:96
The Village Labourer,
1760–1832, 3:404
The Village Minstrel, 1:285
The Village of Stepanchikovo
and Its Inhabitants, 2:714
A Village Romeo and Juliet,
2:597
A Village That Chose Prog-
ress: Chan Kom Revisited,
3:39
The Village Witch Doctor
and Other Stories, 2:150
Villa Magdalena, 2:333, 2:334
The Villas of Le Corbusier
1920–1930, 3:778
Ville Cruelle, 2:132
Villette, 1:334, 1:335
Vinayapitaka, 2:315

Vincent Van Gogh, 3:795
Vincent Van Gogh: Biogra-
phy, 3:795
Vincent Van Gogh: Paintings
and Drawings, 3:795
Vindication of the Rights of
Women, 1:300
Vinegar Tom, 1:458
Vineland, 1:1035
Vineyard Tales, 3:858
The Vinland Map and the
Tartar Relation, 3:900
The Vinland Sagas, 2:640
Vintage and Historic Racing
Cars, 5:247
Vintage Mencken, 1:859
The Vintage Turgenev, 2:770
Violence against Women,
3:218
Violence and Religious Com-
mitment, 4:867
Violence and Responsibility:
The Individual, the Family
and Society, 5:423
Violence and the Sacred,
4:429
Violence in Colombia, 3:635
The Violent Bear It Away,
1:1023
The Violent Face of Nature:
Severe Phenomena and
Natural Disasters, 5:636
The Violent Land, 2:891,
2:892
A Violent Life, 2:431, 2:432
Violent Origins, 4:429
The Violent World of Hugh
Greene, 1:567
The Violet Fairy Book, 3:883
Violette Leduc, 2:486
Viper's Tangle, 2:489
Virgil, 2:397
Virgil: Father of the West,
2:397
Virgil's Aeneid and the Tra-
dition of Hellenistic Poet-
ry, 2:397
Virgil's Augustan Epic, 2:397
Virgil's Eclogues: Landscapes
of Experience, 2:397
Virgil's Georgics: A New In-
terpretation, 2:397
Virgil's Iliad: An Essay on
Epic Narrative, 2:397
Virgil's Mind at Work, 2:397
The Virginal Conception and
Bodily Resurrection of
Jesus, 4:685, 4:887
The Virgin and the Mouse-
trap: Essays in Search of
the Soul of Science, 5:10
Virginia, 1:843

The Virginian, 1:789, 1:1210, 1:1211, 1:1218

The Virginians, 1:403

Virginians at Home: Family Life in the Eighteenth Century, 3:588

The Virginia Report of 1799–1800, Touching the Alien and Sedition Laws, 3:161

Virginia Woolf: A Biography, 1:570

Virginia Woolf: A Guide to Research, 1:570

Virginia Woolf: A Study of the Short Fiction, 1:569

Virginia Woolf: A Writer's Life, 1:570

Virginia Woolf: Centennial Papers, 1:570

Virginia Woolf: Dramatic Novelist, 1:570

Virginia Woolf: New Critical Essays, 1:570

Virginia Woolf: The Major Novels, 1:570

Virginia Woolf and Postmodernism, 1:570

Virginia Woolf and the Languages of Patriarchy, 1:570

Virginia Woolf and the Madness of Language, 1:570

Virginia Woolf and the Poetry of Fiction, 1:570

Virginia Woolf and War: Fiction, Reality, and Myth, 1:570

Virginia Woolf's Rediscovered Essays: Sources and Allusions, 1:570

Virginie: Her Two Lives, 1:984, 1:985

The Virgin in the Garden, 1:455

Virgin Land: The American West as Symbol and Myth, 1:652, 3:533

Virgin Soil, 2:768, 2:769

Virgin Soil Upturned, 2:755

Virology, 5:760

The Virtual Classroom: A New Option for Learning, 5:307

Virtual Reality, 5:565

Virtual Reality: A Selected Bibliography, 5:565

Virtue's Hero: Emerson, Antislavery, and Reform, 1:670

Virtuoso, the Instrumentalist as Superstar, 3:657

The Virtuous Journalist, 5:132

Virtuous Woman: Reflections on Christian Feminist Ethics, 4:749

Virtuous Women: Three Masterpieces of Traditional Korean Fiction, 2:299

Virus Hunting: AIDS, Cancer and the Human Retrovirus, 5:387, 5:783

A Virus of Love and Other Tales of Medical Detection, 5:389

The Visible and the Invisible, 4:311

Visible Fictions, 1:1157

The Visible Hand: The Managerial Revolution in American Business, 3:49

Visible Saints: The History of a Puritan Idea, 3:588

Visio, 1:153

Vision and Aging, 5:384

Vision and Certitude in the Age of Ockham, 4:121

Vision and Style in Patrick White: A Study of Five Novels, 2:966

The Visionary, 2:376

The Visionary Company, 1:267, 1:1137

Visionary Film, The American Avant-Garde, 1:1158

Visionary Science, 5:207

The Vision in God: Malebranche's Scholastic Sources, 4:182

Vision in Motion, 3:760

A Vision of Battlements, 1:453

The Vision of Columbus: A Poem in Nine Books, 1:633

A Vision of Dynamic Space, Rudolf Laban, 3:746

The Vision of Piers Plowman, 1:153

The Vision of Piers Plowman: A Complete Edition of the B-Text, 1:153

Vision of the Vedic Poets, 4:501

The Vision of the Void, 1:1065

The Vision of This Land, 1:855

Vision of William Concerning Piers the Plowman, in Three Parallel Texts, 1:153

Visions, 2:548

Visions: Stories and Photographs, 2:699

Visions, Images and Dreams: Yiddish Film Past and Present, 2:31

Visions and Heat: The Making of the Indonesian Revolution, 3:491

Visions and Revisions: Essays on African Literature and Criticism, 2:111

Visions from San Francisco Bay, 2:818

Visions of Caliban: Of Chimpanzees, Humans and the Honored Shape, 5:833

Visions of Cody, 1:998

Visions of Desire: Tanizaki's Fictional Worlds, 2:294

Visions of Excess: Selected Writings 1927–1939, 2:456

Visions of Gerard, 1:998

Visions of Glory: A History and a Memory of Jehovah's Witnesses, 4:863

Visions of Symmetry, 5:495

Visions of the End: Apocalyptic Traditions in the Middle Ages, 4:700

Visions of Virtue in Tokugawa Japan, 3:475

The Visit, 2:577

The Visitants, 2:964

The Visitors, 1:1262

Visit to a Small Plant, 1:1062

A Visit to Germany, Italy and Malta 1840–1841, 2:647

A Visit to Italy, 1:408

Visnuism and Sivaism: A Comparison, 4:504

Vistas of History, 3:590

A Visual Art of Jean Cocteau, 2:469, 3:834

The Visual Arts: A History, 3:757

The Visual Display of Quantitative Information, 1:11, 5:524, 5:558

Visual Languages, 5:550

Visual Perception: An Introduction, 3:177

Vita, 1:153

Vita: A Bibliography of Vita Sackville-West, 1:542

The Vital Balance: The Life Process in Mental Health and Illness, 5:464

The Vital Center: The Politics of Freedom, 3:597

Vital Circuits, 5:342

The Vital Few: The Entrepreneur and American Economic Progress, 3:51

Vital Involvement in Old
  Age, 5:442
The Vitality of the Lyric
  Voice, 2:190
Vital Parts, 1:948, 1:949
Vital Signs: Medical Realism
  in Nineteenth-Century Fic-
  tion, 1:319
Vital Signs 1993: The Trends
  That Are Shaping Our Fu-
  ture, 5:828
The Vital South: How Presi-
  dents Are Elected, 3:542
The Vitamin C Connection,
  5:345
Vitamin Politics, 5:345
Vitamins and Health Foods:
  The Great American Hus-
  tle, 5:346
Vitamins and Minerals: Help
  or Harm, 5:346
Vita Nuova (New Life),
  1:391, 2:416
Vita Sexualis, 2:290
Vittorino Da Feltre and Oth-
  er Humanist Educators,
  4:132
Vittorio Alfieri, 2:405
Viva, 1:825
Vivaldi, 3:727
Vivat! Vivat Regina!, 1:445
A Vives Bibliography, 4:156
Vives' Introduction to Wis-
  dom: A Renaissance Text-
  book, 4:156
Vivian Grey, 1:351
The Viviporous Quadrupeds
  of North America, 5:786
The Vivisector, 2:965, 2:966
Vivo o Povo Brasileiro, 2:898
The Vixens, 1:1225
Vjenceslav Novak, 2:785
Vladimir Country Roads,
  2:759
Vladimir Medem: The Life
  and Soul of a Legendary
  Jewish Socialist, 4:656
Vladimir Nabokov (Bloom),
  2:741
Vladimir Nabokov (Sharpe),
  1:1020, 2:742
Vladimir Nabokov (Wood),
  2:742
Vladimir Nabokov: A Critical
  Study of the Novels, 2:742
Vladimir Nabokov: A De-
  scriptive Bibliography,
  1:1020
Vladimir Nabokov: A Pictori-
  al Biography, 2:741
Vladimir Nabokov: A Refer-
  ence Guide, 1:1020

Vladimir Nabokov: The
  American Years, 2:741
Vladimir Nabokov: The Rus-
  sian Years, 2:741
Vladimir Nabokov's Lolita,
  2:741
V-Letter and Other Poems,
  1:1045
VNR's Encyclopedia of Hos-
  pitality and Tourism, 3:890
Vocabulary of Modern Spo-
  ken Greek (English-Greek
  and Greek-English), 1:99
The Vocabulary of Organic
  Chemistry, 5:726
The Vocal Songs in the
  Plays of Shakespeare,
  1:221
A Vocation and a Voice: Sto-
  ries, 1:740
Vocation and Identity in the
  Fiction of Muriel Spark,
  1:552
The Vocation of Man, 4:198
The Voice, 2:141
A Voice Crying in the Wil-
  derness, 5:110
Voice/Data Telecommunica-
  tions for Business, 5:297
Voice-Data Telecommunica-
  tions Systems, 5:296
A Voice from the Chorus,
  2:757
A Voice from the Factories,
  1:384
The Voice in the Margin,
  1:714, 1:631
Voice of a Native Son: The
  Poetics of Richard Wright,
  1:906
Voice of Conscience, 2:81
The Voice of Experience,
  5:459
Voice of Norway, 3:381
The Voice of Prose: Early
  Prose and Autobiography,
  2:746
The Voice of the Desert: A
  Naturalist's Interpretation,
  5:834
The Voice of the Earth,
  5:175, 5:176
The Voice of the Folk: Folk-
  lore and American Liter-
  ary Theory, 3:868
The Voice of the Masters,
  2:846
The Voice of the People,
  1:843
The Voice of the Poor: Es-
  says in Economics and
  Political Persuasion, 3:79

The Voice of the Silence,
  4:874
Voice of the Voiceless: The
  Four Pastoral Letters and
  Other Statements, 4:748
The Voice of Things, 2:494
The Voice of Truth, 4:553
Voices and Instruments of
  the Middle Ages, 3:662
Voices and Visions: The Poet
  in America, 1:800
Voices at the Late Hour,
  2:658
Voices from Ancient Egypt:
  an Anthology of Middle
  Kingdom Writings, 2:53
Voices from Summerland:
  An Anthology of Jamaican
  Poetry, 2:931
Voices from the Iron House:
  A Study of Lu Xun, 2:256
Voices from the Jungle: Bur-
  mese Youth in Transition,
  2:314
Voices from the Thai Coun-
  tryside: The Short Stories
  of Samruan Singh, 2:336
Voices from the Whirlwind,
  2:244
Voices from the Yiddish: Es-
  says, Memoirs, Diaries,
  2:33, 4:657
Voices from Twentieth Cen-
  tury Africa: Griots and
  Town-Criers, 2:113
Voices in Black and White,
  1:809
Voices in Exile, 2:931
Voices in Exile: The Decem-
  brist Memoirs, 3:395
Voices in Summer, 1:621
Voices in the Evening, 2:422
Voices of a People: The Sto-
  ry of Yiddish Folksong,
  2:32, 3:852
Voices of Change in the
  Spanish American Theater:
  An Anthology, 2:849
Voices of Israel, 2:8
The Voices of Matthew Ar-
  nold, 1:328
Voices of Modern Greece,
  2:371
Voices of Our Kind: An An-
  thology of Contemporary
  Scottish Verse, 1:418
Voices of Protest: Huey
  Long, Father Coughlin,
  and the Great Depression,
  3:534
Voices of Silence: Lives of
  the Trappists Today, 4:752

The Voices of Silence: Man and His Art, 2:487
Voices of Spring, 2:267
Voices of the Past, 3:808
Voices of the Poor, 1:377
Voices of Wisdom: Jewish Ideals and Ethics for Everyday Living, 4:598
Voices within the Ark: The Modern Jewish Poets, 2:10, 2:34
The Voice That Is Great within Us, 1:801, 1:915
The Volcano, 2:333, 2:334
Volcanoes, 5:629
Volcanoes of the Earth, 5:629
Volcanoes of the World, 5:630
Volcanology, 5:630
The Volcano Lover, 1:1053
Volcano Weather: The Story of 1816, the Year without a Summer, 5:634
Volga Falls to the Caspian Sea, 2:747
Vollständige Konkordanz zum griechischen Neuen Testament, 4:817
Volpone, 1:183
Völsunga Saga, 2:639
Voltaire (Ayer), 4:273
Voltaire (Lanson), 4:218, 4:273
Voltaire (Morley), 2:516
Voltaire: A Biographical Fantasy, 1:875
Voltaire: Historian, 2:516
Voltaire, Pascal, and Human Destiny, 4:218
Voltaire and Leibniz, 4:218
Voltaire and the English Deists, 4:218
Voltaire's Old Testament Criticism, 4:218
Voltaire's Politics, 4:218, 2:516
Voluntary Associations: Perspectives on the Literature, 3:210
The Voluntary Church, 4:754
Volunteers, 1:479
The Volunteers: Means and Ends in a National Organization, 3:210
A Volunteer's Adventures, 1:744
The Von Balthasar Reader, 4:891
Voodoo in Haiti, 4:467
Voodoo in New Orleans, 4:868

Voodoo Tales, as Told among the Negroes of the Southwest, 3:867
The Vortex (Coward), 1:465
The Vortex (Rivera), 2:881
Voss, 2:958, 2:965, 2:966
Voters, Patrons and Parties, 3:362
Voting: A Study of Opinion Formation in a Presidential Campaign, 3:230
Vox Clamantis, 1:152
A Voyage around the World with the Romazov Exploring Expedition in the Years 1815–18, 2:576
Voyage de Humboldt et Bonplaud, 3:131
Voyage of Argo, 2:352
The Voyage of Captain Popanilla, 1:351
The Voyage of Christopher Columbus, 3:916
Voyage of the Beagle, 5:638
The Voyage of the Discovery, 3:936
The Voyage of the Liberdade, 3:937
The Voyage of the Sanderling, 3:897
Voyage of the Spaceship Beagle, 5:135
The Voyage Out, 1:569
The Voyage Perilous: Willa Cather's Romanticism, 1:822
Voyager, 5:220
Voyager: A Life of Hart Crane, 1:823
Voyagers to the West, 3:564
Voyages and Discoveries, 3:923
Voyages and Discoveries of the Companions of Columbus, 1:679, 1:680
Voyages and Documents, 3:923
The Voyages and Explorations of Samuel de Champlain, 1604–1616, 3:908
Voyages of Discovery, 3:917
Voyages of Samuel de Champlain, 1604–1618, 1:631
Voyages to the New World, 3:335
The Voyage That Never Ends, 2:919
A Voyage to Pagany, 1:900
Voyage to Windward: The Life of Robert Louis Stevenson, 1:397
The Voyeur, 2:430, 2:500

Vril: The Power of the Coming Race (The Coming Race), 1:340
Vsevolod Garshin, 2:719
V. S. Naipaul (Hamner), 2:939
V. S. Naipaul (Hughes), 2:939
V. S. Naipaul (King), 2:939
V. S. Naipaul (Thorpe), 2:939
V. S. Naipaul (Walsh), 2:939
V. S. Naipaul: A Critical Introduction, 2:939
V. S. Naipaul: A Materialist Reading, 2:939
V. S. Naipaul: An Introduction to His Work, 2:939
V. S. Naipaul: A Study in Expatriate Sensibility, 2:939
V. S. Naipaul's Fiction: In Quest of the Enemy, 2:939
V. S. Pritchett, 1:538
V. S. Pritchett: A Study of the Short Fiction, 1:538
V. Sackville-West, 1:542
V. Sackville-West: A Critical Biography, 1:542
Vulnerable People: A View of American Fiction since 1945, 1:918
V Was for Victory: Politics and American Culture during World War II, 3:534
Vyakhyayukti, 4:514

W

Wagner: A Biography, 1813–1833, 3:729
Wagner and Beethoven: Richard Wagner's Reception of Beethoven, 3:728
Wagner and the Romantic Disaster, 3:728
The Wagner Compendium: A Guide to Wagner's Life and Music, 3:729
Wagnerism in European Culture and Politics, 3:728
The Wagner Operas, 3:729
Wagner's "Ring" and Its Symbols, 2:605
Wagner's Siegfried: Its Drama, History, and Music, 3:728
Wagonmaster, 1:1165
Wahhabiyya: Islamic Reform and Politics in French West Africa, 4:570
Waiariki, 2:976

Waiting for God, 2:516, 4:788

Waiting for Godot, 1:439, 2:459

Waiting for Lefty, 1:1105, 1:1106

Waiting for Prime Time: The Women of Television News, 3:808

Waiting for Sheila, 1:449

Waiting for the Barbarians, 2:160

Waiting for the Boat, 1:536

Waiting for the Dawn: Mircea Eliade in Perspective, 4:474

Waiting for the Morning Train: An American Boyhood, 3:572

Waiting for the Party: The Life of Frances Hodgson Burnett, 1:1201

Waiting for the Verdict, 1:743

Waiting for the Wind: Thirty-six Poets of Japan's Late Middle Ages, 2:274

Waiting for Winter, 1:867

The Waiting Land: A Spell in Nepal, 3:905

The Waiting Years, 2:286

The Wakefield Mystery Plays, 1:159

The Wakefield Pageants in the Towneley Cycle, 1:159

The Wake of Jamey Foster, 1:1094

The Wake of the Gods: Melville's Mythology, 1:688

The Wake of the Great Sealers, 3:906

The Waking, 1:1038

Waking Giants: The Presence of the Past in Modernism, 1:795

Waking Up Dry: How to End Bedwetting Forever, 5:406

Walden, 1:659, 1:700, 1:701

Walden: Volatile Truths, 1:701

Walden; or Life in the Woods, 5:837

Walden Two, 3:193, 3:194

Waldheim: The Missing Years, 3:375

Wales: A New Study, 3:369

Wales in British Politics, Eighteen Sixty Eight to Nineteen Twenty Two, 3:367

Walford's Guide to Reference Material, 1:62, 1:74, 3:327

A Walk across America, 3:892

A Walker in the City, 1:996

Walker Percy, 1:1029

Walker Percy: An American Search, 1:1029

Walker Percy, Nineteen Thirty to Nineteen Eighty-Four, 1:1029

Walker Percy and the Old Modern Age, 1:1029

Walker's Mammals of the World, 5:761, 5:769

Walker's Rhyming Dictionary of the English Language, 1:95

Walkin' and Talkin' Revisited, 3:862

Walking: A Complete Guide to the Complete Exercise, 5:326

Walking Down the Stairs: Selections from Interviews, 1:1001

Walking Europe from Top to Bottom, 3:899

Walking North with Keats, 1:295

Walking Westward in the Morning, 2:318

Walking with the Great Apes: Jane Goodall, Dian Fossey, and Birute Galdikas, 3:909, 5:833,

Walkin' over Medicine, 5:331

Walk in Peace: Legends and Stories of the Michigan Indians, 3:862

A Walk in the Night, 2:164

A Walk in the Night and Other Stories, 2:165

Walks in the World, 1:798

A Walk through Britain, 3:899

A Walk through Wales, 3:898

The Walk West: A Walk across America 2, 3:892

The Wall: Intimacy, 2:507

Wallace Stevens, 1:887, 1:888

Wallace Stevens: A Celebration, 1:887

Wallace Stevens: A Faber Student Guide, 1:888

Wallace Stevens: A Mythology of Self, 1:887

Wallace Stevens: A Poet's Growth, 1:888

Wallace Stevens: Images and Judgments, 1:887

Wallace Stevens: Imagination and Faith, 1:888

Wallace Stevens: Musing the Obscure, 1:888

Wallace Stevens: The Critical Heritage, 1:887

Wallace Stevens: The Early Years, 1879–1923, 1:888

Wallace Stevens: The Intensest Rendezvous, 1:887

Wallace Stevens: The Later Years, 1925–1955, 1:888

Wallace Stevens: The Plain Sense of Things, 1:888

Wallace Stevens: The Poetics of Modernism, 1:887

Wallace Stevens and Poetic Theory: Conceiving the Supreme Fiction, 1:888

Wallace Stevens and the Actual World, 1:887

The Wallace Stevens Case: Law and the Practice of Poetry, 1:887

Wallace Stevens' Supreme Fiction: A New Romanticism, 1:887

Wallenstein & Mary Stuart, 2:609

The Walnut Trees of Altenberg, 2:487

Walpole and the Whig Supremacy, 3:362

Walt Disney: A Guide to References and Resources, 1:1165

Walt Disney, The Art of Animation, 1:1165

Walter Crane, 1:584

Walter Crane as a Book Illustrator, 1:583

Walter de la Mare, 1:467

Walter de la Mare: An Exploration, 1:467

Walter Gropius, 3:777

Walter Lippmann: A Study in Personal Journalism, 3:809, 3:815

Walter Lippmann: Cosmopolitanism in the Century of Total War, 3:158

Walter Lippmann and the American Century, 3:158, 3:815

Walter Pater, 1:387

Walter Pater: The Aesthetic Moment, 1:387

Walter Pater: The Critic as Artist of Ideas, 1:387

Walter Pater and His Reading, 1874–1877, 1:387

Walter Pater and the Gods of Disorder, 1:387

Walter Pater's Art of Autobiography, 1:388

Walter Reed: A Biography, 5:312

Walter Savage Landor, 1:296

Walter Scott, 1:300

The Walton War and Tales of the Great Smoky Mountains, 3:860
Walt Whitman, 1:708
Walt Whitman: A Life, 1:707
Walt Whitman, the Critical Heritage, 1:707
Walt Whitman and Emily Dickinson: Poetry of the Central Consciousness, 1:748
Walt Whitman and the American Reader, 1:707
Walt Whitman and the Body Beautiful, 1:707
Walt Whitman's Language Experiment, 1:708
Walt Whitman's "Song of Myself": A Mosaic of Interpretations, 1:707
The Waltz of the Toreadors, 2:450
Wampeters, Foma and Granfalloons, 1:1063
Wanasema: Conversations with African Writers, 2:107
Wanda Gág: The Story of an Artist, 1:1203
The Wanderer (Burney), 1:235
The Wanderer (Hamsun), 2:664
The Wanderers (Mphahlele), 2:166
Wanderers Twain, 2:822
Wandering, 2:256, 2:590
The Wandering Fool, 2:101
Wandering Ghost: The Odyssey of Lafcadio Hearn, 3:908
Wandering in the Garden, Waking from a Dream, 2:232, 2:260
The Wandering Jew, 2:590
The Wandering Minstrel, 1:376, 1:378
Wanderings: Chaim Potok's History of the Jews, 1:1032
Wanderings in West Africa from Liverpool to Fernando Po, 3:914
Wandering Star, 2:45
Wandering through Winter, 5:818
Wang An-shih: Practical Reformer?, 2:225
Wang An-shih, Chinese Statesman and Educationalist of the Sung Dynasty, 2:225
Wang Ch'ang-ling, 2:226
Wang Wei, 2:228

Wang Wei, Li Po, Tu Fu, Li Ho: Four T'ang Poets, 2:191
Wang Wei, the Painter-Poet, 2:228
The Waning of the Middle Ages, 3:331, 4:691
The Want Bone, 1:1030
The Wanting Seed, 1:453, 1:454
The Wapshot Chronicle, 1:960
The Wapshot Scandal, 1:960, 1:961
The War: A Memoir, 2:474
War: Ends and Means, 3:280
War, Economy and Society, 1939–1945, 3:280
War, Taxation, and Rebellion in Early Tudor England, 3:358
The War against Nuclear Power, 5:112
War against the Idols: The Reformation of Worship from Erasmus to Calvin, 4:737
The War against the Jews, 1933–1945, 4:635
War and American Thought: From the Revolution to the Monroe Doctrine, 3:522
War and Children, 5:444
War and Exile: A Vietnamese Anthology, 2:339
War and Ideology, 3:278
War and Imperialism in Republican Rome, 327–70 B.C., 3:308
War and Peace, 2:755, 2:763, 2:764
War and Peace in the Law of Islam, 4:895
War and Peace in the World's Religions, 4:895
War and Peace since 1945, 3:277
War and Society in Africa, 3:418
War and Society in Ancient Mesoamerica, 3:628
War and Society in the Greek World, 3:308
War and Society in the Roman World, 3:308
War and the Christian Conscience, 5:112
War and the German Mind, 2:565
War and the World, 2:739
War and Welfare, 3:532

War as a Spiritual Experience, 2:595
The War Between the Tates, 1:1007
War by Other Means, 3:491
War Crimes, 2:951
War Crimes in Vietnam, 4:324
The Warden, 1:405
The War Diaries, 2:962
Ward Number Six and Other Stories, 2:708
The Ward of Our Lady of Mercy, 2:836
The Ward of Thorpe-Combe, 1:408
Ward Ritchie: The Lagune Verde Imprenta Years, 1975–1990, 1:45
The Ward Ritchie Press and Anderson, Ritchie and Simon, 1:45
Warhol, 3:796
War in the Age of Intelligent Machines, 3:278
War in the Ancient World, 3:308
War in the Land of Egypt, 2:59
The Warlord of Mars, 1:1256
The War Lords, 3:410
Warlords, Artists, and Commoners: Japan in the Sixteenth Century, 3:474
War Lords of Washington, 3:572
War Machine: The Rationalization of Slaughter in the Modern Age, 3:343
The Warmup: Life as a Warmup Comic, 3:872
Warned by a Ghost, 1:619
Warning, 5:354
Warning to the West, 2:761
The War of Atonement, October 1973, 3:440
The War of Dreams, 1:455
War of Illusions: German Policies from 1911 to 1914, 3:278
The War of the American Revolution, 3:509
The War of the End of the World, 2:887, 2:894
The War of the Revolution, 3:522
The War of the Worlds, 1:564, 1:611, 1:1178
The War of Time, 2:859, 2:860
The War on Land: The British Army in World War II, 3:279

War Plays, 1:446
The War Poems of Siegfried Sassoon, 1:542
The War Prayer, 1:781, 1:1201
The Warrior and the Priest, 3:531, 3:595
The Warriors, 1:1247
Warriors against Israel, 3:440
Warriors at Suez, 3:440
The Warrior's Cinema: The Cinema of Akira Kurosawa, 3:839
Warriors for Jerusalem, 3:440
The Warriors of God: Jihad and the Fundamentalism of Islam, 4:577
Warriors of Mars, 1:617
The Wars, 2:910, 2:911
Wars I Have Seen, 1:881
The Wars of America, 3:546
The Wars of the Roses: Military Activity and English Society, 1452–1497, 3:357
The Wars of Watergate: The Last Crisis of Richard Nixon, 3:539
War Stories and Poems, 1:371
Wartime and Aftermath, 1:420
Wartime Journalism, 1939–1943, 1:1143
Wartime Letters of Rainer Maria Rilke, 1914–1921, 2:607
Wartime Writings, 2:504
The War to End All Wars, 3:531
The War Wife: Vietnamese Poetry, 2:339
The War with Hannibal, 3:317
The War without a Name: France in Algeria, 1954–1962, 3:374
War without Mercy: Race and Power in the Pacific War, 3:477, 3:534
The War with Spain in 1898, 3:533
The War with the Newts, 2:789, 2:790
Was Einstein Right? Putting General Relativity to the Test, 5:49
Washi: The World of Japanese Paper, 1:5
The Washing of the Spears, 3:424

Washing Silk: The Life and Selected Poetry of Wei Chuang, 2:228
Washington, D.C., 1:1062
The Washington Black Book, 3:806
Washington Goes to War, 3:534
Washington Information Directory 1992–93, 1:105
Washington Irving, 1:681
Washington Irving: An American Study, 1802–1832, 1:681
Washington Square, 1:763
The Waste Land, 1:412, 1:413, 1:416, 1:471, 1:795, 1:797, 1:963, 1:980, 3:878
The Waste Land: A Facsimile and Transcript of the Original Drafts, Including the Annotations of Ezra Pound, 1:472
Waste of Timelessness: And Other Early Stories, 1:866
The Waste Package, 5:177
Was the Red Flag Flying There?, 3:439
The Watcher and Other Stories, 2:412
Watch It Come Down, 1:532
Watch on the Rhine, 1:1092, 1:1093
Water: A Primer, 5:632
Water: The Nature, Uses, and Future of Our Most Abused Resource, 5:632
Water and Dreams: An Essay on Imagination of Matter, 4:274
Water Atlas of the United States, 5:631
The Water-Babies, 1:369
Water Babies: The Igor Tjarkovsky Method for Delivering in Water, 5:359
The Water Encyclopedia, 5:618
The Water Engine: An American Fable, 1:1101
The Waterfall, 1:468
Water from the Rock: Black Resistance in a Revolutionary Age, 3:520
Waterlily Fire: Poems 1935–1962, 1:1042
The Waterman, 2:631
Water Margin, 2:218, 2:219
Watermark, 2:704, 3:898
The Water-Method Man, 1:991, 1:992
Water Music, 1:953
The Water of Babylon, 1:433

Waters and Lands, 2:437
The Watershed: A Biography of Johannes Kepler, 4:161, 5:608
Watershed Hydrology, 5:631
Water Supply, 5:245
The Water-Witch; or, The Skimmer of the Seas: A Tale, 1:664
The Watsons, 1:275
Watt, 1:439, 2:459
Watteau's Shepherds: The Detective Novel in Britain, 1914–1940, 1:604
Waugh in Abyssinia, 1:561
Waugh on Women, 1:563
A Wave, 1:936
Wave Mechanics and Its Applications, 5:704
Wave Optics, 5:666
Waverly, or, Sixty Years Since, 1:298
The Waverley Dictionary, 1:300
The Waverley Novels and Their Critics, 1:300
Waves (Ibuse), 2:287
The Waves (Kang Shin-jae), 2:303
The Waves (Woolf), 1:569
Waves: Stories, 2:261
Waves and Beaches: The Dynamics of the Ocean Surface, 5:631
The Way and Its Power, 4:528
Way Down East, 1:1167
Wayfarers, 2:664
The Way Home, 2:961
The Way of All Flesh, 1:342
A Way of Being, 5:468
The Way of Heaven: An Introduction to the Confucian Religious Life, 4:526
The Way of Individuation, 5:456
The Way of Korean Zen, 4:538
A Way of Life, 5:54
Way of Perfection, 2:550
A Way of Seeing: A Critical Study of James Agee, 1:933
The Way of Tea, 4:537
The Way of the Faithful: An Anthology of Jewish Mysticism, 4:629
The Way of the Masks, 3:34
The Way of the Pilgrim and the Pilgrim Continues His Way, 4:755
The Way of the World, 1:237

The Way of Torah. An Introduction to Judaism, 4:596
Way of Zen, 4:860, 4:881
Ways and Crossways, 2:468
The Ways and Means of Statistics, 5:524
Wayside Courtships, 1:751
The Wayside Motor Inn, 1:1091
Ways of Escape, 1:489
The Ways of Paradox, 4:412
The Ways of Paradox and Other Essays, 5:100
The Ways of Peace, 4:388
The Ways of Philosophy, 4:23
The Ways of the Hour: A Tale, 1:664
Ways of Thinking of Eastern Peoples: India, China, Tibet, Japan, 4:350
The Ways of White Folks, 1:848
Ways of Worldmaking, 4:403
Way Station, 1:1262
Ways with Words, 3:250
The Way the Future Was: A Memoir, 1:1261
The Way Things Work, 5:12, 5:193
The Way to Chaeronea, 2:355
The Way to Rainy Mountain, 1:1016
The Way to the Western Sea: Lewis and Clark across the Continent, 3:521, 3:928
The Way to Wisdom: An Introduction to Philosophy, 4:21, 4:300, 5:138
The Way Upstream, 1:436
The Wayward Bus, 1:884
The Wayward Pressman, 3:814
Wayward Reporter: The Life of A. J. Liebling, 3:814
Wayward Youth, 5:416
Waywaya: Eleven Filipino Short Stories, 2:332
The Way We Live Now, 1:405, 1:1052
The Way We Never Were: American Families and the Nostalgia Trap, 3:206
The Way West, 1:1214
W. B. Yeats and the Emergence of the Irish Free State, 1918–1939, 1:572
W. D. Howells: Selected Criticism, 1:760
We (Lindbergh), 3:929
We (Zamyatin), 2:774
We, the Tikopia, 3:19, 3:25, 3:29, 3:30

Weak Foundations, 3:637
Wealth and Poverty, 3:66
The Wealth of Nations, 3:106, 3:107, 4:215
The Wealth of Nature, 5:117
The Wealth of the Solomons, 3:495
We Always Treat Women Too Well, 2:496
Weapons and Hope, 5:110, 5:133
Weapons of Happiness, 1:449, 1:450
The Weary Blues, 1:847
Weather, 5:634
Weather Almanac, 1:83, 5:7
The Weather Book: An Easy to Understand Guide to the USA's Weather, 5:634
Weather Forecasting, 5:647
The Weather Handbook, 5:633
Weathering, 5:628
The Weather Machine: How Our Weather Works and Why It Is Changing, 5:633
Weather of U.S. Cities, 5:633
The Weather Tomorrow: Why Can't They Get It Right?, 5:633
The Weavers, 2:586
The Web: Stories by Argentine Women, 2:849
The Web and the Rock, 1:903
The Webbs and Their Work, 3:113
W.E.B. Du Bois (McKissack), 1:832
W.E.B. Du Bois (Tuttle), 3:579
W.E.B. Du Bois: A Bibliography of His Published Writings, 3:578
W.E.B. Du Bois: A Bibliography of Writings about Him, 1:832
W.E.B. Du Bois: Black Radical Democrat, 1:832
W.E.B. Du Bois: Negro Leader in a Time of Crisis, 3:578
We Believe in One God, 4:572
The Web of Belief, 4:412, 5:100
The Web of Progress, 3:525
A Web of Relationships, 1:750
Webster: The Critical Heritage, 1:201
Webster's Collegiate Thesaurus, 1:94

Webster's First New Intergalactic Wickedary of the English Language, 1:1187, 4:765
Webster's Medical Desk Dictionary, 5:367
Webster's New Biographical Dictionary, 1:86, 3:7
Webster's New Dictionary of Synonyms, 1:95
Webster's New Geographical Dictionary, 1:85, 5:618
Webster's New World Dictionary of Media and Communications, 3:802
Webster's New World Dictionary of Acronyms and Abbreviations, 1:93
Webster's New World Dictionary of the American Language, College Edition, 1:91
Webster's New World German Dictionary: A Collins Concise Dictionary, 1:99
Webster's New World Hebrew-English Dictionary, 1:99
Webster's New World Kenkyusha Japanese-English Character Reading Dictionary, 1:100
Webster's New World Thesaurus, 1:94
Webster's Third New International Dictionary of the English Language Unabridged, 1:91
The Web That Has No Weaver: Understanding Chinese Medicine, 5:319
We Called It Music: A Generation of Jazz, 3:668
We Can't Pay? We Won't Pay! 2:421
The Wedding, 2:709
The Wedding of a Poet: A One-Act Comedy (1859), 2:96
The Wedding of Zein, 2:72
Wedding Song, 2:68
Wedlock of the Gods, 2:147
We Drink from Our Own Wells: The Spiritual Journey of a People, 4:769
We Eat the Mines and the Mines Eat Us, 3:22, 3:633
Weekly Chronicles, 2:819
A Week on the Concord and Merrimack Rivers, 1:659, 1:700, 1:701, 5:837

A Week on the Concord and Merrimack Rivers; Walden; The Maine Woods; Cape Cod, 1:701
Weep Not, Child, 2:151, 2:153, 2:154
WEESKA Electronic Communication Systems, 5:305
We Have Always Lived in the Castle, 1:992
We Have Never Been Modern, 5:166, 5:167
Weh Dem, Der Lügt, 2:583
We Hold These Truths, 4:271
Weighing Chances, 5:523
The Weight of the World, 2:586
Weimar: A Cultural History, 3:377
Weimar Culture, 2:565
Weimar Culture: The Outsider as Insider, 3:376
Weird Tales, 2:591
Weird Tales from the Northern Seas, 2:666
The Weir of Hermiston, 1:396
Welcome to Hard Times, 1:969
Welcome to Our City, 1:903, 1:904
Welcome to the Monkey House, 1:1063
Welcoming Disaster, 2:919
Welfare: The Social Issues in Philosophical Perspective, 4:318
Welfare Economics: Ten Introductory Essays, 3:64
Welfare Economics and the Theory of the State, 3:64
The Welfare State in Britain: A Political History since 1945, 3:366
We Lived There Too, 1630–1930, 4:640
We Live Too Short and Die Too Long, 5:316
The Well, 2:39, 2:956
The Well and the Tree: World and Time in Early Germanic Culture, 4:437
Well-Being, 4:389
Well Body, Well Earth: The Sierra Club Environmental Health Sourcebook, 5:342
The Well Child Book, 5:323
The Well Dressed Explorer, 2:950
The Wellesley Index to Victorian Periodicals, 1824–1900, 1:319

The Wellfleet Whale and Companion Poems, 1:1003
The Wellness Book, 5:400
The Wellness Encyclopedia, 5:312
The Well of Loneliness, 1:492
The Well of the Saints, 1:555
The Wellsprings of Music, 3:667
Well-Tempered Clavier, 3:675
The Well-Wrought Urn: Studies in the Structure of Poetry, 1:248, 1:924, 1:953
We Love Glenda So Much and Other Stories, 2:861
The Welsh in Their History, 3:369
Welsh Nationalism in the Twentieth Century, 3:369
Welty, 1:895
Welty: A Life in Literature, 1:895
The Welty Collection, 1:896
Wendell Berry, 5:269
We of the Mountains, 2:77
The Wept of Wishton-Wish, 1:664, 1:1244
We're No Angels, 1:1101
Werner, 1:271
Werther, 2:421
Wesker on File, 1:565
Wesker the Playwright, 1:565
Wesley and Sanctification: A Study in the Doctrine of Salvation, 4:790
Wesley Mitchell (1874–1948), John Commons, Clarence Ayers, 3:74, 3:97
Wessex Tales, 1:361
West Africa: An Introduction to Its History, 3:420
West Africa, the Former French States, 3:420
West Africa and the Atlantic Slave Trade, 3:430
West African Folk-Tales, 2:126
West African Kingdoms in the Nineteenth Century, 3:420
West African Poetry: A Critical History, 2:126
West African Resistance: The Military Response to Colonial Occupation, 3:420
The West African Village Novel, 2:126
West Africa Partitioned, 3:420
West Africa under Colonial Rule, 3:420

The West and Reconstruction, 3:531
The West and the Nation: Essays in Honour of W. L. Morton, 3:622
The West beyond the West: A History of British Columbia, 3:609
West Coast Jazz: Modern Jazz in California, 3:668
The Western Church in the Later Middle Ages, 4:691, 4:721
Western Europe in the Middle Ages: 300–1475, 3:332
Western Europe in the Middle Ages: A Short History, 3:332
The Western Films of John Ford, 1:1166
The Western Impact on World Music, 3:667
The Western Intellectual Tradition: From Leonardo to Hegel, 4:159, 5:162
A Western Journal, 1:904
Western Man and Environmental Ethics, 5:160, 5:161
Western Mysticism: Neglected Chapters in the History of Religion, 4:111
The Western Response to Zoroaster, 4:444
Western Septet: Seven Stories of the American West, 2:821
The Western Slave Coast and Its Rulers, 3:421
Western Society and the Church in the Middle Ages, 4:691
Western Theatre: Revolution and Revival, 1:272
Western Trails: A Collection of Short Stories, 1:733
Western Union, 1:1213
The Western Way of War: Infantry Battle in Classical Greece, 3:308
The Western World and Japan, 3:502
Western Writing Implements in the Age of the Quill Pen, 1:15
West from Home, 1:1208
West Indian Folk Tales, 2:931
West Indian Literature, 2:930
West Indian Narrative: An Introductory Anthology, 2:931

The West Indian Novel,
2:930

The West Indian Novel and
Its Background, 2:930

West Indian Poetry, 2:930

West Indian Stories, 2:931,
2:941

The West Indies and the
Spanish Main, 1:406

West Indies Limited, 2:869

West Malaysia and Singapore: A Selected Bibliography, 3:492

The Westminster Dictionary
of Christian Ethics, 4:2,
4:718, 4:893

The Westminster Dictionary
of Christian Spirituality,
4:676, 4:718

The Westminster Dictionary
of Christian Theology,
4:676

Westminster Dictionary of
Church History, 4:675,
4:719

The Westminster Review,
1:323, 1:386, 4:190

The West of Owen Wister:
Selected Short Stories,
1:789

West of Suez, 1:532

Westview Special Studies on
the Middle East, 4:568

West Virginia Folk Music,
3:860

Westward, Ha!: Around the
World in 80 Clichés, 1:868

Westward Ho!, 1:369

Westward the Tide, 1:1215

Westward to Vinland, 3:380,
3:610, 3:899

We the People: The Economic Origins of the Constitution, 3:543

We the People: Vol. 1 Foundations, 3:141

Wetherby, 1:493

The W.E.T. Workout, 5:326

We Who Are about To . . .,
1:1262

The Whale and Other Uncollected Translations, 1:1066

The Whale and the Reactor,
5:73, 5:131, 5:145, 5:146,
5:148

Whale Watcher's Handbook,
5:760

Whanau, 2:977

What a Man's Gotta Do: The
Masculine Myth in Popular Culture, 3:207

What Are My Chances? 5:405

What Are People For? 5:269

What a Way to Go, 1:1017

What Can She Know? 4:391

What Computers Can't Do: A
Critique of Artificial Reason, 5:571

What Computers Still Can't
Do: A Critique of Artificial
Reason, 5:74

"What Do You Care What
Other People Think?"
3:908

What Do You Say after You
Say Hello: The Psychology
of Human Destiny, 5:434

The What D'Ye Call It: A
Tragi-Comical Pastoral
Farce, 1:246

What Engineers Know and
How They Know It, 5:49,
5:257

What Every Engineer Should
Know about Engineering
Information Sources, 5:217

What Every Woman Knows,
1:329, 1:438

What Happened, 1:881

What Happens during Business Cycles: A Progress
Report, 3:97

What Happens in Book Publishing, 1:47

What Has Government Done
to Our Health Care? 5:333

What I Believe, 4:324, 5:165

What I Did Last Summer,
1:1091

What If? A User's Guide to
Spreadsheets on the IBM
PC, 5:558

What If You Died Tomorrow, 2:967

What Is a Law of Nature?
5:62

What Is a Masterpiece? 3:756

What Is an Editor? Saxe
Commins at Work, 1:40

What Is Art? 2:765

What Is a Thing? 4:292, 5:90

What Is Calculus About?
5:491

What Is Called Thinking?
4:292, 5:90

What Is Christianity? 4:741

What Is Cinema, 1:1156,
3:827

What Is Dance: Readings in
Theory and Criticism,
3:732

What Is English, 1:1127

What Is History? 3:275

What Is Life? Mind and Matter, 5:714

What Is Life? The Physical
Aspects of a Living Cell,
5:714

What Is Literature? 4:329

What Is Literature and Other
Essays, 2:507

What Is Man? and Other
Philosophical Writings,
1:780

What Is Mathematics? An
Elementary Approach to
Ideas and Methods, 5:480

What Is Midrash? 4:612

What Is Philosophy? 4:292,
4:315, 5:96

What Is Property? 3:140

What Is Religion? 4:747

What Is Remembered, 1:881

What Is Sufism? 4:575

What Is Surrealism? Selected
Writings, 2:462

What Is Theatre?: Incorporating—the Dramatic Event,
1:1071

What Is This Jewish Heritage? 4:596

What Is to Be Done? (Chernyshevsky), 2:711

What Is to Be Done? (Peck),
3:52, 3:287

What Jung Really Said, 5:455

What Kind of Life: The Limits of Medical Progress,
5:84

What Life Should Mean to
You, 5:431

What Mad Pursuit: A Personal View of Scientific Discovery, 5:9, 5:784, 5:791

What Maisie Knew, 1:763

What Man Can Make of
Man, 4:296

What Manner of Man, 4:772

What Model for Europe?
3:345

What Nietzsche Means, 4:247

What Philosophy Can Do,
4:379

What Poetry Is, 2:628

What Price Glory, 1:1081

What Remains and Other
Stories, 2:616

What's Bred in the Bone,
2:910

What Schools Are For, 3:250

What's Left to Eat? 5:12,
5:345

What's News: The Media in
American Society, 3:802

What's O'Clock, 1:856

What Sort of People Should
There Be? 5:120

The Whig Ascendancy: Colloquies on Hanoverian Eng-
land, 3:361

Whigs and Hunters, 3:410

While England Slept: A Survey of World Affairs,
1932–1938, 3:401

While Messiah Tarried: Jewish Socialist Movements,
1871–1917, 3:349

While Six Million Died: A
Chronicle of American Ap-
athy, 4:640

While the Sun Shines, 1:540

Whilomville Stories, 1:742

Whipperginny, 1:485

The Whirlpool, 1:359

A Whir of Gold, 2:925

The Whisper of Star: A Siberian Journey, 3:906

Whispers from the Carib-
bean: I Going Away, I Go-
ing Home, 2:930

Whisper to the Earth, 1:991

Whistle, 1:994

Whistle: Chapter One of a
Work-in-Progress, 1:995

The Whistleblowers: Exposing Corruption in Govern-
ment and Industry, 3:49

Whitaker's Almanac, 1:83

Whitaker's Books in Print,
1:71

Whitaker's Cumulative Books
List, 1:71

The White Album, 1:968

White Attitudes toward Black
People, 3:208

White Book, 2:793

White Buildings, 1:823

The White Castle: A Novel,
2:96

White Collar, 3:235

White Collar Crime, 3:205

White Collar Fictions, 1:805

The White Company, 1:607

White Deer, 1:891

The White Devil, 1:200

The White Devil Discover'd,
1:201

White Fang, 1:773, 1:774

The White Goddess, 1:485

The White Guard, 2:705,
2:706

The White-Haired Lover,
1:1045

Whitehead, Process Philosophy, and Education, 4:341

Whitehead and the Modern
World: Science, Metaphys-
ics, and Civilization, 4:342

Whitehead's American Essays
in Social Philosophy,
4:341

Whitehead's Metaphysics of
Extension and Solidarity,
4:342

Whitehead's Ontology, 4:342

Whitehead's Philosophical
Development, 4:342

Whitehead's Philosophy: Selected Essays, 1935–1970,
4:289, 4:342

Whitehead's Theory of
Knowledge, 4:341

A White Heron, 1:770

A White Heron and Other
Stories, 1:769

White House Doctor, 5:315

White House Years, 3:539

White-Jacket, 1:686, 1:687

White Lies: Melville's Narratives of Facts, 1:689

White Man, Listen! 1:905,
1:906

White Man's Country, 3:422

The White Man's Indian,
3:554

White Mythologies: Writing,
History, and the West,
3:277, 1:1133

The White Nile, 3:419

White over Black: American
Attitudes toward the Ne-
gro, 1550–1812, 3:556

The White Peacock, 1:509

White Shroud: Poems,
1980–1985, 1:981

White Stones and Fir Trees,
2:781

The White Terror and the
Red: A Novel of Revolu-
tionary Russia, 1:737, 2:37

White Violence and Black
Response from Recon-
struction to Montgomery,
3:557

The White Witch of Rose-
hall, 2:934, 2:935

White Wolf Woman, 3:865

Whitfield's University Rhyming Dictionary, 1:95

Whither? and Other Stories,
2:17

Whither Mankind, 3:565

Whitman and Han Yong-un,
2:301

Whitman and the American
Idiom, 1:707

Whitman and Tradition: The
Poet in His Century, 1:708

Whitman in His Own Time,
1:708

Whitman's Poetry of the
Body: Sexuality, Politics,
and the Text, 1:707

Whitman the Political Poet,
1:707

Whitney's Star Finder, 5:591

The Whitsun Weddings,
1:507

Who Built America? 3:552

Who Can Be Happy and
Free in Russia? 2:742

Who Do You Think You
Are? 2:921

Who Framed Roger Rabbit,
1:1164

Who Is a Sikh? The Problem
of Sikh Identity, 4:516

Who Is She? Images of
Women in Australian Fic-
tion, 2:947

Who Is Teddy Villanova?
1:949

Who Is to Blame? 2:727

Who Is Who, Government,
Politics, Banking and In-
dustry in Latin America,
3:624

Who Killed CBS? The Undo-
ing of America's Number-
One News Network, 3:805

Who Knows: Information in
the Age of the Fortune
500, 5:558

The Whole Armour and The
Secret Ladder, 2:936

The Whole Birth Catalog: A
Sourcebook for Choices in
Childbirth, 5:357

Whole Days in the Trees,
2:474

Whole Earth Software Catalog 1986, 5:539

The Whole Internet User's
Guide & Catalog, 5:547

Whole Language: What's the
Difference, 3:254

Whole Motion: Collected
Poems, 1945–1992, 1:967

The Wholeness of Life, 4:555

A Whole New Ball Game: An
Interpretation of American
Sports, 3:552

The Whole World Is Watch-
ing, 3:203

The Whole World Over,
2:757

Whom to Marry and How to
Get Married, 1:377, 1:378

Who Remembers the Sea,
2:119

Who Rides with Wyatt?
1:1213

Whoroscope, 1:439

Who's Afraid of Virginia Woolf? 1:1080, 1:1081, 2:679

Whose Body? 1:610

Whose Justice? Which Rationality? 4:407

Whose Little Boy Are You? 2:15

Whose Science? Whose Knowledge? Thinking from Women's Lives, 4:40, 5:154, 5:187

Who Should Decide? Paternalism in Health Care, 5:119

Who Survives Cancer? 5:372

Who's Who, 1:86, 1:516

Who's Who among Black Americans, 1:86

Who's Who in Africa? Leaders for the Nineteen Nineties, 3:418

Who's Who in America, 1:86, 1:128

Who's Who in America 1994, 3:507

Who's Who in American Art, 1:86

Who's Who in American Film Now, 3:826

Who's Who in American Law, 1:86

Who's Who in American Music: Classical, 3:658

Who's Who in American Politics, 1:86

Who's Who in American Politics 1993–94, 3:507

Who's Who in British History, 3:355

Who's Who in Early Hanoverian England, 3:363

Who's Who in Engineering, 5:4

Who's Who in Faulkner, 1:836

Who's Who in H. G. Wells, 1:564

Who's Who in Religion, 1992–93, 4:7

Who's Who in Rock, 3:654

Who's Who in Science and Engineering, 1992-1993, 5:4

Who's Who in Science in Europe, 5:4

Who's Who in Scottish History, 3:368

Who's Who in Stuart Britain, 3:360

Who's Who in Technology, 5:4

Who's Who in Technology Today, 5:218

The Who's Who in the History of Philosophy, 4:14

Who's Who in Tudor England, 3:359

Who's Who in Wagner: An A to Z Look at His Life and Work, 3:728

Who's Who in Writers, Editors and Poets, 1:128

Who's Who of American Women, 1:86

Who's Who of Jazz, 3:668

Who's Who of Nobel Prize Winners, 1901–1990, 5:4

Who's Who of Southern Africa, 1991–92, 3:424

Who Wants a Cheap Rhinoceros? 1:1207

Who Was a Jew, 4:621

Who Was When? A Dictionary of Contemporaries, 1:88

Who Was Who in America, 3:507

Who Was Who in American History: Science and Technology, 5:30

Who Was Who in the Roman World, 3:298

Who Won What When, 1:135

Why Americans Don't Vote, 3:144

Why Are We in Vietnam? 1:1011, 1:1012

Why Are We So Blest? 2:130, 2:131

Why Buildings Fall Down: How Structures Fail, 5:12

Why Came Ye Not to Court, 1:196

Why Doesn't My Funny Bone Make Me Laugh? 5:343

Why Do I Write? 1:448

Why Do Jews Need a Land of Their Own? 2:46

Why God Became Man and the Virgin Conception and Original Sin, 4:108

Why Gorbachev Happened: His Triumphs and His Failures, 3:346

Why I Am Not a Christian and Other Essays on Religion and Related Subjects, 4:324

Why in the World, 3:891

Why Men Fight: A Method of Abolishing the International Duel, 4:324

Why Noah Chose the Dove, 1:1050

Why Preserve Natural Variety? 5:115

Why the Confederacy Lost, 3:586

Why the South Lost the Civil War, 3:526

Why Things Don't Work: The Anthropology of Daily Life, 3:32

A Wicked Irony: The Rhetoric of Lermontov's "A Hero of Our Time," 2:735

The Wide, Wide World, 1:1219

Wide Awake at 3:00 A.M.: By Choice or by Chance, 5:340

Wide-Body: The Triumph of the 747, 5:219

Wide Fields, 1:1089

The Wide Net and Other Stories, 1:895

The Wider Sea, 1:393, 1:395

Wide Sargasso Sea, 2:940

Widow, Nun and Courtesan, 2:211

The Widow Barnaby, 1:408

The Widow Married: A Sequel to "The Widow Barnaby," 1:408

Widows, 2:864

The Widows of Russia, Nabokov's Style and Other Essays, 2:689

The Widow's Tears, 1:175

Wieland, 1:635, 1:636, 1:1239

Wierook en Tranen, 2:630

The Wife, and Woman's Reward, 1:384

The Wife of His Youth and Other Stories, 1:738, 1:739

Wife of Light, 1:931

Wife to Mr. Milton, 1:485

The Wigwam and the Cabin, 1:696, 1:697

Wigwam Evenings, 1:749

The Wild Beach and Other Stories, 2:692

Wild Berries, 2:774

The Wild Body, 1:514

Wild Bouquet, 2:678

The Wild Boy of Burundi, 5:422

The Wild Boys: A Book of the Dead, 1:957

Wild Cat Falling, 2:960, 2:961

A Wild Civility: Interactions in the Poetry and Thought of Robert Graves, 1:486

Wild Conquest, 2:158

Wild Dogs: The Natural History of the Nondomestic Canidae, 5:771
The Wild Duck, 2:665, 2:666
The Wilderness, 2:266
Wilderness: A Tale of the Civil War, 1:892
Wilderness and the American Mind, 3:550, 5:824
The Wilderness and the City, 4:36
The Wilderness Hunter, 3:594
Wilderness Road, 1:1089
Wildfire, 1:1214
Wildfire: Grassroots Revolts in Israel in the Post-Socialist Era, 4:642
Wild Freedom, 1:1212
Wild Geese (Hwang Sun-wŏn), 2:302
The Wild Geese (Ōgai), 2:290
The Wild Goats of Ein Gedi, 4:643
Wild Grass, 2:256
Wild Honey, 2:708
Wild Hunter in the Bush of Ghosts, 2:150
Wildlife Ecology and Management, 5:820
Wild Lilies, Poisonous Weeds, 2:233
Wild Mountain Thyme, 1:621
Wild Palms, 1:835
A Wild Patience Has Taken Me This Far: Poems, 1978-1981, 1:1037
A Wild Sheep Chase: A Novel, 2:290
Wild Thorns, 2:59
Wild Women in the Whirlwind, 1:910
Wiley: 175 Years of Publishing, 1:45
Wilfred Owen, 1:533
Wilhelm Conrad Röntgen and the Early History of the Röntgen Rays, 5:711
Wilhelm Meister (Carlyle), 1:343
Wilhelm Meister (Goethe), 2:580, 2:581
Wilhelm Wundt and the Making of a Scientific Psychology, 3:197
Wilkie Collins: A Biography, 1:346
Wilkie Collins: A Critical and Bibliographical Study, 1:346

Wilkie Collins: A Critical Survey of His Prose Fiction with a Bibliography, 1:346
Wilkie Collins: The Critical Heritage, 1:346
The Will, 1:329
Willa: The Life of Willa Cather, 1:821
Willa Cather, 1:821, 1:822, 1:972
Willa Cather: A Critical Biography, 1:821
Willa Cather: A Literary Life, 1:822
Willa Cather: A Memoir, 1:822
Willa Cather: A Study of the Short Fiction, 1:822
Willa Cather: Double Lives, 1:821
Willa Cather and the Art of Conflict, 1:822
Willa Cather in Person: Interviews, Speeches, and Letters, 1:821
Willa Cather Living: A Personal Record, 1:821
Willa Cather on Writing: Critical Studies on Writing as an Art, 1:821
Willa Cather's Collected Short Fiction 1892-1912, 1:821
Willa Cather's Modernism: A Study of Style of Technique, 1:821
Willa Cather's My Antonia, 1:821
Will and Circumstance, 4:210
The Will and the Word: The Poetry of Edward Taylor, 1:644
Willehalm, 2:616, 2:617
Will Henry-Clay Fisher, 1:1213
William Auvergne and Robert Grosseteste, 4:115
William Balston, Paper Maker, 1759-1849, 1:4
William Blake, 1:279
William Blake: A Critical Essay, 1:279
William Blake: A Man without a Mask, 1:278
William Blake: His Philosophy and Symbols, 1:279
William Blake: The Critical Heritage, 1:278
William Blake: The Politics of Vision, 1:279
William Blake and His Circle, 1:279

William Blake's Circle of Destiny, 1:279
William Bradford, 1:634
William Bradford: The Collected Verse, 1:634
William Burroughs: Algebra of Need, 1:958
William Carlos Williams, 1:900, 1:901
William Carlos Williams: An American Artist, 1:900
William Carlos Williams: A New World Naked, 1:901
William Carlos Williams: Man and Poet, 1:901
William Carlos Williams: The Critical Heritage, 1:901
William Carlos Williams: The Poet and His Critics, 1:901
William Carlos Williams, the Arts, and Literary Tradition, 1:901
William Carlos Williams and Autobiography: The Woods of His Own Nature, 1:901
William Carlos Williams and Romantic Idealism, 1:901
William Carlos Williams and the Ethics of Painting, 1:901
William Carlos Williams and Transcendentalism: Fitting the Crab in a Box, 1:900
William Carlos Williams' Paterson: A Critical Appraisal, 1:901
William Caslon, 1693-1766, 1:13
William Collins, 1:236
William Collins and 18th-Century Poetry, 1:236
William Cowper, 1:238
William Cowper: A Biography, 1:238
William Cowper: A Critical Life, 1:238
William Cowper of the Inner Temple, 1:238
William Cullen Bryant (Bigelow), 1:661
William Cullen Bryant (Brown), 1:661
William Cullen Bryant (McClean), 1:662
William Cullen Bryant and His America, 1:661
William Dean Howells, 1:759
William Dean Howells: A Bibliography, 1:759
William Dean Howells: A Study, 1:759
William Dean Howells: The Friendly Eye, 1:760

William Edwin Rudge, 1:8
William Faulkner, 1:836,
  1:837
William Faulkner: A Bibliog-
  raphy of Secondary
  Works, 1:838
William Faulkner: A Critical
  Study, 1:837
William Faulkner: American
  Writer, 1:837
William Faulkner: First En-
  counters, 1:836
William Faulkner: Four Dec-
  ades of Criticism, 1:838
William Faulkner: His Life
  and Work, 1:837
William Faulkner: The Mak-
  ing of a Novelist, 1:837
William Faulkner: The Yok-
  napatawpha Country, 1:836
William Faulkner: Toward
  Yoknapatawpha and Be-
  yond, 1:836
William Fitzhugh and His
  Chesapeake World,
  1676-1701, 3:517
William Foxwell Albright: A
  Twentieth-Century Genius,
  4:828
William Fulbright and the
  Vietnam War, 3:544
William Gilmore Simms,
  1:697
William Golding, 1:484
William Golding: A Structur-
  al Reading of His Fiction,
  1:484
William Golding: Some Criti-
  cal Considerations, 1:484
William Golding: The Man
  and His Books, 1:484
William Harvey: The Man,
  the Physician, and the Sci-
  entist, 5:361
William Harvey: Trailblazer
  of Medicine, 5:362
William Harvey and His Age,
  5:361
William Harvey and the Cir-
  culation of the Blood,
  5:362
William Harvey's Biological
  Ideas, 5:362
William Hazlitt, Critic of
  Power, 1:291
William Heinesen, 2:656
William Heytesbury: Medieval
  Logic and the Rise of
  Mathematical Physics,
  4:104
William Hickling Prescott,
  1:695, 3:649

William Hickling Prescott: A
  Memorial, 3:649
William James (Bird), 1:768,
  4:237
William James (Brennan),
  1:769, 3:188
William James: A Biography,
  1:768
William James: A Reference
  Guide, 1:769
William James: His Life and
  Thought, 1:769, 3:188,
  4:238
William James: The Center
  of His Vision, 1:769,
  3:188, 4:237
William James, Public Phi-
  losopher, 1:769, 4:237
William James and Henri
  Bergson: A Study in Con-
  trasting Theories, 4:237
William James and Pheno-
  menology (Edie), 3:188
William James and Pheno-
  menology: A Study of
  "The Principles of Psy-
  chology" (Wilshire), 3:188,
  5:454
William James on Exception-
  al Mental States: The 1896
  Lowell Lectures, 1:769,
  3:188
William James's Philosophy:
  A New Perspective, 4:237
William James's Radical Re-
  construction of Philoso-
  phy, 4:238
William Langland: Piers
  Plowman: An Alliterative
  Verse Translation, 1:153
William Lloyd's Life of Py-
  thagoras, with a New The-
  sis on the Origin of the
  New Testament, 5:514
William Lyon Mackenzie
  King: A Political Biogra-
  phy, 3:614
William Makepeace Thacker-
  ay, 1:404
William Makepeace Thacker-
  ay: An Annotated Bibliog-
  raphy, 1976-1987, 1:404
William Makepeace Thacker-
  ay's "Vanity Fair," 1:404
William Morris, 1:383
William Morris: Design and
  Enterprise in Victorian
  England, 1:383
William Morris: His Art, His
  Writings, and His Public
  Life: A Record, 1:383
William Morris: His Life and
  Work, 1:383

William Morris: Romantic to
  Revolutionary, 1:383, 3:410
William Morris: The Con-
  struction of the Male Self,
  1856-1872, 1:383
William Morris: The Critical
  Heritage, 1:382
William Morris and the Art
  of the Book, 1:12, 1:383
William Morris Full Color
  Patterns and Designs,
  1:383
William Ockham, 4:120
William of Sherwood's Trea-
  tise on Syncategorematic
  Words, 4:103
William Posters, 1:547
William S. Burroughs: An
  Annotated Bibliography of
  His Works and Criticism,
  1:958
William S. Burroughs,
  1953-1973: A Bibliogra-
  phy, 1:958
William Shakespeare, 1:209
William Shakespeare: A Com-
  pact Documentary Life,
  1:205
William Shakespeare: A Doc-
  umentary Life, 1:205
William Shakespeare: A Lit-
  erary Life, 1:204
William Shakespeare: A
  Reader's Guide, 1:222
William Shakespeare: A
  Study of Facts and Prob-
  lems, 1:204
William Shakespeare: A Tex-
  tual Companion, 1:207
William Shakespeare: His
  World, His Work, His In-
  fluence, 1:221
William Shakespeare: Rec-
  ords and Images, 1:205
William Shakespeare: The
  Complete Works, 1:206
William Shakespeare: The
  Poems, 1:206
William Shakespeare the
  Man, 1:205
William Stanley Jevons: Criti-
  cal Assessments, 3:85
William Styron, 1:1057
William Sydney Porter (O.
  Henry): A Reference
  Guide, 1:757
William Tell, 2:609
William the Conqueror,
  1:370
William Vaughn Moody,
  1:775
William Vaughn Moody: A
  Study, 1:775

William Whewell: A Composite Portrait, 4:258, 5:58
William Whewell, Philosopher of Science, 4:258, 5:57
William Wordsworth, 1:307
William Wordsworth: A Life, 1:307
William Wordsworth: His Doctrine and Art in Their Historical Relations, 1:306
William Wordsworth: His Life, Works and Influence, 1:307
William Wordsworth: Intensity and Achievement, 1:307
William Wordsworth and the Age of English Romanticism, 1:266
William Wycherley: A Reference Guide, 1:263
Willie Master's Lonesome Wife, 1:980
Willing and Unwilling, 4:256
Willis E. Lamb, Jr.: A Festschrift on the Occasion of his 65th Birthday, 5:698
Williwaw, 1:1061, 1:1062
Will My Baby Be Normal? 5:359
Will Rogers, 3:887
Will Rogers: A Biography, 3:887
Will Rogers' Daily Telegrams: The Coolidge Years, 1926–1929, 3:887
Will's Boy, 1:1017
Will Therapy and Truth and Reality, 5:466
The Will to Be Human, 5:420
The Will to Believe, 1:768, 3:187
The Will to Believe: Novelists of the 1930s, 1:421
The Will to Believe and Human Immortality, 4:237
The Will to Change: Poems 1968–70, 1:1037
The Will to Meaning: Foundations and Applications of Logotherapy, 5:444
The Will to Power, 4:245, 4:246
Will Warburton: A Romance of Real Life, 1:359
Willy Brandt: Portrait of a Statesman, 3:377
Will You Please Be Quiet, Please? 1:960
Wilson Harris, 2:936
Wilson Harris and the Caribbean Novel, 2:936

Wilson Harris and the Modern Tradition, 2:936
The Winchester Malory: A Facsimile, 1:155
The Wind, 2:509
Wind, Sand and Stars, 2:504
A Wind across the Grass, 2:233
Wind and Sand, 5:220
Wind and Stone: A Novel, 2:293
Wind and Waves, 2:287
The Wind and the Waves: Four Modern Korean Poets, 2:299
Wind Fall: The End of the Affair, 3:907
The Wind from the Plain, 2:100
The Wind from the Sun: Stories of the Space Age, 1:614
The Wind in the Rose-bush: And Other Stories of the Supernatural, 1:750
The Wind in the Willows (Grahame), 1:578, 1:584, 1:588
Wind in the Willows (Landesbergis), 2:806
The Windmill of Love, 1:619
Windmills, Bridges and Old Machines: Discovering Our Industrial Past, 5:232
Windmills of the Gods, 1:1223
The Window and the Garden, 2:546
A Window in Thrums, 1:329, 1:438
The Window of Memory: The Literary Career of Thomas Wolfe, 1:904
A Window on Provence: One Summer's Sojourn into the Simple Life, 3:900
Windows: The Official Guide to Microsoft's Operating Environment, 5:554
Window Shopping: Cinema and the Postmodern, 3:827
Windows on Japanese Education, 3:248
Windows on the Mind, 5:341
Windows that Open Inward: Images of Chile, 2:875
A Window to Criticism: Shakespeare's Sonnets and Modern Poetics, 1:215
Windsor Forest, 1:251
The Windward Road, 5:817
Windy McPherson's Son, 1:811

Wine, Women and Death: Medieval Hebrew Poems on the Good Life, 2:10
The Wine-Dark Sea, 2:438
Winesburg, Ohio, 1:811, 1:858
Winesburg, Ohio: An Exploration, 1:812
The Wing-and-Wing; or, Le Feu-Follet: A Tale, 1:664
The Winged Colt, 2:800
The Winged Gospel: America's Romance with Aviation, 1900–1950, 3:547
The Winged Serpent: American Indian Prose and Poetry, 1:631
Wings (Kopit), 1:1098
Wings (Kuzmin), 2:733
The Wings of the Dove, 1:763
The Winners (Cortázar), 2:862
Winners (Friel), 1:479
Winners: The Blue Ribbon Encyclopedia of Awards, 1:88
Winner Take Nothing, 1:845
Winnie, 1:954
Winnie-the-Pooh, 1:587, 1:588
The Winning of the Midwest: Social and Political Conflict, 1888–1896, 3:532
The Winning of the West, 3:594
Winning Pulitzers, 3:821
Winning the Brain Race, 3:250
Winning with Statistics, 5:524
Winning Women into Mathematics, 5:479
The Winslow Boy, 1:540
Winter: Notes from Montana, 5:817
Winter Garden, 2:875
Winter in Majorca, 2:505
Winter Notes on Summer Impressions, 2:714
Winter of Artifice, 1:864, 1:865
The Winter of Our Discontent, 1:884
Winter Plum: Contemporary Chinese Fiction, 2:235
Winterset, 1:1081
The Winter's Tale, 1:205, 1:206, 2:461
Wired Cities: Shaping the Future of Communications, 5:297
Wisconsin Folklore, 3:862
Wisconsin Lore, 3:861

Wisdom, 1:161

Wisdom, Madness and Folly: The Making of a Psychiatrist, 1927–1957, 5:459

Wisdom and Love in St. Thomas Aquinas, 4:286

Wisdom as Moderation: A Philosophy of the Middle Way, 4:289

Wisdom of Insecurity, 4:881

The Wisdom of Life, 4:256

The Wisdom of Marcus Aurelius, 4:76

The Wisdom of Pierre Charron, 4:125

The Wisdom of Science, 4:384

The Wisdom of the Heart, 1:861

The Wisdom of the Outlaw, 4:436

Wisdom of the Prophets, 4:583

The Wisdom of the Upanishads, 4:501, 4:550

Wisdom of the West, 4:324

The Wisdom Symposium, 1:161

Wise Blood, 1:1023

Wise Blood (and The Violent Bear It Away and Everything That Rises Must Converge), 1:1024

Wise Child, 1:486

Wise Children, 1:455

Wise Guy, Solomon, 2:21

Wise Men Fish Here, 1:44

A Wish Comes True, 1:619

Wishes, Lies and Dreams, 1:1001, 1:1002

The Wissenschaftslehre nova methodo, 4:198

Wit and Wisdom of G. K. Chesterton, 1:458

Witchcraft, Oracles, and Magic among the Azande, 3:29, 4:475, 4:476

Witchcraft in Old and New England, 3:858

Witchcraft in the Middle Ages, 3:332, 4:700

Witchcraft Today. Bk 1: The Modern Craft Movement, 4:865

Witches, Ghosts and Signs: Folklore of the Southern Appalachians, 3:860

The Witches of Eastwick, 1:1059, 1:1060

The Witches' Way: Principles, Rituals and Beliefs of Modern Witchcraft, 4:865

The Witch Herbalist of the Remote Town, 2:150

Witch Hunting in Southwest Germany, 1562–1684, 4:730

The Witching of Elspie, 2:926

Witching Times, 1:744

The Witch of Edmonton, 1:176, 1:179

With All My Might: An Autobiography, 1:819

With Brendan Behan, 1:442

With Ears Opening like Morning Glories, 1:896

With Eisenstein in Hollywood, 3:835

With Fire and Sword, 2:821

Within Human Experience: The Philosophy of William Ernest Hocking, 4:297

Within Our Reach: Breaking the Cycle of Disadvantage, 3:252

Within the Gates, 1:526

Within the Plantation Household, 3:524

W. I. Thomas on Social Organization and Social Personality, 3:242

Without a Dowry and Other Plays, 2:744

Without Consent: Mass-Elite Linkages in Presidential Politics, 3:144

Without Fear or Favor, 3:822

Without Feathers, 1:933

Without Me You're Nothing: The Essential Guide to Home Computers, 5:537

With Perfect Faith: The Foundations of Jewish Belief, 4:629

With Reference to Reference, 4:382, 4:403

With the Bark On: Popular Humor of the Old South, 3:870

With the Swamis in America and India, 4:563

With Walker in Nicaragua and Other Early Poems, 2:859

Witi Ihimaera and the Bicultural Vision, 2:978

A Witkacy Reader: The Life and Work of Stanislaw Ignacy Witkiewicz, 2:822

Witness against War: Pacifism in Canada, 1900–1945, 3:608

Witnesses at the Creation, 3:521

Witnesses for Oil, 5:278

Witnesses to a Vanishing America: The Nineteenth-Century Response, 3:550

The Witness for the Prosecution, 1:606

The Witness of Poetry, 2:818

Witness to Illness: Strategies for Caregiving and Coping, 5:377

Witness to the Future, 2:653

Witness to War: A Biography of Marguerite Higgins, 3:807

Witold Gombrowicz, 2:814

Wittgenstein (Ayer), 4:273, 4:344

Wittgenstein (Grayling), 4:245

Wittgenstein (Von Wright), 4:338

Wittgenstein: A Life: Young Ludwig, 1889–1921, 4:346

Wittgenstein: An Introduction, 4:347

Wittgenstein: Conversations, 1949–1951, 4:345

Wittgenstein: From Mysticism to Ordinary Language, 4:346

Wittgenstein: Language and World, 4:345

Wittgenstein: Lectures and Conversations on Aesthetics, Psychology, and Religious Belief, 4:344

Wittgenstein: Meaning and Mind, 4:345

Wittgenstein, Ethics and Aesthetics: The View from Eternity, 4:347

Wittgenstein and Derrida, 4:398

Wittgenstein and His Times, 4:346

Wittgenstein and Kierkegaard, 4:345

Wittgenstein and Modern Philosophy, 4:345

Wittgenstein and Political Philosophy, 4:345

Wittgenstein and the Turning Point in the History of Mathematics, 4:347

Wittgenstein Centenary Essays, 4:345

Wittgenstein on Ethics and Religious Belief, 4:344

Wittgenstein on Language: Meaning, Use, and Truth, 4:346

Wittgenstein on Rules and Private Language, 4:301

Wittgenstein's Early Philosophy: Three Sides of the Mirror, 4:346

Wittgenstein's Later Philosophy, 4:345

Wittgenstein's Lectures on the Foundations of Mathematics, 5:493

Wittgenstein's Nephew: A Friendship, 2:569

Wittgenstein's Philosophy of Psychology, 4:345

Wittgenstein's Tractatus: A Critical Exposition of Its Main Lines on Thought, 4:347

Wittgenstein's Tractatus: An Introduction, 4:346

Wittgenstein—Toward a Re-Evaluation, 4:345

Wives and Daughters, 1:355

Wives at War and Other Stories, 2:140

Wives of the God-King: The Rituals of Devadasis of Puri, 4:505

Wizard from Vienna: Franz Anton Mesmer, 4:847

A Wizard of Earthsea, 1:1260

Wizard of Law, 2:147

The Wizard of Oz, 1:1194, 1:1200

The Wizard of Oz and Who He Was, 1:1200

The Wizard of Tuskegee, 1901–1915, 3:270

Wizardry and Wild Romance, 1:616

Wodwo, 1:498

The Woes of Wit, 2:726

Wole Soyinka, 2:149

Wole Soyinka: An Introduction to His Writing, 2:149

Wolf and Bear Stories, 3:862

The Wolf and the Lamb, 3:372

Wolfe Tone: Prophet of Irish Independence, 3:370

Wolfgang Pauli, 5:708

Wolfram von Eschenbach, 2:617

Wolf to the Slaughter, 1:609

Wolfwatching, 1:498

Wolves and Other Love Stories of Ivan Bunin, 2:707

The Woman, 1:446

Woman: Dependent or Independent Variable? 3:179

Woman, Culture, and Society, 3:25

A Woman Alone: Autobiographical Writings, 2:163

Woman and Society in the Spanish Drama of the Golden Age, 2:524

The Woman and the Myth: Margaret Fuller's Life and Writings, 1:673

Woman as Image in Medieval Literature from the Twelfth Century to Dante, 4:698

Woman at Point Zero, 2:71, 2:120

The Woman at the Washington Zoo, 1:993

Woman at War, 2:427

The Woman beneath the Skin, 5:136, 5:187

Woman Doctor: The Education of Jane Patterson, M.D., 5:314

The Woman from Sarajevo, 2:828

Womanguides: Readings toward a Feminist Theology, 4:785, 4:905

Woman in a Lampshade, 2:956

Woman in Christian Tradition, 4:679

Woman in Mind, 1:436, 1:437

Woman in Science, 5:10

The Woman in the Dunes, 2:284, 2:285

Woman in the Mists, 3:909

Woman in the Nineteenth Century, 1:672, 1:673

Woman Invisible: A Personal Odyssey in Christian Feminism, 4:749

The Woman in White, 1:346

A Woman Killed with Kindness, 1:182

A Woman like You, 5:402

A Woman Making History: Mary Ritter Beard through Her Letters, 3:566

The Woman of Andros, 1:898

A Woman of Genius (Austin), 1:732, 1:733

A Woman of Genius (Cruz), 2:862

Woman of Letters: A Life of Virginia Woolf, 1:570, 1:1039

A Woman of No Importance, 1:409, 1:410

The Woman of Rome, 2:429, 2:430

A Woman on Paper, 3:785

A Woman on the Shore, 2:923

A Woman Rice Planter, 3:532

Woman Running in the Mountains, 2:294

The Woman's Bible Commentary, 4:819

Woman's Body, Woman's Word, 2:56

A Woman's Choice: New Options in the Treatment of Breast Cancer, 5:373

A Woman's Decision: Breast Care, Treatment and Reconstruction, 5:371

Woman's Fiction, 1:657, 1:1224

The Woman's Guide to Business Travel, 3:893

A Woman's Guide to the Prevention, Detection and Treatment of Cancer, 5:373

A Woman's Kingdom and Other Stories, 2:708

Woman's Life, 2:489

The Woman's Part: Feminist Criticism of Shakespeare, 1:208

Womanspirit Rising: A Feminist Reader in Religion, 4:650

Woman's Place in Pope's World, 1:252

A Woman's Revenge, 2:489

Woman's Rights Tracts, 1:380

Woman's "True" Profession: Voices from the History of Teaching, 3:255

Woman's Voice in Latin American Literature, 2:847

Woman the Gatherer, 4:431

The Woman Warrior, 1:1000, 3:909

The Woman Who Could Not Read, and Other Tales, 2:775

The Woman Who Had Two Navels, 2:330

The Woman Who Owned the Shadows, 1:1135

The Woman Within, 1:843

A Woman without a Name, 1:1099

Woman-Work: Women and the Party in Revolutionary China, 3:469

Woman—Image—Text: Readings in Pre-Raphaelite Art and Literature, 1:315

The Womb of Space: The Cross-cultural Imagination, 2:930, 2:936

Women, AIDS, and Activism,
5:388
Women, Androgynes, and
Other Mythical Beasts,
4:505, 4:890
Women, Art and Society,
3:759
Women, Branch Stories, and
Religious Rhetoric in a
Tamil Buddhist Text, 4:514
Women, Crime, and Custody
in Victorian England,
1:313, 3:365
Women, Crime and Criminal
Justice, 3:205
Women, Drinking, and Preg-
nancy, 5:402
Women, Ethnics, and Exot-
ics, 1:657
Women, Freedom, and Cal-
vin, 4:761
Women, Health, and Heal-
ing: Toward a New Per-
spective, 5:355
Women, Health and Medi-
cine, 5:13
Women, Knowledge, and Re-
ality, 4:391
Women, Men, and the Bible,
4:749
Women, Nature, and Psyche,
4:391
Women, Power, and Subver-
sion, 1:319
Women, Race and Class,
3:218
Women, Religion, and Sexu-
ality, 4:894
Women, Religion, and Social
Change, 4:426, 4:504,
4:513, 4:529, 4:532
Women, Technology and In-
novation, 5:205
Women, Writing, History
1640–1740, 1:225
Women against her Sex, 2:72
Women and Appletrees,
2:672
Women and Authority: Re-
emerging Mormon Femi-
nism, 4:892
Women and Economics,
1:752, 1:753
Women and Folklore: Images
and Genres, 3:848
Women and Gender: A Fe-
minist Psychology, 3:178
Women and Geography: A
Comprehensive Bibliogra-
phy, 3:119
Women and Heart Disease,
5:374

Women and Jewish Law,
4:650
Women and Literature, 1:924
Women and Medicine, 5:314
Women and Men: An An-
thropologist's View, 3:17
Women and Music: A His-
tory, 3:662
Women and Music in Cross-
Cultural Perspective, 3:666
Women and Party Politics in
Peninsular Malaysia, 3:492
Women and Politics in
Islam: The Trial of Bena-
zir Bhutto, 3:487
Women and Print Culture,
1:231
Women and Reason, 4:391
Women and Religion in
America, 4:749
Women and Sacrifice: Male
Narcissism and the Psy-
chology of Religion, 4:892
Women and Sex, 2:120
Women and Social Action in
Victorian and Edwardian
England, 3:343, 3:364
Women and Substance Use,
5:403
Women and the Ancestors:
Black Carib Kinship and
Ritual, 4:466
Women and the Environ-
ment, 5:188
Women and the Law of
Property in Early America,
3:557
Women and the Mass Media:
A Sourcebook for Re-
search and Action, 3:802
Women and the Priesthood:
Essays from the Orthodox
Tradition, 4:693
Women and the Work of Be-
nevolence, 3:555
Women and Work, 1:330,
1:331
Women and World Religions,
4:892
Women Anthropologists: A
Biographical Dictionary,
3:10
Women Are Different, 2:140
Women Artists: Fifteen Fifty
to Nineteen Fifty, 3:761
Women Artists, Women Ex-
iles, "Miss Grief" and
Other Stories, 1:790
Women as a Force in His-
tory: A Study in Traditions
and Realities, 3:565
The Women at the Pump,
2:664

Women at War: The Story of
Fifty Military Nurses Who
Served in Vietnam, 3:539
Women at War with Ameri-
ca: Private Lives in a Pa-
triotic Era, 3:534
Women Beware Women,
1:190
Women-Church, 4:785
Women Composers, Conduc-
tors, and Musicians of the
Twentieth Century, 3:656,
3:671
Women in African Literature
Today, 2:109
Women in American Music:
A Bibliography of Music
and Literature, 3:654
Women in Buddhism, 4:514
Women in Chinese Society,
3:472
Women in Cross-Cultural
Perspective, 3:178
Women in Engineering:
Women, Power, and
Workplace Culture, 5:188
Women in Frankish Society:
Marriage and the Cloister,
500–900, 4:701
Women in Greek Myth,
4:447
Women in Hispanic Litera-
ture: Icons and Fallen
Idols, 2:522
Women in Indian Society: A
Reader, 4:508
Women in Islam, 4:578,
4:580
Women in Love, 1:509
Women in Mathematics,
5:29, 5:494
Women in Modern America:
A Brief History, 3:554
Women in Motion, 3:825
Women in Muslim Family
Law, 3:442
Women in Popular Culture:
A Reference Guide, 3:873
Women in Psychology, 3:181
Women in Public: Between
Banners and Ballots,
1825–1880, 3:557
Women in Revolutionary
Russia, 3:397
Women in Russian Litera-
ture. Seventeen Eighty to
Eighteen Sixty-Three, 2:684
Women in Science: Antiquity
through the Nineteenth
Century, 5:4, 5:29
Women in Science: Portraits
from a World in Transi-
tion, 5:10

Women in Shaker Community and Worship, 4:849
Women in Soviet Fiction, 1917–1964, 2:686
Women in Spiritual Communitarian Societies in the United States, 4:843
Women in the Air, 5:219
Women in the Early Church, 4:678
Women in the Field: America's Pioneering Women Naturalists, 5:817
Women in the Global Factory, 3:218
Women in the Middle Ages, 3:331, 4:699
Women in the Poetry of T. S. Eliot: A Psychoanalytic Approach, 1:473
Women in the Reformation in France and England, 4:749
Women in Utopia, 4:844
Women in Western European History, 3:326
Women in World Religions, 4:506, 4:514, 4:526, 4:528, 4:892
Women Leaders in the Ancient Synagogue, 4:614
Women Making Music: The Western Art Tradition, 1150–1950, 3:659
Women Novelists in Spain and Spanish America, 2:524
Women of Algiers in their Apartment, 2:120
The Women of Brewster Place, 1:1020, 1:1021
The Women of England from Anglo-Saxon Times to the Present, 3:354, 3:355
Women of Letters: A Life of Virginia Woolf, 1:1039
Women of Mathematics: A Bibliographic Sourcebook, 5:494
Women of Messina, 2:443
The Women of Muriel Spark, 1:552
Women of Sand and Myrrh, 2:59
Women of Science: Righting the Record, 5:187
Women of Spirit, 4:679, 4:785
The Women of Suye Mura, 3:480
Women of the Klan: Racism and Gender in the 1920s, 3:217

Women of the Shtetl: Through the Eye of Y. L. Peretz, 2:43
Women of the World: The Great Foreign Correspondents, 3:806
Women of Trachis, 2:368
Women of Wisdom, 4:543
Women on the Color Line, 1:740
The Women on the Porch, 1:983
Women on Women: An Anthology of American Lesbian Short Fiction, 1:1184
Women Philosophers, 4:391
Women Philosophers: A Bio-Critical Sourcebook, 4:6, 4:161
Women Poets of Japan (The Burning Heart: Women Poets of Japan), 2:274
Women Romantic Poets, 1770–1838: An Anthology, 1:268
Women's America: Refocusing the Past, 3:513
Women Scientists from Antiquity to the Present: An Index, 5:28
Women Scientists in America: Struggles and Strategies to 1940, 5:49
Women's Fiction, 1:627, 1:722, 1:945
Women's Fiction from Latin America, 2:849
Women's Folklore, Women's Culture, 3:869
Women Silversmiths, 1685–1845, 3:767
Women's Life and Work in the Southern Colonies, 3:518
Women's Life in Greece and Rome, 3:309
Women's Lives: Themes and Variations in Gender Learning, 3:178
Women's Lives and the 18th-Century English Novel, 1:229
Women's Pictures: Feminism and Cinema, 1:1157
Women's Rights Movement in Iran, 3:448
The Women's Suffrage Movement and Irish Society in the Early Twentieth Century, 3:371
Women's Voices on Africa: A Century of Travel Writings, 3:905

Women's Work, Markets and Economic Development in Nineteenth-Century Ontario, 3:613
Women under the Knife: A Gynecologist's Report on Hazardous Medicine, 5:355
Women under the Knife: A History of Surgery, 5:312
Women War Correspondents of World War II, 3:809
The Women Who Knew Too Much, 1:1169
Women Writers and Poetic Identity, 1:336
Women Writers in Black Africa: Contributions in Women's Studies, 2:106
Women Writers in Russian Modernism: An Anthology, 2:693
Women Writers of Black Africa, 2:163
Women Writers of Contemporary Spain, 2:522
Women Writers of the Middle Ages, 4:698
A Wonder Book and Tanglewood Tales, 1:675
A Wonder-Book for Girls and Boys, 1:676, 1:1194
The Wonderful Adventures of Nils, 2:676, 2:677
The Wonderful Dog and Other Tales, 2:775
Wonderful Farm, 2:452
Wonderful Fool: A Novel, 2:286
Wonderful Life: The Burgess Shale and the Nature of History, 5:818
The Wonderful O., 1:891
Wonderful Wizard Marvelous Land, 1:1200
Wonderful Words, Silent Truths: Essays on Poetry and a Memoir, 1:1048
The Wonderful Year and Other Pamphlets, 1:176
Wonderland, 1:1023
The Wonder of Philosophy, 4:21
The Wonder Ring, 1:1159
The Wonder That Was India, 3:483, 4:351, 4:498
Wonderwoman and Superman: The Ethics of Human Biotechnology, 5:120
The Wood beyond the World, 1:617
The Woodblock Engravers, 1:29

Woodcraft; or, Hawks about the Dovecote, 1:697
Woodcutters, 2:569
Wood Engraving, 1:27
The Wooden Shepherdess, 1:496
The Woodlanders, 1:361
Woodrow Wilson: Revolution, War, and Peace, 3:532
Woodrow Wilson, World Statesman, 3:544
Woodrow Wilson and a Revolutionary World, 1913–1921, 3:532
Woodrow Wilson and World Politics, 3:546
The Woods, 1:1101
The Woods, Lakeboat, and Edmond, 1:1101
The Woods Hole Cantata: Essays on Science and Society, 5:766
Woodstock, 1:299
Woody Allen (McCann), 3:830
Woody Allen (Pogel), 3:830
Woody Allen: A Biography, 3:830
Woody Allen: His Films and Career, 3:829
A Woody Allen Encyclopedia, 3:829
The Wooing of Earth, 5:795
The Wool Trade in English Medieval History, 3:358
The Word, 2:652
Word and Object, 4:412, 5:99, 5:100
Word and Object in Husserl, Frege, and Russell, 4:324, 5:103
Word and Story in C. S. Lewis, 1:513
The Word and the Stone, 2:876
Word and Work in the Poetry of Juan Ramón Jiménez, 2:542
A Word Child, 1:523
Word Crazy: Broadway Lyricists from Cohan to Sondheim, 1:798
Word for Word: A Dictionary of Etymological Cognates, 1:96
The Word in Black and White, 1:629, 1:651
The Word of God in the Ethics of Jacques Ellul, 5:165
The Word of Life. Systematic Theology, 4:885

Word Perfect: Literacy in the Computer Age, 5:574
Wordplays Five: New American Drama, 1:1079
Wordplays Two: New American Drama, 1:1079
The Word Processing Book, 5:562
The Word Remains: A Life of Oscar Romero, 4:747
The Words, 2:506, 2:507
Words about Pictures: The Narrative Art of Children's Picture Books, 1:1196
Words and Faces, 1:41
Words and Music in the Middle Ages, 3:663
Words and Music in the Novels of Andrey Bely, 2:701
Words and the Poet, 2:397
Words for All Seasons, 2:494
Words for the Wind, 1:1038
Words in Stone: Pierre Écrite, 2:461, 2:462
Words into Type, 1:118
Words like Arrows: A Collection of Yiddish Folk Sayings, 2:32
Words of Eternity: Blake and the Poetics of the Sublime, 1:279
Words of Farewell: Stories by Korean Women Writers, 2:298
Words of Love: A Complete Guide to Romance Fiction, 1:618
The Words of My Roaring, 2:915
Words with Power: Being a Secondary Study of the Bible and Literature, 1:977
Wordsworth: A Collection of Critical Essays, 1:306
Wordsworth: A Re-interpretation, 1:306
Wordsworth: Lectures and Essays, 1:307
Wordsworth: The Sense of History, 1:307
Wordsworth and the Enlightenment, 1:307
Wordsworth and the Lake District, 3:899
Wordsworth and "The Recluse," 1:307
Wordsworth and the Vocabulary of Emotion, 1:307
Wordsworth's Great Period Poems: Four Essays, 1:307
Wordsworth's Historical Imagination, 1:308

Wordsworth's Poetry, 1785–1814, 1:307
Wordsworth's Second Nature: A Study of the Poetry and Politics, 1:307
Word Watcher's Handbook, 1:92
The Wordworthy Computer, 5:561
Work: A Story of Experience, 1:1198
Work, Culture, and Society in Industrializing America, 3:531
Work, Inc.: A Philosophical Inquiry, 5:73
Work, Society, and Politics, 3:364
Work, Study, Travel Abroad, 1992–1993, 3:891
Work 1961–73, 1:1175
Work and Personality: An Inquiry into the Impact of Social Stratification, 3:214
Worker Cooperatives in America, 3:218
Workers and Their Wages: Changing Patterns in the United States, 3:60
Workers at Risk: Voices from the Workplace, 5:75
Workers in Industrial America, 3:547
Workers in the Dawn, 1:358, 1:359
The Workers of Tianjin, 1900–1949, 3:470
Work Hard and You Shall Be Rewarded, 3:868
Work Hazards and Industrial Conflict, 5:353
Working and Caring, 5:322
Working-Class Experience, 3:607
Working-Class Fiction in Theory and Practice, 1:547
Working Classics: Poems on Industrial Life, 1:801
Working Days: The "Journals of the Grapes of Wrath," 1:885
Working in T.V. News: The Insider's Guide, 3:806
Working Press of the Nation, 1:72
Workings of the Spirit, 1:938, 1:1137
Working with Families: An Introduction to Family Therapy, 5:419
Working with Mentally Handicapped Persons in Their Residences, 5:420

Working with Structuralism, 1:422, 1:515

Working with Vaughan, 3:726

Work in Progress: Joyce Centenary Essays, 1:505

The Work of a Common Woman, 1:1187

The Work of Angels, 3:767

Work of Art, 1:854

The Work of Brian W. Aldiss: An Annotated Bibliography and Guide, 1:613

The Work of Human Hands, 5:314

The Work of Self-Representation: Lyric Poetry in Colonial New England, 1:629

The Work of the Afro-American Woman, 1:725

The Work of the Digestive Glands, 5:364

The Work of the Gods in Tikopia, 3:30, 4:461

The Work of William Morris, 1:383

Work on Myth, 2:581

Works (Bunyan), 1:174

Works (Malory), 1:155

Works (Stevenson), 1:397

Works and Days (Hesiod), 2:342, 2:357, 2:358, 4:481

Works and Lives: The Anthropologist as Author, 3:31, 4:478

Works in Prose and Verse (Bradstreet), 1:634

Works-Made-for-Hire Under the 1976 Copyright Act, 1:55

Works of Attila József, 2:800

The Works of Carl P. Rollins, 1:12

The Works of Charles Babbage, 5:575

The Works of Edmund Burke, 3:152

The Works of Isambard Kingdom Brunel, 5:250

The Works of Ivan Bunin, 2:707

The Works of Jean Sibelius, 3:718

The Works of Jeremy Bentham, 3:150

The Works of Karlheinz Stockhausen, 3:721

The Works of Louis L'Amour, 1:1216

The Works of Love, 1:1017

Works of Love: Some Christian Reflections in the Form of Discourses, 4:239

Works of Man, 5:231

Works of Mark Twain, 1:1201

Works of Plato, 3:163

The Works of Seyyed Hossein Nasr through His Fortieth Birthday, 4:902

The Works of W. Somerset Maugham, 1:520

Works on Vision, 4:191

The World, 2:818

The World, the Text, and the Critic, 1:926, 1:1042

The World about Us, 2:509

The World according to Garp, 1:991, 1:992

World Aflame, 4:768

The World after Oil: The Shifting Axis of Power and Wealth, 5:214

World Agricultural Statistics, 5:262

World Almanac and Book of Facts, 1:83

The World and Africa, 1:832, 3:578

The World and Language in Wittgenstein's Philosophy, 4:346

The World and the Individual, 4:249, 4:250

The World and the Sickle-Cell Gene: A Study in Health Education, 5:385

A World Apart, 2:814

World Architecture: An Illustrated History from the Earliest Times, 3:761

The World as a Total System, 3:53, 3:72

The World as I See It, 5:682

The World as Will and Idea, 4:254

The World as Will and Representation, 4:256

The World at Play in Boccaccio's Decameron, 2:410

World Authors, 1950–1970, 1:128, 2:4

World Authors 1970-1975, 1:128, 2:4

World Authors 1975–1980, 2:3

World Authors 1980–1985, 1:128, 2:3

World Bibliography of Bibliographies, 1:63, 1:120

A World Bibliography of Bibliographies, 1964–1974, 1:63

The World Book Encyclopedia, 1:107

The World Book Encyclopedia of Science, 5:3

The World Book of Odds, 5:523

A World by Itself: The Pastoral Moment in Cooper's Fiction, 1:665

World Christian Encyclopedia, 4:3, 4:716, 4:742

World Chronology of Music History, 3:655

World Cinema since 1945: An Encyclopedic History, 3:826

World Communication: Threat or Promise? 5:306

World Communications: A Handbook, 3:801

The World Crisis in Education: A View from the Eighties, 3:249

World Databases in Medicine, 5:3

World Deforestation in the Twentieth Century, 5:824

A World Destroyed, 3:280, 3:535

World Dictionary of Awards and Prizes, 1:135

World Directory of Social Science Institutions, 3:6

The World Doesn't End: Prose Poems, 1:1048

World Drama, 2:4

A World Elsewhere: The Place of Style in American Literature, 1:651

World Energy Outlook, 5:186

World Enough and Space Time, 5:67

World Enough and Time, 1:892

World Fact File, 1:83

World Folktales: A Scribner Resource Collection, 3:847

The World Food Problem: Present and Future, 5:270

The World from Brown's Lounge, 3:866

World Furniture: An Illustrated Survey, 3:766

World Guide to Libraries, 1:70

World Guide to Scientific Associations and Learned Societies, 5:4

World Guide to Special Libraries, 1:70

World Handbook of Political and Social Indicators, 3:157, 3:138

World Historical Fiction Guide, 1:122, 1:125

A World History (McNeill),
3:288
World History (Upshur),
3:275
World History: The Destiny-
Idea and the Causality-
Principle, 3:291
World History in the Twenti-
eth Century, 3:274
The World History Made in
the Present, 3:276
A World History of Photogra-
phy, 5:37
World History of the Dance,
3:732
A World I Never Made,
1:833
The World in Miniature,
4:520, 4:523, 4:534, 4:544
The World in the Attic,
1:1017
The World in the Twentieth
Century, 3:274
The World Is a Room, 2:14
The World Is My Home: A
Memoir, 3:932
The World Is Round, 1:882
World Light, 2:642
World List of Mammalian
Species, 5:759
World Literature Today,
2:436
Worldly Hopes: Poems, 1:934
The Worldly Philosophers,
3:45, 3:87, 3:92, 3:95,
3:101, 3:107
Worldly Power: The Making
of the Wall Street Journal,
3:809
The World Ocean: An Intro-
duction to Oceanography,
5:631
The World of Ancient Rome,
2:380
The World of a Renaissance
Jew, 4:624
World of Art, 4:340
The World of Ballet, 3:736
The World of Biblical Litera-
ture, 4:822
The World of C. Wright
Mills, 3:235
A World of Change: Britain
in the Early Modern Age,
1450–1700, 3:354
The World of Charles Dick-
ens, 1:351, 1:567
The World of Count Basie,
3:677
The World of Dreams, 5:440
The World of Duke Elling-
ton, 3:695

The World of Elia: Charles
Lamb's Essayistic Romanti-
cism, 1:296
The World of George Sand,
2:505
A World of Grace, 4:904
World of Gwendolyn Brooks,
1:954
The World of Hesiod, 2:358
The World of Humanism,
1453–1517, 4:696
World of Islam, 3:444
The World of John of Salis-
bury, 4:116
The World of Josephus,
4:666
The World of K'ung Shang-
jen: A Man of Letters in
Early Ch'ing China, 2:191
The World of Late Antiquity:
150–750, 3:303
The World of Lawrence: A
Passionate Appreciation,
1:861
World of Learning, 1:83,
1:105
World of Learning 1993,
5:726
The World of Leonardo da
Vinci, 3:780
The World of Luis Buñuel:
Essays in Criticism, 3:832
The World of Mathematics
(Neuman), 5:482
The World of Mathematics
(von Neumann), 5:583
World of Melodrama, 1:1075
World of Modern Chinese
Fiction, 2:235
The World of Musical Come-
dy, 1:1073, 3:655
The World of Myth: An An-
thology, 3:855, 4:427
The World of Odysseus,
2:361, 3:301
A World of Order and Light:
The Fiction of John Gard-
ner, 1:979
World of Our Fathers, 1:989,
1:990, 2:30, 3:555, 4:639
The World of Physics, 5:678
The World of Plácido Do-
mingo, 3:693
A World of Profit, 1:937
World of Ptavvs, 1:1261
The World of Rafael Salas,
2:330
The World of Ramón y Ca-
jal, with Selections from
His Nonscientific Writings,
5:811
The World of Richard
Wright, 1:906

The World of Samuel Beck-
ett, 1:440
World of Sholom Aleichem,
2:46
The World of Sports Statis-
tics, 5:522
A World of Strangers (Gordi-
mer), 2:162
A World of Strangers (Lof-
land), 3:216, 3:231
The World of Swing, 3:668
The World of the Ancient
Maya, 4:455
The World of the Cell, 5:775
The World of the Polyne-
sians Seen through Their
Myths and Legends, Poetry
and Art, 2:970, 4:461
The World of the Shining
Prince: Court Life in An-
cient Japan, 3:475
The World of the Talmud,
4:620
The World of the Ten Thou-
sand Things: Poems
1980–1990, 1:1067
World of the Yeshiva, 4:654
The World of Thought in
Ancient China, 3:468,
4:525
The World of Titian,
c.1488–1576, 3:793
A World of Watchers, 5:818
World of Wonders, 2:910
A World of Words, 1:694
The World of Yesterday: An
Autobiography, 2:617
World Oil Prices: Demand,
Supply and Substitutes,
5:280
The World Petroleum Mar-
ket, 5:283, 5:290
World Philosophy, 4:7, 4:38
World Philosophy: Essays
and Reviews of 225 Major
Works, 4:266
World Politics and Personal
Insecurity, 3:157
World Politics and the Arab-
Israeli Conflict, 3:439
World Power or Decline,
3:278
World Prehistory: A Brief In-
troduction, 4:432
The World Refinery Industry:
Need for Restructuring,
5:286
World Regional Geography:
Issues for Today, 3:125
World Religions and Ecolo-
gy, 5:199
World Religions and World
Community, 4:573

World Resources: 1992–93, 5:817
World Resources 1986, 3:273
A World Restored, 3:341
A World Ruled by Number, 3:85
The World's Best Books: Homer to Hemingway, 1:75
The World's Best Essays, 1:728
The World's Best Essays from the Earliest Period to the Present Time, 1:727
World's Best Poetry, 1:720
World's Best Poetry, Supplement VI, 2:113
World's Debt to Pasteur, 5:409, 5:809
The World's Discoverers, 3:909
World Security and Equity, 3:64
The World Seen at Eighty: Impressions of an Ateriosclerotic, 5:810
World's End, 1:952, 1:953
World's Fair, 1:969
The World's Greatest Scriptures, 4:5
The World's Great Religions, 4:6
Worlds in Regression: Some Novels of Vladimir Nabokov, 2:741
Worlds of Dust and Jade, 2:224
The Worlds of Existentialism: A Critical Reader, 4:264
Worlds of Music: An Introduction to the Music of the World's Peoples, 3:670
The Worlds of Plato and Aristotle, 4:71
Worlds of Wonder, Days of Judgment, 3:517
World So Wide, 1:854
The World's Perspective: John Webster and the Jacobean Drama, 1:200
World Spirituality: An Encyclopedic History of the Religious Quest, 4:888
A World Split Apart, 2:761
Worlds within Worlds: The Novels of Ivan Turgenev, 2:770
The World Theater of Wagner, 3:729
The World the Slaveholders Made: Two Essays in Interpretation, 3:524, 3:580

The World Trading System, 3:61
World Travel and Tourism Review, 3:891
The World Treasury of Science Fiction, 1:612
The World Turned Upside Down, 3:404
World War I: An Outline History, 3:277
World War I and the Origin of Civil Liberties in the United States, 3:532
World War Two German Military Studies, 3:376
The Worldwatch Reader, 5:828
World Who's Who in Science, 5:28
Worldwide Government Directory, 1:105
Worldwide Science and Technology Advice to the Highest Levels of Governments, 5:181
The World within the Word (Gass), 1:980
The World within the World (Barrow), 5:11
World within Walls: Japanese Literature of the Pre-Modern Era 1600–1867, 2:272
World within World (Spender), 1:552
Worship and Ethics: A Study in Rabbinic Judaism, 4:600, 4:620
Worship in the World's Religions, 4:898
The Worship of Nature, 4:477
Wörterbuch . . . Dictionary of Bookbinding and Restauration of Papyri, Manuscripts . . . Bindings, and Globes in German, English, French and Italian, 1:24
The Would-Be Gentleman, 2:490
The Wound and the Bow, 1:370
The Wounded Spirit: T. E. Lawrence's Seven Pillars of Wisdom, 3:926
Wounds in the Rain, 1:742
Woyzeck, 2:573, 2:574
Wrath of John Steinbeck, 1:885
A Wreath for the Maidens, 2:139
A Wreath for Udomo, 2:158, 2:159

The Wreckage of Agathon, 1:978
The Wrecker, 1:396
The Wreck of the Deutschland, 1:364
The Wreck of the Zephyr, 1:1207, 1:1208
The Wrestling Match, 2:137
The Wretched of the Earth, 2:121
Wright Morris, 1:1018
Wright Morris: Memory and Imagination, 1:1017
A Wrinkle in Time, 1:1194
The Writer and His Milieu, 2:328
The Writer as Shaman: The Pilgrimages of Conrad Aiken and Walker Percy, 1:810
The Writer at His Craft, 1:812
A Writer at War: Arnold Bennett, 1914–1918, 1:444
The Writer in the Catastrophe of Our Time, 2:883
A Writer's America: Landscape in Literature, 1:996
Writers and Politics in Modern Italy, 2:401
Writers and Politics in Modern Spain, 2:522
Writers and Society in Contemporary Italy: A Collection of Essays, 2:400
Writers and Their Milieu, 2:328
Writers and Their Work Series, 1:127
Writers at Work: Third Series, 1:1075
A Writer's Diary (Dostoyevsky), 2:712, 2:714
A Writer's Diary (Woolf), 1:569
The Writer's Directory: 1980-1982, 1:126
The Writer's Divided Self in Bulgakov's The Master and Margarita, 2:706
Writers from the South Pacific, 2:971
A Writer's Guide to Copyright, 1:55
Writers in Arms: The Literary Impact of the Spanish Civil War, 2:522
Writers in Politics. Studies in African Literature, 2:155
Writers in Revolt: An Anthology, 1:130
Writers in Russia: 1917–1978, 2:687

Writer's Market, 1:118

A Writer's Notebook, 1:520

Writers of the Caribbean and Central America: A Bibliography, 2:931

Writers of the Modern South: The Faraway Country, 1:919

Writers of the Purple Sage: An Anthology of Recent Western Writing, 1:921

Writers on the Left, 1:803

The Writer's Point of View, 1:520

Writer's Survival Manual, 1:48

Writing about Canada: A Handbook for Modern Canadian History, 3:607

Writing about Science, 5:9

Writing about Vietnam, 2:339

Writing American History: Essays on Modern Scholarship, 3:515

Writing and Difference, 4:398

Writing and Illuminating and Lettering, 1:17

Writing and Reading Differently, 1:1128

The Writing and Selling of Fiction, 1:48

Writing and Sexual Difference, 1:923

Writing a Novel, 1:449

Writing Books for Children and Young People, 1:46

The Writing Business: A Poets and Writers Handbook, 1:48

Writing by Numbers: Trollope's Serial Fiction, 1:407

Writing Culture: The Poetics and Politics of Ethnography, 1:1133, 3:12, 4:426

Writing Degree Zero, 2:446

Writing from the Fringe: A Study of Modern Aboriginal Literature, 2:946

The Writing Game, 1:515

Writing in England Today: The Last Fifteen Years, 1:423

Writing in the Computer Age, 5:561

Writing in the New Nation, 3:516

Writing like a Woman, 1:926

Writing Lives: Principia Biographica, 1:87, 1:727, 1:928, 1:972

Writing Materials of the East, 1:5

The Writing of American History, 3:515

The Writing of Canadian History, 3:618

The Writing of East and Central Africa, 2:152

The Writing of Fiction, 1:786

The Writing of Wole Soyinka, 2:149

Writing on Religion, 3:213

Writing on the Tongue, 2:317

The Writing on the Wall: An Anthology of Czechoslovak Literature Today, 2:789, 2:833

Writing Realism: Howells, James, and Norris in the Mass Market, 1:712

Writings from Ancient Israel, 4:812

Writings from the New Yorker: 1927–1976, 1:898

The Writings of a Savage, 3:775

The Writings of Brendan Behan, 1:442

The Writings of Jean-Paul Sartre, 4:330

Writings of Leon Trotsky, 3:295

The Writings of Martin Buber, 4:662

The Writings of Nathanael West, 1:897

The Writings of the New Testament: An Interpretation, 4:813

Writings on Civil Disobedience and Nonviolence, 2:765

Writings on Economics, 4:201

Writings on Wright: Selected Comments on Frank Lloyd Wright, 3:798

Writing Space: The Computer, Hypertext, and the History of Writing, 5:561

Writing the American Classics, 1:722

Writing the Margins, 1:844

Writing with a Word Processor, 5:538

Writing with Scripture, 4:607

Writing Women's History: International Perspectives, 3:276

Written History as an Act of Faith, 3:565

Written on a Body, 2:884

Written on Bamboo and Silk, 2:187

Written on the Wind, 1:1175

Written Out of History: Our Jewish Foremothers, 4:650

W. Robertson Smith and the Sociological Study of Religion, 4:492

Wrong: Stories, 1:1186

The Wrong Box, 1:396

The Wrong Set, 1:567

W. S. Gilbert, 1:358

W. S. Gilbert: His Life and Letters, 1:357

W. Somerset Maugham, 1:520, 1:521

W. Somerset Maugham: An Annotated Bibliography of Writings about Him, 1:521

W. Somerset Maugham: The Critical Heritage, 1:520

Wu Ching-tzu, 2:230

Wuthering Heights, 1:335, 1:336

Wyandotté, or, The Hutted Knoll: A Tale, 1:664

Wyatt: The Critical Heritage, 1:201

Wyclif and the Oxford Schools, 4:104

Wycliffe Biographical Dictionary of the Church, 4:720

The Wycliffe Historical Geography of the Bible Lands, 3:437

The Wyclyf Tradition, 4:714

Wylder's Hand, 1:601

Wyndham Lewis: Religion and Modernism, 1:514

Wyndham Lewis and Western Man, 1:514

Wyndham Lewis's Pictorial Integer, 1:514

X

Xaipe, 1:825

Xala, 2:145

Xenakis, 3:731

Xenophanes of Colophon: Fragments, 4:52

Xenophon, 3:324, 4:91

Xenophon's Socratic Discourse: An Interpretation of the Oeconomicus, 4:91

Xenophon the Athenian, 4:91

The X-Ray Information Book, 5:397

X-Rays: Health Effects of Common Exams, 5:397

X-Rays and Electrons: An Outline of Recent X-Ray Theory, 5:678

Y

The Yage Letters, 1:957, 1:981

Yahweh and the Gods of Canaan, 4:445, 4:822, 4:828

Yaki Bud, Yaki Nabud, 2:91

The Yale Critics: Deconstruction in America, 1:1133

Yale University School of Medicine Heart Book, 5:375

The Yalu Flows, 2:305

Yama: The Pit, 2:733

Yangtze: Nature, History, and the River, 3:467

Yang Wan-li, 2:231

Yankee Bookseller, 1:41

Yankee Leviathan, 3:542

Yankev Glatshteyn, 2:38

Yanomamo: The Fierce People, 3:25

A Yard of Sun, 1:480

Yawar Fiesta, 2:852

Yeager: An Autobiography, 5:220

The Year 1905, 2:745

The Yearbook of American and Canadian Churches, 4:5, 4:752

The Yearbook of the United Nations, 1:83, 1:111

The Year Fifteen, 2:897

A Year in Provence, 3:900

The Year in San Fernando, 2:932

The Year of Decision: 1846, 3:576

The Year of Liberty: The Story of the Great Rebellion of 1798, 3:370

The Year of the Bull, 2:658

Year of the Elephant, 2:58

The Year of Three Popes, 4:744

The Years, 1:569

The Years and Hours of Emily Dickinson, 1:748

The Years as Catches: First Poems, 1:971

A Year's Letters, 1:398

Years of Childhood, 2:697

The Years of Lyndon Johnson, Vol. 1: The Path to Power, 3:537

The Years of Lyndon Johnson, Vol. 2: Means of Ascent, 3:537

Years of My Youth, 1:758

The Years with Ross, 1:889, 1:890

The Year's Work in English Studies, 1:120

Year Two Thousand: A Critical Biography of Edward Bellamy, 1:734

Yeast, 1:369, 5:211

Yeats, 1:974

Yeats: The Man and the Masks, 1:975

Yeats, Ireland and Fascism, 1:572

Yeats and American Poetry: The Traditional of the Self, 1:798

Yeats and Postmodernism, 1:572

Yeats and the Beginning of the Irish Renaissance, 1:572

Yeats and the Poetics of Hate, 1:572

Yeats and the Poetry of Death: Elegy, Self-Elegy, and the Sublime, 1:572

Yeats at Songs and Choruses, 1:572

Yeats' Myth of Self: The Autobiographical Prose, 1:572

Yeats's Interaction with Tradition, 1:572

Yeats the Initiate, 1:572

Yekaterina Voronina, 2:754

Yekl, 1:737, 2:37

Yellow Dwarf, 1:583

The Yellow Earth Road, 2:303

The Yellow Fairy Book, 3:883

Yellow Flowers in the Antipodean Room, 2:974

The Yellow Heart, 2:875

The Yellow House on the Corner, 1:970

Yellowstone Ecology: A Road Guide, 5:759

Yellowstone Kelly, 1:1213

Yellow Wallpaper and Other Writing, 1:752

The Yellow Wind, 2:19

The Yemassee, 1:695, 1:697, 1:1244

Yemen, 3:454

The Yemen Arab Republic: Development and Change in an Ancient Land, 3:451

Yemen in Early Islam, 3:454

Yemenite Jews: A Photographic Essay, 4:644

Yenne Velt: The Great Works of Jewish Fantasy and Occult, 2:34

Yentl the Yeshiva Boy, 2:48

Yerma, 2:538

Yertle the Turtle and Other Stories, 1:1204

Yerushalmi: The Talmud of the Land of Israel: An Introduction, 4:613

Yes and No: The Intimate Folklore of Africa, 2:108

The Yeshiva, 2:39

Yes Is for a Very Young Man, 1:881

Yesterday's Faces, 1:593

Yet Other Waters, 1:833

Yiddish: A Survey and a Grammar, 2:31

Yiddish: Turning to Life, 2:30

Yiddish and English: A Century of Yiddish in America, 2:30

Yiddish Culture in Britain: A Guide, 2:30

The Yiddish Dictionary Sourcebook, 2:30

A Yiddish Dictionary in Transliteration, 2:29

Yiddish-English-Hebrew Dictionary, 1:103

Yiddish in America: Social and Cultural Foundations, 2:31

Yiddish in America: Socio-Linguistic Description and Analysis, 2:31

Yiddish Language and Folklore: A Selective Bibliography for Research, 2:33

Yiddish Literature: Its Scope and Major Writers, 2:32

Yiddish Literature in English Translation: Books Published 1945–1967, 2:31

Yiddish Literature in English Translation: List of Books in Print, 2:31

The Yiddish Press: An Americanizing Agency, 2:32

Yiddish Stories Old and New, 2:34

Yiddish Tales, 2:33

Yi Jing, 4:524

Yingl, Tsingl Khvat, 2:41

Yoga: Immortality and Freedom, 4:474, 4:503

Yoga for Health: The Total Program, 5:319

Yoga Sutras, 4:550

Yokomitsu Riichi, Modernist, 2:295

Yom Kippur and After, 3:436

Yom Kippur Anthology, 4:599

Yonnondio: From the Thirties, 1:1026

Yordan Yovkov, 2:783

Yorick and the Critics: Sterne's Reputation in England, 1760–1868, 1:259

York Cycle, 1:158

York Mystery Plays: A Selection in Modern Spelling, 1:159

The Yorkshire Tragedy, 1:204

Yoruba Warfare in the Nineteenth Century, 3:425

The Yosemite, 5:836

Yoshe Kalb, 2:49

Yoshitsune: A Fifteenth-Century Japanese Chronicle, 2:275

You, I, and the Others, 4:340

You and Neurosis, 5:426

You and Your Hearing: How to Protect It, Preserve It, and Restore It, 5:380

You Are the World, 4:555

You Can Fool All of the People All the Time, 3:870

You Can Have a Baby: Everything You Need to Know about Fertility, 5:357

You Can't Drown the Fire: Latin American Women Writing in Exile, 2:850

You Can't Get There from Here, 2:913, 2:914

You Can't Go Home Again, 1:903

You Can't Take It with You, 1:1097

You Don't Have to Live with Cystitis!, 5:406

You Don't Need a Hysterectomy, 5:356

You Have Seen Their Faces, 1:819

You Know I Can't Hear You When the Water's Running, 1:1082, 1:1083

You Know Me, Al, 1:852

You Might As Well Live: The Life and Times of Dorothy Parker, 1:868

You Must Know Everything, 2:700

You Never Can Tell, 1:545

The Young Adult Reader's Adviser, 1:75, 1:1195

The Young Assassins, 2:540

The Young Athlete's Health Handbook, 5:400

Young Charles Lamb, 1775–1802, 1:296

Young Children's Thinking: Studies of Some Aspects of Piaget's Theory, 3:267

Young Coleridge and the Philosophers of Nature, 1:288

The Young Duke: A Moral Tale, though Gay, 1:351

Young England, 1:317

The Youngest Science: Notes of a Medicine Watcher, 5:19, 5:315

Young Frederick Douglass: The Maryland Years, 1:668

Young George Farquhar, 1:243

A Young Girl's Diary, 5:447

Young Hamlet: Essays on Shakespeare's Tragedies, 1:213

The Young Heiress, 1:408

The Young Hemingway, 1:847

Young Henry of Navarre, 2:601

The Young Hölderlin, 2:594

Young John Dewey: An Essay in American Intellectual History, 4:225

Young La Fontaine, 2:485

The Young Lloyd George, 3:366

Young Longfellow (1807–1843), 1:683

Young Lorenzo: The Early Life of D. H. Lawrence, 1:510

Young Love, 1:408

A Young Man in Search of Love, 2:48

Young Man Luther, 3:182, 3:334, 4:778, 5:442

Young Man Thoreau, 1:702

Young Mr. Lincoln, 1:1165

The Young Mr. Wesley, 4:790

Young Philip Sidney: 1572–1577, 1:196

The Young Reader's Companion, 1:1195

Young Shakespeare, 1:204

The Young Shelley: Genesis of a Radical, 1:303

Young Törless, 2:604

You Only Live Once: Memories of Ian Fleming, 1:594

You Only Live Twice, 1:594

Your Aching Back: A Doctor's Guide to Relief, 5:394

Your Baby and Child, 5:323

Your Child Has a Disability, 5:375

You're Not Watching Me, Mommy, 1:532

Your Health, Your Moods, and the Weather, 5:341

Your Personal Vitamin Profile, 5:345

Your Premature Baby, 5:322

Your Resource Guide to Environmental Organizations, 5:816

Your Skin and How to Live in It, 5:399

Your Telephone: Operation, Selection and Installation, 5:229

Your Thwarts in Pieces, Your Mooring Rope Cut, 2:53

Your Thyroid: A Home Reference, 5:382

Your Word Is Fire: The Hasidic Masters on Contemplative Prayer, 4:632

You Shall Be as Gods, 5:451

Youth, Identity, Power: The Chicano Movement, 3:557

Youth and America's Future, 3:253

Youth and the Bright Medusa, 1:821

The Youth of James Whitcomb Riley, 1:778

Youth Restored, 2:775, 2:776

Youth without Youth, and Other Novellas, 2:825

Ysengrimus, 2:629

The Yüan Chen Variations, 2:216

Yüan Hung-tao and the Kung-an School, 2:189

Yugoslav Popular Ballads, 2:828

Yugoslav Story, 1843–1983, 3:393

Yukon Wild, 3:895

Yunus Emre and His Mystical Poetry, 2:102

Yurok Myths, 3:33

Yury Trifonov: A Critical Study, 2:767

Yūsuf Idrīs: Changing Visions, 2:65

Yu-t'ai Hsin Yung, 2:201

Yvain, or The Knight with the Lion, 2:467

Yves Bonnefoy, 2:462

Yvonne: Princess of Burgundia, 2:813

Z

Zaddik, 4:632

Zadig, or Destiny, 4:217

The Zaehnsdorfs (1842–1947): Craft Bookbinders, 1:22

Zakhor: Jewish History and Jewish Memory, 4:595

Zalmen, or the Madness of God, 1:1065

Zamani: A Survey of East African History, 3:422

The Zambesi Expedition, 1858–1863, 3:930

Zami, a New Spelling of My Name, 1:1189, 1:1190

Zamyatin's We: A Collection of Critical Essays, 2:775

Zane Grey, 1:1214

Zane Grey: A Biography, 1:1214

Zanoni: A Rosicrucian Tale, 1:340

Zanzibar: City, Island, and Coast, 3:914

Zarathustra's Sister: The Case of Elizabeth and Friedrich Nietzsche, 4:247

Zayni Barakat, 2:59

Zazie in the Metro, 2:496

Zeami's Style: The Noh Plays of Zeami Motokiyo, 2:280

The Zebra-Striped Hearse, 1:1235

Zen: Traditions and Transition, 4:538

Zen Action/Zen Person, 4:537

Zen and American Thought, 4:33, 4:859

Zen and Japanese Culture, 3:476, 4:558

Zen and the Art of Motorcycle Maintenance: An Inquiry into Values, 5:72, 5:157

Zen and the Art of the Internet: A Beginner's Guide, 5:547

Zen and Western Thought, 4:364

Zen Awakening and Society, 4:537

Zen Buddhism, 4:558

Zen Buddhism and Psychoanalysis, 4:558

Zen Buddhism in the Twentieth Century, 4:537, 4:558

Zen Effects: The Life of Alan Watts, 4:859, 4:881

A Zen Life: D. T. Suzuki Remembered, 4:558

Zen Mind, Beginner's Mind, 4:538

Zeno of Elea: A Text with Translation and Notes, 4:52

A Zen Wave: Bashō's Haiku and Zen, 2:276

Zeph: A Posthumous Story, 1:760

Zero, 2:894

Zero Hour: A Summons to the Free, 1:815

Zero Hour and Other Documentary Poems, 2:859

Zettel, 4:344

Zhenia's Childhood, 2:746

Zima Junction, 2:773

Zimbabwe Prose and Poetry, 2:158

Zimmerman's Complete Guide to Nonprescription Drugs, 5:312

The Zimmerman Telegram, 3:411, 3:412

Zion before Zionism, 4:657

Zion in America, 4:639

Zionism: The Crucial Phase, 4:658

Zionism: The Formative Years, 4:643

Zionism in Germany, 1897–1933, 3:350, 4:658

Zionism in Poland: The Formative Years, 1915–1926, 3:349, 4:658

The Zionist Dream Revisited: From Herzl to Gush Emunim and Back, 4:658

Zionist Idea: A Historical Analysis and Reader, 3:348, 4:658

Zip: A Novel of the Left and the Right, 1:935

Zlateh the Goat and Other Stories, 2:47

The Zodiac, 1:967

Zodiac Arch, 3:939

Zohar: The Book of Enlightenment, 4:630

The Zohar in Moslem and Christian Spain, 4:629

Zohar—The Book of Splendor: Basic Readings from the Kabbalah, 4:672

Zohrab: An Introduction, 2:81

Zola and the Craft of Fiction, 2:518

Zola and the Dreyfus Case, 2:518

Zola's Crowds, 2:518

The Zone: A Prison Camp Guard's Story, 2:716

Zoological Philosophy, 5:802

Zoo Station: Adventures in East and West Berlin, 3:901

The Zoo Story, 1:1080

Zora in Florida, 1:850

Zora Neale Hurston, 1:850, 1:851

Zora Neale Hurston: A Literary Biography, 1:850

Zora Neale Hurston: A Reference Guide, 1:850

Zora Neale Hurston: A Storyteller's Life, 1:851

Zora Neale Hurston's Their Eyes Were Watching God, 1:850

Zora! Zora Neale Hurston: A Woman and Her Community, 1:850

Zorba the Greek, 2:374

Zoroastrianism: A Beleaguered Faith, 4:518, 4:548

Zoroastrianism: The Rediscovery of Missing Chapters in Man's Religious History, 4:547

Zoroastrianism and the Parsis, 4:444, 4:517

Zoroastrians, 4:444

Zoroastrians: Their Religious Beliefs and Practices, 4:547

Zuckerman Bound: A Trilogy and Epilogue, 1:1041

Zuckerman Unbound, 1:1040, 1:1041

Zukofsky's "A." An Introduction, 1:1068

Zuleika Dobson, 1:440, 1:441

The Zulu Aftermath, 3:424

Zulu Poems, 2:164

Zuni Folk Tales, 3:864

Zuñi Mythology, 3:27

The Z was Zapped, 1:1207, 1:1208

Zwingli, 4:791

Zwingli: An Introduction to His Thought, 3:334, 4:791

Zwingli: A Reformed Theologian, 4:791

Zwingli: Third Man of the Reformation, 4:791

Zwingli and Bullinger, 4:791

Zwingli and the Arts, 4:737

A Zwingli Bibliography, 4:791

Zwingli the Reformer: His Life and Work, 4:791

Zygmunt Krasiński, Romantic Universalist: An International Tribute, 2:815

Subject Index

This index cumulates in alphabetical sequence the Subject Indexes of the five preceding volumes. The number of the volume in which the subject appears is given with a colon followed by the page number(s) on which the subjects can be located.

This index provides detailed, multiple-approach access to the subject content of the volumes. Arrangement is alphabetical. The names of profiled, main-entry authors are not included in this index; the reader is reminded to use the Name Index to locate these individuals. For additional information, the reader should refer to the detailed Table of Contents at the front of each of the five preceding volumes.

A

Abbey Theatre, 1:423, 1:424, 1:441, 1:479, 1:490, 1:526, 1:555, 1:571
Abolition, *See* Antislavery movement
Aboriginals, Australian, *See* Australian culture and society, Koori Aboriginals; Australian literature, Koori authors
Abortion, 5:117, 5:134
contemporary religious issues, 4:894
Absolute idealism, 4:249
Absolute nothing, 4:290
Abstracting and indexing, 1:111–15
Abstracts
historical, 3:8
social-scientific, 3:5–6
Abuse
drama, American, 1:1111, 1:1116
middle to late twentieth-century American literature, 1:1002, 1:1064
modern British and Irish literature, 1:463
slave writings, 1:681
Academic life, contemporary philosophical issues, 4:378
Académie Française, 2:146

Academy Award, 1:1165, 1:1166, 1:1168
Academy, Greek, *See* Greek Academy
Acculturation, 3:13–14
Achaemenid Persia, 3:315
Achievement through Action Award, 5:291
Acid rain, 5:277
Acids and bases, 5:733, 5:749
Acmeists, 2:683, 2:696, 2:733, 2:737
Acronym and abbreviation dictionaries, 1:93
Action theory, Western philosophy, twentieth-century, 4:282
Actors and actresses
filmmaking, 1:1167, 1:1170, 1:1172
films, 1:1177, 1:1178
gangster, 1:1176
silent, 1:1160
westerns, 1:1165
medieval British drama, 1:157
itinerant performers, 1:161
Renaissance drama, 1:168
cross-dressing, 1:168
mobile troupes, 1:168
Restoration comedy
women's roles, 1:228
Shakespeare, 1:217
twentieth-century American drama, 1:1069

Victorian period, 1:389
Acts of Union (Great Britain, 1536 and 1543), 3:353
Actual idealism, Western philosophy, twentieth-century, 4:284
Adenosine triphosphate, 5:611
Adventure story
authors, 1:593–98
British popular literature, 1:591, 1:592–98
children's literature
American, 1:1194
British, 1:576, 1:577, 1:590
early nineteenth-century American literature, 1:659
sea tales, 1:662, 1:666, 1:685
historical fiction, 1:1244
middle to late nineteenth-century American literature, 1:773, 1:776
middle to late twentieth-century American literature, 1:1054
sea tales, 1:964
modern British and Irish literature, 1:463
Renaissance British literature, 1:167
Restoration and eighteenth-century literature, 1:256

Adventure story (*cont.*)
  Victorian period, 1:329,
    1:395
    sea tales, 1:374
    westerns, 1:1215
Aeronautics and aviation,
  5:218–20
Aesthetics, *See also* Art
  views
  African literatures, 2:105
  Chinese literature, 2:206
  contemporary philosophical
    issues, 4:392
  East African literature,
    2:152
  film studies, 1:1155
  French literature, 2:445,
    2:475, 2:482, 2:513
  Hebrew literature, 2:15
  Hungarian literature, 2:801
  Italian literature, 2:414,
    2:442
  Japanese literature, 2:293
  Latin American literatures,
    2:855
  middle to late nineteenth-
    century American liter-
    ature, 1:762
  modern British and Irish
    literature, 1:412, 1:413,
    1:478
  Russian literature, 2:704,
    2:733, 2:738
  Spanish literature, 2:521,
    2:553
  Victorian period, 1:314,
    1:316, 1:324
  Western philosophy
    1700–1800, 4:192, 4:203,
      4:204, 4:207
    1800–1900, 4:253, 4:255
    twentieth-century, 4:326
Afghanistan, 3:454
Africa
  anthropology of, 3:32
  European imperialism in,
    3:340
  exploration of, 3:929,
    3:932, 3:937–38, 3:941
  travel in, 3:901–6
African American culture
  and society
  American dream, early
    twentieth-century,
    1:797
  folk, 1:849
  folklore, middle to late
    twentieth-century,
    1:954
  ghetto life
    drama, 1:1086
    fiction, 1:802
  Gullah film, 1:1162

jazz, 1:793
literary theory, 1:1137
middle to late twentieth-
  century American liter-
  ature, 1:937, 1:939,
  1:1064
movements, early twenti-
  eth-century, 1:831
romances, 1:1225
the South, early twentieth-
  century, 1:816, 1:905
African Americans, 3:554–58,
  3:576–80, 3:585
anthropology of, 3:32
black militancy, 1:807,
  1:831
children's literature, 1:1194
Civil War, 1:667
drama, American,
  1:1069–70, 1:1071,
  1:1083–85, 1:1086,
  1:1088, 1:1090, 1:1092,
  1:1100, 1:1119
early nineteenth-century
  American literature,
  1:681
early twentieth-century
  American literature,
  1:792, 1:802, 1:824,
  1:831, 1:834, 1:879,
  1:881, 1:905
education of, 3:269
filmmakers, 1:1162, 1:1170,
  1:1171
folklore of, 3:866–67
gay literature, 1:1188–89
Harlem Renaissance, 1:797,
  1:816, 1:817, 1:848,
  1:849, 1:852, 1:856,
  1:891, 1:1137
historical fiction, 1:1245
intelligence of, 3:188
Islam, 4:566, 4:876
late Christianity, 4:762,
  4:771
liberation theology, 4:748
literary theory, 1:1136,
  1:1144
middle to late nineteenth-
  century American liter-
  ature, 1:721, 1:726,
  1:736, 1:738, 1:753,
  1:754, 1:771, 1:785
middle to late twentieth-
  century American liter-
  ature, 1:934, 1:937–39,
  1:940, 1:953–54, 1:973,
  1:1009, 1:1014, 1:1018,
  1:1020, 1:1029, 1:1032,
  1:1036, 1:1056, 1:1064

middle to late twentieth-
  century American poet-
  ry, 1:911, 1:970, 1:984,
  1:986, 1:1044
Myrdal's study of, 3:98,
  3:235
religious movements, twentieth-century, 4:861,
  4:867
science fiction, 1:1256
slaves, 3:522
slave writings, 1:646, 1:666,
  1:681
sociology of, 3:226, 3:244
women authors, 1:1137,
  1:1139, 1:1144
African Arts Prize, 2:143
African culture and society
  Akan, 2:131
  animism, 2:124
  Arabic literature, 2:66
  assimilation, 2:138
  Caribbean literature, 2:929
  colonialism affecting,
    2:104, 2:121, 2:130
  Danish literature, 2:648
  Igbo, 2:127, 2:130, 2:136,
    2:139
  Ijaw, 2:133
  Morocco, 2:117
  ritual and performance,
    2:103, 2:114, 2:115
  slavery affecting, 2:104,
    2:125, 2:137
  traditional, 2:146
  urban, 2:135
  white-settler problem,
    2:151, 2:153, 2:157
African history, 3:414–32,
  See also Middle
  Eastern history.
  authors, 3:424–32
  East Africa, 3:422–23
  European imperialism and,
    3:340
  North Africa and Sahel,
    3:418–19
  reference works, 3:415–16
  Southern Africa, 3:423–24
  surveys and general works,
    3:416–18
  West and Central Africa,
    3:419–21
African influence
  Brazilian literature, 2:890
  Caribbean literature, 2:933
  Latin American literatures,
    2:869
African literatures, 2:103–68
  African versus colonial lan-
    guages, 2:103, 2:105,
    2:131

authors, chronology,
2:113–14
collections, 2:113
East African, *See* East African literature
history and criticism,
2:106–12
North African, *See* North African literature
praises and boasts, 2:103
South African, *See* South African literature
West African, *See* West African literature
women authors, 2:105
African philosophy, 4:26,
4:367–71
authors, 4:350, 4:369–71
general works, 4:368
African religions, indigenous,
4:459, 4:462
African studies, 3:414–15
Afrikaans literature, *See*
South African literature
Agassiz, Louis, 3:130
Agassiz Professorship, *See*
Alexander Agassiz Professorship
Age and aging, 3:200–1,
5:315–18
Age of Johnson, 1:249
Age of Reason, 1:224
Christianity in the eighteenth century,
4:738–40
Age of Revolution, Christianity in the nineteenth
century, 4:740–42
health care, 5:84
nutrition and, 5:348–49
Agesilaus (king, Sparta),
3:323
Aggression, 3:170, 3:190,
3:204
animal behavior, 5:835
Agricultural economics,
3:47–48, 3:85
Agricultural Experiment Stations, 5:260
Agriculture, *See also* Agriculture and food technology
ancient history, 3:304
chemistry, agricultural,
5:742
food engineering, 5:220–21
medieval Europe, 3:329
molecular biology and,
5:766
research, statistics, 5:529,
5:530
science, 5:179

Agriculture and food
technology, 5:258–75
alternative agriculture,
5:265–66
authors, 5:267–75
food technology, 5:266–67
general reference works,
5:260–62
production agriculture,
5:262–64
technological innovations,
5:260, 5:264
traditional agriculture,
5:264–65
AIDS, 1:1180, 5:366,
5:386–88
documentary, 1:1188
Air pollution, energy concerns, 5:277
Air transportation systems,
5:246
Albania, 3:391, 3:392
Albanian literature, 2:778–80
authors, 2:777, 2:779
Albany, New York, Shakers,
4:849
Alchemy, 5:722, 5:739
Renaissance philosophy,
4:149
Alcoholism, 5:401–3
fetal alcohol syndrome,
5:375
Aldington, Richard, 1:826,
3:926
Aldiss lamp, 5:303
Alexander (the Great; king,
Macedon), 3:312, 3:446
Alexander Agassiz Professorship, 5:14
Alexandrian school, 4:61
medieval philosophy, 4:116
Algebra
linear, 5:512
literature, 5:482–85
polynomial equations,
5:483
Algonquian Bible, 4:801
Algonquin Round Table,
1:814, 1:867
Alienation, *See also* Isolation
Australian literature, 2:960
Canadian literature, 2:911,
2:916
Caribbean literature, 2:933,
2:934, 2:936, 2:940,
2:942
Chinese literature, 2:255
Danish literature, 2:654
detective story, 1:1226,
1:1227
drama, American, 1:1080,
1:1082

early twentieth-century
American literature,
1:802, 1:826, 1:853
French literature, 2:510
Frisian literature, 2:635
Hebrew literature, 2:8,
2:11
Japanese literature, 2:290
Korean literature, 2:300
Latin American literatures,
2:870, 2:885
middle to late twentieth-century American poetry, 1:1004, 1:1067
modern British and Irish
drama, 1:524, 1:565
modern British and Irish
literature, 1:412, 1:420,
1:433, 1:463
New Zealand literature,
2:972
North African literature,
2:115, 2:118
romantic period, British,
1:266
science fiction, 1:1254
West African literature,
2:146
Allegory
Arabic literature, 2:67, 2:75
Caribbean literature, 2:940
children's literature, British, 1:576, 1:587
Chinese literature, 2:186,
2:187, 2:196, 2:202,
2:207, 2:222, 2:231,
2:267, 2:268
drama, American, 1:1080
early nineteenth-century
American literature,
1:686
early twentieth-century
American literature,
1:834, 1:869, 1:892
French literature, 2:483,
2:501
German literature, 2:582,
2:586
high fantasy, British, 1:611
Italian literature, 2:409,
2:411, 2:416
Latin American literatures,
2:853, 2:872, 2:885
Middle English poetry,
1:145
Middle English, 1:149,
1:152, 1:153, 1:155
middle to late twentieth-century American literature, 1:942, 1:1060
modern British and Irish
literature, 1:496, 1:512
Persian drama, 2:93

Allegory (cont.)
Portuguese literature, 2:556
Renaissance literature,
1:173, 1:196, 1:197
Restoration and eighteenth-
century poetry, 1:227
Russian literature, 2:772
South African literature,
2:160
Spanish literature, 2:543
Victorian period, 1:365
West African literature,
2:125, 2:131, 2:133,
2:138, 2:148
Allergies and asthma, 5:386
Alliluyeva, Svetlana, 3:292
Almanacs, 1:81–83
Alpha rays, 5:711
Alternative agriculture,
5:265–66
Alternative health care sys-
tems, 5:318–21
Alzheimer's Disease, 5:391
Amana community, 4:843
America, See also United
States
Christian religion, 4:750–54
French and Spanish col-
onies, 4:752–54
American Biograph, 1:1166
American Book Award
African American literary
theory, 1:1144
middle to late twentieth-
century American liter-
ature, 1:960, 1:1020,
1:1064
middle to late twentieth-
century American poet-
ry, 1:1000, 1:1066
American civilization, ancient
religions and philoso-
phies, 4:453–58
American culture and society
American dream
drama, 1:1102, 1:1111
middle to late nine-
teenth-century, 1:711,
1:737
middle to late twentieth-
century, 1:940, 1:1033
analyses, middle to late
twentieth-century,
1:968
communism, early twenti-
eth-century, 1:808,
1:831
Creole, middle to late
nineteenth-century,
1:721, 1:736, 1:739
criticism, early twentieth-
century, 1:807

decline, middle to late
twentieth-century,
1:993
Disneyland, 1:1164
diversity
literary theory, 1:1136
middle to late nine-
teenth-century, 1:711,
1:712
middle to late twentieth-
century, 1:910
expatriates, 1:793
film industry, 1:1155–79
films, 1:792, 1:933
Great Tradition, changes,
1:1124, 1:1125
Jews, drama, 1:1094,
1:1103, 1:1105, 1:1112
junk, detective story,
1:1234
literary theory, 1:1148
mass-production effects,
1:792
materialism
middle to late nine-
teenth-century, 1:721
middle-class, 1:853,
1:1059
middle to late twentieth-
century American liter-
ature, 1:989, 1:991
mobility rise, early twentieth-century, 1:792
nationalism, early nine-
teenth-century, 1:648,
1:682
New England life, 1:695,
1:698, 1:700, 1:708
oppressed southerner, drama, 1:1088
reform
early nineteenth-century,
1:659
early twentieth-century,
1:879
middle to late nine-
teenth-century, 1:711,
1:730, 1:733
reportage, middle to late
twentieth-century,
1:958
South
early nineteenth-century,
1:684, 1:696
early twentieth-century,
1:802, 1:807, 1:818,
1:834, 1:843, 1:892,
1:894
historical fiction, 1:1249
middle to late nine-
teenth-century, 1:721,
1:736, 1:738, 1:744,
1:753, 1:771, 1:790

middle to late twentieth-
century, 1:982, 1:1009,
1:1024, 1:1029
suburban, middle to late
twentieth-century,
1:960
Tarzan, science fiction,
1:1255
technological advances,
middle to late twenti-
eth-century, 1:908
tenement life drama,
1:1109
transient labor, early twentieth-century, 1:883
upper class
comedy, 1:1085
vignettes, 1:1090
urban, middle to late
twentieth-century,
1:908, 1:1004
utilitarianism, early nineteenth-century, 1:649,
1:656
Victorian period, 1:374,
1:407
westward expansion, mid-
dle to late twentieth-
century, 1:1053
working class, middle to
late twentieth-century,
1:960, 1:1026
American dance, 3:733
American Farm Bureau Fed-
eration, 5:268
American history
Civil War diary, 1:738
literature, 1:741, 1:744,
1:771, 1:982
participants, 1:667
poetry, 1:686, 1:703,
1:815
colonies, 1:625, 1:626,
1:632, 1:638, 1:639,
1:645
Depression-era
drama, 1:1105
fiction, 1:793, 1:818
early nineteenth-century
American literature,
1:690
historical fiction, 1:1244
McCarthyism, 1:1103,
1:1105
Revolution, 1:641, 1:658,
1:983, 1:1192, 1:1202,
1:1244
South, 1:695
American influence
modern British and Irish
poetry, 1:415–16
modern British drama,
1:458, 1:1104

American Institute of Psychoanalysis, 5:452
American literature
anthologies, 1:129–30
bibliographies, 1:121
fiction, 1:122
poetry, 1:123
biographical references,
1:127–28
children's, popular, 1:1192,
1:1193–1209
authors, 1:1197–1209
collections, 1:1196–97
history and criticism,
1:1195–96
women authors, 1:1197,
1:1200–1202, 1:1204,
1:1208
drama, twentieth-century,
1:1069–1123
early American, 1:625–47
early nineteenth-century,
1:648–709
early twentieth-century,
1:791–907
film studies, 1:1155–79
guides, handbooks,
1:132–33
history of, 1:133–34
homosexuality, 1:1179–91
lesbianism, 1:1179–91
literary theory, 1:922,
1:1126, 1:1129–55
authors, 1:1134–55
collections, 1:1133–34
history and criticism,
1:1130–33
women authors,
1:1135–36, 1:1139–40,
1:1143, 1:1145–46,
1:1151–52
middle to late nineteenth-
century, 1:710–90
middle to late twentieth-
century, 1:908–1068
new directions, 1:1124–91
collections, 1:1128–29
history and criticism,
1:1126–28
popular modes,
1:1192–1263
children's, 1:1193–1209
detective story,
1:1225–38
historical fiction,
1:1244–51
horror story, 1:1238–44
romances, 1:1219–25
science fiction,
1:1251–63
westerns, 1:1210–19
reference works, 1:119

American Philosophical Association, 4:378
American Philosophical Soci-
ety Library, 1:638
American Physical Society,
5:291
American Psychological Asso-
ciation Award, 5:469
American Revolution,
3:519–22
American Social History
Project, 3:530–31
American Statistical Association, 5:519
Americas, indigenous religions, 4:463–66
Americium, 5:754
Amherst, Massachusetts,
1:745, 1:760
Ammonium chloride,
5:733–34
Amorality
detective story, 1:1227
middle to late twentieth-
century American liter-
ature, 1:956
Ampere Prize, 5:744
Anabaptists, 4:723, 4:732
Analytical chemistry,
5:735–36
Analytic geometry, Western
philosophy, 1600–1700,
4:168
Analytic philosophy
contemporary issues, 4:376,
4:377, 4:381, 4:395,
4:410, 4:412
Western philosophy, twen-
tieth-century, 4:261,
4:262, 4:271, 4:282,
4:311, 4:333
Anatomy, 5:339–43, 5:360–61,
5:772–73, 5:791, 5:810
Ancestor worship, 2:104
Chinese religion, 4:521
indigenous religions, 4:462
Mediterranean ancient ur-
ban civilization, 4:438
West African literature,
2:151
Ancient and classical period,
bibliography, 5:38–39
Ancient civilizations, urban
Mediterranean religions,
4:419, 4:438–53
New World religions,
4:419, 4:453–58
Ancient history, 3:297
agriculture, science, and
technology, 3:304
archaeology in, 3:304–5
art in, 3:755
authors, 3:309–24

European civilization,
3:327–28
general works, 3:298–99
Greece and Hellenic
world, 3:301–2
law, 3:305–6
numismation in, 3:306
philosophy, religion, education, 3:306–7
reference works, 3:298
Rome and Roman Empire,
3:302–3
society, economy, and
trade, 3:307–8
sources and documents,
3:299–300
war, peace, and diplomacy,
3:308–9
Western Asia and Egypt,
3:300–301
women, family, and sexuality, 3:309
Ancient Period (Middle East),
3:433, 3:434
Ancient religions and
philosophies, 4:419–94
authors, 4:468–94
Canaanite, 4:444
Egyptian, 4:441
Greek, 4:445
Hittite, 4:444
indigenous, 4:419, 4:458–66
Iranian, 4:443
prehistoric religions,
4:431–37
Roman, 4:447
study of, 4:420–31
urban civilizations
Mediterranean, 4:419,
4:438–53
New World, 4:419,
4:453–58
women authors, 4:478
Andrew W. Mellon Professorship, 5:55
Anesthesiology, 5:369–70,
5:408
Angevin England
(1154–1216), 3:356–57
Anglican Church, 4:776
Anglo-Saxons, 1:140
Angry Young Men, 1:419,
1:432, 1:433, 1:449,
1:531, 1:1087
Animal behavior, 3:190,
3:194, 5:798, 5:825–27,
5:835
Animal locomotion, 5:361
Animal rights, 4:43
Animism
ancient religion, 4:421
Chinese religion, 4:521

Animism (*cont.*)
  Eastern religions, 4:495,
    4:496
  Hinduism, 4:502
  Japan and Korea popular
    religion, 4:538
Annales school of history,
    3:283, 3:372, 3:620
Anomie, 3:225
Anonymous works
  Chinese literature, 2:187,
    2:194, 2:226
  early nineteenth-century
    American literature,
    1:662
  early twentieth-century
    American literature,
    1:812
  French literature, 2:452,
    2:479, 2:509
  identification of, 1:77
  Japanese literature,
    2:274–75
  Middle English, 1:145,
    1:146, 1:148, 1:155
  middle to late nineteenth-
    century American liter-
    ature, 1:743
  Netherlandic literature,
    2:619
  Old Norse-Icelandic litera-
    ture, 2:639, 2:642
  Restoration and eighteenth-
    century literature,
    1:259
  romantic period, British,
    1:275, 1:298, 1:305
  Spanish literature, 2:544
  Western philosophy,
    1600–1700, 4:178
    1700–1800, 4:197
    1800–1900, 4:227
Anorexia nervosa, 5:394
Antarctica, travel in, 3:906–7,
    3:912, 3:914–15, 3:936
Anthologies, 1:128–30
Anthrax, 5:801
Anthropocentricity, 4:43
Anthropological archaeology,
    3:12–13
Anthropological jurispru-
    dence, 3:34
Anthropological linguistics,
    3:10, 3:20–21, 3:27,
    3:42
Anthropology, 3:4, 3:10–42
  anthropological archaeol-
    ogy, 3:12–13
  authors, 3:26–42
  culture and acculturation,
    3:13–14
  culture and personality,
    3:15

economic, 3:16
ethnology, 3:16–17
evolution and, 3:17–19
folklore, 3:846
histories and surveys, 3:11
kinship and caste, 3:19–20
language, 3:20–21
methodology and issues,
    3:11–12
modern societies, 3:21–23
reference works, 3:10–11
religion, 3:23–24
social structure, 3:24–25
study of religion, 4:425,
    4:426
tribal societies, 3:25–26
Western philosophy, twen-
    tieth-century, 4:335
Anthroposophy, 2:700, 4:852,
    4:858, 4:880
Anti-establishment, *See also*
    Dissent, writers of
  Netherlandic literature,
    2:622, 2:623, 2:632
Anti-Semitism, 1:871, 5:81,
    5:142, 5:675
  contemporary issues, 4:394
  deconstruction, 1:1142
  European Jews, 4:634
  French literature, 2:465
  German literature, 2:579,
    2:610
  Italian literature, 2:407
  modern British and Irish
    literature, 1:507, 1:513
  modern Judaism, 4:655
  Western philosophy,
    1800–1900, 4:220
  Zionism, 4:657
Anti-technology, 5:166
Antibiotics, 5:795
Antigua authors, *See* Carib-
    bean literature
Antihero
  Brazilian literature, 2:898
  German literature, 2:582
  Spanish literature, 2:544
Antipoetry
  Latin American literatures,
    2:862, 2:870, 2:877
Antiquarks, 5:690
Antiromanticism
  Italian literature, 2:421,
    2:424
Antislavery movement
  early nineteenth-century
    American literature,
    1:659, 1:666, 1:667,
    1:681, 1:698, 1:708
  middle to late nineteenth-
    century American liter-
    ature, 1:753
Antitoxins, 5:738

Anxiety, 5:90
  early twentieth-century
    American literature,
    1:796, 1:807
Apocrypha
  extracanonical materials,
    4:809–10
  historical background,
    4:806, 4:807
Apollo moon landing, 5:113,
    5:612, 5:614
Apologists, 4:62
Apothegms, *See* Proverbs
Applied anthropology, 3:10
Applied folklore, 3:867–70
Applied psychology, 3:167
Arabian Peninsula, 3:450–52
Arabic (language), 3:444–45
Arabic influence
  East African literature,
    2:151
  North African literature,
    2:114, 2:115
  Persian literature, 2:81
Arabic literature, 2:54–75
  authors, 2:60–75
  children's, 2:74
  classical, 2:54, 2:62, 2:65,
    2:69
  collections, 2:56–57
  drama, 2:63
  general reading, 2:58–59
  history and criticism,
    2:54–56
  language, 2:54
  modern, 2:54
  North African literature,
    2:116, 2:118
  West African literature,
    2:124
  women authors, 2:54, 2:71
Arabs, *See also* Palestinians
  African contacts of, 3:414
  Arabic literature, 2:54, 2:64
  Hebrew literature, 2:24
  Israel (modern) and, 3:439
  North African literature,
    2:118, 2:119, 2:120,
    2:122
  Palestine and, 3:438
Archaeology, 3:12–13,
    3:304–5
Architecture, 3:755–56
  authors, 3:768–98
  biographies in, 3:764
  general reading list,
    3:761–62
  special aspects of,
    3:762–64
Arctic region, travel in,
    3:906–7, 3:912, 3:915,
    3:921, 3:932–33, 3:939
Argentina, 3:633, 3:649

Argentine authors, *See* Latin American literatures
Argentine culture and society
  authoritarianism, 2:872
  disappeared persons, 2:883
  Gaucho motifs, 2:844, 2:869, 2:884
  Italians, 2:844
Argon, 5:754
Argument, contemporary issues, 4:379
Arianism, early Christianity, 4:684
Aristotelianism
  books, 4:66–72
  medieval philosophy, 4:93, 4:112, 4:117
  Renaissance philosophy, 4:123, 4:152, 4:153
Armenian history
  deportation, 2:75, 2:79, 2:81
  massacres, 2:80
Armenian literature, 2:75–81
  authors, 2:77–81
  collections, 2:76–77
  general background, 2:76
  history and criticism, 2:76
  women authors, 2:78, 2:80
Arminianism, 4:731
Arrhenius theory of acids and bases, 5:733
Art, 3:755–56
  authors, 3:768–98
  biographies in, 3:761
  decorative, 3:764–65
    ceramics and glassware, 3:765–66
    furniture, 3:766
    illustrated books and manuscripts, 3:766–67
    metal arts, 3:767
    rugs and textiles, 3:767
  general reading list, 3:756–58
  philosophy of, contemporary issues, 4:403, 4:407
  science and technology, 5:189–95, 5:203
  sociology of, 3:202
  special aspects of, 3:758–61
Art theory, 3:755
Art views, *See also* Aesthetics
  drama, American, 1:1120
  literary theory, 1:1149
  middle to late nineteenth-century American literature, 1:722

middle to late twentieth-century American literature, 1:1052
  Victorian period, 1:324, 1:393
Arthritis, 5:398
Arthurian legend
  middle to late twentieth-century American literature, 1:949
  Victorian period, 1:400
Arthurian romance
  French literature, 2:466
  German literature, 2:586
  Middle English, 1:145, 1:146, 1:154, 1:155
Artifice
  Chinese literature, 2:217
  Greek theater, 2:355
  Russian literature, 2:740
Artificial intelligence, 3:174–75
  anthologies, 5:569–70
  background and introductory works, 5:567–72
  collections, 5:569–70
  contemporary philosophical issue, 4:382
  developments, philosophical studies of, 5:73–77
  philosophy, background, context, 5:570–72
Artificial organs, 5:370–71
Artificial satellites, 5:619, 5:633
Asceticism
  early and medieval Christianity, 4:674
  Jainism, 4:509
  medieval Judaism, 4:629
  Western philosophy, twentieth-century, 4:305
Asia
  European imperialism in, 3:340
  exploration of, 3:933–34
  travel in, 3:901–6
  Western, ancient history of, 3:300–301
Asian Americans
  drama, 1:1094
  middle to late nineteenth-century American literature, 1:721
  middle to late twentieth-century American literature, 1:1000
Asian history, 3:461–503, *See also* Middle Eastern history
  authors, 3:496–503
  East Asia, 3:463–82
    China, 3:465–72

Japan, 3:472–80
    Korea, 3:480–82
    reference works, 3:463–65
  reference works, 3:462–63
  South Asia, 3:482–88
    Bangladesh, 3:486–87
    general works, 3:482–83
    India, 3:483–86
    Pakistan, 3:487
    reference works, 3:482
    Sri Lanka (Ceylon), 3:487–88
  Southeast Asia, 3:488–93
    Burma, 3:489
    Indonesia, 3:491
    Malaysia, Singapore, and Brunei Darussalam, 3:492
    Philippines, 3:492–93
    reference works, 3:488
    surveys and general works, 3:488–89
    Thailand, 3:490
    Vietnam, Cambodia, and Laos, 3:490–91
  surveys and general works, 3:463
Asian philosophy, modern, 4:348–67, 4:372–75
  Chinese, 4:357–62
  general works, 4:349
  Indian, 4:350–55
  Islam, 4:372–75
  Japanese, 4:363–67
  Tibetan, 4:355–57
Aspen Award, 2:894
Association for Computing Machinery, 5:307
Association for Humanistic Psychology, 5:437
Association of Southeast Asian Nations (ASEAN), 3:488
Assyro-Babylonian religious tradition, 4:544
Asthma, 5:386
Astrology
  oikoumene world, 4:451
  religious movements, twentieth-century, 4:860
Astronomy, 5:585–613
  authors, 5:599–613
  "big bang," 5:594, 5:605, 5:606
  cosmic harmony, 5:608
  cosmology, 5:594–96
  galaxies, 5:593–94
  heliocentric solar system, 5:601
  history of, 5:31–32, 5:589–90
  nuclear fission, 5:602

Astronomy (*cont.*)
  pendulums, research, 5:603
  planets and solar system,
      5:592–93, 5:601,
      5:603–604
  reference and general
      books, 5:587–89
  spectroheliograph, 5:605
  stars, 5:593–94, 5:610
  stellar energy, 5:602
  stellar motion, 5:606
  telescopes, 5:589–90,
      5:607–609
  without instruments,
      5:590–92
Astrophysics, 5:653–57
  general works, 5:654–56
  history, 5:656–57
Atheism
  Danish literature, 2:651
  French literature, 2:506
  Renaissance drama, 1:199
  romantic period, British,
      1:301
  Western philosophy, twen-
      tieth-century, 4:328
Atlases, 1:83–85
  historical, 3:8–9
  social-scientific, 3:6
Atmosphere, 3:125
Atmospheric science,
      5:632–34
Atom, structure of, 5:712
Atomic and nuclear physics,
      5:657–58
  general works, 5:658
  history, 5:658
Atomic bomb
  construction of, 5:684,
      5:693
  detonation device, 5:582
  development of, 5:133,
      5:657, 5:671, 5:678,
      5:706–707, 5:813
  production of, 5:179
  radioactive fallout, 5:751
  reports on effects of, 5:161
  research on, 5:142, 5:677
  testing, 5:541, 5:751
Atomic clocks, 5:717
Atomic Energy Commission,
      5:707
Atomic theory, 5:56, 5:741
Atomism
  Greek philosophy, 4:73
  modern Western philoso-
      phy, 4:158
  pre-Socratic philosophy,
      4:52
  Roman philosophy, 4:75
  Western philosophy,
      1600–1700, 4:172

Western philosophy, twen-
      tieth-century, 4:320,
      4:333, 4:343
Atoms for Peace Conference,
      5:673
Atonement, traditional issues,
      4:885
Attitudes, 3:176–77
Attraction, animal behavior,
      5:835
Audubon Medal, 5:829
Augustan Age, 1:224
  Restoration and eighteenth-
      century poetry, 1:227
Augustinians
  medieval philosophy, 4:108
  Renaissance philosophy,
      4:138
Australia, 3:493–94
  indigenous religions, 4:460,
      4:461
Australian culture and
      society
  aristocracy, 2:950
  Koori Aboriginals, 2:944,
      2:954, 2:960, 2:968
  penal settlements, 2:948
  rural life, 2:959
  transportation of convicts,
      2:944
Australian literature,
      2:944–68
  authors, 2:947–68
  collections, 2:947
  drama, 2:967
  history and criticism, 2:946
  Koori authors, 2:945, 2:960
  women authors, 2:948–49,
      2:952, 2:953, 2:955,
      2:961, 2:963, 2:968
Austria, 3:374–76
Austrian-Hungarian Empire,
      3:374, 3:387, 3:388
Auteur theory, 3:824
Author's Club Prize, 1:547
Authorship
  literary theory, 1:1145–46
  Shakespeare controversy,
      1:203, 1:204
Autobiography, 3:768
  Arabic literature, 2:74
  Australian literature, 2:950
  Canadian literature, 2:920
  Caribbean literature, 2:936
  children's literature, Brit-
      ish, 1:584
  Chinese literature, 2:185,
      2:218, 2:250, 2:253,
      2:259, 2:268
  Danish literature, 2:651
  drama, American, 1:1106,
      1:1112, 1:1117

early American literature,
      1:637
early nineteenth-century
      American literature,
      1:666, 1:667, 1:681
early twentieth-century
      American literature,
      1:810, 1:829, 1:843,
      1:853, 1:861, 1:871,
      1:881, 1:894, 1:903
French literature, 2:466,
      2:479, 2:485, 2:499,
      2:504, 2:506, 2:508,
      2:510
German literature, 2:585,
      2:591, 2:597
Greek modern literature,
      2:372
Hungarian literature, 2:799
Italian literature, 2:421,
      2:430
Japanese literature
  classical, 2:279
  modern, 2:281, 2:285,
      2:289
Latin American literatures,
      2:860, 2:870, 2:872,
      2:874, 2:887
literary theory, 1:1144
Middle English, 1:146,
      1:152, 1:153
middle to late nineteenth-
      century American liter-
      ature, 1:726, 1:729–30,
      1:733, 1:749, 1:751–52,
      1:754, 1:758, 1:762,
      1:773, 1:785
middle to late twentieth-
      century American liter-
      ature, 1:923, 1:934,
      1:946, 1:969, 1:994,
      1:998, 1:1000, 1:1031,
      1:1036, 1:1046, 1:1049
modern British and Irish
      drama, 1:524
modern British and Irish
      literature, 1:447, 1:452,
      1:456, 1:483–84, 1:487,
      1:500, 1:506, 1:508,
      1:511, 1:518, 1:520–21,
      1:535, 1:540, 1:547,
      1:552, 1:562–63, 1:569
modern Irish literature,
      1:527, 1:528
Netherlandic literature,
      2:623, 2:631
New Zealand literature,
      2:973
North African literature,
      2:119, 2:123
Norwegian literature,
      2:667, 2:668

Old Norse-Icelandic literature, 2:641, 2:643
popular American litera-
ture, 1:1198
Portuguese literature, 2:560
Renaissance literature,
1:173
Restoration and eighteenth-
century literature,
1:229, 1:258
romantic period, British,
1:305
Russian literature, 2:700–1,
2:716, 2:720, 2:724,
2:729, 2:732, 2:736,
2:743, 2:745, 2:767
Serbian literature, 2:829
slave narrative, 2:137
South African literature,
2:158, 2:163, 2:166,
2:167
Victorian period, 1:310,
1:329, 1:341, 1:358,
1:365, 1:374–75, 1:380,
1:385, 1:405
West African literature,
2:130, 2:136, 2:138,
2:148
Western philosophy, twen-
tieth-century, 4:272,
4:280, 4:320, 4:321,
4:329
writing, reference works,
1:86–87
Automobiles
gasoline mileage, 5:279
production, 5:233, 5:242
Automotive engineering, See
Transportation
Averroism, medieval philosophy, 4:96
Aviation, 5:218–20
Aztecs, 4:456, 4:457

B

Babylon, 3:438
Bacteria, 5:800, 5:801, 5:803
Baghdad, 3:449
Baha'i faith, religious move-
ments, twentieth-cen-
tury, 4:860
Balfour Declaration, 3:347
Balkans, 3:390–93
Ballad
Chinese literature, 2:187,
2:205, 2:215, 2:216,
2:224, 2:225
Danish literature, 2:644

East African literature,
2:156
Faroese literature, 2:655
French literature, 2:514
Middle English, 1:145,
1:148, 1:152
middle to late nineteenth-
century American liter-
ature, 1:754
corridos, 1:718
Old Norse-Icelandic rimur,
2:639
Renaissance literature,
1:177
romantic period, British,
1:267
Slovak literature, 2:832
Spanish literature, 2:542
Victorian period, 1:390
Ballad opera
Restoration and eighteenth-
century drama, 1:246
Ballet, 3:733
Ballooning, 5:218
Balzan Prize, 5:796
Bancroft, George, 1:1176
Bangladesh, 3:486–87
Banting Institute, 5:407
Banting Research Founda-
tion, 5:406
Barbados authors, See Carib-
bean literature
Barcelona Seix Barral Prize,
2:857
Barium platinocyanide, 5:710
Baroque influence
French drama, 2:470
Latin American literatures,
2:860
Mexican authors, 2:844
Polish literature, 2:809
Baryons, 5:661
Bauhaus, 3:776
Bayesian statistics, 5:530
Bayley, John, 1:523
Be-bop jazz, 3:708
Bean Professorship, See
Winifred and Atherton
Bean Professorship
Beat Generation, 2:909
gay literature, 1:1190
middle to late twentieth-
century American liter-
ature, 1:909, 1:911,
1:956, 1:963, 1:980,
1:997, 1:1051
religious movements, twen-
tieth-century, 4:853,
4:859
Beck Depression Inventory,
5:432
Beck Hopelessness Scale,
5:432

Bedouins (people), 3:450
Bees, "language" of, 5:796
Behavior, 3:166, See also
Psychology
aggression, 3:170
animal behavior, 3:190,
3:194
biological bases of,
3:170–71, 3:224
sociobiology, 3:199
conditioned reflexes, 3:191
sociological study of, 3:233
collective behavior,
3:202–3
conflict and conflict resolution, 3:204
dramaturgical approach
to, 3:228
ethnomethodology, 3:227
Behavioral therapy, 5:412
Behaviorism, 3:166, 3:193–96
political science, 3:155,
3:162
Western philosophy, twen-
tieth-century, 4:309
Being
celebration of, 2:541
concept of, 5:435
Western philosophy, twen-
tieth-century, 4:290,
4:304
Belgium, 3:379, 3:380, 3:382
Belief, 3:176–77, 3:228
African philosophy, 4:371
early Christianity, 4:684–87
Islamic philosophy, 4:372
Islamic religion, 4:564
Belisarius, 3:319
Bell-shaped curve, 5:529
Bellevue-Wechsler I and II
(intelligence tests),
3:196
Benelux countries, 3:380
Benoist Prize, 5:744
Berlin Epic Theater, 2:572
Berliner Ensemble, 2:572
Beta decay, 5:708
Beta rays, 5:711
Bhakti movement, 2:170
medieval Indian literature,
2:173–74
Bhopal, 5:243
Bialik Prize, 2:11, 2:16, 2:26
Bible, 4:792–838
authors, 4:827–38
books of, See individual
books
general works, 4:793–96
access tools, 4:794
bibliographies, 4:795
critical editions of origi-
nal texts, 4:794

Bible (*cont.*)
historical background,
4:806–12
archaeology, 4:808
extracanonical materials,
4:809–12
geography, 4:809
Judaism and early Christianity, 4:806–8
languages, 4:792–93
New Testament, *See* New
Testament
Old Testament, *See* Old
Testament
study of, 4:793, 4:812–27
commentaries, 4:819–22
dictionaries and concordances, 4:817–19
interpretation histories,
4:813
introduction, 4:815–17
methods and principles,
4:814
theologies, 4:826
topic and author masterworks, 4:822–26
versions, *See* Versions of
the Bible
Biblical drama, *See* Religious
drama
Bibliography
analytical, 1:58, 1:59
readings, 1:62
enumerative, 1:58, 1:59,
1:63–68
general, 1:64
national, 1:64–68
readings, 1:61–62
general readings, 1:60–63
geographic, 3:117
historical, 1:58, 1:60, 3:8
readings, 1:63
social-scientific, 3:6
United States history,
3:509–11
Bibliophilia, *See* Book collecting
"Big bang," 5:594, 5:605,
5:606, 5:654, 5:689
Bildungsroman
Australian literature, 2:958,
2:963
Canadian literature, 2:906
early twentieth-century
American literature,
1:903
German literature, 2:560
middle to late nineteenth-century American literature, 1:773
middle to late twentieth-century American literature, 1:1056

Russian literature, 2:723
Victorian period, 1:372
Bing Professor of Population
Studies, 5:831
Binomial distribution, 5:528
Biochemistry, 5:732,
5:773–74
Bioclimatology, 5:774–75
Bioethics, *See also*
Biomedicine; Medicine
genetic engineering,
5:781–83
Biogeography, 3:125
Biographical directories, 5:4
Biographical reference,
1:85–86
literature, 1:126–28
writing biography, 1:86–87
Biographies
architects, 3:764
artists, 3:755, 3:761, 3:768
Biological sciences,
5:757–813, *See also*
specific topics for
detailed treatment
anatomy, 5:772–73, 5:791
authors, 5:784–813
biochemistry, 5:773–74
bioclimatology, 5:774–75
biology, 5:758–66
biophysics, 5:775
botany, 5:757, 5:766–68,
5:802, 5:811
cell biology, 5:775–76
classification schedules for
plants and animals,
5:804–805
developmental biology,
5:776–77
ethology, 5:798
genetics, 5:757, 5:777–83
histology, 5:772–73
history of, 5:33–34
horticulture, 5:786
microbiology, 5:783, 5:795
molecular biology, 5:689,
5:757, 5:766, 5:783–84
neuroanatomy, 5:810
ornithology, 5:786
paleontology, 5:802
physiology, 5:772–73
taxonomy, 5:804–805
uniform taxonomic systems, 5:805
virology, 5:783, 5:789–90
zoology, 5:757, 5:768–72,
5:802, 5:832
Biology, 5:758–66
behavior, 3:170–71, 3:224
animal behavior, 3:190
sociobiology, 3:199
general bibliography,
5:762–66

history of, 5:33–34
mathematics and, 5:797
philosophical treatments
of, 4:384, 5:67–68
reference works, 5:758–62
statistics and, 5:797
Biomedicine, 5:93, 5:106
Biophysics, 5:775
Biosphere, 3:125
Biotechnology, 5:73–77,
5:221–22
Birth defects, 5:375
Bishop's Bible, 4:800
Black Aesthetic movement,
1:1044, 1:1137
Black comedy
American drama, 1:1071,
1:1080, 1:1086, 1:1117
middle to late twentieth-century American literature, 1:948, 1:1012,
1:1040
Renaissance drama, 1:199
Black consciousness movements, 2:105
Black Death, plague, 2:409
Black Filmmaker Foundation, 1:1162
Black holes, 5:606, 5:677,
5:691, 5:708–709, 5:719
Black humor
early twentieth-century
American literature,
1:896
middle to late twentieth-century American literature, 1:987, 1:991
modern British and Irish
drama, 1:524
modern British and Irish
literature, 1:414, 1:453
Black Legend, 3:623, 3:642
Black militancy
early twentieth-century
American literature,
1:807, 1:831
middle to late twentieth-century American literature, 1:940, 1:941
middle to late twentieth-century American poetry, 1:1044
Black Mountain poets, 1:909,
1:911, 1:965, 1:969,
1:971, 1:1026
Black Muslims, religious
movements, twentieth-century, 4:566, 4:861
Black nationalism, 1:831,
1:941, 1:1137, 1:1189
Black-body radiation, 5:709

Blackface
  twentieth-century American
    drama, 1:1069, 1:1070
  Jim Crow routine,
    1:1070
Blacks, *See also* African
    Americans
  African literatures, 2:104
  apartheid, 2:157, 2:159,
    2:161, 2:164
  Brazilian culture and soci-
    ety, 2:889
  Caribbean literature, 2:929,
    2:933, 2:937
  Latin American literatures,
    2:869
  North African literature,
    2:115
  South African literature,
    2:163, 2:166
  Spanish American culture
    and society, 2:844
Blank verse
  drama, American, 1:1081
  early nineteenth-century
    American literature,
    1:653, 1:654, 1:661
  early twentieth-century
    American literature,
    1:815
  opera, Victorian period,
    1:356
  poetry, Victorian period,
    1:360
  Renaissance
    drama, 1:186
    literature, 1:191
  Restoration and eighteenth-
    century poetry, 1:237
  romantic period, British,
    1:277
Blindness, *See* Eye disorders
Blood diseases, *See* Hematol-
    ogy
Bloomsbury Group, 1:542,
    1:568, 1:569, 4:312
Blue Heron Press, 1:1245
Bly, Nellie, 3:820
Bohemia, 3:387
"Bok globules," 5:599
Bolivia, 3:633–34
Bollingen Prize
  early twentieth-century
    American poetry,
    1:810, 1:825, 1:857,
    1:874, 1:886, 1:889,
    1:899
  middle to late twentieth-
    century American po-
    etry, 1:952, 1:971,
    1:1005, 1:1038, 1:1044,
    1:1061

modern British and Irish
    literature, 1:435
Bon religion, 4:542
Bonding, organic chemistry,
    5:730, 5:749
Bone diseases, *See* Orthope-
    dics
Book collecting, 1:75–76
  bibliography, 1:59
  introduction, manuals, 1:76
  language of, 1:76
  rare books, 1:78
    bibliographies and check-
      lists, 1:78–79
    middle to late twentieth-
      century American liter-
      ature, 1:979
  reading, 1:30–34
Book industry, *See also*
    Publishing industry
  bestsellers, 1:51
  companies and organiza-
    tions, biographies,
    1:39–45
  education, 1:45–48
  history, 1:4, 1:36–37
    British, 1:36–37
    North American, 1:37–39
  issues and commentary,
    1:48–51
  operations, 1:45–48
  persons, biographies,
    1:39–45
  reference materials,
    1:51–53
  trends, 1:48–51
Book production
  arts and crafts of, 1:3–30
  binding and conservation,
    1:21–27
  illustration, 1:27–30
  ink and rollers, 1:21
  printing, 1:6–12
  printing types
    calligraphy, 1:12–20
    letterforms, 1:12–20
  writing surfaces, 1:4–6
Book selection tools, 1:72–75
  best lists, 1:75
  children's, 1:74–75
Book trade, 1:68–75
  bibliographies, 1:70–71
  directories, 1:69–70
  language of, 1:69
Booker Prize
  African literatures, 2:105
  Australian literature, 2:951,
    2:957
  modern British and Irish
    literature, 1:432, 1:451,
    1:454
  New Zealand literature,
    2:976

South African literature,
    2:160
  West African literature,
    2:143
Books, illustrated, 3:755,
    3:766–67
Boolean logic, 5:542
Border subject, literary theo-
    ry, 1:1136, 1:1147
Boston Pops Orchestra,
    1:1099
Botany, 5:766–68
  general works, 5:767–78
  history of, 5:33–34
  reference works, 5:767
  research, 5:802
  subdivisions, 5:757
  vascular plants, 5:811
Bourke-White, Margaret,
    1:819
Brahmanism, 4:496
Brandeis Award, 1:899, 1:952
Brandywine School of Art,
    1:1194, 1:1205
Brazil, 3:634, 3:645
Brazilian Academy of Letters,
    2:891, 2:899, 2:900
Brazilian culture and society
  backlands, 2:898, 2:899
  Japanese, 2:889
  shamans and Yorube gods,
    2:892
  synchretism, 2:889, 2:894
Brazilian literature,
    2:888–901
  authors, 2:891–901
  children's, 2:900
  collections, 2:890–91
  history and criticism, 2:890
  Portuguese language,
    2:888–89, 2:899
  women authors, 2:889,
    2:895, 2:897, 2:900
Bread Loaf School, Middle-
    bury, Vermont, 1:841
Breeding, crops, 5:259
Bridges, engineering, 5:249,
    5:254, 5:256
British influence
  American literature,
    1:1192, 1:1193
  children's, 1:1193
  early nineteenth-century
    poetry, 1:654
British Isles, 3:351–53
  England, 3:353–68
    general histories,
      3:355–56
    Hanoverian (1717–1837),
      3:361–63
    later Middle Ages
      (1216–1485), 3:357–58

British Isles (*cont.*)
Norman and Angevin
(1066–1216), 3:356–57
pre-1066, 3:356
reference works,
3:353–55
revolution, 3:336
Stuart (1603–1714),
3:359–61
Tudor (1485–1603),
3:358–59
twentieth-century,
3:365–68
Victorian (1837–1901),
3:363–65
Ireland
Northern Ireland, 3:371
prehistory to 1800, 3:370
reference works and
general histories,
3:369–70
since 1800, 3:370–71
Scotland, 3:368
Wales, 3:369
British literature
anthologies, 1:129
bibliographies, 1:121
fiction, 1:122
biographical references,
1:127
children's, popular, 1:573,
1:574–90
authors, 1:580–90
collections, 1:579
history and criticism,
1:578–79
women authors, 1:585,
1:588, 1:590
guides, 1:132
Irish literature, *See* Modern British and Irish
literature
literary history, 1:133
medieval, 1:139–61
popular modes, 1:573–622
adventure/thriller,
1:592–98
children's, 1:574–90
detective story, 1:604–11
Gothic/horror, 1:598–604
romances, 1:617–22
science fiction/fantasy,
1:611–17
reference works, 1:119
Renaissance, 1:162–201
Restoration and eighteenth-
century, 1:223–63
romantic period,
1:264–308, *See also*
Romanticism
Shakespeare, 1:202–22
Victorian period, 1:309–411

British Psychoanalytic Soci-
ety, 5:457
British-English dictionaries,
1:91
Bronze, mining, 5:237
Brookings Institution,
5:183–84
Brown v. Board of Educa-
tion (U.S., 1954), 3:188
Brownian motion, 5:681
Browning Society, 1:338
Brunei Darussalam, 3:492
Brunei literature, *See* Malay
literature
Büchner Prize, 2:569, 2:585,
2:594, 2:614
Buddha, 4:511, 4:512
Buddhism
Cambodian literature,
2:315
Chinese literature, 2:187,
2:198, 2:199, 2:201,
2:209, 2:223, 2:227
Chinese religion, 4:521,
4:529
Eastern religions, 4:496
Japanese philosophy, 4:365
Japanese religion,
4:536–38, 4:540
Korean religion, 4:536–38,
4:540
Lao literature, 2:321
Latin American literatures,
2:878
modern developments,
4:515
religious movements, twen-
tieth-century, 4:859
South Asian religion,
4:510–15
Southeast Asian religion,
4:519
Thai literature, 2:334
Tibet, 4:542
Tibetan philosophy, 4:356,
4:357
Vietnam, 4:520
Buffalo Bill, 1:1098
Bulgaria, 3:391, 3:392
Bulgarian history
nationalism, 2:781, 2:782
Turkish occupation, 2:780
Bulgarian literature, 2:780–82
authors, 2:777, 2:781–82
collections, 2:781
history and criticism,
2:780–81
women authors, 2:781
Burma, 3:489
Burmese history
Myanmar, 2:312
nationalism, 2:313

Burmese literature, 2:312–14
authors, chronology, 2:312
collections, 2:313–14
history and criticism, 2:313
women authors, 2:313,
2:314
Business administration,
3:48–49
Business cycles and
fluctuations, 3:49–50,
3:81–82, 3:84–85, 3:97,
3:104
Kuznets cycle, 3:90
Business economics, 3:48–49
Business ethics, contemporary philosophical is-
sues, 4:387
Byelorussian literature,
2:783–84
author, 2:777, 2:783
Byzantine Empire, 3:329,
3:390–91

C

Cabala
medieval Judaism, 4:629
Renaissance philosophy,
4:152
Western philosophy,
1600–1700, 4:167
Cable television, 3:800
Calculus, 5:489–91, 5:511
Western philosophy,
1600–1700, 4:176,
4:183
Caldecott Medal
children's literature, Ameri-
can, 1:580, 1:1207
Callaway Professorship, 5:51
Calvinism, 2:630, 3:334,
4:731
Cambodia, 3:490–91
Cambodian literature,
2:314–15
Cambridge Platonism
modern Western philoso-
phy, 4:157
Western philosophy,
1600–1700, 4:166,
4:167, 4:182
Canaanite religions, 4:444
Canada, folklore of, 3:874–75
Canadian culture and society
multicultural, 2:903, 2:920
Parsee community, 2:919
Canadian history, 3:604–22
authors, 3:617–22
British North America (to
1867), 3:612–14

Confederation and Dominion, 3:614–15
cultural and regional, 3:609–10
diplomatic, 3:607–8
discovery, exploration, and indigenous peoples, 3:610–11
early, and New France, 3:611–12
modern, 3:616
reference works, 3:605–6
social, 3:608–9
surveys and general works, 3:606–7
Canadian literature, 2:902–28
authors, 2:905–28
collections, 2:904
English language, 2:902
history and criticism, 2:904
women authors, 2:906, 2:911, 2:914, 2:916, 2:919, 2:920–21, 2:926
Canal building, 5:231, 5:248–49, 5:253, 5:255, 5:256
Cancer, 5:371–73
Cannes Prix International des Femmes, 2:900
Cao Dai religion, 4:520
religious movements, twentieth-century, 4:867
Capitalism, 3:50–51, 3:76, 3:78, 3:82, 3:94–95, 3:104–7, 3:243, 3:340
muckraking and, 3:823
Captivity narrative
historical fiction, 1:1244
westerns, 1:1211
Carbon dioxide, 5:277, 5:288
Carboxylic acid, 5:731
Cardiovascular diseases, 5:373–75
Careers
dentistry, 5:335–36
engineering, 5:227–28
medicine, 5:336
nursing, 5:337–38, 5:362
statistics, 5:519
Cargo cults, 4:466, 4:467
Caribbean culture and society
analysis, 2:938
Creole, Jamaica, 2:933
folk and popular influences, 2:941
miscegenation, 2:934
revindication efforts, 2:941
variety, 2:929
Caribbean history
effects of colonialism, 2:929, 2:934, 2:938, 2:940

Caribbean literature, 2:929–43
Antigua authors, 2:936
authors, 2:932–43
Barbados authors, 2:933, 2:936
collections, 2:931
diversity of language, 2:929
patois, 2:929
Dominican authors, 2:940
Guyanese authors, 2:935, 2:937
Haitian authors, 2:929, 2:941
history and criticism, 2:930
Jamaican authors, 2:934, 2:937, 2:940, 2:941
Saint Lucia author, 2:942
Trinidadian authors, 2:932, 2:935, 2:938, 2:942
women authors, 2:936, 2:940
Caribbean religions, indigenous, 4:464, 4:466
Carnegie Foundation, 5:363
Cartesianism
modern Western philosophy, 4:157, 4:158
Western philosophy, 1600–1700, 4:164, 4:181
Cartography, 3:120–21, 3:134
Carvings, prehistoric religion, 4:432, 4:433
Caste, 3:19–20
Hinduism, 4:502
South Asian religions, 4:500
Catacombs, early Christianity, 4:687
Catapults, 5:498
Cathode rays, 5:715
Catholic literary award, 1:488
Causality, modern Western philosophy, 4:157–58
Cavalier poets, 1:181, 1:183
Cave art, 1:625
prehistoric religion, 4:432
CBS (Columbia Broadcasting System), 3:818
CD-ROMs, 5:533, 5:535–36, 5:539, 5:545, 5:554
bibliography, 1:64
dictionaries, 1:89
encyclopedias, 1:105
general reference, 1:80
statistics, 1:108
Celibacy
Shakers, 4:848, 4:849
Unification Church, 4:870
Cell biology, 5:775–76
Cell metabolism, 5:801
Cell physiology, 5:772

Celtic religion, prehistoric, 4:436
Censorship
Albanian literature, 2:779
Brazilian literature, 2:894
Bulgarian literature, 2:780
Burmese literature, 2:313
Byelorussian literature, 2:783
children's literature, American, 1:1203
Chinese literature, 2:203, 2:232
Czech literature, 2:788, 2:793, 2:794, 2:795
drama
American, 1:1087
romantic period, 1:270, 1:271
Victorian period, 1:367
early twentieth-century American literature, 1:861
East African literature, 2:154
French literature, 2:451
German literature, 2:569
Indonesian literature, 2:321
Italian literature, 2:443
Korean literature, 2:302
Latin American literatures, 2:872, 2:886
middle to late twentieth-century American literature, 1:957
middle to late twentieth-century American poetry, 1:981
modern British and Irish drama, 1:445, 1:532
modern British and Irish literature, 1:476, 1:492, 1:504, 1:508
modern Irish literature, 1:459
Persian drama, 2:82
Persian literature, 2:85, 2:93
reference books, 1:56–57
Renaissance philosophy, 4:142
Restoration theater, 1:228, 1:244
Russian literature, 2:683, 2:705, 2:720, 2:727, 2:743, 2:745, 2:747–48, 2:750, 2:760, 2:772, 2:775
Serbian literature, 2:829
South African literature, 2:157, 2:159, 2:161, 2:166, 2:168

Censorship (*cont.*)
Southeast Asian literatures, 2:310
Spanish literature, 2:520, 2:521, 2:529, 2:530, 2:532, 2:540
Ukrainian literature, 2:837, 2:838, 2:839
Victorian period, 1:360
West African literature, 2:145
Western philosophy
1600–1700, 4:171, 4:182
1800–1900, 4:231
Census taking, 5:526, 5:576
Center of the Philosophy of Science, 5:100
Central Africa, 3:419–21
Central Asian religion, 4:541–44
Tibetan, 4:542–44
Centre 42, 1:565
Ceramics, 3:765–66
Ceremonials, primitive, Mediterranean ancient urbancivilization, 4:438
Cervantes Prize, 2:532
Ceylon (Sri Lanka), 3:487–88
Challenger, 5:243
Chamberlain, Neville, 3:400
Channeling, 4:865, See also Correspondences
Characters, literary, See Literary characters
Charlemagne (the Great; Charles I; emperor, Holy Roman Empire), 3:328, 3:374
Charm quarks, 5:690
Chemical engineering, 5:222–23
Chemistry, 5:722–56
agricultural chemistry, 5:742
analytical chemistry, 5:735–36
antitoxins, 5:738
applications of, 5:736–37
atomic weights, 5:740
authors, 5:737–56
biochemistry, 5:732
chemical industry, history, 5:31–32, 5:727–29
chemical reaction theory, 5:748
chemical thermodynamics, 5:746
cyanamide, 5:741
dating techniques, 5:750
dictionaries, 5:723–26
directories, 5:723–26
ekaaluminum, 5:750

electrochemical equivalents, 5:744
electron pairs, 5:749
empirical formulas, 5:723
encyclopedias, 5:723–26
environmental chemistry, 5:736–37
equilibrium theories, 5:734
general bibliography, 5:723–27
general chemistry, 5:729–30
guides to chemical literature, 5:727
history of chemistry and chemical industry, 5:31–32, 5:727–29
inorganic chemistry, 5:732–34, 5:754, 5:755
instrument design and manufacture, 5:738
iron, magnetization of, 5:711
isomers, 5:723
macromolecules, 5:746
magnetic resonance imaging, 5:743–44
molecular formulas, 5:723
nomenclature, 5:738
oral contraceptives, 5:743
organic chemistry, 5:730–32, 5:754, 5:755
organic synthesis, 5:741
osmosis, 5:738
periodic table, 5:722
periodicity, law of, 5:750
physical chemistry, 5:734–35, 5:754
polymers, 5:745–46
radiocarbon dating, 5:750
reaction rate coefficient, 5:738
reaction theory, 5:748
reproductive hazards, 5:737
structural formulas, 5:723
tin, calcination, 5:739
toxins, 5:738
Chernobyl, 5:108, 5:243
Chi-square goodness-of-fit test, 5:531
Chiang Kai-shek, 3:816
Chicago Critics, 1:1138
Chicago School of Economics, 3:107
Chicago School of Sociology, 3:199, 3:222, 3:236, 3:244
Chicano, See Latin American literatures, Mexican American authors, Mexican Americans

Child psychology, 3:164, 3:191–92
children's literature
American, 1:1206
British, 1:575, 1:576
literary theory, 1:1140
Victorian period, 1:329
Childbirth, 5:357–60
Children
child care and development, 5:321–23
childrearing, studies on, 5:204
illness and disease, 5:375–76
infantile sexual instinct, 5:445
intellectual development of, 3:266
Montessori Method for, 3:265
nutrition, 5:348
psychiatry and psychology, 3:183, 3:191–92, 5:416–17, 5:434–35, 5:444, 5:456–57
Children's literature, See American literature; British literature
Chile, 3:634–35
Chilean authors, See Latin American literatures
Chilean culture and society
disappeared persons, 2:864
Chimpanzees, studies of, 5:832–33
China, 3:465, 3:816
art in, 3:755
exploration of, 3:933–34
geometry, ancient China, 5:485
health care systems, 5:318
modern, 3:469–72
oil, politics, 5:280
reference works, 3:465–66
surveys and general works, 3:466–67
twentieth century, before, 3:467–69
China, People's Republic of, 3:465
Chinese culture and society
land reform, 2:264
Manchuria, 2:245, 2:246
peasant, 2:249, 2:262
rural, 2:258
seventeenth-century, 2:197
Taiwan, 2:232, 2:240, 2:241, 2:247, 2:251
twelfth-century, 2:226
Chinese history
communism, 2:232, 2:248, 2:256

Tiananmen Square,
2:232, 2:255, 2:267
Cultural Revolution, 2:236,
2:241, 2:244, 2:249,
2:254, 2:259, 2:263
dynasties, 2:186
Ch'ing, 2:188, 2:218
Han, 2:187, 2:194, 2:195,
2:230
Liang, 2:231
Ming, 2:188, 2:202, 2:226
Sung, 2:188, 2:214,
2:215, 2:219
T'ang, 2:187, 2:206,
2:209, 2:214, 2:224,
2:227, 2:228
Yuan, 2:188, 2:203
Chinese influence
Japanese literature, 2:269
Korean literature, 2:296
Chinese literature, 2:184-268
classical language, 2:185
history and criticism, 2:186
Mandarin dialect, 2:247
modern, 2:185, 2:231-68
"Literature of the
Wounded," 232, 2:254
authors, 2:236-68
collections, 2:235
drama, 2:265, 2:268
history and criticism,
2:233-34
women authors, 2:238,
2:240-41, 2:246, 2:248,
2:251, 2:261-64,
2:266-67
Peking dialect, 2:250
traditional, 2:185,
2:187-231
authors, 2:193-231
ch'ü, 2:188
collections, 2:192-93
drama, 2:188
fourteenth-century,
2:203
seventeenth-century,
2:209, 2:221
thirteenth-century,
2:226
fu, 2:187, 2:200, 2:212,
2:220, 2:230, 2:231
history and criticism,
2:188-92
hsiao p'in, 2:218
lü shih, 2:187
sao, 2:187
shih, 2:187, 2:197, 2:199,
2:202, 2:213, 2:215,
2:220, 2:224-25, 2:231
tz'u, 2:188, 2:204, 2:209,
2:213, 2:215, 2:220,
2:228, 2:257
women authors, 2:204

Western influence, 2:185,
2:232, 2:242, 2:253
written language, 2:184
Chinese philosophy, 4:357-62
authors, 4:350, 4:359-62
general works, 4:358
Chinese religion
ancient tradition and classics, 4:524
Buddhism, 4:529
Confucianism, 4:521, 4:525
East Asia, 4:521-33
general works, 4:522-24
popular, 4:530
reference works and an-
thologies, 4:521
Taoism, 4:521, 4:526-29
Western influence and
modern era, 4:531-33
Chivalry
French literature, 2:444
Italian literature, 2:406,
2:413, 2:439
Netherlandic literature,
2:620
Spanish literature, 2:520,
2:534
Cholera, 5:801
Cholmondeley Award, 1:549
Choreographers, 3:734-35
Christian Church
early centuries, 4:687-90
late centuries, 4:716-18,
4:719
Christian Churches of the
East
Crusades, 4:692-94
medieval Christianity, 4:691
Christian Science, 4:842
Christianity, See also
Religion
Age of Reason, 4:738-40
Age of Revolution,
4:740-42
Albanian literature, 2:778
ancient Judaism, 4:616,
4:619
Armenian literature, 2:75
atonement, 4:886
Australian literature, 2:957
Canadian literature, 2:908
Chinese literature, 2:242,
2:253
contemporary issues, 4:883
early and medieval,
4:674-714
authors, 4:701-14
histories, 4:676-78, 4:681
reference works, 4:675
source collections,
4:679-81
topical studies, 4:678
women authors, 4:706

early thinkers, 4:62
general works, 4:63
early twentieth-century
American literature,
1:889
environmental ethics and,
5:113
European Jews and, 3:346
1500 to the present,
4:715-91
authors, 4:756-91
dictionaries, encyclope-
dias, handbooks,
4:716-20
ethics and theology,
4:718
general reference works,
4:716
women authors,
4:764-65, 4:784-85,
4:788
French literature, 2:460,
2:466, 2:468, 2:482,
2:489, 2:516
gay literature, 1:1186
German literature, 2:577
Greek and Roman philoso-
phy, 4:45
history of, 4:806-8
European civilization,
3:327, 3:329
Ireland, 3:352
medieval Europe, 3:329,
3:330
Middle East, 3:434
Reformation, 3:333-34
Roman Empire, 3:310
indigenous religions, 4:463
Italian literature, 2:409,
2:416, 2:429, 2:430
Judaism and, 4:602
Latin literature, 2:379
Marxism and, 5:163
medieval Judaism,
4:623-25
medieval literature, British,
1:139, 1:140
medieval philosophy,
4:92-121
medieval, 4:690-701
Eastern churches and
Crusades, 4:692-94
emperors, popes, and
councils, 4:694
life and culture,
4:698-701
special histories,
4:690-92
thought and doctrine,
4:695-98
Middle English, 1:153

Christianity (*cont.*)
  middle to late twentieth-
    century American liter-
    ature, 1:1029
  middle to late twentieth-
    century American poet-
    ry, 1:1005
  modern British and Irish
    literature, 1:435, 1:442,
    1:457, 1:460, 1:471,
    1:473, 1:488, 1:492,
    1:501–2, 1:515, 1:551,
    1:560
  modern Irish literature,
    1:459, 1:494, 1:506,
    1:528
  mystery cults, 4:450
  1914 to the present,
    4:742–50
  liberation theology,
    4:747–50
  North African literature,
    2:115, 2:116
  Renaissance literature,
    1:172, 1:175, 1:180
  Restoration and eighteenth-
    century poetry, 1:251
  romantic period, British,
    1:277–78
  Russian literature, 2:712,
    2:721, 2:763
  South African literature,
    2:157, 2:166
  Spanish literature, 2:519,
    2:550, 2:551
  theological study of reli-
    gion, 4:422
  Victorian period, 1:363
  West African literature,
    2:124, 2:125, 2:127,
    2:132
  Western philosophy,
    1800–1900, 4:238,
    4:253
Christmas carol, 1:148
Chromosomes, 5:806–808
Chronic diseases, 5:376–78
Church and state
  late Christianity,
    1500–1560, 4:723
  medieval Christianity, 4:690
Church Fathers, *See* Fathers
    of the Church
Church of England, 4:725,
    4:763
Cinema, *See* Film studies
Cistercians, medieval philoso-
    phy, 4:111
Cities
  medieval Europe, 3:329,
    3:407
  urban geography, 3:123–24,
    3:127, 3:129

urban life, 3:199, 3:216–17
Citric acid cycle, 5:801
City life, *See* Urban life
City-state, Greek civilization,
    4:446
Civil engineering, 5:223–24
Civil liberties, 3:139
Civil rights, 3:139
  drama, American, 1:1083
  early nineteenth-century
    American literature,
    1:667, 1:682
  early twentieth-century
    American literature,
    1:831
  middle to late twentieth-
    century American liter-
    ature, 1:939, 1:1064
  Victorian period, 1:341
Civil War (United States),
    3:526–30, 3:571, 3:574,
    3:585
Clarence H. Robinson Profes-
    sorship, 5:19
Class, *See* Social class
Classical economics, 3:106
Classical electrodynamics,
    5:673
Classical mechanics, 5:705
  general works, 5:659–61
  history, 5:661
Classicism
  French literature, 2:479,
    2:502
  German literature, 2:560,
    2:563, 2:593, 2:609
  Polish literature, 2:819
Clean Air Act, 5:277
Client centered theory of
    psychotherapy, 5:467
Clifton Suspension Bridge,
    5:249
Climatology, *See* Meteorology
Clinical judgment in medi-
    cine, analyses of,
    5:78–80
Clinical psychology,
    5:411–73, 3:167
  abnormal psychology,
    5:412
  "adjustment," 5:460
  art and neurosis, 5:465
  authors, 5:429–73
  BASIC I.D., 5:460
  behavioral therapy, 5:412
  child psychology, 5:416–17,
    5:434–35, 5:444
  children, 5:456–57
  client centered theory of
    psychotherapy, 5:467
  cognitive psychology, 5:412
  depression, treatment,
    5:432

disorders, literature,
    5:425–29
emotional development,
    theories of, 5:472
empathy, 5:457
Eupsychian approach,
    5:461
existentialism and, 5:436,
    5:462
general psychology litera-
    ture, 5:413–14
Gestalt psychology, 5:411,
    5:412, 5:464
humanistic psychology,
    5:412, 5:437–38, 5:461,
    5:462
identity crisis, 5:441
image, role of, 5:458
intensive individual psycho-
    therapy, 5:437–38
intrapsychic conflict, 5:457
introverts and extroverts,
    5:454
logotherapy, 5:443
"metabletic" method, 5:471
milieu therapy, 5:458
multimodal assessment,
    5:460
personality disorders, 5:430
rational-emotive therapy
    movement, 5:438
self-psychology, 5:457
sexuality, 5:429, 5:430,
    5:440, 5:445
social attitudes, study of,
    5:431
special reading lists,
    5:416–24
therapy and counseling,
    methods and ap-
    proaches, 5:417–26
war veterans, work with,
    5:470
Club of Rome, 5:167
CNN (Cable News Network),
    3:805
Coal
  burning of, 5:277
  oil and gas, and, 5:285–86
  tar, 5:752
Cobra group, 2:623
Coeducation, 3:265
Cognition, 3:171–72, 5:90,
    5:178
  contemporary philosophical
    issues, 4:381, 4:382,
    4:396
  development of, 3:191–92
  modern Western philoso-
    phy, 4:157
Cognitive psychology, 5:412
Cold war, 3:277, 3:291,
    3:400, 5:109

Collaborative works, *See also*
Collectively composed
works
Chinese literature, 2:211
detective story, 1:1236
drama, American, 1:1096
early twentieth-century
American literature,
1:859, 1:884
filmmaking, 1:1156, 1:1162,
1:1163
French literature, 2:472
Irish drama, 1:490
Latin American literatures,
2:878
literary theory, 1:1136,
1:1154
modern British and Irish
drama, 1:449, 1:450,
1:492, 1:493
modern British and Irish
literature, 1:435, 1:474,
1:500, 1:517, 1:521,
1:538, 1:547, 1:563
opera, Victorian period,
1:356
Renaissance drama, 1:172,
1:200
Restoration and eighteenth-
century literature,
1:252
romances, 1:1221
Russian literature, 2:729
Victorian period, 1:377,
1:399
Collage
film studies, 1:1159
Collective behavior, 3:202-3
Collectively composed works
ancient Near Eastern literature, 2:51
Hebrew literature, 2:8
Collegiants, Western philosophy, 1600-1700, 4:186
Colombia, 3:635
Colombian authors, *See* Lat-
in American literatures
Colonial history (United
States, 1606-1763),
3:516-19
Colonialism, 3:335
Africa, 3:414
African philosophy, 4:348
Asian philosophy, modern,
4:348
India, 3:484-85
Indian philosophy, 4:350
indigenous religions affect-
ed by, 4:466
Italian, 3:383
Latin America, 3:623,
3:628-30, 3:642

religion in America,
4:752-54
Southeast Asia, 3:488
Color vision, 3:189
and color blindness, 5:692,
5:741
Comédie Française, 2:450
Comedy
American drama, 1:1081,
1:1109, 1:1111
cabaret, 1:1100
drawing room, 1:1085
drama, Victorian period,
1:367, 1:409
films, 1:1160
Irish drama, 1:490, 1:526
middle to late twentieth-
century American liter-
ature, 1:933
modern British and Irish
drama, 1:465, 1:486,
1:554
drawing room, 1:471
modern British and Irish
literature, 1:483
Renaissance drama, 1:175,
1:183, 1:185, 1:189
Restoration drama, 1:228,
1:232, 1:237, 1:242-43,
1:246, 1:254, 1:261,
1:263
Shakespeare, 1:210
Victorian period, 1:378,
1:389, 1:399
drawing room, 1:311
Comitatus, 1:142, 1:143
Commedia dell'arte, 2:399,
2:420, 2:422
French drama, 2:490
Turkish drama, 2:95
Common-sense school
early American literature,
1:637, 1:641
early nineteenth-century
American literature,
1:656
Western philosophy,
1700-1800, 4:211
Communal groups, religious
movements, nine-
teenth-century, 4:843
Communes, 3:217
Communicable diseases, *See*
Infectious diseases
Communications, *See also*
Mass media
sociological study of,
3:203-4, 3:229-30
Communications technology,
5:294-308
agriculture, effects on,
5:260
authors, 5:305-308

data communications,
5:301-303
fiber optics, 5:303-304
general works, 5:295-98
switching systems, 5:301
technical references,
5:304-305
transmission systems and
methods, 5:298-301
Communism
Balkans, 3:391
Chinese philosophy, 4:361
decline in, 3:342
Eastern Europe, 3:388
Soviet Union, 3:393-98
Western philosophy, twen-
tieth-century, 4:286
Community life, 3:216-17,
3:220, 3:225, 3:229-31,
3:242
Comparative economic sys-
tems, 3:51-52
Comparative literature,
2:981-91
genres, 2:982
Germany, 2:610
history and principles,
2:983-84
influences, 2:982, 2:990
interrelations, 2:982,
2:987-90
art and music, 2:987-88
general, 2:987
myth, 2:988
philosophy, 2:988
politics, 2:988-89
psychoanalysis, 2:989
religion, 2:989
science, 2:989-90
Italian, 2:419
Japan, 2:281
literary movements,
2:985-87
themes and motifs, 2:981,
2:984-85
translation, 2:982, 2:990-91
Comparative philosophy,
4:36-38
East-West, 4:37
general, 4:37
Indian, 4:353
Comparative political ideologies, 3:139-41
Comparative political systems, 3:141
Compton effect, 5:678
Computer applications
business and professional,
5:555-59
creativity in the arts,
5:564-66
cyberpunk fiction, 5:562

Computer applica-
    tions (*cont.*)
  data communications,
    5:559–60
  databases, 5:559–60
  education, 5:566–67
  fiction and computers,
    5:562–63
  hypertext, 5:560–63
Computer programming
  environments, 5:551–53
  general programming,
    5:549–51
  introductions, 5:549–51
  languages, 5:551–53
  media, 5:551–53
  operating systems and en-
    vironments, 5:553–55
  structural engineering,
    5:245
  surveys, 5:549–51
Computers and computer
    science, 3:111, 5:532–84,
    See also Computer
    applications; Computer
    programming
  artificial intelligence,
    3:174–75, 5:567–62
  authors, 5:575–84
  automatic digital computer,
    5:575
  beginner's guides, 5:536–38
  biographies, 5:541–43
  census analysis, 5:576
  collections, 5:539–41
  compiler, development of,
    5:577
  cultural issues, 5:572–75
  dictionaries, 5:539–41
  difference engine, 5:575,
    5:578
  digital computer, 5:581
  electronic mail (e-mail),
    5:301, 5:532
  ethical issues, 5:124–27
  future, 5:533
  general accounts and biog-
    raphies, 5:542–43
  geographic information sys-
    tems, 3:117, 3:120
  health care and technolo-
    gy, 5:366
  historical bibliography,
    5:541–43
  history of, 5:533, 5:541–42
  introduction to computing,
    5:536–38
  languages, computer,
    5:535, 5:548, 5:551–53,
    5:566
  mainframe computers,
    5:553
  mathematics and, 5:581

  Microsoft Windows,
    5:553–54
  MS-DOS, 5:553–54
  periodicals, 5:535–56
  personal computers, 5:542
  privacy and, 5:572
  programming, 5:548–55
  reference works, 5:539–41
  social issues, 5:572–75
  statistics and, 5:518
Conceptism, 2:539
Conceptual pragmatism,
    Western philosophy,
    twentieth-century,
    4:301
Concrete imagery
  Canadian literature, 2:907
  Chinese literature, 2:237
  Russian literature, 2:683
  South African literature,
    2:164
Condensed matter, 5:668
Conditioned reflexes, 3:191
Conductors (orchestral),
    3:671
Confessing Church, 4:757,
    4:759
Confessional poetry
  middle to late twentieth-
    century American poet-
    ry, 1:909, 1:911, 1:950,
    1:1005, 1:1030, 1:1045,
    1:1051
  modern British and Irish
    poetry, 1:501
Confessional style
  Japanese literature, 2:292
  Russian literature, 2:734
Conflict and conflict resolu-
    tion, 3:204
Confraternity Version, *See*
    New American Bible
Confucianism, 4:496
  Chinese philosophy, 4:358,
    4:359, 4:360, 4:362
  Chinese religion, 4:521,
    4:525
Congenital deformities, 5:776
Congress of Vienna (1815),
    3:379, 3:388
Connecticut Wits, The, 1:632
Consciencism
  African philosophy, 4:370
Consciousness, 3:166
  Japanese philosophy, 4:364
  studies of, 5:411
Conservative Judaism, 4:651,
    4:654
Constitution (U.S.), 3:161,
    3:541
Constitutional history of
    United States, 3:541–44
Constitutionalism, 3:141–42

Construction and mainte-
    nance engineering,
    5:224–25
Consumer advocacy move-
    ment, 5:127
Consumerism
  health care, 5:331–32
  medicine and health, 5:309
Contemplation, late Chris-
    tianity, 4:780, 4:786
Contemporary music,
    3:665–66
Contemporary Period (Middle
    East), 3:433
Continental theory, 1:1125,
    1:1141, 1:1148, *See
    also* Deconstruction
Control engineering,
    5:242–43
Conversational works
  early nineteenth-century
    American literature,
    1:672, 1:677
  Victorian period, 1:381
Conway Suspension Bridge,
    5:256
Cooperative communities,
    See Communal groups
Copernican system, Renais-
    sance philosophy,
    4:134, 4:135, 4:141,
    4:142
Copper, mining, 5:237
Copyright, 1:31–55
Corn, 5:258, 5:259, 5:270
Corn Laws (England), 3:100
Correspondence principle,
    5:673
Correspondences, religious
    movements, nine-
    teenth-century, 4:840.
    See also Channeling
Cosmetic surgery, *See* Plastic
    surgery
Cosmic censorship, 5:708
Cosmic consciousness, 2:410
Cosmogony, Western philoso-
    phy, 1600–1700, 4:167
Cosmology, 5:594–96,
    5:653–57
  general works, 5:654–56
  history of, 5:656–57
  philosophical treatments
    of, 5:67–68
  Renaissance philosophy,
    4:134, 4:135, 4:148
  Western philosophy,
    twentieth-century,
    4:260, 4:340
  research, 5:689
Cost-benefit analysis, 3:69–70
Costa Rica, 3:635–36

Cotton gin, invention of,
  5:259
Council of Trent, *See* Trent,
  Council of
Councils of the Church
  early Christianity, 4:681
  medieval Christianity, 4:694
Counseling psychology, 3:167
Counter Reformation,
  4:727–29, 4:736
Court cases, ethical issues,
  5:106
Court life
  Chinese literature, 2:187,
    2:195, 2:200, 2:215,
    2:230
  French literature, 2:466,
    2:485, 2:492
  Italian literature, 2:412,
    2:413, 2:436
  Japanese literature, 2:279,
    2:280, 2:293
  Korean literature, 2:297,
    2:301
  Persian drama, 2:82
  Renaissance British litera-
    ture, 1:164
  Renaissance drama, 1:185
    masque, 1:168
  Renaissance literature,
    1:195, 1:196, 1:201
  Spanish literature, 2:532,
    2:539, 2:547
Court life, medieval philoso-
  phy, 4:115
Court literature
  Lao, 2:321
  Thai literature, 2:334
  Vietnamese literature,
    2:337
Court poetry
  Arabic literature, 2:73
  Burmese literature, 2:313
  Chinese literature, 2:194,
    2:198, 2:200, 2:201
  Japanese literature, 2:277
  Malay literature, 2:323
  Persian literature, 2:89
  Thai literature, 2:337
  Turkish literature, 2:95
  Urdu literature, 2:175
Court Theatre, 1:423, 1:544
Courtly legend
  German literature, 2:586,
    2:617
Courtly love
  German literature, 2:562,
    2:581, 2:604
  Italian literature, 2:433
  Middle English, 1:146,
    1:149
  Netherlandic literature,
    2:626

Spanish literature, 2:548
Coverdale Bible, 4:799
Cowboy westerns, 1:1009,
  1:1218
Crafoord Prize, 5:831
Creationism, 2:870
Creative film foundation,
  1:1163
Creativity
  art, science and technolo-
    gy, 5:186
  computer applications, cre-
    ativity in the arts,
    5:564–66
  history of studies of, 5:56
  mathematics, 5:494
  philosophy of, 5:85
Crime, 3:204–5
Crime Writers Association,
  1:608, 1:609
Criminology, 5:463
Critical idealism, Western
  philosophy, twentieth-
  century, 4:274
Critical realism, Western philosophy, twentieth-cen-
  tury, 4:260, 4:302,
  4:326
Criticism
  dance, 3:731–32
  film, 3:827
  music, 3:658–64
Croatian literature, 2:784–87
  authors, 2:777, 2:786–87
  collections, 2:785–86
  drama, 2:786
  history and criticism, 2:785
  women authors, 2:787
Cromwell, Oliver, 3:336
Crops, *See* Agriculture and
  food technology
Crude oil, 5:241
Crusades
  Eastern Orthodox Church,
    4:755
  medieval Christianity,
    4:692–94
Crystalline solids, 5:668
Crystallography, 4:257
Cuba, 3:636
Cuban Americans, 1:988
Cuban authors, *See under*
  Latin American litera-
  tures
Cuban Casa de las Americas
  Prize, 2:870
Culteranism, 2:539
Cults
  cargo, 4:466, 4:467
  imperial, 4:451
  mystery, 4:446, 4:450
  prehistoric religion, 4:433

religious movements, twentieth-century, 4:856,
  4:857
Cultural anthropology (ethnology), 3:10, 3:16–17
Cultural configuration, 3:32
Cultural critiques, philosophy
  of science, 5:65–67
Cultural deprivation, 5:413
Cultural evolution, 3:39,
  3:239
Cultural geography, 3:121–22
Cultural history, 3:462
  Canada, 3:609–10
  United States, 3:558–61
Cultural materialism, 3:31
Culture
  acculturation, 3:13–14
  anthropological archaeol-
    ogy, 3:13
  anthropological, 3:10
  definition of, 3:39
  geographic, 3:121–22
  history of, 3:399
  Islamic, 3:442–44
  language, 3:42
  personality, 3:15
  popular, 3:846, 3:872–74
    authors, 3:874–88
  poverty, 3:34
  pre-Columbian, 3:626–28
Culture, philosophy of, *See*
  Historicism
Cuneiform writing, Mesopota-
  mian ancient urban
  civilization, 4:440
Curium, 5:754
Cyanamide, 5:741
Cyberpunk fiction, 5:562
Cyborg, 1:1147
Cycle plays, 1:156, 1:158
  Renaissance, British, 1:167
Cynicism, Greek philosophy,
  4:89
Cyprus, 3:391
Cyrenaic school, 4:89
Cyrus the Younger (prince,
  Persia), 3:323
Cystic fibrosis, 5:780
Cytochemistry, *See* Cell biol-
  ogy
Cytophysiology, 5:775
Czech literature, 2:787–95
  authors, 2:777, 2:789–95
  collections, 2:789
  drama, 2:789, 2:791
  history and criticism,
    2:788–89
Czech Republic, 3:389
Czechoslovakia, 3:387–89
Czechs (people), 3:387

D

Da Gama, Vasco, 3:384
Dag Hammarskjold International Prize, 2:135
Dalai Lama, 4:356, 4:558
  contemporary religious issues, 4:905
Dali, Salvador, 3:832
Dams, 5:231
Dance, 3:653, 3:731–54, *See also* Music
  American, 3:733
  authors, 3:735–54
  ballet, 3:733
  choreographers, 3:734–35
  companies, 3:734
  ethnic, 3:733–34
  folk song and dance, 3:850–53
  general reference, 3:732–33
  history and criticism of, 3:731–32
Dance companies, 3:734
Dancing Dervishes, *See* Whirling Dervishes
Danilevsky, Nikolai, 3:393
Danish literature, 2:644–54
  authors, 2:638, 2:646–54
  children's, 2:646
  collections, 2:645
  drama, 2:650, 2:652
  history and criticism, 2:645
  women authors, 2:645, 2:648, 2:649, 2:654
Dark Ages, 3:328
Darwinian philosophy, 2:652
Darwinian theory of evolution, 5:757, 5:792, 5:799, 5:811
Data communications, 5:301–303, 5:559–60
Databases, 5:546, 5:559–60
Dates, *See* Facts
DDT, *See* Dichloro-diphenyl-trichloroethane
Dead Sea Scrolls, 4:792, 4:794
Deafness, 5:379–80
Death and dying, 5:144, 5:378–79
Death customs and rites
  Egypt, ancient religion, 4:441
  indigenous religions, 4:461
  prehistoric religion, 4:432
  Zoroastrianism, 4:517
Debauchery
  Chinese literature, 2:207, 2:265
  French literature, 2:455, 2:478

German literature, 2:601
  Latin literature, 2:390
  Renaissance literature, 1:180
  Victorian period, 1:398
Decadence
  Chinese literature, 2:206, 2:265
  detective story, 1:1228
  French literature, 2:456, 2:465, 2:478, 2:513, 2:514
  Italian literature, 2:399, 2:405
  middle to late nineteenth-century American literature, 1:761
  modern British and Irish literature, 1:414, 1:440, 1:463, 1:500
  Restoration and eighteenth-century poetry, 1:227
  romantic period, British, 1:281
  Spanish literature, 2:553
  Victorian period, 1:309, 1:324, 1:391
Decision-making
  computers and, 5:125
  medicine, philosophy, 5:78–80
Declaration of Independence (U.S.), 3:154, 3:159, 3:541
Deconstructionism, 1:1130, 1:1142, 1:1150
  contemporary philosophical issues, 4:390–92, 4:396
  current theological method, 4:889
  middle to late twentieth-century American literature, 1:966
  modern British and Irish literature, 1:463
  Western philosophy, twentieth-century, 4:262
Decorative arts, 3:756, 3:764–65
  ceramics and glassware, 3:765–66
  furniture, 3:766
  illustrated books and manuscripts, 3:766–67
  metal arts, 3:767
  rugs and textiles, 3:767
Deep sea exploration, 5:640–41, 5:642
Democracy, 3:142–43, 3:163, 3:340
Democratic socialism, Western philosophy, twentieth-century, 4:297

Demographic economics, 3:59–60
Demography, 3:241
  statistics and, 5:520
Denmark, 3:379, 3:381
Dental care, 5:335–43
Dentistry as a profession, 5:335–36
Deoxyribonucleic acid (DNA)
  alteration of, 5:781
  discovery of, 5:757
  double helix structure, 5:775
  mechanism for coding, 5:605
  molecular structure, 5:777, 5:812
  recombinant technology, 5:804
  structure of, 5:689, 5:774, 5:790
  viruses and, 5:783
  X-ray studies of, 5:813
Depression, treatment of, 5:432
Dermatology, 5:339–43
Design, engineering and technology, 5:225–27
Detective story
  American popular literature, 1:1209, 1:1225–38
  authors, 1:605–11, 1:1227–38
  British popular literature, 1:591, 1:604–11
  early nineteenth-century American literature, 1:691
  middle to late twentieth-century American literature, 1:949
  modern British and Irish literature, 1:457, 1:511, 1:543, 1:568
  Victorian period, 1:346
  women authors, 1:605, 1:608–9, 1:1229, 1:1231, 1:1235, 1:1238
Determinism, 5:95
Developing countries
  agriculture, 5:270
  oil, 5:276–77, 5:280
  technology, 5:136
Development, economic, 3:53–54, 3:104
  geographic, 3:122
Development, individual, 3:173–74, 3:181–82, 3:191–92
  age and aging, 3:200–1
  intellectual, 3:266
Developmental biology, 5:776–77

Deviance, 3:204–5
Dexter Prize, 5:50
Diabetes, 5:381–82, 5:406
Diagnostic testing, 5:324
Dialectic
  Greek philosophy, 4:88
  medieval philosophy, 4:107
  Western philosophy, twentieth-century, 4:269, 4:281
Dialectical materialism, 3:271, 3:289
  Western philosophy, 1800–1900, 4:227
Dialogues
  Plato, 4:77–78, 4:89
  Socrates, 4:89
Dianetics, 4:869
Diary
  early twentieth-century American literature, 1:864
  middle to late nineteenth-century American literature, 1:738, 1:761
Diaspora
  Hebrew Bible, 4:796
  Jews, 4:591, 4:607
Dichloro-diphenyl-trichloroethane, 5:259
Dictionaries, 1:89–103, 3:755
  chemistry, 5:723–26
  choice guidebooks, 1:89
  computers and computer science, 5:539–41
  general reference work, 5:2–3
  historical, 3:7–8
  illness and disease, 5:367
  literature, 1:131–33
  social-scientific, 3:4–5
  United States history, 3:508–9
Diet, See Nutrition and diet
Dietrich, Marlene, 1:1176
Difference engine, 5:575, 5:578
Dime novel
  American popular literature, 1:1211
    romances, 1:1219
  detective story, 1:1226
  middle to late nineteenth-century American literature, 1:720
Dinosaurs, 5:615
Dionysiac movements, Greek ancient religion, 4:446
Dionysiac spirit
  festivals, 2:342
  poetry, 2:370, 2:376
Diplomacy
  ancient history, 3:308–9

Canada, 3:607–8
  United States history, 3:544–47, 3:567, 3:583, 3:601
  world history, 3:277–81
Directories, 1:103–5 See also under specific topics
  biographical directories, 5:4
  chemistry, 5:723–26
  historical, 3:8–9
  illness and disease, 5:367–68
  information science, 5:545–46
  organizational directories, 5:3–4
  social-scientific, 3:6
Directors (film), 3:824, 3:827–29
Disabilities, 3:201–2
Disasters, technological, 5:127
Discrimination, See also Race relations
  economic study of, 3:66–67
  Myrdal's study of, 3:98, 3:235
Disease, See Illness and disease
Disneyland, 1:1164
Disordered materials, 5:704
Display (animal behavior), 5:825
Dissent, writers of, See also Anti-establishment
  African literatures, 2:104
  Albanian literature, 2:779
  Arabic literature, 2:63, 2:65
  Armenian literature, 2:78, 2:80
  Brazilian literature, 2:889
  Burmese literature, 2:314
  Canadian literature, 2:909
  Chinese literature, 2:232, 2:237, 2:244, 2:249, 2:254, 2:259, 2:263
  Croatian literature, 2:787
  Czech literature, 2:788, 2:791, 2:793, 2:794, 2:795
  early twentieth-century American literature, 1:905
  East African literature, 2:154
  French literature, 2:464
  gay literature, 1:1179–91
  German literature, 2:596, 2:606, 2:613
  Greek modern literature, 2:375

Indian literature, 2:181
Indian subcontinent literature, 2:176
Indonesian literature, 2:319, 2:321
Korean literature, 2:303
Latin American literatures, 2:859, 2:862, 2:864, 2:877, 2:886
Latin literature, 2:379
Malay literature, 2:326
middle to late twentieth-century American literature, 1:938, 1:941, 1:951, 1:989
modern British and Irish drama, 1:424
North African literature, 2:121
Persian literature, 2:88, 2:93
Philippine literature, 2:332
Polish literature, 2:812, 2:814, 2:815
Russian literature, 2:683, 2:696, 2:698–99, 2:711, 2:724, 2:727, 2:732, 2:734, 2:737, 2:747–48, 2:753, 2:757, 2:760, 2:771–72
Serbian literature, 2:829
Slovak literature, 2:833
South African literature, 2:157
Southeast Asian literatures, 2:311
Spanish literature, 2:521, 2:552
Turkish literature, 2:98, 2:100
twentieth-century American drama, 1:1071
Ukrainian literature, 2:838
Vietnamese literature, 2:338, 2:340
West African literature, 2:125, 2:133, 2:143, 2:144, 2:145, 2:148
Distinguished Service Award, U.S. Department of Interior, 5:829
Divine Light Mission, 4:872
DNA, See Deoxyribonucleic acid (DNA)
Doctrine
  early Christianity, 4:681, 4:684–87
  medieval Christianity, 4:695–98
Documentarism, 2:673

Documentary
  ancient history, 3:299–300
  early twentieth-century
    American literature,
    1:827
  filmmaking, 1:1164, 1:1166
  gay literature, 1:1188,
    1:1191
  middle to late twentieth-
    century American liter-
    ature, 1:932
  United States, 3:511–12
Dollard, John, 3:190
Dolphin language, 5:768
Dominican authors, *See* Ca-
    ribbean literature
Dominican Republic, 3:636
Dominicans, Renaissance phi-
    losophy, 4:134, 4:136,
    4:137
Donatism, early Christianity,
    4:684
Douay Version, 4:800
Double helix, 5:775
Doubt, critical method of,
    5:502
Drama
  bibliographies, 1:123
  censorship, Victorian peri-
    od, 1:367
  early American literature,
    1:642, 1:645
  indexes, 1:124
  Irish theater, 1:423
  medieval, British, 1:156–61
  middle to late twentieth-
    century American,
    1:936
    bibliography and refer-
      ence, 1:427–28 :543,
      1:544, 1:553, 1:565
    collections, 1:427 :543,
      1:544, 1:553, 1:565
    history and criticism,
      1:425–26 :543, 1:544,
      1:553, 1:565
    theaters and companies,
      1:426–27 :543, 1:544,
      1:553, 1:565
  modern Irish, 1:423, 1:441,
    1:478, 1:490, 1:525,
    1:526, 1:555, 1:571
  Renaissance, British,
    1:167–71
  Restoration and eighteenth-
    century, 1:241, 1:257
    ballad opera, 1:246
  Restoration comedy, 1:223,
    1:228, 1:232, 1:237,
    1:242, 1:243, 1:246,
    1:254, 1:261, 1:263
  Restoration tragedy, 1:251

  romantic period, British,
    1:270–72, 1:276–77
  Shakespeare, 1:202–22
  twentieth-century Ameri-
    can, 1:857, 1:890,
    1:898, 1:903,
    1:1069–1123
    authors, 1:1079–1123
    collections, 1:1076–79
    history and criticism,
      1:1071–76
    minstrel show, Jim Crow
      routine, 1:1070
    Tom shows, 1:1070
    women authors, 1:1071,
      1:1092–93, 1:1100,
      1:1105, 1:1113, 1:1114
  Victorian period, 1:311,
    1:320–23, 1:329, 1:331,
    1:347, 1:366–67, 1:376,
    1:388–89, 1:398, 1:409
Dramaturgical approach,
    3:228
Dreaming, the, 4:460, 4:461
Dreams, 3:183
  psychology, 5:411
Dreyfus, Alfred, 2:518
Drug addiction, 2:613
  middle to late twentieth-
    century American liter-
    ature, 1:956
  modern British and Irish
    literature, 1:491, 1:499
  romantic period, British,
    1:286, 1:290
Drugs
  abuse, 5:403–404
  indigenous religions, 4:464
  psychopharmacology,
    5:412–13
Druids, Celtic religion, 4:436
Drury Lane Theater, 1:254,
    1:270, 1:320
Dualism
  African literatures, 2:103
  contemporary philosophical
    issues, 4:396
  French literature, 2:460,
    2:473, 2:482
  German literature, 2:589
  gnosticism, 4:453
  Iranian ancient religions,
    4:443
  middle to late twentieth-
    century American poet-
    ry, 1:1001
  modern British and Irish
    literature, 1:488
  Russian literature, 2:758
  Western philosophy,
    1600–1700, 4:168
    twentieth-century, 4:277,
      4:302, 4:320, 4:325

Duff Cooper Prize, 1:469
Dunamis, 4:339
Dutch East Indies, 3:379,
    3:380
Dutch literature, *See* Nether-
    landic literature
Dwarf stars, 5:677
Dyes, 5:733, 5:752

E

Ear and throat disorders,
    5:379–80
Early American literature,
    1:625–47
  authors, 1:632–47
  collections, 1:630–32
    Native Americans, 1:631
    nature writing, 1:631
    travel narrative, 1:631
  drama, 1:642, 1:645
  history and criticism,
    1:627–30
  women authors, 1:634,
    1:642, 1:646
Early Modern Period (Middle
    East), 3:433, 3:434
Early nineteenth-century
    American literature,
    1:648–709
  authors, 1:660–709
  collections, 1:653
  fiction, 1:656–58
    history and criticism,
      1:657–58
  history and criticism,
    1:649–52
  nonfiction, 1:658–60
    collections, 1:660
    history and criticism,
      1:659–60
  poetry, 1:653–56
    collections, 1:655–56
    history and criticism,
      1:654–55
  women authors, 1:671–72,
    1:695, 1:697
Early twentieth-century
    American literature,
    1:791–907
  authors, 1:809–907
  children's, 1:897
  collections, 1:795
  fiction, 1:801–6
    collections, 1:805–6
    history and criticism,
      1:803–5
  history and criticism,
    1:793–95
  nonfiction, 1:806–9

collections, 1:808–9
history and criticism,
1:808
poetry, 1:795–801
collections, 1:800–801
history and criticism,
1:797–800
women authors, 1:802,
1:812, 1:819, 1:826,
1:842, 1:849, 1:852,
1:855, 1:860, 1:863–64,
1:867, 1:869, 1:875,
1:880, 1:894
Earth sciences, 5:614–48, See
also specific topics for
more detailed
treatment
applied science, 5:634–37
atmospheric science,
5:632–34
authors, 5:640–48
geochemistry, 5:627–29
geography, 5:618–21
geology, 5:621–25,
5:643–48
geomorphology, 5:625–27,
5:643
geophysics, 5:627–29
history of, 5:32–33
hydrology, 5:630–32
landscape, 5:625–27, 5:643
marine biology, 5:630
meteorology, 5:633,
5:641–42, 5:647
minerology, 5:627–29
natural resources and ap-
plied science, 5:634–37
oceanography, 5:630–32,
5:640–41, 5:648
paleontology, 5:637–40
physiography, 5:643
reference and general
books, 5:615–18
seismology, 5:646–47
East Africa, 3:422–23
East African literature,
2:151–56
authors, 2:114, 2:152–56
collections, 2:152
drama, 2:153, 2:156
history and criticism, 2:152
languages, 2:151, 2:152,
2:153
ajami, Swahili, 2:151
Gikuyu, 2:153
women authors, 2:155
East Asian religion, 4:520–41
Chinese, 4:521–33
Japanese and Korean,
4:533–41

East European literatures,
2:777–841
Albanian, See Albanian literature
authors, chronology,
2:777–78
Bulgarian, See Bulgarian
literature
Byelorussian, See Byelorussian literature
Croatian, See Croation literature
Czech, See Czech literature
Estonian, See Estonian literature
German, See German liter-
ature
Hungarian, See Hungarian
literature
Latvian, See Latvian litera-
ture
Lithuanian, See Lithuanian
literature
Macedonian, See Macedo-
nian literature
Polish, See Polish litera-
ture
Rumanian, See Rumanian
literature
Serbian, See Serbian literature
Slovak, See Slovak litera-
ture
Slovenian, See Slovenian
literature
Ukrainian, See Ukrainian
literature
Eastern churches, See Chris-
tian Churches of the
East; Eastern Orthodox
Church
Eastern European history,
3:387–89
Czechoslovakia, Czech Re-
public, and Slovakia,
3:389
Hungary, 3:389–90
Jews in, 3:346
Poland, 3:390
political map, change in,
2:2
Romania, 3:390
surveys and general works,
3:389
Eastern Orthodox Church
Crusades, 4:692–94, 4:755
early Christianity, 4:681
late Christianity, 4:754–56
Eastern religions
authors, 4:548–63
Central Asia, 4:541–44
East Asia, 4:520–41

non-Islamic and non-Jew-
ish of the Middle East
and North Africa,
4:544–48
religious movements, twentieth-century, 4:853,
4:871, 4:872, 4:880
South Asia, 4:497–518
Southeast Asia, 4:518–20
women authors, 4:548
Eckankar, 4:872
Eclecticism, 4:59
E. Coli, 5:800
Ecology, 5:814–38
animal behavior, 5:825–27
authors, 5:827–38
environmentalism,
5:821–25
evolution, theories of,
5:830
glaciers, 5:836
human, 3:236–37
natural history, 5:817–19
reference books, 5:815–17
science fiction, 1:1258
wilderness, threats to,
5:827, 5:833, 5:834
Econometrics, 3:63–64,
3:87–88
Economic anthropology, 3:16
Economic development,
3:53–54, 3:104
Economic geography,
3:122–23
Economic history, 3:54–55
Great Depression, 3:533–36
United States, 3:47–49
Economics, 3:4, 3:43–115
agriculture, natural re-
sources, and environ-
mental, 3:47–48
Asia and Pacific, 3:461,
3:462
authors, 3:68–115
business administration
and business, 3:48–49
business cycles and fluctuations, 3:49–50
capitalism and accumula-
tion of capital, 3:50–51
comparative economic sys-
tems, 3:51–52
economic development,
technological change,
and growth, 3:53–54
economic history, 3:54–55
energy, 5:283–85
European Economic Com-
munity, 3:325, 3:342,
3:385
financial, 3:55–56
geographic, 3:122–23

Economics (*cont.*)
  health, education, and
    welfare, 3:56–57
  health care, 5:332–33,
    5:366
  histories and surveys of
    economic thought,
    3:45–46
  history, 3:289–90
    ancient, 3:307–8
    Industrial Revolution,
      3:340
    industrialization, 3:339
    medieval Europe, 3:329,
      3:330
  industrial organization,
    3:57–58
  international, 3:58–59
  labor and demographic,
    3:59–60
  law and, 3:60–61
  macroeconomics and fiscal
    policy, 3:61–63
  mathematical and quantita-
    tive methods, 3:63–64
  methodology and issues,
    3:46–47
  microeconomics, 3:64–65
  Middle Eastern
    Egypt, 3:445
    Iran, 3:447
    Iraq, 3:449
    Saudi Arabia, 3:450
  monetary economics and
    policy, 3:65
  poverty, discrimination,
    and the distribution of
    income, 3:66–67
  public, 3:67–68
  reference works, 3:44–45
Economics, Western philosophy, 1800–1900, 4:227,
  4:241, 4:244
Ecophilosophy, 4:38
Ecstasy
  Shakers, 4:848
  shamanism, 4:430
Ecuador, 3:636
Ecumenical movement
  Bible study, 4:812, 4:832
  late Christianity, 4:774
  theological study of reli-
    gion, 4:423
Eddystone Lighthouse, 5:254
Edison Company, 1:1166,
  1:1173, 5:251
Education, 3:246–70
  ancient history, 3:306–7
  authors, 3:258–70
  bibliography
    lay public, 3:248–53
    professional educators,
      3:253–58

Coleman Report, on race
  and, 3:223
computer applications,
  5:566–67
economic study, 3:56–57
engineering, 5:227–28
geographic, 3:117–18
theory of, 3:164
Education, philosophy of,
  Western philosophy,
  1800–1900, 4:223
Educational psychology,
  3:187
Edward I (King of England),
  3:353
Efficiency, 3:43
EGF, *See* Epidermal growth
  factor
Ego, evolvement of, 5:441
Egypt, 3:444–46
  ancient history of, 3:297,
    3:300–301, 3:434
  ancient religion, 4:441
  geometry, 5:485
  ancient, North African tra-
    dition, 4:548
  Israel (modern) and, 3:439
Egyptian culture
  ancient Near Eastern liter-
    ature, 2:51
  Arab renaissance, 2:54
Egyptian literature, *See* Ara-
  bic literature
Eichmann, Adolf, 3:281
Eight T'ang and Sung Mas-
  ters of Prose, 2:225
Eight-fold way, 5:690
Eighteenth century
  aeronautics and aviation,
    5:218
  bibliography, 5:43–45
  biological sciences, 5:757
  calculus, 5:489–90
  ethics, 5:105
  Europe, 3:337–38
  geometry, 5:485
  physiology, 5:772
Eighteenth-century Europe,
  3:337–38
Ekaaluminum, 5:750
El Salvador, 3:636–37
Eleatic school, 4:51
Electoral politics, 3:143–44
Electric power industry,
  5:286–88
Electrical engineering,
  5:228–31
Electrochemical equivalents,
  5:744
Electrodynamics, 5:692
Electrolysis, laws of, 5:683
Electromagmetic induction,
  5:683

Electromagnetic force, 5:713,
  5:718
Electromagnetic interactions,
  5:685
Electromagnetic radiation,
  5:665
Electromagnetic spectrum,
  5:593
Electromagnetic theory,
  5:699
Electromagnetic waves,
  5:694, 5:700
Electron orbits, 5:673
Electron pairs, 5:749
Electron spin, 5:679
Electronic information
  technology
  ethical issues, 5:124–27
Electronic mail (e-mail),
  5:301, 5:532
Electronic publishing, 1:3
Electronics, 5:228–31
Electrons, 5:699, 5:702
  missing energy, 5:708
Elegy
  Middle English, 1:149
  modern British and Irish
    literature, 1:435
  Old English, 1:142
  Restoration and eighteenth-
    century poetry, 1:248
  romantic period, British,
    1:267, 1:302
Elementary particle physics
  contributions to field,
    5:686, 5:690, 5:713,
    5:720
  fundamental particle, 5:661
  general works, 5:661–62
  history of, 5:662–63
  measurement of, 5:657
Elitism
  drama, American, 1:1091
  great tradition in American
    literature, 1:1124
  modern British and Irish
    literature, 1:414
  Western philosophy, twen-
    tieth-century, 4:314
Elizabethan drama, 1:168,
  1:170, 1:172, 1:183,
  1:184
Ellesmere Canal Company,
  5:255
Ellipsoidal figures of equilibrium, 5:677
Embryology, 5:776
Emergency medicine,
  5:380–81
Emigration, *See also* Exile;
  Immigration
  Australian authors, 2:945,
    2:961, 2:962

Canadian authors, 2:909,
  2:924
Caribbean authors, 2:937
Czech authors, 2:794
Czech literature, 2:788
film studies, 1:1175, 1:1177
Hebrew authors, 2:7
Latvian authors, 2:803
Lithuanian authors, 2:805
middle to late twentieth-
  century American liter-
  ature, 1:1002, 1:1048
Polish authors, 2:809,
  2:813, 2:814, 2:817
Rumanian authors, 2:824
Russian authors, 2:707,
  2:719–20, 2:724, 2:736,
  2:757, 2:772, See also
  under Russian litera-
  ture, émigré before
  1939
Ukrainian authors, 2:838
Yiddish authors, 2:28, 2:37,
  2:40
Emotional development,
  theories of, 5:472
Empathy, 5:457
Empiricism
  contemporary issues, 4:408,
    4:411
  modern Western philoso-
    phy, 4:157
  Restoration and eighteenth-
    century literature,
    1:224, 1:229
  Western philosophy
    1600–1700, 4:164, 4:169
    1700–1800, 4:195
    1800–1900, 4:244
Encyclopedias, 1:105–7, 3:755
  See also under specific
    topics
  historical, 3:7–8
  literature, 1:131
  social-scientific, 3:4–5
  United States history,
    3:508–9
Encyclopedists, 3:372
  Western philosophy,
    1700–1800, 4:195
Endocrine diseases, 5:381–82,
  5:406
Energy, 5:276–93, See also
  Natural gas; Oil
  authors, 5:290–93
  coal, oil, and gas, 5:285–86
  economic considerations,
    5:283–85
  electric power industry,
    5:286–88
  general bibliography,
    5:278–79

policy, United States,
  5:281–83
renewable technologies,
  5:288–90
Energy Agency, 5:186
Energy transfer, 5:673
Engineering, See also
  specific topics for
  more detailed
  treatment
  aeronautics, 5:218–20
  agricultural food engineer-
    ing, 5:220–21
  anti-technological backlash,
    5:166
  authors, 5:248–57
  automotive engineering,
    5:246–48
  aviation, 5:218–20
  biotechnology, 5:221–22
  careers, 5:227–28
  chemical engineering,
    5:222–23
  civil engineering, 5:223–24
  construction and mainte-
    nance, 5:224–25
  control engineering,
    5:242–43
  defined, 5:211
  design, 5:225–27
  developments, philosophi-
    cal studies of, 5:73–77
  education, 5:227–28
  electrical engineering,
    5:228–31
  electronics, 5:228–31
  ethical issues, 5:127–31
  flight, 5:218–20
  general reference works,
    5:215–18
  general works, 5:212–15
  geology, 5:241–42
  guides, 5:215–18
  history of, 5:36–37,
    5:231–33
  holography, 5:234–35
  industrial engineering,
    5:233–34
  inventors and inventing,
    5:225–27
  lasers and holography,
    5:234–35
  management, 5:233–34
  mechanical engineering,
    5:235–36
  metallurgy, 5:237–38
  military engineering,
    5:236–37
  mining, 5:237–38
  naval engineering,
    5:238–39, 5:249
  nuclear engineering,
    5:239–41

patents, 5:241–42
petroleum engineering,
  5:241–42 .
psychology, 3:167
robotics, 5:242–43
safety engineering,
  5:243–44
sanitary engineering,
  5:244–45
structural engineering,
  5:245–46
technology and, 5:211–57
transportation and automotive engineering,
  5:246–48
England, 3:330, 3:353–68
  folk ballads of, 3:77
  general histories, 3:355–56
  Hanoverian (1717–1837),
    3:361–63
  later Middle Ages
    (1216–1485), 3:357–58
  Norman and Angevin
    (1066–1216), 3:356–57
  pre-1066, 3:356
  reference works, 3:353–55
  Reformation, 4:725–27,
    4:733–35
  Stuart (1603–1714),
    3:359–61
    English Revolution, 3:336
  Tudor (1485–1603),
    3:358–59
  twentieth-century, 3:365–68
  Victorian (1837–1901),
    3:363–65
English culture and society
  bleakness, in modern liter-
    ature, 1:414
  castle tales, 1:575
  class system, 1:476
  detective fiction, 1:604
  divorce and custody, Victo-
    rian period, 1:383–84
  farces and spoofs, 1:311
  folk tales, 1:573
  Gothic novel, 1:591
  London, Victorian period,
    1:347, 1:377
  manners and morals, Vic-
    torian period, 1:403,
    1:405
  medieval literature,
    1:139–40
  Middle English, 1:149,
    1:153
  middle-class
    Restoration and eigh-
      teenth-century, 1:229
  Old English, 1:143
  Renaissance, 1:162–64
  social commentary

English culture and society (*cont.*)
   modern British and Irish drama, 1:437
   modern British and Irish literature, 1:419
   spoof, 1:311
   television, 1:535
   upper-class spoof, 1:522
   utilitarianism, Victorian period, 1:323
   Victorian Age, 1:577
   Victorian aristocracy, 1:461
   working class
      Victorian period drama, 1:321
      Victorian period, 1:309, 1:310, 1:317, 1:341, 1:344, 1:355, 1:368, 1:377
English Revised Version, 4:801
English Revolution, 3:336
English Stage Company, 1:424, 1:531
English-language dictionaries, 1:89–91
English-usage dictionaries, 1:91–92
Enlightenment
   Danish literature, 2:650
   early American literature, 1:637
   French literature, 2:471
   German literature, 2:563
   late Christianity, 4:716
   modern Judaism, 4:646
   modern Western philosophy, 4:158
   Restoration and eighteenth-century literature, 1:224
   Western philosophy
      1600–1700, 4:166
      1700–1800, 4:198, 4:204, 4:208
Environment, *See also* entries beginning Environmental
   energy concerns, 5:277
   geographic, 3:116–17
   physical, 3:125–26
   health and, 5:352–54
   problems, philosophical studies of, 5:73–77
   sanitary engineering, 5:244–45
   sociological study of, 3:205–6
Environmental chemistry, 5:736–37

Environmental degradation
   contemporary philosophical issues, 4:388
   religious movements, twentieth-century, 4:854
Environmental Directorate, 5:186
Environmental economics, 3:47–48
Environmental ethics, 5:105, 5:113–17
Environmental history, 3:549–51
Environmental science, 5:814–38
   animal behavior, 5:825–27
   authors, 5:827–38
   environmentalism, 5:821–25
   global early warning system, 5:828
   landscape, destruction of, 5:827
   natural history, 5:817–19
   ocean, studies of, 5:828–29
   reference books, 5:815–17
   wilderness, threats to, 5:827, 5:833, 5:834
Epic novel
   French literature, 2:502
   Latin American literatures, 2:866
   Russian literature, 2:755
   West African literature, 2:142
   Yiddish literature, 2:35
Epic poetry, *See also* Narrative poetry
   Armenian literature, 2:75, 2:78
   Cambodian literature, 2:315
   Canadian literature, 2:923
   children's literature, British, 1:575
   Czech literature, 2:788
   early American literature, 1:644
   early twentieth-century American literature, 1:797, 1:815
   East African literature, 2:151
   Estonian literature, 2:795
   Finnish literature, 2:659
   French literature, 2:509
   German literature, 2:562, 2:604
   Greek classical literature, 2:341, 2:357, 2:358
   Greek Hellenistic literature, 2:352

Greek modern literature, 2:370
Hungarian literature, 2:800
Indian literature, ancient, 2:171
Italian literature, 2:416, 2:439
Laotian literature, 2:321
Latin American literatures, 2:854, 2:869, 2:874
Latin literature, 2:379, 2:387, 2:396
   medieval literature, 2:398
   middle to late twentieth-century American poetry, 1:1015
Netherlandic literature, 2:619
Old English, 1:143
Persian literature, 2:82, 2:89
Polish literature, 2:817
Portuguese literature, 2:556, 2:558
Renaissance literature, 1:164, 1:179, 1:191, 1:197
romantic period, British, 1:293, 1:305
Russian literature, 2:682, 2:702
Serbian literature, 2:826, 2:831
Slovak literature, 2:832
Slovenian literature, 2:836
South African literature, 2:164
Spanish literature, 2:519, 2:537
Thai literature, 2:334
Ukrainian literature, 2:837, 2:839
Yiddish literature, 2:28
Epicureanism, 4:54
   Greek philosophy, 4:73
   Roman philosophy, 4:58, 4:75
Epidemics, 5:801
Epidemiology, 5:382–83
Epidermal growth factor, 5:790
Epigram
   Greek Hellenistic literature, 2:368
   Latin literature, 2:379, 2:388
Epistemology, 5:61–65
   contemporary issues, 4:380, 4:395, 4:399, 4:403, 4:411
   medieval philosophy, 4:98
   Western philosophy
      1600–1700, 4:178

twentieth-century, 4:275, 4:302, 4:312, 4:320, 4:332
Epitaph, 1:858
Erie Canal, 5:231
Ernest Hemingway Award, 1:844
Eroticism
Arabic literature, 2:65
Chinese literature, 2:185, 2:187, 2:200, 2:201, 2:226
early twentieth-century American literature, 1:865, 1:901
French literature, 2:451, 2:455
gay literature, 1:1190
Greek modern literature, 2:372
horror story, British, 1:602
Japanese literature, 2:293
Latin American literatures, 2:878
modern British and Irish literature, 1:491
Renaissance drama, 1:186
Renaissance literature, 1:166, 1:194
romances, 1:1224
Spanish literature, 2:520, 2:553
Victorian period, 1:310, 1:398
Espionage, See Thriller
Essay, See also Periodical essay
middle to late twentieth-century American literature, 1:922, 1:933, 1:966, 1:1008
modern British and Irish literature, 1:428, 1:447, 1:457, 1:477
romantic period, British, 1:272–73, 1:290, 1:292, 1:295
Victorian period, 1:324, 1:373, 1:386, 1:393
Essenes, 4:616
Estonian literature, 2:795–97
authors, chronology, 2:777
women authors, 2:797
Ethics, See also Ethics in science, technology, and medicine
animal rights, 4:43
Arabic literature, 2:61
children's literature
American, 1:1194, 1:1204
British, 1:576, 1:587
Chinese literature, 2:186, 2:194, 2:195

contemporary issues, 4:406
philosophical issues, 4:387–89
religious issues, 4:892–95, 4:897
early American literature, 1:635
early nineteenth-century American literature, 1:674
French drama, 2:490
French literature, 2:460, 2:471, 2:485, 2:487, 2:489, 2:516
Greek classical drama, 2:350
Greek classical literature, 2:343
Islamic philosophy, 4:374
Japanese philosophy, 4:367
Judaism, 4:597
late Christianity, 4:718
1914 to present, 4:742–47
middle to late nineteenth-century American literature, 1:722, 1:758, 1:761, 1:768, 1:786
middle to late twentieth-century American literature, 1:968, 1:975, 1:1007, 1:1054, 1:1056
modern British and Irish literature, 1:448, 1:463, 1:482–83, 1:488, 1:493, 1:498, 1:523, 1:551
Modern Western philosophy, 4:158
Old Norse-Icelandic literature, 2:642
Renaissance, 1:163, 4:122
Restoration and eighteenth-century literature, 1:224, 1:232, 1:244, 1:249, 1:253
Russian literature, 2:713, 2:726, 2:760, 2:763
Victorian period, 1:353
Western philosophy
1700–1800, 4:193–94, 4:196, 4:204, 4:210–11, 4:214–15
1800–1900, 4:230, 4:244, 4:253, 4:256
twentieth-century, 4:301, 4:311, 4:316, 4:332, 4:338
Ethics in science, technology, and medicine, 5:105–146
authors, 5:131–46
bioethics, 5:117–24
biomedicine, 5:93, 5:106

computer technology, 5:124–27
electronic information technology, 5:124–27
engineering ethics, 5:127–31
environmental ethics, 5:105, 5:113–17
genetic engineering, 5:105
information technology, 5:105, 5:124–27
medicine, general, 5:117–24
nuclear ethics, 5:105, 5:108–113
science, general, 5:106–108
technology, general, 5:127–31
Ethnic dance, 3:733–34
Ethnic music, 3:666–67
Ethnicity, 3:212, 3:554–58
African American folklore and, 3:866–67
Asia and Pacific, 3:462
intergroup relations, 3:208–9
Native American folklore and, 3:864–66
Ethnographic realism, 2:839
Ethnography, study of religion, 4:425
Ethnology (cultural anthropology), 3:10, 3:16–17
Ethnomethodology, 3:227
Ethnophilosophy, African, 4:367, 4:369, 4:370, 4:371
Ethology, 3:190, 3:194
ancient religion, 4:421
Etymological dictionaries, 1:95–96
Euclidean geometry, See Geometry
Euphuism, 1:185
Europe
African studies in, 3:414
modern Judaism, 4:634–38
modern philosophy, 4:157
philosophy, 4:27–33
travel in, 3:898–901
European Centre for Nuclear Research, 5:673
European civilization, 3:327–29
Asia and Pacific viewed by, 3:461
Jews in, 3:346
medieval, 3:329–32
Pirenne thesis on, 3:407
Reformation, 3:333–34
Renaissance, 3:332–33

European Economic Commu-
nity, 3:325, 3:342,
3:352, 3:385
European history, 3:325-413
authors, 3:398-413
Balkans and Greece (mod-
ern), 3:390-93
British Isles, 3:351-53
England, 3:353-68
Ireland, 3:369-71
Scotland, 3:368
Wales, 3:369
during revolutionary period
(1789-1832), 3:338-40
Eastern Europe, 3:387-89
Czechoslovakia, Czech
Republic, and Slovakia,
3:389
Hungary, 3:389-90
Poland, 3:390
Romania, 3:390
surveys and general
works, 3:389
eighteenth century,
3:337-38
European civilization, foun-
dations of, 3:327-29
expansion and exploration,
3:334-36
France, 3:371-74
general studies and reference works, 3:325-27
Germanic, 3:374-75
Austria, 3:375-76
Germany, 3:376-78
Switzerland, 3:378
· Jewish, 3:346-51
medieval, 3:329-32
nineteenth century,
3:340-41
Northern Europe, 3:378-80
Low Countries, 3:382-83
Scandinavia, 3:381-82
surveys and general
works, 3:380-81
Reformation, 3:333-34
Renaissance, 3:332-33
Russia, Eurasian republics,
and Baltic states,
3:393-94
general works, 3:394-95
post-Soviet era, 3:398
Soviet era, 3:395-98
tsarist era, 3:395
science and the Enlightenment, 3:337
seventeenth century, 3:336
Southern Europe, 3:383-85
Italy, 3:385-86
Portugal, 3:386
Spain, 3:386-87
twentieth-century
1900-1920, 3:343

1920-1945, 3:344-45
since 1945, 3:345-46
Euthanasia, 5:117
Evan Pugh Professorship,
5:176
Evangelical groups, 4:742,
4:780
religious movements, twentieth-century, 4:864
Evangelical Rationalists,
4:723
Evangelism, 4:767
religious movements, twentieth-century, 4:863
Evidence, philosophical,
Western philosophy,
1700-1800, 4:208
Evil, problem of
medieval philosophy, 4:116
Western philosophy,
1700-1800, 4:217
Evolution, 3:17-19, 5:637,
5:779-80, 5:802, 5:830
cultural, 3:39, 3:239
Darwinian theory, 5:757,
5:792, 5:799, 5:811
Western philosophy
1800-1900, 4:219
twentieth-century, 4:336
Exclusion principle, 5:708
Excommunication
late Christianity, 4:727,
4:777, 4:780
medieval Christianity, 4:692
medieval philosophy, 4:119
Western philosophy,
1600-1700, 4:186
Exercise, 5:325-27
Exhibitionism, 2:917
Exile, See also Emigration;
Immigration
Arabic authors, 2:63, 2:73
Armenian authors, 2:75,
2:78, 2:79, 2:80
Australian literature, 2:953
Brazilian authors, 2:898
Cambodian authors, 2:315
Caribbean literature, 2:929,
2:934, 2:936, 2:938,
2:940, 2:942
Chinese authors, 2:196,
2:199, 2:201, 2:211,
2:220, 2:225, 2:236,
2:250, 2:255, 2:261,
2:264, 2:267
Chinese literature, 2:260
Czech authors, 2:788
Danish authors, escaping
Nazism, 2:652
East African literature,
2:151, 2:153
Estonian authors, 2:796
film stars, 1:1161

French authors, 2:482,
2:492, 2:514
German authors, 2:569,
2:612
escaping Nazism, 2:564,
2:571, 2:576, 2:578,
2:590, 2:601, 2:608,
2:611, 2:615, 2:617
Greek classical authors,
2:354
Hungarian authors, 2:798,
2:801
Italian authors, 2:421,
2:424
Italian literature, 2:416
Laotian authors, 2:322
Latin American authors,
2:842-43, 2:854, 2:858,
2:862, 2:864, 2:871,
2:877, 2:881, 2:883,
2:885
Latin authors, 2:389
Lithuanian authors, 2:806
modern British and Irish
authors, 1:462, 1:504,
1:526, 1:528
North African literature,
2:121
Norwegian authors, 2:668
Persian authors, 2:86, 2:93
Polish authors, 2:810,
2:816, 2:822
Portuguese authors, 2:557,
2:560
Russian authors, 2:683,
2:697, 2:703, 2:716,
2:732, 2:737, 2:749,
2:753, 2:759
South African literature,
2:157-60, 2:163-64,
2:166
Spanish authors, 2:521,
2:528, 2:540, 2:549,
2:552
Swedish authors, 2:672
Turkish authors, 2:98
Ukrainian authors, 2:840
Vietnamese authors, 2:340
West African authors,
2:138
Yiddish authors, escaping
Nazism, 2:38
Existentialism, 5:96, 5:436,
5:462
Brazilian literature, 2:895
contemporary issues, 4:376
drama, American, 1:1085
French literature, 2:445,
2:464, 2:487, 2:494,
2:506
Latin American literatures,
2:853, 2:870

middle to late nineteenth-
century American liter-
ature, 1:741
middle to late twentieth-
century American liter-
ature, 1:942, 1:966
modern British and Irish
drama, 1:439
modern British and Irish
literature, 1:412
Netherlandic literature,
2:627
Polish literature, 2:813,
2:820
Russian literature, 2:699
Spanish literature, 2:552
Ukrainian literature, 2:840
Western philosophy, twen-
tieth-century, 4:261,
4:290, 4:298–99, 4:304,
4:309, 4:328, 4:334
Exotic cultures
Russian literature, 2:729
Exotic literature
adventure/thriller, 1:592,
1:593, 1:596
Gothic/horror, 1:598
historical fiction, 1:1248
horror story, 1:1242
middle to late twentieth-
century American liter-
ature, 1:1034, 1:1042
romantic period, British,
1:269, 1:281, 1:304
science fiction, 1:1251
Exotic locales
North African literature,
2:117
Russian literature, 2:706,
2:749, 2:755
Exotic themes
Latin American literatures,
2:845, 2:863
Expanding universe, discovery, 5:653
Expatriates, See also
Emigration; Exile
early twentieth-century
American authors,
1:793, 1:812, 1:844–45,
1:861, 1:864, 1:870,
1:881, 1:896, 1:905
middle to late nineteenth-
century American au-
thors, 1:786
middle to late nineteenth-
century American liter-
ature, 1:790
middle to late twentieth-
century American liter-
ature, 1:938
modern British and Irish
literature, 1:420, 1:566

Experimental phenomenol-
ogy, 5:92
Experimental psychology,
3:197, 4:382
Exploration, 3:889–90, See
also Travel
authors, 3:911–42
Canada, 3:610–11
European, 3:334–36
individual accounts of,
3:907–11
Portuguese and Spanish,
3:384
Explorers
deep sea exploration,
5:640–41, 5:642
glaciers, 5:836
Expressionism
drama, American, 1:1070,
1:1106, 1:1109, 1:1116
film studies, 1:1155,
1:1168, 1:1176, 1:1178
German literature, 2:564,
2:597
modern British and Irish
drama, 1:458, 1:537
modern British and Irish
literature, 1:568
Netherlandic literature,
2:629
Serbian literature, 2:827
Slovak literature, 2:833
Swedish literature, 2:679
Extension Service, 5:260
Extraterrestial life, 4:257,
5:597–98, 5:608–9
Extremism, Islamic religion,
4:565
Extroverts and introverts,
5:454
Eye disorders, 5:383–84

F

Fabian socialism, 3:112–13
Fabius (Quintus Fabius Maxi-
mus Cunctator), 3:112
Fable
Arabic literature, 2:75
Australian literature, 2:964
early twentieth-century
American literature,
1:889
French literature, 2:445,
2:452, 2:484
German literature, 2:574
Greek classical literature,
2:351
Latin American literatures,
2:853

Latin literature, 2:379
middle to late twentieth-
century American liter-
ature, 1:979
modern British and Irish
literature, 1:530
Netherlandic literature,
2:620, 2:629
Persian literature, 2:91,
2:93
Polish literature, 2:818
Russian literature, 2:719
South African literature,
2:160
Factorial ecology, 3:126
Facts
almanacs and yearbooks,
1:81–83
directories, 1:103–5
reference-tool access,
1:87–88
Fairy, Germanic religion,
4:437
Fairy tale, 3:845, 3:879–80,
3:883, See also
Folklore
children's literature, British, 1:576, 1:577, 1:587
Chinese literature, 2:217,
2:237
Danish literature, 2:646
early nineteenth-century
American literature,
1:656
fantasy, British, 1:615
German literature, 2:584,
2:612
Latvian literature, 2:803
Lithuanian literature, 2:805
middle to late twentieth-
century American liter-
ature, 1:943, 1:963
modern British and Irish
literature, 1:455, 1:558
Russian literature, 2:743
Victorian period, 1:347
Faith
early and medieval Chris-
tianity, 4:674, 4:695
medieval philosophy, 4:107,
4:108
Renaissance philosophy,
4:151, 4:153
Western philosophy, twen-
tieth-century, 4:285
Faith healing
Christian Science, 4:842
indigenous religions, 4:462
Mesmerism, 4:846
oikoumene world, 4:450
shamanism, 4:430
Families
ancient history, 3:309

Families (*cont.*)
  anthropology, 3:19–20
  sociology of, 3:206–7
Famine, 5:828
Fantasy, *See also* High
    fantasy
  adventure/thriller, 1:593
  Australian literature, 2:951
  Brazilian literature, 2:899
  children's literature
    American, 1:1194,
      1:1199, 1:1203, 1:1206,
      1:1207
    British, 1:574, 1:577,
      1:578, 1:586, 1:590
  Chinese literature, 2:196,
    2:217, 2:230
  Czech literature, 2:789
  drama, American, 1:1110,
    1:1116
  early twentieth-century
    American literature,
    1:879, 1:894
  Faroese literature, 2:656
  Greek Hellenistic litera-
    ture, 2:363
  horror story, 1:1239
  Hungarian literature, 2:799
  Indian literature, 2:180
  Irish drama, 1:490, 1:526
  Italian literature, 2:411
  Latin American literatures,
    2:852, 2:853, 2:855,
    2:861, 2:872, 2:881
  Lithuanian literature, 2:805
  middle to late nineteenth-
    century American liter-
    ature, 1:733
  middle to late twentieth-
    century American liter-
    ature, 1:942, 1:948,
    1:952, 1:1013, 1:1029,
    1:1062
  modern British and Irish
    drama, 1:544
  modern British and Irish
    literature, 1:412, 1:476,
    1:477, 1:500, 1:512,
    1:522, 1:558, 1:561,
    1:563
  New Zealand literature,
    2:974
  North African literature,
    2:118
  opera, Victorian period,
    1:357
  Polish literature, 2:818
  Portuguese literature, 2:559
  Russian literature, 2:697,
    2:704, 2:705, 2:721,
    2:729, 2:740, 2:753,
    2:757, 2:769
  science fiction, 1:1259,
    1:1262
  Serbian literature, 2:831
  South African literature,
    2:163, 2:165
  Spanish literature, 2:531
  Swedish literature, 2:676
  Victorian period, 1:347,
    1:409
  Yiddish literature, 2:37,
    2:47
Farce, *See also* Satire
  drama, Victorian period,
    1:311, 1:347, 1:376
  French drama, 2:483, 2:490
  French literature, 2:479
  German literature, 2:608
  modern British and Irish
    drama, 1:424, 1:529
  modern British and Irish
    literature, 1:414
  Renaissance drama, 1:168,
    1:199
  Restoration drama, 1:228
  Russian literature, 2:717
  West African drama, 2:140
Faroese literature, 2:655–57
  authors, 2:638, 2:656
  collections, 2:655
  history and criticism, 2:655
Farrington Daniels Award,
    5:291
Fatalism
  Chinese literature, 2:237
  early twentieth-century
    American literature,
    1:802, 1:829, 1:876,
    1:898
  French literature, 2:509
  westerns, 1:1214
Fathers of the Church
  early Christianity, 4:690
  medieval philosophy, 4:93,
    4:108, 4:112
  patristic period, 4:98–100
Fauna, 5:768
Faust legend, 2:853
  popular American litera-
    ture, 1:1198
  Renaissance drama, 1:186
Feasts and festivals
  Greek ancient religion,
    4:446
  Hittite and Canaanite reli-
    gions, 4:444
Federal Occupational Safety
    and Health Act,
    5:243–44
Federal Reserve System,
    3:65, 3:76, 3:77
Federalism, 3:141–42, 3:161
Federalist Papers, 3:541
  Feeling
  Western philosophy
    1700–1800, 4:215
    1800–1900, 4:253
Female-male complementar-
    ity, 5:136
Feminism, 3:846
  African Americans, 1:1139
  African literatures, 2:105
  Arabic literature, 2:60,
    2:70, 2:71
  Australian literature, 2:952,
    2:963
  Brazilian literature, 2:889,
    2:897
  Canadian literature, 2:906,
    2:921
  Chinese literature, 2:239,
    2:246, 2:251, 2:264
  contemporary philosophical
    issues, 4:390
  contemporary religious is-
    sues, 4:891, 4:904
  detective story, 1:1238
  early nineteenth-century
    American literature,
    1:671, 1:672, 1:681
  early twentieth-century
    American literature,
    1:793, 1:802, 1:812,
    1:843, 1:860, 1:864
  film studies, 1:1156,
    1:1169, 1:1174, 1:1176
  French literary theory,
    1:1143
  French literature, 2:458,
    2:467, 2:469, 2:492,
    2:504
  gay literature, 1:1186–91
  gender studies and,
    5:178–79, 5:186–89,
    5:201
  Italian literature, 2:426
  late Christianity, 4:764,
    4:784
  Latin American literatures,
    2:860, 2:873, 2:885
  liberation theology, 4:749
  literary theory, 1:1140,
    1:1145–46, 1:1147
  Mexican Americans, 1:1136
  middle to late nineteenth-
    century American liter-
    ature, 1:711, 1:752,
    1:786
  middle to late twentieth-
    century American liter-
    ature, 1:922, 1:948,
    1:1026, 1:1037, 1:1039,
    1:1046, 1:1052, 1:1064

middle to late twentieth-century American poetry, 1:911, 1:1031, 1:1045
modern British and Irish drama, 1:458, 1:493
modern British and Irish literature, 1:412–13, 1:454, 1:468, 1:540, 1:565
modern Judaism, 4:649
new directions in American literature, 1:1126
New Zealand literature, 2:976
North African literature, 2:116, 2:119, 2:120
Norwegian literature, 2:665, 2:668, 2:670
Persian literature, 2:88, 2:91
philosophy of science, 5:66
philosophy, 4:40
popular American literature, 1:1198
religious movements, twentieth-century, 4:854, 4:865
Restoration comedy, 1:232
Restoration drama, 1:242
romances, 1:618, 1:1151, 1:1221, 1:1223
Russian literature, 2:711
science fiction, 1:1262
sociology, 3:221
Spanish literature, 2:521
Swedish literature, 2:672
theological study of religion, 4:423
twentieth-century American drama, 1:1071, 1:1115
Victorian period, 1:330, 1:334, 1:341, 1:353, 1:355, 1:375, 1:380
West African literature, 2:132, 2:144
Western philosophy, 1800–1900, 4:244
Ferdinand (King of Spain), 3:384
Fertilizer, 5:259, 5:272–73
Fetal alcohol syndrome, 5:375
Fetus
experimentation, 5:117
illnesses, 5:776
Fiber optics, 5:303–304
Fibers, growth of, See Epidermal growth factor
Fiction and computers, 5:562–63
Field theory (psychology), 3:189, 5:649

Filipino literature, See Philippine literature
Film, 3:799–800, 3:823–24
authors, 3:829–44
criticism and theory, 3:827
dance in, 3:736
directors, 3:827–29
general reference and history, 3:824–27
music for, 3:667
sociological study of, 3:203–4
Film studies, 1:1155–79
authors, 1:1159–79
children's, 1:1163, 1:1164
collage, 1:1159
collections, 1:1158–59
distancing, 1:1174
editing techniques, 1:1173
history and criticism, 1:1156–58
middle to late twentieth-century American literature, 1:933
mise en scène, 1:1155, 1:1161
montage, 1:1155, 1:1168
nickelodeon, 1:1173
special effects, 1:1171
westerns, 1:1165
women, 1:1162, 1:1174
Financial economics, 3:55–56
Finland, 3:381
Finland Literary Prize, 2:661
Finnish literature, 2:657–61
authors, 2:638, 2:658–61
children's, 2:658
collections, 2:658
women authors, 2:658, 2:660
First aid, See Emergency medicine
Fiscal policy, 3:61–63
Fish classification, 5:785
Fitzgerald, Zelda, 1:838, 1:839
Flies, research on, 5:807, 5:808
Flight engineering, See Aeronautics and aviation; Aviation
Florentine Academy, 4:140
Fluxions, method of, 5:705
Folk humor, 3:870–72
Folklore, 3:845–47
African Americans, 1:848, 1:849, 1:891
authors, 3:874–88
children's literature, American, 1:1194
Chinese literature, 2:249
East African literature, 2:156

Finnish literature, 2:659
folk and popular humor, 3:870–72
folk song and dance, 3:850–53
folk tales, legends, and myths, 3:853–57
general works, 3:847–49
German literature, 2:584
Gothic/horror, 1:598
Greek classical literature, 2:357
indigenous religions, 4:459
Latvian literature, 2:803
Lithuanian literature, 2:804, 2:806
middle to late nineteenth-century American literature, 1:754
middle to late twentieth-century American literature, 1:954
miscellaneous and applied, 3:867–70
modern Irish drama, 1:423, 1:526
modern Irish literature, 1:490
North African literature, 2:117
Polish literature, 2:822
reference works, 3:849–50
Rumanian literature, 2:823
Russian drama, 2:744
Russian literature, 2:718, 2:720, 2:721, 2:742, 2:747, 2:752, 2:753
Slovenian literature, 2:837
Turkish literature, 2:99
Ukrainian literature, 2:841
United States regional and ethnic
African American, 3:866–67
Mid-Atlantic states, 3:858–59
Midwest, 3:861–62
Native American, 3:864–66
New England, 3:857–58
South, 3:860–61
West, 3:862–64
Vietnamese literature, 2:338
West African literature, 2:127, 2:150
Yiddish literature, 2:35, 2:37
Folk poetry
Armenian literature, 2:75, 2:79
Chinese literature, 2:224

Folk poetry (*cont.*)
Greek Byzantine literature,
2:344
Hungarian literature, 2:797
Latin American literatures,
2:871
Latvian literature, 2:803
Rumanian literature, 2:822
Turkish literature, 2:101
Yiddish literature, 2:50
Folk song and dance,
3:850–53
Folk songs
African literatures, 2:103
American literature, 1:1193
Chinese literature, 2:187,
2:194, 2:237
drama, American, 1:1088
early twentieth-century
American literature,
1:878
Estonian literature, 2:795
Finnish literature, 2:657,
2:659
Latvian literature, 2:803
Ukrainian literature, 2:840
Yiddish literature, 2:50
Folk tales, 3:853–57
African literatures, 2:103
Caribbean literature, 2:941
children's literature, Brit-
ish, 1:573, 1:574,
1:577, 1:583
early twentieth-century
American literature,
1:817, 1:851
East African literature,
2:152
Frisian literature, 2:634,
2:636
middle to late twentieth-
century American liter-
ature, 1:1049
Norwegian literature, 2:661
Persian literature, 2:91
Swedish literature, 2:676
West African literature,
2:125, 2:138, 2:151
Foner, Eric, 3:526
Food technology, *See* Agri-
culture and food tech-
nology
Foreign relations, 3:544–47,
3:583
Foreign-language dictionaries,
1:96–103
Forensic medicine, 5:343–44
Forgery
book, 1:35–36
Renaissance philosophy,
4:155
Formentor Prize, 2:426

Fortune telling and
divination
Chinese religion, 4:521
Hittite and Canaanite religions, 4:444
Inca religion, 4:458
indigenous religions, 4:461
Mesopotamian ancient ur-
ban civilization, 4:440
oikoumene world, 4:450
religious movements, twentieth-century, 4:860
47 Workshop, 1:903, 1:1070,
1:1085
Fossil fuels
alternatives to use of,
5:281
dependence on, 5:285
emissions, 5:277
industrial economics and,
5:276
nuclear engineering, 5:239
prices of, 5:288
Fossils, *See* Paleontology
Fountain Grove community,
4:843
Fourier-transform nuclear
magnetic resonance,
5:744
Fox Films, 1:1165
France
film in, 3:823–24
history of, 3:371–74
Revolution, 3:338–40
Jews in, 3:347
New France (Canada) and,
3:604, 3:611–12
philosophy, 4:27
Frances K. Hutchinson Me-
dal, 5:829
Franciscans, medieval philosophy, 4:93, 4:110,
4:112, 4:119
Franco, Francisco, 3:385
Frankfurt School, 3:199,
3:229, 4:262, 4:392,
4:403, 4:407
Fraser, Lady Antonia, 1:534
Fraud
romantic period author,
1:284
Free will
medieval philosophy, 4:108,
4:113, 4:114, 4:116
Renaissance philosophy,
4:122, 4:152, 4:155
Western philosophy
1600–1700, 4:168
1700–1800, 4:210
1800–1900, 4:254
Freemasons, 4:840
French Academy, 2:444,
2:517

French culture and society
Ancient Régime, 2:515
bohemian, 2:504
bourgeoisie, 2:475, 2:479
nineteenth-century, 2:453
peasantry, 2:480
seventeenth-century, 2:507
the masses, 2:502, 2:518
French language
modern British and Irish
drama, 1:439
French literature, 2:444–518
authors, 2:449–518
children's, 2:485
collections, 2:448
history and criticism,
2:446–48
language, 2:444, 2:446
theater history, 2:444–45,
2:448–49
eighteenth-century, 2:457
seventeenth-century,
2:470, 2:490, 2:497
twentieth-century, 2:450,
2:451, 2:459, 2:468,
2:481, 2:483
unities, 2:498
women authors, 2:458,
2:467, 2:469, 2:473,
2:484–85, 2:492,
2:504–5, 2:507, 2:510,
2:516–17
French Revolution, 3:338–40,
3:347
Freudian psychology, 3:15,
3:846
basis of, 5:411
child psychoanalysis, 5:444
ego, evolvement of, 5:441
influence of, 5:445
libido, theories of, 5:454,
5:457
personality theories, 5:431
sexuality, emphasis on,
5:430
"talking cure," 5:458
Friends, Religious Society of
Shakers, 4:849
Western philosophy,
1600–1700, 4:167
Frisian literature, 2:619,
2:633–36
authors, 2:635–36
children's, 2:636
women authors, 2:636
Frontier life
American literature, 1:1193
American popular litera-
ture, 1:1209
westerns, 1:1210, 1:1214,
1:1215
Canadian literature, 2:903,
2:920

children's literature, American, 1:1208
early American literature, 1:625, 1:637
early nineteenth-century American literature, 1:648, 1:656–57, 1:662, 1:683, 1:690, 1:695, 1:702
films, westerns, 1:1165
middle to late nineteenth-century American literature, 1:750
New Zealand literature, 2:970
Norwegian literature, 2:667
Renaissance literature, 1:173
Swedish literature, 2:678
twentieth-century American drama, 1:1069
Frothingham Professorship, Logic and Metaphysics, 5:82
Fruit flies, research on, 5:807, 5:808
Fulbright professorship, 5:200
Fulbright-Hayes Scholarship, 5:250, 5:291
Functionalism
  anthropological, 3:35
  sociological, 3:223
Fundamentalism
  Islamic philosophy, 4:372
  Islamic religion, 4:566, 4:577
Furniture, 3:766
Fusion reactions, 5:667
Future life, beliefs in
  mystery cults, 4:450
  Tibetan Buddhism, 4:543
Futurism
  Canadian literature, 2:906
  Italian literature, 2:427, 2:430, 2:440
  middle to late twentieth-century American literature, 1:948
  modern British and Irish literature, 1:530
  Russian literature, 2:683, 2:731, 2:738, 2:774

G

Galaxies
  astronomy, 5:593–94
  measurement of distances, 5:653
  physics, 5:677

Gambler's ruin, 5:527
Game theory, 3:111
Gamma absorption, 5:703
Gamma radiation, 5:703
Gamma rays, 5:711
Gas, See Natural gas
Gases, thermal expansion of, 5:747
Gastrointestinal diseases, 5:384–85
Gauge theory, 5:654
Gauls, See Celtic religion
Gaussian curve, 5:507, 5:529
Gays, See Homosexuality; Lesbianism
Gazetteers, 1:83–85
Gender, 3:554–58
  sex differences, 3:185
  sociology of, 3:207, 3:221
Gender bending, 2:883
Gender roles
  drama, American, 1:1113
  science fiction, 1:1258
Gender studies, 5:178–79, 5:186–89, 5:201
Gene enzyme hypothesis, 5:788
Gene therapy, 5:781
General adaptation syndrome, 5:400
General reference works
  agriculture and food technology, 5:260–62
  biographical directories, 5:4
  dictionaries and encyclopedias, 5:2–3
  directories, 5:3–5
  engineering and technology, 5:215–18
  guides and indexes, 5:5
  medicine, 5:5–6, 5:12–13
  organizational directories, 5:3–4
  philosophy of science, technology, and medicine, 5:60–61
  physical sciences, 5:11
  society and science, technology and medicine, 5:148–49
  technology, 5:11–12
General science, general reference works, 5:9–11
Generalization, contemporary issues, 4:383
Generation of '27
  Spanish literature, 2:529, 2:531, 2:540
Generation of '45
  Indonesian literature, 2:316, 2:319

Generation of '50
  Malay literature, 2:323, 2:325, 2:326
Generation of '66
  Indonesian literature, 2:316
Generation of '98
  Spanish literature, 2:521, 2:530, 2:545, 2:551
Genetic engineering, 5:105, 5:781–83, 5:804
Genetics, 5:757, 5:777–83
  bioethics, 5:781–83
  chromosomes, 5:806–808
  counseling, genetic, 5:780–81
  dominant and recessive characteristics, 5:806–807
  evolution, 5:779–80
  gene enzyme hypothesis, 5:788
  general bibliography, 5:777–79
  genetic engineering, 5:105, 5:781–83, 5:804
  medical genetics, 5:780–81
  oncogene, 5:790
Geneva Bible, 4:799
Genocide, 2:28
  European Jews, 4:634, 4:635
Geochemistry, 5:627–29
Geographic information systems (GIS), 3:117, 3:120–21, 5:619
Geography, 3:116–36
  authors, 3:126–36
  cartography and geographic information systems, 3:120–21
  European, 3:325
  history of, 5:32–33
  human, 3:121
    cultural, 3:121–22
    economic, 3:122–23
    political, 3:123
    urban, 3:123–24
  literature, 5:618–21
  methodology and issues, 3:119–20
  physical, 3:125–26
  reference works, surveys, and collections, 3:118–19
  regional, 3:124–25
Geology, 5:621–25, 5:643–48, See also Geophysics; Petroleum engineering and engineering geology
Geometrodynamics, 5:719
Geometry
  algebraic, 5:512

Geometry (*cont.*)
 analytic geometry, 5:485,
  5:486
 Euclidean, 5:477, 5:504,
  5:511, 5:529
 harpedonaptai, 5:485
 literature, 5:485–87
 "method of exhaustion,"
  5:498
 non-Euclidean, 5:477,
  5:486, 5:529
 parallel postulate, 5:486
 plane geometry, 5:485
 projective, 5:509
 Pythagorean theorem,
  5:504, 5:514
 solid geometry, 5:485,
  5:504
 trigonometry, 5:486
Geomorphology, 3:125,
  5:625–27, 5:643
Geophysics, 5:627–29, 5:631
Geopolitics, 3:133
George Kreis (George Cir-
  cle), 2:579
George Sarton Medal, 5:14
German culture and society
 bourgeoisie, 2:608
 fin de siècle Vienna, 2:611
 realistic novel, 2:578
 rural life, 2:606
German history
 reunification, 2:564, 2:606,
  2:616
 Thirty Years War, 2:563,
  2:585
German literature, 2:562–618
 authors, 2:567–618
 background reading,
  2:173–4, 2:564–65
 children's, 2:574, 2:584,
  2:592
 collections, 2:566
 drama
  eighteenth-century, 2:599,
   2:609
  nineteenth-century, 2:573,
   2:580, 2:583, 2:587,
   2:598, 2:609, 2:614
  twentieth-century, 2:570,
   2:571, 2:577, 2:579,
   2:585–86, 2:591, 2:596,
   2:603, 2:614
 East German, 2:564, 2:569,
  2:590, 2:606, 2:612,
  2:615
 history and criticism,
  2:565–66
 women authors, 2:576,
  2:598, 2:608, 2:612,
  2:615

Germanic history, 3:328,
  3:374–75
 Austria, 3:375–76
 Germany, 3:376–78
 Switzerland, 3:378
Germanic influence
 Old English, 1:143
Germanic religion, prehis-
  toric, 4:437
Germany, 3:374–78
 Lutheranism, late Christian-
  ity, 4:730
 philosophy, 4:28
Gerontology, 5:315–18
Gestalt psychology, 3:187,
  3:189, 3:195, 5:411,
  5:412, 5:464
Gifford Lectures, 5:160, 5:202
Gift of tongues, *See* Glossola-
  lia
GIS, *See* Geographic Infor-
  mation Systems
Glaciers, 5:836
Glasnost, 3:394
Glassware, 3:765–66
Global climate, 5:113, 5:288
Global early warning system,
  5:828
Glossolalia, Shakers, 4:849
Gluons, 5:661
Gnosticism
 early Christianity, 4:684
 oikoumene world, 4:452
God, *See also* Theism
 early Christianity, 4:684
 Italian literature, 2:416
 medieval philosophy, 4:113,
  4:116
 middle to late twentieth-
  century American liter-
  ature, 1:1022, 1:1023,
  1:1065
 modern British and Irish
  literature, 1:488
 Portuguese literature, 2:561
 Restoration and eighteenth-
  century literature,
  1:224, 1:255
 Spanish literature, 2:543
 Swedish literature, 2:675
 traditional issues, 4:884,
  4:900
 Western philosophy
  1600–1700, 4:167, 4:169,
   4:181, 4:182
  1700–1800, 4:194
  twentieth-century, 4:285,
   4:288
Gods
 Aztecs, 4:456
 Celtic religion, 4:436
 Egypt, ancient religion,
  4:441

Germanic religion, 4:437
 Greek ancient religion,
  4:445
 Hinduism, 4:502
 Hittite and Canaanite reli-
  gions, 4:444
 Inca religion, 4:458
 indigenous religions, 4:461,
  4:463
 Iranian ancient religions,
  4:443
 Japanese religion, 4:535
 Mediterranean ancient ur-
  ban civilization, 4:438,
  4:440
 mystery cults, 4:450
 religious movements, twen-
  tieth-century, 4:868
 Roman religion, 4:447
 South Asian religions,
  4:499, 4:500
 Taoism, 4:527
Godwin, William, 3:92
Gold Medalist Pi-Tau-Sigma,
  5:257
Golden mean, 2:385
Gongorist style, 2:528, 2:540,
  2:541
Good
 Western philosophy
  1600–1700, 4:168
  1800–1900, 4:241
Goodman, Mitchell, 1:1003
Gorbachev, Mikhail, 3:388
Gospels
 ancient Judaism, 4:615,
  4:616, 4:617
 Bible study, 4:829
Gothic influence
 Australian literature, 2:956
 Canadian literature, 2:913
 children's literature, American, 1:1197
 detective story, 1:1238
 early nineteenth-century
  American literature,
  1:679, 1:692
 German literature, 2:591
 horror story, 1:1239,
  1:1243
 Japanese literature, classical, 2:280
 middle to late twentieth-
  century American liter-
  ature, 1:1022, 1:1033
 romances, British, 1:617,
  1:621
Gothic story
 British popular literature,
  1:598–604
 authors, 1:599–604
 authors, chronology,
  1:599

British/American compared, 1:598
modern British and Irish literature, 1:469
Restoration and eighteenth-century literature, 1:262
romantic period, British, 1:269, 1:275, 1:301
Gothic tradition
British literature, popular modes, 1:590, 1:591
early American literature, 1:635
Victorian period, 1:335
Government, See also Political science
economics, 3:78, 3:79, 3:107
Keynesian, 3:86
medieval Europe, 3:329–30
political science, 3:137, 3:158–59
constitutionalism and federalism, 3:141–42
electoral politics, 3:143–44
legislative behavior, 3:146
presidency, 3:146–47
public administration, 3:147
seventeenth-century Europe, 3:336
state and local, 3:148
educational support by, 3:247
Government publications, 1:107–11
statistics, 1:107–8
Governor General's Award, 2:919, 2:921
Graça Aranha Foundation Prize, 2:897
Grace, Western philosophy, 1600–1700, 4:181
Grail legends
French literature, 2:466
German literature, 2:616
Grand Prix du Roman, 2:511
Graphics, See Illustration
Gravitation, 5:663–65, 5:705
general works, 5:664–65
histories, 5:665
Great Awakening, 1:636
Great Bible, 4:799
Great books series, 4:269
Great Britain (United Kingdom), 3:330, 3:353–68, See also British Isles; England
Canada and, 3:604, 3:612–14

general histories, 3:355–56
Hanoverian (1717–1837), 3:361–63
later Middle Ages (1216–1485), 3:357–58
Norman and Angevin (1066–1216), 3:356–57
philosophy, 4:29
pre-1066, 3:356
reference works, 3:353–55
Reformation, 4:733–36
Stuart (1603–1714), 3:359–61
English Revolution, 3:336
Tudor (1485–1603), 3:358–59
twentieth-century, 3:365–68
Arabian Peninsula under, 3:451
Balfour Declaration, 3:347
World War II, 3:400
Victorian (1837–1901), 3:363–65
Great Chain of Being, religious movements, nineteenth-century, 4:840
Great Depression, 3:76, 3:81, 3:533–36
Great Peloponnesian War, 3:321–23
Great Western Railway, 5:250
Greece (ancient), 3:297, 3:301–2, 3:311, 3:315, 3:321–24
art in, 3:755
European civilization and, 3:327
medieval theology and, 3:330
Greece (modern), 3:391, 3:393
Greek Academy, 4:77
books, 4:78–85
Greek civilization
Minoans and Mycenaeans, 4:445
oikoumene world, 4:448
Western philosophy, 1800–1900, 4:245
Greek influence
Bulgarian literature, 2:780
Croatian literature, 2:784
Macedonian literature, 2:807
Greek literature, 2:341–77
Byzantine period, 2:341, 2:344
history and criticism, 2:344–48
women authors, 2:344
classical period, 2:341–69

authors, 2:349–69
collections, general, 2:348
Dionysiac festival drama, 2:342
dithyramb, 2:342
drama, See Greek theater
history and criticism, 2:344–48
Pindaric ode, 2:365
Sapphic meter, 2:366
women authors, 2:366
German literature, influence, 2:593
Hellenistic period, 2:341, 2:343
history and criticism, 2:344–48
Latin literature, influence, 2:378
modern period, 2:341, 2:370–77
authors, 2:371–77
collections, 2:371
history and criticism, 2:371
women authors, 2:372, 2:377
Greek philosophy, 4:29, 4:44–91
authors, 4:64–91
classical period, 2:343
general works, 4:46–49
Hellenistic period, 2:343
pre-Socratic, 4:49–53
Sophists, 4:53–54
Western philosophy, 1800–1900, 4:221
Greek religion, ancient, 4:445
Greek theater
classical
chorus, 2:342, 2:355, 2:367
collections, 2:349
comedy, 2:342, 2:352
festival drama, 2:342
tragedy, 2:342, 2:350, 2:355, 2:366
Hellenistic, 2:343
comedy, 2:364
Greeks, ancient
biological sciences, 5:757
calculus, 5:489
ecology, 5:814
mathematics, 5:477
number theory, 5:488
"Green revolution," 5:259, 5:270
Greenhouse effect, 5:277, 5:288

Greenwich Village, New York City, 1:812, 1:822, 1:824, 1:860
Greta Hall, 1:304
Grierson, Sir George, 2:169
Gross national product, 5:220
Group 47 prize, 2:568
Group theory, atomic nucleus, 5:720
Groups
  psychological study of, 3:172–73
  sociological study of
    collective behavior, 3:202–3
    intergroup relations, 3:208–9
Grove Press, 1:861, 1:957
Growth, economic, 3:53–54, 3:83, 3:89, 3:90, 3:104
Guatemala, 3:637
Guatemalan authors, See Latin American literatures
Guggenheim Fellowship, 5:200, 5:257, 5:269
  early twentieth-century American literature, 1:823, 1:824
  middle to late twentieth-century American literature, 1:944–45, 1:954, 1:989–90, 1:993, 1:995, 1:1000, 1:1025–26, 1:1044, 1:1047–48, 1:1057, 1:1067
Guides and indexes, See also under specific topics
  chemistry, 5:727
  engineering, 5:215–18
  general reference work, 5:5
  historical, 3:8
  social-scientific, 3:5
  society and science, technology and medicine, 5:5
Gulag literature, 2:753, 2:755, 2:757, 2:759
Gulls, behavior, 5:835
Guru
  religious movements, twentieth-century, 4:853, 4:872
  Sikhism, 4:515
  South Asian religions, 4:500
Gustavian poets, 2:670
Guyana, 3:637
Guyanese authors, See Caribbean literature
Gynecology, 5:354–60

H

Haiti, 3:637–38
Haitian authors, See Caribbean literature
Halley's Comet, 5:606
Hamilton, Alexander, 3:161
Hampstead Child Therapy Clinic, 5:444
Handbooks
  historical, 3:8
  social-scientific, 3:5
Handicaps, 3:201–2
Hanoverian England (1717–1837), 3:361–63
Hans Christian Andersen prize, 2:658
Hapsburg Empire, 3:374, 3:379
Hare Krishna movement, 4:862
Harlem Renaissance, 1:797, 1:816–17, 1:848–49, 1:852, 1:856, 1:891, 1:1137
Harlequin Books, 1:1220
Harmon Prize, 1:824
Harmony
  Chinese religion, 4:524
  Eastern religions, 4:495, 4:496
Harpedonaptai, 5:485
Haruspicy, 4:450
Harvard Project Physics, 5:17
Hashemites (people), 3:454
Hasidism, 4:631–33
  medieval Judaism, 4:629
Hawthornden Prize, 1:542, 1:547
HDTV, See High-definition television
Health, 3:56–57
Health care, 3:201–2, 5:327–35, See also Illness and disease; Medicine; Medicine and health
  alternative systems, 5:318–21
  comparative studies, 5:330–31
  concepts and theories, philosophy, 5:77–78
  consumerism and, 5:331–32
  distinction between medicine and, 5:79
  economics, 5:332–33, 5:366
  government role, 5:333
  history of, 5:35–36
  home health care, 5:334
  legislation, 5:333
  limits on spending, 5:84
  long-term care, 5:376–78
  nursing homes, 5:334
  spending, 5:117
  trends, 5:334–35
Health professions, 5:335–39
  dentistry, 5:335–36
  general works, 5:335
  medicine, 5:336
  nursing, 5:337–38
Hearing disorders, See Ear and throat disorders
Heart diseases, See Cardiovascular diseases
Hebrew Bible, 4:792, 4:793, 4:801, 4:802
  ancient Judaism, 4:608
  commentaries, 4:628
  Hittites and Canaanites, 4:444
  versions, 4:796
Hebrew literature, 2:6–27, 4:647, See also Jewish literature, Yiddish literature
  authors, 2:10–27
  collections, 2:9–10
  history and criticism, 2:8–9
  periods, 2:6
    Haskalah movement, 2:6, 2:25
    Israel, 2:8
    modern European, 2:7, 2:15
    Palestine, 2:7, 2:13
  women authors, 2:8, 2:18, 2:19
Hebrews (ancient), 3:438
Hedonism, 2:497
Hegel Prize, 5:88
Hegelian philosophy, 3:74, 3:94, 3:284–85, 3:289
  Western philosophy, twentieth-century, 4:303
Helium, 5:697, 5:710, 5:754
Hellenic World, 3:301–2
Hellenistic Age
  Greek philosophy, 4:44, 4:45
  Jewish literature, 4:607
  oikoumene world, 4:448–53
  philosophies, 4:54–58
  Skepticism, 4:57
  Stoicism, 4:56
Hematology, 5:339–43, 5:385
Henry VIII (king, England), 3:353
Henslowe, Philip, 1:175, 1:176, 1:182
Hepatoscopy, 4:440
Heredity, See also Genetics
  evolution and, 5:779–80

fruit flies, research on, 5:807
theory of, 5:777
Heresy
early Christianity, 4:684–87
late Christianity, 4:764
medieval Christianity, 4:691, 4:698
medieval philosophy, 4:119
Renaissance philosophy, 4:133, 4:135, 4:137
Hermeneutics
contemporary issues, 4:401
Western philosophy, 1800–1900, 4:226
twentieth-century, 4:262, 4:283, 4:290, 4:318
Hermetics, 2:437, 2:441
Heroic theme
Middle English, 1:145
Old English, 1:141–42, 1:143
Hertz unit of frequency, 5:694
Herzl, Theodore, 3:347
Heteronyms, 2:560
Hicks, Granville, 3:586
High fantasy, See also Fantasy
adventure story, British, 1:594
British popular literature, 1:591, 1:611–17
children's literature
American, 1:1195
British, 1:578
horror story, British, 1:600
High-definition television, 5:294
Hinduism, 4:502–9
animism, 4:496
Indian philosophy, 4:351, 4:353, 4:354, 4:355
modern British and Irish literature, 1:500
religious movements, twentieth-century, 4:862, 4:871, 4:872
Western influences, 4:507–9
Hippocratic Oath, 5:105
Hiroshima bombing, 5:714
Histology, 5:339–43, 5:772–73
Historical drama
American, 1:1081, 1:1099
outdoor pageant, 1:1088
modern British and Irish, 1:445, 1:458
modern Irish, 1:490
Renaissance, 1:168, 1:172, 1:179
Shakespeare, 1:211

Victorian period, 1:311, 1:399
Historical fiction
American popular literature, 1:1209, 1:1244–51
authors, 1:1245–51
children's literature
American, 1:1195, 1:1202, 1:1204, 1:1208
British, 1:574
early twentieth-century American literature, 1:816, 1:820, 1:843
middle to late nineteenth-century American literature, 1:786
middle to late twentieth-century American literature, 1:908–9
modern British and Irish literature, 1:484, 1:496, 1:536
Renaissance literature, 1:177
romantic period, British, 1:269, 1:298
Victorian period, 1:317, 1:340, 1:353, 1:368, 1:385–86, 1:389, 1:403
women authors, 1:1246, 1:1248
Historical geography, 3:133
Historical linguistics, 3:20
Historical literature
middle to late nineteenth-century American, 1:729
Old English, 1:142
Renaissance, 1:179, 1:193
Victorian period, 1:375
Historical novel
Arabic literature, 2:67
Australian literature, 2:957
Bulgarian literature, 2:780
Caribbean literature, 2:934, 2:940
Chinese literature, 2:211, 2:244
Croatian literature, 2:787
Finnish literature, 2:657, 2:661
German literature, 2:578
Italian literature, 2:423, 2:426
Japanese literature, 2:290
Netherlandic literature, 2:625, 2:631
Norwegian literature, 2:668
Philippine literature, 2:331
Polish literature, 2:810, 2:821
Russian literature, 2:743
Spanish literature, 2:546

Ukrainian literature, 2:838
Yiddish literature, 2:42, 2:50
Historical-interpretive approach, study of religion, 4:425
Historicism
modern Western philosophy, 4:158
Western philosophy
1800–1900, 4:226
twentieth-century, 4:261, 4:279, 4:340
Historiography, 1:1153, 1:1154, 3:275–77
Latin American, 3:643
United States, 3:514–16
History
African, 3:414–32
authors, 3:424–32
East Africa, 3:422–23
North Africa and Sahel, 3:418–19
reference works, 3:415–16
Southern Africa, 3:423–24
surveys and general works, 3:416–18
West and Central Africa, 3:419–21
ancient, 3:297
agriculture, science, and technology, 3:304
archaeology in, 3:304–5
authors, 3:309–24
general works, 3:298–99
Greece and Hellenic world, 3:301–2
law, 3:305–6
numismation in, 3:306
philosophy, religion, education, 3:306–7
reference works, 3:298
Rome and Roman Empire, 3:302–3
society, economy, and trade, 3:307–8
sources and documents, 3:299–300
war, peace, and diplomacy in, 3:308–9
Western Asia and Egypt, 3:300–301
women, family, and sexuality, 3:309
arts
dance, 3:731–32
film, 3:824–27
music, 3:658–64
Asian and Pacific
Australia, New Zealand,

History (*cont.*)
    and Pacific Island nations, 3:493–96
    authors, 3:496–503
    East Asia, 3:463–82
    reference works, 3:462–63
    South Asia, 3:482–88
    Southeast Asia, 3:488–93
    surveys and general works, 3:463
    Australia, 3:494
    Austria, 3:375–76
    Balkans, 3:390–93
    Bangladesh, 3:486–87
    British Isles, 3:351–53
    Burma, 3:489
    Canadian, 3:604–22
    authors, 3:617–22
    British North America (to 1867), 3:612–14
    Confederation and Dominion, 3:614–15
    cultural and regional, 3:609–10
    diplomatic, 3:607–8
    discovery, exploration, and indigenous peoples, 3:610–11
    early, and New France, 3:611–12
    modern, 3:616
    reference works, 3:605–6
    social, 3:608–9
    surveys and general works, 3:606–7
    China, 3:465–72
    before 1900, 3:467–69
    modern, 3:469–72
    reference works, 3:465–66
    surveys and general works, 3:466–67
    Czechoslovakia, 3:389
    economic, 3:54–55
    economic thought, 3:45–46
    Egypt, 3:444–46
    England, 3:353–68
    European, 3:325–413
    authors, 3:398–413
    Balkans and Greece, 3:390–93
    Eastern Europe, 3:387–90
    eighteenth century, 3:337–38
    European civilization, foundations of, 3:327–29
    expansion and exploration, 3:334–36
    general studies and reference works, 3:325–27
    Jewish, 3:346–51

medieval, 3:329–32
nineteenth-century, 3:340–41
northern Europe, 3:378–83
Reformation, 3:333–34
Renaissance, 3:332–33
revolutionary period (1789–1832), 3:338–40
science and enlightenment, 3:336
seventeenth century, 3:336
southern Europe, 3:383–87
twentieth-century, 3:342–46
France, 3:371–74
general references, 3:3–9
    atlases, directories, and yearbooks, 3:8–9
    bibliographies, 3:8
    dictionaries and encyclopedias, 3:7–8
    handbooks and guides, 3:8
    indexes and abstracts, 3:8
    methods of historical research, 3:9
Germanic, 3:374–78
Germany, 3:376–78
Greece (ancient), *See* Ancient history
Greece (modern), 3:393
Hungary, 3:389–90
India, 3:483–86
Indonesia, 3:491
Iran (Persia), 3:446–49
Iraq, 3:449–50
Ireland, 3:369–71
Italy, 3:385–86
Japan, 3:472–80
    modern, 3:476–80
    premodern, 3:474–76
    reference works, 3:473
    surveys and general works, 3:473–74
Korea, 3:480–82
Latin American, 3:623–50
    authors, 3:641–50
    conquest and colonial era, 3:628–30
    individual countries, 3:633–41
    modern, 3:630–31
    pre-Columbian peoples and cultures, 3:626–28
    reference works, 3:624–25
    regional studies, 3:631–32

surveys and general works, 3:625–26
Low Countries (Europe), 3:382–83
Malaysia, Singapore, and Brunei Darussalam, 3:492
Middle Eastern, 3:433–60
    authors, 3:455–60
    general reference works and surveys, 3:434–38
    Islamic culture and nations, 3:441–55
    Israel and Jewish history, 3:438–41
    Saudi Arabia and Arabian Peninsula, 3:450–52
    Turkey, 3:452–53
New Zealand, 3:494–95
Oceania (Pacific Island nations), 3:495–96
Pakistan, 3:387
Philippines, 3:492–93
Poland, 3:390
political science, 3:138–39
Portugal, 3:386
psychology, 3:167–68
Roman Empire, *See* Ancient history
Romania, 3:390
Russian, Eurasian, and Baltic, 3:393–94
    general works, 3:394–95
    post-Soviet era, 3:398
    Soviet era, 3:395–98
    tsarist era, 3:395
Scandinavia, 3:381–82
Scotland, 3:368
sociology, 3:199–200
Spain, 3:386–87
Sri Lanka (Ceylon), 3:487–88
Switzerland, 3:378
Thailand, 3:490
United States, 3:504–603
    authors, 3:561–603
    bibliographies, 3:509–11
    Civil War and sectional conflict (1850–1877), 3:526–30
    colonial period, 3:516–19
    cultural and intellectual, 3:558–61
    Declaration of Independence, Constitution, and Federalist Papers, 3:541
    diplomacy and foreign relations, 3:544–47
    documentary histories, 3:511–12
    economic, 3:547–49

encyclopedias and dictionaries, 3:508–9
environmental, 3:549–51
gender, race, and ethnicity, 3:554–58
Great Depression and World War II (1920–1945), 3:533–36
historiography of, 3:514–16
middle period (1815–1850), 3:522–26
modern (1945–present), 3:536–40
political and constitutional, 3:541–44
pre-world power (1877–1920), 3:530–33
reference works, 3:505–8
Revolution and early period (1763–1815), 3:519–22
social change and, 3:551–53
surveys and general works, 3:512–14
world, 3:271–324
authors, 3:281–96
reference works, 3:272–73
surveys and general works, 3:273–75
war and peace, 3:277–81
writing and philosophy of, 3:275–77
Vietnam, Cambodia, and Laos, 3:490–91
Wales, 3:369
History of Science Society, 5:55
History of science, technology, and medicine, 5:23–58
ancient and classical period, 5:38–39
art and, 5:186
astronomy, 5:31–32
astrophysics, 5:656–57
atomic and nuclear physics, 5:658
authors, 5:50–58
biological sciences, 5:33–34
biology, 5:33–34
botany, 5:33–34
chemistry, 5:31–32, 5:727–29
chronological divisions, 5:37–49
classical mechanics, 5:661
cosmology, 5:656–57
earth sciences, 5:32–33
eighteenth century, 5:41–43

elementary particle physics, 5:662–63
engineering history, 5:231–33
general works, 5:24–27
geography, 5:32–33
geology, 5:32–33
gravitation, 5:665
health, 5:312–15
health care, 5:35–36
mathematics, 5:30–31
medicine, 5:35–36, 5:312–15
medieval times, 5:39–40, 5:58
meteorology, 5:32–33
middle ages, 5:39–40, 5:231
nineteenth century, 5:45–47
nuclear physics, 5:658
oceanography, 5:32–33
optics, 5:666–67
philosophy of science, historical critiques, 5:65–67
physical sciences, 5:31–32
physics, 5:31–32, 5:651–52
plasma physics, 5:667
quantum mechanics, 5:661
reference works, 5:27–30
relativity, 5:665
renaissance and reformation, 5:1450–1600, 5:40–41, 5:58
seventeenth century, 5:41–43
social sciences, 5:34–35
solid-state physics, 5:669
"special sciences," 5:30–36
technology and engineering, 5:36–37
twentieth century, 5:47–49
zoology, 5:33–34
History, philosophy of
contemporary issues, 4:401
Western philosophy, 1700–1800, 4:204, 4:216
Hitler, Adolf, 1:513, 3:133, 3:840
Hittite religions, 4:444
Holism
contemporary philosophical issues, 4:411
Western philosophy
1700–1800, 4:198
1800–1900, 4:221, 4:226
Holland, See Netherlands
Hollywood, 1:1156, 1:1161, 1:1163, 1:1166–67, 1:1175–78, 3:799, 3:810, 3:824

Holocaust, 3:438
contemporary philosophical issues, 4:386
contemporary religious issues, 4:900
European Jews, 4:635
Jewish history, 4:593
Jewish literature, 4:663
theology after, 4:647
Holocaust literature
German, 2:575, 2:591
Hebrew, 2:8, 2:14, 2:15, 2:23
Italian, 2:425
middle to late twentieth-century American literature, 1:1027, 1:1049, 1:1056, 1:1064, 1:1065
Russian, 2:773
Yiddish, 2:29, 2:37, 2:38, 2:50
Holography, See Lasers and holography
Holy Roman Empire, 3:328
Home health care, 5:334
Homeostasis, 5:789
Homily, See Sermon
Homosexuality
American literature, 1:1179–91
authors, 1:1185–91
collections, 1:1183–85
history and criticism, 1:1181–83
Chinese literature, 2:260
Danish literature, 2:647
early twentieth-century American literature, 1:812
Finnish literature, 2:659
French literature, 2:478, 2:479
gay literature, 1:1179–91
Greek modern literature, 2:372
Italian literature, 2:431
Latin American literatures, 2:843, 2:880, 2:888
middle to late twentieth-century American literature, 1:910, 1:938, 1:957, 1:961, 1:1025, 1:1061
modern British and Irish literature, 1:434, 1:453, 1:465, 1:474, 1:476, 1:491–92, 1:495, 1:500, 1:529, 1:532
new directions in American literature, 1:1124, 1:1126
Russian literature, 2:733
Victorian period, 1:409

Honduras, 3:638
Honor
    Brazilian literature, 2:898
    Latin American literatures,
        2:866
    Spanish drama, 2:554
    Spanish literature, 2:532,
        2:538
Hornbook
    children's literature
        American, 1:1193
        British, 1:575
Horror story
    American popular litera-
        ture, 1:1193, 1:1209,
        1:1238–44
    authors, 1:599–604,
        1:1239–44
    British popular literature,
        1:590, 1:591, 1:598–604
    children's literature,
        1:1239
    early nineteenth-century
        American literature,
        1:692
    middle to late nineteenth-
        century American liter-
        ature, 1:734
    middle to late twentieth-
        century American liter-
        ature, 1:948, 1:958,
        1:1024
    Restoration and eighteenth-
        century literature,
        1:256
    romances, British, 1:617
    romantic period, British,
        1:269, 1:300
    science fiction, 1:1251
    Victorian period, 1:335,
        1:374
    women authors, 1:1239,
        1:1242
Horticulture, 5:786
Horwitz Prize, 5:744
Hubble Space Telescope,
    5:585, 5:589
Hugo Award for science fic-
    tion, 1:1251, 1:1253,
    1:1261
Human development,
    3:173–74, 3:181–82,
    3:191–92
    age and aging, 3:200–201
    intellectual development,
        3:266
Human ecology, 3:236–37
Human evolution, 3:17–19
Human genome project,
    5:812
Human geography, 3:121
    cultural, 3:121–22
    economic, 3:122–23

political, 3:123
urban, 3:123–24
Human Relations Area Files,
    3:38
Human rights
    Burmese literature, 2:314
    early American literature,
        1:641
    Russian literature, 2:683,
        2:752, 2:757
    Ukrainian authors, 2:839
    West African literature,
        2:133
Human sexuality, 3:207–8,
    3:309
Humanism, 5:55
    Chinese philosophy, 4:362
    Croatian literature, 2:787
    early twentieth-century
        American literature,
        1:889
    French literature, 2:491,
        2:497
    German literature, 2:588
    Indonesian literature, 2:316
    Italian literature, 2:398,
        2:409, 2:433
    Korean literature, 2:302,
        2:306, 2:307
    Malay literature, 2:326
    middle to late twentieth-
        century American liter-
        ature, 1:1029
    modern British and Irish
        literature, 1:476
    Portuguese literature, 2:558
    Renaissance literature,
        1:193
    Renaissance philosophy,
        4:122, 4:138, 4:145,
        4:147–48, 4:150, 4:152,
        4:154–55
    Restoration and eighteenth-
        century literature,
        1:261
    Russian literature, 2:732,
        2:748
    Western philosophy,
        1800–1900, 4:222
Humanistic psychology,
    5:412, 5:437–38, 5:461,
    5:462
Humanistic psychotherapy,
    3:193
Humanistic sociology, 3:221
Humor, 3:847, 3:870–72
    adventure/thriller, 1:597
    American literature, 1:1193
    Arabic literature, 2:66
    Brazilian literature, 2:896,
        2:899
    Canadian literature, 2:912,
        2:913, 2:918

Caribbean literature, 2:942
children's literature
    American, 1:1194, 1:1206
    British, 1:580, 1:586
Chinese drama, 2:221,
    2:227
Chinese literature, 2:229,
    2:240, 2:243, 2:250,
    2:257
Chinese traditional drama,
    2:188
Czech literature, 2:789,
    2:790
Danish literature, 2:646
drama, American, 1:1087,
    1:1093, 1:1096–97,
    1:1099, 1:1101, 1:1115,
    1:1122
early nineteenth-century
    American literature,
    1:673, 1:678, 1:679,
    1:683, 1:684, 1:702
early twentieth-century
    American literature,
    1:813, 1:814, 1:819,
    1:852, 1:868, 1:890
East African literature,
    2:155
fantasy, British, 1:615
film animation, 1:1164
French drama, 2:450,
    2:483, 2:490
French literature, 2:452,
    2:494, 2:496, 2:497
German literature, 2:575
Greek classical drama,
    2:342
Hebrew literature, 2:21
Japanese literature, 2:278,
    2:287
Latin American literatures,
    2:861, 2:866, 2:868,
    2:877
middle to late nineteenth-
    century American liter-
    ature, 1:718, 1:721,
    1:732, 1:738, 1:749,
    1:756, 1:761, 1:777,
    1:779–80
middle to late twentieth-
    century American liter-
    ature, 1:935, 1:942,
    1:948, 1:952, 1:963,
    1:972–73, 1:985, 1:987,
    1:992, 1:1007, 1:1013,
    1:1020, 1:1024,
    1:1033–34, 1:1049,
    1:1057, 1:1061
modern British and Irish
    drama, 1:529

modern British and Irish
literature, 1:432, 1:442,
1:448, 1:457, 1:476,
1:494, 1:507, 1:513,
1:516, 1:522–23, 1:536,
1:538, 1:551, 1:561
modern Irish literature,
1:525
Netherlandic literature,
2:625
Old Norse-Icelandic literature, 2:644
Persian drama, 2:82
Persian literature, 2:85,
2:91, 2:94
Restoration and eighteenth-
century literature,
1:232, 1:244, 1:246,
1:252, 1:253, 1:256,
1:258
Restoration comedy, 1:243,
1:247, 1:262
romantic period, British,
1:271, 1:275
Russian drama, 2:726
Russian literature, 2:698,
2:728–30, 2:732, 2:762,
2:772, 2:775
Spanish literature, 2:549
Turkish drama, 2:95
Turkish literature, 2:97,
2:98, 2:100
Victorian period drama,
1:321, 1:347
Victorian period opera,
1:357
Victorian period, 1:360,
1:374, 1:377, 1:378,
1:403, 1:405
West African literature,
2:138, 2:144, 2:145
Yiddish literature, 2:35,
2:45, 2:47
Hungarian culture and
society
populist movement, 2:798,
2:799, 2:802
Hungarian literature,
2:797–803
authors, 2:777, 2:799–803
collections, 2:798–99
drama, 2:802
history and criticism, 2:798
Hungary, 3:387–90
Hunger, world, 5:134
Huntington's disease, 5:780
Hussein, Saddam, 3:449,
3:454
Hutchins Heuristic, 1:80
Hybrid cereal crops, 5:270
Hybridization, 5:259
Hydrocarbons, 5:731
Hydrochloric acid, 5:733

Hydrodynamics, 5:692
Hydrogen bomb, See also
Atomic bomb
development of, 5:143,
5:657
opposition to, 5:707
Hydrogen spectrum, 5:697
Hydrology, 3:125, 5:630–32
Hydrosphere, 3:125
Hypertext, 5:560–62, 5:563
Hypnotism, See Mesmerism

I

IAEE, See International Asso-
ciation of Energy
Economists
Iberia, 3:384–85
Jews in, 3:346
Muslims in, 3:441
Portugal, 3:386
Spain, 3:386–87
Ice Age, 5:785
Iceland, 3:381
Icelandic literature, See Old
Norse-Icelandic litera-
ture
Iconclastic controversy, 4:692
Iconoclasm
Russian literature, 2:697
Slovenian literature, 2:836
Iconography
early Christianity, 4:687
medieval Christianity, 4:692
Idealism
modern Western philoso-
phy, 4:158
Norwegian literature,
2:663, 2:665
Polish literature, 2:817
Western philosophy
1700–1800, 4:191, 4:197
1800–1900, 4:220, 4:230,
4:231, 4:249, 4:251,
4:252, 4:255
twentieth-century, 4:259,
4:281, 4:284, 4:303,
4:304, 4:317
Ideas, history of
medieval philosophy, 4:96
Western philosophy, twen-
tieth-century, 4:302
Identity and identity crisis,
5:441
Ideological State Apparatuses
(ISAs), 1:1125
Ideologies, comparative,
3:139–41

IEEE, See Institute of Electrical and Electronic
Engineers
Illness and disease,
5:366–410, 5:400–401
AIDS epidemic, 5:366
alcoholism, 5:401–403
anesthesiology, 5:369–70,
5:408
arthritis, 5:398
artificial organs, 5:370–71
authors, 5:406–410
biographies, 5:368–69
blindness, 5:383–84
cancer, 5:371–73
cardiovascular diseases,
5:373–75
childhood diseases,
5:375–76
chronic diseases, 5:376–78
deafness, 5:379–80
death and dying, 5:378–79
diabetes, 5:381–82, 5:406
dictionaries, 5:367
directories, 5:367–68
drug abuse, 5:403–404
ear and throat disorders,
5:379–80
emergency medicine,
5:380–81
encyclopedias, 5:368
endocrine diseases,
5:381–82, 5:406
epidemiology, 5:382–83
eye disorders, 5:383–84
gastrointestinal diseases,
5:384–85
hematologic diseases, 5:385
immunology, 5:385–88
implants, 5:370–71
infectious diseases,
5:389–90
long-term care, 5:376–78
musculoskeletal disorders,
5:396, 5:399–400
neurological diseases,
5:391–94
nutritional disorders,
5:394–95
orthopedics, 5:396
plastic surgery, 5:396–97
prostheses, 5:370–71
radiology, 5:397
reference works, 5:367–68
respiratory diseases,
5:397–98
rheumatic diseases, 5:398
skin diseases, 5:399
smoking, 5:404
spontaneous generation of
disease, 5:809
sports medicine, 5:399–400
substance abuse, 5:401–404

Illness and disease (*cont.*)
  surgery, 5:404–405, 5:408
  therapeutics, 5:405
  transplantation of organs,
    5:117, 5:370–71
  urologic diseases, 5:406
Illustration, 3:755, 3:766–67,
    See also Picture book
  animation, cartoon, film,
    1:1163
  children's literature
    American, 1:1194, 1:1205
    British, 1:577, 1:578,
      1:580, 1:583, 1:585,
      1:588
  comic strips, American lit-
    erature, 1:1193
  early twentieth-century
    American literature,
    1:889
  middle to late twentieth-
    century American liter-
    ature, 1:943
  modern British and Irish
    literature, 1:440, 1:549
  poetry, 1:855
  reference works, 1:27–30
  romantic period, British,
    1:277
  Victorian period, 1:352,
    1:409
Imagination theory
  Restoration and eighteenth-
    century literature,
    1:224, 1:248
  romantic period, British,
    1:265, 1:266, 1:267
Imagism
  early twentieth-century
    American poetry,
    1:796, 1:826, 1:855,
    1:870, 1:899
  middle to late twentieth-
    century American poet-
    ry, 1:1036, 1:1066
  modern British and Irish
    literature, 1:412
Immanence, modern Western
  philosophy, 4:157,
  4:158
Immigration, 3:581, *See also*
  Emigration; Exile
  Canadian authors, 2:919,
    2:920
  Caribbean authors, 2:932
  European Jews to United
    States, 3:347
  Hebrew authors, 2:11–26
  Israel, 3:439
  Korean authors, 2:304
  middle to late nineteenth-
    century American liter-
    ature, 1:710, 1:721

Jews, 1:737
  settlement house, 1:730
  middle to late twentieth-
    century American liter-
    ature, 1:988
  Norwegian authors, 2:667
  Philippine authors, 2:328,
    2:333
  sociological study of, 3:241
  Swedish literature, 2:678
Immortality, *See also* Life
  after death
  Renaissance philosophy,
    4:140
  Western philosophy,
    1700–1800, 4:208
Immunology, 5:385–88
  AIDS, 5:366, 5:386–88
  allergies and asthma, 5:386
Imperial cult, oikoumene
  world, 4:451
Imperialism, 3:340
Implants, 5:370–71
Impressionism, 3:780, 3:781,
    3:783, 3:789
  Hebrew literature, 2:7
  Lithuanian literature, 2:805
Imprinting
  animal behavior, 5:825,
    5:835
  psychological, 3:190
In vitro fertilization, 5:117
Inca calendar, 4:458
Inca religion, New World,
    4:458
Incarnation, traditional is-
    sues, 4:885
Incest
  horror story, 1:1239
  Renaissance drama, 1:173,
    1:179
  romantic period, British,
    1:271, 1:281
Income
  distribution of, 3:66–67,
    3:100–101
  national, 3:89–90
Indeterminism, 5:95
Indexes, *See also under*
    specific topics
  abstracting sources,
    1:111–15
  drama, 1:124
  encyclopedias, 1:106
  fiction, 1:124–25
  gazetteer, 1:84
  historical, 3:8
  literature reference works,
    1:124–25
  newspaper, 1:111
  periodical, 1:111
  poetry, 1:125
  quotations, 1:116

  social-scientific, 3:5–6
India, 3:295, 3:483–86,
    3:498–500
Indian culture and society
  diversity, 2:169, 2:175
  languages, 2:169
    Bengali, 2:182
    Dravidian, 2:169
    English, 2:170
    Indo-European, 2:169
    Sanskrit, 2:169, 2:171
    synthesis, 2:170, 2:171
Indian philosophy, 4:350–55
  authors, 4:351–55
  authors, chronology, 4:350
  general works, 4:351
Indian religion
  South Asian traditions,
    4:497–518
  Western philosophy,
    1800–1900, 4:255
Indian Statistical Institute,
    5:526
Indian subcontinent,
    literature of, 2:169–83
  ancient Indian, 2:171
    general reference works,
      2:171–73
  authors, 2:178–83
    general reference works,
      2:170–71
  medieval: Bhakti move-
    ment, 2:173–74
  modern fiction, 2:176–83
    general reference works,
      2:176–78
  modern poetry, 2:174–76
    anthologies, 2:175
    regional language, 2:176
Indians, American, *See* Na-
    tive Americans
Indigenous peoples, *See also*
    Native Americans
  of Canada, 3:610–11
Indigenous religions, 4:419,
    4:458–66
  Africa, 4:459, 4:462
  Americas, 4:463–66
  Australia, 4:460, 4:461
  Caribbean, 4:464, 4:466
  Mesoamerica, 4:463, 4:465
  North America, 4:463,
    4:464
  Oceania, 4:461
  South America, 4:464,
    4:465
  Western influence, 4:466
Individual development,
    3:173–74, 3:181–82,
    3:191–92
  age and aging, 3:200–1
  intellectual development,
    3:266

Individualism
  medieval philosophy, 4:93, 4:113
  modern Western philosophy, 4:158
  Renaissance philosophy, 4:122
  Western philosophy, twentieth-century, 4:275, 4:303
Indo-European religions, prehistoric, 4:434
Indonesia, 3:491
Indonesian literature, 2:315–21
  authors, 2:312, 2:318–21
  collections, 2:317–18
  history and criticism, 2:317
Inductive inference, 5:103
Indus Valley civilization, South Asian religions, 4:499
Industrial engineering, 5:233–34
Industrial fermentation, 5:221
Industrial health and safety, 5:106, 5:127
Industrial Light and Magic Laboratory, 1:1171
Industrial organization, 3:57–58
Industrial Revolution, 3:339, 3:340
  energy for, 5:276
  ethics and, 5:105
  transportation system, 5:253
Industrialization, 3:94, 3:112, 3:339
  economic growth and, 5:179
  history of, 5:56
Inertia, 5:687
Infectious diseases, 5:389–90, 5:801
Infinity, Renaissance philosophy, 4:135
Information science, 5:532–84, See also Computers and computer science; Information technology
  abstracts, 5:545–46
  authors, 5:575–84
  bibliographies, 5:545–46
  databases, 5:546
  directories, 5:545–46
  guides and introductions, 5:543–45
  handbooks, 5:545–46
  indexes, 5:545–46

introduction to information and library science, 5:543–48
on-line sources and information utilities, 5:546–48
Information, sociology of, 3:219–20
Information technology
  engineering, 5:228
  ethical issues, 5:105, 5:124–27
Initiation rites, See also Rites of passage
  mystery cults, 4:450
  religious movements, twentieth-century, 4:868
  shamanism, 4:430
Inorganic chemistry, 5:732–34, 5:754, 5:755
  acids and bases, 5:733, 5:749
  ammonium chloride, 5:733–34
  dyes, 5:733, 5:752
  hydrochloric acid, 5:733
  sulfuric acid, 5:733, 5:751
Input-output analysis, 3:90–91
Insects, studies on, 5:796
Instincts, 3:194
Institute for Daseinanalytic Psychotherapy and Psychodynamics, 5:435
Institute for Nuclear Studies, 5:717
Institute for Theoretical Physics, 5:673
Institute of Electrical and Electronic Engineers, 5:286
Institute of Energy Conversion, 5:290
Institution of Civil Engineers, 5:254, 5:256
Instruction
  children's literature, British book types, 1:575
  early nineteenth-century American literature, 1:658, 1:659, 1:695
  modern British and Irish literature, 1:512
  Renaissance drama, 1:183
  Renaissance literature, 1:195
  Victorian period, 1:375
Instrumentalism, 4:223
Instrumentation, 5:92, 5:95
Instruments, musical, 3:671–72
Insulin, 5:406

Integrated service digital networks, 5:294, 5:295
Intellectual development, 3:266
Intellectual history of United States, 3:558–61
Intellectual life, 3:202, 3:231
Intelligence, 3:174–75
  race and, 3:188
  testing of, 3:180, 3:196, 3:268
Intentionality, theory of, 4:221
Interaction, social, 3:208
Interactive television, 3:800, 3:810
Interdisciplinary studies
  science and technology, 5:147–48, 5:169
Intergroup relations, 3:208–9
International Association of Energy Economists, 5:290
International Center for Theoretical Physicists, 5:713
International economics, 3:58–59, 3:110
  geographic, 3:122–23
International organization publications, 1:111
International Poet's Association Award, 2:304
International Publishers Prize
  German literature, 2:594
  Latin American literatures, 2:855
International relations, 3:133, 3:144–45
International Solar Energy Society, 5:291
Internet, 5:533, 5:543
Intertestamental period of the Bible, See Apocrypha
Intertextuality, 2:623
Interview, 2:420
Introspection, 3:166
Introverts and extroverts, 5:454
Inventors and inventing, 5:225–27
  cotton gin, 5:259
  historical forces, 5:56
  reaper, 5:259
Investiture controversy, 4:694
Iran (Persia), 3:446–49
Iranian culture and society
  underclass, 2:87, 2:91
Iranian literature, See Persian literature
Iranian religions, ancient, 4:443

Iraq, 3:449–50
Ireland
  history of, 3:328, 3:352
    Northern Ireland, 3:371
    prehistory to 1800, 3:370
    reference works and
      general histories,
      3:369–70
    since 1800, 3:370–71
Irish literature, *See* Modern
    British and Irish litera-
    ture
Irish National Theatre Soci-
    ety, 1:490
Iron Curtain, 3:400
Iron, magnetization of, 5:711
Irony
  American literature, 1:1193
  Australian literature, 2:949,
    2:956
  Brazilian literature, 2:896
  Canadian literature, 2:924
  Caribbean literature, 2:933,
    2:938
  children's literature, Ameri-
    can, 1:1203
  Chinese modern drama,
    2:268
  Czech literature, 2:789
  early twentieth-century
    American literature,
    1:841, 1:843, 1:851,
    1:867, 1:869, 1:874,
    1:892
  French literature, 2:479,
    2:514
  German literature, 2:606
  Italian literature, 2:430
  Latin American literatures,
    2:853, 2:866
  Latin literature, 2:391
  middle to late nineteenth-
    century American liter-
    ature, 1:786
  middle to late twentieth-
    century American liter-
    ature, 1:953, 1:962,
    1:993, 1:995, 1:1007,
    1:1023, 1:1033, 1:1036,
    1:1049
  modern British and Irish
    literature, 1:413, 1:416,
    1:476, 1:482, 1:494,
    1:500–1, 1:503, 1:507,
    1:523–24, 1:541, 1:549,
    1:561
  modern Irish literature,
    1:506
  Netherlandic literature,
    2:626, 2:627
  Restoration and eighteenth-
    century drama, 1:263

Restoration and eighteenth-
    century literature,
    1:239, 1:244, 1:258
  romances, 1:620
  Russian literature, 2:727,
    2:769, 2:772
  Spanish literature, 2:549,
    2:552
  Victorian period, 1:347
  West African literature,
    2:139
Isabella (Queen of Spain),
    3:384
ISDNs, *See* Integrated ser-
    vice digital networks
ISES, *See* International Solar
    Energy Society
Islam, 3:441
  Arabic literature, 2:54
  Indian literature, 2:180
  North African literature,
    2:115
  Persian literature, 2:81
  Turkish literature, 2:101
  West African literature,
    2:124, 2:125, 2:134,
    2:144
Islamic culture and nations,
    3:433, 3:434, 3:441–55
  Egypt, 3:444–46
  Iran (Persia), 3:446–49
  Iraq, 3:449–50
  Islamic culture, 3:442–44
  Saudi Arabia and Arabian
    Peninsula, 3:450–52
  Turkey, 3:452–53
Islamic culture and society
  philosophy, 4:372
  religion, 4:577–80
Islamic law, 4:564, 4:566
Islamic philosophy, 4:372–75
  authors, 4:350, 4:374–75
  general works, 4:372
  medieval philosophy, 4:96
Islamic religion, 4:564–90
  authors, 4:580–90
  contemporary religious is-
    sues, 4:902
  dictionaries, encyclopedias,
    and literature, 4:566
  general histories and com-
    parative studies,
    4:567–74
  Jews in Muslim lands,
    4:625
  mysticism, philosophy, and
    theology, 4:574–77
  philosophy, 4:374, 4:375
Isolation
  Australian literature, 2:956
  Brazilian literature, 2:895
  Canadian literature, 2:916,
    2:925

Caribbean literature, 2:938
  drama, American, 1:1082,
    1:1095, 1:1100, 1:1122
  early twentieth-century
    American literature,
    1:796, 1:875
  Frisian literature, 2:635
  German literature, 2:573,
    2:595, 2:601
  Japanese literature, 2:291
  Latin American literatures,
    2:886
  middle to late nineteenth-
    century American liter-
    ature, 1:741, 1:752,
    1:769
  middle to late twentieth-
    century American liter-
    ature, 1:933, 1:990,
    1:992, 1:1035
  modern British and Irish
    drama, 1:486
  modern British and Irish
    literature, 1:435, 1:444,
    1:538, 1:540
  Netherlandic literature,
    2:625, 2:630
  New Zealand literature,
    2:972, 2:974
  Restoration and eighteenth-
    century literature,
    1:239
  Restoration and eighteenth-
    century poetry, 1:237
  romantic period, British,
    1:277
  Russian literature, 2:737,
    2:767
  Swedish literature, 2:679
  Victorian period, 1:358
  West African literature,
    2:138, 2:146
Isomers, 5:723
Israel, 3:347, 3:438–41
  Egypt and, 3:445
Israel, land of
  history of, 4:806, 4:836
  Judaism, 4:595
    ancient, 4:603, 4:604,
      4:606, 4:614
  sites of the Bible, 4:808,
    4:809
Israel, state of
  modern Judaism, 4:641–43
  Zionism, 4:657
Israel Prize, 2:11, 2:13, 2:17,
    2:19
Israeli culture and society
  Hebrew literature, 2:24,
    2:25
  kibbutz, 2:22, 2:23
Israeli literature, *See* Hebrew
    literature

Italian influence
Renaissance drama, 1:200
Renaissance literature,
1:166, 1:201
Italian literature, 2:398–443
authors, 2:403–43
collections, 2:402–3
drama, modern, 2:418,
2:420, 2:435
history and criticism,
2:400–2
Latin language, 2:409,
2:431, 2:433
linguistic experimentation,
2:426
national unification, 2:399
periods, 2:398
Tuscan language, 2:413
women authors, 2:400,
2:419–21, 2:426, 2:428
Italians
Argentine authors, 2:844
Italy, 3:383–86
Renaissance in, 3:332,
3:399, 3:755
Italy, philosophy, 4:29

J

Jainism, 4:509
Jamaica, 3:638
Jamaican authors, See under
Caribbean literature
James family, 1:761–69
James Hogg Society, 1:291
James I (King of England),
3:353
James R. Killian, Jr. Faculty
Achievement Award,
5:293
James VI (King of Scotland),
3:353
James Tait Black Memorial
Award, 1:461, 1:476,
1:493, 1:567
Jansenism, Western philoso-
phy, 1600–1700, 4:163,
4:185
Japan, 3:26–27, 3:472–73,
3:500–501
film in, 3:839
modern, 3:476–80
premodern, 3:474–76
reference works, 3:473
surveys and general works,
3:473–74
Japanese drama, 2:269
Bunraku puppet theater,
2:269, 2:276

history and criticism,
2:272–73
Kabuki theater, 2:269,
2:271, 2:276
Noh, 2:269, 2:270, 2:271,
2:280
Japanese influence
children's literature, American, 1:1204
Japanese literature, 2:269–95
anonymous works,
2:274–75
classical, 2:269, 2:270–80
authors, 2:275–80
collections, 2:273–74
history and criticism,
2:271–73
periods, 2:270–71
women authors, 2:270,
2:277, 2:278, 2:279
haiku, 2:269, 2:271, 2:276,
2:277, 2:278, 2:280,
2:288, 2:291
modern, 2:270, 2:280–95
authors, 2:284–95
collections, 2:283
history and criticism,
2:282
women authors, 2:281,
2:285, 2:286, 2:287,
2:294, 2:295
tanka, 2:269, 2:280
uncertainty, transitory
views, 2:269, 2:270,
2:278, 2:288
Western influence, 2:281
Japanese philosophy,
4:363–67
authors, 4:350, 4:363–67
general works, 4:363
Japanese religion, 4:496,
4:533–41
ancient tradition and Shinto, 4:535
Buddhism, 4:536–38, 4:540
general works, 4:534
popular, 4:538–40
reference works and an-
thologies, 4:533
Western influence, 4:533,
4:540
Jay, John, 3:161
Jazz, 3:667–69
drama, American, 1:1119
early twentieth-century
American literature,
1:793
middle to late twentieth-
century American liter-
ature, 1:910, 1:998
middle to late twentieth-
century American poet-
ry, 1:1028

modern British and Irish
literature, 1:507
Jazz Age, 1:793
Jehovah's Witnesses, 4:863
Jena period system
Western philosophy
1700–1800, 4:197, 4:218
1800–1900, 4:228, 4:231,
4:251, 4:252
twentieth-century, 4:278
Jerusalem, 3:438
Jerusalem Bible, 4:803
Jesuits
late Christianity, 4:728,
4:770
Renaissance philosophy,
4:154
Jesus Christ
ancient Judaism, 4:619
early and medieval Chris-
tianity, 4:674
early Christianity, 4:684
incarnation, traditional issues, 4:885
religious movements, twentieth-century, 4:864
Jesus movement, 4:864
Jewish Bible, See Hebrew
Bible
Jewish culture and society,
See also Israeli culture
and society
Yiddish role, 2:28, 2:39
folkways, 2:39, 2:41
ghetto, 2:36, 2:42
shtetl, 2:36, 2:40
sweatshop, 2:29, 2:44
Jewish law, codes of
medieval Judaism, 4:626
Rabbinic literature, 4:609
Jewish literature, See also
Hebrew literature
ancient Judaism, 4:607–13
religious, 4:601
Jewish philosophy
Judaism, 4:600
medieval Judaism, 4:628
modern Judaism, 4:645
Rabbinic literature, 4:609
Western philosophy,
1700–1800, 4:208
Jewish religion, See Judaism
Jewish Version, 4:801
Jews, See also Anti-Semitism;
Holocaust literature
ancient history, 3:316
Brazilian literature, 2:889,
2:899
Canadian literature, 2:903,
2:915, 2:924, 2:926
drama, American, 1:1103,
1:1105, 1:1112, 1:1115
Europe, 3:346–51

Jews (cont.)
    folklore of, 3:881
    expelled from Iberia, 3:384
    German literature, 2:578,
        2:590, 2:600, 2:608
    Hebrew literature, 2:6–27
        Ashkenazi, 2:6
        Sephardic, 2:8
    Italian literature, 2:425
    Latin American literatures,
        2:844, 2:864, 2:868,
        2:876
    Middle Eastern history,
        3:438–41
    middle to late nineteenth-
        century American liter-
        ature, 1:721, 1:737,
        1:773
    middle to late twentieth-
        century American liter-
        ature, 1:935, 1:973,
        1:987, 1:1012–13,
        1:1027, 1:1032,
        1:1039–40, 1:1048,
        1:1064–65
    Portuguese literature,
        2:556, 2:557
    Russian literature, 2:699,
        2:727, 2:754, 2:773
    Spanish literature, 2:20,
        2:519, 2:520, 2:548
    Yiddish literature, 2:28–50
        Ashkenazi, 2:28
Jews, history of
    Judaism, 4:591–673
        ancient, 4:603–7
        medieval, 4:622–26
        modern, 4:633–45
John Burroughs Medal, 5:829
John Gamble Kirkwood Me-
    dal, 5:744
John Llewellyn Rhys Prize,
    1:455
Johnson, Lyndon B., 3:296,
    3:583
Jones, John Paul, 3:588
Jordan, 3:454
Josephson effects, 5:695
Journal, See Periodical
Journalism, 3:799, 3:804–9
    authors, 3:812–23
Judaism, 4:591–673
    ancient, 4:603–21
        art and archaeology,
            4:613
        Jews, history of, 4:603–7
        literature, 4:607–13
        religious movements,
            4:614–21
    art and music, 4:597
    atonement, 4:886
    authors, 4:660–73
    authors, chronology, 4:660

Bible, 4:801
Christianity, 4:602
contemporary religious is-
    sues, 4:900
ethics, 4:597
historical background,
    4:806–8
liturgy, 4:598–600
medieval, 4:622–33
    Jews, history of,
        4:622–26
    religious movements,
        4:630–33
    thought, 4:626–30
modern, 4:633–59
    Jews, history of,
        4:633–45
    religious movements,
        4:650–59
    thought, 4:645–50
practice, 4:601
religious movements, twen-
    tieth-century, 4:864
Western philosophy,
    1700–1800, 4:208
Julian (Roman emperor),
    3:310
Julius II (pope), 3:781–82
Jungle story
    Brazilian literature, 2:900
    Latin American literatures,
        2:881, 2:886, 2:887
Jupiter, 5:615
Jurisprudence, See Law
Justice
    contemporary issues,
        4:385–87
    Western philosophy, twen-
        tieth-century, 4:315

K

Kaiser Wilhelm Institute,
    5:709
Kalinga Prize, 5:796
Kantianism, Western philoso-
    phy, 1700–1800, 4:197
Karaites, 4:628, 4:630
Karl W. Boer Solar Energy
    Award, 5:291
Karma
    Buddhism, 4:529
    South Asian religions,
        4:500
Kate Greenaway Medal,
    1:585
Kemal Ataturk, 3:452
Kennedy, John F., 3:103,
    3:500, 3:570, 3:597,
    3:804, 3:819

Keynesian economics, 3:77,
    3:80–81, 3:83, 3:85–87,
    3:102
Keystone Studio, 1:1160
Khomeini, Ruhollah (Ayatol-
    lah), 2:181, 3:447
Khrushchev, Nikita, 3:292
Kievan era (Russia), 3:393
Kinetic theory of gases,
    5:674
King James Version, 4:800
Kinship, 3:19–20
Knowledge, See also
    Epistemology
    medieval philosophy, 4:108,
        4:117
    Renaissance philosophy,
        4:148
    Western philosophy,
        1700–1800, 4:199
Knowledge, sociology of,
    3:202, 3:219–21,
    3:231–32
Knox Version, 4:802
Koch's Postulates, 5:801
Koran
    Islamic philosophy, 4:374
    Islamic religion, 4:564,
        4:587
Korea, 3:480–82
Korean history
    Japanese occupation,
        2:302, 2:305
Korean literature, 2:296–309
    authors, 2:300–9
    collections, 2:298–99
    history and criticism, 2:298
    languages, 2:296, 2:297
        English, 2:305
    periods, 2:296–97
    scribes, 2:297
    universality, 2:306
    women authors, 2:297,
        2:301, 2:303
Korean religion, 4:533–41
    Buddhism, 4:536–38, 4:540
    general works, 4:534
    popular, 4:538–40
    reference works and an-
        thologies, 4:533
    Western influence, 4:540
Krypton, 5:754
Ku Klux Klan, 1:710, 1:792,
    1:1167
Kulturgeschichte (history of
    culture), 3:399
Künstlerroman, 1:451
Kuwait, 3:449, 3:454
Kuznets cycle, 3:90
Kyoto School, 4:363, 4:364,
    4:365, 4:366

L

Labor economics, 3:59–60,
        3:73, 3:83, 3:112–13
Lac operon, 5:800
Lake poets, 1:264, 1:286,
        1:290–91, 1:304, 1:305
Lamb shift, 5:697
"Land ethic," 5:834
Land Grant Colleges, 5:260
Land Institute, 5:272
Landscape
    destruction of, 5:827,
        5:833, 5:834
    science of, 5:625–27, 5:643
Langley Porter Neuropsychi-
        atric Institute, 5:433
Language, contemporary
        philosophical issues,
        4:390, 4:396, 4:402,
        4:411, 4:413
Language, function of, 5:99
Language, philosophy of,
        Western philosophy,
        1700–1800, 4:190
Language poetry, 1:912
Languages
    anthropological linguistics,
        3:10, 3:20–21, 3:27
    culture and, 3:42
    European, 3:328
    in Switzerland, 3:375
    Native American, 3:39
Laos, 3:490–91
Laotian literature, 2:321–22
    collections, 2:322
    history and criticism, 2:322
Laplace equation, 5:698
Laplace transform, 5:530
Large-number coincidences,
        5:680
Lasers and holography,
        5:234–35, 5:303
Lasso, Hamilton, 3:923
Latin America
    education in, 3:261–62
    liberation theology, 4:747,
        4:768
    modern Judaism, 4:644
    philosophy, 4:33
    regional geography of,
        3:124
    religious movements, twen-
        tieth-century, 4:867
Latin American culture and
        society
    diversity, 2:844
    oppression, 2:851
Latin American history,
        3:623–50
    authors, 3:641–50

conquest and colonial era,
        3:628–30
    modern, 3:630–31
    individual countries,
        3:633–41
    regional studies,
        3:631–32
    pre-Columbian peoples and
        cultures, 3:626–28
    reference works, 3:624–25
    surveys and general works,
        3:625–26
Latin American literatures,
        2:842–901
    Argentine authors, 2:844,
        2:853, 2:855, 2:861,
        2:869–70, 2:872,
        2:880–82, 2:884
        women, 2:879, 2:885
    authors, 2:850–88
    Brazilian literature, See
        Brazilian literature
    Chilean authors, 2:863–64,
        2:869–70, 2:877, 2:885,
        2:887
        women, 2:851, 2:873
    collections, 2:848–50
    Colombian authors, 2:866,
        2:881
    Cuban authors, 2:842,
        2:843, 2:852, 2:857,
        2:859, 2:869, 2:871,
        2:877, 2:883
        "Spanglish," 2:857
    drama, 2:858, 2:887
    Guatemalan authors, 2:853
    history and criticism,
        2:845–48
    Mexican American authors,
        2:842
        Spanish language, 2:872
    Mexican authors, 2:843,
        2:844, 2:852–54, 2:858,
        2:860, 2:865 2:868,
        2:876, 2:878, 2:882,
        2:888
        women, 2:860, 2:862,
        2:868
    Nicaraguan authors, 2:858,
        2:863
    Paraguayan authors, 2:881
    Peruvian authors, 2:852,
        2:868, 2:885–86
    Puerto Rican authors,
        2:842, 2:843, 2:870,
        2:883
    Salvadoran authors, 2:862
    Spanish American litera-
        ture, 2:842
        indigenous cultures,
        2:844
        language diversity, 2:843
    Uruguayan authors, 2:876

Latin literature, 2:378–97
    authors, 2:382–97
    collections, 2:382
    history and criticism,
        2:380–82
    women authors, 2:395
Latter-Day Saints, 4:844–46
Latvian literature, 2:803–4
Laurentian (St. Lawrence
        River-based) histories
        of Canada, 3:604,
        3:618, 3:621
Law
    ancient history, 3:305–6
    anthropological jurispru-
        dence, 3:34
    economic, 3:60–61
    legislative behavior, 3:146
    political science, 3:145
Law of large numbers, 5:527
Law of the Minimum, 5:274
Law, philosophy of
    Renaissance, 4:154
    Western philosophy
        1600–1700, 4:186
        1700–1800, 4:190, 4:209
Learning, 3:175–76, 3:190,
        See also Education
    behaviorism, 3:196
    cognition, 3:171–72
    cognitive development,
        3:191–92
    conditioned reflexes, 3:191
    intellectual development,
        3:266
    intelligence, 3:174–75
Least squares, method of,
        5:529
Leatherstocking Tales, 1:662
Lebanon, 3:454
Legends, 3:853–57
Legislative behavior, 3:146
Lenin Peace Prize, 2:854
Leonardo da Vinci Medal,
        5:50, 5:55
Leptons, 5:661
Lesbianism
    American literature,
        1:1179–91
        authors, 1:1185–91
        collections, 1:1183–85
        history and criticism,
        1:1181–83
    drama, American, 1:1092
    early twentieth-century
        American authors,
        1:881
    early twentieth-century
        American literature,
        1:812
    French literature, 2:486
    gay literature, 1:1179–91

Lesbianism (*cont.*)
  Latin American authors,
    2:880
  Mexican Americans, 1:1136
  middle to late twentieth-
    century American liter-
    ature, 1:910, 1:911,
    1:1037
  middle to late twentieth-
    century American poet-
    ry, 1:1042
  modern British and Irish
    literature, 1:492, 1:540,
    1:541
  Native Americans, 1:1135
  new directions in Ameri-
    can literature, 1:1124,
    1:1126
Lessons, *See* Instruction
Lever, law of, 5:498
Levinson Prize, 1:823, 1:965,
  1:971
Liberal education, 3:263
Liberalism, 3:340
  Islamic philosophy, 4:372
Liberation theology, 2:858,
  2:862, 4:467, 4:747-50
  authors, 4:763, 4:764, 4:768
  contemporary issues, 4:896
  study of religion, 4:423
Libido, theories of, 5:454,
  5:457
Libraries, computerization,
  5:533, 5:534
Library directories, 1:70
Library of Congress, 3:154
Library of Congress consul-
  tant, 1:888, 1:986,
  1:993, 1:1045
Library science, 5:543-48,
  See also Information
  science
Life Achievement Award
  film studies, 1:1161,
    1:1166, 1:1169, 1:1178
Life after death, 4:886-87,
  See also Immortality;
  Incarnation
Life experience, Western phi-
  losophy, 1800-1900,
  4:226
Light, speed of, 5:701
Light bulb, 5:748
Light waves, 5:701
Lighthouses, construction,
  5:254
Likelihood ratio test, 5:530
Limerick
  children's literature, Brit-
    ish, 1:586
Lincoln, Abraham, 3:573
Lincoln Film Company,
  1:1172

Linear B script, Greek civilization, 4:445
Linguistic analysis, Western
  philosophy, twentieth-
  century, 4:261, 4:271,
  4:278, 4:282, 4:325
Linguistics
  anthropological, 3:10,
    3:20-21, 3:27, 3:42
  history of, Western philoso-
    phy, 1700-1800, 4:198
  phonemic theory, 3:39
Linnaean Society, 5:811
Liquid helium, 5:697
Literary characters
  adventure story, British,
    1:594
  adventure/thriller, 1:592,
    1:593
  Arabic literature, 2:67
  Canadian literature, 2:912,
    2:914
  cartoon animation, film,
    1:1163
  children's literature, Brit-
    ish, 1:581, 1:588, 1:590
  detective story, 1:1226,
    1:1228-31, 1:1233-37
  detective story, British,
    1:605, 1:606, 1:607,
    1:609, 1:610
  early nineteenth-century
    American literature,
    1:657, 1:662, 1:673,
    1:674
  early twentieth-century
    American literature,
    1:801-3, 1:828-29,
    1:833, 1:834, 1:852,
    1:869, 1:879, 1:883-84,
    1:892, 1:903
  French drama, 2:458
  French literature, 2:469,
    2:497, 2:508, 2:512,
    2:517
  German literature, 2:581
  Greek modern literature,
    2:373
  historical fiction, 1:1246-48
  horror story, 1:602-3
  Italian literature, 2:433
  Latin American literatures,
    2:851
  Latin literature, 2:383
  middle to late nineteenth-
    century American liter-
    ature, 1:711, 1:739,
    1:741, 1:754, 1:779
  middle to late twentieth-
    century American liter-
    ature, 1:943, 1:948,
    1:968, 1:972, 1:977,
    1:982, 1:987, 1:994,

  1:996, 1:998, 1:1029,
    1:1040, 1:1042, 1:1059
  modern British and Irish
    drama, 1:531, 1:565
  modern British and Irish
    literature, 1:453, 1:457,
    1:482, 1:558
  New Zealand literature,
    2:975
  North African literature,
    2:123
  Polish literature, 2:814
  Restoration and eighteenth-
    century literature,
    1:253, 1:256, 1:258,
    1:259
  Restoration comedy, 1:232,
    1:247, 1:254
  romances, 1:1221
  Russian literature, 2:700,
    2:702, 2:723, 2:728,
    2:734, 2:772
  science fiction, 1:1255,
    1:1257
  science fiction/fantasy,
    British, 1:616
  Spanish literature, 2:519,
    2:529, 2:534, 2:537,
    2:548, 2:551
  thriller, 1:595, 1:596
  Victorian period, 1:329,
    1:351, 1:352, 1:386,
    1:400, 1:403, 1:405
  West African literature,
    2:136
  westerns, 1:1211, 1:1212,
    1:1215
  Yiddish literature, 2:45
Literature, *See also under*
  specific topics
  anthologies, 1:128-30
  bibliographies, 1:119-23
  biographical references,
    1:126-28
  criticism, literary, 1:134-35
  new directions, Ameri-
    can, 1:1125
  guides, handbooks, diction-
    aries, 1:131-33
  history, literary, 1:133-34
  interpretation of, 2:461,
    2:476
  reference works, 1:119-35
  sociology of, 3:202
  theory, literary, 1:922,
    1:1126, 1:1129-55
Lithography, 3:755
Lithosphere, 3:125
Lithuanian literature, 2:804-7
  authors, 2:778, 2:805-7
  drama, 2:806
  history and criticism, 2:805

Liturgical drama, *See* Religious drama
Local government, 3:148
  educational support by, 3:247
Local-color authors
  American literature, 1:1193
  early nineteenth-century American literature, 1:673, 1:683, 1:698
  middle to late nineteenth-century American literature, 1:732, 1:738-39, 1:749, 1:754-55, 1:769, 1:789
Logic
  contemporary issues, 4:379, 4:380
  medieval philosophy, 4:97, 4:107, 4:120
  Western philosophy
    1600-1700, 4:164, 4:176
    1800-1900, 4:228, 4:243, 4:248
    twentieth-century, 4:261
"Logic of relations," 5:84
Logical empiricism, 5:103
  Western philosophy, twentieth-century, 4:261, 4:272, 4:278, 4:313, 4:343
Logical positivism, Western philosophy, twentieth-century, 4:261, 4:272, 4:278, 4:332, 4:337, 4:343
Logotherapy, 5:443
Loines Award, 1:874, 1:899, 1:949
London Bridge, 5:254
Loneliness, *See* Alienation; Isolation
Longitudinal data, 3:3
Lost generation, 1:793, 1:822, 1:838, 1:844, 1:881
Love poetry
  Arabic literature, 2:62, 2:70
  Burmese literature, 2:313
  Chinese literature, 2:188, 2:200, 2:208, 2:216
  Danish literature, 2:653
  early twentieth-century American, 1:860
  French literature, 2:452, 2:474, 2:501, 2:502, 2:512
  Frisian literature, 2:634
  German literature, 2:586, 2:614
  Greek classical literature, 2:366
  Indian subcontinent literature, 2:170

Italian literature, 2:416
Korean literature, 2:301
Latin American literatures, 2:852, 2:873
Middle English, 1:145, 1:148, 1:150
middle to late nineteenth-century American, 1:745
middle to late twentieth-century American poetry, 1:1045
Portuguese literature, 2:556
Renaissance literature, 1:164, 1:177
Russian literature, 2:756, 2:771
Slovenian literature, 2:836
Spanish literature, 2:549
Urdu literature, 2:175
Love, psychology of, 5:449
Love, types of
  Chinese literature, 2:196, 2:226
  French drama, 2:488, 2:498
  French literature, 2:484
  Greek Hellenistic drama, 2:364
  Greek Hellenistic literature, 2:363
  Russian literature, 2:707
  Spanish literature, 2:549, 2:551
Love songs
  Chinese literature, 2:196, 2:200
  Italian literature, 2:413, 2:424
Love story, *See* Romances
Low Countries (Europe), 3:379-80, 3:382-83
Lumière brothers (Louis Jean and Auguste Marie Louis Nicolas), 3:823
Lutheranism, 2:637
Lutherans, late Christianity, 4:730
Luxembourg, 3:380
Lyceum, Athens, *See* Peripatetic school
Lyric
  ballad opera, 1:246
  film animation, 1:1163
  Middle English, 1:145, 1:148
  middle to late nineteenth-century American literature, 1:754, 1:771
  Native American, 1:718
  Renaissance literature, 1:174, 1:181

Restoration and eighteenth-century literature, 1:261
romantic period, British, 1:279, 1:280
Lyric poetry
  Armenian literature, 2:78
  Caribbean literature, 2:942
  Chinese literature, 2:194, 2:231
  East African literature, 2:156
  French literature, 2:444, 2:445, 2:468, 2:502, 2:514
  German literature, 2:588, 2:593, 2:603
  Greek classical literature, 2:342, 2:366
  Greek Hellenistic literature, 2:365
  Hebrew literature, 2:16
  Italian literature, 2:406, 2:424, 2:426, 2:440
  Korean literature, 2:305
  Latin American literatures, 2:862
  Latin literature, 2:394
  Portuguese literature, 2:558
  Rumanian literature, 2:823
  Russian literature, 2:696, 2:702, 2:703, 2:731, 2:742, 2:750, 2:758
  Serbian literature, 2:830
  Slovak literature, 2:832
  Slovenian literature, 2:836
  Spanish literature, 2:519, 2:520, 2:528, 2:531, 2:542

M

MacAlpin, Kenneth (King of the Scots), 3:352-53
MacArthur Foundation Award, 1:984, 1:996, 1:1001, 1:1035, 1:1047, 1:1144
Maccabees, 3:316
Macedonian literature, 2:807-9
  authors, 2:778, 2:808-9
  collections, 2:808
  drama, 2:809
  history and criticism, 2:807-8
  language, 2:808
  Prilep dialect, 2:807
Mach principle, 5:699
Macroeconomics, 3:61-63

Macromolecules, 5:746
Magazine, See Periodical
Magazines, 3:804
Magic
  oikoumene world, 4:448,
    4:450, 4:451
  religious movements
    nineteenth-century, 4:840
    twentieth-century, 4:864
  Renaissance philosophy,
    4:133–35, 4:137, 4:149
  shamanism, 4:430
  South Asian religions,
    4:500
Magic realism
  Brazilian literature, 2:890,
    2:893
  Canadian literature, 2:913
  Chinese literature, 2:259
  Italian literature, 2:411
  Latin American literatures,
    2:866
  middle to late twentieth-
    century American liter-
    ature, 1:988
  Netherlandic literature,
    2:627
Magnetic fields, 5:672, 5:699
Magnetic monopole, 5:679
Magnetic resonance imaging,
  5:743–44
Magyars (people), 3:387
Mahayana Buddhism, 4:511
Mainau Declaration of Nobel
  Laureates, 5:751
Malapropisms, 1:254
Malay literature, 2:322–27
  authors, 2:312, 2:325–27
  collections, 2:324–25
  history and criticism, 2:324
  languages, 2:324
Malaysia, 3:492
Manhattan Project, 5:179,
  5:671, 5:678, 5:720
Manichaeism, 4:443
Manoralism, 3:329
Manuscripts, illustrated,
  3:766–67
Mao Tun Prize, 2:238, 2:249
Maoism, 4:358, 4:359, 4:361
Maori (people), 3:493
Maori authors, See under
  New Zealand literature
Mapplethorpe, Robert, 1:1189
Maps, 3:116, See also
  Geography
  cartography, 3:134
  geographic information sys-
    tems, 3:117, 3:120–21
Marconi International Fel-
  lowship, 5:305
Marine biology, 5:630

Marine exploration, 3:918,
  3:920
Marriage, sociology of,
  3:206–7
Mars
  canyons of, 5:615
  intelligent life, ideas on,
    5:608–609
Martyrdom
  early and medieval Chris-
    tianity, 4:674
  Renaissance philosopher,
    4:135, 4:147
Marvelous reality theory,
  2:859
Marxism and Marxists,
  3:74–75, 3:94–95, 3:340
  African philosophy, 4:370
  African studies, 3:430
  anthropology, 3:37
  anti-Marxism, 5:69
  Christianity and, 5:163
  contemporary philosophical
    issues, 4:393, 4:407
  economics, 3:102
  education, 3:261–62
  Fabian socialism, 3:112
  folklore, 3:846
  geography, 3:122, 3:123
  history, 3:271, 3:286–87,
    3:289–95, 3:352,
    3:404–5, 3:408, 3:410,
    3:580, 3:601, 3:647
  neo-Marxism, 5:88
  political science, 3:155–56
  sociology, 3:198, 3:199,
    3:222
  Soviet Union, 3:393–98
  Western philosophy
    1800–1900, 4:227, 4:241
    twentieth-century, 4:261
Maser (microwave amplifica-
  tion by stimulated
  emission of radiation),
  5:717
Masoretes, 4:794
Masque
  Renaissance drama, 1:168
Mass media, 3:799–844
  film, 3:823–24
    authors, 3:829–44
    criticism and theory,
      3:827
    directors, 3:827–29
    general reference and
      history, 3:824–27
  general works, 3:802–4
  journalism, 3:804–9
  music and, 3:653
  radio and television,
    3:809–12
    authors, 3:812–23
  reference works, 3:801–2

  sociological study of,
    3:203–4
Materialism, modern Western
  philosophy, 4:159
Mathematical economics,
  3:63–64, 3:87–88
Mathematics, 5:477–517
  Abelian functions, 5:517
  algebra, 5:482–85
  astronomy and, 5:512
  authors, 5:497–517
  axioms, 5:508, 5:510
  biology and, 5:797
  calculus, 5:489–91
  complex functions, theory
    of, 5:501
  computers and, 5:581
  continuum hypothesis,
    5:508
  creativity, 5:494
  determinate equations,
    5:503
  different approaches to,
    5:494–95
  doubt, critical method of,
    5:502
  elliptic functions, 5:517
  Gaussian curve, 5:507
  general mathematics,
    5:480–82
  geometry, 5:477, 5:485–87
  handbooks, 5:478–80
  history of, 5:30–31,
    5:491–92
  hyperelliptic functions,
    5:517
  indeterminate equations,
    5:503
  infinitesimal calculus,
    5:511
  logic, 5:508
  mind-body problem, 5:502
  nonstandard analysis,
    5:490, 5:515
  number theory, 5:488–89,
    5:506–508
  philosophy of, 5:492–94
  physics, 5:512
  prime numbers, 5:506
  probability theory, 5:506
  puzzle books, 5:495–97
  recreational mathematics,
    5:495–97
  reference books, 5:478–80
  "significant form," study
    of, 5:478
  symbolic logic, 5:499
  transfinite set theory,
    5:500, 5:509
  universalist mathemati-
    cians, 5:509, 5:513

Mathematics, history of
  contemporary philosophical
    issues, 4:410
  Greek philosophy, 4:87
  Western philosophy
    1600–1700, 4:183, 4:185
    1800–1900, 4:229, 4:257
    twentieth-century,
      4:260–61, 4:320
Matriarchy, 2:851
Matrix mechanics, 5:675
Matter, theory of, 5:56
Matthew effect, 3:233
Matthew's Bible, 4:799
Maya, 4:454, 4:455
Maya calendar, 4:455
McArthur Foundation Fellow-
    ship, 5:831
McAuley Clinic, 5:433
McCarthyism, 3:263
McDowell Colony, 1:876
McKinley, William, 3:935
Meaning
  contemporary issues, 4:376
  Western philosophy, twen-
    tieth-century, 4:310
Mechanical engineering,
    5:235–36
Mechanics, 5:649
Mechanism, modern Western
    philosophy, 4:157,
    4:158
Mechanization, agriculture,
    5:259
Medical ethics
  contemporary philosophical
    issues, 4:387
  contemporary religious is-
    sues, 4:893
Medical genetics, 5:780–81
Medici circle, Renaissance
    philosophy, 4:140,
    4:144, 4:152
Medicine. See also
    Biomedicine; general
    headings of science,
    technology, and
    medicine; Illness and
    disease; Medicine and
    health; Psychiatry;
    specific topics
  AIDS, health care, and dis-
    abling conditions,
    3:201–2
  bioethics, 5:117–24
  careers in, 5:336
  clinical judgment, analyses
    of, 5:78–80
  concepts and theories, phi-
    losophy, 5:77–78
  decision-making, 5:78–80
  ethical issues, 5:117–24

general reference works,
    5:5–6, 5:12–13
  history of, 5:35–36
  illness and disease, See Ill-
    ness and disease
  mind in medicine, philoso-
    phy, 5:80–81
  philosophy of, generally,
    5:77–81
  psychoanalysis, 3:182–83,
    3:193
  sixteenth century, 5:751
  society and, See Society
    and science, technol-
    ogy and medicine
  sports medicine, 5:399–400
Medicine and health,
    5:309–365, 5:325–27
  aging, 5:315–18, 5:348–49
  alternative health care sys-
    tems, 5:318–21
  anatomy, 5:339–43
  authors, 5:360–65
  biography, 5:312–15
  body and health, 5:339–43
  child care and develop-
    ment, 5:321–23
  dental care, 5:335–43
  dermatology, 5:339–43
  diagnostic testing, 5:324
  diet, 5:344–49, 5:394–95
  environmental health,
    5:352–54
  exercise, 5:325–27
  forensic medicine,
    5:343–44
  gerontology, 5:315–18
  gynecology, 5:354–60
  health care, See Health
    care
  health professions, See
    Health professions
  hematology, 5:339–43
  histology, 5:339–43
  history of medicine,
    5:312–15
  law and medicine,
    5:343–44
  neurology, 5:339–43
  neurophysiology, 5:364
  nutrition and diet,
    5:344–49, 5:394–95
  obstetrics, 5:354–60
  occupational health,
    5:352–54
  ophthalmology, 5:339–43
  pediatrics, 5:321–23
  pharmacology, 5:349–52
  physical fitness, 5:325–27
  physiology, 5:339–43
  poisons, 5:349–52
  public health, 5:352–54,
    5:366

radiology, 5:324
  reference books, 5:310–12
  toxicology, 5:349–52
  women's health, 5:354–60
Medicine men, See Shaman-
    ism
Medieval European history,
    3:329–32
  England, 3:357–58
  Northern Europe, 3:379
  urban development in,
    3:407
Medieval literature
  Armenian, 2:78, 2:79
  British, 1:139–61
    history and criticism,
      1:141
  children's literature, British
    castle tales, 1:575
  Chinese, 2:211, 2:219
  drama, British, 1:156–61
    chronology, 1:158
    collections, 1:158
    cycle plays, 1:156, 1:158
    history and criticism,
      1:157
    miracle plays, 1:156,
      1:160
    morality plays, 1:156,
      1:160
  French, 2:452, 2:466,
    2:501, 2:509, 2:512,
    2:514
  German, 2:581, 2:594,
    2:604, 2:614, 2:616
  Hebrew, 2:20, 2:23
  high fantasy, British, 1:611,
    1:617
  Italian, 2:398, 2:409, 2:416
  Korean, 2:296
  Middle English, 1:140,
    1:144–55
  middle to late twentieth-
    century American liter-
    ature, 1:978
  Netherlandic, 2:619, 2:626
  Norwegian, 2:661, 2:668
  Old English, 1:141–44
  Old Norse-Icelandic, 2:639
  Russian, 2:682
  Spanish, 2:548
Medieval Period (Middle
    East), 3:433, 3:434
Medieval philosophy,
    4:92–121
  authors, 4:105–21
  Averroism, 4:96
  fourteenth and fifteenth
    centuries, 4:103–5
  general works, 4:93
  ideas, history, 4:96
  Islamic thought, 4:96
  method of study, 4:95

Medieval philosophy (cont.)
   special topics, 4:95–98
   text collections, 4:94
   twelfth and thirteenth cen-
      turies, 4:101–3
   Western philosophy, twen-
      tieth-century, 4:285
Medieval times, bibliography,
   5:39–40, 5:58
Meditation, 5:400
   Buddhism, Chinese, 4:529
   Confucianism, 4:525
   Indian philosophy, 4:352
   religious movements, twen-
      tieth-century, 4:858,
      4:859, 4:872
   Tibetan Buddhism, 4:542
   Tibetan philosophy, 4:357
   Western philosophy, twen-
      tieth-century, 4:313
Mediterranean world
   ancient religions and phi-
      losophies, 4:419,
      4:438–53
   Eastern Orthodox Church,
      4:754
Megalithic monuments, pre-
   historic religion, 4:433
Megalopolises, 3:129
Megarian school, 4:89
Mellon Professorship, See
   Andrew W. Mellon
   Professorship
Melodrama, 2:422
   early twentieth-century
      American literature,
      1:894
   film studies, 1:1172,
      1:1174, 1:1175
   Gothic romance, British,
      1:622
   Gothic story, British, 1:603
   middle to late nineteenth-
      century American liter-
      ature, 1:790
   modern British and Irish
      drama, 1:445, 1:543
   modern British and Irish
      literature, 1:461
   modern Irish drama, 1:526
   romantic period, British,
      1:271
   twentieth-century American
      drama, 1:1070, 1:1092
   Victorian period, 1:311,
      1:320, 1:374
Memory, 3:182–83
Mendel's laws, 5:806, 5:807
Mendelian genetics, 5:766
Menninger Clinic, 5:463
Mennonites, 2:927, 4:780
Mental health, philosophy,
   5:80–81

Mental illness, 5:137, 5:412
Mercury Theatre of the Air,
   1:1178
Mesmerism, 4:846
Mesoamerica religions
   indigenous, 4:463, 4:465
   Maya, 4:454, 4:455
   New World, 4:454–57
   Olmecs, 4:454, 4:455
Mesons, 5:661
   neutral K-meson, 5:679,
      5:686
Mesopotamia, 3:449
Mesopotamian religions,
   Mediterranean ancient
   urbancivilization, 4:440
Mesopotamian-Anatolian cul-
   ture, 2:51
Messiah
   ancient Judaism, 4:620
   religious movements, twen-
      tieth-century, 4:864
   Sabbateanism, 4:631
Messianism, 2:810, 2:817
Mestizo history, 3:646
Mestizos
   Latin American authors,
      2:885
   Spanish American culture
      and society, 2:844
Meta-ethics, contemporary
   philosophical issues,
   4:387
Metafiction, 1:909, 1:942
Metal arts, 3:767
Metallurgy, 5:237–38, 5:722
Metaphysical poets
   Renaissance literature,
      1:175, 1:177, 1:180,
      1:188
   Restoration and eighteenth-
      century poetry, 1:227
Metaphysics
   early American literature,
      1:643
   Greek philosophy, 4:64
   medieval philosophy, 4:120
   middle to late nineteenth-
      century American liter-
      ature, 1:768
   modern British and Irish
      literature, 1:469
   Renaissance philosophy,
      4:135, 4:154
   science fiction, 1:1256–57
   Western philosophy
      1600–1700, 4:168
      1700–1800, 4:219
      twentieth-century, 4:302,
         4:305, 4:314, 4:333,
         4:338
Meteorology, 5:32–33, 5:633,
   5:641–42, 5:647

Methodism, 4:738
Methodology
   anthropology, 3:11–12
   economics, 3:46–47
      game theory, 3:111
      input-output analysis in,
         3:90–91
      mathematical and quanti-
         tative, 3:63–64
   geography, 3:119–20
      quantitative, 3:117
   history, 3:9, 3:275–77,
      3:374–75
      Annales school of, 3:372
      in ancient history, 3:299,
         3:322
      Marxist, 3:289
      Namierism, 3:406
      Soviet, 3:393–94
      United States, 3:504,
         3:514–16
   philosophy of science,
      5:61–65
   political science, 3:138
   psychology, 3:166, 3:168–69
   social sciences, 3:6–7
      participant observation,
         3:10
   sociology, 3:200
      ethnomethodology, 3:227
      values in, 3:231
Mexican American authors,
   See under Latin Ameri-
   can literatures
Mexican Americans
   early twentieth-century
      American literature,
      1:883
   gay literature, 1:1190
   literary theory, 1:1136
   middle to late nineteenth-
      century American liter-
      ature, 1:710, 1:718
Mexican authors, See under
   Latin American litera-
   tures
Mexican culture and society
   Aztecs, 2:853, 2:868
   identity, 2:865, 2:878
   indigenous, 2:860
   rural life, 2:882
Mexico, 3:34, 3:638–39, 3:644
   Mesoamerica religions,
      4:456
Microbial activity, discovery
   of, 5:221
Microbiology, 5:783, 5:795
Microeconomics, 3:64–65
Microfiche, 1:65
Microformat, 1:108
Microscope, 5:803
Microwave radar, 5:697

Mid-Atlantic states, folklore of, 3:858–59
Middle Ages, *See also* Medieval European history
bibliography, 5:39–40
Christianity, 4:690–701
Danish literature, 2:644
ecology, 5:814
engineering, 5:231
French literature, 2:444, 2:501
Frisian literature, 2:633
German literature, 2:562
Italian literature, 2:398, 2:420
Judaism, 4:622–33
medieval philosophy, 4:92–121
mind in medicine, 5:411
Old Norse-Icelandic literature, 2:642
Portuguese literature, 2:556
Scandinavian literatures, 2:637
Spanish literature, 2:537, 2:548, 2:549
Western philosophy, 1800–1900, 4:253
Middle America, *See* Mesoamerica
Middle East, non-Islamic and non-Jewish tradition, 4:544–48
Middle Eastern history, 3:433–60
authors, 3:455–60
general reference works and surveys, 3:434–38
Islamic culture and nations, 3:441–55
Egypt, 3:444–46
Iran (Persia), 3:446–49
Iraq, 3:449–50
Islamic culture, 3:442–44
Saudi Arabia and Arabian Peninsula, 3:450–52
Turkey, 3:452–53
Israel and Jewish history, 3:438–41
Middle Eastern literatures, 2:51–52
ancient Near Eastern, 2:51–53
collections, 2:52
general background, 2:52
individual texts, 2:53
Arabic literature, *See* Arabic literature
Armenian literature, *See* Armenian literature

Persian literature, *See* Persian literature
Turkish literature, *See* Turkish literature
Middle Eastern studies, 3:434
Middle English, 1:140, 1:144–55
authors and works, 1:148–55
collections, 1:147
history and criticism, 1:146–47
women authors, 1:146, 1:152
Middle Platonism, 4:59
Middle to late nineteenth-century American literature, 1:710–90
authors, 1:728–90
children's literature, 1:749, 1:760
collections, 1:717
fiction, 1:720–25
collections, 1:725
history and criticism, 1:722–25
history and criticism, 1:712–17
nonfiction, 1:726–28
collections, 1:727–28
history and criticism, 1:726–27
poetry, 1:717–20
collections, 1:719–20
history and criticism, 1:718–19
women authors, 1:721, 1:732, 1:738, 1:739, 1:743, 1:745, 1:749, 1:752–53, 1:760–61, 1:769, 1:772, 1:786, 1:789
Middle to late twentieth-century American literature, 1:908–1068
authors, 1:929–1068
children's, 1:1049, 1:1055
fiction, 1:915–22
collections, 1:921–22
history and criticism, 1:916–21
history and criticism, 1:910–11
nonfiction, 1:922–29
autobiography, 1:923, 1:927–28
biography, 1:923, 1:928–29
criticism, 1:923–27
poetry, 1:911–15
collections, 1:914–15
history and criticism, 1:912–14

women authors, 1:916, 1:931, 1:934, 1:939, 1:944–45, 1:950, 1:952–53, 1:962, 1:970, 1:981–82, 1:992, 1:1000–001, 1:1003, 1:1007, 1:1009, 1:1014, 1:1018, 1:1020–23, 1:1025, 1:1027, 1:1029–30, 1:1037, 1:1039, 1:1041, 1:1044–47, 1:1050, 1:1052, 1:1055, 1:1057–58, 1:1061, 1:1064
Middle-school movement, 3:247
Midrash, 4:609
Midwest (United States), folklore of, 3:861–62
Miles Franklin Award, 2:952, 2:964
Milesian school, 4:51
Milieu interieur, 5:789
Milieu therapy, 5:458
Militancy
Islamic religion, 4:564
late Christianity, 4:762
religious movements, twentieth-century, 4:861, 4:876
Sikhism, 4:516
Military, *See also* Atomic bomb; Hydrogen bomb
civil engineering, 5:223
computers and computer science, 5:533
destructiveness of, 5:170
engineering, 5:236–37
strategy, 5:184
World War II, research following, 5:161
Military ethics, contemporary philosophical issues, 4:388
Military history, 3:271, 3:287–88
ancient, 3:310, 3:321–22
Milky Way galaxy, 5:598, 5:603, 5:612, 5:680
Mind, nature of, *See also* Dualism
contemporary issues, 4:395, 4:396
contemporary philosophical issues, 4:381–83
Mind in medicine, *See also* Clinical psychology; Psychiatry
philosophy, 5:80–81
Mind-body problem, 5:502
Minerals, *See* minerology
Minerology, 5:627–29

Minimalism, 3:696
  middle to late twentieth-
    century American liter-
    ature, 1:916, 1:940,
    1:945
  modern British and Irish
    drama, 1:412, 1:439,
    1:534
Mining, 5:237–38
Minority religions
  religious movements,
    4:839–81
    authors, 4:873–81
    women authors, 4:873–74
  religious movements, nine-
    teenth-century,
    4:840–53
  religious movements, twen-
    tieth-century, 4:853–73
    controversial issues,
      4:856
    descriptive and historical
      works, 4:855
    directories, encyclope-
      dias, and bibliogra-
      phies, 4:854
    theological and philo-
      sophical response,
      4:857
    Theosophy, 4:858
Miracle plays, 1:156, 1:160
Mishnah, 4:609, 4:619
Missionaries
  American colonies, 4:752
  early Christianity, 4:681
  late Christianity, 4:715,
    4:728, 4:740, 4:770
Missionary influence
  North African literature,
    2:115
  West African literature,
    2:124, 2:125, 2:132
Mithraism, 4:443
Mock epic
  Brazilian literature, 2:900
  early American literature,
    1:632
  Italian literature, 2:406
  Restoration and eighteenth-
    century literature,
    1:223
  Restoration and eighteenth-
    century poetry, 1:252
Modal logic, Western philos-
    ophy, twentieth-cen-
    tury, 4:300, 4:301
Modern British and Irish
    literature, 1:412–572
  authors, 1:430–572
  Celtic, 1:459, 1:555, 1:571
  children's, 1:442, 1:466,
    1:467, 1:497, 1:512
  collections, 1:415

drama, 1:423–28
fiction, 1:419–23
  collections, 1:422–23
  history and criticism,
    1:420–22
Gaelic, 1:459, 1:525, 1:527,
  1:528
history and criticism,
  1:414–15
Irish poetry, 1:416
Irish renaissance, 1:460,
  1:490, 1:555
nonfiction, 1:428–30
  collections, 1:430
  history and criticism,
    1:429
poetry, 1:415–19
  collections, 1:418–19
  history and criticism,
    1:417–18
Scottish dialect, 1:516
Vikings, and tribal culture,
  1:494
women authors, 1:412,
  1:447, 1:451, 1:454–55,
  1:458, 1:461, 1:467,
  1:489, 1:492, 1:501,
  1:523, 1:538, 1:540–41,
  1:547–48, 1:550, 1:565,
  1:568
Modernism, 3:769
  Brazilian literature, 2:889,
    2:892
  Canadian literature, 2:922,
    2:925
  Croatian literature, 2:785
  Danish literature, 2:653
  early twentieth-century
    American literature,
    1:812
  Finnish literature, 2:657,
    2:660
  French literature, 2:450,
    2:468
  Hebrew literature, 2:7,
    2:18, 2:27
  Hungarian literature, 2:797
  Italian literature, 2:414,
    2:428, 2:431
  Latin American literatures,
    2:863, 2:871, 2:881,
    2:884
  Lithuanian literature, 2:804
  middle to late twentieth-
    century American liter-
    ature, 1:995, 1:1052
  middle to late twentieth-
    century American poet-
    ry, 1:1015
  modern British and Irish
    literature, 1:413, 1:462
  modern British and Irish
    poetry, 1:452

New Zealand literature,
  2:973
Persian literature, 2:87
Restoration and eighteenth-
  century literature,
  1:225
Russian literature, 2:698
Serbian literature, 2:827,
  2:830, 2:831, 2:832
Slovak literature, 2:833
Slovenian literature, 2:834,
  2:837
Swedish literature, 2:671
Ukrainian literature, 2:840
Yiddish literature, 2:29
Modernization, 3:209
"Modes of living," 5:814
Modleski, Tania, 1:1151
Moe, Jorgen, 3:845
Molecular biology, 5:783–84
  agricultural research, 5:766
  classification of animals,
    5:768
  contributions to, 5:689
  defined, 5:757
  DNA structure, 5:790
Molecular chemistry, 5:740,
  5:741
Molecular genetics, contem-
  porary philosophical is-
  sues, 4:384
Monad, Western philosophy,
  1600–1700, 4:167
Monasticism
  early Christianity, 4:687
  medieval Christianity, 4:698
  medieval philosophy, 4:111
Monetarism, 3:76, 3:77
Monetary economics and
  policy, 3:65
Monism
  Hinduism, 4:502
  Western philosophy,
    1800–1900, 4:221
  Western philosophy, twen-
    tieth-century, 4:283,
    4:320
Monopolies, 3:110
Monotheism
  ancient religion, 4:421
  Eastern religions, 4:496
  Egypt, ancient religion,
    4:442
  Hinduism, 4:502
  Iranian ancient religions,
    4:443
  Islamic religion, 4:564
  Zoroastrianism, 4:546,
    4:547
Montage
  film studies, 1:1155, 1:1168

middle to late twentieth-century American literature, 1:957, 1:985
prosody, 1:909
Montage technique
Chinese literature, 2:241
German literature, 2:576
Montessori Method, 3:265
Moonies, *See* Unification Church
Moors, 3:384
Moral philosophy, history of, 5:56
Morality, *See also* Ethics
modern Western philosophy, 4:158
Western philosophy
1700–1800, 4:193, 4:203
1800–1900, 4:254
twentieth-century, 4:277, 4:299
Morality plays, 1:156, 1:160
modern British and Irish drama, 1:480
Renaissance, British, 1:167
Morality tale
Brazilian literature, 2:898
Yiddish literature, 2:41
Mormons, *See* Latter-Day Saints
Morrill Act of 1862, 5:260
Motherhood, studies on, 5:204
Motion, laws of, 5:705
Motion picture, *See* Film studies
Motion pictures, *See* Film
Motivation, 3:175–76
Mott transistors, 5:704
Movement poetic school, 1:416, 1:466, 1:481, 1:491, 1:497, 1:501, 1:507
Movements, social, 3:215
Movie-going, 2:880
MRI, *See* Magnetic resonance imaging
Muckraking, 3:823
Mudge Method, *See* Hutchins Heuristic
Multiculturalism, reference works, 1:119
Multidisciplinary approach, contemporary philosophicalissues, 4:376
Muons, 5:721
Musculoskeletal disorders, 5:396, 5:399–400
Music, 3:653–731, *See also* Dance
appreciation of, 3:664–65
authors, 3:673–731

folk song and dance, 3:850–53
general reference, 3:653–58
history and criticism of, 3:658–64
instruments, 3:671–72
singers, 3:672
types of
conductors, 3:671
contemporary, 3:665–66
ethnic, 3:666–67
film, 3:667
jazz, 3:667–69
non-Western, 3:669–70
opera, 3:670–71
Music, contemporary philosophical issues, 4:392
Music appreciation, 3:664–65
Musical instruments, 3:671–72
Musical theater
modern British and Irish drama, 1:531
twentieth-century American, 1:1071
rock, 1:1113
Victorian period, 1:321, 1:356
Muslims, 3:441, 3:450, *See also* Islamic culture and nations
Egypt conquered by, 3:444–45
expelled from Iberia, 3:384
Indian literature, 2:181
Islamic religion, 4:564, 4:565, 4:566
medieval Judaism, 4:625
Mesopotamia conquered by, 3:449
Persia conquered by, 3:447
society and politics, 4:577
Spanish literature, 2:519, 2:520
Mussolini, Benito, 3:99
Mutations
defined, 5:779
enzyme blocking and, 5:788
radiation and, 5:808
Myanmar (Burma), 3:489
Myrdal, Alva, 3:235
Mystery cults
Greek ancient religion, 4:446
oikoumene world, 4:450
Mystery play, *See* Cycle plays
Mystery story, *See* Detective story
Mystery Writers of America, 1:608–9, 1:619, 1:1227–228, 1:1233, 1:1236, 1:1238

Mysticism, *See also* Sufism
Arabic literature, 2:64
Bengali literature, 2:182
Chinese literature, 2:201
early nineteenth-century American literature, 1:704
early twentieth-century American literature, 1:823
French literature, 2:492, 2:514
Hebrew literature, 2:11, 2:15
Islamic philosophy, 4:375
Islamic religion, 4:574–77
late Christianity, 4:786, 4:788
Latin American literatures, 2:855
Lithuanian literature, 2:805
medieval Christianity, 4:695
medieval Judaism, 4:629
medieval philosophy, 4:111, 4:112
Middle English, 1:146, 1:152, 1:155
middle to late nineteenth-century American literature, 1:768
modern British and Irish drama, 1:423
modern British and Irish literature, 1:469
modern British and Irish poetry, 1:560
Netherlandic literature, 2:626
Old Norse-Icelandic literature, 2:643
Persian literature, 2:82, 2:86, 2:92
Portuguese literature, 2:556
Renaissance philosophy, 4:133, 4:149
romantic period, British, 1:305
Russian literature, 2:700, 2:702, 2:721
Spanish literature, 2:520, 2:542, 2:543, 2:550
Swedish literature, 2:673, 2:675
Turkish literature, 2:99, 2:101
Urdu literature, 2:175
Victorian period, 1:390
West African literature, 2:138
Western philosophy, 1600–1700, 4:185
Myth
African literatures, 2:103

Myth (cont.)
Armenian literature, 2:78
Australian literature, 2:955, 2:958
Caribbean literature, 2:935
children's literature, American, 1:1194
British, 1:575
Chinese literature, 2:198
comparative literature, 2:988
Danish literature, 2:652
drama, American, 1:1111
Finnish literature, 2:659
French drama, 2:450, 2:451, 2:468
French literature, 2:512
gay literature, 1:1187, 1:1189
German literature, 2:584, 2:586, 2:604
Germanic religion, 4:437
gnosticism, 4:453
Greek classical drama, 2:342, 2:350
Greek classical literature, 2:341, 2:357, 2:360
Greek modern literature, 2:373
guides, handbooks, dictionaries, 1:133
Hinduism, 4:502
Hittite and Canaanite religions, 4:444
Indian literature, ancient, 2:171
Indian subcontinent literature, 2:170, 2:176
indigenous religions, 4:460, 4:461, 4:463
Irish drama, 1:490
Italian literature, 2:424, 2:437
Japanese literature, 2:290
classical, 2:270
Japanese religion, 4:535
Korean literature, 2:296
Latin American literatures, 2:853, 2:858, 2:868, 2:878
Latin literature, 2:379, 2:389
Lithuanian literature, 2:804
Mesopotamian ancient urban civilization, 4:440
Mexico, 4:456
middle to late nineteenth-century American literature, 1:726
Native American, 1:718

middle to late twentieth-century American literature, 1:942, 1:962, 1:963, 1:976, 1:1009, 1:1013, 1:1018, 1:1022, 1:1036
modern British and Irish literature, 1:455, 1:484–85, 1:502, 1:521
modern Irish drama, 1:423
Native Americans, 1:1135
Netherlandic literature, 2:628
New Zealand literature, 2:976, 2:980
North African literature, 2:114, 2:115
Old English, 1:143
Old Norse-Icelandic literature, 2:639, 2:643
Persian literature, 2:89
popular literature, British, 1:574
Renaissance literature, 1:185
Restoration and eighteenth-century literature, 1:248
romantic period, British, 1:267, 1:277
Russian literature, 2:758
Serbian literature, 2:831, 2:832
Spanish literature, 2:538
study of religion, 4:427
West African literature, 2:124, 2:130, 2:133, 2:140, 2:142, 2:148, 2:150
Mythology, 3:847, 3:853–57, 3:876, See also Folklore
folklore and, 3:846
general works, 3:847–49
reference works, 3:849–50
Mythopoeic school, 2:919

N

Namierism, 3:406
Napoleon, 2:813
Naropa Institute, Colorado, 4:357
Narrative poetry
Caribbean literature, 2:942
Chinese literature, 2:196, 2:216
early nineteenth-century American literature, 1:682

East African literature, 2:151
French literature, 2:509
Greek classical literature, 2:341, 2:360
Lithuanian literature, 2:805
modern British and Irish poetry, 1:518
Philippine literature, 2:327
romantic period, British, 1:293, 1:296
Russian literature, 2:734, 2:738, 2:742, 2:750
Thai literature, 2:337
Victorian period, 1:382, 1:400
Vietnamese literature, 2:338
Nasser, Gamal Abdul, 3:445
NASTS, See National Association of Science, Technology, and Society
Nation of Islam, See Black Muslims
National anthem, 2:657
National Association for the Advancement of Colored People (NAACP), 3:577
National Association of Science, Technology, and Society, 5:51, 5:176
National Book Award
children's literature, American, 1:1204
early twentieth-century American literature, 1:835, 1:857, 1:866, 1:869, 1:898
early twentieth-century American poetry, 1:825, 1:886, 1:900
middle to late twentieth-century American poetry, 1:933, 1:950, 1:970, 1:993, 1:1005, 1:1015, 1:1025, 1:1038
modern British and Irish literature, 1:435
science fiction, 1:1259
National Book Critics Circle Award
middle to late twentieth-century American literature, 1:979, 1:996, 1:1018, 1:1040, 1:1050
middle to late twentieth-century American poetry, 1:984
National Bureau of Economic Research, 3:97
National Council of Churches, 5:177

National Farmers Union, 5:268
National income, 3:89–90
National Institute of Arts and Letters Literary Award, 5:269
National literatures
comparative, 2:981
cultural identity, 2:2
relationships, 2:1
National Psychological Association for Psychoanalysis, 5:466
National Socialists, *See* Nazism
National Theatre, English, 1:424, 1:449, 1:464, 1:479, 1:524, 1:553
Nationalism, 3:340, 3:375, 3:605
Native Americans, 3:554–58
Bible, 4:801
Brazilian literature, 2:891, 2:898
Canadian literature, 2:903, 2:914, 2:926, 2:927
captivity narrative, 1:1211, 1:1244
detective story, 1:1231
drama, American, 1:1069, 1:1098
early American literature, 1:625
collections, 1:631
early nineteenth-century American literature, 1:682, 1:690, 1:696
folklore of, 3:864–66
indigenous religions, 4:463–66
languages of, 3:39
Latin American literatures, 2:852–53, 2:860, 2:865, 2:868, 2:878, 2:881, 2:885
literary theory, 1:1135
middle to late nineteenth-century American literature, 1:710, 1:718, 1:726, 1:749, 1:760
middle to late twentieth-century American literature, 1:1016, 1:1046, 1:1051
westerns, 1:1215, 1:1217
Natural gas
coal, oil, and gas, 5:285–86
petroleum engineering, 5:241
political concerns, 5:280
shortages, 5:276–77
Natural history, 5:817–19
Natural law, 3:337

Natural philosophy, modern Western philosophy, 4:157
Natural resources, 3:47–48
applied science, 5:634–37
Natural rights, Western philosophy, 1600–1700, 4:186
Natural selection, 5:792, 5:811
Naturalism, 5:95
Australian drama, 2:967
Australian literature, 2:961
Danish literature, 2:651
drama, American, 1:1080
early twentieth-century American literature, 1:802, 1:829, 1:833, 1:861
Finnish literature, 2:660
French literature, 2:445, 2:517
German literature, 2:564, 2:586, 2:614
Hungarian literature, 2:902
Italian literature, 2:419
Japanese literature, 2:292
middle to late nineteenth-century American literature, 1:712, 1:721, 1:773, 1:776
middle to late twentieth-century American literature, 1:994
modern British and Irish literature, 1:419
Netherlandic literature, 2:625
Norwegian literature, 2:668
Polish literature, 2:810
Serbian literature, 2:830
Slovak literature, 2:833
Spanish literature, 2:521, 2:527, 2:546
Victorian period, 1:380
Western philosophy, twentieth-century, 4:259
Yiddish literature, 2:42
Nature, *See also* Pastoral theme
Arabic literature, 2:69
Brazilian literature, 2:900
Chinese literature, traditional, 2:197, 2:201, 2:214, 2:227
French literature, 2:466
German literature, 2:595
Greek modern literature, 2:373
Japanese literature
classical, 2:270
modern, 2:281

Latin American literatures, 2:881
Lithuanian literature, 2:805
Russian literature, 2:749, 2:771
Nature, in Renaissance philosophy, 4:123, 4:133, 4:137
Nature writing
children's literature, British, 1:584
early American literature, 1:626, 1:631, 1:640
early nineteenth-century American literature, 1:661, 1:669, 1:699, 1:703, 1:704
middle to late nineteenth-century American poetry, 1:745
middle to late twentieth-century American literature, 1:983, 1:1021, 1:1051
middle to late twentieth-century American poetry, 1:934
modern British and Irish literature, 1:491, 1:521, 1:557
Renaissance literature, 1:188, 1:199
Restoration and eighteenth-century poetry, 1:261
Victorian period, 1:365
Naval engineering, 5:238–39, 5:249
Nazism, 3:183, 3:189, 3:281, 3:291, 3:342, 3:375
American dramatists affected by, 1:1103
Bauhaus under, 3:776
Christian authors affected by, 4:757, 4:759, 4:787, 4:788
Danish authors influenced by, 2:652
deconstruction, 1:966, 1:1142
European Jews under, 3:347, 4:635, 4:642
film studies, 1:1175
French authors influenced by, 2:450, 2:464, 2:465, 2:473, 2:489, 2:492, 2:506
Frisian literature, 2:634
German authors influenced by, 2:564, 2:568–69, 2:570–71, 2:575–76, 2:582, 2:587, 2:590–91, 2:600–1, 2:608, 2:611–12, 2:614–15, 2:617

Nazism (*cont.*)
German philosophers af-
fected by, 4:298, 4:299
association with, 4:290
escaping, 4:392, 4:394,
4:407
Greek authors influenced
by, 2:372, 2:376, 2:377
Italian authors influenced
by, 2:409, 2:421, 2:425,
2:429
Jewish authors affected by,
4:660, 4:663, 4:664,
4:900
Jewish philosophers affected by, 4:220, 4:234
Jewish scholars affected
by, 4:493
middle to late twentieth-
century American liter-
ature, 1:1063, 1:1064
music under, 3:729
Netherlandic literature,
2:626, 2:628, 2:630
Norwegian authors influ-
enced by, 2:664
Polish authors influenced
by, 2:812, 2:813, 2:815,
2:820
Swedish authors aiding escape, 2:676
Yiddish authors
escaping, 2:38
influenced by, 2:49
Yiddish literature, 2:28
Nebula Award for science
fiction, 1:1253, 1:1261,
1:1263
Nebular hypothesis, 5:698
Negritude movement
African literatures, 2:104
Caribbean literature, 2:929
West African literature,
2:146
Neo-Kantian ethics, 5:93
modern Western philoso-
phy, 4:159
Western philosophy, twen-
tieth-century, 4:279
Neo-Thomism, Western phi-
losophy, twentieth-cen-
tury, 4:260, 4:269,
4:285
Neoclassical economics, 3:93
Neoclassicism
Arabic literature, 2:73
French drama, 2:470, 2:498
French literature, 2:515
Neolithic period, prehistoric
religion, 4:433
Neon, 5:754
Neoplatonism, 4:60–62
Greek philosophy, 4:77

medieval philosophy, 4:114
Roman philosophy, 4:86
Neorealism
Italian literature, 2:411,
2:429, 2:431, 2:438,
2:442
Latin American literatures,
2:870
Portuguese literature,
2:557, 2:560
Russian literature, 2:749,
2:774
Neoricans, *See under* Latin
American literatures,
Puerto Rican authors
Neoromanticism, 2:7
modern British and Irish
poetry, 1:416
Nerve growth factor, 5:790,
5:804
Netherlandic culture and
society
criticism, 2:626, 2:629,
2:632–33
Netherlandic literature,
2:619–36
authors, 2:622–33
collections, 2:622
drama, 2:632
English language, 2:621
Frisian, *See* Frisian litera-
ture
history and criticism, 2:621
women authors, 2:625,
2:626, 2:627
Netherlands, 3:379–80,
3:382–83
Jews in, 3:346
seventeenth century, 3:336
Neuroanatomy, 5:810
Neurological diseases,
5:391–94
Neurology, 5:339–43
Neuron theory, 5:810
Neurophysiology, 5:364
Neurospora Crassa fungus,
5:788
Neustadt International Prize
for Literature
Czech literature, 2:794
Polish literature, 2:817
Neutral K-meson, 5:679,
5:686
Neutrinos, 5:708
Neutron bomb, 5:133
Neutron bombardment, 5:684
Neutron stars, 5:677
New Age movement, reli-
gious movements,
twentieth-century,
4:854, 4:857, 4:865
New American Bible,
4:803–4

New Criticism
early twentieth-century
American literature,
1:806, 1:808, 1:816,
1:874, 1:888, 1:892
literary theory, American
literature, 1:1129,
1:1130, 1:1137, 1:1154
middle to late twentieth-
century American liter-
ature, 1:953, 1:993
modern British and Irish
literature, 1:467, 1:471
New Deal, 5:184
New England
early nineteenth-century
American literature,
1:660, 1:665, 1:668–69,
1:672, 1:674, 1:677,
1:682, 1:684, 1:695,
1:698, 1:700, 1:704,
1:708
early twentieth-century
American literature,
1:796, 1:841
Gothic fiction, 1:598
middle to late nineteenth-
century American liter-
ature, 1:718, 1:721,
1:731, 1:733, 1:745,
1:749, 1:760, 1:769,
1:770, 1:786
middle to late twentieth-
century American liter-
ature, 1:1005
popular American litera-
ture, 1:1197
New England, folklore of,
3:857–58
New English Bible, 4:803,
4:804
New France (Canada), 3:604,
3:611–12
New Harmony, Indiana,
communal groups,
4:843
"New Humanism," 5:55
New journalism, 1:916,
1:1011
New Left, 5:94
New novelists
French literature, 2:445,
2:473, 2:493, 2:500,
2:505
New poetry movement
Arabic literature, 2:63, 2:72
Persian literature, 2:94
Turkish literature, 2:98
New Realism, Western phi-
losophy, twentieth-cen-
tury, 4:260

New Revised Standard Version, 4:804
New Testament, 4:792
  historical background, 4:806, 4:807
  introduction to study of, 4:815–17
  theological study, 4:826, 4:829–34
  topic and author masterworks, 4:824–26
New Thought movement, 4:847
New Wave (film), 3:824, 3:837, 3:842
New World civilization, See American civilization
New World religions
  ancient urban civilization, 4:419, 4:453–58
  Inca, 4:458
  Mesoamerica, 4:454–57
New York City
  Yiddish authors, 2:36, 2:37, 2:39
  Yiddish literature, 2:42, 2:44
New York Drama Critics Circle Award
  early twentieth-century American drama, 1:883, 1:903
  middle to late twentieth-century American drama, 1:1080, 1:1081
  modern British and Irish drama, 1:445, 1:480, 1:500, 1:553
  twentieth-century American drama, 1:1089, 1:1093, 1:1095, 1:1102–3, 1:1107–8, 1:1112, 1:1115, 1:1117, 1:1119, 1:1121–22
New York Film Critics Award, 1:1166
New York Institute for Gestalt Therapy, 5:464
New York Psychoanalytic Institute, 5:433
New York school, 1:911, 1:935, 1:1002, 1:1025
New York Stock Exchange, 5:251
New York Times (newspaper), 3:822
New York World (newspaper), 3:820
New York Zoological Society Gold Medal, 5:829
New Zealand, 3:493–95

New Zealand culture and society
  colonialism, 2:969
  Polynesians, Maoris, 2:969, 2:975, 2:976, 2:977
  Samoan, 2:979
New Zealand literature, 2:969–80
  authors, 2:971–80
  children's, 2:975
  collections, 2:971
  history and criticism, 2:970–71
  Maori authors, 2:970, 2:975–77
  Samoan author, 2:979
  women authors, 2:973, 2:975, 2:976, 2:978
Newbery Award for children's literature, 1:1204
Newbery, John, 1:576
Newgate novel, 1:316
Newspaper, 3:799, 3:800, 3:820, 3:822
  British popular literature, 1:591
  early nineteenth-century American literature, 1:658, 1:667, 1:671–72, 1:683
  identification tools, 1:72
  journalism and, 3:804–9
  indexes, 1:111
  Victorian period, 1:311
Newtonianism, modern Western philosophy, 4:157
NGF, See Nerve growth factor
Niagara Movement, 3:577
Nicaragua, 3:639
Nicaraguan authors, See under Latin American literatures
Nihilism
  Bulgarian literature, 2:781
  early twentieth-century American poetry, 1:841
  French literature, 2:503
  German literature, 2:595, 2:603
  Japanese philosophy, 4:365
  Korean literature, 2:306
  modern British and Irish drama, 1:449
  modern British and Irish literature, 1:412, 1:547
  Netherlandic literature, 2:622, 2:626
  Spanish literature, 2:548
  Western philosophy, 1800–1900, 4:246

1960s, dissident culture, 5:175
Nineteenth century
  aeronautics and aviation, 5:218
  agriculture and food technology, 5:259
  algebra, 5:483
  bibliography, 5:45–47
  biological sciences, 5:757
  botany, 5:766
  calculus, 5:490
  geometry, 5:486
  zoology, 5:768
Nineteenth-century American literature, See Early nineteenth-century American literature; Middle to late nineteenth-century American literature
Nineteenth-century Europe, 3:340–41
Nirvana, Buddhism, 4:510
Nitrogen, 5:731, 5:748
NMR, See Nuclear magnetic resonance imaging
Noah's Ark, 2:911
Nobel Prize
  African literatures, 2:104
  Arabic literature, 2:67
  Australian literature, 2:945, 2:964
  biological sciences, 5:788, 5:789–91, 5:796, 5:800, 5:800–802, 5:804, 5:806–8, 5:810, 5:812–13, 5:837
  Burmese literature, 2:314
  Caribbean literature, 2:942
  chemistry, 5:710–11, 5:738, 5:740–41, 5:743, 5:745–46, 5:748–49, 5:751 5:753–55
  contemporary religious issues, 4:905
  Czech literature, 2:788, 2:794
  Danish literature, 2:645, 2:651
  early twentieth-century American literature, 1:834, 1:844, 1:853
  Eastern religions, 4:558
  economics, 3:68–70, 3:76–78, 3:81–84, 3:87–91, 3:98–99, 3:103–4, 3:107–8, 5:519
  Finnish literature, 2:657, 2:660

Nobel Prize (*cont.*)
French literature, 2:459,
2:463, 2:477, 2:479,
2:489, 2:492, 2:501,
2:509
German literature, 2:569,
2:574, 2:586, 2:589,
2:601, 2:608
Greek literature, 2:370,
2:373, 2:376
Hebrew literature, 2:11
Indian literature, 2:182
Italian literature, 2:399,
2:412, 2:419, 2:427,
2:434, 2:437
Japanese literature, 2:281,
2:288
late Christianity, 4:771
Latin American literatures,
2:842–43, 2:853, 2:866,
2:873, 2:878
literature, 3:400–1
middle to late nineteenth-
century American liter-
ature, 1:730, 1:731
middle to late twentieth-
century American liter-
ature, 1:945, 1:1048,
1:1049, 1:1064, 1:1965
modern British and Irish
literature, 1:438, 1:470,
1:472, 1:481, 1:483,
1:544–45, 1:570, 1:571
Norwegian literature,
2:662, 2:663, 2:664,
2:668
Old Norse-Icelandic literature, 2:640, 2:641
peace, 3:235, 3:935–36
physics, 5:664, 5:670–73,
5:675–82, 5:684–86,
5:690, 5:693, 5:695–98,
5:701–704, 5:707–710,
5:712–21
physiology or medicine,
3:190–91, 3:194–95,
5:18, 5:364, 5:406,
5:407–8, 5:789–91,
5:796 5:800–2, 5:804,
5:812–13, 5:825, 5:832,
5:835
Polish literature, 2:810,
2:817, 2:820, 2:821
Russian literature, 2:703,
2:706, 2:745, 2:755,
2:759
Scandinavian literatures,
2:638
Serbian literature, 2:827,
2:828
South African literature,
2:161

Spanish literature, 2:529,
2:531, 2:533, 2:542
Swedish literature, 2:671,
2:675, 2:676, 2:677
Tibetan philosophy, 4:356
twentieth-century American
drama, 1:1106
Victorian period, 1:369,
1:370
West African literature,
2:147
Western philosophy
1800–1900, 4:219
twentieth-century, 4:320,
4:321, 4:328
Yiddish literature, 2:46
Noma Award, 2:132
Nominalism
contemporary philosophical
issues, 4:402
medieval philosophy, 4:93,
4:120
Western philosophy,
1700–1800, 4:190
Non-Western music, 3:669–70
Nonconservation of parity,
5:720
Noncrystalline solids, 5:668
Nonfiction novel, 1:916,
1:958
Nonsense poetry
children's literature
American, 1:1207
British, 1:581, 1:586
Nonviolence
contemporary religious issues, 4:895
Indian philosophy, 4:351
Jainism, 4:509
late Christianity, 4:772
Noogenesis, 4:336
Norman England
(1066–1154), 3:356–57
Norse mythology, Germanic
religion, 4:437
North Africa, 3:418–19
non-Islamic and non-Jew-
ish tradition, 4:544–48
North African literature,
2:114–23
authors, 2:113, 2:117–23
collections, 2:117
drama, 2:121
history and criticism, 2:117
languages, 2:116
Amharic, 2:121
Arabic, 2:120
French, 2:118, 2:119,
2:122, 2:123
Somali, 2:121
praises and boasts, 2:114
Western influence, 2:116

women authors, 2:116,
2:119, 2:120
North America
Columbus's voyages to,
3:915–17
exploration of, 3:922–23,
3:941–42
indigenous religions, 4:459,
4:463, 4:464
modern Judaism, 4:638–41
regional geography of,
3:124
travel in, 3:894–98
North Pole, 3:912, 3:914–15,
3:932–33
Northern European history,
3:378–80
Low Countries, 3:382–83
Scandinavia, 3:381–82
surveys and general works,
3:380–81
Northern Ireland, 3:352,
3:371
Norway, 3:379, 3:381–82
Norwegian literature,
2:661–70
authors, 2:639, 2:663–70
collections, 2:662
drama, 2:665
history and criticism, 2:662
women authors, 2:662,
2:667, 2:668, 2:670
Nubian literature, *See* North
African literature
Nuclear Energy Agency,
5:186
Nuclear engineering,
5:239–41
Nuclear fission, 5:142, 5:602,
5:657, 5:719
Nuclear gamma radiation,
5:703
Nuclear magnetic resonance
imaging, 5:672
Nuclear physics, 5:657–58
contributions to, 5:689,
5:710
general works, 5:658
group theory, 5:720
history of, 5:658
Nuclear power
anti-nuclear movements,
5:172
control of plants, 5:242
developments, philosophi-
cal studies of, 5:73–77
ethical issues, 5:105,
5:108–113, 5:133
plant construction, 5:286
Nuclear reactors, 5:671,
5:684
Nuclear safety, 5:277, 5:286
Nuclear submarines, 5:238

Nuclear test ban treaty of 1963, 5:108
Nuclear waste, 5:239
Nuclear weapons, *See also* Atomic bomb; Hydrogen bomb; Neutron bomb
consequences of nuclear war, 5:831
ethical issues, 5:108–113
plutonium, 5:719
radar-controlled bombing systems, 5:717
test ban treaties, 5:133
Nucleic acids, 5:813
Number theory, 4:229, 5:488–89, 5:506–508
Numismation, 3:306
Nursery rhymes
children's literature, British, 1:580, 1:583
Nursing as a profession, 5:337–38, 5:362
Nursing homes, 5:334
Nutrition and diet, 5:344–49, 5:394–95

O

Obie Award
early twentieth-century American drama, 1:881
modern British drama, 1:458
twentieth-century American drama, 1:1087, 1:1089, 1:1094, 1:1099, 1:1110, 1:1121–22
Objectification, 2:500
Objective poetry, 2:446, 2:494
Objectivism
early twentieth-century American poetry, 1:899, 1:900
middle to late twentieth-century American poetry, 1:1036
modern British and Irish poetry, 1:560
Obstetrics, 5:354–60
Occasional verse, 1:255, 1:678, 1:934, 1:966
Occasionalism, Western philosophy, 1600–1700, 4:181
Occult, 2:666
adventure/thriller, 1:596
horror story, 1:1243
modern British and Irish literature, 1:570

religious movements, twentieth-century, 4:853, 4:854, 4:860
Rosicrucianism, 4:848
Victorian period, 1:340
Occupational health and safety, 5:243–44, 5:352–54
Ocean, studies of, 5:828–29
Oceania (Pacific Island nations), 3:493–96
indigenous religions, 4:461
travel in, 3:901–6
Oceanography, 5:630–32, 5:640–41, 5:648
history of, 5:32–33
Oceans, exploration of, 3:918, 3:920
Ode
romantic period, British, 1:267, 1:293, 1:302, 1:305
OECD, *See* The Organization for Economic Cooperation and Development
Oedipus complex, 5:445, 5:457
Oedipus legend
German literature, 2:586
Spanish literature, 2:532
OEEC, *See* Organization for European Economic Cooperation
O. Henry Award, 1:867, 1:1025, 1:1225
Oikoumene world
faith healing, 4:450
gnosticism, 4:452
Hellenistic world, 4:448–53
imperial cult, 4:451
magic, 4:448, 4:450, 4:451
mystery cults, 4:450
Roman Empire, 4:448–53
Oil
coal, oil, and gas, 5:285–86
crisis, 5:1970s, 5:276–77, 5:288
crude oil, 5:241
political concerns, 5:279–81, 5:290
Old English, 1:140, 1:141–44
collections, 1:143
conventional devices, 1:141–42, 1:143
history and criticism, 1:142–43
middle to late twentieth-century American literature, 1:978
Old Norse-Icelandic literature, 2:639–44
authors, 2:638, 2:641–44
collections, 2:640
history and criticism, 2:640

Old Stone Age, *See* Paleolithic period
Old Testament, 4:792
introduction to study of, 4:815–17
texts, 4:794
theological study, 4:826, 4:834, 4:837
topic and author masterworks, 4:822–24
Olmecs, 4:454, 4:455
On-line service
bibliography, 1:64
dictionaries, 1:89
encyclopedias, 1:105
general reference, 1:80
Oncogene, 5:790
Oncology, *See* Cancer
Oneida community, 4:843
Onitsha market literature
East African literature, 2:151
West African literature, 2:135, 2:140
Ontological argument, Western philosophy, twentieth-century, 4:288
Ontology
contemporary issues, 4:380
Western philosophy, twentieth-century, 4:283
OPEC, *See* Organization of Petroleum Exporting Countries
Opera, 3:670–71
Victorian period, travesties, 1:356
Ophthalmology, 5:339–43
Opinions, 3:176
public opinion, 3:147–48, 3:157
Optics, 5:665–67
general works, 5:666
history, 5:666–67
Oral biography, 240
Oral contraceptives, 5:743
Oral tradition
African literatures, 2:103
American literature, 1:1193
Armenian literature, 2:75, 2:78
Australian literature, 2:944
Bible, 4:792, 4:796, 4:835
Canadian literature, 2:903
Caribbean literature, 2:933
Celtic religion, 4:436
children's literature, British, 1:574, 1:575, 1:577
Chinese literature, 2:216
early American literature, 1:625
East African literature, 2:152

Oral tradition (*cont.*)
  Eastern religions, 4:496
  Frisian literature, 2:633
  German literature, 2:584
  Greek Byzantine literature,
    2:344
  Greek literature, 2:341
  indigenous religions, 4:459
  Japanese religion, 4:535
  Korean literature, 2:296,
    2:297
  Laotian literature, 2:322
  Macedonian literature,
    2:807
  Malay literature, 2:323
  medieval literature, British,
    1:140
  Middle English, 1:148
  middle to late nineteenth-
    century American liter-
    ature, 1:754
  modern British and Irish
    literature, 1:515
  North African literature,
    2:104, 2:114, 2:122
  Old English, 1:141
  Philippine literature, 2:327
  Rabbinic Judaism, 4:619
  Rumanian literature, 2:823
  Serbian literature, 2:826
  South African literature,
    2:156
  Southeast Asian literatures,
    2:310
  Spanish literature, 2:537
  Turkish literature, 2:95
  Ukrainian literature, 2:837
  Vietnamese literature,
    2:338
  West African literature,
    2:131, 2:133, 2:142,
    2:150
Oral traditions, in African
  history, 3:431
Oratory
  early nineteenth-century
    American literature,
    1:667
  Greek classical literature,
    2:343, 2:354
  Latin literature, 2:384,
    2:392
  middle to late twentieth-
    century American liter-
    ature, 1:948
  Roman philosophy, 4:72
Orbital symmetry, conversion
  of, 5:755
Orchestral music
  conductors of, 3:671
  instruments of, 3:671–72

Organic chemistry, 5:730–32,
    5:754
  bonds, 5:730, 5:749
  carboxylic acid, 5:731
  classification schedules,
    5:731
  hydrocarbons, 5:731
  medicinal properties of,
    5:731
  molecules, 5:740, 5:741
  nitrogen, 5:731, 5:748
  orbital symmetry, conver-
    sion of, 5:755
  radioisotope carbon-14,
    5:740
  synthesizing, 5:741
Organic synthesis, 5:741
"Organicism," principle of,
    5:169
Organization for European
  Economic Cooperation,
    5:185
Organization of Petroleum
  Exporting Countries,
    5:276–77, 5:279–80,
    5:290
Organizational directories,
    5:3–4
Organizations, 3:210, 3:234
  industrial, 3:57–58
  social structure of,
    3:215–16
Oriental philosophy, *See*
  Asian philosophy; Chi-
  nese philosophy; Indi-
  an philosophy; Islamic
  philosophy
Ornithology, 5:786
Orphism, Greek ancient reli-
  gion, 4:446
Orthodox Church, Eastern,
  See Eastern Orthodox
  Church
Orthodox Judaism, 4:651,
    4:653
  medieval period, 4:626,
    4:627
Orthopedics, 5:396
Oscar, 1:1166, 1:1178
Osmosis, 5:738
OTA, *See* The U.S. Congres-
  sional Office of Tech-
  nological Assessment
Ottoman Empire, 3:433,
    3:445, 3:452
Out-of-print titles, 1:39, 1:119
Overpopulation, 5:828
Overspecialization, 5:186
Oxford Bible, *See* New En-
  glish Bible
Oxford Playhouse, 1:479
Oxygen, discovery of,
    5:52–53

Oz books, 1:1200
Ozone layer, 5:113

P

Pacific history, 3:461–62,
    3:493, *See also* Asian
    history
  Australia, 3:494
  authors, 3:496–503
  general works, 3:493–94
  Indonesia, 3:491
  Japan, 3:472–80
  New Zealand, 3:494–95
  Oceania, 3:495–96
  Philippines, 3:492–93
  reference works, 3:462–63
  surveys and general works,
    3:463
Pacific Island nations
  (Oceania), 3:493–96
  travel in, 3:901–6
Pacifism, 2:927
  Indian philosophy, 4:351
  Western philosophy, twen-
    tieth-century, 4:320,
    4:321
Paganism
  religious movements, twen-
    tieth-century, 4:864
  Renaissance philosophy,
    4:150, 4:151
Pageant
  drama,
    American outdoor,
      1:1088
    medieval, 1:157
      cycle plays, 1:158
    modern British, 1:471
Pahlavi, Mohammad Reza
  (shah, Iran), 3:447
Pakistan, 3:487
Paleoarchaeology, 3:13
Paleolithic period, prehistoric
  religions, 4:432
Paleontology, 5:637–40, 5:802
  reconstruction of fossils,
    5:791
  Western philosophy, twen-
    tieth-century, 4:335
Palestine, 3:438
  Zionism, 3:347
Palestinians, 3:438–39
  Arabic literature, 2:54,
    2:67, 2:70
  Hebrew literature, 2:7, 2:8,
    2:18
Palomar Observatory, 5:605
Pan-Africanism, 1:831
Panama, 3:639–40

Pancreas and fat metabolism, 5:789
Panpsychism, Western philosophy, twentieth-century, 4:288
Pantheism
  Western philosophy
    1600–1700, 4:186
    twentieth-century, 4:288
Papacy
  late Christianity, 4:740, 4:770
  medieval Christianity, 4:694
Parable
  Canadian literature, 2:911
  German literature, 2:592
  Latin American literatures, 2:866
  middle to late twentieth-century American literature, 1:962
  modern British and Irish drama, 1:446
  North African literature, 2:123
Paradigm, 4:406, 5:53
"Paradoxes of confirmation," 5:91
Paraguay, 3:640
Paraguayan authors, See Latin American literatures
Parallel postulate, 5:486
Parapsychology
  Spiritualism, 4:850
  Theosophy, 4:858
Pareto optimality, 3:99
Pareto's Law, 3:99
Paris, France
  expatriates, 1:566, 1:786, 1:793, 1:812, 1:839, 1:844–45, 1:861, 1:864, 1:881, 1:896, 1:905, 1:938
Parmenidean absolute, Western philosophy, 1800–1900, 4:221
Parnassians, 2:370
Parody
  drama, American, 1:1087, 1:1098
  early twentieth-century American literature, 1:890
  German literature, 2:571
  Greek Hellenistic literature, 2:363
  horror story, 1:599
  Latin American literatures, 2:858, 2:865
  middle to late twentieth-century American literature, 1:949

modern British and Irish drama, 1:544
modern British and Irish literature, 1:412, 1:414, 1:440, 1:503, 1:515, 1:529
North African literature, 2:118
opera, Victorian period, 1:357
Renaissance literature, 1:194
Restoration and eighteenth-century literature, 1:229
romantic period, British, 1:264, 1:275, 1:291, 1:297
Russian literature, 2:730, 2:755, 2:758, 2:772, 2:775
West African drama, 2:148
Participant observation, 3:10
Particle physics, See Elementary particle physics
Pasteurization, 5:409, 5:809
Pastoral theme, See also Nature; Nature writing
  Chinese literature, 2:214, 2:262
  early twentieth-century American poetry, 1:796, 1:841
  French literature, 2:504
  Greek classical literature, 2:359
  Greek Hellenistic literature, 2:343, 2:363, 2:368
  Italian drama, 2:440
  Lithuanian literature, 2:804
  modern British and Irish poetry, 1:450, 1:496
  Renaissance, 1:163–64, 1:167, 1:185, 1:191, 1:195
  Restoration and eighteenth-century poetry, 1:227
  Spanish literature, 2:520
  Victorian period, 1:382
Patents, See Inventors and inventing
Patrick White Prize, 2:949
Patristic philosophy, medieval thought, 4:98–100
Peace, 3:148–49
  ancient history, 3:308–9
  history, 3:277–81
Peas, breeding of, 5:806
Pediatrics, 5:321–23
Pelagianism, early Christianity, 4:685
Peloponnesian War, 3:321–23

PEN Freedom-to-Write Award, 2:321
Pen name, See Pseudonym
Pendulum clock, 5:695
Pendulums, research, 5:603
Penicillin, 5:221, 5:407–408
Penny dreadful, 1:575, 1:591, 1:602
Pentateuch, 4:792, 4:836
Pentecostal movements, 4:467
  late Christianity, 4:715
People's Temple, 4:867
People's theater, 2:501
Perception
  contemporary issues, 4:395
  philosophical issues, 4:382
  medieval philosophy, 4:108
  Western philosophy
    1600–1700, 4:164
    1700–1800, 4:211
    1800–1900, 4:254
    twentieth-century, 4:277, 4:309
Perception, psychology of, 5:411
Perceptions, 3:177, 3:241
Percy, Thomas, 1:148
Pereval group, 2:748
Performance arts
  African literatures, 2:103
  Chinese literature, 2:185
  film studies, 1:1155–79
  dance, 1:1162, 1:1174
  modern British and Irish drama, 1:424
  modern British and Irish literature, 1:547
  dance and song, television, 1:535
  dance, 1:504
  modern British and Irish poetry, 1:492
  poet's theater, 1:1008, 1:1025
  poetry reading, 1:854, 1:912, 1:1028
  Russian poetry, 2:743
  West African drama, 2:133
Pericles, 3:322
Periodic table of elements, 5:708
Periodical
  African American literary theory, 1:1145
  early nineteenth-century American literature, 1:659, 1:672, 1:673, 1:677, 1:702

Periodical (*cont.*)
early twentieth-century
American literature,
1:792, 1:807–8, 1:817,
1:867, 1:888–89, 1:897,
1:901
expatriates, 1:822
identification tools, 1:72
indexes, 1:111
middle to late nineteenth-
century American liter-
ature, 1:721, 1:744,
1:749, 1:758
middle to late twentieth-
century American liter-
ature, 1:980
modern British and Irish
literature, 1:474
Restoration and eighteenth-
century literature,
1:232, 1:257
romantic period, British,
1:273
Victorian period, 1:311,
1:323–24, 1:376
Periodical essay, *See also*
Essay
modern British and Irish
literature, 1:428
Restoration and eighteenth-
century literature,
1:230–31, 1:232–33,
1:249, 1:257
Periodicity, law of, 5:750
Peripatetic school, 4:64, 4:65
books, 4:66–72
membership, 4:90
Perkins, Maxwell, 1:903
Persia (Iran), 3:446–49
Persian Gulf War, 3:805,
5:279
Persian literature, 2:81–94
authors, 2:85–94
children's, 2:94
collections, 2:83–84
general reading, 2:84
history and criticism,
2:82–83
language, 2:81
women authors, 2:87, 2:88,
2:90
Personalism, Western philosophy, twentieth-cen-
tury, 4:259, 4:299
Personality, 3:177–78, *See
also* Psychology
anthropology, 3:15
psychoanalysis, 3:182–83
socialization, 3:216
sociological study of, 3:238
Perspective, light, and color,
5:186

Perspectivism, philosophy of,
2:546
Peru, 3:640
Peruvian authors, *See* Latin
American literatures
Peruvian culture and society
hypocrisy, 2:887
intermingling, Quechua,
2:852
oppressed Indians, 2:885
Pessimism
Western philosophy
1700–1800, 4:192, 4:217
twentieth-century, 4:281
Pesticides, 5:829
Petroleum engineering and
engineering geology,
5:241–42
Pharisees, 4:615
Pharmacology, 5:349–52
Phenomenalism, Western philosophy, twentieth-cen-
tury, 4:320
Phenomenology, 1:1150,
3:227, 5:90, 5:92
contemporary issues, 4:376
modern Western philoso-
phy, 4:159
Western philosophy
1800–1900, 4:234
twentieth-century, 4:261,
4:290, 4:309, 4:318,
4:331
Philip II (King of Macedon),
3:314
Philip II (King of Spain),
3:384, 3:648
Philippine literature,
2:327–34
authors, 2:312, 2:329–34
collections, 2:329
history and criticism, 2:328
Tagalog and other lan-
guages, 2:327, 2:328
Philippines, 3:492–93
Philosophical Radicals, 4:190
Philosophy
African, modern, 4:367–71
ancient history, 3:306–7
ancient religion and,
4:419–94
Asian, modern, 4:348–67,
4:372–75
contemporary issues,
4:376–415
authors, 4:392–415
deconstruction and
postmodernism,
4:390–92
ethics, 4:387–89
general works, 4:378–79
mind, nature of,
4:381–83

problems, state of,
4:379–81
rights and justice,
4:385–87
science, philosophy of,
4:383–85
women authors, 4:394,
4:405
encyclopedias and dictionaries, 4:2, 4:12–15
general histories and surveys, 4:2
general reference, 4:1–8
general, 4:11–43
authors, 4:38–43
women authors, 4:39
geographic area, 4:25–36
Greek and Roman, 4:44–91
handbooks, sourcebooks,
and guides, 4:5–7
Hegelian, 3:74, 3:94,
3:284–85
histories, 3:275–77, 4:15–18
indexes, 4:7, 4:12–15
introductions, 4:19–25
Islam, modern, 4:372–75
Islamic religion, 4:574–77
medieval, 4:92–121
Renaissance, 4:122–56
sociology and, 3:199
Western
1600–1900, 4:157–258
twentieth-century,
4:259–347
Philosophy, comparative, *See*
Comparative philoso-
phy
Philosophy of science,
technology, and
medicine, 5:59–104
artificial intelligence,
5:73–77
attacks on philosophy of
science, 5:61
authors, 5:81–104
biology, 5:67–68
clinical judgment in medicine, 5:78–80
cosmology, 5:67–68
cultural critiques, 5:65–67
decision-making in medi-
cine, 5:78–80
developments, studies of,
5:73–77
engineering, 5:73–77
environmental problems,
5:73–77
epistemological issues,
5:61–65
general reference works,
5:60–61
historical critiques, 5:65–67
medicine, general, 5:77–81

methodological issues,
5:61–65
mind in medicine, 5:80–81
nuclear power, 5:73–77
quantum mechanics,
5:67–68
relativity, 5:67–68
risk assessment, 5:73–77
science, general, 5:61
social critiques, 5:65–67
social sciences, 5:67–68
technology, general,
5:69–77
Phonemic theory, 3:39
Phosphate fertilizer, 5:272–73
Photoelectric effect, 5:664,
5:681–82, 5:702
Photograph book
children's literature, British, 1:581
Depression era, 1:819
early twentieth-century
American literature,
1:825, 1:884
middle to late twentieth-
century American literature, 1:932
modern British and Irish
literature, 1:538
Victorian period, 1:329
Photography, 5:187
Physical anthropology, 3:10,
5:410
Physical chemistry, 5:734–35,
5:754
chemical equilibrium,
5:734
thermodynamics, 5:734–35,
5:746
Physical geography, 3:125–26
Physical geology, See Geophysics
Physical sciences
general reference works,
5:11
history of, 5:31–32
Physics, 5:649–721
astrophysics, 5:653–57
atomic and nuclear phys-
ics, 5:657–58
authors, 5:669–721
beta decay, 5:708
black-body radiation, 5:709
cathode rays, 5:715
classical electrodynamics,
5:673
classical mechanics,
5:659–61, 5:705
condensed matter, 5:668
correspondence principle,
5:673
cosmology, 5:653–57, 5:689
crystalline solids, 5:668

disordered materials, 5:704
eight-fold way, 5:690
electrodynamics, 5:692
electrolysis, laws of, 5:683
electromagmetic induction,
5:683
electromagnetic force,
5:713, 5:718
electromagnetic interac-
tions, 5:685
electromagnetic theory,
5:699
electromagnetic waves,
5:694, 5:700
electrons, 5:673, 5:679,
5:699, 5:702
elementary particle phys-
ics, 5:661–63, 5:686,
5:690, 5:713, 5:720
ellipsoidal figures of equilibrium, 5:677
energy transfer, 5:673
exclusion principle, 5:708
field theory, 5:649
fluxions, method of, 5:705
gamma absorption, 5:703
gamma radiation, 5:703
general physics, 5:650–53
geometrodynamics, 5:719
gravitation, 5:663–665,
5:705
hertz unit of frequency,
5:694
high pressure physics,
5:676
history of, 5:31–32,
5:651–52
hydrodynamics, 5:692
inertia, 5:687
Josephson effects, 5:695
kinetic theory of gases,
5:674
Lamb shift, 5:697
Laplace equation, 5:698
large-number coincidences,
5:680
light waves, 5:701
liquid helium, 5:697
Mach principle, 5:699
magnetic fields, 5:672,
5:699
magnetic monopole, 5:679
mathematical analysis
branch, 5:649
matrix mechanics, 5:675
mechanics, 5:649
microwave radar, 5:697
motion, laws of, 5:705
Mott transistors, 5:704
muons, 5:721
nebular hypothesis, 5:698
neutral K-meson, 5:679,
5:686

neutrinos, 5:708
neutron bombardment,
5:684
neutron stars, 5:677
"no-hair" theorem, 5:691
nonconservation of parity,
5:720
noncrystalline solids, 5:668
nuclear gamma radiation,
5:703
nuclear physics, 5:657–58,
5:689, 5:720
optics, 5:665–67
pendulum clock, 5:695
photoelectric effect,
5:681–82, 5:702
pi-mesons, 5:721
pions, 5:721
plasma physics, 5:667
polarized light, 5:683
quantum electrodynamics
(QED), 5:672, 5:679,
5:685, 5:697, 5:715,
5:717
quantum mechanics,
5:659–61, 5:693, 5:706,
5:716
quantum theory, 5:673,
5:675, 5:678, 5:680,
5:709, 5:714, 5:719
quarks and antiquarks,
5:690
radio waves, 5:694
radio-frequency spectroscopy, 5:697
radioactivity, 5:679, 5:684,
5:710–12
reference works, 5:652–53
relativity, 5:663–65,
5:681–82, 5:703
scanning tunneling micros-
copy, 5:672
semiconductors, 5:704
shock waves, 5:699
solid-state physics,
5:668–69, 5:670
space travel and, 5:670
space-time singularities,
5:691
statistical mechanics, 5:720
stellar evolution, 5:686
stellar movement, 5:680
subatomic particle physics,
5:715
superconductivity,
5:670–71, 5:695–96
synchroton radiation, 5:715
thermodynamics, 5:676
transistor, development of,
5:670
uncertainty principle, 5:693
virtual photons, 5:685
vortex rings, 5:715

Physics (*cont.*)
  wave mechanics, 5:714
  weak currents, 5:690,
    5:713, 5:718
  white dwarf stars, 5:677
Physiography, 5:643
Physiological psychology,
  3:167
Physiology, 5:339–43,
  5:772–73
Pi-mesons, 5:721
Picaresque
  early twentieth-century
    American literature,
    1:884, 1:898
  Renaissance British litera-
    ture, 1:167
  Renaissance literature,
    1:194
Picaresque novel
  Chinese literature, 2:229
  detective story, 1:1226
  early twentieth-century
    American literature,
    1:861
  German literature, 2:585
  Japanese literature, 2:271
  Latin American literatures,
    2:888
  middle to late twentieth-
    century American liter-
    ature, 1:942, 1:946
  Restoration and eighteenth-
    century literature,
    1:256
  Spanish literature, 2:520,
    2:529, 2:544, 2:548
Picture book, *See also*
  Illustration
  children's literature
    American, 1:1194,
      1:1202–3, 1:1206
    British, 1:574, 1:577,
      1:578, 1:580, 1:583
Pilgrim
  Middle English literature,
    1:149
  Renaissance literature,
    1:173
Pioneer life, *See* Frontier life
Pirenne thesis, 3:407
Planetary motion, Western
  philosophy, 1600–1700,
  4:171
Planning
  economic, 3:78
  policy planning and formu-
    lation, 3:146
  social, 3:244
  urban, 3:124
Plasma physics, 5:657
  general works, 5:667
  history of, 5:667

Plastic surgery, 5:396–97
Plate tectonics, 5:648
Platonism
  books, 4:77–85
  Middle Platonism, 4:59
  Neoplatonism, 4:60–62
  Renaissance philosophy,
    4:122–23, 4:140
Play techniques, psycho-
  therapy, 5:457
Pleasure
  Greek philosophy, 4:73
  Renaissance philosophy,
    4:155
  Roman philosophy, 4:75
Pléiade, the, 2:502
Pluralism
  contemporary philosophical
    issues, 4:377, 4:380
  pre-Socratic philosophy,
    4:52
Plutonium, 5:719, 5:754
Poet laureate
  early twentieth-century
    American poetry, 1:841
  middle to late twentieth-
    century American po-
    etry, 1:954, 1:970,
    1:1021, 1:1061
  modern British and Irish
    poetry, 1:444, 1:497,
    1:511, 1:519
  Restoration and eighteenth-
    century poetry, 1:240
  romantic period, British,
    1:304
  United States, 2:704
  Victorian period, 1:313,
    1:314, 1:399
Poetry reading , 1:854, 1:912,
  1:1028
Poet's Corner in Westminster
  Abbey, 1:150, 1:400
Poisons, *See* Toxicology
Poland, 3:388, 3:390
  immigrants in United
    States from, 3:241
  Jews in, 3:346
  philosophy, 4:30
Polarized light, 5:683
Policy planning and formula-
  tion, 3:146
Policy sciences, 3:156–57
Policy-making, science and
  technology, 5:178,
  5:179–86
  energy policy, U.S.,
    5:281–83
  oil, geopolitics, 5:279–81
  public policy, 5:335
  research institutions,
    5:183–86

Polish literature, 2:809–22
  authors, 2:778, 2:812–22
  collections, 2:811
  drama, 2:813, 2:815, 2:818,
    2:820, 2:822
  history and criticism, 2:811
Political economy, 3:92,
  3:106
Political geography, 3:123
Political history of United
  States, 3:541–44
Political ideologies, 3:139–41
Political parties, 3:234
Political science, 3:4,
  3:137–65, *See also*
    Political Science and
    Philosophy
  authors, 3:149–65
  civil liberties and civil
    rights, 3:139
  comparative political ideol-
    ogies, 3:139–41
  comparative political sys-
    tems, 3:141
  constitutionalism and fed-
    eralism, 3:141–42
  democratic theory and
    practice, 3:142–43
  electoral politics, 3:143–44
  histories and surveys,
    3:138–39
  international relations,
    3:144–45
  law and society, 3:145
  legislative behavior, 3:146
  policy planning and formu-
    lating, 3:146
  presidency, 3:146–47
  public administration,
    3:147
  public opinion, 3:147–48
  reference and methodol-
    ogy, 3:138
  state and local govern-
    ment, 3:148
  war and peace, 3:148–49
Political science and
  philosophy
  contemporary issues, 4:377,
    4:386, 4:394, 4:407
  medieval thought, 4:98
  modern Western philoso-
    phy, 4:158
  Renaissance, 4:133–34,
    4:144
  Western philosophy
    1600–1700, 4:173, 4:178
    1700–1800, 4:204, 4:210,
      4:213
    1800–1900, 4:227,
      4:230–31, 4:241
    twentieth-century, 4:313
Political systems, 3:141

Pollution
  air pollution, energy concerns, 5:277
  pesticides, 5:829
Polygamy, Latter-Day Saints, 4:845
Polymers, 5:745–46
Pop art, 3:795
Pop culture, 2:880
Pope, *See* Papacy
Popular culture, 3:624, 3:846, 3:872–74
  authors, 3:874–88
Popular humor, 3:870–72
Population, 3:92
  demography, 3:241
  geography, 3:127
  growth, 5:134, 5:247
  industrialization and, 3:339
  sociological study of, 3:205–6
Pornography
  Chinese literature, 2:209, 2:226
  French literature, 2:455
  middle to late twentieth-century American literature, 1:1004
  romances, 1:618
Portugal, 3:384–86, 3:414, 3:623
Portuguese literature, 2:556–61
  authors, 2:558–61
  drama, 2:561
  general bibliography, 2:557
Positive thinking, *See* New Thought movement
Positivism, 5:84, 5:91, 5:95, 5:98, 5:99
  modern Western philosophy, 4:159
  Western philosophy, 1800–1900, 4:222
Posthumous awards
  early twentieth-century American poetry, 1:900
  middle to late twentieth-century American literature, 1:932, 1:960
  middle to late twentieth-century American poetry, 1:1025
Posthumous literature
  Arabic, 2:72
  Canadian, 2:919
  children's literature, American, 1:1208
  contemporary philosophical issues, 4:377
  early nineteenth-century American literature, 1:686

early twentieth-century American literature, 1:829, 1:839
early twentieth-century American poetry, 1:856
Faroese, 2:656
French, 2:492, 2:495
Italian, 2:423
middle to late nineteenth-century American literature, 1:744, 1:776
middle to late twentieth-century American literature, 1:959 1:961, 1:992
middle to late twentieth-century American poetry, 1:1031
modern British and Irish drama, 1:441
modern British and Irish literature, 1:476, 1:518, 1:530, 1:538, 1:540
modern British and Irish poetry, 1:541
romantic period, British, 1:275
Renaissance philosophy, 4:144, 4:153
Russian, 2:767
South African, 2:165
Victorian period, 1:396, 1:405
West African, 2:141
Western philosophy
  1600–1700, 4:168, 4:173
  1700–1800, 4:195, 4:200, 4:213
  1800–1900, 4:227, 4:230, 4:238, 4:244, 4:248
  twentieth-century, 4:280, 4:308, 4:336
Postimpressionism, 3:780–81, 3:794
Postmodernism, 3:199, 3:211
  contemporary philosophical issues, 4:390–92, 4:399, 4:412
  current theological method, 4:889
  Italian literature, 2:400, 2:420
  literary theory, 1:1149
  middle to late twentieth-century American literature, 1:909, 1:935, 1:938, 1:952
  modern British and Irish literature, 1:535
  New Zealand literature, 2:977
  West African literature, 2:143

Poststructuralism, 1:1130, 1:1141
  French feminism, 1:1143
  middle to late twentieth-century American literature, 1:922
Poverty
  anthropological study of, 3:34
  economic study of, 3:66–67, 3:80, 3:112
  sociological study of, 3:211–12
Pragmatism, 2:430, 5:92, 5:95, 5:96
  Chinese philosophy, 4:360
  modern Western philosophy, 4:159
  Western philosophy, 1800–1900, 4:223, 4:235
  Western philosophy, twentieth-century, 4:260, 4:308, 4:317
Prayer, Islamic religion, 4:565
Prayer wheels, 4:543
Pre-Columbian Latin American history, 3:626–28
Pre-Raphaelite Brotherhood, 1:310, 1:314, 1:391, 1:397, 1:474
Pre-Socratic philosophy, 4:49–53
  Atomism, 4:52
  Eleatic school, 4:51
  general works, 4:50
  Milesian school, 4:51
  pluralism, 4:52
Preanimism, ancient religion, 4:421
Pregnancy and childbirth, 5:357–60
Prehistoric religions, 4:419, 4:431–37
  Celtic, 4:436
  Germanic, 4:437
  Indo-European, 4:434
  Neolithic period, 4:433
  Paleolithic period, 4:432
  Proto-Indo-European, 4:434, 4:435
Prejudice, 5:431
Premio Xavier Villaurrutia, 2:868
Presbyterianism, late Christianity, 4:773
Preservation, historical, 2:759
Presidency, 3:146–47
Presidential Medal of Freedom, 1:897
Primatology, 1:1147

Primitive religions, *See* Prehistoric religions
Printing, 3:755
Printing industry
  early nineteenth-century American literature, 1:649
  reference works, 1:6–21
Prison experience
  Chinese literature, 2:200, 2:209, 2:237, 2:239, 2:263
  Christian author, 4:759
  East African literature, 2:153, 2:154
  French literature, 2:476, 2:478, 2:509
  Greek modern literature, 2:375
  Italian literature, 2:423, 2:425
  middle to late nineteenth-century American literature, 1:757
  modern British and Irish literature, 1:441
  Polish literature, 2:812, 2:814
  Renaissance philosophy, 4:147
  Russian literature, 2:683, 2:696, 2:698–99, 2:711–12, 2:734, 2:737, 2:753, 2:755, 2:757, 2:759
  South African literature, 2:157, 2:164, 2:165
  Spanish literature, 2:532, 2:541
  Victorian period, 1:409
  Vietnamese literature, 2:338
  West African literature, 2:131, 2:146, 2:147
  Western philosophy, twentieth-century, 4:286
Privacy issues, 5:124–25, 5:572
Prix des Critiques, 2:493
Prix Femina, 2:493
Prix Goncourt, 2:487, 2:512
  North African literature, 2:117
Prix Médicis
  Czech literature, 2:793
  Hebrew literature, 2:24
Prix Théophraste Renaudot, 2:463
Prizes and awards, *See also* individual prizes, such as Nobel Prize
  African American literary theory, 1:1144

Australian literature, 2:949, 2:961
children's literature, American, 1:1202
Danish literature, 2:653
detective story, British, 1:608, 1:609
drama, American, 1:1080, 1:1084, 1:1086–87, 1:1089, 1:1094, 1:1096, 1:1099, 1:1112, 1:1115, 1:1119–20, 1:1122
early twentieth-century American literature, 1:810, 1:826, 1:835, 1:878, 1:897
early twentieth-century American poetry, 1:841, 1:863, 1:874, 1:899–900
filmmaking, 1:1162, 1:1164, 1:1166
gay literature, 1:1190
German literature, 2:575
Greek literature, 2:372
Hebrew literature, 2:11, 2:17, 2:18, 2:21
horror story, 1:1240
Indonesian literature, 2:319
Italian literature, 2:420
Korean literature, 2:302, 2:303, 2:307, 2:308
Latin American literatures, 2:870
literary theory, 1:1148, 1:1151
Malay literature, 2:325, 2:326
middle to late twentieth-century American literature, 1:931, 1:945, 1:964, 1:973, 1:1021, 1:1025, 1:1030, 1:1034–35, 1:1051, 1:1055, 1:1065
middle to late twentieth-century American poetry, 1:934, 1:936, 1:949, 1:965, 1:971, 1:981, 1:990, 1:995, 1:1000, 1:1004–5, 1:1015, 1:1036, 1:1038, 1:1044–45, 1:1047, 1:1048, 1:1057, 1:1067
modern British and Irish literature, 1:455, 1:476, 1:482, 1:499, 1:516
New Zealand literature, 2:976
Norwegian literature, 2:669
Philippine literature, 2:330, 2:331, 2:333
reference books, 1:135

romances, 1:1222
science fiction, British, 1:612, 1:613
science fiction/fantasy, British, 1:616
screenplay, American, 1:1090
South African literature, 2:162, 2:165
Swedish literature, 2:673
thriller, British, 1:595
Turkish literature, 2:98
West African literature, 2:144
Western philosophy, twentieth-century, 4:282, 4:297, 4:299, 4:301, 4:305, 4:313–14, 4:338
westerns, 1:1214
Yiddish literature, 2:47
Probability theory, 5:518–31
  authors, 5:527–31
  binomial distribution, 5:528
  contributions to, 5:506
  gambler's ruin, 5:527
  general bibliography, 5:521–25
  historical surveys, 5:526–27
  history of, 5:525–26
  law of large numbers, 5:527
  random walk, 5:527
  reference works, 5:520–21
Process philosophy
  Western philosophy, twentieth-century, 4:260, 4:275, 4:288, 4:340
Production agriculture, 5:262–64
Progression d'effet, 1:475
Progressive education, 3:259–60
Propaganda
  Chinese literature, 2:186, 2:237
  Estonian literature, 2:796
  film studies, 1:1164
  German literature, 2:601
  Renaissance drama, 1:168, 1:172
  Russian literature, 2:712, 2:724
Prosody
  Arabic literature, 2:62
  Arabic meter, 2:20
  Australian literature, 2:955
  Canadian literature, 2:907
  children's literature, American, 1:1203
  Chinese traditional literature, 2:187, 2:188

early nineteenth-century
American literature,
1:653–54, 1:691
blank verse, 1:653, 1:654,
1:661
free verse, 1:705
occasional verse, 1:678
sonnet, 1:704
early twentieth-century
American poetry, 1:825
epitaph, 1:858
French drama
Alexandrine, 2:498
French literature, 2:451,
2:502
Greek classical literature,
2:354, 2:359, 2:360
dithyramb, 2:342
Pindaric ode, 2:365
Sapphic meter, 2:366
Italian literature, 2:430
Petrarchan sonnet, 2:433
terza rima, 2:406
Japanese literature, 2:269,
2:271
literary theory, 1:1137
Middle English forms,
1:144–45
Middle English, 1:150
middle to late nineteenth-
century American liter-
ature, 1:717–18
dialect, 1:777
free verse, 1:718
middle to late twentieth-
century American liter-
ature, 1:909
middle to late twentieth-
century American poet-
ry catalytic theory,
1:1026
modern British and Irish
poetry, 1:452,
1:466–67, 1:548, 1:556
pararhyme, 1:533
modern Irish poetry, 1:459
Old English forms,
1:141–42
Old Norse-Icelandic literature
eddic lays, 2:639, 2:642,
2:643, 2:644
skaldic verse, 2:638,
2:643
Persian literature, 2:89,
2:92, 2:93
Portuguese literature, 2:556
ottava rima, 2:558
Renaissance literature,
1:164, 1:177, 1:180
sonnet types, 1:201
Restoration and eighteenth-
century poetry

couplet, 1:241
heroic couplet, 1:227
rhyming dictionaries, 1:95
romantic period, British,
1:266–67
couplet, 1:289, 1:293
metrics, 1:298
ode, 1:293
sonnet, 1:305
Spanish literature, 2:519,
2:528, 2:539, 2:541
Turkish literature, 2:95,
2:99
Urdu literature, 2:175
Victorian period, 1:363–64
blank verse, 1:360
idyl, 1:400
sonnet, 1:336
Prostheses, 5:370–71
Protest, See Dissent, writers
of
Protestant Reformation,
3:333–34
Protestantism
Bible, 4:802, 4:803, 4:804
late Christianity,
4:1500–1560, 4:720,
4:725
theological study of religion, 4:423
Proto-Indo-European reli-
gions, prehistoric,
4:434, 4:435
Protons, 5:661
Protoplasm, 5:811
Proverbs, 1:115
Judaism, 4:598
ancient, 4:615, 4:619
Provincetown Players, 1:860,
1:1106
Pseudonym
Arabic literature, 2:62,
2:65, 2:70
Australian authors, 2:950,
2:952
books on, 1:77
children's literature
American, 1:1194, 1:1203
British, 1:581
Chinese literature, 2:185,
2:251
detective story, 1:1233,
1:1236
British, 1:605
early nineteenth-century
American literature,
1:671, 1:681
early twentieth-century
American literature,
1:811, 1:856
French literature, 2:508
gay literature, 1:1189
Greek authors, 2:373

historical fiction, 1:1247
horror story, 1:1240,
1:1242
Italian authors, 2:407
Japanese authors, 2:271
Malay literature, 2:326
middle to late nineteenth-
century American liter-
ature, 1:757, 1:777,
1:779
middle to late twentieth-
century American liter-
ature, 1:937, 1:956,
1:1022, 1:1031
modern British and Irish
literature, 1:511, 1:522,
1:548, 1:565
modern Irish literature,
1:525, 1:527
Persian authors, 2:89, 2:93
Philippine authors, 2:329
Renaissance literature,
1:197
romances, 1:1221
British, 1:620
romantic period, British,
1:291, 1:295
Russian literature, 2:757
science fiction/fantasy,
British, 1:615
Southeast Asian authors,
2:311
thriller, 1:595, 1:596
Victorian period, 1:333,
1:352, 1:369, 1:373,
1:383
West African literature,
2:132
Western philosophy
1700–1800, 4:217
1800–1900, 4:238
westerns, 1:1212, 1:1215,
1:1218
Yiddish literature, 2:41,
2:45
Pseudoscience
popular works on, 5:8
psychoanalysis as, 5:83
work against influence of,
5:14, 5:16, 5:61
Psoriasis, See Skin diseases
Psychiatry, 5:411–73, See
also Freudian
psychology;
Psychoanalysis
art and neurosis, 5:465
authors, 5:429–73
children, 5:416–17,
5:434–35, 5:444,
5:456–57
client centered theory of
psychotherapy, 5:467

Psychiatry (*cont.*)
depression, treatment,
5:432
disorders, literature,
5:425–29
emotional development,
theories of, 5:472
empathy, 5:457
existentialism and, 5:436,
5:462
general literature, 5:414–15
identity crisis, 5:441
image, role of, 5:458
intensive individual psychotherapy, 5:437
intrapsychic conflict, 5:457
introverts and extroverts,
5:454
libido, theories of, 5:454,
5:457
logotherapy, 5:443
love, 5:449
mental illness, diagnoses,
5:137
"metabletic" method, 5:471
milieu therapy, 5:458
Oedipus complex, 5:445,
5:457
personality disorders, 5:430
rational-emotive therapy
movement, 5:438
schizophrenia, studies of,
5:459, 5:470
self-psychology, 5:457
sexuality, 5:429, 5:430,
5:440, 5:445
social attitudes, study of,
5:431
special reading lists,
5:416–24
therapy and counseling,
methods and ap-
proaches, 5:417–26
Psychoanalysis, 3:182–83,
3:193
archaeological psychoanalysis, 5:466
conventional, 5:451
early twentieth-century
American literature,
1:826
Freudian, 5:435–36, 5:452
literature, 5:424–25
modified approaches, 5:432
pseudoscience, 5:83
Psychoanalytic theory
feminism, 1:1140, 1:1143
Psycho-drama, 1:1095
Psychological anthropology,
3:15
Psychological lifespace, 3:189
Psychological novel
detective story, 1:1231

French literature, 2:445,
2:495
modern British and Irish
literature, 1:469, 1:477
Netherlandic literature,
2:631
romantic period, British,
1:291
Russian literature, 2:712,
2:734
Victorian period, 1:334
Psychologism, Western philosophy, 1800–1900,
4:229, 4:234
Psychology, 3:4, 3:153,
3:166–97, *See also*
Clinical psychology
aggression, 3:170
anthropological, 3:15
authors, 3:179–97
biological bases of behavior, 3:170–71
child psychology, 3:164
cognition, 3:171–72
drama, American, 1:1106
early twentieth-century
American literature,
1:838, 1:894
groups, 3:172–73
history of, 3:167–68
individual development,
3:173–74
intellectual development,
3:266
intelligence and artificial
intelligence, 3:174–75
learning and motivation,
3:175–76
methodology, 3:168–69
middle to late nineteenth-
century American liter-
ature, 1:741, 1:768
middle to late twentieth-
century American liter-
ature, 1:992, 1:1022,
1:1024
modern British and Irish
literature, 1:447, 1:451,
1:494
opinions, attitudes, and beliefs, 3:176
perception, 3:177
personality, 3:177–78
popular literature, British,
1:574
reference works, 3:169–70
Renaissance drama, 1:179
social, 3:232
study of religion, 4:423,
4:424
contemporary issues,
4:890
surveys, 3:168

westerns, 1:1217
women, 3:178–79
Psychotherapy, *See* Clinical
psychology; Psychiatry
humanistic, 3:193
psychoanalysis, 3:182–83
Public access to information,
5:124
Public administration, 3:147
Public economics, 3:67–68
Public health, 5:352–54,
5:366
Public Health Institute, 5:470
Public opinion, 3:147–48,
3:157
Public policy, relation of sci-
ence to, 5:144
Public Utilities Regulatory
Policies Act, 5:286
Publishing, contemporary
philosophical issues,
4:378
Publishing industry, *See also*
Book industry
biographies of persons,
companies, and organi-
zations, 1:39–45
British popular literature,
1:591
romances, statistics, 1:617
Victorian period, 1:317
Puerto Rican authors, *See*
under Latin American
literatures
Puerto Rico, 3:640–41, 3:935
Pugh Professorship, *See* Evan
Pugh Professorship
Pugwash movement, 5:108
Pulitzer Prize
children's literature, American, 1:1203
drama, American, 1:857,
1:903, 1:1080–81,
1:1088, 1:1093, 1:1095,
1:1097, 1:1102–103,
1:1105, 1:1107,
1:1109–110,
1:1115–117, 1:1119,
1:1121–122
early twentieth-century
American literature,
1:810, 1:815, 1:835,
1:843, 1:853, 1:869,
1:877, 1:879, 1:883,
1:892, 1:897–98
early twentieth-century
American poetry,
1:841, 1:856, 1:860,
1:876, 1:878, 1:886,
1:900
historical fiction, 1:1247,
1:1249
history of, 5:50

middle to late nineteenth-century American literature, 1:751, 1:786
middle to late twentieth-century American literature, 1:932, 1:945–46, 1:960–61, 1:964, 1:972, 1:988, 1:996, 1:1007, 1:1013, 1:1016, 1:1018, 1:1021, 1:1047, 1:1050, 1:1053, 1:1064, 1:1066
middle to late twentieth-century American poetry, 1:949–50, 1:970–71, 1:987, 1:995, 1:1001, 1:1003, 1:1005, 1:1031, 1:1038, 1:1045, 1:1048, 1:1051, 1:1061, 1:1067
modern British and Irish poetry, 1:434, 1:435
nonfiction, 5:293
westerns, 1:1214
Pulp fiction
adventure/thriller, 1:598
detective story, 1:1226, 1:1232, 1:1233
science fiction, 1:1252
westerns, 1:1214, 1:1215
Pun
children's literature, British, 1:586, 1:587
Chinese drama, 2:221
French literature, 2:494, 2:496
gay literature, 1:1188
Latin American literatures, 2:857
literary theory, 1:1144
middle to late twentieth-century American literature, 1:1019
modern British and Irish drama, 1:439
modern British and Irish literature, 1:503, 1:504
Renaissance literature, 1:193
Restoration and eighteenth-century literature, 1:256
Swedish literature, 2:678
Punishment, contemporary issues, 4:386
Puppet theater
Indonesia, 2:320
Japanese Bunraku, 2:269, 2:276
Persian drama, 2:82
Spanish literature, 2:531
Pure Land Buddhism, 4:511, 4:512
Chinese religion, 4:529
Eastern religions, 4:496

Japan and Korea, 4:536
Vietnam, 4:520
Puritans
children's literature, 1:1193–94
British, 1:576
early American literature, 1:625–26, 1:633–34, 1:636
early nineteenth-century American literature, 1:648, 1:682
late Christianity, 4:766
Reformation, 4:733
Renaissance literature, 1:173
PURPA, See Public Utilities Regulatory Policies Act
Puzzle books, 5:495–97
Pyramids, 4:441
Mexico, 4:456
Pyrrhonism, 4:58
Pythagorean theorem, 5:504, 5:514

Q

QED, See Quantum electrodynamics (QED)
Quakers, See Friends, Religious Society of
early American literature, 1:626
early nineteenth-century American literature, 1:708
Qualitative analysis, 3:238
Qualitative methods, 3:3
Quantitative methods
economic, 3:63–64
geographic, 3:117, 3:135
Quantum electrodynamics (QED)
contributions to, 5:672, 5:697, 5:715
development of, 5:679, 5:717
interaction among electrons, 5:685
Quantum mechanics, 5:659–61
development of, 5:706, 5:746
founder of, 5:693
general works, 5:659–61
history of, 5:661
philosophical treatments of, 5:67–68
research on, 5:716
Quantum optics, 5:665

Quantum physics, 5:678, 5:680
Quantum theory, 5:673, 5:675, 5:709, 5:714, 5:719
Quarks, 5:661, 5:690
Queen's Gold Medal, 1:549
Quesnay, François, 3:106
Quotations, 1:116–17

R

Rabbi
ancient Judaism, 4:606
Rabbinic Judaism, 4:618–21
Rabbinic literature, 4:609–13
Midrash, 4:609
Mishnah, 4:609, 4:619
Talmuds, 4:609, 4:619
Tosefta, 4:609, 4:619
Rabbinic period, ancient Judaism, 4:606
Rabies, treatment for, 5:409
Race, 3:212, 3:554–58, See also Race relations
Coleman Report on, 3:223
intelligence and, 3:188
intergroup relations, 3:208–9
Myrdal's study of, 3:98, 3:235
United States
sociology of, 3:244
Race relations
adventure/thriller, 1:596
African Americans, 1:1139
African literatures, 2:104, 2:105
Australian literature, 2:960, 2:968
Canadian literature, 2:914, 2:922, 2:927
Caribbean literature, 2:934, 2:935, 2:940, 2:942
children's literature, American, 1:1194
drama, American, 1:1083, 1:1085–86, 1:1090, 1:1096, 1:1119
early twentieth-century American literature, 1:792, 1:797, 1:802, 1:807, 1:831, 1:847, 1:853, 1:856, 1:879, 1:892, 1:905
East African literature, 2:151
filmmaking, 1:1167, 1:1170, 1:1172
gay literature, 1:1188–89

Race relations *(cont.)*
  Latin American literatures,
    2:872
  middle to late nineteenth-
    century American liter-
    ature, 1:710, 1:721,
    1:736, 1:738, 1:760,
    1:771, 1:785
  middle to late twentieth-
    century American liter-
    ature, 1:922, 1:938,
    1:940, 1:1009, 1:1018,
    1:1029
  middle to late twentieth-
    century American poet-
    ry, 1:970
  Native Americans, 1:1135
  Netherlandic literature,
    2:625, 2:628
  New Zealand literature,
    2:970, 2:975, 2:977,
    2:979
  North African literature,
    2:118
  Philippine literature, 2:332
  romances, 1:1225
  science fiction, 1:1258
  Serbian literature, 2:828
  South African literature,
    2:158, 2:160–61,
    2:163–64
    apartheid, 2:157, 2:159,
      2:167
  Swedish literature, 2:679
  West African literature,
    2:125, 2:136
Racism, 3:623
Radar screens, 5:813
Radiation
  effect on human beings,
    5:751
  electromagnetic radiation,
    5:665
  magnetic fields and, 5:699
  mutation and, 5:808
Radiative transfer, 5:677
"Radical monopolies," 5:136
Radical movements, 1960s,
    5:175
Radio, 3:800, 3:809–12
  authors, 3:812–23
  journalism and, 3:804–9
Radio engineering, 5:228
Radio waves, 5:694
Radio-frequency spectro-
    scopy, 5:697
Radioactivity, 5:710–12
  decay, 5:679
  fallout, 5:751
  isotopes, 5:684
  waste, disposal, 5:176
Radiocarbon dating, chemis-
    try, 5:750

Radioisotope carbon-14,
    5:740
Radiology, 5:324, 5:397
Radon, 5:754
Rags-to-riches genre
  children's literature, Ameri-
    can, 1:1193–94
Railroads, engineering, 5:246,
    5:250, 5:254
Ramakrishna Mission, 4:354,
    4:871
Rare books, 1:77–79
  anonymous, keys to,
    1:77–79
  bibliographies and check-
    lists, 1:66, 1:78–79
  collectors and dealers, 1:77
  prices, 1:78
Rational-emotive therapy
  movement, 5:438
Rationalism
  Chinese literature, 2:238
  French literature, 2:477,
    2:510
  Hebrew literature, 2:6,
    2:12
  Jewish thought, 4:646
  modern Western philoso-
    phy, 4:158
  Western philosophy
    1700–1800, 4:209, 4:218
    twentieth-century, 4:280
Reaction rate coefficient,
    5:738
Reading, love of, 1:30–34
  censorship, 1:56–57
Realism, *See also* Social re-
    alism
  African literatures, 2:105
  Armenian literature, 2:79
  Australian literature, 2:957
  Brazilian literature, 2:899
  Burmese literature, 2:313
  Caribbean literature, 2:941
  children's literature,
    American, 1:1195
    British, 1:574, 1:577
  Chinese literature, 2:214,
    2:217, 2:232, 2:239,
    2:255
  Croatian literature, 2:785
  Danish literature, 2:649,
    2:654
  detective story, 1:1227,
    1:1230
  early twentieth-century
    American literature,
    1:818, 1:833, 1:843,
    1:853
  Finnish literature, 2:657
  French literature, 2:475
  German literature, 2:564

  Hebrew literature, 2:7,
    2:15, 2:22
  Italian literature, 2:419,
    2:437, 2:441
  Japanese literature, 2:271,
    2:287, 2:288
  Korean literature, 2:298
  Latin American literatures,
    2:852, 2:853
  Lithuanian literature, 2:806
  middle to late nineteenth-
    century American liter-
    ature, 1:711, 1:721,
    1:737, 1:739, 1:743–44,
    1:749–50, 1:757
  middle to late twentieth-
    century American liter-
    ature, 1:916, 1:940,
    1:988, 1:1002, 1:1022
  middle to late twentieth-
    century American poet-
    ry, 1:1048
  modern British and Irish
    drama, 1:565
  modern British and Irish
    literature, 1:419, 1:482,
    1:515, 1:536, 1:563
  modern Irish drama, 1:526
  North African literature,
    2:119
  Norwegian literature,
    2:662, 2:665, 2:669
  Persian literature, 2:93,
    2:94
  Philippine literature, 2:327
  Polish literature, 2:810,
    2:820
  Portuguese literature, 2:557
  Renaissance drama, 1:176
  Restoration and eighteenth-
    century literature,
    1:239, 1:244
  Rumanian literature, 2:823
  Russian literature, 2:683,
    2:698, 2:706, 2:721,
    2:723, 2:732, 2:742,
    2:752, 2:755, 2:768
  Serbian literature, 2:827
  Slovak literature, 2:833
  Slovenian literature, 2:834
  South African literature,
    2:165
  Spanish literature, 2:521,
    2:537, 2:547
  Swedish literature, 2:671,
    2:679
  thriller, 1:595
  Turkish literature, 2:101
  twentieth-century American
    drama, 1:1070, 1:1071,
    1:1092, 1:1110
  Victorian period, 1:317,
    1:336, 1:348, 1:353

West African literature,
2:139
Western philosophy, twen-
tieth-century, 4:259,
4:280, 4:283, 4:312,
4:332
Yiddish literature, 2:37
Reality
Western philosophy
1800–1900, 4:251
twentieth-century, 4:259
Reaper, invention of, 5:259
Reason
early and medieval Chris-
tianity, 4:674, 4:695
modern Western philoso-
phy, 4:158
Western philosophy
1700–1800, 4:205, 4:210
twentieth-century, 4:276,
4:285
Reason, philosophical studies, 5:88
Reasoning
Japanese philosophy, 4:366
Western philosophy,
1700–1800, 4:199
Reclusiveness
early twentieth-century
American authors,
1:812, 1:891
horror story author, British, 1:601
middle to late nineteenth-
century American
poets, 1:745
middle to late twentieth-
century American au-
thors, 1:1035, 1:1042
Restoration and eighteenth-
century authors, 1:248
romance author, British,
1:621
Reconstruction, 3:526
Reconstructionism, 4:659
Reference works, See also
under specific topics
bibliography, 1:58–79
books about books, 1:3–57
general, 1:89–118
literature, 1:119–35
Reflexes, conditioned, 3:191
Reflexive sociology, 3:228
Reform Judaism, 4:600,
4:651, 4:652
Reformation, 2:585, 3:333–34
late Christianity, 4:716
English, 4:725–27
1500–1560, 4:720–29
radical elements, 4:723–25
Roman Catholic,
4:727–29

late Christianity,
1560–1648, 4:729–38
after Calvin, 4:731
art and music, 4:737
Great Britain, 4:733–36
Lutheranism in Germany
and Scandinavia, 4:730
radical elements, 4:732
Regency poets, 1:264, 1:281
Regional geography,
3:124–25, 3:134
Regional history, of Canada,
3:609–10
Regional literature, See Local-color authors
Regional studies, in Latin
America, 3:631–32
Regression or reversion,
5:529
Regulation, 3:107, See also
Government
Reincarnation, See Trans-
migration
Relativity, 5:663–65,
5:681–82, 5:703
general works, 5:664–65
history of, 5:665
philosophical treatments
of, 5:67–68
Religion, See also names of
religions, such as
Christianity; specific
religion, such as
Quakers
African literatures, 2:103,
2:105
American literature, 1:1192
historical fiction, 1:1244,
1:1250
ancient, and philosophies,
4:419–94
anthropology of, 3:23–24
Arabic literature, 2:61
Armenian literature, 2:75
Bible, 4:792–838
Burmese literature, 2:313
Cambodian literature,
2:315
Canadian literature, 2:919,
2:927
Chinese literature, 2:196,
2:210, 2:211
Christianity, early and medieval, 4:674–714
Christianity, late, 4:1500 to
the present, 4:715–91
comparative literature,
2:989
contemporary issues,
4:882–906
authors, 4:899–906
character, affections, and
virtues, 4:897

ethics, 4:892–95
interreligious dialogue,
4:898
liberation theology, 4:896
ritual, worship, and religious community,
4:897
Roman Catholic thought,
4:890–91
social sciences, 4:889–90
theological method,
4:888–89
traditional, 4:884–88
women authors, 4:904
women, 4:891
drama, American, 1:1083
early American literature,
1:625, 1:626, 1:636,
1:644
early twentieth-century
American literature,
1:889
Eastern, 4:495–563
encyclopedias, dictionaries,
and atlases, 4:2–5
European Jews, 3:346–51
French literature, 2:514,
2:516
gay literature, 1:1186
general histories and surveys, 4:2
general reference, 4:1–8
Greek Byzantine literature,
2:344
Greek modern literature,
2:373
handbooks, sourcebooks,
and guides, 4:5–7
Hebrew literature, 2:6,
2:11–12, 2:15–16
history of
ancient, 3:306–7, 3:310
European, 3:327
medieval Europe, 3:329,
3:330
Reformation, 3:333–34
indexes, 4:7
introductions to, 4:883
Islam, 3:441, 3:447,
4:564–90
Japanese literature, 2:286
Judaism, 4:591–673
Korean literature, 2:306
Laotian literature, 2:321
Latin literature, 2:379
medieval philosophy,
4:92–121
Middle Eastern history
and, 3:434
Middle English, 1:146,
1:148

Religion (cont.)
   middle to late nineteenth-
      century American liter-
      ature, 1:741
   middle to late twentieth-
      century American liter-
      ature, 1:962, 1:986,
      1:1023–24, 1:1032
   modern British and Irish
      literature, 1:471, 1:488,
      1:500–2, 1:548, 1:560
   Netherlandic literature,
      2:620
   Norwegian literature, 2:668
   Persian drama, 2:82
   Philippine literature, 2:329
   philosophy of, see Reli-
      gion, philosophy of
   psychology of, 3:187
   Renaissance literature,
      1:172, 1:191
   Renaissance, 1:162–63
   Restoration and eighteenth-
      century literature,
      1:224, 1:229, 1:255
   Restoration and eighteenth-
      century poetry, 1:237,
      1:251
   romantic period, British,
      1:277
   Russian literature,
      2:682–83, 2:700, 2:702,
      2:705, 2:712, 2:718,
      2:728, 2:735, 2:745,
      2:763
   science and, 5:160, 5:163,
      5:178, 5:195–99
   science fiction, 1:1260
   sociology of, 3:212, 3:220
   Spanish literature, 2:519
   technology and, 5:195–99
   Thai literature, 2:334
   Turkish literature, 2:95
   Victorian period, 1:309,
      1:342, 1:345, 1:368,
      1:375
   West African literature,
      2:141, 2:144
   Western philosophy
      1700–1800, 4:208
      1800–1900, 4:241, 4:253
   Yiddish literature, 2:28,
      2:39
Religion, philosophy of
   contemporary issues,
      4:882–906
   contemporary philosophical
      issues, 4:380
   Western philosophy,
      1700–1800, 4:200
Religious drama
   French literature, 2:492
   German literature, 2:596

Lithuanian literature, 2:806
medieval, British, 1:156–61
Netherlandic literature,
   2:623, 2:632
Renaissance, British, 1:167
Spanish literature, 2:532
Religious movements
   ancient Judaism, 4:614–21
   contemporary issues, 4:883
   Indian philosophy, 4:354
   indigenous religions, 4:466
   late Christianity, 4:716
   medieval Judaism,
      4:630–33
   minority religions,
      4:839–81
      authors, 4:873–81
      women authors, 4:873–74
   modern Judaism, 4:650–59
   nineteenth-century,
      4:840–53
   twentieth-century, 4:853–73
      controversial issues,
         4:856
      descriptive and historical
         works, 4:855
      directories, encyclope-
         dias, and bibliogra-
         phies, 4:854
      theological and philo-
         sophical response,
         4:857
      Theosophy, 4:858
Religious poetry
   Middle English, 1:145,
      1:148
   Old English, 1:142
   Renaissance, 1:199
   Victorian period, 1:390
Religious sects
   ancient Judaism, 4:614
   Islamic religion, 4:565
Religious socialism, 5:206
Renaissance 3:332–33, 3:399,
   5:1450–1600
   algebra, 5:483
   American literature, 1:1192
   Arabic literature, 2:54
   bibliography, 5:40–41, 5:58
   British literature,
      1:162–201
      authors, 1:171–201
      poetry, 1:164–66
      prose fiction, 1:166–67
      women authors, 1:163
   Byelorussian literature,
      2:783
   drama, British, 1:167–71
      collections, 1:170–71
      history and criticism,
         1:169–70
   ethics, 5:105

French literature, 2:492,
   2:497
historical fiction, 1:1246
Italian literature, 2:398,
   2:404, 2:406, 2:408–10,
   2:433
Italy, 3:383, 3:755
Netherlandic literature,
   2:620
Polish literature, 2:809
Portuguese literature,
   2:556, 2:558
science, technology, and
   art, 5:189–95, 5:203
Spanish literature, 2:548
women authors, 1:163
Renaissance philosophy,
   4:122–56
   authors, 4:132–56
   general works, 4:123–32
Renewable energy technol-
   ogies, 5:288–90
Reproductive hazards and
   chemicals, 5:737
Research institutions, science
   and technology policy,
   5:183–86
Respiratory diseases,
   5:397–98
Responsa literature, 4:626
Responsible caution, ethic of,
   5:93
Restoration and eighteenth-
   century literature,
   1:223–63
   authors, 1:231–63
   children's, 1:260
   collections, 1:227
   drama, 1:228
   fiction, 1:229–30
   history and criticism,
      1:225–26
   nonfiction, 1:230–31
   poetry, 1:227
   women authors, 1:232,
      1:235, 1:250
Resurrection, traditional issues, 4:886, 4:887
Revelation
   early and medieval Chris-
      tianity, 4:674, 4:695
   Western philosophy, twen-
      tieth-century, 4:285
Revenge tragedy
   Renaissance drama, 1:168,
      1:184, 1:185, 1:199
Reversionary Judaism, 4:659
Revised English Bible, 4:804
Revised Standard Version,
   4:802
Revolutions
   American, 3:519–22
   English, 3:336

French, 3:338–40, 3:347
Industrial, 3:340
Iranian, 3:447
Russian, 3:286–87, 3:294, 3:393, 3:835
Rhetoric
African literatures, 2:103
Chinese literature, 2:230
East African literature, 2:156
French literature, 2:456
Greek classical literature, 2:342
Italian literature, 2:442
Latin literature, 2:379, 2:387, 2:392
West African literature, 2:132, 2:137
Rheumatic diseases, 5:398
Rhind Papyrus, 5:477
Rhyming dictionaries, 1:95
Richter scale, 5:646
Rights, contemporary issues, 4:385–87
Risk assessment
developments, philosophical studies of, 5:73–77
probabilistic, 5:141
Rites of passage
indigenous religions, 4:462
study of religion, 4:429
Ritual
Aztecs, 4:456
contemporary religious issues, 4:897
Egypt, ancient religion, 4:441
indigenous religions, 4:460–61, 4:463–64
Islamic religion, 4:565–66
Japanese religion, 4:535
Maya, 4:455
medieval Christianity, 4:698
Mediterranean ancient urban civilization, 4:438
prehistoric religion, 4:432
study of religion, 4:427–30
RKO, 1:1178
Robin Hood stories
children's literature, 1:1194, 1:1205
Robinson Professorship, See Clarence H. Robinson Professorship
Robinson projection, 3:134
Robot, 2:789
science fiction, American, 1:1209, 1:1253
Robotics, 5:242–43
introduction of term, 5:14
Rockefeller Foundation, 5:269, 5:605

Rockefeller Public Service Award, 5:257
Rocks, See Minerology
Rodale Award for Creative Achievement, 5:307
Roe v. Wade, 5:134
Roman Catholic Church, 3:329, 3:383, See also Christianity
Apocrypha, 4:810
Bible, 4:800, 4:802–3
contemporary issues, 4:890–91, 4:902, 4:904
early Christianity, 4:681
late Christianity, 4:1500–1560, 4:720, 4:727–29
theological study of religion, 4:423
Roman Empire, 3:297, 3:302–3, 3:310–14, 3:316–21, 3:374
early Christianity, 4:681, 4:682–84
European civilization, 3:327–28
fall of, 3:390
Iberia, 3:384
Jews in, 3:438
oikoumene world, 4:448–53
Roman literature, See Latin literature
Roman philosophy
authors, 4:64–91
Epicureanism, 4:58
Greek influence, 4:44–91
general works, 4:46–49
Stoicism, 4:56, 4:58, 4:59
Roman religion, ancient, 4:447
Romances
American popular literature, 1:1193, 1:1209, 1:1219–25
authors, 1:618–22, 1:1220–25
British popular literature, 1:591, 1:617–22
detective story, 1:1238
early twentieth-century American literature, 1:801
historical fiction, 1:1244
literary theory, 1:1151
Middle English poetry, 1:145
middle to late nineteenth-century American literature, 1:760
middle to late twentieth-century American literature, 1:1022

Renaissance literature, 1:185, 1:195
romantic period, British, 1:292, 1:298
sea tales, 1:685–86
Victorian period, 1:365, 1:382, 1:385, 1:389
women authors, 1:617, 1:618–21, 1:1219, 1:1220–21, 1:1223–24
Romania, 3:388, 3:390
Romanov era (Russia), 3:393
Romansh (language), 3:378
Romantic movement, 3:845
Romanticism
Albanian literature, 2:779
American literature, 1:1192
Brazilian literature, 2:891
British literature, 1:264–308
authors, 1:274–308
drama, 1:270–72
fiction, 1:269–70
nonfiction, 1:272–74
poetry, 1:266–69
women authors, 1:269, 1:271, 1:274, 1:276, 1:300
Byelorussian literature, 2:783
children's literature, British, 1:295, 1:576, 1:577
Croatian literature, 2:785
Czech literature, 2:788
Danish literature, 2:644
early nineteenth-century American literature, 1:649
early twentieth-century American literature, 1:843
Estonian literature, 2:796
French literature, 2:445, 2:466, 2:472, 2:504, 2:510
Frisian literature, 2:634
German literature, 2:563, 2:575, 2:577, 2:591, 2:605, 2:610, 2:612
Gothic/horror, 1:598
Hungarian literature, 2:797
Italian literature, 2:421
Japanese literature, 2:292
literary theory, 1:1137
Lithuanian literature, 2:804
middle to late nineteenth-century American literature, 1:732
modern British and Irish literature, 1:437
modern British and Irish poetry, 1:556
modern Irish drama, 1:555

Romanticism (*cont.*)
Netherlandic literature,
2:630
Old Norse-Icelandic litera-
ture, 2:639
Polish literature, 2:809,
2:815, 2:817
Portuguese literature, 2:557
religious movements, nine-
teenth-century, 4:840
Restoration and eighteenth-
century poetry, 1:227
Russian literature, 2:720,
2:771
Serbian literature, 2:826
Slovak literature, 2:832
Slovenian literature, 2:834
Spanish literature, 2:521,
2:530
Swedish literature, 2:670,
2:672
Ukrainian literature, 2:840
Victorian period, 1:310,
1:313–14, 1:316, 1:327,
1:335, 1:343
Western philosophy,
1800–1900, 4:252,
4:253
Rome, ancient, 3:302–3,
3:755, *See also* Roman
Empire
ecology, 5:814
Röntgen rays, 5:710
Roosevelt, Franklin D., 3:400,
3:570, 3:810
Rosenbach Museum, Phila-
delphia, 1:863
Rosicrucianism, 4:847
Royal Court Theatre, 1:424,
1:433, 1:449, 1:458,
1:564
Royal Society, 5:255, 5:256,
5:742
Royal Swedish Academy of
Sciences, 5:831
Rugs, 3:767
Rumanian literature,
2:822–26
authors, 2:778, 2:824–26
Rumanian State Prize for Literature, 2:824
Runic inscriptions, Germanic
religion, 4:437
Russell Paradox, 4:229
Russia, 3:330, 3:393–94,
3:412–13, *See also*
Russian culture and
society; Soviet Union
general works, 3:394–95
geography, 3:131
philosophy, 4:30
post-Soviet era, 3:398
Soviet era, 3:395–98

tsarist era, 3:395
Russian culture and society
Abkhazians, Georgia, 2:729
bureaucracy, 2:772
ethnic diversity, 2:684
Kirghiz, 2:695
nineteenth-century trends,
2:768
outcasts, 2:724
peasant, 2:748
peasant/elite gap, 2:683,
2:712
provincial life, 2:697, 2:707
Ukrainian, 2:720
urban life, 2:767, 2:773
village life, 2:752, 2:756,
2:759
Russian literature, 2:682–776
authors, 2:694–776
children's, 2:712
collections, 2:691–94
communism affecting,
2:683
drama
nineteenth-century, 2:720,
2:726, 2:744, 2:750,
2:769
twentieth-century, 2:705,
2:707, 2:724
émigré, before 1939, 2:683,
2:701, 2:739, 2:753,
2:774
history and criticism,
2:684–91
linguistic experimentation,
2:731
Western philosophy, twen-
tieth-century, 4:335
women authors, 2:695,
2:696, 2:701, 2:711,
2:726, 2:728, 2:744,
2:752, 2:762, 2:767
Russian Revolution,
3:286–87, 3:294, 3:393,
3:835

S

Sabbateanism, 4:631
Sacrament, early Christianity,
4:684
Sacrifice
Aztecs, 4:456
Celtic religion, 4:436
Inca religion, 4:458
Mesopotamian ancient ur-
ban civilization, 4:440
prehistoric religion, 4:432
South Asian religions,
4:500
study of religion, 4:428

Sadducees, 4:616
Sadism
French literature, 2:475,
2:503
Netherlandic literature,
2:627
Sadomasochism, 1:1242
Safavids (people), 3:447
Safety
engineering, 5:243–44
industrial accidents, 5:106
nuclear safety, 5:277, 5:286
Saga
Old Norse-Icelandic litera-
ture, 2:639, 2:641,
2:642, 2:643, 2:644
Sage philosophy
African, 4:371
Chinese religion, 4:524,
4:525, 4:527
Sahel (Africa), 3:418–19
Sahitya Akademi Award,
2:178
Saint Lucia author, *See* Ca-
ribbean literature
Saint-singers, 2:173, 2:174
women, 2:173
Saints plays, *See* Miracle
plays
Salon
early twentieth-century
American literature,
1:881
French literature, 2:486,
2:488, 2:495, 2:510
romantic period, British,
1:292
Russian literature, 2:728
Salt Lake City, Utah, Latter-
Day Saints, 4:845
Salvadoran authors, *See* Lat-
in American literatures
Salvation
Western philosophy
1800–1900 4:253, 4:255
twentieth-century, 4:305
Salzburg Festival, 2:592
Samaritans, 4:618
Samizdat, 2:683, 2:695, 2:698,
2:702, 2:716–17, 2:720,
2:727, 2:762, 2:772
Samoa, 3:36
San Francisco renaissance,
1:971, 1:1008
Sanitary engineering,
5:244–45
Sanskrit, Indian religion,
4:497
Santería
religious movements, twen-
tieth-century, 4:867
sacrifice, 4:428, 4:868
Sarris, Andrew, 3:824

Sarton Medal, *See* George
Sarton Medal
Satanism, 4:868
Satellites, 5:228
Satire
American literature, 1:1193
Armenian literature, 2:77,
2:81
Australian literature, 2:948
Brazilian literature, 2:896
Bulgarian literature, 2:780
Canadian literature, 2:912,
2:913
Caribbean literature, 2:942
children's literature
American, 1:1203
British, 1:576, 1:580,
1:584
Chinese literature, 2:188,
2:202, 2:205, 2:208,
2:210, 2:216, 2:229,
2:240, 2:253, 2:255
Czech literature, 2:788,
2:789, 2:790, 2:793
Danish literature, 2:650
drama, American, 1:1087,
1:1089, 1:1097,
1:1101–2
early American literature,
1:632, 1:638
early nineteenth-century
American literature,
1:660, 1:671, 1:679,
1:684
early twentieth-century
American literature,
1:807, 1:844, 1:868,
1:879, 1:890, 1:901
East African literature,
2:155
film studies, 1:1161
French drama, 2:450,
2:458, 2:490
French literature, 2:452,
2:471, 2:479, 2:506,
2:515
German literature, 2:571,
2:574, 2:582
Greek classical drama,
2:352, 2:367
Greek Hellenistic litera-
ture, 2:343, 2:363,
2:369
Hebrew literature, 2:21
Italian literature, 2:406,
2:430
Korean literature, 2:304
Latin American literatures,
2:853, 2:877, 2:887
Latin literature, 2:379,
2:386, 2:390
Malay literature, 2:326
Middle English, 1:153

middle to late nineteenth-
century American liter-
ature, 1:729, 1:738,
1:752, 1:779–80, 1:786
middle to late twentieth-
century American liter-
ature, 1:948–49, 1:969,
1:992, 1:1005, 1:1007,
1:1013, 1:1022, 1:1029,
1:1040, 1:1056, 1:1059,
1:1061, 1:1063
modern British and Irish
drama, 1:554
modern British and Irish
literature, 1:419, 1:440,
1:448, 1:453, 1:461,
1:469, 1:498, 1:513,
1:515, 1:530, 1:547,
1:561, 1:567
modern Irish drama, 1:479,
1:526, 1:555
modern Irish literature,
1:525
Netherlandic literature,
2:620, 2:625, 2:629
opera, Victorian period,
1:357
Persian drama, 2:82
Persian literature, 2:87,
2:93, 2:94
Polish literature, 2:818
Renaissance drama,
1:183, 1:187, 1:189,
1:199
Renaissance literature,
1:172, 1:177, 1:188,
1:194, 1:196
Renaissance philosophy,
4:138
Restoration and eighteenth-
century drama, 1:241,
1:242, 1:246
Restoration and eighteenth-
century literature,
1:223, 1:232, 1:244,
1:259
Restoration and eighteenth-
century poetry, 1:227,
1:241
romantic period, British,
1:275, 1:281, 1:292
Russian drama, 2:720,
2:726, 2:739
Russian literature, 2:705,
2:716–17, 2:719,
2:728–30, 2:735, 2:740,
2:742–43, 2:754,
2:757–58, 2:768, 2:770,
2:772, 2:774–75
Slovak literature, 2:833
Spanish literature, 2:520,
2:534, 2:548, 2:549,
2:553

Turkish drama, 2:101
Turkish literature, 2:100
Victorian period, 1:317,
1:329, 1:334, 1:342–43,
1:347, 1:366, 1:369,
1:376, 1:403, 1:405
West African literature,
2:132, 2:145
Western philosophy,
1700–1800, 4:209,
4:217
Yiddish literature, 2:40
Saudi Arabia, 3:450–52
oil and gas, 5:280
Savoy opera, 1:357
Scandinavia, 3:379, 3:381–82
Lutheranism, late Christianity, 4:730
philosophy, 4:31
Scandinavian literatures,
2:637–81
authors, chronology,
2:638–39
collections, 2:638
Danish, *See* Danish literature
Faroese, *See* Faroese literature
Finnish, *See* Finnish literature
history and criticism, 2:638
Norwegian, *See* Norwegian
literature
Old Norse-Icelandic, *See*
Old Norse-Icelandic lit-
erature
relationships, 2:1
Swedish, *See* Swedish liter-
ature
Scanning tunneling micros-
copy, 5:672
Scarcity, 3:43
Scatology
Chinese literature, 2:265
Russian literature, 2:698,
2:717
Schism, medieval Christianity, 4:692, 4:694
Schizophrenia, studies of,
5:459, 5:470
Scholasticism
medieval Christianity, 4:695
Renaissance philosophy,
4:136, 4:152
Western philosophy, twen-
tieth-century, 4:305
Schoolroom poets, 1:653,
1:717
Schools, 3:246–48, *See also*
Education

Science, *See also* general
   headings of science,
   technology, and
   medicine; specific
   topics
ancient, 3:304
art and, 5:189–95
astronomy, 5:585–613
biological sciences,
   5:757–813
chemistry, 5:722–56
computer science,
   5:532–84
earth sciences, 5:614–48
ecology, 5:814–38
environmental science,
   5:814–38
ethical issues, 5:106–108
European, 3:337
feminist and gender stud-
   ies, 5:186–89
information science,
   5:532–84
mathematics, 5:477–517
philosophy of, 5:61, *See
   also* Philosophy of science, technology, and
   medicine
physics, 5:649–721
policy-making, 5:179–86
probability theory,
   5:518–31
progress, 5:179
religion and, 5:195–99
social problems and, 3:223
society and, 5:147–207, *See
   also* Society and sci-
   ence, technology and
   medicine
sociology of, 3:213–14,
   3:239
space science, 5:585–613
statistics, 5:518–31
theology and, 5:160, 5:163
Science, history of
medieval philosophy, 4:97
Renaissance philosophy,
   4:134, 4:141
Science, philosophy of
contemporary issues,
   4:383–85, 4:398, 4:405,
   4:406, 4:409
Greek philosophy, 4:64,
   4:65
medieval philosophy, 4:110
modern Western philoso-
   phy, 4:159
Western philosophy
   1600–1700, 4:164
   1800–1900, 4:257
   twentieth-century, 4:273,
      4:313, 4:340

Science, technology, and
   public policy, 5:148
Science, technology, and society studies, 5:147–48,
   5:177
Science, Western philosophy,
   1600–1700, 4:169,
   4:171, 4:172
Science fiction
American popular litera-
   ture, 1:1193, 1:1209,
   1:1251–63
authors, 1:612–17,
   1:1252–63
British popular literature,
   1:591, 1:611–17
children's literature, American, 1:1199
filmmaking, 1:1171
Hungarian literature, 2:799
middle to late twentieth-
   century American literature, 1:1062, 1:1063
modern British and Irish
   literature, 1:469, 1:563
Polish literature, 2:815
Russian literature, 2:704,
   2:762
women authors, 1:1259,
   1:1261
Science of Judaism, 4:647
"Science policy" defined,
   5:179
Scientific method, 5:86
contemporary philosophical
   issues, 4:383, 4:402,
   4:405
Greek philosophy, 4:64
Judaism, 4:647
Renaissance philosophy,
   4:141, 4:142
Western philosophy
   1600–1700, 4:165
   twentieth-century, 4:259,
      4:261, 4:280
Scientific theory, contempo-
   rary issues, 4:383
"Scientific-rationalistic" mod-
   el, 5:69
Scientology, 4:869
Scotland, 3:352–53, 3:368
folk ballads of, 3:877
philosophy, 4:32
Reformation, 4:735, 4:773
Scriblerus Club, 1:246, 1:252
Sea tales, *See* Adventure
   story; Romances
Seance, 4:850
Second Temple period, an-
   cient Judaism, 4:603–6
Security issues, 5:124–25

Seduction
middle to late twentieth-
   century American liter-
   ature, 1:1019
romances, 1:1219
"Seeking Roots" group,
   2:249, 2:266
Seers, Celtic religion, 4:436
Seismology, 5:646–47
Selection as key to evolu-
   tion, 5:792, 5:811
Self-Concept Test, 5:432
Self-fulfilling prophecies,
   3:233
Self-psychology, 5:457
Self-Realization Fellowship,
   4:872
Semiconductors, 5:704, 5:735
Semiotics
French literature, 2:454,
   2:478
Italian literature, 2:400,
   2:419
literary theory, 1:1141
Sennett, Mack, 1:1160
Sensation
psychology of, 5:411
Western philosophy,
   1700–1800, 4:195
Sensuality
Chinese drama, 2:227
Chinese literature, 2:205,
   2:208, 2:230, 2:238
early twentieth-century
   American poetry, 1:886
French literature, 2:482,
   2:484, 2:513
Japanese literature, 2:293,
   2:295
middle to late nineteenth-
   century American literature, 1:739
Renaissance literature,
   1:175, 1:177
romantic period, British,
   1:292
South African literature,
   2:160
Spanish literature, 2:549,
   2:552
Victorian period, 1:310
West African literature,
   2:146
Septuagint, 4:796
Serapion Brotherhood, 2:729,
   2:731
Serapionsabende, 2:591
Serbia, 3:392–93
Serbian literature, 2:826–32
authors, 2:778, 2:828–32
collections, 2:828
drama, 2:827
history and criticism, 2:827

Sermon
  American literature, 1:1192
  early American literature,
    1:636, 1:644
  early nineteenth-century
    American literature,
    1:656, 1:658, 1:659
  Middle English, 1:146
  Old English, 1:142
  Renaissance British litera-
    ture, 1:166
  Restoration and eighteenth-
    century literature,
    1:224, 1:258
Seven Sages of the Bamboo
  Grove, 2:199, 2:202
Seventeenth century
  bibliography, 5:41–43
  Europe, 3:336
Sex differences, 3:185
Sexism
  late Christianity, 4:764
  philosophy, 4:40
Sexuality, 3:207–8
  Arabic literature, 2:60
  ancient history, 3:309
  Australian literature, 2:948,
    2:963
  Caribbean literature, 2:938
  Chinese literature, 2:188,
    2:200, 2:203, 2:211,
    2:226, 2:239, 2:249,
    2:251, 2:254, 2:263,
    2:266
  clinical psychology and
    psychiatry, 5:429,
    5:430, 5:440, 5:445
  contemporary religious is-
    sues, 4:894
  Danish literature, 2:648,
    2:651
  detective story, 1:1227,
    1:1233, 1:1237
  drama, :
    American, 1:1082,
      1:1101, 1:1120
    Victorian period, 1:367,
      1:389
  early twentieth-century
    American literature,
    1:811, 1:819, 1:853
  film studies, 1:1177
  French literature, 2:471,
    2:475, 2:477, 2:484,
    2:501, 2:503
  gay literature, 1:1188
    literary theory, 1:1179–80
  German literature, 2:587
  Gothic story, 1:602
  horror story, 1:599, 1:602
  Italian literature, 2:426
  Japanese literature, 2:271,
    2:290

Latin American literatures,
  2:883
Latin literature, 2:389
literary theory, 1:1144,
  1:1146
middle to late nineteenth-
  century American liter-
  ature, 1:739
middle to late twentieth-
  century American liter-
  ature, 1:975, 1:985,
  1:1018, 1:1022, 1:1064
middle to late twentieth-
  century American poet-
  ry, 1:1042, 1:1045,
  1:1046
modern British and Irish
  drama, 1:458
modern British and Irish
  literature, 1:455, 1:508,
  1:567
Netherlandic literature,
  2:624
North African literature,
  2:120
Norwegian literature, 2:668
prehistoric religion, 4:433
religious movements, twentieth-century, 4:867
Renaissance drama, 1:187,
  1:190
romances, 1:1220, 1:1222
romantic period, British,
  1:281
Russian literature, 2:698,
  2:707, 2:735, 2:736,
  2:758
science fiction, 1:1257,
  1:1258
Spanish literature, 2:546,
  2:548
Victorian period, 1:341,
  1:391
West African literature,
  2:135
Western philosophy,
  1800–1900, 4:228,
  4:255
westerns, 1:1217
Shadow play, 2:95
Shakers, 4:848–50
Shakespeare, 1:202–22
  biographies, 1:204–5
  critical studies, 1:207–15
  comedies, 1:210
  history plays, 1:211
  poetry, nondramatic,
    1:215
  tragedies, 1:212–14
  general reference, 1:220–22
  language and style,
    1:215–16
  source studies, 1:219

texts, editions, 1:170,
  1:205–7
textual studies, 1:207
theater and stagecraft,
  1:217
Shamanism
  Eastern religions, 4:495,
    4:496
  indigenous religions, 4:463,
    4:464
  study of religion, 4:430
Shelmore Bank, 5:256
Shi'ite, 2:81
Shiite sect, Islamic religion,
  4:564, 4:565
Shinto, Japanese religion,
  4:535, 4:538, 4:540
Ship construction, See Naval
  engineering
Shock therapy, 5:412
Shock waves, 5:699
Short-focus lenses, 5:803
SHOT, See Society for the
  History of Technology
Shrine, prehistoric religion,
  4:433
Siberia, 2:800
SIDS, See Sudden infant
  death syndrome
Sierra Club, 5:141–42
Sight, literature on, 5:186
Sikhism, 2:170, 4:515–17
Sin, doctrines of, medieval
  philosophy, 4:116
Singapore, 3:492
Singapore literature, See Ma-
  lay literature
Singers, 3:672
Sixteenth century
  astronomy, 5:600
  medicine, 5:751
Skaz technique, 2:735
Skepticism
  contemporary philosophical
    issues, 4:384
  Hellenistic Age, 4:57
  Jewish thought, 4:646
  Renaissance philosophy,
    4:133, 4:146, 4:151
  Western philosophy
    1600–1700, 4:166, 4:172
    1700–1800, 4:199, 4:200
Skin diseases, 5:399
Skyscrapers, 3:783, 3:792
Slang and colloquial diction-
  aries, 1:92–93
Slave narrative, 2:137
Slave writings
  early American literature,
    1:626, 1:646
  early nineteenth-century
    American literature,
    1:666, 1:681

Slave writings (*cont.*)
  early twentieth-century
    American literature,
    1:817
  middle to late nineteenth-
    century American liter-
    ature, 1:785
  middle to late twentieth-
    century American liter-
    ature, 1:916, 1:937,
    1:1018
Slavery, 3:335, 3:426, 3:522,
    3:580, 3:598, 3:929
  African history, 3:419–21
  Brazilian culture and soci-
    ety, 2:889
  child sex, Victorian period,
    1:341
  drama, American, 1:1119
  middle to late nineteenth-
    century American liter-
    ature, 1:743
  Spanish American culture
    and society, 2:844
  twentieth-century American
    drama, 1:1070
Slavic people, 3:387
Slovak literature, 2:832–34
  authors, chronology, 2:778
Slovakia, 3:387, 3:389
Slovenian literature, 2:834–37
  authors, 2:778, 2:835–37
  collections, 2:835
  history and criticism, 2:835
Smoking and health, 5:404
Social anthropology, 3:38
Social attitudes, study of,
    5:431
Social behaviorism, 4:308
  contemporary philosophical
    issues, 4:414
Social change, 3:209,
    3:219–20, 3:236,
    3:551–53
Social choice, theory of, 3:68
Social class, 3:211–12, 3:214
  caste and, 3:19
Social constructionism,
    1:1179
Social contract, 3:164
  contemporary issues,
    4:385–87
Social control, 3:204–5
Social critiques, philosophy
    of science, 5:65–67
Social Darwinism, 3:185
Social evolution, 5:88–89
Social history, 3:3, 3:352,
    3:462
  of Canada, 3:608–9
Social movements, 3:215
Social philosophy
  modern Judaism, 4:655

Renaissance, 4:136
Western philosophy, twen-
    tieth-century, 4:313,
    4:314, 4:316
Social planning, 3:244
Social psychology, 3:167,
    3:232
Social realism
  Albanian literature, 2:779
  Arabic literature, 2:63
  Australian literature, 2:944
  Brazilian literature, 2:890
  Bulgarian literature, 2:780,
    2:782
  Byelorussian literature,
    2:783
  Danish literature, 2:645
  early twentieth-century
    American literature,
    1:866
  Estonian literature, 2:796
  German literature, 2:603,
    2:612
  Hungarian literature, 2:798
  Indian subcontinent litera-
    ture, 2:176
  Indonesian literature, 2:316
  Latvian literature, 2:803
  Lithuanian literature, 2:805
  modern Irish drama, 1:423
  Polish literature, 2:812
  Russian literature, 2:720,
    2:724, 2:730
  Swedish literature, 2:679
  Turkish literature, 2:97,
    2:100
  Ukrainian literature, 2:838,
    2:839
Social sciences, 3:3–9
  contemporary philosophical
    issues, 4:384
  contemporary religious is-
    sues, 4:889–90
  general references, 3:3–4
    atlases, directories, and
      yearbooks, 3:6
    bibliographies, 3:6
    dictionaries and encyclo-
      pedias, 3:4–5
    handbooks and guides,
      3:5
    indexes and abstracts,
      3:5–6
    methods of social re-
      search, 3:6–7
  history of, 5:34–35
  philosophical treatments
    of, 5:67–68
  study of religion, 4:423
Social space, 3:189
Social structure, 3:215–16
  anthropology, 3:24–25

Socialism, 3:74–75, 3:82,
    3:94–95, 3:104, 3:340
  Fabian, 3:112–13
  in Czechoslovakia, 3:388
Socialization, 3:216
Societies, *See also*
    Anthropology;
    Sociology
  ancient, 3:307–8
  modern, 3:21–23
  pre-Columbian, 3:626–28
  tribal, 3:25–26
Society and science,
    technology and
    medicine, 5:147–77
  art, science, and technol-
    ogy, 5:189–95
  authors, 5:13–20, 5:159–76,
    5:199–207
  directories, 5:3–5
  feminist and gender stud-
    ies, 5:186–89
  general bibliography,
    5:149–59
  general reference works,
    5:2–3, 5:148–49
  guides and indexes, 5:5
  medicine, general refer-
    ence work, 5:5
  overviews, 5:148–49
  policy-making, science and
    technology, 5:179–86
  religion, science and tech-
    nology, 5:195–99
  special issues, 5:178–207
Society for Scientific Philoso-
    phy, 5:91
Society for Social Responsi-
    bility in Science, 5:20
Society for the History of
    Technology, 5:51
Society of Philosophy and
    Technology, 5:51
Sociobiology, 3:199, 5:796
Sociology, 3:4, 3:198–245
  age and aging, 3:200–1
  AIDS, health care, and dis-
    abling conditions,
    3:201–2
  art, literature, and intellec-
    tual life, 3:202
  authors, 3:218–45
  collective behavior,
    3:202–3
  communications, film, and
    television, 3:203–4
  conflict and conflict reso-
    lution, 3:204
  crime, deviance, and social
    control, 3:204–5
  environment, technology,
    and population,
    3:205–6

family and marriage,
3:206-7
founders of, 3:162, 3:163
gender, 3:207
history and surveys of,
3:199-200
human sexuality, 3:207-8
interaction, 3:208
intergroup relations,
3:208-9
methodology of, 3:200
modernization and social
change, 3:209
organizations, 3:210
postmodernism, 3:211
poverty and social class,
3:211-12
race and ethnicity, 3:212
religion, 3:212-13
science, 3:213-14
social change, 3:551-53
social class, 3:214
social movements, 3:215
social structure, 3:215-16
socialization, 3:216
study of religion, 4:423,
4:424
contemporary issues,
4:890
urban and community life,
3:216-17
utopianism and communes,
3:217
Western philosophy
1800-1900, 4:222, 4:223,
4:228, 4:241
twentieth-century, 4:331
women and women's is-
sues, 3:217-18
work, 3:218
Solar system
collapse of, 5:698
Western philosophy
1600-1700, 4:169, 4:184
1700-1800, 4:204
Solid-state physics, 5:668-69,
5:670
general works, 5:668-69
history of, 5:669
Somerset Maugham Award,
1:432, 1:455
Songs, See also Folk songs;
Love songs
popular
Armenian literature, 2:78
Canadian literature,
2:909
French literature, 2:494
Russian literature, 2:698,
2:719, 2:742-43
saint-singers, 2:173
Sonnet

early nineteenth-century
American poetry, 1:704
early twentieth-century
American poetry, 1:860
French literature, 2:502
gay literature, 1:1187
Italian literature, 2:408,
2:433
Latin American literatures,
2:873
middle to late nineteenth-
century American poet-
ry, 1:772
modern British and Irish
poetry, 1:450, 1:556
Portuguese literature, 2:556
Renaissance literature,
1:191, 1:195, 1:197,
1:201
romantic period, British,
1:267, 1:305
Spanish literature, 2:528,
2:541
Victorian period, 1:336,
1:390, 1:391
Sophists, 3:322, 4:53-54
Soul
medieval philosophy, 4:117
Renaissance philosophy,
4:134, 4:140
Western philosophy,
1600-1700, 4:169,
4:182
South (United States), folklore of, 3:860-61
South African literature,
2:156-68
authors, 2:114, 2:158-68
collections, 2:158
drama, 2:160
history and criticism,
2:157-58
languages, 2:157
Sesotho, 2:166
Zulu, 2:164
praises and boasts, 2:156
women authors, 2:161,
2:163, 2:168
South America, See also
Latin American history
exploration of, 3:941-42
indigenous religions, 4:464,
4:465
travel in, 3:894-98
South Asia, 3:482-88
Bangladesh, 3:486-87
general works, 3:482-83
India, 3:483-86
Pakistan, 3:487
reference works, 3:482
Sri Lanka (Ceylon),
3:487-88

South Asian religions,
4:497-518
ancient heritage, 4:499-501
Buddhism, 4:510-15
general works, 4:498
Hinduism, 4:502-9
Jainism, 4:509
reference works and an-
thologies, 4:497
Sikhism, 4:515-17
Zoroastrianism, 4:517
South Pole, 3:912, 3:914-15,
3:936
Southeast Asia, 3:488-93
Burma, 3:489
Indonesia, 3:491
Malaysia, Singapore, and
Brunei Darussalam,
3:492
Philippines, 3:492-93
reference works, 3:488
surveys and general works,
3:488-89
Thailand, 3:490
Vietnam, Cambodia, and
Laos, 3:490-91
Southeast Asian literatures,
2:310-40
authors, chronology, 2:311
Burmese, See Burmese lit-
erature
Cambodian, See Cambodi-
an literature
connections, 2:2
history and criticism,
2:311-12
Indonesian, See Indonesian
literature
Laotian, See Laotian litera-
ture
Malaysia, Brunei, and Sin-
gapore, See Malay lit-
erature
Philippine, See Philippine
literature
Thai, See Thai literature
Vietnamese, See Vietnam-
ese literature
Southeast Asian religion,
4:518-20
Buddhism, 4:519
general works, 4:518
popular, 4:518
Vietnam, 4:520
Southern Africa, 3:423-24
Southern Authors Award,
1:892
Southern European history,
3:383-85
Italy, 3:385-86
Portugal, 3:386
Spain, 3:386-87

Southwest, American
  early nineteenth-century
    American literature,
    1:673, 1:679, 1:683,
    1:702
  early twentieth-century
    American literature,
    1:802
  middle to late nineteenth-
    century American liter-
    ature, 1:732
Sovereignty, 3:164
Soviet Union, 3:342,
    3:393–98, See also
    Russia
  breakup, 5:279–80
  collapse of, 3:325
  Eastern Europe and, 3:388
  end of cold war, 3:277
  film in, 3:835
  music in, 3:710, 3:717
  Russian Revolution,
    3:286–87, 3:294
  space program, 5:592,
    5:596
  under Stalin, 3:291–92
Space age, 2:678
Space and time
  Western philosophy
    1600–1700, 4:184
    twentieth-century, 4:302
Space foam, 5:719
Space program, 5:596–97
Space science, 5:585–613
  authors, 5:599–613
  extraterrestrial intelligence,
    search for, 5:597–98,
    5:608–609
Space travel, 3:911–12,
    3:934–35
  science fiction, 1:1251,
    1:1252, 1:1255, 1:1258
Spain, 3:384–87, 3:648
  Columbus's voyages for,
    3:915–17
  Latin America and, 3:623
Spanish American literature,
    See Latin American lit-
    eratures
Spanish Civil War, 3:384–85,
    3:786
Spanish culture and society
  French influence, 2:520
  gypsies, 2:538
  lower classes, 2:530
  Middle Ages, 2:537
  Muslim, Jewish, and Chris-
    tian influence, 2:519
  rural life, 2:538
Spanish history
  civil war, 2:521, 2:532,
    2:538, 2:540–41
  decline of Spain, 2:521

  dictatorship, 2:521
  effects of Inquisition, 2:520
Spanish literature, 2:519–55
  authors, 2:527–55
  children's, 2:542
  collections, 2:526–27
  drama, 2:520
    collections, 2:523–24,
      2:526
    seventeenth-century,
      2:532, 2:551, 2:553
    sixteenth-century, 2:548
    twentieth-century, 2:531,
      2:532, 2:538, 2:553
  Hebrew literature, 2:19,
    2:23
  history and criticism,
    2:522–26
  Philippine literature influ-
    ence, 2:327
  regional
    Andalusian, 2:552
    Catalan, 2:521
    Galician, 2:533
  women authors, 2:521,
    2:533, 2:545, 2:550
Sparta (ancient), 3:323
Spectroheliograph, 5:605
Speculative philosophy
  contemporary issues, 4:377
  Western philosophy, twen-
    tieth-century, 4:338,
    4:340
Speeches, See Oratory
Spelling dictionaries, 1:95
Spingarn Medal, 1:738
Spinozism, Western philoso-
    phy, 1700–1800, 4:208
Spirits
  indigenous religions, 4:463
  Japanese religion, 4:535
  religious movements, nine-
    teenth-century, 4:840
  Renaissance philosophy,
    4:134
  shamanism, 4:430
  Western philosophy,
    1600–1700, 4:167
Spiritualism
  communal groups, 4:843
  Mesmerism, 4:846
  religious movements
    nineteenth-century, 4:840,
      4:850
    twentieth-century, 4:868
  Shakers, 4:849
  Swedenborgianism, 4:851
Spiritualists, 4:723
Spirituality
  religious movements, twen-
    tieth-century, 4:853,
    4:854
  traditional issues, 4:887

Spontaneous generation of
    disease, 5:809
Sports medicine, 5:399–400
Sputnik, 5:596
Spy story, See Thriller
Sri Lanka (Ceylon), 3:487–88
St. Louis Post-Dispatch
    (newspaper), 3:820
Stalin Prize
  Chinese literature, 2:264
  Russian literature, 2:744,
    2:754
Standard deviation, 5:529
Stanford-Binet Intelligence
    Test, 3:180
Stars
  astronomy, 5:593–94, 5:610
  collapsed, 5:691
  neutron stars, 5:677
  white dwarf stars, 5:677
State, 3:137, 3:159, 3:164,
    See also Political
    science
  Hegelian philosophy and,
    3:285
  in Asia and Pacific, 3:461
  Islamic, 3:447
  medieval Europe, 3:329
State government, 3:148
Statistical mechanics, 5:720
Statistics, 5:518–31
  agricultural research,
    5:529, 5:530
  authors, 5:527–31
  Bayesian, 5:530
  bell-shaped curve, 5:529
  biology and, 5:797
  chi-square goodness-of-fit
    test, 5:530
  computers and, 5:518
  contingency table analysis,
    5:530
  correlation coefficient,
    5:530
  demography and, 5:520
  errors, 5:530
  Gaussian curve, 5:507,
    5:529
  general bibliography,
    5:521–25
  historical surveys, 5:526–27
  history of, 5:525–26
  Laplace transform, 5:530
  least squares, method of,
    5:529
  life tables, 5:520
  likelihood ratio test, 5:530
  maximum likelihood func-
    tion, 5:530
  numbers, theory of, 5:530
  reference works, 5:520–21
  regression or reversion,
    5:529

standard deviation, 5:529
Statistics, economic, 3:63–64
Statue of Liberty, 1:772
Steam engine, 5:276
Steam power, 5:248–49
Stellar evolution, 5:686
Stellar motion, 5:606, 5:680
Stereoscopies, 2:463
Sterilization, 5:221
Stock tickers and printers, 5:251
Stockholm School of Economics, 3:114
Stoicism
    French literature, 2:464, 2:491
    Hellenistic Age, 4:56
    Latin literature, 2:390, 2:393
    Roman philosophy, 4:58, 4:59, 4:76, 4:88
Stonehenge, 4:433
Storm and Stress, 2:563, 2:580, 2:609
Strategic Defense Initiative, 5:108
Stratemeyer Syndicate, 1:1193
Strawberry Hill, 1:262, 1:603
Stream-of-consciousness
    Chinese literature, 2:263
    early twentieth-century American literature, 1:826, 1:834
    French literature, 2:509
    German literature, 2:610
    Latin American literatures, 2:870
    middle to late nineteenth-century American literature, 1:762, 1:768
    middle to late twentieth-century American literature, 1:1022
    modern British and Irish literature, 1:503, 1:540, 1:568
    Russian literature, 2:758
    Spanish literature, 2:533
    Swedish literature, 2:679
Strega Prize, 2:423, 2:432
Stress and disease, 5:400–401
Structural anthropology, 3:33
Structural engineering, 5:245–46
Structuralism, 1:1130, 1:1140–41
    film studies, 1:1156
    French literature, 2:454, 2:476
    Russian literature, 2:770
    study of religion, 4:426

STS studies, See Science, technology, and society studies
Stuart England (1603–1714), 3:359–61
Subatomic matter, 5:672
Subatomic particle physics, 5:715
Substance abuse, 5:401–4
    alcoholism, 5:401–3
    drug abuse, 5:403–4
    smoking, 5:404
Subway systems, 5:246
Success story, See Rags-to-riches genre
Sudden infant death syndrome, 5:375
Suez Canal, 3:445
Sufism
    Islamic philosophy, 4:375
    Islamic religion, 4:566
    Persian literature, 2:82, 2:86, 2:89, 2:92
    Turkish literature, 2:101
    Urdu literature, 2:175
Suicide, 3:225
    authors, romantic period, 1:284
    Caribbean literature, 2:938
    Chinese authors, 2:196, 2:263
    drama
        American, 1:1095, 1:1099, 1:1100, 1:1105
        Victorian period, 1:388
    early twentieth-century American authors, 1:823, 1:845
    early twentieth-century American literature, 1:802
    German authors, 2:575, 2:599, 2:613, 2:617
    German literature, 2:615
    Greek classical authors, 2:354
    Greek philosopher, 4:89
    Italian authors, 2:425, 2:432
    Japanese authors, 2:285, 2:288, 2:289
    Korean authors, 2:306
    Latin American authors, 2:852, 2:879, 2:881
    Latin authors, 2:387, 2:388, 2:390, 2:393
    middle to late twentieth-century American authors, 1:950, 1:1002, 1:1030, 1:1045
    modern British and Irish authors, 1:569

modern British and Irish literature, 1:469
Netherlandic literature, 2:626
Persian authors, 2:90
Polish authors, 2:812
religious movements, twentieth-century, 4:867
Roman philosopher, 4:88
Russian authors, 2:718, 2:719, 2:738, 2:767
Sulfuric acid, 5:733, 5:751
Sunni sect, Islamic religion, 4:564, 4:565
Superconductivity, 5:670–71, 5:695–96
Superstition, 5:14
Suprarealism, 2:855
Supreme Court, U.S., 3:188
Surgery, 5:404–5, 5:408
Surha Gold Medal, 5:292
Surrealism
    Arabic literature, 2:65
    Australian literature, 2:964
    Canadian literature, 2:915, 2:922
    children's literature, American, 1:1207
    Chinese literature, 2:265
    drama, American, 1:1110
    early twentieth-century American literature, 1:812, 1:868, 1:896
    French literature, 2:445, 2:462, 2:465, 2:468, 2:474
    German literature, 2:571
    Greek modern literature, 2:370, 2:373
    Hebrew literature, 2:26
    Japanese literature, 2:284
    Latin American literatures, 2:853, 2:858, 2:859, 2:873
    middle to late twentieth-century American literature, 1:943, 1:952, 1:1002, 1:1055
    middle to late twentieth-century American poetry, 1:990, 1:1015, 1:1047
    modern British and Irish drama, 1:445
    modern British and Irish literature, 1:412
    Persian literature, 2:94
    Polish literature, 2:813
    Russian literature, 2:739, 2:757, 2:762
    Spanish literature, 2:521, 2:528–29, 2:534
Surrogate motherhood, 5:117

Survival of the fittest, 5:792,
    5:811
Swami, religious movements,
    twentieth-century,
    4:853, 4:862, 4:871
Sweden, 3:379, 3:382
Swedenborgianism, 4:851
Swedish literature, 2:670–81
    authors, 2:639, 2:672–81
    children's, 2:676, 2:677
    collections, 2:671–72
    drama, 2:675, 2:679
    history and criticism, 2:671
    women authors, 2:676,
        2:677
Switching systems, 5:301
Switzerland, 3:375, 3:378
Symbolic forms, theory of,
    Western philosophy,
    twentieth-century,
    4:279
Symbolic interaction theory,
    3:221
Symbolic logic, 5:85, 5:499
    Western philosophy, twen-
        tieth-century, 4:301,
        4:320
Symbolism
    African literatures, 2:105
    Arabic literature, 2:72
    Australian literature, 2:964
    Bulgarian literature, 2:780
    Caribbean literature, 2:937
    Chinese literature, 2:196,
        2:206, 2:208, 2:222,
        2:265
    Czech literature, 2:788
    Danish literature, 2:648,
        2:650
    drama, American, 1:1106
    early nineteenth-century
        American literature,
        1:674, 1:686
    Estonian literature, 2:796
    French drama, 2:450
    French literature, 2:445,
        2:468, 2:499, 2:501,
        2:512, 2:513
    German literature
        blue flower, 2:605
    Greek modern literature,
        2:370
    Hebrew literature, 2:14
    Latin American literatures,
        2:868, 2:880, 2:885
    Lithuanian literature, 2:804
    Middle English, 1:155
    middle to late nineteenth-
        century American liter-
        ature, 1:741

middle to late twentieth-
    century American liter-
    ature, 1:955, 1:962,
    1:994, 1:1005, 1:1018,
    1:1023, 1:1035
modern British and Irish
    literature, 1:412, 1:419,
    1:447, 1:487, 1:503
North African literature,
    2:123
Norwegian literature, 2:665
Rumanian literature, 2:823
Russian literature, 2:683,
    2:700, 2:704, 2:721,
    2:728, 2:758, 2:774
South African literature,
    2:160
Spanish literature, 2:532,
    2:538, 2:542–43
Swedish literature, 2:675,
    2:676, 2:678–79, 2:681
Victorian period, 1:390
West African drama, 2:148
West African literature,
    2:130, 2:138, 2:141,
    2:148
Yiddish literature, 2:29,
    2:35, 2:37, 2:41
Synagogue, 4:796
Synchroton radiation, 5:715
Synonym, antonym, and
    homonym dictionaries,
    1:93–95
Syria, 3:453–54
Syro-Palestinian culture, 2:51
System theory, 3:38

T

Taboo
    detective story, 1:604
    Gothic story, 1:602
    science fiction, 1:1257
Taiwan
    nativist movement, 2:232,
        2:241, 2:247, 2:251
Tall tale
    American literature, 1:1193
    early nineteenth-century
        American literature,
        1:673, 1:702
    middle to late twentieth-
        century American liter-
        ature, 1:949
Talmuds, 4:609, 4:619
Tantric Buddhism, 4:542
Taoism, 4:496
    Chinese literature, 2:186,
        2:199–200, 2:223

Chinese religion, 4:521,
    4:526–29
Taormina Prize, 2:696
Targums, 4:608, 4:796
Taxes, 3:80, 3:86, 3:247
Taxonomy, 5:804–5
Teaching, See Instruction
"Technique," notion of,
    5:163
"Techno-science," 5:23
Technocapitalism, 5:72
Technological change,
    3:53–54
Technology, See also general
    headings of science,
    technology, and medi-
    cine; specific topics
    agriculture and food,
        5:258–75
    ancient history, 3:304
    art and, 5:189–95
    biotechnology, 5:221–22
    communications, 5:294–308
    defined, 5:211
    developments, philosophi-
        cal studies of, 5:73–77
    economic study of change
        in, 3:53–54
    energy resources, 5:276–93
    engineering and, 5:36–37,
        5:211–57
    ethical issues, 5:127–31
    feminist and gender stud-
        ies, 5:186–89
    food, 5:258–75
    general reference works,
        5:11–12
    mass media, 3:800, 3:810
    medieval Europe, 3:330
    music and, 3:653
    nature of, general, 5:69–72
    philosophy of, 5:69, See
        also Philosophy of sci-
        ence, technology, and
        medicine
    policy-making, 5:179–86
    politics of, 5:72–73
    progress, 5:179
    religion and, 5:195–99
    society and, 5:147–207, See
        also Society and sci-
        ence, technology and
        medicine
    sociology of, 3:205–6,
        3:236
Technology Assessment Act
    of 1972, 5:184
"Technology policy" defined,
    5:179
Teleconferencing, 5:298
Telegraph, invention of,
    5:251

Teleology
modern Western philosophy, 4:158
Western philosophy, 1700–1800, 4:204
Telephone, 5:294–95
Telephone directory, 1:85
Telescopes, See Astronomy
Television, 3:800, 3:809–12
artificial intelligence, programs on, 5:603
"Ascent of Man" series, 5:161–62
astronomy, 5:611
authors, 3:812–23
engineering, 5:228
film and, 3:824
high-definition, 5:294
journalism and, 3:804–9
music on, 3:653
sociological study of, 3:203–4
Temples
Hittite and Canaanite religions, 4:444
Inca religion, 4:458
Maya, 4:455
Mediterranean ancient urban civilization, 4:438, 4:440
Mexico, 4:456
religious movements, twentieth-century, 4:862
Templeton Prize for Progress in Religion, 5:202
Ten Friends of the Northern Quarter, 2:202
Teotihuacan, Mexico, 4:456, 4:457
Territoriality (animal behavior), 5:825
Testing
educational, 3:247
intelligence, 3:268
psychological, 3:180
Textile industry, 5:221, 5:222
Textiles, 3:767
Thai literature, 2:334–37
authors, 2:312, 2:336–37
collections, 2:335
history and criticism, 2:335
Thailand, 3:490
Theater, See also Drama
alternative, twentieth-century American, 1:1113
Broadway, 1:1071
censorship
Restoration, 1:228, 1:244
romantic period, 1:270, 1:271
community, twentieth-century American, 1:1112, 1:1123

little theater movement, twentieth-century American, 1:1070
Living Theater appraisal, 1:1109
modern British and Irish, 1:423–25, 1:426–27, 1:441, 1:449, 1:458, 1:467, 1:492, 1:529, 1:532
off-Broadway, 1:1002, 1:1015, 1:1087, 1:1120
off-off-Broadway, 1:1101, 1:1110
poet's theater, 1:1008, 1:1025
public
modern British and Irish drama, 1:458
Renaissance drama, 1:168
twentieth-century American, 1:1087
regional, twentieth-century American, 1:1071, 1:1087–88, 1:1095, 1:1115
Renaissance drama, 1:167–69
repertory
modern British and Irish, 1:424, 1:531, 1:564
twentieth-century American, 1:1071, 1:1087, 1:1096
Restoration comedy, 1:223, 1:228
Shakespeare, 1:217
Victorian period, 1:311, 1:320–21, 1:356
Theater, music for, 3:667
Theater of cruelty
Australian drama, 2:967
French drama, 2:451
Theater of the Absurd
American drama, 1:1080, 1:1087, 1:1094, 1:1098
Czech drama, 2:789, 2:791
French drama, 2:445, 2:478
Persian drama, 2:93
Polish drama, 2:813, 2:820, 2:822
Theatre Hall of Fame, 1:1082
Theism
Western philosophy
1600–1700, 4:168
twentieth-century, 4:260, 4:271, 4:332
Theodore Roethke Memorial Foundation, 1:1038
Theodore Roethke Prize, 1:990, 1:1021

Theology, 3:330, See also Religion
Bible study, 4:826
Christian, study of religion, 4:422
contemporary traditional issues, 4:884–88
current method, 4:888–89
postmodernism and deconstruction, 4:889
religion, language, and knowledge, 4:888
Islamic religion, 4:574–77
Judaism, 4:592, 4:595
late Christianity, 4:718
1914 to present, 4:742–47
medieval philosophy, 4:92–121
modern Judaism, 4:645, 4:648
modern Western philosophy, 4:157
post-Holocaust, 4:647
Western philosophy, 1700–1800, 4:207
Theology and science, See Religion
Theosophy
religious movements
nineteenth-century, 4:852
twentieth-century, 4:858
Therapeutics, 5:405
Theravada Buddhism
Eastern religions, 4:510
religious movements, twentieth-century, 4:859
Thermodynamics, 5:676, 5:734–35, 5:746
Thermonuclear crisis, 1949–50, 5:719
Thermonuclear reactions, 5:667
Third world countries, See Developing countries
Thomism
contemporary issues, 4:376
medieval philosophy, 4:93
Renaissance philosophy, 4:136
Western philosophy, twentieth-century, 4:260, 4:305
Three Mile Island, 5:108
Thriller
authors, 1:593–98
British popular literature, 1:592–98
children's popular American literature, 1:1197
early twentieth-century American literature, 1:898

Thriller (*cont.*)
  film studies, 1:1168, 1:1175
  modern British and Irish
      drama, 1:450
  modern British and Irish
      literature, 1:432, 1:469,
      1:477, 1:488, 1:566–67
Throat disorders, 5:379–80
Tibetan philosophy, 4:355–57
  authors, 4:350, 4:356–57
  general works, 4:356
Tibetan religion, 4:542–44
Time (magazine), 3:815–16
Time, concept of
  Caribbean literature, 2:940
  Greek modern literature,
      2:372
  Latin American literatures,
      2:859, 2:861, 2:870
  Netherlandic literature,
      2:623
  Russian literature, 2:718
  Spanish literature, 2:544
Time travel
  middle to late twentieth-
      century American liter-
      ature, 1:1063
  science fiction, 1:1252
Tin, calcination, 5:739
Tin oxide, 5:748
Titanic, 5:640–41
Toklas, Alice B., 1:881
Toltecs, 4:456, 4:457
Tony Award
  drama, American, 1:1094,
      1:1112, 1:1115, 1:1119
  modern British and Irish
      drama, 1:500
Torah, 4:593, 4:597
  Orthodox Judaism, 4:653
  Rabbinic Judaism,
      4:618–20
Tosefta, 4:609, 4:619
Totalitarianism, 5:449
Totemism, ancient religion,
      4:421, 4:429
Tourism, 3:889, *See also*
      Travel
Toxicology, 5:349–52, 5:738
Toy book, *See* Picture book
Trade
  between Africa and Arab
      nations, 3:414
  in ancient history, 3:307–8
Tragedy
  Renaissance drama, 1:168,
      1:175, 1:182–83, 1:190,
      1:200
  Restoration drama, 1:228,
      1:251
  Shakespeare, 1:212–14

Tragicomedy
  Renaissance drama, 1:173,
      1:189
  Restoration drama, 1:228
Trance
  Mesmerism, 4:846
  shamanism, 4:430
  Spiritualism, 4:850
Transactional Analysis, 5:433
Transcendental meditation,
      4:872
Transcendentalism, 5:836–37
  early nineteenth-century
      American literature,
      1:659, 1:668, 1:672,
      1:699, 1:704
  popular American litera-
      ture, 1:1197
  religious movements, nine-
      teenth-century, 4:840
Transfinite set theory, 5:500,
      5:509
Transgression, 2:455
Translations of the Bible,
      See Versions of the Bi-
      ble
Transmigration
  South Asian religions,
      4:500
  traditional issues, 4:886,
      4:887
Transplantation of organs,
      5:117, 5:370–71
Transportation
  automotive engineering
      and, 5:246–48
  innovations, agriculture
      and, 5:260
Transposition, 5:806
Transvestism
  American drama, 1:1094
  literary theory, 1:1146
  middle to late twentieth-
      century American liter-
      ature, 1:991, 1:1061
Travel, 3:889–90
  Africa, Asia, and Oceania,
      3:901–6
  Americas, North and
      South, 3:894–98
  Arctic and Antarctica,
      3:906–7
  authors, 3:911–42
  Europe, 3:898–901
  individual accounts of,
      3:907–11
  reference works
      general, 3:891–94
      scholarly, 3:890–91
Travel book
  American literature, 1:1192
  early American literature,
      1:625

  collections, 1:631
  early nineteenth-century
      American literature,
      1:656, 1:659, 1:685
  early twentieth-century
      American literature,
      1:861
  middle to late nineteenth-
      century American liter-
      ature, 1:721
  middle to late twentieth-
      century American liter-
      ature, 1:1008
  modern British and Irish
      literature, 1:565
  Restoration and eighteenth-
      century literature,
      1:233, 1:244, 1:256
  Victorian period, 1:324,
      1:342, 1:395, 1:407
Travel guides, 3:889
Trent, Council of, 4:727,
      4:728
Triage, 5:117
Tribal religions, *See* Indige-
      nous religions
Tribal societies, 3:25–26
Trigonometry, 5:486
Trinidad-Tobago, 3:641, 3:647
Trinidadian authors, *See un-
      der* Caribbean litera-
      ture
Trinity
  early Christianity, 4:684
  Western philosophy,
      1600–1700, 4:167
Tristan legend, 2:512
Trojan War, 3:315
Tropisms, 2:505
Trotskyism, 3:294, 3:647
Truth
  contemporary philosophical
      issues, 4:376
  Western philosophy, twen-
      tieth-century, 4:276
Tsarist Russia, 3:395
Tuberculosis, 5:801
Tudor England (1485–1603),
      3:358–59
Turing Machine, 5:541
Turing Test, 5:541, 5:581
Turkey, 3:452–53
  Byzantine Empire con-
      quered by, 3:391
  World War I, 3:434, 3:445
Turkish literature, 2:94–101
  authors, 2:96–101
  collections, 2:96
  general reading, 2:96
  history and criticism,
      2:95–96
  modern, 2:94
  Ottoman, 2:94

women authors, 2:97
Twentieth century, bibliography, 5:47–49
Twentieth-century American literature, See Early twentieth-century American literature; Middle to late twentieth-century American literature
Twentieth-century China, 3:469–72
Twentieth-century Europe, 3:342
1900–1920, 3:343
1920–1945, 3:344–45
England, 3:365–68
general works, 3:342–43
since 1945, 3:345–46
Twentieth-century United States
Great Depression to World War II (1920–1945), 3:533–36
modern (1945–present), 3:536–40
pre-World War I (1877–1920), 3:530–33
Tyndale Bible, 4:799
Type A personalities, 5:400
Typesetting machines, 1:13
Tyrothricin, 5:795

U

UFOs, See Unidentified flying objects (UFOs)
Ukrainian literature, 2:837–41
authors, 2:778, 2:838–41
collections, 2:838
drama, 2:839
history and criticism, 2:838
languages, 2:837
women authors, 2:840
Umbanda, 4:867
Uncertainty principle, 5:693
Unconscious, psychology, 5:411
Underground publishing, 2:838, See also Samizdat
Undersea exploration, 5:640–41, 5:642
Unidentified flying objects (UFOs), 4:869, 5:454, 5:598
Unification Church, 4:870, 4:877
Union catalogs
bibliography, 1:64, 1:65

Union of Soviet Socialist Republics (USSR), See Soviet Union
United Artists, 1:1161, 1:1167
United Kingdom, See Great Britain
United Nations publications, 1:111
United Productions America (UPA), 1:1164
United States, See also America; United States history
African studies in, 3:414–15
Canada and, 3:604
emigration of European Jews to, 3:347
end of cold war, 3:277
Europe and, 3:342
exploration of, 3:927–28
geography, 3:128
journalism in, 3:804
minority religious movements, 4:839–81
Myrdal's study of race in, 3:98, 3:235
philosophy, 4:33–36
political science, 3:137, 3:151, 3:154, 3:164–65
civil liberties and civil rights, 3:139
constitutionalism and federalism, 3:141–42
democratic theory and practice, 3:142–43
electoral politics, 3:143–44
law and society, 3:145
legislative behavior, 3:146
policy planning and formulation, 3:146
presidency, 3:146–47
state and local government, 3:148
Puerto Rico, 3:640–41
regional and ethnic folklore of
African American, 3:866–67
Mid-Atlantic states, 3:858–59
Midwest, 3:861–62
Native American, 3:864–66
New England, 3:857–58
South, 3:860–61
West, 3:862–64
sociological study of, 3:231, 3:234
travel in, 3:894–98
war with Iraq, 3:449

World War I, 3:434
United States Conference of Catholic Bishops, 5:109
United States history, 3:504–603
authors, 3:561–603
bibliographies, 3:509–11
Civil War and sectional conflict (1850–1877), 3:526–30
colonial period (1606–1763), 3:516–19
cultural and intellectual, 3:558–61
Declaration of Independence, Constitution, and Federalist Papers, 3:541
diplomacy and foreign relations, 3:544–47
documentary histories, 3:511–12
economic, 3:547–49
encyclopedias and dictionaries, 3:508–9
environmental, 3:549–51
gender, race, and ethnicity, 3:554–58
Great Depression and World War II (1920–1945), 3:533–36
historiography of, 3:514–16
middle period (1815–1850), 3:522–26
modern (1945–present), 3:536–40
political and constitutional, 3:541–44
pre-world power (1877–1920), 3:530–33
reference works, 3:505–8
Revolution and early period (1763–1815), 3:519–22
social change and, 3:551–53
surveys and general works, 3:512–14
Unity of science movement, See Logical positivism
Universal pragmatics, 5:88
Universalist mathematicians, 5:509, 5:513
University Wits, 1:194
Unknown works, See Anonymous works
Up-Biblum God, 4:801
Upanishads, Vedanta religion, 4:500, 4:501
Uranium, 5:754
Urban geography, 3:123–24, 3:127, 3:129

Urban life, 3:199, 3:216–17,
    3:238
  human ecology of,
    3:236–37
  Industrial Revolution and,
    3:340
  medieval Europe, 3:329,
    3:407
  Mediterranean world, an-
    cient civilizations,
    4:438–53
  New World, ancient civili-
    zations, 4:419,
    4:453–58
Urdu literature, 2:175
Urea, 5:755
Urologic diseases, 5:406
Uruguay, 3:641
Uruguayan authors, See Latin
    American literatures
Usher Prize, 5:257
U.S. National Academy of
    Engineering, 5:256
U.S. Natural Environmental
    Policy Act of 1969,
    5:106
U.S. Office of Scientific Re-
    search and Develop-
    ment, 5:199
Utilitarianism, 3:150
  modern Western philoso-
    phy, 4:158
  Western philosophy
    1700–1800, 4:190
    1800–1900, 4:243–44,
    4:256
Utopian views, 3:198, 3:217,
    3:232
  Chinese philosophy,
    4:360–61
  communal groups, 4:843
  Indian philosophy, 4:352
  religious movements, nine-
    teenth-century, 4:840
  Renaissance philosophy,
    4:137, 4:147
  Theosophy, 4:858
  Western philosophy, twen-
    tieth-century, 4:276
Utopias, studies of, 5:169

V

Vaccinations, development
    of, 5:409
Vachel Lindsay Prize, 5:269
Valens (Roman emperor),
    3:310

Vampire
  horror story, 1:601–2,
    1:1239, 1:1242
Vedanta, Indian philosophy,
    4:353
Vedanta religion
  religious movements, twen-
    tieth-century, 4:871
  Upanishads, 4:501
Vedic literature
  Aranyakas, 4:500
  Brahmanas, 4:500
  Hinduism, 4:502
  Upanishads, 4:500–1
  Vedas, 4:500
Vedic religion, 4:500
Venetian school of painting,
    3:793
Venezuela, 3:641
Venus, 5:615
Verne, Jules, 1:563
Verse drama
  American, 1:1070, 1:1081
  Arabic literature, 2:73
  early twentieth-century
    American literature,
    1:812, 1:857
  German literature, 2:571,
    2:586, 2:593, 2:609
  Hungarian literature, 2:902
  middle to late nineteenth-
    century American liter-
    ature, 1:775
  modern British and Irish,
    1:423, 1:469, 1:471,
    1:480, 1:500
  modern Irish, 1:459
  Norwegian literature, 2:665
  Polish literature, 2:815
  romantic period, British,
    1:271, 1:281, 1:302
  Russian literature, 2:682,
    2:726
  Serbian literature, 2:827,
    2:831
Versions of the Bible
  ancient, 4:796–806
  chronology, 4:799–805
  English, 4:797–98
  textual criticism, 4:805
Victorian England
    (1837–1901), 3:363–65
Victorian period
  adventure story, British,
    1:594
  authors, 1:326–411
  British literature,
    1:309–411
  children's literature, 1:329,
    1:370, 1:374, 1:395,
    1:403
  British, 1:577
  drama, 1:320–23

  collections, 1:323
  history and criticism,
    1:322–23
  history and criticism,
    1:311–13
  horror story, British, 1:602
  middle to late twentieth-
    century American liter-
    ature, 1:989, 1:1039
  modern British and Irish
    literature, 1:412, 1:454,
    1:477
  nonfiction, 1:323–26
  collections, 1:326
  history and criticism,
    1:325
  novel, 1:316–20
  history and criticism,
    1:318–20
  poetry, 1:313–16
  collections, 1:316
  history and criticism,
    1:315
  Scottish dialect, 1:329
  women authors, 1:310,
    1:317, 1:324, 1:330,
    1:332–36, 1:340,
    1:352–55, 1:375, 1:379,
    1:383–85, 1:390, 1:407
Vienna (Austria), 3:391
Vienna Circle, 4:409
  Western philosophy, twen-
    tieth-century, 4:272,
    4:278, 4:332, 4:337,
    4:343
Vienna Circle of Logical Po-
    sitivists, 5:84, 5:91,
    5:98
Vienna Psychoanalytic Insti-
    tute, 5:466
Vietnam, 3:490–91
Vietnam War, 3:488, 3:583,
    3:804, 3:822
Vietnamese literature,
    2:337–40
  authors, chronology, 2:312
  collections, 2:339
  history and criticism, 2:339
Vietnamese religious tradi-
    tions, 4:520
Viking Age, 2:637
Vikings, 3:378–79
Vinci, Leonardo da, Medal,
    See Leonardo da Vinci
    Medal
Virology, 5:783, 5:789–90
Virtual photons, 5:685
Vision, 3:189
Visual arts, 5:205
Vitruvius, 3:756
Von Neumann architecture,
    5:541, 5:582
Vortex rings, 5:715

Vorticism
  modern British and Irish
    literature, 1:412, 1:513
Voudon, 4:867

W

Waka, See Japanese litera-
  ture, tanka
Wales, 3:353, 3:369
Wall paintings, ancient Juda-
  ism, 4:613
Wallace Stegner Writing Fel-
  lowship, 5:268
War, 3:148–49, See also
  Diplomacy
  aggression, 3:170, 3:190
  ancient history, 3:308–9
  conflict and conflict reso-
    lution, 3:204
  history, 3:277–81
War experience
  Australian literature, 2:958,
    2:962
  Byelorussian literature,
    2:784
  Chinese literature, 2:206
  Czech literature, 2:791
  Danish literature, 2:650
  drama, American, 1:1108
  early twentieth-century
    American literature,
    1:828, 1:844, 1:881
  French literature, 2:465,
    2:480, 2:487
  German literature, 2:595,
    2:598, 2:606
  Hebrew literature, 2:14,
    2:23, 2:25
  Italian literature, 2:409,
    2:425, 2:429
  Korean literature, 2:300
  Lithuanian literature, 2:806
  middle to late twentieth-
    century American liter-
    ature, 1:951, 1:987,
    1:994, 1:1011, 1:1056,
    1:1061–64
  middle to late twentieth-
    century American poet-
    ry, 1:970, 1:990,
    1:1005, 1:1048
  modern British and Irish
    drama, 1:493, 1:544
  modern British and Irish
    literature, 1:413–14,
    1:456, 1:475, 1:481,
    1:485, 1:515, 1:561

modern British and Irish
  poetry, 1:416, 1:533,
  1:541–42
Netherlandic literature,
  2:621, 2:623, 2:626,
  2:628, 2:630
North African literature,
  2:119
Polish literature, 2:820,
  2:822
Russian literature, 2:699,
  2:718, 2:719, 2:727,
  2:742, 2:756
science fiction, 1:1260
Serbian literature, 2:829
Vietnamese literature,
  2:339
West African literature,
  2:127, 2:130, 2:141,
  2:143, 2:146
War poets
  modern British and Irish,
    1:416, 1:450, 1:481,
    1:533, 1:541–42
Warfare
  contemporary philosophical
    issues, 4:388
  contemporary religious is-
    sues, 4:895, 4:900
Waste
  nuclear waste, 5:239
  treatment of, 5:221
Watergate scandal, 3:804–5
Waterways, 5:246
Wave mechanics, 5:714
Waverley novels, 1:298
Weak currents, 5:690, 5:713,
  5:718, 5:720
Weather forecasting, See Meteorology
Wechsler Intelligence Scale
  for Children (WISC),
  3:196
Welfare, 3:56–57
Wellness, See Medicine and
  health
West (United States), folklore
  of, 3:862–64
West Africa, 3:419–21
West African literature,
  2:124–51
  authors, 2:113, 2:126–51
  children's, 2:135, 2:139
  collections, 2:126
  drama, 2:133, 2:143,
    2:147–48
  history and criticism, 2:126
  languages
    ajami, 2:124, 2:134
    Arabic, 2:124–25, 2:134
    French, 2:146
    Hausa, 2:125
    pidgin English, 2:150

women authors, 2:129,
  2:132, 2:136, 2:139,
  2:143, 2:147
West Indian literature, See
  Caribbean literature
Western civilization, Western
  philosophy, 4:158
Western influence
  Chinese philosophy, 4:360
  Chinese religion, 4:531
  Hinduism, 4:507–9
  indigenous religions, 4:466
  Islamic philosophy, 4:372
  Japanese philosophy, 4:363
  Japanese religion, 4:533,
    4:540
  Korean religion, 4:540
Western literature
  comparative literature,
    2:981, 2:990
  influence on Czech litera-
    ture, 2:788
  influence on Philippine lit-
    erature, 2:327
  influence on Southeast
    Asian literatures, 2:310
  influence on Turkish litera-
    ture, 2:95
Western philosophy,
    seventeenth to
    twentieth centuries,
    4:157–258
  1600–1700, 4:157
    authors, 4:163–89
    women authors, 4:166
  1700–1800, 4:157–58
    authors, 4:190–219
  1800–1900, 4:158–59
    authors, 4:219–58
  general bibliography,
    4:159–63
Western philosophy,
    twentieth-century,
    4:259–347
  authors, 4:269–349
  general works, 4:262–68
Westernization
  African philosophy, 4:348
  Asian philosophy, modern,
    4:348
  Indian philosophy, 4:350
Westerns
  American popular litera-
    ture, 1:1209,
    1:1210–19, 1:1232
  authors, 1:1211–19
  middle to late nineteenth-
    century American liter-
    ature, 1:721, 1:789
  middle to late twentieth-
    century American poet-
    ry, 1:969, 1:1053
Whales' songs, 5:768

Whig Interpretation of History, 3:351–52
Whimsy
  children's literature, British, 1:587
  early twentieth-century American literature, 1:807, 1:811, 1:814
  modern British and Irish literature, 1:437, 1:494
  Victorian period drama, 1:321
Whirling Dervishes, 4:566, 4:589
White dwarf stars, 5:677
Wicca, See Witchcraft
Wilderness, threats to, 5:827, 5:833, 5:834
William I (the Conqueror; King of England), 3:353
Wilson, Woodrow, 3:815
Winifred and Atherton Bean Professorship, 5:160
Winifred Holtby Memorial Prize, 2:178
Witchcraft, religious movements, twentieth-century, 4:864
Women, See also Gender studies
  ancient history, 3:309
  Asian and Pacific history, 3:462
  engineering careers, 5:227–28
  John Stuart Mill on, 3:96
  nineteenth-century United States, 3:522
  psychology of, 3:178–79, 3:185
  sociology of, 3:217–18
    gender, 3:207
    human sexuality, 3:207–8
  United States, 3:554–58, 3:596
Women authors, See national literatures, such as German literature
Women's health, 5:354–60
  pregnancy and childbirth, 5:357–60
Women's Press Collective, 1:1187
Women's studies, 3:596
Woods Hole Marine Biological Laboratory, 5:828
Woods Hole Oceanographic Institute, 5:640
Woodward-Hoffman rules of conversion of orbital symmetry, 5:755
Work, sociology of, 3:218

Working-class movement, Western philosophy, 1800–1900, 4:227, 4:241
World Bank, 5:292
World Council of Churches, 5:163
World economy
  history of development of, 5:56
World history, 3:271–324
  adventure/thriller, 1:592
  authors, 3:281–96
  middle to late twentieth-century, 1:908
  reference works, 3:272–73
  surveys and general works, 3:273–75
  thriller, 1:595
  war and peace, 3:277–81
  writing and philosophy of, 3:275–77
World literature, 2:1–5
  anthologies, 1:130
  bibliographies, 1:121–22
  biographical references, 1:128
  collections, 2:4–5
  comparative, 2:981
  East European literatures contribution, 2:777
  general reference, 2:2–4
  genres, 2:1
  reference works, 1:119
  universality, 2:2
World War I, 3:342–43, 3:815
  Balkans, 3:391
  biotechnology, 5:221
  Canada in, 3:604
  Eastern Europe, 3:388
  Germany in, 3:375
  Middle East, 3:434, 3:445, 3:450
  Italy in, 3:383
  Turkey in, 3:452
  United States in, 3:530–33
World War II, See also
  Atomic bomb, 3:342, 3:344–45, 3:461
  aeronautics and aviation, expansion following, 5:218
  Balkans, 3:391
  biotechnology, 5:221
  Brookings Institution, 5:184
  communications technology, 5:294
  concentration camps, 5:434, 5:443
  earth sciences, 5:614

  Eastern Europe, 3:387, 3:388
  Germany in, 3:375
  government funding of science and technology, 5:179
  Great Britain during, 3:400
  information science following, 5:580–81
  Jews during, 3:347, 3:438
  Manhattan Project, 5:179
  military engineering, 5:237
  military research, 5:161
  Nazism, 5:84, 5:93, 5:138, 5:443, 5:709, 5:714
  penicillin, discovery of, 5:408
  radio during, 3:800, 3:818
  support for science following, 5:199
  United States in, 3:533–36
Worship
  Celtic religion, 4:436
  contemporary religious issues, 4:897
  Islamic religion, 4:565
  Judaism, 4:598–600
  medieval Christianity, 4:698
  Roman religion, 4:447
Writer's Project, 1:905
Writing guides, 1:117–18
Wyclif Bible, 4:799

X

X-rays
  Compton effect, 5:678
  diffraction, 5:775, 5:813
  discovery of, 5:710
  exploratory surgery, 5:743
  optics, 5:665
  research on, 5:672, 5:703
Xenon, 5:754
Xerxes (Persian emperor), 3:315

Y

Yale Psychiatric Clinic, 5:433
Yale School of Drama, 1:1070
Yale School of literary criticism, 1:1141, 1:1150
Yearbooks, 1:81–83
  historical, 3:8–9
  social-scientific, 3:6
Yerkes Observatory, 5:605, 5:607

Yeshiva, Orthodox Judaism,
    4:653
Yiddish literature, 2:28–50,
    4:655, 4:656, *See also*
    Hebrew literature; Jew-
    ish literature
  authors, 2:34–50
  children's, 2:40, 2:47
  collections, 2:30–34
  general reading, 2:29
  Haskalah movement, 2:29
  history and criticism,
    2:30–33
  language fusion and assi-
    milation, 2:28
  Russian, 2:699
  women authors, 2:38–40
Yin and Yang, Chinese reli-
    gion, 4:521, 4:524–25
Yoga
  Buddhism, 4:511
  Hinduism, 4:502
  Indian philosophy, 4:352
  religious movements, twen-
    tieth-century, 4:872
Yogacara, 4:511

Young Germany movement,
    2:587
Young Hegelians, Western
    philosophy, 1800–1900,
    4:227–28, 4:241
Young Ones, The
    Yiddish literature, 2:29,
    2:36, 2:39
Youth culture, religious
    movements, twentieth-
    century, 4:853–54
Yugoslavia, 3:391–93
Yugoslavia (former), philoso-
    phy, 4:33

Z

Zen
    Chinese Buddhism, 4:529
    Japan and Korea, 4:536
    Japanese philosophy, 4:364
    religious movements, twen-
    tieth-century, 4:853,
    4:859

Vietnam, 4:520
Zero Population Growth,
    5:831
Zero volume, 5:708
Ziggurat, 4:440
    Inca religion, 4:458
Zionism, 3:347, 4:641, 4:655,
    4:657
    Hebrew literature, 2:8,
    2:12, 2:16
    Yiddish literature, 2:43
Zoology, 5:757, 5:768–72,
    5:802
    chimpanzees, studies of,
    5:832–33
    general works, 5:769–72
    history of, 5:33–34
    reference works, 5:769
Zora Neale Hurston Society
    Award, 1:1144
Zoroastrianism
    Indian religion, 4:497
    Parsis, 4:517, 4:546
    Iran, 4:546–48
    Iranian ancient religions,
    4:443